P9-DTF-022

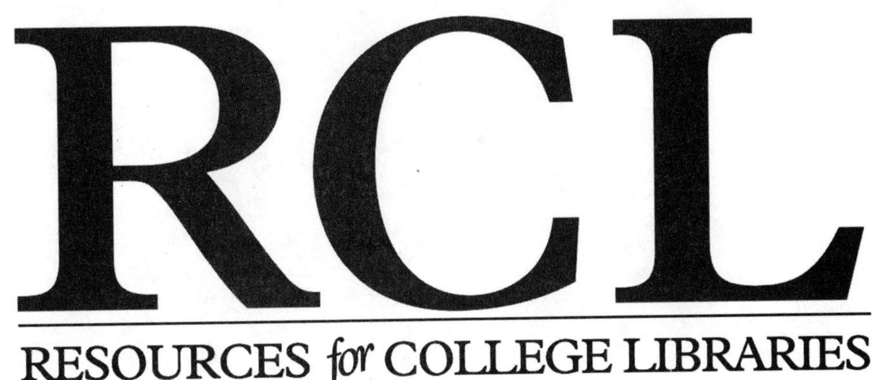

2007

This Edition of ***Resources for College Libraries*** was prepared by:

ACRL & Choice:
Project Editor: Marcus Elmore
Editorial Director, Choice: Francine Graf
Editor & Publisher, Choice: Irving Rockwood

Special Thanks to Our Proofreaders:
Monika Maslowski, Jinna Anderson, Chris Sullivan, Jennifer Donahue, Judith Douville, Rebecca Bartlett, and Carolyn Wilcox

Record Entry Completed By:
Monika Maslowski, Laurie Trulock, and Sheila Laverty

R. R. Bowker LLC:
John Krafty: Product Manager, RCL
Ashley Ludwig: Managing Editor, RCL
Frank Morris: IT Director
Minh Huynh: Senior Programmer Analyst
Robert Zeisler: Senior Programmer Analyst

Editorial Staff:
Ian Singer: Vice President, Data Services
Roy Crego: Senior Managing Director, Editorial
Eleanor Schubauer: Managing Editor
Michael Olenick: Managing Editor
Beverly Palacio: Associate Editor

Production Department:
Doreen Gravesande: Senior Director, Production
Ralph Coviello, Manager, Manufacturing Services
Myriam Nunez: Project Manager, Product Development & Content Integrity
Kennard McGill: Production Consultant

Research Completed By:
Pat Diaz, Bobbie Ferraro, Kathy Griner, Becky Housel, and Diane Johnson.

Record Entry Completed By:
Jenny Marie DeJesus, Dorothy Perry-Gilchrist, Anthony Giuffra, and Steven Zaffuto

RESOURCES *for* COLLEGE LIBRARIES

2007

Volume 3:
History

Mary Ellen Davis, Executive Director, ACRL

Published by
R. R. Bowker LLC
630 Central Avenue, New Providence
New Jersey 07974

Annie Callanan, President and CEO

URL: http://www.rclweb.net
E-mail address: rclfeedback@bowker.com

Readers may send any corrections and/or updates to the information in this work to:
rclfeedback@bowker.com

International Standard Book Number:

7 Volume Set:	ISBN: 0-8352-4855-0 ISBN13: 978-0-8352-4855-6
Vol. 1: Humanities:	ISBN: 0-8352-4856-9 ISBN13: 978-0-8352-4856-3
Vol. 2: Language & Literature:	ISBN: 0-8352-4857-7 ISBN13: 978-0-8352-4857-0
Vol. 3: History:	ISBN: 0-8352-4858-5 ISBN13: 978-0-8352-4858-7
Vol. 4: Social Sciences:	ISBN: 0-8352-4859-3 ISBN13: 978-0-8352-4859-4
Vol. 5: Science and Technology:	ISBN: 0-8352-4860-7 ISBN13: 978-0-8352-4860-0
Vol. 6: Interdisciplinary & Area Studies:	ISBN: 0-8352-4861-5 ISBN13: 978-0-8352-4861-7
Vol. 7: Indexes:	ISBN: 0-8352-4862-3 ISBN13: 978-0-8352-4862-4

Printed and bound in the United States of America

Table of Contents

Resources for College Libraries: General Introduction

Like its predecessors, the three editions of *Books for College Libraries* (BCL) that appeared in 1988, 1975, and 1964, *Resources for College Libraries* (RCL) is a bibliography of carefully selected works spanning the college curriculum and comprising a recommended core collection for all academic libraries. In the tradition of its predecessors, which drew on the such sources as the published catalog of Harvard's Lamont Library (1954), the shelflist of the undergraduate library of the University of Michigan, and, crucially, Charles Shaw's *List of Books for College Libraries* (1931), RCL attempts to balance multiple, often contradictory demands. It seeks to provide a balanced set of recommendations that take note of the weight of the various academic disciplines within the undergraduate curriculum, the degree to which those various disciplines depend on book materials for their essential teaching and research resources, and the extensive pattern of changes that have reshaped the academic curriculum since 1988, the year in which BCL3, the most recent edition of *Books for College Libraries,* appeared.

Of necessity, RCL also embodies a paradox identified by the late Virginia Clark, editor of BCL3: it "can fully succeed only by failing. It would be disastrous should the collection it suggests serve perfectly to ratify the finished work of book selection in any library."[1] Not only will individual institutions create collections significantly larger than the roughly 65,000 titles recommended by RCL, but they will tailor those collections to reflect the size and strength of their own individual departments, majors, and programs. RCL attempts to make general recommendations, within individual subject areas, of those titles most necessary for teaching the subject to undergraduates. In many cases, this means a foundation to which the smallest institutions should aspire but which larger collections will far surpass.

We describe RCL as a successor to, rather than a new edition of, BCL for two reasons. The first is formal, and lies behind the change in nomenclature: RCL includes in its recommendations a variety of electronic resources, including Web sites, subscription databases, e-books, and other electronic materials. The second, procedural reason follows from this: unlike its predecessors, RCL will appear as both a multivolume print edition and a searchable, continuously updated electronic database. In addition, there is a third, tacit distinction which may be made between RCL and the various editions of BCL: although bibliographers compiling subject lists for RCL often took the titles listed in BCL3 as a starting point, our bibliographic work emphasized building a comprehensive, retrospective list of titles by reference to the current undergraduate curriculum, and thus much of the work on RCL was from scratch. In contrast, the relationship between the various editions of BCL was demonstrably that of revision; from one edition to the next, there was an expectation that a title would be retained unless it was actively removed (if, for instance, it had been superseded by a more recent work). Because so much more time had passed between the appearance of BCL3 and the development of RCL than between any successive editions of BCL, bibliographers faced the simultaneously daunting and liberating prospect of creating a subject list *de novo.* That this same period (1988-2006) has seen momentous sea changes in many of the academic disciplines in the humanities and the sciences, as well as the growth of interdisciplinary study across all the academic disciplines, made this an opportunity to take measure of the way subjects are taught to undergraduates, as well as the sorts of subjects which are taught, when developing our core list.

One result of this reassessment was the decision to recognize and include as separate subject divisions in RCL a number of interdisciplinary fields, e.g., Environmental Studies and Gender Studies. The decision about which fields to include was based primarily on the degree to which those subjects function as areas of formal study at undergraduate institutions in the U.S., whether as major programs, academic minors, or areas of concentration housed within another department (film studies, for instance, is often offered as a program or concentration within the departments of English, Comparative Literature, or Theater). We recognized that the lists of titles recommended for teaching interdisciplinary subjects, e.g., Asian American Studies, might overlap significantly with the corresponding title lists for related traditional fields, e.g., American Literature. At the same time, we were confident that many of the recommended interdisciplinary titles would be unique, and so it has proved. The degree of overlap between the various sections of RCL is, throughout, fortuitous and reflects actual overlap between various undergraduate curricula. Effort was made to regularize the editions selected, but the work of compiling the various subject lists proceeded on an independent basis.

1. Virginia Clark, "Introduction," *Books for College Libraries: A Core Collection of 50,000 Titles,* (3rd ed., Chicago: American Library Association, 1988), vii.

The other dramatic difference between RCL and BCL is the decision to move away from Library of Congress classification as the primary framework for the selection and classification of titles. Though this is bound to be regarded by many librarians as a controversial decision, we are confident that it will prove in retrospect to be a sound one. The rationale for doing so is the desire to have titles classified in a fashion which closely follows the contours of the undergraduate curriculum. While LC accomplishes this for some subjects (for instance, British or American Literature, which are taught by chronological periods, and within periods by major authors and by forms such as poetry or drama), other curricula fail to mesh well with LC classification: Business Administration, for example, is responsible for the largest portion of baccalaureate degrees conferred by U.S. colleges and universities,[2] yet the classification of materials in the business curriculum in LC class HB-HJ, while sufficient for cataloging purposes, offers no insight on the relationship between materials so classified and the curriculum in which they are used. It is, furthermore, an arrangement which makes perfect sense to, but only to, librarians. Not all copies of BCL resided in technical services departments, but it seems unlikely that they were much consulted by students or faculty. Our hope is that the new classification scheme will work to the advantage of all the academic library's constituencies: librarians, especially those lacking strong background in a given subject, will be able to see not only the recommended titles but also, in the subject taxonomy, a map of the undergraduate curriculum; faculty will find recommendations of essential works in a form more accessible than LC, and bearing a closer correspondence to the way their courses and departments are organized; students, searching for a place to begin research on a particular topic, will also be able to recognize in the classification scheme something corresponding to their own encounter with the subject matter in the classroom and laboratory. Finally, since each entry in RCL retains its LC classification, those who prefer to search for materials in this fashion will still be able to.

RCL is the result of the collaborative efforts of 332 contributors, almost exclusively teaching faculty or librarians at U.S. colleges and universities. There were three kinds of contributors: subject editors, bibliographers, and referees. Subject editors were selected on the basis of their subject expertise and teaching or collection development experience: eighteen hold doctorates, four are members of the teaching faculty at research universities, two are independent scholars, and the remainder are academic librarians. Many have previously contributed to or authored major bibliographies in their subject areas. They were responsible for developing the subject classification taxonomy for their respective subject areas, for recruiting bibliographers and coordinating their efforts, and for reviewing the results. The subject editors represented a change from the various editions of BCL, where the bibliographers (mainly Choice reviewers) dealt directly with the project editor. By inserting a layer of subject experts we sought to ensure that the titles selected and the taxonomies in which they were classified reflected as much as possible the realities of the contemporary undergraduate curriculum. The second class of RCL contributors, bibliographers, was responsible for the bulk of the actual selection of titles. Like the subject editors, they were faculty and librarians selected for their subject knowledge, often with particular expertise in one specific aspect of a field. Finally, a pool of sixty-four referees, senior faculty or subject-specialist librarians, provided independent assessment of the initial lists developed by the bibliographers; the subject editors used this feedback to further refine their lists prior to publication.

The development of RCL had presumed from the beginning that bibliographers would be manipulating electronic bibliographic records in some sort of online environment, but the decision of the Association of College and Research Libraries (ACRL) Board of Directors to partner with publisher R. R. Bowker to produce RCL allowed us access to Bowker's massive database of bibliographic records, as well as the extensive technical support and expertise Bowker deployed on behalf of the project. Bibliographers selected titles in Bowker's *booksinprint.com* database, in a particular edition, and then imported them to the online RCL Authoring System, where they assigned subject headings and recommended audience levels. In those instances where no bibliographic record existed for a desired title, one was created from a reliable source (preferably with book in hand, though this was not always possible). At the same time, bibliographers submitted corrections to Bowker records when they identified errors or inconsistencies. While this system allowed us to avoid much of the brute effort which was expended on the creation of bibliographic records for the various editions of BCL, it also meant that bibliographers spent thousands of person-hours in the *booksinprint.com* database, identifying the most recent and reliable edition of particular works; in some cases, editors elected to include multiple editions, especially where the differences between them are significant for undergraduate teaching (see, for instance, the decision to include multiple, equally worthwhile translations of Dante's *Divine Comedy* in the Italian literature section).

The use of an online system for the manipulation of electronic bibliographic records was in part a matter of efficiency, but more importantly, it finally addresses one longstanding issue faced by BCL, that of obsolescence.

2. http://nces.ed.gov/fastfacts/display.asp?id=37: U.S. Department of Education, National Center for Education Statistics. (2006). *Digest of Education Statistics, 2005* (NCES 2006-030), chapter 3.

When *Choice* magazine was founded in 1964, it was envisioned as, among other things, an ongoing supplement to BCL1. This approach did not prove practical, and the second and third editions of BCL were required. In contrast, RCL will be updated on an ongoing basis beginning almost immediately after its initial publication; bibliographic records will reflect changes in print status, and new titles will be introduced at regular intervals, to supplement or replace extant titles.

In addition to the tireless efforts of the contributors, on whom I cannot lavish sufficient praise, special thanks to the ACRL Board of Directors and Mary Ellen Davis, ACRL Executive Director, without whose approval and generous support this project would not have been possible. Oversight and advice were provided throughout the project by the RCL Editorial Board: Carolyn Sheehy, North Central College, Chair; and other members Joan Ellen Broome, Georgia Southern University; Barbara Burd, College Misericordia; Brian E. Coutts, Western Kentucky University; Bradford Lee Eden, University of California, Santa Barbara; Stacey Marien, American University; and Richard Shaw, Technical College of the Lowcountry.

Thanks are also due the editorial staff of *Choice*, all of whom contributed effort and advice to the production of this work in varying degrees (and all of whom exhibited tremendous kindness in their efforts, especially in the final days): Becky Bartlett, Judith Douville, Fran Graf, Lisa Mitten, and Carolyn Wilcox. Fran Graf and Irv Rockwood, the Publisher of *Choice*, deserve another helping of praise for their advice, encouragement, and oversight of the project, as well as for handling negotiations of our partnership with R. R. Bowker. Judith Douville made superhuman contributions to a number of subject areas in addition to her own responsibilities in Chemistry. Although almost every member of the *Choice* office staff contributed to this work, Sheila Laverty deserves special praise for her work on the Dance section. Finally, the work would not have been completed if it had not been for the tireless effort of a small cadre of freelance staff, namely Jennifer Donahue, Monika Maslowski, Teri Staab, and Laurie Trulock, who proofread and edited subject headings and section notes, entered titles, cataloged records, and helped maintain communication with subject editors, with extraordinary care, intelligence, and persistence.

With our partners at R. R. Bowker, we enjoyed the highest degree of collegiality and cooperation. Special thanks are due to Angela D'Agostino, Vice-President of Marketing; John Krafty, Product Manager of *Books In Print*; Ashley Ludwig, Managing Editor; Todd Rudloff, Project Manager of *Books In Print*; Frank Morris, Senior Programmer; Minh Huynh, Senior Programmer Analyst, all of whom made significant contributions to bringing this work to the light of day.

Finally, my deep thanks to my family, Colleen and Graham, for their patience and support throughout this project.

Marcus Elmore,

Editor

A Note on the RCL Subject Taxonomy

One of the distinctive features of *Resources for College Libraries* is the subject taxonomy used to organize the titles included in RCL. Developed specifically for RCL by the RCL editorial team, and in particular by the subject editors, the RCL taxonomy reflects the contours of today's undergraduate curriculum. The RCL taxonomy's major headings, therefore, generally correspond to academic majors, departments, or courses of study, e.g., anthropology, business administration, or physics. (In some cases an academic discipline has been further subdivided in order to create sections of manageable size, e.g., the subdivision of History by geographical region.) The goal is a classification scheme, which organizes materials as they would be taught by faculty and encountered in the classroom and the laboratory by undergraduate students.

In some subject areas, e.g. British and American literature, the RCL subject taxonomy closely resembles the Library of Congress classification scheme used in *Books for College Libraries,* 3rd edition. In most cases, however, the differences between LC and today's undergraduate curriculum, have been so substantial as to require the development of a new taxonomy from scratch. This has been especially true for the interdisciplinary subjects such as African American Studies, Criminal Justice, and Native American Studies, which draw upon materials from a dizzying range of LC classes. Gender Studies, for example, draws from a large array of academic disciplines, including (but not limited to) psychology, sociology, literature, philosophy, political science, medicine, and history.

The coverage of interdisciplinary subjects in RCL is another of its distinguishing features, and one deemed essential from the very inception of the project. Although there is some overlap between the interdisciplinary title lists and those of related traditional subjects, e.g., American literature and Chicano/a literature (a subsection of Latino Studies), the interdisciplinary sections inevitably include many unique titles. In addition, the inclusion of the interdisciplinary subjects makes it possible to distinguish those titles which have been selected as essential resources for a traditional subject such as American literature (e.g., Carson McCullers' *Collected Novels*), from those selected for an interdisciplinary area (e.g., Pat Mora's *Communion,* selected for Latino Studies > Humanities > Literature > Chicano/a Literature), and also from those selected for both (e.g., Mora's *Borders*).

By making the ways in which titles are actually used in the classroom the focus for our classification of titles in RCL, we hope to both dramatically increase its usefulness to students and faculty members and also to underscore the extent to which titles were selected on the basis of their importance to undergraduate study and teaching.

RCL Contributors

John Abbott, Graduate Student, GSLIS, University of Illinois, Urbana-Champaign.
Subject Editor: European History.

Randy Abbott, Head Reference Librarian, University of Evansville.
Referee.

Anthony Adam, Assistant Director, John B. Coleman Library, Prairie View A&M University.
Bibliographer: GLBT Studies.

Jan Adamczyk, Slavic Reference Service, University of Illinois.
Bibliographer: Russian Languages and Literatures.

Michael Adams, Librarian, CUNY Graduate Center.
Bibliographer: American Literature.

Paulita Aguilar, Curator, Indigenous Nations Library Program, University of New Mexico.
Bibliographer: Native American Studies.

Flavia Alaya, Professor of English, Ramapo College of New Jersey.
Referee.

Jean Alexander, Head of Reference, Hunt Library, Carnegie Mellon University.
Referee.

Duncan Alford, Head of Reference, Law Library, Georgetown University.
Bibliographer: Law.

Karen Antell, Head, Reference Department, University of Oklahoma.
Bibliographer: Technology and Engineering.

Ralph Arcari, Director Emeritus, Health Center Library, University of Connecticut.
Subject Editor: Medicine.

Susan Ariew, University Librarian, University of South Florida.
Bibliographer: Education.

Jan Armstrong, Professor of Education, University of New Mexico.
Referee.

Teresa Arrington, Associate Professor of Modern Languages, Blue Mountain College.
Bibliographer: Spanish Language and Literature.

Susan Awe, Director of Parish Memorial Library, University of New Mexico.
Referee.

David Azzolina, Reference librarian, University of Pennsylvania.
Bibliographer: General Language and Literature.

Pete Banholzer, Technical Information Specialist, NASA.
Bibliographer: Geology.

Ron Banks, Human Subjects Coordinator, Institutional Review Board, University of Illinois.
Bibliographer: Education.

David Bantz, Chief Information Architect, University of Alaska.
Referee.

Adele Barsh, Business and Economics Librarian, Carnegie Mellon University.
Bibliographer: Business Administration.

Jennifer Bartlett, Head of Research & Instructional Services, Murray State University.
Bibliographer: American Literature.

Edwin Battistella, Dean of Arts and Letters and Professor of English, University of Southern Oregon.
Bibliographer: General Language and Literature.

Frederic Baumgartner, Professor of History, Virginia Tech University.
Bibliographer: European History.

Robert Beauregard, Professor, Urban Policy Analysis and Management, New School University.
Referee.

Linda Behrend, Cataloging Librarian, University of Tennessee, Knoxville.
Bibliographer: American Literature.

Penny Beile, Head, Curriculum Materials Center, University of Central Florida.
Bibliographer: Education.

Dean Bell, Dean and Chief Academic Officer, Spertus Institute of Jewish Studies.
Bibliographer: European History.

Dennis Benamati, Director, Ryan-Matura Library, Sacred Heart University.
Referee.

Riva Berleant-Schiller, Professor emerita of Anthropology, University of Connecticut, emerita.
Subject Editor: Anthropology.

Jay Bernstein, Reader Services Librarian, Kingsborough Community College.
Referee.

John Berry, Native American Studies Librarian, University of California, Berkeley.
Subject Editor: Native American Studies.

Sharon Black, Librarian, Annenberg School for Communication, University of Pennsylvania.
Bibliographer: Journalism and Communication.

Steve Blackburn, Library Director, Hartford Seminary.
Referee.

Robert Bland, Associate University Librarian Automation and Technical Services, University of North Carolina, Asheville.
Bibliographer: Philosophy.

Richard Bleiler, Humanities Bibliographer, University of Connecticut.
Bibliographer: General Language and Literature.

Laurel Blewett, Manager of Library Services, Edward Hospital.
Referee.

Christopher Bloss, Instructional Services Librarian, University of South Dakota.
Bibliographer: American Literature.

Ellen Bosman, Head of Technical Services, New Mexico State University.
Subject Editor: GLBT Studies.

Jesús Bottaro, Instructor, CUNY / Medgar Evers College.
Bibliographer: Spanish Language and Literature.

Steven Botterill, Professor of Italian, University of California, Berkeley.
Referee.

Sally Bowdoin, Head of Serials, Brooklyn College.
Subject Editor: British Literature.

Linda Bowles-Adarkwa, Subject Specialist, Black Studies and Women Studies, San Francisco State University.
Bibliographer: African American Studies.

James Boxall, Director, GIS Centre, Dalhousie University.
Subject Editor: Geography.

James Bracken, Assistant Director for Main Library Research and Reference Services, Ohio State University.
Subject Editor: Other Literatures in English.

Laura Braunstein, Research and Reference Services, Dartmouth University.
Bibliographer: General Language and Literature.

Tony Bremholm, Life Sciences Librarian, Texas A&M University.
Referee.

Karl Bridges, Coordinator of Electronic Instruction Resources, University of Vermont.
Bibliographer: U.S. and Canadian History.

JoEllen Broome, Reference Specialist, Georgia Southern University.
Subject Editor: Environmental Studies.

Mitchell Brown, Research Librarian for Chemistry and Earth System Sciences, University of California, Irvine.
Referee.

Mary Jane Brustman, Bibliographer for Social Welfare and Criminal Justice, SUNY Albany.
Subject Editor: Criminal Justice.

Mark Bullock, Graduate Student, History Department, University of Illinois at Chicago.
Bibliographer: European History.

Merry Burlingham, Chief Bibliographer and Collections Officer, University of Texas.
Bibliographer: Asian History, Languages, and Literatures.

Angela Cannon, Reference Librarian, Library of Congress.
Bibliographer: Russian Languages and Literatures.

Karen Cary, Head, Collection Management, Virginia Commonwealth University.
Bibliographer: Sociology.

Melissa Cast, Reference Librarian and Subject Specialist for Education, University of Nebraska Omaha.
Bibliographer: Education.

Rafaela Castro, Bibliographer, University of California, Davis.
Subject Editor: Latino Studies.

Tina Ching, Reference Librarian, Arizona State University.
Referee.

Diana Chlebek, English and Modern Languages and Literature Bibliographer, University of Akron.
Bibliographer: French Language and Literature.

Michael Chromey, Humanities Librarian, Atlanta University Center.
Bibliographer: African American Studies.

Hui Hua Chua, US Documents Librarian, Michigan State University.
Bibliographer: Journalism and Communication.

Alan Church, Professor of English, University of Texas at Brownsville.
Referee.

Janet Clarke, Asian American Studies Selector, Stony Brook University.
Bibliographer: Asian American Studies.

Kim Clarke, Assistant Librarian, Selector for Women's Studies, University of Minnesota, Twin Cities.
Subject Editor: Gender Studies.

Rudolph Clay, Subject Librarian, African and African-American Studies, Washington University.
Bibliographer: African American Studies.

Ana Maria Cobos, Library Department Chair, Saddleback College.
Subject Editor: Latino Studies.

Francesca Colecchia, Professor of Spanish, Duquesne University.
Referee.

Gerardo Colmenar, Associate Librarian, Asian American Studies, University of California, Santa Barbara.
Subject Editor: Asian American Studies.

Mark Connell, Director, Center for Advancement of Technology in Education, SUNY College at Cortland.
Referee.

Paul Connors, Research Analyst, Michigan Legislative Service Bureau.
Bibliographer: U.S. and Canadian History.

Miriam Conteh-Morgan, Collection Manager for African Studies, Ohio State University.
Bibliographer: African American Studies.

Kate Corby, Education and Psychology Bibliographer, Michigan State University.
Subject Editor: Education.

Ronald Cormier, Professor of French, Longwood College.
Referee.

Alice Crosetto, Acquisitions Librarian, University of Toledo.
Bibliographer: British Literature.

Cynthia Crosser, Social Sciences and Humanities Librarian, University of Maine.
Bibliographer: Education.

Gwyneth Crowley, Coordinator of Collection Development, Social Science Libraries, Yale University.
Subject Editor: Economics.

Alice Daugherty, Reference Librarian, Louisiana State University.
Bibliographer: American Literature.

Stephanie Davis, Librarian, Spring Arbor University.
Bibliographer: Education.

Judith de Luce, Professor of Classics, Miami University of Ohio.
Referee.

Kathy Dean, Humanities Bibliographer, Ohio State University.
Bibliographer: Other Literatures in English.

Louise Deis, Science & Technology Reference Librarian, Princeton University.
Subject Editor: Environmental Sciences; General Science.

JoAnn DeVries, Associate Librarian, Reference/Bibliographer, University of Minnesota.
Bibliographer: Agriculture.

Jan Dixon, Reference Librarian, University of Arkansas.
Bibliographer: Geology.

Deborah Dolan, Social Science Librarian, Hofstra University.
Bibliographer: Psychology.

Travis Dolence, Instruction Librarian, Minnesota State University Moorhead.
Referee.

Michael Doorley, Associate Lecturer in Humanities, American College, Dublin.
Bibliographer: European History.

Judith Douville, Visual Arts, Science and Technology Editor, CHOICE.
Subject Editor: Chemistry.

Bill Drew, Associate Librarian, Systems and Reference, SUNY – Morrisville.
Referee.

Heather Dubnick, Field Bibliographer, Modern Language Assoc.
Subject Editor: Spanish Language and Literature.

Dana Dunn, Professor of Psychology, Moravian College.
Referee.

Lisa Dunn, Head of Reference, Colorado School of Mines.
Bibliographer: Geology.

Karin Durán, Teacher Curriculum Center Librarian, California State University Northridge.
Bibliographer: Latino Studies.

David Eastman, Doctoral Candidate, Department of Religious Studies, Yale University.
Bibliographer: Religion.

Mary Edsall, Professor of Library and Information Science, Catholic University of America.
Subject Editor: Dance.

Marcus Elmore, CHOICE.
Subject Editor: General Language and Literature.

Robert Elsie, Independent scholar.
Bibliographer: European History.

Kimberly Embelton, Literature and Languages Librarian, California State University Northridge.
Bibliographer: British Literature.

Michael Emery, Professor of English, Cottey College.
Bibliographer: GLBT Studies.

Mark Emmons, Head, Instruction Services, University of New Mexico.
Subject Editor: Film.

Carlene Engstrom, Director, D'Arcy McNickle Library, Salish Kootenai College.
Bibliographer: Native American Studies.

Pam Enrici, Associate Librarian, University of Maryland.
Bibliographer: Technology and Engineering.

Robert Entenmann, Professor of History, St. Olaf College.
Referee.

Isabel Espinal, Librarian for Afro American Studies, Anthropology, Native American Indian Studies, University of Massachussetts.
Bibliographer: African American Studies.

James Allan Evans, Professor Emeritus of Classical Near Eastern and Religious Studies, University of British Columbia.
Bibliographer: European History.

Angel Falcon, Harvard University, formerly.
Bibliographer: African American Studies.

David Feldman, Professor of Mathematics, University of New Hampshire.
Referee.

Robert Fernekes, Information Services Librarian, Business Specialist, Georgia Southern University.
Bibliographer: Business Administration.

Anne Fields, OSU Libraries Coordinator for Research and Reference, Ohio State University.
Bibliographer: Education.

Jenifer Flaxbart, Head Librarian, Reference and Information Services, University of Texas, Austin.
Bibliographer: Journalism and Communication.

Adonna Fleming, GIS / Maps Librarian, University of Nebraska – Lincoln.
Bibliographer: Geology.

Nicole Fluhr, Professor of English, Southern Connecticut State University.
Referee.

Michael Fosmire, Science Librarian, Purdue University.
Subject Editor: Physics.

Stephen Foster, University Librarian, Wright State University.
Referee.

Gerri Foudy, Government and Politics, Public Affairs, and Law Librarian, University of Maryland.
Bibliographer: Political Science.

Kathleen Fountain, Political Science and Social Work Librarian, California State University, Chico.
Bibliographer: Political Science.

Kristine Fowler, Mathematics Librarian, University of Minnesota, Twin Cities.
Subject Editor: Mathematics.

Stephen Fowlkes, Bibliographer for Sociology, Social Work and Reference, Tulane University.
Bibliographer: Sociology.

Ann Fox, Professor of English, Davidson College.
Referee.

Joe Fugate, Professor of German, Kalamazoo College.
Referee.

Steve Fullwood, Manuscripts Librarian, Schomburg Center for Research in Black Culture, New York Public Library.
Bibliographer: African American Studies.

Ronald Ganze, Professor of English, Valparaiso University.
Bibliographer: Medieval Studies.

Bill Gargan, Reference Librarian and Bibliographer, Brooklyn College.
Bibliographer: British Literature.

Meryle Gaston, Islamic and Middle Eastern Studies Librarian, University of California, Santa Barbara.
Subject Editor: Middle Eastern History, Languages, and Literatures.

Cameron Gearen, Lecturer in English, Yale University.
Bibliographer: General Language and Literature.

Caroline Geck, Librarian, Kean University.
Referee.

Jennifer Geddes, Research Associate Professor of Religious Studies, University of Virginia.
Bibliographer: General Language and Literature.

Mary Gilles, Business Reference Librarian, Washington State University.
Subject Editor: Law.

David Giovacchini, Arabic Librarian, Middle East Collection, Stanford University.
Referee.

Ed Goedeken, Humanities Bibliographer, Iowa State University.
Subject Editor: U.S. and Canadian History.

Melissa Goldsmith, Lecturer, Louisiana State University.
Referee.

Millie Gonzalez, Reference Librarian, Framingham State College.
Bibliographer: Business Administration.

Olympia Gonzalez, Professor of Spanish, Loyola University of Chicago.
Referee.

David Goodman, Professor of Library and Information Science, Long Island University.
Subject Editor: Biology.

Candice Goucher, Professor of History, Washington State University, Vancouver.
Referee.

Malaika Grant, Reference/Instruction Librarian, University of Minnesota, Twin Cities.
Bibliographer: Gender Studies.

Laura Graves, Professor of History, South Plains College.
Bibliographer: Native American Studies.

Chip Green, Professor of Geology, University of South Carolina Upstate.
Referee.

Susan Green, Professor of History, California State University, Chico.
Referee.

Cheryl Grossman, Electronic Services Supervisor, LearningWork Connection, Ohio State University.
Bibliographer: Education.

Anna Marie Guengerich, Librarian, College of Education, University of Iowa.
Bibliographer: Psychology.

Richard Hacken, European Studies Bibliographer, Brigham Young University.
Referee.

Michael Handis, Associate Librarian for Collection Management, CUNY Graduate Center.
Bibliographer: European History.

Shaun Hardy, Librarian, Carnegie Institution of Washington.
Bibliographer: Geology.

Sara Harrington, Art Librarian, Rutgers University.
Referee.

Jon Harrison, Social Sciences Collections Coordinator, Missouri State University.
Bibliographer: Criminal Justice.

Elizabeth Hartung, Professor of Sociology, California Sate University Channel Islands.
Bibliographer: Sociology.

Laurence Hauptman, Professor of History, SUNY New Paltz.
Bibliographer: Native American Studies.

Peter Hayes, Professor of History, Northwestern University.
Bibliographer: European History.

Charles Hayford, Research Fellow, Department of History, Northwestern University.
Subject Editor: Asian History, Languages, and Literatures.

Jeremy Hein, Professor of Sociology, University of Wisconsin – Eau Claire.
Referee.

Eileen Herring, Agriculture Librarian, University of Hawaii.
Bibliographer: Agriculture.

Martin Hewitt, Head of History Department, Trinity and All Saints College, University of Leeds.
Referee.

Terry Hill, Customer Representative for North America, OTTO HARRASSOWITZ GmbH & Co. KG.
Bibliographer: Political Science.

Baraba Hillson, Public and International Affairs and Psychology Liaison Librarian, George Mason University.
Referee.

Lee Hilyer, Mathematics Subject Librarian, University of Houston.
Bibliographer: Education.

Keith Hitchins, Professor of History, University of Illinois.
Bibliographer: European History.

Adrian Ho, Assistant Librarian, University of Houston.
Bibliographer: Journalism and Communication.

David Hogg, Astronomer, National Radio Astronomy Observatory.
Referee.

Jane Holmquist, Astrophysics Librarian, Princeton University.
Subject Editor: Astronomy.

Emily Horning, Librarian for Philosophy, Religious Studies and Anthropology, Yale University.
Subject Editor: Religion.

John Hunter, Science/Engineering Librarian, Rice University.
Bibliographer: Geology.

Carol Hutchins, Head Librarian, Courant Institute of Mathematical Sciences, New York University.
Subject Editor: Computing.

Robin Imhof, Reference Librarian, University of the Pacific.
Bibliographer: GLBT Studies.

Richard Irving, Associate Librarian, SUNY Albany.
Bibliographer: Criminal Justice.

Kristin Jacobi, Head, Catologing Department, Eastern Connecticut State University.
Bibliographer: Native American Studies.

James Jaffe, Professor of History, University of Wisconsin – Whitewater.
Bibliographer: European History.

Arif Jamal, Social Sciences Bibliographer, University of Pittsburgh.
Bibliographer: African American Studies.

Sylvia James, Sylvia James Consultancy.
Bibliographer: Business Administration.

Fred Jenkins, Head of Collection Management, University of Dayton.
Subject Editor: Ancient History; Classics.

Donald Clay Johnson, Curator, Ames Library of South Asia, University of Minnesota.
Bibliographer: Asian History, Languages, and Literatures.

Melissa Johnson, Reference and Instruction Librarian, Lynn University.
Bibliographer: European History.

Sarah Johnson, Librarian, Eastern Illinois University.
Bibliographer: General Language and Literature.

Lisa Johnston, Head of Public Services, Sweet Briar College.
Bibliographer: British Literature.

Scott Johnston, Librarian, CUNY Graduate Center.
Subject Editor: Urban Studies.

David P. Jordan, Professor of History, University of Illinois at Chicago.
Bibliographer: European History.

Jonathan Judaken, Professor of History, University of Memphis.
Bibliographer: European History.

Jeannie Kamerman, Director, Curriculum Materials Library, University of West Florida.
Bibliographer: Education.

James Kelly, Humanities Bibliographer, University of Massachussetts.
Subject Editor: American Literature.

Marcia Keyser, Instruction and Reference Librarian, Drake University.
Bibliographer: Education.

Shayee Khanaka, Librarian, Middle Eastern Collection, University of California Berkeley.
Bibliographer: Middle Eastern History, Languages, and Literatures.

Sherise Kimura, Reference Librarian, University of San Francisco.
Bibliographer: Asian American Studies.

Douglas King, Librarian, University of South Carolina.
Bibliographer: American Literature.

Laura Kinner, Coordinator, Cataloging Services, University of Toledo.
Bibliographer: British Literature.

Harold Kirkwood, Librarian, Purdue University.
Bibliographer: Business Administration.

Patricia Kirkwood, Science Librarian, University of Arkansas.
Bibliographer: Technology and Engineering.

Sheila Kirven, Education Services Librarian, New Jersey City University.
Bibliographer: Education.

Linda Klein, Reference Librarian, Eastern Kentucky University.
Bibliographer: British Literature.

Michael Knee, Science Bibliographer and Reference Librarian, University of Albany.
Bibliographer: Computing.

Norma Kobzina, Head of Information Services, Marian Koshland Bioscience and Natural Resources Library, University of California, Berkeley.
Subject Editor: Agriculture.

David Koenigstein, Librarian, Brooklyn College.
Bibliographer: British Literature.

Gayla Koerting, Special Collections Librarian, University of South Dakota.
Bibliographer: U.S. and Canadian History.

Laura Koltutsky, Information Services Librarian, University of Houston.
Bibliographer: Education.

Kwasi Konadu, Professor of History, Winston Salem State University.
Bibliographer: African History, Languages, and Literatures.

Svetlana Korolev, Science Librarian, University of Wisconsin, Madison.
Referee.

Wade Kotter, Social Sciences Librarian, Weber State University.
Bibliographer: Criminal Justice.

Joe Kraus, Science Librarian, University of Denver.
Referee.

Eiko Kuwana, Professor of History, University of the Sacred Heart, Tokyo.
Bibliographer: European History.

Sharon Ladenson, Gender Studies and Communications Bibliographer, Michigan State University.
Bibliographer: Journalism and Communication.

Carolyn Laffoon, Earth and Atmospheric Sciences Librarian, Purdue University.
Bibliographer: Geology.

Blake Landor, Bibliographer for Philosophy, Classics, and Religion, University of Florida.
Subject Editor: Philosophy.

Jeffry Larson, Librarian for Romance Languages and Literatures, Linguistics, and Classics, Yale University.
Subject Editor: French Language and Literature; Italian Language and Literature.

Jason E. Lavery, Professor of History, Oklahoma State University.
Bibliographer: European History.

Bernadette Lear, Behavioral Sciences and Education Librarian, Pennsylvania State University.
Bibliographer: Psychology.

Patrick Leary, Research Fellow, Department of History, Northwestern University.
Subject Editor: Victorian Studies.

Richard S. Levy, Professor of History, University of Illinois at Chicago.
Bibliographer: European History.

Kevin Lindstrom, Behavioral Sciences and Education Librarian, University of British Columbia.
Bibliographer: Geology.

Ken Liss, Communication Librarian, Boston College.
Bibliographer: Journalism and Communication.

Carol Loranger, Professor of English, Wright State University.
Referee.

Jack Lynch, Professor of English, Rutgers University.
Bibliographer: British Literature.

Karen MacDonald, Business Subject Specialist Librarian, Texas A&M University.
Bibliographer: Business Administration.

Peter Magierski, Librarian for the Middle East Studies, New York University.
Bibliographer: Middle Eastern History, Languages, and Literatures.

Diane Maher, University Archivist, University of San Diego.
Bibliographer: American Literature; British Literature.

Janice Mathews, Librarian for Urban Studies and Social Work, University of Connecticut.
Referee.

Rhonda McGinnis, Business and Economics Librarian, Wayne State University.
Bibliographer: Business Administration.

Glenn McGuigan, Business Reference Librarian, Penn State University.
Subject Editor: Business Administration.

Peter McKay, Business Librarian, University of Florida.
Bibliographer: Business Administration.

Paula McMillen, Social Sciences Librarian, Oregon State University.
Bibliographer: Education.

Lori Mestre, Digital Learning Librarian, University of Illinois.
Bibliographer: Education.

Sue Metcalf, Social Sciences Librarian, New Mexico State University.
Referee.

Marion Miller, Professor of History, University of Illinois at Chicago, emerita.
Bibliographer: European History.

Lisa Mitten, CHOICE.
Subject Editor: Native American Studies.

Sandy Mooney, Design Librarian, Louisiana State University.
Referee.

Fred Muratori, Bibliographer for Anglo-American and Comparative Literature and Film, Cornell University.
Bibliographer: Drama and Theater.

Paula Murphy, Library Consultant.
Referee.

Linda Musser, Head, Fletcher L. Byrom Earth and Mineral Sciences Library, Pennsylvania State University.
Bibliographer: Geology.

Theodore Natsoulas, Professor of History, University of Toledo.
Bibliographer: European History.

Sharon Naylor, Education, Psychology and TMC Division Head, Illinois State University.
Bibliographer: Education.

Antoinette Nelson, Branch Manager, Science and Engineering Library, University of Texas Arlington.
Subject Editor: Technology and Engineering.

Jan Newberry, Professor of Anthropology, University of Lethbridge.
Referee.

Shawn Nicholson, Bibliographer for Sociology, Social Work, Urban Planning, Michigan State University.
Referee.

Jim Niessen, World History Librarian, Rutgers University.
Bibliographer: European History.

Byron Nordstrom, Professor of History, Gustavus Adolphus University.
Bibliographer: European History.

Akilah Nosakhere, Manager, Reference and Research Division, Auburn Avenue Research Library of African American Culture and History.
Subject Editor: African American Studies.

Nancy O'Brien, Head, Education and Social Science Library, University of Illinois.
Subject Editor: Education.

Darby Orcutt, Collection Manager for the Humanities and Data Analysis, North Carolina State University.
Bibliographer: Journalism and Communication.

Harriet Ottenheimer, Professor of Anthropology, Kansas State University.
Bibliographer: Anthropology.

Mark Padnos, Coordinator of Public Services, Bronx Community College.
Subject Editor: Germanic Languages and Literatures.

John Page, Associate Dean, Learning Resources Division, University of the District of Columbia.
Bibliographer: African American Studies.

Tim Parrish, Professor of English, Southern Connecticut State University.
Bibliographer: General Language and Literature.

Lucy Patrick, Head of Special Collections, Florida State University.
Referee.

Christopher Peebles, Associate Vice President for Information Technology and Professor of Anthropology, Indiana University.
Bibliographer: Anthropology.

Ed Peters, Professor of History, University of Pennsylvania.
Bibliographer: European History.

Carmelita Pickett, African American Studies Librarian, Emory University.
Bibliographer: African American Studies.

Lisa Pillow, Collection Development Librarian, University of Wisconsin – River Falls.
Bibliographer: African American Studies.

Chestalene Pintozzi, Science-Engineering Librarian, University of Arizona.
Bibliographer: Geology.

Don Polzella, Professor of Psychology and Associate Dean for Faculty Development and Graduate Programs, University of Dayton.
Subject Editor: Psychology.

Diethelm Prowe, Professor of History, Carleton College.
Bibliographer: European History.

Eleanor Randall, Reference Librarian, Edinboro University of Pennsylvania.
Bibliographer: Biology.

Brenda Reed, Public Services Librarian, Education Library, Queen's University.
Bibliographer: Education.

Ira Revels, Instruction Librarian, Cornell University.
Bibliographer: African American Studies.

Leslie Reynolds, Director of Policy Sciences and Economics Library, Texas A&M University.
Bibliographer: Business Administration.

Amy Robb, Field Librarian for Women's Studies and Communication, University of Michigan.
Bibliographer: Journalism and Communication.

Gloria Roberson, Reference Librarian, Adelphi University.
Bibliographer: African American Studies.

Beth Roberts, Earth and Mineral Sciences Librarian, Pennsylvania State University.
Bibliographer: Geology.

Elizabeth Robertson, Professor of English, University of Colorado.
Bibliographer: British Literature.

Martin Roden, Professor emeritus of Engineering, UCLA.
Bibliographer: Technology and Engineering.

Raquel Rodriguez, Librarian for the African American Collection, University of Pittsburgh.
Bibliographer: African American Studies.

Lisa Romero, Communications Librarian, University of Illinois.
Subject Editor: Journalism and Communication.

Lana Kay Rosenberg, Director, Dance Theatre, Miami University of Ohio.
Referee.

Tony Rosso, Professor of English, Southern Connecticut State University.
Bibliographer: British Literature.

Dana Roth, Chemistry Librarian, Caltech.
Bibliographer: Chemistry.

Linda Salem, Education Librarian, San Diego State University.
Bibliographer: British Literature.

Mark Sanders, Student Outreach Reference Librarian, East Carolina University.
Bibliographer: Environmental Studies.

Rachel Sandoval, Historical Records Project Archivist, University of California, Irvine.
Bibliographer: Latino Studies.

Victoria Santana, Electronic Services Librarian, Oklahoma City University.
Bibliographer: Native American Studies.

Román Santillán, Reference/Instruction Librarian, CUNY / College of Staten Island.
Bibliographer: Spanish Language and Literature.

Vernon Schlotzhauer, Social Science Librarian, Pennsylvania State University.
Bibliographer: Psychology.

Geoff Schmidt, Professor of English, Illinois State University – Edwardsville.
Bibliographer: General Language and Literature.

Alan Schroeder, Business Librarian, California State University Northridge.
Bibliographer: Business Administration.

Kate Schroeder, Doctoral Candidate, History Department, Indiana University.
Subject Editor: African History, Languages, and Literatures.

Friedrich Schuler, Professor of History, Portland State University.
Subject Editor: Latin American History.

Katrin Schultheiss, Professor of History, University of Illinois at Chicago.
Bibliographer: European History.

Jason Schultz, Communications Librarian, Georgia State University.
Bibliographer: African American Studies.

Catherine Shreve, Librarian for Public Policy and Political Science, Duke University.
Subject Editor: Political Science.

Jack Shreve, Professor of English, Allegany College.
Bibliographer: GLBT Studies.

Adam Siegel, Reference Librarian, University of California, Davis.
Bibliographer: Native American Studies.

Dorothy Siles, Librarian, Taylorville Public Library.
Bibliographer: Native American Studies.

Jane Sloan, Media Librarian, Rutgers University.
Subject Editor: Film.

Becky Smith, Head, Business and Economics Library, University of Illinois.
Bibliographer: Business Administration.

Helen Smith, Life Sciences Librarian, Penn State University.
Bibliographer: Agriculture.

Michael Smith, Business Librarian, Texas A&M University.
Bibliographer: Business Administration.

Jacqueline Snider, Librarian, ACT.
Bibliographer: Education.

Doug Southard, DRA International.
Bibliographer: Business Administration.

Roland Spickermann, Professor of History, University of Texas, Permian Basin.
Bibliographer: European History.

Jill Spreitzer, Assistant Librarian, Public Services, University of Detroit Mercy.
Bibliographer: Technology and Engineering.

Jennifer Stevens, Humanities Liaison Librarian, George Mason University.
Bibliographer: Other Literatures in English.

David Stoloff, Professor of Education, Eastern Connecticut State University.
Referee.

Fred Stoss, Biological Science Librarian, SUNY Buffalo.
Subject Editor: Biology.

Stephen Stratton, Head of Collection Development, California State University, Channel Islands.
Subject Editor: Sociology.

Cindy Stretch, Professor of English, Southern Connecticut State University.
Referee.

Leanne Strum, Library Liaison to the School of Business, Regent University.
Bibliographer: Business Administration.

Mila Su, Coordinator of Reference Services, Pennsylvania State University.
Subject Editor: Sport and Recreation.

Helen Sullivan, Head, Slavic Reference Service, University of Illinois.
Subject Editor: Russian Languages and Literatures.

Sarah Sussman, Curator, French and Italian Collections, Stanford University.
Bibliographer: European History.

Marek Suszko, Professor of History, Purdue University North Central.
Bibliographer: European History.

Laura Taddeo, Reference Librarian, SUNY Buffalo.
Bibliographer: British Literature.

Kornelia Tancheva, Director of Instructional Services, Cornell University.
Subject Editor: Drama and Theater.

Wendy Tann, Librarian, Federal Reserve Bank.
Bibliographer: Business Administration.

Cornelia Akins Taylor, Special Collections Librarian, Florida A & M University.
Bibliographer: African American Studies.

Betty Taylor-Thompson, Professor of English, Texas Southern University.
Referee.

Edward Teague, Head, Architecture & Allied Arts Library, University of Oregon.
Subject Editor: Visual Arts.

Samantha Teplitzky, Earth Sciences Librarian and Bibliographer, Stanford University.
Bibliographer: Geology.

Stephen Thompson, Co-Leader, Technical Services Department, Brown University.
Bibliographer: American Literature.

Erik Thomson, Collegiate Assistant Professor, Social Sciences, University of Chicago.
Bibliographer: European History.

Charles Thurston, Reference Librarian and Bibliographer, University of Texas at San Antonio.
Bibliographer: Education.

Judie Triplehorn, Librarian, Geophysical Institute, University of Alaska.
Bibliographer: Geology.

Markel Tumlin, English and American Literature Librarian, San Diego State University.
Bibliographer: American Literature.

Andrea Twiss-Brooks, Bibliographer for Chemical and Geophysical Sciences, University of Chicago.
Subject Editor: Geology.

Kent Underwood, Music Librarian, New York University.
Subject Editor: Music.

Alan Unsworth, Reference Librarian, University of Rochester.
Referee.

David Vaccari, Professor of Engineering, Stevens Institute of Technology.
Bibliographer: Technology and Engineering.

Susan Vega Garcia, Reference & Instruction Librarian, Bibliographer, Iowa State University.
Bibliographer: Latino Studies.

Tom Volkening, Engineering Librarian, Michigan State University.
Bibliographer: Technology and Engineering.

Heather Ward, University of Oregon, formerly.
Subject Editor: Medieval Studies.

Diane Warner, Monographs and Special Formats Cataloger, Texas Tech University.
Bibliographer: American Literature.

Gary Wasdin, Library Director, New School University.
Referee.

Matthew Wayman, Instruction Coordinator, Penn State University.
Bibliographer: U.S. and Canadian History.

Jeneen Willemssen, Librarian, Conserve School.
Bibliographer: Education.

Wendy Williamson, Economics Librarian, University of Minnesota.
Referee.

Suzanne Wise, Collection Development Librarian, Appalachia State University.
Referee.

Ada Woods, Reference Librarian, Towson University.
Bibliographer.

Peng Xu, Reference Librarian, Michigan State University.
Bibliographer: Business Administration.

Lisa Yuro, Reference Librarian/Humanities and Social Sciences Coordinator, University of Alabama.
Bibliographer: Journalism and Communication.

Ann Zawistoski, Reference and Instruction Librarian, Carleton College.
Bibliographer: Geology.

Linda Zellmer, Head, Geology Library, Indiana University.
Subject Editor: Geology.

HOW TO USE
RESOURCES FOR COLLEGE LIBRARIES

Resources for College Libraries (RCL) was designed to be easily searchable by author, title, and the RCL subject taxonomy. The set consists of seven volumes, Volumes 1-6 arranged by RCL Subject, and sorted alphabetically by author. Volume 7 is a comprehensive author, title and subject index. The volumes are arranged by *Resources for College Library* Subject Headings, a full listing of which is present in the Subject Headings Index in volume 7.

Each title in *Resources for College Libraries* has been classified with a specific RCL Subject and/or subjects. Titles can and often do appear within more than one RCL Subject area. Titles have been given a specific readership level through audience code: g=general, l=lower-division undergraduate, u=upper-division undergraduate graduate, and/or f=faculty level resources. Titles previously mentioned in *Books for College Libraries, 3rd Edition*, have been noted with a specific BCL3 icon B. Non-book entries can be easily identified with the icons for Web, Ebook, or CD/DVD-ROM.

Classification Number, Dewey Decimal Number, Library of Congress Control Number, Audience Code, and whether it has been reviewed in Choice Magazine.

Entries in the Author Index can include the following bibliographic information when available: author, co-author, editor, co-editor, translator, co-translator, along with page number(s) and volume number(s) of the selected works within the 6-volume set. Entries are not cross-referenced by other than primary author and/or first contributor. Entries in the Title Index include the title, page number(s) and volume number(s) of the selected works within the 6-volume set.

Titles in *Resources for College Libraries* have been alphabetized using the following rules:

- Initial articles of titles in English, French, German, Italian, and Spanish are not included for sorting purposes.
- Titles beginning with acronyms appear before those beginning with words. For example, B E A M A Directory would precede Baal, Babylon.
- As a general rule, U.S. and UN are filed in strict alphabetical order.

SAMPLE RCL ENTRY

1 DRAMA AND THEATER > Western Drama > United States

2 **Wilmeth, Don B. & Bigsby, Christopher (Editors)** **PN2221**
3 The Cambridge History of American Theater: 4 1870-1945. 5 Ed. 2
6 Don B. Wilmeth & Christopher Bigsby (Contribution by). 7 Trade Paper.
8 Cambridge University Press. 9 New York, NY. 10 2006. 11 608p.
12 Cambridge History of American Theater Ser. 13 ISBN: 0-521-67984-2, ISBN13: 978-0-521-67984-8. 14 Dewey:792/.0973.
15 LCCN: 00-000000
16 Audience: l,u,f. 17 *Choice, 2005* B

1. RCL Subject Heading
2. Author/First Contributor
3. Title
4. Subtitle
5. Ed. Info
6. Additional Contributors
7. Binding Type
8. Publisher
9. Publisher Location
10. Publication Date
11. Number of Pages
12. Series Title
13. ISBN, ISBN-13
14. Dewey
15. LCCN
16. Audience Code
17. Choice Review and Date

Title entries can include the following bibliographic information, when available: author, co-author, editor, co-editor, translator, co-translator, title, number of volumes, edition, series information, binding type, publisher, publisher location, date of publication, number of pages, ISBN, ISBN-13, Library of Congress

- Numeric Titles may be found near the end of the Title Index

Authors in *Resources for College Libraries* have been alphabetized using the following rules:

- Proper names beginning with "Mc" and "Mac" are filed in strict alphabetical order. For example, entries for contributors' names such as MacAdam, MacAvory, and MacCarthy are located prior to the pages with entries for names such as McAdam, McCoy, and McDermott.
- When author names are represented with initials, they are alphabetized before author first names. For example, Smith, H. C. appears before Smith, Harold A.

Any errors in bibliographic data should be E-mailed directly to: rclwebfeedback@bowker.com

ABBREVIATIONS AND CODE LIST:

BCL3	*Books for College Libraries, 3rd Edition*
Bk.(s.)	Book(s)
Ed.	Edition
F	Faculty
G	General
Inc.	Incorporated
Jr.	Junior
ISBN	International Standard Book Number
L	Lower-Division Undergraduate
LCCN	Library of Congress Control Number
p.	Pages
RCL	Resources for College Libraries
Ser.	Series
Sr.	Senior
U	Upper-Division Undergraduate

Geographical Abbreviations

AL	Alabama
AK	Alaska
AB	Alberta
AE	American Europe
AS	American Samoa
AZ	Arizona
AR	Arkansas
ACT	Australian Capital Territory
BC	British Columbia
CA	California
CM	Central Marianas
CO	Colorado
CT	Connecticut
DE	Delaware
DC	District Of Columbia
FM	Federated States Of Micronesia
FL	Florida
GA	Georgia
GU	Guam
HI	Hawaii
ID	Idaho
IL	Illinois
IN	Indiana
IA	Iowa
KS	Kansas
KY	Kentucky
LA	Louisiana
ME	Maine
MB	Manitoba
MH	Marshall Islands
MD	Maryland
MA	Massachusetts
MI	Michigan
MP	Middle Pacific
MN	Minnesota
MS	Mississippi
MO	Missouri
MT	Montana
NE	Nebraska
NV	Nevada
NB	New Brunswick
NH	New Hampshire
NJ	New Jersey
NM	New Mexico
NSW	New South Wales
NY	New York
NF	Newfoundland
NC	North Carolina
ND	North Dakota
NP	Northern Marianas
N.T.	Northern Territory (Australia)
NT	Northwest Territory
NS	Nova Scotia
NU	Nunavut
OH	Ohio
OK	Oklahoma
ON	Ontario
OR	Oregon
TT	Pacific Territories
PW	Pacific West
PA	Pennsylvania
PE	Prince Edward Island
PR	Puerto Rico
PQ	Quebec
QLD	Queensland
RI	Rhode Island
SK	Saskatchewan
SA	South Australia
SC	South Carolina
SD	South Dakota
TAS	Tasmania
TN	Tennessee
TX	Texas
UT	Utah
VT	Vermont
VIC	Victoria
VI	Virgin Islands
VA	Virginia
WA	Washington
WV	West Virginia
W.A.	Western Australia
WI	Wisconsin
WY	Wyoming
YT	Yukon Territory

ANCIENT HISTORY

This section covers the history of the ancient Near East (Mesopotamia, the Hittites, ancient Palestine, Persia, and Egypt), Greece, and Rome. The reference and general works sections cover general histories, encyclopedias, bibliographies, and the like covering more than one ancient civilization. The major civilization of the ancient Mediterranean and Near East are covered geographically in order of their rise to prominence. Egypt, Greece, and Rome are subdivided by topic and period. "Sources" sections under Greece and Rome include both general discussions of primary source materials and collections of them. Works of the Greek and Roman historical writers may be found in the author listings under Classics.

— Fred Jenkins

General and Reference Works

G1033

☐ Ancient World Mapping Center.
http://www.unc.edu/awmc/

Audience: **g,l,u,f.**

HQ1127

☐ Diotima: Materials for the Study of Women and Gender in the Ancient World.
http://www.stoa.org/diotima/

Audience: **g,l,u,f.**

Bickerman, Elias J. **D54.5 .B5 1980**
Chronology of the Ancient World. Ed. 2. Trade Cloth. Cornell University Press. Ithaca, NY. 1980. 260p. Aspects of Greek and Roman Life Ser. ISBN:0-8014-1282-X, ISBN13: 978-0-8014-1282-0. Dewey:529/.32. LCCN:78-058899.
Audience: **f.**

Boardman, John (Editor), et al. **DE59.O94 1986**
The Oxford History of the Classical World. Jasper Griffin & Oswyn Murray (Editors). Trade Cloth. Oxford University Press, Inc. New York, NY. 1986. 892p. ISBN:0-19-872112-9, ISBN13: 978-0-19-872112-3. Dewey:937. LCCN:85-021774.
Audience: **g,l,u,f.** B *Choice, 1987.*

Bowman, Alan K. & Woolf, Greg (Editors) **LC149.L4958 1996**
Literacy and Power in the Ancient World. Trade Paper. Cambridge University Press. New York, NY. 1996. 259p. ISBN:0-521-58736-0, ISBN13: 978-0-521-58736-5. Dewey:302.2/244/093.
Audience: **u,f.**

Braudel, Fernand **DE71.B6813 2001**
Mediterranean in the Ancient World. Trade Cloth. Penguin Group (USA) Inc. New York, NY. 2001. 416p. ISBN:0-7139-9331-6, ISBN13: 978-0-7139-9331-8. Dewey:930/.09822. LCCN:2001-431163.
Audience: **g,u,f.**

Braudel, Fernand **DE71.B6813 2001**
Memory and the Mediterranean. Roselyne de Ayala & Paule Braudel (Editors), Sian Reynolds (Translator). Trade Cloth. Alfred A. Knopf Inc. New York, NY. 2001. 400p. ISBN:0-375-40426-0, ISBN13: 978-0-375-40426-9. Dewey:930.091822. LCCN:2001-091011.
Audience: **g,u,f.** *Choice, 2002.*

Cambridge University Press Staff **D57**
The Cambridge Ancient History, Set. Ed. 2. Cloth Text. Cambridge University Press. New York, NY. 2005. 16552p. The Cambridge Ancient History Ser. ISBN:0-521-85073-8, ISBN13: 978-0-521-85073-5. Dewey:930.
Audience: **u,f.**

Casson, Lionel **VK16.C37 1991**
The Ancient Mariners: Seafarers and Sea Fighters of the Mediterranean in Ancient Times. Ed. 2. Trade Paper. Princeton University Press. Princeton, NJ. 1991. 299p. ISBN:0-691-01477-9, ISBN13: 978-0-691-01477-7. Dewey:387.5/093. LCCN:90-047717.
Audience: **g,u,f.** B

Casson, Lionel **Z722.C37 2001**
Libraries in the Ancient World. Cloth over Boards. Yale University Press. Cumberland, RI. 2001. 192p. ISBN:0-300-08809-4, ISBN13: 978-0-300-08809-0. Dewey:027/.03. LCCN:00-011668.
Audience: **g,u,f.**

Finley, M. I. **HC31.F5 1999**
Ancient Economy. Trade Paper. University of California Press. Berkeley, CA. 1999. 290p. Sather Classical Lectures, Vol. 48:No. 30 ISBN:0-520-21946-5, ISBN13: 978-0-520-21946-5. Dewey:330.938. LCCN:99-461792.
Audience: **u,f.**

Freeman, Charles **DE71**
Egypt, Greece and Rome: Civilizations of the Ancient Mediterranean. Ed. 2. Paper Text. Oxford University Press, Inc. New York, NY. 2004. 732p. ISBN:0-19-926364-7, ISBN13: 978-0-19-926364-6. Dewey:930/.09822. LCCN:2004-041505.
Audience: **g,l,u.**

Haywood, John **G141**
The Penguin Historical Atlas of Ancient Civilizations. Simon Hall (Editor). Trade Paper. Penguin Group (USA) Inc. New York, NY. 2005. 144p. ISBN:0-14-101448-2, ISBN13: 978-0-14-101448-7. Dewey:911.0901.
Audience: **g,l,u.**

Isaac, Benjamin H. **DF135.I82 2004**
The Invention of Racism in Classical Antiquity. Trade Cloth. Princeton University Press. Princeton, NJ. 2004. 592p. ISBN:0-691-11691-1, ISBN13: 978-0-691-11691-4. Dewey:320.5/6/0938. LCCN:2003-048610.
Audience: **f.** *Choice, 2004.*

Kitzinger, Rachel & Grant, Michael (Editors) **DE59.C55 1988**
Civilization of the Ancient Mediterranean: Greece and Rome, Set. Trade Cloth. Thomson Gale. Farmington Hills, MI. 1988. 1980p. Civilization of the Ancient Mediterranean Ser., Vol. 3 ISBN:0-684-17594-0, ISBN13: 978-0-684-17594-2. Dewey:938. LCCN:87-023465.
Audience: **g,l,u.** *Choice, 1989.*

McEvedy, Colin **G1033**
The New Penguin Atlas of Ancient History. Ed. 2. John Woodcock (Illustrator). Trade Paper. Penguin Group (USA) Inc. New York, NY. 2003. 128p. ISBN:0-14-051348-5, ISBN13: 978-0-14-051348-6. Dewey:911.
Audience: **g,l,u.**

Scarre, Christopher **D54.5**
Smithsonian Timelines of the Ancient World: A Visual Chronology from the Origins of Life to A. D. 1500. Trade Cloth. Dorling Kindersley Publishing, Inc. New York, NY. 1993. 256p. ISBN:1-56458-305-8, ISBN13: 978-1-56458-305-5. Dewey:930/.02/02. LCCN:93-018480.
Audience: **g,l,u.**

Snowden, Frank M. Jr. **GN496**
Before Color Prejudice: The Ancient View of Blacks. Trade Paper. Harvard University Press. Cambridge, MA. 1991. 176p. ISBN:0-674-06381-3, ISBN13: 978-0-674-06381-5. Dewey:305.8/96/03. LCCN:82-011852.
Audience: **g,u,f.**

Speake, Graham (Editor) **DE5.D53 1994**
A Dictionary of Ancient History. Trade Cloth. Blackwell

Publishing, Inc. Malden, MA. 1994. 768p. ISBN:0-631-18069-9, ISBN13: 978-0-631-18069-2. Dewey:930.03. LCCN:93-001437.
Audience: **g,l,u.**

Starr, Chester G. Jr. (Editor) **D59.S75 1991**
A History of the Ancient World. Ed. 4. Cloth Text. Oxford University Press, Inc. New York, NY. 1991. 800p. ISBN:0-19-506629-4, ISBN13: 978-0-19-506629-6. Dewey:930. LCCN:90-034970.
Audience: **g,l.**

Ancient Near East > General

DS62.2
ABZU: A Guide to Information Related to the Study of the Ancient Near East on the Web.
http://www.etana.org/abzu/
Jones, Charles E. (Editor).
Audience: **g,l,u,f.**

Aruz, Joan (Editor) **N5335**
Art of the First Cities: The Third Millennium B. C. from the Mediterranean to the Indus. Ronald Wallenfels (Contribution by). Cloth over Boards. Yale University Press. Cumberland, RI. 2003. 564p. Metropolitan Museum of Art Ser. ISBN:0-300-09883-9, ISBN13: 978-0-300-09883-9. Dewey:709.5/6/09013. LCCN:2003-044482.
Audience: **g,l,u,f.** *Choice, 2004.*

Bienkowski, Piotr **DS56.D5 2000**
Dictionary of the Ancient Near East. Book, Other. University of Pennsylvania Press. Philadelphia, PA. 2000. 352p. ISBN:0-8122-3557-6, ISBN13: 978-0-8122-3557-9. Dewey:939.4. LCCN:00-021715.
Audience: **g,l,u,f.** *Choice, 2000.*

Bryce, Trevor (Revised by) **DS62.23.B79 2003**
Letters of the Great Kings of the Ancient near East: The Royal Correspondence of the Late Bronze Age. Paper over Boards. Routledge. New York, NY. 2003. 272p. ISBN:0-415-25857-X, ISBN13: 978-0-415-25857-9. Dewey:935/.02. LCCN:2003-009879.
Audience: **u,f.**

Chavalas, Mark W. & Younger, K. Lawson Jr. (Editors) **BS73.2**
Mesopotamia and the Bible. Trade Paper. Continuum International Publishing Group, Ltd. London, 2003. 320p. Journal for the Study of the Old Testament Supplement, Vol. 341 ISBN:0-567-08231-8, ISBN13: 978-0-567-08231-2. Dewey:220.95.
Audience: **u,f.**

Chavalas, Mark & Mark Chavalas, Professor (Editors) **DS62.2.A63 2005**
Ancient near East: Historical Sources in Translation. Trade Cloth. Blackwell Publishing, Inc. Malden, MA. 2006. 472p. Blackwell Sourcebooks in Ancient History ISBN:0-631-23580-9, ISBN13: 978-0-631-23580-4. Dewey:939/.4. LCCN:2005-013796.
Audience: **l,u,f.**

Frankfort, Henri A. **BL325.K5 F7 1978**
Kingship and the Gods: A Study of Ancient near Eastern Religion as the Integration of Society and Nature. Samuel N. Kramer (Preface by). Trade Paper. University of Chicago Press. Chicago, IL. 1978. 470p. Oriental Institute Essay Ser. ISBN:0-226-26011-9, ISBN13: 978-0-226-26011-2. Dewey:299/.3/1. LCCN:48-005158.
Audience: **u,f.**

Frankfort, Henri A., et al. **DS57**
The Intellectual Adventure of Ancient Man: An Essay of Speculative Thought in the Ancient Near East. John A. Wilson, Thorkild Jacobsen & William A. Irwin (Authors). Trade Paper. University of Chicago Press. Chicago, IL. 1977. 410p. Oriental Institute Essays Ser. ISBN:0-226-26008-9, ISBN13: 978-0-226-26008-2. Dewey:181. LCCN:47-001318.
Audience: **g,u,f.**

Kuhrt, Amelie **DS62.23**
Ancient Near East 3000-330 B. C. Trade Paper. Routledge. New York, NY. 1997. 840p. History of the Ancient World Ser. ISBN:0-415-16762-0, ISBN13: 978-0-415-16762-8. Dewey:939.4.
Audience: **u,f.**

Liverani, Mario **DS62.23 .L583 2001**
International Relations in the Ancient near East, 1600-1100 B. C. Cloth over Boards. Palgrave Macmillan. New York, NY. 2002. 261p. Studies in Diplomacy ISBN:0-333-76153-7, ISBN13: 978-0-333-76153-3. Dewey:327/.0939/409013. LCCN:2001-032784.
Audience: **u,f.** *Choice, 2002.*

Lloyd, Seton **PS3554.O798Z474**
The Art of the Ancient near East. Paper Text. Textbook Publishers. Temecula, CA. 2003. 303p. ISBN:0-7581-6295-2, ISBN13: 978-0-7581-6295-3. Dewey:811/.54.
Audience: **g,l,u,f.**

Pritchard, James B. (Editor) **BS1180**
Ancient near Eastern Texts Relating to the Old Testament with Supplement, Set. Ed. 3. Trade Cloth. Princeton University Press. Princeton, NJ. 1969. 548p. Princeton Studies on the near East Ser. ISBN:0-691-03503-2, ISBN13: 978-0-691-03503-1.
Audience: **g,l,u,f.**

Richard, Suzanne (Editor) **DS56.N395 2003**
Near Eastern Archaeology: A Reader. Trade Cloth. Eisenbrauns, Inc. Winona Lake, IN. 2004. 486p. ISBN:1-57506-083-3, ISBN13: 978-1-57506-083-5. Dewey:939/.4. LCCN:2003-012571.
Audience: **u,f.** *Choice, 2004.*

Snell, Daniel (Editor) **DS57.C56 2005**
A Companion to the Ancient near East. Trade Cloth. Blackwell Publishing, Inc. Malden, MA. 2005. 528p. Blackwell Companions to the Ancient World Ser. ISBN:0-631-23293-1, ISBN13: 978-0-631-23293-3. Dewey:939/.4. LCCN:2004-012928.
Audience: **u,f.** *Choice, 2005.*

Snell, Daniel C. **DS62.23.S65 1997**
Life in the Ancient near East, 3100-332 B. C. E. Cloth over Boards. Yale University Press. Cumberland, RI. 1997. 288p. ISBN:0-300-06615-5, ISBN13: 978-0-300-06615-9. LCCN:96-032549.
Audience: **g,l,u.** *Choice, 1997.*

Van de Mieroop, Marc **DS62.2.V36 2003**
A History of the Ancient near East, c. 3000-323 BC. Trade Paper. Blackwell Publishing, Inc. Malden, MA. 2003. 336p. Blackwell History of the Ancient World Ser., Vol. 1 ISBN:0-631-22552-8, ISBN13: 978-0-631-22552-2. Dewey:939/.4. LCCN:2002-028113.
Audience: **g,u,f.** *Choice, 2003.*

von Soden, Wolfram **DS57.S5813 1994**
The Ancient Orient: An Introduction to the Study of the Ancient Near East. Donald J. Schley (Translator). Trade Paper. William B. Eerdmans Publishing Company. Grand Rapids, MI. 1994. 283p. ISBN:0-8028-0142-0, ISBN13: 978-0-8028-0142-5. Dewey:939/.4. LCCN:93-036268.
Audience: **g,l,u,f.**

Ancient Near East > Mesopotamia

Black, Jeremy (Editor), et al. **PJ3953**
The Literature of Ancient Sumer. Graham Cunningham, Eleanor Robson & Gabor Zolyomi (Editors). Trade Cloth. Oxford University Press, Inc. New York, NY. 2005. 320p. ISBN:0-19-926311-6, ISBN13: 978-0-19-926311-0. Dewey:899/.9508. LCCN:2005-295986.
Audience: **u,f.** *Choice, 2005.*

Bottero, Jean **TX725.I72B68 2004**
The Oldest Cuisine in the World: Cooking in Mesopotamia. Teresa Lavender Fagan (Translator). Trade Cloth. University of Chicago Press. Chicago, IL. 2004. 152p. ISBN:0-226-06735-1, ISBN13: 978-0-226-06735-3. Dewey:641.5935. LCCN:2003-061292.
Audience: **g,u,f.** *Choice, 2004.*

Bottero, Jean, et al. **DS57.B6813 2000**
Ancestor of the West: Writing, Reasoning, and Religion in Mesopotamia, Elam, and Greece. Clarisse Herrenschmidt & Jean-Pierre Vernant (Authors), Teresa Lavender Fagan (Translator). Trade Cloth. University of Chicago Press. Chicago, IL. 2000. 208p. ISBN:0-226-06715-7, ISBN13: 978-0-226-06715-5. Dewey:939./4. LCCN:99-023113.
Audience: **g,u,f.**

Bottéro, Jean **DS72**
Everyday Life in Ancient Mesopotamia. Trade Paper. Johns Hopkins University Press. Baltimore, MD. 2001. 288p. ISBN:0-8018-6864-5, ISBN13: 978-0-8018-6864-1. Dewey:935/.01.
Audience: **g,l,u,f.**

Brackman, Arnold C. **DS70.88.L3 B7**
The Luck of Nineveh. Trade Cloth. McGraw-Hill Companies, The. New York, NY. 1978. ISBN:0-07-007030-X, ISBN13: 978-0-07-007030-1. Dewey:935. LCCN:78-001893.
Audience: **g,l,u,f.**

Dalley, Stephanie (Author, Editor, Introduction by, Notes by) **BL1620**
Myths from Mesopotamia: Creation, the Flood, Gilgamesh, and Others. Trade Paper. Oxford University Press, Inc. New York, NY. 1998. 368p. Oxford World's Classics Ser. ISBN:0-19-283589-0, ISBN13: 978-0-19-283589-5. Dewey:299/.21.
Audience: **g,l,u.** *Choice, 1990.*

Dalley, Stephanie (Author, Editor) **DS56.D33**
The Legacy of Mesopotamia. A. T. Reyes, David Pingree, Alison Salvesen & Henrietta McCall (Authors), Marion Cox (Illustrator). Trade Paper. Oxford University Press, Inc. New York, NY. 2006. 246p. Legacy Ser. ISBN:0-19-929158-6, ISBN13: 978-0-19-929158-8. Dewey:935.
Audience: **g,l,u,f.**

Glassner, Jean-Jacques **P211.G5413 2003**
Writing in Sumer: The Invention of Cuneiform. Zainab Bahrani & Marc Van de Mieroop (Editor, Translators). Trade Cloth. Johns Hopkins University Press. Baltimore, MD. 2003. 288p. ISBN:0-8018-7389-4, ISBN13: 978-0-8018-7389-8. Dewey:492/.1. LCCN:2002-154025.
Audience: **g,l,u,f.** *Choice, 2004.*

Kramer, Samuel N. **DS72**
History Begins at Sumer: Thirty-Nine "Firsts" in Man's Recorded History. Ed. 3. Book, Other. University of Pennsylvania Press. Philadelphia, PA. 1981. 448p. ISBN:0-8122-1276-2, ISBN13: 978-0-8122-1276-1. Dewey:935/.01. LCCN:81-051144.
Audience: **g,l,u,f.** B

Kramer, Samuel N. **BL1615.K73 1997**
Sumerian Mythology: A Study of Spiritual and Literary Achievement in the Third Millenium B.C. Ed. 2. Book, Other. University of Pennsylvania Press. Philadelphia, PA. 1972. 152p. ISBN:0-8122-1047-6, ISBN13: 978-0-8122-1047-7. Dewey:299/.9295. LCCN:97-037348.
Audience: **g,l,u,f.**

Kramer, Samuel N. **DS72**
The Sumerians: Their History, Culture, and Character. Trade Paper. University of Chicago Press. Chicago, IL. 1971. 372p. ISBN:0-226-45238-7, ISBN13: 978-0-226-45238-8. Dewey:913.3/5. LCCN:63-011398.
Audience: **g,l,u,f.** B

Layard, Austen **DS70.5.N47**
Discoveries in the Ruins of Nineveh and Babylon. Trade Cloth. Gorgias Press, LLC. Piscataway, NJ. 2002. 740p. ISBN:1-931956-50-2, ISBN13: 978-1-931956-50-5. Dewey:913.35.
Audience: **g,u,f.**

Layard, Henry Austin **DS70.L42**
Nineveh and Its Remains: With a New Introduction by Stephanie Dalley. Trade Cloth. Gorgias Press, LLC. Piscataway, NJ. 2004. ISBN:1-59333-128-2, ISBN13: 978-1-59333-128-3. Dewey:913.5/03/3.
Audience: **g,u,f.**

Leick, Gwendolyn **DS70.5.B3L45 2003**
The Babylonians: An Introduction. Paper over Boards. Routledge. New York, NY. 2002. 192p. ISBN:0-415-25314-4, ISBN13: 978-0-415-25314-7. Dewey:935.
Audience: **g,l,u.**

Leick, Gwendolyn **DS69.5**
Mesopotamia: The Invention of the City. Trade Paper. Penguin Group (USA) Inc. New York, NY. 2003. 384p. ISBN:0-14-026574-0, ISBN13: 978-0-14-026574-3. Dewey:935. LCCN:2003-270094.
Audience: **g,l,u.**

Matthews, Roger **DS69.5.M37 2003**
The Archaeology of Mesopotamia: Theories and Approaches. Trade Paper. Routledge. New York, NY. 2003. 256p. Approaching the Ancient World Ser. ISBN:0-415-25317-9, ISBN13: 978-0-415-25317-8. Dewey:935/.001. LCCN:2002-068224.
Audience: **g,u,f.** *Choice, 2004.*

Oates, Joan & Oates, David **DS70.5.C3O255 2001**
Nimrud: An Assyrian Imperial City Revealed. Trade Paper. British School of Archaeology in Iraq. London, 2001. 200p. ISBN:0-903472-25-2, ISBN13: 978-0-903472-25-8. Dewey:935.03. LCCN:2002-437244.
Audience: **u,f.** *Choice, 2002.*

Pollock, Susan **DS73.1 .P65 1999**
Ancient Mesopotamia. Rita P. Wright (Contribution by). Cloth Text. Cambridge University Press. New York, NY. 1999. 272p. Case Studies in Early Societies ISBN:0-521-57334-3, ISBN13: 978-0-521-57334-4. Dewey:935. LCCN:00-507311.
Audience: **u,f.** *Choice, 1999.*

Potts, D. T. **DS57**
Mesopotamia: The Material Foundations. Trade Cloth. Continuum International Publishing Group, Ltd. London, 340p. Athlone Publications in Egyptology and Ancient near Eastern Studies Ser. ISBN:0-485-93001-3, ISBN13: 978-0-485-93001-6. Dewey:935. LCCN:96-034832.
Audience: **u,f.**

Potts, D. T. **DS70.7**
Mesopotamian Civilization: The Material Foundations. Trade Paper. Continuum International Publishing Group, Ltd. London, 2004. 400p. Athlone Publications in Egyptology and Ancient near Eastern Studies Ser. ISBN:0-8264-6727-X, ISBN13: 978-0-8264-6727-0. Dewey:935.
Audience: **u,f.** *Choice, 1997.*

Potts, D. T. **DS65 .P68 1999**
The Archaeology of Elam: Formation and Transformation of an Ancient Iranian State. Norman Yoffee, Susan Alcock, Tom Dillehay, Stephen Shennan & Carla Sinopoli (Contribution by). Trade Paper. Cambridge University Press. New York, NY. 1999. 520p. World Archaeology Ser. ISBN:0-521-56496-4, ISBN13: 978-0-521-56496-0. Dewey:935. LCCN:98-041051.
Audience: **g,u,f.** *Choice, 2000.*

Russell, John M. **DS70.5.N47R86 1998**
The Final Sack of Nineveh: The Discovery, Documentation, and Destruction of Sennacherib's Palace at Nineveh, Iraq. Cloth over Boards. Yale University Press. Cumberland, RI. 1998. 248p. ISBN:0-300-07418-2, ISBN13: 978-0-300-07418-5. Dewey:935. LCCN:98-015067.
Audience: **u,f.** *Choice, 1999.*

Van de Mieroop, Marc **DS69.5**
The Ancient Mesopotamian City. Paper Text. Oxford University Press, Inc. New York, NY. 1999. 286p. ISBN:0-19-815286-8, ISBN13: 978-0-19-815286-6. Dewey:935/.009732. LCCN:97-008199.
Audience: **u,f.** *Choice, 1998.*

Van de Mieroop, Marc **DS73.35.V36 2004**
King Hammurabi of Babylon: A Biography. Trade Cloth. Blackwell Publishing, Inc. Malden, MA. 2004. 184p. Blackwell Ancient Lives Ser. ISBN:1-4051-2659-0, ISBN13: 978-1-4051-2659-5. Dewey:935/.02/092 B. LCCN:2004-013272.
Audience: **g,u,f.** *Choice, 2006.*

Woolley, Leonard **DS70.5.U7 W63 1982**
Ur 'of the Chaldees': A Revised and Updated Edition of Sir Leonard Woolley's Excavations at Ur by P. R. S. Moorey. Book, Other. Cornell University Press. Ithaca, NY. 1982. ISBN:0-8014-1518-7, ISBN13: 978-0-8014-1518-0. Dewey:935. LCCN:81-086557.
Audience: **u,f.**

Ancient Near East > Hittites

Bryce, Trevor **DS66**
Kingdom of the Hittites. Ed. 2. Trade Cloth. Oxford University Press, Inc. New York, NY. 2006. 576p. ISBN:0-19-927908-X, ISBN13: 978-0-19-927908-1. Dewey:939/.2. LCCN:2005-021643.
Audience: **g,l,u,f.**

Bryce, Trevor **DS66.B755 2004**
Life and Society in the Hittite World. Trade Paper. Oxford University Press, Inc. New York, NY. 2004. 328p. ISBN:0-19-927588-2, ISBN13: 978-0-19-927588-5. Dewey:909/.49199.
Audience: **g,l,u,f.** *Choice, 2003.*

Ceram, C. W. **DS66.C35 2001**
The Secret of the Hittites: The Discovery of an Ancient Empire. Trade Paper. Sterling Publishing Co., Inc. New York, NY. 2001. 320p. Phoenix Press Ser. ISBN:1-84212-295-9, ISBN13: 978-1-84212-295-2. Dewey:939/.203. LCCN:2001-276572.
Audience: **g,l,u.**

Gurney, O. R. **DS155**
The Hittites. Paper Text. Textbook Publishers. Temecula, CA. 2003. 239p. ISBN:0-7581-6590-0, ISBN13: 978-0-7581-6590-9. Dewey:939/.2.
Audience: **g,l,u,f.** B

Macqueen, J. G. **DS66**
The Hittites: And Their Contemporaries in Asia Minor. Ed. 4. Trade Paper. Thames & Hudson. New York, NY. 1996. 176p. Ancient Peoples and Places Ser. ISBN:0-500-27887-3, ISBN13: 978-0-500-27887-1. Dewey:939.2. LCCN:85-051750.
Audience: **u,f.**

Ancient Near East > Israel, Phoenicia, and Syria

Ahlstrom, Gosta W. **DS117 .A545 1993**
The History of Ancient Palestine. Trade Paper. Augsburg Fortress, Publishers. Minneapolis, MN. 2003. 990p. ISBN:0-8006-2770-9, ISBN13: 978-0-8006-2770-6. Dewey:933. LCCN:93-016628.
Audience: **g,l,u,f.**

Avi-Yonah, Michael **DS124 .A9413 1976**
The Jews of Palestine: A Political History from the Bar Kokhba War to the Arab Conquest. Trade Cloth. Blackwell Publishing, Inc. Malden, MA. xviii, 286p. ISBN:0-631-14740-3, ISBN13: 978-0-631-14740-4. Dewey:956.94/004/924. LCCN:77-351181.
Audience: **l,u,f.**

Ben-Tor, Amnon (Editor) **DS111.A2M3513**
The Archaeology of Ancient Israel. R. Greenberg (Translator). Trade Paper. Yale University Press. Cumberland, RI. 1994. 419p. ISBN:0-300-05919-1, ISBN13: 978-0-300-05919-9. Dewey:933.
Audience: **l,u,f.** *Choice, 1993.*

Cohen, Shaye J. D. **BM176 .C615**
From the Maccabees to the Mishnah. Wayne A. Meeks (Editor). Trade Paper. Westminster John Knox Press. Louisville, KY. 1987. 252p. Library of Early Christianity, Vol. 7 ISBN:0-664-25017-3, ISBN13: 978-0-664-25017-1. Dewey:296/.09/014. LCCN:86-028077.
Audience: **u,f.** *Choice, 1987.*

Coogan, Michael D. **BS635.2.O94 2001**
The Oxford History of the Biblical World. Trade Cloth. Oxford University Press, Inc. New York, NY. 1999. 656p. ISBN:0-19-508707-0, ISBN13: 978-0-19-508707-9. Dewey:220.9/5. LCCN:00-060612.
Audience: **g,l,u,f.**

Cross, Frank Moore Jr. **BM155.2**
Canaanite Myth and Hebrew Epic: Essays in the History of the Religion of Israel. Trade Cloth. Harvard University Press. Cambridge, MA. 1973. 394p. ISBN:0-674-09175-2, ISBN13: 978-0-674-09175-7. Dewey:296/.09. LCCN:72-076564.
Audience: **l,u,f.**

Cross, Frank Moore Jr. **BS1171.2**
From Epic to Canon: History and Literature in Ancient Israel. Trade Paper. Johns Hopkins University Press. Baltimore, MD. 2000. 280p. ISBN:0-8018-6533-6, ISBN13: 978-0-8018-6533-6. Dewey:221.6.
Audience: **l,u,f.** *Choice, 1999.*

Dothan, Trude **DS90.D63 1992**
People of the Sea: The Search for the Philistines. Children's Board Books. Simon & Schuster. New York, NY. 1992. 256p. ISBN:0-02-532261-3, ISBN13: 978-0-02-532261-5. Dewey:933. LCCN:91-047880.
Audience: **g,l,u,f.**

Dothan, Trude K. **DS90 .D613**
The Philistines and Their Material Culture. Trade Paper. Books on Demand. Ann Arbor, MI. 332p. ISBN:0-7837-2501-9, ISBN13: 978-0-7837-2501-7. Dewey:933. LCCN:80-022060.
Audience: **u,f.**

Hayes, John H. & Miller, J. Maxwell **DS117.M6 1986**
History of Ancient Israel and Judah. Trade Cloth. Westminster John Knox Press. Louisville, KY. 1986. 524p. ISBN:0-664-21262-X, ISBN13: 978-0-664-21262-9. Dewey:933. LCCN:85-011468.
Audience: **g,u.** *Choice, 1986.*

Hoffmeier, James K. **BS680.E9**
Israel in Egypt: The Evidence for the Authenticity of the Exodus Tradition. Trade Paper. Oxford University Press, Inc. New York, NY. 1999. 264p. ISBN:0-19-513088-X, ISBN13: 978-0-19-513088-1. Dewey:222/.12095.
Audience: **u,f.**

Kamm, Antony **DS121.K23 1999**
Israelites: Introduction. Trade Paper. Routledge. New York, NY. 1999. 256p. ISBN:0-415-18096-1, ISBN13: 978-0-415-18096-2. Dewey:933. LCCN:98-053884.
Audience: **g,l,u.**

Markoe, Glenn **DS154.9.P48P49 2003**
Petra Rediscovered: Lost City of the Nabataeans. Trade Cloth. Harry N. Abrams, Inc. New York, NY. 2003. 288p. ISBN:0-8109-4537-1, ISBN13: 978-0-8109-4537-1. Dewey:939/.48. LCCN:2003-006209.
Audience: **g,l,u,f.**

Markoe, Glenn **DS81.M23 2000**
Phoenicians. Trade Paper. University of California Press. Berkeley, CA. 2001. 224p. Peoples of the Past Ser. ISBN:0-520-22614-3, ISBN13: 978-0-520-22614-2. Dewey:939.4/4. LCCN:00-711588.
Audience: **l,u,f.**

Pettinato, Giovanni **DS0099.E25P4**
Ebla: A New Look at History. C. Faith Richardson (Translator). Trade Paper. Books on Demand. Ann Arbor, MI. 1991. 303p. ISBN:0-608-03673-0, ISBN13: 978-0-608-03673-1. Dewey:939/.43. LCCN:90-020907.
Audience: **l,u,f.** *Choice, 1992.*

Pitard, Wayne T. **DS99.D3 P58 1987**
Ancient Damascus: A Historical Study of the Syrian City-State from Earliest Times until Its Fall to the Assyrians in 732 B.C. Cloth Text. Eisenbrauns, Inc. Winona Lake, IN. 1987. ix, 230p. ISBN:0-931464-29-3, ISBN13: 978-0-931464-29-4. Dewey:956.91/4. LCCN:86-024360.
Audience: **u,f.** *Choice, 1987.*

Redford, Donald B. **DT82.5.P19**
Egypt, Canaan, and Israel in Ancient Times. Trade Paper. Princeton University Press. Princeton, NJ. 1993. 512p. ISBN:0-691-00086-7, ISBN13: 978-0-691-00086-2. Dewey:303.48/26205694.
Audience: **u,f.** *Choice, 1992.*

Sandars, N. K. **DE73.2.S4**
The Sea Peoples: Warriors of the Ancient Mediterranean, 1250-1150 BC. Trade Cloth. Thames & Hudson. New York, NY. 1978. 224p. ISBN:0-500-02085-X, ISBN13: 978-0-500-02085-2. Dewey:930/.09/822. LCCN:77-083798.
Audience: **g,l,u,f.** B

Taylor, Jane **DS154.9.P48T39 2002**
Petra and the Lost Kingdom of the Nabataeans. Trade Cloth. Harvard University Press. Cambridge, MA. 2002. 224p. ISBN:0-674-00849-9, ISBN13: 978-0-674-00849-6. Dewey:939.48. LCCN:2002-512890.
Audience: **g,l,u,f.**

Tubb, Jonathan N. **DS121.4.T83 1998**
Canaanites. Trade Cloth. University of Oklahoma Press. Norman, OK. 1999. 160p. Peoples of the Past Ser., Vol. 2 ISBN:0-8061-3108-X, ISBN13: 978-0-8061-3108-5. Dewey:939.4/004/926. LCCN:98-008841.
Audience: **g,l,u,f.** *Choice, 1999.*

Wilhelm, Gernot **DS56**
The Hurrians: Ancient Near East. Trade Cloth. Aris & Phillips. Oxford, 1989. 139p. ISBN:0-85668-489-9, ISBN13: 978-0-85668-489-0. Dewey:939/.4.
Audience: **u,f.** *Choice, 1990.*

Egypt (PreDynastic to Arab Conquest) > Pharaonic Egypt

Aldred, Cyril **DT83.A65 1998**
The Egyptians. Ed. 3. Aidan Dodson (Revised by). Trade Paper. Thames & Hudson. New York, NY. 1998. 224p. ISBN:0-500-28036-3, ISBN13: 978-0-500-28036-2. Dewey:932/.01. LCCN:98-060040.
Audience: **g,l,u,f.**

Andrews, Carol **DT62.M7**
Egyptian Mummies. Trade Paper. Harvard University Press. Cambridge, MA. 2004. 96p. British Museum Paperbacks Ser. ISBN:0-674-01391-3, ISBN13: 978-0-674-01391-9. Dewey:393/.3/0932.
Audience: **g,l,u.**

Andrews, Carol (Editor) **PJ1555.E5 F38 1990**
The Ancient Egyptian Book of the Dead. Raymond Oliver Faulkner (Translator). Trade Paper. University of Texas Press. Austin, TX. 1990. 192p. ISBN:0-292-70425-9, ISBN13: 978-0-292-70425-1. Dewey:299/.31. LCCN:90-070343.
Audience: **u,f.**

Assmann, Jan **BS580.M6A79 1997**
Moses the Egyptian: The Memory of Egypt in Western Monotheism. Trade Cloth. Harvard University Press. Cambridge, MA. 1997. 288p. ISBN:0-674-58738-3, ISBN13: 978-0-674-58738-0. Dewey:222/.1/092. LCCN:96-051600.
Audience: **u,f.** *Choice, 1997.*

Assmann, Jan **DT83.A8813 2002**
The Mind of Egypt: History and Meaning in the Time of the Pharaohs. Andrew Jenkins (Translator). Trade Cloth. Henry Holt & Company. New York, NY. 2002. 528p. ISBN:0-8050-5462-6, ISBN13: 978-0-8050-5462-0. Dewey:932/.01. LCCN:2001-044504.
Audience: **u,f.**

Assmann, Jan **BL2450.E8A8813 2005**
Death and Salvation in Ancient Egypt. David Lorton (Translator). Saddle Stitched, Cloth over Boards, Dust Jacket. Cornell University Press. Ithaca, NY. 2005. 490p. ISBN:0-8014-4241-9, ISBN13: 978-0-8014-4241-4. Dewey:299.3123. LCCN:2005-002783.
Audience: **g,l,u,f.**

Assmann, Jan **BL2441.2.A8713 2001**
The Search for God in Ancient Egypt. David Lorton (Translator). Book, Other. Cornell University Press. Ithaca, NY. 2001. 288p. ISBN:0-8014-3786-5, ISBN13: 978-0-8014-3786-1. Dewey:292.2/11. LCCN:00-012577.
Audience: **g,l,u,f.**

Breasted, James H. (Editor) **DT57 .B76**
Ancient Records of Egypt: Historical Documents from the Earliest Times to the Persian Conquest. Trade Cloth. Russell & Russell Publishers. New York, NY. 1962. ISBN:0-8462-0134-8, ISBN13: 978-0-8462-0134-2. Dewey:932. LCCN:62-013827.
Audience: **u,f.**

Carter, Howard **DT87.5**
The Tomb of TutAnkhAmen: The Burial Chamber. Trade Paper. Gerald Duckworth & Company, Ltd. London, 2001. 400p. ISBN:0-7156-3075-X, ISBN13: 978-0-7156-3075-4. Dewey:932/.014.
Audience: **g,l,u,f.**

Carter, Howard & Mace, A. C. **DT60**
The Tomb of Tut Ankh Amen: Search, Discovery and the Clearance of the Antechamber. Trade Paper. Gerald Duckworth & Company, Ltd. London, 2003. 192p. Duckworth Egyptology Ser. ISBN:0-7156-3172-1, ISBN13: 978-0-7156-3172-0. Dewey:932/.014.
Audience: **g,l,u,f.**

Carter, Howard **DT87.5**
The Tomb of TutAnkhAmen: The Annexe and Treasury. Nicholas Reeves (Editor). Trade Paper. Gerald Duckworth & Company, Ltd. London, 2000. 256p. ISBN:0-7156-2964-6, ISBN13: 978-0-7156-2964-2. Dewey:932/.014.
Audience: **g,l,u,f.**

Casson, Lionel **DT61.C34 2001**
Everyday Life in Ancient Egypt. Ed. 2. Trade Paper. Johns Hopkins University Press. Baltimore, MD. 2001. 176p. ISBN:0-8018-6601-4, ISBN13: 978-0-8018-6601-2. Dewey:932. LCCN:00-059091.
Audience: **g,l,u,f.**

Collier, Mark & Manley, Bill **PJ1097**
How to Read Egyptian Hieroglyphs: A Step-by-Step Guide to Teach Yourself. Trade Cloth. University of California Press. Berkeley, CA. 2003. 191p. ISBN:0-520-23949-0, ISBN13: 978-0-520-23949-4. Dewey:493.111. LCCN:2003-279067.
Audience: **u,f.**

David, Rosalie **DT83.D23 1999**
The Handbook to Life in Ancient Egypt. Trade Paper. Oxford University Press, Inc. New York, NY. 1999. 400p. ISBN:0-19-513215-7, ISBN13: 978-0-19-513215-1. Dewey:932. LCCN:99-010264.
Audience: **g,l,u,f.**

David, Rosalie **DT61**
The Pyramid Builders of Ancient Egypt: A Modern Investigation of Pharaoh's Workforce. Trade Paper. Routledge. New York, NY. 1997. 304p. ISBN:0-415-15292-5, ISBN13: 978-0-415-15292-1. Dewey:932/.01.
Audience: **g,l,u,f.**

Edwards, I. E. S. **DT63**
The Pyramids of Egypt. Ed. 3. Trade Paper. Penguin Group (USA) Inc. New York, NY. 1986. 352p. ISBN:0-14-013634-7, ISBN13: 978-0-14-013634-0. Dewey:932.
Audience: **g,l,u,f.** B

Gardiner, Alan Henderson **PA2087**
Egypt of the Pharaohs: An Introduction. Paper Text. Oxford University Press, Inc. New York, NY. 1966. 461p. ISBN:0-19-500267-9, ISBN13: 978-0-19-500267-6. Dewey:475.
Audience: **u,f.** B

Hoffman, Michael A. **GN865.E3**
Egypt Before the Pharaohs. Trade Paper. Kazi Publications, Inc. Chicago, IL. 1996. 430p. ISBN:0-614-21624-9, ISBN13: 978-0-614-21624-0. Dewey:932/.011.
Audience: **u,f.** B

Hornung, Erik & Bryan, Betsy **N5350.H67 2002**
The Quest for Immortality: Hidden Treasures of Egypt. Trade Cloth. Prestel Publishing. New York, NY. 2002. 288p. ISBN:3-7913-2735-6, ISBN13: 978-3-7913-2735-8. Dewey:709/.32/074753. LCCN:2002-018847.
Audience: **g,l,u,f.** *Choice, 2003, 2002.*

Hornung, Erik **BL2441.2**
Akhenaten and the Religion of Light. David Lorton (Translator). Trade Paper. Cornell University Press. Ithaca, NY. 2001. 160p. ISBN:0-8014-8725-0, ISBN13: 978-0-8014-8725-5. Dewey:299/.31.
Audience: **g,l,u,f.** *Choice, 2000.*

Hornung, Erik **PJ1551.H67 1999**
The Ancient Egyptian Books of the Afterlife. David Lorton (Translator). Book, Other. Cornell University Press. Ithaca, NY. 1999. 224p. ISBN:0-8014-3515-3, ISBN13: 978-0-8014-3515-7. Dewey:299/.31. LCCN:99-010888.
Audience: **u,f.**

Hornung, Erik **DT83 .H5813 1999**
History of Ancient Egypt: An Introduction. David Lorton (Translator). Trade Paper. Cornell University Press. Ithaca, NY. 1999. 224p. ISBN:0-8014-8475-8, ISBN13: 978-0-8014-8475-9. Dewey:932. LCCN:98-044396.
Audience: **g,l,u.**

Hornung, Erik **BF1434.E3H6713 2001**
The Secret Lore of Egypt: Its Impact on the West. David Lorton (Translator). Trade Cloth. Cornell University Press. Ithaca, NY. 2002. 240p. ISBN:0-8014-3847-0, ISBN13: 978-0-8014-3847-9. Dewey:135/.4. LCCN:2001-004361.
Audience: **g,l,u,f.** *Choice, 2002.*

James, T. G. H. **DT61**
Pharaoh's People: Scenes from Life in Imperial Egypt. Trade Paper. I. B. Tauris & Company, Ltd. London, 2003. 282p. ISBN:1-86064-832-0, ISBN13: 978-1-86064-832-8. Dewey:932.
Audience: **g,l,u,f.**

James, T. G. H. **DT61**
A Short History of Ancient Egypt. Trade Cloth. International Book Centre, Inc. Troy, MI. 1995. 167p. ISBN:0-86685-720-6, ISBN13: 978-0-86685-720-8. Dewey:932/.01.
Audience: **g,l,u.**

Lichtheim, Miriam **PJ1943 .L5 2006**
Ancient Egyptian Literature: New Kingdom. Ed. 2. Trade Paper. University of California Press. Berkeley, CA. 2006. 265p. ISBN:0-520-24843-0, ISBN13: 978-0-520-24843-4. Dewey:893/.108. LCCN:2005-046681.
Audience: **g,l,u,f.**

Lichtheim, Miriam **PJ1943**
Ancient Egyptian Literature: Old and Middle Kingdoms. Ed. 2. Trade Paper. University of California Press. Berkeley, CA. 2006. 280p. ISBN:0-520-24842-2, ISBN13: 978-0-520-24842-7. Dewey:893/.108. LCCN:2005-046681.
Audience: **g,l,u,f.**

Lichtheim, Miriam **PJ1943 .L5 2006**
Ancient Egyptian Literature: Late Period. Ed. 2. Trade Paper. University of California Press. Berkeley, CA. 2006. 260p. ISBN:0-520-24844-9, ISBN13: 978-0-520-24844-1. Dewey:893/.108. LCCN:2005-046681.
Audience: **g,l,u,f.**

Manley, Bill **G2491.S2M3 1996**
Ancient Egypt. Trade Paper. Penguin Group (USA) Inc. New York, NY. 1997. 144p. Hist Atlas Ser. ISBN:0-14-051331-0, ISBN13: 978-0-14-051331-8. Dewey:911.3/2. LCCN:97-675187.
Audience: **g,l,u.**

Manley, Bill (Editor) **DT60**
Seventy Great Mysteries of Ancient Egypt. Trade Cloth. Thames & Hudson. New York, NY. 2003. 304p. ISBN:0-500-05123-2, ISBN13: 978-0-500-05123-8. Dewey:932. LCCN:2003-100123.
Audience: **g,l,u.**

Manniche, Lise **DT73.T3M36 1987**
City of the Dead: Thebes in Egypt. Trade Cloth. University of Chicago Press. Chicago, IL. 1987. 160p. British Museum Publications ISBN:0-226-50339-9, ISBN13: 978-0-226-50339-4. Dewey:932. LCCN:87-005022.
Audience: **g,l,u,f.**

Manniche, Lise **DT62.T5M36 1999**
Sacred Luxuries: Fragrance, Aromatherapy, and Cosmetics in Ancient Egypt. Werner Forman (Photographer). Trade Cloth. Cornell University Press. Ithaca, NY. 1999. 160p. ISBN:0-8014-3720-2, ISBN13: 978-0-8014-3720-5. Dewey:391.6/3/0932. LCCN:99-027112.
Audience: **g,l,u,f.**

Mertz, Barbara **DT61**
Temples, Tombs and Hieroglyphs: A Popular History of Ancient Egypt. Trade Cloth. Brockhampton Press. London, 2001. 335p. ISBN:1-86019-910-0, ISBN13: 978-1-86019-910-3. Dewey:932/.01.
Audience: **g,l,u.**

Parkinson, Richard **DT60**
Rosetta Stone. Trade Paper. British Museum Press. London, 2005. 64p. British Museum Objects in Focus Ser. ISBN:0-7141-5021-5, ISBN13: 978-0-7141-5021-5. Dewey:493/.111. LCCN:2005-363526.
Audience: **g,l,u.**

Redford, Donald B. **DT59.B598**
Akhenaten: The Heretic King. Trade Paper. Princeton University Press. Princeton, NJ. 1987. 288p. ISBN:0-691-00217-7, ISBN13: 978-0-691-00217-0. Dewey:932/.014/0924. LCCN:83-022960.
Audience: **u,f.**

Redford, Donald B. (Editor) **BL2428.A53 2002**
The Ancient Gods Speak: A Guide to Egyptian Religion. Trade Cloth. Oxford University Press, Inc. New York, NY. 2002. 428p. ISBN:0-19-515401-0, ISBN13: 978-0-19-515401-6. Dewey:299/.31/03. LCCN:2002-072411.
Audience: **g,l,u,f.**

Redford, Donald B. **DT82.5.P19**
Egypt, Canaan, and Israel in Ancient Times. Trade Paper. Princeton University Press. Princeton, NJ. 1993. 512p. ISBN:0-691-00086-7, ISBN13: 978-0-691-00086-2. Dewey:303.48/26205694.
Audience: **u,f.** *Choice, 1992.*

Redford, Donald B. **DT83.R4 2004**
From Slave to Pharaoh: The Black Experience of Ancient Egypt. Trade Cloth. Johns Hopkins University Press. Baltimore, MD. 2004. 232p. ISBN:0-8018-7814-4, ISBN13: 978-0-8018-7814-5. Dewey:932/.015. LCCN:2003-010639.
Audience: **u,f.** *Choice, 2005.*

Redford, Donald B. (Editor) **DT58.O94 2001**
The Oxford Encyclopedia of Ancient Egypt, Set. Trade Cloth. Oxford University Press, Inc. New York, NY. 2001. 1,656p. ISBN:0-19-510234-7, ISBN13: 978-0-19-510234-5. Dewey:932. LCCN:99-054801.
Audience: **g,l,u,f.** *Choice, 2001.*

Roehrig, Catharine H. (Editor), et al. **DT87.15.H378 2005**
Hatshepsut: From Queen to Pharaoh. Cathleen A. Keller & Renee Dreyfus (Editors). Saddle Stitched, Cloth over Boards, Dust Jacket. Yale University Press. Cumberland, RI. 2005. 356p. Metropolitan Museum of Art Ser. ISBN:0-300-11139-8, ISBN13: 978-0-300-11139-2. Dewey:932/.014/092. LCCN:2005-020286.
Audience: **g,l,u,f.**

Shaw, Ian (Editor) **DT83.O95 2000**
The Oxford History of Ancient Egypt. Trade Cloth. Oxford University Press, Inc. New York, NY. 2000. 554p. Oxford Illustrated Histories Ser. ISBN:0-19-815034-2, ISBN13: 978-0-19-815034-3. Dewey:932. LCCN:2001-274677.
Audience: **g,l,u,f.** *Choice, 2001.*

Ucko **DT74-107.87DT1-3415**
Encounters with Ancient Egypt. Trade Paper. Taylor & Francis Group. Abingdon, 2003. 1810p. Ucl Ser. ISBN:1-84472-008-X, ISBN13: 978-1-84472-008-8. Dewey:300.
Audience: **u,f.** *Choice, 2004.*

Wilkinson, Toby **DT43**
Genesis of the Pharaohs. Trade Cloth. Thames & Hudson. New York, NY. 2003. 208p. ISBN:0-500-05122-4, ISBN13: 978-0-500-05122-1. Dewey:932/.01. LCCN:2002-110322.
Audience: **u,f.**

Wilkinson, Toby A. **DT85.W49 1999**
Early Dynastic Egypt. Paper over Boards. Routledge. New York, NY. 1999. 440p. ISBN:0-415-18633-1, ISBN13: 978-0-415-18633-9. Dewey:932/.012. LCCN:98-035836.
Audience: **u,f.** *Choice, 2000.*

Wilson, John A. **DT61**
The Culture of Ancient Egypt. Trade Paper. University of Chicago Press. Chicago, IL. 1956. 352p. ISBN:0-226-90152-1, ISBN13: 978-0-226-90152-7. Dewey:913.32. LCCN:56-004923.
Audience: **g,l,u,f.**

Egypt (PreDynastic to Arab Conquest) > Greco-Roman Egypt

PA3611 .A88
Papyri. Trade Cloth. Harvard University Press. Cambridge, MA. Loeb Classical Library, Nos. 266, 282, 360 ISBN:0-318-53132-1, ISBN13: 978-0-318-53132-8. Dewey:481.7.
Audience: **u,f.**

Bagnall, Roger S. **DT93**
Egypt in Late Antiquity. Trade Paper. Princeton University Press. Princeton, NJ. 1995. 382p. ISBN:0-691-01096-X, ISBN13: 978-0-691-01096-0. Dewey:932/.022.
Audience: **u,f.** *Choice, 1994.*

Bagnall, Roger S. & Rathbone, Dominic W. (Editors) **DT92**
Egypt from Alexander to the Early Christians: An Archaeological and Historical Guide. Saddle Stitched, Cloth over Boards, Dust Jacket. Getty Conservation Institute. Los Angeles, CA. 2005. 319p. ISBN:0-89236-796-2, ISBN13: 978-0-89236-796-2. Dewey:932. LCCN:2004-110573.
Audience: **g,l,u.**

Bagnall, Roger & Cribiore, Raffaella **HQ1137.E3**
Women's Letters from Ancient Egypt, 300 BC - AD 800. Trade Cloth. University of Michigan Press. Chicago, IL. 2006. 440p. ISBN:0-472-11506-5, ISBN13: 978-0-472-11506-8. Dewey:932/.02. LCCN:2005-055947.
Audience: **g,l,u,f.**

Bowman, Alan K. **DT0061.B67**
Egypt after the Pharaohs, 332 BC-AD 642: From Alexander to the Arab Conquest. Trade Paper. Books on Demand. Ann Arbor, MI. 264p. ISBN:0-7837-4835-3, ISBN13: 978-0-7837-4835-1. Dewey:932/.02. LCCN:86-011355.
Audience: **g,l,u,f.**

Chauveau, Michel (Contribution by) **DT61.C4613 2000**
Egypt in the Age of Cleopatra: History and Society under the Ptolemies. Book, Other. Cornell University Press. Ithaca, NY. 2000. 240p. ISBN:0-8014-3597-8, ISBN13: 978-0-8014-3597-3. Dewey:932/.021. LCCN:99-049898.
Audience: **g,l,u,f.** *Choice, 2000.*

Fraser, P M **DT73.A4**
Ptolemaic Alexandria. Oxford University Press, Inc. 1985. ISBN:0-19-814278-1, ISBN13: 978-0-19-814278-2.
Audience: **u,f.** B

Grant, Michael **DT92.7**
Cleopatra. Trade Cloth. Book Sales, Inc. Edison, NJ. 2004. 344p. ISBN:0-7858-1828-6, ISBN13: 978-0-7858-1828-1. Dewey:932/.02/0924.
Audience: **g,l,u.**

Haas, Christopher **DT154.A4H36 1997**
Alexandria in Late Antiquity: Topography and Social Conflict. Trade Cloth. Johns Hopkins University Press. Baltimore, MD. 1996. 520p. Ancient Society and History Ser. ISBN:0-8018-5377-X, ISBN13: 978-0-8018-5377-7. Dewey:932. LCCN:96-021424.
Audience: **u,f.** *Choice, 1997.*

Kleiner, Diana E. E. **N5763.K58 2005**
Cleopatra and Rome. Trade Cloth. Harvard University Press. Cambridge, MA. 2005. 352p. ISBN:0-674-01905-9, ISBN13: 978-0-674-01905-8. Dewey:932/.021/092. LCCN:2005-041015.
Audience: **u,f.** *Choice, 2006.*

Lewis, Naphtali **DT72.G7L49 2001**
Greeks in Ptolemaic Egypt: Case Studies in the Social History of the Hellenistic World. Ed. 2. Trade Paper. American Society of Papyrologists. Cincinnati, OH. 2001. 182p. Classics in Papyrology Ser., Vol. 2 ISBN:0-9700591-2-4, ISBN13: 978-0-9700591-2-3. Dewey:932/.02. LCCN:2001-022491.
Audience: **l,u,f.** *Choice, 1987.*

Lewis, Naphtali **DT61.L646 1999**
Life in Egypt under Roman Rule. Ed. 2. Library Binding. Scholars Press. Atlanta, GA. 1999. 240p. Classics in Papyrology

ISBN:0-7885-0560-2, ISBN13: 978-0-7885-0560-7. Dewey:932/.02. LCCN:99-026772.
Audience: **l,u,f.**

Rousseau, Philip **BR1720.P23**
Pachomius: The Making of a Community in Fourth-Century Egypt. Trade Cloth. University of California Press. Berkeley, CA. 1985. xvi, 217p. The Transformation of the Classical Heritage Ser., Vol. VI ISBN:0-520-05048-7, ISBN13: 978-0-520-05048-8. Dewey:271/.0092. LCCN:83-009285.
Audience: **u,f.** *Choice, 1986.*

Rowlandson, Jane (Editor) **HQ1137.E3 W65 1998**
Women and Society in Greek and Roman Egypt: A Sourcebook. Cloth Text. Cambridge University Press. New York, NY. 1998. 432p. ISBN:0-521-58212-1, ISBN13: 978-0-521-58212-4. Dewey:305.42/0932. LCCN:97-032001.
Audience: **l,u,f.**

Verbrugghe, Gerald P. & Wickersham, John M. **DS73.2.V47**
Berossos and Manetho, Introduced and Translated: Native Traditions in Ancient Mesopotamia and Egypt. Trade Paper. University of Michigan Press. Chicago, IL. 2001. 256p. ISBN:0-472-08687-1, ISBN13: 978-0-472-08687-0. Dewey:932.
Audience: **l,u,f.**

Egypt (PreDynastic to Arab Conquest) > Egyptology

Adkins, Lesley & Adkins, Roy A. **PJ1097.A35 2000**
The Keys of Egypt: The Obsession to Decipher Egyptian Hieroglyphs. Trade Cloth. HarperCollins Publishers. New York, NY. 2000. 352p. ISBN:0-06-019439-1, ISBN13: 978-0-06-019439-0. Dewey:493/.111. LCCN:00-038320.
Audience: **g,l,u.**

Belzoni, Giovanni Battista **DT60.B44 2000**
Belzoni's Travels: Narrative of Ther Operations and Recent Discoveries in Egypt and Nubia. Alberto Siliotti (Editor). Trade Cloth. British Museum Press. London, 2001. 336p. ISBN:0-7141-1940-7, ISBN13: 978-0-7141-1940-3. Dewey:916.204/3. LCCN:2001-535723.
Audience: **g,l,u,f.**

David, Rosalie **DT56.9.D39 1994**
Discovering Ancient Egypt. Trade Cloth. Facts On File, Inc. New York, NY. 1994. 192p. ISBN:0-8160-3105-3, ISBN13: 978-0-8160-3105-4. Dewey:932. LCCN:93-038601.
Audience: **g,l,u,f.**

Drower, Margaret (Editor) **CC115.P4**
Letters from the Desert: The Correspondence of Flinders and Hilda Petrie. Trade Paper. Aris & Phillips. Oxford, 2003. 224p. ISBN:0-85668-748-0, ISBN13: 978-0-85668-748-8. Dewey:930.1/0922.
Audience: **g,l,u,f.**

Drower, Margaret S. **PJ1064.P47D7 1995**
Flinders Petrie: A Life in Archaeology. Ed. 2. Library Binding. University of Wisconsin Press. Chicago, IL. 1995. 522p. Studies in Classics ISBN:0-299-14620-0, ISBN13: 978-0-299-14620-7. Dewey:932/.007202 B. LCCN:94-042111.
Audience: **g,l,u,f.** *Choice, 1986.*

Edwards, Amelia **DT54**
A Thousand Miles up the Nile. Ed. 2. Trade Cloth. Darf Publishers, Ltd. London, 1993. 499p. ISBN:1-85077-227-4, ISBN13: 978-1-85077-227-9. Dewey:916.2043.
Audience: **g,l,u,f.**

James, T. G. H. **PJ1064.C3J3 2002**
Howard Carter: The Path to Tutankhamun. Trade Paper. I. B. Tauris & Company, Ltd. London, 2001. 406p. Tauris Parke Paperbacks Ser. ISBN:1-86064-615-8, ISBN13: 978-1-86064-615-7. Dewey:932.007202. LCCN:2001-271661.
Audience: **g,l,u,f.**

Mayes, Stanley **DT76.9.B4 M33 2003**
The Great Belzoni: The Circus Strongman Who Discovered Egypt's Ancient Treasures. Trade Paper. I. B. Tauris & Company, Ltd. London, 2003. 360p. Tauris Parke Paperbacks Ser. ISBN:1-86064-877-0, ISBN13: 978-1-86064-877-9. Dewey:930.1/092. LCCN:2004-268431.
Audience: **g,l,u,f.**

Thompson, Jason **PJ1064.W55T46 1992**
Sir Gardner Wilkinson and His Circle. Trade Cloth. University of Texas Press. Austin, TX. 1992. 326p. ISBN:0-292-77643-8, ISBN13: 978-0-292-77643-2. Dewey:932/.007202. LCCN:91-047636.
Audience: **g,l,u,f.**

Wilson, John A. **DT0060.W65**
Signs and Wonders upon Pharaoh: A History of American Egyptology. Trade Paper. Books on Demand. Ann Arbor, MI. 269p. ISBN:0-608-09568-0, ISBN13: 978-0-608-09568-4. Dewey:913.32. LCCN:64-023535.
Audience: **u,f.**

Persia

Allen, Lindsay **DS281.A58 2005**
The Persian Empire. Trade Cloth. University of Chicago Press. Chicago, IL. 2005. 224p. ISBN:0-226-01447-9, ISBN13: 978-0-226-01447-0. Dewey:935/.05. LCCN:2005-043096.
Audience: **g,u,f.** *Choice, 2006.*

Briant, Pierre **DS281.B7513 2002**
From Cyrus to Alexander: A History of the Persian Empire. Trade Cloth. Eisenbrauns, Inc. Winona Lake, IN. 2004. 196p. ISBN:1-57506-031-0, ISBN13: 978-1-57506-031-6. Dewey:935/.01. LCCN:2001-055736.
Audience: **u,f.**

Brosius, Maria **HQ1130**
Women in Ancient Persia, 559-331 BC. Trade Paper. Oxford University Press, Inc. New York, NY. 1998. 278p. Oxford Classical Monographs ISBN:0-19-815255-8, ISBN13: 978-0-19-815255-2. Dewey:305.4/0935.
Audience: **u,f.**

Dodgeon, Michael L. **DG271.R56 1990**
The Roman Eastern Frontier and the Persian Wars, A. D. 226-363: A Documentary History. Samuel N. Lieu (Editor). Cloth Text. Routledge. New York, NY. 1991. 288p. ISBN:0-415-00342-3, ISBN13: 978-0-415-00342-1. Dewey:937/.08. LCCN:89-010376.
Audience: **u,f.**

Greatrex, Geoffrey & Lieu, Samuel N. C. (Editors) **DG271**
The Roman Eastern Frontier and Persian Wars: 368-628 A. D. Narrative Sourcebook. Paper over Boards. Routledge. New York, NY. 2002. 408p. ISBN:0-415-14687-9, ISBN13: 978-0-415-14687-6. Dewey:949.5/013.
Audience: **u,f.** *Choice, 2003.*

Olmstead, Arthur T. **DS281**
History of the Persian Empire. Trade Paper. University of Chicago Press. Chicago, IL. 1959. 600p. ISBN:0-226-62777-2, ISBN13: 978-0-226-62777-9. Dewey:935.05. LCCN:48-007317.
Audience: **g,l,u,f.**

Greece > General

Adkins, Lesley & Adkins, Roy **DF77.A35 2005**
Handbook to Life in Ancient Greece. Ed. 2. Trade Cloth. Facts On File, Inc. New York, NY. 2005. 528p. Handbook to Life Ser. ISBN:0-8160-5659-5, ISBN13: 978-0-8160-5659-0. Dewey:938. LCCN:2004-047105.
Audience: **g,l,u.**

Bernal, Martin **DF78 .B398 1987**
Black Athena: The Archaeological and Documentary Evidence. Cloth Text. Rutgers University Press. Piscataway, NJ. 1991. 750p. ISBN:0-8135-1583-1, ISBN13: 978-0-8135-1583-0. Dewey:949.5.
Audience: **u,f.** *Choice, 1992.*

Bernal, Martin **DF78 .B398 1987**
Black Athena: The Afroasiatic Roots of Classical Civilization: The Fabrication of Ancient Greece, 1785-1985. Paper Text. Rutgers University Press. Piscataway, NJ. 1987. 575p. ISBN:0-8135-1277-8, ISBN13: 978-0-8135-1277-8. Dewey:949.5. LCCN:87-016408.
Audience: **u,f.** *Choice, 1988.*

Bernal, Martin **PR6029.C33F4**
Black Athena: The Afroasiatic Roots of Classical Civilization: The Linguistic Evidence. Trade Cloth. Rutgers University Press. Piscataway, NJ. 2006. 704p. ISBN:0-8135-3655-3, ISBN13: 978-0-8135-3655-2. Dewey:822.912.
Audience: **g,u,f.**

Bernal, Martin **DF78.B3984 2001**
Black Athena Writes Back: Martin Bernal Responds to His Critics. David Chioni Moore (Editor). Trade Paper. Duke University Press. Durham, NC. 2001. 640p. ISBN:0-8223-2717-1, ISBN13: 978-0-8223-2717-2. Dewey:938. LCCN:2001-023173.
Audience: **u,f.** *Choice, 2002.*

Burckhardt, Jacob **DF77.B94213**
The Greeks and Greek Civilization. Oswyn Murray (Editor), Sheila Stern (Translator). Trade Paper. St. Martin's Press. Gordonville, VA. 1999. 504p. ISBN:0-312-24447-9, ISBN13: 978-0-312-24447-7. Dewey:938.
Audience: **u,f.**

Burkert, Walter **PA3070.B75 2004**
Babylon, Memphis, Persepolis: Eastern Contexts of Greek Culture. Trade Cloth. Harvard University Press. Cambridge, MA. 2004. 192p. ISBN:0-674-01489-8, ISBN13: 978-0-674-01489-3. Dewey:880/.9001. LCCN:2004-047412.
Audience: **g,u,f.** *Choice, 2005.*

Camp, John & Fisher, Elizabeth **DF77**
The World of the Ancient Greeks. Trade Cloth. Thames & Hudson. New York, NY. 2002. 224p. ISBN:0-500-05112-7, ISBN13: 978-0-500-05112-2. Dewey:938. LCCN:2002-100571.
Audience: **g,l,u.**

Cartledge, Paul (Editor) **DF77 .C32 1998**
The Cambridge Illustrated History of Ancient Greece. Cloth Text. Cambridge University Press. New York, NY. 1997. 400p. Illustrated Histories Ser. ISBN:0-521-48196-1, ISBN13: 978-0-521-48196-0. Dewey:938. LCCN:96-051545.
Audience: **g,l,u.**

Habicht, Christian **DF27.P383H33 1998**
Pausanias' Guide to Ancient Greece. Trade Paper. University of California Press. Berkeley, CA. 1999. 232p. Sather Classical Lectures, Vol. 50:No. 30 ISBN:0-520-06170-5, ISBN13: 978-0-520-06170-5. Dewey:913.804/9. LCCN:99-187467.
Audience: **u,f.** *Choice, 1986.*

Hammond, Nicholas G. **DF214.H28 1986**
A History of Greece to 322 B. C. Ed. 3. Paper Text. Oxford University Press, Inc. New York, NY. 1986. 716p. ISBN:0-19-873095-0, ISBN13: 978-0-19-873095-8. Dewey:938. LCCN:86-005222.
Audience: **g,l,u.** B

Hanson, Victor Davis & Keegan, John **DF89.H36 2004**
Wars of the Ancient Greeks. Trade Paper. Smithsonian Institution Press. Washington, DC. 2004. 240p. Smithsonian History of Warfare Ser. ISBN:1-58834-189-5, ISBN13: 978-1-58834-189-1. Dewey:355/.00938. LCCN:2004-049101.
Audience: **g,l,u,f.**

Larsen, Jakob Aall Ottesen **JC73 .L3**
Representative Government in Greek and Roman History. Paper Text. Textbook Publishers. Temecula, CA. 2003. 249p. ISBN:0-7581-2646-8, ISBN13: 978-0-7581-2646-7. Dewey:321.4/0938.
Audience: **u,f.** B

Lefkowitz, Mary **DT14.L44 1996**
Not Out of Africa: How Afrocentrism Became an Excuse to Teach Myth as History. Trade Cloth. Basic Books. New York, NY. 1996. 240p. ISBN:0-465-09837-1, ISBN13: 978-0-465-09837-8. Dewey:949.5. LCCN:95-049109.
Audience: **g,u,f.** *Choice, 1996.*

Lefkowitz, Mary R. & Rogers, Guy (Editors) **DF78.B54 1996**
Black Athena Revisited. Trade Paper. University of North Carolina Press. Chapel Hill, NC. 1996. 544p. ISBN:0-8078-4555-8, ISBN13: 978-0-8078-4555-4. Dewey:938. LCCN:95-008903.
Audience: **u,f.**

Martin, Thomas R. **DF77.M3 2000**
Ancient Greece: From Prehistoric to Hellenistic Times. Cloth over Boards. Yale University Press. Cumberland, RI. 1996. 288p. Yale Nota Bene Ser. ISBN:0-300-06767-4, ISBN13: 978-0-300-06767-5. Dewey:938. LCCN:2001-277145.
Audience: **g,l,u.**

Morkot, Robert **G2001.S1M6 1996**
Penguin Historical Atlas of Ancient Greece. Trade Paper. Penguin Group (USA) Inc. New York, NY. 1997. 144p. History

Atlas Ser. ISBN:0-14-051335-3, ISBN13: 978-0-14-051335-6. Dewey:911.3/8. LCCN:97-675026.
Audience: **g,l,u.**

Murray, Oswyn & Price, Simon (Editors) **DF82**
The Greek City: From Homer to Alexander. Trade Paper. Oxford University Press, Inc. New York, NY. 1991. 388p. ISBN:0-19-814791-0, ISBN13: 978-0-19-814791-6. Dewey:938.
Audience: **u,f.**

Pomeroy, Sarah B., et al. **DF214.B74 2004**
A Brief History of Ancient Greece: Politics, Society, and Culture. Stanley M. Burstein, Walter Donlan & Jennifer Tolbert Roberts (Authors). Cloth Text. Oxford University Press, Inc. New York, NY. 2004. 384p. ISBN:0-19-515680-3, ISBN13: 978-0-19-515680-5. Dewey:938/.09. LCCN:2003-060873.
Audience: **g,l,u.**

Sealey, Raphael **DF222**
A History of the Greek City States, 700-338 BC. Trade Cloth. University of California Press. Berkeley, CA. 1976. 540p. ISBN:0-520-03177-6, ISBN13: 978-0-520-03177-7. Dewey:938.
Audience: **g,l,u.**

Speake, Graham (Editor) **DF757.E53 2000**
Encyclopedia of Greece and the Hellenic Tradition, Set. Trade Cloth. Fitzroy Dearborn Publishers, Inc. Chicago, IL. 2000. 1919p. ISBN:1-57958-141-2, ISBN13: 978-1-57958-141-1. Dewey:938/.003. LCCN:2001-267772.
Audience: **g,l,u,f.** *Choice, 2001.*

Greece > Sources

Bodel, John P. (Editor) **CN350.E77 2001**
Epigraphic Evidence: Ancient History from Inscriptions. Paper over Boards. Routledge. New York, NY. 2001. 272p. History of Linguistic Thought Ser. ISBN:0-415-11623-6, ISBN13: 978-0-415-11623-7. Dewey:938. LCCN:00-059202.
Audience: **u,f.**

Crawford, Michael **DE86**
Sources for Ancient History. Trade Paper. Cambridge University Press. New York, NY. 1983. 250p. Sources of History Ser. ISBN:0-521-28958-0, ISBN13: 978-0-521-28958-0. Dewey:938. LCCN:82-023656.
Audience: **g,l,u,f.**

Crawford, Michael & Whitehead, David (Editors) **DF12 .C7 1983**
Archaic and Classical Greece: A Selection of Ancient Sources in Translation. Trade Cloth. Cambridge University Press. New York, NY. 1983. 660p. ISBN:0-521-22775-5, ISBN13: 978-0-521-22775-9. Dewey:938. LCCN:82-004355.
Audience: **g,l,u.**

Dillon, Matthew & Garland, Lynda **DF75.D55 2000**
Ancient Greece: Social and Historical Documents from Archaic Times to Death of Socrates. Ed. 2. Paper over Boards. Routledge. New York, NY. 2000. 560p. ISBN:0-415-21754-7, ISBN13: 978-0-415-21754-5. Dewey:932. LCCN:99-032499.
Audience: **g,l,u.**

Lefkowitz, Mary R. & Fant, Maureen Brown **HQ1127.W653 2005**
Women's Life in Greece and Rome: A Source Book in Translation. Ed. 3. Trade Cloth. Johns Hopkins University Press. Baltimore, MD. 2005. 464p. ISBN:0-8018-8309-1, ISBN13: 978-0-8018-8309-5. Dewey:305.40938. LCCN:2005-928766.
Audience: **g,l,u,f.**

Stanton, G. R. **DF277.A84 1990**
Athenian Politics C. 800-500 B. C.: A Sourcebook. Trade Paper. Routledge. New York, NY. 1990. 240p. Studies in Ancient Civilization ISBN:0-415-04061-2, ISBN13: 978-0-415-04061-7. Dewey:938/.5. LCCN:89-071345.
Audience: **g,l,u.**

Woodhead, A. G. **CN350.W65 1992**
The Study of Greek Inscriptions. Ed. 2. E-Book. NetLibrary, Inc. Boulder, CO. 1992. ISBN:0-585-14884-8, ISBN13: 978-0-585-14884-7. Dewey:481/.7.
Audience: **u,f.**

Greece > Social History

Archibald, Zosia (Editor), et al. **HC31.H455 2000**
Hellenistic Economies. John Davies, Graham J. Oliver & Vincent Gabrielsen (Editors). Paper over Boards. Routledge. New York, NY. 2001. 416p. ISBN:0-415-23466-2, ISBN13: 978-0-415-23466-5. Dewey:330.9/01. LCCN:00-030819.
Audience: **u,f.**

Blundell, Sue **HQ1134.B58 1995**
Women in Ancient Greece. Trade Paper. Harvard University Press. Cambridge, MA. 1995. 224p. ISBN:0-674-95473-4, ISBN13: 978-0-674-95473-1. Dewey:938/.0082. LCCN:93-036217.
Audience: **g,l,u,f.** *Choice, 1995.*

Burkert, Walter **BL96**
Ancient Mystery Cults. Trade Paper. Harvard University Press. Cambridge, MA. 1987. 192p. Carl Newell Jackson Lectures ISBN:0-674-03387-6, ISBN13: 978-0-674-03387-0. Dewey:291/.093.
Audience: **g,u,f.** *Choice, 1988.*

Burkert, Walter **BL782**
Greek Religion: Archaic and Classical. Trade Paper. Blackwell Publishing, Inc. Malden, MA. 2002. 504p. ISBN:0-631-15624-0, ISBN13: 978-0-631-15624-6. Dewey:292/.08.
Audience: **u,f.**

Cartledge, Paul (Editor), et al. **HC37.M66 2001**
Money, Labour and Land: Approaches to the Economies of Ancient Greece. Edward E. Cohen & Lin Foxhall (Editors). Paper over Boards. Routledge. New York, NY. 2001. 288p. Routledge Classical Monographs ISBN:0-415-19649-3, ISBN13: 978-0-415-19649-9. Dewey:330.938. LCCN:2001-031918.
Audience: **u,f.**

Cohen, Edward E. **HG237**
Athenian Economy and Society: A Banking Perspective. Trade Paper. Princeton University Press. Princeton, NJ. 1997. 306p. ISBN:0-691-01592-9, ISBN13: 978-0-691-01592-7. Dewey:332.1.
Audience: **g,l,u,f.**

Cox, Cheryl A. **HQ662.5.A15 1998**
Household Interests: Property, Marriage Strategies, and Family Dynamics in Ancient Athens. Trade Cloth. Princeton University Press. Princeton, NJ. 1997. 276p. ISBN:0-691-01572-4, ISBN13: 978-0-691-01572-9. Dewey:306.85/09385. LCCN:97-011775.
Audience: **u,f.** *Choice, 1998.*

Davidson, James **DF275 .D23**
Courtesans and Fishcakes: The Consuming Passions of Classical Athens. Trade Cloth. DIANE Publishing Company. Collingdale, PA. 2001. 371p. ISBN:0-7881-9829-7, ISBN13: 978-0-7881-9829-8. Dewey:938.
Audience: **g,l,u,f.**

Dover, Kenneth J. **HQ76.3.G8D68 1989**
Greek Homosexuality: Updated and with a New Postscript. Trade Paper. Harvard University Press. Cambridge, MA. 1989. 256p. ISBN:0-674-36270-5, ISBN13: 978-0-674-36270-3. Dewey:306.76/6/09495. LCCN:89-034289.
Audience: **l,u,f.**

Dover, Kenneth J. **BJ182.D68 1994**
Greek Popular Morality in the Time of Plato and Aristotle. Trade Cloth. Hackett Publishing Company, Inc. Indianapolis, IN. 1994. 352p. ISBN:0-87220-246-1, ISBN13: 978-0-87220-246-7. Dewey:170/.938. LCCN:93-042840.
Audience: **g,l,u,f.** B

Finley, Moses I. **HC37.F56**
Economy and Society of Ancient Greece. Brent D. Shaw & Richard P. Saller (Editors). Trade Cloth. Penguin Group (USA) Inc. New York, NY. 1982. 352p. ISBN:0-670-28847-0, ISBN13: 978-0-670-28847-2. Dewey:330.938. LCCN:81-051886.
Audience: **l,u,f.** B

Golden, Mark **GV23**
Sport and Society in Ancient Greece. P. A. Cartledge & P. D. A. Garnsey (Contribution by). Trade Paper. Cambridge University Press. New York, NY. 1998. 230p. Key Themes in Ancient History Ser. ISBN:0-521-49790-6, ISBN13: 978-0-521-49790-9. Dewey:306.4/83/0938. LCCN:98-003004.
Audience: **g,l,u,f.** *Choice, 1999.*

Hall, Jonathan M. **DF135.H33 1997**
Ethnic Identity in Greek Antiquity. Cloth Text. Cambridge University Press. New York, NY. 1997. 246p. ISBN:0-521-58017-X, ISBN13: 978-0-521-58017-5. Dewey:305.8/00938. LCCN:96-009563.
Audience: **u,f.** *Choice, 1998.*

Hubbard, Thomas K. (Editor) **HQ76.3.G8 H66 2003**
Homosexuality in Greece and Rome: A Sourcebook of Basic Documents. Trade Cloth. University of California Press. Berkeley, CA. 2003. 600p. Joan Palevsky Imprint in Classical Literature Ser. ISBN:0-520-22381-0, ISBN13: 978-0-520-22381-3. Dewey:306.76/6/0937. LCCN:2002-013904.
Audience: **l,u,f.** *Choice, 2003.*

Keuls, Eva C. **HQ1134.K48 1993**
The Reign of the Phallus: Sexual Politics in Ancient Athens. Trade Cloth. University of California Press. Berkeley, CA. 1993. 477p. ISBN:0-520-07928-0, ISBN13: 978-0-520-07928-1. Dewey:306.709385. LCCN:92-032765.
Audience: **u,f.** *Choice, 1985.*

Loraux, Nicole **HQ1075.5.G8.L6713**
The Children of Athena: Athenian Ideas about Citizenship and the Division Between the Sexes. Caroline Levine (Translator). Trade Cloth. Princeton University Press. Princeton, NJ. 1993. 320p. ISBN:0-691-03272-6, ISBN13: 978-0-691-03272-6. Dewey:305.309385. LCCN:92-039325.
Audience: **u,f.** *Choice, 1994.*

Mikalson, Jon D. **BL793.A76 M55 1998**
Religion in Hellenistic Athens. Trade Cloth. University of California Press. Berkeley, CA. 1998. 376p. Hellenistic Culture and Society Ser., Vol. 29 ISBN:0-520-21023-9, ISBN13: 978-0-520-21023-3. Dewey:292/.00938/5. LCCN:97-035407.
Audience: **u,f.**

Miller, Stephen **GV21**
Ancient Greek Athletics. Trade Paper. Yale University Press. Cumberland, RI. 2006. 304p. ISBN:0-300-11529-6, ISBN13: 978-0-300-11529-1. Dewey:796/.09495.
Audience: **g,l,u,f.**

Miller, Stephen G. **GV21.A73 1991**
Arete: Greek Sports from Ancient Sources. Ed. 2. Trade Cloth. University of California Press. Berkeley, CA. 1991. 239p. ISBN:0-520-07508-0, ISBN13: 978-0-520-07508-5. Dewey:796/.0938. LCCN:90-028646.
Audience: **l,u.**

Nevett, Lisa C. **DF99.N48 1999**
House and Society in the Ancient Greek World. Trade Cloth. Cambridge University Press. New York, NY. 1999. xi, 220p. New Studies in Archaeology ISBN:0-05-216439-X, ISBN13: 978-0-05-216439-4. Dewey:306/.0938. LCCN:98-038089.
Audience: **u,f.** *Choice, 2000.*

Patterson, Cynthia B. **HQ510**
The Family in Greek History. Trade Paper. Harvard University Press. Cambridge, MA. 2001. 308p. ISBN:0-674-00568-6, ISBN13: 978-0-674-00568-6. Dewey:306.85/09495.
Audience: **l,u,f.** *Choice, 1999.*

Pomeroy, Sarah B. **HQ510**
Families in Classical and Hellenistic Greece: Representations and Realities. Trade Paper. Oxford University Press, Inc. New York, NY. 1999. 272p. ISBN:0-19-815260-4, ISBN13: 978-0-19-815260-6. Dewey:306.8/5/0938.
Audience: **l,u,f.** *Choice, 1998.*

Pomeroy, Sarah B. **HQ1134.P64 1995**
Goddesses, Whores, Wives and Slaves: Women in Classical Antiquity. Trade Paper. Knopf Publishing Group. New York, NY. 1995. 304p. ISBN:0-8052-1030-X, ISBN13: 978-0-8052-1030-9. Dewey:305.4/2/0938. LCCN:95-109446.
Audience: **g,l,u,f.** B

Pomeroy, Sarah B. **HQ1134.P66 2002**
Spartan Women. Trade Paper. Oxford University Press, Inc. New York, NY. 2002. 216p. ISBN:0-19-513067-7, ISBN13: 978-0-19-513067-6. Dewey:305.4/09389. LCCN:2001-055961.
Audience: **l,u,f.** *Choice, 2003.*

Rostovtzeff, Mikhail I **HN650.5.A8**
Social and Economic History of the Hellenistic World. Oxford University Press, Inc. 1986. ISBN:0-19-814230-7, ISBN13: 978-0-19-814230-0.
Audience: **u,f.**

Spivey, Nigel **GV23.S69 2004**
The Ancient Olympics: A History. Trade Cloth. Oxford University Press, Inc. New York, NY. 2004. 304p. ISBN:0-19-280433-2, ISBN13: 978-0-19-280433-4. Dewey:796.48. LCCN:2004-046147.
Audience: **g,l,u,f.** *Choice, 2005.*

Starr, Chester G. **HC37.S7**
The Economic and Social Growth of Early Greece: 800-500 B.C. Trade Cloth. Oxford University Press, Inc. New York, NY. 1977. 280p. ISBN:0-19-502223-8, ISBN13: 978-0-19-502223-0. Dewey:330.9/38/02. LCCN:76-057265.
Audience: **g,l,u,f.**

Tyrrell, William B. & Brown, Frieda S. **BL793.A76T97 1991**
Athenian Myths and Institutions: Words in Action. Paper Text. Oxford University Press, Inc. New York, NY. 1991. 240p. ISBN:0-19-506719-3, ISBN13: 978-0-19-506719-4. Dewey:292.1/3. LCCN:90-043853.
Audience: **u,f.** *Choice, 1991.*

Valavanis, Panos **BL795.S47 V35 2004**
Games and Sanctuaries in Ancient Greece: Olympia, Delphi, Isthmia, Nemea, Athens. John Boardman (Foreword by). Trade Cloth. Oxford University Press, Inc. New York, NY. 2004. 500p. Antiquities Ser. ISBN:0-89236-762-8, ISBN13: 978-0-89236-762-7. Dewey:796.093. LCCN:2004-103080.
Audience: **u,f.** *Choice, 2005.*

Vernant, Jean-Pierre **DF78.V4713 1988**
Myth and Society in Ancient Greece. Ed. 2. Janet Lloyd (Translator). Trade Cloth. Zone Books. Brooklyn, NY. 1988. 280p. ISBN:0-942299-16-7, ISBN13: 978-0-942299-16-8. Dewey:938. LCCN:87-033786.
Audience: **g,l,u,f.**

Wiedemann, Thomas E.J. **HT863**
Slavery. Oxford University Press. 1997. Greece & Rome. New Surveys in the Classics ISBN:0-19-922321-1, ISBN13: 978-0-19-922321-3.
Audience: **l,u,f.**

Xenophon **PA4494.O43**
Oeconomicus: A Social and Historical Commentary. Sarah B. Pomeroy (Editor, Translator, Commentaries by, Introduction by). Paper Text. Oxford University Press, Inc. New York, NY. 1995. 400p. ISBN:0-19-815025-3, ISBN13: 978-0-19-815025-1. Dewey:888.0108.
Audience: **u,f.**

Greece > By Period > Bronze Age

Allen, Susan Heuck **DF212.S4**
Finding the Walls of Troy: Frank Calvert and Heinrich Schliemann at Hisarlik. Trade Cloth. DIANE Publishing Company. Collingdale, PA. 1999. 409p. ISBN:0-7567-6268-5, ISBN13: 978-0-7567-6268-1. Dewey:930.1/092.
Audience: **g,u,f.** *Choice, 1999.*

Bryce, Trevor **DF221.T8B79 2005**
Trojans and Their Neighbours. Paper over Boards. Routledge. New York, NY. 2006. 240p. Ancient Peoples Ser. ISBN:0-415-34959-1, ISBN13: 978-0-415-34959-8. Dewey:939/.21. LCCN:2005-003604.
Audience: **g,l,u,f.**

Cadogan, Gerald **DF221.C8**
Palaces of Minoan Crete. Routledge. 1980. ISBN:0-416-73160-0, ISBN13: 978-0-416-73160-6.
Audience: **g,l,u.**

Castleden, Rodney **DF220.5.C38 2005**
Mycenaeans. Paper over Boards. Routledge. New York, NY. 2005. 296p. Ancient Peoples Ser. ISBN:0-415-24923-6, ISBN13: 978-0-415-24923-2. Dewey:938/.8. LCCN:2004-019550.
Audience: **g,l,u,f.**

Chadwick, John **DF220 .C43**
The Mycenaean World. Trade Paper. Cambridge University Press. New York, NY. 1976. 218p. ISBN:0-521-29037-6, ISBN13: 978-0-521-29037-1. Dewey:939/.18. LCCN:75-036021.
Audience: **g,l,u,f.**

Dickinson, Oliver **DF220 .D49 1994**
The Aegean Bronze Age. Norman Yoffee, Susan Alcock, Tom Dillehay, Stephen Shennan & Carla Sinopoli (Contribution by). Trade Paper. Cambridge University Press. New York, NY. 1994. 364p. World Archaeology Ser. ISBN:0-521-45664-9, ISBN13: 978-0-521-45664-7. Dewey:939.1. LCCN:93-002666.
Audience: **g,u,f.** *Choice, 1995.*

Doumas, Christos G. **DF261.T4**
Thera, Pompeii of the Ancient Aegean: Excavations at Akrotiri, 1967-1979. Trade Cloth. Thames & Hudson. New York, NY. 1983. 168p. New Aspects of Antiquity Ser. ISBN:0-500-39016-9, ISBN13: 978-0-500-39016-0. Dewey:939/.15. LCCN:81-086685.
Audience: **g,l,u,f.**

Drews, Robert **DF220.D73**
The Coming of the Greeks: Indo-European Conquests in the Aegean and the near East. Trade Paper. Princeton University Press. Princeton, NJ. 1994. 276p. ISBN:0-691-02951-2, ISBN13: 978-0-691-02951-1.
Audience: **u,f.**

Drews, Robert **GN778.3.A1D74**
The End of the Bronze Age: Changes in Warfare and the Catastrophe Ca. 1200 B. C. Trade Paper. Princeton University Press. Princeton, NJ. 1995. 264p. ISBN:0-691-02591-6, ISBN13: 978-0-691-02591-9. Dewey:930.091822.
Audience: **u,f.** *Choice, 1994.*

Finley, M. I. **PA4037.F48 2002**
The World of Odysseus. Bernard Knox (Introduction by). Trade Paper. New York Review of Books, Incorporated, The. New York, NY. 2002. 232p. New York Review Books Classics Ser. ISBN:1-59017-017-2, ISBN13: 978-1-59017-017-5. Dewey:883/.01. LCCN:2002-002882.
Audience: **g,l,u,f.**

Fitton, J. Lesley **DF220.F54 1996**
The Discovery of the Greek Bronze Age. Trade Cloth. Harvard University Press. Cambridge, MA. 1996. 192p. British Museum Paperbacks Ser. ISBN:0-674-21188-X, ISBN13: 978-0-674-21188-9. Dewey:938/.01. LCCN:95-079880.
Audience: **g,l,u,f.** *Choice, 1996.*

Fitton, J. Lesley **DF220.3.F57 2002**
Minoans. Trade Cloth. British Museum Press. London, 2002. 232p. Peoples of the Past Ser. ISBN:0-7141-2140-1, ISBN13: 978-0-7141-2140-6. Dewey:939.1/8. LCCN:2003-428050.
Audience: **g,l,u,f.**

Graham, James W. **DF221.C8G7 1987**
The Palaces of Crete. Trade Cloth. Princeton University Press. Princeton, NJ. 1987. 320p. ISBN:0-691-03585-7, ISBN13: 978-0-691-03585-7. Dewey:939/.18. LCCN:85-043376.
Audience: **u,f.**

Higgins, Reynold **N5660.H5 1997**
Minoan and Mycenaean Art. Ed. 2. Lyvia Morgan (Revised by). Trade Paper. Thames & Hudson. New York, NY. 1997. 216p. World of Art Ser. ISBN:0-500-20303-2, ISBN13: 978-0-500-20303-3. Dewey:709.3/918. LCCN:97-060252.
Audience: **g,l,u,f.**

MacGillivray, Joseph Alexander **DF212.E82M33 2000**
Minotaur: Sir Arthur Evans and the Archaeology of the Minoan Myth. Trade Paper. Farrar, Straus & Giroux. New York, NY. 2000. viii, 373p. ISBN:0-8090-3035-7, ISBN13: 978-0-8090-3035-4. Dewey:939/.18. LCCN:00-033606.
Audience: **g,l,u,f.** *Choice, 2001.*

Mylonas, George E. **DF0221.M9M93**
Mycenae and the Mycenaean Age. Trade Paper. Books on Demand. Ann Arbor, MI. 340p. ISBN:0-8357-6229-7, ISBN13: 978-0-8357-6229-8. Dewey:913.391031. LCCN:65-017154.
Audience: **u,f.**

Pendlebury, J.D.S. **DF 221 C86 P3**
Handbook to the Palace of Minos at Knoss. Trade Paper. Kessinger Publishing, LLC. Whitefish, MT. 2003. ISBN:0-7661-3916-6, ISBN13: 978-0-7661-3916-9. Dewey:939.18.
Audience: **u,f.**

Schliemann, Heinrich **DF221.T8**
Ilios: City of the Trojans. Trade Cloth. Athena Publications, Inc. Naples, FL. 1996. 854p. Original Sources in Exploration Ser. ISBN:1-887954-01-5, ISBN13: 978-1-887954-01-3. Dewey:913.3/9/2103.
Audience: **g,l,u,f.**

Schliemann, Heinrich **DF221.T8 S2513**
Troy and Its Remains. Trade Cloth. Peter Smith Publisher, Inc. Magnolia, MA. 1995. ISBN:0-8446-6862-1, ISBN13: 978-0-8446-6862-8. Dewey:939/.21.
Audience: **g,l,u,f.**

Taylour, William **DF221.M9**
The Mycenaeans. Ed. 2. Trade Paper. Thames & Hudson. New York, NY. 1990. 180p. Ancient Peoples and Places Ser. ISBN:0-500-27586-6, ISBN13: 978-0-500-27586-3. Dewey:938. LCCN:82-050813.
Audience: **g,l,u,f.** B

Traill, David A. **DF212.S4**
Schliemann of Troy: Treasure and Deceit. Trade Paper. St. Martin's Press. Gordonville, VA. 1997. 384p. ISBN:0-312-15647-2, ISBN13: 978-0-312-15647-3. Dewey:930.1/092.
Audience: **g,l,u,f.**

Vermeule, Emily T. **DF220 .V4**
Greece in the Bronze Age. Paper Text. University of Chicago Press. Chicago, IL. 1999. 428p. ISBN:0-226-85354-3, ISBN13: 978-0-226-85354-3. Dewey:938. LCCN:64-023427.
Audience: **g,l,u,f.** B

Willetts, R. F. **DF261.C8W55 2004**
The Civilization of Ancient Crete. Trade Paper. Phoenix Press, WC2. London, 2004. 280p. Phoenix Press Ser. ISBN:1-84212-746-2, ISBN13: 978-1-84212-746-9. Dewey:939.18.
Audience: **g,u,f.** B

Greece > By Period > Archaic Greece

Andrewes, Anthony **DF222**
The Greek Tyrants. Trade Paper. Brill Academic Publishers, Inc. Boston, MA. 1956. ISBN:0-09-029564-1, ISBN13: 978-0-09-029564-7. Dewey:938.
Audience: **g,l,u,f.**

Boardman, John **DF251.B6 1999**
The Greeks Overseas: Their Early Colonies and Trade. Ed. 4. Trade Paper. Thames & Hudson. New York, NY. 1999. 304p. ISBN:0-500-28109-2, ISBN13: 978-0-500-28109-3. Dewey:930/.09/822. LCCN:98-061437.
Audience: **g,u,f.** B

Burkert, Walter **DF78.B8513 1992**
The Orientalizing Revolution: Near Eastern Influence on Greek Culture in the Early Archaic Age. Trade Cloth. Harvard University Press. Cambridge, MA. 1992. 238p. Revealing Antiquity Ser., No. 5 ISBN:0-674-64363-1, ISBN13: 978-0-674-64363-5. Dewey:938. LCCN:92-008923.
Audience: **g,u,f.** *Choice, 1993.*

Cerchiai, Luca, et al. **DG55.M3C4713 2004**
The Greek Cities of Magna Graecia and Sicily. Lorena Jannelli & Fausto Longo (Authors). Trade Cloth. Oxford University Press, Inc. New York, NY. 2004. 288p. Antiquities Ser. ISBN:0-89236-751-2, ISBN13: 978-0-89236-751-1. Dewey:937/.701. LCCN:2003-023715.
Audience: **u,f.**

Coldstream, J. N. **DF221.5.C65 2003**
Geometric Greece: 900-700 BC. Ed. 2. Trade Paper. Routledge. New York, NY. 2003. 456p. ISBN:0-415-29899-7, ISBN13: 978-0-415-29899-5. Dewey:938/.01. LCCN:2003-041421.
Audience: **u,f.**

Hurwit, Jeffrey M. **NX448.5**
The Art and Culture of Early Greece: 1100-480 B. C. Trade Paper. Cornell University Press. Ithaca, NY. 1987. 368p. ISBN:0-8014-9401-X, ISBN13: 978-0-8014-9401-7. Dewey:700/.938. LCCN:85-004204.
Audience: **g,l,u,f.** *Choice, 1986.*

Kelly, Thomas **DF0221.A8K44**
A History of Argos to 500 B. C. Trade Paper. Books on Demand. Ann Arbor, MI. 226p. Minnesota Monographs in the Humanities, Vol. 9 ISBN:0-608-15968-9, ISBN13: 978-0-608-15968-3. Dewey:938/.8. LCCN:76-011500.
Audience: **u,f.**

Morgan, Catherine **DF135.M67 2003**
Early Greek States Beyond the Polis. Paper over Boards. Routledge. New York, NY. 2003. 336p. ISBN:0-415-08996-4, ISBN13: 978-0-415-08996-8. Dewey:321/.00938. LCCN:2002-032623.
Audience: **u,f.** *Choice, 2004.*

Murray, Oswyn **DF77.M82 1993**
Early Greece. Ed. 2. Trade Paper. Harvard University Press. Cambridge, MA. 1993. 368p. ISBN:0-674-22132-X, ISBN13: 978-0-674-22132-1. Dewey:938/.02. LCCN:93-015040.
Audience: **g,l,u,f.** *B*

Pearson, Lionel **DF212.A2 P4 1975**
Early Ionian Historians. Trade Cloth. Greenwood Publishing Group, Inc. Portsmouth, NH. 1975. 240p. ISBN:0-8371-5314-X, ISBN13: 978-0-8371-5314-8. Dewey:938/.007/2022. LCCN:75-136874.
Audience: **u,f.**

Starr, Chester G. **JC73.S68 1986**
Individual and Community: The Rise of the Polis, 800-500 B. C. Trade Cloth. Oxford University Press, Inc. New York, NY. 1986. 144p. ISBN:0-19-503971-8, ISBN13: 978-0-19-503971-9. Dewey:320.938. LCCN:85-015360.
Audience: **g,l,u.** *B* *Choice, 1986.*

Greece > By Period > Classical Greece

Boedeker, Deborah & Raaflaub, Kurt A. (Editors) **DF277**
Democracy, Empire, and the Arts in Fifth-Century Athens. Trade Paper. Harvard University Press. Cambridge, MA. 2003. 512p. ISBN:0-674-01258-5, ISBN13: 978-0-674-01258-5. Dewey:938.5/04.
Audience: **u,f.**

Boegehold, Alan L. & Scafuro, Adele C. **JC75.C5.A85**
Athenian Identity and Civic Ideology. Trade Paper. Johns Hopkins University Press. Baltimore, MD. 2002. 248p. ISBN:0-8018-6970-6, ISBN13: 978-0-8018-6970-9. Dewey:323.609385.
Audience: **u,f.** *Choice, 1994.*

Camp, John M. **DF275.C28 2004**
The Archaeology of Athens. Trade Paper. Yale University Press. Cumberland, RI. 2004. 352p. ISBN:0-300-10151-1, ISBN13: 978-0-300-10151-5. Dewey:938/.5.
Audience: **g,l,u,f.** *Choice, 2002.*

Camp, John M. **DF287.A23C36 1992**
The Athenian Agora: Excavations In The Heart of Classical Athens. Ed. 2. Trade Paper. Thames & Hudson. New York, NY. 1998. 232p. New Aspects of Antiquity Ser. ISBN:0-500-27683-8, ISBN13: 978-0-500-27683-9. Dewey:938.5. LCCN:85-051469.
Audience: **g,l,u,f.**

Cartledge, Paul **DF78**
The Greeks: A Portrait of Self and Others. Ed. 2. Trade Paper. Oxford University Press, Inc. New York, NY. 2002. 248p. ISBN:0-19-280388-3, ISBN13: 978-0-19-280388-7. Dewey:938. LCCN:2003-265319.
Audience: **u,f.**

Cartledge, Paul **DF261.S8C37 2001**
Sparta and Lakonia: A Regional History, 1300-362 BC. Ed. 2. Paper over Boards. Routledge. New York, NY. 2001. 376p. ISBN:0-415-26356-5, ISBN13: 978-0-415-26356-6. Dewey:938.9. LCCN:2001-034888.
Audience: **u,f.**

Cartledge, Paul **DF261.S8 C375 2001**
Spartan Reflections. Trade Cloth. University of California Press. Berkeley, CA. 2001. 288p. ISBN:0-520-23123-6, ISBN13: 978-0-520-23123-8. Dewey:938/.9. LCCN:2001-033205.
Audience: **u,f.** *Choice, 2002.*

Cohen, Edward E. **HN10.A74**
The Athenian Nation. Trade Paper. Princeton University Press. Princeton, NJ. 2002. 272p. ISBN:0-691-09490-X, ISBN13: 978-0-691-09490-8. Dewey:306/.09385.
Audience: **u,f.**

Demand, Nancy H. **DF261.T3**
Thebes in the Fifth Century. Trade Cloth. Routledge. New York, NY. 1983. 208p. States and Cities of Ancient Greece Ser. ISBN:0-7100-9288-1, ISBN13: 978-0-7100-9288-5. Dewey:938/.4. LCCN:82-016702.
Audience: **u,f.**

Ehrenberg, Victor L. **DF77**
From Solon to Socrates: Greek History and Civilization During the 6th and 5th Centuries B.C. Ed. 2. Trade Cloth. Routledge. New York, NY. 1990. 528p. ISBN:0-415-04024-8, ISBN13: 978-0-415-04024-2. Dewey:913.38/03.
Audience: **g,l,u.**

Forsdyke, Sara **JC75.E9F67 2005**
Exile, Ostracism and Democracy: The Politics of Expulsion in Ancient Greece. Trade Cloth. Princeton University Press. Princeton, NJ. 2005. 376p. ISBN:0-691-11975-9, ISBN13: 978-0-691-11975-5. Dewey:364.6/8. LCCN:2004-065773.
Audience: **u,f.**

Green, Peter **DF225.6.G7 1996**
The Year of the Salamis, 480-479 B.C.: The Greco-Persian Wars. Trade Paper. University of California Press. Berkeley, CA. 1998. 374p. ISBN:0-520-20313-5, ISBN13: 978-0-520-20313-6. Dewey:938/.03. LCCN:95-046654.
Audience: **g,u,f.**

Hammond, Nicholas G. **DF214.H28 1986**
A History of Greece to 322 B. C. Ed. 3. Paper Text. Oxford University Press, Inc. New York, NY. 1986. 716p. ISBN:0-19-873095-0, ISBN13: 978-0-19-873095-8. Dewey:938. LCCN:86-005222.
Audience: **g,l,u.** *B*

Hanson, Victor Davis (Editor) **U33 .H66 1993**
Hoplites: Classical Greek Battle Experience. Trade Paper. Routledge. New York, NY. 1993. 304p. ISBN:0-415-09816-5, ISBN13: 978-0-415-09816-8. Dewey:355.00938.
Audience: **u,f.**

Hanson, Victor Davis **HD133 .H36 1999**
The Other Greeks: The Family Farm and the Agrarian Roots of Western Civilization. Ed. 2. Trade Paper. University of California Press. Berkeley, CA. 1999. 596p. ISBN:0-520-20935-4, ISBN13: 978-0-520-20935-0. Dewey:338.1/6. LCCN:99-018181.
Audience: **u,f.** *Choice, 1995.*

Hanson, Victor Davis **DF229.H36 2005**
A War Like No Other: How the Athenians and Spartans Fought the Peloponnesian War. Trade Cloth. Alfred A. Knopf Inc. New York, NY. 2005. 416p. ISBN:1-4000-6095-8, ISBN13: 978-1-4000-6095-5. Dewey:938/.05. LCCN:2004-062892.
Audience: **g,l,u,f.**

Hanson, Victor Davis **UA929.95.A35 H27**
Warfare and Agriculture in Classical Greece. Ed. 2. Trade Cloth. University of California Press. Berkeley, CA. 1998. 300p. Biblioteca di Studi Antichi Ser. ISBN:0-520-21596-6, ISBN13: 978-0-520-21596-2. Dewey:338.1/4. LCCN:97-052207.
Audience: **u,f.**

Hanson, Victor Davis **U33 .H36 2000**
The Western Way of War: Infantry Battle in Classical Greece. Ed. 2. Trade Paper. University of California Press. Berkeley, CA. 2000. 308p. ISBN:0-520-21911-2, ISBN13: 978-0-520-21911-3. Dewey:355/.00938. LCCN:99-029002.
Audience: **g,u,f.** *Choice, 1989.*

Hurwit, Jeffrey M. **DF287.A2**
The Athenian Acropolis: History, Mythology, and Archaeology from the Neolithic Era to the Present. Trade Paper. Cambridge University Press. New York, NY. 2000. 408p. ISBN:0-521-42834-3, ISBN13: 978-0-521-42834-7. Dewey:938/.5.
Audience: **u,f.** *Choice, 1999.*

Jones, Nicholas F. **DF261.A8J65 2004**
Rural Athens under the Democracy. Book, Other. University of Pennsylvania Press. Philadelphia, PA. 2004. 344p. ISBN:0-8122-3774-9, ISBN13: 978-0-8122-3774-0. Dewey:307.72/09385/09014. LCCN:2003-061794.
Audience: **u,f.** *Choice, 2004.*

Kagan, Donald **DF229.3.K33 1990**
The Archidamian War. Trade Paper. Cornell University Press. Ithaca, NY. 1990. 400p. ISBN:0-8014-9714-0, ISBN13: 978-0-8014-9714-8. Dewey:938/.05. LCCN:89-028639.
Audience: **u,f.** B

Kagan, Donald **DF229.T6**
The Fall of the Athenian Empire. Trade Paper. Cornell University Press. Ithaca, NY. 1991. 480p. ISBN:0-8014-9984-4, ISBN13: 978-0-8014-9984-5. Dewey:938/.05. LCCN:86-032946.
Audience: **u,f.** *Choice, 1988.*

Kagan, Donald **DF229.T6**
The Outbreak of the Peloponnesian War. Trade Paper. Cornell University Press. Ithaca, NY. 1989. 420p. ISBN:0-8014-9556-3, ISBN13: 978-0-8014-9556-4. Dewey:938/.05. LCCN:69-018212.
Audience: **u,f.** B

Kagan, Donald **DF229.T6**
The Peace of Nicias and the Sicilian Expedition. Trade Paper. Cornell University Press. Ithaca, NY. 1991. 400p. ISBN:0-8014-9940-2, ISBN13: 978-0-8014-9940-1. Dewey:938/.05. LCCN:81-003150.
Audience: **u,f.** B

Kagan, Donald **DF229.T6**
The Peloponnesian War. Trade Paper. Penguin Group (USA) Inc. New York, NY. 2004. 544p. ISBN:0-14-200437-5, ISBN13: 978-0-14-200437-1. Dewey:938/.05.
Audience: **g,l,u.**

Meier, Christian **DF277**
Athens: A Portrait of the City in Its Golden Age. Trade Cloth. John Murray. London, 1999. vii, 628p. ISBN:0-7195-5959-6, ISBN13: 978-0-7195-5959-4. Dewey:938.5/04.
Audience: **g,l,u.**

Meiggs, Russell **DF227.M44 1979**
The Athenian Empire. Paper Text. Oxford University Press, Inc. New York, NY. 1979. 648p. ISBN:0-19-814843-7, ISBN13: 978-0-19-814843-2. Dewey:938/.04. LCCN:80-456017.
Audience: **u,f.** B

Meiggs, Russell & Lewis, David M. (Editors) **CN360**
A Selection of Greek Historical Inscriptions to the End of the Fifth Century B. C. Ed. 2. Paper Text. Oxford University Press, Inc. New York, NY. 1989. 338p. ISBN:0-19-814487-3, ISBN13: 978-0-19-814487-8. Dewey:487.1.
Audience: **f.**

Miller, Margaret Christina **DF227.5 .M56 1997**
Athens and Persia in the Fifth Century BC: A Study in Cultural Receptivity. Trade Paper. Cambridge University Press. New York, NY. 2004. 405p. ISBN:0-521-60758-2, ISBN13: 978-0-521-60758-2. Dewey:938.5/04.
Audience: **u,f.**

Munn, Mark D. **DF277**
The School of History: Athens in the Age of Socrates. Trade Paper. University of California Press. Berkeley, CA. 2003. 538p. A Joan Palevsky Book in Classical Literature Ser. ISBN:0-520-23685-8, ISBN13: 978-0-520-23685-1. Dewey:938/.04. LCCN:99-046451.
Audience: **u,f.**

Ober, Josiah **JC75.D36O24 1996**
The Athenian Revolution: Essays on Ancient Greek Democracy and Political Theory. Trade Cloth. Princeton University Press. Princeton, NJ. 1996. 224p. ISBN:0-691-01095-1, ISBN13: 978-0-691-01095-3. Dewey:321.8/09385. LCCN:96-019341.
Audience: **u,f.** *Choice, 1997.*

Ober, Josiah **JC79.A8 O24**
Mass and Elite in Democratic Athens: Rhetoric, Ideology, and the Power of the People. Trade Paper. Princeton University Press. Princeton, NJ. 1991. 408p. ISBN:0-691-02864-8, ISBN13: 978-0-691-02864-4. Dewey:306/.2/0938.
Audience: **u,f.** *Choice, 1989.*

Ober, Josiah **DF275.O33 1998**
Political Dissent in Democratic Athens: Intellectual Critics of Popular Rule. Cloth Text. Princeton University Press. Princeton, NJ. 1998. 440p. Martin Classical Lectures ISBN:0-691-00122-7, ISBN13: 978-0-691-00122-7. Dewey:938.5/06. LCCN:98-007110.
Audience: **u,f.** *Choice, 1999.*

Osborne, Robin
The Old Oligarch: Pseudo-Xenophon's Constitution of the Athenians. Ed. 2. Robin Osborne (Translator). LACTORs. 2004. ISBN:0-903625-31-8, ISBN13: 978-0-903625-31-9.
Audience: **g,l,u.**

Pearson, Lionel **DF211**
The Local Historians of Attica. Trade Paper. Oxford University Press, Inc. New York, NY. 1981. 167p. American Philological Association Philological Monographs ISBN:0-89130-540-8, ISBN13: 978-0-89130-540-8. Dewey:938/.5/0072. LCCN:81-016556.
Audience: **u,f.** B

Raaflaub, Kurt A. **JC599.G73R3313 2004**
The Discovery of Freedom in Ancient Greece. Renate Franciscono (Translator). Trade Cloth. University of Chicago

Press. Chicago, IL. 2004. 427p. ISBN:0-226-70101-8, ISBN13: 978-0-226-70101-1. Dewey:323.44/0938. LCCN:2003-012786.
Audience: **u,f.** *Choice, 2004.*

Rhodes, P. J. **JC75.D36A768 2004**
Athenian Democracy. Trade Cloth. Oxford University Press, Inc. New York, NY. 2004. 384p. Edinburgh Readings on the Ancient World Ser. ISBN:0-19-522139-7, ISBN13: 978-0-19-522139-8. Dewey:320.938/5/09014. LCCN:2004-002169.
Audience: **u,f.**

Rhodes, P. J. **JC71.A1R46 1986**
The Greek City States: A Source Book. Trade Cloth. University of Oklahoma Press. Norman, OK. 1986. 286p. ISBN:0-8061-2010-X, ISBN13: 978-0-8061-2010-2. Dewey:321.06/0938. LCCN:86-003375.
Audience: **l,u.** *Choice, 1987.*

Rhodes, P. J. (Author, Editor) **JC75.D36A768 2004**
Athenian Democracy. Trade Paper. Oxford University Press, Inc. New York, NY. 2004. 384p. Edinburgh Readings on the Ancient World Ser. ISBN:0-19-522140-0, ISBN13: 978-0-19-522140-4. Dewey:320.938/5/09014. LCCN:2004-002169.
Audience: **u,f.**

Strauss, Barry S. **DF225.6.S76 2004**
The Battle of Salamis: The Naval Encounter That Saved Greece — and Western Civilization. Trade Cloth. Simon & Schuster, Inc. New York, NY. 2004. 320p. ISBN:0-7432-4450-8, ISBN13: 978-0-7432-4450-3. Dewey:938/.03. LCCN:2004-045341.
Audience: **g,u,f.** *Choice, 2005.*

Thomas, Rosalind **PA227.T47 1989**
Oral Tradition and Written Record in Classical Athens. Peter Burke & Ruth Finnegan (Contribution by). Cloth Text. Cambridge University Press. New York, NY. 1989. 328p. Cambridge Studies in Oral and Literate Culture, No. 18 ISBN:0-521-35025-5, ISBN13: 978-0-521-35025-9. Dewey:480/.938/5. LCCN:88-022918.
Audience: **u,f.**

Tomlinson, R. A. **DF261.A67 T64**
Argos and the Argolid. Trade Cloth. Cornell University Press. Ithaca, NY. 1972. 280p. ISBN:0-8014-0713-3, ISBN13: 978-0-8014-0713-0. Dewey:913.3/8/8. LCCN:78-038286.
Audience: **u,f.**

Whitley, James **DF77 .W537 2001**
The Archaeology of Ancient Greece. Norman Yoffee, Susan Alcock, Tom Dillehay, Stephen Shennan & Carla Sinopoli (Contribution by). Cloth Text. Cambridge University Press. New York, NY. 2001. 512p. World Archaeology Ser. ISBN:0-521-62205-0, ISBN13: 978-0-521-62205-9. Dewey:938. LCCN:2001-018438.
Audience: **g,u,f.** *Choice, 2003, 2002.*

Wycherley, R. E. **DF275**
The Stones of Athens. Trade Cloth. Princeton University Press. Princeton, NJ. 1978. 312p. ISBN:0-691-03553-9, ISBN13: 978-0-691-03553-6. Dewey:938/.5. LCCN:77-072142.
Audience: **g,l,u,f.**

Greece > By Period > Fourth Century and Alexander

Bosworth, A. B. **BF1589 .B8 1993**
Conquest and Empire: The Reign of Alexander the Great. Trade Paper. Cambridge University Press. New York, NY. 1993. 346p. A Canto Book Ser. ISBN:0-521-40679-X, ISBN13: 978-0-521-40679-6. Dewey:938/.07/0924 B.
Audience: **u,f.** *Choice, 1989.*

Buckler, John **DF231.2**
The Theban Hegemony, 371-362 B. C. Trade Cloth. Harvard University Press. Cambridge, MA. 1980. 360p. Historical Studies, No. 98 ISBN:0-674-87645-8, ISBN13: 978-0-674-87645-3. Dewey:938/.06. LCCN:79-024928.
Audience: **u,f.** B

Cartledge, Paul **DF234.C285 2004**
Alexander the Great: A New Life. Trade Cloth. Overlook Press, The. New York, NY. 2004. 352p. ISBN:1-58567-565-2, ISBN13: 978-1-58567-565-4. Dewey:938/.07/092 B. LCCN:2004-054747.
Audience: **g,l,u,f.** *Choice, 2005.*

Errington, Malcolm **DF261.M2E7713 1990**
A History of Macedonia. Catherine Errington (Translator). Trade Cloth. University of California Press. Berkeley, CA. 1990. 325p. Hellenistic Culture and Society Ser., No. 5 ISBN:0-520-06319-8, ISBN13: 978-0-520-06319-8. Dewey:938/.1. LCCN:89-020193.
Audience: **u,f.** *Choice, 1991.*

Fox, Robin Lane **DF234**
Alexander the Great. Trade Paper. Penguin Group (USA) Inc. New York, NY. 2004. 576p. ISBN:0-14-303513-4, ISBN13: 978-0-14-303513-8. Dewey:921.
Audience: **g,l,u,f.**

Green, Peter **DF234.G68 1991**
Alexander of Macedon, 356-323 B.C.: A Historical Biography. Trade Paper. University of California Press. Berkeley, CA. 1992. 656p. ISBN:0-520-07166-2, ISBN13: 978-0-520-07166-7. Dewey:938/.07/092 B. LCCN:91-007292.
Audience: **g,l,u,f.**

Hammond, N. G. L. **DF233.8.P59H35 1994**
Philip of Macedon. Trade Cloth. Johns Hopkins University Press. Baltimore, MD. 1971. 248p. ISBN:0-8018-4927-6, ISBN13: 978-0-8018-4927-5. Dewey:938/.07/092 B. LCCN:94-001067.
Audience: **u,f.** *Choice, 1995.*

Hammond, Nicholas G. **DF261.M2**
The Macedonian State: Origins, Institutions, and History. Paper Text. Oxford University Press, Inc. New York, NY. 1993. 434p. ISBN:0-19-814927-1, ISBN13: 978-0-19-814927-9. Dewey:938.1. LCCN:89-008575.
Audience: **u,f.**

Heckel, Waldemar **DF234**
Who's Who in Age of Alexander the Great: Prosopography of Alexander's Empire. Trade Cloth. Blackwell Publishing, Inc. Malden, MA. 2006. 416p. ISBN:1-4051-1210-7, ISBN13: 978-1-4051-1210-9. Dewey:938/.07/0922 B. LCCN:2005-010995.
Audience: **g,l,u,f.** *Choice, 2006.*

Heckel, Waldemar & Yardley, John (Editors) **DF234.A1A45 2003**
Alexander the Great: Historical Sources in Translation. Trade Cloth. Blackwell Publishing, Inc. Malden, MA. 2003. 376p. Blackwell Sourcebooks in Ancient History ISBN:0-631-22820-9, ISBN13: 978-0-631-22820-2. Dewey:938/.07/092 B. LCCN:2002-153417.
Audience: **g,l,u.** *Choice, 2004.*

Holt, Frank Lee **DF234.57**
Into the Land of Bones: Alexander the Great in Afghanistan. Trade Cloth. University of California Press. Berkeley, CA. 2005. 232p. Hellenistic Culture and Society Ser., Vol. 47 ISBN:0-520-24553-9, ISBN13: 978-0-520-24553-2. Dewey:939/.6. LCCN:2004-024131.
Audience: **g,u,f.** *Choice, 2006.*

Loraux, Nicole **DF231.3.L6713 2001**
The Divided City: On Memory and Forgetting in Ancient Athens. Jeff Fort & Corinne Pache (Translators). Trade Paper. Zone Books. Brooklyn, NY. 2006. 360p. ISBN:1-890951-09-9, ISBN13: 978-1-890951-09-2. Dewey:938.506. LCCN:2001-017970.
Audience: **u,f.** *Choice, 2002.*

Munn, Mark D. **DF277**
The School of History: Athens in the Age of Socrates. Trade Paper. University of California Press. Berkeley, CA. 2003. 538p. A Joan Palevsky Book in Classical Literature Ser. ISBN:0-520-23685-8, ISBN13: 978-0-520-23685-1. Dewey:938/.04. LCCN:99-046451.
Audience: **u,f.**

Rhodes, P. J. & Osborne, Robin (Editor, Translators) **CN365.G74 2003**
Greek Historical Inscriptions, 404-323 BC. Trade Cloth. Oxford University Press, Inc. New York, NY. 2004. 632p. ISBN:0-19-815313-9, ISBN13: 978-0-19-815313-9. Dewey:938/.06. LCCN:2002-042552.
Audience: **f.**

Sealey, Raphael **DF277.S315 1993**
Demosthenes and His Time: A Study in Defeat. Cloth Text. Oxford University Press, Inc. New York, NY. 1993. 352p. ISBN:0-19-507928-0, ISBN13: 978-0-19-507928-9. Dewey:938/.5. LCCN:92-018540.
Audience: **u,f.** *Choice, 1993.*

Stewart, Andrew **DF234.2 .S74 1993**
Faces of Power: Alexander's Image and Hellenistic Politics. Trade Cloth. University of California Press. Berkeley, CA. 1994. 616p. Hellenistic Culture and Society Ser., Vol. 11 ISBN:0-520-06851-3, ISBN13: 978-0-520-06851-3. Dewey:938.107092. LCCN:92-010205.
Audience: **g,u,f.**

Strauss, Barry S. **DF277.S77 1987**
Athens after the Peloponnesian War: Class, Faction and Policy, 403-386 B.C. Trade Cloth. Cornell University Press. Ithaca, NY. 1987. 191p. ISBN:0-8014-1942-5, ISBN13: 978-0-8014-1942-3. Dewey:938/.5. LCCN:86-016677.
Audience: **u,f.**

Tarn, W. W. **DF234**
Alexander the Great: Sources and Studies, Vol. 2. Trade Paper. Cambridge University Press. New York, NY. 2003. 495p. ISBN:0-521-53137-3, ISBN13: 978-0-521-53137-5. Dewey:938.07.
Audience: **u,f.**

Tarn, William W. **DF234**
Alexander the Great: Narrative. Trade Cloth. Cambridge University Press. New York, NY. 1979. 176p. ISBN:0-521-22584-1, ISBN13: 978-0-521-22584-7. Dewey:938/.07/0924. LCCN:78-074533.
Audience: **u,f.**

Wilcken, Ulrich **DF234 .W713 1967**
Alexander the Great. Eugene N. Borza (Editor), G. C. Richards (Translator). Trade Paper. W. W. Norton & Company, Inc. New York, NY. 1967. 400p. ISBN:0-393-00381-7, ISBN13: 978-0-393-00381-9. Dewey:938/.07. LCCN:67-015823.
Audience: **g,l,u,f.** B

Wolpert, Andrew **DF231.3.W65 2002**
Remembering Defeat: Civil War and Civic Memory in Ancient Athens. Trade Cloth. Johns Hopkins University Press. Baltimore, MD. 2002. 208p. ISBN:0-8018-6790-8, ISBN13: 978-0-8018-6790-3. Dewey:938. LCCN:2001-000950.
Audience: **u,f.** *Choice, 2002.*

Worthington, Ian (Editor) **DF234**
Alexander the Great: A Reader. Paper over Boards. Routledge. New York, NY. 2003. 352p. ISBN:0-415-29186-0, ISBN13: 978-0-415-29186-6. Dewey:938/.07/092 B. LCCN:2002-037151.
Audience: **g,l,u.** *Choice, 2003.*

Greece > By Period > Hellenistic and Roman (323 B.C.-A.D. 565)

Austin, M. M. **DF235.A1**
The Hellenistic World from Alexander to the Roman Conquest: A Selection of Ancient Sources in Translation. Ed. 2. Cloth Text. Cambridge University Press. New York, NY. 2006. 656p. ISBN:0-521-82860-0, ISBN13: 978-0-521-82860-4. Dewey:938/.07.
Audience: **g,l,u.** B

Bagnall, Roger S. & Derow, Peter (Editors) **DE86.H38 2003**
The Hellenistic Period: Historical Sources in Translation. Ed. 2. Trade Cloth. Blackwell Publishing, Inc. Malden, MA. 2003. 352p. Blackwell Sourcebooks in Ancient History, Vol. 1 ISBN:1-4051-0132-6, ISBN13: 978-1-4051-0132-5. Dewey:938/.08. LCCN:2002-153416.
Audience: **g,l,u.**

Bosworth, A. B. **DE86.B67 2005**
Legacy of Alexander: Politics, Warfare, and Propaganda under the Successors. Trade Paper. Oxford University Press, Inc. New York, NY. 2005. 336p. ISBN:0-19-928515-2, ISBN13: 978-0-19-928515-0. Dewey:938.08.
Audience: **u,f.**

Bugh, Glenn R. (Editor) **DE86.C35 2006**
The Cambridge Companion to the Hellenistic World. Cloth Text. Cambridge University Press. New York, NY. 2006. 402p. Cambridge Companions to the Ancient World Ser. ISBN:0-521-82879-1, ISBN13: 978-0-521-82879-6. Dewey:938/.08. LCCN:2005-028730.
Audience: **u,f.**

Cartledge, Paul, et al. **DF77.H5463 1997**
Hellenistic Constructs: Essays in Culture, History, and Historiography. Peter Garnsey & Erich S. Gruen (Authors).

Trade Cloth. University of California Press. Berkeley, CA. 1997. 330p. Hellenistic Culture and Society Ser., Vol. 26 ISBN:0-520-20676-2, ISBN13: 978-0-520-20676-2. Dewey:938. LCCN:97-007317.
Audience: **u,f.**

Cartledge, Paul & Spawforth, Antony **DF261**
Hellenistic and Roman Sparta. Ed. 2. Trade Paper. Routledge. New York, NY. 2001. 328p. ISBN:0-415-26277-1, ISBN13: 978-0-415-26277-4. Dewey:938.9/08.
Audience: **u,f.**

Engels, Donald W. **HC37.E54 1990**
Roman Corinth: An Alternative Model for the Classical City. Trade Cloth. University of Chicago Press. Chicago, IL. 1990. 248p. ISBN:0-226-20870-2, ISBN13: 978-0-226-20870-1. Dewey:307.76/0938/7. LCCN:89-027004.
Audience: **u,f.**

Green, Peter **DE86.G738 1990**
Alexander to Actium: The Historical Evolution of the Hellenistic Age. Trade Cloth. University of California Press. Berkeley, CA. 1990. 970p. Hellenistic Culture and Society Ser., Vol. 1 ISBN:0-520-05611-6, ISBN13: 978-0-520-05611-4. Dewey:938. LCCN:86-004339.
Audience: **g,l,u.** *Choice, 1991.*

Green, Peter (Editor) **DF77.H5464 1993**
Hellenistic History and Culture. Trade Cloth. University of California Press. Berkeley, CA. 1993. 293p. Hellenistic Culture and Society Ser., Vol. 9 ISBN:0-520-07564-1, ISBN13: 978-0-520-07564-1. Dewey:938. LCCN:91-031398.
Audience: **u,f.** *Choice, 1994.*

Gruen, Erich S. **DS121.65.G78 2002**
Diaspora: Jews Amidst Greeks and Romans. Trade Cloth. Harvard University Press. Cambridge, MA. 2002. 400p. ISBN:0-674-00750-6, ISBN13: 978-0-674-00750-5. Dewey:933. LCCN:2001-052767.
Audience: **u,f.** *Choice, 2002.*

Gruen, Erich S. **BM176**
Heritage and Hellenism. Trade Paper. University of California Press. Berkeley, CA. 2002. 356p. Hellenistic Culture and Society Ser. ISBN:0-520-23506-1, ISBN13: 978-0-520-23506-9. Dewey:296.09014. LCCN:97-038808.
Audience: **u,f.**

Habicht, Christian **DF285.H313 1997**
Athens from Alexander to Antony. Deborah L. Schneider (Translator). Trade Cloth. Harvard University Press. Cambridge, MA. 1997. 408p. ISBN:0-674-05111-4, ISBN13: 978-0-674-05111-9. Dewey:938/.5. LCCN:97-005180.
Audience: **g,u,f.** *Choice, 1998.*

Kuhrt, Amelie & Sherwin-White, Susan (Editors) **DS57.H388 1987**
Hellenism in the East: The Interaction of Greek and Non-Greek Civilizations from Syria to Central Asia After Alexander. Trade Cloth. University of California Press. Berkeley, CA. 1988. 300p. Hellenistic Culture and Society Ser., Vol. 2 ISBN:0-520-06054-7, ISBN13: 978-0-520-06054-8. Dewey:939/.4. LCCN:87-005033.
Audience: **u,f.** *Choice, 1988.*

Larsen, Jakob Aall Ottesen **JC75.F3.L3**
Greek Federal States: Their Institutions and History. Trade Cloth. Oxford University Press, Inc. New York, NY. 1968. xxviii, 537p. ISBN:0-19-814265-X, ISBN13: 978-0-19-814265-2. Dewey:321/.02/0938. LCCN:68-080903.
Audience: **u,f.**

Ma, John **DS155**
Antiochos III and the Cities of Western Asia Minor: With New Preface and Addenda. Trade Paper. Oxford University Press, Inc. New York, NY. 2002. 425p. ISBN:0-19-925051-0, ISBN13: 978-0-19-925051-6. Dewey:939.2. LCCN:99-023236.
Audience: **u,f.**

MacLeod, Roy **Z722.5**
The Library of Alexandria: Centre of Learning in the Ancient World. Trade Paper. I. B. Tauris & Company, Ltd. London, 2002. 256p. ISBN:1-86064-821-5, ISBN13: 978-1-86064-821-2. Dewey:027.032.
Audience: **g,l,u,f.**

Momigliano, Arnaldo D. **DF78**
Alien Wisdom: The Limits of Hellenization. Trade Paper. Cambridge University Press. New York, NY. 1990. 184p. ISBN:0-521-38761-2, ISBN13: 978-0-521-38761-3. Dewey:938.
Audience: **u,f.** B

Oliver, James H. **DF0240.O44**
The Civic Tradition and Roman Athens. Trade Paper. Books on Demand. Ann Arbor, MI. 182p. ISBN:0-7837-0338-4, ISBN13: 978-0-7837-0338-1. Dewey:938/.5. LCCN:82-016180.
Audience: **u,f.**

Pearson, Lionel **DG55.M3.P32 1987**
The Greek Historians of the West: Timaeus and His Predecessors. Trade Paper. Oxford University Press, Inc. New York, NY. 1988. 305p. American Philological Association Philological Monographs ISBN:1-55540-078-7, ISBN13: 978-1-55540-078-1. Dewey:945/.755. LCCN:87-004877.
Audience: **u,f.** *Choice, 1988.*

Peters, F. E. **DS57 .P46**
Harvest of Hellenism. Trade Paper. Simon & Schuster. New York, NY. 1971. ISBN:0-671-20659-1, ISBN13: 978-0-671-20659-8. Dewey:939. LCCN:74-116509.
Audience: **g,u,f.**

Sherwin-White, Susan & Kuhrt, Amelie **DS96.S53 1993**
From Samarkhand to Sardis: A New Approach to the Seleucid Empire. Trade Cloth. University of California Press. Berkeley, CA. 1993. 261p. Hellenistic Culture and Society Ser., No. 13 ISBN:0-520-08183-8, ISBN13: 978-0-520-08183-3. Dewey:939/.43. LCCN:92-025624.
Audience: **u,f.** *Choice, 1994.*

Shipley, Graham **DF235.S54 2000**
The Greek World after Alexander: 323-30 B. C. Paper over Boards. Routledge. New York, NY. 2000. 600p. History of the Ancient World Ser. ISBN:0-415-04617-3, ISBN13: 978-0-415-04617-6. Dewey:938/.08. LCCN:99-036098.
Audience: **g,l,u.** *Choice, 2000.*

Tarn, William W. **DS451.T3 1997**
Greeks in Bactria and India. Ed. 3. Trade Cloth. Ares Publishers, Inc. Golden, CO. 1984. 628p. ISBN:0-89005-524-6, ISBN13: 978-0-89005-524-3. Dewey:934. LCCN:98-112690.
Audience: **u,f.** B

Tarn, William W. **DF77**
Hellenistic Civilization. Trade Paper. Penguin Group (USA) Inc. New York, NY. 1989. ISBN:0-317-02815-4, ISBN13: 978-0-317-02815-7. Dewey:938.
Audience: **g,u,f.**

Tcherikover, Victor **DS122.T313 1999**
Hellenistic Civilization and the Jews. Trade Paper. Hendrickson Publishers, Inc. Peabody, MA. 1999. 584p. ISBN:1-56563-476-4, ISBN13: 978-1-56563-476-3. Dewey:938/.09. LCCN:99-047101.
Audience: **g,u,f.** B

Rome > General

Adkins, Lesley & Adkins, Roy **DG75.A35 2004**
Handbook to Life in Ancient Rome. Ed. 2. Trade Cloth. Facts On File, Inc. New York, NY. 2004. 464p. Facts on File Library of World History ISBN:0-8160-5026-0, ISBN13: 978-0-8160-5026-0. Dewey:937. LCCN:2003-049255.
Audience: **g,l,u.** *Choice, 1994.*

Boatwright, Mary T., et al. **DG209.B58 2004**
The Romans: From Village to Empire. Daniel Gargola & Richard J. A. Talbert (Authors). Trade Cloth. Oxford University Press, Inc. New York, NY. 2004. 544p. ISBN:0-19-511875-8, ISBN13: 978-0-19-511875-9. Dewey:937. LCCN:2003-053670.
Audience: **g,u,f.** *Choice, 2004.*

Bowman, Alan K. (Editor), et al. **AS122.L5 VOL.114**
Representations of Empire: Rome and the Mediterranean World. Hannah M. Cotton, Martin Goodman & Simon Price (Editors). Trade Cloth. Oxford University Press, Inc. New York, NY. 2003. 208p. Proceedings of the British Academy Ser., Vol. 114 ISBN:0-19-726276-7, ISBN13: 978-0-19-726276-4. Dewey:937.06. LCCN:2003-275602.
Audience: **u,f.**

Burns, Thomas S. **DG254.2.B87 2003**
Rome and the Barbarians, 100 B. C. - A. D. 400. Trade Cloth. Johns Hopkins University Press. Baltimore, MD. 2003. 480p. Ancient Society and History Ser. ISBN:0-8018-7306-1, ISBN13: 978-0-8018-7306-5. Dewey:303.48/2360397/09015. LCCN:2002-015858.
Audience: **u,f.** *Choice, 2004.*

Edwards, Catharine & Woolf, Greg (Editors) **DG63.R65 2003**
Rome the Cosmopolis. Trade Cloth. Cambridge University Press. New York, NY. 2003. 266p. ISBN:0-521-80005-6, ISBN13: 978-0-521-80005-1. Dewey:937.6. LCCN:2002-031207.
Audience: **g,l,u,f.** *Choice, 2003.*

Goldsworthy, Adrian **U35.G65 2005**
Roman Warfare. Trade Paper. HarperCollins Publishers. New York, NY. 2005. 240p. Smithsonian History of Warfare Ser. ISBN:0-06-083852-3, ISBN13: 978-0-06-083852-2. Dewey:355.00937. LCCN:2005-053791.
Audience: **g,l,u,f.**

Scarre, Christopher **G1033.S28 1995**
Ancient Rome. Trade Paper. Penguin Group (USA) Inc. New York, NY. 1995. 144p. History Atlas Ser. ISBN:0-14-051329-9, ISBN13: 978-0-14-051329-5. Dewey:911.3/7. LCCN:95-220804.
Audience: **g,l,u.**

Vagi, David L. **CJ833.V34 1999**
Coinage and History of the Roman Empire, C. 82 B.C.—A.D. 480, Set. Trade Cloth. Amos Press, Inc. Sidney, OH. 1999. ISBN:0-944945-31-7, ISBN13: 978-0-944945-31-5. Dewey:332.4/937. LCCN:00-698949.
Audience: **g,l,u,f.**

Woolf, Greg (Editor) **DG63**
The Cambridge Illustrated History of the Roman World. Cloth Text. Cambridge University Press. New York, NY. 2003. 384p. Cambridge Illustrated Histories Ser. ISBN:0-521-82775-2, ISBN13: 978-0-521-82775-1. Dewey:937. LCCN:2004-298480.
Audience: **g,l,u.**

Rome > Sources

Keppie, Lawrence J. **CN510.K46 1991**
Understanding Roman Inscriptions. Trade Paper. Johns Hopkins University Press. Baltimore, MD. 1978. 160p. ISBN:0-8018-4352-9, ISBN13: 978-0-8018-4352-5. Dewey:980. LCCN:91-019853.
Audience: **g,l,u,f.** *Choice, 1992.*

Lewis, Naphtali & Reinhold, Meyer **DG13.L4 1990**
Roman Civilization, Vols. I & II. Ed. 3. Cloth Text. Columbia University Press. New York, NY. 1990. 1348p. ISBN:0-231-07054-3, ISBN13: 978-0-231-07054-6. Dewey:937. LCCN:90-033405.
Audience: **l,u.**

Mellor, Ronald (Editor) **DG207.H57 2004**
The Historians of Ancient Rome: An Anthology of the Major Writings. Ed. 2. UK-B Format Paperback. Routledge. New York, NY. 2004. 632p. ISBN:0-415-97108-X, ISBN13: 978-0-415-97108-9. Dewey:937/.0072/037. LCCN:2004-011920.
Audience: **g,l,u.**

Rome > Social History

Auguet, Roland **GV31.A9213 1972**
Cruelty and Civilization: The Roman Games. Paper over Boards. Routledge. New York, NY. 1994. 224p. ISBN:0-415-10452-1, ISBN13: 978-0-415-10452-4. Dewey:394.3/0937. LCCN:94-191303.
Audience: **g,l,u,f.**

Balsdon, J. P. V. D. **DG90**
Life and Leisure in Ancient Rome. Trade Paper. Phoenix Press, WC2. London, 2002. 464p. ISBN:1-84212-593-1, ISBN13: 978-1-84212-593-9. Dewey:390/.0937/6.
Audience: **g,l,u,f.**

Beard, Mary, et al. **BL802 .B43 1998**
Religions of Rome: A Sourcebook. John North & Simon Price (Authors). Trade Paper. Cambridge University Press. New York, NY. 1998. 430p. ISBN:0-521-45646-0, ISBN13: 978-0-521-45646-3. Dewey:200/.937/6. LCCN:97-021302.
Audience: **u,f.**

Beard, Mary, et al. **BL802 .B43 1998**
Religions of Rome: A History. John North & Simon Price (Authors). Trade Paper. Cambridge University Press. New York, NY. 1998. 478p. ISBN:0-521-31682-0, ISBN13: 978-0-521-31682-8. Dewey:200/.937/6. LCCN:97-021302.
Audience: **u,f.** *Choice, 1999.*

Bonner, Stanley F. **LA81 .B56**
Education in Ancient Rome: From the Elder Cato to the Younger Pliny. Trade Cloth. University of California Press. Berkeley, CA. 1977. ISBN:0-520-03439-2, ISBN13: 978-0-520-03439-6. Dewey:370/.937/6. LCCN:76-052023.
Audience: **u,f.**

Bradley, Keith R. **HQ511.B73 1991**
Discovering the Roman Family: Studies in Roman Social History. Paper Text. Oxford University Press, Inc. New York, NY. 1991. 240p. ISBN:0-19-505858-5, ISBN13: 978-0-19-505858-1. Dewey:306/.0945/632. LCCN:90-034248.
Audience: **u,f.**

Bradley, Keith R. **HT863.B72 1987**
Slaves and Masters in the Roman Empire: A Study in Social Control. Paper Text. Oxford University Press, Inc. New York, NY. 1987. 164p. ISBN:0-19-520607-X, ISBN13: 978-0-19-520607-4. Dewey:306/.363/0937. LCCN:87-015331.
Audience: **u,f.**

Bradley, Keith **HT863 .B7 1994**
Slavery and Society at Rome. P. A. Cartledge & P. D. A. Garnsey (Contribution by). Trade Paper. Cambridge University Press. New York, NY. 1994. 216p. Key Themes in Ancient History Ser. ISBN:0-521-37887-7, ISBN13: 978-0-521-37887-1. Dewey:306.3/62/09376. LCCN:93-042802.
Audience: **u,f.** *Choice, 1995.*

Carcopino, Jerome **DG69**
Daily Life in Ancient Rome: The People and the City at the Height of the Empire. Ed. 2. Trade Paper. Yale University Press. Cumberland, RI. 2003. 368p. ISBN:0-300-10186-4, ISBN13: 978-0-300-10186-7. Dewey:913.76.
Audience: **g,l,u,f.** B

Dixon, Suzanne **HQ1136.D59 2001**
Reading Roman Women: Sources, Genres, and Real Life. Trade Paper. Gerald Duckworth & Company, Ltd. London, 2002. 256p. ISBN:0-7156-2981-6, ISBN13: 978-0-7156-2981-9. Dewey:305.4/2/0937. LCCN:2001-409328.
Audience: **u,f.**

Dixon, Suzanne **HQ511.D59 1991**
The Roman Family. Trade Paper. Johns Hopkins University Press. Baltimore, MD. 1978. 296p. Ancient Society and History Ser. ISBN:0-8018-4200-X, ISBN13: 978-0-8018-4200-9. Dewey:306.85/0945/632. LCCN:91-025876.
Audience: **u,f.** *Choice, 1993.*

Duncan-Jones, Richard **HC39 .D886 1990**
Structure and Scale in the Roman Economy. Trade Paper. Cambridge University Press. New York, NY. 2002. 261p. ISBN:0-521-89289-9, ISBN13: 978-0-521-89289-6. Dewey:330.9/37.
Audience: **u,f.** *Choice, 1990.*

Fagan, Garrett G. **DG97**
Bathing in Public in the Roman World. Trade Paper. University of Michigan Press. Chicago, IL. 2002. 480p. ISBN:0-472-08865-3, ISBN13: 978-0-472-08865-2. Dewey:391.64.
Audience: **u,f.**

Flower, Harriet I. **DG103.F56 1996**
Ancestor Masks and Aristocratic Power in Roman Culture. Cloth Text. Oxford University Press, Inc. New York, NY. 1997. 428p. ISBN:0-19-815018-0, ISBN13: 978-0-19-815018-3. Dewey:393/.09376. LCCN:96-008168.
Audience: **u,f.** *Choice, 1997.*

Gardner, Jane F. & Wiedemann, Thomas **HQ511.R66 1991**
The Roman Household: A Sourcebook. Trade Cloth. Routledge. New York, NY. 1991. 240p. ISBN:0-415-04421-9, ISBN13: 978-0-415-04421-9. Dewey:306.85/0945/632. LCCN:90-008691.
Audience: **l,u.**

Grubbs, Judith E. **KJA2192**
Women and the Law in the Roman Empire: A Sourcebook on Marriage, Divorce and Widowhood. Paper over Boards. Routledge. New York, NY. 2002. 376p. ISBN:0-415-15240-2, ISBN13: 978-0-415-15240-2. Dewey:346.370134.
Audience: **u.**

MacMullen, Ramsay **DG78**
Roman Social Relations, 50 B. C to A. D. 284. Trade Paper. Yale University Press. Cumberland, RI. 1981. 212p. ISBN:0-300-02702-8, ISBN13: 978-0-300-02702-0. Dewey:937/.07. LCCN:73-086909.
Audience: **u,f.**

Meijer, Fik **GV35.M45 2005**
The Gladiators: History's Most Deadly Sport. Trade Cloth. St. Martin's Press. Gordonville, VA. 2005. 272p. ISBN:0-312-34874-6, ISBN13: 978-0-312-34874-8. Dewey:796/.0937. LCCN:2005-049380.
Audience: **g,u,f.** *Choice, 2006.*

Meijer, Fik J. & Van Nifj, Onno **HF373.M45 1992**
Trade, Transport and Society in the Ancient World: A Sourcebook. Cloth Text. Routledge. New York, NY. 1992. 272p. ISBN:0-415-00344-X, ISBN13: 978-0-415-00344-5. Dewey:330.093. LCCN:91-046010.
Audience: **u,f.** *Choice, 1993.*

Morgan, Teresa **LA71 .M85 1998**
Literate Education in the Hellenistic and Roman Worlds. P. D. Garnsey, G. C. Horrocks, R. L. Hunter, M. Millett, R. G. Osborne, M. D. Reeve & D. N. Sedley (Contribution by). Trade Cloth. Cambridge University Press. New York, NY. 1999. 384p. Cambridge Classical Studies ISBN:0-521-58466-3, ISBN13: 978-0-521-58466-1. Dewey:370/.938. LCCN:98-013857.
Audience: **u,f.**

Plass, Paul **GV31.P53 1995**
The Game of Death in Ancient Rome: Arena Sport and Political Suicide. Library Binding. University of Wisconsin Press. Chicago, IL. 1995. 296p. Studies in Classics ISBN:0-299-14570-0, ISBN13: 978-0-299-14570-5. Dewey:306.4/83/09376. LCCN:94-040884.
Audience: **u,f.** *Choice, 1996.*

Potter, D. S. & Mattingly, D. J. (Editors) **DG272.L54 1999**
Life, Death, and Entertainment in the Roman Empire. Trade Cloth. University of Michigan Press. Chicago, IL. 1999. 368p.

ISBN:0-472-10924-3, ISBN13: 978-0-472-10924-1. Dewey:937/.06. LCCN:98-040201.
Audience: **u,f.**

Rostovtzeff, Mikhail I. **DG271**
Social and Economic History of the Roman Empire. Ed. 2. P. M. Fraser (Editor). Trade Cloth. Oxford University Press, Inc. New York, NY. 1956. 890p. ISBN:0-19-814231-5, ISBN13: 978-0-19-814231-7. Dewey:301.44.
Audience: **f.**

Scheid, John **BL803.S3413 2003**
An Introduction to Roman Religion. Janet Lloyd (Translator). Trade Paper. Indiana University Press. Bloomington, IN. 2003. 240p. ISBN:0-253-21660-5, ISBN13: 978-0-253-21660-1. Dewey:292.07. LCCN:2003-007470.
Audience: **g,l,u,f.** *Choice, 2004.*

Shelton, Jo-Ann **HN10.R7S45 1998**
As the Romans Did: A Sourcebook in Roman Social History. Ed. 2. Paper Text. Oxford University Press, Inc. New York, NY. 1997. 512p. ISBN:0-19-508974-X, ISBN13: 978-0-19-508974-5. Dewey:306/.0945/632. LCCN:96-035257.
Audience: **l,u.**

Treggiari, Susan M. **DG205.T74 2001**
Roman Social History. Paper over Boards. Routledge. New York, NY. 2001. 192p. Classical Foundations Ser. ISBN:0-415-19521-7, ISBN13: 978-0-415-19521-8. Dewey:937/.007/2. LCCN:2001-034794.
Audience: **u,f.**

Wiedemann, Thomas E. J. **HT863**
Slavery. Oxford University Press. 1997. Greece & Rome. New Surveys in the Classics ISBN:0-19-922321-1, ISBN13: 978-0-19-922321-3.
Audience: **l,u,f.**

Zanker, Paul **DG70.P7Z3613 1998**
Pompeii: Public and Private Life. Deborah L. Schneider (Translator). Trade Paper. Harvard University Press. Cambridge, MA. 1999. 262p. Revealing Antiquity Ser., Vol. 11 ISBN:0-674-68967-4, ISBN13: 978-0-674-68967-1. Dewey:937.7. LCCN:98-024720.
Audience: **g,u,f.** *Choice, 1999.*

Rome > By Period > Origins (to 509 B.C.)

Banti, Luisa **DG223.B313**
The Etruscan Cities and Their Culture. Erika Bizzari (Translator). Trade Cloth. University of California Press. Berkeley, CA. 1974. ISBN:0-520-01910-5, ISBN13: 978-0-520-01910-2. Dewey:913.37/5.
Audience: **u,f.**

Cornell, Tim **DG233.C67 1995**
Beginnings of Rome: Italy and Rome from the Bronze Age to the Punic Wars (c. 1000-264 B. C.). Trade Paper. Routledge. New York, NY. 1995. 528p. History of the Ancient World Ser. ISBN:0-415-01596-0, ISBN13: 978-0-415-01596-7. Dewey:937/.01. LCCN:94-043757.
Audience: **u,f.**

Gabba, Emilio **DG233.G33 1991**
Dionysius and "The History of Archaic Rome". Trade Cloth. University of California Press. Berkeley, CA. 1991. 271p. Sather Classical Lectures, No. 56 ISBN:0-520-07302-9, ISBN13: 978-0-520-07302-9. Dewey:937. LCCN:90-011138.
Audience: **u,f.** *Choice, 1992.*

Grandazzi, Alexandre **DG65.G7313 1997**
The Foundation of Rome: Myth and History. Jane M. Todd (Translator). Book, Other. Cornell University Press. Ithaca, NY. 1997. 272p. ISBN:0-8014-3114-X, ISBN13: 978-0-8014-3114-2. Dewey:937. LCCN:97-017341.
Audience: **u,f.** *Choice, 1998.*

Holloway, R. Ross **DG63.H57**
Archaeology of Early Rome and Latium. Trade Paper. Routledge. New York, NY. 1996. 224p. ISBN:0-415-14360-8, ISBN13: 978-0-415-14360-8. Dewey:937.6.
Audience: **u,f.** *Choice, 1995.*

Scullard, Howard H. **DG55.E87S35 1998**
Etruscan Cities and Rome. Trade Paper. Johns Hopkins University Press. Baltimore, MD. 1998. 384p. ISBN:0-8018-6072-5, ISBN13: 978-0-8018-6072-0. Dewey:937/.5. LCCN:98-008777.
Audience: **u,f.**

Wiseman, Timothy Peter (Editor) **BL805 .W57 1995**
Remus: A Roman Myth. Cloth Text. Cambridge University Press. New York, NY. 1995. 259p. ISBN:0-521-41981-6, ISBN13: 978-0-521-41981-9. Dewey:398.209. LCCN:94-042523.
Audience: **u,f.** *Choice, 1996.*

Rome > By Period > Early Republic (509 B.C.- 146 B.C.)

Astin, A. E. **DG261**
Scipio Aemilianus. Trade Cloth. Oxbow Books, Ltd. Oxford, 2002. 392p. ISBN:0-19-814257-9, ISBN13: 978-0-19-814257-7. Dewey:937/.05/092.
Audience: **u,f.** B

Astin, Alan E. **DG253.C3A87 2000**
Cato the Censor. Cloth Text. Oxford University Press, Inc. New York, NY. 2000. 344p. Oxford Scholarly Classics Ser. ISBN:0-19-814809-7, ISBN13: 978-0-19-814809-8. Dewey:937/.04/092 B. LCCN:2001-266328.
Audience: **u,f.** B

Crawford, Michael **DG235**
The Roman Republic. Ed. 2. Trade Paper. Harvard University Press. Cambridge, MA. 1993. 256p. ISBN:0-674-77927-4, ISBN13: 978-0-674-77927-3. Dewey:937/.02. LCCN:93-001102.
Audience: **g,l,u.**

Forsythe, Gary **DG209 .F735 2005**
A Critical History of Early Rome: From Prehistory to the First Punic War. Trade Cloth. University of California Press. Berkeley, CA. 2005. 416p. ISBN:0-520-22651-8, ISBN13: 978-0-520-22651-7. Dewey:937. LCCN:2004-008505.
Audience: **u,f.** *Choice, 2005.*

Goldsworthy, Adrian **DG242.G65 2001**
The Punic Wars. Sterling Publishing Co., Inc. 2002. ISBN:0-304-35967-X, ISBN13: 978-0-304-35967-7.
Audience: **g,l,u,f.**

Gruen, Erich S. **DG77.G78 1992**
Culture and National Identity in Republican Rome. Trade Cloth. Cornell University Press. Ithaca, NY. 1992. 336p. Townsend Lectures - Cornell Studies ISBN:0-8014-2759-2, ISBN13: 978-0-8014-2759-6. Dewey:937. LCCN:92-052756.
Audience: **u,f.** *Choice, 1993.*

Gruen, Erich S. **DG241.2.G78 1986**
The Hellenistic World and the Coming of Rome. Trade Paper. University of California Press. Berkeley, CA. 1986. 800p. ISBN:0-520-05737-6, ISBN13: 978-0-520-05737-1. Dewey:937/.06. LCCN:82-008581.
Audience: **u,f.**

Harris, William V. **JV98**
War and Imperialism in Republican Rome: 327-70 B. C. Paper Text. Oxford University Press, Inc. New York, NY. 1985. 310p. ISBN:0-19-814866-6, ISBN13: 978-0-19-814866-1. Dewey:937/.02.
Audience: **u,f.**

Heurgon, Jacques **DG231 .H4613 1973**
The Rise of Rome. Trade Cloth. University of California Press. Berkeley, CA. 1973. ISBN:0-520-01795-1, ISBN13: 978-0-520-01795-5. Dewey:913.37/6. LCCN:70-126762.
Audience: **u,f.**

Hoyos, Dexter **DG249**
Hannibal: Rome's Greatest Enemy. Trade Cloth. Bristol Phoenix Press. Exeter, 2006. 128p. ISBN:1-904675-46-8, ISBN13: 978-1-904675-46-4. Dewey:937.04092.
Audience: **g,l,u,f.**

Hoyos, Dexter **DG247**
Hannibal's Dynasty: Power and Politics in the Western Mediterranean, 247-183 BC. Paper over Boards. Routledge. New York, NY. 2003. 288p. ISBN:0-415-29911-X, ISBN13: 978-0-415-29911-4. Dewey:939.7/3.
Audience: **g,u,f.** *Choice, 2003.*

Lazenby, J. F. **DG247.L39 1998**
Hannibal's War: A Military History of the Second Punic War. Trade Paper. University of Oklahoma Press. Norman, OK. 1998. 368p. ISBN:0-8061-3004-0, ISBN13: 978-0-8061-3004-0. Dewey:937/.04. LCCN:97-038302.
Audience: **g,u,f.**

Lazenby, John **DG243.L39 1996**
The First Punic War. Trade Cloth. Stanford University Press. Palo Alto, CA. 1996. 224p. ISBN:0-8047-2673-6, ISBN13: 978-0-8047-2673-3. Dewey:937/.04. LCCN:95-078817.
Audience: **g,u,f.** *Choice, 1996.*

Lintott, Andrew **JC88.L588 2003**
The Constitution of the Roman Republic. Trade Paper. Oxford University Press, Inc. New York, NY. 2003. 310p. ISBN:0-19-926108-3, ISBN13: 978-0-19-926108-6. Dewey:342.3/7/029.
Audience: **u,f.** *Choice, 1999.*

Raaflaub, Kurt A. **DG83.3.S59**
Social Struggles in Archaic Rome: New Perspectives on the Conflict of the Orders. Ed. 2. Trade Cloth. Blackwell Publishing, Inc. Malden, MA. 2005. 448p. ISBN:1-4051-0060-5, ISBN13: 978-1-4051-0060-1. Dewey:937/.02. LCCN:2005-006167.
Audience: **u,f.**

Salmon, E. T. **DG87**
Roman Colonization under the Republic. Trade Cloth. Cornell University Press. Ithaca, NY. 1970. Aspects of Greek and Roman Life Ser. ISBN:0-8014-0547-5, ISBN13: 978-0-8014-0547-1. Dewey:325.337. LCCN:72-087009.
Audience: **u,f.**

Salmon, E. T. **DG190.S3 S3**
Samnium and the Samnites. Trade Cloth. Cambridge University Press. Cambridge, 1967. 460p. ISBN:0-521-06185-7, ISBN13: 978-0-521-06185-8. Dewey:913.7/7.
Audience: **u,f.**

Scullard, Howard H. **DG231**
A History of the Roman World 753 to 146 BC. Ed. 4. Trade Paper. Routledge. New York, NY. 1991. 576p. ISBN:0-415-05915-1, ISBN13: 978-0-415-05915-2. Dewey:937.02.
Audience: **g,l,u.**

Scullard, Howard H. **DG250 .S3 1981**
Roman Politics, 220-150 B. C. Trade Cloth. Greenwood Publishing Group, Inc. Portsmouth, NH. 1982. 325p. ISBN:0-313-23296-2, ISBN13: 978-0-313-23296-1. Dewey:320.937. LCCN:81-013434.
Audience: **u,f.**

Taylor, Lily R. **JC85.E4T3**
Roman Voting Assemblies: From the Hannibalic War to the Dictatorship of Caesar. Trade Paper. University of Michigan Press. Chicago, IL. 1991. 194p. Jerome Lectures; Ann Arbor Paperbacks Ser. ISBN:0-472-08125-X, ISBN13: 978-0-472-08125-7. Dewey:320.937.
Audience: **u,f.**

Walbank, Frank W. **D58.P8W35 2002**
Polybius, Rome and the Hellenistic World: Essays and Reflections. Trade Cloth. Cambridge University Press. New York, NY. 2002. 368p. ISBN:0-521-81208-9, ISBN13: 978-0-521-81208-5. Dewey:930/.07/2. LCCN:2002-020170.
Audience: **u,f.**

Rome > By Period > Late Republic (146-27 B.C.)

Badian, E. (Editor) **DG59.A2B33 2000**
Foreign Clientele, Two Hundred Sixty-Four to Seventy BC. Cloth Text. Oxford University Press, Inc. New York, NY. 2006. 332p. Oxford Scholarly Classics Ser. ISBN:0-19-814204-8, ISBN13: 978-0-19-814204-1. Dewey:937/.04. LCCN:2001-266327.
Audience: **u,f.**

Badian, E. **HC39 .B33**
Publicans and Sinners: Private Enterprise in the Service of the Roman Republic. Trade Cloth. Cornell University Press. Ithaca, NY. 1972. 158p. ISBN:0-8014-0676-5, ISBN13: 978-0-8014-0676-8. Dewey:338/.04/0937. LCCN:70-164712.
Audience: **u,f.**

Badian, E. **DG266**
Roman Imperialism in the Late Republic. Ed. 2. Trade Cloth. Cornell University Press. Ithaca, NY. 1971. 129p. ISBN:0-8014-0024-4, ISBN13: 978-0-8014-0024-7. Dewey:937.05.
Audience: **u,f.** B

Bradley, Keith R. **HT1191.B73 1989**
Slavery and Rebellion in the Roman World, 140 B.C.-70 B.C. Trade Cloth. Indiana University Press. Bloomington, IN. 1989. 202p. ISBN:0-253-31259-0, ISBN13: 978-0-253-31259-4. Dewey:937/.05. LCCN:88-045757.
Audience: **u,f.** *Choice, 1990.*

Gabba, Emilio **DG254.G3132**
Republican Rome, the Army and the Allies. P. J. Cuff (Translator). Trade Cloth. University of California Press. Berkeley, CA. 1977. 281p. ISBN:0-520-03259-4, ISBN13: 978-0-520-03259-0. Dewey:355/.00937. LCCN:76-014307.
Audience: **u,f.** B

Goldsworthy, Adrian K. **U35**
The Roman Army at War 100 BC - AD 200. Trade Paper. Oxford University Press, Inc. New York, NY. 1998. 326p. Oxford Classical Monographs ISBN:0-19-815090-3, ISBN13: 978-0-19-815090-9. Dewey:355/.00937.
Audience: **u,f.**

Gruen, Erich S. **DG254**
The Last Generation of the Roman Republic. Trade Paper. University of California Press. Berkeley, CA. 1995. 624p. ISBN:0-520-20153-1, ISBN13: 978-0-520-20153-8. Dewey:937.06. LCCN:72-089244.
Audience: **u,f.**

Gruen, Erich S. **JC0085.J9G7**
Roman Politics and the Criminal Courts, 149-78 B. C. Trade Paper. Books on Demand. Ann Arbor, MI. 351p. ISBN:0-598-23385-7, ISBN13: 978-0-598-23385-1. Dewey:343/.0937/03. LCCN:68-029179.
Audience: **u,f.**

Keaveney, Arthur **DG250.5 .K42 1987B**
Rome and the Unification of Italy. Library Binding. Croom Helm, Ltd. London, 1987. 226p. ISBN:0-7099-3121-2, ISBN13: 978-0-7099-3121-8. Dewey:937. LCCN:88-186626.
Audience: **u,f.**

Keaveney, Arthur **DG256.7.K42 2005**
Sulla, the Last Republican. Ed. 2. Trade Cloth. Routledge. New York, NY. 2005. ISBN:0-203-37104-6, ISBN13: 978-0-203-37104-6. Dewey:937/.05/092 B. LCCN:2004-020916.
Audience: **u,f.**

Lintott, Andrew **DG211 .L5 1999**
Violence in Republican Rome. Ed. 2. Trade Paper. Oxford University Press, Inc. New York, NY. 1999. 268p. ISBN:0-19-815282-5, ISBN13: 978-0-19-815282-8. Dewey:303.6/0937. LCCN:2001-278025.
Audience: **u,f.**

Millar, Fergus **DG254.2.M55 1998**
The Crowd in Rome in the Late Republic. Trade Cloth. University of Michigan Press. Chicago, IL. 1998. 256p. Jerome Lectures, Vol. 22 ISBN:0-472-10892-1, ISBN13: 978-0-472-10892-3. Dewey:937/.05. LCCN:97-050351.
Audience: **u,f.** *Choice, 1999.*

Mouritsen, Henrik **DG241.2 .M68 2001**
Plebs and Politics in the Late Roman Republic. Cloth Text. Cambridge University Press. New York, NY. 2001. 170p. ISBN:0-521-79100-6, ISBN13: 978-0-521-79100-7. Dewey:320.93709014. LCCN:2001-275248.
Audience: **u,f.** *Choice, 2002.*

Rosenstein, Nathan S. **DG83.5.I6R67 1990**
Imperatores Victi: Military Defeat and Aristocratic Competition in the Middle and Late Republic. Trade Cloth. University of California Press. Berkeley, CA. 1990. 208p. ISBN:0-520-06939-0, ISBN13: 978-0-520-06939-8. Dewey:321/.14/0937. LCCN:89-020653.
Audience: **u,f.** *Choice, 1991.*

Rosenstein, Nathan Stewart **S431.R67 2004**
Rome at War: Farms, Families, and Death in the Middle Republic. Trade Cloth. University of North Carolina Press. Chapel Hill, NC. 2004. 312p. Studies in the History of Greece and Rome ISBN:0-8078-2839-4, ISBN13: 978-0-8078-2839-7. Dewey:630/.937/6. LCCN:2003-008542.
Audience: **u,f.** *Choice, 2004.*

Scullard, Howard H. **DG266**
From the Gracchi to Nero: A History of Rome from 133 B. C. to A. D. 68. Ed. 5. Trade Paper. Routledge. New York, NY. 1982. 528p. ISBN:0-415-02527-3, ISBN13: 978-0-415-02527-0. Dewey:937/.05. LCCN:81-022286.
Audience: **g,l,u,f.**

Seager, Robin **DG258.S42 2002**
Pompey the Great. Ed. 2. Trade Paper. Blackwell Publishing, Inc. Malden, MA. 2002. 288p. ISBN:0-631-22721-0, ISBN13: 978-0-631-22721-2. Dewey:937/.05/092 B. LCCN:2002-022773.
Audience: **u,f.**

Stockton, David **DG254.5**
The Gracchi. Paper Text. Oxford University Press, Inc. New York, NY. 1979. 268p. ISBN:0-19-872105-6, ISBN13: 978-0-19-872105-5. Dewey:937/.05/0922. LCCN:78-041143.
Audience: **u,f.**

Syme, Ronald **DG254.S9 2002**
The Roman Revolution. Trade Paper. Oxford University Press, Inc. New York, NY. 2002. 592p. ISBN:0-19-280320-4, ISBN13: 978-0-19-280320-7. Dewey:937/.05. LCCN:2002-725567.
Audience: **u,f.**

Taylor, Lily R. **DG81**
Party Politics in the Age of Caesar. Trade Paper. University of California Press. Berkeley, CA. 1949. 272p. Sather Classical Lectures, No. 22:No. 30 ISBN:0-520-01257-7, ISBN13: 978-0-520-01257-8. Dewey:937.05.
Audience: **u,f.**

Ward, Allen M. **DG260.C73**
Marcus Crassus and the Late Roman Republic. Trade Cloth. University of Missouri Press. Columbia, MO. 1977. 320p. ISBN:0-8262-0216-0, ISBN13: 978-0-8262-0216-1. Dewey:937'.05'0924. LCCN:76-056794.
Audience: **u,f.** B

Rome > By Period > Early Empire (27 B.C.- A.D. 284)

DG274

☐ De Imperatoribus Romanis.
http://www.roman-emperors.org/startup.htm
Audience: **g,l,u,f.**

Ando, Clifford **DG59.A2 A64 2000**
Imperial Ideology and Provincial Loyalty in the Roman Empire. Trade Cloth. University of California Press. Berkeley, CA. 2000. 518p. Classics and Contemporary Thought Ser., Vol. 6 ISBN:0-520-22067-6, ISBN13: 978-0-520-22067-6. Dewey:937/.06. LCCN:99-041499.
Audience: **u,f.** *Choice, 2001.*

Barrett, Anthony A. **DG282.6.B37 1996**
Agrippina: Sex, Power, and Politics in the Early Empire. Cloth over Boards. Yale University Press. Cumberland, RI. 1996. 352p. ISBN:0-300-06598-1, ISBN13: 978-0-300-06598-5. Dewey:937/.07/092 B. LCCN:96-060318.
Audience: **g,u,f.** *Choice, 1997.*

Barrett, Anthony A. **DG279**
Caligula: The Corruption of Power. Trade Paper. Yale University Press. Cumberland, RI. 1998. 360p. ISBN:0-300-07429-8, ISBN13: 978-0-300-07429-1. Dewey:937/.07/092.
Audience: **g,u,f.** *Choice, 1990.*

Barrett, Anthony A. **DG291.7.L5B37 2002**
Livia: First Lady of Imperial Rome. Cloth over Boards. Yale University Press. Cumberland, RI. 2002. 450p. ISBN:0-300-09196-6, ISBN13: 978-0-300-09196-0. Dewey:937/.07/092 B. LCCN:2002-003073.
Audience: **g,u,f.** *Choice, 2003.*

Birley, Anthony **DG300.B57 1999**
Septimus Severus: The African Emperor. Ed. 2. Trade Paper. Routledge. New York, NY. 1999. 320p. Key Guides ISBN:0-415-16591-1, ISBN13: 978-0-415-16591-4. Dewey:937/.07/092 B. LCCN:00-269156.
Audience: **g,u,f.**

Birley, Anthony R. **DG295.B57 1997**
Hadrian: The Restless Emperor. Paper over Boards. Routledge. New York, NY. 1997. 424p. Roman Imperial Biographies Ser. ISBN:0-415-16544-X, ISBN13: 978-0-415-16544-0. Dewey:[B]. LCCN:96-049232.
Audience: **g,u,f.** *Choice, 1998.*

Birley, Anthony R. **DG297.B5 2000**
Marcus Aurelius. Ed. 2. Trade Paper. Routledge. New York, NY. 2000. 352p. Roman Imperial Biographies Ser. ISBN:0-415-17125-3, ISBN13: 978-0-415-17125-0. Dewey:937/.07/092 B. LCCN:00-711200.
Audience: **g,u,f.**

Boatwright, Mary T. **DG295.B63 1987**
Hadrian and the City of Rome. Trade Cloth. Princeton University Press. Princeton, NJ. 1987. 315p. ISBN:0-691-03588-1, ISBN13: 978-0-691-03588-8. Dewey:937/.07. LCCN:86-030440.
Audience: **u,f.** *Choice, 1988.*

Boatwright, Mary Taliaferro **DG295.B62 2000**
Hadrian and the Cities of the Roman Empire. Trade Cloth. Princeton University Press. Princeton, NJ. 2000. 262p. ISBN:0-691-04889-4, ISBN13: 978-0-691-04889-5. Dewey:937.07/092 B. LCCN:99-041096.
Audience: **u,f.** *Choice, 2000.*

Bowersock, Glen W. **DS62.2**
Roman Arabia. Trade Cloth. Harvard University Press. Cambridge, MA. 1983. 242p. ISBN:0-674-77755-7, ISBN13: 978-0-674-77755-2. Dewey:939/.4. LCCN:82-023274.
Audience: **u,f.** B

Boyle, Anthony James & Dominik, William J. **DG286.F53 2003**
Flavian Rome: Culture, Image, Text. Trade Cloth. Brill Academic Publishers. Leiden, 2002. xviii, 754p. ISBN:90-04-11188-3, ISBN13: 978-90-04-11188-2. Dewey:937/.07. LCCN:2003-272841.
Audience: **u,f.** *Choice, 2003.*

Butcher, Kevin **DS96.2.B87 2003**
Roman Syria and the Near East. Trade Cloth. Oxford University Press, Inc. New York, NY. 2004. 474p. Antiquities Ser. ISBN:0-89236-715-6, ISBN13: 978-0-89236-715-3. Dewey:939/.43. LCCN:2003-006252.
Audience: **u,f.** *Choice, 2005.*

Campbell, J. B. **DG276.5.C26 1984**
The Emperor and the Roman Army: Thirty-One B.C. to A.D. Two Hundred Thirty-Five. Trade Cloth. Oxford University Press, Inc. New York, NY. 1984. 482p. ISBN:0-19-814834-8, ISBN13: 978-0-19-814834-0. Dewey:322/.5/0937. LCCN:83-019353.
Audience: **u,f.** B

Champlin, Edward **DG285.C53 2003**
Nero. Trade Cloth. Harvard University Press. Cambridge, MA. 2003. 360p. ISBN:0-674-01192-9, ISBN13: 978-0-674-01192-2. Dewey:937/.07/092 B. LCCN:2003-045268.
Audience: **u,f.** *Choice, 2004.*

Eck, Werner & Takacs, Sarolta A. **DG279.E2513 2003**
The Age of Augustus. Deborah Lucas Schneider (Translator). Trade Cloth. Blackwell Publishing, Inc. Malden, MA. 2002. 176p. ISBN:0-631-22957-4, ISBN13: 978-0-631-22957-5. Dewey:937/.07/092 B. LCCN:2002-005373.
Audience: **g,l,u.** *Choice, 2003.*

Galinsky, Karl (Editor) **DG279.C35 2005**
The Cambridge Companion to the Age of Augustus. Cloth Text. Cambridge University Press. New York, NY. 2005. 432p. Cambridge Companion to the Classics Ser. ISBN:0-521-80796-4, ISBN13: 978-0-521-80796-8. Dewey:937/.07. LCCN:2005-010513.
Audience: **u,f.**

Grainger, John D. **DG293.G73 2002**
The Roman Succession Crisis of AD 96-99 and the Reign of Nerva. Paper over Boards. Routledge. New York, NY. 2002. 192p. Roman Imperial Biographies Ser. ISBN:0-415-28917-3, ISBN13: 978-0-415-28917-7. Dewey:937/.07/092 B. LCCN:2002-067991.
Audience: **g,l,u,f.** *Choice, 2003.*

Grant, Michael **DG292.G73 1994**
The Antonines: The Roman Empire in Transition. Paper over Boards. Routledge. New York, NY. 1994. 248p. ISBN:0-415-10754-7, ISBN13: 978-0-415-10754-9. Dewey:937/.07. LCCN:94-000597.
Audience: **g,l,u.** *Choice, 1995.*

Grant, Michael **DG206.G5**
Nero. Trade Cloth. Dorset Press. New York, NY. 1989. 240p. Reprints Ser. ISBN:0-88029-311-X, ISBN13: 978-0-88029-311-2. Dewey:937/.06/0924.
Audience: **g,l,u.**

Grant, Michael **DG298.G73 1996**
The Severans: The Changed Roman Empire. Paper over Boards. Routledge. New York, NY. 1996. 160p. ISBN:0-415-12772-6, ISBN13: 978-0-415-12772-1. Dewey:937/.07. LCCN:95-045816.
Audience: **g,l,u.** *Choice, 1997.*

Griffin, Miriam T. **DG285.G75 2000**
[e] Nero: The End of a Dynasty. E-Book. Routledge. New York, NY. ISBN:0-203-13309-9, ISBN13: 978-0-203-13309-5. Dewey:937/.07.
Audience: **g,l,u,f.**

Jones, A. H. M. **DG279**
Augustus. Trade Paper. W. W. Norton & Company, Inc. New York, NY. 1971. 208p. Ancient Culture and Society Ser. ISBN:0-393-00584-4, ISBN13: 978-0-393-00584-4. Dewey:937/.06/0924.
Audience: **g,l,u.**

Keppie, Lawrence **DG89.K47 1998**
The Making of the Roman Army: From Republic to Empire. Trade Paper. University of Oklahoma Press. Norman, OK. 1998. 272p. ISBN:0-8061-3014-8, ISBN13: 978-0-8061-3014-9. Dewey:355/.00937. LCCN:97-030610.
Audience: **g,l,u,f.**

Levick, Barbara **DG279**
Claudius: The Corruption of Power. Trade Paper. Yale University Press. Cumberland, RI. 1993. 272p. ISBN:0-300-05831-4, ISBN13: 978-0-300-05831-4. Dewey:937/.07/092. LCCN:89-051800.
Audience: **g,u,f.** *Choice, 1990.*

Levick, Barbara **DG282.L58 1999**
Tiberius the Politician. Ed. 2. Trade Paper. Routledge. New York, NY. 1999. 336p. Roman Imperial Biographies Ser. ISBN:0-415-21753-9, ISBN13: 978-0-415-21753-8. Dewey:937/.07/0924. LCCN:00-266955.
Audience: **g,u,f.**

Levick, Barbara **DG289.L48 1999**
Vespasian. Paper over Boards. Routledge. New York, NY. 1999. 376p. Routledge Key Guides ISBN:0-415-16618-7, ISBN13: 978-0-415-16618-8. Dewey:937/.06/092 B. LCCN:98-052448.
Audience: **g,u,f.**

Luttwak, Edward N. **U35.L8 1979**
The Grand Strategy of the Roman Empire: From the First Century A. D. to the Third. Trade Paper. Johns Hopkins University Press. Baltimore, MD. 1952. 272p. ISBN:0-8018-2158-4, ISBN13: 978-0-8018-2158-5. Dewey:355/.033037/09015. LCCN:76-017232.
Audience: **g,u,f.** B

MacMullen, Ramsay **BR195.E9M33 1984**
[e] Christianizing the Roman Empire: (A. D. 100-400). E-Book. NetLibrary, Inc. Boulder, CO. 1984. ISBN:0-585-38120-8, ISBN13: 978-0-585-38120-6. Dewey:270.1.
Audience: **g,u,f.**

MacMullen, Ramsay **MT145.B14**
Corruption and the Decline of Rome. Trade Paper. Yale University Press. Cumberland, RI. 1990. 331p. ISBN:0-300-04799-1, ISBN13: 978-0-300-04799-8. Dewey:786.4/0421.
Audience: **u,f.** *Choice, 1989.*

MacMullen, Ramsay **DG270 .M34 1992**
Enemies of the Roman Order: Treason Unrest and Alienation in the Empire. Trade Paper. Routledge. New York, NY. 1993. 384p. ISBN:0-415-08621-3, ISBN13: 978-0-415-08621-9. Dewey:937.06. LCCN:92-018399.
Audience: **u,f.**

MacMullen, Ramsay **DG0306.M3**
Roman Government's Response to Crisis, A.D. 235-337. Trade Paper. Books on Demand. Ann Arbor, MI. 320p. ISBN:0-8357-8311-1, ISBN13: 978-0-8357-8311-8. Dewey:354/.37. LCCN:75-043324.
Audience: **l,u,f.** B

MacMullen, Ramsay **DG273.M33 2000**
Romanization in the Time of Augustus. Cloth over Boards. Yale University Press. Cumberland, RI. 2000. 240p. ISBN:0-300-08254-1, ISBN13: 978-0-300-08254-8. Dewey:937/.07. LCCN:00-028108.
Audience: **u,f.** *Choice, 2001.*

Malitz, Jürgen **DG285.M3513 2005**
Nero. Trade Cloth. Blackwell Publishing, Inc. Malden, MA. 2005. 192p. Blackwell Ancient Lives Ser. ISBN:1-4051-2177-7, ISBN13: 978-1-4051-2177-4. Dewey:937/.07/092 B. LCCN:2004-027395.
Audience: **g,l,u.** *Choice, 2006.*

Mattern, Susan P. **DG311**
Rome and the Enemy: Imperial Strategy in the Principate. Trade Paper. University of California Press. Berkeley, CA. 2002. 278p. ISBN:0-520-23683-1, ISBN13: 978-0-520-23683-7. Dewey:937.06. LCCN:98-040630.
Audience: **u,f.**

Millar, Fergus **KJA2880**
The Emperor in the Roman World. Trade Cloth. Cornell University Press. Ithaca, NY. 1977. 696p. ISBN:0-8014-1058-4, ISBN13: 978-0-8014-1058-1. Dewey:354.3703/12. LCCN:76-020059.
Audience: **u,f.**

Millar, Fergus **DS62.25 .M53 1993**
The Roman Near East, 31 B. C. - A. D. 337. Trade Cloth. Harvard University Press. Cambridge, MA. 1993. 624p. ISBN:0-674-77885-5, ISBN13: 978-0-674-77885-6. Dewey:939.4. LCCN:93-018174.
Audience: **u,f.** *Choice, 1994.*

Millar, Fergus & Segal, Erich (Editors) **DG279**
Caesar Augustus: Seven Aspects. Trade Cloth. Oxford University Press, Inc. New York, NY. 1984. x, 221p. ISBN:0-19-814851-8, ISBN13: 978-0-19-814851-7. Dewey:937/.07/0924. LCCN:83-020976.
Audience: **u,f.**

Moore, J. M. & Brunt, P. A. (Editors) **DG279**
Res Gestae Divi Augusti. Paper Text. Oxford University Press, Inc. New York, NY. 1969. 96p. ISBN:0-19-831772-7, ISBN13: 978-0-19-831772-2. Dewey:937./07/092.
Audience: **u,f.**

Morgan, M. Gwyn **DG286.M64 2005**
69 A.D.: The Year of Four Emperors. Trade Cloth. Oxford University Press, Inc. New York, NY. 2005. 336p. ISBN:0-19-512468-5, ISBN13: 978-0-19-512468-2. Dewey:937/.05. LCCN:2005-047271.
Audience: **g,u,f.**

Packer, James E. **NA2515**
The Forum of Trajan in Rome: A Study of the Monuments in Brief. Trade Paper. University of California Press. Berkeley, CA. 2001. 252p. ISBN:0-520-22673-9, ISBN13: 978-0-520-22673-9. Dewey:722.7/0937.
Audience: **g,u,f.**

Potter, David S. **DG271.P68 2004**
The Roman Empire at Bay: AD 180-395. Paper over Boards. Routledge. New York, NY. 2004. 784p. Routledge History of the Ancient World Ser. ISBN:0-415-10057-7, ISBN13: 978-0-415-10057-1. Dewey:937/.07. LCCN:2003-013171.
Audience: **g,l,u.**

Scullard, Howard H. **DA145**
Roman Britain: Outpost of the Empire. Trade Paper. Thames & Hudson. New York, NY. 1986. 192p. ISBN:0-500-27405-3, ISBN13: 978-0-500-27405-7. Dewey:936.1/04. LCCN:78-063042.
Audience: **g,u.**

Southern, Pat **DG298.S67 2001**
The Roman Empire from Severus to Constantine. Ed. 2. Paper over Boards. Routledge. New York, NY. 2001. 416p. ISBN:0-415-23943-5, ISBN13: 978-0-415-23943-1. Dewey:937/.06. LCCN:2001-019483.
Audience: **g,l,u.** *Choice, 2002.*

Watson, Alaric **DG308.W37 1999**
Aurelian and the Third Century. Paper over Boards. Routledge. New York, NY. 1999. 328p. ISBN:0-415-07248-4, ISBN13: 978-0-415-07248-9. Dewey:937/.07/092 B. LCCN:98-023382.
Audience: **u,f.** *Choice, 1999.*

Webster, Graham **U35.W48 1998**
The Roman Imperial Army of the First and Second Centuries A. D. Ed. 3. Hugh Elton (Introduction by). Trade Paper. University of Oklahoma Press. Norman, OK. 1998. 400p. ISBN:0-8061-3000-8, ISBN13: 978-0-8061-3000-2. Dewey:355/.00937. LCCN:97-041776.
Audience: **u,f.**

Wellesley, Kenneth **DG286.W44 2000**
The Year of the Four Emperors. Ed. 3. Barbara Levick (Introduction by). Paper over Boards. Routledge. New York, NY. 2004. 272p. Roman Imperial Biographies Ser. ISBN:0-415-23228-7, ISBN13: 978-0-415-23228-9. Dewey:937/.06/0922. LCCN:00-032209.
Audience: **g,u,f.**

Wells, Colin **DG311**
The Roman Empire. Trade Cloth. Stanford University Press. Palo Alto, CA. 1984. 368p. ISBN:0-8047-1237-9, ISBN13: 978-0-8047-1237-8. Dewey:937/.06. LCCN:83-040699.
Audience: **g,l,u.**

Wells, Peter S. **DG59.E8W45 1999**
The Barbarians Speak: How the Conquered Peoples Shaped Roman Europe. Cloth Text. Princeton University Press. Princeton, NJ. 1999. xii, 335p. ISBN:0-691-05871-7, ISBN13: 978-0-691-05871-9. Dewey:936. LCCN:99-012193.
Audience: **u,f.** *Choice, 2000.*

Wells, Peter S. **DD123.W45 2003**
The Battle That Stopped Rome: Emperor Augustus Arminius and Slaughter of Legions in Teutoburg Forest. Trade Cloth. W. W. Norton & Company, Inc. New York, NY. 2003. 224p. ISBN:0-393-02028-2, ISBN13: 978-0-393-02028-1. Dewey:936.3/02. LCCN:2003-010789.
Audience: **g,l,u,f.**

Whittaker, C. R. **DG311**
Frontiers of the Roman Empire: A Social and Economic Study. Trade Paper. Johns Hopkins University Press. Baltimore, MD. 1997. 360p. Ancient Society and History Ser. ISBN:0-8018-5785-6, ISBN13: 978-0-8018-5785-0. Dewey:937/.06. LCCN:93-031342.
Audience: **u,f.** *Choice, 1995.*

Woolf, Greg **DC33.2.W66 1998**
Becoming Roman: The Origins of Provincial Civilization in Gaul. Trade Cloth. Cambridge University Press. New York, NY. 1998. 314p. ISBN:0-521-41445-8, ISBN13: 978-0-521-41445-6. Dewey:944. LCCN:97-047263.
Audience: **u,f.** *Choice, 1999.*

Zanker, Paul **N5760**
The Power of Images in the Age of Augustus. Alan Shapiro (Translator). Trade Paper. University of Michigan Press. Chicago, IL. 1990. 396p. Thomas Spencer Jerome Lectures ISBN:0-472-08124-1, ISBN13: 978-0-472-08124-0. Dewey:709/.37.
Audience: **u,f.** *Choice, 1989.*

Rome > By Period > Late Empire (A.D. 284-565)

DG274
De Imperatoribus Romanis.
http://www.roman-emperors.org/startup.htm
Audience: **g,l,u,f.**

Augustae **DG274**
Scriptores Historiae Augustae: The Two Valerians, the Two Gallieni, the Thirty Pretenders, the Deified Claudius, the Deified Aurelian, Tacitus, Probus, Firmus, Saturninus, Proculus and Bonosus, Carus, Carinus and Numerian. E. H. Warmington (Editor), David Magie (Translator). Trade Cloth. Harvard University Press. Cambridge, MA. 1932. 544p. Loeb Classical Library, No. 139-140, 263 ISBN:0-674-99290-3, ISBN13: 978-0-674-99290-0. Dewey:870.
Audience: **u,f.**

Barnes, Timothy D. **DG316.B37 1998**
Ammianus Marcellinus and the Representation of Historical Reality. Book, Other. Cornell University Press. Ithaca, NY. 1998. 336p. Studies in Classical Philology ISBN:0-8014-3526-9, ISBN13: 978-0-8014-3526-3. Dewey:937/.007/202. LCCN:98-019791.
Audience: **u,f.** *Choice, 1999.*

Barnes, Timothy D. **BR1720.A7**
Athanasius and Constantius: Theology and Politics in the Constantinian Empire. Trade Paper. Harvard University Press. Cambridge, MA. 2001. 364p. ISBN:0-674-00549-X, ISBN13: 978-0-674-00549-5. Dewey:270.2092. LCCN:92-033050.
Audience: **u,f.**

Barnes, Timothy D. **BR170**
Constantine and Eusebius. Trade Cloth. Harvard University Press. Cambridge, MA. 1981. 466p. ISBN:0-674-16530-6, ISBN13: 978-0-674-16530-4. Dewey:937/.08/0922. LCCN:81-004248.
Audience: **u,f.** BCL3

Barnes, Timothy D. **DG0313.B3**
The New Empire of Diocletian and Constantine. Trade Paper. Books on Demand. Ann Arbor, MI. 324p. ISBN:0-7837-2221-4, ISBN13: 978-0-7837-2221-4. Dewey:937/.08/0922. LCCN:81-006569.
Audience: **u,f.**

Bowersock, G. W. **DF240.B69 1996**
Hellenism in Late Antiquity. Trade Paper. University of Michigan Press. Chicago, IL. 1996. 132p. Thomas Spencer Jerome Lectures ISBN:0-472-06418-5, ISBN13: 978-0-472-06418-2. Dewey:292.0091822.
Audience: **l,u,f.**

Bowersock, G. W. (Editor), et al. **DE5.L29 1999**
Late Antiquity: A Guide to the Postclassical World. Peter Brown & Oleg Grabar (Editors). Trade Cloth. Harvard University Press. Cambridge, MA. 1999. 802p. Harvard University Press Reference Library ISBN:0-674-51173-5, ISBN13: 978-0-674-51173-6. Dewey:938/.003. LCCN:99-025639.
Audience: **l,u,f.** *Choice, 2000.*

Bowersock, Glen W. **DG317 .B68**
Julian the Apostate. Trade Cloth. Harvard University Press. Cambridge, MA. 1978. 152p. ISBN:0-674-48881-4, ISBN13: 978-0-674-48881-6. Dewey:937/.08/0924. LCCN:77-022769.
Audience: **l,u,f.**

Brown, Peter **BR170.B72 1992**
Authority and the Sacred: Aspects of the Christianisation of the Roman World. Cloth Text. Cambridge University Press. New York, NY. 1995. 105p. ISBN:0-521-49557-1, ISBN13: 978-0-521-49557-8. Dewey:270.1. LCCN:94-042652.
Audience: **l,u,f.** *Choice, 1996.*

Brown, Peter **BR195.C45B76 1988**
The Body and Society: Men, Women, and Sexual Renunciation in Early Christianity. Trade Cloth. Columbia University Press. New York, NY. 1988. 504p. Lectures on the History of Religions Ser., No. 13 ISBN:0-231-06100-5, ISBN13: 978-0-231-06100-1. Dewey:241.6/6. LCCN:87-030941.
Audience: **u,f.** *Choice, 1989.*

Brown, Peter **BL805.B74 1982**
Society and the Holy in Late Antiquity. Trade Cloth. University of California Press. Berkeley, CA. 1982. 350p. ISBN:0-520-04305-7, ISBN13: 978-0-520-04305-3. Dewey:261.109. LCCN:80-039862.
Audience: **g,l,u,f.** BCL3

Brown, Peter **DG77**
World of Late Antiquity. Trade Paper. W. W. Norton & Company, Inc. New York, NY. 1989. 216p. Library of World Civilization ISBN:0-393-95803-5, ISBN13: 978-0-393-95803-4. Dewey:930.5.
Audience: **g,l,u,f.**

Burns, Thomas S. **U35.B79 1994**
Barbarians Within the Gates of Rome: A Study of Roman Military Policy and the Barbarians, ca. 375-425 A. D. Trade Cloth. Indiana University Press. Bloomington, IN. 1995. 452p. ISBN:0-253-31288-4, ISBN13: 978-0-253-31288-4. Dewey:937/.08. LCCN:94-012788.
Audience: **u,f.** *Choice, 1995.*

Burns, Thomas S. **D157**
A History of the Ostrogoths. Trade Paper. Indiana University Press. Bloomington, IN. 1991. 320p. ISBN:0-253-20600-6, ISBN13: 978-0-253-20600-8. Dewey:909.07. LCCN:83-049286.
Audience: **l,u,f.**

Burns, Thomas S. **D51; D138**
Ostrogoths. Kinship and Society. Trade Paper. Coronet Books. Philadelphia, PA. 1980. 153p. ISBN:3-515-02967-2, ISBN13: 978-3-515-02967-4. Dewey:940.1.
Audience: **u,f.**

Burns, Thomas S. & Eadie, John W. **HT114.U725 2001**
Urban Centers and Rural Contexts in Late Antiquity. Trade Paper. Michigan State University Press. East Lansing, MI. 2001. xxvii, 379p. ISBN:0-87013-585-6, ISBN13: 978-0-87013-585-9. Dewey:307.76/0937. LCCN:00-013228.
Audience: **u,f.**

Bury, John B. **DG311**
History of the Later Roman Empire: From the Death of Theodosius I to the Death of Justinian. Trade Paper. Dover Publications, Inc. Mineola, NY. 1958. 503p. 0 ISBN:0-486-20399-9, ISBN13: 978-0-486-20399-7. Dewey:DG311.
Audience: **g,l,u,f.**

Bury, John B. **DG311**
History of the Later Roman Empire: From the Death of Theodosius I to the Death of Justinian. Trade Paper. Dover Publications, Inc. Mineola, NY. 1958. 496p. 0 ISBN:0-486-20398-0, ISBN13: 978-0-486-20398-0. Dewey:937.08.
Audience: **g,l,u,f.**

Cameron, Alan & Long, Jacqueline **PA4441.S9C36 1993**
Barbarians and Politics at the Court of Arcadius. Sherry Lee (Contribution by). Trade Cloth. University of California Press. Berkeley, CA. 1993. 456p. The Transformation of the Classical Heritage Ser., Vol. XIX ISBN:0-520-06550-6, ISBN13: 978-0-520-06550-5. Dewey:949.5/01/072. LCCN:91-016486.
Audience: **u,f.**

Cameron, Averil **DG311 .C36 1993**
The Later Roman Empire. Trade Paper. Harvard University Press. Cambridge, MA. 1993. 256p. ISBN:0-674-51194-8, ISBN13: 978-0-674-51194-1. Dewey:937/.06. LCCN:92-041000.
Audience: **g,l,u.**

Cameron, Averil **DE71.C25 1993**
The Mediterranean World in Late Antiquity, AD 395-600. Trade Paper. Routledge. New York, NY. 1993. 272p. Routledge History of the Ancient World Ser. ISBN:0-415-01421-2, ISBN13: 978-0-415-01421-2. Dewey:930. LCCN:92-034600.
Audience: **g,l,u.**

Eusebius **DG315**
Life of Constantine. Averil Cameron & Stuart Hall (Editors). Trade Cloth. Oxford University Press, Inc. New York, NY. 1999. 414p. Clarendon Ancient History Ser. ISBN:0-19-814917-4,

ISBN13: 978-0-19-814917-0. Dewey:937/.08/092 B. LCCN:99-021397.
Audience: **u,f.**

Gibbon, Edward **DG311**
The History of the Decline and Fall of the Roman Empire, Set. John B. Bury (Editor). Trade Cloth. A M S Press, Inc. New York, NY. ISBN:0-404-02820-9, ISBN13: 978-0-404-02820-6. Dewey:937/.06. LCCN:78-168113.
Audience: **g,l,u,f.**

Goffart, Walter A. **D121**
Barbarians and Romans, A. D. 418-584: The Techniques of Accommodation. Trade Paper. Princeton University Press. Princeton, NJ. 1987. 296p. ISBN:0-691-10231-7, ISBN13: 978-0-691-10231-3. Dewey:940.1/2.
Audience: **u,f.**

Heather, Peter **DG311.H43 2005**
The Fall of the Roman Empire: A New History of Rome and the Barbarians. Trade Cloth. Oxford University Press, Inc. New York, NY. 2005. 576p. ISBN:0-19-515954-3, ISBN13: 978-0-19-515954-7. Dewey:937/.09. LCCN:2005-047345.
Audience: **g,l,u,f.**

Heather, Peter **D137.H425 1996**
The Goths. Trade Cloth. Blackwell Publishing, Inc. Malden, MA. 1996. 376p. The Peoples of Europe Ser. ISBN:0-631-16536-3, ISBN13: 978-0-631-16536-1. Dewey:936.3/02. LCCN:96-006725.
Audience: **g,l,u,f.** *Choice, 1997.*

Heather, Peter J. **D137.H43 1991**
Goths and Romans AD 332-489. Trade Cloth. Oxford University Press, Inc. New York, NY. 1992. 394p. Oxford Historical Monographs ISBN:0-19-820234-2, ISBN13: 978-0-19-820234-9. Dewey:936. LCCN:91-012261.
Audience: **u,f.** *Choice, 1993.*

Holum, Kenneth G. **DG312**
Theodosian Empresses: Women and Imperial Dominion in Late Antiquity. Trade Paper. University of California Press. Berkeley, CA. 1989. 325p. Transformation of the Classical Heritage Ser., Vol. III ISBN:0-520-06801-7, ISBN13: 978-0-520-06801-8. Dewey:937/.09/0922. LCCN:81-043690.
Audience: **u,f.**

Jones, A. H. M. **DG511**
The Later Roman Empire, 284-602: A Social, Economic, and Administrative Survey, Vol. 1. Trade Paper. Johns Hopkins University Press. Baltimore, MD. 1986. 772p. ISBN:0-8018-3353-1, ISBN13: 978-0-8018-3353-3. Dewey:945/.01. LCCN:85-024077.
Audience: **u,f.**

Jones, A. H. M. **DG511**
The Later Roman Empire, 284-602: A Social, Economic, and Administrative Survey, Vol. 2. Trade Paper. Johns Hopkins University Press. Baltimore, MD. 1986. 772p. ISBN:0-8018-3354-X, ISBN13: 978-0-8018-3354-0. Dewey:945/.01. LCCN:85-024077.
Audience: **u,f.**

Kelly, Christopher **DG83.5.K45 2004**
Ruling the Later Roman Empire. Trade Cloth. Harvard University Press. Cambridge, MA. 2004. 352p. Revealing Antiquity Ser., Vol. 15 ISBN:0-674-01564-9, ISBN13: 978-0-674-01564-7. Dewey:937/.09. LCCN:2004-047664.
Audience: **u,f.** *Choice, 2005.*

Lenski, Noel (Editor) **DG315.C36 2005**
The Cambridge Companion to the Age of Constantine. Cloth Text. Cambridge University Press. New York, NY. 2005. 488p. ISBN:0-521-81838-9, ISBN13: 978-0-521-81838-4. Dewey:937/.08/092. LCCN:2005-011724.
Audience: **g,u,f.**

Lenski, Noel Emmanuel **DF559 .L46 2002**
Failure of Empire: Valens and the Roman State in the Fourth Century A.D. Trade Cloth. University of California Press. Berkeley, CA. 2003. 460p. The Transformation of the Classical Heritage Ser. ISBN:0-520-23332-8, ISBN13: 978-0-520-23332-4. Dewey:949.5/9013. LCCN:2002-009716.
Audience: **u,f.** *Choice, 2003.*

Lieu, Samuel N. & Montserrat, Dominic **BR180.F76 1996**
From Constantine to Julian: A Source History. Paper over Boards. Routledge. New York, NY. 1995. 320p. ISBN:0-415-09335-X, ISBN13: 978-0-415-09335-4. Dewey:937/.08. LCCN:95-000283.
Audience: **u,f.**

Lieu, Samuel & Montserrat, Dominic (Editors) **DG315.C65 1998**
Constantine: History Historiography and Legend. Paper over Boards. Routledge. New York, NY. 1998. 264p. ISBN:0-415-10747-4, ISBN13: 978-0-415-10747-1. Dewey:937/.08/092 B. LCCN:97-045571.
Audience: **g,l,u.**

Maas, Michael (Editor) **DF572.C35 2004**
The Cambridge Companion to the Age of Justinian. Cloth Text. Cambridge University Press. New York, NY. 2005. 672p. Cambridge Companions to the Ancient World Ser. ISBN:0-521-81746-3, ISBN13: 978-0-521-81746-2. Dewey:949.5/013. LCCN:2004-049266.
Audience: **g,u,f.** *Choice, 2006.*

MacCormack, Sabine **DG124**
Art and Ceremony in Late Antiquity. Trade Cloth. University of California Press. Berkeley, CA. 1981. 450p. The Transformation of the Classical Heritage Ser., Vol. 1 ISBN:0-520-03779-0, ISBN13: 978-0-520-03779-3. Dewey:390.220937. LCCN:78-062864.
Audience: **l,u,f.**

MacMullen, Ramsay **BR170.M33 1997**
Christianity and Paganism in the Fourth to Eighth Centuries. Cloth over Boards. Yale University Press. Cumberland, RI. 1997. 288p. ISBN:0-300-07148-5, ISBN13: 978-0-300-07148-1. Dewey:270.2. LCCN:97-007786.
Audience: **l,u,f.** *Choice, 1998.*

MacMullen, Ramsay **DG0306.M3**
Roman Government's Response to Crisis, A.D. 235-337. Trade Paper. Books on Demand. Ann Arbor, MI. 320p. ISBN:0-8357-8311-1, ISBN13: 978-0-8357-8311-8. Dewey:354/.37. LCCN:75-043324.
Audience: **l,u,f.**

Matthews, J. F. **DG319.M37**
Western Aristocracies and Imperial Court, A. D. 364-425. Trade Cloth. Oxford University Press, Inc. New York, NY. 1975. xiv, 445p. ISBN:0-19-814817-8, ISBN13: 978-0-19-814817-3. Dewey:322.4/3/0937. LCCN:75-309538.
Audience: **u,f.**

Matthews, John F. **KJA457.M38 2000**
Laying down the Law: A Study of the Theodosian Code. Cloth over Boards. Yale University Press. Cumberland, RI. 2000. 336p. ISBN:0-300-07900-1, ISBN13: 978-0-300-07900-5. Dewey:340.5/4. LCCN:00-035198.
Audience: **u,f.**

McLynn, Neil **BR1720.A5M37 1994**
Ambrose of Milan: Church and Court in a Christian Capital. Trade Cloth. University of California Press. Berkeley, CA. 1994. 430p. The Transformation of the Classical Heritage Ser., Vol. 22 ISBN:0-520-08461-6, ISBN13: 978-0-520-08461-2. Dewey:270.2/092 B. LCCN:94-002261.
Audience: **u,f.** *Choice, 1995.*

Millar, Fergus **DF562 .M55 2006**
A Greek Roman Empire: Power and Belief under Theodosius II. Trade Cloth. University of California Press. Berkeley, CA. 2006. 304p. Sather Classical Lectures, Vol. 64 ISBN:0-520-24703-5, ISBN13: 978-0-520-24703-1. Dewey:949.5/013. LCCN:2006-003042.
Audience: **u,f.**

Nixon, C. E. & Rodgers, Barbara S. **PA6166.P36 1994**
In Praise of Later Roman Emperors: The Panegyrici Latini. Trade Cloth. University of California Press. Berkeley, CA. 1995. 748p. Transformation of the Classical Heritage Ser., Vol. 21 ISBN:0-520-08326-1, ISBN13: 978-0-520-08326-4. Dewey:875/.0108. LCCN:93-027872.
Audience: **u,f.**

Salzman, Michele R. **CE46.S25 1990**
On Roman Time: The Codex-Calendar of 354 and the Rhythms of Urban Life in Late Antiquity. Trade Cloth. University of California Press. Berkeley, CA. 1991. 335p. The Transformation of the Classical Heritage Ser., Vol. 17 ISBN:0-520-06566-2, ISBN13: 978-0-520-06566-6. Dewey:529/.3/0937. LCCN:89-005116.
Audience: **u,f.**

Salzman, Michele Renee **BR195.C6S35 2002**
The Making of a Christian Aristocracy: Social and Religious Change in the Western Roman Empire. Trade Cloth. Harvard University Press. Cambridge, MA. 2002. 368p. ISBN:0-674-00641-0, ISBN13: 978-0-674-00641-6. Dewey:270.2/086/21. LCCN:2001-047075.
Audience: **u,f.** *Choice, 2002.*

Van Dam, Raymond **DC62**
Leadership and Community in Late Ancient Gaul. Trade Cloth. University of California Press. Berkeley, CA. 1985. 400p. The Transformation of the Classical Heritage Ser., Vol. VIII ISBN:0-520-05162-9, ISBN13: 978-0-520-05162-1. Dewey:936.402. LCCN:83-024321.
Audience: **u,f.**

Ward-Perkins, Bryan **DG311**
The Fall of Rome: And the End of Civilization. Trade Cloth. Oxford University Press, Inc. New York, NY. 2005. 248p. ISBN:0-19-280564-9, ISBN13: 978-0-19-280564-5. Dewey:945/.6301. LCCN:2005-299925.
Audience: **g,l,u,f.** *Choice, 2006.*

Warmington, E. H. (Editor) **DG274**
Scriptores Historiae Augustae: Hadrian, Aelius, Antoninus Pius, Marcus Aurelius, L. Verus, Avidius Cassius, Commodus, Pertinax, Didius Julianus, Septimius Severus, Pescennius Niger, Clodius Albinus. David Magie (Translator). Trade Cloth. Harvard University Press. Cambridge, MA. 1991. 544p. Loeb Classical Library, No. 139-140, 263 ISBN:0-674-99154-0, ISBN13: 978-0-674-99154-5. Dewey:870.
Audience: **u,f.**

Warmington, E. H. (Editor) **DG274**
Scriptores Historiae Augustae: Caracalla. Geta. Opellius Macrinus. Diadumenianus. Elagabalus. Severus Alexander. The Two Maximini. The Three Gordians. Maximus and Balbinus, Vol. 2. David Magie (Translator). Trade Cloth. Harvard University Press. Cambridge, MA. 1969. 528p. Loeb Classical Library, No. 139-140, 263 ISBN:0-674-99155-9, ISBN13: 978-0-674-99155-2. Dewey:870.
Audience: **u,f.**

EUROPEAN HISTORY

The world has changed greatly since BCL3, and so have the questions we ask of history. The collapse of the Soviet bloc in 1989 recast the historical landscape in far-reaching ways, as once-closed archives started revealing their secrets and long-suppressed peoples began reclaiming their history. The fading of old divisions between "East" and "West" Europe, meanwhile, refocused challenges to the heavily Western-oriented approaches that informed so much historical writing of the last century. Still other trends, notably the accelerating rush of globalization, have greatly broadened the frames of reference by which another twentieth-century construct, Western Civilization, might be revisited and reconsidered.

Invigorating times, in other words, but also a bit disorienting. The Cold War and Atlanticist rationales for teaching European history have lost much of their force, and while there is no lack of (arguably better) conceptual arguments to take their place, the academy has yet to sort these out.

All of this bears upon the bibliographies that follow for European history. Western Europe still casts the longest shadows, but the peoples and regions of Eastern and East Central Europe have gained new definition and clarity, in part through a greatly modified taxonomy more attuned to that historical experience. The introduction of some new fields, such as Communications and Media, reflects the continued drift of social history onto more cultural tracks. Other fields, including Imperialism, Women's History and Jewish History, have been greatly expanded and reworked, in keeping with their growing curricular importance.

Alongside this revamped taxonomy, the RCL offers a substantially new roster of book titles, though the degree of turnover varies according to region and subject matter. The bibliographies for Russia and former Soviet lands, for example, draw heavily from more recent literature, reflecting the new historiographical directions made possible over the past decade or so.

This section includes a wide range of works, most of which fall under one of these categories:

1) Historical monographs (the great majority of titles)

2) Essay collections; especially those that announce (or given limitations will have to stand in for) important historical departures, controversies or trends.

3) Primary documents. Teaching history to undergraduates means promoting their capacity for sympathetic imagination, and I have tried to include, alongside several primary document readers, a variety of memoirs, autobiographies, letter collections and the like.

4) Novels and other fictive works. While the possibilities here of course are endless, selection has been restricted to a handful of worthy but less well-known titles.

— John Abbott

General History > European History, General Works

Bayly, C. A. **D295.B28 2003**
The Birth of the Modern World, 1780-1914: Global Connections and Comparisons. Trade Paper. Blackwell Publishing, Inc. Malden, MA. 2003. 568p. Blackwell History of the World Ser. ISBN:0-631-23616-3, ISBN13: 978-0-631-23616-0. Dewey:909.8. LCCN:2003-001453.
Audience: **g,l,u,f.** *Choice, 2004.*

Mikkeli, Heikki **D104.M49 1998**
Europe As an Idea and an Identity. Cloth over Boards. Palgrave Macmillan. New York, NY. 1998. 280p. ISBN:0-312-21039-6, ISBN13: 978-0-312-21039-7. Dewey:940. LCCN:97-027133.
Audience: **g,l,u,f.**

Palmer, R. R., et al.
A History of the Modern World, with PowerWeb. Ed. 10. Joel Colton & Lloyd Kramer (Authors). Trade Cloth. McGraw-Hill Higher Education. Burr Ridge, IL. 2006. ISBN:0-07-325500-9, ISBN13: 978-0-07-325500-2.
Audience: **g,l,u,f.**

Pounds, Norman J. G. **D21.5.P62 1990**
An Historical Geography of Europe. Cloth Text. Cambridge University Press. New York, NY. 1990. 498p. ISBN:0-521-32217-0, ISBN13: 978-0-521-32217-1. Dewey:911/.4. LCCN:89-023968.
Audience: **g,l,u,f.** *Choice, 1991.*

Wolf, Eric R. **D208.W64 1982**
Europe and the People Without History. Trade Paper. University of California Press. Berkeley, CA. 1997. 534p. ISBN:0-520-04898-9, ISBN13: 978-0-520-04898-0. Dewey:940.2. LCCN:81-024031.
Audience: **g,l,u,f.** *B*

General History > Historiography

Chakrabarty, Dipesh **D13.5.E85C43 2000**
Provincializing Europe: Postcolonial Thought and Historical Difference. Trade Paper. Princeton University Press. Princeton, NJ. 2000. 320p. Reprints of Economics Classics Ser. ISBN:0-691-04909-2, ISBN13: 978-0-691-04909-0. Dewey:901. LCCN:99-087722.
Audience: **u,f.**

Cohen, Deborah & O'Connor, Maura (Editors) **D13.5.E85**
Comparison and History: Europe in Cross National Perspective. Paper over Boards. Routledge. New York, NY. 2004. 232p. ISBN:0-415-94442-2, ISBN13: 978-0-415-94442-7. Dewey:940/.01. LCCN:2004-015901.
Audience: **g,l,u,f.**

Evans, Richard J. **D16.8.E847 1999**
In Defense of History. Trade Cloth. W. W. Norton & Company, Inc. New York, NY. 1999. 288p. ISBN:0-393-04687-7, ISBN13: 978-0-393-04687-8. Dewey:907. LCCN:98-024422.
Audience: **g,l,u,f.** *Choice, 1999.*

Fontana, Josep **D13.5.E85F66 1995**
The Distorted Past: A Re-Interpretation of Europe. Colin Smith (Translator). Trade Cloth. Blackwell Publishing, Inc. Malden, MA. 1995. 232p. ISBN:0-631-17622-5, ISBN13: 978-0-631-17622-0. Dewey:940/.072. LCCN:94-039077.
Audience: **u,f.** *Choice, 1995.*

Winks, Robin & Louis, Roger (Editors) **DA16 .O95 1998**
The Oxford History of the British Empire: Historiography. Trade Cloth. Oxford University Press, Inc. New York, NY. 1999. 756p. Oxford History of the British Empire Ser., Vol. V ISBN:0-19-820566-X, ISBN13: 978-0-19-820566-1. Dewey:909/.0971241. LCCN:97-036299.
Audience: **u,f.** *Choice, 2000.*

General History > Military and Naval history

Brodie, Bernard **U21.2**
War and Politics. Trade Paper. Longman Publishing. Boston, MA. 1974. 514p. ISBN:0-02-315020-3, ISBN13: 978-0-02-315020-3. Dewey:355/.02.
Audience: **g,l,u,f.**

Contamine, Philippe **UA646**
War in the Middle Ages. Michael Jones (Translator). Trade Paper. Blackwell Publishing, Inc. Malden, MA. 1992. 424p. ISBN:0-631-14469-2, ISBN13: 978-0-631-14469-4. Dewey:355/.0094.
Audience: **g,l,u,f.** *B*

Delbruck, Hans **U27**
History of the Art of War Within the Framework of Political History: The Middle Ages. Walter J. Renfroe Jr. (Translator). Trade Cloth. Greenwood Publishing Group, Inc. Portsmouth, NH. 1982. 711p. Contributions in Military History Ser., No. 26 ISBN:0-8371-8164-X, ISBN13: 978-0-8371-8164-6. Dewey:355/.02/09. LCCN:72-000792.
Audience: **g,u,f.**

Delbruck, Hans **U27**
History of the Art of War Within the Framework of Political History: The Modern Era. Walter J. Renfroe Jr. (Translator). Book, Other. Greenwood Publishing Group, Inc. Portsmouth, NH. 1985. 487p. Contributions in Military History Ser., No. 39 ISBN:0-8371-8165-8, ISBN13: 978-0-8371-8165-3. Dewey:355/.02/09. LCCN:72-000792.
Audience: **g,u,f.** *Choice, 1985.*

Freedman, Lawrence (Editor) **U21.2.W357 1994**
War. Paper Text. Oxford University Press, Inc. New York, NY. 1994. 400p. Oxford Readers Ser. ISBN:0-19-289254-1, ISBN13: 978-0-19-289254-6. Dewey:355.02. LCCN:93-021348.
Audience: **g,l,u,f.**

Glete, Jan **D27.G55 2000**
Warfare at Sea, 1500-1650: Maritime Conflicts and the Transformation of Europe. Paper over Boards. Routledge. New York, NY. 1999. 256p. Warfare and History Ser. ISBN:0-415-21454-8, ISBN13: 978-0-415-21454-4. Dewey:359.0094. LCCN:00-689213.
Audience: **g,l,u,f.**

Hale, J. R. **U43.E95**
War and Society in Renaissance Europe, 1450-1620. Trade Paper. McGill-Queen's University Press. Montreal, PQ. 1998.

288p. War and European Society Ser. ISBN:0-7735-1765-0, ISBN13: 978-0-7735-1765-3. Dewey:355/.02/094.
Audience: **g,u,f.**

Howard, Michael **U43**
War in European History. Ed. 2. Trade Paper. Oxford University Press, Inc. New York, NY. 2001. 176p. ISBN:0-19-280208-9, ISBN13: 978-0-19-280208-8. Dewey:940.
Audience: **g,l,u,f.**

Huntington, Samuel P. **JK330**
The Soldier and the State: The Theory and Politics of Civil-Military Relations. Trade Paper. Harvard University Press. Cambridge, MA. 1981. 560p. ISBN:0-674-81736-2, ISBN13: 978-0-674-81736-4. Dewey:322.5/0973. LCCN:57-006349.
Audience: **u,f.**

Hutchinson, John F. **HV568**
Champions of Charity: War and the Rise of the Red Cross. Trade Paper. Westview Press. Boulder, CO. 1997. 496p. ISBN:0-8133-3367-9, ISBN13: 978-0-8133-3367-0. Dewey:361.7/7. LCCN:95-026628.
Audience: **g,l,u,f.** *Choice, 1996.*

Keegan, John **D25.K43**
The Face of Battle. Trade Cloth. Peter Smith Publisher, Inc. Magnolia, MA. 2000. ISBN:0-8446-7126-6, ISBN13: 978-0-8446-7126-0. Dewey:909.08.
Audience: **g,l,u.**

Kennedy, Paul M. (Editor) **U162.G68 1991**
Grand Strategies in War and Peace. Cloth over Boards. Yale University Press. Cumberland, RI. 1991. 224p. ISBN:0-300-04944-7, ISBN13: 978-0-300-04944-2. Dewey:355.02/0722. LCCN:90-023410.
Audience: **g,l,u,f.** *Choice, 1991.*

Kennedy, Paul M. **D210.K46 1989**
The Rise and Fall of the Great Powers: Economic Change and Military Conflict from 1500 to 2000. Trade Cloth. Knopf Publishing Group. New York, NY. 1989. 704p. ISBN:0-679-72019-7, ISBN13: 978-0-679-72019-5. Dewey:909.82. LCCN:88-040123.
Audience: **g,l,u,f.** *Choice, 1988.*

Liddell-Hart, Basil H. **D25.L45 1991**
Strategy. Ed. 2. Trade Paper. Penguin Group (USA) Inc. New York, NY. 1991. 448p. ISBN:0-452-01071-3, ISBN13: 978-0-452-01071-0. Dewey:355.4. LCCN:90-025082.
Audience: **g,l,u,f.**

Mahan, Alfred Thayer **D246**
The Influence of Sea Power upon History, 1660-1783. Library Binding. Reprint Services Company. Temecula, CA. 1999. Notable American Authors Ser. ISBN:0-7812-3915-X, ISBN13: 978-0-7812-3915-8. Dewey:909/.6.
Audience: **g,l,u,f.**

McNeill, William H. **U37.M38 1999**
The Pursuit of Power: Technology, Armed Force, and Society since A. D. 1000. Trade Paper. University of Chicago Press. Chicago, IL. 1984. 416p. ISBN:0-226-56158-5, ISBN13: 978-0-226-56158-5. Dewey:355.0209. LCCN:81-024095.
Audience: **u,f.**

Murphey, Rhoads **U43.T9M87 1999**
Ottoman Warfare, 1500-1700. Cloth Text. Rutgers University Press. Piscataway, NJ. 1999. xxii, 278p. ISBN:0-8135-2684-1, ISBN13: 978-0-8135-2684-3. Dewey:355/.00956/0903. LCCN:98-045274.
Audience: **u,f.** *Choice, 1999.*

Paret, Peter (Editor), et al. **U162.M25 1986**
Makers of Modern Strategy: From Machiavelli to the Nuclear Age. Gordon A. Craig & Felix Gilbert (Editors). Trade Paper. Princeton University Press. Princeton, NJ. 1986. 950p. ISBN:0-691-02764-1, ISBN13: 978-0-691-02764-7. Dewey:355/.02. LCCN:85-017029.
Audience: **u,f.**

Parker, Geoffrey **U39 .P37 1996**
The Military Revolution: Military Innovation and the Rise of the West, 1500-1800. Ed. 2. Trade Paper. Cambridge University Press. New York, NY. 1996. 285p. ISBN:0-521-47958-4, ISBN13: 978-0-521-47958-5. Dewey:355/.009. LCCN:95-024970.
Audience: **u,f.**

Ropp, Theodore **U39.R6 2000**
War in the Modern World. Alex Roland (Introduction by). Trade Paper. Johns Hopkins University Press. Baltimore, MD. 2000. 424p. ISBN:0-8018-6445-3, ISBN13: 978-0-8018-6445-2. Dewey:355/.009/03. LCCN:99-087565.
Audience: **g,l,u,f.**

Small, Melvin & Singer, J. David **U21.2**
Resort to Arms: International and Civil Wars, 1816-1980. Ed. 2. Trade Cloth. SAGE Publications, Inc. Thousand Oaks, CA. 1982. 372p. ISBN:0-8039-1776-7, ISBN13: 978-0-8039-1776-7. Dewey:303.6/6. LCCN:81-018518.
Audience: **u,f.**

Vagts, Alfred **UA10 .V3 1981**
A History of Militarism: Civilian and Military. Trade Cloth. Greenwood Publishing Group, Inc. Portsmouth, NH. 1981. 542p. ISBN:0-313-22961-9, ISBN13: 978-0-313-22961-9. Dewey:355/.0213. LCCN:81-004918.
Audience: **l,u.**

Von Clausewitz, Carl **U102.C65 1984**
On War. Michael C. Howard & Peter Paret (Editor, Translators), Bernard Brodie (Introduction by). Paper Text. Princeton University Press. Princeton, NJ. 1989. 752p. ISBN:0-691-01854-5, ISBN13: 978-0-691-01854-6. Dewey:355.02. LCCN:84-003401.
Audience: **u,f.**

Wright, Quincy **U21.2 .W75 1983**
A Study of War. Ed. 2. Trade Paper. University of Chicago Press. Chicago, IL. 1983. 474p. Midway Reprint Ser. ISBN:0-226-91001-6, ISBN13: 978-0-226-91001-7. Dewey:303.6/6. LCCN:83-050443.
Audience: **g,u,f.**

General History > Communications and Media

Altick, Richard D. **Z1003.5.G7A53 1998**
The English Common Reader: A Social History of the Mass Reading Public, 1800-1900. Ed. 2. Cloth Text. Ohio State University Press. Columbus, OH. 1998. 468p.

ISBN:0-8142-0793-6, ISBN13: 978-0-8142-0793-2. Dewey:028/.9/0941. LCCN:98-019581.
Audience: **g,l,u,f.**

Briggs, Asa & Burke, Peter **P90.B695 2005**
A Social History of the Media: From Gutenberg to the Internet. Ed. 2. Trade Paper, Perfect. Polity Press. Cambridge, 2005. 400p. ISBN:0-7456-3512-1, ISBN13: 978-0-7456-3512-5. Dewey:302.2309.
Audience: **g,l,u,f.** *Choice, 2006.*

Chappell, Warren & Bringhurst, Robert **Z124.C47 1999**
A Short History of the Printed Word. Ed. 2. Trade Paper. Hartley & Marks, Inc. Point Roberts, WA. 2000. xx, 312p. ISBN:0-88179-154-7, ISBN13: 978-0-88179-154-9. Dewey:686.2/09. LCCN:98-011931.
Audience: **g,l,u,f.**

Crowley, David & Heyer, Paul **P90.C62945 2007**
Communication in History: Technology, Culture, Society. Ed. 5. Trade Paper. Allyn & Bacon, Inc. Boston, MA. 2006. 368p. ISBN:0-205-48388-7, ISBN13: 978-0-205-48388-4. Dewey:302.209. LCCN:2006-043220.
Audience: **g,l,u,f.**

Daniell, David **BS455.D27 2003**
The Bible in English: Its History and Influence. Cloth over Boards. Yale University Press. Cumberland, RI. 2003. 962p. ISBN:0-300-09930-4, ISBN13: 978-0-300-09930-0. Dewey:220.52009. LCCN:2002-153177.
Audience: **u,f.** *Choice, 2004.*

de Hamel, Christopher **ND2900.D36 1994**
A History of Illuminated Manuscripts. Ed. 2. Trade Cloth. Phaidon Press, Inc. New York, NY. 1994. 240p. ISBN:0-7148-2949-8, ISBN13: 978-0-7148-2949-4. Dewey:745.6/7/094. LCCN:95-150977.
Audience: **g,l,u,f.**

Diringer, David **Z6 .D57 1982**
The Book Before Printing: Ancient, Medieval and Oriental. Trade Paper. Dover Publications, Inc. Mineola, NY. 1982. 604p. ISBN:0-486-24243-9, ISBN13: 978-0-486-24243-9. Dewey:002. LCCN:81-017290.
Audience: **g,l,u,f.**

Eisenstein, Elizabeth L. **Z124.E374 2005**
The Printing Revolution in Early Modern Europe. Ed. 2. Cloth Text. Cambridge University Press. New York, NY. 2005. 406p. ISBN:0-521-84543-2, ISBN13: 978-0-521-84543-4. Dewey:686.2/094. LCCN:2005-003961.
Audience: **g,l,u,f.** B

Febvre, Lucien **Z4**
The Coming of the Book: The Impact of Printing, 1450-1800. Trade Paper. Analytical Psychology Club of San Francisco, Inc. San Francisco, CA. 1997. 384p. Classics Ser. ISBN:1-85984-108-2, ISBN13: 978-1-85984-108-2. Dewey:002/.094.
Audience: **g,l,u,f.**

Howsam, Leslie **BV2370.B8 H69 1991**
Cheap Bibles: Nineteenth-Century Publishing and the British and Foreign Bible Society. Terry Belanger & David McKitterick (Contribution by). Trade Paper. Cambridge University Press. New York, NY. 2002. 263p. Cambridge Studies in Publishing and Printing History Ser. ISBN:0-521-52212-9, ISBN13: 978-0-521-52212-0. Dewey:070.5/0941/09034.
Audience: **g,l,u,f.**

Manguel, Alberto **Z1003**
A History of Reading. Trade Paper. Penguin Group (USA) Inc. New York, NY. 1997. 384p. ISBN:0-14-016654-8, ISBN13: 978-0-14-016654-5. Dewey:028.9/09.
Audience: **g,l,u,f.** *Choice, 1997.*

Martin, Henri-Jean **Z40.M3713 1994**
The History and Power of Writing. Lydia G. Cochrane (Translator). Trade Paper. University of Chicago Press. Chicago, IL. 1995. 608p. ISBN:0-226-50836-6, ISBN13: 978-0-226-50836-8. Dewey:302.2/244/09. LCCN:93-026718.
Audience: **u,f.**

McKitterick, David **Z124.M39 2003**
Print, Manuscript and the Search for Order, 1450-1830. Trade Cloth. Cambridge University Press. New York, NY. 2003. 328p. ISBN:0-521-82690-X, ISBN13: 978-0-521-82690-7. Dewey:002/.094. LCCN:2002-035178.
Audience: **u,f.**

Ong, Walter J. **P35.O5 2002**
Orality and Literacy: The Technologizing of the Word. Ed. 2. Trade Paper. Routledge. New York, NY. 2002. 216p. New Accents Ser. ISBN:0-415-28129-6, ISBN13: 978-0-415-28129-4. Dewey:808/.0082. LCCN:2002-069913.
Audience: **g,l,u,f.**

Parkes, M. B. **P301.5.P86P37 1993**
Pause and Effect: An Introduction to the History of Punctuation in the West. Trade Cloth. University of California Press. Berkeley, CA. 1993. 400p. ISBN:0-520-07941-8, ISBN13: 978-0-520-07941-0. Dewey:411. LCCN:91-041770.
Audience: **g,l,u,f.**

Popkin, Jeremy D. (Editor) **PN4751.M43 1995**
Media and Revolution. Cloth Text. University Press of Kentucky. Lexington, KY. 1995. 256p. ISBN:0-8131-1899-9, ISBN13: 978-0-8131-1899-4. Dewey:070. LCCN:94-031808.
Audience: **g,l,u,f.** *Choice, 1995.*

Rose, Mark **KD1289**
Authors and Owners: The Invention of Copyright. Trade Cloth. Harvard University Press. Cambridge, MA. 1993. 190p. ISBN:0-674-05308-7, ISBN13: 978-0-674-05308-3. Dewey:346.4/1/0482. LCCN:92-043010.
Audience: **g,l,u,f.**

Standage, Tom **HE7631.S677 1998**
The Victorian Internet: The Remarkable Story of the Telegraph and the Nineteenth Century's On-Line Pioneers. Trade Cloth. Walker & Company. New York, NY. 1998. 224p. ISBN:0-8027-1342-4, ISBN13: 978-0-8027-1342-1. Dewey:384.1/09. LCCN:98-024959.
Audience: **g,l,u,f.**

Vincent, David **LC156.A2V55 2000**
The Rise of Mass Literacy: Reading and Writing in Modern Europe. Trade Cloth. Polity Press. Cambridge, 2000. 208p. ISBN:0-7456-1444-2, ISBN13: 978-0-7456-1444-1. Dewey:302.2/244/094. LCCN:00-027871.
Audience: **g,l,u,f.** *Choice, 2001.*

General History > Economic History

HC240
Cambridge Economic History of Europe. Trade Cloth. Cambridge University Press. New York, NY. 1978. 1456p. The Cambridge Economic History of Europe Ser., Vol. 7 ISBN:0-521-21124-7, ISBN13: 978-0-521-21124-6. Dewey:330.94.
Audience: **u,f.**

HC240.C312
Cambridge Economic History of Europe. Trade Cloth. Cambridge University Press. New York, NY. 1965. 450p. The Cambridge Economic History of Europe Ser., Vol. 6 ISBN:0-521-04508-8, ISBN13: 978-0-521-04508-7. Dewey:330.94.
Audience: **u,f.**

Anderson, J. L. **HC59**
Explaining Long-Term Economic Change. London: Macmillan Press. 1991. Studies in Economic and Social History ISBN:0-333-42068-3, ISBN13: 978-0-333-42068-3.
Audience: **u,f.**

Aston, Trevor (Editor) **HN373.A8716**
Crisis in Europe, 1560-1660: Essays from "Past and Present". Trade Paper. Routledge. New York, NY. 1983. 376p. ISBN:0-7100-6889-1, ISBN13: 978-0-7100-6889-7. Dewey:940.22.
Audience: **u,f.**

Bonney, Richard (Editor) **HJ1000.R57 1999**
The Rise of the Fiscal State in Europe, c. 1200-1815. Trade Cloth. Oxford University Press, Inc. New York, NY. 1999. 540p. ISBN:0-19-820402-7, ISBN13: 978-0-19-820402-2. Dewey:336.4. LCCN:98-049345.
Audience: **u,f.** *Choice, 2000.*

Brady, Thomas A. Jr. (Editor), et al. **D203.H36 1996**
Handbook of European History, 1400-1600: Late Middle Ages Renaissence and Reformation. Heiko A. Oberman & James D. Tracy (Editors). Trade Paper. William B. Eerdmans Publishing Company. Grand Rapids, MI. 1996. 733p. Handbook of European History, 1400-1600 Late Middle Ages ISBN:0-8028-4194-5, ISBN13: 978-0-8028-4194-0. Dewey:940.2. LCCN:95-050652.
Audience: **l,u,f.**

Braudel, Fernand **HC45 .B7132**
Capitalism and Material Life, 1400-1800. Trade Paper. HarperCollins Publishers. New York, NY. 1974. ISBN:0-06-131836-1, ISBN13: 978-0-06-131836-8. Dewey:309.1/03.
Audience: **u,f.**

Braudel, Fernand **DE80.B7713 1995**
The Mediterranean and the Mediterranean World in the Age of Philip II. Ed. 2. Trade Paper. University of California Press. Berkeley, CA. 1996. 732p. Mediterranean and the Mediterranean World in the Age of Philip Ser., Vol. 2 ISBN:0-520-20330-5, ISBN13: 978-0-520-20330-3. Dewey:909/.0982205. LCCN:95-037581.
Audience: **u,f.**

Braudel, Fernand **HC51.B67413 1992**
Civilization and Capitalism, 15th-18th Century: The Wheels of Commerce. Sian Reynolds (Translator). Trade Paper. University of California Press. Berkeley, CA. 1992. 670p. Civilization and Capitalism, 15th-18th Century Ser., Vol. 2 ISBN:0-520-08115-3, ISBN13: 978-0-520-08115-4. Dewey:909.08. LCCN:92-010173.
Audience: **u,f.**

Braudel, Fernand **DE80.B7713 1995**
The Mediterranean and the Mediterranean World in the Age of Philip II. Sian Reynolds (Translator). Trade Paper. University of California Press. Berkeley, CA. 1996. 644p. Mediterranean and the Mediterranean World in the Age of Philip Ser., Vol. 1 ISBN:0-520-20308-9, ISBN13: 978-0-520-20308-2. Dewey:909/.0982205. LCCN:95-037581.
Audience: **u,f.**

Braudel, Fernand **HC51.B67413 1992**
The Perspective of the World: Civilization and Capitalism, 15th-18th Century. Sian Reynolds (Translator). Trade Paper. University of California Press. Berkeley, CA. 1992. 700p. Civilization and Capitalism, 15th-18th Century Ser., Vol. 3 ISBN:0-520-08116-1, ISBN13: 978-0-520-08116-1. LCCN:92-010173.
Audience: **u,f.**

Braudel, Fernand **HC51.B67413 1992**
The Structures of Everyday Life - The Limits of the Possible. Sian Reynolds (Translator). Trade Paper. University of California Press. Berkeley, CA. 1992. 624p. Civilization and Capitalism, 15th-18th Century Ser., Vol. 1 ISBN:0-520-08114-5, ISBN13: 978-0-520-08114-7. Dewey:909.08. LCCN:92-010173.
Audience: **u,f.**

Burke, Peter **HC240.B88**
Economy and Society in Early Modern Europe; Essays from Annales. Trade Cloth. Harper & Row Ltd. London, 1972. 169p. ISBN:0-06-136074-0, ISBN13: 978-0-06-136074-9. Dewey:330.9/4/02. LCCN:79-184873.
Audience: **u,f.**

Cameron, Rondo **HC21.C33 1997**
A Concise Economic History of the World: From Paleolithic Times to the Present. Ed. 3. Paper Text. Oxford University Press, Inc. New York, NY. 1997. 480p. ISBN:0-19-510782-9, ISBN13: 978-0-19-510782-1. Dewey:330.9. LCCN:96-033657.
Audience: **l,u,f.** *Choice, 1998, 1990.*

Cameron, Rondo & Neal, Larry **HC21.C33 2002**
A Concise Economic History of the World: From Paleolithic Times to the Present. Ed. 4. Paper Text. Oxford University Press, Inc. New York, NY. 2002. 480p. ISBN:0-19-512705-6, ISBN13: 978-0-19-512705-8. Dewey:330.9. LCCN:2001-051380.
Audience: **g,l,u.** *Choice, 1998, 1990.*

Carus-Wilson, Eleanora Mary **HC12 .C3**
Essays in Economic History: Reprints,. Paper Text. Textbook Publishers. Temecula, CA. 2003. ISBN:0-7581-3575-0, ISBN13: 978-0-7581-3575-9. Dewey:330.82.
Audience: **u,f.**

Chandler, Alfred D. **HD2356.U5C44 1994**
Scale and Scope: The Dynamics of Industrial Capitalism. Trade Paper. Harvard University Press. Cambridge, MA. 1994. 780p.

ISBN:0-674-78995-4, ISBN13: 978-0-674-78995-1. Dewey:338.64409. LCCN:94-132234.
Audience: **u,f.**

Cipolla, Carlo M. **HC240.C49513 1993**
Before the Industrial Revolution: European Society and Economy, 1000-1700. Ed. 3. Trade Paper. W. W. Norton & Company, Inc. New York, NY. 1994. 348p. ISBN:0-393-31198-8, ISBN13: 978-0-393-31198-3. Dewey:330.94/01. LCCN:94-002708.
Audience: **g,l,u,f.** *B*

Cipolla, Carlo M. **HF1025**
Between Two Cultures: An Introduction to Economic History. Trade Paper. W. W. Norton & Company, Inc. New York, NY. 1992. 224p. ISBN:0-393-30816-2, ISBN13: 978-0-393-30816-7. Dewey:330.9.
Audience: **g,l,u.** *Choice, 1992.*

Cipolla, Carlo M. **HC39.C53**
The Economic Decline of Empires. Trade Cloth. Methuen & Company, Ltd. London, 1970. 280p. ISBN:0-416-16090-5, ISBN13: 978-0-416-16090-1. Dewey:330/.09. LCCN:79-019611.
Audience: **u,f.**

Cipolla, Carlo M. (Editor) **HC240**
The Fontana Economic History of Europe. Cloth Text. Barnes & Noble Books-Imports. Lanham, MD. 1977. 408p. Fontana Economic History of Europe Ser., Vol. 5, Pt. 2 ISBN:0-06-492182-4, ISBN13: 978-0-06-492182-4. Dewey:330.9/4/05. LCCN:75-026207.
Audience: **u,f.**

Cipolla, Carlo M. (Editor) **HC240**
The Fontana Economic History of Europe. Cloth Text. Barnes & Noble Books-Imports. Lanham, MD. 1977. 404p. Fontana Economic History of Europe Ser., Vol. 6 Pt. 2 ISBN:0-06-492184-0, ISBN13: 978-0-06-492184-8. Dewey:330.9/4/05. LCCN:75-026207.
Audience: **u,f.**

Cipolla, Carlo M. (Editor) **HC240**
The Fontana Economic History of Europe: The Middle Ages. Cloth Text. Barnes & Noble Books-Imports. Lanham, MD. 1976. 389p. Fontana Economic History of Europe Ser., Vol. 1 ISBN:0-06-492176-X, ISBN13: 978-0-06-492176-3. Dewey:330.9/4/01. LCCN:75-026027.
Audience: **u,f.**

Cipolla, Carlo M. (Editor) **HC240**
The Fontana Economic History of Europe. Cloth Text. Barnes & Noble Books-Imports. Lanham, MD. 1977. 640p. Fontana Economic History of Europe Ser., Vol. 2 ISBN:0-06-492177-8, ISBN13: 978-0-06-492177-0. Dewey:330.9/4/05. LCCN:75-026207.
Audience: **u,f.**

Cipolla, Carlo M. (Editor) **HC240**
The Fontana Economic History of Europe. Cloth Text. Barnes & Noble Books-Imports. Lanham, MD. 1976. 479p. Fontana Economic History of Europe Ser., Vol. 4, Pt. 2 ISBN:0-06-492180-8, ISBN13: 978-0-06-492180-0. Dewey:330.9/4/05. LCCN:75-026027.
Audience: **u,f.**

Cipolla, Carlo M. (Editor) **HC240**
The Fontana Economic History of Europe. Cloth Text. Barnes & Noble Books-Imports. Lanham, MD. 1976. 366p. Fontana Economic History of Europe Ser., Vol. 4, Pt. 1 ISBN:0-06-492179-4, ISBN13: 978-0-06-492179-4. Dewey:330.9/4/05. LCCN:75-026027.
Audience: **u,f.**

Cipolla, Carlo M. (Editor) **HC240**
The Fontana Economic History of Europe. Cloth Text. Barnes & Noble Books-Imports. Lanham, MD. 1977. vii, 376p. Fontana Economic History of Europe Ser., Vol. 6, Pt. 1 ISBN:0-06-492183-2, ISBN13: 978-0-06-492183-1. Dewey:330.9/4/05.
Audience: **u,f.**

Cipolla, Carlo M. (Editor) **HC240**
The Fontana Economic History of Europe: The Twentieth Century. Cloth Text. Barnes & Noble Books-Imports. Lanham, MD. 1977. 402p. Fontana Economic History of Europe Ser., Vol. 5, Pt. 1 ISBN:0-06-492181-6, ISBN13: 978-0-06-492181-7. Dewey:330.9/4/05. LCCN:75-026207.
Audience: **u,f.**

Cipolla, Carlo M. (Editor) **HC240**
The Industrial Revolution, 1700 - 1914. Cloth Text. Barnes & Noble Books-Imports. Lanham, MD. 1976. 624p. Fontana Economic History of Europe Ser., Vol. 3 ISBN:0-06-492178-6, ISBN13: 978-0-06-492178-7. Dewey:330.9/4/05. LCCN:75-026027.
Audience: **u,f.**

Cipolla, Carlo M. **HD9999.C58C5 2003**
Clocks and Culture, 1300-1700. Anthony Grafton (Introduction by). Trade Paper. W. W. Norton & Company, Inc. New York, NY. 2003. 192p. The Norton Library ISBN:0-393-32443-5, ISBN13: 978-0-393-32443-3. Dewey:338.4/768111/09. LCCN:2004-301201.
Audience: **l,u,f.**

Davis, Ralph **HC240**
The Rise of the Atlantic Economies. Charles Wilson (Editor). Trade Paper. Cornell University Press. Ithaca, NY. 1973. 340p. World Economic History Ser. ISBN:0-8014-9143-6, ISBN13: 978-0-8014-9143-6. Dewey:330.9/4.
Audience: **u,f.**

Day, John **HC240.D343 1999**
Money and Finance in the Age of Merchant Capitalism. Trade Paper. Blackwell Publishing, Inc. Malden, MA. 1998. 176p. ISBN:0-631-21225-6, ISBN13: 978-0-631-21225-6. Dewey:332.1/094. LCCN:98-025561.
Audience: **u,f.**

Earle, Peter (Editor) **HC240**
Essays in European Economic History 1500-1800. Trade Cloth. Oxford University Press, Inc. New York, NY. 1974. 282p. ISBN:0-19-877054-5, ISBN13: 978-0-19-877054-1. Dewey:330.94/022.
Audience: **u,f.**

Eichengreen, Barry J. **HG3881**
Globalizing Capital: A History of the International Monetary System. Trade Paper. Princeton University Press. Princeton, NJ.

1998. 236p. ISBN:0-691-00245-2, ISBN13: 978-0-691-00245-3. Dewey:332/.042.
Audience: **u,f.** *Choice, 1997.*

Flinn, Michael W. & Smout, T. C. (Editors) **HN383**
Essays in Social History. Trade Cloth. Oxford University Press, Inc. New York, NY. 1974. xiii, 289p. ISBN:0-19-877017-0, ISBN13: 978-0-19-877017-6. Dewey:941.07.
Audience: **u,f.**

Floud, Roderick (Editor, Introduction by) **HC253**
Essays in Quantitative Economic History. Trade Cloth. Oxford University Press, Inc. New York, NY. 1974. 258p. ISBN:0-19-877018-9, ISBN13: 978-0-19-877018-3. Dewey:330.941.
Audience: **u,f.**

Gerschenkron, Alexander **HC335.G386**
Economic Backwardness in Historical Perspective. Trade Cloth. Harvard University Press. Cambridge, MA. 1962. 468p. ISBN:0-674-22600-3, ISBN13: 978-0-674-22600-5. Dewey:330.947. LCCN:62-017217.
Audience: **u,f.**

Glass, D. V. (Editor) **HB881**
Population in History: Essays in Historical Demography. Eversley, D. E. C. (Editor). London: Edward Arnold. 1965.
Audience: **u,f.**

Hatcher, John & Bailey, Mark **HC254.H37 2001**
Modelling the Middle Ages: The History and Theory of England's Economic Development. Cloth Text. Oxford University Press, Inc. New York, NY. 2001. 272p. ISBN:0-19-924411-1, ISBN13: 978-0-19-924411-9. Dewey:330.94/01. LCCN:00-066922.
Audience: **u,f.** *Choice, 2002.*

Heilbroner, Robert L. **HB76 .H4 1986**
The Worldly Philosophers: The Lives, Times, and Ideas of the Great Economic Thinkers. Ed. 6. Trade Cloth. Simon & Schuster. New York, NY. 1986. 365p. A Touchstone Book Ser. ISBN:0-671-63482-8, ISBN13: 978-0-671-63482-7. Dewey:330.1/0922. LCCN:86-022003.
Audience: **l,u,f.**

Hunt, Edwin S. & Murray, James M. **HF3495.H86 1999**
A History of Business in Medieval Europe, 1200-1550. Cloth Text. Cambridge University Press. New York, NY. 1999. 298p. Medieval Textbooks Ser. ISBN:0-521-49581-4, ISBN13: 978-0-521-49581-3. Dewey:330.94/01. LCCN:98-038599.
Audience: **u,f.** *Choice, 1999.*

Jenkins, David (Editor) **NK8906.C36 2002**
The Cambridge History of Western Textiles, Set. Quantity Pack, Trade Cloth. Cambridge University Press. New York, NY. 2003. 1400p. ISBN:0-521-34107-8, ISBN13: 978-0-521-34107-3. Dewey:338.4/7677/009. LCCN:2001-052958.
Audience: **g,l,u,f.** *Choice, 2004.*

Jones, Eric **HC240.J57 2003**
The European Miracle: Environments, Economies and Geopolitics in the History of Europe and Asia. Ed. 3. Cloth Text. Cambridge University Press. New York, NY. 2003. 344p. ISBN:0-521-82094-4, ISBN13: 978-0-521-82094-3. Dewey:330.94/02. LCCN:2002-035083.
Audience: **l,u,f.** *Choice, 2004.*

Kamen, Henry Arthur Francis **HN373.K293 2000**
Early Modern European Society. Ed. 2. Paper over Boards. Routledge. New York, NY. 2000. 304p. ISBN:0-415-15864-8, ISBN13: 978-0-415-15864-0. Dewey:306/.094. LCCN:99-037008.
Audience: **l,u,f.** *Choice, 2000.*

Kellenbenz, Hermann **HC240.K387**
The Rise of the European Economy: An Economic History of Continental Europe from Fifteenth Hundred to Seventeen Fifty. Trade Cloth. Holmes & Meier Publishers, Inc. Teaneck, NJ. 1976. 350p. ISBN:0-8419-0273-9, ISBN13: 978-0-8419-0273-2. Dewey:330.9/4/02. LCCN:76-007487.
Audience: **u,f.**

Landes, David S. **HC240.L26 2003**
The Unbound Prometheus: Technological Change and Industrial Development in Western Europe from 1750 to Present. Ed. 2. Cloth Text. Cambridge University Press. New York, NY. 2003. 588p. ISBN:0-521-82666-7, ISBN13: 978-0-521-82666-2. Dewey:338.094. LCCN:2002-041539.
Audience: **u,f.** B

Landes, David S. **HC240.Z9W45 1998**
The Wealth and Poverty of Nations: Why Some Are So Rich and Some So Poor. Trade Cloth. W. W. Norton & Company, Inc. New York, NY. 1998. 544p. ISBN:0-393-04017-8, ISBN13: 978-0-393-04017-3. Dewey:330.1/6. LCCN:97-027508.
Audience: **u,f.** *Choice, 1998.*

Lane, Frederick C. (Editor) **HB75**
Enterprise and Secular Change: Readings in Economic History. Riermersma, Jelle C. (Editor). Homewood, Ill.: Richard D. Irwin, Inc. 1953.
Audience: **u,f.**

Mathias, Peter & Postan, M. M. (Editors) **HC240**
The Cambridge Economic History of Europe: The Industrial Economies: Capital Labour and Enterprise, Part 1, Britain, France, Germany and Scandinavia. Trade Paper. Cambridge University Press. New York, NY. 1982. 852p. The Cambridge Economic History of Europe Ser., Vol. 7 ISBN:0-521-28800-2, ISBN13: 978-0-521-28800-2. Dewey:330.94. LCCN:41-003509.
Audience: **u,f.**

Mathias, Peter & Postan, M. M. (Editors) **HC240.C3**
The Cambridge Economic History of Europe from the Decline of the Roman Empire: The Industrial Economies: Capital, Labour and Enterprise, the United States, Japan and Russia. Trade Paper. Cambridge University Press. New York, NY. 1982. 651p. The Cambridge Economic History of Europe Ser. ISBN:0-521-28801-0, ISBN13: 978-0-521-28801-9. Dewey:330.94. LCCN:41-003509.
Audience: **u,f.**

Mathias, Peter & Postan, M. M. (Editors) **HC240.C3**
The Industrial Economies: Capital, Labour and Enterprise: The United States, Japan and Russia, Vol. 7, Pt. 2. Trade Cloth.

Cambridge University Press. New York, NY. 1978. 670p. The Cambridge Economic History of Europe Ser., Vol. 7 ISBN:0-521-21591-9, ISBN13: 978-0-521-21591-6. Dewey:330.94.
Audience: **u,f.**

Mathias, P. & Pollard, Sidney (Editors) **HC240.C312 1989**
The Cambridge Economic History of Europe: The Industrial Economies: The Development of Economic and Social Policies, Vol. 8. Trade Cloth. Cambridge University Press. New York, NY. 1989. 1280p. The Cambridge Economic History of Europe Ser. ISBN:0-521-22504-3, ISBN13: 978-0-521-22504-5. Dewey:330.94.
Audience: **u,f.** *Choice, 1990.*

McCloskey, Deirdre N. **PE1479.E35M33 2000**
Economical Writing. Ed. 2. Paper Text. Waveland Press, Inc. Prospect Heights, IL. 1999. 98p. ISBN:1-57766-063-3, ISBN13: 978-1-57766-063-7. Dewey:808/.06633. LCCN:00-710407.
Audience: **u,f.**

Miskimin, Harry A. **HC240**
The Economy of Early Renaissance Europe, 1300-1460. Trade Paper. Cambridge University Press. New York, NY. 1975. 204p. ISBN:0-521-29021-X, ISBN13: 978-0-521-29021-0. Dewey:330.9/4/017. LCCN:75-016607.
Audience: **u,f.**

Miskimin, Harry A. **HC240**
The Economy of the Later Renaissance Europe, 1460-1600. Trade Paper. Cambridge University Press. New York, NY. 1975. x, 222p. ISBN:0-521-29208-5, ISBN13: 978-0-521-29208-5. Dewey:330.9/4/02. LCCN:75-017120.
Audience: **u,f.**

Mokyr, Joel **HC79.T4**
The Lever of Riches: Technological Creativity and Economic Progress. Paper Text. Oxford University Press, Inc. New York, NY. 1992. 368p. ISBN:0-19-507477-7, ISBN13: 978-0-19-507477-2. Dewey:338/.064. LCCN:89-028298.
Audience: **u,f.** *Choice, 1990.*

Mokyr, Joel (Editor) **HC15**
The Oxford Encyclopedia of Economic History, Set. Trade Cloth. Oxford University Press, Inc. New York, NY. 2003. 2806p. ISBN:0-19-510507-9, ISBN13: 978-0-19-510507-0. Dewey:330/.03. LCCN:2003-008992.
Audience: **g,l,u,f.** *Choice, 2004.*

Musgrave, Peter **HC240.M793 1999**
The Early Modern European Economy. Trade Paper. Palgrave Macmillan. New York, NY. 1999. 248p. ISBN:0-312-22332-3, ISBN13: 978-0-312-22332-8. Dewey:330.9/4. LCCN:99-012189.
Audience: **u,f.** *Choice, 1999.*

Nicholas, David **D202.8.N53 1999**
The Transformation of Europe 1300-1600. Trade Paper. Oxford University Press, Inc. New York, NY. 1999. 496p. Arnold History of Europe Ser. ISBN:0-340-66208-5, ISBN13: 978-0-340-66208-3. Dewey:940.1. LCCN:98-051966.
Audience: **u,f.**

North, Douglass Cecil **HC21**
Structure and Change in Economic History. Trade Paper. W. W. Norton & Company, Inc. New York, NY. 1982. 240p. ISBN:0-393-95241-X, ISBN13: 978-0-393-95241-4. Dewey:330.9. LCCN:81-038368.
Audience: **u,f.**

North, Douglass C. & Thomas, Robert Paul **HC240**
The Rise of the Western World: A New Economic History. Trade Paper. Cambridge University Press. New York, NY. 1976. 179p. ISBN:0-521-29099-6, ISBN13: 978-0-521-29099-9. Dewey:330.9. LCCN:73-077258.
Audience: **l,u.**

Parker, Geoffrey & Smith, Lesley M. **D246.G24 1997**
The General Crisis of the Seventeenth Century. Ed. 2. Paper over Boards. Routledge. New York, NY. 1997. 320p. ISBN:0-415-16518-0, ISBN13: 978-0-415-16518-1. Dewey:940.2/52. LCCN:96-045505.
Audience: **g,u,f.**

Parker, William N. & Jones, Eric L. (Editors) **HD1917**
European Peasants and Their Markets: Essays in Agrarian Economic History. Trade Cloth. Princeton University Press. Princeton, NJ. 1976. 376p. ISBN:0-691-05230-1, ISBN13: 978-0-691-05230-4. Dewey:338.1/094. LCCN:75-015281.
Audience: **u,f.**

Polanyi, Karl **HC53.P6 2001**
The Great Transformation: The Political and Economic Origins of Our Time. Ed. 2. Trade Paper. Beacon Press. Boston, MA. 2001. 328p. ISBN:0-8070-5643-X, ISBN13: 978-0-8070-5643-1. Dewey:330.9. LCCN:00-064156.
Audience: **l,u.**

Postan, M. M. (Editor) **HD1917**
The Cambridge Economic History of Europe from the Decline of the Roman Empire: The Agrarian Life of the Middle Ages. Ed. 2. Cloth Text. Cambridge University Press. New York, NY. 1966. 888p. The Cambridge Economic History of Europe Ser., Vol. 1 ISBN:0-521-04505-3, ISBN13: 978-0-521-04505-6. Dewey:338.1/094/0902.
Audience: **l,u.**

Postan, M. M. & Miller, E (Editors) **HC240**
The Cambridge Economic History of Europe: Trade and Industry in the Middle Ages. Ed. 2. Cloth Text. Cambridge University Press. New York, NY. 1987. 1024p. The Cambridge Economic History of Europe Ser. ISBN:0-521-08709-0, ISBN13: 978-0-521-08709-4. Dewey:330.94.
Audience: **l,u.**

Postan, M. M. (Editor), et al. **HC240**
The Cambridge Economic History of Europe from the Decline of the Roman Empire: Economic Organisation and Policies in the Middle Ages. E. E. Rich & E Miller (Editors). Trade Cloth. Cambridge University Press. New York, NY. 1963. 712p. The Cambridge Economic History of Europe Ser. ISBN:0-521-04506-1, ISBN13: 978-0-521-04506-3. Dewey:338.1/094/0902.
Audience: **l,u.**

Prak, Maarten Roy **HC240.E233 2000**
Early Modern Capitalism: Economic and Social Change in Europe 1400-1800. Paper over Boards. Routledge. New York, NY. 2001. 256p. Routledge Explorations in Economic History Ser., Vol. 21 ISBN:0-415-21714-8, ISBN13: 978-0-415-21714-9. Dewey:338.94/009. LCCN:00-035308.
Audience: **l,u.**

Rich, E. E. & Wilson, C. H. (Editors) **HC240**
The Cambridge Economic History of Europe: The Economy of Expanding Europe in the 16th and 17th Centuries, Vol. 4. Trade Cloth. Cambridge University Press. New York, NY. 1967. 674p. The Cambridge Economic History of Europe Ser. ISBN:0-521-04507-X, ISBN13: 978-0-521-04507-0. Dewey:330.94.
Audience: **u,f.**

Rich, E. E. (Editor), et al. **HC240**
The Cambridge Economic History of Europe from the Decline of the Roman Empire: The Economic Organization of Early Modern Europe. C. H. Wilson, D. C. Coleman, P. Mathias & M. M. Postan (Editors). Trade Cloth. Cambridge University Press. New York, NY. 1977. 750p. The Cambridge Economic History of Europe Ser. ISBN:0-521-08710-4, ISBN13: 978-0-521-08710-0. Dewey:330.94. LCCN:41-003509.
Audience: **u,f.**

Vries, Jan De **HC240 1976**
The Economy of Europe in an Age of Crisis, 1600-1750. Trade Paper. Cambridge University Press. New York, NY. 1976. 295p. ISBN:0-521-29050-3, ISBN13: 978-0-521-29050-0. Dewey:330.9/4/0252. LCCN:75-030438.
Audience: **l,u.**

Wallerstein, Immanuel **HC240**
The Modern World System: Mercantilism and the Consolidation of the European World-Economy, 1600-1750. Ed. 2. Paper Text. Elsevier Science & Technology Books. Saint Louis, MO. 1980. 384p. Studies in Social Discontinuity Ser. ISBN:0-12-785924-1, ISBN13: 978-0-12-785924-8. Dewey:330.9/4/021. LCCN:73-005318.
Audience: **u,f.**

Wallerstein, Immanuel **HC51.W28 1974 VOL. 3**
The Modern World-System: The Second Era of Great Expansion of the Capitalist World-Economy, 1730s-1840s. Cloth Text. Elsevier Science & Technology Books. Saint Louis, MO. 1988. 372p. Studies in Social Discontinuity Ser. ISBN:0-12-785925-X, ISBN13: 978-0-12-785925-5. Dewey:330.94/02 s. LCCN:88-010457.
Audience: **u,f.**

Wallerstein, Immanuel **HC21**
The Modern World System: Capitalist Agriculture and the Origins of the European World-Economy in the 16th Century. Edward Shorter & Charles Tilly (Contribution by). Paper Text. Elsevier Science & Technology Books. Saint Louis, MO. 1980. 410p. Studies in Social Discontinuity Ser. ISBN:0-12-785919-5, ISBN13: 978-0-12-785919-4. Dewey:330.9. LCCN:73-005318.
Audience: **u,f.**

Winter, J. M. **HC240**
War and Economic Development. Trade Cloth. Cambridge University Press. Cambridge, 1975. 305p. ISBN:0-521-20535-2, ISBN13: 978-0-521-20535-1. Dewey:330.94. LCCN:74-082219.
Audience: **u,f.**

Youngson, A. J. (Editor) **HC51 .E26**
Economic Development in the Long Run. Cloth Text. Palgrave Macmillan. New York, NY. 1973. ISBN:0-312-22890-2, ISBN13: 978-0-312-22890-3. Dewey:330.9. LCCN:72-079503.
Audience: **u,f.**

General History > Economic History > Demographic and Agrarian History

Ambrosoli, Mauro **SB87.E8 A5313 1997**
The Wild and the Sown: Botany and Agriculture in Western Europe, 1350-1850. Mary Salvatorelli (Translator). Trade Cloth. Cambridge University Press. New York, NY. 1997. 487p. Past and Present Publications ISBN:0-521-46509-5, ISBN13: 978-0-521-46509-0. Dewey:630.9/4. LCCN:96-000300.
Audience: **u,f.**

Astill, Grenville & Langdon, John (Editors) **S452.M43 1997**
Medieval Farming and Technology: The Impact of Agricultural Change in Northwest Europe. Trade Cloth. Brill Academic Publishers, Inc. Boston, MA. 1997. "xii, 321"p. Technology and Change in History Ser., No. 1 ISBN:90-04-10582-4, ISBN13: 978-90-04-10582-9. Dewey:630/.94/0902. LCCN:97-007623.
Audience: **u,f.**

Aston, T. H. & Philpin, C. H. E. (Editors) **HN373**
The Brenner Debate: Agrarian Class Structure and Economic Development in Pre-Industrial Europe. Lyndal Roper (Contribution by). Trade Paper. Cambridge University Press. New York, NY. 1987. 350p. Past and Present Publications ISBN:0-521-34933-8, ISBN13: 978-0-521-34933-8. Dewey:338.1/094.
Audience: **u,f.**

Benedictow, Ole J. **RC172.B46 2004**
The Black Death, 1346-1353: The Complete History. Trade Cloth. Boydell & Brewer, Ltd. Woodbridge, 2004. 454p. ISBN:0-85115-943-5, ISBN13: 978-0-85115-943-0. Dewey:614.5/732. LCCN:2003-024313.
Audience: **l,u,f.** *Choice, 2005.*

Borsch, Stuart J. **RC179.E3B67 2005**
The Black Death in Egypt and England: A Comparative Study. Trade Cloth. University of Texas Press. Austin, TX. 2005. 207p. ISBN:0-292-70617-0, ISBN13: 978-0-292-70617-0. Dewey:330.962/024. LCCN:2004-023691.
Audience: **u,f.**

Boserup, Ester **HB871**
Population and Technological Change: A Study of Long-Term Trends. Paper Text. University of Chicago Press. Chicago, IL. 1983. 268p. ISBN:0-226-06674-6, ISBN13: 978-0-226-06674-5. Dewey:304.6/2. LCCN:80-021116.
Audience: **u,f.**

Cipolla, Carlo M. (Editor) **HB871**
The Economic History of World Population. Ed. 7. Cloth Text. Barnes & Noble Books-Imports. Lanham, MD. 1978. 155p. ISBN:0-06-491138-1, ISBN13: 978-0-06-491138-2. Dewey:304.6/2.
Audience: **u,f.**

Cohn, Sam **RC178**
The Black Death Transformed: Disease and Culture in Early Renaissance Europe. Trade Paper. Oxford University Press, Inc. New York, NY. 2003. 336p. A Hodder Arnold Publication ISBN:0-340-70647-3, ISBN13: 978-0-340-70647-3. Dewey:362.1/9232/094.
Audience: **l,u,f.** *Choice, 2003.*

Grigg, David B. **HD1415.G684 1992**
The Transformation of Agriculture in the West. Paper Text. Blackwell Publishing, Inc. Malden, MA. 1992. 176p. New Perspectives on the Past Ser. ISBN:0-631-17094-4, ISBN13: 978-0-631-17094-5. Dewey:338.109. LCCN:92-130360.
Audience: **l,u.** *Choice, 1992.*

Herlihy, David **RC178.A1H47 1997**
The Black Death and the Transformation of the West. Samuel K. Cohn Jr. (Editor, Introduction by). Trade Paper. Harvard University Press. Cambridge, MA. 1997. 128p. ISBN:0-674-07613-3, ISBN13: 978-0-674-07613-6. Dewey:940.1/92. LCCN:96-054637.
Audience: **u,f.**

Hopcroft, Rosemary L. **HD1333.E85H66 1999**
Regions, Institutions, and Agrarian Change in European History. Trade Cloth. University of Michigan Press. Chicago, IL. 1999. 288p. Economics, Cognition, and Society Ser. ISBN:0-472-11023-3, ISBN13: 978-0-472-11023-0. Dewey:338.1/094. LCCN:99-006089.
Audience: **u,f.**

Houston, Rab A. **HB3583.H63 1995**
The Population History of Britain and Ireland 1500-1750. Maurice Kirby (Contribution by). Cloth Text. Cambridge University Press. New York, NY. 1995. 105p. New Studies in Economic and Social History, No. 18 ISBN:0-521-55277-X, ISBN13: 978-0-521-55277-6. Dewey:304.6/0941. LCCN:95-018507.
Audience: **u,f.**

Jordan, William C. **RC178.A1**
The Great Famine: Northern Europe in the Early Fourteenth Century. Trade Paper. Princeton University Press. Princeton, NJ. 1997. 328p. ISBN:0-691-05891-1, ISBN13: 978-0-691-05891-7. Dewey:940.1/92.
Audience: **u,f.** *Choice, 1996.*

Rotberg, Robert I. & Robb, Theodore K. (Editors) **HB3585.P658 1986**
Population and Economy: From the Traditional to the Modern World. Cloth Text. Cambridge University Press. New York, NY. 1986. 229p. Studies in Interdisciplinary History ISBN:0-521-32540-4, ISBN13: 978-0-521-32540-0. Dewey:304.6/0941. LCCN:85-026945.
Audience: **u,f.** *Choice, 1987.*

Scott, Tom (Editor) **HD1531.5.P4 1998**
The Peasantries of Europe: From the Fourteenth to the Eighteenth Centuries. Trade Paper. Addison-Wesley Longman, Inc. Boston, MA. 1998. 432p. ISBN:0-582-10131-X, ISBN13: 978-0-582-10131-9. Dewey:305.5/633/094. LCCN:97-041897.
Audience: **u,f.**

Sweeney, Del **S452.A47 1995**
Agriculture in the Middle Ages: Technology, Practice, and Representation. Trade Paper. University of Pennsylvania Press. Philadelphia, PA. 1995. 416p. Middle Ages Ser. ISBN:0-8122-1511-7, ISBN13: 978-0-8122-1511-3. Dewey:306.3/49/0940902. LCCN:95-024416.
Audience: **u,f.**

Thirsk, Joan **S455.T48 1997**
Alternative Agriculture: A History: From the Black Death to the Present Day. Trade Cloth. Oxford University Press, Inc. New York, NY. 1997. 376p. ISBN:0-19-820662-3, ISBN13: 978-0-19-820662-0. Dewey:630.9/41/0903. LCCN:98-115344.
Audience: **g,l,u,f.** *Choice, 1998.*

Walter, John & Schofield, Roger S. (Editors) **HC260.F3**
Famine, Disease and the Social Order in Early Modern Society. Jan De Vries, Paul Johnson, Richard Smith & Keith Wrightson (Contribution by). Trade Paper. Cambridge University Press. New York, NY. 1991. 349p. Studies in Population, Economy and Society in Past Time ISBN:0-521-40613-7, ISBN13: 978-0-521-40613-0. Dewey:363.8/0942/0903.
Audience: **u,f.** *Choice, 1990.*

Wrigley, E. Anthony, et al. **HB3585 .E54 1997**
English Population History from Family Reconstitution 1580-1837. R. S. Davies, J. E. Oeppen & R. S. Schofield (Authors), Jan De Vries, Paul Johnson, Richard Smith & Keith Wrightson (Contribution by). Cloth Text. Cambridge University Press. New York, NY. 1997. 681p. Cambridge Studies in Population, Economy and Society in Past Time, No. 32 ISBN:0-521-59015-9, ISBN13: 978-0-521-59015-0. Dewey:304.6/0942. LCCN:96-047524.
Audience: **u,f.** *Choice, 1998.*

Wrigley, E. Anthony & Schofield, Roger S. **HB3585 .W74 1989**
The Population History of England, 1541-1871. Jan De Vries, Paul Johnson, Richard Smith & Keith Wrightson (Contribution by). Trade Paper. Cambridge University Press. New York, NY. 1989. 830p. Cambridge Studies in Population, Economy and Society in Past Time Ser. ISBN:0-521-35688-1, ISBN13: 978-0-521-35688-6. Dewey:304.6/0942. LCCN:88-028368.
Audience: **u,f.**

General History > Economic History > Urban History

Boone, M., et al. **HJ8615.U77 2003**
Urban Public Debts, Urban Governments and the Market for Annuities in Western Europe. K. Davids & P. Janssesns (Authors). Trade Paper. Brepols Publishers. B-2300 Turnhout, 2003. 256p. Studies in European Urban History Ser., Vol. 3 ISBN:2-503-51383-2, ISBN13: 978-2-503-51383-6. LCCN:2004-412093.
Audience: **u,f.**

Clark, Peter (Editor, Contribution by) **D210 .S62 1995**
Small Towns in Early Modern Europe. David Reeder (Contribution by). Trade Cloth. Cambridge University Press. New York, NY. 1995. 330p. Themes in International Urban History Ser., No. 3 ISBN:0-521-46463-3, ISBN13: 978-0-521-46463-5. Dewey:940.2. LCCN:94-010674.
Audience: **u,f.**

Cowan, Alexander **CB351.C65 1998**
Urban Europe, 1500-1700. Paper Text. Oxford University Press, Inc. New York, NY. 1998. 240p. A Hodder Arnold Publication Ser. ISBN:0-340-71981-8, ISBN13: 978-0-340-71981-7. Dewey:940.2. LCCN:98-019577.
Audience: **u,f.**

De Vries, Jan **HT131.D4 1984**
European Urbanization: 1500-1800. Trade Cloth. Harvard University Press. Cambridge, MA. 1984. 432p. Harvard Studies in Urban History ISBN:0-674-27015-0, ISBN13: 978-0-674-27015-2. Dewey:307.7/6/094. LCCN:84-010774.
Audience: **u,f.**

Friedrichs, Christopher R. **HT131.F75 1995**
The Early Modern City, 1450-1750. Trade Paper. Longman Publishing Group. White Plains, NY. 1995. 392p. A History of Urban Society in Europe Ser. ISBN:0-582-01320-8, ISBN13: 978-0-582-01320-9. Dewey:307.76/094/0903. LCCN:94-021545.
Audience: **u,f.**

Hohenberg, Paul M. & Lees, Lynn H. **HT131.H58 1995**
The Making of Urban Europe, 1000-1994. Ed. 2. Trade Paper. Harvard University Press. Cambridge, MA. 1995. 448p. ISBN:0-674-54362-9, ISBN13: 978-0-674-54362-1. Dewey:307.7/6/094. LCCN:95-009303.
Audience: **u,f.**

Nicholas, David **HT115.N53 1997**
Growth of the Medieval City: From Late Antiquity to the Early Fourteenth Century. Trade Paper. Addison-Wesley Longman, Inc. Boston, MA. 1997. 432p. History of Urban Society in Europe Ser. ISBN:0-582-29906-3, ISBN13: 978-0-582-29906-1. Dewey:307.7/6/094/0902. LCCN:96-027185.
Audience: **l,u,f.** *Choice, 1997.*

Nicholas, David **HT115.N55 1997**
The Later Medieval City 1300-1500. Paper Text. Longman Publishing Group. White Plains, NY. 1997. 536p. A History of Urban Society in Europe Ser. ISBN:0-582-01317-8, ISBN13: 978-0-582-01317-9. Dewey:307.7/6/094/0902. LCCN:96-027175.
Audience: **u,f.** *Choice, 1997.*

Nicholas, David **CB351.N55 2003**
Urban Europe, 1100-1700. Cloth over Boards. Palgrave Macmillan. New York, NY. 2003. 256p. ISBN:0-333-94982-X, ISBN13: 978-0-333-94982-5. Dewey:940/.091732. LCCN:2003-051934.
Audience: **u,f.** *Choice, 2004.*

Tilly, Charles & Blockmans, Wim P. (Editors) **D200.C57 1994**
Cities and the Rise of States in Europe, A. D. 1000-1800. Trade Paper. Westview Press. Boulder, CO. 1994. 290p. ISBN:0-8133-8849-X, ISBN13: 978-0-8133-8849-6. Dewey:940. LCCN:94-017378.
Audience: **u,f.**

Van der Woude, Ad (Editor), et al.
Urbanization in History: A Process of Dynamic Interactions. Jan De Vries & Akira Hayami (Editors). Paper Text. Oxford University Press, Inc. New York, NY. 1995. 386p. International Studies in Demography ISBN:0-19-828958-8, ISBN13: 978-0-19-828958-6.
Audience: **u,f.**

General History > History of Science

Asma, Stephen T. **QH70.A1A75 2003**
Stuffed Animals and Pickled Heads: The Culture and Evolution of Natural History Museums. Trade Paper. Oxford University Press, Inc. New York, NY. 2003. 320p. ISBN:0-19-516336-2, ISBN13: 978-0-19-516336-0. Dewey:508/.074.
Audience: **g,l,u,f.**

Brown Reference Group **Q124.97**
Medieval Science, Technology and Medicine: An Encyclopedia. Steven J. Livesey, Thomas F. Glick, Faith Wallis & Daniel A. Stout (Editors). Paper over Boards. Routledge. New York, NY. 2005. 624p. The Routledge Encyclopedias of the Middle Ages Ser., Vol. 11 ISBN:0-415-96930-1, ISBN13: 978-0-415-96930-7. Dewey:509/.02. LCCN:2005-022223.
Audience: **g,l,u.** *Choice, 2006.*

Cobb, Cathy & Goldwhite, Harold **QD11 .C59 1995**
Creations of Fire: Chemistry's Lively History from Alchemy to the Atomic Age. Trade Paper. Perseus Books Group. New York, NY. 2001. 496p. ISBN:0-7382-0594-X, ISBN13: 978-0-7382-0594-6. Dewey:540.9.
Audience: **g,l,u,f.** *Choice, 1996.*

Cohen, Claudine **QE882.P8C6413 2002**
The Fate of the Mammoth: Fossils, Myth, and History. William Rodarmor (Translator). Trade Cloth. University of Chicago Press. Chicago, IL. 2002. 336p. ISBN:0-226-11292-6, ISBN13: 978-0-226-11292-3. Dewey:569/.67. LCCN:2001-048011.
Audience: **g,l,u,f.** *Choice, 2003, 2002.*

Daston, Lorraine & Park, Katharine (Editors) **Q125.2**
The Cambridge History of Science: Early Modern Science. David C. Lindberg & Ronald L. Numbers (Contribution by). Trade Cloth. Cambridge University Press. New York, NY. 2006. 894p. The Cambridge History of Science Ser. ISBN:0-521-57244-4, ISBN13: 978-0-521-57244-6. Dewey:509.409031.
Audience: **g,l,u,f.**

Dean, Dennis R. **QE22.M32 D43 1999**
Gideon Mantell and the Discovery of Dinosaurs. Trade Cloth. Cambridge University Press. New York, NY. 1999. 310p. ISBN:0-521-42048-2, ISBN13: 978-0-521-42048-8. Dewey:560/.92 B. LCCN:98-016448.
Audience: **g,l,u,f.** *Choice, 1999.*

Dohrn-van Rossum, Gerhard **QB107.D6413 1996**
History of the Hour: Clocks and Modern Temporal Orders. Thomas Dunlap (Translator). Trade Cloth. University of Chicago Press. Chicago, IL. 1996. 463p. ISBN:0-226-15510-2, ISBN13: 978-0-226-15510-4. Dewey:529/.7/09. LCCN:95-047660.
Audience: **g,l,u,f.** *Choice, 1996.*

Farber, Paul Lawrence **QH15.F27 2000**
Finding Order in Nature: The Naturalist Tradition from Linnaeus to E. O. Wilson. Trade Cloth. Johns Hopkins University Press. Baltimore, MD. 2000. 152p. Johns Hopkins Introductory Studies in the History of Science ISBN:0-8018-6389-9, ISBN13: 978-0-8018-6389-9. Dewey:508/.09. LCCN:99-089621.
Audience: **g,l,u,f.** *Choice, 2001.*

Gordin, Michael D. **QD22.M43G67 2004**
A Well-Ordered Thing: Dmitrii Mendeleev and the Shadow of the Periodic Table. Trade Cloth. Basic Books. New York, NY. 2004. 384p. ISBN:0-465-02775-X, ISBN13: 978-0-465-02775-0. Dewey:540/.92 B. LCCN:2003-025533.
Audience: **g,l,u,f.** *Choice, 2004.*

Graham, Loren R. **Q127.S696 G729 1993**
Science in Russia and the Soviet Union: A Short History. George Basalla & Owen Hannaway (Contribution by). Trade Paper. Cambridge University Press. New York, NY. 1994. 351p.

Cambridge Studies in the History of Science Ser. ISBN:0-521-28789-8, ISBN13: 978-0-521-28789-0. Dewey:509.47. LCCN:92-005087.
Audience: **g,u,f.** *Choice, 1993.*

Hassenbruch, Arne (Editor) **Q125.R335 2000**
Reader's Guide to the History of Science. Trade Cloth. Fitzroy Dearborn Publishers, Inc. Chicago, IL. 2000. 964p. ISBN:1-884964-29-X, ISBN13: 978-1-884964-29-9. Dewey:509. LCCN:2001-270888.
Audience: **g,l,u.** *Choice, 2001.*

Heilbron, John L. (Editor) **Q125**
The Oxford Companion to the History of Modern Science. Trade Cloth. Oxford University Press, Inc. New York, NY. 2003. 972p. ISBN:0-19-511229-6, ISBN13: 978-0-19-511229-0. Dewey:509. LCCN:2002-153783.
Audience: **g,l,u,f.** *Choice, 2003.*

Krebs, Robert E. **Q124.97.K73 2004**
Groundbreaking Scientific Experiments, Inventions, and Discoveries of the Middle Ages and the Renaissance. Cloth Text. Greenwood Publishing Group, Inc. Portsmouth, NH. 2004. 344p. Groundbreaking Scientific Experiments, Inventions, and Discoveries Through the Ages Ser. ISBN:0-313-32433-6, ISBN13: 978-0-313-32433-8. Dewey:509.4/0902. LCCN:2003-060075.
Audience: **g,l,u.** *Choice, 2004.*

Krebs, Robert E. & Krebs, Carolyn A. **Q124**
Groundbreaking Scientific Experiments, Inventions, and Discoveries of the Ancient World. Cloth Text. Greenwood Publishing Group, Inc. Portsmouth, NH. 2003. 400p. Groundbreaking Scientific Experiments, Inventions, and Discoveries Through the Ages Ser. ISBN:0-313-31342-3, ISBN13: 978-0-313-31342-4. Dewey:509.3. LCCN:2003-045530.
Audience: **g,l,u.**

Losee, John **Q175.L666 2005**
Theories on the Scrap Heap: Scientists and Philosophers on the Falsification, Rejection, and Replacement of Theories. Trade Paper, Perfect. University of Pittsburgh Press. Pittsburgh, PA. 2005. 206p. Fields Institute Communications Ser., Vol. 45 ISBN:0-8229-5873-2, ISBN13: 978-0-8229-5873-4. Dewey:501. LCCN:2004-062747.
Audience: **g,l,u,f.** *Choice, 2005.*

Martin, Geoffrey J. **G80.M38 2004**
All Possible Worlds: A History of Geographical Ideas. Ed. 4. Trade Cloth. Oxford University Press, Inc. New York, NY. 2005. 605p. ISBN:0-19-516870-4, ISBN13: 978-0-19-516870-9. Dewey:910/.9. LCCN:2004-057559.
Audience: **u,f.** *Choice, 2005.*

McAllister, James W. **Q175.M415 1996**
Beauty and Revolution in Science. Book, Other. Cornell University Press. Ithaca, NY. 1996. 248p. ISBN:0-8014-3240-5, ISBN13: 978-0-8014-3240-8. Dewey:501. LCCN:96-003910.
Audience: **g,l,u,f.** *Choice, 1997.*

McKusick, James C. **PR590**
Green Writing: Romanticism and Ecology. Cloth over Boards. Palgrave Macmillan. New York, NY. 2000. 272p. ISBN:0-312-23448-1, ISBN13: 978-0-312-23448-5. Dewey:821.7/09.
Audience: **l,u,f.** *Choice, 2001.*

Nyhart, Lynn K. **QL799.5.N94 1995**
Biology Takes Form: Animal Morphology and the German Universities, 1800-1900. Trade Cloth. University of Chicago Press. Chicago, IL. 1995. 428p. Science and Its Conceptual Foundations Ser. ISBN:0-226-61086-1, ISBN13: 978-0-226-61086-3. Dewey:591.4/0943/09034. LCCN:95-003227.
Audience: **u,f.** *Choice, 1996.*

Nyhart, Lynn K. & Broman, Thomas H. (Editors) **T14.5**
Science and Civil Society, Vol. 17. Trade Cloth. University of Chicago Press. Chicago, IL. 2002. 350p. Osiris Ser. ISBN:0-226-07371-8, ISBN13: 978-0-226-07371-2. Dewey:303.483.
Audience: **u,f.**

Olby, Robert C. (Editor), et al. **Q125.C565 1990**
Companion to the History of Modern Science. Geoffrey Cantor, John Christie & Jonathon Hodge (Editors). Paper over Boards. Routledge. New York, NY. 1989. 1080p. ISBN:0-415-01988-5, ISBN13: 978-0-415-01988-0. Dewey:509. LCCN:89-010483.
Audience: **g,l,u,f.** *Choice, 1990.*

Rezun, Miron **Q127**
Science, Technology, and Ecopolitics in the U. S. S. R. Trade Cloth. Greenwood Publishing Group, Inc. Portsmouth, NH. 1996. 240p. ISBN:0-275-95383-1, ISBN13: 978-0-275-95383-6. Dewey:306.4/5/0947. LCCN:95-022010.
Audience: **u,f.** *Choice, 1996.*

Schlagel, Richard H. **Q174.8.S335 1995**
From Myth to Modern Mind: From Copernicus to Quantum Mechanics. Paper Text. Peter Lang Publishing, Inc. New York, NY. 1996. 580p. American University Studies, Vol. 171:Philosophy ISBN:0-8204-2699-7, ISBN13: 978-0-8204-2699-0. Dewey:509. LCCN:94-047030.
Audience: **g,l,u.** *Choice, 1997.*

Schlagel, Richard H. **Q124.95.S35 1985**
From Myth to the Modern Mind: A Study of the Origins and Growth of Scientific Thought: Animism to Archimedes. Cloth Text. Peter Lang Publishing, Inc. New York, NY. 1985. 283p. American University Studies, Ser. V, Vol. 12:Philosophy ISBN:0-8204-0219-2, ISBN13: 978-0-8204-0219-2. Dewey:509/.3. LCCN:84-023361.
Audience: **l,u,f.** B

Shectman, Jonathan **Q125**
Groundbreaking Scientific Experiments, Inventions and Discoveries of the 18th Century. Cloth Text. Greenwood Publishing Group, Inc. Portsmouth, NH. 2003. 368p. Groundbreaking Scientific Experiments, Inventions, and Discoveries Through the Ages Ser. ISBN:0-313-32015-2, ISBN13: 978-0-313-32015-6. Dewey:509/.033. LCCN:2002-075306.
Audience: **g.** *Choice, 2004.*

Vucinich, Alexander S. **AS262.A68**
Empire of Knowledge: Academy of Sciences of the U. S. S. R. (1917-1970). Trade Cloth. University of California Press. Berkeley, CA. 1984. 480p. ISBN:0-520-04871-7, ISBN13: 978-0-520-04871-3. Dewey:067. LCCN:83-003484.
Audience: **u,f.** B

Wallace, David Rains **QE707.C63W35 1999**
The Bonehunters' Revenge: Dinosaurs, Greed, and the Greatest Scientific Feud of the Gilded Age. Trade Cloth. Houghton Mifflin Company Trade & Reference Division. Boston, MA. 1999. 366p. ISBN:0-395-85089-4, ISBN13: 978-0-395-85089-3. Dewey:560/.978/09034. LCCN:99-031904.
Audience: **g,l,u,f.** *Choice, 2000.*

Windelspecht, Michael **Q125**
Groundbreaking Scientific Experiments, Inventions and Discoveries of the 17th Century. Cloth Text. Greenwood Publishing Group, Inc. Portsmouth, NH. 2001. 304p. Groundbreaking Scientific Experiments, Inventions and Discoveries Through the Ages Ser. ISBN:0-313-31501-9, ISBN13: 978-0-313-31501-5. Dewey:509/.032. LCCN:2001-023316.
Audience: **g.** *Choice, 2002.*

Windelspecht, Michael **Q125**
Groundbreaking Scientific Experiments, Inventions and Discoveries of the 19th Century. Cloth Text. Greenwood Publishing Group, Inc. Portsmouth, NH. 2003. 304p. Groundbreaking Scientific Experiments, Inventions, and Discoveries Through the Ages Ser. ISBN:0-313-31969-3, ISBN13: 978-0-313-31969-3. Dewey:509.034. LCCN:2002-075305.
Audience: **g.** *Choice, 2003.*

General History > History of Science > Einstein and his Age

Folsing, Albrecht **QC16.E5**
Albert Einstein: A Biography. Ewald Osers (Translator). Trade Paper. Penguin Group (USA) Inc. New York, NY. 1998. 928p. ISBN:0-14-023719-4, ISBN13: 978-0-14-023719-1. Dewey:530/.092. LCCN:96-026341.
Audience: **g,l.** *Choice, 1997.*

Holton, Gerald **Q173.H7342 1995**
Einstein, History and Other Passions. Cloth Text. Springer. New York, NY. 1995. 320p. AIP Masters of Modern Physics Ser. ISBN:1-56396-333-7, ISBN13: 978-1-56396-333-9. Dewey:500. LCCN:94-037483.
Audience: **g,l,u,f.** *Choice, 1995.*

Holton, Gerald **Q180.A3H65 2005**
Victory and Vexation in Science: Einstein, Bohr, Heisenberg, and Others. Trade Cloth. Harvard University Press. Cambridge, MA. 2005. 244p. ISBN:0-674-01519-3, ISBN13: 978-0-674-01519-7. Dewey:500. LCCN:2004-060572.
Audience: **g,l,u,f.** *Choice, 2005.*

Pais, Abraham **QC16.E5**
Subtle Is the Lord: The Science and the Life of Albert Einstein. Roger Penrose (Foreword by). Trade Paper, Perfect. Oxford University Press, Inc. New York, NY. 2005. 576p. ISBN:0-19-280672-6, ISBN13: 978-0-19-280672-7. Dewey:530.092 B. LCCN:2005-285161.
Audience: **g,l.** B

General History > History of Science > Scientific Revolution

Biagioli, Mario **QB36.G2B54 1993**
Galileo, Courtier: The Practice of Science in the Culture of Absolutism. Trade Cloth. University of Chicago Press. Chicago, IL. 1993. 416p. Science and Its Conceptual Foundations Ser. ISBN:0-226-04559-5, ISBN13: 978-0-226-04559-7. Dewey:509.2. LCCN:92-033736.
Audience: **u,f.** *Choice, 1994.*

Butterfield, Herbert **Q125**
The Origins of Modern Science. Trade Paper. Simon & Schuster. New York, NY. 1997. 256p. ISBN:0-684-83637-8, ISBN13: 978-0-684-83637-9. Dewey:509.
Audience: **g,l,u,f.**

Christianson, John Robert **QB36.B8 C54 1999**
On Tycho's Island: Tycho Brahe and His Assistants, 1570-1601. Trade Cloth. Cambridge University Press. New York, NY. 1999. 463p. ISBN:0-521-65081-X, ISBN13: 978-0-521-65081-6. Dewey:520/.92 B. LCCN:99-033118.
Audience: **u,f.**

Cohen, H. Floris **Q125.C538 1994**
The Scientific Revolution: A Historiographical Inquiry. Trade Paper. University of Chicago Press. Chicago, IL. 1994. 680p. ISBN:0-226-11280-2, ISBN13: 978-0-226-11280-0. Dewey:509.4/09032. LCCN:93-041784.
Audience: **u,f.** *Choice, 1995.*

Dear, Peter **Q127.E8D433 2001**
Revolutionizing the Sciences: European Knowledge and Its Ambitions, 1500-1700. Cloth Text. Princeton University Press. Princeton, NJ. 2001. 365p. ISBN:0-691-08859-4, ISBN13: 978-0-691-08859-4. Dewey:509.4/09/031. LCCN:00-109720.
Audience: **g,l,u,f.** *Choice, 2001.*

Debus, Allen G. **QD14.D43 2002**
The Chemical Philosophy. Trade Paper. Dover Publications, Inc. Mineola, NY. 2002. 624p. ISBN:0-486-42175-9, ISBN13: 978-0-486-42175-9. Dewey:540/.9/031. LCCN:2002-017457.
Audience: **u,f.**

Drake, Stillman **QB36.G2.D688 2001**
Galileo: A Very Short Introduction. Trade Paper. Oxford University Press, Inc. New York, NY. 2001. 152p. Very Short Introductions Ser. ISBN:0-19-285456-9, ISBN13: 978-0-19-285456-8. Dewey:520/.92 B. LCCN:2001-269133.
Audience: **g,l,u,f.**

Fantoli, Annibale **QB41.F31513 2003**
Galileo: For Copernicanism and for the Church. Ed. 3. Trade Paper. Libreria Editrice Vaticana. Citta del Vaticano, 2003. 624p. ISBN:88-209-7427-4, ISBN13: 978-88-209-7427-5. Dewey:520/.94/09032. LCCN:2004-397975.
Audience: **u,f.**

Fauvel, John (Editor), et al. **QC16.N7.L47 1988**
Let Newton Be!. Raymond Flood, Michael Shortland & Robin J. Wilson (Editors). Trade Cloth. Oxford University Press, Inc. New York, NY. 1989. 280p. ISBN:0-19-853924-X, ISBN13: 978-0-19-853924-7. Dewey:509.2/4. LCCN:88-009911.
Audience: **g,l,u,f.** *Choice, 1989.*

Feingold, Mordechai **Q183.4.G7**
The Mathematicians' Apprenticeship: Science, Universities and Society in England, 1560-1640. Trade Cloth. Cambridge University Press. New York, NY. 1984. 256p. ISBN:0-521-25133-8, ISBN13: 978-0-521-25133-4. Dewey:507/.042. LCCN:83-001911.
Audience: **u,f.**

Feingold, Mordechai **QC16.N54F45 2004**
The Newtonian Moment: Isaac Newton and the Making of Modern Culture. New York Public Library, Humanities and Social Sciences Library Staff (Contribution by). Trade Cloth. Oxford University Press, Inc. New York, NY. 2004. 240p. ISBN:0-19-517735-5, ISBN13: 978-0-19-517735-0. Dewey:530/.092. LCCN:2004-018090.
Audience: **u,f.** *Choice, 2005.*

Funkenstein, Amos **BT130 .F86**
Theology and the Scientific Imagination from the Middle Ages to the Seventeenth Century. Trade Paper. Princeton University Press. Princeton, NJ. 1989. 460p. ISBN:0-691-02425-1, ISBN13: 978-0-691-02425-7. Dewey:261.5. LCCN:85-043281.
Audience: **u,f.** *Choice, 1987.*

Gingerich, Owen **QB41.G38 2004**
The Book Nobody Read: Chasing the Revolutions of Nicolaus Copernicus. Cloth over Boards. Walker & Company. New York, NY. 2004. 256p. ISBN:0-8027-1415-3, ISBN13: 978-0-8027-1415-2. Dewey:520. LCCN:2003-068879.
Audience: **u,f.** *Choice, 2004.*

Gingerich, Owen **QB15.G563 1993**
The Eye of Heaven: Ptolemy, Copernicus, Kepler. Cloth Text. Springer. New York, NY. 1997. 300p. Masters of Modern Physics Ser., Vol. 7 ISBN:0-88318-863-5, ISBN13: 978-0-88318-863-7. Dewey:520/.9. LCCN:91-026227.
Audience: **g,l,u,f.** *Choice, 1993.*

Grafton, Anthony **B785.C34G73 1999**
Cardano's Cosmos: The Worlds and Works of a Renaissance Astrologer. Trade Cloth. Harvard University Press. Cambridge, MA. 2000. 304p. ISBN:0-674-09555-3, ISBN13: 978-0-674-09555-7. Dewey:133.5/092. LCCN:99-030238.
Audience: **u,f.** *Choice, 2000.*

Hall, A. Rupert **Q125**
The Revolution in Science, 1500-1750. Ed. 3. Trade Paper. Longman Publishing Group. White Plains, NY. 1989. 384p. ISBN:0-582-49133-9, ISBN13: 978-0-582-49133-5. Dewey:509/.03. LCCN:82-008978.
Audience: **g,l,u,f.** B

Hall, A. Rupert **QC16.N7 H35 1996**
Isaac Newton: Adventurer in Thought. Sally Gregory Kohlstedt (Contribution by), David Knight (Contribution by, Preface by). Trade Paper. Cambridge University Press. New York, NY. 1996. 484p. Science Biographies Ser. ISBN:0-521-56669-X, ISBN13: 978-0-521-56669-8. Dewey:509.2. LCCN:96-176355.
Audience: **g,l,u,f.**

Heilbron, J. L. **QB29.H33 1999**
The Sun in the Church: Cathedrals as Solar Observatories. Trade Cloth. Harvard University Press. Cambridge, MA. 1999. 8 color illustrations in an 8 page insert, 43 halftones, 75 geometric line illustrations, 12 digital line illustrations, 15 tables 384p. ISBN:0-674-85433-0, ISBN13: 978-0-674-85433-8. Dewey:520/.94. LCCN:99-023123.
Audience: **u,f.** *Choice, 2000.*

Hoyle, Fred **QB36.C8 H75 1973B**
Nicolaus Copernicus: An Essay on His Life and Work. Trade Cloth. Heinemann. Portsmouth, NH. 1973. x, 84p. ISBN:0-435-54425-X, ISBN13: 978-0-435-54425-6. Dewey:520/.92/4. LCCN:73-163684.
Audience: **g,l,u,f.**

Jardine, Lisa **Q143.H7J37 2004**
The Curious Life of Robert Hooke: The Man Who Measured London. Trade Cloth. HarperCollins Publishers. New York, NY. 2004. 432p. ISBN:0-06-053897-X, ISBN13: 978-0-06-053897-2. Dewey:509.2 B. LCCN:2003-056993.
Audience: **u,f.**

Jardine, Lisa **D231**
Ingenious Pursuits: Building the Scientific Revolution. Trade Paper. Doubleday Publishing. New York, NY. 2000. 464p. ISBN:0-385-72001-7, ISBN13: 978-0-385-72001-4. Dewey:940.2/2.
Audience: **g,l,u,f.**

Joseph, George G. **QA22 .J67 2000**
The Crest of the Peacock: The Non-European Roots of Mathmatics. Ed. 2. Trade Paper. Princeton University Press. Princeton, NJ. 2000. 416p. ISBN:0-691-00659-8, ISBN13: 978-0-691-00659-8. Dewey:510/.9. LCCN:00-102425.
Audience: **g,l,u,f.**

Koestler, Arthur **BL245.K63 1959**
The Sleepwalkers: A History of Man's Changing Vision of the Universe. Herbert Butterfield (Introduction by). Trade Paper. Penguin Group (USA) Inc. New York, NY. 1990. 624p. ISBN:0-14-019246-8, ISBN13: 978-0-14-019246-9. Dewey:523.1/09. LCCN:90-183553.
Audience: **u,f.**

Koyre, Alexandre **QB29 .K6913 1992**
The Astronomical Revolution: Copernicus - Kepler - Borelli. Trade Paper. Dover Publications, Inc. Mineola, NY. 1992. 531p. ISBN:0-486-27095-5, ISBN13: 978-0-486-27095-1. Dewey:520/.9/03. LCCN:92-010477.
Audience: **u,f.**

Kuhn, Thomas S. **Q175.K95 1996**
The Structure of Scientific Revolutions. Ed. 3. Trade Paper. University of Chicago Press. Chicago, IL. 1996. 226p. ISBN:0-226-45808-3, ISBN13: 978-0-226-45808-3. Dewey:509. LCCN:96-013195.
Audience: **g,l,u,f.** B

Lindemann, Mary **RA418.3.E85 L55 1999**
Medicine and Society in Early Modern Europe. William Beik, T. C. W. Blanning & Brendan Simms (Contribution by). Cloth Text. Cambridge University Press. New York, NY. 1999. 263p. New Approaches to European History Ser., No. 16 ISBN:0-521-41254-4, ISBN13: 978-0-521-41254-4. Dewey:306.4/61/094. LCCN:99-017819.
Audience: **u,f.** *Choice, 2000.*

Nebelsick, Harold P. **BL240.2.N424 1992**
Renaissance and Reformation and the Rise of Science. Paper Text. Continuum International Publishing Group, Ltd. London, 1992. 320p. ISBN:0-567-09604-1, ISBN13: 978-0-567-09604-3. Dewey:261.5/5/094. LCCN:92-229876.
Audience: **u,f.**

Rogers, John **PR438.P65**
The Matter of Revolution: Science, Poetry, and Politics in the Age of Milton. Book, Other. Cornell University Press. Ithaca, NY. 1998. 280p. ISBN:0-8014-8525-8, ISBN13: 978-0-8014-8525-1. Dewey:820.9/358.
Audience: **u,f.** *Choice, 1996.*

Rosen, Edward **QB35.R67 1986**
Three Imperial Mathematicians. Library Binding. OPAL Publishing Corporation. Norwalk, CT. 1986. 367p. ISBN:0-89835-242-8, ISBN13: 978-0-89835-242-9. Dewey:520/.92/2 B. LCCN:86-199074.
Audience: **u,f.** *Choice, 1986.*

Rosen, Edward **QB36.C8R63 1995**
Copernicus and His Successors. Erna Hilfstein (Editor). Trade Cloth. Continuum International Publishing Group, Ltd. London, 2003. 256p. ISBN:1-85285-071-X, ISBN13: 978-1-85285-071-5. Dewey:520/.92. LCCN:95-020560.
Audience: **u,f.**

Ruderman, David B. **BM538.S3R818 1995**
Jewish Thought and Scientific Discovery in Early Modern Europe. Cloth over Boards. Yale University Press. Cumberland, RI. 1995. 404p. ISBN:0-300-06112-9, ISBN13: 978-0-300-06112-3. Dewey:296.3/75/094. LCCN:94-030520.
Audience: **u,f.** *Choice, 1995.*

Schiebinger, Londa **Q130**
The Mind Has No Sex?: Women in the Origins of Modern Science. Trade Paper. Harvard University Press. Cambridge, MA. 1991. 368p. ISBN:0-674-57625-X, ISBN13: 978-0-674-57625-4. Dewey:500/.82. LCCN:88-034945.
Audience: **u,f.** *Choice, 1990.*

Shapin, Steven **Q125.S5166 1996**
The Scientific Revolution. Trade Cloth. University of Chicago Press. Chicago, IL. 1996. 232p. Science * Culture Ser. ISBN:0-226-75020-5, ISBN13: 978-0-226-75020-0. Dewey:509. LCCN:96-013196.
Audience: **g,l,u,f.** *Choice, 1997.*

Shapin, Steven & Schaffer, Simon **Q175**
Leviathan and the Air-Pump: Hobbes, Boyle, and the Experimental Life. Trade Paper. Princeton University Press. Princeton, NJ. 1989. 456p. ISBN:0-691-02432-4, ISBN13: 978-0-691-02432-5. Dewey:501. LCCN:85-042705.
Audience: **u,f.**

Smith, Pamela H. **Q125.2**
The Business of Alchemy: Science and Culture in the Holy Roman Empire. Trade Paper. Princeton University Press. Princeton, NJ. 1997. 320p. ISBN:0-691-01599-6, ISBN13: 978-0-691-01599-6. Dewey:306.4/5/0943/09032.
Audience: **u,f.**

Webster, Charles **Q125.W347 2005**
From Paracelsus to Newton: Magic and the Making of Modern Science. Trade Paper. Dover Publications, Inc. Mineola, NY. 2005. 128p. ISBN:0-486-43833-3, ISBN13: 978-0-486-43833-7. Dewey:509.
Audience: **g,l,u,f.**

Westfall, Richard S. **N56.W52**
The Life of Isaac Newton. Trade Paper. Cambridge University Press. New York, NY. 1994. 350p. A Canto Book Ser. ISBN:0-521-47737-9, ISBN13: 978-0-521-47737-6. Dewey:530.092. LCCN:92-003377.
Audience: **g,l,u,f.** *Choice, 1993.*

Yates, Frances A. **B783.Z7Y3 1999**
Giordano Bruno and the Hermetic Tradition. Library Binding. Routledge. New York, NY. 1999. 273p. Selected Works, Vol. 2 ISBN:0-415-22045-9, ISBN13: 978-0-415-22045-3. Dewey:195. LCCN:99-015949.
Audience: **u,f.**

Zagorin, Perez **B1197**
Francis Bacon. Trade Paper. Princeton University Press. Princeton, NJ. 1999. 304p. ISBN:0-691-00966-X, ISBN13: 978-0-691-00966-7. Dewey:192. LCCN:97-041404.
Audience: **u,f.** *Choice, 1998.*

General History > History of Science > Darwin and Darwinism

Banton, Michael P. **QH367**
Darwinism and the Study of Society: A Centenary Symposium. Paper Text. Textbook Publishers. Temecula, CA. 2003. xx, 191p. ISBN:0-7581-3240-9, ISBN13: 978-0-7581-3240-6. Dewey:575.082.
Audience: **u,f.**

Bowlby, John **QH31.D2B742**
Charles Darwin: A New Life. Trade Paper. W. W. Norton & Company, Inc. New York, NY. 1992. 528p. ISBN:0-393-30930-4, ISBN13: 978-0-393-30930-0. Dewey:575/.0092 B.
Audience: **g,l,u,f.** *Choice, 1992.*

Browne, Janet **QH31.D2B84 1996**
Charles Darwin: Voyaging. Trade Paper. Princeton University Press. Princeton, NJ. 1996. 632p. ISBN:0-691-02606-8, ISBN13: 978-0-691-02606-0. Dewey:575/.0092 B. LCCN:95-053319.
Audience: **g,l,u,f.** *Choice, 1995.*

Browne, Janet **QH31.D2 B84 1995**
Charles Darwin: The Power of Place. Trade Cloth. Alfred A. Knopf Inc. New York, NY. 2002. 608p. ISBN:0-679-42932-8, ISBN13: 978-0-679-42932-6. Dewey:575/.0092. LCCN:94-006598.
Audience: **g,l,u,f.** *Choice, 2003.*

Darwin, Charles **QH31.D2A4 1985**
The Correspondence of Charles Darwin: 1861. Frederick Burkhardt, Duncan M. Porter, Janet Browne & Marsha Richmond (Editors). Trade Cloth. Cambridge University Press. New York, NY. 1994. 645p. The Correspondence of Charles Darwin Ser., Vol. 9 ISBN:0-521-45156-6, ISBN13: 978-0-521-45156-7. Dewey:575.0092. LCCN:84-045347.
Audience: **u,f.** *Choice, 1995.*

Darwin, Charles **QH31.D2A33 1985**
The Correspondence of Charles Darwin: 1860, Vol. 8. Frederick Burkhardt, Duncan M. Porter, Janet Browne & Marsha Richmond (Editors). Trade Cloth. Cambridge University Press. New York, NY. 1993. 808p. The Correspondence of Charles Darwin Ser., Vol. 8 ISBN:0-521-44241-9, ISBN13: 978-0-521-44241-1. Dewey:575/.0092 B. LCCN:84-045347.
Audience: **u,f.**

Darwin, Charles & Darwin, Charles **QH365.A1 2006**
From So Simple a Beginning: Darwin's Four Great Books. Edward Osborne Wilson (Editor). Trade Cloth. W. W. Norton & Company, Inc. New York, NY. 2005. 1504p. ISBN:0-393-06134-5, ISBN13: 978-0-393-06134-5. Dewey:576.8/2. LCCN:2005-025825.
Audience: **g,l,u,f.**

Hawkins, Mike **HM106.H38 1997**
Social Darwinism in European and American Thought, 1860-1945: Nature as Model and Nature as Threat. Trade Cloth. Cambridge University Press. New York, NY. 1997. 351p. ISBN:0-521-57400-5, ISBN13: 978-0-521-57400-6. Dewey:304.5. LCCN:96-020946.
Audience: **l,u,f.** *Choice, 1998.*

Kelly, Alfred H. **DD67 .K4**
The Descent of Darwin: The Popularization of Darwinism in Germany, 1860-1914. Trade Cloth. University of North Carolina Press. Chapel Hill, NC. 1981. xi, 185p. ISBN:0-8078-1460-1, ISBN13: 978-0-8078-1460-4. Dewey:001.1/0943. LCCN:80-019445.
Audience: **u,f.**

Mayr, Ernst W. **QH366.2**
One Long Argument: Charles Darwin and the Genesis of Modern Evolutionary Thought. Trade Paper. Harvard University Press. Cambridge, MA. 1993. 214p. Questions of Science Ser. ISBN:0-674-63906-5, ISBN13: 978-0-674-63906-5. Dewey:575.
Audience: **g,l,u,f.** *Choice, 1992.*

McGowan, Christopher **QE705.G7 M3**
The Dragon Seekers: How an Extraordinary Circle of Fossilists Discovered the Dinosaurs and Paved the Way for Darwin. Trade Paper. Perseus Books Group. New York, NY. 2002. 272p. ISBN:0-7382-0673-3, ISBN13: 978-0-7382-0673-8. Dewey:560.9/22/42.
Audience: **g,l,u,f.** *Choice, 2001.*

Ruse, Michael **QH360.5.R874 1999**
Mystery of Mysteries: Is Evolution a Social Construction? Trade Cloth. Harvard University Press. Cambridge, MA. 1999. 320p. ISBN:0-674-46706-X, ISBN13: 978-0-674-46706-4. Dewey:576.8/01. LCCN:98-041969.
Audience: **g,l,u,f.** *Choice, 1999.*

Weikart, Richard **HX273**
Socialist Darwinism: Evolution in German Socialist Thought from Marx to Bernstein. Trade Cloth. International Scholars Publications. Lanham, MD. 1998. 324p. ISBN:1-57309-290-8, ISBN13: 978-1-57309-290-6. Dewey:335/.001. LCCN:98-047354.
Audience: **u,f.**

General History > History of Science > Nuclear Age

Angelo, Joseph A. **TK9145**
Nuclear Technology. Cloth Text. Greenwood Publishing Group, Inc. Portsmouth, NH. 2004. 656p. Sourcebooks in Modern Technology ISBN:1-57356-336-6, ISBN13: 978-1-57356-336-9. Dewey:621.48. LCCN:2004-011238.
Audience: **u,f.** *Choice, 2005.*

Boorse, Henry, et al. **QC773.B66 1989**
The Atomic Scientists: A Biographical History. Lloyd Motz & Jefferson H. Weaver (Authors). Trade Cloth. John Wiley & Sons, Inc. Hoboken, NJ. 1989. 472p. ISBN:0-471-50455-6, ISBN13: 978-0-471-50455-9. Dewey:539/.09. LCCN:88-035181.
Audience: **g,l,u,f.** *Choice, 1989.*

Holloway, David **UA770.H632 1994**
Stalin and the Bomb: The Soviet Union and Atomic Energy, 1939-56. Cloth over Boards. Yale University Press. Cumberland, RI. 1994. 480p. ISBN:0-300-06056-4, ISBN13: 978-0-300-06056-0. Dewey:355.8/25119. LCCN:94-008216.
Audience: **u,f.** *Choice, 1995.*

Holton, Gerald **Q180.A3H65 2005**
Victory and Vexation in Science: Einstein, Bohr, Heisenberg, and Others. Trade Cloth. Harvard University Press. Cambridge, MA. 2005. 244p. ISBN:0-674-01519-3, ISBN13: 978-0-674-01519-7. Dewey:500. LCCN:2004-060572.
Audience: **g,l,u,f.** *Choice, 2005.*

Powers, Thomas **QC16.H35P69 2000**
Heisenberg's War: The Secret History of the German Bomb. Trade Paper. Da Capo Press, Inc. Cambridge, MA. 2000. 640p. ISBN:0-306-81011-5, ISBN13: 978-0-306-81011-4. Dewey:623.451190943. LCCN:00-055577.
Audience: **g,l,u,f.** *Choice, 1993.*

Rayner-Canham, Marelene F. & Rayner-Canham, Geoffrey W. (Author, Editors) **QC15**
A Devotion to Their Science: Pioneer Women of Radioactivity. Trade Cloth. McGill-Queen's University Press. Montreal, PQ. 1997. 320p. ISBN:0-7735-1608-5, ISBN13: 978-0-7735-1608-3. Dewey:539.7/52/0922.
Audience: **g,l,u,f.** *Choice, 1997.*

General History > History of Science > Science and Technology

Heller, Henry **HC280.T4 H45 1996**
Labour, Science and Technology in France, 1500-1620. Trade Cloth. Cambridge University Press. New York, NY. 1995. 270p. Studies in Early Modern History ISBN:0-521-55031-9, ISBN13: 978-0-521-55031-4. Dewey:338/.064/0944/09031. LCCN:95-006125.
Audience: **u,f.** *Choice, 1996.*

Hughes, Thomas P. **TK1005.H83 1983**
Networks of Power: Electrification in Western Society, 1880-1930. Trade Cloth. Johns Hopkins University Press. Baltimore, MD. 1993. 488p. ISBN:0-8018-2873-2, ISBN13: 978-0-8018-2873-7. Dewey:333.7932. LCCN:82-014858.
Audience: **g,l,u,f.** ℞

McGowan, Christopher **TJ603.4.G7M43 2004**
Rail, Steam, and Speed: The Rocket and the Birth of Steam Locomotion. Trade Cloth. Columbia University Press. New York, NY. 2004. 400p. ISBN:0-231-13474-6, ISBN13: 978-0-231-13474-3. Dewey:625.26/1/094209034. LCCN:2004-049411.
Audience: **g,l,u,f.** *Choice, 2005.*

General History > History of Science > History of Medicine

R133
Companion Eencyclopedia of the History of Medicine. Ed. 1. Bynum, W. F.; Porter, Roy (Editors). Routledge. 1997. ISBN:0-415-16418-4, ISBN13: 978-0-415-16418-4.
Audience: **g,l,u,f.**

Jacquart, Danielle & Thomasset, Claude **R141.J3313 1988**
Sexuality and Medicine in the Middle Ages. Matthew Adamson (Translator). Cloth Text. Princeton University Press. Princeton, NJ. 1988. 232p. ISBN:0-691-05550-5, ISBN13: 978-0-691-05550-3. Dewey:612.6/0094. LCCN:88-025311.
Audience: **u,f.** *Choice, 1989.*

Lindemann, Mary **RA418.3.E85 L55 1999**
Medicine and Society in Early Modern Europe. William Beik, T. C. W. Blanning & Brendan Simms (Contribution by). Cloth Text. Cambridge University Press. New York, NY. 1999. 263p. New Approaches to European History Ser., No. 16 ISBN:0-521-41254-4, ISBN13: 978-0-521-41254-4. Dewey:306.4/61/094. LCCN:99-017819.
Audience: **u,f.** *Choice, 2000.*

Porter, Roy (Editor) **R131 .C232**
The Cambridge History of Medicine. Cloth Text. Cambridge University Press. New York, NY. 2006. 414p. ISBN:0-521-86426-7, ISBN13: 978-0-521-86426-8. Dewey:610/.9.
Audience: **g,l,u,f.**

Porter, Roy **R131.P59 1998**
The Greatest Benefit to Mankind: A Medical History of Humanity from Antiquity to the Present. Trade Cloth. W. W. Norton & Company, Inc. New York, NY. 1998. 800p. ISBN:0-393-04634-6, ISBN13: 978-0-393-04634-2. Dewey:610.9. LCCN:98-010219.
Audience: **g,l,u,f.**

Siraisi, Nancy G. **R141.S546 1990**
Medieval and Early Renaissance Medicine: An Introduction to Knowledge and Practice. Trade Paper. University of Chicago Press. Chicago, IL. 1990. 264p. ISBN:0-226-76130-4, ISBN13: 978-0-226-76130-5. Dewey:610/.902. LCCN:89-020368.
Audience: **l,u.** *Choice, 1991.*

Wellman, Kathleen **R507.L193W46 1992**
La Mettrie: Medicine, Philosophy, and Enlightenment. Cloth Text. Duke University Press. Durham, NC. 1992. 358p. ISBN:0-8223-1204-2, ISBN13: 978-0-8223-1204-8. Dewey:610/.92 B. LCCN:91-023992.
Audience: **u,f.** *Choice, 1992.*

General History > Social and Cultural History

Di Scala, Spencer M. **D424.D5 2004**
Twentieth Century Europe. Paper Text. McGraw-Hill Higher Education. Burr Ridge, IL. 2003. 816p. ISBN:0-07-016052-X, ISBN13: 978-0-07-016052-1. Dewey:940.5. LCCN:2003-045930.
Audience: **g,l,u,f.**

Rietbergen, Peter **D20.R42 2006**
Europe: A Cultural History. Ed. 2. Cloth Text. Routledge. New York, NY. 2006. 576p. ISBN:0-415-32358-4, ISBN13: 978-0-415-32358-1. Dewey:940. LCCN:2005-012198.
Audience: **g,l,u,f.**

General History > Social and Cultural History > Women

☐ Women in World History.
http://chnm.gmu.edu/wwh/index.html
Center for History and New Media, George Mason University.
Audience: **g,l,u,f.**

Anderson, Bonnie S. & Zinsser, Judith P. **HQ1587.A53 2000**
A History of Their Own: Women in Europe from Prehistory to the Present, Vol. 1. Paper Text. Oxford University Press, Inc. New York, NY. 1999. 608p. ISBN:0-19-512838-9, ISBN13: 978-0-19-512838-3. Dewey:305.4/094. LCCN:98-046743.
Audience: **g,l,u,f.** *Choice, 1989.*

Anderson, Bonnie S. & Zinsser, Judith P. **HQ1587.A53 2000**
A History of Their Own: Women in Europe from Prehistory to the Present. Paper Text. Oxford University Press, Inc. New York, NY. 1999. 601p. ISBN:0-19-512839-7, ISBN13: 978-0-19-512839-0. Dewey:305.4/094. LCCN:98-046743.
Audience: **g,l,u,f.** *Choice, 1989.*

Bock, Gisela **HQ1587.B63 2001**
Women in European History. Trade Paper. Blackwell Publishing, Inc. Malden, MA. 2001. 320p. The Making of Europe Ser. ISBN:0-631-19145-3, ISBN13: 978-0-631-19145-2. Dewey:305.4/094. LCCN:2001-002364.
Audience: **g,l,u,f.**

Boxer, Marilyn J. & Quataert, Jean H. **HQ1150.B63 2000**
Connecting Spheres: European Women in a Globalizing World, 1500 to the Present. Ed. 2. Joan Scott (Foreword by). Paper Text. Oxford University Press, Inc. New York, NY. 1999. 352p. ISBN:0-19-510951-1, ISBN13: 978-0-19-510951-1. Dewey:305.4/094. LCCN:99-019863.
Audience: **u,f.**

Bridenthal, Renate, et al. **HQ1588.B43 1998**
Becoming Visible: Women in European History. Ed. 3. Susan Mosher Stuard & Merry E. Wiesner (Authors). Paper Text. Houghton Mifflin College Division. Boston, MA. 1997. 594p. ISBN:0-395-79625-3, ISBN13: 978-0-395-79625-2. Dewey:305.4/094. LCCN:97-072450.
Audience: **g,l,u,f.**

DiCaprio, Lisa & Wiesner, Merry E. **HQ1587.D53 2000**
Lives and Voices: Sources in European Women's History. Paper Text. Houghton Mifflin College Division. Boston, MA. 2000. 633p. ISBN:0-395-97052-0, ISBN13: 978-0-395-97052-2. Dewey:305.4/094. LCCN:00-104431.
Audience: **g,l,u,f.**

Eller, Cynthia **GN799.W66E49**
The Myth of Matriarchal Prehistory: Why an Invented Past Will Not Give Women a Future. Trade Paper. Beacon Press. Boston, MA. 2001. 304p. ISBN:0-8070-6793-8, ISBN13: 978-0-8070-6793-2. Dewey:306.83. LCCN:99-057360.
Audience: **g,l,u,f.** *Choice, 2001.*

Lerner, Gerda **HQ1121**
The Creation of Feminist Consciousness: From the Middle Ages to Eighteen-Seventy. Trade Paper. Oxford University Press, Inc. New York, NY. 1994. 416p. ISBN:0-19-509060-8, ISBN13: 978-0-19-509060-4. Dewey:305.4/09. LCCN:92-020411.
Audience: **g,l,u,f.** *Choice, 1993.*

Lerner, Gerda **HQ1121**
The Creation of Patriarchy. Trade Paper. Oxford University Press, Inc. New York, NY. 1987. 344p. Women and History Ser. ISBN:0-19-505185-8, ISBN13: 978-0-19-505185-8. Dewey:305.4/09. LCCN:85-021578.
Audience: **g,l,u,f.** *Choice, 1986.*

Simonton **HQ1587.R68 2006**
Women in Europe Since 1700. Trade Cloth. Routledge. New York, NY. 2006. 416p. ISBN:0-415-30103-3, ISBN13: 978-0-415-30103-9. Dewey:305.4/094. LCCN:2005-014215.
Audience: **g,l,u,f.**

Wiesner-Hanks, Merry E. **HQ1075.W526 2001**
Gender in History. Trade Paper. Blackwell Publishing, Inc. Malden, MA. 2001. 256p. New Perspectives on the Past Ser. ISBN:0-631-21036-9, ISBN13: 978-0-631-21036-8. Dewey:305.3/09. LCCN:00-013063.
Audience: **g,l,u,f.** *Choice, 2002.*

General History > Social and Cultural History > Women > Medieval

Bitel, Lisa M. **HQ1143**
Women in Early Medieval Europe, 400-1100. Cloth Text. Cambridge University Press. New York, NY. 2002. 344p. Cambridge Medieval Textbooks Ser. ISBN:0-521-59207-0, ISBN13: 978-0-521-59207-9. Dewey:305.42/094/0902. LCCN:2003-544740.
Audience: **u,f.**

Bloch, R. Howard **HQ1143.B56 1991**
Medieval Misogyny and the Invention of Western Romantic Love. Trade Paper. University of Chicago Press. Chicago, IL. 1992. 308p. ISBN:0-226-05973-1, ISBN13: 978-0-226-05973-0. Dewey:305.4/09/02. LCCN:91-012699.
Audience: **u,f.** *Choice, 1992.*

Brubaker, Leslie & Smith, Julia M. H. (Editors) **HQ1075.5.E85G46 2004**
Gender in the Early Medieval World: East and West, 300-900. Trade Paper. Cambridge University Press. New York, NY. 2004. 346p. ISBN:0-521-01327-5, ISBN13: 978-0-521-01327-7. Dewey:305.3/094. LCCN:2003-069751.
Audience: **u,f.** *Choice, 2005.*

Brundage, James A. **KJ985.S48**
Law, Sex, and Christian Society in Medieval Europe. Trade Paper. University of Chicago Press. Chicago, IL. 1990. 698p. ISBN:0-226-07784-5, ISBN13: 978-0-226-07784-0. Dewey:344.4054. LCCN:87-010759.
Audience: **u,f.**

Bynum, Caroline W. **BV4509.5**
Holy Feast and Holy Fast: The Religious Significance of Food to Medieval Women. Trade Paper. University of California Press. Berkeley, CA. 1988. 300p. The New Historicism Ser., No. 1:Studies in Cultural Poetics ISBN:0-520-06329-5, ISBN13: 978-0-520-06329-7. Dewey:248.4/6. LCCN:85-028896.
Audience: **g,u,f.** *Choice, 1987.*

Duby, Georges & Pantel, Pauline S. (Editors) **HQ1121.S79513 1992**
A History of Women: From Ancient Goddesses to Christian Saints. Arthur Goldhammer (Translator). Trade Cloth. Harvard University Press. Cambridge, MA. 1992. 600p. Women in the West Ser., Vol. 1 ISBN:0-674-40370-3, ISBN13: 978-0-674-40370-3. Dewey:305.4094. LCCN:91-034134.
Audience: **g,l,u,f.** *Choice, 1992.*

Grossman, Avraham **BM729.W6G7613 2004**
Pious and Rebellious: Jewish Women in Medieval Europe. Trade Cloth. University Press of New England. Lebanon, NH. 2004. 352p. Tauber Institute for the Study of European Jewry Ser. ISBN:1-58465-391-4, ISBN13: 978-1-58465-391-2. Dewey:305.48/892404/0902. LCCN:2004-003029.
Audience: **u,f.** *Choice, 2005.*

Herlihy, David **HD6134.H47 1990**
Opera Muliebria: Women and Work in Medieval Europe. Trade Paper. McGraw-Hill Higher Education. Burr Ridge, IL. 1989. 288p. New Perspectives on European History Ser. ISBN:0-07-557744-5, ISBN13: 978-0-07-557744-7. Dewey:331.4/094/0902. LCCN:89-013191.
Audience: **g,l,u,f.** *Choice, 1990.*

Jochens, Jenny **HQ1147.N8J63 1995**
Women in Old Norse Society. Book, Other. Cornell University Press. Ithaca, NY. 1996. 328p. ISBN:0-8014-3165-4, ISBN13: 978-0-8014-3165-4. Dewey:305.4/09/02. LCCN:95-031506.
Audience: **g,l,u,f.** *Choice, 1996.*

Johnson, Penelope D. **BX4220.F8**
Equal in Monastic Profession: Religious Women in Medieval France. Catherine R. Stimpson (Foreword by). Trade Paper. University of Chicago Press. Chicago, IL. 1994. 310p. Women in Culture and Society Ser. ISBN:0-226-40186-3, ISBN13: 978-0-226-40186-7. Dewey:271/.90044/09021. LCCN:90-045510.
Audience: **u,f.** *Choice, 1991.*

Ward, Jennifer **HQ1147.E9W37 2002**
Women in Medieval Europe: 1200 - 1500. Trade Paper. Longman Publishing. Boston, MA. 2003. 336p. ISBN:0-582-28827-4, ISBN13: 978-0-582-28827-0. Dewey:305.4/2/094/0902.
Audience: **g,l,u,f.**

General History > Social and Cultural History > Women > Early Modern

Davis, Natalie Zemon **CT3233.D38 1995**
Women on the Margins: Three Seventeenth-Century Lives. Trade Cloth. Harvard University Press. Cambridge, MA. 1995. 372p. ISBN:0-674-95520-X, ISBN13: 978-0-674-95520-2. Dewey:920.7/2/09032. LCCN:97-013765.
Audience: **g,l,u,f.**

Duby, Georges (Editor), et al. **HQ1121.S79513 1992**
Renaissance and Enlightenment Paradoxes. Michelle Perrot, Natalie Zemon Davis & Arlette Farge (Editors). Trade Cloth. Harvard University Press. Cambridge, MA. 1993. 608p. Women in the West Ser. ISBN:0-674-40372-X, ISBN13: 978-0-674-40372-7. Dewey:305.4094. LCCN:91-034134.
Audience: **g,l,u,f.** *Choice, 1993.*

Gowing, Laura **HQ1599.E5G69 2003**
Common Bodies: Women, Touch and Power in Seventeenth-Century England. Cloth over Boards. Yale University Press. Cumberland, RI. 2003. 272p. ISBN:0-300-10096-5, ISBN13: 978-0-300-10096-9. Dewey:305.42/0942/09032. LCCN:2003-012939.
Audience: **u,f.** *Choice, 2004.*

Hufton, Olwen **HQ1587**
The Prospect Before Her, Vol. 2. Trade Paper. Alfred A. Knopf Inc. New York, NY. 1998. ISBN:0-679-76819-X, ISBN13: 978-0-679-76819-7. Dewey:305.4/094.
Audience: **g,l,u,f.**

King, Margaret L. **HQ1148.K56 1991**
Women of the Renaissance. Catherine R. Stimpson (Foreword by). Trade Paper. University of Chicago Press. Chicago, IL. 1991. 350p. Women in Culture and Society Ser. ISBN:0-226-43618-7, ISBN13: 978-0-226-43618-0. Dewey:305.4/094. LCCN:91-019960.
Audience: **u,f.** *Choice, 1992.*

Mendelson, Sara & Crawford, Patricia **HQ1599.E5M46 1998**
Women in Early Modern England 1550-1720. Trade Cloth. Oxford University Press, Inc. New York, NY. 1998. 480p. ISBN:0-19-820124-9, ISBN13: 978-0-19-820124-3. Dewey:305.4/0942. LCCN:97-033337.
Audience: **u,f.** *Choice, 1999.*

Roper, Lyndal **HQ1630.A84**
The Holy Household: Women and Morals in Reformation Augsburg. Paper Text. Oxford University Press, Inc. New York, NY. 1991. 306p. Oxford Studies in Social History ISBN:0-19-820280-6, ISBN13: 978-0-19-820280-6. Dewey:305.4/2/0943375. LCCN:89-009413.
Audience: **u,f.**

Roper, Lyndal **BF1583**
Witch Craze: Terror and Fantasy in Baroque Germany. Cloth over Boards. Yale University Press. Cumberland, RI. 2004. 376p. ISBN:0-300-10335-2, ISBN13: 978-0-300-10335-9. Dewey:133.4/3/0943/09031. LCCN:2004-111947.
Audience: **u,f.** *Choice, 2005.*

Spring, Eileen **93-590 [KD]**
Law, Land, and Family: Aristocratic Inheritance in England, 1300 to 1800. Trade Paper. University of North Carolina Press. Chapel Hill, NC. 1997. 212p. Studies in Legal History Ser. ISBN:0-8078-4642-2, ISBN13: 978-0-8078-4642-1. Dewey:346.4/2/052. LCCN:93-000590.
Audience: **u,f.** *Choice, 1994.*

Wiesner, Merry E. **HQ1587 .W54 2000**
Women and Gender in Early Modern Europe. Ed. 2. William Beik, T. C. W. Blanning & Brendan Simms (Contribution by). Cloth Text. Cambridge University Press. New York, NY. 2000. 342p. New Approaches to European History Ser., No. 20 ISBN:0-521-77105-6, ISBN13: 978-0-521-77105-4. Dewey:305.4/094. LCCN:00-022070.
Audience: **g,l,u,f.** *Choice, 1994.*

Wunder, Heide **HQ1623.W85 1998**
He Is the Sun, She Is the Moon: Women in Early Modern Germany. Trade Cloth. Harvard University Press. Cambridge, MA. 1998. 320p. ISBN:0-674-38321-4, ISBN13: 978-0-674-38321-0. Dewey:305.4/0943. LCCN:97-038959.
Audience: **u,f.** *Choice, 1998.*

General History > Social and Cultural History > Women > Modern

Allen, Ann T. **HQ759.A42 1991**
Feminism and Motherhood in Germany, 1800-1914. Cloth Text. Rutgers University Press. Piscataway, NJ. 1991. 275p. ISBN:0-8135-1686-2, ISBN13: 978-0-8135-1686-8. Dewey:305.42/0943. LCCN:90-021164.
Audience: **g,l,u,f.** *Choice, 1992.*

Anderson, Bonnie S. **HQ1154**
Joyous Greetings: The First International Women's Movement, 1830-1860. Trade Cloth. HarperCollins Publishers. New York, NY. 1999. 256p. ISBN:0-06-017072-7, ISBN13: 978-0-06-017072-1. Dewey:305.42/09/034.
Audience: **u,f.** *Choice, 2000.*

Bell, Susan G. & Offen, Karen M. (Editors) **HQ1588.W645 1983**
Women, the Family, and Freedom: The Debate in Documents, 1880-1950, Vol. II. Trade Paper. Stanford University Press. Palo Alto, CA. 1983. 490p. ISBN:0-8047-1173-9, ISBN13: 978-0-8047-1173-9. Dewey:305.4/09. LCCN:82-061081.
Audience: **g,l,u,f.**

Bell, Susan G. & Offen, Karen M. (Editors) **HQ1154**
Women, the Family, and Freedom: The Debate in Documents, 1750-1880, Vol. I. Trade Paper. Stanford University Press. Palo Alto, CA. 1983. 577p. ISBN:0-8047-1171-2, ISBN13: 978-0-8047-1171-5. Dewey:305.4/2/09. LCCN:82-061081.
Audience: **g,l,u,f.**

Boxer, Marilyn J. & Quataert, Jean H. (Editors) **HX546**
Socialist Women: European Socialist Feminism in the Nineteenth and Early Twentieth-Centuries. Trade Paper. Elsevier. New York, NY. 1978. 272p. ISBN:0-444-99050-X, ISBN13: 978-0-444-99050-1. Dewey:335/.0094. LCCN:77-016618.
Audience: **u,f.**

Canning, Kathleen **HD6150.N67C36 1996**
Languages of Labor and Gender: Female Factory Work in Germany, 1850-1914. Book, Other. Cornell University Press. Ithaca, NY. 1996. 352p. ISBN:0-8014-3123-9, ISBN13: 978-0-8014-3123-4. Dewey:331.4/87/09435509043. LCCN:96-000793.
Audience: **u,f.** *Choice, 1997.*

Clark, Anna **HD8390**
Struggle for the Breeches: Gender and the Making of the British Working Class. Trade Paper. University of California Press. Berkeley, CA. 1997. 432p. Studies on the History of Society and Culture, Vol. 23 ISBN:0-520-20883-8, ISBN13: 978-0-520-20883-4. Dewey:305.5/62/0941. LCCN:93-050835.
Audience: **u,f.**

Clements, Barbara Evans **HX313.7 .C64 1997**
Bolshevik Women. Trade Cloth. Cambridge University Press. New York, NY. 1997. 352p. ISBN:0-521-45403-4, ISBN13: 978-0-521-45403-2. Dewey:947/.084/082. LCCN:96-050036.
Audience: **g,l,u,f.** *Choice, 1998.*

Cole, Joshua **HB3593.C614 2000**
The Power of Large Numbers: Population, Politics and Gender in Nineteenth-Century France. Trade Cloth. Cornell University Press. Ithaca, NY. 2000. 272p. ISBN:0-8014-3701-6, ISBN13: 978-0-8014-3701-4. Dewey:304.6/0944/09034. LCCN:99-046229.
Audience: **u,f.** *Choice, 2000.*

Davies, Llewelyn **HD3423 .D17 1977**
Life As We Have Known It. Virginia Woolf (Introduction by). Trade Cloth. Random House, Inc. New York, NY. 1994. 141p. ISBN:0-86068-000-2, ISBN13: 978-0-86068-000-0. Dewey:942.081/092/2. LCCN:78-322722.
Audience: **g,l,u,f.**

De Grazia, Victoria **HQ1638.D4 1991**
How Fascism Ruled Women: Italy, 1922-1945. Trade Cloth. University of California Press. Berkeley, CA. 1992. 384p. ISBN:0-520-07456-4, ISBN13: 978-0-520-07456-9. Dewey:305.42/0945. LCCN:91-008901.
Audience: **u,f.** *Choice, 1992.*

Engel, Barbara Alpern **HV1662.E54 2003**
Women in Russia, 1700-2000. Cloth Text. Cambridge University Press. New York, NY. 2003. 304p. ISBN:0-521-80270-9, ISBN13: 978-0-521-80270-3. Dewey:305.4/0947. LCCN:2003-043017.
Audience: **g,l,u,f.** *Choice, 2004.*

Flanders, Judith **HQ615.F58 2004**
Inside the Victorian Home: A Portrait of Domestic Life in Victorian England. Trade Cloth. W. W. Norton & Company, Inc. New York, NY. 2004. 416p. ISBN:0-393-05209-5, ISBN13: 978-0-393-05209-1. Dewey:306/.0942/09034. LCCN:2003-027693.
Audience: **g,l,u,f.** *Choice, 2005.*

Frader, Laura L. & Rose, Sonya O. (Editors) **HD6134.C58 1996**
Gender and Class in Modern Europe. Book, Other. Cornell University Press. Ithaca, NY. 1996. 376p. ISBN:0-8014-2922-6, ISBN13: 978-0-8014-2922-4. Dewey:331.4/094. LCCN:95-052529.
Audience: **g,l,u,f.**

Fuchs, Rachel & Thompson, Victoria **HQ1587.F83 2005**
Women in Nineteenth-Century Europe. Cloth over Boards. Palgrave Macmillan. New York, NY. 2005. 176p. ISBN:0-333-67605-X, ISBN13: 978-0-333-67605-9. Dewey:305.4/094/09034. LCCN:2004-054938.
Audience: **g,l,u,f.**

Goldman, Wendy Z. **KLA540 .G65 1993**
Women, the State and Revolution: Soviet Family Policy and Social Life, 1917-1936. Trade Paper. Cambridge University Press. New York, NY. 1993. 363p. Cambridge Russian, Soviet and Post-Soviet Studies, No. 90 ISBN:0-521-45816-1, ISBN13: 978-0-521-45816-0. Dewey:305.420947. LCCN:92-047481.
Audience: **u,f.** *Choice, 1994.*

Grayzel, Susan R. **D639.W7G73 2002**
Women and the First World War. Trade Paper. Longman Publishing. Boston, MA. 2002. 216p. ISBN:0-582-41876-3, ISBN13: 978-0-582-41876-9. Dewey:940.3/082.
Audience: **g,l,u,f.**

Grayzel, Susan R. **D639.W7G57 1999**
Women's Identities at War: Gender, Motherhood and Politics in Britain and France During the First World War. Trade Paper. University of North Carolina Press. Chapel Hill, NC. 1999. 360p. ISBN:0-8078-4810-7, ISBN13: 978-0-8078-4810-4. Dewey:940.53/082. LCCN:98-047607.
Audience: **u,f.**

Gullace, Nicoletta F. **JN906.G85 2002**
The Blood of Our Sons: Men, Women, and the Renegotiation of British Citizenship During the Great War. Cloth over Boards. Palgrave Macmillan. New York, NY. 2002. 288p. ISBN:0-312-29446-8, ISBN13: 978-0-312-29446-5. Dewey:940.3/1/0941. LCCN:2002-016917.
Audience: **u,f.** *Choice, 2003.*

Heineman, Elizabeth D. **HQ800.2 .H45 1999**
What Difference Does a Husband Make?: Women and Marital Status in Nazi and Postwar Germany. Trade Cloth. University of California Press. Berkeley, CA. 1999. 392p. Studies on the History of Society and Culture, Vol. 33 ISBN:0-520-21425-0, ISBN13: 978-0-520-21425-5. Dewey:306.8/153/0943/09043. LCCN:98-028003.
Audience: **u,f.**

Horn, Pamela **HQ1593.H77 1991**
Victorian Countrywomen. Trade Cloth. Blackwell Publishing, Inc. Malden, MA. 1991. 288p. ISBN:0-631-15522-8, ISBN13: 978-0-631-15522-5. Dewey:305.4/0942. LCCN:90-038582.
Audience: **g,l,u,f.** *Choice, 1991.*

Hufton, Olwen H. **DC158.8**
Women and the Limits of Citizenship in the French Revolution. Trade Cloth. University of Toronto Press. Toronto, ON. 1992. 440p. Donald G. Creighton Lectures ISBN:0-8020-5898-1, ISBN13: 978-0-8020-5898-0. Dewey:944.04082.
Audience: **g,l,u,f.**

Jordan, Ellen R. **HD6135.J667 1999**
Women's Movement and Women's Employment in Nineteenth Century Britain. Paper over Boards. Routledge. New York, NY. 1999. 288p. Research in Gender and History Ser. ISBN:0-415-18951-9, ISBN13: 978-0-415-18951-4. Dewey:331.4/0941/09034. LCCN:98-051633.
Audience: **u,f.** *Choice, 2000.*

Kent, Susan K. **JN979.K43 1987**
Sex and Suffrage in Britain, 1860-1914. Cloth Text. Princeton University Press. Princeton, NJ. 1987. 336p. ISBN:0-691-05497-5, ISBN13: 978-0-691-05497-1. Dewey:324.6/23/0941. LCCN:86-025307.
Audience: **g,l,u,f.** *Choice, 1987.*

Koonz, Claudia **HQ1623.K66 1987**
Mothers in the Fatherland: Women, Family Life and Nazi Ideology, 1919-1945. Trade Cloth. St. Martin's Press. Gordonville, VA. 1987. 640p. ISBN:0-312-54933-4, ISBN13: 978-0-312-54933-6. Dewey:306/.0943. LCCN:86-013815.
Audience: **g,l,u,f.** *Choice, 1987.*

Koven, Seth **HV4085.L6K68 2004**
Slumming: Sexual and Social Politics in Victorian London. Trade Cloth. Princeton University Press. Princeton, NJ. 2004.

368p. ISBN:0-691-11592-3, ISBN13: 978-0-691-11592-4. Dewey:306.7/086/94209421. LCCN:2003-060514.
Audience: **g,l,u,f.**

Maynes, Mary Jo, et al. **HQ777.S4 2004**
Secret Gardens, Satanic Mills: Placing Girls in European History, 1750-1960. Birgitte Soland & Christina Benninghaus (Authors). Trade Cloth. Indiana University Press. Bloomington, IN. 2004. 344p. ISBN:0-253-34449-2, ISBN13: 978-0-253-34449-6. Dewey:305.23/082/094. LCCN:2004-002658.
Audience: **g,l,u,f.** *Choice, 2006.*

Meyer, Alfred G. **HQ1625.B73M49 1985**
The Feminism and Socialism of Lily Braun. Trade Cloth. Indiana University Press. Bloomington, IN. 1986. 256p. ISBN:0-253-32169-7, ISBN13: 978-0-253-32169-5. Dewey:305.4/2/0924. LCCN:84-043077.
Audience: **g,l,u,f.** *Choice, 1986.*

Owings, Alison **D811.5.O885 1993**
Frauen: German Women Recall the Third Reich. Trade Cloth. Rutgers University Press. Piscataway, NJ. 1993. 550p. ISBN:0-8135-1992-6, ISBN13: 978-0-8135-1992-0. Dewey:943/.086/0922. LCCN:92-042097.
Audience: **g,l,u,f.** *Choice, 1994.*

Pedersen, Susan **HV700.G7**
Family, Dependence, and the Origins of the Welfare State: Britain and France, 1914-1945. Trade Paper. Cambridge University Press. New York, NY. 1995. 478p. ISBN:0-521-55834-4, ISBN13: 978-0-521-55834-1. Dewey:362.82/8/094109041.
Audience: **u,f.**

Reagin, Nancy Ruth **HQ1623.R43 1995**
A German Women's Movement: Class and Gender in Hanover, 1880-1933. Trade Paper. University of North Carolina Press. Chapel Hill, NC. 1995. 336p. ISBN:0-8078-4525-6, ISBN13: 978-0-8078-4525-7. Dewey:305.42/0943. LCCN:94-039348.
Audience: **u,f.** *Choice, 1996.*

Roberts, Mary L. **HQ1075.5.F8.R63 1994**
Civilization Without Sexes: Reconstructing Gender in Postwar France, 1917-1927. Trade Cloth. University of Chicago Press. Chicago, IL. 1994. 352p. Women in Culture and Society Ser. ISBN:0-226-72121-3, ISBN13: 978-0-226-72121-7. Dewey:305.3/0944. LCCN:93-026899.
Audience: **u,f.** *Choice, 1994.*

Roberts, Mary Louise **HQ1617.R55 2002**
Disruptive Acts: The New Woman in Fin-de-Siecle France. Trade Cloth. University of Chicago Press. Chicago, IL. 2002. 364p. ISBN:0-226-72124-8, ISBN13: 978-0-226-72124-8. Dewey:305.42/0944. LCCN:2002-004194.
Audience: **u,f.** *Choice, 2003.*

Roessler, Shirley **DC158.8.E57 1996**
Out of the Shadows: Women and Politics in the French Revolution, 1789-95. Cloth Text. Peter Lang Publishing, Inc. New York, NY. 1996. 288p. Studies in Modern European History, Vol. 14 ISBN:0-8204-2565-6, ISBN13: 978-0-8204-2565-8. Dewey:944.04/082. LCCN:94-040970.
Audience: **u,f.** *Choice, 1997.*

Ross, Ellen **HQ759.R66 1993**
Love and Toil: Motherhood in Outcast London, 1870-1918. Trade Cloth. Oxford University Press, Inc. New York, NY. 1993. 326p. ISBN:0-19-503957-2, ISBN13: 978-0-19-503957-3. Dewey:306.874/3/094212. LCCN:92-040849.
Audience: **g,l,u,f.** *Choice, 1994.*

Scott, Joan W. **HQ1613**
Only Paradoxes to Offer: French Feminists and the Rights of Man. Trade Paper. Harvard University Press. Cambridge, MA. 1997. 246p. ISBN:0-674-63931-6, ISBN13: 978-0-674-63931-7. Dewey:305.4/2/0944.
Audience: **u,f.** *Choice, 1996.*

Scott, Joan Wallach **HQ1154.S335 1999**
Gender and the Politics of History. Ed. 2. Trade Paper. Columbia University Press. New York, NY. 1999. 242p. Gender and Culture Ser. ISBN:0-231-11857-0, ISBN13: 978-0-231-11857-6. Dewey:305.4/09. LCCN:99-028686.
Audience: **u,f.**

Shapiro, Ann-Louise **HV6046.S46 1996**
Breaking the Codes: Female Criminality in Fin-de-Siecle Paris. Trade Cloth. Stanford University Press. Palo Alto, CA. 1996. 296p. ISBN:0-8047-1663-3, ISBN13: 978-0-8047-1663-5. Dewey:364.3/74/0944. LCCN:95-037867.
Audience: **u,f.** *Choice, 1996.*

Slaughter, Jane **D802.I8S53 1997**
Women and the Italian Resistance, 1943-45. Trade Cloth. Arden Press, Inc. Denver, CO. 1997. 201p. Women and Modern Revolution Ser. ISBN:0-912869-13-5, ISBN13: 978-0-912869-13-1. Dewey:940.53/45. LCCN:97-004937.
Audience: **g,l,u,f.** *Choice, 1998.*

Stewart, Mary L. **HQ1613.S68 2001**
For Health and Beauty: Physical Culture for Frenchwomen, 1880s-1930s. Trade Cloth. Johns Hopkins University Press. Baltimore, MD. 2001. 288p. ISBN:0-8018-6483-6, ISBN13: 978-0-8018-6483-4. Dewey:305.4/0944. LCCN:00-041258.
Audience: **u,f.** *Choice, 2002.*

Taylor, Barbara **HQ1154**
Eve and the New Jerusalem: Socialism and Feminism in the Nineteenth Century. Trade Paper. Harvard University Press. Cambridge, MA. 1993. 402p. ISBN:0-674-27023-1, ISBN13: 978-0-674-27023-7. Dewey:305.4/2/09034. LCCN:92-031980.
Audience: **u,f.** B

Taylor, Therese **BX4700.S65**
Bernadette of Lourdes: Her Life, Death and Visions. Trade Cloth. Continuum International Publishing Group, Ltd. London, 2003. 352p. ISBN:0-86012-337-5, ISBN13: 978-0-86012-337-8. Dewey:271.9/1/02.
Audience: **g,l,u,f.** *Choice, 2004.*

Tiersten, Lisa **HC280.C6 T54 2001**
Marianne in the Market: Envisioning Consumer Society in Fin-de-Siècle France. Trade Cloth. University of California Press. Berkeley, CA. 2001. 336p. ISBN:0-520-22529-5, ISBN13: 978-0-520-22529-9. Dewey:339.4/7/0820944. LCCN:00-066629.
Audience: **u,f.** *Choice, 2002.*

Walkowitz, Judith R. **HQ72.G7W33**
City of Dreadful Delight: Narratives of Sexual Danger in Late-Victorian London. Catherine R. Stimpson (Foreword by). Trade Paper. University of Chicago Press. Chicago, IL. 1992. 368p. Women in Culture and Society Ser. ISBN:0-226-87146-0, ISBN13: 978-0-226-87146-2. Dewey:305.4/2/09421/09034. LCCN:91-048153.
Audience: **g,l,u,f.**

Wood, Elizabeth A. **HX546.W67 1997**
[e] The Baba and the Comrade: Gender and Politics in Revolutionary Russia. E-Book. Indiana University Press. Bloomington, IN. 1997. 336p. Indiana-Michigan Series in Russian and East European Studies ISBN:0-253-33311-3, ISBN13: 978-0-253-33311-7. Dewey:321.9/2/0820947. LCCN:97-002290.
Audience: **g,u,f.** *Choice, 1998.*

Yalom, Marilyn (Author, Introduction by) **DC158.8**
Blood Sisters: The French Revolution in Women's Memory. Trade Paper. Rivers Oram Press/Pandora. London, 1995. 308p. ISBN:0-04-440918-4, ISBN13: 978-0-04-440918-2. Dewey:944.04082.
Audience: **u,f.** *Choice, 1994.*

Zedner, Lucia **HV9649.E5.Z43 1991**
Women, Crime, and Custody in Victorian England. Trade Cloth. Oxford University Press, Inc. New York, NY. 1992. 372p. ISBN:0-19-820264-4, ISBN13: 978-0-19-820264-6. Dewey:364.3/74/082. LCCN:92-136980.
Audience: **g,l,u,f.** *Choice, 1992.*

Zweiniger-Bargielowska, Ina **HQ1593.P65 1990**
Women in Twentieth-Century Britain: Social, Cultural and Political Change. Trade Paper. Longman Publishing Group. White Plains, NY. 2001. 392p. ISBN:0-582-40480-0, ISBN13: 978-0-582-40480-9. Dewey:305.4/2/0941/0904.
Audience: **g,l,u,f.** *Choice, 2001.*

General History > Social and Cultural History > Children

Schultz, James A. **HQ792.G3S376 1995**
The Knowledge of Childhood in the German Middle Ages, 1100-1350. Trade Cloth. University of Pennsylvania Press. Philadelphia, PA. 1995. 336p. Middle Ages Ser. ISBN:0-8122-3297-6, ISBN13: 978-0-8122-3297-4. Dewey:305.23/0943/0902. LCCN:95-017057.
Audience: **g,u,f.** *Choice, 1996.*

General History > Social and Cultural History > Gender and Sexuality

Abrams, Lynn **HQ1587.A27 2002**
The Making of Modern Woman. Trade Paper. Longman Publishing Group. White Plains, NY. 2002. 392p. ISBN:0-582-41410-5, ISBN13: 978-0-582-41410-5. Dewey:940.2/8/082. LCCN:2001-054702.
Audience: **u,f.** *Choice, 2003.*

Foucault, Michel **HQ16**
A History of Sexuality: An Introduction, Vol. 1. Trade Paper. Knopf Publishing Group. New York, NY. 1990. 176p. ISBN:0-679-72469-9, ISBN13: 978-0-679-72469-8. Dewey:306.7/091821. LCCN:79-007460.
Audience: **u,f.**

Haliczer, Stephen **BX2263.S7H35 1996**
Sexuality in the Confessional: A Sacrament Profaned. Cloth Text. Oxford University Press, Inc. New York, NY. 1996. 280p. Studies in the History of Sexuality ISBN:0-19-509656-8, ISBN13: 978-0-19-509656-9. Dewey:264/.020862/09460903. LCCN:94-047094.
Audience: **u,f.** *Choice, 1996.*

Hall, Lesley & Porter, Roy **HQ18.G7P67 1995**
The Facts of Life: The Creation of Sexual Knowledge in Britain, 1650-1950. Cloth over Boards. Yale University Press. Cumberland, RI. 1995. 428p. ISBN:0-300-06221-4, ISBN13: 978-0-300-06221-2. Dewey:306.7/0941. LCCN:94-021091.
Audience: **g,l,u,f.** *Choice, 1995.*

Hull, Isabel V. **HQ18.G3H84 1996**
Sexuality, State, and Civil Society in Germany, 1700-1815. Trade Cloth. Cornell University Press. Ithaca, NY. 1996. 536p. ISBN:0-8014-3126-3, ISBN13: 978-0-8014-3126-5. Dewey:306.7/0943. LCCN:95-031511.
Audience: **u,f.** *Choice, 1996.*

Karras R M Staff **HQ14.K37 2005**
Sexuality in Medieval Europe. Perfect, Paper over Boards. Routledge. New York, NY. 2005. 200p. ISBN:0-415-28962-9, ISBN13: 978-0-415-28962-7. Dewey:306.7/09/02. LCCN:2004-021794.
Audience: **g,l,u,f.**

Shoemaker, Robert & Vincent, Mary (Editors) **D13.5.E85G45 1998**
Gender and History in Western Europe. Cloth Text. Oxford University Press, Inc. New York, NY. 1998. 400p. Arnold Readers in History Ser. ISBN:0-340-67693-0, ISBN13: 978-0-340-67693-6. Dewey:940/.07/2. LCCN:98-014555.
Audience: **u,f.**

Tamagne, Florence
A History of Homosexuality in Europe, 1919-1939. Trade Cloth. Algora Publishing. New York, NY. 2004. 596p. ISBN:0-87586-356-6, ISBN13: 978-0-87586-356-6.
Audience: **g,l,u,f.**

Trumbach, Randolph **HQ18.G7T785 1998**
Sex and the Gender Revolution: Heterosexuality and the Third Gender in Enlightenment London. Trade Cloth. University of Chicago Press. Chicago, IL. 1998. 528p. Chicago Series on Sexuality, History and Society ISBN:0-226-81290-1, ISBN13: 978-0-226-81290-8. Dewey:306.76/4/09421. LCCN:97-052615.
Audience: **u,f.** *Choice, 1999.*

General History > Religious History > Medieval Christendom

Abelard, Peter **BJ1240.A2313 1995**
Ethical Writings: The Complete Texts of Ethics and Dialogue Between a Philosopher, a Jew, and a Christian. Paul V. Spade (Translator), Marilyn M. Adams (Introduction by). Trade Cloth. Hackett Publishing Company, Inc. Indianapolis, IN. 1995. 208p. Hackett Classics Ser. ISBN:0-87220-323-9, ISBN13: 978-0-87220-323-5. Dewey:241. LCCN:95-024270.
Audience: **u,f.**

Alexander, Paul J. **BR238.A4 1980**
The Patriarch Nicephorus of Constantinople: Ecclesiastical Policy and Image Worship in the Byzantine Empire. Trade Cloth. A M S Press, Inc. New York, NY. Heresies of the Early Christian and Medieval Era Ser., No. II ISBN:0-404-16195-2, ISBN13: 978-0-404-16195-8. Dewey:270/.3/0924. LCCN:78-063177.
Audience: **u,f.**

Aquinas, Thomas **BX1749**
Aquinas's Shorter Summa: St. Thomas's Own Concise Version of His Summa Theologica. Cyril Vollert (Translator). Perfect. Sophia Institute Press. Manchester, NH. 2002. 432p. ISBN:1-928832-43-1, ISBN13: 978-1-928832-43-0. Dewey:230/.2.
Audience: **u,f.**

Augustine **BR65.A5**
City of God. Gill Evans (Editor), Henry Bettenson (Translator). Trade Paper. Penguin Group (USA) Inc. New York, NY. 2004. 1168p. ISBN:0-14-044894-2, ISBN13: 978-0-14-044894-8. Dewey:230/.01.
Audience: **g,l,u.**

Barraclough, Geoffrey **BX955.2**
The Medieval Papacy. Trade Cloth. W. W. Norton & Company, Inc. New York, NY. 1979. 216p. Library of World Civilization ISBN:0-393-95100-6, ISBN13: 978-0-393-95100-4. Dewey:262.130902.
Audience: **g,l,u.** B

Benedict of Nursia **BX3004.A2 1982**
The Rule of St. Benedict: The Abingdon Copy. John Chamberlin (Editor). Trade Paper. Pontifical Institute of Mediaeval Studies, Department of Publications. Toronto, ON. 1982. 95p. Toronto Medieval Latin Texts Ser., Vol. 13 ISBN:0-88844-463-X, ISBN13: 978-0-88844-463-9. Dewey:255/.106. LCCN:82-205899.
Audience: **u,f.**

Bettenson, Henry & Maunder, Chris (Editors) **BR141.D63 1999**
Documents of the Christian Church. Ed. 3. Paper Text. Oxford University Press, Inc. New York, NY. 1999. 488p. ISBN:0-19-288071-3, ISBN13: 978-0-19-288071-0. Dewey:270. LCCN:00-267728.
Audience: **g,l,u,f.**

Brown, Peter **BR1720.A9B7 2000**
Augustine of Hippo: A Biography with a New Epilogue. Trade Paper. University of California Press. Berkeley, CA. 2000. 562p. ISBN:0-520-22757-3, ISBN13: 978-0-520-22757-6. LCCN:2001-268207.
Audience: **g,l,u,f.**

Brown, Peter **BR162.3.B76 2002**
The Rise of Western Christendom: Triumph and Diversity 200-1000 AD. Ed. 2. Trade Paper. Blackwell Publishing, Inc. Malden, MA. 2002. 640p. The Making of Europe Ser. ISBN:0-631-22138-7, ISBN13: 978-0-631-22138-8. Dewey:274. LCCN:2002-003526.
Audience: **l,u,f.** *Choice, 1996.*

Butler, Edward Cuthbert **BX3002**
Benedictine Monachism: Studies in Benedictine Life and Rule. Paper Text. Textbook Publishers. Temecula, CA. 2003. 424p. ISBN:0-7581-3633-1, ISBN13: 978-0-7581-3633-6. Dewey:271.1.
Audience: **u,f.** B

Bynum, Caroline Walker **BT872**
Resurrection of the Body in Western Christianity, 200-1336. Trade Paper. Columbia University Press. New York, NY. 1996. 224p. ACLS Lectures on the History of Religions Ser. ISBN:0-231-08127-8, ISBN13: 978-0-231-08127-6. Dewey:236.8/09.
Audience: **u,f.**

Christiansen, Eric **D173.C47 1997**
Northern Crusades. Ed. 2. Trade Paper. Penguin Group (USA) Inc. New York, NY. 1998. 320p. ISBN:0-14-026653-4, ISBN13: 978-0-14-026653-5. Dewey:909/.07. LCCN:98-161230.
Audience: **u,f.**

Duckett, Eleanor S. **D135**
The Gateway to the Middle Ages: Monasticism. Paper Text. DIANE Publishing Company. Collingdale, PA. 1999. 262p. ISBN:0-7881-6390-6, ISBN13: 978-0-7881-6390-6. Dewey:940.11.
Audience: **l,u.**

Ehler, Sidney Z. & Morrall, John B. **BV630.A1**
Church and State Through the Centuries. Trade Paper. Biblo & Tannen Booksellers & Publishers, Inc. Cheshire, CT. 1988. ISBN:0-8196-0189-6, ISBN13: 978-0-8196-0189-6. Dewey:261.7/08. LCCN:66-030406.
Audience: **l,u.**

Evans, G. R. **BR65.G56**
The Thought of Gregory the Great. Christine Carpenter, Rosamond McKitterick & Jonathan Shepard (Contribution by). Trade Paper. Cambridge University Press. New York, NY. 1988. 176p. Studies in Medieval Life and Thought, No. 2 ISBN:0-521-36826-X, ISBN13: 978-0-521-36826-1. Dewey:230.140.
Audience: **g,l,u.** *Choice, 1987.*

Evans, G. R. (Translator, Foreword by) **BX1751.2**
Bernard of Clairvaux: Selected Works. Jean Leclercq (Introduction by), Ewert Cousins (Preface by). Trade Cloth. Paulist Press. Mahwah, NJ. 1987. 352p. Classics of Western Spirituality Ser. ISBN:0-8091-2917-5, ISBN13: 978-0-8091-2917-1. Dewey:282. LCCN:87-020093.
Audience: **u,f.**

Gilson, Etienne **B72.G48**
History of Christian Philosophy in the Middle Ages. Paper Text. Textbook Publishers. Temecula, CA. 2003. 829p. ISBN:0-7581-5033-4, ISBN13: 978-0-7581-5033-2. Dewey:189.
Audience: **g,u.** B

Harnack, Adolf **BT21 .H33**
History of Dogma. Trade Paper. Wipf & Stock Publishers. Eugene, OR. 1997. 2504p. ISBN:1-57910-067-8, ISBN13: 978-1-57910-067-4. Dewey:230.09.
Audience: **u,f.**

Hussey, Joan M. **BX324.3**
The Orthodox Church in the Byzantine Empire. Trade Paper. Oxford University Press, Inc. New York, NY. 1990. 440p. Oxford History of the Christian Church Ser.

ISBN:0-19-826456-9, ISBN13: 978-0-19-826456-9. Dewey:281.9/09/02.
Audience: **u,f.** *Choice, 1986.*

Kempe, Margery B. **PR2007.K4A199 1996**
The Book of Margery Kempe. Lynn Staley (Editor). Trade Paper. Medieval Institute Publications. Kalamazoo, MI. 1998. viii, 263p. Middle English Texts ISBN:1-879288-72-9, ISBN13: 978-1-879288-72-0. Dewey:[B]. LCCN:96-027254.
Audience: **u,f.**

Knowles, Dom David **BX2592**
The Monastic Order in England: A History of Its Development from the Times of St. Dunstan to the Fourth Lateran Council, 940-1216. Trade Paper. Cambridge University Press. New York, NY. 2004. 804p. ISBN:0-521-54808-X, ISBN13: 978-0-521-54808-3. Dewey:271/.00942/0902.
Audience: **u,f.**

Lambert, Malcolm **BT1319.L35 2002**
Medieval Heresy: Popular Movements from the Gregorian Reform to the Reformation. Ed. 3. Trade Paper. Blackwell Publishing, Inc. Malden, MA. 2002. 504p. ISBN:0-631-22276-6, ISBN13: 978-0-631-22276-7. Dewey:273/.6. LCCN:2001-043102.
Audience: **u,f.**

Lebreton, Jules & Zeiller, Jacques **BR0165.L34**
The History of the Primitive Church, Vol. 3. Ernest C. Messenger (Translator). Trade Paper. Books on Demand. Ann Arbor, MI. 263p. ISBN:0-598-53256-0, ISBN13: 978-0-598-53256-5. Dewey:270.1. LCCN:44-001453.
Audience: **u,f.**

Leclercq, Jean **BX2470.L413 1982**
Love of Learning and Desire for God: A Study of Monastic Culture. Ed. 3. Trade Paper. Fordham University Press. Bronx, NY. 1982. 282p. ISBN:0-8232-0407-3, ISBN13: 978-0-8232-0407-6. Dewey:255. LCCN:60-053004.
Audience: **u,f.** B

Luebke, David M. (Editor) **BR430.L84 1999**
The Counter-Reformation: The Essential Readings. Trade Paper. Blackwell Publishing, Inc. Malden, MA. 1999. 240p. Essential Readings in History Ser. ISBN:0-631-21104-7, ISBN13: 978-0-631-21104-4. Dewey:270.6. LCCN:99-019862.
Audience: **l,u,f.**

Luther, Martin **BJ1460 .L8**
The Bondage of the Will. Trade Paper. Lulu.com. Morrisville, NC. 2005. 295p. ISBN:1-4116-4319-4, ISBN13: 978-1-4116-4319-2. Dewey:234.9.
Audience: **g,l,u,f.**

Luther, Martin **BR332**
Luther's Ninety-Five Theses. C. M. Jacobs (Translator), Harold J. Grimm (Revised by). Trade Paper. Augsburg Fortress, Publishers. Minneapolis, MN. 2003. 18p. ISBN:0-8006-1265-5, ISBN13: 978-0-8006-1265-8. Dewey:270.6.
Audience: **u,f.**

Lynch, Joseph H. **BR252.L96 1992**
The Medieval Church: A Brief History. Trade Paper. Longman Publishing. Boston, MA. 1995. 400p. ISBN:0-582-49467-2, ISBN13: 978-0-582-49467-1. Dewey:270.094. LCCN:91-045261.
Audience: **l,u,f.**

MacCulloch, Diarmaid **BR305.3.M33 2004**
The Reformation. Trade Paper. Penguin Group (USA) Inc. New York, NY. 2005. 864p. ISBN:0-14-303538-X, ISBN13: 978-0-14-303538-1. Dewey:270.6. LCCN:2003-061607.
Audience: **g,l,u.** *Choice, 2004.*

Marenbon, John **B765.A24 M37 1997**
The Philosophy of Peter Abelard. Trade Paper. Cambridge University Press. New York, NY. 1999. 396p. ISBN:0-521-66399-7, ISBN13: 978-0-521-66399-1. Dewey:194.
Audience: **u,f.**

Morris, Colin (Editor) **CB351**
Sepulchre of Christ and the Medieval West: From the Beginning to 1600. Trade Cloth. Oxford University Press, Inc. New York, NY. 2005. 454p. ISBN:0-19-826928-5, ISBN13: 978-0-19-826928-1. Dewey:232.96/4. LCCN:2004-027967.
Audience: **u,f.** *Choice, 2006.*

Netanyahu, Benjamin **BX1735.N48 1995**
The Origins of the Inquisition in Fifteenth Century Spain. Trade Cloth. Random House, Inc. New York, NY. 1995. 1,384p. ISBN:0-679-41065-1, ISBN13: 978-0-679-41065-2. Dewey:272/.2/0946. LCCN:92-053643.
Audience: **u,f.** *Choice, 1996.*

Pamphilus, Eusebius **BR160.E55**
Eusebius' Ecclesiastical History: A Third Century Historian Looks at the Early Church. Trade Cloth. Hendrickson Publishers, Inc. Peabody, MA. 1998. 528p. ISBN:1-56563-371-7, ISBN13: 978-1-56563-371-1. Dewey:270.
Audience: **u,f.**

Pelikan, Jaroslav J. **BT21.2**
Emergence of the Catholic Tradition, 100-600. Trade Cloth. University of Chicago Press. Chicago, IL. 1997. 442p. The Christian Tradition Ser., Vol. 1:A History of the Development of Christian Doctrine ISBN:0-226-65370-6, ISBN13: 978-0-226-65370-9. Dewey:230/.09. LCCN:79-142042.
Audience: **u,f.** B

Pelikan, Jaroslav J. **BT21.2**
The Spirit of Eastern Christendom, 600-1700. Trade Cloth. University of Chicago Press. Chicago, IL. 1996. 358p. The Christian Tradition Ser., Vol. 2:A History of the Development of Christian Doctrine Ser. ISBN:0-226-65372-2, ISBN13: 978-0-226-65372-3. Dewey:230/.09. LCCN:79-142042.
Audience: **u,f.**

Peters, Edward M. **BX1712.P48 1989**
Inquisition. Trade Cloth. University of California Press. Berkeley, CA. 1989. vi, 362p. ISBN:0-520-06630-8, ISBN13: 978-0-520-06630-4. Dewey:272/.2. LCCN:88-007832.
Audience: **g,l,u,f.** *Choice, 1989.*

Robinson, I. S. **BX1210.R63 1990**
The Papacy, 1073-1198: Continuity and Innovation. Trade Paper. Cambridge University Press. New York, NY. 1990. 571p. Cambridge Medieval Textbooks ISBN:0-521-31922-6, ISBN13: 978-0-521-31922-5. Dewey:261/.13/0902. LCCN:89-034126.
Audience: **l,u.** *Choice, 1991.*

Runciman, Steven **BX303**
The Eastern Schism: A Study of the Papacy and the Eastern Churches During the XIth and XIIth Centuries. Trade Paper, Perfect. Wipf & Stock Publishers. Eugene, OR. 2005. 189p. ISBN:1-59752-096-9, ISBN13: 978-1-59752-096-6. Dewey:270.38.
Audience: **u,f.**

Runciman, Steven **BT1319 .R86 1982**
The Medieval Manichee: A Study of the Christian Dualist Heresy. Trade Paper. Cambridge University Press. New York, NY. 1982. 224p. ISBN:0-521-28926-2, ISBN13: 978-0-521-28926-9. Dewey:273. LCCN:82-004123.
Audience: **u,f.** *B*

Schaff, Philip **BR145.S3 1996**
History of the Christian Church, Set. Ed. 3. Box or Slipcased. Hendrickson Publishers, Inc. Peabody, MA. 1996. 7120p. ISBN:1-56563-196-X, ISBN13: 978-1-56563-196-0. Dewey:270. LCCN:96-028348.
Audience: **u,f.** *B*

Southern, R. W. **BR145.2**
Western Society and the Church in the Middle Ages. Trade Paper. Penguin Group (USA) Inc. New York, NY. 1990. 384p. History of the Church Ser. ISBN:0-14-013755-6, ISBN13: 978-0-14-013755-2. Dewey:270.
Audience: **g,l,u.**

Staniforth, Maxwell (Translator) **BR60.A62 1987**
Early Christian Writings: The Apostolic Fathers. Andrew Louth (Introduction by, Revised by). Trade Paper. Penguin Group (USA) Inc. New York, NY. 1987. 208p. Classics Ser. ISBN:0-14-044475-0, ISBN13: 978-0-14-044475-9. Dewey:270.1. LCCN:87-176711.
Audience: **u,f.**

Tanner, Norman P. (Editor) **BX825.A1990**
Decrees of the Ecumenical Councils: From Nicea I to Vatican II. Trade Cloth. Georgetown University Press. Washington, DC. 1990. 2,528p. ISBN:0-87840-490-2, ISBN13: 978-0-87840-490-2. Dewey:262/.52. LCCN:90-003209.
Audience: **u,f.**

Thompson, E. A. **BR1720.P26T48 1999**
(e) Who Was Saint Patrick? E-Book. NetLibrary, Inc. Boulder, CO. 1999. ISBN:0-585-21071-3, ISBN13: 978-0-585-21071-1. Dewey:270.2/092/4.
Audience: **l,u.**

Tierney, Brian **BX1790**
The Crisis of Church and State 1050-1300. Trade Paper. University of Toronto Press. Toronto, ON. 1988. 210p. Medieval Academy Reprints for Teaching Ser., Vol. 21 ISBN:0-8020-6701-8, ISBN13: 978-0-8020-6701-2. Dewey:261.709021. LCCN:89-124004.
Audience: **u,f.**

Ullmann, Walter **BX955.2.U5 1970**
The Growth of Papal Government in the Middle Ages; a Study in the Ideological Relation of Clerical to Lay Power. Ed. 3. Trade Cloth. Methuen & Company, Ltd. London, 1970. xxiv, 496p. ISBN:0-416-15890-0, ISBN13: 978-0-416-15890-8. Dewey:262/.13/09021. LCCN:72-476873.
Audience: **u,f.** *B*

General History > Religious History > Judaism, European Jews > Medieval and Early Modern

Beinart, Haim & Green, Jeffrey M. **DS135.S7B41413 2001**
The Expulsion of the Jews from Spain. Trade Cloth. Littman Library of Jewish Civilization, The. London, 2002. 612p. ISBN:1-874774-41-2, ISBN13: 978-1-874774-41-9. Dewey:946/.004924. LCCN:2001-038026.
Audience: **u,f.** *Choice, 2002.*

Dubin, Lois C. **DS135.I85T735 1999**
The Port Jews of Habsburg Trieste: Absolutist Politics and Enlightenment Culture. Trade Cloth. Stanford University Press. Palo Alto, CA. 1999. 2p. Stanford Studies in Jewish History and Culture ISBN:0-8047-3320-1, ISBN13: 978-0-8047-3320-5. Dewey:945.3/93/004924. LCCN:98-043111.
Audience: **u,f.** *Choice, 1999.*

Grossman, Avraham **BM729.W6G7613 2004**
Pious and Rebellious: Jewish Women in Medieval Europe. Trade Cloth. University Press of New England. Lebanon, NH. 2004. 352p. Tauber Institute for the Study of European Jewry Ser. ISBN:1-58465-391-4, ISBN13: 978-1-58465-391-2. Dewey:305.48/892404/0902. LCCN:2004-003029.
Audience: **u,f.** *Choice, 2005.*

Meyerson, Mark D. **DS135.S7M485 2004**
A Jewish Renaissance in Fifteenth-Century Spain. Trade Cloth. Princeton University Press. Princeton, NJ. 2004. 272p. Jews, Christians, and Muslims from the Ancient to the Modern World Ser. ISBN:0-691-11749-7, ISBN13: 978-0-691-11749-2. Dewey:946/.004924. LCCN:2003-056329.
Audience: **g,u,f.** *Choice, 2005.*

Meyerson, Mark D. **DS135.S75S2365 2004**
Jews in an Iberian Frontier Kingdom: Society, Economy, and Politics in Morvedre, 1248-1391. Trade Cloth. Brill Academic Publishers. Leiden, 2004. xx, 308p. The Medieval and Early Modern Iberian World Ser., Vol. 20 ISBN:90-04-13739-4, ISBN13: 978-90-04-13739-4. Dewey:946/.763. LCCN:2004-040771.
Audience: **u,f.** *Choice, 2005.*

General History > Religious History > Judaism, European Jews > Modern

Beller, Steven **DS135.A92V5213 1990**
Vienna and the Jews, 1867-1938: A Cultural History. Trade Paper. Cambridge University Press. New York, NY. 1991. 281p. ISBN:0-521-40727-3, ISBN13: 978-0-521-40727-4. Dewey:943.6/13/004924.
Audience: **g,u,f.** *Choice, 1990.*

Meyerson, Mark D. **DS135.S7M485 2004**
A Jewish Renaissance in Fifteenth-Century Spain. Trade Cloth. Princeton University Press. Princeton, NJ. 2004. 272p. Jews, Christians, and Muslims from the Ancient to the Modern World Ser. ISBN:0-691-11749-7, ISBN13: 978-0-691-11749-2. Dewey:946/.004924. LCCN:2003-056329.
Audience: **g,u,f.** *Choice, 2005.*

Meyerson, Mark D. **DS135.S75S2365 2004**
Jews in an Iberian Frontier Kingdom: Society, Economy, and Politics in Morvedre, 1248-1391. Trade Cloth. Brill Academic Publishers. Leiden, 2004. xx, 308p. The Medieval and Early Modern Iberian World Ser., Vol. 20 ISBN:90-04-13739-4, ISBN13: 978-90-04-13739-4. Dewey:946/.763. LCCN:2004-040771.
Audience: **u,f.** *Choice, 2005.*

General History > Religious History > Catholic Reformation

Haliczer, Stephen **BX2263.S7H35 1996**
Sexuality in the Confessional: A Sacrament Profaned. Cloth Text. Oxford University Press, Inc. New York, NY. 1996. 280p. Studies in the History of Sexuality ISBN:0-19-509656-8, ISBN13: 978-0-19-509656-9. Dewey:264/.020862/09460903. LCCN:94-047094.
Audience: **u,f.** *Choice, 1996.*

Homza, Lu Ann **BX1584**
Religious Authority in the Spanish Renaissance. Trade Paper. Johns Hopkins University Press. Baltimore, MD. 2004. 344p. The Johns Hopkins University Studies in Historical and Political Science Ser. ISBN:0-8018-7904-3, ISBN13: 978-0-8018-7904-3. Dewey:274.6/06.
Audience: **u,f.** *Choice, 2000.*

General History > Religious History > Anti-Judaism and Antisemitism > Modern

Aronson, I. Michael **DS135.R9A74 1990**
Troubled Waters: The Origins of the 1881 Anti-Jewish Pogroms in Russia. Cloth Text. University of Pittsburgh Press. Pittsburgh, PA. 1991. 286p. Russian and East European Studies Ser. ISBN:0-8229-3656-9, ISBN13: 978-0-8229-3656-5. Dewey:947/.004924. LCCN:90-033957.
Audience: **g,u,f.** *Choice, 1991.*

Aschheim, Steven E. **DS135.G33A76 1999**
Brothers and Strangers: The East European Jew in German and German Jewish Consciousness, 1800-1923. Trade Cloth. University of Wisconsin Press. Chicago, IL. 1983. 368p. Mark H. Ingraham Prize ISBN:0-299-09114-7, ISBN13: 978-0-299-09114-9. Dewey:306/.08924043. LCCN:81-069812.
Audience: **u,f.**

Beller, Steven **DS135.A92V5213 1990**
Vienna and the Jews, 1867-1938: A Cultural History. Trade Paper. Cambridge University Press. New York, NY. 1991. 281p. ISBN:0-521-40727-3, ISBN13: 978-0-521-40727-4. Dewey:943.6/13/004924.
Audience: **g,u,f.** *Choice, 1990.*

Bredin, Jean-Denis **E743.5.H55**
The Affair: The Case of Alfred Dreyfus. Trade Paper. George Braziller Inc. New York, NY. 1987. ISBN:0-8076-1175-1, ISBN13: 978-0-8076-1175-3. Dewey:364.131. LCCN:85-022374.
Audience: **g,l,u,f.**

Burns, Michael **DC354.B88 1999**
France and the Dreyfus Affair: A Documentary History. Cloth over Boards. Palgrave Macmillan. New York, NY. 1998. 224p. Bedford Series in History and Culture ISBN:0-312-21813-3, ISBN13: 978-0-312-21813-3. Dewey:944/.004924. LCCN:98-086157.
Audience: **l,u,f.**

Frankel, Jonathan **HX550.J4**
Prophecy and Politics: Socialism, Nationalism, and the Russian Jews, 1862-1917. Trade Paper. Cambridge University Press. New York, NY. 1984. 708p. ISBN:0-521-26919-9, ISBN13: 978-0-521-26919-3. Dewey:335/.0089924. LCCN:80-014414.
Audience: **l,u.**

Frankel, Jonathan & Zipperstein, Steven J. (Editors) **DS135.E83**
Assimilation and Community: The Jews in Nineteenth-Century Europe. Trade Paper. Cambridge University Press. New York, NY. 2004. 396p. ISBN:0-521-52601-9, ISBN13: 978-0-521-52601-2. Dewey:305.8/92/40409034.
Audience: **u,f.** *Choice, 1992.*

Friedlander, Saul **DS135.G3315**
Nazi Germany and the Jews: The Years of Persecution, 1933-1939. Trade Paper. HarperCollins Publishers. New York, NY. 1998. 464p. Nazi Germany and the Jews Ser., Vol. 1 ISBN:0-06-092878-6, ISBN13: 978-0-06-092878-0. Dewey:940.53/18.
Audience: **g,u,f.**

Gordon, Sarah **D810.J4**
Hitler, Germans, and the Jewish Question. Trade Paper. Princeton University Press. Princeton, NJ. 1984. 432p. ISBN:0-691-10162-0, ISBN13: 978-0-691-10162-0. Dewey:940.53/15/03924. LCCN:83-043073.
Audience: **g,l,u,f.**

Katz, Jacob **DS147.K37 1998**
Out of the Ghetto: The Social Background of Jewish Emancipation, 1770-1870. Trade Cloth. Syracuse University Press. Syracuse, NY. 1998. 272p. Modern Jewish History Ser. ISBN:0-8156-0532-3, ISBN13: 978-0-8156-0532-4. Dewey:305.892/4. LCCN:98-025601.
Audience: **g,l,u,f.**

Kauders, Anthony D. **D802.G3**
Democratization and the Jews: Munich, 1945-1965. Cloth Text. University of Nebraska Press. Lincoln, NE. 2004. 336p. Studies in Antisemitism Ser. ISBN:0-8032-2763-9, ISBN13: 978-0-8032-2763-7. Dewey:305.892/4043/09045. LCCN:2003-111393.
Audience: **u,f.** *Choice, 2005.*

Kertzer, David I. **DS135.I8**
The Kidnapping of Edgardo Mortara: The Extraordinary Story of How a Jewish Child, Made a Prisoner of the Vatican in 1858, Ended the Rule of the Popes in Italy. Trade Cloth. Random House Value Publishing. New York, NY. 1998. RHVP-Remainder Ser. ISBN:0-517-28897-4, ISBN13: 978-0-517-28897-9. Dewey:945/.004924.
Audience: **g,l,u,f.** *Choice, 1997.*

Kertzer, David I. **BM535.K43 2001**
The Popes Against the Jews: The Vatican's Role in the Rise of Modern Anti-Semitism. Trade Cloth. Alfred A. Knopf Inc. New York, NY. 2001. 368p. ISBN:0-375-40623-9, ISBN13: 978-0-375-40623-2. Dewey:261.2/6/09. LCCN:2001-033728.
Audience: **u,f.** *Choice, 2002.*

Klier, John Doyle & Lambroza, Shlomo (Editors) **DS135.R9 P55 1991**
Pogroms: Anti-Jewish Violence in Modern Russian History. Trade Cloth. Cambridge University Press. New York, NY. 1992. 413p. ISBN:0-521-40532-7, ISBN13: 978-0-521-40532-4. Dewey:947/.004924. LCCN:90-025617.
Audience: **u,f.** *Choice, 1992.*

Kostyrchenko, Gennadi V. **DS146.S65K68 1995**
Out of the Red Shadows: Anti-Semitism in Stalin's Russia. Trade Cloth. Prometheus Books, Publishers. Amherst, NY. 1995. 333p. Russian Studies Ser. ISBN:0-87975-930-5, ISBN13: 978-0-87975-930-8. Dewey:947/.004924. LCCN:94-039151.
Audience: **u,f.**

Lazare, Bernard **DS145.L413 1995**
Antisemitism, Its History and Causes. Robert S. Wistrich (Introduction by). Trade Paper. University of Nebraska Press. Lincoln, NE. 1995. 200p. ISBN:0-8032-7954-X, ISBN13: 978-0-8032-7954-4. Dewey:305.892/4. LCCN:95-005651.
Audience: **g,l,u,f.**

Levy, Richard S. **DS145.A642 1991**
Antisemitism in the Modern World: An Anthology of Texts. Ed. 1. Paper Text. Houghton Mifflin College Division. Boston, MA. 1990. 270p. Sources in Modern History Ser. ISBN:0-669-24340-X, ISBN13: 978-0-669-24340-6. Dewey:305.8/924. LCCN:90-081852.
Audience: **g,l,u,f.**

Levy, Richard S. **DS146.E8A58 2005**
Antisemitism: A Historical Encyclopedia of Prejudice and Persecution. Robert Levy (Editor). Library Binding. ABC-CLIO, Inc. Santa Barbara, CA. 2005. 1000p. ISBN:1-85109-439-3, ISBN13: 978-1-85109-439-4. Dewey:305.892/4/009. LCCN:2005-009480.
Audience: **g,l,u,f.** *Choice, 2005.*

Marrus, Michael R. **DS135.F83**
The Politics of Assimilation: The French Jewish Community at the Time of the Dreyfus Affair. Trade Paper. Oxford University Press, Inc. New York, NY. 1981. 314p. ISBN:0-19-822591-1, ISBN13: 978-0-19-822591-1. Dewey:305.8/924/044. LCCN:75-563429.
Audience: **u,f.**

Marrus, Michael R. & Paxton, Robert O. **DS135.F83M3813 1983**
Vichy France and the Jews. Stanley Hoffmann (Foreword by). Trade Paper. Stanford University Press. Palo Alto, CA. 1995. 454p. ISBN:0-8047-2499-7, ISBN13: 978-0-8047-2499-9. Dewey:944/.0816/089924. LCCN:94-068126.
Audience: **u,f.**

Massing, Paul W. **DS0135.G33M3**
Rehearsal for Destruction: A Study of Political Anti-Semitism in Imperial Germany. Trade Paper. Books on Demand. Ann Arbor, MI. 360p. Studies in Prejudice, Amer. Jewish Comm., Soc. Studies Ser. Publ. 2 ISBN:0-598-77903-5, ISBN13: 978-0-598-77903-8. Dewey:296. LCCN:49-050156.
Audience: **g,l,u,f.**

Mosse, George L. **D1056**
Toward the Final Solution: A History of European Racism. Trade Cloth. Howard Fertig Inc. New York, NY. 1978. ISBN:0-86527-194-1, ISBN13: 978-0-86527-194-4. Dewey:305.8/0094. LCCN:77-024356.
Audience: **u,f.**

Nathans, Benjamin **DS135.R92**
Beyond the Pale: The Jewish Encounter with Late Imperial Russia. Trade Paper. University of California Press. Berkeley, CA. 2004. 426p. Studies on the History of Society and Culture Ser. ISBN:0-520-24232-7, ISBN13: 978-0-520-24232-6. Dewey:947/.004924. LCCN:2001-003513.
Audience: **u,f.** *Choice, 2003.*

Niewyk, Donald L. **DS135.G33N44 2001**
Jews in Weimar Germany. Trade Paper. Transaction Publishers. Somerset, NJ. 2000. 229p. ISBN:0-7658-0692-4, ISBN13: 978-0-7658-0692-5. Dewey:943/.004924. LCCN:00-044713.
Audience: **u,f.**

Pauley, Bruce F. **91-50249 [DS]**
From Prejudice to Persecution: A History of Austrian Anti-Semitism. Trade Paper. University of North Carolina Press. Chapel Hill, NC. 1998. 456p. ISBN:0-8078-4713-5, ISBN13: 978-0-8078-4713-8. Dewey:305.892/40436. LCCN:91-050249.
Audience: **g,u,f.** *Choice, 1992.*

Poliakov, Leon **DS145.P4613 2003**
The History of Anti-Semitism. Book, Other. University of Pennsylvania Press. Philadelphia, PA. 2003. 352p. ISBN:0-8122-3766-8, ISBN13: 978-0-8122-3766-5. Dewey:305.892/4/009. LCCN:2003-057081.
Audience: **g,l,u,f.**

Pulzer, Peter **DS135.G33P85 2003**
Jews and the German State: The Political History of a Minority, 1848-1933. Trade Paper. Wayne State University Press. Detroit, MI. 2002. 394p. ISBN:0-8143-3130-0, ISBN13: 978-0-8143-3130-9. Dewey:943/.004924. LCCN:2003-041116.
Audience: **u,f.** *Choice, 1992.*

Pulzer, Peter **DS146.G4P8 1988**
The Rise of Political Anti-Semitism in Germany and Austria. Trade Paper. Harvard University Press. Cambridge, MA. 1988. 384p. ISBN:0-674-77166-4, ISBN13: 978-0-674-77166-6. Dewey:323.1/1924/043. LCCN:88-015062.
Audience: **g,l,u,f.**

Ranki, Vera **DS135.H9R36 1999**
The Politics of Inclusion and Exclusion: Jews and Nationalism in Hungary. Cloth Text. Holmes & Meier Publishers, Inc. Teaneck, NJ. 1999. 274p. ISBN:0-8419-1401-X, ISBN13: 978-0-8419-1401-8. Dewey:943.9/004924. LCCN:98-045937.
Audience: **g,l,u,f.** *Choice, 1999.*

Reinharz, Jehuda & Mendes-Flohr, Paul R. (Editors) **DS102.J43 1995**
The Jew in the Modern World: A Documentary History. Ed. 2. Paper Text. Oxford University Press, Inc. New York, NY. 1995. 766p. ISBN:0-19-507453-X, ISBN13: 978-0-19-507453-6. Dewey:909/.04924. LCCN:94-009181.
Audience: **g,l,u,f.**

Rogger, Hans **DS135.R9R64 1986**
Jewish Policies and Right-Wing Politics in Imperial Russia. Trade Cloth. University of California Press. Berkeley, CA. 1985. ISBN:0-520-04596-3, ISBN13: 978-0-520-04596-5. Dewey:947/.004924. LCCN:85-001006.
Audience: **u,f.** *Choice, 1986.*

Segel, Binjamin W. **DS145.P7**
A Lie and a Libel: The History of the Protocols of the Elders of Zion. Richard S. Levy (Editor, Translator). Trade Cloth. University of Nebraska Press. Lincoln, NE. 1995. 148p.

ISBN:0-8032-9245-7, ISBN13: 978-0-8032-9245-1. Dewey:305.892/4. LCCN:95-010034.
Audience: **u,f.**

Shapiro, James **PN3235**
Oberammergau: The Troubling Story of the World's Most Famous Passion Play. UK-Trade Paper. Knopf Publishing Group. New York, NY. 2001. 272p. Vintage Bks. ISBN:0-375-70852-9, ISBN13: 978-0-375-70852-7. Dewey:792.1/6.
Audience: **g,l,u,f.** *Choice, 2001.*

Wilson, Stephen **DS146.F8**
Ideology and Experience: Antisemitism in France at the Time of the Dreyfus Affair. Trade Cloth. Oxford University Press, Inc. New York, NY. 1985. 832p. Littman Library of Jewish Civilization ISBN:0-19-710052-X, ISBN13: 978-0-19-710052-3. Dewey:305.8/924/044. LCCN:81-065467.
Audience: **u,f.** B

Winock, Michel **DC369.W5613 1998**
Nationalism, Antisemitism, and Fascism in France. Jane Marie Todd (Translator). Trade Paper. Stanford University Press. Palo Alto, CA. 2001. 360p. ISBN:0-8047-3287-6, ISBN13: 978-0-8047-3287-1. Dewey:944.081. LCCN:98-011298.
Audience: **g,l,u,f.** *Choice, 1999.*

General History > Nationalism

Anderson, Benedict **JC311**
Imagined Communities: Reflections on the Origin and Spread of Nationalism. Trade Cloth. Analytical Psychology Club of San Francisco, Inc. San Francisco, CA. 1983. 160p. ISBN:0-86091-059-8, ISBN13: 978-0-86091-059-6. Dewey:320.5/4. LCCN:84-152806.
Audience: **g,l,u,f.**

Balakrishnan, Gopal (Editor) **JC311**
Mapping the Nation. Trade Paper. Analytical Psychology Club of San Francisco, Inc. San Francisco, CA. 1996. 288p. Mapping Ser. ISBN:1-85984-060-4, ISBN13: 978-1-85984-060-3. Dewey:320.5/4.
Audience: **g,l,u,f.**

Brubaker, Rogers **JN2919.B78 1992**
Citizenship and Nationhood in France and Germany. Trade Paper. Harvard University Press. Cambridge, MA. 1998. 288p. ISBN:0-674-13178-9, ISBN13: 978-0-674-13178-1. Dewey:323.6/0943. LCCN:91-042897.
Audience: **g,l,u,f.** *Choice, 1993.*

Connor, Walker **GN380**
Ethnonationalism: The Quest for Understanding. Trade Paper. Princeton University Press. Princeton, NJ. 1993. 248p. ISBN:0-691-02563-0, ISBN13: 978-0-691-02563-6. Dewey:323.1/1. LCCN:93-017829.
Audience: **g,l,u,f.** *Choice, 1994.*

Deutsch, Karl Wolfgang **JC311**
Nationalism and Social Communication: An Inquiry into the Foundations of Nationality. Paper Text. Textbook Publishers. Temecula, CA. 2003. x, 292p. ISBN:0-7581-5311-2, ISBN13: 978-0-7581-5311-1. Dewey:320.15.
Audience: **u,f.** B

Eley, Geoffrey & Suny, Ronald G. (Editors) **JC311.B4125 1996**
Becoming National: A Reader. Paper Text. Oxford University Press, Inc. New York, NY. 1996. 528p. ISBN:0-19-509661-4, ISBN13: 978-0-19-509661-3. Dewey:320.5/4. LCCN:95-034438.
Audience: **u,f.**

Gellner, Ernest **JC311.G483 2006**
Nations and Nationalism. Ed. 2. Trade Paper. Blackwell Publishing Ltd. Oxford, 2006. 204p. New Perspectives on the Past Ser. ISBN:1-4051-3442-9, ISBN13: 978-1-4051-3442-2. Dewey:320.54. LCCN:2005-031819.
Audience: **g,l,u,f.**

Greenfeld, Liah **JC311**
Nationalism: Five Roads to Modernity. Trade Paper. Harvard University Press. Cambridge, MA. 1992. 400p. ISBN:0-674-60319-2, ISBN13: 978-0-674-60319-6. Dewey:320.54.
Audience: **u,f.** *Choice, 1993.*

Hobsbawm, E. J. **JC311 .H577 1992**
Nations and Nationalism since 1780: Programme, Myth, Reality. Ed. 2. Trade Paper. Cambridge University Press. New York, NY. 1992. 214p. A Canto Book Ser. ISBN:0-521-43961-2, ISBN13: 978-0-521-43961-9. Dewey:320.5/4. LCCN:92-014949.
Audience: **g,l,u,f.**

Hobsbawm, Eric J. & Ranger, Terence (Editors) **HM201**
The Invention of Tradition. Trade Paper. Cambridge University Press. New York, NY. 1992. 328p. A Canto Book Ser. ISBN:0-521-43773-3, ISBN13: 978-0-521-43773-8. Dewey:303.3/72. LCCN:82-014711.
Audience: **g,l,u,f.** B

Hroch, Miroslav **D359.H77 2000**
Social Preconditions of National Revival in Europe: A Comparative Analysis of the Social Composition of Patriotic Groups among the Smaller European Nations. Ben Fowkes (Translator). Trade Paper. Columbia University Press. New York, NY. 1999. 220p. ISBN:0-231-11771-X, ISBN13: 978-0-231-11771-5. Dewey:320.54/094. LCCN:99-031410.
Audience: **u,f.**

Hutchinson, John & Smith, Anthony D. **JC311.N3228 2000**
Nationalism: Critical Concepts in Political Science. Children's Board Books. Routledge. New York, NY. 2000. 2096p. Critical Concepts in Political Science Ser. ISBN:0-415-20109-8, ISBN13: 978-0-415-20109-4. Dewey:320.54. LCCN:99-020802.
Audience: **g,l,u,f.** *Choice, 2001.*

Llobera, Josep R. **JC311.L725 1994**
The God of Modernity: The Development of Nationalism in Western Europe. Brian Nelson (Editor). Cloth over Boards. Berg Publishers. Oxford, 1994. 229p. European Studies ISBN:0-85496-921-7, ISBN13: 978-0-85496-921-0. Dewey:320.5/4/094. LCCN:94-028884.
Audience: **g,l,u,f.**

Mosse, George L. **DD76 .M65 1991**
The Nationalization of the Masses: Political Symbolism and Mass Movements in Germany, from the Napoleonic Wars Through the Third Reich. Book, Other. Cornell University Press. Ithaca, NY. 1991. 272p. ISBN:0-8014-9978-X, ISBN13: 978-0-8014-9978-4. Dewey:320.943. LCCN:91-055260.
Audience: **g,l,u,f.**

Senelick, Laurence (Editor) **PN2570.N38 1990**
National Theater in Northern and Eastern Europe, 1746-1900. W. D. Howarth, John Northam & Glynne W. Wickham (Contribution by). Cloth Text. Cambridge University Press. New York, NY. 1991. 510p. Theatre in Europe Ser., :A Documentary History ISBN:0-521-24446-3, ISBN13: 978-0-521-24446-6. Dewey:792/.094/09034. LCCN:90-001651.
Audience: **u,f.** *Choice, 1991.*

Seton-Watson, Hugh **D32.S47**
Nations and States: An Enquiry into the Origins of Nations and the Politics of Nationalism. Paper Text. Westview Press. Boulder, CO. 1977. 563p. ISBN:0-89158-227-4, ISBN13: 978-0-89158-227-4. Dewey:320.5/4/09. LCCN:77-004237.
Audience: **u,f.** B

Smith, Anthony D. **JC311**
Chosen Peoples: Sacred Sources of National Identity. Trade Cloth. Oxford University Press, Inc. New York, NY. 2004. 360p. ISBN:0-19-210017-3, ISBN13: 978-0-19-210017-7. Dewey:320.5/4. LCCN:2004-298484.
Audience: **g,l,u,f.** *Choice, 2004.*

Smith, Anthony D. **JC11**
The Ethnic Origins of Nations. Trade Paper. Blackwell Publishing, Inc. Malden, MA. 1988. 336p. ISBN:0-631-16169-4, ISBN13: 978-0-631-16169-1. Dewey:320.5/4/09.
Audience: **u,f.**

Tilly, Charles **JN94.A2T54 1990**
Coercion, Capital, and European States, AD 990-1990. Cloth Text. Blackwell Publishing, Inc. Malden, MA. 1990. 288p. ISBN:1-55786-067-X, ISBN13: 978-1-55786-067-5. Dewey:940. LCCN:89-017730.
Audience: **u,f.** *Choice, 1990.*

General History > By period > Medieval History (476-1453)

Anderson, Roberta & Bellenger, Dominic Aidan (Editors) **D113.5.A585 2003**
Medieval Worlds: A Sourcebook. Paper over Boards. Routledge. New York, NY. 2003. 368p. ISBN:0-415-25308-X, ISBN13: 978-0-415-25308-6. Dewey:940.1. LCCN:2002-154819.
Audience: **g,l,u,f.**

Bull, Marcus **D116**
Thinking Medieval: An Introduction to the Study of the Middle Ages. Cloth over Boards. Palgrave Macmillan. New York, NY. 2005. 224p. ISBN:1-4039-1294-7, ISBN13: 978-1-4039-1294-7. Dewey:909.07. LCCN:2005-051167.
Audience: **g,l,u,f.**

Crouch, David **HT653.G7C75 2005**
The Birth of Nobility: Constructing Aristocracy in England and France, 900-1300. Trade Paper, Perfect. Longman Publishing Group. White Plains, NY. 2005. 384p. ISBN:0-582-36981-9, ISBN13: 978-0-582-36981-8. Dewey:305.520941. LCCN:2004-060072.
Audience: **g,l,u,f.** *Choice, 2006.*

Deliyannis, Deborah Mauskopf (Editor) **D116**
Historiography in the Middle Ages. Trade Cloth. Brill Academic Publishers. Leiden, 2003. viii, 464p. ISBN:90-04-11881-0, ISBN13: 978-90-04-11881-2. Dewey:909.07/07/2. LCCN:2002-028389.
Audience: **u,f.** *Choice, 2003.*

Hunt, Edwin S. & Murray, James M. **HF3495.H86 1999**
A History of Business in Medieval Europe, 1200-1550. Cloth Text. Cambridge University Press. New York, NY. 1999. 298p. Medieval Textbooks Ser. ISBN:0-521-49581-4, ISBN13: 978-0-521-49581-3. Dewey:330.94/01. LCCN:98-038599.
Audience: **u,f.** *Choice, 1999.*

Reeves, Marjorie **D13.R366 1999**
The Prophetic Sense of History in Medieval and Renaissance Europe: From Jerusalem to Cyprus. Trade Cloth. Ashgate Publishing, Ltd. Aldershot, 1999. 316p. Variorum Collected Studies, No. 660 ISBN:0-86078-805-9, ISBN13: 978-0-86078-805-8. Dewey:907/.204. LCCN:99-031184.
Audience: **u,f.**

Rosenwein, Barbara H. **D117.R67 2002**
A Short History of the Middle Ages. Trade Paper. Broadview Press. Peterborough, ON. 2002. 220p. ISBN:1-55111-290-6, ISBN13: 978-1-55111-290-9. Dewey:940.1. LCCN:2002-282702.
Audience: **l,u.** *Choice, 2002.*

General History > By period > Medieval History (476-1453) > Migrations

Christie, Neil **DG511**
The Lombards. Trade Paper. Blackwell Publishing, Inc. Malden, MA. 1998. 288p. The Peoples of Europe Ser. ISBN:0-631-21197-7, ISBN13: 978-0-631-21197-6. Dewey:945/.01.
Audience: **l,u.** *Choice, 1995.*

Clover, Frank M. **DG312.C54 1993**
The Late Roman West and the Vandals. Trade Cloth. Ashgate Publishing, Ltd. Aldershot, 1993. 296p. Collected Studies, No. CS401 ISBN:0-86078-354-5, ISBN13: 978-0-86078-354-1. Dewey:937.09. LCCN:93-018599.
Audience: **u,f.**

Curta, Florin **DR49.26 .C87 2001**
The Making of the Slavs: History and Archaeology of the Lower Danube Region, c. 500-700. Christine Carpenter, Rosamond McKitterick & Jonathan Shepard (Contribution by). Trade Cloth. Cambridge University Press. New York, NY. 2001. 492p. Studies in Medieval Life and Thought ISBN:0-521-80202-4, ISBN13: 978-0-521-80202-4. Dewey:949.601. LCCN:00-052915.
Audience: **u,f.** *Choice, 2002.*

Heather, Peter **D137.H43**
Goths and Romans AD 332-489. Trade Paper. Oxford University Press, Inc. New York, NY. 1994. 396p. Historical Monographs ISBN:0-19-920535-3, ISBN13: 978-0-19-920535-6. Dewey:936.
Audience: **u,f.**

Jones, Gwyn **DL31.J6 1984**
A History of the Vikings. Ed. 2. Trade Paper. Oxford University Press, Inc. New York, NY. 2001. 522p. ISBN:0-19-280134-1, ISBN13: 978-0-19-280134-0. Dewey:914.8/03/1. LCCN:83-013303.
Audience: **l,u.** B

Jones, Michael E. **DA145**
The End of Roman Britain. Trade Paper. Cornell University Press. Ithaca, NY. 1998. 336p. ISBN:0-8014-8530-4, ISBN13: 978-0-8014-8530-5. Dewey:936.1/04.
Audience: **l,u,f.** *Choice, 1996.*

Jordanes **D137.J9 2006**
The Gothic History of Jordanes: In English Version with an Introduction and a Commentary. Charles Christopher Mierow (Editor, Translator). Paper Text. Arx Publishing. Bristol, PA. 2005. 188p. The Christian Roman Empire Ser., Vol. 2 ISBN:1-889758-77-9, ISBN13: 978-1-889758-77-0. Dewey:909/.0439. LCCN:2006-011974.
Audience: **u,f.**

Loyn, Henry **DA158.L68**
The Vikings in Britain. Trade Cloth. Blackwell Publishing, Inc. Malden, MA. 1999. 136p. ISBN:0-631-18711-1, ISBN13: 978-0-631-18711-0. Dewey:942.01.
Audience: **g,l,u.**

Macartney, Carlile A. **DB927 .M3**
The Magyars in the Ninth Century. Trade Paper. Books on Demand. Ann Arbor, MI. 253p. ISBN:0-608-12055-3, ISBN13: 978-0-608-12055-3. Dewey:943.91. LCCN:31-019298.
Audience: **u,f.**

Thompson, E. A. **D141**
The Huns. Trade Paper. Blackwell Publishing, Inc. Malden, MA. 1999. 336p. The Peoples of Europe Ser. ISBN:0-631-21443-7, ISBN13: 978-0-631-21443-4. Dewey:936.
Audience: **l,u,f.**

Wolfram, Herwig **D137.W6213 1988**
History of the Goths. Thomas J. Dunlap (Translator, Illustrator). Trade Paper. University of California Press. Berkeley, CA. 1990. 580p. ISBN:0-520-06983-8, ISBN13: 978-0-520-06983-1. Dewey:940.1.
Audience: **g,l,u.** *Choice, 1989.*

General History > By period > Medieval History (476-1453) > Crusades

Barber, Malcolm C. **XR473.B27 1994**
The New Knighthood: A History of the Order of the Temple. Trade Paper. Cambridge University Press. New York, NY. 1995. 465p. A Canto Book Ser. ISBN:0-521-55872-7, ISBN13: 978-0-521-55872-3. Dewey:271.7/913. LCCN:92-420415.
Audience: **g,l,u,f.** *Choice, 1994.*

Christiansen, Eric **D173.C47 1997**
Northern Crusades. Ed. 2. Trade Paper. Penguin Group (USA) Inc. New York, NY. 1998. 320p. ISBN:0-14-026653-4, ISBN13: 978-0-14-026653-5. Dewey:909/.07. LCCN:98-161230.
Audience: **u,f.**

Comnena, Anna **DF605**
The Alexiad. Trade Paper. Kessinger Publishing, LLC. Whitefish, MT. 2004. ISBN:1-4191-5186-X, ISBN13: 978-1-4191-5186-6. Dewey:949.5/03/092 B.
Audience: **g,l,u,f.**

De Villehardouin, Geoffroi & De Joinville, Jean **D151**
Chronicles of the Crusades. Margaret R. Shaw (Translator, Introduction by). Trade Paper. Penguin Group (USA) Inc. New York, NY. 1963. 368p. Penguin Classics Ser. ISBN:0-14-044124-7, ISBN13: 978-0-14-044124-6. Dewey:940.18.
Audience: **g,l,u,f.**

Gabrieli, Francesco **D151**
Arab Historians of the Crusades. Trade Paper. Kazi Publications, Inc. Chicago, IL. 1996. 365p. ISBN:0-614-21098-4, ISBN13: 978-0-614-21098-9. Dewey:909.07.
Audience: **u,f.**

Hillenbrand, Carole **DS38.6.H55 2000**
The Crusades: Islamic Perspectives. Trade Paper. Routledge. New York, NY. 2000. 720p. ISBN:0-415-92914-8, ISBN13: 978-0-415-92914-1. Dewey:909/.097671. LCCN:00-044642.
Audience: **u,f.** *Choice, 2001.*

Nicholson, Helen **CR4701**
Templars, Hospitallers and Teutonic Knights: The Image of the Military Orders, 1128-1291. Trade Paper. St. Martin's Press. Gordonville, VA. 1995. 224p. ISBN:0-7185-2277-X, ISBN13: 978-0-7185-2277-3. Dewey:271.7/91.
Audience: **l,u,f.**

Phillips, Jonathan **D162.E96 2001**
Conquest of Lisbon: De Expugnatione Lyxbonesi. Charles Wendell David (Translator). Trade Paper. Columbia University Press. New York, NY. 2001. 224p. Records of Western Civilization Ser. ISBN:0-231-12123-7, ISBN13: 978-0-231-12123-1. Dewey:946.9/42502. LCCN:00-060327.
Audience: **g,l,u,f.**

Queller, Donald E. **D164**
Fourth Crusade: The Conquest of Constantinople. Ed. 2. Book, Other. University of Pennsylvania Press. Philadelphia, PA. 1999. 368p. Middle Ages Ser. ISBN:0-8122-1713-6, ISBN13: 978-0-8122-1713-1. Dewey:949.6/18/013.
Audience: **g,l,u.**

Riley-Smith, Jonathan **D161.2**
The First Crusade and the Idea of Crusading. Trade Paper. Continuum International Publishing Group, Ltd. London, 240p. ISBN:0-485-12094-1, ISBN13: 978-0-485-12094-3. Dewey:940.1/8.
Audience: **l,u.** *Choice, 1987.*

Riley-Smith, Jonathan Simon Christopher **D157.R54 2002**
What Were the Crusades? Ed. 3. Trade Paper. Palgrave Macmillan. New York, NY. 2002. 128p. ISBN:0-333-94904-8, ISBN13: 978-0-333-94904-7. Dewey:909.07. LCCN:2002-075297.
Audience: **l,u.**

Runciman, Steven **D161.2**
A History of the Crusades, Set. Quantity Pack, Trade Cloth. Cambridge University Press. New York, NY. 1987. 466p. ISBN:0-521-20554-9, ISBN13: 978-0-521-20554-2. Dewey:940.1/8.
Audience: **u,f.** B

Setton, Kenneth M. **Q11.BX955.2**
The Papacy and the Levant, 1204-1571: The Sixteenth Century, Vol. 3. Trade Cloth. American Philosophical Society. Canton, MA. 1984. Memoirs Ser., Vol. 161 ISBN:0-87169-161-2, ISBN13: 978-0-87169-161-3. Dewey:081 s 270.5. LCCN:75-025476.
Audience: **u,f.**

Setton, Kenneth M. **Q11. BX955.2**
The Papacy and the Levant, 1204-1571: The Fifteenth Century. Trade Cloth. American Philosophical Society. Canton, MA. 1978. Memoirs Ser., Vol. 127 ISBN:0-87169-127-2, ISBN13: 978-0-87169-127-9. Dewey:081 s 270.5. LCCN:75-025476.
Audience: **u,f.**

Setton, Kenneth M. **Q11 .P612 VOL. 114**
The Papacy and the Levant, 1204-1571: The Thirteenth and Fourteenth Centuries. Trade Cloth. American Philosophical Society. Canton, MA. 1976. Memoirs Ser., Vol. 114 ISBN:0-87169-114-0, ISBN13: 978-0-87169-114-9. Dewey:081. LCCN:75-025476.
Audience: **u,f.**

Setton, Kenneth M. & Baldwin, Marshall W. (Editors) **D157.S482**
A History of the Crusades: The First Hundred Years. Ed. 2. Trade Paper. University of Wisconsin Press. Chicago, IL. 1969. 740p. ISBN:0-299-04834-9, ISBN13: 978-0-299-04834-1. Dewey:940.1/8.
Audience: **l,u.**

Setton, Kenneth M. & Hazard, Harry W. (Editors) **D157.S482**
A History of the Crusades: The Art and Architecture of the Crusader States, Vol. 4. Trade Paper. University of Wisconsin Press. Chicago, IL. 1977. 448p. ISBN:0-299-06824-2, ISBN13: 978-0-299-06824-0. Dewey:940.1/8.
Audience: **u,f.**

Setton, Kenneth M. & Hazard, Harry W. (Editors) **D157.S482 1975**
A History of the Crusades: Fourteenth and Fifteenth Centuries. Trade Paper. University of Wisconsin Press. Chicago, IL. 1975. 836p. ISBN:0-299-06674-6, ISBN13: 978-0-299-06674-1. Dewey:909.07.
Audience: **l,u.**

Setton, Kenneth M. (Editor), et al. **D157.S482 1989**
A History of the Crusades: The Impact of the Crusades on Europe. Harry W. Hazard & Norman P. Zacour (Editors). Trade Paper. University of Wisconsin Press. Chicago, IL. 1990. 728p. ISBN:0-299-10744-2, ISBN13: 978-0-299-10744-4. Dewey:940.1/8.
Audience: **u,f.**

Setton, Kenneth M. (Editor), et al. **D157 .S482**
A History of the Crusades: The Later Crusades, 1189-1311. Ed. 2. Robert Lee Wolff & Harry W. Hazard (Editors). Trade Paper. University of Wisconsin Press. Chicago, IL. 1969. 896p. ISBN:0-299-04844-6, ISBN13: 978-0-299-04844-0. Dewey:940.1/8.
Audience: **u,f.**

Setton, Kenneth M. (Editor), et al. **D157.S482 1985**
A History of the Crusades: The Impact of the Crusades on the near East. Norman P. Zacour & Harry W. Hazard (Editors). Trade Paper. University of Wisconsin Press. Chicago, IL. 1985. 624p. ISBN:0-299-09144-9, ISBN13: 978-0-299-09144-6. Dewey:909.07.
Audience: **u,f.**

General History > By period > Medieval History (476-1453) > Latin Kingdom of Jerusalem

Edbury, Peter W. **D175.E33 1999**
Kingdoms of the Crusaders: From Jerusalem to Cyprus. Trade Cloth. Ashgate Publishing, Ltd. Aldershot, 1999. 364p. Variorum Collected Studies, Vol. 653 ISBN:0-86078-792-3, ISBN13: 978-0-86078-792-1. Dewey:956/.014. LCCN:99-072354.
Audience: **u,f.**

Hamilton, Bernard **D184.4 .H36 2000**
The Leper King and his Heirs: Baldwin IV and the Crusader Kingdom of Jerusalem. Trade Paper. Cambridge University Press. New York, NY. 2005. 314p. ISBN:0-521-01747-5, ISBN13: 978-0-521-01747-3. Dewey:956.944203092.
Audience: **u,f.**

Holt, P. M. **DS38.6**
The Age of the Crusades: The Near East from 11th C-1517. Paper Text. Longman Publishing. Boston, MA. 1989. 250p. History of the Near East Ser. ISBN:0-582-49302-1, ISBN13: 978-0-582-49302-5. Dewey:956/.01. LCCN:84-027801.
Audience: **l,u,f.**

Holt, P. M. **D157**
The Crusader States and their Neighbours: 1098-1291. Trade Paper. Longman Publishing. Boston, MA. 2004. 120p. ISBN:0-582-36931-2, ISBN13: 978-0-582-36931-3. Dewey:909/.07.
Audience: **u,f.**

LaMonte, J. L. **D182.L3**
Feudal Monarchy in the Latin Kingdom of Jerusalem, 1100-1291. Trade Cloth. Periodicals Service Company. Germantown, NY. 1932. Mediaeval Academy of America Publications, Vol. 11 ISBN:0-527-01685-3, ISBN13: 978-0-527-01685-2. Dewey:956.9.
Audience: **u,f.**

Phillips, Johnthan P. **D183.P45 1996**
Defenders of the Holy Land: Relations Between the Latin East and the West, 1119-1187. Trade Cloth. Oxford University Press, Inc. New York, NY. 1996. 326p. ISBN:0-19-820540-6, ISBN13: 978-0-19-820540-1. Dewey:909.07. LCCN:95-043444.
Audience: **u,f.** *Choice, 1997.*

Riley-Smith, Jonathan **D183**
The Feudal Nobility and the Kingdom of Jerusalem, 1174-1277. Trade Cloth. Shoe String Press, Inc. North Haven, CT. 1973. xiv, 351p. ISBN:0-208-01348-2, ISBN13: 978-0-208-01348-4. Dewey:321.3/095694/4. LCCN:73-000526.
Audience: **u,f.**

Tibble, Steven **D183.T53 1989**
Monarchy and Lordships in the Latin Kingdom of Jerusalem, 1099-1291. Trade Cloth. Oxford University Press, Inc. New York, NY. 1990. 224p. ISBN:0-19-822731-0, ISBN13: 978-0-19-822731-1. Dewey:956.94/4203. LCCN:89-023093.
Audience: **u,f.**

General History > By period > Medieval History (476-1453) > Islamic World and Europe. Islamic Spain. Spanish Reconquista

Abulafia, David **HF3750.7.A543 2000**
Mediterranean Encounters, Economic, Religious, Political, 1100-1550. Trade Cloth. Ashgate Publishing, Ltd. Aldershot, 2000. 370p. Variorum Collected Studies, No. 694 ISBN:0-86078-841-5, ISBN13: 978-0-86078-841-6. Dewey:382/.09182/2. LCCN:00-061793.
Audience: **u,f.**

Baer, Yitzhak **DS135.S7B343 1992**
A History of the Jews in Christian Spain, Vol. I. Louis Schoffman (Translator), Benjamin Gampel (Introduction by). Paper Text. Jewish Publication Society. Dulles, VA. 1993. 470p. ISBN:0-8276-0425-4, ISBN13: 978-0-8276-0425-4. Dewey:946/.004924. LCCN:61-016852.
Audience: **u,f.**

Barton, Simon & Fletcher, Richard (Editors) **DP99**
The World of el Cid: Chronicles of the Spanish Reconquest. Trade Paper. Manchester University Press. Manchester, 2001. 304p. Manchester Medieval Sources Ser. ISBN:0-7190-5226-2, ISBN13: 978-0-7190-5226-2. Dewey:946/.02.
Audience: **u,f.**

Burns, Robert Ignatius **DP0302.V205D**
Foundations of Crusader Valencia: Revolt and Recovery, 1257-1263. Trade Paper. Books on Demand. Ann Arbor, MI. 1991. 456p. Diplomatarium Regni Valentiae = Diplomatarium of the Crusader Kingdom of Valencia; 2 Ser., Vol. 2 ISBN:0-608-07178-1, ISBN13: 978-0-608-07178-7. Dewey:946/.76302. LCCN:90-008837.
Audience: **u,f.**

Chejne, Anwar G. **DP0103.C46**
Muslim Spain, Its History and Culture. Trade Paper. Books on Demand. Ann Arbor, MI. 587p. ISBN:0-608-15949-2, ISBN13: 978-0-608-15949-2. Dewey:946/.02. LCCN:73-087254.
Audience: **l,u.**

Collins, Roger **DP96.C649 1995**
Early Medieval Spain: Unity in Diversity, 400-1000. Ed. 2. Trade Paper. Palgrave Macmillan. New York, NY. 1995. 344p. New Studies in Medieval History ISBN:0-312-12662-X, ISBN13: 978-0-312-12662-9. Dewey:946/.01. LCCN:95-004155.
Audience: **g,l,u,f.**

Constable, Olivia Remie **HF3685.C66 1996**
Trade and Traders in Muslim Spain: The Commercial Realignment of the Iberian Peninsula, 900-1500. Christine Carpenter, Rosamond McKitterick & Jonathan Shepard (Contribution by). Trade Paper. Cambridge University Press. New York, NY. 1996. 348p. Studies in Medieval Life and Thought, No. 24 ISBN:0-521-56503-0, ISBN13: 978-0-521-56503-5. Dewey:382/.0946.
Audience: **u,f.**

Glick, Thomas F. **DP99.G47 2005**
Islam and Christian Spain. Ed. 2. Cloth Text. Brill Academic Publishers. Leiden, 2005. xxii, 402p. The Medieval and Early Modern Iberian World Ser., Vol. 27 ISBN:90-04-14771-3, ISBN13: 978-90-04-14771-3. Dewey:946/.02. LCCN:2005-016467.
Audience: **u,f.**

James I of Aragon **DP0129.J2**
The Chronicle of James I, King of Aragon, Surnamed the Conqueror, (Written by Himself). with an Historical Introduction, Notes, Appendix, Glossary, and General Index, by Pascual de Gayangos, Vol. 2. John Forster (Translator). Trade Paper. Books on Demand. Ann Arbor, MI. 330p. ISBN:0-598-01362-8, ISBN13: 978-0-598-01362-0. Dewey:946.5502.
Audience: **u,f.**

Kamen, Henry **DP161.K35 2005**
Spain, 1469-1714: A Society of Conflict. Ed. 3. Trade Paper. Longman Publishing Group. White Plains, NY. 2005. 368p. ISBN:0-582-78464-6, ISBN13: 978-0-582-78464-2. Dewey:946. LCCN:2005-045833.
Audience: **g,l,u,f.**

Kennedy, Hugh **DP102.K46 1996**
Muslim Spain and Portugal: A Political History of Al-Andalus. Trade Paper. Longman Publishing Group. White Plains, NY. 1997. 360p. ISBN:0-582-49515-6, ISBN13: 978-0-582-49515-9. Dewey:946/.02. LCCN:96-022764.
Audience: **g,l,u,f.** *Choice, 1997.*

Lomax, Derek W. **DP99.L69**
The Reconquest of Spain. Trade Cloth. Longman Publishing Group. White Plains, NY. 1978. xii, 212p. ISBN:0-582-50209-8, ISBN13: 978-0-582-50209-3. Dewey:946/.02. LCCN:77-003030.
Audience: **l,u.** B

Menéndez Pidal, Ramón **DP0099.M43**
The Cid and His Spain. Harold Sunderland (Translator). Trade Paper. Books on Demand. Ann Arbor, MI. 576p. ISBN:0-598-54833-5, ISBN13: 978-0-598-54833-7. Dewey:946.02. LCCN:35-005208.
Audience: **u,f.**

O'Callaghan, Joseph F. **DP140.3.O25 1993**
The Learned King: The Reign of Alfonso X of Castile. Trade Cloth. University of Pennsylvania Press. Philadelphia, PA. 1993. 408p. Middle Ages Ser. ISBN:0-8122-3226-7, ISBN13: 978-0-8122-3226-4. Dewey:946/.02/092. LCCN:93-013417.
Audience: **u,f.** *Choice, 1994.*

O'Callaghan, Joseph F. **DP99.O33 2002**
Reconquest and Crusade in Medieval Spain. Trade Cloth. University of Pennsylvania Press. Philadelphia, PA. 2002. 344p. The Middle Ages Ser. ISBN:0-8122-3696-3, ISBN13: 978-0-8122-3696-5. Dewey:946/.02. LCCN:2002-028952.
Audience: **u,f.** *Choice, 2003.*

Reilly, Bernard F. **DP0137.6.R44**
The Kingdom of Leon-Castilla under King Alfonso VI, 1065-1109. Trade Paper. Books on Demand. Ann Arbor, MI. 1988. 427p. ISBN:0-608-01601-2, ISBN13: 978-0-608-01601-6. Dewey:946/.202. LCCN:87-003502.
Audience: **u,f.** *Choice, 1989.*

Reilly, Bernard F. **DP138.3.R45 1998**
Kingdom of Leon-Castilla under King Alfonso VII, 1126-1157. Trade Cloth. University of Pennsylvania Press. Philadelphia, PA. 1998. 416p. Middle Ages Ser. ISBN:0-8122-3452-9, ISBN13: 978-0-8122-3452-7. Dewey:946/.202. LCCN:98-006677.
Audience: **u,f.** *Choice, 1999.*

Reilly, Bernard F. **DP99 .R375 1993**
The Medieval Spains. Cloth Text. Cambridge University Press. New York, NY. 1993. 240p. Cambridge Medieval Textbooks ISBN:0-521-39436-8, ISBN13: 978-0-521-39436-9. Dewey:946.02. LCCN:92-023379.
Audience: **g,l,u,f.**

Roth, Norman **DS135.S7R68 1994**
Jews, Visigoths, and Muslims in Medieval Spain: Cooperation and Conflict. Trade Cloth. Brill Academic Publishers, Inc. Boston, MA. 1994. 367p. Medieval Iberian Peninsula Ser., Vol. 10:Texts and Studies ISBN:90-04-09971-9, ISBN13: 978-90-04-09971-5. Dewey:946/.004924. LCCN:94-018401.
Audience: **u,f.** *Choice, 1995.*

Watt, W. Montgomery **D199.3 .I8**
Islamic Philosophy and Theology. Paper Text. Textbook Publishers. Temecula, CA. 2003. xxiii, 196p. ISBN:0-7581-1360-9, ISBN13: 978-0-7581-1360-3. Dewey:181.947.
Audience: **g,l,u.**

General History > By period > Medieval History (476-1453) > Early Middle Ages

Bede **BR749**
Ecclesiastical History of the English People. Leo Sherley-Price (Translator), D. H. Farmer (Introduction by, Notes by), Ronald E. Latham (Revised by). Trade Paper. Penguin Group (USA) Inc. New York, NY. 1991. 400p. Penguin Classics Ser. ISBN:0-14-044565-X, ISBN13: 978-0-14-044565-7. Dewey:274.2.
Audience: **l,u.**

Boethius, Ancius **B659**
The Consolation of Philosophy. P. G. Walsh (Editor). Trade Paper. Oxford University Press, Inc. New York, NY. 2000. 240p. Oxford World's Classics Ser. ISBN:0-19-283883-0, ISBN13: 978-0-19-283883-4. Dewey:100. LCCN:98-030457.
Audience: **l,u,f.**

Cantor, Norman F. **CB351**
Civilization of the Middle Ages. Trade Paper. HarperCollins Publishers. New York, NY. 1994. 624p. ISBN:0-06-092553-1, ISBN13: 978-0-06-092553-6. Dewey:940.1. LCCN:92-056237.
Audience: **g,l.**

Dawson, Christopher **CB353.D3 2002**
The Making of Europe: An Introduction to the History of European Unity. Trade Paper. Catholic University of America Press. Washington, DC. 2002. 282p. ISBN:0-8132-1083-6, ISBN13: 978-0-8132-1083-4. Dewey:940.1. LCCN:2002-007079.
Audience: **g,l,u,f.** B

de Brakelond, Jocelin **BX2596.B78.J6**
Chronicle of the Abbey of Bury St. Edmunds. Diana Greenway & Jane Sayers (Translator, Introduction by, Notes by). Trade Paper. Oxford University Press, Inc. New York, NY. 1998. 182p. Oxford World's Classics Ser. ISBN:0-19-283895-4, ISBN13: 978-0-19-283895-7. Dewey:271/.1042644. LCCN:99-186649.
Audience: **u,f.**

Easton, Stewart C. & Wieruszowski, Helene **DC73.E2 1979**
The Era of Charlemagne: Frankish State and Society. Trade Paper. Krieger Publishing Company. Melbourne, FL. 1979. 192p. Anvil Ser. ISBN:0-88275-905-1, ISBN13: 978-0-88275-905-0. Dewey:944/.01. LCCN:79-004518.
Audience: **l,u,f.**

Einhard **DC0073.32.G7**
Early Lives of Charlemagne. A. J. Grant (Editor). Trade Paper. Books on Demand. Ann Arbor, MI. 208p. ISBN:0-598-90818-8, ISBN13: 978-0-598-90818-6. Dewey:944/.01092 B. LCCN:22-019805.
Audience: **g,l,u,f.**

Fouracre, Paul (Editor) **D117**
The New Cambridge Medieval History, Set. Rosamond McKitterick (Editor, Contribution by), Timothy Reuter, David Luscombe & Jonathan Riley-Smith (Editors), David Abulafia (Editor, Contribution by), Michael Jones & Christopher Allmand (Editors), Martin Brett, Edward Powell, Simon Keynes, Jonathan Shepard, Peter Linehan & Peter Spufford (Contribution by). Quantity Pack, Trade Cloth. Cambridge University Press. New York, NY. 2005. 8186p. The New Cambridge Medieval History Ser. ISBN:0-521-85360-5, ISBN13: 978-0-521-85360-6. Dewey:909.07. LCCN:93-039643.
Audience: **g,l,u,f.**

Gregory of Tours **DC64.G8P46 2005**
A History of the Franks. Lewis Thorpe (Translator, Introduction by). Trade Paper. Penguin Group (USA) Inc. New York, NY. 1976. 720p. Classics Ser. ISBN:0-14-044295-2, ISBN13: 978-0-14-044295-3. Dewey:944.01. LCCN:75-311930.
Audience: **g,l,u,f.**

Lawrence, C. H. **BX2470.L39 2001**
Medieval Monasticism: Forms of Religious Life in Western Europe in the Middle Ages. Ed. 3. Trade Paper. Longman Publishing. Boston, MA. 2000. 336p. ISBN:0-582-40427-4, ISBN13: 978-0-582-40427-4. Dewey:271/.0094/0902. LCCN:2001-268236.
Audience: **g,l,u,f.**

McCormick, Michael **HF3495.M333 2001**
Origins of the European Economy: Communications and Commerce AD 300-900. Trade Cloth. Cambridge University Press. New York, NY. 2002. 1130p. ISBN:0-521-66102-1, ISBN13: 978-0-521-66102-7. Dewey:380/.094. LCCN:00-064142.
Audience: **l,u.** *Choice, 2003, 2002.*

Moss, Henry S. **D121.M6 1980**
The Birth of the Middle Ages, 395-814. Trade Cloth. Greenwood Publishing Group, Inc. Portsmouth, NH. 1980. 291p. ISBN:0-313-22708-X, ISBN13: 978-0-313-22708-0. Dewey:940.1/2. LCCN:80-024038.
Audience: **u,f.**

Ostrogorsky, George **DF552.5.O8153**
History of the Byzantine State. Paper Text. Rutgers University Press. Piscataway, NJ. 1986. 624p. ISBN:0-8135-1198-4, ISBN13: 978-0-8135-1198-6. Dewey:949.5.
Audience: **u,f.** B

Painter, Sidney **CB351 .P3**
Medieval Society. Book, Other. Cornell University Press. Ithaca, NY. 1951. 109p. ISBN:0-8014-9850-3, ISBN13: 978-0-8014-9850-3. Dewey:940.1.
Audience: **l,u.** B

Pamphili, Eusebius **BR60.F3**
Ecclesiastical History, Bks. 6-10. Ray J. Deferrari (Translator). Trade Cloth. Catholic University of America Press. Washington, DC. 1955. 325p. Fathers of the Church Ser., Vol. 29 ISBN:0-8132-0029-6, ISBN13: 978-0-8132-0029-3. Dewey:281.1. LCCN:65-027501.
Audience: **u,f.**

Pirenne, Henri **JS61**
Medieval Cities: Their Origins and the Revival of Trade. Frank D. Halsey (Translator). Trade Cloth. Princeton University Press. Princeton, NJ. 1969. 253p. ISBN:0-691-00760-8, ISBN13: 978-0-691-00760-1. Dewey:913.
Audience: **u,f.**

Procopius **DF72**
History of the Wars. Secret History. Trade Cloth. Harvard University Press. Cambridge, MA. Loeb Classical Library, Nos. 48, 81, 107, 173, 217, 290, 343 ISBN:0-318-53074-0, ISBN13: 978-0-318-53074-1. Dewey:949.5.
Audience: **g,l,u,f.**

Tacitus, Cornelius **PA6707.G4R58 1999**
Germania. James Rives (Translator, Introduction by, Commentaries by). Paper Text. Oxford University Press, Inc. New York, NY. 1999. 360p. Clarendon Ancient History Ser. ISBN:0-19-924000-0, ISBN13: 978-0-19-924000-5. Dewey:936.3. LCCN:98-052883.
Audience: **l,u.**

Vasiliev, Alexander A. **DF552.V3**
History of the Byzantine Empire, 324-1453. Ed. 2. Trade Paper. University of Wisconsin Press. Chicago, IL. 1958. 382p. History of the Byzantine Empire, 324-1453 Ser., Vol. 1 ISBN:0-299-80925-0, ISBN13: 978-0-299-80925-6. Dewey:949.5.
Audience: **u,f.**

Wallace-Hadrill, J. M. **D121.W32 1996**
The Barbarian West: 400-1000. Ed. 4. Trade Paper. Blackwell Publishing, Inc. Malden, MA. 1996. 184p. ISBN:0-631-20292-7, ISBN13: 978-0-631-20292-9. Dewey:940.1. LCCN:96-030693.
Audience: **u,f.**

Wood, Ian **DC65 .W48 1994**
The Merovingian Kingdoms, 450-751. Trade Paper. Longman Publishing Group. White Plains, NY. 1995. 408p. ISBN:0-582-49372-2, ISBN13: 978-0-582-49372-8. Dewey:944.01. LCCN:92-046027.
Audience: **u,f.**

General History > By period > Medieval History (476-1453) > High Middle Ages

Artz, Frederick B. **CB351.A56 1980**
The Mind of the Middle Ages: An Historical Survey. Ed. 3. Trade Paper. University of Chicago Press. Chicago, IL. 1980. 600p. ISBN:0-226-02840-2, ISBN13: 978-0-226-02840-8. Dewey:909.07. LCCN:79-016259.
Audience: **l,f.**

Barber, Malcolm **CB351.B239 2004**
Two Cities: Medieval Europe, 1050-1320. Ed. 2. Paper over Boards. Routledge. New York, NY. 2004. 560p. ISBN:0-415-17414-7, ISBN13: 978-0-415-17414-5. Dewey:940.1/7. LCCN:2003-019889.
Audience: **l,u.**

Barraclough, Geoffrey **DD89.B27 1984**
The Origins of Modern Germany. Trade Paper. W. W. Norton & Company, Inc. New York, NY. 1984. 504p. ISBN:0-393-30153-2, ISBN13: 978-0-393-30153-3. Dewey:943. LCCN:84-001624.
Audience: **g,l,u,f.**

Bartlett, Robert Merrill **D200**
The Making of Europe: Conquest, Colonization, and Cultural Change, 9500-1350. Trade Paper. Princeton University Press. Princeton, NJ. 1994. 447p. ISBN:0-691-03780-9, ISBN13: 978-0-691-03780-6. Dewey:940.1.
Audience: **l,u.**

Bloch, Marc **D131.B513**
Feudal Society, Vol. 2. L. A. Manyon (Translator). Trade Paper. University of Chicago Press. Chicago, IL. 1964. 229p. ISBN:0-226-05979-0, ISBN13: 978-0-226-05979-2. Dewey:940.14. LCCN:61-004322.
Audience: **l,u,f.**

Bloch, Marc **D131.B513 1961**
Feudal Society, Vol. 1. L. A. Manyon (Translator). Trade Paper. University of Chicago Press. Chicago, IL. 1964. 287p. ISBN:0-226-05978-2, ISBN13: 978-0-226-05978-5. Dewey:940.14. LCCN:61-004322.
Audience: **l,u.**

Boissonnade, P. **HD4847.B63 2002**
Life and Work in Medieval Europe. Trade Paper. Dover Publications, Inc. Mineola, NY. 2002. 416p. ISBN:0-486-41987-8, ISBN13: 978-0-486-41987-9. Dewey:305.5620940902. LCCN:2001-042346.
Audience: **l,u.**

Cohen, Mark R. **DS118**
Under Crescent and Cross: The Jews in the Middle Ages. Trade Paper. Princeton University Press. Princeton, NJ. 1995. 302p. ISBN:0-691-01082-X, ISBN13: 978-0-691-01082-3. Dewey:909/.04924.
Audience: **l,u,f.** *Choice, 1994.*

Davis, William Stearns **CB355 .D3**
Life on a Mediaeval Barony: A Picture of a Typical Feudal Community in the Thirteenth Century. Trade Paper. University Press of the Pacific. Miami, FL. 2004. 448p. ISBN:1-4102-1918-6, ISBN13: 978-1-4102-1918-3. Dewey:940.14.
Audience: **u,f.**

Duby, Georges **DC33.2**
France in the Middle Ages, 987-1460: From Hugh Capet to Joan of Arc. Juliet Vale (Translator). Trade Paper. Blackwell Publishing, Inc. Malden, MA. 1993. 360p. History of France Ser. ISBN:0-631-18945-9, ISBN13: 978-0-631-18945-9. Dewey:944/.02. LCCN:91-007753.
Audience: **g,l,u,f.** *Choice, 1992.*

Ganshof, F. L. **JC111.G3213 1996**
Feudalism. Ed. 3. Trade Paper. University of Toronto Press. Toronto, ON. 1996. 176p. Medieval Academy Reprints for Teaching Ser., No. 34 ISBN:0-8020-7158-9, ISBN13: 978-0-8020-7158-3. Dewey:321/.3. LCCN:96-164675.
Audience: **g,l,u,f.**

Haskins, Charles H. **PA8035**
The Renaissance of the Twelfth Century. Trade Paper. Harvard University Press. Cambridge, MA. 1927. 439p.

ISBN:0-674-76075-1, ISBN13: 978-0-674-76075-2. Dewey:879.09.
Audience: **u,f.**

Holt, J. C. **JN147.H642 1985**
Magna Carta and Medieval Government. Trade Cloth. Continuum International Publishing Group, Ltd. London, 2003. 328p. ISBN:0-907628-38-9, ISBN13: 978-0-907628-38-5. Dewey:942.03/3. LCCN:85-005542.
Audience: **u,f.**

Lynch, Joseph H. **BR252.L96 1992**
The Medieval Church: A Brief History. Trade Paper. Longman Publishing. Boston, MA. 1995. 400p. ISBN:0-582-49467-2, ISBN13: 978-0-582-49467-1. Dewey:270.094. LCCN:91-045261.
Audience: **l,u,f.**

McLaughlin, Mary Martin **BX4655.2**
The Letters of Heloise and Abelard: A Translation of Their Complete Correspondence. Trade Cloth. Palgrave Macmillan. New York, NY. 2003. 400p. ISBN:0-312-22935-6, ISBN13: 978-0-312-22935-1. Dewey:282.0922.
Audience: **u,f.**

Moore, R. I. **D201.M66 2000**
The First European Revolution: 970-1215. Trade Paper. Blackwell Publishing, Inc. Malden, MA. 2000. 256p. The Making of Europe Ser. ISBN:0-631-22277-4, ISBN13: 978-0-631-22277-4. Dewey:943/.02. LCCN:00-031022.
Audience: **g,l,u,f.** *Choice, 2001.*

Prestwich, Michael **DA60.P74 1996**
Armies and Warfare in the Middle Ages: The English Experience. Cloth over Boards. Yale University Press. Cumberland, RI. 1996. 406p. ISBN:0-300-06452-7, ISBN13: 978-0-300-06452-0. Dewey:355.3/0942/0902. LCCN:95-036142.
Audience: **g,l,u,f.** *Choice, 1996.*

Reynolds, Susan **D117**
Fiefs and Vassals: The Medieval Evidence Reinterpreted. Paper Text. Oxford University Press, Inc. New York, NY. 1996. 560p. ISBN:0-19-820648-8, ISBN13: 978-0-19-820648-4. Dewey:321.3/0902.
Audience: **u,f.** *Choice, 1995.*

Southern, R. W. **CB351**
The Making of the Middle Ages. Paper Text. Textbook Publishers. Temecula, CA. 2003. 280p. ISBN:0-7581-0032-9, ISBN13: 978-0-7581-0032-0. Dewey:940.1.
Audience: **g,l,u,f.** B

Stephenson, Carl **D131**
Mediaeval Feudalism. Julia E. Edmondson (Illustrator). Trade Paper. Cornell University Press. Ithaca, NY. 1956. 127p. ISBN:0-8014-9013-8, ISBN13: 978-0-8014-9013-2. Dewey:321.3.
Audience: **l,u.** B

Strayer, Joseph R. **JN7.S7 2005**
On the Medieval Origins of the Modern State. Ed. 2. William Chester Jordan & Charles Tilly (Foreword by). Trade Paper. Princeton University Press. Princeton, NJ. 2005. 136p. Princeton Classic Editions Ser. ISBN:0-691-12185-0, ISBN13: 978-0-691-12185-7. Dewey:320.1/1/094. LCCN:2005-043957.
Audience: **l,u,f.**

Tierney, Brian **BX1790**
The Crisis of Church and State 1050-1300. Trade Paper. University of Toronto Press. Toronto, ON. 1988. 210p. Medieval Academy Reprints for Teaching Ser., Vol. 21 ISBN:0-8020-6701-8, ISBN13: 978-0-8020-6701-2. Dewey:261.709021. LCCN:89-124004.
Audience: **u,f.**

Tierney, Brian **D113.M49 1999**
The Middle Ages: Readings in Medieval History. Ed. 5. Paper Text. McGraw-Hill Higher Education. Burr Ridge, IL. 1998. 360p. ISBN:0-07-303290-5, ISBN13: 978-0-07-303290-0. Dewey:909.07. LCCN:98-016808.
Audience: **l,u.**

Tierney, Brian **D113.M49 1999**
The Middle Ages: Sources of Medieval History. Ed. 6. Paper Text. McGraw-Hill Higher Education. Burr Ridge, IL. 1998. 384p. ISBN:0-07-303289-1, ISBN13: 978-0-07-303289-4. Dewey:909.07. LCCN:98-016808.
Audience: **l,u.**

White, Lynn Jr. **CB353**
Medieval Technology and Social Change. Paper Text. Oxford University Press, Inc. New York, NY. 1966. 216p. ISBN:0-19-500266-0, ISBN13: 978-0-19-500266-9. Dewey:901.92.
Audience: **l,u,f.**

General History > By period > Medieval History (476-1453) > Late Middle Ages

Allen, Mark & Fisher, John H. **PR9275.A583**
The Complete Canterbury Tales of Geoffrey Chaucer. Paper Text. Thomson Wadsworth. Belmont, CA. 2005. 528p. ISBN:0-8384-5708-8, ISBN13: 978-0-8384-5708-5. Dewey:813.
Audience: **g,l,u,f.**

Allmand, Christopher **DC96.A44 1988**
The Hundred Years War: England and France at War c.1300 - c.1450. Trade Paper. Cambridge University Press. New York, NY. 1988. 224p. Cambridge Medieval Textbooks ISBN:0-521-31923-4, ISBN13: 978-0-521-31923-2. Dewey:944/.025. LCCN:87-013251.
Audience: **g,l,u,f.**

Bean, J.M.W. **JN141**
From Lord to Patron: Lordship in Late Medieval England. Trade Cloth. Manchester University Press. Manchester, 1989. xii, 279p. ISBN:0-7190-2855-8, ISBN13: 978-0-7190-2855-7. Dewey:321.3/0942. LCCN:89-004777.
Audience: **l,u,f.**

Bennett, Judith M. & Hollister, C. Warren **D118.H624 2002**
Medieval Europe: A Short History. Ed. 9. Paper Text. McGraw-Hill Higher Education. Burr Ridge, IL. 2001. 456p. ISBN:0-07-234657-4, ISBN13: 978-0-07-234657-2. Dewey:940.1. LCCN:2001-044875.
Audience: **g,l,u.**

Byrne, Joseph Patrick **RC172**
The Black Death. Cloth Text. Greenwood Publishing Group, Inc. Portsmouth, NH. 2004. 272p. Greenwood Guides to Historic Events of the Medieval World Ser.

ISBN:0-313-32492-1, ISBN13: 978-0-313-32492-5. Dewey:614.5/732. LCCN:2004-043640.
Audience: **l,u.** *Choice, 2005.*

Dante Alighieri **NC248.P5**
Inferno, Esolen Translation. Anthony Esolen (Translator). Trade Paper. Ballantine Books. New York, NY. 2005. 560p. ISBN:0-345-48357-X, ISBN13: 978-0-345-48357-7.
Audience: **g,l,u,f.**

Froissart, Jean **D113.F75**
The Chronicles of Froissart. Trade Paper. Kessinger Publishing, LLC. Whitefish, MT. 2004. ISBN:1-4191-5672-1, ISBN13: 978-1-4191-5672-4. Dewey:940.1.
Audience: **u,f.**

Giovanni, Boccaccio **PQ4272.S5**
Decameron. Trade Paper. Lectorum, S.A. de C.V.. Coyoacan, D.F., 2005. 174p. ISBN:970-732-072-9, ISBN13: 978-970-732-072-7. Dewey:853/.1.
Audience: **g,l,u,f.**

Hamilton, Bernard **BX1712.H26 1981**
Medieval Inquisition. Paper Text. Holmes & Meier Publishers, Inc. Teaneck, NJ. 1981. 111p. ISBN:0-8419-0695-5, ISBN13: 978-0-8419-0695-2. Dewey:272/.2. LCCN:80-027997.
Audience: **g,l,u.**

Holmes, George **DA175 .H58**
The Later Middle Ages, 1272-1485. Paper Text. Textbook Publishers. Temecula, CA. 2003. 276p. ISBN:0-7581-3296-4, ISBN13: 978-0-7581-3296-3. Dewey:914.2/03/3.
Audience: **l,u.**

Horrox, Rosemary (Translator) **RC178.A1B58 1994**
The Black Death. Trade Paper. Manchester University Press. Manchester, 1994. 384p. Manchester Medieval Sources Ser., Vol. 1 ISBN:0-7190-3498-1, ISBN13: 978-0-7190-3498-5. Dewey:614.4/94. LCCN:93-050558.
Audience: **g,l,u,f.** *Choice, 1995.*

Itzkowitz, Norman **DR486.I89 1980**
Ottoman Empire and Islamic Tradition. Trade Paper. University of Chicago Press. Chicago, IL. 1980. 128p. Phoenix Book Ser. ISBN:0-226-38806-9, ISBN13: 978-0-226-38806-9. Dewey:956.1/01. LCCN:79-023386.
Audience: **l,u,f.** *B*

Jordan, William C. **RC178.A1**
The Great Famine: Northern Europe in the Early Fourteenth Century. Trade Paper. Princeton University Press. Princeton, NJ. 1997. 328p. ISBN:0-691-05891-1, ISBN13: 978-0-691-05891-7. Dewey:940.1/92.
Audience: **u,f.** *Choice, 1996.*

Kaeuper, Richard W. **DA225.K34 1988**
War, Justice, and Public Order: England and France in the Later Middle Ages. Trade Cloth. Oxford University Press, Inc. New York, NY. 1988. 462p. ISBN:0-19-822873-2, ISBN13: 978-0-19-822873-8. Dewey:942.03. LCCN:87-020409.
Audience: **u,f.** *Choice, 1989.*

Kantorowicz, Ernst H. **JC375**
The King's Two Bodies: A Study in Mediaeval Political Theology. Trade Paper. Princeton University Press. Princeton, NJ. 1997. 592p. ISBN:0-691-01704-2, ISBN13: 978-0-691-01704-4. Dewey:321.60940902. LCCN:57-005448.
Audience: **u,f.**

Lambert, Malcolm **BT1319.L35 2002**
Medieval Heresy: Popular Movements from the Gregorian Reform to the Reformation. Ed. 3. Trade Paper. Blackwell Publishing, Inc. Malden, MA. 2002. 504p. ISBN:0-631-22276-6, ISBN13: 978-0-631-22276-7. Dewey:273/.6. LCCN:2001-043102.
Audience: **u,f.**

Lopez, Robert S. & Raymond, Irving W. (Translators) **HF395**
Medieval Trade in the Mediterranean World: Illustrative Documents. Ed. 2. Olivia Remie Constable (Foreword by). Trade Paper. Columbia University Press. New York, NY. 2001. 496p. Records of Western Civilization Ser. ISBN:0-231-12357-4, ISBN13: 978-0-231-12357-0. Dewey:382/.09182/2. LCCN:2002-278336.
Audience: **u,f.**

Lucas, Henry S. **CB359**
The Renaissance and the Reformation. Trade Cloth. A M S Press, Inc. New York, NY. ISBN:0-404-19815-5, ISBN13: 978-0-404-19815-2. Dewey:901.93. LCCN:83-045665.
Audience: **l,u.**

Oman, Charles William Chadwick **U37.O6 1998**
A History of the Art of War in the Middle Ages. Trade Paper. Greenhill Books/Lionel Leventhal, Ltd. London, 1998. 502p. Greenhill Military Paperbacks Ser. ISBN:1-85367-332-3, ISBN13: 978-1-85367-332-0. Dewey:355/.0094/0902. LCCN:98-004145.
Audience: **g,l,u,f.**

Ozment, Steven **BR270**
The Age of Reform, 1250-1550: An Intellectual and Religious History of Late Medieval and Reformation Europe. Trade Paper. Yale University Press. Cumberland, RI. 1981. 458p. ISBN:0-300-02760-5, ISBN13: 978-0-300-02760-0. Dewey:274. LCCN:79-024162.
Audience: **u,f.** *B*

Phillips, J. R. **G89.P48 1998**
The Medieval Expansion of Europe. Ed. 2. Trade Paper. Oxford University Press, Inc. New York, NY. 1998. 342p. ISBN:0-19-820740-9, ISBN13: 978-0-19-820740-5. Dewey:910/.9. LCCN:99-179710.
Audience: **l,u.** *Choice, 1989.*

Pirenne, Henri **HC41**
Economic and Social History of Medieval Europe. I. E. Clegg (Translator). Trade Paper. Harcourt Trade Publishers. New York, NY. 1956. 252p. ISBN:0-15-627533-3, ISBN13: 978-0-15-627533-0. Dewey:330.9. LCCN:37-028587.
Audience: **g,l,u,f.**

Strayer, Joseph R. **JN7.S7 2005**
On the Medieval Origins of the Modern State. Ed. 2. William Chester Jordan & Charles Tilly (Foreword by). Trade Paper. Princeton University Press. Princeton, NJ. 2005. 136p. Princeton Classic Editions Ser. ISBN:0-691-12185-0, ISBN13: 978-0-691-12185-7. Dewey:320.1/1/094. LCCN:2005-043957.
Audience: **l,u,f.**

Ullmann, Walter **BX1301.U55**
The Origins of the Great Schism: A Study in the Fourteenth-Century Ecclesiastical History. Trade Paper. Books on Demand. Ann Arbor, MI. 268p. ISBN:0-598-80888-4, ISBN13: 978-0-598-80888-2. Dewey:270.5. LCCN:49-002953.
Audience: **u,f.**

Waley, Daniel Philip & Denley, Peter **D202.W3 2001**
Later Medieval Europe: 1250-1520. Ed. 3. Trade Paper. Longman Publishing. Boston, MA. 2001. 372p. ISBN:0-582-25831-6, ISBN13: 978-0-582-25831-0. Dewey:940.1. LCCN:2001-038457.
Audience: **g,l,u,f.**

General History > By period > Early Modern History (1453-1789)

Kamen, Henry Arthur Francis **HN373.K293 2000**
Early Modern European Society. Ed. 2. Paper over Boards. Routledge. New York, NY. 2000. 304p. ISBN:0-415-15864-8, ISBN13: 978-0-415-15864-0. Dewey:306/.094. LCCN:99-037008.
Audience: **l,u,f.** *Choice, 2000.*

Kors, Alan C. **BF1566.W739 2001**
Witchcraft in Europe, 400-1700: A Documentary History. Ed. 2. Trade Paper. University of Pennsylvania Press. Philadelphia, PA. 2000. 480p. Middle Ages Ser. ISBN:0-8122-1751-9, ISBN13: 978-0-8122-1751-3. Dewey:133.4/3/094. LCCN:00-064934.
Audience: **g,l,u,f.** *Choice, 2001.*

Musgrave, Peter **HC240.M793 1999**
The Early Modern European Economy. Trade Paper. Palgrave Macmillan. New York, NY. 1999. 248p. ISBN:0-312-22332-3, ISBN13: 978-0-312-22332-8. Dewey:330.9/4. LCCN:99-012189.
Audience: **u,f.** *Choice, 1999.*

General History > By period > Early Modern History (1453-1789) > Renaissance

Bouwsma, William J. **CB401.E94 2000**
The Waning of the Renaissance, 1550-1640. Cloth over Boards. Yale University Press. Cumberland, RI. 2001. 304p. Yale Intellectual History of the West Ser. ISBN:0-300-08537-0, ISBN13: 978-0-300-08537-2. Dewey:940.2/1. LCCN:00-049538.
Audience: **u,f.** *Choice, 2001.*

Brotton, Jerry **CB361.B75 2003**
The Renaissance Bazaar: From the Silk Road to Michelangelo. Trade Paper. Oxford University Press, Inc. New York, NY. 2003. 256p. ISBN:0-19-280265-8, ISBN13: 978-0-19-280265-1. Dewey:940.2/1.
Audience: **g,u,f.** *Choice, 2003.*

Bull, Malcolm **N7760.B85 2005**
Mirror of the Gods. Trade Cloth. Oxford University Press, Inc. New York, NY. 2005. 496p. ISBN:0-19-521923-6, ISBN13: 978-0-19-521923-4. Dewey:704.9/4892/09024. LCCN:2004-063136.
Audience: **g,u,f.** *Choice, 2005.*

Burckhardt, Jacob **DG445.B813**
The Civilization of the Renaissance in Italy. Trade Paper. BiblioBazaar. Charleston, SC. 2006. 430p. ISBN:1-4264-0093-4, ISBN13: 978-1-4264-0093-3. Dewey:945/.05.
Audience: **g,l,u,f.**

Burke, Peter (Editor) **D13 .B78**
The Renaissance Sense of the Past. Cloth Text. Palgrave Macmillan. New York, NY. 1970. Documents of Modern History Ser. ISBN:0-312-67375-2, ISBN13: 978-0-312-67375-8. Dewey:907.2/04.
Audience: **g,l,u,f.**

Chartier, Roger (Editor), et al. **CB245**
A History of Private Life: Passions of the Renaissance. Philippe Aries & Georges Duby (Editors), Arthur Goldhammer (Translator). Trade Cloth. Harvard University Press. Cambridge, MA. 1989. 655p. ISBN:0-674-39977-3, ISBN13: 978-0-674-39977-8. Dewey:909/.09821. LCCN:86-018286.
Audience: **g,l,u,f.** *Choice, 1989.*

Cohn, Sam **RC178.A1C63 2002**
The Black Death Transformed: Disease and Culture in Early Renaissance Europe. Trade Cloth. Oxford University Press, Inc. New York, NY. 2002. 320p. ISBN:0-340-70646-5, ISBN13: 978-0-340-70646-6. Dewey:362.1/9232/094. LCCN:2002-319324.
Audience: **u,f.** *Choice, 2003.*

Crosby, Alfred W. **D202 .C76 1997**
The Measure of Reality: Quantification in Western Europe, 1250-1600. Cloth Text. Cambridge University Press. New York, NY. 1996. 257p. ISBN:0-521-55427-6, ISBN13: 978-0-521-55427-5. Dewey:940. LCCN:96-003092.
Audience: **u,f.** *Choice, 1997.*

Edgerton, Samuel Y. Jr. **N7430**
The Heritage of Giotto's Geometry: Art and Science on the Eve of the Scientific Revolution. Book, Other. Cornell University Press. Ithaca, NY. 1994. 336p. ISBN:0-8014-8198-8, ISBN13: 978-0-8014-8198-7. Dewey:701/.8. LCCN:91-012301.
Audience: **u,f.** *Choice, 1992.*

Gille, Bertrand **TA18.G5413**
Engineers of the Renaissance. Trade Cloth. MIT Press. Cambridge, MA. 1966. ISBN:0-262-07022-7, ISBN13: 978-0-262-07022-5. Dewey:620.0094.
Audience: **u,f.**

Gilmore, Myron P. **D228.G48 1983**
The World of Humanism, 1453-1517. Cloth Text. Greenwood Publishing Group, Inc. Portsmouth, NH. 1983. xv, 326p. The Rise of Modern Europe Ser. ISBN:0-313-24081-7, ISBN13: 978-0-313-24081-2. Dewey:940.2. LCCN:83-010718.
Audience: **u,f.**

Hale, J. R. **U43.E95**
War and Society in Renaissance Europe, 1450-1620. Trade Paper. McGill-Queen's University Press. Montreal, PQ. 1998. 288p. War and European Society Ser. ISBN:0-7735-1765-0, ISBN13: 978-0-7735-1765-3. Dewey:355/.02/094.
Audience: **g,u,f.**

Hale, John **CB367.H35 1994**
Civilization of Europe in the Renaissance. Trade Cloth. Simon & Schuster. New York, NY. 1994. 672p. ISBN:0-689-12200-4, ISBN13: 978-0-689-12200-2. Dewey:940.21. LCCN:93-046246.
Audience: **g,l,u,f.** *Choice, 1994.*

Jardine, Lisa **CB361**
Worldly Goods: A New History of the Renaissance. Trade Paper. W. W. Norton & Company, Inc. New York, NY. 1998. 480p.

ISBN:0-393-31866-4, ISBN13: 978-0-393-31866-1. Dewey:940.2/1. LCCN:98-008710.
Audience: **g,l,u,f.**

Kristeller, Paul Oskar **B775 .K73**
Renaissance Thought and Its Sources. Michael Mooney (Editor). Trade Paper. Columbia University Press. New York, NY. 1981. 347p. ISBN:0-231-04513-1, ISBN13: 978-0-231-04513-1. Dewey:190/.9/024. LCCN:79-015521.
Audience: **u,f.**

Mattingly, Garrett **JX1641.M27 1988**
Renaissance Diplomacy. Trade Paper. Dover Publications, Inc. Mineola, NY. 1988. 284p. ISBN:0-486-25570-0, ISBN13: 978-0-486-25570-5. Dewey:327/.2/094. LCCN:87-027288.
Audience: **g,u,f.**

Porter, Roy & Teich, Mikulas (Editors) **CB361 .R387 1991**
The Renaissance in National Context. Cloth Text. Cambridge University Press. New York, NY. 1991. 249p. ISBN:0-521-36181-8, ISBN13: 978-0-521-36181-1. Dewey:940.2/1. LCCN:90-002561.
Audience: **g,l,u,f.** *Choice, 1992.*

Potter, G. R. (Editor) **D208**
The Renaissance, 1493-1520. Trade Paper. Cambridge University Press. New York, NY. 1975. 568p. The New Cambridge Modern History Ser., Vol.1 ISBN:0-521-09974-9, ISBN13: 978-0-521-09974-5. Dewey:909.
Audience: **u,f.**

Rabb, Theodore K. **D247**
The Last Days of the Renaissance: The March to Modernity. Trade Cloth. Basic Books. New York, NY. 2006. 280p. ISBN:0-465-06801-4, ISBN13: 978-0-465-06801-2. Dewey:940.2/1. LCCN:2005-030382.
Audience: **g,l,u,f.**

Rowland, Ingrid D. **DG797.8.R68 1998**
The Culture of the High Renaissance: Ancients and Moderns in Sixteenth-Century Rome. Cloth Text. Cambridge University Press. New York, NY. 1998. 446p. ISBN:0-521-58145-1, ISBN13: 978-0-521-58145-5. Dewey:945/.06. LCCN:97-029765.
Audience: **u,f.** *Choice, 1999.*

Schmitt, C. B. (Editor), et al. **B775.C25 1988**
The Cambridge History of Renaissance Philosophy. Quentin Skinner, Eckhard Kessler & Jill Kraye (Editors). Trade Cloth. Cambridge University Press. New York, NY. 1988. 922p. ISBN:0-521-25104-4, ISBN13: 978-0-521-25104-4. Dewey:190/.9/024. LCCN:87-005212.
Audience: **u,f.** *Choice, 1988.*

Schmitt, Charles B. **B485**
Aristotle and the Renaissance. Trade Cloth. Harvard University Press. Cambridge, MA. 1983. 208p. Martin Classical Lectures, No. 27 ISBN:0-674-04525-4, ISBN13: 978-0-674-04525-5. Dewey:189. LCCN:82-015388.
Audience: **u,f.**

Thomson, J. K. J. **D118.T49 1998**
Decline in History: The European Experience. Trade Cloth. Polity Press. Cambridge, 1998. 240p. Themes in History Ser. ISBN:0-7456-1424-8, ISBN13: 978-0-7456-1424-3. Dewey:909/.0982201. LCCN:98-039778.
Audience: **u,f.** *Choice, 1999.*

General History > By period > Early Modern History (1453-1789) > Age of Enlightenment

Beales, Derek **D286**
Enlightenment and Reform in Eighteenth-Century Europe. Hamish Scott (Introduction by). Cloth over Boards. I. B. Tauris & Company, Ltd. London, 2005. 256p. International Library of Historical Studies, Vol. 29 ISBN:1-86064-949-1, ISBN13: 978-1-86064-949-3. Dewey:940.2/53. LCCN:2005-298531.
Audience: **l,u.** *Choice, 2006.*

Becker, Carl L. **B802.B4 1991**
Heavenly City of the Eighteenth-Century Philosophers. Trade Paper. Yale University Press. Cumberland, RI. 1959. 192p. Storrs Lectures ISBN:0-300-00017-0, ISBN13: 978-0-300-00017-7. Dewey:190/.9/033. LCCN:91-023968.
Audience: **g,l,u,f.**

Broadie, Alexander (Editor) **B1402.E55C36 2002**
The Companion to the Scottish Enlightenment. Cloth Text. Cambridge University Press. New York, NY. 2003. 382p. Cambridge Companions to Philosophy Ser. ISBN:0-521-80273-3, ISBN13: 978-0-521-80273-4. Dewey:001/.09411/09033. LCCN:2002-067261.
Audience: **g,l,u,f.**

Burns, William E. **Q121.B87 2003**
Science in the Enlightenment: An Encyclopedia. Library Binding. ABC-CLIO, Inc. Santa Barbara, CA. 2003. 400p. ABC-CLIO's History of Science Ser. ISBN:1-57607-886-8, ISBN13: 978-1-57607-886-0. Dewey:509/.033. LCCN:2003-011342.
Audience: **g,l,u,f.** *Choice, 2004.*

Canizares-Esguerra, Jorge **F1412.C25 2001**
How to Write the History of the New World: Histories, Epistemologies, and Identities in the Eighteenth-Century Atlantic World. Trade Cloth. Stanford University Press. Palo Alto, CA. 2001. xviii, 450p. Cultural Sitings Ser. ISBN:0-8047-4084-4, ISBN13: 978-0-8047-4084-5. Dewey:980. LCCN:00-050486.
Audience: **u,f.** *Choice, 2002.*

Cassirer, Ernst **B802**
The Philosophy of the Enlightenment. James P. Pettegrove (Editor), Fritz C. A. Koelin (Translator). Trade Paper. Princeton University Press. Princeton, NJ. 1968. 384p. ISBN:0-691-01963-0, ISBN13: 978-0-691-01963-5. Dewey:190.
Audience: **u,f.**

Craveri, Benedetta **DC121.7.C73 2005**
The Age of Conversation. Teresa Waugh (Translator). Trade Cloth. New York Review of Books, Incorporated, The. New York, NY. 2005. 600p. ISBN:1-59017-141-1, ISBN13: 978-1-59017-141-7. Dewey:305.48/96/094409033. LCCN:2005-003059.
Audience: **l,u,f.** *Choice, 2006.*

Delon, Michel (Editor) **CB411**
Encyclopedia of the Enlightenment, Set. Philip Stewart (Translator). Trade Cloth. Fitzroy Dearborn Publishers, Inc. Chicago, IL. 2001. 1500p. ISBN:1-57958-246-X, ISBN13: 978-1-57958-246-3. Dewey:940.2/53.
Audience: **l,u,f.** *Choice, 2002.*

Gay, Peter **B802 .G3**
The Enlightenment: The Rise of Modern Paganism. Trade Cloth. Peter Smith Publisher, Inc. Magnolia, MA. 1996. ISBN:0-8446-6891-5, ISBN13: 978-0-8446-6891-8. Dewey:190.9033.
Audience: **g,u,f.**

Gay, Peter **B29**
The Enlightenment - An Interpretation: The Science of Freedom. Trade Paper. W. W. Norton & Company, Inc. New York, NY. 1996. 744p. Enlightenment Ser., Vol. 2 ISBN:0-393-31366-2, ISBN13: 978-0-393-31366-6. Dewey:190. LCCN:77-024671.
Audience: **g,u,f.**

Hazard, Paul **D273.5 .H32**
The European Mind, the Critical Years 1680: 1715. Paper Text. Textbook Publishers. Temecula, CA. 2003. xx, 454p. ISBN:0-7581-0078-7, ISBN13: 978-0-7581-0078-8. Dewey:914.
Audience: **u,f.**

Israel, Jonathan I. **B802**
Radical Enlightenment: Philosophy and the Making of Modernity 1650-1750. Trade Paper. Oxford University Press, Inc. New York, NY. 2002. 832p. ISBN:0-19-925456-7, ISBN13: 978-0-19-925456-9. Dewey:940.2/5.
Audience: **u,f.**

Kors, Alan Charles **B802.E53 2002**
Encyclopedia of the Enlightenment 1670-1815, Set. Trade Cloth. Oxford University Press, Inc. New York, NY. 2002. 1,874p. ISBN:0-19-510430-7, ISBN13: 978-0-19-510430-1. Dewey:940.2/5. LCCN:2002-003766.
Audience: **g,l,u,f.** *Choice, 2003.*

Kramnick, Isaac (Editor) **B802.P59 1995**
The Portable Enlightenment Reader. Trade Paper. Penguin Group (USA) Inc. New York, NY. 1995. 704p. Portable Library ISBN:0-14-024566-9, ISBN13: 978-0-14-024566-0. Dewey:940.2/5. LCCN:95-016720.
Audience: **g,l,u,f.**

Mah, Harold **B1925.E5M34 2003**
Enlightenment Phantasies: Cultural Identity in France and Germany, 1750-1914. Trade Cloth. Cornell University Press. Ithaca, NY. 2003. 232p. ISBN:0-8014-4144-7, ISBN13: 978-0-8014-4144-8. Dewey:940.2. LCCN:2003-009504.
Audience: **u,f.** *Choice, 2004.*

McMahon, Darrin M. **DC146**
Enemies of the Enlightenment: The French Counter-Enlightenment and the Making of Modernity. Trade Paper. Oxford University Press, Inc. New York, NY. 2002. 276p. ISBN:0-19-515893-8, ISBN13: 978-0-19-515893-9. Dewey:944.04.
Audience: **l,u,f.** *Choice, 2002.*

Melton, James Van Horn **D286.M44 2001**
The Rise of the Public in Enlightenment Europe. Cloth Text. Cambridge University Press. New York, NY. 2001. 298p. New Approaches to European History Ser., Vol. 22 ISBN:0-521-46573-7, ISBN13: 978-0-521-46573-1. Dewey:940.28. LCCN:2001-025456.
Audience: **l,u,f.** *Choice, 2002.*

Munck, Thomas **B802.M82 2000**
The Enlightenment: A Comparative Social History, 1721-1794. Trade Cloth. Oxford University Press, Inc. New York, NY. 2000. 264p. An Arnold Publication Ser. ISBN:0-340-66326-X, ISBN13: 978-0-340-66326-4. Dewey:940.2/53. LCCN:2001-265415.
Audience: **u,f.** *Choice, 2001.*

Munck, Thomas **B802.M82 2000**
The Enlightenment: A Comparative Social History 1721-1794. Trade Paper. Oxford University Press, Inc. New York, NY. 2000. 264p. A Hodder Arnold Publication ISBN:0-340-66325-1, ISBN13: 978-0-340-66325-7. Dewey:940.25. LCCN:2001-265415.
Audience: **u,f.** *Choice, 2001.*

Muthu, Sankar **JC359.M87 2003**
Enlightenment Against Empire. Trade Cloth. Princeton University Press. Princeton, NJ. 2003. 376p. ISBN:0-691-11516-8, ISBN13: 978-0-691-11516-0. Dewey:325/.32/01. LCCN:2002-042717.
Audience: **u,f.** *Choice, 2004.*

Outram, Dorinda **B802.O98 2005**
The Enlightenment. Ed. 2. William Beik, T. C. W. Blanning & Brendan Simms (Contribution by). Cloth Text. Cambridge University Press. New York, NY. 2005. 182p. New Approaches to European History Ser., Vol. 31 ISBN:0-521-83776-6, ISBN13: 978-0-521-83776-7. Dewey:001.1/094/09033. LCCN:2004-065043.
Audience: **l,u,f.**

Porter, Roy **B1302.E65P67 2000**
The Creation of the Modern World: The Untold Story of the British Enlightenment. Trade Cloth. W. W. Norton & Company, Inc. New York, NY. 2000. 608p. ISBN:0-393-04872-1, ISBN13: 978-0-393-04872-8. Dewey:941.07. LCCN:00-049632.
Audience: **l,u,f.** *Choice, 2001.*

Rothschild, Emma **HB83.R68 2001**
Economic Sentiments: Adam Smith, Condorcet, and the Enlightenment. Trade Cloth. Harvard University Press. Cambridge, MA. 2001. 368p. ISBN:0-674-00489-2, ISBN13: 978-0-674-00489-4. Dewey:330.15/3. LCCN:00-053943.
Audience: **u,f.** *Choice, 2001.*

Schmidt, James (Editor) **B802.W47 1996**
What Is Enlightenment?: Eighteenth-Century Answers and Twentieth-Century Questions. Trade Paper. University of California Press. Berkeley, CA. 1996. 578p. Philosophical Traditions Ser., Vol. 7 ISBN:0-520-20226-0, ISBN13: 978-0-520-20226-9. Dewey:190. LCCN:95-046975.
Audience: **l,u,f.**

Wolff, Larry **DJK13.W65 1994**
Inventing Eastern Europe: The Map of Civilization on the Mind of the Enlightenment. Trade Cloth. Stanford University Press. Palo Alto, CA. 1994. xvi, 419p. ISBN:0-8047-2314-1, ISBN13: 978-0-8047-2314-5. Dewey:306.2/0947. LCCN:93-032774.
Audience: **l,u,f.** *Choice, 1995.*

General History > By period > Early Modern History (1453-1789) > Age of Exploration

Bergreen, Laurence **G420.M2B47 2003**
Over the Edge of the World: Magellan's Terrifying Circumnavigation of the Globe. Trade Paper. HarperCollins

Publishers. New York, NY. 2004. 512p. P. S. Ser. ISBN:0-06-093638-X, ISBN13: 978-0-06-093638-9. Dewey:910/.92 B. LCCN:2003-050143.

Audience: **g,l,u,f.**

Boxer **JV4203**
Portuguese Seaborne Empire. Ed. 2. Trade Cloth. Carcanet Press, Ltd. Manchester, 456p. ISBN:0-85635-962-9, ISBN13: 978-0-85635-962-0. Dewey:325.3469.

Audience: **u,f.**

Ishikawa, Chiyo (Editor, Introduction by) **N7104.S73 2004**
Spain in the Age of Exploration, 1492-1819. Jesus Carrillo, Richard Kagan, Javier Morales, Ben Schmidt, Sarah Schroth, Andrew Schulz & Jose de la Sota (Contribution by). Trade Cloth. University of Nebraska Press. Lincoln, NE. 2005. 300p. ISBN:0-8032-2505-9, ISBN13: 978-0-8032-2505-3. Dewey:709/.46/074797772. LCCN:2004-012309.

Audience: **g,l,u,f.** *Choice, 2005.*

Kendrick, John **G286.M2**
Alejandro Malaspina: Portrait of a Visionary. Trade Cloth. McGill-Queen's University Press. Montreal, PQ. 208p. ISBN:0-7735-1830-4, ISBN13: 978-0-7735-1830-8. Dewey:910.9/2.

Audience: **g,u,f.** *Choice, 1999.*

Levenson, Jay (Editor) **CB367.C57 1991**
Circa, 1492: Art in the Age of Exploration. Cloth over Boards. Yale University Press. Cumberland, RI. 1991. 512p. ISBN:0-300-05167-0, ISBN13: 978-0-300-05167-4. Dewey:910.9. LCCN:91-050590.

Audience: **g,u,f.** *Choice, 1992.*

Parry, J. H. **G80**
The Age of Reconnaissance: Discovery, Exploration, and Settlement, 1450-1650. Trade Cloth. University of California Press. Berkeley, CA. 1982. 400p. ISBN:0-520-04235-2, ISBN13: 978-0-520-04235-3. Dewey:910/.94. LCCN:81-051175.

Audience: **g,u,f.**

Phillips, William D. Jr. & Phillips, Carla Rahn **E111.P67 1991**
The Worlds of Christopher Columbus. Cloth Text. Cambridge University Press. New York, NY. 1991. 336p. ISBN:0-521-35097-2, ISBN13: 978-0-521-35097-6. Dewey:970.01/5. LCCN:91-018790.

Audience: **g,l,u,f.** *Choice, 1992.*

Russell, Peter E. **G286.H5R879 2000**
Prince Henry "The Navigator": A Life. Cloth over Boards. Yale University Press. Cumberland, RI. 2000. 464p. ISBN:0-300-08233-9, ISBN13: 978-0-300-08233-3. Dewey:946.9/02/092 B. LCCN:99-049569.

Audience: **g,l,u,f.** *Choice, 2001.*

Smith, Roger C. **VM83.S65 1993**
Vanguard of Empire: Ships of Exploration in the Age of Columbus. Cloth Text. Oxford University Press, Inc. New York, NY. 1993. 328p. ISBN:0-19-507357-6, ISBN13: 978-0-19-507357-7. Dewey:623.8/22/094609024. LCCN:91-040929.

Audience: **u,f.** *Choice, 1993.*

Subrahmanyam, Sanjay **G286.G2S83 1997**
The Career and Legend of Vasco da Gama. Trade Paper. Cambridge University Press. New York, NY. 1998. 424p. ISBN:0-521-64629-4, ISBN13: 978-0-521-64629-1. Dewey:910.9/2.

Audience: **u,f.**

Subrahmanyam, Sanjay **DS34**
The Portuguese Empire in Asia, 1500-1700: A Political and Economic History. Trade Cloth. Addison-Wesley Longman, Ltd. Harlow, 1993. 384p. ISBN:0-582-05069-3, ISBN13: 978-0-582-05069-3. Dewey:950.3. LCCN:92-010236.

Audience: **g,l,u,f.**

General History > By period > Early Modern History (1453-1789) > European Overseas Expansion

Abernethy, David B. **D210.A19 2000**
The Dynamics of Global Dominance: European Overseas Empires, 1415-1980. Cloth over Boards. Yale University Press. Cumberland, RI. 2000. 544p. ISBN:0-300-07304-6, ISBN13: 978-0-300-07304-1. Dewey:940. LCCN:00-033472.

Audience: **g,u,f.**

Baber, Zaheer **GN635.I4**
The Science of Empire: Scientific Knowledge, Civilization, and Colonial Rule in India. Cloth Text. State University of New York Press. Albany, NY. 1996. 299p. SUNY Series in Science, Technology, and Society ISBN:0-7914-2919-9, ISBN13: 978-0-7914-2919-8. Dewey:306.450954. LCCN:95-030116.

Audience: **u,f.** *Choice, 1996.*

Crosby, Alfred W. (Author, Contribution by) **GF50.C76 2004**
Ecological Imperialism: The Biological Expansion of Europe, 900-1900. Ed. 2. Donald Worster (Contribution by). Cloth Text. Cambridge University Press. New York, NY. 2004. 390p. Studies in Environment and History Ser. ISBN:0-521-83732-4, ISBN13: 978-0-521-83732-3. Dewey:302.4. LCCN:2004-040401.

Audience: **g,l,u,f.** *Choice, 1987.*

Dorn, Walter Louis **D289**
Competition for Empire, 1740-1763. New York: Harper & Row. 1963. Rise of Modern Europe Ser.

Audience: **g,u,f.**

Elliott, J. H. **E18.82.E44 2006**
Empires of the Atlantic World: Britain and Spain in America 1492-1830. Cloth over Boards. Yale University Press. Cumberland, RI. 2006. 560p. ISBN:0-300-11431-1, ISBN13: 978-0-300-11431-7. Dewey:970/.02. LCCN:2005-034842.

Audience: **g,l,u,f.** *Choice, 2006.*

Elliott, J. H. **CB203**
The Old World and the New: 1492-1650. Trade Paper. Cambridge University Press. New York, NY. 1992. 134p. A Canto Book Ser. ISBN:0-521-42709-6, ISBN13: 978-0-521-42709-8. Dewey:303.482407.

Audience: **g,l,u,f.**

Fuentes, Carlos **DP99**
The Buried Mirror: Reflections on Spain and the New World. Trade Cloth. Peter Smith Publisher, Inc. Magnolia, MA. 1999. ISBN:0-8446-7012-X, ISBN13: 978-0-8446-7012-6. Dewey:946/.02.

Audience: **g,l,u,f.**

Hobson, John M. **CB251.H63 2004**
The Eastern Origins of Western Civilisation. Cloth Text. Cambridge University Press. New York, NY. 2004. 392p. ISBN:0-521-83835-5, ISBN13: 978-0-521-83835-1. Dewey:909/.09821. LCCN:2003-063549.
Audience: **u,f.**

Kamen, Henry **DP164.K36 2003**
Empire: How Spain Became a World Power, 1492-1763. Trade Cloth. HarperCollins Publishers. New York, NY. 2003. 640p. ISBN:0-06-019476-6, ISBN13: 978-0-06-019476-5. Dewey:946.03. LCCN:2002-038748.
Audience: **g,u,f.**

Lach, Donald **CB203**
Asia in the Making of Europe. Chicago, University of Chicago Press. 1965.
Audience: **u,f.**

Marshall, P. J. **JV1016**
Making and Unmaking of Empires: Britain, India, and America c.1750-1783. Trade Cloth. Oxford University Press, Inc. New York, NY. 2005. 408p. ISBN:0-19-927895-4, ISBN13: 978-0-19-927895-4. Dewey:325.3410954.
Audience: **u,f.** *Choice, 2006.*

Muldoon, James **JC359.M86 1999**
Empire and Order: The Concept of Empire, 800-1800. Cloth over Boards. Palgrave Macmillan. New York, NY. 1999. 219p. Studies in Modern History Ser. ISBN:0-312-22226-2, ISBN13: 978-0-312-22226-0. Dewey:325.3/2/09. LCCN:99-013305.
Audience: **u,f.** *Choice, 2000.*

Pagden, Anthony **CB203**
European Encounter with the New World: From Renaissance to Romanticism. Trade Paper. Yale University Press. Cumberland, RI. 1994. 216p. ISBN:0-300-05950-7, ISBN13: 978-0-300-05950-2. Dewey:303.482407. LCCN:92-021947.
Audience: **g,u,f.** *Choice, 1993.*

Pagden, Anthony **D359.7**
Lords of All the World: Ideologies of Empire in Spain, Britain, and France, 1492-1830. Trade Paper. Yale University Press. Cumberland, RI. 1998. 244p. ISBN:0-300-07449-2, ISBN13: 978-0-300-07449-9. Dewey:325.3/2/094. LCCN:95-013867.
Audience: **g,l,u,f.**

Pagden, Anthony **D135**
Peoples and Empires: A Short History of European Migration, Exploration, and Conquest, from Greece to the Present. Trade Paper. Random House Adult Trade Publishing Group. New York, NY. 2003. 256p. Modern Library Chronicles, Vol. 6 ISBN:0-8129-6761-5, ISBN13: 978-0-8129-6761-6. Dewey:909. LCCN:2003-269730.
Audience: **g,l,u,f.** *Choice, 2001.*

Parry, J. H. **F1412.P25 1990**
The Spanish Seaborne Empire. Trade Paper. University of California Press. Berkeley, CA. 1990. 417p. ISBN:0-520-07140-9, ISBN13: 978-0-520-07140-7. Dewey:980/.01. LCCN:90-034818.
Audience: **g,l,u,f.**

Raudzens, George **D228.R38 1999**
Empires: Europe and Globalization, 1492-1788. Trade Cloth. Sutton Publishing. New York, NY. 1999. 214p. ISBN:0-7509-1986-8, ISBN13: 978-0-7509-1986-9. Dewey:940.2/2. LCCN:00-361747.
Audience: **g,l,u,f.**

Scammell, Geoffrey V. **D217**
The First Imperial Age: European Overseas Expansion 1400-1715. Cloth Text. Routledge. New York, NY. 1990. 288p. ISBN:0-685-46024-X, ISBN13: 978-0-685-46024-5. Dewey:325/.34/05.
Audience: **g,l,u,f.**

General History > By period > Modern Era (1789-present)

Biagini, Eugenio F.
Liberty, Retrenchment and Reform: Popular Liberalism in the Age of Gladstone, 1860-1880. Trade Paper. Cambridge University Press. New York, NY. 2004. 488p. ISBN:0-521-54886-1, ISBN13: 978-0-521-54886-1. Dewey:941.081.
Audience: **u,f.** *Choice, 1993.*

Crozier, Andrew J. **JV2018.C76 1988**
Appeasement and Germany's Last Bid for Colonies. Cloth Text. Palgrave Macmillan. New York, NY. 1988. 368p. ISBN:0-312-01546-1, ISBN13: 978-0-312-01546-6. Dewey:909/.09712430823. LCCN:87-023060.
Audience: **u,f.** *Choice, 1989.*

Elson Roessler, Shirley & Miklos, Reinhold **D299.E47 2003**
Europe 1715-1919: From Enlightenment to World War. Book, Other. Rowman & Littlefield Publishers, Inc. Lanham, MD. 2003. 320p. ISBN:0-7425-2766-2, ISBN13: 978-0-7425-2766-9. Dewey:940.2/53. LCCN:2003-010251.
Audience: **g,l,u,f.** *Choice, 2004.*

Emsley, Clive **HV8203.E47 1999**
Gendarmes and the State in Nineteenth-Century Europe. Trade Cloth. Oxford University Press, Inc. New York, NY. 1999. 300p. ISBN:0-19-820798-0, ISBN13: 978-0-19-820798-6. Dewey:363.2/0944/09034. LCCN:99-023234.
Audience: **g,l,u,f.** *Choice, 2000.*

Goldstein, Robert Justin **Z658.E85**
The War for the Public Mind: Political Censorship in Nineteenth-Century Europe. Westport, Conn.: Praeger. 2000. ISBN:0-275-96461-2, ISBN13: 978-0-275-96461-0.
Audience: **g,l,u,f.**

Haythornthwaite, Philip J.
The Napoleonic Source Book. Trade Paper. Arms & Armour Press. London, 1997. 414p. ISBN:1-85409-287-1, ISBN13: 978-1-85409-287-8. Dewey:940.27.
Audience: **g,l,u,f.** *Choice, 1991.*

Kier, Elizabeth **UA700.K54 1997**
Imagining War: French and British Military Doctrine Between the Wars. Trade Cloth. Princeton University Press. Princeton, NJ. 1997. 288p. Princeton Studies in International History and Politics ISBN:0-691-01191-5, ISBN13: 978-0-691-01191-2. Dewey:355/.033544. LCCN:96-046302.
Audience: **g,l,u,f.** *Choice, 1998.*

Kocka, Jurgen & Mitchell, Allan (Editors)
Bourgeois Society in 19th Century Europe. Trade Paper. Berg Publishers. Oxford, 1993. 480p. ISBN:0-85496-414-2, ISBN13: 978-0-85496-414-7. Dewey:305.5/5/094/09034. LCCN:91-017753.
Audience: **u,f.**

Pereboom, Maarten **DA47.1.P47 1995**
Democracies at the Turning Point: Britain, France and the End of the Postware Order, 1928-1933. Cloth Text. Peter Lang Publishing, Inc. New York, NY. 1995. 256p. Studies in Modern European History, Vol. 13 ISBN:0-8204-2535-4, ISBN13: 978-0-8204-2535-1. Dewey:940.5/1. LCCN:94-013004.
Audience: **g,l,u,f.** *Choice, 1996.*

Perry, Marvin (Author, Compiled by), et al. **D411.S65 2000**
Sources of Twentieth-Century Europe. Matthew Berg & James Krukones (Author, Compiled by). Paper Text. Houghton Mifflin College Division. Boston, MA. 1999. 493p. ISBN:0-395-92568-1, ISBN13: 978-0-395-92568-3. Dewey:940.5. LCCN:99-071911.
Audience: **g,l,u,f.**

Schroeder, Paul W. **D295.T73 1994**
The Transformation of European Politics 1763-1848. Trade Cloth. Oxford University Press, Inc. New York, NY. 1994. 916p. History of Modern Europe Ser. ISBN:0-19-822119-3, ISBN13: 978-0-19-822119-7. Dewey:940.2/53. LCCN:93-026439.
Audience: **u,f.** *Choice, 1994.*

Venturi, Franco
The End of the Old Regime in Europe, 1776-1789: The Great States of the West, Pt. I, Vols. I & II. R. Burr Litchfield (Translator). Trade Cloth. Princeton University Press. Princeton, NJ. 1991. 1094p. ISBN:0-691-03158-4, ISBN13: 978-0-691-03158-3. Dewey:940.2/53.
Audience: **u,f.** *Choice, 1991.*

General History > By period > Modern Era (1789-present) > French Revolution and Napoleonic Wars (1789-1815)

Connelly, Owen **DC202.C6 1990**
Napoleon's Satellite Kingdoms: Managing Conquered Peoples. Trade Cloth. Krieger Publishing Company. Melbourne, FL. 1990. 400p. ISBN:0-89464-416-5, ISBN13: 978-0-89464-416-0. Dewey:940.2/7. LCCN:89-019917.
Audience: **u,f.**

Esdaile, Charles J. **DC231.E833 2004**
Fighting Napoleon: Guerrillas, Bandits, and Adventurers in Spain, 1808-1814. Cloth over Boards. Yale University Press. Cumberland, RI. 2004. 288p. ISBN:0-300-10112-0, ISBN13: 978-0-300-10112-6. Dewey:940.2/742/0946. LCCN:2003-026237.
Audience: **g,u,f.** *Choice, 2005.*

Esdaile, Charles J. **DC231.E834 2003**
The Peninsular War: A New History. Cloth over Boards. Palgrave Macmillan. New York, NY. 2003. 640p. ISBN:1-4039-6231-6, ISBN13: 978-1-4039-6231-7. Dewey:940.2/742. LCCN:2003-273462.
Audience: **g,u,f.** *Choice, 2004.*

Palmer, R. R. (Robert Roswell) **D295**
The Age of the Democratic Revolution: A Political History of Europe and America, 1760-1800. Princeton, N.J.: Princeton University Press. 1974. ISBN:0-691-00569-9, ISBN13: 978-0-691-00569-0.
Audience: **u,f.**

Palmer, Robert R. (Author, Preface by) **D295.P3**
Age of the Democratic Revolution: The Challenge. Trade Paper. Princeton University Press. Princeton, NJ. 1969. 544p. ISBN:0-691-00569-9, ISBN13: 978-0-691-00569-0. Dewey:940.25. LCCN:59-010068.
Audience: **g,u,f.**

Palmer, Robert R. (Author, Preface by) **D295 .P3**
Age of the Democratic Revolution: The Struggle, Vol. 2. Trade Paper. Princeton University Press. Princeton, NJ. 1970. 596p. ISBN:0-691-00570-2, ISBN13: 978-0-691-00570-6. Dewey:940.25. LCCN:59-010068.
Audience: **g,u,f.**

Stone, Bailey **DC138.S77 2002**
Reinterpreting the French Revolution: A Global-Historical Perspective. Trade Cloth. Cambridge University Press. New York, NY. 2002. 300p. ISBN:0-521-81147-3, ISBN13: 978-0-521-81147-7. Dewey:944.04. LCCN:2002-071509.
Audience: **u,f.** *Choice, 2003.*

Tone, John Lawrence **DC231.T63 1994**
The Fatal Knot: The Guerrilla War in Navarre and the Defeat of Napoleon in Spain. University of North Carolina Press. 1994. ISBN:0-8078-2169-1, ISBN13: 978-0-8078-2169-5.
Audience: **g,u,f.**

Woolf, Stuart J. **D308.W66 1991**
Napoleon's Integration of Europe. Paper over Boards. Routledge. New York, NY. 1991. 336p. ISBN:0-415-04961-X, ISBN13: 978-0-415-04961-0. Dewey:940.2/7. LCCN:90-024135.
Audience: **u,f.** *Choice, 1992.*

General History > By period > Modern Era (1789-present) > Restoration. Vienna Congress. Metternich's Europe (1815-1848)

Clark, T. J. **N6847**
The Absolute Bourgeois: Artists and Politics in France 1848-1851. University of California Press. 1999. ISBN:0-520-21744-6, ISBN13: 978-0-520-21744-7.
Audience: **g,l,u,f.**

Dowe, Dieter **D387.E8713 2001**
Europe in 1848: Revolution and Reform. Dieter Langewiesche, Jonathan Sperber & Heinz-Gerhard Haupt (Editors). Trade Cloth. Berghahn Books, Inc. New York, NY. 2001. 976p. ISBN:1-57181-164-8, ISBN13: 978-1-57181-164-6. Dewey:940.2/85. LCCN:00-027750.
Audience: **u,f.** *Choice, 2001.*

Duveau, Georges **DC270.D853 1984**
Eighteen Forty-Eight: The Making of a Revolution. Trade Paper. Harvard University Press. Cambridge, MA. 1984. 288p. ISBN:0-674-54348-3, ISBN13: 978-0-674-54348-5. Dewey:944.06/3.
Audience: **g,l,u,f.**

Evans, Robert & Pogge von Strandmann, Hartmut (Editors) **D387.R429 2000**
The Revolutions in Europe, 1848-1849: From Reform to Reaction. Trade Cloth. Oxford University Press, Inc. New York, NY. 2000. 264p. ISBN:0-19-820840-5, ISBN13: 978-0-19-820840-2. Dewey:940.2/84. LCCN:2001-278123.
Audience: **u,f.**

Jennings, Lawrence Charles **DC272.5**
France and Europe in 1848: A Study of French Foreign Affairs in Time of Crisis. Trade Cloth. Oxford University Press, Inc. New York, NY. 1973. ix, 280p. ISBN:0-19-822514-8, ISBN13: 978-0-19-822514-0. Dewey:327.44/04. LCCN:73-173775.
Audience: **u,f.**

Kissinger, Henry A. **D383**
A World Restored: Europe after Napoleon. Trade Cloth. Peter Smith Publisher, Inc. Magnolia, MA. 1990. ISBN:0-8446-2384-9, ISBN13: 978-0-8446-2384-9. Dewey:940.28.
Audience: **u,f.**

Namier, Lewis B. **D387**
1848: The Revolution of the Intellectuals. Trade Paper. Oxford University Press, Inc. New York, NY. 1992. 138p. ISBN:0-19-726111-6, ISBN13: 978-0-19-726111-8. Dewey:940.284.
Audience: **g,l,u,f.**

Robertson, Priscilla **D387.R6**
Revolutions of 1848: A Social History. Trade Paper. Textbook Publishers. Temecula, CA. 2003. xi, 464p. ISBN:0-7581-5659-6, ISBN13: 978-0-7581-5659-4. Dewey:940.28.
Audience: **g,l,u,f.**

Sperber, Jonathan **D363**
The European Revolutions, 1848-1851. Ed. 2. William Beik & T. C. W. Blanning (Contribution by). Cloth Text. Cambridge University Press. New York, NY. 2005. 334p. New Approaches to European History Ser., Vol. 29 ISBN:0-521-83907-6, ISBN13: 978-0-521-83907-5. Dewey:940.2/84. LCCN:2004-057071.
Audience: **g,l,u,f.**

Stearns, Peter N. **D387.S7 1974**
1848: The Revolutionary Tide in Europe. Trade Cloth. Norton. Farnborough, 1974. 278p. ISBN:0-393-05510-8, ISBN13: 978-0-393-05510-8. Dewey:940.2/84. LCCN:73-016474.
Audience: **g,u,f.**

General History > By period > Modern Era (1789-present) > European Imperialism and Colonialism

Bates, Darrel **DT156.6**
The Fashoda Incident of 1898: An Encounter on the Nile. Trade Cloth. Oxford University Press, Inc. New York, NY. 1984. xiii, 194p. ISBN:0-19-211771-8, ISBN13: 978-0-19-211771-7. Dewey:962.9/3. LCCN:83-008176.
Audience: **u,f.**

Baumgart, Winfried **JC359**
Imperialism: The Idea and Reality of British and French Colonial Expansion, 1880-1914. Ben V. Mast (Translator). Trade Cloth. Oxford University Press, Inc. New York, NY. 1982. 252p. ISBN:0-19-873040-3, ISBN13: 978-0-19-873040-8. Dewey:325/.32/09. LCCN:81-022434.
Audience: **l,u.**

Betts, Raymond F. **JV105.B47**
The False Dawn. Trade Paper. University of Minnesota Press. Minneapolis, MN. 1978. Europe and the World in the Age of Expansion Ser. ISBN:0-8166-0852-0, ISBN13: 978-0-8166-0852-2. Dewey:325/.34. LCCN:75-014683.
Audience: **g,l,u,f.**

Darby, Phillip **JC359.D28 1987**
Three Faces of Imperialism: British and American Approaches to Asia and Africa, 1870-1970. Cloth over Boards. Yale University Press. Cumberland, RI. 1987. 267p. ISBN:0-300-03748-1, ISBN13: 978-0-300-03748-7. Dewey:325/.32. LCCN:86-024665.
Audience: **g,u,f.** *Choice, 1988.*

Feis, Herbert **HG0171**
Europe, the World's Banker 1870-1914. Trade Paper. Books on Demand. Ann Arbor, MI. 494p. ISBN:0-598-91830-2, ISBN13: 978-0-598-91830-7. LCCN:30-029459.
Audience: **g,u,f.**

Gifford, Prosser (Editor) **DT32**
France and Britain in Africa: Imperial Rivalry and Colonial Rule. Trade Cloth. Yale University Press. Cumberland, RI. 1972. xix, 989p. ISBN:0-300-01289-6, ISBN13: 978-0-300-01289-7. Dewey:960. LCCN:70-151574.
Audience: **u,f.** B

Gifford, Prosser & Louis, Roger W. (Editors) **DT0032.B73**
Britain and Germany in Africa: Imperial Rivalry and Colonial Rule. Trade Paper. Books on Demand. Ann Arbor, MI. 847p. ISBN:0-8357-7405-8, ISBN13: 978-0-8357-7405-5. Dewey:325.6. LCCN:67-024500.
Audience: **u,f.**

Graham, Gerald S. **DS757**
The China Station: War and Diplomacy 1830-1860. Trade Cloth. Oxford University Press, Inc. New York, NY. 1978. 464p. ISBN:0-19-822472-9, ISBN13: 978-0-19-822472-3. Dewey:951/.03. LCCN:78-040070.
Audience: **g,u,f.**

Hart, Jonathan **JV105.H33 2003**
Comparing Empires: European Colonialism from Portuguese Expansion to the Spanish-American War. Cloth over Boards. Palgrave Macmillan. New York, NY. 2003. 288p. ISBN:1-4039-6188-3, ISBN13: 978-1-4039-6188-4. Dewey:325/.3/094. LCCN:2003-054897.
Audience: **u,f.** *Choice, 2004.*

Headrick, Daniel R. **JC359**
The Tools of Empire: Technology and European Imperialism in the Nineteenth Century. Paper Text. Oxford University Press, Inc. New York, NY. 1981. 232p. ISBN:0-19-502832-5, ISBN13: 978-0-19-502832-4. Dewey:303.4/83/09034. LCCN:80-018099.
Audience: **g,l,u,f.**

Hobsbawm, Eric J. **D359.7 .H63**
The Age of Empire. Trade Cloth. Peter Smith Publisher, Inc. Magnolia, MA. 1989. ISBN:0-8446-6925-3, ISBN13: 978-0-8446-6925-0. Dewey:909.81.
Audience: **g,u,f.**

Hobsbawm, Eric J. **HC253.H6**
Industry and Empire: The Birth of the Industrial Revolution. Trade Cloth. Peter Smith Publisher, Inc. Magnolia, MA. 2000. ISBN:0-8446-7122-3, ISBN13: 978-0-8446-7122-2. Dewey:330.942.
Audience: **u,f.**

Hochschild, Adam **DT655 .H63**
King Leopold's Ghost. Trade Paper. Houghton Mifflin Company. New York, NY. 2006. 384p. ISBN:0-618-71167-8, ISBN13: 978-0-618-71167-3. Dewey:967.51/022.
Audience: **g,l,u,f.**

Ingram, Edward **DS33.4.G7**
The Beginning of the Great Game in Asia, 1828-1834. Trade Cloth. Oxford University Press, Inc. New York, NY. 1979. xv, 361p. ISBN:0-19-822470-2, ISBN13: 978-0-19-822470-9. Dewey:327.41/05. LCCN:78-040078.
Audience: **u,f.**

Ingram, Edward **DS63.2.G7**
In Defence of British India: Great Britain in the Middle East, 1775-1842. Trade Paper. Taylor & Francis Group. Abingdon, 1984. 236p. ISBN:0-7146-3246-5, ISBN13: 978-0-7146-3246-9. Dewey:327.41056.
Audience: **u,f.**

Judd, Denis **DA16.J88**
Empire: The British Imperial Experience from 1765 to the Present. Trade Paper. Basic Books. New York, NY. 1998. 568p. ISBN:0-465-01954-4, ISBN13: 978-0-465-01954-0. Dewey:941.
Audience: **g,u,f.** *Choice, 1997.*

Landes, David S. **HG3386.A6 L36 1979**
Bankers and Pashas: International Finance and Economic Imperialism in Egypt. Trade Paper. Harvard University Press. Cambridge, MA. 1980. 370p. ISBN:0-674-06165-9, ISBN13: 978-0-674-06165-1. Dewey:332.1/5/0962.
Audience: **g,u,f.**

Louis, William Roger, et al. **JV246.I43**
Imperialism: The Robinson and Gallagher Controversy. Ronald E. Robinson & John Gallagher (Authors). Trade Cloth. Scholastic Library Publishing. Danbury, CT. 1976. 252p. Modern Scholarship on European History Ser. ISBN:0-531-05375-X, ISBN13: 978-0-531-05375-1. Dewey:325/.341/096. LCCN:75-026730.
Audience: **u,f.**

Pakenham, Thomas **DT1896**
The Boer War. Trade Cloth. Random House, Inc. New York, NY. 1994. ISBN:0-679-43047-4, ISBN13: 978-0-679-43047-6. Dewey:968.04/8. LCCN:93-026234.
Audience: **g,l,u,f.**

Pakenham, Thomas **DT28.P34 1991**
The Scramble for Africa: White Man's Conquest of the Dark Continent from 1876 to 1912. Trade Cloth. Random House, Inc. New York, NY. 1991. 784p. ISBN:0-394-51576-5, ISBN13: 978-0-394-51576-2. Dewey:960.3/12. LCCN:91-052681.
Audience: **g,u,f.**

Robinson, R. **DT32**
Africa and the Victorians: The Official Mind of Imperialism. Ed. 2. Trade Paper. Palgrave Macmillan. New York, NY. 1997. 544p. ISBN:0-333-31006-3, ISBN13: 978-0-333-31006-9. Dewey:325/.32/0941.
Audience: **u,f.**

Schultz, Kirsten **F2534.S324 2001**
Tropical Versailles: Empire, Monarchy, and the Portuguese Royal Court in Rio de Janeiro, 1808-1821. Paper over Boards. Routledge. New York, NY. 2001. 320p. New World in the Atlantic World Ser. ISBN:0-415-92987-3, ISBN13: 978-0-415-92987-5. Dewey:981/.53033. LCCN:00-068741.
Audience: **u,f.**

Semmel, Bernard **JC359**
The Liberal Ideal and the Demons of Empire: Theories of Imperialism from Adam Smith to Lenin. Trade Cloth. Johns Hopkins University Press. Baltimore, MD. 1977. 240p. ISBN:0-8018-4540-8, ISBN13: 978-0-8018-4540-6. Dewey:325.32. LCCN:92-036270.
Audience: **g,u,f.**

Smith, Woodruff D. **D299**
European Imperialism in the Nineteenth and Twentieth Centuries. Paper Text. Thomson Wadsworth. Belmont, CA. 1982. 288p. ISBN:0-88229-812-7, ISBN13: 978-0-88229-812-2. Dewey:940.2/8. LCCN:82-007859.
Audience: **g,l,u,f.**

Wesseling, H. L. **D359.7.W47 2004**
The European Colonial Empires, 1815-1919. Trade Paper. Longman Publishing Group. White Plains, NY. 2004. 304p. ISBN:0-582-09551-4, ISBN13: 978-0-582-09551-9. Dewey:325/.32/094. LCCN:2004-044403.
Audience: **g,l,u,f.** *Choice, 2005.*

Wesseling, H. L. **D539**
Imperialism and Colonialism: Essays on the History of European Expansion. Book, Other. Greenwood Publishing Group, Inc. Portsmouth, NH. 1997. 224p. Contributions in Comparative Colonial Studies, Vol. 32 ISBN:0-313-30431-9, ISBN13: 978-0-313-30431-6. Dewey:325/.32/091821. LCCN:96-053847.
Audience: **u,f.**

Wesseling, H. L. **DT28**
Divide and Rule: The Partition of Africa, 1880-1914. Arnold J. Pomerans (Translator). Trade Cloth. Greenwood Publishing Group, Inc. Portsmouth, NH. 1996. 464p. ISBN:0-275-95137-5, ISBN13: 978-0-275-95137-5. Dewey:960.3/12. LCCN:95-038253.
Audience: **g,l,u,f.** *Choice, 1996.*

Yapp, M. E. **DS446.5**
Strategies of British India: Britain, Iran, and Afghanistan, 1798-1850. Trade Cloth. Oxford University Press, Inc. New York, NY. 1980. 690p. ISBN:0-19-822481-8, ISBN13: 978-0-19-822481-5. Dewey:327.54. LCCN:79-041089.
Audience: **u,f.**

General History > By period > Modern Era (1789-present) > Racism and Social Darwinism

Hawkins, Mike **HM106.H38 1997**
Social Darwinism in European and American Thought, 1860-1945: Nature as Model and Nature as Threat. Trade Cloth. Cambridge University Press. New York, NY. 1997. 351p. ISBN:0-521-57400-5, ISBN13: 978-0-521-57400-6. Dewey:304.5. LCCN:96-020946.
Audience: **l,u,f.** *Choice, 1998.*

Kiernan, Victor **JV305.K53 1995**
The Lords of Human Kind: European Attitudes to Other Cultures in the Imperial Age. Ed. 4. Trade Paper. Serif. London, 2001. 354p. ISBN:1-897959-23-0, ISBN13: 978-1-897959-23-7. Dewey:325.32. LCCN:96-180106.
Audience: **g,u,f.**

Lauren, Paul Gordon **HT1521.L33 1996**
Power and Prejudice: The Politics and Diplomacy of Racial Discrimination. Ed. 2. Trade Paper. Westview Press. Boulder, CO. 1996. 448p. ISBN:0-8133-2143-3, ISBN13: 978-0-8133-2143-1. Dewey:305.8/00973. LCCN:95-045848.
Audience: **g,u,f.**

Mosse, George L. **HT1521.M63 1997**
Toward the Final Solution: A History of European Racism. Trade Paper. Howard Fertig Inc. New York, NY. 1997. xvi, 277p. ISBN:0-86527-428-2, ISBN13: 978-0-86527-428-0. Dewey:305.8/0094. LCCN:97-180711.
Audience: **g,l,u,f.**

Weikart, Richard **HQ755.5.G3W435 2004**
From Darwin to Hitler: Evolutionary Ethics, Eugenics, and Racism in Germany. Cloth over Boards. Palgrave Macmillan. New York, NY. 2004. 324p. ISBN:1-4039-6502-1, ISBN13: 978-1-4039-6502-8. Dewey:305.8/00943. LCCN:2003-065613.
Audience: **g,l,u,f.** *Choice, 2005.*

General History > By period > Modern Era (1789-present) > World War I. Causes. Diplomacy. Social Impact. Military Operations

Audoin-Rouzeau, Stephane & Becker, Annette **D524.5.A8813 2002**
14 - 18: Understanding the Great War. Catherine Temerson (Translator). Cloth over Boards. Farrar, Straus & Giroux. New York, NY. 2002. 288p. ISBN:0-8090-4642-3, ISBN13: 978-0-8090-4642-3. Dewey:940.3. LCCN:2002-111422.
Audience: **g,l,u,f.** *Choice, 2003.*

Bell, Peter **DA565.C4B45 1996**
Chamberlain, Germany, and Japan. Trade Cloth. Palgrave Macmillan. New York, NY. 1996. 304p. Studies in Military and Strategic History ISBN:0-312-15883-1, ISBN13: 978-0-312-15883-5. Dewey:941.084. LCCN:95-053264.
Audience: **u,f.** *Choice, 1996.*

Bond, Brian (Editor) **D522.42.F56 1991**
The First World War and British Military History. Trade Cloth. Oxford University Press, Inc. New York, NY. 1991. 344p. ISBN:0-19-822299-8, ISBN13: 978-0-19-822299-6. Dewey:940.4/072. LCCN:91-010894.
Audience: **g,u,f.** *Choice, 1992.*

Bourke, Joanna **U22.3**
An Intimate History of Killing: Face-to-Face Killing in Twentieth Century Warfare. Trade Paper. Basic Books. New York, NY. 2000. 544p. ISBN:0-465-00738-4, ISBN13: 978-0-465-00738-7. Dewey:355.13.
Audience: **g,l,u,f.**

Brose, Eric Dorn **UA712.B76 2001**
The Kaiser's Army: The Politics of Military Technology in Germany during the Machine Age, 1870-1918. Trade Cloth. Oxford University Press, Inc. New York, NY. 2001. 336p. ISBN:0-19-514335-3, ISBN13: 978-0-19-514335-5. Dewey:355.4/0943. LCCN:00-061121.
Audience: **g,l,u,f.** *Choice, 2002.*

Brown, Malcolm **D568.4**
Lawrence of Arabia: The Life, the Legend. Saddle Stitched, Cloth over Boards, Dust Jacket. Thames & Hudson. New York, NY. 2005. 208p. ISBN:0-500-51238-8, ISBN13: 978-0-500-51238-8. Dewey:940.415092. LCCN:2005-900274.
Audience: **g,l,u,f.**

Brown, Malcolm **D568.4**
T. E. Lawrence in War and Peace: An Anthology of the Military Writings of Lawrence of Arabia. Michael Clarke (Foreword by). Cloth over Boards. Greenhill Books/Lionel Leventhal, Ltd. London, 2006. 280p. ISBN:1-85367-653-5, ISBN13: 978-1-85367-653-6. Dewey:940.4/15. LCCN:2006-296148.
Audience: **g,u,f.**

Burgwyn, H. James **D617**
The Legend of the Mutilated Victory: Italy, the Great War, and the Paris Peace Conference, 1915-1919, 38. Trade Cloth. Greenwood Publishing Group, Inc. Portsmouth, NH. 1993. 368p. Contributions to the Study of World History Ser., No. 38 ISBN:0-313-28885-2, ISBN13: 978-0-313-28885-2. Dewey:940.32245. LCCN:92-045082.
Audience: **u,f.** *Choice, 1994.*

Cassar, George H. **D569.A2C236 1998**
The Forgotten Front: The British Campaign in Italy 1917-18. Trade Cloth. Continuum International Publishing Group, Ltd. London, 1998. 288p. ISBN:1-85285-166-X, ISBN13: 978-1-85285-166-8. Dewey:940.4/145. LCCN:97-032575.
Audience: **u,f.** *Choice, 1999.*

Cornwall, Mark **D639.P7A93 2000**
The Undermining of Austria-Hungary: The Battle for Hearts and Minds. Cloth over Boards. Palgrave Macmillan. New York, NY. 2000. 503p. ISBN:0-312-23151-2, ISBN13: 978-0-312-23151-4. Dewey:940.4/09436. LCCN:99-059429.
Audience: **g,u,f.** *Choice, 2001.*

Ferguson, Niall **D521**
The Pity of War: Explaining World War I. Trade Cloth. Penguin Group (USA) Inc. New York, NY. 1998. 304p. ISBN:0-7139-9246-8, ISBN13: 978-0-7139-9246-5. Dewey:940.3.
Audience: **u,f.** *Choice, 1999.*

Grayzel, Susan R. **D639.W7G73 2002**
Women and the First World War. Trade Paper. Longman Publishing. Boston, MA. 2002. 216p. ISBN:0-582-41876-3, ISBN13: 978-0-582-41876-9. Dewey:940.3/082.
Audience: **g,l,u,f.**

Grieves, Keith **HD5765.A6G77 1988**
The Politics of Manpower, 1914-18. Cloth Text. Palgrave Macmillan. New York, NY. 1988. 256p. War, Armed Forces, and Society Ser., Vol. 1 ISBN:0-312-01320-5, ISBN13: 978-0-312-01320-2. Dewey:355.2/23/0941. LCCN:87-020511.
Audience: **u,f.** *Choice, 1988.*

Gullace, Nicoletta F. **JN906.G85 2002**
The Blood of Our Sons: Men, Women, and the Renegotiation of British Citizenship During the Great War. Cloth over Boards. Palgrave Macmillan. New York, NY. 2002. 288p. ISBN:0-312-29446-8, ISBN13: 978-0-312-29446-5. Dewey:940.3/1/0941. LCCN:2002-016917.
Audience: **u,f.** *Choice, 2003.*

Hamilton, Richard F. & Herwig, Holger H. (Editors) **D511.O68 2003**
The Origins of World War I. Cloth Text. Cambridge University Press. New York, NY. 2003. 552p. ISBN:0-521-81735-8, ISBN13: 978-0-521-81735-6. Dewey:940.3/11. LCCN:2002-067092.
Audience: **u,f.** *Choice, 2003.*

Hanna, Martha **D639.P88F743 1996**
The Mobilization of Intellect: French Scholars and Writers During the Great War. Trade Cloth. Harvard University Press. Cambridge, MA. 1996. 304p. ISBN:0-674-57755-8, ISBN13: 978-0-674-57755-8. Dewey:940.4/0944. LCCN:95-042544.
Audience: **u,f.** *Choice, 1997.*

Herwig, Holger H. **D531.H464 1997**
The First World War: Germany and Austria-Hungary 1914-1918. Paper Text. Oxford University Press, Inc. New York, NY. 1996. 512p. Modern Wars Ser. ISBN:0-340-57348-1, ISBN13: 978-0-340-57348-8. Dewey:940.4147. LCCN:96-028152.
Audience: **u,f.** *Choice, 1997.*

Hitchcock, William I. **DC404.H53 1998**
France Restored: Cold War Diplomacy and the Quest for Leadership in Europe, 1944-1954. John L. Gaddis (Foreword by). Trade Cloth. University of North Carolina Press. Chapel Hill, NC. 1998. 312p. The New Cold War History Ser. ISBN:0-8078-2428-3, ISBN13: 978-0-8078-2428-3. Dewey:327.44. LCCN:97-051123.
Audience: **u,f.** *Choice, 1999.*

Horne, John N. & Kramer, Alan **D626.G3H67 2001**
German Atrocities, 1914: A History of Denial. Cloth over Boards. Yale University Press. Cumberland, RI. 2001. 624p. ISBN:0-300-08975-9, ISBN13: 978-0-300-08975-2. Dewey:940.4/05. LCCN:2001-026884.
Audience: **g,u,f.**

Howard, Michael **D521.H645 2002**
The First World War. Trade Cloth. Oxford University Press, Inc. New York, NY. 2002. 176p. Very Short Introductions Ser. ISBN:0-19-285362-7, ISBN13: 978-0-19-285362-2. Dewey:940.3. LCCN:2002-283851.
Audience: **g,l,u,f.**

Hughes-Wilson, John & Corns, Cathryn M. **D639**
Blindfold and Alone: British Military Executions in the Great War. Trade Paper. Cassell P L C. London, 2005. 544p. Cassell Military Paperbacks Ser. ISBN:0-304-36696-X, ISBN13: 978-0-304-36696-5. Dewey:940.480941. LCCN:2005-482020.
Audience: **u,f.**

Hynes, Samuel **D523.H96 1991**
A War Imagined: The First World War and English Culture. Trade Cloth. Simon & Schuster. New York, NY. 1991. 512p. ISBN:0-689-12128-8, ISBN13: 978-0-689-12128-9. Dewey:940.3. LCCN:90-021873.
Audience: **u,f.** *Choice, 1991.*

Joll, James **D511**
Origins of the First World War. Ed. 2. Trade Paper. Longman Publishing. Boston, MA. 2004. ISBN:0-321-27657-4, ISBN13: 978-0-321-27657-5. Dewey:940.3/11.
Audience: **g,l,u,f.**

Keynes, John Maynard **HB95.K35 2004**
The End of Laissez Faire and the Economic Consequences of the Peace. Trade Cloth. Prometheus Books, Publishers. Amherst, NY. 2004. 330p. Great Minds Ser. ISBN:1-59102-268-1, ISBN13: 978-1-59102-268-8. Dewey:330.15/6. LCCN:2004-020143.
Audience: **g,l,u,f.**

Langdon, John W. **D511.L225 1990**
July, 1914: The Long Debate, 1918-1990. Trade Cloth. Berg Publishers. Oxford, 1991. 206p. ISBN:0-85496-680-3, ISBN13: 978-0-85496-680-6. Dewey:940.3/11. LCCN:90-033210.
Audience: **u,f.** *Choice, 1991.*

Le Naour, Jean-Yves **DC373.M2356L413 2004**
The Living Unknown Soldier: A Story of Grief and the Great War. Penny Allen (Translator). Cloth over Boards. Henry Holt & Company. New York, NY. 2004. 240p. ISBN:0-8050-7522-4, ISBN13: 978-0-8050-7522-9. Dewey:940.4/1244/092 B. LCCN:2004-040276.
Audience: **g,l,u,f.**

Liddle, Peter & Cecil, Hugh **D641**
The Eleventh Hour: The Eightieth Anniversary of Armistice Day. Trade Cloth. Pen & Sword Books Ltd. Barnsley, 1998. 386p. ISBN:0-85052-609-4, ISBN13: 978-0-85052-609-7. Dewey:940.4/39.
Audience: **g,u,f.**

Macdonald, Lyn **D544.M22 1999**
To the Last Man: Spring 1918. Trade Cloth. Avalon Publishing Group. New York, NY. 1999. 416p. ISBN:0-7867-0663-5, ISBN13: 978-0-7867-0663-1. Dewey:940.4/34.
Audience: **g,l,u,f.**

Millett, Allan R. & Murray, Williamson R. (Editor, Contribution by) **U42 .M556 1996**
Military Innovation in the Interwar Period. Richard R. Muller, Geoffrey Till, Holger H. Herwig, Alan Beyerchen & Barry Watts (Contribution by). Trade Paper. Cambridge University Press. New York, NY. 1998. 448p. ISBN:0-521-63760-0, ISBN13: 978-0-521-63760-2. Dewey:355/.02/09041.
Audience: **g,u,f.**

Parker, Robert A. **DA47.2.P37 1993**
Chamberlain and Appeasement: British Policy and the Coming of the Second World War. Cloth Text. Palgrave Macmillan. New York, NY. 1993. 320p. ISBN:0-312-09659-3, ISBN13: 978-0-312-09659-5. Dewey:327.41043. LCCN:93-016656.
Audience: **u,f.** *Choice, 1994.*

Roberts, Mary L. **HQ1075.5.F8.R63 1994**
Civilization Without Sexes: Reconstructing Gender in Postwar France, 1917-1927. Trade Cloth. University of Chicago Press. Chicago, IL. 1994. 352p. Women in Culture and Society Ser. ISBN:0-226-72121-3, ISBN13: 978-0-226-72121-7. Dewey:305.3/0944. LCCN:93-026899.
Audience: **u,f.** *Choice, 1994.*

Roshwald, Aviel & Stites, Richard (Editors) **D523**
European Culture in the Great War: The Arts, Entertainment and Propaganda, 1914-1918. Cloth Text. Cambridge University Press. New York, NY. 1999. 442p. Studies in the Social and Cultural History of Modern Warfare, No. 6
ISBN:0-521-57015-8, ISBN13: 978-0-521-57015-2. Dewey:940.3/1. LCCN:98-027978.
Audience: **u,f.** *Choice, 1999.*

Samuels, Martin **UA647.S182 1995**
Command or Control: Command, Training and Tactics in the German and British Armies, 1888-1918. Cloth Text. Taylor & Francis Group. Abingdon, 1996. 340p. ISBN:0-7146-4570-2, ISBN13: 978-0-7146-4570-4. Dewey:355/.033541. LCCN:95-007053.
Audience: **u,f.** *Choice, 1996.*

Schollgen, Gregor (Editor) **DD221.5.E8 1990**
Escape into War?: The Foreign Policy of Imperial Germany. Trade Cloth. Berg Publishers. Oxford, 1990. 185p. German Historical Perspectives Ser., Vol. 6 ISBN:0-85496-275-1, ISBN13: 978-0-85496-275-4. Dewey:327.43. LCCN:90-000345.
Audience: **u,f.** *Choice, 1991.*

Stevenson, David **D511.S815 1996**
Armaments and the Coming of War: Europe, 1904-1914. Trade Cloth. Oxford University Press, Inc. New York, NY. 1996. 474p. ISBN:0-19-820208-3, ISBN13: 978-0-19-820208-0. Dewey:940.3/1/12. LCCN:95-040415.
Audience: **u,f.** *Choice, 1997.*

Stone, Norman **D550.S76**
The Eastern Front, 1914-1917. Trade Cloth. Simon & Schuster. New York, NY. 1975. 348p. ISBN:0-684-14492-1, ISBN13: 978-0-684-14492-4. Dewey:940.4/147. LCCN:75-018914.
Audience: **g,u,f.**

Strachan, Hew **D251**
The First World War. New York : Viking. 2004. ISBN:0-670-03295-6, ISBN13: 978-0-670-03295-2.
Audience: **g,l,u,f.**

Strachan, Hew **D251**
The First World War, Vol. 1: To Arms. Oxford : Oxford University Press. 2003. ISBN:0-19-926191-1, ISBN13: 978-0-19-926191-8.
Audience: **u,f.**

Thies, Jochen **D511.A574 2005**
The Origins of the War of 1914. Trade Paper. Enigma Books. New York, NY. 2005. 2100p. ISBN:1-929631-26-X, ISBN13: 978-1-929631-26-1. Dewey:940.311.
Audience: **u,f.**

Williamson, Samuel R. Jr. **DB86.W515 1990**
Austria-Hungary and the Origins of the First World War. Trade Cloth. Palgrave Macmillan. New York, NY. 1991. 292p. The Making of the 20th Century Ser. ISBN:0-312-05239-1, ISBN13: 978-0-312-05239-3. Dewey:943.6/044. LCCN:90-041895.
Audience: **g,u,f.** *Choice, 1991.*

Winter, Jay **D523 .W58 1995**
Sites of Memory, Sites of Mourning: The Great War in European Cultural History. Paul Kennedy, Antoine Prost & Emmanuel Sivan (Contribution by). Cloth Text. Cambridge University Press. New York, NY. 1995. 320p. Studies in the Social and Cultural History of Modern Warfare, No. 1 ISBN:0-521-49682-9, ISBN13: 978-0-521-49682-7. Dewey:940.3. LCCN:94-044586.
Audience: **g,u,f.** *Choice, 1996.*

Woodward, David **DA577**
Lloyd George and the Generals. Cloth Text. Taylor & Francis Group. Abingdon, 2003. 368p. ISBN:0-7146-5507-4, ISBN13: 978-0-7146-5507-9. Dewey:941.083.
Audience: **u,f.**

General History > By period > Modern Era (1789-present) > World War II. Causes. Diplomacy. Social Impact. Military Operations

Barnett, Correlli (Editor) **D757.H546 2003**
Hitler's Generals. Trade Paper. Grove/Atlantic, Inc. New York, NY. 2003. 528p. ISBN:0-8021-3994-9, ISBN13: 978-0-8021-3994-8. Dewey:940.54/1343/0922 B. LCCN:2003-272429.
Audience: **g,l,u,f.**

Bennett, Ralph Francis **D756.5.N6.B44 1980**
Ultra in the West: The Normandy Campaign, 1944-45. Trade Cloth. Simon & Schuster. New York, NY. 1980. xvi, 336p. ISBN:0-684-16704-2, ISBN13: 978-0-684-16704-6. Dewey:940.54/21. LCCN:80-050912.
Audience: **g,u,f.**

Bonn, Keith E. (Editor) **D764**
Slaughterhouse: The Handbook of the Eastern Front. David Glantz, Marc J. Rikmenspoel, Scott McMichael, Hugh Foster, Steven Myers, Yuri Khonko & Natalya Khonko (Contribution by). Trade Paper. Aegis Consulting Group. Bedford, PA. 2004. 520p. ISBN:0-9717650-9-X, ISBN13: 978-0-9717650-9-2. Dewey:940.5421.
Audience: **g,l,u,f.**

Calvocoressi, Peter, et al. **D743.C24 1989**
Total War: Causes and Courses of the Second World War. Guy Wint & John Pritchard (Authors). Trade Cloth. Knopf Publishing Group. New York, NY. 1989. xxviii, 1315p. ISBN:0-394-57811-2, ISBN13: 978-0-394-57811-8. Dewey:940.53. LCCN:88-043278.
Audience: **g,l,u,f.**

Dear, I. C. **D740.O94 1995**
The Oxford Companion to the Second World War. Trade Cloth. Oxford University Press, Inc. New York, NY. 2000. 1268p. ISBN:0-19-214168-6, ISBN13: 978-0-19-214168-2. Dewey:940.53/03. LCCN:95-148182.
Audience: **g,u,f.**

Garrett, Stephen A. **D786.G36 1993**
Ethics and Airpower in World War II: The British Bombing of German Cities. Trade Cloth. Palgrave Macmillan. New York, NY. 1993. 288p. ISBN:0-312-08683-0, ISBN13: 978-0-312-08683-1. Dewey:940.5/44941. LCCN:92-037119.
Audience: **g,l,u,f.** *Choice, 1993.*

Harrison, Mark (Editor) **D734**
The Economics of World War II: Six Great Powers in International Comparison. Michael D. Bordo, Forrest Capie & Angela Redish (Contribution by). Trade Paper. Cambridge University Press. New York, NY. 2000. 332p. Studies in Macroeconomic History ISBN:0-521-78503-0, ISBN13: 978-0-521-78503-7. Dewey:940.53/14.
Audience: **g,l,u,f.**

Hasegawa, Tsuyoshi **D813.J3H37 2005**
Racing the Enemy: Stalin, Truman, and the Surrender of Japan. Trade Cloth. Harvard University Press. Cambridge, MA. 2005. 432p. ISBN:0-674-01693-9, ISBN13: 978-0-674-01693-4. Dewey:940.53/2452. LCCN:2004-059786.
Audience: **g,l,u,f.** *Choice, 2006.*

Heiber, Helmut **D757**
Hitler and His Generals: Miltary Conferences 1942-1945: The First Complete Stenographic Record of the Military Conferences from Stalingrad to Berlin. Trade Paper. Enigma Books. New York, NY. 2004. 1211p. ISBN:1-929631-28-6, ISBN13: 978-1-929631-28-5. Dewey:940.5/4/0943.
Audience: **u,f.**

Hough, Richard & Richards, Denis **D756.5.B7H67 1989**
The Battle of Britain: The Greatest Air Battle of World War II. Trade Cloth. W. W. Norton & Company, Inc. New York, NY. 1989. 397p. ISBN:0-393-02766-X, ISBN13: 978-0-393-02766-2. Dewey:940.54/211. LCCN:89-012697.
Audience: **g,l,u,f.** *Choice, 1990.*

Knox, MacGregor **DG571.K63 2000**
Common Destiny: Dictatorship, Foreign Policy, and War in Fascist Italy and Nazi Germany. Cloth Text. Cambridge University Press. New York, NY. 2000. 276p. ISBN:0-521-58208-3, ISBN13: 978-0-521-58208-7. Dewey:943.08. LCCN:99-016896.
Audience: **g,l,u,f.** *Choice, 2000.*

Levine, Alan J. **D790**
The Strategic Bombing of Germany, 1940-1945. Trade Cloth. Greenwood Publishing Group, Inc. Portsmouth, NH. 1992. 248p. ISBN:0-275-94319-4, ISBN13: 978-0-275-94319-6. Dewey:940.5442. LCCN:91-045610.
Audience: **g,l,u,f.** *Choice, 1993.*

Liddell-Hart, Basil H. **D757**
German Generals Talk. Trade Paper. HarperCollins Publishers. New York, NY. 1971. 320p. ISBN:0-688-06012-9, ISBN13: 978-0-688-06012-1. Dewey:940.54/13/430922.
Audience: **g,l,u.**

Milward, Alan S. **HC58.M53**
War, Economy and Society, Nineteen Thirty-Nine to Nineteen Forty-Five. Trade Cloth. Peter Smith Publisher, Inc. Magnolia, MA. 1983. ISBN:0-8446-5966-5, ISBN13: 978-0-8446-5966-4. Dewey:940.53/14.
Audience: **g,l,u,f.**

Murray, Williamson & Millett, Allan R. **D767.98.M87 2000**
A War to Be Won: Fighting the Second World War, 1937-1945. Trade Cloth. Harvard University Press. Cambridge, MA. 2000. 736p. Belknap Press Ser. ISBN:0-674-00163-X, ISBN13: 978-0-674-00163-3. Dewey:940.53. LCCN:99-086624.
Audience: **g,u,f.** *Choice, 2000.*

Neillands, Robin
The Conquest of the Reich: D-Day to VE Day - A Soldier's History. Trade Paper. New York University Press. New York, NY. 1997. 304p. ISBN:0-8147-5789-8, ISBN13: 978-0-8147-5789-5. Dewey:940.54/21/0922.
Audience: **g,l,u,f.**

Overy, Richard **D743**
Why the Allies Won. Cloth Text. DIANE Publishing Company. Collingdale, PA. 1998. 396p. ISBN:0-7881-5869-4, ISBN13: 978-0-7881-5869-8. Dewey:940.5/4.
Audience: **g,l,u,f.** *Choice, 1996.*

Porch, Douglas **D766.P67 2004**
The Path to Victory: The Mediterranean Theater in World War II. Cloth over Boards. Farrar, Straus & Giroux. New York, NY. 2004. 816p. ISBN:0-374-20518-3, ISBN13: 978-0-374-20518-8. Dewey:940.54/29. LCCN:2003-060845.
Audience: **g,u,f.** *Choice, 2005.*

Prazmowska, Anita J. **D750.P68 1995**
Britain and Poland, 1939-1943: The Betrayed Ally. Trade Cloth. Cambridge University Press. New York, NY. 1995. 250p. Cambridge Russian, Soviet and Post-Soviet Studies, 97 ISBN:0-521-40309-X, ISBN13: 978-0-521-40309-2. Dewey:940.53/2. LCCN:94-026412.
Audience: **g,u,f.** *Choice, 1996.*

Richards, Pamela S. **D810**
Scientific Information in Wartime: An Allied-German Rivalry, 1939-1945. Trade Cloth. Greenwood Publishing Group, Inc. Portsmouth, NH. 1994. 192p. Contributions in Military Studies Ser., No. 151 ISBN:0-313-29062-8, ISBN13: 978-0-313-29062-6. Dewey:940.5485. LCCN:93-025050.
Audience: **u,f.** *Choice, 1995.*

Rose, Sonya O. **DA587**
Which People's War?: National Identity and Citizenship in Wartime Britain 1939-1945. Trade Cloth. Oxford University Press, Inc. New York, NY. 2003. 342p. ISBN:0-19-925572-5, ISBN13: 978-0-19-925572-6. Dewey:941.084. LCCN:2003-273343.
Audience: **g,u,f.** *Choice, 2004.*

Syrett, David **D780.S96 1994**
The Defeat of the German U-Boats: The Battle of the Atlantic. Cloth Text. University of South Carolina Press. Columbia, SC. 1994. 330p. Studies in Maritime History ISBN:0-87249-984-7, ISBN13: 978-0-87249-984-3. Dewey:940.54/516/09163. LCCN:93-044333.
Audience: **g,u,f.** *Choice, 1994.*

Thomas **D761.9.A1T48 1998**
French Empire at War, 1940-1945. Trade Cloth. Manchester University Press. Manchester, 1998. 336p. Studies in Imperialism ISBN:0-7190-5034-0, ISBN13: 978-0-7190-5034-3. Dewey:940.3/44. LCCN:98-010253.
Audience: **g,u,f.** *Choice, 1998.*

Weinberg, Gerhard L. **DD256.5**
Hitler's Foreign Policy: The Road to World War II 1933-1939. Trade Cloth. Enigma Books. New York, NY. 2005. 1200p. ISBN:1-929631-27-8, ISBN13: 978-1-929631-27-8. Dewey:327.43009043.
Audience: **u,f.**

Weinberg, Gerhard L. **D743.W424 2005**
A World at Arms: A Global History of World War II. Ed. 2. Trade Cloth. Cambridge University Press. New York, NY. 2005.

1208p. ISBN:0-521-85316-8, ISBN13: 978-0-521-85316-3. Dewey:941.54. LCCN:2005-041954.
Audience: **g,u,f.**

Wilt, Alan F. **D757.W545 1990**
War from the Top: German and British Military Decision Making During World War II. Trade Cloth. Indiana University Press. Bloomington, IN. 1990. 400p. ISBN:0-253-36455-8, ISBN13: 978-0-253-36455-5. Dewey:940.54/01. LCCN:89-045566.
Audience: **u,f.** *Choice, 1991.*

Young, Robert J. **D742.F7Y68 1996**
France and the Origins of the Second World War. Trade Cloth. Palgrave Macmillan. New York, NY. 1996. 200p. ISBN:0-312-16185-9, ISBN13: 978-0-312-16185-9. Dewey:944/.0815. LCCN:96-010410.
Audience: **g,l,u,f.** *Choice, 1997.*

General History > By period > Modern Era (1789-present) > Holocaust. Jews

Abzug, Robert H. **D804.19.A25 1999**
America Views the Holocaust, 1933-1945: A Brief Documentary History. Cloth over Boards. Palgrave Macmillan. New York, NY. 1999. 256p. Bedford Series in History and Culture ISBN:0-312-21819-2, ISBN13: 978-0-312-21819-5. Dewey:940.53/18. LCCN:98-087517.
Audience: **g,l,u.**

Aly, Gotz **D804.3.A45813 1999**
Final Solution: Nazi Population Policy and the Murder of the European Jew. Cloth Text. Oxford University Press, Inc. New York, NY. 1999. 384p. A Hodder Arnold Publication ISBN:0-340-67757-0, ISBN13: 978-0-340-67757-5. Dewey:940.5/318. LCCN:98-036599.
Audience: **g,l,u,f.** *Choice, 1999.*

Arad, Yitzhak (Editor), et al. **D804.19.D63 1999**
Documents on the Holocaust: Selected Sources on the Destruction of the Jews of Germany and Austria, Poland, and the Soviet Union. Ed. 8. Israel Gutman & Abraham Margaliot (Editors). Paper Text. University of Nebraska Press. Lincoln, NE. 1999. 508p. ISBN:0-8032-5937-9, ISBN13: 978-0-8032-5937-9. Dewey:940.5318. LCCN:99-032577.
Audience: **g,l,u,f.**

Arendt, Hannah **K5301**
Eichmann in Jerusalem: A Report on the Banality of Evil. Trade Cloth. Peter Smith Publisher, Inc. Magnolia, MA. 1983. ISBN:0-8446-5977-0, ISBN13: 978-0-8446-5977-0. Dewey:341.6/9.
Audience: **g,u,f.** B

Bajohr, Frank **DS135.G4H3274 2001**
"Aryanization" in Hamburg. George Wilkes (Translator). Trade Cloth. Berghahn Books, Inc. New York, NY. 2002. 300p. Monographs in German History, Vol. 7 ISBN:1-57181-484-1, ISBN13: 978-1-57181-484-5. Dewey:943/.515004924. LCCN:2001-043586.
Audience: **u,f.** *Choice, 2002.*

Baldwin, Peter (Editor) **DD256.5.R436 1990**
Reworking the Past: Hitler, the Holocaust, and the Historians' Debate. Trade Cloth. Beacon Press. Boston, MA. 1990. 316p. ISBN:0-8070-4302-8, ISBN13: 978-0-8070-4302-8. Dewey:943/004924. LCCN:88-043073.
Audience: **g,l,u,f.**

Bankier, David **DD256.5.B32 1992**
The Germans and the Final Solution: Public Opinion under Nazism. Cloth Text. Blackwell Publishing, Inc. Malden, MA. 1992. 224p. Jewish Society and Culture Ser. ISBN:0-631-17968-2, ISBN13: 978-0-631-17968-9. Dewey:940.5/318. LCCN:91-017503.
Audience: **g,l,u,f.** *Choice, 1992.*

Bankier, David (Editor) **DS146.G4P75 2000**
Probing the Depths of German Antisemitism: German Society and the Persecution of the Jews, 1933-1941. Trade Cloth. Berghahn Books, Inc. New York, NY. 2000. 592p. ISBN:1-57181-238-5, ISBN13: 978-1-57181-238-4. Dewey:940.53/18. LCCN:99-056222.
Audience: **g,l,u,f.** *Choice, 2001.*

Barnett, Victoria **BR856**
For the Soul of the People: Protestant Protest Against Hitler. Trade Paper. Oxford University Press, Inc. New York, NY. 1998. 368p. ISBN:0-19-512118-X, ISBN13: 978-0-19-512118-6. Dewey:280.4/0943/09043.
Audience: **g,l,u,f.** *Choice, 1993.*

Bauer, Yehuda **DS135.G3315B38 1994**
Jews for Sale?: Nazi-Jewish Negotiations, 1939-1945. Cloth over Boards. Yale University Press. Cumberland, RI. 1994. 320p. ISBN:0-300-05913-2, ISBN13: 978-0-300-05913-7. Dewey:940.53/18/0943. LCCN:94-027780.
Audience: **u,f.** *Choice, 1995.*

Bauer, Yehuda **D804.3.B37 1989**
Out of the Ashes: The Impact of American Jews on Post-Holocaust European Jewry. Trade Cloth. Elsevier Science & Technology Books. Saint Louis, MO. 1989. 344p. ISBN:0-08-036504-3, ISBN13: 978-0-08-036504-6. Dewey:940.53/15/0392404. LCCN:88-025412.
Audience: **g,l,u,f.** *Choice, 1989.*

Bauer, Yehuda & Keren, Nili **D804.34.B38 2001**
A History of the Holocaust. Trade Cloth. Scholastic Library Publishing. Danbury, CT. 2001. 432p. Single Titles Social Studies Ser. ISBN:0-531-11884-3, ISBN13: 978-0-531-11884-9. Dewey:940.53/18. LCCN:00-033033.
Audience: **g,l,u,f.**

Bergen, Doris L. **BR856.B398 1996**
Twisted Cross: The German Christian Movement in the Third Reich. Trade Paper. University of North Carolina Press. Chapel Hill, NC. 1996. 360p. ISBN:0-8078-4560-4, ISBN13: 978-0-8078-4560-8. Dewey:261.7/0943/09043. LCCN:95-017954.
Audience: **u,f.** *Choice, 1996.*

Bergen, Doris L. **DD256.5B3916 2002**
War and Genocide: A Concise History of the Holocaust. Trade Cloth. Rowman & Littlefield Publishers, Inc. Lanham, MD. 2002. 280p. Critical Issues in History Ser. ISBN:0-8476-9630-8, ISBN13: 978-0-8476-9630-7. Dewey:943.086. LCCN:2002-008963.
Audience: **g,l,u,f.** *Choice, 2003.*

Braham, Randolph L. **DS135.H9B74 2000**
The Politics of Genocide: The Holocaust in Hungary. Ed. 2. Trade Cloth. Wayne State University Press. Detroit, MI. 2000.

321p. ISBN:0-8143-2690-0, ISBN13: 978-0-8143-2690-9. Dewey:940.53/18/09439. LCCN:99-020739.
Audience: **u,f.**

Breitman, Richard **DD247.H46B74 1992**
The Architect of Genocide: Himmler and the Final Solution. Trade Paper. University Press of New England. Lebanon, NH. 1992. 348p. Tauber Institute for the Study of European Jewry Ser., Vol. 14 ISBN:0-87451-596-3, ISBN13: 978-0-87451-596-1. Dewey:943.086092. LCCN:92-053857.
Audience: **u,f.**

Breitman, Richard, et al. **D810.S7**
U. S. Intelligence and the Nazis. Norman J. W. Goda, Timothy Naftali & Robert Wolfe (Authors). Cloth Text. Cambridge University Press. New York, NY. 2005. 508p. ISBN:0-521-85268-4, ISBN13: 978-0-521-85268-5. Dewey:940.548673.
Audience: **u,f.** *Choice, 2006, 2005.*

Brenner, Michael **DS135.G33B7513 1997**
After the Holocaust: Rebuilding Jewish Lives in Postwar Germany. Barbara Harshav (Translator). Trade Cloth. Princeton University Press. Princeton, NJ. 1997. 208p. ISBN:0-691-02665-3, ISBN13: 978-0-691-02665-7. Dewey:943/.004924. LCCN:97-001149.
Audience: **u,f.** *Choice, 1998.*

Browning, Christopher R. **D804.3 .B769 2000**
Nazi Policy, Jewish Workers, German Killers. Trade Paper. Cambridge University Press. New York, NY. 2000. 198p. ISBN:0-521-77490-X, ISBN13: 978-0-521-77490-1. Dewey:940.53/18. LCCN:99-040042.
Audience: **g,l,u,f.**

Browning, Christopher R. **D804.3.B77 1992**
Ordinary Men: Reserve Battalion 101 and the Final Solution in Poland. Trade Cloth. HarperCollins Publishers. New York, NY. 1992. 224p. ISBN:0-06-019013-2, ISBN13: 978-0-06-019013-2. Dewey:940.53/18. LCCN:91-050471.
Audience: **g,l,u,f.** *Choice, 1992.*

Browning, Christopher R. **D804.3.B773 2004**
The Origins of the Final Solution: The Evolution of Nazi Jewish Policy, September 1939-March 1942. Jurgen Matthaus (Contribution by). Trade Cloth. University of Nebraska Press. Lincoln, NE. 2004. 640p. Comprehensive History of the Holocaust Ser. ISBN:0-8032-1327-1, ISBN13: 978-0-8032-1327-2. Dewey:940.53/1811. LCCN:2003-060813.
Audience: **l,u,f.** *Choice, 2004.*

Bukey, Evan Burr **99-21475 [DB]**
Hitler's Austria: Popular Sentiment in the Nazi Era, 1938-1945. Trade Paper. University of North Carolina Press. Chapel Hill, NC. 2002. 336p. ISBN:0-8078-5363-1, ISBN13: 978-0-8078-5363-4. Dewey:943.605/22.
Audience: **u,f.** *Choice, 2000.*

Burrin, Philippe **D804.3.B8713 1994**
Hitler and the Jews: The Genesis of the Holocaust. Patsy Southgate (Translator), Saul Friedlander (Introduction by). Paper Text. Oxford University Press, Inc. New York, NY. 1994. 192p. An Arnold Publication Ser. ISBN:0-340-59362-8, ISBN13: 978-0-340-59362-2. Dewey:940.53/18. LCCN:93-034024.
Audience: **g,l,u.**

Curtis, Michael **DC397.C87 2003**
Verdict on Vichy: Power and Prejudice in the Vichy France Regime. Trade Cloth. Arcade Publishing, Inc. New York, NY. 2003. 440p. ISBN:1-55970-689-9, ISBN13: 978-1-55970-689-6. Dewey:944.081/6. LCCN:2002-044055.
Audience: **u,f.** *Choice, 2004.*

Czerniakow, Adam **DS135.P62W2613 1999**
The Warsaw Diary of Adam Czerniakow: Prelude to Doom. Raul Hilberg, Stanislaw Staron & Josef Kermisz (Editors). Trade Paper. Ivan R. Dee Publisher. Blue Ridge Summit, PA. 1999. 444p. ISBN:1-56663-230-7, ISBN13: 978-1-56663-230-0. Dewey:940.53/18094384. LCCN:98-042718.
Audience: **g,l,u,f.**

Delbo, Charlotte **D805.P7 D413 1978**
None of Us Will Return: Auschwitz and After. Trade Paper. Beacon Press. Boston, MA. 1978. ISBN:0-8070-6371-1, ISBN13: 978-0-8070-6371-2. Dewey:940.54/7243/094386. LCCN:77-088586.
Audience: **g,l,u,f.**

Dobroszycki, Lucjan **DS135.P62**
The Chronicle of the Lodz Ghetto, 1941-1944. Trade Paper. Yale University Press. Cumberland, RI. 1987. 565p. ISBN:0-300-03924-7, ISBN13: 978-0-300-03924-5. Dewey:943.8/4. LCCN:84-003614.
Audience: **u,f.**

Dwork, Deborah & Jan van Pelt, Robert **D805.P7D89 1996**
Auschwitz, 1270 to the Present. Trade Cloth. W. W. Norton & Company, Inc. New York, NY. 1996. 416p. ISBN:0-393-03933-1, ISBN13: 978-0-393-03933-7. Dewey:940.53/18. LCCN:95-040275.
Audience: **g,l,u,f.** *Choice, 1997.*

Evans, Richard J. **DD256.5.E92 1989**
In Hitler's Shadow: West German Historians and the Attempt to Escape from the Nazi Past. Trade Cloth. Knopf Publishing Group. New York, NY. 1989. x, 196p. ISBN:0-394-57686-1, ISBN13: 978-0-394-57686-2. Dewey:943.086. LCCN:88-043239.
Audience: **g,l,u.** *Choice, 1990.*

Evans, Richard J. **KD379.5.I78E95 2002**
Lying about Hitler: History, Holocaust and the David Irving Trial. Trade Paper. Basic Books. New York, NY. 2002. 336p. ISBN:0-465-02153-0, ISBN13: 978-0-465-02153-6. Dewey:940.53/18.
Audience: **g,l,u,f.**

Ezergailis, Andrew **DS135.L3.E94 1996**
The Holocaust in Latvia, 1941-1944: The Missing Center. Trade Cloth. Bow Historical Books. New Providence, NJ. 1996. xxi, 465p. ISBN:9984-9054-3-8, ISBN13: 978-9984-9054-3-3. Dewey:940.53/18/094743. LCCN:95-042583.
Audience: **g,l,u,f.** *Choice, 1997.*

Friedlander, Henry **94-40941 [DD]**
The Origins of Nazi Genocide: From Euthanasia to the Final Solution. Trade Paper. University of North Carolina Press. Chapel Hill, NC. 1997. 448p. ISBN:0-8078-4675-9, ISBN13: 978-0-8078-4675-9. Dewey:943/.086. LCCN:94-040941.
Audience: **g,l,u,f.** *Choice, 1996.*

Friedlander, Saul **DS135.G3315F75 1997**
The Years of Persecution, 1933-1939. Trade Cloth. HarperCollins Publishers. New York, NY. 1997. 448p. Nazi

Germany and the Jews Ser., Vol. 1 ISBN:0-06-019042-6, ISBN13: 978-0-06-019042-2. Dewey:940.53/18. LCCN:96-021915.
Audience: **g,l,u,f.** *Choice, 1997.*

Friedman, Jonathan **DS135.G4F664 1998**
The Lion and the Star: Gentile-Jewish Relations in Three Hessian Towns, 1919-1945. Cloth Text. University Press of Kentucky. Lexington, KY. 1998. 292p. ISBN:0-8131-2043-8, ISBN13: 978-0-8131-2043-0. Dewey:943/.4164. LCCN:97-033201.
Audience: **u,f.** *Choice, 1998.*

Gellately, Robert **DS135.G33**
The Gestapo and German Society: Enforcing Racial Policy, 1933-1945. Paper Text. Oxford University Press, Inc. New York, NY. 1992. 314p. ISBN:0-19-820297-0, ISBN13: 978-0-19-820297-4. Dewey:943/.004924.
Audience: **u,f.** *Choice, 1991.*

Gellately, Robert **DS135.G3315G45 1990**
The Gestapo and German Society: Enforcing Racial Policy, 1933-1945. Trade Cloth. Oxford University Press, Inc. New York, NY. 1990. 320p. ISBN:0-19-822869-4, ISBN13: 978-0-19-822869-1. Dewey:943/.004924. LCCN:89-026534.
Audience: **u,f.** *Choice, 1991.*

Gellately, Robert & Stoltzfus, Nathan (Editors) **DD256.5**
Social Outsiders in Nazi Germany. Trade Paper. Princeton University Press. Princeton, NJ. 2001. 338p. ISBN:0-691-08684-2, ISBN13: 978-0-691-08684-2. Dewey:323.1/43/09043.
Audience: **g,l,u,f.**

Gerlach, Wolfgang **DS146.G4G4813 2000**
And the Witnesses Were Silent: The Confessing Church and the Persecution of the Jews. Victoria J. Barnett (Editor, Translator). Cloth Text. University of Nebraska Press. Lincoln, NE. 2000. 304p. ISBN:0-8032-2165-7, ISBN13: 978-0-8032-2165-9. Dewey:261.8/348924043. LCCN:99-044916.
Audience: **g,l,u,f.** *Choice, 2000.*

Grau, Gunter & Shoppmann, Claudia (Editors) **HQ76.3.G4H6613 1995**
A Hidden Holocaust: Lesbian and Gay Persecution in Germany, 1933-1945. Cloth Text. Fitzroy Dearborn Publishers, Inc. Chicago, IL. 1997. 336p. ISBN:1-884964-15-X, ISBN13: 978-1-884964-15-2. Dewey:306.7660943. LCCN:98-113406.
Audience: **g,l,u,f.**

Gross, Jan T. **DS135.P62J444 2001**
Neighbors: The Destruction of the Jewish Community in Jedwabne, Poland. Trade Cloth. Princeton University Press. Princeton, NJ. 2001. 272p. ISBN:0-691-08667-2, ISBN13: 978-0-691-08667-5. Dewey:940.53/18/0943843. LCCN:00-051685.
Audience: **u,f.** *Choice, 2002.*

Grynberg, Michal (Editor) **D810.J4P2713 2002**
Words to Outlive Us: Eyewitness Accounts from the Warsaw Ghetto. Philip Boehm (Translator). Cloth over Boards. Henry Holt & Company. New York, NY. 2002. 480p. ISBN:0-8050-5833-8, ISBN13: 978-0-8050-5833-8. Dewey:940.5/318/092243841. LCCN:2001-051387.
Audience: **g,l,u,f.**

Gutman, Israel **DS135.P63**
Resistance: The Warsaw Ghetto Uprising. Trade Paper. Houghton Mifflin Company Trade & Reference Division. Boston, MA. 1998. 328p. ISBN:0-395-90130-8, ISBN13: 978-0-395-90130-4. Dewey:943.8/4. LCCN:93-046767.
Audience: **g,l,u.** *Choice, 1994.*

Haar, Ingo & Fahlbusch, Michael (Editors) **DD238.G39 2004**
German Scholars and Ethnic Cleansing, 1920-1945. Trade Cloth. Berghahn Books, Inc. New York, NY. 2004. 320p. Austrian and Habsburg Studies ISBN:1-57181-435-3, ISBN13: 978-1-57181-435-7. Dewey:323.143/09/041. LCCN:2004-047674.
Audience: **g,l,u,f.** *Choice, 2005.*

Hayes, Peter **HD9654.9.I5 H39 2001**
Industry and Ideology: I. G. Farben in the Nazi Era. Ed. 2. Trade Cloth. Cambridge University Press. New York, NY. 2000. 432p. ISBN:0-521-78110-8, ISBN13: 978-0-521-78110-7. Dewey:338.7/66/009409043. LCCN:00-023560.
Audience: **u,f.** *Choice, 1987.*

Heger, Heinz **HQ75.7.H4313 1994**
The Men with the Pink Triangle: The True Life and Death Story of Homosexuals in the Nazi Death Camps. Ed. 2. Trade Paper. Alyson Publications. Los Angeles, CA. 1994. 120p. ISBN:1-55583-006-4, ISBN13: 978-1-55583-006-9. Dewey:940.54/7243. LCCN:94-029646.
Audience: **g,l.**

Hoess, Rudolf **D805.G3H553 2000**
Commandant of Auschwitz: The Autobiography of Rudolf Hess. Ed. 2. Constantine FitzGibbon & Joachim Neugroschel (Translators), Primo Levi (Introduction by). Trade Paper. Phoenix Press, WC2. London, 2000. 252p. Phoenix Press Ser. ISBN:1-84212-024-7, ISBN13: 978-1-84212-024-8. Dewey:940.54/7243/094386. LCCN:00-702547.
Audience: **g,l,u,f.**

Hoffman, Eva **D804.348.H64 2004**
After Such Knowledge: Memory, History, and the Legacy of the Holocaust. Trade Cloth. PublicAffairs. New York, NY. 2003. 320p. ISBN:1-58648-046-4, ISBN13: 978-1-58648-046-2. LCCN:2003-066443.
Audience: **u,f.**

Ioanid, Radu **DS135.R7I6513 2000**
The Holocaust in Romania: The Destruction of Jews and Gypsies under the Antonescu Regime, 1940-1944. Trade Cloth. Ivan R. Dee Publisher. Blue Ridge Summit, PA. 2000. 416p. ISBN:1-56663-256-0, ISBN13: 978-1-56663-256-0. Dewey:940.53/18/09498. LCCN:99-043229.
Audience: **g,l,u,f.** *Choice, 2000.*

Kershaw, Ian **DD247.H5K462 1999**
Hitler, 1889-1936: Hubris. Trade Cloth. W. W. Norton & Company, Inc. New York, NY. 1999. 845p. Hitler Ser., Vol. 1 ISBN:0-393-04671-0, ISBN13: 978-0-393-04671-7. Dewey:943.086/092 B. LCCN:98-029569.
Audience: **g,u,f.**

Kershaw, Ian **DD247.H5**
Hitler, 1936-1945: Nemesis. Trade Cloth. W. W. Norton & Company, Inc. New York, NY. 2000. 1161p. ISBN:0-393-04994-9, ISBN13: 978-0-393-04994-7. Dewey:943/.086/092. LCCN:98-029569.
Audience: **g,u,f.** *Choice, 2001.*

Klee, Ernst, et al. **D804.3**
The Good Old Days: The Holocaust As Seen by Its Perpetrators and Bystanders. Willi Dressen & Volker Reiss (Authors). Trade Cloth. William S. Konecky Associates, Inc. Old Saybrook, CT. 1997. 336p. ISBN:1-56852-133-2, ISBN13: 978-1-56852-133-6. Dewey:940.5318.
Audience: **g,l,u,f.**

Kluger, Ruth **DS135.A93K58513 2001**
Still Alive: A Holocaust Girlhood Remembered. Lore Segal (Foreword by). Trade Cloth. Feminist Press at The City University of New York. New York, NY. 2001. 272p. Helen Rose Schever Jewish Women Ser. ISBN:1-55861-271-8, ISBN13: 978-1-55861-271-6. Dewey:940.53/18/092. LCCN:2001-040459.
Audience: **g,l,u,f.**

Kruk, Herman **DS135.L52V554813**
The Last Days of the Jerusalem of Lithuania: Chronicles from the Vilna Ghetto and the Camps, 1939-1944. Benjamin Harshav (Editor), Barbara Harshav (Translator). Cloth over Boards. Yale University Press. Cumberland, RI. 2002. 816p. ISBN:0-300-04494-1, ISBN13: 978-0-300-04494-2. Dewey:940.53/18/092 B. LCCN:2002-016736.
Audience: **u,f.** *Choice, 2003.*

Langer, Lawrence L. **D804.3.L36**
Holocaust Testimonies: The Ruins of Memory. Trade Paper. Yale University Press. Cumberland, RI. 1993. 235p. ISBN:0-300-05247-2, ISBN13: 978-0-300-05247-3. Dewey:940.53/18. LCCN:90-044768.
Audience: **g,l,u,f.** *Choice, 1991.*

Lanzmann, Claude **D804.3.L36813 1995**
Shoah: The Complete Text of the Acclaimed Holocaust Film. Ed. 10. Trade Paper. Da Capo Press, Inc. Cambridge, MA. 1995. 196p. ISBN:0-306-80665-7, ISBN13: 978-0-306-80665-0. Dewey:940.53/18/0922. LCCN:95-035137.
Audience: **g,l,u,f.**

Laqueur, Walter (Editor) **D804.25.H66 2001**
The Holocaust Encyclopedia. Judith Tydor Baumel (Contribution by). Cloth over Boards. Yale University Press. Cumberland, RI. 2001. 816p. ISBN:0-300-08432-3, ISBN13: 978-0-300-08432-0. Dewey:940.53/18/03. LCCN:00-106567.
Audience: **g,l,u,f.** *Choice, 2001.*

Lazare, Lucien **DS135.F83L3613 1996**
Rescue as Resistance: How Jewish Organizations Fought the Holocaust in France. Jeffrey M. Green (Translator). Trade Cloth. Columbia University Press. New York, NY. 1996. 352p. ISBN:0-231-10124-4, ISBN13: 978-0-231-10124-0. Dewey:944/.004924. LCCN:95-050615.
Audience: **u,f.** *Choice, 1996.*

Levi, Primo **D805.P7L4413**
Survival in Auschwitz. Trade Paper. Simon & Schuster. New York, NY. 1995. 192p. U Ser. ISBN:0-684-82680-1, ISBN13: 978-0-684-82680-6. LCCN:86-013656.
Audience: **g,l,u,f.**

Levi, Primo **D804.3.L4813 1989**
The Drowned and the Saved. Raymond Rosenthal (Translator). Trade Paper. Knopf Publishing Group. New York, NY. 1989. 208p. International Ser. ISBN:0-679-72186-X, ISBN13: 978-0-679-72186-4. Dewey:940.5/318. LCCN:88-040375.
Audience: **g,l,u,f.**

Levin, Dov **DS135.P6L47613 1995**
The Lesser of Two Evils: Eastern European Jewry under Soviet Rule 1939-1941. Trade Cloth. Jewish Publication Society. Dulles, VA. 1995. 424p. ISBN:0-8276-0518-8, ISBN13: 978-0-8276-0518-3. Dewey:943.8/004924. LCCN:95-018725.
Audience: **g,u,f.** *Choice, 1996.*

Lewin, Abraham **DS135.P62W314 1988**
A Cup of Tears: A Diary of the Warsaw Ghetto. Antony Polonsky (Editor), Chris Hutton (Translator). Trade Cloth. Blackwell Publishing, Inc. Malden, MA. 1988. 224p. ISBN:0-631-16215-1, ISBN13: 978-0-631-16215-5. Dewey:940.53/15/0392404384. LCCN:88-016762.
Audience: **g,l,u,f.** *Choice, 1989.*

Lewy, Guenter **BX1536.L4 1999**
The Catholic Church and Nazi Germany. Trade Paper. Da Capo Press, Inc. Cambridge, MA. 2000. 448p. ISBN:0-306-80931-1, ISBN13: 978-0-306-80931-6. Dewey:282/.43. LCCN:99-042093.
Audience: **u,f.** B

Lewy, Guenter **D810.G9**
The Nazi Persecution of the Gypsies. Trade Paper. Oxford University Press, Inc. New York, NY. 2001. 318p. ISBN:0-19-514240-3, ISBN13: 978-0-19-514240-2. Dewey:940.53/18/08991497.
Audience: **g,l,u,f.** *Choice, 2000.*

Marrus, Michael R. **D804.3.M37 1989**
The Holocaust in History. Trade Paper. Penguin Group (USA) Inc. New York, NY. 1989. 28p. ISBN:0-452-00953-7, ISBN13: 978-0-452-00953-0. Dewey:940.53/15/03924. LCCN:88-021790.
Audience: **g,l,u,f.** *Choice, 1988.*

Marrus, Michael R. **D804.G42N87 1997**
The Nuremberg War Crimes Trial, 1945-46: A Documentary History. Trade Paper. Bedford/Saint Martin's. New York, NY. 1997. 276p. The Bedford Series in History and Culture ISBN:0-312-13691-9, ISBN13: 978-0-312-13691-8. Dewey:341.6/9/0268. LCCN:96-086777.
Audience: **g,l,u,f.**

Melson, Robert **DS195.5.M45 1992**
Revolution and Genocide: On the Origins of the Armenian Genocide and the Holocaust. Leo Kuper (Foreword by). Trade Cloth. University of Chicago Press. Chicago, IL. 1992. 386p. ISBN:0-226-51990-2, ISBN13: 978-0-226-51990-6. Dewey:956.6015. LCCN:91-047944.
Audience: **g,l,u,f.** *Choice, 1993.*

Mishell, William W. **DS135.R93.K286 1988**
Kaddish for Kovno: Life and Death in a Lithuanian Ghetto, 1941-1945. Trade Cloth. Chicago Review Press, Inc. Chicago, IL. 1988. vii, 398p. ISBN:1-55652-033-6, ISBN13: 978-1-55652-033-4. Dewey:947/.5. LCCN:88-002587.
Audience: **g,l,u,f.**

Muller, Filip **D805.5.A96M85 1999**
Eyewitness Auschwitz: Three Years in the Gas Chambers. Trade Paper. Ivan R. Dee Publisher. Blue Ridge Summit, PA. 1999. 192p. ISBN:1-56663-271-4, ISBN13: 978-1-56663-271-3. Dewey:940.54/7243/094386. LCCN:99-032041.
Audience: **g,l,u,f.**

Niewyk, Donald L. (Editor) **D804.195.F74 1998**
Fresh Wounds: Early Narratives of Holocaust Survival. Trade Cloth. University of North Carolina Press. Chapel Hill, NC.

1998. 432p. ISBN:0-8078-2393-7, ISBN13: 978-0-8078-2393-4. Dewey:940.53/18. LCCN:97-017725.
Audience: **u,f.** *Choice, 1998.*

Novick, Peter **D804.45.U55N68 2000**
The Holocaust in American Life. Trade Paper. Houghton Mifflin Company Trade & Reference Division. Boston, MA. 2000. 382p. ISBN:0-618-08232-8, ISBN13: 978-0-618-08232-2. Dewey:940.53/18. LCCN:99-020074.
Audience: **g,l,u.** *Choice, 1999.*

Owings, Alison **D811.5.O885 1993**
Frauen: German Women Recall the Third Reich. Trade Cloth. Rutgers University Press. Piscataway, NJ. 1993. 550p. ISBN:0-8135-1992-6, ISBN13: 978-0-8135-1992-0. Dewey:943/.086/0922. LCCN:92-042097.
Audience: **g,l,u,f.** *Choice, 1994.*

Patterson, David (Editor, Translator) **DS135.R92C647 2002**
The Complete Black Book of Russian Jewry. Helen Segall (Introduction by), Irving Louis Horowitz (Foreword by). Trade Cloth. Transaction Publishers. Somerset, NJ. 2001. 579p. ISBN:0-7658-0069-1, ISBN13: 978-0-7658-0069-5. Dewey:940.5/318/0947. LCCN:2001-052299.
Audience: **g,l,u,f.** *Choice, 2002.*

Phayer, Michael **BX1378.P49 2000**
[e] The Catholic Church and the Holocaust, 1930-1965. E-Book. Indiana University Press. Bloomington, IN. 2000. xviii, 301p. ISBN:0-253-33725-9, ISBN13: 978-0-253-33725-2. Dewey:282/.09/044. LCCN:99-087415.
Audience: **u,f.** *Choice, 2001.*

Pinchuk, Ben-Cion **DS135.P6P49 1991**
Eastern Poland on the Eve of the Holocaust: Shtetl Jews under Soviet Rule 1939-1941. Cloth Text. Blackwell Publishing, Inc. Malden, MA. 1990. 256p. ISBN:0-631-17469-9, ISBN13: 978-0-631-17469-1. Dewey:943.8/004924. LCCN:90-000126.
Audience: **u,f.** *Choice, 1991.*

Polonsky, Antony & Davies, Norman (Editors) **DS135.R93G3436 1991**
Jews in Eastern Poland and the U. S. S. R., 1939-46. Cloth Text. Palgrave Macmillan. New York, NY. 1991. 440p. ISBN:0-312-06200-1, ISBN13: 978-0-312-06200-2. Dewey:947/.718004924. LCCN:91-012028.
Audience: **l,u,f.** *Choice, 1992.*

Polonsky, Antony & Michlic, Joanna B. (Editors) **DS135.P62J4458 2004**
The Neighbors Respond: The Controversy over the Jedwabne Massacre in Poland. Trade Paper. Princeton University Press. Princeton, NJ. 2003. 432p. ISBN:0-691-11306-8, ISBN13: 978-0-691-11306-7. Dewey:940.53/18/09438. LCCN:2003-043366.
Audience: **u,f.** *Choice, 2004.*

Ranki, Vera **DS135.H9R36 1999**
The Politics of Inclusion and Exclusion: Jews and Nationalism in Hungary. Cloth Text. Holmes & Meier Publishers, Inc. Teaneck, NJ. 1999. 274p. ISBN:0-8419-1401-X, ISBN13: 978-0-8419-1401-8. Dewey:943.9/004924. LCCN:98-045937.
Audience: **g,l,u,f.** *Choice, 1999.*

Roland, Charles G. **DS135.P62.W3355 1992**
Courage under Siege: Starvation, Disease and Death in the Warsaw Ghetto. Trade Cloth. Oxford University Press, Inc. New York, NY. 1992. 320p. Studies in Jewish History ISBN:0-19-506285-X, ISBN13: 978-0-19-506285-4. Dewey:940.53/18/094384. LCCN:91-045644.
Audience: **u,f.** *Choice, 1993.*

Roth, John K. & Rittner, Carol (Editors) **BX1378.P57 2001**
Pope Pius XII and the Holocaust. Trade Cloth. Continuum International Publishing Group, Ltd. London, 2002. 256p. Leicester History of Religions Ser. ISBN:0-7185-0274-4, ISBN13: 978-0-7185-0274-4. Dewey:282/.092. LCCN:2001-038319.
Audience: **u,f.** *Choice, 2003.*

Schleunes, Karl A. **DS135.G3315S34 1990**
The Twisted Road to Auschwitz: Nazi Policy Toward German Jews, 1933-1939. Hans Mommsen (Foreword by). Trade Paper. University of Illinois Press. Champaign, IL. 1990. 304p. ISBN:0-252-06147-0, ISBN13: 978-0-252-06147-9. Dewey:943/.004924. LCCN:90-035944.
Audience: **g,l,u,f.**

Schulte, Theo **D802.S75S38 1989**
The German Army and Nazi Policies in Occupied Russia. Trade Cloth. Berg Publishers. Oxford, 1989. 406p. ISBN:0-85496-160-7, ISBN13: 978-0-85496-160-3. Dewey:940.53/37. LCCN:87-025599.
Audience: **g,u,f.** *Choice, 1989.*

Sereny, Gitta **D805.G3 S456 1983**
Into That Darkness: An Examination of Conscience. Trade Paper. Knopf Publishing Group. New York, NY. 1983. 400p. ISBN:0-394-71035-5, ISBN13: 978-0-394-71035-8. Dewey:940.54/72/4304355. LCCN:82-040049.
Audience: **u,f.**

Shermer, Michael & Grobman, Alex **D804.3**
Denying History: Who Says the Holocaust Never Happened and Why Do They Say It? Arthur Hertzberg (Foreword by). Trade Paper. University of California Press. Berkeley, CA. 2002. 332p. ISBN:0-520-23469-3, ISBN13: 978-0-520-23469-7. Dewey:940.5318. LCCN:00-028690.
Audience: **g,l,u,f.** *Choice, 2001.*

Sierakowiak, Dawid **DS135.P63**
The Diary of Dawid Sierakowiak: Five Notebooks from the Lodz Ghetto. Alan Adelson (Editor), Kamil Turowski (Translator). Trade Paper. Oxford University Press, Inc. New York, NY. 1998. 288p. ISBN:0-19-512285-2, ISBN13: 978-0-19-512285-5. Dewey:940.5/318/092.
Audience: **g,l,u,f.**

Sofsky, Wolfgang **D805.G3**
The Order of Terror: The Concentration Camp. William Templer (Translator). Trade Paper. Princeton University Press. Princeton, NJ. 1999. 368p. ISBN:0-691-00685-7, ISBN13: 978-0-691-00685-7. Dewey:940.54/7243.
Audience: **u,f.** *Choice, 1997.*

Soros, Tivadar **DS135.H93S67713 2001**
Masquerade: Dancing Around Death in Nazi Occupied Hungary. Humphrey Tonkin (Translator), Paul Soros & George Soros (Foreword by). Trade Cloth. Arcade Publishing, Inc. New York, NY. 2001. 275p. ISBN:1-55970-581-7, ISBN13: 978-1-55970-581-3. Dewey:943.9/004924. LCCN:2001-022626.
Audience: **g,l,u,f.**

Spiegelman, Art **DS135.P62**
Maus: A Survivor's Tale: My Father Bleeds History. Trade Cloth. Knopf Publishing Group. New York, NY. 1991. ISBN:0-394-54155-3, ISBN13: 978-0-394-54155-6. Dewey:940.53/15/03924024.
Audience: **g,l,u,f.**

Sprecher, Drexel A. **KZ1176.S68 1999**
Inside the Nuremberg Trial: A Prosecutor's Comprehensive Account. Claiborne Pell & William E. Jackson (Preface by). Trade Cloth. University Press of America, Inc. Lanham, MD. 1999. 1626p. ISBN:0-7618-1284-9, ISBN13: 978-0-7618-1284-5. Dewey:341.6/9. LCCN:98-031583.
Audience: **g.** *Choice, 1999.*

Stolzfus, Nathan **DS135.G4B476 1996**
Resistance of the Heart. Trade Cloth. W. W. Norton & Company, Inc. New York, NY. 1996. 352p. ISBN:0-393-03904-8, ISBN13: 978-0-393-03904-7. Dewey:305.8/924043155. LCCN:95-050107.
Audience: **g,l,u,f.** *Choice, 1997.*

Stone, Dan (Editor) **D804.348.H57 2004**
The Historiography of the Holocaust. Cloth over Boards. Palgrave Macmillan. New York, NY. 2004. 512p. ISBN:0-333-99745-X, ISBN13: 978-0-333-99745-1. Dewey:940.53/18/072. LCCN:2003-055637.
Audience: **g,l,u,f.** *Choice, 2004.*

Szpilman, Wladyslaw **DS135.P63S94713 1999**
The Pianist: The Extraordinary True Story of One Man's Survival in Warsaw, 1939-1945. Cloth over Boards. Picador. New York, NY. 1999. 240p. ISBN:0-312-24415-0, ISBN13: 978-0-312-24415-6. Dewey:940.53'18'092. LCCN:99-036033.
Audience: **g,l,u,f.** *Choice, 2000.*

Trunk, Isaiah **DS135.E83T78 1996**
Judenrat: The Jewish Councils in Eastern Europe under Nazi Occupation. Steven T. Katz (Introduction by). Trade Cloth. University of Nebraska Press. Lincoln, NE. 1996. 663p. ISBN:0-8032-9428-X, ISBN13: 978-0-8032-9428-8. Dewey:940.53/1503/924. LCCN:95-049993.
Audience: **u,f.** B

Zabarko, Boris (Editor) **DS135.U43A154 2005**
Holocaust in the Ukraine. Trade Cloth. Vallentine Mitchell Publishers. Middlesex, 2004. 394p. Library of Holocaust Testimonies Ser. ISBN:0-85303-612-8, ISBN13: 978-0-85303-612-8. Dewey:940.53/18/0922477. LCCN:2005-297198.
Audience: **g,u,f.** *Choice, 2005.*

General History > By period > Modern Era (1789-present) > Decolonization

Carruthers, Susan L. **DA16.C34 1995**
Winning Hearts and Minds: British Governments, the Media and Colonial Counter-Insurgency, 1944-1960. Trade Cloth. Continuum International Publishing Group, Ltd. London, 1995. 256p. ISBN:0-7185-0027-X, ISBN13: 978-0-7185-0027-6. Dewey:325.3/1/41. LCCN:95-007954.
Audience: **u,f.** *Choice, 1996.*

Low, D. A. **DA16.L8684 1993**
Eclipse of Empire. Trade Cloth. Cambridge University Press. New York, NY. 1991. 391p. ISBN:0-521-38329-3, ISBN13: 978-0-521-38329-5. Dewey:325/.341. LCCN:89-022286.
Audience: **u,f.** *Choice, 1992.*

General History > By period > Modern Era (1789-present) > Postwar Europe (1945-1989). Cold War

af Malmborg, Mikael **CB203.M386 2002**
The Meaning of Europe. Bo Strath (Editor). Cloth over Boards. Berg Publishers. Oxford, 2002. 224p. ISBN:1-85973-576-2, ISBN13: 978-1-85973-576-3. Dewey:940. LCCN:2002-002835.
Audience: **u,f.**

Caute, David **D857**
The Dancer Defects: The Struggle for Cultural Supremacy During the Cold War. Trade Cloth. Oxford University Press, Inc. New York, NY. 2003. 824p. ISBN:0-19-924908-3, ISBN13: 978-0-19-924908-4. Dewey:306/.0973. LCCN:2004-297973.
Audience: **g,u,f.**

Daddow, Oliver J. **HC241**
Britain and Europe since 1945: Historiographical Perspectives on Integration. Cloth over Boards. Manchester University Press. Manchester, 2004. 288p. ISBN:0-7190-6137-7, ISBN13: 978-0-7190-6137-0. Dewey:337.1/4. LCCN:2003-064862.
Audience: **u,f.**

Graham, Brian **D209.M683 1998**
Modern Europe: Place, Culture and Identity. Paper Text. Oxford University Press, Inc. New York, NY. 1998. 336p. An Arnold Publication Ser. ISBN:0-340-67698-1, ISBN13: 978-0-340-67698-1. Dewey:940. LCCN:98-028788.
Audience: **g,u,f.**

Hasegawa, Tsuyoshi **D813.J3H37 2005**
Racing the Enemy: Stalin, Truman, and the Surrender of Japan. Trade Cloth. Harvard University Press. Cambridge, MA. 2005. 432p. ISBN:0-674-01693-9, ISBN13: 978-0-674-01693-4. Dewey:940.53/2452. LCCN:2004-059786.
Audience: **g,l,u,f.** *Choice, 2006.*

Mastny, Vojtech **DK267.M3567 1996**
The Cold War and Soviet Insecurity: The Stalin Years. Trade Cloth. Oxford University Press, Inc. New York, NY. 1996. 304p. ISBN:0-19-510616-4, ISBN13: 978-0-19-510616-9. Dewey:947/.0842. LCCN:95-049341.
Audience: **g,u,f.** *Choice, 1997.*

McCormick, John **JN30.M38 2005**
Understanding the European Union: A Concise Introduction. Ed. 3. Cloth over Boards. Palgrave Macmillan. New York, NY. 2005. 288p. The European Union Ser. ISBN:1-4039-4450-4, ISBN13: 978-1-4039-4450-4. Dewey:341.242/2. LCCN:2005-041047.
Audience: **g,l,u,f.** *Choice, 2000.*

Nelsen, Brent F. & Stubb, Alexander (Editors) **JN15.E889 2003**
The European Union: Readings on the Theory and Practice of European Integration. Ed. 3. Paper Text. Lynne Rienner

Publishers, Inc. Boulder, CO. 2003. 375p. ISBN:1-58826-231-6, ISBN13: 978-1-58826-231-8. Dewey:341.242/2. LCCN:2003-043221.
Audience: **g,l,u,f.**

Rougemont, Denis de **D104**
The Idea of Europe. Guterman, Norbert (Translated by). New York, Macmillan. 1966.
Audience: **g,u,f.**

Salmon, Trevor C. & Nicoll, William (Editors) **JN15.B79 1997**
Building European Union: A Documentary History and Analysis. Trade Paper. Manchester University Press. Manchester, 1997. 240p. Europe in Change Ser. ISBN:0-7190-4446-4, ISBN13: 978-0-7190-4446-5. Dewey:337.1/4. LCCN:96-026854.
Audience: **g,l,u,f.**

Britain > Historiography

Z2016
☐ Royal Historical Society Bibliography.
http://www.rhs.ac.uk/bibl/
Royal Historical Society, Institute of Historical Research, University of London.
Audience: **g,l,u,f.**

Clive, John **DA3.M3**
Macaulay: The Shaping of the Historian. Trade Cloth. Random House, Inc. New York, NY. 1986. ISBN:0-394-47278-0, ISBN13: 978-0-394-47278-2. Dewey:907/.2024.
Audience: **u,f.**

Hamburger, Joseph **DA3.M3**
Macaulay and the Whig Tradition. Library Binding. University of Chicago Press. Chicago, IL. 1996. 288p. ISBN:0-226-31472-3, ISBN13: 978-0-226-31472-3. Dewey:941.081/092/4. LCCN:75-027892.
Audience: **u,f.**

Pares, Richard **DA505.P3 1988**
King George III and the Politicians. Trade Cloth. Oxford University Press, Inc. New York, NY. 1988. 224p. ISBN:0-19-821240-2, ISBN13: 978-0-19-821240-9. Dewey:941.07/3. LCCN:87-014064.
Audience: **g,l,u,f.**

Richardson, R. C. **DA403.R53 1999**
The Debate on the English Revolution. Ed. 3. Trade Cloth. Manchester University Press. Manchester, 1999. 262p. Issues in Historiography Ser. ISBN:0-7190-4739-0, ISBN13: 978-0-7190-4739-8. Dewey:941.06/3/072. LCCN:98-028825.
Audience: **u,f.**

Taylor, Arthur J. (Editor) **HD7023**
The Standard of Living in Britain in the Industrial Revolution. Trade Cloth. Routledge. New York, NY. 1975. 271p. Debates in Economic History Ser. ISBN:0-416-08250-5, ISBN13: 978-0-416-08250-0. Dewey:339.4/7/0880623.
Audience: **g,l,u,f.**

Woolf, D. R. **DA1**
The Idea of History in Early Stuart England: Erudition, Ideology, and the Light of Truth from the Accession of James I to the Civil War. Trade Cloth. University of Toronto Press. Toronto, ON. 1990. 377p. ISBN:0-8020-5862-0, ISBN13: 978-0-8020-5862-1. Dewey:907/.2042.
Audience: **l,u,f.** *Choice, 1991.*

Britain > British Empire. Commonwealth of Nations

Andrews, Kenneth R. **DA86.A74 1991**
Ships, Money and Politics: Seafaring and Naval Enterprise in the Reign of Charles I. Trade Cloth. Cambridge University Press. New York, NY. 1991. 250p. ISBN:0-521-40116-X, ISBN13: 978-0-521-40116-6. Dewey:359/.00941. LCCN:90-040407.
Audience: **u,f.** *Choice, 1992.*

Barnett, Correlli **DA578.B33 1986**
The Collapse of British Power. Trade Paper. Brill Academic Publishers, Inc. Boston, MA. 1986. 656p. ISBN:0-391-03439-1, ISBN13: 978-0-391-03439-6. Dewey:941/.083. LCCN:86-003032.
Audience: **g,l,u,f.**

Beasley, Edward **JV1016**
Mid-Victorian Imperialists: British Gentlemen and the Empire of the Mind. Paper over Boards. Routledge. New York, NY. 2005. 256p. British and Foreign and Colonial Policy Ser. ISBN:0-7146-5698-4, ISBN13: 978-0-7146-5698-4. Dewey:909/.0971241081. LCCN:2004-028868.
Audience: **u,f.**

Brown, Judith M. & Louis, Roger (Editors) **DA18**
The Oxford History of the British Empire: The Twentieth Century. Trade Cloth. Oxford University Press, Inc. New York, NY. 1999. 800p. Oxford History of the British Empire Ser., Vol. IV ISBN:0-19-820564-3, ISBN13: 978-0-19-820564-7. Dewey:325.3/41/0904.
Audience: **u,f.** *Choice, 2000.*

Canny, Nicholas (Editor) **DA16**
The Oxford History of the British Empire: The Origins of Empire: British Overseas Enterprise to the Close of the Seventeenth Century. Trade Cloth. Oxford University Press, Inc. New York, NY. 1998. 554p. Oxford History of the British Empire Ser. ISBN:0-19-820562-7, ISBN13: 978-0-19-820562-3. Dewey:325.3/41.
Audience: **u,f.**

Douglas, Roy **DA16.D68 2002**
Liquidation of Empire: The Decline of the British Empire. Cloth over Boards. Palgrave Macmillan. New York, NY. 2002. 190p. ISBN:0-333-80454-6, ISBN13: 978-0-333-80454-4. Dewey:909/.09712410825. LCCN:2002-019599.
Audience: **u,f.** *Choice, 2003.*

Eldridge, C. C. **PR478.I53E43 1996**
The Imperial Experience: From Carlyle to Forster. Cloth over Boards. Palgrave Macmillan. New York, NY. 1996. 232p. ISBN:0-312-16136-0, ISBN13: 978-0-312-16136-1. Dewey:820/.09/008. LCCN:96-033917.
Audience: **g,l,u,f.**

Etherington, Norman (Contribution by) **BV2059**
Missions and Empire. Trade Cloth. Oxford University Press, Inc.

New York, NY. 2005. 330p. Oxford History of the British Empire Companion Ser. ISBN:0-19-925347-1, ISBN13: 978-0-19-925347-0. Dewey:266.009. LCCN:2005-282368.
Audience: **g,l,u,f.**

Gilmour, David **DS475.G55 2006**
The Ruling Caste: Imperial Lives in the Victorian Raj. Cloth over Boards. Farrar, Straus & Giroux. New York, NY. 2006. 416p. ISBN:0-374-28354-0, ISBN13: 978-0-374-28354-4. Dewey:954.03/508621. LCCN:2005-044679.
Audience: **u,f.**

Hobsbawm, Eric J. **D359.7 .H63**
The Age of Empire. Trade Cloth. Peter Smith Publisher, Inc. Magnolia, MA. 1989. ISBN:0-8446-6925-3, ISBN13: 978-0-8446-6925-0. Dewey:909.81.
Audience: **g,u,f.**

Hobsbawm, Eric J. **HC253.H6**
Industry and Empire: The Birth of the Industrial Revolution. Trade Cloth. Peter Smith Publisher, Inc. Magnolia, MA. 2000. ISBN:0-8446-7122-3, ISBN13: 978-0-8446-7122-2. Dewey:330.942.
Audience: **u,f.**

James, Lawrence **DA16.J26 1996**
The Rise and Fall of the British Empire. Trade Cloth. St. Martin's Press. Gordonville, VA. 1995. 720p. ISBN:0-312-14039-8, ISBN13: 978-0-312-14039-7. Dewey:909/.0971241. LCCN:95-038774.
Audience: **g,u,f.**

Judd, Denis **DA16.J88**
Empire: The British Imperial Experience from 1765 to the Present. Trade Paper. Basic Books. New York, NY. 1998. 568p. ISBN:0-465-01954-4, ISBN13: 978-0-465-01954-0. Dewey:941.
Audience: **g,u,f.** *Choice, 1997.*

Levine, Philippa (Editor) **HQ1593**
Gender and Empire. Trade Cloth. Oxford University Press, Inc. New York, NY. 2004. 320p. Oxford History of the British Empire Companion Ser. ISBN:0-19-924951-2, ISBN13: 978-0-19-924951-0. Dewey:305.3/09171/241. LCCN:2004-044614.
Audience: **u,f.**

Lloyd, T. O. **DA300.L58 1984**
The British Empire, Fifteen Fifty-Eight to Nineteen Eighty-Three. Trade Cloth. Oxford University Press, Inc. New York, NY. 1984. xvi, 430p. Short Oxford History of the Modern World Ser. ISBN:0-19-873024-1, ISBN13: 978-0-19-873024-8. Dewey:909/.0971241. LCCN:83-019481.
Audience: **g,l,u,f.**

Lloyd, T. O. **DA566.7**
Empire, Welfare State, Europe: History of the United Kingdom, 1906-2001. Ed. 5. Paper Text. Oxford University Press, Inc. New York, NY. 2002. 568p. Short Oxford History of the Modern World Ser. ISBN:0-19-870067-9, ISBN13: 978-0-19-870067-8. Dewey:941.082. LCCN:2002-282243.
Audience: **g,u,f.**

Lloyd, Trevor Owen **DA16.L84 1996**
The British Empire, 1558-1995. Ed. 2. Paper Text. Oxford University Press, Inc. New York, NY. 1997. 468p. Short Oxford History of the Modern World Ser. ISBN:0-19-873133-7, ISBN13: 978-0-19-873133-7. Dewey:909/.0971241. LCCN:97-188661.
Audience: **g,u,f.**

Long, Roger D. (Editor) **DA16**
The Man on the Spot: Essays on British Empire History, 31. Book, Other. Greenwood Publishing Group, Inc. Portsmouth, NH. 1995. 256p. Contributions in Comparative Colonial Studies, Vol. 31 ISBN:0-313-29524-7, ISBN13: 978-0-313-29524-9. Dewey:941. LCCN:95-009667.
Audience: **g,l,u,f.** *Choice, 1996.*

Mackenzie, John M. (Editor) **DA533.I46 1989**
Imperialism and Popular Culture. Trade Paper. Manchester University Press. Manchester, 1989. 256p. Studies in Imperialism ISBN:0-7190-1868-4, ISBN13: 978-0-7190-1868-8. Dewey:941.082. LCCN:85-013657.
Audience: **u,f.** *Choice, 1986.*

Magnus, Philip Sir (Philip Montefiore) **DA68.32.K6**
Kitchener: Portrait of an Imperialist. Harmondsworth, Penguin. 1968.
Audience: **g,l,u,f.**

Mansergh, Nicholas **DA18.M3285**
Survey of British Commonwealth Affairs: Problems of Wartime Cooperation and Post-War Change, 1939-1952. Cloth Text. Taylor & Francis Group. Abingdon, 1968. 469p. ISBN:0-7146-1496-3, ISBN13: 978-0-7146-1496-0. Dewey:327/.09171/242.
Audience: **g,l,u,f.**

Marshall, P. J. (Editor) **DA16.M29 1996**
The Cambridge Illustrated History of the British Empire. Trade Paper. Cambridge University Press. New York, NY. 2001. 400p. Cambridge Illustrated Histories Ser. ISBN:0-521-00254-0, ISBN13: 978-0-521-00254-7. Dewey:909/.09712/41.
Audience: **u,f.**

Marshall, P. J. & Low, Alaine (Editors) **DA16**
The Oxford History of the British Empire: The Eighteenth Century. Trade Cloth. Oxford University Press, Inc. New York, NY. 1998. 662p. Oxford History of the British Empire Ser. ISBN:0-19-820563-5, ISBN13: 978-0-19-820563-0. Dewey:325.3/41.
Audience: **u,f.**

Porter, Andrew **JV1017**
The Oxford History of the British Empire: The Nineteenth Century. Trade Cloth. Oxford University Press, Inc. New York, NY. 1999. 796p. Oxford History of the British Empire Ser., Vol. 3 ISBN:0-19-820565-1, ISBN13: 978-0-19-820565-4. Dewey:325.3/41/09034.
Audience: **u,f.**

Porter, Bernard **DA16.P67 2004**
The Lion's Share: A Short History of British Imperialism, 1850-2004. Ed. 4. Trade Paper. Longman Publishing Group. White Plains, NY. 2004. 496p. ISBN:0-582-77252-4, ISBN13: 978-0-582-77252-6. Dewey:909/.0971241. LCCN:2004-040108.
Audience: **g,l,u,f.**

Pottinger, George **DS363.P67**
The Afghan Connection: The Extraordinary Adventures of Major Eldred Pottinger. Edinburgh: Scottish Academic Press. 1983. ISBN:0-7073-0286-2, ISBN13: 978-0-7073-0286-7.
Audience: **u,f.**

Samson, Jane (Editor) **DA16.B69 2001**
The British Empire. Paper Text. Oxford University Press, Inc. New York, NY. 2001. 344p. Oxford Readers Ser. ISBN:0-19-289293-2, ISBN13: 978-0-19-289293-5. Dewey:909/.0971/241. LCCN:00-069296.
Audience: **g,u,f.**

Thompson, Andrew **JV1011.T46 2005**
Empire Strikes Back: The Impact of Imperialism on Britain from the Mid-Nineteenth Century. Trade Paper. Longman Publishing Group. White Plains, NY. 2005. 392p. ISBN:0-582-43829-2, ISBN13: 978-0-582-43829-3. Dewey:941.08. LCCN:2004-060192.
Audience: **u,f.**

Trench, Charles C. **DA68.32.G6**
The Road to Khartoum: A Life of General Charles Gordon. Trade Cloth. Dorset Press. New York, NY. 1988. 289p. ISBN:0-88029-152-4, ISBN13: 978-0-88029-152-1. Dewey:962.4/03/0924.
Audience: **g,l,u,f.**

Winks, Robin & Louis, Roger (Editors) **DA16 .O95 1998**
The Oxford History of the British Empire: Historiography. Trade Cloth. Oxford University Press, Inc. New York, NY. 1999. 756p. Oxford History of the British Empire Ser., Vol. V ISBN:0-19-820566-X, ISBN13: 978-0-19-820566-1. Dewey:909/.0971241. LCCN:97-036299.
Audience: **u,f.** *Choice, 2000.*

Britain > England > History, General Works

DA28
☐ Oxford DNB: Oxford Dictionary of National Biography. http://www.oxforddnb.com/
Oxford University Press.
Audience: **g,l,u,f.**

Beckett, John V. **HD1923.B43 1990**
The Agricultural Revolution. Paper Text. Blackwell Publishing, Inc. Malden, MA. 1990. 96p. Historical Association Studies ISBN:0-631-16287-9, ISBN13: 978-0-631-16287-2. Dewey:338.1/0941. LCCN:89-017702.
Audience: **g,l,u,f.**

Berg, Maxine **HD9720.5**
The Age of Manufactures: Industry, Innovation, and Work in Britain, 1700-1820. Totowa, N.J.: Barnes & Noble. 1985. ISBN:0-389-20584-2, ISBN13: 978-0-389-20584-5.
Audience: **l,u.**

Clarkson, L. A. **HD2329.C56 1985**
Proto-Industrialization: The First Phase of Industrialization? Trade Paper. Macmillan Publishers Ltd. London, 1985. 87p. Studies in Economic and Social History ISBN:0-333-34392-1, ISBN13: 978-0-333-34392-0. Dewey:338.094. LCCN:85-244461.
Audience: **g,l,u,f.**

Harrison, J. F. **HN398.E5H37 1984**
The English Common People: A Social History from the Norman Conquest to the Present. Trade Cloth. Barnes & Noble Books-Imports. Lanham, MD. 1984. 446p. ISBN:0-389-20470-6, ISBN13: 978-0-389-20470-1. Dewey:306/.0942. LCCN:84-000437.
Audience: **l,u.** B

Porter, Roy **DA485**
English Society in the Eighteenth Century. Ed. 2. Trade Paper. Penguin Group (USA) Inc. New York, NY. 1990. 448p. Penguin Social History of Britain Ser. ISBN:0-14-013819-6, ISBN13: 978-0-14-013819-1. Dewey:942/.07. LCCN:91-121132.
Audience: **g,l,u,f.**

Routh, C. R. & Birley, R. (Foreword by) **DA310.T48 1984**
They Saw It Happen: An Anthology of Eye-Witnesses' Accounts of Events in British History, 1465-1688. Library Binding. Greenwood Publishing Group, Inc. Portsmouth, NH. 1984. xvi, 220p. ISBN:0-313-24301-8, ISBN13: 978-0-313-24301-1. Dewey:941.05. LCCN:84-006585.
Audience: **g,l,u,f.**

Trevelyan, George Macaulay **DA32**
Illustrated English Social History. London, New York, Longmans, Green. 1949.
Audience: **l,u.**

Walton, Izaak **PR3757.W6**
The Lives of Dr. John Donne, Sir Henry Wotton, Mr. Richard Hooker, Mr. George Herbert: 1670. Trade Cloth. Scolar Press. Aldershot, 1969. 431p. ISBN:0-85417-165-7, ISBN13: 978-0-85417-165-1. Dewey:821.309. LCCN:75-473305.
Audience: **u,f.**

Wrigley, E. Anthony & Schofield, Roger S. **HB3585.W74**
The Population History of England, 1541-1871: A Reconstruction. Trade Cloth. Harvard University Press. Cambridge, MA. 1981. 779p. Studies in Social and Demographic History ISBN:0-674-69007-9, ISBN13: 978-0-674-69007-3. Dewey:304.6/0942. LCCN:81-005010.
Audience: **l,u,f.**

Britain > England > Military and Diplomatic History

Barnett, Correlli **DA578.B33 1986**
The Collapse of British Power. Trade Paper. Brill Academic Publishers, Inc. Boston, MA. 1986. 656p. ISBN:0-391-03439-1, ISBN13: 978-0-391-03439-6. Dewey:941/.083. LCCN:86-003032.
Audience: **g,l,u,f.**

Black, J. **DA498.B53 1985**
British Foreign Policy in the Age of Walpole. Cloth Text. Brill Academic Publishers, Inc. Boston, MA. 1985. 256p. ISBN:0-85976-126-6, ISBN13: 978-0-85976-126-0. Dewey:941.07/1. LCCN:85-213381.
Audience: **u,f.** *Choice, 1985.*

Blake, Robert **DA576.B53 1985**
The Decline of Power, Nineteen Fifteen to Nineteen Sixty-Four. Trade Cloth. Oxford University Press, Inc. New York, NY. 1985.

400p. Paladin History of England Ser. ISBN:0-19-520480-8, ISBN13: 978-0-19-520480-3. Dewey:941.082. LCCN:85-004909.
Audience: **l,u,f.** *Choice, 1985.*

Bourne, Kenneth **DA550.B68 1970**
The Foreign Policy of Victorian England, 1830-1902. Trade Cloth. Oxford University Press, Inc. New York, NY. 1970. xii, 531p. ISBN:0-19-873007-1, ISBN13: 978-0-19-873007-1. Dewey:327.42. LCCN:75-543411.
Audience: **l,u,f.**

Cobban, Alfred (Editor) **DA42**
The Debate on the French Revolution, 1789-1800. Ed. 2. London: A. and C. Black. 1963. The British Political Tradition, Bk. 2
Audience: **u,f.**

Hough, Richard **DA89.1.M59.H68**
Mountbatten. Trade Cloth. Random House, Inc. New York, NY. 1981. xv, 302p. ISBN:0-394-51162-X, ISBN13: 978-0-394-51162-7. Dewey:941.082/092/4. LCCN:80-006023.
Audience: **l,u,f.**

Kennedy, Paul M. **DA47.2**
The Rise of the Anglo-German Antagonism, 1860-1914. Paper Text. Routledge. New York, NY. 1982. 604p. ISBN:0-04-940064-9, ISBN13: 978-0-04-940064-1. Dewey:327.41043. LCCN:80-040461.
Audience: **l,u,f.**

Kennedy, Paul M. **DA560**
The Realities Behind Diplomacy: Background Influences on British External Policy, 1865-1980. London: Fontana Press. 1985. ISBN:0-00-686004-4, ISBN13: 978-0-00-686004-4.
Audience: **u,f.**

Longford, Elizabeth **DA68.12.W4.L62**
Wellington. Trade Cloth. Harper & Row Ltd. London, 1970. ISBN:0-06-012669-8, ISBN13: 978-0-06-012669-8. Dewey:942.07/092/4. LCCN:75-095973.
Audience: **g,l,u,f.**

Mattingly, Garrett **DA360**
The Armada. Trade Paper, Perfect. Houghton Mifflin Company Trade & Reference Division. Boston, MA. 2005. 464p. ISBN:0-618-56591-4, ISBN13: 978-0-618-56591-7. Dewey:942.05/5.
Audience: **l,u,f.**

Rogers, Clifford J. **DA233.R64 2000**
War Cruel and Sharp: English Strategy under Edward III, 1327-1360. Trade Cloth. Boydell & Brewer, Ltd. Woodbridge, 2000. 480p. Warfare in History Ser. ISBN:0-85115-804-8, ISBN13: 978-0-85115-804-4. Dewey:944/.025. LCCN:00-042922.
Audience: **g,l,u,f.** *Choice, 2001.*

Sacks, David H. **HC258.B76**
The Widening Gate: Bristol and the Atlantic Economy, 1450-1700. Trade Paper. University of California Press. Berkeley, CA. 1993. 492p. The New Historicism Ser., No. 15:Studies in Cultural Poetics ISBN:0-520-08449-7, ISBN13: 978-0-520-08449-0. Dewey:330.9423/93. LCCN:90-019878.
Audience: **u,f.** *Choice, 1992.*

Speck, W. A. **DA814.5**
Stability and Strife: England 1714-1760. Trade Paper. Harvard University Press. Cambridge, MA. 1979. 224p. New History of England Ser. ISBN:0-674-83350-3, ISBN13: 978-0-674-83350-0. Dewey:942.07/2.
Audience: **l,u,f.**

Terraine, John **DA88.5**
Trafalgar. Trade Cloth. Mason/Charter Publishers, Inc. New York, NY. 1976. 205p. ISBN:0-88405-387-3, ISBN13: 978-0-88405-387-3. Dewey:940.2/7. LCCN:76-011423.
Audience: **l,u,f.**

Thomas, Donald **DA88.1.D9.T44 1978**
Cochrane: Brittania's Last Sea King. Trade Cloth. Penguin Group (USA) Inc. New York, NY. 1978. 383p. ISBN:0-670-22644-0, ISBN13: 978-0-670-22644-3. Dewey:359.3/31/0924. LCCN:78-006940.
Audience: **l,u,f.**

Woodham Smith, Cecil Blanche Fitz Gerald **DA564.B3**
The Reason Why. Paper Text. Textbook Publishers. Temecula, CA. 2003. 287p. ISBN:0-7581-8689-4, ISBN13: 978-0-7581-8689-8. Dewey:942.081/0924.
Audience: **l,u,f.**

Britain > England > Social Life and Customs. Ethnography

Bailey, Peter **GV75.B33 1987**
Leisure and Class in Victorian England: Rational Recreation and the Contest for Control, 1830-1885. Trade Paper. Routledge. New York, NY. 1987. 288p. ISBN:0-416-02142-5, ISBN13: 978-0-416-02142-4. Dewey:790/.0941. LCCN:87-005467.
Audience: **l,u,f.**

Briggs, Asa **HN398.E5B74**
A Social History of England. Ed. 3. Trade Cloth. Weidenfeld & Nicolson, Ltd. London, 1995. 352p. ISBN:0-297-83262-X, ISBN13: 978-0-297-83262-1. Dewey:942.
Audience: **g,l,u,f.**

Briggs, Asa **DA533**
Victorian Things. Trade Paper. Sutton Publishing, Ltd. Stroud, 2003. 448p. ISBN:0-7509-3339-9, ISBN13: 978-0-7509-3339-1. Dewey:942.081.
Audience: **g,l,u,f.** *Choice, 1989.*

Briggs, Asa **HT133**
Victorian Cities. Andrew Lees & Lynn H. Lees (Introduction by). Trade Paper. University of California Press. Berkeley, CA. 1993. 411p. Classics in Urban History Ser., Vol. 2 ISBN:0-520-07922-1, ISBN13: 978-0-520-07922-9. Dewey:307.7/6/0942/09034. LCCN:92-030443.
Audience: **g,l,u,f.**

Briggs, Asa **DA560**
Victorian People: A Reassessment of Persons and Themes, 1851-67. Ruari McLean (Illustrator). Trade Paper. University of Chicago Press. Chicago, IL. 1975. 324p. Chicago Collectors Editions Ser. ISBN:0-226-07488-9, ISBN13: 978-0-226-07488-7. Dewey:942.081. LCCN:55-005118.
Audience: **g,l,u,f.** *B*

Burn, W. L. (William Laurence) **DA550**
The Age of Equipoise: A Study of the Mid-Victorian Generation. Aldershot: Gregg Revivals. 1993. Modern Revivals

in History Ser. ISBN:0-7512-0296-7, ISBN13: 978-0-7512-0296-0.
Audience: **u,f.**

Byrne, Muriel S. & Boland, Bridget (Editors) **DA335.L5.L572 1983**
The Lisle Letters: An Abridgement. Hugh T. Roper (Foreword by). Trade Cloth. University of Chicago Press. Chicago, IL. 1983. 462p. ISBN:0-226-08800-6, ISBN13: 978-0-226-08800-6. Dewey:942.05. LCCN:82-015914.
Audience: **u,f.**

Clark, Pete A. **GT3843**
The English Alehouse: A Social History, 1200-1830. Ed. 1. Trade Paper. Longman Publishing Group. White Plains, NY. 1983. 384p. ISBN:0-582-50835-5, ISBN13: 978-0-582-50835-4. Dewey:306/.48.
Audience: **u,f.**

Davidoff, Leonore **HQ1596**
The Best Circles: Society Etiquette and the Season. Glendinning, Victoria (Introduction by). London: Cresset Library. 1986. ISBN:0-09-168761-6, ISBN13: 978-0-09-168761-8.
Audience: **l,u,f.**

Kent, Susan K. **JN979.K43 1987**
Sex and Suffrage in Britain, 1860-1914. Cloth Text. Princeton University Press. Princeton, NJ. 1987. 336p. ISBN:0-691-05497-5, ISBN13: 978-0-691-05497-1. Dewey:324.6/23/0941. LCCN:86-025307.
Audience: **g,l,u,f.** *Choice, 1987.*

Laslett, Peter **HN398.E5**
The World We Have Lost: Further Explored. Smith, Richard (Introduction by). London: Routledge. 2005. ISBN:0-415-22833-6, ISBN13: 978-0-415-22833-6.
Audience: **u,f.**

Lorimer, Douglas A. **DA125.N4.L67 1978**
Colour, Class and the Victorians: English Attitudes Toward the Negro in the Mid-Nineteenth Century. Trade Cloth. Holmes & Meier Publishers, Inc. Teaneck, NJ. 1978. 330p. ISBN:0-8419-0392-1, ISBN13: 978-0-8419-0392-0. Dewey:305.8/96/042. LCCN:78-006396.
Audience: **u,f.**

Malcolmson, Malcolm **GV75**
Popular Recreations English Society. Trade Cloth. Cambridge University Press. New York, NY. 1973. 198p. ISBN:0-521-20147-0, ISBN13: 978-0-521-20147-6. Dewey:301.5/7/0942. LCCN:72-091958.
Audience: **g,l,u,f.**

Manning, Brian **DA415**
The English People and the English Revolution, 1640-1649. Trade Cloth. Heinemann. Portsmouth, NH. 1976. x, 390p. ISBN:0-435-32565-5, ISBN13: 978-0-435-32565-7. Dewey:942.06/2. LCCN:76-370634.
Audience: **g,l,u,f.**

Marshall, Rosalind K. **HQ1147.G7**
Virgins and Viragos: A History of Women in Scotland from 1080-1980. Trade Cloth. Academy Chicago Publishers, Ltd. Chicago, IL. 1983. 340p. ISBN:0-89733-075-7, ISBN13: 978-0-89733-075-6. Dewey:305.4/09411. LCCN:82-024439.
Audience: **g,l,u,f.**

Pollock, Linda A. **HQ767.87 .P64 1983**
Forgotten Children: Parent-Child Relations from 1500 to 1900. Trade Paper. Cambridge University Press. New York, NY. 1983. 352p. ISBN:0-521-27133-9, ISBN13: 978-0-521-27133-2. Dewey:306.8/74/0941. LCCN:83-005315.
Audience: **l,u,f.** B

Porter, Roy **DA485**
English Society in the Eighteenth Century. Ed. 2. Trade Paper. Penguin Group (USA) Inc. New York, NY. 1990. 448p. Penguin Social History of Britain Ser. ISBN:0-14-013819-6, ISBN13: 978-0-14-013819-1. Dewey:942/.07. LCCN:91-121132.
Audience: **g,l,u,f.**

Read, Donald **DA533.R37**
England, 1868-1914: The Age of Urban Democracy. Trade Cloth. Longman Publishing Group. White Plains, NY. 1979. 530p. ISBN:0-582-48278-X, ISBN13: 978-0-582-48278-4. Dewey:942.081. LCCN:78-041034.
Audience: **u,f.**

Roberts, Elizabeth **HQ1599.E5R62 1984**
A Woman's Place: An Oral History of Working Class Women, 1890-1940. Trade Cloth. Blackwell Publishing, Inc. Malden, MA. 1984. 272p. ISBN:0-631-13572-3, ISBN13: 978-0-631-13572-2. Dewey:305.4/2/0942. LCCN:84-016785.
Audience: **u,f.** *Choice, 1985.*

Rowse, A. L. **DA670.C8**
Tudor Cornwall. Trade Cloth. Dyllansow Truran. Truro, 1989. 462p. ISBN:1-85022-058-1, ISBN13: 978-1-85022-058-9. Dewey:942.3705.
Audience: **g,l,u,f.**

Seaver, Paul S. **BX9339.W26S4 1985**
Wallington's World: A Puritan Artisan in Seventeenth-Century London. Trade Cloth. Stanford University Press. Palo Alto, CA. 1985. 272p. ISBN:0-8047-1267-0, ISBN13: 978-0-8047-1267-5. Dewey:941.06. LCCN:84-040447.
Audience: **u,f.** *Choice, 1986.*

Smith, F. B. **HD4145**
The People's Health, 1830-1910. Trade Cloth. Ashgate Publishing, Ltd. Aldershot, 1993. 442p. Modern Revivals in History Ser. ISBN:0-7512-0185-5, ISBN13: 978-0-7512-0185-7. Dewey:363/.0941.
Audience: **g,l,u,f.**

Stone, Lawrence **HQ613.S76**
The Family, Sex and Marriage. Trade Cloth. HarperCollins Publishers. New York, NY. 1977. xxxi, 800p. ISBN:0-06-014142-5, ISBN13: 978-0-06-014142-4. Dewey:306.850941. LCCN:77-000050.
Audience: **g,l,u,f.**

Thompson, Flora **S522.G7**
Lark Rise to Candleford: A Trilogy. Julie Neild (Illustrator), H. J. Massingham (Introduction by). Trade Cloth. Oxford University Press, Inc. New York, NY. 1980. 576p. ISBN:0-19-211759-9, ISBN13: 978-0-19-211759-5. Dewey:942.5/7081/0924.
Audience: **u,f.**

Trevelyan, George Macaulay **DA32**
Illustrated English Social History. London, New York, Longmans, Green. 1949.
Audience: **l,u.**

Walvin, James **DA125.N4**
The Black Presence. Trade Cloth. Knopf Publishing Group. New York, NY. 1972. 228p. Sourcebooks in the Negro History Ser. ISBN:0-8052-3434-9, ISBN13: 978-0-8052-3434-3. Dewey:301.45/1/96042. LCCN:75-169829.
Audience: **g,l,u,f.**

Wiener, Martin J. **HN385**
English Culture and the Decline of the Industrial Spirit, 1850-1980. Trade Cloth. Cambridge University Press. New York, NY. 1981. 250p. ISBN:0-521-23418-2, ISBN13: 978-0-521-23418-4. Dewey:306.3/4/0942/0904. LCCN:80-022684.
Audience: **l,u,f.**

Williams, Raymond **DA533.W6 1983**
Culture and Society, 1780-1950. Ed. 2. Trade Cloth. Columbia University Press. New York, NY. 1983. 363p. A Morningside Bk. ISBN:0-231-02287-5, ISBN13: 978-0-231-02287-3. Dewey:306/.4/0941. LCCN:85-005195.
Audience: **g,u,f.** B

Winter, J. M. **HB3583.A3W56 2003**
The Great War and the British People. Ed. 2. Trade Paper. Palgrave Macmillan. New York, NY. 2003. 376p. ISBN:1-4039-0695-5, ISBN13: 978-1-4039-0695-3. Dewey:304.6/0941/09041. LCCN:2002-042822.
Audience: **l,u,f.** *Choice, 1986.*

Britain > England > Politics

JN210
Growth of Political Stability. Trade Paper. Brill Academic Publishers, Inc. Boston, MA. 1987. ISBN:0-391-01908-2, ISBN13: 978-0-391-01908-9. Dewey:320.9/42.
Audience: **l,u,f.**

Andrews, Kenneth R. **DA86.A74 1991**
Ships, Money and Politics: Seafaring and Naval Enterprise in the Reign of Charles I. Trade Cloth. Cambridge University Press. New York, NY. 1991. 250p. ISBN:0-521-40116-X, ISBN13: 978-0-521-40116-6. Dewey:359/.00941. LCCN:90-040407.
Audience: **u,f.** *Choice, 1992.*

Blake, Robert **DA554**
Disraeli. Ed. 2. Trade Paper. Prion. London, 1998. 850p. Lost Treasures Ser. ISBN:1-85375-275-4, ISBN13: 978-1-85375-275-9. Dewey:941/.081/092.
Audience: **g,l,u,f.**

Bourne, Kenneth **DA536.P2**
Palmerston, the Early Years, 1784-1841. New York: Macmillan. 1982. ISBN:0-02-903740-9, ISBN13: 978-0-02-903740-9.
Audience: **u,f.**

Brewer, John **JN210**
Party Ideology and Popular Politics at the Accession of George Third. Trade Cloth. Cambridge University Press. New York, NY. 1976. 391p. ISBN:0-521-21049-6, ISBN13: 978-0-521-21049-2. Dewey:320.941. LCCN:76-014773.
Audience: **u,f.**

Brewer, John **DA480.B74 1990**
The Sinews of Power: War, Money and the English State, 1688-1783. Trade Paper. Harvard University Press. Cambridge, MA. 1990. 320p. ISBN:0-674-80930-0, ISBN13: 978-0-674-80930-7. Dewey:941.07. LCCN:90-004414.
Audience: **u,f.**

Castle, Barbara **DA591.C3/**
The Castle Diaries 1964-70. Trade Cloth. Weidenfeld & Nicolson, Ltd. London, 1984. xvi, 858p. ISBN:0-297-78374-2, ISBN13: 978-0-297-78374-9. Dewey:941.085/6/0924. LCCN:84-252672.
Audience: **u,f.**

Cecil, David **DA538.A1**
Melbourne. Trade Cloth. Macmillan Publishing Company, Inc. Old Tappan, NJ. 1974. 450p. ISBN:0-672-52038-9, ISBN13: 978-0-672-52038-9. Dewey:942.0740924. LCCN:54-009486.
Audience: **g,l,u,f.**

Churchill, Winston S. **DA565.C6**
Lord Randolph Churchill. Paper Text. Textbook Publishers. Temecula, CA. 2003. 840p. ISBN:0-7581-7414-4, ISBN13: 978-0-7581-7414-7. Dewey:923.242.
Audience: **g,l,u,f.**

Clark, J. C. **JN175.C58 1985**
English Society, 1688-1832: Ideology, Social Structure and Political Practice During the Ancien Regime. Cloth Text. Cambridge University Press. New York, NY. 1985. 449p. Cambridge Studies in the History and Theory of Politics ISBN:0-521-30922-0, ISBN13: 978-0-521-30922-6. Dewey:320.941. LCCN:85-010995.
Audience: **l,u,f.** *Choice, 1986.*

Colley, Linda **JN1129.T72**
In Defiance of Oligarchy: The Tory Party 1714-60. Trade Paper. Cambridge University Press. New York, NY. 1985. 383p. ISBN:0-521-31311-2, ISBN13: 978-0-521-31311-7. Dewey:324.241/02. LCCN:81-010004.
Audience: **u,f.**

Crossman, R. H. S. (Richard Howard Stafford) **DA591.C76 A34 1975**
The Diaries of a Cabinet Minister. London: Hamilton: Cape. 1975. ISBN:0-241-89110-8, ISBN13: 978-0-241-89110-0.
Audience: **u,f.**

De Krey, Gary S. **JS3566.D45 1985**
A Fractured Society: The Politics of London in the First Age of Party, 1688-1715. Trade Cloth. Oxford University Press, Inc. New York, NY. 1985. 420p. ISBN:0-19-820067-6, ISBN13: 978-0-19-820067-3. Dewey:942.106. LCCN:85-234226.
Audience: **u,f.** *Choice, 1986.*

Elton, Geoffrey R. **JN515**
The Parliament of England, 1559-1581. Trade Paper. Cambridge University Press. New York, NY. 1989. 416p. ISBN:0-521-38988-7, ISBN13: 978-0-521-38988-4. Dewey:328.42/09.
Audience: **u,f.** *Choice, 1987.*

Elton, Geoffrey R. **JN181 .T85 1982**
The Tudor Constitution: Documents and Commentary. Ed. 2. Trade Paper. Cambridge University Press. New York, NY. 1982. 542p. ISBN:0-521-28757-X, ISBN13: 978-0-521-28757-9. Dewey:942/.05. LCCN:81-015216.
Audience: **u,f.**

Fisher, Nigel **DA590**
Harold Macmillan: A Biography. Trade Cloth. St. Martin's Press. Gordonville, VA. 1982. 416p. ISBN:0-312-36322-2,

ISBN13: 978-0-312-36322-2. Dewey:941.085/092/4. LCCN:81-048509.
Audience: **g,l,u,f.**

Gash, Norman **DA522.L7G37 1984**
Lord Liverpool: The Life and Political Career of Robert Banks Jenkinson, Second Earl of Liverpool, 1770-1828. Trade Cloth. Harvard University Press. Cambridge, MA. 1985. 296p. ISBN:0-674-53910-9, ISBN13: 978-0-674-53910-5. Dewey:941.07/3/0924. LCCN:84-012842.
Audience: **g,l,u,f.**

Gash, Norman **DA536.P3**
Mr. Secretary Peel: The Life of Sir Robert Peel to 1830. Ed. 2. Cloth Text. Longman Publishing Group. White Plains, NY. 1985. 712p. ISBN:0-582-49723-X, ISBN13: 978-0-582-49723-8. Dewey:941.081/092/4. LCCN:85-007751.
Audience: **u,f.**

Gash, Norman **DA559.7**
Reaction and Reconstruction in English Politics, 1832 to 1852. Trade Cloth. Greenwood Publishing Group, Inc. Portsmouth, NH. 1981. 227p. ISBN:0-313-22927-9, ISBN13: 978-0-313-22927-5. Dewey:941.07/5. LCCN:81-001813.
Audience: **u,f.**

Gash, Norman **DA536.P3G32 1986**
Sir Robert Peel: The Life of Sir Robert Peel After 1830. Ed. 2. Paper Text. Longman Publishing Group. White Plains, NY. 1986. 745p. ISBN:0-582-49722-1, ISBN13: 978-0-582-49722-1. Dewey:941.081/092/4 B. LCCN:85-023934.
Audience: **g,l,u,f.**

Goodwin, Albert **DA520.G6 1979**
The Friends of Liberty: The English Democratic Movement in the Age of the French Revolution. Trade Cloth. Harvard University Press. Cambridge, MA. 1979. 594p. ISBN:0-674-32339-4, ISBN13: 978-0-674-32339-1. Dewey:320.9/41/073. LCCN:78-015673.
Audience: **g,l,u,f.**

Greville, Charles **DA536.G8**
The Great World. Garden City, N.Y., Doubleday. 1963.
Audience: **g,l,u,f.**

Grigg, John **DA566.9.L5.G78 1978**
Lloyd George: The People's Champion, 1902-1911. Trade Cloth. University of California Press. Berkeley, CA. 1978. 391p. ISBN:0-520-03634-4, ISBN13: 978-0-520-03634-5. Dewey:941.083/092/4. LCCN:77-091762.
Audience: **l,u,f.**

Grigg, John **DA566.9.L5G777 1985**
Lloyd George: From Peace to War, 1912-1916. Trade Cloth. University of California Press. Berkeley, CA. 1985. 512p. ISBN:0-520-05417-2, ISBN13: 978-0-520-05417-2. Dewey:941.083/092/4. LCCN:84-016150.
Audience: **u,f.** *Choice, 1985.*

Grigg, John **DA566.9.L5.G8 1974**
The Young Lloyd George. Trade Cloth. University of California Press. Berkeley, CA. 1978. 320p. ISBN:0-520-02677-2, ISBN13: 978-0-520-02677-3. Dewey:942.081/092/4. LCCN:73-091067.
Audience: **l,u,f.**

Harris, Tim **DA445.H24 2003**
London Crowds in the Reign of Charles II: Propaganda and Politics from the Restoration until the Exclusion Crisis. Anthony Fletcher, John Guy & John Morrill (Contribution by). Trade Paper. Cambridge University Press. New York, NY. 1990. 280p. Cambridge Studies in Early Modern British History ISBN:0-521-39845-2, ISBN13: 978-0-521-39845-9. Dewey:942.1/066.
Audience: **u,f.** *Choice, 1988.*

Hirst, Derek **DA390.H57 1986**
Authority and Conflict: England, 1603-1658. Trade Cloth. Harvard University Press. Cambridge, MA. 1986. 400p. New History of England Ser. ISBN:0-674-05290-0, ISBN13: 978-0-674-05290-1. Dewey:941.06. LCCN:85-024957.
Audience: **u,f.** *Choice, 1986.*

Hirst, Derek **DA390**
Authority and Conflict: England, 1603-1658. Cambridge, Mass.: Harvard University Press. 1986. The New History of England Ser. ISBN:0-674-05290-0, ISBN13: 978-0-674-05290-1.
Audience: **u,f.**

Holmes, Geoffrey S. **DA495.H59 1987**
British Politics in the Age of Anne. Ed. 2. Trade Cloth. Continuum International Publishing Group, Ltd. London, 2003. 620p. ISBN:0-907628-73-7, ISBN13: 978-0-907628-73-6. Dewey:941.06/9. LCCN:87-014833.
Audience: **u,f.**

Hutton, Ronald **DA375**
The Restoration: A Political and Religious History of England and Wales, 1658-1667. Paper Text. Oxford University Press, Inc. New York, NY. 1993. 388p. ISBN:0-19-820392-6, ISBN13: 978-0-19-820392-6. Dewey:942.06.
Audience: **l,u,f.** *Choice, 1986, 1985.*

James, Robert Rhodes **DA564.R7J3**
Rosebery, a Biography of Archibald Philip, Fifth Earl of Rosebery. New York: Macmillan. 1964.
Audience: **g,l,u,f.**

Jay, Richard **DA565.C4.J39**
Joseph Chamberlain: A Political Study. Trade Cloth. Oxford University Press, Inc. New York, NY. 1981. ix, 383p. ISBN:0-19-822623-3, ISBN13: 978-0-19-822623-9. Dewey:941.081/092/4. LCCN:80-040812.
Audience: **u,f.**

Kronenberger, Louis **DA512.W6.K76**
The Extraordinary Mr. Wilkes: His Life and Times. Trade Cloth. Doubleday Publishing. New York, NY. 1974. xv, 269p. ISBN:0-385-05131-X, ISBN13: 978-0-385-05131-6. Dewey:328.42/092/4. LCCN:73-079686.
Audience: **g,l,u,f.**

Miller, John **DA448.M54**
Popery and Politics in England, 1660-1688. Trade Cloth. Cambridge University Press. New York, NY. 1973. 296p. ISBN:0-521-20236-1, ISBN13: 978-0-521-20236-7. Dewey:322/.1/0942. LCCN:73-079306.
Audience: **u,f.**

Morgan, Kenneth O. **DA576.M67**
Consensus and Disunity: The Lloyd George Coalition Government, 1918-1922. Trade Cloth. Oxford University Press, Inc. New York, NY. 1979. 448p. ISBN:0-19-822497-4, ISBN13: 978-0-19-822497-6. Dewey:320.9/41/083. LCCN:79-040263.
Audience: **u,f.**

Morgan, Kenneth O. **DA588.M637 1985**
Labour in Power, 1945-1951. Trade Paper. Oxford University Press, Inc. New York, NY. 1985. 564p. ISBN:0-19-285150-0, ISBN13: 978-0-19-285150-5. Dewey:941.085/4. LCCN:85-003003.
Audience: **u,f.**

Morley, John M. **DA563**
The Life of William Ewart Gladstone, Set. Trade Cloth. Greenwood Publishing Group, Inc. Portsmouth, NH. 1971. ISBN:0-8371-0576-5, ISBN13: 978-0-8371-0576-5. Dewey:941.0810924. LCCN:68-057630.
Audience: **g,l,u,f.**

Neale, J. E. Sir (John Ernest) **DA356**
Elizabeth I and Her Parliaments, 1584-1601. New York: St. Martin's Press. 1958.
Audience: **u,f.**

Pares, Richard **DA505.P3 1988**
King George III and the Politicians. Trade Cloth. Oxford University Press, Inc. New York, NY. 1988. 224p. ISBN:0-19-821240-2, ISBN13: 978-0-19-821240-9. Dewey:941.07/3. LCCN:87-014064.
Audience: **g,l,u,f.**

Peck, Linda Levy **DA390**
Court Patronage and Corruption in Early Stuart England. Boston; London: Unwin Hyman. 1990. ISBN:0-04-942195-6, ISBN13: 978-0-04-942195-0.
Audience: **u,f.**

Pelling, Henry **DA588.P44 1984**
The Labour Governments, 1945-51. Cloth Text. Palgrave Macmillan. New York, NY. 1984. 301p. ISBN:0-312-46288-3, ISBN13: 978-0-312-46288-8. Dewey:320.9/41/09044. LCCN:83-022977.
Audience: **u,f.**

Prest, John **DA564.R8.P73 1972**
Lord John Russell. Trade Cloth. University of South Carolina Press. Columbia, SC. 1972. xvi, 568p. ISBN:0-87249-269-9, ISBN13: 978-0-87249-269-1. Dewey:942.081/0924. LCCN:72-005340.
Audience: **g,l,u,f.**

Pugh, Martin **DA566.7**
The Making of Modern British Politics, 1867-1939. Ed. 2. Trade Paper. Blackwell Publishing, Inc. Malden, MA. 1993. 344p. ISBN:0-631-17928-3, ISBN13: 978-0-631-17928-3. Dewey:941.08. LCCN:92-022093.
Audience: **u,f.**

Read, Donald **DA536.C6**
Cobden and Bright: a Victorian Political Partnership. New York: St. Martin's Press. 1968. ISBN:0-7131-5306-7, ISBN13: 978-0-7131-5306-4.
Audience: **u,f.**

Read, Donald **DA533.R37**
England, 1868-1914: The Age of Urban Democracy. Trade Cloth. Longman Publishing Group. White Plains, NY. 1979. 530p. ISBN:0-582-48278-X, ISBN13: 978-0-582-48278-4. Dewey:942.081. LCCN:78-041034.
Audience: **u,f.**

Robbins, Keith **DA565.B8**
John Bright. London ; Boston: Routledge & K. Paul. 1979. ISBN:0-7100-8992-9, ISBN13: 978-0-7100-8992-2.
Audience: **g,l,u,f.**

Rude, George **DA510**
Wilkes and Liberty. Trade Paper. Lawrence & Wishart, Ltd. London, 1983. 240p. ISBN:0-85315-579-8, ISBN13: 978-0-85315-579-9. Dewey:941.07/3.
Audience: **l,u,f.**

Russell, Conrad **DA315**
The Crisis of Parliaments: English History, 1509-1660. Paper Text. Oxford University Press, Inc. New York, NY. 1971. 450p. Short Oxford History of the Modern World Ser. ISBN:0-19-913034-5, ISBN13: 978-0-19-913034-4. Dewey:941.05.
Audience: **u,f.**

Sommerville, Johann P. (Introduction by) **JA84.G7**
Politics and Ideology in England 1603-1640. Ed. 1. Trade Paper. Longman Publishing Group. White Plains, NY. 1989. 254p. ISBN:0-582-49432-X, ISBN13: 978-0-582-49432-9. Dewey:320.5/0942. LCCN:85-005165.
Audience: **u,f.**

Southgate **DA533**
Passing of the Whigs 1832-1886. Trade Cloth. Ashgate Publishing Company. Williston, VT. 1993. 520p. ISBN:0-7512-0217-7, ISBN13: 978-0-7512-0217-5. Dewey:941.081.
Audience: **u,f.**

Underdown, David **DA415.U5 1985**
Pride's Purge: Politics in the Puritan Revolution. Paper Text. Routledge. New York, NY. 1985. 440p. ISBN:0-04-822045-0, ISBN13: 978-0-04-822045-5. Dewey:942.06/3. LCCN:85-001218.
Audience: **l,u,f.**

Underdown, David **DA425**
Pride's Purge: Politics in the Puritan Revolution. Trade Cloth. Oxford University Press, Inc. New York, NY. 1971. xi, 424p. ISBN:0-19-822342-0, ISBN13: 978-0-19-822342-9. Dewey:942.06/3. LCCN:78-853456.
Audience: **l,u,f.**

Underdown, David **DA390**
Revel, Riot, and Rebellion: Popular Politics and Culture in England 1603-1660. Paper Text. Oxford University Press, Inc. New York, NY. 1987. 340p. ISBN:0-19-285193-4, ISBN13: 978-0-19-285193-2. Dewey:942/.06.
Audience: **u,f.** *Choice, 1986.*

Wilson, Harold **DA592**
A Personal Record: The Labour Government, 1964-1970. Boston: Little, Brown. 1971.
Audience: **u,f.**

Britain > English History > Early (to 1066)

Geoffrey of Monmouth **DA140**
The History of the Kings of Britain. Thorpe Lewis (Introduction by). Trade Paper. Penguin Group (USA) Inc. New York, NY.

1977. 384p. Classics Ser. ISBN:0-14-044170-0, ISBN13: 978-0-14-044170-3. Dewey:942/.01.
Audience: **g,l,u,f.**

Merrifield, Ralph **DA677.1.M46 1983**
London: City of the Romans. Trade Cloth. University of California Press. Berkeley, CA. 1983. 288p. ISBN:0-520-04922-5, ISBN13: 978-0-520-04922-2. Dewey:936.2/1204. LCCN:82-040412.
Audience: **u,f.**

Poole, Austin Lane (Editor) **DA130**
Medieval England. Oxford, Clarendon Press. 1958.
Audience: **g,l,u,f.**

Britain > English History > Early (to 1066) > Celts

Laing, Lloyd Robert **DA140.L33 1979**
Celtic Britain. Trade Cloth. Simon & Schuster. New York, NY. 1979. xi, 190p. ISBN:0-684-16225-3, ISBN13: 978-0-684-16225-6. Dewey:936.1. LCCN:78-066127.
Audience: **l,u,f.**

Britain > English History > Early (to 1066) > Saxons

Alcock, Leslie **DA152.A7**
Arthur's Britain: History and Archaeology, AD 367-634. Trade Cloth. Penguin Group (USA) Inc. New York, NY. 1971. xviii, 415p. ISBN:0-7139-0245-0, ISBN13: 978-0-7139-0245-7. Dewey:914.2. LCCN:72-176453.
Audience: **u,f.**

Campbell, James (Editor) **DA152.C28 1982**
The Anglo-Saxons. Eric John & Patrick Wormwald (Contribution by). Book, Other. Cornell University Press. Ithaca, NY. 1982. 272p. ISBN:0-8014-1482-2, ISBN13: 978-0-8014-1482-4. Dewey:942.01. LCCN:81-070710.
Audience: **l,u,f.**

Whitelock, Dorothy (Editor, Introduction by) **DA150**
The Anglo-Saxon Chronicle. David C. Douglas & Susie I. Tucker (Editors). Trade Cloth. Greenwood Publishing Group, Inc. Portsmouth, NH. 1986. 272p. ISBN:0-313-25214-9, ISBN13: 978-0-313-25214-3. Dewey:942.01. LCCN:86-000364.
Audience: **g,l,u,f.**

Britain > English History > Medieval (1066-1485)

Brown, Andrew **BR744.B76 2003**
Church and Society in England, 1000-1500. Cloth over Boards. Palgrave Macmillan. New York, NY. 2003. 256p. Social History in Perspective Ser. ISBN:0-333-69144-X, ISBN13: 978-0-333-69144-1. Dewey:274.2/04. LCCN:2003-049832.
Audience: **u,f.**

Campbell, Bruce M. S. **S455 .C26 2000**
English Seignorial Agriculture, 1250-1450. Alan R. H. Baker, Richard Dennis & Deryck Holdworth (Contribution by). Trade Cloth. Cambridge University Press. New York, NY. 2000. 546p. Studies in Historical Geography, No. 31 ISBN:0-521-30412-1, ISBN13: 978-0-521-30412-2. Dewey:630/.942. LCCN:99-039384.
Audience: **u,f.**

Hatcher, John & Bailey, Mark **HC254.H37 2001**
Modelling the Middle Ages: The History and Theory of England's Economic Development. Cloth Text. Oxford University Press, Inc. New York, NY. 2001. 272p. ISBN:0-19-924411-1, ISBN13: 978-0-19-924411-9. Dewey:330.94/01. LCCN:00-066922.
Audience: **u,f.** *Choice, 2002.*

Kaeuper, Richard W. **DA225.K34 1988**
War, Justice, and Public Order: England and France in the Later Middle Ages. Trade Cloth. Oxford University Press, Inc. New York, NY. 1988. 462p. ISBN:0-19-822873-2, ISBN13: 978-0-19-822873-8. Dewey:942.03. LCCN:87-020409.
Audience: **u,f.** *Choice, 1989.*

Lloyd, T. H. **HF455**
England and the German Hanse, 1157-1611: A Study of Their Trade and Commercial Diplomacy. Trade Paper. Cambridge University Press. New York, NY. 2002. 411p. ISBN:0-521-52214-5, ISBN13: 978-0-521-52214-4. Dewey:382/.0942043.
Audience: **u,f.** *Choice, 1992.*

Myers, A. R. **DA680**
London in the Age of Chaucer. Trade Paper. University of Oklahoma Press. Norman, OK. 1988. 248p. Centers of Civilization Ser., Vol. 31 ISBN:0-8061-2111-4, ISBN13: 978-0-8061-2111-6. Dewey:942.103/7. LCCN:73-177342.
Audience: **g,l,u,f.** B

Wood, Charles T. **DA250**
Joan of Arc and Richard III: Sex, Saints, and Government in the Middle Ages. Paper Text. Oxford University Press, Inc. New York, NY. 1991. 288p. ISBN:0-19-506951-X, ISBN13: 978-0-19-506951-8. Dewey:942.04. LCCN:87-035023.
Audience: **u,f.** *Choice, 1989.*

Britain > English History > Medieval (1066-1485) > Normans

Alecto Historical Editions Board Staff, et al. **DA190**
Domesday Book: A Complete Translation. Geoffrey Martin & Ann Williams (Authors). Trade Paper. Penguin Group (USA) Inc. New York, NY. 2004. 1456p. ISBN:0-14-143994-7, ISBN13: 978-0-14-143994-5. Dewey:333.3/22/0942.
Audience: **g,l,u,f.**

Barlow, Frank **BR750.B37**
The English Church, 1066-1154: A History of the Anglo-Norman Church. Trade Cloth. Longman Publishing Group. White Plains, NY. 1979. xii, 340p. ISBN:0-582-50236-5, ISBN13: 978-0-582-50236-9. Dewey:274.2. LCCN:78-040458.
Audience: **u,f.** B

Bates Staff **DC611.N856 B37**
Normandy Before 1066. Ed. 2. Paper Text. Longman Publishing Group. White Plains, NY. 1996. ISBN:0-582-08410-5, ISBN13: 978-0-582-08410-0. Dewey:944/.2.
Audience: **u,f.**

Brown, Reginald A. **DA195.B7**
The Normans and the Norman Conquest. Trade Cloth. Constable & Robinson Ltd. London, 1969. xvi, 292p. ISBN:0-09-456260-1, ISBN13: 978-0-09-456260-8. Dewey:942.02/1. LCCN:77-366379.
Audience: **l,u.**

Chibnall, Marjorie **DA195.C47 1987**
Anglo-Norman England, 1066-1166. Trade Cloth. Blackwell Publishing, Inc. Malden, MA. 1986. 248p. ISBN:0-631-13234-1, ISBN13: 978-0-631-13234-9. Dewey:942.02. LCCN:85-011255.
Audience: **u,f.** *Choice, 1986.*

Chibnall, Marjorie **DA195.C47 1987**
Anglo-Norman England, 1066-1166. Trade Paper. Blackwell Publishing, Inc. Malden, MA. 1987. 256p. ISBN:0-631-15439-6, ISBN13: 978-0-631-15439-6. Dewey:942.02. LCCN:85-011255.
Audience: **l,u.** *Choice, 1986.*

Douglas, David C. **DA197**
William the Conqueror: The Norman Impact upon England. Trade Paper. University of California Press. Berkeley, CA. 1967. 488p. English Monarchs Ser., No. 1 ISBN:0-520-00350-0, ISBN13: 978-0-520-00350-7. Dewey:942/.021/092.
Audience: **u,f.**

Douglas, David C. & Greenaway, G. W. (Editors) **DA26.E55 1979**
English Historical Documents, 1042-1189. Ed. 2. Library Binding. Routledge. New York, NY. 1996. 1110p. English Historical Documents Ser., Vol. 2 ISBN:0-415-14367-5, ISBN13: 978-0-415-14367-7. Dewey:941. LCCN:78-017965.
Audience: **u,f.**

Fleming, Robin **DA197**
Kings and Lords in Conquest England. Christine Carpenter, D. E. Luscombe, Rosamond McKitterick & Jonathan Shepard (Contribution by). Trade Paper. Cambridge University Press. New York, NY. 2004. 279p. Cambridge Studies in Medieval Life and Thought, Vol. 4 ISBN:0-521-52694-9, ISBN13: 978-0-521-52694-4. Dewey:942.02/1.
Audience: **l,u.** *Choice, 1992.*

Golding, Brian **DA197.G65 2001**
Conquest and Colonisation: The Normans in Britain, 1066-1100. Ed. 2. Cloth over Boards. Palgrave Macmillan. New York, NY. 2001. 243p. British History in Perspective Ser. ISBN:0-333-96152-8, ISBN13: 978-0-333-96152-0. Dewey:942.02/1. LCCN:00-053073.
Audience: **u,f.** *Choice, 1995.*

Hollister, C. Warren **DA198.H65 2001**
Henry I. Amanda Clark Frost (Editor). Cloth over Boards. Yale University Press. Cumberland, RI. 2001. 576p. The English Monarchs Ser. ISBN:0-300-08858-2, ISBN13: 978-0-300-08858-8. Dewey:942/.023/092. LCCN:2002-280779.
Audience: **g,l,u,f.** *Choice, 2002.*

Hollister, C. Warren, et al. **DA30.H652 2001 VOL.1**
The Making of England: To 1399. Ed. 8. Robert C. Stacey & Robin Chapman Stacey (Authors). Paper Text. Houghton Mifflin College Division. Boston, MA. 2000. 406p. History of England Ser., Vol. 1 ISBN:0-618-00101-8, ISBN13: 978-0-618-00101-9. Dewey:941 s 942. LCCN:00-133911.
Audience: **u,f.**

Hudson, John **DA195**
Land, Law, and Lordship in Anglo-Norman England. Trade Paper. Oxford University Press, Inc. New York, NY. 1997. 330p. Oxford Historical Monographs ISBN:0-19-820688-7, ISBN13: 978-0-19-820688-0. Dewey:333.3/22/0942/09021. LCCN:93-013962.
Audience: **u,f.** *Choice, 1995.*

Lawson, M. K. **DA196**
The Battle of Hastings 1066. Trade Cloth. Tempus Publishing, Ltd. Stroud, Gloucestershire, 2004. 304p. ISBN:0-7524-2689-3, ISBN13: 978-0-7524-2689-1. Dewey:942/.019.
Audience: **l,u,f.** *Choice, 2004.*

Matthew, Donald **D34.G7**
Britain and the Continent 1000-1300: The Impact of the Norman Conquest. Trade Cloth. Hodder Education. London, 2005. 336p. A Hodder Arnold Publication ISBN:0-340-74060-4, ISBN13: 978-0-340-74060-6. Dewey:942.03. LCCN:2005-296612.
Audience: **u,f.**

Thorn, Frank **DA190**
Domesday Book: A Survey of the Counties of England. Parker, Celia; Morris, John (Editors). Chichester: Phillimore. 1986. History from the Sources Ser. ISBN:0-85033-585-X, ISBN13: 978-0-85033-585-9.
Audience: **g,l,u,f.**

Wilson, David M. **NK3049**
The Bayeux Tapestry. Trade Cloth. Thames & Hudson. New York, NY. 2004. 234p. ISBN:0-500-25122-3, ISBN13: 978-0-500-25122-5. Dewey:746.3/944.
Audience: **u,f.**

Britain > English History > Medieval (1066-1485) > Angevins

Alecto Historical Editions Board Staff, et al. **DA190**
Domesday Book: A Complete Translation. Geoffrey Martin & Ann Williams (Authors). Trade Paper. Penguin Group (USA) Inc. New York, NY. 2004. 1456p. ISBN:0-14-143994-7, ISBN13: 978-0-14-143994-5. Dewey:333.3/22/0942.
Audience: **g,l,u,f.**

Bartlett, Robert Merrill **DA195.B28**
England under the Norman and Angevin Kings, 1075-1225. Trade Paper. Oxford University Press, Inc. New York, NY. 2002. 808p. New Oxford History of England Ser. ISBN:0-19-925101-0, ISBN13: 978-0-19-925101-8. Dewey:942.02. LCCN:99-016108.
Audience: **u,f.** *Choice, 2000.*

Carpenter, D. A. **DA227.C375 1996**
The Reign of Henry III. Trade Cloth. Continuum International Publishing Group, Ltd. London, 1996. 420p. ISBN:1-85285-137-6, ISBN13: 978-1-85285-137-8. Dewey:941.03/4. LCCN:96-005798.
Audience: **g,l,u,f.**

Church, S. D. (Editor) **DA208.K557 2003**
King John: New Interpretations. Trade Paper. Boydell & Brewer, Ltd. Woodbridge, 2003. 392p. ISBN:0-85115-947-8, ISBN13: 978-0-85115-947-8. Dewey:942/.033/092.
Audience: **g,l,u,f.**

De Hoveden, Roger **DA200.H842**
Annals of Roger De Hoveden. H. T. Riley (Translator). Trade Cloth. A M S Press, Inc. New York, NY. Bohn's Antiquarian Library ISBN:0-404-50060-9, ISBN13: 978-0-404-50060-3. Dewey:942.03/1. LCCN:68-057865.
Audience: **u,f.**

Douglas, David C. **DA197**
William the Conqueror: The Norman Impact upon England. Trade Paper. University of California Press. Berkeley, CA. 1967. 488p. English Monarchs Ser., No. 1 ISBN:0-520-00350-0, ISBN13: 978-0-520-00350-7. Dewey:942/.021/092.
Audience: **u,f.**

Gillingham, John **DA205.G55 2001**
The Angevin Empire. Ed. 2. Trade Paper. Oxford University Press, Inc. New York, NY. 2001. 160p. A Hodder Arnold Publication ISBN:0-340-74115-5, ISBN13: 978-0-340-74115-3. Dewey:940.1/8. LCCN:2001-268753.
Audience: **l,u.**

Hall, G. D. (Editor) **KD600.G5513 1993**
The Treatise on the Laws and Customs of the Realm of England Commonly Called Glanvill. Trade Cloth. Oxford University Press, Inc. New York, NY. 1994. 300p. Oxford Medieval Texts ISBN:0-19-822179-7, ISBN13: 978-0-19-822179-1. Dewey:344.2. LCCN:93-023844.
Audience: **u,f.**

Hollister, C. Warren **DA198.H65 2001**
Henry I. Amanda Clark Frost (Editor). Cloth over Boards. Yale University Press. Cumberland, RI. 2001. 576p. The English Monarchs Ser. ISBN:0-300-08858-2, ISBN13: 978-0-300-08858-8. Dewey:942/.023/092. LCCN:2002-280779.
Audience: **g,l,u,f.** *Choice, 2002.*

Hollister, C. Warren, et al. **DA30.H652 2001 VOL.1**
The Making of England: To 1399. Ed. 8. Robert C. Stacey & Robin Chapman Stacey (Authors). Paper Text. Houghton Mifflin College Division. Boston, MA. 2000. 406p. History of England Ser., Vol. 1 ISBN:0-618-00101-8, ISBN13: 978-0-618-00101-9. Dewey:941 s 942. LCCN:00-133911.
Audience: **u,f.**

Holt, J. C. **JN147 .H64 1991**
Magna Carta. Ed. 2. Trade Paper. Cambridge University Press. New York, NY. 1992. 575p. ISBN:0-521-27778-7, ISBN13: 978-0-521-27778-5. Dewey:942.03. LCCN:91-019456.
Audience: **l,u,f.**

Hudson, John **KD671.H83 1996**
The Formation of English Common Law: Law and Society in England from the Norman Conquest to Magna Carta. Ed. 1. Trade Paper. Longman Publishing. Boston, MA. 1996. 280p. The Medieval World Ser., : ISBN:0-582-07026-0, ISBN13: 978-0-582-07026-4. Dewey:344.2/009. LCCN:95-049759.
Audience: **l,u,f.** *Choice, 1997.*

Hudson, John **DA195**
Land, Law, and Lordship in Anglo-Norman England. Trade Paper. Oxford University Press, Inc. New York, NY. 1997. 330p. Oxford Historical Monographs ISBN:0-19-820688-7, ISBN13: 978-0-19-820688-0. Dewey:333.3/22/0942/09021. LCCN:93-013962.
Audience: **u,f.** *Choice, 1995.*

Kelley, Amy **DA209.E6**
Eleanor of Aquitaine and the Four Kings. Trade Paper. Harvard University Press. Cambridge, MA. 1991. 442p. ISBN:0-674-24254-8, ISBN13: 978-0-674-24254-8. Dewey:942.031. LCCN:50-006545.
Audience: **g,l,u,f.**

Lawson, M. K. **DA196**
The Battle of Hastings 1066. Trade Cloth. Tempus Publishing, Ltd. Stroud, Gloucestershire, 2004. 304p. ISBN:0-7524-2689-3, ISBN13: 978-0-7524-2689-1. Dewey:942/.019.
Audience: **l,u,f.** *Choice, 2004.*

Norgate, Kate **DA175**
England under the Angevin Kings. Library Binding. Burt Franklin Publisher. New York, NY. 1969. ISBN:0-8337-2576-9, ISBN13: 978-0-8337-2576-9. Dewey:942/.03.
Audience: **l,u,f.**

Painter, Sidney **DA209.P4 P3 1982**
William Marshal: Knight-Errant, Baron and Regent of England, Vol. 13. Trade Paper. University of Toronto Press. Toronto, ON. 1982. 305p. Medieval Academy Reprints for Teaching Ser., No. 13 ISBN:0-8020-6498-1, ISBN13: 978-0-8020-6498-1. Dewey:942.03/4/0924. LCCN:82-188876.
Audience: **u,f.** B

Pollock, Frederick & Maitland, Frederic William **KD532.P64 1996**
The History of English Law Before the Time of Edward I 1898, Set. Ed. 2. Trade Cloth. Lawbook Exchange, Limited, The. Clark, NJ. 1996. 706p. ISBN:1-886363-22-6, ISBN13: 978-1-886363-22-9. Dewey:349.42. LCCN:96-016003.
Audience: **u,f.**

Prestwich, Michael **DA229.P73 2003**
The Three Edwards: War and State in England, 1272-1377. Ed. 2. Paper over Boards. Routledge. New York, NY. 2003. 304p. ISBN:0-415-30308-7, ISBN13: 978-0-415-30308-8. Dewey:942.03. LCCN:2002-036780.
Audience: **g,l,u.** B

Prestwich, Michael **DA225**
English Politics in the Thirteenth Century. Jeremy Black (Editor). Trade Paper. St. Martin's Press. Gordonville, VA. 160p. British History in Perspective Ser. ISBN:0-333-41434-9, ISBN13: 978-0-333-41434-7. Dewey:320.942. LCCN:92-221275.
Audience: **l,u,f.**

Staunton, M. (Editor) **DA209.T4L58 2001**
The Lives of Thomas Becket. Cloth over Boards. Manchester University Press. Manchester, 2001. 272p. Manchester Medieval Sources Ser. ISBN:0-7190-5454-0, ISBN13: 978-0-7190-5454-9. Dewey:942.03/1/092 B. LCCN:2001-044104.
Audience: **g,l,u,f.**

Turner, Ralph V. **JN147**
Magna Carta. Cloth Text. Longman Publishing. Boston, MA. 2003. 288p. ISBN:0-582-43826-8, ISBN13: 978-0-582-43826-2. Dewey:942/.033.
Audience: **l,u,f.** *Choice, 2004.*

Turner, Ralph V. & Heiser, Richard R. **DA207.T87 2000**
The Reign of Richard Lionheart. Trade Cloth. Longman Publishing Group. White Plains, NY. 2001. 304p. ISBN:0-582-25660-7, ISBN13: 978-0-582-25660-6. Dewey:942.03/2/092 B. LCCN:00-022160.
Audience: **g,l,u,f.** *Choice, 2000.*

Vaughan, Richard (Editor) **BV1561.W770**
The Illustrated Chronicles of Matthew Paris: Observations of the Thirteenth-Century Life. Ian Cannell (Photographer). Trade Paper. DIANE Publishing Company. Collingdale, PA. 2000. 210p. ISBN:0-7881-9505-0, ISBN13: 978-0-7881-9505-1. Dewey:940.1.
Audience: **u,f.**

Warren, W. L. **DA206**
Henry II. Trade Paper. University of California Press. Berkeley, CA. 1977. 350p. Yale English Monarchs Ser., No. 4 ISBN:0-520-03494-5, ISBN13: 978-0-520-03494-5. Dewey:942.031092.
Audience: **g,l,u,f.** ℬ

Warren, W. L. **DA208.W38 1997**
King John. D. A. Carpenter (Foreword by). Trade Cloth. Yale University Press. Cumberland, RI. 1998. 376p. English Monarchs Ser. ISBN:0-300-07373-9, ISBN13: 978-0-300-07373-7. Dewey:942.03/3/092 b. LCCN:97-061405.
Audience: **g,l,u,f.** ℬ

Britain > English History > Medieval (1066-1485) > Lancaster-York

Bennett, H. S. **DA240 .B4 1990**
The Pastons and Their England: Studies in an Age of Transition. Trade Paper. Cambridge University Press. New York, NY. 1990. 304p. A Canto Book Ser. ISBN:0-521-39826-6, ISBN13: 978-0-521-39826-8. Dewey:942.04/092/2 B. LCCN:90-034447.
Audience: **u,f.**

Fenn, John **DA240**
The Paston Letters. Archer-Hind; Laura Pocock (Editors). London, Dent; New York, Dutton. 1956. Everyman's Llibrary
Audience: **u,f.**

Gillingham, John **DA250.G54 1981**
The Wars of the Roses: Peace and Conflict in Fifteenth-Century England. Cloth Text. Louisiana State University Press. Baton Rouge, LA. 1982. 278p. ISBN:0-8071-1005-1, ISBN13: 978-0-8071-1005-8. Dewey:942.04. LCCN:81-000819.
Audience: **l,u,f.**

Britain > English History > Modern (1485-)

Houston, Rab A. **HB3583.H63 1995**
The Population History of Britain and Ireland 1500-1750. Maurice Kirby (Contribution by). Cloth Text. Cambridge University Press. New York, NY. 1995. 105p. New Studies in Economic and Social History, No. 18 ISBN:0-521-55277-X, ISBN13: 978-0-521-55277-6. Dewey:304.6/0941. LCCN:95-018507.
Audience: **u,f.**

Britain > English History > Modern (1485-) > Tudors (1485-1603). Elizabethan Age

Barry, Jonathan (Editor) **HT133**
The Tudor and Stuart Town: A Reader in English Urban History, 1530-1688. Paper Text. Longman Publishing Group. White Plains, NY. 1990. 272p. Readers in Urban History Ser. ISBN:0-685-72459-X, ISBN13: 978-0-685-72459-0. Dewey:307.76/0942.
Audience: **g,l,u,f.**

Byrne, Muriel S. & Boland, Bridget (Editors) **DA335.L5.L572 1983**
The Lisle Letters: An Abridgement. Hugh T. Roper (Foreword by). Trade Cloth. University of Chicago Press. Chicago, IL. 1983. 462p. ISBN:0-226-08800-6, ISBN13: 978-0-226-08800-6. Dewey:942.05. LCCN:82-015914.
Audience: **u,f.**

Collinson, Patrick **BX9333.C62 1989**
The Elizabethan Puritan Movement. Trade Paper. Oxford University Press, Inc. New York, NY. 1990. 528p. ISBN:0-19-822298-X, ISBN13: 978-0-19-822298-9. Dewey:285/.9. LCCN:89-022977.
Audience: **u,f.**

Cressy, David **LC156.G7**
Literacy and the Social Order: Reading and Writing in Tudor and Stuart England. Cloth Text. Cambridge University Press. New York, NY. 1980. 256p. ISBN:0-521-22514-0, ISBN13: 978-0-521-22514-4. Dewey:302.2/0942. LCCN:79-041767.
Audience: **l,u,f.**

Dickens, A.G. **BR375.D5 1991**
The English Reformation. Ed. 2. Trade Paper. Pennsylvania State University Press. University Park, PA. 1991. 600p. ISBN:0-271-00798-2, ISBN13: 978-0-271-00798-4. Dewey:274.2/06. LCCN:91-013618.
Audience: **u,f.**

Dyer, Alan **HT133.D84 1995**
Decline and Growth in English Towns, 1400-1640. Cloth Text. Cambridge University Press. New York, NY. 1995. 90p. New Studies in Economic and Social History, Vol. 13 ISBN:0-521-55272-9, ISBN13: 978-0-521-55272-1. Dewey:942/.009732. LCCN:95-018411.
Audience: **u,f.**

Elton, Geoffrey R. **DA315.E6 1991**
England under the Tudors. Ed. 3. Trade Paper. Routledge. New York, NY. 1991. 544p. ISBN:0-415-06533-X, ISBN13: 978-0-415-06533-7. Dewey:942.05. LCCN:91-008187.
Audience: **l,u.**

Elton, Geoffrey R. **JN515**
The Parliament of England, 1559-1581. Trade Paper. Cambridge University Press. New York, NY. 1989. 416p. ISBN:0-521-38988-7, ISBN13: 978-0-521-38988-4. Dewey:328.42/09.
Audience: **u,f.** *Choice, 1987.*

Elton, Geoffrey R. **DA332.E497 1977**
Reform and Reformation: England, 1509-1558. Trade Cloth. Harvard University Press. Cambridge, MA. 1978. 432p. Harvard

Paperbacks Ser., No. 146, The New History of England ISBN:0-674-75245-7, ISBN13: 978-0-674-75245-0. Dewey:941.05/092/2. LCCN:77-006464.
Audience: **u,f.**

Elton, Geoffrey R. **JN181 .T85 1982**
The Tudor Constitution: Documents and Commentary. Ed. 2. Trade Paper. Cambridge University Press. New York, NY. 1982. 542p. ISBN:0-521-28757-X, ISBN13: 978-0-521-28757-9. Dewey:942/.05. LCCN:81-015216.
Audience: **u,f.**

Ferguson, Arthur B. **DA314.F47**
Clio Unbound: Perception of the Social and Cultural Past in Renaissance England. Trade Cloth. Duke University Press. Durham, NC. 1979. xv, 442p. Monographs in Medieval and Renaissance Studies, No. 2 ISBN:0-8223-0417-1, ISBN13: 978-0-8223-0417-3. Dewey:907/.2042. LCCN:78-067198.
Audience: **u,f.**

Fox, Alistair **DA334.M8**
Thomas More: History and Providence. Trade Cloth. Yale University Press. Cumberland, RI. 1983. 288p. ISBN:0-300-02951-9, ISBN13: 978-0-300-02951-2. Dewey:942.05/2/0924. LCCN:82-011178.
Audience: **g,l,u,f.**

Gillingham, John **DA0250.G54**
The Wars of the Roses: Peace and Conflict in Fifteenth-Century England. Trade Paper. Books on Demand. Ann Arbor, MI. 1981. 308p. ISBN:0-7837-9868-7, ISBN13: 978-0-7837-9868-4. Dewey:942.04. LCCN:81-083851.
Audience: **u,f.**

Guy, John S. **DA315**
Tudor England. Paper Text. Oxford University Press, Inc. New York, NY. 1990. 596p. ISBN:0-19-285213-2, ISBN13: 978-0-19-285213-7. Dewey:942.05. LCCN:88-005371.
Audience: **g,l,u,f.** *Choice, 1989.*

Haigh **DA355.H17 1988**
Elizabeth I. Ed. 1. Cloth Text. Addison-Wesley Longman, Inc. Boston, MA. 1989. 212p. ISBN:0-582-02390-4, ISBN13: 978-0-582-02390-1. Dewey:942.05/5/0924 B. LCCN:87-029853.
Audience: **g,l,u,f.**

Haigh, Christopher (Editor) **BR375.E54 1987**
The English Reformation Revised. Trade Paper. Cambridge University Press. New York, NY. 1987. 240p. ISBN:0-521-33631-7, ISBN13: 978-0-521-33631-4. Dewey:274.2/06.
Audience: **g,l,u,f.**

Kenny, Anthony **DA334.M8**
Thomas More. Trade Cloth. Oxford University Press, Inc. New York, NY. 1983. Past Masters Ser. ISBN:0-19-287574-4, ISBN13: 978-0-19-287574-7. Dewey:942.05/2/0924.
Audience: **g,l,u,f.**

Levine, David A. & Wrightson, Keith **HC258.W47L48 1991**
The Making of an Industrial Society: Whickham, 1560-1765. Cloth Text. Oxford University Press, Inc. New York, NY. 1991. 480p. Oxford Studies in Social History ISBN:0-19-820066-8, ISBN13: 978-0-19-820066-6. Dewey:330.9428/73. LCCN:90-039320.
Audience: **u,f.** *Choice, 1992.*

Loades, David M. **DA347.L58 1991**
The Reign of Mary Tudor: Politics, Government and Religion in England, 1553-58. Ed. 1. Paper Text. Longman Publishing Group. White Plains, NY. 1991. 448p. ISBN:0-582-05759-0, ISBN13: 978-0-582-05759-3. Dewey:942.05/4/092. LCCN:90-042615.
Audience: **u,f.**

MacCaffrey, Wallace T. **DA360**
Elizabeth I. Trade Paper. Oxford University Press, Inc. New York, NY. 1994. 496p. A Hodder Arnold Publication ISBN:0-340-61455-2, ISBN13: 978-0-340-61455-6. Dewey:942.055. LCCN:93-003568.
Audience: **g,l,u,f.**

MacCaffrey, Wallace T. **DA0355.M26**
Queen Elizabeth and the Making of Policy, 1572-1588. Trade Paper. Books on Demand. Ann Arbor, MI. 540p. ISBN:0-608-06420-3, ISBN13: 978-0-608-06420-8. Dewey:354.4207/2/09. LCCN:80-008564.
Audience: **u,f.**

MacCaffrey, Wallace T. **DA0355.M27**
Shaping of the Elizabethan Regime. Trade Cloth. Books on Demand. Ann Arbor, MI. 517p. ISBN:0-8357-9513-6, ISBN13: 978-0-8357-9513-5. Dewey:942.055092. LCCN:68-027409.
Audience: **u,f.**

Marius, Richard **DA334.M8**
Thomas More: A Biography. Trade Paper. Harvard University Press. Cambridge, MA. 1999. 592p. ISBN:0-674-88525-2, ISBN13: 978-0-674-88525-7. Dewey:942.05/2/0924.
Audience: **g,l,u,f.**

Mattingly, Garrett **DA360**
The Armada. Trade Paper, Perfect. Houghton Mifflin Company Trade & Reference Division. Boston, MA. 2005. 464p. ISBN:0-618-56591-4, ISBN13: 978-0-618-56591-7. Dewey:942.05/5.
Audience: **l,u,f.**

Mattingly, Garrett **DA333.A6**
Catherine of Aragon. Trade Cloth. A M S Press, Inc. New York, NY. ISBN:0-404-20169-5, ISBN13: 978-0-404-20169-2. Dewey:942.05/2/092. LCCN:83-045808.
Audience: **g,l,u,f.**

Neale, J. E. Sir (John Ernest) **DA356**
Elizabeth I and Her Parliaments, 1584-1601. New York: St. Martin's Press. 1958.
Audience: **u,f.**

Neale, John E. **DA355**
Queen Elizabeth the First. Trade Cloth. Academy Chicago Publishers, Ltd. Chicago, IL. 1992. 424p. ISBN:0-89733-362-4, ISBN13: 978-0-89733-362-7. Dewey:923.142.
Audience: **g,l,u,f.**

Pollard, Albert F. **DA334.W8 P6 1978**
Wolsey. Library Binding. Greenwood Publishing Group, Inc. Portsmouth, NH. 1978. ISBN:0-8371-7997-1, ISBN13: 978-0-8371-7997-1. Dewey:942.05/2/0924. LCCN:74-033897.
Audience: **g,l,u,f.**

Quinn, D. B. & Ryan, A. N. **DA86**
England's Sea Empire. Cloth Text. Routledge. New York, NY.

1983. 256p. Early Modern Europe Today Ser. ISBN:0-04-942179-4, ISBN13: 978-0-04-942179-0. Dewey:387.5/0942. LCCN:83-011755.
Audience: **g,l,u,f.**

Ridley, Jasper **DA334.A1.R52 1983**
Statesman and Saint: Wolsey and More, a Study in Contrast. Trade Cloth. Penguin Group (USA) Inc. New York, NY. 1983. 384p. ISBN:0-670-48905-0, ISBN13: 978-0-670-48905-3. Dewey:942.05/2/0922. LCCN:82-070122.
Audience: **u,f.**

Ridley, Jasper Godwin **DA317.8.C8**
Thomas Cranmer. Oxford: Clarendon Press. 1962.
Audience: **g,l,u,f.**

Rowse, A. L. **DA670.C8**
Tudor Cornwall. Trade Cloth. Dyllansow Truran. Truro, 1989. 462p. ISBN:1-85022-058-1, ISBN13: 978-1-85022-058-9. Dewey:942.3705.
Audience: **g,l,u,f.**

Russell, Conrad **DA315**
The Crisis of Parliaments: English History, 1509-1660. Paper Text. Oxford University Press, Inc. New York, NY. 1971. 450p. Short Oxford History of the Modern World Ser. ISBN:0-19-913034-5, ISBN13: 978-0-19-913034-4. Dewey:941.05.
Audience: **u,f.**

Scarisbrick, J. J. **DA334.M8**
Henry VIII. Trade Cloth. University of California Press. Berkeley, CA. 1968. English Monarchs Ser., No. 2 ISBN:0-520-01129-5, ISBN13: 978-0-520-01129-8. Dewey:942.05/2/0924. LCCN:68-010995.
Audience: **g,l,u,f.**

Slavin, Arthur Joseph **DA315**
The Precarious Balance: English Government and Society, 1450-1640. Ed. 1. New York, Knopf; [distributed by Random House]. 1973. The Borzoi history of England, v. 3 ISBN:0-394-47951-3, ISBN13: 978-0-394-47951-4.
Audience: **u,f.**

Smith, Lacey Baldwin **DA355**
Elizabeth Tudor: Portrait of a Queen. Boston: Little, Brown. 1975. The Library of World Biography ISBN:0-316-80152-6, ISBN13: 978-0-316-80152-2.
Audience: **g,l,u,f.**

Stone, Lawrence **DA356**
The Crisis of the Aristocracy, 1558 to 1641. Trade Cloth. Oxford University Press, Inc. New York, NY. 1965. 378p. ISBN:0-19-821314-X, ISBN13: 978-0-19-821314-7. Dewey:914.2.
Audience: **u,f.**

Thirsk, Joan **HC260.I53.T48**
Economic Policy and Projects: The Development of a Consumer Society in Early Modern England. Trade Cloth. Oxford University Press, Inc. New York, NY. 1978. 208p. ISBN:0-19-828274-5, ISBN13: 978-0-19-828274-7. Dewey:338/.0941. LCCN:78-315763.
Audience: **u,f.**

Wernham, R. B. **DA356.W47 1984**
After the Armada: Elizabethan England and the Struggle for Western Europe, 1588-1595. Trade Cloth. Oxford University Press, Inc. New York, NY. 1984. 634p. ISBN:0-19-822753-1, ISBN13: 978-0-19-822753-3. Dewey:940.2/32. LCCN:83-008281.
Audience: **u,f.**

Wernham, R. B. **DA360.W37 1994**
The Return of the Armadas: The Last Years of the Elizabethan War Against Spain, 1595-1603. Trade Cloth. Oxford University Press, Inc. New York, NY. 1994. 466p. ISBN:0-19-820443-4, ISBN13: 978-0-19-820443-5. Dewey:942.05/5. LCCN:93-024130.
Audience: **g,u,f.** *Choice, 1995.*

Britain > English History > Modern (1485-) > Early Stuarts (1603-1642)

JN210
Growth of Political Stability. Trade Paper. Brill Academic Publishers, Inc. Boston, MA. 1987. ISBN:0-391-01908-2, ISBN13: 978-0-391-01908-9. Dewey:320.9/42.
Audience: **l,u,f.**

Akrigg, G. P. V. **DA391**
Jacobean Ppageant; or, The Court of King James I. Cambridge: Harvard University Press. 1962.
Audience: **l,u,f.**

Andrews, Kenneth R. **DA86.A74 1991**
Ships, Money and Politics: Seafaring and Naval Enterprise in the Reign of Charles I. Trade Cloth. Cambridge University Press. New York, NY. 1991. 250p. ISBN:0-521-40116-X, ISBN13: 978-0-521-40116-6. Dewey:359/.00941. LCCN:90-040407.
Audience: **u,f.** *Choice, 1992.*

Aylmer, G. E. **JN425**
The King's Servants: The Civil Service of Charles I, 1625-1642. London; Boston : Routledge & Kegan Paul. 1974. ISBN:0-7100-7894-3, ISBN13: 978-0-7100-7894-0.
Audience: **u,f.**

Barry, Jonathan (Editor) **HT133**
The Tudor and Stuart Town: A Reader in English Urban History, 1530-1688. Paper Text. Longman Publishing Group. White Plains, NY. 1990. 272p. Readers in Urban History Ser. ISBN:0-685-72459-X, ISBN13: 978-0-685-72459-0. Dewey:307.76/0942.
Audience: **g,l,u,f.**

Bridenbaugh, Carl **DA390**
Vexed and Troubled Englishmen, 1590-1642. Trade Cloth. Oxford University Press, Inc. New York, NY. 1968. 512p. ISBN:0-19-500493-0, ISBN13: 978-0-19-500493-9. Dewey:942.06.
Audience: **u,f.**

Coward, Barry **DA375**
The Stuart Age. Paper Text. Longman Publishing Group. White Plains, NY. 1980. 493p. A History of England Ser. ISBN:0-582-48833-8, ISBN13: 978-0-582-48833-5. Dewey:942.06. LCCN:79-042887.
Audience: **g,l,u,f.**

Cressy, David **LC156.G7**
Literacy and the Social Order: Reading and Writing in Tudor and Stuart England. Cloth Text. Cambridge University Press. New York, NY. 1980. 256p. ISBN:0-521-22514-0, ISBN13: 978-0-521-22514-4. Dewey:302.2/0942. LCCN:79-041767.
Audience: **l,u,f.**

Hexter, Jack H. **DA0396.P9H4**
The Reign of King Pym. Trade Paper. Books on Demand. Ann Arbor, MI. 1941. 255p. Harvard Historical Studies, Vol. 48 ISBN:0-608-01603-9, ISBN13: 978-0-608-01603-0. Dewey:923.242. LCCN:41-004164.
Audience: **u,f.**

Hibbard, Caroline M. **DA0395.H46**
Charles the First and the Popish Plot. Trade Paper. Books on Demand. Ann Arbor, MI. 354p. ISBN:0-8357-3906-6, ISBN13: 978-0-8357-3906-1. Dewey:941.062. LCCN:81-023075.
Audience: **g,l,u,f.**

Hill, Christopher **DA375**
The Century of Revolution, 1603-1714. Ed. 2. Trade Paper. W. W. Norton & Company, Inc. New York, NY. 1982. 304p. ISBN:0-393-30016-1, ISBN13: 978-0-393-30016-1. Dewey:942.06.
Audience: **g,l,u,f.**

Hill, Christopher **DA375.H54 1985**
The Collected Essays of Christopher Hill: Writing and Revolution in Seventeenth-Century England, Vol. 1. Cloth Text. University of Massachusetts Press. Amherst, MA. 1985. 352p. ISBN:0-87023-467-6, ISBN13: 978-0-87023-467-5. Dewey:082. LCCN:84-016446.
Audience: **u,f.** *Choice, 1985.*

Hirst, Derek **DA390**
Authority and Conflict: England, 1603-1658. Cambridge, Mass.: Harvard University Press. 1986. The New History of England Ser. ISBN:0-674-05290-0, ISBN13: 978-0-674-05290-1.
Audience: **u,f.**

Peck, Linda Levy **DA390**
Court Patronage and Corruption in Early Stuart England. Boston; London: Unwin Hyman. 1990. ISBN:0-04-942195-6, ISBN13: 978-0-04-942195-0.
Audience: **u,f.**

Quinn, D. B. & Ryan, A. N. **DA86**
England's Sea Empire. Cloth Text. Routledge. New York, NY. 1983. 256p. Early Modern Europe Today Ser. ISBN:0-04-942179-4, ISBN13: 978-0-04-942179-0. Dewey:387.5/0942. LCCN:83-011755.
Audience: **g,l,u,f.**

Reay, Barry (Editor) **DA380.P67 1985**
Popular Culture in Seventeenth Century England. Cloth Text. Palgrave Macmillan. New York, NY. 1985. 319p. ISBN:0-312-63036-0, ISBN13: 978-0-312-63036-2. Dewey:306/.4/0942. LCCN:85-002496.
Audience: **g,l,u,f.** *Choice, 1985.*

Sommerville, Johann P. (Introduction by) **JA84.G7**
Politics and Ideology in England 1603-1640. Ed. 1. Trade Paper. Longman Publishing Group. White Plains, NY. 1989. 254p. ISBN:0-582-49432-X, ISBN13: 978-0-582-49432-9. Dewey:320.5/0942. LCCN:85-005165.
Audience: **u,f.**

Stone, Lawrence **DA356**
The Crisis of the Aristocracy, 1558 to 1641. Trade Cloth. Oxford University Press, Inc. New York, NY. 1965. 378p. ISBN:0-19-821314-X, ISBN13: 978-0-19-821314-7. Dewey:914.2.
Audience: **u,f.**

Thirsk, Joan **HC260.I53.T48**
Economic Policy and Projects: The Development of a Consumer Society in Early Modern England. Trade Cloth. Oxford University Press, Inc. New York, NY. 1978. 208p. ISBN:0-19-828274-5, ISBN13: 978-0-19-828274-7. Dewey:338/.0941. LCCN:78-315763.
Audience: **u,f.**

Watt, Tessa **PR428.C48W38 1994**
Cheap Print and Popular Piety, 1550-1640. Anthony Fletcher, John Guy & John Morrill (Contribution by). Trade Paper. Cambridge University Press. New York, NY. 1993. 390p. Cambridge Studies in Early Modern British History ISBN:0-521-45827-7, ISBN13: 978-0-521-45827-6. Dewey:820.9/382/09031.
Audience: **l,u,f.** *Choice, 1992.*

Woolf, D. R. **DA1**
The Idea of History in Early Stuart England: Erudition, Ideology, and the Light of Truth from the Accession of James I to the Civil War. Trade Cloth. University of Toronto Press. Toronto, ON. 1990. 377p. ISBN:0-8020-5862-0, ISBN13: 978-0-8020-5862-1. Dewey:907/.2042.
Audience: **l,u,f.** *Choice, 1991.*

Zagorin, Perez **DA395**
Court and the Country: The Beginning of the English Revolution. Paper Text. Simon & Schuster Children's Publishing. New York, NY. 1971. ISBN:0-689-70275-2, ISBN13: 978-0-689-70275-4. Dewey:320.9/42. LCCN:72-104129.
Audience: **g,l,u,f.**

Britain > English History > Modern (1485-) > Civil War and Commonwealth (1642-1660). Cromwell

Aylmer, G. E. **JN425**
The State's Servants: The Civil Service of the English Republic, 1649-1660. Trade Cloth. Routledge. New York, NY. 1973. 498p. ISBN:0-7100-7637-1, ISBN13: 978-0-7100-7637-3. Dewey:354/.42/00100932.
Audience: **u,f.**

Barry, Jonathan (Editor) **HT133**
The Tudor and Stuart Town: A Reader in English Urban History, 1530-1688. Paper Text. Longman Publishing Group. White Plains, NY. 1990. 272p. Readers in Urban History Ser. ISBN:0-685-72459-X, ISBN13: 978-0-685-72459-0. Dewey:307.76/0942.
Audience: **g,l,u,f.**

Brailsford, Henry Noel **DA425 .B7**
The Levellers and the English Revolution. Paper Text. Textbook Publishers. Temecula, CA. 2003. xvi, 715p. ISBN:0-7581-3458-4, ISBN13: 978-0-7581-3458-5. Dewey:942.062.
Audience: **l,u,f.**

Brewer, John & Styles, John (Editors) **KD612**
An Ungovernable People: The English and Their Law in the Seventeenth and Eighteenth Centuries. Trade Cloth. Rutgers University Press. Piscataway, NJ. 1980. 400p. ISBN:0-8135-0891-6, ISBN13: 978-0-8135-0891-7. Dewey:340/.115/0942.
Audience: **g,l,u,f.**

Capp, B. S. **DA425**
The Fifth Monarchy Men; A Study in Seventeenth-Century English Millenarianism. Totowa, New Jersey, Rowman and Littlefield. 1972.
Audience: **u,f.**

Gardiner, Samuel Rawson **DA390**
History of the Commonwealth and Protectorate, 1649-1656. New York: AMS Press. 1965.
Audience: **u,f.**

Gardiner, Samuel Rawson **DA390**
History of the Great Civil War, 1642-1649. New York: AMS Press. 1965.
Audience: **u,f.**

Gentles, Ian **DA405.G46 1991**
The New Model Army: In England, Ireland and Scotland, 1645-1653. Cloth Text. Blackwell Publishing, Inc. Malden, MA. 1991. 608p. ISBN:0-631-15869-3, ISBN13: 978-0-631-15869-1. Dewey:941.06/2. LCCN:90-028320.
Audience: **u,f.** *Choice, 1992.*

Haller, William & Davies, Godfrey **DA400.H3**
The Leveller Tracts: 1647-1653. Trade Cloth. Peter Smith Publisher, Inc. Magnolia, MA. 1979. ISBN:0-8446-1218-9, ISBN13: 978-0-8446-1218-8. Dewey:942.063.
Audience: **l,u,f.**

Harris, R. W. **DA447.C6.H37 1983**
Clarendon and the English Revolution. Trade Cloth. Stanford University Press. Palo Alto, CA. 1983. 464p. ISBN:0-8047-1216-6, ISBN13: 978-0-8047-1216-3. Dewey:942.06/092/4. LCCN:83-040092.
Audience: **g,l,u,f.**

Hexter, Jack H. **DA0396.P9H4**
The Reign of King Pym. Trade Paper. Books on Demand. Ann Arbor, MI. 1941. 255p. Harvard Historical Studies, Vol. 48 ISBN:0-608-01603-9, ISBN13: 978-0-608-01603-0. Dewey:923.242. LCCN:41-004164.
Audience: **u,f.**

Hill, Christopher **DA375**
The Century of Revolution, 1603-1714. Ed. 2. Trade Paper. W. W. Norton & Company, Inc. New York, NY. 1982. 304p. ISBN:0-393-30016-1, ISBN13: 978-0-393-30016-1. Dewey:942.06.
Audience: **g,l,u,f.**

Hill, Christopher **DA375.H54 1985**
The Collected Essays of Christopher Hill: Writing and Revolution in Seventeenth-Century England, Vol. 1. Cloth Text. University of Massachusetts Press. Amherst, MA. 1985. 352p. ISBN:0-87023-467-6, ISBN13: 978-0-87023-467-5. Dewey:082. LCCN:84-016446.
Audience: **u,f.** *Choice, 1985.*

Hill, Christopher **DA405.H49 1984**
The Experience of Defeat: Milton and Some Contemporaries. Trade Cloth. Penguin Group (USA) Inc. New York, NY. 1984. 320p. ISBN:0-670-30208-2, ISBN13: 978-0-670-30208-6. Dewey:941.06. LCCN:83-040211.
Audience: **u,f.**

Hill, Christopher **DA426**
God's Englishman: Oliver Cromwell and the English Revolution. Trade Paper. HarperCollins Publishers. New York, NY. 1972. 324p. ISBN:0-06-131666-0, ISBN13: 978-0-06-131666-1. Dewey:941/.064/092.
Audience: **g,l,u,f.**

Hill, Christopher **DA380.H48 1997**
Intellectual Origins of the English Revolution—Revisited. Ed. 2. Trade Cloth. Oxford University Press, Inc. New York, NY. 1997. 438p. ISBN:0-19-820668-2, ISBN13: 978-0-19-820668-2. Dewey:942.06/21. LCCN:96-051165.
Audience: **l,u,f.**

Hill, Christopher **DA380 .H5**
Puritanism and Revolution: Studies in Interpretation of the English Revolution of the 17th Century. Paper Text. Textbook Publishers. Temecula, CA. 2003. 402p. ISBN:0-7581-3969-1, ISBN13: 978-0-7581-3969-6. Dewey:942.062.
Audience: **l,u,f.**

Hill, Christopher **DA380**
A World Turned Upside Down: Radical Ideas During the English Revolution. Trade Paper. Penguin Group (USA) Inc. New York, NY. 1984. 432p. ISBN:0-14-013732-7, ISBN13: 978-0-14-013732-3. Dewey:322.42094209032.
Audience: **g,l,u,f.**

Hill, Christopher **DA380**
The World Turned Upside Down. Trade Cloth. Penguin Group (USA) Inc. New York, NY. 1972. ISBN:0-670-78975-5, ISBN13: 978-0-670-78975-7. Dewey:914.2/03/62.
Audience: **g,l,u,f.**

Hirst, Derek **DA390**
Authority and Conflict: England, 1603-1658. Cambridge, Mass.: Harvard University Press. 1986. The New History of England Ser. ISBN:0-674-05290-0, ISBN13: 978-0-674-05290-1.
Audience: **u,f.**

Hughes, Anne **DA415.H83 1998**
The Causes of the English Civil War. Ed. 2. Cloth over Boards. Palgrave Macmillan. New York, NY. 1998. 216p. British History in Perspective Ser. ISBN:0-312-21708-0, ISBN13: 978-0-312-21708-2. Dewey:941/.062. LCCN:98-024042.
Audience: **g,l,u,f.**

Hunt, William **DA670.E7**
The Puritan Moment: The Coming of Revolution in an English County. Trade Paper. Harvard University Press. Cambridge, MA. 1984. 376p. Harvard Historical Studies, No. 102 ISBN:0-674-73904-3, ISBN13: 978-0-674-73904-8. Dewey:942.6/7/062.
Audience: **l,u,f.**

Hyde, Edward **DA415**
The History of the Rebellion and Civil Wars in England Begun in the Year 1641, Set. W. Dunn Macray (Editor). Trade Cloth. Oxford University Press, Inc. New York, NY. 1993. 3094p. ISBN:0-19-821206-2, ISBN13: 978-0-19-821206-5. Dewey:941.06/2.
Audience: **l,u,f.**

Manning, Brian **DA415**
The English People and the English Revolution, 1640-1649. Trade Cloth. Heinemann. Portsmouth, NH. 1976. x, 390p. ISBN:0-435-32565-5, ISBN13: 978-0-435-32565-7. Dewey:942.06/2. LCCN:76-370634.
Audience: **g,l,u,f.**

McGregor, J. F. **BR757.R33 1984**
Radical Religion in the English Revolution. B. Reay (Editor). Trade Cloth. Oxford University Press, Inc. New York, NY. 1984. 219p. ISBN:0-19-873044-6, ISBN13: 978-0-19-873044-6. Dewey:274.2/07. LCCN:85-116178.
Audience: **l,u,f.**

Morrill, John **DA426.O45 1990**
Oliver Cromwell and the English Revolution. Other. Addison-Wesley Longman, Inc. Boston, MA. 1990. 312p. ISBN:0-582-01675-4, ISBN13: 978-0-582-01675-0. Dewey:941.06/4/092 B. LCCN:89-035960.
Audience: **l,u,f.**

Morrill, John (Editor) **DA415.R38 1983**
Reactions to the English Civil War, 1642-1649. Cloth Text. Palgrave Macmillan. New York, NY. 1984. 257p. ISBN:0-312-66443-5, ISBN13: 978-0-312-66443-5. Dewey:941.06/2. LCCN:82-025538.
Audience: **l,u,f.**

Notestein, Wallace **DA380.N6**
English People on the Eve of Colonization: 1603-1630. Mass Market. HarperCollins Publishers. New York, NY. 1985. New American Nation Ser. ISBN:0-06-133006-X, ISBN13: 978-0-06-133006-3. Dewey:942.061.
Audience: **g,l,u,f.**

Reay, Barry (Editor) **DA380.P67 1985**
Popular Culture in Seventeenth Century England. Cloth Text. Palgrave Macmillan. New York, NY. 1985. 319p. ISBN:0-312-63036-0, ISBN13: 978-0-312-63036-2. Dewey:306/.4/0942. LCCN:85-002496.
Audience: **g,l,u,f.** *Choice, 1985.*

Reay, Barry **BX7676.2.R4 1985**
The Quakers and the English Revolution. Christopher R. Hill (Foreword by). Cloth Text. Palgrave Macmillan. New York, NY. 1985. 200p. ISBN:0-312-65808-7, ISBN13: 978-0-312-65808-3. Dewey:289.6/42. LCCN:84-022355.
Audience: **l,u,f.** *Choice, 1985.*

Richardson, R. C. **DA403.R53 1999**
The Debate on the English Revolution. Ed. 3. Trade Cloth. Manchester University Press. Manchester, 1999. 262p. Issues in Historiography Ser. ISBN:0-7190-4739-0, ISBN13: 978-0-7190-4739-8. Dewey:941.06/3/072. LCCN:98-028825.
Audience: **u,f.**

Russell, Conrad **DA415.R78 1990**
The Causes of the English Civil War. Paper Text. Oxford University Press, Inc. New York, NY. 1990. 256p. Ford Lectures ISBN:0-19-822141-X, ISBN13: 978-0-19-822141-8. Dewey:941.06/2. LCCN:90-030543.
Audience: **l,u.** *Choice, 1991.*

Russell, Conrad (Editor) **DA415**
The Origins of the English Civil War. Trade Cloth. Pan Macmillan. London, 1973. "x, 286"p. Problems in Focus Ser. ISBN:0-333-12399-9, ISBN13: 978-0-333-12399-7. Dewey:942.06/2. LCCN:73-165920.
Audience: **g,l,u,f.**

Solt, Leo F. (Leo Frank) **DA415**
Saints in Arms; Puritanism and Democracy in Cromwell's Army. New York, AMS Press. 1971. Stanford Studies in History, Economics, and Political Science; Vol. 18 ISBN:0-404-50976-2, ISBN13: 978-0-404-50976-7.
Audience: **u,f.**

Stone, Lawrence **DA390.S85 2001**
The Causes of the English Revolution 1529-1642. Ed. 2. Trade Paper. Routledge. New York, NY. 2001. 208p. ISBN:0-415-26673-4, ISBN13: 978-0-415-26673-4. Dewey:942.06/2. LCCN:2001-049100.
Audience: **l,u.**

Underdown, David **DA415.U5 1985**
Pride's Purge: Politics in the Puritan Revolution. Paper Text. Routledge. New York, NY. 1985. 440p. ISBN:0-04-822045-0, ISBN13: 978-0-04-822045-5. Dewey:942.06/3. LCCN:85-001218.
Audience: **l,u,f.**

Underdown, David **DA425**
Pride's Purge: Politics in the Puritan Revolution. Trade Cloth. Oxford University Press, Inc. New York, NY. 1971. xi, 424p. ISBN:0-19-822342-0, ISBN13: 978-0-19-822342-9. Dewey:942.06/3. LCCN:78-853456.
Audience: **l,u,f.**

Underdown, David **DA390**
Revel, Riot, and Rebellion: Popular Politics and Culture in England 1603-1660. Paper Text. Oxford University Press, Inc. New York, NY. 1987. 340p. ISBN:0-19-285193-4, ISBN13: 978-0-19-285193-2. Dewey:942/.06.
Audience: **u,f.** *Choice, 1986.*

Wedgwood, C. V. **DA405**
King's Peace 1637-1641. Paper Text. Textbook Publishers. Temecula, CA. 2003. 510p. ISBN:0-7581-8941-9, ISBN13: 978-0-7581-8941-7.
Audience: **l,u,f.**

Wedgwood, C. V. **DA405**
King's War: 1641. Paper Text. Textbook Publishers. Temecula, CA. 2003. 702p. ISBN:0-7581-8944-3, ISBN13: 978-0-7581-8944-8. Dewey:942.062.
Audience: **l,u,f.**

Wedgwood, Cicely V. **DA396.S8.W4 1970**
Strafford, 1593-1641. Library Binding. Greenwood Publishing Group, Inc. Portsmouth, NH. 1970. 366p. ISBN:0-8371-4566-X, ISBN13: 978-0-8371-4566-2. Dewey:942.06/2/0924. LCCN:76-110882.
Audience: **u,f.**

Woolf, D. R. **DA1**
The Idea of History in Early Stuart England: Erudition, Ideology, and the Light of Truth from the Accession of James I to the Civil War. Trade Cloth. University of Toronto Press. Toronto, ON. 1990. 377p. ISBN:0-8020-5862-0, ISBN13: 978-0-8020-5862-1. Dewey:907/.2042.
Audience: **l,u,f.** *Choice, 1991.*

Woolrych, Austin **DA425.W59 1982**
Commonwealth to Protectorate. Trade Cloth. Oxford University Press, Inc. New York, NY. 1982. 458p. ISBN:0-19-822659-4,

ISBN13: 978-0-19-822659-8. Dewey:941.06/3.
LCCN:82-167677.
Audience: **g,l,u,f.**

Zagorin, Perez **DA395**
Court and the Country: The Beginning of the English Revolution. Paper Text. Simon & Schuster Children's Publishing. New York, NY. 1971. ISBN:0-689-70275-2, ISBN13: 978-0-689-70275-4. Dewey:320.9/42. LCCN:72-104129.
Audience: **g,l,u,f.**

Britain > English History > Modern (1485-) > Later Stuarts

Cressy, David **LC156.G7**
Literacy and the Social Order: Reading and Writing in Tudor and Stuart England. Cloth Text. Cambridge University Press. New York, NY. 1980. 256p. ISBN:0-521-22514-0, ISBN13: 978-0-521-22514-4. Dewey:302.2/0942. LCCN:79-041767.
Audience: **l,u,f.**

De Krey, Gary S. **JS3566.D45 1985**
A Fractured Society: The Politics of London in the First Age of Party, 1688-1715. Trade Cloth. Oxford University Press, Inc. New York, NY. 1985. 420p. ISBN:0-19-820067-6, ISBN13: 978-0-19-820067-3. Dewey:942.106. LCCN:85-234226.
Audience: **u,f.** *Choice, 1986.*

Defoe, Daniel **DA620.D31 1928**
A Tour Through England and Wales; Divided into Circuits or Journies. London, J.M. Dent; New York, E.P. Dutton. 1928. Everyman's Library: Travel and Topography
Audience: **g,l,u,f.**

Earle, Peter **HT690.G7E27 1989**
The Making of the English Middle Class: Business, Society and Family Life in London 1660-1730. Trade Cloth. University of California Press. Berkeley, CA. 1989. xiii, 446p. ISBN:0-520-06826-2, ISBN13: 978-0-520-06826-1. Dewey:305.5/5/0942109032. LCCN:89-004976.
Audience: **g,l,u,f.** *Choice, 1990.*

Earle, Peter **DA448.9.E17 1978**
Monmouth's Rebels. Trade Cloth. Palgrave Macmillan. New York, NY. 1977. xi, 236p. ISBN:0-312-54512-6, ISBN13: 978-0-312-54512-3. Dewey:942.06/7. LCCN:77-084928.
Audience: **l,u.**

Evelyn, John **DA378.P4**
The Diary of John Evelyn. Library Binding. Routledge. New York, NY. 1997. 1342p. Great British Diarists Ser. ISBN:0-415-14954-1, ISBN13: 978-0-415-14954-9. Dewey:942/.06/092.
Audience: **g,l,u,f.**

Harris, R. W. **DA447.C6.H37 1983**
Clarendon and the English Revolution. Trade Cloth. Stanford University Press. Palo Alto, CA. 1983. 464p. ISBN:0-8047-1216-6, ISBN13: 978-0-8047-1216-3. Dewey:942.06/092/4. LCCN:83-040092.
Audience: **g,l,u,f.**

Harris, Tim **DA445.H24 2003**
London Crowds in the Reign of Charles II: Propaganda and Politics from the Restoration until the Exclusion Crisis. Anthony Fletcher, John Guy & John Morrill (Contribution by). Trade Paper. Cambridge University Press. New York, NY. 1990. 280p. Cambridge Studies in Early Modern British History ISBN:0-521-39845-2, ISBN13: 978-0-521-39845-9. Dewey:942.1/066.
Audience: **u,f.** *Choice, 1988.*

Hutton, Ronald **DA375**
The Restoration: A Political and Religious History of England and Wales, 1658-1667. Paper Text. Oxford University Press, Inc. New York, NY. 1993. 388p. ISBN:0-19-820392-6, ISBN13: 978-0-19-820392-6. Dewey:942.06.
Audience: **l,u,f.** *Choice, 1986, 1985.*

Jones, J. R. **DA435.J66**
Country and Court: England, Sixteen Fifty-Eight to Seventeen Fourteen. Trade Cloth. Harvard University Press. Cambridge, MA. 1978. 377p. New History of England Ser. ISBN:0-674-17525-5, ISBN13: 978-0-674-17525-9. Dewey:942.06. LCCN:78-005362.
Audience: **u,f.**

Kenyon, J. P. (John Philipps) **DA448**
The Popish Plot. New York, St. Martin's Press. 1972.
Audience: **u,f.**

Macaulay, Thomas Babington, el al. **DA435**
History of England from the Accession of James II. Macaulay, Baron (Author). London, Dent; New York, Dutton. 1953. Everyman's Library, 34-37. History
Audience: **g,l,u,f.**

Miller, John **DA448.M54**
Popery and Politics in England, 1660-1688. Trade Cloth. Cambridge University Press. New York, NY. 1973. 296p. ISBN:0-521-20236-1, ISBN13: 978-0-521-20236-7. Dewey:322/.1/0942. LCCN:73-079306.
Audience: **u,f.**

Pepys, Samuel **DA447.P4**
The Diary of Samuel Pepys: A New and Complete Transcription. Latham, Robert ; Matthews, William (Editors). Berkeley, University of California Press. 1970. ISBN:0-520-01575-4, ISBN13: 978-0-520-01575-3.
Audience: **u,f.**

Pepys, Samuel **DA447.P4A425 1985**
The Shorter Pepys. Robert A. Latham (Editor, Selected by). Trade Cloth. University of California Press. Berkeley, CA. 1985. 1152p. ISBN:0-520-03426-0, ISBN13: 978-0-520-03426-6. Dewey:941.06/6/0924 B. LCCN:85-040210.
Audience: **g,l,u,f.**

Reay, Barry (Editor) **DA380.P67 1985**
Popular Culture in Seventeenth Century England. Cloth Text. Palgrave Macmillan. New York, NY. 1985. 319p. ISBN:0-312-63036-0, ISBN13: 978-0-312-63036-2. Dewey:306/.4/0942. LCCN:85-002496.
Audience: **g,l,u,f.** *Choice, 1985.*

Seaward, Paul **DA445.S43 1990**
The Restoration, 1660-1688: British History in Perspective. Trade Cloth. Palgrave Macmillan. New York, NY. 1991. 173p. ISBN:0-312-04929-3, ISBN13: 978-0-312-04929-4. Dewey:941.06/6. LCCN:90-040585.
Audience: **u,f.**

Steele, Ian K. **HE202.S74 1986**
The English Atlantic, 1675-1740: An Exploration of Communication and Community. Trade Cloth. Oxford University Press, Inc. New York, NY. 1986. 414p. ISBN:0-19-503968-8, ISBN13: 978-0-19-503968-9. Dewey:380.3/09171/241. LCCN:85-025828.
Audience: **u,f.** *Choice, 1987.*

Britain > English History > Modern (1485-) > Glorious Revolution. William and Mary

JN210
Growth of Political Stability. Trade Paper. Brill Academic Publishers, Inc. Boston, MA. 1987. ISBN:0-391-01908-2, ISBN13: 978-0-391-01908-9. Dewey:320.9/42.
Audience: **l,u,f.**

Beresford, John (Editor) **DA485**
James Woodforde: The Diary of a Country Parson, 1758-1802. Trade Paper. Canterbury Press Norwich. London, 1996. 622p. ISBN:1-85311-138-4, ISBN13: 978-1-85311-138-9. Dewey:942.0730924.
Audience: **u,f.**

Black, J. **DA498.B53 1985**
British Foreign Policy in the Age of Walpole. Cloth Text. Brill Academic Publishers, Inc. Boston, MA. 1985. 256p. ISBN:0-85976-126-6, ISBN13: 978-0-85976-126-0. Dewey:941.07/1. LCCN:85-213381.
Audience: **u,f.** *Choice, 1985.*

Brewer, John **DA480.B74 1990**
The Sinews of Power: War, Money and the English State, 1688-1783. Trade Paper. Harvard University Press. Cambridge, MA. 1990. 320p. ISBN:0-674-80930-0, ISBN13: 978-0-674-80930-7. Dewey:941.07. LCCN:90-004414.
Audience: **u,f.**

Brewer, John & Styles, John (Editors) **KD612**
An Ungovernable People: The English and Their Law in the Seventeenth and Eighteenth Centuries. Trade Cloth. Rutgers University Press. Piscataway, NJ. 1980. 400p. ISBN:0-8135-0891-6, ISBN13: 978-0-8135-0891-7. Dewey:340/.115/0942.
Audience: **g,l,u,f.**

Burns, J. H. (Editor) **JA81.C283 1990**
The Cambridge History of Political Thought, 1450-1700. Mark Goldie (As told to). Trade Cloth. Cambridge University Press. New York, NY. 1991. 810p. The Cambridge History of Political Thought Ser. ISBN:0-521-24716-0, ISBN13: 978-0-521-24716-0. Dewey:320/.09. LCCN:89-022282.
Audience: **u,f.**

Chesterfield, Philip Dormer Stanhope, Earl of **DA501.C5**
The Letters of Philip Dormer Stanhope, 4th Earl of Chesterfield. Dobrée, Bonamy (Editor). London, Eyre & Spottiswoode; New York, Viking Press. 1932.
Audience: **u,f.**

Clark, J. C. **JN175.C58 1985**
English Society, 1688-1832: Ideology, Social Structure and Political Practice During the Ancien Regime. Cloth Text. Cambridge University Press. New York, NY. 1985. 449p. Cambridge Studies in the History and Theory of Politics ISBN:0-521-30922-0, ISBN13: 978-0-521-30922-6. Dewey:320.941. LCCN:85-010995.
Audience: **l,u,f.** *Choice, 1986.*

Colley, Linda **JN1129.T72**
In Defiance of Oligarchy: The Tory Party 1714-60. Trade Paper. Cambridge University Press. New York, NY. 1985. 383p. ISBN:0-521-31311-2, ISBN13: 978-0-521-31311-7. Dewey:324.241/02. LCCN:81-010004.
Audience: **u,f.**

De Krey, Gary S. **JS3566.D45 1985**
A Fractured Society: The Politics of London in the First Age of Party, 1688-1715. Trade Cloth. Oxford University Press, Inc. New York, NY. 1985. 420p. ISBN:0-19-820067-6, ISBN13: 978-0-19-820067-3. Dewey:942.106. LCCN:85-234226.
Audience: **u,f.** *Choice, 1986.*

Dunn, John **B1297**
Locke. Trade Cloth. Oxford University Press, Inc. New York, NY. 1984. xii, 97p. ISBN:0-19-287561-2, ISBN13: 978-0-19-287561-7. Dewey:192. LCCN:83-013169.
Audience: **u,f.**

Earle, Peter **HT690.G7E27 1989**
The Making of the English Middle Class: Business, Society and Family Life in London 1660-1730. Trade Cloth. University of California Press. Berkeley, CA. 1989. xiii, 446p. ISBN:0-520-06826-2, ISBN13: 978-0-520-06826-1. Dewey:305.5/5/0942109032. LCCN:89-004976.
Audience: **g,l,u,f.** *Choice, 1990.*

George, M. Dorothy **HN398.L7G4 1999**
London Life in the Eighteenth Century. Ed. 2. Trade Cloth. Academy Chicago Publishers, Ltd. Chicago, IL. 1999. 458p. ISBN:0-89733-147-8, ISBN13: 978-0-89733-147-0. Dewey:306/.09421. LCCN:99-010241.
Audience: **g,l,u,f.**

Gregg, Edward **DA495**
Queen Anne. Ed. 2. Trade Paper. Yale University Press. Cumberland, RI. 2001. 512p. Yale English Monarchs Ser. ISBN:0-300-09024-2, ISBN13: 978-0-300-09024-6. Dewey:941.06/9/092 B. LCCN:2001-093245.
Audience: **g,l,u,f.**

Hatton, Ragnhild H. **DA501.A2.H4**
George the First, Elector and King. Trade Cloth. Harvard University Press. Cambridge, MA. 1978. 416p. ISBN:0-674-34935-0, ISBN13: 978-0-674-34935-3. Dewey:941.07/1/0924. LCCN:77-015058.
Audience: **g,l,u,f.**

Holmes, Geoffrey S. **DA495.H59 1987**
British Politics in the Age of Anne. Ed. 2. Trade Cloth. Continuum International Publishing Group, Ltd. London, 2003. 620p. ISBN:0-907628-73-7, ISBN13: 978-0-907628-73-6. Dewey:941.06/9. LCCN:87-014833.
Audience: **u,f.**

Hoppit, Julian **HG3769.G73E54 1987**
Risk and Failure in English Business, 1700-1800. Trade Cloth. Cambridge University Press. New York, NY. 1987. 240p.

ISBN:0-521-32624-9, ISBN13: 978-0-521-32624-7. Dewey:332.7/5/0942. LCCN:87-000743.
Audience: **u,f.** *Choice, 1988.*

Jones, J. R. **DA435.J66**
Country and Court: England, Sixteen Fifty-Eight to Seventeen Fourteen. Trade Cloth. Harvard University Press. Cambridge, MA. 1978. 377p. New History of England Ser. ISBN:0-674-17525-5, ISBN13: 978-0-674-17525-9. Dewey:942.06. LCCN:78-005362.
Audience: **u,f.**

Jones, James R. **DA452**
The Revolution of 1688 in England. Trade Paper. W. W. Norton & Company, Inc. New York, NY. 1973. Revolutions in the Modern World Ser. ISBN:0-393-09998-9, ISBN13: 978-0-393-09998-0. Dewey:942.06/7.
Audience: **g,l,u,f.**

Kramnick, Isaac **DA501.B6**
Bolingbroke and His Circle: The Politics of Nostalgia in the Age of Walpole. Trade Paper. Cornell University Press. Ithaca, NY. 1992. 336p. ISBN:0-8014-8001-9, ISBN13: 978-0-8014-8001-0. Dewey:941.06/9/092. LCCN:92-004257.
Audience: **u,f.**

Langford, Paul **DA480**
A Polite and Commercial People: England, 1727-1783. Trade Cloth. Oxford University Press, Inc. New York, NY. 1998. 824p. ISBN:0-19-820733-6, ISBN13: 978-0-19-820733-7. Dewey:942/.07. LCCN:91-031628.
Audience: **u,f.**

Malcolmson, Malcolm **GV75**
Popular Recreations English Society. Trade Cloth. Cambridge University Press. New York, NY. 1973. 198p. ISBN:0-521-20147-0, ISBN13: 978-0-521-20147-6. Dewey:301.5/7/0942. LCCN:72-091958.
Audience: **g,l,u,f.**

Marshall, Dorothy **HV245**
The English Poor in the Eighteenth Century: A Study in Social and administrative History. New York: Kelley. 1989.
Audience: **u,f.**

Monod, Paul K. **DA813.M86 1989**
Jacobitism and the English People, 1688-1788. Trade Cloth. Cambridge University Press. New York, NY. 1989. 424p. ISBN:0-521-33534-5, ISBN13: 978-0-521-33534-8. Dewey:941/.07. LCCN:88-036743.
Audience: **u,f.** *Choice, 1990.*

Montagu, Lady Mary Wortley **DA501.M7**
The Complete Letters of Lady Mary Wortley Montagu. Robert Halsband (Editor). Other. Oxford University Press, Inc. New York, NY. ISBN:0-318-54813-5, ISBN13: 978-0-318-54813-5. Dewey:826/.5.
Audience: **g,l,u,f.**

Namier, Lewis B. **DA480.N3 1970**
Crossroads of Power. Trade Cloth. Ayer Company Publishers, Inc. Manchester, NH. 1977. viii, 234p. Essay Index Reprint Ser. ISBN:0-8369-1690-5, ISBN13: 978-0-8369-1690-4. Dewey:942.07/08. LCCN:77-119604.
Audience: **u,f.**

Pares, Richard **F1621 .P32**
War and Trade in West Indies. Trade Paper. Taylor & Francis Group. Abingdon, 1963. 631p. ISBN:0-7146-1943-4, ISBN13: 978-0-7146-1943-9. Dewey:972.9.
Audience: **g,l,u,f.**

Plumb, J. H. **DA480**
The First Four Georges. Paper Text. Textbook Publishers. Temecula, CA. 2003. 208p. ISBN:0-7581-9592-3, ISBN13: 978-0-7581-9592-0. Dewey:941/.07/0922.
Audience: **g,l,u,f.**

Plumb, J. H. (John Harold) **DA501.W2**
Sir Robert Walpole. Clifton [N.J.] A.M. Kelley. 1973. Houghton Mifflin Reprint Editions Ser. ISBN:0-678-03551-2, ISBN13: 978-0-678-03551-1.
Audience: **g,l,u,f.**

Pocock, J. G. **JA84.G7 P635 1985**
Virtue, Commerce, and History: Essays on Political Thought and History, Chiefly in the Eighteenth Century. Trade Cloth. Cambridge University Press. New York, NY. 1985. 336p. Ideas in Context Ser. ISBN:0-521-25701-8, ISBN13: 978-0-521-25701-5. Dewey:320/.01. LCCN:84-015626.
Audience: **g,l,u,f.**

Rude, George **DA682.R8**
Hanoverian London, Seventeen Fourteen to Eighteen Eight. Trade Cloth. University of California Press. Berkeley, CA. 1971. xvi, 271p. History of London Ser. ISBN:0-520-01778-1, ISBN13: 978-0-520-01778-8. Dewey:914.21/03/7. LCCN:69-010590.
Audience: **u,f.**

Schwoerer, Lois G. **DA452**
The Declaration of Rights, 1689. Trade Cloth. Johns Hopkins University Press. Baltimore, MD. 1972. 407p. ISBN:0-8018-2430-3, ISBN13: 978-0-8018-2430-2. Dewey:941.067. LCCN:81-002942.
Audience: **u,f.**

Schwoerer, Lois G. **DA0452.S3**
The Declaration of Rights, Sixteen Eighty-Nine. Trade Paper. Books on Demand. Ann Arbor, MI. 407p. ISBN:0-8357-8090-2, ISBN13: 978-0-8357-8090-2. Dewey:344.202/85. LCCN:81-002942.
Audience: **u,f.**

Shellabarger, Samuel **DA501.C5 S52**
Lord Chesterfield and His World. Trade Cloth. Biblo & Tannen Booksellers & Publishers, Inc. Cheshire, CT. 1971. ISBN:0-8196-0271-X, ISBN13: 978-0-8196-0271-8. Dewey:942.07/1/0924. LCCN:72-156737.
Audience: **u,f.**

Steele, Ian K. **HE202.S74 1986**
The English Atlantic, 1675-1740: An Exploration of Communication and Community. Trade Cloth. Oxford University Press, Inc. New York, NY. 1986. 414p. ISBN:0-19-503968-8, ISBN13: 978-0-19-503968-9. Dewey:380.3/09171/241. LCCN:85-025828.
Audience: **u,f.** *Choice, 1987.*

Thompson, Edward P. **HV6943.A54 1975**
Albion's Fatal Tree: Crime and Society in Eighteenth-Century England. Trade Cloth. Knopf Publishing Group. New York, NY.

1976. 352p. ISBN:0-394-47120-2, ISBN13: 978-0-394-47120-4. Dewey:364/.942. LCCN:75-023256.
Audience: **u,f.**

Trevelyan, George Macaulay **DA452**
The English Revolution, 1688-1689. New York: Oxford University Press. 1977. ISBN:0-19-500263-6, ISBN13: 978-0-19-500263-8.
Audience: **g,l,u,f.**

Walpole, Horace **DA483.W2**
Correspondence: Yale Edition of Horace Walpole's Correspondence. Lewis, W. S. (Wilmarth Sheldon) (Editor). New Haven: Yale University Press. 1937. ISBN:0-300-02717-6, ISBN13: 978-0-300-02717-4.
Audience: **l,u,f.**

Walpole, Horace **DA506.W2**
Selected Letters of Horace Walpole. W. S. Lewis (Editor). Trade Cloth. Yale University Press. Cumberland, RI. 1973. 344p. ISBN:0-300-01643-3, ISBN13: 978-0-300-01643-7. Dewey:826/.6. LCCN:72-091300.
Audience: **u,f.**

Britain > English History > Modern (1485-) > George III (1760-1820). Regency (1801-1837)

Beresford, John (Editor) **DA485**
James Woodforde: The Diary of a Country Parson, 1758-1802. Trade Paper. Canterbury Press Norwich. London, 1996. 622p. ISBN:1-85311-138-4, ISBN13: 978-1-85311-138-9. Dewey:942.0730924.
Audience: **u,f.**

Bourne, Kenneth **DA554**
Palmerston: The Early Years 1784-1841. Trade Cloth. Macmillan Publishing Company, Inc. Old Tappan, NJ. 1982. 749p. ISBN:0-318-54242-0, ISBN13: 978-0-318-54242-3. Dewey:941.081/092/4.
Audience: **g,l,u,f.**

Brewer, John **JN210**
Party Ideology and Popular Politics at the Accession of George Third. Trade Cloth. Cambridge University Press. New York, NY. 1976. 391p. ISBN:0-521-21049-6, ISBN13: 978-0-521-21049-2. Dewey:320.941. LCCN:76-014773.
Audience: **u,f.**

Brewer, John & Styles, John (Editors) **KD612**
An Ungovernable People: The English and Their Law in the Seventeenth and Eighteenth Centuries. Trade Cloth. Rutgers University Press. Piscataway, NJ. 1980. 400p. ISBN:0-8135-0891-6, ISBN13: 978-0-8135-0891-7. Dewey:340/.115/0942.
Audience: **g,l,u,f.**

Burns, J. H. (Editor) **JA81.C283 1990**
The Cambridge History of Political Thought, 1450-1700. Mark Goldie (As told to). Trade Cloth. Cambridge University Press. New York, NY. 1991. 810p. The Cambridge History of Political Thought Ser. ISBN:0-521-24716-0, ISBN13: 978-0-521-24716-0. Dewey:320/.09. LCCN:89-022282.
Audience: **u,f.**

Butterfield, Herbert, Sir **DA505**
George III and the Historians. New York, Macmillan. 1959. Cassell History Ser.
Audience: **l,u,f.**

Clark, J. C. **JN175.C58 1985**
English Society, 1688-1832: Ideology, Social Structure and Political Practice During the Ancien Regime. Cloth Text. Cambridge University Press. New York, NY. 1985. 449p. Cambridge Studies in the History and Theory of Politics ISBN:0-521-30922-0, ISBN13: 978-0-521-30922-6. Dewey:320.941. LCCN:85-010995.
Audience: **l,u,f.** *Choice, 1986.*

Cobbett, William **DA625.C654 1932**
Rural Rides. London, J.M. Dent & Sons, Ltd.; New York, E.P. Dutton & Co., Inc. 1932.
Audience: **g,l,u,f.**

Gash, Norman **DA522.L7G37 1984**
Lord Liverpool: The Life and Political Career of Robert Banks Jenkinson, Second Earl of Liverpool, 1770-1828. Trade Cloth. Harvard University Press. Cambridge, MA. 1985. 296p. ISBN:0-674-53910-9, ISBN13: 978-0-674-53910-5. Dewey:941.07/3/0924. LCCN:84-012842.
Audience: **g,l,u,f.**

George, M. Dorothy **HN398.L7G4 1999**
London Life in the Eighteenth Century. Ed. 2. Trade Cloth. Academy Chicago Publishers, Ltd. Chicago, IL. 1999. 458p. ISBN:0-89733-147-8, ISBN13: 978-0-89733-147-0. Dewey:306/.09421. LCCN:99-010241.
Audience: **g,l,u,f.**

Goodwin, Albert **DA520.G6 1979**
The Friends of Liberty: The English Democratic Movement in the Age of the French Revolution. Trade Cloth. Harvard University Press. Cambridge, MA. 1979. 594p. ISBN:0-674-32339-4, ISBN13: 978-0-674-32339-1. Dewey:320.9/41/073. LCCN:78-015673.
Audience: **g,l,u,f.**

Gregg, Edward **DA495**
Queen Anne. Ed. 2. Trade Paper. Yale University Press. Cumberland, RI. 2001. 512p. Yale English Monarchs Ser. ISBN:0-300-09024-2, ISBN13: 978-0-300-09024-6. Dewey:941.06/9/092 B. LCCN:2001-093245.
Audience: **g,l,u,f.**

Hoppit, Julian **HG3769.G73E54 1987**
Risk and Failure in English Business, 1700-1800. Trade Cloth. Cambridge University Press. New York, NY. 1987. 240p. ISBN:0-521-32624-9, ISBN13: 978-0-521-32624-7. Dewey:332.7/5/0942. LCCN:87-000743.
Audience: **u,f.** *Choice, 1988.*

Jarrett, Derek **DA485**
England in the Age of Hogarth. Cloth over Boards. Yale University Press. Cumberland, RI. 1986. 213p. ISBN:0-300-03608-6, ISBN13: 978-0-300-03608-4. Dewey:942.07. LCCN:85-052071.
Audience: **g,l,u,f.**

Kronenberger, Louis **DA512.W6.K76**
The Extraordinary Mr. Wilkes: His Life and Times. Trade Cloth. Doubleday Publishing. New York, NY. 1974. xv, 269p. ISBN:0-385-05131-X, ISBN13: 978-0-385-05131-6. Dewey:328.42/092/4. LCCN:73-079686.
Audience: **g,l,u,f.**

Langford, Paul **DA480**
A Polite and Commercial People: England, 1727-1783. Trade Cloth. Oxford University Press, Inc. New York, NY. 1998. 824p. ISBN:0-19-820733-6, ISBN13: 978-0-19-820733-7. Dewey:942/.07. LCCN:91-031628.
Audience: **u,f.**

Malcolmson, Malcolm **GV75**
Popular Recreations English Society. Trade Cloth. Cambridge University Press. New York, NY. 1973. 198p. ISBN:0-521-20147-0, ISBN13: 978-0-521-20147-6. Dewey:301.5/7/0942. LCCN:72-091958.
Audience: **g,l,u,f.**

Marshall, Dorothy **HV245**
The English Poor in the Eighteenth Century: A Study in Social and administrative History. New York: Kelley. 1989.
Audience: **u,f.**

Monod, Paul K. **DA813.M86 1989**
Jacobitism and the English People, 1688-1788. Trade Cloth. Cambridge University Press. New York, NY. 1989. 424p. ISBN:0-521-33534-5, ISBN13: 978-0-521-33534-8. Dewey:941/.07. LCCN:88-036743.
Audience: **u,f.** *Choice, 1990.*

Namier, Lewis B. **DA480.N3 1970**
Crossroads of Power. Trade Cloth. Ayer Company Publishers, Inc. Manchester, NH. 1977. viii, 234p. Essay Index Reprint Ser. ISBN:0-8369-1690-5, ISBN13: 978-0-8369-1690-4. Dewey:942.07/08. LCCN:77-119604.
Audience: **u,f.**

Namier, Lewis B. **DA505 .N25**
England in the Age of the American Revolution. Ed. 2. Cloth Text. Palgrave Macmillan. New York, NY. 1974. ISBN:0-312-25270-6, ISBN13: 978-0-312-25270-0. Dewey:942.072.
Audience: **g,l,u,f.**

Pares, Richard **DA505.P3 1988**
King George III and the Politicians. Trade Cloth. Oxford University Press, Inc. New York, NY. 1988. 224p. ISBN:0-19-821240-2, ISBN13: 978-0-19-821240-9. Dewey:941.07/3. LCCN:87-014064.
Audience: **g,l,u,f.**

Plumb, J. H. **DA480**
The First Four Georges. Paper Text. Textbook Publishers. Temecula, CA. 2003. 208p. ISBN:0-7581-9592-3, ISBN13: 978-0-7581-9592-0. Dewey:941/.07/0922.
Audience: **g,l,u,f.**

Pollock, John **DA522.W6**
Wilberforce. Ed. 2. Trade Paper. Lion Publishing. Colorado Springs, CO. 1986. 384p. ISBN:0-7459-1061-0, ISBN13: 978-0-7459-1061-1. Dewey:322.4/4/0924.
Audience: **u,f.**

Rude, George **DA682.R8**
Hanoverian London, Seventeen Fourteen to Eighteen Eight. Trade Cloth. University of California Press. Berkeley, CA. 1971. xvi, 271p. History of London Ser. ISBN:0-520-01778-1, ISBN13: 978-0-520-01778-8. Dewey:914.21/03/7. LCCN:69-010590.
Audience: **u,f.**

Rude, George **DA510**
Wilkes and Liberty. Trade Paper. Lawrence & Wishart, Ltd. London, 1983. 240p. ISBN:0-85315-579-8, ISBN13: 978-0-85315-579-9. Dewey:941.07/3.
Audience: **l,u,f.**

Schwartz, Richard B. **DA682**
Daily Life in Johnson's London. Trade Paper. University of Wisconsin Press. Chicago, IL. 1983. 216p. ISBN:0-299-09494-4, ISBN13: 978-0-299-09494-2. Dewey:942.107. LCCN:83-050080.
Audience: **u,f.**

Spater, George **PR3325**
William Cobbett: The Poor Man's Friend. Trade Cloth. Cambridge University Press. New York, NY. 1982. 653p. ISBN:0-521-24538-9, ISBN13: 978-0-521-24538-8. Dewey:828/.608. LCCN:81-003859.
Audience: **g,l,u,f.**

Speck, W. A. **DA814.5**
Stability and Strife: England 1714-1760. Trade Paper. Harvard University Press. Cambridge, MA. 1979. 224p. New History of England Ser. ISBN:0-674-83350-3, ISBN13: 978-0-674-83350-0. Dewey:942.07/2.
Audience: **l,u,f.**

Thomas, Peter D. **DA506.N7 T48**
Lord North. Cloth Text. Palgrave Macmillan. New York, NY. 1975. 175p. British Political Biography Ser. ISBN:0-312-49840-3, ISBN13: 978-0-312-49840-5. Dewey:941.07/3/0924. LCCN:75-029819.
Audience: **g,l,u,f.**

Thompson, Edward P. **HV6943.A54 1975**
Albion's Fatal Tree: Crime and Society in Eighteenth-Century England. Trade Cloth. Knopf Publishing Group. New York, NY. 1976. 352p. ISBN:0-394-47120-2, ISBN13: 978-0-394-47120-4. Dewey:364/.942. LCCN:75-023256.
Audience: **u,f.**

Thompson, Edward P. **KD7852.B55**
Whigs and Hunters. Trade Paper. Knopf Publishing Group. New York, NY. 1976. ISBN:0-394-73086-0, ISBN13: 978-0-394-73086-8. Dewey:328.42/07/78. LCCN:75-023168.
Audience: **u,f.**

Thompson, Flora **S522.G7**
Lark Rise to Candleford: A Trilogy. Julie Neild (Illustrator), H. J. Massingham (Introduction by). Trade Cloth. Oxford University Press, Inc. New York, NY. 1980. 576p. ISBN:0-19-211759-9, ISBN13: 978-0-19-211759-5. Dewey:942.5/7081/0924.
Audience: **u,f.**

Walpole, Horace **DA483.W2**
Correspondence: Yale Edition of Horace Walpole's Correspondence. Lewis, W. S. (Wilmarth Sheldon) (Editor). New Haven: Yale University Press. 1937. ISBN:0-300-02717-6, ISBN13: 978-0-300-02717-4.
Audience: **l,u,f.**

Walpole, Horace **DA506.W2**
Selected Letters of Horace Walpole. W. S. Lewis (Editor). Trade Cloth. Yale University Press. Cumberland, RI. 1973. 344p. ISBN:0-300-01643-3, ISBN13: 978-0-300-01643-7. Dewey:826/.6. LCCN:72-091300.
Audience: **u,f.**

Wiener, Joel H. **DA470.W48**
Great Britain: The Lion at Home; a Documentary History of Domestic Policy, 1689-1973. Trade Cloth. Chelsea House Publishers. Langhorne, PA. 1974. ISBN:0-8352-0776-5, ISBN13: 978-0-8352-0776-8. Dewey:942. LCCN:74-007447.
Audience: **g,l,u,f.**

Wordsworth, William **DA670**
Guide Through the District of the Lakes in the North of England: With a Description of the Scenery for the Use of Tourists and Residents. Trade Cloth. Greenwood Publishing Group, Inc. Portsmouth, NH. 1969. 174p. ISBN:0-8371-0764-4, ISBN13: 978-0-8371-0764-6. Dewey:914.28. LCCN:68-055639.
Audience: **g,l,u,f.**

Britain > English History > Modern (1485-) > Victorian Era (1837-1901)

Altick, Richard D. **DA533**
Victorian People and Ideas. Trade Paper. W. W. Norton & Company, Inc. New York, NY. 1974. 338p. ISBN:0-393-09376-X, ISBN13: 978-0-393-09376-6. Dewey:942.081.
Audience: **g,l,u.**

Anderson, Olive **HV6548.G7A53 1987**
Suicide in Victorian and Edwardian England. Trade Cloth. Oxford University Press, Inc. New York, NY. 1987. 489p. ISBN:0-19-820101-X, ISBN13: 978-0-19-820101-4. Dewey:362.2. LCCN:87-005613.
Audience: **l,u,f.** *Choice, 1988.*

Arnstein, Walter L. **KD4354**
The Bradlaugh Case: Atheism, Sex, and Politics among the Late Victorians. Cloth Text. University of Missouri Press. Columbia, MO. 1984. 388p. ISBN:0-8262-0425-2, ISBN13: 978-0-8262-0425-7. Dewey:342.41/055/0264. LCCN:83-006814.
Audience: **u,f.**

Bailey, Peter **GV75.B33 1987**
Leisure and Class in Victorian England: Rational Recreation and the Contest for Control, 1830-1885. Trade Paper. Routledge. New York, NY. 1987. 288p. ISBN:0-416-02142-5, ISBN13: 978-0-416-02142-4. Dewey:790/.0941. LCCN:87-005467.
Audience: **l,u,f.**

Belchem, John **DA536.H75**
Orator Hunt: Henry Hunt and English Working-Class Radicalism. Trade Cloth. Oxford University Press, Inc. New York, NY. 1985. 320p. ISBN:0-19-822759-0, ISBN13: 978-0-19-822759-5. Dewey:322.4/4/0924.
Audience: **u,f.** *Choice, 1986.*

Blake, Robert **DA554**
Disraeli. Ed. 2. Trade Paper. Prion. London, 1998. 850p. Lost Treasures Ser. ISBN:1-85375-275-4, ISBN13: 978-1-85375-275-9. Dewey:941/.081/092.
Audience: **g,l,u,f.**

Bourne, Kenneth **DA550.B68 1970**
The Foreign Policy of Victorian England, 1830-1902. Trade Cloth. Oxford University Press, Inc. New York, NY. 1970. xii, 531p. ISBN:0-19-873007-1, ISBN13: 978-0-19-873007-1. Dewey:327.42. LCCN:75-543411.
Audience: **l,u,f.**

Bourne, Kenneth **DA554**
Palmerston: The Early Years 1784-1841. Trade Cloth. Macmillan Publishing Company, Inc. Old Tappan, NJ. 1982. 749p. ISBN:0-318-54242-0, ISBN13: 978-0-318-54242-3. Dewey:941.081/092/4.
Audience: **g,l,u,f.**

Bourne, Kenneth **DA536.P2**
Palmerston, the Early Years, 1784-1841. New York: Macmillan. 1982. ISBN:0-02-903740-9, ISBN13: 978-0-02-903740-9.
Audience: **u,f.**

Briggs, Asa **DA530.B68**
The Age of Improvement. Paper Text. Textbook Publishers. Temecula, CA. 2003. xii, 547p. ISBN:0-7581-9471-4, ISBN13: 978-0-7581-9471-8. Dewey:941.07.
Audience: **g,l,u,f.** B

Briggs, Asa **DA533**
Victorian Things. Trade Paper. Sutton Publishing, Ltd. Stroud, 2003. 448p. ISBN:0-7509-3339-9, ISBN13: 978-0-7509-3339-1. Dewey:942.081.
Audience: **g,l,u,f.** *Choice, 1989.*

Briggs, Asa **HT133**
Victorian Cities. Andrew Lees & Lynn H. Lees (Introduction by). Trade Paper. University of California Press. Berkeley, CA. 1993. 411p. Classics in Urban History Ser., Vol. 2 ISBN:0-520-07922-1, ISBN13: 978-0-520-07922-9. Dewey:307.7/6/0942/09034. LCCN:92-030443.
Audience: **g,l,u,f.**

Briggs, Asa **DA560**
Victorian People: A Reassessment of Persons and Themes, 1851-67. Ruari McLean (Illustrator). Trade Paper. University of Chicago Press. Chicago, IL. 1975. 324p. Chicago Collectors Editions Ser. ISBN:0-226-07488-9, ISBN13: 978-0-226-07488-7. Dewey:942.081. LCCN:55-005118.
Audience: **g,l,u,f.** B

Buckley, Jerome H. **PR461.B75 1969**
Victorian Temper: A Study in Literary Culture. Trade Cloth. Harvard University Press. Cambridge, MA. 1969. x, 282p. ISBN:0-674-93680-9, ISBN13: 978-0-674-93680-5. Dewey:820.9/009/8. LCCN:74-089967.
Audience: **u,f.**

Burn, W. L. (William Laurence) **DA550**
The Age of Equipoise: A Study of the Mid-Victorian Generation. Aldershot: Gregg Revivals. 1993. Modern Revivals in History Ser. ISBN:0-7512-0296-7, ISBN13: 978-0-7512-0296-0.
Audience: **u,f.**

Cannadine, David **HT653.G7C358 1990**
The Decline and Fall of the British Aristocracy. Trade Cloth. Yale University Press. Cumberland, RI. 1990. 832p. ISBN:0-300-04761-4, ISBN13: 978-0-300-04761-5. Dewey:305.5/2/0941. LCCN:90-012303.
Audience: **l,u,f.** *Choice, 1991.*

Cecil, David **DA538.A1**
Melbourne. Trade Cloth. Macmillan Publishing Company, Inc. Old Tappan, NJ. 1974. 450p. ISBN:0-672-52038-9, ISBN13: 978-0-672-52038-9. Dewey:942.0740924. LCCN:54-009486.
Audience: **g,l,u,f.**

Chadwick, Owen **BR759**
The Victorian Church. London: SCM Press. 1987. ISBN:0-334-02409-9, ISBN13: 978-0-334-02409-5.
Audience: **u,f.**

Churchill, Winston S. **DA565.C6**
Lord Randolph Churchill. Paper Text. Textbook Publishers. Temecula, CA. 2003. 840p. ISBN:0-7581-7414-4, ISBN13: 978-0-7581-7414-7. Dewey:923.242.
Audience: **g,l,u,f.**

Clark, G. Kitson **DA533**
The Making of Victorian England. Trade Paper. Simon & Schuster. New York, NY. 1972. ISBN:0-689-70049-0, ISBN13: 978-0-689-70049-1. Dewey:942. LCCN:62-051827.
Audience: **g,u,f.**

Collini, Stefan **DA550.C62 1993**
Public Moralists: Political Thought and Intellectual Life in Britain, 1850-1930. Paper Text. Oxford University Press, Inc. New York, NY. 1993. 388p. ISBN:0-19-820422-1, ISBN13: 978-0-19-820422-0. Dewey:941.08. LCCN:92-041294.
Audience: **g,l,u,f.** *Choice, 1992.*

Collini, Stefan, et al. **JA84.G7**
That Noble Science of Politics: A Study in Nineteenth-Century Intellectual History. John Burrow & Donald Winch (Authors). Trade Paper. Cambridge University Press. New York, NY. 1983. 400p. ISBN:0-521-27770-1, ISBN13: 978-0-521-27770-9. Dewey:320/.0941. LCCN:83-007697.
Audience: **u,f.**

Crouzet, Francois **HC255.C7313 1982**
The Victorian Economy. A. S. Forster (Translator). Cloth Text. Columbia University Press. New York, NY. 1982. 400p. ISBN:0-231-05542-0, ISBN13: 978-0-231-05542-0. Dewey:330.941/081. LCCN:82-001292.
Audience: **l,u.**

Davidoff, Leonore **HQ1596**
The Best Circles: Society Etiquette and the Season. Glendinning, Victoria (Introduction by). London: Cresset Library. 1986. ISBN:0-09-168761-6, ISBN13: 978-0-09-168761-8.
Audience: **l,u,f.**

Davidoff, Leonore & Hall, Catherine **HT690.G7D38 1987**
Family Fortunes: Men and Women of the English Middle Class, 1780-1850. Trade Cloth. University of Chicago Press. Chicago, IL. 1987. 576p. Women in Culture and Society Ser. ISBN:0-226-13732-5, ISBN13: 978-0-226-13732-2. Dewey:305.5/5/094209033. LCCN:86-030874.
Audience: **l,u,f.** *Choice, 1988.*

Dyhouse, Carol **HQ798 .D85**
Girls Growing up in Late Victorian and Edwardian England. Trade Cloth. Routledge. New York, NY. 1981. 224p. Studies in Social History ISBN:0-7100-0821-X, ISBN13: 978-0-7100-0821-3. Dewey:305.2/3/0941. LCCN:81-008578.
Audience: **l,u,f.**

Dyos, H. J. & Wolff, Michael (Editors) **DA533**
The Victorian City: Images and Realities. Paper over Boards. Routledge. New York, NY. 2000. 1352p. ISBN:0-415-19325-7, ISBN13: 978-0-415-19325-2. Dewey:941/.081.
Audience: **l,u.**

Ehrlich, Cyril **ML652.E4 1990**
The Piano: A History. Ed. 2. Trade Cloth. Oxford University Press, Inc. New York, NY. 1990. 272p. ISBN:0-19-816181-6, ISBN13: 978-0-19-816181-3. Dewey:786.2/1/09. LCCN:89-023161.
Audience: **g,l,u,f.** *Choice, 1990.*

Floud, Roderick & McCloskey, Donald N. (Editors) **HC254.5 .E27**
The Economic History of Britain since 1700, Set. Ed. 2. Quantity Pack, Paper Text. Cambridge University Press. New York, NY. 1994. 1368p. ISBN:0-521-45961-3, ISBN13: 978-0-521-45961-7. Dewey:330.941/07.
Audience: **u,f.** *Choice, 1995.*

Gash, Norman **DA535**
Aristocracy and People: Britain, 1815-1865. Trade Paper. Harvard University Press. Cambridge, MA. 1981. 383p. New History of England Ser. ISBN:0-674-04491-6, ISBN13: 978-0-674-04491-3. Dewey:309.1/41/07.
Audience: **u,f.**

Gash, Norman **DA536.P3**
Mr. Secretary Peel: The Life of Sir Robert Peel to 1830. Ed. 2. Cloth Text. Longman Publishing Group. White Plains, NY. 1985. 712p. ISBN:0-582-49723-X, ISBN13: 978-0-582-49723-8. Dewey:941.081/092/4. LCCN:85-007751.
Audience: **u,f.**

Gash, Norman **JN223**
Politics in the Age of Peel: A Study in the Technique of Parliamentary representation, 1830-1850. Ed. 2. Hassocks, Sussex, Eng. : Harvester Press ; Atlantic Highlands, N.J. : Humanities Press. 1977. ISBN:0-391-00676-2, ISBN13: 978-0-391-00676-8.
Audience: **u,f.**

Gash, Norman **DA559.7**
Reaction and Reconstruction in English Politics, 1832 to 1852. Trade Cloth. Greenwood Publishing Group, Inc. Portsmouth, NH. 1981. 227p. ISBN:0-313-22927-9, ISBN13: 978-0-313-22927-5. Dewey:941.07/5. LCCN:81-001813.
Audience: **u,f.**

Gash, Norman **DA536.P3G32 1986**
Sir Robert Peel: The Life of Sir Robert Peel After 1830. Ed. 2. Paper Text. Longman Publishing Group. White Plains, NY. 1986. 745p. ISBN:0-582-49722-1, ISBN13: 978-0-582-49722-1. Dewey:941.081/092/4 B. LCCN:85-023934.
Audience: **g,l,u,f.**

Gillett, Paula **ND467.5.V52G55 1990**
Worlds of Art: Painters in Victorian Society. Cloth Text. Rutgers University Press. Piscataway, NJ. 1989. 275p. ISBN:0-8135-1459-2, ISBN13: 978-0-8135-1459-8. Dewey:759.2. LCCN:89-030373.
Audience: **g,l,u,f.** *Choice, 1990.*

Girouard, Mark **NA7620**
The Victorian Country House. Trade Cloth. Yale University Press. Cumberland, RI. 1979. 448p. ISBN:0-300-02390-1,

ISBN13: 978-0-300-02390-9. Dewey:728.8/3/0942. LCCN:79-064077.
Audience: **g,l,u,f.**

Greville, Charles **DA536.G8**
The Great World. Garden City, N.Y., Doubleday. 1963.
Audience: **g,l,u,f.**

Gross, John **PR63.G7 1992**
The Rise and Fall of the Man of Letters: English Literary Life since 1800. Trade Paper. Ivan R. Dee Publisher. Blue Ridge Summit, PA. 1992. 372p. ISBN:1-56663-000-2, ISBN13: 978-1-56663-000-9. Dewey:820.9. LCCN:92-016011.
Audience: **u,f.**

Haig, Alan **BX5175**
The Victorian Clergy. Trade Cloth. Croom Helm, Ltd. London, 1984. 380p. ISBN:0-7099-1230-7, ISBN13: 978-0-7099-1230-9. Dewey:262/.14342.
Audience: **u,f.**

Halévy, Elie **DA530.H443**
A History of the English People in the Nineteenth Century. Ed. 2. Watkin, E.I. (Translator). London, E. Benn. 1949.
Audience: **g,l,u,f.**

Halévy, Elie **DA530.H444**
A History of the English People in the Nineteenth Century. Watkin, E.I. (Translator); Barker, D.A. (Translator); McCallum, R.B. (Introduction by). New York: Barnes & Noble. 1960.
Audience: **l,u.**

Harrison, Brian **DA530.H446 1982**
Peaceable Kingdom: Stability and Change in Modern Britain. Trade Cloth. Oxford University Press, Inc. New York, NY. 1983. 504p. ISBN:0-19-822603-9, ISBN13: 978-0-19-822603-1. Dewey:306/.0941. LCCN:82-006400.
Audience: **l,u.**

Harrison, Brian H. **HV5446.H35**
Drink and the Victorians: The Temperance Question in England, 1815-1872. Trade Cloth. Edinburgh University Press. Edinburgh, 1998. 528p. ISBN:1-85331-046-8, ISBN13: 978-1-85331-046-1. Dewey:178.
Audience: **g,l,u,f.**

Hawkins, Angus **DA560**
Parliament, Party, and the Art of Politics in Britain, 1855-1859. Trade Cloth. Stanford University Press. Palo Alto, CA. 1987. xiv, 415p. ISBN:0-8047-1317-0, ISBN13: 978-0-8047-1317-7. Dewey:941.081. LCCN:85-051801.
Audience: **u,f.**

Heyck, T. W. **DA533.H48 1982**
The Transformation of Intellectual Life in Victorian England. Cloth Text. Palgrave Macmillan. New York, NY. 1982. 262p. ISBN:0-312-81427-5, ISBN13: 978-0-312-81427-4. Dewey:942.081. LCCN:82-000840.
Audience: **g,l,u,f.** *B*

Hilton, Boyd **HC256.5**
The Age of Atonement: The Influence of Evangelicalism on Social and Economic Thought 1785-1865. Paper Text. Oxford University Press, Inc. New York, NY. 1992. 428p. ISBN:0-19-820295-4, ISBN13: 978-0-19-820295-0. Dewey:306/.3/0941.
Audience: **g,l,u,f.**

Himmelfarb, Gertrude **HC255**
The Idea of Poverty: England in the Early Industrial Age. Trade Cloth. Alfred A. Knopf Inc. New York, NY. 1983. 596p. ISBN:0-394-53062-4, ISBN13: 978-0-394-53062-8. Dewey:305.5/69/0941. LCCN:83-047964.
Audience: **u,f.**

Himmelfarb, Gertrude **DA533.H55 1995**
Victorian Minds. Trade Paper. Ivan R. Dee Publisher. Blue Ridge Summit, PA. 1995. 420p. ISBN:1-56663-077-0, ISBN13: 978-1-56663-077-1. Dewey:941.07. LCCN:94-043053.
Audience: **l,u.**

Hobsbawm, E. J. (Eric John), et al. **HD1534**
Captain Swing. Rudé, George F. E. (Author). London: Phoenix. 2001. ISBN:1-84212-235-5, ISBN13: 978-1-84212-235-8.
Audience: **u,f.**

Hoggart, Richard **DA566.4.H54 1998**
The Uses of Literacy. Trade Paper. Transaction Publishers. Somerset, NJ. 1998. 320p. Classics in Communication and Mass Culture Ser. ISBN:0-7658-0421-2, ISBN13: 978-0-7658-0421-1. Dewey:302.2/3/08623/0942. LCCN:97-013291.
Audience: **l,u,f.**

Holmes, Colin **JV7624**
John Bull's Island: Immigration and British society, 1871-1971. Houndmills, Basingstoke, Hampshire: Macmillan. 1988. ISBN:0-333-28209-4, ISBN13: 978-0-333-28209-0.
Audience: **u,f.**

Honey, J. R. **LA631.7.H64 1977**
Tom Brown's Universe: The Development of the English Public School of the 19th Century. Trade Cloth. Crown Publishing Group. New York, NY. 1978. ISBN:0-8129-0689-6, ISBN13: 978-0-8129-0689-9. Dewey:370/.942. LCCN:76-056585.
Audience: **g,u,f.**

Houghton, Walter Edwards **DA533**
The Victorian Frame of Mind 1830-1870. Paper Text. Textbook Publishers. Temecula, CA. 2003. 467p. ISBN:0-7581-5322-8, ISBN13: 978-0-7581-5322-7. Dewey:942.081.
Audience: **u,f.**

Houghton, Walter Edwards **DA533**
The Victorian Frame of Mind, 1830-1870. New Haven : Published for Wellesley College by Yale University Press. 1985. ISBN:0-300-00122-3, ISBN13: 978-0-300-00122-8.
Audience: **u,f.**

Inglis, Kenneth Stanley **BR759**
Churches and the Working Classes in Victorian England. London, Routledge and K. Paul. 1963. Studies in Social History ISBN:0-7100-4556-5, ISBN13: 978-0-7100-4556-0.
Audience: **l,u.**

Jalland, Pat **HQ1593.J34 1986**
Women, Marriage, and Politics, 1860-1914. Trade Cloth. Oxford University Press, Inc. New York, NY. 1987. 380p. ISBN:0-19-822668-3, ISBN13: 978-0-19-822668-0. Dewey:305.4/0941. LCCN:85-028406.
Audience: **l,u,f.** *Choice, 1987.*

James, Robert Rhodes **DA564.R7J3**
Rosebery, a Biography of Archibald Philip, Fifth Earl of Rosebery. New York: Macmillan. 1964.
Audience: **g,l,u,f.**

Jay, Richard **DA565.C4.J39**
Joseph Chamberlain: A Political Study. Trade Cloth. Oxford University Press, Inc. New York, NY. 1981. ix, 383p. ISBN:0-19-822623-3, ISBN13: 978-0-19-822623-9. Dewey:941.081/092/4. LCCN:80-040812.
Audience: **u,f.**

Jenkyns, Richard **DA550 .J46**
The Victorians and Ancient Greece. Trade Cloth. Harvard University Press. Cambridge, MA. 1990. 398p. ISBN:0-674-93686-8, ISBN13: 978-0-674-93686-7. Dewey:941.081. LCCN:79-025487.
Audience: **u,f.**

Jones, Andrew **DA560**
The Politics of Reform, 1884. Cloth Text. Cambridge University Press. New York, NY. 1972. 295p. Cambridge Studies in the History and Theory of Politics Ser. ISBN:0-521-08376-1, ISBN13: 978-0-521-08376-8. Dewey:942.081. LCCN:72-172832.
Audience: **u,f.**

Jones, Gareth Stedman **HC110.P6**
Outcast London: A Study in the Relationship Between Classes in Victorian Society. Trade Paper. Knopf Publishing Group. New York, NY. 1984. ISBN:0-394-72547-6, ISBN13: 978-0-394-72547-5. Dewey:301.44/1.
Audience: **u,f.**

Joyce, Patrick **HC255.J69 1980**
Work, Society, and Politics: The Culture of the Factory in Later Victorian England. Trade Cloth. Rutgers University Press. Piscataway, NJ. 1980. xxv, 356p. ISBN:0-8135-0899-1, ISBN13: 978-0-8135-0899-3. Dewey:303.48309427. LCCN:79-093087.
Audience: **u,f.**

Kitson Clark, G. S. R. (George Sidney Roberts) **DA533**
The Making of Victorian England. Routledge. 1991. ISBN:0-415-06591-7, ISBN13: 978-0-415-06591-7.
Audience: **l,u.**

Laqueur, Thomas W. **BV1517.G7**
Religion and Respectability: Sunday Schools and English Working Class Culture, 1780-1850. Trade Cloth. Yale University Press. Cumberland, RI. 1976. ISBN:0-300-01859-2, ISBN13: 978-0-300-01859-2. Dewey:301.5/8. LCCN:74-029728.
Audience: **u,f.**

Lewis, Jane **HQ1599.E5L49 1984**
Women in England, 1870-1950: Sexual Divisons and Social Change. Trade Cloth. Indiana University Press. Bloomington, IN. 1985. 288p. ISBN:0-253-36608-9, ISBN13: 978-0-253-36608-5. Dewey:305.4/0942. LCCN:84-048437.
Audience: **u,f.**

Longford, Elizabeth **DA554**
Queen Victoria: Born to Succeed. New York: Harper & Row. 1965.
Audience: **g,l,u,f.**

MacDonagh, Oliver **JN216.M15 1977**
Early Victorian Government, 1830-1870. Trade Cloth. Holmes & Meier Publishers, Inc. Teaneck, NJ. 1977. 242p. ISBN:0-8419-0304-2, ISBN13: 978-0-8419-0304-3. Dewey:300/.942. LCCN:76-057957.
Audience: **u,f.**

Machin, G. I. **BR759**
Politics and the Churches in Great Britain, 1832-1868. Trade Cloth. Oxford University Press, Inc. New York, NY. 1978. ix, 438p. ISBN:0-19-826436-4, ISBN13: 978-0-19-826436-1. Dewey:322/.1/0941. LCCN:77-030296.
Audience: **u,f.**

Machin, G. I. **BR759.M27 1987**
Politics and the Churches in Great Britain, 1869-1921. Trade Cloth. Oxford University Press, Inc. New York, NY. 1987. 388p. ISBN:0-19-820106-0, ISBN13: 978-0-19-820106-9. Dewey:322/.1/0941. LCCN:87-001620.
Audience: **u,f.** *Choice, 1988.*

Mandler, Peter **DA550.M34 1990**
Aristocratic Government in the Age of Reform: Whigs and Liberals, 1830-1852. Trade Cloth. Oxford University Press, Inc. New York, NY. 1990. 320p. ISBN:0-19-821781-1, ISBN13: 978-0-19-821781-7. Dewey:320.941/09/034. LCCN:89-026535.
Audience: **u,f.**

Mathias, Peter **HC255**
The First Industrial Nation: An Economic History of Britain, 1700-1914. Ed. 2. Trade Cloth. Routledge. New York, NY. 1983. 480p. ISBN:0-416-33290-0, ISBN13: 978-0-416-33290-2. Dewey:330.9/42. LCCN:82-022898.
Audience: **l,u,f.**

Matthew, H. C. G. (Henry Colin Gray) **DA563.4**
Gladstone 1809-1898. Oxford University Press. 1997. ISBN:0-19-820696-8, ISBN13: 978-0-19-820696-5.
Audience: **g,l,u,f.**

McCalman, Iain **HN400.R3**
Radical Underworld: Prophets, Revolutionaries and Pornographers in London, 1795-1840. Paper Text. Oxford University Press, Inc. New York, NY. 1993. 358p. ISBN:0-19-812286-1, ISBN13: 978-0-19-812286-9. Dewey:320.9421. LCCN:87-011770.
Audience: **g,l,u,f.** *Choice, 1988.*

McCord, Norman **HF2044**
The Anti-Corn Law League 1838-1846. Ed. 2. London: Allen & Unwin. 1968. Unwin university books, 62
Audience: **u,f.**

McCord, Norman **HF2044**
The Anti-Corn Law League 1838-1846. Trade Cloth. Ashgate Publishing, Ltd. Aldershot, 1993. 224p. Modern Revivals in History Ser. ISBN:0-7512-0147-2, ISBN13: 978-0-7512-0147-5. Dewey:322.43094109034.
Audience: **u,f.**

McCord, Norman **DA530.M43 1991**
British History, 1815-1906. Paper Text. Oxford University Press, Inc. New York, NY. 1991. 538p. Short Oxford History of the Modern World Ser. ISBN:0-19-822858-9, ISBN13: 978-0-19-822858-5. Dewey:941.081. LCCN:90-019697.
Audience: **g,l,u,f.**

Meacham, Standish **HD8386.M4 1977**
A Life Apart: The English Working Class, 1890-1914. Trade Cloth. Harvard University Press. Cambridge, MA. 1977. 320p.

ISBN:0-674-53075-6, ISBN13: 978-0-674-53075-1. Dewey:301.44/42/0942. LCCN:77-072673.
Audience: **u,f.**

Miles, Dudley H. **HN400.R3P576 1988**
Francis Place, 1771-1854: The Life of a Remarkable Radical. Cloth Text. Palgrave Macmillan. New York, NY. 1988. 256p. ISBN:0-312-01953-X, ISBN13: 978-0-312-01953-2. Dewey:363.9/6/0941. LCCN:87-035324.
Audience: **u,f.** *Choice, 1988.*

Moore, David Cresap **JN955.M56**
The Politics of Deference: A Study of the Mid-Nineteenth Century English Political System. Trade Cloth. Bow Historical Books. New Providence, NJ. 1976. 529p. ISBN:0-06-494932-X, ISBN13: 978-0-06-494932-3. Dewey:324/.41. LCCN:74-026187.
Audience: **u,f.**

Morley, John M. **DA563**
The Life of William Ewart Gladstone, Set. Trade Cloth. Greenwood Publishing Group, Inc. Portsmouth, NH. 1971. ISBN:0-8371-0576-5, ISBN13: 978-0-8371-0576-5. Dewey:941.0810924. LCCN:68-057630.
Audience: **g,l,u,f.**

Morrell, Jack & Thackray, Arnold W. **Q41.B85.M67 1981**
Gentlemen of Science: Early Years of the British Association for the Advancement of Science. Trade Cloth. Oxford University Press, Inc. New York, NY. 1981. xxiii, 592p. ISBN:0-19-858163-7, ISBN13: 978-0-19-858163-5. Dewey:506/.041. LCCN:81-201474.
Audience: **g,f.** B

Morris, R. J. **HN400.S6**
Class and Class Consciousness in the Industrial Revolution, 1780-1850. Paper Text. Brill Academic Publishers, Inc. Boston, MA. 1979. 80p. Studies in Economic and Social History ISBN:0-333-15454-1, ISBN13: 978-0-333-15454-0. Dewey:301.44/0941.
Audience: **u,f.**

Morris, R. J. **HT690.G7M67 1990**
Class, Sect and Party: The Making of the British Middle Class, Leeds, 1820-1850. Cloth Text. Manchester University Press. Manchester, 1990. ISBN:0-7190-2225-8, ISBN13: 978-0-7190-2225-8. Dewey:305.5/5/094281909034. LCCN:89-039337.
Audience: **u,f.**

Namier, Lewis Bernstein, Sir **JN210**
The Structure of Politics at the Accession of George III. Ed. 2. [London] Macmillan; [New York] St. Martin's Press. 1970.
Audience: **u,f.**

Newbould, Ian **DA539.N48 1990**
Whiggery and Reform, 1830-41: The Politics of Government. Trade Cloth. Stanford University Press. Palo Alto, CA. 1991. 410p. ISBN:0-8047-1759-1, ISBN13: 978-0-8047-1759-5. Dewey:941.07/5. LCCN:89-062180.
Audience: **u,f.** *Choice, 1991.*

Newsome, David **LA632**
Godliness and Good Learning: Four Studies on a Victorian Ideal. Trade Cloth. Transatlantic Arts, Inc. Albuquerque, NM. 1961. ISBN:0-7195-1015-5, ISBN13: 978-0-7195-1015-1. Dewey:370/.942.
Audience: **g,l,u,f.**

O'Gorman, Frank **JN951.O46 1989**
Voters, Patrons, and Parties: The Unreformed Electorate of Hanoverian England 1734-1832. Trade Cloth. Oxford University Press, Inc. New York, NY. 1989. 460p. ISBN:0-19-820056-0, ISBN13: 978-0-19-820056-7. Dewey:324.241/009. LCCN:88-030304.
Audience: **g,l,u,f.** *Choice, 1990.*

Olsen, Donald J. **HT169.G72.L6474 1976**
The Growth of Victorian London. Cloth Text. Holmes & Meier Publishers, Inc. Teaneck, NJ. 1976. 348p. ISBN:0-8419-0284-4, ISBN13: 978-0-8419-0284-8. Dewey:720/.9421. LCCN:76-025164.
Audience: **l,u,f.**

Oppenheim, Janet **BF1242.G7 O66 1985**
The Other World: Spiritualism and Psychical Research in England, 1850-1914. Trade Paper. Cambridge University Press. New York, NY. 1988. 518p. ISBN:0-521-34767-X, ISBN13: 978-0-521-34767-9. Dewey:133.9/0942.
Audience: **g,l,u,f.** *Choice, 1985.*

Perkin, Harold **HN400.S6P47 1989**
The Rise of Professional Society: England since 1880. Trade Cloth. Routledge. New York, NY. 1989. 480p. ISBN:0-415-00890-5, ISBN13: 978-0-415-00890-7. Dewey:305.5/0942. LCCN:88-010113.
Audience: **u,f.** *Choice, 1989.*

Perkin, Harold J. **HN385 .P46**
The Origins of Modern English Society: 1780-1880. Trade Paper. University of Toronto Press. Toronto, ON. 1969. ISBN:0-8020-6141-9, ISBN13: 978-0-8020-6141-6. Dewey:309.1/42. LCCN:76-384509.
Audience: **u,f.**

Peterson, M. Jeanne **R488.L/**
The Medical Profession in Mid-Victorian London. Trade Cloth. University of California Press. Berkeley, CA. 1978. x, 406p. ISBN:0-520-03343-4, ISBN13: 978-0-520-03343-6. Dewey:610.69/52/09421. LCCN:76-048362.
Audience: **g,l,u,f.**

Pottinger, George **DS363.P67**
The Afghan Connection: The Extraordinary Adventures of Major Eldred Pottinger. Edinburgh: Scottish Academic Press. 1983. ISBN:0-7073-0286-2, ISBN13: 978-0-7073-0286-7.
Audience: **u,f.**

Prest, John **DA564.R8.P73 1972**
Lord John Russell. Trade Cloth. University of South Carolina Press. Columbia, SC. 1972. xvi, 568p. ISBN:0-87249-269-9, ISBN13: 978-0-87249-269-1. Dewey:942.081/0924. LCCN:72-005340.
Audience: **g,l,u,f.**

Pugh, Martin **DA566.7**
The Making of Modern British Politics, 1867-1939. Ed. 2. Trade Paper. Blackwell Publishing, Inc. Malden, MA. 1993. 344p. ISBN:0-631-17928-3, ISBN13: 978-0-631-17928-3. Dewey:941.08. LCCN:92-022093.
Audience: **u,f.**

Read, Donald **DA536.C6**
Cobden and Bright: a Victorian Political Partnership. New York: St. Martin's Press. 1968. ISBN:0-7131-5306-7, ISBN13: 978-0-7131-5306-4.
Audience: **u,f.**

Read, Donald **DA533.R37**
England, 1868-1914: The Age of Urban Democracy. Trade Cloth. Longman Publishing Group. White Plains, NY. 1979. 530p. ISBN:0-582-48278-X, ISBN13: 978-0-582-48278-4. Dewey:942.081. LCCN:78-041034.
Audience: **u,f.**

Reader, W. J. (William Joseph) **HT687**
Professional Men: The Rise of the Professional Classes in Nineteenth-Century England. New York, Basic Books. 1966.
Audience: **g,l,u,f.**

Reid, Alastair J. **HN400.S6 R45 1995**
Social Classes and Social Relations in Britain, 1850-1914. Cloth Text. Cambridge University Press. New York, NY. 1995. 82p. New Studies in Economic and Social History, No. 19 ISBN:0-521-55278-8, ISBN13: 978-0-521-55278-3. Dewey:305.5/0941. LCCN:95-017013.
Audience: **u,f.**

Richardson, Ruth **GT3243.R53 2001**
Death, Dissection and the Destitute. Ed. 2. Trade Cloth. University of Chicago Press. Chicago, IL. 2001. 453p. ISBN:0-226-71239-7, ISBN13: 978-0-226-71239-0. Dewey:393/.0941. LCCN:00-062029.
Audience: **u,f.**

Robbins, Keith **DA565.B8**
John Bright. London ; Boston: Routledge & K. Paul. 1979. ISBN:0-7100-8992-9, ISBN13: 978-0-7100-8992-2.
Audience: **g,l,u,f.**

Robbins, Keith **DA533**
Nineteenth-Century Britain: Integration and Diversity. Trade Paper. Oxford University Press, Inc. New York, NY. 1995. 212p. Ford Lectures ISBN:0-19-820585-6, ISBN13: 978-0-19-820585-2. Dewey:941.081. LCCN:87-023951.
Audience: **u,f.**

Roberts, Elizabeth **HQ1599.E5R62 1984**
A Woman's Place: An Oral History of Working Class Women, 1890-1940. Trade Cloth. Blackwell Publishing, Inc. Malden, MA. 1984. 272p. ISBN:0-631-13572-3, ISBN13: 978-0-631-13572-2. Dewey:305.4/2/0942. LCCN:84-016785.
Audience: **u,f.** *Choice, 1985.*

Robson, John M. **JC223.M66**
Improvement of Mankind: The Social and Political Thought of John Stuart Mill. Trade Cloth. University of Toronto Press. Toronto, ON. 1968. ISBN:0-8020-1529-8, ISBN13: 978-0-8020-1529-7. Dewey:300/.924. LCCN:68-140051.
Audience: **u,f.**

Rothblatt, Sheldon **LF118**
The Revolution of the Dons: Cambridge and Society in Victorian England. Trade Cloth. Cambridge University Press. New York, NY. 1981. 328p. ISBN:0-521-23958-3, ISBN13: 978-0-521-23958-5. Dewey:378.426/59. LCCN:80-041865.
Audience: **u,f.**

Rubinstein, W. D. **HC260.W4**
Men of Property: The Very Wealthy in Britain Since the Industrial Revolution. Trade Cloth. Rutgers University Press. Piscataway, NJ. 1981. 256p. ISBN:0-8135-0927-0, ISBN13: 978-0-8135-0927-3. Dewey:305.5/2.
Audience: **u,f.**

Samuel, Raphael (Editor) **HD60.5.U5**
Village Life and Labour. Trade Cloth. Routledge. New York, NY. 1975. xxii, 278p. History Workshop Ser. ISBN:0-7100-7499-9, ISBN13: 978-0-7100-7499-7. Dewey:301.5/5.
Audience: **g,l,u,f.**

Semple, Janet **HV8978.F7**
Bentham's Prison: A Study of the Panopticon Penitentiary. Trade Cloth. Oxford University Press, Inc. New York, NY. 1993. 354p. ISBN:0-19-827387-8, ISBN13: 978-0-19-827387-5. Dewey:365.92. LCCN:92-041295.
Audience: **u,f.** *Choice, 1994.*

Shannon, Richard **DA563.5**
Gladstone and the Bulgarian Agitation, 1876. Ed. 2. Trade Cloth. Shoe String Press, Inc. North Haven, CT. 1975. xxviii, 308p. ISBN:0-208-01487-X, ISBN13: 978-0-208-01487-0. Dewey:941.081. LCCN:74-022945.
Audience: **u,f.**

Sheppard, Francis **HC258.L6.S5 1971**
London, 1808-1870: The Infernal wen. Trade Cloth. University of California Press. Berkeley, CA. 1971. xx, 427p. History of London Ser. ISBN:0-520-01847-8, ISBN13: 978-0-520-01847-1. Dewey:309.1/421/07. LCCN:71-142067.
Audience: **u,f.**

Simmons, Jack **HE3018.S58 1991**
The Victorian Railway. Trade Cloth. Thames & Hudson. New York, NY. 1991. 416p. ISBN:0-500-25110-X, ISBN13: 978-0-500-25110-2. Dewey:385/.0941. LCCN:90-070206.
Audience: **g,l,u,f.** *Choice, 1991.*

Smith, F. B. **JN543**
The Making of the Second Reform Bill. Trade Cloth. Ashgate Publishing, Ltd. Aldershot, 1993. 320p. Modern Revivals in History Ser. ISBN:0-7512-0113-8, ISBN13: 978-0-7512-0113-0. Dewey:942.081.
Audience: **u,f.**

Smith, F. B. **HD4145**
The People's Health, 1830-1910. Trade Cloth. Ashgate Publishing, Ltd. Aldershot, 1993. 442p. Modern Revivals in History Ser. ISBN:0-7512-0185-5, ISBN13: 978-0-7512-0185-7. Dewey:363/.0941.
Audience: **g,l,u,f.**

Soffer, Reba N. **H53.G7**
Ethics and Society in England: The Revolution in the Social Sciences, 1870-1914. Trade Cloth. University of California Press. Berkeley, CA. 1978. 304p. ISBN:0-520-03521-6, ISBN13: 978-0-520-03521-8. Dewey:300/.1/8. LCCN:77-079239.
Audience: **l,u,f.**

Somervell, D. C. (David Churchill) **DA533**
English Thought in the Nineteenth Century. Westport, Conn.: Greenwood Press. 1977. ISBN:0-8371-9793-7, ISBN13: 978-0-8371-9793-7.
Audience: **l,u,f.**

Southgate **DA533**
Passing of the Whigs 1832-1886. Trade Cloth. Ashgate Publishing Company. Williston, VT. 1993. 520p. ISBN:0-7512-0217-7, ISBN13: 978-0-7512-0217-5. Dewey:941.081.
Audience: **u,f.**

Spiers, Edward M. **UA649.S73**
The Army and Society, 1815-1914. Trade Cloth. Longman Publishing Group. White Plains, NY. 1980. 318p. ISBN:0-582-48565-7, ISBN13: 978-0-582-48565-5. Dewey:301.5/93/0941. LCCN:79-040042.
Audience: **u,f.**

Stedman-Jones, Gareth **HD8390 .J8 1983**
Languages of Class: Studies in English Working Class History 1832-1982. Cloth Text. Cambridge University Press. New York, NY. 1984. 268p. ISBN:0-521-25648-8, ISBN13: 978-0-521-25648-3. Dewey:305.5/62/0942. LCCN:83-007721.
Audience: **u,f.**

Steele, E. D. **DA536.P2S74 1991**
Palmerston and Liberalism, 1855-1865. Trade Cloth. Cambridge University Press. New York, NY. 1991. 483p. ISBN:0-521-40045-7, ISBN13: 978-0-521-40045-9. Dewey:941.081/092. LCCN:90-040491.
Audience: **u,f.** *Choice, 1992.*

Strachey, Lytton **PR6037.T73N67 2005**
Eminent Victorians Definitive Edition. Trade Paper. Continuum International Publishing Group, Ltd. London, 2005. 424p. ISBN:0-8264-7618-X, ISBN13: 978-0-8264-7618-0. Dewey:941.0810922. LCCN:2004-266934.
Audience: **g,l,u,f.**

Strachey, Lytton **DA554.S7 1969**
Queen Victoria. Trade Cloth. Random House. London, 1969. 257p. ISBN:0-7011-1131-3, ISBN13: 978-0-7011-1131-1. Dewey:941/.081/092. LCCN:72-435370.
Audience: **g,l,u,f.**

Taylor, Arthur J. (Editor) **HD7023**
The Standard of Living in Britain in the Industrial Revolution. Trade Cloth. Routledge. New York, NY. 1975. 271p. Debates in Economic History Ser. ISBN:0-416-08250-5, ISBN13: 978-0-416-08250-0. Dewey:339.4/7/0880623.
Audience: **g,l,u,f.**

Taylor, Barbara **HQ1154**
Eve and the New Jerusalem: Socialism and Feminism in the Nineteenth Century. Trade Paper. Harvard University Press. Cambridge, MA. 1993. 402p. ISBN:0-674-27023-1, ISBN13: 978-0-674-27023-7. Dewey:305.4/2/09034. LCCN:92-031980.
Audience: **u,f.** B

Thompson, Dorothy **HV6485.G7**
The Chartists: Popular Politics in the Industrial Revolution. Trade Paper. Knopf Publishing Group. New York, NY. 1984. ISBN:0-394-72474-7, ISBN13: 978-0-394-72474-4. Dewey:322.4/4/0941.
Audience: **u,f.**

Thompson, E. P. **HD8389**
The Making of the English Working Class. Trade Cloth. Peter Smith Publisher, Inc. Magnolia, MA. 1999. ISBN:0-8446-6993-8, ISBN13: 978-0-8446-6993-9. Dewey:301.44/42/0942.
Audience: **l,u,f.** B

Thompson, F. M. **DA550.T53 1988**
The Rise of Respectable Society: A Social History of Victorian Britain, 1830-1900. Trade Cloth. Harvard University Press. Cambridge, MA. 1988. 382p. ISBN:0-674-77285-7, ISBN13: 978-0-674-77285-4. Dewey:941.081. LCCN:88-014802.
Audience: **g,l,u,f.** *Choice, 1989.*

Thompson, F. M. L. (Francis Michael Longstreth) **HN385**
English Landed Society in the Nineteenth Century. London: Routledge & Kegan Paul; Toronto: University of Toronto Press. 1963. Studies in Social History
Audience: **l,u,f.**

Thompson, Flora **S522.G7**
Lark Rise to Candleford: A Trilogy. Julie Neild (Illustrator), H. J. Massingham (Introduction by). Trade Cloth. Oxford University Press, Inc. New York, NY. 1980. 576p. ISBN:0-19-211759-9, ISBN13: 978-0-19-211759-5. Dewey:942.5/7081/0924.
Audience: **u,f.**

Trench, Charles C. **DA68.32.G6**
The Road to Khartoum: A Life of General Charles Gordon. Trade Cloth. Dorset Press. New York, NY. 1988. 289p. ISBN:0-88029-152-4, ISBN13: 978-0-88029-152-1. Dewey:962.4/03/0924.
Audience: **g,l,u,f.**

Turner, Frank M. **DA533**
The Greek Heritage in Victorian Britain. Trade Cloth. Yale University Press. Cumberland, RI. 1981. 475p. ISBN:0-300-02480-0, ISBN13: 978-0-300-02480-7. Dewey:941.08. LCCN:80-024013.
Audience: **u,f.**

Vicinus, Martha (Editor) **HQ1593**
Suffer and Be Still: Women in the Victorian Age. Trade Cloth. Indiana University Press. Bloomington, IN. 1972. 256p. ISBN:0-253-35572-9, ISBN13: 978-0-253-35572-0. Dewey:305.4/2/0941. LCCN:71-184524.
Audience: **l,u,f.**

Vincent, David **HD8388**
Bread, Knowledge and Freedom: A Study of Nineteenth-Century Working Class Autobiography. Trade Paper. Routledge. New York, NY. 1983. 221p. ISBN:0-416-34670-7, ISBN13: 978-0-416-34670-1. Dewey:305.5/62/0941. LCCN:82-014163.
Audience: **g,l,u,f.**

Vincent, David **LC156.G72E58 1989**
Literacy and Popular Culture: England, 1750-1914. Peter Burke & Ruth Finnegan (Contribution by). Trade Paper. Cambridge University Press. New York, NY. 1993. 374p. Studies in Oral and Literate Culture, No. 19 ISBN:0-521-45771-8, ISBN13: 978-0-521-45771-2. Dewey:302.2/244/0942/09034.
Audience: **g,l,u,f.** *Choice, 1990.*

Webb, R. K. (Robert Kiefer) **HD8389**
The British Working Class Reader, 1790-1848; Literacy and Social Tension. New York: Kelley. 1971. ISBN:0-678-00578-8, ISBN13: 978-0-678-00578-1.
Audience: **u,f.**

Webb, Robert K. **DA470**
Modern England: From the Eighteenth Century to the Present. Ed. 2. Trade Paper. Addison-Wesley Educational Publishers, Inc. Boston, MA. 1997. 685p. ISBN:0-06-046974-9, ISBN13: 978-0-06-046974-0. Dewey:941.07.
Audience: **l,u.**

Wiener, Martin J. **HN385**
English Culture and the Decline of the Industrial Spirit, 1850-1980. Trade Cloth. Cambridge University Press. New York, NY. 1981. 250p. ISBN:0-521-23418-2, ISBN13: 978-0-521-23418-4. Dewey:306.3/4/0942/0904. LCCN:80-022684.
Audience: **l,u,f.**

Wiener, Martin Joel **HV6022.G7 W54 1990**
Reconstructing the Criminal: Culture, Law, and Policy in England, 1830-1914. Trade Paper. Cambridge University Press. New York, NY. 1994. 400p. ISBN:0-521-47882-0, ISBN13: 978-0-521-47882-3. Dewey:364.9/42/09034.
Audience: **u,f.** *Choice, 1991.*

Williams, Raymond **DA533.W6 1983**
Culture and Society, 1780-1950. Ed. 2. Trade Cloth. Columbia University Press. New York, NY. 1983. 363p. A Morningside Bk. ISBN:0-231-02287-5, ISBN13: 978-0-231-02287-3. Dewey:306/.4/0941. LCCN:85-005195.
Audience: **g,u,f.** B

Wohl, Anthony S. **HD4145**
Endangered Lives: Public Health in Victorian Britain. Trade Cloth. Harvard University Press. Cambridge, MA. 1983. 416p. ISBN:0-674-25241-1, ISBN13: 978-0-674-25241-7. Dewey:363/.0941.
Audience: **g,l,u,f.**

Woodham Smith, Cecil Blanche Fitz Gerald **DA564.B3**
The Reason Why. Paper Text. Textbook Publishers. Temecula, CA. 2003. 287p. ISBN:0-7581-8689-4, ISBN13: 978-0-7581-8689-8. Dewey:942.081/0924.
Audience: **l,u,f.**

Young, G. M. (George Malcolm) **DA550**
Portrait of an Age: Victorian England. Ed. 2. London: Phoenix. 2002. ISBN:1-84212-598-2, ISBN13: 978-1-84212-598-4.
Audience: **g,l,u,f.**

Young, Robert M. **QH361.Y68 1985**
Darwin's Metaphor: Nature's Place in Victorian Culture. Cloth Text. Cambridge University Press. New York, NY. 1985. 368p. ISBN:0-521-30083-5, ISBN13: 978-0-521-30083-4. Dewey:575.01/62/09. LCCN:84-021377.
Audience: **u,f.**

Ziegler, Philip **DA539**
King William IV. Trade Cloth. Cresset Press, Inc. Sarasota, FL. 1960. 335p. ISBN:0-00-211934-X, ISBN13: 978-0-00-211934-4. Dewey:941.07/5/0924. LCCN:61-001297.
Audience: **g,l,u,f.**

Britain > English History > Modern (1485-) > Edwardian Era

DA688.B65 1975
The Bloomsbury Group: A Collection of Memoirs, Commentary, and Criticism. Trade Cloth. University of Toronto Press. Toronto, ON. 1975. xxi, 444p. ISBN:0-8020-2182-4, ISBN13: 978-0-8020-2182-3. Dewey:942.1/082. LCCN:75-331714.
Audience: **l,u,f.**

Barnett, Correlli **DA578.B33 1986**
The Collapse of British Power. Trade Paper. Brill Academic Publishers, Inc. Boston, MA. 1986. 656p. ISBN:0-391-03439-1, ISBN13: 978-0-391-03439-6. Dewey:941/.083. LCCN:86-003032.
Audience: **g,l,u,f.**

Bernstein, George L. **JC599.G7**
Liberalism and Liberal Politics in Edwardian England. Paper Text. Routledge. New York, NY. 1986. 256p. ISBN:0-04-942199-9, ISBN13: 978-0-04-942199-8. Dewey:941.082. LCCN:85-022877.
Audience: **g,l,u,f.** *Choice, 1987.*

Dangerfield, George **DA576.D3 1997**
The Strange Death of Liberal England. Peter Stansky (Foreword by). Trade Paper. Stanford University Press. Palo Alto, CA. 1997. 364p. ISBN:0-8047-2930-1, ISBN13: 978-0-8047-2930-7. Dewey:941/.083. LCCN:96-070279.
Audience: **g,l,u,f.**

Gadd, David **DA688.G23 1975**
The Loving Friends: A Portrait of Bloomsbury. Trade Cloth. Harcourt College Publishers. Fort Worth, TX. 1975. xii, 210p. ISBN:0-15-154740-8, ISBN13: 978-0-15-154740-1. Dewey:700/.92/2. LCCN:74-026596.
Audience: **l,u,f.**

Grigg, John **DA566.9.L5.G78 1978**
Lloyd George: The People's Champion, 1902-1911. Trade Cloth. University of California Press. Berkeley, CA. 1978. 391p. ISBN:0-520-03634-4, ISBN13: 978-0-520-03634-5. Dewey:941.083/092/4. LCCN:77-091762.
Audience: **l,u,f.**

Grigg, John **DA566.9.L5.G8 1974**
The Young Lloyd George. Trade Cloth. University of California Press. Berkeley, CA. 1978. 320p. ISBN:0-520-02677-2, ISBN13: 978-0-520-02677-3. Dewey:942.081/092/4. LCCN:73-091067.
Audience: **l,u,f.**

Hynes, Samuel **DA570.H9 1991**
The Edwardian Turn of Mind. Trade Cloth. Random House of Canada, Ltd. Mississauga, ON. 1992. 427p. ISBN:0-7126-5028-8, ISBN13: 978-0-7126-5028-1. Dewey:941.0823. LCCN:93-140915.
Audience: **l,u,f.**

Rosen, Andrew **JN979**
Rise up, Women!: The Militant Campaign of the Women's Social and Political Union, 1903-1914. Trade Cloth. Ashgate Publishing, Ltd. Aldershot, 1993. 340p. Modern Revivals in History Ser. ISBN:0-7512-0173-1, ISBN13: 978-0-7512-0173-4. Dewey:324/.3/0941.
Audience: **g,l,u,f.**

Taylor, A. J. P. **DA566.4**
English History, 1914-1945. Trade Cloth. Oxford University Press, Inc. New York, NY. 1978. 737p. Oxford History of England Ser., Vol. 15 ISBN:0-19-821715-3, ISBN13: 978-0-19-821715-2. Dewey:941.082.
Audience: **g,l,u,f.**

Britain > English History > Modern (1485-) > World War I

Barnett, Correlli **DA578.B33 1986**
The Collapse of British Power. Trade Paper. Brill Academic Publishers, Inc. Boston, MA. 1986. 656p. ISBN:0-391-03439-1, ISBN13: 978-0-391-03439-6. Dewey:941/.083. LCCN:86-003032.
Audience: **g,l,u,f.**

Gilbert, Martin **DA566.9.C5.G463 1982**
Winston S. Churchill: The Wilderness Years. Trade Cloth. Houghton Mifflin Company. New York, NY. 1982. 279p. ISBN:0-395-31869-6, ISBN13: 978-0-395-31869-0. Dewey:941.082/092/4. LCCN:82-009279.
Audience: **g,l,u,f.**

Grigg, John **DA566.9.L5G777 1985**
Lloyd George: From Peace to War, 1912-1916. Trade Cloth. University of California Press. Berkeley, CA. 1985. 512p. ISBN:0-520-05417-2, ISBN13: 978-0-520-05417-2. Dewey:941.083/092/4. LCCN:84-016150.
Audience: **u,f.** *Choice, 1985.*

Manchester, William **DA566.9.C5.M26 1983**
The Last Lion: Winston Churchill Visions of Glory, 1874-1932. Trade Cloth. Little Brown & Company. New York, NY. 1983. 973p. ISBN:0-316-54503-1, ISBN13: 978-0-316-54503-7. Dewey:941.084/092/4. LCCN:82-024972.
Audience: **u,f.**

Marwick, Arthur **DA577.M37**
The Deluge: British Society and the First World War. Ed. 2. Basingstoke: Palgrave Macmillan. 2006. ISBN:0-230-00245-5, ISBN13: 978-0-230-00245-6.
Audience: **g,l,u,f.**

Taylor, A. J. P. **DA566.4**
English History, 1914-1945. Trade Cloth. Oxford University Press, Inc. New York, NY. 1978. 737p. Oxford History of England Ser., Vol. 15 ISBN:0-19-821715-3, ISBN13: 978-0-19-821715-2. Dewey:941.082.
Audience: **g,l,u,f.**

Winter, J. M. **HB3583.A3W56 2003**
The Great War and the British People. Ed. 2. Trade Paper. Palgrave Macmillan. New York, NY. 2003. 376p. ISBN:1-4039-0695-5, ISBN13: 978-1-4039-0695-3. Dewey:304.6/0941/09041. LCCN:2002-042822.
Audience: **l,u,f.** *Choice, 1986.*

Britain > English History > Modern (1485-) > Interwar England

Annan, Noel Gilroy, et al. **DA566.4**
Our Age: Portrait of a Generation. Annan, Baron (Author). London: Weidenfeld and Nicolson. 1990. ISBN:0-297-81129-0, ISBN13: 978-0-297-81129-9.
Audience: **g,l,u,f.**

Barnett, Correlli **DA578.B33 1986**
The Collapse of British Power. Trade Paper. Brill Academic Publishers, Inc. Boston, MA. 1986. 656p. ISBN:0-391-03439-1, ISBN13: 978-0-391-03439-6. Dewey:941/.083. LCCN:86-003032.
Audience: **g,l,u,f.**

Dangerfield, George **DA576.D3 1997**
The Strange Death of Liberal England. Peter Stansky (Foreword by). Trade Paper. Stanford University Press. Palo Alto, CA. 1997. 364p. ISBN:0-8047-2930-1, ISBN13: 978-0-8047-2930-7. Dewey:941/.083. LCCN:96-070279.
Audience: **g,l,u,f.**

Gilbert, Martin **DA566.9.C5.G463 1982**
Winston S. Churchill: The Wilderness Years. Trade Cloth. Houghton Mifflin Company. New York, NY. 1982. 279p. ISBN:0-395-31869-6, ISBN13: 978-0-395-31869-0. Dewey:941.082/092/4. LCCN:82-009279.
Audience: **g,l,u,f.**

Graves, Robert **DA566.4**
The Long Week-End: A Social History of Great Britain, 1918-1939. Trade Paper. W. W. Norton & Company, Inc. New York, NY. 2001. 480p. ISBN:0-393-31136-8, ISBN13: 978-0-393-31136-5. Dewey:941.083.
Audience: **g,l,u,f.**

Morgan, Kenneth O. **DA576.M67**
Consensus and Disunity: The Lloyd George Coalition Government, 1918-1922. Trade Cloth. Oxford University Press, Inc. New York, NY. 1979. 448p. ISBN:0-19-822497-4, ISBN13: 978-0-19-822497-6. Dewey:320.9/41/083. LCCN:79-040263.
Audience: **u,f.**

Mowat, Charles Loch **DA578**
Britain Between the Wars, 1918-1940. Boston: Beacon Press. 1971. Europe in the Twentieth Century Ser.; 381
Audience: **g,l,u,f.**

Taylor, A. J. P. **DA566.4**
English History, 1914-1945. Trade Cloth. Oxford University Press, Inc. New York, NY. 1978. 737p. Oxford History of England Ser., Vol. 15 ISBN:0-19-821715-3, ISBN13: 978-0-19-821715-2. Dewey:941.082.
Audience: **g,l,u,f.**

Britain > English History > Modern (1485-) > World War II

Barnett, Correlli **DA578.B33 1986**
The Collapse of British Power. Trade Paper. Brill Academic Publishers, Inc. Boston, MA. 1986. 656p. ISBN:0-391-03439-1, ISBN13: 978-0-391-03439-6. Dewey:941/.083. LCCN:86-003032.
Audience: **g,l,u,f.**

Gilbert, Martin **DA566.9.C5.G463 1982**
Winston S. Churchill: The Wilderness Years. Trade Cloth. Houghton Mifflin Company. New York, NY. 1982. 279p. ISBN:0-395-31869-6, ISBN13: 978-0-395-31869-0. Dewey:941.082/092/4. LCCN:82-009279.
Audience: **g,l,u,f.**

Manchester, William **DA566.9.C5.M26 1983**
The Last Lion: Winston Churchill Visions of Glory, 1874-1932. Trade Cloth. Little Brown & Company. New York, NY. 1983. 973p. ISBN:0-316-54503-1, ISBN13: 978-0-316-54503-7. Dewey:941.084/092/4. LCCN:82-024972.
Audience: **u,f.**

Skidelsky, Robert Jacob Alexander **DA574.M6.S55**
Oswald Mosley. Trade Cloth. Holt, Rinehart & Winston. Austin, TX. 1975. 578p. ISBN:0-03-086580-8, ISBN13: 978-0-03-086580-0. Dewey:942.084/092/4. LCCN:74-006941.
Audience: **g,l,u,f.**

Taylor, A. J. P. **DA566.4**
English History, 1914-1945. Trade Cloth. Oxford University Press, Inc. New York, NY. 1978. 737p. Oxford History of England Ser., Vol. 15 ISBN:0-19-821715-3, ISBN13: 978-0-19-821715-2. Dewey:941.082.
Audience: **g,l,u,f.**

Britain > English History > Modern (1485-) > Postwar England

Bartlett, C. J. **DA588.B28**
A History of Postwar Britain, 1945-1974. Trade Cloth. Longman Publishing Group. White Plains, NY. 1977. viii, 360p. ISBN:0-582-48319-0, ISBN13: 978-0-582-48319-4. Dewey:941.085. LCCN:77-003000.
Audience: **u,f.**

Castle, Barbara **DA591.C3/**
The Castle Diaries 1964-70. Trade Cloth. Weidenfeld & Nicolson, Ltd. London, 1984. xvi, 858p. ISBN:0-297-78374-2, ISBN13: 978-0-297-78374-9. Dewey:941.085/6/0924. LCCN:84-252672.
Audience: **u,f.**

Crossman, R. H. S. (Richard Howard Stafford) **DA591.C76 A34 1975**
The Diaries of a Cabinet Minister. London: Hamilton: Cape. 1975. ISBN:0-241-89110-8, ISBN13: 978-0-241-89110-0.
Audience: **u,f.**

Fisher, Nigel **DA590**
Harold Macmillan: A Biography. Trade Cloth. St. Martin's Press. Gordonville, VA. 1982. 416p. ISBN:0-312-36322-2, ISBN13: 978-0-312-36322-2. Dewey:941.085/092/4. LCCN:81-048509.
Audience: **g,l,u,f.**

Lloyd, T. O. **DA566**
Empire to Welfare State: English History, 1906-1985. Ed. 3. Trade Cloth. Oxford University Press, Inc. New York, NY. 1986. 560p. Short History of the Modern World Ser. ISBN:0-19-822135-5, ISBN13: 978-0-19-822135-7. Dewey:942.082.
Audience: **u,f.**

Longford, Elizabeth **DA590.L64 1983**
The Queen: The Life of Elizabeth II. Trade Cloth. Alfred A. Knopf Inc. New York, NY. 1983. xi, 415p. ISBN:0-394-52328-8, ISBN13: 978-0-394-52328-6. Dewey:941.085/092/4. LCCN:83-048115.
Audience: **g,l,u,f.**

Morgan, Kenneth O. **DA588.M637 1985**
Labour in Power, 1945-1951. Trade Paper. Oxford University Press, Inc. New York, NY. 1985. 564p. ISBN:0-19-285150-0, ISBN13: 978-0-19-285150-5. Dewey:941.085/4. LCCN:85-003003.
Audience: **u,f.**

Morgan, Kenneth O. **DA592.M67 1992**
The People's Peace: British History, 1945-1990. Trade Paper. Oxford University Press, Inc. New York, NY. 1992. 584p. ISBN:0-19-285252-3, ISBN13: 978-0-19-285252-6. Dewey:941.085. LCCN:91-029757.
Audience: **u,f.**

Pelling, Henry **DA588.P44 1984**
The Labour Governments, 1945-51. Cloth Text. Palgrave Macmillan. New York, NY. 1984. 301p. ISBN:0-312-46288-3, ISBN13: 978-0-312-46288-8. Dewey:320.9/41/09044. LCCN:83-022977.
Audience: **u,f.**

Wilson, Harold **DA592**
A Personal Record: The Labour Government, 1964-1970. Boston: Little, Brown. 1971.
Audience: **u,f.**

Britain > English History > Special Topics

Beale, Philip O. **HE6945.B4 1998**
A History of the Post in England from the Romans to the Stuarts. Trade Cloth. Ashgate Publishing, Ltd. Aldershot, 1998. 288p. ISBN:1-85928-404-3, ISBN13: 978-1-85928-404-9. Dewey:383.494. LCCN:97-038528.
Audience: **u,f.** *Choice, 1999.*

Cross, Nigel **PR451 .C76 1985**
The Common Writer: Life in Nineteenth-Century Grub Street. Trade Cloth. Cambridge University Press. New York, NY. 1985. 271p. ISBN:0-521-24564-8, ISBN13: 978-0-521-24564-7. Dewey:820/.9/008. LCCN:84-029247.
Audience: **g,l,u,f.** *Choice, 1986.*

Dooley, Allan C. **PR0468.T48D6**
Author and Printer in Victorian England. Trade Paper. Books on Demand. Ann Arbor, MI. 206p. Victorian Literature and Culture Ser. ISBN:0-608-08554-5, ISBN13: 978-0-608-08554-8. Dewey:820.9008. LCCN:92-010420.
Audience: **l,u.** *Choice, 1993.*

Erickson, Lee **PR451.E75 1999**
Economy of Literary Form: English Literature and the Industrialization of Publishing, 1800-1850. Trade Paper. Johns Hopkins University Press. Baltimore, MD. 2000. 224p. ISBN:0-8018-6358-9, ISBN13: 978-0-8018-6358-5. Dewey:820.9/007. LCCN:95-017054.
Audience: **u,f.**

Feather, John P. **Z325.F414 1988B**
A History of British Publishing. Trade Paper. Routledge. New York, NY. 1989. 304p. ISBN:0-415-02654-7, ISBN13: 978-0-415-02654-3. Dewey:070.5/0941. LCCN:88-028715.
Audience: **g,l,u,f.**

Griest, Guinevere L. **Z792.M84**
Mudie's Circulating Library and the Victorian Novel. Mudie's Select Library Staff (Contribution by). Trade Cloth. David & Charles Publishers. Newton Abbot, 1971. xiv, 272p. ISBN:0-7153-5309-8, ISBN13: 978-0-7153-5309-7. Dewey:027/.2/421.
Audience: **l,u,f.**

Gross, John **PR63.G7 1992**
The Rise and Fall of the Man of Letters: English Literary Life since 1800. Trade Paper. Ivan R. Dee Publisher. Blue Ridge Summit, PA. 1992. 372p. ISBN:1-56663-000-2, ISBN13: 978-1-56663-000-9. Dewey:820.9. LCCN:92-016011.
Audience: **u,f.**

Kernan, Alvin **PR3534**
Samuel Johnson and the Impact of Print. Trade Paper. Princeton University Press. Princeton, NJ. 1989. 375p. ISBN:0-691-01475-2, ISBN13: 978-0-691-01475-3. Dewey:828.609. LCCN:86-042842.
Audience: **u,f.**

Patten, Robert L. **PR4583.P29 1978**
Charles Dickens and His Publishers. Cloth Text. Oxford University Press, Inc. New York, NY. 1978. 518p. ISBN:0-19-812076-1, ISBN13: 978-0-19-812076-6. Dewey:823/.8. LCCN:77-030164.
Audience: **g,l,u,f.** B

Rose, Jonathan **Z1039.L3R67 2001**
The Intellectual Life of the British Working Classes. Cloth over Boards. Yale University Press. Cumberland, RI. 2001. 544p. ISBN:0-300-08886-8, ISBN13: 978-0-300-08886-1. Dewey:028/.9/0941. LCCN:00-068562.
Audience: **g,l,u,f.** *Choice, 2002.*

Slack, Paul A. **KD3299 .S57 1995**
The English Poor Law, 1531-1782. Ed. 2. Maurice Kirby (Contribution by). Cloth Text. Cambridge University Press. New York, NY. 1995. 84p. New Studies in Economic and Social History, No. 9 ISBN:0-521-55268-0, ISBN13: 978-0-521-55268-4. Dewey:362.5/8/0942. LCCN:95-018728.
Audience: **u,f.**

Sparrow, Andrew **JN508**
Obscure Scribblers: A History of Parliamentary Reporting. Trade Cloth. Politico's Publishing Ltd. Tunbridge Wells, 2003. 356p. ISBN:1-84275-061-5, ISBN13: 978-1-84275-061-2. Dewey:070.4/49941. LCCN:2003-501380.
Audience: **u,f.** *Choice, 2004.*

Vincent, David **LC156.A2V55 2000**
The Rise of Mass Literacy: Reading and Writing in Modern Europe. Trade Cloth. Polity Press. Cambridge, 2000. 208p. ISBN:0-7456-1444-2, ISBN13: 978-0-7456-1444-1. Dewey:302.2/244/094. LCCN:00-027871.
Audience: **g,l,u,f.** *Choice, 2001.*

Britain > English History > Special Topics > Religious Conflict. Puritanism

Arnstein, Walter L. **KD4354**
The Bradlaugh Case: Atheism, Sex, and Politics among the Late Victorians. Cloth Text. University of Missouri Press. Columbia, MO. 1984. 388p. ISBN:0-8262-0425-2, ISBN13: 978-0-8262-0425-7. Dewey:342.41/055/0264. LCCN:83-006814.
Audience: **u,f.**

Bossy, John **BX1492.B67X 1976**
The English Catholic Community, 1570-1850. Trade Cloth. Oxford University Press, Inc. New York, NY. 1976. xii, 446p. ISBN:0-19-519847-6, ISBN13: 978-0-19-519847-8. Dewey:282/.42. LCCN:84-672164.
Audience: **u,f.**

Chadwick, Owen **BR759**
The Victorian Church. London: SCM Press. 1987. ISBN:0-334-02409-9, ISBN13: 978-0-334-02409-5.
Audience: **u,f.**

Collinson, Patrick **BX9333.C62 1989**
The Elizabethan Puritan Movement. Trade Paper. Oxford University Press, Inc. New York, NY. 1990. 528p. ISBN:0-19-822298-X, ISBN13: 978-0-19-822298-9. Dewey:285/.9. LCCN:89-022977.
Audience: **u,f.**

Dickens, A.G. **BR375.D5 1991**
The English Reformation. Ed. 2. Trade Paper. Pennsylvania State University Press. University Park, PA. 1991. 600p. ISBN:0-271-00798-2, ISBN13: 978-0-271-00798-4. Dewey:274.2/06. LCCN:91-013618.
Audience: **u,f.**

Fox, Alistair **DA334.M8**
Thomas More: History and Providence. Trade Cloth. Yale University Press. Cumberland, RI. 1983. 288p. ISBN:0-300-02951-9, ISBN13: 978-0-300-02951-2. Dewey:942.05/2/0924. LCCN:82-011178.
Audience: **g,l,u,f.**

Haig, Alan **BX5175**
The Victorian Clergy. Trade Cloth. Croom Helm, Ltd. London, 1984. 380p. ISBN:0-7099-1230-7, ISBN13: 978-0-7099-1230-9. Dewey:262/.14342.
Audience: **u,f.**

Haigh, Christopher (Editor) **BR375.E54 1987**
The English Reformation Revised. Trade Paper. Cambridge University Press. New York, NY. 1987. 240p. ISBN:0-521-33631-7, ISBN13: 978-0-521-33631-4. Dewey:274.2/06.
Audience: **g,l,u,f.**

Hibbard, Caroline M. **DA0395.H46**
Charles the First and the Popish Plot. Trade Paper. Books on Demand. Ann Arbor, MI. 354p. ISBN:0-8357-3906-6, ISBN13: 978-0-8357-3906-1. Dewey:941.062. LCCN:81-023075.
Audience: **g,l,u,f.**

Hill, Christopher **DA380.H48 1997**
Intellectual Origins of the English Revolution—Revisited. Ed. 2. Trade Cloth. Oxford University Press, Inc. New York, NY. 1997. 438p. ISBN:0-19-820668-2, ISBN13: 978-0-19-820668-2. Dewey:942.06/21. LCCN:96-051165.
Audience: **l,u,f.**

Hill, Christopher **DA380 .H5**
Puritanism and Revolution: Studies in Interpretation of the English Revolution of the 17th Century. Paper Text. Textbook Publishers. Temecula, CA. 2003. 402p. ISBN:0-7581-3969-1, ISBN13: 978-0-7581-3969-6. Dewey:942.062.
Audience: **l,u,f.**

Hill, Christopher **DA380.H52 1997**
Society and Puritanism in Pre-Revolutionary England. Trade Cloth. Palgrave Macmillan. New York, NY. 1997. 464p. ISBN:0-312-17431-4, ISBN13: 978-0-312-17431-6. Dewey:941.06/2. LCCN:97-032014.
Audience: **l,u.**

Hill, Christopher **DA380**
A World Turned Upside Down: Radical Ideas During the English Revolution. Trade Paper. Penguin Group (USA) Inc. New York, NY. 1984. 432p. ISBN:0-14-013732-7, ISBN13: 978-0-14-013732-3. Dewey:322.42094209032.
Audience: **g,l,u,f.**

Hill, Christopher **DA380**
The World Turned Upside Down. Trade Cloth. Penguin Group (USA) Inc. New York, NY. 1972. ISBN:0-670-78975-5, ISBN13: 978-0-670-78975-7. Dewey:914.2/03/62.
Audience: **g,l,u,f.**

Hilton, Boyd **HC256.5**
The Age of Atonement: The Influence of Evangelicalism on Social and Economic Thought 1785-1865. Paper Text. Oxford University Press, Inc. New York, NY. 1992. 428p. ISBN:0-19-820295-4, ISBN13: 978-0-19-820295-0. Dewey:306/.3/0941.
Audience: **g,l,u,f.**

Hirst, Derek **DA390.H57 1986**
Authority and Conflict: England, 1603-1658. Trade Cloth. Harvard University Press. Cambridge, MA. 1986. 400p. New History of England Ser. ISBN:0-674-05290-0, ISBN13: 978-0-674-05290-1. Dewey:941.06. LCCN:85-024957.
Audience: **u,f.** *Choice, 1986.*

Hirst, Derek **DA390**
Authority and Conflict: England, 1603-1658. Cambridge, Mass.: Harvard University Press. 1986. The New History of England Ser. ISBN:0-674-05290-0, ISBN13: 978-0-674-05290-1.
Audience: **u,f.**

Hunt, William **DA670.E7**
The Puritan Moment: The Coming of Revolution in an English County. Trade Paper. Harvard University Press. Cambridge, MA. 1984. 376p. Harvard Historical Studies, No. 102 ISBN:0-674-73904-3, ISBN13: 978-0-674-73904-8. Dewey:942.6/7/062.
Audience: **l,u,f.**

Hutton, Ronald **DA375**
The Restoration: A Political and Religious History of England and Wales, 1658-1667. Paper Text. Oxford University Press, Inc. New York, NY. 1993. 388p. ISBN:0-19-820392-6, ISBN13: 978-0-19-820392-6. Dewey:942.06.
Audience: **l,u,f.** *Choice, 1986, 1985.*

Inglis, Kenneth Stanley **BR759**
Churches and the Working Classes in Victorian England. London, Routledge and K. Paul. 1963. Studies in Social History ISBN:0-7100-4556-5, ISBN13: 978-0-7100-4556-0.
Audience: **l,u.**

Kenyon, J. P. (John Philipps) **DA448**
The Popish Plot. New York, St. Martin's Press. 1972.
Audience: **u,f.**

Laqueur, Thomas W. **BV1517.G7**
Religion and Respectability: Sunday Schools and English Working Class Culture, 1780-1850. Trade Cloth. Yale University Press. Cumberland, RI. 1976. ISBN:0-300-01859-2, ISBN13: 978-0-300-01859-2. Dewey:301.5/8. LCCN:74-029728.
Audience: **u,f.**

Loades, David M. **DA347.L58 1991**
The Reign of Mary Tudor: Politics, Government and Religion in England, 1553-58. Ed. 1. Paper Text. Longman Publishing Group. White Plains, NY. 1991. 448p. ISBN:0-582-05759-0, ISBN13: 978-0-582-05759-3. Dewey:942.05/4/092. LCCN:90-042615.
Audience: **u,f.**

Machin, G. I. **BR759**
Politics and the Churches in Great Britain, 1832-1868. Trade Cloth. Oxford University Press, Inc. New York, NY. 1978. ix, 438p. ISBN:0-19-826436-4, ISBN13: 978-0-19-826436-1. Dewey:322/.1/0941. LCCN:77-030296.
Audience: **u,f.**

Machin, G. I. **BR759.M27 1987**
Politics and the Churches in Great Britain, 1869-1921. Trade Cloth. Oxford University Press, Inc. New York, NY. 1987. 388p. ISBN:0-19-820106-0, ISBN13: 978-0-19-820106-9. Dewey:322/.1/0941. LCCN:87-001620.
Audience: **u,f.** *Choice, 1988.*

McGregor, J. F. **BR757.R33 1984**
Radical Religion in the English Revolution. B. Reay (Editor). Trade Cloth. Oxford University Press, Inc. New York, NY. 1984. 219p. ISBN:0-19-873044-6, ISBN13: 978-0-19-873044-6. Dewey:274.2/07. LCCN:85-116178.
Audience: **l,u,f.**

Miller, John **DA448.M54**
Popery and Politics in England, 1660-1688. Trade Cloth. Cambridge University Press. New York, NY. 1973. 296p. ISBN:0-521-20236-1, ISBN13: 978-0-521-20236-7. Dewey:322/.1/0942. LCCN:73-079306.
Audience: **u,f.**

Newsome, David **LA632**
Godliness and Good Learning: Four Studies on a Victorian Ideal. Trade Cloth. Transatlantic Arts, Inc. Albuquerque, NM. 1961. ISBN:0-7195-1015-5, ISBN13: 978-0-7195-1015-1. Dewey:370/.942.
Audience: **g,l,u,f.**

Notestein, Wallace **DA380.N6**
English People on the Eve of Colonization: 1603-1630. Mass Market. HarperCollins Publishers. New York, NY. 1985. New American Nation Ser. ISBN:0-06-133006-X, ISBN13: 978-0-06-133006-3. Dewey:942.061.
Audience: **g,l,u,f.**

Pollard, Albert F. **DA334.W8 P6 1978**
Wolsey. Library Binding. Greenwood Publishing Group, Inc. Portsmouth, NH. 1978. ISBN:0-8371-7997-1, ISBN13: 978-0-8371-7997-1. Dewey:942.05/2/0924. LCCN:74-033897.
Audience: **g,l,u,f.**

Reay, Barry **BX7676.2.R4 1985**
The Quakers and the English Revolution. Christopher R. Hill (Foreword by). Cloth Text. Palgrave Macmillan. New York, NY. 1985. 200p. ISBN:0-312-65808-7, ISBN13: 978-0-312-65808-3. Dewey:289.6/42. LCCN:84-022355.
Audience: **l,u,f.** *Choice, 1985.*

Richardson, R. C. **DA403.R53 1999**
The Debate on the English Revolution. Ed. 3. Trade Cloth. Manchester University Press. Manchester, 1999. 262p. Issues in Historiography Ser. ISBN:0-7190-4739-0, ISBN13: 978-0-7190-4739-8. Dewey:941.06/3/072. LCCN:98-028825.
Audience: **u,f.**

Ridley, Jasper Godwin **DA317.8.C8**
Thomas Cranmer. Oxford: Clarendon Press. 1962.
Audience: **g,l,u,f.**

Russell, Conrad **DA315**
The Crisis of Parliaments: English History, 1509-1660. Paper Text. Oxford University Press, Inc. New York, NY. 1971. 450p. Short Oxford History of the Modern World Ser. ISBN:0-19-913034-5, ISBN13: 978-0-19-913034-4. Dewey:941.05.
Audience: **u,f.**

Seaver, Paul S. **BX9339.W26S4 1985**
Wallington's World: A Puritan Artisan in Seventeenth-Century London. Trade Cloth. Stanford University Press. Palo Alto, CA. 1985. 272p. ISBN:0-8047-1267-0, ISBN13: 978-0-8047-1267-5. Dewey:941.06. LCCN:84-040447.
Audience: **u,f.** *Choice, 1986.*

Solt, Leo F. (Leo Frank) **DA415**
Saints in Arms; Puritanism and Democracy in Cromwell's Army. New York, AMS Press. 1971. Stanford Studies in History, Eonomics, and Political Science; Vol. 18 ISBN:0-404-50976-2, ISBN13: 978-0-404-50976-7.
Audience: **u,f.**

Tauney, R. H. **BR115.C3T38 1998**
Religion and the Rise of Capitalism. Adam B. Seligman (Introduction by). Trade Paper. Transaction Publishers. Somerset, NJ. 1998. 337p. ISBN:0-7658-0455-7, ISBN13: 978-0-7658-0455-6. Dewey:330.12/2. LCCN:98-009644.
Audience: **l,u.**

Thomas, Keith **BR377.T48 1997**
Religion and the Decline of Magic: Studies in Popular Beliefs in Sixteenth and Seventeenth Century England. Trade Paper. Oxford University Press, Inc. New York, NY. 1997. 736p. ISBN:0-19-521360-2, ISBN13: 978-0-19-521360-7. Dewey:133. LCCN:97-002365.
Audience: **u,f.**

Tyacke, Nicholas **BX5073.T93 1989**
Anti-Calvinists: The Rise of English Arminianism c. 1590-1640. Trade Paper. Oxford University Press, Inc. New York, NY. 1990. 328p. Oxford Historical Monographs ISBN:0-19-820184-2, ISBN13: 978-0-19-820184-7. Dewey:283/.42/09031. LCCN:89-035135.
Audience: **u,f.**

Underdown, David **DA425**
Pride's Purge: Politics in the Puritan Revolution. Trade Cloth. Oxford University Press, Inc. New York, NY. 1971. xi, 424p. ISBN:0-19-822342-0, ISBN13: 978-0-19-822342-9. Dewey:942.06/3. LCCN:78-853456.
Audience: **l,u,f.**

Watt, Tessa **PR428.C48W38 1994**
Cheap Print and Popular Piety, 1550-1640. Anthony Fletcher, John Guy & John Morrill (Contribution by). Trade Paper. Cambridge University Press. New York, NY. 1993. 390p. Cambridge Studies in Early Modern British History ISBN:0-521-45827-7, ISBN13: 978-0-521-45827-6. Dewey:820.9/382/09031.
Audience: **l,u,f.** *Choice, 1992.*

Wormald, Jennifer **DA783.41**
Court, Kirk and Community: Scotland, 1470-1625. Trade Paper. Edinburgh University Press. Edinburgh, 1991. 216p. ISBN:0-7486-0276-3, ISBN13: 978-0-7486-0276-6. Dewey:941.103.
Audience: **u,f.**

Britain > English History > Special Topics > Industrial Revolution

Ashton, T. S. **HC254.5.A78 1997**
The Industrial Revolution, 1760-1830. Ed. 2. Pat Hudson (Preface by, Contribution by). Paper Text. Oxford University Press, Inc. New York, NY. 1998. 154p. ISBN:0-19-289289-4, ISBN13: 978-0-19-289289-8. Dewey:338/.0941. LCCN:98-134894.
Audience: **u,f.** B

Berg, Maxine **HD9720.5**
The Age of Manufactures, 1700-1820: Industry, Innovation, and Work in Britain. Ed. 2. Trade Paper. Routledge. New York, NY. 1994. 352p. ISBN:0-415-06935-1, ISBN13: 978-0-415-06935-9. Dewey:338.4/767/09033. LCCN:93-023364.
Audience: **u,f.**

Brewer, John **DA480.B74 1990**
The Sinews of Power: War, Money and the English State, 1688-1783. Trade Paper. Harvard University Press. Cambridge, MA. 1990. 320p. ISBN:0-674-80930-0, ISBN13: 978-0-674-80930-7. Dewey:941.07. LCCN:90-004414.
Audience: **u,f.**

Clarkson, L. A. **HD2329.C56 1985**
Proto-Industrialization: The First Phase of Industrialization? Trade Paper. Macmillan Publishers Ltd. London, 1985. 87p. Studies in Economic and Social History ISBN:0-333-34392-1, ISBN13: 978-0-333-34392-0. Dewey:338.094. LCCN:85-244461.
Audience: **g,l,u,f.**

Crafts, N.F.R. **HC254.5.C73 1985**
British Economic Growth During the Industrial Revolution. Trade Cloth. Bow Historical Books. New Providence, NJ. 1985. 220p. ISBN:0-19-873066-7, ISBN13: 978-0-19-873066-8. Dewey:338.941. LCCN:85-002926.
Audience: **l,u,f.** B

Floud, Roderick & McCloskey, Donald N. (Editors) **HC254.5 .E27 1994**
The Economic History of Britain since 1700: 1700-1860. Ed. 2. Trade Cloth. Cambridge University Press. New York, NY. 1994. 432p. ISBN:0-521-41498-9, ISBN13: 978-0-521-41498-2. Dewey:330.941/07. LCCN:93-020093.
Audience: **u,f.** B

Floud, Roderick & McCloskey, Donald N. (Editors) **HC254.5.E27 1994**
The Economic History of Britain since 1700: 1939-1992. Ed. 2. Cloth Text. Cambridge University Press. New York, NY. 1994. 400p. ISBN:0-521-41500-4, ISBN13: 978-0-521-41500-2. Dewey:330.94107. LCCN:93-020093.
Audience: **u,f.**

Floud, Roderick (Editor), et al. **HC254.5.E27 1993**
The Economic History of Britain since 1700: 1860-1939. Ed. 2. Donald N. McCloskey & Deirdre N. McCloskey (Editors).

Trade Paper. Cambridge University Press. New York, NY. 1994. 448p. ISBN:0-521-42521-2, ISBN13: 978-0-521-42521-6. Dewey:330.941/07. LCCN:93-020093.

Audience: **u,f.**

Hobsbawm, Eric J. **HC253.H6**
Industry and Empire: The Birth of the Industrial Revolution. Trade Cloth. Peter Smith Publisher, Inc. Magnolia, MA. 2000. ISBN:0-8446-7122-3, ISBN13: 978-0-8446-7122-2. Dewey:330.942.

Audience: **u,f.**

Levine, David A. & Wrightson, Keith **HC258.W47L48 1991**
The Making of an Industrial Society: Whickham, 1560-1765. Cloth Text. Oxford University Press, Inc. New York, NY. 1991. 480p. Oxford Studies in Social History ISBN:0-19-820066-8, ISBN13: 978-0-19-820066-6. Dewey:330.9428/73. LCCN:90-039320.

Audience: **u,f.** *Choice, 1992.*

McKendrick, Neil, et al. **HC260.C6**
The Birth of a Consumer Society: Commercialization of Eighteenth Century England. John Brewer & J.H. Plumb (Authors). Trade Cloth. Taylor & Francis Group. Abingdon, 1982. 342p. ISBN:0-905118-00-6, ISBN13: 978-0-905118-00-0. Dewey:306/.3.

Audience: **u,f.**

McKendrick, Neil, et al. **HC257.E5.M37 1982**
The Birth of a Consumer Society: The Commercialization of Eighteenth-Century England. John Brewer & John H. Plumb (Authors). Trade Cloth. Indiana University Press. Bloomington, IN. 1982. 345p. ISBN:0-253-31205-1, ISBN13: 978-0-253-31205-1. Dewey:306/.3. LCCN:82-047953.

Audience: **g,l,u,f.**

Mokyr, Joel (Editor) **HC254.5.B88 1993**
The British Industrial Revolution: An Economic Perspective. Trade Paper. Westview Press. Boulder, CO. 1993. 362p. ISBN:0-8133-8510-5, ISBN13: 978-0-8133-8510-5. Dewey:338.0941. LCCN:92-021167.

Audience: **l,u,f.** *Choice, 1994.*

Rubinstein, W. D. **HC260.W4**
Men of Property: The Very Wealthy in Britain Since the Industrial Revolution. Trade Cloth. Rutgers University Press. Piscataway, NJ. 1981. 256p. ISBN:0-8135-0927-0, ISBN13: 978-0-8135-0927-3. Dewey:305.5/2.

Audience: **u,f.**

Thirsk, Joan **HC260.I53.T48**
Economic Policy and Projects: The Development of a Consumer Society in Early Modern England. Trade Cloth. Oxford University Press, Inc. New York, NY. 1978. 208p. ISBN:0-19-828274-5, ISBN13: 978-0-19-828274-7. Dewey:338/.0941. LCCN:78-315763.

Audience: **u,f.**

Thompson, Dorothy **HV6485.G7**
The Chartists: Popular Politics in the Industrial Revolution. Trade Paper. Knopf Publishing Group. New York, NY. 1984. ISBN:0-394-72474-7, ISBN13: 978-0-394-72474-4. Dewey:322.4/4/0941.

Audience: **u,f.**

Wiener, Martin J. **HN385**
English Culture and the Decline of the Industrial Spirit, 1850-1980. Trade Cloth. Cambridge University Press. New York, NY. 1981. 250p. ISBN:0-521-23418-2, ISBN13: 978-0-521-23418-4. Dewey:306.3/4/0942/0904. LCCN:80-022684.

Audience: **l,u,f.**

Britain > English History > Special Topics > Law and Custom

Anderson, Olive **HV6548.G7A53 1987**
Suicide in Victorian and Edwardian England. Trade Cloth. Oxford University Press, Inc. New York, NY. 1987. 489p. ISBN:0-19-820101-X, ISBN13: 978-0-19-820101-4. Dewey:362.2. LCCN:87-005613.

Audience: **l,u,f.** *Choice, 1988.*

Beattie, J. M. **KD7876.B43 1986**
Crime and the Courts in England, 1660-1800. Trade Cloth. Princeton University Press. Princeton, NJ. 1986. 768p. ISBN:0-691-05437-1, ISBN13: 978-0-691-05437-7. Dewey:364/.942. LCCN:84-042875.

Audience: **u,f.**

Brewer, John & Styles, John (Editors) **KD612**
An Ungovernable People: The English and Their Law in the Seventeenth and Eighteenth Centuries. Trade Cloth. Rutgers University Press. Piscataway, NJ. 1980. 400p. ISBN:0-8135-0891-6, ISBN13: 978-0-8135-0891-7. Dewey:340/.115/0942.

Audience: **g,l,u,f.**

Burns, J. H. (Editor) **JA81.C283 1990**
The Cambridge History of Political Thought, 1450-1700. Mark Goldie (As told to). Trade Cloth. Cambridge University Press. New York, NY. 1991. 810p. The Cambridge History of Political Thought Ser. ISBN:0-521-24716-0, ISBN13: 978-0-521-24716-0. Dewey:320/.09. LCCN:89-022282.

Audience: **u,f.**

Clark, Pete A. **GT3843**
The English Alehouse: A Social History, 1200-1830. Ed. 1. Trade Paper. Longman Publishing Group. White Plains, NY. 1983. 384p. ISBN:0-582-50835-5, ISBN13: 978-0-582-50835-4. Dewey:306/.48.

Audience: **u,f.**

Davidoff, Leonore **HQ1596**
The Best Circles: Society Etiquette and the Season. Glendinning, Victoria (Introduction by). London: Cresset Library. 1986. ISBN:0-09-168761-6, ISBN13: 978-0-09-168761-8.

Audience: **l,u,f.**

Harrison, Brian H. **HV5446.H35**
Drink and the Victorians: The Temperance Question in England, 1815-1872. Trade Cloth. Edinburgh University Press. Edinburgh, 1998. 528p. ISBN:1-85331-046-8, ISBN13: 978-1-85331-046-1. Dewey:178.

Audience: **g,l,u,f.**

Herrup, Cynthia B. **KD8276**
The Common Peace: Participation and the Criminal Law in Seventeenth-Century England. Anthony Fletcher, John Guy &

John Morrill (Contribution by). Trade Paper. Cambridge University Press. New York, NY. 1989. 256p. Cambridge Studies in Early Modern British History ISBN:0-521-37587-8, ISBN13: 978-0-521-37587-0. Dewey:345.41/01.
Audience: **g,l,u,f.** *Choice, 1988.*

Marshall, Rosalind K. **HQ1147.G7**
Virgins and Viragos: A History of Women in Scotland from 1080-1980. Trade Cloth. Academy Chicago Publishers, Ltd. Chicago, IL. 1983. 340p. ISBN:0-89733-075-7, ISBN13: 978-0-89733-075-6. Dewey:305.4/09411. LCCN:82-024439.
Audience: **g,l,u,f.**

Prest, Wilfrid R. **KD463.P74 1986**
The Rise of the Barristers: A Social History of the English Bar, 1590-1640. Trade Cloth. Oxford University Press, Inc. New York, NY. 1987. 458p. Oxford Studies in Social History ISBN:0-19-821764-1, ISBN13: 978-0-19-821764-0. Dewey:340/.023/42. LCCN:86-002238.
Audience: **u,f.** *Choice, 1987.*

Richardson, Ruth **GT3243.R53 2001**
Death, Dissection and the Destitute. Ed. 2. Trade Cloth. University of Chicago Press. Chicago, IL. 2001. 453p. ISBN:0-226-71239-7, ISBN13: 978-0-226-71239-0. Dewey:393/.0941. LCCN:00-062029.
Audience: **u,f.**

Samuel, Raphael (Editor) **HD60.5.U5**
Village Life and Labour. Trade Cloth. Routledge. New York, NY. 1975. xxii, 278p. History Workshop Ser. ISBN:0-7100-7499-9, ISBN13: 978-0-7100-7499-7. Dewey:301.5/5.
Audience: **g,l,u,f.**

Stone, Lawrence **HQ613.S76**
The Family, Sex and Marriage. Trade Cloth. HarperCollins Publishers. New York, NY. 1977. xxxi, 800p. ISBN:0-06-014142-5, ISBN13: 978-0-06-014142-4. Dewey:306.850941. LCCN:77-000050.
Audience: **g,l,u,f.**

Thompson, E. P. (Edward Palmer) **HN398.E5**
Customs in Common. New York: New Press; Distributed by W.W. Norton. 1991. Studies in Traditional Popular Cuulture ISBN:1-56584-003-8, ISBN13: 978-1-56584-003-4.
Audience: **l,u,f.**

Thompson, Edward P. **HV6943.A54 1975**
Albion's Fatal Tree: Crime and Society in Eighteenth-Century England. Trade Cloth. Knopf Publishing Group. New York, NY. 1976. 352p. ISBN:0-394-47120-2, ISBN13: 978-0-394-47120-4. Dewey:364/.942. LCCN:75-023256.
Audience: **u,f.**

Wiener, Martin Joel **HV6022.G7 W54 1990**
Reconstructing the Criminal: Culture, Law, and Policy in England, 1830-1914. Trade Paper. Cambridge University Press. New York, NY. 1994. 400p. ISBN:0-521-47882-0, ISBN13: 978-0-521-47882-3. Dewey:364.9/42/09034.
Audience: **u,f.** *Choice, 1991.*

Britain > English History > Special Topics > Imperialism

Bayly, C. A. **DA16.B36 1989**
Imperial Meridian: The British Empire and the World 1780-1830. Ed. 1. Trade Paper. Longman Publishing Group. White Plains, NY. 1989. 312p. Studies in Modern History ISBN:0-582-49438-9, ISBN13: 978-0-582-49438-1. Dewey:909.7. LCCN:88-008435.
Audience: **g,l,u,f.**

Beasley, Edward **JV1016**
Mid-Victorian Imperialists: British Gentlemen and the Empire of the Mind. Paper over Boards. Routledge. New York, NY. 2005. 256p. British and Foreign and Colonial Policy Ser. ISBN:0-7146-5698-4, ISBN13: 978-0-7146-5698-4. Dewey:909/.0971241081. LCCN:2004-028868.
Audience: **u,f.**

Brown, Judith M. & Louis, Roger (Editors) **DA18**
The Oxford History of the British Empire: The Twentieth Century. Trade Cloth. Oxford University Press, Inc. New York, NY. 1999. 800p. Oxford History of the British Empire Ser., Vol. IV ISBN:0-19-820564-3, ISBN13: 978-0-19-820564-7. Dewey:325.3/41/0904.
Audience: **u,f.** *Choice, 2000.*

Canny, Nicholas (Editor) **DA16**
The Oxford History of the British Empire: The Origins of Empire: British Overseas Enterprise to the Close of the Seventeenth Century. Trade Cloth. Oxford University Press, Inc. New York, NY. 1998. 554p. Oxford History of the British Empire Ser. ISBN:0-19-820562-7, ISBN13: 978-0-19-820562-3. Dewey:325.3/41.
Audience: **u,f.**

Cell, John Whitson **DA17.H3**
Hailey: A Study in British Imperialism, 1872-1969. Cambridge; New York: Cambridge University Press. 1992. ISBN:0-521-41107-6, ISBN13: 978-0-521-41107-3.
Audience: **u,f.**

Douglas, Roy **DA16.D68 2002**
Liquidation of Empire: The Decline of the British Empire. Cloth over Boards. Palgrave Macmillan. New York, NY. 2002. 190p. ISBN:0-333-80454-6, ISBN13: 978-0-333-80454-4. Dewey:909/.09712410825. LCCN:2002-019599.
Audience: **u,f.** *Choice, 2003.*

Eldridge, C. C. **PR478.I53E43 1996**
The Imperial Experience: From Carlyle to Forster. Cloth over Boards. Palgrave Macmillan. New York, NY. 1996. 232p. ISBN:0-312-16136-0, ISBN13: 978-0-312-16136-1. Dewey:820/.09/008. LCCN:96-033917.
Audience: **g,l,u,f.**

Etherington, Norman (Contribution by) **BV2059**
Missions and Empire. Trade Cloth. Oxford University Press, Inc. New York, NY. 2005. 330p. Oxford History of the British Empire Companion Ser. ISBN:0-19-925347-1, ISBN13: 978-0-19-925347-0. Dewey:266.009. LCCN:2005-282368.
Audience: **g,l,u,f.**

Hobsbawm, Eric J. **D359.7 .H63**
The Age of Empire. Trade Cloth. Peter Smith Publisher, Inc. Magnolia, MA. 1989. ISBN:0-8446-6925-3, ISBN13: 978-0-8446-6925-0. Dewey:909.81.
Audience: **g,u,f.**

Hobsbawm, Eric J. **HC253.H6**
Industry and Empire: The Birth of the Industrial Revolution. Trade Cloth. Peter Smith Publisher, Inc. Magnolia, MA. 2000. ISBN:0-8446-7122-3, ISBN13: 978-0-8446-7122-2. Dewey:330.942.
Audience: **u,f.**

Howe, Stephen **DA18.H714 1993**
Anticolonialism in British Politics: The Left and the End of Empire 1918-1964. Cloth Text. Oxford University Press, Inc. New York, NY. 1993. 392p. Oxford Historical Monographs ISBN:0-19-820423-X, ISBN13: 978-0-19-820423-7. Dewey:325.341. LCCN:93-010369.
Audience: **u,f.** *Choice, 1994.*

Hyam, Ronald **JV1017.H92 2002**
Britain's Imperial Century 1815-1914: A Study of Empire and Expansion. Ed. 3. Trade Paper. Palgrave Macmillan. New York, NY. 2003. 416p. Cambridge Imperial and Post-Colonial Studies ISBN:0-333-99311-X, ISBN13: 978-0-333-99311-8. Dewey:325/.341/09034. LCCN:2002-072332.
Audience: **g,l,u,f.**

James, Lawrence **DA16.J26 1996**
The Rise and Fall of the British Empire. Trade Cloth. St. Martin's Press. Gordonville, VA. 1995. 720p. ISBN:0-312-14039-8, ISBN13: 978-0-312-14039-7. Dewey:909/.0971241. LCCN:95-038774.
Audience: **g,u,f.**

Judd, Denis **DA16.J88**
Empire: The British Imperial Experience from 1765 to the Present. Trade Paper. Basic Books. New York, NY. 1998. 568p. ISBN:0-465-01954-4, ISBN13: 978-0-465-01954-0. Dewey:941.
Audience: **g,u,f.** *Choice, 1997.*

Levine, Philippa (Editor) **HQ1593**
Gender and Empire. Trade Cloth. Oxford University Press, Inc. New York, NY. 2004. 320p. Oxford History of the British Empire Companion Ser. ISBN:0-19-924951-2, ISBN13: 978-0-19-924951-0. Dewey:305.3/09171/241. LCCN:2004-044614.
Audience: **u,f.**

Lloyd, T. O. **DA566.7**
Empire, Welfare State, Europe: History of the United Kingdom, 1906-2001. Ed. 5. Paper Text. Oxford University Press, Inc. New York, NY. 2002. 568p. Short Oxford History of the Modern World Ser. ISBN:0-19-870067-9, ISBN13: 978-0-19-870067-8. Dewey:941.082. LCCN:2002-282243.
Audience: **g,u,f.**

Lloyd, Trevor Owen **DA16.L84 1996**
The British Empire, 1558-1995. Ed. 2. Paper Text. Oxford University Press, Inc. New York, NY. 1997. 468p. Short Oxford History of the Modern World Ser. ISBN:0-19-873133-7, ISBN13: 978-0-19-873133-7. Dewey:909/.0971241. LCCN:97-188661.
Audience: **g,u,f.**

Long, Roger D. (Editor) **DA16**
The Man on the Spot: Essays on British Empire History, 31. Book, Other. Greenwood Publishing Group, Inc. Portsmouth, NH. 1995. 256p. Contributions in Comparative Colonial Studies, Vol. 31 ISBN:0-313-29524-7, ISBN13: 978-0-313-29524-9. Dewey:941. LCCN:95-009667.
Audience: **g,l,u,f.** *Choice, 1996.*

Mackenzie, John M. (Editor) **DA533.I46 1989**
Imperialism and Popular Culture. Trade Paper. Manchester University Press. Manchester, 1989. 256p. Studies in Imperialism ISBN:0-7190-1868-4, ISBN13: 978-0-7190-1868-8. Dewey:941.082. LCCN:85-013657.
Audience: **u,f.** *Choice, 1986.*

Magnus, Philip Sir (Philip Montefiore) **DA68.32.K6**
Kitchener: Portrait of an Imperialist. Harmondsworth, Penguin. 1968.
Audience: **g,l,u,f.**

Marshall, P. J. (Editor) **DA16.M29 1996**
The Cambridge Illustrated History of the British Empire. Trade Paper. Cambridge University Press. New York, NY. 2001. 400p. Cambridge Illustrated Histories Ser. ISBN:0-521-00254-0, ISBN13: 978-0-521-00254-7. Dewey:909/.09712/41.
Audience: **u,f.**

Marshall, P. J. & Low, Alaine (Editors) **DA16**
The Oxford History of the British Empire: The Eighteenth Century. Trade Cloth. Oxford University Press, Inc. New York, NY. 1998. 662p. Oxford History of the British Empire Ser. ISBN:0-19-820563-5, ISBN13: 978-0-19-820563-0. Dewey:325.3/41.
Audience: **u,f.**

Porter, A. N. & Stockwell, A. J. **JV1018.P66 1987**
British Imperial Policy and Decolonization, 1938-64: 1938-51, Vol. 1. Cloth Text. Palgrave Macmillan. New York, NY. 1987. 270p. ISBN:0-312-00554-7, ISBN13: 978-0-312-00554-2. Dewey:325/.31/41. LCCN:87-004272.
Audience: **u,f.** *Choice, 1988.*

Porter, A. N. & Stockwell, A. J. **JV1018 .P66**
British Imperial Policy and Decolonization, 1938-64: Nineteen Fifty-One to Nineteen Sixty-Four, Vol. 2. Cloth Text. Palgrave Macmillan. New York, NY. 1989. 424p. ISBN:0-312-02364-2, ISBN13: 978-0-312-02364-5. Dewey:325/.31/41. LCCN:87-004272.
Audience: **u,f.** *Choice, 1990.*

Porter, Andrew **JV1017**
The Oxford History of the British Empire: The Nineteenth Century. Trade Cloth. Oxford University Press, Inc. New York, NY. 1999. 796p. Oxford History of the British Empire Ser., Vol. 3 ISBN:0-19-820565-1, ISBN13: 978-0-19-820565-4. Dewey:325.3/41/09034.
Audience: **u,f.**

Porter, Bernard **DA16.P67 2004**
The Lion's Share: A Short History of British Imperialism, 1850-2004. Ed. 4. Trade Paper. Longman Publishing Group. White Plains, NY. 2004. 496p. ISBN:0-582-77252-4, ISBN13: 978-0-582-77252-6. Dewey:909/.0971241. LCCN:2004-040108.
Audience: **g,l,u,f.**

Rotberg, Robert I. **DT776.R4R66 1988**
The Founder: Cecil Rhodes and the Pursuit of Power. Cloth Text. Oxford University Press, Inc. New York, NY. 1988. 854p. ISBN:0-19-504968-3, ISBN13: 978-0-19-504968-8. Dewey:968.04/092/4. LCCN:88-005960.
Audience: **u,f.** *Choice, 1989.*

Streets, Heather **DA68**
Martial Races: The Military, Race, and Masculinity in British Imperial Culture, 1857-1914. Manchester; New York: Manchester University Press. 2004. ISBN:0-7190-6962-9, ISBN13: 978-0-7190-6962-8.
Audience: **u,f.**

Thornton, A. P. **DA16**
The Imperial Idea and Its Enemies: A Study in British Power. Paper Text. Textbook Publishers. Temecula, CA. 2003. xiv, 370p. ISBN:0-7581-8832-3, ISBN13: 978-0-7581-8832-8. Dewey:325/.32/0941.
Audience: **g,l,u,f.**

Britain > English History > Special Topics > Decolonization

Douglas, Roy **DA16.D68 2002**
Liquidation of Empire: The Decline of the British Empire. Cloth over Boards. Palgrave Macmillan. New York, NY. 2002. 190p. ISBN:0-333-80454-6, ISBN13: 978-0-333-80454-4. Dewey:909/.09712410825. LCCN:2002-019599.
Audience: **u,f.** *Choice, 2003.*

James, Lawrence **DA16.J26 1996**
The Rise and Fall of the British Empire. Trade Cloth. St. Martin's Press. Gordonville, VA. 1995. 720p. ISBN:0-312-14039-8, ISBN13: 978-0-312-14039-7. Dewey:909/.0971241. LCCN:95-038774.
Audience: **g,u,f.**

Thompson, Andrew **JV1011.T46 2005**
Empire Strikes Back: The Impact of Imperialism on Britain from the Mid-Nineteenth Century. Trade Paper. Longman Publishing Group. White Plains, NY. 2005. 392p. ISBN:0-582-43829-2, ISBN13: 978-0-582-43829-3. Dewey:941.08. LCCN:2004-060192.
Audience: **u,f.**

Britain > English History > Local History

Beresford, M. W. **DA610 .B4**
Medieval England, an Aerial Survey. Paper Text. Textbook Publishers. Temecula, CA. 2003. xiii, 274p. ISBN:0-7581-1233-5, ISBN13: 978-0-7581-1233-0. Dewey:942.
Audience: **g,l,u,f.**

Clark, Peter **DA670.K3.C494 1977**
English Provincial Society from the Reformation to the Revolution: Religion, Politics and Society in Kent, 1500-1640. Trade Cloth. Fairleigh Dickinson University Press. Cranbury, NJ. 1978. xiii, 504p. ISBN:0-8386-2075-2, ISBN13: 978-0-8386-2075-5. Dewey:942.2/3/05. LCCN:76-053900.
Audience: **u,f.**

Cobbett, William **DA625.C654 1932**
Rural Rides. London, J.M. Dent & Sons, Ltd.; New York, E.P. Dutton & Co., Inc. 1932.
Audience: **g,l,u,f.**

Darby, H. C. & Versey, G. R. **HD604**
Domesday Gazetteer. Trade Cloth. Cambridge University Press. New York, NY. 1975. 552p. Domesday Geography of England Ser. ISBN:0-521-20666-9, ISBN13: 978-0-521-20666-2. Dewey:333.3/22/0942. LCCN:75-019532.
Audience: **g,l,u,f.**

Darby, H. C. (Henry Clifford) **DA600.D35**
A New Historical Geography of England. Cambridge; New York: Cambridge University Press. 1973. ISBN:0-521-20116-0, ISBN13: 978-0-521-20116-2.
Audience: **g,l,u,f.**

Defoe, Daniel **DA620.D31 1928**
A Tour Through England and Wales; Divided into Circuits or Journies. London, J.M. Dent; New York, E.P. Dutton. 1928. Everyman's Library: Travel and Topography
Audience: **g,l,u,f.**

Ekwall, Eilert **DA645.E38**
The Concise Oxford Dictionary of English Place-Names. Oxford: Clarendon Press. 1987.
Audience: **g,l,u,f.**

Hoskins, W.G. **DA600.H6 1970**
Making of the English Landscape. Trade Paper. Penguin Group (USA) Inc. New York, NY. 1970. 328p. ISBN:0-14-021035-0, ISBN13: 978-0-14-021035-4. Dewey:911/.42. LCCN:77-021107.
Audience: **g,l,u,f.**

Merrifield, Ralph **DA677.1.M46 1983**
London: City of the Romans. Trade Cloth. University of California Press. Berkeley, CA. 1983. 288p. ISBN:0-520-04922-5, ISBN13: 978-0-520-04922-2. Dewey:936.2/1204. LCCN:82-040412.
Audience: **u,f.**

Myers, A. R. **DA680**
London in the Age of Chaucer. Trade Paper. University of Oklahoma Press. Norman, OK. 1988. 248p. Centers of Civilization Ser., Vol. 31 ISBN:0-8061-2111-4, ISBN13: 978-0-8061-2111-6. Dewey:942.103/7. LCCN:73-177342.
Audience: **g,l,u,f.** B

Priestley, J. B. **DA630.P7 1984**
English Journey: Jubilee Edition. Trade Cloth. University of Chicago Press. Chicago, IL. 1997. 320p. ISBN:0-226-68212-9, ISBN13: 978-0-226-68212-9. Dewey:914.20483. LCCN:83-040619.
Audience: **g,l,u,f.**

Rowse, A. L. **DA670.C8**
Tudor Cornwall. Trade Cloth. Dyllansow Truran. Truro, 1989. 462p. ISBN:1-85022-058-1, ISBN13: 978-1-85022-058-9. Dewey:942.3705.
Audience: **g,l,u,f.**

Rude, George **DA682.R8**
Hanoverian London, Seventeen Fourteen to Eighteen Eight. Trade Cloth. University of California Press. Berkeley, CA. 1971. xvi, 271p. History of London Ser. ISBN:0-520-01778-1,

ISBN13: 978-0-520-01778-8. Dewey:914.21/03/7. LCCN:69-010590.
Audience: **u,f.**

Stow, John **DA680.S87x**
Survey of London. Wheatley, H. B. (Introduction by). London: Dent; New York: Dutton. 1965.
Audience: **l,u.**

Thompson, Flora **S522.G7**
Lark Rise to Candleford: A Trilogy. Julie Neild (Illustrator), H. J. Massingham (Introduction by). Trade Cloth. Oxford University Press, Inc. New York, NY. 1980. 576p. ISBN:0-19-211759-9, ISBN13: 978-0-19-211759-5. Dewey:942.5/7081/0924.
Audience: **u,f.**

Wordsworth, William **DA670**
Guide Through the District of the Lakes in the North of England: With a Description of the Scenery for the Use of Tourists and Residents. Trade Cloth. Greenwood Publishing Group, Inc. Portsmouth, NH. 1969. 174p. ISBN:0-8371-0764-4, ISBN13: 978-0-8371-0764-6. Dewey:914.28. LCCN:68-055639.
Audience: **g,l,u,f.**

Britain > English History > Cultural Life

DA688.B65 1975
The Bloomsbury Group: A Collection of Memoirs, Commentary, and Criticism. Trade Cloth. University of Toronto Press. Toronto, ON. 1975. xxi, 444p. ISBN:0-8020-2182-4, ISBN13: 978-0-8020-2182-3. Dewey:942.1/082. LCCN:75-331714.
Audience: **l,u,f.**

Annan, Noel Gilroy, et al. **DA566.4**
Our Age: Portrait of a Generation. Annan, Baron (Author). London: Weidenfeld and Nicolson. 1990. ISBN:0-297-81129-0, ISBN13: 978-0-297-81129-9.
Audience: **g,l,u,f.**

Brown, Lucy M. **PN5117.B76 1985**
Victorian News and Newspapers. Trade Cloth. Oxford University Press, Inc. New York, NY. 1985. 300p. ISBN:0-19-822624-1, ISBN13: 978-0-19-822624-6. Dewey:072. LCCN:86-142738.
Audience: **u,f.** *Choice, 1986.*

Buckley, Jerome H. **PR461.B75 1969**
Victorian Temper: A Study in Literary Culture. Trade Cloth. Harvard University Press. Cambridge, MA. 1969. x, 282p. ISBN:0-674-93680-9, ISBN13: 978-0-674-93680-5. Dewey:820.9/009/8. LCCN:74-089967.
Audience: **u,f.**

Burns, J. H. (Editor) **JA81.C283 1990**
The Cambridge History of Political Thought, 1450-1700. Mark Goldie (As told to). Trade Cloth. Cambridge University Press. New York, NY. 1991. 810p. The Cambridge History of Political Thought Ser. ISBN:0-521-24716-0, ISBN13: 978-0-521-24716-0. Dewey:320/.09. LCCN:89-022282.
Audience: **u,f.**

Butler, Marilyn **PR457**
Romantics, Rebels and Reactionaries: English Literature and Its Background, 1760-1830. Paper Text. Oxford University Press, Inc. New York, NY. 1985. 220p. Opus Ser. ISBN:0-19-289132-4, ISBN13: 978-0-19-289132-7. Dewey:820.9/145. LCCN:80-042404.
Audience: **u,f.**

Cannon, John **HT653.G7 1987**
Aristocratic Century: The Peerage of Eighteenth-Century England. Trade Paper. Cambridge University Press. New York, NY. 1987. 204p. ISBN:0-521-33566-3, ISBN13: 978-0-521-33566-9. Dewey:305.5/2/0942/09033. LCCN:84-007721.
Audience: **u,f.**

Chesterfield, Philip Dormer Stanhope, Earl of **DA501.C5**
The Letters of Philip Dormer Stanhope, 4th Earl of Chesterfield. Dobrée, Bonamy (Editor). London, Eyre & Spottiswoode; New York, Viking Press. 1932.
Audience: **u,f.**

Clark, G. Kitson **DA533**
The Making of Victorian England. Trade Paper. Simon & Schuster. New York, NY. 1972. ISBN:0-689-70049-0, ISBN13: 978-0-689-70049-1. Dewey:942. LCCN:62-051827.
Audience: **g,u,f.** B

Clark, J. C. **JN175.C58 1985**
English Society, 1688-1832: Ideology, Social Structure and Political Practice During the Ancien Regime. Cloth Text. Cambridge University Press. New York, NY. 1985. 449p. Cambridge Studies in the History and Theory of Politics ISBN:0-521-30922-0, ISBN13: 978-0-521-30922-6. Dewey:320.941. LCCN:85-010995.
Audience: **l,u,f.** *Choice, 1986.*

Collini, Stefan **DA550.C62 1993**
Public Moralists: Political Thought and Intellectual Life in Britain, 1850-1930. Paper Text. Oxford University Press, Inc. New York, NY. 1993. 388p. ISBN:0-19-820422-1, ISBN13: 978-0-19-820422-0. Dewey:941.08. LCCN:92-041294.
Audience: **g,l,u,f.** *Choice, 1992.*

Collini, Stefan, et al. **JA84.G7**
That Noble Science of Politics: A Study in Nineteenth-Century Intellectual History. John Burrow & Donald Winch (Authors). Trade Paper. Cambridge University Press. New York, NY. 1983. 400p. ISBN:0-521-27770-1, ISBN13: 978-0-521-27770-9. Dewey:320/.0941. LCCN:83-007697.
Audience: **u,f.**

Cressy, David **LC156.G7**
Literacy and the Social Order: Reading and Writing in Tudor and Stuart England. Cloth Text. Cambridge University Press. New York, NY. 1980. 256p. ISBN:0-521-22514-0, ISBN13: 978-0-521-22514-4. Dewey:302.2/0942. LCCN:79-041767.
Audience: **l,u,f.**

Ehrlich, Cyril **ML652.E4 1990**
The Piano: A History. Ed. 2. Trade Cloth. Oxford University Press, Inc. New York, NY. 1990. 272p. ISBN:0-19-816181-6, ISBN13: 978-0-19-816181-3. Dewey:786.2/1/09. LCCN:89-023161.
Audience: **g,l,u,f.** *Choice, 1990.*

Ford, Boris (Editor) **NX543**
The Cambridge Guide to the Arts in Britain: The Augustan Age. Trade Cloth. Cambridge University Press. New York, NY. 1991. 384p. The Cambridge Guide to the Arts in Britain Ser., Vol. 5 ISBN:0-521-30978-6, ISBN13: 978-0-521-30978-3. Dewey:700.941.
Audience: **u,f.**

Ford, Boris (Editor) **NX543.A1**
The Cambridge Guide to the Arts in Britain: The Seventeenth Century. Trade Cloth. Cambridge University Press. New York, NY. 1990. 368p. The Cambridge Guide to the Arts in Britain Ser., Vol. 4 ISBN:0-521-30977-8, ISBN13: 978-0-521-30977-6. Dewey:700/.941.
Audience: **u,f.** *Choice, 1991.*

Ford, Boris (Editor) **NX543.A1**
The Cambridge Guide to the Arts in Britain: Renaissance and Reformation. Trade Cloth. Cambridge University Press. New York, NY. 1989. 368p. The Cambridge Guide to the Arts in Britain Ser. ISBN:0-521-30976-X, ISBN13: 978-0-521-30976-9. Dewey:700/.941.
Audience: **u,f.** *Choice, 1991.*

Gadd, David **DA688.G23 1975**
The Loving Friends: A Portrait of Bloomsbury. Trade Cloth. Harcourt College Publishers. Fort Worth, TX. 1975. xii, 210p. ISBN:0-15-154740-8, ISBN13: 978-0-15-154740-1. Dewey:700/.92/2. LCCN:74-026596.
Audience: **l,u,f.**

Gillett, Paula **ND467.5.V52G55 1990**
Worlds of Art: Painters in Victorian Society. Cloth Text. Rutgers University Press. Piscataway, NJ. 1989. 275p. ISBN:0-8135-1459-2, ISBN13: 978-0-8135-1459-8. Dewey:759.2. LCCN:89-030373.
Audience: **g,l,u,f.** *Choice, 1990.*

Goodwin, Albert **DA520.G6 1979**
The Friends of Liberty: The English Democratic Movement in the Age of the French Revolution. Trade Cloth. Harvard University Press. Cambridge, MA. 1979. 594p. ISBN:0-674-32339-4, ISBN13: 978-0-674-32339-1. Dewey:320.9/41/073. LCCN:78-015673.
Audience: **g,l,u,f.**

Greenblatt, Stephen **PR421**
Renaissance Self-Fashioning: From More to Shakespeare. Library Binding. University of Chicago Press. Chicago, IL. 1980. 272p. ISBN:0-226-30653-4, ISBN13: 978-0-226-30653-7. Dewey:820.9/384. LCCN:80-013837.
Audience: **u,f.**

Gross, John **PR63.G7 1992**
The Rise and Fall of the Man of Letters: English Literary Life since 1800. Trade Paper. Ivan R. Dee Publisher. Blue Ridge Summit, PA. 1992. 372p. ISBN:1-56663-000-2, ISBN13: 978-1-56663-000-9. Dewey:820.9. LCCN:92-016011.
Audience: **u,f.**

Heyck, T. W. **DA533.H48 1982**
The Transformation of Intellectual Life in Victorian England. Cloth Text. Palgrave Macmillan. New York, NY. 1982. 262p. ISBN:0-312-81427-5, ISBN13: 978-0-312-81427-4. Dewey:942.081. LCCN:82-000840.
Audience: **g,l,u,f.** BCL3

Hill, Christopher **DA380**
A World Turned Upside Down: Radical Ideas During the English Revolution. Trade Paper. Penguin Group (USA) Inc. New York, NY. 1984. 432p. ISBN:0-14-013732-7, ISBN13: 978-0-14-013732-3. Dewey:322.42094209032.
Audience: **g,l,u,f.**

Himmelfarb, Gertrude **DA533.H55 1995**
Victorian Minds. Trade Paper. Ivan R. Dee Publisher. Blue Ridge Summit, PA. 1995. 420p. ISBN:1-56663-077-0, ISBN13: 978-1-56663-077-1. Dewey:941.07. LCCN:94-043053.
Audience: **l,u.**

Hoggart, Richard **DA566.4.H54 1998**
The Uses of Literacy. Trade Paper. Transaction Publishers. Somerset, NJ. 1998. 320p. Classics in Communication and Mass Culture Ser. ISBN:0-7658-0421-2, ISBN13: 978-0-7658-0421-1. Dewey:302.2/3/08623/0942. LCCN:97-013291.
Audience: **l,u,f.**

Honey, J. R. **LA631.7.H64 1977**
Tom Brown's Universe: The Development of the English Public School of the 19th Century. Trade Cloth. Crown Publishing Group. New York, NY. 1978. ISBN:0-8129-0689-6, ISBN13: 978-0-8129-0689-9. Dewey:370/.942. LCCN:76-056585.
Audience: **g,u,f.**

Houghton, Walter Edwards **DA533**
The Victorian Frame of Mind 1830-1870. Paper Text. Textbook Publishers. Temecula, CA. 2003. 467p. ISBN:0-7581-5322-8, ISBN13: 978-0-7581-5322-7. Dewey:942.081.
Audience: **u,f.**

Houghton, Walter Edwards **DA533**
The Victorian Frame of Mind, 1830-1870. New Haven : Published for Wellesley College by Yale University Press. 1985. ISBN:0-300-00122-3, ISBN13: 978-0-300-00122-8.
Audience: **u,f.**

Houston, Rab A. **LC156.G7**
Scottish Literacy and the Scottish Identity: Illiteracy and Society in Scotland and Northern England, 1600-1800. Trade Cloth. Cambridge University Press. New York, NY. 1985. 336p. Cambridge Studies in Population, Economy and Society in Past Time, No. 4 ISBN:0-521-26598-3, ISBN13: 978-0-521-26598-0. Dewey:302.2/0941. LCCN:85-007800.
Audience: **l,u,f.**

Jarrett, Derek **DA485**
England in the Age of Hogarth. Cloth over Boards. Yale University Press. Cumberland, RI. 1986. 213p. ISBN:0-300-03608-6, ISBN13: 978-0-300-03608-4. Dewey:942.07. LCCN:85-052071.
Audience: **g,l,u,f.**

Jenkyns, Richard **DA550 .J46**
The Victorians and Ancient Greece. Trade Cloth. Harvard University Press. Cambridge, MA. 1990. 398p. ISBN:0-674-93686-8, ISBN13: 978-0-674-93686-7. Dewey:941.081. LCCN:79-025487.
Audience: **u,f.**

Langford, Paul **DA480**
A Polite and Commercial People: England, 1727-1783. Trade Cloth. Oxford University Press, Inc. New York, NY. 1998. 824p.

ISBN:0-19-820733-6, ISBN13: 978-0-19-820733-7. Dewey:942/.07. LCCN:91-031628.
Audience: **u,f.**

Martin, Julian **B1198.M36 1992**
Francis Bacon, the State and the Reform of Natural Philosophy. Trade Cloth. Cambridge University Press. New York, NY. 1991. 250p. ISBN:0-521-38249-1, ISBN13: 978-0-521-38249-6. Dewey:192. LCCN:90-024242.
Audience: **u,f.**

McKendrick, Neil, et al. **HC257.E5.M37 1982**
The Birth of a Consumer Society: The Commercialization of Eighteenth-Century England. John Brewer & John H. Plumb (Authors). Trade Cloth. Indiana University Press. Bloomington, IN. 1982. 345p. ISBN:0-253-31205-1, ISBN13: 978-0-253-31205-1. Dewey:306/.3. LCCN:82-047953.
Audience: **g,l,u,f.**

Montagu, Lady Mary Wortley **DA501.M7**
The Complete Letters of Lady Mary Wortley Montagu. Robert Halsband (Editor). Other. Oxford University Press, Inc. New York, NY. ISBN:0-318-54813-5, ISBN13: 978-0-318-54813-5. Dewey:826/.5.
Audience: **g,l,u,f.**

Oppenheim, Janet **BF1242.G7 O66 1985**
The Other World: Spiritualism and Psychical Research in England, 1850-1914. Trade Paper. Cambridge University Press. New York, NY. 1988. 518p. ISBN:0-521-34767-X, ISBN13: 978-0-521-34767-9. Dewey:133.9/0942.
Audience: **g,l,u,f.** *Choice, 1985.*

Passmore, John **B803**
A Hundred Years of Philosophy. Ed. 2. Trade Paper. Penguin Group (USA) Inc. New York, NY. 1978. 640p. ISBN:0-14-020927-1, ISBN13: 978-0-14-020927-3. Dewey:190/.9/034.
Audience: **l,u.**

Paulson, Ronald **N6766.P38 1975B**
Emblem and Expression: Meaning in English Art of the Eighteenth Century. Trade Cloth. Harvard University Press. Cambridge, MA. 1975. 288p. ISBN:0-674-24778-7, ISBN13: 978-0-674-24778-9. Dewey:700/.942. LCCN:74-031988.
Audience: **u,f.**

Phillipson, N. T. (Nicholas T.) **DA30.H93**
Hume. New York: St. Martin's Press. 1989. Historians on Historians Ser. ISBN:0-312-03076-2, ISBN13: 978-0-312-03076-6.
Audience: **g,l,u,f.**

Reay, Barry (Editor) **DA380.P67 1985**
Popular Culture in Seventeenth Century England. Cloth Text. Palgrave Macmillan. New York, NY. 1985. 319p. ISBN:0-312-63036-0, ISBN13: 978-0-312-63036-2. Dewey:306/.4/0942. LCCN:85-002496.
Audience: **g,l,u,f.** *Choice, 1985.*

Robson, John M. **JC223.M66**
Improvement of Mankind: The Social and Political Thought of John Stuart Mill. Trade Cloth. University of Toronto Press. Toronto, ON. 1968. ISBN:0-8020-1529-8, ISBN13: 978-0-8020-1529-7. Dewey:300/.924. LCCN:68-140051.
Audience: **u,f.**

Rothblatt, Sheldon **LF118**
The Revolution of the Dons: Cambridge and Society in Victorian England. Trade Cloth. Cambridge University Press. New York, NY. 1981. 328p. ISBN:0-521-23958-3, ISBN13: 978-0-521-23958-5. Dewey:378.426/59. LCCN:80-041865.
Audience: **u,f.**

Schwartz, Richard B. **DA682**
Daily Life in Johnson's London. Trade Paper. University of Wisconsin Press. Chicago, IL. 1983. 216p. ISBN:0-299-09494-4, ISBN13: 978-0-299-09494-2. Dewey:942.107. LCCN:83-050080.
Audience: **u,f.**

Semple, Janet **HV8978.F7**
Bentham's Prison: A Study of the Panopticon Penitentiary. Trade Cloth. Oxford University Press, Inc. New York, NY. 1993. 354p. ISBN:0-19-827387-8, ISBN13: 978-0-19-827387-5. Dewey:365.92. LCCN:92-041295.
Audience: **u,f.** *Choice, 1994.*

Shellabarger, Samuel **DA501.C5 S52**
Lord Chesterfield and His World. Trade Cloth. Biblo & Tannen Booksellers & Publishers, Inc. Cheshire, CT. 1971. ISBN:0-8196-0271-X, ISBN13: 978-0-8196-0271-8. Dewey:942.07/1/0924. LCCN:72-156737.
Audience: **u,f.**

Soffer, Reba N. **H53.G7**
Ethics and Society in England: The Revolution in the Social Sciences, 1870-1914. Trade Cloth. University of California Press. Berkeley, CA. 1978. 304p. ISBN:0-520-03521-6, ISBN13: 978-0-520-03521-8. Dewey:300/.1/8. LCCN:77-079239.
Audience: **l,u,f.**

Somervell, D. C. (David Churchill) **DA533**
English Thought in the Nineteenth Century. Westport, Conn.: Greenwood Press. 1977. ISBN:0-8371-9793-7, ISBN13: 978-0-8371-9793-7.
Audience: **l,u,f.**

Spufford, Margaret **PR963**
Small Books and Pleasant Histories: Popular Fiction and Its Readership in Seventeenth-Century England. Lyndal Roper (Contribution by). Trade Paper. Cambridge University Press. New York, NY. 1985. 296p. Past and Present Publications ISBN:0-521-31218-3, ISBN13: 978-0-521-31218-9. Dewey:302.2/32.
Audience: **u,f.**

Strachey, Lytton **PR6037.T73N67 2005**
Eminent Victorians Definitive Edition. Trade Paper. Continuum International Publishing Group, Ltd. London, 2005. 424p. ISBN:0-8264-7618-X, ISBN13: 978-0-8264-7618-0. Dewey:941.0810922. LCCN:2004-266934.
Audience: **g,l,u,f.**

Turner, Frank M. **DA533**
The Greek Heritage in Victorian Britain. Trade Cloth. Yale University Press. Cumberland, RI. 1981. 475p. ISBN:0-300-02480-0, ISBN13: 978-0-300-02480-7. Dewey:941.08. LCCN:80-024013.
Audience: **u,f.**

Vincent, David **LC156.G72E58 1989**
Literacy and Popular Culture: England, 1750-1914. Peter Burke & Ruth Finnegan (Contribution by). Trade Paper. Cambridge

University Press. New York, NY. 1993. 374p. Studies in Oral and Literate Culture, No. 19 ISBN:0-521-45771-8, ISBN13: 978-0-521-45771-2. Dewey:302.2/244/0942/09034.
Audience: **g,l,u,f.** *Choice, 1990.*

Walpole, Horace **DA483.W2**
Correspondence: Yale Edition of Horace Walpole's Correspondence. Lewis, W. S. (Wilmarth Sheldon) (Editor). New Haven: Yale University Press. 1937. ISBN:0-300-02717-6, ISBN13: 978-0-300-02717-4.
Audience: **l,u,f.**

Walpole, Horace **DA506.W2**
Selected Letters of Horace Walpole. W. S. Lewis (Editor). Trade Cloth. Yale University Press. Cumberland, RI. 1973. 344p. ISBN:0-300-01643-3, ISBN13: 978-0-300-01643-7. Dewey:826/.6. LCCN:72-091300.
Audience: **u,f.**

Watt, Ian P. **PR851**
The Rise of the Novel. W. B. Carnochan (Foreword by). Trade Paper. University of California Press. Berkeley, CA. 2001. 339p. ISBN:0-520-23069-8, ISBN13: 978-0-520-23069-9. Dewey:823.509.
Audience: **g,l,u,f.**

Watt, Tessa **PR428.C48W38 1994**
Cheap Print and Popular Piety, 1550-1640. Anthony Fletcher, John Guy & John Morrill (Contribution by). Trade Paper. Cambridge University Press. New York, NY. 1993. 390p. Cambridge Studies in Early Modern British History ISBN:0-521-45827-7, ISBN13: 978-0-521-45827-6. Dewey:820.9/382/09031.
Audience: **l,u,f.** *Choice, 1992.*

Westfall, Richard S. **QC16.E5**
Never at Rest: A Biography of Isaac Newton. Trade Paper. Cambridge University Press. New York, NY. 1983. 928p. ISBN:0-521-27435-4, ISBN13: 978-0-521-27435-7. Dewey:530/.092. LCCN:79-026294.
Audience: **g.** B

Wiener, Martin J. **HN385**
English Culture and the Decline of the Industrial Spirit, 1850-1980. Trade Cloth. Cambridge University Press. New York, NY. 1981. 250p. ISBN:0-521-23418-2, ISBN13: 978-0-521-23418-4. Dewey:306.3/4/0942/0904. LCCN:80-022684.
Audience: **l,u,f.**

Williams, Raymond **DA533.W6 1983**
Culture and Society, 1780-1950. Ed. 2. Trade Cloth. Columbia University Press. New York, NY. 1983. 363p. A Morningside Bk. ISBN:0-231-02287-5, ISBN13: 978-0-231-02287-3. Dewey:306/.4/0941. LCCN:85-005195.
Audience: **g,u,f.** B

Williams, Raymond **DA566**
The Long Revolution. Trade Cloth. Greenwood Publishing Group, Inc. Portsmouth, NH. 1975. 369p. ISBN:0-8371-8244-1, ISBN13: 978-0-8371-8244-5. Dewey:941.082. LCCN:75-016613.
Audience: **l,u.**

Young, G. M. (George Malcolm) **DA550**
Portrait of an Age: Victorian England. Ed. 2. London: Phoenix. 2002. ISBN:1-84212-598-2, ISBN13: 978-1-84212-598-4.
Audience: **g,l,u,f.**

Britain > English History > Class

Amussen, Susan D. **HQ615.A49 1988**
An Ordered Society: Family and Village in England, 1560-1725. Cloth Text. Blackwell Publishing, Inc. Malden, MA. 1988. 256p. ISBN:0-631-15521-X, ISBN13: 978-0-631-15521-8. Dewey:306.8/5/0942. LCCN:87-025952.
Audience: **u,f.** *Choice, 1988.*

Bailey, Peter **GV75.B33 1987**
Leisure and Class in Victorian England: Rational Recreation and the Contest for Control, 1830-1885. Trade Paper. Routledge. New York, NY. 1987. 288p. ISBN:0-416-02142-5, ISBN13: 978-0-416-02142-4. Dewey:790/.0941. LCCN:87-005467.
Audience: **l,u,f.**

Belchem, John **DA536.H75**
Orator Hunt: Henry Hunt and English Working-Class Radicalism. Trade Cloth. Oxford University Press, Inc. New York, NY. 1985. 320p. ISBN:0-19-822759-0, ISBN13: 978-0-19-822759-5. Dewey:322.4/4/0924.
Audience: **u,f.** *Choice, 1986.*

Cannadine, David **HT653.G7C358 1990**
The Decline and Fall of the British Aristocracy. Trade Cloth. Yale University Press. Cumberland, RI. 1990. 832p. ISBN:0-300-04761-4, ISBN13: 978-0-300-04761-5. Dewey:305.5/2/0941. LCCN:90-012303.
Audience: **l,u,f.** *Choice, 1991.*

Davidoff, Leonore & Hall, Catherine **HT690.G7D38 1987**
Family Fortunes: Men and Women of the English Middle Class, 1780-1850. Trade Cloth. University of Chicago Press. Chicago, IL. 1987. 576p. Women in Culture and Society Ser. ISBN:0-226-13732-5, ISBN13: 978-0-226-13732-2. Dewey:305.5/5/094209033. LCCN:86-030874.
Audience: **l,u,f.** *Choice, 1988.*

Earle, Peter **HT690.G7E27 1989**
The Making of the English Middle Class: Business, Society and Family Life in London 1660-1730. Trade Cloth. University of California Press. Berkeley, CA. 1989. xiii, 446p. ISBN:0-520-06826-2, ISBN13: 978-0-520-06826-1. Dewey:305.5/5/0942109032. LCCN:89-004976.
Audience: **g,l,u,f.** *Choice, 1990.*

Gash, Norman **DA535**
Aristocracy and People: Britain, 1815-1865. Trade Paper. Harvard University Press. Cambridge, MA. 1981. 383p. New History of England Ser. ISBN:0-674-04491-6, ISBN13: 978-0-674-04491-3. Dewey:309.1/41/07.
Audience: **u,f.**

Girouard, Mark **NA7620**
The Victorian Country House. Trade Cloth. Yale University Press. Cumberland, RI. 1979. 448p. ISBN:0-300-02390-1, ISBN13: 978-0-300-02390-9. Dewey:728.8/3/0942. LCCN:79-064077.
Audience: **g,l,u,f.**

Hill, Christopher **DA375**
The Century of Revolution, 1603-1714. Ed. 2. Trade Paper. W. W. Norton & Company, Inc. New York, NY. 1982. 304p. ISBN:0-393-30016-1, ISBN13: 978-0-393-30016-1. Dewey:942.06.
Audience: **g,l,u,f.**

Hill, Christopher **DA375.H54 1985**
The Collected Essays of Christopher Hill: Writing and Revolution in Seventeenth-Century England, Vol. 1. Cloth Text. University of Massachusetts Press. Amherst, MA. 1985. 352p. ISBN:0-87023-467-6, ISBN13: 978-0-87023-467-5. Dewey:082. LCCN:84-016446.
Audience: **u,f.** *Choice, 1985.*

Hobsbawm, E. J. (Eric John), et al. **HD1534**
Captain Swing. Rudé, George F. E. (Author). London: Phoenix. 2001. ISBN:1-84212-235-5, ISBN13: 978-1-84212-235-8.
Audience: **u,f.**

Jones, Gareth Stedman **HC110.P6**
Outcast London: A Study in the Relationship Between Classes in Victorian Society. Trade Paper. Knopf Publishing Group. New York, NY. 1984. ISBN:0-394-72547-6, ISBN13: 978-0-394-72547-5. Dewey:301.44/1.
Audience: **u,f.**

Mandler, Peter **DA550.M34 1990**
Aristocratic Government in the Age of Reform: Whigs and Liberals, 1830-1852. Trade Cloth. Oxford University Press, Inc. New York, NY. 1990. 320p. ISBN:0-19-821781-1, ISBN13: 978-0-19-821781-7. Dewey:320.941/09/034. LCCN:89-026535.
Audience: **u,f.**

McCalman, Iain **HN400.R3**
Radical Underworld: Prophets, Revolutionaries and Pornographers in London, 1795-1840. Paper Text. Oxford University Press, Inc. New York, NY. 1993. 358p. ISBN:0-19-812286-1, ISBN13: 978-0-19-812286-9. Dewey:320.9421. LCCN:87-011770.
Audience: **g,l,u,f.** *Choice, 1988.*

Meacham, Standish **HD8386.M4 1977**
A Life Apart: The English Working Class, 1890-1914. Trade Cloth. Harvard University Press. Cambridge, MA. 1977. 320p. ISBN:0-674-53075-6, ISBN13: 978-0-674-53075-1. Dewey:301.44/42/0942. LCCN:77-072673.
Audience: **u,f.**

Miles, Dudley H. **HN400.R3P576 1988**
Francis Place, 1771-1854: The Life of a Remarkable Radical. Cloth Text. Palgrave Macmillan. New York, NY. 1988. 256p. ISBN:0-312-01953-X, ISBN13: 978-0-312-01953-2. Dewey:363.9/6/0941. LCCN:87-035324.
Audience: **u,f.** *Choice, 1988.*

Morris, R. J. **HN400.S6**
Class and Class Consciousness in the Industrial Revolution, 1780-1850. Paper Text. Brill Academic Publishers, Inc. Boston, MA. 1979. 80p. Studies in Economic and Social History ISBN:0-333-15454-1, ISBN13: 978-0-333-15454-0. Dewey:301.44/0941.
Audience: **u,f.**

Morris, R. J. **HT690.G7M67 1990**
Class, Sect and Party: The Making of the British Middle Class, Leeds, 1820-1850. Cloth Text. Manchester University Press. Manchester, 1990. ISBN:0-7190-2225-8, ISBN13: 978-0-7190-2225-8. Dewey:305.5/5/094281909034. LCCN:89-039337.
Audience: **u,f.**

Reader, W. J. (William Joseph) **HT687**
Professional Men: The Rise of the Professional Classes in Nineteenth-Century England. New York, Basic Books. 1966.
Audience: **g,l,u,f.**

Reid, Alastair J. **HN400.S6 R45 1995**
Social Classes and Social Relations in Britain, 1850-1914. Cloth Text. Cambridge University Press. New York, NY. 1995. 82p. New Studies in Economic and Social History, No. 19 ISBN:0-521-55278-8, ISBN13: 978-0-521-55278-3. Dewey:305.5/0941. LCCN:95-017013.
Audience: **u,f.**

Roberts, Elizabeth **HQ1599.E5R62 1984**
A Woman's Place: An Oral History of Working Class Women, 1890-1940. Trade Cloth. Blackwell Publishing, Inc. Malden, MA. 1984. 272p. ISBN:0-631-13572-3, ISBN13: 978-0-631-13572-2. Dewey:305.4/2/0942. LCCN:84-016785.
Audience: **u,f.** *Choice, 1985.*

Spater, George **PR3325**
William Cobbett: The Poor Man's Friend. Trade Cloth. Cambridge University Press. New York, NY. 1982. 653p. ISBN:0-521-24538-9, ISBN13: 978-0-521-24538-8. Dewey:828/.608. LCCN:81-003859.
Audience: **g,l,u,f.**

Stedman-Jones, Gareth **HD8390 .J8 1983**
Languages of Class: Studies in English Working Class History 1832-1982. Cloth Text. Cambridge University Press. New York, NY. 1984. 268p. ISBN:0-521-25648-8, ISBN13: 978-0-521-25648-3. Dewey:305.5/62/0942. LCCN:83-007721.
Audience: **u,f.**

Stone, Lawrence **DA356**
The Crisis of the Aristocracy, 1558 to 1641. Trade Cloth. Oxford University Press, Inc. New York, NY. 1965. 378p. ISBN:0-19-821314-X, ISBN13: 978-0-19-821314-7. Dewey:914.2.
Audience: **u,f.**

Stone, Lawrence **DA356**
Family and Fortune: Studies in Aristocratic Finance in the Sixteenth and Seventeenth Centuries. Trade Cloth. Oxford University Press, Inc. New York, NY. 1973. xviii, 315p. ISBN:0-19-822401-X, ISBN13: 978-0-19-822401-3. Dewey:332/.024/0942. LCCN:73-175161.
Audience: **u,f.**

Thompson, E. P. **HD8389**
The Making of the English Working Class. Trade Cloth. Peter Smith Publisher, Inc. Magnolia, MA. 1999. ISBN:0-8446-6993-8, ISBN13: 978-0-8446-6993-9. Dewey:301.44/42/0942.
Audience: **l,u,f.** B

Thompson, Edward P. **HV6943.A54 1975**
Albion's Fatal Tree: Crime and Society in Eighteenth-Century England. Trade Cloth. Knopf Publishing Group. New York, NY. 1976. 352p. ISBN:0-394-47120-2, ISBN13: 978-0-394-47120-4. Dewey:364/.942. LCCN:75-023256.
Audience: **u,f.**

Thompson, Edward P. **KD7852.B55**
Whigs and Hunters. Trade Paper. Knopf Publishing Group. New York, NY. 1976. ISBN:0-394-73086-0, ISBN13: 978-0-394-73086-8. Dewey:328.42/07/78. LCCN:75-023168.
Audience: **u,f.**

Thompson, F. M. **DA550.T53 1988**
The Rise of Respectable Society: A Social History of Victorian Britain, 1830-1900. Trade Cloth. Harvard University Press. Cambridge, MA. 1988. 382p. ISBN:0-674-77285-7, ISBN13: 978-0-674-77285-4. Dewey:941.081. LCCN:88-014802.
Audience: **g,l,u,f.** *Choice, 1989.*

Thompson, F. M. L. (Francis Michael Longstreth) **HN385**
English Landed Society in the Nineteenth Century. London: Routledge & Kegan Paul; Toronto: University of Toronto Press. 1963. Studies in Social History
Audience: **l,u,f.**

Vincent, David **HD8388**
Bread, Knowledge and Freedom: A Study of Nineteenth-Century Working Class Autobiography. Trade Paper. Routledge. New York, NY. 1983. 221p. ISBN:0-416-34670-7, ISBN13: 978-0-416-34670-1. Dewey:305.5/62/0941. LCCN:82-014163.
Audience: **g,l,u,f.**

Webb, R. K. (Robert Kiefer) **HD8389**
The British Working Class Reader, 1790-1848; Literacy and Social Tension. New York: Kelley. 1971. ISBN:0-678-00578-8, ISBN13: 978-0-678-00578-1.
Audience: **u,f.**

Britain > Wales

Morgan, Kenneth O. **DA722**
Rebirth of a Nation: Wales, 1880-1980. Trade Cloth. Oxford University Press, Inc. New York, NY. 1981. 476p. History of Wales Ser., Vol. VI ISBN:0-19-821736-6, ISBN13: 978-0-19-821736-7. Dewey:942.9082. LCCN:80-040337.
Audience: **u,f.**

Morgan, Kenneth O. **DA722.M63 1991**
Wales in British Politics: 1868-1922. Ed. 4. Trade Paper. University of Wales Press. Cardiff, 1991. 360p. ISBN:0-7083-1124-5, ISBN13: 978-0-7083-1124-0. Dewey:320.9429.
Audience: **u,f.**

Britain > Wales > General

Jones, Gareth E. **DA714.J585 1984**
Modern Wales: A Concise History, C. 1485-1979. Cloth Text. Cambridge University Press. New York, NY. 1984. 376p. ISBN:0-521-24232-0, ISBN13: 978-0-521-24232-5. Dewey:942.9. LCCN:84-009590.
Audience: **u,f.**

Britain > Wales > History

Davies, R. R. **DA715.D37 1987**
Conquest, coexistence, and change: Wales, 1063-1415. Oxford: Clarendon Press; [Cardiff] : University of Wales Press. 1987. ISBN:0-19-821732-3, ISBN13: 978-0-19-821732-9.
Audience: **u,f.**

Jones, Gareth E. **DA714.J585 1984**
Modern Wales: A Concise History, C. 1485-1979. Cloth Text. Cambridge University Press. New York, NY. 1984. 376p. ISBN:0-521-24232-0, ISBN13: 978-0-521-24232-5. Dewey:942.9. LCCN:84-009590.
Audience: **u,f.**

Morgan, Kenneth O. **DA722.M62 1998**
Rebirth of a Nation: Wales 1880-1980. Trade Paper. Oxford University Press, Inc. New York, NY. 1987. 480p. Oxford History of Wales Ser., Vol. VI ISBN:0-19-821760-9, ISBN13: 978-0-19-821760-2. Dewey:942.9082. LCCN:97-034376.
Audience: **u,f.**

Thomas, David & Morgan, Prys **DA714**
Wales: The Shaping of a Nation. Trade Cloth. Trafalgar Square. North Pomfret, VT. 1984. 256p. ISBN:0-7153-8418-X, ISBN13: 978-0-7153-8418-3. Dewey:942.9. LCCN:86-109841.
Audience: **l,u.**

Williams, Gwyn A. **DA720.W496 1980; DA720 W56 1980**
The Search for Beulah Land: The Welsh and the Atlantic Revolution. New York: Holmes & Meier. 1980. ISBN:0-8419-0589-4, ISBN13: 978-0-8419-0589-4.
Audience: **u,f.**

Britain > Wales > Description and Local History

Peate, Iorwerth C. **DA725**
Tradition and Folk Life. Trade Cloth. Faber & Faber, Ltd. London, 1972. 148p. ISBN:0-571-09804-5, ISBN13: 978-0-571-09804-0. Dewey:914.29/03.
Audience: **l,u.**

Britain > Scotland > General

Houston, Rab A. **LC156.G7**
Scottish Literacy and the Scottish Identity: Illiteracy and Society in Scotland and Northern England, 1600-1800. Trade Cloth. Cambridge University Press. New York, NY. 1985. 336p. Cambridge Studies in Population, Economy and Society in Past Time, No. 4 ISBN:0-521-26598-3, ISBN13: 978-0-521-26598-0. Dewey:302.2/0941. LCCN:85-007800.
Audience: **l,u,f.**

Marshall, Rosalind K. **HQ1147.G7**
Virgins and Viragos: A History of Women in Scotland from 1080-1980. Trade Cloth. Academy Chicago Publishers, Ltd. Chicago, IL. 1983. 340p. ISBN:0-89733-075-7, ISBN13: 978-0-89733-075-6. Dewey:305.4/09411. LCCN:82-024439.
Audience: **g,l,u,f.**

Smout, T. C. **DA815**
A Century of the Scottish People: 1830-1950. Trade Cloth. Yale University Press. Cumberland, RI. 1986. 310p. ISBN:0-300-03774-0, ISBN13: 978-0-300-03774-6. Dewey:941.108.
Audience: **u,f.** *Choice, 1987.*

Smout, T. C. (Thomas Christopher) **DA772.S63 1998**
A History of the Scottish People, 1560-1830. London: Fontana. 1998. ISBN:0-00-686027-3, ISBN13: 978-0-00-686027-3.
Audience: **l,u.**

Wormald, Jennifer **DA783.41**
Court, Kirk and Community: Scotland, 1470-1625. Trade Paper. Edinburgh University Press. Edinburgh, 1991. 216p. ISBN:0-7486-0276-3, ISBN13: 978-0-7486-0276-6. Dewey:941.103.
Audience: **u,f.**

Britain > Scotland > History

Harvie, Christopher T. **DA765**
Scotland and Nationalism: Scottish Society and Politics, 1707-1977. Trade Paper. State Mutual Book & Periodical Service, Ltd. Bridgehampton, NY. 1986. 318p. ISBN:0-7855-2150-X, ISBN13: 978-0-7855-2150-1. Dewey:320.5/4/09411.
Audience: **u,f.**

Smout, T. C. **DA815**
A Century of the Scottish People: 1830-1950. Trade Cloth. Yale University Press. Cumberland, RI. 1986. 310p. ISBN:0-300-03774-0, ISBN13: 978-0-300-03774-6. Dewey:941.108.
Audience: **u,f.** *Choice, 1987.*

Britain > Scotland > History > 1603-1745. The Union and Jacobite movements

Lenman, Bruce **DA813.L4**
The Jacobite Risings in Britain, 1689-1746. Trade Cloth. Methuen Publishing Ltd. London, 1980. 320p. ISBN:0-413-39650-9, ISBN13: 978-0-413-39650-1. Dewey:941.07. LCCN:80-496548.
Audience: **u,f.**

Mitchison, Rosalind **DA800**
Lordship to Patronage: Scotland 1603-1745. Trade Paper. Hodder Education. London, 1983. 198p. ISBN:0-7131-6313-5, ISBN13: 978-0-7131-6313-1. Dewey:941.106. LCCN:83-217946.
Audience: **u,f.**

Mitchison, Rosalind **DA800**
Lordship to Patronage: Scotland 1603 - 1745. Trade Paper. Edinburgh University Press. Edinburgh, 1991. 200p. ISBN:0-7486-0233-X, ISBN13: 978-0-7486-0233-9. Dewey:941.106.
Audience: **u,f.**

Speck, William A. **DA814.5**
Butcher: The Duke of Cumberland and the Suppression of the Forty-Five. Trade Cloth. Blackwell Publishing, Inc. Malden, MA. 1983. 240p. ISBN:0-631-10501-8, ISBN13: 978-0-631-10501-5. Dewey:941.07/2. LCCN:81-169642.
Audience: **u,f.**

Britain > Scotland > History > Scottish Enlightenment

Daiches, David **DA812.D3**
The Paradox of Scottish Culture: The Eighteenth-Century Experience. London, New York, Oxford University Press. 1964. The Whidden Lectures, 1964
Audience: **u,f.**

Britain > Scotland > History > 19th and 20th Centuries

Harvie, Christopher **DA821**
No Gods and Precious Few Heroes: Scotland, 1914-1980. Trade Cloth. University of Toronto Press. Toronto, ON. 1981. 192p. New History of Scotland Ser. ISBN:0-8020-2450-5, ISBN13: 978-0-8020-2450-3. Dewey:941.1083.
Audience: **u,f.**

Britain > Scotland > History > Local History and Description

Boswell, James & Johnson, Samuel **DA880.H4.J6 1970**
Johnson's Journey to the Western Islands of Scotland and Boswell's Journal of a Tour to the Hebrides with Samuel Johnson. R. W. Chapman (Editor). Trade Paper. Oxford University Press, Inc. New York, NY. 1970. 494p. Oxford Standard Authors Ser. ISBN:0-19-281072-3, ISBN13: 978-0-19-281072-4. Dewey:914.11/7/047. LCCN:75-507901.
Audience: **g,l,u,f.**

Ireland. Northern Ireland.

Z2016
Royal Historical Society Bibliography.
http://www.rhs.ac.uk/bibl/
Royal Historical Society, Institute of Historical Research, University of London.
Audience: **g,l,u,f.**

Akenson, Donald Harman **JV7711.A34**
The Irish Diaspora: A Primer. Trade Paper. P. D. Meany Publishers. Lombard, IL. 1997. 319p. ISBN:0-88835-001-5, ISBN13: 978-0-88835-001-5. Dewey:304.809415.
Audience: **f.** *Choice, 1994.*

Barnard, T. C. **DA940**
The Kingdom of Ireland, 1641-1760. Trade Paper. Palgrave Macmillan. New York, NY. 2004. 216p. British History in Perspective Ser. ISBN:0-333-61077-6, ISBN13: 978-0-333-61077-0. Dewey:941.507. LCCN:2004-044501.
Audience: **g,l.** *Choice, 2005.*

Bartlett, Thomas **DA947**
Fall and Rise of the Irish Nation: The Catholic Question,1690-1830. Trade Cloth. Gill & MacMillan, Ltd. Dublin, 1992. 452p. ISBN:0-7171-1577-1, ISBN13: 978-0-7171-1577-8. Dewey:941.507.
Audience: **g,u.**

Bartlett, Thomas & Hayton, David **DA947 .P46**
Penal ERA and Golden Age: Essays in Irish History, 1690-1800. Ulster Historical Foundation Staff (Contribution by). Trade Paper. Ulster Historical Foundation. Belfast, 1979. ix, 232p. ISBN:0-901905-23-2, ISBN13: 978-0-901905-23-9. Dewey:941.507. LCCN:80-488545.
Audience: **u,f.**

Bell, J.Bowyer **DA990.U46**
Irish Troubles: A Generation of Violence,1967-92. Trade Paper. Gill & MacMillan, Ltd. Dublin, 1994. 872p. ISBN:0-7171-2201-8, ISBN13: 978-0-7171-2201-1. Dewey:941.60824.
Audience: **u,f.**

Boyce, David George **DA950**
Nineteenth Century Ireland: The Search for Stability. Trade Paper. Gill & MacMillan, Ltd. Dublin, 2005. 352p. New Gill History of Ireland Ser., Vol. 5 ISBN:0-7171-3299-4, ISBN13: 978-0-7171-3299-7. Dewey:941.5081. LCCN:2006-386413.
Audience: **g,u.**

Brady, Ciaran (Editor) **DA908.I58 1999**
Interpreting Irish History: The Debate on Historical Revisionism. Trade Cloth. Irish Academic Press. Dublin, 1999. 360p. ISBN:0-7165-2499-6, ISBN13: 978-0-7165-2499-1. Dewey:941.5/007/20415. LCCN:99-036788.
Audience: **u,f.**

Brady, Ciaran & Gillespie, Raymond (Editors) **HC260.5**
Natives and Newcomers: The Making of Irish Colonial Society 1534-1641. Trade Cloth. Irish Academic Press. Dublin, 1986. 260p. ISBN:0-7165-2378-7, ISBN13: 978-0-7165-2378-9. Dewey:941.505.
Audience: **u,f.**

Canny, Nicholas P. **DA935 .C365 1987**
From Reformation to Restoration: Ireland 1534-1660. Trade Paper. Helicon Publishing, Ltd. Oxon, 1987. viii, 238p. ISBN:0-86167-061-2, ISBN13: 978-0-86167-061-1. Dewey:941.505. LCCN:88-200874.
Audience: **l,u.**

Coogan **DA965.D4C66 1993**
De Valera. Trade Cloth. Random House. London, 1993. 704p. ISBN:0-09-175030-X, ISBN13: 978-0-09-175030-5. Dewey:941.5082/2/092 B. LCCN:93-238760.
Audience: **g,u.**

Cosgrove, Art **DA933**
Late Medieval Ireland, 1370-1541. Trade Paper. Educational Company of Ireland, The. Dublin, 1981. ISBN:0-86167-059-0, ISBN13: 978-0-86167-059-8. Dewey:941.5.
Audience: **g,l.**

Doorley, Michael **HS61**
Irish-American Diaspora Nationalism: The Friends of Irish Freedom, 1916-35. Trade Cloth. Four Courts Press. Dublin 8, 2005. 240p. ISBN:1-85182-830-3, ISBN13: 978-1-85182-830-2. Dewey:366.00899162073. LCCN:2006-365462.
Audience: **g,u.**

Duffy, Patrick (Editor), et al. **DA933.G34 2001**
Gaelic Ireland C.1350-1600: Land, Lordship and Settlement. David Edwards & Elizabeth FitzPatrick (Editors). Trade Cloth. Four Courts Press. Dublin 8, 2001. 454p. ISBN:1-85182-547-9, ISBN13: 978-1-85182-547-9. Dewey:941.5. LCCN:2001-273055.
Audience: **g,u.**

Duffy, Patrick (Editor), et al. **DA920**
Gaelic Ireland, C 1250-C 1650: Land, Lordship and Settlement. David Edwards & Elizabeth Fitzpatrick (Editors). Trade Paper. Four Courts Press. Dublin 8, 2004. 454p. ISBN:1-85182-800-1, ISBN13: 978-1-85182-800-5. Dewey:941.5/04.
Audience: **u,f.**

Duffy, Sean (Editor) **DA911**
Atlas of Irish History. Trade Paper. Gill & MacMillan, Ltd. Dublin, 1996. 144p. ISBN:0-7171-2479-7, ISBN13: 978-0-7171-2479-4. Dewey:941.5.
Audience: **g,l.**

Foster, R. F. **DA938.F67 1988**
Modern Ireland, 1600-1972. Trade Cloth. Penguin Group (USA) Inc. New York, NY. 1989. 704p. ISBN:0-7139-9010-4, ISBN13: 978-0-7139-9010-2. Dewey:941.5. LCCN:89-118698.
Audience: **g,u.** *Choice, 1989.*

Garvin **DA963.G37 1996**
1922: The Birth of Irish Democracy. Trade Cloth. Palgrave Macmillan. New York, NY. 1996. 320p. ISBN:0-312-16477-7, ISBN13: 978-0-312-16477-5. Dewey:941.5082/2. LCCN:96-009801.
Audience: **u,f.** *Choice, 1997.*

Garvin, Tom **DA963.G37 2005**
1922: the Birth of Irish Democracy. Trade Paper. Gill & MacMillan, Ltd. Dublin, 2005. 256p. ISBN:0-7171-3969-7, ISBN13: 978-0-7171-3969-9. Dewey:941.70822.
Audience: **g,u.**

Hopkinson, Michael **DA962**
The Irish War of Independence. Trade Cloth. Gill & MacMillan, Ltd. Dublin, 2004. 288p. ISBN:0-7171-3741-4, ISBN13: 978-0-7171-3741-1. Dewey:941.7082/1.
Audience: **g,u.** *Choice, 2003.*

Houston, Rab A. **HB3583.H63 1995**
The Population History of Britain and Ireland 1500-1750. Maurice Kirby (Contribution by). Cloth Text. Cambridge University Press. New York, NY. 1995. 105p. New Studies in Economic and Social History, No. 18 ISBN:0-521-55277-X, ISBN13: 978-0-521-55277-6. Dewey:304.6/0941. LCCN:95-018507.
Audience: **u,f.**

Kenny, Kevin **E184.I6K47 2000**
The American Irish: A History. Trade Cloth. Longman Publishing Group. White Plains, NY. 2000. 352p. ISBN:0-582-27818-X, ISBN13: 978-0-582-27818-9. Dewey:973/.049162. LCCN:00-021234.
Audience: **g,u.** *Choice, 2001.*

Lennon, Colm **DA935.L46 1995**
Sixteenth Century Ireland: The Incomplete Conquest. Trade Cloth. Palgrave Macmillan. New York, NY. 1995. 390p. ISBN:0-312-12462-7, ISBN13: 978-0-312-12462-5. Dewey:941.505. LCCN:94-032460.
Audience: **g,u.** *Choice, 1995.*

Lydon, James F. **DA910.L87 1998**
The Making of Ireland: A History. Trade Paper. Routledge. New York, NY. 1998. 440p. ISBN:0-415-01348-8, ISBN13: 978-0-415-01348-2. Dewey:941.5. LCCN:98-013707.
Audience: **g,l.**

Lyons, F. S. **HN400.3.A8**
Ireland since the Famine. Ed. 2. Trade Paper. HarperCollins Publishers Ltd. London, 1985. 880p. ISBN:0-00-686005-2, ISBN13: 978-0-00-686005-1. Dewey:941.5081.
Audience: **g,l,u.**

MacRaild, Donald M. & Hepburn, A. C. (Editors) **DA125.I7G74 2000**
The Great Famine and Beyond: Irish Immigrants in Britain in the Nineteenth and Twentieth Centuries. Trade Cloth. Irish Academic Press. Dublin, 2000. 303p. ISBN:0-7165-2706-5, ISBN13: 978-0-7165-2706-0. Dewey:941.004/9162. LCCN:99-047584.
Audience: **u,f.**

Mallie & McKittrick **DA990.U46**
Endgame in Ireland. Trade Paper. Hodder General Publishing Division. London, 2002. 320p. ISBN:0-340-82169-8, ISBN13: 978-0-340-82169-5. Dewey:941.6/0824.
Audience: **g,l.**

McKay, Susan **DA990.U46M144 2005**
Northern Protestants: An Unsettled People. Ed. 2. Trade Paper. Blackstaff Press, Ltd. Antrim, 2006. 407p. ISBN:0-85640-771-2, ISBN13: 978-0-85640-771-0. Dewey:941.6/00882044. LCCN:2006-361678.
Audience: **g,u.**

Moody, T. W. & Martin, F. X. (Editors) **DA910**
The Course of Irish History. Radio Telefis Eireann Staff (Contribution by). Trade Paper. Mercier Press, Limited, The. Dublin 2, 2003. xv, 462p. ISBN:1-85635-370-2, ISBN13: 978-1-85635-370-0. Dewey:941.5.
Audience: **g,l.**

Morgan, Hiram **DA937.3.M66 1993**
Tyrone's Rebellion: The Outbreak of the Nine Years War in Tudor Ireland. Trade Cloth. Royal Historical Society. London, 1993. 264p. Royal Historical Society Studies in History, Vol. 67 ISBN:0-86193-224-2, ISBN13: 978-0-86193-224-5. Dewey:941.5/05. LCCN:93-020043.
Audience: **f.**

Nolan, Janet A. **HQ1600.3.N65 1989**
Ourselves Alone: Women's Emigration from Ireland, 1885-1920. Cloth Text. University Press of Kentucky. Lexington, KY. 1989. 152p. ISBN:0-8131-1684-8, ISBN13: 978-0-8131-1684-6. Dewey:304.8/3730415. LCCN:89-035145.
Audience: **u,f.** *Choice, 1990.*

O'Day, Alan **DA908.M34 1996**
The Making of Modern Irish History: Revisionism and the Revisionist Controversy. D. George Boyce (Editor). Paper over Boards. Routledge. New York, NY. 1996. 256p. ISBN:0-415-09819-X, ISBN13: 978-0-415-09819-9. Dewey:941.5/07. LCCN:95-036523.
Audience: **u,f.**

Owens, Rosemary Cullen **HQ1600.3.O94 2005**
A Social History of Women in Ireland 1870-1970. Trade Cloth. Gill & MacMillan, Ltd. Dublin, 2005. 432p. ISBN:0-7171-3681-7, ISBN13: 978-0-7171-3681-0. Dewey:305.4209/034009417. LCCN:2005-482844.
Audience: **u,f.**

Pakenhaam, Thomas **PR9387.9.A486**
The Year of Liberty. Ed. 2. Trade Paper. Little, Brown Book Group Ltd. London, 2000. 432p. ISBN:0-349-11252-5, ISBN13: 978-0-349-11252-7. Dewey:941.507.
Audience: **g,l.**

Townshend, Charles **DA962**
Easter 1916: The Irish Rebellion. Trade Cloth. Penguin Books, Ltd. London, 2005. 464p. ISBN:0-7139-9690-0, ISBN13: 978-0-7139-9690-6. Dewey:941.50821. LCCN:2006-372767.
Audience: **g,u.**

Ward, Margaret **HQ1600.3 .W37**
Unmanageable Revolutionaries: Women and Irish Nationalism. Trade Paper. Pluto Press. London, 1995. 320p. ISBN:0-7453-1084-2, ISBN13: 978-0-7453-1084-8. Dewey:322.4209415.
Audience: **g,u.**

Ireland. Northern Ireland. > Ireland > General

Cullen, L. M. **DA906**
The Emergence of Modern Ireland 1600-1900. Trade Cloth. Holmes & Meier Publishers, Inc. Teaneck, NJ. 1981. 292p. ISBN:0-8419-0727-7, ISBN13: 978-0-8419-0727-0. Dewey:941.5. LCCN:81-006548.
Audience: **u,f.**

Cullen, L. M. (Louis M.) **HC260.5**
An Economic History of Ireland since 1660. Ed. 2. London: B.T. Batsford. 1987. ISBN:0-7134-5808-9, ISBN13: 978-0-7134-5808-4.
Audience: **u,f.**

Duffy, Sean (Editor) **DA911**
Atlas of Irish History. Trade Paper. Gill & MacMillan, Ltd. Dublin, 1996. 144p. ISBN:0-7171-2479-7, ISBN13: 978-0-7171-2479-4. Dewey:941.5.
Audience: **g,l.**

Lyons, F. S. **HN400.3.A8**
Ireland since the Famine. Ed. 2. Trade Paper. HarperCollins Publishers Ltd. London, 1985. 880p. ISBN:0-00-686005-2, ISBN13: 978-0-00-686005-1. Dewey:941.5081.
Audience: **g,l,u.**

Lyons, F. S. L. (Francis Stewart Leland) **DA958.P2**
Charles Stewart Parnell. Dublin: Gill & MacMillan. 2005. ISBN:0-7171-3939-5, ISBN13: 978-0-7171-3939-2.
Audience: **g,l,u,f.**

MacDonagh, Oliver **DA950.22.M235 1991**
O'Connell: The Life of Daniel O'Connell, 1775-1847. London: Weidenfeld and Nicolson. 1991. ISBN:0-297-82017-6, ISBN13: 978-0-297-82017-8.
Audience: **u,f.**

MacDonagh, Oliver **DA950**
States of Mind: Two cCnturies of Anglo-Irish Conflict, 1780-1980. London: Pimlico. 1992. ISBN:0-7126-5039-3, ISBN13: 978-0-7126-5039-7.
Audience: **u,f.**

Moody, T. W. & Martin, F. X. (Editors) **DA910**
The Course of Irish History. Radio Telefis Eireann Staff (Contribution by). Trade Paper. Mercier Press, Limited, The. Dublin 2, 2003. xv, 462p. ISBN:1-85635-370-2, ISBN13: 978-1-85635-370-0. Dewey:941.5.
Audience: **g,l.** B

Ireland. Northern Ireland. > Ireland > History > Early and Medieval to 1603

Bradshaw, Brendan (Editor), et al. **PR129.I7R47 1993**
Representing Ireland: Literature and the Origins of Conflict 1534-1660. Andrew Hadfield & Willy Maley (Editors). Trade Cloth. Cambridge University Press. New York, NY. 1993. 259p. ISBN:0-521-41634-5, ISBN13: 978-0-521-41634-4. Dewey:820.932415. LCCN:92-037859.
Audience: **u,f.**

Brady, Ciaran **DA935.B69 1994**
The Chief Governors: The Rise and Fall of Reform Government in Tudor Ireland 1536-1588. Anthony Fletcher, John Guy & John Morrill (Contribution by). Trade Paper. Cambridge University Press. New York, NY. 2002. 343p. Cambridge Studies in Early Modern British History Ser. ISBN:0-521-52004-5, ISBN13: 978-0-521-52004-1. Dewey:941.5/05.
Audience: **u,f.**

Brady, Ciaran & Gillespie, Raymond (Editors) **HC260.5**
Natives and Newcomers: The Making of Irish Colonial Society 1534-1641. Trade Cloth. Irish Academic Press. Dublin, 1986. 260p. ISBN:0-7165-2378-7, ISBN13: 978-0-7165-2378-9. Dewey:941.505.
Audience: **u,f.**

Canny, Nicholas **DA947.C34 1988**
Kingdom and Colony: Ireland in the Atlantic World, 1560-1800. Trade Cloth. Johns Hopkins University Press. Baltimore, MD. 1973. 159p. Studies in Atlantic History and Culture ISBN:0-8018-3603-4, ISBN13: 978-0-8018-3603-9. Dewey:941.5. LCCN:87-046309.
Audience: **u,f.**

Canny, Nicholas P. **DA935 .C365 1987**
From Reformation to Restoration: Ireland 1534-1660. Trade Paper. Helicon Publishing, Ltd. Oxon, 1987. viii, 238p. ISBN:0-86167-061-2, ISBN13: 978-0-86167-061-1. Dewey:941.505. LCCN:88-200874.
Audience: **l,u.**

Canny, Nicholas P. **DA935**
From Reformation to Restoration: Ireland, 1534-1660. Dublin: Helicon; Distributed by the Educational Company of Ireland. 1987. Helicon History of Ireland Ser. ISBN:0-86167-061-2, ISBN13: 978-0-86167-061-1.
Audience: **u,f.**

Cosgrove, Art **DA933**
Late Medieval Ireland, 1370-1541. Trade Paper. Educational Company of Ireland, The. Dublin, 1981. ISBN:0-86167-059-0, ISBN13: 978-0-86167-059-8. Dewey:941.5.
Audience: **g,l.**

Cosgrove, Art (Editor) **DA912**
A New History of Ireland: Medieval Ireland, 1169-1534. Ed. 2. Trade Cloth. Oxford University Press, Inc. New York, NY. 1993. 1,064p. New History of Ireland Ser., Vol. 2 ISBN:0-19-821755-2, ISBN13: 978-0-19-821755-8. Dewey:941.5. LCCN:76-376168.
Audience: **g,l,u,f.** *Choice, 1993.*

Duffy, Patrick (Editor), et al. **DA933.G34 2001**
Gaelic Ireland C.1350-1600: Land, Lordship and Settlement. David Edwards & Elizabeth FitzPatrick (Editors). Trade Cloth. Four Courts Press. Dublin 8, 2001. 454p. ISBN:1-85182-547-9, ISBN13: 978-1-85182-547-9. Dewey:941.5. LCCN:2001-273055.
Audience: **g,u.**

Duffy, Sean (Editor) **DA934.5.R63 2002**
Robert the Bruce's Irish Wars: The Invasion of Ireland 1306-1329. Trade Cloth. Tempus Publishing, Ltd. Stroud, Gloucestershire, 2002. 240p. ISBN:0-7524-1974-9, ISBN13: 978-0-7524-1974-9. Dewey:941.5/03. LCCN:2002-391376.
Audience: **f.**

Ellis, Steven G. **DA935.E58 1998**
Ireland in the Age of the Tudors, 1447-1603: English Expansion and the End of Gaelic Rule. Ed. 2. Trade Paper. Longman Publishing Group. White Plains, NY. 1998. 464p. Longman History of Ireland Ser. ISBN:0-582-01901-X, ISBN13: 978-0-582-01901-0. Dewey:941.505. LCCN:98-023157.
Audience: **u,f.**

Harbison, Peter **DA930**
Pre-Christian Ireland: From the First Settlers to the Early Celts. Trade Paper. Thames & Hudson. New York, NY. 1995. 208p. Ancient Peoples and Places Ser. ISBN:0-500-27809-1, ISBN13: 978-0-500-27809-3. Dewey:941.501. LCCN:87-051301.
Audience: **g,u.**

Lennon, Colm **DA935.L46 1995**
Sixteenth Century Ireland: The Incomplete Conquest. Trade Cloth. Palgrave Macmillan. New York, NY. 1995. 390p. ISBN:0-312-12462-7, ISBN13: 978-0-312-12462-5. Dewey:941.505. LCCN:94-032460.
Audience: **g,u.** *Choice, 1995.*

Moody, T. W. (Editor) **DA910**
Early Modern Ireland, 1534-1691. Trade Cloth. Oxford University Press, Inc. New York, NY. 1976. 800p. New History of Ireland Ser., No. 3 ISBN:0-19-821739-0, ISBN13: 978-0-19-821739-8. Dewey:941.5. LCCN:76-376168.
Audience: **u,f.**

Morgan, Hiram **DA937.3.M66 1993**
Tyrone's Rebellion: The Outbreak of the Nine Years War in Tudor Ireland. Trade Cloth. Royal Historical Society. London, 1993. 264p. Royal Historical Society Studies in History, Vol. 67 ISBN:0-86193-224-2, ISBN13: 978-0-86193-224-5. Dewey:941.5/05. LCCN:93-020043.
Audience: **f.**

O'Croinin, Daibhi (Editor) **DA930.O2 1995**
Early Medieval Ireland, 400-1200. Trade Paper. Pearson Education. Boston, MA. 1995. 400p. A History of England Ser. ISBN:0-582-01565-0, ISBN13: 978-0-582-01565-4. Dewey:941.5/01. LCCN:94-043307.
Audience: **g,u.**

Richter, Michael **DA930.R5313**
Medieval Ireland: The Enduring Tradition. Brian Stone & Adrian Keogh (Translators). Trade Paper. Palgrave Macmillan. New York, NY. 1996. 226p. ISBN:0-312-15812-2, ISBN13: 978-0-312-15812-5. Dewey:941.5.
Audience: **u,f.** *Choice, 1989.*

Ireland. Northern Ireland. > Ireland > History > 1603-1800. Union

Barnard, T. C. **DA940**
The Kingdom of Ireland, 1641-1760. Trade Paper. Palgrave Macmillan. New York, NY. 2004. 216p. British History in Perspective Ser. ISBN:0-333-61077-6, ISBN13: 978-0-333-61077-0. Dewey:941.507. LCCN:2004-044501.
Audience: **g,l.** *Choice, 2005.*

Bartlett, Thomas **DA947**
Fall and Rise of the Irish Nation: The Catholic Question,1690-1830. Trade Cloth. Gill & MacMillan, Ltd. Dublin, 1992. 452p. ISBN:0-7171-1577-1, ISBN13: 978-0-7171-1577-8. Dewey:941.507.
Audience: **g,u.**

Bartlett, Thomas & Hayton, David **DA947 .P46**
Penal ERA and Golden Age: Essays in Irish History, 1690-1800. Ulster Historical Foundation Staff (Contribution by). Trade Paper. Ulster Historical Foundation. Belfast, 1979. ix, 232p. ISBN:0-901905-23-2, ISBN13: 978-0-901905-23-9. Dewey:941.507. LCCN:80-488545.
Audience: **u,f.**

Bottigheimer, Karl S. **DA944.4**
English Money and Irish Land; The Adventurers in the Cromwellian settlement of Ireland. Oxford [Eng.] Clarendon Press. 1971.
Audience: **l,u,f.**

Canny, Nicholas **DA947.C34 1988**
Kingdom and Colony: Ireland in the Atlantic World, 1560-1800. Trade Cloth. Johns Hopkins University Press. Baltimore, MD. 1973. 159p. Studies in Atlantic History and Culture ISBN:0-8018-3603-4, ISBN13: 978-0-8018-3603-9. Dewey:941.5. LCCN:87-046309.
Audience: **u,f.**

Canny, Nicholas P. **DA935**
From Reformation to Restoration: Ireland, 1534-1660. Dublin: Helicon; Distributed by the Educational Company of Ireland. 1987. Helicon History of Ireland Ser. ISBN:0-86167-061-2, ISBN13: 978-0-86167-061-1.
Audience: **u,f.**

Ciardha, Eamonn O. **DA948.A2O28 2002**
Ireland and the Jacobite Cause, 1685-1766: A Fatal Attachment. Trade Cloth. Four Courts Press. Dublin 8, 2002. 468p. ISBN:1-85182-534-7, ISBN13: 978-1-85182-534-9. Dewey:941.506. LCCN:2002-282232.
Audience: **f.** *Choice, 2002.*

Connolly, Sean **BX1504**
Priests and People in Pre-Famine Ireland, 1780-1845. Cloth Text. Palgrave Macmillan. New York, NY. 1982. 340p. ISBN:0-312-64411-6, ISBN13: 978-0-312-64411-6. Dewey:261.1/09415. LCCN:81-016526.
Audience: **u,f.**

Dickson, David **DA940.D54 2000**
New Foundations: Ireland, 1660-1800. Ed. 2. Trade Cloth. Irish Academic Press. Dublin, 2000. 240p. ISBN:0-7165-2632-8, ISBN13: 978-0-7165-2632-2. Dewey:941.507. LCCN:99-036787.
Audience: **u,f.**

Elliott, Marianne **DA948.5**
Partners in Revolution: The United Irishmen and France. Trade Cloth. Yale University Press. Cumberland, RI. 1982. 430p. ISBN:0-300-02770-2, ISBN13: 978-0-300-02770-9. Dewey:322.4/2/09415. LCCN:82-050441.
Audience: **u,f.**

Elliott, Marianne **DA948.6.T6E45 1989**
Wolfe Tone: Prophet of Irish Independence. Cloth over Boards. Yale University Press. Cumberland, RI. 1990. 492p. ISBN:0-300-04637-5, ISBN13: 978-0-300-04637-3. Dewey:941.507/092 B. LCCN:89-036283.
Audience: **g,l.** *Choice, 1990.*

McLoughlin, Thomas **PR8749.M37 1999**
Contesting Ireland: Irish Voices Against England in the Eighteenth-Century. Trade Paper. Four Courts Press. Dublin 8, 1999. 240p. ISBN:1-85182-449-9, ISBN13: 978-1-85182-449-6. Dewey:820.9/358. LCCN:99-197826.
Audience: **f.**

Moody, T. W. (Editor) **DA910**
Early Modern Ireland, 1534-1691. Trade Cloth. Oxford University Press, Inc. New York, NY. 1976. 800p. New History of Ireland Ser., No. 3 ISBN:0-19-821739-0, ISBN13: 978-0-19-821739-8. Dewey:941.5. LCCN:76-376168.
Audience: **u,f.**

Moody, T. W. (Editor), et al. **DA910**
New History of Ireland: Eighteenth Century Ireland, 1691-1800. F. X. Martin & F. J. Byrne (Editors). Trade Cloth. Oxford University Press, Inc. New York, NY. 1986. 914p. New History of Ireland Ser., No. 4 ISBN:0-19-821742-0, ISBN13: 978-0-19-821742-8. Dewey:941.5. LCCN:76-376168.
Audience: **u,f.** *Choice, 1986.*

Pakenhaam, Thomas **PR9387.9.A486**
The Year of Liberty. Ed. 2. Trade Paper. Little, Brown Book Group Ltd. London, 2000. 432p. ISBN:0-349-11252-5, ISBN13: 978-0-349-11252-7. Dewey:941.507.
Audience: **g,l.**

Simms, J. G. **DA945**
Jacobite Ireland, 1685-91. Trade Paper. Four Courts Press. Dublin 8, 2000. 320p. ISBN:1-85182-553-3, ISBN13: 978-1-85182-553-0. Dewey:941.56.
Audience: **u,f.**

Ireland. Northern Ireland. > Ireland > History > 19th and 20th Centuries. Irish Question. Famine. Republic and Free State

Boyce, David George **DA950**
Nineteenth Century Ireland: The Search for Stability. Trade Paper. Gill & MacMillan, Ltd. Dublin, 2005. 352p. New Gill History of Ireland Ser., Vol. 5 ISBN:0-7171-3299-4, ISBN13: 978-0-7171-3299-7. Dewey:941.5081. LCCN:2006-386413.
Audience: **g,u.**

Campbell, Colm **KDK1340.C36 1994**
Emergency Law in Ireland, 1918-1925. Trade Cloth. Oxford University Press, Inc. New York, NY. 1994. 456p. ISBN:0-19-825675-2, ISBN13: 978-0-19-825675-5. Dewey:344.15031. LCCN:93-008767.
Audience: **u,f.** *Choice, 1995.*

Coogan **DA965.D4C66 1993**
De Valera. Trade Cloth. Random House. London, 1993. 704p. ISBN:0-09-175030-X, ISBN13: 978-0-09-175030-5. Dewey:941.5082/2/092 B. LCCN:93-238760.
Audience: **g,u.**

Coogan, Tim Pat **DA965.C6C66 2002**
Michael Collins: The Man Who Made Ireland. Trade Paper. Palgrave Macmillan. New York, NY. 2002. 524p. ISBN:0-312-29511-1, ISBN13: 978-0-312-29511-0. Dewey:941.5082/1/092 B. LCCN:2002-282940.
Audience: **g,l.**

Cormac, O'Grada **DA950.7.O366 1998**
Black '47 and Beyond: The Great Irish Famine in History, Economy, and Memory. Trade Cloth. Princeton University Press. Princeton, NJ. 1999. 320p. Princeton Economic History of the Western World Ser. ISBN:0-691-01550-3, ISBN13: 978-0-691-01550-7. Dewey:941.508. LCCN:98-027291.
Audience: **u,f.** *Choice, 1999.*

Cote, Jane M. **DA958.P24C67 1991**
Fanny and Anna Parnell: Ireland's Patriot Sisters. Cloth Text. Palgrave Macmillan. New York, NY. 1991. 352p. ISBN:0-312-06089-0, ISBN13: 978-0-312-06089-3. Dewey:941.5/0922 B. LCCN:90-026393.
Audience: **u,f.** *Choice, 1992.*

Donnelly, James S. **DA950.7**
The Great Irish Potato Famine. Trade Paper. Sutton Publishing, Ltd. Stroud, 2003. 304p. ISBN:0-7509-2928-6, ISBN13: 978-0-7509-2928-8. Dewey:941.5/081.
Audience: **g,u.**

Dwyer, T. Ryle **DA965.D4.D868**
De Valera: The Man and the Myths. Trade Paper. Poolbeg Press. Dublin, 1992. 370p. ISBN:1-85371-180-2, ISBN13: 978-1-85371-180-0. Dewey:941.7082092.
Audience: **u,f.** *Choice, 1992.*

Ferriter, Diarmaid **DA959.F47 2005**
The Transformation of Ireland. Perfect, Paper over Boards, Dust Jacket. Overlook Press, The. New York, NY. 2005. 884p. ISBN:1-58567-681-0, ISBN13: 978-1-58567-681-1. Dewey:941.5082. LCCN:2005-049849.
Audience: **u,f.**

Foster, R. F. **DA925.F63 1993**
Paddy and Mr. Punch: Connections in Irish and English History. Trade Cloth. Penguin Group (USA) Inc. New York, NY. 1994. 400p. ISBN:0-7139-9095-3, ISBN13: 978-0-7139-9095-9. Dewey:941. LCCN:94-128325.
Audience: **u,f.**

Garvin, Tom **DA963.G37 2005**
1922: the Birth of Irish Democracy. Trade Paper. Gill & MacMillan, Ltd. Dublin, 2005. 256p. ISBN:0-7171-3969-7, ISBN13: 978-0-7171-3969-9. Dewey:941.70822.
Audience: **g,u.**

Geary, Laurence M. & Kelleher, Margaret **DA950**
New Views of Nineteenth-Century Ireland: A Guide to Recent Research. Trade Paper. University College Dublin Press. Dublin, 2005. 34p. ISBN:1-904558-28-3, ISBN13: 978-1-904558-28-6. Dewey:941.5081072. LCCN:2005-415869.
Audience: **u,f.**

Gray, Peter **DA950.7**
Famine, Land and Politics: British Government and Irish Society, 1843-1850. Trade Paper. Irish Academic Press. Dublin, 2001. 400p. ISBN:0-7165-2642-5, ISBN13: 978-0-7165-2642-1. Dewey:941.5/081.
Audience: **f.**

Hopkinson, Michael **DA962**
The Irish War of Independence. Trade Cloth. Gill & MacMillan, Ltd. Dublin, 2004. 288p. ISBN:0-7171-3741-4, ISBN13: 978-0-7171-3741-1. Dewey:941.7082/1.
Audience: **g,u.** *Choice, 2003.*

Hopkinson, Michael **DA963**
Green Against Green: The Irish Civil War. Ed. 2. Trade Paper. Gill & MacMillan, Ltd. Dublin, 2004. 336p. ISBN:0-7171-3760-0, ISBN13: 978-0-7171-3760-2. Dewey:941.5082/2.
Audience: **g,u.**

Jeffery, Keith **D549.5.I73 J44 2001**
Ireland and the Great War. Cloth Text. Cambridge University Press. New York, NY. 2000. 221p. ISBN:0-521-77323-7, ISBN13: 978-0-521-77323-2. Dewey:940.3/415. LCCN:99-087299.
Audience: **u,f.**

Keogh, Dermot **BX1505.K46 1995**
Ireland and the Vatican. Trade Cloth. Cork University Press. Cork, 1995. 410p. ISBN:0-902561-83-9, ISBN13: 978-0-902561-83-0. Dewey:327.4170456/34. LCCN:95-121165.
Audience: **f.**

Kinealy, Christine **HC260.5.Z9F347 1995**
This Great Calamity: The Irish Famine 1845-52. Cloth Text. Roberts Rinehart Publishers. Boulder, CO. 1995. 472p. ISBN:1-57098-034-9, ISBN13: 978-1-57098-034-3. Dewey:363.8/09415/09034. LCCN:95-067332.
Audience: **g,u.** *Choice, 1996.*

Kissane, Bill **DA963**
Politics of the Irish Civil War. Trade Cloth. Oxford University Press, Inc. New York, NY. 2005. 276p. ISBN:0-19-927355-3, ISBN13: 978-0-19-927355-3. Dewey:941.50822. LCCN:2005-296335.
Audience: **f.**

Kissane, Noel (Editor) **DA950.7.I75 1995**
The Irish Famine: A Documentary History. Trade Cloth. Syracuse University Press. Syracuse, NY. 1996. 188p. ISBN:0-907328-25-3, ISBN13: 978-0-907328-25-4. Dewey:941.508. LCCN:96-105841.
Audience: **u,f.**

Laffan, Michael **JN1571.5.S56 L34 19**
The Resurrection of Ireland: The Sinn Féin Party, 1916-1923. Cloth Text. Cambridge University Press. New York, NY. 1999. 530p. ISBN:0-521-65073-9, ISBN13: 978-0-521-65073-1. Dewey:324.241508309. LCCN:99-011331.
Audience: **u,f.** *Choice, 2000.*

Larkin, Emmet **DA957.9 .L36 1990B**
The Roman Catholic Church and the Home Rule Movement in Ireland, 1870-1874. Trade Cloth. Gill & MacMillan, Ltd. Dublin, 1990. xxi, 416p. ISBN:0-7171-1760-X, ISBN13: 978-0-7171-1760-4. Dewey:941.5081. LCCN:91-115719.
Audience: **u,f.**

Lee, Joseph **DA951**
The Modernization of Irish Society. Ed. 2. Trade Paper. Gill & MacMillan, Ltd. Dublin, 1989. 181p. ISBN:0-7171-1693-X, ISBN13: 978-0-7171-1693-5. Dewey:309.1/415/08.
Audience: **g,l.**

Lee, Joseph J. **DA963.L44 1989**
Ireland, 1912-1985: Politics and Society. Trade Paper. Cambridge University Press. New York, NY. 1990. 776p. ISBN:0-521-37741-2, ISBN13: 978-0-521-37741-6. Dewey:941.5082. LCCN:88-023763.
Audience: **g,u.** *Choice, 1990.*

Maume, Patrick **DA960.M38 1999**
The Long Gestation: Irish Nationalist Life 1891-1918. Cloth over Boards. Palgrave Macmillan. New York, NY. 2000. 348p. ISBN:0-312-22549-0, ISBN13: 978-0-312-22549-0. Dewey:941.5082/1. LCCN:99-022052.
Audience: **u,f.**

McGee, Owen **DA954**
The Irish Republican Brotherhood: From the Land League to Sinn Fein. Trade Cloth. Four Courts Press. Dublin 8, 2005. 288p. ISBN:1-85182-921-0, ISBN13: 978-1-85182-921-7. Dewey:322.4209415. LCCN:2006-386075.
Audience: **u,f.**

O'Day, Alan **DA957.O24 1998**
Irish Home Rule, 1867-1921. Trade Cloth. Manchester University Press. Manchester, 1998. 360p. New Frontiers in History Ser. ISBN:0-7190-3775-1, ISBN13: 978-0-7190-3775-7. Dewey:941.508. LCCN:97-047404.
Audience: **g,u.** *Choice, 1999.*

O'Grada, Cormac **HD1930.3**
Ireland Before and after the Famine: Explorations in Economic History, 1800-1925. Ed. 2. Cloth Text. Manchester University Press. Manchester, 1993. 224p. ISBN:0-7190-4035-3, ISBN13: 978-0-7190-4035-1. Dewey:330.9415/08.
Audience: **u,f.** *Choice, 1988.*

O'Grada, Cormac **HC260.5.O436 1997**
Rocky Road: The Irish Economy since the 1920s. Trade Paper. Manchester University Press. Manchester, 1997. 272p. ISBN:0-7190-4584-3, ISBN13: 978-0-7190-4584-4. Dewey:330.9/417/082. LCCN:97-012986.
Audience: **u,f.**

Owens, Rosemary Cullen **HQ1600.3.O94 2005**
A Social History of Women in Ireland 1870-1970. Trade Cloth. Gill & MacMillan, Ltd. Dublin, 2005. 432p. ISBN:0-7171-3681-7, ISBN13: 978-0-7171-3681-0. Dewey:305.4209/034009417. LCCN:2005-482844.
Audience: **u,f.**

Regan, John **DA963.R44 1999**
The Irish Counter-Revolution, 1921-36: Treatyite Politics and Settlement in Independent Ireland. Cloth over Boards. Palgrave Macmillan. New York, NY. 2000. 494p. ISBN:0-312-22727-2, ISBN13: 978-0-312-22727-2. Dewey:941.5082/2. LCCN:99-022263.
Audience: **f.** *Choice, 2000.*

Townshend, Charles **DA962**
Easter 1916: The Irish Rebellion. Trade Cloth. Penguin Books, Ltd. London, 2005. 464p. ISBN:0-7139-9690-0, ISBN13: 978-0-7139-9690-6. Dewey:941.50821. LCCN:2006-372767.
Audience: **g,u.**

Ward, Margaret **HQ1600.3 .W37**
Unmanageable Revolutionaries: Women and Irish Nationalism. Trade Paper. Pluto Press. London, 1995. 320p. ISBN:0-7453-1084-2, ISBN13: 978-0-7453-1084-8. Dewey:322.4209415.
Audience: **g,u.**

Woodham-Smith, Cecil **DA950.7 .W6 1991**
The Great Hunger: Ireland, 1845-1849. Trade Paper. Penguin Group (USA) Inc. New York, NY. 1992. 528p. ISBN:0-14-014515-X, ISBN13: 978-0-14-014515-1. Dewey:363.8.
Audience: **g,l.**

Ireland. Northern Ireland. > Northern Ireland

Bardon, Jonathan **DA990.U46.B2254 1992**
A History of Ulster. Trade Cloth. Blackstaff Press, The. 1993. 924p. ISBN:0-85640-466-7, ISBN13: 978-0-85640-466-5. Dewey:941.6. LCCN:92-225896.
Audience: **g,u.** *Choice, 1993.*

Bell, J.Bowyer **DA990.U46**
Irish Troubles: A Generation of Violence,1967-92. Trade Paper. Gill & MacMillan, Ltd. Dublin, 1994. 872p. ISBN:0-7171-2201-8, ISBN13: 978-0-7171-2201-1. Dewey:941.60824.
Audience: **u,f.**

Hennessey, Thomas **DA990.U46.H43 1997**
A History of Northern Ireland, 1920-1996. Trade Cloth. Gill & MacMillan, Ltd. Dublin, 1997. 300p. ISBN:0-7171-2400-2, ISBN13: 978-0-7171-2400-8. Dewey:941.60824. LCCN:98-117510.
Audience: **g,l.**

Mallie & McKittrick **DA990.U46**
Endgame in Ireland. Trade Paper. Hodder General Publishing Division. London, 2002. 320p. ISBN:0-340-82169-8, ISBN13: 978-0-340-82169-5. Dewey:941.6/0824.
Audience: **g,l.**

McKay, Susan **DA990.U46M144 2005**
Northern Protestants: An Unsettled People. Ed. 2. Trade Paper. Blackstaff Press, Ltd. Antrim, 2006. 407p. ISBN:0-85640-771-2, ISBN13: 978-0-85640-771-0. Dewey:941.6/00882044. LCCN:2006-361678.
Audience: **g,u.**

Miller, David **DA990.U46R47 1998**
Rethinking Northern Ireland: Culture, Ideology and Colonialism. Trade Paper. Longman Publishing Group. White Plains, NY. 1998. 344p. ISBN:0-582-30287-0, ISBN13: 978-0-582-30287-7. Dewey:941.6. LCCN:98-028732.
Audience: **u,f.**

Ruane, Joseph & Todd, Jennifer **DA990.U46 R83 1996**
The Dynamics of Conflict in Northern Ireland: Power, Conflict and Emancipation. Trade Paper. Cambridge University Press. New York, NY. 1996. 381p. ISBN:0-521-56879-X, ISBN13: 978-0-521-56879-1. Dewey:941.6/082. LCCN:95-052013.
Audience: **f.** *Choice, 1997.*

Ireland. Northern Ireland. > Northern Ireland > General

Duffy, Sean (Editor) **DA911**
Atlas of Irish History. Trade Paper. Gill & MacMillan, Ltd. Dublin, 1996. 144p. ISBN:0-7171-2479-7, ISBN13: 978-0-7171-2479-4. Dewey:941.5.
Audience: **g,l.**

France > History, General Works

Agulhon, Maurice **DC335.A3813 1993**
The French Republic, 1879-1992. Antonia Nevill (Translator). Trade Cloth. Blackwell Publishing, Inc. Malden, MA. 1993. 592p. History of France Ser. ISBN:0-631-17031-6, ISBN13: 978-0-631-17031-0. Dewey:944/.08. LCCN:92-045622.
Audience: **g,u,f.** *Choice, 1994.*

Atkin, Nicholas & Tallatt, Frank (Editors) **DC252 .R54 1998**
The Right in France: Nationalism and the State, 1789-1996. Cloth over Boards. I. B. Tauris & Company, Ltd. London, 1997. 250p. International Library of Historical Studies ISBN:1-86064-197-0, ISBN13: 978-1-86064-197-8. Dewey:320.52/0944.
Audience: **u,f.** *Choice, 1998.*

Birnbaum, Pierre **DC36.9.B5713 2001**
The Idea of France. Malcolm DeBevoise (Translator). Cloth over Boards. Farrar, Straus & Giroux. New York, NY. 2001. 352p. ISBN:0-8090-4650-4, ISBN13: 978-0-8090-4650-8. Dewey:944. LCCN:00-063430.
Audience: **g,u,f.** *Choice, 2002.*

Bloch, Marc **GF127.E852**
French Rural History: An Essay on Its Basic Characteristics. Janet Sondheimer (Translator). Trade Paper. University of California Press. Berkeley, CA. 1970. ISBN:0-520-01660-2, ISBN13: 978-0-520-01660-6. Dewey:333.7/6/0944. LCCN:66-015483.
Audience: **l,u,f.**

Cobban, Alfred **DC110**
History of Modern France: 1871-1962. Trade Paper. Penguin Group (USA) Inc. New York, NY. 1990. 272p. ISBN:0-14-013827-7, ISBN13: 978-0-14-013827-6. Dewey:944.08.
Audience: **g,l,u,f.**

Cobban, Alfred **DC110 .C57**
History of Modern France: 1715-1799. Trade Paper. Penguin Group (USA) Inc. New York, NY. 1991. 304p. ISBN:0-14-013825-0, ISBN13: 978-0-14-013825-2. Dewey:944.034.
Audience: **g,l,u,f.**

Cobban, Alfred **DC110**
A History of Modern France: From the First Empire to the Second Empire. Ed. 2. Harmondsworth, Middlesex, England; New York : Penguin Books. 1986. ISBN:0-14-020525-X, ISBN13: 978-0-14-020525-1.
Audience: **g,l,u,f.**

Hazareesingh, Sudhir **JN2451.H39 1994**
Political Traditions in Modern France. Paper Text. Oxford University Press, Inc. New York, NY. 1994. 364p. ISBN:0-19-878075-3, ISBN13: 978-0-19-878075-5. Dewey:320.944. LCCN:93-039461.
Audience: **g,l,u,f.** *Choice, 1995.*

Kedward, H. R. (Harry Roderick) **DC361**
France and the French: A Modern History. Ed. 1. Woodstock, NY: Overlook Press. 2006. ISBN:1-58567-733-7, ISBN13: 978-1-58567-733-7.
Audience: **g,l,u,f.**

Kritzman, Lawrence D. & Nora, Pierre **DC33.L6513 1996**
Realms of Memory: The Construction of the French Past. Arthur Goldhammer (Translator). Trade Cloth. Columbia University Press. New York, NY. 1996. 642p. Realms of Memory Ser. ISBN:0-231-08404-8, ISBN13: 978-0-231-08404-8. Dewey:944. LCCN:95-049349.
Audience: **u,f.**

Lebovics, Herman **DC33.7**
True France: The Wars over Cultural Identity, 1900-1945. Trade Paper. Cornell University Press. Ithaca, NY. 1994. 248p. The Wilder House Series in Politics, History, and Culture ISBN:0-8014-8193-7, ISBN13: 978-0-8014-8193-2. Dewey:944.081.
Audience: **u,f.** *Choice, 1993.*

Morrissey, Robert John **DC73.M7513 2003**
Charlemagne and France: A Thousand Years of Mythology. Catherine Thanyi (Translator). Trade Cloth. University of Notre Dame Press. Notre Dame, IN. 2003. 456p. The Laura Shannon Series in French Medieval Studies ISBN:0-268-02277-1, ISBN13: 978-0-268-02277-8. Dewey:944/.014/092 B. LCCN:2002-013900.
Audience: **u,f.** *Choice, 2003.*

Nora, Pierre **DC33**
Rethinking France: Les Lieux de Memoire: Space. David P. Jordan (Translator). Trade Cloth. University of Chicago Press. Chicago, IL. 2006. 300p. ISBN:0-226-59133-6, ISBN13: 978-0-226-59133-9. Dewey:944.
Audience: **u,f.**

Nora, Pierre & Kritzman, Lawrence D. **DC33**
Realms of Memory: The Construction of the French Past. Arthur Goldhammer (Translator). Trade Cloth. Columbia University Press. New York, NY. 1998. 688p. Realms of Memory Ser. ISBN:0-231-10926-1, ISBN13: 978-0-231-10926-0. Dewey:944. LCCN:95-049349.
Audience: **u,f.**

Nora, Pierre & Kritzman, Lawrence D. **DC33.L6513 1996**
Realms of Memory: The Construction of the French Past. Arthur Goldhammer (Translator). Trade Cloth. Columbia University Press. New York, NY. 1997. 576p. Realms of Memory Ser., Vol. 2 ISBN:0-231-10634-3, ISBN13: 978-0-231-10634-4. Dewey:944. LCCN:95-049349.
Audience: **u,f.**

Sowerwine, Charles **DC335.S66 2000**
France since 1870: Culture, Politics and Society. Cloth over Boards. Palgrave Macmillan. New York, NY. 2001. 544p. ISBN:0-333-65836-1, ISBN13: 978-0-333-65836-9. Dewey:944.081. LCCN:00-034522.
Audience: **g,l,u,f.** *Choice, 2002.*

France > Military and Diplomatic History

Barker, Nancy N. **DC0059.8.M6B**
The French Experience in Mexico, 1821-1861: A History of Constant Misunderstanding. Trade Paper. Books on Demand. Ann Arbor, MI. 284p. ISBN:0-8357-3891-4, ISBN13: 978-0-8357-3891-0. Dewey:327.72044. LCCN:78-012935.
Audience: **u,f.**

Bell, P. M. **DC59.8.G7B45 1996**
France and Britain 1900-1940. Ed. 1. Cloth Text. Longman Publishing Group. White Plains, NY. 1996. 256p. ISBN:0-582-22954-5, ISBN13: 978-0-582-22954-9. Dewey:327.4/1/044. LCCN:95-041012.
Audience: **g,l,u,f.**

Bell, P. M. **DA589.8.B45 1997**
France and Britain, 1940-1994: The Long Separation. Trade Paper. Longman Publishing Group. White Plains, NY. 1997. 328p. ISBN:0-582-28920-3, ISBN13: 978-0-582-28920-8. Dewey:327.41044. LCCN:96-043210.
Audience: **g,l,u,f.** *Choice, 1997.*

Cox, Gary P. **UA700.C68 1994**
The Halt in the Mud: French Strategic Planning from Waterloo to Sedan. Trade Paper. Westview Press. Boulder, CO. 1994. 258p. History and Warfare Ser. ISBN:0-8133-1536-0, ISBN13: 978-0-8133-1536-2. Dewey:355.033544. LCCN:93-025458.
Audience: **u,f.** *Choice, 1994.*

Keiger, John **DC341.K44 1983**
France and the Origins of the First World War. Cloth Text. Palgrave Macmillan. New York, NY. 1983. 240p. ISBN:0-312-30292-4, ISBN13: 978-0-312-30292-4. Dewey:327.73. LCCN:83-008660.
Audience: **g,l,u,f.**

Keiger, John **DC369.K45 2001**
France and the World since 1870. Paper Text. Oxford University Press, Inc. New York, NY. 2001. 272p. International Relations and the Great Powers Ser. ISBN:0-340-59507-8, ISBN13: 978-0-340-59507-7. Dewey:327.44. LCCN:2001-277679.
Audience: **g,l,u,f.** *Choice, 2002.*

Rynning, Sten **UA700**
Changing Military Doctrine: Presidents and Military Power in Fifth Republic France, 1958-2000. Trade Cloth. Greenwood Publishing Group, Inc. Portsmouth, NH. 2001. 256p. ISBN:0-275-97286-0, ISBN13: 978-0-275-97286-8. Dewey:355/.033544. LCCN:2001-021169.
Audience: **u,f.** *Choice, 2002.*

Young, Robert J. **D742.F7Y68 1996**
France and the Origins of the Second World War. Ed. 1. Trade Paper. Palgrave Macmillan. New York, NY. 1996. 200p. The Making of the 20th Century Ser. ISBN:0-312-16186-7, ISBN13: 978-0-312-16186-6. Dewey:944/.0815. LCCN:96-010410.
Audience: **g,l,u,f.** *Choice, 1997.*

France > Social Life and Customs. Ethnography

Mendras, Henri & Cole, Alistair **GN585.F8M46 1991**
Social Change in Modern France: Towards a Cultural Anthropology of the Fifth Republic. Cloth Text. Cambridge University Press. New York, NY. 1991. 262p. ISBN:0-521-39108-3, ISBN13: 978-0-521-39108-5. Dewey:306/.0944. LCCN:90-001493.
Audience: **u,f.** *Choice, 1991.*

Vigarello, Georges **GT2846.F7V5413 1988**
Concepts of Cleanliness: Changing Attitudes in France since the Middle Ages. Jean Birrell (Translator). Trade Cloth. Cambridge University Press. New York, NY. 1988. 256p. Past and Present Publications ISBN:0-521-34248-1, ISBN13: 978-0-521-34248-3. Dewey:391/.64/0944. LCCN:88-004125.
Audience: **g,l,u,f.** *Choice, 1989.*

Wylie, Laurence William **DC611.V357**
Village in the Vaucluse. Ed. 3. Cambridge, Mass. : Harvard University Press. 1974. ISBN:0-674-93937-9, ISBN13: 978-0-674-93937-0.
Audience: **g,l,u,f.**

Zeldin, Theodore **DC34.Z45 1996**
The French. Philip Turner (Editor). Trade Paper. Kodansha America, Inc. New York, NY. 1996. 544p. Kodansha Globe Ser. ISBN:1-56836-157-2, ISBN13: 978-1-56836-157-4. Dewey:944.083/8. LCCN:96-034603.
Audience: **g,l,u,f.**

France > History > Early and Medieval to 1515

Kibler, William W. (Editor), et al. **DC33.2.M44 1995**
Medieval France: An Encyclopedia. Grover A. Zinn, John Bell Henneman Jr. & Lawrence Earp (Editors). Trade Cloth. Garland

Publishing, Inc. New York, NY. 1995. 1080p. Encyclopedias of the Middle Ages Ser., Vol. 2 ISBN:0-8240-4444-4, ISBN13: 978-0-8240-4444-2. Dewey:944/.003. LCCN:95-002617.
Audience: **g,l,u,f.** *Choice, 1995.*

Reyerson, Kathryn L. & Drendel, J. (Editors)
Urban and Rural Communities in Medieval France: Provence and Languedoc, 1000-1500. Trade Cloth. Brill Academic Publishers, Inc. Boston, MA. 1998. xxiv, 336p. The Medieval Mediterranean Ser., Vol. 18 ISBN:90-04-10850-5, ISBN13: 978-90-04-10850-9. LCCN:98-035745.
Audience: **u,f.**

France > History > Early and Medieval to 1515 > Gauls. Celts. Franks

Drinkwater, J. F. **DC62**
Roman Gaul. Trade Cloth. Cornell University Press. Ithaca, NY. 1983. 272p. ISBN:0-8014-1642-6, ISBN13: 978-0-8014-1642-2. Dewey:936.4. LCCN:83-045143.
Audience: **u,f.**

Drinkwater, John & Elton, Hugh (Editors) **DC62.F54 1992**
Fifth-Century Gaul: A Crisis of Identity? Trade Cloth. Cambridge University Press. New York, NY. 1992. 398p. ISBN:0-521-41485-7, ISBN13: 978-0-521-41485-2. Dewey:936.4. LCCN:91-018375.
Audience: **u,f.**

King, Anthony **DC63.K56 1990**
Roman Gaul and Germany. Trade Cloth. University of California Press. Berkeley, CA. 1990. 240p. Exploring the Roman World Ser. ISBN:0-520-06989-7, ISBN13: 978-0-520-06989-3. Dewey:936.302. LCCN:89-020546.
Audience: **u,f.** *Choice, 1991.*

Woolf, Greg **DC33.2.W66 1998**
Becoming Roman: The Origins of Provincial Civilization in Gaul. Trade Cloth. Cambridge University Press. New York, NY. 1998. 314p. ISBN:0-521-41445-8, ISBN13: 978-0-521-41445-6. Dewey:944. LCCN:97-047263.
Audience: **u,f.** *Choice, 1999.*

France > History > Early and Medieval to 1515 > 476-1328. Merovingians, Carolingians. Capetians

Baldwin, John W. **DC91**
The Government of Philip Augustus: Foundations of French Royal Power in the Middle Ages. Trade Cloth. University of California Press. Berkeley, CA. 1991. 632p. ISBN:0-520-07391-6, ISBN13: 978-0-520-07391-3. Dewey:944.023092. LCCN:84-023930.
Audience: **u,f.** *Choice, 1986.*

Barber, Malcolm C. **BX4891.2.B37 2000**
The Cathars: Dualist Heretics in Languedoc in the High Middle Ages. Trade Paper. Longman Publishing Group. White Plains, NY. 2000. 304p. The Medieval World Ser. ISBN:0-582-25661-5, ISBN13: 978-0-582-25661-3. Dewey:273/.6. LCCN:00-022125.
Audience: **u,f.** *Choice, 2001.*

Barbero, Alessandro **DC73 .B3613 2004**
Charlemagne: Father of a Continent. Allan Cameron (Translator). Trade Cloth. University of California Press. Berkeley, CA. 2004. 438p. ISBN:0-520-23943-1, ISBN13: 978-0-520-23943-2. Dewey:944/.0142/092 B. LCCN:2003-017208.
Audience: **g,l,u,f.** *Choice, 2005.*

Becher, Matthias **DC73.B39 2003**
Charlemagne. Cloth over Boards. Yale University Press. Cumberland, RI. 2003. 176p. ISBN:0-300-09796-4, ISBN13: 978-0-300-09796-2. Dewey:944/.014/092 B. LCCN:2003-007858.
Audience: **g,l,u,f.** *Choice, 2004.*

Bouchard, Constance B. **DC33.2.B59 1998**
Strong of Body, Brave and Noble: Chivalry and Society in Medieval France. Book, Other. Cornell University Press. Ithaca, NY. 1998. 232p. ISBN:0-8014-3097-6, ISBN13: 978-0-8014-3097-8. Dewey:944/.02. LCCN:97-038906.
Audience: **g,l,u,f.** *Choice, 1999.*

Drew, Katherine F. (Translator, Introduction by) **KJ336.E5 1991**
The Laws of the Salian Franks. Trade Cloth. University of Pennsylvania Press. Philadelphia, PA. 1991. 276p. Middle Ages Ser. ISBN:0-8122-8256-6, ISBN13: 978-0-8122-8256-6. Dewey:340.5/5. LCCN:90-021755.
Audience: **u,f.** *Choice, 1991.*

Dunbabin, Jean **DC70.D86 2000**
France in the Making 843-1180. Ed. 2. Paper Text. Oxford University Press, Inc. New York, NY. 2000. 476p. ISBN:0-19-820846-4, ISBN13: 978-0-19-820846-4. Dewey:944/.21. LCCN:00-266935.
Audience: **g,l,u,f.**

Einhard, et al. **DC73.32.T45 1969B**
Two Lives of Charlemagne. Notker & Notker the Stammerer Staff (Authors), Lewis Thorpe (Translator, Introduction by). Trade Paper. Penguin Group (USA) Inc. New York, NY. 1969. 240p. Classics Ser., 13 ISBN:0-14-044213-8, ISBN13: 978-0-14-044213-7. Dewey:944/.01/0924. LCCN:72-473993.
Audience: **g,l,u,f.**

Farmer, Sharon A. **HC278.P3F37 2001**
Surviving Poverty in Medieval Paris: Gender, Ideology, and the Daily Lives of the Poor. Book, Other. Cornell University Press. Ithaca, NY. 2005. 224p. Conjunctions of Religion and Power in the Medieval Past Ser. ISBN:0-8014-3836-5, ISBN13: 978-0-8014-3836-3. Dewey:362.5/8/09443610902. LCCN:2001-003585.
Audience: **g,l,u,f.** *Choice, 2002.*

Fawtier, Robert **DC82.F313**
The Capetian Kings of France: Monarchy and Nation, 987. Paper Text. Textbook Publishers. Temecula, CA. 2003. 242p. ISBN:0-7581-8818-8, ISBN13: 978-0-7581-8818-2. Dewey:944.021.
Audience: **u,f.**

Fouracre, Paul **DC71**
Age of Charles Martel. Trade Cloth. Longman Publishing Group. White Plains, NY. 2000. 224p. ISBN:0-582-06475-9, ISBN13: 978-0-582-06475-1. Dewey:[B].
Audience: **u,f.**

Geary, Patrick J. **DC65.G43 1988**
Before France and Germany: The Creation and Transformation of the Merovingian World. Paper Text. Oxford University Press, Inc. New York, NY. 1988. 272p. ISBN:0-19-504458-4, ISBN13: 978-0-19-504458-4. Dewey:943/.01. LCCN:87-007927.
Audience: **g,l,u,f.** *Choice, 1988.*

Hallam, Elizabeth M. & Everard, Judith **DC82.H34 2001**
Capetian France 987-1328. Ed. 2. Trade Paper. Longman Publishing Group. White Plains, NY. 2001. 496p. ISBN:0-582-40428-2, ISBN13: 978-0-582-40428-1. Dewey:944/.021. LCCN:00-061499.
Audience: **u,f.**

Hummer, Hans J. **DC61**
Politics and Power in Early Medieval Europe: Alsace and the Frankish Realm, 600-1000. Rosamond McKitterick, Christine Carpenter & Jonathan Shepard (Contribution by). Trade Cloth. Cambridge University Press. New York, NY. 2006. 318p. Cambridge Studies in Medieval Life and Thought Ser., Vol. 65:Fourth Ser. ISBN:0-521-85441-5, ISBN13: 978-0-521-85441-2. Dewey:944.3901. LCCN:2006-296130.
Audience: **u,f.**

Johnson, Penelope D. **BX4220.F8**
Equal in Monastic Profession: Religious Women in Medieval France. Catherine R. Stimpson (Foreword by). Trade Paper. University of Chicago Press. Chicago, IL. 1994. 310p. Women in Culture and Society Ser. ISBN:0-226-40186-3, ISBN13: 978-0-226-40186-7. Dewey:271/.90044/09021. LCCN:90-045510.
Audience: **u,f.** *Choice, 1991.*

Kaeuper, Richard W. **DA225.K34 1988**
War, Justice, and Public Order: England and France in the Later Middle Ages. Trade Cloth. Oxford University Press, Inc. New York, NY. 1988. 462p. ISBN:0-19-822873-2, ISBN13: 978-0-19-822873-8. Dewey:942.03. LCCN:87-020409.
Audience: **u,f.** *Choice, 1989.*

Ladurie, Emmanuel Le Roy **DC801.M753**
Montaillou: The Promised Land of Error. Barbara Bray (Translator). UK-Trade Paper. Knopf Publishing Group. New York, NY. 1979. 416p. ISBN:0-394-72964-1, ISBN13: 978-0-394-72964-0. Dewey:944/.88.
Audience: **g,l,u,f.**

Maddicott, J. R. **DA228.M7M33 1994**
Simon de Montfort. Trade Paper. Cambridge University Press. New York, NY. 1996. 430p. ISBN:0-521-37636-X, ISBN13: 978-0-521-37636-5. Dewey:942/.034/092.
Audience: **g,l,u,f.** *Choice, 1995.*

McKitterick, Rosamond **P211.3.E85M35 1989**
The Carolingians and the Written Word. Trade Paper. Cambridge University Press. New York, NY. 1989. 308p. ISBN:0-521-31565-4, ISBN13: 978-0-521-31565-4. Dewey:001.54/3/094. LCCN:88-029232.
Audience: **u,f.**

McKitterick, Rosamond **DC70**
History and Memory in the Carolingian World. Cloth Text. Cambridge University Press. New York, NY. 2004. 354p. ISBN:0-521-82717-5, ISBN13: 978-0-521-82717-1. Dewey:940.1. LCCN:2005-297210.
Audience: **l,u,f.** *Choice, 2005.*

Poly, Jean-Pierre & Bournazel, Eric **DC82.P6513 1990**
The Feudal Transformation, 900-1200. Trade Cloth. Holmes & Meier Publishers, Inc. Teaneck, NJ. 1991. x, 424p. Europe Past and Present Ser. ISBN:0-8419-1167-3, ISBN13: 978-0-8419-1167-3. Dewey:944/.02. LCCN:90-042094.
Audience: **u,f.** *Choice, 1992.*

Power, Daniel **DC611.N854P68 2004**
The Norman Frontier in the Twelfth and Early Thirteenth Centuries. Christine Carpenter, D. E. Luscombe, Rosamond McKitterick & Jonathan Shepard (Contribution by). Trade Cloth. Cambridge University Press. New York, NY. 2004. 664p. Cambridge Studies in Medieval Life and Thought, Vol. 6 ISBN:0-521-57172-3, ISBN13: 978-0-521-57172-2. Dewey:944/.2023. LCCN:2004-045704.
Audience: **u,f.**

Richard, Jean **DC91.R5313 1992**
Saint Louis: Crusader King of France. Simon Lloyd (Editor), Jean Birrell (Translator). Trade Cloth. Cambridge University Press. New York, NY. 1992. 384p. ISBN:0-521-38156-8, ISBN13: 978-0-521-38156-7. Dewey:944.023092. LCCN:91-002621.
Audience: **g,l,u,f.** *Choice, 1992.*

Riche, Pierre **DC70**
The Carolingians: A Family Who Forged Europe. Michael I. Allen (Translator). Trade Cloth. University of Pennsylvania Press. Philadelphia, PA. 1993. 424p. Middle Ages Ser. ISBN:0-8122-3062-0, ISBN13: 978-0-8122-3062-8. Dewey:944/.01. LCCN:91-303532.
Audience: **u,f.** *Choice, 1993.*

France > History > Early and Medieval to 1515 > 1339-1453. Hundred Years' War. Joan of Arc

Astell, Ann W. & Wheeler, Bonnie (Editors) **DC103.J629 2003**
Joan of Arc and Spirituality. Cloth over Boards. Palgrave Macmillan. New York, NY. 2003. 308p. The New Middle Ages Ser. ISBN:1-4039-6222-7, ISBN13: 978-1-4039-6222-5. Dewey:282/.092. LCCN:2003-050576.
Audience: **u,f.** *Choice, 2004.*

Curry, Anne **DC96.C87 2003**
The Hundred Years War. Ed. 2. Cloth over Boards. Palgrave Macmillan. New York, NY. 2003. 240p. British History in Perspective Ser. ISBN:1-4039-0816-8, ISBN13: 978-1-4039-0816-2. Dewey:944/.025. LCCN:2003-040483.
Audience: **g,l,u,f.** *Choice, 1993.*

Denieul-Cormier, Anne **DC36.6.D4613**
Wise and Foolish Kings: The House of Valois. Trade Cloth. Doubleday Publishing. New York, NY. 1980. viii, 398p. ISBN:0-385-04903-X, ISBN13: 978-0-385-04903-0. Dewey:944/.025. LCCN:77-175365.
Audience: **g,l,u,f.**

Fraioli, Deborah A. **DC104.F73 2000**
Joan of Arc: The Early Debate. Trade Cloth. Suffolk Records Society. Ipswich, 1999. 256p. ISBN:0-85115-572-3, ISBN13: 978-0-85115-572-2. Dewey:944/.026/092. LCCN:99-038918.
Audience: **u,f.** *Choice, 2000.*

Gies, Frances **DC103**
Joan of Arc: The Legend and the Reality. Trade Cloth. Thomas Y. Crowell Company. New York, NY. 1981. 256p. ISBN:0-690-01942-4, ISBN13: 978-0-690-01942-1. Dewey:944/.026/0924. LCCN:80-007900.
Audience: **g,l,u,f.**

Henneman, John B. **DC97.C54H46 1996**
Olivier de Clisson and Political Society in France under Charles V and Charles VI. Book, Other. University of Pennsylvania Press. Philadelphia, PA. 1996. 360p. Middle Ages Ser. ISBN:0-8122-3353-0, ISBN13: 978-0-8122-3353-7. Dewey:944/.025/092 B. LCCN:96-011190.
Audience: **u,f.** *Choice, 1997.*

Kaeuper, Richard W. **DA225.K34 1988**
War, Justice, and Public Order: England and France in the Later Middle Ages. Trade Cloth. Oxford University Press, Inc. New York, NY. 1988. 462p. ISBN:0-19-822873-2, ISBN13: 978-0-19-822873-8. Dewey:942.03. LCCN:87-020409.
Audience: **u,f.** *Choice, 1989.*

Rogers, Clifford J. **DA233.R64 2000**
War Cruel and Sharp: English Strategy under Edward III, 1327-1360. Trade Cloth. Boydell & Brewer, Ltd. Woodbridge, 2000. 480p. Warfare in History Ser. ISBN:0-85115-804-8, ISBN13: 978-0-85115-804-4. Dewey:944/.025. LCCN:00-042922.
Audience: **g,l,u,f.** *Choice, 2001.*

Sumption, Jonathan **DC96.S86 1991**
The Hundred Years War: Trial by Battle. Trade Cloth. University of Pennsylvania Press. Philadelphia, PA. 1992. 672p. Middle Ages Ser. ISBN:0-8122-3147-3, ISBN13: 978-0-8122-3147-2. Dewey:944/.025. LCCN:91-025816.
Audience: **g,u,f.** *Choice, 1992.*

Wood, Charles T. **DA250**
Joan of Arc and Richard III: Sex, Saints, and Government in the Middle Ages. Paper Text. Oxford University Press, Inc. New York, NY. 1991. 288p. ISBN:0-19-506951-X, ISBN13: 978-0-19-506951-8. Dewey:942.04. LCCN:87-035023.
Audience: **u,f.** *Choice, 1989.*

France > History > Early Modern (1515-1789)

Crawford, Katherine **DC36.1.C73 2004**
Perilous Performances: Gender and Regency in Early Modern France. Trade Cloth. Harvard University Press. Cambridge, MA. 2004. 310p. Harvard Historical Studies, Vol. 145 ISBN:0-674-01541-X, ISBN13: 978-0-674-01541-8. Dewey:320.444. LCCN:2004-052386.
Audience: **u,f.** *Choice, 2005.*

Martin, Henri-Jean **Z305 .M27**
The French Book: Religion, Absolutism and Readership, 1585-1715. Paul Saenger & Nadine Saenger (Translators). Trade Paper. Johns Hopkins University Press. Baltimore, MD. 1996. 136p. Symposia in Comparative History Ser. ISBN:0-8018-5419-9, ISBN13: 978-0-8018-5419-4. Dewey:381/.45002/0944.
Audience: **g,l,u,f.**

Potter, David **DC611.P588 P68 1993**
War and Government in the French Provinces: Picardy, 1470-1560. Trade Cloth. Cambridge University Press. New York, NY. 1993. 409p. ISBN:0-521-43189-1, ISBN13: 978-0-521-43189-7. Dewey:944.2/6/09024. LCCN:92-011887.
Audience: **u,f.** *Choice, 1994.*

France > History > Early Modern (1515-1789) > 16th Century. Henri IV. Louis XIII. Louis XIV

Baumgartner, Frederic J. **DC96**
France in the Sixteenth Century. Trade Paper. St. Martin's Press. Gordonville, VA. 1995. 368p. ISBN:0-312-09964-9, ISBN13: 978-0-312-09964-0. Dewey:944/.025.
Audience: **g,l,u.**

Baumgartner, Frederic J. **DC114.B38 1988**
Henry II: King of France 1547-1559. Library Binding. Duke University Press. Durham, NC. 1988. xiv, 359p. ISBN:0-8223-0795-2, ISBN13: 978-0-8223-0795-2. Dewey:944/.028 B. LCCN:87-019955.
Audience: **g,l,u,f.** *Choice, 1988.*

Beik, William **DC611.L319 1988**
Absolutism and Society in Seventeenth-Century France: State Power and Provincial Aristocracy in Languedoc. John Elliott, Olwen Hufton, H. G. Koenigsberger & H. M. Scott (Contribution by). Trade Paper. Cambridge University Press. New York, NY. 1989. 398p. Cambridge Studies in Early Modern History ISBN:0-521-36782-4, ISBN13: 978-0-521-36782-0. Dewey:321.6/09448/09032. LCCN:84-009561.
Audience: **u,f.**

Benedict, Philip **DC801.R86B46**
Rouen During the Wars of Religion. John Elliott, Olwen Hufton, H. G. Koenigsberger & H. M. Scott (Contribution by). Trade Paper. Cambridge University Press. New York, NY. 2004. 317p. Cambridge Studies in Early Modern History Ser. ISBN:0-521-54797-0, ISBN13: 978-0-521-54797-0. Dewey:944.2/52/028.
Audience: **u,f.**

Berger, Robert W. **NA1046 .B47 1994**
A Royal Passion: Louis XIV as Patron of Architecture. Trade Cloth. Cambridge University Press. New York, NY. 1994. 224p. ISBN:0-521-44029-7, ISBN13: 978-0-521-44029-5. Dewey:720.9/44. LCCN:92-017172.
Audience: **u,f.** *Choice, 1995.*

Bergin, Joseph **DC123.9.R5B44 1991**
The Rise of Richelieu. Trade Cloth. Yale University Press. Cumberland, RI. 1991. 256p. ISBN:0-300-04992-7, ISBN13: 978-0-300-04992-3. Dewey:944/.032/092 B. LCCN:90-050943.
Audience: **g,l,u,f.** *Choice, 1991.*

Davis, Natalie Zemon **GT3041.F8D38 2000**
The Gift in Sixteenth-Century France. Trade Cloth. University of Wisconsin Press. Chicago, IL. 2000. x, 185p. Curti Lectures ISBN:0-299-16880-8, ISBN13: 978-0-299-16880-3. Dewey:394. LCCN:00-008913.
Audience: **u,f.** *Choice, 2001.*

Davis, Natalie Zemon **DC33.D33**
Society and Culture in Early Modern France: Eight Essays by Natalie Zemon Davis. Trade Cloth. Stanford University Press. Palo Alto, CA. 1975. xx, 364p. ISBN:0-8047-0868-1, ISBN13: 978-0-8047-0868-5. Dewey:944/.027. LCCN:74-082777.
Audience: **u,f.**

Diefendorf, Barbara **DC719.D54 1991**
Beneath the Cross: Catholics and Huguenots in Sixteenth-Century Paris. Paper Text. Oxford University Press, Inc. New York, NY. 1991. 288p. ISBN:0-19-507013-5, ISBN13: 978-0-19-507013-2. Dewey:944/.361029. LCCN:90-020737.
Audience: **l,u,f.**

Elliott, John H. **DC123.9.RS 1989**
Richelieu and Olivares. Trade Paper. Cambridge University Press. New York, NY. 1991. 197p. A Canto Book Ser. ISBN:0-521-40674-9, ISBN13: 978-0-521-40674-1. Dewey:944/.032/0924.
Audience: **u,f.**

Garrisson, Janine **DC33.3.G36 1995**
A History of Sixteenth-Century France, 1483-1598: Renaissance, Reformation, and Rebellion. Richard Rex (Translator). Cloth Text. Palgrave Macmillan. New York, NY. 1995. 448p. European Studies ISBN:0-312-12612-3, ISBN13: 978-0-312-12612-4. Dewey:944/.028. LCCN:94-047567.
Audience: **u,f.** *Choice, 1996.*

Goubert, Pierre **DC126**
Louis XIV and Twenty Million Frenchmen. Trade Paper. Knopf Publishing Group. New York, NY. 1972. 352p. ISBN:0-394-71751-1, ISBN13: 978-0-394-71751-7. Dewey:944/.033.
Audience: **g,l,u,f.**

Greengrass, Mark **DC122.G73 1995**
France in the Age of Henry IV: The Struggle for Stability. Ed. 2. Trade Paper. Addison-Wesley Longman, Inc. Boston, MA. 1995. 344p. Studies in Modern History ISBN:0-582-08721-X, ISBN13: 978-0-582-08721-7. Dewey:944/.031. LCCN:94-006451.
Audience: **g,l.**

Harding, Robert R. **JS7353.A8**
Anatomy of a Power Elite: The Provincial Governors of Early Modern France. Cloth over Boards. Yale University Press. Cumberland, RI. 1978. 320p. Historical Publications, No. 120 ISBN:0-300-02202-6, ISBN13: 978-0-300-02202-5. Dewey:352/.0073. LCCN:78-004125.
Audience: **u,f.**

Heller, Henry **HC280.T4 H45 1996**
Labour, Science and Technology in France, 1500-1620. Trade Cloth. Cambridge University Press. New York, NY. 1995. 270p. Studies in Early Modern History ISBN:0-521-55031-9, ISBN13: 978-0-521-55031-4. Dewey:338/.064/0944/09031. LCCN:95-006125.
Audience: **u,f.** *Choice, 1996.*

Holt, Mack P. **DC111.3**
The French Wars of Religion, 1562-1629. Ed. 2. William Beik, T. C. W. Blanning & Brendan Simms (Contribution by). Cloth Text. Cambridge University Press. New York, NY. 2005. 258p. New Approaches to European History Ser., Vol. 36 ISBN:0-521-83872-X, ISBN13: 978-0-521-83872-6. Dewey:944.029. LCCN:2006-277383.
Audience: **u,f.**

Kingdon, Robert McCune **DC111**
Geneva and the Coming of the Wars of Religion in France, 1555-1563. Librairie E. Droz. 1956. Travaux d'humanisme et renaissance; 22
Audience: **u,f.**

Knecht, R. J. **DC111.3.K55 2000**
The French Civil Wars, 1562-1598. Trade Cloth. Longman Publishing Group. White Plains, NY. 2000. 360p. Modern Wars in Perspective Ser. ISBN:0-582-09548-4, ISBN13: 978-0-582-09548-9. Dewey:944/.029. LCCN:00-026013.
Audience: **g,l,u,f.** *Choice, 2001.*

Knecht, R. J. **DC113.K58 1994**
Renaissance Warrior and Patron: The Reign of Francis I. Ed. 2. Trade Paper. Cambridge University Press. New York, NY. 1996. 638p. ISBN:0-521-57885-X, ISBN13: 978-0-521-57885-1. Dewey:944/.028/092.
Audience: **u,f.**

Ladurie, Emmanuel Le Roy **DC126.L4613 2001**
Saint-Simon and the Court of Louis XIV. Arthur Goldhammer (Translator), Jean-Fancois Fitou (Contribution by). Trade Cloth. University of Chicago Press. Chicago, IL. 2001. 448p. ISBN:0-226-47320-1, ISBN13: 978-0-226-47320-8. Dewey:944/.033. LCCN:00-013227.
Audience: **u,f.** *Choice, 2002.*

Ladurie, LeRoy **HD1536.F8 L4**
French Peasantry, Fourteen Fifty to Sixteen Fifty. Trade Cloth. University of California Press. Berkeley, CA. 1986. ISBN:0-685-19370-5, ISBN13: 978-0-685-19370-9. Dewey:305.56.
Audience: **u,f.**

Lewis, W. H. **DC128**
The Splendid Century: Life in the France of Louis XIV. Paper Text. Waveland Press, Inc. Prospect Heights, IL. 1997. 306p. ISBN:0-88133-921-0, ISBN13: 978-0-88133-921-5. Dewey:944.033.
Audience: **g,l,u,f.**

Love, Ronald S. **DC122.8.L68 2001**
Blood and Religion: The Conscience of Henri IV, 1553-1593. Trade Cloth. McGill-Queen's University Press. Montreal, PQ. 2001. xii, 457p. ISBN:0-7735-2124-0, ISBN13: 978-0-7735-2124-7. Dewey:944/.031/092 B. LCCN:2002-421711.
Audience: **u,f.** *Choice, 2002.*

Lux, David S. **Q46.L89 1989**
Patronage and Royal Science in 17th-Century France: The Academie de Physique in Caen. Book, Other. Cornell University Press. Ithaca, NY. 1989. 256p. ISBN:0-8014-2334-1, ISBN13: 978-0-8014-2334-5. Dewey:506/.044. LCCN:89-001002.
Audience: **u,f.** *Choice, 1990.*

Lynn, John A. **UA702 .L9523 1997**
Giant of the Grand Siècle: The French Army, 1610-1715. Trade Cloth. Cambridge University Press. New York, NY. 1997. 651p. ISBN:0-521-57273-8, ISBN13: 978-0-521-57273-6. Dewey:355/.00944/09032. LCCN:96-022239.
Audience: **u,f.** *Choice, 1998.*

Major, J. Russell **JN2413**
Representative Government in Early Modern France. Trade Cloth. Yale University Press. Cumberland, RI. 1980. 752p.

ISBN:0-300-02300-6, ISBN13: 978-0-300-02300-8. Dewey:321.8/7/0944. LCCN:79-014711.
Audience: **l,u,f.**

Martin, A. Lynn **BX3731**
Henry III and the Jesuit Politicians. Librairie E. Droz. 1973. Travaux d'humanisme et Renaissance; 134
Audience: **u,f.**

McGowan, Margaret M. **DC33.3.M39 2000**
The Vision of Rome in Late Renaissance France. Cloth over Boards. Yale University Press. Cumberland, RI. 2000. 476p. ISBN:0-300-08535-4, ISBN13: 978-0-300-08535-8. Dewey:944. LCCN:00-033556.
Audience: **u,f.** *Choice, 2001.*

Muchembled, Robert **DC0033.M8813**
Popular Culture and Elite Culture in France, 1400-1750. Trade Paper. Books on Demand. Ann Arbor, MI. 336p. ISBN:0-7837-8813-4, ISBN13: 978-0-7837-8813-5. Dewey:306/.4/0944. LCCN:84-025078.
Audience: **l,u,f.** *Choice, 1986.*

Potter, David **DC95.6.P68 1995**
A History of France, 1460-1560: The Emergence of a Nation-State. Trade Paper. Palgrave Macmillan. New York, NY. 1995. 456p. New Studies in Medieval History ISBN:0-312-12480-5, ISBN13: 978-0-312-12480-9. Dewey:944/.02. LCCN:94-032239.
Audience: **u,f.** *Choice, 1995.*

Ranum, Orest A. **DC124.4.R36 1993**
The Fronde: A French Revolution, 1648-1652. Trade Cloth. W. W. Norton & Company, Inc. New York, NY. 1993. 386p. ISBN:0-393-03550-6, ISBN13: 978-0-393-03550-6. Dewey:944.033. LCCN:93-006816.
Audience: **g,l,u,f.** *Choice, 1994.*

Ranum, Orest A. **DC729.R3 2003**
Paris in the Age of Absolutism. Ed. 2. Trade Paper. Pennsylvania State University Press. University Park, PA. 2002. 416p. ISBN:0-271-02221-3, ISBN13: 978-0-271-02221-5. Dewey:394.261. LCCN:2002-009846.
Audience: **u,f.**

Roelker, Nancy L. **DC33.3.R64 1996**
One King, One Faith: The Parlement of Paris and the Religious Reformations of the Sixteenth Century. Trade Cloth. University of California Press. Berkeley, CA. 1996. 532p. A Centennial Bk. ISBN:0-520-08626-0, ISBN13: 978-0-520-08626-5. Dewey:944/.029. LCCN:94-040396.
Audience: **u,f.** *Choice, 1996.*

Salmon, J. H. M. **DC116.5.S25 1979**
Society in Crisis: France in the Sixteenth Century. Trade Cloth. Routledge. New York, NY. 1979. 384p. University Paperbacks Ser. ISBN:0-416-73050-7, ISBN13: 978-0-416-73050-0. Dewey:944/.028. LCCN:79-040748.
Audience: **g,l,u.**

Sonnino, Paul **D246**
Louis XIV and the Origins of the Dutch War. John Elliott, Olwen Hufton, H. G. Koenigsberger & H. M. Scott (Contribution by). Trade Paper. Cambridge University Press. New York, NY. 2003. 249p. Cambridge Studies in Early Modern History Ser. ISBN:0-521-53134-9, ISBN13: 978-0-521-53134-4. Dewey:940.2/52.
Audience: **u,f.** *Choice, 1989.*

Sutherland, Nicola M. **BX9454.2.S9**
The Huguenot Struggle for Recognition. Trade Paper. Books on Demand. Ann Arbor, MI. 314p. ISBN:0-7837-2991-X, ISBN13: 978-0-7837-2991-6. Dewey:272/.4. LCCN:79-064070.
Audience: **l,u,f.**

Taylor, Larissa J. **BV4208.F8T38 1992**
Soldiers of Christ: Preaching in Late Medieval and Reformation France. Cloth Text. Oxford University Press, Inc. New York, NY. 1992. 368p. ISBN:0-19-506993-5, ISBN13: 978-0-19-506993-8. Dewey:251/.00944/09024. LCCN:91-026715.
Audience: **u,f.** *Choice, 1992.*

Treasure, Geoffrey **DC129**
Louis XIV. Trade Paper. Longman Publishing Group. White Plains, NY. 2001. 392p. ISBN:0-582-27958-5, ISBN13: 978-0-582-27958-2. Dewey:944/.033/092.
Audience: **g,l,u.** *Choice, 2002.*

Treasure, Geoffrey **DC129**
Mazarin: Crisis of Absolutism. Trade Paper. Routledge. New York, NY. 1997. 432p. ISBN:0-415-16211-4, ISBN13: 978-0-415-16211-1. Dewey:944/.033/092.
Audience: **g,l,u,f.**

Wolf, John B. (Editor) **DC129**
Louis the Fourteenth: A Profile. Trade Cloth. Farrar, Straus & Giroux. New York, NY. 1972. World Profiles Ser. ISBN:0-8090-6683-1, ISBN13: 978-0-8090-6683-4. Dewey:944/.033/0924; B. LCCN:73-163574.
Audience: **g,l,u.**

Wolfe, Michael **DC122.3.W65 1993**
The Conversion of Henri the Fourth: Politics, Power and Religious Belief in Early Modern France. Trade Cloth. Harvard University Press. Cambridge, MA. 1993. 265p. Historical Studies, Vol. 114 ISBN:0-674-17031-8, ISBN13: 978-0-674-17031-5. Dewey:944.031. LCCN:92-024881.
Audience: **g,l,u,f.**

Wood, James B. **DC116.5 .W66 1996**
The King's Army: Warfare, Soldiers and Society During the Wars of Religion in France, 1562-76. John Elliott, Olwen Hufton, H. G. Koenigsberger & H. M. Scott (Contribution by). Trade Cloth. Cambridge University Press. New York, NY. 1996. 365p. Studies in Early Modern History ISBN:0-521-55003-3, ISBN13: 978-0-521-55003-1. Dewey:944/.028. LCCN:95-040713.
Audience: **u,f.** *Choice, 1997.*

France > History > Early Modern (1515-1789) > 1715-1789. Louis XV. Louis XVI. Enlightenment

Alder, Ken **DC151.A58 1997**
Engineering the Revolution: Arms and Enlightenment in France, 1763-1815. Trade Cloth. Princeton University Press. Princeton, NJ. 1997. 494p. ISBN:0-691-02671-8, ISBN13: 978-0-691-02671-8. Dewey:944.04. LCCN:96-025139.
Audience: **u,f.** *Choice, 1997.*

Brockliss, Laurence **DC33.4.B76 2002**
Calvet's Web: Enlightenment and the Republic of Letters in Eighteenth-Century France. Trade Cloth. Oxford University

Press, Inc. New York, NY. 2002. 492p. ISBN:0-19-924748-X, ISBN13: 978-0-19-924748-6. Dewey:610/.92 B. LCCN:2002-512708.
Audience: **u,f.** *Choice, 2003.*

Cranston, Maurice W. **PQ2045.C7 1991**
Jean-Jacques: The Early Life and Work of Jean-Jacques Rousseau, 1712-1754. Trade Paper. University of Chicago Press. Chicago, IL. 1991. 382p. ISBN:0-226-11862-2, ISBN13: 978-0-226-11862-8. Dewey:848/.509 B. LCCN:90-045994.
Audience: **g,u,f.**

Cranston, Maurice W. **PQ2043.C73 1991**
The Noble Savage: Jean-Jacques Rousseau, 1754-1762. Trade Cloth. University of Chicago Press. Chicago, IL. 1991. 413p. ISBN:0-226-11863-0, ISBN13: 978-0-226-11863-5. Dewey:848/.509 B. LCCN:90-028111.
Audience: **g,u,f.** *Choice, 1991.*

Cranston, Maurice **PQ2047.C73 1997**
The Solitary Self: Jean-Jacques Rousseau in Exile and Adversity. Sanford Lakoff (Foreword by). Trade Cloth. University of Chicago Press. Chicago, IL. 1997. 267p. ISBN:0-226-11865-7, ISBN13: 978-0-226-11865-9. Dewey:194. LCCN:96-012922.
Audience: **g,u,f.** *Choice, 1997.*

Damrosch, Leo **PQ2043.D36 2005**
Jean-Jacques Rousseau: Restless Genius. Trade Cloth. Houghton Mifflin Company Trade & Reference Division. Boston, MA. 2005. 480p. ISBN:0-618-44696-6, ISBN13: 978-0-618-44696-4. Dewey:848/.509 B. LCCN:2005-013579.
Audience: **g,l,u,f.** *Choice, 2006.*

Darnton, Robert **PQ265**
The forbidden best-sellers of pre-revolutionary France. New York : W.W. Norton. 1995. ISBN:0-393-03720-7, ISBN13: 978-0-393-03720-3.
Audience: **g,l,u,f.**

Darnton, Robert **DC33.4**
The Great Cat Massacre: And Other Episodes in French Cultural History. Trade Paper. Knopf Publishing Group. New York, NY. 1985. 320p. ISBN:0-394-72927-7, ISBN13: 978-0-394-72927-5. Dewey:944/.034.
Audience: **g,l,u,f.**

Darnton, Robert **Z1028**
The Literary Underground of the Old Regime. Trade Paper. Harvard University Press. Cambridge, MA. 1982. 272p. ISBN:0-674-53657-6, ISBN13: 978-0-674-53657-9. Dewey:070.5/9.
Audience: **g,l,u,f.**

Diderot, Denis **PQ1979**
Rameau's Nephew and D'Alembert's Dream. Leonard W. Tancock (Translator, Introduction by). Trade Paper. Penguin Group (USA) Inc. New York, NY. 1976. 240p. Classics Ser. ISBN:0-14-044173-5, ISBN13: 978-0-14-044173-4. Dewey:848.5/09. LCCN:77-357900.
Audience: **g,l,u,f.**

Doyle, William (Editor) **DC125.O53 2001**
Old Regime France: 1648-1788. Paper Text. Oxford University Press, Inc. New York, NY. 2001. 293p. Short Oxford History of France Ser. ISBN:0-19-873129-9, ISBN13: 978-0-19-873129-0. Dewey:944/.03. LCCN:00-069286.
Audience: **u,f.** *Choice, 2002.*

Garrioch, David **DC729 .G33 2002**
The Making of Revolutionary Paris. Trade Cloth. University of California Press. Berkeley, CA. 2002. 412p. ISBN:0-520-23253-4, ISBN13: 978-0-520-23253-2. Dewey:944/.36. LCCN:2001-008255.
Audience: **l,u,f.** *Choice, 2003.*

Goodman, Dena **PQ618.G66 1996**
The Republic of Letters: A Cultural History of the French Enlightenment. Trade Paper. Cornell University Press. Ithaca, NY. 1996. 336p. ISBN:0-8014-8174-0, ISBN13: 978-0-8014-8174-1. Dewey:944/.034.
Audience: **u,f.** *Choice, 1995.*

Hardman, John **DC137.1**
Louis XVI: The Silent King. Paper Text. Oxford University Press, Inc. New York, NY. 2000. 224p. Reputations Ser. ISBN:0-340-70650-3, ISBN13: 978-0-340-70650-3. Dewey:944/.035/092.
Audience: **g,l,u,f.** *Choice, 2001.*

Jones, Colin **DC131**
The Great Nation: France from Louis XV to Napoleon. Trade Paper. Penguin Group (USA) Inc. New York, NY. 2003. 688p. ISBN:0-14-013093-4, ISBN13: 978-0-14-013093-5. Dewey:944/.034.
Audience: **l,u,f.**

Lever, Evelyne **DC137.1**
Marie Antoinette: The Last Queen of France. Catherine Temerson (Translator). Trade Paper. St. Martin's Press. Gordonville, VA. 2001. 352p. ISBN:0-312-28333-4, ISBN13: 978-0-312-28333-9. Dewey:944/.035/092.
Audience: **g,l,u,f.**

Lough, John **DC25**
France on the Eve of Revolution: British Travellers' Observations, 1763-1788. Trade Cloth. Lyceum Books, Inc. University Park, IL. 1988. 354p. ISBN:0-925065-04-8, ISBN13: 978-0-925065-04-9. Dewey:914.403. LCCN:87-070642.
Audience: **g,l,u,f.**

Montesquieu, Charles de Secondat **PQ2011.L5E53 2004**
The Persian Letters. C. J. Betts (Translator, Introduction by). Trade Paper. Penguin Group (USA) Inc. New York, NY. 1973. 1p. Classics Ser. ISBN:0-14-044281-2, ISBN13: 978-0-14-044281-6. Dewey:843.5. LCCN:73-163802.
Audience: **g,l,u,f.**

Peabody, Sue **HT1178**
There Are No Slaves in France: The Political Culture of Race and Slavery in the Ancien Regime. Trade Paper. Oxford University Press, Inc. New York, NY. 2002. 220p. ISBN:0-19-515866-0, ISBN13: 978-0-19-515866-3. Dewey:326/.0944. LCCN:95-039056.
Audience: **u,f.**

Pearson, Roger **PQ2099.P43 2005**
Voltaire Almighty: A Life in Pursuit of Freedom. Cloth over Boards. Bloomsbury Publishing. New York, NY. 2005. 384p. ISBN:1-58234-630-5, ISBN13: 978-1-58234-630-4. Dewey:848/.509 B. LCCN:2005-053027.
Audience: **g,l,u,f.** *Choice, 2006.*

Rapley, Elizabeth **BX2347.8.W6R36 1990**
The Dévotes: Women and Church in Seventeenth-Century France. Trade Cloth. McGill-Queen's University Press.

Montreal, PQ. 1990. 320p. Studies in the History of Religion ISBN:0-7735-0727-2, ISBN13: 978-0-7735-0727-2. Dewey:271/.90044/09032. LCCN:90-162427.
Audience: **g,l,u,f.** *Choice, 1990.*

Roche, Daniel **DC715.R6413 1985**
People of Paris: An Essay in Popular Culture in the 18th Century. M. Evans & G. Lewis (Translators). Cloth over Boards. Berg Publishers. Oxford, 1987. 288p. ISBN:0-907582-46-X, ISBN13: 978-0-907582-46-5. Dewey:306/.0944/36. LCCN:85-021436.
Audience: **l,u,f.**

Rousseau, Jean-Jacques **JC575**
A Discourse on Inequality. Maurice Cranston (Translator, Annotations by, Introduction by). Trade Paper. Penguin Group (USA) Inc. New York, NY. 1985. 192p. Classics Ser. ISBN:0-14-044439-4, ISBN13: 978-0-14-044439-1. Dewey:320/.011. LCCN:85-121076.
Audience: **g,l,u,f.**

Rousseau, Jean-Jacques & Wu, Michael **LB512**
Emile: Or on Education. Allan Bloom (Translator, Introduction by, Notes by). Trade Paper. Basic Books. New York, NY. 1979. 512p. ISBN:0-465-01931-5, ISBN13: 978-0-465-01931-1. Dewey:370. LCCN:78-073765.
Audience: **u,f.**

Swann, Julian **KJV3747 .S93 1995**
Politics and the Parlement of Paris under Louis XV, 1754-1774. Trade Paper. Cambridge University Press. New York, NY. 1995. 400p. ISBN:0-521-48362-X, ISBN13: 978-0-521-48362-9. Dewey:328.44/071/09033. LCCN:94-019471.
Audience: **u,f.** *Choice, 1996.*

Voltaire **PQ2082.C3E5 1999**
Candide. Daniel Gordon (Editor). Trade Paper. Bedford/Saint Martin's. New York, NY. 1998. 138p. The Bedford Series in History and Culture Ser. ISBN:0-312-14854-2, ISBN13: 978-0-312-14854-6. Dewey:843/.5. LCCN:98-085192.
Audience: **g,l,u,f.**

Vyverberg, Henry **B1925.E5V93 1989**
Human Nature, Cultural Diversity, and the French Enlightenment. Trade Cloth. Oxford University Press, Inc. New York, NY. 1989. 234p. ISBN:0-19-505864-X, ISBN13: 978-0-19-505864-2. Dewey:194. LCCN:89-002971.
Audience: **g,l,u,f.** *Choice, 1990.*

Wellman, Kathleen **R507.L193W46 1992**
La Mettrie: Medicine, Philosophy, and Enlightenment. Cloth Text. Duke University Press. Durham, NC. 1992. 358p. ISBN:0-8223-1204-2, ISBN13: 978-0-8223-1204-8. Dewey:610/.92 B. LCCN:91-023992.
Audience: **u,f.** *Choice, 1992.*

France > History > Modern (1789-)

Cole, Joshua **HB3593.C614 2000**
The Power of Large Numbers: Population, Politics and Gender in Nineteenth-Century France. Trade Cloth. Cornell University Press. Ithaca, NY. 2000. 272p. ISBN:0-8014-3701-6, ISBN13: 978-0-8014-3701-4. Dewey:304.6/0944/09034. LCCN:99-046229.
Audience: **u,f.** *Choice, 2000.*

France > History > Modern (1789-) > Long Nineteenth Century (1789-1914)

Accampo, Elinor A. **HQ623.A15 1989**
Industrialization, Family Life, and Class Relations: Saint Chamond, 1815-1914. Trade Cloth. University of California Press. Berkeley, CA. 1989. 320p. ISBN:0-520-06095-4, ISBN13: 978-0-520-06095-1. Dewey:306.8/5/0944581. LCCN:88-000459.
Audience: **u,f.** *Choice, 1990.*

Ackerman, Evelyn Bernette **RA771.7.F8A28 1990**
Health Care in the Parisian Countryside, 1800-1914. Cloth Text. Rutgers University Press. Piscataway, NJ. 1990. 258p. ISBN:0-8135-1548-3, ISBN13: 978-0-8135-1548-9. Dewey:610/.944. LCCN:89-070063.
Audience: **u,f.** *Choice, 1991.*

Agulhon, Maurice **HN438.V3**
The Republic in the Village: The People of the War from the French Revolution to the Second Republic. Ed. 2. Janet Lloyd (Translator). Trade Cloth. Cambridge University Press. New York, NY. 1982. 431p. Past and Present Publications ISBN:0-521-23693-2, ISBN13: 978-0-521-23693-5. Dewey:944/.9306. LCCN:81-017095.
Audience: **u,f.**

Aminzade, Ronald **DC252.A46 1993**
Ballots and Barricades: Class Formation and Republican Politics in France, 1830-1871. Trade Cloth. Princeton University Press. Princeton, NJ. 1993. 368p. ISBN:0-691-09479-9, ISBN13: 978-0-691-09479-3. Dewey:944.06. LCCN:93-018279.
Audience: **g,u,f.** *Choice, 1994.*

Cole, Joshua **HB3593.C614 2000**
The Power of Large Numbers: Population, Politics and Gender in Nineteenth-Century France. Trade Cloth. Cornell University Press. Ithaca, NY. 2000. 272p. ISBN:0-8014-3701-6, ISBN13: 978-0-8014-3701-4. Dewey:304.6/0944/09034. LCCN:99-046229.
Audience: **u,f.** *Choice, 2000.*

Cubitt, Geoffrey **BX3731.C83 1993**
The Jesuit Myth: Conspiracy Theory and Politics in Nineteenth-Century France. Trade Cloth. Oxford University Press, Inc. New York, NY. 1993. 360p. ISBN:0-19-822868-6, ISBN13: 978-0-19-822868-4. Dewey:271/.53044/09034. LCCN:93-018391.
Audience: **u,f.** *Choice, 1994.*

Ehrenberg, John **HX893.7.P78E47 1996**
Proudhon and His Age. Trade Cloth. Brill Academic Publishers, Inc. Boston, MA. 1996. 216p. ISBN:0-391-03891-5, ISBN13: 978-0-391-03891-2. Dewey:335.2 B. LCCN:95-019461.
Audience: **g,l,u,f.** *Choice, 1996.*

Gibson, Ralph **BX1530.G45 1989**
A Social History of French Catholicism, 1789-1914. Trade Cloth. Routledge. New York, NY. 1989. 352p. ISBN:0-415-01619-3, ISBN13: 978-0-415-01619-3. Dewey:282/.44. LCCN:88-028652.
Audience: **u,f.** *Choice, 1990.*

Goldstein, Jan Ellen **RC450.F7P67 2005**
The Post-Revolutionary Self: Politics and Psyche in France, 1750-1850. Trade Cloth. Harvard University Press. Cambridge, MA. 2005. 430p. ISBN:0-674-01680-7, ISBN13:

978-0-674-01680-4. Dewey:155.2/0944/09033. LCCN:2005-040206.
Audience: **u,f.** *Choice, 2006.*

Hazareesingh, Sudhir **E99.C9P55 2004**
The Saint-Napoleon: Celebrations of Sovereignty in Nineteenth-Century France. Trade Cloth. Harvard University Press. Cambridge, MA. 2004. 322p. ISBN:0-674-01341-7, ISBN13: 978-0-674-01341-4. Dewey:944.07. LCCN:2004-040512.
Audience: **u,f.** *Choice, 2005.*

Jennings, Lawrence C. **HT1178 .J46 2000**
French Anti-Slavery: The Movement for the Abolition of Slavery in France, 1802-1848. Trade Cloth. Cambridge University Press. New York, NY. 2000. 330p. ISBN:0-521-77249-4, ISBN13: 978-0-521-77249-5. Dewey:326/.8/094409034. LCCN:99-045555.
Audience: **u,f.** *Choice, 2001.*

Liu, Tessie P. **HD9865.F73C484 1994**
The Weaver's Knot: The Contradictions of Class Struggle and Family Solidarity in Western France, 1750-1914. Book, Other. Cornell University Press. Ithaca, NY. 1994. 312p. ISBN:0-8014-8019-1, ISBN13: 978-0-8014-8019-5. Dewey:338.4/7677/0094418. LCCN:93-043802.
Audience: **g,l,u,f.** *Choice, 1994.*

Mansel, Philip **DC33.5**
The Court of France 1789-1830. Trade Paper. Cambridge University Press. New York, NY. 1991. 355p. ISBN:0-521-42398-8, ISBN13: 978-0-521-42398-4. Dewey:944/.00880621.
Audience: **g,u,f.** *Choice, 1989.*

Maza, Sarah C. **HT690.F8**
The Myth of the French Bourgeoisie: An Wssay on the Social Imaginary, 1750-1850. Cambridge, Mass. :; Harvard University Press. 2003. ISBN:0-674-01046-9, ISBN13: 978-0-674-01046-8.
Audience: **u,f.**

Merriman, John (Editor) **HT135.F76 1981**
French Cities in the Nineteenth Century: Class, Power, and Urbanization. Trade Cloth. Holmes & Meier Publishers, Inc. Teaneck, NJ. 1982. 256p. ISBN:0-8419-0464-2, ISBN13: 978-0-8419-0464-4. Dewey:307.7/6/0944. LCCN:81-002520.
Audience: **u,f.** B

Merriman, John M. **HT352.F8M47 1991**
The Margins of City Life: Explorations on the French Urban Frontier, 1815-1851. Cloth Text. Oxford University Press, Inc. New York, NY. 1991. 336p. ISBN:0-19-506438-0, ISBN13: 978-0-19-506438-4. Dewey:307.76/0944. LCCN:90-034841.
Audience: **u,f.** *Choice, 1991.*

Nord, Philip G. **DC340.N67 1995**
The Republican Moment: Struggles for Democracy in Nineteenth-Century France. Trade Cloth. Harvard University Press. Cambridge, MA. 1995. 352p. ISBN:0-674-76271-1, ISBN13: 978-0-674-76271-8. Dewey:944.07. LCCN:95-010445.
Audience: **u,f.** *Choice, 1996.*

Palmer, Robert R. (Editor, Translator) **DC255.T3**
From Jacobin to Liberal: Marc-Antoine Jullien, 1775-1848. Trade Cloth. Princeton University Press. Princeton, NJ. 1993. 272p. ISBN:0-691-03299-8, ISBN13: 978-0-691-03299-3. Dewey:944.06092. LCCN:92-046872.
Audience: **u,f.**

Sewell, William H. Jr. **HD8429 .S48**
Work and Revolution in France: The Language of Labor from the Old Regime to 1848. Trade Paper. Cambridge University Press. New York, NY. 1980. 352p. ISBN:0-521-29951-9, ISBN13: 978-0-521-29951-0. Dewey:335/.2/0944. LCCN:80-012103.
Audience: **u,f.**

France > History > Modern (1789-) > French Revolution (1789-1799). Causes, Antecedents, Events.

Baker, Keith Michael **DC138.B23 1990**
Inventing the French Revolution: Essays on French Political Culture in the Eighteenth Century. Lorraine Daston, Dorothy Ross, Quentin Skinner & James Tully (Contribution by). Trade Paper. Cambridge University Press. New York, NY. 1990. 382p. Ideas in Context Ser. ISBN:0-521-38578-4, ISBN13: 978-0-521-38578-7. Dewey:944/.034. LCCN:89-023943.
Audience: **u,f.**

Bertaud, Jean-Paul **DC151.B4313 1988**
The Army of the French Revolution: From Citizen-Soldiers to Instrument of Power. Robert R. Palmer (Translator). Trade Cloth. Princeton University Press. Princeton, NJ. 1988. 384p. ISBN:0-691-05537-8, ISBN13: 978-0-691-05537-4. Dewey:944.04. LCCN:88-015098.
Audience: **u,f.** *Choice, 1989.*

Blanning, T. C. W. **DC151.B62 1996**
The French Revolutionary Wars, 1787-1802. Paper Text. Oxford University Press, Inc. New York, NY. 1996. 304p. Modern Wars Ser. ISBN:0-340-56911-5, ISBN13: 978-0-340-56911-5. Dewey:944/.04. LCCN:95-048313.
Audience: **l,u.**

Chartier, Roger **DC138.C4813 1991**
The Cultural Origins of the French Revolution. Keith M. Baker & Steven L. Kaplan (Editors), Lydia G. Cochrane (Translator). Trade Cloth. Duke University Press. Durham, NC. 1991. 260p. Bicentennial Reflections on the French Revolution Ser. ISBN:0-8223-0981-5, ISBN13: 978-0-8223-0981-9. Dewey:944.04. LCCN:90-024404.
Audience: **l,u.** *Choice, 1992.*

Cobb, Richard C. **HN425 .C6 1972**
Police and the People: French Popular Protest, 1789-1820. Trade Cloth. Oxford University Press, Inc. New York, NY. 1972. 416p. ISBN:0-19-881297-3, ISBN13: 978-0-19-881297-5. Dewey:322.4/4/0944. LCCN:73-153045.
Audience: **u,f.**

Cobb, Richard **DC148 .C63 1998**
The French and Their Revolution: Selected Writings. David Gilmour (Editor, Introduction by). Trade Paper. New Press, The. New York, NY. 1999. 480p. ISBN:1-56584-540-4, ISBN13: 978-1-56584-540-4. Dewey:944.04. LCCN:2004-296529.
Audience: **u,f.**

Desan, Suzanne **BL875.F8D47 1990**
Reclaiming the Sacred: Lay Religion and Popular Politics in Revolutionary France. David Laitin (Editor). Book, Other. Cornell University Press. Ithaca, NY. 1990. 272p. The Wilder House Series in Politics, History, and Culture ISBN:0-8014-2404-6, ISBN13: 978-0-8014-2404-5. Dewey:261.7/0944/09033. LCCN:90-055120.
Audience: **u,f.**

Doyle, William **DC147.8.D69 1999**
Origins of the French Revolution. Ed. 3. Paper Text. Oxford University Press, Inc. New York, NY. 1999. 248p. ISBN:0-19-873174-4, ISBN13: 978-0-19-873174-0. Dewey:944.04/07/2. LCCN:98-039031.
Audience: **l,u.** B

Doyle, William **DC139**
The Oxford History of the French Revolution. Ed. 2. Paper Text. Oxford University Press, Inc. New York, NY. 2003. 496p. ISBN:0-19-925298-X, ISBN13: 978-0-19-925298-5. Dewey:944/.04. LCCN:2002-029004.
Audience: **g,l,u,f.** *Choice, 1989.*

Egret, Jean **DC136.5**
The French Pre-Revolution, 1787-1788. Wesley D. Camp (Translator), J. F. Bosher (Introduction by). Library Binding. University of Chicago Press. Chicago, IL. 1978. xxii, 314p. ISBN:0-226-19142-7, ISBN13: 978-0-226-19142-3. Dewey:944/.035. LCCN:77-078776.
Audience: **l,u.** B

Forrest, Alan **DC148**
Paris, the Provinces and the French Revolution. Trade Paper. Oxford University Press, Inc. New York, NY. 2004. 272p. A Hodder Arnold Publication ISBN:0-340-56434-2, ISBN13: 978-0-340-56434-9. Dewey:944.04. LCCN:2004-301196.
Audience: **u,f.** *Choice, 2005.*

Forrest, Alan **DC195.A625F67 1996**
The Revolution in Provincial France: Aquitaine, 1789-1799. Trade Cloth. Oxford University Press, Inc. New York, NY. 1996. 388p. ISBN:0-19-820616-X, ISBN13: 978-0-19-820616-3. Dewey:944.7/04. LCCN:96-005762.
Audience: **u,f.** *Choice, 1997.*

Forrest, Alan **DC151.F68 1990**
Soldiers of the French Revolution. Keith M. Baker & Steven L. Kaplan (Editors). Cloth Text. Duke University Press. Durham, NC. 1989. 207p. Bicentennial Reflections on the French Revolution Ser. ISBN:0-8223-0909-2, ISBN13: 978-0-8223-0909-3. Dewey:944.04. LCCN:89-035875.
Audience: **u,f.** *Choice, 1990.*

Furet, Francois **DC148**
Revolutionary France, 1770-1880. Antonia Nevill (Translator). Trade Paper. Blackwell Publishing, Inc. Malden, MA. 1995. 640p. History of France Ser. ISBN:0-631-19808-3, ISBN13: 978-0-631-19808-6. Dewey:944/.04.
Audience: **u,f.** *Choice, 1993.*

Furet, Francois **DC148.D5313 1989**
A Critical Dictionary of the French Revolution. Mona Ozouf (Editor), Arthur Goldhammer (Translator). Trade Cloth. Harvard University Press. Cambridge, MA. 1989. 1120p. ISBN:0-674-17728-2, ISBN13: 978-0-674-17728-4. Dewey:944.04. LCCN:89-030656.
Audience: **u,f.** *Choice, 1990.*

Gershoy, Leo **DC0146.B2G43**
Bertrand Barere: A Reluctant Terrorist. Paper Text. Textbook Publishers. Temecula, CA. 2003. 459p. ISBN:0-7581-5676-6, ISBN13: 978-0-7581-5676-1. Dewey:923.244.
Audience: **u,f.** B

Hufton, Olwen H. **DC158.8**
Women and the Limits of Citizenship in the French Revolution. Trade Cloth. University of Toronto Press. Toronto, ON. 1992. 440p. Donald G. Creighton Lectures ISBN:0-8020-5898-1, ISBN13: 978-0-8020-5898-0. Dewey:944.04082.
Audience: **g,l,u,f.**

Hunt, Lynn A. **DC148.H86 1992**
The Family Romance of the French Revolution. Trade Cloth. University of California Press. Berkeley, CA. 1992. 213p. ISBN:0-520-07741-5, ISBN13: 978-0-520-07741-6. Dewey:944.04. LCCN:91-026852.
Audience: **u,f.** *Choice, 1992.*

Jordan, David P. **DC137.08 .J68**
The King's Trial: Louis XVI vs. the French Revolution. Ed. 25. Trade Paper. University of California Press. Berkeley, CA. 2004. 300p. ISBN:0-520-23697-1, ISBN13: 978-0-520-23697-4. Dewey:345/.44/0231.
Audience: **u,f.** B

Jordan, David P. **DC146.R6J67 1989**
The Revolutionary Career of Maximilien Robespierre. Trade Paper. University of Chicago Press. Chicago, IL. 1989. 315p. ISBN:0-226-41037-4, ISBN13: 978-0-226-41037-1. Dewey:944.04. LCCN:89-004908.
Audience: **g,l,u,f.** B *Choice, 1985.*

Kaplan, Steven L. **DC160**
Farewell, Revolution: The Historian's Feud, France, 1789-1989. Book, Other. Cornell University Press. Ithaca, NY. 1996. 256p. ISBN:0-8014-8271-2, ISBN13: 978-0-8014-8271-7. Dewey:944.04.
Audience: **u,f.**

Kaplan, Steven L. **DC160.K35 1995**
Farewell, Revolution: Disputed Legacies, France, 1789 - 1989. Book, Other. Cornell University Press. Ithaca, NY. 1995. 608p. ISBN:0-8014-2718-5, ISBN13: 978-0-8014-2718-3. Dewey:944.04. LCCN:94-024107.
Audience: **u,f.** *Choice, 1996.*

Lefebvre, Georges **DC142.R67**
The French Revolution. Paper Text. Textbook Publishers. Temecula, CA. 2003. ISBN:0-7581-4613-2, ISBN13: 978-0-7581-4613-7. Dewey:944.04.
Audience: **l,u,f.** B

Lefebvre, Georges **DC138.L4513 2005**
The Coming of the French Revolution: By Georges Lefebvre: Translated and with a Preface by R. R. Palmer. R. R. Palmer (Translator), Timothy Tackett (Introduction by). Trade Paper. Princeton University Press. Princeton, NJ. 2005. 280p. Princeton Classic Editions Ser. ISBN:0-691-12188-5, ISBN13: 978-0-691-12188-8. Dewey:944.04/1. LCCN:2005-040861.
Audience: **l,u.**

Lucas, Colin R. **DC611.L808**
The Structure of the Terror. Trade Cloth. Oxford University Press, Inc. New York, NY. 1973. 428p. Oxford Historical Monographs ISBN:0-19-821843-5, ISBN13: 978-0-19-821843-2. Dewey:944/.58/044. LCCN:73-164199.
Audience: **u,f.** B

Mason, Laura & Rizzo, Tracey **DC141.M37 1999**
The French Revolution: A Document Collection. Paper Text. Houghton Mifflin College Division. Boston, MA. 1998. 357p. ISBN:0-669-41780-7, ISBN13: 978-0-669-41780-7. Dewey:944.04. LCCN:98-072059.
Audience: **g,l,u,f.**

McManners, John **DC158**
The French Revolution and the Church. Trade Cloth. Greenwood Publishing Group, Inc. Portsmouth, NH. 1982. 161p. ISBN:0-313-23074-9, ISBN13: 978-0-313-23074-5. Dewey:322/.1/0944. LCCN:82-015532.
Audience: **g,l,u,f.** B

Palmer, R. R. **DC177.P33 2005**
Twelve Who Ruled: The Year of the Terror in the French Revolution. Isser Woloch (Foreword by). Trade Paper. Princeton University Press. Princeton, NJ. 2005. 280p. Princeton Classic Editions Ser. ISBN:0-691-12187-7, ISBN13: 978-0-691-12187-1. Dewey:944.04/0922. LCCN:2005-045401.
Audience: **u,f.** B

Popkin, Jeremy D. **PN5176.P59 1990**
Revolutionary News: The Press in France, 1789-1799. Keith M. Baker & Steven L. Kaplan (Editors). Cloth Text. Duke University Press. Durham, NC. 1990. 239p. Bicentennial Reflections on the French Revolution Ser. ISBN:0-8223-0984-X, ISBN13: 978-0-8223-0984-0. Dewey:074/.09/033. LCCN:89-028511.
Audience: **u,f.** *Choice, 1990.*

Roessler, Shirley **DC158.8.E57 1996**
Out of the Shadows: Women and Politics in the French Revolution, 1789-95. Cloth Text. Peter Lang Publishing, Inc. New York, NY. 1996. 288p. Studies in Modern European History, Vol. 14 ISBN:0-8204-2565-6, ISBN13: 978-0-8204-2565-8. Dewey:944.04/082. LCCN:94-040970.
Audience: **u,f.** *Choice, 1997.*

Rose, R. B. **DC155**
The Enragés: Socialists of the French Revolution? Melbourne University Press on behalf of the Australian Humanities Research Council; [New York, Cambridge University Press] 1965. Australian Humanities Research Council. Monographs; 12; Variation: Australian Humanities Research Council; Monographs; 12.
Audience: **u,f.**

Schaeper, Thomas J. **E265.C5S34 1995**
France and America During the Revolutionary Era: The Life of Jacques-Donatien Leray de Chaumont, 1725-1803. Trade Cloth. Berghahn Books, Inc. New York, NY. 1995. 396p. ISBN:1-57181-050-1, ISBN13: 978-1-57181-050-2. Dewey:973.3/47. LCCN:94-030422.
Audience: **g,l,u,f.** *Choice, 1996.*

Scott, John A. (Editor) **DC187.8; KJV130.B32**
The Defense of Gracchus Babeuf. Thomas Cornell (Illustrator). Trade Paper. Knopf Publishing Group. New York, NY. 1988. 120p. Studies in the Libertarian and Utopian Tradition Ser ISBN:0-8052-0342-7, ISBN13: 978-0-8052-0342-4. Dewey:347.99/44. LCCN:67-011244.
Audience: **u,f.**

Soboul, Albert **DC158.8**
The Sans-Culottes: The Popular Movement and Revolutionary Government, 1793-1794. Remy Inglis Hall (Translator). Trade Paper. Princeton University Press. Princeton, NJ. 1981. 318p. ISBN:0-691-00782-9, ISBN13: 978-0-691-00782-3. Dewey:944.04.
Audience: **u,f.**

Sutherland, D. M. **DC148.S855 1986**
France Seventeen Eighty-Nine to Eighteen Fifteen: Revolution and Counterrevolution. Paper Text. Oxford University Press, Inc. New York, NY. 1986. 494p. ISBN:0-19-520513-8, ISBN13: 978-0-19-520513-8. Dewey:944.04. LCCN:86-000719.
Audience: **u,f.**

Sydenham, M. J. **DC148.S985 1974**
The First French Republic, Seventeen Ninety-Two to Eighteen Four. Trade Cloth. University of California Press. Berkeley, CA. 1974. xi, 360p. ISBN:0-520-02577-6, ISBN13: 978-0-520-02577-6. Dewey:944.04. LCCN:73-085796.
Audience: **u,f.** B

Sydenham, Michael J. **DC146.B814**
Leonard Bourdon: The Career of a Revolutionary, 1754-1807. Trade Cloth. Wilfrid Laurier University Press. Waterloo, ON. 1999. 448p. ISBN:0-88920-319-9, ISBN13: 978-0-88920-319-8. Dewey:944.04/092. LCCN:98-093282.
Audience: **g,l,u,f.** *Choice, 2000.*

Tackett, Timothy **DC137.05.T33 2003**
When the King Took Flight. Trade Cloth. Harvard University Press. Cambridge, MA. 2003. 288p. ISBN:0-674-01054-X, ISBN13: 978-0-674-01054-3. Dewey:944/.035/092. LCCN:2002-027334.
Audience: **g,l,u,f.** *Choice, 2003.*

Thompson, J. M. **DC146.R6T45**
Robespierre and the French Revolution. Paper Text. Textbook Publishers. Temecula, CA. 2003. vii, 180p. ISBN:0-7581-9014-X, ISBN13: 978-0-7581-9014-7. Dewey:923.244.
Audience: **l,u,f.**

Tilly, Charles **DC183.5**
The Vendee: A Sociological Analysis of the Counter-Revolution of 1793. Trade Cloth. Harvard University Press. Cambridge, MA. 1976. ISBN:0-674-93303-6, ISBN13: 978-0-674-93303-3. Dewey:944.04/4. LCCN:64-021247.
Audience: **u,f.**

Van Kley, Dale K. **DC33.4**
The Religious Origins of the French Revolution: From Calvin to the Civil Constitution, 1560-1791. Trade Paper. Yale University Press. Cumberland, RI. 1999. 400p. ISBN:0-300-08085-9, ISBN13: 978-0-300-08085-8. Dewey:944/.03. LCCN:95-047072.
Audience: **l,u,f.** *Choice, 1997.*

Yalom, Marilyn (Author, Introduction by) **DC158.8**
Blood Sisters: The French Revolution in Women's Memory. Trade Paper. Rivers Oram Press/Pandora. London, 1995. 308p. ISBN:0-04-440918-4, ISBN13: 978-0-04-440918-2. Dewey:944.04082.
Audience: **u,f.** *Choice, 1994.*

France > History > Modern (1789-) > Napoleonic France (1799-1815). Napoleonic Wars. Congress of Vienna

Alexander, R. S. **DC203.A5 2001**
Napoleon. Trade Paper. Oxford University Press, Inc. New York, NY. 2001. 288p. Reputations Ser. ISBN:0-340-71916-8, ISBN13: 978-0-340-71916-9. Dewey:944.05/092 B. LCCN:2001-276686.
Audience: **g,l,u,f.** *Choice, 2002.*

Chandler, David G. **DC151**
The Campaigns of Napoleon: The Mind and Method of History's Greatest Soldier. Trade Cloth. Simon & Schuster. New York, NY. 1973. 1216p. ISBN:0-02-523660-1, ISBN13: 978-0-02-523660-8. Dewey:940.27. LCCN:66-012970.
Audience: **g,l,u,f.**

de Caulaincourt, Armand **DC198.C35A3 2005**
With Napoleon in Russia. Jean Hanoteau & George Libaire (Editors). Trade Paper, Perfect. Dover Publications, Inc. Mineola, NY. 2005. 464p. ISBN:0-486-44013-3, ISBN13: 978-0-486-44013-2. Dewey:940.2/742/092 B. LCCN:2004-065692.
Audience: **g,l,u,f.**

Esdaile, Charles J. **DC231.E834 2003**
The Peninsular War: A New History. Cloth over Boards. Palgrave Macmillan. New York, NY. 2003. 640p. ISBN:1-4039-6231-6, ISBN13: 978-1-4039-6231-7. Dewey:940.2/742. LCCN:2003-273462.
Audience: **g,u,f.** *Choice, 2004.*

Esdaile, Charles J. **DC151.E7 1995**
The Wars of Napoleon. Trade Paper. Longman Publishing Group. White Plains, NY. 1995. 417p. Modern Wars in Perspective Ser. ISBN:0-582-05955-0, ISBN13: 978-0-582-05955-9. Dewey:940.2/7. LCCN:94-044377.
Audience: **l,u,f.**

Forrest, Alan **DC235**
Napoleon's Men: The Soldiers of the Revolution and Empire. Trade Cloth. Continuum International Publishing Group, Ltd. London, 2003. 274p. ISBN:1-85285-269-0, ISBN13: 978-1-85285-269-6. Dewey:940.2/7.
Audience: **u,f.** *Choice, 2003.*

Heckscher, Eli Filip **HF1543.H43**
The Continental System, an Economic Interpretation. Charles Scott Fearenside (Translator). Trade Paper. Books on Demand. Ann Arbor, MI. 436p. ISBN:0-598-97117-3, ISBN13: 978-0-598-97117-3. Dewey:382.3. LCCN:23-005314.
Audience: **l,u,f.**

Herold, J. Christopher **DC146**
Mistress to an Age: A Life of Madame de Stael. Trade Cloth. Greenwood Publishing Group, Inc. Portsmouth, NH. 1975. 500p. ISBN:0-8371-8339-1, ISBN13: 978-0-8371-8339-8. Dewey:848/.609 B. LCCN:75-018399.
Audience: **u,f.** B

Holtman, Robert B. **DC202.5.H65 1969**
Napoleonic Propaganda. Library Binding. Greenwood Publishing Group, Inc. Portsmouth, NH. 1985. xv, 272p. ISBN:0-8371-2140-X, ISBN13: 978-0-8371-2140-6. Dewey:944/.04/6. LCCN:78-090530.
Audience: **u,f.** B

Horne, Alistair **DA87.1.N4**
How Far from Austerlitz?: Napoleon 1805-1815. Trade Paper. St. Martin's Press. Gordonville, VA. 1998. 464p. ISBN:0-312-18724-6, ISBN13: 978-0-312-18724-8. Dewey:940.2/7/092.
Audience: **u,f.**

Kauffmann, Jean-Paul **DC211.K3813 1999**
The Black Room at Longwood: Napoleon's Exile on Saint Helena. Patricia Marie Clancy (Translator). Trade Cloth. Avalon Publishing Group. New York, NY. 1999. 304p. ISBN:1-56858-128-9, ISBN13: 978-1-56858-128-6. Dewey:944/.05/092. LCCN:99-018168.
Audience: **g,l,u,f.**

Latimer, Elizabeth Wormeley (Translator) **DC211**
Talks of Napoleon at St. Helena with General Baron Gourgaud. Trade Paper. Kessinger Publishing, LLC. Whitefish, MT. 2004. ISBN:1-4179-4832-9, ISBN13: 978-1-4179-4832-1. Dewey:944.05.
Audience: **u,f.**

Lefebvre, Georges **DC201**
Napoleon, Set. Henry F. Stockhold & J. E. Anderson (Translators). Paper Text. Columbia University Press. New York, NY. 1990. 776p. ISBN:0-231-07387-9, ISBN13: 978-0-231-07387-5. Dewey:940.270924.
Audience: **g,l,u,f.**

Markham, Felix M. **DC201 .M18**
Napoleon and the Awakening of Europe. Trade Cloth. Lawrence Verry Inc. Mystic, CT. 1972. Men and Their Times Ser. ISBN:0-340-08366-2, ISBN13: 978-0-340-08366-6. Dewey:944.04.
Audience: **g,l,u,f.**

Nicolson, Harold **DC249.N5 2000**
The Congress of Vienna: A Study in Allied Unity, 1812-1822. Trade Paper. Grove/Atlantic, Inc. New York, NY. 2000. 312p. ISBN:0-8021-3744-X, ISBN13: 978-0-8021-3744-9. Dewey:940.2/7. LCCN:00-041709.
Audience: **u,f.**

Roberts, Andrew **DC203 .R6824 2001**
Napoleon and Wellington: The Battle of Waterloo - And the Great Comanders Who Fought It. Trade Cloth. Simon & Schuster. New York, NY. 2002. 384p. ISBN:0-7432-2832-4, ISBN13: 978-0-7432-2832-9. Dewey:940.2/74/0922. LCCN:2003-545018.
Audience: **g,l,u,f.** *Choice, 2003.*

Roseberry, Lord **DC211 .R79**
Napoleon: The Last Phase. Trade Paper. Kessinger Publishing, LLC. Whitefish, MT. 2003. ISBN:0-7661-7331-3, ISBN13: 978-0-7661-7331-6. Dewey:944.05092.
Audience: **u,f.**

Stael, Germaine de & Berger, Morroe **PQ2431.A23 2000**
Politics, Literature and National Character. Trade Paper. Transaction Publishers. Somerset, NJ. 2000. 371p. ISBN:0-7658-0645-2, ISBN13: 978-0-7658-0645-1. Dewey:848/.609. LCCN:00-023400.
Audience: **g,l,u,f.**

Stael, Germaine de **DC146.S7A25 2000**
Ten Years of Exile. Avriel H. Goldberger (Translator). Trade Cloth. Northern Illinois University Press. DeKalb, IL. 2003. 327p. ISBN:0-87580-255-9, ISBN13: 978-0-87580-255-8. Dewey:944.04/092 B. LCCN:99-023994.
Audience: **g,l,u,f.** *Choice, 2001.*

Woloch, Isser **DC155.W65 1994**
The New Regime: Transformations of the French Civic Order, 1789-1820s. Trade Cloth. W. W. Norton & Company, Inc. New York, NY. 1994. 536p. ISBN:0-393-03591-3, ISBN13: 978-0-393-03591-9. Dewey:944/.04. LCCN:93-001917.
Audience: **u,f.** *Choice, 1994.*

Zamoyski, Adam **DC235.Z35 2004**
Moscow 1812: Napoleon's Fatal March. Trade Cloth. HarperCollins Publishers. New York, NY. 2004. 672p. ISBN:0-06-107558-2, ISBN13: 978-0-06-107558-2. Dewey:940.2/742/0947. LCCN:2004-047575.
Audience: **g,l,u,f.**

France > History > Modern (1789-) > Restoration (1815-1830)

Alexander, R. S. & Alexander, Robert **DC256.A43 2003**
Re-Writing the French Revolutionary Tradition: Liberal Opposition and the Fall of the Bourbon Monarchy. Peter Baldwin, Christopher Clark, James B. Collins, Mia Rodriguez-Salgado & Lyndal Roper (Contribution by). Trade Cloth. Cambridge University Press. New York, NY. 2003. 402p. New Studies in European History Ser. ISBN:0-521-80122-2, ISBN13: 978-0-521-80122-5. Dewey:944/.06. LCCN:2003-043812.
Audience: **u,f.** *Choice, 2004.*

Kroen, Sheryl **DC256.8 .K76 2000**
Politics and Theater: The Crisis of Legitimacy in Restoration France, 1815-1830. Trade Cloth. University of California Press. Berkeley, CA. 2000. 410p. Studies on the History of Society and Culture, Vol. 40 ISBN:0-520-22214-8, ISBN13: 978-0-520-22214-4. Dewey:944.06. LCCN:99-048330.
Audience: **u,f.** *Choice, 2001.*

Reddy, William M. **DC252.R38 1997**
The Invisible Code: Honor and Sentiment in Postrevolutionary France, 1814-1848. Trade Cloth. University of California Press. Berkeley, CA. 1997. 292p. ISBN:0-520-20536-7, ISBN13: 978-0-520-20536-9. Dewey:944.04. LCCN:96-021675.
Audience: **u,f.** *Choice, 1997.*

Spitzer, Alan B. **DC0256.8.S66**
The French Generation of 1820. Trade Paper. Books on Demand. Ann Arbor, MI. 1987. 352p. ISBN:0-608-02869-X, ISBN13: 978-0-608-02869-9. Dewey:944.06. LCCN:86-025471.
Audience: **u,f.**

France > History > Modern (1789-) > July Monarchy (1830-1848)

Collingham, H. A. **DC266.5**
July Monarchy. Ed. 1. Paper Text. Addison-Wesley Longman, Inc. Boston, MA. 1989. 470p. ISBN:0-582-02186-3, ISBN13: 978-0-582-02186-0. Dewey:944.06/3. LCCN:87-024490.
Audience: **u,f.** *Choice, 1989.*

Loyrette, Henry & Pantazzi, Michael **N6853.P5**
Daumier: 1808-1879. Cloth over Boards. Yale University Press. Cumberland, RI. 2000. 600p. ISBN:0-300-08359-9, ISBN13: 978-0-300-08359-0. Dewey:709/.2. LCCN:00-340799.
Audience: **g,l,u,f.** *Choice, 2000.*

Popkin, Jeremy D. **PN5177.P67 2002**
Press, Revolution and Social Identities in France, 1830-1835. Trade Cloth. Pennsylvania State University Press. University Park, PA. 2001. x, 329p. ISBN:0-271-02152-7, ISBN13: 978-0-271-02152-2. Dewey:074/.09/034. LCCN:2001-021545.
Audience: **u,f.** *Choice, 2002.*

Robb, Graham **PQ2178**
Balzac: A Biography. Trade Paper. W. W. Norton & Company, Inc. New York, NY. 2003. 572p. ISBN:0-393-31387-5, ISBN13: 978-0-393-31387-1. Dewey:843.7. LCCN:94-018614.
Audience: **g,l,u,f.**

France > History > Modern (1789-) > 1848 Revolution and Second Republic (1848-1852)

Agulhon, Maurice **DC272 .A3513 1983**
The Republican Experiment, 1848-1852. Janet Lloyd (Translator). Trade Paper. Cambridge University Press. New York, NY. 1983. 225p. History of Modern France Ser., No. 2 ISBN:0-521-28988-2, ISBN13: 978-0-521-28988-7. Dewey:944.07. LCCN:82-023461.
Audience: **u,f.** B

Clark, T. J. **N6847**
The absolute bourgeois: artists and politics in France, 1848-1851. Berkeley : University of California Press. 1999. ISBN:0-520-21744-6, ISBN13: 978-0-520-21744-7.
Audience: **g,l,u,f.**

de Tocqueville, Alexis **DC270.T652 1986**
Recollections: The French Revolution of 1848. J. P. Mayer (Editor, Introduction by), Fernand Braude (Preface by). Trade Paper. Transaction Publishers. Somerset, NJ. 1987. 333p. ISBN:0-88738-658-X, ISBN13: 978-0-88738-658-9. Dewey:944.07. LCCN:86-001485.
Audience: **g,l,u,f.**

Jennings, Lawrence Charles **DC272.5**
France and Europe in 1848: A Study of French Foreign Affairs in Time of Crisis. Trade Cloth. Oxford University Press, Inc. New York, NY. 1973. ix, 280p. ISBN:0-19-822514-8, ISBN13: 978-0-19-822514-0. Dewey:327.44/04. LCCN:73-173775.
Audience: **u,f.**

Margadant, Ted W. **DC276**
French Peasants in Revolt: The Insurrection of 1851. Trade Cloth. Princeton University Press. Princeton, NJ. 1980. 408p. ISBN:0-691-05284-0, ISBN13: 978-0-691-05284-7. Dewey:944.07. LCCN:79-084001.
Audience: **u,f.**

Price, Roger (Editor) **DC271.5.E53 1996**
Documents on the French Revolution 1848. Trade Cloth. Palgrave Macmillan. New York, NY. 1997. 240p. Documents in

History Ser. ISBN:0-312-16128-X, ISBN13: 978-0-312-16128-6. Dewey:944.07. LCCN:96-007530.
Audience: **g,l,u,f.**

Watkins, Sharon B. **JC229.T8W38 2003**
Alexis de Tocqueville and the Second Republic, 1848-1852: A Study in Political Practice and Principles. Trade Paper. University Press of America, Inc. Lanham, MD. 2003. 614p. ISBN:0-7618-2505-3, ISBN13: 978-0-7618-2505-0. Dewey:944.07/092 B. LCCN:2003-040237.
Audience: **u,f.** *Choice, 2003.*

France > History > Modern (1789-) > Second Empire. Franco-German War (1852-1871)

Edwards, Stewart (Editor) **DC316**
The Communards of Paris, 1871. Trade Cloth. Cornell University Press. Ithaca, NY. 1973. 180p. ISBN:0-8014-0779-6, ISBN13: 978-0-8014-0779-6. Dewey:944/.36/081. LCCN:72-013387.
Audience: **g,l,u,f.**

Jordan, David P. **HT178.F72P345 1995**
Transforming Paris: The Life and Labors of Baron Haussmann. Trade Cloth. Simon & Schuster. New York, NY. 1995. 455p. ISBN:0-02-916531-8, ISBN13: 978-0-02-916531-7. Dewey:307.1/216/092 B. LCCN:94-030089.
Audience: **u,f.**

Plessis, Alain **944.07**
The Rise and Fall of the Second Empire, 1852-1871. Jonathan Mandelbaum (Translator). Trade Paper. Cambridge University Press. New York, NY. 1988. 218p. Cambridge History of Modern France Ser., No. 3 ISBN:0-521-35856-6, ISBN13: 978-0-521-35856-9. Dewey:944.07.
Audience: **g,l,u,f.** *Choice, 1985.*

Price, Roger **DC280 .P74 2001**
The French Second Empire: An Anatomy of Political Power. Peter Baldwin, Christopher Clark, James B. Collins, Mia Rodr¡guez-Salgado & Lyndal Roper (Contribution by). Trade Cloth. Cambridge University Press. New York, NY. 2001. 518p. New Studies in European History ISBN:0-521-80830-8, ISBN13: 978-0-521-80830-9. Dewey:944.07092 B. LCCN:2001-025954.
Audience: **u,f.** *Choice, 2003, 2002.*

Price, Roger **DC272.5.P75 2004**
People and Politics in France, 1848-1870. Peter Baldwin, Christopher Clark, James B. Collins, Mia Rodr¡guez-Salgado & Lyndal Roper (Contribution by). Trade Cloth. Cambridge University Press. New York, NY. 2004. 488p. New Studies in European History Ser. ISBN:0-521-83706-5, ISBN13: 978-0-521-83706-4. Dewey:944/.07. LCCN:2003-065206.
Audience: **u,f.** *Choice, 2005.*

Taylor, Therese **BX4700.S65**
Bernadette of Lourdes: Her Life, Death and Visions. Trade Cloth. Continuum International Publishing Group, Ltd. London, 2003. 352p. ISBN:0-86012-337-5, ISBN13: 978-0-86012-337-8. Dewey:271.9/1/02.
Audience: **g,l,u,f.** *Choice, 2004.*

Wawro, Geoffrey **DC293.W38 2003**
The Franco-Prussian War: The German Conquest of France in 1870-1871. Trade Cloth. Cambridge University Press. New York, NY. 2003. 344p. ISBN:0-521-58436-1, ISBN13: 978-0-521-58436-4. Dewey:943.08/2. LCCN:2002-041685.
Audience: **g,l,u,f.** *Choice, 2004.*

France > History > Modern (1789-) > Third Republic (1875-1940)

Audoin-Rouzeau, Stephane **D548 .A8313 1992**
Men at War 1914-1918: National Sentiment and Trench Journalism in France during the First World War. Helen McPhail (Translator). Cloth over Boards. Berg Publishers. Oxford, 1992. 207p. Reports from the French Trenches ISBN:0-85496-673-0, ISBN13: 978-0-85496-673-8. Dewey:940.41244. LCCN:91-045272.
Audience: **u,f.**

Bredin, Jean-Denis **E743.5.H55**
The Affair: The Case of Alfred Dreyfus. Trade Paper. George Braziller Inc. New York, NY. 1987. ISBN:0-8076-1175-1, ISBN13: 978-0-8076-1175-3. Dewey:364.131. LCCN:85-022374.
Audience: **g,l,u,f.**

Carles, Emilie & Destanque, Robert **DC801.B853**
A Life of Her Own: The Transformation of a Countrywoman in 20th-Century France. Auriel H. Goldberger (Translator). Trade Paper. Penguin Group (USA) Inc. New York, NY. 1992. 304p. ISBN:0-14-016965-2, ISBN13: 978-0-14-016965-2. Dewey:944/.97.
Audience: **g,l,u,f.**

Caron, Vicki **DS135.F63**
Uneasy Asylum: France and the Jewish Refugee Crisis, 1933-1942. Trade Paper. Stanford University Press. Palo Alto, CA. 1999. 605p. Studies in Jewish History and Culture ISBN:0-8047-4377-0, ISBN13: 978-0-8047-4377-8. Dewey:944/.004924.
Audience: **u,f.** *Choice, 1999.*

Duroselle, Jean Baptiste **DC396**
France and the Nazi Threat 1932-1939: The Collapse of French Diplomacy. Trade Paper. Enigma Books. New York, NY. 2004. 545p. ISBN:1-929631-15-4, ISBN13: 978-1-929631-15-5. Dewey:327.4404309043.
Audience: **g,u,f.** *Choice, 2004.*

Fink, Carole **D15.B596 F56 1989**
Marc Bloch: A Life in History. Cloth Text. Cambridge University Press. New York, NY. 1989. 400p. ISBN:0-521-37300-X, ISBN13: 978-0-521-37300-5. Dewey:944.007202. LCCN:88-032216.
Audience: **u,f.** *Choice, 1990.*

Ford, Caroline **DC611.F498F67 1993**
Creating the Nation in Provincial France: Religion and Political Identity in Brittany. Trade Cloth. Princeton University Press. Princeton, NJ. 1993. 272p. ISBN:0-691-05667-6, ISBN13: 978-0-691-05667-8. Dewey:944.11. LCCN:92-020828.
Audience: **u,f.** *Choice, 1993.*

Guillaumin, Emile **PQ2631.R63**
The Life of a Simple Man. Ed. 3. Eugen Weber (Editor, Introduction by), Margaret Crosland (Translator). Trade Paper. University Press of New England. Lebanon, NH. 1982. 231p. ISBN:0-87451-246-8, ISBN13: 978-0-87451-246-5. Dewey:843/.912. LCCN:82-040339.
Audience: **g,l,u,f.**

Hanna, Martha **D639.P88F743 1996**
The Mobilization of Intellect: French Scholars and Writers During the Great War. Trade Cloth. Harvard University Press. Cambridge, MA. 1996. 304p. ISBN:0-674-57755-8, ISBN13: 978-0-674-57755-8. Dewey:940.4/0944. LCCN:95-042544.
Audience: **u,f.** *Choice, 1997.*

Hyman, Paula **DS135.F8 H96 1998**
The Jews of Modern France. Trade Paper. University of California Press. Berkeley, CA. 1998. 278p. Jewish Communities in the Modern World Ser., Vol. 1 ISBN:0-520-20925-7, ISBN13: 978-0-520-20925-1. Dewey:944/.004924. LCCN:97-039349.
Audience: **u,f.** *Choice, 1999.*

Johansen, Anja **HV6485.F8J64 2004**
Soldiers As Police: The French and Prussian Armies and the Policing of Popular Protest, 1889-1914. Trade Cloth. Ashgate Publishing, Ltd. Aldershot, 2005. 340p. ISBN:0-7546-3376-4, ISBN13: 978-0-7546-3376-1. Dewey:363.32. LCCN:2004-008258.
Audience: **u,f.** *Choice, 2005.*

Jordan, Nicole **DC369**
The Popular Front and Central Europe: The Dilemmas of French Impotence 1918-1940. Trade Paper. Cambridge University Press. New York, NY. 2002. 366p. ISBN:0-521-52242-0, ISBN13: 978-0-521-52242-7. Dewey:327.4/4043/09041.
Audience: **u.**

Kiesling, Eugenia C. **D761.K54 1996**
Arming Against Hitler: France and the Limits of Military Planning. Trade Cloth. University Press of Kansas. Lawrence, KS. 1996. 264p. Modern War Studies ISBN:0-7006-0764-1, ISBN13: 978-0-7006-0764-8. Dewey:940.534. LCCN:95-053924.
Audience: **u,f.** *Choice, 1997.*

Lacouture, Jean **DC342.8.P4**
De Gaulle: The Rebel, 1890-1944. Patrick O'Brian (Translator). Trade Paper. W. W. Norton & Company, Inc. New York, NY. 1993. 640p. ISBN:0-393-30999-1, ISBN13: 978-0-393-30999-7. Dewey:944.083/6/092 B.
Audience: **u,f.** *Choice, 1991.*

Morowitz, Laura & Emery, Elizabeth **DC33.6.M67 2003**
Consuming the Past: The Medieval Revival in Fin-De-Siecle France. Trade Cloth. Ashgate Publishing, Ltd. Aldershot, 2003. 308p. ISBN:0-7546-0319-9, ISBN13: 978-0-7546-0319-1. Dewey:944.081/2. LCCN:2002-027801.
Audience: **g,l,u,f.** *Choice, 2004.*

Roberts, Mary L. **HQ1075.5.F8.R63 1994**
Civilization Without Sexes: Reconstructing Gender in Postwar France, 1917-1927. Trade Cloth. University of Chicago Press. Chicago, IL. 1994. 352p. Women in Culture and Society Ser. ISBN:0-226-72121-3, ISBN13: 978-0-226-72121-7. Dewey:305.3/0944. LCCN:93-026899.
Audience: **u,f.** *Choice, 1994.*

Roberts, Mary Louise **HQ1617.R55 2002**
Disruptive Acts: The New Woman in Fin-de-Siecle France. Trade Cloth. University of Chicago Press. Chicago, IL. 2002. 364p. ISBN:0-226-72124-8, ISBN13: 978-0-226-72124-8. Dewey:305.42/0944. LCCN:2002-004194.
Audience: **u,f.** *Choice, 2003.*

Shapiro, Ann-Louise **HV6046.S46 1996**
Breaking the Codes: Female Criminality in Fin-de-Siecle Paris. Trade Cloth. Stanford University Press. Palo Alto, CA. 1996. 296p. ISBN:0-8047-1663-3, ISBN13: 978-0-8047-1663-5. Dewey:364.3/74/0944. LCCN:95-037867.
Audience: **u,f.** *Choice, 1996.*

Smith, Leonard V., et al. **D516.S65 2002**
France and the Great War. Stiphane Audoin-Rouzeau & Annette Becker (Authors). Cloth Text. Cambridge University Press. New York, NY. 2003. 222p. New Approaches to European History Ser. ISBN:0-521-66176-5, ISBN13: 978-0-521-66176-8. Dewey:940.3/44. LCCN:2002-031202.
Audience: **g,l,u,f.**

Stuart, Robert C. **HX263 .S78 1992**
Marxism at Work: Ideology, Class and French Socialism During the Third Republic. Trade Cloth. Cambridge University Press. New York, NY. 1992. 535p. ISBN:0-521-41526-8, ISBN13: 978-0-521-41526-2. Dewey:335.4/0944/09034. LCCN:91-027093.
Audience: **u,f.** *Choice, 1993.*

Taithe, Bertrand **DC320.T35 2001**
Defeated Flesh: Medicine, Society and the Birth of Modern France. Trade Cloth. Rowman & Littlefield Publishers, Inc. Lanham, MD. 1999. 304p. ISBN:0-7425-0048-9, ISBN13: 978-0-7425-0048-8. Dewey:944.081/2. LCCN:2001-019879.
Audience: **u,f.** *Choice, 2000.*

Watson, Donald R. **DC342.8.C6W34 1976**
Georges Clemenceau: A Political Biography. Trade Cloth. David McKay Company, Inc. New York, NY. 1976. 463p. ISBN:0-679-50703-5, ISBN13: 978-0-679-50703-1. Dewey:944.0814092. LCCN:76-028607.
Audience: **g,l,u,f.**

Weber, Eugen **HN426.W4 1976**
Peasants into Frenchmen: The Modernization of Rural France, 1870-1914. Trade Cloth. Stanford University Press. Palo Alto, CA. 1976. xvi, 616p. ISBN:0-8047-0898-3, ISBN13: 978-0-8047-0898-2. Dewey:301.29/44. LCCN:75-007486.
Audience: **u,f.** B

Williams, Charles **DC420.W535 1993**
The Last Great Frenchman: A Life of General de Gaulle. Ed. 1. Trade Cloth. John Wiley & Sons, Inc. Hoboken, NJ. 1995. 544p. ISBN:0-471-11711-0, ISBN13: 978-0-471-11711-7. Dewey:944/.082/092. LCCN:94-042881.
Audience: **g,l,u,f.**

Zola, Emile **DC354.8.Z6513 1996**
The Dreyfus Affair: J'Accuse and Other Writings. Alain Pages (Editor), Eleanor Levieux (Translator). Cloth over Boards. Yale University Press. Cumberland, RI. 1996. 244p. ISBN:0-300-06689-9, ISBN13: 978-0-300-06689-0. Dewey:944/.0812/092. LCCN:96-001735.
Audience: **g,l,u,f.** *Choice, 1997.*

France > History > Modern (1789-) > Defeat, Vichy and Occupation (1940-1946)

Bloch, Marc **D802.F8**
Strange Defeat: A Statement of Evidence Written in 1940. Trade Paper. W. W. Norton & Company, Inc. New York, NY. 1999. 200p. ISBN:0-393-31911-3, ISBN13: 978-0-393-31911-8. Dewey:940.5344.
Audience: **g,l,u,f.**

Doughty, Robert A. **D756.5.M4D68 1990**
The Breaking Point: Sedan and the Fall of France, 1940. Trade Cloth. Shoe String Press, Inc. North Haven, CT. 1990. xiv, 374p. ISBN:0-208-02281-3, ISBN13: 978-0-208-02281-3. Dewey:940.54/21431. LCCN:90-032505.
Audience: **u,f.** *Choice, 1991.*

Footitt, Hilary & Simmonds, John **D761.F65 1988**
France, 1943-1945. Trade Cloth. Holmes & Meier Publishers, Inc. Teaneck, NJ. 1988. 335p. Politics of Liberation Ser. ISBN:0-8419-1175-4, ISBN13: 978-0-8419-1175-8. Dewey:940.53/44. LCCN:88-003086.
Audience: **g,u,f.** *Choice, 1989.*

Jackson, Julian **DC397**
The Fall of France: The Nazi Invasion of 1940. Trade Cloth. Oxford University Press, Inc. New York, NY. 2003. 256p. The Making of the Modern World Ser. ISBN:0-19-280300-X, ISBN13: 978-0-19-280300-9. Dewey:940.54/214. LCCN:2002-044697.
Audience: **g,l,u,f.** *Choice, 2004.*

Kaplan, Alice **D802.F8B6985 2000**
The Collaborator: The Trial and Execution of Robert Brasillach. Trade Cloth. University of Chicago Press. Chicago, IL. 2000. 336p. ISBN:0-226-42414-6, ISBN13: 978-0-226-42414-9. Dewey:848/.91209 B. LCCN:99-048291.
Audience: **u,f.** *Choice, 2000.*

Kedward, Harry R. **D802.F8**
Resistance in Vichy France: A Study of Ideas and Motivation in the Southern Zone, 1940-42. Trade Cloth. Oxford University Press, Inc. New York, NY. 1984. ix, 311p. ISBN:0-19-821956-3, ISBN13: 978-0-19-821956-9. Dewey:940.53/448. LCCN:83-017269.
Audience: **g,l,u,f.**

Marrus, Michael R. & Paxton, Robert O. **DS135.F83M3813 1983**
Vichy France and the Jews. Stanley Hoffmann (Foreword by). Trade Paper. Stanford University Press. Palo Alto, CA. 1995. 454p. ISBN:0-8047-2499-7, ISBN13: 978-0-8047-2499-9. Dewey:944/.0816/089924. LCCN:94-068126.
Audience: **u,f.**

Morgan, Ted **D802.F82L9454 1990**
An Uncertain Hour: The French, the Germans, the Jews, and the City of Lyon, 1940-1945. Trade Cloth. HarperCollins Publishers. New York, NY. 1990. 384p. ISBN:0-87795-989-7, ISBN13: 978-0-87795-989-2. Dewey:940.53/44. LCCN:89-034066.
Audience: **g,l,u,f.**

Paxton, Robert O. **DC397**
Vichy France: Old Guard and New Order. Ed. 2. Trade Paper. Columbia University Press. New York, NY. 2001. 438p. ISBN:0-231-12469-4, ISBN13: 978-0-231-12469-0. Dewey:944.081/6. LCCN:2002-319326.
Audience: **g,l,u,f.**

Poznanski, Renie **DS135.F83P7913 2001**
Jews in France During World War II. Library Binding. University Press of New England. Lebanon, NH. 2002. 768p. Tauber Institute for the Study of European Jewry Ser. ISBN:0-87451-896-2, ISBN13: 978-0-87451-896-2. Dewey:940.53/18/0944. LCCN:2001-004982.
Audience: **u,f.**

Sweets, John F. **D802.F8**
Choices in Vichy France: The French under Nazi Occupation. Paper Text. Oxford University Press, Inc. New York, NY. 1994. 320p. ISBN:0-19-509052-7, ISBN13: 978-0-19-509052-9. Dewey:940.53/44. LCCN:85-010579.
Audience: **g,l,u,f.** *Choice, 1986.*

Thomas **D761.9.A1T48 1998**
French Empire at War, 1940-1945. Trade Cloth. Manchester University Press. Manchester, 1998. 336p. Studies in Imperialism ISBN:0-7190-5034-0, ISBN13: 978-0-7190-5034-3. Dewey:940.3/44. LCCN:98-010253.
Audience: **g,u,f.** *Choice, 1998.*

Young, Robert J. **D742.F7Y68 1996**
France and the Origins of the Second World War. Trade Cloth. Palgrave Macmillan. New York, NY. 1996. 200p. ISBN:0-312-16185-9, ISBN13: 978-0-312-16185-9. Dewey:944/.0815. LCCN:96-010410.
Audience: **g,l,u,f.** *Choice, 1997.*

Zaretsky, Robert **DC611.G217Z37 1995**
Nimes at War: Religion, Politics, and Public Opinion in the Gard, 1938-1944. Cloth Text. Pennsylvania State University Press. University Park, PA. 1995. 328p. ISBN:0-271-01326-5, ISBN13: 978-0-271-01326-8. Dewey:944/.830815. LCCN:93-041182.
Audience: **g,l,u,f.** *Choice, 1995.*

Zuccotti, Susan **DS135.F83Z83 1999**
The Holocaust, the French, and the Jews. Trade Paper. University of Nebraska Press. Lincoln, NE. 1999. 408p. ISBN:0-8032-9914-1, ISBN13: 978-0-8032-9914-6. Dewey:940.53/18/0944. LCCN:99-010662.
Audience: **g,l,u,f.** *Choice, 1994.*

France > History > Modern (1789-) > Fourth and Fifth Republics (1947-). Algeria Crisis

Bess, Michael D. **GE199.F8B47 2003**
The Light-Green Society: Ecology and Technological Modernity in France, 1960-2000. Trade Cloth. University of Chicago Press. Chicago, IL. 1995. 387p. ISBN:0-226-04417-3, ISBN13: 978-0-226-04417-0. Dewey:333.7/2/0944. LCCN:2003-009664.
Audience: **u,f.** *Choice, 2004.*

Gildea, Robert **DC404.G5 2002**
France since 1945. Ed. 2. Trade Paper. Oxford University Press, Inc. New York, NY. 2002. 368p. ISBN:0-19-280131-7, ISBN13: 978-0-19-280131-9. Dewey:944.083. LCCN:2002-281075.
Audience: **g,l,u,f.**

Hitchcock, William I. **DC404.H53 1998**
France Restored: Cold War Diplomacy and the Quest for Leadership in Europe, 1944-1954. Trade Paper. University of North Carolina Press. Chapel Hill, NC. 1998. 312p. The New Cold War History Ser. ISBN:0-8078-4747-X, ISBN13: 978-0-8078-4747-3. Dewey:327.44. LCCN:97-051123.
Audience: **g,l,u,f.** *Choice, 1999.*

Horne, Alistair **DT295.H64 2006**
A Savage War of Peace: Algeria 1954-1962. Trade Paper. New York Review of Books, Incorporated, The. New York, NY. 2006. 600p. New York Review Books Classics ISBN:1-59017-218-3, ISBN13: 978-1-59017-218-6. Dewey:965/.046. LCCN:2006-003506.
Audience: **g,u,f.**

Khilnani, Sunil **JA84.F8K5 1993**
Arguing Revolution: The Intellectual Left in Post-War France. Cloth over Boards. Yale University Press. Cumberland, RI. 1993. 256p. ISBN:0-300-05745-8, ISBN13: 978-0-300-05745-4. Dewey:320.50944. LCCN:93-017376.
Audience: **u,f.** *Choice, 1994.*

Lacouture, Jean **DC420.L313 1990**
De Gaulle: The Ruler 1945-1970, Vol. II. Alan Sheridan (Translator). Trade Cloth. W. W. Norton & Company, Inc. New York, NY. 1992. 700p. ISBN:0-393-03084-9, ISBN13: 978-0-393-03084-6. Dewey:944.083/6/092 B. LCCN:90-037997.
Audience: **g,u,f.** *Choice, 1992.*

Maran, Rita **DT295**
Torture: The Role of Ideology in the French-Algerian War. Trade Cloth. Greenwood Publishing Group, Inc. Portsmouth, NH. 1989. 230p. ISBN:0-275-93248-6, ISBN13: 978-0-275-93248-0. Dewey:965/.04. LCCN:88-037478.
Audience: **g,l,u,f.** *Choice, 1990.*

Revel, Jacques & Naddabb, Ramona (Editors) **D13.5.F8 H57**
Histories: French Constructions of the Postwar French Thought. Trade Paper. New Press, The. New York, NY. 1998. 684p. Postwar French Thought Ser. ISBN:1-56584-435-1, ISBN13: 978-1-56584-435-3. Dewey:944/.081/0722. LCCN:95-071802.
Audience: **u,f.**

Ross, Kristin **DC33.7**
Fast Cars, Clean Bodies: Decolonization and the Reordering of French Culture. Trade Paper. MIT Press. Cambridge, MA. 1996. 274p. October Bks. ISBN:0-262-68091-2, ISBN13: 978-0-262-68091-2. Dewey:944.083.
Audience: **u,f.** *Choice, 1995.*

Rousso, Henry **DC397**
The Vichy Syndrome: History and Memory in France since 1944. Goldhammer, Arthur (Translator). Cambridge, Mass. : Harvard University Press. 1994. ISBN:0-674-93538-1, ISBN13: 978-0-674-93538-9.
Audience: **g,l,u,f.**

Young, John W. **DC404.Y68 1990**
France, the Cold War and the Western Alliance, 1944-1949: French Foreign Policy and Post-War Europe. Cloth Text. Palgrave Macmillan. New York, NY. 1990. 384p. ISBN:0-312-04193-4, ISBN13: 978-0-312-04193-9. Dewey:327.44. LCCN:89-029481.
Audience: **g,u,f.** *Choice, 1990.*

France > Special topics > Immigration

MacMaster, Neil (Editor) **DC34.5.A4M33 1996**
Colonial Migrants and Racism: Algerians in France, 1900-62. Cloth over Boards. Palgrave Macmillan. New York, NY. 1997. 320p. ISBN:0-312-16501-3, ISBN13: 978-0-312-16501-7. Dewey:305.8/92765/044. LCCN:96-003247.
Audience: **u,f.** *Choice, 1997.*

Ogden, Philip E. & White, Paul E. (Editors) **HB2053.M53 1988**
Migrants in Modern France. Paper over Boards. Routledge. New York, NY. 2003. 256p. ISBN:0-04-301209-4, ISBN13: 978-0-04-301209-3. Dewey:304.8/0944. LCCN:88-017108.
Audience: **u,f.** *Choice, 1990.*

Phillips, Peggy A. **DC417**
Republican France: Divided Loyalties. Book, Other. Greenwood Publishing Group, Inc. Portsmouth, NH. 1993. 208p. Contributions in Political Science Ser., No. 325 ISBN:0-313-27503-3, ISBN13: 978-0-313-27503-6. Dewey:320.944. LCCN:92-045075.
Audience: **g,l,u,f.** *Choice, 1994.*

France > Special topics > Colonialism, Decolonization

Aldrich, Robert **JV1811**
Greater France: A History of French Overseas Expansion. Trade Paper. Palgrave Macmillan. New York, NY. 1996. 385p. European Studies ISBN:0-312-16000-3, ISBN13: 978-0-312-16000-5. Dewey:909/.0971244.
Audience: **u,f.** *Choice, 1997.*

Aldrich, Robert & Connell, John **HC276.3 .A64 1991**
France's Overseas Frontier: Les Departements et Territoires d'Outre-Mer. Trade Cloth. Cambridge University Press. New York, NY. 1992. 367p. ISBN:0-521-39061-3, ISBN13: 978-0-521-39061-3. Dewey:909/.0971244. LCCN:91-009067.
Audience: **u,f.** *Choice, 1992.*

Thomas, Martin **JV1818**
The French Empire Between the Wars: Imperialism, Politics and Society. Cloth over Boards. Manchester University Press. Manchester, 2005. 384p. Studies in Imperialism Ser. ISBN:0-7190-6518-6, ISBN13: 978-0-7190-6518-7. Dewey:909/.09712440822. LCCN:2005-279837.
Audience: **u,f.** *Choice, 2006.*

France > Special topics > Historiography > French Revolution

de Tocqueville, Alexis **DC138.T6313 1998**
The Old Regime and the Revolution: Notes on the French Revolution and Napolean. Francois Furet & Francoise Melonio (Editors), Alan S. Kahan (Translator). Trade Cloth. University of Chicago Press. Chicago, IL. 2001. 512p. ISBN:0-226-80533-6, ISBN13: 978-0-226-80533-7. Dewey:944.04. LCCN:97-043814.
Audience: **g,l,u,f.**

Furet, Francois & Marx, Karl **DC148.F8613 1988**
Marx and the French Revolution. Lucien Calvie (Editor), Deborah K. Furet (Translator). Trade Cloth. University of Chicago Press. Chicago, IL. 1988. 247p. ISBN:0-226-27338-5, ISBN13: 978-0-226-27338-9. Dewey:944.04. LCCN:88-020439.
Audience: **u,f.**

Furet, Francois **DC148.D5313 1989**
A Critical Dictionary of the French Revolution. Mona Ozouf (Editor), Arthur Goldhammer (Translator). Trade Cloth. Harvard University Press. Cambridge, MA. 1989. 1120p. ISBN:0-674-17728-2, ISBN13: 978-0-674-17728-4. Dewey:944.04. LCCN:89-030656.
Audience: **u,f.** *Choice, 1990.*

Hobsbawm, Eric J. **DC148.H56 1990**
Echoes of the Marseillaise: Two Centuries Look Back on the French Revolution. Cloth Text. Rutgers University Press. Piscataway, NJ. 1990. 185p. ISBN:0-8135-1523-8, ISBN13: 978-0-8135-1523-6. Dewey:944.04/072. LCCN:89-039351.
Audience: **g,l,u,f.**

Khilnani, Sunil **JA84.F8K5 1993**
Arguing Revolution: The Intellectual Left in Post-War France. Cloth over Boards. Yale University Press. Cumberland, RI. 1993. 256p. ISBN:0-300-05745-8, ISBN13: 978-0-300-05745-4. Dewey:320.50944. LCCN:93-017376.
Audience: **u,f.** *Choice, 1994.*

Michelet, Jules **DC161.M51532**
History of the French Revolution. Gordon Wright (Editor, Introduction by), Charles Cocks (Translator). Paper Text. University of Chicago Press. Chicago, IL. 1997. xxii, 476p. Classic European Historians Ser. ISBN:0-226-52333-0, ISBN13: 978-0-226-52333-0. Dewey:944.04. LCCN:67-015315.
Audience: **u,f.** B

Roessler, Shirley **DC158.8.E57 1996**
Out of the Shadows: Women and Politics in the French Revolution, 1789-95. Cloth Text. Peter Lang Publishing, Inc. New York, NY. 1996. 288p. Studies in Modern European History, Vol. 14 ISBN:0-8204-2565-6, ISBN13: 978-0-8204-2565-8. Dewey:944.04/082. LCCN:94-040970.
Audience: **u,f.** *Choice, 1997.*

Yalom, Marilyn (Author, Introduction by) **DC158.8**
Blood Sisters: The French Revolution in Women's Memory. Trade Paper. Rivers Oram Press/Pandora. London, 1995. 308p. ISBN:0-04-440918-4, ISBN13: 978-0-04-440918-2. Dewey:944.04082.
Audience: **u,f.** *Choice, 1994.*

France > Special topics > Historiography > Napoleon

Butterfield, Herbert, Sir **DC203**
Napoleon. Collier Books. 1962.
Audience: **g,l,u.**

Geyl, Pieter **DC203.8**
Napoleon, For and Against. Renier, Olive (Translator). New Haven, Yale University Press. 1967.
Audience: **u,f.**

France > Local History > Regions and Provinces

Cope, Christopher **DC611.B775C66 1987**
The Lost Kingdom of Burgundy. Trade Cloth. W. Clement Stone, P M A Communications, Inc. Northbrook, IL. 1987. 296p. ISBN:0-396-08955-0, ISBN13: 978-0-396-08955-1. Dewey:944/.4. LCCN:86-019761.
Audience: **u,f.**

Galliou, Patrick & Jones, Michael **DC611.B851**
The Bretons. Trade Paper. Blackwell Publishing, Inc. Malden, MA. 1996. 352p. The Peoples of Europe Ser. ISBN:0-631-20105-X, ISBN13: 978-0-631-20105-2. Dewey:944.1.
Audience: **g,l,u,f.** *Choice, 1992.*

Jacob, James E. **DC611.B318J33 1994**
Hills of Conflict: Basque Nationalism in France. Cloth Text. University of Nevada Press. Reno, NV. 1994. 568p. The Basque Ser., : ISBN:0-87417-220-9, ISBN13: 978-0-87417-220-1. Dewey:946/.6. LCCN:93-014730.
Audience: **u,f.** *Choice, 1995.*

Johnson, Christopher H. **HC277.L2J64 1995**
The Life and Death of Industrial Languedoc, 1700-1920. Trade Cloth. Oxford University Press, Inc. New York, NY. 1995. 322p. ISBN:0-19-504508-4, ISBN13: 978-0-19-504508-6. Dewey:338.4/767/09448. LCCN:94-029309.
Audience: **u,f.** *Choice, 1995.*

France > Local History > Paris

Benjamin, Walter **PT2603.E455P33513**
The Arcades Project. Howard Eiland & Kevin McLaughlin (Translators). Trade Paper. Harvard University Press. Cambridge, MA. 2002. 1088p. Belknap Press Ser. ISBN:0-674-00802-2, ISBN13: 978-0-674-00802-1. Dewey:944/.361081.
Audience: **u,f.** *Choice, 2000.*

Garrioch, David **DC729 .G33 2002**
The Making of Revolutionary Paris. Trade Cloth. University of California Press. Berkeley, CA. 2002. 412p. ISBN:0-520-23253-4, ISBN13: 978-0-520-23253-2. Dewey:944/.36. LCCN:2001-008255.
Audience: **l,u,f.** *Choice, 2003.*

Gluck, Mary **NX549.P2G58 2004**
Popular Bohemia: Modernism and Urban Culture in Nineteenth-Century Paris. Trade Cloth. Harvard University Press. Cambridge, MA. 2005. 238p. ISBN:0-674-01530-4, ISBN13: 978-0-674-01530-2. Dewey:700/.1/0/30944361034. LCCN:2004-054379.
Audience: **u,f.** *Choice, 2006.*

Harvey, David **DC715.H337 2003**
Paris, Capital of Modernity. Paper over Boards. Routledge. New York, NY. 2003. 384p. ISBN:0-415-94421-X, ISBN13: 978-0-415-94421-2. Dewey:944/.36107. LCCN:2003-004067.
Audience: **u,f.**

Jones, Colin **DC707.J66 2005**
Paris: The Biography of a City. Trade Cloth. Penguin Group (USA) Inc. New York, NY. 2005. 592p. ISBN:0-670-03393-6, ISBN13: 978-0-670-03393-5. Dewey:944/.361. LCCN:2004-053608.
Audience: **g,l,u,f.**

Jordan, David P. **HT178.F72P345 1995**
Transforming Paris: The Life and Labors of Baron Haussmann. Trade Cloth. Simon & Schuster. New York, NY. 1995. 455p. ISBN:0-02-916531-8, ISBN13: 978-0-02-916531-7. Dewey:307.1/216/092 B. LCCN:94-030089.
Audience: **u,f.**

Germany > General Works and Histories

Allen, Ann T. **HQ759.A42 1991**
Feminism and Motherhood in Germany, 1800-1914. Cloth Text. Rutgers University Press. Piscataway, NJ. 1991. 275p. ISBN:0-8135-1686-2, ISBN13: 978-0-8135-1686-8. Dewey:305.42/0943. LCCN:90-021164.
Audience: **g,l,u,f.** *Choice, 1992.*

Barclay, David E. & Weitz, Eric D. (Editors) **HX273**
Between Reform and Revolution: German Socialism and Communism from 1840 to 1990. Trade Cloth. Berghahn Books, Inc. New York, NY. 2003. 600p. ISBN:1-57181-120-6, ISBN13: 978-1-57181-120-2. Dewey:335/.00943. LCCN:97-022088.
Audience: **u,f.**

Berger, Stefan **DD89**
Germany. Trade Paper. Oxford University Press, Inc. New York, NY. 2004. 288p. A Hodder Arnold Publication ISBN:0-340-70584-1, ISBN13: 978-0-340-70584-1. Dewey:321/.05/0943. LCCN:2004-304822.
Audience: **g,l,u,f.** *Choice, 2005.*

Blackbourn, David **TC73.B53 2006**
The Conquest of Nature: Water, Landscape, and the Making of Modern Germany. Trade Cloth. W. W. Norton & Company, Inc. New York, NY. 2006. 608p. ISBN:0-393-06212-0, ISBN13: 978-0-393-06212-0. Dewey:627.0943. LCCN:2006-001386.
Audience: **u,f.**

Blackbourn, David **DD203.B6 2002**
History of Germany, 1780-1918: The Long Nineteenth Century. Ed. 2. Trade Cloth. Blackwell Publishing, Inc. Malden, MA. 2002. 480p. Blackwell Classic Histories of Europe Ser. ISBN:0-631-23195-1, ISBN13: 978-0-631-23195-0. Dewey:943.07. LCCN:2002-066700.
Audience: **u,f.**

Blackbourn, David & Eley, Geoffrey **DD204.B5213 1984**
The Peculiarities of German History: Bourgeois Society and Politics in Nineteenth-Century Germany. Paper Text. Oxford University Press, Inc. New York, NY. 1984. 308p. ISBN:0-19-873057-8, ISBN13: 978-0-19-873057-6. Dewey:943/.07. LCCN:84-010051.
Audience: **u,f.** B

Cioc, Mark & Cronon, William **GF540.C56 2005**
The Rhine: An Eco-Biography, 1815-2000. Trade Paper. University of Washington Press. Seattle, WA. 2005. 272p. ISBN:0-295-98500-3, ISBN13: 978-0-295-98500-8. Dewey:333.91/62/09434.
Audience: **l,u,f.** *Choice, 2003.*

Cioc, Mark **GF540.C56 2002**
The Rhine: An Eco-Biography, 1815-2000. William Cronon (Foreword by). Trade Cloth. University of Washington Press. Seattle, WA. 2002. 272p. Weyerhaeuser Environmental Bks. ISBN:0-295-98254-3, ISBN13: 978-0-295-98254-0. Dewey:333.91/62/09434. LCCN:2002-072694.
Audience: **g,u,f.** *Choice, 2003.*

Cocks, Geoffrey & Jarausch, Konrad H. (Editors) **HT690.G3G46 1990**
German Professions, 1800-1950. Trade Cloth. Oxford University Press, Inc. New York, NY. 1990. 350p. ISBN:0-19-505596-9, ISBN13: 978-0-19-505596-2. Dewey:305.5/53/0943. LCCN:89-034784.
Audience: **g,l,u,f.** *Choice, 1991.*

Craig, Gordon A. **DD259.C7 1991**
The Germans. Trade Paper. Penguin Group (USA) Inc. New York, NY. 1991. 368p. ISBN:0-452-01085-3, ISBN13: 978-0-452-01085-7. Dewey:943. LCCN:91-012814.
Audience: **g,l,u,f.**

Crawshaw, Steve **DD290.25**
Easier Fatherland: Germany in the Twenty-First Century. Trade Cloth. Continuum International Publishing Group, Ltd. London, 2004. 288p. ISBN:0-8264-6320-7, ISBN13: 978-0-8264-6320-3. Dewey:943.088. LCCN:2005-279388.
Audience: **g,l,u,f.** *Choice, 2005.*

Flippo, Hyde **DD60.F55**
The German Way: Aspects of Behavior, Attitudes and Customs in the German-Speaking World. Paper Text. McGraw-Hill/Contemporary. Lincolnwood, IL. 1997. 128p. Dewey:943.087/9.
Audience: **g,l,u,f.**

Frevert, Ute **HQ1627.F69713 1989**
Women in German History: From Bourgeois Emancipation to Sexual Liberation. Stuart McKinnon-Evans, Barbara Norden & Terry Bond (Translators). Cloth over Boards. Berg Publishers. Oxford, 1990. 346p. ISBN:0-85496-233-6, ISBN13: 978-0-85496-233-4. Dewey:305.4/2/0943. LCCN:88-013123.
Audience: **u,f.** *Choice, 1989.*

Herf, Jeffrey **DD238**
Reactionary Modernism: Technology, Culture, and Politics in Weimar and the Third Reich. Trade Paper. Cambridge University Press. New York, NY. 1986. 272p. ISBN:0-521-33833-6, ISBN13: 978-0-521-33833-2. Dewey:943.086.
Audience: **u,f.**

Koshar, Rudy **DD222 .K67 2000**
From Monuments to Traces: Artifacts of German Memory, 1870-1990. Trade Cloth. University of California Press. Berkeley, CA. 2000. 368p. Weimar and Now Ser., Vol. 24:German Cultural Criticism ISBN:0-520-21768-3, ISBN13: 978-0-520-21768-3. Dewey:943.08. LCCN:99-088549.
Audience: **u,f.** *Choice, 2001.*

Koshar, Rudy **85-28958**
Social Life, Local Politics, and Nazism: Marburg, 1880-1935. Trade Paper. University of North Carolina Press. Chapel Hill, NC. 1990. 413p. ISBN:0-8078-4287-7, ISBN13: 978-0-8078-4287-4. Dewey:943/.41. LCCN:85-028958.
Audience: **u,f.** *Choice, 1987.*

McClelland, Charles E. **HD8038.G3**
The German Experience of Professionalization: Modern Learned Professions and Their Organizations from the Early Nineteenth Century to the Hitler Era. Trade Paper. Cambridge University Press. New York, NY. 2002. 265p. ISBN:0-521-52253-6, ISBN13: 978-0-521-52253-3. Dewey:331.7/12/0943.
Audience: **u,f.** *Choice, 1992.*

Pulzer, Peter **DS135.G33P85 2003**
Jews and the German State: The Political History of a Minority, 1848-1933. Trade Paper. Wayne State University Press. Detroit, MI. 2002. 394p. ISBN:0-8143-3130-0, ISBN13: 978-0-8143-3130-9. Dewey:943/.004924. LCCN:2003-041116.
Audience: **u,f.** *Choice, 1992.*

Reagin, Nancy Ruth **HQ1623.R43 1995**
A German Women's Movement: Class and Gender in Hanover, 1880-1933. Trade Paper. University of North Carolina Press. Chapel Hill, NC. 1995. 336p. ISBN:0-8078-4525-6, ISBN13: 978-0-8078-4525-7. Dewey:305.42/0943. LCCN:94-039348.
Audience: **u,f.** *Choice, 1996.*

Ryan, Judith (Editor) **PT91.N49 2004**
A New History of German Literature. David E. Wellbery, Hans Ulrich Gumbrecht, Anton Kaes, Joseph Koerner & Dorothea E. von MŸcke (Contribution by). Trade Cloth. Harvard University Press. Cambridge, MA. 2005. 1032p. Harvard University Press Reference Library ISBN:0-674-01503-7, ISBN13: 978-0-674-01503-6. Dewey:830.9. LCCN:2004-059590.
Audience: **g,l,u,f.** *Choice, 2005.*

Schulze, Hagen & Schneider, Deborah L. **DD17**
Germany: A New History. Trade Paper. Harvard University Press. Cambridge, MA. 2001. 368p. ISBN:0-674-00545-7, ISBN13: 978-0-674-00545-7. Dewey:943.
Audience: **g,l,u,f.**

Sheehan, James J. **DD204.S53 2001**
German Liberalism in the 19th Century. Trade Cloth. Prometheus Books, Publishers. Amherst, NY. 1995. 421p. German Studies ISBN:1-57392-606-X, ISBN13: 978-1-57392-606-5. Dewey:320.512094309034.
Audience: **g,l,u,f.**

Turk, Eleanor L. **DD90**
The History of Germany. Cloth Text. Greenwood Publishing Group, Inc. Portsmouth, NH. 1999. 256p. The Histories of the Modern Nations Ser. ISBN:0-313-30274-X, ISBN13: 978-0-313-30274-9. Dewey:943. LCCN:98-035258.
Audience: **g,l,u,f.** *Choice, 1999.*

Germany > Military and Diplomatic History

Brechtefeld, Jorg **DAW1045.G3B74 1996**
Mitteleuropa and German Politics: 1848 to the Present. Trade Cloth. Palgrave Macmillan. New York, NY. 1996. 240p. ISBN:0-312-15841-6, ISBN13: 978-0-312-15841-5. Dewey:327/.0943. LCCN:95-052081.
Audience: **u,f.** *Choice, 1997.*

Brose, Eric Dorn **UA712**
The Kaiser's Army: The Politics of Military Technology in Germany during the Machine Age, 1870-1918. Trade Paper. Oxford University Press, Inc. New York, NY. 2004. 336p. ISBN:0-19-517945-5, ISBN13: 978-0-19-517945-3. Dewey:355.4/0943.
Audience: **g,u,f.** *Choice, 2002.*

Bucholz, Arden **U155.G3B83 1991**
Moltke, Schlieffen and Prussian War Planning. Trade Cloth. Berg Publishers. Oxford, 1991. 368p. ISBN:0-85496-653-6, ISBN13: 978-0-85496-653-0. Dewey:355/.033543. LCCN:90-039333.
Audience: **u,f.** *Choice, 1992.*

Citino, Robert Michael **DD101.C58 2005**
The German Way of War: From the Thirty Years' War to the Third Reich. Saddle Stitched, Cloth over Boards, Dust Jacket. University Press of Kansas. Lawrence, KS. 2005. 428p. Modern War Studies ISBN:0-7006-1410-9, ISBN13: 978-0-7006-1410-3. Dewey:355.02/0943. LCCN:2005-024615.
Audience: **g,u,f.** *Choice, 2006.*

Corum, James S. **UA710.C67 1992**
The Roots of Blitzkrieg: Hans von Seeckt and German Military Reform. Trade Cloth. University Press of Kansas. Lawrence, KS. 1992. xviii, 276p. Modern War Studies ISBN:0-7006-0541-X, ISBN13: 978-0-7006-0541-5. Dewey:355.02/0943. LCCN:92-005178.
Audience: **g,u,f.** *Choice, 1993.*

Craig, Gordon A. **DD221**
The Politics of the Prussian Army: 1640-1945. Paper Text. Oxford University Press, Inc. New York, NY. 1964. 556p. ISBN:0-19-500257-1, ISBN13: 978-0-19-500257-7. Dewey:943.08.
Audience: **u,f.**

Echevarria, Antulio Joseph **U43.G3E28 2000**
After Clausewitz: German Military Thinkers Before the Great War. Trade Cloth. University Press of Kansas. Lawrence, KS. 2004. x, 346p. Modern War Studies ISBN:0-7006-1071-5, ISBN13: 978-0-7006-1071-6. Dewey:355.02/0943/09034. LCCN:00-010228.
Audience: **g,u,f.** *Choice, 2001.*

Foley, Robert T. **D545.V3F65 2004**
German Strategy and the Path to Verdun: Erich von Falkenhayn and the Development of Attrition, 1870-1916. Hew Strachan & Geoffrey Wawro (Contribution by). Cloth Text. Cambridge University Press. New York, NY. 2005. 316p. Cambridge Military Histories Ser. ISBN:0-521-84193-3, ISBN13: 978-0-521-84193-1. Dewey:940.4/013. LCCN:2004-045708.
Audience: **u,f.** *Choice, 2006.*

Frevert, Ute **DD103**
Nation in Barracks: Modern Germany, Military Conscription and Civil Society. Andrew Boreham (Translator). Cloth over Boards. Berg Publishers. Oxford, 2004. 288p. ISBN:1-85973-881-8, ISBN13: 978-1-85973-881-8. Dewey:355.2/25/0943. LCCN:2004-020617.
Audience: **g,l,u,f.** *Choice, 2005.*

Herwig, Holger H. **D531.H464 1997**
The First World War: Germany and Austria-Hungary 1914-1918. Paper Text. Oxford University Press, Inc. New York, NY. 1996. 512p. Modern Wars Ser. ISBN:0-340-57348-1, ISBN13: 978-0-340-57348-8. Dewey:940.4147. LCCN:96-028152.
Audience: **u,f.** *Choice, 1997.*

Horne, John N. & Kramer, Alan **D626.G3H67 2001**
German Atrocities, 1914: A History of Denial. Cloth over Boards. Yale University Press. Cumberland, RI. 2001. 624p. ISBN:0-300-08975-9, ISBN13: 978-0-300-08975-2. Dewey:940.4/05. LCCN:2001-026884.
Audience: **g,u,f.**

Hull, Isabel V. **DD103.H85 2004**
Absolute Destruction. Book, Other. Cornell University Press. Ithaca, NY. 2004. 408p. ISBN:0-8014-4258-3, ISBN13: 978-0-8014-4258-2. Dewey:355.02/13/094309034. LCCN:2004-013387.
Audience: **u,f.** *Choice, 2005.*

Liulevicius, Vejas Gabriel **D551 .L58 2000**
War Land on the Eastern Front: Culture, National Identity, and German Occupation in World War I. Paul Kennedy, Antoine Prost, Emmanuel Sivan & Jay Winter (Contribution by). Trade Cloth. Cambridge University Press. New York, NY. 2000. 318p. Studies in the Social and Cultural History of Modern Warfare, Vol. 9 ISBN:0-521-66157-9, ISBN13: 978-0-521-66157-7. Dewey:940.4143. LCCN:00-693294.
Audience: **u,f.** *Choice, 2001.*

Muhle, Eduard (Editor) **DD232**
Germany and the European East in the Twentieth Century. Cloth over Boards. Berg Publishers. Oxford, 2003. 224p. German Historical Perspectives Ser. ISBN:1-85973-710-2, ISBN13: 978-1-85973-710-1. Dewey:327.43047/09/04. LCCN:2003-000660.
Audience: **u,f.** *Choice, 2004.*

Nekrich, Aleksandr M. & Freeze, Gregory L. **DD120.S65N45 1997**
Pariahs, Partners, Predators: German-Soviet Relations, 1922-1941. Trade Cloth. Columbia University Press. New York, NY. 1997. 320p. ISBN:0-231-10676-9, ISBN13: 978-0-231-10676-4. Dewey:327.43047/09/042. LCCN:96-029605.
Audience: **u,f.** *Choice, 1998.*

Schollgen, Gregor (Editor) **DD221.5.E8 1990**
Escape into War?: The Foreign Policy of Imperial Germany. Trade Cloth. Berg Publishers. Oxford, 1990. 185p. German Historical Perspectives Ser., Vol. 6 ISBN:0-85496-275-1, ISBN13: 978-0-85496-275-4. Dewey:327.43. LCCN:90-000345.
Audience: **u,f.** *Choice, 1991.*

Germany > History > Early (to 481). Germanic tribes

King, Anthony **DC63.K56 1990**
Roman Gaul and Germany. Trade Cloth. University of California Press. Berkeley, CA. 1990. 240p. Exploring the Roman World Ser. ISBN:0-520-06989-7, ISBN13: 978-0-520-06989-3. Dewey:936.302. LCCN:89-020546.
Audience: **u,f.** *Choice, 1991.*

Tacitus, Cornelius **DG291.7.A2T313 1999**
Agricola and Germany. Anthony Birley (Translator). Trade Paper. Oxford University Press, Inc. New York, NY. 1999. 216p. Oxford World's Classics Ser. ISBN:0-19-283300-6, ISBN13: 978-0-19-283300-6. Dewey:936.1/03. LCCN:98-034569.
Audience: **g,l,u.**

Todd, Malcolm **DD75.T62 2004**
Early Germans. Ed. 2. Trade Paper. Blackwell Publishing, Inc. Malden, MA. 2004. 288p. The Peoples of Europe Ser. ISBN:1-4051-1714-1, ISBN13: 978-1-4051-1714-2. Dewey:936.3. LCCN:2004-055089.
Audience: **g,l,u,f.**

Germany > History > Medieval Kingdoms and Empires (to 1519)

Arnold, Benjamin **JN3249.A76**
Count and Bishop in Medieval Germany: A Study of Regional Power, 1100-1350. Trade Paper. Books on Demand. Ann Arbor, MI. 230p. Middle Ages Ser. ISBN:0-608-07303-2, ISBN13: 978-0-608-07303-3. Dewey:320.943. LCCN:91-024938.
Audience: **u,f.** *Choice, 1992.*

Barraclough, Geoffrey **DD89.B27 1984**
The Origins of Modern Germany. Trade Paper. W. W. Norton & Company, Inc. New York, NY. 1984. 504p. ISBN:0-393-30153-2, ISBN13: 978-0-393-30153-3. Dewey:943. LCCN:84-001624.
Audience: **g,l,u,f.**

Fuhrmann, Horst **DD141 .F8313 1986**
Germany in the High Middle Ages: C. 1050-1200. Timothy Reuter (Translator). Trade Paper. Cambridge University Press. New York, NY. 1986. 195p. Cambridge Medieval Textbooks ISBN:0-521-31980-3, ISBN13: 978-0-521-31980-5. Dewey:943/.02. LCCN:85-029988.
Audience: **g,l,u,f.**

Hampe, Karl & Baethgen, Friedrich **DD126 .H313 1973**
Germany Under the Salian and Hohenstaufen Emperors. Ralph F. Bennett (Translator). Trade Cloth. Rowman & Littlefield Publishers, Inc. Lanham, MD. 1973. 306p. ISBN:0-87471-173-8, ISBN13: 978-0-87471-173-8. Dewey:943/.02. LCCN:71-185304.
Audience: **u,f.**

Haverkamp, Alfred **DD126.H3813 1992**
Medieval Germany, 1056-1273. Ed. 2. Helga Braun & Richard Mortimer (Translators). Paper Text. Oxford University Press, Inc. New York, NY. 1992. 440p. ISBN:0-19-822172-X, ISBN13: 978-0-19-822172-2. Dewey:943/.02. LCCN:93-187306.
Audience: **u,f.**

Huffman, Joseph P. **DA47.2.H84 2000**
The Social Politics of Medieval Diplomacy: Anglo-German Relations, 1066-1307. Trade Cloth. University of Michigan Press. Chicago, IL. 2000. 376p. Studies in Medieval and Early Modern Civilization Ser. ISBN:0-472-11061-6, ISBN13: 978-0-472-11061-2. Dewey:327.41043. LCCN:99-051933.
Audience: **u,f.** *Choice, 2001.*

Jeep, John M. (Editor) **DD126.M43 2001**
Medieval Germany: An Encyclopedia. Trade Cloth. Garland Publishing, Inc. New York, NY. 2001. 800p. Routledge Encyclopedias of the Middle Ages Ser. ISBN:0-8240-7644-3, ISBN13: 978-0-8240-7644-3. Dewey:943/.02/03. LCCN:00-061780.
Audience: **g,l,u,f.** *Choice, 2001.*

Lloyd, T. H. **HF455**
England and the German Hanse, 1157-1611: A Study of Their Trade and Commercial Diplomacy. Trade Paper. Cambridge

University Press. New York, NY. 2002. 411p. ISBN:0-521-52214-5, ISBN13: 978-0-521-52214-4. Dewey:382/.0942043.
Audience: **u,f.** *Choice, 1992.*

Scaglione, Aldo **GT3520.S34 1991**
Knights at Court: Courtliness, Chivalry, and Courtesy from Ottonian Germany to the Italian Renaissance. Trade Cloth. University of California Press. Berkeley, CA. 1992. 440p. ISBN:0-520-07270-7, ISBN13: 978-0-520-07270-1. Dewey:940.1. LCCN:91-006703.
Audience: **u,f.** *Choice, 1992.*

Schultz, James A. **HQ792.G3S376 1995**
The Knowledge of Childhood in the German Middle Ages, 1100-1350. Trade Cloth. University of Pennsylvania Press. Philadelphia, PA. 1995. 336p. Middle Ages Ser. ISBN:0-8122-3297-6, ISBN13: 978-0-8122-3297-4. Dewey:305.23/0943/0902. LCCN:95-017057.
Audience: **g,u,f.** *Choice, 1996.*

Germany > History > Medieval Kingdoms and Empires (to 1519) > Merovingians. Carolingians (481-918)

Barbero, Alessandro **DC73 .B3613 2004**
Charlemagne: Father of a Continent. Allan Cameron (Translator). Trade Cloth. University of California Press. Berkeley, CA. 2004. 438p. ISBN:0-520-23943-1, ISBN13: 978-0-520-23943-2. Dewey:944/.0142/092 B. LCCN:2003-017208.
Audience: **g,l,u,f.** *Choice, 2005.*

Becher, Matthias **DC73.B39 2003**
Charlemagne. Cloth over Boards. Yale University Press. Cumberland, RI. 2003. 176p. ISBN:0-300-09796-4, ISBN13: 978-0-300-09796-2. Dewey:944/.014/092 B. LCCN:2003-007858.
Audience: **g,l,u,f.** *Choice, 2004.*

Drew, Katherine F. (Translator, Introduction by) **KJ336.E5 1991**
The Laws of the Salian Franks. Trade Cloth. University of Pennsylvania Press. Philadelphia, PA. 1991. 276p. Middle Ages Ser. ISBN:0-8122-8256-6, ISBN13: 978-0-8122-8256-6. Dewey:340.5/5. LCCN:90-021755.
Audience: **u,f.** *Choice, 1991.*

Einhard, et al. **DC73.32.T45 1969B**
Two Lives of Charlemagne. Notker & Notker the Stammerer Staff (Authors), Lewis Thorpe (Translator, Introduction by). Trade Paper. Penguin Group (USA) Inc. New York, NY. 1969. 240p. Classics Ser., 13 ISBN:0-14-044213-8, ISBN13: 978-0-14-044213-7. Dewey:944/.01/0924. LCCN:72-473993.
Audience: **g,l,u,f.**

Geary, Patrick J. **DC65.G43 1988**
Before France and Germany: The Creation and Transformation of the Merovingian World. Paper Text. Oxford University Press, Inc. New York, NY. 1988. 272p. ISBN:0-19-504458-4, ISBN13: 978-0-19-504458-4. Dewey:943/.01. LCCN:87-007927.
Audience: **g,l,u,f.** *Choice, 1988.*

Gregory, Saint Bishop of Tours **DC65**
Gregory of Tours : the Merovingians. Murray, Alexander C. (Editor). Broadview Press. 2006. Readings in medieval civilizations and cultures ISBN:1-55111-523-9, ISBN13: 978-1-55111-523-8.
Audience: **g,l,u,f.**

McKitterick, Rosamond **P211.3.E85M35 1989**
The Carolingians and the Written Word. Trade Paper. Cambridge University Press. New York, NY. 1989. 308p. ISBN:0-521-31565-4, ISBN13: 978-0-521-31565-4. Dewey:001.54/3/094. LCCN:88-029232.
Audience: **u,f.**

McKitterick, Rosamond **DC70**
History and Memory in the Carolingian World. Cloth Text. Cambridge University Press. New York, NY. 2004. 354p. ISBN:0-521-82717-5, ISBN13: 978-0-521-82717-1. Dewey:940.1. LCCN:2005-297210.
Audience: **l,u,f.** *Choice, 2005.*

Riche, Pierre **DC70**
The Carolingians: A Family Who Forged Europe. Michael I. Allen (Translator). Trade Cloth. University of Pennsylvania Press. Philadelphia, PA. 1993. 424p. Middle Ages Ser. ISBN:0-8122-3062-0, ISBN13: 978-0-8122-3062-8. Dewey:944/.01. LCCN:91-303532.
Audience: **u,f.** *Choice, 1993.*

Germany > History > Medieval Kingdoms and Empires (to 1519) > Houses of Saxony and Franconia (919-1125)

Adam of Bremen **BX1538.H35A3313 2002**
History of the Archbishops of Hamburg-Bremen. Francis Joseph Tschan (Translator, Introduction by, Notes by), Timothy Reuter (Translator). Trade Cloth. Columbia University Press. New York, NY. 2002. 288p. Records of Western Civilization Ser. ISBN:0-231-12574-7, ISBN13: 978-0-231-12574-1. Dewey:282/.43515/0902. LCCN:2001-053731.
Audience: **g,l,u,f.**

Althoff, Gerd **DD140.4.A4813 2003**
Otto III. Phyllis G. Jestice (Translator). Trade Cloth. Pennsylvania State University Press. University Park, PA. 2003. 232p. ISBN:0-271-02232-9, ISBN13: 978-0-271-02232-1. Dewey:943/.022/092 B. LCCN:2003-009373.
Audience: **g,l,u,f.** *Choice, 2004.*

Robinson, I. S. **DD143 .R68 1999**
Henry IV of Germany 1056-1106. Trade Paper. Cambridge University Press. New York, NY. 2003. 418p. ISBN:0-521-54590-0, ISBN13: 978-0-521-54590-7. Dewey:943.023092 B.
Audience: **u,f.**

Thietmar **DD136.T48 2000**
Ottonian Germany: The Chronicon of Thietmar of Merseburg. David Warner (Translator). Cloth over Boards. Manchester University Press. Manchester, 2001. 432p. Manchester Medieval Sources Ser. ISBN:0-7190-4925-3, ISBN13: 978-0-7190-4925-5. Dewey:943/.022. LCCN:2001-030102.
Audience: **g,l,u,f.**

Weinfurter, Stefan **DD143.W46 1999**
The Salian Century: Main Currents in an Age of Transition. Book, Other. University of Pennsylvania Press. Philadelphia, PA. 1999. 248p. Middle Ages Ser. ISBN:0-8122-3508-8, ISBN13: 978-0-8122-3508-1. Dewey:943/.023. LCCN:99-025597.
Audience: **g,l,u,f.** *Choice, 2000.*

Germany > History > Medieval Kingdoms and Empires (to 1519) > Hohenstaufen period (1125-1273)

Abulafia, David **DD151 .A28 1988**
Frederick Second: A Medieval Emperor. Trade Cloth. Penguin Group (USA) Inc. New York, NY. 1988. 480p. ISBN:0-7139-9004-X, ISBN13: 978-0-7139-9004-1. Dewey:943.0250924. LCCN:88-060417.
Audience: **g,l,u,f.**

Abulafia, David **HF411 .A28**
The Two Italies: Economic Relations Between the Norman Kingdom of Sicily and the Northern Communes. Trade Paper. Cambridge University Press. New York, NY. 2005. 330p. Cambridge Studies in Medieval Life and Thought Ser., Vol. 9:Third Ser. ISBN:0-521-02306-8, ISBN13: 978-0-521-02306-1. Dewey:382/.0945/10458.
Audience: **u,f.**

Kantorowicz, Ernst Hartwig **DD151**
Frederick the Second, 1194-1250. Ungar. 1967.
Audience: **u,f.**

Otto, et al. **DD149.O78413 2004**
The Deeds of Frederick Barbarossa. Rahewin & Charles Christopher Mierow (Authors). Trade Cloth. Columbia University Press. New York, NY. 2004. 384p. Records of Western Civilization Ser. ISBN:0-231-13418-5, ISBN13: 978-0-231-13418-7. Dewey:943/.024/092. LCCN:2004-045583.
Audience: **g,l,u,f.**

Germany > History > Medieval Kingdoms and Empires (to 1519) > 1273-1519

Benecke, Gerhard **DD174**
Maximillian I, 1459-1519. Trade Cloth. Routledge. New York, NY. 1982. 224p. ISBN:0-7100-9023-4, ISBN13: 978-0-7100-9023-2. Dewey:943/.029/0924. LCCN:82-000608.
Audience: **g,l,u,f.**

Du Boulay, F. R. H. **DD156 .D83X 1983B**
Germany in the Later Middle Ages. Trade Paper. Continuum International Publishing Group, Ltd. London, 1991. 180p. ISBN:0-485-12042-9, ISBN13: 978-0-485-12042-4. Dewey:943/.02. LCCN:84-672301.
Audience: **g,u,f.**

Scott, Tom **HC283.S27 2001**
Society and Economy in Germany, 1300-1600. Cloth over Boards. Palgrave Macmillan. New York, NY. 2002. 304p. European Studies ISBN:0-333-58531-3, ISBN13: 978-0-333-58531-3. Dewey:943/.02. LCCN:2001-053167.
Audience: **u,f.** *Choice, 2002.*

Strauss, Gerald (Introduction by) **DD174**
Manifestations of Discontent in Germany on the Eve of the Reformation: A Collection of Documents Selected, Translated, and Introduced by Gerald Strauss. Trade Cloth. Indiana University Press. Bloomington, IN. 1971. 276p. ISBN:0-253-33670-8, ISBN13: 978-0-253-33670-5. Dewey:943/.02. LCCN:75-135014.
Audience: **g,l,u,f.**

Germany > History > Modern (1815-)

Anderson, Margaret Lavinia **JN3838.A54 2000**
Practicing Democracy: Elections and Political Culture in Imperial Germany. Trade Paper. Princeton University Press. Princeton, NJ. 2000. 504p. ISBN:0-691-04854-1, ISBN13: 978-0-691-04854-3. Dewey:324.7/0943/09034. LCCN:99-045803.
Audience: **u,f.** *Choice, 2000.*

Barkin, Kenneth D. **HC0285.B35**
The Controversy over German Industrialization, 1890-1902. Trade Paper. Books on Demand. Ann Arbor, MI. 317p. ISBN:0-8357-8852-0, ISBN13: 978-0-8357-8852-6. Dewey:382/.7/0943. LCCN:78-101359.
Audience: **u,f.**

Blackbourn, David **DD203.B6 2002**
History of Germany, 1780-1918: The Long Nineteenth Century. Ed. 2. Trade Cloth. Blackwell Publishing, Inc. Malden, MA. 2002. 480p. Blackwell Classic Histories of Europe Ser. ISBN:0-631-23195-1, ISBN13: 978-0-631-23195-0. Dewey:943.07. LCCN:2002-066700.
Audience: **u,f.**

Blackbourn, David **BT660.M37B57 1994**
Marpingen: Apparitions of the Virgin Mary in Bismarckian Germany. Trade Cloth. Alfred A. Knopf Inc. New York, NY. 1994. ISBN:0-679-41843-1, ISBN13: 978-0-679-41843-6. Dewey:232.91/7/094342. LCCN:93-037733.
Audience: **u,f.**

Canning, Kathleen **HD6150.N67C36 1996**
Languages of Labor and Gender: Female Factory Work in Germany, 1850-1914. Book, Other. Cornell University Press. Ithaca, NY. 1996. 352p. ISBN:0-8014-3123-9, ISBN13: 978-0-8014-3123-4. Dewey:331.4/87/09435509043. LCCN:96-000793.
Audience: **u,f.** *Choice, 1997.*

Chickering, Roger **DD228**
Imperial Germany and the Great War, 1914-1918. Ed. 2. William Beik, T. C. W. Blanning & Brendan Simms (Contribution by). Trade Paper. Cambridge University Press. New York, NY. 2004. 248p. New Approaches to European History Ser., Vol. 27 ISBN:0-521-54780-6, ISBN13: 978-0-521-54780-2. Dewey:940.3/43. LCCN:2004-274268.
Audience: **g,l,u,f.**

Craig, Gordon A. **DD220**
Germany, 1866-1945. Paper Text. Oxford University Press, Inc. New York, NY. 1980. 825p. History of Modern Europe Ser. ISBN:0-19-502724-8, ISBN13: 978-0-19-502724-2. Dewey:943/.08.
Audience: **g,l,u.**

Davis, Belinda J. **D538.5.B47D38 2000**
Home Fires Burning: Food, Politics and Everyday Life in World War I Berlin. Trade Paper. University of North Carolina Press. Chapel Hill, NC. 2000. 349p. ISBN:0-8078-4837-9, ISBN13: 978-0-8078-4837-1. Dewey:943/.155084. LCCN:99-032578.
Audience: **g,l,u,f.** *Choice, 2000.*

Feldman, Gerald D. **HC286.2 .F4 1992**
Army, Industry and Labour in Germany, 1914-1918. Trade Paper. Berg Publishers. Oxford, 1992. 586p. Legacy of the Great War Ser. ISBN:0-85496-764-8, ISBN13: 978-0-85496-764-3. Dewey:338.0943. LCCN:92-012579.
Audience: **u,f.**

Gagliardo, John G. **DD175.G34 1991**
Germany under the Old Regime, 1600-1790. Trade Paper. Longman Publishing Group. White Plains, NY. 1995. 464p. Longman History of Germany Ser. ISBN:0-582-49106-1, ISBN13: 978-0-582-49106-9. Dewey:943. LCCN:90-046361.
Audience: **u,f.** *Choice, 1992.*

Gall, Lothar **DD218.G2213 1986**
Bismarck: 1815-1871, Vol. 1. J. A. Underwood (Translator). Paper Text. Routledge. New York, NY. 1990. 284p. ISBN:0-04-445779-0, ISBN13: 978-0-04-445779-4. Dewey:943.08/092/4 B. LCCN:85-026658.
Audience: **u,f.** *Choice, 1987.*

Gall, Lothar & Underwood, J. A. **DD218**
Bismarck: White Revolutionary 1815-1871, Vol. 2. Trade Paper. Routledge. New York, NY. 1990. 284p. ISBN:0-415-09457-7, ISBN13: 978-0-415-09457-3. Dewey:943.08/092/4 B.
Audience: **u,f.**

Kaplan, Marion A. **DS135.G33**
The Making of the Jewish Middle Class: Women, Family, and Identity in Imperial Germany. Trade Paper. Oxford University Press, Inc. New York, NY. 1994. 368p. Studies in Jewish History ISBN:0-19-509396-8, ISBN13: 978-0-19-509396-4. Dewey:943/.004924. LCCN:90-045234.
Audience: **l,u,f.** *Choice, 1992.*

Kelly, Alfred H. **DD67 .K4**
The Descent of Darwin: The Popularization of Darwinism in Germany, 1860-1914. Trade Cloth. University of North Carolina Press. Chapel Hill, NC. 1981. xi, 185p. ISBN:0-8078-1460-1, ISBN13: 978-0-8078-1460-4. Dewey:001.1/0943. LCCN:80-019445.
Audience: **u,f.**

Lees, Andrew **HT137.L354 2002**
Cities, Sin, and Social Reform in Imperial Germany. Trade Cloth. University of Michigan Press. Chicago, IL. 2002. 448p. Social History, Popular Culture and Politics in Germany Ser. ISBN:0-472-11258-9, ISBN13: 978-0-472-11258-6. Dewey:307.76/0943/09034. LCCN:2001-006516.
Audience: **u,f.**

Martel, Gordon (Editor) **DD220**
Modern Germany Reconsidered. Trade Cloth. Routledge. New York, NY. 1992. 304p. ISBN:0-415-07811-3, ISBN13: 978-0-415-07811-5. Dewey:943/.08.
Audience: **u,f.**

Mommsen, Wolfgang J. **DD220.M5613 1995**
Imperial Germany 1867-1918: Politics, Culture, and Society in an Authoritarian State. Richard Deveson (Translator). Trade Paper. Oxford University Press, Inc. New York, NY. 1995. 320p. An Arnold Publication Ser. ISBN:0-340-59360-1, ISBN13: 978-0-340-59360-8. Dewey:943.08. LCCN:95-031744.
Audience: **g,l,u,f.** *Choice, 1996.*

Nipperdey, Thomas **DD203.N5513 1996**
Germany from Napoleon to Bismarck, 1800-1866. Daniel Nolan (Translator). Trade Cloth. Princeton University Press. Princeton, NJ. 1996. 760p. ISBN:0-691-02636-X, ISBN13: 978-0-691-02636-7. Dewey:943/.07. LCCN:95-004498.
Audience: **g,u,f.** *Choice, 1996.*

Ogilvie, Sheilagh (Editor) **DD17**
Germany: A New Social and Economic History 1630-1800, Vol. 2. Paper Text. Oxford University Press, Inc. New York, NY. 1996. 448p. A Hodder Arnold Publication Ser. ISBN:0-340-65216-0, ISBN13: 978-0-340-65216-9. Dewey:943.
Audience: **u,f.**

Overy, Richard & Ogilvie, Sheilagh (Author, Editors) **DD89**
Germany: A New Social and Economic History, since 1800, Vol. 3. Trade Paper. Oxford University Press, Inc. New York, NY. 2003. 448p. An Arnold Publication ISBN:0-340-65214-4, ISBN13: 978-0-340-65214-5. Dewey:943.
Audience: **g,u,f.**

Pflanze, Otto **DD0218.P44**
Bismarck and the Development of Germany: The Period of Consolidation, 1871-1880, Vol. 2. Trade Paper. Books on Demand. Ann Arbor, MI. 572p. ISBN:0-608-09104-9, ISBN13: 978-0-608-09104-4. Dewey:943/.07. LCCN:89-011004.
Audience: **u,f.**

Pflanze, Otto **DD0218.P44**
Bismarck and the Development of Germany: The Period of Unification, 1815-1871, Vol. 1. Ed. 2. Trade Paper. Books on Demand. Ann Arbor, MI. 548p. ISBN:0-608-09103-0, ISBN13: 978-0-608-09103-7. Dewey:943/.07. LCCN:89-011004.
Audience: **u,f.**

Pflanze, Otto **DD0218.P44**
Bismarck and the Development of Germany: The Period of Fortification, 1880-1898, Vol. 3. Ed. 2. Trade Paper. Books on Demand. Ann Arbor, MI. 486p. ISBN:0-608-09105-7, ISBN13: 978-0-608-09105-1. Dewey:943/.07. LCCN:89-011004.
Audience: **u,f.** B

Pinson, Koppel S. **DD203**
Modern Germany: Its History and Civilization. Ed. 2. Paper Text. Waveland Press, Inc. Prospect Heights, IL. 1989. 682p. ISBN:0-88133-434-0, ISBN13: 978-0-88133-434-0. Dewey:943.08.
Audience: **g,u,f.**

Röhl, John C. G. **DD229.R6413 1996**
The Kaiser and His Court: Wilhelm II and the Government of Germany. Terence F. Cole (Translator). Trade Paper. Cambridge University Press. New York, NY. 1996. 287p. ISBN:0-521-56504-9, ISBN13: 978-0-521-56504-2. Dewey:943.08/4/092.
Audience: **u,f.**

Scribner, Bob **HN445.G472 1996**
Germany: A New Social and Economic History, 1450-1630, Vol. 1. Paper Text. Oxford University Press, Inc. New York, NY. 1995. 416p. A Hodder Arnold Publication ISBN:0-340-65217-9,

ISBN13: 978-0-340-65217-6. Dewey:943/.028.
LCCN:95-017543.
Audience: **u,f.** *Choice, 1996.*

Scribner, R. W. **BR852.S34 2001**
Religion and Culture in Germany, 1400-1800. Lyndal Roper (Editor). Trade Cloth. Brill Academic Publishers. Leiden, 2004. xviii, 382p. Studies in Medieval and Reformation Thought Ser., Vol. 81 ISBN:90-04-11457-2, ISBN13: 978-90-04-11457-9. Dewey:274.3. LCCN:2001-037614.
Audience: **u,f.**

Sheehan, James J. **DD17**
German History, 1770-1866. Trade Paper. Oxford University Press, Inc. New York, NY. 1993. 986p. History of Modern Europe Ser. ISBN:0-19-820432-9, ISBN13: 978-0-19-820432-9. Dewey:943. LCCN:89-023023.
Audience: **u,f.** *Choice, 1991.*

Smith, Helmut W. **DD204.S57 1995**
German Nationalism and Religious Conflict: Culture, Ideology, Politics, 1870-1914. Cloth Text. Princeton University Press. Princeton, NJ. 1995. 256p. ISBN:0-691-03624-1, ISBN13: 978-0-691-03624-3. Dewey:320.5/4/0943. LCCN:94-016983.
Audience: **u,f.** *Choice, 1995.*

Stern, Fritz Richard **DD67**
The Politics of Cultural Despair: A Study in the Rise of the Germanic Ideology. Paper Text. Textbook Publishers. Temecula, CA. 2003. 367p. ISBN:0-7581-2681-6, ISBN13: 978-0-7581-2681-8. Dewey:943.08/07/2022.
Audience: **u,f.** B

Tipton, Frank B. **DD203 .T56 2003C**
A History of Modern Germany since 1815. Trade Cloth. University of California Press. Berkeley, CA. 2003. 751p. ISBN:0-520-24050-2, ISBN13: 978-0-520-24050-6. Dewey:943/.07. LCCN:2003-048449.
Audience: **u,f.** *Choice, 2004.*

Von Treitschke, Heinrich G. **DD206**
History of Germany in the Nineteenth Century. Library Binding. University of Chicago Press. Chicago, IL. 1993. xxx, 411p. Classic European Historians Ser. ISBN:0-226-81278-2, ISBN13: 978-0-226-81278-6. Dewey:943/.07. LCCN:75-005072.
Audience: **u,f.**

Wehler, Hans-Ulrich **DD220.W413 1985**
The German Empire, 1871-1918. Kim Traynor (Translator). Trade Paper. Berg Publishers. Oxford, 1997. 293p. ISBN:0-907582-32-X, ISBN13: 978-0-907582-32-8. Dewey:943.08/3. LCCN:84-073484.
Audience: **u,f.** B *Choice, 1986.*

Weikart, Richard **HQ755.5.G3W435 2006**
From Darwin to Hitler: Evolutionary Ethics, Eugenics, and Racism in Germany. Trade Paper. Palgrave Macmillan. New York, NY. 2006. 328p. ISBN:1-4039-7201-X, ISBN13: 978-1-4039-7201-9. Dewey:305.8/00943.
Audience: **g,l,u,f.** *Choice, 2005.*

Wilson, Peter H. **DD175.W54 2004**
From Reich to Revolution: German History 1600-1806. Cloth over Boards. Palgrave Macmillan. New York, NY. 2004. 456p. European History in Perspective Ser. ISBN:0-333-65243-6, ISBN13: 978-0-333-65243-5. Dewey:943. LCCN:2004-044502.
Audience: **u,f.** *Choice, 2005.*

Wunder, Heide **HQ1623.W85 1998**
He Is the Sun, She Is the Moon: Women in Early Modern Germany. Trade Cloth. Harvard University Press. Cambridge, MA. 1998. 320p. ISBN:0-674-38321-4, ISBN13: 978-0-674-38321-0. Dewey:305.4/0943. LCCN:97-038959.
Audience: **u,f.** *Choice, 1998.*

Germany > History > Modern (1815-) > Reformation and Counter reformation. Thirty Years War (1519-1648)

Asch, Ronald G. **D258.A83 1997**
The Thirty Years War: The Holy Roman Empire and Europe, 1618 to 1648. Trade Paper. Palgrave Macmillan. New York, NY. 1997. 259p. European History in Perspective Ser. ISBN:0-312-16585-4, ISBN13: 978-0-312-16585-7. Dewey:940.2/4. LCCN:96-041029.
Audience: **g,l,u,f.** *Choice, 1997.*

Behringer, Wolfgang **BF1583 .B4413 1997**
Witchcraft Persecutions in Bavaria: Popular Magic, Religious Zealotry and Reason of State in Early Modern Europe. J. C. Grayson & David Lederer (Translators), Lyndal Roper (Contribution by). Trade Cloth. Cambridge University Press. New York, NY. 1997. 503p. Past and Present Publications ISBN:0-521-48258-5, ISBN13: 978-0-521-48258-5. Dewey:133.4/3/09433. LCCN:96-043846.
Audience: **u,f.** *Choice, 1998.*

Blickle, Peter **BR307.B527 1998**
From the Communal Reformation to the Revolution of the Common Man. Trade Cloth. Brill Academic Publishers, Inc. Boston, MA. 1998. "x, 226"p. Studies in Medieval and Reformation Thought, Vol. 65 ISBN:90-04-10770-3, ISBN13: 978-90-04-10770-0. Dewey:274/.06. LCCN:98-018525.
Audience: **u,f.**

Blickle, Peter **DD182**
The Revolution of 1525: The German Peasants' War from a New Perspective. Thomas A. Brady Jr. (Author, Translator), H. C. Midelfort (Translator). Trade Cloth. Johns Hopkins University Press. Baltimore, MD. 1982. 272p. ISBN:0-8018-2472-9, ISBN13: 978-0-8018-2472-2. Dewey:943/.031. LCCN:81-047603.
Audience: **u,f.**

Brady, Thomas A. **BR350.S78**
The Politics of the Reformation in Germany: Jacob Sturm (1489-1553) of Strasbourg. Trade Cloth. Prometheus Books, Publishers. Amherst, NY. 280p. German Studies ISBN:1-57392-293-5, ISBN13: 978-1-57392-293-7. Dewey:944/.38353028/092.
Audience: **g,l,u,f.**

Dixon, C. Scott (Editor) **BR305.2.G45 1999**
The German Reformation: The Essential Readings. Trade Cloth. Blackwell Publishing, Inc. Malden, MA. 1999. 304p. Essential Readings in History Ser. ISBN:0-631-20810-0, ISBN13: 978-0-631-20810-5. Dewey:274.3/06. LCCN:98-056639.
Audience: **g,l,u,f.**

Dixon, C. Scott **BR305.3.D58 2002**
The Reformation in Germany. Trade Cloth. Blackwell Publishing, Inc. Malden, MA. 2002. 240p. Historical Association

Studies ISBN:0-631-20252-8, ISBN13: 978-0-631-20252-3. Dewey:274.3/06. LCCN:2001-003372.
Audience: **g,l,u,f.** *Choice, 2002.*

Forster, Marc R. **BX1538.S6 F67 1992**
The Counter-Reformation in the Villages: Religion and Reform in the Bishopric of Speyer, 1560-1720. Book, Other. Cornell University Press. Ithaca, NY. 1992. 288p. ISBN:0-8014-2566-2, ISBN13: 978-0-8014-2566-0. Dewey:282/.43435. LCCN:91-055564.
Audience: **u,f.**

Forster, Marc R. **BX1537.G3 F67 2001**
Catholic Revival in the Age of the Baroque: Religious Identity in Southwest Germany, 1550-1750. Peter Baldwin, Christopher Clark, James B. Collins, Mia Rodr¡guez-Salgado & Lyndal Roper (Contribution by). Trade Cloth. Cambridge University Press. New York, NY. 2001. 282p. New Studies in European History ISBN:0-521-78044-6, ISBN13: 978-0-521-78044-5. Dewey:282.4340903. LCCN:00-036305.
Audience: **u,f.**

Harrington, Joel F. **HQ728 .H293 1995**
Reordering Marriage and Society in Reformation Germany. Trade Cloth. Cambridge University Press. New York, NY. 1995. 333p. ISBN:0-521-46483-8, ISBN13: 978-0-521-46483-3. Dewey:306.8/1/0943/09031. LCCN:94-010919.
Audience: **u,f.** *Choice, 1996.*

Hsia, R. Po-chia **BR735**
Social Discipline in the Reformation: Central Europe, 1550-1750. Trade Paper. Routledge. New York, NY. 1992. 218p. Christianity and Society in the Modern World Ser. ISBN:0-415-01149-3, ISBN13: 978-0-415-01149-5. Dewey:274.
Audience: **u,f.**

Kittleson, James M. **BR325.K455 2003**
Luther the Reformer: The Story of the Man and His Career. Trade Cloth. Augsburg Fortress, Publishers. Minneapolis, MN. 2004. 334p. ISBN:0-8006-3597-3, ISBN13: 978-0-8006-3597-8. Dewey:284.1/092.
Audience: **g,l,u,f.**

Lull, Timothy F. & Russell, William R. (Editors) **BR331.E5 3004**
Martin Luther's Basic Theological Writings. Ed. 2. CD-ROM, Trade Paper. Augsburg Fortress, Publishers. Minneapolis, MN. 2004. 512p. ISBN:0-8006-3680-5, ISBN13: 978-0-8006-3680-7. Dewey:230/.41.
Audience: **g,l,u,f.** *Choice, 1990.*

Matheson, Peter (Editor, Translator) **BX4946.M8 A25 1988**
The Collected Works of Thomas Muntzer. Trade Cloth. Continuum International Publishing Group, Ltd. London, 1988. 544p. ISBN:0-567-09495-2, ISBN13: 978-0-567-09495-7. Dewey:284.3. LCCN:92-202173.
Audience: **g,l,u,f.**

McKim, Donald K. (Editor) **BR325.C26 2003**
The Cambridge Companion to Martin Luther. Trade Cloth. Cambridge University Press. New York, NY. 2003. 338p. Cambridge Companions to Religion Ser. ISBN:0-521-81648-3, ISBN13: 978-0-521-81648-9. Dewey:284.1/092. LCCN:2002-035077.
Audience: **g,l,u,f.** *Choice, 2004.*

Mortimer, Geoff **D270.A2M67 2002**
Eyewitness Accounts of the Thirty Years War 1618-48. Cloth over Boards. Palgrave Macmillan. New York, NY. 2002. 224p. ISBN:0-333-98404-8, ISBN13: 978-0-333-98404-8. Dewey:940.2/4/0922. LCCN:2001-056137.
Audience: **g,l,u,f.** *Choice, 2003.*

Oberman, Heiko **BR325**
Luther: Man Between God and the Devil. Eileen Walliser-Schwarzbart (Translator). Trade Paper. Yale University Press. Cumberland, RI. 2006. 400p. ISBN:0-300-10313-1, ISBN13: 978-0-300-10313-7. Dewey:284.1092.
Audience: **g,l,u,f.**

Ozment, Steven **CT1097.B44T47 1990**
Three Behaim Boys: Growing Up in Early Modern Germany - A Chronicle of Their Lives. Trade Cloth. Yale University Press. Cumberland, RI. 1990. 312p. ISBN:0-300-04670-7, ISBN13: 978-0-300-04670-0. Dewey:943/.32403/0922 B. LCCN:89-027312.
Audience: **g,l,u,f.** *Choice, 1990.*

Robisheaux, Thomas **HN458.L3 R63 1989**
Rural Society and the Search for Order in Early Modern Germany. Trade Cloth. Cambridge University Press. New York, NY. 1989. 320p. ISBN:0-521-35626-1, ISBN13: 978-0-521-35626-8. Dewey:307.7/2/094347. LCCN:88-027450.
Audience: **u,f.** *Choice, 1990.*

Scott, Tom **BX4946.M8S35 1989**
Thomas Muntzer: Theology and Revolution in the German Reformation. Cloth Text. Palgrave Macmillan. New York, NY. 1989. 160p. ISBN:0-312-02679-X, ISBN13: 978-0-312-02679-0. Dewey:284/.3/0924 B. LCCN:88-028183.
Audience: **g,l,u,f.** *Choice, 1990.*

Scott, Tom **HC288.R66S36 2005**
Town, Country, and Regions in Reformation Germany. Trade Cloth. Brill Academic Publishers. Leiden, 2005. 464p. Studies in Medieval and Reformation Traditions : History, Culture, Religion, Ideas, Vol. 106 ISBN:90-04-14321-1, ISBN13: 978-90-04-14321-0. Dewey:943/.031. LCCN:2004-062924.
Audience: **u,f.**

Wedgwood, C. V. & Kennedy, Paul **D258.W4 2005**
The Thirty Years War. Anthony Grafton (Introduction by). Trade Paper. New York Review of Books, Incorporated, The. New York, NY. 2005. 536p. New York Review Books Classics ISBN:1-59017-146-2, ISBN13: 978-1-59017-146-2. Dewey:940.2/4. LCCN:2004-027336.
Audience: **g,l,u,f.**

Germany > History > Modern (1815-) > Baroque. Enlightenment. Napoleonic Wars. (1648-1815)

Beiser, Frederick C. **DD419.B45 1992**
Enlightenment, Revolution, and Romanticism: The Genesis of Modern German Political Thought, 1790-1800. Trade Cloth. Harvard University Press. Cambridge, MA. 1992. 448p. ISBN:0-674-25727-8, ISBN13: 978-0-674-25727-6. Dewey:320.50943. LCCN:91-040026.
Audience: **u,f.** *Choice, 1993.*

Beiser, Frederick C. **B2748.R37B45 1987**
The Fate of Reason: German Philosophy from Kant to Fichte. Trade Cloth. Harvard University Press. Cambridge, MA. 1987. 419p. ISBN:0-674-29502-1, ISBN13: 978-0-674-29502-5. Dewey:193. LCCN:86-014303.
Audience: **u,f.** *Choice, 1987.*

Blanning, Timothy C. W. **DD801.R682**
The French Revolution in Germany: Occupation and Resistance in the Rhineland 1792-1802. Trade Cloth. Oxford University Press, Inc. New York, NY. 1983. 362p. ISBN:0-19-822564-4, ISBN13: 978-0-19-822564-5. Dewey:943/.406. LCCN:83-003960.
Audience: **u,f.**

Bruford, Walter H. **DD193 .B74**
Germany in the Eighteenth Century. Trade Cloth. Cambridge University Press. New York, NY. 1935. 364p. ISBN:0-521-04354-9, ISBN13: 978-0-521-04354-0. Dewey:943.05.
Audience: **g,l,u,f.**

Epstein, Klaus W. **DD0065.E6**
The Genesis of German Conservatism. Trade Paper. Books on Demand. Ann Arbor, MI. 747p. ISBN:0-7837-6777-3, ISBN13: 978-0-7837-6777-2. Dewey:943. LCCN:66-011970.
Audience: **u,f.**

Gray, Marion W. **HQ1075.5.E8525G73**
Productive Men and Reproductive Women: The Agrarian Household and the Emergence of Separate Spheres during the German Enlightenment. Trade Cloth. Berghahn Books, Inc. New York, NY. 2000. 256p. ISBN:1-57181-171-0, ISBN13: 978-1-57181-171-4. Dewey:305.3/094. LCCN:99-019028.
Audience: **u,f.** *Choice, 2000.*

Hull, Isabel V. **HQ18.G3H84 1996**
Sexuality, State, and Civil Society in Germany, 1700-1815. Trade Cloth. Cornell University Press. Ithaca, NY. 1996. 536p. ISBN:0-8014-3126-3, ISBN13: 978-0-8014-3126-5. Dewey:306.7/0943. LCCN:95-031511.
Audience: **u,f.** *Choice, 1996.*

Kant, Immanuel **JC181 .K29513 1990**
Kant: Political Writings. Ed. 2. H. S. Reiss (Editor), H. B. Nisbet (Translator). Cloth Text. Cambridge University Press. New York, NY. 1991. 327p. Texts in the History of Political Thought ISBN:0-521-39185-7, ISBN13: 978-0-521-39185-6. Dewey:320/.01. LCCN:90-001453.
Audience: **u,f.**

Kuehn, Manfred **B2797 .K86 2001**
Kant: A Biography. Cloth Text. Cambridge University Press. New York, NY. 2001. 566p. ISBN:0-521-49704-3, ISBN13: 978-0-521-49704-6. Dewey:193 B. LCCN:00-033671.
Audience: **u,f.** *Choice, 2001.*

Lindemann, Mary **HV280.H3L56 1990**
Patriots and Paupers: Hamburg, 1712-1830. Cloth Text. Oxford University Press, Inc. New York, NY. 1990. 352p. ISBN:0-19-506140-3, ISBN13: 978-0-19-506140-6. Dewey:361.6/0943/51509033. LCCN:89-016302.
Audience: **u,f.** *Choice, 1991.*

Melton, James Van Horn **LC135.G32 P785 1988**
Absolutism and the Eighteenth-Century Origins of Compulsory Schooling in Prussia and Austria. Trade Cloth. Cambridge University Press. New York, NY. 1988. 288p. ISBN:0-521-34668-1, ISBN13: 978-0-521-34668-9. Dewey:379/.23. LCCN:87-033022.
Audience: **u,f.** *Choice, 1989.*

Raeff, Marc **KK190**
The Well-Ordered Police State: Social and Institutional Change Through Law in the Germanies and Russia, 1660-1800. Trade Cloth. Yale University Press. Cumberland, RI. 1983. 304p. ISBN:0-300-02869-5, ISBN13: 978-0-300-02869-0. Dewey:340/.115/0943. LCCN:82-019980.
Audience: **u,f.**

Ritter, Gerhard A. **DD404**
Frederick the Great: A Historical Profile. Peter Paret (Translator, Introduction by). Trade Cloth. University of California Press. Berkeley, CA. 1975. 268p. ISBN:0-520-02775-2, ISBN13: 978-0-520-02775-6. Dewey:943.053.
Audience: **g,l,u,f.**

Rosenberg, Hans **JN4431.R76 1958**
Bureaucracy, Aristocracy, and Autocracy. Harvard University Press. 1958.
Audience: **u,f.**

Simms, Brendan **DD420 .S56 1997**
The Impact of Napoleon: Prussian High Politics, Foreign Policy and the Crisis of the Executive, 1797-1806. Trade Cloth. Cambridge University Press. New York, NY. 1997. 408p. ISBN:0-521-45360-7, ISBN13: 978-0-521-45360-8. Dewey:943/.073. LCCN:96-006483.
Audience: **u,f.** *Choice, 1998.*

Vierhaus, Rudolf **HC285 .V5313 1988**
Germany in the Age of Absolutism. Jonathan B. Knudsen (Translator). Cloth Text. Cambridge University Press. New York, NY. 1989. 192p. ISBN:0-521-32686-9, ISBN13: 978-0-521-32686-5. Dewey:943.04. LCCN:87-031970.
Audience: **g,l,u,f.**

Germany > History > Modern (1815-) > Vormarz (1815-1848)

Beiser, Frederick C. (Editor) **B2948 .C28 1993**
The Cambridge Companion to Hegel. Trade Paper. Cambridge University Press. New York, NY. 1993. 528p. Cambridge Companions to Philosophy Ser. ISBN:0-521-38711-6, ISBN13: 978-0-521-38711-8. Dewey:193. LCCN:92-015572.
Audience: **u,f.** *Choice, 1993.*

Berdahl, Robert M. **DD419.B47 1988**
The Politics of the Prussian Nobility: The Development of a Conservative Ideology, 1770-1848. Cloth Text. Princeton University Press. Princeton, NJ. 1988. 512p. ISBN:0-691-05536-X, ISBN13: 978-0-691-05536-7. Dewey:943. LCCN:88-017616.
Audience: **u,f.** *Choice, 1989.*

Brose, Eric D. **DD420.B76 1993**
Out of the Shadow of Antiquity: The Politics of Technological Change in Prussia, 1809-1848. Cloth Text. Princeton University Press. Princeton, NJ. 1992. 312p. ISBN:0-691-05685-4, ISBN13: 978-0-691-05685-2. Dewey:338.0943. LCCN:92-015232.
Audience: **u,f.** *Choice, 1993.*

Hamerow, Theodore S. **HC285**
Restoration, Revolution, Reaction: Economics and Politics in Germany, 1815-1871. Trade Paper. Princeton University Press. Princeton, NJ. 1966. 360p. ISBN:0-691-00755-1, ISBN13: 978-0-691-00755-7. Dewey:330.943.
Audience: **u,f.**

Heine, Heinrich **PT2309.D413 1986**
Deutschland: A Winter's Tale. T. J. Reed (Translator). Trade Cloth. Angel Books. London, 1987. 96p. ISBN:0-946162-21-2, ISBN13: 978-0-946162-21-5. Dewey:831/.7. LCCN:86-082062.
Audience: **g,l,u,f.** *Choice, 1987.*

Heine, Heinrich **B2523.H413 1986**
Religion and Philosophy in Germany. John Snodgrass (Translator). Paper Text. State University of New York Press. Albany, NY. 1986. 177p. ISBN:0-88706-283-0, ISBN13: 978-0-88706-283-4. Dewey:193. LCCN:85-027675.
Audience: **g,l,u,f.**

Herzog, Dagmar **DD801.B18H47 1996**
Intimacy and Exclusion: Religious Politics in Pre-Revolutionary Baden. Trade Cloth. Princeton University Press. Princeton, NJ. 1996. 264p. Studies in Culture - Power - History ISBN:0-691-04493-7, ISBN13: 978-0-691-04493-4. Dewey:320.943/46/09034. LCCN:95-019577.
Audience: **u,f.** *Choice, 1996.*

Heuvel, Jon Vanden **DD205.G6V36 2001**
A German Life in the Age of Revolution: Joseph Gorres, 1776-1848. Henry A. Kissinger (Foreword by). Trade Cloth. Catholic University of America Press. Washington, DC. 2000. xxv, 408p. ISBN:0-8132-0948-X, ISBN13: 978-0-8132-0948-7. Dewey:943/.06/092 B. LCCN:99-014598.
Audience: **u,f.** *Choice, 2002.*

Levinger, Matthew **DD347.L45 2000**
Enlightened Nationalism: The Transformation of Prussian Political Culture, 1806-1848. Trade Cloth. Oxford University Press, Inc. New York, NY. 2000. 332p. ISBN:0-19-513185-1, ISBN13: 978-0-19-513185-7. Dewey:943/.07. LCCN:99-032583.
Audience: **u,f.** *Choice, 2001.*

Pinkard, Terry **B2947 .P56 2000**
Hegel: A Biography. Trade Cloth. Cambridge University Press. New York, NY. 2000. 800p. ISBN:0-521-49679-9, ISBN13: 978-0-521-49679-7. Dewey:193 B. LCCN:99-034812.
Audience: **u,f.** *Choice, 2000.*

Rowe, Michael **DD801.R682**
From 'Reich' to State: The Rhineland in the Revolutionary Age, 1780-1830. Trade Cloth. Cambridge University Press. New York, NY. 2003. 344p. New Studies in European History Ser. ISBN:0-521-82443-5, ISBN13: 978-0-521-82443-9. Dewey:943.4306. LCCN:2003-273876.
Audience: **u,f.**

Germany > History > Modern (1815-) > German Unification (1848-1871)

Beck, Hermann **HV279.P9B43 1995**
The Origins of the Authoritarian Welfare State in Prussia: Conservatives, Bureaucracy, and the Social Question, 1815-70. Trade Cloth. University of Michigan Press. Chicago, IL. 1995. 320p. Social History, Popular Culture, and Politics in Germany Ser. ISBN:0-472-10546-9, ISBN13: 978-0-472-10546-5. Dewey:361.943. LCCN:94-035186.
Audience: **u,f.** *Choice, 1995.*

Brophy, James M. **HE3079.P7B76 1998**
Capitalism, Politics and Railroads in Prussia, 1830-1870. Cloth Text. Ohio State University Press. Columbus, OH. 1998. 272p. Historical Perspectives on Business Enterprise Ser. ISBN:0-8142-0751-0, ISBN13: 978-0-8142-0751-2. Dewey:385/.0943/09034. LCCN:97-029251.
Audience: **u,f.** *Choice, 1998.*

Bucholz, Arden **DD219.M7B83 2001**
Moltke and the German Wars, 1864-1871. Cloth over Boards. Palgrave Macmillan. New York, NY. 2001. 252p. European History in Perspective Ser. ISBN:0-333-68757-4, ISBN13: 978-0-333-68757-4. Dewey:355/.0092 B. LCCN:00-062613.
Audience: **u,f.** *Choice, 2002.*

Eyck, Frank **DD207.5.E87**
The Frankfurt Parliament. St. Martins. 1969. ISBN:0-312-30345-9, ISBN13: 978-0-312-30345-7.
Audience: **u,f.**

Sperber, Jonathan **DD801.R74**
Rhineland Radicals: The Democratic Movement and the Revolution of 1848-1849. Trade Paper. Princeton University Press. Princeton, NJ. 1992. 544p. ISBN:0-691-00866-3, ISBN13: 978-0-691-00866-0. Dewey:943/.4. LCCN:91-000127.
Audience: **u,f.** *Choice, 1992.*

Vick, Brian E. **DD207.5.V48 2002**
Defining Germany: The 1848 Frankfurt Parliamentarians and National Identity. Trade Cloth. Harvard University Press. Cambridge, MA. 2002. 302p. Harvard Historical Studies, Vol. 143 ISBN:0-674-00911-8, ISBN13: 978-0-674-00911-0. Dewey:320.943/09/034. LCCN:2002-024073.
Audience: **u,f.** *Choice, 2003.*

Wawro, Geoffrey **DD438 .W39 1996**
The Austro-Prussian War: Austria's War with Prussia and Italy in 1866. Trade Cloth. Cambridge University Press. New York, NY. 1996. 368p. ISBN:0-521-56059-4, ISBN13: 978-0-521-56059-7. Dewey:943/.076. LCCN:95-050529.
Audience: **u,f.** *Choice, 1997.*

Wawro, Geoffrey **DC293.W38 2003**
The Franco-Prussian War: The German Conquest of France in 1870-1871. Trade Cloth. Cambridge University Press. New York, NY. 2003. 344p. ISBN:0-521-58436-1, ISBN13: 978-0-521-58436-4. Dewey:943.08/2. LCCN:2002-041685.
Audience: **g,l,u,f.** *Choice, 2004.*

Wetzel, David **DC292.W48 2001**
A Duel of Giants: Bismarck, Napoleon III, and the Origins of the Franco-Prussian War. Trade Cloth. University of Wisconsin Press. Chicago, IL. 2001. 240p. ISBN:0-299-17490-5, ISBN13: 978-0-299-17490-3. Dewey:943.08/2. LCCN:2001-002003.
Audience: **u,f.** *Choice, 2002.*

Ziblatt, Daniel **JC201.Z53 2006**
Structuring the State: The Formation of Italy and Germany and the Puzzle of Federalism. Trade Cloth. Princeton University Press. Princeton, NJ. 2006. 288p. ISBN:0-691-12167-2, ISBN13: 978-0-691-12167-3. Dewey:320.443/049. LCCN:2005-043378.
Audience: **u,f.**

Germany > History > Modern (1815-) > Imperial Germany. World War I (1871-1918)

Abrams, Lynn **HD7395**
Workers' Culture in Imperial Germany. Paper over Boards. Routledge. New York, NY. 1992. 224p. ISBN:0-415-07635-8, ISBN13: 978-0-415-07635-7. Dewey:305.5620943. LCCN:91-012748.
Audience: **u,f.** *Choice, 1992.*

Anderson, Margaret L. **DD205.W4**
Windthorst: A Political Biography. Trade Cloth. Oxford University Press, Inc. New York, NY. 1981. 534p. ISBN:0-19-822578-4, ISBN13: 978-0-19-822578-2. Dewey:943.08/092/4. LCCN:80-041313.
Audience: **u,f.**

Berghahn, Volker **HC285.B395 2004**
Imperial Germany 1871-1918: Economy, Society, Culture and Politics. Ed. 2. Paper Text. Berghahn Books, Inc. New York, NY. 2005. 400p. ISBN:1-84545-011-6, ISBN13: 978-1-84545-011-3. Dewey:943.08/3. LCCN:2004-056003.
Audience: **g,l,u,f.**

Clark, Christopher **DD229.C53 2000**
Kaiser Wilhelm II. Trade Paper. Longman Publishing. Boston, MA. 2000. 288p. ISBN:0-582-24559-1, ISBN13: 978-0-582-24559-4. Dewey:943.08/4/092 B. LCCN:00-030939.
Audience: **g,l,u,f.** *Choice, 2001.*

Ferguson, Niall **HC289.H2 F47 1995**
Paper and Iron: Hamburg Business and German Politics in the Era of Inflation, 1897-1927. Trade Cloth. Cambridge University Press. New York, NY. 1995. 553p. ISBN:0-521-47016-1, ISBN13: 978-0-521-47016-2. Dewey:338.943/515. LCCN:94-013455.
Audience: **u,f.** *Choice, 1996.*

Jefferies, Matthew **DD67.J44 2003**
Imperial Culture in Germany, 1871-1918. Cloth over Boards. Palgrave Macmillan. New York, NY. 2003. 368p. European Studies ISBN:1-4039-0420-0, ISBN13: 978-1-4039-0420-1. Dewey:943.08/3. LCCN:2003-040478.
Audience: **g,l,u,f.** *Choice, 2004.*

Johansen, Anja **HV6485.F8J64 2004**
Soldiers As Police: The French and Prussian Armies and the Policing of Popular Protest, 1889-1914. Trade Cloth. Ashgate Publishing, Ltd. Aldershot, 2005. 340p. ISBN:0-7546-3376-4, ISBN13: 978-0-7546-3376-1. Dewey:363.32. LCCN:2004-008258.
Audience: **u,f.** *Choice, 2005.*

Ladd, Brian **HT169.G3L24 1990**
Urban Planning and Civic Order in Germany, 1860-1914. Trade Cloth. Harvard University Press. Cambridge, MA. 1990. 326p. Harvard Historical Studies, Vol. 105 ISBN:0-674-93115-7, ISBN13: 978-0-674-93115-2. Dewey:307.1/216/0943. LCCN:89-029433.
Audience: **g,u,f.** *Choice, 1990.*

McAleer, Kevin **CR4595.G3M35 1994**
Dueling: The Cult of Honor in Fin-de-Siecle Germany. Trade Cloth. Princeton University Press. Princeton, NJ. 1994. 288p. ISBN:0-691-03462-1, ISBN13: 978-0-691-03462-1. Dewey:394/.8/0943. LCCN:94-004401.
Audience: **g,l,u,f.** *Choice, 1995.*

Repp, Kevin **DD228.5.R38 2000**
Reformers, Critics, and the Paths of German Modernity: Anti-Politics and the Search for Alternatives, 1890-1914. Trade Cloth. Harvard University Press. Cambridge, MA. 2000. 368p. ISBN:0-674-00057-9, ISBN13: 978-0-674-00057-5. Dewey:943.08/4. LCCN:00-020603.
Audience: **u,f.** *Choice, 2000.*

Smith, Helmut Walser **DS146.G4S57 2002**
The Butcher's Tale: Murder and Anti-Semitism in a German Town. Trade Cloth. W. W. Norton & Company, Inc. New York, NY. 2002. 288p. ISBN:0-393-05098-X, ISBN13: 978-0-393-05098-1. Dewey:305.892/404382. LCCN:2002-022883.
Audience: **g,l,u,f.** *Choice, 2003.*

Germany > History > Modern (1815-) > Revolution and Weimar Republic (1918-1933)

Allen, William S. **DD256.5**
The Nazi Seizure of Power: The Experience of a Single German Town, 1922-1945. Trade Paper. Scholastic Library Publishing. Danbury, CT. 1984. 388p. Single Titles-Adult Ser. ISBN:0-531-05633-3, ISBN13: 978-0-531-05633-2. Dewey:943.085. LCCN:83-027340.
Audience: **g,l,u,f.**

Balderston, Theo **HC286.3 .B249 2002**
Economics and Politics in the Weimar Republic. Maurice Kirby (Contribution by). Trade Paper. Cambridge University Press. New York, NY. 2002. 138p. New Studies in Economic and Social History Ser. ISBN:0-521-77760-7, ISBN13: 978-0-521-77760-5. Dewey:330.943085. LCCN:2002-073751.
Audience: **l,u,f.**

Baranowski, Shelley O. **DD453.B37 1995**
The Sanctity of Rural Life: Nobility, Protestantism, and Nazism in Weimar Prussia. Trade Cloth. Oxford University Press, Inc. New York, NY. 1995. 278p. ISBN:0-19-506881-5, ISBN13: 978-0-19-506881-8. Dewey:943.085. LCCN:94-019307.
Audience: **u,f.** *Choice, 1995.*

Bessel, Richard **HN445**
Germany after the First World War. Paper Text. Oxford University Press, Inc. New York, NY. 1995. 340p. ISBN:0-19-820586-4, ISBN13: 978-0-19-820586-9. Dewey:306/.0943/09042. LCCN:92-040025.
Audience: **g,l,u,f.** *Choice, 1994.*

Brenner, Michael **DS135.G33B74 1996**
The Renaissance of Jewish Culture in Weimar Germany. Cloth over Boards. Yale University Press. Cumberland, RI. 1996. 320p. ISBN:0-300-06262-1, ISBN13: 978-0-300-06262-5. Dewey:943/.085/089924. LCCN:95-030449.
Audience: **g,u,f.** *Choice, 1996.*

Broszat, Martin & Bestard-Camps, Joan **DD256.5**
Hitler and the Collapse of Weimar Germany. Volker R. Berghahn (Translator, Foreword by). Cloth over Boards. Berg

Publishers. Oxford, 1987. 168p. ISBN:0-85496-509-2, ISBN13: 978-0-85496-509-0. Dewey:943.085. LCCN:86-026857.
Audience: **g,l,u,f.** *Choice, 1987.*

Childers, Thomas **83-5924**
The Nazi Voter: The Social Foundations of Fascism in Germany, 1919-1933. Trade Paper. University of North Carolina Press. Chapel Hill, NC. 1985. 383p. ISBN:0-8078-4147-1, ISBN13: 978-0-8078-4147-1. Dewey:324.943/085. LCCN:83-005924.
Audience: **g,l,u.**

Dobson, Sean **DD901.L58D63 2000**
Authority and Upheaval in Leipzig, 1910-1920: The Story of a Relationship. Trade Cloth. Columbia University Press. New York, NY. 2001. 352p. ISBN:0-231-12076-1, ISBN13: 978-0-231-12076-0. Dewey:943/.2122087. LCCN:00-055460.
Audience: **u,f.**

Feldman, Gerald D. **DD240**
The Great Disorder: Politics, Economics, and Society in the German Inflation, 1914-1924. Trade Paper. Oxford University Press, Inc. New York, NY. 1997. 1040p. ISBN:0-19-510114-6, ISBN13: 978-0-19-510114-0. Dewey:943/.085.
Audience: **u,f.** *Choice, 1994.*

Fritzsche, Peter **DD238.F74 1998**
Germans into Nazis. Trade Cloth. Harvard University Press. Cambridge, MA. 1998. 288p. ISBN:0-674-35091-X, ISBN13: 978-0-674-35091-5. Dewey:943.085. LCCN:97-023453.
Audience: **g,l,u,f.** *Choice, 1998.*

Fritzsche, Peter **DD240.F75 1990**
Rehearsals for Fascism: Populism and Political Mobilization in Weimar Germany. Trade Cloth. Oxford University Press, Inc. New York, NY. 1990. 320p. ISBN:0-19-505780-5, ISBN13: 978-0-19-505780-5. Dewey:943.085. LCCN:89-034096.
Audience: **l,u,f.**

Gay, Peter **DD239**
The Weimar Culture: The Outsider as Insider. Trade Paper. W. W. Norton & Company, Inc. New York, NY. 2001. 224p. ISBN:0-393-32239-4, ISBN13: 978-0-393-32239-2. Dewey:943.085.
Audience: **u,f.**

Guttsman, Willi **NX180.S6G88 1990**
Workers' Culture in Weimar Germany: Between Tradition and Commitment. Cloth over Boards. Berg Publishers. Oxford, 1990. 332p. ISBN:0-907582-59-1, ISBN13: 978-0-907582-59-5. Dewey:700/.1/03. LCCN:89-038853.
Audience: **u,f.** *Choice, 1991.*

Hong, Young-Sun **HV275.H664 1998**
Welfare, Modernity, and the Weimar State. Trade Cloth. Princeton University Press. Princeton, NJ. 1998. 306p. Princeton Studies in Culture/Power/History ISBN:0-691-05674-9, ISBN13: 978-0-691-05674-6. Dewey:362.5/8/094309041. LCCN:97-034249.
Audience: **u,f.**

Kaes, Anton, et al. **DD240.W3927**
The Weimar Republic Sourcebook. Martin Jay & Edward Dimendberg (Authors). Trade Paper. University of California Press. Berkeley, CA. 1995. 828p. Weimar and Now: German Cultural Criticism Ser. ISBN:0-520-06775-4, ISBN13: 978-0-520-06775-2. Dewey:943.085. LCCN:93-042108.
Audience: **l,u,f.**

Kolb, Eberhard **DD237.K6713 2004**
The Weimar Republic. Ed. 2. Paper over Boards. Routledge. New York, NY. 2004. 304p. ISBN:0-415-34441-7, ISBN13: 978-0-415-34441-8. Dewey:943.085. LCCN:2004-046839.
Audience: **l,u.**

Maier, Charles S. **D727**
Recasting Bourgeois Europe: Stabilization in France, Germany and Italy in the Decade after World War I. Trade Paper. Princeton University Press. Princeton, NJ. 1975. 664p. ISBN:0-691-10025-X, ISBN13: 978-0-691-10025-8. Dewey:320.9/4/051. LCCN:73-002488.
Audience: **u,f.**

Merkl, Peter H. **DD253.25**
Political Violence under the Swastika: 581 Early Nazis. Trade Cloth. Princeton University Press. Princeton, NJ. 1975. 752p. ISBN:0-691-07561-1, ISBN13: 978-0-691-07561-7. Dewey:324.243/038. LCCN:74-012143.
Audience: **u,f.**

Mommsen, Hans **DD237.M5713 1996**
The Rise and Fall of Weimar Democracy. Elborg Forster & Larry E. Jones (Translators). Trade Paper. University of North Carolina Press. Chapel Hill, NC. 1998. 624p. ISBN:0-8078-4721-6, ISBN13: 978-0-8078-4721-3. Dewey:943/.085. LCCN:95-008902.
Audience: **l,u,f.** *Choice, 1996.*

Nolan, Mary **HD70.G2N64 1994**
Visions of Modernity: American Business and the Modernization of Germany. Trade Cloth. Oxford University Press, Inc. New York, NY. 1994. 336p. ISBN:0-19-507021-6, ISBN13: 978-0-19-507021-7. Dewey:338.943. LCCN:93-020943.
Audience: **u,f.** *Choice, 1995.*

Peukert, Detlev J. **DD237**
The Weimar Republic. Trade Paper. Farrar, Straus & Giroux. New York, NY. 1993. 216p. ISBN:0-8090-1556-0, ISBN13: 978-0-8090-1556-6. Dewey:943.086.
Audience: **l,u.**

Rabinbach, Anson **DD239**
In the Shadow of Catastrophe: German Intellectuals Between Apocalypse and Enlightenment. Trade Paper. University of California Press. Berkeley, CA. 2001. 272p. Weimar and Now: German Cultural Criticism Ser., Vol. 14 ISBN:0-520-22690-9, ISBN13: 978-0-520-22690-6. Dewey:943.085/086/31.
Audience: **u,f.** *Choice, 1998.*

Turner, Henry A. Jr. **HD3616.G35**
German Big Business and the Rise of Hitler. Trade Paper. Oxford University Press, Inc. New York, NY. 1987. 525p. ISBN:0-19-504235-2, ISBN13: 978-0-19-504235-1. Dewey:943.085. LCCN:84-005645.
Audience: **g,l,u,f.** B

von Ankum, Katharina (Editor) **HQ1623.W66 1997**
Women in the Metropolis: Gender and Modernity in Weimar Culture. Trade Paper. University of California Press. Berkeley, CA. 1997. 244p. Weimar and Now Ser., Vol. II:German Cultural Criticism ISBN:0-520-20465-4, ISBN13: 978-0-520-20465-2. Dewey:305.4/0943. LCCN:96-003118.
Audience: **u,f.**

Wright, Jonathan **DD231.S83.W75 2004**
Gustav Stresemann: Weimar's Greatest Statesman. Trade Paper. Oxford University Press, Inc. New York, NY. 2004. 588p.

ISBN:0-19-927329-4, ISBN13: 978-0-19-927329-4. Dewey:943/.085/092.
Audience: **u,f.**

Germany > History > Modern (1815-) > Nazi Germany (1933-1945)

Abel, Theodore **DD247.H5A75 1986**
Why Hitler Came into Power. Thomas Childers (Foreword by). Trade Paper. Harvard University Press. Cambridge, MA. 1986. 346p. ISBN:0-674-95200-6, ISBN13: 978-0-674-95200-3. Dewey:943.086. LCCN:86-011998.
Audience: **g,l,u,f.**

Allen, Michael Thad **DD253.6.A65 2002**
The Business of Genocide: The SS, Slave Labor and the Concentration Camps. Trade Cloth. University of North Carolina Press. Chapel Hill, NC. 2002. 392p. ISBN:0-8078-2677-4, ISBN13: 978-0-8078-2677-5. Dewey:940.53/18. LCCN:2001-041474.
Audience: **g,u,f.** *Choice, 2002.*

Baird, Jay W. **DD243.B35 1990**
To Die for Germany: Heroes in the Nazi Pantheon. Trade Cloth. Indiana University Press. Bloomington, IN. 1990. 350p. ISBN:0-253-31125-X, ISBN13: 978-0-253-31125-2. Dewey:943.086/0922 B. LCCN:89-045189.
Audience: **g,l,u,f.** *Choice, 1990.*

Bajohr, Frank **DS135.G4H3274 2001**
"Aryanization" in Hamburg. George Wilkes (Translator). Trade Cloth. Berghahn Books, Inc. New York, NY. 2002. 300p. Monographs in German History, Vol. 7 ISBN:1-57181-484-1, ISBN13: 978-1-57181-484-5. Dewey:943/.515004924. LCCN:2001-043586.
Audience: **u,f.** *Choice, 2002.*

Barnett, Victoria **BX4844.55.A4B37 1992**
For the Soul of the People: Protestant Protest Against Hitler. Trade Cloth. Oxford University Press, Inc. New York, NY. 1992. 384p. ISBN:0-19-505306-0, ISBN13: 978-0-19-505306-7. Dewey:280.4/0943/09043. LCCN:91-031024.
Audience: **g,u,f.** *Choice, 1993.*

Biesold, Horst **HV2748.B5413 1999**
Crying Hands: Eugenics and Deaf People in Nazi Germany. Henry Friedlander (Introduction by). Trade Cloth. Gallaudet University Press. Washington, DC. 1999. 208p. ISBN:1-56368-077-7, ISBN13: 978-1-56368-077-9. Dewey:362.4/2094309043. LCCN:99-027291.
Audience: **g,u,f.** *Choice, 2000.*

Broszat, Martin **JN3952**
The Hitler State: The Foundation and Development of the Internal Structure of the Third Reich. John Hiden (Translator). Trade Paper. Longman Publishing Group. White Plains, NY. 1989. 378p. ISBN:0-582-48997-0, ISBN13: 978-0-582-48997-4. Dewey:320.943. LCCN:80-040302.
Audience: **u,f.**

Burleigh, Michael **R726.B87 1994**
Death and Deliverance: "Euthansasia" in Germany c. 1900-1945. Cloth Text. Cambridge University Press. New York, NY. 1994. 400p. ISBN:0-521-41613-2, ISBN13: 978-0-521-41613-9. Dewey:179/.7. LCCN:93-048229.
Audience: **u,f.** *Choice, 1995.*

Burleigh, Michael **DD256.5**
The Third Reich: A New History. Trade Paper. Farrar, Straus & Giroux. New York, NY. 2001. 992p. ISBN:0-8090-9326-X, ISBN13: 978-0-8090-9326-7. Dewey:943/.086.
Audience: **g,l,u,f.** *Choice, 2001.*

Burleigh, Michael & Wippermann, Wolfgang **DD256.5 .B93 1991**
The Racial State: Germany 1933-1945. Trade Paper. Cambridge University Press. New York, NY. 1991. 402p. ISBN:0-521-39802-9, ISBN13: 978-0-521-39802-2. Dewey:323.1/43/09043. LCCN:90-020209.
Audience: **u,f.**

Bytwerk, Randall
▢ Nazi and East German Propaganda Guide. http://www.calvin.edu/academic/cas/gpa/ Calvin College.
Audience: **g,l,u,f.**

Engelmann, Bernt **DD256.5.E5313 1986**
In Hitler's Germany: Everyday Life in the Third Reich. Krishna Winston (Translator). Trade Cloth. Knopf Publishing Group. New York, NY. 1986. 320p. ISBN:0-394-52449-7, ISBN13: 978-0-394-52449-8. Dewey:943.086/092/4. LCCN:86-042626.
Audience: **g,l,u,f.** *Choice, 1987.*

Feldman, Gerald D. & Seibel, Wolfgang **D804.3.N483 2004**
Networks of Nazi Persecution: Bureaucracy, Business, and the Organization of the Holocaust. Trade Cloth. Berghahn Books, Inc. New York, NY. 2004. 388p. ISBN:1-57181-177-X, ISBN13: 978-1-57181-177-6. Dewey:940.53/181. LCCN:2004-043734.
Audience: **u,f.** *Choice, 2005.*

Friedlander, Saul **DS135.G3315**
Nazi Germany and the Jews: The Years of Persecution, 1933-1939. Trade Paper. HarperCollins Publishers. New York, NY. 1998. 464p. Nazi Germany and the Jews Ser., Vol. 1 ISBN:0-06-092878-6, ISBN13: 978-0-06-092878-0. Dewey:940.53/18.
Audience: **g,u,f.**

Gellately, Robert **DD256.5**
Backing Hitler: Consent and Coercion in Nazi Germany. Trade Paper. Oxford University Press, Inc. New York, NY. 2002. 378p. ISBN:0-19-280291-7, ISBN13: 978-0-19-280291-0. Dewey:943/.086.
Audience: **g,u,f.** *Choice, 2002.*

Gellately, Robert **DS135.G33**
The Gestapo and German Society: Enforcing Racial Policy, 1933-1945. Paper Text. Oxford University Press, Inc. New York, NY. 1992. 314p. ISBN:0-19-820297-0, ISBN13: 978-0-19-820297-4. Dewey:943/.004924.
Audience: **u,f.** *Choice, 1991.*

Haar, Ingo & Fahlbusch, Michael (Editors) **DD238.G39 2004**
German Scholars and Ethnic Cleansing, 1920-1945. Trade Cloth. Berghahn Books, Inc. New York, NY. 2004. 320p. Austrian and Habsburg Studies ISBN:1-57181-435-3, ISBN13: 978-1-57181-435-7. Dewey:323.143/09/041. LCCN:2004-047674.
Audience: **g,l,u,f.** *Choice, 2005.*

Hamerow, Theodore S. **DD256.3.H335 1997**
On the Road to the Wolf's Lair: German Resistance to Hitler. Trade Cloth. Harvard University Press. Cambridge, MA. 1997.

454p. ISBN:0-674-63680-5, ISBN13: 978-0-674-63680-4. Dewey:943.086. LCCN:96-044364.
Audience: **g,l,u,f.**

Hardach, Karl **HC286.H3613**
Political Economy of Germany in the 20th Century. Trade Cloth. University of California Press. Berkeley, CA. 1980. 240p. ISBN:0-520-03809-6, ISBN13: 978-0-520-03809-7. Dewey:330.943/08. LCCN:78-064754.
Audience: **u,f.**

Hayes, Peter **HD9536.G44D42 2004**
From Cooperation to Complicity: Degussa in the Third Reich. Cloth Text. Cambridge University Press. New York, NY. 2004. 368p. ISBN:0-521-78227-9, ISBN13: 978-0-521-78227-2. Dewey:940.53/1813. LCCN:2004-049742.
Audience: **u,f.** *Choice, 2005.*

Hayes, Peter **HD9654.9.I5 H39 2001**
Industry and Ideology: I. G. Farben in the Nazi Era. Ed. 2. Trade Cloth. Cambridge University Press. New York, NY. 2000. 432p. ISBN:0-521-78110-8, ISBN13: 978-0-521-78110-7. Dewey:338.7/66/009409043. LCCN:00-023560.
Audience: **u,f.** *Choice, 1987.*

Heineman, Elizabeth D. **HQ800.2 .H45 1999**
What Difference Does a Husband Make?: Women and Marital Status in Nazi and Postwar Germany. Trade Cloth. University of California Press. Berkeley, CA. 1999. 392p. Studies on the History of Society and Culture, Vol. 33 ISBN:0-520-21425-0, ISBN13: 978-0-520-21425-5. Dewey:306.8/153/0943/09043. LCCN:98-028003.
Audience: **u,f.**

Herbert, Ulrich **HD8450 .H43213 1997**
Hitler's Foreign Workers: Enforced Foreign Labor in Germany under the Third Reich. William Templer (Translator). Trade Cloth. Cambridge University Press. New York, NY. 1997. 529p. ISBN:0-521-47000-5, ISBN13: 978-0-521-47000-1. Dewey:331.1/1734/0943. LCCN:97-145431.
Audience: **u,f.** *Choice, 1997.*

Hitler, Adolf **DD247**
Hitler's Second Book: The Unpublished Sequel to Mein Kampf. Gerhard L. Weinberg (Editor), Krista Smith (Translator). Trade Cloth. Enigma Books. New York, NY. 2003. 325p. ISBN:1-929631-16-2, ISBN13: 978-1-929631-16-2. Dewey:943.085.
Audience: **u,f.** *Choice, 2004.*

Hoffmann, Peter **DD256.3.H613 1996**
The History of the German Resistance, 1933-1945. Ed. 3. Trade Paper. McGill-Queen's University Press. Montreal, PQ. 1996. 872p. ISBN:0-7735-1531-3, ISBN13: 978-0-7735-1531-4. Dewey:322.4/2/0943/09043. LCCN:97-189058.
Audience: **u,f.**

Johnson, Eric & Reuband, Karl-Heinz **DD256.5**
What We Knew: Terror, Mass Murder, and Everyday Life in Nazi Germany. Cloth Text. Basic Books. New York, NY. 2005. 464p. ISBN:0-465-08571-7, ISBN13: 978-0-465-08571-2. Dewey:943.086.
Audience: **g,l,u,f.** *Choice, 2006.*

Kamenetsky, Christa **PT1021**
Children's Literature in Hitler's Germany: The Cultural Policy of National Socialism. Trade Paper. Ohio University Press. Athens, OH. 1986. xvi, 359p. ISBN:0-8214-0843-7, ISBN13: 978-0-8214-0843-8. Dewey:830.9/9282. LCCN:83-008220.
Audience: **g,l,u,f.**

Kater, Michael H. **DD253.5.K28 2004**
Hitler Youth. Trade Cloth. Harvard University Press. Cambridge, MA. 2004. 368p. ISBN:0-674-01496-0, ISBN13: 978-0-674-01496-1. Dewey:943.086/0835. LCCN:2004-047359.
Audience: **g,l,u,f.** *Choice, 2005.*

Kershaw, Ian **DD247.H5K462 1999**
Hitler, 1889-1936: Hubris. Trade Cloth. W. W. Norton & Company, Inc. New York, NY. 1999. 845p. Hitler Ser., Vol. 1 ISBN:0-393-04671-0, ISBN13: 978-0-393-04671-7. Dewey:943.086/092 B. LCCN:98-029569.
Audience: **g,u,f.**

Kershaw, Ian **DD247.H5**
Hitler, 1936-1945: Nemesis. Trade Cloth. W. W. Norton & Company, Inc. New York, NY. 2000. 1161p. ISBN:0-393-04994-9, ISBN13: 978-0-393-04994-7. Dewey:943/.086/092. LCCN:98-029569.
Audience: **g,u,f.** *Choice, 2001.*

Kershaw, Ian **DD256.5.K47 1989**
The Nazi Dictatorship: Problems and Perspectives of Interpretation. Ed. 2. Trade Cloth. Hodder Education. London, 1989. 224p. ISBN:0-340-49008-X, ISBN13: 978-0-340-49008-2. Dewey:943.086. LCCN:88-033350.
Audience: **g,u,f.**

Koonz, Claudia **HQ1623.K66 1987**
Mothers in the Fatherland: Women, Family Life and Nazi Ideology, 1919-1945. Trade Cloth. St. Martin's Press. Gordonville, VA. 1987. 640p. ISBN:0-312-54933-4, ISBN13: 978-0-312-54933-6. Dewey:306/.0943. LCCN:86-013815.
Audience: **g,l,u,f.** *Choice, 1987.*

Koonz, Claudia **HQ1623.K66**
Mothers in the Fatherland: Women, the Family and Nazi Politics. Trade Paper. St. Martin's Press. Gordonville, VA. 1988. 600p. ISBN:0-312-02256-5, ISBN13: 978-0-312-02256-3. Dewey:305.4/0943/09043.
Audience: **g,u,f.**

Lehmann-Haupt, Hellmut **N8725.L4 1973**
Art under a Dictatorship. Octagon Books. 1973. ISBN:0-374-94896-8, ISBN13: 978-0-374-94896-2.
Audience: **g,l,u,f.**

Levi, Erik **ML240**
Music in the Third Reich. Trade Paper. Palgrave Macmillan. New York, NY. 1996. 320p. ISBN:0-312-12948-3, ISBN13: 978-0-312-12948-4. Dewey:780.943.
Audience: **g,l,u,f.** *Choice, 1994.*

Lifton, Robert J. **R853**
The Nazi Doctors: Medical Killing and the Psychology of Genocide. Trade Paper. Basic Books. New York, NY. 1988. 576p. ISBN:0-465-04905-2, ISBN13: 978-0-465-04905-9. Dewey:940.54/05. LCCN:85-073874.
Audience: **g,u,f.** *Choice, 1987.*

Mandell, Richard D. **GV722 1936.M3 1986**
The Nazi Olympics. Trade Paper. University of Illinois Press. Champaign, IL. 1987. 360p. Sport and Society Ser.

ISBN:0-252-01325-5, ISBN13: 978-0-252-01325-6. Dewey:796.4/8/09043. LCCN:86-019347.
Audience: **l,u,f.**

Mommsen, Hans **DD256.3.M67313 2003**
Alternatives to Hitler: German Resistance under the Third Reich. Angus McGeoch (Translator), Jeremy Noakes (Introduction by). Cloth Text. Princeton University Press. Princeton, NJ. 2003. 320p. ISBN:0-691-11693-8, ISBN13: 978-0-691-11693-8. Dewey:943.086. LCCN:2003-102879.
Audience: **u,f.** *Choice, 2004.*

Naokes, Jeremy & Pridham, G. (Editors) **JN3971.A98**
The German Home Front in World War II: A Documentary Reader. Ed. 192. Trade Paper. University of Exeter Press. Exeter, 1998. 698p. Nazism 1919-1945, a Documentary Reader Ser., Vol. 4 ISBN:0-85989-311-1, ISBN13: 978-0-85989-311-4. Dewey:324.2/43/038.
Audience: **g,l,u,f.**

Neumann, Franz L. **DD253**
Behemoth: The Structure and Practice of National Socialism, 1933-1944. Ed. 2. Library Binding. Hippocrene Books, Inc. New York, NY. 1963. ISBN:0-88254-844-1, ISBN13: 978-0-88254-844-9. Dewey:943.086.
Audience: **u,f.**

Nicosia, Francis R. & Huener, Jonathan **HD2859**
Business and Industry in Nazi Germany. Trade Cloth. Berghahn Books, Inc. New York, NY. 2004. 176p. Studies in Business History and Political Economy Ser. ISBN:1-57181-653-4, ISBN13: 978-1-57181-653-5. Dewey:338.0943/09/043. LCCN:2003-062961.
Audience: **u,f.** *Choice, 2004.*

Noakes, Jeremy & Pridham, G. (Editors) **DD240**
The Rise to Power, 1919-1934: A Documentary Reader. Ed. 2. Trade Cloth. University of Exeter Press. Exeter, 1998. 220p. Nazism 1919-1945, a Documentary Reader Ser., Vol. 1 ISBN:0-85989-598-X, ISBN13: 978-0-85989-598-9. Dewey:943.085.
Audience: **g,l,u,f.**

Noakes, Jeremy & Pridham, Geoffrey (Editors) **DD256.5**
Foreign Policy, War and Racial Extermination: A Documentary Reader. Ed. 3. Trade Paper. University of Exeter Press. Exeter, 2001. 688p. Nazism 1919-1945 Ser., Vol. 3 ISBN:0-85989-602-1, ISBN13: 978-0-85989-602-3. Dewey:324.2/43/038.
Audience: **g,l,u,f.**

Noakes, Jeremy & Pridham, Geoffrey (Editors) **DD256.5**
State, Economy and Society 1933-39: A Documentary Reader. Ed. 5. Trade Cloth. University of Exeter Press. Exeter, 2000. 448p. Nazism 1919-1945, a Documentary Reader Ser., Vol. 2 ISBN:0-85989-599-8, ISBN13: 978-0-85989-599-6. Dewey:324.2/43038.
Audience: **g,l,u,f.**

Overy, R. J. **HC286.7**
War and Economy in the Third Reich. Trade Paper. Oxford University Press, Inc. New York, NY. 1995. 404p. ISBN:0-19-820599-6, ISBN13: 978-0-19-820599-9. Dewey:338.9/43.
Audience: **g,u,f.**

Owings, Alison **D811.5.O885 1993**
Frauen: German Women Recall the Third Reich. Trade Cloth. Rutgers University Press. Piscataway, NJ. 1993. 550p. ISBN:0-8135-1992-6, ISBN13: 978-0-8135-1992-0. Dewey:943/.086/0922. LCCN:92-042097.
Audience: **g,l,u,f.** *Choice, 1994.*

Petropoulos, Jonathan **95-11738 [N]**
Art As Politics in the Third Reich. Trade Paper. University of North Carolina Press. Chapel Hill, NC. 1999. 464p. ISBN:0-8078-4809-3, ISBN13: 978-0-8078-4809-8. Dewey:701/.03/0943/09044. LCCN:98-011738.
Audience: **u,f.** *Choice, 1996.*

Petropoulos, Jonathan **N6868.5.N37P4823**
The Faustian Bargain: The Art World in Nazi Germany. Trade Cloth. Oxford University Press, Inc. New York, NY. 2000. 416p. ISBN:0-19-512964-4, ISBN13: 978-0-19-512964-9. Dewey:701/.03/0943/09044. LCCN:99-033372.
Audience: **u,f.** *Choice, 2000.*

Peuckert, Detley J. & Peukert, Detlev J. K. **DD256.5**
Inside Nazi Germany: Conformity, Opposition, and Racism in Everyday Life. Richard Deveson (Translator). Trade Paper. Yale University Press. Cumberland, RI. 1989. 288p. ISBN:0-300-04480-1, ISBN13: 978-0-300-04480-5. Dewey:943.086. LCCN:86-051431.
Audience: **g,l,u,f.** *Choice, 1987.*

Pine, Lisa **HQ625.P56 1997**
Nazi Family Policy, 1933-1945. Cloth over Boards. Berg Publishers. Oxford, 1997. 256p. ISBN:1-85973-902-4, ISBN13: 978-1-85973-902-0. Dewey:306.8/5/0943/09044. LCCN:98-116485.
Audience: **g,u,f.**

Reck-Malleczewen, Freidrich **DD247.H5**
Diary of a Man in Despair: A Masterpiece about the Comprehension of Evil. Paul Rubens (Translator). Trade Cloth. Gerald Duckworth & Company, Ltd. London, 2001. 240p. Duck Editions ISBN:0-7156-3000-8, ISBN13: 978-0-7156-3000-6. Dewey:943/.086/092.
Audience: **g,u,f.**

Schleunes, Karl A. **DS135.G3315S34 1990**
The Twisted Road to Auschwitz: Nazi Policy Toward German Jews, 1933-1939. Hans Mommsen (Foreword by). Trade Paper. University of Illinois Press. Champaign, IL. 1990. 304p. ISBN:0-252-06147-0, ISBN13: 978-0-252-06147-9. Dewey:943/.004924. LCCN:90-035944.
Audience: **g,l,u,f.**

Schoenbaum, David **DD256.5**
Hitler's Social Revolution: Class and Status in Nazi Germany, 1933-1939. Trade Paper. W. W. Norton & Company, Inc. New York, NY. 1997. 350p. ISBN:0-393-31554-1, ISBN13: 978-0-393-31554-7. Dewey:943.086. LCCN:80-011579.
Audience: **g,l,u,f.**

Spicer, Kevin P. **BX1538.B4S65 2004**
Resisting the Third Reich: The Catholic Clergy in Hitler's Berlin. Trade Cloth. Northern Illinois University Press. DeKalb,

IL. 2004. 268p. ISBN:0-87580-330-X, ISBN13: 978-0-87580-330-2. Dewey:282/.43155/09043. LCCN:2004-001437.
Audience: **g,l,u,f.** *Choice, 2005.*

Stackelberg, Roderick **DD256.48.S73 1999**
Hitler's Germany: Origins, Interpretations, Legacies. Trade Paper. Routledge. New York, NY. 1999. 320p. ISBN:0-415-20115-2, ISBN13: 978-0-415-20115-5. Dewey:943.086/072. LCCN:98-048166.
Audience: **g,l,u,f.**

Steigmann-Gall, Richard **BR856.S66 2003**
The Holy Reich: Nazi Conceptions of Christianity, 1919-1945. Cloth Text. Cambridge University Press. New York, NY. 2003. 310p. ISBN:0-521-82371-4, ISBN13: 978-0-521-82371-5. Dewey:943.086. LCCN:2002-031341.
Audience: **u,f.** *Choice, 2004.*

Steinweis, Alan E. **NX550.A1S75 1993**
Art, Ideology, and Economics in Nazi Germany: The Reich Chambers of Music, Theater, and the Visual Arts. Trade Paper. University of North Carolina Press. Chapel Hill, NC. 1996. 243p. ISBN:0-8078-4607-4, ISBN13: 978-0-8078-4607-0. Dewey:700.9/43/09043. LCCN:93-007059.
Audience: **g,u,f.** *Choice, 1993.*

Steinweis, Alan E. **DS146.G4S73 2006**
Studying the Jew: Scholarly Antisemitism in Nazi Germany. Trade Cloth. Harvard University Press. Cambridge, MA. 2006. 214p. ISBN:0-674-02205-X, ISBN13: 978-0-674-02205-8. Dewey:940.53/180943. LCCN:2005-052831.
Audience: **u,f.**

Stolleis, Michael **KK190.S7613 1998**
The Law under Swastika: Studies on Legal History in Nazi Germany. Thomas Dunlap (Translator), Marcus Zimmerman (Foreword by). Trade Cloth. University of Chicago Press. Chicago, IL. 1998. 280p. ISBN:0-226-77525-9, ISBN13: 978-0-226-77525-8. Dewey:349.43/09/043. LCCN:97-036021.
Audience: **g,u,f.** *Choice, 1998.*

Turner, Henry Ashby **HD9710.G44O648 2005**
General Motors and the Nazis: The Struggle for Control of Opel, Europe's Biggest Carmaker. Saddle Stitched, Cloth over Boards, Dust Jacket. Yale University Press. Cumberland, RI. 2005. 208p. ISBN:0-300-10634-3, ISBN13: 978-0-300-10634-3. Dewey:338.7/629222. LCCN:2005-001370.
Audience: **g,u,f.**

Von Klemperer, Klemens **DD256.5**
German Resistance Against Hitler: The Search for Allies Abroad, 1938-1945. Paper Text. Oxford University Press, Inc. New York, NY. 1994. 502p. ISBN:0-19-820551-1, ISBN13: 978-0-19-820551-7. Dewey:943.086. LCCN:91-034961.
Audience: **g,u,f.**

Wachsmann, Nikolaus **HV9677.W33 2004**
Hitler's Prisons: Legal Terror in Nazi Germany. Cloth over Boards. Yale University Press. Cumberland, RI. 2004. 560p. ISBN:0-300-10250-X, ISBN13: 978-0-300-10250-5. Dewey:365/.943/09043. LCCN:2003-021218.
Audience: **u,f.** *Choice, 2005.*

Whealey, Robert H. **DP269**
Hitler and Spain: The Nazi Role in the Spanish Civil War, 1936-1939. Trade Paper. University Press of Kentucky. Lexington, KY. 2005. 280p. ISBN:0-8131-9139-4, ISBN13: 978-0-8131-9139-3. Dewey:946.081.
Audience: **u,f.** *Choice, 1990.*

Germany > History > Modern (1815-) > Germany in World War Two

Barnett, Correlli (Editor) **D757.H546 2003**
Hitler's Generals. Trade Paper. Grove/Atlantic, Inc. New York, NY. 2003. 528p. ISBN:0-8021-3994-9, ISBN13: 978-0-8021-3994-8. Dewey:940.54/1343/0922 B. LCCN:2003-272429.
Audience: **g,l,u,f.**

Bartov, Omer **D764.B233 2001**
The Eastern Front, 1941-1945: German Troops and the Barbarisation of Warfare. Ed. 2. Trade Paper. Palgrave Macmillan. New York, NY. 2001. 248p. St. Antony's Ser. ISBN:0-333-94944-7, ISBN13: 978-0-333-94944-3. Dewey:940.54/1343. LCCN:2001-021231.
Audience: **u,f.**

Beevor, Antony **D757.9.B418 2002**
The Fall of Berlin 1945. Trade Cloth. Penguin Group (USA) Inc. New York, NY. 2002. 512p. ISBN:0-670-03041-4, ISBN13: 978-0-670-03041-5. Dewey:940.5421. LCCN:2002-510674.
Audience: **g,l,u,f.** *Choice, 2002.*

Beevor, Antony **D764.3.S7B37 1998**
Stalingrad: The Fateful Siege, 1942-1943. Trade Paper. Penguin Group (USA) Inc. New York, NY. 1999. 560p. ISBN:0-14-028458-3, ISBN13: 978-0-14-028458-4. Dewey:940.54/21785. LCCN:98-019346.
Audience: **g,l,u,f.**

Dallin, Alexander **D802.S75.D34 1981**
German Rule in Russia 1941-1945. Ed. 2. Library Binding. Westview Press. Boulder, CO. 1985. 700p. A Study of Occupation Policies ISBN:0-86531-102-1, ISBN13: 978-0-86531-102-2. Dewey:940.53/47. LCCN:80-052877.
Audience: **u,f.**

Deist, Wilhelm & Messerschmidt, Manfred **D743**
Germany and the Second World War: The Build-Up of German Aggression, Vol. I. P. S. Falla (Editor, Translator), Ewald Osers & Dean S. McMurry (Translators). Trade Cloth. Oxford University Press, Inc. New York, NY. 1991. 828p. ISBN:0-19-822866-X, ISBN13: 978-0-19-822866-0. Dewey:940.53. LCCN:90-007134.
Audience: **g,l,u,f.** *Choice, 1992.*

Fritz, Stephen G. **D757.85**
Frontsoldaten: The German Soldier in World War II. Trade Cloth. University Press of Kentucky. Lexington, KY. 1995. 312p. ISBN:0-8131-0943-4, ISBN13: 978-0-8131-0943-5. Dewey:940.54/1343.
Audience: **g,l,u,f.** *Choice, 1996.*

Glantz, David M. **D764.3**
Before Stalingrad: Barbarossa, Hitler's Invasion of Russia 1941. Trade Cloth. Tempus Publishing, Ltd. Stroud, Gloucestershire,

2004. 272p. ISBN:0-7524-2692-3, ISBN13: 978-0-7524-2692-1. Dewey:940.5/4217.
Audience: **g,l,u,f.**

Glantz, David M. & House, Jonathan M. **D764**
When Titans Clashed: How the Red Army Stopped Hitler. Trade Cloth. University Press of Kansas. Lawrence, KS. 2004. xiv, 418p. Modern War Studies ISBN:0-7006-0899-0, ISBN13: 978-0-7006-0899-7. Dewey:940.5/4217. LCCN:95-024588.
Audience: **g,l,u,f.** *Choice, 1996.*

Hastings, Max **D743.H36 2004**
Armageddon: The Battle for Germany, 1944-1945. Trade Cloth. Alfred A. Knopf Inc. New York, NY. 2004. 640p. ISBN:0-375-41433-9, ISBN13: 978-0-375-41433-6. Dewey:940.54/21. LCCN:2004-046468.
Audience: **g,l,u,f.** *Choice, 2005.*

Heiber, Helmut & Glantz, David M. (Editors) **D743.5**
Hitler and His Generals: Military Conferences, 1942-1945. Gerhard L. Weinberg (Introduction by). Trade Cloth. Enigma Books. New York, NY. 2003. 1211p. Ser. ISBN:1-929631-09-X, ISBN13: 978-1-929631-09-4. Dewey:940.530202.
Audience: **g,u,f.** *Choice, 2003.*

Levine, Alan J. **D790**
The Strategic Bombing of Germany, 1940-1945. Trade Cloth. Greenwood Publishing Group, Inc. Portsmouth, NH. 1992. 248p. ISBN:0-275-94319-4, ISBN13: 978-0-275-94319-6. Dewey:940.5442. LCCN:91-045610.
Audience: **g,l,u,f.** *Choice, 1993.*

Liddell-Hart, Basil H. **D757**
German Generals Talk. Trade Paper. HarperCollins Publishers. New York, NY. 1971. 320p. ISBN:0-688-06012-9, ISBN13: 978-0-688-06012-1. Dewey:940.54/13/430922.
Audience: **g,l,u.**

Maier, Klaus A., et al. **D743**
Germany and the Second World War: Germany's Initial Conquests in Europe, Vol. II. Horst Rohde, Bernd Stegeman & Hans Umbreit (Authors), Dean S. McMurry & Ewald Osers (Translators). Trade Cloth. Oxford University Press, Inc. New York, NY. 1991. 460p. ISBN:0-19-822885-6, ISBN13: 978-0-19-822885-1. Dewey:940.53.
Audience: **g,l,u,f.** *Choice, 1992.*

Muller, Richard & Corum, James S. (Translators) **UG635.G3C6823 1997**
The Luftwaffe's Way of War: German Air Force Doctrine, 1911-1945. Trade Cloth. Nautical & Aviation Publishing Company of America, Incorporated, The. Mount Pleasant, SC. 1998. 320p. ISBN:1-877853-47-X, ISBN13: 978-1-877853-47-0. Dewey:358.4/00943. LCCN:97-011252.
Audience: **g,l,u,f.** *Choice, 1999.*

Nossack, Hans Erich & Drenttel, William **D757.9.H3N68 2005**
The End: Hamburg 1943. Joel Agee (Translator), Erich Andres (Photographer), David Rieff (Foreword by). Trade Cloth. University of Chicago Press. Chicago, IL. 2004. 112p. ISBN:0-226-59556-0, ISBN13: 978-0-226-59556-6. Dewey:940.54/213515. LCCN:2004-005284.
Audience: **g,l,u,f.**

Reese, Willy Peter **D764.R41713 2005**
A Stranger to Myself: The Inhumanity of War: Russia, 1941-44. Stefan Schmitz (Editor), Michael Hofmann (Translator), Max Hastings (Foreword by). Cloth over Boards. Farrar, Straus & Giroux. New York, NY. 2005. 208p. ISBN:0-374-13978-4, ISBN13: 978-0-374-13978-0. Dewey:940.54/217/092 B. LCCN:2005-047893.
Audience: **g,l,u,f.**

Schoenhals, Kai P. **DD256**
The Free Germany Movement: A Case of Patriotism or Treason? Trade Cloth. Greenwood Publishing Group, Inc. Portsmouth, NH. 1989. 176p. Contributions to the Study of World History Ser., No. 12 ISBN:0-313-26390-6, ISBN13: 978-0-313-26390-3. Dewey:940.53/43. LCCN:88-021396.
Audience: **g,l,u.** *Choice, 1989.*

Schreiber, Gerhard, et al. **DD256.5.D43413 1990**
Germany and the Second World War: The Mediterranean, South-East Europe, and North Africa 1939-1941 (from Italy's Declaration of Non-Belligerence to the Entry of the United States into the War). Bernard Stegemann & Detlef Vogel (Authors), P. S. Falla (Editor, Translator), Dean S. McMurry, Ewald Osers & Louise Wilmott (Translators). Trade Cloth. Oxford University Press, Inc. New York, NY. 1995. 840p. ISBN:0-19-822884-8, ISBN13: 978-0-19-822884-4. Dewey:940.5/3. LCCN:90-007135.
Audience: **g,l,u,f.** *Choice, 1996.*

Schulte, Theo **D802.S75S38 1989**
The German Army and Nazi Policies in Occupied Russia. Trade Cloth. Berg Publishers. Oxford, 1989. 406p. ISBN:0-85496-160-7, ISBN13: 978-0-85496-160-3. Dewey:940.53/37. LCCN:87-025599.
Audience: **g,u,f.** *Choice, 1989.*

Taylor, Frederick **D757.9.D7T39 2004**
Dresden: Tuesday, February 13 1945. Trade Cloth. HarperCollins Publishers. New York, NY. 2004. 544p. ISBN:0-06-000676-5, ISBN13: 978-0-06-000676-1. Dewey:940.54/2132142. LCCN:2003-057139.
Audience: **g,l,u,f.**

Thamm, Gerhardt B. **D811.T4386 2000**
Boy Soldier: A German Teenager at the Nazi Twilight. Cloth Text. McFarland & Company, Incorporated Publishers. Jefferson, NC. 2000. 188p. ISBN:0-7864-0660-7, ISBN13: 978-0-7864-0660-9. Dewey:940.54/8243. LCCN:99-53098.
Audience: **g,l,u,f.**

Weinberg, Gerhard L. **D757 .W384 1995**
Germany, Hitler, and World War II: Essays in Modern German and World History. Cloth Text. Cambridge University Press. New York, NY. 1995. 353p. ISBN:0-521-47407-8, ISBN13: 978-0-521-47407-8. Dewey:940.5/3/43. LCCN:94-027076.
Audience: **u,f.**

Germany > History > Modern (1815-) > Allied Occupation (1945-1949)

Gimbel, John **Q149.U5G53 1990**
Science, Technology, and Reparations: Exploitation and Plunder in Postwar Germany. Trade Cloth. Stanford University Press. Palo Alto, CA. 1990. 304p. ISBN:0-8047-1761-3, ISBN13: 978-0-8047-1761-8. Dewey:940.53/1422. LCCN:89-037835.
Audience: **g,l,u,f.** *Choice, 1991.*

Glaser, Hermann **DD259.25**
The rubble years: the cultural roots of postwar Germany. Paragon House. 1986. ISBN:0-913729-26-4, ISBN13: 978-0-913729-26-7.
Audience: **g,l,u,f.**

Jackson, Robert H. **JX6731.W3 J33 1971**
Nuremberg Case. Trade Cloth. Cooper Square Publishers, Inc. New York, NY. 1972. 268p. ISBN:0-8154-0403-4, ISBN13: 978-0-8154-0403-3. Dewey:341.6/9. LCCN:73-166584.
Audience: **g,l,u,f.**

Marrus, Michael R. **D804.G42N87 1997**
The Nuremberg War Crimes Trial, 1945-46: A Documentary History. Trade Paper. Bedford/Saint Martin's. New York, NY. 1997. 276p. The Bedford Series in History and Culture ISBN:0-312-13691-9, ISBN13: 978-0-312-13691-8. Dewey:341.6/9/0268. LCCN:96-086777.
Audience: **g,l,u,f.**

Naimark, Norman M. **DD285.N35 1995**
The Russians in Germany: A History of the Soviet Zone of Occupation, 1945-1949. Trade Cloth. Harvard University Press. Cambridge, MA. 1995. 608p. ISBN:0-674-78405-7, ISBN13: 978-0-674-78405-5. Dewey:943/.0874. LCCN:95-007725.
Audience: **g,u,f.** *Choice, 1996.*

Overy, Richard **D757**
Interrogations: The Nazi Elite in Allied Hands 1945. Trade Paper. Penguin Group (USA) Inc. New York, NY. 2002. 672p. ISBN:0-14-200158-9, ISBN13: 978-0-14-200158-5. Dewey:940.5/40943.
Audience: **g,u,f.**

Peterson, Edward N. **D757.P48 1990**
The Many Faces of Defeat: The German People's Experience in 1945. Cloth Text. Peter Lang Publishing, Inc. New York, NY. 1991. 480p. American University Studies, Ser. IX, Vol. 88:History ISBN:0-8204-1351-8, ISBN13: 978-0-8204-1351-8. Dewey:940.53. LCCN:90-005829.
Audience: **g,l,u,f.** *Choice, 1991.*

Schivelbusch, Wolfgang **DD866.S34 1998**
In a Cold Crater: Cultural and Intellectual Life in Berlin, 1945-1948. Trade Cloth. University of California Press. Berkeley, CA. 1998. 248p. Weimar and Now Ser., Vol. 18 ISBN:0-520-20366-6, ISBN13: 978-0-520-20366-2. Dewey:943/.155. LCCN:97-040067.
Audience: **u,f.** *Choice, 1999.*

Schwartz, Thomas A. **E183.8.G3S513 1991**
America's Germany: John J. McCloy and the Federal Republic of Germany. Trade Cloth. Harvard University Press. Cambridge, MA. 1991. 418p. ISBN:0-674-03115-6, ISBN13: 978-0-674-03115-9. Dewey:327.73043. LCCN:90-039849.
Audience: **g,l,u,f.** *Choice, 1991.*

Germany > History > Modern (1815-) > German Federal Republic. German Democratic Republic (1949-1989)

Bark, Dennis L. & Gress, David R. **DD258.7.B37 1989**
A History of West Germany, Vol. II: Democracy & Its Discontents, 1963-1988. Trade Cloth. Blackwell Publishing, Inc. Malden, MA. 1989. 352p. ISBN:0-631-16788-9, ISBN13: 978-0-631-16788-4. Dewey:943.087. LCCN:88-038212.
Audience: **u,f.** *Choice, 1990.*

Bark, Dennis L. & Gress, David R. **DD258.7.B37 1989**
A History of West Germany, Vol. I: From Shadow to Substance, 1945-1963. Trade Cloth. Blackwell Publishing, Inc. Malden, MA. 1989. 352p. ISBN:0-631-16787-0, ISBN13: 978-0-631-16787-7. Dewey:943.087. LCCN:88-038212.
Audience: **u,f.** *Choice, 1990.*

Bartee, Wayne C. **DD901**
A Time to Speak Out: The Leipzig Citizen Protests and the Fall of East Germany. Uwe Schwabe (Foreword by). Trade Cloth. Greenwood Publishing Group, Inc. Portsmouth, NH. 2000. 224p. ISBN:0-275-96982-7, ISBN13: 978-0-275-96982-0. Dewey:943/.21220878. LCCN:00-038560.
Audience: **g,l,u,f.**

Bytwerk, Randall
☐ Nazi and East German Propaganda Guide. http://www.calvin.edu/academic/cas/gpa/
Calvin College.
Audience: **g,l,u,f.**

Dennis, Mike **HN460.5.A8D46 1993**
Social and Economic Modernization in Eastern Germany: From Honecker to Kohl. Trade Cloth. St. Martin's Press. Gordonville, VA. 1993. 272p. ISBN:0-86187-166-9, ISBN13: 978-0-86187-166-7. Dewey:306.09431. LCCN:93-008747.
Audience: **u,f.** *Choice, 1994.*

Diefendorf, Jeffry M. **HT178.G4D54 1993**
In the Wake of War: The Reconstruction of German Cities after World War II. Trade Cloth. Oxford University Press, Inc. New York, NY. 1993. 424p. ISBN:0-19-507219-7, ISBN13: 978-0-19-507219-8. Dewey:307.76/0943/09045. LCCN:92-028145.
Audience: **u,f.** *Choice, 1995.*

Diehl, James M. **UB359.G3D5 1993**
The Thanks of the Fatherland: German Veterans after the Second World War. Trade Cloth. University of North Carolina Press. Chapel Hill, NC. 1993. xiv, 346p. ISBN:0-8078-2077-6, ISBN13: 978-0-8078-2077-3. Dewey:362.86/0943. LCCN:92-050811.
Audience: **u,f.** *Choice, 1993.*

Fehrenbach, Heide **HQ777.9.F44 2005**
Race after Hitler: Black Occupation Children in Postwar Germany and America. Trade Cloth. Princeton University Press. Princeton, NJ. 2005. 272p. ISBN:0-691-11906-6, ISBN13: 978-0-691-11906-9. Dewey:943/.004059073031. LCCN:2004-043162.
Audience: **g,l,u,f.** *Choice, 2006.*

Frei, Norbert **DD259.4.F72413**
Adenauer's Germany and the Nazi Past: The Politics of Amnesty and Integration. Joel Golb (Translator). Trade Cloth. Columbia University Press. New York, NY. 2002. 365p. ISBN:0-231-11882-1, ISBN13: 978-0-231-11882-8. Dewey:940.53/144/0943. LCCN:2002-073502.
Audience: **u,f.** *Choice, 2003.*

Fulbrook, Mary **DD258.7.F86 2000**
Interpretations of the Two Germanies, 1945-1990. Ed. 2. Trade Paper. Palgrave Macmillan. New York, NY. 2000. 119p. Studies

in European History Ser. ISBN:0-312-23190-3, ISBN13: 978-0-312-23190-3. Dewey:943.087. LCCN:99-089381.
Audience: **g,l,u,f.**

Gray, William Glenn **DD259.5.G46 2003**
Germany's Cold War: The Global Campaign to Isolate East Germany, 1949-1969. Trade Cloth. University of North Carolina Press. Chapel Hill, NC. 2003. 368p. The New Cold War History Ser. ISBN:0-8078-2758-4, ISBN13: 978-0-8078-2758-1. Dewey:327.430431/09/045. LCCN:2002-006444.
Audience: **u,f.** *Choice, 2003.*

Jarausch, Konrad H. & Gransow, Volker **DD290.22.D4813 1994**
Uniting Germany: Documents and Debates, 1944-1993. Ed. 4. Trade Cloth. Berghahn Books, Inc. New York, NY. 2003. 320p. ISBN:1-57181-011-0, ISBN13: 978-1-57181-011-3. Dewey:943.087. LCCN:94-020694.
Audience: **g,l,u,f.** *Choice, 1995.*

Maier, Charles S. **DD289**
Dissolution: The Crisis of Communism and the End of East Germany. Trade Cloth. Princeton University Press. Princeton, NJ. 1997. ISBN:0-614-27831-7, ISBN13: 978-0-614-27831-6. Dewey:943.10878.
Audience: **g,l,u.**

Moeller, Robert G. **HQ1236.5**
Protecting Motherhood: Women and the Family in the Politics of Postwar West Germany. Trade Cloth. University of California Press. Berkeley, CA. 1993. 346p. ISBN:0-520-07903-5, ISBN13: 978-0-520-07903-8. Dewey:305.4/2/0943/09045. LCCN:92-006622.
Audience: **u,f.**

Moeller, Robert G. (Editor) **DD259.2.W475 1997**
West Germany under Construction: Politics, Society, and Culture in the Adenauer Era. Trade Paper. University of Michigan Press. Chicago, IL. 1997. 472p. Social History, Popular Culture, and Politics In Germany Ser. ISBN:0-472-06648-X, ISBN13: 978-0-472-06648-3. Dewey:943/.087. LCCN:96-038008.
Audience: **u,f.** *Choice, 1998.*

Nicholls, A. J. **HC286.5**
Freedom with Responsibility: The Social Market Economy in Germany, 1918-1963. Paper Text. Oxford University Press, Inc. New York, NY. 2000. 436p. ISBN:0-19-820852-9, ISBN13: 978-0-19-820852-5. Dewey:338.9/43/09041.
Audience: **g,u,f.** *Choice, 1995.*

Ross, Corey **HX280.5.A6R67 2000**
Constructing Socialism at the Grass-Roots: The Transformation of East Germany, 1945-1965. Cloth over Boards. Palgrave Macmillan. New York, NY. 2000. 278p. ISBN:0-312-23041-9, ISBN13: 978-0-312-23041-8. Dewey:335.43/0943/109045. LCCN:99-049746.
Audience: **g,l,u,f.** *Choice, 2000.*

Schissler, Hanna **DD258.7.M57 2001**
The Miracle Years: A Cultural History of West Germany, 1949-1968. Cloth Text. Princeton University Press. Princeton, NJ. 2000. 448p. ISBN:0-691-05819-9, ISBN13: 978-0-691-05819-1. Dewey:943.087. LCCN:00-039974.
Audience: **g,l,u,f.**

Schwarz, Hans P. **DD259.7.A3**
Konrad Adenauer: The Statesman, 1952-1967. Geoffrey Penny (Translator). Trade Cloth. Berghahn Books, Inc. New York, NY. 1997. 910p. ISBN:1-57181-960-6, ISBN13: 978-1-57181-960-4. Dewey:943/.087/092. LCCN:95-037776.
Audience: **g,u,f.**

Schwarz, Hans-Peter **DD259.7.A3S3313 1995**
Konrad Adenauer: From the German Empire to the Federal Republic, 1876-1952. Trade Cloth. Berghahn Books, Inc. New York, NY. 1995. 760p. ISBN:1-57181-870-7, ISBN13: 978-1-57181-870-6. Dewey:943/.08/092. LCCN:95-037776.
Audience: **g,u,f.** *Choice, 1996.*

Smyser, W. R. **DD257.25**
From Yalta to Berlin: The Cold War Struggle over Germany. Trade Paper. Palgrave Macmillan. New York, NY. 2000. 496p. ISBN:0-312-23340-X, ISBN13: 978-0-312-23340-2. Dewey:943/.087. LCCN:98-055304.
Audience: **g,l,u,f.** *Choice, 1999.*

Thomas, Nick **HM881**
Protest Movements in 1960s West Germany: A Social History of Dissent and Democracy. Cloth over Boards. Berg Publishers. Oxford, 2003. 288p. ISBN:1-85973-645-9, ISBN13: 978-1-85973-645-6. Dewey:303.48/4/0943. LCCN:2002-151465.
Audience: **g,l,u,f.** *Choice, 2003.*

Wiesen, S. Jonathan **HC286.5**
West German Industry and the Challenge of the Nazi Past, 1945-1955. Trade Paper. University of North Carolina Press. Chapel Hill, NC. 2004. 352p. ISBN:0-8078-5543-X, ISBN13: 978-0-8078-5543-0. Dewey:338.0943/09045. LCCN:2001-023566.
Audience: **g,u,f.** *Choice, 2002.*

Germany > History > Modern (1815-) > Reunified Germany (1989-)

Borneman, John **DD881.B675 1990**
After the Wall: East Meets West in the New Berlin. Trade Cloth. Basic Books. New York, NY. 1991. 464p. ISBN:0-465-00083-5, ISBN13: 978-0-465-00083-8. Dewey:943.1/55. LCCN:90-055589.
Audience: **g,l,u,f.**

Darnton, Robert **DD289**
Berlin Journal, 1989-1990. Trade Paper. W. W. Norton & Company, Inc. New York, NY. 1993. 352p. ISBN:0-393-31018-3, ISBN13: 978-0-393-31018-4. Dewey:943.1087/8.
Audience: **g,l,u,f.** *Choice, 1991.*

Young, Brigitte **HQ1623**
Triumph of the Fatherland: German Unification and the Marginalization of Women. Trade Cloth. University of Michigan Press. Chicago, IL. 1999. 296p. Social History, Popular Culture, and Politics in Germany Ser. ISBN:0-472-10948-0, ISBN13: 978-0-472-10948-7. Dewey:305.42/0943. LCCN:98-040080.
Audience: **g,l,u,f.** *Choice, 2000.*

Germany > Special Topics > Contending with the Nazi past. Historical Controversies

Evans, Richard J. **DD256.5.E92 1989**
In Hitler's Shadow: West German Historians and the Attempt to Escape from the Nazi Past. Trade Paper. Knopf Publishing Group. New York, NY. 1989. 196p. ISBN:0-679-72348-X, ISBN13: 978-0-679-72348-6. Dewey:943.086. LCCN:88-043239.
Audience: **g,l,u,f.** *Choice, 1990.*

Herf, Jeffrey **D804.3.H474 1997**
Divided Memory: The Nazi Past in the Two Germanys. Trade Cloth. Harvard University Press. Cambridge, MA. 1997. 560p. ISBN:0-674-21303-3, ISBN13: 978-0-674-21303-6. Dewey:940.53/18/0943. LCCN:97-011231.
Audience: **u,f.** *Choice, 1998.*

Holborn, Hajo **D424 .H6 1982**
The Political Collapse of Europe. Library Binding. Greenwood Publishing Group, Inc. Portsmouth, NH. 1982. 207p. ISBN:0-313-23031-5, ISBN13: 978-0-313-23031-8. Dewey:940.2/8. LCCN:82-011839.
Audience: **g,l,u,f.**

Jarausch, Konrad Hugo & Geyer, Michael **DD86.J253 2003**
Shattered Past: Reconstructing German Histories. Trade Paper. Princeton University Press. Princeton, NJ. 2002. 336p. ISBN:0-691-05936-5, ISBN13: 978-0-691-05936-5. Dewey:943.08/07/2043. LCCN:2002-016933.
Audience: **u,f.** *Choice, 2003.*

Jaspers, Karl **DD256.48.J3713 2001**
The Question of German Guilt. Ed. 2. Trade Paper. Fordham University Press. Bronx, NY. 2001. 117p. Perspectives in Continental Philosophy Ser., Vol. 16 ISBN:0-8232-2069-9, ISBN13: 978-0-8232-2069-4. Dewey:943.086. LCCN:00-029375.
Audience: **g,u,f.**

Knowlton, James & Cates, Truett (Translators) **D804.3**
Forever in the Shadow of Hitler?: The Dispute about the Germans' Understanding of Hisotry: Original Documents of the Historikerstreit, the Controversy Concerning the Singularity of the Holocaust. Trade Cloth. Prometheus Books, Publishers. Amherst, NY. 286p. ISBN:1-57392-321-4, ISBN13: 978-1-57392-321-7. Dewey:940.53/18/072.
Audience: **u,f.**

Maier, Charles S. **D804.3.M35 1988**
The Unmasterable Past: History, Holocaust, and German National Identity. Trade Cloth. Harvard University Press. Cambridge, MA. 1988. 240p. ISBN:0-674-92975-6, ISBN13: 978-0-674-92975-3. Dewey:940.53/15/03924. LCCN:88-011690.
Audience: **u,f.** *Choice, 1989.*

Meinecke, Friedrich **DD256.5**
German Catastrophe: Reflections and Recollections. Trade Paper. Beacon Press. Boston, MA. 1963. ISBN:0-8070-5667-7, ISBN13: 978-0-8070-5667-7. Dewey:943.086.
Audience: **g,l,u,f.**

Sereny, Gitta **DD256.5.S443 2001**
Healing Wound: Experiences and Reflections, Germany, 1938-2001. Trade Cloth. W. W. Norton & Company, Inc. New York, NY. 2001. 320p. ISBN:0-393-04428-9, ISBN13: 978-0-393-04428-7. Dewey:943.087. LCCN:2001-044006.
Audience: **g,l,u,f.** *Choice, 2002.*

Germany > Special Topics > Culture and Politics

Applegate, Celia **ML410.B13A7 2005**
Bach in Berlin: Nation and Culture in Mendelssohn' Revival of the St. Matthew Passion. Book, Other. Cornell University Press. Ithaca, NY. 2005. 304p. ISBN:0-8014-4389-X, ISBN13: 978-0-8014-4389-3. Dewey:780/.943/09034. LCCN:2005-013205.
Audience: **g,l,u,f.** *Choice, 2006.*

Applegate, Celia & Potter, Pamela Maxine **ML275.M933 2002**
Music and German National Identity. Trade Cloth. University of Chicago Press. Chicago, IL. 2002. 329p. ISBN:0-226-02130-0, ISBN13: 978-0-226-02130-0. Dewey:780/.943. LCCN:2001-007534.
Audience: **u,f.**

Dennis, David **ML410.B4 D34**
Beethoven in German Politics, 1870-1989. Trade Paper. Yale University Press. Cumberland, RI. 1996. 264p. ISBN:0-300-10529-0, ISBN13: 978-0-300-10529-2. Dewey:780/.92.
Audience: **g,l,u,f.**

Jelavich, Peter **PN1968.G3J45 1993**
Berlin Cabaret. Trade Cloth. Harvard University Press. Cambridge, MA. 1993. 336p. Studies in Cultural History, Vol. 9 ISBN:0-674-06761-4, ISBN13: 978-0-674-06761-5. Dewey:792.7/0943155. LCCN:93-016096.
Audience: **g,l,u,f.** *Choice, 1994.*

Katz, Jacob **ML410.V4**
The Darker Side of Genius: Richard Wagner's Anti-Semitism. Perfect. University Press of New England. Lebanon, NH. 2002. 172p. ISBN:1-58465-240-3, ISBN13: 978-1-58465-240-3. Dewey:782.1/092/4. LCCN:85-040935.
Audience: **g,l,u,f.** *Choice, 1986.*

Kreimeier, Klaus **PN1999.U35 K713 1999**
The UFA Story: A History of Germany's Greatest Film Company, 1918-1945. Trade Paper. University of California Press. Berkeley, CA. 1999. 459p. Weimar and Now Ser., Vol. 23 ISBN:0-520-22069-2, ISBN13: 978-0-520-22069-0. Dewey:791.43/0943. LCCN:99-014017.
Audience: **u,f.**

Lepenies, Wolf **DD97.L47 2006**
The Seduction of Culture in German History. Trade Cloth. Princeton University Press. Princeton, NJ. 2006. 248p. ISBN:0-691-12131-1, ISBN13: 978-0-691-12131-4. Dewey:943. LCCN:2005-048907.
Audience: **g,u,f.**

Marchand, Suzanne L. **DD193.5.M37 1996**
Down from Olympus: Archaeology and Philhellenism in Germany, 1750-1970. Trade Cloth. Princeton University Press.

Princeton, NJ. 1996. 416p. ISBN:0-691-04393-0, ISBN13: 978-0-691-04393-7. Dewey:938/.0072/043. LCCN:95-053324.
Audience: **g,u,f.** *Choice, 1997.*

McClelland, Charles E. **LA727**
State, Society and University in Germany, Seventeen Hundred to Nineteen Fourteen. Cloth Text. Cambridge University Press. New York, NY. 1980. 448p. ISBN:0-521-22742-9, ISBN13: 978-0-521-22742-1. Dewey:378.43. LCCN:79-013575.
Audience: **g,u,f.**

Mosse, George L. **DD232.M6 1997**
The Crisis of German Ideology: Intellectual Origins of the Third Reich. Trade Paper. Howard Fertig Inc. New York, NY. 1998. x, 373p. ISBN:0-86527-426-6, ISBN13: 978-0-86527-426-6. Dewey:320.54/0943. LCCN:97-026819.
Audience: **u,f.**

Ringer, Fritz K. **LA727.R47 1990**
The Decline of the German Mandarins: The German Academic Community, 1890-1933. Trade Paper. Wesleyan University Press. Middletown, CT. 1990. 548p. ISBN:0-8195-6235-1, ISBN13: 978-0-8195-6235-7. Dewey:301.445. LCCN:90-050315.
Audience: **u,f.**

Spotts, Frederic **ML410.W2**
Bayreuth: A History of the Wagner Festival. Trade Paper. Yale University Press. Cumberland, RI. 1996. 344p. ISBN:0-300-06665-1, ISBN13: 978-0-300-06665-4. Dewey:782.1/079/43315.
Audience: **g,l,u,f.** *Choice, 1994.*

Stern, Fritz R. **DD67**
The Politics of Cultural Despair: A Study in the Rise of the Germanic Ideology. Trade Cloth. University of California Press. Berkeley, CA. 1961. 367p. California Library Reprint Ser. ISBN:0-520-02626-8, ISBN13: 978-0-520-02626-1. Dewey:943.08/07/2022. LCCN:61-007517.
Audience: **u,f.**

Wingler, Hans **N332.B38**
Bauhaus: Weimar, Dessau, Berlin, Chicago. Trade Paper. MIT Press. Cambridge, MA. 1978. 700p. ISBN:0-262-73047-2, ISBN13: 978-0-262-73047-1. Dewey:707/.1/5.
Audience: **g,u,f.**

Zuhlsdorff, Volkmar **DD68**
Hitler's Exiles: The German Cultural Resistance in America and Europe. Martin H. Bott (Translator). Trade Cloth. Continuum International Publishing Group, Ltd. London, 2004. 240p. ISBN:0-8264-7324-5, ISBN13: 978-0-8264-7324-0. Dewey:369/.243/097309043. LCCN:2004-300859.
Audience: **g,l,u,f.** *Choice, 2005.*

Germany > Special Topics > Nation and Nationalism

Fritsch-Bournazel, Renata **DD257.25.F7713 1988**
Confronting the German Question: Germans on the East-West Divide. Trade Cloth. Berg Publishers. Oxford, 1988. 176p. ISBN:0-85496-100-3, ISBN13: 978-0-85496-100-9. Dewey:943.087. LCCN:87-026886.
Audience: **g,l,u,f.** *Choice, 1988.*

Schulze, Hagen **DD204 .S3413 1990**
The Course of German Nationalism: From Frederick the Great to Bismarck, 1763-1867. Sarah Hanbury-Tenison (Translator). Trade Paper. Cambridge University Press. New York, NY. 1991. 188p. ISBN:0-521-37759-5, ISBN13: 978-0-521-37759-1. Dewey:943. LCCN:89-077388.
Audience: **g,l,u,f.** *Choice, 1991.*

Germany > Special Topics > German Jews

Barkai, Avraham **DS135.G33**
From Boycott to Annihilation: The Economic Struggle of German Jews, 1933-1943. Perfect. University Press of New England. Lebanon, NH. 2002. 256p. Tauber Institute for the Study of European Jewry Ser. ISBN:1-58465-223-3, ISBN13: 978-1-58465-223-6. Dewey:943/.004924. LCCN:89-040228.
Audience: **u,f.** *Choice, 1990.*

Barkai, Avraham **DS135.G33**
German-Jewish History in Modern Times: Renewal and Destruction, 1918-1945. Michael Brenner & Michael A. Meyer (Editors). Trade Cloth. Columbia University Press. New York, NY. 1998. 384p. ISBN:0-231-07478-6, ISBN13: 978-0-231-07478-0. Dewey:943.004924. LCCN:96-013900.
Audience: **g,u,f.** *Choice, 1999.*

Brenner, Michael **DS135.G33B74 1996**
The Renaissance of Jewish Culture in Weimar Germany. Cloth over Boards. Yale University Press. Cumberland, RI. 1996. 320p. ISBN:0-300-06262-1, ISBN13: 978-0-300-06262-5. Dewey:943/.085/089924. LCCN:95-030449.
Audience: **g,u,f.** *Choice, 1996.*

Brenner, Michael **DS135.G33**
After the Holocaust: Rebuilding Jewish Lives in Postwar Germany. Barbara Harshav (Translator). Trade Paper. Princeton University Press. Princeton, NJ. 1999. 208p. ISBN:0-691-00679-2, ISBN13: 978-0-691-00679-6. Dewey:943/.004924.
Audience: **g,u,f.** *Choice, 1998.*

Broder, Henryk **DS135.G332B76 2003**
A Jew in the New Germany. Sander L. Gilman & Lilian M. Friedberg (Editors), Broder Translators' Collective Staff (Translator). Trade Cloth. University of Illinois Press. Champaign, IL. 2003. 176p. Humanities Laboratory Ser. ISBN:0-252-02856-2, ISBN13: 978-0-252-02856-4. Dewey:305.892/4043/09045. LCCN:2002-153958.
Audience: **g,l,u,f.** *Choice, 2004.*

Feiner, Shmuel **DS113.F4413 2003**
The Jewish Enlightenment. Book, Other. University of Pennsylvania Press. Philadelphia, PA. 2003. 456p. Jewish Culture and Contexts Ser. ISBN:0-8122-3755-2, ISBN13: 978-0-8122-3755-9. Dewey:296/.094/09033. LCCN:2003-061057.
Audience: **u,f.** *Choice, 2004.*

Geller, Jay Howard **DS135.G332G39 2004**
Jews in Post-Holocaust Germany, 1945-1953. Cloth Text. Cambridge University Press. New York, NY. 2004. 344p. ISBN:0-521-83353-1, ISBN13: 978-0-521-83353-0. Dewey:305.892/4043/09045. LCCN:2004-045672.
Audience: **g,l,u,f.**

Gluckel of Hameln Staff **DS135.G5 H33813 1977**
The Memoirs of Gluckel of Hamelin. Marvin Lowenthal (Translator), Robert Rosen (Introduction by). Trade Paper. Knopf Publishing Group. New York, NY. 1987. 336p. ISBN:0-8052-0572-1, ISBN13: 978-0-8052-0572-5. Dewey:943/.515004924/0092. LCCN:77-075290.
Audience: **g,l,u,f.**

Hess, Jonathan M. **DS135**
Germans, Jews and the Claims of Modernity. Cloth over Boards. Yale University Press. Cumberland, RI. 2002. 272p. ISBN:0-300-09701-8, ISBN13: 978-0-300-09701-6. Dewey:305.892/4043/09033. LCCN:2002-001452.
Audience: **u,f.** *Choice, 2003.*

Jersch-Wenzel, Stefi **DS135.G32B48 1996**
German-Jewish History in Modern Times: Emancipation and Acculturation, 1870-1871. Michael A. Meyer & Michael Brenner (Editors). Trade Cloth. Eastern European Monographs. Bradenton, FL. 1997. 392p. ISBN:0-231-07474-3, ISBN13: 978-0-231-07474-2. Dewey:943/.004924. LCCN:96-013900.
Audience: **u,f.** *Choice, 1998.*

Kaplan, Marion A. **DS135.G32J49 2004**
Jewish Daily Life in Germany, 1618-1945. Trade Cloth. Oxford University Press, Inc. New York, NY. 2005. 541p. ISBN:0-19-517164-0, ISBN13: 978-0-19-517164-8. Dewey:943/.004924. LCCN:2004-041471.
Audience: **u,f.** *Choice, 2006.*

Kaplan, Marion A. **DS135.G33K292 1991**
The Making of the Jewish Middle Class: Women, Family, and Identity in Imperial Germany. Cloth Text. Oxford University Press, Inc. New York, NY. 1991. 368p. Studies in Jewish History ISBN:0-19-503952-1, ISBN13: 978-0-19-503952-8. Dewey:943/.004924. LCCN:90-045234.
Audience: **g,l,u,f.** *Choice, 1992.*

Kauders, Anthony **DS146.G4K38 1996**
German Politics and the Jews: Dusseldorf and Nuremberg, 1910-1933. Cloth Text. Oxford University Press, Inc. New York, NY. 1996. 224p. Oxford Historical Monographs ISBN:0-19-820631-3, ISBN13: 978-0-19-820631-6. Dewey:943/.004924. LCCN:96-012141.
Audience: **g,u,f.** *Choice, 1997.*

Levenson, Alan T. **DS141.L6435 2004**
Between Philosemitism and Antisemitism: Defenses of Jews and Judaism in Germany, 1871-1932. Cloth Text. University of Nebraska Press. Lincoln, NE. 2004. 304p. ISBN:0-8032-2957-7, ISBN13: 978-0-8032-2957-0. Dewey:305.892/4043/09034. LCCN:2003-023385.
Audience: **g,u,f.** *Choice, 2005.*

Lowenstein, Steven M. **DS135.G4B46725 1994**
The Berlin Jewish Community: Enlightenment, Family and Crisis, 1770-1830. Trade Cloth. Oxford University Press, Inc. New York, NY. 1994. 312p. Studies in Jewish History ISBN:0-19-508326-1, ISBN13: 978-0-19-508326-2. Dewey:943.1/55004924. LCCN:92-039884.
Audience: **g,l,u,f.** *Choice, 1995.*

Meyer, Michael A. (Editor), et al. **DS135.G32B48 1996**
German-Jewish History in Modern Times: Tradition and Enlightenment 1600-1780. Michael Brenner, Mordechai Breuer & Michael Graetz (Editors). Trade Cloth. Eastern European Monographs. Bradenton, FL. 1996. 436p. ISBN:0-231-07472-7, ISBN13: 978-0-231-07472-8. Dewey:943/.004924. LCCN:96-013900.
Audience: **u,f.** *Choice, 1997.*

Mosse, W. E. **DS135.G5A155 1989**
The German-Jewish Economic Elite, 1820-1935: A Socio-Cultural Profile. Trade Cloth. Oxford University Press, Inc. New York, NY. 1989. 380p. ISBN:0-19-822990-9, ISBN13: 978-0-19-822990-2. Dewey:943/.004924. LCCN:88-015934.
Audience: **g,u,f.** *Choice, 1990.*

Niewyk, Donald L. **DS135.G33N44 2001**
Jews in Weimar Germany. Trade Paper. Transaction Publishers. Somerset, NJ. 2000. 229p. ISBN:0-7658-0692-4, ISBN13: 978-0-7658-0692-5. Dewey:943/.004924. LCCN:00-044713.
Audience: **u,f.**

Roemer, Nils H. **DS135.G33R54 2005**
Jewish Scholarship and Culture in Nineteenth-Century Germany: Between History and Faith. Trade Cloth. University of Wisconsin Press. Chicago, IL. 2005. 254p. Studies in German Jewish Cultural History and Literature ISBN:0-299-21170-3, ISBN13: 978-0-299-21170-7. Dewey:907/.2/023924043. LCCN:2005-001337.
Audience: **u,f.** *Choice, 2006.*

Strauss, Herbert A. **DS135.G5S76 1999**
In the Eye of the Storm: Growing up Jewish in Germany, 1918-1943, a Memoir. Trade Cloth. Fordham University Press. Bronx, NY. 1999. 262p. ISBN:0-8232-1916-X, ISBN13: 978-0-8232-1916-2. Dewey:943/.155004924/0092. LCCN:99-016618.
Audience: **g,l,u,f.** *Choice, 2000.*

Germany > Special Topics > German Middle Classes

Augustine, Dolores L. **HC285**
Patricians and Parvenus: Wealth and High Society in Wilhelmine Germany. Cloth over Boards. Berg Publishers. Oxford, 1994. 350p. ISBN:0-85496-397-9, ISBN13: 978-0-85496-397-3. Dewey:305.550943. LCCN:93-029862.
Audience: **u,f.** *Choice, 1995.*

Blackbourn, David (Editor) **HT690.G3**
German Bourgeoisie: Essays on the Social History of the German Middle Class. Trade Paper. Routledge. New York, NY. 1993. 368p. ISBN:0-415-09358-9, ISBN13: 978-0-415-09358-3. Dewey:305.550943. LCCN:90-035016.
Audience: **u,f.**

Jarausch, Konrad H. **HD8038.G3J37 1990**
The Unfree Professions: German Lawyers, Teachers, and Engineers, 1900-1950. Trade Cloth. Oxford University Press, Inc. New York, NY. 1990. 366p. ISBN:0-19-504482-7, ISBN13: 978-0-19-504482-9. Dewey:331.7/12/09430904. LCCN:89-036827.
Audience: **u,f.** *Choice, 1991.*

Lebovics, Herman **DD238.L43**
Social Conservatism and the Middle Classes in Germany, 1914-1933. Princeton Univesity Press. 1969.
Audience: **u,f.**

Germany > Regional, Provincial, and Local History > Berlin

Elkins, T. H. & Hofmeister, B. **DD866.E44 1988**
Berlin: Spatial Structure of a Divided City. Paper over Boards. Routledge. New York, NY. 1988. 296p. ISBN:0-416-92220-1, ISBN13: 978-0-416-92220-2. Dewey:943.1/55. LCCN:87-021722.
Audience: **g,u,f.** *Choice, 1988.*

Friedrich, Otto **DD880.F75 1995**
Before the Deluge: A Portrait of Berlin in the 1920s. Trade Paper. HarperCollins Publishers. New York, NY. 1995. 464p. ISBN:0-06-092679-1, ISBN13: 978-0-06-092679-3. Dewey:943.1/5508. LCCN:96-103399.
Audience: **g,l,u,f.**

Hagen, William W. **DD801.B687H34 2002**
Ordinary Prussians: Brandenburg Junkers and Villagers, 1500-1840. Peter Baldwin, Christopher Clark, James B. Collins, Mia Rodr¡guez-Salgado & Lyndal Roper (Contribution by). Trade Cloth. Cambridge University Press. New York, NY. 2002. 712p. New Studies in European History ISBN:0-521-81558-4, ISBN13: 978-0-521-81558-1. Dewey:943/.15. LCCN:2002-017502.
Audience: **u,f.** *Choice, 2003.*

Ladd, Brian **HT169.G32B4127 1997**
The Ghosts of Berlin: Confronting German History in the Urban Landscape. Trade Cloth. University of Chicago Press. Chicago, IL. 1997. 282p. ISBN:0-226-46761-9, ISBN13: 978-0-226-46761-0. Dewey:307.121. LCCN:96-028562.
Audience: **g,l,u,f.**

Large, David Clay **DD860**
Berlin. Trade Paper. Basic Books. New York, NY. 2001. 736p. ISBN:0-465-02632-X, ISBN13: 978-0-465-02632-6. Dewey:943/.155.
Audience: **g,l,u,f.** *Choice, 2001.*

Richie, Alexandra **DD881.R5 1998**
Faust's Metropolis: A History of Berlin. Trade Cloth. Avalon Publishing Group. New York, NY. 1998. 984p. ISBN:0-7867-0510-8, ISBN13: 978-0-7867-0510-8. Dewey:943.1/55. LCCN:98-016802.
Audience: **u,f.** *Choice, 1998.*

Till, Karen E. **DD881.T55 2005**
The New Berlin: Memory, Politics, Place. Trade Cloth. University of Minnesota Press. Minneapolis, MN. 2005. 296p. ISBN:0-8166-4010-6, ISBN13: 978-0-8166-4010-2. Dewey:943/.155088. LCCN:2004-028616.
Audience: **g,u,f.** *Choice, 2006.*

Austria. Austro-Hungarian Empire > General Histories

Brook-Shepherd, Gordon **DB17**
The Austrians: A Thousand Year Odyssey. Trade Paper. HarperCollins World. New York, NY. 1997. 483p. ISBN:0-00-638255-X, ISBN13: 978-0-00-638255-3. Dewey:943.6.
Audience: **g,l,u,f.**

Bucur, Maria & Wingfield, Nancy Merriwether **DAW1048.S73 2001**
Staging the Past: The Politics of Commemoration in Habsburg Central Europe, 1848 to the Present. Trade Paper. Purdue University Press. West Lafayette, IN. 2001. 337p. Central European Studies ISBN:1-55753-161-7, ISBN13: 978-1-55753-161-2. Dewey:943.06. LCCN:00-068422.
Audience: **u,f.**

Evans, R. J. **D228**
The Making of the Hapsburg Monarchy, 1550-1700: An Interpretation. Trade Paper. Oxford University Press, Inc. New York, NY. 1984. 556p. ISBN:0-19-873085-3, ISBN13: 978-0-19-873085-9. Dewey:943.6/03. LCCN:79-040616.
Audience: **g,u,f.**

Fichtner, Paula S. **DB36.3.H3F53 2003**
The Habsburg Monarchy 1490-1848: Attributes of Empire. Cloth over Boards. Palgrave Macmillan. New York, NY. 2003. 240p. European History in Perspective Ser. ISBN:0-333-73727-X, ISBN13: 978-0-333-73727-9. Dewey:943.6/03. LCCN:2002-044804.
Audience: **l,u,f.** *Choice, 2004.*

Good, David F. **HC264**
The Economic Rise of the Hapsburg Empire 1750-1914. Trade Cloth. University of California Press. Berkeley, CA. 1984. 288p. ISBN:0-520-05094-0, ISBN13: 978-0-520-05094-5. Dewey:330.94. LCCN:83-017959.
Audience: **u,f.**

Ingrao, Charles W. **DB36.3.H3 I54 1994**
The Habsburg Monarchy, 1618-1815. Ed. 2. Cloth Text. Cambridge University Press. New York, NY. 2000. 284p. New Approaches to European History Ser., No. 3 ISBN:0-521-78034-9, ISBN13: 978-0-521-78034-6. Dewey:943.6/03. LCCN:00-712309.
Audience: **g,l,u,f.**

Ingrao, Charles W. (Editor) **DB65.5.S73 1994**
State and Society in Early Modern Austria. Cloth Text. Purdue University Press. West Lafayette, IN. 1994. 360p. ISBN:1-55753-047-5, ISBN13: 978-1-55753-047-9. Dewey:943.6/03. LCCN:93-033879.
Audience: **u,f.** *Choice, 1995.*

Johnston, William M. **DB30.J64**
The Austrian Mind: An Intellectual and Social History, 1848-1938. Trade Paper. University of California Press. Berkeley, CA. 1976. 531p. ISBN:0-520-04955-1, ISBN13: 978-0-520-04955-0. Dewey:914.36/03/4. LCCN:75-111418.
Audience: **u,f.**

Kann, Robert A. **DB36.3.H3**
A History of the Habsburg Empire, 1526-1918. Trade Paper. University of California Press. Berkeley, CA. 1974. xiv, 646p. ISBN:0-520-04206-9, ISBN13: 978-0-520-04206-3. Dewey:943.6/03. LCCN:72-097733.
Audience: **u,f.**

Okey, Robin **DB36.3.H3O44 2000**
The Habsburg Monarchy, C. 1765-1918: From Enlightenment to Eclipse. Cloth over Boards. Palgrave Macmillan. New York, NY. 2000. 464p. ISBN:0-312-23375-2, ISBN13: 978-0-312-23375-4. Dewey:943.6. LCCN:00-039007.
Audience: **g,u,f.** *Choice, 2001.*

Sked, Alan **DB80.S58 2001**
The Decline and Fall of the Habsburg Empire, 1815-1918. Ed. 2. Paper Text. Longman Publishing Group. White Plains, NY. 2001. 368p. ISBN:0-582-35666-0, ISBN13: 978-0-582-35666-5. Dewey:943.6/04. LCCN:2001-022348.
Audience: **g,l,u,f.**

Tapié, Victor Lucien **DB47**
The Rise and Fall of the Habsburg Monarchy. New York, Praeger. 1971.
Audience: **g,l,u.**

Taylor, A. J. P. **DB80**
The Habsburg Monarchy, 1809-1918: A History of the Austrian Empire and Austria-Hungary. Trade Paper. University of Chicago Press. Chicago, IL. 1976. 280p. Phoenix Book, P683 Ser. ISBN:0-226-79145-9, ISBN13: 978-0-226-79145-6. Dewey:943.6/04. LCCN:76-368919.
Audience: **g,u,f.**

Austria. Austro-Hungarian Empire > Military and Diplomatic History

Bridge, F. R. **DB80**
The Habsburg Monarchy among the Great Powers, 1815-1918. Trade Cloth. Berg Publishers. Oxford, 1991. 430p. ISBN:0-85496-413-4, ISBN13: 978-0-85496-413-0. Dewey:943.6/04. LCCN:89-028947.
Audience: **u,f.** *Choice, 1991.*

Deak, Istvan **UB415.A8D43 1990**
Beyond Nationalism: A Social and Political History of the Habsburg Officer Corps, 1848-1918. Trade Cloth. Oxford University Press, Inc. New York, NY. 1990. 288p. ISBN:0-19-504505-X, ISBN13: 978-0-19-504505-5. Dewey:306.2/7/09436. LCCN:89-009389.
Audience: **u,f.** *Choice, 1991.*

Hochedlinger, Michael **DB66**
Austria's Wars of Emergence, 1683-1797. Trade Paper. Longman Publishing. Boston, MA. 2003. 488p. ISBN:0-582-29084-8, ISBN13: 978-0-582-29084-6. Dewey:943.6/03.
Audience: **u,f.** *Choice, 2004.*

Lackey, Scott A. **UA672**
The Rebirth of the Habsburg Army: Friedrich Beck and the Rise of the General Staff. Book, Other. Greenwood Publishing Group, Inc. Portsmouth, NH. 1995. 272p. Contributions in Military Studies Ser., 161 ISBN:0-313-29361-9, ISBN13: 978-0-313-29361-0. Dewey:355/.009436. LCCN:95-007897.
Audience: **u,f.** *Choice, 1996.*

Reinerman, Alan J. **BX1517.R44**
Austria and the Papacy in the Age of Metternich: Between Conflict and Cooperation, 1809-1830, Vol. 1. Trade Cloth. Catholic University of America Press. Washington, DC. 1979. 254p. ISBN:0-8132-0548-4, ISBN13: 978-0-8132-0548-9. Dewey:327.436/045/6. LCCN:79-000774.
Audience: **u,f.** *Choice, 1990.*

Reinerman, Alan J. **BX1517.R44**
Austria and the Papacy in the Age of Metternich II: Revolution and Reaction, 1830-1838. Trade Cloth. Catholic University of America Press. Washington, DC. 1989. 429p. ISBN:0-8132-0669-3, ISBN13: 978-0-8132-0669-1. Dewey:327.436/045/6. LCCN:79-000774.
Audience: **u,f.** *Choice, 1990.*

Wawro, Geoffrey **DD438 .W39 1996**
The Austro-Prussian War: Austria's War with Prussia and Italy in 1866. Trade Paper. Cambridge University Press. New York, NY. 1997. 329p. ISBN:0-521-62951-9, ISBN13: 978-0-521-62951-5. Dewey:943/.076.
Audience: **g,l,u,f.** *Choice, 1997.*

Austria. Austro-Hungarian Empire > By Period > Early Modern to 1792

Beales, Derek **DB74.B42 1986**
Joseph II: In the Shadow of Maria Theresa, 1741-1780, Vol. 1. Trade Cloth. Cambridge University Press. New York, NY. 1987. 546p. Joseph Ii Ser. ISBN:0-521-24240-1, ISBN13: 978-0-521-24240-0. Dewey:943/.057/0924. LCCN:86-017103.
Audience: **u,f.** *Choice, 1988.*

Benecke, Gerhard **DD174**
Maximilian I (1459-1519): An Analytical biography. London ; Boston : Routledge & Kegan Paul. 1982. ISBN:0-7100-9023-4, ISBN13: 978-0-7100-9023-2.
Audience: **u,f.**

Bernard, Paul P. **DB74.7.P47B47 1991**
From the Enlightenment to the Police State: The Public Life of Johann Anton Pergen. Trade Cloth. University of Illinois Press. Champaign, IL. 1991. 264p. ISBN:0-252-01745-5, ISBN13: 978-0-252-01745-2. Dewey:363.2/83/092 B. LCCN:90-038594.
Audience: **u,f.** *Choice, 1991.*

Bernard, Paul P. **DB74.3.B397 1971**
Jesuits and Jacobins: Enlightenment and Enlightened Despotism in Austria. Trade Cloth. University of Illinois Press. Champaign, IL. 1971. 207p. ISBN:0-252-00180-X, ISBN13: 978-0-252-00180-2. Dewey:914.36/03/3. LCCN:78-151997.
Audience: **u,f.**

Bernard, Paul P. **HV6953**
The Limits of Enlightenment: Joseph II and the Law. Trade Cloth. University of Illinois Press. Champaign, IL. 1979. 160p. ISBN:0-252-00735-2, ISBN13: 978-0-252-00735-4. Dewey:364/.9436. LCCN:79-012030.
Audience: **u,f.**

Blanning, Timothy C. W. **DB71**
Joseph II. Ed. 1. Trade Cloth. Addison-Wesley Longman, Ltd. Harlow, 1994. 256p. Profiles in Power Ser. ISBN:0-582-05273-4, ISBN13: 978-0-582-05273-4. Dewey:943.603092. LCCN:93-029516.
Audience: **g,l,u,f.**

Brandi, Karl **DD180.5 .B72**
Emperor Charles V: The Growth and Destiny of a Man and of a World-Empire. Paper Text. Brill Academic Publishers, Inc. Boston, MA. 1968. ISBN:0-224-60916-5, ISBN13: 978-0-224-60916-6. Dewey:943.031092.
Audience: **u,f.**

Dickson, P. G. M. (Peter George Muir); Maria Theresa, Empress of Austria **HJ1059**
Finance and Government under Maria Theresa, 1740-1780, Vol. II Finance and Credit. Oxford [Oxfordshire] : Clarendon Press ; New York : Oxford University Press. 1987. ISBN:0-19-822882-1, ISBN13: 978-0-19-822882-0.
Audience: **u,f.**

Dickson, P. G. M. (Peter George Muir); Maria Theresa, Empress of Austria **HJ1059**
Finance and Government under Maria Theresia, 1740-1780. Vol. 1 Society and Government. Oxford University Press. 1987. ISBN:0-19-822570-9, ISBN13: 978-0-19-822570-6.
Audience: **u,f.**

Dubin, Lois C. **DS135.I85T735 1999**
The Port Jews of Habsburg Trieste: Absolutist Politics and Enlightenment Culture. Trade Cloth. Stanford University Press. Palo Alto, CA. 1999. 2p. Stanford Studies in Jewish History and Culture ISBN:0-8047-3320-1, ISBN13: 978-0-8047-3320-5. Dewey:945.3/93/004924. LCCN:98-043111.
Audience: **u,f.** *Choice, 1999.*

Fichtner, Paula S. **DB65.3.F48**
Ferdinand I of Austria. Trade Cloth. Eastern European Monographs. Bradenton, FL. 1982. 362p. East European Monographs, No. 100 ISBN:0-914710-94-X, ISBN13: 978-0-914710-94-3. Dewey:943.6/032/0924.
Audience: **u,f.**

Macartney, C. A. **DB71.M28**
Maria Theresa and the House of Austria. Trade Cloth. Lawrence Verry Inc. Mystic, CT. 1969. Men and Their Times Ser. ISBN:0-8426-0002-7, ISBN13: 978-0-8426-0002-6. Dewey:943.053/0924.
Audience: **g,l,u,f.**

Melton, James Van Horn **LC135.G32 P785 1988**
Absolutism and the Eighteenth-Century Origins of Compulsory Schooling in Prussia and Austria. Trade Cloth. Cambridge University Press. New York, NY. 1988. 288p. ISBN:0-521-34668-1, ISBN13: 978-0-521-34668-9. Dewey:379/.23. LCCN:87-033022.
Audience: **u,f.** *Choice, 1989.*

Roider, Karl A. Jr. **DB49.T8**
Austria's Eastern Question, 1700-1970. Trade Cloth. Princeton University Press. Princeton, NJ. 1982. 246p. ISBN:0-691-05355-3, ISBN13: 978-0-691-05355-4. Dewey:327.4056. LCCN:81-048141.
Audience: **u,f.**

Spielman, John P. **DB67.S68**
Leopold the First of Austria. Trade Cloth. Rutgers University Press. Piscataway, NJ. 1977. ISBN:0-8135-0836-3, ISBN13: 978-0-8135-0836-8. Dewey:943.6/03/0924.
Audience: **g,u,f.**

Wangermann, Ernst **DB74**
From Joseph Second to the Jacobin Trials: Government Policy and Public Opinion in the Habsburg Dominions in the Period of the French Revolution. Ed. 2. Trade Cloth. Greenwood Publishing Group, Inc. Portsmouth, NH. 1979. 218p. Oxford Historical Monographs ISBN:0-313-20852-2, ISBN13: 978-0-313-20852-2. LCCN:78-026290.
Audience: **u,f.**

Austria. Austro-Hungarian Empire > By Period > 19th Century (to 1914)

Beller, Steven **DB87.B45 1996**
Francis Joseph. Ed. 1. Paper Text. Longman Publishing Group. White Plains, NY. 1996. 280p. Profiles in Power Ser. ISBN:0-582-06089-3, ISBN13: 978-0-582-06089-0. Dewey:943.6/043/092. LCCN:96-019897.
Audience: **g,l,u,f.**

Beller, Steven **DS135.A92V5213 1990**
Vienna and the Jews, 1867-1938: A Cultural History. Trade Paper. Cambridge University Press. New York, NY. 1991. 281p. ISBN:0-521-40727-3, ISBN13: 978-0-521-40727-4. Dewey:943.6/13/004924.
Audience: **g,u,f.** *Choice, 1990.*

Boyer, John W. **DB854.B67 1995**
Culture and Political Crisis in Vienna: Christian Socialism in Power, 1897-1918. Trade Cloth. University of Chicago Press. Chicago, IL. 1995. 718p. ISBN:0-226-06960-5, ISBN13: 978-0-226-06960-9. Dewey:320.94361309034. LCCN:94-036240.
Audience: **u,f.** *Choice, 1996.*

Boyer, John W. **DB30**
Political Radicalism in Late Imperial Vienna: Origins of the Christian Social Movement, 1848-1897. Trade Paper. University of Chicago Press. Chicago, IL. 1995. 592p. ISBN:0-226-06956-7, ISBN13: 978-0-226-06956-2. Dewey:943.6/13/04. LCCN:19-970900.
Audience: **u,f.**

Bucur, Maria & Wingfield, Nancy Merriwether **DAW1048.S73 2001**
Staging the Past: The Politics of Commemoration in Habsburg Central Europe, 1848 to the Present. Trade Paper. Purdue University Press. West Lafayette, IN. 2001. 337p. Central European Studies ISBN:1-55753-161-7, ISBN13: 978-1-55753-161-2. Dewey:943.06. LCCN:00-068422.
Audience: **u,f.**

De Sauvigny, Guillaume **DB80.8.M57 B43**
Metternich and His Times. Cloth Text. Brill Academic Publishers, Inc. Boston, MA. 1962. ISBN:0-232-48202-0, ISBN13: 978-0-232-48202-7. Dewey:943.6042092.
Audience: **u,f.**

Hamann, Brigitte **DD247.H5**
Hitler's Vienna: A Dictator's Apprenticeship. Thomas Thornton (Translator). Trade Paper. Oxford University Press, Inc. New York, NY. 2000. 490p. ISBN:0-19-514053-2, ISBN13: 978-0-19-514053-8. Dewey:943.6/13051/092 B.
Audience: **g,u,f.**

Jaszi, Oazkar **DB91.J3**
The Dissolution of the Habsburg Monarchy. Paper Text. Textbook Publishers. Temecula, CA. 2003. 482p. ISBN:0-7581-2531-3, ISBN13: 978-0-7581-2531-6. Dewey:943.604.
Audience: **u,f.**

Kraehe, Enno E. **DD80.8.M57**
Metternich's German Policy: The Contest with Napoleon, 1799-1814. Trade Cloth. Princeton University Press. Princeton,

NJ. 1963. ISBN:0-691-05134-8, ISBN13: 978-0-691-05134-5. Dewey:943.6/03/0924.
Audience: **u,f.**

Kraehe, Enno E. **DB0080.8.M57**
Metternich's German Policy: The Congress of Vienna, 1814-1815, Vol. 2. Trade Paper. Books on Demand. Ann Arbor, MI. 1983. 458p. ISBN:0-608-04650-7, ISBN13: 978-0-608-04650-1. LCCN:63-009994.
Audience: **u,f.**

Le Rider, Jacques **BF697.L3913 1993**
Modernity and Crises of Identity: Culture and Society in Fin-de-Siecle Vienna. Trade Cloth. Continuum International Publishing Group, Ltd. London, 1993. 448p. ISBN:0-8264-0631-9, ISBN13: 978-0-8264-0631-6. Dewey:155.2/09436/13. LCCN:59-015520.
Audience: **u,f.** *Choice, 1994.*

Morton, Frederic **DB851**
A Nervous Splendor: Vienna, 1888-1889. Trade Paper. Penguin Group (USA) Inc. New York, NY. 1980. 352p. ISBN:0-14-005667-X, ISBN13: 978-0-14-005667-9. Dewey:943.6/04/0924. LCCN:80-017493.
Audience: **g,l,u,f.**

Morton, Frederic **DB851**
Thunder at Twilight: Vienna, 1913-1914. Trade Cloth. Peter Smith Publisher, Inc. Magnolia, MA. 2003. ISBN:0-8446-7256-4, ISBN13: 978-0-8446-7256-4. Dewey:943.6/13/044.
Audience: **g,l,u,f.**

Redlich, Josef **DB87**
Emperor Francis Joseph of Austria; A Biography. Hamden, Conn., Archon Books. 1965.
Audience: **u,f.**

Roth, Joseph **PZ33**
The Radetzky March. Trade Paper. Overlook Press, The. New York, NY. 2002. 352p. ISBN:1-58567-326-9, ISBN13: 978-1-58567-326-1. Dewey:833/.9/1.
Audience: **g,l,u,f.**

Schorske, Carl E. **DB851**
Fin-de-siècle Vienna: Politics and Culture. New York :; Vintage Books. 1981. ISBN:0-394-74478-0, ISBN13: 978-0-394-74478-0.
Audience: **g,l,u,f.**

Sweet, Paul R. **DB80.8.G4 S9**
Friedrich Von Gentz, Defender of the Old Order. Library Binding. Greenwood Publishing Group, Inc. Portsmouth, NH. 1985. ISBN:0-8371-2560-X, ISBN13: 978-0-8371-2560-2. Dewey:940.2/7/0924.
Audience: **u,f.**

von Metternich, Prince Clemens **DB80.8.M57A3 2004**
Metternich: The Autobiography, 1773-1815. Trade Paper. Ravenhall. Welwyn Garden City, 2004. 265p. ISBN:1-905043-01-5, ISBN13: 978-1-905043-01-9. Dewey:943.6/04/092. LCCN:2006-540025.
Audience: **g,l,u,f.**

Whiteside, Andrew G. **BP223.Z8**
The Socialism of Fools: Georg Ritter Von Schonerer and Austrian Pan-Germanism. Trade Cloth. University of California Press. Berkeley, CA. 1975. 512p. ISBN:0-520-02434-6, ISBN13: 978-0-520-02434-2. Dewey:320.5/4/0924. LCCN:73-076097.
Audience: **g,u,f.**

Zweig, Stefan **PT2653.W42 Z5 1964**
The World of Yesterday. Harry Zohn (Introduction by). Paper Text. University of Nebraska Press. Lincoln, NE. 1964. 463p. ISBN:0-8032-5224-2, ISBN13: 978-0-8032-5224-0. Dewey:838/.91209. LCCN:43-005821.
Audience: **g,l,u,f.**

Austria. Austro-Hungarian Empire > By Period > World War I and Republic (1914-1938)

Brook-Shepherd, Gordon **DB89.F7**
Victims at Sarajevo: the romance and tragedy of Franz Ferdinand and Sophie. London : Harville Press : Distributed by W. Collins. 1984. ISBN:0-00-272007-8, ISBN13: 978-0-00-272007-6.
Audience: **g,l,u,f.**

Bukey, Evan B. **DB879.L6B84 1986**
Hitler's Hometown: Linz, Austria, 1908-1945. Trade Cloth. Indiana University Press. Bloomington, IN. 1986. 308p. ISBN:0-253-32833-0, ISBN13: 978-0-253-32833-5. Dewey:943.6/2. LCCN:85-045762.
Audience: **g,u,f.** *Choice, 1987.*

Carsten, F. L. **DB96**
The First Austrian Republic Nineteen Eighteen to Nineteen Thirty-Eight: A Study Based on British and Austrian Documents. Trade Cloth. Ashgate Publishing, Ltd. Aldershot, 1986. 380p. ISBN:0-566-05162-1, ISBN13: 978-0-566-05162-3. Dewey:943.6/051. LCCN:86-219029.
Audience: **u,f.**

Cornwall, Mark **D639.P7A93 2000**
The Undermining of Austria-Hungary: The Battle for Hearts and Minds. Cloth over Boards. Palgrave Macmillan. New York, NY. 2000. 503p. ISBN:0-312-23151-2, ISBN13: 978-0-312-23151-4. Dewey:940.4/09436. LCCN:99-059429.
Audience: **g,u,f.** *Choice, 2001.*

Crankshaw, Edward **DB85.C7 1983**
The Fall of the House of Habsburg. Trade Paper. Penguin Group (USA) Inc. New York, NY. 1983. 420p. ISBN:0-14-006459-1, ISBN13: 978-0-14-006459-9. Dewey:943.6040922. LCCN:82-018071.
Audience: **g,l,u,f.**

Gruber, Helmut **HN418.V5G78 1991**
Red Vienna: Experiment in Working-Class Culture, 1919-1934. Trade Cloth. Oxford University Press, Inc. New York, NY. 1991. 288p. ISBN:0-19-506914-5, ISBN13: 978-0-19-506914-3. Dewey:306/.09436/13. LCCN:90-024065.
Audience: **u,f.** *Choice, 1992.*

Herwig, Holger H. **D531.H464 1997**
The First World War: Germany and Austria-Hungary 1914-1918. Paper Text. Oxford University Press, Inc. New York, NY. 1996. 512p. Modern Wars Ser. ISBN:0-340-57348-1, ISBN13: 978-0-340-57348-8. Dewey:940.4147. LCCN:96-028152.
Audience: **u,f.** *Choice, 1997.*

Low, Alfred D. **DB97.L68 1985**
The Anschluss Movement, 1931-1938. Trade Cloth. Eastern European Monographs. Bradenton, FL. 1985. 507p. ISBN:0-88033-078-3, ISBN13: 978-0-88033-078-7. Dewey:943.6/051. LCCN:85-070774.
Audience: **u,f.** *Choice, 1986.*

Pauley, Bruce F. **91-50249 [DS]**
From Prejudice to Persecution: A History of Austrian Anti-Semitism. Trade Paper. University of North Carolina Press. Chapel Hill, NC. 1998. 456p. ISBN:0-8078-4713-5, ISBN13: 978-0-8078-4713-8. Dewey:305.892/40436. LCCN:91-050249.
Audience: **g,u,f.** *Choice, 1992.*

Rabinbach, Anson **PT8895**
The Crisis of Austrian Socialism: From Red Vienna to Civil War, 1927-1934. Trade Cloth. University of Chicago Press. Chicago, IL. 1994. 312p. ISBN:0-226-70121-2, ISBN13: 978-0-226-70121-9. Dewey:839.8/226. LCCN:82-010919.
Audience: **u,f.**

Wegs, J. Robert **HD8420.V52W45 1989**
Growing up Working Class: Continuity and Change among Viennese Youth 1890-1938. Cloth Text. Pennsylvania State University Press. University Park, PA. 1989. 224p. ISBN:0-271-00637-4, ISBN13: 978-0-271-00637-6. Dewey:305.2/35/0943613. LCCN:87-043188.
Audience: **u,f.** *Choice, 1989.*

Williamson, Samuel R. Jr. **DB86.W515 1990**
Austria-Hungary and the Origins of the First World War. Trade Cloth. Palgrave Macmillan. New York, NY. 1991. 292p. The Making of the 20th Century Ser. ISBN:0-312-05239-1, ISBN13: 978-0-312-05239-3. Dewey:943.6/044. LCCN:90-041895.
Audience: **g,u,f.** *Choice, 1991.*

Austria. Austro-Hungarian Empire > By Period > German Annexation, World War II and Aftermath

Bukey, Evan Burr **99-21475 [DB]**
Hitler's Austria: Popular Sentiment in the Nazi Era, 1938-1945. Trade Paper. University of North Carolina Press. Chapel Hill, NC. 2002. 336p. ISBN:0-8078-5363-1, ISBN13: 978-0-8078-5363-4. Dewey:943.605/22.
Audience: **u,f.** *Choice, 2000.*

Luza, Radomir V. **DB49.G3**
Austro-German Relations in the Anschluss Era. Trade Cloth. Princeton University Press. Princeton, NJ. 1975. 432p. ISBN:0-691-07568-9, ISBN13: 978-0-691-07568-6. Dewey:327.436/043. LCCN:74-025619.
Audience: **u,f.**

Whitnah, Donald R. & Erickson, Edgar L. **DB99**
The American Occupation of Austria: Planning and Early Years. Book, Other. Greenwood Publishing Group, Inc. Portsmouth, NH. 1985. 352p. Contributions in Military Studies Ser., No. 46 ISBN:0-313-24894-X, ISBN13: 978-0-313-24894-8. Dewey:355.4/9/09436. LCCN:85-005428.
Audience: **u,f.** *Choice, 1986.*

Hungary > General History

DB925
☐ Corvinus Library Hungarian History. http://hungarianhistory.com/
Hungary.network and Hunyadi Ocs.mk.
Audience: **g,l,u,f.**

Hoensch, J **DB945.H5613 1988**
History of Modern Hungary, 1867-1986. Trade Cloth. Longman Publishing Group. White Plains, NY. 1988. 340p. ISBN:0-582-01484-0, ISBN13: 978-0-582-01484-8. Dewey:943.9/05. LCCN:87-004170.
Audience: **g,l,u,f.** *Choice, 1989.*

Kontler, Laszlo **DB925.1.K57 2002**
A History of Hungary: Millennium in Central Europe. Cloth over Boards. Palgrave Macmillan. New York, NY. 2003. 544p. ISBN:1-4039-0316-6, ISBN13: 978-1-4039-0316-7. Dewey:943.9. LCCN:2002-075298.
Audience: **g,l,u,f.** *Choice, 2003.*

Lendvai, Paul **DB925.L4613 2003**
The Hungarians: A Thousand Years of Victory in Defeat. Trade Cloth. Princeton University Press. Princeton, NJ. 2003. 608p. ISBN:0-691-11406-4, ISBN13: 978-0-691-11406-4. Dewey:943.9. LCCN:2002-110218.
Audience: **u,f.** *Choice, 2003.*

Molnar, Miklos **DB925.1 .M6413 2001**
A Concise History of Hungary. Anna Magyar (Translator). Cloth Text. Cambridge University Press. New York, NY. 2001. 388p. Cambridge Concise Histories Ser. ISBN:0-521-66142-0, ISBN13: 978-0-521-66142-3. Dewey:943.9. LCCN:00-041408.
Audience: **g,l,u,f.** *Choice, 2002.*

Sugar, Peter F. (Editor), et al. **DB925.3.H57 1990**
A History of Hungary. Peter Hanak & Tibor Frank (Editors). Trade Cloth. Indiana University Press. Bloomington, IN. 1990. 438p. ISBN:0-253-35578-8, ISBN13: 978-0-253-35578-2. Dewey:943.9. LCCN:88-046215.
Audience: **g,l,u.** *Choice, 1991.*

Hungary > Social Life. Ethnography

Hollos, Marida C. **HN420.5.A8H65 2001**
Scandal in a Small Town: Understanding Modern Hungary Though the Stories of Three Families. Cloth Text. M. E. Sharpe Inc. Armonk, NY. 2001. 230p. ISBN:0-7656-0740-9, ISBN13: 978-0-7656-0740-9. Dewey:943.9. LCCN:2001-032822.
Audience: **g,l,u,f.** *Choice, 2002.*

Verdery, Katherine **DR280.4 .V47 1983**
Transylvanian Villagers: Three Centuries of Political, Economic and Ethnic Change. Trade Cloth. University of California Press. Berkeley, CA. 1983. 400p. ISBN:0-520-04879-2, ISBN13: 978-0-520-04879-9. Dewey:949.8/4. LCCN:82-017411.
Audience: **g,l,u,f.**

Hungary > By Period > Early to 1792

Balazs, Eva H. **DB920.5**
Hungary and the Habsburgs, 1765-1800. Trade Cloth. Central European University Press. Herndon, VA. 1997. 430p.

ISBN:963-9116-03-3, ISBN13: 978-963-9116-03-0. Dewey:943.9/042.
Audience: **u,f.** *Choice, 1998.*

Bayerle, Gustav **DB932.3**
Ottoman Diplomacy in Hungary. Cloth Text. Taylor & Francis Group. Philadelphia, PA. 1997. 204p. ISBN:0-7007-0901-0, ISBN13: 978-0-7007-0901-4. Dewey:327.439/0496.
Audience: **u,f.**

Engel, Pal **DB929.E545 2001**
Realm of St. Stephen: A History of Medieval Hungary, 895-1526. Andrew Ayton (Editor), Tamas Palosfalvi (Translator). Cloth over Boards. I. B. Tauris & Company, Ltd. London, 2001. 416p. International Library of Historical Studies ISBN:1-86064-061-3, ISBN13: 978-1-86064-061-2. Dewey:943.9/02. LCCN:95-062314.
Audience: **g,l,u,f.** *Choice, 2002.*

Gates-Coon, Rebecca **DB932.7.G38 1994**
The landed estates of the Esterházy princes : Hungary during the reforms of Maria Theresia and Joseph II. Johns Hopkins University Press. 1994. The Johns Hopkins University studies in historical and political science; 112th ser. (1994); Variation: Johns Hopkins University studies in historical and political science; 112th ser. ISBN:0-8018-4785-0, ISBN13: 978-0-8018-4785-1.
Audience: **u,f.**

Hungary > By Period > 1792-1867. Revolutions of 1848. Creation of Dual Monarchy

Barany, George **DB933.3.S8**
Stephen Széchenyi and the awakening of Hungarian nationalism, 1791-1841. Princeton University Press. 1968.
Audience: **u,f.**

Deak, Istvan **DB937**
The Lawful Revolution: Louis Kossuth and the Hungarians, 1848-1849. Cloth Text. Columbia University Press. New York, NY. 1979. 415p. ISBN:0-231-04602-2, ISBN13: 978-0-231-04602-2. Dewey:943.9/04/0924. LCCN:78-022063.
Audience: **g,l,u,f.**

Freifeld, Alice **DB933.F74 2000**
Nationalism and the Crowd in Liberal Hungary, 1848-1914. Trade Cloth. Johns Hopkins University Press. Baltimore, MD. 2000. 416p. ISBN:0-8018-6462-3, ISBN13: 978-0-8018-6462-9. Dewey:943.9/042. LCCN:00-008814.
Audience: **g,l,u,f.** *Choice, 2001.*

Janos, A. C. **JN2063**
The Politics of Backwardness in Hungary, 1825-1945. Trade Cloth. Princeton University Press. Princeton, NJ. 1982. 372p. ISBN:0-691-07633-2, ISBN13: 978-0-691-07633-1. Dewey:320.9439. LCCN:81-047137.
Audience: **u,f.**

Roberts, Ian W. **DK210.R62 1991**
Nicholas the First and the Russian Intervention in Hungary. Cloth Text. Palgrave Macmillan. New York, NY. 1991. 310p. ISBN:0-312-04897-1, ISBN13: 978-0-312-04897-6. Dewey:327.470439/09/034. LCCN:90-034608.
Audience: **u,f.** *Choice, 1991.*

Hungary > By Period > 1867-1918. Dual Monarchy. World War I

Freifeld, Alice **DB933.F74 2000**
Nationalism and the Crowd in Liberal Hungary, 1848-1914. Trade Cloth. Johns Hopkins University Press. Baltimore, MD. 2000. 416p. ISBN:0-8018-6462-3, ISBN13: 978-0-8018-6462-9. Dewey:943.9/042. LCCN:00-008814.
Audience: **g,l,u,f.** *Choice, 2001.*

Gero, Andras **DB87.G4513 2001**
Emperor Francis Joseph, King of the Hungarians. Trade Cloth. Eastern European Monographs. Bradenton, FL. 2000. 280p. ISBN:0-88033-464-9, ISBN13: 978-0-88033-464-8. Dewey:943.604092. LCCN:00-134924.
Audience: **g,u,f.**

Gero, Andras **JN2121 .G47 1997**
Hungarian Parliament, 1867-1918: A Mirage of Power. Trade Cloth. Eastern European Monographs. Bradenton, FL. 1997. 240p. ISBN:0-88033-367-7, ISBN13: 978-0-88033-367-2. Dewey:328.439/072/09034. LCCN:96-061478.
Audience: **u,f.**

Gyani, Gabor **HT145.H8G9313 2002**
Parlor and Kitchen: Housing and Domestic Culture in Budapest, 1870-1940. Trade Cloth. Central European University Press. Herndon, VA. 2002. 220p. ISBN:963-9241-27-X, ISBN13: 978-963-9241-27-5. Dewey:307.76/09439/12. LCCN:2002-000678.
Audience: **u,f.** *Choice, 2003.*

Hanak, Peter **DB847**
The Garden and the Workshop: Essays on the Cultural History of Vienna and Budapest. Paper Text. Princeton University Press. Princeton, NJ. 1999. 250p. ISBN:0-691-00965-1, ISBN13: 978-0-691-00965-0. Dewey:943.6/13.
Audience: **u,f.**

Lukacs, John **DB988**
Budapest 1900: A Historical Portrait of a City and Its Culture. Trade Paper. Grove/Atlantic, Inc. New York, NY. 1994. 304p. ISBN:0-8021-3250-2, ISBN13: 978-0-8021-3250-5. Dewey:943.912. LCCN:88-015290.
Audience: **g,l,u,f.**

Nemes, Robert **DB991.N46 2005**
The Once and Future Budapest. Saddle Stitched, Cloth over Boards, Dust Jacket. Northern Illinois University Press. DeKalb, IL. 2005. 247p. ISBN:0-87580-337-7, ISBN13: 978-0-87580-337-1. Dewey:943.912. LCCN:2004-023579.
Audience: **g,l,u,f.** *Choice, 2006.*

Ranki, Vera **DS135.H9R36 1999**
The Politics of Inclusion and Exclusion: Jews and Nationalism in Hungary. Cloth Text. Holmes & Meier Publishers, Inc. Teaneck, NJ. 1999. 274p. ISBN:0-8419-1401-X, ISBN13: 978-0-8419-1401-8. Dewey:943.9/004924. LCCN:98-045937.
Audience: **g,l,u,f.** *Choice, 1999.*

Hungary > By Period > 1918-1945. Revolution. Regency. World War II

Barany, Zoltan D. **DB956.B37 1993**
Soldiers and Politics in Eastern Europe, 1945-1990: The Case of Hungary. Cloth Text. Palgrave Macmillan. New York, NY. 1993. 240p. ISBN:0-312-09722-0, ISBN13: 978-0-312-09722-6. Dewey:943.905. LCCN:93-016624.
Audience: **g,l,u,f.** *Choice, 1994.*

Borhi, Laszlo **DB956.4.B67 2004**
Hungary in the Cold War: 1945-1956. Trade Cloth. Central European University Press. Herndon, VA. 2004. 384p. ISBN:963-9241-80-6, ISBN13: 978-963-9241-80-0. Dewey:943.905/2. LCCN:2004-009360.
Audience: **g,u,f.** *Choice, 2005.*

Gati, Charles **DK67.5.H8G37 1986**
Hungary and the Soviet Bloc. Trade Cloth. Duke University Press. Durham, NC. 1986. x, 244p. ISBN:0-8223-0684-0, ISBN13: 978-0-8223-0684-9. Dewey:327.470439. LCCN:86-019739.
Audience: **g,u,f.** *Choice, 1987.*

Gyani, Gabor **HT145.H8G9313 2002**
Parlor and Kitchen: Housing and Domestic Culture in Budapest, 1870-1940. Trade Cloth. Central European University Press. Herndon, VA. 2002. 220p. ISBN:963-9241-27-X, ISBN13: 978-963-9241-27-5. Dewey:307.76/09439/12. LCCN:2002-000678.
Audience: **u,f.** *Choice, 2003.*

Kadarkay, Arpad **B4815.L84K34 1991**
Georg Lukacs: Life, Thought and Politics. Cloth Text. Blackwell Publishing, Inc. Malden, MA. 1991. 384p. ISBN:1-55786-114-5, ISBN13: 978-1-55786-114-6. Dewey:199/.439 B. LCCN:90-001243.
Audience: **u,f.** *Choice, 1992.*

Sakmyster, Thomas L. **DB955.6.H67 S25 1994**
Hungary's Admiral on Horseback: Miklo's Horthy, 1918-1944. Trade Cloth. Eastern European Monographs. Bradenton, FL. 1994. 476p. ISBN:0-88033-293-X, ISBN13: 978-0-88033-293-4. Dewey:943.9105.
Audience: **u,f.** *Choice, 1995.*

Siklos, Andras **DB955 .S57 1988**
Revolution in Hungary and the Dissolution of the Multinational State 1918. Cloth Text. Brill Academic Publishers, Inc. Boston, MA. 1988. 172p. Studia Historica ISBN:963-05-4466-0, ISBN13: 978-963-05-4466-5. Dewey:943.9051. LCCN:88-166855.
Audience: **u,f.** *Choice, 1989.*

Soros, Tivadar **DS135.H93S67713 2001**
Masquerade: Dancing Around Death in Nazi Occupied Hungary. Humphrey Tonkin (Translator), Paul Soros & George Soros (Foreword by). Trade Cloth. Arcade Publishing, Inc. New York, NY. 2001. 275p. ISBN:1-55970-581-7, ISBN13: 978-1-55970-581-3. Dewey:943.9/004924. LCCN:2001-022626.
Audience: **g,l,u,f.**

Ungvary, Krisztian **D765.562.B8U5413**
The Siege of Budapest: One Hundred Days in World War II. Ladislaus Lob (Translator), John Lukacs (Foreword by). Cloth over Boards. Yale University Press. Cumberland, RI. 2005. 512p. ISBN:0-300-10468-5, ISBN13: 978-0-300-10468-4. Dewey:940.54/213912. LCCN:2004-015687.
Audience: **g,l,u,f.** *Choice, 2006.*

Wallenberg, Raoul **D809.S8W32 1995**
Letters and Dispatches 1924-1944. Kjersti Board (Translator). Trade Cloth. Arcade Publishing, Inc. New York, NY. 1995. 286p. ISBN:1-55970-275-3, ISBN13: 978-1-55970-275-1. Dewey:940.54/77943912/092. LCCN:94-033217.
Audience: **g,l,u,f.** *Choice, 1995.*

Hungary > By Period > 1945-1989. Hungarian Uprising of 1956

Kiraly, Bela K. & Jonas, Paul **DB957 .H84**
The Hungarian Revolution of 1956 in Retrospect. Trade Cloth. Eastern European Monographs. Bradenton, FL. 1978. Eastern European Monographs, No. 40 ISBN:0-914710-33-8, ISBN13: 978-0-914710-33-2. Dewey:943.9/05. LCCN:77-082394.
Audience: **u,f.**

Roman, Eric **DB956.R66 1996**
Hungary and the Victor Powers, 1945-1950. Trade Cloth. Palgrave Macmillan. New York, NY. 1996. 275p. ISBN:0-312-15891-2, ISBN13: 978-0-312-15891-0. Dewey:943.9/052. LCCN:95-052046.
Audience: **u,f.** *Choice, 1996.*

Hungary > By Period > 1989-

Konrad, George **DB958.3.K6613 1995**
The Melancholy of Rebirth: Essays from Post-Communist Central Eruope, 1989-1994. Trade Paper. Harcourt Trade Publishers. New York, NY. 1995. 176p. ISBN:0-15-600252-3, ISBN13: 978-0-15-600252-3. Dewey:943.905/3. LCCN:94-039650.
Audience: **u.**

Czechoslovakia. Czech Republic. Slovakia. Bohemia. Moravia > General History

Cornej, Petr & Pokorny, Jiri **DB2063 .C668 2000**
Brief History of the Czech Lands To 2004. Anna Bryson (Translator). Trade Paper. Prah Press. Praha 5, 2003. 96p. ISBN:80-7252-026-1, ISBN13: 978-80-7252-026-8. Dewey:943.7. LCCN:2001-376779.
Audience: **g,l.**

Crane, John O. & Crane, Sylvia **DB2188**
Czechoslovakia: Anvil of the Cold War. Trade Cloth. Greenwood Publishing Group, Inc. Portsmouth, NH. 1990. 384p. ISBN:0-275-93577-9, ISBN13: 978-0-275-93577-1. Dewey:943.7/03. LCCN:90-039146.
Audience: **u,f.** *Choice, 1991.*

Skilling, H. Gordon (Editor) **DB2186.C94 1990**
Czechoslovakia, 1918-88: Seventy Years from Independence. Cloth Text. Palgrave Macmillan. New York, NY. 1991. 215p. ISBN:0-312-05785-7, ISBN13: 978-0-312-05785-5. Dewey:943.7/03. LCCN:90-020269.
Audience: **u,f.**

Steiner, Peter **PG5011.S74 2000**
The Deserts of Bohemia: Czech Fiction and Its Social Context. Trade Cloth. Cornell University Press. Ithaca, NY. 2000. 272p. ISBN:0-8014-3717-2, ISBN13: 978-0-8014-3717-5. Dewey:891.8/6305. LCCN:99-055905.
Audience: **u,f.** *Choice, 2000.*

Stone, Norman & Strouhal, Eduard (Editors) **DB2187.5.C94 1989**
Czechoslovakia: Crossroads and Crises, 1918-88. Cloth Text. Palgrave Macmillan. New York, NY. 1989. 336p. ISBN:0-312-03201-3, ISBN13: 978-0-312-03201-2. Dewey:943.7/03. LCCN:89-006068.
Audience: **g,l,u,f.** *Choice, 1990.*

Czechoslovakia. Czech Republic. Slovakia. Bohemia. Moravia > By Period > Early and Medieval to 1526

Bartos, F. M. **DB2106.B3713 1986**
The Hussite Revolution: 1424-1437. Trade Cloth. Eastern European Monographs. Bradenton, FL. 1986. 204p. ISBN:0-88033-097-X, ISBN13: 978-0-88033-097-8. Dewey:943.7/1022. LCCN:85-082135.
Audience: **u,f.** *Choice, 1987.*

Fudge, Thomas A. **DB2105.F83 2002**
The Crusade Against Heretics in Bohemia, 1418-1437: Sources and Documents for the Hussite Crusades. Trade Cloth. Ashgate Publishing, Ltd. Aldershot, 2002. 446p. Crusade Texts in Translation Ser., Vol. 9 ISBN:0-7546-0801-8, ISBN13: 978-0-7546-0801-1. Dewey:943.71/0224. LCCN:2002-101557.
Audience: **u,f.**

Fudge, Thomas A. **BX4915.2.F83 1998**
The Magnificent Ride: The First Reformation in Hussite Bohemia. Trade Cloth. Ashgate Publishing, Ltd. Aldershot, 1998. 315p. St Andrews Studies in Reformation History ISBN:1-85928-372-1, ISBN13: 978-1-85928-372-1. Dewey:284/.3. LCCN:97-039853.
Audience: **u,f.**

Wolverton, Lisa **DB2082.5.W65 2001**
Hastening Toward Prague: Power and Society in the Medieval Czech Lands. Book, Other. University of Pennsylvania Press. Philadelphia, PA. 2001. 406p. Middle Ages Ser. ISBN:0-8122-3613-0, ISBN13: 978-0-8122-3613-2. Dewey:943.71/6223. LCCN:2001-027490.
Audience: **u,f.** *Choice, 2002.*

Czechoslovakia. Czech Republic. Slovakia. Bohemia. Moravia > By Period > Habsburg Rule (1526-1918)

Agnew, Hugh L. **DB2168 .A34 1993**
Origins of the Czech National Renascence. Cloth Text. University of Pittsburgh Press. Pittsburgh, PA. 1994. 338p. Russian and East European Studies ISBN:0-8229-3742-5, ISBN13: 978-0-8229-3742-5. Dewey:943.7. LCCN:92-036909.
Audience: **l,u,f.**

Cohen, Gary B. **DB2624.G4**
The Politics of Ethnic Survival : Germans in Prague, 1861-1914. Ed. 2. Purdue University Press. 2006. Central European studies ISBN:1-55753-404-7, ISBN13: 978-1-55753-404-0.
Audience: **u,f.**

Glassheim, Eagle **DB2178.7.G59 2005**
Noble Nationalists: The Transformation of the Bohemian Aristocracy. Trade Cloth. Harvard University Press. Cambridge, MA. 2005. 316p. ISBN:0-674-01889-3, ISBN13: 978-0-674-01889-1. Dewey:943.71/024. LCCN:2005-046322.
Audience: **u,f.** *Choice, 2006.*

Kieval, Hillel J. **DS135.C96B638 1988**
The Making of Czech Jewry: National Conflict and Jewish Society in Bohemia, 1870-1918. Trade Cloth. Oxford University Press, Inc. New York, NY. 1988. 296p. Studies in Jewish History ISBN:0-19-504057-0, ISBN13: 978-0-19-504057-9. Dewey:305.8/924/04371. LCCN:87-001597.
Audience: **u,f.** *Choice, 1989.*

Orton, Lawrence D. **DB214**
The Prague Slav Congress of 1848. Trade Cloth. Eastern European Monographs. Bradenton, FL. 1978. 187p. East European Monographs, No. 46 ISBN:0-914710-39-7, ISBN13: 978-0-914710-39-4. Dewey:320.54.
Audience: **u,f.**

Pech, Stanley Z. **DB214**
The Czech Revolution of 1848. University of North Carolina Press. 1969.
Audience: **g,l,u,f.**

Pursell, Brennan C. **D801.P47**
The Winter King: Frederick V of the Palatinate and the Coming of the Thirty Years' War. Trade Cloth. Ashgate Publishing, Ltd. Aldershot, 2003. 338p. ISBN:0-7546-3401-9, ISBN13: 978-0-7546-3401-0. Dewey:943/.435041/092 B. LCCN:2002-032986.
Audience: **l,u,f.**

Skilling, H. Gordon **DB2191.M38S58 1994**
T. G. Masaryk: Against the Current, 1882-1914. Cloth Text. Pennsylvania State University Press. University Park, PA. 1994. 478p. ISBN:0-271-01042-8, ISBN13: 978-0-271-01042-7. Dewey:943.7/032/092. LCCN:93-029636.
Audience: **u,f.** *Choice, 1995.*

Unterberger, Betty Miller **D619.U63 1989**
The United States, Revolutionary Russia,and the Rise of Czechoslovakia. University of North Carolina Press. 1989. ISBN:0-8078-1853-4, ISBN13: 978-0-8078-1853-4.
Audience: **l,u,f.**

Czechoslovakia. Czech Republic. Slovakia. Bohemia. Moravia > By Period > Czechoslovak Republic (1918-1939)

Capek, Karel **DB2191.M38A513 1995**
Talks with T. G. Masaryk. Michael H. Heim (Translator). Trade Cloth. Catbird Press. North Haven, CT. 1995. 272p. ISBN:0-945774-26-5, ISBN13: 978-0-945774-26-6. Dewey:943.7/032/092 B. LCCN:94-042805.
Audience: **g,l,u,f.**

Lukes, Igor **DB2078.G3L85 1996**
Czechoslovakia Between Stalin and Hitler: The Diplomacy of Edvard Benes in the 1930s. Cloth Text. Oxford University Press, Inc. New York, NY. 1996. 352p. ISBN:0-19-510266-5, ISBN13: 978-0-19-510266-6. Dewey:943.7/032. LCCN:95-009284.
Audience: **g,l,u,f.** *Choice, 1996.*

Prochazka, Theodore Sr. **DB2196.P76**
The Second Republic. Cloth Text. Eastern European Monographs. Bradenton, FL. 1981. 231p. East European Monographs, No. 90 ISBN:0-914710-84-2, ISBN13: 978-0-914710-84-4. Dewey:943.7/03. LCCN:81-065161.
Audience: **u,f.**

Smelser, Ronald M. **DB205.8.G4 S55**
The Sudeten Problem, 1933-1938: "Volkstumpolitik" and the Formulation of Nazi Foreign Policy. Trade Cloth. Wesleyan University Press. Middletown, CT. 1975. 324p. ISBN:0-8195-4077-3, ISBN13: 978-0-8195-4077-5. Dewey:327.43/0437. LCCN:74-005912.
Audience: **u,f.**

Taborsky, Edward **DB2191.B45 T3**
President Edvard Benes, Between East and West, 1938-1948. Trade Cloth. Hoover Institution Press. Stanford, CA. 1981. 312p. Publication Ser., No. 246 ISBN:0-8179-7461-X, ISBN13: 978-0-8179-7461-9. Dewey:943.7/03/0924. LCCN:80-083829.
Audience: **u,f.**

Wingfield, Nancy M. **DB2198.7.W56 1989**
Minority Party Politics in a Multinational State: The German Social Democrats of Czechoslovakia, 1918-1938. Trade Cloth. Eastern European Monographs. Bradenton, FL. 1989. 238p. ISBN:0-88033-156-9, ISBN13: 978-0-88033-156-2. Dewey:943.7/03. LCCN:88-072222.
Audience: **u,f.**

Czechoslovakia. Czech Republic. Slovakia. Bohemia. Moravia > By Period > German Occupation, World War II (1939-1945)

Luza, Radomir & Vella, Christina **D802**
The Hitler Kiss: A Memoir of the Czech Resistance. Trade Paper. Louisiana State University Press. Baton Rouge, LA. 2004. 312p. ISBN:0-8071-3030-3, ISBN13: 978-0-8071-3030-8. Dewey:940.54/82437.
Audience: **g,l,u,f.**

MacDonald, Callum **DD247.H42M33 1998**
The Killing of Reinhard Heydrich: The Ss Butcher of Prague. Trade Paper. Da Capo Press, Inc. Cambridge, MA. 1998. 264p. ISBN:0-306-80860-9, ISBN13: 978-0-306-80860-9. Dewey:943.086/092 B. LCCN:98-007844.
Audience: **g,l,u,f.**

Mastny, Vojtech **DB215.3**
The Czechs under Nazi Rule: The Failure of National Resistance, 1939-42. Cloth Text. Columbia University Press. New York, NY. 1971. xiii, 274p. East Central European Studies of the Russian Institute ISBN:0-231-03303-6, ISBN13: 978-0-231-03303-9. Dewey:940.53437. LCCN:72-132065.
Audience: **u,f.**

Czechoslovakia. Czech Republic. Slovakia. Bohemia. Moravia > By Period > 1945-1989. Postwar and Communist Eras

Abrams, Bradley F. **HX528.A25 2004**
The Struggle for the Soul of the Nation: Czech Culture and the Rise of Communism. Book, Other. Rowman & Littlefield Publishers, Inc. Lanham, MD. 2004. 372p. The Harvard Cold War Studies Book ISBN:0-7425-3023-X, ISBN13: 978-0-7425-3023-2. Dewey:943.704. LCCN:2003-026054.
Audience: **l,u,f.** *Choice, 2004.*

Dubcek, Alexander **DB2221.D93**
Hope Dies Last: The Autobiography of Alexander Dubcek. Jiri Hochman (Editor, Translator). Trade Paper. Kodansha America, Inc. New York, NY. 1995. 368p. ISBN:1-56836-039-8, ISBN13: 978-1-56836-039-3. Dewey:943.704092.
Audience: **g,l,u,f.**

Frommer, Benjamin **KJP43.F76 2004**
National Cleansing: Retribution against Nazi Collaborators in Postwar Czechoslovakia. Paul Kennedy, Antoine Prost, Emmanuel Sivan & Jay Winter (Contribution by). Trade Cloth. Cambridge University Press. New York, NY. 2004. 108p. Studies in the Social and Cultural History of Modern Warfare Ser., Vol. 20 ISBN:0-521-81067-1, ISBN13: 978-0-521-81067-8. Dewey:341.6/9. LCCN:2004-041848.
Audience: **u,f.** *Choice, 2005.*

Havel, Václav **DJK50.P68 1985**
The Power of the Powerless: Citizens Against the State in Central Eastern Europe. John Keane (Editor), Steven Lukes (Introduction by). Cloth Text. M. E. Sharpe Inc. Armonk, NY. 1985. 228p. ISBN:0-87332-370-X, ISBN13: 978-0-87332-370-3. Dewey:323.4/4/0947. LCCN:85-024978.
Audience: **u,f.**

Klima, Ivan **PG5038.L85**
Waiting for the Dark, Waiting for the Light: A Novel. Paul Wilson (Translator). Trade Paper. Grove/Atlantic, Inc. New York, NY. 2006. 256p. ISBN:0-8021-4243-5, ISBN13: 978-0-8021-4243-6. Dewey:891.8/6354.
Audience: **g,l,u,f.**

Korbel, Josef **DB215.5 .K68**
Communist Subversion of Czechoslovakia, 1938-1948: The Failure of Coexistence. Trade Cloth. Princeton University Press. Princeton, NJ. 1959. ISBN:0-691-08705-9, ISBN13: 978-0-691-08705-4. Dewey:943.703.
Audience: **g,l,u,f.**

Kovaly, Heda **DB2211.K68**
Under a Cruel Star : A Life in Prague, 1941-1968. Epstein, Francis and Helen (translators). Holmes & Meier. 1997. ISBN:0-8419-1377-3, ISBN13: 978-0-8419-1377-6.
Audience: **g,l,u,f.**

Czechoslovakia. Czech Republic. Slovakia. Bohemia. Moravia > By Period > 1989-1993. "Velvet Revolution"

Shepherd, Robin E. H. **DB2244.7.S44 2000**
Czechoslovakia: The Velvet Revolution and Beyond. Cloth over Boards. Palgrave Macmillan. New York, NY. 2000. 216p. ISBN:0-312-23068-0, ISBN13: 978-0-312-23068-5. Dewey:943.705. LCCN:99-051860.
Audience: **g,l,u,f.** *Choice, 2000.*

Czechoslovakia. Czech Republic. Slovakia. Bohemia. Moravia > By Period > 1993- . Czech Republic. Slovak Republic

Innes, Abby **DB2238.7.I55 2001**
Czechoslovakia: The Short Goodbye. Cloth over Boards. Yale University Press. Cumberland, RI. 2001. 352p. ISBN:0-300-09063-3, ISBN13: 978-0-300-09063-5. Dewey:943.705. LCCN:2001-039024.
Audience: **u,f.** *Choice, 2002.*

Leff, Carol **DB2238.7.L44 1996**
The Czech and Slovak Republics. Trade Paper. Westview Press. Boulder, CO. 1996. 320p. Nations of the Modern World Ser., :Europe ISBN:0-8133-2921-3, ISBN13: 978-0-8133-2921-5. Dewey:320.9437. LCCN:96-012080.
Audience: **u,f.** *Choice, 1997.*

Czechoslovakia. Czech Republic. Slovakia. Bohemia. Moravia > Ethnicity and Region

Iggers, Wilma (Editor, Translator) **DS135.C95J8313 1992**
The Jews of Bohemia and Moravia: A Historical Reader. Ilse Barker, Kaca Polackova-Kenley & Kathrine Talbot (Translators). Cloth Text. Wayne State University Press. Detroit, MI. 1992. 412p. ISBN:0-8143-2228-X, ISBN13: 978-0-8143-2228-4. Dewey:943.7/004924. LCCN:92-037151.
Audience: **g,l,u.**

Kieval, Hillel J. **99-053814**
Languages of Community: The Jewish Experience in the Czech Lands. Trade Cloth. University of California Press. Berkeley, CA. 2000. 326p. ISBN:0-520-21410-2, ISBN13: 978-0-520-21410-1. LCCN:99-053814.
Audience: **u,f.** *Choice, 2001.*

King, Jeremy **DB2650.C463**
Budweisers into Czechs and Germans: A Local History of Bohemian Politics. Trade Paper. Princeton University Press. Princeton, NJ. 2005. 304p. ISBN:0-691-12234-2, ISBN13: 978-0-691-12234-2. Dewey:305.83104371.
Audience: **u,f.**

Luza, Radomir **AS36**
The Transfer of the Sudeten Germans. Trade Cloth. New York University Press. New York, NY. 1964. 336p. ISBN:0-8147-0269-4, ISBN13: 978-0-8147-0269-7. Dewey:338.43. LCCN:64-012558.
Audience: **u,f.**

Wiskemann, Elizabeth **DB200.7**
Czech & Germans : A Study of the Struggle in the Historic Provinces of Bohemia and Moravia. Ed. 2. St. Martin, issued under the auspices of the Royal Institute of International Affairs by Macmillan. 1967.
Audience: **u,f.**

Czechoslovakia. Czech Republic. Slovakia. Bohemia. Moravia > Ethnicity and Region > Slovakia

Kirschbaum, Stanislav J. **DB2763.K57 1995**
A History of Slovakia: The Struggle for Survival. Cloth over Boards. Palgrave Macmillan. New York, NY. 1995. 368p. ISBN:0-312-10403-0, ISBN13: 978-0-312-10403-0. Dewey:943.73. LCCN:94-022501.
Audience: **g,l,u,f.** *Choice, 1995.*

Czechoslovakia. Czech Republic. Slovakia. Bohemia. Moravia > Ethnicity and Region > Bohemia and Prague

Boehm, Barbara Drake & Fajt, Jiri (Editors) **N6833.P72P73 2005**
Prague, the Crown of Bohemia, 1347-1437. Saddle Stitched, Cloth over Boards, Dust Jacket. Yale University Press. Cumberland, RI. 2005. 384p. Metropolitan Museum of Art Ser. ISBN:0-300-11138-X, ISBN13: 978-0-300-11138-5. Dewey:709/.4371/20747471. LCCN:2005-022954.
Audience: **g,l,u,f.** *Choice, 2006.*

Iggers, Wilma A. **HQ1610.3.Z9P754 1995**
Women of Prague: Ethnic Diversity and Social Change from the 18th Century to the Present. Trade Cloth. Berghahn Books, Inc. New York, NY. 1995. 400p. ISBN:1-57181-008-0, ISBN13: 978-1-57181-008-3. Dewey:305.4/09437/12. LCCN:95-001636.
Audience: **u,f.**

Knox, Brian **NA1023**
The Architecture of Prague and Bohemia. Faber and Faber. 1962.
Audience: **g,l,u,f.**

Sayer, Derek **DB2063.S28 1998**
The Coasts of Bohemia: A Czech History. Cloth Text. Princeton University Press. Princeton, NJ. 1998. 413p. ISBN:0-691-05760-5, ISBN13: 978-0-691-05760-6. Dewey:943.71. LCCN:97-041418.
Audience: **l,u,f.** *Choice, 1998.*

Teich, Mikulas (Editor, Contribution by) **DB2005 .B64 1998**
Bohemia in History. Jiri Slama, Jaroslav Meznik, Zdenek Merinsky, Frantisek Kavka, Frantisek Smahel, Josef Macek & Josef Valka (Contribution by). Cloth Text. Cambridge University Press. New York, NY. 1998. 410p. ISBN:0-521-43155-7, ISBN13: 978-0-521-43155-2. Dewey:943.71. LCCN:97-023902.
Audience: **u,f.** *Choice, 1999.*

Czechoslovakia. Czech Republic. Slovakia. Bohemia. Moravia > Ethnicity and Region > Moravia

Dekan, Jan **DB2386**
Moravia Magna : The Great Moravian Empire, its Art and Times. Trebaticka, Heather (translator). Control Data Arts. 1981. ISBN:0-89893-084-7, ISBN13: 978-0-89893-084-9.
Audience: **g,l,u,f.**

Greece > General History

Finlay, George **DF757 .F5 1970**
History of Greece. Trade Cloth. A M S Press, Inc. New York, NY. 1970. ISBN:0-404-02390-8, ISBN13: 978-0-404-02390-4. Dewey:949.5. LCCN:72-115399.
Audience: **g,l,u,f.**

Vacalopoulos, Apostolos E. **DF801.B3313**
The Greek Nation, 1453-1669. Trade Cloth. Rutgers University Press. Piscataway, NJ. 1976. 472p. ISBN:0-8135-0810-X, ISBN13: 978-0-8135-0810-8. Dewey:949.5/05. LCCN:75-023273.
Audience: **g,l,u,f.**

Vacalopoulos, Apostolos E. **DF631.B313 1970**
Origins of the Greek Nation: The Byzantine Period 1204-1461. Ian N. Moles (Translator). Trade Cloth. Rutgers University Press. Piscataway, NJ. 1970. xxviii, 401p. Byzantine Ser. ISBN:0-8135-0659-X, ISBN13: 978-0-8135-0659-3. Dewey:949.5/04. LCCN:75-119511.
Audience: **g,l,u,f.**

Greece > Civilization and Legacies

Burckhardt, Jacob **DF77.B94213**
The Greeks and Greek Civilization. Oswyn Murray (Editor), Sheila Stern (Translator). Trade Paper. St. Martin's Press. Gordonville, VA. 1999. 504p. ISBN:0-312-24447-9, ISBN13: 978-0-312-24447-7. Dewey:938.
Audience: **u,f.**

Fitton, J. Lesley **DF220**
The Discovery of the Greek Bronze Age. Trade Paper. Harvard University Press. Cambridge, MA. 1998. 192p. British Museum Paperbacks Ser. ISBN:0-674-21189-8, ISBN13: 978-0-674-21189-6. Dewey:938/.01.
Audience: **g,l,u,f.** *Choice, 1996.*

Marchand, Suzanne L. **DD193.5.M37 1996**
Down from Olympus: Archaeology and Philhellenism in Germany, 1750-1970. Trade Cloth. Princeton University Press. Princeton, NJ. 1996. 416p. ISBN:0-691-04393-0, ISBN13: 978-0-691-04393-7. Dewey:938/.0072/043. LCCN:95-053324.
Audience: **g,u,f.** *Choice, 1997.*

Rawson, Elizabeth **AZ321**
The Spartan Tradition in European Thought. Trade Paper. Oxford University Press, Inc. New York, NY. 1991. 400p. ISBN:0-19-814733-3, ISBN13: 978-0-19-814733-6. Dewey:001.2094.
Audience: **u,f.**

Tournikiotis, Panayotis (Editor) **NA281**
The Parthenon and Its Impact in Modern Times. Melissa. 1994. ISBN:960-204-019-X, ISBN13: 978-960-204-019-5.
Audience: **g,l,u,f.**

Yiannias, John L. (Editor) **DJK24.B985 1991**
The Byzantine Tradition after the Fall of Constantinople. Cloth Text. University Press of Virginia. Charlottesville, VA. 1991. 400p. ISBN:0-8139-1329-2, ISBN13: 978-0-8139-1329-2. Dewey:947. LCCN:91-008474.
Audience: **u,f.** *Choice, 1992.*

Greece > By Period > Eastern Empire (323-565). Constantine. Justinian

Alcock, Susan E. **DF222**
Graecia Capta: The Landscapes of Roman Greece. Trade Paper. Cambridge University Press. New York, NY. 1995. 330p. ISBN:0-521-56819-6, ISBN13: 978-0-521-56819-7. Dewey:938/.09.
Audience: **g,l,u,f.**

Baker, G. P. **DF572.B34 2002**
Justinian: The Last Roman Emperor. Trade Paper. Cooper Square Publishers, Inc. New York, NY. 2002. 384p. ISBN:0-8154-1217-7, ISBN13: 978-0-8154-1217-5. Dewey:949.5/013/092 B. LCCN:2002-276805.
Audience: **g,l,u,f.**

Baker, George P. **DG315.B3 2001**
Constantine the Great and the Christian Revolution. Trade Paper. Cooper Square Publishers, Inc. New York, NY. 2001. 384p. ISBN:0-8154-1158-8, ISBN13: 978-0-8154-1158-1. Dewey:937/.08/0924. LCCN:2003-265703.
Audience: **g,l,u,f.**

Bowersock, G. W. (Editor), et al. **DE5.L29 1999**
Late Antiquity: A Guide to the Postclassical World. Peter Brown & Oleg Grabar (Editors). Trade Cloth. Harvard University Press.

Cambridge, MA. 1999. 802p. Harvard University Press Reference Library ISBN:0-674-51173-5, ISBN13: 978-0-674-51173-6. Dewey:938/.003. LCCN:99-025639.
Audience: **l,u,f.** *Choice, 2000.*

Bury, John B. **DG311**
History of the Later Roman Empire: From the Death of Theodosius I to the Death of Justinian. Trade Paper. Dover Publications, Inc. Mineola, NY. 1958. 503p. 0 ISBN:0-486-20399-9, ISBN13: 978-0-486-20399-7. Dewey:DG311.
Audience: **g,l,u,f.**

Bury, John B. **DG311**
History of the Later Roman Empire: From the Death of Theodosius I to the Death of Justinian. Trade Paper. Dover Publications, Inc. Mineola, NY. 1958. 496p. 0 ISBN:0-486-20398-0, ISBN13: 978-0-486-20398-0. Dewey:937.08.
Audience: **g,l,u,f.**

Cameron, Averil **DE71.C25 1993**
The Mediterranean World in Late Antiquity, AD 395-600. Trade Paper. Routledge. New York, NY. 1993. 272p. Routledge History of the Ancient World Ser. ISBN:0-415-01421-2, ISBN13: 978-0-415-01421-2. Dewey:930. LCCN:92-034600.
Audience: **g,l,u.**

Evans, James A. **DF568.E83 1996**
The Age of Justinian: The Circumstances of Imperial Power. Paper over Boards. Routledge. New York, NY. 1996. 360p. ISBN:0-415-02209-6, ISBN13: 978-0-415-02209-5. Dewey:949.5/01/0922. LCCN:95-036732.
Audience: **g,l,u,f.**

Evans, James Allan **DF572.5**
The Empress Theodora: Partner of Justinian. Trade Paper. University of Texas Press. Austin, TX. 2003. 172p. ISBN:0-292-70270-1, ISBN13: 978-0-292-70270-7. Dewey:949.5/013/092.
Audience: **g,u,f.** *Choice, 2003.*

Fowden, Garth **DF531.F69 1993**
Empire to Commonwealth: Consequences of Monotheism in Late Antiquity. Trade Cloth. Princeton University Press. Princeton, NJ. 1993. 224p. ISBN:0-691-06989-1, ISBN13: 978-0-691-06989-0. Dewey:949.501. LCCN:92-037903.
Audience: **u,f.** *Choice, 1993.*

Harries, Jill & Wood, Ian (Editors) **KJA459**
The Theodosian Code. Trade Cloth. Cornell University Press. Ithaca, NY. 1993. 264p. ISBN:0-8014-2946-3, ISBN13: 978-0-8014-2946-0. Dewey:340.5/4. LCCN:93-017596.
Audience: **u,f.** *Choice, 1994.*

Jones, A. H. M. **DG511**
The Later Roman Empire, 284-602: A Social, Economic, and Administrative Survey, Vol. 1. Trade Paper. Johns Hopkins University Press. Baltimore, MD. 1986. 772p. ISBN:0-8018-3353-1, ISBN13: 978-0-8018-3353-3. Dewey:945/.01. LCCN:85-024077.
Audience: **u,f.**

Jones, A. H. M. **DG511**
The Later Roman Empire, 284-602: A Social, Economic, and Administrative Survey, Vol. 2. Trade Paper. Johns Hopkins University Press. Baltimore, MD. 1986. 772p. ISBN:0-8018-3354-X, ISBN13: 978-0-8018-3354-0. Dewey:945/.01. LCCN:85-024077.
Audience: **u,f.**

Kousoulas, D. G. **DG315 .K65 1997**
The Life and Times of Constantine the Great: The First Christian Emperor. Trade Cloth. Rutledge Books, Inc. Danbury, CT. 1997. 511p. ISBN:1-887750-61-4, ISBN13: 978-1-887750-61-5. Dewey:937/.08/092. LCCN:97-066794.
Audience: **g,l,u,f.**

Lenski, Noel (Editor) **DG315.C36 2005**
The Cambridge Companion to the Age of Constantine. Cloth Text. Cambridge University Press. New York, NY. 2005. 488p. ISBN:0-521-81838-9, ISBN13: 978-0-521-81838-4. Dewey:937/.08/092. LCCN:2005-011724.
Audience: **g,u,f.**

Maas, Michael (Editor) **DF572.C35 2004**
The Cambridge Companion to the Age of Justinian. Cloth Text. Cambridge University Press. New York, NY. 2005. 672p. Cambridge Companions to the Ancient World Ser. ISBN:0-521-81746-3, ISBN13: 978-0-521-81746-2. Dewey:949.5/013. LCCN:2004-049266.
Audience: **g,u,f.** *Choice, 2006.*

Greece > By Period > Byzantine Empire (565-1453). Theme system. Palaeologi. Fall of Constantinople

Angold, Michael **BX300**
Church and Society in Byzantium under the Comneni, 1081-1261. Trade Paper. Cambridge University Press. New York, NY. 2000. 620p. ISBN:0-521-26986-5, ISBN13: 978-0-521-26986-5. Dewey:274.9/504. LCCN:94-012146.
Audience: **g,l,u,f.** *Choice, 1996.*

Comnena, Anna **DF605 .C6 1978**
The Alexiad of the Princess Anna Comnena. Elizabeth A. Dawes (Translator). Trade Cloth. A M S Press, Inc. New York, NY. ISBN:0-404-15414-X, ISBN13: 978-0-404-15414-1. Dewey:949.5/03/0924. LCCN:76-029821.
Audience: **g,l,u,f.**

Curta, Florin **DR49.26 .C87 2001**
The Making of the Slavs: History and Archaeology of the Lower Danube Region, c. 500-700. Christine Carpenter, Rosamond McKitterick & Jonathan Shepard (Contribution by). Trade Cloth. Cambridge University Press. New York, NY. 2001. 492p. Studies in Medieval Life and Thought ISBN:0-521-80202-4, ISBN13: 978-0-521-80202-4. Dewey:949.601. LCCN:00-052915.
Audience: **u,f.** *Choice, 2002.*

Geanakoplos, Deno John **DF531**
Interaction of the. Yale University Press. 1976. ISBN:0-300-01831-2, ISBN13: 978-0-300-01831-8.
Audience: **u,f.**

Greene, Molly **DF901.C83**
A Shared World: Christians and Muslims in the Early Modern Mediterranean. Trade Paper. Princeton University Press. Princeton, NJ. 2002. 242p. Modern Greek Studies

ISBN:0-691-09542-6, ISBN13: 978-0-691-09542-4. Dewey:949.5/905.
Audience: **u,f.** *Choice, 2000.*

Gregory, Timothy **DF552.G68 2005**
A History of Byzantium. Blackwell. 2005. ISBN:0-631-23512-4, ISBN13: 978-0-631-23512-5.
Audience: **g,l,u,f.**

Haldon, John F. **DF571 .H35 1997**
Byzantium in the Seventh Century: The Transformation of a Culture. Ed. 2. Trade Paper. Cambridge University Press. New York, NY. 1997. 520p. ISBN:0-521-31917-X, ISBN13: 978-0-521-31917-1. Dewey:949.5/02. LCCN:97-224707.
Audience: **g,l,u,f.** *Choice, 1991.*

Harris, Jonathan **DF601**
Byzantium and the Crusades. Trade Cloth. Continuum International Publishing Group, Ltd. London, 2003. 256p. Crusader Worlds Ser. ISBN:1-85285-298-4, ISBN13: 978-1-85285-298-6. Dewey:949.503. LCCN:2004-296243.
Audience: **g,l,u,f.** *Choice, 2004.*

Laiou, Angeliki E. (Editor) **KJA1350**
Law and Society in Byzantium, 9th-12th Centuries. Simon, Dieter (Editor). Dumbarton Oaks Research Library and Collection : Distributed by Harvard University Press. 1994. ISBN:0-88402-222-6, ISBN13: 978-0-88402-222-0.
Audience: **u,f.**

Lock, Peter **DF609.L63 1995**
The Franks in the Aegean, 1204-1500. Trade Cloth. Longman Publishing Group. White Plains, NY. 1995. 400p. ISBN:0-582-05140-1, ISBN13: 978-0-582-05140-9. Dewey:949.5/02. LCCN:94-039822.
Audience: **g,l,u,f.** *Choice, 1995.*

Magdalino, Paul **DF607.M34 1993**
The Empire of Manuel I Komnenos, 1143-1180. Trade Cloth. Cambridge University Press. New York, NY. 1993. 583p. ISBN:0-521-30571-3, ISBN13: 978-0-521-30571-6. Dewey:949.503. LCCN:92-013501.
Audience: **u,f.** *Choice, 1994.*

Maguire, Henry **DF521**
Byzantine Court Culture from 829 To 1204. Trade Paper. Harvard University Press. Cambridge, MA. 2004. 372p. Dumbarton Oaks Research Library and Collection ISBN:0-88402-308-7, ISBN13: 978-0-88402-308-1. Dewey:949.5.
Audience: **u,f.**

Nicol, Donald M. **DF631 .N5 1993**
The Last Centuries of Byzantium, 1261-1453. Ed. 2. Trade Paper. Cambridge University Press. New York, NY. 1993. 483p. ISBN:0-521-43991-4, ISBN13: 978-0-521-43991-6. Dewey:949.504. LCCN:92-046203.
Audience: **g,l,u,f.**

Nicol, Donald M. **DF631 .N5 1993**
The Last Centuries of Byzantium, 1261-1453. Ed. 2. Cloth Text. Cambridge University Press. New York, NY. 1993. 483p. ISBN:0-521-43384-3, ISBN13: 978-0-521-43384-6. Dewey:949.504. LCCN:92-046203.
Audience: **g,l,u,f.**

Norwich, John Julius **DF521**
Byzantium: The Apogee. Trade Cloth. Alfred A. Knopf Inc. New York, NY. 1992. 416p. Byzantium Ser., Vol. 2 ISBN:0-394-53779-3, ISBN13: 978-0-394-53779-5. Dewey:949.502. LCCN:91-053119.
Audience: **g,l,u,f.**

Norwich, John Julius **DF553.N67 1989**
Byzantium: The Early Centuries. Trade Cloth. Alfred A. Knopf Inc. New York, NY. 1989. 416p. Byzantium Ser., Vol. 1 ISBN:0-394-53778-5, ISBN13: 978-0-394-53778-8. Dewey:949.5. LCCN:88-045508.
Audience: **g,l,u,f.** *Choice, 1989.*

Norwich, John Julius **D164**
Byzantium: The Decline and Fall. Trade Cloth. Alfred A. Knopf Inc. New York, NY. 1995. 528p. Byzantium Ser. ISBN:0-679-41650-1, ISBN13: 978-0-679-41650-0. Dewey:949.5/03.
Audience: **g,l,u,f.**

Obolensky, Dimitri **DF717**
The Byzantine Commonwealth: Eastern Europe, 500-1453. Trade Paper. Saint Vladimir's Seminary Press. Yonkers, NY. 1983. 552p. ISBN:0-913836-98-2, ISBN13: 978-0-913836-98-9. Dewey:949.5. LCCN:82-016970.
Audience: **u,f.**

Ostrogorsky, George **DF552.5.O8153**
History of the Byzantine State. Paper Text. Rutgers University Press. Piscataway, NJ. 1986. 624p. ISBN:0-8135-1198-4, ISBN13: 978-0-8135-1198-6. Dewey:949.5.
Audience: **u,f.** B

Psellus, Michael **DF591**
Fourteen Byzantine Rulers: The Chronographia of Michael Psellus. E. R. Sewter (Translator), Joan M. Hussey (Introduction by). Trade Paper. Penguin Group (USA) Inc. New York, NY. 1979. 400p. Classics Ser. ISBN:0-14-044169-7, ISBN13: 978-0-14-044169-7. Dewey:949.5/02.
Audience: **g,l,u,f.**

Rice, Tamara T. **DF531**
Everyday Life in Byzantium. Trade Cloth. Dorset Press. New York, NY. 1987. ISBN:0-88029-145-1, ISBN13: 978-0-88029-145-3. Dewey:913.395.
Audience: **g,l,u,f.**

Runciman, Steven **DR502 .R86 1990**
The Fall of Constantinople 1453. Trade Paper. Cambridge University Press. New York, NY. 1990. 270p. A Canto Book Ser. ISBN:0-521-39832-0, ISBN13: 978-0-521-39832-9. Dewey:949.5/04. LCCN:90-033079.
Audience: **g,l,u,f.**

Treadgold, Warren T. **DF581.T73 1988**
The Byzantine Revival, 780-842. Trade Cloth. Stanford University Press. Palo Alto, CA. 1988. 528p. ISBN:0-8047-1462-2, ISBN13: 978-0-8047-1462-4. Dewey:949.5/02. LCCN:87-037392.
Audience: **g,l,u,f.** *Choice, 1989.*

Treadgold, Warren T. **DF552.T65 1997**
A History of the Byzantine State and Society. Trade Cloth. Stanford University Press. Palo Alto, CA. 1997. 874p. ISBN:0-8047-2421-0, ISBN13: 978-0-8047-2421-0. Dewey:949.5/02. LCCN:97-023492.
Audience: **g,l,u,f.** *Choice, 1998.*

Vasiliev, Alexander Alexandrovich **DF552**
History of the Byzantine Empire, 324-1453, Vol. 2. University of Wisconsin Press. 1964.
Audience: **g,l,u,f.**

Vasiliev, Alexander Alexandrovich **DF522**
History of the Byzantine Empire, 324-1453, Vol. 1. University of Wisconsin Press. 1964.
Audience: **g,l,u,f.**

Vryonis, Speros **DF545.V78**
The Decline of Medieval Hellenism in Asia Minor and the Process of Islamization from the Eleventh Through the Fifteenth Century. Trade Cloth. University of California Press. Berkeley, CA. 1971. xvii, 532p. ISBN:0-520-01597-5, ISBN13: 978-0-520-01597-5. Dewey:913.3/95/03. LCCN:75-094984.
Audience: **u,f.**

Whittow, Mark **DF556.W45 1996**
The Making of Byzantium, 600-1025. Trade Paper. University of California Press. Berkeley, CA. 1996. 480p. ISBN:0-520-20497-2, ISBN13: 978-0-520-20497-3. Dewey:949.5. LCCN:95-044924.
Audience: **g,l,u,f.** *Choice, 1997.*

Greece > By Period > Modern Greece

Clogg, Richard **DF802**
A Concise History of Greece. Ed. 2. Trade Cloth. Cambridge University Press. New York, NY. 2002. 308p. Cambridge Concise Histories Ser. ISBN:0-521-80872-3, ISBN13: 978-0-521-80872-9. Dewey:949.5. LCCN:2002-725551.
Audience: **g,l,u,f.** *Choice, 1993.*

Dakin, Douglas **DF801**
The Unification of Greece. Cloth Text. Palgrave Macmillan. New York, NY. 1972. ISBN:0-312-83300-8, ISBN13: 978-0-312-83300-8. Dewey:949.5/06. LCCN:76-187329.
Audience: **l,u,f.**

Koliopoulos, Giannaes & Veremaes, Thanos **DF802.K647 2002**
Greece: The Modern Sequel. Trade Cloth. New York University Press. New York, NY. 2002. 407p. ISBN:0-8147-4766-3, ISBN13: 978-0-8147-4766-7. Dewey:949.507. LCCN:2002-016551.
Audience: **g,l,u,f.** *Choice, 2003.*

Mazower, Mark **DF951.T45M39 2005**
Salonica, City of Ghosts: Christians, Muslims, and Jews, 1430-1950. Trade Cloth. Alfred A. Knopf Inc. New York, NY. 2005. 528p. ISBN:0-375-41298-0, ISBN13: 978-0-375-41298-1. Dewey:949.5/65. LCCN:2004-057690.
Audience: **g,l,u,f.** *Choice, 2006.*

Woodhouse, C. M. **DF717**
Modern Greece: A Short History. Ed. 5. Trade Paper. Faber & Faber, Inc. New York, NY. 2000. 384p. ISBN:0-571-19794-9, ISBN13: 978-0-571-19794-1. Dewey:949.5.
Audience: **g,l,u,f.**

Greece > By Period > Modern Greece > Turkish Rule (1453-1821)

Gourgouris, Stathis **JC311.G657 1996**
Dream Nation: Enlightenment, Colonization, and the Institution of Modern Greece. Trade Cloth. Stanford University Press. Palo Alto, CA. 1996. 358p. ISBN:0-8047-2638-8, ISBN13: 978-0-8047-2638-2. Dewey:949.507. LCCN:95-050865.
Audience: **u,f.** *Choice, 1997.*

Kitromilides, Paschalis M. **LA2375.G82 I573 1992**
The Enlightenment As Social Criticism: Iosipos Moisiodax and Greek Culture in the Eighteenth Century. Trade Cloth. Princeton University Press. Princeton, NJ. 1992. 199p. Princeton Modern Greek Studies ISBN:0-691-07383-X, ISBN13: 978-0-691-07383-5. Dewey:306.09495. LCCN:91-023998.
Audience: **g,l,u,f.**

Runciman, Steven **BX410**
The Great Church in Captivity: A Study of the Patriarchate of Constantinople from the Eve of the Turkish Conquest to the Greek War of Independence. Trade Paper. Cambridge University Press. New York, NY. 1985. 455p. ISBN:0-521-31310-4, ISBN13: 978-0-521-31310-0. Dewey:281.9.
Audience: **g,l,u,f.**

Greece > By Period > Modern Greece > 1821-1913. War of Independence. Kapodistrias

Bastéa, Eleni **NA9202.A8 B37 2000**
The Creation of Modern Athens: Planning the Myth. Trade Cloth. Cambridge University Press. New York, NY. 1999. 300p. ISBN:0-521-64120-9, ISBN13: 978-0-521-64120-3. Dewey:711/.4/094951209034. LCCN:99-010717.
Audience: **u,f.** *Choice, 2000.*

Carabott, Philip (Editor) **DF825**
Greek society in the making, 1863-1913 : realities, symbols, and visions. Variorum. 1997. ISBN:0-86078-612-9, ISBN13: 978-0-86078-612-2.
Audience: **u,f.**

Clogg, Richard (Editor) **DF804.7 .S8**
The Struggle for Greek Independence: Essays to Mark the 150th Anniversary of the Greek War of Independence. Trade Cloth. Shoe String Press, Inc. North Haven, CT. 1973. vi, 259p. ISBN:0-208-01303-2, ISBN13: 978-0-208-01303-3. Dewey:949.5/06. LCCN:73-012073.
Audience: **g,l,u,f.**

Dakin, Douglas **DF805**
The Greek Struggle for Independence, 1821-1833. Trade Cloth. University of California Press. Berkeley, CA. 1973. ISBN:0-520-02342-0, ISBN13: 978-0-520-02342-0. Dewey:949.5/06. LCCN:72-089798.
Audience: **g,l,u,f.**

Gallant, Thomas W. **DF901.I65G35 2002**
Experiencing Dominion: Culture, Identity and Power in the British Mediterranean. Trade Cloth. University of Notre Dame Press. Notre Dame, IN. 2002. 272p. ISBN:0-268-02801-X,

ISBN13: 978-0-268-02801-5. Dewey:303.482. LCCN:2002-510495.
Audience: **u,f.**

Gondicas, Dimitri & Issawi, Charles P. (Editors) **DR435.G8O88 1999**
Ottoman Greeks in the Age of Nationalism: Politics, Economy and Society in the Nineteenth Century. Trade Cloth. Darwin Press, Inc. Princeton, NJ. 1999. 229p. ISBN:0-87850-096-0, ISBN13: 978-0-87850-096-3. Dewey:956.1/00489. LCCN:99-028792.
Audience: **g,l,u,f.**

Koliopoulos, John S. **HV6453.G8**
Brigands with a Cause: Brigandage and Irredentism in Modern Greece 1821-1912. Trade Cloth. Oxford University Press, Inc. New York, NY. 1987. 352p. ISBN:0-19-822863-5, ISBN13: 978-0-19-822863-9. Dewey:364.1/55. LCCN:88-154957.
Audience: **u,f.** *Choice, 1988.*

Kolokotrones, Theodoros ; Tertsetes, Georgios **DF815.K64**
Memoirs from the Greek War of Independence, 1821-1883. Argonaut Publishers. 1969.
Audience: **g,l,u,f.**

Petropoulos, John Anthony **DF823**
Politics and Statecraft in the Kingdom of Greece, 1833-1843. Princeton University Press. 1968.
Audience: **u,f.**

St. Clair, William **DF807**
That Greece Might Still Be Free: the Philhellenes in the War of Independence. Oxford University Press. 1972. ISBN:0-19-215194-0, ISBN13: 978-0-19-215194-0.
Audience: **g,l,u,f.**

Greece > By Period > Modern Greece > 20th Century. Republic (1924-1935). World War II. Communist Insurgency. Junta

Saraphes, Stephanos G. **D802.G8**
ELAS: Greek Resistance Army. Humanities Press. 1981. ISBN:0-391-02505-8, ISBN13: 978-0-391-02505-9.
Audience: **g,l,u,f.**

Cassimatis, Louis P. **DF787.U5C37 1988**
American Influence in Greece, 1917-1929. Trade Cloth. Kent State University Press. Kent, OH. 1988. 320p. ISBN:0-87338-357-5, ISBN13: 978-0-87338-357-8. Dewey:303.4/8273/0495. LCCN:88-003012.
Audience: **u,f.** *Choice, 1989.*

Clogg, Richard **DF787.G7C56 2000**
Anglo-Greek Attitudes: Studies in History. Cloth over Boards. Palgrave Macmillan. New York, NY. 2000. 217p. St. Antony's Ser. ISBN:0-312-23523-2, ISBN13: 978-0-312-23523-9. Dewey:303.48/2495041. LCCN:00-031116.
Audience: **u,f.**

Clogg, Richard **JN5185.A1.C56 1987**
Parties and Elections in Greece: The Search for Legitimacy. Cloth Text. Duke University Press. Durham, NC. 1988. xvii, 268p. ISBN:0-8223-0794-4, ISBN13: 978-0-8223-0794-5. Dewey:320.9495. LCCN:87-030376.
Audience: **g,u,f.** *Choice, 1988.*

Close, David **DF850.C55 2002**
Greece Since 1945: Politics, Economy and Society. Trade Paper. Longman Publishing Group. White Plains, NY. 2002. 328p. The Post War World Ser. ISBN:0-582-35667-9, ISBN13: 978-0-582-35667-2. Dewey:949.507/6. LCCN:2002-023574.
Audience: **l,u.** *Choice, 2003, 2002.*

Eudes, Dominique **D802.G8 E913 1973**
The Kapetanios. John Howe (Translator). Trade Cloth. Monthly Review Press. New York, NY. 1973. 400p. ISBN:0-85345-275-X, ISBN13: 978-0-85345-275-1. Dewey:940.53/495. LCCN:72-092032.
Audience: **u,f.**

Frazier, Robert **E183.8.G8F73 1991**
Anglo-American Relations with Greece: The Coming of the Cold War, 1942-47. Ed. 1. Trade Cloth. Palgrave Macmillan. New York, NY. 1991. 256p. ISBN:0-312-06142-0, ISBN13: 978-0-312-06142-5. Dewey:327.495. LCCN:90-026877.
Audience: **u,f.** *Choice, 1992.*

Hondros, John L. **D802.G8**
Occupation and Resistance: The Greek Agony, 1941-1944. Cloth Text. Pella Publishing Company, Inc. New York, NY. 1983. 340p. ISBN:0-918618-24-X, ISBN13: 978-0-918618-24-5. Dewey:940.53/495.
Audience: **u,f.**

Iatrides, John O. (Editor) **DF849**
Greece in the 1940s: A Nation in Crisis. Trade Cloth. University Press of New England. Lebanon, NH. 1981. 462p. ISBN:0-87451-198-4, ISBN13: 978-0-87451-198-7. Dewey:949.5/074. LCCN:80-054472.
Audience: **l,u,f.**

Karakasidou, Anastasia N. **DF901.A75K37 1997**
Fields of Wheat, Hills of Blood: Passages to Nationhood in Greek Macedonia, 1870-1990. Trade Paper. University of Chicago Press. Chicago, IL. 1997. 358p. ISBN:0-226-42494-4, ISBN13: 978-0-226-42494-1. Dewey:949.5/607. LCCN:96-034475.
Audience: **u,f.** *Choice, 1998.*

Kofas, Jon V. **HC295.K565 1989**
Intervention and Underdevelopment: Greece During the Cold War. Cloth Text. Pennsylvania State University Press. University Park, PA. 1989. 227p. ISBN:0-271-00661-7, ISBN13: 978-0-271-00661-1. Dewey:330.9495/07. LCCN:88-026572.
Audience: **u,f.** *Choice, 1990.*

Loizos, Peter & Papataxiarchis, Evthmios (Editors) **GN585.G85C66 1991**
Contested Identities: Gender and Kinship in Modern Greece. Trade Paper. Princeton University Press. Princeton, NJ. 1991. 272p. Princeton Modern Greek Studies ISBN:0-691-02859-1, ISBN13: 978-0-691-02859-0. Dewey:306.83/09495. LCCN:90-047780.
Audience: **g,u,f.** *Choice, 1992.*

Mazower, Mark **DF849.5.A48 2000**
After the War Was Over: Reconstructing the Family, Nation, and State in Greece, 1943-1960. Cloth Text. Princeton University Press. Princeton, NJ. 2000. 352p. Princeton Modern Greek

Studies ISBN:0-691-05841-5, ISBN13: 978-0-691-05841-2. Dewey:949.507/4. LCCN:00-036680.
Audience: **u,f.**

Mazower, Mark **HC295.M38 1991**
Greece and the Inter-War Economic Crisis. Trade Cloth. Oxford University Press, Inc. New York, NY. 1991. 348p. Oxford Historical Monographs ISBN:0-19-820205-9, ISBN13: 978-0-19-820205-9. Dewey:330.9495/07. LCCN:91-009620.
Audience: **u,f.**

Mazower, Mark **D802.E9**
Inside Hitler's Greece: The Experience of Occupation,1941-1944. Trade Paper. Yale University Press. Cumberland, RI. 2001. 464p. ISBN:0-300-08923-6, ISBN13: 978-0-300-08923-3. Dewey:940.5/337.
Audience: **l,u,f.**

Mitrakos, Alexander S. **DB65.3.F48**
France in Greece in World War I: A Study in the Politics of Power. Trade Cloth. Eastern European Monographs. Bradenton, FL. 1982. 258p. ISBN:0-914710-95-8, ISBN13: 978-0-914710-95-0. Dewey:943.6/032/0924. LCCN:82-126190.
Audience: **u,f.**

Papacosma, S. Victor **DF831.P36**
The Military in Greek Politics: The 1909 Coup D'Etat. Trade Cloth. Kent State University Press. Kent, OH. 1977. 254p. ISBN:0-87338-208-0, ISBN13: 978-0-87338-208-3. Dewey:949.5/07. LCCN:77-022391.
Audience: **u,f.**

Papandreou, Andreas George **DF852**
Democracy at Gunpoint: the Greek Front. Doubleday. 1970.
Audience: **g,l,u,f.**

Smith, Michael L. **DF845.S58 1998**
Ionian Vision: Greece in Asia Minor, 1919-1922. Cloth over Boards. University of Michigan Press. Chicago, IL. 1999. 424p. ISBN:0-472-10990-1, ISBN13: 978-0-472-10990-6. Dewey:949.507/2. LCCN:98-039700.
Audience: **u,f.**

Sutton, David **CR4731.G82**
Memories Cast in Stone: The Relevance of the Past in Everyday Life. Cloth over Boards. Berg Publishers. Oxford, 1998. 224p. Mediterranea Ser. ISBN:1-85973-943-1, ISBN13: 978-1-85973-943-3. Dewey:949.5/87.
Audience: **l,u,f.** *Choice, 1999.*

Vatikiotis, Panayiotis J. **DF849.58.M48**
Popular Autocracy in Greece, 1936-41: A Political Biography of General Loannis Metaxas. Frank Cass. 1998. ISBN:0-7146-4869-8, ISBN13: 978-0-7146-4869-9.
Audience: **g,l,u,f.**

Vlavianos, Haris **JN5185.K6V56 1991**
Greece, 1941-1949: From Resistance to Civil War: The Strategy of the Greek Communist Party. Cloth Text. Palgrave Macmillan. New York, NY. 1992. 320p. ISBN:0-312-06573-6, ISBN13: 978-0-312-06573-7. Dewey:324.2495/075/09. LCCN:91-012136.
Audience: **l,u.** *Choice, 1992.*

Wittner, Lawrence S. **E143.8.G8**
American Intervention in Greece: 1943-1949. Cloth Text. Columbia University Press. New York, NY. 1982. 432p. Contemporary American History Ser. ISBN:0-231-04196-9, ISBN13: 978-0-231-04196-6. Dewey:327.730495. LCCN:81-038521.
Audience: **u,f.**

Greece > Local History and Description > Athens

Smith, Michael Llewellyn **DF920.S65 2004**
Athens: A Cultural and Literary History. Trade Paper. Interlink Publishing Group, Inc. Northampton, MA. 2004. 256-264p. Cities of the Imagination Ser. ISBN:1-56656-540-5, ISBN13: 978-1-56656-540-0. Dewey:949.5/12. LCCN:2004-003243.
Audience: **g,l,u,f.**

Staikos, K. (Editor), et al. **NA1100.A845 2002**
Athens: From the Classical Period to the Present Day (5th Century B. C. -A. D. 2000). Charalampos Bouras, M. Sakellariou & E. Touloupa (Editors). Trade Cloth. Oak Knoll Press. New Castle, DE. 2002. 540p. ISBN:1-58456-091-6, ISBN13: 978-1-58456-091-3. Dewey:949.5/12. LCCN:2002-030712.
Audience: **g,l,u,f.** *Choice, 2003.*

Stoneman, Richard **DF921.S76 2004**
A Traveller's History of Athens. Trade Cloth. Interlink Publishing Group, Inc. Northampton, MA. 2004. 304p. The Traveller's History Ser. ISBN:1-56656-533-2, ISBN13: 978-1-56656-533-2. Dewey:949.5/12. LCCN:2003-023720.
Audience: **g,l,u,f.**

Zinovieff, Sofka **DF920**
Eurydice Street: A Place in Athens. Trade Cloth. Granta Books. London, 2004. 288p. ISBN:1-86207-681-2, ISBN13: 978-1-86207-681-5. Dewey:914.95/120476. LCCN:2004-426235.
Audience: **g,l,u,f.**

Greece > Local History and Description > Crete

Herzfeld, Michael **DF951.R4H47 1991**
A Place in History: Social and Monumental Time in a Cretan Town. Trade Paper. Princeton University Press. Princeton, NJ. 1991. 330p. Princeton Studies in Culture/Power/History ISBN:0-691-02855-9, ISBN13: 978-0-691-02855-2. Dewey:949.9/8. LCCN:90-028755.
Audience: **u,f.** *Choice, 1992.*

Hopkins, Adam **DF901.C82**
Crete: Its Past, Present and People. Victor Shreeve (Illustrator). Trade Paper. Faber & Faber, Inc. New York, NY. 1979. 250p. ISBN:0-571-11361-3, ISBN13: 978-0-571-11361-3. Dewey:949.98.
Audience: **g,l,u,f.**

Smith, Michael L. **DF901.C82**
The Great Island. Trade Cloth. Penguin Group (USA) Inc. New York, NY. 1975. ix, 182p. ISBN:0-7139-0510-7, ISBN13: 978-0-7139-0510-6. Dewey:914.998.
Audience: **g,l,u,f.**

Cyprus

Calotychos, Vangelis (Editor) **DS54.5.C97 1998**
Cyprus and Its People: Nation, Identity, and Experience in an Unimaginable Community, 1955-1997. Trade Cloth. Westview Press. Boulder, CO. 1998. 344p. ISBN:0-8133-3515-9, ISBN13: 978-0-8133-3515-5. Dewey:956.9304. LCCN:98-019812.
Audience: **u,f.** *Choice, 1999.*

Hannay, Lord **DS54.9**
Cyprus: The Search for a Solution. Cloth over Boards. I. B. Tauris & Company, Ltd. London, 2005. 256p. ISBN:1-85043-665-7, ISBN13: 978-1-85043-665-2. Dewey:320.9/5693/090511. LCCN:2005-295113.
Audience: **g,l,u,f.** *Choice, 2005.*

Kelling, George H. **DS54.8**
Countdown to Rebellion: British Policy in Cyprus, 1939-1955, 27. Trade Cloth. Greenwood Publishing Group, Inc. Portsmouth, NH. 1990. 200p. Contributions in Comparative Colonial Studies, No. 27 ISBN:0-313-26848-7, ISBN13: 978-0-313-26848-9. Dewey:956.45/03. LCCN:89-026002.
Audience: **g,l,u,f.** *Choice, 1990.*

O'Malley, Brendan & Craig, Ian **DS54.9**
The Cyprus Conspiracy: America, Espionage and the Turkish Invasion. Trade Paper. I. B. Tauris & Company, Ltd. London, 2001. 288p. ISBN:1-86064-737-5, ISBN13: 978-1-86064-737-6. Dewey:956.4503.
Audience: **g,l,u,f.**

Papadakis, Yiannis **DS54.9**
Echoes from the Dead Zone: Across the Cyprus Divide. Cloth over Boards. I. B. Tauris & Company, Ltd. London, 2005. 224p. ISBN:1-85043-428-X, ISBN13: 978-1-85043-428-3. Dewey:956.9304. LCCN:2005-298948.
Audience: **g,l,u,f.**

Italy > Regional History. Mezzogiorno, Sicily

Astarita, Tommaso **DG826.A78 2005**
Between Salt Water and Holy Water. Trade Cloth. W. W. Norton & Company, Inc. New York, NY. 2005. 352p. ISBN:0-393-05864-6, ISBN13: 978-0-393-05864-2. Dewey:945/.7. LCCN:2005-006085.
Audience: **u,f.**

Finley, Moses I., et al. **DG866 .F5 1987**
A History of Sicily. Mack Smith & Duggan (Authors). Trade Cloth. Penguin Group (USA) Inc. New York, NY. 1987. ISBN:0-670-81725-2, ISBN13: 978-0-670-81725-2. Dewey:945/.8. LCCN:86-040426.
Audience: **g,l,u,f.**

Levi, Carlo **DG975.B3L4813 2006**
Christ Stopped at Eboli: The Story of a Year. Frances Frenaye (Translator), Mark Rotella (Introduction by). Trade Paper. Farrar, Straus & Giroux. New York, NY. 2006. 272p. ISBN:0-374-53009-2, ISBN13: 978-0-374-53009-9. Dewey:945/.74. LCCN:2005-044677.
Audience: **g,l,u,f.**

Moe, Nelson **DG825 .M64**
View from Vesuvius: Italian Culture and the Southern Question. Trade Paper. University of California Press. Berkeley, CA. 2006. 380p. Studies on the History of Society and Culture Ser. ISBN:0-520-24826-0, ISBN13: 978-0-520-24826-7. Dewey:945.708. LCCN:2001-005018.
Audience: **u,f.**

Italy > Urban History

Brucker, Gene **DG737 .B7351 1998**
Florence: The Golden Age, 1138-1737. Trade Paper. University of California Press. Berkeley, CA. 1998. 278p. ISBN:0-520-21522-2, ISBN13: 978-0-520-21522-1. Dewey:945/.51. LCCN:2004-268176.
Audience: **u,f.**

Crouzet-Pavan, Elisabeth **DG676.C8813 2002**
Venice Triumphant: The Horizons of a Myth. Lydia G. Cochrane (Translator). Trade Cloth. Johns Hopkins University Press. Baltimore, MD. 2002. 424p. ISBN:0-8018-6958-7, ISBN13: 978-0-8018-6958-7. Dewey:945/.31. LCCN:2001-006617.
Audience: **u,f.** *Choice, 2003.*

Davis, Robert C. & Marvin, Garry R. **DG674.2 .D34 2004**
Venice, the Tourist Maze: A Cultural Critique of the World's Most Touristed City. Trade Cloth. University of California Press. Berkeley, CA. 2004. 368p. ISBN:0-520-23803-6, ISBN13: 978-0-520-23803-9. Dewey:945/.31. LCCN:2003-007854.
Audience: **g,l,u,f.** *Choice, 2005.*

Krautheimer, Richard **DG811.K7 2000**
Rome: Profile of a City, 312-1308. Marvin Trachtenberg (Foreword by). Trade Paper. Princeton University Press. Princeton, NJ. 2000. 418p. ISBN:0-691-04961-0, ISBN13: 978-0-691-04961-8. Dewey:945/.632. LCCN:99-053723.
Audience: **g,l,u,f.** B

Lancaster, Jordan **DG845.6**
In the Shadow of Vesuvius : A Cultural History of Naples. I. B. Tauris ; distributed in the U.S.A. by Palgrave Macmillan. 2005. ISBN:1-85043-764-5, ISBN13: 978-1-85043-764-2.
Audience: **l,u.**

Martin, John **DG675.6.V39 2000**
Venice Reconsidered: The History and Civilization of an Italian City-State, 1297-1797. Dennis Romano (Editor). Trade Cloth. Johns Hopkins University Press. Baltimore, MD. 2000. 560p. ISBN:0-8018-6312-0, ISBN13: 978-0-8018-6312-7. Dewey:945/.31. LCCN:00-021349.
Audience: **u,f.**

Painter, Borden **DG813.P28 2005**
Mussolini's Rome: Rebuilding the Eternal City. Saddle Stitched, Cloth over Boards, Dust Jacket. Palgrave Macmillan. New York, NY. 2005. 224p. Italian and Italian American Studies ISBN:1-4039-6604-4, ISBN13: 978-1-4039-6604-9. Dewey:945/.632091. LCCN:2004-043153.
Audience: **g,l,u,f.**

Italy > General History

Di Scala, Spencer **DG545.D5 2004**
Italy: From Revolution to Republic, 1700 to the Present. Ed. 3. Trade Paper. Westview Press. Boulder, CO. 2004. 520p.

ISBN:0-8133-4177-9, ISBN13: 978-0-8133-4177-4. Dewey:945. LCCN:2003-020236.
Audience: **g,l,u,f.**

Hearder, Harry **DG467 .H43 2001**
Italy: A Short History. Ed. 2. Jonathan Morris (Editor). Cloth Text. Cambridge University Press. New York, NY. 2001. 306p. ISBN:0-521-80613-5, ISBN13: 978-0-521-80613-8. Dewey:945. LCCN:2001-035695.
Audience: **g,l,u,f.**

Italy > Foreign policy, Diplomacy

Palumbo, Patrizia **DT35 .P56 2003**
A Place in the Sun: Africa in Italian Colonial Culture from Post-Unification to the Present. Trade Cloth. University of California Press. Berkeley, CA. 2003. 400p. ISBN:0-520-23232-1, ISBN13: 978-0-520-23232-7. Dewey:303.48/24506. LCCN:2003-005685.
Audience: **u,f.**

Italy > By Period > Early Medieval

Abulafia, David **DD151 .A28 1988**
Frederick Second: A Medieval Emperor. Trade Cloth. Penguin Group (USA) Inc. New York, NY. 1988. 480p. ISBN:0-7139-9004-X, ISBN13: 978-0-7139-9004-1. Dewey:943.0250924. LCCN:88-060417.
Audience: **g,l,u,f.**

Abulafia, David (Editor) **DG527**
Italy in the Central Middle Ages, 1000-1300. Paper Text. Oxford University Press, Inc. New York, NY. 2004. 280p. Short Oxford History of Italy Ser. ISBN:0-19-924704-8, ISBN13: 978-0-19-924704-2. Dewey:945/.03. LCCN:2004-041470.
Audience: **u,f.**

Abulafia, David **HF411 .A28**
The Two Italies: Economic Relations Between the Norman Kingdom of Sicily and the Northern Communes. Trade Paper. Cambridge University Press. New York, NY. 2005. 330p. Cambridge Studies in Medieval Life and Thought Ser., Vol. 9:Third Ser. ISBN:0-521-02306-8, ISBN13: 978-0-521-02306-1. Dewey:382/.0945/10458.
Audience: **u,f.**

Brentano, Robert **DG811.B73 1990**
Rome Before Avignon: A Social History of Thirteenth-Century Rome. Trade Paper. University of California Press. Berkeley, CA. 1991. 357p. ISBN:0-520-06952-8, ISBN13: 978-0-520-06952-7. Dewey:945/.632/04. LCCN:90-015493.
Audience: **u,f.**

Dameron, George W. **BX1548.F55D33 1991**
Episcopal Power and Florentine Society, 1000-1320. Trade Cloth. Harvard University Press. Cambridge, MA. 1991. 284p. Harvard Historical Studies, No. 107 ISBN:0-674-25891-6, ISBN13: 978-0-674-25891-4. Dewey:945/.5103. LCCN:90-036715.
Audience: **u,f.** *Choice, 1991.*

Dunbabin, Jean **DG847.2.D86 1998**
Charles I of Anjou: Power, Kingship and State-Making in Thirteenth-Century Europe. Trade Paper. Addison-Wesley Longman, Inc. Boston, MA. 1998. 224p. The Medieval World Ser., : ISBN:0-582-25370-5, ISBN13: 978-0-582-25370-4. Dewey:[B]. LCCN:97-037576.
Audience: **u,f.**

Dyson, Stephen L. **DG77**
Community and Society in Roman Italy. Trade Paper. Johns Hopkins University Press. Baltimore, MD. 2001. 400p. Ancient Society and History Ser. ISBN:0-8018-6760-6, ISBN13: 978-0-8018-6760-6. Dewey:937. LCCN:91-020070.
Audience: **u,f.** *Choice, 1992.*

Foote, David **BX1547.O78F66 2004**
Lordship, Reform, and the Development of Civil Society in Medieval Italy: The Bishopric of Orvieto, 1100-1250. Trade Cloth. University of Notre Dame Press. Notre Dame, IN. 2004. 272p. ISBN:0-268-02871-0, ISBN13: 978-0-268-02871-8. Dewey:282/.45652/09021. LCCN:2004-011375.
Audience: **u,f.** *Choice, 2005.*

Hyde, J. K. **DG523**
Society and Politics in Medieval Italy. Paper Text. St. Martin's Press. Gordonville, VA. 1973. ISBN:0-312-73920-6, ISBN13: 978-0-312-73920-1. Dewey:309.1/45.
Audience: **g,l,u,f.**

La Rocca, Cristina (Editor) **DF503.I8 2002**
Italy in the Early Middle Ages, 476-1000. Paper Text. Oxford University Press, Inc. New York, NY. 2002. 288p. Short Oxford History of Italy Ser. ISBN:0-19-870048-2, ISBN13: 978-0-19-870048-7. Dewey:945/.03. LCCN:2002-072552.
Audience: **g,l,u,f.**

Lane, Frederic C. **DG676**
Venice: A Maritime Republic. Trade Paper. Johns Hopkins University Press. Baltimore, MD. 1973. 528p. ISBN:0-8018-1460-X, ISBN13: 978-0-8018-1460-0. Dewey:945/.31. LCCN:72-012342.
Audience: **u,f.** B

Lopez, Robert S. & Raymond, Irving W. (Translators) **HF395.M43 2001**
Medieval Trade in the Mediterranean World: Illustrative Documents. Ed. 2. Olivia Remie Constable (Foreword by). Trade Cloth. Columbia University Press. New York, NY. 2001. 496p. Records of Western Civilization Ser. ISBN:0-231-12356-6, ISBN13: 978-0-231-12356-3. Dewey:382/.09182/2. LCCN:2002-278336.
Audience: **l,u,f.**

Loud, G. A. **DG867.215.R64L68**
The Age of Robert Guiscard: Southern Italy and the Norman Conquest. Trade Cloth. Longman Publishing Group. White Plains, NY. 2000. 344p. The Medieval World Ser. ISBN:0-582-04528-2, ISBN13: 978-0-582-04528-6. Dewey:945/.8. LCCN:00-042126.
Audience: **u,f.**

Loud, G. A. & Metcalfe, A. (Editors) **HN488.S68S63 2002**
The Society of Norman Italy. Trade Cloth. Brill Academic Publishers. Leiden, 2002. xxii, 384p. The Medieval Mediterranean Ser., Vol. 38 ISBN:90-04-12541-8, ISBN13: 978-90-04-12541-4. Dewey:301/.09457. LCCN:2002-025418.
Audience: **u,f.** *Choice, 2003.*

Madden, Thomas F. & Rees, Ronald **DG677.64.M33 2003**
Enrico Dandolo and the Rise of Venice. Trade Cloth. Johns Hopkins University Press. Baltimore, MD. 2003. 352p. ISBN:0-8018-7317-7, ISBN13: 978-0-8018-7317-1. Dewey:945/.3104/092 B. LCCN:2002-013623.
Audience: **g,l,u,f.** *Choice, 2004.*

Noble, Thomas F. **DG797.1**
The Republic of St. Peter: The Birth of the Papal State, 680-825. Book, Other. University of Pennsylvania Press. Philadelphia, PA. 1986. 412p. Middle Ages Ser. ISBN:0-8122-1239-8, ISBN13: 978-0-8122-1239-6. Dewey:945/.6. LCCN:83-021870.
Audience: **g,l,u,f.**

Partner, Peter **DG797.P37 1972**
The Lands of St. Peter. Trade Cloth. University of California Press. Berkeley, CA. 1972. 494p. ISBN:0-520-02181-9, ISBN13: 978-0-520-02181-5. Dewey:945/.6. LCCN:73-182793.
Audience: **u,f.** B

Thompson, Augustine **BX1210**
Cities of God: The Religion of the Italian Communes, 1125-1325. Trade Cloth. Pennsylvania State University Press. University Park, PA. 2006. 520p. ISBN:0-271-02909-9, ISBN13: 978-0-271-02909-2. Dewey:282/.45/09022.
Audience: **u,f.** *Choice, 2006.*

Wickham, Chris **DG737**
Courts and Conflict in Twelfth-Century Tuscany. Trade Cloth. Oxford University Press, Inc. New York, NY. 2004. 376p. ISBN:0-19-926586-0, ISBN13: 978-0-19-926586-2. Dewey:945.504. LCCN:2004-270317.
Audience: **u,f.** *Choice, 2004.*

Wickham, Chris **DG503.W52 1989**
Early Medieval Italy: Central Power and Local Society 400-1000. Trade Paper. University of Michigan Press. Chicago, IL. 1990. 256p. Ann Arbor Paperbacks Ser. ISBN:0-472-08099-7, ISBN13: 978-0-472-08099-1. Dewey:945. LCCN:89-032476.
Audience: **g,l,u,f.**

Italy > By Period > City-states and Renaissance (1268-1526)

Brucker, Gene **DG737 .B7351 1998**
Florence: The Golden Age, 1138-1737. Trade Paper. University of California Press. Berkeley, CA. 1998. 278p. ISBN:0-520-21522-2, ISBN13: 978-0-520-21522-1. Dewey:945/.51. LCCN:2004-268176.
Audience: **u,f.**

Celenza, Christopher S. **DG445.C38 2004**
The Lost Italian Renaissance: Humanists, Historians, and Latin's Legacy. Trade Cloth. Johns Hopkins University Press. Baltimore, MD. 2004. 232p. ISBN:0-8018-7815-2, ISBN13: 978-0-8018-7815-2. Dewey:945/.05/072. LCCN:2003-012858.
Audience: **u,f.** *Choice, 2005.*

Chojnacki, Stanley **HQ630.15.V47C48 2000**
Women and Men in Renaissance Venice: Twelve Essays on Patrician Society. Trade Paper. Johns Hopkins University Press. Baltimore, MD. 2000. 384p. ISBN:0-8018-6395-3, ISBN13: 978-0-8018-6395-0. Dewey:306.7/0945/31. LCCN:99-038575.
Audience: **g,l,u,f.**

Cohn, Samuel K. Jr. **HD1536.I8 C576 1999**
Creating the Florentine State: Peasants and Rebellion, 1348-1434. Trade Cloth. Cambridge University Press. New York, NY. 1999. 322p. ISBN:0-521-66337-7, ISBN13: 978-0-521-66337-3. Dewey:945.510508863. LCCN:99-020440.
Audience: **u,f.** *Choice, 2000.*

Cohn, Samuel K. Jr. **HN475.C59 1992**
The Cult of Remembrance and the Black Death: Six Renaissance Cities in Central Italy. Trade Cloth. Johns Hopkins University Press. Baltimore, MD. 1992. 448p. ISBN:0-8018-4303-0, ISBN13: 978-0-8018-4303-7. Dewey:393.0945. LCCN:91-045267.
Audience: **u,f.** *Choice, 1993.*

Dameron, George W. **BX1548.F55D334 2004**
Florence and Its Church in the Age of Dante. Trade Cloth. University of Pennsylvania Press. Philadelphia, PA. 2004. 328p. The Middle Ages Ser. ISBN:0-8122-3823-0, ISBN13: 978-0-8122-3823-5. Dewey:274.5/5105. LCCN:2004-049601.
Audience: **u,f.** *Choice, 2006.*

Davis, Charles T. **PQ4422 .D33 1984**
Dante's Italy and Other Essays. Trade Cloth. University of Pennsylvania Press. Philadelphia, PA. 1984. 352p. Middle Ages Ser. ISBN:0-8122-7883-6, ISBN13: 978-0-8122-7883-5. Dewey:851/.1. LCCN:83-003600.
Audience: **u,f.**

Epstein, Steven A. **95-26585 [DG]**
Genoa and the Genoese, 958-1528. Trade Paper. University of North Carolina Press. Chapel Hill, NC. 2001. 416p. ISBN:0-8078-4992-8, ISBN13: 978-0-8078-4992-7. Dewey:945/.182.
Audience: **u,f.** *Choice, 1997.*

Grendler, Paul F. **LA797.G74 2001**
The Universities of the Italian Renaissance. Trade Cloth. Johns Hopkins University Press. Baltimore, MD. 2002. 616p. ISBN:0-8018-6631-6, ISBN13: 978-0-8018-6631-9. Dewey:378.45. LCCN:00-011287.
Audience: **u,f.** *Choice, 2002.*

Lansing, Carol **HT653.I8L36 1991**
The Florentine Magnates: Lineage and Faction in a Medieval Commune. Trade Cloth. Princeton University Press. Princeton, NJ. 1991. 285p. ISBN:0-691-03154-1, ISBN13: 978-0-691-03154-5. Dewey:305.5/223/0945510902. LCCN:91-006867.
Audience: **u,f.** *Choice, 1992.*

Lansing, Carol **BT1319**
Power and Purity: Cathar Heresy in Medieval Italy. Trade Paper. Oxford University Press, Inc. New York, NY. 2001. 288p. ISBN:0-19-514980-7, ISBN13: 978-0-19-514980-7. Dewey:273.6.
Audience: **u,f.**

Larner, John **NX552.A1.L3 1971**
Culture and Society in Italy, 1290-1420. Trade Cloth. Simon & Schuster. New York, NY. 1971. xi, 399p. ISBN:0-684-12367-3, ISBN13: 978-0-684-12367-7. Dewey:914.5/03/4. LCCN:72-110680.
Audience: **g,l,u.**

Larner, John **DG531**
Italy in the Age of Dante and Petrarch, 1216-1380. Trade Cloth. Longman Publishing Group. White Plains, NY. 1980. 288p.

ISBN:0-582-49149-5, ISBN13: 978-0-582-49149-6. Dewey:945/.04. LCCN:79-041509.
Audience: **g,l,u.**

Martines, Lauro **DG737.9.M376 2003**
April Blood: Florence and the Plot Against the Medici. Trade Cloth. Oxford University Press, Inc. New York, NY. 2003. 320p. ISBN:0-19-515295-6, ISBN13: 978-0-19-515295-1. Dewey:945/.5105. LCCN:2002-153155.
Audience: **u,f.**

Tabacco, Giovanni **DG503.T2913 1989**
The Struggle for Power in Medieval Italy: Structures of Political Rule, 400-1400. Rosalind B. Jensen (Translator). Trade Cloth. Cambridge University Press. New York, NY. 1990. 359p. Cambridge Medieval Textbooks Ser. ISBN:0-521-33469-1, ISBN13: 978-0-521-33469-3. Dewey:945. LCCN:89-009771.
Audience: **u,f.**

Tuohy, Thomas **DG975.F42 T86 1996**
Herculean Ferrara: Ercole d'Este (1471-1505) and the Invention of a Ducal Capital. Trade Cloth. Cambridge University Press. New York, NY. 1996. 566p. Studies in Italian History and Culture ISBN:0-521-46471-4, ISBN13: 978-0-521-46471-0. Dewey:945/.4. LCCN:96-185795.
Audience: **u,f.** *Choice, 1997.*

Italy > By Period > High Renaissance

Burckhardt, Jacob **DG445**
The Civilization of the Renaissance in Italy. Middlemore, S. G. C. ; (Samuel George Chetwynd) (Translator). Modern Library. 2002. The Modern Library classics ISBN:0-375-75926-3, ISBN13: 978-0-375-75926-0.
Audience: **g,l,u,f.**

Cellini, Benvenuto **NB623.C3A2 1998**
The Autobiography of Benvenuto Cellini. George Bull (Translator, Introduction by, Notes by). Trade Paper. Penguin Group (USA) Inc. New York, NY. 1999. 1p. Classics Ser. ISBN:0-14-044718-0, ISBN13: 978-0-14-044718-7. Dewey:730.9/2. LCCN:00-501056.
Audience: **g,l,u,f.** B

Cohen, Thomas V. & Cohen, Elizabeth S. **KKH38.C64 1993**
Words and Deeds in Renaissance Rome: Trials Before the Papal Magistrates. Trade Cloth. University of Toronto Press. Toronto, ON. 1993. 590p. ISBN:0-8020-2825-X, ISBN13: 978-0-8020-2825-9. Dewey:347.45/63207. LCCN:94-149427.
Audience: **g,l,u,f.** *Choice, 1994.*

Fiorani, Francesca **DG445.F56 2005**
The Marvel of Maps: Art, Cartography, and Politics in Renaissance Italy. Cloth over Boards. Yale University Press. Cumberland, RI. 2005. 360p. ISBN:0-300-10727-7, ISBN13: 978-0-300-10727-2. Dewey:526/.0945/09031. LCCN:2004-023964.
Audience: **g,l,u,f.** *Choice, 2006.*

King, Ross **NA5621.F7K56 2001**
Brunelleschi's Dome: How a Renaissance Genius Reinvented Architecture. Trade Paper. Penguin Group (USA) Inc. New York, NY. 2001. 208p. ISBN:0-14-200015-9, ISBN13: 978-0-14-200015-1. Dewey:726.6/0945/51. LCCN:2001-280068.
Audience: **g,l,u,f.** *Choice, 2001.*

King, Ross **ND623.B9.K55 2003**
Michelangelo and the Pope's Ceiling. Trade Paper. Penguin Group (USA) Inc. New York, NY. 2003. 384p. ISBN:0-14-200369-7, ISBN13: 978-0-14-200369-5. Dewey:759.5. LCCN:2003-283284.
Audience: **g,l,u,f.**

Martines, Lauro **DG737.97.M3 2006**
Fire in the City: Savonarola and the Struggle for the Soul of Renaissance Florence. Trade Cloth. Oxford University Press, Inc. New York, NY. 2006. 360p. ISBN:0-19-517748-7, ISBN13: 978-0-19-517748-0. Dewey:945/.5105092 B. LCCN:2005-031802.
Audience: **g,l,u,f.**

Martines, Lauro **DG494.M37 1988**
Power and Imagination: City-States in Renaissance Italy. Trade Paper. Johns Hopkins University Press. Baltimore, MD. 1988. 400p. ISBN:0-8018-3643-3, ISBN13: 978-0-8018-3643-5. Dewey:945. LCCN:87-029843.
Audience: **g,l,u,f.** B

McClure, George W. **DG445.M42 2004**
The Culture of Profession in Late Renaissance Italy. Trade Cloth. University of Toronto Press. Toronto, ON. 2004. 390p. ISBN:0-8020-8970-4, ISBN13: 978-0-8020-8970-0. Dewey:945/.07. LCCN:2004-557570.
Audience: **u,f.** *Choice, 2005.*

Partner, Peter **DG812.12**
Renaissance Rome: A Portrait of a Society, 1500-1559. Trade Cloth. University of California Press. Berkeley, CA. 1980. 248p. ISBN:0-520-03945-9, ISBN13: 978-0-520-03945-2. Dewey:945/.632/06.
Audience: **g,l,u,f.** B

Stinger, Charles L. **DG812.1.S75 1998**
The Renaissance in Rome. Trade Cloth. Indiana University Press. Bloomington, IN. 1998. 472p. ISBN:0-253-33491-8, ISBN13: 978-0-253-33491-6. Dewey:945/.63205. LCCN:98-007343.
Audience: **g,l,u,f.** B *Choice, 1985.*

Viroli, Maurizio **DG738.14.M2**
Niccolo's Smile: A Biography of Machiavelli. Antony Shugaar (Translator). Trade Paper. Farrar, Straus & Giroux. New York, NY. 2002. 288p. ISBN:0-374-52800-4, ISBN13: 978-0-374-52800-3. Dewey:945.5/1/06/092.
Audience: **g,l,u,f.** *Choice, 2001.*

Italy > By Period > 1550-1796

Black, Christopher F. **BX1543.B55 2004**
Church, Religion and Society in Early Modern Italy. Cloth over Boards. Palgrave Macmillan. New York, NY. 2004. 352p. European Studies ISBN:0-333-61844-0, ISBN13: 978-0-333-61844-8. Dewey:274.5/06. LCCN:2004-050022.
Audience: **u,f.** *Choice, 2005.*

Ginzburg, Carlo **BR877.F74G5613**
The Cheese and the Worms: The Cosmos of a Sixteenth-Century Miller. Anne Tedeschi & John Tedeschi (Translators). Trade Paper. Johns Hopkins University Press. Baltimore, MD. 1978. 208p. ISBN:0-8018-4387-1, ISBN13: 978-0-8018-4387-7. Dewey:344.505/288.
Audience: **u,f.** B

Ginzburg, Carlo GR177.F75
The Night Battles: Witchcraft and Agrarian Cults in the Sixteenth and Seventeenth Centuries. John Tedeschi & Anne C. Tedeschi (Translators). Trade Paper. Johns Hopkins University Press. Baltimore, MD. 1992. 232p. ISBN:0-8018-4386-3, ISBN13: 978-0-8018-4386-0. Dewey:398.4/1/094539.
Audience: **u,f.**

Gross, Hanns DG797.8
Rome in the Age of Enlightenment: The Post-Tridentine Syndrome and the Ancien Régime. John Elliott, Olwen Hufton, H. G. Koenigsberger & H. M. Scott (Contribution by). Trade Paper. Cambridge University Press. New York, NY. 2004. 422p. Cambridge Studies in Early Modern History Ser. ISBN:0-521-89378-X, ISBN13: 978-0-521-89378-7. Dewey:945.6/32/07.
Audience: **u,f.**

Marino, John A. (Editor) DG538.E17 2002
Early Modern Italy: 1550-1796. Paper Text. Oxford University Press, Inc. New York, NY. 2002. 330p. Short Oxford History of Italy Ser. ISBN:0-19-870042-3, ISBN13: 978-0-19-870042-5. Dewey:945.07. LCCN:2002-514900.
Audience: **g,l,u,f.**

Matter, E. Ann & Coakley, John (Editors) BV639.W7C69 1994
Creative Women in Medieval and Early Modern Italy: A Religious and Artistic Renaissance. Trade Cloth. University of Pennsylvania Press. Philadelphia, PA. 1994. 376p. Middle Ages Ser. ISBN:0-8122-3236-4, ISBN13: 978-0-8122-3236-3. Dewey:274.5/05/082. LCCN:94-027864.
Audience: **u,f.** *Choice, 1995.*

Italy > By Period > Napoleonic Era (1796-1815)

Acton, Harold DG848.3
The Bourbons of Naples. Trade Paper. Prion. London, 1998. 750p. Lost Treasures Ser. ISBN:1-85375-291-6, ISBN13: 978-1-85375-291-9. Dewey:945.7/3/08/0922.
Audience: **l,u.**

Broers, Michael DC202.5.B763 2004
The Napoleonic Empire in Italy, 1796-1814: Cultural Imperialism in a European Context? Cloth over Boards. Palgrave Macmillan. New York, NY. 2005. 320p. ISBN:1-4039-0565-7, ISBN13: 978-1-4039-0565-9. Dewey:945/.082. LCCN:2004-052347.
Audience: **u,f.**

Nicassio, Susan VanDiver DG812.7
Imperial City: Rome, Romans and Napoleon, 1796-1815. Trade Cloth. Ravenhall. Welwyn Garden City, 2005. 255p. ISBN:1-905043-06-6, ISBN13: 978-1-905043-06-4. Dewey:945.632082. LCCN:2006-404595.
Audience: **u,f.**

Italy > By Period > Risorgimento (1815-1871)

Ascoli, Albert Russell (ed), Von Henneberg, Krystyna (ed) DG552
Making and Remaking Italy : The Cultivation of National Identity Around the Risorgimento. Berg. 2001. ISBN:1-85973-447-2, ISBN13: 978-1-85973-447-6.
Audience: **u,f.**

Ascoli, Albert Russell & von Henneberg, Krystyna (Editors) DG552
Making and Remaking Italy: The Cultivation of National Identity Around the Risorgimento. Cloth over Boards. Berg Publishers. Oxford, 2001. 320p. ISBN:1-85973-447-2, ISBN13: 978-1-85973-447-6. Dewey:945/.083.
Audience: **u,f.**

Hearder, Harry DG552.8.C3H42 1994
Cavour. Cloth Text. Longman Publishing Group. White Plains, NY. 1995. 224p. Profiles in Power Ser. ISBN:0-582-01899-4, ISBN13: 978-0-582-01899-0. Dewey:945/.08/0924. LCCN:93-038424.
Audience: **g,l,u,f.** *Choice, 1995.*

Kertzer, David I. DS135.I9M595 1997
The Kidnapping of Edgardo Mortara: The Extraordinary Story of How a Jewish Child, Made a Prisoner of the Vatican in 1858, Ended the Rule of the Popes in Italy. Trade Cloth. Random House, Inc. New York, NY. 1997. 350p. ISBN:0-679-45031-9, ISBN13: 978-0-679-45031-3. Dewey:945/.004924. LCCN:96-039159.
Audience: **g,l,u,f.** *Choice, 1997.*

Kertzer, David I. DG798.7 .K47
Prisoner of the Vatican: The Popes, the Kings, and Garibaldi's Rebels in the Struggle to Rule Modern Italy. Trade Paper. Houghton Mifflin Company Trade & Reference Division. Boston, MA. 2006. 368p. ISBN:0-618-61919-4, ISBN13: 978-0-618-61919-1. Dewey:945/.63084.
Audience: **g,l,u.**

Patriarca, Silvana HA19 .P37 1996
Numbers and Nationhood: Writing Statistics in Nineteenth-Century Italy. Trade Cloth. Cambridge University Press. New York, NY. 1996. 294p. Studies in Italian History and Culture ISBN:0-521-46296-7, ISBN13: 978-0-521-46296-9. Dewey:945/.08. LCCN:95-004328.
Audience: **u,f.**

Pick, Daniel DG813.15
Rome or Death: The Diversion of General Garibaldi. Trade Cloth. Random House. London, 2005. 160p. ISBN:0-224-07179-3, ISBN13: 978-0-224-07179-6. Dewey:945.632084092. LCCN:2005-482142.
Audience: **g,l,u,f.**

Riall, Lucy DG552.R46 1994
The Italian Risorgimento: State, Society and National Unification. Trade Paper. Routledge. New York, NY. 1994. 128p. Historical Connections Ser. ISBN:0-415-05775-2, ISBN13: 978-0-415-05775-2. Dewey:945/.08. LCCN:93-033882.
Audience: **g,l,u,f.**

Sarti, Roland DG552
Mazzini: A Life for the Religion of Politics. Trade Cloth. Greenwood Publishing Group, Inc. Portsmouth, NH. 1997. 264p.

ISBN:0-275-95080-8, ISBN13: 978-0-275-95080-4. Dewey:945/.08. LCCN:96-037112.
Audience: **g,l,u,f.** *Choice, 1997.*

Italy > By Period > Unified Italy (1871-1922). Rise of Fascism

Bosworth, Richard **DG568.5.B66 1983**
Italy and the Approach of the First World War. Cloth Text. Palgrave Macmillan. New York, NY. 1983. 174p. The Making of the 20th Century Ser. ISBN:0-312-43924-5, ISBN13: 978-0-312-43924-8. Dewey:945.08. LCCN:82-016841.
Audience: **g,l,u,f.** ℬ

Burgwyn, H. James **D617**
The Legend of the Mutilated Victory: Italy, the Great War, and the Paris Peace Conference, 1915-1919, 38. Trade Cloth. Greenwood Publishing Group, Inc. Portsmouth, NH. 1993. 368p. Contributions to the Study of World History Ser., No. 38 ISBN:0-313-28885-2, ISBN13: 978-0-313-28885-2. Dewey:940.32245. LCCN:92-045082.
Audience: **u,f.** *Choice, 1994.*

Cinel, Dino **JV8132 .C56 1991**
The National Integration of Italian Return Migration, 1870-1929. Robert Fogel & Stephan Thernstrom (Contribution by). Trade Cloth. Cambridge University Press. New York, NY. 1991. 288p. Interdisciplinary Perspectives on Modern History Ser. ISBN:0-521-40058-9, ISBN13: 978-0-521-40058-9. Dewey:304.8/45/073. LCCN:91-006989.
Audience: **u,f.** *Choice, 1992.*

De Grand, Alexander **DG575**
The Hunchback's Tailor: Giovanni Giolitti and Liberal Italy from the Challenge of Mass Politics to the Rise of Fascism, 1882-1922. Trade Cloth. Greenwood Publishing Group, Inc. Portsmouth, NH. 2000. 312p. Italian and Italian-American Studies ISBN:0-275-96874-X, ISBN13: 978-0-275-96874-8. Dewey:945.09. LCCN:00-025126.
Audience: **u,f.** *Choice, 2001.*

Drake, Richard **HX286.5.D73 2003**
Apostles and Agitators: Italy's Marxist Revolutionary Tradition. Trade Cloth. Harvard University Press. Cambridge, MA. 2003. 292p. ISBN:0-674-01036-1, ISBN13: 978-0-674-01036-9. Dewey:335.43/092/245. LCCN:2002-191344.
Audience: **u,f.** *Choice, 2004.*

Lyttelton, Adrian (Editor) **DG571.L49 2002**
Liberal and Fascist Italy: 1900-1945. Paper Text. Oxford University Press, Inc. New York, NY. 2002. 314p. Short Oxford History of Italy Ser. ISBN:0-19-873198-1, ISBN13: 978-0-19-873198-6. Dewey:945.091. LCCN:2002-512772.
Audience: **g,l,u,f.**

Lyttelton, Adrian **DG571.L95 1987**
The Seizure of Power: Fascism in Italy, 1919-1929. Ed. 2. Trade Paper. Princeton University Press. Princeton, NJ. 1988. 546p. ISBN:0-691-02278-X, ISBN13: 978-0-691-02278-9. Dewey:321.9/4/0945. LCCN:87-007309.
Audience: **u,f.** ℬ *Choice, 1988.*

Lyttelton, Adrian **DG568.5**
Italian Fascisms from Pareto to Gentile. Harper & Row. 1975. Roots of the Right ISBN:0-06-131884-1, ISBN13: 978-0-06-131884-9.
Audience: **g,l,u,f.**

Lyttelton, Adrian (editor) **DG571**
Liberal and fascist Italy : 1900-1945. Oxford University Press. 2002. The short Oxford history of Italy ISBN:0-19-873197-3, ISBN13: 978-0-19-873197-9.
Audience: **u,f.**

Mack-Smith, Denis M. **DG450**
Italy and Its Monarchy. Trade Paper. Yale University Press. Cumberland, RI. 1992. 413p. ISBN:0-300-05132-8, ISBN13: 978-0-300-05132-2. Dewey:945/.084.
Audience: **g,l,u,f.** *Choice, 1990.*

Pernicone, Nunzio **HX902.P47 1993**
Italian Anarchism, 1864-1892. Cloth Text. Princeton University Press. Princeton, NJ. 1993. 336p. ISBN:0-691-05692-7, ISBN13: 978-0-691-05692-0. Dewey:335.830945. LCCN:92-046661.
Audience: **u,f.** *Choice, 1994.*

Reeder, Linda **HQ1644.55**
Widows in White: Migration and the Transformation of Rural Italian Women, Sicily, 1880-1928. Cloth over Boards. University of Toronto Press. Toronto, ON. 2003. 304p. Studies in Gender and History, Vol. 22 ISBN:0-8020-3731-3, ISBN13: 978-0-8020-3731-2. Dewey:305.42/09458/091734. LCCN:2003-271534.
Audience: **u,f.** *Choice, 2003.*

Snowden, Frank M. **HD679.P83S66 1986**
Violence and Great Estates in the South of Italy: Apulia, 1900-1922. Trade Cloth. Cambridge University Press. New York, NY. 1986. 255p. ISBN:0-521-30731-7, ISBN13: 978-0-521-30731-4. Dewey:322.4/409457509041. LCCN:2005-277508.
Audience: **u,f.** *Choice, 1986.*

Ziblatt, Daniel **JC201.Z53 2006**
Structuring the State: The Formation of Italy and Germany and the Puzzle of Federalism. Trade Cloth. Princeton University Press. Princeton, NJ. 2006. 288p. ISBN:0-691-12167-2, ISBN13: 978-0-691-12167-3. Dewey:320.443/049. LCCN:2005-043378.
Audience: **u,f.**

Italy > By Period > Fascist Italy (1922-43)

Ben-Ghiat, Ruth **99-087279**
Fascist Modernities: Italy, 1922-1945. Trade Cloth. University of California Press. Berkeley, CA. 2001. 332p. Studies on the History of Society and Culture, Vol. 42 ISBN:0-520-22363-2, ISBN13: 978-0-520-22363-9. Dewey:945/.091. LCCN:99-087279.
Audience: **u,f.**

Berezin, Mabel **DG571.B444 1997**
Making the Fascist Self: The Political Culture of Interwar Italy. Book, Other. Cornell University Press. Ithaca, NY. 1997. 296p. The Wilder House Series in Politics, History, and Culture ISBN:0-8014-3202-2, ISBN13: 978-0-8014-3202-6. Dewey:306.2/0945/09041. LCCN:96-053410.
Audience: **u,f.** *Choice, 1997.*

Bosworth, R. J. B. **DG575.M8**
Mussolini. Trade Paper. Oxford University Press, Inc. New York, NY. 2003. 624p. An Arnold Publication ISBN:0-340-80988-4, ISBN13: 978-0-340-80988-4. Dewey:945/.091/092.
Audience: **g,l,u,f.** *Choice, 2003.*

Cooke, Philip (Editor) **D802.I8I85 1997**
Italian Resistance: An Anthology: Manchester New Italian Texts. Trade Cloth. Manchester University Press. Manchester, 1998. 208p. Manchester New Italian Texts ISBN:0-7190-5172-X, ISBN13: 978-0-7190-5172-2. Dewey:850.8/0358. LCCN:97-014285.
Audience: **g,l,u,f.**

De Grand, Alexander **DG571.D37 2000**
Italian Fascism: Its Origins and Development. Ed. 3. Paper Text. University of Nebraska Press. Lincoln, NE. 2000. 191p. ISBN:0-8032-6622-7, ISBN13: 978-0-8032-6622-3. Dewey:320.53/3/0945. LCCN:99-047948.
Audience: **g,l,u,f.**

De Grazia, Victoria **HQ1638.D4 1991**
How Fascism Ruled Women: Italy, 1922-1945. Trade Cloth. University of California Press. Berkeley, CA. 1992. 384p. ISBN:0-520-07456-4, ISBN13: 978-0-520-07456-9. Dewey:305.42/0945. LCCN:91-008901.
Audience: **u,f.** *Choice, 1992.*

Delzell, Charles F. **DG0571**
Mussolini's Enemies: The Italian Anti-Fascist Resistance. Trade Paper. Books on Demand. Ann Arbor, MI. 641p. ISBN:0-608-09164-2, ISBN13: 978-0-608-09164-8. Dewey:945.091. LCCN:61-007406.
Audience: **u,f.**

Delzell, Charles F. **DG571.D4**
Mussolini's Enemies: The Italian Anti-Fascist Resistance. Princeton University Press. 1961.
Audience: **u,f.**

Diggins, John P. **DG499.U5.D5**
Mussolini and Fascism: The View from America. Trade Cloth. Princeton University Press. Princeton, NJ. 1972. 544p. ISBN:0-691-04604-2, ISBN13: 978-0-691-04604-4. Dewey:914.5/03/91. LCCN:78-153845.
Audience: **g,l,u,f.** B

Fogu, Claudio **DG571.F548 2003**
The Historic Imaginary: Politics of History in Fascist Italy. Trade Cloth. University of Toronto Press. Toronto, ON. 2003. 288p. Toronto Italian Studies ISBN:0-8020-8764-7, ISBN13: 978-0-8020-8764-5. Dewey:945.091. LCCN:2004-270180.
Audience: **u,f.**

Gentile, Emilio **DG571.G3913 1996**
The Sacralization of Politics in Fascist Italy. Keith Botsford (Translator). Trade Cloth. Harvard University Press. Cambridge, MA. 1996. 222p. ISBN:0-674-78475-8, ISBN13: 978-0-674-78475-8. Dewey:945.091. LCCN:96-005074.
Audience: **u,f.** *Choice, 1997.*

Gregor, A. James **DG571.G734 2005**
Mussolini's Intellectuals: Fascist Social and Political Thought. Trade Cloth. Princeton University Press. Princeton, NJ. 2004. 288p. ISBN:0-691-12009-9, ISBN13: 978-0-691-12009-6. Dewey:320.53/3/094509042. LCCN:2004-049133.
Audience: **u,f.** *Choice, 2005.*

Ipsen, Carl **HB3599 .I67 1996**
Dictating Demography: The Problem of Population in Fascist Italy. Jan DeVries, Paul Johnson, Richard Smith & Keith Wrightson (Contribution by). Trade Cloth. Cambridge University Press. New York, NY. 1996. 301p. Cambridge Studies in Population, Economy and Society in Past Time, No. 28 ISBN:0-521-55452-7, ISBN13: 978-0-521-55452-7. Dewey:363.9/1/0945. LCCN:95-048989.
Audience: **u,f.** *Choice, 1997.*

Knox, MacGregor **DG572 .K56 1986**
Mussolini Unleashed, 1939-1941: Politics and Strategy in Fascist Italy's Last War. Cloth Text. Cambridge University Press. New York, NY. 1982. 400p. ISBN:0-521-23917-6, ISBN13: 978-0-521-23917-2. Dewey:945/.091/092. LCCN:81-038508.
Audience: **u,f.**

Passerini, Luisa **HD6957.I8T8**
Fascism in Popular Memory: The Cultural Experience of the Turin Working Class. Robert Lumley & Jude Bloomfield (Translators). Trade Cloth. Cambridge University Press. New York, NY. 1987. 254p. Studies in Modern Capitalism ISBN:0-521-30290-0, ISBN13: 978-0-521-30290-6. Dewey:305.5/62/094512. LCCN:86-017179.
Audience: **u,f.** *Choice, 1987.*

Pollard, John F. **DG499.V3**
Vatican and Italian Fascism, 1929-32: A Study in Conflict. Trade Paper. Cambridge University Press. New York, NY. 2005. 255p. ISBN:0-521-02366-1, ISBN13: 978-0-521-02366-5. Dewey:327.45045/634.
Audience: **g,l,u,f.**

Slaughter, Jane **D802.I8S53 1997**
Women and the Italian Resistance, 1943-45. Trade Cloth. Arden Press, Inc. Denver, CO. 1997. 201p. Women and Modern Revolution Ser. ISBN:0-912869-13-5, ISBN13: 978-0-912869-13-1. Dewey:940.53/45. LCCN:97-004937.
Audience: **g,l,u,f.** *Choice, 1998.*

Stone, Marla **NX750.I8S76 1998**
The Patron State: Culture and Politics in Fascist Italy. Cloth Text. Princeton University Press. Princeton, NJ. 1998. 360p. ISBN:0-691-02969-5, ISBN13: 978-0-691-02969-6. Dewey:700/.945/09043. LCCN:98-009449.
Audience: **u,f.** *Choice, 1999.*

Willson, Perry R. **HQ1236.5.I8W54 2002**
Peasant Women and Politics in Fascist Italy: The Massaie Rurali Section of the PNF. Paper over Boards. Routledge. New York, NY. 2002. 240p. ISBN:0-415-29170-4, ISBN13: 978-0-415-29170-5. Dewey:324.245/02. LCCN:2002-074322.
Audience: **u,f.**

Italy > By Period > Postwar Italy

Brucker, Gene **DG737 .B7351 1998**
Florence: The Golden Age, 1138-1737. Trade Paper. University of California Press. Berkeley, CA. 1998. 278p. ISBN:0-520-21522-2, ISBN13: 978-0-520-21522-1. Dewey:945/.51. LCCN:2004-268176.
Audience: **u,f.**

Crouzet-Pavan, Elisabeth **DG676.C8813 2002**
Venice Triumphant: The Horizons of a Myth. Lydia G. Cochrane (Translator). Trade Cloth. Johns Hopkins University Press. Baltimore, MD. 2002. 424p. ISBN:0-8018-6958-7, ISBN13: 978-0-8018-6958-7. Dewey:945/.31. LCCN:2001-006617.
Audience: **u,f.** *Choice, 2003.*

Davis, Robert C. & Marvin, Garry R. **DG674.2 .D34 2004**
Venice, the Tourist Maze: A Cultural Critique of the World's Most Touristed City. Trade Cloth. University of California Press. Berkeley, CA. 2004. 368p. ISBN:0-520-23803-6, ISBN13: 978-0-520-23803-9. Dewey:945/.31. LCCN:2003-007854.
Audience: **g,l,u,f.** *Choice, 2005.*

Ginsborg, Paul **JN5451**
A History of Contemporary Italy: Society and Politics, 1943-1988. Trade Paper. Palgrave Macmillan. New York, NY. 2003. 592p. ISBN:1-4039-6153-0, ISBN13: 978-1-4039-6153-2. Dewey:945/.0928.
Audience: **u,f.**

Krautheimer, Richard **DG811.K7 2000**
Rome: Profile of a City, 312-1308. Marvin Trachtenberg (Foreword by). Trade Paper. Princeton University Press. Princeton, NJ. 2000. 418p. ISBN:0-691-04961-0, ISBN13: 978-0-691-04961-8. Dewey:945/.632. LCCN:99-053723.
Audience: **g,l,u,f.** B

Lancaster, Jordan **DG846**
In the Shadow of Vesuvius: A Cultural History of Naples. Saddle Stitched, Cloth over Boards, Dust Jacket. I. B. Tauris & Company, Ltd. London, 2005. 288p. ISBN:1-85043-764-5, ISBN13: 978-1-85043-764-2. Dewey:945/.73. LCCN:2005-299706.
Audience: **g,l,u,f.** *Choice, 2006.*

Martin, John **DG675.6.V39 2000**
Venice Reconsidered: The History and Civilization of an Italian City-State, 1297-1797. Dennis Romano (Editor). Trade Cloth. Johns Hopkins University Press. Baltimore, MD. 2000. 560p. ISBN:0-8018-6312-0, ISBN13: 978-0-8018-6312-7. Dewey:945/.31. LCCN:00-021349.
Audience: **u,f.**

Miller, James Edward **DG738**
Politics in a Museum: Governing Post-War Florence. Trade Cloth. Greenwood Publishing Group, Inc. Portsmouth, NH. 2002. 280p. Italian and Italian-American Studies ISBN:0-275-97231-3, ISBN13: 978-0-275-97231-8. Dewey:945/.51092. LCCN:2001-059084.
Audience: **u,f.** *Choice, 2003.*

Painter, Borden **DG813.P28 2005**
Mussolini's Rome: Rebuilding the Eternal City. Saddle Stitched, Cloth over Boards, Dust Jacket. Palgrave Macmillan. New York, NY. 2005. 224p. Italian and Italian American Studies ISBN:1-4039-6604-4, ISBN13: 978-1-4039-6604-9. Dewey:945/.632091. LCCN:2004-043153.
Audience: **g,l,u,f.**

Putnam, Robert D., et al. **JN5477.R35**
Making Democracy Work: Civic Traditions in Modern Italy. Robert Leonardi & Raffaella Y. Nanetti (Authors). Trade Paper. Princeton University Press. Princeton, NJ. 1994. 274p. ISBN:0-691-03738-8, ISBN13: 978-0-691-03738-7. Dewey:306.2/0945/09045.
Audience: **g,l,u,f.** *Choice, 1993.*

Schneider, Jane & Schneider, Peter T. **HV6453.I83 M376432**
Reversible Destiny: Mafia, Antimafia, and the Struggle for Palermo. Trade Cloth. University of California Press. Berkeley, CA. 2003. 364p. ISBN:0-520-22100-1, ISBN13: 978-0-520-22100-0. Dewey:364.1/06/0945823. LCCN:2002-013905.
Audience: **g,l,u,f.** *Choice, 2003.*

Netherlands (Low Countries) > General Histories

Blom, J. C. & Lamberts, E. (Editors) **DH131.G4713 1998**
History of the Low Countries. James C. Kennedy (Translator). Trade Cloth. Berghahn Books, Inc. New York, NY. 1999. 492p. ISBN:1-57181-084-6, ISBN13: 978-1-57181-084-7. Dewey:949.3. LCCN:98-022708.
Audience: **g,l,u,f.** *Choice, 2000.*

Hooker, Mark T. **DJ111**
The History of Holland. Cloth Text. Greenwood Publishing Group, Inc. Portsmouth, NH. 1999. 264p. The Greenwood Histories of the Modern Nations Ser. ISBN:0-313-30658-3, ISBN13: 978-0-313-30658-7. Dewey:949.2. LCCN:98-051895.
Audience: **g,l,u,f.**

Netherlands (Low Countries) > By Period > Early Modern (to 1780)

De Vries, Jan & Van der Woude, Ad **HC324 .V72 1997**
The First Modern Economy: Success, Failure, and Perseverance of the Dutch Economy, 1500-1815. Trade Cloth. Cambridge University Press. New York, NY. 1997. 791p. ISBN:0-521-57061-1, ISBN13: 978-0-521-57061-9. Dewey:330.9/492. LCCN:96-003298.
Audience: **u,f.** *Choice, 1998.*

Geyl, Pieter **DJ156**
The Revolt of the Netherlands, 1555 to 1609. Ed. 2. Paper Text. Barnes & Noble Books-Imports. Lanham, MD. 1980. ISBN:0-06-492383-5, ISBN13: 978-0-06-492383-5. Dewey:949.2/03. LCCN:79-053235.
Audience: **u,f.**

Huizinga, Johan H. **DJ71**
Dutch Civilization in the Seventeenth Century. Pieter Geyl & F. W. Hugenholtz (Editors), Arnold Pomerans (Translator). Trade Cloth. Continuum International Publishing Group, Ltd. London, 1968. ISBN:0-8044-1411-4, ISBN13: 978-0-8044-1411-1. Dewey:914.92/03. LCCN:68-022778.
Audience: **u,f.**

Israel, Jonathan I. **DH186**
The Dutch Republic: Its Rise, Greatness, and Fall 1477-1806. Paper Text. Oxford University Press, Inc. New York, NY. 1998. 1,262p. Oxford History of Early Modern Europe Ser. ISBN:0-19-820734-4, ISBN13: 978-0-19-820734-4. Dewey:949.2/.02.
Audience: **u,f.** *Choice, 1995.*

Israel, Jonathan Irvine **D231.I55 1997**
Conflicts of Empires: Spain, the Low Countries and the Struggle for World Supremacy, 1585-1713. Trade Cloth. Continuum International Publishing Group, Ltd. London, 1997. 504p. ISBN:1-85285-161-9, ISBN13: 978-1-85285-161-3. Dewey:940. LCCN:97-016021.
Audience: **u,f.** *Choice, 1998.*

North, Michael **ND646**
Art and Commerce in the Dutch Golden Age: A Social History of Seventeenth-Century Netherlandish Painting. Catherine Hill (Translator). Trade Paper. Yale University Press. Cumberland, RI. 1999. 176p. ISBN:0-300-08131-6, ISBN13: 978-0-300-08131-2. Dewey:759.9492/09/032. LCCN:96-046135.
Audience: **g,l,u,f.** *Choice, 1997.*

Parker, Geoffrey **DH186.5**
The Dutch Revolt. Trade Paper. Penguin Group (USA) Inc. New York, NY. 1989. 336p. ISBN:0-14-055233-2, ISBN13: 978-0-14-055233-1. Dewey:949.2/03.
Audience: **g,l,u,f.**

Parker, Geoffrey **DH186.5.P28 2004**
The Army of Flanders and the Spanish Road, 1567-1659: The Logistics of Spanish Victory and Defeat in the Low Countries' Wars. Ed. 2. John Elliott, Olwen Hufton, H. G. Koenigsberger & H. M. Scott (Contribution by). Trade Cloth. Cambridge University Press. New York, NY. 2004. 324p. Cambridge Studies in Early Modern History Ser. ISBN:0-521-83600-X, ISBN13: 978-0-521-83600-5. Dewey:949.2/03. LCCN:2005-279821.
Audience: **u,f.**

Price, J. L. **DJ401.H6P75 1994**
Holland and the Dutch Republic in the Seventeenth Century: The Politics of Particularism. Cloth Text. Oxford University Press, Inc. New York, NY. 1994. 320p. ISBN:0-19-820383-7, ISBN13: 978-0-19-820383-4. Dewey:949.2/3. LCCN:93-027130.
Audience: **u,f.** *Choice, 1995.*

Rowen, Herbert H. **DJ182**
The Princes of Orange: The Stadholders in the Dutch Republic. John Elliot, Olwen Hufton, H. G. Koenigsberger, H. M. Scott & John Elliott (Contribution by). Trade Paper. Cambridge University Press. New York, NY. 1990. 264p. Studies in Early Modern History ISBN:0-521-39653-0, ISBN13: 978-0-521-39653-0. Dewey:949.2/04.
Audience: **u,f.** *Choice, 1989.*

Schama, Simon **DJ182**
The Embarrassment of Riches: An Interpretation of Dutch Culture in the Golden Age. Trade Paper. Knopf Publishing Group. New York, NY. 1997. 720p. ISBN:0-679-78124-2, ISBN13: 978-0-679-78124-0. Dewey:949.2/04.
Audience: **g,u,f.** *Choice, 1987.*

Sicking, Louis **DJ135.S52 2004**
Neptune and the Netherlands: State, Economy, and War at Sea in the Renaissance. Trade Cloth. Brill Academic Publishers. Leiden, 2004. xxxii, 552p. History of Warfare Ser., Vol. 23 ISBN:90-04-13850-1, ISBN13: 978-90-04-13850-6. Dewey:359/.009492. LCCN:2004-043504.
Audience: **u,f.** *Choice, 2005.*

Tracy, James D. **DJ401.H64T73 1990**
Holland under Habsburg Rule, 1506-1566: The Formation of a Body Politic. Trade Cloth. University of California Press. Berkeley, CA. 1990. 320p. ISBN:0-520-06882-3, ISBN13: 978-0-520-06882-7. LCCN:90-010856.
Audience: **u,f.** *Choice, 1991.*

Van Deursen, A. **HN513.D4813 1991**
Plain Lives in a Golden Age: Popular Culture, Religion and Society in Seventeenth-Century Holland. Maarten Ultee (Translator). Cloth Text. Cambridge University Press. New York, NY. 1991. 418p. ISBN:0-521-36606-2, ISBN13: 978-0-521-36606-9. Dewey:306/.09492/09032. LCCN:90-001684.
Audience: **g,l,u,f.** *Choice, 1992.*

Wedgwood, Cicely V. **DH188.W7**
William the Silent: William of Nassau, Prince of Orange, 1533-1584. Cloth Text. Brill Academic Publishers, Inc. Boston, MA. 1960. 256p. ISBN:0-224-60761-8, ISBN13: 978-0-224-60761-2. Dewey:949.2030924.
Audience: **g,l,u,f.**

Zumthor, Paul **DJ172**
Daily Life in Rembrandt's Holland. Simon W. Taylor (Translator). Trade Cloth. Stanford University Press. Palo Alto, CA. 1993. 374p. ISBN:0-8047-2200-5, ISBN13: 978-0-8047-2200-1. Dewey:949.2/04. LCCN:93-027947.
Audience: **g,l,u,f.**

Netherlands (Low Countries) > By Period > Modern (1780-)

Kossman, E. H. **DJ202**
The Low Countries, 1780-1940. Trade Cloth. Oxford University Press, Inc. New York, NY. 1978. 790p. History of Modern Europe Ser. ISBN:0-19-822108-8, ISBN13: 978-0-19-822108-1. Dewey:949.2. LCCN:77-030291.
Audience: **g,u,f.**

Sander, Gordon **D805.N4**
The Frank Family That Survived. UK-B Format Paperback. Random House. London, 2005. 320p. ISBN:0-09-944329-5, ISBN13: 978-0-09-944329-2. Dewey:940.53180922.
Audience: **g,l,u,f.** *Choice, 2005.*

Schama, Simon **DJ182**
Patriots and Liberators: Revolution in the Netherlands, 1780-1813. Trade Paper. Knopf Publishing Group. New York, NY. 1992. 768p. ISBN:0-679-72949-6, ISBN13: 978-0-679-72949-5. Dewey:949.2/04.
Audience: **g,u,f.**

Warmbrunn, Werner **DJ287 .W3**
The Dutch under German Occupation, 1940-1945. Trade Cloth. Stanford University Press. Palo Alto, CA. 1963. viii, 338p. ISBN:0-8047-0152-0, ISBN13: 978-0-8047-0152-5. Dewey:940.5337.
Audience: **g,u,f.**

Netherlands (Low Countries) > Belgium, 1830 to present

Boudart, Marina (Editor), et al. **DH418.M6 1990**
Modern Belgium. Michel Boudart & Rene Bryssinck (Editors).

Trade Cloth. Society for the Promotion of Science & Scholarship, Inc. Palo Alto, CA. 1990. 592p. ISBN:0-930664-10-8, ISBN13: 978-0-930664-10-7. Dewey:949.304. LCCN:90-061813.
Audience: **u,f.** *Choice, 1991.*

Conway, Martin **DH689.D4.C66 1993**
Collaboration in Belgium: Leon Degrelle and the Rexist Movement, 1940-1944. Cloth over Boards. Yale University Press. Cumberland, RI. 1993. 384p. ISBN:0-300-05500-5, ISBN13: 978-0-300-05500-9. Dewey:949.3042092. LCCN:93-010870.
Audience: **g,u,f.** *Choice, 1994.*

Cook, Bernard A. **DH521.C66 2002**
Belgium: A History. Trade Paper. Peter Lang Publishing, Inc. New York, NY. 2005. xviii, 205p. Studies in Modern European History, Vol. 50 ISBN:0-8204-5824-4, ISBN13: 978-0-8204-5824-3. Dewey:949.3. LCCN:2001-050655.
Audience: **g,l,u,f.** *Choice, 2003.*

Deprez, Kas & Vos, Louis (Editors) **DH491.N325 1998**
Nationalism in Belgium: Shifting Identities, 1780-1995. Trade Cloth. Palgrave Macmillan. New York, NY. 1998. 299p. ISBN:0-312-21249-6, ISBN13: 978-0-312-21249-0. Dewey:949.3. LCCN:97-038683.
Audience: **u,f.** *Choice, 1999.*

Hermans, T. J. (Editor) **DH491.F48 1992**
The Flemish Movement: A Documentary History 1780-1980. Cloth Text. Continuum International Publishing Group, Ltd. London, 1992. 360p. ISBN:0-485-11368-6, ISBN13: 978-0-485-11368-6. Dewey:949.3. LCCN:91-022810.
Audience: **u,f.** *Choice, 1992.*

Hochschild, Adam **DT655.H63 1998**
King Leopold's Ghost: A Story of Greed, Terror, and Heroism in Colonial Africa. Trade Cloth. Houghton Mifflin Company Trade & Reference Division. Boston, MA. 1998. 384p. ISBN:0-395-75924-2, ISBN13: 978-0-395-75924-0. Dewey:967.5/102. LCCN:98-016813.
Audience: **g,l,u,f.** *Choice, 1999.*

Keyes, Roger **DH687**
Outrageous fortune: the tragedy of Leopold III of the Belgians, 1901-1941. London: Secker & Warburg. 1984. ISBN:0-436-23320-7, ISBN13: 978-0-436-23320-3.
Audience: **u,f.**

Kieft, David Owen **DH566**
Belgium's Return to Neutrality: An Essay in the Frustrations of Small Power Diplomacy. Trade Cloth. Oxford University Press, Inc. New York, NY. 1972. xv, 201p. ISBN:0-19-821497-9, ISBN13: 978-0-19-821497-7. Dewey:327.493. LCCN:72-183279.
Audience: **u,f.**

Rooney, John W. Jr. **DH651**
Revolt in the Netherlands: Brussels, 1830. David H. Pinkney (Introduction by), John W. Rooney (Preface by). Paper Text. Coronado Press, Inc. Lawrence, KS. 1982. 250p. ISBN:0-87291-156-X, ISBN13: 978-0-87291-156-7. Dewey:949.303.
Audience: **u,f.**

Strikwerda, Carl **DH671.S17 1997**
A House Divided: Catholics, Socialists, and Flemish Nationalists in Nineteenth Century Belgium. Book, Other. Rowman & Littlefield Publishers, Inc. Lanham, MD. 1998. 420p. ISBN:0-8476-8526-8, ISBN13: 978-0-8476-8526-4. Dewey:320.9493/09/034. LCCN:97-018816.
Audience: **u,f.** *Choice, 1998.*

Warmbrunn, Werner **D802.B4.W37 1993**
The German Occupation of Belgium 1940-1944. Trade Cloth. Peter Lang Publishing, Inc. New York, NY. 1993. xv, 366p. American University Studies, Vol. 122:History ISBN:0-8204-1773-4, ISBN13: 978-0-8204-1773-8. Dewey:940.53/37. LCCN:91-035882.
Audience: **g,u,f.** *Choice, 1994.*

Zuckerman, Larry **D615.Z83 2003**
The Rape of Belgium: The Untold Story of World War I. Trade Cloth. New York University Press. New York, NY. 2004. 350p. ISBN:0-8147-9704-0, ISBN13: 978-0-8147-9704-4. Dewey:940.3/493. LCCN:2003-015217.
Audience: **g,u,f.** *Choice, 2004.*

Central and Eastern Europe > General Histories and Geographies

Frucht, Richard (Editor) **DJK6.E53 2000**
Encyclopedia of Eastern Europe: From the Congress of Vienna to the Fall of Communism. Trade Cloth. Garland Publishing, Inc. New York, NY. 2000. 800p. Reference Library of Social Science, Vol. 751 ISBN:0-8153-0092-1, ISBN13: 978-0-8153-0092-2. Dewey:947/.0003. LCCN:00-021517.
Audience: **g,l,u,f.** *Choice, 2000.*

Halecki, Oscar **DK4249.5.H35 1991**
Jadwiga of Anjou and the Rise of East Central Europe. Thaddeus V. Gromada (Editor). Trade Cloth. Eastern European Monographs. Bradenton, FL. 1991. 400p. ISBN:0-88033-206-9, ISBN13: 978-0-88033-206-4. Dewey:943.8/023/092. LCCN:91-061035.
Audience: **u,f.** *Choice, 1992.*

Halecki, Oskar **DR36.H3**
Borderlands of Western Civilization: A History of East Central Europe. Paper Text. Textbook Publishers. Temecula, CA. 2003. xvi, 503p. ISBN:0-7581-4683-3, ISBN13: 978-0-7581-4683-0. Dewey:940.
Audience: **u,f.**

Johnson, Lonnie R. **DAW1038.J64 2001**
Central Europe: Enemies, Neighbors, Friends. Ed. 2. Paper Text. Oxford University Press, Inc. New York, NY. 2001. 368p. ISBN:0-19-514825-8, ISBN13: 978-0-19-514825-1. Dewey:943. LCCN:2001-021342.
Audience: **g,l,u,f.** *Choice, 1997.*

Magocsi, Paul Robert **G1881**
Historical Atlas of Central Europe. Ed. 2. Trade Cloth. University of Washington Press. Seattle, WA. 2003. 288p. History of East Central Europe Ser., 1 ISBN:0-295-98146-6, ISBN13: 978-0-295-98146-8. Dewey:911/.43. LCCN:2001-027907.
Audience: **g,l,u,f.** *Choice, 2003.*

Snyder, Timothy **DJK48.5.S66 2003**
The Reconstruction of Nations: Poland, Ukraine, Lithuania, Belarus, 1569-1999. Cloth over Boards. Yale University Press. Cumberland, RI. 2003. 384p. ISBN:0-300-09569-4, ISBN13: 978-0-300-09569-2. Dewey:947.084. LCCN:2002-066356.
Audience: **g,u,f.** *Choice, 2003.*

Turncock, David **GF645.E92T868 2002**
Human Geography of East-Central Europe. Paper over Boards. Routledge. New York, NY. 2002. 448p. ISBN:0-415-12191-4, ISBN13: 978-0-415-12191-0. Dewey:304.2/0943. LCCN:2002-068016.
Audience: **g,u,f.** *Choice, 2003.*

Wandycz, Piotr Stefan **DJK38.W36 2001**
The Price of Freedom: A History of East Central Europe from the Middle Ages to the Present. Ed. 2. Trade Paper. Routledge. New York, NY. 2001. 360p. ISBN:0-415-25491-4, ISBN13: 978-0-415-25491-5. Dewey:943. LCCN:00-054873.
Audience: **g,l,u,f.**

Wolff, Larry **JN6581**
Inventing Eastern Europe: The Map of Civilization on the Mind of the Enlightenment. Trade Paper. Stanford University Press. Palo Alto, CA. 1996. 435p. ISBN:0-8047-2702-3, ISBN13: 978-0-8047-2702-0. Dewey:306.2/0947. LCCN:93-032774.
Audience: **u,f.** *Choice, 1995.*

Central and Eastern Europe > By Period > 20th Century

Crampton, R. J. **DJK38.C73 1997**
Eastern Europe in the Twentieth Century and After. Ed. 2. Paper over Boards. Routledge. New York, NY. 1997. 532p. ISBN:0-415-16422-2, ISBN13: 978-0-415-16422-1. Dewey:947.084. LCCN:97-000665.
Audience: **g,l,u,f.**

Eberhardt, Piotr **HB3582.7.A3**
Ethnic Groups and Population Changes in Twentieth-Century Central-Eastern Europe : History, Data, and Analysis. Armonk, N.Y. : M.E. Sharpe. 2003. ISBN:0-7656-0665-8, ISBN13: 978-0-7656-0665-5.
Audience: **u,f.**

Petersen, Roger Dale **DJK26.P48 2002**
Understanding Ethnic Violence: Fear, Hatred, and Resentment in Twentieth-Century Eastern Europe. Cloth Text. Cambridge University Press. New York, NY. 2002. 312p. Cambridge Studies in Comparative Politics ISBN:0-521-80986-X, ISBN13: 978-0-521-80986-3. Dewey:305.8/00947/0904. LCCN:2002-017403.
Audience: **g,l,u,f.** *Choice, 2003.*

Pittaway, Mark **DJK50**
Eastern Europe, 1939-2000. Cloth Text. Oxford University Press, Inc. New York, NY. 2004. 224p. A Hodder Arnold Publication ISBN:0-340-76220-9, ISBN13: 978-0-340-76220-2. Dewey:947.0009045. LCCN:2004-541429.
Audience: **g,u,f.** *Choice, 2005.*

White, Stephen (Editor), et al. **DJK51**
Developments in Central and East European Politics 3. Judy Batt & Paul G. Lewis (Editors). Trade Cloth. Duke University Press. Durham, NC. 2003. ISBN:0-8223-3082-2, ISBN13: 978-0-8223-3082-0. Dewey:320.94/09171/7.
Audience: **u,f.** *Choice, 2004.*

Central and Eastern Europe > By Period > Interwar Era

Kofman, Jan **HC244.K595 1997**
Economic Nationalism and Development: Central and Eastern Europe Between the Two World Wars. Trade Cloth. Westview Press. Boulder, CO. 1997. 256p. ISBN:0-8133-8725-6, ISBN13: 978-0-8133-8725-3. Dewey:382.7/0943. LCCN:97-008090.
Audience: **l,u.** *Choice, 1998.*

Rothschild, Joseph **DJK4.S93 VOL. 9**
East Central Europe Between the Two World Wars. Trade Paper. University of Washington Press. Seattle, WA. 2004. "xvii, 420"p. A History of East Central Europe Ser., Vol. 9 ISBN:0-295-95350-0, ISBN13: 978-0-295-95350-2. Dewey:943. LCCN:74-008327.
Audience: **g,u,f.**

Seton-Watson, Hugh **DJK49.S47 1986**
Eastern Europe Between the Wars: 1918-1941. Paper Text. Westview Press. Boulder, CO. 1986. 425p. Encore Edition Ser. ISBN:0-8133-7092-2, ISBN13: 978-0-8133-7092-7. Dewey:947. LCCN:85-051672.
Audience: **l,u.**

Central and Eastern Europe > By Period > 1945-1989

Connelly, John **LC178.G29C66 2000**
Captive University: The Sovietization of East German, Czech and Polish Higher Education, 1945-1956. Trade Paper. University of North Carolina Press. Chapel Hill, NC. 2000. 456p. ISBN:0-8078-4865-4, ISBN13: 978-0-8078-4865-4. Dewey:379.431. LCCN:00-030262.
Audience: **u,f.**

Deak, Istvan (Editor), et al. **D802.E9P65 2000**
The Politics of Retribution in Europe: World War II and Its Aftermath. Jan T. Gross & Tony Judt (Editors). Cloth Text. Princeton University Press. Princeton, NJ. 2000. 368p. ISBN:0-691-00953-8, ISBN13: 978-0-691-00953-7. Dewey:940.53163. LCCN:99-069400.
Audience: **g,u,f.**

Naimark, Norman & Gibianskii, Leonid (Editors) **DK267**
Establishment of Communist Regimes in Eastern Europe, 1944-1949. Trade Paper. Westview Press. Boulder, CO. 1998. 328p. ISBN:0-8133-3534-5, ISBN13: 978-0-8133-3534-6. Dewey:947/.0842.
Audience: **g,u,f.**

Rothschild, Joseph **DJK50.R67 2000**
Return to Diversity: A Political History of East Central Europe since World War II. Ed. 3. Paper Text. Oxford University Press, Inc. New York, NY. 1999. 352p. ISBN:0-19-511993-2, ISBN13: 978-0-19-511993-0. Dewey:949. LCCN:98-029737.
Audience: **u,f.** *Choice, 1989.*

Swain, Geoffrey & Swain, Nigel **HX240.7.A6S93 2003**
Eastern Europe Since 1945. Ed. 3. Trade Paper. Palgrave Macmillan. New York, NY. 2003. 224p. Making of the Modern World Ser. ISBN:1-4039-0417-0, ISBN13: 978-1-4039-0417-1. Dewey:320.94709045. LCCN:2003-041021.
Audience: **g,l,u,f.**

Tismaneanu, Vladimir **DK40**
Reinventing Politics: Eastern Europe from Stalin to Havel. Trade Paper. Simon & Schuster. New York, NY. 2000. 320p. ISBN:0-7432-1282-7, ISBN13: 978-0-7432-1282-3. Dewey:947. LCCN:91-042878.
Audience: **g,l,u,f.**

Central and Eastern Europe > By Period > 1989-

Adam, Jan **HX240.7.A6A33 1996**
Why Did the Socialist System Collapse in Central and East European Countries?: The Case of Poland, the Former Czechoslovakia and Hungary. Cloth over Boards. Palgrave Macmillan. New York, NY. 1996. 258p. ISBN:0-312-12879-7, ISBN13: 978-0-312-12879-1. Dewey:335.43/0943. LCCN:95-034283.
Audience: **g,u,f.** *Choice, 1996.*

Ash, Timothy Garton **DK274**
The Magic Lantern: The Revolution of '89 Witnessed in Warsaw, Budapest, Berlin and Prague. Trade Paper. David McKay Company, Inc. New York, NY. 1993. 176p. ISBN:0-679-74048-1, ISBN13: 978-0-679-74048-3. Dewey:947.085. LCCN:92-050611.
Audience: **g,l,u,f.** *Choice, 1991.*

Kenney, Padraic **DJK51.K465 2002**
A Carnival of Revolution: Central Europe 1989. Trade Cloth. Princeton University Press. Princeton, NJ. 2002. 352p. ISBN:0-691-05028-7, ISBN13: 978-0-691-05028-7. Dewey:943/.0009/048. LCCN:2001-036866.
Audience: **g,l,u,f.** *Choice, 2003, 2002.*

Levesque, Jacques **DJK45.S65L4813 1997**
Enigma of 1989: The U. S. S. R. and the Liberation of Eastern Europe. Keith Martin (Translator). Trade Cloth. University of California Press. Berkeley, CA. 1997. 275p. ISBN:0-520-20631-2, ISBN13: 978-0-520-20631-1. Dewey:327.47047/09048. LCCN:96-052426.
Audience: **g,u,f.** *Choice, 1998.*

Rosenberg, Tina **DK288**
The Haunted Land: Facing Europe's Ghosts after Communism. Trade Paper. Knopf Publishing Group. New York, NY. 1996. 464p. ISBN:0-679-74499-1, ISBN13: 978-0-679-74499-3. Dewey:947/.0854.
Audience: **g,l,u,f.** *Choice, 1995.*

Saxonberg, Steven **HX240.7.A6**
Fall: A Comparative Study of the End of Communism in Czechoslovakia, East Germany, Hungary and Poland. Cloth Text. Gordon & Breach Publishing Group. New York, NY. 2000. 452p. International Studies in Global Change ISBN:90-5823-097-X, ISBN13: 978-90-5823-097-3. Dewey:320.532.
Audience: **g,l,u,f.** *Choice, 2001.*

Stokes, Gale **DJK50.F76 1996**
From Stalinism to Pluralism: A Documentary History of Eastern Europe since 1945. Ed. 2. Paper Text. Oxford University Press, Inc. New York, NY. 1996. 304p. ISBN:0-19-509446-8, ISBN13: 978-0-19-509446-6. Dewey:947/.084. LCCN:95-005924.
Audience: **g,l,u,f.** *Choice, 1991.*

Stokes, Gale **DJK51**
The Walls Came Tumbling Down: The Collapse of Communism in Eastern Europe. Paper Text. Oxford University Press, Inc. New York, NY. 1993. 328p. ISBN:0-19-506645-6, ISBN13: 978-0-19-506645-6. Dewey:940/.09717. LCCN:92-044862.
Audience: **g,l,u,f.** *Choice, 1994.*

Verdery, Katherine **HX373.5.V47 1996**
What Was Socialism, and What Comes Next?: Princeton Studies in Culture - Power - History. Cloth Text. Princeton University Press. Princeton, NJ. 1996. 256p. ISBN:0-691-01133-8, ISBN13: 978-0-691-01133-2. Dewey:338.9498. LCCN:95-032123.
Audience: **u,f.** *Choice, 1996.*

Russia

Goldman, Wendy Z. **KLA540 .G65 1993**
Women, the State and Revolution: Soviet Family Policy and Social Life, 1917-1936. Trade Paper. Cambridge University Press. New York, NY. 1993. 363p. Cambridge Russian, Soviet and Post-Soviet Studies, No. 90 ISBN:0-521-45816-1, ISBN13: 978-0-521-45816-0. Dewey:305.420947. LCCN:92-047481.
Audience: **u,f.** *Choice, 1994.*

Grayzel, Susan R. **D639.W7G73 2002**
Women and the First World War. Trade Paper. Longman Publishing. Boston, MA. 2002. 216p. ISBN:0-582-41876-3, ISBN13: 978-0-582-41876-9. Dewey:940.3/082.
Audience: **g,l,u,f.**

Higonnet, Margaret R. (Editor) **D640.A2N87 2001**
Nurses at the Front: Writing the Wounds of the Great War. Trade Paper. Northeastern University Press. Boston, MA. 2001. 161p. ISBN:1-55553-484-8, ISBN13: 978-1-55553-484-4. Dewey:940.4/7573/092. LCCN:2001-018013.
Audience: **g,l,u,f.**

Holloway, David **UA770.H632 1994**
Stalin and the Bomb: The Soviet Union and Atomic Energy, 1939-56. Cloth over Boards. Yale University Press. Cumberland, RI. 1994. 480p. ISBN:0-300-06056-4, ISBN13: 978-0-300-06056-0. Dewey:355.8/25119. LCCN:94-008216.
Audience: **u,f.** *Choice, 1995.*

Rezun, Miron **Q127**
Science, Technology, and Ecopolitics in the U. S. S. R. Trade Cloth. Greenwood Publishing Group, Inc. Portsmouth, NH. 1996. 240p. ISBN:0-275-95383-1, ISBN13: 978-0-275-95383-6. Dewey:306.4/5/0947. LCCN:95-022010.
Audience: **u,f.** *Choice, 1996.*

Russia > General History

Brown, Archie (Editor), et al. **DK14.C35 1994**
The Cambridge Encyclopedia of Russia: And the Former Soviet Union. Ed. 2. Michael C. Kaser & Gerry Smith (Editors). Cloth Text. Cambridge University Press. New York, NY. 1994. 622p. Cambridge World Encyclopedias Ser. ISBN:0-521-35593-1, ISBN13: 978-0-521-35593-3. Dewey:947/.003. LCCN:94-024668.
Audience: **g,l,u,f.** *Choice, 1995.*

Dukes, Paul **DK40.D84 1998**
A History of Russia: Medieval, Modern, Contemporary, c. 882-1996. Ed. 3. Trade Cloth. Duke University Press. Durham, NC. 1997. 430p. ISBN:0-8223-2082-7, ISBN13: 978-0-8223-2082-1. Dewey:947. LCCN:97-015047.
Audience: **g,l,u,f.**

Hosking, Geoffrey **DK40.H66 2001**
Russia and the Russians: A History. Trade Paper. Harvard University Press. Cambridge, MA. 2003. 768p. ISBN:0-674-01114-7, ISBN13: 978-0-674-01114-4. Dewey:947. LCCN:00-065085.
Audience: **g,u,f.** *Choice, 2001.*

Lawrence, John T. **DK40 .L38 1993**
The History of Russia. Ed. 7. Trade Paper. Penguin Group (USA) Inc. New York, NY. 1993. 368p. ISBN:0-452-01084-5, ISBN13: 978-0-452-01084-0. Dewey:947. LCCN:92-044548.
Audience: **g,l,u,f.**

Malia, Martin **DK32.M18 1999**
Russia under Western Eyes: From the Bronze Horseman to the Lenin Mausoleum. Trade Cloth. Harvard University Press. Cambridge, MA. 1999. 528p. ISBN:0-674-78120-1, ISBN13: 978-0-674-78120-7. Dewey:947. LCCN:98-039769.
Audience: **u,f.** *Choice, 1999.*

Milner-Gulland, Robin R. **DK32.M626 1997**
The Russians. Trade Cloth. Blackwell Publishing, Inc. Malden, MA. 1997. 272p. The Peoples of Europe Ser. ISBN:0-631-18805-3, ISBN13: 978-0-631-18805-6. Dewey:947. LCCN:96-051542.
Audience: **g,l,u,f.** *Choice, 1998.*

Moss, Walter **DK40.M67 1997**
A History of Russia since 1855. Trade Paper. McGraw-Hill Higher Education. Burr Ridge, IL. 1996. 576p. History of Russia Ser., Vol. 2 ISBN:0-07-043482-4, ISBN13: 978-0-07-043482-0. Dewey:947. LCCN:96-034845.
Audience: **g,l,u,f.** *Choice, 1997.*

Moss, Walter G. **DK40**
History of Russia: To 1917. Paper Text. McGraw-Hill Higher Education. Burr Ridge, IL. 2001. 622p. ISBN:0-07-253624-1, ISBN13: 978-0-07-253624-9. Dewey:947.
Audience: **g,l,u,f.**

Obolonsky, Alexander V. **DK61.O2613 2003**
The Drama of Russian Political History: System Against Individuality. Vincent Ostrom (Foreword by). Trade Cloth. Texas A&M University Press. College Station, TX. 2002. 288p. Eastern European Studies, 19 ISBN:1-58544-224-0, ISBN13: 978-1-58544-224-9. Dewey:947. LCCN:2002-012708.
Audience: **u,f.**

Poe, Marshall T. **DK49.P64 2003**
The Russian Moment in World History: An Essay in Historical. Trade Cloth. Princeton University Press. Princeton, NJ. 2003. 144p. ISBN:0-691-11612-1, ISBN13: 978-0-691-11612-9. Dewey:947/.001. LCCN:2002-044717.
Audience: **g,l,u,f.** *Choice, 2004.*

Pokrovskii, M. N. **DK5.P653 1970**
Russia in World History; Selected Essays. Trade Cloth. University of Michigan Press. Chicago, IL. 1970. 241p. ISBN:0-472-08737-1, ISBN13: 978-0-472-08737-2. Dewey:947.084/1. LCCN:75-107981.
Audience: **u,f.**

Riasanovsky, Nicholas Valentine & Steinberg, Mark D. **DK40.R5 2004**
A History of Russia. Ed. 7. Trade Paper. Oxford University Press, Inc. New York, NY. 2004. 792p. ISBN:0-19-515394-4, ISBN13: 978-0-19-515394-1. Dewey:947. LCCN:2004-049594.
Audience: **g,u,f.**

Service, Robert **DK266.S494 2005**
A History of Modern Russia: From Nicholas II to Vladimir Putin. Ed. 2. Trade Paper. Harvard University Press. Cambridge, MA. 2005. 704p. ISBN:0-674-01801-X, ISBN13: 978-0-674-01801-3. Dewey:947.084. LCCN:2004-060610.
Audience: **g,u,f.**

Wheatcroft, Stephen G. (Editor) **DK38.C38 2002**
Challenging Traditional Views of Russian History. Cloth over Boards. Palgrave Macmillan. New York, NY. 2002. 264p. Studies in Russian and East European History and Society ISBN:0-333-75461-1, ISBN13: 978-0-333-75461-0. Dewey:947/.007/2. LCCN:2001-059829.
Audience: **u,f.**

Russia > Primary Source Collections

Cracraft, James **DK127.M35 1993**
Major Problems in the History of Imperial Russia. Ed. 1. Paper Text. Houghton Mifflin College Division. Boston, MA. 1994. 661p. ISBN:0-669-21497-3, ISBN13: 978-0-669-21497-0. Dewey:947. LCCN:93-070549.
Audience: **g,l,u,f.**

Marker, Gary (Editor) **DK40**
Reinterpreting Russian History: Readings, 860-1860s. Daniel H. Kaiser (Compiled by). Trade Paper. Oxford University Press, Inc. New York, NY. 1994. 462p. ISBN:0-19-507858-6, ISBN13: 978-0-19-507858-9. Dewey:947. LCCN:92-046294.
Audience: **g,l,u,f.**

Riha, Thomas (Editor) **DK4 .R5**
Readings in Russian Civilization: Imperial Russia, 1700-1917. Ed. 2. Trade Paper. University of Chicago Press. Chicago, IL. 1969. 294p. ISBN:0-226-71855-7, ISBN13: 978-0-226-71855-2. Dewey:914. LCCN:69-014825.
Audience: **g,l,u,f.**

Riha, Thomas (Editor) **DK4 .R5**
Readings in Russian Civilization: Russia Before Peter the Great, 900-1700. Ed. 2. Trade Paper. University of Chicago Press. Chicago, IL. 1969. 266p. Russia Before Peter the Great, 900-1700 Ser., Vol. 1 ISBN:0-226-71853-0, ISBN13: 978-0-226-71853-8. Dewey:947.085. LCCN:69-014825.
Audience: **g,l,u,f.**

Riha, Thomas (Editor) **DK4.R54**
Readings in Russian Civilization: Soviet Russia, 1917 - Present, Vol. 3. Ed. 2. Trade Paper. University of Chicago Press. Chicago, IL. 1969. 378p. Soviet Russia, 1917 - Present Ser., Vol. 3 ISBN:0-226-71857-3, ISBN13: 978-0-226-71857-6. Dewey:947. LCCN:69-014825.
Audience: **g,l,u,f.**

Vernadsky, George (Editor), et al. **DK3**
A Source Book for Russian History from Early Times to 1917. Ralph T. Fisher, Alan D. Ferguson, Andrew Lossky & Sergei Pushkarev (Editors). Trade Cloth. Yale University Press. Cumberland, RI. 1972. 1248p. ISBN:0-300-01625-5, ISBN13: 978-0-300-01625-3. Dewey:947/.008. LCCN:70-011536.
Audience: **g,l,u,f.**

Russia > Cultural and Intellectual History

Baron, Samual H. & Kollmann, Nancy S. (Editors) **BL65.C8R442 1997**
Religion and Culture in Early Modern Russia. Library Binding. Northern Illinois University Press. DeKalb, IL. 1997. 240p. ISBN:0-87580-218-4, ISBN13: 978-0-87580-218-3. Dewey:306.6/0947. LCCN:96-022921.
Audience: **u,f.**

Berdiaev, Nikolai A. & Berdyaev, Nicolas **DK189.2**
The Russian Idea. Reginald M. French (Translator). Trade Cloth. Greenwood Publishing Group, Inc. Portsmouth, NH. 1979. 255p. ISBN:0-313-20968-5, ISBN13: 978-0-313-20968-0. Dewey:947/.07. LCCN:78-032021.
Audience: **u,f.**

Berlin, Isaiah **DK189**
Russian Thinkers. Trade Cloth. Peter Smith Publisher, Inc. Magnolia, MA. 1992. ISBN:0-8446-6604-1, ISBN13: 978-0-8446-6604-4. Dewey:947/.07.
Audience: **u,f.**

Billington, James H. **DK32.7 .B5**
The Icon and the Axe: An Interpretive History of Russian Culture. Trade Cloth. Peter Smith Publisher, Inc. Magnolia, MA. 1994. ISBN:0-8446-6754-4, ISBN13: 978-0-8446-6754-6. Dewey:914.703.
Audience: **g,u,f.**

David-Fox, Michael (Editor), et al. **DK38.A46 2004**
After the Fall: Essays in Russian and Soviet Historiography. Peter Holquist, Marshall Poe & Alexander Martin (Editors). Trade Paper. Slavica Publishers. Bloomington, IN. 2004. 261p. Kritika Historical Studies, Vol. 2 ISBN:0-89357-321-3, ISBN13: 978-0-89357-321-8. Dewey:947/.0072. LCCN:2004-026229.
Audience: **u,f.**

Figes, Orlando **DK32**
Natasha's Dance: A Cultural History of Russia. Trade Cloth. Penguin Group (USA) Inc. New York, NY. 2002. 672p. ISBN:0-7139-9517-3, ISBN13: 978-0-7139-9517-6. Dewey:947.
Audience: **g,u,f.**

Graham, Loren R. **Q127.S696 G729 1993**
Science in Russia and the Soviet Union: A Short History. George Basalla & Owen Hannaway (Contribution by). Trade Paper. Cambridge University Press. New York, NY. 1994. 351p. Cambridge Studies in the History of Science Ser. ISBN:0-521-28789-8, ISBN13: 978-0-521-28789-0. Dewey:509.47. LCCN:92-005087.
Audience: **g,u,f.** *Choice, 1993.*

Kelly, Catriona **BJ1943.K45 2001**
Refining Russia: Advice Literature, Polite Culture, and Gender from Catherine to Yeltsin. Trade Cloth. Oxford University Press, Inc. New York, NY. 2001. 482p. ISBN:0-19-815987-0, ISBN13: 978-0-19-815987-2. Dewey:646.7/00947. LCCN:2001-275935.
Audience: **g,u,f.** *Choice, 2002.*

Lovell, Stephen **DK32.L79 2003**
Summerfolk: A History of the Dacha, 1710-2000. Trade Cloth. Cornell University Press. Ithaca, NY. 2003. 254p. ISBN:0-8014-4071-8, ISBN13: 978-0-8014-4071-7. Dewey:643.2. LCCN:2002-012234.
Audience: **g,u,f.** *Choice, 2003.*

Masaryk, Tomas G. **DK32**
The Spirit of Russia: Studies in History, Literature and Philosophy. Ed. 2. Paul, Eden (Translator); Paul, Cedar (Translator). Macmillan. 1968.
Audience: **u,f.**

Mazour, Anatole G. **DK38**
Modern Russian Historiography. Trade Cloth. Greenwood Publishing Group, Inc. Portsmouth, NH. 1976. 224p. ISBN:0-8371-8285-9, ISBN13: 978-0-8371-8285-8. Dewey:947/.007/2047. LCCN:75-016962.
Audience: **u,f.**

Raeff, Marc **DK32.7.R877 1999**
Russian Intellectual History: An Anthology. Isaiah Berlin (Introduction by). Trade Cloth. Prometheus Books, Publishers. Amherst, NY. 1986. 416p. ISBN:1-57392-294-3, ISBN13: 978-1-57392-294-4. Dewey:947.06. LCCN:98-050380.
Audience: **u,f.**

Rzhevsky, Nicholas (Editor) **DK32 .C33 1998**
The Cambridge Companion to Modern Russian Culture. Dean Worth, Dmitry S. Likhachev, Mark Bassin, Pierre Hart, Abbott Gleason, Catriona Kelly, David Bethea & John Bowlt (Contribution by). Cloth Text. Cambridge University Press. New York, NY. 1999. 400p. Cambridge Companions to Culture Ser. ISBN:0-521-47218-0, ISBN13: 978-0-521-47218-0. Dewey:947.08. LCCN:98-003850.
Audience: **g,l,u.**

Stites, Richard **DK266.4 .S76 1992**
Russian Popular Culture: Entertainment and Society Since 1900. Mary McAuley (Contribution by). Trade Paper. Cambridge University Press. New York, NY. 1992. 287p. Cambridge Russian Paperbacks Ser., No. 7 ISBN:0-521-36986-X, ISBN13: 978-0-521-36986-2. Dewey:306.0947. LCCN:91-033592.
Audience: **g,u,f.** *Choice, 1993.*

Taruskin, Richard F. **ML300.T37 2000**
Defining Russia Musically: Historical and Hermeneutical Essays. Trade Paper. Princeton University Press. Princeton, NJ. 2000. 594p. ISBN:0-691-07065-2, ISBN13: 978-0-691-07065-0. Dewey:780/.947.
Audience: **u,f.** *Choice, 1997.*

Walicki, Andrzej **HN523.W3413**
A History of Russian Thought: From the Enlightenment to Marxism. Hilda Andrews-Rusiecka (Translator). Trade Cloth. Stanford University Press. Palo Alto, CA. 1979. xviii, 456p. ISBN:0-8047-1026-0, ISBN13: 978-0-8047-1026-8. Dewey:320.5/0947. LCCN:78-066181.
Audience: **u,f.**

Wortman, Richard **DK127.W67 2006**
Scenarios of Power: Myth and Ceremony in Russian Monarchy from Peter the Great to the Abdication of Nicholas II. Trade Paper. Princeton University Press. Princeton, NJ. 2006. 480p. ISBN:0-691-12374-8, ISBN13: 978-0-691-12374-5. Dewey:394/.4/09470903. LCCN:2005-021463.
Audience: **u,f.**

Purlevskii, Savva Dmitrievich **HT807.P87 2005**
A Life under Russian Serfdom: The Memoirs of Savva Dmitrievich Purlevskii, 1800-1868. Trade Cloth. Central European University Press. Herndon, VA. 2005. 119p. ISBN:963-9241-99-7, ISBN13: 978-963-9241-99-2. Dewey:306.3/65/092. LCCN:2004-027453.
Audience: **g,l,u,f.**

Roosevelt, Priscilla **DK142.R66 1995**
Life on the Russian Country Estate: A Social and Cultural History. William C. Brumfield (Photographer). Cloth over Boards. Yale University Press. Cumberland, RI. 1995. 384p. ISBN:0-300-05595-1, ISBN13: 978-0-300-05595-5. Dewey:947. LCCN:94-042337.
Audience: **u,f.**

Russia > Social History

Balzer, Harley D. (Editor) **HT690.R9R866 1996**
Russia's Missing Middle Class: The Professions in Russian History. Cloth Text. M. E. Sharpe Inc. Armonk, NY. 1996. 352p. ISBN:1-56324-707-0, ISBN13: 978-1-56324-707-1. Dewey:305.5/5/0947. LCCN:95-042117.
Audience: **u,f.**

Blum, Jerome **HT807**
Lord and Peasant in Russia: From the 9th to the 19th Century. Trade Paper. Princeton University Press. Princeton, NJ. 1971. 688p. ISBN:0-691-00764-0, ISBN13: 978-0-691-00764-9. Dewey:947.
Audience: **u,f.**

Engel, Barbara Alpern **HV1662.E54 2003**
Women in Russia, 1700-2000. Cloth Text. Cambridge University Press. New York, NY. 2003. 304p. ISBN:0-521-80270-9, ISBN13: 978-0-521-80270-3. Dewey:305.4/0947. LCCN:2003-043017.
Audience: **g,l,u,f.** *Choice, 2004.*

Levin, Eve **HQ18.E852L48**
Sex and Society in the World of the Orthodox Slavs, 900-1700. Book, Other. Cornell University Press. Ithaca, NY. 1989. 344p. ISBN:0-8014-8304-2, ISBN13: 978-0-8014-8304-2. Dewey:306.7/0947.
Audience: **g,u,f.** *Choice, 1990.*

Mironov, Boris N. & Eklof, Ben **HN523.M547 1999**
Social History of Imperial Russia, 1700-1917, Vol. 2. Ed. 2. Trade Paper. Westview Press. Boulder, CO. 1999. 408p. ISBN:0-8133-3665-1, ISBN13: 978-0-8133-3665-7. Dewey:306/.0947. LCCN:99-019884.
Audience: **u,f.**

Mironov, Boris N. & Eklof, Ben **HN523.M547 1999**
A Social History of Imperial Russia, 1700-1917, Vol. 1. Trade Paper. Westview Press. Boulder, CO. 1999. 600p. ISBN:0-8133-8598-9, ISBN13: 978-0-8133-8598-3. Dewey:306/.0947. LCCN:99-019884.
Audience: **u,f.** *Choice, 2000.*

Russia > Military and Diplomatic History

Adomeit, Hannes **DD120.S65A34 1998**
Imperial Overstretch: Germany in Soviet Policy from Stalin to Gorbachev: an Analysis Based on New Archival Evidence, Memoirs, and Interviews. Trade Cloth. Nomos Verlagsgesellschaft. Baden-Baden, 1998. 609p. Internationale Politik und Sicherheit Ser. ISBN:3-7890-5133-0, ISBN13: 978-3-7890-5133-3. Dewey:303.48/243047. LCCN:98-208539.
Audience: **u,f.**

Andrew, Christopher & Gordievsky, Oleg **JN6529.I6A53 1990**
KGB: The Inside Story of Its Foreign Operations from Lenin to Gorbachev. Trade Cloth. HarperCollins Publishers. New York, NY. 1990. 24p. ISBN:0-06-016605-3, ISBN13: 978-0-06-016605-2. Dewey:327.1/247/009. LCCN:90-055525.
Audience: **u,f.** *Choice, 1991.*

Harrison, Richard W. **U163.H38 2001**
The Russian Way of War: Operational Art, 1904-1940. Trade Cloth. University Press of Kansas. Lawrence, KS. 2004. xii, 352p. Modern War Studies ISBN:0-7006-1074-X, ISBN13: 978-0-7006-1074-7. Dewey:355.4/0947/0904. LCCN:00-047775.
Audience: **u,f.** *Choice, 2001.*

Higham, Robin & Kagan, Frederick W. (Editors) **DK51.M548 2001**
The Military History of Tsarist Russia. Cloth over Boards. Palgrave Macmillan. New York, NY. 2002. 272p. ISBN:0-312-22635-7, ISBN13: 978-0-312-22635-0. Dewey:355/.00947. LCCN:2001-018541.
Audience: **u,f.**

Jelavich, Barbara **DR38.3.S65 J45 1991**
Russia's Balkan Entanglements, 1806-1914. Trade Cloth. Cambridge University Press. New York, NY. 1991. 304p. ISBN:0-521-40126-7, ISBN13: 978-0-521-40126-5. Dewey:949.6. LCCN:90-020036.
Audience: **u,f.** *Choice, 1992.*

Kennan, George F. **DK266.5.K46 1978**
Soviet Foreign Policy, 1917-1941. Trade Cloth. Greenwood Publishing Group, Inc. Portsmouth, NH. 1978. 192p. ISBN:0-313-20355-5, ISBN13: 978-0-313-20355-8. Dewey:327.47. LCCN:78-001568.
Audience: **u,f.**

LeDonne, John P. **DK43.L4 2003**
The Grand Strategy of the Russian Empire, 1650-1831. Trade Cloth. Oxford University Press, Inc. New York, NY. 2003. 278p. ISBN:0-19-516100-9, ISBN13: 978-0-19-516100-7. Dewey:947. LCCN:2002-044695.
Audience: **u,f.** *Choice, 2004.*

Lohr, Eric & Poe, Marshall T. (Editors) **DK51.M546 2002**
The Military and Society in Russia, 1450-1917. Trade Cloth. Brill Academic Publishers. Leiden, 2002. xxiv, 552p. History of Warfare Ser., Vol. 14 ISBN:90-04-12273-7, ISBN13: 978-90-04-12273-4. Dewey:947. LCCN:2002-025411.
Audience: **u,f.** *Choice, 2003.*

Lukin, Alexander **DK68.7.C5L85 2002**
The Bear Watches the Dragon: Russia's Perceptions of China and the Evolution of Russian-Chinese Relations since the Eighteenth Century. Trade Cloth. M. E. Sharpe Inc. Armonk, NY. 2003. 440p. ISBN:0-7656-1025-6, ISBN13: 978-0-7656-1025-6. Dewey:327.47051/09. LCCN:2002-066947.
Audience: **u,f.** *Choice, 2003.*

Lynch, Allen C. **DJK45.S65**
The Soviet Study of International Relations. Trade Paper. Cambridge University Press. New York, NY. 1989. 241p. Soviet and East European Studies ISBN:0-521-36763-8, ISBN13: 978-0-521-36763-9. Dewey:327/.0947.
Audience: **g,u,f.** *Choice, 1988.*

Menning, Bruce W. **UA770.M467 1992**
Bayonets Before Bullets: The Imperial Russian Army, 1861-1914. Library Binding. Indiana University Press. Bloomington, IN. 1992. 352p. Indiana-Michigan Series in Russian and East European Studies ISBN:0-253-33745-3, ISBN13: 978-0-253-33745-0. Dewey:355.3/0947. LCCN:92-008233.
Audience: **u,f.** *Choice, 1993.*

Nekrich, Aleksandr M. & Freeze, Gregory L. **DD120.S65N45 1997**
Pariahs, Partners, Predators: German-Soviet Relations, 1922-1941. Trade Cloth. Columbia University Press. New York, NY. 1997. 320p. ISBN:0-231-10676-9, ISBN13: 978-0-231-10676-4. Dewey:327.43047/09/042. LCCN:96-029605.
Audience: **u,f.** *Choice, 1998.*

Ouimet, Matthew J. **DJK45.S65O89 2003**
The Rise and Fall of the Brezhnev Doctrine in Soviet Foreign Policy. Trade Cloth. University of North Carolina Press. Chapel Hill, NC. 2003. 384p. New Cold War History Ser. ISBN:0-8078-2740-1, ISBN13: 978-0-8078-2740-6. Dewey:327.47. LCCN:2002-008796.
Audience: **g,u,f.** *Choice, 2003.*

Ragsdale, Hugh (Editor) **DK66 .I48 1993**
Imperial Russian Foreign Policy. Valeri Nikolaevich Ponomarev (Assisted by), Lee H. Hamilton (Contribution by). Trade Cloth. Cambridge University Press. New York, NY. 1993. 471p. Woodrow Wilson Center Press Ser. ISBN:0-521-44229-X, ISBN13: 978-0-521-44229-9. Dewey:327.47. LCCN:93-004306.
Audience: **u,f.**

Richard, David A. **UB225.R9R53 1998**
The Tsar's Colonels: Professionalism, Strategy, and Subversion in Late Imperial Russia. Ed. 674. Trade Cloth. Harvard University Press. Cambridge, MA. 1999. 570p. ISBN:0-674-91111-3, ISBN13: 978-0-674-91111-6. Dewey:355/.033547/09034. LCCN:98-019400.
Audience: **u,f.** *Choice, 1999.*

Rohwer, Jurgen & Monakov, Mikhail **VA573.R54 2001**
Stalin's Ocean-Going Fleet: Soviet Naval Strategy and Shipbuilding Programs 1935-1953. Paper over Boards. Taylor & Francis Group. Philadelphia, PA. 2001. 352p. Naval Policy and History Ser., Vol. 11 ISBN:0-7146-4895-7, ISBN13: 978-0-7146-4895-8. Dewey:359/.00947/09041. LCCN:2001-017494.
Audience: **u,f.** *Choice, 2002.*

Shiraev, Eric & Zubok, Vladislav **E183.8.S65S544 2000**
Anti-Americanism in Russia: From Stalin to Putin. Cloth over Boards. Palgrave Macmillan. New York, NY. 2000. 192p. ISBN:0-312-22979-8, ISBN13: 978-0-312-22979-5. Dewey:327.47073. LCCN:00-040463.
Audience: **g,l,u,f.** *Choice, 2001.*

Stoecker, Sally W. **UA772.S824**
Forging Stalin's Army: Marshal Tukhachevsky and the Politics of Military Innovation. David Glantz (Foreword by). Trade Paper. Westview Press. Boulder, CO. 1999. 208p. ISBN:0-8133-3735-6, ISBN13: 978-0-8133-3735-7. Dewey:355/.00947/09041.
Audience: **g,u,f.** *Choice, 1998.*

Westad, Odd Arne (Editor) **DK68.7.C5B75 1998**
Brothers in Arms: The Rise and Fall of the Sino-Soviet Alliance, 1945-1963. Trade Paper. Stanford University Press. Palo Alto, CA. 1999. 426p. Cold War International History Project Ser. ISBN:0-8047-3485-2, ISBN13: 978-0-8047-3485-1. Dewey:327.4/7/051. LCCN:98-042422.
Audience: **u,f.** *Choice, 1999.*

Russia > Colonization and Empire

Allworth, Edward (Editor) **DK508.9.K78T37 1988**
The Tatars of Crimea: Their Struggle for Survival. Cloth Text. Duke University Press. Durham, NC. 1988. xv, 396p. Central Asia Book Ser. ISBN:0-8223-0758-8, ISBN13: 978-0-8223-0758-7. Dewey:323.1/194388047/0904. LCCN:87-033186.
Audience: **u,f.** *Choice, 1989.*

Barrett, Thomas M. **DK35.B375 1999**
At the Edge of Empire: The Terek Cossacks and the North Caucasus Frontier, 1700-1860. Trade Paper. Westview Press. Boulder, CO. 1999. 264p. ISBN:0-8133-3671-6, ISBN13: 978-0-8133-3671-8. Dewey:947. LCCN:99-028671.
Audience: **g,l,u,f.** *Choice, 1999.*

Benningsen, Alexandre A. & Wimbush, Enders S. **DK34.M8B46 1986**
Muslims of the Soviet Empire: A Guide. Trade Cloth. Indiana University Press. Bloomington, IN. 1986. 308p. ISBN:0-253-33958-8, ISBN13: 978-0-253-33958-4. Dewey:947/.00882971. LCCN:86-045517.
Audience: **g,u,f.** *Choice, 1987.*

Brower, Daniel R. **DK856.B76 2003**
Turkestan and the Fate of the Russian Empire. Paper over Boards. Routledge. New York, NY. 2003. 240p. ISBN:0-415-29744-3, ISBN13: 978-0-415-29744-8. Dewey:958.408. LCCN:2002-068285.
Audience: **u,f.** *Choice, 2003.*

Brower, Daniel R. & Lazzerini, Edward J. (Editors) **DK33.R88 1997**
Russia's Orient: Imperial Borderlands and Peoples, 1700-1917. Trade Cloth. Indiana University Press. Bloomington, IN. 1997. 364p. Indiana-Michigan Series in Russian and East European Studies ISBN:0-253-33274-5, ISBN13: 978-0-253-33274-5. Dewey:323.1/47. LCCN:96-039473.
Audience: **u,f.**

Fisher, Alan W. **DK508.9.K78**
The Crimean Tatars: Studies of Nationalities in the U. S. S. R. Trade Paper. Hoover Institution Press. Stanford, CA. 1978. 264p. Publication Ser., No. 166 ISBN:0-8179-6662-5, ISBN13: 978-0-8179-6662-1. Dewey:947.717. LCCN:76-041085.
Audience: **u,f.**

Gvosdev, Nikolas K. **DK68.7.G28G88 2000**
Imperial Policies and Perspectives Towards Georgia, 1760-1819. Cloth over Boards. Palgrave Macmillan. New York, NY. 2000. 220p. St. Antony's Series ISBN:0-312-22990-9, ISBN13: 978-0-312-22990-0. Dewey:327.4704758. LCCN:99-048655.
Audience: **u,f.** *Choice, 2000.*

Hirsch, Francine **DK33.H57 2005**
Empire of Nations: Ethnographic Knowledge and the Making of the Soviet Union. Book, Other. Cornell University Press. Ithaca, NY. 2005. 392p. Culture and Society after Socialism Ser. ISBN:0-8014-4273-7, ISBN13: 978-0-8014-4273-5. Dewey:323.147/09/04. LCCN:2005-002722.
Audience: **u,f.** *Choice, 2006.*

Hosking, Geoffrey Alan **DK49.H68 1997**
Russia: People and Empire, 1552-1917. Trade Cloth. Harvard University Press. Cambridge, MA. 1997. 576p. ISBN:0-674-78118-X, ISBN13: 978-0-674-78118-4. Dewey:947/.04. LCCN:97-005069.
Audience: **g,u,f.** *Choice, 1997.*

Jersild, Austin **DK511.C2J47 2002**
Orientalism and Empire: North Caucasus Mountain Peoples and the Georgian Frontier, 1845-1917. Trade Cloth. McGill-Queen's University Press. Montreal, PQ. 2002. 272p. ISBN:0-7735-2328-6, ISBN13: 978-0-7735-2328-9. Dewey:947.5/2. LCCN:2002-491752.
Audience: **u,f.** *Choice, 2002.*

Khodarkovsky, Michael **DK43.K485 2001**
Russia's Steppe Frontier: The Making of a Colonial Empire, 1500-1800. Trade Cloth. Indiana University Press. Bloomington, IN. 2002. 272p. Indiana-Michigan Series in Russian and East European Studies ISBN:0-253-33989-8, ISBN13: 978-0-253-33989-8. Dewey:947.04. LCCN:2001-003581.
Audience: **u,f.** *Choice, 2002.*

Martin, Terry **JN6520.M5M27 2001**
The Affirmative Action Empire: Nations and Nationalism in the Soviet Union, 1923-1939. Book, Other. Cornell University Press. Ithaca, NY. 2001. 528p. Wilder House Series in Politics, History, and Culture Ser. ISBN:0-8014-3813-6, ISBN13: 978-0-8014-3813-4. Dewey:947.084/2. LCCN:2001-003232.
Audience: **g,u,f.**

Miller, Alexei & Rieber, Alfred J. (Editors) **JC359.I67 2004**
Imperial Rule. Saddle Stitched, Cloth over Boards, Dust Jacket. Central European University Press. Herndon, VA. 2005. 212p. Pasts Incorporated Ser., Vol. 1 ISBN:963-9241-92-X, ISBN13: 978-963-9241-92-3. Dewey:325/.32/09034. LCCN:2004-020458.
Audience: **g,u,f.**

Nahaylo, Bohdan & Swoboda, Victor **DK33.N26 1990**
Soviet Disunion: A History of the Nationalities Problem in the U. S. S. R. Reinforced. Simon & Schuster. New York, NY. 1990. 432p. ISBN:0-02-922401-2, ISBN13: 978-0-02-922401-4. Dewey:947/.004. LCCN:89-071502.
Audience: **g,u,f.** *Choice, 1991.*

Northrop, Douglas **HX546.N67 2003**
Veiled Empire: Gender and Power in Stalinist Central Asia. Book, Other. Cornell University Press. Ithaca, NY. 2004. 448p. ISBN:0-8014-3944-2, ISBN13: 978-0-8014-3944-5. Dewey:305.48/697. LCCN:2003-020316.
Audience: **u,f.** *Choice, 2004.*

Polvinen, Tuomo **DL1065.5.B62P6413**
Imperial Borderland: Bobrikov and the Attempted Russification of Finland, 1898-1904. Steven Huxley (Translator). Cloth Text. Duke University Press. Durham, NC. 1995. 272p. ISBN:0-8223-1563-7, ISBN13: 978-0-8223-1563-6. Dewey:948.97/02. LCCN:94-038507.
Audience: **u,f.** *Choice, 1996.*

Rorlich, Azade-Ayse **DK511.T17R67 1986**
The Volga Tatars: A Profile in National Resilience. Cloth Text. Hoover Institution Press. Stanford, CA. 1986. 288p. Publication Ser., No. 339:Studies of Nationalities in the U. S. S. R. ISBN:0-8179-8391-0, ISBN13: 978-0-8179-8391-8. Dewey:947/.83. LCCN:86-018631.
Audience: **u,f.** *Choice, 1987.*

Sunderland, Willard **DK113.S86 2004**
Taming the Wild Field: Colonization and Empire on the Russian Steppe. Trade Cloth. Cornell University Press. Ithaca, NY. 2004. 264p. ISBN:0-8014-4209-5, ISBN13: 978-0-8014-4209-4. Dewey:947. LCCN:2004-001132.
Audience: **g,l,u,f.** *Choice, 2005.*

Suny, Ronald Grigor & Martin, Terry (Editors) **DK266.S8 2002**
A State of Nations: Empire and Nation-Making in the Age of Lenin and Stalin. Trade Paper. Oxford University Press, Inc. New York, NY. 2001. 320p. ISBN:0-19-514423-6, ISBN13: 978-0-19-514423-9. Dewey:947. LCCN:2001-021712.
Audience: **u,f.**

Uehling, Greta **DK508.9.K78U35 2004**
Beyond Memory: The Crimean Tatars' Deportation and Return. Cloth over Boards. Palgrave Macmillan. New York, NY. 2004. 320p. Anthropology, History, and Critical Imagination Ser. ISBN:1-4039-6264-2, ISBN13: 978-1-4039-6264-5. Dewey:947.7/100494388. LCCN:2003-063697.
Audience: **u,f.** *Choice, 2005.*

Williams, Brian Glyn **DK508.9.K78W55 2001**
The Crimean Tatars: The Diaspora Experience and the Forging of a Nation. Trade Cloth. Brill Academic Publishers. Leiden, 2001. xxviii, 520p. Brill's Inner Asian Library, Vol. 2 ISBN:90-04-12122-6, ISBN13: 978-90-04-12122-5. Dewey:305.89/4388. LCCN:2001-035369.
Audience: **u,f.** *Choice, 2002.*

Russia > Local and Regional History > St. Petersburg

Clark, Katerina **DK557.C57 1995**
Petersburg: Crucible of Cultural Revolution. Trade Cloth. Harvard University Press. Cambridge, MA. 1995. 392p. ISBN:0-674-66335-7, ISBN13: 978-0-674-66335-0. Dewey:947.2/1/084. LCCN:95-017161.
Audience: **u,f.** *Choice, 1996.*

George, Arthur L. & George, Elena **DK561.G46 2003**
St. Petersburg: Russia's Window to the Future—The First Three Centuries. Trade Cloth. Taylor Trade Publishing. Blue Ridge Summit, PA. 2003. 512p. ISBN:1-58979-017-0, ISBN13: 978-1-58979-017-9. Dewey:947/.21. LCCN:2003-001138.
Audience: **g,u,f.** *Choice, 2004.*

Lincoln, W. Bruce **DK552.L56 2001**
Sunlight at Midnight: St. Petersburg and the Rise of Modern Russia. Trade Cloth. Basic Books. New York, NY. 2001. 432p. ISBN:0-465-08323-4, ISBN13: 978-0-465-08323-7. Dewey:947/.21. LCCN:00-049795.
Audience: **g,l,u,f.** *Choice, 2002.*

Shvidkovsky, Dmitri **NA1196.S5613 1996**
St. Petersburg: Architecture of the Tsars. Alexander Orloff (Photographer). Trade Cloth. Abbeville Press, Inc. New York, NY. 1996. 360p. ISBN:0-7892-0217-4, ISBN13: 978-0-7892-0217-8. Dewey:720/.947/4530903. LCCN:96-017849.
Audience: **g,l,u,f.** *Choice, 1997.*

Russia > Local and Regional History > Siberia

Forsyth, James **DK758.F67 1994**
A History of the Peoples of Siberia: Russia's North Asian Colony, 1581-1990. Trade Cloth. Cambridge University Press. New York, NY. 1992. 475p. ISBN:0-521-40311-1, ISBN13: 978-0-521-40311-5. Dewey:957/.004. LCCN:91-008137.
Audience: **u,f.** *Choice, 1993.*

Hudgins, Sharon **DK756.2.H83 2003**
The Other Side of Russia: A Slice of Life in Siberia and the Russian Far East. Trade Cloth. Texas A&M University Press. College Station, TX. 2003. 352p. Eastern European Studies, No. 21 ISBN:1-58544-237-2, ISBN13: 978-1-58544-237-9. Dewey:915.704/86. LCCN:2002-013749.
Audience: **g,l,u,f.** *Choice, 2003.*

Jordan, Bella Bychkova & Jordan, Terry G. **DK781.D98B96 2001**
Siberian Village: Land and Life in the Sakha Republic. Trade Cloth. University of Minnesota Press. Minneapolis, MN. 2001. 208p. ISBN:0-8166-3569-2, ISBN13: 978-0-8166-3569-6. Dewey:957/.5. LCCN:00-013104.
Audience: **g,u,f.** *Choice, 2001.*

Kotkin, Stephen & Wolff, David (Editors) **DK761.R43 1995**
Rediscovering Russia in Asia: Siberia and the Russian Far East. Trade Cloth. M. E. Sharpe Inc. Armonk, NY. 1995. 380p. ISBN:1-56324-546-9, ISBN13: 978-1-56324-546-6. Dewey:957. LCCN:95-001849.
Audience: **u,f.**

Lincoln, W. Bruce **DK761.L56 1994**
The Conquest of a Continent: Siberia and the Russians. Trade Cloth. Fodor's Travel Publications. New York, NY. 1993. xxii, 500p. ISBN:0-679-41214-X, ISBN13: 978-0-679-41214-4. Dewey:957. LCCN:93-022342.
Audience: **g,l,u,f.** *Choice, 1994.*

Mote, Victor L. **DK761.M68 1998**
Siberia: Worlds Apart. Trade Paper. Westview Press. Boulder, CO. 1998. 256p. Series on the Post-Soviet Republics ISBN:0-8133-1298-1, ISBN13: 978-0-8133-1298-9. Dewey:957. LCCN:98-014843.
Audience: **g,l,u,f.** *Choice, 1998.*

Rasputin, Valentin **DK753.R3713 1996**
Siberia, Siberia. Margaret Winchell & Gerald Mikkelson (Translator, Introduction by). Trade Cloth. Northwestern University Press. Evanston, IL. 1996. 438p. ISBN:0-8101-1287-6, ISBN13: 978-0-8101-1287-2. Dewey:957. LCCN:96-007098.
Audience: **g,l,u,f.** *Choice, 1997.*

Russia > By period > Early and Medieval (to 1613)

Berry, Lloyd E. & Crummey, Robert O. (Editors) **DK19**
Rude and Barbarous Kingdom: Russia in the Accounts of Sixteenth-Century English Voyagers. Trade Cloth. University of Wisconsin Press. Chicago, IL. 1972. 416p. ISBN:0-299-04760-1, ISBN13: 978-0-299-04760-3. Dewey:914.7/03/408. LCCN:68-016059.
Audience: **g,l,u,f.**

Curta, Florin **DR49.26 .C87 2001**
The Making of the Slavs: History and Archaeology of the Lower Danube Region, c. 500-700. Christine Carpenter, Rosamond McKitterick & Jonathan Shepard (Contribution by). Trade Cloth. Cambridge University Press. New York, NY. 2001. 492p. Studies in Medieval Life and Thought ISBN:0-521-80202-4, ISBN13: 978-0-521-80202-4. Dewey:949.601. LCCN:00-052915.
Audience: **u,f.** *Choice, 2002.*

De Hartog, Leo **DK90.H35 1996**
Russia and the Mongol Yoke: The History of Russian Principalities and the Golden Horde, 1221-. Cloth Text. I. B. Tauris & Company, Ltd. London, 1996. 256p. ISBN:1-85043-961-3, ISBN13: 978-1-85043-961-5. Dewey:947/.043. LCCN:95-060223.
Audience: **g,l,u,f.** *Choice, 1996.*

De Madariaga, Isabel **DK106.D4 2005**
Ivan the Terrible: First Tsar of Russia. Cloth over Boards. Yale University Press. Cumberland, RI. 2005. 526p. ISBN:0-300-09757-3, ISBN13: 978-0-300-09757-3. Dewey:947/.043/092 B. LCCN:2004-029807.
Audience: **g,u,f.** *Choice, 2005.*

Dvornik, Francis **D147**
The Slavs in European History and Civilization. Cloth Text. Rutgers University Press. Piscataway, NJ. 1975. 696p. ISBN:0-8135-0799-5, ISBN13: 978-0-8135-0799-6. Dewey:940/.04918.
Audience: **u,f.**

Fennell, John **BX485.F45 1995**
A History of the Russian Church to 1448. Cloth Text. Longman Publishing. Boston, MA. 1995. 272p. ISBN:0-582-08068-1, ISBN13: 978-0-582-08068-3. Dewey:281.947/09/02. LCCN:94-016348.
Audience: **g,l,u,f.** *Choice, 1995.*

Franklin, S. & Shepard, J. **DK73.F73 1996**
The Emergence of Russia, 750-1200. Trade Cloth. Longman Publishing Group. White Plains, NY. 1996. 472p. History of Russia Ser. ISBN:0-582-49090-1, ISBN13: 978-0-582-49090-1. Dewey:947/.02. LCCN:95-049326.
Audience: **g,l,u,f.** *Choice, 1996.*

Halperin, Charles J. **DK90**
Russia and the Golden Horde: The Mongol Impact on Medieval Russian History. Trade Paper. Indiana University Press. Bloomington, IN. 1987. 192p. ISBN:0-253-20445-3, ISBN13: 978-0-253-20445-5. Dewey:947/.03. LCCN:84-048254.
Audience: **u,f.**

Kollmann, Nancy S. **DK62.K57 1987**
Kinship and Politics: The Making of the Muscovite Political System, 1345-1547. Trade Cloth. Stanford University Press. Palo Alto, CA. 1987. 344p. ISBN:0-8047-1340-5, ISBN13: 978-0-8047-1340-5. Dewey:947/.04. LCCN:86-005923.
Audience: **u,f.** *Choice, 1987.*

Kollmann, Nancy Shields **KLA285.H65K65 1999**
By Honor Bound: State and Society in Early Modern Russia. Trade Cloth. Cornell University Press. Ithaca, NY. 1999. 320p. ISBN:0-8014-3435-1, ISBN13: 978-0-8014-3435-8. Dewey:345.47/0256. LCCN:99-013343.
Audience: **u,f.** *Choice, 2000.*

Martin, Janet L. B. **DK71 .M29 1995**
Medieval Russia, 980-1584. Trade Paper. Cambridge University Press. New York, NY. 1995. 477p. Medieval Textbooks Ser. ISBN:0-521-36832-4, ISBN13: 978-0-521-36832-2. Dewey:947/.02. LCCN:94-042360.
Audience: **g,l,u,f.**

Perrie, Maureen & Pavlov, Andrei **DK106**
Ivan the Terrible. Trade Paper. Longman Publishing. Boston, MA. 2003. 248p. ISBN:0-582-09948-X, ISBN13: 978-0-582-09948-7. Dewey:947/.043/092.
Audience: **g,u,f.** *Choice, 2004.*

Platonov, Sergei Fedorovich **DK0109**
Boris Godunov. Trade Paper. Books on Demand. Ann Arbor, MI. 160p. ISBN:0-598-87529-8, ISBN13: 978-0-598-87529-7. Dewey:947.040924. LCCN:27-001627.
Audience: **g,u,f.**

Platonov, Sergei Fedorovich **DK111.P5813**
Time of Troubles: A Historical Study of the Internal Crisis and Social Struggles in Sixteenth and Seventeenth-Century Muscovy. John T. Alexander (Translator). Trade Paper. University Press of Kansas. Lawrence, KS. 1970. xviii, 198p. ISBN:0-7006-0062-0, ISBN13: 978-0-7006-0062-5. Dewey:947/.04. LCCN:79-097029.
Audience: **g,u,f.**

Pouncy, Carolyn J. (Editor, Translator) **PG3300.D613 1994**
The "Domostroi": Rules for Russian Households in the Time of Ivan the Terrible. Book, Other. Cornell University Press. Ithaca, NY. 1994. 296p. ISBN:0-8014-2410-0, ISBN13: 978-0-8014-2410-6. Dewey:640/.947/09031. LCCN:93-048474.
Audience: **g,l,u,f.**

Vernadsky, George **DK73**
Kievan Russia. Trade Paper. Yale University Press. Cumberland, RI. 1973. 426p. History of Russia Ser., No. 2 ISBN:0-300-01647-6, ISBN13: 978-0-300-01647-5. Dewey:947. LCCN:43-001903.
Audience: **u,f.**

Russia > By period > 17th 18th Centuries

Aksakov, Sergei **DK37.8.A3**
A Russian Gentleman. Edward Crankshaw (Editor), J. D. Duff (Translator). Trade Paper. Oxford University Press, Inc. New York, NY. 1982. 288p. Oxford World's Classics Ser. ISBN:0-19-281573-3, ISBN13: 978-0-19-281573-6. Dewey:891.73/3. LCCN:81-022327.
Audience: **g,l,u,f.**

Anisimov, Evgenii V. **DK127**
Five Empresses: Court Life in Eighteenth-Century Russia. Kathleen Carroll (Translator). Trade Cloth. Greenwood Publishing Group, Inc. Portsmouth, NH. 2004. 384p. ISBN:0-275-98464-8, ISBN13: 978-0-275-98464-9. Dewey:947/.06/092 B. LCCN:2004-050588.
Audience: **g,u,f.** *Choice, 2005.*

Avrich, Paul **DK43**
Russian Rebels, 1600-1800. Schocken Books. 1972. ISBN:0-8052-3458-6, ISBN13: 978-0-8052-3458-9.
Audience: **g,u,f.**

Cross, Anthony **DK34.B7 C76 1997**
By the Banks of the Neva: Chapters from the Lives and Careers of the British in Eighteenth-Century Russia. Cloth Text. Cambridge University Press. New York, NY. 1996. 490p. ISBN:0-521-55293-1, ISBN13: 978-0-521-55293-6. Dewey:947/.0042. LCCN:96-003825.
Audience: **u,f.** *Choice, 1997.*

Dixon, Simon **DK127 .D59 1999**
The Modernisation of Russia, 1676-1825. William Beik, T. C. W. Blanning & Brendan Simms (Contribution by). Cloth Text. Cambridge University Press. New York, NY. 1999. 286p. New Approaches to European History Ser., No. 15 ISBN:0-521-37100-7, ISBN13: 978-0-521-37100-1. Dewey:947. LCCN:98-046739.
Audience: **g,l,u,f.** *Choice, 2000.*

Dukes, Paul **DK114.D84 1990**
The Making of Russian Absolutism, 1613-1801. Ed. 2. Trade Paper. Longman Publishing Group. White Plains, NY. 1990. 256p. Longman History of Russia Ser. ISBN:0-582-00324-5, ISBN13: 978-0-582-00324-8. Dewey:947/.046. LCCN:90-005496.
Audience: **g,l,u,f.**

Hughes, Lindsey A. **DK125.H84 1990**
Sophia, Regent of Russia, Sixteen Fifty-Seven to Seventeen Hundred Four. Cloth over Boards. Yale University Press. Cumberland, RI. 1990. 368p. ISBN:0-300-04790-8, ISBN13: 978-0-300-04790-5. Dewey:947/.049/092 B. LCCN:90-012288.
Audience: **u,f.** *Choice, 1991.*

Klier, John **DS135.R9K53 1986**
Russia Gathers Her Jews: The Origins of the "Jewish Question" in Russia, 1772-1825. Trade Cloth. Northern Illinois University Press. DeKalb, IL. 1986. 275p. ISBN:0-87580-117-X, ISBN13: 978-0-87580-117-9. Dewey:947/.004924. LCCN:86-002473.
Audience: **u,f.**

LeDonne, John P. **DK127.L43 1991**
Absolutism and Ruling Class: The Formation of the Russian Political Order, 1700-1825. Cloth Text. Oxford University Press, Inc. New York, NY. 1991. 400p. ISBN:0-19-506805-X, ISBN13: 978-0-19-506805-4. Dewey:306.2/0947. LCCN:90-020057.
Audience: **u,f.** *Choice, 1992.*

Leonard, Carol S. **DK166.L64 1993**
[e] Reform and Regicide: The Reign of Peter III of Russia. E-Book. Indiana University Press. Bloomington, IN. 1993. 244p. Indiana-Michigan Series in Russian and East European Studies ISBN:0-253-33322-9, ISBN13: 978-0-253-33322-3. Dewey:947/.062. LCCN:92-005176.
Audience: **u,f.** *Choice, 1993.*

Marrese, Michelle Lamarche **HQ1662.M367 2002**
A Woman's Kingdom: Noblewomen and the Control of Property in Russia, 1700-1861. Trade Cloth. Cornell University Press. Ithaca, NY. 2002. 336p. ISBN:0-8014-3911-6, ISBN13: 978-0-8014-3911-7. Dewey:305.4/0947. LCCN:2001-007531.
Audience: **u,f.** *Choice, 2003.*

McGrew, Roderick E. **DK186.M39 1992**
Paul I of Russia, 1754-1801. Trade Cloth. Oxford University Press, Inc. New York, NY. 1992. 424p. ISBN:0-19-822567-9, ISBN13: 978-0-19-822567-6. Dewey:947/.07/092. LCCN:91-039188.
Audience: **g,u,f.** *Choice, 1993.*

Montefiore, Sebag **DK170**
The Prince of Princes: The Life of Potemkin. Trade Paper. St. Martin's Press. Gordonville, VA. ISBN:0-312-30419-6, ISBN13: 978-0-312-30419-5. Dewey:947/.063/092 B.
Audience: **g,u,f.** *Choice, 2002.*

Porshnev, B. F. & Dukes, Paul **D271.R8 P67 1995**
Muscovy and Sweden in the Thirty Years' War, 1630-1635. Brian Pearce (Translator). Trade Cloth. Cambridge University Press. New York, NY. 1995. 278p. ISBN:0-521-45139-6, ISBN13: 978-0-521-45139-0. Dewey:940.2/4. LCCN:95-010293.
Audience: **u,f.** *Choice, 1997.*

Radishchev, Alexander **HN525**
Journey from Petersburg to Moscow. Trade Paper. Bookking International. Paris, 1999. World Classic Literature Ser. ISBN:2-87714-258-2, ISBN13: 978-2-87714-258-8. Dewey:891.7/4/2.
Audience: **u,f.**

Raeff, Marc **DK127**
Imperial Russia 1682-1825: The Coming of Age of Modern Russia. Knopf. 1971. ISBN:0-394-30305-9, ISBN13: 978-0-394-30305-5.
Audience: **g,u,f.**

Raeff, Marc **HT647**
Origins of the Russian Intelligensia: The Eighteenth-Century Nobility. Trade Paper. Harcourt Trade Publishers. New York, NY. 1966. 260p. ISBN:0-15-670150-2, ISBN13: 978-0-15-670150-1. Dewey:301.44. LCCN:66-019152.
Audience: **u,f.**

Rostislavov, Dmitriaei Ivanovich **DK651.R495R6713 2002**
Provincial Russia in the Age of Enlightenment: The Memoir of a Priest's Son. Alexander M. Martin (Editor, Translator, Introduction by). Trade Cloth. Northern Illinois University Press. DeKalb, IL. 2003. 279p. ISBN:0-87580-285-0, ISBN13: 978-0-87580-285-5. Dewey:947/.33. LCCN:2001-044495.
Audience: **g,u,f.** *Choice, 2003, 2002.*

Russia > By period > 17th 18th Centuries > Peter the Great (1682-1725)

Anderson, M. S. **DK131.A49 1995**
Peter the Great. Ed. 2. Cloth Text. Addison-Wesley Longman, Ltd. Harlow, 1995. 240p. Profiles in Power Ser. ISBN:0-582-08412-1, ISBN13: 978-0-582-08412-4. Dewey:947/.05/0924. LCCN:94-044378.
Audience: **g,l,u,f.**

Bushkovitch, Paul **DK133 .B87 2001**
Peter the Great: The Struggle for Power, 1671-1725. Peter Baldwin, Christopher Clark, James B. Collins, Lyndal Roper & Mia Rodr¡guez-Salgado (Contribution by). Trade Cloth. Cambridge University Press. New York, NY. 2001. 498p. New Studies in European History ISBN:0-521-80585-6, ISBN13: 978-0-521-80585-8. Dewey:947.05. LCCN:00-069919.
Audience: **g,u,f.** *Choice, 2002.*

Cracraft, James **DK133.C74 2004**
The Petrine Revolution in Russian Culture. Trade Cloth. Harvard University Press. Cambridge, MA. 2004. 576p. ISBN:0-674-01316-6, ISBN13: 978-0-674-01316-2. Dewey:947/.05. LCCN:2004-040581.
Audience: **u,f.** *Choice, 2005.*

Cracraft, James **N6986.C73 1997**
The Petrine Revolution in Russian Imagery. Trade Cloth. University of Chicago Press. Chicago, IL. 1997. 394p. ISBN:0-226-11665-4, ISBN13: 978-0-226-11665-5. Dewey:709/.47/09032. LCCN:97-006309.
Audience: **u,f.** *Choice, 1998.*

Cracraft, James **DK131.C73 2003**
The Revolution of Peter the Great. Trade Cloth. Harvard University Press. Cambridge, MA. 2003. 214p. ISBN:0-674-01196-1, ISBN13: 978-0-674-01196-0. Dewey:947/.05. LCCN:2003-049917.
Audience: **g,l,u,f.** *Choice, 2004.*

Cracraft, James E. **NA1186.C73 1988**
The Petrine Revolution in Russian Architecture. Trade Cloth. University of Chicago Press. Chicago, IL. 1988. 402p.

ISBN:0-226-11664-6, ISBN13: 978-0-226-11664-8. Dewey:720/.947. LCCN:87-034293.
Audience: **u,f.** *Choice, 1989.*

Hughes, Lindsey **DK131.H84 1998**
Russia in the Age of Peter the Great. Cloth over Boards. Yale University Press. Cumberland, RI. 1998. 656p. ISBN:0-300-07539-1, ISBN13: 978-0-300-07539-7. Dewey:947/.05. LCCN:98-018667.
Audience: **g,l,u,f.** *Choice, 1999.*

Massie, Robert K. **DK131.M28 1991**
Peter the Great. Trade Cloth. Random House Value Publishing. New York, NY. 1993. 928p. ISBN:0-517-06483-9, ISBN13: 978-0-517-06483-2. Dewey:947/.05/092 B. LCCN:91-023069.
Audience: **g,l,u,f.**

Phillips, Edward J. **DK57**
The Founding of Russia's Navy: Peter the Great and the Azov Fleet, 1688-1714. Trade Cloth. Greenwood Publishing Group, Inc. Portsmouth, NH. 1995. 232p. Contributions in Military Studies Ser., No. 159 ISBN:0-313-29520-4, ISBN13: 978-0-313-29520-1. Dewey:359/.0947. LCCN:94-046941.
Audience: **u,f.** *Choice, 1995.*

Zitser, Ernest A. (Editor) **DK133.Z58 2004**
The Transfigured Kingdom: Sacred Parody and Charismatic Authority at the Court of Peter the Great. Trade Cloth. Cornell University Press. Ithaca, NY. 2004. 280p. ISBN:0-8014-4147-1, ISBN13: 978-0-8014-4147-9. Dewey:947/.05. LCCN:2004-000816.
Audience: **u,f.** *Choice, 2005.*

Russia > By period > 17th 18th Centuries > Catherine the Great (1762-1796)

Alexander, John T. **DK170.A58**
Catherine the Great: Life and Legend. Trade Paper. Oxford University Press, Inc. New York, NY. 1989. 432p. ISBN:0-19-506162-4, ISBN13: 978-0-19-506162-8. Dewey:947/.063/0924 B.
Audience: **g,l,u,f.** *Choice, 1989.*

Catherine II **DK170.C3213 2005**
The Memoirs of Catherine the Great. Hilde Hoogenboom & Markus I. Cruse (Translators). Trade Cloth. Random House Adult Trade Publishing Group. New York, NY. 2005. 247p. ISBN:0-679-64299-4, ISBN13: 978-0-679-64299-2. Dewey:947/.063/092 B. LCCN:2004-061107.
Audience: **g,u,f.** *Choice, 2005.*

De Madariaga, Isabel **DK171**
Catherine the Great: A Short History. Ed. 2. Trade Paper. Yale University Press. Cumberland, RI. 2002. 262p. ISBN:0-300-09722-0, ISBN13: 978-0-300-09722-1. Dewey:947/.063/092.
Audience: **g,l,u,f.** *Choice, 1991.*

Kaplan, Herbert H. **HF3628.G7K37 1995**
Russian Overseas Commerce with Great Britain During the Reign of Catherine II. Trade Cloth. American Philosophical Society. Canton, MA. 1996. 301p. Memoirs Ser., Vol. 218 ISBN:0-87169-218-X, ISBN13: 978-0-87169-218-4. Dewey:382.0941047. LCCN:94-078517.
Audience: **u,f.** *Choice, 1996.*

Madariaga, Isabel de **DK170**
Russia in the Age of Catherine the Great. Saddle Stitched. Phoenix Press, WC2. London, 2002. 720p. Phoenix Press Ser. ISBN:1-84212-511-7, ISBN13: 978-1-84212-511-3. Dewey:947.063092.
Audience: **u,f.**

Russia > By period > 19th Century

Brooks, Jeffrey **Z1003.5.S62B76 2003**
When Russia Learned to Read: Literacy and Popular Literature, 1861-1917. Trade Paper. Northwestern University Press. Evanston, IL. 2003. 488p. Studies in Russian Literature and Theory ISBN:0-8101-1897-1, ISBN13: 978-0-8101-1897-3. Dewey:028/.9/0947. LCCN:2003-044153.
Audience: **u,f.** *Choice, 1986.*

Engel, Barbara Alpern **HQ1662 .E54 1994**
Between the Fields and the City: Women, Work, and Family in Russia, 1861-1914. Cloth Text. Cambridge University Press. New York, NY. 1994. 266p. ISBN:0-521-44236-2, ISBN13: 978-0-521-44236-7. Dewey:305.5/633/082/0947. LCCN:93-031191.
Audience: **u,f.** *Choice, 1994.*

Frierson, Cathy A. (Editor, Translator) **HD1521**
Aleksandr Nikolaevich Engelgardt's Letters from the Country, 1872-1887. Trade Paper. Oxford University Press, Inc. New York, NY. 1993. 288p. ISBN:0-19-507621-4, ISBN13: 978-0-19-507621-9. Dewey:305.5633. LCCN:92-039426.
Audience: **g,u,f.**

Herzen, Alexander **D209.6.H4**
My Past and Thoughts: The Memoirs of Alexander Herzen. Dwight MacDonald & Dwight Macdonald (Editors). Trade Paper. University of California Press. Berkeley, CA. 1999. 752p. ISBN:0-520-04210-7, ISBN13: 978-0-520-04210-0. Dewey:947/.07/0924. LCCN:73-015933.
Audience: **g,u,f.**

Hoch, Stephen L. **HT807**
Serfdom and Social Control in Russia: Petrovskoe, a Village in Tambov. Trade Paper. University of Chicago Press. Chicago, IL. 1989. 230p. ISBN:0-226-34585-8, ISBN13: 978-0-226-34585-7. Dewey:306/.365/094735. LCCN:86-006915.
Audience: **u,f.** *Choice, 1987.*

Hunter, C. G. **DK25.H85**
Russia; Being a Complete Picture of That Empire; Including a Full Description of Their Government, Laws, Religion, Commerce, Manners, Customs. Adamant Media. 2005. Elibron Classics ISBN:1-4021-6273-1, ISBN13: 978-1-4021-6273-2.
Audience: **g,l,u,f.**

Kerans, David **S469.R9 K39 2001**
Mind and Labor on the Farm in Black-Earth Russia. Trade Cloth. Central European University Press. Herndon, VA. 2001. 510p. ISBN:963-9116-94-7, ISBN13: 978-963-9116-94-8. Dewey:338.10947. LCCN:00-051329.
Audience: **u,f.** *Choice, 2002.*

Malia, Martin **DK209.6.H4**
Alexander Herzen and the Birth of Russian Socialism, 1812-1855. Trade Cloth. Harvard University Press. Cambridge, MA. 1961. 496p. ISBN:0-674-01500-2, ISBN13: 978-0-674-01500-5. Dewey:335.0947.
Audience: **u,f.**

Mazour, Anatole G. **DK212 .M3**
The First Russian Revolution, 1825: The Decembrist Movement. Trade Cloth. Stanford University Press. Palo Alto, CA. 1937. xvi, 328p. ISBN:0-8047-0081-8, ISBN13: 978-0-8047-0081-8. Dewey:947.07.
Audience: **u,f.**

Mosse, W. E. **DK189.M68 1992**
Perestroika under the Tsars. Cloth Text. I. B. Tauris & Company, Ltd. London, 1993. 300p. ISBN:1-85043-519-7, ISBN13: 978-1-85043-519-8. Dewey:330.947. LCCN:91-068023.
Audience: **g,u,f.** *Choice, 1993.*

Nathans, Benjamin **DS135.R9 .N38 2001**
Beyond the Pale: The Jewish Encounter with Late Imperial Russia. Trade Cloth. University of California Press. Berkeley, CA. 2002. 426p. Studies on the History of Society and Culture, Vol. 45 ISBN:0-520-20830-7, ISBN13: 978-0-520-20830-8. Dewey:947/.004924. LCCN:2001-003513.
Audience: **g,u,f.** *Choice, 2003.*

Nikitenko, Aleksandr **PG2947.N5A3 2001**
Up from Serfdom: My Childhood and Youth in Russia, 1804-1824. Helen Saltz Jacobson (Translator), Peter Kolchin (Foreword by). Cloth over Boards. Yale University Press. Cumberland, RI. 2001. 256p. ISBN:0-300-08414-5, ISBN13: 978-0-300-08414-6. Dewey:891.709 B. LCCN:00-043866.
Audience: **g,l,u,f.**

Polunov, Alexander **DK189.P64**
Russia in the Nineteenth Century: Autocracy, Reform, and Social Change, 1814-1914. Larissa Zakharova & Thomas C. Owen (Editors), Marshall S. Shatz (Translator). Cloth Text. M. E. Sharpe Inc. Armonk, NY. 2005. 272p. The New Russian History Ser. ISBN:0-7656-0671-2, ISBN13: 978-0-7656-0671-6. Dewey:947/.07. LCCN:2005-007919.
Audience: **u,f.** *Choice, 2006.*

Pomper, Philip **HN523**
The Russian Revolutionary Intelligentsia. Ed. 2. Keith Eubank (Editor). Trade Paper. Harlan Davidson Inc. Wheeling, IL. 1993. 256p. European History Ser. ISBN:0-88295-895-X, ISBN13: 978-0-88295-895-8. Dewey:305.5/52/0947. LCCN:92-005628.
Audience: **u,f.**

Riasanovsky, Nicholas V. **HT690.R/**
A Parting of the Ways: Government and the Educated Public in Russia, 1801-1855. Trade Cloth. Oxford University Press, Inc. New York, NY. 1977. 334p. ISBN:0-19-822533-4, ISBN13: 978-0-19-822533-1. Dewey:323.3/2.
Audience: **u,f.**

Ruud, Charles A. & Stepanov, S. A. **HV8225.7.O54R8813**
Fontanka 16: The Tsars' Secret Police. Trade Cloth. McGill-Queen's University Press. Montreal, PQ. 1997. ix, 394p. ISBN:0-7735-1787-1, ISBN13: 978-0-7735-1787-5. Dewey:363.2/83/0947. LCCN:00-340629.
Audience: **u,f.** *Choice, 1999.*

Schrader, Abby M. **HV8621.R9S37 2002**
Languages of the Lash: Corporal Punishment and Identity in Imperial Russia. Trade Cloth. Northern Illinois University Press. DeKalb, IL. 2003. 271p. ISBN:0-87580-289-3, ISBN13: 978-0-87580-289-3. Dewey:364.6/7/0947. LCCN:2001-044453.
Audience: **u,f.** *Choice, 2002.*

Seton-Watson, Hugh **DK189**
The Russian Empire, 1801-1917. Trade Cloth. Oxford University Press, Inc. New York, NY. 1967. 834p. Oxford History of Modern Europe Ser. ISBN:0-19-822103-7, ISBN13: 978-0-19-822103-6. Dewey:947.08.
Audience: **u,f.**

Worobec, Christine D. **HN530.R87W67 1991**
Peasant Russia: Family and Community in the Post-Emancipation Period. Cloth Text. Princeton University Press. Princeton, NJ. 1991. 272p. ISBN:0-691-03151-7, ISBN13: 978-0-691-03151-4. Dewey:305.5/633/0947. LCCN:90-041811.
Audience: **u,f.** *Choice, 1991.*

Russia > By period > 19th Century > Alexander I (1801-1825)

Palmer, Alan Warwick **DK191**
Alexander I: Tsar of War and Peace. Phoenix Giant. 1997. ISBN:1-85799-866-9, ISBN13: 978-1-85799-866-5.
Audience: **u,f.**

Strakhovsky, Leonid I. **DK191.S75 1970**
Alexander I of Russia, the Man Who Defeated Napoleon. Library Binding. Greenwood Publishing Group, Inc. Portsmouth, NH. 1971. 302p. ISBN:0-8371-4034-X, ISBN13: 978-0-8371-4034-6. Dewey:947/.07/0924. LCCN:77-100245.
Audience: **g,u,f.**

Troubetzkoy, Alexis S. **DK192.T767 2002**
Imperial Legend: The Mysterious Disappearance of Tsar Alexander I. Trade Cloth. Arcade Publishing, Inc. New York, NY. 2002. 312p. ISBN:1-55970-608-2, ISBN13: 978-1-55970-608-7. Dewey:947/.072/092 B. LCCN:2001-045750.
Audience: **g,l,u,f.** *Choice, 2003, 2002.*

Whittaker, Cynthia H. **LA2375.S592U939 1984**
The Origins of Modern Russian Education: An Intellectual Biography of Count Sergei Uvarov, 1786-1855. Trade Cloth. Northern Illinois University Press. DeKalb, IL. 1984. 348p. ISBN:0-87580-100-5, ISBN13: 978-0-87580-100-1. Dewey:370/.92/4 B. LCCN:84-007471.
Audience: **u,f.**

Russia > By period > 19th Century > Nicholas I (1825-1855)

Haywood, Richard **HE3138.H385 1998**
Russia Enters the Railway Age, 1842-1855. Trade Cloth. Eastern European Monographs. Bradenton, FL. 1998. 650p. ISBN:0-88033-390-1, ISBN13: 978-0-88033-390-0. Dewey:385/.0947. LCCN:98-070323.
Audience: **u,f.** *Choice, 2000.*

Kagan, Frederick W. **UA772.K24 1999**
The Military Reforms of Nicholas I: The Origins of the Modern Russian Army. Cloth over Boards. Palgrave Macmillan. New York, NY. 1999. 352p. ISBN:0-312-21928-8, ISBN13: 978-0-312-21928-4. Dewey:355.3/0947/09034. LCCN:98-044711.
Audience: **u,f.** *Choice, 2000.*

Lincoln, W. Bruce **DK210.L56 1989**
Nicholas I: Emperor and Autocrat of All the Russias. Trade Paper. Northern Illinois University Press. DeKalb, IL. 2003. 424p. ISBN:0-87580-548-5, ISBN13: 978-0-87580-548-1. Dewey:947/.073/092. LCCN:89-016304.
Audience: **g,u,f.**

Presniakov, Alexander E. **DK210.P713**
Emperor Nicholas the First of Russia: The Apogee of Autocracy, 1825-1855. Judith C. Zacek (Translator). Trade Cloth. Academic International Press. Gulf Breeze, FL. 1974. xl, 102p. Russian Ser., No. 23 ISBN:0-87569-053-X, ISBN13: 978-0-87569-053-7. Dewey:320.9/47/07. LCCN:73-090779.
Audience: **g,u,f.**

Rich, Norman M. **DK215.R53 1985**
Why the Crimean War?: A Cautionary Tale. Library Binding. University Press of New England. Lebanon, NH. 1985. 280p. ISBN:0-87451-328-6, ISBN13: 978-0-87451-328-8. Dewey:947/.073. LCCN:84-040593.
Audience: **g,u,f.** *Choice, 1985.*

Roberts, Ian W. **DK210.R62 1991**
Nicholas the First and the Russian Intervention in Hungary. Cloth Text. Palgrave Macmillan. New York, NY. 1991. 310p. ISBN:0-312-04897-1, ISBN13: 978-0-312-04897-6. Dewey:327.470439/09/034. LCCN:90-034608.
Audience: **u,f.** *Choice, 1991.*

Stanislawski, Michael **DS135.R9.S77 1983**
Tsar Nicholas I and the Jews: The Transformation of Jewish Society in Russia, 1825-1855. Trade Cloth. Jewish Publication Society. Dulles, VA. 1983. 272p. ISBN:0-8276-0216-2, ISBN13: 978-0-8276-0216-8. Dewey:947/.004924. LCCN:82-016199.
Audience: **u,f.**

Russia > By period > 19th Century > Alexander II (1855-1881). Alexander III (1881-1894)

Aronson, I. Michael **DS135.R9A74 1990**
Troubled Waters: The Origins of the 1881 Anti-Jewish Pogroms in Russia. Cloth Text. University of Pittsburgh Press. Pittsburgh, PA. 1991. 286p. Russian and East European Studies Ser. ISBN:0-8229-3656-9, ISBN13: 978-0-8229-3656-5. Dewey:947/.004924. LCCN:90-033957.
Audience: **g,u,f.** *Choice, 1991.*

Engel, Barbara A. (Editor), et al. **HN530.Z9R328 1987**
Five Sisters: Women Against the Tsar. Cliford N. Roesenthal & Alix K. Shulman (Editors). Paper Text. Routledge. New York, NY. 1987. 304p. ISBN:0-04-445034-6, ISBN13: 978-0-04-445034-4. Dewey:322.4/2/0922. LCCN:87-017584.
Audience: **g,l,u,f.**

Klier, John D. **DS135.R9 K534 1995**
Imperial Russia's Jewish Question, 1855-1881. Trade Cloth. Cambridge University Press. New York, NY. 1995. 555p. Russian, Soviet and Post-Soviet Studies, No. 96 ISBN:0-521-46035-2, ISBN13: 978-0-521-46035-4. Dewey:947/.004924. LCCN:94-009145.
Audience: **u,f.** *Choice, 1996.*

Lincoln, W. Bruce **DK220.L56 1990**
The Great Reforms: Autocracy, Bureaucracy, and the Politics of Change in Imperial Russia. Trade Cloth. Northern Illinois University Press. DeKalb, IL. 2003. 302p. ISBN:0-87580-155-2, ISBN13: 978-0-87580-155-1. Dewey:947.08. LCCN:90-007186.
Audience: **g,u,f.** *Choice, 1991.*

Mosse, W. E. **DK220.M6 1992**
Alexander II and the Modernization of Russia. Ed. 2. Cloth over Boards. I. B. Tauris & Company, Ltd. London, 1992. 216p. ISBN:1-85043-513-8, ISBN13: 978-1-85043-513-6. Dewey:947.081. LCCN:91-068022.
Audience: **u,f.**

Radzinsky, Edvard **DK220.R33 2005**
Alexander II: The Last Great Tsar. Antonina W. Bouis (Translator). Trade Cloth. Simon & Schuster. New York, NY. 2005. 480p. ISBN:0-7432-7332-X, ISBN13: 978-0-7432-7332-9. Dewey:947.08/1/092 B. LCCN:2005-049413.
Audience: **g,u,f.**

Ulam, Adam B. **DK221.U38 1977**
In the Name of the People: Prophets and Conspirators in Prerevolutionary Russia. Trade Cloth. Penguin Group (USA) Inc. New York, NY. 1977. xii, 418p. ISBN:0-670-39691-5, ISBN13: 978-0-670-39691-7. Dewey:947.08. LCCN:76-042221.
Audience: **g,u,f.**

Wcislo, Francis W. **DK221.W25 1990**
Reforming Rural Russia: State, Local Society, and National Politics, 1855-1914. Cloth Text. Princeton University Press. Princeton, NJ. 1990. 376p. Studies of the Harriman Institute, Columbia University ISBN:0-691-05574-2, ISBN13: 978-0-691-05574-9. Dewey:947.08/09734. LCCN:89-070242.
Audience: **u,f.** *Choice, 1991.*

Russia > By period > Revolutionary Russia. Nicholas II (1894-1917)

Alexandra, Tsaritsa **DK254.A5A3 1997**
Last Diary of Tsaritsa Alexandra. Alexandra Raskina, Vladimir A. Kozlov & Vladimir M. Khrustalev (Editors), Robert K. Massie (Introduction by). Cloth over Boards. Yale University Press. Cumberland, RI. 1997. 326p. Annals of Communism Ser. ISBN:0-300-07212-0, ISBN13: 978-0-300-07212-9. Dewey:947.08/3/092 B. LCCN:97-015675.
Audience: **u,f.** *Choice, 1998.*

Ascher, Abraham **DK254.S595A9 2001**
P. A. Stolypin: The Search for Stability in Late Imperial Russia. Trade Paper. Stanford University Press. Palo Alto, CA. 2002. 482p. ISBN:0-8047-4547-1, ISBN13: 978-0-8047-4547-5. Dewey:947.08/3/092 B.
Audience: **u,f.** *Choice, 2001.*

Ascher, Abraham **DK263**
The Revolution Of 1905: Authority Restored. Trade Cloth. Stanford University Press. Palo Alto, CA. 1992. 472p.

ISBN:0-8047-1972-1, ISBN13: 978-0-8047-1972-8. Dewey:947/.083. LCCN:87-026697.
Audience: **u,f.** *Choice, 1993.*

Ascher, Abraham **DK263.A9 1988**
The Revolution of 1905: Russia in Disarray. Trade Cloth. Stanford University Press. Palo Alto, CA. 1988. xvi, 424p. ISBN:0-8047-1436-3, ISBN13: 978-0-8047-1436-5. Dewey:947/.083. LCCN:87-026657.
Audience: **u,f.** *Choice, 1988.*

Bonnell, Victoria E. **HD6735.L4**
Roots of Rebellion: Workers' Politics and Organizations in St. Petersburg and Moscow, 1900-1914. Trade Cloth. University of California Press. Berkeley, CA. 1983. 528p. ISBN:0-520-04740-0, ISBN13: 978-0-520-04740-2. Dewey:331.8/0947312. LCCN:83-001084.
Audience: **g,l,u,f.**

Bonnell, Victoria E. (Editor) **HD8526**
The Russian Worker: Life and Labor under the Tsarist Regime. Trade Cloth. University of California Press. Berkeley, CA. 1983. 240p. ISBN:0-520-05059-2, ISBN13: 978-0-520-05059-4. Dewey:305.5/62/0922. LCCN:83-047856.
Audience: **g,l,u,f.**

Carrere D'Encausse, Helene **DK258.C3713 2000**
Nicholas II. George Holoch (Translator). Trade Cloth. Holmes & Meier Publishers, Inc. Teaneck, NJ. 2000. xiii, 321p. ISBN:0-8419-1397-8, ISBN13: 978-0-8419-1397-4. Dewey:947.08/3/092 B. LCCN:99-048898.
Audience: **g,u,f.** *Choice, 2000.*

Clowes, Edith W. (Editor), et al. **DK220.B48 1991**
Between Tsar and People: Educated Society and the Quest for Public Identity in Late Imperial Russia. Samuel D. Kassow & James L. W. West III (Editors). Trade Cloth. Princeton University Press. Princeton, NJ. 1991. 367p. ISBN:0-691-03153-3, ISBN13: 978-0-691-03153-8. Dewey:947.08/1. LCCN:90-009079.
Audience: **u,f.** *Choice, 1991.*

Cockfield, Jamie H. **DK254**
White Crow: The Life and Times of the Grand Duke Nicholas Mikhailovich Romanov, 1859-1919. Trade Cloth. Greenwood Publishing Group, Inc. Portsmouth, NH. 2002. 328p. ISBN:0-275-97778-1, ISBN13: 978-0-275-97778-8. Dewey:947.08/3/092 B. LCCN:2002-025209.
Audience: **g,u,f.** *Choice, 2003.*

Economakis, Evel G. **HD8526.E25 1998**
From Peasant to Petersburger. Cloth over Boards. Palgrave Macmillan. New York, NY. 1999. 226p. ISBN:0-312-21497-9, ISBN13: 978-0-312-21497-5. Dewey:305.5/62/094721. LCCN:98-013558.
Audience: **g,l,u,f.** *Choice, 1999.*

Fuhrmann, Joseph T. (Editor) **DK258**
The Complete Wartime Correspondence of Tsar Nicholas II and the Empress Alexandra: April 1914-March 1917. Cloth Text. Greenwood Publishing Group, Inc. Portsmouth, NH. 1999. 784p. Documentary Reference Collections ISBN:0-313-30511-0, ISBN13: 978-0-313-30511-5. Dewey:947.08/3/092. LCCN:97-018193.
Audience: **g,u,f.** *Choice, 1999.*

Gatrell, Peter **HC334.5.G378 2005**
Russia's First World War: A Social and Economic History. Trade Paper. Longman Publishing Group. White Plains, NY. 2005. 344p. ISBN:0-582-32818-7, ISBN13: 978-0-582-32818-1. Dewey:940.3/47. LCCN:2004-060071.
Audience: **g,u,f.** *Choice, 2006.*

Haimson, Leopold H. **HX313 .H3**
Russian Marxists and the Origins of Bolshevism. Trade Cloth. Harvard University Press. Cambridge, MA. 1955. Russian Research Center Studies, No. 19 ISBN:0-674-78225-9, ISBN13: 978-0-674-78225-9. Dewey:335.4. LCCN:55-010972.
Audience: **u,f.**

Jahn, Hubertus F. **D639.P7R85 1995**
Patriotic Culture in Russia During World War I. Book, Other. Cornell University Press. Ithaca, NY. 1995. 256p. ISBN:0-8014-3131-X, ISBN13: 978-0-8014-3131-9. Dewey:940.3/47. LCCN:95-008512.
Audience: **g,u,f.** *Choice, 1996.*

Kassow, Samuel D. **HT690.R/**
Students, Professors, and the State in Tsarist Russia. Trade Cloth. University of California Press. Berkeley, CA. 1989. 480p. California Studies on the History of Society and Culture, No. 5 ISBN:0-520-05760-0, ISBN13: 978-0-520-05760-9. Dewey:323.3231. LCCN:88-040237.
Audience: **u,f.** *Choice, 1990.*

Lieven, Dominic C. **DK262.L48 1983**
Russia and the Origins of the First World War. Cloth Text. Palgrave Macmillan. New York, NY. 1983. 225p. The Making of the 20th Century Ser. ISBN:0-312-69608-6, ISBN13: 978-0-312-69608-5. Dewey:947/.08/3. LCCN:82-024095.
Audience: **u,f.**

Lieven, Dominic C. **DK253.L54 1989**
Russia's Rulers Before the Old Regime. Cloth over Boards. Yale University Press. Cumberland, RI. 1989. 429p. ISBN:0-300-04371-6, ISBN13: 978-0-300-04371-6. Dewey:947.08/092/2. LCCN:88-038155.
Audience: **u,f.** *Choice, 1990.*

Radzinsky, Edvard **DK258**
The Last Tsar: The Life and Death of Nicholas II. Marian Schwartz (Translator). UK-Trade Paper. Doubleday Publishing. New York, NY. 1993. 496p. ISBN:0-385-46962-4, ISBN13: 978-0-385-46962-3. Dewey:947.08/3 20. LCCN:93-016757.
Audience: **g,u,f.**

Rogger, Hans **DK241**
Russia in the Age of Modernisation and Revolution, 1881-1917. Trade Paper. Longman Publishing. Boston, MA. 1989. 323p. Longman History of Russia Ser. ISBN:0-582-48912-1, ISBN13: 978-0-582-48912-7. Dewey:947.08. LCCN:83-000714.
Audience: **g,u,f.**

Steinberg, Mark D. & Khrustalev, Vladimir M. **DK258.S74 1995**
The Fall of the Romanovs: Political Dreams and Personal Struggles in a Time of Revolution. Elizabeth Tucker (Translator). Cloth over Boards. Yale University Press. Cumberland, RI. 1995. 464p. Annals of Communism Ser. ISBN:0-300-06557-4, ISBN13: 978-0-300-06557-2. Dewey:947/.083/0922. LCCN:95-000477.
Audience: **g,l,u,f.** *Choice, 1996.*

Thatcher, Ian D. **DK254.T6T49 2000**
Leon Trotsky and World War One: August 1914 - February 1917. Cloth over Boards. Palgrave Macmillan. New York, NY. 2000. 272p. ISBN:0-312-23487-2, ISBN13: 978-0-312-23487-4. Dewey:940.3. LCCN:00-027151.
Audience: **g,l,u,f.** *Choice, 2001.*

Tomaszewski, Fiona K. **DK262.T63 2002**
A Great Russia: Russia and the Triple Entente, 1905-1914. Trade Cloth. Greenwood Publishing Group, Inc. Portsmouth, NH. 2002. 208p. ISBN:0-275-97366-2, ISBN13: 978-0-275-97366-7. Dewey:327.47041/09/041. LCCN:2001-053083.
Audience: **g,u,f.** *Choice, 2002.*

Verner, Andrew M. **DK258.V44 1990**
The Crisis of Russian Autocracy: Nicholas II and the 1905 Revolution. Trade Cloth. Princeton University Press. Princeton, NJ. 1990. 392p. ISBN:0-691-04773-1, ISBN13: 978-0-691-04773-7. Dewey:947.08/3. LCCN:89-010710.
Audience: **u,f.** *Choice, 1990.*

Von Laue, Theodore H. **HC334.5**
Sergei Witte and the Industrialization of Russia. Paper Text. Simon & Schuster Children's Publishing. New York, NY. 1969. ISBN:0-689-70196-9, ISBN13: 978-0-689-70196-2. Dewey:338.947. LCCN:63-010520.
Audience: **u,f.**

Weinberg, Robert **DK264.2.O3W45 1993**
The Revolution of 1905 in Odessa: Blood on the Steppes. Trade Cloth. Indiana University Press. Bloomington, IN. 1993. 272p. Indiana-Michigan Series in Russian and East European Studies ISBN:0-253-36381-0, ISBN13: 978-0-253-36381-7. Dewey:947/.717. LCCN:92-023096.
Audience: **u,f.** *Choice, 1993.*

Zuckerman, Frederic S. **HV8225.7.O54Z83 1996**
The Tsarist Secret Police and Russian Society, 1880-1917. Trade Cloth. New York University Press. New York, NY. 1996. 400p. ISBN:0-8147-9673-7, ISBN13: 978-0-8147-9673-3. Dewey:363.2/83/0947. LCCN:95-016138.
Audience: **g,u,f.** *Choice, 1997.*

Russia > By period > 1917 Revolution

Abraham, Richard **DK254.K3A64**
Alexander Kerensky: The First Love of the Revolution. Trade Paper. Columbia University Press. New York, NY. 1990. 503p. ISBN:0-231-06109-9, ISBN13: 978-0-231-06109-4. Dewey:947.084/1/0924 B.
Audience: **g,u,f.** *Choice, 1987.*

Acton, Edward (Editor), et al. **DK265.C68 1997**
Critical Companion to the Russian Revolution, 1914-1921. V. I. Cherniaev & William G. Rosenberg (Editors). Trade Cloth. Indiana University Press. Bloomington, IN. 1997. 800p. ISBN:0-253-33333-4, ISBN13: 978-0-253-33333-9. Dewey:947/.0841. LCCN:97-006945.
Audience: **u,f.** *Choice, 1998.*

Chamberlin, William H. **DK265.C43 1987**
The Russian Revolution, Nineteen Seventeen to Nineteen Twenty-One, Vol. 1: 1917-1918: From the Overthrow of the Tsar to the Assumption of Power by the Bolsheviks. Diane P. Koenker (Editor). Trade Cloth. Princeton University Press. Princeton, NJ. 1987. 536p. ISBN:0-691-05492-4, ISBN13: 978-0-691-05492-6. Dewey:947.084/1. LCCN:87-003719.
Audience: **g,u,f.**

Chamberlin, William H. **DK265.C43 1987**
The Russian Revolution, Nineteen Seventeen to Nineteen Twenty-One, Vol. II: 1918-1921: From the Civil War to the Consolidation of Power. Diane P. Koenker (Editor). Trade Cloth. Princeton University Press. Princeton, NJ. 1987. 612p. ISBN:0-691-05493-2, ISBN13: 978-0-691-05493-3. Dewey:947.084/1. LCCN:87-003719.
Audience: **g,u,f.**

Judson, William V. **DK265.7.J83 1998**
Russia in War and Revolution: General William V. Judson's Accounts from Petrograd, 1917-1918. Neil V. Salzman (Editor). Trade Cloth. Kent State University Press. Kent, OH. 1998. 350p. ISBN:0-87338-597-7, ISBN13: 978-0-87338-597-8. Dewey:947.084/1. LCCN:97-035946.
Audience: **g,l,u,f.** *Choice, 1998.*

Read, Christopher **DK265.R3718 1996**
From Tsar to Soviets: The Russian People and Their Revolution, 1917-1921. Cloth Text. Oxford University Press, Inc. New York, NY. 1996. 336p. ISBN:0-19-521242-8, ISBN13: 978-0-19-521242-6. Dewey:947.084/1. LCCN:96-138387.
Audience: **g,l,u,f.** *Choice, 1996.*

Reed, John **DK265**
Ten Days That Shook the World. A. J. P. Taylor & V. I. Lenin (Introduction by). Trade Paper. Penguin Group (USA) Inc. New York, NY. 1990. 368p. Twentieth Century Classics Ser. ISBN:0-14-018293-4, ISBN13: 978-0-14-018293-4. Dewey:947/.0841.
Audience: **g,l,u,f.**

Steinberg, Mark D. **DK265.A544 2001**
Voices of Revolution, 1917. Marian Schwartz (Translator). Cloth over Boards. Yale University Press. Cumberland, RI. 2001. 432p. Annals of Communism Ser. ISBN:0-300-09016-1, ISBN13: 978-0-300-09016-1. Dewey:947/.0841. LCCN:2001-026309.
Audience: **g,l,u,f.**

Sukhanov, N. N. **DK265.7.S8813 1984**
The Russian Revolution, Nineteen Seventeen. Joel Carmichael (Editor). Trade Cloth. Princeton University Press. Princeton, NJ. 1984. 744p. ISBN:0-691-05406-1, ISBN13: 978-0-691-05406-3. Dewey:947.0841092. LCCN:83-043102.
Audience: **g,u,f.**

Wade, Rex A. **DK265.W24 2005**
The Russian Revolution 1917. Ed. 2. William Beik & T. C. W. Blanning (Contribution by). Cloth Text. Cambridge University Press. New York, NY. 2005. 368p. New Approaches to European History Ser. ISBN:0-521-84155-0, ISBN13: 978-0-521-84155-9. Dewey:947.084/1. LCCN:2004-062849.
Audience: **g,l,u,f.** *Choice, 2001.*

Russia > By period > Soviet Union (1918-1991)

Bonnell, Victoria E. **DK266**
Iconography of Power: Soviet Political Posters under Lenin and Stalin. Trade Paper. University of California Press. Berkeley,

CA. 1999. 386p. Studies on the History of Society and Culture Ser. ISBN:0-520-22153-2, ISBN13: 978-0-520-22153-6. Dewey:947.084. LCCN:96-036252.
Audience: **g,u,f.** *Choice, 1998.*

Bukharin, Nikolai **PG3476.B776.V7413**
How It All Began: The Prison Novel. George Shriver (Translator), Stephen F. Cohen (Foreword by). Trade Cloth. Eastern European Monographs. Bradenton, FL. 1998. 416p. ISBN:0-231-10730-7, ISBN13: 978-0-231-10730-3. Dewey:891.73/42. LCCN:97-038428.
Audience: **u,f.** *Choice, 1998.*

Chumachenko, Tatiana A. **BX492.C4813 2002**
Church and State in Soviet Russia: Russian Orthodoxy from World War II to the Khrushchev Years. Edward E. Roslof (Editor, Translator). Trade Cloth. M. E. Sharpe Inc. Armonk, NY. 2002. 256p. The New Russian History Ser. ISBN:0-7656-0748-4, ISBN13: 978-0-7656-0748-5. Dewey:322/.1/094709044. LCCN:2002-066946.
Audience: **u,f.** *Choice, 2003.*

Clements, Barbara Evans **HX313.7 .C64 1997**
Bolshevik Women. Trade Cloth. Cambridge University Press. New York, NY. 1997. 352p. ISBN:0-521-45403-4, ISBN13: 978-0-521-45403-2. Dewey:947/.084/082. LCCN:96-050036.
Audience: **g,l,u,f.** *Choice, 1998.*

Cohen, Stephen F. **DK268.B76**
Bukharin and the Bolshevik Revolution: A Political Biography, 1888-1938. Trade Paper. Oxford University Press, Inc. New York, NY. 1980. 560p. ISBN:0-19-502697-7, ISBN13: 978-0-19-502697-9. Dewey:947.0840924.
Audience: **g,u,f.**

Cohen, Stephen F. **JN6511**
Rethinking the Soviet Experience: Politics and History since 1917. Paper Text. Oxford University Press, Inc. New York, NY. 1986. 235p. ISBN:0-19-504016-3, ISBN13: 978-0-19-504016-6. Dewey:947/.0072. LCCN:84-000749.
Audience: **g,u,f.**

Daniels, Robert V. (Editor, Translator, Introduction by) **HX313 .D644 1993**
A Documentary History of Communism in Russia: From Lenin to Gorbachev. Ed. 3. Trade Paper. University Press of New England. Lebanon, NH. 1993. 428p. ISBN:0-87451-616-1, ISBN13: 978-0-87451-616-6. Dewey:335.43/0947. LCCN:92-056902.
Audience: **g,u,f.**

Davies, Richard W. (Editor), et al. **HC335 .T7362 1994**
The Economic Transformation of the Soviet Union, 1913-1945. Mark Harrison & Stephen G. Wheatcroft (Editors). Trade Cloth. Cambridge University Press. New York, NY. 1993. 413p. ISBN:0-521-45152-3, ISBN13: 978-0-521-45152-9. Dewey:330.947084. LCCN:93-025112.
Audience: **u,f.**

Engel, Barbara A. & Posadskaia-Vanderbeck, Anastasia (Editors) **HQ1662.R43 1998**
A Revolution of Their Own: Voices of Women in Soviet History. Sona Hoisington (Translator). Trade Paper. Westview Press. Boulder, CO. 1997. 256p. ISBN:0-8133-3365-2, ISBN13: 978-0-8133-3365-6. Dewey:947/.084/082. LCCN:97-026662.
Audience: **g,l,u,f.**

Goldman, Wendy Z. **KLA540 .G65 1993**
Women, the State and Revolution: Soviet Family Policy and Social Life, 1917-1936. Cloth Text. Cambridge University Press. New York, NY. 1993. 363p. Cambridge Russian, Soviet and Post-Soviet Studies, No. 90 ISBN:0-521-37404-9, ISBN13: 978-0-521-37404-0. Dewey:305.420947. LCCN:92-047481.
Audience: **u,f.** *Choice, 1994.*

Gorsuch, Anne E. **HX313.G666 2000**
Youth in Revolutionary Russia: Enthusiasts, Bohemians, Delinquents. Trade Cloth. Indiana University Press. Bloomington, IN. 2000. x, 274p. Indiana-Michigan Series in Russian and East European Studies ISBN:0-253-33766-6, ISBN13: 978-0-253-33766-5. Dewey:305.235/0947/09041. LCCN:00-024181.
Audience: **g,l,u,f.** *Choice, 2001.*

Graham, Loren R. **TA140.P25G73 1993**
The Ghost of the Executed Engineer: Technology and the Fall of the Soviet Union. Trade Cloth. Harvard University Press. Cambridge, MA. 1993. 154p. Russian Research Center Studies, No. 87 ISBN:0-674-35436-2, ISBN13: 978-0-674-35436-4. Dewey:620/.0092. LCCN:93-001119.
Audience: **g,l,u,f.** *Choice, 1994.*

Husband, William **BL2765.S65H87 2000**
Godless Communists: Atheism and Society in Soviet Russia, 1917-1932. Trade Cloth. Northern Illinois University Press. DeKalb, IL. 2003. 258p. ISBN:0-87580-257-5, ISBN13: 978-0-87580-257-2. Dewey:211/.8/0947. LCCN:99-033412.
Audience: **u,f.** *Choice, 2000.*

Kenez, Peter **PN1993.5.R9K39 2001**
Cinema and Soviet Society: From the Revolution to the Death of Stalin. Cloth over Boards, Trade Cloth. I. B. Tauris & Company, Ltd. London, 2001. 288p. KINO - the Russian Cinema Ser. ISBN:1-86064-632-8, ISBN13: 978-1-86064-632-4. Dewey:791.43/0947. LCCN:2001-270261.
Audience: **g,l,u,f.**

Levesque, Jacques **DJK45.S65L4813 1997**
Enigma of 1989: The U. S. S. R. and the Liberation of Eastern Europe. Keith Martin (Translator). Trade Cloth. University of California Press. Berkeley, CA. 1997. 275p. ISBN:0-520-20631-2, ISBN13: 978-0-520-20631-1. Dewey:327.47047/09048. LCCN:96-052426.
Audience: **g,u,f.** *Choice, 1998.*

Levin, Nora **DS135.R92L48 1988**
The Jews in the Soviet Union since 1917. Cloth Text. New York University Press. New York, NY. 1988. 864p. ISBN:0-8147-5018-4, ISBN13: 978-0-8147-5018-6. Dewey:947.004924. LCCN:87-021951.
Audience: **g,u,f.** *Choice, 1989.*

Lewin, Moshe **DK266.L474 2005**
Soviet Century. Trade Cloth. Verso Books. London, 2005. 352p. ISBN:1-84467-016-3, ISBN13: 978-1-84467-016-1. Dewey:947.084. LCCN:2004-015478.
Audience: **g,l,u,f.** *Choice, 2006.*

Mawdsley, Evan & White, Stephen **JN6549.E9M39 2000**
The Soviet Elite from Lenin to Gorbachev: The Central Committee and Its Members, 1917-1991. Trade Cloth. Oxford University Press, Inc. New York, NY. 2000. 348p. ISBN:0-19-829738-6, ISBN13: 978-0-19-829738-3. Dewey:324.247/075/0922. LCCN:99-053199.
Audience: **u,f.** *Choice, 2001.*

McCannon, John **DK501.5.M38 1998**
Red Arctic: Polar Exploration and the Myth of the North in the Soviet Union, 1932-1939. Cloth Text. Oxford University Press, Inc. New York, NY. 1998. 256p. ISBN:0-19-511436-1, ISBN13: 978-0-19-511436-2. Dewey:947. LCCN:97-013937.
Audience: **g,l,u,f.** *Choice, 1998.*

Peterson, D. J. **GE190.E852**
Troubled Lands: The Legacy of Soviet Environmental Destruction. Trade Paper. Westview Press. Boulder, CO. 1993. 276p. A Rand Corporation Research Study ISBN:0-8133-1674-X, ISBN13: 978-0-8133-1674-1. Dewey:363.700947. LCCN:92-030796.
Audience: **g,l,u,f.** *Choice, 1993.*

Roslof, Edward E. **BX492.R66 2002**
[e] Red Priests: Renovationism, Russian Orthodoxy, and Revolution, 1905-1946. E-Book. Indiana University Press. Bloomington, IN. 2002. 288p. Indiana-Michigan Series in Russian and East European Studies ISBN:0-253-34128-0, ISBN13: 978-0-253-34128-0. Dewey:261.7/0947/09041. LCCN:2001-008456.
Audience: **u,f.** *Choice, 2003.*

Shlapentokh, Vladimir **HN523.5.S434 1989**
Public and Private Life of the Soviet People: Changing Values in Post-Stalin Russia. Cloth Text. Oxford University Press, Inc. New York, NY. 1989. 296p. ISBN:0-19-504266-2, ISBN13: 978-0-19-504266-5. Dewey:306/.0947. LCCN:87-034962.
Audience: **u,f.** *Choice, 1989.*

Siegelbaum, Lewis H. & Suny, Ronald G. (Editors) **HD8524.M35 1994**
Making Workers Soviet: Power, Class, and Identity. Book, Other. Cornell University Press. Ithaca, NY. 1995. 416p. ISBN:0-8014-3022-4, ISBN13: 978-0-8014-3022-0. Dewey:305.5/62/0947. LCCN:94-021989.
Audience: **u,f.**

Stites, Richard **DK266.4.S75 1989**
Revolutionary Dreams: Utopian Vision and Experimental Life in the Russian Revolution. Cloth Text. Oxford University Press, Inc. New York, NY. 1988. 324p. ISBN:0-19-505536-5, ISBN13: 978-0-19-505536-8. Dewey:947.084. LCCN:88-005263.
Audience: **u,f.** *Choice, 1989.*

Suny, Ronald G. **DK266.S94 1998**
The Soviet Experiment: Russia, the U. S. S. R., and the Successor States. Paper Text. Oxford University Press, Inc. New York, NY. 1997. 560p. ISBN:0-19-508105-6, ISBN13: 978-0-19-508105-3. Dewey:947. LCCN:97-019996.
Audience: **g,u,f.**

Ulam, Adam B. **HX313.U39 1998**
The Bolsheviks: The Intellectual and Political History of the Triumph of Communism in Russia. Trade Paper. Harvard University Press. Cambridge, MA. 1998. 598p. ISBN:0-674-07830-6, ISBN13: 978-0-674-07830-7. Dewey:947/.084. LCCN:98-135587.
Audience: **g,u,f.**

Von Laue, Theodore H. **DK246 .V58 1993**
Why Lenin? Why Stalin? Why Gorbachev?: The Rise and Fall of the Soviet System. Ed. 3. Trade Paper. Longman Publishing. Boston, MA. 1997. 194p. ISBN:0-06-501111-2, ISBN13: 978-0-06-501111-1. Dewey:947.084. LCCN:92-015870.
Audience: **g,l,u,f.**

Vucinich, Alexander S. **AS262.A68**
Empire of Knowledge: Academy of Sciences of the U. S. S. R. (1917-1970). Trade Cloth. University of California Press. Berkeley, CA. 1984. 480p. ISBN:0-520-04871-7, ISBN13: 978-0-520-04871-3. Dewey:067. LCCN:83-003484.
Audience: **u,f.** B

Xenakis, Christopher I. **DK266**
What Happened to the Soviet Union?: How and Why American Sovietologists Were Caught by Surprise. Trade Cloth. Greenwood Publishing Group, Inc. Portsmouth, NH. 2002. 248p. ISBN:0-275-97527-4, ISBN13: 978-0-275-97527-2. Dewey:947/.007/2. LCCN:2002-022439.
Audience: **g,u,f.** *Choice, 2003.*

Yurchak, Alexei **DK266.4.Y87 2005**
Everything Was Forever, until It Was No More: The Last Soviet Generation. Trade Cloth. Princeton University Press. Princeton, NJ. 2005. 336p. In-Formation Ser. ISBN:0-691-12116-8, ISBN13: 978-0-691-12116-1. Dewey:947.085. LCCN:2004-042384.
Audience: **u,f.** *Choice, 2006.*

Russia > By period > Soviet Union (1918-1991) > Biography. Lenin. Stalin

Brackman, Roman **DK268.S8B69 2001**
The Secret File of Joseph Stalin: A Hidden Life. Cloth Text. Taylor & Francis Group. Abingdon, 2001. 466p. ISBN:0-7146-5050-1, ISBN13: 978-0-7146-5050-0. Dewey:947.084. LCCN:00-050861.
Audience: **g,u,f.** *Choice, 2001.*

d'Encausse, Helene Carrere **DK254.L4C2813 2001**
Lenin. George Holoch (Translator). Trade Cloth. Holmes & Meier Publishers, Inc. Teaneck, NJ. 2001. xi, 371p. ISBN:0-8419-1412-5, ISBN13: 978-0-8419-1412-4. Dewey:947.084/1/092 B. LCCN:2001-024537.
Audience: **g,l,u,f.** *Choice, 2002.*

Lourie, Richard **DK275.S25L68 2002**
Sakharov: A Biography. Trade Cloth. University Press of New England. Lebanon, NH. 2005. 480p. ISBN:1-58465-207-1, ISBN13: 978-1-58465-207-6. Dewey:323/.092 B. LCCN:2001-005246.
Audience: **g,l,u,f.**

Montefiore, Simon Sebag **DK268.S8M573 2004**
Stalin: The Court of the Red Tsar. Trade Cloth. Alfred A. Knopf Inc. New York, NY. 2004. 816p. ISBN:1-4000-4230-5, ISBN13: 978-1-4000-4230-2. Dewey:947.084/2/092 B. LCCN:2003-027390.
Audience: **g,u,f.** *Choice, 2004.*

Service, Robert **DK254.L4S4323 2000**
Lenin: A Biography. Trade Cloth. Harvard University Press. Cambridge, MA. 2000. 587p. ISBN:0-674-00330-6, ISBN13: 978-0-674-00330-9. Dewey:947/.0841/092. LCCN:00-021394.
Audience: **g,u,f.** *Choice, 2001.*

Service, Robert **DK268.S8S4237 2005**
Stalin: A Biography. Trade Cloth. Harvard University Press. Cambridge, MA. 2005. 736p. ISBN:0-674-01697-1, ISBN13:

978-0-674-01697-2. Dewey:947.084/1/092 B. LCCN:2004-061115.
Audience: **g,u,f.** *Choice, 2005.*

Thatcher, Ian D. **DK254.T6T5 2002**
Trotsky. Paper over Boards. Routledge. New York, NY. 2002. 264p. Historical Biographies Ser. ISBN:0-415-23250-3, ISBN13: 978-0-415-23250-0. Dewey:947.084/092 B. LCCN:2002-028469.
Audience: **g,l,u,f.** *Choice, 2003.*

Tucker, Robert C. **DK268.S8T86 1990**
Stalin in Power: An Interpretive History. Trade Cloth. W. W. Norton & Company, Inc. New York, NY. 1990. 707p. ISBN:0-393-02881-X, ISBN13: 978-0-393-02881-2. Dewey:947.084/2/092. LCCN:89-078047.
Audience: **g,u,f.**

Volkogonov, Dmitri **DK254.L4V587 1994**
Lenin: A New Biography. Trade Cloth. Simon & Schuster. New York, NY. 1994. 529p. ISBN:0-02-933435-7, ISBN13: 978-0-02-933435-5. Dewey:947.084/1/092 B. LCCN:94-031752.
Audience: **g,u,f.** *Choice, 1995.*

Volkogonov, Dmitri **DK254.T6V6513 1996**
Trotsky: The Eternal Revolutionary. Reinforced. Simon & Schuster. New York, NY. 1996. 560p. ISBN:0-684-82293-8, ISBN13: 978-0-684-82293-8. Dewey:947.084/092 B. LCCN:95-042315.
Audience: **g,u,f.** *Choice, 1996.*

White, James D. **DK254.L4W375 2001**
Lenin: The Practice and Theory of Revolution. Cloth over Boards. Palgrave Macmillan. New York, NY. 2001. 274p. European History in Perspective Ser. ISBN:0-333-72156-X, ISBN13: 978-0-333-72156-8. Dewey:947.084/1/092 B. LCCN:00-062593.
Audience: **g,l,u,f.** *Choice, 2002.*

Russia > By period > Soviet Union (1918-1991) > Memoirs

Andreev-Khomiakov, Gennady **DK268.A54A3 1997**
Bitter Waters: Life and Work in Stalin's Russia. Ann E. Healy (Translator). Trade Cloth. Westview Press. Boulder, CO. 1997. 224p. ISBN:0-8133-2390-8, ISBN13: 978-0-8133-2390-9. Dewey:947.084/2/092. LCCN:96-053092.
Audience: **g,l,u,f.** *Choice, 1998.*

Bek, Anna Nikolaevna & Rassweiler, Anne Dickason **R534.B368A3 2004**
[e] The Life of a Russian Woman Doctor: A Siberian Memoir, 1869-1954. E-Book. Indiana University Press. Bloomington, IN. 2004. 176p. ISBN:0-253-34460-3, ISBN13: 978-0-253-34460-1. Dewey:610/.92. LCCN:2004-006413.
Audience: **g,l,u,f.** *Choice, 2005.*

Dune, Eduard M. **DK254.D78.A3 1993**
Notes of a Red Guard. Diane P. Koenker & S. A. Smith (Editor, Translators). Trade Cloth. University of Illinois Press. Champaign, IL. 1993. 328p. ISBN:0-252-01972-5, ISBN13: 978-0-252-01972-2. Dewey:947.084/1/092. LCCN:92-018937.
Audience: **g,u,f.** *Choice, 1994.*

Ginzburg, Eugenia S. **DK268.3 .G513**
Journey into the Whirlwind. Ed. 1. Trade Paper. Harcourt Trade Publishers. New York, NY. 2002. 432p. ISBN:0-15-602751-8, ISBN13: 978-0-15-602751-9. Dewey:365/.6/0924.
Audience: **g,l,u,f.**

Khrushchev, Nikita Sergeevich & Khrushchev, Sergeaei (Editors) **DK275.K5A3 2004**
Memoirs of Nikita Khrushchev. Trade Cloth. Pennsylvania State University Press. University Park, PA. 2004. 752p. ISBN:0-271-02332-5, ISBN13: 978-0-271-02332-8. Dewey:947.085/2/092 B. LCCN:2003-007060.
Audience: **g,u,f.** *Choice, 2006.*

Kopelev, Lev Z. **PG3482.7.P4 Z51613**
The Education of a True Believer. Gary Kern (Translator). Trade Cloth. HarperCollins Publishers. New York, NY. 1980. ISBN:0-06-012476-8, ISBN13: 978-0-06-012476-2. Dewey:365/.45/0924. LCCN:79-003397.
Audience: **g,l,u,f.**

Kravchenko, Viktor Andreevich **DK0268.K7A3**
I Chose Freedom: The Personal and Political Life of a Soviet Official. Trade Paper. Books on Demand. Ann Arbor, MI. 522p. ISBN:0-598-74953-5, ISBN13: 978-0-598-74953-6. Dewey:947.084. LCCN:46-002999.
Audience: **g,u,f.**

Scott, John **DK781.M3S35 1989**
Behind the Urals: An American Worker in Russias City of Steel. Perfect, Paper over Boards. Indiana University Press. Bloomington, IN. 1989. 306p. ISBN:0-253-35125-1, ISBN13: 978-0-253-35125-8. Dewey:947.87. LCCN:88-046214.
Audience: **g,l,u,f.**

Russia > By period > Soviet Union (1918-1991) > Early Soviet Regime (1918-1928). Civil War. New Economic Policy

Babel, Isaac **PG3476.B2K613 2003**
Red Cavalry. Nathalie Constantine (Translator), Michael Dirda (Introduction by). Trade Paper. W. W. Norton & Company, Inc. New York, NY. 2003. 352p. ISBN:0-393-32423-0, ISBN13: 978-0-393-32423-5. Dewey:891.73/42. LCCN:2003-000682.
Audience: **g,l,u,f.**

Ball, Alan M. **HV887.R8**
Now My Soul Is Hardened: Abandoned Children in Soviet Russia, 1918-1930. Trade Paper. University of California Press. Berkeley, CA. 1996. 362p. ISBN:0-520-20694-0, ISBN13: 978-0-520-20694-6. Dewey:362.730947.
Audience: **g,u,f.** *Choice, 1994.*

Gladkov, Fyodor Vasilievich **PG3476.G53T813 1994**
Cement. A. S. Arthur & C. Ashleigh (Translators). Trade Cloth. Northwestern University Press. Evanston, IL. 1994. 312p. European Classics Ser. ISBN:0-8101-1175-6, ISBN13: 978-0-8101-1175-2. Dewey:891.73/42. LCCN:94-022785.
Audience: **g,l,u,f.**

Lincoln, W. Bruce **DK265.L449 1999**
Red Victory: A History of the Russian Civil War, 1918-1921. Trade Paper. Da Capo Press, Inc. Cambridge, MA. 1999. 640p. ISBN:0-306-80909-5, ISBN13: 978-0-306-80909-5. Dewey:947.084/1. LCCN:98-054830.
Audience: **g,u,f.**

Mawdsley, Evan **DK265.M372 1987**
The Russian Civil War. Cloth Text. Routledge. New York, NY. 1987. 320p. ISBN:0-04-947024-8, ISBN13: 978-0-04-947024-8. Dewey:947.084/1. LCCN:87-001113.
Audience: **g,l,u,f.** *Choice, 1988.*

Tucker, Robert C. (Editor) **DK254.L3 A5787**
The Lenin Anthology. Paper Text. W. W. Norton & Company, Inc. New York, NY. 1975. ISBN:0-393-09236-4, ISBN13: 978-0-393-09236-3. Dewey:335.43/092/4.
Audience: **u,f.**

Wood, Elizabeth A. **HX546.W67 1997**
e The Baba and the Comrade: Gender and Politics in Revolutionary Russia. E-Book. Indiana University Press. Bloomington, IN. 1997. 336p. Indiana-Michigan Series in Russian and East European Studies ISBN:0-253-33311-3, ISBN13: 978-0-253-33311-7. Dewey:321.9/2/0820947. LCCN:97-002290.
Audience: **g,u,f.** *Choice, 1998.*

Russia > By period > Soviet Union (1918-1991) > Stalin Era (to 1953)

Brandenberger, David **DK266.4.B73 2002**
National Bolshevism: Stalinist Mass Culture and the Formation of Modern Russian National Identity, 1931-1956. Trade Cloth. Harvard University Press. Cambridge, MA. 2002. 400p. Russian Research Center Studies, Vol. 93 ISBN:0-674-00906-1, ISBN13: 978-0-674-00906-6. Dewey:306/.0947. LCCN:2002-068801.
Audience: **u,f.** *Choice, 2003.*

Brooks, Jeffrey **DK40**
Thank You, Comrade Stalin!: Soviet Public Culture from Revolution to Cold War. Trade Paper. Princeton University Press. Princeton, NJ. 2001. 340p. ISBN:0-691-08867-5, ISBN13: 978-0-691-08867-9. Dewey:947.
Audience: **u,f.** *Choice, 2000.*

Conquest, Robert **DK267**
The Great Terror: A Reassessment. Paper Text. Oxford University Press, Inc. New York, NY. 1991. 584p. ISBN:0-19-507132-8, ISBN13: 978-0-19-507132-0. Dewey:947.084/2.
Audience: **g,u,f.**

Conquest, Robert **HD1492.R9**
The Harvest of Sorrow: Soviet Collectivization and the Terror-Famine. Trade Paper. Oxford University Press, Inc. New York, NY. 1987. 430p. ISBN:0-19-505180-7, ISBN13: 978-0-19-505180-3. Dewey:338.7/63/0947.
Audience: **g,u,f.** *Choice, 1987.*

Conquest, Robert **HV8224**
Inside Stalin's Secret Police: NKVD Politics, 1936-1939. Trade Cloth. Hoover Institution Press. Stanford, CA. 1985. ix, 222p. Publication Ser., No. 324 ISBN:0-8179-8241-8, ISBN13: 978-0-8179-8241-6. Dewey:363.2/83/0947. LCCN:84-029765.
Audience: **u,f.**

Dallin, Alexander & Firsov, Fridrikh I. (Editors) **DK268.S8A4 2000**
Dimitrov and Stalin, 1934-1943: Letters from the Soviet Archives. Vadim A. Staklo (Translator). Cloth over Boards. Yale University Press. Cumberland, RI. 2000. 312p. Annals of Communism Ser. ISBN:0-300-08021-2, ISBN13: 978-0-300-08021-6. Dewey:947.084/2. LCCN:99-039083.
Audience: **u,f.**

Davies, R. W. & Wheatcroft, Stephen G. **HD1492.R9Y4 2003**
The Years of Hunger: Soviet Agriculture, 1931-1933. Cloth over Boards. Palgrave Macmillan. New York, NY. 2004. 624p. The Industrialization of Soviet Russia Ser. ISBN:0-333-31107-8, ISBN13: 978-0-333-31107-3. Dewey:338.1/0947/09043. LCCN:2003-050925.
Audience: **u,f.** *Choice, 2004.*

Fitzpatrick, Sheila **DK267**
Everyday Stalinism: Ordinary Life in Extraordinary Times: Soviet Russia in the 1930s. Trade Paper. Oxford University Press, Inc. New York, NY. 2000. 300p. ISBN:0-19-505001-0, ISBN13: 978-0-19-505001-1. Dewey:947/.0842.
Audience: **g,u,f.** *Choice, 1999.*

Fitzpatrick, Sheila **HD1492.S65F58 1994**
Stalin's Peasants: Collectiveness and Popular Resistance in Russia. Trade Cloth. Oxford University Press, Inc. New York, NY. 1994. 416p. ISBN:0-19-506982-X, ISBN13: 978-0-19-506982-2. Dewey:306.3/64/0947. LCCN:93-004786.
Audience: **u,f.** *Choice, 1994.*

Garros, Veronique (Editor), et al. **DK268.A1I54 1995**
Intimacy and Terror: Soviet Diaries of The 1930s. Natalia Korenevskaya & Thomas Lahusen (Editors), Carol A. Flath (Translator). Trade Cloth. New Press, The. New York, NY. 1995. 416p. ISBN:1-56584-200-6, ISBN13: 978-1-56584-200-7. Dewey:920.047. LCCN:95-001967.
Audience: **u,f.**

Goldman, Wendy Z. **HD6166 .G65 2002**
Women at the Gates: Gender and Industry in Stalin's Russia. Cloth Text. Cambridge University Press. New York, NY. 2002. 314p. ISBN:0-521-78064-0, ISBN13: 978-0-521-78064-3. Dewey:331.40947. LCCN:2001-035060.
Audience: **u,f.**

Gorlizki, Yoram, et al. **DK268.4.G67 2003**
Cold Peace: Stalin and the Soviet Ruling Circle, 1945-1953. O. V. Khlevneiiuk & Oleg V. Khlevniuk (Authors). Trade Cloth. Oxford University Press, Inc. New York, NY. 2004. 272p. ISBN:0-19-516581-0, ISBN13: 978-0-19-516581-4. Dewey:947.084/2/092. LCCN:2003-048081.
Audience: **g,u,f.** *Choice, 2004.*

Hoffmann, David L. **HX313.H58 2003**
Stalinist Values: The Cultural Norms of Soviet Modernity, 1917-1941. Trade Cloth. Cornell University Press. Ithaca, NY. 2003. 264p. ISBN:0-8014-4089-0, ISBN13: 978-0-8014-4089-2. Dewey:947.084/1. LCCN:2002-155926.
Audience: **u,f.** *Choice, 2004.*

Holloway, David **DK267**
Stalin and the Bomb: The Soviet Union and Atomic Energy, 1939-1956. Trade Paper. Yale University Press. Cumberland, RI. 1996. 480p. ISBN:0-300-06664-3, ISBN13: 978-0-300-06664-7. Dewey:947/.0842.
Audience: **g,l,u,f.**

Khlevniuk, Oleg V. **HV8964.S65K48 2004**
The History of the Gulag: From Collectivization to the Great Terror. Vadim A. Staklo (Translator), Robert Conquest (Foreword by). Cloth over Boards. Yale University Press. Cumberland, RI. 2004. 464p. Annals of Communism Ser. ISBN:0-300-09284-9, ISBN13: 978-0-300-09284-4. Dewey:365/.45/094709043. LCCN:2004-010969.
Audience: **u,f.** *Choice, 2005.*

Koestler, Arthur **PT2621.A26**
Darkness at Noon. Library Binding. Sagebrush Education Resources. Caledonia, MN. 1968. ISBN:0-8085-7636-4, ISBN13: 978-0-8085-7636-5. Dewey:833.9/12.
Audience: **g,l,u,f.**

Kostyrchenko, Gennadi V. **DS146.S65K68 1995**
Out of the Red Shadows: Anti-Semitism in Stalin's Russia. Trade Cloth. Prometheus Books, Publishers. Amherst, NY. 1995. 333p. Russian Studies Ser. ISBN:0-87975-930-5, ISBN13: 978-0-87975-930-8. Dewey:947/.004924. LCCN:94-039151.
Audience: **u,f.**

Kotkin, Stephen **DK651.M159K675 1995**
Magnetic Mountain: Stalinism as a Civilization. Trade Cloth. University of California Press. Berkeley, CA. 1995. 690p. ISBN:0-520-06908-0, ISBN13: 978-0-520-06908-4. Dewey:947/.87. LCCN:94-011839.
Audience: **g,u,f.** *Choice, 1995.*

Levin, Dov **DS135.P6L47613 1995**
The Lesser of Two Evils: Eastern European Jewry under Soviet Rule 1939-1941. Trade Cloth. Jewish Publication Society. Dulles, VA. 1995. 424p. ISBN:0-8276-0518-8, ISBN13: 978-0-8276-0518-3. Dewey:943.8/004924. LCCN:95-018725.
Audience: **g,u,f.** *Choice, 1996.*

Mastny, Vojtech **DK267.M3567 1996**
The Cold War and Soviet Insecurity: The Stalin Years. Trade Cloth. Oxford University Press, Inc. New York, NY. 1996. 304p. ISBN:0-19-510616-4, ISBN13: 978-0-19-510616-9. Dewey:947/.0842. LCCN:95-049341.
Audience: **g,u,f.** *Choice, 1997.*

Merridale, Catherine **JN6598.K7M42637 1990**
Moscow Politics and the Rise of Stalin: The Communist Party in the Capital, 1925-32. Cloth Text. Palgrave Macmillan. New York, NY. 1991. 297p. ISBN:0-312-04799-1, ISBN13: 978-0-312-04799-3. Dewey:324.247/075/0947312. LCCN:90-008360.
Audience: **g,u,f.** *Choice, 1991.*

Perrie, Maureen **DK269.5.P47 2000**
The Cult of Ivan the Terrible in Stalin's Russia. Cloth over Boards. Palgrave Macmillan. New York, NY. 2002. 273p. Studies in Russian and Eastern European History Ser. ISBN:0-333-65684-9, ISBN13: 978-0-333-65684-6. Dewey:947/.043/092. LCCN:2001-032718.
Audience: **g,u,f.** *Choice, 2002.*

Read, Anthony & Fisher, David **D749.5.R8R43 1988**
Deadly Embrace: Hitler, Stalin and the Nazi-Soviet Pact, 1939-1941. Trade Cloth. W. W. Norton & Company, Inc. New York, NY. 1988. xxi, 687p. ISBN:0-393-02528-4, ISBN13: 978-0-393-02528-6. Dewey:940.53/2. LCCN:88-018123.
Audience: **g,u,f.** *Choice, 1989.*

Read, Christopher (Editor) **DK267.S6937 2002**
The Stalin Years: A Reader. Cloth over Boards. Palgrave Macmillan. New York, NY. 2003. 240p. ISBN:0-333-96342-3, ISBN13: 978-0-333-96342-5. Dewey:947.084/2. LCCN:2002-035909.
Audience: **g,l,u,f.**

Shearer, David R. **HD3616.S472S5 1996**
Industry, State, and Society in Stalin's Russia, 1926-1934. Book, Other. Cornell University Press. Ithaca, NY. 1997. 312p. ISBN:0-8014-3207-3, ISBN13: 978-0-8014-3207-1. Dewey:338.947/009/042. LCCN:96-008178.
Audience: **u,f.** *Choice, 1997.*

Siegelbaum, Lewis H. & Sokolov, Andrei (Editors) **DK267.S69386 2000**
Stalinism as a Way of Life: A Narrative in Documents. Thomas H. Hoisington & Steven Shabad (Translators). Cloth over Boards. Yale University Press. Cumberland, RI. 2000. 480p. Annals of Communism Ser. ISBN:0-300-08480-3, ISBN13: 978-0-300-08480-1. Dewey:947.084. LCCN:00-032074.
Audience: **g,u,f.** *Choice, 2001.*

Straus, Kenneth M. **HD8526.S87 1997**
Factory and Community in Stalin's Russia: The Making of an Industrial Working Class. Cloth Text. University of Pittsburgh Press. Pittsburgh, PA. 1998. 480p. Series in Russian and East European Studies ISBN:0-8229-4048-5, ISBN13: 978-0-8229-4048-7. Dewey:305.5/62/0947. LCCN:97-021046.
Audience: **u,f.**

Witkin, Zara **TA140.W59A3 1991**
An American Engineer in Stalin's Russia: The Memoirs of Zara Witkin, 1932-1934. Michael Gelb (Introduction by). Trade Cloth. University of California Press. Berkeley, CA. 1991. 352p. ISBN:0-520-07134-4, ISBN13: 978-0-520-07134-6. Dewey:624/.092 B. LCCN:91-014405.
Audience: **g,l,u,f.** *Choice, 1992.*

Russia > By period > Soviet Union (1918-1991) > The Great Patriotic War (1941-1945). Legacies and Popular Memory

Beevor, Antony **D764.3.S7B37 1998**
Stalingrad: The Fateful Siege, 1942-1943. Trade Paper. Penguin Group (USA) Inc. New York, NY. 1999. 560p. ISBN:0-14-028458-3, ISBN13: 978-0-14-028458-4. Dewey:940.54/21785. LCCN:98-019346.
Audience: **g,l,u,f.**

Dallin, Alexander **D802.S75.D34 1981**
German Rule in Russia 1941-1945. Ed. 2. Library Binding. Westview Press. Boulder, CO. 1985. 700p. A Study of Occupation Policies ISBN:0-86531-102-1, ISBN13: 978-0-86531-102-2. Dewey:940.53/47. LCCN:80-052877.
Audience: **u,f.**

Dallin, Alexander **DK508.9.T73D35 1998**
Odessa, 1941-1944: A Case Study of Soviet Territory under Foreign Rule. Larry L. Watts (Introduction by). Trade Cloth. Center for Romanian Studies, The. Iali, 1998. 296p. ISBN:973-98391-1-8, ISBN13: 978-973-98391-1-2. Dewey:947.7/2. LCCN:98-208730.
Audience: **u,f.** *Choice, 1998.*

Erickson, John **D764.E737 1999**
The Road to Berlin: Stalin's War with Germany. Trade Paper. Yale University Press. Cumberland, RI. 1999. 896p. Road to Berlin Ser., Vol. 2 ISBN:0-300-07813-7, ISBN13: 978-0-300-07813-8. Dewey:940.5/4217. LCCN:98-089037.
Audience: **g,l,u,f.**

Erickson, John **D764.E737 1999**
Stalin's War with Germany. Trade Paper. Yale University Press. Cumberland, RI. 1999. 606p. Stalin's War with Germany Ser., Vol. 1 ISBN:0-300-07812-9, ISBN13: 978-0-300-07812-1. Dewey:940.5421. LCCN:98-089037.
Audience: **g,l,u,f.**

Glantz, David M. **D764.G5558 2005**
Colossus Reborn: The Red Army at War: 1941-1943. Trade Cloth. University Press of Kansas. Lawrence, KS. 2005. 816p. Modern War Studies ISBN:0-7006-1353-6, ISBN13: 978-0-7006-1353-3. Dewey:940.54/1247. LCCN:2004-013594.
Audience: **g,u,f.** *Choice, 2005.*

Gorodetsky, Gabriel **D754.S65G67 1999**
Grand Delusion: Stalin and the German Invasion of Russia. Cloth over Boards. Yale University Press. Cumberland, RI. 1999. 424p. ISBN:0-300-07792-0, ISBN13: 978-0-300-07792-6. Dewey:940.54/0947. LCCN:99-012728.
Audience: **g,u,f.** *Choice, 1999.*

Grossman, Vasily Semenovich **PG3476.G7Z3513 2006**
Life and Fate. Robert Chandler (Introduction by). Trade Paper. New York Review of Books, Incorporated, The. New York, NY. 2006. 896p. New York Review Books Classics ISBN:1-59017-201-9, ISBN13: 978-1-59017-201-8. Dewey:891.73/42. LCCN:2005-022739.
Audience: **g,l,u,f.**

Grossman, Vasily **D764.G772 2006**
A Writer at War: Vasily Grossman with the Red Army, 1941-1945. Antony Beevor (Editor), Luba Vinogradova (Translator). Trade Cloth. Knopf Publishing Group. New York, NY. 2006. 400p. ISBN:0-375-42407-5, ISBN13: 978-0-375-42407-6. Dewey:940.54/217/092 B. LCCN:2005-051033.
Audience: **g,l,u,f.** *Choice, 2006.*

Hasegawa, Tsuyoshi **D813.J3H37 2005**
Racing the Enemy: Stalin, Truman, and the Surrender of Japan. Trade Cloth. Harvard University Press. Cambridge, MA. 2005. 432p. ISBN:0-674-01693-9, ISBN13: 978-0-674-01693-4. Dewey:940.53/2452. LCCN:2004-059786.
Audience: **g,l,u,f.** *Choice, 2006.*

Merridale, Catherine **D764.M395 2006**
Ivan's War: Life and Death in the Red Army, 1939-1945. Cloth over Boards. Henry Holt & Company. New York, NY. 2006. 480p. ISBN:0-8050-7455-4, ISBN13: 978-0-8050-7455-0. Dewey:940.54/217. LCCN:2005-050457.
Audience: **g,u,f.**

Murphy, David E. **D764.M845 2005**
What Stalin Knew: The Enigma of Barbarossa. Cloth over Boards. Yale University Press. Cumberland, RI. 2005. 340p. ISBN:0-300-10780-3, ISBN13: 978-0-300-10780-7. Dewey:940.54/217. LCCN:2004-065916.
Audience: **g,u,f.** *Choice, 2006.*

Noggle, Anne **D792.S65N64 1994**
A Dance with Death: Soviet Airwomen in World War II. Christine A. White (Introduction by). Trade Cloth. Texas A&M University Press. College Station, TX. 1994. 336p. ISBN:0-89096-601-X, ISBN13: 978-0-89096-601-3. Dewey:940.54/4947. LCCN:94-001301.
Audience: **g,l,u,f.** *Choice, 1995.*

Overy, Richard **D764.O94 1997**
Russia's War: Blood upon the Snow. Trade Cloth. Simon & Schuster. New York, NY. 1998. 432p. ISBN:1-57500-051-2, ISBN13: 978-1-57500-051-0. Dewey:940.54/0947. LCCN:97-213178.
Audience: **g,l,u,f.** *Choice, 1998.*

Pleshakov, Constantine **D764.P5317 2005**
Stalin's Folly: The Tragic First Ten Days of World War Two on the Eastern Front. Trade Cloth. Houghton Mifflin Company Trade & Reference Division. Boston, MA. 2005. 320p. ISBN:0-618-36701-2, ISBN13: 978-0-618-36701-6. Dewey:940.54/217. LCCN:2004-065133.
Audience: **g,u,f.**

Rotundo, L. **D764.3.S7B33 1989**
Battle for Stalingrad: The 1943 Soviet General Staff Study. Trade Cloth. Potomac Books, Inc. Dulles, VA. 1989. 342p. ISBN:0-08-035974-4, ISBN13: 978-0-08-035974-8. Dewey:940.54/21. LCCN:88-023503.
Audience: **g,u,f.** *Choice, 1990.*

Simmons, Cynthia & Perlina, Nina **D764.3.L4S56 2002**
Writing the Siege of Leningrad: Women's Diaries, Memoirs, and Documentary Prose. Trade Cloth. University of Pittsburgh Press. Pittsburgh, PA. 2002. 304p. ISBN:0-8229-4183-X, ISBN13: 978-0-8229-4183-5. Dewey:940.54/21721. LCCN:2001-006540.
Audience: **g,l,u,f.** *Choice, 2003, 2002.*

Stites, Richard (Editor) **DK273.R78 1995**
Culture and Entertainment in Wartime Russia. Trade Cloth. Indiana University Press. Bloomington, IN. 1995. 256p. ISBN:0-253-35403-X, ISBN13: 978-0-253-35403-7. Dewey:947.084/2. LCCN:94-027315.
Audience: **u,f.** *Choice, 1995.*

Thurston, Robert W. & Bonwetsch, Bernd **D764.P45 2000**
The People's War: Responses to World War II in the Soviet Union. Trade Cloth. University of Illinois Press. Champaign, IL. 2000. 288p. ISBN:0-252-02600-4, ISBN13: 978-0-252-02600-3. Dewey:947.084/2. LCCN:00-008493.
Audience: **g,l,u,f.** *Choice, 2001.*

Tumarkin, Nina **D764.T855 1994**
The Living and the Dead. Trade Cloth. Basic Books. New York, NY. 1994. 256p. ISBN:0-465-07159-7, ISBN13: 978-0-465-07159-3. Dewey:947.084. LCCN:94-002964.
Audience: **g,l,u,f.** *Choice, 1995.*

Weeks, Albert Loren **DK268.5.W44 2002**
Stalin's Other War: Soviet Grand Strategy, 1939-1941. Book, Other. Rowman & Littlefield Publishers, Inc. Lanham, MD. 2002. 224p. ISBN:0-7425-2191-5, ISBN13: 978-0-7425-2191-9. Dewey:940.53/2247. LCCN:2002-001793.
Audience: **g,u,f.** *Choice, 2003.*

Werth, Alexander **D764**
Russia at War, 1941-1945. Trade Paper. Avalon Publishing Group. New York, NY. 1999. 1136p. ISBN:0-7867-0722-4, ISBN13: 978-0-7867-0722-5. Dewey:940.5421.
Audience: **g,u,f.**

Werth, Alexander **D764**
The Year of Stalingrad: A Historical Record and a Study of Russian Mentality, Methods and Policies. Trade Paper. Simon Publications, Inc. 2002. 478p. ISBN:1-931541-76-0, ISBN13: 978-1-931541-76-3. Dewey:940.542. LCCN:47-002255.
Audience: **g,u,f.**

Zubkova, Elena **HN523.5.Z8 1998**
Russia after the War: Hopes, Illusions and Disappointments, 1945-1957. Hugh Ragsdale (Editor, Translator). Trade Cloth. M. E. Sharpe Inc. Armonk, NY. 1999. 250p. The New Russian History Ser. ISBN:0-7656-0227-X, ISBN13: 978-0-7656-0227-5. Dewey:306/.0947. LCCN:98-017042.
Audience: **g,l,u,f.** *Choice, 1999.*

Russia > By period > Soviet Union (1918-1991) > Post Stalin Era (1953-1964). Khrushchev

Fursenko, Aleksandr & Naftali, Timothy **E841.F86**
One Hell of a Gamble: Khruschev, Castro and Kennedy, 1958-1964. Trade Cloth. DIANE Publishing Company. Collingdale, PA. 2001. 420p. ISBN:0-7881-9758-4, ISBN13: 978-0-7881-9758-1. Dewey:973.922.
Audience: **g,l,u,f.**

Kozlov, Vladimir A. **DK274.K6513 2002**
Mass Uprisings in the U. S. S. R.: Protest and Rebellion in the Post-Stalin Years. Elaine McClarnand McKinnon (Editor, Translator). Trade Cloth. M. E. Sharpe Inc. Armonk, NY. 2002. 368p. The New Russian History Ser. ISBN:0-7656-0667-4, ISBN13: 978-0-7656-0667-9. Dewey:947.085. LCCN:2001-049843.
Audience: **g,u,f.** *Choice, 2003.*

Kulavig, Erik **DK274.K828 2002**
Dissent in the Years of Krushchev: Nine Stories about Disobedient Russians. Cloth over Boards. Palgrave Macmillan. New York, NY. 2003. 192p. ISBN:0-333-99037-4, ISBN13: 978-0-333-99037-7. Dewey:947.085. LCCN:2002-022417.
Audience: **g,u,f.** *Choice, 2003.*

Taubman, William **DK275.K5T38 2003**
Khrushchev: The Man and His Era. Trade Cloth. W. W. Norton & Company, Inc. New York, NY. 2003. 768p. ISBN:0-393-05144-7, ISBN13: 978-0-393-05144-5. Dewey:947.085/2/092 B. LCCN:2002-026404.
Audience: **g,u,f.** *Choice, 2003.*

Russia > By period > Soviet Union (1918-1991) > Brezhnev Era (1964-1982)

Bacon, Edwin & Sandle, Mark (Editors) **DK275.B7B74 2002**
Brezhnev Reconsidered. Cloth over Boards. Palgrave Macmillan. New York, NY. 2003. 288p. Studies in Russian and East European History and Society ISBN:0-333-79463-X, ISBN13: 978-0-333-79463-0. Dewey:947.085/3/092. LCCN:2002-072321.
Audience: **u,f.** *Choice, 2003.*

Brezhneva, Luba **DK275.B73A3 1995**
The World I Left Behind: Pieces of a Past. Trade Cloth. Random House, Inc. New York, NY. 1995. 392p. ISBN:0-679-43911-0, ISBN13: 978-0-679-43911-0. Dewey:947.085/3/092 B. LCCN:94-041088.
Audience: **g,l,u,f.** *Choice, 1996.*

Russia > By period > Soviet Union (1918-1991) > 1982-1991. Gorbachev. Collapse of Soviet Union

Alexievich, Svetlana **TD186.5.B35 A4413**
Voices from Chernobyl: The Oral History of a Nuclear Disaster. Keith Gessen (Translator). Trade Paper. Picador. New York, NY. 2006. 256p. ISBN:0-312-42584-8, ISBN13: 978-0-312-42584-5. Dewey:363.17/99/094776.
Audience: **g,l,u,f.**

Braithwaite, Rodric **DK510.763.B73 2002**
Across the Moscow River: The World Turned Upside Down. Cloth over Boards. Yale University Press. Cumberland, RI. 2002. 384p. ISBN:0-300-09496-5, ISBN13: 978-0-300-09496-1. Dewey:947.086. LCCN:2001-007277.
Audience: **g,l,u,f.** *Choice, 2003.*

Dobbs, Michael **DK274.D63 1997**
Down with Big Brother: The Fall of the Soviet Empire. Trade Cloth. Alfred A. Knopf Inc. New York, NY. 1997. 503p. ISBN:0-679-43179-9, ISBN13: 978-0-679-43179-4. Dewey:947/.0854. LCCN:96-021607.
Audience: **g,l,u,f.** *Choice, 1997.*

Graffy, Julian & Hosking, Geoffrey Alan (Editors) **P92.S65C85 1989**
Culture and the Media in the U. S. S. R. Today. Cloth Text. Palgrave Macmillan. New York, NY. 1989. 208p. ISBN:0-312-03457-1, ISBN13: 978-0-312-03457-3. Dewey:302.23/0947. LCCN:89-033421.
Audience: **g,u,f.** *Choice, 1990.*

Hewett, Ed A. & Winston, Victor H. (Editors) **HC336.26.M555 1991**
Milestones in Glasnost and Perestroyka: Politics and People. Trade Cloth. Brookings Institution Press. Washington, DC. 1991. 546p. ISBN:0-8157-3624-X, ISBN13: 978-0-8157-3624-0. Dewey:338.947/009/048. LCCN:91-015304.
Audience: **g,u,f.** *Choice, 1992.*

Lewin, Moshe **DK286.L48 1991**
The Gorbachev Phenomenon: A Historical Interpretation. Trade Paper. University of California Press. Berkeley, CA. 1991. 208p. ISBN:0-520-07429-7, ISBN13: 978-0-520-07429-3. Dewey:947.085. LCCN:90-046995.
Audience: **g,l,u,f.** *Choice, 1988.*

Remnick, David **DK288.R46 1993**
Lenin's Tomb: The Last Days of the Soviet Empire. Trade Cloth. Random House, Inc. New York, NY. 1993. 512p.

ISBN:0-679-42376-1, ISBN13: 978-0-679-42376-8.
Dewey:947.085/4. LCCN:92-056841.
Audience: **g,l,f.** *Choice, 1993.*

White, Stephen **HV5515.15 .W48 1996**
Russia Goes Dry: Alcohol, State and Society. Cloth Text. Cambridge University Press. New York, NY. 1995. 264p. ISBN:0-521-55211-7, ISBN13: 978-0-521-55211-0. Dewey:363.4/1/0947. LCCN:95-013221.
Audience: **g,u,f.** *Choice, 1996.*

Russia > Commonwealth of Independent States (CIS)

Batalden, Stephen K. & Batalden, Sandra L. **DK17.B34 1997**
The Newly Independent States of Eurasia: Handbook of Former Soviet Republics. Ed. 2. Paper Text. Greenwood Publishing Group, Inc. Portsmouth, NH. 1997. 248p. ISBN:0-89774-940-5, ISBN13: 978-0-89774-940-4. Dewey:947.086. LCCN:97-003893.
Audience: **g,l,u,f.** *Choice, 1994.*

Buckley, Mary (Editor) **HQ1665.15 .P67 1997**
Post-Soviet Women: From the Baltic to Central Asia. Cloth Text. Cambridge University Press. New York, NY. 1997. 334p. ISBN:0-521-56320-8, ISBN13: 978-0-521-56320-8. Dewey:305.4/2/0947. LCCN:96-036259.
Audience: **g,l,u,f.** *Choice, 1998.*

Smith, Graham **DK293 .N36 1998**
Nation-Building in the Post-Soviet Borderlands: The Politics of National Identities. Trade Cloth. Cambridge University Press. New York, NY. 1998. 307p. ISBN:0-521-59045-0, ISBN13: 978-0-521-59045-7. Dewey:305.8/00947. LCCN:97-032113.
Audience: **u,f.**

Russia > Commonwealth of Independent States (CIS) > Russia (1991 to present)

Baker, Peter & Glasser, Susan **DK510.763.B35 2005**
Kremlin Rising: Vladimir Putin's Russia and the End of Revolution. Trade Cloth. Simon & Schuster. New York, NY. 2005. 464p. ISBN:0-7432-6431-2, ISBN13: 978-0-7432-6431-0. Dewey:947.086. LCCN:2005-044157.
Audience: **g,l,u,f.** *Choice, 2006.*

Davies, R. W. **DK266.D28 1997**
Soviet History in the Yeltsin Era. Cloth over Boards. Palgrave Macmillan. New York, NY. 1997. 272p. Studies in Russian and Eastern European History Ser. ISBN:0-312-17372-5, ISBN13: 978-0-312-17372-2. Dewey:947.084/07/2047. LCCN:96-029714.
Audience: **u,f.** *Choice, 1997.*

Dunlop, John B. **DK511.C37 D86 1998**
Russia Confronts Chechnya: Roots of a Separatist Conflict. Trade Cloth. Cambridge University Press. New York, NY. 1998. 248p. ISBN:0-521-63184-X, ISBN13: 978-0-521-63184-6. Dewey:947.5/2. LCCN:97-051840.
Audience: **g,u,f.** *Choice, 1999.*

Meier, Andrew **DK510.76.M44 2003**
Black Earth: A Journey Through Russia after the Fall. Trade Cloth. W. W. Norton & Company, Inc. New York, NY. 2003. 512p. ISBN:0-393-05178-1, ISBN13: 978-0-393-05178-0. Dewey:914.704/86. LCCN:2003-006562.
Audience: **g,l,u,f.**

Strayer, Robert **DK286.S77 1998**
Why Did the Soviet Union Collapse?: Understanding Historical Change. Trade Cloth. M. E. Sharpe Inc. Armonk, NY. 1998. 240p. ISBN:0-7656-0003-X, ISBN13: 978-0-7656-0003-5. Dewey:947.085/4. LCCN:97-046087.
Audience: **g,l,u,f.**

Tishkov, Valery **DK511.C37 T572 2004**
Chechnya: Life in a War-Torn Society. Trade Cloth. University of California Press. Berkeley, CA. 2004. 302p. California Series in Public Anthropology, Vol. 6 ISBN:0-520-23887-7, ISBN13: 978-0-520-23887-9. Dewey:947.5/2. LCCN:2003-017330.
Audience: **g,u,f.** *Choice, 2005.*

Troxel, Tiffany A. **JN6697.8.T76 2002**
Parliamentary Power in Russia, 1994-2001: A New Era. Cloth over Boards. Palgrave Macmillan. New York, NY. 2003. 272p. St. Antony's Ser. ISBN:0-333-99283-0, ISBN13: 978-0-333-99283-8. Dewey:328.47. LCCN:2002-028746.
Audience: **l,u,f.** *Choice, 2003.*

Russia > Commonwealth of Independent States (CIS) > Ukraine

Berkhoff, Karel C. **DK508.833.B47 2004**
Harvest of Despair: Life and Death in Ukraine under Nazi Rule. Trade Cloth. Harvard University Press. Cambridge, MA. 2004. 480p. ISBN:0-674-01313-1, ISBN13: 978-0-674-01313-1. Dewey:940.53/477. LCCN:2003-062870.
Audience: **g,u,f.** *Choice, 2004.*

Gross, Jan T. **DK4415.G76 1988**
Revolution from Abroad: The Soviet Conquest of Poland's Western Ukraine and Western Belorussia. Cloth Text. Princeton University Press. Princeton, NJ. 1988. 380p. ISBN:0-691-09433-0, ISBN13: 978-0-691-09433-5. Dewey:943.8/053. LCCN:87-045520.
Audience: **u,f.** *Choice, 1988.*

Marples, David R. **DK508.833.M37 1992**
Stalinism in Ukraine in the 1940s. Cloth over Boards. Palgrave Macmillan. New York, NY. 1992. 248p. ISBN:0-312-08401-3, ISBN13: 978-0-312-08401-1. Dewey:947.710842. LCCN:92-002295.
Audience: **g,u,f.** *Choice, 1993.*

Plokhy, Serhii **DK508.47**
Unmaking Imperial Russia: Mykhailo Hrushevsky and the Writing of Ukrainian History. Dust Jacket. University of Toronto Press. Toronto, ON. 2005. 700p. ISBN:0-8020-3937-5, ISBN13: 978-0-8020-3937-8. Dewey:947.7/0072/02. LCCN:2005-278322.
Audience: **u,f.** *Choice, 2005.*

Procyk, Anna M. **D265.2**
Russian Nationalism and Ukraine: The Nationality Policy of the Volunteer Army During the Civil War. Trade Cloth. Ukrainian Academic Press. Littleton, CO. 1995. xvi, 202p. ISBN:1-895571-04-9, ISBN13: 978-1-895571-04-2. Dewey:947.084/1.
Audience: **u,f.** *Choice, 1996.*

Subtelny, Orest **DK508**
Ukraine: A History. Cloth Text. University of Toronto Press. Toronto, ON. 1988. 678p. ISBN:0-8020-5808-6, ISBN13: 978-0-8020-5808-9. Dewey:947.7.
Audience: **g,u,f.** *Choice, 1989.*

Szporluk, Roman **DK67.5.U38S98 2000**
Russia, Ukraine and the Breakup of the Soviet Union. Trade Paper. Hoover Institution Press. Stanford, CA. 2000. xlix, 437p. Publication Ser., No. 467 ISBN:0-8179-9542-0, ISBN13: 978-0-8179-9542-3. Dewey:947.085/4. LCCN:99-050309.
Audience: **u,f.** *Choice, 2001.*

Zabarko, Boris (Editor) **DS135.U43A154 2005**
Holocaust in the Ukraine. Trade Cloth. Vallentine Mitchell Publishers. Middlesex, 2004. 394p. Library of Holocaust Testimonies Ser. ISBN:0-85303-612-8, ISBN13: 978-0-85303-612-8. Dewey:940.53/18/0922477. LCCN:2005-297198.
Audience: **g,u,f.** *Choice, 2005.*

Russia > Commonwealth of Independent States (CIS) > Belarus (Belorussia)

Marsh, Rosalind & Korosteleva, Elena **DK507.817**
Contemporary Belarus: Between Democracy and Dictatorship. Paper over Boards. Taylor & Francis Group. Abingdon, 2002. 224p. ISBN:0-7007-1613-0, ISBN13: 978-0-7007-1613-5. Dewey:947.8/086.
Audience: **u,f.** *Choice, 2004.*

Zaprudnik, Jan **DK507.54.Z37 1993**
Belarus: At the Crossroads in History. Trade Paper. Westview Press. Boulder, CO. 1993. 278p. ISBN:0-8133-1339-2, ISBN13: 978-0-8133-1339-9. Dewey:947.65084. LCCN:92-042923.
Audience: **g,l,u,f.** *Choice, 1994.*

Russia > Commonwealth of Independent States (CIS) > Georgia

Braund, David **DK677.1.B7 1994**
Georgia in Antiquity: A History of Colchis and Transcaucasian Iberia, 550 BC-AD 562. Trade Cloth. Oxford University Press, Inc. New York, NY. 1994. 378p. ISBN:0-19-814473-3, ISBN13: 978-0-19-814473-1. Dewey:947/.95. LCCN:93-040486.
Audience: **u,f.** *Choice, 1995.*

Suny, Ronald G. **DK511.G4S78 1988**
The Making of the Georgian Nation. Trade Cloth. Indiana University Press. Bloomington, IN. 1988. 416p. Hoover Institute Studies ISBN:0-253-33623-6, ISBN13: 978-0-253-33623-1. Dewey:947/.95. LCCN:87-021367.
Audience: **g,l,u,f.** *Choice, 1989.*

Russia > Commonwealth of Independent States (CIS) > Moldova

King, Charles **DK509.54.K56 2000**
The Moldovans: Romania, Russia and the Politics of Culture. Trade Cloth. Hoover Institution Press. Stanford, CA. 2000. xxix, 303p. Publication Ser., Vol. 471:Studies of Nationalities ISBN:0-8179-9791-1, ISBN13: 978-0-8179-9791-5. Dewey:947.6. LCCN:99-041906.
Audience: **g,u,f.** *Choice, 2000.*

Mitrasca, Marcel **D619**
Moldova: Diplomatic History from the Archives of the Great Powers: a Romanian Province under Russian Rule. Trade Cloth. Algora Publishing. New York, NY. 2002. 320p. ISBN:1-892941-87-2, ISBN13: 978-1-892941-87-9. Dewey:940.3/22. LCCN:2002-005746.
Audience: **u,f.** *Choice, 2003.*

Russia > Commonwealth of Independent States (CIS) > Central Asia

Abazov, Rafis **DK918.12.A23 2004**
Historical Dictionary of Kyrgyzstan. Trade Cloth. Scarecrow Press, Inc. Lanham, MD. 2003. 416p. Asian/Oceanian Historical Dictionaries Ser., No. 49 ISBN:0-8108-4868-6, ISBN13: 978-0-8108-4868-9. Dewey:958.43/003. LCCN:2003-019174.
Audience: **g,l,u,f.** *Choice, 2004.*

Allworth, Edward A. **DK948.62.A45 1990**
The Modern Uzbeks: From the Fourteenth Century to the Present, a Cultural History. Trade Paper. Hoover Institution Press. Stanford, CA. 1990. 410p. Publication Series: Studies of Nationalities in the U. S. S. R., No. 373 ISBN:0-8179-8732-0, ISBN13: 978-0-8179-8732-9. Dewey:958/.7. LCCN:89-019899.
Audience: **u,f.** *Choice, 1991.*

Glenn, John **DK859.56.G57 1999**
The Soviet Legacy in Central Asia. Cloth over Boards. Palgrave Macmillan. New York, NY. 1999. 212p. ISBN:0-312-22218-1, ISBN13: 978-0-312-22218-5. Dewey:320.9/58. LCCN:98-055307.
Audience: **u,f.** *Choice, 2000.*

Grousset, Rene **DS329.4**
The Empire of the Steppes: A History of Central Asia. Trade Paper. Rutgers University Press. Piscataway, NJ. 1988. 687p. ISBN:0-8135-1304-9, ISBN13: 978-0-8135-1304-1. Dewey:958.
Audience: **g,u,f.**

Jones Luong, Pauline **HN670.22.A8T73 2003**
The Transformation of Central Asia: States and Societies from Soviet Rule to Independence. Book, Other. Cornell University Press. Ithaca, NY. 2003. 400p. ISBN:0-8014-4151-X, ISBN13: 978-0-8014-4151-6. Dewey:306/.0958. LCCN:2003-011825.
Audience: **u,f.** *Choice, 2004.*

Keller, Shoshana **DK948**
To Moscow, Not Mecca: The Soviet Campaign Against Islam in Central Asia, 1917-1941. Trade Cloth. Greenwood Publishing Group, Inc. Portsmouth, NH. 2001. 300p. ISBN:0-275-97238-0, ISBN13: 978-0-275-97238-7. Dewey:958/.041/0882971. LCCN:2001-021665.
Audience: **g,u,f.** *Choice, 2002.*

Landau, Jacob M., et al. **P119.32.A783L36 2001**
Politics of Language in the Ex-Soviet Muslim States: Azerbaijan, Uzbekistan, Kazakhstan, Kyrgyzstan, Turkmenistan, Tajikistan. Barbara Kellner-Heinkele & C. Hurst & Co. (Publishers) Ltd. Staff (Authors). Trade Cloth. University of

Michigan Press. Chicago, IL. 2001. 274p. ISBN:0-472-11226-0, ISBN13: 978-0-472-11226-5. Dewey:306.44/958. LCCN:2001-027390.
Audience: **u,f.** *Choice, 2002.*

Olcott, Martha Brill **HC420.3.O43 2005**
Central Asia's Second Chance. Trade Cloth. Carnegie Endowment for International Peace. Washington, DC. 2005. 250p. ISBN:0-87003-217-8, ISBN13: 978-0-87003-217-2. Dewey:320.958/09/051. LCCN:2005-013327.
Audience: **u,f.** *Choice, 2006.*

Olcott, Martha Brill **DK908.8675.O43 2002**
Kazakhstan: Unfulfilled Promise. Cloth Text. Carnegie Endowment for International Peace. Washington, DC. 2002. 320p. ISBN:0-87003-189-9, ISBN13: 978-0-87003-189-2. Dewey:958.45/086. LCCN:2001-008724.
Audience: **u,f.** *Choice, 2002.*

Payne, Matthew J. **HE3140.T87P39 2001**
Stalin's Railroad: Turksib and the Building of Socialism. Trade Cloth. University of Pittsburgh Press. Pittsburgh, PA. 2001. 400p. Series in Russian and East European Studies ISBN:0-8229-4166-X, ISBN13: 978-0-8229-4166-8. Dewey:385/.0957. LCCN:2001-003342.
Audience: **u,f.** *Choice, 2002.*

Ro'i, Yaacov **BP63.A34R65 2000**
Islam in the Soviet Union: From the Second World War to Gorbachev. Trade Cloth. Columbia University Press. New York, NY. 2000. 600p. ISBN:0-231-11954-2, ISBN13: 978-0-231-11954-2. Dewey:297/.0947. LCCN:99-041848.
Audience: **g,u,f.** *Choice, 2001.*

Schatz, Edward **DK907.S34 2004**
Modern Clan Politics: The Power of "Blood" in Kazakhstan and Beyond. Trade Cloth. University of Washington Press. Seattle, WA. 2004. 256p. ISBN:0-295-98446-5, ISBN13: 978-0-295-98446-9. Dewey:306.2/095845. LCCN:2004-013607.
Audience: **u,f.** *Choice, 2005.*

Russia > Commonwealth of Independent States (CIS) > Armenia

Bournoutian, George A. **DS175.B65 2002**
A Concise History of the Armenian People. Paper Text. Mazda Publishers, Inc. Costa Mesa, CA. 2002. 510p. ISBN:1-56859-141-1, ISBN13: 978-1-56859-141-4. Dewey:909/.0491992. LCCN:2002-021898.
Audience: **l,u,f.** *Choice, 2003.*

De Waal, Thomas **DK699.N34D4 2003**
Black Garden: Armenia and Azerbaijan Through Peace and War. Trade Cloth. New York University Press. New York, NY. 2003. 352p. ISBN:0-8147-1944-9, ISBN13: 978-0-8147-1944-2. Dewey:947.54085/4. LCCN:2002-153482.
Audience: **u,f.** *Choice, 2003.*

Hovannisian, Richard G. **DS195.5R46 1999**
Remembrance and Denial: The Case of the Armenian Genocide. Trade Cloth. Wayne State University Press. Detroit, MI. 1999. 304p. ISBN:0-8143-2777-X, ISBN13: 978-0-8143-2777-7. Dewey:956.6/2015. LCCN:98-028282.
Audience: **l,u,f.**

Somakian, Manoug **DS195.S56 1995**
Empires in Conflict: Armenia and the Great Powers, 1912-1920. Ed. 1. Cloth over Boards. I. B. Tauris & Company, Ltd. London, 1995. 256p. International Library of Historical Studies, Vol. 2 ISBN:1-85043-912-5, ISBN13: 978-1-85043-912-7. Dewey:956.6/202. LCCN:95-223129.
Audience: **u,f.** *Choice, 1996.*

Suny, Ronald G. **DK687**
Looking Toward Ararat: Armenia in Modern History. Trade Cloth. Indiana University Press. Bloomington, IN. 1993. 304p. ISBN:0-253-35583-4, ISBN13: 978-0-253-35583-6. Dewey:956.6/2. LCCN:92-019420.
Audience: **g,u,f.**

Russia > Commonwealth of Independent States (CIS) > Azerbaijan

Altstadt, Audrey L. **DK696.6.A48 1992**
The Azerbaijani Turks: Power and Identity under Russian Rule. Cloth Text. Hoover Institution Press. Stanford, CA. 1992. 334p. Publication Ser., No. 410:Studies of Nationalities in the U. S. S. R. ISBN:0-8179-9181-6, ISBN13: 978-0-8179-9181-4. Dewey:947/.91. LCCN:91-041684.
Audience: **u,f.** *Choice, 1992.*

De Waal, Thomas **DK699.N34D4 2003**
Black Garden: Armenia and Azerbaijan Through Peace and War. Trade Cloth. New York University Press. New York, NY. 2003. 352p. ISBN:0-8147-1944-9, ISBN13: 978-0-8147-1944-2. Dewey:947.54085/4. LCCN:2002-153482.
Audience: **u,f.** *Choice, 2003.*

Russia > Independent Successor States > Turkmenistan

Abazov, Rafis **DK938.12.A2 2005**
Historical Dictionary of Turkmenistan. Trade Cloth. Scarecrow Press, Inc. Lanham, MD. 2005. 344p. Historical Dictionaries of Asia, Oceania, and the Middle East Ser., Vol. 53 ISBN:0-8108-5362-0, ISBN13: 978-0-8108-5362-1. Dewey:958.5/003. LCCN:2004-016829.
Audience: **g,l,u,f.** *Choice, 2005.*

Edgar, Adrienne Lynn **DK938.85.E35 2004**
Tribal Nation: The Making of Soviet Turkmenistan. Trade Cloth. Princeton University Press. Princeton, NJ. 2004. 304p. ISBN:0-691-11775-6, ISBN13: 978-0-691-11775-1. Dewey:958.5/084. LCCN:2004-043423.
Audience: **g,l,u,f.** *Choice, 2005.*

Scandinavia > General Histories

Allardt, Erik, et. al. (editor) **JN7042**
Nordic Democracy : Ideas, Issues, and Institutions in Politics, Economy, Education, Social and Cultural Affairs of Denmark, Finland, Iceland, Norway, and Sweden. Det Danske Selskab. 1981.
Audience: **u,f.**

Arter, David **JN7056.A77 1984**
The Nordic Parliaments: A Comparative Analysis. Cloth Text. Palgrave Macmillan. New York, NY. 1985. 432p. ISBN:0-312-57767-2, ISBN13: 978-0-312-57767-4. Dewey:328/.3/0948. LCCN:84-009803.
Audience: **u,f.**

Barton, H. Arnold **DL78.B37 1986**
Scandinavia in the Revolutionary Era, 1760-1815. Cloth Text. University of Minnesota Press. Minneapolis, MN. 1986. 477p. ISBN:0-8166-1392-3, ISBN13: 978-0-8166-1392-2. Dewey:948/.05. LCCN:84-026972.
Audience: **u,f.** *Choice, 1987.*

Derry, T. K. **DL46.D43**
A History of Scandinavia. Trade Cloth. University of Minnesota Press. Minneapolis, MN. 1979. x, 447p. ISBN:0-8166-0835-0, ISBN13: 978-0-8166-0835-5. Dewey:948. LCCN:78-014284.
Audience: **g,l,u.**

Einhorn, Eric S. **JN7042**
Modern Welfare States : Politics and Policies in Social Democratic Scandinavia. Logue, John. Praeger. 1989. ISBN:0-275-92450-5, ISBN13: 978-0-275-92450-8.
Audience: **l,u.**

Geyer, Robert (Editor), et al. **HX318.5.G58 2000**
Globalization, Europeanization, and the End of Scandinavian Social Democracy? Christine Ingebritsen & Jonathon Wayne Moses (Editors). Trade Cloth. St. Martin's Press. Gordonville, VA. 2000. xiv, 265p. ISBN:0-333-72710-X, ISBN13: 978-0-333-72710-2. Dewey:335/.00948. LCCN:99-023360.
Audience: **u,f.**

Haetta, Odd Mathis **DL42.L36**
The Sami, an Indigenous People of the Arctic. Gurholt, Ole Petter (translator). D. Girji. 1966. ISBN:82-7374-305-5, ISBN13: 978-82-7374-305-3.
Audience: **u,f.**

Helle, Knut (Editor, Contribution by) **DL61**
The Cambrdige History of Scandinavia: Prehistory to 1520. E. I. Kouri, Torkel Jansson & E. L. Petersen (Contribution by). Cloth Text. Cambridge University Press. New York, NY. 2003. 892p. The Cambridge History of Scandinavia Ser. ISBN:0-521-47299-7, ISBN13: 978-0-521-47299-9. Dewey:948/.02. LCCN:2004-298829.
Audience: **g,l,u,f.** *Choice, 2004.*

Ingebritsen, Christine **HC240.25.S34**
Nordic States and European Unity. Book, Other. Cornell University Press. Ithaca, NY. 2000. 240p. Cornell Studies in Political Economy ISBN:0-8014-8659-9, ISBN13: 978-0-8014-8659-3. Dewey:337.1/42.
Audience: **u,f.**

Mead, W. R. **DL7**
An Historical Geography of Scandinavia. Trade Cloth. Elsevier Science & Technology Books. Saint Louis, MO. 1981. 313p. ISBN:0-12-487420-7, ISBN13: 978-0-12-487420-6. Dewey:911/.48. LCCN:81-066377.
Audience: **l,u,f.**

Mead, W. R. & Hall, Wendy **DL11**
Scandinavia. Trade Cloth. Walker & Company. New York, NY. 1972. Nations and Peoples Library ISBN:0-8027-2125-7, ISBN13: 978-0-8027-2125-9. Dewey:914.8/03/8.
Audience: **g,l.**

Murray, Alan V. (Editor) **D162.2.C78 2001**
Crusade and Conversation on the Baltic Frontier 1150-1500. Trade Cloth. Ashgate Publishing, Ltd. Aldershot, 2001. 320p. ISBN:0-7546-0325-3, ISBN13: 978-0-7546-0325-2. Dewey:947/.0009/02. LCCN:2001-088803.
Audience: **u,f.**

Nissen, Henrik S. (Editor) **D754.S29.S27 1983**
Scandinavia During the Second World War. Thomas Munch-Petersen (Translator). Trade Cloth. University of Minnesota Press. Minneapolis, MN. 1983. x, 398p. Nordic Ser., Vol. 9 ISBN:0-8166-1110-6, ISBN13: 978-0-8166-1110-2. Dewey:940.53/48. LCCN:82-002779.
Audience: **l,u,f.**

Nordstrom, Byron J. (Editor) **DL43**
Dictionary of Scandinavian History. Cloth Text. Greenwood Publishing Group, Inc. Portsmouth, NH. 1986. 724p. ISBN:0-313-22887-6, ISBN13: 978-0-313-22887-2. Dewey:948/.003/21. LCCN:83-025204.
Audience: **g,l,u,f.** *Choice, 1986.*

Nordstrom, Byron J. **DL46.N7 2000**
Scandinavia since 1500. Trade Cloth. University of Minnesota Press. Minneapolis, MN. 2000. 400p. ISBN:0-8166-2098-9, ISBN13: 978-0-8166-2098-2. Dewey:948. LCCN:99-089029.
Audience: **l,u,f.** *Choice, 2001.*

Nyberg, Tore **BX2640.N94 2000**
Monasticism in North-Western Europe, 800-1200. Trade Cloth. Ashgate Publishing, Ltd. Aldershot, 2000. 308p. ISBN:1-85928-212-1, ISBN13: 978-1-85928-212-0. Dewey:271/.00648/09021. LCCN:00-026602.
Audience: **u,f.**

Sawyer, Birgit & Sawyer, Peter **DL65**
Medieval Scandinavia: From Conversion to Reformation, Circa 800-1500. Trade Paper. University of Minnesota Press. Minneapolis, MN. 1993. 284p. Nordic Ser., Vol. 16 ISBN:0-8166-1739-2, ISBN13: 978-0-8166-1739-5. Dewey:948.02. LCCN:93-003511.
Audience: **u,f.** *Choice, 1994.*

Scott, Franklin Daniel **DL5**
Scandinavia. Harvard University Press. 1975. The American foreign policy library ISBN:0-674-79000-6, ISBN13: 978-0-674-79000-1.
Audience: **g,l,u,f.**

Somme, Axel (Editor) **DL5 .S6 1968B**
A Geography of Norden. Trade Cloth. International Publications Service. Levittown, PA. 1968. 400p. ISBN:0-435-34820-5, ISBN13: 978-0-435-34820-5. Dewey:914.8. LCCN:71-409716.
Audience: **u,f.**

Tagil, Sven **DL41.E85 1995**
Ethnicity and Nation-Building in the Nordic World. Trade Cloth. Southern Illinois University Press. Carbondale, IL. 1995. 343p. ISBN:0-8093-1974-8, ISBN13: 978-0-8093-1974-9. Dewey:305.8/00948. LCCN:94-013163.
Audience: **u,f.**

Scandinavia > History

Arter, David **JN7056.A77 1984**
The Nordic Parliaments: A Comparative Analysis. Cloth Text. Palgrave Macmillan. New York, NY. 1985. 432p. ISBN:0-312-57767-2, ISBN13: 978-0-312-57767-4. Dewey:328/.3/0948. LCCN:84-009803.
Audience: **u,f.**

Barton, H. Arnold **DL78.B37 1986**
Scandinavia in the Revolutionary Era, 1760-1815. Cloth Text. University of Minnesota Press. Minneapolis, MN. 1986. 477p. ISBN:0-8166-1392-3, ISBN13: 978-0-8166-1392-2. Dewey:948/.05. LCCN:84-026972.
Audience: **u,f.** *Choice, 1987.*

Derry, T. K. **DL46.D43**
A History of Scandinavia. Trade Cloth. University of Minnesota Press. Minneapolis, MN. 1979. x, 447p. ISBN:0-8166-0835-0, ISBN13: 978-0-8166-0835-5. Dewey:948. LCCN:78-014284.
Audience: **g,l,u.**

Geyer, Robert (Editor), et al. **HX318.5.G58 2000**
Globalization, Europeanization, and the End of Scandinavian Social Democracy? Christine Ingebritsen & Jonathon Wayne Moses (Editors). Trade Cloth. St. Martin's Press. Gordonville, VA. 2000. xiv, 265p. ISBN:0-333-72710-X, ISBN13: 978-0-333-72710-2. Dewey:335/.00948. LCCN:99-023360.
Audience: **u,f.**

Helle, Knut (Editor, Contribution by) **DL61**
The Cambrdige History of Scandinavia: Prehistory to 1520. E. I. Kouri, Torkel Jansson & E. L. Petersen (Contribution by). Cloth Text. Cambridge University Press. New York, NY. 2003. 892p. The Cambridge History of Scandinavia Ser. ISBN:0-521-47299-7, ISBN13: 978-0-521-47299-9. Dewey:948/.02. LCCN:2004-298829.
Audience: **g,l,u,f.** *Choice, 2004.*

Ingebritsen, Christine **HC240.25.S34**
Nordic States and European Unity. Book, Other. Cornell University Press. Ithaca, NY. 2000. 240p. Cornell Studies in Political Economy ISBN:0-8014-8659-9, ISBN13: 978-0-8014-8659-3. Dewey:337.1/42.
Audience: **u,f.**

Mead, W. R. **DL7**
An Historical Geography of Scandinavia. Trade Cloth. Elsevier Science & Technology Books. Saint Louis, MO. 1981. 313p. ISBN:0-12-487420-7, ISBN13: 978-0-12-487420-6. Dewey:911/.48. LCCN:81-066377.
Audience: **l,u,f.**

Mead, W. R. & Hall, Wendy **DL11**
Scandinavia. Trade Cloth. Walker & Company. New York, NY. 1972. Nations and Peoples Library ISBN:0-8027-2125-7, ISBN13: 978-0-8027-2125-9. Dewey:914.8/03/8.
Audience: **g,l.**

Nissen, Henrik S. (Editor) **D754.S29.S27 1983**
Scandinavia During the Second World War. Thomas Munch-Petersen (Translator). Trade Cloth. University of Minnesota Press. Minneapolis, MN. 1983. x, 398p. Nordic Ser., Vol. 9 ISBN:0-8166-1110-6, ISBN13: 978-0-8166-1110-2. Dewey:940.53/48. LCCN:82-002779.
Audience: **l,u,f.**

Nordstrom, Byron J. (Editor) **DL43**
Dictionary of Scandinavian History. Cloth Text. Greenwood Publishing Group, Inc. Portsmouth, NH. 1986. 724p. ISBN:0-313-22887-6, ISBN13: 978-0-313-22887-2. Dewey:948/.003/21. LCCN:83-025204.
Audience: **g,l,u,f.** *Choice, 1986.*

Nordstrom, Byron J. **DL46.N7 2000**
Scandinavia since 1500. Trade Cloth. University of Minnesota Press. Minneapolis, MN. 2000. 400p. ISBN:0-8166-2098-9, ISBN13: 978-0-8166-2098-2. Dewey:948. LCCN:99-089029.
Audience: **l,u,f.** *Choice, 2001.*

Nyberg, Tore **BX2640.N94 2000**
Monasticism in North-Western Europe, 800-1200. Trade Cloth. Ashgate Publishing, Ltd. Aldershot, 2000. 308p. ISBN:1-85928-212-1, ISBN13: 978-1-85928-212-0. Dewey:271/.00648/09021. LCCN:00-026602.
Audience: **u,f.**

Sawyer, Birgit & Sawyer, Peter **DL65**
Medieval Scandinavia: From Conversion to Reformation, Circa 800-1500. Trade Paper. University of Minnesota Press. Minneapolis, MN. 1993. 284p. Nordic Ser., Vol. 16 ISBN:0-8166-1739-2, ISBN13: 978-0-8166-1739-5. Dewey:948.02. LCCN:93-003511.
Audience: **u,f.** *Choice, 1994.*

Somme, Axel (Editor) **DL5 .S6 1968B**
A Geography of Norden. Trade Cloth. International Publications Service. Levittown, PA. 1968. 400p. ISBN:0-435-34820-5, ISBN13: 978-0-435-34820-5. Dewey:914.8. LCCN:71-409716.
Audience: **u,f.**

Tagil, Sven **DL41.E85 1995**
Ethnicity and Nation-Building in the Nordic World. Trade Cloth. Southern Illinois University Press. Carbondale, IL. 1995. 343p. ISBN:0-8093-1974-8, ISBN13: 978-0-8093-1974-9. Dewey:305.8/00948. LCCN:94-013163.
Audience: **u,f.**

Scandinavia > Denmark

Davidson, Hilda Ellis **DL147.S2413 1998**
Saxo Grammaticus : The History of the Danes, Books I - IX: I. English text; II. Commentary. Fisher, Peter (translator). D.S. Brewer. 2006. ISBN:0-85991-502-6, ISBN13: 978-0-85991-502-1.
Audience: **g,l,u,f.**

Gold, Carol **LC2185 .G65**
Educating Middle Class Daughters: Private Girls Schools in Copenhagen 1790-1820. Trade Cloth. Museum Tusculanum Press. Copenhagen S, 1996. 272p. ISBN:87-7289-355-9, ISBN13: 978-87-7289-355-6. Dewey:370.19345.
Audience: **u,f.**

Lauring, Palle **DL148**
History of Denmark. Trade Cloth. Dorset Press. New York, NY. 1991. 274p. Reprints Ser. ISBN:0-88029-608-9, ISBN13: 978-0-88029-608-3. Dewey:948.9.
Audience: **g,l,u.**

Logue, John **JN7365.S7**
Socialism and Abundance: Radical Socialism in the Danish Welfare State. Trade Cloth. University of Minnesota Press. Minneapolis, MN. 1983. 400p. Nordic Ser., Vol. 8 ISBN:0-8166-1131-9, ISBN13: 978-0-8166-1131-7. Dewey:324.248907. LCCN:81-014819.
Audience: **u,f.**

Oakley, Stewart P. **DL148**
A Short History of Denmark. Praeger. 1972.
Audience: **g,l,u.**

West, John F. **DL271.F2.W43 1972**
Faroe: The Emergence of a Nation. Trade Cloth. Paul S. Eriksson Publisher. Forest Dale, VT. 1973. x, 312p. ISBN:0-8397-2063-7, ISBN13: 978-0-8397-2063-8. Dewey:914.91/5. LCCN:77-151438.
Audience: **g,l,u,f.**

Scandinavia > Iceland

Byock, Jesse **DL352.B96 2001**
Viking Age Iceland. Trade Paper. Penguin Group (USA) Inc. New York, NY. 2001. 480p. ISBN:0-14-029115-6, ISBN13: 978-0-14-029115-5. Dewey:949.1/01. LCCN:2001-275355.
Audience: **g,l,u,f.**

Karlsson, Gunnar **DL338.H849 2000**
The History of Iceland. Trade Cloth. University of Minnesota Press. Minneapolis, MN. 2000. xiii, 418p. ISBN:0-8166-3588-9, ISBN13: 978-0-8166-3588-7. Dewey:949.12. LCCN:99-054536.
Audience: **g,l,u,f.** *Choice, 2001.*

Whitehead, Por **DL375**
The Ally Who Came in from the Cold: A Survey of Icelandic Foreign Policy 1946-1956. Trade Paper. University of Iceland Press. IS-101 Reykjavik, 1998. 125p. ISBN:9979-54-245-4, ISBN13: 978-9979-54-245-2. Dewey:303.4824912.
Audience: **u,f.**

Scandinavia > Norway

Barton, H. Arnold **DL805.B37 2002**
Sweden and Visions of Norway: Politics and Culture, 1814-1905. Trade Cloth. Southern Illinois University Press. Carbondale, IL. 2002. 224p. ISBN:0-8093-2441-5, ISBN13: 978-0-8093-2441-5. Dewey:948.1/03. LCCN:2002-024663.
Audience: **g,l,u,f.** *Choice, 2003.*

Danielsen, Rolf, et al. **DL448 .N77 1998**
Norway: A History from the Vikings to Our Own Times. Stale Dyrvik, Tore Gronlie, Knut Helle & Edgar Hovland (Authors). Trade Cloth. Scandinavian University Press North America. Cambridge, MA. 1995. 486p. ISBN:82-00-21803-1, ISBN13: 978-82-00-21803-6. Dewey:948.1. LCCN:00-296045.
Audience: **g,l,u.**

Derry, T. K. **DL506.D47**
A History of Modern Norway, 1814-1972. Trade Cloth. Oxford University Press, Inc. New York, NY. 1973. xiii, 506p. ISBN:0-19-822503-2, ISBN13: 978-0-19-822503-4. Dewey:948.1/03. LCCN:73-168733.
Audience: **l,u,f.**

Derry, Thomas K. **DL448 .D4 1979**
A Short History of Norway. Trade Cloth. Greenwood Publishing Group, Inc. Portsmouth, NH. 1979. 281p. ISBN:0-313-21467-0, ISBN13: 978-0-313-21467-7. Dewey:948.1. LCCN:79-010688.
Audience: **g,l,u.**

Hoidal, Oddvar K. **DL529.Q5**
Quisling : A Study in Treason. Norwegian University Press. 1989. ISBN:82-00-18400-5, ISBN13: 978-82-00-18400-3.
Audience: **u,f.**

Larsen, Karen **DL448.L3**
History of Norway. Trade Cloth. Princeton University Press. Princeton, NJ. 1948. 604p. American-Scandinavian Foundation Ser. ISBN:0-691-05127-5, ISBN13: 978-0-691-05127-7. Dewey:948.1. LCCN:48-009017.
Audience: **l,u,f.**

Riste, Olav **DL458**
Norway's Foreign Relations : A History. Universitetsforlaget. 2001. ISBN:82-15-00051-7, ISBN13: 978-82-15-00051-0.
Audience: **l,u,f.**

Sturluson, Snorri **PT7277.E5**
Heimskringla : History of the Kings of Norway. Hollander, Lee M. (translator). University of Texas Press. 1991. ISBN:0-292-73061-6, ISBN13: 978-0-292-73061-8.
Audience: **g,l,u,f.**

Scandinavia > Sweden

Akerman, Susanna **DL719.A44 1991**
Queen Christina of Sweden and Her Circle: The Transformation of a Seventeenth-Century Philosophical Libertine. Trade Cloth. Brill Academic Publishers, Inc. Boston, MA. 1991. xv, 339p. BSIH Ser., No. 21 ISBN:90-04-09310-9, ISBN13: 978-90-04-09310-2. Dewey:948.5/02/092 B. LCCN:90-042995.
Audience: **u,f.** *Choice, 1992.*

Barton, H. Arnold **DL805.B37 2002**
Sweden and Visions of Norway: Politics and Culture, 1814-1905. Trade Cloth. Southern Illinois University Press. Carbondale, IL. 2002. 224p. ISBN:0-8093-2441-5, ISBN13: 978-0-8093-2441-5. Dewey:948.1/03. LCCN:2002-024663.
Audience: **g,l,u,f.** *Choice, 2003.*

Childs, Marquis William **HD3616.S53**
Sweden ; The Middle Way. Yale University Press. 1936.
Audience: **l,u,f.**

Gustavson, Carl G. **HC375**
The Small Giant : Sweden Enters the Industrial Era. Ohio University Press. 1986. ISBN:0-8214-0825-9, ISBN13: 978-0-8214-0825-4.
Audience: **u,f.**

Hadenius, Stig **DL658.8**
Swedish Politics During the 20th Century. Swedish Institute. 1985. ISBN:91-520-0168-7, ISBN13: 978-91-520-0168-4.
Audience: **u,f.**

Lockhart, Paul **DL713.L63 2004**
Sweden in the Seventeenth Century. Cloth over Boards. Palgrave Macmillan. New York, NY. 2004. 256p. European History in Perspective Ser. ISBN:0-333-73156-5, ISBN13: 978-0-333-73156-7. Dewey:948.5/034. LCCN:2003-067752.
Audience: **u,f.** *Choice, 2005.*

Magnusson, Lars **HC375.M3413 2000**
An Economic History of Sweden. Paper over Boards. Routledge. New York, NY. 2000. 328p. Explorations in Economic History Ser., Vol. 16 ISBN:0-415-18167-4, ISBN13: 978-0-415-18167-9. Dewey:330.9485. LCCN:99-039725.
Audience: **g,l,u.** *Choice, 2000.*

Milner, Henry **HC375**
Sweden: Social Democracy in Practice. Trade Paper. Oxford University Press, Inc. New York, NY. 1990. 280p. ISBN:0-19-827856-X, ISBN13: 978-0-19-827856-6. Dewey:361.6/5/09485.
Audience: **u,f.**

Moberg, Vilhelm **DL648**
A History of the Swedish People: From Renaissance to Revolution. Paul Britten Austin (Translator). Trade Paper. University of Minnesota Press. Minneapolis, MN. 2005. 288p. ISBN:0-8166-4657-0, ISBN13: 978-0-8166-4657-9. Dewey:948.5.
Audience: **l,u.**

Moberg, Vilhelm **DL648.M6213 2005**
A History of the Swedish People: From Prehistory to the Renaissance. Paul Britten Austin (Translator), Gunnar Myrdal (Foreword by). Trade Paper. University of Minnesota Press. Minneapolis, MN. 2005. 224p. ISBN:0-8166-4656-2, ISBN13: 978-0-8166-4656-2. Dewey:948.5. LCCN:2005-002141.
Audience: **l,u.**

Nordstrom, Byron J. **DL648**
The History of Sweden. Ed. 1. Greenwood Press. 2002. Greenwood histories of the modern nations ISBN:0-313-31258-3, ISBN13: 978-0-313-31258-8.
Audience: **g,l,u.**

Roberts, Michael **DL748.R63 1986**
The Age of Liberty: Sweden 1719-1772. Trade Cloth. Cambridge University Press. New York, NY. 1986. 244p. ISBN:0-521-32092-5, ISBN13: 978-0-521-32092-4. Dewey:948.5/03. LCCN:85-012745.
Audience: **u,f.** *Choice, 1986.*

Roberts, Michael **DL648**
Essays in Swedish History. Trade Cloth. University of Minnesota Press. Minneapolis, MN. 1968. ISBN:0-8166-0476-2, ISBN13: 978-0-8166-0476-0. Dewey:948.5.
Audience: **u,f.**

Roberts, Michael **DL706**
Gustavus Adolphus and the Rise of Sweden. English Universities Press. 1973. ISBN:0-340-12414-8, ISBN13: 978-0-340-12414-7.
Audience: **u,f.**

Scobbie, Irene **DL643.S37 1995**
Historical Dictionary of Sweden. Trade Cloth. Scarecrow Press, Inc. Lanham, MD. 1995. 341p. European Historical Dictionaries Ser., No. 7 ISBN:0-8108-2922-3, ISBN13: 978-0-8108-2922-0. Dewey:948.5003. LCCN:94-020482.
Audience: **g,l,u,f.**

Scott, Franklin Daniel **DL648**
Sweden, the Nation's History. Koblik, Steven (epilogue). Southern Illinois University Press. 1988. ISBN:0-8093-1513-0, ISBN13: 978-0-8093-1513-0.
Audience: **l,u.**

Scandinavia > Foreign Relations, Diplomacy

Holst, Johan Jorgen (editor) **DL55**
Five Roads to Nordic Security. Universitetsforlaget. 1973. Norwegian foreign policy studies ISBN:82-00-04756-3, ISBN13: 978-82-00-04756-8.
Audience: **u,f.**

Rystad, Goran (editor) **D271.S34**
Europe and Scandinavia : Aspects of the Process of Integration in the 17th Century. Esselte Studium. 1983. Lund studies in international history ISBN:91-24-32785-9, ISBN13: 978-91-24-32785-9.
Audience: **u,f.**

Salmon, Patrick **DL83.S35 1997**
Scandinavia and the Great Powers 1890-1940. Trade Cloth. Cambridge University Press. New York, NY. 1997. 445p. ISBN:0-521-41161-0, ISBN13: 978-0-521-41161-5. Dewey:327.4/8. LCCN:96-053310.
Audience: **l,u,f.** *Choice, 1998.*

Sundelius, Bengt (Editor) **DL55**
The Foreign Policies of Northern Europe. Cloth Text. Westview Press. Boulder, CO. 1982. 239p. Special Studies in International Relations ISBN:0-89158-909-0, ISBN13: 978-0-89158-909-9. Dewey:327.48. LCCN:81-024062.
Audience: **g,l,u.**

Scandinavia > Vikings

Brondsted, Johannes **DL65**
The Vikings. Skov, Kalle (translator). Penguin Books. 1965.
Audience: **g,l,u.**

Chibnall, Marjorie **D148.C48 2001**
The Normans. Trade Cloth. Blackwell Publishing, Inc. Malden, MA. 2000. 208p. The Peoples of Europe Ser. ISBN:0-631-18671-9, ISBN13: 978-0-631-18671-7. Dewey:909/.04395. LCCN:00-033665.
Audience: **g,l,u,f.** *Choice, 2001.*

Jones, Gwyn **DL65**
A History of the Vikings. Trade Cloth. Oxford University Press, Inc. New York, NY. 1985. xviii, 504p. ISBN:0-19-215882-1, ISBN13: 978-0-19-215882-6. Dewey:914.8/03/1. LCCN:83-013303.
Audience: **g,l,u,f.**

Roesdahl, Else **DL65**
The VIkings. Margeson, Susan M. ; Williams, Kirsten (translators). Allen Lane. 1991. ISBN:0-7139-9048-1, ISBN13: 978-0-7139-9048-5.
Audience: **g,l,u.**

Salmon, Patrick **DL83.S35 1997**
Scandinavia and the Great Powers 1890-1940. Trade Cloth. Cambridge University Press. New York, NY. 1997. 445p. ISBN:0-521-41161-0, ISBN13: 978-0-521-41161-5. Dewey:327.4/8. LCCN:96-053310.
Audience: **l,u,f.** *Choice, 1998.*

Sawyer, Birgit (Editor), et al. **BR972.C48 1987**
The Christianization of Scandinavia. Peter Sawyer & Ian Wood (Editors). Trade Paper. Coronet Books. Philadelphia, PA. 1987. xi, 130p. ISBN:91-86708-04-X, ISBN13: 978-91-86708-04-7. Dewey:274.8/03. LCCN:88-114592.
Audience: **u,f.**

Sawyer, P. H. **DL65.S254 1982**
Kings and Vikings: Scandinavia and Europe, A. Trade Cloth. Methuen & Company, Ltd. London, 1982. x, 182p. ISBN:0-416-74180-0, ISBN13: 978-0-416-74180-3. Dewey:940/.04395. LCCN:82-012539.
Audience: **l,u.**

Sundelius, Bengt (Editor) **DL55**
The Foreign Policies of Northern Europe. Cloth Text. Westview Press. Boulder, CO. 1982. 239p. Special Studies in International Relations ISBN:0-89158-909-0, ISBN13: 978-0-89158-909-9. Dewey:327.48. LCCN:81-024062.
Audience: **g,l,u.**

Scandinavia > Finland

Aunesluoma, Juhana **DA47.9.F5**
From War to Cold War : Anglo-Finnish Relations in the 20th Century. SKS. 2005. Studia historica (Helsinki, Finland) ISBN:951-746-702-8, ISBN13: 978-951-746-702-5.
Audience: **u,f.**

Jakobson, Max **DL1046**
Finland : Myth and Reality. Otava Publishing Company. 1987. ISBN:951-1-08601-4, ISBN13: 978-951-1-08601-7.
Audience: **g,l,u.**

Jutikkala, Eino **DL1032**
A History of Finland. Pirinen, Kauko (author) ; Sjoblom, Paul (translator). Pareger. 1962. Books that matter
Audience: **g,l,u.**

Polvinen, Tuomo **DL1065.5.B62P6413**
Imperial Borderland: Bobrikov and the Attempted Russification of Finland, 1898-1904. Steven Huxley (Translator). Cloth Text. Duke University Press. Durham, NC. 1995. 272p. ISBN:0-8223-1563-7, ISBN13: 978-0-8223-1563-6. Dewey:948.97/02. LCCN:94-038507.
Audience: **u,f.** *Choice, 1996.*

Puntila, L. A. **DL1044 .P8513**
The Political History of Finland, 1809-1966. Trade Cloth. Taylor & Francis Group. Philadelphia, PA. 1976. 248p. ISBN:0-8448-0913-6, ISBN13: 978-0-8448-0913-7. Dewey:947.1.
Audience: **g,l,u.**

Schoolfield, George C. **DL1175.46.S36 1996**
Helsinki of the Czars Finland's Capital, 1808-1918. Trade Cloth. Camden House. Elizabethtown, NY. 1996. 336p. Studies in Scandinavian Literature and Culture Ser. ISBN:1-57113-026-8, ISBN13: 978-1-57113-026-6. Dewey:948.97/1. LCCN:95-018982.
Audience: **u,f.** *Choice, 1996.*

Singleton, Fred **DL1032 .S55 1998**
A Short History of Finland. Ed. 2. Cloth Text. Cambridge University Press. New York, NY. 1998. 221p. ISBN:0-521-64069-5, ISBN13: 978-0-521-64069-5. Dewey:948.97. LCCN:99-158605.
Audience: **g,l,u.** *Choice, 1990.*

Trotter, William R. **DL1097.T76 1991**
A Frozen Hell: The Russo-Finnish Winter War of, 1939-1940. Trade Cloth. Algonquin Books of Chapel Hill. Chapel Hill, NC. 1991. 320p. ISBN:0-945575-22-X, ISBN13: 978-0-945575-22-1. Dewey:948.9703/2. LCCN:90-019968.
Audience: **g,l,u,f.** *Choice, 1991.*

Vloyantes, John P. **JX1555.3.Z7 R88**
Silk Glove Hegemony - Finnish Soviet Relations, 1944-1974. Trade Cloth. Kent State University Press. Kent, OH. 1975. 200p. ISBN:0-87338-174-2, ISBN13: 978-0-87338-174-1. Dewey:327.471/047. LCCN:74-027387.
Audience: **u,f.**

Wuorinen, John Henry **DL1032**
A History of Finland. Published for American-Scandinavian Foundation by Columbia University PRess. 1965.
Audience: **g,l,u.**

Spain. Portugal > Spain > Culture and Civilization

Bango Torviso, Isidro Gonzalo **DS135.S7**
Remembering Sepharad: Jewish Culture in Medieval Spain. State Corp. for Spanish Cultural Action Abroad. 2003. ISBN:84-96008-27-4, ISBN13: 978-84-96008-27-4.
Audience: **g,l,u,f.**

Dodds, Jerrilynn **NA1303.D63 1989**
Architecture and Ideology in Early Medieval Spain. Library Binding. Pennsylvania State University Press. University Park, PA. 1994. 256p. ISBN:0-271-00671-4, ISBN13: 978-0-271-00671-0. Dewey:720/.946/09021. LCCN:88-043437.
Audience: **g,u,f.** *Choice, 1991.*

Jayyusi, Salma K. (Editor) **DP103 .L38 1994C**
The Legacy of Muslim Spain. Manuela Marin (Contribution by). Trade Cloth. Brill Academic Publishers, Inc. Boston, MA. 1994. xx, 1106p. Handbook of Oriental Studies, Vol. 12:Near and Middle East ISBN:90-04-09599-3, ISBN13: 978-90-04-09599-1. Dewey:946/.02. LCCN:92-029604.
Audience: **g,u,f.** *Choice, 1993.*

Moffitt, John F. **NX562.A1M65 1999**
The Arts of Spain: From Prehistory to Postmodernism. Trade Paper. Thames & Hudson. New York, NY. 1999. 240p. World of Art Ser. ISBN:0-500-20315-6, ISBN13: 978-0-500-20315-6. Dewey:709/.46. LCCN:98-060192.
Audience: **g,l,u,f.** *Choice, 1999.*

Nash, Elizabeth **DP362.N37 2000**
Madrid: A Cultural and Literary Companion. Trade Paper. Interlink Publishing Group, Inc. Northampton, MA. 2004. 256-264p. Cities of the Imagination Ser. ISBN:1-56656-368-2, ISBN13: 978-1-56656-368-0. Dewey:946/.41. LCCN:00-058055.
Audience: **g,l,u,f.**

Spain. Portugal > Spain > By Period > To 711. Visigoth Kingdom

Collins, Roger **DP96.C653 2004**
Visigothic Spain, 409-711. Trade Cloth. Blackwell Publishing, Inc. Malden, MA. 2004. 272p. A History of Spain Ser. ISBN:0-631-18185-7, ISBN13: 978-0-631-18185-9. Dewey:946/.01. LCCN:2003-017277.
Audience: **u,f.** *Choice, 2005.*

Curchin, Leonard A. **DP94.C87 1991**
Roman Spain: Conquest and Assimilation. Trade Cloth. Routledge. New York, NY. 1991. 240p. ISBN:0-415-06451-1, ISBN13: 978-0-415-06451-4. Dewey:936.6/03. LCCN:90-021723.
Audience: **g,l,u,f.** *Choice, 1992.*

James, Edward **DP96.V57**
Visigothic Spain: New Approaches. Trade Cloth. Oxford University Press, Inc. New York, NY. 1980. 328p. ISBN:0-19-822543-1, ISBN13: 978-0-19-822543-0. Dewey:946/.01. LCCN:79-040337.
Audience: **u,f.**

Keay, S. J. **DP94.K4 1988**
Roman Spain. Trade Cloth. University of California Press. Berkeley, CA. 1988. 240p. Exploring the Roman World Ser., Vol. 2 ISBN:0-520-06380-5, ISBN13: 978-0-520-06380-8. Dewey:936.6/03. LCCN:87-035722.
Audience: **g,l,u,f.** *Choice, 1988.*

Spain. Portugal > Spain > By Period > Muslim Spain. Reconquista (8th to 15th centuries)

Barton, Simon & Fletcher, R. A. (Editors) **DP99**
The World of el Cid: Chronicles of the Spanish Reconquest. Cloth over Boards. Manchester University Press. Manchester, 2001. 304p. Manchester Medieval Sources Ser. ISBN:0-7190-5225-4, ISBN13: 978-0-7190-5225-5. Dewey:946/.02.
Audience: **g,l,u,f.**

Collins, Roger **DP99**
Arab Conquest of Spain: 710-797. Trade Paper. Blackwell Publishing, Inc. Malden, MA. 1995. 256p. ISBN:0-631-19405-3, ISBN13: 978-0-631-19405-7. Dewey:946/.02. LCCN:88-033356.
Audience: **g,u,f.** *Choice, 1990.*

Constable, Olivia R. (Editor) **DP97.4.M43 1997**
Medieval Iberia: Readings from Christian, Muslim, and Jewish Sources. Trade Cloth. University of Pennsylvania Press. Philadelphia, PA. 1997. 448p. Middle Ages Ser. ISBN:0-8122-3333-6, ISBN13: 978-0-8122-3333-9. Dewey:946/.02. LCCN:97-004097.
Audience: **g,l,u,f.**

Constable, Olivia R. **HF3685.C66 1996**
Trade and Traders in Muslim Spain: The Commercial Realignment of the Iberian Peninsula, 900-1500. Trade Cloth. Cambridge University Press. New York, NY. 1994. 348p. Studies in Medieval Life and Thought, No. 24 ISBN:0-521-43075-5, ISBN13: 978-0-521-43075-3. Dewey:382/.0946. LCCN:93-015165.
Audience: **u,f.** *Choice, 1995.*

Fletcher, Richard **DP99 .F56**
Moorish Spain. Ed. 2. Trade Paper. University of California Press. Berkeley, CA. 2006. 224p. ISBN:0-520-24840-6, ISBN13: 978-0-520-24840-3. Dewey:946/.02.
Audience: **g,u,f.**

Glick, Thomas F. **DP99.G46 1995**
From Muslim Fortress to Christian Castle: Social and Cultural Change in Medieval Spain. Cloth Text. Manchester University Press. Manchester, 1996. 224p. ISBN:0-7190-3349-7, ISBN13: 978-0-7190-3349-0. Dewey:946/.02. LCCN:95-002195.
Audience: **u,f.** *Choice, 1996.*

Glick, Thomas F. **DP99.G47 2005**
Islam and Christian Spain. Ed. 2. Cloth Text. Brill Academic Publishers. Leiden, 2005. xxii, 402p. The Medieval and Early Modern Iberian World Ser., Vol. 27 ISBN:90-04-14771-3, ISBN13: 978-90-04-14771-3. Dewey:946/.02. LCCN:2005-016467.
Audience: **u,f.**

Harvey, L. P. **DP99**
Islamic Spain, 1250 to 1500. Trade Paper. University of Chicago Press. Chicago, IL. 1992. 386p. ISBN:0-226-31962-8, ISBN13: 978-0-226-31962-9. Dewey:946/.02. LCCN:90-030225.
Audience: **g,l,u,f.** *Choice, 1991.*

Hillgarth, J. N. **DP99**
The Spanish Kingdoms, 1250-1516: 250-1410 Precarious Balance. Trade Cloth. Oxford University Press, Inc. New York, NY. 1976. 476p. ISBN:0-19-822530-X, ISBN13: 978-0-19-822530-0. Dewey:946/.02. LCCN:76-364728.
Audience: **u,f.**

Hillgarth, J. N. **DP99**
The Spanish Kingdoms, 1250-1560: Castilian Hegemony, 1410-1516. Trade Cloth. Oxford University Press, Inc. New York, NY. 1978. 728p. ISBN:0-19-822531-8, ISBN13: 978-0-19-822531-7. Dewey:946/.02.
Audience: **u,f.**

Kagan, Richard L. **DP178**
Lucrecia's Dreams: Politics and Prophecy in Sixteenth-Century Spain. Trade Paper. University of California Press. Berkeley, CA. 1995. 244p. ISBN:0-520-20158-2, ISBN13: 978-0-520-20158-3. Dewey:946/.043/092 B. LCCN:89-020607.
Audience: **g,u,f.** *Choice, 1991.*

Kennedy, Hugh **DP102.K46 1996**
Muslim Spain and Portugal: A Political History of Al-Andalus. Trade Cloth. Longman Publishing Group. White Plains, NY. 1997. 360p. ISBN:0-582-29968-3, ISBN13: 978-0-582-29968-9. Dewey:946/.02. LCCN:96-022764.
Audience: **g,u,f.** *Choice, 1997.*

Kosto, Adam J. **HN590.C36 K67 2001**
Making Agreements in Medieval Catalonia: Power, Order, and the Written Word, 1000-1200. Christine Carpenter, D. E. Luscombe, Rosamond McKitterick & Jonathan Shepard (Contribution by). Trade Cloth. Cambridge University Press. New York, NY. 2001. 390p. Studies in Medieval Life and Thought, Vol. 4 ISBN:0-521-79239-8, ISBN13: 978-0-521-79239-4. Dewey:303.3. LCCN:00-062162.
Audience: **u,f.** *Choice, 2001.*

Lowney, Christopher **DP99.L695 2005**
A Vanished World: Medieval Spain's Golden Age of Enlightenment. Trade Cloth. Simon & Schuster. New York, NY. 2005. 336p. ISBN:0-7432-4359-5, ISBN13: 978-0-7432-4359-9. Dewey:946/.02. LCCN:2004-056362.
Audience: **g,l,u,f.** *Choice, 2006.*

MacKay, Angus **DP99.M23 1977**
Spain in the Middle Ages: From Frontier to Empire, 1000-1500. Trade Cloth. Palgrave Macmillan. New York, NY. 1977. xii, 245p. New Studies in Medieval History ISBN:0-312-74978-3, ISBN13: 978-0-312-74978-1. Dewey:946/.02. LCCN:76-052257.
Audience: **g,l,u,f.**

Menocal, Maria Rosa **DP99.M465 2002**
The Ornament of the World: How Muslims, Jews, and Christians Created a Culture of Tolerance in Medieval Spain. Harold Bloom (Preface by). Trade Cloth. Little Brown & Company. New York, NY. 2002. 336p. ISBN:0-316-56688-8, ISBN13: 978-0-316-56688-9. Dewey:946/.01. LCCN:2002-512742.
Audience: **g,l,u,f.** *Choice, 2003.*

O'Callaghan, Joseph F. **DP96**
A History of Medieval Spain. Ithaca: Cornell University Press. 1983. ISBN:0-8014-9264-5, ISBN13: 978-0-8014-9264-8.
Audience: **g,u,f.**

O'Callaghan, Joseph F. **DP99.O33 2002**
Reconquest and Crusade in Medieval Spain. Trade Cloth. University of Pennsylvania Press. Philadelphia, PA. 2002. 344p. The Middle Ages Ser. ISBN:0-8122-3696-3, ISBN13: 978-0-8122-3696-5. Dewey:946/.02. LCCN:2002-028952.
Audience: **u,f.** *Choice, 2003.*

Phillips, Jonathan **D162.E96 2001**
Conquest of Lisbon: De Expugnatione Lyxbonesi. Charles Wendell David (Translator). Trade Paper. Columbia University Press. New York, NY. 2001. 224p. Records of Western Civilization Ser. ISBN:0-231-12123-7, ISBN13: 978-0-231-12123-1. Dewey:946.9/42502. LCCN:00-060327.
Audience: **g,l,u,f.**

Reilly, Bernard F. **DP137.6.R44 1988**
The Kingdom of Leon-Castilla under King Alfonso VI, 1065-1109. Trade Cloth. Princeton University Press. Princeton, NJ. 1988. 410p. ISBN:0-691-05515-7, ISBN13: 978-0-691-05515-2. Dewey:946/.202. LCCN:87-003502.
Audience: **u,f.** *Choice, 1989.*

Reilly, Bernard F. **DP138.3.R45 1998**
Kingdom of Leon-Castilla under King Alfonso VII, 1126-1157. Trade Cloth. University of Pennsylvania Press. Philadelphia, PA. 1998. 416p. Middle Ages Ser. ISBN:0-8122-3452-9, ISBN13: 978-0-8122-3452-7. Dewey:946/.202. LCCN:98-006677.
Audience: **u,f.** *Choice, 1999.*

Reilly, Bernard F. **DP99 .R375 1993**
The Medieval Spains. Cloth Text. Cambridge University Press. New York, NY. 1993. 240p. Cambridge Medieval Textbooks ISBN:0-521-39436-8, ISBN13: 978-0-521-39436-9. Dewey:946.02. LCCN:92-023379.
Audience: **g,l,u,f.**

Reilly, Bernard F. (Author, Preface by) **DP99**
The Contest of Christian and Muslim Spain: 1031-1157. John Lynch (Editor). Cloth Text. Blackwell Publishing, Inc. Malden, MA. 1995. 284p. A History of Spain Ser. ISBN:0-631-16913-X, ISBN13: 978-0-631-16913-0. Dewey:946.02.
Audience: **g,l,u,f.** *Choice, 1992.*

Spain. Portugal > Spain > By Period > Catholic Monarchs. Habsburg Spain (1459-1700)

Beinart, Haim & Green, Jeffrey M. **DS135.S7B41413 2001**
The Expulsion of the Jews from Spain. Trade Cloth. Littman Library of Jewish Civilization, The. London, 2002. 612p. ISBN:1-874774-41-2, ISBN13: 978-1-874774-41-9. Dewey:946/.004924. LCCN:2001-038026.
Audience: **u,f.** *Choice, 2002.*

Edwards, John **DP164.E39 2000**
The Spain of the Catholic Monarchs, 1474-1520. Trade Paper. Blackwell Publishing, Inc. Malden, MA. 2001. 336p. A History of Spain Ser. ISBN:0-631-22143-3, ISBN13: 978-0-631-22143-2. Dewey:946/.03. LCCN:00-009574.
Audience: **g,u,f.** *Choice, 2001.*

Eire, Carlos M. N. **BX1584 .E57 1995**
From Madrid to Purgatory: The Art and Craft of Dying in Sixteenth-Century Spain. John Elliott, Olwen Hufton, H. G. Koenigsberger & H. M. Scott (Contribution by). Trade Paper. Cambridge University Press. New York, NY. 2002. 587p. Cambridge Studies in Early Modern History Ser. ISBN:0-521-52942-5, ISBN13: 978-0-521-52942-6. Dewey:236/.0946/09031.
Audience: **u,f.**

Elliott, J. H. **DP185.9.O6**
The Count-Duke of Olivares: The Statesman in an Age of Decline. Trade Paper. Yale University Press. Cumberland, RI. 1989. 738p. ISBN:0-300-04499-2, ISBN13: 978-0-300-04499-7. Dewey:946/.05/0924 B. LCCN:85-026450.
Audience: **u,f.** *Choice, 1987.*

Elliott, John Huxtable **DP171**
Imperial Spain 1469-1716. London : Penguin. 2002. ISBN:0-14-100703-6, ISBN13: 978-0-14-100703-8.
Audience: **g,l,u,f.**

Feros, Antonio **DP183 .F47 2000**
Kingship and Favoritism in the Spain of Philip III, 1598-1621. John Elliott, Olwen Hufton, H. G. Koenigsberger & H. M. Scott (Contribution by). Trade Cloth. Cambridge University Press. New York, NY. 2000. 318p. Studies in Early Modern History ISBN:0-521-56113-2, ISBN13: 978-0-521-56113-6. Dewey:946/.043. LCCN:99-054217.
Audience: **u,f.** *Choice, 2001.*

Giles, Mary E. **BX1735.W59 1998**
Women in the Inquisition: Spain and the New World. Trade Cloth. Johns Hopkins University Press. Baltimore, MD. 1998. 416p. ISBN:0-8018-5931-X, ISBN13: 978-0-8018-5931-1. Dewey:272/.2/082. LCCN:98-003998.
Audience: **g,u,f.** *Choice, 1999.*

Goodman, David S. **T26.S7G66 1988**
Power and Penury: Government, Technology and Science in Philip II's Spain. Trade Cloth. Cambridge University Press. New York, NY. 1988. 287p. ISBN:0-521-30532-2, ISBN13: 978-0-521-30532-7. Dewey:338.94606. LCCN:87-024630.
Audience: **u,f.** *Choice, 1989.*

Goodman, David **DP81.5 .G6 1997**
Spanish Naval Power, 1589-1665: Reconstruction and Defeat. John Elliott, Olwen Hufton, H. G. Koenigsberger & H. M. Scott (Contribution by). Trade Paper. Cambridge University Press. New York, NY. 2003. 326p. Cambridge Studies in Early Modern History Ser. ISBN:0-521-52257-9, ISBN13: 978-0-521-52257-1. Dewey:359/.00946/09031.
Audience: **u,f.** *Choice, 1997.*

Haliczer, Stephen **BX2263.S7H35 1996**
Sexuality in the Confessional: A Sacrament Profaned. Cloth Text. Oxford University Press, Inc. New York, NY. 1996. 280p. Studies in the History of Sexuality ISBN:0-19-509656-8, ISBN13: 978-0-19-509656-9. Dewey:264/.020862/09460903. LCCN:94-047094.
Audience: **u,f.** *Choice, 1996.*

Harvey, L. P. **DP104.H37 2005**
Muslims in Spain, 1500 To 1614. Trade Cloth. University of Chicago Press. Chicago, IL. 2005. 462p. ISBN:0-226-31963-6, ISBN13: 978-0-226-31963-6. Dewey:946/.04/088297. LCCN:2004-015747.
Audience: **g,u,f.** *Choice, 2006.*

Herzog, Tamar **JN8399.C26**
Defining Nations:Iimmigrants and Citizens in Early Modern Spain and Spanish America. New Haven: Yale University Press. 2003. ISBN:0-300-09253-9, ISBN13: 978-0-300-09253-0.
Audience: **u,f.**

Hillgarth, J. N. **DP171.5.H54 2000**
The Mirror of Spain, 1500-1700: The Formation of a Myth. Trade Cloth. University of Michigan Press. Chicago, IL. 2000. 608p. History, Languages and Cultures of the Spanish and Portuguese Worlds Ser. ISBN:0-472-11092-6, ISBN13: 978-0-472-11092-6. Dewey:946/.04. LCCN:00-008541.
Audience: **g,u,f.** *Choice, 2001.*

Homza, Lu Ann **BX1584**
Religious Authority in the Spanish Renaissance. Trade Paper. Johns Hopkins University Press. Baltimore, MD. 2004. 344p. The Johns Hopkins University Studies in Historical and Political Science Ser. ISBN:0-8018-7904-3, ISBN13: 978-0-8018-7904-3. Dewey:274.6/06.
Audience: **u,f.** *Choice, 2000.*

Ishikawa, Chiyo (Editor, Introduction by) **N7104.S73 2004**
Spain in the Age of Exploration, 1492-1819. Jesus Carrillo, Richard Kagan, Javier Morales, Ben Schmidt, Sarah Schroth, Andrew Schulz & Jose de la Sota (Contribution by). Trade Cloth. University of Nebraska Press. Lincoln, NE. 2005. 300p. ISBN:0-8032-2505-9, ISBN13: 978-0-8032-2505-3. Dewey:709/.46/074797772. LCCN:2004-012309.
Audience: **g,l,u,f.** *Choice, 2005.*

Israel, Jonathan Irvine **D231.I55 1997**
Conflicts of Empires: Spain, the Low Countries and the Struggle for World Supremacy, 1585-1713. Trade Cloth. Continuum International Publishing Group, Ltd. London, 1997. 504p. ISBN:1-85285-161-9, ISBN13: 978-1-85285-161-3. Dewey:940. LCCN:97-016021.
Audience: **u,f.** *Choice, 1998.*

Kamen, Henry **DP164.K36 2003**
Empire: How Spain Became a World Power, 1492-1763. Trade Cloth. HarperCollins Publishers. New York, NY. 2003. 640p. ISBN:0-06-019476-6, ISBN13: 978-0-06-019476-5. Dewey:946.03. LCCN:2002-038748.
Audience: **g,u,f.**

Kamen, Henry **DP178.K36 1997**
Philip of Spain. Cloth over Boards. Yale University Press. Cumberland, RI. 1997. 412p. ISBN:0-300-07081-0, ISBN13: 978-0-300-07081-1. Dewey:946. LCCN:96-052421.
Audience: **g,l,u,f.** *Choice, 1997.*

Kamen, Henry **DP194.K3613 2001**
Philip V of Spain: The King Who Reigned Twice. Cloth over Boards. Yale University Press. Cumberland, RI. 2001. 288p. ISBN:0-300-08718-7, ISBN13: 978-0-300-08718-5. Dewey:946/.055/092 B. LCCN:00-067192.
Audience: **g,u,f.** *Choice, 2001.*

Kamen, Henry **DP161.K35 2005**
Spain, 1469-1714: A Society of Conflict. Ed. 3. Trade Paper. Longman Publishing Group. White Plains, NY. 2005. 368p. ISBN:0-582-78464-6, ISBN13: 978-0-582-78464-2. Dewey:946. LCCN:2005-045833.
Audience: **g,l,u,f.**

Kamen, Henry A. **BX1735**
The Spanish Inquisition: A Historical Revision. Trade Paper. Yale University Press. Cumberland, RI. 1999. 392p. ISBN:0-300-07880-3, ISBN13: 978-0-300-07880-0. Dewey:272/.2/0946.
Audience: **g,u,f.** *Choice, 1998.*

Kamen, Henry Arthur Francis **DP191.A6K36 2004**
The Duke of Alba. Cloth over Boards. Yale University Press. Cumberland, RI. 2004. 216p. ISBN:0-300-10283-6, ISBN13: 978-0-300-10283-3. Dewey:949.2/03/092 B. LCCN:2004-001543.
Audience: **u,f.**

Meyerson, Mark D. **DS135.S7M485 2004**
A Jewish Renaissance in Fifteenth-Century Spain. Trade Cloth. Princeton University Press. Princeton, NJ. 2004. 272p. Jews, Christians, and Muslims from the Ancient to the Modern World Ser. ISBN:0-691-11749-7, ISBN13: 978-0-691-11749-2. Dewey:946/.004924. LCCN:2003-056329.
Audience: **g,u,f.** *Choice, 2005.*

Meyerson, Mark D. **DS135.S75S2365 2004**
Jews in an Iberian Frontier Kingdom: Society, Economy, and Politics in Morvedre, 1248-1391. Trade Cloth. Brill Academic Publishers. Leiden, 2004. xx, 308p. The Medieval and Early Modern Iberian World Ser., Vol. 20 ISBN:90-04-13739-4, ISBN13: 978-90-04-13739-4. Dewey:946/.763. LCCN:2004-040771.
Audience: **u,f.** *Choice, 2005.*

Nader, Helen **JS6320.C296N33 1990**
Liberty in Absolutist Spain: The Hapsburg Sale of Towns, 1516-1700. Trade Cloth. Johns Hopkins University Press. Baltimore, MD. 1990. 328p. Studies in Historical and Political Science, 108th Series, No. 1 ISBN:0-8018-3850-9, ISBN13: 978-0-8018-3850-7. Dewey:320.8/0946/2. LCCN:89-024503.
Audience: **u,f.** *Choice, 1991.*

Netanyahu, Benjamin **BX1735.N48 1995**
The Origins of the Inquisition in Fifteenth Century Spain. Trade Cloth. Random House, Inc. New York, NY. 1995. 1,384p. ISBN:0-679-41065-1, ISBN13: 978-0-679-41065-2. Dewey:272/.2/0946. LCCN:92-053643.
Audience: **u,f.** *Choice, 1996.*

Parker, Geoffrey **DP178**
The Grand Strategy of Philip II. Trade Paper. Yale University Press. Cumberland, RI. 2000. 472p. ISBN:0-300-08273-8, ISBN13: 978-0-300-08273-9. Dewey:946/.043/092.
Audience: **u,f.** *Choice, 1999.*

Parker, Geoffrey **DH186.5.P28 2004**
The Army of Flanders and the Spanish Road, 1567-1659: The Logistics of Spanish Victory and Defeat in the Low Countries' Wars. Ed. 2. John Elliott, Olwen Hufton, H. G. Koenigsberger & H. M. Scott (Contribution by). Trade Cloth. Cambridge University Press. New York, NY. 2004. 324p. Cambridge Studies in Early Modern History Ser. ISBN:0-521-83600-X, ISBN13: 978-0-521-83600-5. Dewey:949.2/03. LCCN:2005-279821.
Audience: **u,f.**

Perez, Joseph **BX1735.P4713**
The Spanish Inquisition: A History. Janet Lloyd (Translator). Cloth over Boards. Yale University Press. Cumberland, RI. 2005. 256p. ISBN:0-300-10790-0, ISBN13: 978-0-300-10790-6. Dewey:272/.2.
Audience: **g,u,f.** *Choice, 2006.*

Perry, M. E. **DP104.P475 2005**
Handless Maiden: Moriscos and the Politics of Religion in Early Modern Spain. Trade Cloth. Princeton University Press. Princeton, NJ. 2005. 192p. Jews, Christians, and Muslims from the Ancient to the Modern World Ser. ISBN:0-691-11358-0, ISBN13: 978-0-691-11358-6. Dewey:946/.04/088297. LCCN:2004-044675.
Audience: **g,l,u,f.** *Choice, 2006.*

Pike, Ruth **DS135.S75S455 2000**
Linajudos and Conversos in Seville: Greed and Prejudice in Sixteenth and Seventeenth Century Spain. Trade Cloth. Peter Lang Publishing, Inc. New York, NY. 2000. xiii, 217p. American University Studies, Vol. 195:History ISBN:0-8204-4964-4, ISBN13: 978-0-8204-4964-7. Dewey:946/.86004924. LCCN:99-087558.
Audience: **g,u,f.** *Choice, 2001.*

Rodriquez, M. J. & Adams, Simon **DA360.E54 1991**
England, Spain and the Grand Armada, 1585-1604. Trade Cloth. Rowman & Littlefield Publishers, Inc. Lanham, MD. 1991. 324p. ISBN:0-389-20955-4, ISBN13: 978-0-389-20955-3. Dewey:942.05/5. LCCN:91-000506.
Audience: **u,f.** *Choice, 1992.*

Rodríguez-Salgado, Maria J. **DD179.R62 1988**
The Changing Face of Empire: Charles V, Philip II, and Habsburg Authority, 1551-1559. John Elliott, Olwen Hufton, H. G. Koenigsberger & H. M. Scott (Contribution by). Trade Cloth. Cambridge University Press. New York, NY. 1988. 392p. Studies in Early Modern History ISBN:0-521-30346-X, ISBN13: 978-0-521-30346-0. Dewey:943/.031. LCCN:87-032647.
Audience: **u,f.** *Choice, 1989.*

Sánchez, Magdalena S. **DP182**
The Empress, the Queen, and the Nun: Women and Power at the Court of Philip III of Spain. Trade Paper. Johns Hopkins University Press. Baltimore, MD. 2003. 296p. The Johns Hopkins University Studies in Historical and Political Science Ser. ISBN:0-8018-7243-X, ISBN13: 978-0-8018-7243-3. Dewey:946/.051. LCCN:97-042171.
Audience: **g,u,f.** *Choice, 1999.*

Thompson, I. A. A. & Casalilla, Bartolomi Yun (Editors) **HC384 .C34 1994**
The Castilian Crisis of the Seventeenth Century: New Perspectives on the Economic and Social History of Seventeenth-Century Spain. Lyndal Roper (Contribution by). Trade Cloth. Cambridge University Press. New York, NY. 1994. 345p. Past and Present Publications ISBN:0-521-41624-8, ISBN13: 978-0-521-41624-5. Dewey:330.946. LCCN:93-027991.
Audience: **u,f.** *Choice, 1995.*

Spain. Portugal > Spain > By Period > Bourbon Spain (1700-1931). Peninsular War. Constitutional Monarchy

Esdaile, Charles J. **DC231.E833 2004**
Fighting Napoleon: Guerrillas, Bandits, and Adventurers in Spain, 1808-1814. Cloth over Boards. Yale University Press. Cumberland, RI. 2004. 288p. ISBN:0-300-10112-0, ISBN13: 978-0-300-10112-6. Dewey:940.2/742/0946. LCCN:2003-026237.
Audience: **g,u,f.** *Choice, 2005.*

Esdaile, Charles J. **DC231.E834 2003**
The Peninsular War: A New History. Cloth over Boards. Palgrave Macmillan. New York, NY. 2003. 640p. ISBN:1-4039-6231-6, ISBN13: 978-1-4039-6231-7. Dewey:940.2/742. LCCN:2003-273462.
Audience: **g,u,f.** *Choice, 2004.*

Herr, Richard **DP192**
The Eighteenth Century Revolution in Spain. Paper Text. Textbook Publishers. Temecula, CA. 2003. 484p. ISBN:0-7581-5708-8, ISBN13: 978-0-7581-5708-9. Dewey:946.054.
Audience: **u,f.**

Kendrick, John **G286.M2**
Alejandro Malaspina: Portrait of a Visionary. Trade Cloth. McGill-Queen's University Press. Montreal, PQ. 208p. ISBN:0-7735-1830-4, ISBN13: 978-0-7735-1830-8. Dewey:910.9/2.
Audience: **g,u,f.** *Choice, 1999.*

Martin, Benjamin **HD8584.M28 1990**
The Agony of Modernization: Labor and Industrialization in Spain. Book, Other. Cornell University Press. Ithaca, NY. 1990. 576p. Cornell International Industrial and Labor Relations Reports, No. 16 ISBN:0-87546-165-4, ISBN13: 978-0-87546-165-6. Dewey:331/.0946. LCCN:89-077909.
Audience: **g,u,f.** *Choice, 1991.*

Ringrose, David R. **HC385 .R514 1996**
Spain, Europe, and the 'Spanish Miracle', 1700-1900. Cloth Text. Cambridge University Press. New York, NY. 1996. 455p. ISBN:0-521-43486-6, ISBN13: 978-0-521-43486-7. Dewey:946.05. LCCN:96-158113.
Audience: **u,f.** *Choice, 1996.*

Romero Salvadbo, Francisco J. **D520.S8R66 1999**
Spain: Between War and Revolution. Paper over Boards. Routledge. New York, NY. 1999. 256p. Blanch Studies in Contemporary Spain, Vol. 1 ISBN:0-415-21293-6, ISBN13: 978-0-415-21293-9. Dewey:946/.074. LCCN:99-010069.
Audience: **u,f.** *Choice, 2000.*

Schmidt-Nowara, Christopher **HT1078.S38 1999**
Empire and Antislavery: Spain, Cuba and Puerto Rico, 1833-1874. Cloth Text. University of Pittsburgh Press. Pittsburgh, PA. 1999. xiii, 239p. Pitt Latin American Ser. ISBN:0-8229-4089-2, ISBN13: 978-0-8229-4089-0. Dewey:326/.8/09171246. LCCN:99-006423.
Audience: **g,u,f.** *Choice, 1999.*

Sherwood, Joan **HV1245.M332.I537**
Poverty in Eighteenth-Century Spain: The Women and Children of the Inclusa. Cloth Text. University of Toronto Press. Toronto, ON. 1988. 239p. ISBN:0-8020-2662-1, ISBN13: 978-0-8020-2662-0. Dewey:305.5690946. LCCN:89-175362.
Audience: **u,f.** *Choice, 1989.*

Tone, John Lawrence **DC231.T63 1994**
The Fatal Knot: The Guerrilla War in Navarre and the Defeat of Napoleon in Spain. University of North Carolina Press. 1994. ISBN:0-8078-2169-1, ISBN13: 978-0-8078-2169-5.
Audience: **g,u,f.**

Spain. Portugal > Spain > By Period > Second Spanish Republic (1931-1939). Spanish Civil War

Bolloten, Burnett **DP269.B6563 1991**
The Spanish Civil War: Revolution and Counterrevolution. Trade Cloth. University of North Carolina Press. Chapel Hill, NC. 1991. 1107p. ISBN:0-8078-1906-9, ISBN13: 978-0-8078-1906-7. Dewey:946.081. LCCN:89-077911.
Audience: **g,u,f.** *Choice, 1991.*

Brenan, Gerald **DP233 .B7 1990**
The Spanish Labyrinth: An Account of the Social and Political Background of the Spanish Civil War. Ed. 2. Trade Paper. Cambridge University Press. New York, NY. 1990. 404p. A Canto Book Ser. ISBN:0-521-39827-4, ISBN13: 978-0-521-39827-5. Dewey:946. LCCN:90-033310.
Audience: **g,l,u,f.**

de Rivas Cherif, Cipriano **DP268.R513 1995**
Portrait of an Unknown Man: Manuel Azana and Modern Spain. Paul Stewart (Translator), Enrique de Rivas (Introduction by). Trade Cloth. Fairleigh Dickinson University Press. Cranbury, NJ. 1995. 432p. ISBN:0-8386-3584-9, ISBN13: 978-0-8386-3584-1. Dewey:946.081/092 B. LCCN:94-042956.
Audience: **g,l,u,f.** *Choice, 1996.*

Falcoff, Mark & Pike, Fredrick B. (Editors) **DP269.8.P8S6 1982**
The Spanish Civil War, 1936-1939: American Hemispheric Perspectives. Trade Cloth. University of Nebraska Press. Lincoln, NE. 1982. xxiv, 357p. ISBN:0-8032-1961-X, ISBN13: 978-0-8032-1961-8. Dewey:946.081. LCCN:81-014644.
Audience: **u,f.**

Graham, Helen **DP269**
The Spanish Republic at War 1936-1939. Trade Paper. Cambridge University Press. New York, NY. 2002. 486p. ISBN:0-521-45932-X, ISBN13: 978-0-521-45932-7. Dewey:946.081. LCCN:2003-271804.
Audience: **g,l,u,f.** *Choice, 2003.*

Martin, Benjamin **HD8584.M28 1990**
The Agony of Modernization: Labor and Industrialization in Spain. Book, Other. Cornell University Press. Ithaca, NY. 1990. 576p. Cornell International Industrial and Labor Relations Reports, No. 16 ISBN:0-87546-165-4, ISBN13: 978-0-87546-165-6. Dewey:331/.0946. LCCN:89-077909.
Audience: **g,u,f.** *Choice, 1991.*

Orwell, George **PR6029.R8**
Homage to Catalonia. Ed. 1. Trade Paper. Harcourt Trade Publishers. New York, NY. 1969. 264p. Harvest Book Ser. ISBN:0-15-642117-8, ISBN13: 978-0-15-642117-1. Dewey:946/.081. LCCN:52-006442.
Audience: **g,l,u,f.**

Payne, Stanley G. **DP269**
Falange: A History of Spanish Fascism. Paper Text. Textbook Publishers. Temecula, CA. 2003. ix, 316p. ISBN:0-7581-3445-2, ISBN13: 978-0-7581-3445-5. Dewey:946.081.
Audience: **u,f.**

Payne, Stanley G. **DP243.P39 1999**
Fascism in Spain, 1923-1977. Cloth Text. University of Wisconsin Press. Chicago, IL. 1999. xii, 601p. ISBN:0-299-16560-4, ISBN13: 978-0-299-16560-4. Dewey:946.08. LCCN:99-023078.
Audience: **g,l,u,f.** *Choice, 2000.*

Payne, Stanley G. **DP269**
Spain's First Democracy: The Second Republic, 1931-1936. Trade Paper. University of Wisconsin Press. Chicago, IL. 1993. 494p. ISBN:0-299-13674-4, ISBN13: 978-0-299-13674-1. Dewey:946.081. LCCN:92-056925.
Audience: **g,u,f.** *Choice, 1994.*

Preston, Paul **DP269.8.W7P74 2003**
Doves of War: Four Women of Spain. Trade Cloth. Northeastern University Press. Boston, MA. 2003. 480p. ISBN:1-55553-560-7, ISBN13: 978-1-55553-560-5. Dewey:946.081/082. LCCN:2003-001047.
Audience: **g,l,u,f.** *Choice, 2004.*

Preston, Paul **DP264.F7P74 1994**
Franco: A Biography. Trade Cloth. Basic Books. New York, NY. 1994. 1024p. ISBN:0-465-02515-3, ISBN13: 978-0-465-02515-2. Dewey:946.082/092 B. LCCN:94-028636.
Audience: **g,u,f.** *Choice, 1995.*

Seidman, Michael **DP269.8.S65S54 2002**
Republic of Egos: A Social History of the Spanish Civil War. Trade Cloth. University of Wisconsin Press. Chicago, IL. 2002. xi, 304p. ISBN:0-299-17860-9, ISBN13: 978-0-299-17860-4. Dewey:946.081/1. LCCN:2002-002808.
Audience: **g,l,u,f.** *Choice, 2003.*

Seidman, Michael **HD8590.B342S45 1991**
Workers Against Work: Labor in Paris and Barcelona During the Popular Fronts. Trade Cloth. University of California Press. Berkeley, CA. 1990. 384p. ISBN:0-520-06915-3, ISBN13: 978-0-520-06915-2. Dewey:322/.2/094436. LCCN:90-033716.
Audience: **u,f.** *Choice, 1991.*

Thomas, Hugh **DP269.T46 2001**
The Spanish Civil War. Trade Paper. Random House Adult Trade Publishing Group. New York, NY. 2001. 1120p. Modern Library War ISBN:0-375-75515-2, ISBN13: 978-0-375-75515-6. Dewey:946.081. LCCN:2001-030833.
Audience: **g,u,f.**

Townson, Nigel **JN8395.R4T68 2000**
The Crisis of Democracy in Spain: Centrist Politics under the Second Republic (1931-1936). Chris Himsworth & Andrea Loux (Editors). Trade Cloth. Sussex Academic Press. Eastbourne, 2000. 444p. ISBN:1-898723-19-2, ISBN13: 978-1-898723-19-6. Dewey:324.246/02. LCCN:99-059288.
Audience: **u,f.** *Choice, 2001.*

Whealey, Robert H. **DP269**
Hitler and Spain: The Nazi Role in the Spanish Civil War, 1936-1939. Trade Paper. University Press of Kentucky. Lexington, KY. 2005. 280p. ISBN:0-8131-9139-4, ISBN13: 978-0-8131-9139-3. Dewey:946.081.
Audience: **u,f.** *Choice, 1990.*

Spain. Portugal > Spain > By Period > Franco Era (1939-1975)

Anaya, Pilar Ortuno **HX238.5.O77 2001**
European Socialists and Spain: The Transition to Democracy, 1959-1977. Cloth over Boards. Palgrave Macmillan. New York, NY. 2002. 273p. St. Antony's Ser. ISBN:0-333-94927-7, ISBN13: 978-0-333-94927-6. Dewey:320.946/09/045. LCCN:2001-048207.
Audience: **g,l,u,f.** *Choice, 2002.*

Cuevas, Tomasa **HV9742.5.C84.A313**
Prison of Women: Testimonies of War and Resistance in Spain, 1939-1975. Mary E. Giles (Editor, Translator). Cloth Text. State University of New York Press. Albany, NY. 1998. 256p. ISBN:0-7914-3857-0, ISBN13: 978-0-7914-3857-2. Dewey:365/.45/0820946. LCCN:97-033352.
Audience: **g,l,u,f.** *Choice, 1999.*

Morcillo, Aurora G. **HQ1236.5.S7M667 2000**
True Catholic Womanhood: Gender Ideology in Franco's Spain. Trade Cloth. Northern Illinois University Press. DeKalb, IL. 1999. 214p. ISBN:0-87580-256-7, ISBN13: 978-0-87580-256-5. Dewey:305.42/0946. LCCN:99-022907.
Audience: **g,l,u,f.** *Choice, 2000.*

Payne, Stanley G. **DP243.P39 1999**
Fascism in Spain, 1923-1977. Cloth Text. University of Wisconsin Press. Chicago, IL. 1999. xii, 601p. ISBN:0-299-16560-4, ISBN13: 978-0-299-16560-4. Dewey:946.08. LCCN:99-023078.
Audience: **g,l,u,f.** *Choice, 2000.*

Payne, Stanley G. **DP270.P365 2000**
The Franco Regime, 1936-1975. Trade Paper. Sterling Publishing Co., Inc. New York, NY. 2000. 704p. Phoenix Press Ser. ISBN:1-84212-046-8, ISBN13: 978-1-84212-046-0. Dewey:946.081. LCCN:00-690729.
Audience: **g,u,f.** *Choice, 1988.*

Rein, Raanan **F2833.5.S7 R43 1993**
The Franco-Peron Alliance: The Relations Between Spain and Argentina, 1946-1955. Martha Grenzeback (Translator). Cloth Text. University of Pittsburgh Press. Pittsburgh, PA. 1993. 344p. Latin American Ser. ISBN:0-8229-3751-4, ISBN13: 978-0-8229-3751-7. Dewey:327.46082. LCCN:92-035764.
Audience: **u,f.** *Choice, 1994.*

Richards, Michael **JC599.S6**
A Time of Silence: Civil War and the Culture of Repression in Franco's Spain, 1936-1945. Cambridge [England]; New York:; Cambridge University Press. 1998. Studies in the social and cultural history of modern warfare; 4. ISBN:0-521-59401-4, ISBN13: 978-0-521-59401-1.
Audience: **u,f.**

Spain. Portugal > Spain > By Period > Democratic Spain (1975-)

Gilmore, David D. **GT4262.A55G55 1998**
Carnival and Culture: Sex, Symbol, and Status in Spain. Cloth over Boards. Yale University Press. Cumberland, RI. 1998. 256p. ISBN:0-300-07480-8, ISBN13: 978-0-300-07480-2. Dewey:394.25/0946. LCCN:98-016185.
Audience: **g,l,u,f.** *Choice, 1999.*

Jones, Anny Brooksbank **HQ1692.J66 1997**
Women in Contemporary Spain. Trade Cloth. Manchester University Press. Manchester, 1998. 251p. ISBN:0-7190-4756-0, ISBN13: 978-0-7190-4756-5. Dewey:305.4/2/0946/09049. LCCN:97-020797.
Audience: **g,u,f.** *Choice, 1998.*

Ortiz Griffin, Julia & Griffin, William D. **DP272.O784 2002**
Spain and Portugal Today. Trade Paper. Peter Lang Publishing, Inc. New York, NY. 2003. xiii, 242p. Studies in Modern European History, Vol. 32 ISBN:0-8204-4031-0, ISBN13: 978-0-8204-4031-6. Dewey:946.083. LCCN:2001-050303.
Audience: **g,l,u,f.** *Choice, 2004.*

Preston, Paul **DP272.4.J8P738 2004**
Juan Carlos: Steering Spain from Dictatorship to Democracy. Trade Cloth. W. W. Norton & Company, Inc. New York, NY. 2004. 608p. ISBN:0-393-05804-2, ISBN13: 978-0-393-05804-8. Dewey:946.083/092 B. LCCN:2004-047435.
Audience: **g,u,f.**

Spain. Portugal > Spain > General Histories

Boyd, Carolyn P. **LC93.S7B69 1997**
Historia Patria: Politics, History, and National Identity in Spain, 1875-1975. Trade Cloth. Princeton University Press. Princeton, NJ. 1997. 382p. ISBN:0-691-02656-4, ISBN13: 978-0-691-02656-5. Dewey:320.54/0946. LCCN:96-045261.
Audience: **u,f.** *Choice, 1998.*

Carr, Raymond (Editor) **DP66**
Spain: A History. Trade Paper. Oxford University Press, Inc. New York, NY. 2001. 328p. ISBN:0-19-280236-4, ISBN13: 978-0-19-280236-1. Dewey:946. LCCN:99-042639.
Audience: **g,l,u,f.**

Collins, Roger **DP96.C649 1995**
Early Medieval Spain: Unity in Diversity, 400-1000. Ed. 2. Trade Paper. Palgrave Macmillan. New York, NY. 1995. 344p. New Studies in Medieval History ISBN:0-312-12662-X, ISBN13: 978-0-312-12662-9. Dewey:946/.01. LCCN:95-004155.
Audience: **g,l,u,f.**

Cowans, Jon **DP233.M59 2003**
Modern Spain: A Documentary History. Book, Other. University of Pennsylvania Press. Philadelphia, PA. 2003. 320p. ISBN:0-8122-3717-X, ISBN13: 978-0-8122-3717-7. Dewey:946.08. LCCN:2003-040217.
Audience: **g,l,u,f.**

De Oliveira Martins, J. P. **DP48 .O42 1969**
History of Iberian Civilization. Aubrey Fitz Gerald Bell (Translator), S. DeMadariaga (Introduction by). Trade Cloth. Cooper Square Publishers, Inc. New York, NY. 1969. 292p. ISBN:0-8154-0300-3, ISBN13: 978-0-8154-0300-5. Dewey:914.6/03. LCCN:71-081778.
Audience: **u,f.**

Gerber, Jane S. **DS135.S7.G47 1992**
The Jews of Spain: A History of the Sephardic Experience. Trade Cloth. Simon & Schuster. New York, NY. 1992. 320p. ISBN:0-02-911573-6, ISBN13: 978-0-02-911573-2. Dewey:946. LCCN:92-026941.
Audience: **g,l,u,f.** *Choice, 1993.*

Hooper, John **HN583.5.H66 1995**
The New Spaniards: A Portrait of the New Spain. Ed. 2. Trade Paper. Penguin Group (USA) Inc. New York, NY. 1995. 496p. ISBN:0-14-013191-4, ISBN13: 978-0-14-013191-8. Dewey:306/.0946/0904. LCCN:96-106277.
Audience: **g,l,u,f.**

Linehan, Peter **DP96.L56 1993**
History and the Historians of Medieval Spain. Trade Cloth. Oxford University Press, Inc. New York, NY. 1993. 766p. ISBN:0-19-821945-8, ISBN13: 978-0-19-821945-3. Dewey:946. LCCN:92-021842.
Audience: **u,f.** *Choice, 1994.*

Phillips, Carla R. & Phillips, William D. Jr. **HD9905.S822P48 1997**
Spain's Golden Fleece: Wool Production and the Wool Trade from the Middle Ages to the Nineteenth Century. Trade Cloth. Johns Hopkins University Press. Baltimore, MD. 1997. 464p. ISBN:0-8018-5518-7, ISBN13: 978-0-8018-5518-4. Dewey:338.1/763145. LCCN:96-047945.
Audience: **u,f.** *Choice, 1998.*

Sahlins, Peter **DC611.P985S24 1989**
Boundaries: The Making of France and Spain in the Pyrenees. Trade Cloth. University of California Press. Berkeley, CA. 1989. 372p. ISBN:0-520-06538-7, ISBN13: 978-0-520-06538-3. Dewey:946/.52. LCCN:89-004711.
Audience: **u,f.** *Choice, 1990.*

Spain. Portugal > Portugal

Anderson, James Maxwell **DP538**
The History of Portugal. Cloth Text. Greenwood Publishing Group, Inc. Portsmouth, NH. 2000. 248p. The Histories of the Modern Nations Ser. ISBN:0-313-31106-4, ISBN13: 978-0-313-31106-2. Dewey:946.9. LCCN:99-043637.
Audience: **g,l,u,f.**

Birmingham, David **DP538**
A Concise History of Portugal. Ed. 2. Cloth Text. Cambridge University Press. New York, NY. 2003. 240p. Cambridge Concise Histories Ser. ISBN:0-521-83004-4, ISBN13: 978-0-521-83004-1. Dewey:946.9. LCCN:2004-273150.
Audience: **g,l,u,f.**

Costa Gomes, Rita **KKQ250.G6613 2002**
The Making of a Court Society: Kings and Nobles in Late Medieval Portugal. Alison Aiken (Translator). Trade Cloth. Cambridge University Press. New York, NY. 2003. 512p. ISBN:0-521-80011-0, ISBN13: 978-0-521-80011-2. Dewey:305.5/223/09469. LCCN:2002-067727.
Audience: **u,f.**

Costa Pinto, Antonio **DP680**
Salazar's Dictatorship and European Fascism: Problems and Perspectives of Interpretation. Trade Cloth. Eastern European Monographs. Bradenton, FL. 1996. 238p. Social Science Monographs ISBN:0-88033-968-3, ISBN13: 978-0-88033-968-1. Dewey:946.9042. LCCN:94-065458.
Audience: **u,f.**

De Gois, Damiao **DP756 .G68 1996**
Lisbon in the Renaissance. Jeffrey S. Ruth (Translator, Introduction by). Trade Paper. Italica Press. New York, NY. 1996. 88p. Historical Travel Guides Ser. ISBN:0-934977-36-4, ISBN13: 978-0-934977-36-4. Dewey:946.9/425. LCCN:96-025081.
Audience: **g,l,u,f.**

Levenson, Jay (Editor) **N7121**
The Age of the Baroque in Portugal. Cloth over Boards. Yale University Press. Cumberland, RI. 1993. 256p. ISBN:0-300-05841-1, ISBN13: 978-0-300-05841-3. Dewey:709.469. LCCN:93-005425.
Audience: **u,f.**

Livermore, Harold U. **DP538**
New History of Portugal. Ed. 2. Trade Cloth. Cambridge University Press. New York, NY. 1976. 418p. ISBN:0-521-21320-7, ISBN13: 978-0-521-21320-2. Dewey:946.9. LCCN:76-011085.
Audience: **g,l,u,f.**

Marques, A. H. de Oliveira **DP532.3 .M3413**
Daily Life in Portugal in the Late Middle Ages. S. S. Wyatt (Translator), Vitor Andre (Illustrator). Trade Paper. University of Wisconsin Press. Chicago, IL. 1971. 372p. ISBN:0-299-05584-1, ISBN13: 978-0-299-05584-4. Dewey:914.690. LCCN:78-106040.
Audience: **l,u,f.**

Maxwell, Kenneth **DP681 .M39 1995**
The Making of Portuguese Democracy. Trade Paper. Cambridge University Press. New York, NY. 1997. 264p. ISBN:0-521-58596-1, ISBN13: 978-0-521-58596-5. Dewey:946.9/044.
Audience: **g,l,u,f.**

Oliveira, Marques A. **DP538 .M37**
A History of Portugal: From Lusitania to Empire. Trade Cloth. Columbia University Press. New York, NY. 1972. 507p. ISBN:0-231-03159-9, ISBN13: 978-0-231-03159-2. Dewey:946.9. LCCN:77-184748.
Audience: **u,f.** B

Phillips, Jonathan **D162.E96 2001**
Conquest of Lisbon: De Expugnatione Lyxbonesi. Charles Wendell David (Translator). Trade Paper. Columbia University Press. New York, NY. 2001. 224p. Records of Western Civilization Ser. ISBN:0-231-12123-7, ISBN13: 978-0-231-12123-1. Dewey:946.9/42502. LCCN:00-060327.
Audience: **g,l,u,f.**

Robinson, Rachael **DP675**
Contemporary Portugal. Cloth Text. Routledge. New York, NY. 1979. 308p. ISBN:0-04-946013-7, ISBN13: 978-0-04-946013-3. Dewey:946.9/042. LCCN:79-040004.
Audience: **g,l,u,f.** B

Russell, Peter E. **G286.H5R879 2000**
Prince Henry "The Navigator": A Life. Cloth over Boards. Yale University Press. Cumberland, RI. 2000. 464p. ISBN:0-300-08233-9, ISBN13: 978-0-300-08233-3. Dewey:946.9/02/092 B. LCCN:99-049569.
Audience: **g,l,u,f.** *Choice, 2001.*

Schultz, Kirsten **F2534.S324 2001**
Tropical Versailles: Empire, Monarchy, and the Portuguese Royal Court in Rio de Janeiro, 1808-1821. Paper over Boards. Routledge. New York, NY. 2001. 320p. New World in the Atlantic World Ser. ISBN:0-415-92987-3, ISBN13: 978-0-415-92987-5. Dewey:981/.53033. LCCN:00-068741.
Audience: **u,f.**

Switzerland

Bernath, Magdalena, et al. **DQ208.G64 2004**
Swiss Foreign Policy: Foundations and Possibilities. Daniel Schwarz & Laurent Goetschel (Authors). Trade Paper. Routledge. New York, NY. 2004. 224p. ISBN:0-415-34813-7, ISBN13: 978-0-415-34813-3. Dewey:327.494. LCCN:2004-050839.
Audience: **u,f.**

Billigmeier, Robert H. **DQ496 .B54**
A Crisis in Swiss Pluralism: The Romans and Their Relations with the German- and Italian-Swiss in the Perspective of a Millennium. Trade Cloth. Walter de Gruyter GmbH & Co. KG. Berlin, 1979. 450p. Contributions to the Sociology of Language Ser., No. 26 ISBN:90-279-7577-9, ISBN13: 978-90-279-7577-5. Dewey:949.4/7. LCCN:81-462333.
Audience: **g,f.**

Birmingham, David **DQ851.C355B57 2000**
Switzerland: A Village History. Cloth over Boards. Palgrave Macmillan. New York, NY. 2000. 247p. ISBN:0-312-23076-1, ISBN13: 978-0-312-23076-0. Dewey:949.4/53. LCCN:99-051698.
Audience: **g,l,u.**

Butler, Michael (Editor), et al. **DQ69.M35 2000**
The Making of Modern Switzerland, 1848-1998. Malcolm Pender & Joy Charnley (Editors). Cloth over Boards. Palgrave Macmillan. New York, NY. 2000. 179p. New Perspectives in German Studies ISBN:0-312-23459-7, ISBN13: 978-0-312-23459-1. Dewey:949.407. LCCN:00-027824.
Audience: **u,f.** *Choice, 2001.*

Emmanuel, Le Roy Ladurie **DQ398.54.P53.L413**
The Beggar and the Professor: A Sixteenth-Century Family Saga. Arthur Goldhammer (Translator). Trade Cloth. University of Chicago Press. Chicago, IL. 1997. 416p. ISBN:0-226-47323-6, ISBN13: 978-0-226-47323-9. Dewey:949.4/3203/0922 B. LCCN:96-023340.
Audience: **u,f.**

Fossedal, Gregory A. **JN8788.F67**
Direct Democracy in Switzerland. Trade Paper. Transaction Publishers. Somerset, NJ. 2005. 304p. ISBN:1-4128-0505-8, ISBN13: 978-1-4128-0505-6. Dewey:320.4494.
Audience: **g,l,u.** *Choice, 2003, 2002.*

Gabriel, Jurg Martin & Fischer, Thomas (Editors) **DQ75.S85 2003**
Swiss Foreign Policy, 1945-2002. Cloth over Boards. Palgrave Macmillan. New York, NY. 2003. 256p. ISBN:1-4039-1275-0, ISBN13: 978-1-4039-1275-6. Dewey:327.494/09/045. LCCN:2003-045182.
Audience: **u,f.**

Halbrook, Stephen P. **D754.S9**
Target Switzerland: Swiss Armed Neutrality in World War II. Trade Cloth. Spellmount, Limited Publishers. Stroud, 1997. 336p. ISBN:1-86227-056-2, ISBN13: 978-1-86227-056-5. Dewey:940.53/494.
Audience: **g,l.** *Choice, 1999.*

Hinde, John R. **D15.B8H56 2000**
Jacob Burckhardt and the Crisis of Modernity. Trade Cloth. McGill-Queen's University Press. Montreal, PQ. 2000. 224p. McGill-Queen's Studies in the History of Ideas, Vol. 29 ISBN:0-7735-1027-3, ISBN13: 978-0-7735-1027-2. Dewey:907/.202. LCCN:2002-279554.
Audience: **u,f.**

Hughes, Christopher **DQ17.H8 1975**
Switzerland. Trade Cloth. Greenwood Publishing Group, Inc. Portsmouth, NH. 1975. 303p. ISBN:0-275-33320-5, ISBN13: 978-0-275-33320-1. Dewey:914.94/03/7. LCCN:73-015169.
Audience: **g,l.** B

Jenkins, John R. **DQ356.J46 1986**
Jura Separation in Switzerland. Trade Cloth. Oxford University Press, Inc. New York, NY. 1987. 226p. Oxford Research Studies in Geography ISBN:0-19-823247-0, ISBN13: 978-0-19-823247-6. Dewey:949.4/5. LCCN:85-018734.
Audience: **u,f.**

Luck, J. Murray **DQ54.L83 1985**
History of Switzerland: From Before the Beginnings to the Days of the Present. Trade Cloth. Society for the Promotion of Science & Scholarship, Inc. Palo Alto, CA. 1985. 887p. ISBN:0-930664-06-X, ISBN13: 978-0-930664-06-0. Dewey:949.4. LCCN:85-050338.
Audience: **g,l.**

Luck, J. Murray (Editor), et al. **DQ17**
Modern Switzerland. Lukas F. Burckhardt & Hans Haug (Editors). Trade Cloth. Society for the Promotion of Science & Scholarship, Inc. Palo Alto, CA. 1978. 531p. ISBN:0-930664-01-9, ISBN13: 978-0-930664-01-5. Dewey:949.4. LCCN:77-083453.
Audience: **u,f.**

Martin, William, et al. **DQ55 .M34 1971B**
Switzerland: From Roman Times to the Present. Ed. 6. Pierre Béguin & Jocasta Innes (Authors). Trade Cloth. Paul Elek Inc. Salem, NH. 1971. 335p. ISBN:0-236-15402-8, ISBN13: 978-0-236-15402-9. Dewey:914.9403. LCCN:73-583989.
Audience: **g,l.**

Meier, Heinz K. **DQ76.U6 M4**
Friendship under Stress: U. S.-Swiss Relations, 1900-1950. Trade Cloth. Peter Lang Publishing, Inc. New York, NY. 1970. 423p. ISBN:3-261-00611-0, ISBN13: 978-3-261-00611-0. Dewey:327.494/073.
Audience: **g,u.**

Meier, Heinz K. **Z2771.M45 1990**
Switzerland. Library Binding. ABC-CLIO, Inc. Santa Barbara, CA. 1990. 430p. World Bibliographical Ser. ISBN:1-85109-107-6, ISBN13: 978-1-85109-107-2. Dewey:016.9494. LCCN:91-121289.
Audience: **g,u.** *Choice, 1991.*

Milton, John & Potter, G. R. **BR345**
Zwingli. Trade Cloth. Cambridge University Press. New York, NY. 1976. 449p. ISBN:0-521-20939-0, ISBN13: 978-0-521-20939-7. Dewey:270.6/092/4. LCCN:75-046136.
Audience: **u,f.** B

Price, Lorna **NA4828**
The Plan of St. Gall in Brief: An Overview Based on the 3-Volume Work by Walter Horn and Ernest Born. Trade Paper. University of California Press. Berkeley, CA. 1982. 120p. ISBN:0-520-04334-0, ISBN13: 978-0-520-04334-3. Dewey:726/.771. LCCN:82-070215.
Audience: **g,u.**

Remak, Joachim **DQ161.R38 1993**
A Very Civil War: The Swiss Sonderbund War of 1847. Trade Paper. Westview Press. Boulder, CO. 1993. 221p. ISBN:0-8133-1529-8, ISBN13: 978-0-8133-1529-4. Dewey:949.406. LCCN:92-042922.
Audience: **u,f.**

Sauter, Marc Rodolphe **GN841.S27**
Switzerland, from Earliest Times to the Roman Conquest. Trade Cloth. Westview Press. Boulder, CO. 1976. 208p. ISBN:0-89158-543-5, ISBN13: 978-0-89158-543-5. Dewey:936.3. LCCN:76-000977.
Audience: **u,f.** B

Schelbert, Leo (Editor) **D754.S9S95 2000**
Switzerland Under Siege 1939-1945: A Neutral Nation's Struggle for Survival. Trade Paper. Picton Press. Rockport, ME. 2000. 247p. Swiss American Historical Society Special Publication Ser., No. 18 ISBN:0-89725-414-7, ISBN13: 978-0-89725-414-4. Dewey:940.53/494. LCCN:00-108241.
Audience: **u,f.**

Shoumatoff, Nicholas & Shoumatoff, Nina **DQ823.5.S332 2001**
The Alps: Europe's Mountain Heart. Francoise Rebuffat (Foreword by). Trade Cloth. University of Michigan Press. Chicago, IL. 2001. 320p. ISBN:0-472-11111-6, ISBN13: 978-0-472-11111-4. Dewey:949.4/7. LCCN:00-062997.
Audience: **g,l.**

Steinberg, Jonathan **DQ17.S7 1996**
Why Switzerland? Ed. 2. Cloth Text. Cambridge University Press. New York, NY. 1996. 320p. ISBN:0-521-48170-8, ISBN13: 978-0-521-48170-0. Dewey:949.4. LCCN:95-043246.
Audience: **g,l,u.**

Zimmer, Oliver **JN8901**
A Contested Nation: History, Memory and Nationalism in Switzerland, 1761-1891. Trade Cloth. Cambridge University Press. New York, NY. 2003. 290p. Past and Present Publications ISBN:0-521-81919-9, ISBN13: 978-0-521-81919-0. Dewey:320.5/4/09494/09034.
Audience: **u,f.** *Choice, 2004.*

Balkan Peninsula > General Works

Brown, L. Carl (Editor) **DS62.4.B679 1996**
The Imperial Legacy: The Ottoman Imprint on the Balkans and the Middle East. Trade Cloth. Columbia University Press. New York, NY. 1996. 320p. ISBN:0-231-10304-2, ISBN13: 978-0-231-10304-6. Dewey:909/.09712561. LCCN:95-015506.
Audience: **g,l,u,f.** *Choice, 1996.*

Clark, Victoria **BX310.C58 2000**
Why Angels Fall: A Journey Through Orthodox Europe from Byzantium to Kosovo. Cloth over Boards. Palgrave Macmillan. New York, NY. 2000. 432p. ISBN:0-312-23396-5, ISBN13: 978-0-312-23396-9. Dewey:281.9/4. LCCN:00-711570.
Audience: **g,l,u,f.** *Choice, 2001.*

Gerolymatos, Andre **DR36**
The Balkan Wars: Conquest, Revolution and Retribution from the Ottoman Era to the Twentieth Century. Cloth Text. Basic Books. New York, NY. 2002. 320p. ISBN:0-465-02731-8, ISBN13: 978-0-465-02731-6. Dewey:949.6/1014.
Audience: **g,u,f.** *Choice, 2003, 2002.*

Gerolymatos, Andre **DR38.15**
The Balkan Wars. Trade Paper. Basic Books. New York, NY. 2003. 320p. ISBN:0-465-02732-6, ISBN13: 978-0-465-02732-3. Dewey:949.6. LCCN:2003-270045.
Audience: **g,u,f.**

Hupchick, Dennis P. **DR36.H87 2004**
The Balkans: From Constantinople to Communism. Trade Paper. Palgrave Macmillan. New York, NY. 2004. 386p. ISBN:1-4039-6417-3, ISBN13: 978-1-4039-6417-5. Dewey:949.6.
Audience: **g,l,u,f.** *Choice, 2003, 2002.*

Jelavich, Barbara **DR36**
History of the Balkans. Cambridge: Cambridge University Press. 1991. The Joint Committee on Eastern Europe publication series; 12
Audience: **g,l,u,f.**

Milojkovic-Djuric, Jelena **D377.3.M53 1994**
Panslavism and National Identity in Russia and in the Balkans, 1830-1880: Images of the Self and Others. Trade Cloth. Eastern European Monographs. Bradenton, FL. 1994. 177p. ISBN:0-88033-291-3, ISBN13: 978-0-88033-291-0. Dewey:320.5/40947. LCCN:94-072038.
Audience: **u,f.**

Stavrianos, Leften Stavros **DR36.S83 2000**
The Balkans since 1453. Traian Stoianovich (Introduction by). Trade Cloth. New York University Press. New York, NY. 2000. 996p. ISBN:0-8147-9765-2, ISBN13: 978-0-8147-9765-5. Dewey:949.6. LCCN:99-053351.
Audience: **g,u,f.**

Todorova, Maria N. **DR34.T63 1997**
Imagining the Balkans. Trade Paper. Oxford University Press, Inc. New York, NY. 1997. 268p. ISBN:0-19-508751-8, ISBN13: 978-0-19-508751-2. Dewey:949.6/1/015. LCCN:96-007161.
Audience: **g,u,f.** *Choice, 1998.*

White, George W. **DR38.2.W48 2000**
Nationalism and Territory: Constructing Group Identity in Southeastern Europe. Book, Other. Rowman & Littlefield Publishers, Inc. Lanham, MD. 2000. 320p. Geographical Perspectives on the Human Past Ser., : ISBN:0-8476-9808-4, ISBN13: 978-0-8476-9808-0. Dewey:323.1/496. LCCN:99-039940.
Audience: **u,f.** *Choice, 2000.*

Balkan Peninsula > By Period

Crampton, R. J. **DR48.5.C68 2002**
The Balkans since the Second World War. Trade Paper. Longman Publishing. Boston, MA. 2002. 408p. ISBN:0-582-24883-3, ISBN13: 978-0-582-24883-0. Dewey:949.6/055. LCCN:2002-021886.
Audience: **g,l,u,f.** *Choice, 2003, 2002.*

Fine, John V. Jr. **DR36**
The Late Medieval Balkans: A Critical Survey from the Late Twelfth Century to the Ottoman Conquest. Trade Paper. University of Michigan Press. Chicago, IL. 1994. 704p. ISBN:0-472-08260-4, ISBN13: 978-0-472-08260-5. Dewey:949.6.
Audience: **u,f.** *Choice, 1987.*

Jelavich, Barbara **DR36 .J37 1983**
History of the Balkans, Vol. 2. Trade Paper. Cambridge University Press. New York, NY. 1983. 512p. ISBN:0-521-27459-1, ISBN13: 978-0-521-27459-3. Dewey:949.6. LCCN:82-022093.
Audience: **u,f.**

Jelavich, Barbara **DR36 .J37 1983**
History of the Balkans: Eighteenth and Nineteenth Centuries, Vol. 1. Trade Cloth. Cambridge University Press. New York, NY. 1983. 400p. ISBN:0-521-25249-0, ISBN13: 978-0-521-25249-2. Dewey:949.6. LCCN:82-022093.
Audience: **u,f.**

Jelavich, Barbara **DR38.3.S65 J45 1991**
Russia's Balkan Entanglements, 1806-1914. Trade Cloth. Cambridge University Press. New York, NY. 1991. 304p. ISBN:0-521-40126-7, ISBN13: 978-0-521-40126-5. Dewey:949.6. LCCN:90-020036.
Audience: **u,f.** *Choice, 1992.*

Jelavich, Charles & Jelavich, Barbara **DJK38**
The Establishment of the Balkan National States, 1804-1920. Trade Cloth. University of Washington Press. Seattle, WA. 1986. 374p. History of East Central Europe Ser., Vol. 8 ISBN:0-295-95444-2, ISBN13: 978-0-295-95444-8. Dewey:947. LCCN:76-049162.
Audience: **g,u,f.**

Macfie, A. L. **D371**
The Eastern Question 1774-1923. London ; New York : Longman. 1996. ISBN:0-582-29195-X, ISBN13: 978-0-582-29195-9.
Audience: **u,f.**

Sugar, Pete F. **DJK4 .S93**
Southeastern Europe Under Ottoman Rule, 1354-1804. Trade Paper. University of Washington Press. Seattle, WA. 1977. 365p. History of East Central Europe Ser., Vol. 5 ISBN:0-295-96033-7, ISBN13: 978-0-295-96033-3. Dewey:949 s 949.6. LCCN:76-007799.
Audience: **u,f.**

Balkan Peninsula > Yugoslavia

Alexander, Stella **BR966.3**
Church and State in Yugoslavia since 1945. Cambridge ; New York : Cambridge University Press. 1979. Soviet and East European studies ISBN:0-521-21942-6, ISBN13: 978-0-521-21942-6.
Audience: **u,f.**

Banac, Ivo **DR1295**
The National Question in Yugoslavia: Origins, History, Politics. Book, Other. Cornell University Press. Ithaca, NY. 1988. 456p. ISBN:0-8014-9493-1, ISBN13: 978-0-8014-9493-2. Dewey:949.7/021. LCCN:83-045931.
Audience: **g,l,u,f.**

Banac, Ivo **HX365.5.A6B36 1988**
With Stalin Against Tito: Cominformist Splits in Yugoslav Communism. Book, Other. Cornell University Press. Ithaca, NY. 1988. 320p. ISBN:0-8014-2186-1, ISBN13: 978-0-8014-2186-0. Dewey:335.43. LCCN:88-047717.
Audience: **u,f.** *Choice, 1989.*

Burg, Steven L. & Shoup, Paul S. **DR1313.7.P43B87 1998**
The War in Bosnia-Herzegovina: Ethnic Conflict and International Intervention. Cloth Text. M. E. Sharpe Inc. Armonk, NY. 1999. 520p. ISBN:1-56324-308-3, ISBN13: 978-1-56324-308-0. Dewey:949.703. LCCN:98-028005.
Audience: **u,f.** *Choice, 1999.*

Djilas, Milovan **D802.Y8**
Wartime. Trade Paper. Harcourt Trade Publishers. New York, NY. 1980. 496p. ISBN:0-15-694712-9, ISBN13: 978-0-15-694712-1. Dewey:940.53/497/0924. LCCN:80-016174.
Audience: **g,l,u,f.**

Djilas, Milovan **DR312**
Land Without Justice. W. Jovanovich (Introduction by). Trade Paper. Harcourt Trade Publishers. New York, NY. 1972. 366p. ISBN:0-15-648117-0, ISBN13: 978-0-15-648117-5. Dewey:914.97. LCCN:58-008574.
Audience: **g,l,u,f.**

Doder, Dusko **DR370.D62**
The Yugoslavs. Trade Cloth. Random House, Inc. New York, NY. 1978. xiv, 256p. ISBN:0-394-42538-3, ISBN13: 978-0-394-42538-2. Dewey:309/.1/49702. LCCN:77-090287.
Audience: **g,u,f.**

Gagnon, V. P. **DR1313.G34 2004**
The Myth of Ethnic War: Serbia and Croatia in the 1990s. Book, Other. Cornell University Press. Ithaca, NY. 2004. 240p. ISBN:0-8014-4264-8, ISBN13: 978-0-8014-4264-3. Dewey:949.703. LCCN:2004-010399.
Audience: **u,f.** *Choice, 2005.*

Lampe, John R. **DR1246.L36 1996**
Yugoslavia as History: Twice There Was a Country. Cloth Text. Cambridge University Press. New York, NY. 1996. 441p. ISBN:0-521-46122-7, ISBN13: 978-0-521-46122-1. Dewey:949.7. LCCN:96-010390.
Audience: **g,l,u,f.** *Choice, 1997.*

Lederer, Ivo **D651.Y8 L4**
Yugoslavia at the Paris Peace Conference: A Study in Frontiermaking. Trade Cloth. Elliot's Books. Northford, CT. 1963. ISBN:0-685-26674-5, ISBN13: 978-0-685-26674-8. Dewey:940.31425.
Audience: **u,f.**

Lilly, Carol S. **DR1302.L55 2001**
Power and Persuasion: Ideology and Rhetoric in Communist Yugoslavia, 1944-1953. Trade Paper. Westview Press. Boulder, CO. 2000. 284p. ISBN:0-8133-3825-5, ISBN13: 978-0-8133-3825-5. Dewey:949.702. LCCN:00-048470.
Audience: **u,f.**

Malesevic, Sinisa **JN9670.M35 2002**
Ideology, Legitimacy and the New State: Yugoslavia, Serbia and Croatia. Paper over Boards. Taylor & Francis Group. Abingdon, 2002. 352p. Cass Series on Nationalism and Ethnicity, Vol. 4 ISBN:0-7146-5215-6, ISBN13: 978-0-7146-5215-3. Dewey:320.9497. LCCN:2002-020215.
Audience: **l,u,f.** *Choice, 2003.*

Merrill, Christopher **DR1313.8.M48 1999**
Only the Nails Remain: Scenes from the Balkan Wars. Book, Other. Rowman & Littlefield Publishers, Inc. Lanham, MD. 1999. 424p. ISBN:0-8476-9820-3, ISBN13: 978-0-8476-9820-2. Dewey:949.703. LCCN:99-016783.
Audience: **g,l,u,f.** *Choice, 2000.*

Naimark, Norman M. & Case, Holly (Editors) **DR1246.Y83 2003**
Yugoslavia and Its Historians: Understanding the Balkan Wars of the 1990s. Trade Cloth. Stanford University Press. Palo Alto, CA. 2003. 296p. ISBN:0-8047-4594-3, ISBN13: 978-0-8047-4594-9. Dewey:949.6/007/20497. LCCN:2002-015102.
Audience: **g,l,u,f.** *Choice, 2003.*

Ramet, Sabrina P. **DR1308.R36 1992**
Balkan Babel: Politics, Culture, and Religion in Yugoslavia. Trade Paper. Westview Press. Boulder, CO. 1992. 230p. ISBN:0-8133-8184-3, ISBN13: 978-0-8133-8184-8. Dewey:949.702. LCCN:91-033354.
Audience: **g,u,f.** *Choice, 1992.*

Roberts, Walter R. **D754.Y9R6 1987**
Tito, Mihailovic, and the Allies. Paper Text. Duke University Press. Durham, NC. 1987. xxi, 406p. ISBN:0-8223-0773-1, ISBN13: 978-0-8223-0773-0. Dewey:940.53/2. LCCN:87-005357.
Audience: **g,u,f.**

Rusinow, Dennison **DR370**
The Yugoslav Experiment 1948-1974. Trade Cloth. University of California Press. Berkeley, CA. 1977. ISBN:0-520-03304-3, ISBN13: 978-0-520-03304-7. Dewey:309.1/497/02. LCCN:76-020032.
Audience: **u,f.**

West, Rebecca **DR1221**
Black Lamb and Grey Falcon: A Journey Through Yugoslavia. Trade Paper. Penguin Group (USA) Inc. New York, NY. 1995. 1200p. Twentieth Century Classics Ser. ISBN:0-14-018847-9, ISBN13: 978-0-14-018847-9. Dewey:914.9/7/0421.
Audience: **g,l,u,f.**

West, Richard **DR1300**
Tito: And the Rise and Fall of Yugoslavia. Trade Paper. Avalon Publishing Group. New York, NY. 1996. 448p. ISBN:0-7867-0332-6, ISBN13: 978-0-7867-0332-6. Dewey:949.7023092.
Audience: **g,l,u,f.**

Balkan Peninsula > Yugoslavian Successor State

Alexander, Stella **BR966.3**
Church and State in Yugoslavia since Nineteen Forty-Five. Trade Cloth. Cambridge University Press. New York, NY. 1979. 398p. Cambridge Russian, Soviet and Post-Soviet Studies, No. 28 ISBN:0-521-21942-6, ISBN13: 978-0-521-21942-6. Dewey:322/.1/09497. LCCN:77-088668.
Audience: **u,f.**

Banac, Ivo **DR1295**
The National Question in Yugoslavia: Origins, History, Politics. Book, Other. Cornell University Press. Ithaca, NY. 1988. 456p. ISBN:0-8014-9493-1, ISBN13: 978-0-8014-9493-2. Dewey:949.7/021. LCCN:83-045931.
Audience: **g,l,u,f.**

Banac, Ivo **HX365.5.A6B36 1988**
With Stalin Against Tito: Cominformist Splits in Yugoslav Communism. Book, Other. Cornell University Press. Ithaca, NY. 1988. 320p. ISBN:0-8014-2186-1, ISBN13: 978-0-8014-2186-0. Dewey:335.43. LCCN:88-047717.
Audience: **u,f.** *Choice, 1989.*

Burg, Steven L. & Shoup, Paul S. **DR1313.7.P43B87 1998**
The War in Bosnia-Herzegovina: Ethnic Conflict and International Intervention. Cloth Text. M. E. Sharpe Inc. Armonk, NY. 1999. 520p. ISBN:1-56324-308-3, ISBN13: 978-1-56324-308-0. Dewey:949.703. LCCN:98-028005.
Audience: **u,f.** *Choice, 1999.*

Djilas, Milovan **D802.Y8**
Wartime. Trade Paper. Harcourt Trade Publishers. New York, NY. 1980. 496p. ISBN:0-15-694712-9, ISBN13: 978-0-15-694712-1. Dewey:940.53/497/0924. LCCN:80-016174.
Audience: **g,l,u,f.**

Djilas, Milovan **DR312**
Land Without Justice. W. Jovanovich (Introduction by). Trade Paper. Harcourt Trade Publishers. New York, NY. 1972. 366p. ISBN:0-15-648117-0, ISBN13: 978-0-15-648117-5. Dewey:914.97. LCCN:58-008574.
Audience: **g,l,u,f.**

Doder, Dusko **DR370**
The Yugoslavs. Trade Paper. Random House, Inc. New York, NY. 1979. ISBN:0-394-74158-7, ISBN13: 978-0-394-74158-1. Dewey:309/.1/49702. LCCN:79-005027.
Audience: **g,l,u,f.**

Lampe, John R. **DR1246 .L36**
Yugoslavia As History: Twice There Was a Country. Ed. 2. Cloth Text. Cambridge University Press. New York, NY. 2000. 510p. ISBN:0-521-77357-1, ISBN13: 978-0-521-77357-7. Dewey:949.7.
Audience: **g,l,u,f.**

West, Rebecca **DR1221**
Black Lamb and Grey Falcon: A Journey Through Yugoslavia. Trade Paper. Penguin Group (USA) Inc. New York, NY. 1995. 1200p. Twentieth Century Classics Ser. ISBN:0-14-018847-9, ISBN13: 978-0-14-018847-9. Dewey:914.9/7/0421.
Audience: **g,l,u,f.**

West, Richard **DR1300**
Tito: And the Rise and Fall of Yugoslavia. Trade Paper. Avalon Publishing Group. New York, NY. 1996. 448p. ISBN:0-7867-0332-6, ISBN13: 978-0-7867-0332-6. Dewey:949.7023092.
Audience: **g,l,u,f.**

Balkan Peninsula > Yugoslavian Successor State > Serbia and Montenegro

Dragnich, Alex N. **DR1956**
Serbia Through the Ages. Trade Cloth. Eastern European Monographs. Bradenton, FL. 2004. 160p. ISBN:0-88033-541-6, ISBN13: 978-0-88033-541-6. Dewey:949.71. LCCN:2004-108566.
Audience: **g,l,u,f.** *Choice, 2005.*

Hawkesworth, Celia **PG1404.9.W65H39 2000**
Voices in the Shadows. Trade Cloth. Central European University Press. Herndon, VA. 2000. 292p. ISBN:963-9116-62-9, ISBN13: 978-963-9116-62-7. Dewey:891.8/2099287. LCCN:00-022648.
Audience: **g,l,u,f.** *Choice, 2000.*

Laffan, R. G. **DR2007**
The Serbs: Guardians of the Gate. Trade Paper. Dorset Press. New York, NY. 1990. 299p. Reprints Ser. ISBN:0-88029-413-2, ISBN13: 978-0-88029-413-3. Dewey:949.71.
Audience: **g,u,f.**

Matthias, John **PG1465.B38 1999**
The Battle of Kosovo. Vladeta Vuckovic (Contribution by). Trade Paper. Swallow Press. Athens, OH. 1988. 96p. ISBN:0-8040-0897-3, ISBN13: 978-0-8040-0897-6. Dewey:891.8/21001. LCCN:87-010061.
Audience: **g,l,u,f.** *Choice, 1988.*

Ramet, Sabrina P. & Pavlakovic, Vjeran **DR2049.S47 2005**
Serbia since 1989: Politics and Society under Milosevic and After. Trade Cloth. University of Washington Press. Seattle, WA. 2005. 440p. Jackson School Publications in International Studies ISBN:0-295-98538-0, ISBN13: 978-0-295-98538-1. Dewey:949.7103. LCCN:2005-008069.
Audience: **u,f.** *Choice, 2006.*

Stokes, Gale **JN9659.A45S86 1990**
Politics As Development: The Emergence of Political Parties in Nineteenth-Century Serbia. Cloth Text. Duke University Press. Durham, NC. 1990. 416p. ISBN:0-8223-1016-3, ISBN13: 978-0-8223-1016-7. Dewey:324.2497/1/009. LCCN:89-039903.
Audience: **u,f.** *Choice, 1991.*

Thomas, Robert **DR2044.T5 1998**
The Politics of Serbia in the 1990s. Trade Paper. Columbia University Press. New York, NY. 1999. 288p. ISBN:0-231-11381-1, ISBN13: 978-0-231-11381-6. Dewey:949.7103. LCCN:98-017989.
Audience: **g,u,f.** *Choice, 2000.*

Balkan Peninsula > Yugoslavian Successor State > Croatia

Bartlett, William **HN638.A8**
Croatia: between Europe and the Balkans. London ; New York : Routledge. 2003. Postcommunist states and nations; v. 16 ISBN:0-415-27432-X, ISBN13: 978-0-415-27432-6.
Audience: **g,l,u,f.**

Dedijer, Vladimir **D802.Y82C769813 1992**
The Yugoslav Auschwitz and the Vatican: The Croatian Massacre of the Serbs During World War II. Harvey Kendall (Translator). Trade Cloth. Prometheus Books, Publishers. Amherst, NY. 1992. 444p. ISBN:0-87975-752-3, ISBN13: 978-0-87975-752-6. Dewey:940.53/18/094972. LCCN:91-043150.
Audience: **g,u,f.**

Tanner, Marcus **DR1535.T36 1997**
Croatia: A Nation Forged in War. Cloth over Boards. Yale University Press. Cumberland, RI. 1997. 368p. ISBN:0-300-06933-2, ISBN13: 978-0-300-06933-4. Dewey:949.72. LCCN:96-044513.
Audience: **g,l,u,f.** *Choice, 1997.*

Balkan Peninsula > Yugoslavian Successor State > Bosnia and Hercegovina

Bringa, Tone **DR1674.M87.B75 1995**
Being Muslim the Bosnian Way: Identity and Community in a Central Bosnian Village. Trade Cloth. Princeton University Press. Princeton, NJ. 1995. 288p. ISBN:0-691-03453-2, ISBN13: 978-0-691-03453-9. Dewey:305.6/971049742. LCCN:95-018059.
Audience: **g,l,u,f.** *Choice, 1996.*

Burg, Steven L. & Shoup, Paul S. **DR1313.7.P43B87 1998**
The War in Bosnia-Herzegovina: Ethnic Conflict and International Intervention. Cloth Text. M. E. Sharpe Inc. Armonk, NY. 1999. 520p. ISBN:1-56324-308-3, ISBN13: 978-1-56324-308-0. Dewey:949.703. LCCN:98-028005.
Audience: **u,f.** *Choice, 1999.*

Donia, Robert J. **DR1674.M87 D66**
Islam under the Double Eagle: The Muslims of Bosnia and Hercegovina, 1878-1914. Trade Cloth. Eastern European Monographs. Bradenton, FL. 1981. 237p. East European Monographs, No. 78 ISBN:0-914710-72-9, ISBN13: 978-0-914710-72-1. Dewey:949.7/42/00882971. LCCN:80-068441.
Audience: **u,f.**

Donia, Robert J. & Fine, John V. A. Jr. **DR1685.D66 1994**
Bosnia and Hercegovina: A Tradition Betrayed. John C. Hamer (Contribution by). Trade Cloth. Columbia University Press. New York, NY. 1994. 318p. ISBN:0-231-10160-0, ISBN13: 978-0-231-10160-8. Dewey:949.7/42. LCCN:94-016223.
Audience: **g,l,u,f.** *Choice, 1995.*

Hoare, Marko Attila **DR1752**
How Bosnia Armed: The Birth and Rise of the Bosnian Army. Trade Cloth. Saqi Books. London, 2006. 180p. ISBN:0-86356-451-8, ISBN13: 978-0-86356-451-2. Dewey:949.74203. LCCN:2004-445685.
Audience: **u,f.** *Choice, 2005.*

Hoare, Marko Attila **DR1313.3**
How Bosnia Armed. London : Saqi Books in association with the Bosnian Institute. 2004. ISBN:0-86356-451-8, ISBN13: 978-0-86356-451-2.
Audience: **u,f.**

Mahmutcehajic, Rusmir **DR1752.M3313 2000**
The Denial of Bosnia. Ivo Banac (Foreword by). Trade Cloth. Pennsylvania State University Press. University Park, PA. 2000. 440p. Post-Communist Cultural Studies ISBN:0-271-02030-X, ISBN13: 978-0-271-02030-3. Dewey:949.74203. LCCN:99-056307.
Audience: **g,l,u,f.** *Choice, 2001.*

Malcolm, Noel **DR1685.M35 1994**
Bosnia: A Short History. Trade Cloth. New York University Press. New York, NY. 1994. 364p. ISBN:0-8147-5520-8, ISBN13: 978-0-8147-5520-4. Dewey:949.7/42. LCCN:94-011560.
Audience: **g,l,u,f.** *Choice, 1995.*

Malcolm, Noel **DR1685**
Bosnia: A Short History. Trade Paper. New York University Press. New York, NY. 1996. 364p. ISBN:0-8147-5561-5, ISBN13: 978-0-8147-5561-7. Dewey:949.7/42.
Audience: **g,l,u.** *Choice, 1995.*

Pinson, Mark (Editor) **DR1674.M87**
The Muslims of Bosnia - Herzegovina: Their Historic Development from the Middle Ages to the Dissolution of Yugoslavia. Ed. 2. Trade Paper. Harvard University Press. Cambridge, MA. 1996. 223p. ISBN:0-932885-12-8, ISBN13: 978-0-932885-12-8. Dewey:949.7/4200882971.
Audience: **g,u,f.**

Schmitt, Bernadotte Everly **D465**
The Annexation of Bosnia, 1908-1909. New York, H. Fertig. 1970.
Audience: **u,f.**

Balkan Peninsula > Yugoslavian Successor State > Kosovo

Buckley, William Joseph (Editor) **DR2087.C75 2000**
Kosovo: Contending Voices on Balkan Interventions. Trade Cloth. William B. Eerdmans Publishing Company. Grand Rapids, MI. 2000. xix, 528p. ISBN:0-8028-3889-8, ISBN13: 978-0-8028-3889-6. Dewey:949.71. LCCN:99-059275.
Audience: **g,l,u,f.** *Choice, 2001.*

Judah, Tim **DR2078.J83 2002**
Kosovo: War and Revenge. Ed. 2. Trade Paper. Yale University Press. Cumberland, RI. 2002. 408p. ISBN:0-300-09725-5, ISBN13: 978-0-300-09725-2. Dewey:949.703.
Audience: **g,l,u,f.**

Kola, Paulin **DR977.K65 2003**
The Myth of Greater Albania. Trade Cloth. New York University Press. New York, NY. 2003. 320p. ISBN:0-8147-4773-6, ISBN13: 978-0-8147-4773-5. Dewey:949.6503. LCCN:2002-037973.
Audience: **g,u,f.** *Choice, 2004.*

Malcolm, Noel **DR2082**
Kosovo: A Short History. Trade Cloth. New York University Press. New York, NY. 2000. 512p. ISBN:0-8147-5642-5, ISBN13: 978-0-8147-5642-3. Dewey:949.7/1.
Audience: **g,u,f.**

Balkan Peninsula > Yugoslavian Successor State > Slovenia

Ferrar, Marcus & Corsellis, John **DR1445**
Slovenia 1945: Memories of Death and Survival after World War II. Saddle Stitched, Cloth over Boards, Dust Jacket. I. B. Tauris & Company, Ltd. London, 2005. 250p. ISBN:1-85043-840-4, ISBN13: 978-1-85043-840-3. Dewey:949.73023. LCCN:2006-295943.
Audience: **g,l,u,f.**

Gow, James & Carmichael, Cathie **DR1360.G68 2000**
Slovenia and the Slovenes: A Small State and the New Europe. Trade Cloth. Indiana University Press. Bloomington, IN. 2000. xi, 234p. ISBN:0-253-33663-5, ISBN13: 978-0-253-33663-7. Dewey:949.73. LCCN:99-038472.
Audience: **u,f.** *Choice, 2001.*

Balkan Peninsula > Yugoslavian Successor State > Macedonia

Brown, Keith **DR2214.B76 2003**
The Past in Question: Modern Macedonia and the Uncertainties of Nation. Trade Cloth. Princeton University Press. Princeton, NJ. 2003. 320p. ISBN:0-691-09994-4, ISBN13: 978-0-691-09994-1. Dewey:949.76/01. LCCN:2002-074873.
Audience: **u,f.** *Choice, 2004.*

Danforth, Loring M. **DR2185**
The Macedonian Conflict: Ethnic Nationalism in a Transnational World. Trade Paper. Princeton University Press. Princeton, NJ. 1997. 294p. ISBN:0-691-04356-6, ISBN13: 978-0-691-04356-2. Dewey:949.5/6.
Audience: **u,f.** *Choice, 1996.*

Danforth, Loring M. **DR2173.D36 1995**
The Macedonian Conflict: Ethnic Nationalism in a Transnational World. Cloth Text. Princeton University Press. Princeton, NJ. 1995. 288p. ISBN:0-691-04357-4, ISBN13: 978-0-691-04357-9. Dewey:949.5/6. LCCN:95-013319.
Audience: **g,l,u,f.** *Choice, 1996.*

Phillips, John **DR2253**
Macedonia: Warlords and Rebels in the Balkans. Cloth over Boards. Yale University Press. Cumberland, RI. 2004. 240p. ISBN:0-300-10268-2, ISBN13: 978-0-300-10268-0. Dewey:949.7/6/03.
Audience: **g,l,u,f.** *Choice, 2005.*

Pribichevich, Stoyan **DR2185**
Macedonia: Its People and History. Trade Cloth. Pennsylvania State University Press. University Park, PA. 1982. 304p. ISBN:0-271-00315-4, ISBN13: 978-0-271-00315-3. Dewey:949.7/6. LCCN:82-080455.
Audience: **g,u,f.**

Roudometof, Victor **DR2195**
Collective Memory, National Identity, and Ethnic Conflict: Greece, Bulgaria and the Macedonian Question. Trade Cloth. Greenwood Publishing Group, Inc. Portsmouth, NH. 2002. 280p. ISBN:0-275-97648-3, ISBN13: 978-0-275-97648-4. Dewey:949.5/6. LCCN:2002-067937.
Audience: **u,f.** *Choice, 2003.*

Balkan Peninsula > Romania

Behr, Edward **DR267.B39 1991**
Kiss the Hand You Cannot Bite: The Rise and Fall of the Ceausescus. Ryszard Kapuscinski (Foreword by). Trade Cloth. Random House Adult Trade Publishing Group. New York, NY. 1991. ISBN:0-679-40128-8, ISBN13: 978-0-679-40128-5. Dewey:949.8. LCCN:90-022263.
Audience: **g,l,u,f.**

Boia, Lucian **DR217**
Romania: Borderland of Europe. Trade Paper. Reaktion Books, Ltd. London, 2004. 240p. Reaktion Books - Topographics Ser. ISBN:1-86189-103-2, ISBN13: 978-1-86189-103-7. Dewey:949.8.
Audience: **g,l,u,f.** *Choice, 2003, 2002.*

Castellan, Georges **DR217.C34 1989**
A History of the Romanians. Trade Cloth. Eastern European Monographs. Bradenton, FL. 1989. 268p. East European Monographs, No. 257 ISBN:0-88033-154-2, ISBN13: 978-0-88033-154-8. Dewey:949.8. LCCN:88-072221.
Audience: **g,u,f.** *Choice, 1989.*

Deletant, Dennis **DR267.D3713 1999**
Romania under Communist Rule. Ed. 2. Trade Cloth. International Specialized Book Services. Portland, OR. 1999. 203p. ISBN:973-98392-8-2, ISBN13: 978-973-98392-8-0. Dewey:949.803/1. LCCN:00-507298.
Audience: **g,l,u,f.** *Choice, 2000.*

Hitchins, Keith **DR250.H58 1994**
Rumania, 1866-1947. Trade Cloth. Oxford University Press, Inc. New York, NY. 1994. 590p. Oxford History of Modern Europe Ser. ISBN:0-19-822126-6, ISBN13: 978-0-19-822126-5. Dewey:949.8/02. LCCN:93-031575.
Audience: **g,l,u,f.** *Choice, 1995.*

Hlihor, Constantin & Scurtu, Ioan **D766.4.H58 2000**
The Red Army in Romania. Trade Cloth. Center for Romanian Studies, The. Iali, 2000. 288p. ISBN:973-98392-5-8, ISBN13: 978-973-98392-5-9. Dewey:940.54/09498. LCCN:00-340784.
Audience: **u,f.** *Choice, 2001.*

Ioanid, Radu **DS135.R7I6513 2000**
The Holocaust in Romania: The Destruction of Jews and Gypsies under the Antonescu Regime, 1940-1944. Trade Cloth. Ivan R. Dee Publisher. Blue Ridge Summit, PA. 2000. 416p. ISBN:1-56663-256-0, ISBN13: 978-1-56663-256-0. Dewey:940.53/18/09498. LCCN:99-043229.
Audience: **g,l,u,f.** *Choice, 2000.*

Kellogg, Frederick **DR246.K45 1995**
The Road to Romanian Independence. Cloth Text. Purdue University Press. West Lafayette, IN. 1995. 265p. ISBN:1-55753-065-3, ISBN13: 978-1-55753-065-3. Dewey:327.498. LCCN:94-038654.
Audience: **u,f.** *Choice, 1996.*

Livezeanu, Irina **DR264.L58 1995**
Cultural Politics in Greater Romania: Regionalism, Nation Building, and Ethnic Struggle, 1918-1930. Book, Other. Cornell University Press. Ithaca, NY. 1995. 356p. ISBN:0-8014-2445-3, ISBN13: 978-0-8014-2445-8. Dewey:949.8/02. LCCN:94-032401.
Audience: **u,f.** *Choice, 1995.*

Tismaneanu, Vladimir **JN9639.A53 T57 2003**
Stalinism for All Seasons: A Political History of Romanian Communism. Trade Cloth. University of California Press. Berkeley, CA. 2003. 400p. Societies and Culture in East-Central Europe Ser., Vol. 11 ISBN:0-520-23747-1, ISBN13: 978-0-520-23747-6. Dewey:324.2498/075. LCCN:2002-154941.
Audience: **g,l,u,f.** *Choice, 2004.*

Verdery, Katherine **DR267.V47 1991**
National Ideology under Socialism: Identity and Cultural Politics in Ceausescu's Romania. Trade Cloth. University of California Press. Berkeley, CA. 1991. 406p. Societies and Culture in East-Central Europe Ser., No. 7 ISBN:0-520-07216-2, ISBN13: 978-0-520-07216-9. Dewey:306.2/09498. LCCN:90-047727.
Audience: **g,l,u,f.** *Choice, 1992.*

Verdery, Katherine **DR280.4 .V47 1983**
Transylvanian Villagers: Three Centuries of Political, Economic and Ethnic Change. Trade Cloth. University of California Press. Berkeley, CA. 1983. 400p. ISBN:0-520-04879-2, ISBN13: 978-0-520-04879-9. Dewey:949.8/4. LCCN:82-017411.
Audience: **g,l,u,f.**

Verdery, Katherine **HD839.T7V47 2003**
The Vanishing Hectare: Property and Value in Postsocialist Transylvania. Book, Other. Cornell University Press. Ithaca, NY. 2003. 432p. Culture and Society after Socialism Ser. ISBN:0-8014-4197-8, ISBN13: 978-0-8014-4197-4. Dewey:333.3/14984. LCCN:2003-012516.
Audience: **u,f.**

Balkan Peninsula > Bulgaria

Bell, John D. (Editor) **DR93.42**
Bulgaria in Transition: Politics, Economics, Society and Culture after Communism. Trade Paper. Westview Press. Boulder, CO. 1998. 320p. Eastern Europe after Communism Ser. ISBN:0-8133-9010-9, ISBN13: 978-0-8133-9010-9. Dewey:320.9/499.
Audience: **g,u,f.** *Choice, 1999.*

Bristow, John A. **HC403.B75 1996**
The Bulgarian Economy in Transition. Trade Cloth. Edward Elgar Publishing, Inc. Northampton, MA. 1996. 264p. Studies of Communism in Transition ISBN:1-85278-994-8, ISBN13: 978-1-85278-994-7. Dewey:330.9/4977. LCCN:95-036671.
Audience: **u,f.** *Choice, 1996.*

Cellarius, Barbara A. **GF642.B82R463 2004**
In the Land of Orpheus: Rural Livelihoods and Nature Conservation in Post-Socialist Bulgaria. Trade Cloth. University of Wisconsin Press. Chicago, IL. 2004. 278p. ISBN:0-299-20150-3, ISBN13: 978-0-299-20150-0. Dewey:333.72/09499/7. LCCN:2004-007742.
Audience: **u,f.** *Choice, 2005.*

Crampton, R. J. **DR67.C73 1987**
A Short History of Modern Bulgaria. Trade Cloth. Cambridge University Press. New York, NY. 1987. 240p. ISBN:0-521-25340-3, ISBN13: 978-0-521-25340-6. Dewey:949.7/7. LCCN:86-017528.
Audience: **g,l,u,f.** *Choice, 1988.*

Daskalov, Roumen **DR83.D37 2004**
The Making of a Nation in the Balkans: Bulgaria: from History to Historiography. Trade Cloth. Central European University Press. Herndon, VA. 2004. 296p. ISBN:963-9241-83-0, ISBN13: 978-963-9241-83-1. Dewey:949.9/015. LCCN:2004-000869.
Audience: **u,f.** *Choice, 2005.*

Daskalov, Rumen **DR83**
The Making of a Nation in the Balkans: Historiography of the Bulgarian Revival. Budapest; New York:; Central European University Press. 2004. ISBN:963-9241-83-0, ISBN13: 978-963-9241-83-1.
Audience: **u,f.**

Gavrilova, Raina **HT145.B8G38 1999**
Bulgarian Urban Culture in the Eighteenth and Nineteenth Centuries. Trade Cloth. Susquehanna University Press. Cranbury, NJ. 1999. 264p. ISBN:1-57591-015-2, ISBN13: 978-1-57591-015-4. Dewey:307.76/09499. LCCN:98-036205.
Audience: **u,f.** *Choice, 2000.*

Giatzidis, Emile **HN623.5.G5 2002**
An Introduction to Postcommunist Bulgaria: Political, Economic and Social Transformation. Cloth over Boards. Manchester University Press. Manchester, 2002. 224p. Europe in Change Ser. ISBN:0-7190-6094-X, ISBN13: 978-0-7190-6094-6. Dewey:306/.09499. LCCN:2002-026311.
Audience: **g,l,u,f.** *Choice, 2003.*

Hall, Richard C. **D563.A2H35 1996**
Bulgaria's Road to the First World War. Trade Cloth. Eastern European Monographs. Bradenton, FL. 1996. 300p. ISBN:0-88033-357-X, ISBN13: 978-0-88033-357-3. Dewey:940.4/09499. LCCN:96-061470.
Audience: **u,f.**

Miller, Marshall L. **DR89**
Bulgaria During the Second World War. Trade Cloth. Stanford University Press. Palo Alto, CA. 1975. 304p. ISBN:0-8047-0870-3, ISBN13: 978-0-8047-0870-8. Dewey:940.53/4977. LCCN:74-082778.
Audience: **u,f.**

Neuburger, Mary **DR64.2.M8N48 2004**
The Orient Within: Muslim Minorities and the Negotiation of Nationhood in Modern Bulgaria. Trade Cloth. Cornell University Press. Ithaca, NY. 2004. 264p. ISBN:0-8014-4132-3, ISBN13: 978-0-8014-4132-5. Dewey:305.6/97/09499. LCCN:2003-020155.
Audience: **u,f.** *Choice, 2004.*

Perry, Duncan M. **DR2214.P47 1988**
The Politics of Terror: The Macedonian Revolutionary Movements, 1893-1903. R. V. Burks (Introduction by). Cloth Text. Duke University Press. Durham, NC. 1988. 275p. ISBN:0-8223-0813-4, ISBN13: 978-0-8223-0813-3. Dewey:949.5/606. LCCN:87-033062.
Audience: **u,f.** *Choice, 1989.*

Todorov, Tzvetan **D731**
Fragility and Goodness: Why Bulgaria's Jews Survived the Holocaust. Arthur Denner (Translator). Cloth Text. Princeton University Press. Princeton, NJ. 2001. 208p. ISBN:0-691-08832-2, ISBN13: 978-0-691-08832-7. Dewey:940.53/18/09499. LCCN:2001-088186.
Audience: **g,l,u,f.** *Choice, 2002.*

Balkan Peninsula > Albania

Elsie, Robert **PG9603.E438 2005**
Albanian Literature: A Short History. Cloth over Boards. I. B. Tauris & Company, Ltd. London, 2006. 372p. ISBN:1-84511-031-5, ISBN13: 978-1-84511-031-4. Dewey:891/.99109. LCCN:2006-273055.
Audience: **g,l,u,f.**

Fischer, Bernd **D802.A38.F57 1999**
Albania at War, 1939-1945. Trade Paper. Purdue University Press. West Lafayette, IN. 1999. 338p. Central European Studies ISBN:1-55753-141-2, ISBN13: 978-1-55753-141-4. Dewey:949.6/502. LCCN:98-046675.
Audience: **u,f.** *Choice, 1999.*

Fishta, Gjergj **PG9621.F5**
The Highland Lute: The Albanian National Epic. Robert Elsie & Janice Mathie-Heck (Translators). Cloth over Boards. I. B. Tauris & Company, Ltd. London, 2006. 256p. ISBN:1-84511-118-4, ISBN13: 978-1-84511-118-2. Dewey:891/.9911. LCCN:2006-296290.
Audience: **g,l,u,f.**

Jacques, Edwin E. **DR941.J33 1995**
The Albanians: An Ethnic History from Prehistoric Times to the Present. Cloth Text. McFarland & Company, Incorporated Publishers. Jefferson, NC. 1994. 748p. ISBN:0-89950-932-0, ISBN13: 978-0-89950-932-7. Dewey:949.65. LCCN:93-42598.
Audience: **u,f.** *Choice, 1995.*

Schwandner-Sievers, Stephanie & Fischer, Bernd Jurgen (Editors) **DR950.A385 2002**
Albanian Identities: Myth and History. Trade Cloth. Indiana University Press. Bloomington, IN. 2002. xvii, 238p. ISBN:0-253-34189-2, ISBN13: 978-0-253-34189-1. Dewey:949.65. LCCN:2002-068493.
Audience: **g,u,f.**

Tomes, Jason **DR974.Z64T65 2004**
King Zog of Albania: Europe's Self-Made Muslim King. Trade Cloth. New York University Press. New York, NY. 2004. 288p. ISBN:0-8147-8283-3, ISBN13: 978-0-8147-8283-5. Dewey:949.6502. LCCN:2003-061150.
Audience: **g,l,u,f.** *Choice, 2004.*

Vaughan-Whitehead, Daniel **HC402.V38 1999**
Albania in Crisis: The Predictable Fall of the Shining Star. Trade Cloth. Edward Elgar Publishing, Inc. Northampton, MA. 1999. 384p. ISBN:1-84064-070-7, ISBN13: 978-1-84064-070-0. Dewey:338.94965. LCCN:98-042880.
Audience: **u,f.** *Choice, 1999.*

Vickers, Miranda **DR971**
The Albanians: A Modern History. Cloth Text. I. B. Tauris & Company, Ltd. London, 1995. 262p. ISBN:1-85043-749-1, ISBN13: 978-1-85043-749-9. Dewey:949.65/02.
Audience: **g,l,u,f.** *Choice, 1995.*

Poland > General History

Biskupski, Mieczysaw B. **DK4140**
The History of Poland. Cloth Text. Greenwood Publishing Group, Inc. Portsmouth, NH. 2000. 264p. The Histories of the Modern Nations Ser. ISBN:0-313-30571-4, ISBN13: 978-0-313-30571-9. Dewey:943.8. LCCN:99-043162.
Audience: **l,u,f.**

Davies, Norman **DK4140**
God's Playground: A History of Poland in Two Volumes. Ed. 2. Trade Paper. Oxford University Press, Inc. New York, NY. 2005. 616p. ISBN:0-19-925340-4, ISBN13: 978-0-19-925340-1. Dewey:943.8. LCCN:2005-544599.
Audience: **l,u,f.**

Lukowski, Jerzy & Zawadzki, Hubert **DK4140 .L85**
A Concise History of Poland. Ed. 2. Trade Paper. Cambridge University Press. New York, NY. 2006. 408p. Cambridge Concise Histories Ser. ISBN:0-521-61857-6, ISBN13: 978-0-521-61857-1. Dewey:943.8.
Audience: **l.** *Choice, 2002.*

Snyder, Timothy **DJK48.5.S66 2003**
The Reconstruction of Nations: Poland, Ukraine, Lithuania, Belarus, 1569-1999. Cloth over Boards. Yale University Press. Cumberland, RI. 2003. 384p. ISBN:0-300-09569-4, ISBN13: 978-0-300-09569-2. Dewey:947.084. LCCN:2002-066356.
Audience: **g,u,f.** *Choice, 2003.*

Suchodolski, Bogdan **DK4110 .S919 1986**
History of Polish Culture. Trade Cloth. Hippocrene Books, Inc. New York, NY. 1989. 256p. ISBN:83-223-2142-2, ISBN13: 978-83-223-2142-3. Dewey:943.8. LCCN:87-166931.
Audience: **u,f.**

Zamoyski, Adam **DK4140 .Z3**
The Polish Way: A Thousand Year History of the Poles and Their Culture. Trade Cloth. Hippocrene Books, Inc. New York, NY. 1993. 422p. ISBN:0-7818-0200-8, ISBN13: 978-0-7818-0200-0. Dewey:943.8.
Audience: **l,u.**

Poland > By Period > Medieval. Piast Dynasty (966 -1370)

Anonymus, Gallus **DK4190**
Gesta Principum Polonorum: The Deeds of the Princes of the Poles. Janos M. Bak, Paul W. Knoll & Frank Schaer (Translators), Thomas Bisson (Preface by). Trade Cloth. Central European University Press. Herndon, VA. 2003. 374p. Central European Medieval Texts Ser., Vol. 3 ISBN:963-9241-40-7, ISBN13: 978-963-9241-40-4. Dewey:943.8/022. LCCN:2003-007636.
Audience: **g,u,f.**

Poland > By Period > Jagiellonian Dynasty (1382-1572). Polish-Lithuanian Union

Butterwick, Richard (Editor) **DK4179.2.P65 2001**
The Polish-Lithuanian Monarchy in European Context, C. 1500-1795. Cloth over Boards. Palgrave Macmillan. New York, NY. 2001. 271p. ISBN:0-333-77382-9, ISBN13: 978-0-333-77382-6. Dewey:943.8/02. LCCN:00-054533.
Audience: **u,f.**

Segel, Harold B. (Author, Editor, Translator) **JA84.P7P6525 2003**
Political Thought in Renaissance Poland: An Anthology in English. Perfect. Polish Institute of Arts & Sciences of America, Incorporated, The. New York, NY. 2003. 396p. ISBN:0-940962-61-6, ISBN13: 978-0-940962-61-3. Dewey:320/.09438/09031. LCCN:2003-276173.
Audience: **g,u,f.**

Stone, Daniel **DJK4.S93 VOL.4**
The Polish-Lithuanian State, 1386-1795. Trade Cloth. University of Washington Press. Seattle, WA. 2001. xii, 374p. History of East Central Europe Ser., Vol. 4 ISBN:0-295-98093-1, ISBN13: 978-0-295-98093-5. Dewey:943 s 943.8/02. LCCN:00-051179.
Audience: **l,u.** *Choice, 2002.*

Poland > By Period > Polish-Lithuanian Commonwealth (1569-1795)

Butterwick, Richard **DK4330.B88 1998**
Poland's Last King and English Culture: Stanislaw August Poniatowski, 1732-1798. Trade Cloth. Oxford University Press, Inc. New York, NY. 1998. 398p. Oxford Historical Monographs ISBN:0-19-820701-8, ISBN13: 978-0-19-820701-6. Dewey:943.8/025/092. LCCN:97-033338.
Audience: **u,f.** *Choice, 1999.*

Lukowski, Jerzy **DK4329.L85 1998**
Partitions Poland 1772. Ed. 1. Trade Cloth. Longman Publishing Group. White Plains, NY. 1998. 248p. ISBN:0-582-29275-1, ISBN13: 978-0-582-29275-8. Dewey:943.8/025. LCCN:98-008061.
Audience: **u,f.**

Stone, Daniel **DJK4.S93 VOL.4**
The Polish-Lithuanian State, 1386-1795. Trade Cloth. University of Washington Press. Seattle, WA. 2001. xii, 374p. History of East Central Europe Ser., Vol. 4 ISBN:0-295-98093-1, ISBN13: 978-0-295-98093-5. Dewey:943 s 943.8/02. LCCN:00-051179.
Audience: **l,u.** *Choice, 2002.*

Walicki, Andrzej **JN6750.W35 1989**
The Enlightenment and the Birth of Modern Nationhood: Polish Political Thought from Noble Republicanism to Tadeusz Kosciuszko. Cloth Text. University of Notre Dame Press. Notre Dame, IN. 1989. 4p. ISBN:0-268-00618-0, ISBN13: 978-0-268-00618-1. Dewey:320.5/09438. LCCN:88-040318.
Audience: **g,u,f.**

Zamoyski, Adam **DD801.S395**
The Last King of Poland. Trade Cloth. Hippocrene Books, Inc. New York, NY. 1997. 560p. ISBN:0-7818-0603-8, ISBN13: 978-0-7818-0603-9. Dewey:943.8/025/092.
Audience: **l,u,f.**

Poland > By Period > Partitioned Poland (1795-1918)

Kieniewicz, Stefan **HD728**
Emancipation of the Polish Peasantry. Library Binding. University of Chicago Press. Chicago, IL. 1993. xix, 285p. ISBN:0-226-43524-5, ISBN13: 978-0-226-43524-4. Dewey:333.3/2/09438. LCCN:79-092684.
Audience: **g,u,f.** ℬ

Kulczycki, John J. **LA843.7 .K83 1981**
School Strikes in Prussian Poland, 1901 to 1907: The Struggle over Bilingual Education. Trade Cloth. Eastern European Monographs. Bradenton, FL. 1981. 279p. ISBN:0-914710-76-1, ISBN13: 978-0-914710-76-9. Dewey:331.89/28137101/0943. LCCN:80-068445.
Audience: **u,f.**

Porter, Brian **DK4349.3.P67 2000**
When Nationalism Began to Hate: Imagining Modern Politics in Nineteenth-Century Poland. Trade Cloth. Oxford University Press, Inc. New York, NY. 2000. 318p. ISBN:0-19-513146-0, ISBN13: 978-0-19-513146-8. Dewey:320.54/09/034. LCCN:99-020039.
Audience: **u,f.** *Choice, 2000.*

Trzeciakowski, Lech **DK4381.T7913 1990**
The "Kulturkampf" in Prussian Poland. Trade Cloth. Eastern European Monographs. Bradenton, FL. 1990. 223p. East European Monographs ISBN:0-88033-180-1, ISBN13: 978-0-88033-180-7. Dewey:943.8. LCCN:89-081373.
Audience: **u,f.**

Walicki, Andrzej **DK4358.W34 1994**
Philosophy and Romantic Nationalism: The Case of Poland. Paper Text. University of Notre Dame Press. Notre Dame, IN. 1994. 415p. ISBN:0-268-03806-6, ISBN13: 978-0-268-03806-9. Dewey:943.8/03. LCCN:94-019333.
Audience: **g,u,f.**

Walicki, Andrzej **DK189.2.W33 1991**
Russia, Poland, and Universal Regeneration: Studies in Russian and Polish Thought of the Romantic Epoch. Cloth Text. University of Notre Dame Press. Notre Dame, IN. 1991. 232p. ISBN:0-268-01641-0, ISBN13: 978-0-268-01641-8. Dewey:943.8/032. LCCN:90-050972.
Audience: **u,f.**

Wandycz, Piotr **DK434.9**
Stephan, et al.
The Lands of Partitioned Poland 1795-1918. Peter F. Sugar & Donald Warren Treadgold (Authors). Trade Paper. University of Washington Press. Seattle, WA. 1975. 472p. History of East Central Europe Ser., Vol. 7 ISBN:0-295-95358-6, ISBN13: 978-0-295-95358-8. Dewey:943.8/03. LCCN:74-008312.
Audience: **l,u,f.**

Zarnowska, Anna **HD8538.Z375 2004**
Workers, Women, and Social Change in Poland, 1870-1939. Trade Cloth. Ashgate Publishing, Ltd. Aldershot, 2004. 336p. Variorum Collected Studies Ser., :Cs795 Ser. ISBN:0-86078-941-1, ISBN13: 978-0-86078-941-3. Dewey:305.5/62/0943809041. LCCN:2004-007431.
Audience: **u,f.**

Zeromski, Stefan **PG7158.Z4W5514 2002**
The Faithful River. Bill Johnston (Translator). Trade Paper. Northwestern University Press. Evanston, IL. 1999. 179p. European Classics Ser. ISBN:0-8101-1596-4, ISBN13: 978-0-8101-1596-5. Dewey:891.8/536. LCCN:99-027010.
Audience: **g,l,u,f.**

Poland > By Period > Independent Poland (1918-1939)

Davies, Norman **DK4405**
White Eagle, Red Star: The Polish-Soviet War, 1919-20. Trade Paper. Random House. London, 2003. 336p. ISBN:0-7126-0694-7, ISBN13: 978-0-7126-0694-3. Dewey:947.084/1.
Audience: **u,f.**

Stachura, Peter D. **DK4400.S73 2001**
Poland, 1918-1945: An Interpretive and Documentary History of the Second Republic. Trade Paper. Routledge. New York, NY. 2004. 240p. ISBN:0-415-34358-5, ISBN13: 978-0-415-34358-9. Dewey:943.8/04. LCCN:2003-026325.
Audience: **u,f.**

Wandycz, Piotr S. **DK0418.5.R9W**
Soviet-Polish Relations, 1917-1921. Trade Paper. Books on Demand. Ann Arbor, MI. 420p. Russian Research Center

Studies, Vol. 59 ISBN:0-7837-3837-4, ISBN13: 978-0-7837-3837-6. Dewey:327/.470438. LCCN:69-018047.
Audience: **u,f.** BCL3

Wandycz, Piotr S. **DC394.W36 1988**
The Twilight of French Eastern Alliances, 1926-1936: French-Czechoslovak-Polish Relations from Locarno to the Remilitarization of the Rhineland. Trade Cloth. Princeton University Press. Princeton, NJ. 1988. 560p. ISBN:0-691-05528-9, ISBN13: 978-0-691-05528-2. Dewey:327.440437. LCCN:88-005789.
Audience: **u,f.** *Choice, 1989.*

Wat, Aleksander **PG7158.M553**
My Century: The Odyssey of a Polish Intellectual. Richard Lourie (Translator). Trade Paper. W. W. Norton & Company, Inc. New York, NY. 1990. ISBN:0-685-47609-X, ISBN13: 978-0-685-47609-3. Dewey:891.8/517 B.
Audience: **g,f.** *Choice, 1989.*

Zarnowska, Anna **HD8538.Z375 2004**
Workers, Women, and Social Change in Poland, 1870-1939. Trade Cloth. Ashgate Publishing, Ltd. Aldershot, 2004. 336p. Variorum Collected Studies Ser., :Cs795 Ser. ISBN:0-86078-941-1, ISBN13: 978-0-86078-941-3. Dewey:305.5/62/0943809041. LCCN:2004-007431.
Audience: **u,f.**

Poland > By Period > World War Two

Borodziej, Wlodzimierz **D765.2.W3B57713 2005**
The Warsaw Uprising of 1944. Barbara Harshav (Translator). Trade Cloth. University of Wisconsin Press. Chicago, IL. 2006. 196p. ISBN:0-299-20730-7, ISBN13: 978-0-299-20730-4. Dewey:940.53/43841. LCCN:2005-010202.
Audience: **u,f.**

Chodakiewicz, M. **DS135.P62**
Massacre in Jedwabne, July 10 1941: Before During, After. Trade Cloth. Eastern European Monographs. Bradenton, FL. 2005. 224p. ISBN:0-88033-554-8, ISBN13: 978-0-88033-554-6. Dewey:940.531853836. LCCN:2005-935505.
Audience: **u,f.**

Davies, Norman **D765.2.W3**
Rising '44: The Battle for Warsaw. Trade Paper. Penguin Group (USA) Inc. New York, NY. 2005. 784p. ISBN:0-14-303540-1, ISBN13: 978-0-14-303540-4. Dewey:940.53/18/0943841.
Audience: **u,f.**

Gross, Jan T. **DS135.P62**
Neighbors: The Destruction of the Jewish Community in Jedwabne, Poland. Trade Paper. Penguin Group (USA) Inc. New York, NY. 2002. 240p. ISBN:0-14-200240-2, ISBN13: 978-0-14-200240-7. Dewey:940.53/18/0943843.
Audience: **u,f.** *Choice, 2002.*

Hoffman, Eva **DS135.P62**
Shtetl: The Life and Death of a Small Town and the World of Polish Jews. Trade Paper. Houghton Mifflin Company. New York, NY. 1998. 286p. ISBN:0-395-92487-1, ISBN13: 978-0-395-92487-7. Dewey:943.8/05/089924.
Audience: **l.**

Korbonski, Stefan (Introduction by) **D802.P6K6813 2004**
Fighting Warsaw: The Story of the Polish Underground State, 1939-1945. Trade Paper. Hippocrene Books, Inc. New York, NY. 2004. 495p. ISBN:0-7818-1035-3, ISBN13: 978-0-7818-1035-7. Dewey:940.53/438/092 B. LCCN:2004-040602.
Audience: **l,u,f.**

Korbonski, Stefan **D802.P6**
Polish Underground State. Trade Paper. Hippocrene Books, Inc. New York, NY. 1981. 288p. ISBN:0-88254-517-5, ISBN13: 978-0-88254-517-2. Dewey:940.53438.
Audience: **l,u.**

Kozaczuk, Wladyslaw & Straszak, Jerzy **D810.C88K67 2004**
Enigma: How the Poles Broke the Nazi Code. Trade Cloth. Hippocrene Books, Inc. New York, NY. 2004. 164p. ISBN:0-7818-0941-X, ISBN13: 978-0-7818-0941-2. Dewey:940.54/8641. LCCN:2004-040636.
Audience: **l,u,f.**

Lukas, Richard C. **D802.P6L85 1986**
The Forgotten Holocaust: The Poles under German Occupation, 1939-1944. Trade Cloth. University Press of Kentucky. Lexington, KY. 1986. 320p. ISBN:0-8131-1566-3, ISBN13: 978-0-8131-1566-5. Dewey:940.53/438. LCCN:85-013560.
Audience: **l,u,f.** *Choice, 1986.*

Polonsky, Antony & Michlic, Joanna B. (Editors) **DS135.P62J4458 2004**
The Neighbors Respond: The Controversy over the Jedwabne Massacre in Poland. Trade Paper. Princeton University Press. Princeton, NJ. 2003. 432p. ISBN:0-691-11306-8, ISBN13: 978-0-691-11306-7. Dewey:940.53/18/09438. LCCN:2003-043366.
Audience: **u,f.** *Choice, 2004.*

Prazmowska, Anita **DK4410.P73 2004**
Civil War in Poland, 1942-1948. Cloth over Boards. Palgrave Macmillan. New York, NY. 2004. 256p. Studies in Russian and Eastern European History Ser. ISBN:0-333-98212-6, ISBN13: 978-0-333-98212-9. Dewey:943.805/3. LCCN:2003-070077.
Audience: **u,f.** *Choice, 2005.*

Prazmowska, Anita J. **D750**
Britain, Poland and the Eastern Front 1939. Trade Paper. Cambridge University Press. New York, NY. 2004. 239p. Cambridge Russian, Soviet and Post-Soviet Studies ISBN:0-521-52938-7, ISBN13: 978-0-521-52938-9. Dewey:940.5/32.
Audience: **u,f.** *Choice, 1988.*

Rossino, Alexander B. **D765**
Hitler Strikes Poland: Blitzkrieg, Ideology, and Atrocity. Trade Paper. University Press of Kansas. Lawrence, KS. 2005. 360p. ISBN:0-7006-1392-7, ISBN13: 978-0-7006-1392-2. Dewey:940.54/05/09438.
Audience: **l,u,f.** *Choice, 2003.*

Sanford, George **D804.S65S33 2005**
Katyn and the Soviet Massacre of 1940: Truth, Justice and Memory. Paper over Boards. Routledge. New York, NY. 2005. 272p. BASEES/Curzon Series on Russian and East European Studies, Vol. 20 ISBN:0-415-33873-5, ISBN13: 978-0-415-33873-8. Dewey:940.54/7247/0899185. LCCN:2004-065124.
Audience: **l,u,f.**

Siebel-Achenbach, Sebastian **DK4600.S448S54 1994**
Lower Silesia from Nazi Germany to Communist Poland, 1942-1949. Cloth Text. Palgrave Macmillan. New York, NY. 1994. 310p. ISBN:0-312-08533-8, ISBN13: 978-0-312-08533-9. Dewey:943.85. LCCN:92-014070.
Audience: **u,f.**

Szpilman, Wladyslaw **DS135.P63**
The Pianist. Mass Market. St. Martin's Press. Gordonville, VA. 2003. ISBN:0-312-99604-7, ISBN13: 978-0-312-99604-8. Dewey:940.5/318/092.
Audience: **l.**

Zamoyski, Adam **D792.P6**
The Forgotten Few: The Polish Air Force in World War II. Trade Cloth. Pen & Sword Books Ltd. Barnsley, 2004. 256p. ISBN:1-84415-090-9, ISBN13: 978-1-84415-090-8. Dewey:940.54/49438. LCCN:2004-484170.
Audience: **l,u,f.**

Poland > By Period > 1944-1989. Soviet-Polish Relations. Solidarity Movement

Ash, Timothy Garton **DK4442**
The Polish Revolution: Solidarity. Ed. 3. Trade Paper. Yale University Press. Cumberland, RI. 2002. 464p. ISBN:0-300-09568-6, ISBN13: 978-0-300-09568-5. Dewey:943.8/056.
Audience: **u,f.**

Bernhard, Michael H. **JN6752.B37 1993**
The Origins of Democratization in Poland: Workers, Intellectuals, and Oppositional Politics, 1976-1980. Cloth Text. Columbia University Press. New York, NY. 1993. 400p. ISBN:0-231-08092-1, ISBN13: 978-0-231-08092-7. Dewey:943.8055. LCCN:93-002983.
Audience: **u,f.** *Choice, 1994.*

Gomulka, Stanislaw & Polonsky, Anthony **DK4442.P645 1991**
Polish Paradoxes. Cloth Text. Routledge. New York, NY. 1990. 276p. ISBN:0-415-04375-1, ISBN13: 978-0-415-04375-5. Dewey:943.805. LCCN:89-006318.
Audience: **u,f.** *Choice, 1990.*

Gross, Jan T. **DK4415.G76 1988**
Revolution from Abroad: The Soviet Conquest of Poland's Western Ukraine and Western Belorussia. Cloth Text. Princeton University Press. Princeton, NJ. 1988. 380p. ISBN:0-691-09433-0, ISBN13: 978-0-691-09433-5. Dewey:943.8/053. LCCN:87-045520.
Audience: **u,f.** *Choice, 1988.*

Hayden, Jacqueline **JN6769.A52H39 2006**
The Collapse of Communist Power in Poland: Strategic Misperceptions and Unanticipated Outcomes. Trade Cloth. Routledge. New York, NY. 2006. 240p. BASEES/Routledge Series on Russian and East European Studies ISBN:0-415-36805-7, ISBN13: 978-0-415-36805-6. Dewey:320.9438/09/049. LCCN:2005-011140.
Audience: **u,f.**

Milosz, Czeslaw **JN6695**
The Captive Mind. Trade Cloth. Peter Smith Publisher, Inc. Magnolia, MA. 1992. ISBN:0-8446-6615-7, ISBN13: 978-0-8446-6615-0. Dewey:320.9/47/0904.
Audience: **g,u,f.**

Paczkowski, Andrzej **DK4400**
The Spring Will Be Ours: Poland and the Poles from Occupation to Freedom. Jane Cave (Translator). Trade Cloth. Pennsylvania State University Press. University Park, PA. 2003. 600p. ISBN:0-271-02308-2, ISBN13: 978-0-271-02308-3. Dewey:943.805. LCCN:2003-022446.
Audience: **l,u,f.** *Choice, 2004.*

Toranska, Teresa **DK4438**
Them: Stalin's Polish Puppets. Agnieszka Kolakowska (Translator). Trade Paper. HarperCollins Publishers. New York, NY. 1988. 384p. ISBN:0-06-091493-9, ISBN13: 978-0-06-091493-6. Dewey:943.8/05. LCCN:86-045364.
Audience: **u,f.**

Poland > Special Topics > Polish-Jewish Relations

Hoffman, Eva **DS135.P62**
Shtetl: The Life and Death of a Small Town and the World of Polish Jews. Trade Paper. Houghton Mifflin Company. New York, NY. 1998. 286p. ISBN:0-395-92487-1, ISBN13: 978-0-395-92487-7. Dewey:943.8/05/089924.
Audience: **l.**

Polonsky, Anthony (Editor) **DS135.P6**
Polin: Studies in Polish Jewry: Focusing on Jewish Popular Culture and Its Afterlife. Trade Paper. Littman Library of Jewish Civilization, The. London, 2003. 602p. ISBN:1-874774-74-9, ISBN13: 978-1-874774-74-7. Dewey:305.89240438.
Audience: **u,f.**

Polonsky, Antony & Michlic, Joanna B. (Editors) **DS135.P62J4458 2004**
The Neighbors Respond: The Controversy over the Jedwabne Massacre in Poland. Trade Paper. Princeton University Press. Princeton, NJ. 2003. 432p. ISBN:0-691-11306-8, ISBN13: 978-0-691-11306-7. Dewey:940.53/18/09438. LCCN:2003-043366.
Audience: **u,f.** *Choice, 2004.*

Baltic States > General Histories

Hiden, John & Lane, Thomas (Editors) **D741**
The Baltic and the Outbreak of the Second World War. Trade Paper. Cambridge University Press. New York, NY. 2003. 191p. ISBN:0-521-53120-9, ISBN13: 978-0-521-53120-7. Dewey:940.53/11.
Audience: **g,u,f.**

Kahk, Juhan; Tarvel, Enn **HC243**
An Economic History of the Baltic Countries. Almquist & Wiksell. 1997. ISBN:91-22-01778-X, ISBN13: 978-91-22-01778-3.
Audience: **u,f.**

Kirby, David **DK502.7.K57 1995**
The Baltic World, 1772-1993: Europe's Nothern Periphery in an Age of Change. Ed. 1. Trade Cloth. Addison-Wesley Longman, Ltd. Harlow, 1996. 480p. ISBN:0-582-00408-X, ISBN13: 978-0-582-00408-5. Dewey:947.4/07. LCCN:94-022617.
Audience: **g,u,f.** *Choice, 1995.*

Lieven, Anatol **DK502.7.L54 1993**
The Baltic Revolution: Estonia, Latvia, Lithuania and the Path to Independence. Cloth over Boards. Yale University Press. Cumberland, RI. 1993. 496p. ISBN:0-300-05552-8, ISBN13: 978-0-300-05552-8. Dewey:947.4084. LCCN:92-047282.
Audience: **g,l,u,f.** *Choice, 1994.*

Misiunas, Romuald J. & Taagepera, Rein **DK502.7**
The Baltic States, Years of Dependence, 1940-1992. Trade Paper. University of California Press. Berkeley, CA. 1993. 400p. ISBN:0-520-08228-1, ISBN13: 978-0-520-08228-1. Dewey:947/.4. LCCN:92-039806.
Audience: **g,u,f.** *Choice, 1994.*

O'Connor, Kevin **DK502**
The History of the Baltic States. Cloth Text. Greenwood Publishing Group, Inc. Portsmouth, NH. 2003. 248p. The Greenwood Histories of the Modern Nations Ser. ISBN:0-313-32355-0, ISBN13: 978-0-313-32355-3. Dewey:947.9. LCCN:2003-048527.
Audience: **g,l,u,f.** *Choice, 2004.*

Von Rauch, Georg **DK511.B3.R3413**
The Baltic States - Estonia, Latvia, Lithuania: The Years of Independence, 1917-1940. Trade Cloth. University of California Press. Berkeley, CA. 1987. xv, 265p. ISBN:0-520-02600-4, ISBN13: 978-0-520-02600-1. Dewey:947/.4/084. LCCN:73-086849.
Audience: **g,u,f.**

Baltic States > Latvia

Dreifelds, Juris **DK504.8 .D74 1996**
Latvia in Transition. Trade Paper. Cambridge University Press. New York, NY. 1996. 224p. ISBN:0-521-55537-X, ISBN13: 978-0-521-55537-1. Dewey:947.430. LCCN:95-016444.
Audience: **g,l,u,f.** *Choice, 1996.*

Ezergailis, Andrew **DS135.L3.E94 1996**
The Holocaust in Latvia, 1941-1944: The Missing Center. Trade Cloth. Bow Historical Books. New Providence, NJ. 1996. xxi, 465p. ISBN:9984-9054-3-8, ISBN13: 978-9984-9054-3-3. Dewey:940.53/18/094743. LCCN:95-042583.
Audience: **g,l,u,f.** *Choice, 1997.*

Plakans, Andrejs **DK504.54.P57 1995**
The Latvians: A Short History. Trade Cloth. Hoover Institution Press. Stanford, CA. 1995. 257p. Publication Ser., No. 422:Studies of Nationalities in the U. S. S. R. ISBN:0-8179-9301-0, ISBN13: 978-0-8179-9301-6. Dewey:947/.43. LCCN:95-000765.
Audience: **u,f.**

Steimanis, Josifs **DS135.L3S7413 2002**
History of Latvian Jews. Trade Cloth. Eastern European Monographs. Bradenton, FL. 2002. 240p. ISBN:0-88033-493-2, ISBN13: 978-0-88033-493-8. Dewey:947.96/004924. LCCN:2002-101940.
Audience: **g,l,u,f.** *Choice, 2003.*

Baltic States > Estonia

Kasekamp, Andres **JC573.2.E75K37 2000**
The Radical Right in Interwar Estonia. Cloth over Boards. Palgrave Macmillan. New York, NY. 2000. 230p. Studies in Russia and East Europe ISBN:0-312-22598-9, ISBN13: 978-0-312-22598-8. Dewey:320.53/3/09479809043. LCCN:99-044844.
Audience: **g,l,u,f.** *Choice, 2000.*

Raun, Toivo U. **DK503.54.R38 2001**
Estonia and the Estonians. Ed. 2. Trade Paper. Hoover Institution Press. Stanford, CA. 2002. xix, 336p. Publication Ser., P497:Studies of Nationalities ISBN:0-8179-2852-9, ISBN13: 978-0-8179-2852-0. Dewey:947.98. LCCN:2002-279856.
Audience: **u,f.** *Choice, 1987.*

Baltic States > Lithuania

Eidintas, Alfonsas (Editor), et al. **DK505.74**
Lithuania in European Politics: The Years of the First Republic, 1918-1940. Vytautas Tuskenis Zalys & Edvardas Senn (Editors), Alfred Erich (Introduction by). Trade Paper. Palgrave Macmillan. New York, NY. 1999. 272p. ISBN:0-312-22458-3, ISBN13: 978-0-312-22458-5. Dewey:947.9/3/0841.
Audience: **g,l,u,f.** *Choice, 1998.*

Lane, Thomas **DK505.69.R8**
Lithuania: Stepping Westward. Paper over Boards. Routledge. New York, NY. 2002. 288p. Postcommunist States and Nations Ser., 9 ISBN:0-415-26731-5, ISBN13: 978-0-415-26731-1. Dewey:327.4793047.
Audience: **g,u,f.**

Mishell, William W. **DS135.R93.K286 1988**
Kaddish for Kovno: Life and Death in a Lithuanian Ghetto, 1941-1945. Trade Cloth. Chicago Review Press, Inc. Chicago, IL. 1988. vii, 398p. ISBN:1-55652-033-6, ISBN13: 978-1-55652-033-4. Dewey:947/.5. LCCN:88-002587.
Audience: **g,l,u,f.**

Rowell, S. C. **DK505.7 .R68 1994**
Lithuania Ascending: A Pagan Empire Within East-Central Europe, 1295-1345. Christine Carpenter, Rosamond McKitterick & Jonathan Shepard (Contribution by). Trade Cloth. Cambridge University Press. New York, NY. 1994. 415p. Studies in Medieval Life and Thought, No. 25 ISBN:0-521-45011-X, ISBN13: 978-0-521-45011-9. Dewey:947.5. LCCN:92-017442.
Audience: **g,l,u,f.** *Choice, 1995.*

Sabaliunas, Leonas **DK0511.L27S2**
Lithuania in Crisis: Nationalism to Communism, 1939-1940. Trade Paper. Books on Demand. Ann Arbor, MI. 317p. Indiana University Publications International Studies Ser. ISBN:0-598-19308-1, ISBN13: 978-0-598-19308-7. Dewey:947/.5/0842. LCCN:74-143247.
Audience: **u,f.**

Sabaliunas, Leonas **HX315.L77S22 1990**
Lithuanian Social Democracy in Perspective, 1893-1914. Cloth Text. Duke University Press. Durham, NC. 1990. 210p. Duke Press Policy Studies ISBN:0-8223-1015-5, ISBN13: 978-0-8223-1015-0. Dewey:335.5/0947/5. LCCN:89-027306.
Audience: **u,f.** *Choice, 1991.*

LATIN AMERICAN HISTORY

Since the publication of BCL3 in 1988, the study of Latin American history has undergone revolutionary change. Titles selected for this section are organized by a new taxonomy which adds new thematic fields to the more traditional divisions of countries and historical eras. New thematic fields are the historical study of Gender, Popular Culture, Environment, Civil-Military Relations, Drugs, and Afro-Latin America. The titles selected for this section mirror of the ways in which English-language publishers and Anglophone scholars place their emphasis in this dynamic, geographic and thematic area. The texts listed here, while a core selection for undergraduates, should be supplemented with important texts in Spanish and Luso-Brazilian.

Related coverage may be found in other sections of RCL, including Native American Studies and Latino Studies. These works are of profound relevance to Latin America and should also be consulted.

— Friedrich Schuler

Latin America: General

PQ6171
□ Biblioteca Virtual Miguel de Cervantes.
http://www.cervantesvirtual.com/
Audience: **u,f.**

Z7163
□ CARINDEX.
http://www.inasp.info/iah/index.shtml
Audience: **u,f.**

LA555
□ CEDES (Centro de Estudios de Estado y Sociedad).
http://www.cedes.org/index_espaniol.html
Audience: **u,f.**

Z7163
□ Citas Latinoamericanas en Ciencias Sociales y Humanidades (CLASE).
http://ahau.cichcu.unam.mx:8000/ALEPH
Audience: **u,f.**

H62.C58495
□ CLACSO.
http://www.clacso.org/wwwclacso/espanol/html/biblioteca/fbiblioteca.html
Audience: **u,f.**

H61
□ CLACSO (Consejo Latinoamericano de Ciencias Sociales).
http://www.clacso.org/wwwclacso/espanol/html/biblioteca/fbiblioteca.html
Audience: **u,f.**

HC161
□ ECLAC/CEPAL: Economic Commission for Latin America.
http://www.eclac.cl/
Audience: **u,f.**

HF1.A58
□ Economist Intelligence Unit (EIU).
http://www.eiu.com/
Audience: **u,f.**

Z1601
□ Handbook of Latin American Studies (HLAS).
http://lcweb2.loc.gov/hlas/
Audience: **u,f.**

Z1601
□ Hispanic American Periodicals Index (HAPI).
http://hapi.gseis.ucla.edu/
Audience: **l,u,f.**

HG3881.5.I44
□ Inter-American Development Bank-IADB.
http://www.iadb.org/
Audience: **u,f.**

D5
□ Internet Modern History Sourcebook.
http://www.fordham.edu/halsall/mod/modsbook.html
Audience: **l,u,f.**

F1408
□ LANIC (Latin American Network Information Center).
http://lanic.utexas.edu/
Audience: **l,u,f.**

F1401
□ Latin America Data Base (LADB).
http://ladb.unm.edu/
Audience: **l,u,f.**

F1401
□ Latin American Bureau.
http://www.lab.org.uk/
Audience: **l,u,f.**

Z1601
□ Latin American Periodicals Tables of Contents (LAPTOC).
http://lanic.utexas.edu/project/arl/
Audience: **l,u,f.**

Z6944.S3
□ Latindex: Sistema Regional de Información en línea para Revistas Científicas de América Latina,, el Caribe, España y Portugal.
http://www.latindex.unam.mx/
Audience: **u,f.**

F1402.A3
□ Organization of American States (OAS).
http://www.oas.org/
Audience: **u,f.**

JL951
□ Political Database of the Americas.
http://www.georgetown.edu/pdba/
Audience: **u,f.**

SH1
□ Red de revistas Científicas de América Latina y el Caribe, España y Portugal (Red ALyC).
http://redalyc.uaemex.mx/redalyc/index.jsp
Audience: **u,f.**

Q1.A1
□ Scientific Electronic Library Online (Scielo).
http://www.scielo.org/index.php?lang=en
Audience: **u,f.**

Cleary, Edward L. & Stewart-Gambino, Hannah (Editors) BX1426.2
Conflict and Competition: The Latin American Church in a Changing Environment. Library Binding. Lynne Rienner Publishers, Inc. Boulder, CO. 1992. 234p. ISBN:1-55587-251-4, ISBN13: 978-1-55587-251-9. Dewey:282.809049. LCCN:91-044237.
Audience: **g,l,u,f.**

Drake, Paul W. (Editor) HC125.M584 1994
Money Doctors, Foreign Debts and Economic Reforms in Latin America from the 1890s to the Present. Trade Paper. Rowman & Littlefield Publishers, Inc. Lanham, MD. 1994. 304p. Jaguar Books on Latin America, No. 3 ISBN:0-8420-2435-2, ISBN13: 978-0-8420-2435-8. Dewey:338.9/7308. LCCN:93-034563.
Audience: **u,f.** *Choice, 1994.*

Falcoff, Mark & Pike, Fredrick B. (Editors) **DP269.8.P8S6 1982**
The Spanish Civil War, 1936-1939: American Hemispheric Perspectives. Trade Cloth. University of Nebraska Press. Lincoln, NE. 1982. xxiv, 357p. ISBN:0-8032-1961-X, ISBN13: 978-0-8032-1961-8. Dewey:946.081. LCCN:81-014644.
Audience: **u,f.**

Fowler, Will (ed.) **F1413**
Authoritarianism in Latin America Since Independence. Greenwood Press. 1996. Contributions in Latin American Studies, No. 6 ISBN:0-313-29843-2, ISBN13: 978-0-313-29843-1.
Audience: **u,f.**

Greenfield, Gerald M. **HT127**
Latin American Urbanization: Historical Profiles of Major Cities. Cloth Text. Greenwood Publishing Group, Inc. Portsmouth, NH. 1994. 560p. ISBN:0-313-25937-2, ISBN13: 978-0-313-25937-1. Dewey:307.76098. LCCN:93-013015.
Audience: **u,f.**

Haney, Lynne, and Pollard Lisa (eds.) **HQ515**
Families of a New World: Gender, Politics, and State Development In a Global Context. Routledge. 2003. ISBN:0-415-93446-X, ISBN13: 978-0-415-93446-6.
Audience: **u,f.**

Klaiber, Jeffrey **F1414.2**
The Church, Dictatorships and Democracy in Latin America. Trade Cloth. Orbis Books. Maryknoll, NY. 1998. 284p. ISBN:1-57075-214-1, ISBN13: 978-1-57075-214-8. Dewey:322/.1/0980904.
Audience: **u,f.** *Choice, 1999.*

Masur, Gerhard **F2235.3.M39 1969**
Simon Bolivar. Trade Cloth. University of New Mexico Press. Albuquerque, NM. 1969. xiv, 572p. ISBN:0-8263-0131-2, ISBN13: 978-0-8263-0131-4. Dewey:980/.02/0924. LCCN:68-056230.
Audience: **g,l,u,f.**

Molloy, Molly E **F1408**
☐ La Guia:Internet Resources for Latin America. http://lib.nmsu.edu/subject/bord/laguia/
Audience: **l,u,f.**

Roniger, Luis & Herzog, Tamar (Editors) **HN110.5.A8**
The Collective and the Public in Latin America: Cultural Identities and Political Order. Sussex Academic Press. 2000.
Audience: **u,f.**

Schneider, Ben Ross **JL964.P7S36 2004**
Business Politics and the State in Twentieth-Century Latin America. Cloth Text. Cambridge University Press. New York, NY. 2004. 336p. ISBN:0-521-83651-4, ISBN13: 978-0-521-83651-7. Dewey:322/.3/098. LCCN:2004-040684.
Audience: **u,f.** *Choice, 2005.*

Thomson, Guy **F1413**
The European Revolutions of 1848 and the Americas. Institute of Latin American Studies. 2002.
Audience: **u,f.**

Vanden, Harry E. & Prevost, Gary **JL960.V36 2006**
Politics of Latin America: The Power Game. Ed. 2. Paper Text. Oxford University Press, Inc. New York, NY. 2005. 624p. ISBN:0-19-518808-X, ISBN13: 978-0-19-518808-0. Dewey:980. LCCN:2005-048824.
Audience: **g,l,u.**

Weber, David J. & Rausch, Jane M. (Editors) **F1408.3.W47 1994**
Where Cultures Meet: Frontiers in Latin American History. Book, Other. Rowman & Littlefield Publishers, Inc. Lanham, MD. 1997. 222p. Jaguar Books on Latin America, No. 6 ISBN:0-8420-2477-8, ISBN13: 978-0-8420-2477-8. Dewey:980/.001. LCCN:94-001788.
Audience: **l,u,f.**

Latin America: General > Cultural History > Precolombian

Anawalt, Patricia R. **F1219.3.C75**
Indian Clothing Before Cortes: Mesoamerican Costumes from the Codices. Jean C. Sells (Illustrator), H. B. Nicholson (Introduction by). Trade Paper. University of Oklahoma Press. Norman, OK. 1990. 252p. Civilization of the American Indian Ser., Vol. 156 ISBN:0-8061-2288-9, ISBN13: 978-0-8061-2288-5. Dewey:391/.00972. LCCN:80-005942.
Audience: **u,f.**

Bauer, Brian S. **F3429.3.R3B38 1998**
The Sacred Landscape of the Inca: The Cusco Ceque System. Trade Cloth. University of Texas Press. Austin, TX. 1998. 263p. ISBN:0-292-70865-3, ISBN13: 978-0-292-70865-5. Dewey:299/.88323. LCCN:97-049914.
Audience: **u,f.**

Boone, Elizabeth Hill **F1219.54.A98B66 2000**
Stories in Red and Black: Pictorial Histories of the Aztec and Mixtec. Trade Cloth. University of Texas Press. Austin, TX. 2000. 312p. ISBN:0-292-70876-9, ISBN13: 978-0-292-70876-1. Dewey:972/.01. LCCN:99-006214.
Audience: **l,u,f.** *Choice, 2000.*

Braswell, Geoffrey E. (Editor) **F1435.M37 2004**
The Maya and Teotihuacan: Reinterpreting Early Classic Interaction. Trade Paper. University of Texas Press. Austin, TX. 2004. 441p. The Linda Schele Series in Maya and Pre-Columbian Studies ISBN:0-292-70587-5, ISBN13: 978-0-292-70587-6. Dewey:972.5/2.
Audience: **u,f.** *Choice, 2004.*

Burger, Richard L. **F3069**
Chavin: And the Origins of the Andean Civilization. Trade Paper. Thames & Hudson. New York, NY. 1995. 248p. ISBN:0-500-27816-4, ISBN13: 978-0-500-27816-1. Dewey:983.01. LCCN:92-080337.
Audience: **u,f.**

Byland, Bruce E. & Pohl, John M. **F1219.54.M59B95 1994**
In the Realm of Eight Deer: The Archaeology of the Mixtec Codies. Trade Cloth. University of Oklahoma Press. Norman, OK. 1995. 448p. ISBN:0-8061-2612-4, ISBN13: 978-0-8061-2612-8. Dewey:972/.74. LCCN:94-029616.
Audience: **u,f.** *Choice, 1995.*

Carrasco, David **F1219.3.R38**
City of Sacrifice: Violence from the Aztec Empire to the Modern Americas. Trade Paper. Beacon Press. Boston, MA. 2000. 304p. ISBN:0-8070-4643-4, ISBN13: 978-0-8070-4643-2. Dewey:299/.78452.
Audience: **u,f.**

Clark, J. E. **N386.U5.S78**
Olmec Art and Archaeology in Mesoamerica. Mary E. Pye (Editor). Trade Paper. Yale University Press. Cumberland, RI. 2006. 344p. Studies in the History of Art Series, Na Ser. ISBN:0-300-11446-X, ISBN13: 978-0-300-11446-1. Dewey:709 s 704.03/97072. LCCN:2005-028422.
Audience: **u,f.**

Classen, Constance **F3429.3.R3.C53 1993**
Inca Cosmology and the Human Body. Cloth Text. University of Utah Press. Salt Lake City, UT. 1993. 224p. ISBN:0-87480-399-3, ISBN13: 978-0-87480-399-0. Dewey:299/.8. LCCN:92-026079.
Audience: **u,f.** *Choice, 1993.*

Coe, Sophie D. **F1219.76.F67C64 1994**
America's First Cuisines. Trade Paper. University of Texas Press. Austin, TX. 1994. 288p. ISBN:0-292-71159-X, ISBN13: 978-0-292-71159-4. Dewey:394.1/2/08997. LCCN:93-008836.
Audience: **u,f.**

Freidel, David, et al. **F1435.3.R3 F74**
Maya Cosmos. Linda Schele & Joy Parker (Authors). Trade Paper. HarperCollins Publishers. New York, NY. 1995. 544p. ISBN:0-688-14069-6, ISBN13: 978-0-688-14069-4. Dewey:299/.79281.
Audience: **u,f.**

Hassig, Ross **F1219.76.C35H37 2001**
Time, History, and Belief in Aztec and Colonial Mexico. Trade Cloth. University of Texas Press. Austin, TX. 2001. 256p. ISBN:0-292-73139-6, ISBN13: 978-0-292-73139-4. Dewey:529/.32978452. LCCN:00-041783.
Audience: **u,f.** *Choice, 2001.*

Hassig, Ross **F1219**
War and Society in Ancient Mesoamerica. Trade Cloth. University of California Press. Berkeley, CA. 1992. 348p. ISBN:0-520-07734-2, ISBN13: 978-0-520-07734-8. Dewey:972.01. LCCN:91-042635.
Audience: **u,f.**

Kolata, Alan L. **F3319.1.T55K64 1993**
The Tiwanaku: Portrait of an Andean Civilization. Trade Cloth. Blackwell Publishing, Inc. Malden, MA. 1993. 256p. The Peoples of America Ser. ISBN:1-55786-183-8, ISBN13: 978-1-55786-183-2. Dewey:984.12. LCCN:92-039248.
Audience: **u,f.**

Kowalski, Jeff K. (Editor) **F1219.3.A6M48 1999**
Mesoamerican Architecture As a Cultural Symbol. Cloth Text. Oxford University Press, Inc. New York, NY. 1999. 432p. ISBN:0-19-507961-2, ISBN13: 978-0-19-507961-6. Dewey:720.8/9974. LCCN:97-014821.
Audience: **u,f.** *Choice, 1999.*

Leon-Portilla, Miguel **E99.H7**
Aztec Thought and Culture: A Study of the Ancient Nahuatl Mind. Jack E. Davis (Translator). Trade Paper. University of Oklahoma Press. Norman, OK. 1990. 272p. Civilization of the American Indian Ser., Vol. 67 ISBN:0-8061-2295-1, ISBN13: 978-0-8061-2295-3. Dewey:299.784. LCCN:63-011019.
Audience: **u,f.**

Marcus, Joyce **F1219.3.W94.M37 1992**
Mesoamerican Writing Systems: Propaganda, Myth, and History in Four Ancient Civilizations. Cloth Text. Princeton University Press. Princeton, NJ. 1993. 550p. ISBN:0-691-09474-8, ISBN13: 978-0-691-09474-8. Dewey:970.01/072. LCCN:92-009091.
Audience: **u,f.** *Choice, 1993.*

McKeever-Furst, Jill L. **F1219.76.R45M4 1995**
The Natural History of the Soul in Ancient Mexico. Cloth over Boards. Yale University Press. Cumberland, RI. 1995. 240p. ISBN:0-300-06225-7, ISBN13: 978-0-300-06225-0. Dewey:128/.1/0972. LCCN:95-016961.
Audience: **u,f.** *Choice, 1996.*

Miller, Mary E. **F1219.1.C45M55 1986**
The Murals of Bonampak. Trade Cloth. Princeton University Press. Princeton, NJ. 1986. 248p. ISBN:0-691-04033-8, ISBN13: 978-0-691-04033-2. Dewey:751.7/3/097275. LCCN:85-000499.
Audience: **u,f.**

Moctezuma, Eduardo M. **F1219.1.M5M36813**
Life and Death in the Templo Mayor. Bernard R. Ortiz De Montellano & Thelma Ortiz De Montellano (Translators). Trade Paper. University Press of Colorado. Boulder, CO. 1995. 160p. Mesoamerican Worlds Ser. ISBN:0-87081-400-1, ISBN13: 978-0-87081-400-6. Dewey:972/.53. LCCN:95-015700.
Audience: **u,f.**

Morris, Craig & Thompson, Donald E. **F3429.H826M67 1985**
Huanuco Pampa: An Inca City and Its Hinterland. Trade Cloth. Thames & Hudson. New York, NY. 1985. 181p. Ancient Peoples and Places Ser. ISBN:0-500-39020-7, ISBN13: 978-0-500-39020-7. Dewey:985/.22. LCCN:84-052180.
Audience: **u,f.** *Choice, 1986.*

Niles, Susan A. **F3429.3.A65N56 1999**
The Shape of Inca History: Narrative and Architecture in an Andean Empire. Trade Cloth. University of Iowa Press. Iowa City, IA. 1999. 356p. ISBN:0-87745-673-9, ISBN13: 978-0-87745-673-5. Dewey:985/.37. LCCN:98-051181.
Audience: **u,f.** *Choice, 2000.*

Ortiz De Montellano, Bernard R. **F1219.76.M43O78 1990**
Aztec Medicine, Health, and Nutrition. Cloth Text. Rutgers University Press. Piscataway, NJ. 1990. 310p. ISBN:0-8135-1562-9, ISBN13: 978-0-8135-1562-5. Dewey:972/.018. LCCN:89-070142.
Audience: **u,f.** *Choice, 1991.*

Pasztory, Esther **F1219.1.T27P37 1997**
Teotihuacan: An Experiment in Living. Trade Cloth. University of Oklahoma Press. Norman, OK. 1997. 304p. ISBN:0-8061-2847-X, ISBN13: 978-0-8061-2847-4. Dewey:972/.52. LCCN:96-032775.
Audience: **u,f.** *Choice, 1997.*

Paul, Anne **F3429.1.P25P38 1990**
Paracas Ritual Attire: Symbols of Authority in Ancient Peru. Trade Cloth. University of Oklahoma Press. Norman, OK. 1990. 200p. Civilization of the American Indian Ser., No. 195 ISBN:0-8061-2230-7, ISBN13: 978-0-8061-2230-4. Dewey:985/.01. LCCN:89-048729.
Audience: **u,f.** *Choice, 1991.*

Protzen, Jean-Pierre **F3429.1.O44P76 1993**
Inca Architecture and Construction at Ollantaytambo. Robert Batson (Illustrator). Trade Cloth. Oxford University Press, Inc. New York, NY. 1993. 320p. ISBN:0-19-507069-0, ISBN13: 978-0-19-507069-9. Dewey:985/.37. LCCN:91-024152.
Audience: **u,f.** *Choice, 1994.*

Scarborough, Vernon L. & Wilcox, David R. (Editors) **F1219.3.G3**
The Mesoamerican Ballgame. Trade Paper. University of Arizona Press. Tucson, AZ. 1993. 404p. ISBN:0-8165-1360-0, ISBN13: 978-0-8165-1360-4. Dewey:796.3/089/6872. LCCN:90-021890.
Audience: **u,f.** *Choice, 1992.*

Schele, Linda & Freidel, David **F1435.3.K55S34 1992**
A Forest of Kings: The Untold Story of the Ancient Maya. Trade Paper. HarperCollins Publishers. New York, NY. 1992. 544p. ISBN:0-688-11204-8, ISBN13: 978-0-688-11204-2. Dewey:972.81/016. LCCN:91-034069.
Audience: **g,l,u,f.** *Choice, 1991.*

Stevenson, Robert **ML3549**
Music in Aztec and Inca Territory. Trade Cloth. University of California Press. Berkeley, CA. 1977. ISBN:0-520-03169-5, ISBN13: 978-0-520-03169-2. Dewey:781.772.
Audience: **g,l,u,f.**

Stone, Andrea J. **F1435.1.N35S76 1995**
Images from the Underworld: Naj Tunich and the Tradition of Maya Cave Painting. Trade Cloth. University of Texas Press. Austin, TX. 1995. 304p. ISBN:0-292-75552-X, ISBN13: 978-0-292-75552-9. Dewey:972.81. LCCN:94-011145.
Audience: **u,f.** *Choice, 1996.*

Urton, Gary **F3429.U88 1990**
The History of a Myth: Pacariqtambo and the Origin of the Inkas. Trade Cloth. University of Texas Press. Austin, TX. 1990. 184p. ISBN:0-292-73051-9, ISBN13: 978-0-292-73051-9. Dewey:985/.01. LCCN:89-025074.
Audience: **u,f.**

Urton, Gary **F3429.3.Q6U78 2003**
Signs of the Inka Khipu: Binary Coding in the Andean Knotted-String Records. Trade Cloth. University of Texas Press. Austin, TX. 2003. 216p. The Linda Schele Series in Maya and Pre-Columbian Studies ISBN:0-292-78539-9, ISBN13: 978-0-292-78539-7. Dewey:302.2/22. LCCN:2002-012297.
Audience: **u,f.**

Latin America: General > Cultural History > Colonial

Adorno, Rolena **F3430.6.G8A63 2000**
Guaman Poma: Writing and Resistance in Colonial Peru. Ed. 2. Trade Paper. University of Texas Press. Austin, TX. 2000. 256p. ILAS Special Publication Ser. ISBN:0-292-70503-4, ISBN13: 978-0-292-70503-6. Dewey:985/.0072. LCCN:00-041770.
Audience: **u,f.** *Choice, 1987.*

Alban, Juan Pedro Viqueira **F1386.2.V5713 1999**
Propriety and Permissiveness in Bourbon Mexico. Sonya Lipsett-Rivera & Sergio Rivera Ayala (Translators). Book, Other. Rowman & Littlefield Publishers, Inc. Lanham, MD. 1999. 280p. ISBN:0-8420-2466-2, ISBN13: 978-0-8420-2466-2. Dewey:972/.53. LCCN:99-019888.
Audience: **u,f.** *Choice, 2000.*

Bennett, Herman L. **F1386.9.B55B46 2005**
Africans in Colonial Mexico: Absolutism, Christianity, and Afro-Creole Consciousness, 1570-1640. Trade Paper. Indiana University Press. Bloomington, IN. 2005. 288p. Blacks in the Diaspora Ser. ISBN:0-253-21775-X, ISBN13: 978-0-253-21775-2. Dewey:972/.00496.
Audience: **u,f.** *Choice, 2004.*

Boyer, Richard **HQ561.B69 1995**
Lives of the Bigamists: Marriage, Family, and Community in Colonial Mexico. Trade Cloth. University of New Mexico Press. Albuquerque, NM. 1995. 342p. ISBN:0-8263-1571-2, ISBN13: 978-0-8263-1571-7. Dewey:364.1/83/0972. LCCN:94-038576.
Audience: **u,f.**

Brading, D. A. **F1412**
The First America: The Spanish Monarchy, Creole Patriots and the Liberal State, 1492-1866. Trade Paper. Cambridge University Press. New York, NY. 1993. 779p. ISBN:0-521-44796-8, ISBN13: 978-0-521-44796-6. Dewey:980/.013.
Audience: **u,f.** *Choice, 1991.*

Burkhart, Louise M. **F1219.3.R38B78 1989**
The Slippery Earth: Nahua-Christian Moral Dialogue in Sixteenth-Century Mexico. Trade Cloth. University of Arizona Press. Tucson, AZ. 1989. 242p. ISBN:0-8165-1088-1, ISBN13: 978-0-8165-1088-7. Dewey:303.4/8272/046. LCCN:88-038673.
Audience: **u,f.** *Choice, 1989.*

Canizares-Esguerra, Jorge **F1412.C25 2001**
How to Write the History of the New World: Histories, Epistemologies, and Identities in the Eighteenth-Century Atlantic World. Trade Cloth. Stanford University Press. Palo Alto, CA. 2001. xviii, 450p. Cultural Sitings Ser. ISBN:0-8047-4084-4, ISBN13: 978-0-8047-4084-5. Dewey:980. LCCN:00-050486.
Audience: **u,f.** *Choice, 2002.*

Cervantes, Fernando **BF1548 .C48**
The Devil in the New World: The Impact of Diabolism in New Spain. Trade Paper. Yale University Press. Cumberland, RI. 1997. 192p. ISBN:0-300-06889-1, ISBN13: 978-0-300-06889-4. Dewey:133.4/22/0972.
Audience: **u,f.**

Chang-Rodriguez, Raquel **PQ8385.C43 1999**
Hidden Messages: Representation and Resistance in Andean Colonial Drama. Trade Cloth. Bucknell University Press. Cranbury, NJ. 1999. 144p. ISBN:0-8387-5421-X, ISBN13: 978-0-8387-5421-4. Dewey:862. LCCN:98-047707.
Audience: **u,f.** *Choice, 2000.*

Curcio-Nagy, Linda A. **GT4814.M4C87 2004**
The Great Festivals of Colonial Mexico City: Performing Power and Identity. Trade Cloth. University of New Mexico Press. Albuquerque, NM. 2004. 222p. Dialogos Ser. ISBN:0-8263-3166-1, ISBN13: 978-0-8263-3166-3. Dewey:394.26972. LCCN:2003-026972.
Audience: **u,f.** *Choice, 2005.*

Damian, Carol **ND417.C8D36 1995**
The Virgin of the Andes: Art and Ritual In Colonial Cuzco. Trade Cloth. Grassfield Press, Inc. Miami Beach, FL. 1995. 112p. ISBN:0-9628514-8-5, ISBN13: 978-0-9628514-8-3. Dewey:704.9/4855/098537. LCCN:94-073217.
Audience: **u,f.** *Choice, 1996.*

Dean, Carolyn (Contribution by) **GT4995.C6D43 1999**
Inka Bodies and the Body of Christ: Corpus Christi in Colonial Cusco, Peru. Trade Cloth. Duke University Press. Durham, NC. 1999. 264p. ISBN:0-8223-2332-X, ISBN13: 978-0-8223-2332-7. Dewey:394.266. LCCN:98-056544.
Audience: **u,f.** *Choice, 2000.*

Edgerton, Samuel Y. & Perez de Lara, Jorge **N7914.A1E34 2001**
Theaters of Conversion: Religious Architecture and Indian Artisans in Colonial Mexico. Trade Cloth. University of New Mexico Press. Albuquerque, NM. 2004. 368p. ISBN:0-8263-2256-5, ISBN13: 978-0-8263-2256-2. Dewey:704.9/482/0972. LCCN:00-011870.
Audience: **u,f.** *Choice, 2002.*

Fane, Diana **N6553.C66 1996**
Converging Cultures: Art and Identity in Spanish America. Trade Cloth. Harry N. Abrams, Inc. New York, NY. 1996. 328p. ISBN:0-8109-4030-2, ISBN13: 978-0-8109-4030-7. Dewey:709/.72/07474723. LCCN:95-021899.
Audience: **u,f.** *Choice, 1996.*

Few, Martha **HQ1480.A58F49 2002**
Women Who Live Evil Lives: Gender, Religion, and the Politics of Power in Colonial Guatemala, 1650-1750. Trade Cloth. University of Texas Press. Austin, TX. 2002. 208p. ISBN:0-292-72543-4, ISBN13: 978-0-292-72543-0. Dewey:305.42097281. LCCN:2002-003572.
Audience: **u,f.**

Fraser, Valerie **NA913.F73 1990**
The Architecture of Conquest: Building in the Viceroyalty of Peru, 1535-1635. Trade Cloth. Cambridge University Press. New York, NY. 1990. 218p. Cambridge Iberian and Latin American Studies ISBN:0-521-34316-X, ISBN13: 978-0-521-34316-9. Dewey:720/.985. LCCN:88-036548.
Audience: **u,f.** *Choice, 1990.*

Griffiths, Nicholas **F3429.3.R3G74 1996**
The Cross and the Serpent: Religious Repression and Resurgence in Colonial Peru. Trade Cloth. University of Oklahoma Press. Norman, OK. 1996. 362p. ISBN:0-8061-2800-3, ISBN13: 978-0-8061-2800-9. Dewey:299/.895. LCCN:95-024751.
Audience: **u,f.** *Choice, 1996.*

Gruzinksi, Serge **F1219.3.C85**
The Conquest of Mexico: The Incorporation of the Indian Societies into the Western World. Polity Press. 1993.
Audience: **u,f.**

Gruzinksi, Serge **F1408.3**
The Mestizo Mind: The Intellectual Dynamics of Colonization and Globalization. Routledge. 2002. ISBN:0-415-92878-8, ISBN13: 978-0-415-92878-6.
Audience: **u,f.**

Harris, Max **GT4014.A2H37 2000**
Aztecs, Moors, and Christians: Festivals of Reconquest in Mexico and Spain. Trade Cloth. University of Texas Press. Austin, TX. 2000. 319p. ISBN:0-292-73131-0, ISBN13: 978-0-292-73131-8. Dewey:0292731329. LCCN:99-057705.
Audience: **u,f.**

Johnson, Julie G. **PQ7082.S26**
Satire in Colonial Spanish America: Turning the New World Upside Down. Daniel R. Reedy (Foreword by). Trade Cloth. University of Texas Press. Austin, TX. 1993. ISBN:0-292-74028-X, ISBN13: 978-0-292-74028-0. Dewey:867.009/98. LCCN:92-042849.
Audience: **u,f.**

Johnson, Lyman L. & Lipsett-Rivera, Sonya **BJ1533.H8F33 1998**
The Faces of Honor: Sex, Shame, and Violence in Colonial Latin America. Trade Cloth. University of New Mexico Press. Albuquerque, NM. 1998. 240p. Dialogos Ser. ISBN:0-8263-1924-6, ISBN13: 978-0-8263-1924-1. Dewey:306/.098. LCCN:98-018974.
Audience: **u,f.**

Katzew, Ilona **ND1312.M44K37 2004**
Casta Painting: Images of Race in Eighteenth-Century Mexico. Cloth over Boards. Yale University Press. Cumberland, RI. 2004. 252p. ISBN:0-300-10241-0, ISBN13: 978-0-300-10241-3. Dewey:757/.0972/09033. LCCN:2003-017365.
Audience: **u,f.** *Choice, 2004.*

Lewis, Laura A. **HN113.L48 2003**
Hall of Mirrors: Power, Witchcraft, and Caste in Colonial Mexico. Trade Cloth. Duke University Press. Durham, NC. 2003. 280p. Latin America Otherwise Ser. ISBN:0-8223-3111-X, ISBN13: 978-0-8223-3111-7. Dewey:306/.0972. LCCN:2003-005048.
Audience: **u,f.** *Choice, 2004.*

MacCormack, Sabine **F3429.3.R3**
Religion in the Andes: Vision and Imagination in Early Colonial Peru. Trade Paper. Princeton University Press. Princeton, NJ. 1993. 506p. ISBN:0-691-02106-6, ISBN13: 978-0-691-02106-5. Dewey:299/.895.
Audience: **u,f.** *Choice, 1992.*

McKnight, Kathryn Joy **PQ8179.C369Z77 1997**
The Mystic of Tunja: The Writings of Madre Castillo, 1671-1742. Cloth Text. University of Massachusetts Press. Amherst, MA. 1997. 320p. ISBN:1-55849-074-4, ISBN13: 978-1-55849-074-1. Dewey:861. LCCN:96-040881.
Audience: **u,f.** *Choice, 1998.*

Morgan, Ronald J. **BX4659.L3M67 2002**
Spanish American Saints and the Rhetoric of Identity, 1600-1810. Trade Cloth. University of Arizona Press. Tucson, AZ. 2002. 250p. ISBN:0-8165-2140-9, ISBN13: 978-0-8165-2140-1. Dewey:282/.092/28. LCCN:2001-005284.
Audience: **u,f.**

Peterson, Jeanette F. **ND2646.M34P47 1993**
The Paradise Garden Murals of Malinalco: Utopia and Empire in Sixteenth-Century Mexico. Trade Cloth. University of Texas Press. Austin, TX. 1993. 246p. ISBN:0-292-72750-X, ISBN13: 978-0-292-72750-2. Dewey:751.7/3/097252. LCCN:92-007992.
Audience: **u,f.**

Poole, Stafford **BT660.G8**
Our Lady of Guadalupe: The Origins and Sources of a Mexican National Symbol, 1531-1797. Trade Paper. University of Arizona Press. Tucson, AZ. 1996. 325p. ISBN:0-8165-1623-5, ISBN13: 978-0-8165-1623-0. Dewey:232.9/17/097253. LCCN:94-018724.
Audience: **l,u,f.** *Choice, 1995.*

Rabasa, Jose **E123**
Inventing America: Spanish Historiography and the Formation of Eurocentrism. Trade Paper. University of Oklahoma Press. Norman, OK. 1994. 296p. Project for Discourse and Theory Ser., Vol. 11 ISBN:0-8061-2539-X, ISBN13: 978-0-8061-2539-8. Dewey:970.016. LCCN:92-034510.
Audience: **u,f.**

Salles-Reese, Verónica **GR133.T57S35 1997**
From Viracocha to the Virgin of Copacabana: Representation of the Sacred at Lake Titicaca. Trade Cloth. University of Texas Press. Austin, TX. 1997. 220p. ISBN:0-292-77712-4, ISBN13: 978-0-292-77712-5. Dewey:200/.984/12. LCCN:96-021683.
Audience: **u,f.** *Choice, 1997.*

Seed, Patricia **HQ728.S37 1988**
To Love, Honor, and Obey in Colonial Mexico: Conflicts over Marriage Choice, 1574-1821. Trade Cloth. Stanford University Press. Palo Alto, CA. 1988. 333p. ISBN:0-8047-1457-6, ISBN13: 978-0-8047-1457-0. Dewey:306.8/1/097252/0903. LCCN:88-002374.
Audience: **u,f.**

Sigal, Pete **F1435.3.R3S54 2000**
From Moon Goddesses to Virgins: The Colonization of Yucatecan Maya Sexual Desire. Trade Paper. University of Texas Press. Austin, TX. 2000. 344p. ISBN:0-292-77753-1, ISBN13: 978-0-292-77753-8. Dewey:306.7/089/974152. LCCN:00-023488.
Audience: **u,f.** *Choice, 2001.*

Silverblatt, Irene Marsha **F3429.3.S6S55 1987**
Moon, Sun and Witches: Gender Ideologies and Class in Inca and Colonial Peru. Trade Paper. Princeton University Press. Princeton, NJ. 1987. 302p. ISBN:0-691-02258-5, ISBN13: 978-0-691-02258-1. Dewey:985/.01/088042. LCCN:86-022514.
Audience: **u,f.** *Choice, 1987.*

Souza, Laura de Mello e **BF1584.B7S6813 2003**
The Devil and the Land of the Holy Cross: Witchcraft, Slavery, and Popular Religion in Colonial Brazil. Diane Grosklaus Whitty (Translator). Trade Cloth. University of Texas Press. Austin, TX. 2004. 374p. LLILAS Translations from Latin America Ser. ISBN:0-292-70228-0, ISBN13: 978-0-292-70228-8. Dewey:133.4/0981. LCCN:2003-059904.
Audience: **u,f.**

Sweet, James H. **F2659.N4S94 2003**
Recreating Africa: Kinship, Culture, and Religion in the African-Portuguese World, 1441-1770. Trade Cloth. University of North Carolina Press. Chapel Hill, NC. 2003. 336p. ISBN:0-8078-2808-4, ISBN13: 978-0-8078-2808-3. Dewey:981/.00496. LCCN:2003-001194.
Audience: **u,f.** *Choice, 2004.*

Taylor, William B. **BX1428.2.T38 1996**
Magistrates of the Sacred: Priests and Parishioners in Eighteenth-Century Mexico. Trade Cloth. Stanford University Press. Palo Alto, CA. 1996. 984p. ISBN:0-8047-2456-3, ISBN13: 978-0-8047-2456-2. Dewey:972/.02. LCCN:95-022982.
Audience: **u,f.**

Umberger, Emily and Tom Cummins, eds **N6502.2**
Artists and Patrons in Colonial Latin America. Arizona State University Press. 1995.
Audience: **u,f.**

Voekel, Pamela **BX1428.3.V64 2002**
Alone Before God: The Religious Origins of Modernity in Mexico. Trade Cloth. Duke University Press. Durham, NC. 2002. 352p. ISBN:0-8223-2927-1, ISBN13: 978-0-8223-2927-5. Dewey:282/.72. LCCN:2002-001654.
Audience: **u,f.**

Wood, Stephanie **F1221.N3**
Nahua Views of Spanish Colonial Mexico. University of Oklahoma Press. 2003. ISBN:0-8061-3486-0, ISBN13: 978-0-8061-3486-4.
Audience: **u,f.**

Latin America: General > Cultural History > 19th Century

Beezley, William H. **F1233**
Judas at the Jockey Club and Other Episodes of Porfirian Mexico. Ed. 2. Trade Cloth. University of Nebraska Press. Lincoln, NE. 2005. 183p. ISBN:0-8032-6217-5, ISBN13: 978-0-8032-6217-1. Dewey:972.08/14. LCCN:2004-268989.
Audience: **u,f.**

Beezley, William H. (Editor), et al. **GT4814.A2R57 1994**
Rituals of Rule, Rituals of Resistance: Public Celebrations and Popular Culture in Mexico. Cheryl E. Martin & William E. French (Editors). Book, Other. Rowman & Littlefield Publishers, Inc. Lanham, MD. 1994. 374p. Latin American Silhouettes Ser. ISBN:0-8420-2416-6, ISBN13: 978-0-8420-2416-7. Dewey:394.2/6972. LCCN:94-000884.
Audience: **u,f.**

Chasteen, John Charles & Castro-Klarén, Sara (Editors) **F1412.B49 2003**
Beyond Imagined Communities: Reading and Writing the Nation in Nineteenth-Century Latin America. Trade Cloth. Johns Hopkins University Press. Baltimore, MD. 2004. 280p. ISBN:0-8018-7852-7, ISBN13: 978-0-8018-7852-7. Dewey:320.54/098/09034. LCCN:2003-014646.
Audience: **u,f.**

Delpar, Helen **E183.8.M6**
The Enormous Vogue of Things Mexican: Cultural Relations Between the United States and Mexico, 1920-1935. Trade Paper. University of Alabama Press. Tuscaloosa, AL. 1995. 288p. ISBN:0-8173-0811-3, ISBN13: 978-0-8173-0811-7. Dewey:303.48273072. LCCN:92-006125.
Audience: **u,f.** *Choice, 1993.*

French, William E. **HN120.S6.F74 1996**
A Peaceful and Working People: Manners, Morals, and Class Formation in Northern Mexico. Trade Cloth. University of New Mexico Press. Albuquerque, NM. 1996. 263p. ISBN:0-8263-1683-2, ISBN13: 978-0-8263-1683-7. Dewey:305.5/0972/16. LCCN:95-032446.
Audience: **u,f.** *Choice, 1996.*

Garrett, David T. **F3429.1.C9G37 2005**
Shadows of Empire: The Indian Nobility of Cusco, 1750-1825. Alan Knight (Contribution by). Trade Cloth. Cambridge University Press. New York, NY. 2005. 326p. Cambridge Latin American Studies, Vol. 90 ISBN:0-521-84634-X, ISBN13: 978-0-521-84634-9. Dewey:985/37.00498323. LCCN:2005-000259.
Audience: **u,f.**

Gregory, Desmond **F1419.B75G74 1992**
Brute New World: The Rediscovery of Latin America in the Early 19th Century. Cloth over Boards. I. B. Tauris & Company, Ltd. London, 1993. 240p. ISBN:1-85043-567-7, ISBN13: 978-1-85043-567-9. Dewey:980/.00421. LCCN:93-148454.
Audience: **u,f.**

Jaksic, Ivan **PQ8549.B3 Z672 2001**
Andrés Bello: Scholarship and Nation-Building in Nineteenth-Century Latin America. Alan Knight (Contribution by). Trade Cloth. Cambridge University Press. New York, NY. 2001. 278p. Cambridge Latin American Studies, Vol. 87 ISBN:0-521-79195-2, ISBN13: 978-0-521-79195-3. Dewey:861/.5 B. LCCN:00-034273.
Audience: **u,f.** *Choice, 2002.*

Magaldi, Cristina **ML232.8.R5M34 2004**
Music in Imperial Rio de Janeiro: European Culture in a Tropical Milieu. Saddle Stitched, Cloth over Boards. Scarecrow Press, Inc. Lanham, MD. 2004. 187p. ISBN:0-8108-5025-7, ISBN13: 978-0-8108-5025-5. Dewey:780.9815309. LCCN:2004-004745.
Audience: **u,f.** *Choice, 2005.*

Nishida, Mieko **HT1129.S2N57 2003**
Slavery and Identity: Ethnicity, Gender, and Race in Salvador, Brazil, 1808-1888. Trade Cloth. Indiana University Press. Bloomington, IN. 2003. xiii, 255p. Blacks in the Diaspora Ser. ISBN:0-253-21581-1, ISBN13: 978-0-253-21581-9. Dewey:306.3/62/0981. LCCN:2002-010944.
Audience: **u,f.** *Choice, 2003.*

Pessar, Patricia R. (Translator) **BR675.P47 2004**
From Fanatics to Folk: Brazilian Millenarianism and Popular Culture. Trade Cloth, Pictures or Photographs. Duke University Press. Durham, NC. 2004. 296p. ISBN:0-8223-3275-2, ISBN13: 978-0-8223-3275-6. Dewey:209/.0981. LCCN:2003-015047.
Audience: **u,f.** *Choice, 2004.*

Reis, Joao Jose **GT3233.A2R4513 2003**
Death Is a Festival: Funeral Rites and Rebellion in Nineteenth-Century Brazil. H. Sabrina Gledhill (Translator). Trade Cloth. University of North Carolina Press. Chapel Hill, NC. 2003. 448p. Latin America in Translation Ser. ISBN:0-8078-2773-8, ISBN13: 978-0-8078-2773-4. Dewey:393.9/0981/09034. LCCN:2002-011996.
Audience: **u,f.** *Choice, 2004.*

Rugeley, Terry **BL2560.M6R84 2001**
Of Wonders and Wise Men: Religion and Popular Cultures in Southeast Mexico. Trade Paper. University of Texas Press. Austin, TX. 2001. 365p. ISBN:0-292-77107-X, ISBN13: 978-0-292-77107-9. Dewey:277.2/6081. LCCN:00-029909.
Audience: **u,f.**

Sommer, Doris **PQ7082.N7**
Foundational Fictions: The National Romances of Latin America. Trade Paper. University of California Press. Berkeley, CA. 1993. 434p. Latin American Literature and Culture Ser., No. 8 ISBN:0-520-08285-0, ISBN13: 978-0-520-08285-4. Dewey:863. LCCN:90-044240.
Audience: **u,f.**

Tenorio-Trillo, Mauricio **T395.5.M6T46 1996**
Mexico at the World's Fair: Crafting a Modern Nation. Trade Cloth. University of California Press. Berkeley, CA. 1996. 383p. The New Historicism Ser., Vol. 35:Studies in Cultural Poetics ISBN:0-520-20267-8, ISBN13: 978-0-520-20267-2. Dewey:306.4/6. LCCN:95-047068.
Audience: **u,f.** *Choice, 1997.*

Thurner, Mark **F3429.1.A45T58 1997**
From Two Republics to One Divided: Contradictions of Postcolonial Nationmaking in Andean Peru. Library Binding. Duke University Press. Durham, NC. 1997. 224p. Latin America Otherwise Ser. ISBN:0-8223-1805-9, ISBN13: 978-0-8223-1805-7. Dewey:985/.21. LCCN:96-007813.
Audience: **u,f.** *Choice, 1997.*

Vera, Eugenia Roldan **Z151.5**
The British Book Trade and Spanish American Independence: Education and Knowledge Transmission in Transcontinental Perspective. Trade Cloth. Ashgate Publishing Company. Williston, VT. 2003. 304p. ISBN:0-7546-3278-4, ISBN13: 978-0-7546-3278-8. Dewey:381/.45002/0973. LCCN:2003-040356.
Audience: **u,f.**

Walker, Charles **F3451.C9W35 1999**
Smoldering Ashes: Cuzco and the Creation of Republican Peru, 1780-1840. Trade Cloth. Duke University Press. Durham, NC. 1999. xiii, 330p. ISBN:0-8223-2261-7, ISBN13: 978-0-8223-2261-0. Dewey:985/.3704. LCCN:98-030624.
Audience: **u,f.** *Choice, 2000.*

Wasserman, Mark **F1232.W38 2000**
Everyday Life and Politics in Nineteenth Century Mexico: Men, Women, and War. Trade Cloth. University of New Mexico Press. Albuquerque, NM. 2004. 248p. Dialogos Ser. ISBN:0-8263-2170-4, ISBN13: 978-0-8263-2170-1. Dewey:972/.04. LCCN:99-006913.
Audience: **u,f.**

Widdifield, Stacie G. **ND254.W54 1996**
The Embodiment of the National: Politics, Race, and Gender in Late Nineteenth-Century Mexican Painting. Trade Cloth. University of Arizona Press. Tucson, AZ. 1996. 295p. ISBN:0-8165-1561-1, ISBN13: 978-0-8165-1561-5. Dewey:759.972/09/034. LCCN:96-004447.
Audience: **u,f.** *Choice, 1997.*

Zarur, Elizabeth Netto Calil & Lovell, Charles M. (Editors) **ND1432.M45A78 2001**
Art and Faith in Mexico: The Nineteenth-Century Retablo Tradition. Trade Cloth. University of New Mexico Press. Albuquerque, NM. 2004. 360p. ISBN:0-8263-2325-1, ISBN13: 978-0-8263-2325-5. Dewey:755/.2/097207478961. LCCN:00-011009.
Audience: **u,f.** *Choice, 2001.*

Latin America: General > Cultural History > 20th Century

Aching, Gerard **GT4223.A2A25 2002**
Masking and Power: Carnival and Popular Culture in the Caribbean. Trade Paper. University of Minnesota Press. Minneapolis, MN. 2002. 200p. Cultural Studies of the Americas, Vol. 8 ISBN:0-8166-4018-1, ISBN13: 978-0-8166-4018-8. Dewey:394.25/09729. LCCN:2002-005312.
Audience: **u,f.**

Aparicio, Frances R. **ML3535.5.A63 1998**
Listening to Salsa: Gender, Latin Popular Music, and Puerto Rican Cultures. Library Binding. Wesleyan University Press. Middletown, CT. 1998. 302p. Music Culture Ser. ISBN:0-8195-5306-9, ISBN13: 978-0-8195-5306-5. Dewey:781.64. LCCN:97-009121.
Audience: **u,f.** *Choice, 1998.*

Arbena, Joseph & LaFrance, David G. (Editors) **GV586.S64 2002**
Sport in Latin America and the Caribbean. Book, Other. Rowman & Littlefield Publishers, Inc. Lanham, MD. 2002. 241p. Jaguar Books on Latin America, No. 23 ISBN:0-8420-2821-8, ISBN13: 978-0-8420-2821-9. Dewey:796/.098. LCCN:2001-054270.
Audience: **l,u,f.**

Austerlitz, Paul **ML3465.A95 1997**
Merengue: Dominican Music and Dominican Identity. Robert F. Thompson (Foreword by). Trade Cloth. Temple University Press. Philadelphia, PA. 1997. 224p. ISBN:1-56639-483-X, ISBN13: 978-1-56639-483-3. Dewey:784.18/88. LCCN:96-024778.
Audience: **u,f.** *Choice, 1997.*

Baddeley, Oriana & Fraser, Valerie **N6502.5**
Drawing the Line: Art and Cultural Identity in Contemporary Latin America. Verso. 1989. ISBN:0-86091-953-6, ISBN13: 978-0-86091-953-7.
Audience: **u,f.**

Beezley, William H. & Curcio-Nagy, Linda (Editors) **F1408.3.L2743 2000**
Latin American Popular Culture: An Introduction. Book, Other. Rowman & Littlefield Publishers, Inc. Lanham, MD. 2000. 255p. ISBN:0-8420-2710-6, ISBN13: 978-0-8420-2710-6. Dewey:980. LCCN:00-029665.
Audience: **u,f.**

Benjamin, Thomas **F1234.B465 2000**
La Revolucion: Mexico's Great Revolution As Memory, Myth and History. Trade Paper. University of Texas Press. Austin, TX. 2000. 251p. ISBN:0-292-70882-3, ISBN13: 978-0-292-70882-2. Dewey:972.08/16. LCCN:99-046431.
Audience: **u,f.** *Choice, 2000.*

Brandes, Stanley **GT4814.T95B7 1988**
Power and Persuasion: Fiestas and Social Control in Rural Mexico. Trade Cloth. University of Pennsylvania Press. Philadelphia, PA. 1988. 224p. ISBN:0-8122-8077-6, ISBN13: 978-0-8122-8077-7. Dewey:394.2/6972/37. LCCN:87-019205.
Audience: **u,f.** *Choice, 1988.*

Burian, Edward R. (Editor) **NA755.M655 1997**
Modernity and the Architecture of Mexico. Ricardo Legorreta (Foreword by). Trade Cloth. University of Texas Press. Austin, TX. 1997. 232p. ISBN:0-292-70852-1, ISBN13: 978-0-292-70852-5. Dewey:720/.972. LCCN:96-002758.
Audience: **u,f.**

Campbell, Bruce **ND2644.C36 2003**
Mexican Murals in Times of Crisis. Trade Cloth. University of Arizona Press. Tucson, AZ. 2003. 250p. ISBN:0-8165-2239-1, ISBN13: 978-0-8165-2239-2. Dewey:751.7/3/0972. LCCN:2002-010528.
Audience: **u,f.**

Castro, Donald S. **GV1796.T3A74 1991**
The Argentine Tango as Social History, 1880-1955: The Soul of the People. Trade Cloth. Edwin Mellen Press, The. Lewiston, NY. 1991. 274p. Latin American Studies, Vol. 3 ISBN:0-7734-9923-7, ISBN13: 978-0-7734-9923-2. Dewey:793.3/1982. LCCN:90-020558.
Audience: **u,f.**

Chasteen, John Charles **GV1626.C47 2004**
National Rhythms, African Roots: The Deep History of Latin American Popular Dance. Trade Cloth. University of New Mexico Press. Albuquerque, NM. 2004. 257p. Dialogos Ser. ISBN:0-8263-2940-3, ISBN13: 978-0-8263-2940-0. Dewey:792.8/098. LCCN:2003-019742.
Audience: **u,f.** *Choice, 2004.*

Craven, David **N6502.C735 2002**
Art and Revolution in Latin America, 1910-1990. Cloth over Boards. Yale University Press. Cumberland, RI. 2002. 240p. ISBN:0-300-08211-8, ISBN13: 978-0-300-08211-1. Dewey:709/.8/0904. LCCN:2001-006900.
Audience: **g,l,u,f.**

DaMatta, Roberto **GT4233.A2**
Carnivals, Rogues, and Heroes: An Interpretation of the Brazilian Dilemma. John Drury (Translator). Paper Text. University of Notre Dame Press. Notre Dame, IN. 1992. xii, 279p. From the Helen Kellogg Institute for International Studies Ser. ISBN:0-268-00794-2, ISBN13: 978-0-268-00794-2. Dewey:394.2/5/0981. LCCN:90-070861.
Audience: **u,f.** *Choice, 1992.*

Delgado, Celeste F. & Munoz, Jose E. (Editors) **GV1626.E84 1997**
Everynight Life: Culture and Dance in Latino America. Library Binding. Duke University Press. Durham, NC. 1997. 368p. Latin America Otherwise Ser. ISBN:0-8223-1926-8, ISBN13: 978-0-8223-1926-9. Dewey:792.8/098. LCCN:96-043796.
Audience: **u,f.** *Choice, 1998.*

Dennison, Stephanie & Shaw, Lisa **PN1993.5.B6**
Popular Cinema in Brazil: 1930-2001. Cloth over Boards. Manchester University Press. Manchester, 2004. 288p. ISBN:0-7190-6498-8, ISBN13: 978-0-7190-6498-2. Dewey:791.43/0981. LCCN:2005-295547.
Audience: **u,f.** *Choice, 2005.*

Dunn, Christopher **ML3487.B7D86 2001**
Brutality Garden: Tropicalia and the Emergence of a Brazilian Counterculture. Trade Cloth. University of North Carolina Press. Chapel Hill, NC. 2001. 276p. ISBN:0-8078-2651-0, ISBN13: 978-0-8078-2651-5. Dewey:306.4/84. LCCN:2001-035148.
Audience: **u,f.** *Choice, 2002.*

Echevarria, Roberto Gonzalez **GV863.25.A1**
The Pride of Havana: A History of Cuban Baseball. Trade Paper. DIANE Publishing Company. Collingdale, PA. 2004. 464p. ISBN:0-7567-7115-3, ISBN13: 978-0-7567-7115-7. Dewey:796.357/097291.
Audience: **g,l,u,f.** *Choice, 2000.*

Galinsky, Philip **ML3487.B78R43 2002**
Maracatu Atomico: Traditional Modernity and Postmodernity in the Mangue Movement and the New Music Scene of Recife Pernambuco, Brazil. Paper over Boards. Routledge. New York, NY. 2002. 248p. Current Research in Ethnomusicology Ser., Vol. 3 ISBN:0-415-94022-2, ISBN13: 978-0-415-94022-1. Dewey:781.64/0981/34. LCCN:2002-002501.
Audience: **u,f.**

García Canclini, Néstor **HD2346.M4**
Transforming Modernity: Popular Culture in Mexico. Lidia Lozano (Translator). Trade Cloth. University of Texas Press. Austin, TX. 1993. 144p. Translations from Latin America Ser. ISBN:0-292-72758-5, ISBN13: 978-0-292-72758-8. Dewey:338.6/425/0972. LCCN:92-047426.
Audience: **u,f.**

Gordillo, Gaston R. **F2823.T7G67 2004**
Landscapes of Devils: Tensions of Place and Memory in the Argentinean Chaco. Trade Cloth. Duke University Press. Durham, NC. 2004. 312p. ISBN:0-8223-3380-5, ISBN13: 978-0-8223-3380-7. Dewey:304.2/089/987. LCCN:2004-015806.
Audience: **u,f.** *Choice, 2005.*

Guss, David M. **HN363.5.G87 2000**
The Festive State: Race, Ethnicity and Nationalism as Cultural Performance. Trade Paper. University of California Press. Berkeley, CA. 2001. 254p. ISBN:0-520-22331-4, ISBN13: 978-0-520-22331-8. Dewey:306/.0987. LCCN:99-056890.
Audience: **u,f.** *Choice, 2001.*

Hayes, Joy Elizabeth **PN1991.3.M4H59 2000**
Radio Nation: Communication, Popular Culture and Nationalism in Mexico, 1920-1950. Trade Cloth. University of Arizona Press. Tucson, AZ. 2000. 154p. ISBN:0-8165-1852-1, ISBN13: 978-0-8165-1852-4. Dewey:384.54/0972. LCCN:00-008113.
Audience: **u,f.**

Hedrick, Tace **NX501.5**
Mestizo Modernism: Race, Nation and Identity in Latin American Culture, 1900-1940. Rutgers University Press. 2003. ISBN:0-8135-3216-7, ISBN13: 978-0-8135-3216-5.
Audience: **u,f.**

Hendrickson, Carol **F1465.2.C3H46 1995**
Weaving Identities: Construction of Dress and Self in a Highland Guatemala Town. Trade Paper. University of Texas Press. Austin, TX. 1995. 261p. ISBN:0-292-73100-0, ISBN13: 978-0-292-73100-4. Dewey:391/.0089/974. LCCN:95-007296.
Audience: **u,f.** *Choice, 1996.*

Masiello, Francine **PQ7551.M37 2001**
The Art of Transition: Latin American Culture and the Neoliberal Crisis. Trade Cloth. Duke University Press. Durham, NC. 2001. 352p. Latin America Otherwise Ser. ISBN:0-8223-2806-2, ISBN13: 978-0-8223-2806-3. Dewey:860.9/98. LCCN:2001-040217.
Audience: **u,f.** *Choice, 2002.*

McCann, Bryan **ML3487.B7M39 2004**
Hello, Hello Brazil: Popular Music in the Making of Modern Brazil. Trade Cloth, Pictures or Photographs. Duke University Press. Durham, NC. 2004. 312p. ISBN:0-8223-3284-1, ISBN13: 978-0-8223-3284-8. Dewey:781.64/0981. LCCN:2003-024989.
Audience: **u,f.** *Choice, 2004.*

Miller, Marilyn Grace **F1414.M545 2004**
Rise and Fall of the Cosmic Race: The Cult of Mestizaje in Latin America. Trade Cloth. University of Texas Press. Austin, TX. 2004. 216p. ISBN:0-292-70572-7, ISBN13: 978-0-292-70572-2. Dewey:980.03/3. LCCN:2004-002952.
Audience: **u,f.**

Moore, Robin D. **ML3486.C8M66 1997**
Nationalizing Blackness: Afrourbanismo and Artistic Revolution in Havana, 1920-1940. Trade Cloth. University of Pittsburgh Press. Pittsburgh, PA. 1997. 336p. Pitt Latin American Ser. ISBN:0-8229-4040-X, ISBN13: 978-0-8229-4040-1. Dewey:781.63/089/9607291. LCCN:97-021045.
Audience: **u,f.** *Choice, 1998.*

Pacini-Hernandez, Deborah **ML3486.D65P3 1995**
Bachata: Social History of a Dominican Popular Music. Paper Text. Temple University Press. Philadelphia, PA. 1995. 288p. ISBN:1-56639-300-0, ISBN13: 978-1-56639-300-3. Dewey:781.64/097293. LCCN:94-029477.
Audience: **u,f.**

Pilcher, Jeffrey M. **TX716.M4P54 1998**
Que Vivan los Tamales!: Food and the Making of Mexican Identity. Trade Paper. University of New Mexico Press. Albuquerque, NM. 1998. 253p. Dialogos Ser. ISBN:0-8263-1873-8, ISBN13: 978-0-8263-1873-2. Dewey:394.1/0972. LCCN:97-046508.
Audience: **l,u,f.** *Choice, 1998.*

Remedi, Gustavo **GT4240.A2R45 2003**
Carnival Theater: Uruguay's Popular Performers and National Culture. Trade Paper. University of Minnesota Press. Minneapolis, MN. 2003. 312p. Cultural Studies of the Americas, Vol. 15 ISBN:0-8166-3455-6, ISBN13: 978-0-8166-3455-2. Dewey:394.25/09895. LCCN:2003-014542.
Audience: **u,f.**

Roman-Velazquez, Patria **DA676.9.L38R66 1999**
The Making of Latin London: Salsa Music, Place and Identity. Trade Cloth. Ashgate Publishing, Ltd. Aldershot, 1999. vii, 167p. ISBN:1-84014-881-0, ISBN13: 978-1-84014-881-7. Dewey:942.1/00468. LCCN:99-072849.
Audience: **u,f.**

Rubenstein, Anne **PN6790.M48R83 1998**
Bad Language, Naked Ladies and Other Threats to the Nation: A Political History of Comic Books in Mexico. Trade Cloth. Duke University Press. Durham, NC. 1998. 208p. ISBN:0-8223-2108-4, ISBN13: 978-0-8223-2108-8. Dewey:741.5/972. LCCN:98-007517.
Audience: **u,f.** *Choice, 1999.*

Ruck, Rob **GV863.29.A1D657 1999**
The Tropic of Baseball: Baseball in the Dominican Republic. Ed. 2. Trade Cloth. University of Nebraska Press. Lincoln, NE. 1999. 217p. ISBN:0-8032-8978-2, ISBN13: 978-0-8032-8978-9. Dewey:796.357/097293. LCCN:98-045479.
Audience: **g,l,u,f.** *Choice, 1991.*

Salman, Ton (Editor) **F1408.3.L43 1996**
Legacy of the Disinherited: Popular Culture in Latin America: Modernity, Globalisation, Hybridity and Authenticity. Trade Paper. Purdue University Press. West Lafayette, IN. 2003. 278p. ISBN:90-70280-46-9, ISBN13: 978-90-70280-46-8. Dewey:306/.098. LCCN:96-206041.
Audience: **u,f.**

Shaw, Lisa **ML3417.S53 1999**
The Social History of the Brazilian Samba. Trade Cloth. Ashgate Publishing, Ltd. Aldershot, 1999. 211p. Studies in Ethnomusicology ISBN:1-84014-289-8, ISBN13: 978-1-84014-289-1. Dewey:784.18/88. LCCN:98-036992.
Audience: **u,f.** *Choice, 1999.*

Trexler, Richard C. **PN3299.M6T74 2003**
Reliving Golgotha: The Passion Play of Iztapalapa. Trade Cloth. Harvard University Press. Cambridge, MA. 2003. 302p. ISBN:0-674-01064-7, ISBN13: 978-0-674-01064-2. Dewey:792.1/6. LCCN:2002-032743.
Audience: **u,f.**

Waxer, Lise **ML3918.S26W38 2002**
The City of Musical Memory: Salsa, Record Grooves, and Popular Culture in Cali, Colombia. Library Binding. University Press of New England. Lebanon, NH. 2002. 416p. Music Culture Ser. ISBN:0-8195-6441-9, ISBN13: 978-0-8195-6441-2. Dewey:781.64. LCCN:2002-066162.
Audience: **u,f.**

Waxer, Lise (Editor) **ML3535.5.W39 2002**
Situating Salsa: Global Markets and Local Meanings in Latin American Popular Music. Paper over Boards. Routledge. New York, NY. 2002. 336p. Perspectives in Global Pop Ser. ISBN:0-8153-4019-2, ISBN13: 978-0-8153-4019-5. Dewey:781.64. LCCN:2001-043113.
Audience: **u,f.**

Zolov, Eric **F1235.Z65 1999**
Refried Elvis: The Rise of the Mexican Counterculture. Trade Paper. University of California Press. Berkeley, CA. 1999. 364p. ISBN:0-520-21514-1, ISBN13: 978-0-520-21514-6. Dewey:972.08/3. LCCN:98-007968.
Audience: **u,f.** *Choice, 2000.*

Latin America: General > Environmental History

QH541.5.R27
Fate of the Rain Forest, Classroom Set. Trade Cloth. Prentice Hall PTR. Upper Saddle River, NJ. 2002. ISBN:0-13-433621-6, ISBN13: 978-0-13-433621-3. Dewey:372.35.
Audience: **g,l,u.**

Barry, Deborah (Editor), et al. **SD569.C66 2005**
The Community Forests of Mexico: Managing for Sustainable Landscapes. David Barton Bray & Leticia Merino-Pérez (Editors). Trade Cloth. University of Texas Press. Austin, TX. 2005. 390p. ISBN:0-292-70637-5, ISBN13: 978-0-292-70637-8. Dewey:333.75/0972. LCCN:2004-022777.
Audience: **u,f.**

Benson, Elizabeth P. **E59.A7B46 1997**
Birds and Beasts of Ancient Latin America. Trade Cloth. University Press of Florida. Gainesville, FL. 1997. 184p. ISBN:0-8130-1518-9, ISBN13: 978-0-8130-1518-7. Dewey:398.24/52/098. LCCN:97-002976.
Audience: **l,u,f.** *Choice, 1998.*

Cole Christensen, Darryl **HD350.C68C65 1997**
A Place in the Rain Forest: Settling the Costa Rican Frontier. Trade Cloth. University of Texas Press. Austin, TX. 1997. 253p. ISBN:0-292-71190-5, ISBN13: 978-0-292-71190-7. Dewey:333.3/172867. LCCN:96-032321.
Audience: **u,f.**

Collinson, Helen **GE195.L29**
Green Guerrillas: Environmental Conflicts and Intiatives in Latin America and the Caribbean. Trade Cloth. Black Rose Books. Montreal, PQ. 1997. 249p. ISBN:1-55164-067-8, ISBN13: 978-1-55164-067-9. Dewey:333.7097. LCCN:96-079516.
Audience: **u,f.**

Crosby, Alfred W. **E98**
The Columbian Exchange: Biological and Cultural Consequences of 1492. Ed. 30. Trade Cloth. Greenwood Publishing Group, Inc. Portsmouth, NH. 2003. 320p. ISBN:0-275-98073-1, ISBN13: 978-0-275-98073-3. Dewey:614.4/97. LCCN:2003-042858.
Audience: **u,f.**

Dean, Warren **SB291.H4 D43 1987**
Brazil and the Struggle for Rubber: A Study in Environmental History. Alfred W. Crosby & Donald Worster (Contribution by). Trade Cloth. Cambridge University Press. New York, NY. 1987. 256p. Studies in Environment and History ISBN:0-521-33477-2, ISBN13: 978-0-521-33477-8. Dewey:338.1/738952/0981. LCCN:87-005130.
Audience: **u,f.** *Choice, 1988.*

Dean, Warren **SD418.3.B6**
With Broadax and Firebrand: The Destruction of the Brazilian Atlantic Forest. Stuart B. Schwartz (Foreword by). Trade Paper. University of California Press. Berkeley, CA. 1997. 502p. ISBN:0-520-20886-2, ISBN13: 978-0-520-20886-5. Dewey:304.2/8/098109152. LCCN:94-005681.
Audience: **u,f.** *Choice, 1995.*

Diaz-Briquets, Sergio & Perez-Lopez, Jorge **GE160.C9D53 1999**
Conquering Nature: The Environmental Legacy of Socialism in Cuba. Cloth Text. University of Pittsburgh Press. Pittsburgh, PA. 2000. xiii, 328p. Pitt Latin American Ser. ISBN:0-8229-4118-X, ISBN13: 978-0-8229-4118-7. Dewey:363.7/02/097291. LCCN:99-050680.
Audience: **u,f.** *Choice, 2000.*

Evans, Sterling **QH77.C8E935 1999**
The Green Republic: A Conservation History of Costa Rica. Trade Cloth. University of Texas Press. Austin, TX. 1999. 335p. ISBN:0-292-72100-5, ISBN13: 978-0-292-72100-5. Dewey:333.7/2/097286. LCCN:98-025495.
Audience: **l,u,f.**

Faber, Daniel **HC141.Z9.E54 1993**
Environment under Fire: Imperialism and the Ecological Crisis in Central America. Trade Cloth. Monthly Review Press. New York, NY. 1992. 320p. ISBN:0-85345-839-1, ISBN13: 978-0-85345-839-5. Dewey:363.5/06/098. LCCN:92-041825.
Audience: **u,f.** *Choice, 1993.*

Foresta, Ronald A. **QH77.A53F67 1991**
Amazon Conservation in the Age of Development: The Limits of Providence. Trade Cloth. University Press of Florida. Gainesville, FL. 1991. 376p. ISBN:0-8130-1092-6, ISBN13: 978-0-8130-1092-2. Dewey:333.7/2/09811. LCCN:91-000094.
Audience: **u,f.** *Choice, 1992.*

Gade, Daniel W. **F2230.1.B7G33 1999**
Nature and Culture in the Andes. Trade Cloth. University of Wisconsin Press. Chicago, IL. 1999. 312p. ISBN:0-299-16124-2, ISBN13: 978-0-299-16124-8. Dewey:581.6/3/098. LCCN:98-049023.
Audience: **l,u,f.**

Gehlbach, Frederick R. **QH104.5.S6**
Mountain Islands and Desert Seas: A Natural History of the U.S.-Mexican Borderlands. Trade Paper. Texas A&M University Press. College Station, TX. 1993. 340p. Louise Lindsey Merrick Natural Environment Ser., No. 15 ISBN:0-89096-566-8, ISBN13: 978-0-89096-566-5. Dewey:508.78. LCCN:81-040402.
Audience: **l,u,f.**

Hecht, Susanna B. & Cockburn, Alexander **SD418.3.A53H43 1989**
The Fate of the Forest: Developers, Destroyers and Defenders of the Amazon. Trade Cloth. Analytical Psychology Club of San Francisco, Inc. San Francisco, CA. 1989. 224p. ISBN:0-86091-261-2, ISBN13: 978-0-86091-261-3. Dewey:333.75/0981/1. LCCN:89-039145.
Audience: **u,f.**

Heyck, Denis Lynn Daly **HF1480.5.H49 2002**
Surviving Globalization in Three Latin American Communities. Trade Paper. Broadview Press. Peterborough, ON. 2002. 299p. ISBN:1-55111-477-1, ISBN13: 978-1-55111-477-4. Dewey:330.98. LCCN:2002-489833.
Audience: **u,f.** *Choice, 2003.*

Kiy, Richard & Wirth, John D. (Editors) **GE320.N7E58 1998**
Environmental Management on North America's Borders. Trade Cloth. Texas A&M University Press. College Station, TX. 1998. 320p. Environmental History Ser., No. 14 ISBN:0-89096-832-2, ISBN13: 978-0-89096-832-1. Dewey:363.7/056/097. LCCN:98-008291.
Audience: **u,f.** *Choice, 1999.*

Lindsay-Poland, John **E183.8.P2L475 2003**
Emperors in the Jungle: The Hidden History of the U. S. in Panama. Guillermo Castro (Afterword by). Trade Cloth. Duke University Press. Durham, NC. 2003. 256p. American Encounters/Global Interactions Ser. ISBN:0-8223-3100-4, ISBN13: 978-0-8223-3100-1. Dewey:327.7307287/09. LCCN:2002-013820.
Audience: **u,f.** *Choice, 2003.*

Longoria, Arturo **QH107.L675 2000**
Keepers of the Wilderness. Trade Cloth. Texas A&M University Press. College Station, TX. 2004. 128p. Environmental History Ser., Vol. 15 ISBN:0-89096-929-9, ISBN13: 978-0-89096-929-8. Dewey:508.72/12. LCCN:99-053326.
Audience: **l,u,f.**

Maranon, Jon **CT588.M37A3 2001**
The Gringo's Hawk. Trade Cloth, Box or Slipcased. Kenneth Group, The. Eugene, OR. 2001. 320p. ISBN:0-9677787-0-0, ISBN13: 978-0-9677787-0-9. Dewey:333.75/09728. LCCN:99-091873.
Audience: **u,f.**

McCook, Stuart George **S477.A1M33 2002**
States of Nature: Science, Agriculture, and Environment in the Spanish Caribbean, 1760-1940. Trade Cloth. University of Texas Press. Austin, TX. 2002. 216p. ISBN:0-292-75256-3, ISBN13: 978-0-292-75256-6. Dewey:630/.9729. LCCN:2001-052228.
Audience: **u,f.** *Choice, 2002.*

Melville, Elinor G. K. **SF375.5.M6 M45 1994**
A Plague of Sheep: Environmental Consequences of the Conquest of Mexico. Alfred W. Crosby & Donald Worster (Contribution by). Trade Paper. Cambridge University Press. New York, NY. 1997. 219p. Studies in Environment and History Ser. ISBN:0-521-57448-X, ISBN13: 978-0-521-57448-8. Dewey:304.2/7/097246/09031.
Audience: **u,f.**

Miller, Shawn William **SD159.M56 2000**
Fruitless Trees: Portuguese Conservation and Brazil's Colonial Timber. Trade Cloth. Stanford University Press. Palo Alto, CA. 2000. xiii, 325p. ISBN:0-8047-3396-1, ISBN13: 978-0-8047-3396-0. Dewey:338.1/749/0981. LCCN:99-033182.
Audience: **u,f.** *Choice, 2000.*

Murray, Douglas L. **SB950.3.L29M87 1994**
Cultivating Crisis: The Human Cost of Pesticides in Latin America. Ed. 3. Trade Cloth. University of Texas Press. Austin, TX. 1994. 191p. ISBN:0-292-75168-0, ISBN13: 978-0-292-75168-2. Dewey:363.17/92/098. LCCN:94-014278.
Audience: **u,f.** *Choice, 1995.*

Painter, Michael & Durham, William H. (Editors) **GE160.L29S63 1995**
The Social Causes of Environmental Destruction in Latin America. Trade Paper. University of Michigan Press. Chicago, IL. 1995. 288p. Linking Levels of Analysis Ser. ISBN:0-472-06560-2, ISBN13: 978-0-472-06560-8. Dewey:363.7/01/098. LCCN:94-034146.
Audience: **u,f.**

Place, Susan E. (Editor), et al. **SD153.T76 1993**
Tropical Rainforests: Latin American Nature and Society in Transition. William H. Beezley & Colin MacLachlan (Editors). Trade Cloth. Rowman & Littlefield Publishers, Inc. Lanham, MD. 1993. 222p. Jaguar Books on Latin America, No. 2 ISBN:0-8420-2423-9, ISBN13: 978-0-8420-2423-5. Dewey:333.75/16/098. LCCN:93-004335.
Audience: **l,u,f.**

Radding, Cynthia R. **GN560.M6R33 1997**
Wandering Peoples: Colonialism, Ethnic Spaces, and Ecological Frontiers in Northwestern Mexico, 1700-1850. Library Binding. Duke University Press. Durham, NC. 1997. 368p. Latin America Otherwise Ser. ISBN:0-8223-1907-1, ISBN13: 978-0-8223-1907-8. Dewey:305.8/0097217. LCCN:96-035147.
Audience: **u,f.** *Choice, 1997.*

Raffles, Hugh **GN564.B6R34 2002**
In Amazonia: A Natural History. Trade Cloth. Princeton University Press. Princeton, NJ. 2002. 288p. ISBN:0-691-04884-3, ISBN13: 978-0-691-04884-0. Dewey:306/.09811. LCCN:2002-016909.
Audience: **l,u,f.** *Choice, 2003.*

Rival, Laura M. **F3722.1.H83R58 2002**
Trekking Through History: The Huaorani of Amazonian Ecuador. Trade Cloth. Columbia University Press. New York, NY. 2004. 256p. The Historical Ecology Ser.

ISBN:0-231-11844-9, ISBN13: 978-0-231-11844-6. Dewey:986.6/00498. LCCN:2001-042394.
Audience: **u,f.** *Choice, 2003.*

Roberts, J. Timmons & Thanos, Nikki Demetria **GE160.L29**
Trouble in Paradise: Globalization and Environmental Crises in Latin America. Paper over Boards. Routledge. New York, NY. 2003. 304p. ISBN:0-415-92979-2, ISBN13: 978-0-415-92979-0. Dewey:338.98/07. LCCN:2003-011577.
Audience: **u,f.**

Simon, Joel **GE160.M6S55 1997**
Endangered Mexico: An Environment on the Edge. Trade Cloth. Sierra Club Books. San Francisco, CA. 1997. 304p. ISBN:0-87156-351-7, ISBN13: 978-0-87156-351-4. Dewey:363.7/00972. LCCN:96-043720.
Audience: **u,f.** *Choice, 1997.*

Simonian, Lane **S934.M6S55 1995**
Defending the Land of the Jaguar: A History of Conservation in Mexico. Trade Cloth. University of Texas Press. Austin, TX. 1995. 342p. ISBN:0-292-77690-X, ISBN13: 978-0-292-77690-6. Dewey:333.72/0972. LCCN:95-001487.
Audience: **l,u,f.** *Choice, 1996.*

Soluri, John **HD9259.B3H678 2005**
Banana Cultures: Agriculture, Consumption, and Environmental Change in Honduras and the United States. Trade Cloth. University of Texas Press. Austin, TX. 2006. 337p. ISBN:0-292-70957-9, ISBN13: 978-0-292-70957-7. Dewey:306.3/49/097283. LCCN:2005-015808.
Audience: **u,f.**

Steen, Harold K. & Tucker, Richard P. (Editors) **SD247**
Changing Tropical Forests: Historical Perspectives on Today's Challenges in Central and South America. Trade Cloth. Forest History Society, Inc. Durham, NC. 1992. 303p. ISBN:0-8223-1236-0, ISBN13: 978-0-8223-1236-9. Dewey:634.9.
Audience: **u,f.**

Super, John C. **HD9014.L32S87 1988**
Food, Conquest and Colonization in Sixteenth-Century Spanish America. Trade Cloth. University of New Mexico Press. Albuquerque, NM. 1988. 143p. ISBN:0-8263-1049-4, ISBN13: 978-0-8263-1049-1. Dewey:338.1/9/8. LCCN:87-035767.
Audience: **u,f.** *Choice, 1989.*

Townsend, Janet G. **HQ1240.5.S63T68 1995**
Women's Voices from the Rainforest. Paper over Boards. Routledge. New York, NY. 1995. 224p. International Studies of Women and Places ISBN:0-415-10531-5, ISBN13: 978-0-415-10531-6. Dewey:305.42/098. LCCN:94-012466.
Audience: **u,f.** *Choice, 1995.*

Wallace, David Rains **SB484.C8W35 1992**
The Quetzal and the Macaw: The Story of Costa Rica's National Parks. Trade Cloth. Sierra Club Books. San Francisco, CA. 1992. 232p. ISBN:0-87156-585-4, ISBN13: 978-0-87156-585-3. Dewey:333.78/097286. LCCN:91-030500.
Audience: **l,u,f.** *Choice, 1992.*

Ward, Evan R. **TD225.C665W35 2003**
Border Oasis: Water and the Political Ecology of the Colorado River Delta, 1940-1975. Trade Cloth. University of Arizona Press. Tucson, AZ. 2003. 230p. Environmental History of the Borderlands Ser. ISBN:0-8165-2223-5, ISBN13: 978-0-8165-2223-1. Dewey:333.91/009791/3. LCCN:2002-010960.
Audience: **u,f.**

Webster, Fred & Webster, Marie S. **QH77.M6W43 2001**
The Road to el Cielo: Mexico's Forest in the Clouds. Nancy McGowan (Illustrator), Paul S. Martin (Foreword by). Trade Cloth. University of Texas Press. Austin, TX. 2002. 311p. Treasures of Nature Ser. ISBN:0-292-79140-2, ISBN13: 978-0-292-79140-4. Dewey:508.72/12. LCCN:2001-027792.
Audience: **u,f.**

Weinberg, Bill **HC141.Z9E59 1991**
War on the Land: Ecology and Politics in Central America. Trade Paper. Zed Books, Ltd. London, 1991. 224p. ISBN:0-86232-947-7, ISBN13: 978-0-86232-947-1. Dewey:363.7/056/09728. LCCN:91-013782.
Audience: **u,f.** *Choice, 1992.*

Weinstein, Barbara **HD9161.B82 W44 1983**
The Amazon Rubber Boom, 1850-1920. Trade Cloth. Stanford University Press. Palo Alto, CA. 1983. 376p. ISBN:0-8047-1168-2, ISBN13: 978-0-8047-1168-5. Dewey:338.1/738952/0981. LCCN:82-080926.
Audience: **u,f.**

Weisman, Alan **GE160.C7**
Gaviotas: A Village to Reinvent the World. Trade Paper. Chelsea Green Publishing. White River Junction, VT. 2004. 240p. Helen and Scott Nearing Titles Ser. ISBN:1-890132-28-4, ISBN13: 978-1-890132-28-6. Dewey:918.61.
Audience: **u,f.**

Wright, Angus **RC965.A5W75 2006**
The Death of Ramon Gonzalez: The Modern Agricultural Dilemma. Ed. 2. Trade Paper, Perfect. University of Texas Press. Austin, TX. 2005. 416p. ISBN:0-292-71268-5, ISBN13: 978-0-292-71268-3. Dewey:363.17/92/0972. LCCN:2005-009131.
Audience: **u,f.**

Wright, Angus & Wolford, Wendy **HD1333.B6W74 2003**
To Inherit the Earth: Brazil's Landless People and the Struggle to Transform a Nation. Trade Paper. Institute for Food & Development Policy/Food First Books. Oakland, CA. 2003. 400p. ISBN:0-935028-90-0, ISBN13: 978-0-935028-90-4. Dewey:333.3/181. LCCN:2003-014764.
Audience: **u,f.** *Choice, 2004.*

Latin America: General > History of Popular Culture

Schechter, John Mendell **ML199.M86 1999**
Music in Latin American Culture: Regional Traditions. Cloth Text. Thomson Wadsworth. Belmont, CA. 1999. 512p. ISBN:0-02-864750-5, ISBN13: 978-0-02-864750-0. Dewey:780/.98. LCCN:99-013859.
Audience: **g,l,u,f.** *Choice, 1999.*

Latin America: General > History of Popular Culture > Food

Bauer, Arnold J. **HC130.C6 B38 2001**
Goods, Power, History: Latin America's Material Culture. Stuart Schwartz (Contribution by). Trade Cloth. Cambridge University Press. New York, NY. 2001. 266p. New Approaches to the Americas Ser. ISBN:0-521-77208-7, ISBN13: 978-0-521-77208-2. Dewey:339.4/7/098. LCCN:00-064143.
Audience: **u,f.** *Choice, 2002.*

Cabanillas de Rodríguez, Berta **GT2853.P83**
El Puertorriqueño y Su Alimentación a Través de Su Historia (Siglos xvi al xix). Instituto de Cultura Puertorriquena. 1973.
Audience: **u,f.**

Cascudo, Luis da Camara **TX360.B7**
História da Alimentação no Brasil, 2 vols. Editora Itatiaia Limtada. 1982.
Audience: **u,f.**

Clarence-Smith, W. G. & Topik, Steven (Editors) **HD9195.A3512G58 2003**
The Global Coffee Economy in Africa, Asia and Latin America, 1500-1989. Cloth Text. Cambridge University Press. New York, NY. 2003. 504p. ISBN:0-521-81851-6, ISBN13: 978-0-521-81851-3. Dewey:338.1/7373. LCCN:2002-073472.
Audience: **u,f.**

Coe, Sophie D. **F1219.76.F67C64 1994**
America's First Cuisines. Trade Paper. University of Texas Press. Austin, TX. 1994. 288p. ISBN:0-292-71159-X, ISBN13: 978-0-292-71159-4. Dewey:394.1/2/08997. LCCN:93-008836.
Audience: **u,f.**

Crosby, Alfred W. **E98**
The Columbian Exchange: Biological and Cultural Consequences of 1492. Ed. 30. Trade Cloth. Greenwood Publishing Group, Inc. Portsmouth, NH. 2003. 320p. ISBN:0-275-98073-1, ISBN13: 978-0-275-98073-3. Dewey:614.4/97. LCCN:2003-042858.
Audience: **u,f.**

Florescano, Enrique **HD9049.C8**
Precios Del Maíz y Crisis Agrícolas en México (1708-1810). El Colegio de México. 1969.
Audience: **u,f.**

Foster, Nelson & Cordell, Linda S. (Editors) **SB176.A48C45 1992**
Chilies to Chocolate: Foods the Americas Gave the World. Trade Cloth. University of Arizona Press. Tucson, AZ. 1992. 191p. ISBN:0-8165-1324-4, ISBN13: 978-0-8165-1324-6. Dewey:641.3/097. LCCN:92-005243.
Audience: **g,l,u,f.** *Choice, 1993.*

Freyre, Gilberto **F2510.F75243**
The Masters and the Slaves: A Study in the Development of Brazilian Civilization. Samuel Putnam (Translator). Trade Cloth. Alfred A. Knopf Inc. New York, NY. 1964. 432p. Borzoi Books on Latin America Ser. ISBN:0-394-43561-3, ISBN13: 978-0-394-43561-9. Dewey:981. LCCN:64-000395.
Audience: **u,f.**

García Acosta, Virginia **HD9049.W5**
Los Precios del Trigo en La Historia Colonial de México. Centro de Investigaciones y Estudios Superiores en Antropología Social. 1988.
Audience: **u,f.**

Gonzalez, Nancie L. **F1505.2.C3G63 1988**
Sojourners of the Caribbean: Ethnogenesis and Ethnohistory of the Garifuna. Trade Cloth. University of Illinois Press. Champaign, IL. 1987. 272p. ISBN:0-252-01453-7, ISBN13: 978-0-252-01453-6. Dewey:972.8/00497. LCCN:87-006044.
Audience: **u,f.** *Choice, 1988.*

González Casanova, Pablo, ed.
Historia Del Hambre en México. Instituto Nacional de Nutrición. 1986.
Audience: **u,f.**

González de la Vara, Martín **HD9281.M42**
La Historia del Helado en México. Maas y Asociados. 1989.
Audience: **u,f.**

Juárez, José Luis **GT2853.M6**
La Lenta Emergencia de la Comida Mexicana, Ambigüedades Criollas 1750-1800. Editorial Porrúa. 2000.
Audience: **u,f.**

Kiple, Kenneth F. **RA455**
The Caribbean Slave: A Biological History. Alfred W. Crosby & Donald Worster (Contribution by). Trade Paper. Cambridge University Press. New York, NY. 2002. 288p. Studies in Environment and History Ser. ISBN:0-521-52470-9, ISBN13: 978-0-521-52470-4. Dewey:616/.008960729.
Audience: **u,f.** *Choice, 1986.*

Long, Janet, ed **TX716.A1**
Conquista y Comida: Consecuencias del Encuentro de Dos Mundos. UNAM. 1996.
Audience: **u,f.**

Long-Solis, Jane **HD9235.P462**
Capsicum y Cultura: La Historia del Chilli. Trade Paper. Fondo de Cultura Economica USA. San Diego, CA. 1998. 203p. ISBN:968-16-5380-7, ISBN13: 978-968-16-5380-4. Dewey:641.3/384.
Audience: **u,f.**

Lovera, José Rafael **TX360.V4**
Historia de la Alimentación en Venezuela. Monte Avila Editores. 1988.
Audience: **u,f.**

Martin, Patricia P. **GR111.M49 M37 1992**
Songs My Mother Sang to Me: An Oral History of Mexican American Women. Trade Paper. University of Arizona Press. Tucson, AZ. 1992. 224p. ISBN:0-8165-1329-5, ISBN13: 978-0-8165-1329-1. Dewey:398/.0896872073. LCCN:92-006745.
Audience: **l,u,f.**

May, Jacques M. & McLellan, Donna L. (Editors) **TX360.S63**
The Ecology of Malnutrition in Western South America, Vol. 14. Trade Cloth. Hafner Press. Riverside, NJ. 1975. xii, 365p. ISBN:0-02-849070-3, ISBN13: 978-0-02-849070-0. Dewey:338.1/9/8. LCCN:74-004060.
Audience: **u,f.**

Mintz, Sidney W. **GT2850.M58 1996**
Tasting Food, Tasting Freedom: Excursions into Eating, Power, and the Past. Trade Paper. Beacon Press. Boston, MA. 1997. 176p. ISBN:0-8070-4629-9, ISBN13: 978-0-8070-4629-6. Dewey:394.1. LCCN:95-047569.
Audience: **g,l,u,f.**

Mitchell, Kenneth Edward **HD9014.M64C6657 2001**
State-Society Relations in Mexico: Clientelism, Neoliberal State Reform and the Case of Conasupo. Trade Cloth. Ashgate Publishing, Ltd. Aldershot, 2001. 312p. The Political Economy of Latin America Ser. ISBN:0-7546-1718-1, ISBN13: 978-0-7546-1718-1. Dewey:338.1/972. LCCN:2001-089037.
Audience: **u,f.**

Morales, Edmundo **F2230.1.D65M67 1995**
The Guinea Pig: Healing, Food, and Ritual in the Andes. Trade Cloth. University of Arizona Press. Tucson, AZ. 1995. 177p. ISBN:0-8165-1479-8, ISBN13: 978-0-8165-1479-3. Dewey:338.1/7693234. LCCN:95-004343.
Audience: **u,f.** *Choice, 1996.*

Ochoa, Enrique C. **HD9014.M62O24 2000**
Feeding Mexico: The Political Uses of Food since 1910. Trade Cloth. Rowman & Littlefield Publishers, Inc. Lanham, MD. 2000. 267p. Tendencias Hacia el Futuro Comun Ser. ISBN:0-8420-2812-9, ISBN13: 978-0-8420-2812-7. Dewey:363.8/0972. LCCN:99-087310.
Audience: **u,f.** *Choice, 2001.*

Olivas Weston, Rosario **TX716.P4**
La Cocina Cotidiana y Festiva de Los Limeños en el Siglo XIX. Escuela Profesional de Turismo y Hotelería: Universidad de San Martín de Porres. 1999.
Audience: **u,f.**

Olivas Weston, Rosario **TX645**
La Cocina en el Virreinato del Peru. Escuela Profesional de Turismo y Hotelería: Universidad de San Martín de Porres. 1996.
Audience: **u,f.**

Orlove, Benjamin S. (Editor) **HC130.C6A43 1997**
The Allure of the Foreign: Imported Goods in Postcolonial Latin America. Trade Cloth. University of Michigan Press. Chicago, IL. 1997. 240p. Linking Levels of Analysis Ser. ISBN:0-472-10664-3, ISBN13: 978-0-472-10664-6. Dewey:382/.5/0948. LCCN:96-045899.
Audience: **u,f.** *Choice, 1998.*

Pilcher, Jeffrey M. **TX716.M4P54 1998**
Que Vivan los Tamales!: Food and the Making of Mexican Identity. Trade Paper. University of New Mexico Press. Albuquerque, NM. 1998. 253p. Dialogos Ser. ISBN:0-8263-1873-8, ISBN13: 978-0-8263-1873-2. Dewey:394.1/0972. LCCN:97-046508.
Audience: **l,u,f.** *Choice, 1998.*

Remedi, Fernando J. **TX359**
Los Secretos de la Olla. Entre el Gusto y La Necesidad: La Alimentación en la Córdoba de Principios del Siglo XX. Centro de Estudios Históricos. 1998.
Audience: **u,f.**

Rossells, Beatriz **TX641**
La Gastronomia en Potosí y Charcas: Siglos XVIII y XIX, 800 Recetas de la Cocina Criolla. Editora. 1995.
Audience: **u,f.**

Sanderson, Steven E. **HD1793.S26 1986**
The Transformation of Mexican Agriculture: International Structure and the Politics of Rural Change. Trade Cloth. Princeton University Press. Princeton, NJ. 1986. 304p. ISBN:0-691-07693-6, ISBN13: 978-0-691-07693-5. Dewey:338.1/0972. LCCN:85-042701.
Audience: **u,f.** *Choice, 1986.*

Sandstrom, Alan R. **F1371**
Corn Is Our Blood: Culture and Ethnic Identity in a Contemporary Aztec Indian Village. Trade Paper. University of Oklahoma Press. Norman, OK. 1992. 464p. Civilization of the American Indian Ser., Vol. 206 ISBN:0-8061-2403-2, ISBN13: 978-0-8061-2403-2. Dewey:972.62. LCCN:91-050307.
Audience: **u,f.** *Choice, 1992.*

Sanjur, Diva **TX360.U7**
Puerto Rican Food Habits: A Socio-Cultural Approach. Cornell University Press. 1970.
Audience: **u,f.**

Schávelzon, Daniel **TX360.A713**
Historias del Comer y del Beber en Buenos Aires: Arqueología Histórica de la Vajilla de Mesa. Aguilar. 2000.
Audience: **u,f.**

Striffler, Steve & Moberg, Mark **HD9259.B3S683 2003**
Banana Wars: Power, Production, and History in the Americas. Trade Cloth. Duke University Press. Durham, NC. 2003. 360p. American Encounters/Global Interactions Ser. ISBN:0-8223-3159-4, ISBN13: 978-0-8223-3159-9. Dewey:338.1/74772/098. LCCN:2003-008347.
Audience: **u,f.** *Choice, 2004.*

Super, John C. **HD9014.L32S87 1988**
Food, Conquest and Colonization in Sixteenth-Century Spanish America. Trade Cloth. University of New Mexico Press. Albuquerque, NM. 1988. 143p. ISBN:0-8263-1049-4, ISBN13: 978-0-8263-1049-1. Dewey:338.1/9/8. LCCN:87-035767.
Audience: **u,f.** *Choice, 1989.*

Super, John C. **HD9014.L32F66 1985**
Food, Politics and Society in Latin America. Thomas C. Wright (Editor). Trade Cloth. University of Nebraska Press. Lincoln, NE. 1985. 261p. Latin American Studies ISBN:0-8032-4137-2, ISBN13: 978-0-8032-4137-4. Dewey:363.8/098. LCCN:84-015313.
Audience: **u,f.** *Choice, 1986.*

Torres, Felipe, et al, ed. **HD9330.T753**
La Industria de la Masa y la Tortilla: Desarrollo y Tecnología. UNAM. 1996.
Audience: **u,f.**

Vargas, Luis Alberto & Long-Solis, Janet **GT2853**
Food Culture in Mexico. Cloth Text. Greenwood Publishing Group, Inc. Portsmouth, NH. 2005. 216p. Food Culture Around the World Ser. ISBN:0-313-32431-X, ISBN13: 978-0-313-32431-4. Dewey:394.1/2/0972. LCCN:2004-025907.
Audience: **u,f.**

Viola, Herman J. & Margolis, Carolyn J. (Editors) **E112.S45 1991**
Seeds of Change: A Quincentennial Commemoration. Trade Cloth. Smithsonian Institution Press. Washington, DC. 1991. 280p. ISBN:1-56098-035-4, ISBN13: 978-1-56098-035-3. Dewey:970.01/5. LCCN:90-010289.
Audience: **u,f.**

Vizcarra Bordi, Ivonne **F1221.M33**
Entre el Taco Mazahua y el Mundo: La Comida de las Relaciones de Poder, Resistencia e Identidades. Editorial Emahaia. 2002.
Audience: **u,f.**

Warman, Arturo **SB191.M2W34 2003**
Corn and Capitalism: How a Botanical Bastard Grew to Global Dominance. Nancy L. Westrate (Translator). Trade Cloth. University of North Carolina Press. Chapel Hill, NC. 2003. 288p. Latin America in Translation Ser. ISBN:0-8078-2766-5, ISBN13: 978-0-8078-2766-6. Dewey:633.1/5/09. LCCN:2002-010956.
Audience: **g,l,u.** *Choice, 2003.*

Weismantel, Mary J. **F3721.3.F7W45 1988**
Food, Gender, and Poverty in the Ecuadorian Andes. Trade Cloth. University of Pennsylvania Press. Philadelphia, PA. 1989. 242p. ISBN:0-8122-8115-2, ISBN13: 978-0-8122-8115-6. Dewey:394.1/2/0986614. LCCN:88-020480.
Audience: **u,f.** *Choice, 1989.*

Whiteford, Scott & Ferguson, Ann (Editors) **HD9014.C462H37 1991**
Harvest of Want: Hunger and Food Security in Central America and Mexico. Trade Paper. Westview Press. Boulder, CO. 1991. 264p. ISBN:0-8133-7986-5, ISBN13: 978-0-8133-7986-9. Dewey:363.8/09728. LCCN:91-010878.
Audience: **u,f.** *Choice, 1992.*

Latin America: General > History of Civil Military Relations

Aguero, Felipe & Stark, Jeffrey (Editors) **JL966.F38 1998**
Fault Lines of Democracy in Post-Transition Latin America. Trade Paper. University of Miami, North/South Center Press. Coral Gables, FL. 1998. 407p. ISBN:1-57454-046-7, ISBN13: 978-1-57454-046-8. Dewey:320.98/09/048. LCCN:98-042225.
Audience: **l,u,f.** *Choice, 1999.*

Alves, Maria H. **F2538.25.A48 1985**
State and Opposition in Military Brazil. Trade Cloth. University of Texas Press. Austin, TX. 1985. 368p. Latin American Monographs, No. 63 ISBN:0-292-77598-9, ISBN13: 978-0-292-77598-5. Dewey:320.981. LCCN:84-013151.
Audience: **u,f.** *Choice, 1986.*

Anna, Timothy E. **F3446**
The Fall of the Royal Government in Peru. Trade Cloth. University of Nebraska Press. Lincoln, NE. 1980. xiv, 291p. ISBN:0-8032-1004-3, ISBN13: 978-0-8032-1004-2. Dewey:985/.04. LCCN:79-009142.
Audience: **u,f.** B

Anna, Timothy E. **F1412**
Spain and the Loss of America. Trade Cloth. University of Nebraska Press. Lincoln, NE. 1983. xxiv, 343p. ISBN:0-8032-1014-0, ISBN13: 978-0-8032-1014-1. Dewey:980/.02. LCCN:82-011118.
Audience: **u,f.** B

Archer, Christon I. **UA789 .A7**
The Army in Bourbon Mexico, 1760-1810. Trade Cloth. University of New Mexico Press. Albuquerque, NM. 1977. 366p. ISBN:0-8263-0442-7, ISBN13: 978-0-8263-0442-1. Dewey:355.3/52/0946. LCCN:76-057536.
Audience: **u,f.**

Arriagada, Genaro **F3100.A73413 1988**
Pinochet: The Politics of Power. Trade Cloth. Routledge. New York, NY. 1988. 224p. ISBN:0-04-497061-7, ISBN13: 978-0-04-497061-3. Dewey:983/.0647. LCCN:88-001907.
Audience: **u,f.** *Choice, 1989.*

Atkins, G. Pope **F1938.55 .A87**
Arms and Politics in the Dominican Republic. Cloth Text. Westview Press. Boulder, CO. 1981. 158p. Special Studies on Latin America and the Caribbean ISBN:0-86531-112-9, ISBN13: 978-0-86531-112-1. Dewey:322/.5/097293. LCCN:80-028450.
Audience: **u,f.**

Beattie, Peter M. **UB325.B6B43 2001**
The Tribute of Blood: Army, Honor, Race, and Nation in Brazil, 1864-1945. Trade Cloth. Duke University Press. Durham, NC. 2001. 376p. Latin America Otherwise Ser. ISBN:0-8223-2733-3, ISBN13: 978-0-8223-2733-2. Dewey:306.2/7/0981. LCCN:2001-028884.
Audience: **u,f.** *Choice, 2002.*

Bergquist, Charles (Editor), et al. **HN310.Z9V579 1992**
Violence in Colombia: The Contemporary Crisis in Historical Perspective. Ricardo Penaranda & Gonzalo J. Sanchez (Editors). Trade Paper. Rowman & Littlefield Publishers, Inc. Lanham, MD. 1992. 337p. Latin American Silhouettes Ser. ISBN:0-8420-2376-3, ISBN13: 978-0-8420-2376-4. Dewey:303.6/09861. LCCN:91-022992.
Audience: **u,f.**

Biglaiser, Glen **HC167.S67B54 2002**
Guardians of the Nation?: Economists, Generals, and Economic Reform in Latin America. Helen Kellogg Institute for International Studies Staff (Contribution by). Trade Cloth. University of Notre Dame Press. Notre Dame, IN. 2002. xi, 239p. ISBN:0-268-03874-0, ISBN13: 978-0-268-03874-8. Dewey:338.98. LCCN:2002-003991.
Audience: **u,f.** *Choice, 2003.*

Bowman, Kirk S. **HC130.D4B68 2002**
Militarization, Democracy and Development: The Perils of Praetorianism in Latin America. Trade Cloth. Pennsylvania State University Press. University Park, PA. 2002. 289p. ISBN:0-271-02229-9, ISBN13: 978-0-271-02229-1. Dewey:338.98/009/045. LCCN:2002-012190.
Audience: **u,f.** *Choice, 2003.*

Burggraaff, Winfield J. **F2326 .B85**
The Venezuelan Armed Forces in Politics, 1935-1959. Trade Cloth. University of Missouri Press. Columbia, MO. 1972. 252p. ISBN:0-8262-0121-0, ISBN13: 978-0-8262-0121-8. Dewey:320.9/87/063. LCCN:73-185831.
Audience: **u,f.**

Campbell, Leon G. **Q11.P612 VOL. 123**
The Military and Society in Colonial Peru 1750-1810. Trade Paper. American Philosophical Society. Canton, MA. 1978. xviii,

254p. Memoirs Ser., Vol. 123 ISBN:0-87169-123-X, ISBN13: 978-0-87169-123-1. Dewey:081. LCCN:77-091650.
Audience: **u,f.** BCL3

Centeno, Miguel Angel **F1410.5.C46 2002**
Blood and Debt: War and the Nation-State in Latin America. Trade Cloth. Pennsylvania State University Press. University Park, PA. 2002. 344p. ISBN:0-271-02165-9, ISBN13: 978-0-271-02165-2. Dewey:303.6/6/098. LCCN:2001-036764.
Audience: **u,f.** *Choice, 2003.*

Farcau, Bruce W. **F2688**
The Chaco War: Bolivia and Paraguay, 1932-1935. Book, Other. Greenwood Publishing Group, Inc. Portsmouth, NH. 1996. 272p. ISBN:0-275-95218-5, ISBN13: 978-0-275-95218-1. Dewey:989.207/1. LCCN:95-042506.
Audience: **u,f.** *Choice, 1997.*

Farcau, Bruce W. **F3097**
The Ten Cents War: Chile, Peru and Bolivia in the War of the Pacific, 1879-1884. Trade Cloth. Greenwood Publishing Group, Inc. Portsmouth, NH. 2000. 224p. ISBN:0-275-96925-8, ISBN13: 978-0-275-96925-7. Dewey:983.06/16. LCCN:00-036709.
Audience: **u,f.**

Farcau, Bruce W. **JL956**
The Transition to Democracy in Latin America: The Role of the Military. Trade Cloth. Greenwood Publishing Group, Inc. Portsmouth, NH. 1996. 200p. ISBN:0-275-95636-9, ISBN13: 978-0-275-95636-3. Dewey:322/.5/098. LCCN:96-005538.
Audience: **u,f.** *Choice, 1997.*

Fitch, J. Samuel **JL956.C58F57 1998**
The Armed Forces and Democracy in Latin America. Trade Cloth. Johns Hopkins University Press. Baltimore, MD. 1998. 288p. ISBN:0-8018-5917-4, ISBN13: 978-0-8018-5917-5. Dewey:322/.5/098. LCCN:98-016210.
Audience: **u,f.** *Choice, 1999.*

Fitch, John S. 3rd **F3738**
The Military Coup d'Etat as a Political Process: Ecuador, 1948-1966. Trade Cloth. Johns Hopkins University Press. Baltimore, MD. 1988. 264p. Studies in Historical and Political Science, 95th Series, No. 1 ISBN:0-8018-1915-6, ISBN13: 978-0-8018-1915-5. Dewey:322'.5'09866. LCCN:76-047381.
Audience: **u,f.**

Gillespie, Charles Guy **JL3698.A1 G5 1991**
Negotiating Democracy: Politicians and Generals in Uruguay. Alan Knight (Contribution by). Trade Paper. Cambridge University Press. New York, NY. 2006. 282p. Cambridge Latin American Studies ISBN:0-521-02563-X, ISBN13: 978-0-521-02563-8. Dewey:320.9895.
Audience: **u,f.** *Choice, 1992.*

Giraldo, Javier **HV6433.C6G57 1996**
Colombia: The Genocidal Democracy. Noam Chomsky (Introduction by). Trade Cloth. Common Courage Press. Monroe, ME. 1996. 100p. ISBN:1-56751-087-6, ISBN13: 978-1-56751-087-4. Dewey:323.4/9/09861. LCCN:96-014341.
Audience: **u,f.**

Goodman, Louis W., et al. **F1414.2.M537 1990**
The Military and Democracy: The Future of Civil-Military Relations in Latin America. Johanna S. Medelson & Juan Rial (Authors). Trade Cloth. Simon & Schuster. New York, NY. 1989. 352p. ISBN:0-669-21126-5, ISBN13: 978-0-669-21126-9. Dewey:322/.5/098. LCCN:89-036112.
Audience: **u,f.** *Choice, 1990.*

Hayes, Robert A. **F2538.25 H38 1989**
The Armed Nation: The Brazilian Corporate Mystique. Trade Cloth. Arizona State University, Center for Latin American Studies. Tempe, AZ. 1988. 282p. ISBN:0-87918-069-2, ISBN13: 978-0-87918-069-0. Dewey:322/.5/0981. LCCN:87-032558.
Audience: **u,f.**

Helmke, Gretchen **KHA2533.H45 2004**
Courts under Constraints: Judges, Generals, and Presidents in Argentina. Robert H. Bates, Ellen Comisso, Peter Hall, Peter Lange, Joel Migdal & Helen Milner (Contribution by). Trade Cloth. Cambridge University Press. New York, NY. 2004. 240p. Cambridge Studies in Comparative Politics Ser. ISBN:0-521-82059-6, ISBN13: 978-0-521-82059-2. Dewey:347.82/012. LCCN:2004-052120.
Audience: **u,f.** *Choice, 2005.*

Herwig, Holger & Sater, William F. **UA622.S28 1999**
The Grand Illusion: The Prussianization of the Chilean Army. Cloth Text. University of Nebraska Press. Lincoln, NE. 1999. 248p. Studies in War, Society, and the Military ISBN:0-8032-2393-5, ISBN13: 978-0-8032-2393-6. Dewey:355/.00983/09034. LCCN:99-019356.
Audience: **u,f.**

Hunter, Wendy **JL2420.C58H86 1997**
Eroding Military Influence in Brazil: Politicians Against Soldiers. Trade Paper. University of North Carolina Press. Chapel Hill, NC. 1997. 260p. ISBN:0-8078-4620-1, ISBN13: 978-0-8078-4620-9. Dewey:320.981. LCCN:96-022285.
Audience: **u,f.** *Choice, 1997.*

Isaacs, Anita **F3738.I83 1993**
The Politics of Military Rule and Transition in Ecuador, 1972-92: Dancing with the People. Cloth Text. University of Pittsburgh Press. Pittsburgh, PA. 1993. 192p. Latin American Ser. ISBN:0-8229-1173-6, ISBN13: 978-0-8229-1173-9. Dewey:986.607/3. LCCN:92-034039.
Audience: **u,f.** *Choice, 1994.*

Johnson, John J. **F1410 .J7**
The Military and Society in Latin America. Trade Cloth. Stanford University Press. Palo Alto, CA. 1964. x, 308p. ISBN:0-8047-0198-9, ISBN13: 978-0-8047-0198-3. Dewey:980.
Audience: **l,u,f.** BCL3

Kraay, Hendrik **F2651.S1357K73 2001**
Race, State, and Armed Forces in Independence-Era Brazil: Bahia, 1790s-1840s. Trade Cloth. Stanford University Press. Palo Alto, CA. 2002. 376p. ISBN:0-8047-4248-0, ISBN13: 978-0-8047-4248-1. Dewey:306.2/7/098142. LCCN:2001-048429.
Audience: **u,f.** *Choice, 2002.*

Kraay, Hendrik & Whigham, Thomas L. **F2687.I62 2004**
I Die with My Country: Prespectives on the Paraguayan War, 1864-1870. Cloth Text. University of Nebraska Press. Lincoln, NE. 2005. 320p. Studies in War, Society, and the Military Ser. ISBN:0-8032-2762-0, ISBN13: 978-0-8032-2762-0. Dewey:989.2/05. LCCN:2004-007730.
Audience: **u,f.**

Kruijt, Dirk **F3448.2**
Revolution by Decree: Peru, 1968-1975. Thela Publishers. 1994. ISBN:90-5538-004-0, ISBN13: 978-90-5538-004-6.
Audience: **l,u.**

Kuethe, Allan J. **F1779.K84 1986**
Cuba, 1753-1815: Crown, Military and Society. Cloth Text. University of Tennessee Press. Knoxville, TN. 1986. 232p. ISBN:0-87049-487-2, ISBN13: 978-0-87049-487-1. Dewey:972.91/04. LCCN:85-017844.
Audience: **u,f.** *Choice, 1986.*

Kuethe, Allan J. **UA789 .K83**
Military Reform and Society in New Granada, 1773-1808. Trade Cloth. University Press of Florida. Gainesville, FL. 1978. 234p. University of Florida Latin American Monographs, No. 22 ISBN:0-8130-0570-1, ISBN13: 978-0-8130-0570-6. Dewey:355.3/1/0946. LCCN:77-021908.
Audience: **u,f.**

Lewis, Paul H. **F2849**
Guerrillas and Generals: The "Dirty War" in Argentina. Trade Cloth. Greenwood Publishing Group, Inc. Portsmouth, NH. 2001. 280p. ISBN:0-275-97359-X, ISBN13: 978-0-275-97359-9. Dewey:982.06. LCCN:2001-021650.
Audience: **u,f.** *Choice, 2002.*

Lieuwen, Edwin **F1418**
Arms and Politics in Latin America. Paper Text. Textbook Publishers. Temecula, CA. 2003. 335p. ISBN:0-7581-5459-3, ISBN13: 978-0-7581-5459-0. Dewey:355.098.
Audience: **u,f.**

Lieuwen, Edwin **F1414**
Generals vs. Presidents: Neo-Militarism in Latin America. Praeger. 1964.
Audience: **l,u.**

Lieuwen, Edwin **F1234 .L69 1981**
Mexican Militarism: The Political Rise and Fall of the Revolutionary Army, 1910-1940. Trade Cloth. Greenwood Publishing Group, Inc. Portsmouth, NH. 1981. 194p. ISBN:0-313-22911-2, ISBN13: 978-0-313-22911-4. Dewey:972.08/2. LCCN:80-028937.
Audience: **u,f.**

Loveman, Brian **JL952.L68 1993**
The Constitution of Tyranny: Regimes of Exception in Spanish America. Cloth Text. University of Pittsburgh Press. Pittsburgh, PA. 1994. 496p. Latin American Ser. ISBN:0-8229-3766-2, ISBN13: 978-0-8229-3766-1. Dewey:351.003/22/09809034. LCCN:93-028177.
Audience: **u,f.** *Choice, 1994.*

Loveman, Brian **JL956.C58L68 1999**
For la Patria: Politics and the Armed Forces in Latin America. Book, Other. Rowman & Littlefield Publishers, Inc. Lanham, MD. 1999. 333p. Latin American Silhouettes Ser. ISBN:0-8420-2772-6, ISBN13: 978-0-8420-2772-4. Dewey:322/.5/098. LCCN:98-007793.
Audience: **u,f.** *Choice, 1999.*

Loveman, Brian (Editor), et al. **JL956.C58P65 1997**
The Politics of Antipolitics: The Military in Latin America. Ed. 3. Thomas M. Davies Jr., William H. Beezley & Judith Ewell (Editors). Book, Other. Rowman & Littlefield Publishers, Inc. Lanham, MD. 1997. 438p. Latin American Silhouettes Ser. ISBN:0-8420-2609-6, ISBN13: 978-0-8420-2609-3. Dewey:322/.5/098. LCCN:96-009466.
Audience: **u,f.**

Lowenthal, Abraham F. & Fitch, J. Samuel (Editors) **F1414.2.A793 1986**
Armies and Politics in Latin America. Ed. 2. Trade Cloth. Holmes & Meier Publishers, Inc. Teaneck, NJ. 1986. 300p. ISBN:0-8419-0913-X, ISBN13: 978-0-8419-0913-7. Dewey:322/.5/098. LCCN:86-014918.
Audience: **u,f.** B

Mann, Carlos G. **F1566.G85 1996**
Panamanian Militarism: A Historical Interpretation. Paper Text. Ohio University Press. Athens, OH. 1996. 243p. Monographs in International Studies, No. 25 ISBN:0-89680-189-6, ISBN13: 978-0-89680-189-9. Dewey:322/.5/097287. LCCN:95-040747.
Audience: **u,f.**

Mares, David R. (Editor) **JL956.C58 C58**
Civil-Military Relations: Building Democracy and Regional Security in Latin America, Southern Asia, and Central Europe. Trade Paper. Westview Press. Boulder, CO. 1999. 288p. Latin America in Global Perspective Ser. ISBN:0-8133-2422-X, ISBN13: 978-0-8133-2422-7. Dewey:322.5.
Audience: **u,f.**

Masterson, Daniel M. **F3448**
Militarism and Politics in Latin America: Peru from Sanchez Cerro to Sendero Luminoso. Trade Cloth. Greenwood Publishing Group, Inc. Portsmouth, NH. 1991. 360p. Contributions in Military Studies Ser., No. 111 ISBN:0-313-27213-1, ISBN13: 978-0-313-27213-4. Dewey:322/.5/0985. LCCN:90-023010.
Audience: **u,f.** *Choice, 1992.*

Maullin, Richard **F2278**
Soldiers, Guerrillas, and Politics in Colombia. Lexington Books. 1973. ISBN:0-669-88203-8, ISBN13: 978-0-669-88203-2.
Audience: **l,u.**

McAlister, Lyle N. **UB775.M4M3**
The Fuero Militar in New Spain 1764: 1800. Paper Text. Textbook Publishers. Temecula, CA. 2003. vii, 117p. ISBN:0-7581-2289-6, ISBN13: 978-0-7581-2289-6. Dewey:355.1/33/0972.
Audience: **u,f.**

McCann, Frank D. **UA619.M387 2003**
Soldiers of the Patria: A History of the Brazilian Army, 1889-1937. Trade Cloth. Stanford University Press. Palo Alto, CA. 2004. 608p. ISBN:0-8047-3222-1, ISBN13: 978-0-8047-3222-2. Dewey:355/.00981. LCCN:2003-007567.
Audience: **u,f.** *Choice, 2004.*

McSherry, J. Patrice **JL2020.C58M38 1997**
Incomplete Transition: Military Power and Democracy in Argentina. Cloth over Boards. Palgrave Macmillan. New York, NY. 1997. 418p. ISBN:0-312-16252-9, ISBN13: 978-0-312-16252-8. Dewey:982/.06. LCCN:96-048927.
Audience: **u,f.** *Choice, 1997.*

Millett, Richard **F1526.3**
Guardians of the Dynasty: A History of the U. S. Created Guardia Nacional De Nicaragua and the Somoza Family. Trade Paper. Orbis Books. Maryknoll, NY. 1977. ISBN:0-88344-171-3, ISBN13: 978-0-88344-171-8. Dewey:972.85/05. LCCN:76-049499.
Audience: **u,f.**

Millett, Richard & Gold-Biss, Michael (Editors) **UA602.3.M55 1995**
Beyond Praetorianism: The Latin American Military in Transition. Trade Paper. University of Miami, North/South Center Press. Coral Gables, FL. 1996. 332p. ISBN:1-57454-000-9, ISBN13: 978-1-57454-000-0. Dewey:355/.0098. LCCN:95-041548.
Audience: **u,f.**

Morris, James A. **JL1522**
Honduras: Caudillo Politics and Military Rulers. Cloth Text. Westview Press. Boulder, CO. 1984. xiv, 156p. ISBN:0-86531-178-1, ISBN13: 978-0-86531-178-7. Dewey:320.97283. LCCN:83-021789.
Audience: **u,f.** B

Munck, Gerardo L. **JL2031.M78 1998**
Authoritarianism and Democratization: Soldiers and Workers in Argentina, 1976-1983. Trade Cloth. Pennsylvania State University Press. University Park, PA. 1998. 364p. ISBN:0-271-01807-0, ISBN13: 978-0-271-01807-2. Dewey:320.982/09/047. LCCN:98-007195.
Audience: **u,f.** *Choice, 1999.*

Norden, Deborah L. **F2849.2.N67 1996**
Military Rebellion in Argentina: Between Coups and Consolidation. Cloth Text. University of Nebraska Press. Lincoln, NE. 1996. 240p. ISBN:0-8032-3339-6, ISBN13: 978-0-8032-3339-3. Dewey:322/.5/098209045. LCCN:95-032285.
Audience: **u,f.** *Choice, 1996.*

Nun, Jose **F1414.2 .N8**
Latin America: The Hegemonic Crisis and the Military Coup. Trade Paper. University of California, International & Area Studies. Berkeley, CA. 1969. Politics of Modernization Ser., No. 7 ISBN:0-87725-207-6, ISBN13: 978-0-87725-207-8. Dewey:320.9/8.
Audience: **u,f.**

Nunn, Frederick M. **F3099 .N8**
Chilean Politics, 1920-1931: The Honorable Mission of the Armed Forces. Trade Cloth. University of New Mexico Press. Albuquerque, NM. 1970. ISBN:0-8263-0195-9, ISBN13: 978-0-8263-0195-6. Dewey:320.9/83/064. LCCN:70-129808.
Audience: **u,f.**

Nunn, Frederick M. **F3093 .N85**
The Military in Chilean History. Trade Cloth. University of New Mexico Press. Albuquerque, NM. 1976. 364p. ISBN:0-8263-0364-1, ISBN13: 978-0-8263-0364-6. Dewey:322/.5/0983. LCCN:74-027444.
Audience: **u,f.**

Nunn, Frederick M. **F1414.2.N83 1992**
The Time of the Generals: Latin American Professional Militarism in World Perspective. Trade Cloth. University of Nebraska Press. Lincoln, NE. 1992. 340p. ISBN:0-8032-3334-5, ISBN13: 978-0-8032-3334-8. Dewey:322/.5/098. LCCN:91-039896.
Audience: **u,f.** *Choice, 1993.*

Nunn, Frederick M. **UA612.N86 1983**
Yesterday's Soldiers: European Military Professionalism in South America, 1890-1940. Cloth Text. University of Nebraska Press. Lincoln, NE. 1983. 365p. ISBN:0-8032-3305-1, ISBN13: 978-0-8032-3305-8. Dewey:355.5/5/098. LCCN:82-006961.
Audience: **u,f.** B

Perez, Louis A. **UA610.C9**
Army Politics in Cuba, Eighteen Ninety-Eight to Nineteen Fifty-Eight. Trade Cloth. University of Pittsburgh Press. Pittsburgh, PA. 1976. xvi, 240p. Pitt Latin American Ser. ISBN:0-8229-3303-9, ISBN13: 978-0-8229-3303-8. Dewey:322/.5/097291. LCCN:75-035440.
Audience: **u,f.**

Philip, George D. E. **F3448.2**
Rise and Fall of the Peruvian Military Radicals, 1968-1976. Athlone Press. 1978. ISBN:0-485-17709-9, ISBN13: 978-0-485-17709-1.
Audience: **l,u,f.**

Pion-Berlin, David **F2849.2.P565 1997**
Through Corridors of Power: Institutions and Civil-Military Relations in Argentina. Trade Cloth. Pennsylvania State University Press. University Park, PA. 1997. 264p. ISBN:0-271-01705-8, ISBN13: 978-0-271-01705-1. Dewey:322/.5/098209048. LCCN:96-048046.
Audience: **u,f.**

Pion-Berlin, David (Editor) **JL956.C58C583 2001**
Civil-Military Relations in Latin America: New Analytical Perspectives. Abraham F. Lowenthal (Foreword by). Trade Cloth. University of North Carolina Press. Chapel Hill, NC. 2001. 320p. ISBN:0-8078-2656-1, ISBN13: 978-0-8078-2656-0. Dewey:322/.5/098. LCCN:2001-035303.
Audience: **u,f.** *Choice, 2002.*

Potash, Robert A. **UA613**
The Army and Politics in Argentina, 1928-1945: Yrigoyen to Peron. Trade Cloth. Stanford University Press. Palo Alto, CA. 1969. xiv, 314p. ISBN:0-8047-0683-2, ISBN13: 978-0-8047-0683-4. Dewey:320.9/82. LCCN:69-013182.
Audience: **u,f.**

Potash, Robert A. **UA613**
The Army and Politics in Argentina, 1945-1962: Peron to Frondizi. Trade Cloth. Stanford University Press. Palo Alto, CA. 1980. xiv, 418p. ISBN:0-8047-1056-2, ISBN13: 978-0-8047-1056-5. Dewey:320.9/82. LCCN:79-064220.
Audience: **u,f.** B

Potash, Robert A. **UA613 .P67**
The Army and Politics in Argentina, 1962-1973: From Frondizi's Fall to the Peronist Restoration. Trade Cloth. Stanford University Press. Palo Alto, CA. 1996. 592p. ISBN:0-8047-2414-8, ISBN13: 978-0-8047-2414-2. Dewey:320.9/82. LCCN:69-013182.
Audience: **u,f.** *Choice, 1996.*

Rauch, George V. **F2833**
Conflict in the Southern Cone: The Argentine Military and the Boundary Dispute with Chile, 1870-1902. Trade Cloth. Greenwood Publishing Group, Inc. Portsmouth, NH. 1999. 248p. ISBN:0-275-96347-0, ISBN13: 978-0-275-96347-7. Dewey:303.48/282083. LCCN:98-044597.
Audience: **u,f.**

Remmer, Karen L. **JL956.C58R46 1989**
Military Rule in Latin America. Trade Cloth. Routledge. New York, NY. 1989. 208p. ISBN:0-04-445479-1, ISBN13: 978-0-04-445479-3. Dewey:322/.5/098. LCCN:89-032672.
Audience: **l,u,f.** *Choice, 1990.*

Rodriguez, Linda A. (Editor) **UA602.3.R36 1994**
Rank and Privilege: The Military and Society in Latin America. Book, Other. Rowman & Littlefield Publishers, Inc. Lanham, MD. 1997. 239p. Jaguar Books on Latin America, No. 8 ISBN:0-8420-2432-8, ISBN13: 978-0-8420-2432-7. Dewey:306.2/7/098. LCCN:94-014393.
Audience: **u,f.**

Ronfeldt, David F. (Editor) **UA603 .M63**
The Modern Mexican Military: A Reassessment. Trade Cloth. University of California, San Diego, Center for U. S.-Mexican Studies. La Jolla, CA. 1984. 218p. Monographs, No. 15 ISBN:0-935391-52-5, ISBN13: 978-0-935391-52-7. Dewey:355/.00972.
Audience: **u,f.**

Rouquie, Alain **JL956.C58R6813 1987**
The Military and the State in Latin America. Paul E. Sigmund (Translator). Trade Cloth. University of California Press. Berkeley, CA. 1987. 520p. ISBN:0-520-05559-4, ISBN13: 978-0-520-05559-9. Dewey:322/.5/098. LCCN:86-014666.
Audience: **u,f.** *Choice, 1988.*

Sater, William F. **F3097.S26**
Chile and the War of the Pacific. Trade Paper. Books on Demand. Ann Arbor, MI. 1986. 355p. ISBN:0-7837-4205-3, ISBN13: 978-0-7837-4205-2. Dewey:983/.061. LCCN:85-024584.
Audience: **u,f.** *Choice, 1986.*

Sater, William F. **F3097**
The Heroic Image in Chile: Arturo Prat, Secular Saint. Trade Cloth. University of California Press. Berkeley, CA. 1973. ix, 243p. ISBN:0-520-02235-1, ISBN13: 978-0-520-02235-5. Dewey:983/.061/0924. LCCN:70-189221.
Audience: **u,f.**

Scheina, Robert L. **F1413**
Latin America's Wars: The Age of the Professional Soldier, 1900-2001. Trade Cloth. Potomac Books, Inc. Dulles, VA. 2003. 624p. ISBN:1-57488-451-4, ISBN13: 978-1-57488-451-7. Dewey:355/.0098.
Audience: **u,f.**

Scheina, Robert L. **F1413.S34 2002**
Latin America's Wars: The Age of Caudillo, 1791-1899. Trade Cloth. Potomac Books, Inc. Dulles, VA. 2002. 624p. ISBN:1-57488-449-2, ISBN13: 978-1-57488-449-4. Dewey:355/.0098. LCCN:2002-008029.
Audience: **u,f.** *Choice, 2003.*

Schirmer, Jennifer **F1466.5.S33 1998**
The Guatemalan Military Project: A Violence Called Democracy. Trade Cloth. University of Pennsylvania Press. Philadelphia, PA. 1998. 344p. Pennsylvania Studies in Human Rights ISBN:0-8122-3325-5, ISBN13: 978-0-8122-3325-4. Dewey:972.8105/2. LCCN:98-028114.
Audience: **u,f.**

Serbin, Kenneth P. **BX1466.2.S48 2000**
Secret Dialogues: Church-State Relations, Torture and Social Justice in Authoritarian Brazil. Cloth Text. University of Pittsburgh Press. Pittsburgh, PA. 2000. xx, 312p. Pitt Latin American Ser. ISBN:0-8229-4123-6, ISBN13: 978-0-8229-4123-1. Dewey:981.06/3. LCCN:00-009649.
Audience: **u,f.** *Choice, 2001.*

Silva, Patricio (Editor) **JL1856.C58S65 2001**
The Soldier and the State in South America: Essays in Civil-Military Relations. Cloth over Boards. Palgrave Macmillan. New York, NY. 2001. 224p. Latin American Studies ISBN:0-333-93093-2, ISBN13: 978-0-333-93093-9. Dewey:322.5098. LCCN:00-048354.
Audience: **u,f.** *Choice, 2001.*

Smallman, Shawn C. **F2537.S65 2002**
Fear and Memory in the Brazilian Army and Society, 1889-1954. Trade Cloth. University of North Carolina Press. Chapel Hill, NC. 2002. 280p. ISBN:0-8078-2691-X, ISBN13: 978-0-8078-2691-1. Dewey:981.06/4. LCCN:2001-052576.
Audience: **u,f.** *Choice, 2002.*

Stepan, Alfred **F2538.25.S79 1988**
Rethinking Military Politics: Brazil and the Southern Cone. Trade Paper. Princeton University Press. Princeton, NJ. 1988. 192p. ISBN:0-691-02274-7, ISBN13: 978-0-691-02274-1. Dewey:322/.5/0981. LCCN:87-045537.
Audience: **u,f.** *Choice, 1988.*

Stepan, Alfred C. **UA619.S7**
The Military in Politics; Changing Patterns in Brazil. Trade Cloth. Princeton University Press. Princeton, NJ. 1971. xiii, 313p. ISBN:0-691-07537-9, ISBN13: 978-0-691-07537-2. Dewey:322/.5/0981. LCCN:73-132242.
Audience: **u,f.**

Suchlicki, Jaime; Morris, James A; Fernandez, Damian J; Del Aguila, Juan; Suarez, Andres **UA610.C9C83 1989**
The Cuban Military under Castro. Jaime Suchlicki (Editor) ; James A. Morris (Preface by) ; Damian J. Fernandez (Contribution by) ; Juan Del Aguila (Contribution by) ; Andres Suarez (Contribution by). University of Miami, North/South Center Press. 1989. ISBN:0-935501-15-0, ISBN13: 978-0-935501-15-5.
Audience: **u,f.**

Tulchin, Joseph S. **F3448.2.P4735 1994**
Peru in Crisis: Dictatorship or Democracy? Paper Text. Lynne Rienner Publishers, Inc. Boulder, CO. 1994. 200p. Woodrow Wilson Center Current Studies on Latin America ISBN:1-55587-543-2, ISBN13: 978-1-55587-543-5. Dewey:320.985. LCCN:94-014646.
Audience: **u,f.** *Choice, 1995.*

Vale, Brian **F2725.V35 2000**
War Betwixt Englishmen: Brazil Against Argentina on the River Plate. Cloth over Boards. I. B. Tauris & Company, Ltd. London, 2000. 256p. ISBN:1-86064-456-2, ISBN13: 978-1-86064-456-6. Dewey:982/.03. LCCN:00-698573.
Audience: **u,f.**

Waisman, Carlos H. & Peralta-Ramos, Monica (Editors) **F2849.2.F69 1987**
From Military Rule to Liberal Democracy in Argentina. Paper Text. Westview Press. Boulder, CO. 1986. 192p. ISBN:0-8133-7101-5, ISBN13: 978-0-8133-7101-6. Dewey:982/.06. LCCN:86-004068.
Audience: **u,f.** *Choice, 1987.*

Weeks, Gregory **F3100.W43 2003**
The Military and Politics in Postauthoritarian Chile. Trade Cloth. University of Alabama Press. Tuscaloosa, AL. 2003. 248p. ISBN:0-8173-1177-7, ISBN13: 978-0-8173-1177-3. Dewey:320.983/09/049. LCCN:2003-000561.
Audience: **u,f.** *Choice, 2004.*

Whigham, Thomas L. **F2687.W54 2002**
The Paraguayan War: Causes and Early Conduct. Trade Cloth. University of Nebraska Press. Lincoln, NE. 2002. 512p. Studies in War, Society, and the Military ISBN:0-8032-4786-9, ISBN13: 978-0-8032-4786-4. Dewey:989.2/05. LCCN:2001-053461.
Audience: **u,f.** *Choice, 2003.*

Wiarda, Howard J. **JL960 .W5 1978**
Critical Elections and Critical Coups: State, Society and the Military in the Processes of Latin American Development. Trade Paper. Ohio University Press. Athens, OH. 1979. Papers in International Studies: Latin America Ser., No. 5 ISBN:0-89680-082-2, ISBN13: 978-0-89680-082-3. Dewey:322/.5/098. LCCN:79-004433.
Audience: **u,f.**

Williams, Philip J. & Walter, Knut **JL1566.C58W54 1997**
Militarization and Demilitarization in El Salvador's Transition to Democracy. Trade Paper. University of Pittsburgh Press. Pittsburgh, PA. 1998. 260p. Pitt Latin American Ser. ISBN:0-8229-5646-2, ISBN13: 978-0-8229-5646-4. Dewey:322/.5/097284. LCCN:97-004920.
Audience: **u,f.**

Zook, David H., **F3451.B75**
Zarumilla-Marañón: The Ecuador-Peru Dispute. Bookman Associates. 1964.
Audience: **l,u.**

Zook, David H. **F2688.5**
The Conduct of the Chaco War. Ynsfran, Pablo Max (Pref. by); Arnade, Charles W. (Foreword by). Bookman Associates. 1960.
Audience: **l,u.**

Latin America: General > Afro- Latin America

Andrews, George Reid **F1419.N4A63 2004**
Afro-Latin America, 1800-2000. Trade Paper. Oxford University Press, Inc. New York, NY. 2004. 298p. ISBN:0-19-515233-6, ISBN13: 978-0-19-515233-3. Dewey:980/.00496. LCCN:2003-056411.
Audience: **u,f.** *Choice, 2005.*

Appelbaum, Nancy P. (Editor), et al. **F1413.R33 2003**
Race and Nation in Modern Latin America. Anne S. Macpherson & Karin Alejandra Rosemblatt (Editors). Trade Cloth. University of North Carolina Press. Chapel Hill, NC. 2003. 352p. ISBN:0-8078-2769-X, ISBN13: 978-0-8078-2769-7. Dewey:323.1/8/09. LCCN:2002-011044.
Audience: **u,f.** *Choice, 2003.*

Appiah, Anthony & Gates, Henry Louis Jr. **DT14.A37435 2005**
Africana: The Encyclopedia of the African and African American Experience. Ed. 2. Trade Cloth. Oxford University Press, Inc. New York, NY. 2005. 3,950p. ISBN:0-19-517055-5, ISBN13: 978-0-19-517055-9. Dewey:960/.03. LCCN:2004-020222.
Audience: **l,u,f.** *Choice, 2005.*

Brown, David H. **BL2532.S3B76 2003**
Santeria Enthroned: Art, Ritual, and Innovation in an Afro-Cuban Religion. Trade Cloth. University of Chicago Press. Chicago, IL. 2003. 440p. ISBN:0-226-07609-1, ISBN13: 978-0-226-07609-6. Dewey:299/.674. LCCN:2002-073564.
Audience: **u,f.** *Choice, 2004.*

Bueno, Maria de Los Reyes Castillo **F1789.N3C37 2000**
Reyita: The Life of a Black Cuban Woman in the Twentieth Century. Daisy Rubiera Castillo (As told to). Library Binding. Duke University Press. Durham, NC. 2000. 168p. ISBN:0-8223-2579-9, ISBN13: 978-0-8223-2579-6. Dewey:972.9106/092 B. LCCN:99-087007.
Audience: **g,l,u,f.**

Butler, Kim D. **F2651.S2B85 1998**
Freedoms Given, Freedoms Won: Afro-Brazilians in Post-Abolition Sao Paolo and Salvador. Cloth Text. Rutgers University Press. Piscataway, NJ. 1998. 306p. ISBN:0-8135-2503-9, ISBN13: 978-0-8135-2503-7. Dewey:305.896081. LCCN:97-043478.
Audience: **u,f.** *Choice, 1999.*

Chasteen, John Charles **GV1626.C47 2004**
National Rhythms, African Roots: The Deep History of Latin American Popular Dance. Trade Cloth. University of New Mexico Press. Albuquerque, NM. 2004. 257p. Dialogos Ser. ISBN:0-8263-2940-3, ISBN13: 978-0-8263-2940-0. Dewey:792.8/098. LCCN:2003-019742.
Audience: **u,f.** *Choice, 2004.*

Conrad, Robert E. (Editor) **HT1126.C575 1994**
Children of God's Fire: A Documentary History of Black Slavery in Brazil. Ed. 2. Trade Paper. Pennsylvania State University Press. University Park, PA. 1993. 544p. ISBN:0-271-01321-4, ISBN13: 978-0-271-01321-3. Dewey:306.3/62/0981. LCCN:93-038702.
Audience: **u,f.**

De Jesus, Carolina M. **HN290.S33**
Child of the Dark: The Diary of Carolina Maria de Jesus. David St. Clair (Translator), Robert S. Levine (Afterword by). Mass Market. Penguin Group (USA) Inc. New York, NY. 2003. 208p. ISBN:0-451-52910-3, ISBN13: 978-0-451-52910-7. Dewey:306/.0981/61.
Audience: **g,l.**

De La Fuente, Alejandro **F1789.A1F84 2001**
A Nation for All: Race, Inequality, and Politics in Twentieth-Century Cuba. Trade Cloth. University of North Carolina Press. Chapel Hill, NC. 2001. 464p. Envisioning Cuba Ser. ISBN:0-8078-2608-1, ISBN13: 978-0-8078-2608-9. Dewey:305.8/0097291. LCCN:00-046693.
Audience: **u,f.**

Degler, Carl N. **F2659.N4D42 1986**
Neither Black nor White: Slavery and Race Relations in Brazil and the U.S. Trade Paper. University of Wisconsin Press. Chicago, IL. 1986. 324p. ISBN:0-299-10914-3, ISBN13: 978-0-299-10914-1. Dewey:305.8/96081. LCCN:86-040780.
Audience: **u,f.** B

Ferrer, Ada **F1785.F36 1999**
Insurgent Cuba: Race, Nation, and Revolution, 1868-1898. Trade Cloth. University of North Carolina Press. Chapel Hill, NC. 1999. 296p. ISBN:0-8078-2500-X, ISBN13: 978-0-8078-2500-6. Dewey:972.91/05. LCCN:99-013684.
Audience: **u,f.** *Choice, 2000.*

Fryer, Peter **ML232**
Rhythms of Resistance: African Musical Heritage in Brazil. Library Binding. Wesleyan University Press. Middletown, CT. 2000. 281p. ISBN:0-8195-6417-6, ISBN13: 978-0-8195-6417-7. Dewey:780.9/81. LCCN:00-100046.
Audience: **u,f.**

Goldstein, Donna M. **HN290.R5 G58 2003**
Laughter Out of Place: Race, Class, Violence, and Sexuality in a Rio Shantytown. Trade Cloth. University of California Press. Berkeley, CA. 2003. 384p. Public Anthropology Ser. ISBN:0-520-23596-7, ISBN13: 978-0-520-23596-0. Dewey:305.5/68/098153. LCCN:2003-001852.
Audience: **u,f.** *Choice, 2004.*

Hanchard, Michael George **HT1521**
Orpheus and Power: The Movimento Negro of Rio de Janeiro and Sao Paulo, Brazil 1945-1988. Trade Paper. Princeton University Press. Princeton, NJ. 1998. 214p. ISBN:0-691-00270-3, ISBN13: 978-0-691-00270-5. Dewey:305/.800. LCCN:93-038137.
Audience: **u,f.**

Hecht, Tobias **HV887.B82 N674 1998**
At Home in the Street: Street Children of Northeast Brazil. Trade Paper. Cambridge University Press. New York, NY. 1998. 279p. ISBN:0-521-59869-9, ISBN13: 978-0-521-59869-9. Dewey:362.76/0981/3. LCCN:97-034145.
Audience: **u,f.** *Choice, 1998.*

Helg, Aline **F2281.A79H45 2004**
Liberty and Equality in Caribbean Colombia, 1770-1835. Trade Cloth. University of North Carolina Press. Chapel Hill, NC. 2004. 400p. ISBN:0-8078-2876-9, ISBN13: 978-0-8078-2876-2. Dewey:305.896/08611. LCCN:2004-001708.
Audience: **u,f.** *Choice, 2005.*

Helg, Aline **F1789.N3H45 1995**
Our Rightful Share: The Afro-Cuban Struggle for Equality, 1886-1912. Library Binding. University of North Carolina Press. Chapel Hill, NC. 1995. 375p. ISBN:0-8078-2184-5, ISBN13: 978-0-8078-2184-8. Dewey:972.91/00496. LCCN:94-027196.
Audience: **u,f.**

Hellwig, David J. (Editor) **F2659.N4A34 1992**
African-American Reflections on Brazil's Racial Paradise. Trade Cloth. Temple University Press. Philadelphia, PA. 1992. 285p. ISBN:0-87722-892-2, ISBN13: 978-0-87722-892-9. Dewey:981/.00496. LCCN:91-030852.
Audience: **u,f.**

Karasch, Mary C. **HT1129.R53K37 1986**
Slave Life in Rio De Janerio, 1808-1850. Cloth Text. Princeton University Press. Princeton, NJ. 1987. 448p. ISBN:0-691-07708-8, ISBN13: 978-0-691-07708-6. Dewey:305.5/67/098153. LCCN:85-043290.
Audience: **u,f.** *Choice, 1987.*

Klein, Herbert S. **HT1052.5**
African Slavery in Latin America and the Caribbean. Paper Text. Oxford University Press, Inc. New York, NY. 1988. 338p. ISBN:0-19-503838-X, ISBN13: 978-0-19-503838-5. Dewey:306.3/62/098.
Audience: **l,u.**

Lauderdale Graham, Sandra **HT1129.P36L38 2002**
Caetana Says No: Women's Stories from a Brazilian Slave Society. Cloth Text. Cambridge University Press. New York, NY. 2002. 208p. New Approaches to the Americas Ser. ISBN:0-521-81532-0, ISBN13: 978-0-521-81532-1. Dewey:305.48/9625. LCCN:2002-067666.
Audience: **u,f.** *Choice, 2003.*

Levine, Robert M. & Sebebom Meihy, Jose Carlos **F2537.J47 L48**
The Life and Death of Carolina Maria de Jesus. Trade Paper. University of New Mexico Press. Albuquerque, NM. 1996. 176p. Dialogos Ser. ISBN:0-8263-1648-4, ISBN13: 978-0-8263-1648-6. Dewey:981/.61062/092.
Audience: **u,f.** *Choice, 1996.*

Manzano, Juan F. **HT1076.M2813 1996**
The Autobiography of a Slave: A Bilingual Edition. Ivan A. Schulman (Editor, Introduction by), Evelyn P. Garfield (Translator). Trade Cloth. Wayne State University Press. Detroit, MI. 1996. 136p. Latin American Literature and Culture Ser. ISBN:0-8143-2537-8, ISBN13: 978-0-8143-2537-7. Dewey:305.5/67/092 B. LCCN:95-025853.
Audience: **l,u,f.**

Minority Rights Group Staff (Editor) **F1419.N4N6 1995**
No Longer Invisible: Afro-Latin Americans Today. Trade Cloth. Minority Rights Publications. London, 1995. 336p. ISBN:1-873194-80-3, ISBN13: 978-1-873194-80-5. Dewey:980/.00496. LCCN:95-216830.
Audience: **u,f.** *Choice, 1996.*

Montejo, Esteban **HT869.M6 A313 1973**
The Autobiography of a Runaway Slave. Miguel Barnet (Editor). Trade Paper. Random House, Inc. New York, NY. 1983. ISBN:0-394-71832-1, ISBN13: 978-0-394-71832-3. Dewey:917.291/03/50924. LCCN:72-001752.
Audience: **g,l,u,f.**

Moore, Robin D. **ML3486.C8M66 1997**
Nationalizing Blackness: Afrourbanismo and Artistic Revolution in Havana, 1920-1940. Trade Cloth. University of Pittsburgh Press. Pittsburgh, PA. 1997. 336p. Pitt Latin American Ser. ISBN:0-8229-4040-X, ISBN13: 978-0-8229-4040-1. Dewey:781.63/089/9607291. LCCN:97-021045.
Audience: **u,f.** *Choice, 1998.*

Nobles, Melissa **HT1523.N63 2000**
Shades of Citizenship: Race and the Census in Modern Politics. Trade Cloth. Stanford University Press. Palo Alto, CA. 2000. xiv, 248p. ISBN:0-8047-4013-5, ISBN13: 978-0-8047-4013-5. Dewey:305.8/007/2. LCCN:00-026707.
Audience: **u,f.** *Choice, 2001.*

Perez Sarduy, Pedro & Stubbs, Jean **F1789.N3P47 2000**
Afro-Cuban Voices: On Race and Identity in Contemporary Cuba. Manning Marable, James Early & John M. Kirk (Foreword by). Trade Cloth. University Press of Florida. Gainesville, FL. 2000. 312p. Contemporary Cuba Ser. ISBN:0-8130-1735-1, ISBN13: 978-0-8130-1735-8. Dewey:305.896/07291. LCCN:99-053467.
Audience: **u,f.** *Choice, 2000.*

Putnam, Lara **HD1531.C8P88 2002**
The Company They Kept: Migrants and the Politics of Gender in Caribbean Costa Rica, 1870-1960. Trade Cloth. University of North Carolina Press. Chapel Hill, NC. 2002. 320p. ISBN:0-8078-2732-0, ISBN13: 978-0-8078-2732-1. Dewey:306.3/6/097286109034. LCCN:2002-001552.
Audience: **u,f.** *Choice, 2003.*

Reis, João José **HT1129.S24**
Slave Rebellion in Brazil: The Muslim Uprising of 1835 in Bahia. Arthur Brakel (Translator). Trade Paper. Johns Hopkins University Press. Baltimore, MD. 1995. 304p. Studies in Atlantic History and Culture ISBN:0-8018-5250-1, ISBN13: 978-0-8018-5250-3. Dewey:326/.0981/42.
Audience: **u,f.**

Rout, Leslie B. **F1419.N4R68 2003**
The African Experience in Spanish America. Juan Flores & Miriam Jimenez Roman (Introduction by). Trade Paper. Markus Wiener Publishers, Inc. Princeton, NJ. 2003. 420p. ISBN:1-55876-321-X, ISBN13: 978-1-55876-321-0. Dewey:980/.00496. LCCN:2003-049744.
Audience: **u,f.**

Sanders, James E. **F2276.S25 2004**
Contentious Republicans: Popular Politics, Race, and Class in Nineteenth-Century Colombia. Trade Cloth. Duke University Press. Durham, NC. 2004. 320p. ISBN:0-8223-3234-5, ISBN13: 978-0-8223-3234-3. Dewey:986.1/05. LCCN:2003-016426.
Audience: **u,f.** *Choice, 2005.*

Sansone, Carol & Sansone, Livio **F2651.S139N47 2003**
Blackness Without Ethnicity: Constructing Race in Brazil. Cloth over Boards. Palgrave Macmillan. New York, NY. 2003. 256p. ISBN:0-312-29374-7, ISBN13: 978-0-312-29374-1. Dewey:305.896/08142. LCCN:2002-029243.
Audience: **u,f.** *Choice, 2004.*

Scheper-Hughes, Nancy **HV1448.B72**
Death Without Weeping: The Violence of Everyday Life in Brazil. Trade Paper. University of California Press. Berkeley, CA. 1993. 628p. ISBN:0-520-07537-4, ISBN13: 978-0-520-07537-5. Dewey:303.60981.
Audience: **u,f.** *Choice, 1993.*

Schwartz, Stuart B. **HD9114.B7 B347 1985**
Sugar Plantations in the Formation of Brazilian Society: Bahia, 1550-1835. Alan Knight (Contribution by). Trade Paper. Cambridge University Press. New York, NY. 1986. 608p. Cambridge Latin American Studies, No. 52 ISBN:0-521-31399-6, ISBN13: 978-0-521-31399-5. Dewey:306/.0981/42. LCCN:85-006716.
Audience: **u,f.**

Scott, Rebecca J. **E185.93.L6S29 2005**
Degrees of Freedom: Louisiana and Cuba after Slavery. Trade Cloth. Harvard University Press. Cambridge, MA. 2005. 392p. ISBN:0-674-01932-6, ISBN13: 978-0-674-01932-4. Dewey:323.1196/07291/09034. LCCN:2005-047035.
Audience: **u,f.** *Choice, 2006.*

Scott, Rebecca J. **HT1078**
Slave Emancipation in Cuba: The Transition to Free Labor, 1860-1899. Trade Paper. University of Pittsburgh Press. Pittsburgh, PA. 2000. 319p. Pitt Latin American Ser. ISBN:0-8229-5735-3, ISBN13: 978-0-8229-5735-5. Dewey:972.9105.
Audience: **u,f.** *Choice, 1986.*

Sheriff, Robin E. **F2646.9.N4S44 2001**
Dreaming Equality: Color, Race and Racism in Urban Brazil. Trade Cloth. Rutgers University Press. Piscataway, NJ. 2004. 288p. ISBN:0-8135-2999-9, ISBN13: 978-0-8135-2999-8. Dewey:305.896/08153. LCCN:2001-019294.
Audience: **u,f.** *Choice, 2002.*

Skidmore, Thomas E. **F2659.A1S55 1993**
Black into White: Race and Nationality in Brazilian Thought. Paper Text. Duke University Press. Durham, NC. 1993. 334p. ISBN:0-8223-1320-0, ISBN13: 978-0-8223-1320-5. Dewey:305.800981. LCCN:92-028497.
Audience: **u,f.**

Stein, Stanley J. **F2651.V3S7 1985**
Vassouras: A Brazilian Coffee County, 1850-1900: The Roles of Planter and Slave in a Plantation Society. Trade Paper. Princeton University Press. Princeton, NJ. 1986. 336p. ISBN:0-691-02236-4, ISBN13: 978-0-691-02236-9. Dewey:981/.53. LCCN:85-042659.
Audience: **u,f.** B

Stepan, Nancy L. **HQ755.5.L29S74 1991**
The Hour of Eugenics: Race, Gender and Nation in Latin America. Book, Other. Cornell University Press. Ithaca, NY. 1991. 248p. ISBN:0-8014-2569-7, ISBN13: 978-0-8014-2569-1. Dewey:363.92098. LCCN:91-055051.
Audience: **u,f.** *Choice, 1992.*

Sweet, James H. **F2659.N4S94 2003**
Recreating Africa: Kinship, Culture, and Religion in the African-Portuguese World, 1441-1770. Trade Cloth. University of North Carolina Press. Chapel Hill, NC. 2003. 336p. ISBN:0-8078-2808-4, ISBN13: 978-0-8078-2808-3. Dewey:981/.00496. LCCN:2003-001194.
Audience: **u,f.** *Choice, 2004.*

Tannenbaum, Frank **E29.N3T3 1992**
Slave and Citizen: The Classic Comparative Study of Race Relations in the Americas. Franklin Knight (Introduction by). Trade Paper. Beacon Press. Boston, MA. 1992. 160p. ISBN:0-8070-0913-X, ISBN13: 978-0-8070-0913-0. Dewey:973/.0496. LCCN:91-021434.
Audience: **u,f.**

Telles, Edward Eric **F2659.A1T45 2004**
Race in Another America: The Significance of Skin Color in Brazil. Trade Cloth. Princeton University Press. Princeton, NJ. 2004. 336p. ISBN:0-691-11866-3, ISBN13: 978-0-691-11866-6. Dewey:305.896/081. LCCN:2004-044288.
Audience: **u,f.** *Choice, 2005.*

Torres, Arlene & Whitten, Norman E. Jr. (Editors) **F1419.N4B53 1998**
Blackness in Latin America and the Caribbean, Social Dynamics and Cultural Transformations: Eastern South America and the Caribbean. Trade Paper. Indiana University Press. Bloomington, IN. 1998. 456p. ISBN:0-253-21194-8, ISBN13: 978-0-253-21194-1. Dewey:305.89608. LCCN:97-044093.
Audience: **u,f.**

Twine, Frances W. **F2659.N4T86 1998**
Racism in a Racial Democracy: The Maintenance of White Supremacy in Brazil. Trade Cloth. Rutgers University Press. Piscataway, NJ. 1997. 175p. ISBN:0-8135-2364-8, ISBN13: 978-0-8135-2364-4. Dewey:305.896/081. LCCN:97-010768.
Audience: **u,f.** *Choice, 1998.*

Wade, Peter **F2299.B55.W3**
Blackness and Race Mixture: The Dynamics of Racial Identity in Colombia. Trade Paper. Johns Hopkins University Press. Baltimore, MD. 1989. 432p. Studies in Atlantic History and Culture ISBN:0-8018-5251-X, ISBN13: 978-0-8018-5251-0. Dewey:305.8960861. LCCN:92-015581.
Audience: **u,f.** *Choice, 1994.*

Wade, Peter **GN564.L29W33 1997**
Race and Ethnicity in Latin America. Trade Cloth. Pluto Press. London, 1997. 160p. Critical Studies on Latin America ISBN:0-7453-0988-7, ISBN13: 978-0-7453-0988-0. Dewey:305.8/0098. LCCN:96-051820.
Audience: **l,u,f.**

Whitten, Norman E. Jr. & Torres, Arlene (Editors) **F1419.N4B53 1998**
Blackness in Latin America and the Caribbean, Social Dynamics and Cultural Transformations: Central America, Northern, and Western South America. Trade Paper. Indiana University Press. Bloomington, IN. 1998. 432p. ISBN:0-253-21193-X, ISBN13: 978-0-253-21193-4. Dewey:305.89608. LCCN:97-044093.
Audience: **u,f.**

Wright, Winthrop R. **F2349.B55**
Cafe Con Leche: Race, Class, and National Image in Venezuela. Trade Paper. University of Texas Press. Austin, TX. 1993. 184p. ISBN:0-292-79080-5, ISBN13: 978-0-292-79080-3. Dewey:987.00496.
Audience: **u,f.**

Latin America: General > Drugs

Andrews, George & Solomon, David (Editors) **QP981.C14**
The Coca Leaf and Cocaine Papers. Trade Cloth. Harcourt Trade Publishers. New York, NY. 1975. 384p. ISBN:0-15-118237-X, ISBN13: 978-0-15-118237-4. Dewey:615/.782. LCCN:75-012988.
Audience: **u,f.**

Ashley, Richard **RC568.C6**
Cocaine: Its History, Uses and Effects. Mass Market. Warner Books, Inc. New York, NY. 1982. 240p. ISBN:0-446-30500-6, ISBN13: 978-0-446-30500-6. Dewey:613.83.
Audience: **g,l,u,f.**

Astorga Almanza, Luis Alejandro **HV5840.M6**
El Siglo de las Drogas: Usos, Percepciones, y Personajes. Espasa-Calpe Mexicana. 1996. ISBN:968-413-366-9, ISBN13: 978-968-413-366-2.
Audience: **u,f.**

Cotler, Julio **HV5840.P46 C67 1999**
Drogas y Política en el Perú: La Conneción Norteamericana. IEP. 1999. Peru Problema, No. 26
Audience: **u,f.**

Courtwright, David T. **HV5816.C648 2001**
Dark Paradise: A History of Opiate Addiction in America. Ed. 2. Trade Paper. Harvard University Press. Cambridge, MA. 2001. 352p. ISBN:0-674-00585-6, ISBN13: 978-0-674-00585-3. Dewey:362.29/3/0973. LCCN:2001-016547.
Audience: **g,l,u,f.**

Courtwright, David T. **HV4997.C68 2001**
Forces of Habit: Drugs and the Making of the Modern World. Trade Cloth. Harvard University Press. Cambridge, MA. 2001. 288p. ISBN:0-674-00458-2, ISBN13: 978-0-674-00458-0. Dewey:362.29. LCCN:00-061466.
Audience: **g,l,u,f.** *Choice, 2001.*

Friman, H. Richard **HV5801**
Narcodiplomacy: Exporting the U. S. War on Drugs. Trade Cloth. DIANE Publishing Company. Collingdale, PA. 2005. 170p. ISBN:0-7567-9554-0, ISBN13: 978-0-7567-9554-2. Dewey:363.4/5/0973.
Audience: **u,f.**

Gagliano, Joseph A. **HV5840.P46G34 1994**
Coca Prohibition in Peru: The Historical Debates. Trade Cloth. University of Arizona Press. Tucson, AZ. 1994. 245p. ISBN:0-8165-1445-3, ISBN13: 978-0-8165-1445-8. Dewey:363.4/5/0985. LCCN:94-009570.
Audience: **u,f.** *Choice, 1995.*

Goodman, Jordan (Editor), et al. **GT3010.C65 1995**
Consuming Habits: Drugs in History and Anthropology. Paul E. Lovejoy & Andrew Sherratt (Editors). Paper over Boards. Routledge. New York, NY. 1995. 256p. ISBN:0-415-09039-3, ISBN13: 978-0-415-09039-1. Dewey:394.1/4/09. LCCN:94-042752.
Audience: **l,u,f.**

Gootenberg, Paul **HV5810.C645 1999**
Cocaine: Global Histories. Paper over Boards. Routledge. New York, NY. 1999. 240p. ISBN:0-415-19247-1, ISBN13: 978-0-415-19247-7. Dewey:362.29/8. LCCN:99-019400.
Audience: **u,f.**

Grinspoon, Lester & Bakalar, James B. **HV5810.G73**
Cocaine: A Drug and Its Social Evolution. Cloth Text. Basic Books. New York, NY. 1976. x, 308p. ISBN:0-465-01189-6, ISBN13: 978-0-465-01189-6. Dewey:362.2/93. LCCN:76-007675.
Audience: **l,u,f.** B

Henman, Anthony **F2270.2.P3 A57**
ANTONIL, Mama Coca. Hassle Free Press. 1987.
Audience: **u,f.**

Jankowiak, William R. & Bradburd, Daniel (Editors) **HV5824.I48D78 2003**
Drugs, Labor, and Colonial Expansion. Trade Cloth. University of Arizona Press. Tucson, AZ. 2003. viii, 253p. ISBN:0-8165-2351-7, ISBN13: 978-0-8165-2351-1. Dewey:306.3/6. LCCN:2003-005025.
Audience: **u,f.**

Karch, Steven **QP801.C68**
A Brief History of Cocaine. CRC Press. 1996. ISBN:0-8493-4019-5, ISBN13: 978-0-8493-4019-2.
Audience: **g,l,u,f.**

Kennedy, Joseph **HV5822.H4**
Coca Exotica. Trade Cloth. Fairleigh Dickinson University Press. Cranbury, NJ. 1985. 144p. ISBN:0-8386-3103-7, ISBN13: 978-0-8386-3103-4. Dewey:362.2/93. LCCN:82-045861.
Audience: **u,f.** *Choice, 1985.*

McAllister, William B. **HV5801.M335 2000**
Drug Diplomacy in Twentieth Century: International History. Paper over Boards. Routledge. New York, NY. 1999. 368p. ISBN:0-415-17989-0, ISBN13: 978-0-415-17989-8. Dewey:363.45/0904. LCCN:99-018225.
Audience: **u,f.**

Mintz, Sidney W. **GT2850.M58 1996**
Tasting Food, Tasting Freedom: Excursions into Eating, Power, and the Past. Trade Paper. Beacon Press. Boston, MA. 1997. 176p. ISBN:0-8070-4629-9, ISBN13: 978-0-8070-4629-6. Dewey:394.1. LCCN:95-047569.
Audience: **g,l,u,f.**

Morales, Edmundo **HV5840.P46**
Cocaine: White Gold Rush in Peru. Trade Paper. University of Arizona Press. Tucson, AZ. 1990. 228p. ISBN:0-8165-1159-4, ISBN13: 978-0-8165-1159-4. Dewey:363.4/5/0985. LCCN:88-030303.
Audience: **u,f.** *Choice, 1989.*

Mortimer, William Golden **RS165.C5**
Peru and the History of Coca: Divine Plant of the Incas. Library Binding. Gordon Press Publishers. New York, NY. 1976. ISBN:0-8490-0821-2, ISBN13: 978-0-8490-0821-4. Dewey:615.788.
Audience: **u,f.**

Musto, David F. **HV5825.M84 1999**
The American Disease: Origins of Narcotic Control. Ed. 3. Trade Paper. Oxford University Press, Inc. New York, NY. 1999. 430p. ISBN:0-19-512509-6, ISBN13: 978-0-19-512509-2. Dewey:362.29/3/0973. LCCN:98-024976.
Audience: **u,f.**

Nadelmann, Ethan A. **HV8138**
Cops Across Borders: The Internationalization of U. S. Criminal Law Enforcement. Trade Paper. Pennsylvania State University Press. University Park, PA. 1993. 558p. ISBN:0-271-01095-9, ISBN13: 978-0-271-01095-3. Dewey:363.2/0973. LCCN:93-001305.
Audience: **u,f.** *Choice, 1994.*

Pendergrast, Mark **HD9349.S634C674 2000**
For God, Country and Coca-Cola: The Definitive History of the Great American Soft Drink and the Company That Makes It. Ed. 2. Trade Paper. Basic Books. New York, NY. 2000. 640p. ISBN:0-465-05468-4, ISBN13: 978-0-465-05468-8. Dewey:338.7/66362/0973. LCCN:00-701571.
Audience: **g,l,u,f.**

Rudgley, Richard **GN411.R83 1993**
Essential Substances: A Cultural History of Intoxicants in Society. John Urda (Editor), William A. Emboden (Foreword by). Trade Paper. Kodansha America, Inc. New York, NY. 1995. 208p. Kodansha Globe Trade Paperback Ser. ISBN:1-56836-075-4, ISBN13: 978-1-56836-075-1. Dewey:394.1/4. LCCN:93-051053.
Audience: **u,f.**

Sanabria, Harry **HD9019.C632B647 1993**
The Coca Boom and Rural Social Change in Bolivia. Trade Cloth. University of Michigan Press. Chicago, IL. 1993. 296p. Linking Levels of Analysis Ser. ISBN:0-472-10313-X, ISBN13: 978-0-472-10313-3. Dewey:338.1/7374/098423. LCCN:93-023794.
Audience: **u,f.** *Choice, 1994.*

Schivelbusch, Wolfgang **GT2880 .S3613 1993**
Tastes of Paradise: A Social History of Spices, Stimulants, and Intoxicants. David Jacobson (Translator). Trade Paper. Knopf Publishing Group. New York, NY. 1993. 256p. ISBN:0-679-74438-X, ISBN13: 978-0-679-74438-2. Dewey:394.1/2. LCCN:92-050603.
Audience: **g,l,u,f.**

Soux, María Luisa **HD9019.C632 B6473 1993**
La Coca Liberal: Producción y Circulación a Principios del Siglo XX. La Paz. 1993.
Audience: **u,f.**

Spillane, Joseph E. & Kosofsky, Barry E. **HV5825.S597 2000**
Cocaine: From Medical Marvel to Modern Menace in the United States, 1884-1920. Trade Cloth. Johns Hopkins University Press. Baltimore, MD. 2000. 240p. Studies in Industry and Society, Vol. 18 ISBN:0-8018-6230-2, ISBN13: 978-0-8018-6230-4. Dewey:362.29/8/0973. LCCN:99-032725.
Audience: **l,u,f.** *Choice, 2000.*

Taylor, Arnold H. **HV5801 .T3**
American Diplomacy and the Narcotics Traffic, 1900-1939: A Study in International Humanitarian Reform. Trade Cloth. Duke University Press. Durham, NC. 1969. viii, 370p. ISBN:0-8223-0219-5, ISBN13: 978-0-8223-0219-3. Dewey:353.007/65. LCCN:77-086482.
Audience: **u,f.**

Walker **HV5801.W33 1989**
Drug Control in the Americas. Trade Paper. University of New Mexico Press. Albuquerque, NM. 1989. 339p. ISBN:0-8263-1142-3, ISBN13: 978-0-8263-1142-9. Dewey:363.4/5/091812. LCCN:89-004756.
Audience: **u,f.**

Latin America: General > Women and Gender

Alvarez, Sonia E. **HQ1236.5.B6A44 1990**
Engendering Democracy in Brazil: Women's Movements in Transition Politics. Trade Paper. Princeton University Press. Princeton, NJ. 1990. 320p. ISBN:0-691-02325-5, ISBN13: 978-0-691-02325-0. Dewey:305.42/0981. LCCN:90-033837.
Audience: **u,f.** *Choice, 1991.*

Arrom, Silvia M. **HQ1465.M6 A77 1985**
The Women of Mexico City, 1790-1857. Trade Cloth. Stanford University Press. Palo Alto, CA. 1985. 400p. ISBN:0-8047-1233-6, ISBN13: 978-0-8047-1233-0. Dewey:305.4/2/097253/09034. LCCN:83-051324.
Audience: **l,u,f.** *Choice, 1986.*

Burns, Kathryn **F3611.C9B87 1999**
Colonial Habits: Convents and the Spiritual Economy of Cuzco, Peru. Trade Cloth. Duke University Press. Durham, NC. 1999. xi, 307p. ISBN:0-8223-2259-5, ISBN13: 978-0-8223-2259-7. Dewey:985/.37. LCCN:98-008099.
Audience: **u,f.** *Choice, 1999.*

Caufield, Sue Ann **HQ18.B7C38 2000**
In Defense of Honor: Sexual Morality, Modernity and Nation in Early Twentieth Century Brazil. Trade Cloth. Duke University Press. Durham, NC. 1999. xiv, 311p. ISBN:0-8223-2377-X,

ISBN13: 978-0-8223-2377-8. Dewey:306.7/0981/0904. LCCN:99-028323.
Audience: **u,f.** *Choice, 2000.*

Caulfield, Sueann, et al. **KG99.H66 2005**
Honor, Status, and Law in Modern Latin America. Sarah Chambers & Lara Putnam (Authors). Trade Cloth. Duke University Press. Durham, NC. 2005. 360p. ISBN:0-8223-3575-1, ISBN13: 978-0-8223-3575-7. Dewey:340/.115/098. LCCN:2004-029836.
Audience: **u,f.**

Chambers, Sarah **JS2678.A72C48 1999**
From Subjects to Citizens: Honor, Culture and Politics in Arequipa, Peru, 1780-1854. Trade Cloth. Pennsylvania State University Press. University Park, PA. 1999. 296p. ISBN:0-271-01901-8, ISBN13: 978-0-271-01901-7. Dewey:306.2/0985/3209034. LCCN:98-037144.
Audience: **u,f.** *Choice, 2000.*

De Jesus, Carolina M. **HN290.S33**
Child of the Dark: The Diary of Carolina Maria de Jesus. David St. Clair (Translator), Robert S. Levine (Afterword by). Mass Market. Penguin Group (USA) Inc. New York, NY. 2003. 208p. ISBN:0-451-52910-3, ISBN13: 978-0-451-52910-7. Dewey:306/.0981/61.
Audience: **g,l.**

Dore, Elizabeth & Molyneux, Maxine (Editors) **HQ1075.5.L29H53**
Hidden Histories of Gender and the State in Latin America. Cloth Text. Duke University Press. Durham, NC. 2000. 400p. ISBN:0-8223-2434-2, ISBN13: 978-0-8223-2434-8. Dewey:305.3/098. LCCN:99-036543.
Audience: **u,f.**

Findlay, Eileen Suarez **HQ164.A5F56 1999**
Imposing Decency: The Politics of Sexuality and Race in Puerto Rico, 1870-1920. Trade Cloth. Duke University Press. Durham, NC. 1999. 320p. American Encounters/Global Interactions Ser. ISBN:0-8223-2375-3, ISBN13: 978-0-8223-2375-4. Dewey:306/.097295. LCCN:99-025911.
Audience: **u,f.** *Choice, 2000.*

French, John D. & James, Daniel **HD6100.5.G46 1997**
The Gendered Worlds of Latin American Women Workers: From Household and Factory to the Union Hall and Ballot Box. Trade Cloth. Duke University Press. Durham, NC. 1997. 336p. ISBN:0-8223-2000-2, ISBN13: 978-0-8223-2000-5. Dewey:331.4/098. LCCN:97-020053.
Audience: **u,f.** *Choice, 1998.*

Hahner, June E. (Editor) **HQ1460.5.W64**
Women in Latin American History: Their Lives and Views. Paper Text. University of California, Latin American Center. Los Angeles, CA. 1976. Latin American Studies Ser., Vol. 34 ISBN:0-87903-034-8, ISBN13: 978-0-87903-034-6. Dewey:305.4/098. LCCN:75-620131.
Audience: **g,l,u.**

Johnson, Lyman L. & Lipsett-Rivera, Sonya **BJ1533.H8F33 1998**
The Faces of Honor: Sex, Shame, and Violence in Colonial Latin America. Trade Cloth. University of New Mexico Press. Albuquerque, NM. 1998. 240p. Dialogos Ser. ISBN:0-8263-1924-6, ISBN13: 978-0-8263-1924-1. Dewey:306/.098. LCCN:98-018974.
Audience: **u,f.**

Lavrin, Asuncion **HQ1460**
Latin American Women: Historical Perspectives. Trade Cloth. Greenwood Publishing Group, Inc. Portsmouth, NH. 1978. 343p. Contributions in Women's Studies, No. 3 ISBN:0-313-20309-1, ISBN13: 978-0-313-20309-1. Dewey:301.41/2/098. LCCN:77-094758.
Audience: **g,l,u.**

Matto de Turner, Clorinda **PQ8497.M3A913 1996**
Birds without a Nest: A Novel. J. G. H. (Translator), Naomi Lindstrom (Contribution by). Trade Paper. University of Texas Press. Austin, TX. 1996. 205p. Texas Pan American Ser. ISBN:0-292-75195-8, ISBN13: 978-0-292-75195-8. Dewey:863. LCCN:95-044768.
Audience: **g,l,u,f.** *Choice, 1997.*

Nijeholt, Geertje A. & Wieringa, Saskia **HQ1236.W6523 1998**
Women's Movements and Public Policy in Europe, Latin America, and the Caribbean: The Triangle of Empowerment. Virginia Vargas & Chandra Mohanty (Editors). Cloth Text. Garland Publishing, Inc. New York, NY. 1997. 196p. Gender, Culture, and Global Politics Ser., No. 2 ISBN:0-8153-2479-0, ISBN13: 978-0-8153-2479-9. Dewey:305.42. LCCN:97-013518.
Audience: **l,u,f.** *Choice, 1998.*

Shayne, Julie D. **HQ1460.5.S53 2004**
The Revolution Question: Feminisms in el Salvador, Chile, and Cuba Compared. Trade Cloth. Rutgers University Press. Piscataway, NJ. 2004. 240p. ISBN:0-8135-3483-6, ISBN13: 978-0-8135-3483-1. Dewey:305.42. LCCN:2004-003816.
Audience: **u,f.** *Choice, 2005.*

Silverblatt, Irene Marsha **F3429.3.S6S55 1987**
Moon, Sun and Witches: Gender Ideologies and Class in Inca and Colonial Peru. Trade Paper. Princeton University Press. Princeton, NJ. 1987. 302p. ISBN:0-691-02258-5, ISBN13: 978-0-691-02258-1. Dewey:985/.01/088042. LCCN:86-022514.
Audience: **u,f.** *Choice, 1987.*

Socolow, Susan Migden **HQ1460.5 .S64 2000**
The Women of Colonial Latin America. Stuart B. Schwartz (Contribution by). Trade Cloth. Cambridge University Press. New York, NY. 2000. 252p. New Approaches to the Americas Ser. ISBN:0-521-47052-8, ISBN13: 978-0-521-47052-0. Dewey:305.4/098. LCCN:99-029134.
Audience: **g,l,u.** *Choice, 2000.*

Stephen, Lynn **HQ1240.5.L29S74 1997**
Women and Social Movements in Latin America: Power from Below. Trade Cloth. University of Texas Press. Austin, TX. 1997. 352p. ISBN:0-292-77715-9, ISBN13: 978-0-292-77715-6. Dewey:305.42/098. LCCN:96-045788.
Audience: **u,f.** *Choice, 1998.*

Stoll, David **F1465.2.Q5M3885 1999**
Rigoberta Menchu and the Story of All Poor Guatemalans. Trade Paper. Westview Press. Boulder, CO. 1999. 368p. ISBN:0-8133-3694-5, ISBN13: 978-0-8133-3694-7. Dewey:972.81/00497415. LCCN:98-042832.
Audience: **g,l,u,f.**

Tetreault, Mary A. (Editor) **HQ1236.W6364 1994**
Women and Revolution in Africa, Asia, and the New World. Cloth Text. University of South Carolina Press. Columbia, SC. 1994. 472p. ISBN:1-57003-016-2, ISBN13: 978-1-57003-016-1. Dewey:305.42. LCCN:94-018706.
Audience: **g,l,u.** *Choice, 1995.*

Mexico

Britton, John A. **F1234**
Revolution and Ideology: Images of the Mexican Revolution in the United States. University Press of Kentucky, Lexington, KY.. 1995. ISBN:0-8131-1896-4, ISBN13: 978-0-8131-1896-3.
Audience: **u,f.**

Koth, Karl B. **F1371**
Waking the Dictator: Veracruz, the Struggle for Federalism and the Mexican Revolution, 1870-1927. University of Calgary Press, Calgary, Alta.. 2002. Latin American and Caribbean Series ISBN:1-55238-031-9, ISBN13: 978-1-55238-031-4.
Audience: **u,f.**

Meyer, Michael C. & Beezley, William H. (Editors) **F1226.O94 2000**
The Oxford History of Mexico. Trade Cloth. Oxford University Press, Inc. New York, NY. 2000. 736p. ISBN:0-19-511228-8, ISBN13: 978-0-19-511228-3. Dewey:972. LCCN:99-056044.
Audience: **u,f.** *Choice, 2001.*

Mexico > Colonial Mexico

Altman, Ida **F1391.P6A48 2000**
Transatlantic Ties in the Spanish Empire: Brihuega, Spain, and Puebla, Mexico, 1560-1620. Trade Cloth. Stanford University Press. Palo Alto, CA. 2000. viii, 254p. ISBN:0-8047-3663-4, ISBN13: 978-0-8047-3663-3. Dewey:972/.4800461. LCCN:99-047891.
Audience: **u,f.** *Choice, 2001.*

Alvarez de Toledo, Cayetana **F1231**
Politics and Reform in Spain and Viceregal Mexico: The Life and Thought of Juan de Palafox 1600-1659. Trade Cloth. Oxford University Press, Inc. New York, NY. 2004. 354p. Oxford Historical Monographs ISBN:0-19-927028-7, ISBN13: 978-0-19-927028-6. Dewey:972.02. LCCN:2004-300759.
Audience: **u,f.**

Andrien, Kenneth J. & Johnson, Lyman L. **HC124.P65 1994**
[e] The Political Economy of Spanish America in the Age of Revolution, 1750-1850. E-Book. NetLibrary, Inc. Boulder, CO. 1994. ISBN:0-585-17903-4, ISBN13: 978-0-585-17903-2. Dewey:338.98.
Audience: **u,f.**

Archer, Christon I. (Editor) **F1232.B62 2003**
The Birth of Modern Mexico, 1780-1824. Book, Other. Rowman & Littlefield Publishers, Inc. Lanham, MD. 2003. 257p. ISBN:0-8420-5126-0, ISBN13: 978-0-8420-5126-2. Dewey:972/.03. LCCN:2002-155239.
Audience: **u,f.**

Arnold, Linda **JL1246.A76 1988**
Bureaucracy and Bureaucrats in Mexico City, 1742-1835. Trade Cloth. University of Arizona Press. Tucson, AZ. 1988. 202p. ISBN:0-8165-1068-7, ISBN13: 978-0-8165-1068-9. Dewey:354.7201/09. LCCN:88-017226.
Audience: **u,f.** *Choice, 1989.*

Arrom, Silvia M. **HV63.M6A77 2000**
Containing the Poor: The Mexico City Poor House, 1774-1871. Trade Cloth. Duke University Press. Durham, NC. 2000. 408p. ISBN:0-8223-2527-6, ISBN13: 978-0-8223-2527-7. Dewey:362.5/85/097253. LCCN:00-029396.
Audience: **u,f.** *Choice, 2001.*

Bennett, Herman L. **F1386.9.B55B46 2003**
[e] Africans in Colonial Mexico: Absolutism, Christianity, and Afro-Creole Consciousness, 1570-1640. E-Book. Indiana University Press. Bloomington, IN. 2003. 312p. Blacks in the Diaspora Ser. ISBN:0-253-34236-8, ISBN13: 978-0-253-34236-2. Dewey:972/.00496. LCCN:2002-152282.
Audience: **u,f.** *Choice, 2004.*

Boyer, Richard **HQ561.B69 1995**
Lives of the Bigamists: Marriage, Family, and Community in Colonial Mexico. Trade Cloth. University of New Mexico Press. Albuquerque, NM. 1995. 342p. ISBN:0-8263-1571-2, ISBN13: 978-0-8263-1571-7. Dewey:364.1/83/0972. LCCN:94-038576.
Audience: **u,f.**

Boyer, Richard G. & Spurling, Geoffrey (Editors) **F1410.C725 2000**
Colonial Lives: Documents on Latin American History, 1550-1850. Paper Text. Oxford University Press, Inc. New York, NY. 1999. 368p. ISBN:0-19-512512-6, ISBN13: 978-0-19-512512-2. Dewey:980.3/1. LCCN:99-018180.
Audience: **u,f.**

Brading, D. A. **BX1430.M53 B73 1994**
Church and State in Bourbon Mexico: The Diocese of Michoacan, 1749-1810. Trade Cloth. Cambridge University Press. New York, NY. 1994. 314p. ISBN:0-521-46092-1, ISBN13: 978-0-521-46092-7. Dewey:282/.7237. LCCN:93-044303.
Audience: **u,f.**

Brading, D. A. **F1412**
The First America: The Spanish Monarchy, Creole Patriots and the Liberal State, 1492-1866. Trade Paper. Cambridge University Press. New York, NY. 1993. 779p. ISBN:0-521-44796-8, ISBN13: 978-0-521-44796-6. Dewey:980/.013.
Audience: **u,f.** *Choice, 1991.*

Brockington, Lolita G. **HD8119.T44B76 1989**
The Leverage of Labor: Managing the Cortes Haciendas in Tehuantepec, 1588-1688. Cloth Text. Duke University Press. Durham, NC. 1989. xxv, 246p. ISBN:0-8223-0884-3, ISBN13: 978-0-8223-0884-3. Dewey:331/.0972/74. LCCN:88-025717.
Audience: **u,f.** *Choice, 1990.*

Cervantes, Fernando **BF1548 .C48**
The Devil in the New World: The Impact of Diabolism in New Spain. Trade Paper. Yale University Press. Cumberland, RI. 1997. 192p. ISBN:0-300-06889-1, ISBN13: 978-0-300-06889-4. Dewey:133.4/22/0972.
Audience: **u,f.**

Chandler, D. S. **JL1249.S2C48 1991**
Social Assistance and Bureaucratic Politics: The Montepios of Colonial Mexico, 1767-1821. Trade Cloth. University of New Mexico Press. Albuquerque, NM. 1991. 247p. ISBN:0-8263-1306-X, ISBN13: 978-0-8263-1306-5. Dewey:354.72/01/09033. LCCN:91-020369.
Audience: **u,f.** *Choice, 1992.*

Chipman, Donald E. **F1230.C54 2005**
Moctezuma's Children: Aztec Royalty under Spanish Rule, 1520-1700. Trade Cloth. University of Texas Press. Austin, TX. 2005. 224p. ISBN:0-292-70628-6, ISBN13: 978-0-292-70628-6. Dewey:929/.2/0972. LCCN:2004-027640.
Audience: **u,f.**

Chowning, Margaret **F1306.C46 1999**
Wealth and Power in Provincial Mexico: Michoacán from the Late Colony to the Revolution. Trade Cloth. Stanford University Press. Palo Alto, CA. 1999. xiv, 477p. ISBN:0-8047-3428-3, ISBN13: 978-0-8047-3428-8. Dewey:972/.37. LCCN:99-024871.
Audience: **u,f.** *Choice, 2000.*

Clendinnen, Inga **F1219.73**
Aztecs: An Interpretation. Trade Paper. Cambridge University Press. New York, NY. 1995. 414p. A Canto Book Ser. ISBN:0-521-48585-1, ISBN13: 978-0-521-48585-2. Dewey:972/.018.
Audience: **l,u.** *Choice, 1992.*

Clendinnen, Inga **F1376.C55 2003**
Ambivalent Conquests: Maya and Spaniard in Yucatan, 1517-1570. Ed. 2. Alan Knight (Contribution by). Cloth Text. Cambridge University Press. New York, NY. 2003. 264p. Cambridge Latin American Studies, Vol. 61 ISBN:0-521-82031-6, ISBN13: 978-0-521-82031-8. Dewey:972/.6502. LCCN:2002-191144.
Audience: **u,f.** *Choice, 1987.*

Cook, Alexandra P. & Cook, Noble D. **KKT174.N64C66 1991**
Good Faith and Truthful Ignorance: A Case of Transatlantic Bigamy. Trade Cloth. Duke University Press. Durham, NC. 1991. 224p. ISBN:0-8223-1086-4, ISBN13: 978-0-8223-1086-0. Dewey:980/.013/092. LCCN:90-036173.
Audience: **u,f.** *Choice, 1991.*

Cope, R. Douglas **F1386.3 .C66 1994**
The Limits of Racial Domination: Plebeian Society in Colonial Mexico City, 1660-1720. Trade Cloth. University of Wisconsin Press. Chicago, IL. 1994. 220p. ISBN:0-299-14040-7, ISBN13: 978-0-299-14040-3. Dewey:972.5302. LCCN:93-023344.
Audience: **u,f.** *Choice, 1994.*

Couturier, Edith Boorstein **F1231.R72C68 2003**
Silver King: The Remarkable Life of the Count of Regla in Colonial Mexico. Trade Cloth. University of New Mexico Press. Albuquerque, NM. 2003. 224p. ISBN:0-8263-2873-3, ISBN13: 978-0-8263-2873-1. LCCN:2003-007853.
Audience: **u,f.**

Cutter, Charles R. **KF361 .C87**
The Legal Culture of Northern New Spain, 1700-1810. Trade Paper. University of New Mexico Press. Albuquerque, NM. 2001. 227p. ISBN:0-8263-2775-3, ISBN13: 978-0-8263-2775-8. Dewey:349.764/09/033.
Audience: **u,f.**

Deans-Smith, Susan **HD9144.M42D43 1992**
Bureaucrats, Planters, and Workers: The Making of the Tobacco Monopoly in Bourbon Mexico. Trade Cloth. University of Texas Press. Austin, TX. 1992. 384p. ISBN:0-292-70786-X, ISBN13: 978-0-292-70786-3. Dewey:338.1/7371/097209033. LCCN:91-029116.
Audience: **u,f.**

Gerhard, Peter **F1228.9**
The Southeast Frontier of New Spain. Ed. 2. Trade Cloth. University of Oklahoma Press. Norman, OK. 1993. 220p. ISBN:0-8061-2543-8, ISBN13: 978-0-8061-2543-5. Dewey:911/.72. LCCN:92-041923.
Audience: **u,f.**

Gosner, Kevin **F1221.T8.G67 1992**
Soldiers of the Virgin: The Moral Economy of a Colonial Maya Rebellion. Trade Cloth. University of Arizona Press. Tucson, AZ. 1992. 228p. ISBN:0-8165-1293-0, ISBN13: 978-0-8165-1293-5. Dewey:972/.75. LCCN:91-042775.
Audience: **u,f.** *Choice, 1993.*

Guardino, Peter **F1391.O12G83 2005**
Time of Liberty: Popular Political Culture in Oaxaca, 1750-1850. Trade Cloth. Duke University Press. Durham, NC. 2005. 408p. Latin America Otherwise Ser. ISBN:0-8223-3508-5, ISBN13: 978-0-8223-3508-5. Dewey:972/.74. LCCN:2004-027162.
Audience: **u,f.** *Choice, 2006.*

Haber, Stephen, ed. **HC187.H68 1997**
How Latin American Fell Behind: Essays on the Economic Histories of Brazil and Mexico, 1800-1914. Stanford University Press. 1997. ISBN:0-8047-2737-6, ISBN13: 978-0-8047-2737-2.
Audience: **u,f.**

Hamnett, Brian R. **F1231**
Roots of Insurgency: Mexican Regions, 1750-1824. Alan Knight (Contribution by). Trade Paper. Cambridge University Press. New York, NY. 2002. 286p. Cambridge Latin American Studies ISBN:0-521-89324-0, ISBN13: 978-0-521-89324-4. Dewey:972/.02.
Audience: **u,f.** *Choice, 1987.*

Haskett, Robert **F1221.N3H37 1991**
Indigenous Rulers: An Ethnohistory of Town Governments in Colonial Cuernavaca. Trade Cloth. University of New Mexico Press. Albuquerque, NM. 1991. 306p. ISBN:0-8263-1286-1, ISBN13: 978-0-8263-1286-0. Dewey:972/.49. LCCN:91-016324.
Audience: **u,f.** *Choice, 1992.*

Haskett, Robert **F2519.54.A98H37 2004**
Visions of Paradise: Primordial Titles and Mesoamerican History in Cuernavaca. Trade Cloth. University of Oklahoma Press. Norman, OK. 2005. 352p. ISBN:0-8061-3586-7, ISBN13: 978-0-8061-3586-1. Dewey:972/.49. LCCN:2004-055399.
Audience: **u,f.** *Choice, 2006.*

Haslip-Viera, Gabriel **HV6815.M4H37 1999**
Crime and Punishment in Late Colonial Mexico City, 1692-1810. Trade Cloth. University of New Mexico Press. Albuquerque, NM. 1999. xii, 193p. ISBN:0-8263-1875-4, ISBN13: 978-0-8263-1875-6. Dewey:364.972/53. LCCN:98-058106.
Audience: **u,f.** *Choice, 1999.*

Hassig, Ross **F1230 .H37 1994**
Mexico and the Spanish Conquest: Wars in Context. Ed. 1. Trade Paper. Longman Publishing Group. White Plains, NY.

1995. 216p. ISBN:0-582-06829-0, ISBN13: 978-0-582-06829-2. Dewey:972.02. LCCN:92-046022.
Audience: **u,f.**

Hassig, Ross **F1219.76.C35H37 2001**
Time, History, and Belief in Aztec and Colonial Mexico. Trade Cloth. University of Texas Press. Austin, TX. 2001. 256p. ISBN:0-292-73139-6, ISBN13: 978-0-292-73139-4. Dewey:529/.32978452. LCCN:00-041783.
Audience: **u,f.** *Choice, 2001.*

Hecht, Tobias (Editor) **HQ792.L3M56 2002**
Minor Omissions: Children in Latin American History and Society. Trade Cloth. University of Wisconsin Press. Chicago, IL. 2002. 296p. Living in Latin America Ser. ISBN:0-299-18030-1, ISBN13: 978-0-299-18030-0. Dewey:305.23/098. LCCN:2002-003993.
Audience: **u,f.** *Choice, 2003.*

Himmerich Y Valencia, Robert **F1230**
The Encomenderos of New Spain, 1521-1555. Joseph P. Sánchez (Foreword by). Trade Paper. University of Texas Press. Austin, TX. 1996. 364p. ISBN:0-292-73108-6, ISBN13: 978-0-292-73108-0. Dewey:972.02.
Audience: **u,f.**

Hoberman, Loise Schell & Migden Socolow, Susan (Editors) **HN110.5.Z9C626318**
The Countryside in Colonial Latin America. Trade Cloth. University of New Mexico Press. Albuquerque, NM. 1996. 296p. Dialogos Ser. ISBN:0-8263-1710-3, ISBN13: 978-0-8263-1710-0. Dewey:306/.098. LCCN:95-041737.
Audience: **u,f.**

Hoberman, Louisa S. **HF3235.H63 1991**
Mexico's Merchant Elite, 1590-1660: Silver, State, and Society. Cloth Text. Duke University Press. Durham, NC. 1991. 369p. ISBN:0-8223-1134-8, ISBN13: 978-0-8223-1134-8. Dewey:305.5/56. LCCN:90-020659.
Audience: **u,f.** *Choice, 1992.*

Ilarione **F1211.I4213 2000**
Daily Life in Colonial Mexico: The Journey of Friar Ilarione da Bergamo, 1761-1768. Robert Ryal Miller (Editor), William J. Orr (Editor, Translator). Trade Cloth. University of Oklahoma Press. Norman, OK. 2000. 256p. American Exploration and Travel Ser., Vol. 78 ISBN:0-8061-3234-5, ISBN13: 978-0-8061-3234-1. Dewey:972/.02. LCCN:00-025949.
Audience: **u,f.** *Choice, 2001.*

Jaffary, Nora E. **BX1740.M6J34 2004**
False Mystics: Deviant Orthodoxy in Colonial Mexico. Cloth Text. University of Nebraska Press. Lincoln, NE. 2005. 288p. Engendering Latin America Ser. ISBN:0-8032-2599-7, ISBN13: 978-0-8032-2599-2. Dewey:272/.2/0972. LCCN:2004-010511.
Audience: **u,f.** *Choice, 2005.*

Johnson, Lymon L. & Tandeter, Enrique (Editors) **HB235.L25E85 1990**
Essays on the Price History of Eighteenth-Century Latin America. Trade Cloth. University of New Mexico Press. Albuquerque, NM. 1990. 419p. ISBN:0-8263-1163-6, ISBN13: 978-0-8263-1163-4. Dewey:338.5/2/09809033. LCCN:89-036043.
Audience: **u,f.** *Choice, 1990.*

Jones, Grant D. **F1465.2.I87J65 1998**
The Conquest of the Last Maya Kingdom. Trade Cloth. Stanford University Press. Palo Alto, CA. 1998. 550p. ISBN:0-8047-3317-1, ISBN13: 978-0-8047-3317-5. Dewey:972.81/2004974. LCCN:98-016556.
Audience: **u,f.** *Choice, 1999.*

Kellogg, Susan **KDZ480**
Law and the Transformation of Aztec Culture, 1500-1700. Trade Paper. University of Oklahoma Press. Norman, OK. 2005. 320p. ISBN:0-8061-3685-5, ISBN13: 978-0-8061-3685-1. Dewey:325/.3146/09720903.
Audience: **u,f.** *Choice, 1995.*

Kinsbruner, Jay **HT127.5.K56 2005**
The Colonial Spanish-American City: Urban Life in the Age of Atlantic Capitalism. Trade Cloth. University of Texas Press. Austin, TX. 2005. 198p. ISBN:0-292-70621-9, ISBN13: 978-0-292-70621-7. Dewey:307.76098. LCCN:2004-022134.
Audience: **u,f.** *Choice, 2006.*

Leon-Portilla, Miguel **F1231.S33L4613 2002**
Bernardino de Sahagun, First Anthropologist. Trade Cloth. University of Oklahoma Press. Norman, OK. 2002. 224p. ISBN:0-8061-3364-3, ISBN13: 978-0-8061-3364-5. Dewey:972/.02/092. LCCN:2001-053465.
Audience: **l,u,f.** *Choice, 2003.*

Leon-Portilla, Miguel (Editor, Introduction by) **F1230 .V5713**
The Broken Spears: The Aztec Account of the Conquest of Mexico. Lysander Kemp (Translator), J. Jorge Klor de Alva (Foreword by). Trade Paper. DIANE Publishing Company. Collingdale, PA. 2004. 196p. ISBN:0-7567-7964-2, ISBN13: 978-0-7567-7964-1. Dewey:972/.02.
Audience: **l,u,f.**

Lewis, Laura A. **HN113.L48 2003**
Hall of Mirrors: Power, Witchcraft, and Caste in Colonial Mexico. Trade Cloth. Duke University Press. Durham, NC. 2003. 280p. Latin America Otherwise Ser. ISBN:0-8223-3111-X, ISBN13: 978-0-8223-3111-7. Dewey:306/.0972. LCCN:2003-005048.
Audience: **u,f.** *Choice, 2004.*

Lockhart, James **F1221.N3L63 1992**
The Nahuas after the Conquest: A Social and Cultural History of the Indians of Central Mexico, Sixteenth Through Eighteenth Centuries. Trade Cloth. Stanford University Press. Palo Alto, CA. 1992. 672p. ISBN:0-8047-1927-6, ISBN13: 978-0-8047-1927-8. Dewey:972/.02. LCCN:91-029972.
Audience: **u,f.** *Choice, 1993.*

Martin, Cheryl English **E99.A6**
Governance and Society in Colonial Mexico: Chihuahua in the Eighteenth Century. Trade Paper. Stanford University Press. Palo Alto, CA. 2001. 280p. ISBN:0-8047-4168-9, ISBN13: 978-0-8047-4168-2. Dewey:972.1/6/02.
Audience: **u,f.**

Melville, Elinor G. K. **SF375.5.M6 M45 1994**
A Plague of Sheep: Environmental Consequences of the Conquest of Mexico. Alfred W. Crosby & Donald Worster (Contribution by). Trade Paper. Cambridge University Press. New York, NY. 1997. 219p. Studies in Environment and History Ser. ISBN:0-521-57448-X, ISBN13: 978-0-521-57448-8. Dewey:304.2/7/097246/09031.
Audience: **u,f.**

Mundy, Barbara E. **GA481.M86 1996**
The Mapping of New Spain: Indigenous Cartography and the Maps of the Relaciones Geograficas. Trade Cloth. University of Chicago Press. Chicago, IL. 1996. 306p. ISBN:0-226-55096-6, ISBN13: 978-0-226-55096-1. Dewey:912.72. LCCN:96-015824.
Audience: **u,f.** *Choice, 1997.*

Offutt, Leslie Scott **HC138.S25O34 2001**
Town and Region in the Mexican North: Saltillo, 1770-1810. Trade Cloth. University of Arizona Press. Tucson, AZ. 2001. 290p. ISBN:0-8165-2164-6, ISBN13: 978-0-8165-2164-7. Dewey:330.972/14. LCCN:2001-027193.
Audience: **u,f.**

Patch, Robert W. **F1465.P37 2002**
Maya Revolt and Revolution in the Eighteenth Century. Robert M. Levine (Foreword by). Trade Cloth. M. E. Sharpe Inc. Armonk, NY. 2002. 270p. Latin American Realities Ser. ISBN:0-7656-0411-6, ISBN13: 978-0-7656-0411-8. Dewey:972/.6502. LCCN:2002-066518.
Audience: **u,f.**

Pescador, Juan Javier **DP302.O9P47 2003**
The New World Inside a Basque Village: The Oiartzun Valley and Its Atlantic Emigrants, 1550-1800. Cloth Text. University of Nevada Press. Reno, NV. 2003. 200p. The Basque Ser. ISBN:0-87417-570-4, ISBN13: 978-0-87417-570-7. Dewey:303.48/246607. LCCN:2003-006540.
Audience: **u,f.**

Pierce, Donna, et al. **ND253.P54 2004**
Painting a New World: Mexican Art and Life, 1521-1821. Rogelio Ruiz Gomar, Clara Bargellini & Denver Art Museum Staff (Authors), Frederick and Jan Mayer Center for Pre-Columbian and Spanish Colonial Art Staff (Contribution by). Trade Cloth. Denver Art Museum. Denver, CO. 2004. 328p. ISBN:0-914738-49-6, ISBN13: 978-0-914738-49-7. Dewey:759.972/09. LCCN:2003-024691.
Audience: **l,u,f.** *Choice, 2006.*

Poole, Stafford **BT660.G8**
Our Lady of Guadalupe: The Origins and Sources of a Mexican National Symbol, 1531-1797. Trade Paper. University of Arizona Press. Tucson, AZ. 1996. 325p. ISBN:0-8165-1623-5, ISBN13: 978-0-8165-1623-0. Dewey:232.9/17/097253. LCCN:94-018724.
Audience: **l,u,f.** *Choice, 1995.*

Radding, Cynthia R. **GN560.M6R33 1997**
Wandering Peoples: Colonialism, Ethnic Spaces, and Ecological Frontiers in Northwestern Mexico, 1700-1850. Library Binding. Duke University Press. Durham, NC. 1997. 368p. Latin America Otherwise Ser. ISBN:0-8223-1907-1, ISBN13: 978-0-8223-1907-8. Dewey:305.8/0097217. LCCN:96-035147.
Audience: **u,f.** *Choice, 1997.*

Restall, Matthew **F1435**
The Maya World: Yucatec Culture and Society, 1550-1850. Trade Paper. Stanford University Press. Palo Alto, CA. 1997. 474p. ISBN:0-8047-3658-8, ISBN13: 978-0-8047-3658-9. Dewey:972.81/016.
Audience: **l,u,f.** *Choice, 1998.*

Restall, Matthew **F1230.R47 2003**
Seven Myths of the Spanish Conquest. Trade Cloth. Oxford University Press, Inc. New York, NY. 2003. 240p. ISBN:0-19-516077-0, ISBN13: 978-0-19-516077-2. Dewey:980/.013/072. LCCN:2002-192492.
Audience: **u,f.**

Robinson, David J. (Editor) **HB1961.M54 1990**
Migration in Colonial Spanish America. Alan R. H. Baker, Richard Dennis & Deryck Holdworth (Contribution by). Trade Cloth. Cambridge University Press. New York, NY. 1990. 417p. Studies in Historical Geography, No. 16 ISBN:0-521-36281-4, ISBN13: 978-0-521-36281-8. Dewey:304.8/09171/246. LCCN:89-001042.
Audience: **u,f.**

Salvucci, Richard J. **HD9864.M62S25 1987**
Textiles and Capitalism in Mexico: An Economic History of the Obrajes, 1539-1840. Trade Cloth. Princeton University Press. Princeton, NJ. 1988. 240p. ISBN:0-691-07749-5, ISBN13: 978-0-691-07749-9. Dewey:338.4/767702824/0972. LCCN:87-045535.
Audience: **u,f.** *Choice, 1988.*

Schroeder, Susan **F1219.76.P75S37 1991**
Chimalpahin and the Kingdoms of Chalco. Trade Cloth. University of Arizona Press. Tucson, AZ. 1991. 264p. ISBN:0-8165-1182-9, ISBN13: 978-0-8165-1182-2. Dewey:972/.52. LCCN:90-011170.
Audience: **u,f.** *Choice, 1991.*

Schroeder, Susan **F1219.3.W6**
Indian Women of Early Mexico. Trade Paper. University of Oklahoma Press. Norman, OK. 1999. 496p. ISBN:0-8061-2960-3, ISBN13: 978-0-8061-2960-0. Dewey:305.48/897072.
Audience: **l,u,f.** *Choice, 1998.*

Schroeder, Susan (Editor) **F1219.3.G6N37 1998**
Native Resistance and the Pax Colonial in New Spain. Cloth Text. University of Nebraska Press. Lincoln, NE. 1998. 200p. ISBN:0-8032-4266-2, ISBN13: 978-0-8032-4266-1. Dewey:972/.02. LCCN:97-035833.
Audience: **u,f.**

Schwaller, John F. **BX1428.2.S37 1987**
The Church and Clergy in Sixteenth-Century Mexico. Trade Cloth. University of New Mexico Press. Albuquerque, NM. 1987. 280p. ISBN:0-8263-0973-9, ISBN13: 978-0-8263-0973-0. Dewey:282/.72. LCCN:87-005942.
Audience: **u,f.**

Schwartz, Stuart B. (Editor) **F1230.V53 2000**
Victors and Vanquished: Spanish and Nahua Views of the Conquest of Mexico. Cloth over Boards. Palgrave Macmillan. New York, NY. 2000. 288p. Bedford Series in History and Culture ISBN:0-312-22817-1, ISBN13: 978-0-312-22817-0. Dewey:972/.02. LCCN:99-062438.
Audience: **u,f.**

Seed, Patricia **HQ728.S37 1988**
To Love, Honor, and Obey in Colonial Mexico: Conflicts over Marriage Choice, 1574-1821. Trade Cloth. Stanford University Press. Palo Alto, CA. 1988. 333p. ISBN:0-8047-1457-6, ISBN13: 978-0-8047-1457-0. Dewey:306.8/1/097252/0903. LCCN:88-002374.
Audience: **u,f.**

Stafford Poole, C. M. **BX4705.M738P66 1987**
Pedro Moya de Contreras: Catholic Reform and Royal Power in New Spain, 1571-1591. Trade Cloth. University of California

Press. Berkeley, CA. 1987. 350p. ISBN:0-520-05551-9, ISBN13: 978-0-520-05551-3. Dewey:282/.092/4. LCCN:86-001410.
Audience: **u,f.**

Stein, Stanley J. & Stein, Barbara H. **HF3685.S737 2003**
Apogee of Empire: Spain and New Spain in the Age of Charles III, 1759-1789. Trade Cloth. Johns Hopkins University Press. Baltimore, MD. 2003. 480p. ISBN:0-8018-7339-8, ISBN13: 978-0-8018-7339-3. Dewey:382/.0946/08. LCCN:2002-013940.
Audience: **u,f.** *Choice, 2004.*

Stern, Steve J. **F1434.2.S63**
The Secret History of Gender: Women, Men, and Power in Late Colonial Mexico. Trade Paper. University of North Carolina Press. Chapel Hill, NC. 1997. 496p. ISBN:0-8078-4643-0, ISBN13: 978-0-8078-4643-8. Dewey:305.3/0972. LCCN:94-039349.
Audience: **u,f.** *Choice, 1996.*

Taylor, William B. **BX1428.2.T38 1996**
Magistrates of the Sacred: Priests and Parishioners in Eighteenth-Century Mexico. Trade Cloth. Stanford University Press. Palo Alto, CA. 1996. 984p. ISBN:0-8047-2456-3, ISBN13: 978-0-8047-2456-2. Dewey:972/.02. LCCN:95-022982.
Audience: **u,f.**

Terraciano, Kevin **F1219.8.M59T47 2001**
The Mixtecs of Colonial Oaxaca: Ñudzahui History, Sixteenth Through Eighteenth Centuries. Trade Cloth. Stanford University Press. Palo Alto, CA. 2002. 528p. ISBN:0-8047-3756-8, ISBN13: 978-0-8047-3756-2. Dewey:972/.74. LCCN:2001-020022.
Audience: **u,f.** *Choice, 2003, 2002.*

Thomson, Guy P. **HC138.P78T47 1989**
Puebla de Los Angeles: Industry and Society in a Mexican City, 1700-1850. Paper Text. Westview Press. Boulder, CO. 1989. 400p. ISBN:0-8133-7781-1, ISBN13: 978-0-8133-7781-0. Dewey:330.972/48. LCCN:89-037522.
Audience: **u,f.**

Van Young, Eric **F1232**
The Other Rebellion: Popular Violence, Ideology, and the Mexican Struggle for Independence, 1810-1821. Trade Paper. Stanford University Press. Palo Alto, CA. 2001. 720p. ISBN:0-8047-4821-7, ISBN13: 978-0-8047-4821-6. Dewey:972/.03.
Audience: **u,f.**

Vicardo y Guzman, Juan Pablo **F2233.V587 2002**
Letter to the Spanish Americans: A Facsimile of the Second English Edition. John Carter Brown Library. 2002. ISBN:0-916617-58-0, ISBN13: 978-0-916617-58-5.
Audience: **u,f.**

Vinson, Ben **UA605.M55V56 2001**
Bearing Arms for His Majesty: The Free-Colored Militia in Colonial Mexico. Trade Cloth. Stanford University Press. Palo Alto, CA. 2001. 383p. ISBN:0-8047-4229-4, ISBN13: 978-0-8047-4229-0. Dewey:355.3/7/0972. LCCN:2001-020609.
Audience: **u,f.** *Choice, 2002.*

Viqueira Alban, Juan Pedro **F1386.2.V5713 1999**
Property and Permissiveness in Bourbon Mexico. Rowman. 1999. ISBN:0-8420-2466-2, ISBN13: 978-0-8420-2466-2.
Audience: **u,f.**

Voekel, Pamela **BX1428.3.V64 2002**
Alone Before God: The Religious Origins of Modernity in Mexico. Trade Cloth. Duke University Press. Durham, NC. 2002. 352p. ISBN:0-8223-2927-1, ISBN13: 978-0-8223-2927-5. Dewey:282/.72. LCCN:2002-001654.
Audience: **u,f.**

Warren, Richard A. **F1386.3.W37 2001**
Vagrants and Citizens: Politics and the Masses in Mexico City from Colony to Republic. Book, Other. Rowman & Littlefield Publishers, Inc. Lanham, MD. 2001. 202p. Latin American Silhouettes Ser. ISBN:0-8420-2964-8, ISBN13: 978-0-8420-2964-3. Dewey:972/.5304. LCCN:2001-020990.
Audience: **u,f.** *Choice, 2002.*

Whitmore, Thomas M. **F1219.3.P73W47 1992**
Disease and Death in Early Colonial Mexico: Simulating Amerindian Depopulation, Vol. 28. Trade Paper. Westview Press. Boulder, CO. 1992. 261p. ISBN:0-8133-8188-6, ISBN13: 978-0-8133-8188-6. Dewey:305.897/072. LCCN:91-018346.
Audience: **u,f.**

Wood, Stephanie Gail **F1221.N3W66 2003**
Transcending Conquest: Nahua Views of Spanish Colonial Mexico. Trade Cloth. University of Oklahoma Press. Norman, OK. 2003. 224p. ISBN:0-8061-3486-0, ISBN13: 978-0-8061-3486-4. Dewey:972/.02. LCCN:2002-069589.
Audience: **u,f.**

Mexico > 19th Century Mexico

Anna, Timothy E. **F1232.A573 1998**
Forging Mexico, 1821-1835. Trade Cloth. University of Nebraska Press. Lincoln, NE. 1998. 330p. ISBN:0-8032-1047-7, ISBN13: 978-0-8032-1047-9. Dewey:972/.04. LCCN:97-025062.
Audience: **u,f.** *Choice, 1998.*

Arrom, Silvia M. **HV63.M6A77 2000**
Containing the Poor: The Mexico City Poor House, 1774-1871. Trade Cloth. Duke University Press. Durham, NC. 2000. 408p. ISBN:0-8223-2527-6, ISBN13: 978-0-8223-2527-7. Dewey:362.5/85/097253. LCCN:00-029396.
Audience: **u,f.** *Choice, 2001.*

Arrom, Silvia M. **HQ1465.M6 A77 1985**
The Women of Mexico City, 1790-1857. Trade Cloth. Stanford University Press. Palo Alto, CA. 1985. 400p. ISBN:0-8047-1233-6, ISBN13: 978-0-8047-1233-0. Dewey:305.4/2/097253/09034. LCCN:83-051324.
Audience: **l,u,f.** *Choice, 1986.*

Bazant, Jan **BX1428.2 .B38**
Alienation of Church Wealth in Mexico. Cloth Text. Cambridge University Press. New York, NY. 1971. 350p. Cambridge Latin American Studies, No. 11 ISBN:0-521-07872-5, ISBN13: 978-0-521-07872-6. Dewey:333.1/4. LCCN:74-149441.
Audience: **u,f.**

Coatsworth, John H. **HE2818 .C56**
Growth Against Development: The Economic Impact of Railroads in Porfirian Mexico. Trade Cloth. Northern Illinois University Press. DeKalb, IL. 1981. 249p. The Origins of Modern Mexico Ser. ISBN:0-87580-075-0, ISBN13: 978-0-87580-075-2. Dewey:385/.1/0972. LCCN:80-008662.
Audience: **u,f.**

Cosío Villegas, Daniel **F1233.5**
Historia Moderna de México, 10 vols. Editorial Hermes. 1955.
Audience: **l,u.**

de la Barca, Frances Calderon **F1213**
Life in Mexico. Trade Paper. Kessinger Publishing, LLC. Whitefish, MT. 2004. ISBN:1-4191-3023-4, ISBN13: 978-1-4191-3023-6. Dewey:917.2034.
Audience: **l,u,f.**

Diaz Diaz, Fernando **F1232.S2313**
Caudillos y Caciques: Antonio Lopez de Santa Anna y Juan Alvarez. Trade Paper. Books on Demand. Ann Arbor, MI. 365p. Centro de Estudios Historicos. Nueva Serie Ser., Vol. 15 ISBN:0-598-11354-1, ISBN13: 978-0-598-11354-2. Dewey:972.04. LCCN:73-334469.
Audience: **u,f.**

French, William E. **HN120.S6.F74 1996**
A Peaceful and Working People: Manners, Morals, and Class Formation in Northern Mexico. Trade Cloth. University of New Mexico Press. Albuquerque, NM. 1996. 263p. ISBN:0-8263-1683-2, ISBN13: 978-0-8263-1683-7. Dewey:305.5/0972/16. LCCN:95-032446.
Audience: **u,f.** *Choice, 1996.*

González Navarro, Luis **F1376**
Raza y Tierra: La Guerra de Castas y el Heneqén. El Colegio de México. 1970.
Audience: **l,u.**

Guardino, Peter F. **LB875.D4**
Peasants, Politics, and the Formation of Mexico's National State. Paper Text. Stanford University Press. Palo Alto, CA. 336p. ISBN:0-8047-4190-5, ISBN13: 978-0-8047-4190-3. Dewey:370/.1.
Audience: **u,f.**

Haber, Stephen H. **HC135.H17 1989**
Industry and Underdevelopment: The Industrialization of Mexico, 1890-1940. Trade Cloth. Stanford University Press. Palo Alto, CA. 1995. 256p. ISBN:0-8047-1487-8, ISBN13: 978-0-8047-1487-7. Dewey:338.0972. LCCN:88-024863.
Audience: **u,f.** *Choice, 1989.*

Hale, Charles A. **F1232 .H27**
Mexican Liberalism in the Age of Mora, 1821-1853. Trade Cloth. Yale University Press. Cumberland, RI. 1968. Caribbean Ser., No. 11 ISBN:0-300-00531-8, ISBN13: 978-0-300-00531-8. Dewey:320.5/1/0972. LCCN:68-013908.
Audience: **u,f.**

Herrera Serna, Laura **E404**
México en Guerra (1846-1848): Perspectivas Regionales. Consejo Nacional para la Cultura y las Artes. 1997. ISBN:968-29-9718-6, ISBN13: 978-968-29-9718-1.
Audience: **l,u.**

Johns, Michael **F1386.3.J6 1997**
The City of Mexico in the Age of Díaz. Trade Cloth. University of Texas Press. Austin, TX. 1997. 168p. ISBN:0-292-74047-6, ISBN13: 978-0-292-74047-1. Dewey:972/.530814. LCCN:96-044570.
Audience: **u,f.** *Choice, 1998.*

Perry, Laurens B. **F1233.5 .P44**
Juarez and Diaz: Machine Politics in Mexico. Trade Cloth. Northern Illinois University Press. DeKalb, IL. 1978. 467p. The Origins of Modern Mexico Ser. ISBN:0-87580-058-0, ISBN13: 978-0-87580-058-5. Dewey:320.9/71/081. LCCN:76-014671.
Audience: **u,f.**

Reed, Nelson A. **F1376.R43 2001**
The Caste War of Yucatan. Ed. 2. Trade Cloth. Stanford University Press. Palo Alto, CA. 2001. xvi, 428p. ISBN:0-8047-4000-3, ISBN13: 978-0-8047-4000-5. Dewey:972/.6505. LCCN:2001-020019.
Audience: **u,f.** *Choice, 2002.*

Rugeley, Terry **BL2560.M6R84 2001**
Of Wonders and Wise Men: Religion and Popular Cultures in Southeast Mexico. Trade Paper. University of Texas Press. Austin, TX. 2001. 365p. ISBN:0-292-77107-X, ISBN13: 978-0-292-77107-9. Dewey:277.2/6081. LCCN:00-029909.
Audience: **u,f.**

Rugeley, Terry **F1435.3.W2R84 1996**
Yucatán's Maya Peasantry and the Origins of the Caste War. Trade Cloth. University of Texas Press. Austin, TX. 1996. 263p. ISBN:0-292-77074-X, ISBN13: 978-0-292-77074-4. Dewey:972/.606. LCCN:95-042405.
Audience: **u,f.** *Choice, 1997.*

Santoni, Pedro **E407.S26 1996**
Mexicans at Arms: Puro Federalists and the Politics of War, 1845-1848. Trade Cloth. Texas Christian University Press. Fort Worth, TX. 1996. 324p. ISBN:0-87565-158-5, ISBN13: 978-0-87565-158-3. Dewey:973.6/21. LCCN:95-052183.
Audience: **u,f.** *Choice, 1997.*

Stevens, Donald F. **F1232.S74 1991**
Origins of Instability in Early Republican Mexico. Cloth Text. Duke University Press. Durham, NC. 1991. 199p. ISBN:0-8223-1136-4, ISBN13: 978-0-8223-1136-2. Dewey:320.972. LCCN:90-025357.
Audience: **u,f.**

Tenenbaum, Barbara **HJ802.T46 1986**
The Politics of Penury: Debts and Taxes in Mexico, 1821-1856. Trade Cloth. University of New Mexico Press. Albuquerque, NM. 1986. 268p. ISBN:0-8263-0890-2, ISBN13: 978-0-8263-0890-0. Dewey:336.72. LCCN:86-016027.
Audience: **u,f.** *Choice, 1987.*

Vanderwood, Paul J. **HV8161.A2V36 1992**
Disorder and Progress: Bandits, Police, and Mexican Development. Ed. 2. Trade Cloth. Rowman & Littlefield Publishers, Inc. Lanham, MD. 1992. 320p. Latin American Silhouettes Ser. ISBN:0-8420-2438-7, ISBN13: 978-0-8420-2438-9. Dewey:364.1/552/0972. LCCN:92-014784.
Audience: **u,f.**

Vanderwood, Paul J. **BR615.T65V36 1998**
The Power of God Against the Guns of Government: Religious Upheaval in Mexico at the Turn of the Nineteenth Century. Trade Cloth. Stanford University Press. Palo Alto, CA. 1998. 444p. ISBN:0-8047-3038-5, ISBN13: 978-0-8047-3038-9. Dewey:972/.16. LCCN:97-032506.
Audience: **u,f.** *Choice, 1998.*

Wasserman, Mark **F1232.W38 2000**
Everyday Life and Politics in Nineteenth Century Mexico: Men, Women, and War. Trade Cloth. University of New Mexico Press. Albuquerque, NM. 2004. 248p. Dialogos Ser. ISBN:0-8263-2170-4, ISBN13: 978-0-8263-2170-1. Dewey:972/.04. LCCN:99-006913.
Audience: **u,f.**

Mexico > 20th Century Mexico

Aguilar Camín, Héctor & Meyer, Lorenzo **F1234.A22513 1993**
In the Shadow of the Mexican Revolution: Contemporary Mexican History, 1910-1989. Luis A. Fierro (Editor). Trade Paper. University of Texas Press. Austin, TX. 1993. 295p. Translations from Latin America Ser. ISBN:0-292-70451-8, ISBN13: 978-0-292-70451-0. LCCN:93-005168.
Audience: **u,f.**

Alonso, Ana Maria **F1261.A45 1995**
Thread of Blood (H&E): Colonialism, Revolution, and Gender on Mexico's Northern Frontier. Trade Cloth. University of Arizona Press. Tucson, AZ. 1995. 303p. Hegemony and Experience Ser. ISBN:0-8165-1511-5, ISBN13: 978-0-8165-1511-0. Dewey:972/.16. LCCN:95-032475.
Audience: **u,f.** *Choice, 1996.*

Andrews, Gregg **HD6490.F582U613 1991**
Shoulder to Shoulder?: The American Federation of Labor, the United States, and the Mexican Revolution, 1910-1924. Trade Cloth. University of California Press. Berkeley, CA. 1991. 295p. ISBN:0-520-07230-8, ISBN13: 978-0-520-07230-5. Dewey:322/.2/0973. LCCN:91-011343.
Audience: **u,f.** *Choice, 1992.*

Bailey, John J. **JL1281.B34 1988**
Governing Mexico, 1976-88: The Statecraft of Crisis Management. Cloth Text. Palgrave Macmillan. New York, NY. 1988. 272p. ISBN:0-312-01209-8, ISBN13: 978-0-312-01209-0. Dewey:320.972. LCCN:87-028479.
Audience: **u,f.** *Choice, 1989.*

Bailey, John J. & Godson, Roy S. **HV6812.O74 2000**
Organized Crime and Democratic Governability: Mexico and the U.S.-Mexican Borderlands. Trade Cloth. University of Pittsburgh Press. Pittsburgh, PA. 2000. ix, 271p. Pitt Latin American Ser. ISBN:0-8229-5758-2, ISBN13: 978-0-8229-5758-4. Dewey:364.1/06/0972. LCCN:00-011649.
Audience: **u,f.**

Baldwin, Deborah **F1234.B2 1990**
Protestants and the Mexican Revolution: Missionaries, Ministers and Social Change. Trade Cloth. University of Illinois Press. Champaign, IL. 1990. 216p. ISBN:0-252-01659-9, ISBN13: 978-0-252-01659-2. Dewey:972.08/16. LCCN:89-032708.
Audience: **u,f.** *Choice, 1990.*

Becker, Marjorie **F1234.C233B43 1995**
Setting the Virgin on Fire: Lázaro Cárdenas, Michoacán Peasants, and the Redemption of the Mexican Revolution. Trade Paper. University of California Press. Berkeley, CA. 1996. 212p. Twentieth-Century Japan Ser. ISBN:0-520-08419-5, ISBN13: 978-0-520-08419-3. LCCN:94-040327.
Audience: **u,f.** *Choice, 1996.*

Beezley, William H. & Lorey, David E. (Editors) **F1210.V58 2001**
Viva Mexico! Viva la Independencia!: Celebrations of September 16. Book, Other. Rowman & Littlefield Publishers, Inc. Lanham, MD. 2000. xviii, 261p. Latin American Silhouettes Ser. ISBN:0-8420-2914-1, ISBN13: 978-0-8420-2914-8. Dewey:972. LCCN:00-041325.
Audience: **u,f.**

Beezley, William H. (Editor), et al. **GT4814.A2R57 1994**
Rituals of Rule, Rituals of Resistance: Public Celebrations and Popular Culture in Mexico. Cheryl E. Martin & William E. French (Editors). Book, Other. Rowman & Littlefield Publishers, Inc. Lanham, MD. 1994. 374p. Latin American Silhouettes Ser. ISBN:0-8420-2416-6, ISBN13: 978-0-8420-2416-7. Dewey:394.2/6972. LCCN:94-000884.
Audience: **u,f.**

Benjamin, Thomas **F1234.B465 2000**
La Revolucion: Mexico's Great Revolution As Memory, Myth and History. Trade Paper. University of Texas Press. Austin, TX. 2000. 251p. ISBN:0-292-70882-3, ISBN13: 978-0-292-70882-2. Dewey:972.08/16. LCCN:99-046431.
Audience: **u,f.** *Choice, 2000.*

Benjamin, Thomas **HC137.C47B46 1996**
A Rich Land, a Poor People: Politics and Society in Modern Chiapas. Ed. 2. Trade Paper. University of New Mexico Press. Albuquerque, NM. 1996. 376p. ISBN:0-8263-1713-8, ISBN13: 978-0-8263-1713-1. Dewey:338.972/75. LCCN:95-041262.
Audience: **u,f.** *Choice, 1989.*

Benjamin, Thomas & Wasserman, Mark (Editors) **F1234.P96 1990**
Provinces of the Revolution: Essays on Regional Mexican History, 1910-1929. Trade Paper. University of New Mexico Press. Albuquerque, NM. 1990. 400p. ISBN:0-8263-1205-5, ISBN13: 978-0-8263-1205-1. Dewey:972.08/16. LCCN:89-077647.
Audience: **u,f.**

Berger, Dina **G155.M6**
The Development of Mexico's Tourism Industry: Pyramids by Day, Martinis by Night. Trade Cloth. Palgrave Macmillan. New York, NY. 2006. 192p. ISBN:1-4039-6635-4, ISBN13: 978-1-4039-6635-3. Dewey:338.4/79172. LCCN:2005-058652.
Audience: **u,f.** *Choice, 2006.*

Bortz, Jeff & Haber, Stephen H. (Editors) **HC135.M525518 2002**
The Mexican Economy, 1870-1930: Essays on the Economic History of Institutions, Revolution, and Growth. Trade Cloth. Stanford University Press. Palo Alto, CA. 2002. xvii, 348p. Social Science History Ser. ISBN:0-8047-4207-3, ISBN13: 978-0-8047-4207-8. Dewey:330.972. LCCN:2001-049259.
Audience: **u,f.**

Boyer, Christopher R. **HD1531.M6B69 2002**
Becoming Campesinos: Politics, Identity, and Agrarian Struggle in Postrevolutionary Michoacan, 1920-1935. Trade Cloth. Stanford University Press. Palo Alto, CA. 2003. 320p. ISBN:0-8047-4352-5, ISBN13: 978-0-8047-4352-5. Dewey:305.5/633. LCCN:2002-012183.
Audience: **u,f.** *Choice, 2003.*

Brown, Jonathan C. **HD9574.M6B7 1992**
Oil and Revolution in Mexico. Trade Cloth. University of California Press. Berkeley, CA. 1993. 460p. ISBN:0-520-07934-5, ISBN13: 978-0-520-07934-2. Dewey:338.272820972. LCCN:92-025649.
Audience: **u,f.** *Choice, 1993.*

Bruhn, Kathleen **JL1298.A1B78 1997**
Taking on Goliath: Party Formation, Party System Change, and Democratization in Mexico. Trade Paper. Pennsylvania State University Press. University Park, PA. 1996. 520p.

ISBN:0-271-01587-X, ISBN13: 978-0-271-01587-3. Dewey:324/.0972/09049. LCCN:95-047061.
Audience: **u,f.** *Choice, 1997.*

Buchenau, Jürgen **F1231.5.M666 2005**
Mexico Otherwise: Modern Mexico in the Eyes of Foreign Observers. Trade Paper. University of New Mexico Press. Albuquerque, NM. 2005. 285p. ISBN:0-8263-2313-8, ISBN13: 978-0-8263-2313-2. Dewey:972. LCCN:2004-030819.
Audience: **u,f.**

Butler, Edgar W. & Bustamante, Jorge A. (Editors) **JL1292.S874 1991**
Sucesion Presidencial: The Nineteen Eighty-Eight Mexican Presidential Election. Paper Text. Westview Press. Boulder, CO. 1990. 264p. ISBN:0-8133-7886-9, ISBN13: 978-0-8133-7886-2. Dewey:324.972/0834. LCCN:90-025260.
Audience: **u,f.** *Choice, 1991.*

Camp, Roderic A. **BX1428.2.C27 1997**
Crossing Swords: Politics and Religion in Mexico. Trade Cloth. Oxford University Press, Inc. New York, NY. 1997. 350p. ISBN:0-19-510784-5, ISBN13: 978-0-19-510784-5. Dewey:322.1/0972. LCCN:96-000838.
Audience: **u,f.**

Camp, Roderic A. **HC135.C212 1989**
Entrepreneurs and Politics in Twentieth-Century Mexico. Trade Cloth. Oxford University Press, Inc. New York, NY. 1989. 320p. ISBN:0-19-505719-8, ISBN13: 978-0-19-505719-5. Dewey:338/.04/0922. LCCN:88-028745.
Audience: **u,f.** *Choice, 1989.*

Camp, Roderic A. **HN120.Z9**
Intellectuals and the State in Twentieth-Century Mexico. Cloth Text. University of Texas Press. Austin, TX. 1985. 293p. Latin American Monographs, No. 65 ISBN:0-292-73836-6, ISBN13: 978-0-292-73836-2. Dewey:305.5/52/0972.
Audience: **u,f.** *Choice, 1986.*

Camp, Roderic Ai **HN120.Z9 E433 2002**
Mexico's Mandarins: Crafting a Power Elite for the Twenty-First Century. Trade Cloth. University of California Press. Berkeley, CA. 2002. 320p. ISBN:0-520-23343-3, ISBN13: 978-0-520-23343-0. Dewey:305.5/2/0972. LCCN:2001-003643.
Audience: **u,f.**

Camp, Roderic Ai **F1236**
Mexico's Military on the Democratic Stage. Armand B. Peschard-Sverdrup (Foreword by). Trade Cloth. Greenwood Publishing Group, Inc. Portsmouth, NH. 2005. 392p. ISBN:0-275-98810-4, ISBN13: 978-0-275-98810-4. Dewey:972.08/2. LCCN:2005-016705.
Audience: **u,f.** *Choice, 2006.*

Chalkley, John F. **F1234.C478 1998**
Zach Lamar Cobb: El Paso Customs and Intelligence During the Mexican Revolution, 1913-1918. Trade Paper. Texas Western Press. El Paso, TX. 1999. 164p. Southwestern Studies, Vol. 103 ISBN:0-87404-199-6, ISBN13: 978-0-87404-199-6. Dewey:972.08/2. LCCN:96-061730.
Audience: **u,f.**

Chassen-Lopez, Francie R. **F1321.C54 2004**
From Liberal to Revolutionary Oaxaca: The View from the South, Mexico 1867-1911. Trade Paper. Pennsylvania State University Press. University Park, PA. 2005. 512p. ISBN:0-271-02512-3, ISBN13: 978-0-271-02512-4. Dewey:972.74081. LCCN:2003-027047.
Audience: **u,f.**

Coerver, Don M. & Hall, Linda B. **F786.C653 1984**
Texas and the Mexican Revolution: A Study in State and National Border Policy, 1910-1920. Trade Cloth. Trinity University Press. San Antonio, TX. 167p. ISBN:0-939980-06-1, ISBN13: 978-0-939980-06-2. Dewey:976.4/4. LCCN:84-002510.
Audience: **u,f.**

Cook, Maria Lorena **LB2844.53.M6**
Organizing Dissent. Trade Paper. Pennsylvania State University Press. University Park, PA. 1996. 376p. ISBN:0-271-02590-5, ISBN13: 978-0-271-02590-2. Dewey:331.88/113711/0972.
Audience: **u,f.**

Cornelius, Wayne A. **JS2137.A2 C67**
Politics and the Migrant Poor in Mexico City. Trade Cloth. Stanford University Press. Palo Alto, CA. 1975. xiv, 319p. ISBN:0-8047-0880-0, ISBN13: 978-0-8047-0880-7. Dewey:301.5/92/091724. LCCN:75-000179.
Audience: **u,f.**

Cornelius, Wayne A. **JS2117.A2S83 1999**
Subnational Politics and Democratization in Mexico. Trade Paper. University of California, San Diego, Center for U. S.-Mexican Studies. La Jolla, CA. 1999. U. S. - Mexico Contemporary Perspectives Ser., Vol. 13 ISBN:1-878367-39-0, ISBN13: 978-1-878367-39-6. Dewey:320.972/09/049. LCCN:98-054805.
Audience: **u,f.**

Cotter, Joseph S. **S451**
Troubled Harvest: Agronomy and Revolution in Mexico, 1880-2002. Trade Cloth. Greenwood Publishing Group, Inc. Portsmouth, NH. 2003. 424p. Contributions in Latin American Studies, Vol. 22 ISBN:0-313-32515-4, ISBN13: 978-0-313-32515-1. Dewey:630/.972/0904. LCCN:2002-044952.
Audience: **u,f.** *Choice, 2004.*

Crandall, Russell (Editor), et al. **F1236.M4865 2004**
Mexico's Democracy at Work: Political and Economic Dynamics. Guadalupe Paz & Riordan Roett (Editors). Library Binding. Lynne Rienner Publishers, Inc. Boulder, CO. 2004. 200p. ISBN:1-58826-300-2, ISBN13: 978-1-58826-300-1. Dewey:972.08/35. LCCN:2004-009270.
Audience: **u,f.**

Davis, Graham **F395.I6D38 2002**
Land!: Irish Pioneers in Mexican and Revolutionary Texas. Trade Cloth. Texas A&M University Press. College Station, TX. 2002. 320p. Centennial Series of the Association of Former Students, Texas A&M University, No. 92 ISBN:1-58544-189-9, ISBN13: 978-1-58544-189-1. Dewey:976.4/0049162. LCCN:2001-008478.
Audience: **u,f.** *Choice, 2003.*

Dicum, Gregory, et al. **F1219.1.C45R43 1999**
Rebellion in Chiapas: An Historical Reader. Nina Luttinger & John Womack Jr. (Authors). Trade Paper. New Press, The. New York, NY. 1999. 400p. ISBN:1-56584-452-1, ISBN13: 978-1-56584-452-0. Dewey:323.1/19707275. LCCN:98-040702.
Audience: **g,l,u,f.**

Dominguez, Jorge I. & Poire, Alejandro (Editors) **JL1292.T69 1999**
Toward Mexico's Democratization: Parties, Campaigns, Elections and Public Opinion. Trade Paper. Routledge. New York, NY. 1999. 264p. ISBN:0-415-92159-7, ISBN13: 978-0-415-92159-6. Dewey:324.972/0835. LCCN:98-035528.
Audience: **u,f.**

Dulles, John W. F. **F1234 .D9**
Yesterday in Mexico: A Chronicle of the Revolution 1919. Paper Text. Textbook Publishers. Temecula, CA. 2003. 805p. ISBN:0-7581-1562-8, ISBN13: 978-0-7581-1562-1. Dewey:972.082.
Audience: **g,l,u,f.**

Eisenstadt, Todd A. **JL1292.E36 2003**
Courting Democracy in Mexico: Party Strategies and Electoral Institutions. Trade Cloth. Cambridge University Press. New York, NY. 2003. 372p. ISBN:0-521-82001-4, ISBN13: 978-0-521-82001-1. Dewey:324/.0972. LCCN:2003-043473.
Audience: **u,f.** *Choice, 2004.*

Faber, Sebastiaan **F1392.S7F23 2002**
Exile and Cultural Hegemony: Spanish Intellectuals in Mexico, 1939 - 1975. Trade Cloth. Vanderbilt University Press. Nashville, TN. 2002. 344p. ISBN:0-8265-1422-7, ISBN13: 978-0-8265-1422-6. Dewey:305.5/52/097209045. LCCN:2002-011655.
Audience: **u,f.** *Choice, 2003.*

Fagen, Richard R. & Tuohy, William S. **F1391.J2 F3**
Politics and Privilege in a Mexican City. Trade Cloth. Stanford University Press. Palo Alto, CA. 1972. xiv, 210p. ISBN:0-8047-0809-6, ISBN13: 978-0-8047-0809-8. Dewey:320.9/72/6. LCCN:70-183887.
Audience: **u,f.**

Foweraker, Joe & Craig, Ann L. (Editors) **JL1281.P67 1990**
Popular Movements and Political Change in Mexico. Library Binding. Lynne Rienner Publishers, Inc. Boulder, CO. 1990. 312p. ISBN:1-55587-211-5, ISBN13: 978-1-55587-211-3. Dewey:323.3/0972. LCCN:90-034593.
Audience: **l,u.** *Choice, 1991.*

Fowler-Salamini, Heather & Vaughan, Mary K. (Editors) **HQ1462.W66 1994**
Women of the Mexican Countryside, 1850-1990: Creating Spaces, Shaping Transitions. Library Binding. University of Arizona Press. Tucson, AZ. 1994. 253p. ISBN:0-8165-1415-1, ISBN13: 978-0-8165-1415-1. Dewey:305.42/0972. LCCN:94-010179.
Audience: **l,u,f.** *Choice, 1995.*

French, William E. **HN120.S6.F74 1996**
A Peaceful and Working People: Manners, Morals, and Class Formation in Northern Mexico. Trade Cloth. University of New Mexico Press. Albuquerque, NM. 1996. 263p. ISBN:0-8263-1683-2, ISBN13: 978-0-8263-1683-7. Dewey:305.5/0972/16. LCCN:95-032446.
Audience: **u,f.** *Choice, 1996.*

Gabbert, Wolfgang **F1435.3.E72G32 2004**
Becoming Maya: Ethnicity and Social Inequality in Yucatan since 1500. Trade Cloth. University of Arizona Press. Tucson, AZ. 2004. 252p. ISBN:0-8165-2316-9, ISBN13: 978-0-8165-2316-0. Dewey:972/.65. LCCN:2003-014234.
Audience: **u,f.**

Gentleman, Judith A. (Editor) **F1236**
Mexican Politics in Transition. Cloth Text. Westview Press. Boulder, CO. 1987. 320p. Special Studies on Latin America and the Caribbean ISBN:0-8133-7210-0, ISBN13: 978-0-8133-7210-5. Dewey:972.08/32. LCCN:86-004036.
Audience: **u,f.** *Choice, 1988.*

Gilly, Adolfo **F1234.G47413 2005**
The Mexican Revolution: A New Press People's History. Patrick Camiller (Translator). Trade Cloth. New Press, The. New York, NY. 2005. 320p. A New Press People's History Ser. ISBN:1-56584-932-9, ISBN13: 978-1-56584-932-7. Dewey:972.08/1. LCCN:2005-049109.
Audience: **u,f.**

Glade, William P. & Anderson, Charles W. **HC135.G58**
The Political Economy of Mexico, Two Studies. University of Wisconsin Press. 1963.
Audience: **l,u.**

Gonzales, Michael J. **F1234.G6248 2002**
The Mexican Revolution, 1910-1940. Trade Cloth. University of New Mexico Press. Albuquerque, NM. 2002. 307p. Dialogos Ser. ISBN:0-8263-2779-6, ISBN13: 978-0-8263-2779-6. Dewey:972.08/2. LCCN:2001-005644.
Audience: **u,f.**

Green, Rosario; Smith, Peter H. **E183.8.M6**
Dimensions of United States-Mexican Relations. 5 vols. Center for U.S.-Mexican Studies, University of California. 1989. ISBN:0-935391-82-7, ISBN13: 978-0-935391-82-4.
Audience: **u,f.**

Hale, Charles A. **F1233.5.H35 1989**
The Transformation of Liberalism in Late Nineteenth-Century Mexico. Cloth Text. Princeton University Press. Princeton, NJ. 1990. 296p. American History, Literature and Religion Ser. ISBN:0-691-07814-9, ISBN13: 978-0-691-07814-4. Dewey:972.08/12. LCCN:89-032172.
Audience: **u,f.** *Choice, 1990.*

Hall, Linda B. & Coerver, Don M. **E0183.8.M6H**
Revolution on the Border: The United States and Mexico, 1910-1920. Trade Paper. Books on Demand. Ann Arbor, MI. 1990. 217p. ISBN:0-608-04138-6, ISBN13: 978-0-608-04138-4. Dewey:303.4/8273/072. LCCN:88-014222.
Audience: **u,f.** *Choice, 1989.*

Hamilton, Nora **HC135.H27 1982**
The Limits of State Autonomy: Post-Revolutionary Mexico. Princeton University Press. 1982. ISBN:0-691-02211-9, ISBN13: 978-0-691-02211-6.
Audience: **u,f.**

Hansen, Roger D. **HC135**
The Politics of Mexican Development. Trade Cloth. Johns Hopkins University Press. Baltimore, MD. 1971. 298p. ISBN:0-8018-1193-7, ISBN13: 978-0-8018-1193-7. Dewey:330.972/08. LCCN:77-134300.
Audience: **u,f.**

Harris, Charles H. III & Sadler, Louis R. **F786.H3**
The Border and the Revolution: Clandestine Activities of the Mexican Revolution, 1910-1920. Ed. 2. Michael C. Meyer (Introduction by). Trade Paper. High-Lonesome Books. Silver City, NM. 1990. 160p. ISBN:0-944383-07-6, ISBN13: 978-0-944383-07-0. Dewey:972.08/16. LCCN:88-080847.
Audience: **u,f.**

Harris, Charles H. & Sadler, Louis R. **F391.H28 2004**
The Texas Rangers and the Mexican Revolution: The Bloodiest Decade, 1910-1920. Trade Cloth. University of New Mexico Press. Albuquerque, NM. 2004. 673p. ISBN:0-8263-3483-0, ISBN13: 978-0-8263-3483-1. Dewey:972.08/16. LCCN:2004-009059.
Audience: **l,u.** *Choice, 2005.*

Hart, John M. **F1392.A5 H37 2002**
Empire and Revolution: The Americans in Mexico since the Civil War. Trade Cloth. University of California Press. Berkeley, CA. 2002. 688p. ISBN:0-520-22324-1, ISBN13: 978-0-520-22324-0. Dewey:972/.00413. LCCN:2001-027815.
Audience: **u,f.** *Choice, 2002.*

Hart, John M. **F1234**
Revolutionary Mexico: The Coming and Process of the Mexican Revolution. Ed. 10. Trade Paper. University of California Press. Berkeley, CA. 1997. 498p. ISBN:0-520-21531-1, ISBN13: 978-0-520-21531-3. Dewey:972/.081. LCCN:87-005399.
Audience: **u,f.**

Henderson, Peter V. N. **F1235.5.B36H46 1999**
In the Absence of Don Porfirio: Francisco Leon de la Barra and the Mexican Revolution. Book, Other. Rowman & Littlefield Publishers, Inc. Lanham, MD. 1999. 338p. Latin American Silhouettes Ser. ISBN:0-8420-2774-2, ISBN13: 978-0-8420-2774-8. Dewey:972.08/16. LCCN:99-020439.
Audience: **u,f.** *Choice, 2000.*

Hodges, Donald C. **HX851.H63 1995**
Mexican Anarchism after the Revolution. Trade Cloth. University of Texas Press. Austin, TX. 1995. 267p. ISBN:0-292-73093-4, ISBN13: 978-0-292-73093-9. Dewey:335/.83/09720904. LCCN:94-020488.
Audience: **u,f.** *Choice, 1995.*

Horne, Gerald **E185.923.H67 2004**
Black and Brown: African Americans and the Mexican Revolution, 1910-1920. Trade Cloth. New York University Press. New York, NY. 2005. 384p. ISBN:0-8147-3667-X, ISBN13: 978-0-8147-3667-8. Dewey:972.08/16. LCCN:2004-018356.
Audience: **u,f.** *Choice, 2005.*

Inglehart, Ronald F., et al. **E40.I54 1996**
The North American Trajectory: Cultural, Economic, and Political Ties among the United States, Canada, and Mexico. Neil Nevitte & Miguel Basanez (Authors). Trade Cloth. Aldine Transaction. Somerset, NJ. 1996. 198p. Social Institutions and Social Change Ser. ISBN:0-202-30556-2, ISBN13: 978-0-202-30556-1. Dewey:970.05. LCCN:96-008795.
Audience: **u,f.** *Choice, 1997.*

Johnson, Kenneth F. & Bezdek, Robert R. **JL1231**
Mexican Democracy: A Critical View. Ed. 3. Trade Cloth. Greenwood Publishing Group, Inc. Portsmouth, NH. 1984. 279p. ISBN:0-275-91197-7, ISBN13: 978-0-275-91197-3. Dewey:320.972. LCCN:84-011614.
Audience: **u,f.**

Joseph, Gilbert M. **HD9156.H463M65 1988**
Revolution from Without: Yucatán, Mexico, and the United States, 1880-1924. Alan Knight (Introduction by). Paper Text. Duke University Press. Durham, NC. 1988. xviii, 405p. ISBN:0-8223-0822-3, ISBN13: 978-0-8223-0822-5. Dewey:330.972/65081. LCCN:87-032951.
Audience: **u,f.**

Katz, Friedrich **F1234.V63K38 1998**
The Life and Times of Pancho Villa. Trade Cloth. Stanford University Press. Palo Alto, CA. 1998. 985p. ISBN:0-8047-3045-8, ISBN13: 978-0-8047-3045-7. Dewey:972.08/16. LCCN:97-047271.
Audience: **l,u,f.**

Knight, Alan **F1234**
The Mexican Revolution. Trade Cloth. University of Nebraska Press. Lincoln, NE. 1990. ISBN:0-8032-7772-5, ISBN13: 978-0-8032-7772-4. Dewey:972.08/16 20. LCCN:89-028488.
Audience: **u,f.**

Krauze, Enrique **F1231.5**
Mexico: Biography of Power. Trade Paper. HarperCollins Publishers. New York, NY. 1998. 896p. ISBN:0-06-092917-0, ISBN13: 978-0-06-092917-6. Dewey:972.08. LCCN:96-033046.
Audience: **g,l,u,f.**

LaFrance, David G. **F1326.L3 1989**
The Mexican Revolution in Puebla, 1908-1913: The Maderista Movement and the Failure of Liberal Reform. Book, Other. Rowman & Littlefield Publishers, Inc. Lanham, MD. 1989. 272p. ISBN:0-8420-2293-7, ISBN13: 978-0-8420-2293-4. Dewey:972/.48081. LCCN:88-034923.
Audience: **u,f.** *Choice, 1990.*

LaFrance, David G. **F1326.L32 2003**
Revolution in Mexico's Heartland: Politics, War, and State Building in Puebla, 1913-1920. Book, Other. Rowman & Littlefield Publishers, Inc. Lanham, MD. 2003. 305p. Latin American Silhouettes Ser. ISBN:0-8420-5136-8, ISBN13: 978-0-8420-5136-1. Dewey:972/.480816. LCCN:2003-000606.
Audience: **u,f.** *Choice, 2004.*

Lear, John **HD8116.L43 2001**
Workers, Neighbors and Citizens: The Revolution in Mexico City. Cloth Text. University of Nebraska Press. Lincoln, NE. 2001. 441p. Critical Studies in the History of Anthropology ISBN:0-8032-2936-4, ISBN13: 978-0-8032-2936-5. Dewey:972.08/16. LCCN:00-059967.
Audience: **u,f.**

Leighton, George R. (Photographer) **F1234**
The Wind That Swept Mexico: The History of the Mexican Revolution of 1910-1942. Anita Brenner (Text by). Trade Paper. University of Texas Press. Austin, TX. 1984. 310p. Texas Pan American Ser. ISBN:0-292-79024-4, ISBN13: 978-0-292-79024-7. Dewey:972/.0816. LCCN:77-149021.
Audience: **u,f.**

Levy, Daniel C. & Bruhn, Kathleen **JL1281 .L49 2006**
Mexico: The Struggle for Democratic Development. Ed. 2.

Trade Paper. University of California Press. Berkeley, CA. 2006. 382p. ISBN:0-520-24694-2, ISBN13: 978-0-520-24694-2. Dewey:320.972. LCCN:2005-016501.
Audience: **u,f.**

Lewis, Stephen E. **LA429.C42L49 2005**
The Ambivalent Revolution: Forging State and Nation in Chiapas, 1910-1945. Trade Paper, Perfect. University of New Mexico Press. Albuquerque, NM. 2005. 283p. ISBN:0-8263-3601-9, ISBN13: 978-0-8263-3601-9. Dewey:379.72/75/09041. LCCN:2005-001617.
Audience: **u,f.** *Choice, 2006.*

Lieuwen, Edwin **F1234 .L69 1981**
Mexican Militarism: The Political Rise and Fall of the Revolutionary Army, 1910-1940. Trade Cloth. Greenwood Publishing Group, Inc. Portsmouth, NH. 1981. 194p. ISBN:0-313-22911-2, ISBN13: 978-0-313-22911-4. Dewey:972.08/2. LCCN:80-028937.
Audience: **u,f.**

Linhard, Tabea Alexa **F1234.L74 2005**
Fearless Women in the Mexican Revolution and the Spanish Civil War. Perfect, Paper over Boards, Dust Jacket. University of Missouri Press. Columbia, MO. 2005. 282p. ISBN:0-8262-1611-0, ISBN13: 978-0-8262-1611-3. Dewey:946.081. LCCN:2005-016913.
Audience: **u,f.**

Mabry, Donald J. **JL1298.A3.M24**
Mexico's Accion Nacional: A Catholic Alternative to Revolution. Trade Cloth. Syracuse University Press. Syracuse, NY. 1973. 300p. ISBN:0-8156-0096-8, ISBN13: 978-0-8156-0096-1. Dewey:329.9/72. LCCN:73-009975.
Audience: **u,f.** B

Meyers, William K. **F1266.M49 1994**
Forge of Progress, Crucible of Revolt: The Origins of the Mexican Revolution in La Comarca Lagunera, 1880-1911. Trade Paper. University of New Mexico Press. Albuquerque, NM. 1994. 304p. ISBN:0-8263-1470-8, ISBN13: 978-0-8263-1470-3. Dewey:972.08/16. LCCN:94-004349.
Audience: **u,f.** *Choice, 1995.*

Middlebrook, Kevin J. (Editor) **JL1281**
Dilemmas of Political Change in Mexico. Trade Paper. Institute of Latin American Studies. London, 2003. 350p. ISBN:1-900039-45-1, ISBN13: 978-1-900039-45-1. Dewey:320.9/72/09051.
Audience: **u,f.**

Middlebrook, Kevin J. **JL1281.M54 1995**
The Paradox of Revolution: Labor, the State, and Authoritarianism in Mexico. Trade Cloth. Johns Hopkins University Press. Baltimore, MD. 1995. 392p. ISBN:0-8018-4922-5, ISBN13: 978-0-8018-4922-0. Dewey:320.972. LCCN:94-029470.
Audience: **u,f.** *Choice, 1995.*

Middlebrook, Kevin J. (Editor), et al. **F1236**
The Politics of Economic Restructuring in Mexico: State-Society Relations and Regime Change in Mexico. Juan Molinar-Horcasitas & Maria L. Cook (Editors). Trade Paper. University of California, San Diego, Center for U. S.-Mexican Studies. La Jolla, CA. 1994. 351p. U. S. - Mexico Contemporary Perspectives Ser., No. 7 ISBN:1-878367-18-8, ISBN13: 978-1-878367-18-1. Dewey:320.972.
Audience: **u,f.**

Mizrahi, Yemile **JL1298.A3M59 2003**
From Martyrdom to Power: The Partido Accion Nacional in Mexico. Trade Cloth. University of Notre Dame Press. Notre Dame, IN. 2003. xii, 211p. From the Helen Kellogg Institute for International Studies ISBN:0-268-02870-2, ISBN13: 978-0-268-02870-1. Dewey:324.272/04. LCCN:2003-009030.
Audience: **u,f.** *Choice, 2004.*

Morris, Stephen D. **JL1229.C6M69 1991**
Corruption and Politics in Contemporary Mexico. Trade Paper. University of Alabama Press. Tuscaloosa, AL. 1991. 224p. ISBN:0-8173-0525-4, ISBN13: 978-0-8173-0525-3. Dewey:320.972. LCCN:90-047510.
Audience: **u,f.**

Newell, Robert & Rubio, Luis **HC135.N48 1984**
Mexico's Dilemma: The Political Origins of Economic Crisis. Paper Text. Westview Press. Boulder, CO. 1984. 340p. Special Studies on Latin America and the Caribbean ISBN:0-86531-795-X, ISBN13: 978-0-86531-795-6. Dewey:330.972/0834. LCCN:84-003629.
Audience: **u,f.**

Olcott, Jocelyn **HQ1236.5.M6O43 2005**
Revolutionary Women in Postrevolutionary Mexico. Trade Cloth. Duke University Press. Durham, NC. 2005. 328p. Next Wave Ser. ISBN:0-8223-3653-7, ISBN13: 978-0-8223-3653-2. Dewey:320/.082/0972. LCCN:2005-021134.
Audience: **u,f.**

Pasztor, Suzanne B. **F1266.P37 2002**
The Spirit of Hidalgo: The Mexican Revolution in Coahuila. Trade Cloth. Michigan State University Press. East Lansing, MI. 2002. 224p. Latin American and Caribbean Ser. ISBN:0-87013-626-7, ISBN13: 978-0-87013-626-9. Dewey:972/.14. LCCN:2003-269086.
Audience: **u,f.** *Choice, 2003.*

Patch, Robert W. **F1465.P37 2002**
Maya Revolt and Revolution in the Eighteenth Century. Robert M. Levine (Foreword by). Trade Cloth. M. E. Sharpe Inc. Armonk, NY. 2002. 270p. Latin American Realities Ser. ISBN:0-7656-0411-6, ISBN13: 978-0-7656-0411-8. Dewey:972/.6502. LCCN:2002-066518.
Audience: **u,f.**

Paz, Octavio **F1210**
The Labyrinth of Solitude: The Other Mexico and Return to the Labyrinth of Solitude and The U. S. A. and The Philanthropic Ogre. Lysander Kemp (Translator). Trade Paper. Grove/Atlantic, Inc. New York, NY. 1994. 408p. ISBN:0-8021-5042-X, ISBN13: 978-0-8021-5042-4. Dewey:864. LCCN:82-047999.
Audience: **g,l,u,f.**

Peschard-Sverdrup, Armand B. & Rioff, Sara **JL1231.M415 2005**
Mexican Governance: From Single-Party Rule to Divided Government. Paper Text. Center for Strategic & International Studies. Washington, DC. 2005. 400p. Significant Issues Ser., No. 27 ISBN:0-89206-457-9, ISBN13: 978-0-89206-457-1. Dewey:320.972. LCCN:2005-003673.
Audience: **u,f.** *Choice, 2005.*

Purcell, Susan K. **HD2991**
The Mexican Profit-Sharing Decision: Politics and Economic Change in an Authoritarian Regime. Trade Cloth. University of California Press. Berkeley, CA. 1976. 224p. ISBN:0-520-02843-0, ISBN13: 978-0-520-02843-2. Dewey:339.5/2. LCCN:74-084148.
Audience: **u,f.**

Quirk, Robert E. **F1234**
The Mexican Revolution and the Catholic Church, 1910-1929. Trade Cloth. Greenwood Publishing Group, Inc. Portsmouth, NH. 1986. 276p. ISBN:0-313-25121-5, ISBN13: 978-0-313-25121-4. Dewey:972.08/2. LCCN:85-030209.
Audience: **u,f.**

Reich, Peter L. **BX1428.2.R44 1995**
Mexico's Hidden Revolution: The Catholic Church in Law and Politics since 1929. Trade Cloth. University of Notre Dame Press. Notre Dame, IN. 1996. 192p. From the Helen Kellogg Institute for International Studies Ser. ISBN:0-268-01418-3, ISBN13: 978-0-268-01418-6. Dewey:322/.1/09720904. LCCN:95-016516.
Audience: **u,f.**

Rodriguez, Victoria **HQ1236.5.M6W65 1998**
Women's Participation in Mexican Political Life. Trade Paper. Westview Press. Boulder, CO. 1998. 280p. ISBN:0-8133-3529-9, ISBN13: 978-0-8133-3529-2. Dewey:320.0820972. LCCN:98-020771.
Audience: **u,f.** *Choice, 1999.*

Roett, Riordan (Editor) **HC135.M569 1999**
Mexico's Private Sector: Recent History, Future Challenges. Library Binding. Lynne Rienner Publishers, Inc. Boulder, CO. 1998. 252p. ISBN:1-55587-713-3, ISBN13: 978-1-55587-713-2. Dewey:330.972/0836. LCCN:98-025921.
Audience: **u,f.** *Choice, 1999.*

Romanell, Patrick **B1016.R74 1969**
Making of the Mexican Mind: A Study in Recent Mexican Thought. E. S. Brightman (Foreword by). Trade Cloth. Ayer Company Publishers, Inc. Manchester, NH. 1977. ix, 213p. Essay Index Reprint Ser. ISBN:0-8369-1189-X, ISBN13: 978-0-8369-1189-3. Dewey:199/.72. LCCN:76-086778.
Audience: **u,f.**

Romo, David Dorado **F394.E4R66 2005**
Ringside Seat to a Revolution: An Underground Cultural History of el Paso and Juarez: 1893-1923. Trade Paper, Perfect. Cinco Puntos Press. El Paso, TX. 2005. 240p. ISBN:0-938317-91-1, ISBN13: 978-0-938317-91-3. Dewey:972.08/16. LCCN:2005-008283.
Audience: **u,f.** *Choice, 2006.*

Sandos, James A. **F391**
Rebellion in the Borderlands: Anarchism and the Plan of San Diego, 1904-1923. Trade Cloth. University of Oklahoma Press. Norman, OK. 1992. 238p. ISBN:0-8061-2433-4, ISBN13: 978-0-8061-2433-9. Dewey:976.406. LCCN:91-050870.
Audience: **u,f.** *Choice, 1992.*

Schuler, Friedrich E. **F1234.S378**
Mexico Between Hitler and Roosevelt: Mexican Foreign Relations in the Age of Lazaro Cardenas, 1934-1940. Trade Paper. University of New Mexico Press. Albuquerque, NM. 2000. 271p. ISBN:0-8263-2160-7, ISBN13: 978-0-8263-2160-2. Dewey:327.72/009/043.
Audience: **u,f.**

Shirk, David A. **JL1298.A23S55 2004**
Mexico's New Politics: The PAN and Democratic Change. Trade Cloth. Lynne Rienner Publishers, Inc. Boulder, CO. 2004. 275p. ISBN:1-58826-294-4, ISBN13: 978-1-58826-294-3. Dewey:320.972. LCCN:2004-014910.
Audience: **u,f.**

Smith, Peter H. **HN120.Z9E4**
Labyrinths of Power: Political Recruitment in Twentieth-Century Mexico. Trade Cloth. Princeton University Press. Princeton, NJ. 1979. 408p. ISBN:0-691-07592-1, ISBN13: 978-0-691-07592-1. Dewey:301.44/92. LCCN:78-051191.
Audience: **u,f.** B

Snodgrass, Michael **HD8120.M66S658 2003**
Deference and Defiance in Monterrey: Workers, Paternalism, and Revolution in Mexico, 1890-1950. Alan Knight (Contribution by). Cloth Text. Cambridge University Press. New York, NY. 2003. 334p. Cambridge Latin American Studies, Vol. 88 ISBN:0-521-81189-9, ISBN13: 978-0-521-81189-7. Dewey:331/.0972/13. LCCN:2002-034953.
Audience: **u,f.**

Stout, Joseph A. Jr. **F1233.S87 2002**
Schemers and Dreamers: Filibustering in Mexico, 1848-1921. Trade Cloth. Texas Christian University Press. Fort Worth, TX. 2002. 224p. ISBN:0-87565-258-1, ISBN13: 978-0-87565-258-0. Dewey:972/.04. LCCN:2002-002778.
Audience: **u,f.** *Choice, 2003.*

Teichman, Judith A. **HF1956.T45 2001**
The Politics of Freeing Markets in Latin America: Chile, Argentina and Mexico. Trade Cloth. University of North Carolina Press. Chapel Hill, NC. 2001. 296p. ISBN:0-8078-2629-4, ISBN13: 978-0-8078-2629-4. Dewey:382/.71/098. LCCN:2001-023409.
Audience: **u,f.**

Teichman, Judith A. **HD4014.T44 1995**
Privatization and Political Change in Mexico. Trade Paper. University of Pittsburgh Press. Pittsburgh, PA. 1996. 291p. Latin American Ser. ISBN:0-8229-5586-5, ISBN13: 978-0-8229-5586-3. Dewey:338.972. LCCN:95-025839.
Audience: **u,f.** *Choice, 1997.*

Thacker, Strom C. **HF1481 .T43 2000**
Big Business, the State, and Free Trade: Constructing Coalitions in Mexico. Trade Cloth. Cambridge University Press. New York, NY. 2000. 256p. ISBN:0-521-78168-X, ISBN13: 978-0-521-78168-8. Dewey:382/.3/0972. LCCN:00-027890.
Audience: **u,f.**

Tucker, William P. **JL1218.T8**
The Mexican Government Today. University of Minnesota Press. 1957. ISBN:0-8166-0153-4, ISBN13: 978-0-8166-0153-0.
Audience: **g,l,u.**

Turner, Frederick **F1210.T8**
The Dynamic of Mexican Nationalism. University of North Carolina Press. 1968.
Audience: **g,l,u.**

Tutino, John **D16.9**
From Insurrection to Revolution in Mexico: Social Bases of Agrarian Violence, 1750-1940. Trade Paper. Princeton University Press. Princeton, NJ. 1989. 448p. ISBN:0-691-02294-1, ISBN13: 978-0-691-02294-9. Dewey:303.6/4/0972.
Audience: **u,f.** *Choice, 1987.*

Ugalde, Luis Carlos **JL1265.U38 2000**
The Mexican Congress: Old Player, New Power. Armand B. Peschard-Sverdrup (Foreword by). Paper Text. Center for Strategic & International Studies. Washington, DC. 2000. 203p. CSIS Significant Issues Ser., No. 22 ISBN:0-89206-382-3, ISBN13: 978-0-89206-382-6. Dewey:328.72/072. LCCN:00-011772.
Audience: **u,f.** *Choice, 2001.*

Vaughan, Mary Kay (Editor) **F1234**
Eagle and the Virgin. Trade Cloth. Duke University Press. Durham, NC. 2004. 384p. ISBN:0-8223-3657-X, ISBN13: 978-0-8223-3657-0. Dewey:306.0972/09042. LCCN:2005-028220.
Audience: **l,u,f.**

Vernon, Raymond **HC0135.V4**
Dilemma of Mexico's Development: The Roles of the Private and Public Sectors. Trade Cloth. Harvard University Press. Cambridge, MA. 1963. 238p. Center for International Affairs Ser. ISBN:0-674-20650-9, ISBN13: 978-0-674-20650-2. Dewey:338.972. LCCN:63-017214.
Audience: **u,f.** B

Wasserman, Mark **HC137.C46**
Capitalists, Caciques, and Revolution: The Native Elite and Foreign Enterprise in Chihuahua, Mexico, 1854-1911. Trade Cloth. University of North Carolina Press. Chapel Hill, NC. 1984. xii, 232p. ISBN:0-8078-1580-2, ISBN13: 978-0-8078-1580-9. Dewey:330.972/16081. LCCN:83-012481.
Audience: **u,f.**

Weintraub, Sidney **HF1482.5.U5**
A Marriage of Convenience: Relations Between Mexico and the United States: A Twentieth Century Fund Report. Trade Paper. Oxford University Press, Inc. New York, NY. 1991. 288p. ISBN:0-19-507006-2, ISBN13: 978-0-19-507006-4. Dewey:337.72073. LCCN:89-039386.
Audience: **u,f.**

Wood, Andrew G. **HD7288.84.W66 2001**
Revolution in the Street: Women, Workers and Urban Protest in Veracruz, 1870-1927. Book, Other. Rowman & Littlefield Publishers, Inc. Lanham, MD. 2001. 239p. Latin American Silhouettes Ser. ISBN:0-8420-2879-X, ISBN13: 978-0-8420-2879-0. Dewey:322.4/4/097262. LCCN:00-058768.
Audience: **u,f.** *Choice, 2001.*

Yeager, Gertrude M. **HQ1460.5.C66 1994**
Confronting Change, Challenging Tradition: Women in Latin American History. Trade Cloth. Rowman & Littlefield Publishers, Inc. Lanham, MD. 1997. Jaguar Books on Latin America, No. 7 ISBN:0-8420-2479-4, ISBN13: 978-0-8420-2479-2. Dewey:305.4/098. LCCN:94-017441.
Audience: **u,f.**

Young, Elliott **F786.Y565 2004**
Catarino Garza's Revolution on the Texas-Mexico Border. Trade Cloth. Duke University Press. Durham, NC. 2004. 384p. American Encounters/Global Interactions Ser. ISBN:0-8223-3308-2, ISBN13: 978-0-8223-3308-1. Dewey:972/.06. LCCN:2004-002240.
Audience: **u,f.** *Choice, 2005.*

Central America: General

Gossen, Gary H., South and Leon Portilla, Miguel (eds.) **E59.R38**
MesoAmerican Native Spirituality: From the Cult of the Feathered Serpent to the Theology of Liberation. Crossroad. 1997.
Audience: **u,f.**

Central America: General > Belize

Appelbaum, Nancy P. (Editor), et al. **F1413.R33 2003**
Race and Nation in Modern Latin America. Anne S. Macpherson & Karin Alejandra Rosemblatt (Editors). Trade Cloth. University of North Carolina Press. Chapel Hill, NC. 2003. 352p. ISBN:0-8078-2769-X, ISBN13: 978-0-8078-2769-7. Dewey:323.1/8/09. LCCN:2002-011044.
Audience: **u,f.** *Choice, 2003.*

Ardren, Traci **F1435.3.W55A53 2002**
Ancient Maya Women. Trade Cloth. AltaMira Press. Walnut Creek, CA. 2002. 320p. Gender and Archaeology Ser., Vol. 3 ISBN:0-7591-0009-8, ISBN13: 978-0-7591-0009-1. Dewey:305.48/8974152/00901. LCCN:2001-044069.
Audience: **u,f.** *Choice, 2002.*

Bolland, O. Nigel **F1446**
Colonialism and Resistance in Belize: Essays in Historical Sociology. Ed. 2. Trade Paper. University of the West Indies Press. Kingston, 2004. 240p. ISBN:976-640-141-1, ISBN13: 978-976-640-141-2. Dewey:972.82. LCCN:89-144137.
Audience: **u,f.**

Bolland, O. Nigel **HN127**
The Formation of a Colonial Society: Belize, from Conquest to Crown Colony. Trade Cloth. Johns Hopkins University Press. Baltimore, MD. 1990. 256p. Studies in Atlantic History and Culture ISBN:0-8018-1887-7, ISBN13: 978-0-8018-1887-5. Dewey:309.1/7282. LCCN:76-047377.
Audience: **u,f.**

Bolland, O. Nigel **F2175**
Struggles for Freedom: Essays on Slavery, Colonialism, and Culture in the Caribbean and Central America. Ian Randle Publishers. 1997. ISBN:976-8111-16-X, ISBN13: 978-976-8111-16-6.
Audience: **u,f.**

Brady, James **F1219.3.R38I5 2005**
In the Maw of the Earth Monster: Studies of Mesoamerican Ritual Cave Use. Keith M. Prufer (Editor). Trade Cloth. University of Texas Press. Austin, TX. 2005. 448p. The Linda Schele Series in Maya and Pre-Columbian Studies ISBN:0-292-70586-7, ISBN13: 978-0-292-70586-9. Dewey:305.897/42. LCCN:2004-019050.
Audience: **u,f.**

Brown, M. Kathryn & Stanton, Travis W. (Editors) **F1219.3.M55A43 2003**
Ancient Mesoamerican Warfare. Trade Cloth. AltaMira Press. Walnut Creek, CA. 2003. 384p. ISBN:0-7591-0282-1, ISBN13: 978-0-7591-0282-8. Dewey:972/.01. LCCN:2002-154153.
Audience: **l,u,f.** *Choice, 2004.*

Buhler, Richard O. **BX1434.2**
A History of the Catholic Church in Belize. Belize Institute for Social Research and Action. 1976.
Audience: **u,f.**

Clegern, Wayne M. **F1446.3.C4**
British Honduras: Colonial Dead End, 1859-1900. Trade Paper. Books on Demand. Ann Arbor, MI. 223p. Louisiana State University Studies, No. 12:Social Science Ser.
ISBN:0-598-06846-5, ISBN13: 978-0-598-06846-0.
Dewey:972.82/04. LCCN:67-011686.
Audience: **u,f.**

Garber, James (Editor) **F1445.A63 2004**
The Ancient Maya of the Belize Valley: Half a Century of Archaeological Research. Trade Cloth. University Press of Florida. Gainesville, FL. 2003. 512p. Maya Studies
ISBN:0-8130-2685-7, ISBN13: 978-0-8130-2685-5.
Dewey:972.82. LCCN:2003-054096.
Audience: **u,f.** *Choice, 2004.*

Gerhardt, Juliette Cartwright **F1435.1.C84**
Preclassic Maya Architecture at Cuello, Belize. B.A.R.. 1988.
ISBN:0-86054-595-4, ISBN13: 978-0-86054-595-8.
Audience: **u,f.**

Humphreys, Robert A. **F1449.B7A56 1981**
The Diplomatic History of British Honduras, 1638 to 1901. Trade Cloth. Greenwood Publishing Group, Inc. Portsmouth, NH. 1981. 196p. ISBN:0-313-22995-3, ISBN13: 978-0-313-22995-4. Dewey:972.82/03. LCCN:81-004635.
Audience: **u,f.**

Johnson, Howard & Watson, Karl (Editors) **F1629.W47 W5**
The White Minority in the Caribbean. Cloth Text. Markus Wiener Publishers, Inc. Princeton, NJ. 1999. 309p.
ISBN:1-55876-184-5, ISBN13: 978-1-55876-184-1.
Dewey:972.9/004034. LCCN:97-026833.
Audience: **u,f.**

Johnson, Wallace R. **BR625.B42 J64**
A History of Christianity in Belize 1776-1838. Trade Cloth. University Press of America, Inc. Lanham, MD. 1985. 300p.
ISBN:0-8191-4552-1, ISBN13: 978-0-8191-4552-9.
Dewey:209/.7282.
Audience: **u,f.**

Jones, Grant D. **F1435.J76 1989**
Maya Resistance to Spanish Rule: Time and History on a Colonial Frontier. Trade Cloth. University of New Mexico Press. Albuquerque, NM. 1989. 382p. ISBN:0-8263-1161-X, ISBN13: 978-0-8263-1161-0. Dewey:972.81016. LCCN:89-036041.
Audience: **u,f.** *Choice, 1990.*

Killingray, David (Editor), et al. **HF3505.8.M37 2004**
Maritime Empires: British Imperial Maritime Trade in the Nineteenth Century. Margarette Lincoln & Nigel Rigby (Editors). Trade Cloth. Boydell & Brewer, Ltd. Woodbridge, 2004. 242p. ISBN:1-84383-076-0, ISBN13: 978-1-84383-076-4. Dewey:382/.09171/241. LCCN:2004-003934.
Audience: **u,f.**

Lohse, Jon C. & Valdez, Fred (Editors) **F1435.3.S68A53 2004**
Ancient Maya Commoners. American Anthropological Association, Meeting Staff (Contribution by). Trade Cloth. University of Texas Press. Austin, TX. 2004. 311p.
ISBN:0-292-70571-9, ISBN13: 978-0-292-70571-5.
Dewey:972.81/01. LCCN:2004-004631.
Audience: **u,f.**

Moberg, Mark **HD9259.B3B426 1997**
Myths of Ethnicity and Nation: Immigration, Work, and Identity in the Belize Banana Industry. Trade Cloth. University of Tennessee Press. Knoxville, TN. 1997. 256p.
ISBN:0-87049-970-X, ISBN13: 978-0-87049-970-8.
Dewey:338.1/74772/097282. LCCN:96-051261.
Audience: **u,f.** *Choice, 1998.*

Naylor, Robert A. **F1529.M9N39 1989**
Penny Ante Imperialism: The Mosquito Shore and the Bay of Honduras, 1600-1914. Trade Cloth. Fairleigh Dickinson University Press. Cranbury, NJ. 1989. 320p.
ISBN:0-8386-3323-4, ISBN13: 978-0-8386-3323-6.
Dewey:972.83. LCCN:87-045735.
Audience: **u,f.** *Choice, 1989.*

Ranguy, Bismark & Staiano-Ross, Kathryn **F1449.T6**
Tales from a Forgotten Place. Dept. of Anthropology, University of Kansas. 2003. ISBN:0-938332-23-6, ISBN13: 978-0-938332-23-7.
Audience: **u,f.**

Reddock, Rhoda E., ed **BF692.5**
Interrogating Caribbean Masculinities: Theoretical and Empirical Analyses. University of the West Indies Press. 2004.
ISBN:976-640-138-1, ISBN13: 978-976-640-138-2.
Audience: **u,f.**

Simmons, Donald C. **F1457.A5S56 2001**
Confederate Settlements in British Honduras. William F. Winter (Foreword by). Paper Text. McFarland & Company, Incorporated Publishers. Jefferson, NC. 2001. 184p.
ISBN:0-7864-1016-7, ISBN13: 978-0-7864-1016-3.
Dewey:972.82/00413. LCCN:2001-030376.
Audience: **u,f.**

Thomson, P. **F1446**
History of Belize. Trade Paper. Macmillan Caribbean. Oxford, 2004. 174p. ISBN:0-333-77925-8, ISBN13: 978-0-333-77925-5. Dewey:972.8/2.
Audience: **u,f.**

Toledo Maya Cultural Council Staff & Toledo Alcaldes Association Staff **G1561.E1**
Maya Atlas: Fighting for Land Rights in Southern Belize. Trade Paper. North Atlantic Books. Berkeley, CA. 1997. 150p.
ISBN:1-55643-256-9, ISBN13: 978-1-55643-256-9.
Dewey:912.7282. LCCN:97-015801.
Audience: **u,f.**

Weaver, Peter L. **SD397.H67**
Mahogany in Belize: A Historical Perspective. International Institute of Tropical Forestry. 1997.
Audience: **u,f.**

Central America: General > Guatemala

Few, Martha **HQ1480.A58F49 2002**
Women Who Live Evil Lives: Gender, Religion, and the Politics of Power in Colonial Guatemala, 1650-1750. Trade Cloth. University of Texas Press. Austin, TX. 2002. 208p. ISBN:0-292-72543-4, ISBN13: 978-0-292-72543-0. Dewey:305.42097281. LCCN:2002-003572.
Audience: **u,f.**

Hall, Carolyn & Brignoli, Hector Perez **G1551.S1**
Historical Atlas of Central America. Trade Paper. University of Oklahoma Press. Norman, OK. 2005. 336p. ISBN:0-8061-3038-5, ISBN13: 978-0-8061-3038-5. Dewey:911/.728.
Audience: **g,l,u,f.** *Choice, 2004.*

Hill, Robert M. 3rd **F1465.H595 1989**
The Pirir Papers. William Fowler, Ronald M. Spores & John D. Monaghan (Editors). Trade Paper. Vanderbilt University Publications in Anthropology. Nashville, TN. 1989. 109p. Vanderbilt University Publications in Anthropology, No. 37 ISBN:0-935462-28-7, ISBN13: 978-0-935462-28-9. Dewey:972.81. LCCN:89-212270.
Audience: **u,f.**

Hill, Robert M. II **F1465.2.C3H55 1991**
Colonial Cakchiquels: Highland Maya Adaptations to Spanish Rule, 1600-1700. Paper Text. Harcourt College Publishers. Fort Worth, TX. 1992. 235p. Case Studies in Cultural Anthropology ISBN:0-03-073444-4, ISBN13: 978-0-03-073444-1. Dewey:972.81/03. LCCN:91-015326.
Audience: **u,f.**

Jones, Oakah L. Jr. **F1466.4.J66 1994**
Guatemala in the Spanish Colonial Period. Trade Cloth. University of Oklahoma Press. Norman, OK. 1994. 318p. ISBN:0-8061-2603-5, ISBN13: 978-0-8061-2603-6. Dewey:972.81/03. LCCN:93-037914.
Audience: **u,f.**

Kicza, John E. (Editor) **E65.I45 1993**
The Indian in Latin American History: Resistance, Resilience, and Acculturation. Trade Cloth. Rowman & Littlefield Publishers, Inc. Lanham, MD. 1993. 242p. Jaguar Books on Latin America, No. 1 ISBN:0-8420-2421-2, ISBN13: 978-0-8420-2421-1. Dewey:980. LCCN:93-016324.
Audience: **l,u,f.**

Kramer, Wendy **F1465.3.G6K73 1994**
Encomienda Politics in Early Colonial Guatemala, 1524-1544: Dividing the Spoils. Trade Paper. Westview Press. Boulder, CO. 1994. 293p. Dellplain Latin American Studies ISBN:0-8133-8833-3, ISBN13: 978-0-8133-8833-5. Dewey:972.81/02. LCCN:94-018594.
Audience: **u,f.**

Lovell, W. George **F1466.4**
Conquest and survival in colonial Guatemala: A historical geography of the Cuchumatan highlands, 1500-1821. Ed. 3. Trade Paper. McGill-Queen's University Press. Montreal, PQ. 2005. 354p. ISBN:0-7735-2741-9, ISBN13: 978-0-7735-2741-6. Dewey:911/.72817. LCCN:2005-541468.
Audience: **u,f.**

Lutz, Christopher H. **HB3539.A83**
Santiago de Guatemala, 1541-1773: City, Caste, and the Colonial Experience. Trade Paper. University of Oklahoma Press. Norman, OK. 1997. 368p. ISBN:0-8061-2911-5, ISBN13: 978-0-8061-2911-2. Dewey:304.6/097281/62. LCCN:93-046131.
Audience: **u,f.** *Choice, 1995.*

Orellana, Sandra L. **F1435.3.M4O74 1987**
Indian Medicine in Highland Guatemala: The Pre-Hispanic and Colonial Periods. Fred Folger (Illustrator). Trade Cloth. University of New Mexico Press. Albuquerque, NM. 1987. 319p. ISBN:0-8263-0931-3, ISBN13: 978-0-8263-0931-0. Dewey:615.8/82/097281. LCCN:86-024943.
Audience: **u,f.**

Stoll, David **F1465.2.Q5M3885 1999**
Rigoberta Menchu and the Story of All Poor Guatemalans. Trade Paper. Westview Press. Boulder, CO. 1999. 368p. ISBN:0-8133-3694-5, ISBN13: 978-0-8133-3694-7. Dewey:972.81/00497415. LCCN:98-042832.
Audience: **g,l,u,f.**

Van Oss, Adriaan C. **BX1438.2**
Catholic Colonialism: A Parish History of Guatemala, 1524-1821. Alan Knight (Contribution by). Trade Paper. Cambridge University Press. New York, NY. 2002. 268p. Cambridge Latin American Studies ISBN:0-521-52712-0, ISBN13: 978-0-521-52712-5. Dewey:282/.7281.
Audience: **u,f.** *Choice, 1987.*

Central America: General > El Salvador

Bracamonte, Jose A. & Spencer, David E. **F1488**
Strategy and Tactics of the Salvadoran FMLN Guerrillas: Last Battle of the Cold War, Blueprint for Future Conflicts. Trade Cloth. Greenwood Publishing Group, Inc. Portsmouth, NH. 1995. 216p. ISBN:0-275-95018-2, ISBN13: 978-0-275-95018-7. Dewey:972.8405/3. LCCN:94-042844.
Audience: **u,f.** *Choice, 1995.*

Burdick, John (ed.), Hewitt, W.E. (ed.) **BX1426**
The Church at the Grassroots in Latin America: Perspectives on Thirty Years of Activism. Greenwood Publishing. 2000. ISBN:0-275-96659-3, ISBN13: 978-0-275-96659-1.
Audience: **u,f.**

Corr, Edwin G. & Sloan, Stephen (Editors) **D849.L69 1992**
Low Intensity Conflict: Old Threats in a New World. Trade Paper. Westview Press. Boulder, CO. 1992. 317p. Studies in Regional Security ISBN:0-8133-8593-8, ISBN13: 978-0-8133-8593-8. Dewey:355.02. LCCN:92-017572.
Audience: **u,f.**

DeShazer, Mary K. **PN1083.R47D47 1994**
A Poetics of Resistance: Women Writing in el Salvador, South Africa, and the United States. Trade Paper. University of Michigan Press. Chicago, IL. 1994. 368p. ISBN:0-472-06563-7, ISBN13: 978-0-472-06563-9. Dewey:809.1/9358. LCCN:94-006207.
Audience: **u,f.**

Dunkerley, James **F1483**
The Long War: Dictatorship and Revolution in El Salvador. Paper Text. Analytical Psychology Club of San Francisco, Inc. San Francisco, CA. 1985. 318p. ISBN:0-86091-831-9, ISBN13: 978-0-86091-831-8. Dewey:972.84.
Audience: **u,f.**

Ellacuria, Ignacio, et al. **BX1753.T673 1991**
Towards a Society That Serves Its People: The Intellectual Contribution of El Salvador's Murdered Jesuits. Segundo Martes & Ignacio Martin-Bano (Authors), John Hassett & Hugh Lacey (Editors), James Brockman, Phillip Berryman, Adrianno Aron, John Husset & Anne Wallace (Translators). Trade Paper. Georgetown University Press. Washington, DC. 1991. 424p. ISBN:0-87840-523-2, ISBN13: 978-0-87840-523-7. Dewey:261.8/097284. LCCN:91-037465.
Audience: **u,f.** *Choice, 1992.*

Gettleman, Marvin E. (Editor), et al. **F1488.3.E4 1987**
El Salvador: Central America in the New Cold War. Patrick Lacefield, Louis Manashe & David Mermelstein (Editors). Trade Cloth. Grove/Atlantic, Inc. New York, NY. 1987. 480p. ISBN:0-394-55557-0, ISBN13: 978-0-394-55557-7. Dewey:972.84/053. LCCN:86-033499.
Audience: **u,f.**

Gorkin, Michael, et al. **F1488G67 2000**
From Grandmother to Granddaughter: Salvadoran Women's Stories. Marta Pineda & Gloria Leal (Authors). Trade Cloth. University of California Press. Berkeley, CA. 2000. 267p. ISBN:0-520-21165-0, ISBN13: 978-0-520-21165-0. Dewey:972.8405/2. LCCN:99-049789.
Audience: **u,f.**

Grenier, Yvon **F1488.3**
The Emergence of Insurgency in El Salvador: Ideology and Political Will. Cloth Text. University of Pittsburgh Press. Pittsburgh, PA. 1999. 220p. Pitt Latin American Ser. ISBN:0-8229-4094-9, ISBN13: 978-0-8229-4094-4. Dewey:972.84.
Audience: **u,f.** *Choice, 1999.*

Hammond, John L. **LC196.5.S2H36 1998**
Fighting to Learn: Popular Education and Guerrilla War in El Salvador. Trade Cloth. Rutgers University Press. Piscataway, NJ. 1998. 253p. ISBN:0-8135-2525-X, ISBN13: 978-0-8135-2525-9. Dewey:370.11/5. LCCN:97-043068.
Audience: **u,f.**

Juhn, Tricia **F1488.3.J84 1998**
Negotiating Peace in El Salvador: Civil-Military Relations and the Conspiracy to End the War. Cloth over Boards. Palgrave Macmillan. New York, NY. 1998. 182p. International Political Economy Ser. ISBN:0-312-21060-4, ISBN13: 978-0-312-21060-1. Dewey:320.9/7284. LCCN:97-050076.
Audience: **u,f.**

Landau, Saul **F1439**
The Guerrilla Wars of Central America: Nicaragua, El Salvador and Guatemala. Trade Cloth. Institute for Policy Studies. Washington, DC. 1993. 211p. ISBN:0-297-82114-8, ISBN13: 978-0-297-82114-4. Dewey:972.
Audience: **u,f.**

Lauria-Santiago, Aldo & Binford, Leigh **F1488.L36 2004**
Landscapes of Struggle: Politics, Society, and Community in El Salvador. Trade Paper. University of Pittsburgh Press. Pittsburgh, PA. 2004. 296p. Pitt Latin American Ser. ISBN:0-8229-4224-0, ISBN13: 978-0-8229-4224-5. Dewey:972.8405/2. LCCN:2003-021182.
Audience: **u,f.** *Choice, 2005.*

Manwaring, Max G. & Prisk, Court (Editors) **F1488.3 E37**
El Salvador at War: An Oral History of Conflict from the 1979 Insurrection to the Present. Edwin G. Corr (Introduction by). Paper Text. DIANE Publishing Company. Collingdale, PA. 1995. 500p. ISBN:0-7881-2161-8, ISBN13: 978-0-7881-2161-6. Dewey:972.84/053.
Audience: **u,f.**

Océano Staff **F1483.E53 2001**
Enciclopedia de El Salvador, Set. Trade Cloth. Oceano Grupo Editoria, S.A.. Barcelona, 2001. 236p. Enciclopedias de las Naciones Latinoamericanas Ser. ISBN:84-494-1618-3, ISBN13: 978-84-494-1618-7. Dewey:972.84/003. LCCN:2001-354551.
Audience: **u,f.**

Parkman, Patricia **F1487.5.P37 1988**
Nonviolent Insurrection in El Salvador: The Fall of Maximiliano Hernandez Martinez. Trade Cloth. University of Arizona Press. Tucson, AZ. 1988. 168p. ISBN:0-8165-1062-8, ISBN13: 978-0-8165-1062-7. Dewey:972.84/052. LCCN:88-009432.
Audience: **u,f.** *Choice, 1989.*

Peterson, Anna L. (Editor), et al. **BR625.S2C47 2001**
Christianity, Social Change and Globalization in the Americas. Manuel A. Vasquez & Philip J. Williams (Editors). Trade Cloth. Rutgers University Press. Piscataway, NJ. 2004. 259p. ISBN:0-8135-2931-X, ISBN13: 978-0-8135-2931-8. Dewey:261.8/098. LCCN:00-046873.
Audience: **u,f.**

Shayne, Julie D. **HQ1460.5.S53 2004**
The Revolution Question: Feminisms in el Salvador, Chile, and Cuba Compared. Trade Cloth. Rutgers University Press. Piscataway, NJ. 2004. 240p. ISBN:0-8135-3483-6, ISBN13: 978-0-8135-3483-1. Dewey:305.42. LCCN:2004-003816.
Audience: **u,f.** *Choice, 2005.*

Sobrino, Jon & Barr, Robert R. **BX4700.T5**
Archbishop Romero: Memories and Reflections. Trade Paper. Wipf & Stock Publishers. Eugene, OR. 2004. 224p. ISBN:1-59244-977-8, ISBN13: 978-1-59244-977-4. Dewey:282/.092.
Audience: **u,f.**

Stanley, William **HV6433.S2S73 1996**
The Protection Racket State: Elite Politics, Military Extortion, and Civil War in El Salvador. Trade Cloth. Temple University Press. Philadelphia, PA. 1996. 384p. ISBN:1-56639-391-4, ISBN13: 978-1-56639-391-1. Dewey:972.8405. LCCN:95-020998.
Audience: **u,f.** *Choice, 1997.*

Tilley, Virginia Q. **F1505.T55 2005**
Seeing Indians: A Study of Race, Nation, and Power in el Salvador. Trade Paper, Perfect. University of New Mexico Press.

Albuquerque, NM. 2005. 297p. ISBN:0-8263-3925-5, ISBN13: 978-0-8263-3925-6. Dewey:305.897/0728. LCCN:2005-020760.
Audience: **u,f.**

United States, General Accounting Office
El Salvador: Military Assistance has Helped Counter but not Overcome the Insurgency: Report to the Honorable Edward M. Kennedy. U.S. General Accounting Office. 1991.
Audience: **u,f.**

Wade, Christine J., et al. **F1439.B66 2006**
Understanding Central America: Global Forces, Rebellion, and Change. Ed. 4. John A. Booth & Thomas W. Walker (Authors). Trade Paper, Perfect. Westview Press. Boulder, CO. 2005. 304p. ISBN:0-8133-4195-7, ISBN13: 978-0-8133-4195-8. Dewey:972.805. LCCN:2005-004456.
Audience: **u,f.**

Walkowitz, Daniel J. (Editor) **NA9345.M46 2004**
Memory and the Impact of Political Transformation in Public Space. Lisa Maya Knauer (Editor, Contribution by), Barbara Weinstein (Editor), James Carter, John Czaplicka, Kanishka Goonewardena & Anna Krylova (Contribution by). Trade Cloth. Duke University Press. Durham, NC. 2004. 336p. Radical Perspectives Ser. ISBN:0-8223-3377-5, ISBN13: 978-0-8223-3377-7. Dewey:720/.1/03. LCCN:2004-011862.
Audience: **u,f.**

Waller, J. Michael **F1488.3.W35 1991**
The Third Current of Revolution: Inside the North American Front of el Salvador's Guerrilla War. Trade Cloth. University Press of America, Inc. Lanham, MD. 1991. 332p. ISBN:0-8191-8231-1, ISBN13: 978-0-8191-8231-9. Dewey:972.8405/3. LCCN:91-010192.
Audience: **u,f.** *Choice, 1992.*

Whitfield, Teresa **F1488.3.W48 1994**
Paying the Price: Ignacio Ellacuria and the Murdered Jesuits of El Salvador. Alvara De Soto (Foreword by). Cloth Text. Temple University Press. Philadelphia, PA. 1994. 500p. ISBN:1-56639-252-7, ISBN13: 978-1-56639-252-5. Dewey:272/.9/097284. LCCN:94-020361.
Audience: **u,f.**

Wood, Elisabeth J. **F1488.3.W66 2003**
Insurgent Collective Action and Civil War in el Salvador. Trade Cloth. Cambridge University Press. New York, NY. 2003. 328p. Cambridge Studies in Comparative Politics Ser. ISBN:0-521-81175-9, ISBN13: 978-0-521-81175-0. Dewey:972.8405/3. LCCN:2002-041461.
Audience: **u,f.**

Zoomers, A. & Van Den Haar, G. (Editors) **HD1333.L29C87 2000**
Current Land Policy in Latin America: Regularing Land Tenure under Neo-Liberalism. Trade Paper. Royal Tropical Institute Press. 2001. 334p. ISBN:90-6832-137-4, ISBN13: 978-90-6832-137-1. Dewey:333.3/18. LCCN:2002-317662.
Audience: **u,f.**

Central America: General > Honduras

Euraque, Darío A. **F1508.E87 1996**
Reinterpreting the Banana Republic: Region and State in Honduras, 1870-1972. University of North Carolina Press. 1996. ISBN:0-8078-2298-1, ISBN13: 978-0-8078-2298-2.
Audience: **u,f.**

Keogh, Dermot F. (Editor) **BX1426.2.C46 1990**
Church and Politics in Latin America. Graham Greene (Foreword by). Cloth Text. Palgrave Macmillan. New York, NY. 1990. 320p. ISBN:0-312-02815-6, ISBN13: 978-0-312-02815-2. Dewey:261.7/098. LCCN:89-037269.
Audience: **u,f.**

Mahoney, James **JL1410.M34 2001**
The Legacies of Liberalism: Path Dependence and Political Regimes in Central America. Trade Cloth. Johns Hopkins University Press. Baltimore, MD. 2001. 416p. ISBN:0-8018-6552-2, ISBN13: 978-0-8018-6552-7. Dewey:320.9728. LCCN:00-011212.
Audience: **u,f.** *Choice, 2002.*

Murshed, Syed Mansoob (Editor) **HF1418.5.G586 2002**
Globalization, Marginalization, and Development. Paper over Boards. Routledge. New York, NY. 2002. 272p. Routledge Studies in Development Economics, Vol. 28 ISBN:0-415-28850-9, ISBN13: 978-0-415-28850-7. Dewey:337. LCCN:2002-068033.
Audience: **u,f.**

Ronfeldt, David F. **F1436.8.U6**
U.S. Involvement in Central America: Three Views from Honduras. RAND. 1989. ISBN:0-8330-0914-1, ISBN13: 978-0-8330-0914-2.
Audience: **u,f.**

Wade, Christine J., et al. **F1439.B66 2006**
Understanding Central America: Global Forces, Rebellion, and Change. Ed. 4. John A. Booth & Thomas W. Walker (Authors). Trade Paper, Perfect. Westview Press. Boulder, CO. 2005. 304p. ISBN:0-8133-4195-7, ISBN13: 978-0-8133-4195-8. Dewey:972.805. LCCN:2005-004456.
Audience: **u,f.**

Zoomers, A. & Van Den Haar, G. (Editors) **HD1333.L29C87 2000**
Current Land Policy in Latin America: Regularing Land Tenure under Neo-Liberalism. Trade Paper. Royal Tropical Institute Press. 2001. 334p. ISBN:90-6832-137-4, ISBN13: 978-90-6832-137-1. Dewey:333.3/18. LCCN:2002-317662.
Audience: **u,f.**

Central America: General > Nicaragua

Anderson, Leslie E. & Dodd, Lawrence C. **JL1616.A53 2005**
Learning Democracy: Citizen Engagement and Electoral Choice in Nicaragua, 1990-2001. Trade Cloth. University of Chicago Press. Chicago, IL. 2005. 336p. ISBN:0-226-01971-3, ISBN13: 978-0-226-01971-0. Dewey:324.97285/054. LCCN:2004-024387.
Audience: **u,f.** *Choice, 2006.*

Ardon, Patricia **F1439.5**
Post War Reconstruction in Central America: Lessons from El Salvador, Guatemala and Nicaragua. Deborah Eade (Translator, Adapted by). Trade Paper. Oxfam Publishing. Oxford, 2004. 112p. Working Papers ISBN:0-85598-405-8, ISBN13: 978-0-85598-405-2. Dewey:972.8/053.
Audience: **u,f.**

Bayard de Volo, Lorraine **F1527.B39 2001**
Mothers of Heroes and Martyrs: Gender Identity Politics in Nicaragua, 1979-1999. Trade Paper. Johns Hopkins University Press. Baltimore, MD. 2001. 320p. ISBN:0-8018-6764-9, ISBN13: 978-0-8018-6764-4. Dewey:323.3/4/09728509048. LCCN:2001-000239.
Audience: **u,f.**

Belli, Gioconda **PQ6623.I35**
The Country under My Skin: A Memoir of Love and War. Trade Paper. Knopf Publishing Group. New York, NY. 2003. 400p. ISBN:1-4000-3216-4, ISBN13: 978-1-4000-3216-7. Dewey:868/.6409 B.
Audience: **u,f.**

Blakemore, Steven (ed.) **F1528**
Voices Against the State: Nicaraguan Opposition to the FSLN. University of Miami, North-South Center, for the Institute of Interamerican Studies. 1988. ISBN:0-935501-11-8, ISBN13: 978-0-935501-11-7.
Audience: **u,f.**

Burdick, John and Hewitt, W.E. (eds.) **BX1426.2**
The Church at the Grassroots in Latin America: Perspectives on Thirty Years of Activism. Praeger. 2000. ISBN:0-275-96659-3, ISBN13: 978-0-275-96659-1.
Audience: **u,f.**

Clark, George B. **F1526.3.C57 2001**
With the Old Corps in Nicaragua. Trade Cloth. Ballantine Books. New York, NY. 2001. 240p. ISBN:0-89141-737-0, ISBN13: 978-0-89141-737-8. Dewey:972.8505/1. LCCN:00-065248.
Audience: **u,f.**

Cruz, Arturo J. **F1528.22.C78A3 1989**
Memoirs of a Counter-Revolutionary: Life with the Contras, the Sandinistas, and the CIA. Trade Cloth. Doubleday Publishing. New York, NY. 1989. 288p. ISBN:0-385-24879-2, ISBN13: 978-0-385-24879-2. Dewey:972.8505/3/092. LCCN:89-011828.
Audience: **u,f.**

Cruz, Consuelo **JL1456.C78 2005**
Political Culture and Institutional Development in Costa Rica and Nicaragua: World Making in the Tropics. Trade Cloth. Cambridge University Press. New York, NY. 2005. 302p. ISBN:0-521-84203-4, ISBN13: 978-0-521-84203-7. Dewey:306.2/097285. LCCN:2004-026762.
Audience: **u,f.** *Choice, 2006.*

Denevan, William M. (Editor) **E59.P75N37 1992**
The Native Population of the Americas in 1492. Ed. 2. W. George Lovell (Foreword by). Trade Paper. University of Wisconsin Press. Chicago, IL. 1992. 398p. ISBN:0-299-13434-2, ISBN13: 978-0-299-13434-1. Dewey:304.60973. LCCN:91-040042.
Audience: **u,f.**

Dodd, Thomas J. **JL1618 .D63 1992**
Managing Democracy in Central America, a Case Study: United States Election Supervision in Nicaragua, 1927-1933. Trade Paper. University of Miami, North/South Center Press. Coral Gables, FL. 1992. 176p. ISBN:1-56000-631-5, ISBN13: 978-1-56000-631-2. Dewey:324.97285/051. LCCN:92-026327.
Audience: **u,f.**

Dodson, Michael & O'Shaughnessy, Laura N. **F1528.D63 1990**
Nicaragua's Other Revolution: Religious Faith and Political Struggle. Trade Cloth. University of North Carolina Press. Chapel Hill, NC. 1990. xii, 280p. ISBN:0-8078-1881-X, ISBN13: 978-0-8078-1881-7. Dewey:261.7/097285. LCCN:89-035448.
Audience: **u,f.** *Choice, 1991.*

Dye, David R. **F1528**
Democracy Adrift : Caudillo Politics in Nicaragua. The Author. 2004.
Audience: **u,f.**

Fernandez, Damian J. (Editor) **F1436.8.M628C46 1990**
Central America and the Middle East: The Internationalization of the Crises. Trade Cloth. University Press of Florida. Gainesville, FL. 1990. 239p. ISBN:0-8130-1001-2, ISBN13: 978-0-8130-1001-4. Dewey:972.805/3. LCCN:90-003693.
Audience: **u,f.**

Foroohar, Manzar **BX1442.2.F67 1989**
The Catholic Church and Social Change in Nicaragua. Cloth Text. State University of New York Press. Albany, NY. 1989. 262p. ISBN:0-88706-864-2, ISBN13: 978-0-88706-864-5. Dewey:282/.7285. LCCN:88-002144.
Audience: **u,f.** *Choice, 1990.*

Gambone, Michael D. **F1414**
Capturing the Revolution: The United States, Central America and Nicaragua, 1961-1972. Paper Text. Greenwood Publishing Group, Inc. Portsmouth, NH. 2001. 288p. ISBN:0-275-97305-0, ISBN13: 978-0-275-97305-6. Dewey:972.805/2. LCCN:00-069858.
Audience: **u,f.** *Choice, 2002.*

Gilbert, Dennis **JL1619.A52G55 1988**
Sandinistas: The Party and the Revolution. Trade Cloth. Blackwell Publishing, Inc. Malden, MA. 1988. 248p. ISBN:1-55786-006-8, ISBN13: 978-1-55786-006-4. Dewey:324.27285/075. LCCN:88-006591.
Audience: **u,f.** *Choice, 1989.*

Gilbert, Jorge **BR600**
Liberation Theology and Class Struggle in Latin America. Evergreen State College. 1989.
Audience: **u,f.**

Gould, Jeffrey L. **HD1531.N5G68 1990**
To Lead As Equals: Rural Protest and Political Consciousness in Chinandega, Nicaragua, 1912-1979. Trade Paper. University of North Carolina Press. Chapel Hill, NC. 1990. 392p. ISBN:0-8078-4275-3, ISBN13: 978-0-8078-4275-1. Dewey:322.4/4/09728511. LCCN:89-029790.
Audience: **u,f.** *Choice, 1991.*

Graham, Hugh **F1528**
Ploughing the Seas: the Nicaraguan Resistance and the CIA in the Jungles of Southern Nicaragua, 1984-1987. Exile Editions. 2001. ISBN:1-55096-513-1, ISBN13: 978-1-55096-513-1.
Audience: **u,f.**

Griffin-Nolan, Ed **F1528.G74 1991**
Witness for Peace: A Story of Resistance. Jim Wallis (Foreword by). Trade Paper. Westminster John Knox Press. Louisville, KY. 1991. 237p. ISBN:0-664-25179-X, ISBN13: 978-0-664-25179-6. Dewey:972.850. LCCN:90-022812.
Audience: **u,f.**

Guidry, John A. (Editor), et al. **HN16.G57 2000**
Globalizations and Social Movements: Culture, Power and the Transnational Public Sphere. Michael D. Kennedy & Mayer N. Zald (Editors). Trade Cloth. University of Michigan Press. Chicago, IL. 2000. 432p. ISBN:0-472-09721-0, ISBN13: 978-0-472-09721-0. Dewey:303.48/4/09041. LCCN:00-033805.
Audience: **u,f.**

Gullette, David **PQ6657.A6695Z67 1994**
Gaspar! A Spanish Poet-Priest in the Nicaraguan Revolution. Trade Cloth. Bilingual Press/Editorial Bilingue. Tempe, AZ. 1993. 160p. ISBN:0-927534-37-1, ISBN13: 978-0-927534-37-6. Dewey:861. LCCN:93-041109.
Audience: **u,f.** *Choice, 1994.*

Hale, Charles R. **F1529.M9H37 1994**
Resistance and Contradiction: Miskitu Indians and the Nicaraguan State, 1894-1987. Trade Cloth. Stanford University Press. Palo Alto, CA. 1994. xviii, 296p. ISBN:0-8047-2255-2, ISBN13: 978-0-8047-2255-1. Dewey:323.1/1978. LCCN:93-017944.
Audience: **u,f.** *Choice, 1994.*

Hart, Dianne W. **F1528.H36 1990**
Thanks to God and the Revolution: The Oral History of a Nicaraguan Family. Trade Cloth. University of Wisconsin Press. Chicago, IL. 1990. 328p. ISBN:0-299-12610-2, ISBN13: 978-0-299-12610-0. Dewey:972.8505/3. LCCN:90-050090.
Audience: **u,f.** *Choice, 1991.*

Jones, Adam **F1528.J66 2002**
Beyond the Barricades: Nicaragua and the Struggle for the Sandinista Press, 1979-1998. Trade Paper. Ohio University Press. Athens, OH. 2002. 338p. Research in International Studies Ser., Vol. 37:Latin America ISBN:0-89680-223-X, ISBN13: 978-0-89680-223-0. Dewey:070.4/493209. LCCN:2002-022609.
Audience: **u,f.** *Choice, 2003.*

Kodrich, Kris **PN4989.N6K63 2001**
Tradition and Change in the Nicaraguan Press: Newspapers and Journalists in a New Democratic Era. Trade Paper. University Press of America, Inc. Lanham, MD. 2002. 212p. ISBN:0-7618-2171-6, ISBN13: 978-0-7618-2171-7. Dewey:079/.7285. LCCN:2001-054029.
Audience: **u,f.**

Kunzle, David **ND2662.K86 1995**
The Murals of Revolutionary Nicaragua, 1979-1992. Trade Paper. University of California Press. Berkeley, CA. 1995. 222p. ISBN:0-520-08192-7, ISBN13: 978-0-520-08192-5. Dewey:758/.997285053. LCCN:94-049437.
Audience: **u,f.**

Landau, Saul **F1439**
The Guerrilla Wars of Central America: Nicaragua, El Salvador and Guatemala. Trade Cloth. Institute for Policy Studies. Washington, DC. 1993. 211p. ISBN:0-297-82114-8, ISBN13: 978-0-297-82114-4. Dewey:972.
Audience: **u,f.**

Linkogle, Stephanie **BX1442.2.L55 1996**
Gender, Practice and Faith in Nicaragua. Trade Cloth. Ashgate Publishing, Ltd. Aldershot, 1996. 280p. ISBN:1-85972-298-9, ISBN13: 978-1-85972-298-5. Dewey:972.8/5053. LCCN:96-083259.
Audience: **u,f.**

Macaulay, Neill **F1526.3.S244M33**
The Sandino Affair. Ed. 2. Trade Paper. Wacahoota Press. Micanopy, FL. 1998. 320p. ISBN:0-9653864-4-9, ISBN13: 978-0-9653864-4-9. Dewey:972.85/05.
Audience: **u,f.**

Mahoney, James **JL1410.M34 2001**
The Legacies of Liberalism: Path Dependence and Political Regimes in Central America. Trade Cloth. Johns Hopkins University Press. Baltimore, MD. 2001. 416p. ISBN:0-8018-6552-2, ISBN13: 978-0-8018-6552-7. Dewey:320.9728. LCCN:00-011212.
Audience: **u,f.** *Choice, 2002.*

Martin, Randy **PN2401.M38 1994**
Socialist Ensembles: Theater and State in Cuba and Nicaragua. Trade Cloth. University of Minnesota Press. Minneapolis, MN. 1994. 208p. Cultural Politics Ser., Vol. 8 ISBN:0-8166-2480-1, ISBN13: 978-0-8166-2480-5. Dewey:792/.097291/0904. LCCN:94-003925.
Audience: **u,f.**

Meeks, Brian **F2183**
Caribbean Revolutions and Revolutionary Theory: An Assessment of Cuba, Nicaragua and Grenada. Trade Paper. University of the West Indies Press. Kingston, 2001. 220p. ISBN:976-640-104-7, ISBN13: 978-976-640-104-7. Dewey:972.905/2.
Audience: **u,f.**

Montiel-Argüello, Alejandro **F1526.25**
Nicaragua Colonial. Banco Central de Nicaragua. 2000.
Audience: **u,f.**

Moore, John N. **F1528**
The Secret War in Central America: Sandinista Assault on World Order. Trade Cloth. Greenwood Publishing Group, Inc. Portsmouth, NH. 1987. 204p. Foreign Intelligence Book Ser. ISBN:0-313-27041-4, ISBN13: 978-0-313-27041-3. Dewey:972.85053. LCCN:86-028092.
Audience: **u,f.**

Newson, Linda A. **F1525.3.C84N48 1987**
Indian Survival in Colonial Nicaragua. Trade Cloth. University of Oklahoma Press. Norman, OK. 1987. 496p. Civilization of the American Indian Ser., Vol. 175 ISBN:0-8061-2008-8, ISBN13: 978-0-8061-2008-9. Dewey:972.85/00497. LCCN:86-040078.
Audience: **u,f.** *Choice, 1987.*

Nolan, David **F1528**
The Ideology of the Sandinistas and the Nicaraguan Revolution. Institute of Interamerican Studies, Graduate School of International Studies, University of Miami. 1984.
Audience: **u,f.**

Paige, Jeffery M. **HD9199.C42**
Coffee and Power: Revolution and the Rise of Democracy in Central America. Trade Paper. Harvard University Press. Cambridge, MA. 1998. 448p. ISBN:0-674-13649-7, ISBN13: 978-0-674-13649-6. Dewey:338.1/7373/09728.
Audience: **u,f.** *Choice, 1997.*

Pardo-Maurer, R. **F1528**
The Contras, 1980-1989: A Special Kind of Politics. Trade Cloth. Greenwood Publishing Group, Inc. Portsmouth, NH. 1990. 288p. The Washington Papers, No. 147 ISBN:0-275-93817-4, ISBN13: 978-0-275-93817-8. Dewey:972.8505/3. LCCN:90-044608.
Audience: **u,f.** *Choice, 1991.*

Parsa, Misagh **JC491.P36 2000**
States, Ideologies and Social Revolutions: A Comparative Analysis of Iran, Nicaragua and the Philippines. Cloth Text. Cambridge University Press. New York, NY. 2000. 336p. ISBN:0-521-77337-7, ISBN13: 978-0-521-77337-9. Dewey:303.6/4. LCCN:99-087457.
Audience: **u,f.** *Choice, 2001.*

Ratliff, William E. & Miranda, Roger **F1528.M57 1993**
The Civil War in Nicaragua: Inside the Sandinistas. Trade Cloth. Transaction Publishers. Somerset, NJ. 1993. 314p. ISBN:1-56000-064-3, ISBN13: 978-1-56000-064-8. Dewey:972.85053. LCCN:92-001296.
Audience: **u,f.** *Choice, 1993.*

Robinson, William I. **E183.8.N5R64 1992**
A Faustian Bargain: U.S. Intervention in the Nicaraguan Elections and American Foreign Policy in the Post-Cold War Era. Trade Paper. Westview Press. Boulder, CO. 1992. 310p. ISBN:0-8133-8234-3, ISBN13: 978-0-8133-8234-0. Dewey:327.7307285. LCCN:92-004578.
Audience: **u,f.** *Choice, 1993.*

Sabia, Debra **BX2347.72.N5S23 1997**
Contradiction and Conflict: The Popular Church in Nicaragua. Trade Cloth. University of Alabama Press. Tuscaloosa, AL. 1997. 256p. ISBN:0-8173-0873-3, ISBN13: 978-0-8173-0873-5. Dewey:282/.7285/09048. LCCN:96-046304.
Audience: **u,f.** *Choice, 1998.*

Wade, Christine J., et al. **F1439.B66 2006**
Understanding Central America: Global Forces, Rebellion, and Change. Ed. 4. John A. Booth & Thomas W. Walker (Authors). Trade Paper, Perfect. Westview Press. Boulder, CO. 2005. 304p. ISBN:0-8133-4195-7, ISBN13: 978-0-8133-4195-8. Dewey:972.805. LCCN:2005-004456.
Audience: **u,f.**

Walkowitz, Daniel J. (Editor) **NA9345.M46 2004**
Memory and the Impact of Political Transformation in Public Space. Lisa Maya Knauer (Editor, Contribution by), Barbara Weinstein (Editor), James Carter, John Czaplicka, Kanishka Goonewardena & Anna Krylova (Contribution by). Trade Cloth. Duke University Press. Durham, NC. 2004. 336p. Radical Perspectives Ser. ISBN:0-8223-3377-5, ISBN13: 978-0-8223-3377-7. Dewey:720/.1/03. LCCN:2004-011862.
Audience: **u,f.**

Westlake, E. J. **PQ7513.W47 2005**
Our Land Is Made of Courage and Glory: Nationalist Drama of Nicaragua and Guatemala. Trade Cloth. Southern Illinois University Press. Carbondale, IL. 2005. 176p. Theater in the Americas Ser. ISBN:0-8093-2625-6, ISBN13: 978-0-8093-2625-9. Dewey:862/.609358. LCCN:2004-023655.
Audience: **u,f.**

Zarate, Juan C. **F1439.Z37 1994**
Forging Democracy: A Comparative Study of the Effects of U.S. Foreign Policy on Central American Democratization. Trade Cloth. University Press of America, Inc. Lanham, MD. 1994. 174p. ISBN:0-8191-9527-8, ISBN13: 978-0-8191-9527-2. Dewey:327.730728. LCCN:94-009423.
Audience: **u,f.**

Central America: General > Costa Rica

Clarence-Smith, W. G. & Topik, Steven (Editors) **HD9195.A3512G58 2003**
The Global Coffee Economy in Africa, Asia and Latin America, 1500-1989. Cloth Text. Cambridge University Press. New York, NY. 2003. 504p. ISBN:0-521-81851-6, ISBN13: 978-0-521-81851-3. Dewey:338.1/7373. LCCN:2002-073472.
Audience: **u,f.**

Cruz, Consuelo **JL1456.C78 2005**
Political Culture and Institutional Development in Costa Rica and Nicaragua: World Making in the Tropics. Trade Cloth. Cambridge University Press. New York, NY. 2005. 302p. ISBN:0-521-84203-4, ISBN13: 978-0-521-84203-7. Dewey:306.2/097285. LCCN:2004-026762.
Audience: **u,f.** *Choice, 2006.*

Dore, Elizabeth & Molyneux, Maxine (Editors) **HQ1075.5.L29H53**
Hidden Histories of Gender and the State in Latin America. Cloth Text. Duke University Press. Durham, NC. 2000. 400p. ISBN:0-8223-2434-2, ISBN13: 978-0-8223-2434-8. Dewey:305.3/098. LCCN:99-036543.
Audience: **u,f.**

Falola, Toyin & Childs, Matt D. (Editors) **E29.Y67Y67 2004**
The Yoruba Diaspora in the Atlantic World. Trade Cloth. Indiana University Press. Bloomington, IN. 2004. 464p. Blacks in the Diaspora Ser. ISBN:0-253-34458-1, ISBN13: 978-0-253-34458-8. Dewey:970.00496333. LCCN:2004-013528.
Audience: **u,f.** *Choice, 2006.*

Guardia, Ricardo F. **F1547.F387 1978**
History of the Discovery and Conquest of Costa Rica. Harry W. Van Dyke (Translator). Trade Cloth. Gordon Press Publishers. New York, NY. 1978. ISBN:0-8490-1381-X, ISBN13: 978-0-8490-1381-2. Dewey:972.86. LCCN:78-005236.
Audience: **u,f.**

Robinson, David J. (Editor) **HB1961.M54 1990**
Migration in Colonial Spanish America. Alan R. H. Baker, Richard Dennis & Deryck Holdworth (Contribution by). Trade

Cloth. Cambridge University Press. New York, NY. 1990. 417p. Studies in Historical Geography, No. 16 ISBN:0-521-36281-4, ISBN13: 978-0-521-36281-8. Dewey:304.8/09171/246. LCCN:89-001042.

Audience: **u,f.**

Central America: General > Panama

Anderson, Charles L. **E125.B2A5 1970**
Life and Letters of Vasco Nunez De Balboa. Library Binding. Greenwood Publishing Group, Inc. Portsmouth, NH. ISBN:0-8371-3242-8, ISBN13: 978-0-8371-3242-6. Dewey:972.8/02/092. LCCN:70-100140.

Audience: **u,f.**

Anguizola, Gustave **TC774.A67**
Philippe Bunau-Varilla: The Man Behind the Panama Canal. Cloth Text. Rowman & Littlefield Publishers, Inc. Lanham, MD. 1980. 480p. ISBN:0-88229-397-4, ISBN13: 978-0-88229-397-4. Dewey:386/.444/09. LCCN:79-013673.

Audience: **u,f.** B

Briggs, Clarence E. **F1567.B75 1990**
Operation Just Cause. Trade Paper. Stackpole Books. Mechanicsburg, PA. 1990. 176p. ISBN:0-8117-2520-0, ISBN13: 978-0-8117-2520-0. Dewey:972.8705/3. LCCN:90-010079.

Audience: **u,f.**

Carlisle, Rodney P. **HE736.C37**
Sovereignty for Sale. Trade Cloth. Naval Institute Press. Annapolis, MD. 1981. 278p. ISBN:0-87021-668-6, ISBN13: 978-0-87021-668-8. Dewey:387.2/45. LCCN:81-607020.

Audience: **u,f.** B

CODEHUCA **F1567**
Exhumations in Panama: Breaking the Silence, Commission of Defense the Human Rights in Central America. CODEHUCA. 1990.

Audience: **u,f.**

Collazos, Sharon P. **HD8173.5.P47 1991**
Labor and Politics in Panama: The Torrijos Years. Trade Paper. Westview Press. Boulder, CO. 1991. 196p. ISBN:0-8133-8115-0, ISBN13: 978-0-8133-8115-2. Dewey:331.12/042/097287. LCCN:90-021689.

Audience: **u,f.**

Conniff, Michael L. **F1577.B55C67 1985**
Black Labor on a White Canal: Panama, 1904-1981. Trade Cloth. University of Pittsburgh Press. Pittsburgh, PA. 1985. 240p. Latin American Ser. ISBN:0-8229-3509-0, ISBN13: 978-0-8229-3509-4. Dewey:305.8/96/072875. LCCN:84-021970.

Audience: **u,f.** *Choice, 1986.*

Dudden, Arthur P. (Editor) **DU30.A44 2003**
American Empire in the Pacific: Fron Trade to Strategic Balance, 1700-1922. Trade Cloth. Ashgate Publishing, Ltd. Aldershot, 2004. 412p. The Pacific World Ser., No. 9:Lands, Peoples, and History of the Pacific, 1500-1900 ISBN:0-7546-3049-8, ISBN13: 978-0-7546-3049-4. Dewey:303.48/27305. LCCN:2003-052111.

Audience: **u,f.**

Earle, Peter **F1576.P2E18 1982**
The Sack of Panama. Trade Cloth. Penguin Group (USA) Inc. New York, NY. 1982. 320p. ISBN:0-670-61425-4, ISBN13: 978-0-670-61425-7. Dewey:972.8/75. LCCN:81-065267.

Audience: **u,f.**

Habeeb, William M. & Zartman, I. William **F1569.C2**
The Panama Canal Negotiations. Paper Text. Georgetown University, Institute for the Study of Diplomacy. Washington, DC. 1994. 57p. Pew Case Studies in International Affairs ISBN:1-56927-407-X, ISBN13: 978-1-56927-407-1. Dewey:341.446.

Audience: **u,f.**

Harding, Robert C. **F1566.H37 2006**
The History of Panama. Trade Cloth. Greenwood Publishing Group, Inc. Portsmouth, NH. 2006. 176p. The Greenwood Histories of the Modern Nations Ser. ISBN:0-313-33322-X, ISBN13: 978-0-313-33322-4. Dewey:972.87. LCCN:2006-001176.

Audience: **u,f.**

Harding, Robert C. **F1566.5.H37 2001**
The Military Foundations of Panamanian Politics. Trade Cloth. Transaction Publishers. Somerset, NJ. 2001. 233p. ISBN:0-7658-0075-6, ISBN13: 978-0-7658-0075-6. Dewey:322/.5/0978287. LCCN:00-066963.

Audience: **u,f.**

Helms, Mary W. **F1565.2.C8**
Ancient Panama: Chiefs in Search of Power. Cloth Text. University of Texas Press. Austin, TX. 1979. 244p. Texas Pan American Ser. ISBN:0-292-73817-X, ISBN13: 978-0-292-73817-1. Dewey:972.87/00497. LCCN:78-026906.

Audience: **u,f.**

Holmes, James R. **E757**
Theodore Roosevelt and World Order: Police Power in International Relations. Potomac Books. 2006. ISBN:1-57488-883-8, ISBN13: 978-1-57488-883-6.

Audience: **u,f.**

Huchthausen, Peter **E840.4**
America's Splendid Little Wars: A Short History of U. S. Engagements from the Fall of Saigon to Baghdad. Trade Paper. Penguin Group (USA) Inc. New York, NY. 2004. 288p. ISBN:0-14-200465-0, ISBN13: 978-0-14-200465-4. Dewey:973.92.

Audience: **u,f.**

Johns, Christina J. & Johnson, P. Ward **F1567**
State Crime, the Media, and the Invasion of Panama. Trade Cloth. Greenwood Publishing Group, Inc. Portsmouth, NH. 1993. 168p. Criminology and Crime Control Policy Ser. ISBN:0-275-94314-3, ISBN13: 978-0-275-94314-1. Dewey:972.87053. LCCN:93-019092.

Audience: **u,f.**

Kemble, John H. **F865.K32 1990**
The Panama Route, 1848-1869. Cloth Text. University of South Carolina Press. Columbia, SC. 1990. 329p. ISBN:0-87249-697-X, ISBN13: 978-0-87249-697-2. Dewey:383/.142/091641. LCCN:89-028560.

Audience: **u,f.**

La Rosa, Michael & Mejia, German R. (eds.) **F1569.C2**
The United States Discovers Panama: The Writings of Soldiers, Scholars, Scientists, and Scoundrels, 1850-1905. Rowman & Littlefield. 2004. ISBN:0-7425-2721-2, ISBN13: 978-0-7425-2721-8.
Audience: **u,f.**

LaFeber, Walter **E183.8.P2L33 1989**
The Panama Canal: The Crisis in Historical Perspective. Trade Cloth. Oxford University Press, Inc. New York, NY. 1990. 288p. ISBN:0-19-505930-1, ISBN13: 978-0-19-505930-4. Dewey:327.7307287. LCCN:89-036284.
Audience: **u,f.**

Lewis, Lancelot S. **F1577.B55 L48**
The West Indian in Panama. Paper Text. University Press of America, Inc. Lanham, MD. 1980. ISBN:0-8191-0877-4, ISBN13: 978-0-8191-0877-7. Dewey:972.87/004969729. LCCN:79-067449.
Audience: **u,f.**

Lindsay-Poland, John **E183.8.P2L475 2003**
Emperors in the Jungle: The Hidden History of the U. S. in Panama. Guillermo Castro (Afterword by). Trade Cloth. Duke University Press. Durham, NC. 2003. 256p. American Encounters/Global Interactions Ser. ISBN:0-8223-3100-4, ISBN13: 978-0-8223-3100-1. Dewey:327.7307287/09. LCCN:2002-013820.
Audience: **u,f.** *Choice, 2003.*

Mann, Carlos G. **F1566.G85 1996**
Panamanian Militarism: A Historical Interpretation. Paper Text. Ohio University Press. Athens, OH. 1996. 243p. Monographs in International Studies, No. 25 ISBN:0-89680-189-6, ISBN13: 978-0-89680-189-9. Dewey:322/.5/097287. LCCN:95-040747.
Audience: **u,f.**

Markovits, Claude **HF3790.5.Z9S556 20**
The Global World of Indian Merchants, 1750-1947: Traders of Sind from Bukhara to Panama. C. A. Bayly, Rajnarayan Chandavarkar & Gordon Johnson (Contribution by). Trade Cloth. Cambridge University Press. New York, NY. 2000. 344p. Cambridge Studies in Indian History and Society, No. 6 ISBN:0-521-62285-9, ISBN13: 978-0-521-62285-1. Dewey:382.0954918. LCCN:99-047925.
Audience: **u,f.**

McPherson, Alan L. **F1418.M373 2003**
Yankee No!: Anti-Americanism in U. S.- Latin American Relations. Trade Cloth. Harvard University Press. Cambridge, MA. 2003. 272p. ISBN:0-674-01184-8, ISBN13: 978-0-674-01184-7. Dewey:327.7308. LCCN:2003-051118.
Audience: **u,f.** *Choice, 2004.*

Newton, Velma **JV7429**
The Silver Men: West Indian Labour Migration to Panama, 1850-1914. Ian Randle. 2004. ISBN:976-637-132-6, ISBN13: 978-976-637-132-6.
Audience: **u,f.**

Noriega, Manuel & Eisner, Peter **F1567.N67A3 1997**
America's Prisoner: The Memoirs of Manuel Noriega. Trade Cloth. Random House, Inc. New York, NY. 1997. 293p. ISBN:0-679-43227-2, ISBN13: 978-0-679-43227-2. Dewey:972.8705/3/092 B. LCCN:96-027788.
Audience: **u,f.**

Pearcy, Thomas L. **F1566.5.P43 1998**
We Answer Only to God: Politics and the Military in Panama, 1903-1947. Trade Cloth. University of New Mexico Press. Albuquerque, NM. 1998. 232p. ISBN:0-8263-1841-X, ISBN13: 978-0-8263-1841-1. Dewey:972.8705. LCCN:98-014669.
Audience: **u,f.**

Perez-Venero, Alex **F1566.45.P47**
Before the Five Frontiers: Panama from 1821-1903. Trade Cloth. A M S Press, Inc. New York, NY. 1978. xi, 199p. ISBN:0-404-16003-4, ISBN13: 978-0-404-16003-6. Dewey:972.87. LCCN:77-078317.
Audience: **u,f.** B

Petrovich, Sandra Marie **F1576.P2P48 2001**
Henry Morgan's Raid on Panama: Geopolitics and Colonial Ramifications, 1669-1674. Trade Cloth. Edwin Mellen Press, The. Lewiston, NY. 2001. 142p. Caribbean Studies, Vol. 10 ISBN:0-7734-7422-6, ISBN13: 978-0-7734-7422-2. Dewey:972.87/02. LCCN:2001-018667.
Audience: **u,f.**

Phillips, R. Cody **F1567 .O642**
Operation Just Cause: The Incursion into Panama. John S. Brown (Introduction by). Paper Text. DIANE Publishing Company. Collingdale, PA. 2004. 51p. ISBN:0-7567-4318-4, ISBN13: 978-0-7567-4318-5. Dewey:972.8705/3.
Audience: **u,f.**

Priestly, George **F1567.P74 1986**
Military Government and Popular Participation in Panama: The Torrijos Regime, 1968-1975. Paper Text. Westview Press. Boulder, CO. 1986. 166p. Special Studies on Latin America and the Caribbean ISBN:0-8133-7045-0, ISBN13: 978-0-8133-7045-3. Dewey:972.87/052. LCCN:85-003168.
Audience: **u,f.**

Reynolds, Nicholas E. **F1567.R49 1996**
Just Cause: Marine Operations in Panama, 1988-1990. Perfect. United States Government Printing Office. Washington, DC. 1996. 58p. ISBN:0-16-048729-3, ISBN13: 978-0-16-048729-3. Dewey:972.8705/3. LCCN:96-215996.
Audience: **u,f.**

Richardson, Bonham C. **HD8178.5.B37R53 1985**
Panama Money in Barbados, 1900-1920. Cloth Text. University of Tennessee Press. Knoxville, TN. 1986. 308p. ISBN:0-87049-477-5, ISBN13: 978-0-87049-477-2. Dewey:330.97298/1. LCCN:85-006127.
Audience: **u,f.**

Salvador, Mari L., et al. **F1565.2.C8S23 1997**
The Art of Being Kuna: Layers of Meaning among the Kuna of Panama. James Howe, Mac Chapin & Alexander Moore (Authors). Trade Cloth. University of California Los Angeles, Fowler Museum of Cultural History. Los Angeles, CA. 1997. 362p. ISBN:0-930741-60-9, ISBN13: 978-0-930741-60-0. Dewey:306/.0899707287. LCCN:97-036368.
Audience: **u,f.**

Schoonover, Thomas D. **F1436.8.F8S37 2000**
The French in Central America: Culture and Commerce, 1820-1930. Book, Other. Rowman & Littlefield Publishers, Inc. Lanham, MD. 1999. 244p. ISBN:0-8420-2792-0, ISBN13: 978-0-8420-2792-2. Dewey:327.440728. LCCN:99-029226.
Audience: **u,f.**

Siu, Lok C. D. **F1577.C48S58 2005**
Memories of a Future Home: Diasporic Citizenship of Chinese in Panama. Perfect, Paper over Boards, Dust Jacket. Stanford University Press. Palo Alto, CA. 2005. 247p. ISBN:0-8047-5302-4, ISBN13: 978-0-8047-5302-9. Dewey:305.895/107287. LCCN:2005-019787.
Audience: **u,f.**

Skinner, James M. **HE537.4.S65 1989**
France and Panama: The Unknown Years, 1894-1908. Cloth Text. Peter Lang Publishing, Inc. New York, NY. 1988. X, 310p. American University Studies, Ser. IX, Vol. 50:History ISBN:0-8204-0822-0, ISBN13: 978-0-8204-0822-4. Dewey:386/.444. LCCN:88-023656.
Audience: **u,f.**

Sosa, Juan B. **F1567.S67 1999**
In Defiance: The Battle Against General Noriega Fought from Panama's Embassy. Trade Cloth. Francis Press, The. Washington, DC. 1999. 256p. ISBN:0-9665051-1-5, ISBN13: 978-0-9665051-1-5. Dewey:972.8705/3. LCCN:99-040387.
Audience: **u,f.** *Choice, 2000.*

Summ, G. Harvey & Kelly, Tom (Editors) **E183.8.P2G63 1988**
The Good Neighbors: America, Panama and the 1977 Canal Treaties. Paper Text. Ohio University Press. Athens, OH. 1988. 135p. Monographs in International Studies, Latin America Ser., No. 14 ISBN:0-89680-149-7, ISBN13: 978-0-89680-149-3. Dewey:327.7307287. LCCN:87-033956.
Audience: **u,f.**

Taw, Jennifer M. **UH723.T37 1996**
Operation Just Cause: Lessons for Operations Other Than War. Trade Paper. RAND Corporation, The. Santa Monica, CA. 1996. 40p. ISBN:0-8330-2405-1, ISBN13: 978-0-8330-2405-3. Dewey:355.4/9/0973. LCCN:96-023125.
Audience: **u,f.**

Ward, C. **HF3293.S7 W37 1993**
Imperial Panama: Commerce and Conflict in Isthmian America, 1550-1800. Trade Paper. University of New Mexico Press. Albuquerque, NM. 1994. 273p. ISBN:0-8263-1434-1, ISBN13: 978-0-8263-1434-5. Dewey:382/.97287/046. LCCN:93-019493.
Audience: **u,f.**

Caribbean: General > Cuba

S494.5.U72 U73
Urban Agriculture: Food, Jobs and Sustainable Cities. Trade Paper. United Nations Publications. New York, NY. 328p. ISBN:92-1-126047-7, ISBN13: 978-92-1-126047-2. Dewey:630/.9173/2.
Audience: **u,f.** *Choice, 1997.*

Alvarez, Jose & Castellanos, Lazaro Pena **HD9114.C89A6288 2001**
Cuba's Sugar Industry. John M. Kirk (Foreword by). Trade Cloth. University Press of Florida. Gainesville, FL. 2001. 176p. Contemporary Cuba Ser. ISBN:0-8130-2075-1, ISBN13: 978-0-8130-2075-4. Dewey:338.1/7361/097291. LCCN:2001-027454.
Audience: **u,f.**

Ameringer, Charles D. **F1787.5.A6975 2000**
Cuban Democratic Experience: The Autentico Years, 1944-1952. Trade Cloth. University Press of Florida. Gainesville, FL. 2000. 229p. ISBN:0-8130-1755-6, ISBN13: 978-0-8130-1755-6. Dewey:972.9106/3. LCCN:99-087367.
Audience: **u,f.** *Choice, 2000.*

Ayorinde, Christine **BL2532.S3A96 2004**
Afro-Cuban Religiosity, Revolution, and National Identity. Trade Cloth. University Press of Florida. Gainesville, FL. 2004. 304p. The History of African-American Religions Ser. ISBN:0-8130-2755-1, ISBN13: 978-0-8130-2755-5. Dewey:299.6/097291. LCCN:2004-058843.
Audience: **u,f.** *Choice, 2005.*

Azicri, Max **F1788.A93 2000**
Cuba Today and Tomorrow: Reinventing Socialism. Trade Cloth. University Press of Florida. Gainesville, FL. 2000. 416p. Contemporary Cuba Ser. ISBN:0-8130-1756-4, ISBN13: 978-0-8130-1756-3. Dewey:972.9106/4. LCCN:00-044712.
Audience: **u,f.** *Choice, 2001.*

Azicri, Max & Deal, Elsie (Editors) **HX158.5.C85 2004**
Cuban Socialism in a New Century. Trade Cloth. University Press of Florida. Gainesville, FL. 2004. 424p. Contemporary Cuba Ser. ISBN:0-8130-2763-2, ISBN13: 978-0-8130-2763-0. Dewey:335.43/47. LCCN:2004-055474.
Audience: **l,u,f.** *Choice, 2005.*

Baez, Antonio Carmona **HX158.5.C313 2004**
State Resistance to Globalisation in Cuba. Trade Cloth. Pluto Press. London, 2004. 288p. ISBN:0-7453-2146-1, ISBN13: 978-0-7453-2146-2. Dewey:337.7291. LCCN:2003-025964.
Audience: **u,f.**

Behar, Ruth (Editor) **PS508.C83B75 1995**
Bridges to Cuba/Puentes a Cuba. Trade Paper. University of Michigan Press. Chicago, IL. 1996. 448p. ISBN:0-472-06611-0, ISBN13: 978-0-472-06611-7. Dewey:810.8/08687291. LCCN:95-034522.
Audience: **l,u.** *Choice, 1996.*

Benjamin, Jules R. **E183.8.C9B43**
The United States and the Origins of the Cuban Revolution: An Empire of Liberty in an Age of National Liberation. Trade Paper. Princeton University Press. Princeton, NJ. 1992. 248p. ISBN:0-691-02536-3, ISBN13: 978-0-691-02536-0. Dewey:327.7307291.
Audience: **u,f.** *Choice, 1990.*

Berg, Mary (Editor) **PQ7383.5.E5**
Open Your Eyes and Soar: Cuban Women Writing Now. Trade Paper. White Pine Press. Buffalo, NY. 2003. 192p. Secret Weavers Ser. ISBN:1-893996-64-6, ISBN13: 978-1-893996-64-9. Dewey:860.8097291.
Audience: **u,f.**

Bergad, Laird W. **HC152.5.Z7M383 1990**
Cuban Rural Society in the Nineteenth Century: The Social and Economic History of Monoculture in Matanzas. Trade Cloth. Princeton University Press. Princeton, NJ. 1990. 507p. ISBN:0-691-07816-5, ISBN13: 978-0-691-07816-8. Dewey:306/.097291/309034. LCCN:89-036040.
Audience: **u,f.** *Choice, 1990.*

Bergad, Laird W., et al. **HT1077.B47 1995**
The Cuban Slave Market, 1790-1880. Fe Iglesias García & María del Carmen Barcia (Authors), Alan Knight (Contribution

by). Trade Cloth. Cambridge University Press. New York, NY. 1995. 272p. Cambridge Latin American Studies, No. 79 ISBN:0-521-48059-0, ISBN13: 978-0-521-48059-8. Dewey:380.1/44/097291. LCCN:94-038288.
Audience: **u,f.** *Choice, 1996.*

Bethell, Leslie (Editor) **F1776.C8 1993**
Cuba: A Short History. Cloth Text. Cambridge University Press. New York, NY. 1993. 208p. ISBN:0-521-43063-1, ISBN13: 978-0-521-43063-0. Dewey:972.91. LCCN:92-017488.
Audience: **u,f.**

Blight, James G. & Brenner, Philip **F1776.3.S65B65 2002**
Sad and Luminous Days: Cuba's Struggle with the Superpowers after the Missile Crisis. Book, Other. Rowman & Littlefield Publishers, Inc. Lanham, MD. 2002. 352p. ISBN:0-7425-2288-1, ISBN13: 978-0-7425-2288-6. Dewey:327.7291047. LCCN:2002-008626.
Audience: **u,f.** *Choice, 2003.*

Blight, James G. & Kornbluh, Peter **F1788.P575 1998**
Politics of Illusion: The Bay of Pigs Invasion Reexamined. Trade Cloth. Lynne Rienner Publishers, Inc. Boulder, CO. 1997. 284p. Studies in Cuban History ISBN:1-55587-783-4, ISBN13: 978-1-55587-783-5. Dewey:972.9106/4. LCCN:97-023213.
Audience: **u,f.** *Choice, 1998.*

Brenner, Philip **E183.8.C9.B74 1988**
From Confrontation to Negotiation: U. S. Relations with Cuba. Cloth Text. Westview Press. Boulder, CO. 1988. 118p. ISBN:0-8133-7507-X, ISBN13: 978-0-8133-7507-6. Dewey:327.7307291. LCCN:87-033985.
Audience: **u,f.** *Choice, 1989.*

Brock, Lisa & Fuertes, Digna Castraneda (Editors) **E185.61.B474 1998**
Between Race and Empire: African-Americans and Cubans Before the Cuban Revolution. Cloth Text. Temple University Press. Philadelphia, PA. 1998. 256p. ISBN:1-56639-586-0, ISBN13: 978-1-56639-586-1. Dewey:972.9106/4. LCCN:97-020278.
Audience: **u,f.** *Choice, 1998.*

Bronfman, Alejandra **F1789.A1B76 2005**
Measures of Equality. Trade Cloth. University of North Carolina Press. Chapel Hill, NC. 2004. 264p. Envisioning Cuba Ser. ISBN:0-8078-2898-X, ISBN13: 978-0-8078-2898-4. Dewey:305.8/0097291. LCCN:2004-009060.
Audience: **u,f.** *Choice, 2005.*

Bueno, Maria de Los Reyes Castillo **F1789.N3C37 2000**
Reyita: The Life of a Black Cuban Woman in the Twentieth Century. Daisy Rubiera Castillo (As told to). Library Binding. Duke University Press. Durham, NC. 2000. 168p. ISBN:0-8223-2579-9, ISBN13: 978-0-8223-2579-6. Dewey:972.9106/092 B. LCCN:99-087007.
Audience: **g,l,u,f.**

Bunck, Julie M. **F1788.B79 1994**
Fidel Castro and the Quest for a Revolutionary Culture in Cuba. Trade Cloth. Pennsylvania State University Press. University Park, PA. 1994. 254p. ISBN:0-271-01086-X, ISBN13: 978-0-271-01086-1. Dewey:972.9106/4. LCCN:93-013387.
Audience: **u,f.** *Choice, 1994.*

Carbonell, Nestor **F1788.C2566 1989**
And the Russians Stayed...: A Personal Portrait of the Sovietization of Cuba. Trade Cloth. HarperCollins Publishers. New York, NY. 1989. 288p. ISBN:0-688-07213-5, ISBN13: 978-0-688-07213-1. Dewey:972.91/064. LCCN:88-038565.
Audience: **u,f.**

Cardoso, Eliana & Helwege, Ann **F1788.C2575 1992**
Cuba after Communism. Trade Cloth. MIT Press. Cambridge, MA. 1992. 164p. ISBN:0-262-03197-3, ISBN13: 978-0-262-03197-4. Dewey:330.97291. LCCN:92-005663.
Audience: **u,f.**

Carrillo, Justo **F1787.5.C2813 1994**
Cuba, 1933: Students, Yankees, and Soldiers. Trade Paper. University of Miami, North/South Center Press. Coral Gables, FL. 1994. 440p. University of Miami North-South Center Ser. ISBN:1-56000-690-0, ISBN13: 978-1-56000-690-9. Dewey:972.91/06/2. LCCN:93-038233.
Audience: **u,f.**

Centeno, Miguel A. & Font, Mauricio (Editors) **HN210.Z9**
Toward a New Cuba?: Legacies of a Revolution. Trade Paper. Lynne Rienner Publishers, Inc. Boulder, CO. 1998. 245p. ISBN:1-55587-814-8, ISBN13: 978-1-55587-814-6. Dewey:320.97291/09/049. LCCN:96-032581.
Audience: **u,f.**

Centro De Estudios Sobre America Staff (Editor) **F1788.C829 1992**
The Cuban Revolution into the 1990s: Cuban Perspectives. Trade Paper. Westview Press. Boulder, CO. 1992. 197p. ISBN:0-8133-1186-1, ISBN13: 978-0-8133-1186-9. Dewey:972.91064. LCCN:92-014477.
Audience: **u,f.** *Choice, 1993.*

Chaffee, Wilbur R. Jr. & Prevost, Gary (Editors) **F1788.C765 1989**
Cuba: A Different America. Trade Cloth. Rowman & Littlefield Publishers, Inc. Lanham, MD. 1992. 200p. ISBN:0-8476-7503-3, ISBN13: 978-0-8476-7503-6. Dewey:972.9/1/064. LCCN:87-028371.
Audience: **u,f.**

Chaffin, Tom **F1783.C44 1996**
Fatal Glory: Narciso López and the First Clandestine U. S. War Against Cuba. Trade Cloth. University Press of Virginia. Charlottesville, VA. 1996. 280p. ISBN:0-8139-1673-9, ISBN13: 978-0-8139-1673-6. Dewey:972.91/05. LCCN:96-012978.
Audience: **u,f.** *Choice, 1997.*

Chomsky, Aviva (Editor), et al. **F1776.C85 2003**
The Cuba Reader: History, Culture, Politics. Barry Carr & Pamela Maria Smorkaloff (Editors). Trade Cloth. Duke University Press. Durham, NC. 2003. 680p. Latin America Readers Ser. ISBN:0-8223-3184-5, ISBN13: 978-0-8223-3184-1. Dewey:972.91. LCCN:2003-013448.
Audience: **u,f.** *Choice, 2004.*

Cirules, Enrique **HV6453.C9C5713 2004**
The Mafia in Havana: A Caribbean Mob Story. Trade Paper. Ocean Press. New York, NY. 2003. 150p. ISBN:1-876175-42-7, ISBN13: 978-1-876175-42-9. Dewey:364.1/06. LCCN:2001-093727.
Audience: **u,f.**

Corbitt, Duvon Clough **F1789.C53 C6**
A Study of the Chinese in Cuba, 1847-1947. Ashbury College. 1971.
Audience: **u,f.**

Cushing, Lincoln **NC1807.C8C87 2003**
Revolución: Cuban Poster Art. Trade Paper. Chronicle Books LLC. San Francisco, CA. 2003. 132p. ISBN:0-8118-3582-0, ISBN13: 978-0-8118-3582-4. Dewey:741.6/74/09729109046. LCCN:2002-035092.
Audience: **g,l,u,f.** *Choice, 2004.*

Dalton, Thomas C. **HN203.5 .D35 1993**
Everything Within the Revolution: Cuban Strategies for Social Development since 1960. Trade Paper. Westview Press. Boulder, CO. 1993. Series in Political Economy and Economic Development in Latin America ISBN:0-8133-8228-9, ISBN13: 978-0-8133-8228-9. Dewey:361.6/1/097291. LCCN:93-014906.
Audience: **u,f.**

Daniel, Yvonne **GV1769.R8D32 1995**
Rumba: Dance and Social Change in Contemporary Cuba. Trade Cloth. Indiana University Press. Bloomington, IN. 1995. 208p. Blacks in the Diaspora Ser. ISBN:0-253-31605-7, ISBN13: 978-0-253-31605-9. Dewey:784.18/88. LCCN:94-034363.
Audience: **u,f.** *Choice, 1996.*

De La Campa, Roman **E184.C97D4 2001**
Cuba on My Mind: Journeys to a Severed Nation. Trade Cloth. Verso Books. London, 2002. 192p. ISBN:1-85984-790-0, ISBN13: 978-1-85984-790-9. Dewey:973/.04687291/0092 B. LCCN:00-054999.
Audience: **l,u.**

De La Fuente, Alejandro **F1789.A1F84 2001**
A Nation for All: Race, Inequality, and Politics in Twentieth-Century Cuba. Trade Cloth. University of North Carolina Press. Chapel Hill, NC. 2001. 464p. Envisioning Cuba Ser. ISBN:0-8078-2608-1, ISBN13: 978-0-8078-2608-9. Dewey:305.8/0097291. LCCN:00-046693.
Audience: **u,f.**

Del Aguila, Juan M. **F1788**
Cuba: Dilemmas of a Revolution. Ed. 3. Trade Paper. Westview Press. Boulder, CO. 1994. 240p. Nations of Contemporary Latin America Ser. ISBN:0-8133-8665-9, ISBN13: 978-0-8133-8665-2. Dewey:972.91/064. LCCN:94-015158.
Audience: **u,f.**

Diaz, Maria Elena **HT1079.E4**
The Virgin, the King, and the Royal Slaves of el Cobre: Negotiating Freedom in Colonial Cuba, 1670-1780. Trade Paper. Stanford University Press. Palo Alto, CA. 2002. 464p. ISBN:0-8047-4713-X, ISBN13: 978-0-8047-4713-4. Dewey:306.3/62/09729165.
Audience: **u,f.** *Choice, 2001.*

Dimock, Joseph J. **F1763.D56**
Impressions of Cuba in the Nineteenth Century: The Travel Diary of Joseph J. Dimock. Louis A. Perez (Editor). Trade Cloth. DIANE Publishing Company. Collingdale, PA. 2005. 150p. ISBN:0-7567-8679-7, ISBN13: 978-0-7567-8679-3. Dewey:917.29104/5 21.
Audience: **u,f.**

Dominguez, Jorge I. **F1788.D59 1989**
To Make a World Safe for Revolution: Cuba's Foreign Policy. Trade Paper. Harvard University Press. Cambridge, MA. 1989. 382p. Center for International Affairs Ser. ISBN:0-674-89325-5, ISBN13: 978-0-674-89325-2. Dewey:327.7291. LCCN:88-016556.
Audience: **u,f.** *Choice, 1989.*

Dominguez, Jorge I. & Hernandez, Rafael (Editors) **JX1428.C9U18 1989**
U. S. - Cuban Relations in the 1990s. Cloth Text. Westview Press. Boulder, CO. 1989. 324p. ISBN:0-8133-0883-6, ISBN13: 978-0-8133-0883-8. Dewey:327.7291073. LCCN:88-026998.
Audience: **u,f.** *Choice, 1990.*

Dominguez, Jorge I. (Editor), et al. **HC152.5.C8116 2004**
The Cuban Economy at the Start of the Twenty-First Century. Omar Everleny Pérez Villanueva & Lorena Barberia (Editors). Trade Paper. Harvard University Press. Cambridge, MA. 2005. 456p. David Rockefeller Center Series on Latin American Studies ISBN:0-674-01798-6, ISBN13: 978-0-674-01798-6. Dewey:330.97291. LCCN:2004-021019.
Audience: **u,f.**

Echevarria, Roberto Gonzalez **GV863.25.A1**
The Pride of Havana: A History of Cuban Baseball. Trade Paper. DIANE Publishing Company. Collingdale, PA. 2004. 464p. ISBN:0-7567-7115-3, ISBN13: 978-0-7567-7115-7. Dewey:796.357/097291.
Audience: **g,l,u,f.** *Choice, 2000.*

Eckstein, Susan Eva **HX158.5.E35 2003**
Back from the Future: Cuba under Castro. Ed. 2. Alejandro Portes (Foreword by). Paper over Boards. Routledge. New York, NY. 2003. 352p. ISBN:0-415-94793-6, ISBN13: 978-0-415-94793-0. Dewey:338.97291. LCCN:2003-011941.
Audience: **u,f.** *Choice, 1994.*

Erisman, H. Michael **F178.5**
Cuba's Foreign Relations in a Post-Soviet World. Trade Paper. Fordham University Press. Bronx, NY. 2002. 288p. ISBN:0-8130-2587-7, ISBN13: 978-0-8130-2587-2. Dewey:327.7291.
Audience: **u,f.**

Evenson, Debra **KGN327 .E93 2003**
Law and Society in Contemporary Cuba. Ed. 2. Trade Cloth. Kluwer Law International. Biggleswade, 2003. 304p. ISBN:90-411-2165-X, ISBN13: 978-90-411-2165-3. Dewey:347.291.
Audience: **u,f.**

Fermoselle, Rafael **UA610.C9F47 1987**
The Evolution of the Cuban Military, 1492-1986. Trade Cloth. Ediciones Universal. Miami, FL. 2001. 585p. Coleccion Cuba y sus Jueces ISBN:0-89729-428-9, ISBN13: 978-0-89729-428-7. Dewey:355/.0097291. LCCN:86-083093.
Audience: **u,f.**

Fernandez, Alfredo L. **E184.C97F46 2000**
Adrift: The Cuban Raft People. Susan G. Rascon (Translator). Trade Paper. Arte Publico Press. Houston, TX. 2000. 272p. ISBN:1-55885-300-6, ISBN13: 978-1-55885-300-3. Dewey:973/.04687291. LCCN:00-042006.
Audience: **u,f.**

Fernandez, Alina **F1788.22.C3**
Castro's Daughter: An Exile's Memoir of Cuba. Dolores M. Koch (Contribution by). Trade Cloth. DIANE Publishing

Company. Collingdale, PA. 2005. 259p. ISBN:0-7567-8592-8, ISBN13: 978-0-7567-8592-5. Dewey:972.9106/4/092 B.
Audience: **u,f.**

Fernandez, Damian J. & Camara, Madeline **F1760.C835 2000**
Cuba, the Elusive Nation: Interpretations of National Identity. Trade Cloth. University Press of Florida. Gainesville, FL. 2000. 317p. ISBN:0-8130-1800-5, ISBN13: 978-0-8130-1800-3. Dewey:972.91. LCCN:00-027179.
Audience: **u,f.**

Fernandez, Susan J. **HC152.5.Z9C34 2002**
Encumbered Cuba: Capital Markets and Revolt, 1878-1895. Trade Cloth. University Press of Florida. Gainesville, FL. 2002. xii, 203p. ISBN:0-8130-2564-8, ISBN13: 978-0-8130-2564-3. Dewey:330.97291/05. LCCN:2002-072623.
Audience: **u,f.** *Choice, 2003.*

Fernández, Damián J. **JL1010.F47 2000**
Cuba and the Politics of Passion. Trade Cloth. University of Texas Press. Austin, TX. 2000. 192p. ISBN:0-292-72519-1, ISBN13: 978-0-292-72519-5. Dewey:306.2/097291. LCCN:00-024153.
Audience: **u,f.** *Choice, 2001.*

Ferrer, Ada **F1785.F36 1999**
Insurgent Cuba: Race, Nation, and Revolution, 1868-1898. Trade Cloth. University of North Carolina Press. Chapel Hill, NC. 1999. 296p. ISBN:0-8078-2500-X, ISBN13: 978-0-8078-2500-6. Dewey:972.91/05. LCCN:99-013684.
Audience: **u,f.** *Choice, 2000.*

Fitzgerald, Frank T. **HD8038**
Managing Socialism: From Old Cadres to New Professionals in Revolutionary Cuba. Trade Cloth. Greenwood Publishing Group, Inc. Portsmouth, NH. 1990. 176p. ISBN:0-275-93414-4, ISBN13: 978-0-275-93414-9. Dewey:331.25/92/097291. LCCN:89-077246.
Audience: **u,f.**

Fursenko, Aleksandr & Naftali, Timothy **E841.F86**
One Hell of a Gamble: Khruschev, Castro and Kennedy, 1958-1964. Trade Cloth. DIANE Publishing Company. Collingdale, PA. 2001. 420p. ISBN:0-7881-9758-4, ISBN13: 978-0-7881-9758-1. Dewey:973.922.
Audience: **g,l,u,f.**

Garcia-Perez, Gladys M. **F1787.5.G37 1998**
Insurrection and Revolution: Armed Struggle in Cuba, 1952-1959. Louis Perez (Foreword by). Library Binding. Lynne Rienner Publishers, Inc. Boulder, CO. 1998. 138p. Studies in Cuban History ISBN:1-55587-611-0, ISBN13: 978-1-55587-611-1. Dewey:972.9106/3. LCCN:97-049997.
Audience: **u,f.** *Choice, 1998.*

Geldof, Lynn **F1788.G36 1992**
The Cubans: Voices of Change. Trade Paper. St. Martin's Press. Gordonville, VA. 1992. 368p. ISBN:0-312-07689-4, ISBN13: 978-0-312-07689-4. Dewey:972.9106/4. LCCN:92-003627.
Audience: **u,f.**

Geyer, Georgie Anne **F1788.22.C3G48 2001**
Guerrilla Prince: The Untold Story of Fidel Castro. Ed. 3. Trade Paper. Andrews McMeel Publishing. Kansas City, MO. 2002. 496p. ISBN:0-7407-2064-3, ISBN13: 978-0-7407-2064-2. Dewey:972.9106/4/092 B. LCCN:2001-053523.
Audience: **u,f.**

Gimbel, Wendy **F1788.22.B47**
Havana Dreams: A Story of a Cuban Family. Trade Paper. Knopf Publishing Group. New York, NY. 1999. 248p. ISBN:0-679-75070-3, ISBN13: 978-0-679-75070-3. Dewey:972.9/1/064/0922.
Audience: **g,l,u,f.**

Gleijeses, Piero **DT38.9.C9G57 2001**
Conflicting Missions: Havana, Washington and Africa, 1959-1976. Trade Cloth. University of North Carolina Press. Chapel Hill, NC. 2002. 576p. Envisioning Cuba Ser. ISBN:0-8078-2647-2, ISBN13: 978-0-8078-2647-8. Dewey:327.729106/09/046. LCCN:2001-027417.
Audience: **u,f.** *Choice, 2002.*

Gonzalez-Pando, Miguel **E184**
The Cuban Americans. Cloth Text. Greenwood Publishing Group, Inc. Portsmouth, NH. 1998. 224p. The New Americans Ser. ISBN:0-313-29824-6, ISBN13: 978-0-313-29824-0. Dewey:975.9/3004687291. LCCN:97-021448.
Audience: **g,l.**

Gosse, Van **HN90.R3G67 1993**
Where the Boys Are: Cuba, Cold War America, and the Making of a New Left. Trade Cloth. Analytical Psychology Club of San Francisco, Inc. San Francisco, CA. 1993. 260p. Haymarket Ser. ISBN:0-86091-416-X, ISBN13: 978-0-86091-416-7. Dewey:320.5310973. LCCN:94-125612.
Audience: **u,f.** *Choice, 1994.*

Gott, Richard **F1776.G68 2004**
Cuba: A New History. Cloth over Boards. Yale University Press. Cumberland, RI. 2004. 400p. ISBN:0-300-10411-1, ISBN13: 978-0-300-10411-0. Dewey:972.91. LCCN:2004-007556.
Audience: **u,f.** *Choice, 2005.*

Guerra, Lillian **F1783.M38G78 2005**
The Myth of José Martí: Conflicting Nationalisms in Early Twentieth-Century Cuba. Trade Cloth. University of North Carolina Press. Chapel Hill, NC. 2005. 368p. Envisioning Cuba Ser. ISBN:0-8078-2925-0, ISBN13: 978-0-8078-2925-7. Dewey:972.9106/1. LCCN:2004-062098.
Audience: **u,f.** *Choice, 2006.*

Guillermoprieto, Alma **F1765.3.G85 2004**
Dancing with Cuba: A Memoir of the Revolution. Trade Cloth. Knopf Publishing Group. New York, NY. 2004. 304p. ISBN:0-375-42093-2, ISBN13: 978-0-375-42093-1. Dewey:972.9106/4. LCCN:2003-044200.
Audience: **u,f.**

Habel, Janette **F1788.H2313 1991**
Cuba: The Revolution in Peril. Jon Barnes (Translator), Francois Maspero (Foreword by). Trade Cloth. Analytical Psychology Club of San Francisco, Inc. San Francisco, CA. 1991. 280p. ISBN:0-86091-308-2, ISBN13: 978-0-86091-308-5. Dewey:972.9106/4. LCCN:91-002343.
Audience: **u,f.**

Halebsky, Sandor & Kirk, John M. (Editors) **F1788**
Transformation and Struggle: Cuba Faces the 1990s. Trade Cloth. Greenwood Publishing Group, Inc. Portsmouth, NH.

1990. 324p. ISBN:0-275-93227-3, ISBN13: 978-0-275-93227-5. Dewey:972.9106/4. LCCN:89-039648.
Audience: **u,f.** *Choice, 1990.*

Halebsky, Sandor (Editor), et al. **F1788.C816 1992**
Cuba in Transition: Crisis and Transformation. John M. Kirk, Carollee Bengelsdorf, Richard L. Harris, Jean Stubbs & Andrew Zimbalist (Editors). Trade Paper. Westview Press. Boulder, CO. 1992. 244p. ISBN:0-8133-8094-4, ISBN13: 978-0-8133-8094-0. Dewey:320.97291.
Audience: **u,f.**

Halperin, Maurice **HC152.5.H35 1994**
Return to Havana: The Decline of Cuban Society under Castro. Trade Cloth. Vanderbilt University Press. Nashville, TN. 1994. 216p. ISBN:0-8265-1250-X, ISBN13: 978-0-8265-1250-5. Dewey:306/.097291. LCCN:93-041059.
Audience: **u,f.**

Hart, Armando **F1787.5.H3613 2004**
Aldabonazo: Inside the Cuban Revolutionary Underground 1952-58, a participant's Account. Mary-Alice Waters, Roberto Fernández Retamar & Roberto Acosta Matos (Preface by). Trade Paper. Pathfinder Press. New York, NY. 2004. 387p. ISBN:0-87348-968-3, ISBN13: 978-0-87348-968-3. Dewey:972.9106/3. LCCN:2003-114346.
Audience: **u,f.** *Choice, 2004.*

Helg, Aline **F1789.N3H45 1995**
Our Rightful Share: The Afro-Cuban Struggle for Equality, 1886-1912. Library Binding. University of North Carolina Press. Chapel Hill, NC. 1995. 375p. ISBN:0-8078-2184-5, ISBN13: 978-0-8078-2184-8. Dewey:972.91/00496. LCCN:94-027196.
Audience: **u,f.**

Hernandez, Rafael **JL1010.H4713 2003**
Looking at Cuba: Essays on Culture and Civil Society. Trade Cloth. University Press of Florida. Gainesville, FL. 2003. 152p. Contemporary Cuba Ser. ISBN:0-8130-2642-3, ISBN13: 978-0-8130-2642-8. Dewey:300/.97291. LCCN:2003-054075.
Audience: **u,f.** *Choice, 2004.*

Hernández Catá, Ernesto **HG3881.5.I58**
The Fall and Recovery of the Cuban Economy in the 1990s: Mirage or Reality? International Monetary Fund. 2001.
Audience: **l,u.**

Hernández, José M. **E183.8.C9H47 1993**
Cuba and the United States: Intervention and Militarism, 1868-1933. Cloth Text. University of Texas Press. Austin, TX. 1993. 284p. ISBN:0-292-73073-X, ISBN13: 978-0-292-73073-1. Dewey:327.7307291. LCCN:92-021342.
Audience: **u,f.** *Choice, 1993.*

Howard, Philip A. **F1789.N3H68 1998**
Changing History: Afro-Cuban Cabildos and Societies of Color in the Nineteenth Century. Trade Cloth. Louisiana State University Press. Baton Rouge, LA. 1998. xxvi, 228p. ISBN:0-8071-2210-6, ISBN13: 978-0-8071-2210-5. Dewey:972.91/00496. LCCN:98-005449.
Audience: **u,f.** *Choice, 1999.*

Howe, Linda S. **PQ7378.H69 2004**
Transgression and Conformity: Cuban Writers and Artists after the Revolution. Trade Cloth. University of Wisconsin Press. Chicago, IL. 2004. 230p. ISBN:0-299-19730-1, ISBN13: 978-0-299-19730-8. Dewey:860.9/97291/09045. LCCN:2003-020571.
Audience: **u,f.**

Humboldt, Alexander von & Fernandez, Luis Martinez **F1763.H913 2000**
The Island of Cuba: A Political Essay. Trade Cloth. Markus Wiener Publishers, Inc. Princeton, NJ. 2001. 360p. ISBN:1-55876-242-6, ISBN13: 978-1-55876-242-8. Dewey:972.91. LCCN:00-049952.
Audience: **u,f.**

Ibarra, Jorge **HN203.I23 1998**
Prologue to Revolution: Cuba, 1898-1958. Library Binding. Lynne Rienner Publishers, Inc. Boulder, CO. 1998. 235p. Studies in Cuban History ISBN:1-55587-791-5, ISBN13: 978-1-55587-791-0. Dewey:306/.097291. LCCN:97-049324.
Audience: **u,f.** *Choice, 1998.*

Infante, Guillermo Cabrena **PN**
Mea Cuba. Trade Cloth. Santillana USA Publishing Company, Inc. Doral, FL. 2000. 496p. ISBN:84-204-8271-4, ISBN13: 978-84-204-8271-2. Dewey:868.
Audience: **u,f.**

Jensen, Larry R. **F1779.J46 1988**
Children of Colonial Despotism: Press, Politics and Culture in Cuba 1790-1840. Trade Cloth. University Press of Florida. Gainesville, FL. 1988. 224p. ISBN:0-8130-0868-9, ISBN13: 978-0-8130-0868-4. Dewey:972.91/04. LCCN:87-010384.
Audience: **u,f.** *Choice, 1988.*

Johnson, Sherry **HN203.J64 2001**
The Social Transformation of Eighteenth-Century Cuba. Trade Cloth. University Press of Florida. Gainesville, FL. 2001. 320p. ISBN:0-8130-2097-2, ISBN13: 978-0-8130-2097-6. Dewey:306/.097291. LCCN:2001-048074.
Audience: **u,f.** *Choice, 2002.*

Jordan, David C. **F1788.J62 1993**
Revolutionary Cuba and the End of the Cold War. Trade Cloth. University Press of America, Inc. Lanham, MD. 1993. 284p. ISBN:0-8191-8998-7, ISBN13: 978-0-8191-8998-1. Dewey:972.91064. LCCN:92-040550.
Audience: **u,f.** *Choice, 1993.*

Kapcia, Antoni **F1799.H357**
Havana: The Making of Cuban Culture. Cloth over Boards. Berg Publishers. Oxford, 2005. 256p. ISBN:1-85973-832-X, ISBN13: 978-1-85973-832-0. Dewey:972.91/23. LCCN:2005-007951.
Audience: **u,f.**

Kirk, John M. **BR645.C9K57 1989**
Between God and the Party: Religion and Politics in Revolutionary Cuba. Trade Cloth. University Press of Florida. Gainesville, FL. 1989. 256p. ISBN:0-8130-0879-4, ISBN13: 978-0-8130-0879-0. Dewey:322/.1. LCCN:87-016006.
Audience: **u,f.** *Choice, 1989.*

Kuethe, Allan J. **F1779.K84 1986**
Cuba, 1753-1815: Crown, Military and Society. Cloth Text. University of Tennessee Press. Knoxville, TN. 1986. 232p. ISBN:0-87049-487-2, ISBN13: 978-0-87049-487-1. Dewey:972.91/04. LCCN:85-017844.
Audience: **u,f.** *Choice, 1986.*

La Rosa Corzo, Gabino **F1845.L3713 2003**
Runaway Slave Settlements in Cuba: Resistance and Repression. Trade Cloth. University of North Carolina Press. Chapel Hill, NC. 2003. 304p. Envisioning Cuba Ser. ISBN:0-8078-2803-3, ISBN13: 978-0-8078-2803-8. Dewey:973.91/64. LCCN:2003-005071.
Audience: **u,f.** *Choice, 2004.*

Lambert, Francis J. D. **F1783**
Cuba and the Autonomists in the Politics of the First Spanish Restoration, 1878-1898. Institute of Latin American Studies, University of Glasgow. 1996.
Audience: **u,f.**

Leonard, Thomas M. **F1788**
Fidel Castro: A Biography. Cloth Text. Greenwood Publishing Group, Inc. Portsmouth, NH. 2004. 184p. Greenwood Biographies Ser. ISBN:0-313-32301-1, ISBN13: 978-0-313-32301-0. Dewey:972.9106/4/092 B. LCCN:2004-005995.
Audience: **l,u,f.**

Levine, Robert M. **F1763.L65 1990**
Cuba in the 1850's: Through the Lens of Charles DeForest Fredricks. Trade Cloth. University Press of Florida. Gainesville, FL. 1990. 86p. ISBN:0-8130-1010-1, ISBN13: 978-0-8130-1010-6. Dewey:779/.99729105. LCCN:90-034348.
Audience: **u,f.** *Choice, 1991.*

Lowell, Mary Gardner **F1763.L69 2003**
New Year in Cuba: Mary Gardner Lowell's Travel Diary, 1831-1832. Karen Robert (Editor, Introduction by), Laurel Thatcher Ulrich (Preface by). Trade Cloth. Northeastern University Press. Boston, MA. 2005. 208p. The New England Women's Diaries ISBN:1-55553-558-5, ISBN13: 978-1-55553-558-2. Dewey:917.29104/5. LCCN:2002-015463.
Audience: **g,l,u,f.**

Luis, William **F1787**
Culture and Customs of Cuba. Cloth Text. Greenwood Publishing Group, Inc. Portsmouth, NH. 2000. 232p. Culture and Customs of Latin America and the Caribbean Ser. ISBN:0-313-30433-5, ISBN13: 978-0-313-30433-0. Dewey:972.9106. LCCN:00-035324.
Audience: **u,f.**

López, Juan J. **JL1010.L67 2002**
[e] Democracy Delayed: The Case of Castro's Cuba. E-Book. Johns Hopkins University Press. Baltimore, MD. 272p. ISBN:0-8018-7772-5, ISBN13: 978-0-8018-7772-8. Dewey:320.97291.
Audience: **u,f.**

Martinez-Fernandez, Luis **F1783.M386 1998**
Fighting Slavery in the Caribbean: The Life and Times of a British Family in Nineteenth-Century Havana. Robert M. Levine (Foreword by). Trade Cloth. M. E. Sharpe Inc. Armonk, NY. 1998. 216p. Latin American Realities Ser. ISBN:0-7656-0247-4, ISBN13: 978-0-7656-0247-3. Dewey:972.91/05. LCCN:97-032665.
Audience: **u,f.**

Masud-Piloto, Felix **HV640.5.C9M35 1996**
From Welcomed Exiles to Illegal Immigrants: Cuban Migration to the U. S., 1959-1995. Ed. 3. Trade Paper. Rowman & Littlefield Publishers, Inc. Lanham, MD. 1995. 192p. ISBN:0-8476-8149-1, ISBN13: 978-0-8476-8149-5. Dewey:304.8/7307291. LCCN:95-025772.
Audience: **l,u,f.**

Medin, Tzvi **HX523.M43 1990**
Cuba: The Shaping of Revolutionary Consciousness. Library Binding. Lynne Rienner Publishers, Inc. Boulder, CO. 1990. 192p. ISBN:1-55587-187-9, ISBN13: 978-1-55587-187-1. Dewey:972.91064. LCCN:89-039433.
Audience: **u,f.** *Choice, 1991.*

Medina, Pablo **PS3566.L27**
Exiled Memories: A Cuban Childhood. Trade Paper. Persea Books, Inc. New York, NY. 2002. 144p. ISBN:0-89255-280-8, ISBN13: 978-0-89255-280-1. Dewey:811/.54 B.
Audience: **l,u.**

Mendez Rodenas, Adriana **F1799.H3 M4736 1998**
Gender and Nationalism in Colonial Cuba: the Travels of Santa Cruz y Montalvo. Vanderbilt University Press. 1998. ISBN:0-8265-1299-2, ISBN13: 978-0-8265-1299-4.
Audience: **u,f.**

Mendoza, Tony **F1765.3.M46 1999**
Cuba—Going Back. Trade Cloth. University of Texas Press. Austin, TX. 1999. 155p. ISBN:0-292-75232-6, ISBN13: 978-0-292-75232-0. Dewey:917.29104/64. LCCN:98-051938.
Audience: **u,f.**

Mesa-Lago, Carmelo (Editor) **HC152.5.C797 1993**
Cuba after the Cold War. Cloth Text. University of Pittsburgh Press. Pittsburgh, PA. 1993. 408p. Latin American Ser. ISBN:0-8229-3749-2, ISBN13: 978-0-8229-3749-4. Dewey:338.97291. LCCN:92-050847.
Audience: **u,f.** *Choice, 1994.*

Moore, Carlos **F1788.22.C3M66 1988**
Castro, the Blacks, and Africa. Jorge I. Dominguez (Foreword by). Trade Paper. C A A S Publications. Los Angeles, CA. 1988. 472p. Afro-American Culture and Society Monographs, Vol. 8 ISBN:0-934934-33-9, ISBN13: 978-0-934934-33-6. Dewey:972.91/064. LCCN:88-037460.
Audience: **u,f.**

Morley, Morris H. & McGillion, Chris **E183.8.C9M75 2002**
Unfinished Business: America and Cuba after the Cold War, 1989-2001. Cloth Text. Cambridge University Press. New York, NY. 2002. 264p. ISBN:0-521-81716-1, ISBN13: 978-0-521-81716-5. Dewey:327.7307291/09/049. LCCN:2002-017405.
Audience: **u,f.** *Choice, 2003.*

Morris, J. A. **F1788.C635 1993**
Conflict and Change in Cuba. Enrique A. Baloyra (Editor). Trade Paper. University of New Mexico Press. Albuquerque, NM. 1993. 347p. ISBN:0-8263-1465-1, ISBN13: 978-0-8263-1465-9. Dewey:972.9106/4. LCCN:93-002426.
Audience: **u,f.** *Choice, 1994.*

Moses, Catherine **F1765.3.M68 2000**
Real Life in Castro's Cuba. Book, Other. Rowman & Littlefield Publishers, Inc. Lanham, MD. 2000. 184p. Latin American Silhouettes Ser. ISBN:0-8420-2836-6, ISBN13: 978-0-8420-2836-3. Dewey:972.9106/4. LCCN:99-024812.
Audience: **u,f.**

Murray, Mary **F1788.M87 1993**
Cruel and Unusual Punishment: The U. S. Blockade of Cuba. Trade Paper. Ocean Press. New York, NY. 1993. 117p. ISBN:1-875284-78-8, ISBN13: 978-1-875284-78-8. Dewey:337.7307291.
Audience: **u,f.**

Oltuski, Enrique **F1788.O48 2002**
Vida Clandestina: My Life in the Cuban Revolution. Trade Cloth. John Wiley & Sons, Inc. Hoboken, NJ. 2002. 336p. ISBN:0-7879-6169-8, ISBN13: 978-0-7879-6169-5. Dewey:972.9106/4. LCCN:2002-002223.
Audience: **u,f.**

Oppenheimer, Andres **F1788.22.C3O66 1993**
Castro's Final Hour. Trade Paper. Simon & Schuster. New York, NY. 1993. 480p. ISBN:0-671-87299-0, ISBN13: 978-0-671-87299-1. Dewey:972.9106/4. LCCN:93-031433.
Audience: **u,f.**

Padilla, Herberto **PQ7390.P3Z**
Self-Portrait of the Other. Ed. 1. Alexander Coleman (Translator). Trade Paper. Farrar, Straus & Giroux. New York, NY. 1999. 247p. ISBN:0-374-52655-9, ISBN13: 978-0-374-52655-9. Dewey:861. LCCN:89-001263.
Audience: **u,f.**

Palmie, Stephan **BL2566.C9P355 2002**
Wizards and Scientists: Explorations in Afro-Cuban Modernity and Tradition. Trade Cloth. Duke University Press. Durham, NC. 2002. 400p. ISBN:0-8223-2828-3, ISBN13: 978-0-8223-2828-5. Dewey:306/.097291. LCCN:2001-040907.
Audience: **u,f.**

Paquette, Robert L. **F1783.P25 1988**
Sugar Is Made with Blood: The Conspiracy of la Escalera and the Conflict Between Empires over Slavery in Cuba. Trade Cloth. Wesleyan University Press. Middletown, CT. 1988. 365p. ISBN:0-8195-5192-9, ISBN13: 978-0-8195-5192-4. Dewey:972.91/05. LCCN:87-034503.
Audience: **u,f.** *Choice, 1989.*

Paterson, Thomas G. **E183.8.C9P36 1994**
Contesting Castro: The United States and the Triumph of the Cuban Revolution. Trade Cloth. Oxford University Press, Inc. New York, NY. 1994. 384p. ISBN:0-19-508630-9, ISBN13: 978-0-19-508630-0. Dewey:327.7291073. LCCN:93-024260.
Audience: **u,f.** *Choice, 1994.*

Perez Sarduy, Pedro & Stubbs, Jean **F1789.N3P47 2000**
Afro-Cuban Voices: On Race and Identity in Contemporary Cuba. Manning Marable, James Early & John M. Kirk (Foreword by). Trade Cloth. University Press of Florida. Gainesville, FL. 2000. 312p. Contemporary Cuba Ser. ISBN:0-8130-1735-1, ISBN13: 978-0-8130-1735-8. Dewey:305.896/07291. LCCN:99-053467.
Audience: **u,f.** *Choice, 2000.*

Perez, Louis A. Jr. (Editor) **F1783.M38J655 1995**
Jose Marti in the United States: The Florida Experience. Perfect. Arizona State University, Center for Latin American Studies. Tempe, AZ. 1995. 114p. Special Studies, No. 28 ISBN:0-87918-081-1, ISBN13: 978-0-87918-081-2. Dewey:972.91/05/092. LCCN:95-015740.
Audience: **u,f.**

Perez, Louis A. Jr. **F1760.P47 1999**
On Becoming Cuban: Identity, Nationality and Culture. Trade Cloth. University of North Carolina Press. Chapel Hill, NC. 1999. 608p. H. Eugene and Lillian Youngs Lehman Ser. ISBN:0-8078-2487-9, ISBN13: 978-0-8078-2487-0. Dewey:972.91. LCCN:98-042664.
Audience: **u,f.** *Choice, 2000.*

Perez-Lopez, Jorge F. **HD2346.C84P47 1995**
Cuba's Second Economy: From Behind the Scenes to Center Stage. Trade Cloth. Transaction Publishers. Somerset, NJ. 1995. 221p. ISBN:1-56000-189-5, ISBN13: 978-1-56000-189-8. Dewey:330. LCCN:94-030755.
Audience: **u,f.** *Choice, 1995.*

Perez-Lopez, Jorge & Travieso-Diaz, Matias F. **HC152.5.P475 1998**
Perspectives on Cuban Economic Reforms. Trade Paper. Arizona State University, Center for Latin American Studies. Tempe, AZ. 1998. 190p. Special Studies, Vol. 30 ISBN:0-87918-087-0, ISBN13: 978-0-87918-087-4. Dewey:338.97291. LCCN:97-049289.
Audience: **u,f.**

Perez-Stable, Marifeli **F1788.P455 1999**
The Cuban Revolution: Origins, Course, and Legacy. Ed. 2. Trade Paper. Oxford University Press, Inc. New York, NY. 1998. 288p. ISBN:0-19-512749-8, ISBN13: 978-0-19-512749-2. Dewey:972.91064. LCCN:98-020278.
Audience: **u,f.** *Choice, 1994.*

Poyo, Gerald E. **E184.C97P69 1989**
With All and for the Good of All: The Emergence of Popular Nationalism in the Cuban Communities of the United States, 1848-1898. Cloth Text. Duke University Press. Durham, NC. 1989. xvii, 182p. ISBN:0-8223-0881-9, ISBN13: 978-0-8223-0881-2. Dewey:972.91/05. LCCN:88-021129.
Audience: **u,f.** *Choice, 1989.*

Prados-Torreira, Teresa **F1785.P83 2005**
Mambisas. Trade Cloth. University Press of Florida. Gainesville, FL. 2005. 192p. ISBN:0-8130-2852-3, ISBN13: 978-0-8130-2852-1. Dewey:972.91/05/082. LCCN:2005-047072.
Audience: **u,f.** *Choice, 2006.*

Quirk, Robert E. **F1788.22.C3Q57**
Fidel Castro. Trade Paper. W. W. Norton & Company, Inc. New York, NY. 1995. 912p. ISBN:0-393-31327-1, ISBN13: 978-0-393-31327-7. Dewey:972.91064. LCCN:92-039300.
Audience: **l,u,f.** *Choice, 1994.*

Rabkin, Rhoda P. **F1788**
Cuban Politics: The Revolutionary Experiment. Trade Cloth. Greenwood Publishing Group, Inc. Portsmouth, NH. 1990. 256p. Politics in Latin America Ser. ISBN:0-275-93739-9, ISBN13: 978-0-275-93739-3. Dewey:972.9106/4. LCCN:90-038808.
Audience: **u,f.** *Choice, 1991.*

Rice, Donald E. **PN239**
The Rhetorical Uses of the Authorizing Figure: Fidel Castro and Jose Marti. Trade Cloth. Greenwood Publishing Group, Inc. Portsmouth, NH. 1992. 192p. ISBN:0-275-94214-7, ISBN13: 978-0-275-94214-4. Dewey:320.014. LCCN:91-035027.
Audience: **u,f.**

Ritter, Archibald R. M. **HC152.5.R57 2004**
The Cuban Economy. Trade Cloth. University of Pittsburgh Press. Pittsburgh, PA. 2004. 256p. Pitt Latin American Ser.

ISBN:0-8229-4218-6, ISBN13: 978-0-8229-4218-4. Dewey:330.97291. LCCN:2003-021092.
Audience: **u,f.** *Choice, 2004.*

Ritter, Archibald R. M. & Kirk, John M. (Editors) **F1788.2.C8 1995**
Cuba in the International System: Normalization and Integration. Cloth over Boards. Palgrave Macmillan. New York, NY. 1995. 294p. International Political Economy Ser. ISBN:0-312-12653-0, ISBN13: 978-0-312-12653-7. Dewey:327.7291073. LCCN:95-001328.
Audience: **u,f.**

Robins, Nicholas A. **F1776.R595 2003**
The Culture of Conflict in Modern Cuba. Paper Text. McFarland & Company, Incorporated Publishers. Jefferson, NC. 2003. 138p. ISBN:0-7864-1415-4, ISBN13: 978-0-7864-1415-4. Dewey:303.6/097291. LCCN:2002-156686.
Audience: **u,f.**

Rodenas, Adriana M. **F1799.H3M4736 1998**
Gender and Nationalism in Colonial Cuba: The Travels of Santa Cruz y Montalvo, Condesa de Merlin. Trade Cloth. Vanderbilt University Press. Nashville, TN. 1998. 312p. ISBN:0-8265-1299-2, ISBN13: 978-0-8265-1299-4. Dewey:972.91/05. LCCN:97-021193.
Audience: **u,f.** *Choice, 1998.*

Ronning, C. Neale **F1783**
Jose Marti and the Emigre Colony in Key West: Leadership and State Formation. Trade Cloth. Greenwood Publishing Group, Inc. Portsmouth, NH. 1990. 175p. ISBN:0-275-93368-7, ISBN13: 978-0-275-93368-5. Dewey:972.91/05/092. LCCN:89-038802.
Audience: **u,f.** *Choice, 1990.*

Schulz, Donald E. (Editor) **F1788**
Cuba and the Future. Trade Cloth. Greenwood Publishing Group, Inc. Portsmouth, NH. 1994. 208p. Contributions in Latin American Studies, No. 4 ISBN:0-313-28784-8, ISBN13: 978-0-313-28784-8. Dewey:972.91064. LCCN:93-021140.
Audience: **u,f.**

Schwab, Peter **HF1500.5.U5S38 1999**
Cuba: Confronting the U. S. Embargo. Cloth over Boards. Palgrave Macmillan. New York, NY. 1998. 224p. ISBN:0-312-21620-3, ISBN13: 978-0-312-21620-7. Dewey:337.7291073. LCCN:98-044271.
Audience: **u,f.** *Choice, 1999.*

Schwartz, Rosalie **F1785.S38 1989**
The Lawless Liberators: Political Banditry and Cuban Independence. Cloth Text. Duke University Press. Durham, NC. 1989. x, 297p. ISBN:0-8223-0882-7, ISBN13: 978-0-8223-0882-9. Dewey:972.91/05. LCCN:88-022592.
Audience: **u,f.** *Choice, 1989.*

Shacochis, Bob (Foreword by) **F1765.3**
Conversations with Cuba. Trade Paper. University of Georgia Press. Athens, GA. 2001. 272p. ISBN:0-8203-2302-0, ISBN13: 978-0-8203-2302-2. Dewey:972.91064. LCCN:99-016371.
Audience: **g,l,u,f.**

Shaffer, Kirwin R. **HX861.S52 2005**
Anarchism and Countercultural Politics in Early Twentieth-Century Cuba. Trade Cloth. University Press of Florida. Gainesville, FL. 2005. 304p. ISBN:0-8130-2791-8, ISBN13: 978-0-8130-2791-3. Dewey:326.5/7/09729109041. LCCN:2004-054195.
Audience: **u,f.** *Choice, 2006.*

Simons, Geoff **F1776.S55 1996**
Cuba: From Conquistador to Castro. Trade Cloth. Palgrave Macmillan. New York, NY. 1996. 432p. ISBN:0-312-12822-3, ISBN13: 978-0-312-12822-7. Dewey:972.91/00461. LCCN:95-014918.
Audience: **u,f.**

Smith, Wayne S. & Dominguez, Esteban M. (Editors) **F1776.3.U6**
Subject to Solution: Problems in U. S. - Cuban Relations. Library Binding. Lynne Rienner Publishers, Inc. Boulder, CO. 1988. 158p. ISBN:1-55587-127-5, ISBN13: 978-1-55587-127-7. Dewey:327.7291073. LCCN:88-014162.
Audience: **u,f.** *Choice, 1989.*

Staten, Clifford L. **F1787**
The History of Cuba. Cloth Text. Greenwood Publishing Group, Inc. Portsmouth, NH. 2003. 184p. The Greenwood Histories of the Modern Nations Ser. ISBN:0-313-31690-2, ISBN13: 978-0-313-31690-6. Dewey:972.9106. LCCN:2002-035334.
Audience: **l,u,f.**

Sweig, Julia E. **F1787.5.S96 2002**
Inside the Cuban Revolution: Fidel Castro and the Urban Underground. Trade Cloth. Harvard University Press. Cambridge, MA. 2002. 286p. ISBN:0-674-00848-0, ISBN13: 978-0-674-00848-9. Dewey:972.9106/3. LCCN:2002-017151.
Audience: **u,f.**

Thomas, Hugh **F1788 .T47 1998**
Cuba or the Pursuit of Freedom. Ed. 2. Trade Paper. Da Capo Press, Inc. Cambridge, MA. 1998. 1776p. ISBN:0-306-80827-7, ISBN13: 978-0-306-80827-2. Dewey:972.91. LCCN:97-052949.
Audience: **u,f.**

Torres-Cuevas, Eduardo **F1776**
Historia de Cuba: 1492 1898: Formación y Liberación de la Nación. Loyola Vega, Oscar. Editorial Pueblo y Educación. 2001. ISBN:959-13-0745-4, ISBN13: 978-959-13-0745-3.
Audience: **l,u.**

Tulchin, Joseph S. (Editor), et al. **F2177.C83 1997**
Cuba and the Caribbean: Regional Issues and Trends in the Post-Cold War Era. Andres Serbin & Rafael Hernandez (Editors). Book, Other. Rowman & Littlefield Publishers, Inc. Lanham, MD. 1997. 275p. Latin American Silhouettes Ser. ISBN:0-8420-2652-5, ISBN13: 978-0-8420-2652-9. Dewey:303.48/2729. LCCN:96-042491.
Audience: **u,f.**

Valdés Domínguez, Fermín & Stebbins, Consuelo E. **F1785.V162213 2000**
Tragedy in Havana: November 27, 1871. Trade Cloth. University Press of Florida. Gainesville, FL. 2000. 248p. ISBN:0-8130-1747-5, ISBN13: 978-0-8130-1747-1. Dewey:972.91/05. LCCN:99-041381.
Audience: **u,f.**

Vinat de la Mata, Raquel **HQ1507**
Cubanas en la Posguerra (1898-1902): Acercamiento a la Reconstrucción de una Etapa Olvidada. Editora Política. 2001. ISBN:959-01-0452-5, ISBN13: 978-959-01-0452-7.
Audience: **l,u.**

West, Alan **PQ7378**
Tropics of History: Cuba Imagined. Trade Cloth. Greenwood Publishing Group, Inc. Portsmouth, NH. 1997. 232p. ISBN:0-89789-338-7, ISBN13: 978-0-89789-338-1. Dewey:860.9/97291/0904. LCCN:96-047628.
Audience: **u,f.** *Choice, 1998.*

Whitney, Robert **F1787.W58 2001**
State and Revolution in Cuba: Mass Mobilization and Political Change, 1920-1940. Trade Paper. University of North Carolina Press. Chapel Hill, NC. 2001. 272p. Envisioning Cuba Ser. ISBN:0-8078-4925-1, ISBN13: 978-0-8078-4925-5. Dewey:972.9106. LCCN:00-051205.
Audience: **u,f.** *Choice, 2001.*

Yaremko, Jason M. **BV2848.C9Y37 2000**
U. S. Protestant Missions in Cuba: From Independence to Castro. Trade Cloth. University Press of Florida. Gainesville, FL. 2000. xiv, 200p. ISBN:0-8130-1816-1, ISBN13: 978-0-8130-1816-4. Dewey:266/.0237307291. LCCN:00-056387.
Audience: **u,f.**

Zimbalist, Andrew & Brundenius, Claes **HC152.5.Z37 1989**
The Cuban Economy: Measurement and Analysis of Socialist Performance. Trade Cloth. Johns Hopkins University Press. Baltimore, MD. 1989. 240p. Studies in Development ISBN:0-8018-3846-0, ISBN13: 978-0-8018-3846-0. Dewey:330.97291/064. LCCN:89-032029.
Audience: **u,f.** *Choice, 1990.*

Caribbean: General > Jamaica. Haiti.

Balutansky, Kathleen M. & Sourieau, Marie-Agnes (Editors) **PM7834.C37C36 1998**
Caribbean Creolization: Reflections on the Cultural Dynamics of Language, Literature, and Identity. Trade Cloth. University Press of Florida. Gainesville, FL. 1998. 240p. ISBN:0-8130-1558-8, ISBN13: 978-0-8130-1558-3. Dewey:417/.22/09729. LCCN:97-034954.
Audience: **u,f.**

Brown, Gordon S. **E310.7.B76 2005**
Toussaint's Clause: The Founding Fathers and the Haitian Revolution. Trade Cloth. University Press of Mississippi. Jackson, MS. 2006. 240p. ISBN:1-57806-711-1, ISBN13: 978-1-57806-711-4. Dewey:327.7307294/09/033. LCCN:2004-010403.
Audience: **u,f.** *Choice, 2005.*

Burton, Richard D. **F1874**
Afro-Creole: Power, Opposition and Play in the Caribbean. Trade Paper. Cornell University Press. Ithaca, NY. 1997. 320p. ISBN:0-8014-8325-5, ISBN13: 978-0-8014-8325-7. Dewey:303.48/272906. LCCN:96-050046.
Audience: **u,f.** *Choice, 1998.*

Dayan, Joan **F1915.2**
Haiti, History and the Gods. Trade Paper. University of California Press. Berkeley, CA. 1998. 364p. ISBN:0-520-21368-8, ISBN13: 978-0-520-21368-5. Dewey:972.9/4.
Audience: **u,f.** *Choice, 1996.*

Doyle, Laura & Winkiel, Laura A. **PN56.R16G46 2005**
Geomodernisms: Race, Modernism, Modernity. Trade Cloth. Indiana University Press. Bloomington, IN. 2005. 312p. ISBN:0-253-34607-X, ISBN13: 978-0-253-34607-0. Dewey:809/.933552. LCCN:2005-011538.
Audience: **u,f.**

Dubois, Laurent & Garrigus, John **F1923**
Slave Revolution in the Caribbean, 1789-1804: A Brief History with Documents. Cloth over Boards. Palgrave Macmillan. New York, NY. 2006. 208p. The Bedford Series in History and Culture Ser. ISBN:1-4039-7157-9, ISBN13: 978-1-4039-7157-9. Dewey:972.9403.
Audience: **l,u.**

Dupuy, Alex **F1928.2.D86 1997**
Haiti in the New World Order: The Limits of the Democratic Revolution. Trade Paper. Westview Press. Boulder, CO. 1996. 240p. ISBN:0-8133-2113-1, ISBN13: 978-0-8133-2113-4. Dewey:972.9/4/073. LCCN:96-036190.
Audience: **u,f.** *Choice, 1997.*

Fischer, Sibylle **F1923.F57 2004**
Modernity Disavowed: Haiti and the Cultures of Slavery in the Age of Revolution. Trade Cloth. Duke University Press. Durham, NC. 2004. 392p. A John Hope Franklin Center Book Ser. ISBN:0-8223-3252-3, ISBN13: 978-0-8223-3252-7. Dewey:972.94/03. LCCN:2003-017792.
Audience: **u,f.** *Choice, 2005.*

Fleurant, Gerdes **ML3197**
Dancing Spirits: Rhythms and Rituals of Haitian Vodun, the Rada Rite. Trade Cloth. Greenwood Publishing Group, Inc. Portsmouth, NH. 1996. 240p. Contributions to the Study of Music and Dance Ser., Vol. 42 ISBN:0-313-29718-5, ISBN13: 978-0-313-29718-2. Dewey:781.7/96. LCCN:95-046061.
Audience: **u,f.** *Choice, 1997.*

Geggus, David P. **F1923**
[e] Haitian Revolutionary Studies. E-Book. Indiana University Press. Bloomington, IN. 2002. 334p. Blacks in the Diaspora Ser. ISBN:0-253-34104-3, ISBN13: 978-0-253-34104-4. Dewey:972.94/03. LCCN:2001-006201.
Audience: **u,f.** *Choice, 2003.*

Geggus, David P. (Editor) **F1923.I53 2001**
The Impact of the Haitian Revolution in the Atlantic World. Trade Cloth. University of South Carolina Press. Columbia, SC. 2001. 256p. The Carolina Lowcountry and the Atlantic World Ser. ISBN:1-57003-416-8, ISBN13: 978-1-57003-416-9. Dewey:973.5. LCCN:2001-003349.
Audience: **u,f.**

Girard, Philippe **F1928.2.G57 2004**
Clinton in Haiti: The 1994 US Invasion of Haiti. Cloth over Boards. Palgrave Macmillan. New York, NY. 2004. 272p. ISBN:1-4039-6716-4, ISBN13: 978-1-4039-6716-9. Dewey:327.7307294/09/049. LCCN:2004-049760.
Audience: **u,f.**

Goff, Stanley **F1928.2.G64 2000**
Hideous Dream: Special Operations, Racism and Imperialism in the Haiti Invasion of 1994. Trade Paper. Soft Skull Press, Inc. Brooklyn, NY. 2001. 500p. ISBN:1-887128-63-8, ISBN13: 978-1-887128-63-6. Dewey:972.9407/3. LCCN:2001-430137.
Audience: **u,f.**

Goldschmidt, Henry (Author, Editor) **E29.A1R33 2004**
Race, Nation, and Religion in the Americas. Elizabeth A. McAlister (Author), Elizabeth McAlister (Editor). Trade Paper. Oxford University Press, Inc. New York, NY. 2004. 352p. ISBN:0-19-514919-X, ISBN13: 978-0-19-514919-7. Dewey:305.6/0973. LCCN:2003-066225.
Audience: **u,f.** *Choice, 2005.*

Heinl, Robert **F1921.H44**
Written in Blood: Newly Revised Edition. Trade Paper. University Press of America, Inc. Lanham, MD. 2005. 882p. ISBN:0-7618-3177-0, ISBN13: 978-0-7618-3177-8. Dewey:972.94.
Audience: **u,f.**

Henke, Holger & Reno, Fred (Editors) **F2183**
Modern Political Culture in the Caribbean. Trade Paper. University of the West Indies Press. Kingston, 2004. 476p. ISBN:976-640-135-7, ISBN13: 978-976-640-135-1. Dewey:972.9052.
Audience: **u,f.**

Humphrey, Carol Sue **E203**
The Revolutionary Era: Primary Documents on Events from 1776 To 1800. Cloth Text. Greenwood Publishing Group, Inc. Portsmouth, NH. 2003. 384p. Debating Historical Issues in the Media of the Time Ser. ISBN:0-313-32083-7, ISBN13: 978-0-313-32083-5. Dewey:973.3. LCCN:2002-041597.
Audience: **u,f.**

Jenson, Deborah, et al. **F1924**
The Haiti Issue: 1804 and Nineteenth-Century French Studies. Nick Nesbitt, Christopher L. Miller, Chris Bongie, Doris Kadish, Daniel Desormeaux & Albert Valdman (Authors). Trade Paper, Perfect. Yale University Press. Cumberland, RI. 2005. 192p. Yale French Studies Ser. ISBN:0-300-10811-7, ISBN13: 978-0-300-10811-8. Dewey:972.94.
Audience: **u,f.**

Kingsley, Z. **E445.F6K56 2000**
Balancing Evils Judiciously: The Proslavery Writings Zephaniah Kingsley. Daniel M. Stowell (Editor, Annotations by). Trade Cloth. University Press of Florida. Gainesville, FL. 2000. xviii, 127p. Florida History and Culture Ser. ISBN:0-8130-1733-5, ISBN13: 978-0-8130-1733-4. Dewey:306.3/62/09759. LCCN:99-028868.
Audience: **u,f.**

Krenn, Michael L. & Finkelman, Paul (Editors) **E744.R275 1998**
Race and U. S. Foreign Policy from 1900 Through World War II. Library Binding. Garland Publishing, Inc. New York, NY. 1998. 386p. Race and U. S. Foreign Policy from the Colonial Period to the Present Ser., Vol. 3:A Collection of Essays ISBN:0-8153-2957-1, ISBN13: 978-0-8153-2957-2. Dewey:305.8/00973. LCCN:98-021992.
Audience: **u,f.**

Lampe Kingston, Armando **BR655**
Christianity in the Caribbean: Essays on Church History. University of the West Indies Press. 2001. ISBN:976-640-029-6, ISBN13: 978-976-640-029-3.
Audience: **u,f.**

Langley, Lester D. **E18.82.L36 1996**
The Americas in the Age of Revolution, 1750-1850. Cloth over Boards. Yale University Press. Cumberland, RI. 1996. 400p. ISBN:0-300-06613-9, ISBN13: 978-0-300-06613-5. Dewey:970/.03. LCCN:96-011598.
Audience: **u,f.** *Choice, 1997.*

Matibag, Eugenio **F1938.25.H2M38 2002**
Haitian-Dominican Counterpoint. Cloth over Boards. Palgrave Macmillan. New York, NY. 2003. 280p. ISBN:0-312-29432-8, ISBN13: 978-0-312-29432-8. Dewey:972.93. LCCN:2002-029247.
Audience: **u,f.** *Choice, 2004.*

Matthewson, Tim **E183**
A Proslavery Foreign Policy: Haitian-American Relations During the Early Republic. Trade Cloth. Greenwood Publishing Group, Inc. Portsmouth, NH. 2003. 176p. ISBN:0-275-98002-2, ISBN13: 978-0-275-98002-3. Dewey:326/.0973/09033. LCCN:2002-044544.
Audience: **u,f.**

Orizio, Riccardo **JV105.O75 2001**
Lost White Tribes: The End of Privilege and the Last Colonials in Sri Lanka, Jamaica, Brazil, Haiti, Namibia and Guadeloupe. Avril Bardoni (Translator). Trade Cloth. Simon & Schuster. New York, NY. 2001. 288p. ISBN:0-7432-1197-9, ISBN13: 978-0-7432-1197-0. Dewey:908/.6/91. LCCN:2001-023710.
Audience: **u,f.**

Pamphile, Leon D. **E185.P19 2001**
Haitians and African Americans: A Hertiage of Tragedy and Hope. Richard Seckinger (Foreword by). Trade Cloth. University Press of Florida. Gainesville, FL. 2001. 256p. ISBN:0-8130-2119-7, ISBN13: 978-0-8130-2119-5. Dewey:305.896/07294. LCCN:2001-048077.
Audience: **u,f.** *Choice, 2002.*

Renda, Mary A. **F1927.R56 2001**
Taking Haiti: Military Occupation and the Culture of U. S. Imperialism, 1915-1940. Trade Paper. University of North Carolina Press. Chapel Hill, NC. 2001. 440p. Gender and American Culture Ser. ISBN:0-8078-4938-3, ISBN13: 978-0-8078-4938-5. Dewey:972.94/05. LCCN:00-048926.
Audience: **u,f.** *Choice, 2002.*

Rey, Terry **BT652.H2R48 1999**
Our Lady of Class Struggle: The Cult of the Virgin Mary in Haiti. Trade Cloth. Africa World Press. Trenton, NJ. 1998. 400p. ISBN:0-86543-694-0, ISBN13: 978-0-86543-694-7. Dewey:306.6/3291/097294. LCCN:98-031306.
Audience: **u,f.**

San Miguel, Pedro Luis **F1937.5.S2613 2005**
The Imagined Island: History, Identity, and Utopia in Hispaniola. Trade Cloth. University of North Carolina Press. Chapel Hill, NC. 2005. 208p. Latin America in Translation/En Traducción/Em Tradução Ser. ISBN:0-8078-2964-1, ISBN13: 978-0-8078-2964-6. Dewey:972.93/072/2. LCCN:2005-006283.
Audience: **u,f.**

Shannon, Magdaline W **F1927.P75**
Jean Price Mars, the Haitian Elite and the American Occupation, 1915-1935. St. Martin's Press. 1996. ISBN:0-333-65457-9, ISBN13: 978-0-333-65457-6.
Audience: **u,f.**

Sheller, Mimi **F1924.S54 2000**
Democracy after Slavery: Black Publics and Peasant Rebels in Haiti and Jamaica. Trade Cloth. University Press of Florida. Gainesville, FL. 2000. xv, 270p. ISBN:0-8130-1883-8, ISBN13: 978-0-8130-1883-6. Dewey:972.92/04. LCCN:00-057696.
Audience: **u,f.** *Choice, 2001.*

Temperley, Howard (Editor) **DT16.5.R48 2001**
After Slavery: Emancipation and Its Discontents. Trade Paper. Taylor & Francis Group. Abingdon, 2000. 320p. Studies in Slave and Post-Slave Societies and Cultures
ISBN:0-7146-8079-6, ISBN13: 978-0-7146-8079-8. Dewey:981. LCCN:2001-028986.
Audience: **l,u,f.** *Choice, 2001.*

Williamson, Charles T. **E183.8.H2W55 1999**
The U. S. Naval Mission to Haiti, 1959-1963. Victor J. Croizat (Foreword by). Trade Cloth. Naval Institute Press. Annapolis, MD. 1998. 424p. ISBN:1-55750-941-7, ISBN13: 978-1-55750-941-3. Dewey:327.7307294. LCCN:98-029227.
Audience: **u,f.**

Woods, Charles A. and Sergile, Florence E. **QH109.A1**
Biogeography of the West Indies: Patterns and Perspectives. CRC Press. 2001. ISBN:0-8493-2001-1, ISBN13: 978-0-8493-2001-9.
Audience: **u,f.**

Caribbean: General > Dominican Republic

Alvarez, Julia **PZ7.A48BE**
Before We Were Free. Library Binding. Sagebrush Education Resources. Caledonia, MN. 2004. ISBN:0-613-72269-8, ISBN13: 978-0-613-72269-8. Dewey:[Fic].
Audience: **u,f.**

Austerlitz, Paul **ML3465.A95 1997**
Merengue: Dominican Music and Dominican Identity. Robert F. Thompson (Foreword by). Trade Cloth. Temple University Press. Philadelphia, PA. 1997. 224p. ISBN:1-56639-483-X, ISBN13: 978-1-56639-483-3. Dewey:784.18/88. LCCN:96-024778.
Audience: **u,f.** *Choice, 1997.*

Ayala, Cesar J. **HD9114.C89A96 1999**
American Sugar Kingdom: The Plantation Economy of the Spanish Caribbean, 1898-1934. Trade Paper. University of North Carolina Press. Chapel Hill, NC. 1999. 336p. ISBN:0-8078-4788-7, ISBN13: 978-0-8078-4788-6. Dewey:382/.41361/0973. LCCN:99-017349.
Audience: **u,f.** *Choice, 2000.*

Baud, Michiel **HD9144.D63C533 1995**
Peasants and Tobacco in the Dominican Republic, 1870-1930. Cloth Text. University of Tennessee Press. Knoxville, TN. 1995. 336p. ISBN:0-87049-891-6, ISBN13: 978-0-87049-891-6. Dewey:338.1/7371/0972935. LCCN:94-018760.
Audience: **u,f.** *Choice, 1996.*

Bjarkman, Peter **GV862**
Diamonds around the Globe: The Encyclopedia of International Baseball. Cloth Text. Greenwood Publishing Group, Inc. Portsmouth, NH. 2005. 656p. ISBN:0-313-32268-6, ISBN13: 978-0-313-32268-6. Dewey:796.357/09. LCCN:2004-016511.
Audience: **g,l,u,f.**

Bond, George C. (Editor), et al. **RA644.A25A36346 1997**
AIDS in Africa and the Caribbean. John Kreniske, Ida Susser & Joan Vincent (Editors). Trade Paper. Westview Press. Boulder, CO. 1997. 256p. ISBN:0-8133-2879-9, ISBN13: 978-0-8133-2879-9. Dewey:614.5/99392/096. LCCN:97-009642.
Audience: **u,f.** *Choice, 1997.*

Brown, Isabel Zakrzewski **F1938**
Culture and Customs of the Dominican Republic. Cloth Text. Greenwood Publishing Group, Inc. Portsmouth, NH. 1999. 224p. Culture and Customs of Latin America and the Caribbean Ser. ISBN:0-313-30314-2, ISBN13: 978-0-313-30314-2. Dewey:972.93. LCCN:99-027184.
Audience: **u,f.**

Calder, Bruce J. (Author, Introduction by) **F1938.45.C35 2005**
The Impact of Intervention: The Dominican Republic During the U. S. Occupation Of 1916-1924. Perfect. Markus Wiener Publishers, Inc. Princeton, NJ. 2005. 380p. ISBN:1-55876-386-4, ISBN13: 978-1-55876-386-9. Dewey:972.9305/2. LCCN:2005-024909.
Audience: **u,f.**

Camayd-Freixas, Erik & Gonzalez, Jose Eduardo (Editors) **PQ7082.N7P755 2000**
Primitivism and Identity in Latin America: Essays on Art, Literature and Culture. Trade Cloth. University of Arizona Press. Tucson, AZ. 2000. 285p. ISBN:0-8165-2045-3, ISBN13: 978-0-8165-2045-9. Dewey:863/.60911. LCCN:00-008340.
Audience: **u,f.** *Choice, 2001.*

Chester, Eric Thomas **E183.8.D6C48 2001**
Rag-Tags, Scum, Riff-Raff and Commies: The U. S. Intervention in the Dominican Republic, 1965-1966. Trade Cloth. Monthly Review Press. New York, NY. 2001. 353p. ISBN:1-58367-033-5, ISBN13: 978-1-58367-033-0. Dewey:327.7307293. LCCN:00-052090.
Audience: **u,f.** *Choice, 2001.*

Curry, E. R. **E183.8.D6 C87**
Hoover's Dominican Diplomacy and the Origins of the Good Neighbor Policy. Frank Freidel (Editor). Library Binding. Garland Publishing, Inc. New York, NY. 1979. Modern American History Ser., Vol. 5 ISBN:0-8240-3629-8, ISBN13: 978-0-8240-3629-4. Dewey:327.73/07293. LCCN:78-062379.
Audience: **u,f.**

Deagan, Kathleen A. & Cruxent, Jose Maria **F1939.I8D42 2002**
Archaeology at La Isabela: America's First European Town. Cloth over Boards. Yale University Press. Cumberland, RI. 2002. 416p. ISBN:0-300-09041-2, ISBN13: 978-0-300-09041-3. Dewey:972.93. LCCN:2001-057515.
Audience: **u,f.** *Choice, 2003.*

Fischer, Sibylle **F1923.F57 2004**
Modernity Disavowed: Haiti and the Cultures of Slavery in the Age of Revolution. Trade Cloth. Duke University Press.

Durham, NC. 2004. 392p. A John Hope Franklin Center Book Ser. ISBN:0-8223-3252-3, ISBN13: 978-0-8223-3252-7. Dewey:972.94/03. LCCN:2003-017792.
Audience: **u,f.** *Choice, 2005.*

Furst, Peter **PS3556.U765D6 1996**
Don Quixote in Exile. Trade Cloth. Northwestern University Press. Evanston, IL. 1996. 209p. Jewish Lives Ser. ISBN:0-8101-1447-X, ISBN13: 978-0-8101-1447-0. Dewey:813/.54. LCCN:95-026732.
Audience: **u,f.**

Hall, Michael R. **E183**
Sugar and Power in the Dominican Republic: Eisenhower, Kennedy and the Trujillos. Trade Cloth. Greenwood Publishing Group, Inc. Portsmouth, NH. 2000. 176p. Contributions in Latin American Studies ISBN:0-313-31127-7, ISBN13: 978-0-313-31127-7. Dewey:327.7307293/09/045. LCCN:99-016101.
Audience: **u,f.** *Choice, 2000.*

Hartlyn, Jonathan **F1938.55.H37 1998**
The Struggle for Democratic Politics in the Dominican Republic, 1961-1996. Trade Paper. University of North Carolina Press. Chapel Hill, NC. 1998. 400p. H. Eugene and Lillian Youngs Lehman Ser. ISBN:0-8078-4707-0, ISBN13: 978-0-8078-4707-7. Dewey:320.97293/09/045. LCCN:97-036873.
Audience: **u,f.** *Choice, 1998.*

Logan, Rayford Whittingham **F1915**
Haiti and the Dominican Republic. Oxford University Press. 1968.
Audience: **u,f.**

Martinez-Fernandez, Luis **F1741.M37 1994**
Torn Between Empires: Economy, Society, and Patterns of Political Thought in the Hispanic Caribbean, 1840-1878. Trade Cloth. University of Georgia Press. Athens, GA. 1994. 344p. ISBN:0-8203-1568-0, ISBN13: 978-0-8203-1568-3. Dewey:972.904. LCCN:93-014972.
Audience: **u,f.**

Martínez Vergne, Teresita **F1938.4.M338 2005**
Nation and Citizen in the Dominican Republic, 1880-1916. Trade Cloth. University of North Carolina Press. Chapel Hill, NC. 2005. 256p. ISBN:0-8078-2976-5, ISBN13: 978-0-8078-2976-9. Dewey:972.93/04. LCCN:2005-005928.
Audience: **u,f.** *Choice, 2006.*

Matibag, Eugenio **F1938.25.H2M38 2002**
Haitian-Dominican Counterpoint. Cloth over Boards. Palgrave Macmillan. New York, NY. 2003. 280p. ISBN:0-312-29432-8, ISBN13: 978-0-312-29432-8. Dewey:972.93. LCCN:2002-029247.
Audience: **u,f.** *Choice, 2004.*

Morales, Ed **ML3475.M67 2003**
The Latin Beat: The Rhythms and Roots of Latin Music, from Bossa Nova to Salsa and Beyond. Trade Paper. Da Capo Press, Inc. Cambridge, MA. 2003. 400p. ISBN:0-306-81018-2, ISBN13: 978-0-306-81018-3. Dewey:781.64/098. LCCN:2003-016423.
Audience: **g,l,u,f.** *Choice, 2004.*

Moreno Fraginals, Manuel (Editor), et al. **HT1073.B48 1985**
Between Slavery and Free Labor: The Spanish-Speaking Caribbean in the 19th Century. Frank M. Pons & Stanley L. Engerman (Editors). Trade Cloth. Johns Hopkins University Press. Baltimore, MD. 1960. 312p. Studies in Atlantic History and Culture ISBN:0-8018-3224-1, ISBN13: 978-0-8018-3224-6. Dewey:306/.362/09729. LCCN:84-023379.
Audience: **u,f.** *Choice, 1985.*

Moreno, Jose A. **F1938.55 .M66**
Barrios in Arms: Revolution in Santo Domingo. Trade Cloth. University of Pittsburgh Press. Pittsburgh, PA. 1969. Pitt Latin American Ser. ISBN:0-8229-3186-9, ISBN13: 978-0-8229-3186-7. Dewey:972.93/054. LCCN:68-012723.
Audience: **u,f.**

Pacini-Hernandez, Deborah **ML3486.D65P3 1995**
Bachata: Social History of a Dominican Popular Music. Paper Text. Temple University Press. Philadelphia, PA. 1995. 288p. ISBN:1-56639-300-0, ISBN13: 978-1-56639-300-3. Dewey:781.64/097293. LCCN:94-029477.
Audience: **u,f.**

Peguero, Valentina **F1938.4.P44 2004**
The Militarization of Culture in the Dominican Republic, from the Captains General to General Trujillo. Cloth Text. University of Nebraska Press. Lincoln, NE. 2004. 336p. Studies in War, Society, and the Military Ser. ISBN:0-8032-3741-3, ISBN13: 978-0-8032-3741-4. Dewey:972.93. LCCN:2004-011874.
Audience: **u,f.** *Choice, 2005.*

Pons, Frank M. **F1938.M687 1998**
The Dominican Republic: A National History. Ed. 2. Trade Cloth. Markus Wiener Publishers, Inc. Princeton, NJ. 1998. 544p. ISBN:1-55876-191-8, ISBN13: 978-1-55876-191-9. Dewey:972.93. LCCN:98-019818.
Audience: **u,f.**

Roorda, Eric **E183.8.D6R59 1998**
The Dictator Next Door: The Good Neighbor Policy and the Trujillo Regime in the Dominican Republic, 1930-1945. Trade Cloth. Duke University Press. Durham, NC. 1998. 312p. American Encounters/Global Interactions Ser. ISBN:0-8223-2234-X, ISBN13: 978-0-8223-2234-4. Dewey:327.7307293. LCCN:98-012100.
Audience: **u,f.** *Choice, 1999.*

Ruck, Rob **GV863.29.A1D657 1999**
The Tropic of Baseball: Baseball in the Dominican Republic. Ed. 2. Trade Cloth. University of Nebraska Press. Lincoln, NE. 1999. 217p. ISBN:0-8032-8978-2, ISBN13: 978-0-8032-8978-9. Dewey:796.357/097293. LCCN:98-045479.
Audience: **g,l,u,f.** *Choice, 1991.*

Sag'as, Ernesto **F1941.A1S34 2000**
Race and Politics in the Dominican Republic. Trade Cloth. University Press of Florida. Gainesville, FL. 2000. xii, 160p. ISBN:0-8130-1763-7, ISBN13: 978-0-8130-1763-1. Dewey:305.8/0097293. LCCN:99-089361.
Audience: **u,f.** *Choice, 2000.*

Sag'as, Ernesto & Inoa, Orlando (Editors) **F1938**
The Dominican People: A Documentary History. Trade Paper. Markus Wiener Publishers, Inc. Princeton, NJ. 2003. 340p.

ISBN:1-55876-297-3, ISBN13: 978-1-55876-297-8. Dewey:972.93. LCCN:2002-071318.
Audience: **u,f.**

San Miguel, Pedro Luis **F1937.5.S2613 2005**
The Imagined Island: History, Identity, and Utopia in Hispaniola. Trade Cloth. University of North Carolina Press. Chapel Hill, NC. 2005. 208p. Latin America in Translation/En Traducción/Em Tradução Ser. ISBN:0-8078-2964-1, ISBN13: 978-0-8078-2964-6. Dewey:972.93/072/2. LCCN:2005-006283.
Audience: **u,f.**

Sharpe, Kenneth E. **HD430.H34**
Peasant Politics: Struggle in a Dominican Village. Trade Cloth. Johns Hopkins University Press. Baltimore, MD. 1991. 284p. The Johns Hopkins Studies in Atlantic History and Culture Ser. ISBN:0-8018-1952-0, ISBN13: 978-0-8018-1952-0. Dewey:301.44/43. LCCN:77-004782.
Audience: **u,f.**

Turits, Richard Lee **HD1531.D6T87 2003**
Foundations of Despotism: Peasants, the Trujillo Regime, and Modernity in Dominican History. Trade Cloth. Stanford University Press. Palo Alto, CA. 2002. 400p. ISBN:0-8047-4353-3, ISBN13: 978-0-8047-4353-2. Dewey:972.9305/3/092 B. LCCN:2002-010778.
Audience: **u,f.** *Choice, 2003.*

Veeser, Cyrus **HF1502.Z4U57 2002**
A World Safe for Capitalism: Dollar Diplomacy and America's Rise to Global Power. Trade Cloth. Edinburgh University Press. Edinburgh, 2002. 190p. ISBN:0-231-12586-0, ISBN13: 978-0-231-12586-4. Dewey:337.7307292/09/034. LCCN:2002-019283.
Audience: **u,f.** *Choice, 2003.*

Vigil, Ralph H. **KGQ304.Z67V54 1987**
Alonso de Zorita: Royal Judge and Christian Humanist, 1512-1585. Trade Cloth. University of Oklahoma Press. Norman, OK. 1987. 368p. ISBN:0-8061-2061-4, ISBN13: 978-0-8061-2061-4. Dewey:347.7293/014. LCCN:86-040531.
Audience: **u,f.** *Choice, 1988.*

Wiarda, Howard J. **F1938.55**
Dictatorship, Development and Disintegration: Politics and Social Change in the Dominican Republic, Vol. 3. Trade Cloth. University Microfilms, Inc. Ann Arbor, MI. 1975. ISBN:0-8357-0152-2, ISBN13: 978-0-8357-0152-5. Dewey:320.9.
Audience: **u,f.**

Caribbean: General > Other Islands

Alexander, Robert J. **F2131**
Presidents, Prime Ministers and Governors of the English-Speaking Caribbean and Puerto Rico: Conversations and Correspondence. Trade Cloth. Greenwood Publishing Group, Inc. Portsmouth, NH. 1997. 304p. ISBN:0-275-95803-5, ISBN13: 978-0-275-95803-9. Dewey:972.905/2. LCCN:96-033194.
Audience: **u,f.**

Ayala, Cesar J. **HD9114.C89**
American Sugar Kingdom: The Plantation Economy of the Spanish Caribbean, 1898-1934. Trade Paper. DIANE Publishing Company. Collingdale, PA. 2006. 321p. ISBN:0-7567-9948-1, ISBN13: 978-0-7567-9948-9. Dewey:382/.41361/0973.
Audience: **u,f.** *Choice, 2000.*

Baralt, Guillermo A. **HD1471.P92P66313**
Buena Vista: Life and Work on a Puerto Rican Hacienda, 1833-1904. Ed. 2. Trade Paper. University of North Carolina Press. Chapel Hill, NC. 1999. 208p. ISBN:0-8078-4801-8, ISBN13: 978-0-8078-4801-2. Dewey:972.95/7. LCCN:98-037128.
Audience: **u,f.** *Choice, 1999.*

Baver, Sherrie L. **HD3616**
The Political Economy of Colonialism: The State and Industrialization in Puerto Rico. Trade Cloth. Greenwood Publishing Group, Inc. Portsmouth, NH. 1993. 176p. ISBN:0-275-94503-0, ISBN13: 978-0-275-94503-9. Dewey:338.97295. LCCN:92-046553.
Audience: **u,f.** *Choice, 1994.*

Beck, Robert J. **E183.8.G84**
The Grenada Invasion: Politics, Law, and Foreign Policy Decision Making. Westview Press. 1993.
Audience: **u,f.**

Bergad, Laird W. **HD9199.P92**
Coffee and the Growth of Agrarian Capitalism in Nineteenth-Century Puerto Rico. Trade Cloth. Princeton University Press. Princeton, NJ. 1983. 264p. ISBN:0-691-07646-4, ISBN13: 978-0-691-07646-1. Dewey:338.1/7373/097295. LCCN:82-061354.
Audience: **u,f.**

Bishop, Maurice **F2056.83.B57**
Forward Ever!: Three Years of the Grenadian Revolution. Pathfinder Press. 1982. ISBN:0-909196-16-8, ISBN13: 978-0-909196-16-5.
Audience: **u,f.**

Bond, George C. (Editor), et al. **RA644.A25A36346 1997**
AIDS in Africa and the Caribbean. John Kreniske, Ida Susser & Joan Vincent (Editors). Trade Paper. Westview Press. Boulder, CO. 1997. 256p. ISBN:0-8133-2879-9, ISBN13: 978-0-8133-2879-9. Dewey:614.5/99392/096. LCCN:97-009642.
Audience: **u,f.** *Choice, 1997.*

Bosque-Perez, Ramon & Morera, Jose Javier Colon (Editors) **JC599.P9P84 2005**
Puerto Rico under Colonial Rule: Political Persecution and the Quest for Human Rights. Cloth Text. State University of New York Press. Albany, NY. 2005. 288p. ISBN:0-7914-6417-2, ISBN13: 978-0-7914-6417-5. Dewey:325/.373/097295. LCCN:2004-016237.
Audience: **u,f.**

Briggs, Laura **HQ766.5.P8 B75 2002**
Reproducing Empire: Race, Sex, Science and U.S. Imperialism in Puerto Rico. Trade Cloth. University of California Press. Berkeley, CA. 2003. 304p. American Crossroads Ser., Vol. 11 ISBN:0-520-22255-5, ISBN13: 978-0-520-22255-7. Dewey:363.9/6/097295. LCCN:2002-001851.
Audience: **u,f.** *Choice, 2003.*

Brizan, George I. **HD5344.Z9**
The Grenadian Peasantry and Social Revolution, 1930-50. Institute of Social and Economic Research. 1979.
Audience: **u,f.**

Burnett, Christina KF4635.F67 2001
Duffy & Marshall, Burke (Editors)
Foreign in a Domestic Sense: Puerto Rico, American Expansion and the Constitution. Trade Cloth. Duke University Press. Durham, NC. 2001. 464p. American Encounters/Global Interactions Ser. ISBN:0-8223-2689-2, ISBN13: 978-0-8223-2689-2. Dewey:342.73/083. LCCN:00-047644.
Audience: **u,f.** *Choice, 2002.*

Cheng, Pang Guek F2056.C45 2001
Grenada. Library Binding. Marshall Cavendish Corporation. Tarrytown, NY. 2000. 128p. Cultures of the World Ser. ISBN:0-7614-1160-7, ISBN13: 978-0-7614-1160-4. Dewey:972.9845. LCCN:00-047583.
Audience: **l,u,f.**

Chinea, Jorge Luis F1983.W47C45 2005
Race and Labor in the Hispanic Caribbean: The West Indian Immigrant Worker Experience in Puerto Rico, 1800-1850. Trade Cloth. University Press of Florida. Gainesville, FL. 2005. 272p. New Directions in Puerto Rican Studies ISBN:0-8130-2821-3, ISBN13: 978-0-8130-2821-7. Dewey:305.8/0097295. LCCN:2004-066129.
Audience: **u,f.**

Cox, Edward L. HT1105.G84 C69 1984
Free Coloreds in the Slave Societies of St. Kitts and Grenada, 1763-1833. Cloth Text. University of Tennessee Press. Knoxville, TN. 1984. 212p. ISBN:0-87049-414-7, ISBN13: 978-0-87049-414-7. Dewey:305.8/96/072973. LCCN:83-014646.
Audience: **u,f.**

Davidson, J. S. JX4481.D38 1987
Grenada: A Study in Politics and the Limits of International Law. Trade Cloth. Ashgate Publishing Company. Williston, VT. 1986. 200p. ISBN:0-566-05052-8, ISBN13: 978-0-566-05052-7. Dewey:341.5/8. LCCN:86-025783.
Audience: **u,f.**

Davila, Arlene M. F1976.D38 1997
Sponsored Identities: Cultural Politics in Puerto Rico. Trade Cloth. Temple University Press. Philadelphia, PA. 1997. 288p. Puerto Rican Studies ISBN:1-56639-548-8, ISBN13: 978-1-56639-548-9. Dewey:306/.097295. LCCN:97-001942.
Audience: **u,f.** *Choice, 1998.*

De Gutiérrez, Edith PE1068.P8G8 1987
The Movement Against Teaching English in Schools of Puerto Rico. Trade Cloth. University Press of America, Inc. Lanham, MD. 1987. 176p. ISBN:0-8191-6087-3, ISBN13: 978-0-8191-6087-4. Dewey:428/.007/07295. LCCN:86-030763.
Audience: **u,f.**

De Wagenheim, Olga F1973.W33 1997
Jimenez
Puerto Rico: An Interpretive History from Precolumbian Times To 1900. Trade Cloth. Markus Wiener Publishers, Inc. Princeton, NJ. 1998. 320p. ISBN:1-55876-121-7, ISBN13: 978-1-55876-121-6. Dewey:972.95. LCCN:97-036076.
Audience: **u,f.** *Choice, 1998.*

De Wagenheim, Olga F1973.W34 1993
Jimenez
Puerto Rico's Revolt for Independence: El Grito de Lares. Trade Paper. Markus Wiener Publishers, Inc. Princeton, NJ. 1993. 186p. ISBN:1-55876-071-7, ISBN13: 978-1-55876-071-4. Dewey:972.95/04. LCCN:93-015391.
Audience: **u,f.**

Dietz, James L. HC154.5
Economic History of Puerto Rico: Institutional Change and Capitalist Development. Trade Paper. Princeton University Press. Princeton, NJ. 1987. 363p. ISBN:0-691-02248-8, ISBN13: 978-0-691-02248-2. Dewey:330.97295. LCCN:86-012313.
Audience: **u,f.** *Choice, 1987.*

Dorsey, Joseph C. HT1086.D67 2002
Slave Traffic in the Age of Abolition: Puerto Rico, West Africa and the Non-Hispanic Caribbean, 1815-1859. Trade Cloth. University Press of Florida. Gainesville, FL. 2002. xvii, 311p. ISBN:0-8130-2478-1, ISBN13: 978-0-8130-2478-3. Dewey:306.3/62/09729. LCCN:2002-075495.
Audience: **u,f.** *Choice, 2003.*

Duany, Jorge F1975.D83 2002
The Puerto Rican Nation on the Move: Identities on the Island and in the United States. Trade Cloth. University of North Carolina Press. Chapel Hill, NC. 2002. 360p. ISBN:0-8078-2704-5, ISBN13: 978-0-8078-2704-8. Dewey:972.9505. LCCN:2001-057826.
Audience: **u,f.** *Choice, 2003.*

Dujmovic, N. F2056.8.D85 1988
The Grenada Documents: Window on Totalitarianism. Trade Paper. Potomac Books, Inc. Dulles, VA. 1988. 102p. Institute for Foreign Policy Anaylsis Ser. ISBN:0-08-035969-8, ISBN13: 978-0-08-035969-4. Dewey:972.98/45. LCCN:87-032514.
Audience: **u,f.**

Figueroa, Luis A. HT1089.G83F54 2005
Sugar, Slavery, and Freedom in Nineteenth-Century Puerto Rico. Trade Paper, Perfect. University of North Carolina Press. Chapel Hill, NC. 2005. 304p. ISBN:0-8078-5610-X, ISBN13: 978-0-8078-5610-9. Dewey:306.3/62/0972958. LCCN:2005-017471.
Audience: **u,f.**

Findlay, Eileen Suarez HQ164.A5F56 1999
Imposing Decency: The Politics of Sexuality and Race in Puerto Rico, 1870-1920. Trade Cloth. Duke University Press. Durham, NC. 1999. 320p. American Encounters/Global Interactions Ser. ISBN:0-8223-2375-3, ISBN13: 978-0-8223-2375-4. Dewey:306/.097295. LCCN:99-025911.
Audience: **u,f.** *Choice, 2000.*

Flores, Juan (Editor, F128.9.P85
Introduction by)
Puerto Rican Arrival in New York: Narrative of the Migration, 1920-150. Trade Paper. Markus Wiener Publishers, Inc. Princeton, NJ. 2004. 168p. ISBN:1-55876-362-7, ISBN13: 978-1-55876-362-3. Dewey:305.8687. LCCN:2003-047905.
Audience: **u,f.**

Galvin, Miles HX342
The Organized Labor Movement in Puerto Rico. Trade Cloth. Fairleigh Dickinson University Press. Cranbury, NJ. 1979. 248p. ISBN:0-8386-2009-4, ISBN13: 978-0-8386-2009-0. Dewey:335/.0097295. LCCN:77-074389.
Audience: **u,f.**

Gems, Gerald R. GV706.35
The Athletic Crusade: Sport and American Cultural Imperialism. University of Nebraska Press, Lincoln. 2006. ISBN:0-8032-2216-5, ISBN13: 978-0-8032-2216-8.
Audience: **u,f.**

Grosfoguel, Ramon **E184.P85 G68 2003**
Colonial Subjects: Puerto Ricans in a Global Perspective. Trade Cloth. University of California Press. Berkeley, CA. 2003. 272p. ISBN:0-520-23020-5, ISBN13: 978-0-520-23020-0. Dewey:304.8/7307295/09043. LCCN:2003-047327.
Audience: **u,f.** *Choice, 2004.*

Heine, Jorge **F1981.M4.C644 1993**
The Last Cacique: Leadership and Politics in a Puerto Rican City. Cloth Text. University of Pittsburgh Press. Pittsburgh, PA. 1993. 328p. Latin American Ser. ISBN:0-8229-3741-7, ISBN13: 978-0-8229-3741-8. Dewey:320.97295/6. LCCN:92-036910.
Audience: **u,f.** *Choice, 1994.*

Hill, Donald R. **F2061**
The Impact of Migration on the Metropolitan and Folk Society of Carriacou, Grenada. American Museum of Natural History. 1977.
Audience: **u,f.**

Hine, Darlene Clark & McLeod, Jacqueline A. (Editors) **E185.86**
Crossing Boundaries: Comparative History of Black People in Diaspora. Trade Paper. Indiana University Press. Bloomington, IN. 2001. 480p. Blacks in the Diaspora Ser. ISBN:0-253-21450-5, ISBN13: 978-0-253-21450-8. Dewey:305.896/073.
Audience: **u,f.** *Choice, 2000.*

Lewis, Gordon K. **F2056.8.L48 1987**
Grenada: The Jewel Despoiled. Trade Cloth. Johns Hopkins University Press. Baltimore, MD. 1969. 251p. ISBN:0-8018-3422-8, ISBN13: 978-0-8018-3422-6. Dewey:972.98/45. LCCN:86-046282.
Audience: **u,f.** *Choice, 1987.*

MacDonald, Scott B. (Editor), et al. **F2183**
The Caribbean after Grenada: Revolution, Conflict, and Democracy. Harald M. Sandstrom & Paul B. Goodwin Jr. (Editors). Trade Cloth. Greenwood Publishing Group, Inc. Portsmouth, NH. 1988. 304p. ISBN:0-275-92722-9, ISBN13: 978-0-275-92722-6. Dewey:972.9/052. LCCN:88-011986.
Audience: **u,f.** *Choice, 1989.*

Maldonado, Alex W. **F1976.3.M86M37 2006**
Luis Muñoz Marín Puerto Rico's Democratic Revolution. Trade Cloth. University of Puerto Rico Press. Rio Piedras, PR. 2006. 463p. ISBN:0-8477-0163-8, ISBN13: 978-0-8477-0163-6. Dewey:972.9505/2/092. LCCN:2004-053304.
Audience: **u,f.**

Marable, Manning **DT353.M26 1987**
African and Caribbean Politics: From Kwame Nkrumah to the Grenada Revolution. Trade Cloth. Analytical Psychology Club of San Francisco, Inc. San Francisco, CA. 1987. xi, 314p. ISBN:0-86091-172-1, ISBN13: 978-0-86091-172-2. Dewey:320.9182/1. LCCN:87-200127.
Audience: **u,f.**

Martinez-Fernandez, Luis **F1741.M37 1994**
Torn Between Empires: Economy, Society, and Patterns of Political Thought in the Hispanic Caribbean, 1840-1878. Trade Cloth. University of Georgia Press. Athens, GA. 1994. 344p. ISBN:0-8203-1568-0, ISBN13: 978-0-8203-1568-3. Dewey:972.904. LCCN:93-014972.
Audience: **u,f.**

Martinez-Vergne, Teresita **HD9114.P82M37 1992**
Capitalism in Colonial Puerto Rico: Central San Vicente in the Late Nineteenth Century. Trade Cloth. University Press of Florida. Gainesville, FL. 1992. 208p. ISBN:0-8130-1110-8, ISBN13: 978-0-8130-1110-3. Dewey:338.1/7361/097295090. LCCN:91-028358.
Audience: **u,f.**

Matos-Rodriquez, Felix V. & Delgado, Linda C. (Editors) **HQ1522.P84 1998**
Puerto Rican Women's History: New Perspectives. Cloth Text. M. E. Sharpe Inc. Armonk, NY. 1998. 272p. Perspectives on Latin America and the Caribbean Ser. ISBN:0-7656-0245-8, ISBN13: 978-0-7656-0245-9. Dewey:305.4/097295. LCCN:98-010750.
Audience: **u,f.**

McCaffrey, Katherine T. **F1981.V5M33 2002**
Military Power and Popular Protest: The U. S. Navy in Vieques, Puerto Rico. Trade Cloth. Rutgers University Press. Piscataway, NJ. 2004. 224p. ISBN:0-8135-3090-3, ISBN13: 978-0-8135-3090-1. Dewey:972.95/9. LCCN:2001-048838.
Audience: **u,f.** *Choice, 2003.*

Meeks, Brian **F2183**
Caribbean Revolutions and Revolutionary Theory: An Assessment of Cuba, Nicaragua and Grenada. Trade Paper. University of the West Indies Press. Kingston, 2001. 220p. ISBN:976-640-104-7, ISBN13: 978-976-640-104-7. Dewey:972.905/2.
Audience: **u,f.**

Montalvo-Barbot, Alfredo **KGV2919.M66 1997**
Political Conflict and Constitutional Change in Puerto Rico, 1898-1952. Trade Cloth. University Press of America, Inc. Lanham, MD. 1997. 176p. ISBN:0-7618-0901-5, ISBN13: 978-0-7618-0901-2. Dewey:320.97295. LCCN:97-033539.
Audience: **u,f.**

Navarro, Jose-Manuel **E183.8.P9N38 2002**
Creating Tropical Yankees: Social Science Textbooks and U. S. Ideological Control in Puerto Rico, 1898-1908. Paper over Boards. Routledge. New York, NY. 2002. 224p. Latino Studies ISBN:0-415-93116-9, ISBN13: 978-0-415-93116-8. Dewey:325/.37307295/09041. LCCN:2002-017783.
Audience: **u,f.**

Negron-Muntaner, Frances & Grosfoguel, Ramon (Editors) **F1976.P585 1997**
Puerto Rican Jam: Rethinking Colonialism and Nationalism. Book, Other. University of Minnesota Press. Minneapolis, MN. 1997. 256p. ISBN:0-8166-2849-1, ISBN13: 978-0-8166-2849-0. Dewey:972.9505. LCCN:97-009569.
Audience: **u,f.**

Ortiz, Altagracia (Editor) **HD6057.5.U5P84 1996**
Puerto Rican Women and Work: Bridges in Transnational Labor. Trade Cloth. Temple University Press. Philadelphia, PA. 1996. 272p. Puerto Rican Studies ISBN:1-56639-450-3, ISBN13: 978-1-56639-450-5. Dewey:331.4/097295/0904. LCCN:95-043822.
Audience: **u,f.** *Choice, 1997.*

Pico, Fernando **F1975.P47 2004**
Puerto Rico 1898: The War after the War. Sylvia Korwek & P. A. Guzman (Translators). Trade Cloth. Markus Wiener

Publishers, Inc. Princeton, NJ. 2004. xx, 165p. ISBN:1-55876-326-0, ISBN13: 978-1-55876-326-5. Dewey:972.95/04. LCCN:2003-055934.
Audience: **u,f.** *Choice, 2005.*

Pryor, Frederic L. **HC156**
Revolutionary Grenada: A Study in Political Economy. Trade Cloth. Greenwood Publishing Group, Inc. Portsmouth, NH. 1986. 415p. ISBN:0-275-92155-7, ISBN13: 978-0-275-92155-2. Dewey:338.97298/45. LCCN:86-008109.
Audience: **u,f.**

Ramirez de Arellano, Annette B. & Seipp, Conrad **HQ766.5.P8**
Colonialism, Catholicism, and Contraception: A History of Birth Control in Puerto Rico. Trade Cloth. University of North Carolina Press. Chapel Hill, NC. 1983. xiv, 219p. ISBN:0-8078-1544-6, ISBN13: 978-0-8078-1544-1. Dewey:304.6/32/097295. LCCN:82-013646.
Audience: **u,f.**

Rivero, Yeidy M. **PN1992.3.P9R58 2005**
Tuning Out Blackness: Race and Nation in the History of Puerto Rican Television. Lynn Spigel (Editor). Trade Paper, Perfect. Duke University Press. Durham, NC. 2005. 248p. Console-Ing Passions Ser. ISBN:0-8223-3543-3, ISBN13: 978-0-8223-3543-6. Dewey:791.45/65289607295. LCCN:2004-029835.
Audience: **u,f.** *Choice, 2006.*

Rodriguez, Felix V. Matos **HQ1525.S26M38 1999**
Women and Urban Change in San Juan, Puerto Rico, 1820-1868. Trade Cloth. University Press of Florida. Gainesville, FL. 1999. xi, 180p. ISBN:0-8130-1676-2, ISBN13: 978-0-8130-1676-4. Dewey:305.4/097295/1. LCCN:99-017872.
Audience: **u,f.** *Choice, 1999.*

Roy-Fequiere, Magali **F1975.R69 2004**
Women, Creole Identity, and Intellectual Life in Early Twentieth-Century Puerto Rico. Library Binding. Temple University Press. Philadelphia, PA. 2004. 336p. Puerto Rican Studies ISBN:1-59213-230-8, ISBN13: 978-1-59213-230-0. Dewey:305.4/097295/09041. LCCN:2003-053130.
Audience: **u,f.**

Sanchez, Julio **BX4220.P9S36 1983**
The Community of the Holy Spirit: A Movement of Change in a Covent of Nuns in Puerto Rico. Paper Text. University Press of America, Inc. Lanham, MD. 1984. 190p. ISBN:0-8191-3368-X, ISBN13: 978-0-8191-3368-7. Dewey:306/.6.
Audience: **u,f.**

Santiago, Carlos E. **HD5744**
Labor in the Puerto Rican Economy: Postwar Development and Stagnation. Trade Cloth. Greenwood Publishing Group, Inc. Portsmouth, NH. 1992. 192p. ISBN:0-275-94135-3, ISBN13: 978-0-275-94135-2. Dewey:331.1/09729509045. LCCN:91-027268.
Audience: **u,f.** *Choice, 1992.*

Scarano, Francisco A. **HD9114.P83P66**
Sugar and Slavery in Puerto Rico: The Plantation Economy of Ponce, 1800-1850. Trade Cloth. University of Wisconsin Press. Chicago, IL. 1984. 288p. ISBN:0-299-09580-0, ISBN13: 978-0-299-09580-2. Dewey:338.1/7361/0972957. LCCN:83-040271.
Audience: **u,f.**

Seabury, Paul & McDougall, Walter A. (Editors) **F2056.8.G77 1984**
The Grenada Papers. Sidney Hook (Foreword by). Trade Cloth. I C S Press. Oakland, CA. 1984. 364p. ISBN:0-917616-68-5, ISBN13: 978-0-917616-68-6. Dewey:972.98/45. LCCN:84-022356.
Audience: **u,f.** B

Searle, Chris **F2056.8**
Grenada Morning: A Memoir of the "Revo". Karia Press. 1989. ISBN:0-946918-57-0, ISBN13: 978-0-946918-57-7.
Audience: **u,f.**

Siegel, Peter E. (Editor) **F1969.A53 2005**
Ancient Borinquen: Archaeology and Ethnohistory of Native Puerto Rico. Trade Cloth. University of Alabama Press. Tuscaloosa, AL. 2005. 448p. ISBN:0-8173-1471-7, ISBN13: 978-0-8173-1471-2. Dewey:972.95/01. LCCN:2005-002033.
Audience: **u,f.**

Sonesson, Birgit **HF3355.S66 2000**
Puerto Rico's Commerce, 1765-1865: From Regional to Worldwide Market Relations. Trade Cloth. University of California, Latin American Center. Los Angeles, CA. 1999. xiii, 338p. UCLA Latin American Studies, Vol. 85 ISBN:0-87903-085-2, ISBN13: 978-0-87903-085-8. Dewey:380.1/097295/09034. LCCN:99-048897.
Audience: **u,f.**

Steele, Beverley A. **F2056.5**
Grenada: A History of Its People. Trade Paper. Macmillan Caribbean. Oxford, 2003. 496p. ISBN:0-333-93053-3, ISBN13: 978-0-333-93053-3. Dewey:972.9845.
Audience: **u,f.**

Torruella, Juan R. **KGV2919.T67**
The Supreme Court and Puerto Rico: The Doctrine of Separate and Unequal. Trade Cloth. University of Puerto Rico Press. Rio Piedras, PR. 1985. 320p. ISBN:0-8477-3031-X, ISBN13: 978-0-8477-3031-5. Dewey:342.7295/029 347.295. LCCN:84-007572.
Audience: **u,f.**

Valenta, Jiri & Ellison, Herbert J. **F2056.8.G754 1986**
Grenada and Soviet-Cuban Policy: Internal Crisis and U. S. OECS Intervention. Cloth Text. Westview Press. Boulder, CO. 1986. 512p. Special Studies in National Security and Defense Policy ISBN:0-8133-0235-8, ISBN13: 978-0-8133-0235-5. Dewey:972.98/45. LCCN:85-022741.
Audience: **u,f.** *Choice, 1986.*

Villaronga, Gabriel **JL1056**
Toward a Discourse of Consent: Mass Mobilization and Colonial Politics in Puerto Rico, 1932-1948. Trade Cloth. Greenwood Publishing Group, Inc. Portsmouth, NH. 2004. 296p. Contributions in Latin American Studies, No. 23 ISBN:0-313-32423-9, ISBN13: 978-0-313-32423-9. Dewey:324.27295/06. LCCN:2003-070685.
Audience: **u,f.** *Choice, 2005.*

Whalen, Carmen Teresa **F158.9.P85W53 2001**
From Puerto Rico to Philadelphia: Puerto Rican Workers and Postwar Economies. Trade Cloth. Temple University Press. Philadelphia, PA. 2001. xiii, 309p. ISBN:1-56639-835-5, ISBN13: 978-1-56639-835-0. Dewey:305.868/72950748. LCCN:00-034349.
Audience: **u,f.**

Winn, Neil **D1058.W543 1996**
European Crisis Management in the 1980s. Trade Cloth. Ashgate Publishing, Ltd. Aldershot, 1996. 284p. ISBN:1-85521-878-X, ISBN13: 978-1-85521-878-9. Dewey:327/.094. LCCN:96-024593.
Audience: **u,f.**

South America: Individual Countries > Guayanas

Brana-Shute, Gary **HQ1090.7.S78**
On the Corner: Male Social Life in a Paramaribo Creole Neighborhood. Paper Text. Waveland Press, Inc. Prospect Heights, IL. 1989. 123p. ISBN:0-88133-468-5, ISBN13: 978-0-88133-468-5. Dewey:305.3/0988/35.
Audience: **u,f.**

Chin, H. E. **F2425.C48 1987**
Surinam: Politics, Economics and Society. Cloth Text. St. Martin's Press. Gordonville, VA. 1987. 220p. Marxist Regimes Ser. ISBN:0-86187-516-8, ISBN13: 978-0-86187-516-0. Dewey:988/.303. LCCN:87-022041.
Audience: **u,f.** *Choice, 1988.*

Cohen, Robert **F2431.J4C64 1991**
Jews in Another Environment: Surinam in the Second Half of the Eighteenth Century. Trade Cloth. Brill Academic Publishers, Inc. Boston, MA. 1991. xv, 350p. Jewish Studies, No. 1 ISBN:90-04-09373-7, ISBN13: 978-90-04-09373-7. Dewey:988.3/004924. LCCN:91-014402.
Audience: **u,f.** *Choice, 1992.*

Cohen, R. **F2431.J4 J48**
The Jewish Nation in Surinam: Historical Essays. R. Van Lier (Preface by). Trade Paper. Frances Schram. Scranton, PA. 1982. 120p. ISBN:0-8390-0296-3, ISBN13: 978-0-8390-0296-3. Dewey:988/.3004924.
Audience: **u,f.**

Davis, Natalie Zemon **CT3233.D38 1995**
Women on the Margins: Three Seventeenth-Century Lives. Trade Cloth. Harvard University Press. Cambridge, MA. 1995. 372p. ISBN:0-674-95520-X, ISBN13: 978-0-674-95520-2. Dewey:920.7/2/09032. LCCN:97-013765.
Audience: **g,l,u,f.**

De Groot, Silvia W. **F2431.N3**
Djuka Society and Social Change: History of an Attempt to Develop a Bush Negro Community in Surinam, 1917-1926. Cloth Text. Brill Academic Publishers, Inc. Boston, MA. 1969. ISBN:90-232-0108-6, ISBN13: 978-90-232-0108-3. Dewey:988.3.
Audience: **u,f.**

De Groot, Silvia W. **F2431.N3**
From Isolation Towards Integration: The Surinam Maroons and Their Colonial Rulers : Official Documents Relating to the Djukas (1845-1863). Nijhoff. 1977. ISBN:90-247-1962-3, ISBN13: 978-90-247-1962-4.
Audience: **u,f.**

Dew, Edward M. **F2425.D48**
The Difficult Flowering of Surinam: Ethnicity and Politics in a Plural Society. Trade Cloth. Martinus-Nijhoff Publishers (N E). 1978. x, 234p. ISBN:90-247-2057-5, ISBN13: 978-90-247-2057-6. Dewey:320.9/88/3. LCCN:78-012295.
Audience: **u,f.**

Goslinga, Cornelis C. **F2141 .G63**
A Short History of the Netherlands Antilles and Surinam. Paper Text. Springer. New York, NY. 1979. x, 198p. ISBN:90-247-2118-0, ISBN13: 978-90-247-2118-4. Dewey:972.98/6. LCCN:80-453973.
Audience: **u,f.**

Goslinga, Cornelis Cornelis Christiaan **F2141**
The Dutch in the Caribbean and in Surinam, 1791/5-1942. Van Gorcum. 1990. ISBN:90-232-2495-7, ISBN13: 978-90-232-2495-2.
Audience: **u,f.**

Koelewijn, Cees **F2420.1.T7**
Oral Literature of the Trio Indians of Surinam. Foris. 1987. ISBN:90-6765-223-7, ISBN13: 978-90-6765-223-0.
Audience: **u,f.**

Lier, Rudolf **HN330.S8**
A Social Analysis of the History of Surinam. van Yperen, M.J.L. (trans.). Martinus Nijhoof. 1971. ISBN:90-247-5138-1, ISBN13: 978-90-247-5138-9.
Audience: **u,f.**

Marcus, Jacob R. (Editor) **F2423**
Historical Essay on the Colony of Surinam, 1788. Chyet, Stanley F. (Editor). American Jewish Archives. 1974.
Audience: **u,f.**

Panday, R. M. N. (Radjnarain Mohanpersad Nannan) **HD1892**
Agriculture in Surinam, 1650-1950: An Panday, R. M. N. (Radjnarain Mohanpersad Nannan): An Inquiry into the Causes of its Decline. H. J. Paris. 1959.
Audience: **u,f.**

Rice, Anthony **QH15**
Voyages of Discovery: Three Centuries of Natural History Exploration. David Bellamy (Introduction by). Trade Paper. Scriptum Editions. London, 2000. 334p. ISBN:1-902686-06-3, ISBN13: 978-1-902686-06-6. Dewey:508/.09.
Audience: **u,f.**

Sharpe, Jenny **PR9210.O5S47 2003**
Ghosts of Slavery: A Literary Archaeology of Black Women's Lives. Trade Cloth. University of Minnesota Press. Minneapolis, MN. 2003. 208p. ISBN:0-8166-3722-9, ISBN13: 978-0-8166-3722-5. Dewey:810.9/353. LCCN:2002-013315.
Audience: **u,f.**

Shula Marks, and Peter Richardson, eds. **HD5855**
International Labour Migration: Historical Perspectives. Published for the Institute of Commonwealth Studies by M. Temple Smith. 1984. ISBN:0-85117-238-5, ISBN13: 978-0-85117-238-5.
Audience: **u,f.**

Sizer, Nigel & Rice, Richard **QL737.U55**
Backs to the Wall in Suriname: Forest Policy in a Country in Crisis. Trade Cloth. World Resources Institute. Washington, DC. 1995. 46p. ISBN:1-56973-034-2, ISBN13: 978-1-56973-034-8. Dewey:333.7/51/09883.
Audience: **u,f.**

Speckmann, Johan Dirk **F2431.E2**
Marriage and Kinship Among the Indians in Surinam. Van Gorcum. 1965.
Audience: **u,f.**

Stedman, John Gabriel **DA67.1.S7**
The Journal of John Gabriel Stedman, 1744-1797, Soldier and Author, Including an Authentic Account of His Expedition to Surinam in 1772. Mitre Press. 1962.
Audience: **u,f.**

Stedman, John Gabriel **F2410**
Narrative of a Five Years' Expedition Against the Revolted Negroes of Surinam in Guiana on the Wild Coast of South America from the Years 1772 to 1777: Elucidating the History of that Country & Describing its Productions, viz. Quadrupedes, Birds, Reptiles, Trees, Shrubs, Fruits, & Roots; With an Account of the Indians of Guiana and Negroes of Guinea University of Massachusetts Press. 1972.
Audience: u,f.

Stedman, John G. **F2410 .S8152 1992**
Stedman's Surinam: Life in an Eighteenth-Century Slave Society. An Abridged, Modernized Edition of Narrative of a Five Years Expedition against the Revolted Negroes of Surinam. Richard Price & Sally Price (Editors). Trade Paper. Johns Hopkins University Press. Baltimore, MD. 1992. 512p. ISBN:0-8018-4260-3, ISBN13: 978-0-8018-4260-3. Dewey:988.3/01. LCCN:91-027470.
Audience: **u,f.**

South America: Individual Countries > Bolivia

Abercrombie, Thomas A. **F2230.2.A9A24 1997**
Pathways of Memory and Power: Ethnography and History among an Andean People. Trade Cloth. University of Wisconsin Press. Chicago, IL. 1998. 632p. ISBN:0-299-15310-X, ISBN13: 978-0-299-15310-6. Dewey:984/.12. LCCN:96-038814.
Audience: **u,f.** *Choice, 1999.*

Albó, Xavier **F2230.2.A9 A4375 2002**
Pueblos Indios en la Política. La Paz: Plural Editores. 2002. ISBN:99905-64-31-0, ISBN13: 978-99905-64-31-0.
Audience: **u,f.**

Andrien, Kenneth J. **F3429.3.G6A67 2001**
Andean Worlds: Indigenous History, Culture, and Consciousness under Spanish Rule, 1532-1825. Trade Cloth. University of New Mexico Press. Albuquerque, NM. 2001. 290p. ISBN:0-8263-2359-6, ISBN13: 978-0-8263-2359-0. Dewey:980/.00498323. LCCN:2001-001170.
Audience: **u,f.** *Choice, 2002.*

Bakewell, Peter **HD8039.M732B53 1984**
Miners of the Red Mountain: Indian Labor in Potosi, 1545-1650. Trade Cloth. University of New Mexico Press. Albuquerque, NM. 1984. 229p. ISBN:0-8263-0769-8, ISBN13: 978-0-8263-0769-9. Dewey:331.7/6223423/098414. LCCN:84-007582.
Audience: **u,f.**

Bastien, Joseph W. **F3320.2.C3**
Mountain of the Condor: Metaphor and Ritual in an Andean Ayllu. Paper Text. Waveland Press, Inc. Prospect Heights, IL. 1985. 227p. ISBN:0-88133-143-0, ISBN13: 978-0-88133-143-1. Dewey:984.00498.
Audience: **u,f.**

Buechler, Hans C. **F2230.2.A9 B83 1980**
The Masked Media: Aymara Fiestas and Social Interaction in the Bolivian Highlands. Trade Cloth. Walter de Gruyter GmbH & Co. KG. Berlin, 1980. 400p. Approaches to Semiotics Ser., No. 59 ISBN:90-279-7777-1, ISBN13: 978-90-279-7777-9. Dewey:299/.78. LCCN:82-133352.
Audience: **u,f.**

Cole, Jeffrey A. **F3319.1.P6C65 1985**
The Potosi Mita, 1573-1700: Compulsory Indian Labor in the Andes. Trade Cloth. Stanford University Press. Palo Alto, CA. 1985. 224p. ISBN:0-8047-1256-5, ISBN13: 978-0-8047-1256-9. Dewey:331.6/99808414. LCCN:84-040331.
Audience: **u,f.** *Choice, 1986.*

Cook, Noble D. **F3429.3.P68 C66**
Demographic Collapse: Indian Peru, 1520-1620. Trade Cloth. Cambridge University Press. New York, NY. 1982. 320p. Cambridge Latin American Studies, No. 41 ISBN:0-521-23995-8, ISBN13: 978-0-521-23995-0. Dewey:304.6/0985. LCCN:81-009950.
Audience: **u,f.**

Fifer, J. Valerie **F3321.2**
Bolivia: Land, Location and Politics since 1825. Malcolm Deas, Clifford Smith & John Street (Editors). Trade Cloth. Cambridge University Press. New York, NY. 1972. 316p. Cambridge Latin American Studies, Vol. 13 ISBN:0-521-07829-6, ISBN13: 978-0-521-07829-0. Dewey:327.84. LCCN:72-139713.
Audience: **u,f.**

Gill, Lesley **HD6073.D52B514 1994**
Precarious Dependencies: Gender, Class and Domestic Service in Bolivia. Trade Cloth. Columbia University Press. New York, NY. 1994. 186p. ISBN:0-231-09646-1, ISBN13: 978-0-231-09646-1. Dewey:331.4/8164046/0984. LCCN:94-005948.
Audience: **u,f.**

Gill, Lesley **HC183.E4G54 2000**
Teetering on the Rim: Global Restructuring, Daily Life and the Armed Retreat of the Bolivian State. Trade Cloth. Columbia University Press. New York, NY. 2000. 288p. ISBN:0-231-11804-X, ISBN13: 978-0-231-11804-0. Dewey:338.984/12. LCCN:99-055581.
Audience: **u,f.**

Godoy, Ricardo A. **F3320.2.J84 G63**
Mining and Agriculture in Highland Bolivia: Ecology, History, and Commerce among the Jukumanis. Trade Cloth. University of Arizona Press. Tucson, AZ. 1990. 169p. Arizona Studies in Human Ecology ISBN:0-8165-1169-1, ISBN13: 978-0-8165-1169-3. Dewey:305.8/983. LCCN:90-035214.
Audience: **u,f.** *Choice, 1991.*

Goldstein, Daniel M. **HN280.C63G65 2004**
The Spectacular City: Violence and Performance in Urban Bolivia. Trade Cloth. Duke University Press. Durham, NC. 2004. 272p. Latin America Otherwise Ser. ISBN:0-8223-3360-0, ISBN13: 978-0-8223-3360-9. Dewey:306/.0984/23. LCCN:2004-001305.
Audience: **u,f.**

Grindle, Merilee S. & Domingo, Pilar **F3326.P76 2003**
Proclaiming Revolution: Bolivia in Comparative Perspective. Trade Paper. Harvard University Press. Cambridge, MA. 2003. 448p. David Rockefeller Center Series on Latin American Studies, Vol. 10 ISBN:0-674-01141-4, ISBN13: 978-0-674-01141-0. Dewey:984.05/2. LCCN:2003-005161.
Audience: **u,f.**

Healy, Kevin **HN280.Z9C644 2001**
Llamas, Weavings and Organic Chocolate: Multicultural Grassroots Development in the Andes and Amazon of Bolivia. Trade Paper. University of Notre Dame Press. Notre Dame, IN. 2000. xiv, 485p. From the Helen Kellogg Institute for International Studies Ser. ISBN:0-268-01326-8, ISBN13: 978-0-268-01326-4. Dewey:307.1/412/0984. LCCN:00-056801.
Audience: **u,f.**

Jackson, Robert H. **HN280.C6J33 1994**
Regional Markets and Agrarian Transformation in Bolivia: Cochabamba, 1539-1960. Trade Cloth. University of New Mexico Press. Albuquerque, NM. 1994. 284p. ISBN:0-8263-1533-X, ISBN13: 978-0-8263-1533-5. Dewey:306.3/49/098423. LCCN:94-018693.
Audience: **u,f.**

Klein, Herbert S. **HD489.L3.K57 1993**
Haciendas and Ayllus: Rural Society in the Bolivian Andes in the Eighteenth and Nineteenth Centuries. Trade Cloth. Stanford University Press. Palo Alto, CA. 1993. 225p. ISBN:0-8047-2057-6, ISBN13: 978-0-8047-2057-1. Dewey:305.5/0984/12. LCCN:92-019596.
Audience: **u,f.** *Choice, 1994.*

Lagos, Maria L. **F3319.1.T56L34 1994**
Autonomy and Power: The Dynamics of Class and Culture in Rural Bolivia. Book, Other. University of Pennsylvania Press. Philadelphia, PA. 1994. 224p. Ethnohistory Ser. ISBN:0-8122-1500-1, ISBN13: 978-0-8122-1500-7. Dewey:307.7/2/098423. LCCN:93-048809.
Audience: **u,f.** *Choice, 1994.*

Langer, Erick D. **HC183.C48L36 1989**
Economic Change and Rural Resistance in Southern Bolivia, 1880-1930. Trade Cloth. Stanford University Press. Palo Alto, CA. 1989. 288p. ISBN:0-8047-1491-6, ISBN13: 978-0-8047-1491-4. Dewey:303.4/0984/24. LCCN:88-031117.
Audience: **u,f.** *Choice, 1989.*

Larson, Brooke **HD1870.C62L37 1998**
Cochabamba, 1550-1900: Colonialism and Agrarian Transformation in Bolivia. Ed. 2. Trade Cloth. Duke University Press. Durham, NC. 1998. 456p. ISBN:0-8223-2061-4, ISBN13: 978-0-8223-2061-6. Dewey:305.5/633/098423. LCCN:97-029926.
Audience: **u,f.**

Larson, Brooke **F2230.1.G68L37 2003**
Trials of Nation Making: Liberalism, Race, and Ethnicity in the Andes, 1810-1910. Cloth Text. Cambridge University Press. New York, NY. 2004. 318p. ISBN:0-521-56171-X, ISBN13: 978-0-521-56171-6. Dewey:980/.004/98. LCCN:2003-041956.
Audience: **u,f.**

Larson, Brooke (Editor), et al. **F2230.1.C75E85 1995**
Ethnicity, Markets, and Migration in the Andes: At the Crossroads of History and Anthropology. Olivia Harris & Enrique Tandeter (Editors). Cloth Text. Duke University Press. Durham, NC. 1995. 432p. ISBN:0-8223-1633-1, ISBN13: 978-0-8223-1633-6. Dewey:330.98. LCCN:95-000864.
Audience: **u,f.** *Choice, 1996.*

Luykx, Aurolyn **F2230.2.A9L89 1999**
The Citizen Factory: Schooling and Cultural Production in Bolivia. Douglas E. Foley (Foreword by). Cloth Text. State University of New York Press. Albany, NY. 1999. 370p. SUNY Series in Power, Social Identity, and Education ISBN:0-7914-4037-0, ISBN13: 978-0-7914-4037-7. Dewey:305.23/0984. LCCN:98-013843.
Audience: **u,f.**

Murra, John V. **F3429**
Formaciones Económicas y Políticas en el Mundo Andino. Instituto de Estudios Peruanos. 1975. Historia Andina, No. 3
Audience: **u,f.**

Nash, June **HD8039.M72**
We Eat the Mines and the Mines Eat Us: Dependency and Exploitation in Bolivian Tin Mines. Cloth Text. Columbia University Press. New York, NY. 1993. 384p. ISBN:0-231-08050-6, ISBN13: 978-0-231-08050-7. Dewey:331.7/6223453/0984.
Audience: **g,l,u,f.** B

Platt, Tristan **F3319.1.P6**
Estado Boliviano y Ayllu Andino. Tierra y Tributo en el Norte de Potosí. Instituto de Estudios Peruanos. 1982. Historia Andina, No. 9
Audience: **u,f.**

Rasnake, Roger N. **F2230.2.K4R37 1988**
Domination and Cultural Resistance: Authority and Power among Andean People. Cloth Text. Duke University Press. Durham, NC. 1988. xi, 323p. ISBN:0-8223-0809-6, ISBN13: 978-0-8223-0809-6. Dewey:984/.14. LCCN:87-035834.
Audience: **u,f.** *Choice, 1989.*

Rivera Cusicanqui, Silvia **F3320.1.G6 R5713 1987**
Oppressed but Not Defeated. Peasant Struggles among the Aymara and Qechwa in Bolivia. Antezana, Luis H. (prologue). United Nations Research Institute for Social Development. 1987. Report, No. 85.1
Audience: **u,f.**

Salmón, Josefa **F3320.S24 1997**
El Espejo Indígena. El Discurso Indigenista en Bolivia, 1900-1956. La Paz, Bolivia: Plural Editores. 1997. Colecciòn Academia; No. 5 ISBN:84-89891-01-X, ISBN13: 978-84-89891-01-2.
Audience: **u,f.**

Sanjines C, Javier **F3310.S26 2004**
Mestizaje Upside-Down: Aesthetic Politics in Modern Bolivia. Trade Cloth. University of Pittsburgh Press. Pittsburgh, PA. 2004. 240p. ISBN:0-8229-4227-5, ISBN13: 978-0-8229-4227-6. Dewey:320.984/09/0511. LCCN:2003-021374.
Audience: **u,f.** *Choice, 2004.*

Serulnikov, Sergio **F2230.2.A9S46 2003**
Subverting Colonial Authority: Challenges to Spanish Rule in Eighteenth-Century Southern Andes. Trade Cloth. Duke University Press. Durham, NC. 2003. 320p. ISBN:0-8223-3110-1, ISBN13: 978-0-8223-3110-0. Dewey:984/.1403. LCCN:2002-156641.
Audience: **u,f.**

Stephenson, Marcia **F3320.1.W65S74 1999**
Gender and Modernity in Andean Bolivia. Trade Paper. University of Texas Press. Austin, TX. 1999. 271p. ISBN:0-292-77743-4, ISBN13: 978-0-292-77743-9. Dewey:305.48/898084. LCCN:98-042658.
Audience: **u,f.** *Choice, 1999.*

Stern, Steve J. (Editor) **F2230.1.G68R47 1987**
Resistance, Rebellion, and Consciousness in the Andean Peasant World, 18th to 20th Centuries. Cloth Text. University of Wisconsin Press. Chicago, IL. 1987. 416p. ISBN:0-299-11350-7, ISBN13: 978-0-299-11350-6. Dewey:980/.004/98. LCCN:87-040152.
Audience: **u,f.** *Choice, 1988.*

Tandeter, Enrique **HD9536.B63.P68513**
Coercion and Market: Silver Mining in Colonial Potosi, 1692-1826. Trade Cloth. University of New Mexico Press. Albuquerque, NM. 1993. 332p. ISBN:0-8263-1430-9, ISBN13: 978-0-8263-1430-7. Dewey:338.2/7421/098414. LCCN:93-014687.
Audience: **u,f.** *Choice, 1994.*

Thomson, Sinclair **F2230.2.A9**
Colonial Crisis, Community, and Andean Self-Rule: Aymara Politics in the Age of Insurgency: Eighteenth Century La Paz. University of Wisconsin, Madison. 2002.
Audience: **u,f.**

Wachtel, Nathan **F2520.1.C6W3213 1994**
Gods and Vampires: Return to Chipaya. Carol Volk (Translator). Trade Cloth. University of Chicago Press. Chicago, IL. 1994. 164p. ISBN:0-226-86763-3, ISBN13: 978-0-226-86763-2. Dewey:984/.00498. LCCN:93-035865.
Audience: **u,f.**

Zulawski, Ann **HD8275.Z84 1995**
They Eat from Their Labor: Work and Social Change in Colonial Bolivia. Cloth Text. University of Pittsburgh Press. Pittsburgh, PA. 1994. 304p. Latin American Ser. ISBN:0-8229-1183-3, ISBN13: 978-0-8229-1183-8. Dewey:306.3/6/0984. LCCN:94-033040.
Audience: **u,f.**

South America: Individual Countries > Peru > Colonial Peru

Andrien, Kenneth J. **F3429.3.G6A67 2001**
Andean Worlds: Indigenous History, Culture, and Consciousness under Spanish Rule, 1532-1825. Trade Cloth. University of New Mexico Press. Albuquerque, NM. 2001. 290p. ISBN:0-8263-2359-6, ISBN13: 978-0-8263-2359-0. Dewey:980/.00498323. LCCN:2001-001170.
Audience: **u,f.** *Choice, 2002.*

Andrien, Kenneth J. & Adorno, Rolena (Editors) **F3429.3.G6T73 1991**
Transatlantic Encounters: Europeans and Andeans in the Sixteenth Century. Trade Cloth. University of California Press. Berkeley, CA. 1992. 353p. ISBN:0-520-07228-6, ISBN13: 978-0-520-07228-2. Dewey:980/.013. LCCN:91-012232.
Audience: **u,f.** *Choice, 1992.*

Bakewell, Peter (Editor) **TN433.A1M55 1997**
Mines of Silver and Gold in the Americas. Trade Cloth. Ashgate Publishing, Ltd. Aldershot, 1997. 420p. An Expanding World Ser., Vol. 19 ISBN:0-86078-513-0, ISBN13: 978-0-86078-513-2. Dewey:338.2/741/098. LCCN:96-000237.
Audience: **u,f.**

Brown, Kendall W. **HF3470.A73B76 1985**
Bourbons and Brandy: Imperial Reform in Eighteenth-Century Arequipa. Trade Cloth. University of New Mexico Press. Albuquerque, NM. 1986. 331p. ISBN:0-8263-0829-5, ISBN13: 978-0-8263-0829-0. Dewey:330.985/3203. LCCN:85-014104.
Audience: **u,f.**

Burns, Kathryn **F3611.C9B87 1999**
Colonial Habits: Convents and the Spiritual Economy of Cuzco, Peru. Trade Cloth. Duke University Press. Durham, NC. 1999. xi, 307p. ISBN:0-8223-2259-5, ISBN13: 978-0-8223-2259-7. Dewey:985/.37. LCCN:98-008099.
Audience: **u,f.** *Choice, 1999.*

Cahill, David **F3444 .C136 2002**
From Rebellion to Independence in the Andes: Soundings from Southern Peru, 1750-1830. Trade Paper. Transaction Publishers. Somerset, NJ. 2002. 290p. ISBN:90-5260-054-6, ISBN13: 978-90-5260-054-3. Dewey:980. LCCN:2003-488774.
Audience: **u,f.**

Chambers, Sarah **JS2678.A72C48 1999**
From Subjects to Citizens: Honor, Culture and Politics in Arequipa, Peru, 1780-1854. Trade Cloth. Pennsylvania State University Press. University Park, PA. 1999. 296p. ISBN:0-271-01901-8, ISBN13: 978-0-271-01901-7. Dewey:306.2/0985/3209034. LCCN:98-037144.
Audience: **u,f.** *Choice, 2000.*

Cornblit, Oscar **F3351.O7 C67 1995**
Power and Violence in the Colonial City: Oruro from the Mining Renaissance to the Rebellion of Tupac Amaru (1740-1782). Elizabeth Ladd Glick (Translator), Alan Knight (Contribution by). Trade Cloth. Cambridge University Press. New York, NY. 1995. 244p. Cambridge Latin American Studies, No. 76 ISBN:0-521-44148-X, ISBN13: 978-0-521-44148-3. Dewey:984.1303. LCCN:95-228356.
Audience: **u,f.** *Choice, 1996.*

De Cieza De Le On, Pedro, et al. **F3442.C66313 1998**
The Discovery and Conquest of Peru: Chronicles of the New World Encounter. Alexandra P. Cook & David N. Cook (Authors). Trade Cloth. Duke University Press. Durham, NC. 1998. 416p. Latin America in Translation Ser. ISBN:0-8223-2127-0, ISBN13: 978-0-8223-2127-9. Dewey:985/.01. LCCN:98-020158.
Audience: **u,f.**

Dean, Carolyn (Contribution by) **GT4995.C6D43 1999**
Inka Bodies and the Body of Christ: Corpus Christi in Colonial Cusco, Peru. Trade Cloth. Duke University Press. Durham, NC. 1999. 264p. ISBN:0-8223-2332-X, ISBN13: 978-0-8223-2332-7. Dewey:394.266. LCCN:98-056544.
Audience: **u,f.** *Choice, 2000.*

Fisher, John **F3444.F53 2003**
Bourbon Peru 1750-1824. Trade Paper. Liverpool University Press. Liverpool, 2003. 256p. Liverpool Latin American Ser., Vol. 4 ISBN:0-85323-908-8, ISBN13: 978-0-85323-908-6. Dewey:985.033. LCCN:2004-401259.
Audience: **u,f.** *Choice, 2004.*

Griffiths, Nicholas **F3429.3.R3G74 1996**
The Cross and the Serpent: Religious Repression and Resurgence in Colonial Peru. Trade Cloth. University of Oklahoma Press. Norman, OK. 1996. 362p. ISBN:0-8061-2800-3, ISBN13: 978-0-8061-2800-9. Dewey:299/.895. LCCN:95-024751.
Audience: **u,f.** *Choice, 1996.*

Hyland, Sabine **BX4705.V2747H95 2004**
The Jesuit and the Incas: The Extraordinary Life of Padre Blas Valera, S. J. Trade Paper. University of Michigan Press. Chicago, IL. 2004. 272p. History, Languages, and Cultures of the Spanish and Portuguese Worlds Ser. ISBN:0-472-03041-8, ISBN13: 978-0-472-03041-5. Dewey:271.5/302.
Audience: **u,f.** *Choice, 2004.*

Jacobsen, Nils **HC135.E26 1986**
The Economies of Mexico and Peru During the Late Colonial Period, 1760-1810. Puhle, Jurgen, eds.. Colloquium Verlag Berlin. 1986. ISBN:3-7678-0666-5, ISBN13: 978-3-7678-0666-5.
Audience: **u,f.**

Lockhart, James **F3442**
Spanish Peru, 1532-1560: A Social History. Ed. 2. Trade Paper. University of Wisconsin Press. Chicago, IL. 1994. 342p. ISBN:0-299-14164-0, ISBN13: 978-0-299-14164-6. Dewey:985.02. LCCN:93-023338.
Audience: **u,f.**

Mayer, Enrique **F3429.3.E2M38 2001**
The Articulated Peasant: Household Economies in the Andes. Trade Paper. Westview Press. Boulder, CO. 2001. 408p. ISBN:0-8133-3716-X, ISBN13: 978-0-8133-3716-6. Dewey:330.985/0088/63. LCCN:2001-024874.
Audience: **u,f.** *Choice, 2002.*

Mills, Kenneth **F2230.2.K4M56 1997**
Idolatry and Its Enemies: Colonial Andean Religion and Extirpation, 1640-1750. Trade Cloth. Princeton University Press. Princeton, NJ. 1997. 354p. ISBN:0-691-02979-2, ISBN13: 978-0-691-02979-5. Dewey:200/.985/09032. LCCN:96-028847.
Audience: **u,f.** *Choice, 1997.*

Morgan, Ronald J. **BX4659.L3M67 2002**
Spanish American Saints and the Rhetoric of Identity, 1600-1810. Trade Cloth. University of Arizona Press. Tucson, AZ. 2002. 250p. ISBN:0-8165-2140-9, ISBN13: 978-0-8165-2140-1. Dewey:282/.092/28. LCCN:2001-005284.
Audience: **u,f.**

Premo, Bianca **HQ792.P4P74 2005**
Children of the Father King: Youth, Authority, and Legal Minority in Colonial Lima. Trade Cloth. University of North Carolina Press. Chapel Hill, NC. 2005. 368p. ISBN:0-8078-2954-4, ISBN13: 978-0-8078-2954-7. Dewey:305.23/0985/09032. LCCN:2005-000607.
Audience: **u,f.**

Ramirez, Susan E. **HD554.R35 1985**
Provincial Patriarchs: Land Tenure and the Economics of Power in Colonial Peru. Trade Cloth. University of New Mexico Press. Albuquerque, NM. 1986. 481p. ISBN:0-8263-0818-X, ISBN13: 978-0-8263-0818-4. Dewey:333.3/0985. LCCN:85-013934.
Audience: **u,f.** *Choice, 1986.*

Ramirez, Susan Elizabeth **F3442**
The World Upside Down: Cross-Cultural Contact and Conflict in Sixteenth-Century Peru. Trade Paper. Stanford University Press. Palo Alto, CA. 1996. 250p. ISBN:0-8047-3520-4, ISBN13: 978-0-8047-3520-9. Dewey:985/.02.
Audience: **u,f.**

Robins, Nicholas A. **F3444.R59 2002**
Genocide and Millennialism in Upper Peru: The Great Rebellion of 1780-1782. Praeger. 2002. ISBN:0-275-97569-X, ISBN13: 978-0-275-97569-2.
Audience: **u,f.**

Rostworowski de Diez Canseco, Maria **F3429 .R68513 1999**
History of the Inca Realm. Harry B. Iceland (Translator). Cloth Text. Cambridge University Press. New York, NY. 1998. 269p. ISBN:0-521-44266-4, ISBN13: 978-0-521-44266-4. Dewey:980/.00498323. LCCN:98-015504.
Audience: **u,f.**

Silverblatt, Irene Marsha **BX1740.P5S55 2004**
Modern Inquisitions: Peru and the Colonial Origins of the Civilized World. Trade Cloth. Duke University Press. Durham, NC. 2004. 304p. Latin America Otherwise Ser. ISBN:0-8223-3406-2, ISBN13: 978-0-8223-3406-4. Dewey:272/.2/0985. LCCN:2004-011219.
Audience: **u,f.** *Choice, 2005.*

Silverblatt, Irene Marsha **F3429.3.S6S55 1987**
Moon, Sun and Witches: Gender Ideologies and Class in Inca and Colonial Peru. Trade Paper. Princeton University Press. Princeton, NJ. 1987. 302p. ISBN:0-691-02258-5, ISBN13: 978-0-691-02258-1. Dewey:985/.01/088042. LCCN:86-022514.
Audience: **u,f.** *Choice, 1987.*

Stavig, Ward **F3429.1.Q86S73 1999**
The World of Tupac Amaru: Conflict, Community, and Idenity in Colonial Peru. Paper Text. University of Nebraska Press. Lincoln, NE. 1999. 356p. ISBN:0-8032-9255-4, ISBN13: 978-0-8032-9255-0. Dewey:985/.37. LCCN:98-035769.
Audience: **u,f.**

Thomson, Sinclair **F2230.2.K4T54 2002**
We Alone Will Rule: Native Andean Politics in the Age of Insurgency. Trade Cloth. University of Wisconsin Press. Chicago, IL. 2003. 416p. Living in Latin America Ser. ISBN:0-299-17790-4, ISBN13: 978-0-299-17790-4. Dewey:980/.013. LCCN:2002-004975.
Audience: **u,f.** *Choice, 2003.*

Varon Gabar, Rafael **F3442.P776V37 1997**
Francisco Pizarro and His Brothers: The Illusion of Power in Sixteenth-Century Peru. Javier Flores Espinosa (Translator). Trade Cloth. University of Oklahoma Press. Norman, OK. 1997. 368p. ISBN:0-8061-2833-X, ISBN13: 978-0-8061-2833-7. Dewey:985/.02/0922. LCCN:96-041861.
Audience: **u,f.** *Choice, 1997.*

Walker, Charles **F3451.C9W35 1999**
Smoldering Ashes: Cuzco and the Creation of Republican Peru, 1780-1840. Trade Cloth. Duke University Press. Durham, NC. 1999. xiii, 330p. ISBN:0-8223-2261-7, ISBN13: 978-0-8223-2261-0. Dewey:985/.3704. LCCN:98-030624.
Audience: **u,f.** *Choice, 2000.*

South America: Individual Countries > Peru > 19th Century Peru

Aguirre, Carlos **HV9625.L5A48 2005**
The Criminals of Lima and Their Worlds: The Prison Experience, 1850-1935. Trade Cloth. Duke University Press. Durham, NC. 2005. 304p. ISBN:0-8223-3457-7, ISBN13: 978-0-8223-3457-6. Dewey:365/.6/09852509034. LCCN:2004-019864.
Audience: **u,f.**

Billingsley, Edward Baxter **F2235.B676**
In Defense of Neutral Rights; the United States Navy and the Wars of Independence in Chile and Peru. University of North Carolina Press. 1967.
Audience: **u,f.**

Blanchard, Peter **HT1147.B58 1992**
Slavery and Abolition in Early Republican Peru. Book, Other. Rowman & Littlefield Publishers, Inc. Lanham, MD. 1992. 248p. Latin American Silhouettes Ser. ISBN:0-8420-2400-X, ISBN13: 978-0-8420-2400-6. Dewey:306.3/62/0985. LCCN:92-004999.
Audience: **u,f.** *Choice, 1993.*

Chambers, Sarah **JS2678.A72C48 1999**
From Subjects to Citizens: Honor, Culture and Politics in Arequipa, Peru, 1780-1854. Trade Cloth. Pennsylvania State University Press. University Park, PA. 1999. 296p. ISBN:0-271-01901-8, ISBN13: 978-0-271-01901-7. Dewey:306.2/0985/3209034. LCCN:98-037144.
Audience: **u,f.** *Choice, 2000.*

Deere, Carmen D. **HD1531.P4D44 1990**
Household and Class Relations: The Peasant Economy of the Northern Peruvian Highlands, 1900-1980. Trade Cloth. University of California Press. Berkeley, CA. 1990. 384p. ISBN:0-520-06675-8, ISBN13: 978-0-520-06675-5. Dewey:306.3/49/098515. LCCN:89-036110.
Audience: **u,f.**

Deustua, Jose R. **HD9537.P42D48 2000**
The Bewitchment of Silver: The Social Economy of Mining in Nineteenth-Century Peru. Trade Paper. Ohio University Press. Athens, OH. 2000. 306p. Monographs in International Studies, Vol. 31 ISBN:0-89680-209-4, ISBN13: 978-0-89680-209-4. Dewey:338.2/7421/098509034. LCCN:99-034816.
Audience: **u,f.**

Garcia-Bryce, Inigo **HD8350.L562G37 2004**
Crafting the Republic: Lima's Artisans and Nation-Building in Peru, 1221-1879. Trade Cloth. University of New Mexico Press. Albuquerque, NM. 2004. 220p. ISBN:0-8263-3392-3, ISBN13: 978-0-8263-3392-6. Dewey:331.7/94. LCCN:2004-015736.
Audience: **u,f.** *Choice, 2005.*

Gootenberg, Paul **HF1525.G66 1989**
Between Silver and Guano: Commercial Policy and the State in Postindependence Peru. Trade Cloth. Princeton University Press. Princeton, NJ. 1989. 244p. ISBN:0-691-07810-6, ISBN13: 978-0-691-07810-6. Dewey:380.1/3/0985. LCCN:88-035722.
Audience: **u,f.** *Choice, 1990.*

Hunefeldt, Christine **HQ606.15.L5H86 2000**
Liberalism in the Bedroom: Quarreling Spouses in Nineteenth-Century Lima. Trade Cloth. Pennsylvania State University Press. University Park, PA. 2000. 408p. ISBN:0-271-01935-2, ISBN13: 978-0-271-01935-2. Dewey:306.872/0985/2509034. LCCN:98-055336.
Audience: **u,f.** *Choice, 2000.*

Hunefeldt, Christine **HT1148.L56H87 1994**
Paying the Price of Freedom: Family and Labor among Lima's Slaves, 1800-1854. Alexandra M. Stern (Translator). Trade Cloth. University of California Press. Berkeley, CA. 1995. 252p. ISBN:0-520-08235-4, ISBN13: 978-0-520-08235-9. Dewey:306.3/62/098525. LCCN:94-004507.
Audience: **u,f.** *Choice, 1995.*

Jacobsen, Nils **HC228.A93.J3 1993**
Mirages of Transition: The Peruvian Altiplano, 1780-1930. Trade Cloth. University of California Press. Berkeley, CA. 1993. 500p. ISBN:0-520-07938-8, ISBN13: 978-0-520-07938-0. Dewey:338.98536. LCCN:92-033342.
Audience: **u,f.** *Choice, 1994.*

Jacobsen, Nils & Aljovín de Losada, Cristóbal **JL1866.P637 2005**
Political Cultures in the Andes, 1750-1950. Trade Cloth. Duke University Press. Durham, NC. 2005. 376p. Latin America Otherwise Ser. ISBN:0-8223-3503-4, ISBN13: 978-0-8223-3503-0. Dewey:306.20980903. LCCN:2004-025959.
Audience: **u,f.**

Kristal, Efrain **PQ8401.K75 1987**
The Andes Viewed from the City: Literary and Political Discourse on the Indian in Peru, 1848-1930. Cloth Text. Peter Lang Publishing, Inc. New York, NY. 1987. 249p. American University Studies, Ser. XIX, Vol. 6:General Literature ISBN:0-8204-0437-3, ISBN13: 978-0-8204-0437-0. Dewey:863. LCCN:87-017640.
Audience: **u,f.**

Larson, Brooke **F2230.1.G68L37 2003**
Trials of Nation Making: Liberalism, Race, and Ethnicity in the Andes, 1810-1910. Cloth Text. Cambridge University Press. New York, NY. 2004. 318p. ISBN:0-521-56171-X, ISBN13: 978-0-521-56171-6. Dewey:980/.004/98. LCCN:2003-041956.
Audience: **u,f.**

Mallon, Florencia E. **F1231.5.M34 1995**
Peasant and Nation: The Making of Postcolonial Mexico and Peru. Trade Cloth. University of California Press. Berkeley, CA. 1995. 496p. ISBN:0-520-08504-3, ISBN13: 978-0-520-08504-6. Dewey:972/.04. LCCN:93-034677.
Audience: **u,f.** *Choice, 1995.*

Matto de Turner, Clorinda **PQ8497.M3A913 1996**
Birds without a Nest: A Novel. J. G. H. (Translator), Naomi Lindstrom (Contribution by). Trade Paper. University of Texas Press. Austin, TX. 1996. 205p. Texas Pan American Ser. ISBN:0-292-75195-8, ISBN13: 978-0-292-75195-8. Dewey:863. LCCN:95-044768.
Audience: **g,l,u,f.** *Choice, 1997.*

Monaghan, Jay **F865**
Chile, Peru and the California Gold Rush of Eighteen Forty-Nine. Trade Cloth. University of California Press. Berkeley, CA. 1973. ISBN:0-520-02265-3, ISBN13: 978-0-520-02265-2. Dewey:979.4/004/6883. LCCN:72-078946.
Audience: **g,l,u.**

Morner, Magnus **F2212**
The Andean Past: Land Societies, and Conflicts. Cloth Text. Columbia University Press. New York, NY. 1985. xiv, 300p. ISBN:0-231-04726-6, ISBN13: 978-0-231-04726-5. Dewey:306/.098. LCCN:83-023136.
Audience: **u,f.**

Mucke, Ulrich **JL3498.C5M8313 2004**
Political Culture in Nineteenth-Century Peru: The Rise of the Partido Civil. Trade Cloth. University of Pittsburgh Press. Pittsburgh, PA. 2004. 320p. Pitt Latin American Ser. ISBN:0-8229-4229-1, ISBN13: 978-0-8229-4229-0. Dewey:324.285/02. LCCN:2004-001668.
Audience: **u,f.** *Choice, 2005.*

Méndez G, Cecilia **F3451.H79M46 2005**
The Plebeian Republic: The Huanta Rebellion and the Making of the Peruvian State, 1820-1850. Trade Cloth. Duke University Press. Durham, NC. 2005. 368p. ISBN:0-8223-3430-5, ISBN13: 978-0-8223-3430-9. Dewey:985/.05. LCCN:2004-022944.
Audience: **u,f.** *Choice, 2006.*

Nugent, David **JC311.N838 1997**
Modernity at the Edge of Empire: State, Individual and Nation in the Northern Peruvian Andes, 1885-1935. Trade Cloth. Stanford University Press. Palo Alto, CA. 1997. 462p. ISBN:0-8047-2782-1, ISBN13: 978-0-8047-2782-2. Dewey:320.985/46. LCCN:96-049742.
Audience: **u,f.** *Choice, 1998.*

Thurner, Mark **F3429.1.A45T58 1997**
From Two Republics to One Divided: Contradictions of Postcolonial Nationmaking in Andean Peru. Library Binding. Duke University Press. Durham, NC. 1997. 224p. Latin America Otherwise Ser. ISBN:0-8223-1805-9, ISBN13: 978-0-8223-1805-7. Dewey:985/.21. LCCN:96-007813.
Audience: **u,f.** *Choice, 1997.*

Thurner, Mark & Guerrero, Andrés (Editors) **F1413.A43 2003**
After Spanish Rule: Postcolonial Predicaments of the Americas. Trade Cloth. Duke University Press. Durham, NC. 2003. 352p. Latin America Otherwise Ser. ISBN:0-8223-3157-8, ISBN13: 978-0-8223-3157-5. Dewey:980/.03. LCCN:2003-009339.
Audience: **u,f.**

Tristan, Flora **F3423**
Peregrinations of a Pariah. Jean Hawkes (Editor, Translator). Trade Paper. Beacon Press. Boston, MA. 1987. 320p. The Virago-Beacon Traveler Ser. ISBN:0-8070-7027-0, ISBN13: 978-0-8070-7027-7. Dewey:918.5/045. LCCN:86-047873.
Audience: **u,f.**

Walker, Charles **F3451.C9W35 1999**
Smoldering Ashes: Cuzco and the Creation of Republican Peru, 1780-1840. Trade Cloth. Duke University Press. Durham, NC. 1999. xiii, 330p. ISBN:0-8223-2261-7, ISBN13: 978-0-8223-2261-0. Dewey:985/.3704. LCCN:98-030624.
Audience: **u,f.** *Choice, 2000.*

South America: Individual Countries > Peru > 20th Century Peru

Alexander, Robert J. (Editor) **F3448.H2912**
Aprismo: The Ideas and Doctrines of Victor Raul Haya de la Torre. Trade Cloth. Kent State University Press. Kent, OH. 1973. 381p. ISBN:0-87338-125-4, ISBN13: 978-0-87338-125-3. Dewey:320.5/092/4. LCCN:78-181083.
Audience: **u,f.** B

Americas Watch **JC599.P4 P485 1992**
Peru Under Fire: Human Rights Since the Return to Democracy. Yale University Press. 1992. ISBN:0-300-05237-5, ISBN13: 978-0-300-05237-4.
Audience: **u,f.**

Arguedas, Jose Maria **PQ6140.N3**
Deep Rivers. Frances Horning Barraclough (Translator). Paper Text. Waveland Press, Inc. Prospect Heights, IL. 2002. 248p. ISBN:1-57766-244-X, ISBN13: 978-1-57766-244-0. Dewey:863/.6.
Audience: **u,f.** B

Arguedas, José Maria (Editor) **PQ8497.A65**
Yawar Fiesta. Frances Horning Barraclough (Translator). Paper Text. Waveland Press, Inc. Prospect Heights, IL. 2002. 200p. ISBN:1-57766-245-8, ISBN13: 978-1-57766-245-7. Dewey:863.
Audience: **u,f.**

Babb, Florence E. **HD6072.6.P4B23 1989**
Between Field and Cooking Pot: The Political Economy of Marketwomen in Peru. Cloth Text. University of Texas Press. Austin, TX. 1989. 259p. Sourcebooks in Anthropology, No. 15 ISBN:0-292-70775-4, ISBN13: 978-0-292-70775-7. Dewey:331.4/8138118/0985. LCCN:89-004800.
Audience: **u,f.** *Choice, 1990.*

Blanchard, Peter **HD8344**
Origins of the Peruvian Labor Movement, 1883-1919. Trade Cloth. University of Pittsburgh Press. Pittsburgh, PA. 1982. xx, 240p. Latin American Ser. ISBN:0-8229-3455-8, ISBN13: 978-0-8229-3455-4. Dewey:335/.1/0985. LCCN:81-023102.
Audience: **u,f.**

Blanco, Hugo & Camejo, Peter **HD556 .B5513**
Land or Death: The Peasant Struggle in Peru. Trade Paper. Pathfinder Press. New York, NY. 1972. 235p. ISBN:0-87348-266-2, ISBN13: 978-0-87348-266-0. Dewey:333.3/2/0985. LCCN:73-186689.
Audience: **u,f.** B

Bolin, Inge **F2230.2.K4B65 1998**
Rituals of Respect: The Secret of Survival in the High Peruvian Andes. Trade Cloth. University of Texas Press. Austin, TX. 1998. 311p. ISBN:0-292-70866-1, ISBN13: 978-0-292-70866-2. Dewey:813/.54. LCCN:98-008930.
Audience: **u,f.** *Choice, 1999.*

Bourricaud, Francois **F3448.B6813**
Power and Society in Contemporary Peru. Praeger Publishers. 1970.
Audience: **u,f.**

Brown, Michael F. & Fernández, Eduardo **F3430.1.H8**
War of Shadows: The Struggle for Utopia in the Peruvian Amazon. Trade Paper. University of California Press. Berkeley, CA. 1993. 298p. ISBN:0-520-07448-3, ISBN13: 978-0-520-07448-4. Dewey:985/.24. LCCN:90-026076.
Audience: **u,f.** *Choice, 1992.*

Cadena, Marisol de (Contribution by) **F3429.3.M63C33 2000**
Indigenous Mestizos: The Politics of Race and Culture in Cuzco, 1919-1991. Cloth Text. Duke University Press. Durham, NC. 2000. xiii, 408p. Latin America Otherwise Ser. ISBN:0-8223-2385-0, ISBN13: 978-0-8223-2385-3. Dewey:306/.0985/37. LCCN:99-037470.
Audience: **u,f.** *Choice, 2000.*

Cameron, Maxwell A. **JL3481.C36 1994**
Democracy and Authoritarianism in Peru: Political Coalitions and Social Change. Cloth over Boards. Palgrave Macmillan. New York, NY. 1994. 240p. ISBN:0-312-12153-9, ISBN13: 978-0-312-12153-2. Dewey:320.985. LCCN:94-009119.
Audience: **u,f.** *Choice, 1995.*

Cameron, Maxwell A. & Mauceri, Philip (Editors) **JL3481.P47 1997**
The Peruvian Labyrinth. Trade Paper. Pennsylvania State University Press. University Park, PA. 1997. 288p. ISBN:0-271-01661-2, ISBN13: 978-0-271-01661-0. Dewey:320.985/09/045. LCCN:96-042209.
Audience: **u,f.** *Choice, 1998.*

Chaplin, David (Editor) **HN343.5 .P44**
Peruvian Nationalism: A Corporatist Revolution. Trade Cloth. Transaction Publishers. Somerset, NJ. 1976. 600p. The Third World Ser. ISBN:0-87855-077-1, ISBN13: 978-0-87855-077-7. Dewey:301.5/92/0985. LCCN:73-085099.
Audience: **u,f.**

Chavarria, Jesus **HX222.M38 C45**
Jose Carlos Mariategui and the Rise of Modern Peru, 1890-1930. Trade Cloth. University of New Mexico Press. Albuquerque, NM. 1979. ISBN:0-8263-0507-5, ISBN13: 978-0-8263-0507-7. Dewey:335.43/092/4. LCCN:78-021426.
Audience: **u,f.**

Clayton, Lawrence A. **HD9505.P4C43 1986**
Grace - W. R. Grace and Co.: The Formative Years: 1850-1930. Trade Cloth. Jameson Books, Inc. Ottawa, IL. 1986. 416p. ISBN:0-915463-25-3, ISBN13: 978-0-915463-25-1. Dewey:338.8/8885. LCCN:85-014856.
Audience: **u,f.** *Choice, 1987.*

Clayton, Lawrene A. **E193.8.P4C58 1999**
Peru and the United States: The Condor and the Eagle. Trade Paper. University of Georgia Press. Athens, GA. 1999. 376p. The United States and the Americas Ser. ISBN:0-8203-2025-0, ISBN13: 978-0-8203-2025-0. Dewey:327.73085. LCCN:98-033595.
Audience: **u,f.**

Collier, David **HB1951**
Squatters and Oligarchs: Authoritarian Rule and Policy Change in Peru. Trade Cloth. Johns Hopkins University Press. Baltimore, MD. 1993. 200p. ISBN:0-8018-1748-X, ISBN13: 978-0-8018-1748-9. Dewey:301.36/1. LCCN:75-034112.
Audience: **u,f.**

Collins, Jane L. **F2230.2.A9C65 1988**
Unseasonal Migrations: The Effects of Rural Labor Scarcity in Peru. Trade Cloth. Princeton University Press. Princeton, NJ. 1988. 200p. ISBN:0-691-07744-4, ISBN13: 978-0-691-07744-4. Dewey:331.12/798536. LCCN:88-004084.
Audience: **u,f.** *Choice, 1988.*

Crabtree, John **F3448.2.C73 1992**
Peru under Garcia: An Opportunity Lost. Trade Cloth. University of Pittsburgh Press. Pittsburgh, PA. 1992. 240p. Latin American Ser. ISBN:0-8229-1168-X, ISBN13: 978-0-8229-1168-5. Dewey:320.985. LCCN:91-050755.
Audience: **u,f.** *Choice, 1993.*

Davies, Thomas M. Jr. **F3429.3.G6 D38**
Indian Integration in Peru: A Half Century of Experience, 1900-1948. Trade Cloth. University of Nebraska Press. Lincoln, NE. 1974. xii, 204p. ISBN:0-8032-0834-0, ISBN13: 978-0-8032-0834-6. Dewey:980.5. LCCN:73-080965.
Audience: **u,f.**

de Soto, Hernando **HD2346.P4S6713 2002**
The Other Path: The Invisible Revolution in the Third World. Trade Paper. Basic Books. New York, NY. 2002. 352p. ISBN:0-465-01610-3, ISBN13: 978-0-465-01610-5. Dewey:381.
Audience: **u,f.**

Dietz, Henry A. **HN350.L5D54 1998**
Urban Poverty, Political Participation, and the State: Lima, 1970-1990. Trade Paper. University of Pittsburgh Press. Pittsburgh, PA. 1998. 396p. Pitt Latin American Ser. ISBN:0-8229-5667-5, ISBN13: 978-0-8229-5667-9. Dewey:306.2/0985/25. LCCN:98-009054.
Audience: **u,f.** *Choice, 1999.*

Fitzgerald, E. V. K. **HC227 .F53**
The State and Economic Development: Peru since 1968. Cambridge University Press. 1976. ISBN:0-521-21141-7, ISBN13: 978-0-521-21141-3.
Audience: **u,f.**

Fleet, Michael & Smith, Brian H. **BX1468.2.F57 1997**
The Catholic Church and Democracy in Chile and Peru. Cloth Text. University of Notre Dame Press. Notre Dame, IN. 1997. 392p. Helen Kellogg Institute for International Studies Ser. ISBN:0-268-00821-3, ISBN13: 978-0-268-00821-5. Dewey:282/.83/0904. LCCN:96-028967.
Audience: **u,f.** *Choice, 1998.*

Gagliano, Joseph A. **HV5840.P46G34 1994**
Coca Prohibition in Peru: The Historical Debates. Trade Cloth. University of Arizona Press. Tucson, AZ. 1994. 245p. ISBN:0-8165-1445-3, ISBN13: 978-0-8165-1445-8. Dewey:363.4/5/0985. LCCN:94-009570.
Audience: **u,f.** *Choice, 1995.*

Gardiner, C. Harvey **F3434.J3 G37**
The Japanese and Peru, 1873-1973. Trade Cloth. University of New Mexico Press. Albuquerque, NM. 1975. 202p. ISBN:0-8263-0391-9, ISBN13: 978-0-8263-0391-2. Dewey:327.52/085. LCCN:75-017371.
Audience: **u,f.**

Gonzales, Michael J. **HD9114.P52G66 1985**
Plantation Agriculture and Social Control in Northern Peru, 1875-1933. Cloth Text. University of Texas Press. Austin, TX. 1985. 251p. Institute of Latin American Studies, No. 62

ISBN:0-292-76491-X, ISBN13: 978-0-292-76491-0. Dewey:338.1/7361/09851. LCCN:84-002359.
Audience: **u,f.** *Choice, 1986.*

Gootenberg, Paul **HD9484.G9G66 1993**
Imagining Development: Economic Ideas in Peru's "Fictitious Prosperity" of Guano, 1840-1880. Trade Cloth. University of California Press. Berkeley, CA. 1993. 254p. ISBN:0-520-07712-1, ISBN13: 978-0-520-07712-6. Dewey:330.98505. LCCN:92-031679.
Audience: **u,f.** *Choice, 1994.*

Gorriti, Gustavo **F3448.2.G67 1999**
The Shining Path: A History of the Millenarian War in Peru. Library Binding. University of North Carolina Press. Chapel Hill, NC. 1999. 320p. Latin America in Translation Ser. ISBN:0-8078-2373-2, ISBN13: 978-0-8078-2373-6. Dewey:322'.5'0985. LCCN:98-004360.
Audience: **u,f.** *Choice, 2000.*

Graham, Carol **JL3498.A6 G7 1992**
Peru's APRA: Parties, Politics, and the Elusive Quest for Democracy. Library Binding. Lynne Rienner Publishers, Inc. Boulder, CO. 1992. 267p. ISBN:1-55587-306-5, ISBN13: 978-1-55587-306-6. Dewey:324.28507. LCCN:92-000240.
Audience: **u,f.** *Choice, 1993.*

Guillet, David **HD556**
Agrarian Reform and Peasant Economy in Southern Peru. Cloth Text. University of Missouri Press. Columbia, MO. 1979. 244p. ISBN:0-8262-0263-2, ISBN13: 978-0-8262-0263-5. Dewey:333.3/35/09853. LCCN:78-019644.
Audience: **u,f.**

Handelman, Howard **HD1531.P4 H35 1975**
Struggle in the Andes: Peasant Political Mobilization in Peru. Trade Cloth. University of Texas Press. Austin, TX. 1975. 321p. Latin American Monographs, No. 35 ISBN:0-292-77513-X, ISBN13: 978-0-292-77513-8. Dewey:322/.2/0985. LCCN:74-010796.
Audience: **u,f.**

Klaiber, Jeffrey L. **BR720**
Religion and Revolution in Peru, 1824-1976. Cloth Text. University of Notre Dame Press. Notre Dame, IN. 1977. 272p. ISBN:0-268-01599-6, ISBN13: 978-0-268-01599-2. Dewey:322/.1/0985. LCCN:76-051616.
Audience: **u,f.**

Klaren, Peter F. **JL3498.A6.K53**
Modernization, Dislocation, and Aprismo: Origins of the Peruvian Aprista Party, 1870-1932. Trade Cloth. University of Texas Press. Austin, TX. 1973. 213p. Latin American Monographs, No. 32 ISBN:0-292-76001-9, ISBN13: 978-0-292-76001-1. Dewey:329.9/85. LCCN:73-004915.
Audience: **u,f.** B

Klaren, Peter Flindell **F3431.K53 2000**
Peru: Society and Nationhood in the Andes. Trade Paper. Oxford University Press, Inc. New York, NY. 1999. 512p. Latin American Histories Ser. ISBN:0-19-506928-5, ISBN13: 978-0-19-506928-0. Dewey:985. LCCN:99-020062.
Audience: **u,f.**

Kuczynski, P. **HC227**
Peruvian Democracy under Economic Stress: An Account of the Balaunde Administration, 1963-1968. Trade Cloth. Princeton University Press. Princeton, NJ. 1977. 328p. Music-Culture Ser. ISBN:0-691-04213-6, ISBN13: 978-0-691-04213-8. Dewey:330.9/85/063. LCCN:76-024296.
Audience: **u,f.**

Lloyd, Peter **HN350.L5 L56**
The Young Towns of Lima: Aspects of Urbanization in Peru. Cambridge University Press. 1980. ISBN:0-521-29688-9, ISBN13: 978-0-521-29688-5.
Audience: **u,f.**

Lobo, Susan **HT151**
A House of My Own: Social Organization in the Squatter Settlements of Lima, Peru. Trade Paper. University of Arizona Press. Tucson, AZ. 1982. 190p. ISBN:0-8165-0761-9, ISBN13: 978-0-8165-0761-0. Dewey:307.7/6. LCCN:81-016275.
Audience: **u,f.** B

Lowenthal, Abraham F. **HN343.5**
The Peruvian Experiment: Continuity and Change under Military Rule. Cloth Text. Princeton University Press. Princeton, NJ. 1975. 488p. Center for Inter-American Relations Ser. ISBN:0-691-07572-7, ISBN13: 978-0-691-07572-3. Dewey:361.6/1/0985. LCCN:75-002998.
Audience: **u,f.**

Mallon, Florenica E. **HC227**
The Defense of Community in Peru's Central Highlands: Peasant Struggle and Capitalist Transition, 1860-1940. Trade Cloth. Princeton University Press. Princeton, NJ. 1983. 400p. ISBN:0-691-07647-2, ISBN13: 978-0-691-07647-8. Dewey:330.985. LCCN:83-042565.
Audience: **u,f.** B

McClintock, Cynthia & Lowenthal, Abraham F. (Editors) **F3448.2.P49 1983**
The Peruvian Experiment Reconsidered. Trade Cloth. Princeton University Press. Princeton, NJ. 1983. 484p. ISBN:0-691-07648-0, ISBN13: 978-0-691-07648-5. Dewey:320.985. LCCN:82-061377.
Audience: **u,f.** B

Meyerson, Julia **F2230.2.K4M47 1990**
Tambo: Life in an Andean Village. Trade Paper. University of Texas Press. Austin, TX. 1990. 297p. ISBN:0-292-78078-8, ISBN13: 978-0-292-78078-1. Dewey:985.37. LCCN:89-014812.
Audience: **u,f.** *Choice, 1990.*

Morales, Edmundo **HV5840.P46**
Cocaine: White Gold Rush in Peru. Trade Paper. University of Arizona Press. Tucson, AZ. 1990. 228p. ISBN:0-8165-1159-4, ISBN13: 978-0-8165-1159-4. Dewey:363.4/5/0985. LCCN:88-030303.
Audience: **u,f.** *Choice, 1989.*

Oliver-Smith, Anthony **F3611.Y86O44 1986**
The Martyred City: Death and Rebirth in the Andes. Trade Cloth. University of New Mexico Press. Albuquerque, NM. 1986. 291p. ISBN:0-8263-0864-3, ISBN13: 978-0-8263-0864-1. Dewey:985/.21. LCCN:85-020974.
Audience: **u,f.** *Choice, 1986.*

Palmer, David Scott (Editor) **F3448.2.S54 1994**
The Shining Path of Peru. Ed. 2. Trade Paper. Palgrave Macmillan. New York, NY. 1994. 320p. ISBN:0-312-10619-X, ISBN13: 978-0-312-10619-5. Dewey:322.4/2/0985. LCCN:94-025904.
Audience: **u,f.**

Parker, D. S. **HT690.P4P37 1998**
The Idea of the Middle Class: White-Collar Workers and Peruvian Society. Trade Cloth. Pennsylvania State University Press. University Park, PA. 1998. 266p. ISBN:0-271-01743-0, ISBN13: 978-0-271-01743-3. Dewey:305.5/5/0985. LCCN:97-016294.
Audience: **u,f.** *Choice, 1998.*

Parodi, Jorge **HD8039.M52P4613 2000**
To Be a Worker: Identity and Politics in Peru. Catherine M. Conaghan (Editor, Translator, Introduction by), James Alstrum (Translator). Trade Cloth. University of North Carolina Press. Chapel Hill, NC. 2000. 200p. Latin America in Translation Ser. ISBN:0-8078-2548-4, ISBN13: 978-0-8078-2548-8. Dewey:331.7/671/0985. LCCN:99-049579.
Audience: **u,f.**

Peloso, Vincent C. **HD8039.C662P416 1999**
Peasants on Plantations: Subaltern Strategies of Labor and Resistance in the Pisco Valley, Peru. Library Binding. Duke University Press. Durham, NC. 1998. xxi, 251p. Latin America Otherwise Ser. ISBN:0-8223-2229-3, ISBN13: 978-0-8223-2229-0. Dewey:306.3/49. LCCN:98-027846.
Audience: **u,f.** *Choice, 1999.*

Philips, G. **F3448.2**
The Rise and Fall of Peruvian Military Radicals. Athlone Press. 1978. ISBN:0-485-17709-9, ISBN13: 978-0-485-17709-1.
Audience: **u,f.**

Pike, Fredrick B. **F3448.H3P55 1986**
The Politics of the Miraculous in Peru: Haya de la Torre and the Spiritualist Tradition. Cloth Text. University of Nebraska Press. Lincoln, NE. 1986. 391p. ISBN:0-8032-3672-7, ISBN13: 978-0-8032-3672-1. Dewey:985/.063. LCCN:85-001162.
Audience: **u,f.** *Choice, 1986.*

Pike, Fredrick B. **HN260.A5**
The United States and the Andean Republics: Peru, Bolivia, and Ecuador. Edwin O. Reischauer (Foreword by). Trade Cloth. Harvard University Press. Cambridge, MA. 1977. 493p. American Foreign Policy Library ISBN:0-674-92300-6, ISBN13: 978-0-674-92300-3. Dewey:980. LCCN:76-055314.
Audience: **u,f.**

Poole, Deborah **GN347.P66 1997**
Vision, Race, and Modernity: A Visual Economy of the Andean Image World. Trade Paper. Princeton University Press. Princeton, NJ. 1997. 280p. Princeton Studies in Culture/Power/History ISBN:0-691-00645-8, ISBN13: 978-0-691-00645-1. Dewey:305.8/0098/0222. LCCN:96-045561.
Audience: **u,f.** *Choice, 1997.*

Poole, Deborah & Renique, Gerardo **F3448.2**
Peru: Time of Fear. Trade Paper. Latin America Bureau. London, 1992. 200p. Latin America Bureau Ser. ISBN:0-85345-869-3, ISBN13: 978-0-85345-869-2. Dewey:322.420985.
Audience: **u,f.**

Quijano, Anibal **HC227 .Q5313**
Nationalism and Capitalism in Peru: A Study in Neo-Imperialism. Helen R. Lane (Translator). Trade Paper. Monthly Review Press. New York, NY. 1972. 128p. ISBN:0-85345-246-6, ISBN13: 978-0-85345-246-1. Dewey:309.1/85/063. LCCN:78-163117.
Audience: **u,f.**

Quiroz, Alfonso W. **HG185.P4Q56 1993**
Domestic and Foreign Finance in Modern Peru, 1850-1950: Financing Visions of Development. Cloth Text. University of Pittsburgh Press. Pittsburgh, PA. 1993. 312p. Latin American Ser. ISBN:0-8229-1174-4, ISBN13: 978-0-8229-1174-6. Dewey:332.0985. LCCN:92-036947.
Audience: **u,f.**

Rasnake, Roger N. **F2230.2.K4R37 1988**
Domination and Cultural Resistance: Authority and Power among Andean People. Cloth Text. Duke University Press. Durham, NC. 1988. xi, 323p. ISBN:0-8223-0809-6, ISBN13: 978-0-8223-0809-6. Dewey:984/.14. LCCN:87-035834.
Audience: **u,f.** *Choice, 1989.*

Seligmann, Linda J. **HD1333.P42H837 1995**
Between Reform and Revolution: Political Struggles in the Peruvian Andes, 1969-1991. Trade Cloth. Stanford University Press. Palo Alto, CA. 1995. 320p. Program in Agrarian Studies, Yale University ISBN:0-8047-2442-3, ISBN13: 978-0-8047-2442-5. Dewey:322.4/4/098537. LCCN:94-034937.
Audience: **u,f.** *Choice, 1996.*

Sheahan, John **HC227.S435 1999**
Searching for a Better Society: The Peruvian Economy from 1950. Trade Cloth. Pennsylvania State University Press. University Park, PA. 1999. 288p. ISBN:0-271-01872-0, ISBN13: 978-0-271-01872-0. Dewey:338.985. LCCN:98-039335.
Audience: **u,f.** *Choice, 1999.*

Slater, David **HC227.S55 1989**
Territory and State Power in Latin America: The Peruvian Case. Cloth Text. Palgrave Macmillan. New York, NY. 1989. 280p. ISBN:0-312-03073-8, ISBN13: 978-0-312-03073-5. Dewey:330.985. LCCN:89-030608.
Audience: **u,f.** *Choice, 1989.*

Smith, Gavin **HD1536.I8**
Livelihood and Resistance: Peasants and the Politics of Land in Peru. Trade Cloth. University of California Press. Berkeley, CA. 1991. 293p. ISBN:0-520-07662-1, ISBN13: 978-0-520-07662-4. Dewey:305.5/63. LCCN:88-017499.
Audience: **u,f.** *Choice, 1990.*

Starn, Orin **HD1531.P4S73 1999**
Nightwatch: The Politics of Protest in the Peruvian Andes. Trade Cloth. Duke University Press. Durham, NC. 1999. 304p. Latin America Otherwise Ser. ISBN:0-8223-2301-X, ISBN13: 978-0-8223-2301-3. LCCN:98-041295.
Audience: **u,f.** *Choice, 2000.*

Starn, Orin, et al. **F3431.P478 2005**
The Peru Reader: History, Culture, Politics, Vol. 2. Ed. 2. Carlos Iván Degregori & Robin Kirk (Authors). Trade Cloth. Duke University Press. Durham, NC. 2005. 520p. The Latin America Readers Ser. ISBN:0-8223-3655-3, ISBN13: 978-0-8223-3655-6. Dewey:985. LCCN:2005-011391.
Audience: **u,f.**

Stepan, Alfred C. **JL3431.S73**
The State and Society: Peru in Comparative Perspective. Trade Cloth. Princeton University Press. Princeton, NJ. 1978. xix, 348p. ISBN:0-691-07591-3, ISBN13: 978-0-691-07591-4. Dewey:321.9. LCCN:77-085567.
Audience: **u,f.** B

Stephens, Evelyne H. **HD5660.P4 S73**
The Politics of Workers' Participation: The Peruvian Approach in Comparative Perspective. Trade Cloth. Elsevier Science & Technology Books. Saint Louis, MO. 1980. Studies in Social Discontinuity Ser. ISBN:0-12-666250-9, ISBN13: 978-0-12-666250-4. Dewey:658.3/152/0985. LCCN:79-006789.
Audience: **u,f.**

Stern, Steve J. **F3448.2.S53 1998**
Shining and Other Paths: War and Society in Peru, 1980-1995. Trade Cloth. Duke University Press. Durham, NC. 1998. 528p. ISBN:0-8223-2201-3, ISBN13: 978-0-8223-2201-6. Dewey:322.4/2/0985. LCCN:97-043279.
Audience: **u,f.** *Choice, 1999.*

Stokes, Susan C. **HN343.5.S76 1995**
Cultures in Conflict: Social Movements and the State in Peru. Trade Cloth. University of California Press. Berkeley, CA. 1995. 250p. ISBN:0-520-08617-1, ISBN13: 978-0-520-08617-3. Dewey:303.48/4/0985. LCCN:94-011496.
Audience: **u,f.**

Strong, Simon **F3448.2**
Shining Path. Trade Cloth. Random House Value Publishing. New York, NY. 1995. ISBN:0-517-15313-0, ISBN13: 978-0-517-15313-0. Dewey:322.420985.
Audience: **u,f.**

TePaske, John J. (Editor) **Z1656.R47**
Research Guide to Andean History: Bolivia, Chile, Ecuador, and Peru. Cloth Text. Duke University Press. Durham, NC. 1981. xiii, 346p. ISBN:0-8223-0450-3, ISBN13: 978-0-8223-0450-0. Dewey:980. LCCN:80-029365.
Audience: **u,f.**

Thorp, Rosemary **HC227.T484 1991**
Economic Management and Economic Development in Peru and Colombia. Trade Cloth. University of Pittsburgh Press. Pittsburgh, PA. 1991. 240p. Latin American Ser. ISBN:0-8229-1165-5, ISBN13: 978-0-8229-1165-4. Dewey:330.985. LCCN:91-065359.
Audience: **u,f.** *Choice, 1992.*

Thorp, Rosemary, et al. **HC227 .T485 1978**
Peru 1890-1897. Geoffrey Bertram & Bertram Thorp (Authors), Stuart Bruchey (Editor). Trade Cloth. Columbia University Press. New York, NY. 1978. 475p. ISBN:0-231-03433-4, ISBN13: 978-0-231-03433-3. Dewey:330.9/85/063. LCCN:77-027925.
Audience: **u,f.**

Urquidi, Marjory (Translator) **F3408**
Seven Interpretive Essays on Peruvian Reality. Jorge Basadre (Introduction by). Trade Cloth. University of Texas Press. Austin, TX. 2004. xxxvi, 301p. Texas Pan-American Ser. ISBN:0-292-70115-2, ISBN13: 978-0-292-70115-1. Dewey:918.5/03. LCCN:73-156346.
Audience: **u,f.** B

Valderrama Fernández, Ricardo **F2230.2.K4C66313**
Andean Lives: Gregorio Condori Mamani and Asunta Quispe Huamán. Carmen Escalante Gutiérrez (Editor), Gabriela Martínez Escobar (Translator), Paul H. Gelles (Translator, Introduction by), Eulogio Nishiyama (Photographer). Trade Paper. University of Texas Press. Austin, TX. 1996. 213p. ISBN:0-292-72492-6, ISBN13: 978-0-292-72492-1. Dewey:985/.37004983. LCCN:95-032444.
Audience: **u,f.** *Choice, 1996.*

Vargas Llosa, Mario **PQ8498.32.A65P4913**
A Fish in the Water: A Memoir. Helen Lane (Translator). Trade Cloth. Farrar, Straus & Giroux. New York, NY. 1994. 532p. ISBN:0-374-15509-7, ISBN13: 978-0-374-15509-4. Dewey:863. LCCN:93-042603.
Audience: **u,f.**

Weyland, Kurt Gerhard **HC165.W46 2004**
The Politics of Market Reform in Fragile Democracies: Argentina, Brazil, Peru, and Venezuela. Trade Paper. Princeton University Press. Princeton, NJ. 2004. 360p. ISBN:0-691-11787-X, ISBN13: 978-0-691-11787-4. Dewey:338.98.
Audience: **u,f.** *Choice, 2003.*

South America: Individual Countries > Ecuador > Colonial Ecuador

Burt, Jo-Marie & Mauceri, Philip (Editors) **F2212.P615 2004**
Politics in the Andes: Identity, Conflict, Reform. Trade Cloth. University of Pittsburgh Press. Pittsburgh, PA. 2004. 336p. Pitt Latin American Ser. ISBN:0-8229-4225-9, ISBN13: 978-0-8229-4225-2. Dewey:980.03/3. LCCN:2003-015506.
Audience: **u,f.** *Choice, 2004.*

Gauderman, Kimberly **HQ1560.Q58G38 2003**
Women's Lives in Colonial Quito: Gender, Law, and Economy in Spanish America. Trade Cloth. University of Texas Press. Austin, TX. 2003. 195p. ISBN:0-292-70555-7, ISBN13: 978-0-292-70555-5. Dewey:305.4/09866/13. LCCN:2003-004064.
Audience: **u,f.**

Lane, Kris E. **F3781.3.L36 2002**
Quito 1599: City and Colony in Transition. Trade Cloth. University of New Mexico Press. Albuquerque, NM. 2004. 292p. Dialogos Ser. ISBN:0-8263-2356-1, ISBN13: 978-0-8263-2356-9. Dewey:986.6/13. LCCN:2002-004203.
Audience: **u,f.** *Choice, 2003.*

Newson, Linda A. **F3721.3.P76N49 1995**
Life and Death in Early Colonial Equador. Trade Cloth. University of Oklahoma Press. Norman, OK. 1995. 520p. Civilization of the American Indian Ser., Vol. 214 ISBN:0-8061-2697-3, ISBN13: 978-0-8061-2697-5. Dewey:304.6/09866/0903. LCCN:94-041571.
Audience: **u,f.** *Choice, 1995.*

Phelan, John L. **F3733 .P48**
Kingdom of Quito in the Seventeenth Century: Bureaucratic Politics in the Spanish Empire. Trade Cloth. University of Wisconsin Press. Chicago, IL. 1967. 448p. ISBN:0-299-04570-6, ISBN13: 978-0-299-04570-8. Dewey:918.66/03/2.
Audience: **u,f.**

Powers, Karen Vieira **HB3570.Q58P69 1995**
Andean Journeys: Migration, Ethnogenesis and the State in Colonial Quito. Trade Cloth. University of New Mexico, Native American Studies. Albuquerque, NM. 1995. 249p.

ISBN:0-8263-1600-X, ISBN13: 978-0-8263-1600-4. Dewey:304.8/09866/13. LCCN:94-018696.
Audience: **u,f.** *Choice, 1996.*

South America: Individual Countries > Ecuador > 19th Century Ecuador

Goffin, Alvin M. **BV2853.E2G64 1994**
The Rise of Protestant Evangelism in Ecuador, 1895-1990. Trade Cloth. University Press of Florida. Gainesville, FL. 1994. 208p. ISBN:0-8130-1260-0, ISBN13: 978-0-8130-1260-5. Dewey:266/.023708. LCCN:93-036886.
Audience: **u,f.** *Choice, 1994.*

Rodriguez, Linda **HJ953.R62 1985**
The Search for Public Policy: Regional Politics and Government Finances in Ecuador, 1830-1940. Trade Cloth. University of California Press. Berkeley, CA. 1985. 290p. ISBN:0-520-05150-5, ISBN13: 978-0-520-05150-8. Dewey:336.866. LCCN:84-002446.
Audience: **u,f.** *Choice, 1985.*

Sowell, David **RA645.37.A5S69 2001**
The Tale of Healer Miguel Perdomo Neira: Medicine, Ideologies and Power in the Nineteenth-Century Andes. Book, Other. Rowman & Littlefield Publishers, Inc. Lanham, MD. 2001. 171p. Latin American Silhouettes Ser. ISBN:0-8420-2826-9, ISBN13: 978-0-8420-2826-4. Dewey:610/.98/09034. LCCN:00-067984.
Audience: **u,f.**

Townsend, Camilla **HN320.Z9S67 2000**
Tales of Two Cities: Race and Economic Culture in Early Republican North and South America. Trade Cloth. University of Texas Press. Austin, TX. 2000. 344p. ISBN:0-292-78167-9, ISBN13: 978-0-292-78167-2. Dewey:305.5/09752/6. LCCN:99-036415.
Audience: **u,f.**

Van Aken, Mark J. **F3736.F5V36 1989**
King of the Night: Juan Jose Flores and Ecuador, 1824-1864. Trade Cloth. University of California Press. Berkeley, CA. 1989. 328p. ISBN:0-520-06277-9, ISBN13: 978-0-520-06277-1. Dewey:986.6/05. LCCN:88-020606.
Audience: **u,f.** *Choice, 1989.*

South America: Individual Countries > Ecuador > 20th Century Ecuador

Alexander, Robert J. **F2237**
The Bolivarian Presidents: Conversations and Correspondence with Presidents of Bolivia, Peru, and Ecuador. Trade Cloth. Greenwood Publishing Group, Inc. Portsmouth, NH. 1994. 296p. ISBN:0-275-94661-4, ISBN13: 978-0-275-94661-6. Dewey:980.0330922. LCCN:93-011892.
Audience: **u,f.** *Choice, 1995.*

de la Torre, Carlos **JL3081.T67 2000**
Populist Seduction in Latin America: The Ecuadorian Experience. Trade Paper. Ohio University Press. Athens, OH. 2000. 208p. Research in International Studies. Latin America Series / Oh, No. 32 ISBN:0-89680-210-8, ISBN13: 978-0-89680-210-0. Dewey:320.9866. LCCN:99-058922.
Audience: **u,f.** *Choice, 2001.*

Gerlach, Allen **F3738.2.G47 2002**
Indians, Oil and Politics: A Recent History of Ecuador. Book, Other. Rowman & Littlefield Publishers, Inc. Lanham, MD. 2003. 286p. Latin American Silhouettes Ser. ISBN:0-8420-5107-4, ISBN13: 978-0-8420-5107-1. Dewey:986.607/4. LCCN:2002-030656.
Audience: **u,f.** *Choice, 2003.*

Goffin, Alvin M. **BV2853.E2G64 1994**
The Rise of Protestant Evangelism in Ecuador, 1895-1990. Trade Cloth. University Press of Florida. Gainesville, FL. 1994. 208p. ISBN:0-8130-1260-0, ISBN13: 978-0-8130-1260-5. Dewey:266/.023708. LCCN:93-036886.
Audience: **u,f.** *Choice, 1994.*

Isaacs, Anita **F3738.I83 1993**
The Politics of Military Rule and Transition in Ecuador, 1972-92: Dancing with the People. Cloth Text. University of Pittsburgh Press. Pittsburgh, PA. 1993. 192p. Latin American Ser. ISBN:0-8229-1173-6, ISBN13: 978-0-8229-1173-9. Dewey:986.607/3. LCCN:92-034039.
Audience: **u,f.** *Choice, 1994.*

Lucas, Kintto **F3721**
We Will Not Dance on our Grandparents' Tombs: Indigenous Uprisings in Ecuador. Catholic Institute for International Relations (CIIR). 2000. ISBN:1-85287-236-5, ISBN13: 978-1-85287-236-6.
Audience: **u,f.**

Petras, James F. & Veltmeyer, Henry **HB501.P4159 2003**
A System in Crisis: The Dynamics of Free Market Capitalism. Cloth over Boards. Zed Books, Ltd. London, 2004. 224p. ISBN:1-84277-364-X, ISBN13: 978-1-84277-364-2. Dewey:330.9/049. LCCN:2003-045065.
Audience: **u,f.**

Rodriguez, Linda **HJ953.R62 1985**
The Search for Public Policy: Regional Politics and Government Finances in Ecuador, 1830-1940. Trade Cloth. University of California Press. Berkeley, CA. 1985. 290p. ISBN:0-520-05150-5, ISBN13: 978-0-520-05150-8. Dewey:336.866. LCCN:84-002446.
Audience: **u,f.** *Choice, 1985.*

Schodt, David W. **F3738.S34 1987**
Ecuador: An Andean Enigma. Cloth Text. Westview Press. Boulder, CO. 1987. 188p. Profiles - Nations of Contemporary Latin America Ser. ISBN:0-8133-0230-7, ISBN13: 978-0-8133-0230-0. Dewey:986.6/074. LCCN:86-033999.
Audience: **u,f.** *Choice, 1988.*

Striffler, Steve **HD8039.B232E27 2002**
In the Shadows of State and Capital: The United Fruit Company, Popular Struggle and Agrarian Restructuring in Ecuador, 1900-1995. Trade Cloth. Duke University Press. Durham, NC. 2002. 256p. ISBN:0-8223-2836-4, ISBN13: 978-0-8223-2836-0. Dewey:338.7/634772/09866. LCCN:2001-046027.
Audience: **u,f.** *Choice, 2002.*

South America: Individual Countries > Brazil

Deutsch, Sandra McGee **F2847.D483 1999**
Las Derechas: The Extreme Right in Argentina, Brazil, and Chile, 1890-1939. Trade Cloth. Stanford University Press. Palo Alto, CA. 1999. 480p. ISBN:0-8047-3208-6, ISBN13: 978-0-8047-3208-6. Dewey:320.98/09/0413. LCCN:99-019783.
Audience: **u,f.** *Choice, 2000.*

South America: Individual Countries > Brazil > Colonial Brazil

Alden, Dauril **BX3742.A1A53 1996**
The Making of an Enterprise: The Society of Jesus in Portugal, Its Empire, and Beyond, 1540-1750. Trade Cloth. Stanford University Press. Palo Alto, CA. 1996. 936p. ISBN:0-8047-2271-4, ISBN13: 978-0-8047-2271-1. Dewey:255.5/3/009469. LCCN:94-004820.
Audience: **u,f.** *Choice, 1997.*

Alden, Dauril **F2534**
Royal Government in Colonial Brazil: With Special Reference to the Administration of the Marquis of Lavradio, Viceroy, 1769-1779. Trade Cloth. University of California Press. Berkeley, CA. 1968. ISBN:0-520-00008-0, ISBN13: 978-0-520-00008-7. Dewey:981/.03/0924. LCCN:68-026064.
Audience: **u,f.**

Anderson, Robin L. **HD469.A43A53 1999**
Colonization As Exploitation in the Amazon Rain Forest, 1758-1911. Trade Cloth. University Press of Florida. Gainesville, FL. 1999. 192p. ISBN:0-8130-1719-X, ISBN13: 978-0-8130-1719-8. LCCN:99-036929.
Audience: **u,f.** *Choice, 2000.*

Barickman, B. J. **HD1875.R33B37 1998**
A Bahian Counterpoint: Sugar, Tobacco, Cassava, and Slavery in the Recôncavo, 1780-1860. Trade Cloth. Stanford University Press. Palo Alto, CA. 1998. 390p. ISBN:0-8047-2632-9, ISBN13: 978-0-8047-2632-0. Dewey:338.1/0981/42. LCCN:97-042643.
Audience: **u,f.** *Choice, 1998.*

Bethell, Leslie (Editor) **F2524.C56 1987**
Colonial Brazil. Trade Paper. Cambridge University Press. New York, NY. 1987. 408p. ISBN:0-521-34925-7, ISBN13: 978-0-521-34925-3. Dewey:981/.03.
Audience: **u,f.**

Boxer, C. R. **F2532.B7 1973**
The Dutch in Brazil, 1624-1654. Trade Cloth. Shoe String Press, Inc. North Haven, CT. 1973. xiii, 329p. ISBN:0-208-01338-5, ISBN13: 978-0-208-01338-5. Dewey:981/.03. LCCN:73-005701.
Audience: **u,f.** B

Boxer, C. R. **F2528 .B6**
The Golden Age of Brazil 1695: 1750. Paper Text. Textbook Publishers. Temecula, CA. 2003. xiii, 443p. ISBN:0-7581-5316-3, ISBN13: 978-0-7581-5316-6. Dewey:981/.03.
Audience: **u,f.**

Capistrano de Abreu, Joao **F2524.A2413 1997**
Chapters in Brazil's Colonial History, 1500-1800. Stuart Scwartz (Editor), Arthur Brakel (Translator). Trade Cloth. Oxford University Press, Inc. New York, NY. 1997. 272p. Library of Latin America ISBN:0-19-510301-7, ISBN13: 978-0-19-510301-4. Dewey:981/.03. LCCN:96-043461.
Audience: **u,f.**

De Queiros Mattoso, Katia M. **HT1126.M3713 1986**
To Be a Slave in Brazil: 1550-1888. Arthur Goldhammer (Translator), Stuart B. Schwartz (Foreword by). Cloth Text. Rutgers University Press. Piscataway, NJ. 1986. 35p. ISBN:0-8135-1154-2, ISBN13: 978-0-8135-1154-2. Dewey:306/.362/0981. LCCN:85-027760.
Audience: **u,f.** *Choice, 1986.*

Geld, Ellen Bromfield **F2631.G45 2003**
View from the Fazenda: A Tale of the Brazilian Heartlands. Cloth over Boards. Ohio University Press. Athens, OH. 2003. 320p. ISBN:0-8214-1474-7, ISBN13: 978-0-8214-1474-3. Dewey:981/.61. LCCN:2002-027076.
Audience: **u,f.**

Higgins, Kathleen J. **HT1129.S2H53 1999**
"Licentious Liberty" in a Brazilian Gold-Mining Region: Slavery, Gender and Social Control in Eighteenth-Century Sabara, Minas Gerais. Trade Cloth. Pennsylvania State University Press. University Park, PA. 1999. 248p. ISBN:0-271-01910-7, ISBN13: 978-0-271-01910-9. Dewey:306.3/62/098151. LCCN:98-043338.
Audience: **u,f.** *Choice, 2000.*

Letts, Malcolm (Editor) **F2511**
Hans Staden, the True History of His Captivity 1557. Library Binding. Routledge. New York, NY. 2004. 191p. ISBN:0-415-34476-X, ISBN13: 978-0-415-34476-0. Dewey:918.1/0432/092.
Audience: **u,f.**

Lewin, Linda **KHD520.L49 2002**
Surprise Heirs I: Illegitimacy, Patrimonial Rights, and Legal Nationalism in Luso-Brazilian Inheritance, 1750-1821. Trade Cloth. Stanford University Press. Palo Alto, CA. 2003. 240p. ISBN:0-8047-3881-5, ISBN13: 978-0-8047-3881-1. Dewey:346.8105/2. LCCN:2002-010019.
Audience: **u,f.**

Lewin, Linda **KHD520.L49 2003**
Surprise Heirs II: Illegitimacy, Inheritance Rights, and Public Power in the Formation of Imperial Brazil, 1822-1889. Trade Cloth. Stanford University Press. Palo Alto, CA. 2003. 397p. ISBN:0-8047-4606-0, ISBN13: 978-0-8047-4606-9. Dewey:346.8105/2. LCCN:2002-010019.
Audience: **u,f.**

Luna, Francisco Vidal & Klein, Herbert S. **HC188.S3L86 2002**
The Evolution of the Slave Society and Economy of Saao Paulo, from the 1760s to the 1850s. Trade Cloth. Stanford University Press. Palo Alto, CA. 2003. xii, 273p. Social Science History Ser. ISBN:0-8047-4465-3, ISBN13: 978-0-8047-4465-2. Dewey:330.981/61033. LCCN:2002-010785.
Audience: **u,f.** *Choice, 2003.*

Marchant, Alexander N. **H31**
From Barter to Slavery: The Economic Relations of Portuguese and Indians in the Settlement of Brazil, 1500-1580. Trade Cloth. Peter Smith Publisher, Inc. Magnolia, MA. 1942. ISBN:0-8446-1300-2, ISBN13: 978-0-8446-1300-0. Dewey:981.
Audience: **u,f.**

Maxwell, Kenneth **F2534.M29 2004**
Conflicts and Conspiracies: Brazil and Portugal, 1750-1808. Paper over Boards. Routledge. New York, NY. 2004. 320p. ISBN:0-415-94988-2, ISBN13: 978-0-415-94988-0. Dewey:981/.033. LCCN:2004-001858.
Audience: **u,f.**

Metcalf, Alida C. **HQ594.15.S24M48 2005**
Family and Frontier in Colonial Brazil: Santana de Parnaiba, 1580-1822. Trade Paper. University of Texas Press. Austin, TX. 2005. 304p. ISBN:0-292-70652-9, ISBN13: 978-0-292-70652-1. Dewey:306.85/0981/61. LCCN:2004-053553.
Audience: **u,f.** *Choice, 1992.*

Metcalf, Alida C. **F2526.M48 2005**
Go-Betweens and the Colonization of Brazil: 1500-1600. Trade Cloth. University of Texas Press. Austin, TX. 2006. 368p. ISBN:0-292-70970-6, ISBN13: 978-0-292-70970-6. Dewey:981/.032. LCCN:2005-020020.
Audience: **u,f.** *Choice, 2006.*

Russell-Wood, A. J. **F2659.N4.R86 1982**
The Black Man in Slavery and Freedom in Colonial Brazil. Cloth Text. Palgrave Macmillan. New York, NY. 1982. 280p. ISBN:0-312-08326-2, ISBN13: 978-0-312-08326-7. Dewey:981/.00496. LCCN:81-018544.
Audience: **u,f.** B

Russell-Wood, A. J. **HV195.S2 R8**
Fidalgos and Philanthropists: The Santa Casa de Misericordia of Bahia, 1550-1755. Trade Cloth. University of California Press. Berkeley, CA. 1968. ISBN:0-520-01108-2, ISBN13: 978-0-520-01108-3. Dewey:309.1/81/4.
Audience: **u,f.**

Schwartz, Stuart B. **JV4266.R4.S38**
Sovereignty and Society in Colonial Brazil: The High Court of Bahia and Its Judges, 1609-1751. Trade Cloth. University of California Press. Berkeley, CA. 1974. xxvii, 438p. ISBN:0-520-02195-9, ISBN13: 978-0-520-02195-2. Dewey:325/.31/09469. LCCN:76-186112.
Audience: **u,f.** B

Schwartz, Stuart B. **HD9114.B7 B347 1985**
Sugar Plantations in the Formation of Brazilian Society: Bahia, 1550-1835. Alan Knight (Contribution by). Trade Paper. Cambridge University Press. New York, NY. 1986. 608p. Cambridge Latin American Studies, No. 52 ISBN:0-521-31399-6, ISBN13: 978-0-521-31399-5. Dewey:306/.0981/42. LCCN:85-006716.
Audience: **u,f.**

Souza, Laura de Mello e **BF1584.B7S6813 2003**
The Devil and the Land of the Holy Cross: Witchcraft, Slavery, and Popular Religion in Colonial Brazil. Diane Grosklaus Whitty (Translator). Trade Cloth. University of Texas Press. Austin, TX. 2004. 374p. LLILAS Translations from Latin America Ser. ISBN:0-292-70228-0, ISBN13: 978-0-292-70228-8. Dewey:133.4/0981. LCCN:2003-059904.
Audience: **u,f.**

Sweet, James H. **F2659.N4S94 2003**
Recreating Africa: Kinship, Culture, and Religion in the African-Portuguese World, 1441-1770. Trade Cloth. University of North Carolina Press. Chapel Hill, NC. 2003. 336p. ISBN:0-8078-2808-4, ISBN13: 978-0-8078-2808-3. Dewey:981/.00496. LCCN:2003-001194.
Audience: **u,f.** *Choice, 2004.*

South America: Individual Countries > Brazil > 19th Century Brazil

Azevedo, Celia M. **E449.A99 1995**
Abolitionism in the United States and Brazil: A Comparative Perspective. Paper over Boards. Garland Publishing, Inc. New York, NY. 1995. 200p. Studies in African American History and Culture ISBN:0-8153-2332-8, ISBN13: 978-0-8153-2332-7. Dewey:973.7/114. LCCN:95-037819.
Audience: **u,f.** *Choice, 1996.*

Barman, Roderick J. **F2536.P37B37 1999**
Citizen Emperor: Pedro II and the Making of Brazil, 1825-1891. Trade Cloth. Stanford University Press. Palo Alto, CA. 2000. xviii, 548p. ISBN:0-8047-3510-7, ISBN13: 978-0-8047-3510-0. Dewey:981/.04/092. LCCN:99-036776.
Audience: **u,f.** *Choice, 2000.*

Barman, Roderick J. **F2536.I8B37 2002**
Princess Isabel of Brazil: Gender and Power in the Nineteenth Century. Book, Other. Rowman & Littlefield Publishers, Inc. Lanham, MD. 2002. 291p. Latin American Silhouettes Ser. ISBN:0-8420-2845-5, ISBN13: 978-0-8420-2845-5. Dewey:981/.04/092. LCCN:2001-054175.
Audience: **u,f.** *Choice, 2003, 2002.*

Bergad, Laird W. **HT1129.M5 B47 1999**
Slavery and the Demographic and Economic History of Minas Gerais, Brazil, 1720-1888. Alan Knight (Contribution by). Trade Cloth. Cambridge University Press. New York, NY. 1999. 334p. Latin American Studies, Vol. 85 ISBN:0-521-65266-9, ISBN13: 978-0-521-65266-7. Dewey:306.3/62/098151. LCCN:98-050559.
Audience: **u,f.**

Bethell, Leslie (Editor) **F2535.B76 1989**
Brazil: Empire and Republic, 1822-1930. Trade Paper. Cambridge University Press. New York, NY. 1989. 362p. ISBN:0-521-36837-5, ISBN13: 978-0-521-36837-7. Dewey:981/.04. LCCN:88-026736.
Audience: **u,f.**

Bieber, Judy **F2581.B55 1999**
Power, Patronage and Political Violence: State Building on a Brazilian Frontier, 1822-1889. Cloth Text. University of Nebraska Press. Lincoln, NE. 1999. 253p. ISBN:0-8032-1297-6, ISBN13: 978-0-8032-1297-8. Dewey:306.2/0981/5109034. LCCN:99-022581.
Audience: **u,f.** *Choice, 2000.*

Conrad, Robert E. (Editor) **HT1126.C575 1994**
Children of God's Fire: A Documentary History of Black Slavery in Brazil. Ed. 2. Trade Paper. Pennsylvania State University Press. University Park, PA. 1993. 544p. ISBN:0-271-01321-4, ISBN13: 978-0-271-01321-3. Dewey:306.3/62/0981. LCCN:93-038702.
Audience: **u,f.**

Conrad, Robert E. **HT1128 .C66 1993**
The Destruction of Brazilian Slavery, 1850-1888. Ed. 2. Trade Paper. Krieger Publishing Company. Melbourne, FL. 1993. 254p. ISBN:0-89464-750-4, ISBN13: 978-0-89464-750-5. Dewey:322.4/4/0981. LCCN:92-011285.
Audience: **u,f.**

Conrad, Robert E. **HT1126.C58 1986**
World of Sorrow: The African Slave Trade to Brazil. Cloth Text. Louisiana State University Press. Baton Rouge, LA. 1986. 215p. ISBN:0-8071-1245-3, ISBN13: 978-0-8071-1245-8. Dewey:382/.44/0981. LCCN:85-023160.
Audience: **u,f.** *Choice, 1986.*

Da Costa, Emilia Viotti **F2535.C6713 2000**
The Brazilian Empire: Myths and Histories. Ed. 2. Trade Paper. University of North Carolina Press. Chapel Hill, NC. 2000. 352p. ISBN:0-8078-4840-9, ISBN13: 978-0-8078-4840-1. Dewey:981/.04. LCCN:99-042037.
Audience: **u,f.** *Choice, 1986.*

De Jesus, Carolina M. **F2659.N4J4213 1997**
I'm Going to Have a Little House: The Second Diary of Carolina Maria de Jesus. Melvin S. Arrington Jr. (Translator), Robert M. Levine (Translator, Afterword by). Cloth Text. University of Nebraska Press. Lincoln, NE. 1997. 189p. Engendering Latin America Ser. ISBN:0-8032-2583-0, ISBN13: 978-0-8032-2583-1. Dewey:981/.6100496. LCCN:96-053134.
Audience: **u,f.** *Choice, 1998.*

De Jesus, Carolina M. **F2651.S253J47413**
The Unedited Diaries of Carolina Maria De Jesus. Robert M. Levine & Jose C. Meihy (Editors), Nancy P. Naro & Cristina Mehrtens (Translators). Cloth Text. Rutgers University Press. Piscataway, NJ. 1999. xii, 233p. ISBN:0-8135-2569-1, ISBN13: 978-0-8135-2569-3. Dewey:981/.6100496/0092. LCCN:98-004396.
Audience: **u,f.** *Choice, 1999.*

De Jesus, Carolina M. **F2659.N4J47 1998**
Bitita's Diary: The Childhood Memoirs of Carolina Maria de Jesus. Robert M. Levine (Editor, Foreword by), Emanuelle Oliveira & Beth J. Vinkler (Translators). Trade Cloth. M. E. Sharpe Inc. Armonk, NY. 1997. 178p. Latin American Realities Ser. ISBN:0-7656-0211-3, ISBN13: 978-0-7656-0211-4. Dewey:981/.00496/0092 B. LCCN:97-026341.
Audience: **u,f.** *Choice, 1998.*

De Jesus, Carolina M. **HN290.S33**
Child of the Dark: The Diary of Carolina Maria de Jesus. David St. Clair (Translator), Robert S. Levine (Afterword by). Mass Market. Penguin Group (USA) Inc. New York, NY. 2003. 208p. ISBN:0-451-52910-3, ISBN13: 978-0-451-52910-7. Dewey:306/.0981/61.
Audience: **g,l.**

Dean, Warren **HD1531.B7 D42**
Rio Claro: A Brazilian Plantation System, 1820-1920. Trade Cloth. Stanford University Press. Palo Alto, CA. 1976. xx, 234p. ISBN:0-8047-0902-5, ISBN13: 978-0-8047-0902-6. Dewey:331.7/63/37309816. LCCN:75-025149.
Audience: **u,f.**

Degler, Carl N. **F2659.N4D42 1986**
Neither Black nor White: Slavery and Race Relations in Brazil and the U.S. Trade Paper. University of Wisconsin Press. Chicago, IL. 1986. 324p. ISBN:0-299-10914-3, ISBN13: 978-0-299-10914-1. Dewey:305.8/96081. LCCN:86-040780.
Audience: **u,f.** B

Dias, Maria O. **HV1448.B72S26413**
Power and Everyday Life: The Lives of Working Women in Nineteenth-Century Brazil. Ann Frost (Translator). Cloth Text. Rutgers University Press. Piscataway, NJ. 1995. 240p. ISBN:0-8135-2204-8, ISBN13: 978-0-8135-2204-3. Dewey:305.5/69/082. LCCN:94-047497.
Audience: **u,f.** *Choice, 1996.*

do Nascimento, Abdias & do Nascimento, Elisa L. **F2659.N4.N361992**
Africans in Brazil: A Pan-African Perspective. Trade Cloth. Africa World Press. Trenton, NJ. 1992. 218p. ISBN:0-86543-238-4, ISBN13: 978-0-86543-238-3. Dewey:981/.00496. LCCN:91-074122.
Audience: **u,f.** *Choice, 1993.*

Eisenberg, Peter L. **HD9114.B23 P474**
The Sugar Industry in Pernambuco, 1840-1910: Modernization Without Change. Trade Cloth. University of California Press. Berkeley, CA. 1973. ISBN:0-520-01731-5, ISBN13: 978-0-520-01731-3. Dewey:338.1/7/3609813. LCCN:75-117340.
Audience: **u,f.**

Freyre, Gilberto & Horton, Rod W. **F2510 .F754163 1980**
Order and Progress: Brazil from Monarchy to Republic. Trade Cloth. Greenwood Publishing Group, Inc. Portsmouth, NH. 1980. 422p. ISBN:0-313-22363-7, ISBN13: 978-0-313-22363-1. Dewey:981/.05. LCCN:80-011440.
Audience: **u,f.** B

Graham, R. **F2510**
Britain and the Onset of Modernization in Brazil, 1850-1914. Trade Cloth. Cambridge University Press. New York, NY. 1968. 402p. Latin American Studies, No. 4 ISBN:0-521-07078-3, ISBN13: 978-0-521-07078-2. Dewey:301.29/81/042. LCCN:68-021393.
Audience: **u,f.**

Graham, Richard **JL2481.G73 1990**
Patronage and Politics in Nineteenth-Century Brazil. Trade Cloth. Stanford University Press. Palo Alto, CA. 1989. 400p. ISBN:0-8047-1593-9, ISBN13: 978-0-8047-1593-5. Dewey:320.9/81/09034. LCCN:89-021598.
Audience: **u,f.** *Choice, 1990.*

Hahner, June E. **HQ1236.5.B6H34 1990**
Emancipating the Female Sex: The Struggle for Women's Rights in Brazil, 1850-1940. Cloth Text. Duke University Press. Durham, NC. 1990. 328p. ISBN:0-8223-1051-1, ISBN13: 978-0-8223-1051-8. Dewey:305.42/0981. LCCN:90-031833.
Audience: **u,f.** *Choice, 1991.*

Huggins, Martha K. **HV9594.P47 H83 1985**
From Slavery to Vagrancy in Brazil: Crime and Social Control in the Third World. Trade Cloth. Rutgers University Press. Piscataway, NJ. 1985. 190p. Crime, Law and Deviance Ser. ISBN:0-8135-1044-9, ISBN13: 978-0-8135-1044-6. Dewey:364/.981/34. LCCN:83-024611.
Audience: **u,f.** *Choice, 1985.*

Karasch, Mary C. **HT1129.R53K37 1986**
Slave Life in Rio De Janerio, 1808-1850. Cloth Text. Princeton University Press. Princeton, NJ. 1987. 448p. ISBN:0-691-07708-8, ISBN13: 978-0-691-07708-6. Dewey:305.5/67/098153. LCCN:85-043290.
Audience: **u,f.** *Choice, 1987.*

Kirkendall, Andrew J. **KHD196.K57 2002**
Class Mates: Male Student Culture and the Making of a Political Class in Nineteenth-Century Brazil. Cloth Text. University of Nebraska Press. Lincoln, NE. 2002. 270p. Engendering Latin America Ser., Vol. 6 ISBN:0-8032-2748-5, ISBN13: 978-0-8032-2748-4. Dewey:340/.092/2. LCCN:2001-052237.
Audience: **u,f.**

Kraay, Hendrik **F2651.S1357K73 2001**
Race, State, and Armed Forces in Independence-Era Brazil: Bahia, 1790s-1840s. Trade Cloth. Stanford University Press. Palo Alto, CA. 2002. 376p. ISBN:0-8047-4248-0, ISBN13: 978-0-8047-4248-1. Dewey:306.2/7/098142. LCCN:2001-048429.
Audience: **u,f.** *Choice, 2002.*

Lauderdale Graham, Sandra **HD8039.D52 B64 1992**
House and Street: The Domestic World of Servants and Masters in Nineteenth-Century Rio de Janeiro. Trade Paper. University of Texas Press. Austin, TX. 1992. 224p. ISBN:0-292-72757-7, ISBN13: 978-0-292-72757-1. Dewey:331.4/8164046/098153. LCCN:92-026226.
Audience: **u,f.**

Levine, Robert M. **F2537**
Vale of Tears: Revisiting the Canudos Massacre in Northeastern Brazil, 1893-1897. Trade Paper. University of California Press. Berkeley, CA. 1995. 366p. ISBN:0-520-20343-7, ISBN13: 978-0-520-20343-3. Dewey:981/.05. LCCN:91-036011.
Audience: **u,f.** *Choice, 1993.*

Lewin, Linda **JL2499.P372.L48 1987**
Politics and Parentela in Paraiba: A Case Study of Family-Based Oligarchy in Brazil. Trade Cloth. Princeton University Press. Princeton, NJ. 1987. 392p. ISBN:0-691-07719-3, ISBN13: 978-0-691-07719-2. Dewey:306/.2/0981. LCCN:86-042850.
Audience: **u,f.** *Choice, 1988.*

McCann, Frank D. **UA619.M387 2003**
Soldiers of the Patria: A History of the Brazilian Army, 1889-1937. Trade Cloth. Stanford University Press. Palo Alto, CA. 2004. 608p. ISBN:0-8047-3222-1, ISBN13: 978-0-8047-3222-2. Dewey:355/.00981. LCCN:2003-007567.
Audience: **u,f.** *Choice, 2004.*

Naro, Nancy **HT1126**
A Slave's Place, a Master's World: Fashioning Dependency in Rural Brazil. Trade Cloth. Continuum International Publishing Group, Ltd. London, 2001. 256p. ISBN:0-8264-5295-7, ISBN13: 978-0-8264-5295-5. Dewey:306.362. LCCN:99-043275.
Audience: **u,f.**

Naro, Nancy Priscilla (Editor) **F1419.N4**
Blacks, Coloureds and National Identity in Nineteenth-Century Latin America. Trade Paper. Institute of Latin American Studies. London, 2003. 164p. Nineteenth-Century Latin America Ser. ISBN:1-900039-47-8, ISBN13: 978-1-900039-47-5. Dewey:305.89608.
Audience: **u,f.**

Nazzari, Muriel **HQ1017.N39 1991**
Disappearance of the Dowry: Women, Families, and Social Change in São Paulo, Brazil, 1600-1900. Trade Cloth. Stanford University Press. Palo Alto, CA. 1991. 272p. ISBN:0-8047-1928-4, ISBN13: 978-0-8047-1928-5. Dewey:306/.0981/61. LCCN:91-009737.
Audience: **u,f.** *Choice, 1992.*

Needell, Jeffrey D. **HN290.Z9E4543 1987**
A Tropical Belle Epoque: Elite Culture and Society in Turn-of-the-Century Rio de Janeiro. Cloth Text. Cambridge University Press. New York, NY. 1988. 384p. Cambridge Latin American Studies, No. 62 ISBN:0-521-33374-1, ISBN13: 978-0-521-33374-0. Dewey:305.5/2/098153. LCCN:87-009399.
Audience: **u,f.** *Choice, 1988.*

Needell, Jeffrey D. **F2536**
The Party of Order: The Conservatives, the State, and Slavery in the Brazilian Monarchy, 1831-1871. Stanford University Press. 2006. ISBN:0-8047-5369-5, ISBN13: 978-0-8047-5369-2.
Audience: **u,f.**

Nishida, Mieko **HT1129.S2N57 2003**
Slavery and Identity: Ethnicity, Gender, and Race in Salvador, Brazil, 1808-1888. Trade Cloth. Indiana University Press. Bloomington, IN. 2003. xiii, 255p. Blacks in the Diaspora Ser. ISBN:0-253-21581-1, ISBN13: 978-0-253-21581-9. Dewey:306.3/62/0981. LCCN:2002-010944.
Audience: **u,f.** *Choice, 2003.*

Reis, João José **HT1129.S24**
Slave Rebellion in Brazil: The Muslim Uprising of 1835 in Bahia. Arthur Brakel (Translator). Trade Paper. Johns Hopkins University Press. Baltimore, MD. 1995. 304p. Studies in Atlantic History and Culture ISBN:0-8018-5250-1, ISBN13: 978-0-8018-5250-3. Dewey:326/.0981/42.
Audience: **u,f.**

Schultz, Kirsten **F2534.S324 2001**
Tropical Versailles: Empire, Monarchy, and the Portuguese Royal Court in Rio de Janeiro, 1808-1821. Paper over Boards. Routledge. New York, NY. 2001. 320p. New World in the Atlantic World Ser. ISBN:0-415-92987-3, ISBN13: 978-0-415-92987-5. Dewey:981/.53033. LCCN:00-068741.
Audience: **u,f.**

Schwarcz, Lilia Moritz **F2536.P37S3913 2003**
The Emperor's Beard: Dom Pedro II and the Tropical Monarchy of Brazil. John Gledson (Translator). Cloth over Boards. Farrar, Straus & Giroux. New York, NY. 2004. 464p. ISBN:0-8090-4219-3, ISBN13: 978-0-8090-4219-7. Dewey:981/.04/092 B. LCCN:2002-038839.
Audience: **u,f.** *Choice, 2005.*

Scott, Rebecca J., et al. **HT1128.A29 1988**
The Abolition of Slavery and the Aftermath of Emancipation in Brazil. Seymour Drescher, Hebe M. Mattos de Castro, George R. Andrews & Robert M. Levine (Authors), David Bushnell (Introduction by). Paper Text. Duke University Press. Durham, NC. 1988. 180p. ISBN:0-8223-0888-6, ISBN13: 978-0-8223-0888-1. Dewey:326/.0981. LCCN:88-021921.
Audience: **u,f.**

Stein, Stanley J. **F2651.V3S7 1985**
Vassouras: A Brazilian Coffee County, 1850-1900: The Roles of Planter and Slave in a Plantation Society. Trade Paper. Princeton University Press. Princeton, NJ. 1986. 336p. ISBN:0-691-02236-4, ISBN13: 978-0-691-02236-9. Dewey:981/.53. LCCN:85-042659.
Audience: **u,f.** **B**

Topik, Steven C. **E183.8.B7T66 1996**
Trade and Gunboats: The United States and Brazil in the Age of Empire. Trade Cloth. Stanford University Press. Palo Alto, CA. 1997. viii, 301p. ISBN:0-8047-2602-7, ISBN13: 978-0-8047-2602-3. Dewey:327.7/3/081. LCCN:96-010467.
Audience: **u,f.** *Choice, 1997.*

Toussaint-Samson, Adele **F2513.T78 2001**
A Parisian in Brazil: The Travel Account of a Frenchwoman in Nineteenth-Century Rio de Janiero. June Edith Hahner (Editor, Introduction by). Book, Other. Rowman & Littlefield Publishers, Inc. Lanham, MD. 2001. 121p. Latin American Silhouettes Ser. ISBN:0-8420-2854-4, ISBN13: 978-0-8420-2854-7. Dewey:981/.04. LCCN:2001-020631.
Audience: **u,f.**

Weinstein, Barbara **HD9161.B82 W44 1983**
The Amazon Rubber Boom, 1850-1920. Trade Cloth. Stanford University Press. Palo Alto, CA. 1983. 376p. ISBN:0-8047-1168-2, ISBN13: 978-0-8047-1168-5. Dewey:338.1/738952/0981. LCCN:82-080926.
Audience: **u,f.**

South America: Individual Countries > Brazil > 20th Century Brazil

Alexander, Robert J. **F2237**
The ABC Presidents: Conversations and Correspondence with the Presidents of Argentina, Brazil, and Chile. Trade Cloth. Greenwood Publishing Group, Inc. Portsmouth, NH. 1992. 336p. ISBN:0-275-94110-8, ISBN13: 978-0-275-94110-9. Dewey:327.8. LCCN:92-003676.
Audience: **g,l,u,f.**

Alexander, Robert J. **F2538.22.K8A83 1991**
Juscelino Kubitschek and the Development of Brazil. Paper Text. Ohio University Press. Athens, OH. 1991. 500p. Monographs in International Studies, Latin America Ser., No. 16 ISBN:0-89680-163-2, ISBN13: 978-0-89680-163-9. Dewey:981.06/3/0973. LCCN:91-022387.
Audience: **u,f.** *Choice, 1992.*

Alvarez, Sonia E. **HQ1236.5.B6A44 1990**
Engendering Democracy in Brazil: Women's Movements in Transition Politics. Trade Paper. Princeton University Press. Princeton, NJ. 1990. 320p. ISBN:0-691-02325-5, ISBN13: 978-0-691-02325-0. Dewey:305.42/0981. LCCN:90-033837.
Audience: **u,f.** *Choice, 1991.*

Andrews, George R. **F2651.S29**
Blacks and Whites in Sao Paulo, Brazil, 1888-1988. Trade Paper. University of Wisconsin Press. Chicago, IL. 1991. 376p. ISBN:0-299-13104-1, ISBN13: 978-0-299-13104-3. Dewey:305.80098161. LCCN:91-050320.
Audience: **u,f.** *Choice, 1992.*

Archdiocese of São Paulo Staff **HV8599.B7C3813 1998**
Torture in Brazil: A Shocking Report on the Pervasive Use of Torture by Brazilian Military Governments, 1964-1979, Secretly Prepared by the Archiodese of São Paulo. Joan Dassin (Editor, Prologue by), Jaime Wright (Translator). Trade Paper. University of Texas Press. Austin, TX. 1998. 267p. ILAS Special Publication Ser. ISBN:0-292-70484-4, ISBN13: 978-0-292-70484-8. Dewey:365/.644. LCCN:98-013511.
Audience: **u,f.** *Choice, 1999.*

Bastide, Roger **BL2590.B7**
The African Religions of Brazil: Toward a Sociology of the Interpenetration of Civilizations. Helen Sebba (Translator). Trade Cloth. Johns Hopkins University Press. Baltimore, MD. 1978. 494p. Johns Hopkins Studies in Atlantic History and Culture Ser. ISBN:0-8018-2056-1, ISBN13: 978-0-8018-2056-4. Dewey:299/.6/0981. LCCN:78-005421.
Audience: **l,u,f.**

Beattie, Peter M. **UB325.B6B43 2001**
The Tribute of Blood: Army, Honor, Race, and Nation in Brazil, 1864-1945. Trade Cloth. Duke University Press. Durham, NC. 2001. 376p. Latin America Otherwise Ser. ISBN:0-8223-2733-3, ISBN13: 978-0-8223-2733-2. Dewey:306.2/7/0981. LCCN:2001-028884.
Audience: **u,f.** *Choice, 2002.*

Besse, Susan K. **HQ1542**
Restructuring Patriarchy: The Modernization of Gender Inequality in Brazil, 1914-1940. Library Binding. University of North Carolina Press. Chapel Hill, NC. 1996. ISBN:0-614-07953-5, ISBN13: 978-0-614-07953-1. Dewey:305.4/0981. LCCN:95-023353.
Audience: **u,f.** *Choice, 1996.*

Borges, Dain **HQ594.15.B34B67 1992**
The Family in Bahia, Brazil, 1870-1945. Trade Cloth. Stanford University Press. Palo Alto, CA. 1992. 440p. ISBN:0-8047-1921-7, ISBN13: 978-0-8047-1921-6. Dewey:306.85/0981/42. LCCN:91-044471.
Audience: **u,f.** *Choice, 1993.*

Branford, Sue & Rocha, Jan **HD1333.B6**
The Story of the Landless Movement in Brazil. Latin America Bureau. 2002. ISBN:1-899365-51-6, ISBN13: 978-1-899365-51-7.
Audience: **u,f.**

Bresser Pereira, Luiz C. **HC125.P4379 1996**
Economic Crisis and State Reform in Brazil: Toward a New Interpretation of Latin America. Library Binding. Lynne Rienner Publishers, Inc. Boulder, CO. 1996. 258p. ISBN:1-55587-532-7, ISBN13: 978-1-55587-532-9. Dewey:338.98. LCCN:94-028296.
Audience: **u,f.** *Choice, 1996.*

Burdick, John **BR675.B871998**
Blessed Anastacia: Women, Race and Popular Christianity in Brazil. UK-B Format Paperback. Routledge. New York, NY. 1998. 256p. ISBN:0-415-91260-1, ISBN13: 978-0-415-91260-0. Dewey:306.6/7810829/08996. LCCN:98-016293.
Audience: **u,f.**

Burdick, John **BX1466.2**
Looking for God in Brazil: The Progressive Catholic Church in Urban Brazil's Religious Arena. Trade Cloth. University of California Press. Berkeley, CA. 1993. 280p. ISBN:0-520-08000-9, ISBN13: 978-0-520-08000-3. Dewey:261.80981. LCCN:92-032556.
Audience: **u,f.**

Burns, E. Bradford **F2521**
A History of Brazil. Ed. 3. Trade Cloth. Columbia University Press. New York, NY. 1993. 544p. ISBN:0-231-07954-0, ISBN13: 978-0-231-07954-9. Dewey:981. LCCN:93-012216.
Audience: **l,u,f.** *B*

Burns, E. Bradford **E183.8.B7**
The Unwritten Alliance: Riobanco and Brazilian-American Relations. Cloth Text. Columbia University Press. New York, NY. 1966. 305p. Institute of Latin American Studies ISBN:0-231-02855-5, ISBN13: 978-0-231-02855-4. Dewey:327.73081. LCCN:65-025661.
Audience: **u,f.**

Butler, Kim D. **F2651.S2B85 1998**
Freedoms Given, Freedoms Won: Afro-Brazilians in Post-Abolition Sao Paolo and Salvador. Cloth Text. Rutgers University Press. Piscataway, NJ. 1998. 306p. ISBN:0-8135-2503-9, ISBN13: 978-0-8135-2503-7. Dewey:305.896081. LCCN:97-043478.
Audience: **u,f.** *Choice, 1999.*

Cardoso, Fernando E. & Faletto, Enzo **HC125**
Dependency and Development in Latin America. Marjory M. Urquidi (Translator). Trade Cloth. University of California Press. Berkeley, CA. 1979. 227p. ISBN:0-520-03527-5, ISBN13: 978-0-520-03527-0. Dewey:330.9/8/003. LCCN:75-046033.
Audience: **u,f.** *B*

Cardoso, Fernando Henrique **F2538.5.C37A3 2006**
The Accidental President of Brazil: A Memoir. Trade Cloth. PublicAffairs. New York, NY. 2006. 312p. ISBN:1-58648-324-2, ISBN13: 978-1-58648-324-1. Dewey:984.064092 B. LCCN:2005-056385.
Audience: **u,f.**

Castor, Belmiro V. J. **JL2431.C38913 2002**
Brazil Is Not for Amateurs: Patterns of Governance in the Land of Jeitinho. Cloth Text. Xlibris Corporation. Philadelphia, PA. 2003. 265p. ISBN:1-4010-7641-6, ISBN13: 978-1-4010-7641-2. Dewey:351.81. LCCN:2002-094791.
Audience: **u,f.**

Caufield, Sue Ann **HQ18.B7C38 2000**
In Defense of Honor: Sexual Morality, Modernity and Nation in Early Twentieth Century Brazil. Trade Cloth. Duke University Press. Durham, NC. 1999. xiv, 311p. ISBN:0-8223-2377-X, ISBN13: 978-0-8223-2377-8. Dewey:306.7/0981/0904. LCCN:99-028323.
Audience: **u,f.** *Choice, 2000.*

Chandler, Billy J. **F2583.F472 C48**
The Bandit King: Lampiao of Brazil. Trade Cloth. Texas A&M University Press. College Station, TX. 1978. 276p. ISBN:0-89096-050-X, ISBN13: 978-0-89096-050-9. Dewey:364.1/5/0924. LCCN:77-099275.
Audience: **u,f.**

Cunha, Euclides Da **F2537**
Rebellion in the Backlands. Samuel Putnam (Translator). Trade Paper. University of Chicago Press. Chicago, IL. 1957. 562p. ISBN:0-226-12444-4, ISBN13: 978-0-226-12444-5. Dewey:981.
Audience: **u,f.**

Davis, S. H. **F2519.1.A6**
Victims of the Miracle. Trade Cloth. Cambridge University Press. New York, NY. 1977. 240p. ISBN:0-521-21738-5, ISBN13: 978-0-521-21738-5. Dewey:305.8/98/0811. LCCN:77-005132.
Audience: **u,f.**

De Magalhaes De Gandavo, P. **F2526**
The Histories of Brazil. John B. Stetson (Translator). Trade Cloth. Library Reprints, Inc. Temecula, CA. 1922. ISBN:0-7222-2601-2, ISBN13: 978-0-7222-2601-8. Dewey:981.
Audience: **u,f.**

Dean, Warren **HC188.S3.D4**
The Industrialization of Sao Paulo, 1880-1945. Trade Cloth. University of Texas Press. Austin, TX. 1969. x, 263p. ISBN:0-292-70004-0, ISBN13: 978-0-292-70004-8. Dewey:338/.0981/6. LCCN:73-096435.
Audience: **u,f.** *B*

Dean, Warren **SB291.H4 D43 1987**
Brazil and the Struggle for Rubber: A Study in Environmental History. Alfred W. Crosby & Donald Worster (Contribution by). Trade Cloth. Cambridge University Press. New York, NY. 1987. 256p. Studies in Environment and History ISBN:0-521-33477-2, ISBN13: 978-0-521-33477-8. Dewey:338.1/738952/0981. LCCN:87-005130.
Audience: **u,f.** *Choice, 1988.*

Dean, Warren **SD418.3.B6**
With Broadax and Firebrand: The Destruction of the Brazilian Atlantic Forest. Stuart B. Schwartz (Foreword by). Trade Paper. University of California Press. Berkeley, CA. 1997. 502p. ISBN:0-520-20886-2, ISBN13: 978-0-520-20886-5. Dewey:304.2/8/098109152. LCCN:94-005681.
Audience: **u,f.** *Choice, 1995.*

Diacon, Todd A. **F2537.D52 1991**
Millenarian Vision, Capitalist Reality: Brazil's Contestado Rebellion, 1912-1916. Library Binding. Duke University Press. Durham, NC. 1991. 215p. ISBN:0-8223-1157-7, ISBN13: 978-0-8223-1157-7. Dewey:981/.05. LCCN:91-000521.
Audience: **u,f.** *Choice, 1992.*

Diacon, Todd A. **F2537.R66D53 2004**
Stringing Together a Nation: Dido Mariano Da Silva Rondon and the Construction of a Modern Brazil, 1906-1930. Trade Cloth. Duke University Press. Durham, NC. 2004. 240p. ISBN:0-8223-3210-8, ISBN13: 978-0-8223-3210-7. LCCN:2003-013452.
Audience: **u,f.** *Choice, 2004.*

Drogus, Carol A. **BX1466.2.D76 1997**
Women, Religion, and Social Change in Brazil's Popular Church. Trade Cloth. University of Notre Dame Press. Notre Dame, IN. 1997. 226p. Helen Kellogg Institute for International Studies Ser. ISBN:0-268-01951-7, ISBN13: 978-0-268-01951-8. Dewey:282/.81/082. LCCN:97-021492.
Audience: **u,f.** *Choice, 1999.*

Drogus, Carol Ann & Stewart-Gambino, Hannah **BX1466.3.D76 2005**
Activist Faith: Grassroots Women in Democratic Brazil and Chile. Saddle Stitched, Cloth over Boards, Dust Jacket. Pennsylvania State University Press. University Park, PA. 2005. 212p. ISBN:0-271-02549-2, ISBN13: 978-0-271-02549-0. Dewey:261.80820981. LCCN:2004-023769.
Audience: **u,f.** *Choice, 2005.*

Dulles, John W. **F2538.V33**
Vargas of Brazil: A Political Biography. Trade Cloth. University of Texas Press. Austin, TX. 1967. 409p. ISBN:0-292-73655-X, ISBN13: 978-0-292-73655-9. Dewey:981/.06/0924.
Audience: **u,f.**

Dulles, John W. **F2538.22.C37D84**
Castello Branco: The Making of a Brazilian President. Roberto De Oliveira Campos (Foreword by). Trade Cloth. Texas A&M University Press. College Station, TX. 1978. 544p. ISBN:0-89096-043-7, ISBN13: 978-0-89096-043-1. Dewey:981/.06/0924. LCCN:77-099279.
Audience: **u,f.**

Eakin, Marshall C. **HD9536.B83N684 1989**
A British Enterprise in Brazil: The St. John d'el Rey Mining Company and the Morro Velho Gold Mine, 1830-1960. Cloth Text. Duke University Press. Durham, NC. 1989. 336p. ISBN:0-8223-0914-9, ISBN13: 978-0-8223-0914-7. Dewey:338.7/6223422/098151. LCCN:89-033441.
Audience: **u,f.** *Choice, 1991.*

Eakin, Marshall C. **HC189.B4E25 2001**
Tropical Capitalism: The Industrialization of Belo Horizonte, Brazil. Cloth over Boards. Palgrave Macmillan. New York, NY. 2002. 288p. ISBN:0-312-22306-4, ISBN13: 978-0-312-22306-9. Dewey:338.981/51. LCCN:2001-021893.
Audience: **u,f.** *Choice, 2002.*

Fausto, Boris **F2521.F33213 1999**
A Concise History of Brazil. Arthur Brakel (Translator). Trade Cloth. Cambridge University Press. New York, NY. 1999. 376p. Concise Histories Ser. ISBN:0-521-56332-1, ISBN13: 978-0-521-56332-1. Dewey:981. LCCN:98-024722.
Audience: **u,f.**

Font, Mauricio A. **HC187.F6326 2002**
Transforming Brazil: A Reform Era in Perspective. Book, Other. Rowman & Littlefield Publishers, Inc. Lanham, MD. 2003. 288p. ISBN:0-8476-8356-7, ISBN13: 978-0-8476-8356-7. Dewey:320/.6/0981. LCCN:2002-068142.
Audience: **u,f.** *Choice, 2003.*

Foweraker, Joe **HD496 .F68 2002**
The Struggle for Land: A Political Economy of the Pioneer Frontier in Brazil from 1930 to the Present Day. Alan Knight (Contribution by). Trade Paper. Cambridge University Press. New York, NY. 2002. 286p. Cambridge Latin American Studies ISBN:0-521-52600-0, ISBN13: 978-0-521-52600-5. Dewey:333.3/335/0981.
Audience: **u,f.**

Frank, Zephyr L. **HC189.R4F72 2004**
Dutra's World: Wealth and Family in Nineteenth-Century Rio de Janeiro. Trade Cloth. University of New Mexico Press. Albuquerque, NM. 2004. 230p. Dialogos Ser. ISBN:0-8263-3410-5, ISBN13: 978-0-8263-3410-7. Dewey:305.5/234. LCCN:2004-015734.
Audience: **u,f.** *Choice, 2005.*

Freire, Paulo **LC2605**
Pedagogy of the Oppressed. Trade Cloth. The Seabury Press, Inc. New York, NY. 1973. ISBN:0-8164-9132-1, ISBN13: 978-0-8164-9132-2. Dewey:370/.9172/4.
Audience: **u,f.**

Freyre, Gilberto **F2510.F7563 1980**
The Mansions and the Shanties (Sobrados E Mucambos): The Making of Modern Brazil. Harriet De Onis (Translator). Trade Cloth. Greenwood Publishing Group, Inc. Portsmouth, NH. 1980. 431p. ISBN:0-313-22148-0, ISBN13: 978-0-313-22148-4. Dewey:981. LCCN:80-010887.
Audience: **u,f.** B

Freyre, Gilberto **F2510.F75243**
The Masters and the Slaves: A Study in the Development of Brazilian Civilization. Samuel Putnam (Translator). Trade Cloth. Alfred A. Knopf Inc. New York, NY. 1964. 432p. Borzoi Books on Latin America Ser. ISBN:0-394-43561-3, ISBN13: 978-0-394-43561-9. Dewey:981. LCCN:64-000395.
Audience: **u,f.**

Garfield, Seth **F2520.1.A4G37 2001**
Indigenous Struggle at the Heart of Brazil: State Policy, Frontier Expansion and the Xavante Indians, 1937-1988. Trade Cloth. Duke University Press. Durham, NC. 2001. 320p. ISBN:0-8223-2661-2, ISBN13: 978-0-8223-2661-8. Dewey:323.1/1984. LCCN:00-061746.
Audience: **u,f.** *Choice, 2002.*

Gordon, Lincoln **F2538.2.G76 2001**
Brazil's Second Chance: En Route Toward the First World. Trade Paper. Brookings Institution Press. Washington, DC. 2001. xv, 243p. ISBN:0-8157-0032-6, ISBN13: 978-0-8157-0032-6. Dewey:981.06. LCCN:2001-000442.
Audience: **u,f.** *Choice, 2001.*

Graham, Laura R. **F2520.1.A4G73 2003**
Performing Dreams: Discourses of Immortality among the Xavante of Central Brazil. Ed. 2. Trade Paper. Wheatmark. Tucson, AZ. 2003. 304p. ISBN:1-58736-172-8, ISBN13: 978-1-58736-172-2. Dewey:981.00498. LCCN:2002-116088.
Audience: **u,f.**

Hagopian, Frances **JL2481.H34 1996**
Traditional Politics and Regime Change in Brazil. Robert H. Bates, Ellen Comisso, Peter Hall, Peter Lange, Joel S. Migdal & Helen V. Milner (Contribution by). Trade Cloth. Cambridge University Press. New York, NY. 1996. 341p. Studies in Comparative Politics ISBN:0-521-41429-6, ISBN13: 978-0-521-41429-6. Dewey:320.981/09/045. LCCN:95-020453.
Audience: **u,f.** *Choice, 1997.*

Harding, Rachel E. **BL2592.C35H37 2000**
A Refuge in Thunder: Candomble and Alternative Spaces of Blackness. Trade Cloth. Indiana University Press. Bloomington, IN. 2000. 288p. Blacks in the Diaspora Ser. ISBN:0-253-33705-4, ISBN13: 978-0-253-33705-4. Dewey:299/.673/09814209034. LCCN:99-054087.
Audience: **u,f.**

Harter, Eugene C. **F2659.A5H37 2000**
The Lost Colony of the Confederacy. Trade Paper. Texas A&M University Press. College Station, TX. 2000. 160p. Texas A&M University Military History Ser., Vol. 69 ISBN:1-58544-102-3, ISBN13: 978-1-58544-102-0. Dewey:981.004/13. LCCN:00-037803.
Audience: **u,f.**

Hilton, Stanley E. **D810.S7 H47**
Hitler's Secret War in South America, 1939-1945: German Military Espionage and Allied Counterespionage in Brazil. Trade Paper. Louisiana State University Press. Baton Rouge, LA.

1999. 384p. ISBN:0-8071-2436-2, ISBN13: 978-0-8071-2436-9. Dewey:940.54/87/430981. LCCN:80-017726.
Audience: **u,f.**

Hoffman, Paul **TL540.S25H642003**
Wings of Madness: Alberto Santos-Dumont and the Invention of Flight. Trade Cloth. Disney Press. New York, NY. 2003. 380p. ISBN:0-7868-6659-4, ISBN13: 978-0-7868-6659-5. Dewey:629.13/0092. LCCN:2002-032806.
Audience: **u,f.**

Holloway, Thomas H. **JV7462 .H64**
Immigrants on the Land: Coffee and Society in Sao Paulo, 1886-1934. Trade Cloth. University of North Carolina Press. Chapel Hill, NC. 1980. xviii, 218p. ISBN:0-8078-1430-X, ISBN13: 978-0-8078-1430-7. Dewey:301.32/9/816. LCCN:79-024805.
Audience: **u,f.**

Holloway, Thomas H. **HV8185.R5H65 1993**
Policing Rio de Janeiro: Repression and Resistance in a Nineteenth-Century City. Trade Cloth. Stanford University Press. Palo Alto, CA. 1993. 392p. ISBN:0-8047-2056-8, ISBN13: 978-0-8047-2056-4. Dewey:363.2/0981/53. LCCN:92-045685.
Audience: **u,f.** *Choice, 1994.*

Hunter, Wendy **JL2420.C58H86 1997**
Eroding Military Influence in Brazil: Politicians Against Soldiers. Trade Paper. University of North Carolina Press. Chapel Hill, NC. 1997. 260p. ISBN:0-8078-4620-1, ISBN13: 978-0-8078-4620-9. Dewey:320.981. LCCN:96-022285.
Audience: **u,f.** *Choice, 1997.*

Johnson, Ollie Andrew III **F2538.J614 2001**
Brazilian Party Politics and the Coup of 1964. Trade Cloth. University Press of Florida. Gainesville, FL. 2001. xii, 176p. ISBN:0-8130-2079-4, ISBN13: 978-0-8130-2079-2. Dewey:981.06. LCCN:2001-027455.
Audience: **u,f.**

Keck, Margaret E. **JL2498.T7K43 1992**
The Worker's Party and Democratization in Brazil. Cloth over Boards. Yale University Press. Cumberland, RI. 1992. 384p. ISBN:0-300-05074-7, ISBN13: 978-0-300-05074-5. Dewey:324.281/07. LCCN:91-028446.
Audience: **u,f.**

Klein, Herbert & Luna, Francisco Vidal **HC187.L835 2006**
Brazil since 1980. Cloth Text. Cambridge University Press. New York, NY. 2006. 288p. The World Since 1980 Ser. ISBN:0-521-82044-8, ISBN13: 978-0-521-82044-8. Dewey:330.981. LCCN:2006-001012.
Audience: **u,f.**

Lauderdale Graham, Sandra **HT1129.P36L38 2002**
Caetana Says No: Women's Stories from a Brazilian Slave Society. Cloth Text. Cambridge University Press. New York, NY. 2002. 208p. New Approaches to the Americas Ser. ISBN:0-521-81532-0, ISBN13: 978-0-521-81532-1. Dewey:305.48/9625. LCCN:2002-067666.
Audience: **u,f.** *Choice, 2003.*

Leacock, Ruth **E183.8.B7L4 1990**
Requiem for Revolution: The United States and Brazil, 1961-1969. Trade Cloth, Trade Paper. Kent State University Press. Kent, OH. 1990. 329p. American Diplomatic History Ser., No. 3 ISBN:0-87338-401-6, ISBN13: 978-0-87338-401-8. Dewey:327.73081. LCCN:89-020054.
Audience: **u,f.** *Choice, 1990.*

Lesser, Jeff **F2659.A1L47 1999**
Negotiating National Identity: Immigrants, Minorities, and the Struggle for Ethnicity in Brazil. Trade Cloth. Duke University Press. Durham, NC. 1999. 296p. ISBN:0-8223-2260-9, ISBN13: 978-0-8223-2260-3. Dewey:305.8/00981. LCCN:98-038238.
Audience: **u,f.** *Choice, 2000.*

Lesser, Jeffrey **F2659.J5L54 1995**
Welcoming the Undesirables: Brazil and the Jewish Question. Trade Paper. University of California Press. Berkeley, CA. 1995. 300p. ISBN:0-520-08413-6, ISBN13: 978-0-520-08413-1. Dewey:981/.004924. LCCN:93-021199.
Audience: **u,f.** *Choice, 1995.*

Levine, Robert M. **F2521**
The History of Brazil. Cloth Text. Greenwood Publishing Group, Inc. Portsmouth, NH. 1999. 232p. The Histories of the Modern Nations Ser. ISBN:0-313-30390-8, ISBN13: 978-0-313-30390-6. Dewey:981. LCCN:99-021711.
Audience: **l,u,f.** *Choice, 2000.*

Levine, Robert M. **F2358.V33**
The Vargas Regime. Trade Cloth. Columbia University Press. New York, NY. 1970. 270p. Institute of Latin American Studies ISBN:0-231-03370-2, ISBN13: 978-0-231-03370-1. Dewey:981.06/0924. LCCN:78-115222.
Audience: **u,f.**

Lone, Stewart **F2659.J3L66 2001**
The Japanese Community in Brazil, 1908-1940: Between Samurai and Carnival. Cloth over Boards. Palgrave Macmillan. New York, NY. 2002. 221p. ISBN:0-333-63686-4, ISBN13: 978-0-333-63686-2. Dewey:305.8956081. LCCN:2001-035820.
Audience: **u,f.** *Choice, 2002.*

Maxwell, Kenneth R. **F2521.M495 2003**
Naked Tropics: Essays on Empire and Other Rogues. Fouad Ajami (Foreword by). Paper over Boards. Routledge. New York, NY. 2003. 320p. New World in the Atlantic World Ser. ISBN:0-415-94576-3, ISBN13: 978-0-415-94576-9. Dewey:981. LCCN:2003-043129.
Audience: **u,f.**

Meade, Teresa A. **HT178.B72R565 1997**
Civilizing Rio: Reform and Resistance in a Brazilian City, 1889-1930. Trade Paper. Pennsylvania State University Press. University Park, PA. 1996. 224p. ISBN:0-271-01608-6, ISBN13: 978-0-271-01608-5. Dewey:307.76/0981/53. LCCN:96-006452.
Audience: **u,f.** *Choice, 1997.*

O'Dougherty, Maureen **HT690.B7O36 2002**
Consumption Intensified: The Politics of Middle-Class Daily Life in Brazil. Trade Cloth. Duke University Press. Durham, NC. 2002. 224p. ISBN:0-8223-2879-8, ISBN13: 978-0-8223-2879-7. Dewey:305.5//5/0981. LCCN:2001-054304.
Audience: **u,f.** *Choice, 2003, 2002.*

Pang, Eul-Soo **F2551**
The Politics of Coronelismo in Brazil: The Case of Bahia, 1889-1930. University of California Press. 1971.
Audience: **u,f.**

Parker, Phyllis R. **F2538.2**
Brazil and the Quiet Intervention, 1964. Cloth Text. University of Texas Press. Austin, TX. 1979. 161p. Texas Pan American Ser. ISBN:0-292-78507-0, ISBN13: 978-0-292-78507-6. Dewey:327.73/081. LCCN:78-025856.
Audience: **u,f.**

Patai, Daphne **HQ1542.B73 1988**
Brazilian Women Speak: Contemporary Life Stories. Cloth Text. Rutgers University Press. Piscataway, NJ. 1988. 404p. ISBN:0-8135-1300-6, ISBN13: 978-0-8135-1300-3. Dewey:305.4/0981. LCCN:87-023498.
Audience: **u,f.**

Peard, Julyan G. **RC962.B6P43 1999**
Race, Place, and Medicine: The Idea of the Tropics in Nineteenth-Century Brazil. Trade Cloth. Duke University Press. Durham, NC. 1999. 240p. ISBN:0-8223-2376-1, ISBN13: 978-0-8223-2376-1. Dewey:616.9/883/098109034. LCCN:99-034867.
Audience: **u,f.**

Pereira, Anthony W. **HD6614.A29P47 1997**
End of the Peasantry: The Rural Labor Movement in Northeast Brazil, 1961-1988. Trade Paper. University of Pittsburgh Press. Pittsburgh, PA. 1997. 232p. Latin American Ser. ISBN:0-8229-5618-7, ISBN13: 978-0-8229-5618-1. Dewey:331.88/13/09813. LCCN:96-045889.
Audience: **u,f.** *Choice, 1997.*

Pessar, Patricia R. (Translator) **BR675.P47 2004**
From Fanatics to Folk: Brazilian Millenarianism and Popular Culture. Trade Cloth, Pictures or Photographs. Duke University Press. Durham, NC. 2004. 296p. ISBN:0-8223-3275-2, ISBN13: 978-0-8223-3275-6. Dewey:209/.0981. LCCN:2003-015047.
Audience: **u,f.** *Choice, 2004.*

Reichmann, Rebecca L. **F2659.N4R245 1999**
Race in Contemporary Brazil: From Indifference to Inequality. Trade Cloth. Pennsylvania State University Press. University Park, PA. 1999. 304p. ISBN:0-271-01905-0, ISBN13: 978-0-271-01905-5. Dewey:305.896081. LCCN:98-037292.
Audience: **u,f.** *Choice, 2000.*

Reis, Joao Jose **GT3233.A2R4513 2003**
Death Is a Festival: Funeral Rites and Rebellion in Nineteenth-Century Brazil. H. Sabrina Gledhill (Translator). Trade Cloth. University of North Carolina Press. Chapel Hill, NC. 2003. 448p. Latin America in Translation Ser. ISBN:0-8078-2773-8, ISBN13: 978-0-8078-2773-4. Dewey:393.9/0981/09034. LCCN:2002-011996.
Audience: **u,f.** *Choice, 2004.*

Ribeiro, Darcy & Rabassa, Gregory **F2510.R47713 2000**
The Brazilian People: The Formation and Meaning of Brazil. Trade Cloth. University Press of Florida. Gainesville, FL. 2000. xviii, 332p. University of Florida Center for Latin American Studies ISBN:0-8130-1777-7, ISBN13: 978-0-8130-1777-8. Dewey:981. LCCN:99-086541.
Audience: **u,f.** *Choice, 2000.*

Ridings, Eugene **JL2481 .R55 1994**
Business Interest Groups in Nineteenth-Century Brazil. Alan Knight (Contribution by). Trade Cloth. Cambridge University Press. New York, NY. 1994. 395p. Latin American Studies, No. 78 ISBN:0-521-45485-9, ISBN13: 978-0-521-45485-8. Dewey:322.4/3/0981/09034. LCCN:93-032152.
Audience: **u,f.** *Choice, 1995.*

Schwarcz, Lilia **F2699.A1**
The Spectacle of the Races: Scientists, Institutions and the Race Question in Brazil, 1870-1930. Leland Guyer (Translator). Cloth over Boards. Farrar, Straus & Giroux. New York, NY. 1999. 224p. ISBN:0-8090-8789-8, ISBN13: 978-0-8090-8789-1. Dewey:305.8/00981. LCCN:98-042234.
Audience: **u,f.** *Choice, 2000.*

Seidman, Gay W. **HD8286.5.S45 1994**
Manufacturing Militance: Workers' Movements in Brazil and South Africa, 1970-1985. Trade Cloth. University of California Press. Berkeley, CA. 1994. 372p. ISBN:0-520-07519-6, ISBN13: 978-0-520-07519-1. Dewey:331.880968. LCCN:92-035866.
Audience: **u,f.** *Choice, 1994.*

Sheriff, Robin E. **F2646.9.N4S44 2001**
Dreaming Equality: Color, Race and Racism in Urban Brazil. Trade Cloth. Rutgers University Press. Piscataway, NJ. 2004. 288p. ISBN:0-8135-2999-9, ISBN13: 978-0-8135-2999-8. Dewey:305.896/08153. LCCN:2001-019294.
Audience: **u,f.** *Choice, 2002.*

Simpson, Amelia S. **PN1992.6.S48 1993**
Xuxa: The Mega Marketing of Gender, Race, and Modernity. Trade Cloth. Temple University Press. Philadelphia, PA. 1993. 256p. ISBN:1-56639-101-6, ISBN13: 978-1-56639-101-6. Dewey:302.23/45/0981. LCCN:93-018121.
Audience: **u,f.** *Choice, 1994.*

Skidmore, Thomas E. **F2659.A1.S55**
Black into White; Race and Nationality in Brazilian Thought. Trade Cloth. Oxford University Press, Inc. New York, NY. 1974. xvi, 299p. ISBN:0-19-501776-5, ISBN13: 978-0-19-501776-2. Dewey:323.1/81. LCCN:73-090371.
Audience: **u,f.** B

Skidmore, Thomas E. **F2521.S54 1999**
Brazil: Five Centuries of Change. Paper Text. Oxford University Press, Inc. New York, NY. 1999. 272p. Latin American Histories Ser. ISBN:0-19-505810-0, ISBN13: 978-0-19-505810-9. Dewey:981. LCCN:98-023122.
Audience: **u,f.**

Skidmore, Thomas E. **F2538.25.S58 1988**
The Politics of Military Rule in Brazil, 1964-1985. Trade Cloth. Oxford University Press, Inc. New York, NY. 1988. 432p. ISBN:0-19-503898-3, ISBN13: 978-0-19-503898-9. Dewey:981/.063. LCCN:87-011147.
Audience: **u,f.** *Choice, 1988.*

Smallman, Shawn C. **F2537.S65 2002**
Fear and Memory in the Brazilian Army and Society, 1889-1954. Trade Cloth. University of North Carolina Press. Chapel Hill, NC. 2002. 280p. ISBN:0-8078-2691-X, ISBN13: 978-0-8078-2691-1. Dewey:981.06/4. LCCN:2001-052576.
Audience: **u,f.** *Choice, 2002.*

Smith, Joseph **E183.8.B7S55 1991**
Unequal Giants: Diplomatic Relations Between the United States and Brazil, 1889-1930. Cloth Text. University of Pittsburgh Press. Pittsburgh, PA. 1991. 352p. Latin American Ser. ISBN:0-8229-3676-3, ISBN13: 978-0-8229-3676-3. Dewey:327.73081. LCCN:90-025379.
Audience: **u,f.** *Choice, 1992.*

Spitzer, Leo **DS135.A9S65 1989**
Lives in Between: Assimilation and Marginality in Austria, Brazil, and West Africa, 1780-1945. Cloth Text. Cambridge University Press. New York, NY. 1990. 262p. Cambridge Studies in Comparative World History ISBN:0-521-37214-3, ISBN13: 978-0-521-37214-5. Dewey:303.48/2. LCCN:89-024004.
Audience: **u,f.** *Choice, 1990.*

Telles, Edward Eric **F2659.A1T45 2004**
Race in Another America: The Significance of Skin Color in Brazil. Trade Cloth. Princeton University Press. Princeton, NJ. 2004. 336p. ISBN:0-691-11866-3, ISBN13: 978-0-691-11866-6. Dewey:305.896/081. LCCN:2004-044288.
Audience: **u,f.** *Choice, 2005.*

Topik, Steven **HC187.T558 1987**
The Political Economy of the Brazilian State, 1889-1930. Cloth Text. University of Texas Press. Austin, TX. 1987. 255p. Latin American Monographs, No. 71 ISBN:0-292-76500-2, ISBN13: 978-0-292-76500-9. Dewey:338.981. LCCN:87-005835.
Audience: **u,f.** *Choice, 1988.*

Treece, David **F2519**
Exiles, Allies, Rebels: Brazil's Indianist Movement, Indigenist Politics and the Imperial Nation-State. Trade Cloth. Greenwood Publishing Group, Inc. Portsmouth, NH. 2000. 288p. Contributions in Latin American Studies, No. 16 ISBN:0-313-31125-0, ISBN13: 978-0-313-31125-3. Dewey:981/.00498. LCCN:99-049049.
Audience: **u,f.** *Choice, 2000.*

Twine, Frances W. **F2659.N4T86 1998**
Racism in a Racial Democracy: The Maintenance of White Supremacy in Brazil. Trade Cloth. Rutgers University Press. Piscataway, NJ. 1997. 175p. ISBN:0-8135-2364-8, ISBN13: 978-0-8135-2364-4. Dewey:305.896/081. LCCN:97-010768.
Audience: **u,f.** *Choice, 1998.*

Warren, Jonathan W. **F2519.3.E83W37 2001**
Racial Revolutions: Antiracism and Indigenous Resurgence in Brazil. Trade Cloth. Duke University Press. Durham, NC. 2001. 368p. Latin America Otherwise Ser. ISBN:0-8223-2731-7, ISBN13: 978-0-8223-2731-8. Dewey:305.898081. LCCN:2001-033783.
Audience: **u,f.** *Choice, 2002.*

Weinstein, Barbara **HD8289.S282W45 1996**
For Social Peace in Brazil: Industrialists and the Remaking of the Working Class in Sao Paulo, 1920-1964. Trade Paper. University of North Carolina Press. Chapel Hill, NC. 1997. 456p. ISBN:0-8078-4602-3, ISBN13: 978-0-8078-4602-5. Dewey:305.5/62/098161. LCCN:96-010888.
Audience: **u,f.** *Choice, 1997.*

Welch, Cliff **HD6613.5.W45 1999**
The Seed Was Planted: The Sao Paulo Roots of Brazil's Rural Labor Movement, 1888-1988. Trade Cloth. Pennsylvania State University Press. University Park, PA. 1999. 438p. ISBN:0-271-01788-0, ISBN13: 978-0-271-01788-4. Dewey:331.88/0981/61. LCCN:97-049347.
Audience: **u,f.** *Choice, 1999.*

Weyland, Kurt Gerhard **HC165.W46 2004**
The Politics of Market Reform in Fragile Democracies: Argentina, Brazil, Peru, and Venezuela. Trade Paper. Princeton University Press. Princeton, NJ. 2004. 360p. ISBN:0-691-11787-X, ISBN13: 978-0-691-11787-4. Dewey:338.98.
Audience: **u,f.** *Choice, 2003.*

Williams, Daryle **F2538.W55 2001**
Culture Wars in Brazil: The First Vargas Regime, 1930-1945. Trade Cloth. Duke University Press. Durham, NC. 2001. 312p. ISBN:0-8223-2708-2, ISBN13: 978-0-8223-2708-0. Dewey:981.06/1. LCCN:2001-018769.
Audience: **u,f.** *Choice, 2002.*

Wolfe, Joel D. **HD8290.S32**
Working Women, Working Men: Sao Paulo and the Rise of Brazil's Industrial Working Class, 1900-1955. Cloth Text. Duke University Press. Durham, NC. 1993. 328p. ISBN:0-8223-1330-8, ISBN13: 978-0-8223-1330-4. Dewey:305.562098161. LCCN:92-040484.
Audience: **u,f.** *Choice, 1994.*

Wright, Angus & Wolford, Wendy **HD1333.B6W74 2003**
To Inherit the Earth: Brazil's Landless People and the Struggle to Transform a Nation. Trade Paper. Institute for Food & Development Policy/Food First Books. Oakland, CA. 2003. 400p. ISBN:0-935028-90-0, ISBN13: 978-0-935028-90-4. Dewey:333.3/181. LCCN:2003-014764.
Audience: **u,f.** *Choice, 2004.*

South America: Individual Countries > Paraguay > Colonial Paraguay

Ganson, Barbara Anne **F2230.2.G72G35 2003**
The Guarani under Spanish Rule in the Rio de la Plata. Trade Cloth. Stanford University Press. Palo Alto, CA. 2003. xii, 290p. ISBN:0-8047-3602-2, ISBN13: 978-0-8047-3602-2. Dewey:323.1/198382082. LCCN:2002-030455.
Audience: **u,f.** *Choice, 2003.*

Saeger, James Schofield **F2230.2.G78S34 2000**
The Chaco Mission Frontier: The Guaycuruan Experience, 1700-1800. Trade Cloth. University of Arizona Press. Tucson, AZ. 2000. 266p. ISBN:0-8165-2017-8, ISBN13: 978-0-8165-2017-6. Dewey:982/.3. LCCN:00-008254.
Audience: **u,f.**

South America: Individual Countries > Paraguay > 19th Century Paraguay

Enright, Anne **PR6055.N73P58 2003**
The Pleasure of Eliza Lynch. Trade Cloth. Grove/Atlantic, Inc. New York, NY. 2003. 240p. ISBN:0-87113-868-9, ISBN13: 978-0-87113-868-2. Dewey:823/.914. LCCN:2002-035606.
Audience: **u,f.**

Fowler, Will **F1413**
Authoritarianism in Latin America Since Independence. Greenwood Press. 1996. ISBN:0-313-29843-2, ISBN13: 978-0-313-29843-1.
Audience: **u,f.**

Kraay, Hendrik & Whigham, Thomas L. **F2687.I62 2004**
I Die with My Country: Prespectives on the Paraguayan War, 1864-1870. Cloth Text. University of Nebraska Press. Lincoln, NE. 2005. 320p. Studies in War, Society, and the Military Ser. ISBN:0-8032-2762-0, ISBN13: 978-0-8032-2762-0. Dewey:989.2/05. LCCN:2004-007730.
Audience: **u,f.**

Lewis, Paul H. **F2688.L49 1993**
Political Parties and Generations in Paraguay's Liberal Era, 1869-1940. Trade Cloth. University of North Carolina Press. Chapel Hill, NC. 1992. xvi, 228p. ISBN:0-8078-2078-4, ISBN13: 978-0-8078-2078-0. Dewey:989.2/06. LCCN:92-021164.
Audience: **u,f.** *Choice, 1993.*

Renshaw, John **F2679.I5C48**
The Indians of the Paraguayan Chaco: Identity and Economy. Cloth Text. University of Nebraska Press. Lincoln, NE. 2002. 305p. ISBN:0-8032-3938-6, ISBN13: 978-0-8032-3938-8. Dewey:305.8/98/089226. LCCN:2002-108050.
Audience: **u,f.**

Roett, Riordan & Sacks, Richard S. **F2681.R62 1991**
Paraguay: The Personalist Legacy. Trade Paper. Westview Press. Boulder, CO. 1990. 188p. ISBN:0-86531-272-9, ISBN13: 978-0-86531-272-2. Dewey:989.2. LCCN:90-045813.
Audience: **u,f.** *Choice, 1991.*

Schmidt, Kimberly D. (Author, Editor), et al. **BX4931.2.S79 2001**
Strangers at Home: Amish and Mennonite Women in History. Diane Zimmerman Umble & Steven D. Reschly (Author, Editors). Trade Cloth. Johns Hopkins University Press. Baltimore, MD. 2002. 416p. Center Books in Anabaptist Studies ISBN:0-8018-6786-X, ISBN13: 978-0-8018-6786-6. Dewey:289.7/082. LCCN:2001-000580.
Audience: **u,f.** *Choice, 2002.*

Warren, Harris G. **F2688 .W37**
Paraguay and the Triple Alliance: The Postwar Decade, 1869-1878. Trade Cloth. University of Texas Press. Austin, TX. 1978. 388p. Latin American Monographs, No. 44 ISBN:0-292-76445-6, ISBN13: 978-0-292-76445-3. Dewey:989.2/06. LCCN:77-075824.
Audience: **u,f.**

Whigham, Thomas & Cooney, Jerry W. **Z1821**
A Guide to Collections on Paraguay in the United States. Cloth Text. Greenwood Publishing Group, Inc. Portsmouth, NH. 1995. 136p. Reference Guides to Archival and Manuscript Sources in World History Ser., No. 4 ISBN:0-313-29203-5, ISBN13: 978-0-313-29203-3. Dewey:016.9892. LCCN:95-015449.
Audience: **l,u,f.** *Choice, 1996.*

White, Richard A. **F2686 .W48**
Paraguay's Autonomous Revolution, 1810-1840. Trade Cloth. University of New Mexico Press. Albuquerque, NM. 1978. ISBN:0-8263-0486-9, ISBN13: 978-0-8263-0486-5. Dewey:989.2. LCCN:78-055707.
Audience: **u,f.**

Williams, John H. **F2686**
The Rise and Fall of the Paraguayan Republic, 1800-1870. Cloth Text. University of Texas Press. Austin, TX. 1979. 296p. Latin American Monographs, No. 48 ISBN:0-292-77016-2, ISBN13: 978-0-292-77016-4. Dewey:989.2. LCCN:78-620052.
Audience: **u,f.**

South America: Individual Countries > Paraguay > 20th Century Paraguay

Arens, Richard (Editor) **F2679.2.G9 G46**
Genocide in Paraguay. Trade Cloth. Temple University Press. Philadelphia, PA. 1976. 171p. ISBN:0-87722-088-3, ISBN13: 978-0-87722-088-6. Dewey:323.1/19/80892. LCCN:76-005726.
Audience: **u,f.**

Franks, Jeffrey, et al. **HC222**
Paraguay: Corruption, Reform, and the Financial System. International Monetary Fund. 2005. ISBN:1-58906-420-8, ISBN13: 978-1-58906-420-1.
Audience: **u,f.**

Ganson, Barbara Anne **F2230.2.G72G35 2003**
The Guarani under Spanish Rule in the Rio de la Plata. Trade Cloth. Stanford University Press. Palo Alto, CA. 2003. xii, 290p. ISBN:0-8047-3602-2, ISBN13: 978-0-8047-3602-2. Dewey:323.1/198382082. LCCN:2002-030455.
Audience: **u,f.** *Choice, 2003.*

Grow, Michael **HF1524.5.U6 G76**
The Good Neighbor Policy and Authoritarianism in Paraguay: United States Economic Expansion and Great - Power Rivalry in Latin America During World War II. Trade Cloth. University Press of Kansas. Lawrence, KS. 1981. xii, 164p. ISBN:0-7006-0213-5, ISBN13: 978-0-7006-0213-1. Dewey:337.730892. LCCN:81-047797.
Audience: **u,f.**

Keogh, Dermot F. (Editor) **BX1426.2.C46 1990**
Church and Politics in Latin America. Graham Greene (Foreword by). Cloth Text. Palgrave Macmillan. New York, NY. 1990. 320p. ISBN:0-312-02815-6, ISBN13: 978-0-312-02815-2. Dewey:261.7/098. LCCN:89-037269.
Audience: **u,f.**

Kolinski, Charles J. **F2664 .K64**
Historical Dictionary of Paraguay. Trade Cloth. Scarecrow Press, Inc. Lanham, MD. 1973. Latin American Historical Dictionaries Ser., No. 8 ISBN:0-8108-0582-0, ISBN13: 978-0-8108-0582-8. Dewey:989.2/003. LCCN:72-013238.
Audience: **l,u,f.**

Lambert, Peter **F2689.2.T73 1997**
Transition Demo in Paraguay. Andrew Nickson (Editor). Trade Cloth. Palgrave Macmillan. New York, NY. 1997. 240p. Latin American Studies ISBN:0-312-17523-X, ISBN13: 978-0-312-17523-8. Dewey:320.9892/09/049. LCCN:97-009651.
Audience: **u,f.**

Leuchars, Chris **F2687**
To the Bitter End: Paraguay and the War of the Triple Alliance. Trade Cloth. Greenwood Publishing Group, Inc. Portsmouth, NH. 2002. 264p. Contributions in Military Studies, No. 223 ISBN:0-313-32365-8, ISBN13: 978-0-313-32365-2. Dewey:989.2/05. LCCN:2002-069640.
Audience: **u,f.** *Choice, 2003.*

Lewis, Paul H. **F2689 .L48**
Paraguay under Stroessner. Trade Cloth. University of North Carolina Press. Chapel Hill, NC. 1980. xi, 256p. ISBN:0-8078-1437-7, ISBN13: 978-0-8078-1437-6. Dewey:989.2/072. LCCN:79-028554.
Audience: **u,f.**

MacLeod, Murdo J., et al. **F1219.3.M59I53 1989**
Indian-Religious Relations in Colonial Spanish America. James S. Saeger, Susan Schroeder, Stafford Poole & Eric Van Young (Authors), Susan E. Ramirez (Editor, Introduction by). Paper Text. Syracuse University, Foreign & Comparative Studies Program. Syracuse, NY. 1989. Foreign and Comparative Studies Program, Latin American Ser., No. 9 ISBN:0-915984-32-6, ISBN13: 978-0-915984-32-9. Dewey:980/.004/98. LCCN:88-039611.
Audience: **u,f.**

Miranda, Carlos R. **F2689.M54 1990**
The Stroessner Era: Authoritarian Rule in Paraguay. Trade Paper. Westview Press. Boulder, CO. 1990. 177p. ISBN:0-8133-0995-6, ISBN13: 978-0-8133-0995-8. Dewey:989.207/3/092. LCCN:90-030613.
Audience: **u,f.** *Choice, 1991.*

Roett, Riordan & Sacks, Richard S. **F2681.R62 1991**
Paraguay: The Personalist Legacy. Trade Paper. Westview Press. Boulder, CO. 1990. 188p. ISBN:0-86531-272-9, ISBN13: 978-0-86531-272-2. Dewey:989.2. LCCN:90-045813.
Audience: **u,f.** *Choice, 1991.*

Waisman, Carlos H. & Rein, Raanan (Editors) **DP203**
Spanish and Latin American Transitions to Democracy. Trade Cloth. Sussex Academic Press. Eastbourne, 2005. 246p. ISBN:1-903900-73-5, ISBN13: 978-1-903900-73-4. Dewey:320.917/561/09048. LCCN:2005-005583.
Audience: **u,f.**

White, Richard Alan **JC599.P3W48 2004**
Breaking Silence: The Case That Changed the Face of Human Rights. Trade Cloth. Georgetown University Press. Washington, DC. 2004. 320p. Advancing Human Rights Ser. ISBN:1-58901-032-9, ISBN13: 978-1-58901-032-1. Dewey:323/.044/09892. LCCN:2004-004292.
Audience: **u,f.**

South America: Individual Countries > Uruguay > 19th Century Uruguay

Grainger, John D. (Editor) **DA70.A1 VOL. 135**
The Royal Navy in the River Plate, 1806-1807. Trade Cloth. Ashgate Publishing, Ltd. Aldershot, 1996. 398p. Navy Records Ser., Vol. 135 ISBN:1-85928-292-X, ISBN13: 978-1-85928-292-2. Dewey:982/.024. LCCN:95-049047.
Audience: **u,f.**

Johnson, Lyman L. (Editor) **HV6885.B8P76**
The Problem of Order in Changing Societies: Essay on Crime and Policing in Argentina and Uruguay. Trade Paper. Books on Demand. Ann Arbor, MI. 197p. ISBN:0-608-20968-6, ISBN13: 978-0-608-20968-5. Dewey:364.98211. LCCN:89-036709.
Audience: **u,f.**

Kraay, Hendrik & Whigham, Thomas L. **F2687.I62 2004**
I Die with My Country: Prespectives on the Paraguayan War, 1864-1870. Cloth Text. University of Nebraska Press. Lincoln, NE. 2005. 320p. Studies in War, Society, and the Military Ser. ISBN:0-8032-2762-0, ISBN13: 978-0-8032-2762-0. Dewey:989.2/05. LCCN:2004-007730.
Audience: **u,f.**

McLean, David **F2909.M39 1995**
War, Diplomacy, and Informal Empire: Britain, France and Latin America, 1836-1852. Cloth over Boards. I. B. Tauris & Company, Ltd. London, 1995. 224p. ISBN:1-85043-867-6, ISBN13: 978-1-85043-867-0. Dewey:303.48/241082. LCCN:94-060882.
Audience: **u,f.** *Choice, 1995.*

Peloso, Vincent C. & Tenenbaum, Barbara A. (Editors) **F1413.L67 1996**
Liberals, Politics, and Power: State Formation in Nineteenth-Century Latin America. Trade Cloth. University of Georgia Press. Athens, GA. 1996. 352p. ISBN:0-8203-1777-2, ISBN13: 978-0-8203-1777-9. Dewey:980.03/1. LCCN:95-032602.
Audience: **u,f.**

Posada-Carbo, Eduardo, ed. **F1413**
Wars, Parties and Nationalism : Essays on the Politics and Society of Nineteenth-Century Latin America. Institute of Latin American Studies. 1995. ISBN:0-901145-98-X, ISBN13: 978-0-901145-98-7.
Audience: **u,f.**

Whigham, Thomas **HF3375.W48 1991**
The Politics of River Trade: Tradition and Development in the Upper Plata, 1780-1870. Trade Cloth. University of New Mexico Press. Albuquerque, NM. 1991. 292p. ISBN:0-8263-1312-4, ISBN13: 978-0-8263-1312-6. Dewey:382/.0982/12. LCCN:91-003493.
Audience: **u,f.**

South America: Individual Countries > Uruguay > 20th Century Uruguay

Bethell, Leslie (Editor, Contribution by) **F1410.C1834 1984 V**
Latin America since 1930: Spanish South America. Cloth Text. Cambridge University Press. New York, NY. 1991. 935p. The Cambridge History of Latin America Ser. ISBN:0-521-26652-1, ISBN13: 978-0-521-26652-9. Dewey:980 s. LCCN:91-006743.
Audience: **u,f.** *Choice, 1992.*

Drake, Paul W. **HD8259.S65D7 1996**
Labor Movements and Dictatorships: The Southern Cone in Comparative Perspective. Trade Paper. Johns Hopkins University Press. Baltimore, MD. 1996. 240p. ISBN:0-8018-5327-3, ISBN13: 978-0-8018-5327-2. Dewey:322/.2/098. LCCN:96-000790.
Audience: **u,f.** *Choice, 1997.*

Ehrick, Christine **HQ1236.5.U8E47 2005**
Shield of the Weak: Feminism and the State in Uruguay, 1900-1932. Trade Cloth. University of New Mexico Press.

Albuquerque, NM. 2005. 282p. ISBN:0-8263-3468-7, ISBN13: 978-0-8263-3468-8. Dewey:305.42/09895/09041. LCCN:2005-002484.

Audience: **u,f.**

Lavrin, Asuncion **HQ1532.L38 1995**
Women, Feminism and Social Change in Argentina, Chile, and Uruguay, 1890-1940. Cloth Text. University of Nebraska Press. Lincoln, NE. 1995. 491p. Engendering Latin America Ser. ISBN:0-8032-2897-X, ISBN13: 978-0-8032-2897-9. Dewey:305.4/0982. LCCN:95-002729.

Audience: **u,f.** *Choice, 1996.*

Parker, Eldon M. & Alexander, Robert Jackson **HD6647**
A History of Organized Labor in Uruguay and Paraguay. Praeger. 2005. ISBN:0-275-97745-5, ISBN13: 978-0-275-97745-0.

Audience: **u,f.**

Porzecanski, Arturo C. **JL3698.M6**
Uruguay's Tupamaros: The Urban Guerilla. Trade Cloth. Irvington Publishers. New York, NY. 1973. xiii, 80p. Special Studies in International Politics and Government ISBN:0-275-28802-1, ISBN13: 978-0-275-28802-0. Dewey:322.4/2/09895. LCCN:73-013340.

Audience: **u,f.**

Rock, David (Editor) **F1414.2**
Latin America in the 1940's: War and Postwar Transitions. Trade Cloth. University of California Press. Berkeley, CA. 1994. 285p. ISBN:0-520-08416-0, ISBN13: 978-0-520-08416-2. Dewey:980.033. LCCN:93-029798.

Audience: **u,f.**

Weinstein, Martin E. **F2728.W43 1988**
Uruguay: Democracy at the Crossroads. Cloth Text. Westview Press. Boulder, CO. 1988. 160p. Profiles - Nations of Contemporary Latin America Ser. ISBN:0-86531-290-7, ISBN13: 978-0-86531-290-6. Dewey:989.5. LCCN:87-010519.

Audience: **u,f.** *Choice, 1988.*

Whitaker, Arthur Preston **F2232.2.U6**
The United States and the Southern Cone: Argentina, Chile, and Uruguay. Harvard University Press. 1976. ISBN:0-674-92841-5, ISBN13: 978-0-674-92841-1.

Audience: **u,f.**

Whitaker, Arthur Preston **F2232.2.U6**
The United States and the Southern Cone: Argentina, Chile, and Uruguay. Harvard University Press. 1976. ISBN:0-674-92841-5, ISBN13: 978-0-674-92841-1.

Audience: **u,f.**

South America: Individual Countries > Argentina

Bergquist, Charles **HD8256.B47 1986**
Labor in Latin America: Comparative Essays on Chile, Argentina, Venezuela, and Colombia. Trade Cloth. Stanford University Press. Palo Alto, CA. 1986. 416p. Comparative Studies in History, Institutions and Public Policy ISBN:0-8047-1253-0, ISBN13: 978-0-8047-1253-8. Dewey:331/.0968. LCCN:84-051684.

Audience: **u,f.** *Choice, 1986.*

Brown, Jonathan C. **F2831.B882002**
A Brief History of Argentina. Trade Cloth. Facts On File, Inc. New York, NY. 2002. 336p. Brief History Ser. ISBN:0-8160-4959-9, ISBN13: 978-0-8160-4959-2. Dewey:982. LCCN:2002-006459.

Audience: **l,u,f.** *Choice, 2003.*

Della Paolera, Gerardo & Taylor, Alan M. (Editors) **HC175**
A New Economic History of Argentina. Cloth Text. Cambridge University Press. New York, NY. 2003. 416p. ISBN:0-521-82247-5, ISBN13: 978-0-521-82247-3. Dewey:330.982. LCCN:2003-051234.

Audience: **u,f.**

Deutsch, Sandra McGee **F2847.D483 1999**
Las Derechas: The Extreme Right in Argentina, Brazil, and Chile, 1890-1939. Trade Cloth. Stanford University Press. Palo Alto, CA. 1999. 480p. ISBN:0-8047-3208-6, ISBN13: 978-0-8047-3208-6. Dewey:320.98/09/0413. LCCN:99-019783.

Audience: **u,f.** *Choice, 2000.*

Drake, Paul W. **HD8259.S65D7 1996**
Labor Movements and Dictatorships: The Southern Cone in Comparative Perspective. Trade Paper. Johns Hopkins University Press. Baltimore, MD. 1996. 240p. ISBN:0-8018-5327-3, ISBN13: 978-0-8018-5327-2. Dewey:322/.2/098. LCCN:96-000790.

Audience: **u,f.** *Choice, 1997.*

Foster, David William, et al. **F2848**
Culture and Customs of Argentina. Melissa Fitch Lockhart & Darrell B. Lockhart (Authors). Cloth Text. Greenwood Publishing Group, Inc. Portsmouth, NH. 1998. 200p. Culture and Customs of Latin America and the Caribbean Ser. ISBN:0-313-30319-3, ISBN13: 978-0-313-30319-7. Dewey:982.06. LCCN:98-015325.

Audience: **l,u,f.**

Rock, David **F2831.R68 1987**
Argentina, Fifteen-Sixteen to Nineteen Eighty-Two: From Spanish Colonization to the Falklands War. Trade Paper. University of California Press. Berkeley, CA. 1987. ISBN:0-520-06178-0, ISBN13: 978-0-520-06178-1. Dewey:982. LCCN:83-017948.

Audience: **u,f.** *Choice, 1986.*

Whitaker, Arthur Preston **F2232.2.U6**
The United States and the Southern Cone: Argentina, Chile, and Uruguay. Harvard University Press. 1976. ISBN:0-674-92841-5, ISBN13: 978-0-674-92841-1.

Audience: **u,f.**

South America: Individual Countries > Argentina > Colonial Argentina

Brown, Jonathan C. **F2831.B882002**
A Brief History of Argentina. Trade Cloth. Facts On File, Inc. New York, NY. 2002. 336p. Brief History Ser.

ISBN:0-8160-4959-9, ISBN13: 978-0-8160-4959-2. Dewey:982. LCCN:2002-006459.
Audience: **l,u,f.** *Choice, 2003.*

Criscenti, Joseph T. (Editor) **F2846.S26S27 1993**
Sarmiento and His Argentina. Library Binding. Lynne Rienner Publishers, Inc. Boulder, CO. 1993. 216p. ISBN:1-55587-351-0, ISBN13: 978-1-55587-351-6. Dewey:982.04092. LCCN:92-038372.
Audience: **u,f.**

Cushner, Nicholas P. **HD1862 .C87**
Jesuit Ranches and the Agrarian Development of Colonial Argentina, 1650-1767. Paper Text. State University of New York Press. Albany, NY. 1984. 206p. ISBN:0-87395-706-7, ISBN13: 978-0-87395-706-9. Dewey:338.1/0982/43. LCCN:82-019503.
Audience: **u,f.**

Kinsbruner, Jay **HD9325.L29K56 1987**
Petty Capitalism in Spanish America: The Pulperos of Puebla, Mexico City, Caracas, and Buenos Aires, Vol. 21. Paper Text. Westview Press. Boulder, CO. 1986. 161p. Dellplain Latin American Studies ISBN:0-8133-7272-0, ISBN13: 978-0-8133-7272-3. Dewey:381/.456413/0098. LCCN:86-051526.
Audience: **u,f.**

Kinsbruner, Jay **HD9325.L29**
Petty Capitalism in Spanish America: The Pulperos of Puebla, Mexico City, Caracas and Buenos Aires. University of Colorado. 2005.
Audience: **l,u.**

Lynch, John **JL950**
Spanish Colonial Administration, 1782-1810: The Intendant System in the Viceroyalty of the Rio De la Plata, 5. Trade Cloth. Greenwood Publishing Group, Inc. Portsmouth, NH. 1969. 335p. University of London. Historical Studies ISBN:0-8371-0546-3, ISBN13: 978-0-8371-0546-8. Dewey:325.3/1/0946. LCCN:69-013979.
Audience: **u,f.** B

Mata de Lopez, Sara **F2958**
Persistencias y Cambios: Salta y el Noroeste Argentino, 1770-1840. Prohistoria & Manuel Suárez (ed.). Rosario [Argentina]. 1999. ISBN:987-99035-8-7, ISBN13: 978-987-99035-8-2.
Audience: **l,u.**

Socolow, Susan M. **JL2046.S66 1987**
The Bureaucrats of Buenos Aires, 1769-1810: Amor al Real Servicio. Cloth Text. Duke University Press. Durham, NC. 1987. xxi, 356p. ISBN:0-8223-0753-7, ISBN13: 978-0-8223-0753-2. Dewey:306.240982. LCCN:87-009211.
Audience: **u,f.** *Choice, 1988.*

Socolow, Susan M. **HF3390.B8.S62**
Merchants of Buenos Aires, Seventeen Seventy-Eight to Eighteen Hundred and Ten. Trade Cloth. Cambridge University Press. New York, NY. 1978. 272p. Cambridge Latin American Studies, No. 30 ISBN:0-521-21812-8, ISBN13: 978-0-521-21812-2. Dewey:301.44/47. LCCN:77-085216.
Audience: **u,f.** B

South America: Individual Countries > Argentina > 20th C. Argentina

Alexander, Robert J. **F2237**
The ABC Presidents: Conversations and Correspondence with the Presidents of Argentina, Brazil, and Chile. Trade Cloth. Greenwood Publishing Group, Inc. Portsmouth, NH. 1992. 336p. ISBN:0-275-94110-8, ISBN13: 978-0-275-94110-9. Dewey:327.8. LCCN:92-003676.
Audience: **g,l,u,f.**

Andersen, Martin E. **F2848.A6 1993**
Dossier Secreto: Argentina's Desaparecidos and the Myth of the "Dirty War". Cloth Text. Westview Press. Boulder, CO. 1993. 412p. ISBN:0-8133-8212-2, ISBN13: 978-0-8133-8212-8. Dewey:982.06. LCCN:92-033310.
Audience: **u,f.** *Choice, 1994.*

Archetti, Eduardo P. **GV706.34.A73 1999**
Masculinities: Football, Polo and the Tango in Argentina. Cloth over Boards. Berg Publishers. Oxford, 1999. 224p. Global Issues Ser. ISBN:1-85973-261-5, ISBN13: 978-1-85973-261-8. Dewey:305.3/1/0982. LCCN:99-229403.
Audience: **u,f.**

Barnes, John **F2849.P37**
Evita, First Lady: A Biography of Eva Peron. Trade Paper. Grove/Atlantic, Inc. New York, NY. 1996. 224p. ISBN:0-8021-3479-3, ISBN13: 978-0-8021-3479-0. Dewey:982.06/2/092. LCCN:78-003185.
Audience: **l,u,f.**

Brennan, James P. **HD6605.C66B74 1994**
The Labor Wars in Cordoba, 1955-1976: Ideology, Work, and Labor Politics in an Argentine Industrial Society. Trade Cloth. Harvard University Press. Cambridge, MA. 1998. 456p. Harvard Historical Studies, No. 116 ISBN:0-674-50851-3, ISBN13: 978-0-674-50851-4. Dewey:322/.2/098254. LCCN:93-046839.
Audience: **u,f.** *Choice, 1995.*

Brennan, James P. (Editor), et al. **F2849.P492 1998**
Peronism and Argentina. William H. Beezley & Judith Ewell (Editors). Book, Other. Rowman & Littlefield Publishers, Inc. Lanham, MD. 1998. 232p. Latin American Silhouettes Ser. ISBN:0-8420-2706-8, ISBN13: 978-0-8420-2706-9. Dewey:982.06. LCCN:97-046486.
Audience: **u,f.**

Corrales, Javier **HC175.C6684 2002**
Presidents Without Parties: The Politics of Economic Reform in Argentina and Venezuela in the 1990s. Trade Cloth. Pennsylvania State University Press. University Park, PA. 2002. 384p. ISBN:0-271-02194-2, ISBN13: 978-0-271-02194-2. Dewey:338.982. LCCN:2001-055951.
Audience: **u,f.** *Choice, 2003.*

Crawley, Eduardo **F2847.C7 1984**
A House Divided: Argentina, 1880-1980. Rodolfo H. Terragno (Foreword by). Cloth Text. Palgrave Macmillan. New York, NY. 1984. 472p. ISBN:0-312-39254-0, ISBN13: 978-0-312-39254-3. Dewey:982/.05. LCCN:84-017697.
Audience: **u,f.**

Deutsch, Sandra M. **F2847.D48 1986**
Counterrevolution in Argentina, 1900-1932: The Argentine Patriotic League. Cloth Text. University of Nebraska Press.

Lincoln, NE. 1986. 319p. ISBN:0-8032-1669-6, ISBN13: 978-0-8032-1669-3. Dewey:982/.061. LCCN:85-016388.
Audience: **u,f.** *Choice, 1987.*

Dolkhart, Ronald H. (Editor) **F2848.A74 1993**
The Argentine Right: Its History and Intellectual Origins, 1910 to the Present. Sandra F. Deutsch (Compiled by). Book, Other. Rowman & Littlefield Publishers, Inc. Lanham, MD. 1993. 256p. Latin American Silhouettes Ser. ISBN:0-8420-2418-2, ISBN13: 978-0-8420-2418-1. Dewey:320.982. LCCN:92-020368.
Audience: **u,f.**

Dubois, Lindsay **HN270.J67D93 2005**
The Politics of the Past in an Argentine Working-Class Neighbourhood. Trade Paper. University of Toronto Press. Toronto, ON. 2005. 284p. Anthropological Horizons Ser., Vol. 29 ISBN:0-8020-8844-9, ISBN13: 978-0-8020-8844-4. Dewey:306/.0982/11. LCCN:2005-276527.
Audience: **u,f.** *Choice, 2005.*

Francis, Michael J. **E183.8.A7**
The Limits of Hegemony: United States Relations with Argentina and Chile During World War II. Cloth Text. University of Notre Dame Press. Notre Dame, IN. 1977. 304p. International Studies Ser. ISBN:0-268-01260-1, ISBN13: 978-0-268-01260-1. Dewey:940.53/22/73. LCCN:77-089754.
Audience: **u,f.**

Gravil, Robert **HF3388.G7 G73**
The Anglo-Argentine Connection, 1900-1939. Trade Cloth. Westview Press. Boulder, CO. 1985. 300p. Dellplain Latin American Studies, Vol. 16 ISBN:0-317-06876-8, ISBN13: 978-0-317-06876-4. Dewey:382/.0941/082.
Audience: **u,f.**

Guillen, Mauro F. **HD70.A65G84 2003**
The Limits of Convergence: Globalization and Organizational Change in Argentina, South Korea, and Spain. Trade Paper. Princeton University Press. Princeton, NJ. 2003. 304p. ISBN:0-691-11633-4, ISBN13: 978-0-691-11633-4. Dewey:658.4/06.
Audience: **u,f.**

Helmke, Gretchen **KHA2533.H45 2004**
Courts under Constraints: Judges, Generals, and Presidents in Argentina. Robert H. Bates, Ellen Comisso, Peter Hall, Peter Lange, Joel Migdal & Helen Milner (Contribution by). Trade Cloth. Cambridge University Press. New York, NY. 2004. 240p. Cambridge Studies in Comparative Politics Ser. ISBN:0-521-82059-6, ISBN13: 978-0-521-82059-2. Dewey:347.82/012. LCCN:2004-052120.
Audience: **u,f.** *Choice, 2005.*

Hodges, Donald C. **F2849.H6 1988**
Argentina, 1943-1987: The National Revolution and Resistance. Trade Cloth. University of New Mexico Press. Albuquerque, NM. 1988. 360p. ISBN:0-8263-1055-9, ISBN13: 978-0-8263-1055-2. Dewey:982/.06. LCCN:87-035719.
Audience: **u,f.** *Choice, 1989.*

Karush, Matthew B. **F3011.R7K37 2002**
Workers or Citizens: Democracy and Identity in Rosario, Argentina, 1912-1930. Trade Cloth. University of New Mexico Press. Albuquerque, NM. 2004. 264p. ISBN:0-8263-2269-7, ISBN13: 978-0-8263-2269-2. Dewey:320.982/24. LCCN:2001-007539.
Audience: **u,f.**

Kohut, David R. **F2849.2**
Historical Dictionary of the Dirty Wars. Scarecrow Press. 2003.
Audience: **g,l,u,f.**

Lavrin, Asuncion **HQ1532.L38 1995**
Women, Feminism and Social Change in Argentina, Chile, and Uruguay, 1890-1940. Cloth Text. University of Nebraska Press. Lincoln, NE. 1995. 491p. Engendering Latin America Ser. ISBN:0-8032-2897-X, ISBN13: 978-0-8032-2897-9. Dewey:305.4/0982. LCCN:95-002729.
Audience: **u,f.** *Choice, 1996.*

Lewis, Paul H. **89-31350**
The Crisis of Argentine Capitalism. Trade Paper. University of North Carolina Press. Chapel Hill, NC. 1992. 594p. ISBN:0-8078-4356-3, ISBN13: 978-0-8078-4356-7. Dewey:338.982. LCCN:89-031350.
Audience: **u,f.** *Choice, 1990.*

Lewis, Paul H. **F2849**
Guerrillas and Generals: The "Dirty War" in Argentina. Trade Cloth. Greenwood Publishing Group, Inc. Portsmouth, NH. 2001. 280p. ISBN:0-275-97359-X, ISBN13: 978-0-275-97359-9. Dewey:982.06. LCCN:2001-021650.
Audience: **u,f.** *Choice, 2002.*

Manzetti, Luigi **JL2081.M36 1993**
Institutions, Parties, and Coalitions in Argentine Politics. Cloth Text. University of Pittsburgh Press. Pittsburgh, PA. 1994. 408p. Latin American Ser. ISBN:0-8229-3755-7, ISBN13: 978-0-8229-3755-5. Dewey:322.430982. LCCN:93-012872.
Audience: **u,f.** *Choice, 1994.*

Marchak, Patricia **HV6322.3.A7**
God's Assassins: State Terrorism in Argentina in the 1970s. Trade Cloth. McGill-Queen's University Press. Montreal, PQ. 2002. 456p. ISBN:0-7735-2414-2, ISBN13: 978-0-7735-2414-9. Dewey:323/.044/0982/09047.
Audience: **u,f.**

Martínez, Tomás Eloy **PQ**
Santa Evita. Trade Paper. Santillana USA Publishing Company, Inc. Doral, FL. 2005. 426p. ISBN:84-204-6513-5, ISBN13: 978-84-204-6513-5. Dewey:863.
Audience: **u,f.**

Most, Benjamin A. **JL2024.M67 1990**
Changing Authoritarian Rule and Public Policy in Argentina, 1930-1970. Luigi Manzetti (Introduction by). Library Binding. Lynne Rienner Publishers, Inc. Boulder, CO. 1990. 206p. GSIS Monograph in World Affairs ISBN:1-55587-246-8, ISBN13: 978-1-55587-246-5. Dewey:321.9/0982. LCCN:90-042342.
Audience: **u,f.** *Choice, 1991.*

Newton, Ronald C. **F2848.N4 1992**
The Nazi Menace in Argentina, 1931-1947. Trade Cloth. Stanford University Press. Palo Alto, CA. 1992. 540p. ISBN:0-8047-1929-2, ISBN13: 978-0-8047-1929-2. Dewey:982.06/1. LCCN:91-020368.
Audience: **u,f.** *Choice, 1992.*

Norden, Deborah L. **F2849.2.N67 1996**
Military Rebellion in Argentina: Between Coups and Consolidation. Trade Cloth. University of Nebraska Press. Lincoln, NE. 1996. 240p. ISBN:0-8032-8369-5, ISBN13: 978-0-8032-8369-5. Dewey:322/.5/098209045. LCCN:95-032285.
Audience: **u,f.** *Choice, 1996.*

Ortiz, Alicia Dujovne **F2849.22.M44**
Eva Peron: A Biography. Trade Cloth. Santillana USA Publishing Company, Inc. Doral, FL. 1998. ISBN:950-511-205-X, ISBN13: 978-950-511-205-0. Dewey:982/.064/092.
Audience: **l,u,f.**

Peralta-Ramos, Monica **HC175.P42 1991**
The Political Economy of Argentina: Power and Class since 1930. Trade Paper. Westview Press. Boulder, CO. 1991. 191p. ISBN:0-8133-7556-8, ISBN13: 978-0-8133-7556-4. Dewey:338.982. LCCN:91-022385.
Audience: **u,f.** *Choice, 1992.*

Plotkin, Mariano Ben **BF173.P6427 2001**
Freud in the Pampas: The Emergence and Development of a Psychoanalytic Culture in Argentina. Trade Cloth. Stanford University Press. Palo Alto, CA. 2000. xiii, 314p. ISBN:0-8047-4054-2, ISBN13: 978-0-8047-4054-8. Dewey:150.19/5/0982. LCCN:00-040730.
Audience: **u,f.**

Podalsky, Laura **F3001.2.P63 2002**
Specular City: The Transformation of Culture, Consumption, and Space after Peron. Cloth Text. Temple University Press. Philadelphia, PA. 2004. 304p. ISBN:1-56639-947-5, ISBN13: 978-1-56639-947-0. Dewey:306/.0982/11. LCCN:2001-057404.
Audience: **u,f.**

Potash, Robert A. **UA613**
The Army and Politics in Argentina, 1928-1945: Yrigoyen to Peron. Trade Cloth. Stanford University Press. Palo Alto, CA. 1969. xiv, 314p. ISBN:0-8047-0683-2, ISBN13: 978-0-8047-0683-4. Dewey:320.9/82. LCCN:69-013182.
Audience: **u,f.**

Potash, Robert A. **UA613**
The Army and Politics in Argentina, 1945-1962: Peron to Frondizi. Trade Cloth. Stanford University Press. Palo Alto, CA. 1980. xiv, 418p. ISBN:0-8047-1056-2, ISBN13: 978-0-8047-1056-5. Dewey:320.9/82. LCCN:79-064220.
Audience: **u,f.** B

Potash, Robert A. **UA613 .P67**
The Army and Politics in Argentina, 1962-1973: From Frondizi's Fall to the Peronist Restoration. Trade Cloth. Stanford University Press. Palo Alto, CA. 1996. 592p. ISBN:0-8047-2414-8, ISBN13: 978-0-8047-2414-2. Dewey:320.9/82. LCCN:69-013182.
Audience: **u,f.** *Choice, 1996.*

Rein, Monica **LC92.A6R45 1998**
Politics and Education in Argentina, 1946-1962. Martha Grenzeback (Translator), Robert M. Levine (Foreword by). Cloth Text. M. E. Sharpe Inc. Armonk, NY. 1998. 240p. Latin American Realities Ser. ISBN:0-7656-0209-1, ISBN13: 978-0-7656-0209-1. Dewey:379.82. LCCN:97-029381.
Audience: **u,f.** *Choice, 1998.*

Remmer, Karen L. **JL2098.A1 R44 1984**
Party Competition in Argentina and Chile: Political Recruitment and Public Policy, 1890-1930. Cloth Text. University of Nebraska Press. Lincoln, NE. 1984. 296p. ISBN:0-8032-3871-1, ISBN13: 978-0-8032-3871-8. Dewey:324/.0982. LCCN:84-013119.
Audience: **u,f.**

Romero, Luis Alberto **F2848**
A history of Argentina in the Twentieth Century. Pennsylvania State University Press, University Park, Pa.. 2002. ISBN:0-271-02191-8, ISBN13: 978-0-271-02191-1.
Audience: **u,f.**

Spektorowski, Alberto **JC573.2.A7S64 2002**
The Origins of Argentina's Revolution of the Right. Trade Cloth. University of Notre Dame Press. Notre Dame, IN. 2001. 312p. From the Helen Kellogg Institute for International Studies ISBN:0-268-02010-8, ISBN13: 978-0-268-02010-1. Dewey:982.06. LCCN:2001-006427.
Audience: **u,f.** *Choice, 2004.*

Szuchman, Mark D. **HN270.C6**
Mobility and Integration in Urban Argentina: Cordoba in the Liberal Era. Trade Cloth. University of Texas Press. Austin, TX. 1980. 250p. Institute of Latin American Studies, Vol. 52 ISBN:0-292-75057-9, ISBN13: 978-0-292-75057-9. Dewey:305/.0982/54. LCCN:80-014857.
Audience: **u,f.**

Tamarin, David **HD8266.T36 1985**
The Argentine Labor Movement, 1930-1945: A Study in the Origins of Peronism. Trade Cloth. University of New Mexico Press. Albuquerque, NM. 1985. 287p. ISBN:0-8263-0779-5, ISBN13: 978-0-8263-0779-8. Dewey:331.88/0982. LCCN:84-020965.
Audience: **u,f.**

Teichman, Judith A. **HF1956.T45 2001**
The Politics of Freeing Markets in Latin America: Chile, Argentina and Mexico. Trade Cloth. University of North Carolina Press. Chapel Hill, NC. 2001. 296p. ISBN:0-8078-2629-4, ISBN13: 978-0-8078-2629-4. Dewey:382/.71/098. LCCN:2001-023409.
Audience: **u,f.**

Timerman, Jacobo **HV9582.T5513 2002**
Prisoner Without a Name, Cell Without a Number. Toby Talbot (Translator), Ilan Stavans (Introduction by), Arthur Miller (Foreword by). Trade Paper. University of Wisconsin Press. Chicago, IL. 2002. 184p. Wi the Americas Ser. ISBN:0-299-18244-4, ISBN13: 978-0-299-18244-1. Dewey:365/.45/092 B. LCCN:2002-020310.
Audience: **l,u,f.**

Weyland, Kurt Gerhard **HC165.W46 2004**
The Politics of Market Reform in Fragile Democracies: Argentina, Brazil, Peru, and Venezuela. Trade Paper. Princeton University Press. Princeton, NJ. 2004. 360p. ISBN:0-691-11787-X, ISBN13: 978-0-691-11787-4. Dewey:338.98.
Audience: **u,f.** *Choice, 2003.*

South America: Individual Countries > Chile

Bergquist, Charles **HD8256.B47 1986**
Labor in Latin America: Comparative Essays on Chile, Argentina, Venezuela, and Colombia. Trade Cloth. Stanford University Press. Palo Alto, CA. 1986. 416p. Comparative Studies in History, Institutions and Public Policy ISBN:0-8047-1253-0, ISBN13: 978-0-8047-1253-8. Dewey:331/.0968. LCCN:84-051684.
Audience: **u,f.** *Choice, 1986.*

Bethell, Leslie (Editor) **F3093.C546 1993**
Chile since Independence. Cloth Text. Cambridge University Press. New York, NY. 1993. 240p. ISBN:0-521-43375-4, ISBN13: 978-0-521-43375-4. Dewey:983. LCCN:92-017160.
Audience: **u,f.**

Collier, Simon & Sater, William F. **F3081**
A History of Chile, 1808-2002. Ed. 2. Alan Knight (Contribution by). Cloth Text. Cambridge University Press. New York, NY. 2004. 478p. Cambridge Latin American Studies, Vol. 82 ISBN:0-521-82749-3, ISBN13: 978-0-521-82749-2. Dewey:983/.04. LCCN:2003-065454.
Audience: **l,u,f.**

Deutsch, Sandra McGee **F2847.D483 1999**
Las Derechas: The Extreme Right in Argentina, Brazil, and Chile, 1890-1939. Trade Cloth. Stanford University Press. Palo Alto, CA. 1999. 480p. ISBN:0-8047-3208-6, ISBN13: 978-0-8047-3208-6. Dewey:320.98/09/0413. LCCN:99-019783.
Audience: **u,f.** *Choice, 2000.*

Lederman, Daniel **HF1956.L43 2005**
The Political Economy of Protection: Theory and the Chilean Experience. Trade Cloth. Stanford University Press. Palo Alto, CA. 2005. 208p. Social Science History Ser. ISBN:0-8047-4917-5, ISBN13: 978-0-8047-4917-6. Dewey:382/.73/0983. LCCN:2004-024264.
Audience: **u,f.**

Lipp, Solomon **B1049.B54**
Three Chilean Thinkers. McGill University. 1975. ISBN:0-88920-017-3, ISBN13: 978-0-88920-017-3.
Audience: **u,f.**

Loveman, Brian **F3081.L68 2001**
Chile: The Legacy of Hispanic Capitalism. Ed. 3. Trade Paper. Oxford University Press, Inc. New York, NY. 2001. 448p. Latin American Histories Ser. ISBN:0-19-512020-5, ISBN13: 978-0-19-512020-2. Dewey:983. LCCN:00-039938.
Audience: **u,f.** B

Rector, John L. **F3081.R43 2005**
The History of Chile. Trade Paper, Perfect. Palgrave Macmillan. New York, NY. 2005. 336p. ISBN:1-4039-6257-X, ISBN13: 978-1-4039-6257-7. Dewey:983. LCCN:2005-048859.
Audience: **l,u,f.**

Valenzuela, Arturo **JL2611**
Chile. Johns Hopkins University Press. 1978.
Audience: **g,l,u.**

Zeitlin, Maurice **F3095.Z43 1984**
The Civil Wars in Chile, or, the Bourgeois Revolutions That Never Were. Trade Cloth. Princeton University Press. Princeton, NJ. 1984. 264p. ISBN:0-691-07665-0, ISBN13: 978-0-691-07665-2. Dewey:983/.06. LCCN:84-042551.
Audience: **u,f.** B

South America: Individual Countries > Chile > Colonial Chile

Burkholder, Mark A. (Editor) **JV412.A35 1998**
Administrators of Empire. John L. Phelan, Kenneth J. Andrien, D. C. Chandler, Jacques A. Barbier, D. A. Brading, John Lynch, Stuart B. Schwartz & Stephen S. Webb (Contribution by). Trade Cloth. Ashgate Publishing, Ltd. Aldershot, 1998. 406p. An Expanding World Ser., No. 22:The European Impact on World History, 1450-1800 ISBN:0-86078-527-0, ISBN13: 978-0-86078-527-9. Dewey:353.1/5/0970903. LCCN:98-024125.
Audience: **u,f.** *Choice, 1999.*

Cook, N.D. & Lovell, W.George (Editors) **E59.D58**
Secret Judgments of God: Old World Disease in Colonial Spanish America. Trade Paper. University of Oklahoma Press. Norman, OK. 2001. 312p. Civilization of the American Indian Ser., Vol. 205 ISBN:0-8061-3377-5, ISBN13: 978-0-8061-3377-5. Dewey:614.4/28.
Audience: **u,f.**

Flusche, Della M. **HN300.Z9E44 1989**
Two Families in Colonial Chile. Trade Cloth. Edwin Mellen Press, The. Lewiston, NY. 1989. 264p. Latin American Studies, Vol. 2 ISBN:0-88946-491-X, ISBN13: 978-0-88946-491-9. Dewey:305.5/2/0983. LCCN:88-039147.
Audience: **g,l,u,f.**

Flusche, Della M. & Korth, Eugene H. **F3285.B53F48 1983**
Forgotten Females: Women of African and Indian Descent in Colonial Chile, 1535-1800. Trade Cloth. Blaine Ethridge Books. Detroit, MI. 1983. 112p. ISBN:0-87917-085-9, ISBN13: 978-0-87917-085-1. Dewey:920.72/0983. LCCN:82-024269.
Audience: **u,f.**

Korth, Eugene H. **F3091.K6**
Spanish Policy in Colonial Chile: The Struggle for Social Justice, 1535-1700. Trade Cloth. Stanford University Press. Palo Alto, CA. 1968. xi, 320p. ISBN:0-8047-0666-2, ISBN13: 978-0-8047-0666-7. Dewey:323.4/0983. LCCN:68-026779.
Audience: **u,f.** B

South America: Individual Countries > Chile > 19th Century Chile

Agosín, Marjorie & Levison, Julie H. (Editors) **F1409.M22 1999**
Magical Sites: Women Travelers in 19th Century Latin America. Trade Paper. White Pine Press. Buffalo, NY. 1999. 256p. ISBN:1-877727-94-6, ISBN13: 978-1-877727-94-8. Dewey:980. LCCN:99-011291.
Audience: **g,l,u,f.**

Billingsley, Edward Baxter **F2235.B676**
In Defense of Neutral Rights; the United States Navy and the Wars of Independence in Chile and Peru. University of North Carolina Press. 1967.
Audience: **u,f.**

Burr, Robert N. **F3083.5.S/**
By Reason or Force: Chile and the Balancing of Power in South America, 1830-1905. Trade Cloth. University of California Press. Berkeley, CA. 1974. 322p. ISBN:0-520-02644-6, ISBN13: 978-0-520-02644-5. Dewey:327/.098. LCCN:66-063190.
Audience: **u,f.**

Callcott, Maria **F3063.C152003**
Journal of a Residence in Chile During the Year 1822: And, a Voyage from Chile to Brazil in 1823. Jennifer Hayward (Editor).

Trade Cloth. University Press of Virginia. Charlottesville, VA. 2003. 432p. ISBN:0-8139-2215-1, ISBN13: 978-0-8139-2215-7. Dewey:983/.04/092. LCCN:2003-007964.
Audience: **g,l,u,f.**

Clissold, Stephen **F3094**
Bernardo O'Higgins and the Independence of Chile. Praeger. 1969.
Audience: **u,f.**

Garcia, Rigoberto **G25.S7**
Incipient Industrialization in an Underdeveloped Country: The Case of Chile, 1845-1879. Trade Paper. Coronet Books. Philadelphia, PA. 1989. 296p. Institute of Latin American Studies, No. 17 ISBN:91-85894-19-2, ISBN13: 978-91-85894-19-2. Dewey:338.0983. LCCN:89-173024.
Audience: **u,f.**

Herwig, Holger & Sater, William F. **UA622.S28 1999**
The Grand Illusion: The Prussianization of the Chilean Army. Cloth Text. University of Nebraska Press. Lincoln, NE. 1999. 248p. Studies in War, Society, and the Military ISBN:0-8032-2393-5, ISBN13: 978-0-8032-2393-6. Dewey:355/.00983/09034. LCCN:99-019356.
Audience: **u,f.**

Mayo, John **HF3418.G7M39 1987**
British Merchants and Chilean Development, 1851-1886, Vol. 22. Paper Text. Westview Press. Boulder, CO. 1987. 272p. Dellplain Latin American Studies ISBN:0-8133-7278-X, ISBN13: 978-0-8133-7278-5. Dewey:382/.0942/083. LCCN:86-015766.
Audience: **u,f.**

Monaghan, Jay **F865**
Chile, Peru and the California Gold Rush of Eighteen Forty-Nine. Trade Cloth. University of California Press. Berkeley, CA. 1973. ISBN:0-520-02265-3, ISBN13: 978-0-520-02265-2. Dewey:979.4/004/6883. LCCN:72-078946.
Audience: **g,l,u.**

Monteon, Michael **HD9660.N5C5**
Chile in the Nitrate Era: The Evolution of Economic Dependence, 1880-1930. Trade Cloth. University of Wisconsin Press. Chicago, IL. 1982. 284p. ISBN:0-299-08820-0, ISBN13: 978-0-299-08820-0. Dewey:338.4/766165. LCCN:81-070009.
Audience: **u,f.**

O'Brien, Thomas F. **HD9660.N52C5**
The Nitrate Industry and Chile's Crucial Transition. Trade Cloth. New York University Press. New York, NY. 1982. 232p. ISBN:0-8147-6159-3, ISBN13: 978-0-8147-6159-5. Dewey:338.2/764/0983. LCCN:82-002131.
Audience: **u,f.**

Przeworski, Joanne F. **HD9539.C7C5646 1980**
The Decline of the Copper Industry in Chile and the Entrance of North American Capital, 1870 to 1916. Stuart Bruchey (Editor). Library Binding. Ayer Company Publishers, Inc. Manchester, NH. 1981. Multinational Corporations Ser. ISBN:0-405-13379-0, ISBN13: 978-0-405-13379-4. Dewey:338.2/743/0983. LCCN:80-000609.
Audience: **u,f.**

Rosales, Vicente Perez **F3094.P4413 2002**
Times Gone By: Memoirs of a Man of Action. Brian Loveman (Editor), John H. R. Polt (Translator). Trade Paper. Oxford University Press, Inc. New York, NY. 2003. 432p. Library of Latin America ISBN:0-19-511761-1, ISBN13: 978-0-19-511761-5. Dewey:983/.04. LCCN:2002-025115.
Audience: **g,l,u,f.**

Salvatore, Ricardo D. & Aguirre, Carlos (Editors) **HV9510.5.B57 1996**
The Birth of the Penitentiary in Latin America: Essays on Criminology, Prison Reform, and Social Control, 1830-1940. Trade Cloth. University of Texas Press. Austin, TX. 1996. 303p. New Interpretations of Latin America Ser. ISBN:0-292-77706-X, ISBN13: 978-0-292-77706-4. Dewey:365/.98. LCCN:96-003851.
Audience: **u,f.**

Scully, Timothy R. **JL2698.A1S38 1992**
Rethinking the Center: Party Politics in Nineteenth- and Twentieth-Century Chile. Trade Cloth. Stanford University Press. Palo Alto, CA. 1992. 304p. ISBN:0-8047-1913-6, ISBN13: 978-0-8047-1913-1. Dewey:324.283/009. LCCN:91-020367.
Audience: **u,f.** *Choice, 1992.*

Vicuana Mackenna, Benjamin **F3095.V65132002**
The Girondins of Chile: Reminiscences of an Eyewitness. Cristian Gazmuri R & Cristian Gazmuri (Editors), John H.R. Polt (Translator). Trade Paper. Oxford University Press, Inc. New York, NY. 2003. 94p. Library of Latin America ISBN:0-19-515181-X, ISBN13: 978-0-19-515181-7. Dewey:983/.04. LCCN:2002-027415.
Audience: **g,l,u,f.**

Woll, Allen **F3074**
A Functional Past: The Uses of History in Nineteenth-Century Chile. Cloth Text. Louisiana State University Press. Baton Rouge, LA. 1982. xvi, 232p. ISBN:0-8071-0977-0, ISBN13: 978-0-8071-0977-9. Dewey:983/.0072083. LCCN:81-012411.
Audience: **u,f.**

Young, George F. **JV7478.G3Y68**
The Germans in Chile: Immigration and Colonization, 1849-1914. Paper Text. Center for Migration Studies. Staten Island, NY. 1974. 248p. ISBN:0-913256-14-5, ISBN13: 978-0-913256-14-5. Dewey:325/.243/0983. LCCN:73-092118.
Audience: **u,f.**

South America: Individual Countries > Chile > 20th Century Chile

Agosín, Marjorie (Editor) **PQ7081.A1.P37 1999**
Passion, Memory, and Identity: 20th Century Latin American Jewish Women Writers. Trade Cloth. University of New Mexico Press. Albuquerque, NM. 1999. xlii, 217p. Jewish Latin America Ser., : ISBN:0-8263-2045-7, ISBN13: 978-0-8263-2045-2. Dewey:860.9/9287/08992408. LCCN:99-006197.
Audience: **u,f.** *Choice, 2000.*

Aguilera, Pilar & Fredes, Ricardo (Editors) **F3099**
Chile - The Other September 11: An Anthology of Reflections on the 1973 Coup. Ariel Dorfman (Contribution by). Trade Paper. Consortium Book Sales & Distribution. Saint Paul, MN. 2006. 120p. ISBN:1-920888-44-6, ISBN13: 978-1-920888-44-2. Dewey:983.064.
Audience: **g,l,u,f.**

Alexander, Robert J. **F2237**
The ABC Presidents: Conversations and Correspondence with the Presidents of Argentina, Brazil, and Chile. Trade Cloth. Greenwood Publishing Group, Inc. Portsmouth, NH. 1992. 336p. ISBN:0-275-94110-8, ISBN13: 978-0-275-94110-9. Dewey:327.8. LCCN:92-003676.
Audience: **g,l,u,f.**

Allende, Isabel **PQ6613.O79**
My Invented Country: A Memoir. Trade Paper. HarperCollins Publishers. New York, NY. 2004. 224p. ISBN:0-06-054567-4, ISBN13: 978-0-06-054567-3. Dewey:863.6/4.
Audience: **g,l,u,f.**

Arriagada, Genaro **F3100.A73413 1988**
Pinochet: The Politics of Power. Trade Cloth. Routledge. New York, NY. 1988. 224p. ISBN:0-04-497061-7, ISBN13: 978-0-04-497061-3. Dewey:983/.0647. LCCN:88-001907.
Audience: **u,f.** *Choice, 1989.*

Baldez, Lisa **HQ1236.5.C5 B35 2002**
Why Women Protest: Women's Movements in Chile. Cloth Text. Cambridge University Press. New York, NY. 2002. 254p. Cambridge Studies in Comparative Politics ISBN:0-521-81150-3, ISBN13: 978-0-521-81150-7. Dewey:305.420983. LCCN:2001-052842.
Audience: **l,u,f.** *Choice, 2003.*

Barr-Melej, Patrick **HT690.C5B37 2001**
Reforming Chile: Cultural Politics, Nationalism, and the Rise of the Middle Class. Trade Paper. University of North Carolina Press. Chapel Hill, NC. 2001. 312p. ISBN:0-8078-4919-7, ISBN13: 978-0-8078-4919-4. Dewey:305.5/5/0983. LCCN:00-051218.
Audience: **u,f.**

Bauer, Carl J. **HD1696.C5B38 1998**
Against the Current: Privatization, Water Markets and the State in Chile. Trade Cloth. Springer. New York, NY. 1998. 184p. Natural Resource Management and Policy Ser. ISBN:0-7923-8227-7, ISBN13: 978-0-7923-8227-0. Dewey:333.91/00983. LCCN:98-028298.
Audience: **u,f.**

Beckett, Andy **F3101.P56B43 2002**
Pinochet in Piccadilly: Britain and Chile's Secret History. Trade Cloth. Faber & Faber, Inc. New York, NY. 2002. 288p. ISBN:0-571-20241-1, ISBN13: 978-0-571-20241-6. Dewey:303.48/283041/09045. LCCN:2002-483767.
Audience: **g,l,u,f.**

Boeker, Paul H. **F1414.2.L671989**
Lost Illusions: Latin American's Struggle for Democracy, as Recounted by Its Leaders. Richard W. Fisher (Introduction by). Paper Text. Markus Wiener Publishers, Inc. Princeton, NJ. 1990. 360p. ISBN:1-55876-024-5, ISBN13: 978-1-55876-024-0. Dewey:320.98. LCCN:89-027993.
Audience: **u,f.** *Choice, 1990.*

Borzutzky, Silvia **HD7156.B67 2002**
Vital Connections: Politics, Social Security and Inequality in Chile. Helen Kellogg Institute for International Studies Staff (Contribution by). Trade Cloth. University of Notre Dame Press. Notre Dame, IN. 2002. 312p. ISBN:0-268-04356-6, ISBN13: 978-0-268-04356-8. Dewey:368.4/00983. LCCN:2001-004914.
Audience: **u,f.** *Choice, 2003.*

Boyle, Catherine M. **PN2491**
Chilean Theater, 1973-1985: Marginality, Power, Selfhood. Trade Cloth. Fairleigh Dickinson University Press. Cranbury, NJ. 1992. 224p. ISBN:0-685-50340-2, ISBN13: 978-0-685-50340-9. Dewey:792/.0983/09047. LCCN:88-046172.
Audience: **u,f.**

Briones, Claudia Luis & Lanata, Jose L. (Editors) **F2821**
Contemporary Perspectives on the Native Peoples of Pampa, Patagonia, and Tierra del Fuego: Living on the Edge. Trade Cloth. Greenwood Publishing Group, Inc. Portsmouth, NH. 2002. 216p. Native Peoples of the Americas Ser. ISBN:0-89789-830-3, ISBN13: 978-0-89789-830-0. Dewey:305.898/082. LCCN:2002-038591.
Audience: **u,f.**

Carr, Barry & Ellner, Steve (Editors) **JL966**
The Latin American Left: From the Fall of Allende to Perestroika. Trade Paper. Westview Press. Boulder, CO. 1993. 256p. ISBN:0-8133-1201-9, ISBN13: 978-0-8133-1201-9. Dewey:320.98. LCCN:92-028615.
Audience: **u,f.** *Choice, 1993.*

Chavkin, Samuel **F3100**
The Murder of Chile: Eyewitness Accounts of the Coup, The Terror, and the Resistance Today. Everest House. 1982. ISBN:0-89696-137-0, ISBN13: 978-0-89696-137-1.
Audience: **g,l,u,f.**

Dandavati, Annie G. **HQ1236.5.C5D358 2004**
Engendering Democracy in Chile. Trade Cloth. Peter Lang Publishing, Inc. New York, NY. 2005. xii, 153p. American University Studies, Vol. 201 ISBN:0-8204-6143-1, ISBN13: 978-0-8204-6143-4. Dewey:305.42/0983. LCCN:2004-014120.
Audience: **u,f.**

Dandavati, Annie G. **HQ1236.5.C5D361996**
The Women's Movement and the Transition to Democracy in Chile. Paper Text. Peter Lang Publishing, Inc. New York, NY. 1996. XIV, 171p. American University Studies, Series 9, Vol. 172:History ISBN:0-8204-2562-1, ISBN13: 978-0-8204-2562-7. Dewey:320/.0983. LCCN:96-020535.
Audience: **u,f.**

Davies, Matt **P91.5.C5D38 1999**
International Political Economy and Mass Communication in Chile: National Intellectuals and Transnational Hegemony. Cloth over Boards. Palgrave Macmillan. New York, NY. 1999. 226p. International Political Economy Ser. ISBN:0-312-22001-4, ISBN13: 978-0-312-22001-3. Dewey:337.8/3. LCCN:98-049906.
Audience: **u,f.**

Davis, Madeleine (Editor) **JX4292.R4**
The Pinochet Case: Origins, Progress, and Implications. Trade Paper. Institute of Latin American Studies. London, 2003. 245p. ISBN:1-900039-52-4, ISBN13: 978-1-900039-52-9. Dewey:341.488.
Audience: **g,l,u,f.**

De los Reyes, Paulina **HC195.P6 R49 1992**
The Rural Poor: Agrarian Changes and Survival Strategies in Chile 1973-1989. Trade Paper. Uppsala Universitet/Acta Universitatis Uppsaliensis. Uppsala, 1992. 196p. Uppsala Studies in Economic History, No. 34 ISBN:91-554-2961-0,

ISBN13: 978-91-554-2961-4. Dewey:339.460983.
LCCN:92-224445.
Audience: **u,f.**

DeShazo, Peter **HD6617**
Urban Workers and Labor Unions in Chile, 1902-1927. Trade Cloth. University of Wisconsin Press. Chicago, IL. 1983. 384p. ISBN:0-299-09220-8, ISBN13: 978-0-299-09220-7. Dewey:331.88/0983. LCCN:82-070557.
Audience: **u,f.**

Dinges, John **F3100.D565 2005**
The Condor Years: How Pinochet and His Allies Brought Terrorism to Three Continents. Trade Paper. New Press, The. New York, NY. 2005. 336p. ISBN:1-56584-977-9, ISBN13: 978-1-56584-977-8. Dewey:327.1283/009/047.
Audience: **g,l,u,f.**

Dorfman, Ariel & de la Parra, Marco Antonio **F3100.C4722 1990**
Chile from Within, 1973-1988. Susan Meiselas (Editor), Paz Errazuriz (Photographer). Trade Cloth. W. W. Norton & Company, Inc. New York, NY. 1990. 143p. ISBN:0-393-02817-8, ISBN13: 978-0-393-02817-1. Dewey:983.06/5. LCCN:90-036807.
Audience: **g,l,u,f.**

Drake, Paul W. **HD8259.S65D7 1996**
Labor Movements and Dictatorships: The Southern Cone in Comparative Perspective. Trade Paper. Johns Hopkins University Press. Baltimore, MD. 1996. 240p. ISBN:0-8018-5327-3, ISBN13: 978-0-8018-5327-2. Dewey:322/.2/098. LCCN:96-000790.
Audience: **u,f.** *Choice, 1997.*

Drake, Paul W. **F3099**
Socialism and Populism in Chile, 1932-52. Trade Cloth. University of Illinois Press. Champaign, IL. 1978. 416p. ISBN:0-252-00657-7, ISBN13: 978-0-252-00657-9. Dewey:320.9/83/064. LCCN:77-017414.
Audience: **u,f.**

Drake, Paul W. & Jaksic, Ivan (Editors) **F3100.S86 1991**
The Struggle for Democracy in Chile, 1982-1990. Cloth Text. University of Nebraska Press. Lincoln, NE. 1991. xiv, 321p. Latin American Studies ISBN:0-8032-1691-2, ISBN13: 978-0-8032-1691-4. Dewey:983.06/5. LCCN:91-007216.
Audience: **u,f.** *Choice, 1992.*

Drake, Paul **HD8296.5.V53 2004**
Victims of the Chilean Miracle: Workers and Neoliberalism in the Pinochet Era, 1973-2002. Peter Winn (Editor). Trade Cloth. Duke University Press. Durham, NC. 2004. 440p. ISBN:0-8223-3309-0, ISBN13: 978-0-8223-3309-8. Dewey:331/.0983/09045. LCCN:2004-001304.
Audience: **u,f.**

Drogus, Carol Ann & Stewart-Gambino, Hannah **BX1466.3.D76 2005**
Activist Faith: Grassroots Women in Democratic Brazil and Chile. Saddle Stitched, Cloth over Boards, Dust Jacket. Pennsylvania State University Press. University Park, PA. 2005. 212p. ISBN:0-271-02549-2, ISBN13: 978-0-271-02549-0. Dewey:261.80820981. LCCN:2004-023769.
Audience: **u,f.** *Choice, 2005.*

Falcoff, Mark, et al. **F3100.F3 1988**
Chile: Prospects for Democracy. Susan K. Purcell & Arturo Valenzuela (Authors). Trade Paper. Council on Foreign Relations. New York, NY. 1988. 96p. ISBN:0-87609-045-5, ISBN13: 978-0-87609-045-9. Dewey:320.983. LCCN:88-029936.
Audience: **u,f.**

Faundez, Julio **HX198.F38 1988**
Marxism and Democracy in Chile: From 1932 to the Fall of Allende. Cloth over Boards. Yale University Press. Cumberland, RI. 1988. 272p. ISBN:0-300-04024-5, ISBN13: 978-0-300-04024-1. Dewey:324.283/07/09. LCCN:88-009646.
Audience: **u,f.** *Choice, 1989.*

Fiol-Matta, Licia **PQ8097.G6Z556 2002**
A Queer Mother for the Nation: The State and Gabriela Mistral. Trade Cloth. University of Minnesota Press. Minneapolis, MN. 2001. 264p. ISBN:0-8166-3963-9, ISBN13: 978-0-8166-3963-2. Dewey:861/.62. LCCN:2001-005554.
Audience: **u,f.** *Choice, 2002.*

Fischer, Kathleen B. **LC92.C5 F57**
Political Ideology and Educational Reform in Chile, 1964-1976. Trade Cloth. University of California, Latin American Center. Los Angeles, CA. 1979. Latin American Studies, Vol. 46 ISBN:0-87903-046-1, ISBN13: 978-0-87903-046-9. Dewey:379.83. LCCN:79-620018.
Audience: **u,f.**

Fleet, Michael & Smith, Brian H. **BX1468.2.F57 1997**
The Catholic Church and Democracy in Chile and Peru. Cloth Text. University of Notre Dame Press. Notre Dame, IN. 1997. 392p. Helen Kellogg Institute for International Studies Ser. ISBN:0-268-00821-3, ISBN13: 978-0-268-00821-5. Dewey:282/.83/0904. LCCN:96-028967.
Audience: **u,f.** *Choice, 1998.*

Franceschet, Susan **HQ1236.5.C5F73 2005**
Women and Politics in Chile. Trade Cloth. Lynne Rienner Publishers, Inc. Boulder, CO. 2005. 180p. ISBN:1-58826-316-9, ISBN13: 978-1-58826-316-2. Dewey:323.3/4/0983. LCCN:2004-029655.
Audience: **u,f.** *Choice, 2005.*

Francis, Michael J. **E183.8.A7**
The Limits of Hegemony: United States Relations with Argentina and Chile During World War II. Cloth Text. University of Notre Dame Press. Notre Dame, IN. 1977. 304p. International Studies Ser. ISBN:0-268-01260-1, ISBN13: 978-0-268-01260-1. Dewey:940.53/22/73. LCCN:77-089754.
Audience: **u,f.**

Hawkins, Darren G. **JC599.C5H38 2002**
International Human Rights and Authoritarian Rule in Chile. Cloth Text. University of Nebraska Press. Lincoln, NE. 2002. 261p. Human Rights in International Perspective Ser., Vol. 6 ISBN:0-8032-2404-4, ISBN13: 978-0-8032-2404-9. Dewey:323/.0983/09047. LCCN:2001-044597.
Audience: **l,u,f.** *Choice, 2003.*

Hutchison, Elizabeth Q. **HD6126.H88 2001**
Labors Appropriate to Their Sex: Gender, Labor, and Politics in Urban Chile, 1900-1930. Trade Cloth. Duke University Press. Durham, NC. 2001. 360p. Latin America Otherwise Ser. ISBN:0-8223-2732-5, ISBN13: 978-0-8223-2732-5. Dewey:331.4/0983/09041. LCCN:2001-033109.
Audience: **u,f.** *Choice, 2002.*

Jaksic, Ivan **B1046.J35 1989**
Academic Rebels in Chile: The Role of Philosophy in Higher Education and Politics. Paper Text. State University of New York Press. Albany, NY. 1989. 259p. Series in Latin American and Iberian Thought and Culture ISBN:0-88706-879-0, ISBN13: 978-0-88706-879-9. Dewey:199/.83. LCCN:88-012675.
Audience: **u,f.** *Choice, 1989.*

Kamsteeg, Frans H. **BX8762.Z7L395 1998**
Prophetic Pentecostalism in Chile: A Case Study on Religion and Development Policy. Trade Cloth. Scarecrow Press, Inc. Lanham, MD. 1998. 292p. Studies in Evangelicalism, No. 15 ISBN:0-8108-3440-5, ISBN13: 978-0-8108-3440-8. Dewey:289.9/4/0983315. LCCN:97-043226.
Audience: **u,f.**

Kaufman, Edy **F3100**
Crisis in Allende's Chile: New Perspectives. Trade Cloth. Greenwood Publishing Group, Inc. Portsmouth, NH. 1988. 415p. ISBN:0-275-92822-5, ISBN13: 978-0-275-92822-3. Dewey:983/.0647. LCCN:87-012506.
Audience: **u,f.** *Choice, 1988.*

Klubock, Thomas M. **HD8039.M72C55 1998**
Contested Communities: Class, Gender and Politics in Chile's El Teniente Copper Mine, 1904-1948. Trade Cloth. Duke University Press. Durham, NC. 1998. 240p. Comparative and International Working-Class History Ser. ISBN:0-8223-2078-9, ISBN13: 978-0-8223-2078-4. Dewey:331.7/622343/098332. LCCN:97-039535.
Audience: **u,f.** *Choice, 1998.*

Knudson, Jerry W. **F3100**
The Chilean Press During the Allende Years, 1970-1973. Paper Text. State University of New York at Buffalo, Council on International Studies & Programs. Buffalo, NY. 1986. 80p. Council on International Studies and Programs Special Studies, No. 152 ISBN:0-924197-03-X, ISBN13: 978-0-924197-03-1. Dewey:983.0646.
Audience: **u,f.**

Kofas, Jon V. **HJ8589**
The Sword of Damocles: U.S. Financial Hegemony in Columbia and Chile, 1950-1970. Trade Cloth. Greenwood Publishing Group, Inc. Portsmouth, NH. 2002. 264p. ISBN:0-275-97405-7, ISBN13: 978-0-275-97405-3. Dewey:332.1/52. LCCN:2001-059066.
Audience: **u,f.** *Choice, 2003.*

Kohut, David R. **F2849.2**
Historical Dictionary of the Dirty Wars. Scarecrow Press. 2003.
Audience: **g,l,u,f.**

Kornbluh, Peter **F3101.P56K67 2003**
The Pinochet File: A Declassified Dossier on Atrocity and Accountability. Trade Cloth. New Press, The. New York, NY. 2003. 528p. ISBN:1-56584-586-2, ISBN13: 978-1-56584-586-2. Dewey:983.06/5. LCCN:2003-050956.
Audience: **g,l,u,f.**

Lavrin, Asuncion **HQ1532.L38 1995**
Women, Feminism and Social Change in Argentina, Chile, and Uruguay, 1890-1940. Cloth Text. University of Nebraska Press. Lincoln, NE. 1995. 491p. Engendering Latin America Ser. ISBN:0-8032-2897-X, ISBN13: 978-0-8032-2897-9. Dewey:305.4/0982. LCCN:95-002729.
Audience: **u,f.** *Choice, 1996.*

Leon-Dermota, Ken **PN5044**
...And Well Tied Down: Chile's Press under Democracy. Trade Cloth. Greenwood Publishing Group, Inc. Portsmouth, NH. 2003. 224p. ISBN:0-275-97590-8, ISBN13: 978-0-275-97590-6. Dewey:079/.83/09045. LCCN:2002-030719.
Audience: **u,f.** *Choice, 2004.*

Mallon, Florencia E. **F3429.M255 2005**
Courage Tastes of Blood: The Mapuche Community of Nicolas Ailío and the Chilean State, 1906-2001. Trade Cloth. Duke University Press. Durham, NC. 2005. 320p. Radical Perspectives Ser. ISBN:0-8223-3585-9, ISBN13: 978-0-8223-3585-6. Dewey:983/.0049872. LCCN:2005-009918.
Audience: **u,f.** *Choice, 2006.*

Masini, Eleonora and Susan Stratigos **HQ1240.5.D44**
Women, Household and Change. United Nations University Press. 1991.
Audience: **u,f.**

Michaels, Albert L. **F3100**
Background to a Coup: Civil Military Relations in Twentieth Century Chile and the Overthrow of Salvador Allende. Council on International Studies, State University of New York at Buffalo. 1975.
Audience: **u,f.**

O'Shaughnessy, Hugh **F3101.P56O74 2000**
Pinochet: The Politics of Torture. Trade Cloth. New York University Press. New York, NY. 2000. 208p. ISBN:0-8147-6201-8, ISBN13: 978-0-8147-6201-1. Dewey:983/.065/092. LCCN:99-059431.
Audience: **l,u,f.**

Pinochet Ugarte, Augusto **F3101.P56**
A Journey Through Life. Santiago de Chile. 1991.
Audience: **g,l,u,f.**

Pollack, Marcelo **JC573.2.C5P64 1999**
The New Right in Chile, 1973-97. Cloth over Boards. Palgrave Macmillan. New York, NY. 1999. 245p. St. Antony's Series ISBN:0-312-22278-5, ISBN13: 978-0-312-22278-9. Dewey:324.2/83/03. LCCN:99-021776.
Audience: **u,f.**

Power, Margaret **HQ1236.5.C5P69 2002**
Right-Wing Women in Chile: Feminine Power and the Struggle Against Allende, 1964-1973. Trade Cloth. Pennsylvania State University Press. University Park, PA. 2002. 336p. ISBN:0-271-02174-8, ISBN13: 978-0-271-02174-4. Dewey:306/.2/0820983. LCCN:2001-056039.
Audience: **u,f.**

Remmer, Karen L. **JL2098.A1 R44 1984**
Party Competition in Argentina and Chile: Political Recruitment and Public Policy, 1890-1930. Cloth Text. University of Nebraska Press. Lincoln, NE. 1984. 296p. ISBN:0-8032-3871-1, ISBN13: 978-0-8032-3871-8. Dewey:324/.0982. LCCN:84-013119.
Audience: **u,f.**

Reuque Paillalef, Rosa Isolde **F3126.R49A3 2002**
When a Flower Is Reborn: The Life and Times of a Mapuche Feminist. Florencia E. Mallon (Editor, Translator, Introduction

by). Trade Cloth. Duke University Press. Durham, NC. 2002. 384p. ISBN:0-8223-2934-4, ISBN13: 978-0-8223-2934-3. Dewey:983.06/5/092 B. LCCN:2002-001762.
Audience: **g,l,u,f.** *Choice, 2003.*

Rhodes, Sybil **HC130.C63R48 2005**
Social Movements and Free-Market Capitalism in Latin America: Telecommunications Privatization and the Rise of Consumer Protest. Perfect, Paper over Boards. State University of New York Press. Albany, NY. 2005. 228p. ISBN:0-7914-6597-7, ISBN13: 978-0-7914-6597-4. Dewey:384/.041. LCCN:2004-029611.
Audience: **u,f.**

Richard, Nelly **F3100.R52313 2004**
Cultural Residues: Chile in Transition. Trade Cloth. University of Minnesota Press. Minneapolis, MN. 2004. 240p. Cultural Studies of the Americas, Vol. 18 ISBN:0-8166-3641-9, ISBN13: 978-0-8166-3641-9. Dewey:983.06/4. LCCN:2004-012753.
Audience: **u,f.**

Rosemblatt, Karin Alejandra **HQ1075.5.C5R67 2000**
Gendered Compromises: Political Cultures and the State in Chile, 1920-1950. Trade Paper. University of North Carolina Press. Chapel Hill, NC. 2000. 368p. ISBN:0-8078-4881-6, ISBN13: 978-0-8078-4881-4. Dewey:305.3/0983. LCCN:00-039249.
Audience: **u,f.** *Choice, 2001.*

Rytkonen, Paulina **HD1877**
Fruits of Capitalism: Modernisation of Chilean Agriculture 1950-2000. Trade Paper. Almqvist & Wiksell International. Stockholm, 2004. 213p. Lund Studies in Economic History Ser., Vol. 31 ISBN:91-22-02094-2, ISBN13: 978-91-22-02094-3. Dewey:338.10983.
Audience: **u,f.**

Sater, William F. **F3097.S26 1986**
Chile and the War of the Pacific. Trade Cloth. University of Nebraska Press. Lincoln, NE. 1986. xii, 343p. ISBN:0-8032-4155-0, ISBN13: 978-0-8032-4155-8. Dewey:983/.061. LCCN:85-024584.
Audience: **u,f.** *Choice, 1986.*

Sater, William F. **F3100**
The Revolutionary Left and Terrorist Violence in Chile. Rand. 1986. ISBN:1-900039-43-5, ISBN13: 978-1-900039-43-7.
Audience: **u,f.**

Schneider, Cathy L. **HV4076.S26S36 1995**
Shantytown Protest in Pinochet's Chile. Library Binding. Temple University Press. Philadelphia, PA. 1995. 240p. ISBN:1-56639-305-1, ISBN13: 978-1-56639-305-8. Dewey:322.4/4/098331509047. LCCN:95-002098.
Audience: **u,f.** *Choice, 1995.*

Scully, Timothy R. **JL2698.A1S38 1992**
Rethinking the Center: Party Politics in Nineteenth- and Twentieth-Century Chile. Trade Cloth. Stanford University Press. Palo Alto, CA. 1992. 304p. ISBN:0-8047-1913-6, ISBN13: 978-0-8047-1913-1. Dewey:324.283/009. LCCN:91-020367.
Audience: **u,f.** *Choice, 1992.*

Siavelis, Peter **JL2619.S56 2000**
The President and Congress in Post-Authoritarian Chile: Institutional Constraints to Democratic Consolidation. Trade Cloth. Pennsylvania State University Press. University Park, PA. 2000. 272p. ISBN:0-271-01947-6, ISBN13: 978-0-271-01947-5. Dewey:320.483/04. LCCN:98-054921.
Audience: **u,f.** *Choice, 2000.*

Smith, Brian H. **BX1468.2**
The Church and Politics in Chile: Challenges to Modern Catholicism. Trade Cloth. Princeton University Press. Princeton, NJ. 1982. 416p. ISBN:0-691-07629-4, ISBN13: 978-0-691-07629-4. Dewey:282/.83. LCCN:81-047951.
Audience: **u,f.**

Spooner, Mary H. **F3100**
Soldiers in a Narrow Land: The Pinochet Regime in Chile, Updated Edition. Trade Paper. University of California Press. Berkeley, CA. 1999. 318p. ISBN:0-520-22169-9, ISBN13: 978-0-520-22169-7. Dewey:983/.065. LCCN:93-009910.
Audience: **u,f.**

Stern, Steve J. **F3100.S825 2004**
Remembering Pinochet's Chile: On the Eve of London, 1998. Trade Cloth. Duke University Press. Durham, NC. 2004. 280p. Latin America Otherwise Ser. ISBN:0-8223-3354-6, ISBN13: 978-0-8223-3354-8. Dewey:983.06/5. LCCN:2004-001308.
Audience: **l,u,f.** *Choice, 2005.*

Stewart-Gambino, Hannah W. **BX1468.2.S74 1992**
The Church and Politics in the Chilean Countryside. Trade Paper. Westview Press. Boulder, CO. 1992. 200p. ISBN:0-8133-7724-2, ISBN13: 978-0-8133-7724-7. Dewey:261.7/0983. LCCN:91-038076.
Audience: **u,f.**

Teichman, Judith A. **HF1956.T45 2001**
The Politics of Freeing Markets in Latin America: Chile, Argentina and Mexico. Trade Cloth. University of North Carolina Press. Chapel Hill, NC. 2001. 296p. ISBN:0-8078-2629-4, ISBN13: 978-0-8078-2629-4. Dewey:382/.71/098. LCCN:2001-023409.
Audience: **u,f.**

Tinsman, Heidi **HQ1075.5.C5T56 2002**
Partners in Conflict: The Politics of Gender, Sexuality and Labor in the Chilean Agrarian Reform, 1950-1973. Trade Cloth. Duke University Press. Durham, NC. 2002. 352p. Next Wave Ser. ISBN:0-8223-2907-7, ISBN13: 978-0-8223-2907-7. Dewey:305.3/0983. LCCN:2001-007713.
Audience: **u,f.** *Choice, 2003.*

Tulchin, Joseph S. & Varas, Augusto (Editors) **F3100**
From Dictatorship to Democracy: Rebuilding Political Consensus in Chile. Paper Text. Lynne Rienner Publishers, Inc. Boulder, CO. 1991. 91p. Woodrow Wilson Center Current Studies on Latin America ISBN:1-55587-294-8, ISBN13: 978-1-55587-294-6. Dewey:320.983. LCCN:91-034858.
Audience: **u,f.**

Verba, Ericka Kim **BX1468.3.V47 2003**
Catholic Feminism and the Social Question in Chile, 1910-1917: The Liga de Damas Chilenas. Trade Cloth. Edwin Mellen Press, The. Lewiston, NY. 2003. 352p. Roman Catholic Studies, Vol. 19 ISBN:0-7734-6623-1, ISBN13: 978-0-7734-6623-4. Dewey:267.44. LCCN:2003-061494.
Audience: **u,f.**

Vergara, Jose M. & Varas, Florencia **F3100 .V34 1975**
Coup!: The Last Day of Allende. Trade Cloth. Madison Books, Inc. New York, NY. 1974. 192p. ISBN:0-8128-1705-2, ISBN13: 978-0-8128-1705-8. Dewey:983/.064/0924. LCCN:74-080900.
Audience: **u,f.**

Walter, Richard J. **F3271.3.W35 2005**
Politics and Urban Growth in Santiago, Chile, 1891-1941. Trade Cloth. Stanford University Press. Palo Alto, CA. 2005. 352p. ISBN:0-8047-4982-5, ISBN13: 978-0-8047-4982-4. Dewey:983/.315063. LCCN:2004-003970.
Audience: **u,f.** *Choice, 2005.*

Weeks, Gregory **F3100.W43 2003**
The Military and Politics in Postauthoritarian Chile. Trade Cloth. University of Alabama Press. Tuscaloosa, AL. 2003. 248p. ISBN:0-8173-1177-7, ISBN13: 978-0-8173-1177-3. Dewey:320.983/09/049. LCCN:2003-000561.
Audience: **u,f.** *Choice, 2004.*

Whitaker, Arthur Preston **F2232.2.U6**
The United States and the Southern Cone: Argentina, Chile, and Uruguay. Harvard University Press. 1976. ISBN:0-674-92841-5, ISBN13: 978-0-674-92841-1.
Audience: **u,f.**

White, Judy (Editor) **F3100**
Chile's Days of Terror: Eyewitness Accounts of the Military Coup. José Yglesias (Introduction by). Trade Cloth. Pathfinder Press. New York, NY. 1974. 128p. ISBN:0-87348-410-X, ISBN13: 978-0-87348-410-7. Dewey:983/.064/0922. LCCN:74-015529.
Audience: **u,f.**

Winn, Peter **HD9884.C54Y3**
Weavers of Revolution: The Yarur Workers and Chile's Road to Socialism. Paper Text. Oxford University Press, Inc. New York, NY. 1989. 354p. ISBN:0-19-504558-0, ISBN13: 978-0-19-504558-1. Dewey:338.7/67721/098331. LCCN:85-018832.
Audience: **u,f.** *Choice, 1986.*

Zipper, Ricardo Israel **F3100.I87**
Politics and Ideology in Allende's Chile. Cloth Text. Arizona State University, Center for Latin American Studies. Tempe, AZ. 1989. 306p. ISBN:0-87918-064-1, ISBN13: 978-0-87918-064-5. Dewey:983/.0646. LCCN:87-009370.
Audience: **u,f.**

South America: Individual Countries > Colombia

Bergquist, Charles **HD8256.B47 1986**
Labor in Latin America: Comparative Essays on Chile, Argentina, Venezuela, and Colombia. Trade Cloth. Stanford University Press. Palo Alto, CA. 1986. 416p. Comparative Studies in History, Institutions and Public Policy ISBN:0-8047-1253-0, ISBN13: 978-0-8047-1253-8. Dewey:331/.0968. LCCN:84-051684.
Audience: **u,f.** *Choice, 1986.*

South America: Individual Countries > Colombia > Colonial Colombia

Chandler, David L. **HT1133.C46 1981**
Health and Slavery in Colonial Colombia. Stuart Bruchey (Editor). Library Binding. Ayer Company Publishers, Inc. Manchester, NH. 1981. Dissertations in European Economic History Ser. ISBN:0-405-13983-7, ISBN13: 978-0-405-13983-3. Dewey:305.5/6. LCCN:80-002799.
Audience: **u,f.**

Helg, Aline **F2281.A79H45 2004**
Liberty and Equality in Caribbean Colombia, 1770-1835. Trade Cloth. University of North Carolina Press. Chapel Hill, NC. 2004. 400p. ISBN:0-8078-2876-9, ISBN13: 978-0-8078-2876-2. Dewey:305.896/08611. LCCN:2004-001708.
Audience: **u,f.** *Choice, 2005.*

Kuethe, Allan J. **UA789 .K83**
Military Reform and Society in New Granada, 1773-1808. Trade Cloth. University Press of Florida. Gainesville, FL. 1978. 234p. University of Florida Latin American Monographs, No. 22 ISBN:0-8130-0570-1, ISBN13: 978-0-8130-0570-6. Dewey:355.3/1/0946. LCCN:77-021908.
Audience: **u,f.**

McFarlane, Anthony **F2272.M4 1993**
Colombia Before Independence: Economy, Society and Politics under Bourbon Rule. Alan Knight (Contribution by). Trade Cloth. Cambridge University Press. New York, NY. 1993. 415p. Cambridge Latin American Studies, No. 75 ISBN:0-521-41641-8, ISBN13: 978-0-521-41641-2. Dewey:986.1/02. LCCN:92-042299.
Audience: **u,f.** *Choice, 1994.*

Olsen, Margaret M. **BV3500.S2536 2004**
Slavery and Salvation in Colonial Cartagena de Indias. Trade Cloth. University Press of Florida. Gainesville, FL. 2004. 200p. ISBN:0-8130-2757-8, ISBN13: 978-0-8130-2757-9. Dewey:266/.2861/08996. LCCN:2004-049452.
Audience: **u,f.**

Taussig, Michael **F2269.1.P87T38 1987**
Shamanism, Colonialism, and the Wild Man: A Study in Terror and Healing. Trade Cloth. University of Chicago Press. Chicago, IL. 1987. 538p. ISBN:0-226-79012-6, ISBN13: 978-0-226-79012-1. Dewey:986.1/6300498. LCCN:86-011410.
Audience: **l,u,f.** *Choice, 1987.*

Twinam, Ann **HC198.A5.T9 1982**
Miners, Merchants, and Farmers in Colonial Colombia. Cloth Text. University of Texas Press. Austin, TX. 1982. 205p. Latin American Monographs, No. 57 ISBN:0-292-72034-3, ISBN13: 978-0-292-72034-3. Dewey:338/.04/0986126. LCCN:82-011054.
Audience: **l,u,f.** B

Uribe-Uran, Victor M. **KHH207.U75 2000**
Honorable Lives: Lawyers, Families and Politics in Colombia, 1780-1850. Cloth Text. University of Pittsburgh Press. Pittsburgh, PA. 2000. xii, 276p. Pitt Latin American Ser. ISBN:0-8229-4125-2, ISBN13: 978-0-8229-4125-5. Dewey:340/.115/09. LCCN:99-050964.
Audience: **u,f.** *Choice, 2000.*

West, Robert Cooper **PS374.M48N48**
Colonial Placer Mining in Colombia. Paper Text. Textbook Publishers. Temecula, CA. 2003. x, 159p. ISBN:0-7581-9419-6, ISBN13: 978-0-7581-9419-0. Dewey:808.
Audience: **l,u,f.**

South America: Individual Countries > Colombia > 19th Century Colombia

Abel, Christopher **RA467**
Health Care in Colombia, c. 1920-c. 1950: A Preliminary Analysis. Institute of Latin American Studies. 1994. ISBN:0-901145-92-0, ISBN13: 978-0-901145-92-5.
Audience: **u,f.**

Appelbaum, Nancy P. **F2271.9.A66 2003**
Muddied Waters: Race, Region, and Local History in Colombia, 1846-1948. Trade Cloth. Duke University Press. Durham, NC. 2003. 320p. ISBN:0-8223-3080-6, ISBN13: 978-0-8223-3080-6. Dewey:986.1/05. LCCN:2002-151088.
Audience: **u,f.**

Bergquist, Charles W. **F2276.5**
Coffee and Conflict in Colombia 1886-1910. David Bushnell (Prologue by). Paper Text. Duke University Press. Durham, NC. 1986. xiv, 277p. ISBN:0-8223-0735-9, ISBN13: 978-0-8223-0735-8. Dewey:320.9/861/061. LCCN:78-059581.
Audience: **u,f.**

Braun, Herbert **F2291.B6B73 1985**
The Assassination of Gaitan: Public Life and Urban Violence in Columbia. Cloth Text. University of Wisconsin Press. Chicago, IL. 1986. 296p. ISBN:0-299-10360-9, ISBN13: 978-0-299-10360-6. Dewey:986.1/063.1/0924. LCCN:85-040362.
Audience: **u,f.** *Choice, 1986.*

Braun, Herbert **HV6595**
Our Guerrillas, Our Sidewalks: A Journey into the Violence of Colombia. Ed. 2. Book, Other. Rowman & Littlefield Publishers, Inc. Lanham, MD. 2003. 304p. ISBN:0-7425-1859-0, ISBN13: 978-0-7425-1859-9. Dewey:364.1/54/09861. LCCN:2003-043176.
Audience: **g,l,u,f.**

Bushnell, David **F2271.B78 1993**
Making of Modern Colombia: A Nation in Spite of Itself. Trade Cloth. University of California Press. Berkeley, CA. 1993. 384p. ISBN:0-520-07802-0, ISBN13: 978-0-520-07802-4. Dewey:986.1. LCCN:91-046038.
Audience: **g,l,u,f.** *Choice, 1993.*

Delpar, Helen **JL2898.L5 D44**
Red Against Blue: The Liberal Party in Colombian Politics, 1863-1899. Cloth Text. University of Alabama Press. Tuscaloosa, AL. 1981. 304p. ISBN:0-8173-0030-9, ISBN13: 978-0-8173-0030-2. Dewey:320.9/861. LCCN:79-019081.
Audience: **l,u,f.**

Earle, Rebecca A. **F2274**
Spain and the Independence of Colombia, 1808-1825. Trade Cloth. University of Exeter Press. Exeter, 2000. 263p. ISBN:0-85989-612-9, ISBN13: 978-0-85989-612-2. Dewey:986.1/03.
Audience: **u,f.**

Farnsworth-Alvear, Ann **HD6073.T42C854 2000**
Dulcinea in the Factory: Myths, Morals, Men and Women in Colombia's Industrial Experiment, 1905-1960. Trade Cloth. Duke University Press. Durham, NC. 2000. xvi, 303p. Comparative and International Working-Class History Ser. ISBN:0-8223-2461-X, ISBN13: 978-0-8223-2461-4. Dewey:331.4/877/00986126. LCCN:99-044769.
Audience: **l,u,f.** *Choice, 2001.*

Fluharty, Vernon L. **F2277.F58 1975**
Dance of the Millions: Military Rule and the Social Revolution in Colombia, 1930-1956. Trade Cloth. Greenwood Publishing Group, Inc. Portsmouth, NH. 1975. 336p. ISBN:0-8371-8368-5, ISBN13: 978-0-8371-8368-8. Dewey:986.1/063. LCCN:75-026918.
Audience: **l,u,f.**

Green, W. John **F2277.G74 2003**
Gaitanismo, Left Liberalism, and Popular Mobilization in Colombia. Trade Cloth. University Press of Florida. Gainesville, FL. 2003. xiv, 365p. ISBN:0-8130-2598-2, ISBN13: 978-0-8130-2598-8. Dewey:986.106/31. LCCN:2002-035275.
Audience: **u,f.** *Choice, 2003.*

Helg, Aline **F2281.A79H45 2004**
Liberty and Equality in Caribbean Colombia, 1770-1835. Trade Cloth. University of North Carolina Press. Chapel Hill, NC. 2004. 400p. ISBN:0-8078-2876-9, ISBN13: 978-0-8078-2876-2. Dewey:305.896/08611. LCCN:2004-001708.
Audience: **u,f.** *Choice, 2005.*

Henderson, James D. **F2276.5.H46 2001**
Modernization in Colombia: The Laureano Gomez Years, 1889-1965. Trade Cloth. University Press of Florida. Gainesville, FL. 2001. xvii, 508p. ISBN:0-8130-1824-2, ISBN13: 978-0-8130-1824-9. Dewey:986.106/2. LCCN:00-051051.
Audience: **u,f.** *Choice, 2001.*

Henderson, James D. **F2278 .H39 1985**
When Colombia Bled: A History of the Violencia in Tolima. Cloth Text. University of Alabama Press. Tuscaloosa, AL. 1985. 352p. ISBN:0-8173-0212-3, ISBN13: 978-0-8173-0212-2. Dewey:986.1/0632. LCCN:83-018027.
Audience: **l,u,f.**

LeGrand, Catherine **HD515.L44 1986**
Frontier Expansion and Peasant Protest in Columbia, 1850-1936. Trade Cloth. University of New Mexico Press. Albuquerque, NM. 1986. 320p. ISBN:0-8263-0851-1, ISBN13: 978-0-8263-0851-1. Dewey:333.1/6/09861. LCCN:85-024244.
Audience: **l,u,f.**

Londono-Vega, Patricia **F2281.A6L67 2002**
Religion, Society, and Culture in Colombia: Antioquia and Medellin 1850-1930. Trade Cloth. Oxford University Press, Inc. New York, NY. 2002. 416p. Oxford Historical Monographs ISBN:0-19-924953-9, ISBN13: 978-0-19-924953-4. Dewey:986.1/2606. LCCN:2001-054563.
Audience: **u,f.**

McGreevey, W. P. **HC197**
Economic History Colombia. Alan Knight (Contribution by). Cloth Text. Cambridge University Press. New York, NY. 1971. 344p. Cambridge Latin American Studies, Vol. 9 ISBN:0-521-07909-8, ISBN13: 978-0-521-07909-9. Dewey:330.9861/05. LCCN:70-116844.
Audience: **l,u,f.**

Murray, Pamela S. **TN213.C7M87 1997**
Dreams of Development: Colombia's National School of Mines and Its Engineers, 1887-1970. Trade Paper. University of Alabama Press. Tuscaloosa, AL. 1997. 192p. ISBN:0-8173-0839-3, ISBN13: 978-0-8173-0839-1. Dewey:622/.071/1861. LCCN:96-016449.
Audience: **u,f.** *Choice, 1997.*

Oquist, Paul **F2278**
Violence, Conflict, and Politics in Colombia. Trade Cloth. Elsevier Science & Technology Books. Saint Louis, MO. 1980. xiv, 263p. Studies in Social Discontinuity Ser. ISBN:0-12-527750-4, ISBN13: 978-0-12-527750-1. Dewey:986.1/0632. LCCN:79-006778.
Audience: **u,f.**

Palacios, Marco **HD9199.C62**
Coffee in Colombia, Eighteen Hundred to Nineteen Hundred Seventy: An Economic, Social and Political History. Trade Cloth. Cambridge University Press. New York, NY. 1980. 356p. Cambridge Latin American Studies, No. 36 ISBN:0-521-22204-4, ISBN13: 978-0-521-22204-4. Dewey:338.1/7/37309861. LCCN:78-073251.
Audience: **l,u,f.**

Parsons, James J. **F1401.I22 NO. 32**
Antioqueno Colonization in Western Colombia. Trade Cloth. University of California Press. Berkeley, CA. 1968. ISBN:0-520-01464-2, ISBN13: 978-0-520-01464-0. Dewey:986. LCCN:68-058002.
Audience: **u,f.**

Phelan, John L. **F2272**
The People and the King: The Comunero Revolution in Colombia, 1781. Trade Cloth. University of Wisconsin Press. Chicago, IL. 1978. 332p. ISBN:0-299-07290-8, ISBN13: 978-0-299-07290-2. Dewey:986.1/02. LCCN:76-053654.
Audience: **u,f.**

Posada-Carbo, Eduardo **F2281.A79P67 1996**
The Colombian Caribbean: A Regional History, 1870-1950. Trade Cloth. Oxford University Press, Inc. New York, NY. 1996. 314p. Oxford Historical Monographs ISBN:0-19-820628-3, ISBN13: 978-0-19-820628-6. Dewey:986.1. LCCN:95-049561.
Audience: **g,l,u,f.** *Choice, 1997.*

Rappaport, Joanne **F2269.1.C93.R36 1994**
Cumbe Reborn: An Andean Ethnography of History. Trade Cloth. University of Chicago Press. Chicago, IL. 1993. 262p. ISBN:0-226-70525-0, ISBN13: 978-0-226-70525-5. Dewey:986.1062. LCCN:93-004909.
Audience: **u,f.** *Choice, 1994.*

Rappaport, Joanne **F2269.1.C375R36 2005**
Intercultural Utopias: Public Intellectuals, Cultural Experimentation, and Ethnic Pluralism in Colombia. Trade Cloth. Duke University Press. Durham, NC. 2005. 384p. Latin America Otherwise Ser. ISBN:0-8223-3561-1, ISBN13: 978-0-8223-3561-0. Dewey:305.8/009861/53. LCCN:2005-002697.
Audience: **u,f.**

Rappaport, Joanne **F2270.2.P3R36 1990**
The Politics of Memory: Native Historical Interpretation in the Colombian Andes. Trade Cloth. Cambridge University Press. New York, NY. 1990. 240p. Cambridge Latin American Studies, No. 70 ISBN:0-521-37345-X, ISBN13: 978-0-521-37345-6. Dewey:986.1/53004982. LCCN:89-009756.
Audience: **u,f.** *Choice, 1991.*

Rausch, Jane M. **F2277.R29 1999**
Colombia: Territorial Rule and The Llanos Frontier. Trade Cloth. University Press of Florida. Gainesville, FL. 1999. xi, 285p. ISBN:0-8130-1718-1, ISBN13: 978-0-8130-1718-1. Dewey:986.106/3. LCCN:99-022477.
Audience: **u,f.** *Choice, 2000.*

Rausch, Jane M. **F2273.R37 1993**
The Llanos Frontier in Colombian History, 1830-1930. Trade Cloth. University of New Mexico Press. Albuquerque, NM. 1993. 416p. ISBN:0-8263-1396-5, ISBN13: 978-0-8263-1396-6. Dewey:986.1. LCCN:92-000480.
Audience: **l,u,f.** *Choice, 1994.*

Roldan, Mary **HN310.A5R64 2000**
Blood and Fire: La Violencia in Antioquia, Colombia, 1946-1953. Trade Cloth. Duke University Press. Durham, NC. 2002. 400p. Latin America Otherwise Ser. ISBN:0-8223-2903-4, ISBN13: 978-0-8223-2903-9. Dewey:986.1/260632. LCCN:2001-007184.
Audience: **u,f.** *Choice, 2003.*

Safford, Frank **T95**
The Ideal of the Practical: Colombia's Struggle to Form a Technical Elite. Trade Cloth. University of Texas Press. Austin, TX. 1976. 391p. Latin American Monographs, No. 39 ISBN:0-292-73803-X, ISBN13: 978-0-292-73803-4. Dewey:607/.861. LCCN:75-016072.
Audience: **u,f.** B

Sanchez, Gonzalo J. **HN310.Z9V579 1992**
Violence in Colombia: The Contemporary Crisis in Historical Perspective. Trade Cloth. Rowman & Littlefield Publishers, Inc. Lanham, MD. 1992. 337p. Latin American Silhouettes Ser. ISBN:0-8420-2369-0, ISBN13: 978-0-8420-2369-6. Dewey:303.6/09861. LCCN:91-022992.
Audience: **u,f.**

Sanders, James E. **F2276.S25 2004**
Contentious Republicans: Popular Politics, Race, and Class in Nineteenth-Century Colombia. Trade Cloth. Duke University Press. Durham, NC. 2004. 320p. ISBN:0-8223-3234-5, ISBN13: 978-0-8223-3234-3. Dewey:986.1/05. LCCN:2003-016426.
Audience: **u,f.** *Choice, 2005.*

Sharp, William F. **HT1134.C5S5**
Slavery on the Spanish Frontier: The Colombian Choco, 1680-1810. Trade Paper. University of Oklahoma Press. Norman, OK. 1976. 253p. ISBN:0-8061-1759-1, ISBN13: 978-0-8061-1759-1. Dewey:301.44/93/098612. LCCN:76-018767.
Audience: **l,u,f.**

Sharpless, Richard E. **F2277.G24**
Gaitan of Colombia: A Political Biography. Trade Cloth. University of Pittsburgh Press. Pittsburgh, PA. 1977. 236p. Latin American Ser. ISBN:0-8229-3354-3, ISBN13: 978-0-8229-3354-0. Dewey:986.1/063/0924. LCCN:77-074552.
Audience: **l,u,f.**

Sowell, David **HD2346.C72B657 1992**
The Early Colombian Labor Movement: Artisans and Politics in Bogota, 1832-1919. Trade Cloth. Temple University Press. Philadelphia, PA. 1992. 272p. ISBN:0-87722-965-1, ISBN13: 978-0-87722-965-0. Dewey:322/.2/0986148. LCCN:91-045958.
Audience: **u,f.** *Choice, 1993.*

Sánchez, Gonzalo & Meertens, Donny **HV6453.C75S2813 2001**
Bandits, Peasants, and Politics: The Case of la Violencia in Colombia. Alan Hynds (Translator). Trade Cloth. University of Texas Press. Austin, TX. 2001. 247p. Translations from Latin America Ser. ISBN:0-292-77758-2, ISBN13: 978-0-292-77758-3. Dewey:364.9861. LCCN:00-053517.
Audience: **u,f.** *Choice, 2001.*

Twinam, Ann **HC198.A5.T9 1982**
Miners, Merchants, and Farmers in Colonial Colombia. Cloth Text. University of Texas Press. Austin, TX. 1982. 205p. Latin American Monographs, No. 57 ISBN:0-292-72034-3, ISBN13: 978-0-292-72034-3. Dewey:338/.04/0986126. LCCN:82-011054.
Audience: **l,u,f.** ℬ

Twinam, Ann **HQ999.L29T89 1999**
Public Lives, Private Secrets: Gender, Honor, Sexuality and Illegitimacy in Colonial Spanish America. Trade Cloth. Stanford University Press. Palo Alto, CA. 1999. 442p. ISBN:0-8047-3147-0, ISBN13: 978-0-8047-3147-8. Dewey:306.874. LCCN:98-045252.
Audience: **u,f.** *Choice, 2000.*

Uribe-Uran, Victor M. (Editor) **F1412.S85 2001**
State and Society in Spanish America During the Age of Revolution. Book, Other. Rowman & Littlefield Publishers, Inc. Lanham, MD. 2001. 261p. Latin American Silhouettes Ser. ISBN:0-8420-2873-0, ISBN13: 978-0-8420-2873-8. Dewey:980. LCCN:00-058793.
Audience: **l,u,f.**

Urrutia, Miguel **HD6622**
Development of the Colombian Labor Movement. Trade Cloth. Yale University Press. Cumberland, RI. 1969. xi, 297p. ISBN:0-300-01153-9, ISBN13: 978-0-300-01153-1. Dewey:331.88/09861. LCCN:70-081433.
Audience: **l,u,f.**

Wade, Peter **F2299.B55.W3 1993**
Blackness and Race Mixture: The Dynamics of Racial Identity in Colombia. Trade Cloth. Johns Hopkins University Press. Baltimore, MD. 1993. 432p. Johns Hopkins Studies in Atlantic History and Culture Ser. ISBN:0-8018-4458-4, ISBN13: 978-0-8018-4458-4. Dewey:305.8960861. LCCN:92-015581.
Audience: **l,u,f.** *Choice, 1994.*

West, Robert Cooper **PS374.M48N48**
Colonial Placer Mining in Colombia. Paper Text. Textbook Publishers. Temecula, CA. 2003. x, 159p. ISBN:0-7581-9419-6, ISBN13: 978-0-7581-9419-0. Dewey:808.
Audience: **l,u,f.**

Zamosc, Leon **HD516 .Z36 1986**
The Agrarian Question and the Peasant Movement in Colombia: Struggles of the National Peasant Association, 1967-1981. Trade Cloth. Cambridge University Press. New York, NY. 1986. 320p. Cambridge Latin American Studies, No. 58 ISBN:0-521-32010-0, ISBN13: 978-0-521-32010-8. Dewey:322.4/4/09861. LCCN:85-019479.
Audience: **u,f.** *Choice, 1987.*

South America: Individual Countries > Venezuela

Bergquist, Charles **HD8256.B47 1986**
Labor in Latin America: Comparative Essays on Chile, Argentina, Venezuela, and Colombia. Trade Cloth. Stanford University Press. Palo Alto, CA. 1986. 416p. Comparative Studies in History, Institutions and Public Policy ISBN:0-8047-1253-0, ISBN13: 978-0-8047-1253-8. Dewey:331/.0968. LCCN:84-051684.
Audience: **u,f.** *Choice, 1986.*

South America: Individual Countries > Venezuela > Colonial Venezuela

Braveboy-Wagner, Jacqueline A. **F2321.3.G9/**
The Venezuela-Guyana Border Dispute: Britain's Colonial Legacy in Latin America. Paper Text. Westview Press. Boulder, CO. 1984. 200p. A Replica Edition Ser. ISBN:0-86531-953-7, ISBN13: 978-0-86531-953-0. Dewey:341.4/2. LCCN:83-050174.
Audience: **l,u,f.**

Ferry, Robert J. **HN370.Z9E435 1989**
The Colonial Elite of Caracas: Formation and Crisis, 1567-1767. Trade Cloth. University of California Press. Berkeley, CA. 1989. 245p. ISBN:0-520-06399-6, ISBN13: 978-0-520-06399-0. Dewey:305.5/2/09877. LCCN:88-029089.
Audience: **u,f.**

Hussey, Roland D. **HF491.R42 H87 1977**
The Caracas Company, 1728-1784: Study in the History of Spanish Monopolistic Trade. Mira Wilkins (Editor). Library Binding. Ayer Company Publishers, Inc. Manchester, NH. 1977. European Business Ser. ISBN:0-405-09768-9, ISBN13: 978-0-405-09768-3. Dewey:382/.06/546. LCCN:76-029752.
Audience: **u,f.**

Lombardi, John V. **HB3579**
People and Places in Colonial Venezuela. Cathryn L. Lombardi (Illustrator). Trade Cloth. Indiana University Press. Bloomington, IN. 1976. 512p. ISBN:0-253-34330-5, ISBN13: 978-0-253-34330-7. Dewey:301.32/9/87. LCCN:75-025433.
Audience: **g,l,u,f.** ℬ

Pinero, Eugenio **HC237.P55 1994**
The Town of San Felipe and Colonial Cacao Economics. Trade Paper. American Philosophical Society. Canton, MA. 1994. 190p. Transactions Ser., Vol. 84, Pt. 3 ISBN:0-87169-843-9, ISBN13: 978-0-87169-843-8. Dewey:698.8/0704. LCCN:94-071251.
Audience: **u,f.**

Racine, Karen **F2323.M6R332002**
Francisco de Miranda: A Transatlantic Life in the Age of Revolution. Trade Cloth. Rowman & Littlefield Publishers, Inc. Lanham, MD. 2002. 336p. Latin American Silhouettes Ser. ISBN:0-8420-2909-5, ISBN13: 978-0-8420-2909-4. Dewey:987/.04/092. LCCN:2002-070707.
Audience: **g,l,u,f.** *Choice, 2003.*

Whitehead, Neil L. **F2319.2.C3**
Lords of the Tiger Spirit : A History of the Caribs in Colonial Venezuela and Guyana, 1498-1820. Foris Publications. 1988. ISBN:90-6765-240-7, ISBN13: 978-90-6765-240-7.
Audience: **l,u,f.**

Wright, Winthrop R. **F2349.B55W75 1990**
Cafe con Leche: Race, Class, and National Image in Venezuela. Trade Cloth. University of Texas Press. Austin, TX. 1993. 184p. ISBN:0-292-71128-X, ISBN13: 978-0-292-71128-0. Dewey:987/.00496. LCCN:90-032669.
Audience: **l,u,f.** *Choice, 1991.*

South America: Individual Countries > Venezuela > Contemporary Venezuela

Alexander, Robert J. **F2326.B4**
Romulo Betancourt and the Transformation of Venezuela. Trade Cloth. Transaction Publishers. Somerset, NJ. 1982. 750p. ISBN:0-87855-450-5, ISBN13: 978-0-87855-450-8. Dewey:987/.0633/0924. LCCN:81-014684.
Audience: **u,f.** B

Boue, Juan Carlos **HD9574.V42B68 1993**
Venezuela: The Political Economy of Oil. Cloth Text. Oxford University Press, Inc. New York, NY. 1994. 248p. Institute for Energy Studies ISBN:0-19-730012-X, ISBN13: 978-0-19-730012-1. Dewey:338.2/782/0987. LCCN:94-137023.
Audience: **l,u,f.** *Choice, 1994.*

Briggs, Charles L. & Mantini-Briggs, Clara **RA644.C3 B685 2003**
Stories in the Time of Cholera: Racial Profiling During a Medical Nightmare. Trade Cloth. University of California Press. Berkeley, CA. 2003. 390p. ISBN:0-520-23031-0, ISBN13: 978-0-520-23031-6. Dewey:614.5/14/0987. LCCN:2002-016552.
Audience: **l,u,f.** *Choice, 2003.*

Coronil, Fernando **JL3831.C67 1997**
The Magical State: Nature, Money, and Modernity in Venezuela. Trade Cloth. University of Chicago Press. Chicago, IL. 1997. 466p. ISBN:0-226-11601-8, ISBN13: 978-0-226-11601-3. Dewey:306.20987. LCCN:97-008000.
Audience: **u,f.**

Corrales, Javier **HC175.C6684 2002**
Presidents Without Parties: The Politics of Economic Reform in Argentina and Venezuela in the 1990s. Trade Cloth. Pennsylvania State University Press. University Park, PA. 2002. 384p. ISBN:0-271-02194-2, ISBN13: 978-0-271-02194-2. Dewey:338.982. LCCN:2001-055951.
Audience: **u,f.** *Choice, 2003.*

Diaz, Arlene J. **HQ1582.D52 2004**
Female Citizens, Patriarchs, and the Law in Venezuela, 1786-1904. Cloth Text. University of Nebraska Press. Lincoln, NE. 2004. 448p. Engendering Latin America Ser., Vol. 7 ISBN:0-8032-1722-6, ISBN13: 978-0-8032-1722-5. Dewey:305.4/0987. LCCN:2003-059568.
Audience: **l,u,f.** *Choice, 2004.*

Ellner, Steve **HD6652 .E43 1993**
Organized Labor in Venezuela, 1958-1991: Behavior and Concerns in a Democratic Setting. Book, Other. Rowman & Littlefield Publishers, Inc. Lanham, MD. 1993. 312p. Latin American Silhouettes Ser. ISBN:0-8420-2443-3, ISBN13: 978-0-8420-2443-3. Dewey:331.88/0987/09045. LCCN:92-044554.
Audience: **l,u,f.**

Ellner, Steve & Hellinger, Daniel (Editors) **JL3881.V464 2003**
Venezuelan Politics in the Chavez Era: Class, Polarization, and Conflict. Library Binding. Lynne Rienner Publishers, Inc. Boulder, CO. 2002. 260p. ISBN:1-58826-108-5, ISBN13: 978-1-58826-108-3. Dewey:987.06/42. LCCN:2002-073985.
Audience: **l,u,f.** *Choice, 2003.*

Ewell, Judith **F2325.E93 1984**
Venezuela: A Century of Change. Trade Cloth. Stanford University Press. Palo Alto, CA. 1984. 272p. ISBN:0-8047-1213-1, ISBN13: 978-0-8047-1213-2. Dewey:987/.06. LCCN:83-040093.
Audience: **g,l,u,f.** B

Ewell, Judith **E183.8.V3E9 1996**
Venezuela and the United States: From Monroe's Hemisphere to Petroleum's Empire. Cloth Text. University of Georgia Press. Athens, GA. 1996. 267p. The United States and the Americas Ser. ISBN:0-8203-1782-9, ISBN13: 978-0-8203-1782-3. Dewey:327.73087. LCCN:95-002808.
Audience: **u,f.** *Choice, 1996.*

Friedman, Elisabeth J. **HQ1236.5.V4F74 2000**
Unfinished Transitions: Gendered Political Opportunities and Women's Organizing in Latin American Democratization. Trade Cloth. Pennsylvania State University Press. University Park, PA. 2000. 344p. ISBN:0-271-02023-7, ISBN13: 978-0-271-02023-5. Dewey:305.42/0987. LCCN:99-047238.
Audience: **u,f.** *Choice, 2001.*

Guss, David M. **HN363.5.G87 2000**
The Festive State: Race, Ethnicity and Nationalism as Cultural Performance. Trade Paper. University of California Press. Berkeley, CA. 2001. 254p. ISBN:0-520-22331-4, ISBN13: 978-0-520-22331-8. Dewey:306/.0987. LCCN:99-056890.
Audience: **u,f.** *Choice, 2001.*

Karl, Terry L. **HD9574.V42K37 1997**
The Paradox of Plenty: Oil Booms and Petro-States. Trade Paper. University of California Press. Berkeley, CA. 1997. 360p. Studies in International Political Economy ISBN:0-520-20772-6, ISBN13: 978-0-520-20772-1. Dewey:338.2/7282/0987. LCCN:96-053044.
Audience: **u,f.** *Choice, 1998.*

Levine, Daniel H. **BX1470.2**
Popular Voices in Latin American Catholicism. Trade Cloth. Princeton University Press. Princeton, NJ. 1992. 424p. Studies in Church and State ISBN:0-691-08754-7, ISBN13: 978-0-691-08754-2. Dewey:282/.861/09049.
Audience: **l,u,f.**

Lombardi, John V. **F2321.L58 1982**
Venezuela: The Search for Order, the Dream of Progress. Trade Cloth. Oxford University Press, Inc. New York, NY. 1982. 364p. Latin American Histories Ser. ISBN:0-19-503013-3, ISBN13: 978-0-19-503013-6. Dewey:987. LCCN:81-009630.
Audience: **l,u,f.** B

McBeth, B. S. **HD9574.V42**
Juan Vicente Gsmez and the Oil Companies in Venezuela, 1908-1935. Alan Knight (Contribution by). Trade Paper. Cambridge University Press. New York, NY. 2002. 289p. Cambridge Latin American Studies ISBN:0-521-89218-X, ISBN13: 978-0-521-89218-6. Dewey:338.272821.
Audience: **l,u,f.**

McBeth, Brian S. **F2325**
Gunboats, Corruption, and Claims: Foreign Intervention in Venezuela, 1899-1908. Trade Cloth. Greenwood Publishing Group, Inc. Portsmouth, NH. 2001. 320p. Contributions in Latin American Studies, Vol. 20 ISBN:0-313-31356-3, ISBN13: 978-0-313-31356-1. Dewey:987.06/312/092. LCCN:00-035357.
Audience: **g,l,u,f.** *Choice, 2001.*

Myers, David J. **F2329.U67 2004**
The Unraveling of Representative Democracy in Venezuela. Jennifer McCoy (Editor). Trade Cloth. Johns Hopkins University Press. Baltimore, MD. 2004. 376p. ISBN:0-8018-7960-4, ISBN13: 978-0-8018-7960-9. Dewey:320.987. LCCN:2004-005542.
Audience: **l,u,f.** *Choice, 2005.*

Rivas, Darlene **HC237.R569 2002**
Missionary Capitalist: Nelson Rockefeller in Venezuela. Trade Cloth. University of North Carolina Press. Chapel Hill, NC. 2002. 312p. Luther Hartwell Hodges Series on Business, Society and the State ISBN:0-8078-2684-7, ISBN13: 978-0-8078-2684-3. Dewey:338.987/009/045. LCCN:2001-053068.
Audience: **g,l,u,f.**

Roseberry, William **HC238.B58 R67 1983**
Coffee and Capitalism in the Venezuelan Andes. Cloth Text. University of Texas Press. Austin, TX. 1983. 271p. Latin American Monographs, No. 59 ISBN:0-292-71535-8, ISBN13: 978-0-292-71535-6. Dewey:330.987/14. LCCN:83-001350.
Audience: **u,f.** B

Salazar-Carrillo, Jorge & West, Bernadette **HD9574**
Oil and Development in Venezuela During the 20th Century. Trade Cloth. Greenwood Publishing Group, Inc. Portsmouth, NH. 2004. 296p. ISBN:0-275-97262-3, ISBN13: 978-0-275-97262-2. Dewey:330.987/063. LCCN:2003-062252.
Audience: **u,f.** *Choice, 2005.*

Tarver, H. Micheal & Frederick, Julia C. **F2321**
The History of Venezuela. Trade Cloth. Greenwood Publishing Group, Inc. Portsmouth, NH. 2005. 216p. The Greenwood Histories of the Modern Nations Ser. ISBN:0-313-33525-7, ISBN13: 978-0-313-33525-9. Dewey:987. LCCN:2005-018566.
Audience: **g,l,u,f.**

Trinkunas, Harold A. **F2325.T75 2005**
Crafting Civilian Control of the Military in Venezuela: A Comparative Perspective. Trade Cloth. University of North Carolina Press. Chapel Hill, NC. 2005. 312p. ISBN:0-8078-2982-X, ISBN13: 978-0-8078-2982-0. Dewey:322/.5/098709045. LCCN:2005-010252.
Audience: **l,u,f.** *Choice, 2006.*

Weyland, Kurt Gerhard **HC165.W46 2004**
The Politics of Market Reform in Fragile Democracies: Argentina, Brazil, Peru, and Venezuela. Trade Paper. Princeton University Press. Princeton, NJ. 2004. 360p. ISBN:0-691-11787-X, ISBN13: 978-0-691-11787-4. Dewey:338.98.
Audience: **u,f.** *Choice, 2003.*

Wright, Winthrop R. **F2349.B55W75 1990**
Cafe con Leche: Race, Class, and National Image in Venezuela. Trade Cloth. University of Texas Press. Austin, TX. 1993. 184p. ISBN:0-292-71128-X, ISBN13: 978-0-292-71128-0. Dewey:987/.00496. LCCN:90-032669.
Audience: **l,u,f.** *Choice, 1991.*

Yarrington, Douglas **HD9199.V43C748 1997**
A Coffee Frontier in Latin America: Land, Society, and Politics in Duaca, Venezuela, 1830-1936. Trade Paper. University of Pittsburgh Press. Pittsburgh, PA. 1997. 272p. Pitt Latin American Ser. ISBN:0-8229-5632-2, ISBN13: 978-0-8229-5632-7. Dewey:338.1/7373/098725. LCCN:97-004791.
Audience: **l,u,f.** *Choice, 1998.*

UNITED STATES AND CANADIAN HISTORY

The items that appeared in the BCL3 served as the basis for our work. Many of the books recommended earlier were kept because they represent the core or seminal works in the area and remain valuable to future generations of historians. More recently published books were selected if they reflected new historiographic approaches, or treated historical events that were not covered in earlier editions of BCL. In-print items were favored, but we also included out-of-print titles if they were deemed still essential for a basic undergraduate collection. We also included significant collections of reprinted primary sources where available.

— Ed Goedeken

Dumond, Dwight L. (Editor) **E440.5**
Southern Editorials on Secession. Trade Cloth. Peter Smith Publisher, Inc. Magnolia, MA. 1964. ISBN:0-8446-1162-X, ISBN13: 978-0-8446-1162-4. Dewey:973.713.
Audience: **l,u,f.**

Gunderson, Robert Gray **E440.5.G965**
Old Gentlemen's Convention: The Washington Peace Conference Of 1861. Paper Text. Textbook Publishers. Temecula, CA. 2003. xiii, 168p. ISBN:0-7581-1371-4, ISBN13: 978-0-7581-1371-9. Dewey:973.71.
Audience: **l,u,f.**

Perkins, Howard C. **E440.5.P45**
Northern Editorials on Secession, Set. Trade Cloth. Peter Smith Publisher, Inc. Magnolia, MA. 1990. ISBN:0-8446-1347-9, ISBN13: 978-0-8446-1347-5. Dewey:973.68.
Audience: **l,u,f.**

Potter, David M. **E440.5.P856 1995**
Lincoln and His Party in the Secession Crisis. Daniel W. Crofts (Introduction by). Trade Paper. Louisiana State University Press. Baton Rouge, LA. 1995. 440p. ISBN:0-8071-2027-8, ISBN13: 978-0-8071-2027-9. Dewey:973.7/092. LCCN:95-023562.
Audience: **l,u,f.**

Stampp, Kenneth M. **E440**
And the War Came: The North and the Secession Crisis, 1860-1861. Trade Cloth. Greenwood Publishing Group, Inc. Portsmouth, NH. 1980. 331p. ISBN:0-313-22566-4, ISBN13: 978-0-313-22566-6. Dewey:973.7/13. LCCN:80-015742.
Audience: **l,u,f.**

Wooster, Ralph A. **E440.5.W9**
The Secession Conventions of the South. Paper Text. Textbook Publishers. Temecula, CA. 2003. viii, 294p. ISBN:0-7581-5704-5, ISBN13: 978-0-7581-5704-1. Dewey:973.713.
Audience: **l,u,f.**

United States > General Works. Social Life. Customs

Brinkley, Douglas **E178.B838 1998**
The American Heritage History of the United States. Trade Cloth. Penguin Group (USA) Inc. New York, NY. 1998. 640p. ISBN:0-670-86966-X, ISBN13: 978-0-670-86966-4. Dewey:973. LCCN:98-007337.
Audience: **g,l,u,f.**

Brinkley, Douglas & Ambrose, Stephen E. **E173.W78 1999**
Witness to America: An Illustrated Documentary History of the United States from the Revolution to Today. Ed. 2. Trade Cloth. HarperCollins Publishers. New York, NY. 1999. 624p. ISBN:0-06-271611-5, ISBN13: 978-0-06-271611-8. Dewey:973. LCCN:99-023797.
Audience: **g,l,u,f.**

United States > Description. Travel, by Period > 1607-1783

Commager, Henry Steele **E163.C7 2000**
The Empire of Reason: How Europe Imagined and America Realized the Enlightenment. Saddle Stitched. Phoenix Press, WC2. London, 2001. 352p. ISBN:1-84212-076-X, ISBN13: 978-1-84212-076-7. Dewey:973.2. LCCN:2001-430062.
Audience: **u,f.**

Kammen, Michael G. **E162.K2 1990**
People of Paradox: An Inquiry Concerning the Origins of American Civilization. Book, Other. Cornell University Press. Ithaca, NY. 1990. 368p. Cornell Paperbacks Ser. ISBN:0-8014-9755-8, ISBN13: 978-0-8014-9755-1. Dewey:973. LCCN:90-055186.
Audience: **u,f.**

United States > Description. Travel, by Period > 1861-

Birdsall, Stephen S., et al. **GB115**
Regional Landscapes of the United States and Canada. Ed. 6. Jon C. Malinowski, Eugene J. Palka & Margo L. Price (Authors). Trade Cloth. John Wiley & Sons, Inc. Hoboken, NJ. 2004. 408p. ISBN:0-471-15226-9, ISBN13: 978-0-471-15226-2. Dewey:917.3. LCCN:2004-275846.
Audience: **l,u,f.**

United States > Civilization. Intellectual Life

Allen, Frederick L. **E169.1.A4717 1992**
The Big Change: America Transforms Itself: 1900-1950. William L. O'Neill (Introduction by). Trade Paper. Transaction Publishers. Somerset, NJ. 1993. 322p. ISBN:1-56000-639-0, ISBN13: 978-1-56000-639-8. Dewey:973.91. LCCN:92-011261.
Audience: **u,f.**

Baritz, Loren **E169.1.B225 1980**
City on a Hill: A History of Ideas and Myths in America. Trade Cloth. Greenwood Publishing Group, Inc. Portsmouth, NH. 1980. 367p. ISBN:0-313-22268-1, ISBN13: 978-0-313-22268-9. Dewey:973. LCCN:80-011468.
Audience: **f.**

Barth, Gunther **E169.1.B2315 1990**
Fleeting Moments: Nature and Culture in American History. Trade Cloth. Oxford University Press, Inc. New York, NY. 1990. 244p. ISBN:0-19-506296-5, ISBN13: 978-0-19-506296-0. Dewey:973.38. LCCN:90-031526.
Audience: **u,f.** *Choice, 1991.*

Bellah, Robert N. **E169.1.B435 1992**
The Broken Covenant: American Civil Religion in Time of Trial. Ed. 2. Trade Paper. University of Chicago Press. Chicago, IL. 1992. 222p. ISBN:0-226-04199-9, ISBN13: 978-0-226-04199-5. Dewey:306.6/0973. LCCN:74-019479.
Audience: **f.**

Bellah, Robert Neelly **E169.1.B435**
The Broken Covenant: American Civil Religion in a Time of Trial. Trade Cloth. The Seabury Press, Inc. New York, NY. 1975. xvi, 172p. ISBN:0-8164-1161-1, ISBN13: 978-0-8164-1161-0. Dewey:306.6/0973. LCCN:74-019479.
Audience: **u,f.** B

Bellah, Robert N., et al. **E169.12.H29 1985**
Habits of the Heart: Individualism and Commitment in American Life. Richard Madsen, William M. Sullivan, Ann Swidler & Steven M. Tipton (Authors). Trade Cloth. University of California Press. Berkeley, CA. 1985. 376p. ISBN:0-520-05388-5, ISBN13: 978-0-520-05388-5. Dewey:973.92. LCCN:84-016370.
Audience: **g,l,u,f.**

Bercovitch, Sacvan **E169.1**
The Puritan Origins of the American Self. Trade Cloth. Yale University Press. Cumberland, RI. 1977. 260p. ISBN:0-300-01754-5, ISBN13: 978-0-300-01754-0. Dewey:306/.0973. LCCN:74-029713.
Audience: **f.**

Bloom, Allan **LA227.3.B584**
Closing of the American Mind. Library Binding. Sagebrush Education Resources. Caledonia, MN. 1988. ISBN:0-613-18511-0, ISBN13: 978-0-613-18511-0. Dewey:378.73.
Audience: **g,l,u,f.**

Bode, Carl **E166.B635 1983**
The Anatomy of American Popular Culture, 1840-1861. Trade Cloth. Greenwood Publishing Group, Inc. Portsmouth, NH. 1983. 292p. ISBN:0-313-24005-1, ISBN13: 978-0-313-24005-8. Dewey:973.6. LCCN:83-005643.
Audience: **f.**

Bode, Carl **E166.B635**
The Anatomy of American Popular Culture, 1840-1861. Paper Text. Textbook Publishers. Temecula, CA. 2003. xxi, 292p. ISBN:0-7581-2651-4, ISBN13: 978-0-7581-2651-1. Dewey:973.6.
Audience: **f.** B

Bodnar, John (Editor) **E169.1.B695 1996**
Bonds of Affection: Americans Define Their Patriotism. Trade Cloth. Princeton University Press. Princeton, NJ. 1996. 352p. ISBN:0-691-04397-3, ISBN13: 978-0-691-04397-5. Dewey:973. LCCN:95-026683.
Audience: **u,f.**

Boorstin, Daniel J. **E162.B68 1965**
The Americans: The National Experience. Trade Paper. Alfred A. Knopf Inc. New York, NY. 1967. 528p. ISBN:0-394-70358-8, ISBN13: 978-0-394-70358-9. Dewey:917.303. LCCN:95-153525.
Audience: **l,u,f.**

Boorstin, Daniel J. **E169.1.B7513 1974**
The Americans: The Democratic Experience. Trade Paper. Knopf Publishing Group. New York, NY. 1974. 736p. Vintage Ser. ISBN:0-394-71011-8, ISBN13: 978-0-394-71011-2. Dewey:917.3/92. LCCN:74-003298.
Audience: **l,u,f.**

Boorstin, Daniel J. **E188**
The Americans: The Colonial Experience. Paper Text. Textbook Publishers. Temecula, CA. 2003. 434p. ISBN:0-7581-5040-7, ISBN13: 978-0-7581-5040-0. Dewey:973.2.
Audience: **l,u,f.**

Brick, Howard **E169.12.B6946 1998**
Age of Contradiction: American Thought and Culture in the 1960's. Trade Cloth. Thomson Gale. Farmington Hills, MI. 1998. 242p. Twayne's American Thought and Culture Ser. ISBN:0-8057-9080-2, ISBN13: 978-0-8057-9080-1. Dewey:973.92. LCCN:98-018965.
Audience: **u,f.** *Choice, 1999.*

Brogan, D. W. **E169.1.B797**
American Character. Trade Cloth. Peter Smith Publisher, Inc. Magnolia, MA. 1990. ISBN:0-8446-1746-6, ISBN13: 978-0-8446-1746-6. Dewey:917.3.
Audience: **u,f.** B

Brogan, Denis W. **E169.12B699 1980**
America in the Modern World. Trade Cloth. Greenwood Publishing Group, Inc. Portsmouth, NH. 1980. 117p. ISBN:0-313-22254-1, ISBN13: 978-0-313-22254-2. Dewey:973.92. LCCN:79-025851.
Audience: **u,f.**

Browne, Ray B. & Browne, Pat (Editors) **E169.1.D399 2001**
The Guide to United States Popular Culture. Trade Cloth. University of Wisconsin Press. Chicago, IL. 2001. x, 1010p. ISBN:0-87972-821-3, ISBN13: 978-0-87972-821-2. Dewey:306/.0973/03. LCCN:00-057211.
Audience: **g,l,u,f.** *Choice, 2001.*

Campbell-Kelly, Martin & Aspray, William **QA76.17.C36 2004**
Computer: A History of the Information Machine. Ed. 2. Trade Paper. Westview Press. Boulder, CO. 2004. 360p. The Sloan Technology Ser. ISBN:0-8133-4264-3, ISBN13: 978-0-8133-4264-1. Dewey:004/.09. LCCN:2004-006325.
Audience: **g,l,u,f.** *Choice, 2005.*

Carlson, Allan **E169.12**
The American Way: Family and Community in the Shaping of the American Identity. Trade Cloth. ISI Books. Wilmington, DE. 2003. 250p. ISBN:1-932236-11-2, ISBN13: 978-1-932236-11-8. Dewey:973.91. LCCN:2003-109725.
Audience: **f.** *Choice, 2004.*

Carter, Paul A. **E169.1.C286 1989**
Revolt Against Destiny: An Intellectual History of the United States. Trade Cloth. Columbia University Press. New York, NY. 1989. 331p. ISBN:0-231-06616-3, ISBN13: 978-0-231-06616-7. Dewey:973. LCCN:89-007054.
Audience: **u,f.**

Carter, Paul A. **E784.C3 1987**
The Twenties in America. Ed. 2. Abraham S. Eisenstadt & John H. Franklin (Editors). Trade Paper. Harlan Davidson Inc. Wheeling, IL. 2003. 144p. The American History Ser. ISBN:0-88295-717-1, ISBN13: 978-0-88295-717-3. Dewey:973.91. LCCN:74-026538.
Audience: **l,u,f.**

Clark, Michael D. **E169.1.C544 2005**
The American Discovery of Tradition, 1865-1942. Trade Cloth. Louisiana State University Press. Baton Rouge, LA. 2005. 272p.

ISBN:0-8071-3041-9, ISBN13: 978-0-8071-3041-4. Dewey:973.8. LCCN:2004-017537.
Audience: **u,f.** *Choice, 2006.*

Cooney, Terry A. **E169.1.C765 1995**
Balancing Acts: American Thought and Culture in the 1930s. Trade Cloth. Thomson Gale. Farmington Hills, MI. 1995. 288p. Twayne's American Thought and Culture Ser. ISBN:0-8057-9060-8, ISBN13: 978-0-8057-9060-3. Dewey:973.917. LCCN:94-023610.
Audience: **f.**

Cowan, Ruth Schwartz **T21**
A Social History of American Technology. Library Binding. Sagebrush Education Resources. Caledonia, MN. 1996. ISBN:0-613-92161-5, ISBN13: 978-0-613-92161-9. Dewey:609.7/3.
Audience: **g,l,u,f.** *Choice, 1998.*

Crunden, Robert Morse **E169.1.C836**
From Self to Society, 1919-1941. Trade Cloth. Prentice-Hall. Upper Saddle, NJ. 1972. xii, 212p. ISBN:0-13-331421-9, ISBN13: 978-0-13-331421-2. Dewey:301.29/73. LCCN:78-168740.
Audience: **f.**

Crunden, Robert M. (Editor, Introduction by) **E169.1.S964 1999**
The Superfluous Men: Conservative Critics of Modern Culture, 1900-1945. Trade Cloth. ISI Books. Wilmington, DE. 1999. 453p. ISBN:1-882926-30-7, ISBN13: 978-1-882926-30-5. Dewey:973. LCCN:99-064350.
Audience: **f.**

Curti, Merle E. **E169.1**
Growth of American Thought. Ed. 3. Trade Paper. Transaction Publishers. Somerset, NJ. 1981. 949p. ISBN:0-87855-879-9, ISBN13: 978-0-87855-879-7. Dewey:973. LCCN:81-003433.
Audience: **f.**

Curti, Merle E. **E169.1.C87**
Human Nature in American Thought: A History. Trade Paper. Books on Demand. Ann Arbor, MI. 472p. ISBN:0-608-20421-8, ISBN13: 978-0-608-20421-5. Dewey:128/.4. LCCN:79-003965.
Audience: **f.**

Curti, Merle Eugene **E169.1.C86**
American Paradox: The Conflict of Thought and Action. Paper Text. Textbook Publishers. Temecula, CA. 2003. ix, 116p. ISBN:0-7581-4272-2, ISBN13: 978-0-7581-4272-6. Dewey:917.3.
Audience: **f.**

Diggins, John P. **E169.1.D495 1994**
The Promise of Pragmatism: Modernism and the Crisis of Knowledge and Authority. Trade Cloth. University of Chicago Press. Chicago, IL. 1994. 528p. ISBN:0-226-14878-5, ISBN13: 978-0-226-14878-6. Dewey:144.30973. LCCN:93-011686.
Audience: **u,f.** *Choice, 1994.*

Edsforth, Ronald W. & Bennett, Larry (Editors) **E169.1.P5902 1991**
Popular Culture and Political Change in Modern America. Cloth Text. State University of New York Press. Albany, NY. 1991. 232p. SUNY Series in Popular Culture and Political Change ISBN:0-7914-0765-9, ISBN13: 978-0-7914-0765-3. Dewey:306/.0973. LCCN:90-047621.
Audience: **u,f.** *Choice, 1992.*

Fink, Leon **E169.1.F525 1997**
Progressive Intellectuals and the Dilemmas of Democratic Commitment. University of Virginia Library Staff (Photographer). Trade Cloth. Harvard University Press. Cambridge, MA. 1998. 384p. ISBN:0-674-66160-5, ISBN13: 978-0-674-66160-8. Dewey:973/.086/31. LCCN:97-025506.
Audience: **u,f.** *Choice, 1998.*

Frank, Waldo D. **E169.1.F824 1982**
The Re-Discovery of America: An Introduction to the Philosophy of American Life. Library Binding. Greenwood Publishing Group, Inc. Portsmouth, NH. 1982. x, 353p. ISBN:0-313-23451-5, ISBN13: 978-0-313-23451-4. Dewey:973.9. LCCN:81-020286.
Audience: **f.**

Freccero, Carla **E169.12.F717 1999**
Popular Culture: An Introduction. Trade Cloth. New York University Press. New York, NY. 1999. 200p. ISBN:0-8147-2669-0, ISBN13: 978-0-8147-2669-3. Dewey:306/.0973. LCCN:99-006112.
Audience: **l,u,f.**

Gabriel, Ralph Henry **E169.1.G226**
The Course of American Democratic Thought. Paper Text. Textbook Publishers. Temecula, CA. 2003. xiv, 508p. ISBN:0-7581-4701-5, ISBN13: 978-0-7581-4701-1. Dewey:917.3.
Audience: **u,f.**

Gellert, Michael **E169.1.G4514 2001**
The Fate of America: An Inquiry into National Character. Trade Cloth. Potomac Books, Inc. Dulles, VA. 2001. 400p. ISBN:1-57488-356-9, ISBN13: 978-1-57488-356-5. Dewey:973. LCCN:2001-025545.
Audience: **f.** *Choice, 2002.*

Goldfarb, Jeffrey C. **E169.12.G63 1991**
The Cynical Society: The Culture of Politics and the Politics of Culture in American Life. Trade Cloth. University of Chicago Press. Chicago, IL. 1991. 207p. ISBN:0-226-30106-0, ISBN13: 978-0-226-30106-8. Dewey:973.92. LCCN:90-011187.
Audience: **u,f.** *Choice, 1991.*

Handlin, Oscar **E0169.1.H26**
The American People in the Twentieth Century. Ed. 2. Trade Paper. Books on Demand. Ann Arbor, MI. 1966. 256p. The Library of Congress Series in American Civilization ISBN:0-7837-4106-5, ISBN13: 978-0-7837-4106-2. Dewey:917.3. LCCN:66-022368.
Audience: **l,u,f.**

Handlin, Oscar **JV6450**
The Uprooted: The Epic Story of the Great Migrations That Made the American People. Ed. 2. Book, Other. University of Pennsylvania Press. Philadelphia, PA. 2002. 344p. ISBN:0-8122-1788-8, ISBN13: 978-0-8122-1788-9. Dewey:304.8/73. LCCN:2001-048096.
Audience: **u,f.**

Hearn, Charles R. **E169**
The American Dream in the Great Depression. Trade Cloth. Greenwood Publishing Group, Inc. Portsmouth, NH. 1977. 222p. Contributions in American Studies, No. 28 ISBN:0-8371-9478-4, ISBN13: 978-0-8371-9478-3. Dewey:973.917. LCCN:76-056623.
Audience: **f.**

Hofstadter, Richard **E743**
Age of Reform: From Bryan to F. D. R. Mass Market. Knopf Publishing Group. New York, NY. 1960. 352p. Vintage Ser. ISBN:0-394-70095-3, ISBN13: 978-0-394-70095-3. Dewey:973.91.
Audience: **l,u,f.** BCL3

Hofstadter, Richard **E169.1.H74**
Anti-Intellectualism in American Life. Trade Paper. Knopf Publishing Group. New York, NY. 1966. 464p. Vintage Ser. ISBN:0-394-70317-0, ISBN13: 978-0-394-70317-6. Dewey:917.3.
Audience: **u,f.** BCL3

Hofstadter, Richard **HM22.U5H6 1959**
Social Darwinism in American Thought. Trade Cloth. George Braziller Inc. New York, NY. 1959. ISBN:0-8076-0079-2, ISBN13: 978-0-8076-0079-5. Dewey:301/.0973. LCCN:59-009543.
Audience: **f.** BCL3

Hollinger, David A. & Capper, Charles **E169.1.A47218 2005**
The American Intellectual Tradition: 1630-1865. Ed. 5. Cloth Text. Oxford University Press, Inc. New York, NY. 2005. 576p. ISBN:0-19-518337-1, ISBN13: 978-0-19-518337-5. Dewey:973. LCCN:2005-047302.
Audience: **l,u,f.**

Hollinger, David A. & Capper, Charles **E169.1.A47218 2005**
The American Intellectual Tradition: 1865 to the Present. Ed. 5. Trade Cloth. Oxford University Press, Inc. New York, NY. 2005. 592p. ISBN:0-19-518339-8, ISBN13: 978-0-19-518339-9. Dewey:973. LCCN:2005-047302.
Audience: **l,u,f.**

Hounshell, David A. **TS149.H68**
From the American System to Mass Production, 1800-1932: The Development of Manufacturing Technology in the United States. Trade Paper. Johns Hopkins University Press. Baltimore, MD. 1973. 440p. Studies in Industry and Society, No. 4 ISBN:0-8018-3158-X, ISBN13: 978-0-8018-3158-4. Dewey:338.6/5/0973. LCCN:83-016269.
Audience: **u,f.** BCL3

Inge, M. Thomas & Hall, Dennis (Editors) **E169.1.H2643 2002**
Handbook of American Popular Culture, Vol. 3. Ed. 3. Library Binding. Greenwood Publishing Group, Inc. Portsmouth, NH. 2002. liii, 2155p. ISBN:0-313-32369-0, ISBN13: 978-0-313-32369-0. Dewey:306.4/0973. LCCN:2002-071291.
Audience: **l,u,f.** *Choice, 1990.*

Kammen, Michael G. **E169.1.K295 2004**
A Time to Every Purpose: The Four Seasons in American Culture. Trade Cloth. University of North Carolina Press. Chapel Hill, NC. 2004. 416p. ISBN:0-8078-2836-X, ISBN13: 978-0-8078-2836-6. Dewey:700/.4273. LCCN:2003-013734.
Audience: **f.** *Choice, 2004.*

Ketcham, Ralph Louis **E169.1.K417**
From Colony to Country: The Revolution in American Thought, 1750-1820. Trade Cloth. Macmillan Publishing Company, Inc. Old Tappan, NJ. 1974. xiv, 318p. ISBN:0-02-562930-1, ISBN13: 978-0-02-562930-1. Dewey:917.3/03/3. LCCN:73-018763.
Audience: **f.** BCL3

Kirk, Russell **E169**
The American Cause. Trade Cloth. Greenwood Publishing Group, Inc. Portsmouth, NH. 1975. 172p. ISBN:0-8371-7988-2, ISBN13: 978-0-8371-7988-9. Dewey:973. LCCN:75-001122.
Audience: **u,f.** BCL3

Kraus, Michael **E169.1.K688**
Intercolonial Aspects of American Culture on the Eve of the Revolution: With Special Reference to the Northern Towns. Paper Text. Classic Textbooks. Murrieta, CA. 1928. 253p. ISBN:1-4047-6009-1, ISBN13: 978-1-4047-6009-7. Dewey:917.3.
Audience: **f.** BCL3

Kupiec, Mary (Editor), et al. **E169.1.E624 2001**
Encyclopedia of American Cultural and Intellectual History. Peter W. Williams & Mary K. Cayton (Editors). Trade Cloth. Thomson Gale. Farmington Hills, MI. 2001. 2436p. ISBN:0-684-80561-8, ISBN13: 978-0-684-80561-0. Dewey:973/.03. LCCN:2001-020005.
Audience: **g,l,u,f.** *Choice, 2001.*

Laski, Harold J. **E169.1.L38 1977**
American Democracy: A Commentary and an Interpretation. Trade Cloth. Scholar's Bookshelf. Cranbury, NJ. 1977. x, 785p. ISBN:0-678-03165-7, ISBN13: 978-0-678-03165-0. Dewey:917.3/03/91. LCCN:74-122066.
Audience: **f.**

Lears, T. J. Jackson **E169.1.L48 1994**
No Place of Grace: Antimodernism and the Transformation of American Culture, 1880-1920. Trade Paper. University of Chicago Press. Chicago, IL. 1994. 400p. ISBN:0-226-46970-0, ISBN13: 978-0-226-46970-6. Dewey:973.8. LCCN:93-039767.
Audience: **f.**

Leighton, Isabel **E169.1.L526**
Aspirin Age 1919-1941. Library Binding. Amereon, Ltd. Mattituck, NY. ISBN:0-8488-1661-7, ISBN13: 978-0-8488-1661-2. Dewey:917.3.
Audience: **u,f.** BCL3

Lerner, Max **E169.1.L532**
America As a Civilization: Life and Thought in the United States Today. Paper Text. Textbook Publishers. Temecula, CA. 2003. xiii, 1036p. ISBN:0-7581-3796-6, ISBN13: 978-0-7581-3796-8. Dewey:917.3.
Audience: **f.** BCL3

Lieven, Anatol **E169.1.L53949 2004**
America Right or Wrong: An Anatomy of American Nationalism. Trade Cloth. Oxford University Press, Inc. New York, NY. 2004. 288p. ISBN:0-19-516840-2, ISBN13: 978-0-19-516840-2. Dewey:320.54/0973. LCCN:2004-012968.
Audience: **u,f.**

Lipset, Seymour Martin **E169.1.L545 1989**
Continental Divide: The Values and Institutions of the United States and Canada. Trade Cloth. Bow Historical Books. New Providence, NJ. 1989. xviii, 326p. ISBN:0-88806-240-0, ISBN13: 978-0-88806-240-6. Dewey:303.48/273071. LCCN:89-048660.
Audience: **f.**

Lipset, Seymour Martin **E169.1.L546 2003**
The First New Nation: The United States in Historical and Comparative Perspective. Trade Paper. Transaction Publishers.

Somerset, NJ. 2003. 366p. ISBN:0-7658-0522-7, ISBN13: 978-0-7658-0522-5. Dewey:973. LCCN:2003-049219.
Audience: **f.** B

Lukacs, John **E169.1**
A New Republic: A History of the United States in the Twentieth Century. Trade Paper. Yale University Press. Cumberland, RI. 2004. 480p. ISBN:0-300-10429-4, ISBN13: 978-0-300-10429-5. Dewey:973.91. LCCN:2004-109677.
Audience: **l,u,f.**

Lynes, Russell **N6505.L96 1983**
The Tastemakers. Trade Cloth. Greenwood Publishing Group, Inc. Portsmouth, NH. 1983. 362p. ISBN:0-313-23843-X, ISBN13: 978-0-313-23843-7. Dewey:701/.03/0973. LCCN:82-025116.
Audience: **f.** B

Marx, Leo **E169.1.M35 2000**
The Machine in the Garden: Technology and the Pastoral Ideal in America. Ed. 2. Trade Paper. Oxford University Press, Inc. New York, NY. 2000. 414p. ISBN:0-19-513351-X, ISBN13: 978-0-19-513351-6. Dewey:973. LCCN:99-034697.
Audience: **f.** B

May, Henry F. **E169.1.M496 1992**
The End of American Innocence: A Study of the First Years of Our Own Time, 1912-1917. Trade Paper. Columbia University Press. New York, NY. 1994. 470p. ISBN:0-231-09653-4, ISBN13: 978-0-231-09653-9. Dewey:973. LCCN:93-033225.
Audience: **u,f.**

May, Henry F. **E169.1.M496 1992**
The End of American Innocence: A Study of the First Years of Our Own Time, 1912-1917. Trade Cloth. Columbia University Press. New York, NY. 1994. 439p. ISBN:0-231-09652-6, ISBN13: 978-0-231-09652-2. Dewey:973. LCCN:93-033225.
Audience: **f.**

Mead, Margaret **E169.1.M5 1999**
And Keep Your Powder Dry: An Anthropologist Looks at America. Herve Varenne (Introduction by). Trade Cloth. Berghahn Books, Inc. New York, NY. 2000. 256p. Margaret Mead Ser., Vol. 2:The Study of Contemporary Western Cultures ISBN:1-57181-218-0, ISBN13: 978-1-57181-218-6. Dewey:305.8/00973. LCCN:99-029857.
Audience: **u,f.** B

Miller, Perry G. **E169.1.M6273**
Life of the Mind in America: From the Revolution to the Civil War. Trade Paper. Harcourt Trade Publishers. New York, NY. 1970. 300p. ISBN:0-15-651990-9, ISBN13: 978-0-15-651990-8. Dewey:917.303. LCCN:65-019065.
Audience: **u,f.** B

Nagel, Paul C. **E166**
This Sacred Trust: American Nationality, 1778-1898. Trade Cloth. Oxford University Press, Inc. New York, NY. 1971. 392p. ISBN:0-19-501429-4, ISBN13: 978-0-19-501429-7. Dewey:973.6.
Audience: **u,f.** B

Nash, Roderick **E169.1**
Wilderness and the American Mind. Ed. 4. Trade Paper. Yale University Press. Cumberland, RI. 2001. 432p. ISBN:0-300-09122-2, ISBN13: 978-0-300-09122-9. Dewey:333.78/2/0973.
Audience: **u,f.** B

Niebuhr, Reinhold **E169.1.N67**
Pious and Secular America. Paper Text. Textbook Publishers. Temecula, CA. 2003. viii, 150p. ISBN:0-7581-4054-1, ISBN13: 978-0-7581-4054-8. Dewey:917.3.
Audience: **f.** B

Noble, David W. **E0169.1.N7**
The Paradox of Progressive Thought. Trade Paper. Books on Demand. Ann Arbor, MI. 282p. ISBN:0-8357-8979-9, ISBN13: 978-0-8357-8979-0. Dewey:917.3. LCCN:58-008765.
Audience: **u,f.** B

Pells, Richard H. **E169.1.P42 1998**
Radical Visions and American Dreams: Culture and Social Thought in the Depression Years. Trade Paper. University of Illinois Press. Champaign, IL. 1998. 448p. ISBN:0-252-06743-6, ISBN13: 978-0-252-06743-3. Dewey:001.2/0973. LCCN:98-021404.
Audience: **f.**

Perry, Ralph B. **E169.1.P47**
Puritanism and Democracy. Trade Cloth. Random House, Inc. New York, NY. 1980. ISBN:0-8149-0180-8, ISBN13: 978-0-8149-0180-9. Dewey:917.3.
Audience: **f.**

Phalen, Rick, et al. **E169.12.H677 2003**
How We Have Changed: America since 1950. G. Gordon Liddy, Dick Clark & David McCullough (Authors). Trade Cloth. Pelican Publishing Company, Inc. Gretna, LA. 2003. 208p. ISBN:1-58980-110-5, ISBN13: 978-1-58980-110-3. Dewey:973.92. LCCN:2002-015406.
Audience: **l,u,f.**

Phillips, Cabell B. H. **E169.1.P543 2000**
From the Crash to the Blitz, 1929-1939. Herbert Mitgang (Introduction by). Trade Cloth. Fordham University Press. Bronx, NY. 2000. 596p. ISBN:0-8232-1999-2, ISBN13: 978-0-8232-1999-5. Dewey:973.916. LCCN:99-016824.
Audience: **u,f.**

Potter, David M. **E169.1**
People of Plenty: Economic Abundance and the American Character. Trade Paper. University of Chicago Press. Chicago, IL. 1958. 248p. Walgreen Foundation Lectures ISBN:0-226-67633-1, ISBN13: 978-0-226-67633-3. Dewey:917.3. LCCN:54-012797.
Audience: **l,u,f.**

Richard, Carl J. **E169.1.R563 2004**
The Battle for the American Mind: A Brief History of a Nation's Thought. Trade Cloth. Rowman & Littlefield Publishers, Inc. Lanham, MD. 2004. 376p. ISBN:0-7425-3435-9, ISBN13: 978-0-7425-3435-3. Dewey:973. LCCN:2004-004029.
Audience: **u,f.**

Savelle, Max **E169.1.S27**
Seeds of Liberty: The Genesis of the American Mind. Paper Text. Classic Textbooks. Murrieta, CA. 1948. 504p. ISBN:1-4047-4844-X, ISBN13: 978-1-4047-4844-6. Dewey:917.3032.
Audience: **u,f.** B

Schmitt, Peter J. **E169.1.S343 1990**
Back to Nature: The Arcadian Myth in Urban America. Trade Paper. Johns Hopkins University Press. Baltimore, MD. 1990. 264p. ISBN:0-8018-4013-9, ISBN13: 978-0-8018-4013-5. Dewey:973. LCCN:89-043533.
Audience: **f.** B

Schultz, Nancy L. **E169.1.F287 1998**
Fear Itself: Enemies Real and Imagined in American Culture. Cloth Text. Purdue University Press. West Lafayette, IN. 1999. 461p. ISBN:1-55753-114-5, ISBN13: 978-1-55753-114-8. Dewey:973. LCCN:98-013790.
Audience: **u,f.**

Shi, David E. **E169.1.S556 2001**
The Simple Life: Plain Living and High Thinking in American Culture. Trade Paper. University of Georgia Press. Athens, GA. 2001. 342p. ISBN:0-8203-2340-3, ISBN13: 978-0-8203-2340-4. Dewey:973. LCCN:2001-043070.
Audience: **l,u,f.** B

Slater, David & Taylor, Peter (Editors) **E169.1.A471966 1999**
The American Century: Consensus and Coercion in the Projection of American Power. Trade Cloth. Blackwell Publishing, Inc. Malden, MA. 1999. 376p. ISBN:0-631-21221-3, ISBN13: 978-0-631-21221-8. Dewey:973.92. LCCN:99-014781.
Audience: **u,f.**

Stuckey, Mary E. **E169.1.S934 2004**
Defining Americans: The Presidency and National Identity. Trade Cloth. University Press of Kansas. Lawrence, KS. 2004. 336p. ISBN:0-7006-1349-8, ISBN13: 978-0-7006-1349-6. Dewey:973. LCCN:2004-013592.
Audience: **f.** *Choice, 2005.*

Susman, Warren **E169.1.S9733 2003**
Culture As History: The Transformation of American Society in the Twentieth Century. Ed. 2. Trade Paper. Smithsonian Institution Press. Washington, DC. 2003. 352p. ISBN:1-58834-051-1, ISBN13: 978-1-58834-051-1. Dewey:973.91. LCCN:2002-070501.
Audience: **u,f.**

Thompkins, Vincent (Editor) **E169.1.A471979 1997**
Development of the Industrial United States (1878-1899), Vol. 8. Trade Cloth. Thomson Gale. Farmington Hills, MI. 1997. 450p. American Eras Ser. ISBN:0-7876-1485-8, ISBN13: 978-0-7876-1485-0. Dewey:973.8. LCCN:97-003939.
Audience: **f.**

Toynbee, Arnold J. **E169.1.T69**
America and the World Revolution, and Other Lectures. Paper Text. Textbook Publishers. Temecula, CA. 2003. 231p. ISBN:0-7581-6916-7, ISBN13: 978-0-7581-6916-7. Dewey:973.
Audience: **f.**

Weyl, Nathaniel **E169.1.W395**
The Creative Elite in America. Trade Cloth. Public Affairs Press. Washington, DC. 1966. ISBN:0-8183-0160-0, ISBN13: 978-0-8183-0160-5. Dewey:320.1.
Audience: **f.** B

Wylie, Philip **E169.12.W89**
Generation of Vipers. Paper Text. Textbook Publishers. Temecula, CA. 2003. 331p. ISBN:0-7581-4829-1, ISBN13: 978-0-7581-4829-2. Dewey:973.92.
Audience: **f.** B

United States > Civilization. Intellectual Life > Civilization, 1945-

Bell, Daniel **E169.12.B37 1996**
The Cultural Contradictions of Capitalism: 20th Anniversary Edition. Ed. 20. Trade Paper. Basic Books. New York, NY. 1996. 400p. ISBN:0-465-01499-2, ISBN13: 978-0-465-01499-6. Dewey:973.92. LCCN:96-041616.
Audience: **u,f.**

Bellah, Robert N., et al. **E169.12.H29 1985**
Habits of the Heart: Individualism and Commitment in American Life. Richard Madsen, William M. Sullivan, Ann Swidler & Steven M. Tipton (Authors). Trade Cloth. University of California Press. Berkeley, CA. 1985. 376p. ISBN:0-520-05388-5, ISBN13: 978-0-520-05388-5. Dewey:973.92. LCCN:84-016370.
Audience: **g,l,u,f.**

Berger, Arthur A. **E169.12.P65 1998**
The Postmodern Presence: Readings on Postmodernism in American Culture and Society. Trade Cloth. AltaMira Press. Walnut Creek, CA. 1997. 320p. ISBN:0-7619-8979-X, ISBN13: 978-0-7619-8979-0. Dewey:658/.049. LCCN:97-045393.
Audience: **u,f.**

Brick, Howard **E169.12.B6946 1998**
Age of Contradiction: American Thought and Culture in the 1960's. Trade Cloth. Thomson Gale. Farmington Hills, MI. 1998. 242p. Twayne's American Thought and Culture Ser. ISBN:0-8057-9080-2, ISBN13: 978-0-8057-9080-1. Dewey:973.92. LCCN:98-018965.
Audience: **u,f.** *Choice, 1999.*

Brogan, Denis W. **E169.12B699 1980**
America in the Modern World. Trade Cloth. Greenwood Publishing Group, Inc. Portsmouth, NH. 1980. 117p. ISBN:0-313-22254-1, ISBN13: 978-0-313-22254-2. Dewey:973.92. LCCN:79-025851.
Audience: **u,f.**

Carr, David **E169.12.C279 2003**
The Promise of Cultural Institutions. G. Rollie Adams (Contribution by). Trade Cloth. AltaMira Press. Walnut Creek, CA. 2003. 240p. American Association for State and Local History Book Ser. ISBN:0-7591-0291-0, ISBN13: 978-0-7591-0291-0. Dewey:306/.0973/074. LCCN:2002-155808.
Audience: **u,f.**

Ceaser, James W. **E169.12.C38 1997**
Reconstructing America: The Symbol of America in Modern Thought. Cloth over Boards. Yale University Press. Cumberland, RI. 1997. 304p. The Renaissance in Europe Ser., :A Cultural Enquiry ISBN:0-300-07053-5, ISBN13: 978-0-300-07053-8. Dewey:973. LCCN:96-052890.
Audience: **u,f.** *Choice, 1998.*

Combs, James **E169.12.C576 1984**
Polpop: Politics and Popular Culture in America. Trade Cloth. University of Wisconsin Press. Chicago, IL. 1984. 172p. ISBN:0-87972-276-2, ISBN13: 978-0-87972-276-0. Dewey:306/.2/0973. LCCN:83-073574.
Audience: **f.** B

Combs, James **E169.12.C576 1991**
Polpop 2: Politics and Popular Culture in America Today. Trade Cloth. University of Wisconsin Press. Chicago, IL. 1991. 192p.

ISBN:0-87972-541-9, ISBN13: 978-0-87972-541-9. Dewey:306/.2/0973. LCCN:83-073574.
Audience: **u,f.**

Fishwick, Marshall William **E169.12.F64**
Parameters of Popular Culture. Trade Cloth. University of Wisconsin Press. Chicago, IL. 1974. 175p. ISBN:0-87972-064-6, ISBN13: 978-0-87972-064-3. Dewey:917.3/03/9. LCCN:73-089531.
Audience: **f.** *B*

Gans, Herbert J. **E169.12.G36 1999**
Popular Culture and High Culture: An Analysis and Evaluation of Taste. Ed. 2. Trade Paper. Basic Books. New York, NY. 1999. 266p. ISBN:0-465-02609-5, ISBN13: 978-0-465-02609-8. Dewey:306/.01. LCCN:99-040910.
Audience: **u,f.** *B*

Gardner, James **E169.12.G364 1997**
Age of Extremism: The End of Compromise in American Politics, Culture, and Race Relations. Trade Cloth. Carol Publishing Group. Secaucus, NJ. 1997. 240p. ISBN:1-55972-388-2, ISBN13: 978-1-55972-388-6. Dewey:973.929. LCCN:96-051726.
Audience: **u,f.**

Gilman, Nils **E169.12.G55 2003**
Mandarins of the Future: Modernization Theory in Cold War America. Trade Cloth. Johns Hopkins University Press. Baltimore, MD. 2004. 336p. New Studies in American Intellectual and Cultural History ISBN:0-8018-7399-1, ISBN13: 978-0-8018-7399-7. Dewey:303.44/01. LCCN:2002-156769.
Audience: **f.** *Choice, 2004.*

Goldfarb, Jeffrey C. **E169.12.G63 1991**
The Cynical Society: The Culture of Politics and the Politics of Culture in American Life. Trade Cloth. University of Chicago Press. Chicago, IL. 1991. 207p. ISBN:0-226-30106-0, ISBN13: 978-0-226-30106-8. Dewey:973.92. LCCN:90-011187.
Audience: **u,f.** *Choice, 1991.*

Kimball, Roger **E169.12.K467 2000**
The Long March: How the Cultural Revolution of the 1960's Changed America. Trade Cloth. Encounter Books. New York, NY. 2000. 326p. ISBN:1-893554-09-0, ISBN13: 978-1-893554-09-2. Dewey:973.92. LCCN:00-022211.
Audience: **u,f.** *Choice, 2000.*

Knight, Peter (Editor) **E169.12.P6216 2001**
Conspiracy Nation: The Politics of Paranoia in Postwar America. Trade Cloth. New York University Press. New York, NY. 2002. 286p. ISBN:0-8147-4735-3, ISBN13: 978-0-8147-4735-3. Dewey:973.9. LCCN:2001-006231.
Audience: **f.**

May, Lary (Editor) **E169.12.R43 1989**
Recasting America: Culture and Politics in the Age of Cold War. Trade Cloth. University of Chicago Press. Chicago, IL. 1989. 320p. ISBN:0-226-51175-8, ISBN13: 978-0-226-51175-7. Dewey:973.92. LCCN:88-021618.
Audience: **u,f.** *Choice, 1989.*

Nadel, Alan **E169.12.N324 1995**
Containment Culture: American Narratives, Postmodernism, and the Atomic Age. Cloth Text. Duke University Press. Durham, NC. 1995. 336p. New Americanists Ser. ISBN:0-8223-1701-X, ISBN13: 978-0-8223-1701-2. Dewey:973.9. LCCN:95-016631.
Audience: **u,f.** *Choice, 1996.*

Pells, Richard H. **E169.12.P45 1989**
The Liberal Mind in a Conservative Age: American Intellectuals in the 1940s and 1950s. Ed. 2. Trade Paper. Wesleyan University Press. Middletown, CT. 1989. 488p. ISBN:0-8195-6225-4, ISBN13: 978-0-8195-6225-8. Dewey:973.91. LCCN:89-014676.
Audience: **u,f.**

Rieder, Jonathan & Steinlight, Stephen (Editors) **E169.12**
The Fractious Nation?: Unity and Division in Contemporary American Life. Trade Cloth. University of California Press. Berkeley, CA. 2003. 262p. ISBN:0-520-22043-9, ISBN13: 978-0-520-22043-0. Dewey:973.931. LCCN:2003-001858.
Audience: **u,f.** *Choice, 2004.*

Slater, Philip Elliot **E169.12.S53 1970**
The Pursuit of Loneliness; American Culture at the Breaking Point. Trade Cloth. Beacon Press. Boston, MA. 1970. xiii, 154p. ISBN:0-8070-4180-7, ISBN13: 978-0-8070-4180-2. Dewey:917.3/03/92. LCCN:79-101327.
Audience: **f.** *B*

Stearns, Peter N. **E169.12.S82 1999**
Battleground of Desire: The Struggle for Self Control in Modern America. Trade Cloth. New York University Press. New York, NY. 1999. 400p. ISBN:0-8147-8128-4, ISBN13: 978-0-8147-8128-9. Dewey:306/.0973. LCCN:99-006177.
Audience: **u,f.** *Choice, 1999.*

Troy, Gil **E169.12.T765 2005**
Morning in America: How Ronald Reagan Invented the 1980's. Trade Cloth. Princeton University Press. Princeton, NJ. 2005. 400p. Politics and Society in Twentieth Century America Ser. ISBN:0-691-09645-7, ISBN13: 978-0-691-09645-2. Dewey:973.927092.
Audience: **u,f.**

United States > History > Sources. Documents

Allen, Frederick Lewis **E784.A6 2000**
Only Yesterday: An Informal History of the 1920's. Trade Paper. HarperCollins Publishers. New York, NY. 2000. 352p. Perennial Classics Ser. ISBN:0-06-095665-8, ISBN13: 978-0-06-095665-3. Dewey:973.91/3. LCCN:00-028345.
Audience: **u,f.** *B*

Brinkley, Douglas & Ambrose, Stephen E. **E173.W78 1999**
Witness to America: An Illustrated Documentary History of the United States from the Revolution to Today. Ed. 2. Trade Cloth. HarperCollins Publishers. New York, NY. 1999. 624p. ISBN:0-06-271611-5, ISBN13: 978-0-06-271611-8. Dewey:973. LCCN:99-023797.
Audience: **g,l,u,f.**

Colbert, David (Editor) **E173.E9 1997**
Eyewitness to America: 500 Years of American History in the Words of Those Who Saw It Happen. Trade Cloth. Knopf Publishing Group. New York, NY. 1998. 720p. ISBN:0-679-76724-X, ISBN13: 978-0-679-76724-4. Dewey:973.
Audience: **g,l,u,f.**

Ellis, Lewis Ethan **E791.E5**
Frank B. Kellogg and American Foreign Relations 1925-1929. Paper Text. Textbook Publishers. Temecula, CA. 2003. 303p. ISBN:0-7581-4304-4, ISBN13: 978-0-7581-4304-4. Dewey:327.73.
Audience: **f.**

Goldberg, David J. **E784.G65 1999**
Discontented America: The United States in the 1920s. Stanley I. Kutler (Foreword by). Trade Cloth. Johns Hopkins University Press. Baltimore, MD. 1999. 224p. The American Moment Ser. ISBN:0-8018-6004-0, ISBN13: 978-0-8018-6004-1. Dewey:973.91. LCCN:98-036310.
Audience: **l,u,f.** *Choice, 1999.*

Hyser, Raymond M. & Arndt, J. Chris (Compiled by) **E173.V65 2001**
Voices of the American Past: Documents in United States History. Ed. 2. Paper Text. Thomson Wadsworth. Belmont, CA. 2000. 304p. ISBN:0-15-507508-X, ISBN13: 978-0-15-507508-5. Dewey:973. LCCN:00-105422.
Audience: **g,l,u,f.**

Hyser, Raymond M. & Arndt, J. Chris (Compiled by) **E173.V65 2001**
Voices of the American Past: Documents in United States History, Set. Ed. 2. Paper Text. Thomson Wadsworth. Belmont, CA. 2000. 352p. ISBN:0-15-507509-8, ISBN13: 978-0-15-507509-2. Dewey:973. LCCN:00-105422.
Audience: **g,l,u,f.**

Levy, Peter B. (Editor) **E173**
100 Key Documents in American Democracy. Paper Text. Greenwood Publishing Group, Inc. Portsmouth, NH. 1999. 528p. ISBN:0-275-96525-2, ISBN13: 978-0-275-96525-9. Dewey:973. LCCN:93-001137.
Audience: **g,l,u,f.**

Margulies, Phillip (Editor) **E784.R63 2004**
The Roaring Twenties. Trade Paper. Thomson Gale. Farmington Hills, MI. 2004. 267p. Turning Points in World History Ser. ISBN:0-7377-1810-2, ISBN13: 978-0-7377-1810-2. Dewey:973.91/5. LCCN:2003-049370.
Audience: **l,u,f.**

Miller, Nathan **E784.M555 2004**
New World Coming: The 1920s and the Making of Modern America. Trade Paper. Da Capo Press, Inc. Cambridge, MA. 2004. 448p. ISBN:0-306-81379-3, ISBN13: 978-0-306-81379-5. Dewey:973.91/5. LCCN:2004-056140.
Audience: **u,f.**

Miller, Nathan **E784.M555 2003**
New World Coming: The 1920's and the Making of Modern America. Trade Cloth. Simon & Schuster. New York, NY. 2003. 448p. ISBN:0-684-85295-0, ISBN13: 978-0-684-85295-9. Dewey:973.91. LCCN:2003-046001.
Audience: **u,f.**

Morris, Richard B. **E173.M92 1980**
Basic Documents in American History. Paper Text. Krieger Publishing Company. Melbourne, FL. 1980. 194p. Anvil Ser. ISBN:0-89874-202-1, ISBN13: 978-0-89874-202-2. Dewey:973. LCCN:80-012822.
Audience: **g,l,u,f.**

Schlesinger, Arthur M. Jr. **E784.S36 2003**
The Crisis of the Old Order, 1919-1933. Trade Paper. Houghton Mifflin Company Trade & Reference Division. Boston, MA. 2003. 576p. The Age of Roosevelt Ser., Vol. 1 ISBN:0-618-34085-8, ISBN13: 978-0-618-34085-9. Dewey:973.91. LCCN:2003-047884.
Audience: **u,f.**

Shi, David E. & Mayer, Holly A. **E173.S487 2003**
For the Record: A Documentary History of America, Vol. 2. Ed. 2. Trade Paper. W. W. Norton & Company, Inc. New York, NY. 2003. 456p. ISBN:0-393-92445-9, ISBN13: 978-0-393-92445-9. Dewey:973. LCCN:2003-048715.
Audience: **g,l,u,f.**

United States > History > Encyclopedias. Chronologies.

Boyer, Paul S. (Editor) **E174.O94 2001**
The Oxford Companion to United States History. Trade Cloth. Oxford University Press, Inc. New York, NY. 2001. 984p. ISBN:0-19-508209-5, ISBN13: 978-0-19-508209-8. Dewey:973/.03. LCCN:00-055801.
Audience: **g,l,u,f.** *Choice, 2002.*

Brinkley, Douglas **E174.5.N47 2003**
The New York Public Library American History Desk Reference. Ed. 2. New York Public Library Staff (Contribution by). Trade Paper. Hyperion Press. New York, NY. 2003. 576p. ISBN:0-7868-6847-3, ISBN13: 978-0-7868-6847-6. Dewey:973/.02/02. LCCN:2003-056655.
Audience: **g,l,u,f.**

Carruth, Gorton (Editor) **E174.5**
The Encyclopedia of American Facts and Dates. Ed. 7. Trade Cloth. Thomas Y. Crowell Company. New York, NY. 1979. ISBN:0-690-01669-7, ISBN13: 978-0-690-01669-7. Dewey:973/.0202. LCCN:78-004757.
Audience: **g,l,u,f.** B

Cohen, Saul B. **E35.C65 2000**
The Columbia Gazetteer of North America. Trade Cloth. Columbia University Press. New York, NY. 2000. 1250p. ISBN:0-231-11990-9, ISBN13: 978-0-231-11990-0. Dewey:917/.003. LCCN:00-027512.
Audience: **g,l,u,f.** *Choice, 2001.*

Gross, Ernie **E174.5.G753 2003**
The American Years: Chronologies of American History and Experience. Ed. 2. Trade Cloth. Simon & Schuster. New York, NY. 2003. xiii, 902p. Chronologies of American History and Experience Ser. ISBN:0-684-31256-5, ISBN13: 978-0-684-31256-9. Dewey:973/.02/02. LCCN:2002-010006.
Audience: **g,l,u,f.** *Choice, 2003.*

Gross, Ernie **E174.5.G76 2001**
This Day in American History. Ed. 2. Cloth Text. McFarland & Company, Incorporated Publishers. Jefferson, NC. 2001. 348p. ISBN:0-7864-0854-5, ISBN13: 978-0-7864-0854-2. Dewey:973/.02/02. LCCN:00-41120.
Audience: **g,l,u,f.** *Choice, 2001.*

Kutler, Stanley I. **E174.D52 2003**
New Dictionary of American History, Vol. 1. Ed. 3. Trade Cloth. Thomson Gale. Farmington Hills, MI. 2002. ISBN:0-684-80523-5, ISBN13: 978-0-684-80523-8. Dewey:973/.03. LCCN:2002-012433.
Audience: **g,l,u,f.**

Kutler, Stanley I. **E174.D52 2003**
New Dictionary of American History, Vol. 4. Ed. 3. Trade Cloth. Thomson Gale. Farmington Hills, MI. 2002. ISBN:0-684-80526-X, ISBN13: 978-0-684-80526-9. Dewey:973/.03. LCCN:2002-012433.
Audience: **g,l,u,f.**

Kutler, Stanley I. **E174.D52 2003**
New Dictionary of American History, Vol. 2. Ed. 3. Trade Cloth. Thomson Gale. Farmington Hills, MI. 2002. ISBN:0-684-80524-3, ISBN13: 978-0-684-80524-5. Dewey:973/.03. LCCN:2002-012433.
Audience: **g,l,u,f.**

Kutler, Stanley I. **E174.D52 2003**
New Dictionary of American History, Vol. 6. Ed. 3. Trade Cloth. Thomson Gale. Farmington Hills, MI. 2002. ISBN:0-684-80528-6, ISBN13: 978-0-684-80528-3. Dewey:973/.03. LCCN:2002-012433.
Audience: **g,l,u,f.**

Kutler, Stanley I. **E174.D52 2003**
New Dictionary of American History, Vol. 8. Ed. 3. Trade Cloth. Thomson Gale. Farmington Hills, MI. 2002. ISBN:0-684-80530-8, ISBN13: 978-0-684-80530-6. Dewey:973/.03. LCCN:2002-012433.
Audience: **g,l,u,f.**

Kutler, Stanley I. **E174.D52 2003**
New Dictionary of American History, Vol. 10. Ed. 3. Trade Cloth. Thomson Gale. Farmington Hills, MI. 2002. ISBN:0-684-80532-4, ISBN13: 978-0-684-80532-0. Dewey:973/.03. LCCN:2002-012433.
Audience: **g,l,u,f.**

Kutler, Stanley I. **E174.D52 2003**
New Dictionary of American History, Vol. 5. Ed. 3. Trade Cloth. Thomson Gale. Farmington Hills, MI. 2002. ISBN:0-684-80527-8, ISBN13: 978-0-684-80527-6. Dewey:973/.03. LCCN:2002-012433.
Audience: **g,l,u,f.**

Kutler, Stanley I. **E174.D52 2003**
New Dictionary of American History, Vol. 3. Ed. 3. Trade Cloth. Thomson Gale. Farmington Hills, MI. 2002. ISBN:0-684-80525-1, ISBN13: 978-0-684-80525-2. Dewey:973/.03. LCCN:2002-012433.
Audience: **g,l,u,f.**

Kutler, Stanley I. **E174.D52 2003**
New Dictionary of American History, Vol. 7. Ed. 3. Trade Cloth. Thomson Gale. Farmington Hills, MI. 2002. ISBN:0-684-80529-4, ISBN13: 978-0-684-80529-0. Dewey:973/.03. LCCN:2002-012433.
Audience: **g,l,u,f.**

Kutler, Stanley I. **E174.D52 2003**
New Dictionary of American History, Vol. 9. Ed. 3. Trade Cloth. Thomson Gale. Farmington Hills, MI. 2002. ISBN:0-684-80531-6, ISBN13: 978-0-684-80531-3. Dewey:973/.03. LCCN:2002-012433.
Audience: **g,l,u,f.**

Nash, Gary B. (Editor) **E174.E53 2002**
Encyclopedia of American History, Set. Trade Cloth. Facts On File, Inc. New York, NY. 2003. 4864p. Encyclopedia of American History Ser. ISBN:0-8160-4371-X, ISBN13: 978-0-8160-4371-2. Dewey:973/.03. LCCN:2001-051278.
Audience: **g,l,u,f.** *Choice, 2003.*

Yanak, Ted & Cornelison, Pamela **E174.C67 2004**
The Great American History Fact-Finder: The Who, What, Where, When, and Why of American History. Ed. 2. Trade Paper. Houghton Mifflin Company Trade & Reference Division. Boston, MA. 2004. 624p. ISBN:0-618-43941-2, ISBN13: 978-0-618-43941-6. Dewey:973/.03. LCCN:2004-047480.
Audience: **g,l,u,f.** *Choice, 2005.*

United States > History > Historiography. Philosophy.

Adams, Henry **E175.5.A2A3 1999**
The Education of Henry Adams: An Autobiography. Ira B. Nadel (Editor). Trade Paper. Oxford University Press, Inc. New York, NY. 1999. 560p. Oxford World's Classics Ser. ISBN:0-19-282369-8, ISBN13: 978-0-19-282369-4. Dewey:973/.07/202. LCCN:98-046268.
Audience: **u,f.**

Appleby, Joyce Oldham **E175.A668 2004**
A Restless Past: History and the American Public. Trade Cloth. Rowman & Littlefield Publishers, Inc. Lanham, MD. 2005. 200p. ISBN:0-7425-4252-1, ISBN13: 978-0-7425-4252-5. Dewey:973.4/072. LCCN:2004-017213.
Audience: **l,u,f.**

Bernstein, Barton J. **E175.B46 1970**
Towards a New Past: Dissenting Essays in American History. Trade Cloth. Random House. London, 1970. xvi, 364p. ISBN:0-7011-1482-7, ISBN13: 978-0-7011-1482-4. Dewey:973/.072. LCCN:77-852882.
Audience: **u,f.**

Blum, John Morton **E175.5**
Life with History. Trade Cloth. University Press of Kansas. Lawrence, KS. 2004. xiv, 284p. ISBN:0-7006-1338-2, ISBN13: 978-0-7006-1338-0. Dewey:973/.07/202. LCCN:2004-004567.
Audience: **f.** *Choice, 2005.*

Breisach, Ernst A. **E175.B74 1993**
American Progressive History: An Experiment in Modernization. Trade Cloth. University of Chicago Press. Chicago, IL. 1993. 268p. ISBN:0-226-07276-2, ISBN13: 978-0-226-07276-0. Dewey:973.072. LCCN:92-031012.
Audience: **f.** *Choice, 1993.*

Brown, David S. **E175.5.H55B76 2006**
Richard Hofstadter: An Intellectual Biography. Trade Cloth. University of Chicago Press. Chicago, IL. 2006. 320p. ISBN:0-226-07640-7, ISBN13: 978-0-226-07640-9. Dewey:973/.072/02 B. LCCN:2005-017592.
Audience: **f.**

Buhle, Paul & Rice-Maximin, Edward **E175.5.W55B84 1995**
William Appleman Williams: The Tragedy of Empire. UK-B

Format Paperback. Routledge. New York, NY. 1995. 306p. American Radicals Ser. ISBN:0-415-91131-1, ISBN13: 978-0-415-91131-3. Dewey:973.92/092 B. LCCN:95-019420.
Audience: **f.**

Davidson, James West **E175.D38 1982**
After the Fact: The Art of Historical Detection. Trade Cloth. Alfred A. Knopf Inc. New York, NY. 1982. xxxii, 388p. ISBN:0-394-52322-9, ISBN13: 978-0-394-52322-4. Dewey:973. LCCN:81-013737.
Audience: **l,u,f.** BCL3

Diggins, John P. **E175.5.S38L53 1997**
The Liberal Persuasion: Arthur Schlesinger, Jr., and the Challenge of the American Past. Cloth Text. Princeton University Press. Princeton, NJ. 1997. 310p. ISBN:0-691-04829-0, ISBN13: 978-0-691-04829-1. Dewey:973/.072. LCCN:97-018920.
Audience: **f.** *Choice, 1998.*

Fetner, Gerald L. **E175.5.N48F47 2004**
Immersed in Great Affairs: Allan Nevins and the Heroic Age of American History. Trade Cloth. State University of New York Press. Albany, NY. 2004. xii, 243p. ISBN:0-7914-5973-X, ISBN13: 978-0-7914-5973-7. Dewey:973/.07/202 B. LCCN:2003-045655.
Audience: **f.**

Foner, Eric **E175.9.F66 2002**
Who Owns History?: Rethinking the Past in a Changing World. Cloth over Boards. Farrar, Straus & Giroux. New York, NY. 2002. 256p. ISBN:0-8090-9704-4, ISBN13: 978-0-8090-9704-3. Dewey:973/.01. LCCN:2001-051463.
Audience: **l,u,f.** *Choice, 2002.*

Foner, Eric & American Historical Association Staff, Commission on the social studies in the schools (Editors) **E175.N53 1997**
The New American History. Trade Paper. Temple University Press. Philadelphia, PA. 1997. 400p. Critical Perspectives on the Past Ser. ISBN:1-56639-552-6, ISBN13: 978-1-56639-552-6. Dewey:973/.072. LCCN:96-052059.
Audience: **l,u,f.**

Franklin, John Hope **E175.5.F73A3 2005**
Mirror to America: The Autobiography of John Hope Franklin. Cloth over Boards. Farrar, Straus & Giroux. New York, NY. 2005. 416p. ISBN:0-374-29944-7, ISBN13: 978-0-374-29944-6. Dewey:973/.0496073/0092. LCCN:2005-007078.
Audience: **f.** *Choice, 2006.*

Glassberg, David **E175.9.G58 2001**
Sense of History: The Place of the Past in American Life. Trade Paper. University of Massachusetts Press. Amherst, MA. 2001. 288p. ISBN:1-55849-281-X, ISBN13: 978-1-55849-281-3. Dewey:973/.01. LCCN:00-052743.
Audience: **l,u,f.** *Choice, 2002.*

Higham, John (Editor) **E175**
The Reconstruction of American History. Trade Cloth. Greenwood Publishing Group, Inc. Portsmouth, NH. 1980. 244p. ISBN:0-313-22460-9, ISBN13: 978-0-313-22460-7. Dewey:973/.072. LCCN:80-014047.
Audience: **u,f.** BCL3

Higham, John **E175.H654**
Writing American History: Essays on Modern Scholarship. Trade Cloth. Indiana University Press. Bloomington, IN. 1970. x, 207p. ISBN:0-253-19700-7, ISBN13: 978-0-253-19700-9. Dewey:973/.072. LCCN:70-108209.
Audience: **u,f.** BCL3

Hirsch, Jerrold **E175.4.W9H57 2003**
Portrait of America: A Cultural History of the Federal Writers' Project. Trade Cloth. University of North Carolina Press. Chapel Hill, NC. 2003. 328p. ISBN:0-8078-2817-3, ISBN13: 978-0-8078-2817-5. Dewey:973.917. LCCN:2003-006858.
Audience: **f.** *Choice, 2004.*

Johnson, David E. **E175.5.F78J64 2002**
Douglas Southall Freeman. Trade Cloth. Pelican Publishing Company, Inc. Gretna, LA. 2002. 480p. ISBN:1-58980-021-4, ISBN13: 978-1-58980-021-2. Dewey:973.4/1/092 B. LCCN:2001-059802.
Audience: **f.**

Joyce, Davis D. **E175.5.Z56J69 2003**
Howard Zinn: A Radical American Vision. Noam Chomsky (Foreword by). Trade Cloth. Prometheus Books, Publishers. Amherst, NY. 2004. 275p. ISBN:1-59102-131-6, ISBN13: 978-1-59102-131-5. Dewey:973/.072/02. LCCN:2003-016864.
Audience: **f.**

Jumonville, Neil **E175.5.C73J86 1999**
Henry Steele Commager: Midcentury Liberalism and the History of the Present. Trade Cloth. University of North Carolina Press. Chapel Hill, NC. 1999. 352p. ISBN:0-8078-2448-8, ISBN13: 978-0-8078-2448-1. Dewey:973.9/092. LCCN:98-014589.
Audience: **f.**

Lerner, Gerda **E175.5.L47A3 2002**
Fireweed: A Political Autobiography. Trade Cloth. Temple University Press. Philadelphia, PA. 2002. 408p. Critical Perspectives on the Past Ser. ISBN:1-56639-889-4, ISBN13: 978-1-56639-889-3. Dewey:973.91/092. LCCN:2001-054248.
Audience: **f.** *Choice, 2003.*

Palmer, William **E175.45.P35 2001**
Engagement with the Past: The Lives and Works of the World War II Generation of Historians. Trade Cloth. University Press of Kentucky. Lexington, KY. 2001. 368p. ISBN:0-8131-2206-6, ISBN13: 978-0-8131-2206-9. Dewey:973/.07/2022. LCCN:2001-002579.
Audience: **l,u,f.** *Choice, 2002.*

Pfitzer, Gregory M. **E175.P48 1991**
Samuel Eliot Morison's Historical World: In Quest of a New Parkman. Cloth Text. Northeastern University Press. Boston, MA. 1991. 384p. ISBN:1-55553-101-6, ISBN13: 978-1-55553-101-0. Dewey:973/.072. LCCN:90-023592.
Audience: **f.** *Choice, 1992.*

Roper, John Herbert **E175.5.W66C2 1997**
C. Vann Woodward: A Southern Historian and His Critics. Trade Cloth. University of Georgia Press. Athens, GA. 1997. 360p. ISBN:0-8203-1876-0, ISBN13: 978-0-8203-1876-9. Dewey:975/.007202. LCCN:96-021759.
Audience: **f.**

Rutland, Robert Allen (Editor) **E175.45.C58 2000**
Clio's Favorites: Leading Historians of the U. S., 1945-2000. Trade Paper. University of Missouri Press. Columbia, MO. 2001. 216p. ISBN:0-8262-1316-2, ISBN13: 978-0-8262-1316-7. Dewey:973/.07/202273 B. LCCN:00-062847.
Audience: **f.**

Schlesinger, Arthur M. Jr. **E175.5.S38A3 2000**
A Life in the Twentieth Century: Innocent Beginnings, 1917-1950. Trade Cloth. Houghton Mifflin Company Trade & Reference Division. Boston, MA. 2000. 576p. ISBN:0-395-70752-8, ISBN13: 978-0-395-70752-4. Dewey:973.91092. LCCN:00-061322.
Audience: **f.** *Choice, 2001.*

Thelen, David P. (Editor) **E175.M46 1990**
Memory and American History. Trade Cloth. Indiana University Press. Bloomington, IN. 1990. 176p. ISBN:0-253-35940-6, ISBN13: 978-0-253-35940-7. Dewey:973/.01. LCCN:89-024667.
Audience: **l,u,f.**

Tyrrell, Ian R. **E175.T975 2005**
Historians in Public: The Practice of American History, 1890-1970. Trade Paper. University of Chicago Press. Chicago, IL. 2005. 312p. ISBN:0-226-82194-3, ISBN13: 978-0-226-82194-8. Dewey:973/.072/073. LCCN:2005-003459.
Audience: **f.** *Choice, 2006.*

Wilson, Wendy S. & Herman, Gerald **E175.8.W56 2002**
American History on the Screen: Film and Video Resource. Ed. 2. Trade Cloth. Walch Publishing. Portland, ME. 2002. 174p. ISBN:0-8251-4451-5, ISBN13: 978-0-8251-4451-6. Dewey:973/.071/2. LCCN:2003-269739.
Audience: **f.**

Wish, Harvey **E175.W5**
The American Historian: A Social. Paper Text. Textbook Publishers. Temecula, CA. 2003. 366p. ISBN:0-7581-7292-3, ISBN13: 978-0-7581-7292-1. Dewey:973/.072.
Audience: **f.**

Young, James P. **E175.5.A2Y68 2001**
Henry Adams: The Historian as Political Theorist. Trade Cloth. University Press of Kansas. Lawrence, KS. 2001. xiv, 344p. American Political Thought Ser. ISBN:0-7006-1087-1, ISBN13: 978-0-7006-1087-7. Dewey:973/.07/202. LCCN:00-012522.
Audience: **f.** *Choice, 2002.*

United States > History > Historiography. Philosophy. > Historians: Collective Biography

Wilson, Clyde N. (Editor) **E175.45.A48 1984**
American Historians, 1607-1865. Cloth Text. Thomson Gale. Farmington Hills, MI. 1984. 400p. Dictionary of Literary Biography Ser., Vol. 30 ISBN:0-8103-1708-7, ISBN13: 978-0-8103-1708-6. Dewey:973/.072022. LCCN:84-010262.
Audience: **l,u,f.**

Wilson, Clyde N. (Editor) **E175.45.A483 1986**
American Historians, 1866-1912. Cloth Text. Thomson Gale. Farmington Hills, MI. 1986. 350p. Dictionary of Literary Biography Ser., Vol. 47 ISBN:0-8103-1725-7, ISBN13: 978-0-8103-1725-3. Dewey:973/.072022. LCCN:85-029245.
Audience: **l,u,f.**

Wilson, Clyde N. (Editor) **E175.45.T85 1983**
Twentieth-Century American Historians. Cloth Text. Thomson Gale. Farmington Hills, MI. 1983. 536p. Dictionary of Literary Biography Ser., Vol. 17 ISBN:0-8103-1144-5, ISBN13: 978-0-8103-1144-2. Dewey:907/.2022. LCCN:82-024210.
Audience: **l,u,f.** B

United States > History > Historiography. Philosophy. > Methodology. Study. Teaching

Kashatus, William C. **E175.8.K266 2002**
Past, Present and Personal: Teaching Writing in U. S. History. Trade Paper. Heinemann. Portsmouth, NH. 2002. 144p. ISBN:0-325-00449-8, ISBN13: 978-0-325-00449-5. Dewey:973/.07/2. LCCN:2002-005952.
Audience: **f.**

National Archives Staff **E175.8.T43 1989**
Teaching with Documents, Vol. 1. Trade Paper. National Archives & Records Administration. Washington, DC. 1989. 225p. ISBN:0-911333-79-7, ISBN13: 978-0-911333-79-4. Dewey:973/.071/2. LCCN:89-012602.
Audience: **f.**

Percoco, James A. **E175.8.P47 1998**
A Passion for the Past: Creative Teaching of United States History. Trade Paper. Heinemann. Portsmouth, NH. 1998. 176p. ISBN:0-325-00061-1, ISBN13: 978-0-325-00061-9. Dewey:973/.071/273. LCCN:98-021451.
Audience: **f.**

Veccia, Susan H. **E175.8.V43 2004**
Uncovering Our History: Teaching with Primary Sources. Trade Paper. American Library Association. Chicago, IL. 2003. 160p. ISBN:0-8389-0862-4, ISBN13: 978-0-8389-0862-4. Dewey:973/.071. LCCN:2003-019893.
Audience: **f.**

Wheeler, William B. & Becker, Susan D. **E175.8.W47 1994**
Discovering the American Past: A Look at the Evidence: To 1877. Ed. 3. Paper Text. Houghton Mifflin Company. New York, NY. 1993. 320p. ISBN:0-395-66865-4, ISBN13: 978-0-395-66865-8. Dewey:973. LCCN:93-078664.
Audience: **f.**

Wheeler, William B. & Becker, Susan D. **E175.8.W47 2002**
Since 1865: Discovering the American Past: A Look at the Evidence. Ed. 5. Paper Text. Houghton Mifflin College Division. Boston, MA. 2001. 310p. ISBN:0-618-10225-6, ISBN13: 978-0-618-10225-9. Dewey:907.1/173. LCCN:2001-131560.
Audience: **f.**

United States > History > Historiography. Philosophy. > Philosophy of American History

Dawidoff, Robert **E175.9.D39 2000**
Making History Matter. Trade Cloth. Temple University Press. Philadelphia, PA. 2000. 304p. ISBN:1-56639-748-0, ISBN13: 978-1-56639-748-3. Dewey:973. LCCN:99-017037.
Audience: **u,f.**

Foner, Eric **E175.9.F66 2002**
Who Owns History?: Rethinking the Past in a Changing World. Cloth over Boards. Farrar, Straus & Giroux. New York, NY. 2002. 256p. ISBN:0-8090-9704-4, ISBN13: 978-0-8090-9704-3. Dewey:973/.01. LCCN:2001-051463.
Audience: **l,u,f.** *Choice, 2002.*

Fox, Dixon Ryan **E175.9.F69**
Sources of Culture in the Middle West: Backgrounds Versus Frontier. Paper Text. Textbook Publishers. Temecula, CA. 2003. 110p. ISBN:0-7581-4327-3, ISBN13: 978-0-7581-4327-3. Dewey:977.
Audience: **f.** B

Glassberg, David **E175.9.G58 2001**
Sense of History: The Place of the Past in American Life. Trade Paper. University of Massachusetts Press. Amherst, MA. 2001. 288p. ISBN:1-55849-281-X, ISBN13: 978-1-55849-281-3. Dewey:973/.01. LCCN:00-052743.
Audience: **l,u,f.** *Choice, 2002.*

Handlin, Oscar **E175.9.H35 1977**
Chance or Destiny: Turning Points in American History. Trade Cloth. Greenwood Publishing Group, Inc. Portsmouth, NH. 1977. 220p. ISBN:0-8371-9334-6, ISBN13: 978-0-8371-9334-2. Dewey:973/.01. LCCN:76-054255.
Audience: **u,f.** B

Hartz, Louis **E175.9.H37 1991**
The Liberal Tradition in America: An Interpretation of American Political Thought Since the Revolution. Ed. 2. Trade Paper. Harcourt Trade Publishers. New York, NY. 1991. 348p. ISBN:0-15-651269-6, ISBN13: 978-0-15-651269-5. Dewey:973. LCCN:55-005242.
Audience: **f.** B

Niebuhr, Reinhold & Heimert, Alan **E175.9.N5 1983**
A Nation So Conceived: Reflections on the History of America from Its Early Visions to Its Present Power. Marcus Cunliffe (Preface by). Trade Cloth. Greenwood Publishing Group, Inc. Portsmouth, NH. 1983. 155p. ISBN:0-313-23866-9, ISBN13: 978-0-313-23866-6. Dewey:973/.01. LCCN:83-010708.
Audience: **f.** B

Noble, David W. **E175.9.N6**
Historians Against History: The Frontier Thesis and the National Covenant in American Historical Writing since 1830. Trade Paper. Books on Demand. Ann Arbor, MI. 205p. ISBN:0-8357-8898-9, ISBN13: 978-0-8357-8898-4. Dewey:973.01. LCCN:65-022811.
Audience: **u,f.** B

Novick, Peter **D13.5.U6N68 1988**
That Noble Dream: The "Objectivity Question" and the American Historical Profession. Lorraine Daston, Dorothy Ross, Quentin Skinner & James Tully (Contribution by). Trade Cloth. Cambridge University Press. New York, NY. 1988. 670p. Ideas in Context Ser. ISBN:0-521-34328-3, ISBN13: 978-0-521-34328-2. Dewey:907.2/0973. LCCN:88-002606.
Audience: **u,f.** *Choice, 1989.*

Okihiro, Gary Y. **E175.9.O38 2001**
Common Ground: Reimagining American History. Trade Cloth. Princeton University Press. Princeton, NJ. 2001. xvi, 158p. ISBN:0-691-07006-7, ISBN13: 978-0-691-07006-3. Dewey:973. LCCN:00-049112.
Audience: **l,u,f.** *Choice, 2002, 2001.*

Strout, Cushing **E175.9.S8**
The Pragmatic Revolt in American History: Carl Becker and Charles Beard. Paper Text. Textbook Publishers. Temecula, CA. 2003. ix, 182p. ISBN:0-7581-0100-7, ISBN13: 978-0-7581-0100-6. Dewey:973.01.
Audience: **f.**

Yoder, Edwin **E175.9.Y63 1997**
The Historical Present: Uses and Abuses of the Past. Trade Cloth. University Press of Mississippi. Jackson, MS. 1997. 192p. ISBN:0-87805-985-7, ISBN13: 978-0-87805-985-0. Dewey:973/.01. LCCN:96-052057.
Audience: **u,f.** *Choice, 1998.*

United States > History > Biography (General, Collective)

JK1010.A5
Biographical Directory of the United States Congress, 1774-2003. Trade Cloth. Bernan Associates. Lanham, MD. 2002. 2000p. ISBN:0-89059-257-8, ISBN13: 978-0-89059-257-1. Dewey:973.3/12/0922.
Audience: **g,l,u,f.**

Derby, G. **E176.N283**
National Cyclopedia of American Biography. Trade Cloth. New Library Press.Net. Murrieta, CA. 2003. 752p. ISBN:0-7950-4858-0, ISBN13: 978-0-7950-4858-6. Dewey:920/.073.
Audience: **g,l,u,f.**

Garraty, John A. & Carnes, Mark C. (Editors) **CT213.A68 1999**
American National Biography, Set. Trade Cloth. Oxford University Press, Inc. New York, NY. 1999. 22968p. ISBN:0-19-520635-5, ISBN13: 978-0-19-520635-7. Dewey:920.073. LCCN:98-020826.
Audience: **g,l,u,f.** *Choice, 2002, 1999.*

Kennedy, John F. **E176.K4 2003**
Profiles in Courage. Trade Cloth. HarperCollins Publishers. New York, NY. 2003. 272p. ISBN:0-06-053062-6, ISBN13: 978-0-06-053062-4. Dewey:973.099. LCCN:2003-040676.
Audience: **g,l,u,f.** B

McMullin, Thomas A. & Walker, David **E176**
Biographical Directory of American Territorial Governors. Cloth Text. Greenwood Publishing Group, Inc. Portsmouth, NH. 1984. 376p. ISBN:0-313-28101-7, ISBN13: 978-0-313-28101-3. Dewey:973/.09/92. LCCN:84-009095.
Audience: **g,l,u,f.** B

Mullaney, Marie M. **JK2447**
Biographical Directory of the Governors of the United States, 1983-1988. Cloth Text. Greenwood Publishing Group, Inc. Portsmouth, NH. 1989. 408p. ISBN:0-313-28083-5, ISBN13: 978-0-313-28083-2. Dewey:353.9/131/025. LCCN:89-002273.
Audience: **g,l,u,f.**

Raimo, John W. (Editor) **E187**
Biographical Directory of American Colonial and Revolutionary Governors, 1607-1789. Cloth Text. Greenwood Publishing Group, Inc. Portsmouth, NH. 1980. 536p. ISBN:0-313-28133-5, ISBN13: 978-0-313-28133-4. Dewey:973. LCCN:80-013279.
Audience: **g,l,u,f.**

Raimo, John W. (Editor) **E176**
Biographical Directory of the Governors of the United States, 1978-1983. Cloth Text. Greenwood Publishing Group, Inc. Portsmouth, NH. 1985. 400p. ISBN:0-313-28098-3, ISBN13: 978-0-313-28098-6. Dewey:973.926/092/2 B. LCCN:84-020717.
Audience: **g,l,u,f.**

Scribner Reference Staff **E176.C73 1997**
Concise Dictionary of American Biography, Set. Ed. 5. Trade Cloth. Thomson Gale. Farmington Hills, MI. 1997. 1700p. ISBN:0-684-80549-9, ISBN13: 978-0-684-80549-8. Dewey:920.073 B. LCCN:97-034104.
Audience: **g,l,u,f.** *Choice, 1998.*

Scribners Reference Staff **CT103**
Dictionary of American Biography, Set. Trade Cloth. Thomson Gale. Farmington Hills, MI. 1989. 13789p. ISBN:0-684-80540-5, ISBN13: 978-0-684-80540-5. Dewey:920.003.
Audience: **g,l,u,f.**

Sobel, Robert (Editor) **E176**
Biographical Directory of the Governors of the United States, 1789-1978. Cloth Text. Greenwood Publishing Group, Inc. Portsmouth, NH. 1988. 1816p. ISBN:0-313-28093-2, ISBN13: 978-0-313-28093-1. Dewey:973/.0992. LCCN:77-010435.
Audience: **g,l,u,f.** B

United States > History > Biography (General, Collective) > Presidents

Abbott, Philip **E176.1.A29 1996**
Strong Presidents: A Theory of Leadership. Trade Cloth. University of Tennessee Press. Knoxville, TN. 1996. 296p. ISBN:0-87049-931-9, ISBN13: 978-0-87049-931-9. Dewey:973/.099. LCCN:95-041758.
Audience: **u,f.**

Anthony, Carl Sferrazza **E176.1.A68 2000**
America's First Families: An Inside View of 200 Years of Private Life in the White House. Trade Cloth. Simon & Schuster. New York, NY. 2000. 416p. ISBN:0-7432-0303-8, ISBN13: 978-0-7432-0303-6. Dewey:973/.09/9 B. LCCN:00-064936.
Audience: **g,l,u,f.**

Bailey, Thomas A. **E176.1**
Presidential Greatness: The Image and the Man from George Washington to the Present. Trade Cloth. Irvington Publishers. New York, NY. ISBN:0-89197-356-7, ISBN13: 978-0-89197-356-0. Dewey:973/.0992. LCCN:66-019996.
Audience: **g,l,u,f.** B

Bailey, Thomas A. **E176.1**
Presidential Saints and Sinners. Trade Cloth. Simon & Schuster. New York, NY. 1981. 288p. ISBN:0-02-901330-5, ISBN13: 978-0-02-901330-4. Dewey:353.03/1. LCCN:81-067159.
Audience: **g,u,f.**

Beschloss, Michael R. & American Heritage Magazine Staff (Editors) **E176.1.A6515 2000**
The American Heritage Illustrated History of the Presidents: More Than Two Centuries of American Leadership. Trade Cloth. Crown Publishing Group. New York, NY. 2000. 528p. ISBN:0-8129-3249-8, ISBN13: 978-0-8129-3249-2. Dewey:973/.09/9 B. LCCN:99-462173.
Audience: **g,l,u,f.**

Boller, Paul F. Jr. **E176.1.B683 2004**
Presidential Campaigns: From George Washington to George W. Bush. Ed. 2. Trade Cloth. Oxford University Press, Inc. New York, NY. 2004. 496p. ISBN:0-19-516715-5, ISBN13: 978-0-19-516715-3. Dewey:324.973. LCCN:2003-061005.
Audience: **g,l,u,f.** *Choice, 2005.*

Brinkley, Alan & Dyer, Davis (Editors) **E176.1.A653 2004**
The American Presidency. Trade Paper. Houghton Mifflin Company Trade & Reference Division. Boston, MA. 2004. 592p. ISBN:0-618-38273-9, ISBN13: 978-0-618-38273-6. Dewey:973/.09/9. LCCN:2003-062513.
Audience: **g,l,u,f.** *Choice, 2004.*

Brinkley, Alan & Dyer, Davis (Editors) **E176.1.R295 2000**
The Reader's Companion to the American Presidency. Trade Cloth. Houghton Mifflin Company Trade & Reference Division. Boston, MA. 2000. 368p. Reader's Companion Ser. ISBN:0-395-78889-7, ISBN13: 978-0-395-78889-9. Dewey:973. LCCN:99-059638.
Audience: **g,l,u,f.** *Choice, 2000.*

Bunch, Lonnie G. III, et al. **E176.1.A654 2000**
The American Presidency: A Glorious Burden. Spencer R. Crew, Mark G. Hirsch & Harry R. Rubenstein (Authors), Richard Norton Smith (Introduction by). Book, Other. Smithsonian Institution Press. Washington, DC. 2000. xix, 187p. ISBN:1-56098-992-0, ISBN13: 978-1-56098-992-9. Dewey:973/09/9. LCCN:00-061933.
Audience: **g,l,u,f.**

Cornog, Evan & Whelan, Richard **E176.1.C793 2000**
Hats in the Ring: An Illustrated History of American Presidential Campaigns. Trade Cloth. Random House, Inc. New York, NY. 2000. 336p. ISBN:0-679-45730-5, ISBN13: 978-0-679-45730-5. Dewey:324.973. LCCN:00-027578.
Audience: **g,l,u,f.** *Choice, 2001.*

Dallek, Robert **E176.1.D34 2001**
Hail to the Chief: The Making and Unmaking of American Presidents. Trade Paper. Oxford University Press, Inc. New York, NY. 2001. 254p. ISBN:0-19-514582-8, ISBN13: 978-0-19-514582-3. Dewey:973/.09/9. LCCN:00-069878.
Audience: **l,u,f.**

Diller, Daniel C. & Robertson, Stephen L. **E176.1.D56 2001**
Presidents, First Ladies and Vice Presidents: White House Biographies, 1789-2001. Ed. 3. Trade Cloth. CQ Press. Washington, DC. 2000. viii, 271p. ISBN:1-56802-574-2, ISBN13: 978-1-56802-574-2. Dewey:973/.09/9 B. LCCN:00-048649.
Audience: **g,l,u,f.**

Diller, Daniel C. & Robertson, Stephen L. **E176.1.D56 2005**
The Presidents, First Ladies, and Vice Presidents: White House Biographies, 1789-2005. Ed. 2. Trade Cloth. CQ Press. Washington, DC. 2005. 297p. ISBN:1-56802-984-5, ISBN13: 978-1-56802-984-9. Dewey:973/.09/9 B. LCCN:2004-029355.
Audience: **g,u,f.**

Ferrell, Robert H. **E176.1.F475 2005**
Presidential Leadership: From Woodrow Wilson to Harry S. Truman. Trade Cloth. University of Missouri Press. Columbia, MO. 2005. 184p. ISBN:0-8262-1623-4, ISBN13: 978-0-8262-1623-6. Dewey:973.091/09/9. LCCN:2005-023511.
Audience: **u,f.**

Genovese, Michael **E183**
Encyclopedia of the American Presidency. Trade Cloth. Facts On File, Inc. New York, NY. 2004. 560p. ISBN:0-8160-4699-9, ISBN13: 978-0-8160-4699-7. Dewey:973/.09/9. LCCN:2003-049254.
Audience: **g,l,u,f.**

Gould, Lewis L. **E176.1**
The Modern American Presidency. Richard Norton Smith (Foreword by). Trade Paper. University Press of Kansas. Lawrence, KS. 2004. xvi, 302p. ISBN:0-7006-1330-7, ISBN13: 978-0-7006-1330-4. Dewey:973.9/092/2.
Audience: **g,l,u,f.** *Choice, 2003.*

Gould, Lewis L. **E176.1.G68 2003**
The Modern American Presidency. Richard Norton Smith (Foreword by). Trade Cloth. University Press of Kansas. Lawrence, KS. 2003. xvi, 302p. ISBN:0-7006-1252-1, ISBN13: 978-0-7006-1252-9. Dewey:973.9/092/2. LCCN:2002-154108.
Audience: **l,u,f.** *Choice, 2003.*

Graff, Henry F. (Editor) **E176.1.P918 2002**
The Presidents: A Reference History. Ed. 3. Trade Cloth. Thomson Gale. Farmington Hills, MI. 2002. 850p. ISBN:0-684-31226-3, ISBN13: 978-0-684-31226-2. Dewey:973/.09/9. LCCN:2002-001440.
Audience: **g,l,u,f.** B *Choice, 2003, 1997.*

Graff, Henry F. (Editor) **E176.1.P918 1996**
The Presidents: A Reference History. Ed. 2. Trade Cloth. Thomson Gale. Farmington Hills, MI. 1996. 811p. ISBN:0-684-80471-9, ISBN13: 978-0-684-80471-2. Dewey:973/.09/9. LCCN:96-001730.
Audience: **g,l,u,f.** B *Choice, 2003, 1997.*

Greenstein, Fred I. (Editor) **E176.1**
Leadership in the Modern Presidency. Trade Paper. Harvard University Press. Cambridge, MA. 1988. 440p. ISBN:0-674-51855-1, ISBN13: 978-0-674-51855-1. Dewey:973.9/092/2. LCCN:87-027801.
Audience: **u,f.** *Choice, 1989.*

Kane, Joseph N. **E176.1**
Facts about the Presidents. Ed. 6. Trade Cloth. H.W. Wilson. Bronx, NY. 1993. 432p. ISBN:0-8242-0845-5, ISBN13: 978-0-8242-0845-5. Dewey:973/.0992 B. LCCN:93-009207.
Audience: **g,l,u,f.** B

Leuchtenburg, William E. **E176.1**
In the Shadow of FDR: From Harry Truman to Ronald Reagan. Book, Other. Cornell University Press. Ithaca, NY. xii, 346p. ISBN:0-8014-1387-7, ISBN13: 978-0-8014-1387-2. Dewey:973.92. LCCN:83-045147.
Audience: **u,f.** B

McDonald, Forrest **JK511.M34 1994**
The American Presidency: An Intellectual History. Trade Cloth. University Press of Kansas. Lawrence, KS. 1994. viii, 516p. ISBN:0-7006-0652-1, ISBN13: 978-0-7006-0652-8. Dewey:353.03/13/09. LCCN:93-030235.
Audience: **l,u,f.** *Choice, 1994.*

Neustadt, Richard E. **JK516**
Presidential Power and the Modern Presidents: The Politics of Leadership from Roosevelt to Reagan. Trade Paper. Simon & Schuster. New York, NY. 1991. 384p. ISBN:0-02-922796-8, ISBN13: 978-0-02-922796-1. Dewey:352.2/3/0973. LCCN:90-037725.
Audience: **l,u,f.** *Choice, 1991.*

Parmet, Herbert S. **E176.1.P384 2002**
Presidential Power from the New Deal to the New Right. Trade Paper. Krieger Publishing Company. Melbourne, FL. 2002. 232p. Anvil Ser. ISBN:0-89464-837-3, ISBN13: 978-0-89464-837-3. Dewey:973/.09/9 B. LCCN:2001-022533.
Audience: **u,f.**

Pauley, Garth E. **E176.1.P3946 2001**
The Modern Presidency and Civil Rights: Rhetoric on Race from Roosevelt to Nixon. Trade Cloth. Texas A&M University Press. College Station, TX. 2001. 259p. Presidential Rhetoric Ser., Vol. 3 ISBN:1-58544-107-4, ISBN13: 978-1-58544-107-5. Dewey:323.1/73/0904. LCCN:00-010637.
Audience: **f.** *Choice, 2001.*

Shogan, Robert **E176.1.S565 1999**
The Double-Edged Sword: How Character Makes and Ruins Presidents, from Washington to Clinton. Trade Cloth. Westview Press. Boulder, CO. 1998. 304p. ISBN:0-8133-6872-3, ISBN13: 978-0-8133-6872-6. Dewey:973/.09/9. LCCN:98-039828.
Audience: **l,u,f.**

Sidey, Hugh **E176.1.W585 2005**
The White House Remembered. Trade Cloth. White House Historical Association. Washington, DC. 2005. ISBN:0-912308-94-X, ISBN13: 978-0-912308-94-4. Dewey:973.92/092/2. LCCN:2005-023317.
Audience: **u,f.**

Steiner, Franklin **E176.1.S72 1995**
The Religious Beliefs of Our Presidents: From Washington to F. D. R. Trade Paper. Prometheus Books, Publishers. Amherst, NY. 1995. 190p. Freethought Library ISBN:0-87975-975-5, ISBN13: 978-0-87975-975-9. Dewey:973/.099. LCCN:95-010599.
Audience: **u,f.**

Taranto, James & Leo, Leonardo (Editors) **E176.1.P74 2004**
Presidential Leadership: Rating the Best and the Worst in the White House. William J. Bennett (Foreword by). Trade Cloth.

Simon & Schuster. New York, NY. 2004. 304p. A Wall Street Journal Book Ser. ISBN:0-7432-5433-3, ISBN13: 978-0-7432-5433-5. Dewey:973/.09/9. LCCN:2004-040945.

Audience: **l,u,f.**

Urofsky, Melvin I. **E176.1.A6566 2000**
The American Presidents: Critical Essays. Library Binding. Garland Publishing, Inc. New York, NY. 2000. 544p. Reference Library of the Humanities, Vol. 1971 ISBN:0-8153-2184-8, ISBN13: 978-0-8153-2184-2. Dewey:973/.09/9. LCCN:99-038134.

Audience: **l,u,f.**

White, William Allen **E0176.1.W58**
Masks in a Pageant. Paper Text. Classic Textbooks. Murrieta, CA. 1928. 507p. ISBN:1-4047-6033-4, ISBN13: 978-1-4047-6033-2. Dewey:973/.099.

Audience: **f.**

United States > History > American History: General Works

Bailey, Thomas Andrew, et al. **E178.1.B15 2002**
The American Pageant: A Complete History of the Republic. Ed. 12. Lizabeth Cohen & David M. Kennedy (Authors). Cloth Text. Houghton Mifflin College Division. Boston, MA. 2001. 1034p. ISBN:0-618-10349-X, ISBN13: 978-0-618-10349-2. Dewey:973. LCCN:2001-088415.

Audience: **l,u,f.**

Bancroft, George **E178**
History of the United States of America from the Discovery of the Continent, Vol. 1. Trade Paper. Simon Publications, Inc. 2002. 558p. ISBN:0-9725189-0-8, ISBN13: 978-0-9725189-0-1. Dewey:973.

Audience: **f.**

Bancroft, George **E178**
History of the United States of America from the Discovery of the Continent, Vol. 3. Trade Paper. Simon Publications, Inc. 2002. 588p. ISBN:0-9725189-2-4, ISBN13: 978-0-9725189-2-5. Dewey:973. LCCN:07-034341.

Audience: **f.**

Bancroft, George **E178**
History of the United States of America from the Discovery of the Continent, Vol. 5. Trade Paper. Simon Publications, Inc. 2002. 602p. ISBN:0-9725189-4-0, ISBN13: 978-0-9725189-4-9. Dewey:973.

Audience: **f.**

Bancroft, George **E178**
History of the United States of America from the Discovery of the Continent, Vol. 2. Trade Paper. Simon Publications, Inc. 2002. 598p. ISBN:0-9725189-1-6, ISBN13: 978-0-9725189-1-8. Dewey:973. LCCN:07-034341.

Audience: **f.**

Bancroft, George **E178**
History of the United States of America from the Discovery of the Continent, Vol. 4. Trade Paper. Simon Publications, Inc. 2002. 624p. ISBN:0-9725189-3-2, ISBN13: 978-0-9725189-3-2. Dewey:973. LCCN:07-034341.

Audience: **f.**

Bancroft, George **E178**
History of the United States of America from the Discovery of the Continent, Vol. 6. Trade Paper. Simon Publications, Inc. 2002. 635p. ISBN:0-9725189-5-9, ISBN13: 978-0-9725189-5-6. Dewey:973. LCCN:07-034341.

Audience: **f.**

Beard, Charles Austin **E169.1.B33**
The Rise of American Civilization. Paper Text. Classic Textbooks. Murrieta, CA. 1949. 373p. ISBN:1-4047-4848-2, ISBN13: 978-1-4047-4848-4. Dewey:973.

Audience: **u,f.** B

Bender, Thomas **E178.B428 2006**
A Nation among Nations: America's Place in World History. Cloth over Boards. Farrar, Straus & Giroux. New York, NY. 2006. 384p. ISBN:0-8090-9527-0, ISBN13: 978-0-8090-9527-8. Dewey:973. LCCN:2005-052808.

Audience: **g,l,u,f.** *Choice, 2006.*

Burns, James M. **E178.B96 1982**
The American Experiment: Vineyard of Liberty. Trade Cloth. Alfred A. Knopf Inc. New York, NY. 1982. 864p. ISBN:0-394-50546-8, ISBN13: 978-0-394-50546-6. Dewey:973. LCCN:81-047510.

Audience: **f.** B *Choice, 1986.*

Carnes, Mark C. & Garraty, John A. **E178.6.C33 2006**
American Destiny: Narrative of a Nation. Ed. 2. Trade Paper. Longman Publishing. Boston, MA. 2005. 939p. ISBN:0-321-31636-3, ISBN13: 978-0-321-31636-3. Dewey:973. LCCN:2005-040915.

Audience: **g,l,u,f.**

Channing, Edward **E188.C445 1993**
A History of the United States. Davis D. Joyce (Abridged by). Trade Cloth. University Press of America, Inc. Lanham, MD. 1993. 362p. ISBN:0-8191-8914-6, ISBN13: 978-0-8191-8914-1. Dewey:973. LCCN:92-032019.

Audience: **f.** B

Degler, Carl N. **E178**
Out of Our Past: The Forces That Shaped Modern America. Ed. 3. Trade Paper. HarperCollins Publishers. New York, NY. 1983. 672p. ISBN:0-06-131985-6, ISBN13: 978-0-06-131985-3. Dewey:973. LCCN:83-048021.

Audience: **u,f.** B

Divine, Robert A., et al. **E178.1.A4894 2006**
America, Past and Present: Primary Source Edition. Ed. 7. H. W. Brands Jr., T. H. Breen, George M. Fredrickson, Ariela J. Gross & R. Hal Williams (Authors). Trade Paper. Addison-Wesley Longman, Inc. Boston, MA. 2005. 1200p. ISBN:0-321-36570-4, ISBN13: 978-0-321-36570-5. Dewey:973. LCCN:2005-279898.

Audience: **l,u,f.**

Foner, Eric **E178.F66 2006**
Give Me Liberty!: An American History. Trade Paper. W. W. Norton & Company, Inc. New York, NY. 2005. 981p. ISBN:0-393-92782-2, ISBN13: 978-0-393-92782-5. Dewey:973. LCCN:2005-053941.

Audience: **g,l,u,f.**

Hofstadter, Richard **E178.H728**
The United States: The History of a Republic. Paper Text. Textbook Publishers. Temecula, CA. 2003. 812p. ISBN:0-7581-5941-2, ISBN13: 978-0-7581-5941-0. Dewey:973.
Audience: **f.**

Meinig, Donald W. **E178.M57**
The Shaping of America: A Geographical Perspective on 500 Years of History. Cloth over Boards. Yale University Press. Cumberland, RI. 2004. 488p. Shaping of America Ser., Vol. 4:Global America, 1915-2000 ISBN:0-300-10432-4, ISBN13: 978-0-300-10432-5. Dewey:973. LCCN:85-017962.
Audience: **g,l,u,f.** *Choice, 2005, 1999.*

Meinig, Donald W. **E178.M57 1986**
The Shaping of America: A Geographical Prespective on 500 Years of History. Trade Paper. Yale University Press. Cumberland, RI. 1995. 656p. Shaping of America Ser., Vol. 2:Continental America, 1800-1967 ISBN:0-300-06290-7, ISBN13: 978-0-300-06290-8. Dewey:304.20973. LCCN:85-017962.
Audience: **g,l,u,f.**

Meinig, Donald W. **GF503**
The Shaping of America: A Geographical Perspective on 500 Years of History. Trade Paper. Yale University Press. Cumberland, RI. 2000. 480p. Shaping of America Ser., Vol. 3:Transcontinental America, 1850-1915 ISBN:0-300-08290-8, ISBN13: 978-0-300-08290-6. Dewey:973. LCCN:85-017962.
Audience: **g,l,u,f.** *Choice, 2005, 1999.*

Meinig, Donald W. **E178.M57 1986**
The Shaping of America: A Geographical Perspective on 500 Years of History. Trade Paper. Yale University Press. Cumberland, RI. 1988. 504p. Shaping of America Ser., Vol. 1:Atlantic America, 1492-1800 ISBN:0-300-03882-8, ISBN13: 978-0-300-03882-8. Dewey:973. LCCN:85-017962.
Audience: **g,l,u,f.** *Choice, 2005, 1999.*

Morison, Samuel Eliot, et al. **E178**
The Growth of the American Republic, Vol. I. Ed. 7. Henry Steele Commager & William E. Leuchtenburg (Authors). Cloth Text. Oxford University Press, Inc. New York, NY. 1980. 948p. ISBN:0-19-502593-8, ISBN13: 978-0-19-502593-4. Dewey:973. LCCN:79-052432.
Audience: **g,l,u,f.** B

Morison, Samuel Eliot, et al. **E178**
The Growth of the American Republic, Vol. II. Ed. 7. Henry Steele Commager & William E. Leuchtenburg (Authors). Cloth Text. Oxford University Press, Inc. New York, NY. 1980. 946p. ISBN:0-19-502594-6, ISBN13: 978-0-19-502594-1. Dewey:973. LCCN:79-052432.
Audience: **g,l,u,f.** B

Nash, Roderick & Graves, Gregory **E178.N18 2005**
From These Beginnings: A Biographical Approach to American History. Ed. 7. Trade Paper. Longman Publishing Group. White Plains, NY. 2004. 304p. ISBN:0-321-21639-3, ISBN13: 978-0-321-21639-7. Dewey:973/.09/9. LCCN:2004-011058.
Audience: **g,l,u,f.**

Oates, Stephen B. & Errico, Charles J. **E178.1**
From 1865: Portrait of America. Ed. 8. Paper Text. Houghton Mifflin College Division. Boston, MA. 2002. 451p. ISBN:0-618-22024-0, ISBN13: 978-0-618-22024-3. Dewey:973. LCCN:2001-133320.
Audience: **g,l,u,f.**

Oates, Stephen B. & Errico, Charles J. **E178.1**
Portrait of America, Vol. I. Ed. 8. Paper Text. Houghton Mifflin College Division. Boston, MA. 2002. 434p. ISBN:0-618-22023-2, ISBN13: 978-0-618-22023-6. Dewey:973. LCCN:2001-133320.
Audience: **g,l,u,f.**

Zinn, Howard & Arnove, Anthony (Editors) **E178**
Voices of a People's History of the United States. Trade Cloth. Seven Stories Press. New York, NY. 2004. 665p. ISBN:1-58322-647-8, ISBN13: 978-1-58322-647-6. Dewey:973. LCCN:2004-018173.
Audience: **l,u,f.** *Choice, 2005.*

United States > History > Historical Geography

Bial, Raymond **E179.5.B575 2004**
Frontier Settlements. Trade Cloth. Scholastic Library Publishing. Danbury, CT. 2004. 48p. American Community Ser. ISBN:0-516-23705-5, ISBN13: 978-0-516-23705-3. Dewey:978/.02. LCCN:2004-005097.
Audience: **u,f.**

Billington, Ray A. (Editor) **E179.5.B625 1977**
The Frontier Thesis: Valid Interpretation of American History? Trade Paper. Krieger Publishing Company. Melbourne, FL. 1977. 128p. American Problem Studies ISBN:0-88275-586-2, ISBN13: 978-0-88275-586-1. Dewey:973. LCCN:77-009103.
Audience: **l,u,f.**

Billington, Ray Allen **E179.5.B62**
America's Frontier Heritage. Trade Cloth. Holt, Rinehart & Winston. Austin, TX. 1966. xiv, 302p. ISBN:0-03-067045-4, ISBN13: 978-0-03-067045-9. Dewey:973. LCCN:66-013289.
Audience: **l,u,f.** B

Billington, Ray A. & Ridge, Martin **E179.5.B63 2001**
Westward Expansion: A History of the American Frontier. Ed. 6. Trade Paper. University of New Mexico Press. Albuquerque, NM. 2001. 444p. ISBN:0-8263-1981-5, ISBN13: 978-0-8263-1981-4. Dewey:973.5. LCCN:2001-001518.
Audience: **l,u,f.** B

Bradshaw, Michael J. **E179.5.B73 1988**
Regions and Regionalism in the United States. Paper Text. University Press of Mississippi. Jackson, MS. 1988. 186p. ISBN:0-87805-340-9, ISBN13: 978-0-87805-340-7. Dewey:973. LCCN:87-017917.
Audience: **l,u,f.** *Choice, 1988.*

Earle, Carville **E179.5**
The American Way: A Geographical History of Crisis and Recovery. Book, Other. Rowman & Littlefield Publishers, Inc. Lanham, MD. 2003. 472p. ISBN:0-8476-8712-0, ISBN13: 978-0-8476-8712-1. Dewey:911/.73. LCCN:2002-013413.
Audience: **l,u,f.** *Choice, 2004.*

Gilbert, Martin **E179.5**
The Routledge Atlas of American History. Ed. 5. Trade Cloth. Routledge. New York, NY. 2005. 184p. Routledge Historical Atlases Ser. ISBN:0-415-35902-3, ISBN13: 978-0-415-35902-3. Dewey:911.73.
Audience: **g,l,u,f.**

Goetzmann, William H. **E179.5.G63 1995**
New Lands, New Men: America and the Second Great Age of Discovery. Trade Cloth. Texas State Historical Association. Austin, TX. 1995. 536p. Fred H. and Ella Mae Moore Texas History Reprint Ser. ISBN:0-87611-148-7, ISBN13: 978-0-87611-148-2. Dewey:910/.973. LCCN:95-034673.
Audience: **u,f.** *Choice, 1987.*

Graebner, Norman A. **E179.5.G7 1983**
Empire on the Pacific: A Study in American Continental Expansion. Trade Cloth. Regina Books. Claremont, CA. 1983. 278p. Topics in Diplomatic History Ser. ISBN:0-87436-033-1, ISBN13: 978-0-87436-033-2. Dewey:973.6/1. LCCN:82-022680.
Audience: **f.**

Greenberg, Amy S. **E179.5.G79 2005**
Manifest Manhood and the Antebellum American Empire. Cloth Text. Cambridge University Press. New York, NY. 2005. 342p. ISBN:0-521-84096-1, ISBN13: 978-0-521-84096-5. Dewey:973.6. LCCN:2004-020453.
Audience: **u,f.**

Hietala, Thomas R. **E179.5.H54 2003**
Manifest Design: America Exceptionalism and Empire. Trade Paper. Cornell University Press. Ithaca, NY. 2003. xx, 284p. ISBN:0-8014-8846-X, ISBN13: 978-0-8014-8846-7. Dewey:973.5/8. LCCN:2003-269672.
Audience: **u,f.**

Jarnow, Jesse **E179.5.J37 2004**
Manifest Destiny: A Primary Source History of the Settlement of the American Heartland in the Late 19th Century. Library Binding. Rosen Publishing Group, Incorporated, The. New York, NY. 2005. 64p. ISBN:1-4042-0176-9, ISBN13: 978-1-4042-0176-7. Dewey:979/.02. LCCN:2004-003822.
Audience: **f.**

Kane, Joseph Nathan & Aiken, Charles Curry **E180.K3 2005**
American Counties: Origins of County Names Dates of Creation and Population Data 1950-2000. Ed. 5. Trade Cloth. Scarecrow Press, Inc. Lanham, MD. 2004. 560p. ISBN:0-8108-5036-2, ISBN13: 978-0-8108-5036-1. Dewey:917.3/001/4. LCCN:2004-010154.
Audience: **g,l,u,f.** *Choice, 2005.*

Merk, Frederick **E179.5.M4 1995**
Manifest Destiny and Mission in American History. John Mack Faragher (Foreword by). Trade Paper. Harvard University Press. Cambridge, MA. 1995. 286p. ISBN:0-674-54805-1, ISBN13: 978-0-674-54805-3. Dewey:973.6. LCCN:95-220925.
Audience: **u,f.**

Nye, David **E179.5.N94 2004**
America As Second Creation: Technology and Narratives of New Beginnings. Trade Paper. MIT Press. Cambridge, MA. 2004. 383p. ISBN:0-262-64059-7, ISBN13: 978-0-262-64059-6. Dewey:978/.02.
Audience: **f.**

Pletcher, David M. **HF1456.5.P3P56 2001**
The Diplomacy of Involvement: American Economic Expansion across the Pacific, 1784-1900. Trade Paper. University of Missouri Press. Columbia, MO. 2001. 416p. ISBN:0-8262-1315-4, ISBN13: 978-0-8262-1315-0. Dewey:337.7309. LCCN:2001-018917.
Audience: **u,f.** *Choice, 2002.*

Pletcher, David M. **HF1456.5.W45P55 1998**
The Diplomacy of Trade and Investment: American Economic Expansion in the Hemisphere, 1865-1900. Trade Cloth. University of Missouri Press. Columbia, MO. 1998. 440p. ISBN:0-8262-1127-5, ISBN13: 978-0-8262-1127-9. Dewey:337.73. LCCN:97-038825.
Audience: **u,f.**

Roosevelt, Theodore **E179.5.R66 1995**
The Winning of the West: From the Alleghanies to the Mississippi, 1769-1776. John M. Cooper Jr. (Introduction by). Trade Paper. University of Nebraska Press. Lincoln, NE. 1995. 353p. ISBN:0-8032-8954-5, ISBN13: 978-0-8032-8954-3. Dewey:976. LCCN:94-046645.
Audience: **f.**

Roosevelt, Theodore **E179.5.R66 1995**
The Winning of the West: The Founding of the Trans-Alleghany Commonwealths, 1784-1790. Michael N. McConnell (Introduction by). Paper Text. University of Nebraska Press. Lincoln, NE. 1995. 339p. ISBN:0-8032-8956-1, ISBN13: 978-0-8032-8956-7. Dewey:976. LCCN:94-046645.
Audience: **f.**

Roosevelt, Theodore **E179.5.R66 1995**
The Winning of the West: From the Alleghanies to the Mississippi, 1777-1783. Daniel K. Richter (Introduction by). Paper Text. University of Nebraska Press. Lincoln, NE. 1995. 427p. Winning of the West Ser., Vol. 2 ISBN:0-8032-8955-3, ISBN13: 978-0-8032-8955-0. Dewey:976. LCCN:94-046645.
Audience: **f.**

Roosevelt, Theodore **E179.5.R66 1995**
The Winning of the West: Louisiana and the Northwest, 1791-1807. James P. Ronda (Introduction by). Paper Text. University of Nebraska Press. Lincoln, NE. 1995. 363p. ISBN:0-8032-8957-X, ISBN13: 978-0-8032-8957-4. Dewey:976. LCCN:94-046645.
Audience: **f.**

Slotkin, Richard **E179.5.S6 1998**
The Fatal Environment: The Myth of the Frontier in the Age of Industrialization, 1800-1890. Trade Paper. University of Oklahoma Press. Norman, OK. 1998. 656p. ISBN:0-8061-3030-X, ISBN13: 978-0-8061-3030-9. Dewey:973/.072. LCCN:97-038608.
Audience: **f.**

Turner, Frederick J. **E179.5.T956 1996**
The Frontier in American History. Trade Paper. Dover Publications, Inc. Mineola, NY. 1996. 348p. ISBN:0-486-29167-7, ISBN13: 978-0-486-29167-3. Dewey:973. LCCN:95-045209.
Audience: **l,u,f.**

Turner, Frederick J. **E179.5.T9577 1998**
Rereading Frederick Jackson Turner: "The Significance of the Frontier in American History" and Other Essays. John Mack Faragher (Editor). Trade Paper. Yale University Press.

Cumberland, RI. 1999. 276p. ISBN:0-300-07593-6, ISBN13: 978-0-300-07593-9. Dewey:973. LCCN:98-012872.
Audience: **l,u,f.**

Van Alstyne, Richard Warner **E179.5.V32**
The Rising American Empire. Trade Cloth. Oxford University Press, Inc. New York, NY. 1960. 215p. ISBN:0-8129-6212-5, ISBN13: 978-0-8129-6212-3. Dewey:911.73. LCCN:60-052215.
Audience: **u,f.** B

Wall, James T. **E179.5.W33 1999**
The Boundless Frontier: America from Christopher Columbus to Abraham Lincoln. Trade Paper. University Press of America, Inc. Lanham, MD. 1998. 369p. ISBN:0-7618-1302-0, ISBN13: 978-0-7618-1302-6. Dewey:973. LCCN:98-047735.
Audience: **u,f.**

Weeks, William E. **E179.5.W44 1996**
Building the Continental Empire: American Expansion from the Revolution to the Civil War. Book, Other. Ivan R. Dee Publisher. Blue Ridge Summit, PA. 1996. 192p. American Ways Ser. ISBN:1-56663-135-1, ISBN13: 978-1-56663-135-8. Dewey:327.73. LCCN:96-024327.
Audience: **u,f.**

Winks, Robin W. **E179.5.W54 1971**
The Myth of the American Frontier; Its Relevance to America, Canada and Australia. Trade Cloth. Continuum International Publishing Group, Ltd. London, 1971. 39p. ISBN:0-7185-1110-7, ISBN13: 978-0-7185-1110-4. Dewey:917/.03. LCCN:72-185991.
Audience: **l,u,f.** B

Wrobel, David M. **E179.5.W76 1993**
The End of American Exceptionalism: Frontier Anxiety from the Old West to the New Deal. Trade Cloth. University Press of Kansas. Lawrence, KS. 1993. 256p. ISBN:0-7006-0561-4, ISBN13: 978-0-7006-0561-3. Dewey:973.8. LCCN:92-015682.
Audience: **u,f.** *Choice, 1993.*

United States > History > Military and Naval History

Ambrose, Stephen E. **E181.A34 1997**
Americans at War. Trade Cloth. University Press of Mississippi. Jackson, MS. 1997. 240p. ISBN:1-57806-026-5, ISBN13: 978-1-57806-026-9. Dewey:355.009. LCCN:97-018689.
Audience: **g,l,u,f.**

Anderson, Fred & Cayton, Andrew **E181.A53 2005**
The Dominion of War: Empire and Liberty in North America 1500-2000. Trade Cloth. Penguin Group (USA) Inc. New York, NY. 2004. 544p. ISBN:0-670-03370-7, ISBN13: 978-0-670-03370-6. Dewey:973. LCCN:2004-295398.
Audience: **u,f.** *Choice, 2005.*

Black, Jeremy **E181**
America As a Military Power, 1775-1865: From the American Revolution to the Civil War. Paper Text. Greenwood Publishing Group, Inc. Portsmouth, NH. 2002. 248p. Studies in Military History and International Affairs ISBN:0-275-97706-4, ISBN13: 978-0-275-97706-1. Dewey:355/.00973/09033. LCCN:2001-059079.
Audience: **l,u,f.**

Braisted, William R. **E182.B73**
United States Navy in the Pacific, 1897-1909. Trade Cloth. Irvington Publishers. New York, NY. 1958. ISBN:0-8290-0373-8, ISBN13: 978-0-8290-0373-4. Dewey:327.73/018/23. LCCN:70-090473.
Audience: **u,f.** B

Braisted, William R. **E182.B74**
The United States Navy in the Pacific, 1909-1922. Trade Paper. Books on Demand. Ann Arbor, MI. 761p. ISBN:0-608-20098-0, ISBN13: 978-0-608-20098-9. Dewey:359/.00973. LCCN:75-131957.
Audience: **u,f.**

Brinkley, Douglas **D743**
The World War II Desk Reference: With the Eisenhower Center for American Studies. Michael E. Haskew (Editor). Trade Cloth. HarperCollins Publishers. New York, NY. 2004. 592p. ISBN:0-06-052651-3, ISBN13: 978-0-06-052651-1. Dewey:940.53/003. LCCN:2004-301224.
Audience: **l,u,f.**

Chambers, John Whiteclay (Editor) **E181.O94 1999**
The Oxford Companion to American Military History. Trade Cloth. Oxford University Press, Inc. New York, NY. 2000. 950p. ISBN:0-19-507198-0, ISBN13: 978-0-19-507198-6. Dewey:355/.00973. LCCN:99-021181.
Audience: **g,l,u,f.** *Choice, 2000.*

Doughty, Robert, et al. **E181.W275 1996**
American Military History and the Evolution of Warfare in the Western World. Ira Gruber, Roy K. Flint, Mark Grimsley, George C. Herring, Donald D. Horward, John A. Lynn & Williamson Murray (Authors). Paper Text. Houghton Mifflin College Division. Boston, MA. 1996. 793p. ISBN:0-669-41683-5, ISBN13: 978-0-669-41683-1. Dewey:355.00973. LCCN:96-138918.
Audience: **l,u,f.**

Drake, Frederick C. **E182.S564.D7 1984**
The Empire of the Seas: A Biography of Rear Admiral Robert Wilson Shufeldt, USN. University of Hawaii Press. 1984. ISBN:0-8248-0846-0, ISBN13: 978-0-8248-0846-4.
Audience: **f.**

Ekirch, Arthur A. Jr. **E169.1.E49**
Civilian and the Military: A History of the American Anti-Militarist Tradition. Trade Paper. Ralph Myles Publisher, Inc. Colorado Springs, CO. 1972. ISBN:0-87926-007-6, ISBN13: 978-0-87926-007-1. Dewey:973. LCCN:72-080273.
Audience: **u,f.**

Griess, Thomas E. **E181.P5 1986**
Early American Wars and Military Institutions. Trade Paper. Penguin Group (USA) Inc. New York, NY. 1988. 240p. West Point Military History Ser. ISBN:0-89529-324-2, ISBN13: 978-0-89529-324-4. Dewey:973. LCCN:86-017281.
Audience: **f.**

Hagan, Kenneth J. & Roberts, William R. (Editors) **E181**
Against All Enemies: Interpretations of American Military History from Colonial Times to the Present, 51. Trade Cloth. Greenwood Publishing Group, Inc. Portsmouth, NH. 1986. 411p. Contributions in Military Studies Ser., No. 51 ISBN:0-313-21197-3, ISBN13: 978-0-313-21197-3. Dewey:355/.00973. LCCN:85-017660.
Audience: **u,f.**

Heller, Charles E. & Stofft, William A. (Editors) **E181**
America's First Battles, 1776-1965. Trade Cloth. University Press of Kansas. Lawrence, KS. 1986. xiv, 418p. Modern War Studies ISBN:0-7006-0276-3, ISBN13: 978-0-7006-0276-6. Dewey:973. LCCN:86-007825.
Audience: **u,f.** *Choice, 1987.*

Higham, Robin (Editor) **Z1249.M5G83 1975**
A Guide to the Sources of United States Military History. Trade Cloth. Shoe String Press, Inc. North Haven, CT. 1975. xiii, 559p. ISBN:0-208-01499-3, ISBN13: 978-0-208-01499-3. Dewey:016.355/00973. LCCN:75-014455.
Audience: **l,u,f.** *Choice, 1999, 1993.*

Higham, Robin & Mrozek, Donald J. (Editors) **Z1249.M5**
A Guide to the Sources of United States Military History, Supplement I. Trade Cloth. Shoe String Press, Inc. North Haven, CT. 1981. xiv, 332p. ISBN:0-208-01750-X, ISBN13: 978-0-208-01750-5. Dewey:016.355/00973. LCCN:80-000049.
Audience: **l,u,f.** *Choice, 1999, 1993.*

Higham, Robin & Mrozek, Donald J. (Editors) **Z1249.M5G83**
A Guide to the Sources of United States Military History, Supplement IV. Trade Cloth. Shoe String Press, Inc. North Haven, CT. 1998. xiii, 580p. ISBN:0-208-02422-0, ISBN13: 978-0-208-02422-0. Dewey:016.355/00973. LCCN:98-029759.
Audience: **l,u,f.** *Choice, 1999, 1993.*

Higham, Robin & Mrozek, Donald J. (Editors) **Z1249.M5G83**
A Guide to the Sources of United States Military History, Supplement II. Trade Cloth. Shoe String Press, Inc. North Haven, CT. 1986. xiii, 352p. ISBN:0-208-02072-1, ISBN13: 978-0-208-02072-7. Dewey:016.355/00973. LCCN:85-018688.
Audience: **l,u,f.** *Choice, 1999, 1993.*

Higham, Robin & Mrozek, Donald J. (Editors) **Z1249.M5**
A Guide to the Sources of United States Military History, Supplement III. Trade Cloth. Shoe String Press, Inc. North Haven, CT. 1993. xii, 530p. ISBN:0-208-02214-7, ISBN13: 978-0-208-02214-1. Dewey:016.355/00973. LCCN:92-015623.
Audience: **l,u,f.** *Choice, 1999, 1993.*

Kindsvatter, Peter S. **UA28.K55 2003**
American Soldiers: Ground Combat in the World Wars, Korea and Vietnam. Russell F. Weigley (Foreword by). Trade Cloth. University Press of Kansas. Lawrence, KS. 2004. xxiv, 432p. Modern War Studies ISBN:0-7006-1229-7, ISBN13: 978-0-7006-1229-1. Dewey:355/.00973/0904. LCCN:2002-012957.
Audience: **l,u,f.** *Choice, 2003.*

Kohn, Richard H. **UA23**
Eagle and Sword: The Federalists and the Creation of the Military Establishment in America, 1783-1802. Trade Cloth. Simon & Schuster. New York, NY. 1975. xx, 443p. ISBN:0-02-917551-8, ISBN13: 978-0-02-917551-4. Dewey:355.02/13/0973. LCCN:74-033092.
Audience: **f.**

Leckie, Robert **E181**
Great American Battles. Ed. 2. ibooks, Inc. 2003. ISBN:0-7434-5850-8, ISBN13: 978-0-7434-5850-4.
Audience: **g,l,u,f.**

Livezey, William Edmund **E182.M242.L58 1981**
Mahan on Sea Power. University of Oklahoma Press. 1980. ISBN:0-8061-1569-6, ISBN13: 978-0-8061-1569-6.
Audience: **u,f.**

Mahan, A. T. (Alfred Thayer) **E182.M24**
Letters and Papers of Alfred Thayer Mahan. Naval Institute Press. 1975. ISBN:0-87021-339-3, ISBN13: 978-0-87021-339-7.
Audience: **f.**

Mahan, Alfred Thayer **D246**
The Influence of Sea Power upon History, 1660-1783. Trade Paper. Pelican Publishing Company, Inc. Gretna, LA. 2003. 592p. ISBN:1-58980-155-5, ISBN13: 978-1-58980-155-4. Dewey:909/.6.
Audience: **u,f.**

Matloff, Maurice **E181.A44 1996**
American Military History: 1902-1985. Ed. 2. Trade Paper. Da Capo Press, Inc. Cambridge, MA. 1996. 419p. ISBN:0-938289-71-3, ISBN13: 978-0-938289-71-5. Dewey:355.4/0973. LCCN:96-007108.
Audience: **l,u,f.**

Matloff, Maurice **E181.A44 1996**
American Military History, 1775-1902, Vol. 1. Trade Paper. Da Capo Press, Inc. Cambridge, MA. 1996. 396p. ISBN:0-938289-70-5, ISBN13: 978-0-938289-70-8. Dewey:355.4/0973. LCCN:96-007108.
Audience: **l,u,f.**

Millett, Allan R. **VE23.M54 1991**
Semper Fidelis: The History of the United States Marine Corps. Trade Paper. Simon & Schuster. New York, NY. 1991. 845p. The Macmillan Wars of the United States Ser. ISBN:0-02-921596-X, ISBN13: 978-0-02-921596-8. Dewey:359.9/6/0973. LCCN:91-019593.
Audience: **g,l,u,f.**

Millett, Allan R. & Maslowski, Peter **E181.M6986 1994**
For the Common Defense: A Military History of the United States of America. Trade Cloth. Simon & Schuster. New York, NY. 1994. 720p. ISBN:0-02-921597-8, ISBN13: 978-0-02-921597-5. Dewey:973. LCCN:94-005199.
Audience: **g,u,f.**

Millis, Walter **E181.M699**
Arms and Men: A Study in American Military History. Paper Text. Textbook Publishers. Temecula, CA. 2003. 382p. ISBN:0-7581-5253-1, ISBN13: 978-0-7581-5253-4. Dewey:973.
Audience: **f.**

Morison, Samuel Eliot **E207.J7**
John Paul Jones: A Sailor's Biography. Trade Cloth. William S. Konecky Associates, Inc. Old Saybrook, CT. 2004. 496p. ISBN:1-56852-465-X, ISBN13: 978-1-56852-465-8. Dewey:973.3/5/092.
Audience: **u,f.**

Murray, Stuart **E181.M94 2004**
The Facts on File Atlas of American Military History. Trade Cloth. Facts On File, Inc. New York, NY. 2004. 256p. ISBN:0-8160-5578-5, ISBN13: 978-0-8160-5578-4. Dewey:355/.00973/022. LCCN:2004-008994.
Audience: **g,l,u,f.** *Choice, 2005.*

O'Gara, Gordon C. **E182**
Theodore Roosevelt and the Rise of the Modern Navy. Trade Cloth. Greenwood Publishing Group, Inc. Portsmouth, NH. 1970. 138p. ISBN:0-8371-1480-2, ISBN13: 978-0-8371-1480-4. Dewey:359/.00973. LCCN:69-014016.
Audience: **u,f.** B

Prucha, Francis Paul **E0181.P86**
The Sword of the Republic: The United States Army on the Frontier, 1783-1846. Trade Paper. Books on Demand. Ann Arbor, MI. 474p. ISBN:0-608-32524-4, ISBN13: 978-0-608-32524-8. Dewey:977/.02. LCCN:69-010292.
Audience: **l,u,f.** B

Rutman, Darrett Bruce **E181.R87 1979**
A Militant New World, 1607-1640. Richard H. Kohn (Editor). Library Binding. Ayer Company Publishers, Inc. Manchester, NH. 1980. American Military Experience Ser. ISBN:0-405-11890-2, ISBN13: 978-0-405-11890-6. Dewey:973. LCCN:78-022416.
Audience: **u,f.**

Sprout, Harold H. **E182.S79**
Toward a New Order of Sea Power. Library Binding. Reprint Services Company. Temecula, CA. 1993. 336p. History of the United States Ser. ISBN:0-7812-4859-0, ISBN13: 978-0-7812-4859-4. Dewey:359/.009.
Audience: **f.**

Sprout, Harold H. & Sprout, Margaret **E182.S78 1990**
The Rise of American Naval Power, 1776-1918. Jack Sweetman (Editor), Kenneth J. Hagan & Charles C. Campbell (Introduction by). Trade Cloth. Naval Institute Press. Annapolis, MD. 1990. 488p. Classics of Naval Literature Ser. ISBN:0-87021-778-X, ISBN13: 978-0-87021-778-4. Dewey:359/.00973. LCCN:89-048516.
Audience: **u,f.**

Sweetman, Jack **E182.S99 2001**
American Naval History: An Illustrated Chronology of the U. S. Navy and Marine Corps, 1775-Present. Ed. 3. Trade Cloth. Naval Institute Press. Annapolis, MD. 2002. 428p. ISBN:1-55750-867-4, ISBN13: 978-1-55750-867-6. Dewey:359/.00973. LCCN:2001-044870.
Audience: **l,u,f.**

Symonds, Craig L. **E182.S995 2005**
Decision at Sea: Five Naval Battles That Shaped American History. Trade Cloth. Oxford University Press, Inc. New York, NY. 2005. 400p. ISBN:0-19-517145-4, ISBN13: 978-0-19-517145-7. Dewey:359.4/773. LCCN:2004-029394.
Audience: **l,u,f.** *Choice, 2006.*

Vandiver, Frank E. **E181.P575**
Black Jack: The Life and Times of John J. Pershing, Set. Trade Cloth. Texas A&M University Press. College Station, TX. 1977. 1246p. ISBN:0-89096-024-0, ISBN13: 978-0-89096-024-0. Dewey:355.3/31/0924. LCCN:76-051729.
Audience: **u,f.**

VanDiver, Frank E. **E181**
How America Goes to War. Trade Cloth. Greenwood Publishing Group, Inc. Portsmouth, NH. 2005. 176p. Modern Military Tradition Ser. ISBN:0-275-98514-8, ISBN13: 978-0-275-98514-1. Dewey:355/.033073/09. LCCN:2005-004212.
Audience: **u,f.** *Choice, 2006.*

Weigley, Russell F. **UA23**
The American Way of War: A History of United States Military Strategy and Policy. Trade Paper. Indiana University Press. Bloomington, IN. 1960. 602p. ISBN:0-253-28029-X, ISBN13: 978-0-253-28029-9. Dewey:355.4/3/00973. LCCN:77-074434.
Audience: **g,l,u,f.**

Weigley, Russell Frank **UA25**
History of the United States Army. Macmillan. 1974.
Audience: **g,l,u,f.**

Williams, T. Harry **E181**
History of American Wars: From 1745-1918. Trade Paper. Louisiana State University Press. Baton Rouge, LA. 1985. xviii, 435p. ISBN:0-8071-1234-8, ISBN13: 978-0-8071-1234-2. Dewey:973. LCCN:80-002717.
Audience: **u,f.**

United States > History > Political History (General)

Ekirch, Arthur A. Jr. **E183.E4 1967**
Decline of American Liberalism. Paper Text. Simon & Schuster. New York, NY. 1972. 401p. ISBN:0-689-70069-5, ISBN13: 978-0-689-70069-9. Dewey:973. LCCN:67-013171.
Audience: **f.** B

Finkelman, Paul & Wallenstein, Peter (Editors) **E183.E48 2001**
The Encyclopedia of American Political History. Trade Cloth. CQ Press. Washington, DC. 2000. 555p. ISBN:1-56802-511-4, ISBN13: 978-1-56802-511-7. Dewey:973/.03. LCCN:00-066812.
Audience: **g,l,u,f.** *Choice, 2001.*

Gamber, Wendy (Editor), et al. **E183.A495 2003**
American Public Life and the Historical Imagination. Michael Grossberg & Hendrik Hartog (Editors). Trade Cloth. University of Notre Dame Press. Notre Dame, IN. 2003. xi, 308p. ISBN:0-268-02017-5, ISBN13: 978-0-268-02017-0. Dewey:973. LCCN:2003-009068.
Audience: **u,f.**

Girard, Jolyon P. **E183**
America and the World. Cloth Text. Greenwood Publishing Group, Inc. Portsmouth, NH. 2001. 328p. Major Issues in American History Ser. ISBN:0-313-31292-3, ISBN13: 978-0-313-31292-2. Dewey:327.73. LCCN:00-069132.
Audience: **l,u,f.**

Hansen, William P. **E183.H58 2001**
History of American Presidential Elections, 1789-2001, Set. Arthur M. Schlesinger Jr. & Fred L. Israel (Editors). Trade Cloth. Facts On File, Inc. New York, NY. 2001. 4450p. ISBN:0-7910-5713-5, ISBN13: 978-0-7910-5713-1. Dewey:324.973. LCCN:2001-047543.
Audience: **g,l,u,f.**

Jacobs, Meg (Editor), et al. **E183.D46 2003**
The Democratic Experiment: New Directions in American Political History. William J. Novak & Julian E. Zelizer (Editors). Trade Cloth. Princeton University Press. Princeton, NJ. 2003. 464p. ISBN:0-691-11376-9, ISBN13: 978-0-691-11376-0. Dewey:320.973. LCCN:2002-192499.
Audience: **u,f.** *Choice, 2004.*

Jillson, Calvin **E183.J55 2004**
Pursuing the American Dream: Opportunity and Exclusion over Four Centuries. Trade Cloth. University Press of Kansas. Lawrence, KS. 2004. xvi, 348p. American Political Thought Ser. ISBN:0-7006-1342-0, ISBN13: 978-0-7006-1342-7. Dewey:973/.01. LCCN:2004-004568.
Audience: **u,f.** *Choice, 2005.*

Rossiter, Clinton **E183**
Parties and Politics in America. Trade Paper. Cornell University Press. Ithaca, NY. 1964. 212p. ISBN:0-8014-9021-9, ISBN13: 978-0-8014-9021-7. Dewey:329.
Audience: **u,f.**

Smith, William Robertson **E183**
Rhetoric of American Politics: A Study of Documents, 1. Trade Cloth. Greenwood Publishing Group, Inc. Portsmouth, NH. 1970. 464p. Contributions in American Studies ISBN:0-8371-1495-0, ISBN13: 978-0-8371-1495-8. Dewey:320.9/73. LCCN:71-095503.
Audience: **u,f.** B

United States > History > Diplomatic History (General)

Bacevich, Andrew J. **E183.7.B284 2004**
American Empire: The Realities and Consequences of U. S. Diplomacy. Trade Paper. Harvard University Press. Cambridge, MA. 2004. 312p. ISBN:0-674-01375-1, ISBN13: 978-0-674-01375-9. Dewey:327.73.
Audience: **l,u,f.** *Choice, 2003.*

Bailey, Thomas Andrew **E183.7.B33**
The Man In The Street. Paper Text. Classic Textbooks. Murrieta, CA. 1948. 508p. ISBN:1-4047-4837-7, ISBN13: 978-1-4047-4837-8. Dewey:327.73.
Audience: **f.**

Brands, H. W. Jr. **E183.7.B694 1998**
What America Owes the World: The Struggle for the Soul of Foreign Policy. Cloth Text. Cambridge University Press. New York, NY. 1998. 352p. ISBN:0-521-63031-2, ISBN13: 978-0-521-63031-3. Dewey:327.73. LCCN:97-038837.
Audience: **l,u,f.** *Choice, 1999.*

Cohen, Warren I. **E183.7.C24 1993**
The Cambridge History of American Foreign Relations: America in the Age of Soviet Power, 1945-1991. Trade Cloth. Cambridge University Press. New York, NY. 1993. 299p. ISBN:0-521-38193-2, ISBN13: 978-0-521-38193-2. Dewey:327.73. LCCN:92-036165.
Audience: **g,l,u,f.**

Combs, Jerald A. **E183.7.C656 1997**
The History of American Foregn Policy. Ed. 2. Trade Paper. McGraw-Hill Higher Education. Burr Ridge, IL. 1996. 576p. ISBN:0-07-553400-2, ISBN13: 978-0-07-553400-6. Dewey:327.73. LCCN:96-020940.
Audience: **u,f.**

Crabb, Cecil V. Jr. **JX1417**
Policy Makers and Critics: Conflicting Theories of American Foreign Poilicy. Ed. 2. Paper Text. Greenwood Publishing Group, Inc. Portsmouth, NH. 1986. 311p. ISBN:0-275-92210-3, ISBN13: 978-0-275-92210-8. Dewey:941.60824. LCCN:86-016901.
Audience: **u,f.**

Crabb, Cecil V. Jr. **E183.7**
The American Approach to Foreign Policy: A Pragmatic Perspective. Kenneth W. Thompson (Preface by). Trade Cloth. University Press of America, Inc. Lanham, MD. 1985. 102p. The Credibility of Institutions, Policies and Leadership Ser., Vol. 2 ISBN:0-8191-4422-3, ISBN13: 978-0-8191-4422-5. Dewey:327.73. LCCN:84-029087.
Audience: **u,f.**

Ferrell, Robert H. **E183.7.F4 1975**
American Diplomacy: A History. Ed. 3. Trade Cloth. W. W. Norton & Company, Inc. New York, NY. 1975. 900p. ISBN:0-393-09309-3, ISBN13: 978-0-393-09309-4. Dewey:327.73. LCCN:74-022220.
Audience: **l,u,f.** B

Goetzmann, William H. **E183.7.G654 2000**
When the Eagle Screamed: The Romantic Horizon in American Expansionism, 1800-1860. Trade Paper. University of Oklahoma Press. Norman, OK. 2000. 176p. ISBN:0-8061-3223-X, ISBN13: 978-0-8061-3223-5. Dewey:327.73. LCCN:99-055161.
Audience: **f.**

Hogan, Michael J. (Editor) **E183.7.P29 2000**
Paths to Power: The Historiography of American Foreign Relations to 1941. Trade Cloth. Cambridge University Press. New York, NY. 2000. 316p. ISBN:0-521-66287-7, ISBN13: 978-0-521-66287-1. Dewey:327.73/007/2. LCCN:99-028048.
Audience: **f.**

Hogan, Michael J. & Paterson, Thomas G. (Editors) **E183.7.E9 2003**
Explaining the History of American Foreign Relations. Ed. 2. Cloth Text. Cambridge University Press. New York, NY. 2004. 380p. ISBN:0-521-83279-9, ISBN13: 978-0-521-83279-3. Dewey:327.73/001. LCCN:2003-053294.
Audience: **u,f.**

Hunt, Michael H. **E183.7**
Ideology and U. S. Foreign Policy. Trade Paper. Yale University Press. Cumberland, RI. 1988. 237p. ISBN:0-300-04369-4, ISBN13: 978-0-300-04369-3. Dewey:327.73. LCCN:86-015778.
Audience: **u,f.**

Iriye, Akira **E744**
Cambridge History of American Foreign Relations: The Globalizing of America, 1913-1945. Trade Paper. Cambridge University Press. New York, NY. 1995. 254p. ISBN:0-521-48382-4, ISBN13: 978-0-521-48382-7. Dewey:327.7/3.
Audience: **g,l,u,f.**

Jones, Howard **E183.7.J743 2002**
Crucible of Power: A History of American Foreign Relations to 1913. Ed. 2. Trade Paper. Rowman & Littlefield Publishers, Inc. Lanham, MD. 2002. 309p. ISBN:0-8420-2916-8, ISBN13: 978-0-8420-2916-2. Dewey:327.73. LCCN:2001-054183.
Audience: **u,f.**

LaFeber, Walter **E183.7 .C24 1993**
The Cambridge History of American Foreign Relations: The American Search for Opportunity, 1865-1913. Trade Paper.

Cambridge University Press. New York, NY. 1995. 281p. ISBN:0-521-48383-2, ISBN13: 978-0-521-48383-4. Dewey:327.7/3.
Audience: **g,l,u,f.**

Lens, Sidney **E183.7**
The Forging of the American Empire: From the Revolution to Vietnam: A History of American Imperialism. Howard Zinn (Introduction by). Trade Cloth. Pluto Press. London, 2003. 472p. ISBN:0-7453-2101-1, ISBN13: 978-0-7453-2101-1. Dewey:327.73. LCCN:2003-103459.
Audience: **u,f.**

McCormick, James M. **E183.7.M4714 2005**
American Foreign Policy and Process. Ed. 4. Paper Text. Thomson Wadsworth. Belmont, CA. 2004. 640p. ISBN:0-534-61853-7, ISBN13: 978-0-534-61853-7. Dewey:327.73/009/04. LCCN:2004-102432.
Audience: **u,f.**

Merli, Frank J. **E183.7.M472**
Makers of American Diplomacy, from Benjamin Franklin to Henry Kissinger. Trade Cloth. Simon & Schuster. New York, NY. 1974. xix, 728p. ISBN:0-684-13786-0, ISBN13: 978-0-684-13786-5. Dewey:327/.2/0922. LCCN:73-001321.
Audience: **f.** B

Papp, Daniel S., et al. **E183.7.P18 2005**
American Foreign Policy: History, Politics, and Policy. Loch Johnson & John Endicott (Authors). Trade Paper. Addison-Wesley Longman, Inc. Boston, MA. 2004. 560p. ISBN:0-321-07902-7, ISBN13: 978-0-321-07902-2. Dewey:327.73/009. LCCN:2004-016760.
Audience: **u,f.**

Paterson, Thomas G., et al. **E183.7.P28 1988**
American Foreign Policy: A History, Vol. I. Ed. 3. J. Garry Clifford, Kenneth J. Hagen & Robert J. McMahon (Authors). Paper Text. Houghton Mifflin Company Trade & Reference Division. Boston, MA. 1988. 255p. ISBN:0-669-12664-0, ISBN13: 978-0-669-12664-8. Dewey:973. LCCN:87-081183.
Audience: **l,u,f.**

Perkins, Bradford **E183.7.C24 1993**
The Cambridge History of American Foreign Relations: The Creation of a Republican Empire, 1776-1865. Trade Cloth. Cambridge University Press. New York, NY. 1993. 268p. ISBN:0-521-38209-2, ISBN13: 978-0-521-38209-0. Dewey:327.7/3. LCCN:92-036165.
Audience: **g,l,u,f.**

Perkins, Dexter **E183.7**
Foreign Policy and the American Spirit. Glyndon G. Van Deusen & Richard C. Wade (Editors). Trade Cloth. Associated Faculty Press, Inc. New York, NY. 1971. xiii, 254p. ISBN:0-8046-1671-X, ISBN13: 978-0-8046-1671-3. Dewey:327.73. LCCN:73-159076.
Audience: **f.**

Schulzinger, Robert D. (Editor) **E183.7.C658 2003**
A Companion to American Foreign Relations. Trade Cloth. Blackwell Publishing, Inc. Malden, MA. 2003. 576p. Blackwell Companions to American History Ser. ISBN:0-631-22315-0, ISBN13: 978-0-631-22315-3. Dewey:327.73. LCCN:2002-153754.
Audience: **g,l,u,f.** *Choice, 2004.*

Small, Melvin **E183.7.S515 1996**
Democracy and Diplomacy: The Impact of Domestic Politics in U. S. Foreign Policy, 1789-1994. Trade Paper. Johns Hopkins University Press. Baltimore, MD. 1982. 208p. The American Moment Ser. ISBN:0-8018-5178-5, ISBN13: 978-0-8018-5178-0. Dewey:327.73. LCCN:95-008962.
Audience: **f.** *Choice, 1996.*

Thompson, Kenneth W. **E183.7.T47 1992**
Traditions and Values in Politics and Diplomacy: Theory and Practice. Paper Text. Louisiana State University Press. Baton Rouge, LA. 1992. 456p. Political Traditions in Foreign Policy Ser. ISBN:0-8071-1746-3, ISBN13: 978-0-8071-1746-0. Dewey:327.73. LCCN:91-039876.
Audience: **f.**

Thomson Gale Staff (Contribution by) **E183.7.E52 2002**
Encyclopedia of American Foreign Policy, Set. Ed. 2. Trade Cloth. Thomson Gale. Farmington Hills, MI. 2001. 1500p. ISBN:0-684-80657-6, ISBN13: 978-0-684-80657-0. Dewey:327.73/003. LCCN:2001-049800.
Audience: **g,l,u,f.** *Choice, 2002.*

United States > History > Relations with Particular Countries, A-Z

Allison, Graham **E841.A44**
Essence of Decision: Explaining the Cuban Missile Crisis. Trade Cloth. Benjamin-Cummings Publishing Company. San Francisco, CA. 1998. ISBN:0-321-00497-3, ISBN13: 978-0-321-00497-0. Dewey:973.923.
Audience: **u,f.**

Alteras, Isaac **E183.8.I7.A44 1993**
Eisenhower and Israel: United States-Israeli Relations, 1953-1960. Trade Cloth. University Press of Florida. Gainesville, FL. 1993. 408p. ISBN:0-8130-1205-8, ISBN13: 978-0-8130-1205-6. Dewey:327.7305694/09/045. LCCN:92-044703.
Audience: **u,f.** *Choice, 1994.*

Ausland, John C. **E183.8.S65A87 1996**
Kennedy, Khrushchev, and the Berlin-Cuba Crisis, 1961-1964: The 1961-64 Wall. Paul H. Nitze (Foreword by). Trade Cloth. Scandinavian University Press North America. Cambridge, MA. 1996. 256p. ISBN:82-00-22635-2, ISBN13: 978-82-00-22635-2. Dewey:327.73047. LCCN:96-196695.
Audience: **u,f.**

Bain, Kenneth R. **E183.8.I7 B34**
March to Zion: United States Policy and the Founding of Israel. Trade Paper. Texas A&M University Press. College Station, TX. 2000. 256p. ISBN:1-58544-028-0, ISBN13: 978-1-58544-028-3. Dewey:327.73/05694. LCCN:79-007413.
Audience: **u,f.**

Barclay, David E. & Glaser-Schmidt, Elisabeth (Editors) **E183.8.G3T68 1997**
Transatlantic Images and Perceptions: Germany and America since 1776. David Lazar & Christof Mauch (Contribution by). Trade Cloth. Cambridge University Press. New York, NY. 1997. 383p. Publications of the German Historical Institute, Washington, D. C. ISBN:0-521-58091-9, ISBN13: 978-0-521-58091-5. Dewey:327.4/3/073. LCCN:96-031667.
Audience: **f.** *Choice, 1998.*

Bard, Mitchell G. **E183.8.I7B37 1990**
The Water's Edge and Beyond: Defining the Limits to Domestic Influence on United States Middle East Policy. Trade Cloth. Transaction Publishers. Somerset, NJ. 1991. 323p. ISBN:0-88738-346-7, ISBN13: 978-0-88738-346-5. Dewey:327.7305694. LCCN:90-042375.
Audience: **u,f.**

Bartlett, Norman **E183.8.A8.B37**
Australia and America Through 200 Years; 1776-1976. Trade Cloth. Fine Arts Press. Knoxville, TN. 1976. xiv, 258p. ISBN:0-86917-000-7, ISBN13: 978-0-86917-000-7. Dewey:301.29/73/094. LCCN:77-354903.
Audience: **u,f.**

Beichman, Arnold **E183.8.S65B45 1990**
The Long Pretense: Soviet Treaty Diplomacy from Lenin to Gorbachev. William F. Buckley Jr. (Foreword by). Trade Cloth. Transaction Publishers. Somerset, NJ. 1990. 317p. ISBN:0-88738-360-2, ISBN13: 978-0-88738-360-1. Dewey:327.73047. LCCN:90-010815.
Audience: **l,u,f.** *Choice, 1991.*

Bennett, Edward M. **E183.8.S65B46 1985**
Franklin D. Roosevelt and the Search for Security: American-Soviet Relations, 1933-1939. Book, Other. Rowman & Littlefield Publishers, Inc. Lanham, MD. 1985. 243p. America in the Modern World Ser., :Studies in International History ISBN:0-8420-2246-5, ISBN13: 978-0-8420-2246-0. Dewey:973.917/092/4. LCCN:85-010850.
Audience: **u,f.** *Choice, 1986.*

Bermann, Karl **E183.8.N5B46 1986**
Under the Big Stick: Nicaragua and the United States since 1848. Trade Cloth, Box or Slipcased. Compita Publishing. Hampton, VA. 1986. 339p. ISBN:0-89608-324-1, ISBN13: 978-0-89608-324-0. Dewey:327.7285073. LCCN:86-001767.
Audience: **u,f.** *Choice, 1986.*

Bissell, Richard E. **E183**
South Africa and the United States: The Erosion of an Influence Relationship. Trade Cloth. Greenwood Publishing Group, Inc. Portsmouth, NH. 1982. 147p. Studies of Influence in International Relations ISBN:0-275-90764-3, ISBN13: 978-0-275-90764-8. Dewey:327.73068. LCCN:81-022663.
Audience: **u,f.**

Blumenthal, Henry **E183.8.F8.B54**
France and the United States; Their Diplomatic Relation, 1789-1914. Trade Cloth. University of North Carolina Press. Chapel Hill, NC. 1970. xiv, 312p. ISBN:0-8078-1126-2, ISBN13: 978-0-8078-1126-9. Dewey:327.44/073. LCCN:73-080926.
Audience: **u,f.**

Borg, Dorothy & Heinrichs, Waldo H. **E183.8.C5**
Uncertain Years: Chinese-American Relations, 1947-1950. Trade Cloth. Columbia University Press. New York, NY. 1980. 332p. ISBN:0-231-04738-X, ISBN13: 978-0-231-04738-8. Dewey:327.73051. LCCN:79-028297.
Audience: **u,f.**

Caldwell, Dan **E183.8.R9 C28**
American-Soviet Relations: From Nineteen Forty-Seven to the Nixon-Kissinger Grand Design, 61. Trade Cloth. Greenwood Publishing Group, Inc. Portsmouth, NH. 1981. 283p. Contributions in Political Science Ser., No. 69 ISBN:0-313-22538-9, ISBN13: 978-0-313-22538-3. Dewey:327.73047. LCCN:80-027333.
Audience: **u,f.**

Chang, Gordon H. **E183.8.C6C47 1990**
Friends and Enemies: The United States, China, and the Soviet Union, 1948-1972. Trade Cloth. Stanford University Press. Palo Alto, CA. 1990. 416p. Modern America Ser. ISBN:0-8047-1565-3, ISBN13: 978-0-8047-1565-2. Dewey:327.73047. LCCN:89-021865.
Audience: **l,u,f.** *Choice, 1990.*

Chomsky, Noam **E183.8.I7C48 1999**
Fateful Triangle: The United States, Israel, and the Palestinians. Ed. 2. Edward W. Said (Foreword by). Trade Cloth. South End Press. Cambridge, MA. 1999. 600p. South End Press Classics Ser., Vol. 3 ISBN:0-89608-602-X, ISBN13: 978-0-89608-602-9. Dewey:327.7/3/05694. LCCN:98-055140.
Audience: **l,u,f.**

Cohen, Stephen F. **E183.8.R9C56 2000**
Failed Crusade: America and the Tragedy of Post-Communist Russia. Trade Cloth. W. W. Norton & Company, Inc. New York, NY. 2000. 160p. ISBN:0-393-04964-7, ISBN13: 978-0-393-04964-0. Dewey:327.73047. LCCN:00-035501.
Audience: **u,f.** *Choice, 2001.*

Cohen, Warren I. **E183.8.C5C62 2000**
America's Response to China: A History of Sino-American Relations. Ed. 4. Trade Cloth. Columbia University Press. New York, NY. 2000. 270p. ISBN:0-231-11928-3, ISBN13: 978-0-231-11928-3. Dewey:327.73051. LCCN:2001-524810.
Audience: **l,u,f.**

Cortada, James W. **E183**
Two Nations over Time: Spain and the United States, 1776-1977. Trade Cloth. Greenwood Publishing Group, Inc. Portsmouth, NH. 1978. 305p. Contributions in American History Ser., No. 74 ISBN:0-313-20319-9, ISBN13: 978-0-313-20319-0. Dewey:327.73/046. LCCN:77-094752.
Audience: **l,u,f.**

Costigliola, Frank **E183.8.F8C68 1992**
France and the United States: The Cold Alliance since World War II. Cloth Text. Macmillan Publishing Company, Inc. Old Tappan, NJ. 1992. 200p. Twayne's International History Ser., No. 9 ISBN:0-8057-7902-7, ISBN13: 978-0-8057-7902-8. Dewey:327.73044. LCCN:91-041179.
Audience: **u,f.** *Choice, 1992.*

Cuff, Robert D. **E183.8.C2.C87**
Canadian-American Relations in Wartime: From the Great War to the Cold War. Trade Cloth. A. M. Hakkert. Las Palmas G. C., 1975. xiii, 205p. ISBN:0-88866-556-3, ISBN13: 978-0-88866-556-0. Dewey:327.71/073. LCCN:74-080412.
Audience: **f.**

Deatherage, Scott **E183.8.R9R885 1998**
Russia, Friend or Foe: A Critical Analysis of U. S. Foreign Policy Toward Russia. Trade Cloth. McGraw-Hill/Contemporary. Lincolnwood, IL. 1998. x, 196p. ISBN:0-8442-0431-5, ISBN13: 978-0-8442-0431-4. Dewey:327.73047. LCCN:98-212791.
Audience: **l,u,f.**

DeConde, Alexander **E183.8.I8.D4**
Half Bitter, Half Sweet; an Excursion into Italian-American History. Trade Cloth. Simon & Schuster. New York, NY. 1971.

vii, 466p. ISBN:0-684-12366-5, ISBN13: 978-0-684-12366-0. Dewey:301.29/73/045. LCCN:75-123851.
Audience: **f.** B

Delmendo, Sharon **E183.8.P5D45 2004**
The Star-Entangled Banner: One Hundred Years of America in the Philippines. Library Binding. Rutgers University Press. Piscataway, NJ. 2004. 256p. ISBN:0-8135-3410-0, ISBN13: 978-0-8135-3410-7. Dewey:959.9/03. LCCN:2003-018873.
Audience: **u,f.** *Choice, 2005.*

DeTinguy, Anne **E183.8.S65T56 1999**
U. S. - Soviet Relations During the Detente. Trade Cloth. Eastern European Monographs. Bradenton, FL. 1999. 220p. ISBN:0-88033-424-X, ISBN13: 978-0-88033-424-2. Dewey:327.73047. LCCN:99-072634.
Audience: **u,f.**

Dobson, Alan P. **E183.8.G7D63 1995**
Anglo-American Relations in the Twentieth Century: The Politics and Diplomacy of Friendly Superpowers. Paper over Boards. Routledge. New York, NY. 1995. 208p. ISBN:0-415-11942-1, ISBN13: 978-0-415-11942-9. Dewey:327.4/1/073. LCCN:94-039922.
Audience: **l,u,f.** *Choice, 1996.*

Dulles, Foster R. **E183.8.J3**
American Policy Toward Communist China, 1949-1969. Trade Paper. Harlan Davidson Inc. Wheeling, IL. 1972. 288p. ISBN:0-88295-728-7, ISBN13: 978-0-88295-728-9. Dewey:327.73/052. LCCN:70-184974.
Audience: **u,f.**

Dulles, Foster Rhea **E183.8.C5.D79 1972**
American Policy Toward Communist China, 1949-1969. Trade Cloth. Collier Macmillan Canada, Inc. Cambridge, ON. 1972. xiii, 273p. ISBN:0-690-07612-6, ISBN13: 978-0-690-07612-7. Dewey:327.73/052. LCCN:70-184974.
Audience: **f.** B

Dumbrell, John **E183.8.S65**
President Lyndon Johnson and Soviet Communism. Cloth over Boards. Manchester University Press. Manchester, 2004. 240p. ISBN:0-7190-6263-2, ISBN13: 978-0-7190-6263-6. Dewey:327.73047/09/046. LCCN:2004-303644.
Audience: **u,f.** *Choice, 2005.*

Dumbrell, John **E183.8.G7D86 2001**
A Special Relationship: Anglo-American Relations in the Cold War and After. Cloth over Boards. Palgrave Macmillan. New York, NY. 2000. 268p. ISBN:0-333-62249-9, ISBN13: 978-0-333-62249-0. Dewey:327.73041. LCCN:00-040458.
Audience: **u,f.** *Choice, 2001.*

Duric, Mira **E183.8.S65**
The Strategic Defence Initiative: US Policy and the Soviet Union. Trade Cloth. Ashgate Publishing, Ltd. Aldershot, 2003. 198p. ISBN:0-7546-3733-6, ISBN13: 978-0-7546-3733-2. Dewey:358.1/74. LCCN:2003-056048.
Audience: **u,f.**

Eisenberg, Carolyn **E183.8.G3E35 1996**
Drawing the Line: The American Decision to Divide Germany, 1944-1949. Trade Cloth. Cambridge University Press. New York, NY. 1996. 538p. ISBN:0-521-39212-8, ISBN13: 978-0-521-39212-9. Dewey:943/.0874. LCCN:95-010689.
Audience: **u,f.** *Choice, 1996.*

Ewell, Judith **E183.8.V3E9 1996**
Venezuela and the United States: From Monroe's Hemisphere to Petroleum's Empire. Cloth Text. University of Georgia Press. Athens, GA. 1996. 267p. The United States and the Americas Ser. ISBN:0-8203-1782-9, ISBN13: 978-0-8203-1782-3. Dewey:327.73087. LCCN:95-002808.
Audience: **u,f.** *Choice, 1996.*

Fairbank, John K. **DS735.F27 1992**
China: A New History. Ed. 2. Cloth Text. Harvard University Press. Cambridge, MA. 1992. 519p. ISBN:0-674-11670-4, ISBN13: 978-0-674-11670-2. Dewey:951. LCCN:91-044164.
Audience: **f.**

Gaddis, John Lewis **D843.G22 2005**
The Cold War: A New History. Trade Cloth. Penguin Group (USA) Inc. New York, NY. 2005. 352p. ISBN:1-59420-062-9, ISBN13: 978-1-59420-062-5. Dewey:909.82/5. LCCN:2005-053406.
Audience: **g,l,u,f.** *Choice, 2006.*

Gaddis, John Lewis **E183.8.S65G33 1987**
The Long Peace: Inquiries into the History of the Cold War. Oxford University Press, Inc. 1987. ISBN:0-19-504336-7, ISBN13: 978-0-19-504336-5.
Audience: **l,u,f.**

Gaddis, John Lewis **E183.8.S65G34 1990**
Russia, the Soviet Union, and the United States: An Interpretive History. Ed. 2. Paper Text. McGraw-Hill Higher Education. Burr Ridge, IL. 1990. 432p. America and the World Ser. ISBN:0-07-557258-3, ISBN13: 978-0-07-557258-9. Dewey:327.73047. LCCN:89-028784.
Audience: **l,u,f.**

Garrison, Jean A. **E183.8.C5G345 2005**
Making China Policy: From Nixon to G. W. Bush. Library Binding. Lynne Rienner Publishers, Inc. Boulder, CO. 2005. 270p. ISBN:1-58826-360-6, ISBN13: 978-1-58826-360-5. Dewey:327.73051/09/045. LCCN:2005-000411.
Audience: **l,u,f.** *Choice, 2005.*

Gelb, Leslie H. & Betts, Richard K. **E183.8.V5G4 1979**
e The Irony of Vietnam: The System Worked. E-Book. NetLibrary, Inc. Boulder, CO. 1979. ISBN:0-585-34186-9, ISBN13: 978-0-585-34186-6. Dewey:327.73/0597.
Audience: **u,f.** B

Geyer, Alan F. **E183.8.S65G49 1990**
Christianity and the Superpowers: Religion, Politics and History in U. S. - U. S. S. R. Relations. Trade Cloth. Abingdon Press. Nashville, TN. 1990. 192p. ISBN:0-687-07694-3, ISBN13: 978-0-687-07694-9. Dewey:947.084. LCCN:89-078013.
Audience: **f.** *Choice, 1990.*

Goldgeier, James M. & McFaul, Michael **E183.8.R9G626 2004**
Power and Purpose: U. S. Policy Toward Russia after the Cold War. Trade Cloth. Brookings Institution Press. Washington, DC. 2003. 450p. ISBN:0-8157-3174-4, ISBN13: 978-0-8157-3174-0. Dewey:327.73047/09/049. LCCN:2003-019079.
Audience: **u,f.**

Gorbachev, Mikhail **E183.8.S65G67 1987**
Reykjavik: Results and Lessons. Trade Cloth. Sphinx Press. Madison, CT. 1987. 87p. ISBN:0-943071-06-2, ISBN13: 978-0-943071-06-0. Dewey:327.73047. LCCN:86-031438.
Audience: **u,f.**

Grogin, Robert C. **E183.8.S65G756 2001**
Natural Enemies: The United States and the Soviet Union in the Cold War, 1917-1991. Trade Cloth. Lexington Books. Lanham, MD. 2000. 368p. ISBN:0-7391-0139-0, ISBN13: 978-0-7391-0139-1. Dewey:327.73047. LCCN:00-030979.
Audience: **u,f.** *Choice, 2001.*

Haas, Michael **E183.8**
Cambodia, Pol Pot, and the United States: The Faustian Pact. Trade Cloth. Greenwood Publishing Group, Inc. Portsmouth, NH. 1991. 184p. ISBN:0-275-94005-5, ISBN13: 978-0-275-94005-8. Dewey:327.730596. LCCN:90-027548.
Audience: **f.**

Halle, Louis J. **E183.8.P6H35 1985**
The U. S. Acquires the Philippines: Consensus vs. Reality. Trade Cloth. University Press of America, Inc. Lanham, MD. 1985. 72p. The Credibility of Institutions, Policies and Leadership Ser., Vol. 15 ISBN:0-8191-4759-1, ISBN13: 978-0-8191-4759-2. Dewey:327.730599. LCCN:85-009233.
Audience: **f.**

Hart, Parker T. **E183.8.S25H37 1998**
Saudi Arabia and the United States: Birth of a Security Partnership. Trade Cloth. Indiana University Press. Bloomington, IN. 1999. 320p. ISBN:0-253-33460-8, ISBN13: 978-0-253-33460-2. Dewey:327.730538. LCCN:98-035841.
Audience: **u,f.** *Choice, 1999.*

Helmreich, Jonathan E. **E183.8.B4H45 1998**
United States Relations with Belgium and the Congo, 1940-1960. Trade Cloth. University of Delaware Press. Newark, DE. 1998. 288p. ISBN:0-87413-653-9, ISBN13: 978-0-87413-653-1. Dewey:327.730493. LCCN:97-052351.
Audience: **u,f.**

Hirst, Monica **E183.8.B7H58 2004**
The United States and Brazil: A Long Road of Unmet Expectations. Andrew Hurrell (Contribution by). Paper over Boards. Routledge. New York, NY. 2004. 152p. Contemporary Inter-American Relations Ser. ISBN:0-415-95065-1, ISBN13: 978-0-415-95065-7. Dewey:327.73081/09/048. LCCN:2004-011024.
Audience: **u,f.**

Horne, Gerald **E183.8.Z55H67 2001**
From the Barrel of a Gun: The United States and the War Against Zimbabwe, 1965-1980. Trade Paper. University of North Carolina Press. Chapel Hill, NC. 2001. 400p. ISBN:0-8078-4903-0, ISBN13: 978-0-8078-4903-3. Dewey:327.7306891. LCCN:00-039250.
Audience: **f.** *Choice, 2002.*

Houghton, David **E183.8.I55H68 2001**
U. S. Foreign Policy and the Iran Hostage Crisis. Thomas Biersteker, Chris Brown & Phil Cerny (Contribution by). Cloth Text. Cambridge University Press. New York, NY. 2001. 270p. Studies in International Relations, Vol. 75 ISBN:0-521-80116-8, ISBN13: 978-0-521-80116-4. Dewey:955.05/42. LCCN:00-045453.
Audience: **l,u,f.** *Choice, 2002.*

Hulme, Derick L. **E183.8.P19H85 2004**
Palestinian Terrorism and U.S. Foreign Policy, 1969-1977: Dynamics of Response. Trade Cloth. Edwin Mellen Press, The. Lewiston, NY. 2004. 352p. Studies in World Peace, Vol. 17 ISBN:0-7734-6571-5, ISBN13: 978-0-7734-6571-8. Dewey:327.7305694/09/047. LCCN:2003-061533.
Audience: **l,u,f.**

Iriye, Akira **DS518.8.I73 1992**
Across the Pacific: An Inner History of American-East Asian Relations. Trade Cloth. Imprint Publications, Inc. Chicago, IL. 1992. 448p. ISBN:1-879176-08-4, ISBN13: 978-1-879176-08-9. Dewey:305.295. LCCN:92-073114.
Audience: **u,f.**

Jacobs, Seth **E183.8.V5J33 2004**
America's Miracle Man in Vietnam: Ngo Dinh Diem, Religion, Race, and U. S. Intervention in Southeast Asia. Gilbert M. Joseph & Emily S. Rosenberg (Editors). Trade Cloth. Duke University Press. Durham, NC. 2005. 352p. American Encounters/Global Interactions Ser. ISBN:0-8223-3429-1, ISBN13: 978-0-8223-3429-3. Dewey:327.730597/09/045. LCCN:2004-012452.
Audience: **u,f.** *Choice, 2005.*

Jonas, Manfred **E183.8.G3**
The United States and Germany: A Diplomatic History. Book, Other. Cornell University Press. Ithaca, NY. 1985. 336p. ISBN:0-8014-9890-2, ISBN13: 978-0-8014-9890-9. Dewey:327.43073. LCCN:83-015278.
Audience: **u,f.** *B*

Junker, Detlef (Editor) **E183.8.G3U7213 2004**
The United States and Germany in the Era of the Cold War, 1945-1990: A Handbook. Philipp Gassert, Wilfried Mausbach & David B. Morris (Associate Editors), David Lazar & Christof Mauch (Contribution by). Cloth Text. Cambridge University Press. New York, NY. 2004. 608p. Publications of the German Historical Institute ISBN:0-521-83420-1, ISBN13: 978-0-521-83420-9. Dewey:327.43073/09/045. LCCN:2003-060607.
Audience: **u,f.**

Kattenburg, Paul M. **E183.8.V5**
The Vietnam Trauma in American Foreign Policy, 1945-1975. Trade Paper. Transaction Publishers. Somerset, NJ. 1980. 354p. ISBN:0-87855-903-5, ISBN13: 978-0-87855-903-9. Dewey:327.73/0597. LCCN:79-000702.
Audience: **l,u,f.** *B*

Kennan, George F. **DK266.5.K46 1978**
Soviet Foreign Policy, 1917-1941. Trade Cloth. Greenwood Publishing Group, Inc. Portsmouth, NH. 1978. 192p. ISBN:0-313-20355-5, ISBN13: 978-0-313-20355-8. Dewey:327.47. LCCN:78-001568.
Audience: **u,f.**

Kennan, George F. **E183.8.R9**
Soviet-American Relations, 1917-1920: The Decision to Intervene. Trade Paper. Princeton University Press. Princeton, NJ. 1989. 513p. ISBN:0-691-00842-6, ISBN13: 978-0-691-00842-4. Dewey:327.47073. LCCN:56-008382.
Audience: **u,f.**

Kennan, George F. **E183.8.R9**
Soviet-American Relations, 1917-1920: Russia Leaves the War. Trade Paper. Princeton University Press. Princeton, NJ. 1989. 513p. ISBN:0-691-00841-8, ISBN13: 978-0-691-00841-7. Dewey:327.47073. LCCN:56-008382.
Audience: **u,f.**

Kennedy, Robert F. **E183.8**
Thirteen Days: A Memoir of the Cuban Missile Crisis. Arthur M. Schlesinger Jr. (Foreword by). Trade Paper. W. W. Norton & Company, Inc. New York, NY. 1999. 192p.

ISBN:0-393-31834-6, ISBN13: 978-0-393-31834-0. Dewey:973.922. LCCN:73-141589.
Audience: **g,l,u,f.** B

Kennedy, Scott **E183.8.C5C469 2002**
China Cross Talk: The American Debate over China Policy since Normalization, a Reader. Book, Other. Rowman & Littlefield Publishers, Inc. Lanham, MD. 2002. 368p. ISBN:0-7425-1785-3, ISBN13: 978-0-7425-1785-1. Dewey:327.73051/09/045. LCCN:2002-012833.
Audience: **u,f.**

Kirby, William C. (Editor), et al. **E183.8.C5**
Normalization of U. S.-China Relations: An International History. Robert S. Ross & Gong Li (Editors). Trade Cloth. Harvard University Press. Cambridge, MA. 2006. 425p. Harvard East Asian Monographs, Vol. 254 ISBN:0-674-01904-0, ISBN13: 978-0-674-01904-1. Dewey:327.7305109/047. LCCN:2005-028674.
Audience: **l,u,f.**

Krauss, Ellis S. **E183.8.J3B5155 2004**
Beyond Bilateralism: U. S.- Japan Relations in the New Asia-Pacific. Trade Cloth. Stanford University Press. Palo Alto, CA. 2003. 408p. Contemporary Issues in Asia and the Pacific Ser. ISBN:0-8047-4909-4, ISBN13: 978-0-8047-4909-1. Dewey:327.73052. LCCN:2003-018028.
Audience: **u,f.** *Choice, 2004.*

Kusnitz, Leonard A. **E183**
Public Opinion and Foreign Policy: America's China Policy, 1949-1979. Trade Cloth. Greenwood Publishing Group, Inc. Portsmouth, NH. 1984. 191p. Contributions in Political Science Ser., No. 114 ISBN:0-313-24264-X, ISBN13: 978-0-313-24264-9. Dewey:327.73051. LCCN:83-026508.
Audience: **f.** B

Lansford, Tom **E183.8.A3**
A Bitter Harvest: U.S. Foreign Policy and Afghanistan. Trade Cloth. Ashgate Publishing, Ltd. Aldershot, 2003. 212p. US Foreign Policy and Conflict in the Islamic World Ser. ISBN:0-7546-3615-1, ISBN13: 978-0-7546-3615-1. Dewey:327.730581/09/045. LCCN:2003-055321.
Audience: **l,u,f.** *Choice, 2004.*

Larson, Eric V. & Levin, Norman D. **E183.8.K6L37 2004**
Ambivalent Allies?: A Study of South Korean Attitudes Toward the U. S. Trade Paper. RAND Corporation, The. Santa Monica, CA. 2004. 148p. ISBN:0-8330-3584-3, ISBN13: 978-0-8330-3584-4. Dewey:327.5195073/09/0511. LCCN:2004-004736.
Audience: **u,f.**

Lee, Yur-Bok & Patterson, Wayne (Editors) **E183.8.K6K677 1999**
Korean-American Relations: 1866-1997. Cloth Text. State University of New York Press. Albany, NY. 1998. 256p. SUNY Series in Korean Studies ISBN:0-7914-4025-7, ISBN13: 978-0-7914-4025-4. Dewey:303.48/2730519. LCCN:98-003401.
Audience: **u,f.**

Lefebvre, Jeffrey **E183.8.E8L44 1991**
Arms for the Horn: U. S. Security Policy in Ethiopia and Somalia, 1953-1991. Cloth Text. University of Pittsburgh Press. Pittsburgh, PA. 1992. 360p. Policy and Institutional Studies ISBN:0-8229-3680-1, ISBN13: 978-0-8229-3680-0. Dewey:355/.03263. LCCN:90-028360.
Audience: **u,f.** *Choice, 1992.*

Leonard, Thomas M. **E183.8**
Encyclopedia of Cuban-United States Relations. Cloth Text. McFarland & Company, Incorporated Publishers. Jefferson, NC. 2004. 288p. ISBN:0-7864-1521-5, ISBN13: 978-0-7864-1521-2. Dewey:327.7291073/03. LCCN:2003-026010.
Audience: **l,u,f.**

Lippman, Thomas W. **E183.8.S25L57 2004**
Inside the Mirage: America's Fragile Partnership with Saudi Arabia. Trade Cloth. Westview Press. Boulder, CO. 2003. 400p. ISBN:0-8133-4052-7, ISBN13: 978-0-8133-4052-4. Dewey:303.48/2538073. LCCN:2003-017526.
Audience: **u,f.** *Choice, 2004.*

Little, Michael R. **E183.8.S2L58 1994**
A War of Information: The Conflict Between Public and Private U.S. Foreign Policy on El Salvador, 1979-1992. Trade Cloth. University Press of America, Inc. Lanham, MD. 1993. 210p. ISBN:0-8191-9311-9, ISBN13: 978-0-8191-9311-7. Dewey:327.7307284. LCCN:93-031781.
Audience: **f.**

Major, John **E183.8.P2M24 1993**
Prize Possession: The United States Government and the Panama Canal 1903-1979. Trade Cloth. Cambridge University Press. New York, NY. 1993. 454p. ISBN:0-521-43306-1, ISBN13: 978-0-521-43306-8. Dewey:327.7/3/07287. LCCN:92-032406.
Audience: **f.**

Malik, Yogendra K. **E183.8.I4I52 2002**
India and the United States in a Changing World. Ashok Kapur, Harold Gould & Arthur G. Rubinoff (Editors). Trade Cloth. SAGE Publications, Inc. Thousand Oaks, CA. 2002. 560p. ISBN:0-7619-9592-7, ISBN13: 978-0-7619-9592-0. Dewey:327.54073. LCCN:2001-059021.
Audience: **u,f.**

Mann, James H. **E183.8.C5M319 1999**
About Face: A History of America's Curious Relationship with China, from Nixon to Clinton. Trade Cloth. Alfred A. Knopf Inc. New York, NY. 1998. 432p. ISBN:0-679-45053-X, ISBN13: 978-0-679-45053-5. Dewey:327.73051. LCCN:98-006285.
Audience: **u,f.**

Mayers, David **E183.8.S65M373 1995**
The Ambassadors and America's Soviet Policy. Trade Cloth. Oxford University Press, Inc. New York, NY. 1995. 348p. ISBN:0-19-506802-5, ISBN13: 978-0-19-506802-3. Dewey:327.7/3/047. LCCN:94-030032.
Audience: **u,f.** *Choice, 1995.*

McKenzie, Brian Angus **E183.8.F8M38 2005**
Remaking France: Americanization, Public Diplomacy, and the Marshall Plan. Trade Cloth. Berghahn Books, Inc. New York, NY. 2005. 192p. Explorations in Culture and International History Ser., Vol. 2 ISBN:1-84545-154-6, ISBN13: 978-1-84545-154-7. Dewey:327.7304/09/044. LCCN:2005-049340.
Audience: **l,u,f.**

McKercher, B. J. **E183.8.G7M4 1999**
Transition of Power: Britain's Loss of Global Pre-Eminence to the United States, 1930-1945. Trade Cloth. Cambridge

University Press. New York, NY. 1999. 416p. ISBN:0-521-44090-4, ISBN13: 978-0-521-44090-5. Dewey:303.48/273041. LCCN:98-013369.
Audience: **u,f.**

McMahon, Robert J. **E183.8**
The Cold War on the Periphery: The United States, India, and Pakistan. Trade Cloth. Columbia University Press. New York, NY. 1994. 431p. ISBN:0-231-08226-6, ISBN13: 978-0-231-08226-6. Dewey:327.73054. LCCN:93-038724.
Audience: **u,f.** *Choice, 1994.*

Miglietta, John P. **E183.8.S25M54 2001**
American Alliance Policy in the Middle East, 1945-1992: Iran, Israel and Saudi Arabia. Trade Cloth. Lexington Books. Lanham, MD. 2002. 360p. ISBN:0-7391-0304-0, ISBN13: 978-0-7391-0304-3. Dewey:327.73056/09/045. LCCN:2001-048267.
Audience: **u,f.** *Choice, 2003.*

Morley, Morris H. **E183.8.N5M67 1994**
Washington, Somoza and the Sandinistas: State and Regime in U. S. Policy Toward Nicaragua, 1969-1981. Trade Cloth. Cambridge University Press. New York, NY. 1994. 455p. ISBN:0-521-45081-0, ISBN13: 978-0-521-45081-2. Dewey:327.7307285. LCCN:93-034540.
Audience: **f.**

Neumann, William L. **E183.8.J3**
America Encounters Japan: From Perry to MacArthur. Trade Paper. Books on Demand. Ann Arbor, MI. 1963. 365p. Goucher College Ser. ISBN:0-608-04049-5, ISBN13: 978-0-608-04049-3. Dewey:327.73/052. LCCN:63-017667.
Audience: **f.** B

Offner, Arnold A. & Wilson, Theodore A. (Editors) **E183.8.S65V53 2000**
Victory in Europe, 1945: From World War to Cold War. Trade Cloth. University Press of Kansas. Lawrence, KS. 2000. x, 310p. Modern War Studies ISBN:0-7006-1039-1, ISBN13: 978-0-7006-1039-6. Dewey:327.73047. LCCN:00-039873.
Audience: **l,u,f.**

Payne, Richard J. **E183.8.S65P4 1988**
Opportunities and Dangers of Soviet-Cuban Expansion: Towards a Pragmatic U. S. Policy. Roger Fisher (Foreword by). Cloth Text. State University of New York Press. Albany, NY. 1988. 261p. ISBN:0-88706-796-4, ISBN13: 978-0-88706-796-9. Dewey:327.73047. LCCN:87-026778.
Audience: **f.** *Choice, 1989.*

Pease, Neal **E183.8.P7P43 1986**
Poland, the United States, and the Stabilization of Europe, 1919-1933. Cloth Text. Oxford University Press, Inc. New York, NY. 1986. 246p. ISBN:0-19-504050-3, ISBN13: 978-0-19-504050-0. Dewey:327.438073. LCCN:85-031062.
Audience: **f.** *Choice, 1987.*

Pollack, Kenneth M. **E183.8.I55P58 2004**
The Persian Puzzle: The Conflict Between Iran and America. Trade Cloth. Random House Adult Trade Publishing Group. New York, NY. 2004. 576p. ISBN:1-4000-6315-9, ISBN13: 978-1-4000-6315-4. Dewey:327.73054. LCCN:2004-054153.
Audience: **l,u,f.** *Choice, 2005.*

Pollock, David **E183.8**
The Politics of Pressure: American Arms and Israeli Policy Since the Six Day War. Trade Cloth. Greenwood Publishing Group, Inc. Portsmouth, NH. 1982. 328p. Contributions in Political Science Ser., No. 79 ISBN:0-313-22113-8, ISBN13: 978-0-313-22113-2. Dewey:355/.0325694. LCCN:81-023720.
Audience: **u,f.**

Pomeroy, William J. **E183.8.S6P65 1986**
Apartheid, Imperialism and African Freedom. Betty Smith (Editor). Trade Cloth. International Publishers Company, Inc. New York, NY. 1986. 276p. ISBN:0-7178-0640-5, ISBN13: 978-0-7178-0640-9. Dewey:305.8/00968. LCCN:86-010488.
Audience: **f.**

Raat, W. Dirk **E183.8.M6R29 2004**
Mexico and the United States: Ambivalent Vistas. Ed. 3. Trade Cloth. University of Georgia Press. Athens, GA. 2004. 312p. The United States and the Americas Ser. ISBN:0-8203-2595-3, ISBN13: 978-0-8203-2595-8. Dewey:303.48/273072. LCCN:2003-056420.
Audience: **u,f.**

Randall, Stephen J. **E183.8.C7R35 1992**
Colombia and the United States: Hegemony and Interdependence. Trade Cloth. University of Georgia Press. Athens, GA. 1992. 344p. The United States and the Americas Ser. ISBN:0-8203-1401-3, ISBN13: 978-0-8203-1401-3. Dewey:327.730861. LCCN:91-017739.
Audience: **f.** *Choice, 1992.*

Rashid, Al M. **E183.8.J6A4 1993**
Jordan, the United States and the Middle East Peace Process, 1974-1991. Cloth Text. Cambridge University Press. New York, NY. 1993. 301p. Middle East Library, No. 28 ISBN:0-521-41523-3, ISBN13: 978-0-521-41523-1. Dewey:327.7305695. LCCN:91-043477.
Audience: **f.** *Choice, 1993.*

Richard, Alfred **E183.8.P2R53 1990**
Panama Canal in American National Consciousness, 1870-1990. Cloth Text. Garland Publishing, Inc. New York, NY. 1990. 378p. Foreign Economic Policy of the United States Ser. ISBN:0-8240-7471-8, ISBN13: 978-0-8240-7471-5. Dewey:972.87. LCCN:90-003045.
Audience: **u,f.**

Richardson, Louise **E183.8.G7R53 1996**
When Allies Differ: Anglo-American Relations During the Suez and Falklands Crises. Trade Cloth. Palgrave Macmillan. New York, NY. 1996. 352p. ISBN:0-312-15852-1, ISBN13: 978-0-312-15852-1. Dewey:327.4/1/073. LCCN:95-038641.
Audience: **f.**

Roorda, Eric **E183.8.D6R59 1998**
The Dictator Next Door: The Good Neighbor Policy and the Trujillo Regime in the Dominican Republic, 1930-1945. Trade Cloth. Duke University Press. Durham, NC. 1998. 312p. American Encounters/Global Interactions Ser. ISBN:0-8223-2234-X, ISBN13: 978-0-8223-2234-4. Dewey:327.7307293. LCCN:98-012100.
Audience: **u,f.** *Choice, 1999.*

Ross, Robert S. **E183.8.C5R58 1995**
Negotiating Cooperation: The United States and China, 1969-1989. Trade Cloth. Stanford University Press. Palo Alto, CA. 1995. xiv, 350p. ISBN:0-8047-2453-9, ISBN13: 978-0-8047-2453-1. Dewey:327.73051/09/047. LCCN:94-034939.
Audience: **u,f.**

Ross, Robert S. & Jiang, Changbin (Editors) **E183.8.C5R38 2001**
Re-Examining the Cold War: U. S.-China Diplomacy, 1954-1973. Trade Cloth. Harvard University Press. Cambridge, MA. 2002. 528p. Harvard East Asian Monographs, Vol. 203 ISBN:0-674-00524-4, ISBN13: 978-0-674-00524-2. Dewey:327.73051. LCCN:2001-026485.
Audience: **u,f.**

Rossides, Eugene T. (Editor) **E183.8.G8U65 2000**
Handbook on U. S. Relations with Greece and Cyprus. Trade Cloth. American Hellenic Institute. Washington, DC. 1997. ISBN:0-941882-01-2, ISBN13: 978-0-941882-01-9. Dewey:327.730495. LCCN:2002-275273.
Audience: **f.**

Samii, Kuross A. **E183.8.I7S24 1987**
Involvement by Invitation: American Strategies of Containment in Iran. Trade Cloth. Pennsylvania State University Press. University Park, PA. 1987. 208p. ISBN:0-271-00490-8, ISBN13: 978-0-271-00490-7. Dewey:327.73055. LCCN:86-043035.
Audience: **f.** *Choice, 1988.*

Sater, William F. **E183.8.C4S27 1990**
Chile and the United States: Empires in Conflict. Trade Cloth. University of Georgia Press. Athens, GA. 1991. 256p. The United States and the Americas Ser. ISBN:0-8203-1249-5, ISBN13: 978-0-8203-1249-1. Dewey:327.83073. LCCN:90-035055.
Audience: **u,f.** *Choice, 1991.*

Saul, Norman E. **E183.8.R9S383 1996**
Concord and Conflict: The United States and Russia, 1867-1914. Trade Cloth. University Press of Kansas. Lawrence, KS. 1996. 672p. ISBN:0-7006-0754-4, ISBN13: 978-0-7006-0754-9. Dewey:303.48/273047. LCCN:95-025606.
Audience: **u,f.** *Choice, 1996.*

Saul, Norman E. **E183.8.S65S274 1991**
Distant Friends: The United States and Russia, 1763-1867. Trade Cloth. University Press of Kansas. Lawrence, KS. 1991. xii, 448p. ISBN:0-7006-0438-3, ISBN13: 978-0-7006-0438-8. Dewey:303.48/273047. LCCN:90-041807.
Audience: **u,f.** *Choice, 1991.*

Schaller, Michael **E183.8.C5S**
The United States Crusade in China, 1938-1945. Trade Paper. Books on Demand. Ann Arbor, MI. 380p. ISBN:0-8357-3581-8, ISBN13: 978-0-8357-3581-0. Dewey:940.53/22/73. LCCN:78-015032.
Audience: **u,f.**

Schirmer, Daniel B. & Shalom, Stephen R. (Editors) **DS679.P63 1987**
The Philippines Reader: A History of Colonialism, Neocolonialism, Dictatorship, and Resistance. Trade Cloth. South End Press. Cambridge, MA. 1987. 425p. International Studies ISBN:0-89608-276-8, ISBN13: 978-0-89608-276-2. Dewey:959.9/03. LCCN:86-014637.
Audience: **f.**

Schmitt, Karl Michael **E183.8.M6.S35 1974**
Mexico and United States, 1821 1973: Conflict and Coexistence. Ed. 99. Cloth Text. John Wiley & Sons, Inc. Hoboken, NJ. 1974. 288p. ISBN:0-471-76198-2, ISBN13: 978-0-471-76198-3. Dewey:327.72/073. LCCN:73-020327.
Audience: **u,f.** B

Shepard, Robert B. **E183.8.N55S48 1991**
Nigeria, Africa, and the United States: From Kennedy to Reagan. Trade Cloth. Indiana University Press. Bloomington, IN. 1991. 208p. ISBN:0-253-35209-6, ISBN13: 978-0-253-35209-5. Dewey:327.730669. LCCN:90-044509.
Audience: **f.** *Choice, 1992.*

Siegel, Katherine A. **E183.8.S65S56 1996**
Loans and Legitimacy: The Evolution of Soviet-American Relations, 1919-1933. Trade Cloth. University Press of Kentucky. Lexington, KY. 1996. 240p. ISBN:0-8131-1962-6, ISBN13: 978-0-8131-1962-5. Dewey:327,73047/09/041. LCCN:95-026338.
Audience: **u,f.** *Choice, 1996.*

Stanciu, Ion & Cernovodeanu, Paul **E183.8.R8S8 1985**
Distant Lands: The Genesis and Evolution of Romanian-American Relations. Trade Cloth. Eastern European Monographs. Bradenton, FL. 1986. 281p. ISBN:0-88033-088-0, ISBN13: 978-0-88033-088-6. Dewey:327.730498. LCCN:85-070783.
Audience: **f.**

Stephens, Elizabeth **E183.8.I7S74 2005**
U. S. Policy Toward Israel: The Role of Political Culture in Defining the "Special Relationship". Trade Cloth. Sussex Academic Press. Eastbourne, 2006. 339p. ISBN:1-84519-097-1, ISBN13: 978-1-84519-097-2. Dewey:327.7305694. LCCN:2005-009781.
Audience: **u,f.**

Stewart, Gordon T. **E183.8.C2S74 1992**
The American Response to Canada since 1776. Trade Cloth. Michigan State University Press. East Lansing, MI. 1992. 218p. Canadian Ser., No. 3 ISBN:0-87013-312-8, ISBN13: 978-0-87013-312-1. Dewey:327.73071. LCCN:92-053706.
Audience: **u,f.** *Choice, 1993.*

Stieglitz, Perry **E183.8.L28S75 1990**
In a Little Kingdom: The Tragedy of Laos, 1960-1980. Trade Cloth. M. E. Sharpe Inc. Armonk, NY. 1990. 232p. ISBN:0-87332-617-2, ISBN13: 978-0-87332-617-9. Dewey:303.48/2730594. LCCN:90-008069.
Audience: **u,f.**

Stueck, William W. **E183.8.K7**
The Road to Confrontation: American Policy Toward China and Korea, 1947-1950. Trade Paper. Books on Demand. Ann Arbor, MI. 336p. ISBN:0-8357-4402-7, ISBN13: 978-0-8357-4402-7. Dewey:327.73051. LCCN:80-011818.
Audience: **f.**

Swenson-Wright, John **E183.8.J3S94 2005**
Unequal Allies?: United States Security and Alliance Policy Toward Japan, 1945-1960. Trade Cloth. Stanford University Press. Palo Alto, CA. 2005. 400p. ISBN:0-8047-3961-7, ISBN13: 978-0-8047-3961-0. Dewey:327.73052/09/045. LCCN:2004-016215.
Audience: **u,f.** *Choice, 2006.*

Talbott, Strobe **E183.8.I4T35 2004**
Engaging India: Diplomacy, Democracy, and the Bomb. Trade Cloth. Brookings Institution Press. Washington, DC. 2004. 268p. ISBN:0-8157-8300-0, ISBN13: 978-0-8157-8300-8. Dewey:327.73054/09/049. LCCN:2004-012803.
Audience: **u,f.** *Choice, 2005.*

Tate, Merze **E183**
The United States and the Hawaiian Kingdom: A Political History. Trade Cloth. Greenwood Publishing Group, Inc. Portsmouth, NH. 1980. 374p. ISBN:0-313-22441-2, ISBN13: 978-0-313-22441-6. Dewey:996.9/02. LCCN:80-014045.
Audience: **f.** B

Thomas, A. M. **E183.8.S6T46 1997**
The American Predicament: Apartheid and United States Foreign Policy. Trade Cloth. Ashgate Publishing, Ltd. Aldershot, 1997. 144p. ISBN:1-85521-941-7, ISBN13: 978-1-85521-941-0. Dewey:327.73068. LCCN:97-035814.
Audience: **u,f.** *Choice, 1998.*

Tucker, Nancy B. **E183.8.C5T835 2001**
China Confidential: American Diplomats and Sino-American Relations, 1945-1996. Trade Cloth. Columbia University Press. New York, NY. 2000. 638p. ISBN:0-231-10630-0, ISBN13: 978-0-231-10630-6. Dewey:327.73051. LCCN:00-040445.
Audience: **u,f.** *Choice, 2001.*

Tucker, Nancy Bernkopf **E183.8.C5D26 2005**
Dangerous Strait: The U.S.—Taiwan—China Crisis. Trade Cloth. University of Tokyo Press. 2005. 288p. ISBN:0-231-13564-5, ISBN13: 978-0-231-13564-1. Dewey:327.73051/09/045. LCCN:2004-059373.
Audience: **u,f.** *Choice, 2005.*

Tucker, Nancy B. **E183.8.C5**
Patterns in the Dust: Chinese-American Relations and the Recognition Controversy, 1949-1950. William E. Leuchtenburg (Editor). Trade Cloth. Columbia University Press. New York, NY. 1983. 396p. ISBN:0-231-05362-2, ISBN13: 978-0-231-05362-4. Dewey:327.73051. LCCN:82-014724.
Audience: **f.** B

Tulchin, Joseph S. **E183.8.A7T85 1990**
Argentina and the United States: A Conflicted Relationship. Akira Iriye (Editor). Trade Cloth. Thomson Gale. Farmington Hills, MI. 1990. 193p. Twayne's International History Ser., No. 5 ISBN:0-8057-7900-0, ISBN13: 978-0-8057-7900-4. Dewey:327.73082. LCCN:89-026847.
Audience: **f.** *Choice, 1990.*

Ulam, Adam Bruno
Expansion and Coexistence. Ed. 6. Harcourt School Publishers. 1974. ISBN:0-03-038696-9, ISBN13: 978-0-03-038696-1.
Audience: **l,u,f.**

United States, Department of Defense Staff **E183.8.V5.P42**
The Pentagon Papers: The Defense Department History of United States Decisionmaking on Vietnam. Trade Cloth. Beacon Press. Boston, MA. 1971. ISBN:0-8070-0526-6, ISBN13: 978-0-8070-0526-2. Dewey:959.7/0432. LCCN:75-178049.
Audience: **l,u,f.** B

Varg, Paul A. **E183.8.C5V3 1980**
The Making of a Myth: The United States and China, 1897-1912. Trade Cloth. Greenwood Publishing Group, Inc. Portsmouth, NH. 1980. 184p. ISBN:0-313-22125-1, ISBN13: 978-0-313-22125-5. Dewey:327.51073. LCCN:79-025619.
Audience: **f.**

Wandycz, Piotr S. **E183.8.P7.W36**
The United States and Poland. Trade Cloth. Harvard University Press. Cambridge, MA. 1980. 474p. American Foreign Policy Library ISBN:0-674-92685-4, ISBN13: 978-0-674-92685-1. Dewey:327.73/0438. LCCN:79-011998.
Audience: **f.** B

Weihmiller, Gordon R. **E183.8.S65W44 1986**
U. S. - Soviet Summits: An Account of East-West Diplomacy at the Top, 1955-1985. Dusko Doder (Epilogue by), David D. Newsom (Foreword by). Trade Cloth. University Press of America, Inc. Lanham, MD. 1986. 230p. ISBN:0-8191-5442-3, ISBN13: 978-0-8191-5442-2. Dewey:327.73047. LCCN:86-011023.
Audience: **f.** *Choice, 1987.*

Welch, Richard E. Jr. **F259.H72R36 1985**
Response to Revolution: The United States and the Cuban Revolution, 1959-1961. Trade Cloth. University of North Carolina Press. Chapel Hill, NC. 1985. ix, 244p. ISBN:0-8078-1613-2, ISBN13: 978-0-8078-1613-4. Dewey:975.6/041/0924. LCCN:84-025604.
Audience: **f.** B *Choice, 1985.*

Williams, William Appleman **E183.8.R9W63**
American: Russian Relations 1781. Paper Text. Textbook Publishers. Temecula, CA. 2003. 367p. ISBN:0-7581-7445-4, ISBN13: 978-0-7581-7445-1. Dewey:327.73047.
Audience: **f.**

Woods, Randall B. **E183.8.G7W93 1990**
A Changing of the Guard: Anglo-American Relations, 1941-1946. Trade Cloth. University of North Carolina Press. Chapel Hill, NC. 1990. 484p. ISBN:0-8078-1877-1, ISBN13: 978-0-8078-1877-0. Dewey:337.73041/09/044. LCCN:89-022615.
Audience: **f.** *Choice, 1990.*

Woodward, Peter **E183.8.S73W66 2005**
U. S. Foreign Policy and the Horn of Africa. Trade Cloth. Ashgate Publishing, Ltd. Aldershot, 2006. 192p. U. S. Foreign Policy and Conflict in the Islamic World Ser. ISBN:0-7546-3580-5, ISBN13: 978-0-7546-3580-2. Dewey:327.73063. LCCN:2005-023190.
Audience: **u,f.** *Choice, 2006.*

Zhai, Qiang **E183.8.C5Z42 1994**
The Dragon, the Lion and the Eagle: Chinese-British-American Relations, 1949-1958. Trade Cloth. Kent State University Press. Kent, OH. 1994. 296p. American Diplomatic History Ser., No. 7 ISBN:0-87338-490-3, ISBN13: 978-0-87338-490-2. Dewey:951.05. LCCN:93-036348.
Audience: **f.** *Choice, 1994.*

Zi, Zhongyun **E183.8.C5Z54 2002**
No Exit?: The Origin and Evolution of U. S. Policy Toward China, 1945-1950. Ciyun Zhang & Yanli Jia (Translators), Michael H. Hunt (Foreword by). Trade Cloth. EastBridge. Norwalk, CT. 2003. 334p. Voices of Asia Ser. ISBN:1-891936-23-9, ISBN13: 978-1-891936-23-4. Dewey:327.73051/09/044. LCCN:2003-000168.
Audience: **u,f.** *Choice, 2004.*

United States > American History, by Period

Adams, Ephraim Douglass **E469.A25**
Great Britain and the American Civil War. Paper Text. Textbook

Publishers. Temecula, CA. 2003. ISBN:0-7581-4454-7, ISBN13: 978-0-7581-4454-6. Dewey:973.722.
Audience: **u,f.** BCL3

Anbinder, Tyler G. **E453.A52 1992**
Nativism and Slavery: The Northern Know Nothings and the Politics of the 1850s. Cloth Text. Oxford University Press, Inc. New York, NY. 1992. 352p. ISBN:0-19-507233-2, ISBN13: 978-0-19-507233-4. Dewey:320.973/09/034. LCCN:91-043352.
Audience: **f.** *Choice, 1993.*

Ayers, Edward L. **F215.A94 1992**
The Promise of the New South: Life after Reconstruction. Trade Cloth. Oxford University Press, Inc. New York, NY. 1992. 592p. ISBN:0-19-503756-1, ISBN13: 978-0-19-503756-2. Dewey:975/.041. LCCN:91-033070.
Audience: **u,f.** *Choice, 1993.*

Beale, Howard K. **E668.B354**
Critical Year: A Study of Andrew Johnson and Reconstruction. Trade Cloth. Continuum International Publishing Group, Ltd. London, 1958. ISBN:0-8044-1085-2, ISBN13: 978-0-8044-1085-4. Dewey:973.81. LCCN:58-009332.
Audience: **l,u,f.** BCL3

Beisner, Robert L. **E713.B47 1992**
Twelve Against the Empire: The Anti-Imperialists, 1898-1900. Trade Paper. Imprint Publications, Inc. Chicago, IL. 1992. 336p. ISBN:1-879176-10-6, ISBN13: 978-1-879176-10-2. Dewey:327.73. LCCN:93-158081.
Audience: **l,u,f.**

Belz, Herman **E457.2.B38 1997**
Abraham Lincoln: Constitutionalism and Equal Rights in the Civil War Era. Trade Cloth. Fordham University Press. Bronx, NY. 1997. 265p. The North's Civil War Ser., No. 2: ISBN:0-8232-1768-X, ISBN13: 978-0-8232-1768-7. Dewey:973.7. LCCN:97-009935.
Audience: **l,u,f.** *Choice, 1998.*

Belz, Herman **E459**
Reconstructing the Union: Theory and Policy During the Civil War. Trade Cloth. Greenwood Publishing Group, Inc. Portsmouth, NH. 1979. 336p. ISBN:0-313-20862-X, ISBN13: 978-0-313-20862-1. Dewey:973.7/1. LCCN:78-021311.
Audience: **l,u,f.** BCL3

Benedict, Michael L. **E668.B46**
A Compromise of Principle: Congressional Republicans and Reconstruction 1863-1869. Trade Cloth. W. W. Norton & Company, Inc. New York, NY. 1975. 493p. ISBN:0-393-05524-8, ISBN13: 978-0-393-05524-5. Dewey:973.8/1. LCCN:74-010645.
Audience: **l,u,f.** BCL3

Billington, Ray A. **BX1406.B5**
The Protestant Crusade, 1800-1860. Trade Cloth. Peter Smith Publisher, Inc. Magnolia, MA. 1980. ISBN:0-8446-1076-3, ISBN13: 978-0-8446-1076-4. Dewey:282.73.
Audience: **l,u,f.**

Blassingame, John W. **E443.B55 1979**
The Slave Community: Plantation Life in the Antebellum South. Ed. 2. Trade Cloth. Oxford University Press, Inc. New York, NY. 1979. 432p. ISBN:0-19-502562-8, ISBN13: 978-0-19-502562-0. Dewey:975/.00496073. LCCN:78-026890.
Audience: **u,f.** BCL3

Blight, David W. **E468.9.B58 2001**
Race and Reunion: The Civil War in American Memory. Trade Cloth. Harvard University Press. Cambridge, MA. 2001. 526p. Belknap Press Ser. ISBN:0-674-00332-2, ISBN13: 978-0-674-00332-3. Dewey:973.7. LCCN:00-042918.
Audience: **u,f.** *Choice, 2001.*

Botkin, Benjamin A. **PE1408.H393**
Civil War Treasury of Tales, Legends and Folklore. Warren Chapell (Illustrator). Cloth over Boards. BBS Publishing Corporation. Edison, NJ. 1981. 528p. ISBN:0-88394-049-3, ISBN13: 978-0-88394-049-5. Dewey:808.066.
Audience: **u,f.**

Brodsky, Alyn **E697.B84 2000**
Grover Cleveland: A Study in Character. Cloth over Boards. St. Martin's Press. Gordonville, VA. 2000. 512p. ISBN:0-312-26883-1, ISBN13: 978-0-312-26883-1. Dewey:973.8/5/092. LCCN:00-040258.
Audience: **u,f.**

Brown, Dee **E81.B75 2001**
Bury My Heart at Wounded Knee: An Indian History of the American West. Ed. 30. Cloth over Boards. Henry Holt & Company. New York, NY. 2001. 512p. ISBN:0-8050-6634-9, ISBN13: 978-0-8050-6634-0. Dewey:970.5. LCCN:00-040958.
Audience: **g,u,f.**

Cashman, Sean D. **E741.C27 1988**
America in the Age of the Titans: From the Rise of Theodore Roosevelt to the Death of FDR. Trade Cloth. New York University Press. New York, NY. 1988. 622p. ISBN:0-8147-1410-2, ISBN13: 978-0-8147-1410-2. Dewey:973.91. LCCN:87-031563.
Audience: **l,u,f.** *Choice, 1989.*

Cashman, Sean D. **E661.C38 1993**
America in the Gilded Age: From the Death of Lincoln to the Rise of Theodore Roosevelt. Ed. 3. Trade Paper. New York University Press. New York, NY. 1993. 445p. ISBN:0-8147-1495-1, ISBN13: 978-0-8147-1495-9. Dewey:973.8. LCCN:93-012999.
Audience: **l,u,f.**

Castel, Albert **E666.C23**
The Presidency of Andrew Johnson. Trade Cloth. University Press of Kansas. Lawrence, KS. 1979. x, 262p. American Presidency Ser. ISBN:0-7006-0190-2, ISBN13: 978-0-7006-0190-5. Dewey:973.8/1/0924. LCCN:79-011050.
Audience: **l,u,f.** BCL3

Chase, Salmon P. **E415.9.C4 A3**
Inside Lincoln's Cabinet. David Donald (Editor). Trade Cloth. Productivity Press. University Park, IL. 1986. ISBN:0-527-16200-0, ISBN13: 978-0-527-16200-9. Dewey:973.71.
Audience: **u,f.**

Chesnut, Mary Boykin Miller **E487**
Mary Chesnut's Civil War. C. Vann Woodward (Editor). Cloth over Boards. Yale University Press. Cumberland, RI. 1981. 892p. ISBN:0-300-02459-2, ISBN13: 978-0-300-02459-3. Dewey:973.7/82. LCCN:80-036661.
Audience: **u,f.** BCL3

Cole, Arthur C. **E415.7.C69 1971**
The Irrepressible Conflict, 1850-1865. Trade Cloth. Scholarly Press, Inc. Saint Clair Shores, MI. 1971. xv, 468p.

ISBN:0-403-00930-8, ISBN13: 978-0-403-00930-5. Dewey:973.6. LCCN:71-144952.
Audience: **l,u,f.** B

Connelly, Thomas Lawrence **E467.1.L4**
The Marble Man: Robert E. Lee and His Image in American Society. Trade Paper. Louisiana State University Press. Baton Rouge, LA. 1978. 272p. ISBN:0-8071-0474-4, ISBN13: 978-0-8071-0474-3. Dewey:973.7/42/0924. LCCN:76-041778.
Audience: **f.**

Connelly, Thomas Lawrence & Bellows, Barbara L. **E487**
God and General Longstreet: The Lost Cause and the Southern Mind. Trade Cloth. Louisiana State University Press. Baton Rouge, LA. 1995. x, 158p. ISBN:0-8071-2014-6, ISBN13: 978-0-8071-2014-9. Dewey:973.713. LCCN:82-000033.
Audience: **u,f.**

Connelly, Thomas Lawrence & Jones, Archer **E487.C8 1998**
The Politics of Command: Factions and Ideas in Confederate Strategy. Trade Paper. Louisiana State University Press. Baton Rouge, LA. 1998. xvi, 236p. ISBN:0-8071-2349-8, ISBN13: 978-0-8071-2349-2. Dewey:973.7/3013. LCCN:99-160634.
Audience: **u,f.**

Cornish, Dudley T. **E540.N3C77 1987**
The Sable Arm: Black Troops in the Union Army, 1861-1865. Herman Hattaway (Foreword by). Trade Cloth. University Press of Kansas. Lawrence, KS. 2004. xviii, 342p. Modern War Studies ISBN:0-7006-0328-X, ISBN13: 978-0-7006-0328-2. Dewey:973.7/415. LCCN:87-050106.
Audience: **l,u,f.**

Cox, LaWanda **E457.2.C84 1994**
Lincoln and Black Freedom: A Study in Presidential Leadership. James M. McPherson (Foreword by). Trade Paper. University of South Carolina Press. Columbia, SC. 1994. 270p. ISBN:0-87249-997-9, ISBN13: 978-0-87249-997-3. Dewey:973.7/092/4. LCCN:93-037859.
Audience: **u,f.** B

Craven, Avery O. **QA184.2.L39**
The Growth of Southern Nationalism, 1848-1861. Trade Cloth. Louisiana State University Press. Baton Rouge, LA. 1953. x, 434p. A History of the South Ser., Vol. 6 ISBN:0-8071-0006-4, ISBN13: 978-0-8071-0006-6. Dewey:512/.55. LCCN:53-011470.
Audience: **u,f.** B

Craven, Avery O. **E649.C89**
The Repressible Conflict, 1830-1861. Trade Cloth. A M S Press, Inc. New York, NY. ISBN:0-404-20070-2, ISBN13: 978-0-404-20070-1. Dewey:973.711. LCCN:83-045425.
Audience: **l,u,f.**

Crook, D. P. **E469**
The North the South, and the Powers. Cloth Text. John Wiley & Sons, Inc. Hoboken, NJ. 1974. 405p. ISBN:0-471-18855-7, ISBN13: 978-0-471-18855-1. Dewey:973.7/2. LCCN:73-016355.
Audience: **l,u,f.** B

Current, Richard Nelson **E668.C985 1988**
Those Terrible Carpetbaggers: A Reinterpretation. Oxford University Press, Inc. 1988. ISBN:0-19-504872-5, ISBN13: 978-0-19-504872-8.
Audience: **u,f.**

Davis, David Brion **E441.D248 2003**
Challenging the Boundaries of Slavery. Trade Cloth. Harvard University Press. Cambridge, MA. 2003. 128p. The Nathan I. Huggins Lectures ISBN:0-674-01182-1, ISBN13: 978-0-674-01182-3. Dewey:306.3/62/0973. LCCN:2003-041746.
Audience: **u,f.**

Davis, William C. **E487**
The Cause Lost: Myths and Realities of the Confederacy. Trade Paper. University Press of Kansas. Lawrence, KS. 2003. xii, 224p. Modern War Studies ISBN:0-7006-1254-8, ISBN13: 978-0-7006-1254-3. Dewey:973.7/13. LCCN:96-014237.
Audience: **l,u,f.** *Choice, 1997.*

Davis, William C. **E468**
The Commanders of the Civil War. Trade Cloth. Salamander Company. Scotts Valley, CA. 2004. 256p. ISBN:0-86101-395-6, ISBN13: 978-0-86101-395-1. Dewey:973.7/0922.
Audience: **l,u,f.**

Dodd, William E. **E467.1.D26D8 1997**
Jefferson Davis. Steven E. Woodworth (Introduction by). Trade Paper. University of Nebraska Press. Lincoln, NE. 1997. 391p. ISBN:0-8032-6609-X, ISBN13: 978-0-8032-6609-4. Dewey:973.7/13/092. LCCN:97-012862.
Audience: **l,u,f.**

Doenecke, Justus D. **E686.D63**
The Presidencies of James A. Garfield and Chester A. Arthur. Trade Cloth. University Press of Kansas. Lawrence, KS. 1981. xiv, 230p. American Presidency Ser. ISBN:0-7006-0208-9, ISBN13: 978-0-7006-0208-7. Dewey:973.8/4. LCCN:80-018957.
Audience: **l,u,f.** B

Donald, David Herbert **E457.D66 1995**
Lincoln. Trade Cloth. Simon & Schuster. New York, NY. 1995. 720p. ISBN:0-684-80846-3, ISBN13: 978-0-684-80846-8. Dewey:973.7/092. LCCN:95-004782.
Audience: **l,u,f.** *Choice, 1996.*

Donald, David Herbert (Editor) **E462**
Why the North Won the Civil War. Trade Paper. Simon & Schuster. New York, NY. 1996. 128p. ISBN:0-684-82506-6, ISBN13: 978-0-684-82506-9. Dewey:973.7.
Audience: **l,u,f.** B

Dorris, Jonathon T. **KF7221.D6 1977**
Pardon and Amnesty under Lincoln and Johnson: The Restoration of the Confederates to Their Rights and Privileges, 1861-1898. J. C. Randall (Introduction by). Trade Cloth. Greenwood Publishing Group, Inc. Portsmouth, NH. 1977. 459p. ISBN:0-8371-9646-9, ISBN13: 978-0-8371-9646-6. Dewey:343/.73/012. LCCN:77-005940.
Audience: **l,u,f.**

Douglass, Frederick **E449.D749 2000**
Narrative of the Life of Frederick Douglass: An American Slave. Trade Cloth. Holt, Rinehart & Winston. Austin, TX. 2000. xxii, 201p. HRW Library ISBN:0-03-055454-3, ISBN13: 978-0-03-055454-4. Dewey:973.7/092. LCCN:2001-268809.
Audience: **u,f.**

Douglass, Frederick **E449.D738 2003**
The Frederick Douglass Papers: Autobiographical Writings. John W. Blassingame, John R. McKivigan & Peter P. Hinks (Editors). Cloth over Boards. Yale University Press. Cumberland, RI.

2003. 528p. The Frederick Douglas Papers, Vol. 2 ISBN:0-300-09173-7, ISBN13: 978-0-300-09173-1. Dewey:973.7092. LCCN:2003-005833.
Audience: **g,l,u,f.**

DuBois, Ellen Carol **JK1896**
Feminism and Suffrage: The Emergence of an Independent Women's Movement in America 1848-1869. Book, Other. Cornell University Press. Ithaca, NY. 1978. 224p. ISBN:0-8014-1043-6, ISBN13: 978-0-8014-1043-7. Dewey:324/.3/0973. LCCN:77-090902.
Audience: **u,f.** B

Dunning, William A. **E178.A54**
Reconstruction, Political And Economic, 1865-1877. Trade Cloth. Peter Smith Publisher, Inc. Magnolia, MA. 1984. ISBN:0-8446-2010-6, ISBN13: 978-0-8446-2010-7. Dewey:973.8.
Audience: **u,f.**

Eaton, Clement **E467.1.D26**
Jefferson Davis: The Sphinx of the Confederacy. Trade Cloth. Simon & Schuster. New York, NY. 1977. xiii, 334p. ISBN:0-02-908700-7, ISBN13: 978-0-02-908700-8. Dewey:973.7/13/0924. LCCN:77-002512.
Audience: **l,u,f.** B

Fehrenbacher, Don E. **KF4545.S5.F43**
The Dred Scott Case: Its Significance in American Law and Politics. Trade Cloth. Oxford University Press, Inc. New York, NY. 1978. 754p. ISBN:0-19-502403-6, ISBN13: 978-0-19-502403-6. Dewey:342.7/3087. LCCN:78-004665.
Audience: **l,u,f.** B

Fehrenbacher, Don E. & Fehrenbacher, Virginia (Editors) **E457.99.R43 1996**
Recollected Words of Abraham Lincoln. Trade Cloth. Stanford University Press. Palo Alto, CA. 1996. 648p. ISBN:0-8047-2636-1, ISBN13: 978-0-8047-2636-8. Dewey:973.7/092. LCCN:95-037774.
Audience: **l,u,f.**

Fehrenbacher, Don E. **E446.F45 2001**
The Slaveholding Republic: An Account of the United States Government's Relations to Slavery. Ward M. McAfee (Editor). Trade Cloth. Oxford University Press, Inc. New York, NY. 2001. 480p. ISBN:0-19-514177-6, ISBN13: 978-0-19-514177-1. Dewey:326/.0973. LCCN:00-039197.
Audience: **u,f.**

Fellman, Michael, et al. **E470.L72**
Lincoln's Generals. Stephen W. Sears, John Y. Simon & Mark E. Neely Jr. (Authors), Gabor S. Boritt (Editor). Trade Paper. Oxford University Press, Inc. New York, NY. 1995. 272p. ISBN:0-19-510110-3, ISBN13: 978-0-19-510110-2. Dewey:973.7/3.
Audience: **l,u,f.**

Filler, Louis **E449.F493 1986**
Crusade Against Slavery: Friends, Foes, and Reforms 1820-1860. Ed. 2. Keith Irvine (Editor). Trade Cloth. Reference Publications, Inc. Algonac, MI. 1986. 400p. ISBN:0-917256-29-8, ISBN13: 978-0-917256-29-5. Dewey:326/.0973. LCCN:85-030100.
Audience: **f.** B *Choice, 1987.*

Fite, Gilbert C. **S441.F48**
Farmers' Frontier, 1865-1900. Trade Cloth. University of New Mexico Press. Albuquerque, NM. 1966. ISBN:0-318-82388-8, ISBN13: 978-0-318-82388-1. Dewey:333.760973.
Audience: **l,u,f.**

Fitzhugh, George **HN0079.A13F5**
Sociology for the South: Or the Failure of Free Society. Trade Cloth. Ayer Company Publishers, Inc. Manchester, NH. 312p. ISBN:0-8337-1141-5, ISBN13: 978-0-8337-1141-0. Dewey:309.175. LCCN:67-000622.
Audience: **f.**

Fitzhugh, George **E449**
Cannibals All!, or, Slaves Without Masters. C. Vann Woodward (Editor). Trade Paper. Harvard University Press. Cambridge, MA. 1960. 306p. The John Harvard Library ISBN:0-674-09451-4, ISBN13: 978-0-674-09451-2. Dewey:326.973. LCCN:60-005400.
Audience: **l,u,f.**

Foner, Eric **E436**
Free Soil, Free Labor, Free Men: The Ideology of the Republican Party Before the Civil War. Trade Paper. Oxford University Press, Inc. New York, NY. 1971. 366p. ISBN:0-19-501352-2, ISBN13: 978-0-19-501352-8. Dewey:973.6.
Audience: **l,u,f.**

Foner, Eric **E668.F662 1990**
A Short History of Reconstruction. Trade Cloth. HarperCollins Publishers. New York, NY. 1990. 288p. ISBN:0-06-055182-8, ISBN13: 978-0-06-055182-7. Dewey:973.8. LCCN:89-045653.
Audience: **g,l,u,f.**

Foner, Philip S. **E469.8.F66 1981**
British Labor and the American Civil War. Trade Cloth. Holmes & Meier Publishers, Inc. Teaneck, NJ. 1981. 130p. ISBN:0-8419-0671-8, ISBN13: 978-0-8419-0671-6. Dewey:973.7. LCCN:80-026162.
Audience: **l,u,f.** B

Foner, Philip S. **E185**
History of Black Americans: From the Compromise of 1850 to the End of the Civil War. Trade Cloth. Greenwood Publishing Group, Inc. Portsmouth, NH. 1983. 539p. Contributions in American History Ser., No. 103 ISBN:0-8371-7967-X, ISBN13: 978-0-8371-7967-4. Dewey:973/.0496073. LCCN:74-005987.
Audience: **g,l,u,f.** B

Foote, Shelby **E468**
Fort Sumter to Perryville. Trade Cloth. Random House, Inc. New York, NY. 1958. 848p. ISBN:0-394-41948-0, ISBN13: 978-0-394-41948-0.
Audience: **g,l,u,f.**

Foote, Shelby **E468**
Fredericksburg to Meridian. Trade Cloth. Random House, Inc. New York, NY. 1963. 1000p. Civil War Ser., No. 2 ISBN:0-394-41951-0, ISBN13: 978-0-394-41951-0. Dewey:973.7.
Audience: **g,l,u,f.**

Foote, Shelby **E468.F7**
Red River to Appomattox. Trade Cloth. Random House, Inc. New York, NY. 1974. 1120p. Civil War Ser., No. 3 ISBN:0-394-46512-1, ISBN13: 978-0-394-46512-8. Dewey:973.7. LCCN:58-009882.
Audience: **g,l,u,f.**

Fornieri, Joseph **E457.92**
Language of Liberty: Political. Trade Cloth. Regnery Publishing, Incorporated, An Eagle Publishing Company. Washington, DC. 2004. 824p. ISBN:0-89526-176-6, ISBN13: 978-0-89526-176-2. Dewey:973.7.
Audience: **f.**

Fornieri, Joseph R. **E457.2.F73 2003**
Abraham Lincoln's Political Faith. Trade Cloth. Northern Illinois University Press. DeKalb, IL. 2003. 218p. ISBN:0-87580-315-6, ISBN13: 978-0-87580-315-9. Dewey:973.7/092. LCCN:2002-040996.
Audience: **u,f.**

Fredrickson, George M. **E468.9.F83 1993**
The Inner Civil War: Northern Intellectuals and the Crisis of the Union. Trade Paper. University of Illinois Press. Champaign, IL. 1993. 296p. ISBN:0-252-06274-4, ISBN13: 978-0-252-06274-2. Dewey:973.7/15. LCCN:92-036773.
Audience: **u,f.**

Freehling, William W. **E468.9**
The Road to Disunion: Bleeding Kansas to Fort Sumter, Vol. II. Trade Cloth. Oxford University Press, Inc. New York, NY. 2005. 608p. ISBN:0-19-505815-1, ISBN13: 978-0-19-505815-4. Dewey:973.7.
Audience: **u,f.**

Freeman, Douglas Southall **E470.2**
Lee's Lieutenants. Stephen Sears (Abridged by), James M. McPherson (Introduction by). Trade Cloth. William S. Konecky Associates, Inc. Old Saybrook, CT. 2005. 910p. ISBN:1-56852-509-5, ISBN13: 978-1-56852-509-9. Dewey:973.73.
Audience: **l,u,f.**

Fuller, J. F. C. **E468.F96**
Grant and Lee: A Study in Personality and Generalship. Trade Cloth. Indiana University Press. Bloomington, IN. 1957. 336p. ISBN:0-253-13400-5, ISBN13: 978-0-253-13400-4. Dewey:973.7. LCCN:57-010723.
Audience: **l,u,f.**

Gara, Larry **E450.G22 1996**
The Liberty Line: The Legend of the Underground Railroad. Trade Paper. University Press of Kentucky. Lexington, KY. 1996. 216p. ISBN:0-8131-0864-0, ISBN13: 978-0-8131-0864-3. Dewey:973.7/115. LCCN:95-026336.
Audience: **l,u,f.**

Garrison, W. L. **E449**
I Will Be Heard 1822-1835, Vol. 1. Walter M. Merrill (Editor). Trade Cloth. Harvard University Press. Cambridge, MA. 2002. 658p. Letters of William Lloyd Garrison Ser., Vol. 1 ISBN:0-674-52660-0, ISBN13: 978-0-674-52660-0. Dewey:326/.0924. LCCN:75-133210.
Audience: **f.**

Genovese, Eugene D. **E185.6**
Roll, Jordan, Roll: The World the Slaves Made. Trade Cloth. Random House, Inc. New York, NY. 1974. xxii, 823p. ISBN:0-394-49131-9, ISBN13: 978-0-394-49131-8. Dewey:975/.00496073. LCCN:74-004760.
Audience: **g,l,u,f.**

Gienapp, William E. **E457.G46 2001**
Abraham Lincoln and Civil War America: A Biography. Trade Cloth. Oxford University Press, Inc. New York, NY. 2002. 256p. ISBN:0-19-515099-6, ISBN13: 978-0-19-515099-5. Dewey:973.7/092. LCCN:2001-050056.
Audience: **g,l,u,f.**

Gienapp, William E. **JK2357**
The Origins of the Republican Party, 1852-1856. Trade Cloth. Oxford University Press, Inc. New York, NY. 1987. 584p. ISBN:0-19-504100-3, ISBN13: 978-0-19-504100-2. Dewey:324.273/04/09. LCCN:86-008399.
Audience: **u,f.** *Choice, 1987.*

Glad, Paul W. **E664.B87G55**
Trumpet Soundeth: William Jennings Bryan and His Democracy, 1896-1912. Trade Paper. University of Nebraska Press. Lincoln, NE. 1966. xiv, 242p. ISBN:0-8032-5073-8, ISBN13: 978-0-8032-5073-4. Dewey:923.273. LCCN:60-012259.
Audience: **u,f.**

Goodman, Paul **E449.G67 1998**
Of One Blood: Abolitionism and the Origins of Racial Equality. Trade Cloth. University of California Press. Berkeley, CA. 1998. 324p. ISBN:0-520-20794-7, ISBN13: 978-0-520-20794-3. Dewey:973.7/114. LCCN:97-045560.
Audience: **u,f.** *Choice, 1999.*

Goodrich, Thomas **F685.G66 1998**
War to the Knife: Bleeding Kansas, 1854-1861. Trade Cloth. Stackpole Books. Mechanicsburg, PA. 1998. 296p. ISBN:0-8117-1921-9, ISBN13: 978-0-8117-1921-6. Dewey:978.1/02. LCCN:98-009293.
Audience: **f.**

Goodwyn, Lawrence **E661.G67**
Democratic Promise: The Populist Moment in America. Oxford University Press, Inc. 1976. ISBN:0-19-501996-2, ISBN13: 978-0-19-501996-4.
Audience: **l,u,f.**

Gould, Lewis L. **E711.G68**
The Presidency of William McKinley. Trade Cloth. University Press of Kansas. Lawrence, KS. 1981. xiv, 294p. American Presidency Ser. ISBN:0-7006-0206-2, ISBN13: 978-0-7006-0206-3. Dewey:973.8/8/0924. LCCN:80-016022.
Audience: **l,u,f.**

Grimsley, Mark **E487.G78 1995**
The Hard Hand of War: Union Military Policy Toward Southern Civilians, 1861-1865. Trade Cloth. Cambridge University Press. New York, NY. 1995. 256p. ISBN:0-521-46257-6, ISBN13: 978-0-521-46257-0. Dewey:973.7. LCCN:95-022808.
Audience: **f.** *Choice, 1996.*

Grimsley, Mark & Simpson, Brooks D. (Editors) **E487**
The Collapse of the Confederacy. Trade Cloth. University of Nebraska Press. Lincoln, NE. 2005. 201p. Key Issues of the Civil War Era Ser. ISBN:0-8032-7103-4, ISBN13: 978-0-8032-7103-6. Dewey:973.7/13. LCCN:00-059969.
Audience: **l,u,f.**

Hattaway, Herman **E470.H345 1997**
Shades of Blue and Gray: An Introductory Military History of the Civil War. Trade Cloth. University of Missouri Press. Columbia, MO. 1997. 281p. ISBN:0-8262-1107-0, ISBN13: 978-0-8262-1107-1. Dewey:973.7/3. LCCN:97-004455.
Audience: **g,l,u,f.**

Hattaway, Herman & Beringer, Richard E. **E467.1.D26H38 2002**
Jefferson Davis, Confederate President. Trade Cloth. University Press of Kansas. Lawrence, KS. 2002. xxiv, 542p. ISBN:0-7006-1170-3, ISBN13: 978-0-7006-1170-6. Dewey:973.7/13/092. LCCN:2001-007131.
Audience: **l,u,f.** *Choice, 2003.*

Hattaway, Herman & Jones, Archer **E470.H34 1991**
How the North Won: A Military History of the Civil War. Trade Paper. University of Illinois Press. Champaign, IL. 1991. 784p. ISBN:0-252-06210-8, ISBN13: 978-0-252-06210-0. Dewey:973.7/3. LCCN:91-012244.
Audience: **g,l,u,f.**

Helper, Hinton Rowan **E0449.H483**
The Impending Crisis of the South: How to Meet It. Trade Paper. Books on Demand. Ann Arbor, MI. 420p. ISBN:0-598-86479-2, ISBN13: 978-0-598-86479-6. Dewey:326/.0973. LCCN:13-000971.
Audience: **u,f.**

Hesseltine, William B. (Editor) **E464.H4**
The Tragic Conflict. Trade Cloth. George Braziller Inc. New York, NY. 1988. American Epochs Ser. ISBN:0-8076-0169-1, ISBN13: 978-0-8076-0169-3. Dewey:973.7. LCCN:62-009693.
Audience: **l,u,f.**

Hesseltine, William Best **E611.H44**
Civil War Prisons: A Study in War Psychology. Paper Text. Classic Textbooks. Murrieta, CA. 1930. 290p. ISBN:1-4047-6188-8, ISBN13: 978-1-4047-6188-9. Dewey:973.7/7.
Audience: **f.**

Holt, Michael F. **JK201**
Political Crisis of the 1850's. Cloth Text. John Wiley & Sons, Inc. Hoboken, NJ. 1978. 330p. Critical Episodes in American Politics Ser. ISBN:0-471-40840-9, ISBN13: 978-0-471-40840-6. Dewey:320.973. LCCN:77-013564.
Audience: **l,u,f.** B

Holt, Michael F. **E415.7.H75 1991**
Political Parties and American Political Development from the Age of Jackson to the Age of Lincoln. Cloth Text. Louisiana State University Press. Baton Rouge, LA. 1992. 368p. ISBN:0-8071-1728-5, ISBN13: 978-0-8071-1728-6. Dewey:320.973. LCCN:91-031506.
Audience: **u,f.** *Choice, 1993.*

Hoogenboom, Ari **E681.H69 1988**
The Presidency of Rutherford B. Hayes. Trade Cloth. University Press of Kansas. Lawrence, KS. 1988. x, 278p. American Presidency Ser. ISBN:0-7006-0338-7, ISBN13: 978-0-7006-0338-1. Dewey:973.8/3/0924. LCCN:88-005709.
Audience: **l,u,f.** *Choice, 1989.*

Jessup, Philip C. **E664.R7J5**
Elihu Root. Trade Cloth. Shoe String Press, Inc. North Haven, CT. 1964. ISBN:0-208-00492-0, ISBN13: 978-0-208-00492-5. Dewey:923.273.
Audience: **f.** B

Johannsen, Robert W. **E415.9.D73J55 1997**
Stephen A. Douglas. Trade Paper. University of Illinois Press. Champaign, IL. 1997. 993p. ISBN:0-252-06635-9, ISBN13: 978-0-252-06635-1. Dewey:973.6/8/092. LCCN:96-044592.
Audience: **l,u,f.** B

Jones, Archer **E470.J74 1992**
Civil War Command and Strategy: The Process of Victory and Defeat. Trade Cloth. Simon & Schuster. New York, NY. 1992. 338p. ISBN:0-02-916635-7, ISBN13: 978-0-02-916635-2. Dewey:973.7/301. LCCN:91-044224.
Audience: **u,f.**

Jordan, Winthrop D. **E446.J67**
White Man's Burden: Historical Origins of Racism in the United States. Trade Cloth. Oxford University Press, Inc. New York, NY. 1974. xvi, 229p. ISBN:0-19-501742-0, ISBN13: 978-0-19-501742-7. Dewey:301.45/19/6073. LCCN:73-086980.
Audience: **u,f.** B

Klement, Frank L. **E458.8**
Dark Lanterns: Secret Political Societies, Conspiracies and Treason Trials in the Civil War. Trade Paper. Louisiana State University Press. Baton Rouge, LA. 1984. 263p. ISBN:0-8071-1567-3, ISBN13: 978-0-8071-1567-1. Dewey:973.71. LCCN:84-000834.
Audience: **l,u,f.**

Klement, Frank L. **E415.9.V2K55 1998**
The Limits of Dissent: Clement L. Vallandigham and the Civil War. Steven K. Rogstad (Introduction by). Trade Cloth. Fordham University Press. Bronx, NY. 1998. 351p. The North's Civil War Ser., No. 8: ISBN:0-8232-1890-2, ISBN13: 978-0-8232-1890-5. Dewey:973.7/1//092. LCCN:98-047502.
Audience: **f.**

Kraditor, Aileen S. **E449.K7 1989**
Means and Ends in American Abolitionism: Garrison and His Critics on Strategy and Tactics, 1834-1850. Trade Paper. Ivan R. Dee Publisher. Blue Ridge Summit, PA. 1989. 312p. ISBN:0-929587-16-2, ISBN13: 978-0-929587-16-5. Dewey:973.7/114. LCCN:89-012018.
Audience: **l,u,f.** B

LaFeber, Walter **E469**
The New Empire: An Interpretation of American Expansion, 1860-1898. Trade Cloth. Cornell University Press. Ithaca, NY. 1967. 457p. ISBN:0-8014-0241-7, ISBN13: 978-0-8014-0241-8. Dewey:973.7/22.
Audience: **g,l,u,f.** B

Leech, Margaret **E711.6**
In the Days of McKinley: William McKinley. Trade Cloth. American Political Biography. Newtown, CT. 1999. 686p. Signature Ser. ISBN:0-945707-24-X, ISBN13: 978-0-945707-24-0. Dewey:973.8/8/095. LCCN:99-076373.
Audience: **l,u,f.**

Lerner, Gerda **E449.G865L47 2004**
The Grimke Sisters from South Carolina. Ed. 2. Trade Paper. University of North Carolina Press. Chapel Hill, NC. 2004. 464p. ISBN:0-8078-5566-9, ISBN13: 978-0-8078-5566-9. Dewey:326/.8/0922757 B. LCCN:2004-049750.
Audience: **l,u,f.**

Linderman, Gerald F. **E468.9.L56 1987**
Embattled Courage: The Experience of Battle in the American Civil War. Trade Cloth. Simon & Schuster. New York, NY.

1987. 288p. ISBN:0-02-919760-0, ISBN13: 978-0-02-919760-8. Dewey:973.7. LCCN:86-033515.
Audience: **g,l,u,f.** *Choice, 1987.*

McFeely, William S. **E467.1.L4**
Grant: A Biography. Katherine E. Speirs (Editor). Trade Cloth. American Political Biography. Newtown, CT. 1996. 492p. Signature Ser. ISBN:0-945707-15-0, ISBN13: 978-0-945707-15-8. Dewey:973.8/2/0924. LCCN:96-085992.
Audience: **l,u,f.**

McPherson, James M. **E173.O94**
Battle Cry of Freedom: The Era of the Civil War. Trade Cloth. Oxford University Press, Inc. New York, NY. 1988. 928p. Oxford History of the United States Ser., Vol. 6 ISBN:0-19-503863-0, ISBN13: 978-0-19-503863-7. Dewey:973.7/3. LCCN:87-011045.
Audience: **g,l,u,f.** *Choice, 1988.*

McPherson, James M. **E468.M23**
Ordeal by Fire: The Civil War and Reconstruction. Trade Cloth. Alfred A. Knopf Inc. New York, NY. 1982. ISBN:0-394-52470-5, ISBN13: 978-0-394-52470-2. Dewey:973.7.
Audience: **g,l,u,f.**

McPherson, James M. **E449.M176**
Struggle for Equality: Abolitionists and the Negro in the Civil War and Reconstruction. Trade Cloth. Princeton University Press. Princeton, NJ. 1964. 488p. ISBN:0-691-04566-6, ISBN13: 978-0-691-04566-5. Dewey:973.7.
Audience: **l,u,f.**

Millis, Walter **E715.M76 1989**
The Martial Spirit. Trade Paper. Ivan R. Dee Publisher. Blue Ridge Summit, PA. 1989. 444p. ISBN:0-929587-07-3, ISBN13: 978-0-929587-07-3. Dewey:973.88. LCCN:89-123625.
Audience: **f.**

Neely, Mark E. Jr. **E457.N49 1993**
The Last Best Hope of Earth: Abraham Lincoln and the Promise of America. Trade Cloth. Harvard University Press. Cambridge, MA. 1993. 320p. ISBN:0-674-51125-5, ISBN13: 978-0-674-51125-5. Dewey:973.7/092. LCCN:93-022863.
Audience: **u,f.** *Choice, 1994.*

Neely, Mark E. Jr. **E487.N44 1999**
Southern Rights: Political Prisoners and the Myth of Confederate Constitutionalism. Trade Cloth. University Press of Virginia. Charlottesville, VA. 1999. vii, 212p. Nation Divided Ser. ISBN:0-8139-1894-4, ISBN13: 978-0-8139-1894-5. Dewey:973.7/72. LCCN:99-025230.
Audience: **u,f.** *Choice, 2000.*

Neely, Mark E. Jr. **JK2260.N445 2002**
The Union Divided: Party Conflict in the Civil War North. Trade Cloth. Harvard University Press. Cambridge, MA. 2002. 272p. ISBN:0-674-00742-5, ISBN13: 978-0-674-00742-0. Dewey:320.973/09/034. LCCN:2001-039873.
Audience: **u,f.**

Nichols, Roy F. **E0436.N56**
The Disruption of American Democracy. Trade Cloth. A M S Press, Inc. New York, NY. 1983. ISBN:0-404-20190-3, ISBN13: 978-0-404-20190-6. Dewey:973.66. LCCN:83-045826.
Audience: **l,u,f.**

Nichols, Roy F. & Berwanger, Eugene H. **E415.7.N5 1982**
The Stakes of Power: 1845-1877. Trade Cloth. Farrar, Straus & Giroux. New York, NY. 1982. 258p. Making of America Ser. ISBN:0-8090-8801-0, ISBN13: 978-0-8090-8801-0. Dewey:973.6. LCCN:81-013480.
Audience: **u,f.**

Oates, Stephen B. **E451.O17 1984**
To Purge This Land with Blood: A Biography of John Brown. Ed. 2. Trade Paper. University of Massachusetts Press. Amherst, MA. 1984. 448p. ISBN:0-87023-458-7, ISBN13: 978-0-87023-458-3. Dewey:973.6/8/0924. LCCN:84-002635.
Audience: **l,u,f.**

Owsley, Frank L. **JK9887**
State Rights in the Confederacy. Trade Cloth. Peter Smith Publisher, Inc. Magnolia, MA. 1990. ISBN:0-8446-1337-1, ISBN13: 978-0-8446-1337-6. Dewey:973.713.
Audience: **f.**

Owsley, Frank Lawrence **E488.O85**
King Cotton Diplomacy: Foreign Relations of the Confederate States of America. Paper Text. Textbook Publishers. Temecula, CA. 2003. xxiii, 614p. ISBN:0-7581-2509-7, ISBN13: 978-0-7581-2509-5. Dewey:973.721.
Audience: **l,u,f.**

Paludan, Phillip S. **E468.9.P35 1996**
A People's Contest: The Union and Civil War, 1861-1865. Ed. 2. Trade Paper. University Press of Kansas. Lawrence, KS. 1996. 524p. Modern World Studies ISBN:0-7006-0812-5, ISBN13: 978-0-7006-0812-6. Dewey:973.7. LCCN:96-021303.
Audience: **l,u,f.** *Choice, 1989.*

Paludan, Phillip S. **E457.P18 1994**
The Presidency of Abraham Lincoln. Trade Cloth. University Press of Kansas. Lawrence, KS. 1994. xx, 388p. American Presidency Ser. ISBN:0-7006-0671-8, ISBN13: 978-0-7006-0671-9. Dewey:973.7/092. LCCN:93-046830.
Audience: **l,u,f.** *Choice, 1994.*

Patrick, Rembert W. **E487.P3**
Jefferson Davis and His Cabinet. Trade Cloth. A M S Press, Inc. New York, NY. ISBN:0-404-20197-0, ISBN13: 978-0-404-20197-5. Dewey:973.716. LCCN:83-045832.
Audience: **f.**

Perman, Michael **F216.P47**
The Road to Redemption: Southern Politics, 1869-1879. Trade Paper. University of North Carolina Press. Chapel Hill, NC. 1985. 368p. Fred W. Morrison Series in Southern Studies ISBN:0-8078-4141-2, ISBN13: 978-0-8078-4141-9. Dewey:973.8/2. LCCN:83-012498.
Audience: **f.**

Peskin, Allan **E403.1.S4P47 2003**
Winfield Scott and the Profession of Arms. Trade Cloth. Kent State University Press. Kent, OH. 2004. 328p. ISBN:0-87338-774-0, ISBN13: 978-0-87338-774-3. Dewey:355/.0092. LCCN:2003-004414.
Audience: **f.** *Choice, 2004.*

Peskin, Allan & Davis, Jim **E687.P47 1999**
Garfield. Trade Cloth. Kent State University Press. Kent, OH.

1998. 720p. ISBN:0-87338-210-2, ISBN13: 978-0-87338-210-6. Dewey:973.8/4/092 B. LCCN:77-015630.
Audience: **l,u,f.** ℬ

Pletcher, David M. **E686**
Awkward Years: American Foreign Relations Under Garfield and Arthur. Trade Cloth. University of Missouri Press. Columbia, MO. 1962. 400p. ISBN:0-8262-0143-1, ISBN13: 978-0-8262-0143-0. Dewey:973.84. LCCN:62-015589.
Audience: **l,u,f.** ℬ

Pletcher, David M. **HF1456.5.W45P55 1998**
The Diplomacy of Trade and Investment: American Economic Expansion in the Hemisphere, 1865-1900. Trade Cloth. University of Missouri Press. Columbia, MO. 1998. 440p. ISBN:0-8262-1127-5, ISBN13: 978-0-8262-1127-9. Dewey:337.73. LCCN:97-038825.
Audience: **u,f.**

Potter, David M. **E459**
Impending Crisis. Trade Paper. HarperCollins Publishers. New York, NY. 1977. 672p. New American Nation Ser. ISBN:0-06-131929-5, ISBN13: 978-0-06-131929-7. Dewey:973.7/11.
Audience: **l,u,f.**

Potter, David M. **E440.5.P856 1995**
Lincoln and His Party in the Secession Crisis. Daniel W. Crofts (Introduction by). Trade Paper. Louisiana State University Press. Baton Rouge, LA. 1995. 440p. ISBN:0-8071-2027-8, ISBN13: 978-0-8071-2027-9. Dewey:973.7/092. LCCN:95-023562.
Audience: **l,u,f.**

Pratt, Julius **E713.P895**
Expansionists of 1898: The Acquisition of Hawaii and the Spanish Islands. Trade Cloth. Peter Smith Publisher, Inc. Magnolia, MA. 1985. ISBN:0-8446-1364-9, ISBN13: 978-0-8446-1364-2. Dewey:973.88.
Audience: **l,u,f.**

Pratt, Richard H. **E97.6.C2P89 1987**
Battlefield and Classroom: Four Decades with the American Indian, 1876-1904. Robert Marshall Utley (Editor). Trade Cloth. University of Nebraska Press. Lincoln, NE. 1987. xx, 390p. Landmark Edition Ser. ISBN:0-8032-3679-4, ISBN13: 978-0-8032-3679-0. Dewey:973/.0497. LCCN:86-025019.
Audience: **u,f.**

Quarles, Benjamin **E449.Q17 1991**
Black Abolitionists. Trade Paper. Da Capo Press, Inc. Cambridge, MA. 1991. 320p. Quality Paperbacks Ser. ISBN:0-306-80425-5, ISBN13: 978-0-306-80425-0. Dewey:973.7/114. LCCN:90-027218.
Audience: **l,u,f.** ℬ

Quarles, Benjamin **E449.D75**
Frederick Douglass. Trade Cloth. Associated Publishers, Inc. Washington, DC. 1990. ISBN:0-87498-033-X, ISBN13: 978-0-87498-033-2. Dewey:973.8/092.
Audience: **g,l,u,f.**

Quarles, Benjamin **E540.N3Q3**
Negro in the Civil War. Trade Cloth. Russell & Russell Publishers. New York, NY. 1968. ISBN:0-8462-1052-5, ISBN13: 978-0-8462-1052-8. Dewey:973.71/5/30145196. LCCN:68-010941.
Audience: **l,u,f.** ℬ

Rable, George C. **E668.R13 1984**
But There Was No Peace: The Role of Violence in the Politics of Reconstruction. Trade Cloth. University of Georgia Press. Athens, GA. 1984. 270p. ISBN:0-8203-0703-3, ISBN13: 978-0-8203-0703-9. Dewey:973.8. LCCN:83-017883.
Audience: **f.**

Rable, George C. **E487.R18 1994**
The Confederate Republic: A Revolution Against Politics. Trade Cloth. University of North Carolina Press. Chapel Hill, NC. 1994. 430p. Civil War America Ser. ISBN:0-8078-2144-6, ISBN13: 978-0-8078-2144-2. Dewey:973.7/13. LCCN:93-036491.
Audience: **f.** *Choice, 1994.*

Randall, J. G. & Current, Richard Nelson **E457.R212 2000**
Lincoln the President: Last full Measure. Trade Paper. University of Illinois Press. Champaign, IL. 1999. 456p. ISBN:0-252-06872-6, ISBN13: 978-0-252-06872-0. Dewey:973.7/092. LCCN:99-039598.
Audience: **l,u,f.** ℬ

Rawley, James A. **E468.9**
The Politics of Union: Northern Politics During the Civil War. Trade Paper. Books on Demand. Ann Arbor, MI. 1980. 216p. ISBN:0-608-01402-8, ISBN13: 978-0-608-01402-9. Dewey:973.7/1. LCCN:80-017173.
Audience: **f.**

Rawley, James A. **E649.R28 1989**
Turning Points of the Civil War (New Edition). Trade Cloth. University of Nebraska Press. Lincoln, NE. 1989. 230p. ISBN:0-8032-8935-9, ISBN13: 978-0-8032-8935-2. Dewey:973.7. LCCN:89-004873.
Audience: **l,u,f.**

Rhodes, James Ford **E0415.7.R47**
History of the United States from the Compromise of 1850. Allan Nevins (Editor). Trade Paper. Books on Demand. Ann Arbor, MI. 606p. Classic American Historians Ser. ISBN:0-598-15423-X, ISBN13: 978-0-598-15423-1. Dewey:973.6. LCCN:66-023695.
Audience: **l,u,f.**

Roark, James L. **E668.R64 1977**
Masters Without Slaves. Trade Cloth. W. W. Norton & Company, Inc. New York, NY. 1977. xii, 273p. ISBN:0-393-05562-0, ISBN13: 978-0-393-05562-7. Dewey:976/.04. LCCN:76-047689.
Audience: **l,u.** ℬ

Rose, Anne C. **E169.1.R77515 1992**
Victorian America and the Civil War. Trade Cloth. Cambridge University Press. New York, NY. 1992. 320p. ISBN:0-521-41081-9, ISBN13: 978-0-521-41081-6. Dewey:973.8. LCCN:92-002718.
Audience: **u,f.** *Choice, 1993.*

Schoonover, Thomas **E715.S36 2003**
Uncle Sam's War of 1898 and the Origins of Globalization. Walter F. LaFeber (Foreword by). Trade Cloth. University Press of Kentucky. Lexington, KY. 2003. 224p. ISBN:0-8131-2282-1, ISBN13: 978-0-8131-2282-3. Dewey:973.8/91. LCCN:2003-011379.
Audience: **u,f.** *Choice, 2004.*

Schroeder, John Herman **E415.2**
Mr. Polk's War: American Opposition and Dissent, 1846-1848. Trade Cloth. University of Wisconsin Press. Chicago, IL. 1973. xvi, 185p. ISBN:0-299-06160-4, ISBN13: 978-0-299-06160-9. Dewey:973.6/2. LCCN:73-002049.
Audience: **l,u,f.** B

Sears, Stephen W. **E468.9.S43 1999**
Controversies and Commanders of the Civil War: Dispatches from the Army of the Potomac. Trade Cloth. Houghton Mifflin Company Trade & Reference Division. Boston, MA. 1999. 320p. ISBN:0-395-86760-6, ISBN13: 978-0-395-86760-0. Dewey:973.7/3. LCCN:98-037736.
Audience: **f.**

Sears, Stephen W. **E467.1.M2S43 1988**
George B. McClellan: The Young Napoleon. Trade Cloth. Houghton Mifflin Company. New York, NY. 1988. 512p. ISBN:0-89919-264-5, ISBN13: 978-0-89919-264-2. Dewey:973.7/3/0924. LCCN:88-002138.
Audience: **f.** *Choice, 1988.*

Sears, Stephen W. **E474.65**
Landscape Turned Red: The Battle of Antietam. Trade Paper. Houghton Mifflin Company Trade & Reference Division. Boston, MA. 2003. 448p. ISBN:0-618-34419-5, ISBN13: 978-0-618-34419-2. Dewey:973.7/336.
Audience: **u,f.**

Sewell, Richard H. **E449.S49**
Ballots for Freedom: Antislavery Politics in the United States, 1837-1860. Trade Cloth. Oxford University Press, Inc. New York, NY. 1976. xvi, 379p. ISBN:0-19-501997-0, ISBN13: 978-0-19-501997-1. Dewey:322.4/4/0973. LCCN:75-025464.
Audience: **l,u,f.** B

Sewell, Richard H. **E415.7.S525 1988**
A House Divided: Sectionalism and Civil War, 1848-1865. Trade Cloth. Johns Hopkins University Press. Baltimore, MD. 1988. 240p. The American Moment Ser. ISBN:0-8018-3531-3, ISBN13: 978-0-8018-3531-5. Dewey:973.7. LCCN:87-014305.
Audience: **u,f.** *Choice, 1988.*

Simon, John Y. & Stevens, Michael E. **E468.9.N48 1998**
New Perspectives on the Civil War: Myths and Realities of the National Conflict. Trade Cloth. Rowman & Littlefield Publishers, Inc. Lanham, MD. 1999. 395p. ISBN:0-945612-62-1, ISBN13: 978-0-945612-62-9. Dewey:973.7. LCCN:98-018909.
Audience: **l,u,f.** *Choice, 1999.*

Snay, Mitchell **BR535.S63 1997**
Gospel of Disunion: Religion and Separatism in the Antebellum South. Trade Paper. University of North Carolina Press. Chapel Hill, NC. 1997. 280p. ISBN:0-8078-4687-2, ISBN13: 978-0-8078-4687-2. Dewey:277.5/081. LCCN:97-013941.
Audience: **f.**

Stampp, Kenneth M. **E440**
And the War Came: The North and the Secession Crisis, 1860-1861. Trade Cloth. Greenwood Publishing Group, Inc. Portsmouth, NH. 1980. 331p. ISBN:0-313-22566-4, ISBN13: 978-0-313-22566-6. Dewey:973.7/13. LCCN:80-015742.
Audience: **l,u,f.** B

Stampp, Kenneth M. **E668**
Era of Reconstruction, 1865-1877. Trade Cloth. Alfred A. Knopf Inc. New York, NY. 1965. ix, 228p. ISBN:0-394-42355-0, ISBN13: 978-0-394-42355-5. Dewey:973.81.
Audience: **g,l,u,f.** B

Stampp, Kenneth M. **E441.S8**
Peculiar Institution. Trade Cloth. Alfred A. Knopf Inc. New York, NY. 1956. ISBN:0-394-44015-3, ISBN13: 978-0-394-44015-6. Dewey:306.3/62/0975.
Audience: **g,l,u,f.**

Thomas, Emory M. **E487.T48 1991**
The Confederacy As a Revolutionary Experience. Paper Text. University of South Carolina Press. Columbia, SC. 1991. 170p. ISBN:0-87249-780-1, ISBN13: 978-0-87249-780-1. Dewey:973.7/13. LCCN:91-010406.
Audience: **f.**

Thomas, Emory M. **E467.1.L4T48 1995**
Robert E. Lee: A Biography. Trade Cloth. W. W. Norton & Company, Inc. New York, NY. 1995. 576p. ISBN:0-393-03730-4, ISBN13: 978-0-393-03730-2. Dewey:973.7/3/092. LCCN:95-010522.
Audience: **g,l,u,f.** *Choice, 1995.*

Trachtenberg, Alan **E169.1.T72 1982**
The Incorporation of America: Culture and Society in the Gilded Age. Trade Cloth. Farrar, Straus & Giroux. New York, NY. 1982. 247p. American Century Ser. ISBN:0-8090-5827-8, ISBN13: 978-0-8090-5827-3. Dewey:973.8. LCCN:81-013339.
Audience: **u,f.** B

Trask, David F. **E715.T7 1996**
The War with Spain in 1898. Trade Cloth. University of Nebraska Press. Lincoln, NE. 1996. 654p. ISBN:0-8032-9429-8, ISBN13: 978-0-8032-9429-5. Dewey:973.8/9. LCCN:96-021710.
Audience: **l,u,f.** B

Trefousse, Hans **E666.T73 1999**
Impeachment of a President: Andrew Johnson, the Blacks and Reconstruction. Trade Paper. Fordham University Press. Bronx, NY. 1999. 252p. Reconstructing America Ser., Vol. 1 ISBN:0-8232-1923-2, ISBN13: 978-0-8232-1923-0. Dewey:973.8/1/092. LCCN:99-012729.
Audience: **l,u,f.**

Trefousse, Hans L. **E449.T79 1975**
The Radical Republicans: Lincoln's Vanguard for Racial Justice. Trade Paper. Louisiana State University Press. Baton Rouge, LA. 1975. ix, 510p. ISBN:0-8071-0169-9, ISBN13: 978-0-8071-0169-8. Dewey:973.7/1. LCCN:75-331615.
Audience: **l,u,f.**

Trefousse, Hans L. **E415.9.S84T74 1997**
Thaddeus Stevens: Nineteenth-Century Egalitarian. Trade Cloth. University of North Carolina Press. Chapel Hill, NC. 1997. 336p. Civil War America Ser. ISBN:0-8078-2335-X, ISBN13: 978-0-8078-2335-4. Dewey:328.73/092. LCCN:96-035004.
Audience: **f.** *Choice, 1997.*

Trefousse, Hans L. **E83.876**
Andrew Johnson: A Biography. Katherine E. Speirs (Editor). Trade Cloth. American Political Biography. Newtown, CT. 1998. 463p. Signature Ser. ISBN:0-945707-22-3, ISBN13: 978-0-945707-22-6. Dewey:973.8/1/0924. LCCN:98-072938.
Audience: **l,u,f.** *Choice, 1990.*

Trelease, Allen W. **E668**
White Terror: The Ku Klux Klan Conspiracy and Southern Reconstruction. Trade Cloth. Greenwood Publishing Group, Inc. Portsmouth, NH. 1979. 557p. ISBN:0-313-21168-X, ISBN13: 978-0-313-21168-3. Dewey:973.8. LCCN:78-012864.
Audience: **l,u,f.** BCL3

Turner, Frederick J. **E179.5.T958 1984**
The Significance of the Frontier in American History. Martin Ridge (Introduction by), James P. Danky (Contribution by). Trade Cloth. Silver Buckle Press. Madison, WI. 1984. 148p. ISBN:0-931101-01-8, ISBN13: 978-0-931101-01-4. Dewey:973. LCCN:84-014002.
Audience: **g,l,u,f.**

Tyler, Alice **BR516.5.T9 1970**
Freedom's Ferment. Trade Cloth. Ayer Company Publishers, Inc. Manchester, NH. 1977. Essay Index Reprint Ser. ISBN:0-8369-1898-3, ISBN13: 978-0-8369-1898-4. Dewey:309.1/73. LCCN:78-128324.
Audience: **l,u,f.**

Unger, Nancy C. **E664.L16U4 2000**
Fighting Bob la Follette: The Righteous Reformer. Trade Cloth. University of North Carolina Press. Chapel Hill, NC. 2000. 408p. ISBN:0-8078-2545-X, ISBN13: 978-0-8078-2545-7. Dewey:977.5/04/092. LCCN:99-057829.
Audience: **l,u,f.** *Choice, 2001.*

Utley, Robert Marshall **E83.866.U87 1985**
Frontier Regulars: The United States Army and the Indian, 1866-1891. Trade Paper. University of Nebraska Press. Lincoln, NE. 1984. 494p. ISBN:0-8032-9551-0, ISBN13: 978-0-8032-9551-3. Dewey:973.8. LCCN:84-007484.
Audience: **u,f.** BCL3

Utley, Robert Marshall **E81.U747 1984**
The Indian Frontier of the American West, 1846-1890. Trade Cloth. University of New Mexico Press. Albuquerque, NM. 1984. 347p. Histories of the American Frontier Ser. ISBN:0-8263-0715-9, ISBN13: 978-0-8263-0715-6. Dewey:978/.02. LCCN:83-012516.
Audience: **u,f.** BCL3

Utley, Robert Marshall **E99.D1U9**
Last Days of the Sioux Nation. Trade Cloth. Yale University Press. Cumberland, RI. 1963. Western Americana Ser., No. 3 ISBN:0-300-01003-6, ISBN13: 978-0-300-01003-9. Dewey:973/.00497.
Audience: **u,f.**

Van Deburg, William L. **E161**
Slavery and Race in American Popular Culture. Cloth Text. University of Wisconsin Press. Chicago, IL. 1984. 280p. ISBN:0-299-09630-0, ISBN13: 978-0-299-09630-4. Dewey:305.8/96073. LCCN:83-040272.
Audience: **u,f.** BCL3

Vandiver, Frank E. **E467.1.J15V3 1989**
Mighty Stonewall. Trade Cloth. Texas A&M University Press. College Station, TX. 1992. 560p. Texas A&M University Military History Ser., No. 9 ISBN:0-89096-384-3, ISBN13: 978-0-89096-384-5. Dewey:973.7/3/0924. LCCN:88-009642.
Audience: **l,u,f.**

Vandiver, Frank E. **E545.V3 1993**
Rebel Brass: The Confederate Command System. Trade Paper. Louisiana State University Press. Baton Rouge, LA. 1993. 143p. ISBN:0-8071-1862-1, ISBN13: 978-0-8071-1862-7. Dewey:973.713. LCCN:56-009169.
Audience: **l,u,f.** BCL3

Vandiver, Frank E. **E487.V33 1987**
Their Tattered Flags: The Epic of the Confederacy. Trade Paper. Texas A&M University Press. College Station, TX. 1994. 376p. Texas A&M University Military History Ser., No. 5 ISBN:0-89096-355-X, ISBN13: 978-0-89096-355-5. Dewey:975/.03. LCCN:87-006520.
Audience: **f.** BCL3

Vinovskis, Maris A. (Editor) **E468.9**
Toward a Social History of the American Civil War: Exploratory Essays. Trade Cloth. Cambridge University Press. New York, NY. 1990. 213p. ISBN:0-521-39523-2, ISBN13: 978-0-521-39523-6. Dewey:973.7. LCCN:90-036367.
Audience: **f.**

Walters, Ronald G. **HQ1413.C45**
American Reformers, 1815-1860. Trade Cloth. Peter Smith Publisher, Inc. Magnolia, MA. 1997. ISBN:0-8446-6923-7, ISBN13: 978-0-8446-6923-6. Dewey:303.48/4/092.
Audience: **u,f.**

Weeks, Philip **E93.W39 2000**
Farewell, My Nation: The American Indian and the United States in the Nineteenth Century. Ed. 2. Trade Cloth. Harlan Davidson Inc. Wheeling, IL. 2000. xvi, 266p. The American History Ser. ISBN:0-88295-956-5, ISBN13: 978-0-88295-956-6. Dewey:973/.0497. LCCN:00-059635.
Audience: **u,f.**

Widenor, William C. **E664.L7**
Henry Cabot Lodge and the Search for an American Foreign Policy. Trade Cloth. University of California Press. Berkeley, CA. 1980. xi, 389p. ISBN:0-520-03778-2, ISBN13: 978-0-520-03778-6. Dewey:327.73. LCCN:78-062863.
Audience: **l,u,f.** BCL3

Wiebe, Robert H. **E661**
The Search for Order, 1877-1920. Trade Paper. Farrar, Straus & Giroux. New York, NY. 1966. 336p. Making of America Ser. ISBN:0-8090-0104-7, ISBN13: 978-0-8090-0104-0. Dewey:973.8. LCCN:66-027609.
Audience: **l,u,f.** BCL3

Wiley, Bell I. **E607**
The Life of Billy Yank: The Common Soldier of the Union. Trade Cloth. Louisiana State University Press. Baton Rouge, LA. 1971. 480p. ISBN:0-8071-1908-3, ISBN13: 978-0-8071-1908-2. Dewey:973.741. LCCN:75-162619.
Audience: **l,u,f.**

Wiley, Bell I. **E607**
The Life of Johnny Reb: The Common Soldier of the Confederacy. Trade Cloth. Louisiana State University Press. Baton Rouge, LA. 1971. 444p. ISBN:0-8071-1909-1, ISBN13: 978-0-8071-1909-9. Dewey:973.742. LCCN:71-162618.
Audience: **l,u,f.**

Wiley, Bell I. **E487.W65 1994**
Road to Appomattox. Trade Paper. Louisiana State University Press. Baton Rouge, LA. 1994. 152p. ISBN:0-8071-1911-3, ISBN13: 978-0-8071-1911-2. Dewey:973.7/13. LCCN:56-013465.
Audience: **l,u,f.**

Williams, T. Harry **E457.905**
Lincoln and His Generals. Trade Cloth. Dorset Press. New York, NY. 1989. 367p. Reprints Ser. ISBN:0-88029-331-4, ISBN13: 978-0-88029-331-0. Dewey:973.7/092.
Audience: **g,l,u,f.**

Williams, T. Harry **E459**
Lincoln and the Radicals. Trade Paper. University of Wisconsin Press. Chicago, IL. 1960. 432p. ISBN:0-299-00274-8, ISBN13: 978-0-299-00274-9. Dewey:973.9.
Audience: **l,u,f.**

Woodward, C. Vann **F215**
Origins of the New South, 1877-1913. Trade Cloth. Louisiana State University Press. Baton Rouge, LA. 1951. xiv, 656p. History of the South Ser., Vol. 9 ISBN:0-8071-0009-9, ISBN13: 978-0-8071-0009-7. Dewey:975/.041. LCCN:77-014582.
Audience: **g,l,u,f.**

Woodward, C. Vann **E83.877**
Reunion and Reaction: The Compromise of 1877 and the End of Reconstruction. Trade Cloth. Peter Smith Publisher, Inc. Magnolia, MA. 1995. ISBN:0-8446-6871-0, ISBN13: 978-0-8446-6871-0. Dewey:973.8/3.
Audience: **l,u,f.**

Woodward, C. Vann **E664.W337W6**
Tom Watson: Agrarian Rebel. Cloth Text. University Press of Virginia. Charlottesville, VA. 1982. 430p. ISBN:0-8139-0952-X, ISBN13: 978-0-8139-0952-3. Dewey:320.9/758/04. LCCN:73-077845.
Audience: **l,u,f.**

Woodward, C. Vann **E185.61.W86 2002**
The Strange Career of Jim Crow. William S. McFeely (Afterword by). Trade Cloth. Oxford University Press, Inc. New York, NY. 2001. 272p. ISBN:0-19-514689-1, ISBN13: 978-0-19-514689-9. Dewey:305.896/073/09034. LCCN:2001-021668.
Audience: **g,l,u,f.**

Zornow, William Frank **E458.4.Z6 1972**
Lincoln and the Party Divided. Trade Cloth. Greenwood Publishing Group, Inc. Portsmouth, NH. 1972. xi, 264p. ISBN:0-8371-6054-5, ISBN13: 978-0-8371-6054-2. Dewey:973.7/1. LCCN:73-152619.
Audience: **l,u,f.**

United States > American History, by Period > Discovery of America. Early Exploration

Arciniegas, German **E125.V5 A65**
Amerigo and the New World: The Life and Times of Amerigo Vespucci. Paper Text. Textbook Publishers. Temecula, CA. 2003. xvi, 322p. ISBN:0-7581-7433-0, ISBN13: 978-0-7581-7433-8. Dewey:973.19.
Audience: **u,f.**

Bakeless, John Edwin **E162.B3 1961**
The Eyes of Discovery: The Pageant of North America as Seen by the First Explorers. Dover Publications. 1961.
Audience: **u,f.**

Bedini, Silvio A. **E111.C774 1992**
Christopher Columbus Encyclopedia, Vol. I. Trade Cloth. Prentice Hall PTR. Upper Saddle River, NJ. 1995. 787p. Christopher Columbus Encyclopedia Ser., Vol. I ISBN:0-13-142670-2, ISBN13: 978-0-13-142670-2. Dewey:970.01/5/03. LCCN:90-029253.
Audience: **g,l,u,f.**

Bedini, Silvio A. **E111.C774 1992**
Christopher Columbus Encyclopedia, Vol. II. Trade Cloth. Prentice Hall PTR. Upper Saddle River, NJ. 1995. 787p. Christopher Columbus Encyclopedia Ser., Vol. II ISBN:0-13-142688-5, ISBN13: 978-0-13-142688-7. Dewey:970.01/5/03. LCCN:90-029253.
Audience: **g,l,u,f.**

Brebner, John B. **E101.B82**
The Explorers of North America, Fourteen Ninety-Two to Eighteen Hundred Six. Trade Cloth. A M S Press, Inc. New York, NY. ISBN:0-404-20043-5, ISBN13: 978-0-404-20043-5. Dewey:973.1. LCCN:83-045719.
Audience: **u,f.**

Crone, Gerald Roe **E111**
The Discovery of America. Hamilton. 1969. ISBN:0-241-01511-1, ISBN13: 978-0-241-01511-7.
Audience: **l,u,f.**

Flint, Richard & Flint, Shirley Cushing **E125.V3D66 2005**
Documents of the Coronado Expedition, 1539-1542: They Were Not Familiar with His Majesty, nor Did They Wish to Be His Subjects. Saddle Stitched, Cloth over Boards, Dust Jacket. Southern Methodist University Press. Dallas, TX. 2005. 746p. ISBN:0-87074-496-8, ISBN13: 978-0-87074-496-9. Dewey:979.01. LCCN:2004-062562.
Audience: **f.** *Choice, 2005.*

Hallenbeck, Cleve **E125.N9.H3 1970**
Álvar Núñez Cabeza de Vaca; The Journey and Route of the First European to Cross the Continent of North America, 1534-1536. Kennikat Press. 1970. ISBN:0-8046-1377-X, ISBN13: 978-0-8046-1377-4.
Audience: **f.**

Hammond, George P. (Editor, Translator) **E125.V3H4 1977**
Narratives of the Coranado Expedition, 1540-1542. Trade Cloth. A M S Press, Inc. New York, NY. Coronado Cuarto Centennial Publications, 1540-1940, Vol. 2 ISBN:0-404-14669-4, ISBN13: 978-0-404-14669-6. Dewey:979.1/01/0924. LCCN:75-041126.
Audience: **f.**

Ingstad, Anne S; Ingstad, Helge **F1122.9**
The Norse Discovery of America, Set. Ed. 2. Oxford University Press, Inc. 1987. A Scandinavian University Press Publication ISBN:82-00-07562-1, ISBN13: 978-82-00-07562-2.
Audience: **u,f.**

Leonard, Irving A. **E143**
Colonial Travelers in Latin America. William C. Bryant (Editor). Trade Cloth. Juan de la Cuesta-Hispanic Monographs. Newark, DE. 1986. 235p. Estudios de Literatura Latinoamericana Ser., Vol. 1 ISBN:0-936388-30-7, ISBN13: 978-0-936388-30-4. Dewey:918.041.
Audience: **f.**

Maryland Institute for Technology in the Humanities **E18**
Early Americas Digital Archive.
http://narcissus.umd.edu:8080/eada/index.jsp
Maryland Institute for Technology in the Humanities.
Audience: **g,l,u,f.**

McAlister, Lyle N. **E123.M38 1984**
Spain and Portugal in the New World, 1492-1700. University of Minnesota Press. 1984. ISBN:0-8166-1216-1, ISBN13: 978-0-8166-1216-1.
Audience: **u,f.**

McCann, Franklin Thresher **E127.M15**
English Discovery of America To 1585. Paper Text. Textbook Publishers. Temecula, CA. 2003. xiv, 246p. ISBN:0-7581-7442-X, ISBN13: 978-0-7581-7442-0. Dewey:973.17.
Audience: **l,u,f.** B

Morison, Samuel Eliot **E101**
The European Discovery of America: The Southern Voyages, A. D. 1492 - 1616. Trade Paper. Oxford University Press, Inc. New York, NY. 1993. 776p. ISBN:0-19-508272-9, ISBN13: 978-0-19-508272-2. Dewey:970.015. LCCN:93-020183.
Audience: **g,l,u,f.**

Morison, Samuel Eliot **E101**
The European Discovery of America, Vol. 1. Oxford University Press. 1993. ISBN:0-19-508271-0, ISBN13: 978-0-19-508271-5.
Audience: **g,l,u,f.**

Morison, Samuel Eliot; Obregón, Mauricio **E112**
The Caribbean as Columbus Saw It. Little, Brown. 1964.
Audience: **u,f.**

Morison, Samuel Eliot **E111.M86**
Admiral of the Ocean Sea: A Life of Christopher Columbus. Erwin Raisz & Bertram Greene (Illustrators). Trade Cloth. DIANE Publishing Company. Collingdale, PA. 2003. 691p. ISBN:0-7567-6881-0, ISBN13: 978-0-7567-6881-2. Dewey:970.01/5.
Audience: **g,l,u,f.**

Parry, J. H. (John Horace) **E121.P37 1979**
The Discovery of South America. Taplinger Pub. Co. 1979. ISBN:0-8008-2233-1, ISBN13: 978-0-8008-2233-0.
Audience: **u,f.**

Parry, John Horace **JV4062.P3**
The Spanish Theory of Empire in the Sixteenth Century. Trade Paper. Books on Demand. Ann Arbor, MI. 83p. ISBN:0-598-94441-9, ISBN13: 978-0-598-94441-2. Dewey:321/.03. LCCN:41-016610.
Audience: **f.** B

Phillips, William D. Jr. & Phillips, Carla Rahn **E111.P67 1991**
The Worlds of Christopher Columbus. Cloth Text. Cambridge University Press. New York, NY. 1991. 336p. ISBN:0-521-35097-2, ISBN13: 978-0-521-35097-6. Dewey:970.01/5. LCCN:91-018790.
Audience: **g,l,u,f.** *Choice, 1992.*

Quinn, David B. **F229.Q56 1985**
Set Fair for Roanoke: Voyages and Colonies, 1584-1606. Trade Cloth. University of North Carolina Press. Chapel Hill, NC. 1985. 492p. ISBN:0-8078-4123-4, ISBN13: 978-0-8078-4123-5. Dewey:973.1. LCCN:84-002345.
Audience: **u,f.** B

Quinn, David B. **E101**
England and the Discovery of America, 1481-1620. Knopf. 1973. ISBN:0-394-46673-X, ISBN13: 978-0-394-46673-6.
Audience: **l,u,f.**

Quinn, David B. **DA8.22**
Raleigh and the British Empire. Macmillan. 1949.
Audience: **f.**

Sauer, Carl Ortwin **E121.S26**
Sixteenth Century North America; The Land and the People as Seen by the Europeans. University of California Press. 1971. ISBN:0-520-01854-0, ISBN13: 978-0-520-01854-9.
Audience: **u,f.**

Schoenrich, Otto **KKT178.C655L44 2004**
The Legacy of Christopher Columbus: The Historic Litigations Involving His Discoveries, His Will, His Family, and His Descendants. Trade Cloth. Lawbook Exchange, Limited, The. Clark, NJ. 2004. 320p. ISBN:1-58477-404-5, ISBN13: 978-1-58477-404-4. Dewey:346.4605/2. LCCN:2003-058947.
Audience: **u,f.**

Todorov, Tzvetan **E123**
The Conquest of America. Trade Cloth. Peter Smith Publisher, Inc. Magnolia, MA. 1995. ISBN:0-8446-6866-4, ISBN13: 978-0-8446-6866-6. Dewey:970.01/6.
Audience: **u,f.** B

U. S. Institute of Museum and Library Services **E101**
American Journeys: Eyewitness Accounts of Early American Exploration and Settlement: A Digital Library and Learning Center.
http://www.americanjourneys.org
Wisconsin Historical Society.
Audience: **g,l,u,f.**

Vazquez de Espinosa, Antonio **E0143.V33**
Compendium and Description of the West Indies. Charles Upson Clark (Translator). Trade Paper. Books on Demand. Ann Arbor, MI. 874p. Smithsonian Miscellaneous Collections, Vol. 102 ISBN:0-598-39005-7, ISBN13: 978-0-598-39005-9. Dewey:917.29. LCCN:42-038630.
Audience: **f.**

Vega, Garcilaso de la **E125.S7.G26**
The Florida of the Inca; A History of the Adelantado, Hernando de Soto, Governor and Captain General of the Kingdom of Florida, and of Other Heroic Spanish and Indian Cavaliers, Written by the Inca, Garcilaso de la Vega, An Officer of His Majesty, and a Native of the Great City of Cuzco, Capital of the Realms and Provinces of Peru University of Texas Press. 1951.
Audience: f.

United States > American History, by Period > Colonial History

Adams, James T. **F7**
The Founding of New England. Trade Paper. Simon Publications, Inc. 2001. 482p. History of New England Ser., Vol. 1 ISBN:1-931313-50-4, ISBN13: 978-1-931313-50-6. Dewey:974. LCCN:21-009397.
Audience: **f.**

Adams, James Truslow **HD6508.G28**
Provincial Society, 1690-1763. Trade Paper. Simon Publications, Inc. 2001. 374p. ISBN:1-931541-45-0, ISBN13: 978-1-931541-45-9. Dewey:331.880973.
Audience: **f.**

Anderson, Fred **E199.A59 2000**
Crucible of War: The Seven Years' War and the Fate of Empire in British North America, 1754-1766. Trade Paper. Knopf Publishing Group. New York, NY. 2001. 912p. ISBN:0-375-70636-4, ISBN13: 978-0-375-70636-3. Dewey:973.2/6. LCCN:99-018512.
Audience: **l,u,f.** *Choice, 2000.*

Andrews, Charles McLean **E188**
The Colonial Period of American History. Yale University Press. 1964.
Audience: **l,u,f.**

Bedini, Silvio A. **E111.C774 1992**
Christopher Columbus Encyclopedia, Vol. II. Trade Cloth. Prentice Hall PTR. Upper Saddle River, NJ. 1995. 787p. Christopher Columbus Encyclopedia Ser., Vol. II ISBN:0-13-142688-5, ISBN13: 978-0-13-142688-7. Dewey:970.01/5/03. LCCN:90-029253.
Audience: **g,l,u,f.**

Bonomi, Patricia U. **BL2525**
Under the Cope of Heaven: Religion, Society, and Politics in Colonial America. Ed. 2. Trade Cloth. Oxford University Press, Inc. New York, NY. 2003. 328p. ISBN:0-19-516217-X, ISBN13: 978-0-19-516217-2. Dewey:277.3/07. LCCN:2004-271885.
Audience: **u,f.**

Bonomi, Patricia U. **F12**
A Factious People: Politics and Society in Colonial New York. Columbia University Press. 1971. ISBN:0-231-03509-8, ISBN13: 978-0-231-03509-5.
Audience: **f.**

Boorstin, Daniel J. **E162.B68 1964**
The Americans: The Colonial Experience. Trade Paper. Knopf Publishing Group. New York, NY. 1964. 448p. Caravelle Edition Ser., Vol. 1 ISBN:0-394-70513-0, ISBN13: 978-0-394-70513-2. Dewey:973.2. LCCN:75-330427.
Audience: **g,l,u,f.**

Boyer, Paul & Nissenbaum, Stephen **BF1576**
Salem Possessed: The Social Origins of Witchcraft. Trade Paper. Harvard University Press. Cambridge, MA. 1976. 254p. Harvard Paperbacks Ser. ISBN:0-674-78526-6, ISBN13: 978-0-674-78526-7. Dewey:301.2/1. LCCN:73-084399.
Audience: **u,f.**

Bradford, William **F68**
Of Plymouth Plantation. Richard "Little Bear" Wheeler (Preface by). Trade Cloth. FaithWorks. Brentwood, TN. 2003. 353p. ISBN:0-9665233-3-4, ISBN13: 978-0-9665233-3-1. Dewey:974.4.
Audience: **f.**

Brebner, John B. **E101.B82**
The Explorers of North America, Fourteen Ninety-Two to Eighteen Hundred Six. Trade Cloth. A M S Press, Inc. New York, NY. ISBN:0-404-20043-5, ISBN13: 978-0-404-20043-5. Dewey:973.1. LCCN:83-045719.
Audience: **u,f.**

Cave, Alfred A. **E83.63.C37 1996**
The Pequot War. Trade Paper. University of Massachusetts Press. Amherst, MA. 1996. 232p. Native Americans of the Northeast Ser., :Culture, History, and the Contemporary ISBN:1-55849-030-2, ISBN13: 978-1-55849-030-7. Dewey:973.2/2. LCCN:95-047282.
Audience: **g,l,u,f.** *Choice, 1996.*

Eccles, William J. & Cooke, Jacob E. (Editors) **E45.E53 1993**
Encyclopedia of the North American Colonies, Set. Trade Cloth. Thomson Gale. Farmington Hills, MI. 1993. 2397p. ISBN:0-684-19269-1, ISBN13: 978-0-684-19269-7. Dewey:940/.03. LCCN:93-007609.
Audience: **g,l,u.** *Choice, 1994.*

Force, Peter **E187.F69**
Tracts and Other Papers: Relating Principally to the Origin, Settlement, and Progress of the Colonies in North America, from the Discovery of the Country to the Year 1776, Set. Library Binding. Library Reprints, Inc. Temecula, CA. ISBN:0-7222-0913-4, ISBN13: 978-0-7222-0913-4. Dewey:973.2.
Audience: **f.**

Hall, David D. **BR530.H35 1990**
Worlds of Wonder, Days of Judgment: Popular Religious Belief in Early New England. Trade Paper. Harvard University Press. Cambridge, MA. 1990. 336p. ISBN:0-674-96216-8, ISBN13: 978-0-674-96216-3. Dewey:277.4/07. LCCN:90-033425.
Audience: **f.** *Choice, 1989.*

Ingstad, Anne S; Ingstad, Helge **F1122.9**
The Norse Discovery of America, Set. Ed. 2. Oxford University Press, Inc. 1987. A Scandinavian University Press Publication ISBN:82-00-07562-1, ISBN13: 978-82-00-07562-2.
Audience: **u,f.**

Jensen, Merrill **E195.J4 2004**
The Founding of a Nation: A History of the American Revolution, 1763-1776. Trade Cloth. Hackett Publishing Company, Inc. Indianapolis, IN. 2004. 735p. ISBN:0-87220-706-4, ISBN13: 978-0-87220-706-6. Dewey:973.27. LCCN:2003-056880.
Audience: **l,u,f.**

Jones, Alice H. **HC104.J66**
American Colonial Wealth: Documents and Methods, Set. Library Binding. Ayer Company Publishers, Inc. Manchester, NH. 1978. Individual Publications ISBN:0-405-05546-3, ISBN13: 978-0-405-05546-1. Dewey:339.4. LCCN:76-039706.
Audience: **l,u,f.**

Kammen, Michael G. **E195**
A Rope of Sand: The Colonial Agents, British Politics, and the American Revolution. Cornell University Press. 1968.
Audience: **f.**

Labaree, Leonard W. **E188**
Conservatism in Early American History. Trade Paper. Cornell University Press. Ithaca, NY. 1959. 182p. ISBN:0-8014-9008-1, ISBN13: 978-0-8014-9008-8. Dewey:320.520973.
Audience: **u,f.**

Lepore, Jill **E83.67**
The Name of War: King Philip's War and the Origins of American Identity. UK-Trade Paper. Knopf Publishing Group. New York, NY. 1999. 368p. ISBN:0-375-70262-8, ISBN13: 978-0-375-70262-4. Dewey:973.2/4. LCCN:97-002820.
Audience: **u,f.**

Lovejoy, David S. **E191.L68 1987**
The Glorious Revolution in America. Trade Paper. Wesleyan University Press. Middletown, CT. 1987. 423p. ISBN:0-8195-6177-0, ISBN13: 978-0-8195-6177-0. Dewey:973.2. LCCN:86-022482.
Audience: **u,f.** B

Maryland Institute for Technology in the Humanities **E18**
☐ Early Americas Digital Archive.
http://narcissus.umd.edu:8080/eada/index.jsp
Maryland Institute for Technology in the Humanities.
Audience: **g,l,u,f.**

May, Henry F. **E163.M39 1978**
The Enlightenment in America. Paper Text. Oxford University Press, Inc. New York, NY. 1978. 448p. ISBN:0-19-502367-6, ISBN13: 978-0-19-502367-1. Dewey:973. LCCN:78-017451.
Audience: **u,f.**

Miller, Perry G. **F7.M54 1983**
The New England Mind: From Colony to Province. Trade Paper. Harvard University Press. Cambridge, MA. 1983. 528p. ISBN:0-674-61301-5, ISBN13: 978-0-674-61301-0. Dewey:974. LCCN:82-020740.
Audience: **u,f.**

Miller, Perry G. **F7.M56 1983**
The New England Mind: The Seventeenth Century. Trade Paper. Harvard University Press. Cambridge, MA. 1983. 542p. ISBN:0-674-61306-6, ISBN13: 978-0-674-61306-5. Dewey:974/.02. LCCN:82-023291.
Audience: **u,f.**

Nash, Gary B. **E188.N37 1974**
Red, White, and Black: The Peoples of Early America. Trade Cloth. Prentice-Hall. Upper Saddle, NJ. 1974. xvii, 350p. ISBN:0-13-769810-0, ISBN13: 978-0-13-769810-3. Dewey:917.3/03/2. LCCN:74-001003.
Audience: **g,l,u,f.** B

Nash, Gary B. **HN80.B7**
The Urban Crucible: Social Change, Political Consciousness, and the Origins of the American Revolution. Trade Cloth. Harvard University Press. Cambridge, MA. 1979. xix, 548p. ISBN:0-674-93056-8, ISBN13: 978-0-674-93056-8. Dewey:974.4/6102. LCCN:79-012894.
Audience: **l,u,f.** B

Osgood, Herbert L. **E191.O83**
American Colonies in the Seventeenth Century, Vol. 2. Trade Cloth. Peter Smith Publisher, Inc. Magnolia, MA. 1981. ISBN:0-8446-1333-9, ISBN13: 978-0-8446-1333-8. Dewey:973.2.
Audience: **u,f.**

Osgood, Herbert Levi **LA228.C66**
The American Colonies in the Eighteenth Century. Paper Text. Textbook Publishers. Temecula, CA. 2003. ISBN:0-7581-6766-0, ISBN13: 978-0-7581-6766-8. Dewey:378.73.
Audience: **u,f.**

Parkman, Francis **E199**
Montcalm and Wolfe: The French and Indian War. Trade Paper. Da Capo Press, Inc. Cambridge, MA. 2001. 658p. ISBN:0-306-81077-8, ISBN13: 978-0-306-81077-0. Dewey:973.2/6.
Audience: **u,f.**

Phillips, William D. Jr. & Phillips, Carla Rahn **E111.P67 1991**
The Worlds of Christopher Columbus. Cloth Text. Cambridge University Press. New York, NY. 1991. 336p. ISBN:0-521-35097-2, ISBN13: 978-0-521-35097-6. Dewey:970.01/5. LCCN:91-018790.
Audience: **g,l,u,f.** *Choice, 1992.*

Raimo, John W. (Editor) **E187**
Biographical Directory of American Colonial and Revolutionary Governors, 1607-1789. Cloth Text. Greenwood Publishing Group, Inc. Portsmouth, NH. 1980. 536p. ISBN:0-313-28133-5, ISBN13: 978-0-313-28133-4. Dewey:973. LCCN:80-013279.
Audience: **g,l,u,f.**

Rogers, Alan **E210**
Empire and Liberty: American Resistance to British Authority, 1755-1763. Trade Cloth. University of California Press. Berkeley, CA. 1974. xiv, 205p. ISBN:0-520-02275-0, ISBN13: 978-0-520-02275-1. Dewey:322.4/2. LCCN:72-082225.
Audience: **u,f.** B

Rowse, Alfred L. **E188.R885 1978**
The Elizabethans and America. Trade Cloth. Greenwood Publishing Group, Inc. Portsmouth, NH. 1978. 221p. ISBN:0-8371-9350-8, ISBN13: 978-0-8371-9350-2. Dewey:973.2. LCCN:78-005090.
Audience: **f.**

Schoenrich, Otto **KKT178.C655L44 2004**
The Legacy of Christopher Columbus: The Historic Litigations Involving His Discoveries, His Will, His Family, and His Descendants. Trade Cloth. Lawbook Exchange, Limited, The. Clark, NJ. 2004. 320p. ISBN:1-58477-404-5, ISBN13: 978-1-58477-404-4. Dewey:346.4605/2. LCCN:2003-058947.
Audience: **u,f.**

Shifflett, Crandall **F234.J3**
☐ Virtual Jamestown.
http://www.virtualjamestown.org
Audience: **l,u,f.**

Stock, Leo Francis (Editor) **E187.G79 2002**
Proceedings and Debates of the British Parliaments Respecting North America [1924]. Trade Cloth. Lawbook Exchange, Limited, The. Clark, NJ. 2003. ISBN:1-58477-254-9, ISBN13:

978-1-58477-254-5. Dewey:325/.341/0970903. LCCN:2002-025966.
Audience: **u,f.**

Taylor, Alan **E188.T35 2002**
American Colonies: The Settling of North America. Trade Paper. Penguin Group (USA) Inc. New York, NY. 2002. 544p. History of the United States Ser. ISBN:0-14-200210-0, ISBN13: 978-0-14-200210-0. Dewey:973.2.
Audience: **l,u,f.**

U. S. Institute of Museum and Library Services **E101**
☐ American Journeys: Eyewitness Accounts of Early American Exploration and Settlement: A Digital Library and Learning Center.
http://www.americanjourneys.org
Wisconsin Historical Society.
Audience: **g,l,u,f.**

Wertenbaker, Thomas J. **E162.W475X 1977**
The First Americans, 1607-1690. Trade Cloth. Scholarly Press, Inc. Saint Clair Shores, MI. 1927. ISBN:0-403-01269-4, ISBN13: 978-0-403-01269-5. Dewey:973.2. LCCN:84-672765.
Audience: **u,f.**

Wright, Louis B. **E162.W88 1980**
The Atlantic Frontier: Colonial American Civilization, 1607-1763. Trade Cloth. Greenwood Publishing Group, Inc. Portsmouth, NH. 1980. 354p. ISBN:0-313-22320-3, ISBN13: 978-0-313-22320-4. Dewey:973.2. LCCN:79-027846.
Audience: **l,u,f.** B

United States > American History, by Period > American Revolution, 1775-1783

Abernethy, Thomas Perkins **PE64.A78**
Western Lands and the American Revolution. Paper Text. Textbook Publishers. Temecula, CA. 2003. 410p. ISBN:0-7581-4355-9, ISBN13: 978-0-7581-4355-6. Dewey:810.9.
Audience: **u,f.** B

Adams, Randolph Greenfield **E210**
Political Ideas of the American Revolution. Trade Cloth. Library Reprints, Inc. Temecula, CA. 207p. ISBN:0-7222-7632-X, ISBN13: 978-0-7222-7632-7. Dewey:973.31.
Audience: **u,f.**

Albanese, Catherine L. **E20**
Sons of the Fathers: The Civil Religion of the American Revolution. Temple University Press. 1976. ISBN:0-87722-073-5, ISBN13: 978-0-87722-073-2.
Audience: **u,f.**

Andrews, Charles McLean **HF5382.7**
The Colonial Background of the American Revolution: Four Essays in American Colonial History. Paper Text. Textbook Publishers. Temecula, CA. 2003. 220p. ISBN:0-7581-0191-0, ISBN13: 978-0-7581-0191-4. Dewey:650.14.
Audience: **l,u,f.** B

Bailyn, Bernard **E203.B3**
Pamphlets of the American Revolution, 1750-1765, Vol. 1. Jane N. Garrett (Editor). Trade Paper. Harvard University Press. Cambridge, MA. 1965. 787p. The John Harvard Library ISBN:0-674-65250-9, ISBN13: 978-0-674-65250-7. Dewey:973.3082.
Audience: **f.** B

Baldwin, Alice Mary **E210**
The New England Clergy and the American Revolution. F. Ungar Pub. Co.. 1965.
Audience: **f.**

Berkin, Carol **F67**
Jonathan Sewall: Odyssey of an American Loyalist. Trade Paper. iUniverse, Inc. Lincoln, NE. 2000. 220p. ISBN:0-595-00020-7, ISBN13: 978-0-595-00020-3. Dewey:974.4/02/0924.
Audience: **f.** B

Blanco, Richard L. (Editor) **E208.A433 1993**
The American Revolution 1775-1783: An Encyclopedia. Library Binding. Garland Publishing, Inc. New York, NY. 1993. 1896p. Military History of the U. S. Ser., Vol. 1 ISBN:0-8240-5623-X, ISBN13: 978-0-8240-5623-0. Dewey:973.303. LCCN:92-042541.
Audience: **g,l,u,f.** *Choice, 1993.*

Bradley, Patricia **E210**
Slavery, Propaganda, and the American Revolution. Trade Cloth. University Press of Mississippi. Jackson, MS. 1999. 184p. ISBN:1-57806-211-X, ISBN13: 978-1-57806-211-9. Dewey:973.3/88. LCCN:98-012915.
Audience: **u,f.** *Choice, 1999.*

Calhoon, Robert M. **E27**
The Loyalists in Revolutionary America, 1760-1781. Harcourt Brace Jovanovich. 1973. ISBN:0-15-154745-9, ISBN13: 978-0-15-154745-6.
Audience: **u,f.**

Cappon, Lester (Editor) **G1201.S3A8**
Atlas of Early American History: The Revolutionary Era, 1760-1790. Trade Cloth. Princeton University Press. Princeton, NJ. 1976. ISBN:0-911028-00-5, ISBN13: 978-0-911028-00-3. Dewey:911/.73.
Audience: **g,l,u,f.**

Cohen, Lester H. **E20**
The Revolutionary Histories: Contemporary Narratives of the American Revolution. Cornell University Press. 1980. ISBN:0-87754-177-9, ISBN13: 978-0-87754-177-6.
Audience: **f.**

Commager, Henry Steele & Morris, Richard B. (Editors) **E203**
The Spirit of Seventy-Six. Trade Cloth. Book Sales, Inc. Edison, NJ. 1348p. ISBN:0-7858-1463-9, ISBN13: 978-0-7858-1463-4. Dewey:973.3.
Audience: **l,u,f.**

Countryman, Edward **E263.N6**
A People in Revolution: The American Revolution and Political Society in New York, 1760-1790. Johns Hopkins University Press. 1981. ISBN:0-8018-2625-X, ISBN13: 978-0-8018-2625-2.
Audience: **l,u,f.**

Crary, Catherine S. (Compiled by) **E27**
The Price of Loyalty: Tory Writings from the Revolutionary Era. McGraw-Hill. 1973. ISBN:0-07-013460-X, ISBN13: 978-0-07-013460-7.
Audience: **f.**

Davies, K. G. (Editor) **E211**
Documents of the American Revolution, Vol. 12. Trade Cloth. Irish Academic Press. Dublin, 2000. vi, 301p. ISBN:0-7165-2097-4, ISBN13: 978-0-7165-2097-9. Dewey:325/.341/0973.
Audience: **l,u,f.**

Davies, K. G. (Editor) **E211**
Documents of the American Revolution, Vol. 10. Trade Cloth. Irish Academic Press. Dublin, 2000. vi, 516p. ISBN:0-7165-2095-8, ISBN13: 978-0-7165-2095-5. Dewey:325/.341/0973.
Audience: **l,u,f.**

Davies, K. G. (Editor) **E211**
Documents of the American Revolution, Vol. 8. Trade Cloth. Irish Academic Press. Dublin, 2000. vi, 290p. ISBN:0-7165-2093-1, ISBN13: 978-0-7165-2093-1. Dewey:325/.341/0973.
Audience: **l,u,f.**

Davies, K. G. (Editor) **E188**
Documents of the American Revolution, Vol. 6. Trade Cloth. Irish Academic Press. Dublin, 2001. ISBN:0-7165-2091-5, ISBN13: 978-0-7165-2091-7. Dewey:325/.341/0973.
Audience: **l,u,f.**

Davies, K. G. (Editor) **E211**
Documents of the American Revolution, Vol. 18. Trade Cloth. Irish Academic Press. Dublin, vi, 289p. ISBN:0-7165-2103-2, ISBN13: 978-0-7165-2103-7. Dewey:325/.341/0973.
Audience: **l,u,f.**

Davies, K. G. (Editor) **E208**
Documents of the American Revolution, Vol. 2. Trade Cloth. Irish Academic Press. Dublin, 2001. vi, 331p. ISBN:0-7165-2087-7, ISBN13: 978-0-7165-2087-0. Dewey:325/.341/0973.
Audience: **l,u,f.**

Davies, K. G. (Editor) **E211**
Documents of the American Revolution, Vol. 20. Trade Cloth. Irish Academic Press. Dublin, vi, 309p. ISBN:0-7165-2105-9, ISBN13: 978-0-7165-2105-1. Dewey:325/.341/0973.
Audience: **g,l,u,f.**

Davies, K. G. (Editor) **E211**
Documents of the American Revolution, Vol. 16. Trade Cloth. Irish Academic Press. Dublin, vi, 550p. ISBN:0-7165-2101-6, ISBN13: 978-0-7165-2101-3. Dewey:325/.341/0973.
Audience: **l,u,f.**

Davies, K. G. (Editor) **E208**
Documents of the American Revolution, Vol. 3. Trade Cloth. Irish Academic Press. Dublin, 2001. vi, 302p. ISBN:0-7165-2088-5, ISBN13: 978-0-7165-2088-7. Dewey:325/.341/0973.
Audience: **l,u,f.**

Davies, K. G. (Editor) **E211**
Documents of the American Revolution, Vol. 14. Trade Cloth. Irish Academic Press. Dublin, 2000. vi, 299p. ISBN:0-7165-2099-0, ISBN13: 978-0-7165-2099-3. Dewey:325/.341/0973.
Audience: **l,u,f.**

Davies, K. G. (Editor) **E211**
Documents of the American Revolution, Vol. 13. Trade Cloth. Irish Academic Press. Dublin, 2000. vi, 481p. ISBN:0-7165-2098-2, ISBN13: 978-0-7165-2098-6. Dewey:325/.341/0973.
Audience: **l,u,f.**

Davies, K. G. (Editor) **E211**
Documents of the American Revolution, Vol. 11. Trade Cloth. Irish Academic Press. Dublin, 2000. vi, 239p. ISBN:0-7165-2096-6, ISBN13: 978-0-7165-2096-2. Dewey:325/.341/0973.
Audience: **l,u,f.**

Davies, K. G. (Editor) **E211**
Documents of the American Revolution, Vol. 9. Trade Cloth. Irish Academic Press. Dublin, 2000. vi, 237p. ISBN:0-7165-2094-X, ISBN13: 978-0-7165-2094-8. Dewey:325/.341/0973.
Audience: **g,l,u,f.**

Davies, K. G. (Editor) **E211**
Documents of the American Revolution, Vol. 7. Trade Cloth. Irish Academic Press. Dublin, 2001. vi, 432p. ISBN:0-7165-2092-3, ISBN13: 978-0-7165-2092-4. Dewey:325/.341/0973.
Audience: **l,u,f.**

Davies, K. G. (Editor) **E211**
Documents of the American Revolution, Vol. 19. Trade Cloth. Irish Academic Press. Dublin, vii, 541p. ISBN:0-7165-2104-0, ISBN13: 978-0-7165-2104-4. Dewey:325/.341/0973.
Audience: **l,u,f.**

Davies, K. G. (Editor) **E211**
Documents of the American Revolution. Trade Cloth. Irish Academic Press. Dublin, 2001. vi, 523p. ISBN:0-7165-2086-9, ISBN13: 978-0-7165-2086-3. Dewey:325/.341/0973.
Audience: **l,u,f.**

Davies, K. G. (Editor) **E188**
Documents of the American Revolution, Vol. 21. Trade Cloth. Irish Academic Press. Dublin, ISBN:0-7165-2106-7, ISBN13: 978-0-7165-2106-8. Dewey:325/.341/0973.
Audience: **l,u,f.**

Davies, K. G. (Editor) **E211**
Documents of the American Revolution, Vol. 17. Trade Cloth. Irish Academic Press. Dublin, vi, 291p. ISBN:0-7165-2102-4, ISBN13: 978-0-7165-2102-0. Dewey:325/.341/0973.
Audience: **g,l,u,f.**

Davies, K. G. (Editor) **E208**
Documents of the American Revolution, Vol. 4. Trade Cloth. Irish Academic Press. Dublin, 2001. vi, 496p. ISBN:0-7165-2089-3, ISBN13: 978-0-7165-2089-4. Dewey:325/.341/0973.
Audience: **l,u,f.**

Davies, K. G. (Editor) **E211**
Documents of the American Revolution, Vol. 15. Trade Cloth. Irish Academic Press. Dublin, 2000. vi, 320p. ISBN:0-7165-2100-8, ISBN13: 978-0-7165-2100-6. Dewey:325/.341/0973.
Audience: **l,u,f.**

Davies, K. G. (Editor) **E211**
Documents of the American Revolution, Vol. 5. Trade Cloth. Irish Academic Press. Dublin, 2001. vi, 308p. ISBN:0-7165-2090-7, ISBN13: 978-0-7165-2090-0. Dewey:325/.341/0973.
Audience: **l,u,f.**

Fischer, David H. **F69.R43F57 1994**
Paul Revere's Ride. Trade Cloth. Oxford University Press, Inc. New York, NY. 1994. 464p. ISBN:0-19-508847-6, ISBN13: 978-0-19-508847-2. Dewey:973.3/311/092. LCCN:93-025739.
Audience: **l,u,f.** *Choice, 1994.*

Fischer, David Hackett **E263.P4F575 2004**
Washington's Crossing. Trade Cloth. Oxford University Press, Inc. New York, NY. 2004. 576p. Pivotal Moments in American History Ser. ISBN:0-19-517034-2, ISBN13: 978-0-19-517034-4. Dewey:973.3/32. LCCN:2003-019858.
Audience: **l,u,f.** *Choice, 2004.*

Gipson, Lawrence Henry **E209.G5**
The Coming of the Revolution, 1763-1775. Harper. 1954. The New American Nation Series
Audience: **l,u,f.**

Greene, Jack P. & Pole, J. R. (Editors) **E208.B635 1991**
Blackwell Encyclopedia of the American Revolution. Trade Cloth. Blackwell Publishing, Inc. Malden, MA. 1991. 850p. ISBN:1-55786-244-3, ISBN13: 978-1-55786-244-0. Dewey:973.3/03. LCCN:91-003190.
Audience: **g,l,u,f.** *Choice, 1992.*

Gross, Robert A. **F74.C8G76 2001**
The Minutemen and Their World. Alan M. Taylor (Foreword by). Trade Paper. Farrar, Straus & Giroux. New York, NY. 2001. 280p. American Century Ser. ISBN:0-8090-0120-9, ISBN13: 978-0-8090-0120-0. Dewey:974.2/72. LCCN:2001-272032.
Audience: **l,u,f.** B

Hancock, Harold B. **E277.H26**
The Loyalists of Revolutionary Delaware: A University of Delaware Bicentennial Book. Trade Cloth. University of Delaware Press. Newark, DE. 1977. 159p. ISBN:0-87413-116-2, ISBN13: 978-0-87413-116-1. Dewey:973.3/14/09751. LCCN:76-014768.
Audience: **f.** B

Higginbotham, Donald (Editor) **E204**
Reconsiderations on the Revolutionary War: Selected Essays, 14. Trade Cloth. Greenwood Publishing Group, Inc. Portsmouth, NH. 1978. 217p. Contributions in Military History Ser., No. 14 ISBN:0-8371-9846-1, ISBN13: 978-0-8371-9846-0. Dewey:973.3. LCCN:77-084757.
Audience: **u,f.** B

Jameson, John F. **E0209.J33**
The American Revolution Considered As a Social Movement. Library Binding. Reprint Services Company. Temecula, CA. 1991. 105p. U. S. History Ser. ISBN:0-7812-6105-8, ISBN13: 978-0-7812-6105-0. Dewey:973.3.
Audience: **u,f.**

Jones, Alice Hanson **HC10**
Wealth of a Nation to Be: The American Colonies on the Eve of the Revolution. Columbia University Press. 1980. ISBN:0-231-03659-0, ISBN13: 978-0-231-03659-7.
Audience: **u,f.**

Kasson, John F. **T14.5.K37 1999**
Civilizing the Machine: Technology and Republican Values in America, 1776-1900. Trade Paper. Farrar, Straus & Giroux. New York, NY. 1999. 288p. ISBN:0-8090-1620-6, ISBN13: 978-0-8090-1620-4. Dewey:303.48/3/0973. LCCN:98-050621.
Audience: **u,f.** B

Kurtz, Stephen G. & Hutson, James H. (Editors) **E0208.E83**
Essays on the American Revolution. Trade Paper. Books on Demand. Ann Arbor, MI. 332p. ISBN:0-7837-7075-8, ISBN13: 978-0-7837-7075-8. Dewey:973.3/08. LCCN:72-081329.
Audience: **f.** B

Kwasny, Mark V. **E263.N6**
Washington's Partisan War, 1775-1783. Trade Paper. Kent State University Press. Kent, OH. 1996. 444p. ISBN:0-87338-611-6, ISBN13: 978-0-87338-611-1. Dewey:973.3/447. LCCN:96-014559.
Audience: **f.** *Choice, 1997.*

Lambert, Robert Stansbury **E27**
South Carolina Loyalists in the American Revolution. University of South Carolina Press. 1987. ISBN:0-87249-506-X, ISBN13: 978-0-87249-506-7.
Audience: **f.**

Mackesy, Piers **E208.M14 1992**
The War for America, 1775-1783. John W. Shy (Introduction by). Trade Paper. University of Nebraska Press. Lincoln, NE. 1993. 569p. ISBN:0-8032-8192-7, ISBN13: 978-0-8032-8192-9. Dewey:973.3. LCCN:92-037789.
Audience: **g,l,u,f.**

Maier, Pauline **E210.M27 1991**
From Resistance to Revolution: Colonial Radicals and the Development of American Opposition to Britain, 1765-1776. Trade Paper. W. W. Norton & Company, Inc. New York, NY. 1992. 360p. ISBN:0-393-30825-1, ISBN13: 978-0-393-30825-9. Dewey:973.2/7.
Audience: **u,f.** B

Main, Jackson Turner **E208.M33 1973**
The Sovereign States, 1775-1783. Trade Cloth. New Viewpoints. New York, NY. 1973. vii, 502p. ISBN:0-531-06355-0, ISBN13: 978-0-531-06355-2. Dewey:973.3. LCCN:75-190137.
Audience: **u,f.** B

Maryland Institute for Technology in the Humanities **E18**
☐ Early Americas Digital Archive.
http://narcissus.umd.edu:8080/eada/index.jsp
Maryland Institute for Technology in the Humanities.
Audience: **g,l,u,f.**

Middlekauff, Robert **E173.O94**
The Glorious Cause: The American Revolution, 1763-1789. Ed. 2. Trade Cloth. Oxford University Press, Inc. New York, NY. 2005. 750p. The Oxford History of the United States Ser., Vol. 3 ISBN:0-19-516247-1, ISBN13: 978-0-19-516247-9. Dewey:973.3. LCCN:2004-016295.
Audience: **g,l,u,f.** B

Morgan, Edmund S. **E208.M85 1992**
The Birth of the Republic: 1763-89. Ed. 3. Trade Paper. University of Chicago Press. Chicago, IL. 1993. 224p. Chicago History of American Civilization Ser. ISBN:0-226-53757-9, ISBN13: 978-0-226-53757-3. Dewey:973.2/7. LCCN:92-008871.
Audience: **g,l,u,f.**

Morgan, Edmund S. & Morgan, Helen M. **E215.2.M58 1995**
The Stamp Act Crisis: Prologue to Revolution. Trade Cloth. University of North Carolina Press. Chapel Hill, NC. 1995. 342p. Institute of Early American History and Culture Ser. ISBN:0-8078-4513-2, ISBN13: 978-0-8078-4513-4. Dewey:973.3/111. LCCN:94-031357.
Audience: **g,l,u,f.**

Nadelhaft, Jerome J. **E263.S7**
The Disorders of War: The Revolution in South Carolina. Trade Cloth. University of Maine Press. Orono, ME. 1981. 310p. ISBN:0-89101-048-3, ISBN13: 978-0-89101-048-7. Dewey:973.3/09757.
Audience: **f.** B

Noll, Mark A. **E209.N64**
Christians and the American Revolution. Trade Paper. Books on Demand. Ann Arbor, MI. 195p. ISBN:0-8357-9125-4, ISBN13: 978-0-8357-9125-0. Dewey:277.3. LCCN:77-023354.
Audience: **u,f.** B

Paine, Thomas **JC177.A5 1995**
Paine, Collected Writings: Common Sense; the Crisis; Rights of Man; the Age of Reason; Pamphlets, Articles and Letters. Eric Foner (Editor). Trade Cloth. Library of America, The. New York, NY. 1995. 906p. Library of America, Vol. 76 ISBN:1-883011-03-5, ISBN13: 978-1-883011-03-1. Dewey:320.5/1. LCCN:94-025756.
Audience: **l,u,f.**

Pettengill, Ray W. (Translator) **E268.P52**
Letters from America, 1776-1779. Trade Cloth. Associated Faculty Press, Inc. New York, NY. ISBN:0-8046-0366-9, ISBN13: 978-0-8046-0366-9. Dewey:973.38. LCCN:64-025542.
Audience: **f.**

Price, Richard **E0211.P963**
Observations on the Nature of Civil Liberty, the Principles of Government, and the Justice and Policy of the War with America. to Which Is Added an Appendix, Containing a State of the National Debt, an Estimate of the Money Drawn from the Public by the T. Trade Paper. Books on Demand. Ann Arbor, MI. 136p. ISBN:0-608-40572-8, ISBN13: 978-0-608-40572-8. Dewey:973.3/1.
Audience: **f.**

Quarles, Benjamin **E269.N3Q3 1996**
The Negro in the American Revolution. Trade Paper. University of North Carolina Press. Chapel Hill, NC. 1996. 266p. ISBN:0-8078-4603-1, ISBN13: 978-0-8078-4603-2. Dewey:973.3/150396073. LCCN:96-021111.
Audience: **g,l,u,f.** B

Royster, Charles **E259**
A Revolutionary People at War: The Continental Army and American Character, 1775-1783. Trade Paper. University of North Carolina Press. Chapel Hill, NC. 1996. 463p. ISBN:0-8078-4606-6, ISBN13: 978-0-8078-4606-3. Dewey:973.3/4. LCCN:79-010152.
Audience: **l,u,f.** B

Shaffer, Arthur H. **E209.S5**
The Politics of History: Writing the History of the American Revolution, 1783-1815. Trade Cloth. Transaction Publishers. Somerset, NJ. 1975. 228p. ISBN:0-913750-09-3, ISBN13: 978-0-913750-09-4. Dewey:973.3/07/2. LCCN:75-007865.
Audience: **f.** B

Trevelyan, George O. **E208**
The American Revolution, Set. Library Binding. Reprint Services Company. Temecula, CA. 1991. U. S. History Ser. ISBN:0-7812-6107-4, ISBN13: 978-0-7812-6107-4. Dewey:973.3.
Audience: **u,f.**

U. S. Institute of Museum and Library Services **E101**
☐ American Journeys: Eyewitness Accounts of Early American Exploration and Settlement: A Digital Library and Learning Center.
http://www.americanjourneys.org
Wisconsin Historical Society.
Audience: **g,l,u,f.**

Ward, Christopher **E230.W34**
The War of the Revolution. Paper Text. Textbook Publishers. Temecula, CA. 2003. 989p. ISBN:0-7581-9001-8, ISBN13: 978-0-7581-9001-7. Dewey:973.33.
Audience: **l,u,f.**

Willard, Margaret W. (Editor) **E203.W65**
Letters on the American Revolution, 1774-1776. Trade Cloth. Associated Faculty Press, Inc. New York, NY. 1968. ISBN:0-8046-0502-5, ISBN13: 978-0-8046-0502-1. Dewey:973.3/08. LCCN:68-008208.
Audience: **f.**

Wills, Garry **E221**
Inventing America: Jefferson's Declaration of Indepedence. Library Binding. Buccaneer Books, Inc. Cutchogue, NY. 1994. ISBN:1-56849-536-6, ISBN13: 978-1-56849-536-1. Dewey:973.3/13.
Audience: **g,l,u,f.** B

Wood, Gordon S. & Institute of Early American History and Culture Staff **JA84.U5W6 1998**
The Creation of the American Republic, 1776-1787. Trade Paper. University of North Carolina Press. Chapel Hill, NC. 1998. 675p. ISBN:0-8078-4723-2, ISBN13: 978-0-8078-4723-7. Dewey:973.3. LCCN:71-078861.
Audience: **g,l,u,f.** B

Wright, Esmond **E20**
Fabric of Freedom, 1763-1800. Hill and Wang. 1978. ISBN:0-8090-4356-4, ISBN13: 978-0-8090-4356-9.
Audience: **u,f.**

Young, Alfred F. (Editor) **E208.A43**
The American Revolution: Explorations in the History of American Radicalism. Trade Paper. Northern Illinois University Press. DeKalb, IL. 2003. 496p. ISBN:0-87580-519-1, ISBN13: 978-0-87580-519-1. Dewey:973.3. LCCN:75-045359.
Audience: **f.** B

Young, Alfred F. (Editor) **E179.B58 1993**
Beyond the American Revolution: Explorations in the History of American Radicalism. Trade Cloth. Northern Illinois University Press. DeKalb, IL. 2003. 391p. ISBN:0-87580-176-5, ISBN13: 978-0-87580-176-6. Dewey:973.3/1. LCCN:92-042367.
Audience: **u,f.**

Young, Alfred F. **JK2318.N7**
The Democratic Republicans of New York: The Origins, 1763-1797. Trade Paper. Books on Demand. Ann Arbor, MI. 658p. ISBN:0-8357-3920-1, ISBN13: 978-0-8357-3920-7. Dewey:329.3/009747. LCCN:67-023493.
Audience: **f.**

United States > American History, by Period > American Revolution, 1775-1783 > Biography

Alden, John Richard **E207.G23.A6 1969**
General Gage in America: Being Principally a History of His Role in the American Revolution. Greenwood Press. 1969. ISBN:0-8371-2264-3, ISBN13: 978-0-8371-2264-9.
Audience: **u,f.**

Bellesiles, Michael A. **E207.A4B44**
Revolutionary Outlaws: Ethan Allen and the Struggle for Independence on the Early American Frontier. Paper Text. University Press of Virginia. Charlottesville, VA. 1995. 448p. ISBN:0-8139-1603-8, ISBN13: 978-0-8139-1603-3. Dewey:974.303. LCCN:92-031324.
Audience: **u,f.** *Choice, 1994.*

Billias, George A. (Editor) **E206.G46 1994**
George Washington's Generals and Opponents: Their Exploits and Leadership. Trade Paper. Da Capo Press, Inc. Cambridge, MA. 1994. 768p. ISBN:0-306-80560-X, ISBN13: 978-0-306-80560-8. Dewey:973.3/3/0922. LCCN:93-033603.
Audience: **u,f.**

Brodie, Fawn M. **E332.79**
Thomas Jefferson: An Intimate History. Trade Paper. W. W. Norton & Company, Inc. New York, NY. 1998. 608p. ISBN:0-393-31752-8, ISBN13: 978-0-393-31752-7. Dewey:973.4/6/0924. LCCN:73-011348.
Audience: **l,u,f.** B

DeConde, Alexander **E333**
This Affair of Louisiana. Trade Paper. Louisiana State University Press. Baton Rouge, LA. 1979. xii, 325p. ISBN:0-8071-0497-3, ISBN13: 978-0-8071-0497-2. Dewey:976.3/03. LCCN:76-012468.
Audience: **g,l,u,f.**

Fischer, David H. **E331**
The Revolution of American Conservatism. Paper Text. University of Chicago Press. Chicago, IL. 1975. xxii, 456p. Midway Reprint Ser. ISBN:0-226-25135-7, ISBN13: 978-0-226-25135-6. Dewey:973.4. LCCN:75-029561.
Audience: **u,f.**

Gruber, Ira D. **E0267.G86**
The Howe Brothers and the American Revolution. Trade Paper. Books on Demand. Ann Arbor, MI. 416p. ISBN:0-8357-3871-X, ISBN13: 978-0-8357-3871-2. Dewey:973.3/41. LCCN:71-183681.
Audience: **f.** B

Jackson, Donald **E332.2**
Thomas Jefferson and the Stony Mountains: Exploring the West from Monticello. Trade Cloth. University of Illinois Press. Champaign, IL. 1981. 351p. ISBN:0-252-00823-5, ISBN13: 978-0-252-00823-8. Dewey:917.8/042/0924. LCCN:80-010546.
Audience: **l,u,f.** B

Jellison, Charles A. **E207A4 J4**
Ethan Allen: Frontier Rebel. Trade Paper. Syracuse University Press. Syracuse, NY. 1983. 374p. ISBN:0-8156-0189-1, ISBN13: 978-0-8156-0189-0. Dewey:973.30924. LCCN:74-014632.
Audience: **u,f.**

Jones, John Paul **E207.J7**
Memoirs of Rear-Admiral John Paul Jones. Trade Cloth. New Library Press.Net. Murrieta, CA. 399p. ISBN:0-7950-2484-3, ISBN13: 978-0-7950-2484-9. Dewey:973.35/0924.
Audience: **u,f.**

Lafayette, Le Marquis de **DC146.L2**
Lafayette in the Age of the American Revolution, Selected Letters and Papers, 1776-1790: April 27th, 1780-March 29th, 1781. Stanley J. Idzerda, Lloyd S. Cramer, Linda J. Pike & Mary Ann Quinn (Editors). Book, Other. Cornell University Press. Ithaca, NY. 1980. 577p. The Lafayette Papers ISBN:0-8014-1335-4, ISBN13: 978-0-8014-1335-3. Dewey:944/.035/0924. LCCN:76-050268.
Audience: **f.**

Lafayette, Le Marquis de **DC146.L2**
Lafayette in the Age of the American Revolution, Selected Letters and Papers, 1776-1790: January 4th, 1782-December 29th, 1785. Stanley J. Idzerda & Robert R. Crout (Editors). Book, Other. Cornell University Press. Ithaca, NY. 1983. 528p. The Lafayette Papers ISBN:0-8014-1576-4, ISBN13: 978-0-8014-1576-0. Dewey:944/.035/0924. LCCN:76-050268.
Audience: **f.**

Lafayette, Le Marquis de **DC146.L2**
Lafayette in the Age of the American Revolution, Selected Letters and Papers, 1776-1790: April 10th, 1778-March 20th, 1780. Stanley J. Idzerda, Linda J. Pike & Mary A. Quinn (Editors). Book, Other. Cornell University Press. Ithaca, NY. 1979. 520p. The Lafayette Papers ISBN:0-8014-1246-3, ISBN13: 978-0-8014-1246-2. Dewey:944/.035/0924. LCCN:76-050268.
Audience: **f.**

Lafayette, Le Marquis de **DC146.L2**
Lafayette in the Age of the American Revolution, Selected Letters and Papers, 1776-1790, Vol. IV: April 1st, 1781-December 23rd, 1781. Stanley J. Idzerda, Linda J. Pike & Mary A. Quinn (Editors). Trade Cloth. Cornell University Press. Ithaca, NY. 1981. 600p. The Lafayette Papers ISBN:0-8014-1336-2, ISBN13: 978-0-8014-1336-0. Dewey:944.040924. LCCN:76-050268.
Audience: **f.**

Lafayette, Le Marquis de **DC146.L2**
Lafayette in the Age of the American Revolution, Selected Letters and Papers, 1776-1790: December 7th, 1776-March 30th, 1778. Stanley J. Idzerda & Roger E. Smith (Editors). Book, Other. Cornell University Press. Ithaca, NY. 1977. 535p.

The Lafayette Papers ISBN:0-8014-1031-2, ISBN13: 978-0-8014-1031-4. Dewey:944/.035/0924. LCCN:76-050268.
Audience: **f.** 𝐁

Malone, Dumas **E332.M25**
Jefferson and His Time. Trade Cloth. University Press of Virginia. Charlottesville, VA. 2001. 3300p. ISBN:0-8139-2354-9, ISBN13: 978-0-8139-2354-3. Dewey:973.4/6/092.
Audience: **l,u,f.** 𝐁

Malone, Dumas **E332.M25 2005**
Jefferson and the Ordeal of Liberty. Trade Cloth. University Press of Virginia. Charlottesville, VA. 2005. xxx, 545p. ISBN:0-8139-2357-3, ISBN13: 978-0-8139-2357-4. Dewey:973.4/6/092. LCCN:2005-544121.
Audience: **l,u,f.**

Malone, Dumas **E332.M25 2005**
Jefferson and the Rights of Man. Trade Cloth. University Press of Virginia. Charlottesville, VA. 2005. xxix, 506p. ISBN:0-8139-2356-5, ISBN13: 978-0-8139-2356-7. Dewey:973.4/6/092. LCCN:2005-544121.
Audience: **l,u,f.**

Malone, Dumas **E332.M25 2005**
Jefferson the President, First Term, 1801-1805. Trade Cloth. University Press of Virginia. Charlottesville, VA. 2005. ISBN:0-8139-2358-1, ISBN13: 978-0-8139-2358-1. Dewey:973.4/6/092. LCCN:2005-544121.
Audience: **l,u,f.**

Malone, Dumas **E332.M25 2005**
Jefferson the President, Second Term, 1805-1809. Trade Cloth. University Press of Virginia. Charlottesville, VA. 2005. xxxi, 704p. ISBN:0-8139-2359-X, ISBN13: 978-0-8139-2359-8. Dewey:973.4/6/092. LCCN:2005-544121.
Audience: **l,u,f.**

Malone, Dumas **E332.M25 2005**
Jefferson the Virginian. Trade Cloth. University Press of Virginia. Charlottesville, VA. 2005. xxxii, 484p. ISBN:0-8139-2355-7, ISBN13: 978-0-8139-2355-0. Dewey:973.4/6/092. LCCN:2005-544121.
Audience: **l,u,f.**

McDonald, Forrest **E331.M32**
The Presidency of Thomas Jefferson. Trade Cloth. University Press of Kansas. Lawrence, KS. 1986. xii, 204p. American Presidency Ser. ISBN:0-7006-0147-3, ISBN13: 978-0-7006-0147-9. Dewey:320.9/73/046. LCCN:76-000803.
Audience: **l,u,f.** 𝐁

McKee, Christopher **E335.P78M32 1996**
Edward Preble: A Naval Biography, 1761-1807. Ed. 2. Trade Cloth. Naval Institute Press. Annapolis, MD. 1996. 432p. Classics of Naval Literature Ser. ISBN:1-55750-583-7, ISBN13: 978-1-55750-583-5. Dewey:973.4/7. LCCN:96-002679.
Audience: **l,u,f.**

Nelson, Paul David **E207.G3.N44**
General Horatio Gates: A Biography. Louisiana State University Press. 1976. ISBN:0-8071-0159-1, ISBN13: 978-0-8071-0159-9.
Audience: **u,f.**

Peterson, Merrill D. **E210**
Adams and Jefferson: A Revolutionary Dialogue. Paper Text. Oxford University Press, Inc. New York, NY. 1978. 160p. ISBN:0-19-502355-2, ISBN13: 978-0-19-502355-8. Dewey:973.4/4/0924. LCCN:76-001145.
Audience: **l,u,f.**

Peterson, Merrill D. **E332.2**
Jefferson and Madison and the Making of Constitutions. Trade Paper. University Press of Virginia. Charlottesville, VA. 1987. 17p. ISBN:0-8139-1176-1, ISBN13: 978-0-8139-1176-2. Dewey:973.4.
Audience: **l,u,f.**

Peterson, Merrill D. **E211**
Jefferson and the Revolutionary Mind. Trade Cloth. Academy Books. Rutland, VT. 1995. ISBN:1-56715-021-7, ISBN13: 978-1-56715-021-6. Dewey:973.311. LCCN:98-229025.
Audience: **u,f.**

Peterson, Merrill D. **E332.2.P4 1998**
The Jefferson Image in the American Mind. Paper Text. University Press of Virginia. Charlottesville, VA. 1999. 560p. ISBN:0-8139-1851-0, ISBN13: 978-0-8139-1851-8. Dewey:973.4/6/092. LCCN:98-024052.
Audience: **l,u,f.** 𝐁

Peterson, Merrill D. **E332**
The Jefferson Image in the American Mind. Trade Cloth. Oxford University Press, Inc. New York, NY. 1970. 558p. ISBN:0-19-501539-8, ISBN13: 978-0-19-501539-3. Dewey:973.4/6/092.
Audience: **l,u,f.** 𝐁

Peterson, Merrill D. **GV863.A1**
Thomas Jefferson: And the New Nation - to the Vice Presidency, Set. Katherine E. Speirs (Editor). Trade Cloth. American Political Biography. Newtown, CT. 2001. 545p. ISBN:0-945707-30-4, ISBN13: 978-0-945707-30-1. Dewey:796/.357.
Audience: **l,u,f.**

Peterson, Merrill D. **DA220.P2213**
Thomas Jefferson: And the New Nation - Return to Monticello, Vol. 2. Katherine E. Speirs (Editor). Trade Cloth. American Political Biography. Newtown, CT. 2001. 532p. ISBN:0-945707-31-2, ISBN13: 978-0-945707-31-8. Dewey:942.
Audience: **l,u,f.**

Spivak, Burton **E331.S68**
Jefferson's English Crisis, 1803-1809: Commerce, Embargo, and the Republican Revolution. Trade Cloth. University Press of Virginia. Charlottesville, VA. 1979. 250p. ISBN:0-8139-0805-1, ISBN13: 978-0-8139-0805-2. Dewey:973.4/6/0924. LCCN:78-013110.
Audience: **l,u,f.** 𝐁

Wilson, Clyde N. (Editor) **E337.8.C148**
The Papers of John C. Calhoun, 1846. Cloth Text. University of South Carolina Press. Columbia, SC. 1996. 780p. Papers of John C. Calhoun Ser., Vol. XXIII ISBN:1-57003-104-5, ISBN13: 978-1-57003-104-5. Dewey:973.5/092/4. LCCN:59-010351.
Audience: **u,f.**

Wilson, Clyde N. (Editor), et al. **E337.8.C148**
The Papers of John C. Calhoun: 1848-1849. Shirley B. Cook & Alexander Moore (Editors). Trade Cloth. University of South Carolina Press. Columbia, SC. 2001. 576p.

ISBN:1-57003-393-5, ISBN13: 978-1-57003-393-3. Dewey:973.5/092/4. LCCN:59-010351.

Audience: **u,f.**

Wilson, Clyde N. (Editor), et al. **E338.8**
Papers of John C. Calhoun, 1847-1848. Shirley B. Cook & Alexander Moore (Editors). Trade Cloth. University of South Carolina Press. Columbia, SC. 1999. 768p. Papers of John C. Calhoun Ser., Vol. XXV ISBN:1-57003-306-4, ISBN13: 978-1-57003-306-3. Dewey:973.5092. LCCN:59-010351.

Audience: **u,f.**

United States > American History, by Period > American Revolution, 1775-1783 > General Works

Barnes, Ian **E208.B36 2000**
The Historical Atlas of the American Revolution. Charles Royster (Editor). Paper over Boards. Routledge. New York, NY. 2000. 208p. ISBN:0-415-92243-7, ISBN13: 978-0-415-92243-2. Dewey:973.3. LCCN:99-059920.

Audience: **g,l,u,f.** *Choice, 2001.*

Blanco, Richard L. (Editor) **E208.A433 1993**
The American Revolution 1775-1783: An Encyclopedia. Library Binding. Garland Publishing, Inc. New York, NY. 1993. 1896p. Military History of the U. S. Ser., Vol. 1 ISBN:0-8240-5623-X, ISBN13: 978-0-8240-5623-0. Dewey:973.303. LCCN:92-042541.

Audience: **g,l,u,f.** *Choice, 1993.*

Bonwick, Colin **E208**
American Revolution. Ed. 2. Cloth over Boards. Palgrave Macmillan. New York, NY. 2005. 400p. American History in Depth Ser. ISBN:1-4039-9724-1, ISBN13: 978-1-4039-9724-1. Dewey:973.3. LCCN:2005-051386.

Audience: **l,u,f.**

United States > American History, by Period > American Revolution, 1775-1783 > Military and Diplomatic History

Allen, Gardner W. **E271.A42**
A Naval History of the American Revolution, Set. Library Binding. Higginson Book Company. Salem, MA. 1995. 752p. ISBN:0-8328-4503-5, ISBN13: 978-0-8328-4503-1. Dewey:973.35.

Audience: **u,f.**

Baurmeister, Carl Leopold **E268.B4**
Revolution in America: Confidential Letters and Journals 1776. Paper Text. Textbook Publishers. Temecula, CA. 2003. xiv, 640p. ISBN:0-7581-4271-4, ISBN13: 978-0-7581-4271-9. Dewey:973.3.

Audience: **u,f.**

Bemis, Samuel Flagg **E249.B44 1957**
The Diplomacy of the American Revolution. Indiana University Press. 1957. Midland Books, Vol. MB6

Audience: **l,u,f.**

Corwin, E. S. **E249.C83**
French Policy and the American Alliance of, 1778. Trade Cloth. Peter Smith Publisher, Inc. Magnolia, MA. 1990. ISBN:0-8446-0559-X, ISBN13: 978-0-8446-0559-3. Dewey:973.32/4.

Audience: **f.**

Dull, Jonathan R. **E249**
A Diplomatic History of the American Revolution. Trade Paper. Yale University Press. Cumberland, RI. 1987. 236p. ISBN:0-300-03886-0, ISBN13: 978-0-300-03886-6. Dewey:973.3/2. LCCN:85-005306.

Audience: **l,u,f.** *Choice, 1986.*

Fowler, William M. **E271.F68**
Rebels under Sail: The American Navy During the Revolution. Trade Cloth. Simon & Schuster. New York, NY. 1976. xi, 356p. ISBN:0-684-14583-9, ISBN13: 978-0-684-14583-9. Dewey:973.3/5. LCCN:75-038556.

Audience: **u,f.**

Higginbotham, Donald **E210.H63 1983**
The War of American Independence: Military Attitudes, Policies and Practice, 1763-1789. Paper Text. Northeastern University Press. Boston, MA. 1983. 521p. ISBN:0-930350-44-8, ISBN13: 978-0-930350-44-4. Dewey:973.3. LCCN:83-002374.

Audience: **l,u,f.**

Hutson, James H. **E24**
John Adams and the Diplomacy of the American Revolution. University Press of Kentucky. 1980. ISBN:0-8131-1404-7, ISBN13: 978-0-8131-1404-0.

Audience: **u,f.**

Marshall, Douglas W. & Peckham, Howard Henry **G1201.S3**
Campaigns of the American Revolution: An Atlas of Manuscript Maps. University of Michigan Press. 1976. ISBN:0-472-23300-9, ISBN13: 978-0-472-23300-7.

Audience: **l,u.**

Peckham, Howard H. **E230**
The War for Independence: A Military History. Trade Paper. University of Chicago Press. Chicago, IL. 1958. 235p. Chicago History of American Civilization Ser. ISBN:0-226-65316-1, ISBN13: 978-0-226-65316-7. Dewey:973.33. LCCN:58-005685.

Audience: **u,f.**

Rice, Howard C. **E26**
The American Campaigns of Rochambeau's Army, 1780, 1781, 1782, 1783. Brown, Anne K. (Translators & Editors). Princeton University Press. 1972. ISBN:0-691-04610-7, ISBN13: 978-0-691-04610-5.

Audience: **f.**

Royster, Charles **E259**
A Revolutionary People at War: The Continental Army and American Character, 1775-1783. Trade Paper. University of North Carolina Press. Chapel Hill, NC. 1996. 463p. ISBN:0-8078-4606-6, ISBN13: 978-0-8078-4606-3. Dewey:973.3/4. LCCN:79-010152.

Audience: **l,u,f.**

Shy, John **E230.S5 1990**
A People Numerous and Armed: Reflections on the Military Struggle for American Independence. Ed. 2. Trade Paper. University of Michigan Press. Chicago, IL. 1990. 376p. Ann Arbor Paperbacks Ser. ISBN:0-472-06431-2, ISBN13: 978-0-472-06431-1. Dewey:973.3/3. LCCN:89-040806.
Audience: **u,f.**

Shy, John W. **E0210.S5**
Toward Lexington: The Role of the British Army in the Coming of the American Revolution. Trade Paper. Books on Demand. Ann Arbor, MI. 473p. ISBN:0-608-18569-8, ISBN13: 978-0-608-18569-9. Dewey:973.3113. LCCN:65-017160.
Audience: **u,f.** BCL3

Stout, Neil R. **E21**
The Royal Navy in America, 1760-1775: A Study of the Enforcement of British Colonial Policy in the Era of the American Revolution. Naval Institute Press. 1973. ISBN:0-87021-553-1, ISBN13: 978-0-87021-553-7.
Audience: **f.**

Uhlendorf, Bernard A. (Editor) **E241.C4U5**
Siege of Charleston. Trade Cloth. Ayer Company Publishers, Inc. Manchester, NH. 1976. Eyewitness Accounts of the American Revolution Ser. ISBN:0-405-01125-3, ISBN13: 978-0-405-01125-2. Dewey:973.33/6. LCCN:67-029028.
Audience: **u,f.**

United States, Naval History Division **E271.U583**
Naval Documents of the American Revolution. Clark, William Bell (Editor); Kennedy, John F. (Foreword by); Eller, Ernest McNeill (Introduction by). Naval History Division, Dept. of the Navy. 1964.
Audience: **l,u,f.**

Wallace, Willard Mosher **E0230.W3**
Appeal to Arms: A Military History of the American Revolution. Trade Paper. Books on Demand. Ann Arbor, MI. 318p. ISBN:0-598-77857-8, ISBN13: 978-0-598-77857-4. Dewey:973.33. LCCN:51-000348.
Audience: **f.** BCL3

United States > American History, by Period > Revolution to Civil war (1775/1783-1861)

Maryland Institute for Technology in the Humanities **E18**
[Web] Early Americas Digital Archive.
http://narcissus.umd.edu:8080/eada/index.jsp
Maryland Institute for Technology in the Humanities.
Audience: **g,l,u,f.**

U. S. Institute of Museum and Library Services **E101**
[Web] American Journeys: Eyewitness Accounts of Early American Exploration and Settlement: A Digital Library and Learning Center.
http://www.americanjourneys.org
Wisconsin Historical Society.
Audience: **g,l,u,f.**

United States > American History, by Period > Revolution to Civil war (1775/1783-1861) > General Works

Blau, J. L. **E338.S64 2003**
Social Theories of Jacksonian Democracy. Trade Paper. Hackett Publishing Company, Inc. Indianapolis, IN. 2003. 383p. ISBN:0-87220-689-0, ISBN13: 978-0-87220-689-2. Dewey:973.5. LCCN:2003-056169.
Audience: **l,u,f.**

Craven, Avery O. **E338**
The Coming of the Civil War. Ed. 2. Trade Paper. University of Chicago Press. Chicago, IL. 1966. 499p. ISBN:0-226-11894-0, ISBN13: 978-0-226-11894-9. Dewey:973.713. LCCN:57-008572.
Audience: **l,u,f.**

Dangerfield, George **E338.D3**
Awakening of American Nationalism, 1815-1828. Trade Cloth. HarperCollins Publishers. New York, NY. 1965. New American Nation Ser. ISBN:0-06-010945-9, ISBN13: 978-0-06-010945-5. Dewey:973.5.
Audience: **l,u,f.**

Donald, David Herbert **E338.D58 1978**
Liberty and Union. Trade Cloth. Little Brown & Company. New York, NY. 1978. x, 318p. ISBN:0-316-18949-9, ISBN13: 978-0-316-18949-1. Dewey:973. LCCN:78-054090.
Audience: **l,u,f.** BCL3

Livermore, Shaw **E338.L5 1972**
Twilight of Federalism: The Disintegration of the Federalist Party - 1815-1830. Trade Cloth. Gordian Press, Inc. Staten Island, NY. 1972. 302p. ISBN:0-87752-137-9, ISBN13: 978-0-87752-137-2. Dewey:329/.1. LCCN:73-150413.
Audience: **l,u,f.** BCL3

McDonald, Forrest **JA84.U5M43 1985**
Novus Ordo Seclorum: The Intellectual Origins of the Constitution. Trade Cloth. University Press of Kansas. Lawrence, KS. 1985. xiv, 362p. American Political Thought Ser. ISBN:0-7006-0284-4, ISBN13: 978-0-7006-0284-1. Dewey:320/.0973. LCCN:85-013544.
Audience: **u,f.** *Choice, 1986.*

McDonald, Forrest **E311.M12**
The Presidency of George Washington. Trade Paper. University Press of Kansas. Lawrence, KS. 1988. xiv, 210p. American Presidency Ser. ISBN:0-7006-0359-X, ISBN13: 978-0-7006-0359-6. Dewey:973.4/1/0924. LCCN:73-011344.
Audience: **l,u,f.**

Meyers, Marvin **E338.M53**
The Jacksonian Persuasion: Politics and Belief. Paper Text. Textbook Publishers. Temecula, CA. 2003. vi, 231p. ISBN:0-7581-3447-9, ISBN13: 978-0-7581-3447-9. Dewey:973.5.
Audience: **l,u,f.** BCL3

Pessen, Edward **E338.P4 1985**
Jacksonian America: Society, Personality, and Politics. Trade Paper. University of Illinois Press. Champaign, IL. 1985. 400p. ISBN:0-252-01237-2, ISBN13: 978-0-252-01237-2. Dewey:973.5. LCCN:85-001100.
Audience: **l,u,f.** BCL3

Silbey, Joel H. **E338.S55 1985**
The Partisan Imperative: The Dynamics of American Politics Before the Civil War. Trade Cloth. Oxford University Press, Inc. New York, NY. 1985. 234p. ISBN:0-19-503551-8, ISBN13: 978-0-19-503551-3. Dewey:320.973. LCCN:84-020691.
Audience: **l,u,f.** B *Choice, 1985.*

Smelser, Marshall **E338**
The Democratic Republic, 1801-1815. Paper Text. Waveland Press, Inc. Prospect Heights, IL. 1992. 369p. ISBN:0-88133-668-8, ISBN13: 978-0-88133-668-9. Dewey:973.46.
Audience: **l,u,f.** B

Turner, Frederick Jackson **E338.T92**
United States, 1830-1850: The Nation and Its Sections. Paper Text. Classic Textbooks. Murrieta, CA. 1935. 119p. ISBN:1-4047-4886-5, ISBN13: 978-1-4047-4886-6. Dewey:973.56.
Audience: **l,u,f.** B

Wilentz, Sean **E302.1.W55 2005**
The Rise of American Democracy: Jefferson to Lincoln. Trade Cloth. W. W. Norton & Company, Inc. New York, NY. 2005. 992p. ISBN:0-393-05820-4, ISBN13: 978-0-393-05820-8. Dewey:973.5. LCCN:2004-029466.
Audience: **u,f.** *Choice, 2006.*

Wilson, Major L. **E338**
Space, Time, and Freedom: The Quest for Nationality and the Irrepressible Conflict, 1815-1861, 35. Trade Cloth. Greenwood Publishing Group, Inc. Portsmouth, NH. 1974. 309p. Contributions in American History Ser. ISBN:0-8371-7373-6, ISBN13: 978-0-8371-7373-3. Dewey:973. LCCN:74-000287.
Audience: **l,u,f.** B

Young, James S. **JK686**
Washington Community: Eighteen Hundred to Eighteeen Twenty-Eight. Cloth Text. Columbia University Press. New York, NY. 1986. 307p. ISBN:0-231-02901-2, ISBN13: 978-0-231-02901-8. Dewey:353.0009034. LCCN:66-014080.
Audience: **l,u,f.**

United States > American History, by Period > Revolution to Civil war (1775/1783-1861) > Biography

Bartlett, Irving H. **E340.W4.B26 1978**
Daniel Webster. Trade Cloth. W. W. Norton & Company, Inc. New York, NY. 1978. xii, 333p. ISBN:0-393-07524-9, ISBN13: 978-0-393-07524-3. Dewey:973.5/092/4. LCCN:77-027542.
Audience: **l,u,f.** B

Baxter, Maurice G. **E340.W4**
One and Inseparable: Daniel Webster and the Union. Trade Cloth. Harvard University Press. Cambridge, MA. 1984. 668p. Belknap Press Ser. ISBN:0-674-63821-2, ISBN13: 978-0-674-63821-1. Dewey:347.3/0092/4. LCCN:83-026597.
Audience: **l,u,f.** B

Brands, H. W. **E382.B83 2005**
Andrew Jackson: His Life and Times. Trade Cloth. Doubleday Canada, Ltd. Toronto, ON. 2005. 640p. ISBN:0-385-50738-0, ISBN13: 978-0-385-50738-7. Dewey:973.5/6/092. LCCN:2005-042178.
Audience: **g,l,u,f.** *Choice, 2006.*

Capers, Gerald Mortimer **E340.C15**
John C. Calhoun, Opportunist: A Reappraisal. Paper Text. Textbook Publishers. Temecula, CA. 2003. 275p. ISBN:0-7581-2293-4, ISBN13: 978-0-7581-2293-3. Dewey:923.273.
Audience: **l,u,f.** B

Chambers, William Nisbet **E340.B4C5**
Old Bullion Benton, Senator from the New West: Thomas Hart Benton 1782. Paper Text. Textbook Publishers. Temecula, CA. 2003. xv, 517p. ISBN:0-7581-4453-9, ISBN13: 978-0-7581-4453-9. Dewey:923.273.
Audience: **l,u,f.** B

Eaton, Clement **E340.C6E2**
Henry Clay and the Art of American Politics. Paper Text. Textbook Publishers. Temecula, CA. 2003. 209p. ISBN:0-7581-9691-1, ISBN13: 978-0-7581-9691-0. Dewey:923.273.
Audience: **l,u,f.** B

Fuess, Claude M. **E340.W4F95**
Daniel Webster. Ed. 2. Paper Text. Da Capo Press, Inc. Cambridge, MA. 1968. American Scene Ser. ISBN:0-306-71186-9, ISBN13: 978-0-306-71186-2. Dewey:923.273. LCCN:68-008722.
Audience: **l,u,f.** B

Handlin, Lilian **E175.5.B19**
George Bancroft: The Intellectual As Democrat. Trade Cloth. HarperCollins Publishers. New York, NY. 1984. 384p. ISBN:0-06-039033-6, ISBN13: 978-0-06-039033-4. Dewey:973/.072024. LCCN:83-049057.
Audience: **l,u,f.** B

Kirwan, Albert D. **E340.C9K5 1974**
John J. Crittenden: The Struggle for the Union. Trade Cloth. Greenwood Publishing Group, Inc. Portsmouth, NH. 1974. 514p. ISBN:0-8371-6922-4, ISBN13: 978-0-8371-6922-4. Dewey:328.73/092/4. LCCN:73-007309.
Audience: **l,u,f.**

McCullough, David **E322.M38 2001**
John Adams. Trade Cloth. Simon & Schuster. New York, NY. 2001. 752p. ISBN:0-684-81363-7, ISBN13: 978-0-684-81363-9. Dewey:973.4/4/092 B. LCCN:2001-027010.
Audience: **g,l,u,f.**

McDonald, Forrest **E302.6.H2.M32 1979**
Alexander Hamilton: A Biography. Trade Cloth. Norton. Farnborough, 1979. xiii, 464p. ISBN:0-393-01218-2, ISBN13: 978-0-393-01218-7. Dewey:973.4/092/4. LCCN:78-026554.
Audience: **u,f.** B

Nagel, Paul C. **E377**
John Quincy Adams: A Public Life, a Private Life. Trade Paper. Harvard University Press. Cambridge, MA. 1999. 466p. ISBN:0-674-47940-8, ISBN13: 978-0-674-47940-1. Dewey:973.5/5/092 B.
Audience: **l,u,f.**

Wiltse, Charles M. **E340.C15W5**
John C. Calhoun. Trade Cloth. Russell & Russell Publishers. New York, NY. 1968. ISBN:0-8462-1041-X, ISBN13: 978-0-8462-1041-2. Dewey:923.273. LCCN:68-011329.
Audience: **l,u,f.**

United States > American History, by Period > Revolution to Civil war (1775/1783-1861) > By Presidential Administration

Adams, John Q. Jr. **E377.A2 1969**
Memoirs of John Quincy Adams, Comprising Portions of His Diary from 1795 to 1848, Set. Charles Francis Adams Jr. (Editor). Trade Cloth. Ayer Company Publishers, Inc. Manchester, NH. 1969. Select Bibliographies Reprint Ser. ISBN:0-8369-5021-6, ISBN13: 978-0-8369-5021-2. Dewey:973.5/0924. LCCN:71-085454.
Audience: **u,f.**

Adams, John Q. **E377.A214**
Diary of John Quincy Adams: 1794-1845. Allan Nevins (Editor). Trade Cloth. Continuum International Publishing Group, Ltd. London, 1969. American Classics ISBN:0-8044-1010-0, ISBN13: 978-0-8044-1010-6. Dewey:973.5/5/0924. LCCN:68-008892.
Audience: **u,f.**

Ammon, Harry **E372**
James Monroe: The Quest for National Identity. Katherine E. Speirs (Editor). Trade Cloth. American Political Biography. Newtown, CT. 1998. 706p. Signature Ser. ISBN:0-945707-21-5, ISBN13: 978-0-945707-21-9. Dewey:973.5/4/092. LCCN:97-076733.
Audience: **l,u,f.** B

Bemis, Samuel F. **E377.B45 1981**
John Quincy Adams and the Foundations of American Foreign Policy. Library Binding. Greenwood Publishing Group, Inc. Portsmouth, NH. 1981. xix, 588p. ISBN:0-313-22636-9, ISBN13: 978-0-313-22636-6. Dewey:973.5/5/0924. LCCN:80-023039.
Audience: **l,u,f.**

Bemis, Samuel F. **E377.B46 1980**
John Quincy Adams and the Union. Library Binding. Greenwood Publishing Group, Inc. Portsmouth, NH. 1980. xv, 546p. ISBN:0-313-22637-7, ISBN13: 978-0-313-22637-3. Dewey:973.5/5/0924. LCCN:80-020402.
Audience: **l,u,f.**

Bergeron, Paul H. **E416.B47 1987**
The Presidency of James K. Polk. Trade Cloth. University Press of Kansas. Lawrence, KS. 1987. xvi, 312p. American Presidency Ser. ISBN:0-7006-0319-0, ISBN13: 978-0-7006-0319-0. Dewey:973.6/1/0924. LCCN:87-002174.
Audience: **l,u,f.** *Choice, 1987.*

Berton, Pierre **E355.B46 1981**
Flames Across the Border, 1813-1814. Trade Cloth. Little Brown & Company. New York, NY. 1982. 492p. ISBN:0-316-09217-7, ISBN13: 978-0-316-09217-3. Dewey:971.03/4. LCCN:81-082541.
Audience: **l,u,f.** B

Brown, Ralph A. **E321.B84**
The Presidency of John Adams. Trade Cloth. University Press of Kansas. Lawrence, KS. 1975. xii, 248p. American Presidency Ser. ISBN:0-7006-0134-1, ISBN13: 978-0-7006-0134-9. Dewey:973.4/4/0924. LCCN:75-005526.
Audience: **l,u,f.**

Brown, Roger H. **ND588.K5G5**
The Republic in Peril, 1812. Trade Cloth. W. W. Norton & Company, Inc. New York, NY. 1971. 242p. ISBN:0-393-00578-X, ISBN13: 978-0-393-00578-3. Dewey:927.5.
Audience: **l,u,f.**

Cole, Donald B. **E382.C69 1993**
The Presidency of Andrew Jackson. Trade Cloth. University Press of Kansas. Lawrence, KS. 1999. 352p. American Presidency Ser. ISBN:0-7006-0600-9, ISBN13: 978-0-7006-0600-9. Dewey:973.5/6. LCCN:92-043377.
Audience: **l,u,f.** *Choice, 1993.*

Coles, Harry L. **E354**
The War of 1812. Trade Paper. University of Chicago Press. Chicago, IL. 1966. 307p. The Chicago History of American Civilization Ser., Vol. 22 ISBN:0-226-11350-7, ISBN13: 978-0-226-11350-0. Dewey:973.52. LCCN:65-017283.
Audience: **l,u,f.** B

Commager, Henry Steele **HN64.E68 1982**
The Era of Reform, 1830-1860. Trade Paper. Krieger Publishing Company. Melbourne, FL. 1982. 192p. Anvil Ser. ISBN:0-89874-498-9, ISBN13: 978-0-89874-498-9. Dewey:303.4/84. LCCN:82-015190.
Audience: **u,f.** B

Cunningham, Noble E. Jr. **E371.C86 1996**
The Presidency of James Monroe. Trade Cloth. University Press of Kansas. Lawrence, KS. 1996. xvi, 246p. American Presidency Ser. ISBN:0-7006-0728-5, ISBN13: 978-0-7006-0728-0. Dewey:973.5/4. LCCN:95-034157.
Audience: **l,u,f.** *Choice, 1996.*

Dangerfield, George **E371.D3 1989**
The Era of Good Feelings. Trade Paper. Ivan R. Dee Publisher. Blue Ridge Summit, PA. 1989. 530p. ISBN:0-929587-14-6, ISBN13: 978-0-929587-14-1. Dewey:973.5. LCCN:89-012031.
Audience: **l,u,f.** B

Dudley, William S. **E360**
Naval War of 1812: A Documentary History, 1813, Vol. 2. Trade Cloth. United States Government Printing Office. Washington, DC. 1992. 825p. ISBN:0-16-026357-3, ISBN13: 978-0-16-026357-6. Dewey:973.525.
Audience: **u,f.**

Freehling, William W. **E384.3**
Prelude to the Civil War: The Nullification Controversy in South Carolina 1816-1836. Trade Cloth. Peter Smith Publisher, Inc. Magnolia, MA. 1995. ISBN:0-8446-6869-9, ISBN13: 978-0-8446-6869-7. Dewey:973.561.
Audience: **l,u,f.**

Gara, Larry **E432.G37 1991**
The Presidency of Franklin Pierce. Trade Cloth. University Press of Kansas. Lawrence, KS. 1991. xiv, 218p. American Presidency

Ser. ISBN:0-7006-0494-4, ISBN13: 978-0-7006-0494-4. Dewey:973.6/6/092 B. LCCN:91-008367.
Audience: **l,u,f.** *Choice, 1992.*

Hargreaves, Mary W. **E376.H24 1985**
The Presidency of John Quincy Adams. Trade Cloth. University Press of Kansas. Lawrence, KS. 1985. xvi, 400p. American Presidency Ser. ISBN:0-7006-0272-0, ISBN13: 978-0-7006-0272-8. Dewey:973.5/5/0924. LCCN:85-011147.
Audience: **l,u,f.** *Choice, 1986.*

Horsman, Reginald **E357.H72**
The Causes of the War of 1812. Paper Text. Textbook Publishers. Temecula, CA. 2003. 345p. ISBN:0-7581-1645-4, ISBN13: 978-0-7581-1645-1. Dewey:973.521.
Audience: **l,u,f.**

Huff, Archie Vernon **E353.1.C45.H83**
Langdon Cheves of South Carolina. Trade Cloth. Bow Historical Books. New Providence, NJ. 1977. 276p. ISBN:0-87249-256-7, ISBN13: 978-0-87249-256-1. Dewey:328.73/092/4. LCCN:76-049573.
Audience: **l,u,f.**

Jones, Howard **E398.J66**
To the Webster-Ashburton Treaty: A Study in Anglo-American Relations, 1783-1843. Trade Cloth. University of North Carolina Press. Chapel Hill, NC. 1977. xx, 251p. ISBN:0-8078-1306-0, ISBN13: 978-0-8078-1306-5. Dewey:327.73/041. LCCN:76-058341.
Audience: **l,u,f.**

Ketcham, Ralph **E342**
James Madison: A Biography. Katherine E. Speirs (Editor). Trade Cloth. American Political Biography. Newtown, CT. 2003. 737p. Signature Ser. ISBN:0-945707-33-9, ISBN13: 978-0-945707-33-2. Dewey:973.5/1/092.
Audience: **l,u,f.**

Long, David F. **E353.1.B5.L66 1983**
Sailor-Diplomat: A Biography of Commodore James Biddle, 1783-1848. Cloth Text. Northeastern University Press. Boston, MA. 1983. 328p. ISBN:0-930350-39-1, ISBN13: 978-0-930350-39-0. Dewey:973.5/092/4. LCCN:82-022236.
Audience: **l,u,f.**

Mahan, Alfred Thayer **D246**
The Influence of Sea Power upon History, 1660-1783. Trade Paper. Pelican Publishing Company, Inc. Gretna, LA. 2003. 592p. ISBN:1-58980-155-5, ISBN13: 978-1-58980-155-4. Dewey:909/.6.
Audience: **u,f.**

May, Ernest R. **E371**
The Making of the Monroe Doctrine. Trade Cloth. Harvard University Press. Cambridge, MA. 1975. 328p. ISBN:0-674-54340-8, ISBN13: 978-0-674-54340-9. Dewey:327.73. LCCN:75-011619.
Audience: **l,u,f.**

McDonald, Forrest **E311.M12**
The Presidency of George Washington. Trade Paper. University Press of Kansas. Lawrence, KS. 1988. xiv, 210p. American Presidency Ser. ISBN:0-7006-0359-X, ISBN13: 978-0-7006-0359-6. Dewey:973.4/1/0924. LCCN:73-011344.
Audience: **l,u,f.**

Merk, Frederick & Merk, Lois B. **E398**
Fruits of Propaganda in the Tyler Administration. Trade Cloth. Harvard University Press. Cambridge, MA. 1971. 269p. ISBN:0-674-32676-8, ISBN13: 978-0-674-32676-7. Dewey:973.5/8. LCCN:79-135547.
Audience: **l,u,f.**

Moore, Glover **E373.M77**
The Missouri Controversy, 1819-1821. Paper Text. Textbook Publishers. Temecula, CA. 2003. viii, 383p. ISBN:0-7581-2186-5, ISBN13: 978-0-7581-2186-8. Dewey:973.54.
Audience: **l,u,f.**

Morgan, Robert J. **E396.M6 1974**
A Whig Embattled. Trade Cloth. Shoe String Press, Inc. North Haven, CT. 1974. xxi, 199p. ISBN:0-208-01428-4, ISBN13: 978-0-208-01428-3. Dewey:973.5/8/0924. LCCN:74-002004.
Audience: **l,u,f.**

Niven, John **E387**
Martin Van Buren: The Romantic Age of American Politics. Katherine E. Speirs (Editor). Trade Cloth. American Political Biography. Newtown, CT. 2000. 715p. Signature Ser. ISBN:0-945707-25-8, ISBN13: 978-0-945707-25-7. Dewey:973.5/7/0924. LCCN:00-131657.
Audience: **u,f.**

Owsley, Frank L. Jr. **E355.1.N5.O97**
The Struggle for the Gulf Borderlands: The Creek War and the Battle of New Orleans, 1812-1815. Trade Cloth. University Press of Florida. Gainesville, FL. 1981. vii, 255p. ISBN:0-8130-0662-7, ISBN13: 978-0-8130-0662-8. Dewey:973.5/238. LCCN:80-011109.
Audience: **l,u,f.**

Perkins, Bradford **E358.P4**
Castlereagh and Adams: England and the United States, 1812-1823. Trade Cloth. University of California Press. Berkeley, CA. 1964. 374p. ISBN:0-520-00997-5, ISBN13: 978-0-520-00997-4. Dewey:327.73042.
Audience: **l,u,f.**

Perkins, Bradford **E357.P66**
Prologue to War: England and the United States 1805. Paper Text. Textbook Publishers. Temecula, CA. 2003. x, 457p. ISBN:0-7581-2684-0, ISBN13: 978-0-7581-2684-9. Dewey:973.521.
Audience: **l,u,f.**

Peterson, Norma L. **E391.P48 1989**
The Presidencies of William Henry Harrison and John Tyler. Trade Cloth. University Press of Kansas. Lawrence, KS. 1989. xiv, 330p. American Presidency Ser. ISBN:0-7006-0400-6, ISBN13: 978-0-7006-0400-5. Dewey:973.5/8/0922. LCCN:89-005341.
Audience: **l,u,f.** *Choice, 1989.*

Pratt, Julius W. **E357.P9**
Expansionists of Eighteen Twelve. Trade Cloth. Peter Smith Publisher, Inc. Magnolia, MA. 1981. ISBN:0-8446-1363-0, ISBN13: 978-0-8446-1363-5. Dewey:973.521.
Audience: **l,u,f.**

Remini, Robert V. **E382.R4 1998**
Andrew Jackson: The Course of American Empire, 1767-1821. Trade Paper. Johns Hopkins University Press. Baltimore, MD.

1998. 544p. ISBN:0-8018-5911-5, ISBN13: 978-0-8018-5911-3. Dewey:973.5/6/092. LCCN:97-075802.
Audience: **l,u,f.**

Remini, Robert V. **E382.R4 1998**
Andrew Jackson: The Course of American Freedom, 1822-1832. Trade Paper. Johns Hopkins University Press. Baltimore, MD. 1998. 504p. ISBN:0-8018-5912-3, ISBN13: 978-0-8018-5912-0. Dewey:973.5/6/092. LCCN:97-075802.
Audience: **l,u,f.**

Remini, Robert V. **E382.R4 1998**
Andrew Jackson: The Course of American Democracy, 1833-1845. Trade Paper. Johns Hopkins University Press. Baltimore, MD. 1998. 672p. ISBN:0-8018-5913-1, ISBN13: 978-0-8018-5913-7. Dewey:973.5/6/092. LCCN:97-075802.
Audience: **l,u,f.**

Roosevelt, Theodore **E360**
The Naval War of 1812. Trade Paper. Kessinger Publishing, LLC. Whitefish, MT. 2004. ISBN:1-4191-7532-7, ISBN13: 978-1-4191-7532-9. Dewey:973.5/25.
Audience: **l,u,f.**

Rutland, Robert A. **E341**
The Presidency of James Madison. Trade Cloth. University Press of Kansas. Lawrence, KS. 1990. xiv, 234p. American Presidency Ser. ISBN:0-7006-0465-0, ISBN13: 978-0-7006-0465-4. Dewey:973.5/1/092. LCCN:89-070419.
Audience: **l,u,f.** *Choice, 1991.*

Schlesinger, Arthur M. Jr. **E381**
The Age of Jackson. Trade Paper. Little Brown & Company. New York, NY. 1988. 577p. ISBN:0-316-77343-3, ISBN13: 978-0-316-77343-0. Dewey:973.56.
Audience: **l,u,f.**

Sharp, James R. **E386**
Jacksonians vs. the Banks: Politics in the States after the Panic of 1837. Cloth Text. Columbia University Press. New York, NY. 1970. xv, 392p. ISBN:0-231-03260-9, ISBN13: 978-0-231-03260-5. Dewey:332.1/0973. LCCN:70-127783.
Audience: **u,f.** B

Smith, Elbert B. **E421.S65 1988**
The Presidencies of Zachary Taylor and Millard Fillmore. Trade Cloth. University Press of Kansas. Lawrence, KS. 1988. xii, 308p. American Presidency Ser. ISBN:0-7006-0362-X, ISBN13: 978-0-7006-0362-6. Dewey:973.6. LCCN:88-005722.
Audience: **l,u,f.** *Choice, 1989.*

Smith, Elbert B. **E436.S6**
The Presidency of James Buchanan. Trade Cloth. University Press of Kansas. Lawrence, KS. 1975. xvi, 228p. American Presidency Ser. ISBN:0-7006-0132-5, ISBN13: 978-0-7006-0132-5. Dewey:320.9/73/068. LCCN:74-031220.
Audience: **l,u,f.**

Stagg, John C. **E354**
Mr. Madison's War: Politics, Diplomacy and Warfare in the Early American Republic, 1783-1830. Trade Cloth. Princeton University Press. Princeton, NJ. 1983. 560p. ISBN:0-691-04702-2, ISBN13: 978-0-691-04702-7. Dewey:973.5/2. LCCN:82-061386.
Audience: **l,u,f.** B

Van Buren, Martin **E387**
The Autobiography of Martin Van Buren. John C. Fitzpatrick (Editor). Trade Cloth. Scholar's Bookshelf. Cranbury, NJ. 1969. 808p. ISBN:0-678-00531-1, ISBN13: 978-0-678-00531-6. Dewey:973.5/7/0924. LCCN:68-058656.
Audience: **u,f.** B

Ward, John William **E382.W24**
Andrew Jackson, Symbol for an Age. Paper Text. Textbook Publishers. Temecula, CA. 2003. xii, 274p. ISBN:0-7581-6944-2, ISBN13: 978-0-7581-6944-0. Dewey:973.56.
Audience: **l,u,f.** B

Wilson, Major L. **E387.W54 1984**
The Presidency of Martin Van Buren. Trade Cloth. University Press of Kansas. Lawrence, KS. 1984. xiv, 258p. American Presidency Ser. ISBN:0-7006-0238-0, ISBN13: 978-0-7006-0238-4. Dewey:973/.5/7/0924. LCCN:83-017871.
Audience: **l,u,f.** B

United States > American History, by Period > War with Mexico, 1845-1848

Bauer, K. Jack **E404.B37 1993**
The Mexican War, 1846-1848. Robert W. Johannsen (Introduction by). Trade Paper. University of Nebraska Press. Lincoln, NE. 1992. 486p. ISBN:0-8032-6107-1, ISBN13: 978-0-8032-6107-5. Dewey:973.6/2. LCCN:92-013927.
Audience: **l,u,f.** B

Connor, Seymour V. **E404.C8**
North America Divided; the Mexican War, 1846-1848. Trade Cloth. Oxford University Press, Inc. New York, NY. 1971. viii, 300p. ISBN:0-19-501448-0, ISBN13: 978-0-19-501448-8. Dewey:973.6/2. LCCN:77-161885.
Audience: **g,l,u.** B

Johannsen, Robert W. **E404.J64 1985**
To the Halls of the Montezumas: The Mexican War in the American Imagination. Trade Cloth. Oxford University Press, Inc. New York, NY. 1985. 384p. ISBN:0-19-503518-6, ISBN13: 978-0-19-503518-6. Dewey:973.6/2. LCCN:84-020696.
Audience: **l,u,f.** B

Schroeder, John Herman **E415.2**
Mr. Polk's War: American Opposition and Dissent, 1846-1848. Trade Cloth. University of Wisconsin Press. Chicago, IL. 1973. xvi, 185p. ISBN:0-299-06160-4, ISBN13: 978-0-299-06160-9. Dewey:973.6/2. LCCN:73-002049.
Audience: **l,u,f.** B

Singletary, Otis A. **E404.S5**
The Mexican War. Paper Text. Textbook Publishers. Temecula, CA. 2003. 181p. ISBN:0-7581-2522-4, ISBN13: 978-0-7581-2522-4. Dewey:973.62.
Audience: **l,u,f.**

Smith, Justin H. **E404.S66**
War with Mexico. Trade Cloth. Peter Smith Publisher, Inc. Magnolia, MA. 1981. ISBN:0-8446-1413-0, ISBN13: 978-0-8446-1413-7. Dewey:973.62.
Audience: **l,u,f.**

United States > American History, by Period > Middle 19th Century (1845/48-1861)

Abzug, Robert H. **E449**
Passionate Liberator: Theodore Dwight Weld and the Dilemma of Reform. Trade Paper. Oxford University Press, Inc. New York, NY. 1982. 384p. ISBN:0-19-503061-3, ISBN13: 978-0-19-503061-7. Dewey:326/.092/4.
Audience: **l,u,f.** B

Bartlett, Irving H. **E449.P56**
Wendell and Ann Phillips: The Community of Reform, 1840-1880. Trade Cloth. W. W. Norton & Company, Inc. New York, NY. 1981. 249p. ISBN:0-393-01426-6, ISBN13: 978-0-393-01426-6. Dewey:326/.092/4. LCCN:80-027029.
Audience: **l,u,f.**

Birney, James G. **E449**
Letters, 1831-1857, Vols. 1 & 2. Dwight L. Dumond (Editor). Trade Cloth. Peter Smith Publisher, Inc. Magnolia, MA. 1990. ISBN:0-8446-1078-X, ISBN13: 978-0-8446-1078-8. Dewey:326.0973.
Audience: **l,u,f.**

David, Paul A. **E449**
Reckoning with Slavery: Critical Essays in the Quantitative History of American Negro Slavery. Kenneth M. Stampp (Introduction by). Trade Cloth. Oxford University Press, Inc. New York, NY. 1976. ISBN:0-19-502034-0, ISBN13: 978-0-19-502034-2. Dewey:331.1/1734/0973. LCCN:75-038098.
Audience: **u,f.** B

Dick, Robert C. **E449**
Black Protest: Issues and Tactics, 14. Trade Cloth. Greenwood Publishing Group, Inc. Portsmouth, NH. 1974. 338p. Contributions in American Studies ISBN:0-8371-6366-8, ISBN13: 978-0-8371-6366-6. Dewey:322.4/4/0973. LCCN:72-000794.
Audience: **l,u,f.** B

Dillon, Merton L. & Lovejoy, Elijah Parish **E449.L889D5 1980**
Elijah P. Lovejoy, Abolitionist Editor. Trade Cloth. Greenwood Publishing Group, Inc. Portsmouth, NH. 1980. 190p. ISBN:0-313-22352-1, ISBN13: 978-0-313-22352-5. Dewey:326/.092/4. LCCN:80-011000.
Audience: **l,u,f.**

Douglass, Frederick **E449**
The Life and Writings of Frederick Douglass, Vol. 1. Trade Paper. Books on Demand. Ann Arbor, MI. 448p. ISBN:0-598-39939-9, ISBN13: 978-0-598-39939-7. Dewey:322.4/4/0924. LCCN:50-007654.
Audience: **g,l,u,f.**

Douglass, Frederick **E449.D734 1999**
Autobiographical Writings: Narrative. John W. Blassingame, John R. McKigan & Peter P. Hinks (Editors). Cloth over Boards. Yale University Press. Cumberland, RI. 1999. 288p. Frederick Douglass Papers, No. 2 ISBN:0-300-07196-5, ISBN13: 978-0-300-07196-2. Dewey:973.8/092. LCCN:98-026125.
Audience: **l,u,f.** B *Choice, 1999.*

Douglass, Frederick & Foner, Philip S. **E449**
The Life and Writings of Frederick Douglass, Vol. 2. Trade Paper. Books on Demand. Ann Arbor, MI. 578p. ISBN:0-598-39940-2, ISBN13: 978-0-598-39940-3. Dewey:322.4/4/0924. LCCN:50-007654.
Audience: **g,l,u,f.**

Douglass, Frederick & Foner, Philip S. **E0449**
The Life and Writings of Frederick Douglass, Vol. 3. Trade Paper. Books on Demand. Ann Arbor, MI. 448p. ISBN:0-598-39941-0, ISBN13: 978-0-598-39941-0. Dewey:322.4/4/0924. LCCN:50-007654.
Audience: **g,l,u,f.**

Douglass, Frederick & Foner, Philip S. **E449**
The Life and Writings of Frederick Douglass, Vol. 4. Trade Paper. Books on Demand. Ann Arbor, MI. 574p. ISBN:0-598-39942-9, ISBN13: 978-0-598-39942-7. Dewey:322.4/4/0924. LCCN:50-007654.
Audience: **g,l,u,f.**

Douglass, Frederick **E457**
Narrative of the Life of Frederick Douglass: An American Slave, Written by Himself. Alyssa Harad (Contribution by). Mass Market. Simon & Schuster. New York, NY. 2004. 208p. Enriched Classics Ser. ISBN:0-7434-8777-X, ISBN13: 978-0-7434-8777-1. Dewey:973.7/092.
Audience: **g,l,u,f.**

Duberman, Martin (Editor) **E449.D84**
Antislavery Vanguard: New Essays on the Abolitionists. Trade Cloth. Princeton University Press. Princeton, NJ. 1965. 520p. ISBN:0-691-04505-4, ISBN13: 978-0-691-04505-4. Dewey:973.7114.
Audience: **u,f.**

Dumond, Dwight L. (Editor) **E440.5**
Southern Editorials on Secession. Trade Cloth. Peter Smith Publisher, Inc. Magnolia, MA. 1964. ISBN:0-8446-1162-X, ISBN13: 978-0-8446-1162-4. Dewey:973.713.
Audience: **l,u,f.**

Filler, Louis **E449.F493 1986**
Crusade Against Slavery: Friends, Foes, and Reforms 1820-1860. Keith Irvine (Editor). Trade Paper. Reference Publications, Inc. Algonac, MI. 1986. 400p. ISBN:0-917256-30-1, ISBN13: 978-0-917256-30-1. Dewey:326/.0973. LCCN:85-030100.
Audience: **l,u,f.** B *Choice, 1987.*

Fitzhugh, George **E449**
Cannibals All!, or, Slaves Without Masters. C. Vann Woodward (Editor). Trade Paper. Harvard University Press. Cambridge, MA. 1960. 306p. The John Harvard Library ISBN:0-674-09451-4, ISBN13: 978-0-674-09451-2. Dewey:326.973. LCCN:60-005400.
Audience: **l,u,f.**

Fogel, Robert W. & Engerman, Stanley L. **E449**
Time on the Cross: The Economics of American Negro Slavery. Trade Cloth. W. W. Norton & Company, Inc. New York, NY.

1995. 324p. ISBN:0-393-31218-6, ISBN13: 978-0-393-31218-8. Dewey:331.11/734/0973.
Audience: **u,f.**

Foner, Philip S. **E185**
History of Black Americans: From the Compromise of 1850 to the End of the Civil War. Trade Cloth. Greenwood Publishing Group, Inc. Portsmouth, NH. 1983. 539p. Contributions in American History Ser., No. 103 ISBN:0-8371-7967-X, ISBN13: 978-0-8371-7967-4. Dewey:973/.0496073. LCCN:74-005987.
Audience: **g,l,u,f.** B

Foner, R. Eric **E436.F6 1995**
Free Soil, Free Labor, Free Men: The Ideology of the Republican Party Before the Civil War. Trade Cloth. Peter Smith Publisher, Inc. Magnolia, MA. 1996. ISBN:0-8446-6849-4, ISBN13: 978-0-8446-6849-9. Dewey:973.6.
Audience: **l,u,f.**

Friedman, Lawrence J. **E449**
Gregarious Saints: Self and Community in American Abolitionism, 1830-1870. Cloth Text. Cambridge University Press. New York, NY. 1982. 320p. ISBN:0-521-24429-3, ISBN13: 978-0-521-24429-9. Dewey:322.4/4/0973. LCCN:81-015454.
Audience: **l,u,f.** B

Gunderson, Robert Gray **E440.5.G965**
Old Gentlemen's Convention: The Washington Peace Conference Of 1861. Paper Text. Textbook Publishers. Temecula, CA. 2003. xiii, 168p. ISBN:0-7581-1371-4, ISBN13: 978-0-7581-1371-9. Dewey:973.71.
Audience: **l,u,f.** B

Hamilton, Holman **E422.H32**
Zachary Taylor. Trade Cloth. Shoe String Press, Inc. North Haven, CT. 1966. ISBN:0-208-00608-7, ISBN13: 978-0-208-00608-0. Dewey:973.6/3/092.
Audience: **l,u,f.** B

Hamilton, Holman **E423.H2 2005**
Prologue to Conflict: The Crisis and Compromise of 1850. Michael F. Holt (Introduction by). Trade Paper. University Press of Kentucky. Lexington, KY. 2005. 256p. ISBN:0-8131-9136-X, ISBN13: 978-0-8131-9136-2. Dewey:973.7/113. LCCN:2004-027050.
Audience: **l,u,f.**

Helper, Hinton Rowan **E449**
The Impending Crisis of the South: How to Meet It. Trade Cloth. Scholarly Publishing Office, University of Michigan Library. Ann Arbor, MI. 2004. ISBN:1-4181-1640-8, ISBN13: 978-1-4181-1640-8. Dewey:326/.0973.
Audience: **l,u,f.**

Huggins, Nathan Irvin **E449.D75.H83**
Slave and Citizen: The Life of Frederick Douglass. Trade Cloth. Little Brown & Company. New York, NY. 1980. viii, 194p. ISBN:0-316-38000-8, ISBN13: 978-0-316-38000-3. Dewey:326/.092/4. LCCN:79-089336.
Audience: **g,l,u,f.** B

Klein, Philip S. **E437**
President James Buchanan: A President. Katherine E. Speirs (Editor). Trade Cloth. American Political Biography. Newtown, CT. 1995. 506p. Signature Ser. ISBN:0-945707-11-8, ISBN13: 978-0-945707-11-0. Dewey:973.6/8/092. LCCN:95-079749.
Audience: **l,u,f.**

Kraditor, Aileen S. **E449.K7 1989**
Means and Ends in American Abolitionism: Garrison and His Critics on Strategy and Tactics, 1834-1850. Trade Paper. Ivan R. Dee Publisher. Blue Ridge Summit, PA. 1989. 312p. ISBN:0-929587-16-2, ISBN13: 978-0-929587-16-5. Dewey:973.7/114. LCCN:89-012018.
Audience: **l,u,f.** B

Kraut, Alan M. (Editor) **E449.C955 1983**
Crusaders and Compromisers: Essays on the Relationship of the Antislavery Struggle to the Antebellum Party System. Trade Cloth. Greenwood Publishing Group, Inc. Portsmouth, NH. 1983. 286p. Contributions in American History Ser., No. 104 ISBN:0-313-22537-0, ISBN13: 978-0-313-22537-6. Dewey:324.275/09. LCCN:82-021085.
Audience: **u,f.** B

Lerner, Gerda **E449.G865L47 2004**
The Grimke Sisters from South Carolina. Ed. 2. Trade Paper. University of North Carolina Press. Chapel Hill, NC. 2004. 464p. ISBN:0-8078-5566-9, ISBN13: 978-0-8078-5566-9. Dewey:326/.8/0922757 B. LCCN:2004-049750.
Audience: **l,u,f.**

Malin, J. C. **E433.M34**
The Nebraska Question, 1852-1854. Trade Cloth. Peter Smith Publisher, Inc. Magnolia, MA. 1983. ISBN:0-8446-2517-5, ISBN13: 978-0-8446-2517-1. Dewey:973.66.
Audience: **l,u,f.**

Martin, Waldo E. Jr. **E449.D75**
The Mind of Frederick Douglass. Trade Paper. University of North Carolina Press. Chapel Hill, NC. 1986. 346p. ISBN:0-8078-4148-X, ISBN13: 978-0-8078-4148-8. Dewey:973.8/092/4. LCCN:84-005140.
Audience: **l,u,f.** B

McKitrick, Eric L. (Editor) **E449.M16**
Slavery Defended: The Views of the Old South. Trade Cloth. Peter Smith Publisher, Inc. Magnolia, MA. 1980. ISBN:0-8446-1869-1, ISBN13: 978-0-8446-1869-2. Dewey:326/.0973.
Audience: **l,u,f.** B

McKivigan, John R. **E449**
The War Against Proslavery Religion: Abolitionism and the Northern Churches, 1830-1865. Book, Other. Cornell University Press. Ithaca, NY. 1984. 328p. ISBN:0-8014-1589-6, ISBN13: 978-0-8014-1589-0. Dewey:322.4/4/0973. LCCN:83-045933.
Audience: **l,u,f.** B

McPherson, James M. **E449.M176 1995**
The Struggle for Equality: Abolitionists and the Negro in the Civil War and Reconstruction. Ed. 2. Trade Paper. Princeton University Press. Princeton, NJ. 1967. 490p. ISBN:0-691-00555-9, ISBN13: 978-0-691-00555-3. Dewey:973.7114. LCCN:95-151901.
Audience: **g,l,u,f.** B

Merk, Frederick **E416.M4**
The Monroe Doctrine and American Expansionism 1843-1849. Trade Paper. Random House, Inc. New York, NY. 1972. 320p. ISBN:0-394-71760-0, ISBN13: 978-0-394-71760-9. Dewey:973.61.
Audience: **l,u,f.** B

Nichols, Roy F. **E0436.N56**
The Disruption of American Democracy. Trade Cloth. A M S Press, Inc. New York, NY. 1983. ISBN:0-404-20190-3, ISBN13: 978-0-404-20190-6. Dewey:973.66. LCCN:83-045826.
Audience: **l,u,f.**

Perkins, Howard C. **E440.5.P45**
Northern Editorials on Secession, Set. Trade Cloth. Peter Smith Publisher, Inc. Magnolia, MA. 1990. ISBN:0-8446-1347-9, ISBN13: 978-0-8446-1347-5. Dewey:973.68.
Audience: **l,u,f.**

Perry, Lewis & Fellman, Michael (Editors) **E449**
Antislavery Reconsidered: New Perspectives on the Abolitionists. Trade Cloth. Louisiana State University Press. Baton Rouge, LA. 1979. 416p. ISBN:0-8071-0479-5, ISBN13: 978-0-8071-0479-8. Dewey:322.4/4/0973. LCCN:78-010177.
Audience: **u,f.**

Polk, James K. **E416.P77**
Polk: The Diary of a Presidency, 1845-1849, Covering the Mexican War, the Acquisition of Oregon, and the Conquest of California and the Southwest. Library Binding. Reprint Services Company. Temecula, CA. 1991. 412p. American Biography Ser. ISBN:0-7812-8318-3, ISBN13: 978-0-7812-8318-2. Dewey:973.61.
Audience: **l,u,f.**

Potter, David M. **E440.5.P856 1995**
Lincoln and His Party in the Secession Crisis. Daniel W. Crofts (Introduction by). Trade Paper. Louisiana State University Press. Baton Rouge, LA. 1995. 440p. ISBN:0-8071-2027-8, ISBN13: 978-0-8071-2027-9. Dewey:973.7/092. LCCN:95-023562.
Audience: **l,u,f.**

Preston, Dickson J. **E449.D75**
Young Frederick Douglas: The Maryland Years. Trade Paper. Johns Hopkins University Press. Baltimore, MD. 1985. 262p. Maryland Paperback Bookshelf Ser. ISBN:0-8018-2739-6, ISBN13: 978-0-8018-2739-6. Dewey:973.8/092/4. LCCN:80-007992.
Audience: **g,l,u,f.**

Quarles, Benjamin **E449**
Black Abolitionists. Trade Cloth. Oxford University Press, Inc. New York, NY. 1970. ISBN:0-19-500804-9, ISBN13: 978-0-19-500804-3. Dewey:973.7/114.
Audience: **l,u,f.**

Rawley, James A. **F685**
Race and Politics: "Bleeding Kansas" and the Coming of the Civil War. Trade Cloth. University of Nebraska Press. Lincoln, NE. 1979. xvi, 304p. ISBN:0-8032-3854-1, ISBN13: 978-0-8032-3854-1. Dewey:978.1/02. LCCN:79-014856.
Audience: **l,u,f.**

Ripley, C. Peter (Editor) **E449.B624 1985**
The Black Abolitionist Papers: The British Isles, 1830-1865. Trade Cloth. University of North Carolina Press. Chapel Hill, NC. 1985. 639p. ISBN:0-8078-1625-6, ISBN13: 978-0-8078-1625-7. Dewey:973/.0496. LCCN:84-013131.
Audience: **u,f.**

Schor, Joel A. **E449**
Henry Highland Garnet: A Voice of Black Radicalism in the 19th Century. Trade Cloth. Greenwood Publishing Group, Inc. Portsmouth, NH. 1977. 250p. Contributions in American History Ser., No. 54 ISBN:0-8371-8937-3, ISBN13: 978-0-8371-8937-6. Dewey:322.4/4/0924. LCCN:76-008746.
Audience: **l,u,f.**

Sellers, Charles Grier **E417.S4**
James K. Polk, Jacksonian, 1795-1843. Paper Text. Textbook Publishers. Temecula, CA. 2003. ISBN:0-7581-5705-3, ISBN13: 978-0-7581-5705-8. Dewey:973.610924.
Audience: **l,u,f.**

Sewell, Richard H. **E449.S49**
Ballots for Freedom: Antislavery Politics in the United States, 1837-1860. Trade Cloth. Oxford University Press, Inc. New York, NY. 1976. xvi, 379p. ISBN:0-19-501997-0, ISBN13: 978-0-19-501997-1. Dewey:322.4/4/0973. LCCN:75-025464.
Audience: **l,u,f.**

Sorin, Gerald **E449.S697**
Abolitionism: A New Perspective. Trade Paper. Greenwood Publishing Group, Inc. Portsmouth, NH. 1972. 187p. New Perspectives in American History ISBN:0-275-84140-5, ISBN13: 978-0-275-84140-9. Dewey:322.4/4/0973. LCCN:79-143981.
Audience: **u,f.**

Stampp, Kenneth M. **E440**
And the War Came: The North and the Secession Crisis, 1860-1861. Trade Cloth. Greenwood Publishing Group, Inc. Portsmouth, NH. 1980. 331p. ISBN:0-313-22566-4, ISBN13: 978-0-313-22566-6. Dewey:973.7/13. LCCN:80-015742.
Audience: **l,u,f.**

Stowe, Harriet Beecher **PS2384**
Uncle Tom's Cabin. Elizabeth Ammons (Editor). Trade Paper. W. W. Norton & Company, Inc. New York, NY. 1993. 608p. Critical Editions Ser. ISBN:0-393-96303-9, ISBN13: 978-0-393-96303-8. Dewey:813/.3. LCCN:92-040694.
Audience: **g,l,u,f.**

Ten Broek, Jacobus **E0449.T4**
The Antislavery Origins of the Fourteenth Amendment. Trade Paper. Books on Demand. Ann Arbor, MI. 238p. ISBN:0-8357-5639-4, ISBN13: 978-0-8357-5639-6. Dewey:973.7114. LCCN:51-061927.
Audience: **u,f.**

Trefousse, Hans L. **E449.T79 1975**
The Radical Republicans: Lincoln's Vanguard for Racial Justice. Trade Paper. Louisiana State University Press. Baton Rouge, LA. 1975. ix, 510p. ISBN:0-8071-0169-9, ISBN13: 978-0-8071-0169-8. Dewey:973.7/1. LCCN:75-331615.
Audience: **l,u,f.**

Walters, Ronald G. **E449**
The Antislavery Appeal: American Abolitionism after 1830. Trade Cloth. Johns Hopkins University Press. Baltimore, MD. 1994. 216p. ISBN:0-8018-1861-3, ISBN13: 978-0-8018-1861-5. Dewey:322.4/4/0973. LCCN:76-017229.
Audience: **l,u,f.**

Wooster, Ralph A. **E440.5.W9**
The Secession Conventions of the South. Paper Text. Textbook Publishers. Temecula, CA. 2003. viii, 294p. ISBN:0-7581-5704-5, ISBN13: 978-0-7581-5704-1. Dewey:973.713.
Audience: **l,u,f.**

Wyatt-Brown, Bertram **E449.T18W9 1997**
Lewis Tappan and the Evangelical War Against Slavery. Trade Paper. Louisiana State University Press. Baton Rouge, LA. 1997. 376p. ISBN:0-8071-2223-8, ISBN13: 978-0-8071-2223-5. Dewey:326/.8/092 B. LCCN:97-016809.
Audience: **l,u,f.** B

United States > American History, by Period > Middle 19th Century (1845/48-1861) > Biography, A-Z

Abbott, Richard H. **E415.9.W6A64**
Cobbler in Congress: The Life of Henry Wilson, 1812-1875. Trade Cloth. University Press of Kentucky. Lexington, KY. 1972. 308p. ISBN:0-8131-1249-4, ISBN13: 978-0-8131-1249-7. Dewey:973.8/2/0924. LCCN:70-147856.
Audience: **l,u,f.** B

Atherton, Lewis E. **F596.A8**
The Cattle Kings. Trade Paper. University of Nebraska Press. Lincoln, NE. 1972. 324p. ISBN:0-8032-5759-7, ISBN13: 978-0-8032-5759-7. Dewey:978. LCCN:61-013722.
Audience: **u,f.**

Capers, Gerald Mortimer **E415.9.D73C28**
Stephen A. Douglas, Defender of the Union. Paper Text. Textbook Publishers. Temecula, CA. 2003. 239p. ISBN:0-7581-9680-6, ISBN13: 978-0-7581-9680-4. Dewey:923.273.
Audience: **l,u,f.** B

Chase, Salmon Portland **E415.9.C4A3**
Inside Lincoln's Cabinet: The Civil War Diaries of Salmon P. Chase. Paper Text. Textbook Publishers. Temecula, CA. 2003. ix, 342p. ISBN:0-7581-9462-5, ISBN13: 978-0-7581-9462-6. Dewey:973.71.
Audience: **u,f.**

Current, Richard Nelson **E415.9.S84C8 1980**
Old Thad Stevens: A Story of Ambition. Library Binding. Greenwood Publishing Group, Inc. Portsmouth, NH. 1980. v, 344p. ISBN:0-313-22569-9, ISBN13: 978-0-313-22569-7. Dewey:328.73/092/4. LCCN:80-015189.
Audience: **l,u,f.** B

Dana, Richard Henry Jr. **E0415.9.D15**
The Journal, Vol. 1. Robert Francis Lucid (Editor). Trade Paper. Books on Demand. Ann Arbor, MI. 460p. ISBN:0-598-23381-4, ISBN13: 978-0-598-23381-3. Dewey:818/.3/03. LCCN:68-014264.
Audience: **u,f.** B

Donald, David **E415.9.S9D6 1981**
Charles Sumner and the Coming of the Civil War. Paper Text. University of Chicago Press. Chicago, IL. 1981. ISBN:0-226-15633-8, ISBN13: 978-0-226-15633-0. Dewey:973.7/092/4. LCCN:81-011612.
Audience: **l,u,f.**

Donald, David **E415.9.S9**
Charles Sumner and the Rights of Man. Trade Cloth. Random House Children's Books. New York, NY. 1970. ISBN:0-394-41899-9, ISBN13: 978-0-394-41899-5. Dewey:973.7/0924. LCCN:60-009144.
Audience: **l,u,f.**

Douglas, Stephen Arnold **E415.9.D73**
The Letters of Stephen a Douglas. Paper Text. Textbook Publishers. Temecula, CA. 2003. xxxi, 558p. ISBN:0-7581-2230-6, ISBN13: 978-0-7581-2230-8. Dewey:923.273.
Audience: **u,f.**

Durden, Robert F. **E415.9.P53**
James Shepherd Pike: Republicanism and the American Negro 1850-1882. Trade Paper. Duke University Press. Durham, NC. 1957. v, 249p. ISBN:0-8223-0348-5, ISBN13: 978-0-8223-0348-0. Dewey:973.71. LCCN:57-006284.
Audience: **l,u,f.** B

Egan, Ferol **E415.9.F8E33 1985**
Fremont: Explorer for a Restless Nation. Richard Dillon (Foreword by). Trade Paper. University of Nevada Press. Reno, NV. 1985. 612p. Vintage West Ser. ISBN:0-87417-096-6, ISBN13: 978-0-87417-096-2. Dewey:979/.02/0924. LCCN:85-008492.
Audience: **l,u,f.**

Flick, Alexander C. & Lobrano, Gustav **E415.9.T5F5 1973**
Samuel Jones Tilden: A Study in Political Sagacity. Trade Cloth. Greenwood Publishing Group, Inc. Portsmouth, NH. 1973. 597p. ISBN:0-8371-6912-7, ISBN13: 978-0-8371-6912-5. Dewey:973.8/0924. LCCN:73-007103.
Audience: **l,u,f.**

Johannsen, Robert W. **E415.9.D73J55 1997**
Stephen A. Douglas. Trade Paper. University of Illinois Press. Champaign, IL. 1997. 993p. ISBN:0-252-06635-9, ISBN13: 978-0-252-06635-1. Dewey:973.6/8/092. LCCN:96-044592.
Audience: **l,u,f.** B

Logsdon, Joseph **E415.9**
Horace White, Nineteenth Century Liberal. Trade Cloth. Greenwood Publishing Group, Inc. Portsmouth, NH. 1971. 418p. Contributions in American History Ser., No. 10 ISBN:0-8371-3309-2, ISBN13: 978-0-8371-3309-6. Dewey:973.8/0924. LCCN:77-105982.
Audience: **l,u,f.** B

Sewell, Richard H. **E0415.9.H15**
John P. Hale and the Politics of Abolition. Trade Paper. Books on Demand. Ann Arbor, MI. 308p. ISBN:0-7837-4472-2, ISBN13: 978-0-7837-4472-8. Dewey:923.273. LCCN:65-013849.
Audience: **l,u,f.** B

Strong, George Templeton **E415.9.S86**
Diary. Paper Text. Textbook Publishers. Temecula, CA. 2003. ISBN:0-7581-8900-1, ISBN13: 978-0-7581-8900-4. Dewey:974.71.
Audience: **u,f.** B

United States > American History, by Period > Middle 19th Century (1845/48-1861) > By Presidential Administration

Abbott, Richard H. **E415.9.W6A64**
Cobbler in Congress: The Life of Henry Wilson, 1812-1875. Trade Cloth. University Press of Kentucky. Lexington, KY. 1972. 308p. ISBN:0-8131-1249-4, ISBN13: 978-0-8131-1249-7. Dewey:973.8/2/0924. LCCN:70-147856.
Audience: **l,u,f.**

Capers, Gerald Mortimer **E415.9.D73C28**
Stephen A. Douglas, Defender of the Union. Paper Text. Textbook Publishers. Temecula, CA. 2003. 239p. ISBN:0-7581-9680-6, ISBN13: 978-0-7581-9680-4. Dewey:923.273.
Audience: **l,u,f.**

Chase, Salmon Portland **E415.9.C4A3**
Inside Lincoln's Cabinet: The Civil War Diaries of Salmon P. Chase. Paper Text. Textbook Publishers. Temecula, CA. 2003. ix, 342p. ISBN:0-7581-9462-5, ISBN13: 978-0-7581-9462-6. Dewey:973.71.
Audience: **u,f.**

Current, Richard Nelson **E415.9.S84C8 1980**
Old Thad Stevens: A Story of Ambition. Library Binding. Greenwood Publishing Group, Inc. Portsmouth, NH. 1980. v, 344p. ISBN:0-313-22569-9, ISBN13: 978-0-313-22569-7. Dewey:328.73/092/4. LCCN:80-015189.
Audience: **l,u,f.**

Dana, Richard Henry Jr. **E0415.9.D15**
The Journal, Vol. 1. Robert Francis Lucid (Editor). Trade Paper. Books on Demand. Ann Arbor, MI. 460p. ISBN:0-598-23381-4, ISBN13: 978-0-598-23381-3. Dewey:818/.3/03. LCCN:68-014264.
Audience: **u,f.**

Donald, David **E415.9.S9D6 1981**
Charles Sumner and the Coming of the Civil War. Paper Text. University of Chicago Press. Chicago, IL. 1981. ISBN:0-226-15633-8, ISBN13: 978-0-226-15633-0. Dewey:973.7/092/4. LCCN:81-011612.
Audience: **l,u,f.**

Donald, David **E415.9.S9**
Charles Sumner and the Rights of Man. Trade Cloth. Random House Children's Books. New York, NY. 1970. ISBN:0-394-41899-9, ISBN13: 978-0-394-41899-5. Dewey:973.7/0924. LCCN:60-009144.
Audience: **l,u,f.**

Douglas, Stephen Arnold **E415.9.D73**
The Letters of Stephen a Douglas. Paper Text. Textbook Publishers. Temecula, CA. 2003. xxxi, 558p. ISBN:0-7581-2230-6, ISBN13: 978-0-7581-2230-8. Dewey:923.273.
Audience: **u,f.**

Durden, Robert F. **E415.9.P53**
James Shepherd Pike: Republicanism and the American Negro 1850-1882. Trade Paper. Duke University Press. Durham, NC. 1957. v, 249p. ISBN:0-8223-0348-5, ISBN13: 978-0-8223-0348-0. Dewey:973.71. LCCN:57-006284.
Audience: **l,u,f.**

Egan, Ferol **E415.9.F8E33 1985**
Fremont: Explorer for a Restless Nation. Richard Dillon (Foreword by). Trade Paper. University of Nevada Press. Reno, NV. 1985. 612p. Vintage West Ser. ISBN:0-87417-096-6, ISBN13: 978-0-87417-096-2. Dewey:979/.02/0924. LCCN:85-008492.
Audience: **l,u,f.**

Flick, Alexander C. & Lobrano, Gustav **E415.9.T5F5 1973**
Samuel Jones Tilden: A Study in Political Sagacity. Trade Cloth. Greenwood Publishing Group, Inc. Portsmouth, NH. 1973. 597p. ISBN:0-8371-6912-7, ISBN13: 978-0-8371-6912-5. Dewey:973.8/0924. LCCN:73-007103.
Audience: **l,u,f.**

Johannsen, Robert W. **E415.9.D73J55 1997**
Stephen A. Douglas. Trade Paper. University of Illinois Press. Champaign, IL. 1997. 993p. ISBN:0-252-06635-9, ISBN13: 978-0-252-06635-1. Dewey:973.6/8/092. LCCN:96-044592.
Audience: **l,u,f.**

Logsdon, Joseph **E415.9**
Horace White, Nineteenth Century Liberal. Trade Cloth. Greenwood Publishing Group, Inc. Portsmouth, NH. 1971. 418p. Contributions in American History Ser., No. 10 ISBN:0-8371-3309-2, ISBN13: 978-0-8371-3309-6. Dewey:973.8/0924. LCCN:77-105982.
Audience: **l,u,f.**

Nevins, Allan **E468.N428 1992**
Ordeal of the Union: Fruits of Manifest Destiny, 1847-1852. Trade Paper. Macmillan Publishing Company, Inc. Old Tappan, NJ. 1992. 1072p. ISBN:0-02-035441-X, ISBN13: 978-0-02-035441-3. Dewey:973. LCCN:92-003522.
Audience: **l,u,f.**

Nevins, Allan **E415.7**
Ordeal of the Union: A House Dividing, 1852-1857, Vol. 2. Children's Board Books. Simon & Schuster. New York, NY. 1940. ISBN:0-684-10424-5, ISBN13: 978-0-684-10424-9. Dewey:973.
Audience: **l,u,f.**

Nevins, Allan **E468.N428 1992**
Ordeal of the Union, Vol. 2. Trade Paper. Simon & Schuster. New York, NY. 1992. 1072p. ISBN:0-02-035442-8, ISBN13: 978-0-02-035442-0. Dewey:973. LCCN:92-003522.
Audience: **l,u,f.**

Sewell, Richard H. **E0415.9.H15**
John P. Hale and the Politics of Abolition. Trade Paper. Books on Demand. Ann Arbor, MI. 308p. ISBN:0-7837-4472-2, ISBN13: 978-0-7837-4472-8. Dewey:923.273. LCCN:65-013849.
Audience: **l,u,f.**

Strong, George Templeton **E415.9.S86**
Diary. Paper Text. Textbook Publishers. Temecula, CA. 2003.

ISBN:0-7581-8900-1, ISBN13: 978-0-7581-8900-4. Dewey:974.71.
Audience: **u,f.** B

United States > American History, by Period > Civil War Period (1861-1865)

Current, Richard Nelson & Escott, Paul D. (Editors) **E487.E55 1993**
Encyclopedia of the Confederacy, Set. Trade Cloth. Thomson Gale. Farmington Hills, MI. 1993. 1916p. ISBN:0-13-275991-8, ISBN13: 978-0-13-275991-5. Dewey:973.7/13. LCCN:93-004133.
Audience: **g,l,u.** *Choice, 1994.*

Heidler, David S. & Heidler, Jeanne T. **E468.E53 2002**
Encyclopedia of the American Civil War: A Political Social and Military History. Trade Cloth. W. W. Norton & Company, Inc. New York, NY. 2002. 2784p. ISBN:0-393-04758-X, ISBN13: 978-0-393-04758-5. Dewey:973.7/03. LCCN:2002-070280.
Audience: **g,l,u,f.**

Swanson, Mark & Langley, Jacqueline D. (Illustrators) **E470.S94 2004**
Atlas of the Civil War, Month by Month: Major Battles and Troop Movements. Trade Cloth. University of Georgia Press. Athens, GA. 2004. 136p. ISBN:0-8203-2658-5, ISBN13: 978-0-8203-2658-0. Dewey:973.7/3/0223. LCCN:2004-012264.
Audience: **g,l,u,f.** *Choice, 2005.*

United States > American History, by Period > Civil War Period (1861-1865) > Lincoln. Biography. Writings

Andrews, J. Cutler **E609.A62**
South Reports the Civil War. Trade Cloth. Princeton University Press. Princeton, NJ. 1970. xiii, 611p. ISBN:0-691-04597-6, ISBN13: 978-0-691-04597-9. Dewey:973.7. LCCN:75-090942.
Audience: **u,f.** B

Andrews, J. Cutler **E609.A6 1985**
The North Reports the Civil War. Arthur M. Schlesinger Jr. (Foreword by). Trade Paper. University of Pittsburgh Press. Pittsburgh, PA. 1985. 832p. ISBN:0-8229-5370-6, ISBN13: 978-0-8229-5370-8. Dewey:973.7. LCCN:84-022087.
Audience: **u,f.** B

Angle, Paul M. (Editor) **E457**
The Lincoln Reader. Trade Cloth. Amereon, Ltd. Mattituck, NY. ISBN:0-89190-866-8, ISBN13: 978-0-89190-866-1. Dewey:973.7/092.
Audience: **l,u,f.** B

Basler, Roy P. & Sandburg, Carl **E457**
Abraham Lincoln: His Speeches and Writings. Trade Paper. Da Capo Press, Inc. Cambridge, MA. 2001. 888p. ISBN:0-306-81075-1, ISBN13: 978-0-306-81075-6. Dewey:973.7/092.
Audience: **l,u,f.**

Beveridge, Albert J. **E457.3.B576 1971**
Abraham Lincoln: Eighteen Nine to Eighteen Fifty-Eight. Trade Cloth. Scholarly Press, Inc. Saint Clair Shores, MI. 1971. ISBN:0-403-00865-4, ISBN13: 978-0-403-00865-0. Dewey:973.7/0924. LCCN:73-144879.
Audience: **l,u,f.** B

Botkin, B. A. **E655**
Civil War Treasury. Trade Cloth. Book Sales, Inc. Edison, NJ. 1988. ISBN:0-89009-967-7, ISBN13: 978-0-89009-967-4. Dewey:973.7088.
Audience: **u,f.**

Cox, LaWanda **E457.905**
Lincoln and Black Freedom: A Study in Presidential Leadership. Trade Cloth. University of South Carolina Press. Columbia, SC. 1981. 275p. ISBN:0-87249-400-4, ISBN13: 978-0-87249-400-8. Dewey:973.7/092/4. LCCN:81-003350.
Audience: **l,u,f.** B

Craven, Avery O. **E649.C89**
The Repressible Conflict, 1830-1861. Trade Cloth. A M S Press, Inc. New York, NY. ISBN:0-404-20070-2, ISBN13: 978-0-404-20070-1. Dewey:973.711. LCCN:83-045425.
Audience: **l,u,f.**

Current, Richard Nelson & Lincoln, Abraham **E457.C96 1980**
The Lincoln Nobody Knows. Trade Cloth. Greenwood Publishing Group, Inc. Portsmouth, NH. 1980. 314p. ISBN:0-313-22450-1, ISBN13: 978-0-313-22450-8. Dewey:973.7/092/4. LCCN:80-016138.
Audience: **l,u,f.** B

Davis, Jefferson **E467.1.D2596 2004**
The Papers of Jefferson Davis, Vol. 2. Trade Cloth. Louisiana State University Press. Baton Rouge, LA. 2004. 856p. ISBN:0-8071-2909-7, ISBN13: 978-0-8071-2909-8. Dewey:973.7/13/092. LCCN:76-152704.
Audience: **u,f.**

Davis, Jefferson **E664.D28A4 1995**
Jefferson Davis: Private Letters, 1823-1889. Hudson Strode (Editor). Trade Paper. Da Capo Press, Inc. Cambridge, MA. 1995. 580p. ISBN:0-306-80638-X, ISBN13: 978-0-306-80638-4. Dewey:973.7/13/092 B. LCCN:94-047997.
Audience: **u,f.**

Dodd, William E. **E467.1.D26**
Jefferson Davis. Trade Paper. Kessinger Publishing, LLC. Whitefish, MT. 2004. ISBN:1-4179-4460-9, ISBN13: 978-1-4179-4460-6. Dewey:973.7/13/092.
Audience: **l,u,f.**

Donald, David Herbert **E457**
Lincoln Reconsidered: Essays on the Civil War Era. Trade Cloth. Greenwood Publishing Group, Inc. Portsmouth, NH. 1981. 200p. ISBN:0-313-22575-3, ISBN13: 978-0-313-22575-8. Dewey:973.7. LCCN:80-022804.
Audience: **u,f.**

Duberman, Martin **E467.1.A2 D8**
Charles Francis Adams, 1807-1886. Trade Cloth. Stanford University Press. Palo Alto, CA. 1961. xii, 525p. ISBN:0-8047-0625-5, ISBN13: 978-0-8047-0625-4. Dewey:973.7/0924 B. LCCN:68-013742.
Audience: **l,u,f.**

Eaton, Clement **E467.1.D26**
Jefferson Davis: The Sphinx of the Confederacy. Trade Cloth. Simon & Schuster. New York, NY. 1977. xiii, 334p. ISBN:0-02-908700-7, ISBN13: 978-0-02-908700-8. Dewey:973.7/13/0924. LCCN:77-002512.
Audience: **l,u,f.** *B*

Fehrenbacher, Don E. **E457**
Prelude to Greatness: Lincoln in the 1850's. Trade Cloth. Stanford University Press. Palo Alto, CA. 1962. ix, 205p. ISBN:0-8047-0119-9, ISBN13: 978-0-8047-0119-8. Dewey:973.
Audience: **l,u,f.** *B*

Freeman, Douglas S. **E467.1.L4**
R. E. Lee: A Biography. Trade Paper. Simon Publications, Inc. 2001. 647p. ISBN:1-931313-36-9, ISBN13: 978-1-931313-36-0. Dewey:923.573. LCCN:38-034421.
Audience: **l,u,f.**

Freeman, Douglas S. **E467.1.L4**
R. E. Lee: A Biography. Trade Paper. Simon Publications, Inc. 2001. 559p. ISBN:1-931313-38-5, ISBN13: 978-1-931313-38-4. Dewey:923.573. LCCN:38-034421.
Audience: **l,u,f.**

Freeman, Douglas S. **E467.1.L4**
R. E. Lee: A Biography. Trade Paper. Simon Publications, Inc. 2001. 594p. ISBN:1-931313-39-3, ISBN13: 978-1-931313-39-1. Dewey:923.573. LCCN:38-034421.
Audience: **l,u,f.**

Freeman, Douglas S. **E467.1.L4**
R. E. Lee: A Biography. Trade Paper. Simon Publications, Inc. 2001. 621p. ISBN:1-931313-37-7, ISBN13: 978-1-931313-37-7. Dewey:923.573. LCCN:38-034421.
Audience: **l,u,f.**

Hassler, Warren W. Jr. **E467.1.M2H4 1974**
General George B. McClellan: Shield of the Union. Trade Cloth. Greenwood Publishing Group, Inc. Portsmouth, NH. 1974. 350p. ISBN:0-8371-7606-9, ISBN13: 978-0-8371-7606-2. Dewey:923.573. LCCN:74-009619.
Audience: **l,u,f.** *B*

Hendrick, Burton J. **E456**
Lincoln's War Cabinet. Library Binding. Reprint Services Company. Temecula, CA. 1993. 559p. History of the United States Ser. ISBN:0-7812-4896-5, ISBN13: 978-0-7812-4896-9. Dewey:973.71.
Audience: **l,u,f.**

Hesseltine, William B. **E615.H37 1998**
Civil War Prisons: A Study in War Psychology. Trade Cloth. Ohio State University Press. Columbus, OH. 1997. 312p. ISBN:0-8142-0768-5, ISBN13: 978-0-8142-0768-0. Dewey:973.7/7.221. LCCN:98-002980.
Audience: **u,f.** *B*

Hesseltine, William B. **E467.H58 1970**
Confederate Leaders in the New South. Library Binding. Greenwood Publishing Group, Inc. Portsmouth, NH. 1970. xi, 146p. ISBN:0-8371-3686-5, ISBN13: 978-0-8371-3686-8. Dewey:973.71/3. LCCN:71-100230.
Audience: **l,u,f.** *B*

Holzman, Richard S. **E467.1.B87H6**
Stormy Ben Butler. Paper Text. Textbook Publishers. Temecula, CA. 2003. 297p. ISBN:0-7581-9018-2, ISBN13: 978-0-7581-9018-5. Dewey:923.273.
Audience: **l,u,f.** *B*

Howe, Mark Antony de Wolfe (Editor) **E601.H73 2000**
Touched with Fire: Civil War Letters and Diary of Oliver Wendell Holmes, Jr., 1861-1864. Oliver W. Holmes Jr. (Contribution by), David H. Burton (Introduction by). Trade Cloth. Fordham University Press. Bronx, NY. 2000. 158p. The North's Civil War Ser., No. 12: ISBN:0-8232-2016-8, ISBN13: 978-0-8232-2016-8. Dewey:973.7/81. LCCN:99-055152.
Audience: **u,f.**

Jaffa, Harry V. **E457.4.J32**
Crisis of the House Divided: An Interpretation of the Issues in the Lincoln-Douglas Debates. Trade Paper. University of Chicago Press. Chicago, IL. 1999. 460p. ISBN:0-226-39113-2, ISBN13: 978-0-226-39113-7. Dewey:973.6/8.
Audience: **u,f.** *B*

Jarrell, Hampton M. **E467.1.H19J3**
Wade Hampton and the Negro: The Road Not Taken. Trade Cloth. University of South Carolina Press. Columbia, SC. 1969. ISBN:0-87249-017-3, ISBN13: 978-0-87249-017-8. Dewey:923.273. LCCN:50-005796.
Audience: **l,u,f.**

Lewis, Charles L. **E467.1.F23L48 1980**
David Glasgow Farragut. Library Binding. Ayer Company Publishers, Inc. Manchester, NH. 1980. Navies and Men Ser. ISBN:0-405-13043-0, ISBN13: 978-0-405-13043-4. Dewey:973.7/5/0924.. LCCN:79-006115.
Audience: **l,u,f.**

Lewis, Lloyd **E467.1.S55L48 1993**
Sherman: Fighting Prophet. Brooks D. Simpson (Introduction by). Trade Paper. University of Nebraska Press. Lincoln, NE. 1993. 720p. ISBN:0-8032-7945-0, ISBN13: 978-0-8032-7945-2. Dewey:355.0092. LCCN:93-011132.
Audience: **l,u,f.** *B*

Lincoln, Abraham **E457.4.L77**
Created Equal? The Complete Lincoln: Douglas Debates of 1858. Paper Text. Textbook Publishers. Temecula, CA. 2003. xxxiii, 421p. ISBN:0-7581-2529-1, ISBN13: 978-0-7581-2529-3. Dewey:973.68.
Audience: **l,u,f.**

Lincoln, Abraham **E457.91**
The Collected Works of Abraham Lincoln. Roy P. Basler (Editor). Trade Cloth. Rutgers University Press. Piscataway, NJ. 1953. ISBN:0-8135-0172-5, ISBN13: 978-0-8135-0172-7. Dewey:973.7/092 B.
Audience: **u,f.**

Lincoln, Abraham & Basler, Roy Prentice **E457.92**
Lincoln, Abraham, Pres. U. S.: Collected Works Supplement, 1832-1865. Library Binding. Greenwood Publishing Group, Inc. Portsmouth, NH. 1974. xv, 320p. Contributions in American Studies, No. 7 ISBN:0-8371-6492-3, ISBN13: 978-0-8371-6492-2. Dewey:973.7/092/4. LCCN:53-006295.
Audience: **u,f.**

Lincoln, Abraham & Shaw, Archer H. **E457**
The Lincoln Encyclopedia: The Spoken and Written Words of A. Lincoln Arranged for Ready Reference. David C. Mearns (Introduction by). Trade Cloth. Greenwood Publishing Group, Inc. Portsmouth, NH. 1980. 395p. ISBN:0-313-22471-4, ISBN13: 978-0-313-22471-3. Dewey:973.7/092/4. LCCN:80-012651.
Audience: **u,f.** 𝓑

McKinney, Francis F. **E467.1T4M17**
Education in Violence: The Life of George H. Thomas and the History of the Army of the Cumberland. Paper Text. Textbook Publishers. Temecula, CA. 2003. 530p. ISBN:0-7581-0636-X, ISBN13: 978-0-7581-0636-0. Dewey:923.573.
Audience: **l,u,f.** 𝓑

Mitgang, Herbert **E457.15.M5 1980**
Lincoln As They Saw Him. Library Binding. Hippocrene Books, Inc. New York, NY. 1980. xix, 519p. ISBN:0-374-95801-7, ISBN13: 978-0-374-95801-5. Dewey:973.7/092/4. LCCN:80-080031.
Audience: **l,u,f.** 𝓑

Neely, Mark E. **E457.N48**
The Abraham Lincoln Encyclopedia. Trade Cloth. McGraw-Hill Companies, The. New York, NY. 1981. 416p. Louis A. Warren Lincoln Library ISBN:0-07-046145-7, ISBN13: 978-0-07-046145-1. Dewey:973.7/092/4. LCCN:81-007296.
Audience: **u,f.** 𝓑

Nevins, Allan **E415.7**
The Emergence of Lincoln: Prologue to Civil War, 1859-1861, Vol. 4. Children's Board Books. Simon & Schuster. New York, NY. 1950. ISBN:0-684-10416-4, ISBN13: 978-0-684-10416-4. Dewey:973.
Audience: **l,u,f.**

Niven, John **E467.1.W46.N58**
Gideon Welles: Lincoln's Secretary of the Navy. Trade Cloth. Oxford University Press, Inc. New York, NY. 1973. 691p. ISBN:0-19-501693-9, ISBN13: 978-0-19-501693-2. Dewey:973.7/092/4. LCCN:73-082671.
Audience: **l,u,f.** 𝓑

Oates, Stephen B. **E457.O16 1984**
Abraham Lincoln: The Man Behind the Myths. Trade Cloth. HarperCollins Publishers. New York, NY. 1984. 240p. ISBN:0-06-015304-0, ISBN13: 978-0-06-015304-5. Dewey:973.7/092/4. LCCN:83-048798.
Audience: **l,u,f.** 𝓑

Oates, Stephen B. **E457.905**
With Malice Toward None: The Life of Abraham Lincoln. Katherine E. Speirs (Editor). Trade Cloth. American Political Biography. Newtown, CT. 2002. 492p. Signature Ser. ISBN:0-945707-32-0, ISBN13: 978-0-945707-32-5. Dewey:973.7/092/4.
Audience: **l,u,f.** 𝓑

Quarles, Benjamin **E457.2.Q3 1991**
Lincoln and the Negro. Trade Paper. Da Capo Press, Inc. Cambridge, MA. 1991. 288p. Quality Paperbacks Ser. ISBN:0-306-80447-6, ISBN13: 978-0-306-80447-2. Dewey:973.7/092. LCCN:91-018201.
Audience: **l,u,f.** 𝓑

Randall, J. G. & Current, Richard Nelson **E457.R212 2000**
Lincoln the President: Last full Measure. Trade Paper. University of Illinois Press. Champaign, IL. 1999. 456p. ISBN:0-252-06872-6, ISBN13: 978-0-252-06872-0. Dewey:973.7/092. LCCN:99-039598.
Audience: **l,u,f.** 𝓑

Randall, Ruth Painter **E457.25.R3**
Mary Lincoln: Biography of a Marriage. Paper Text. Textbook Publishers. Temecula, CA. 2003. xiv, 555p. ISBN:0-7581-9675-X, ISBN13: 978-0-7581-9675-0. Dewey:973.7/092.
Audience: **l,u,f.** 𝓑

Rawley, James A. **E649.R28 1989**
Turning Points of the Civil War (New Edition). Trade Cloth. University of Nebraska Press. Lincoln, NE. 1989. 230p. ISBN:0-8032-8935-9, ISBN13: 978-0-8032-8935-2. Dewey:973.7. LCCN:89-004873.
Audience: **l,u,f.**

Sandburg, Carl **E457.4.S36**
Abraham Lincoln: The War Years. Cloth over Boards. Harcourt Trade Publishers. New York, NY. 1939. 673p. Abraham Lincoln, the War Years Ser., Vol. 4 ISBN:0-15-101607-0, ISBN13: 978-0-15-101607-5. Dewey:973.7092. LCCN:39-027998.
Audience: **l,u,f.**

Sandburg, Carl **E457.S215 1974**
Abraham Lincoln: The Prairie Years and the War Years. Trade Paper. Harcourt Trade Publishers. New York, NY. 2002. 800p. ISBN:0-15-602752-6, ISBN13: 978-0-15-602752-6. Dewey:973.7/092/4. LCCN:74-008388.
Audience: **l,u,f.**

Sandburg, Carl **E457.3**
Abraham Lincoln the Prairie Years, Vol. 2. Trade Paper. Kessinger Publishing, LLC. Whitefish, MT. 2003. ISBN:0-7661-4609-X, ISBN13: 978-0-7661-4609-9. Dewey:973.7.
Audience: **l,u,f.**

Strong, George Templeton **E601.S888**
Diary of the Civil War 1860: 1865. Paper Text. Textbook Publishers. Temecula, CA. 2003. liii, 664p. ISBN:0-7581-8910-9, ISBN13: 978-0-7581-8910-3. Dewey:973.7.
Audience: **u,f.** 𝓑

Strozier, Charles B. **E457.S897 1982**
Lincoln's Quest for Union: Public and Private Meanings. Cloth Text. Basic Books. New York, NY. 1982. xxiii, 271p. ISBN:0-465-04119-1, ISBN13: 978-0-465-04119-0. Dewey:973.7/092/4. LCCN:81-068406.
Audience: **l,u,f.** 𝓑

Thomas, Benjamin P. **E457.T427**
Abraham Lincoln: A Biography. Trade Cloth. Random House, Inc. New York, NY. 1979. 548p. ISBN:0-394-60468-7, ISBN13: 978-0-394-60468-8. Dewey:973.7/092. LCCN:68-007853.
Audience: **l,u,f.**

Thomas, Benjamin P., et al. **E467.1.S8 T45 1980**
Stanton: The Life and Times of Lincoln's Secretary of War. Harold M. Hyman & Edwin McMasters Stanton (Authors).

Trade Cloth. Greenwood Publishing Group, Inc. Portsmouth, NH. 1980. 642p. ISBN:0-313-22581-8, ISBN13: 978-0-313-22581-9. Dewey:973.7/092/4. LCCN:80-018970.
Audience: **l,u,f.**

Turner, Justin G. & Turner, Linda L. (Editors) **E457.25.T87 1972**
Mary Todd Lincoln: Her Life and Letters. Trade Cloth. Random House Children's Books. New York, NY. 1972. xxv, 750p. ISBN:0-394-46643-8, ISBN13: 978-0-394-46643-9. Dewey:973.7/092/4. LCCN:69-010700.
Audience: **u,f.** B

Turner, Thomas R. **E457.5**
Beware the People Weeping: Public Opinion and the Assassination of Abraham Lincoln. Cloth Text. Louisiana State University Press. Baton Rouge, LA. 1982. xvi, 312p. ISBN:0-8071-0986-X, ISBN13: 978-0-8071-0986-1. Dewey:364.1524092. LCCN:81-014252.
Audience: **l,u,f.** B

Vandiver, Frank E. **E467.1.J15V3 1989**
Mighty Stonewall. Trade Cloth. Texas A&M University Press. College Station, TX. 1992. 560p. Texas A&M University Military History Ser., No. 9 ISBN:0-89096-384-3, ISBN13: 978-0-89096-384-5. Dewey:973.7/3/0924. LCCN:88-009642.
Audience: **l,u,f.**

Von Abele, Rudolph R. **E467.1.S85.V6 1971**
Alexander H. Stephens, a Biography. Cloth Text. Greenwood Publishing Group, Inc. Portsmouth, NH. 1972. 337p. ISBN:0-8371-5201-1, ISBN13: 978-0-8371-5201-1. Dewey:973.7/13/0924. LCCN:74-135614.
Audience: **l,u,f.** B

Wakelyn, Jon L. & Vandiver, Frank E. **E467**
Biographical Dictionary of the Confederacy. Cloth Text. Greenwood Publishing Group, Inc. Portsmouth, NH. 1977. 601p. ISBN:0-8371-6124-X, ISBN13: 978-0-8371-6124-2. Dewey:973.7/13/0922. LCCN:72-013870.
Audience: **u,f.** B

Warner, Ezra J. **E467**
Generals in Blue: Lives of the Union Commanders. Trade Cloth. Louisiana State University Press. Baton Rouge, LA. 1964. xxvi, 680p. ISBN:0-8071-0822-7, ISBN13: 978-0-8071-0822-2. Dewey:920. LCCN:64-021593.
Audience: **l,u,f.** B

Warner, Ezra J. **E467**
Generals in Gray: Lives of the Confederate Commanders. Trade Cloth. Louisiana State University Press. Baton Rouge, LA. 1959. xxviii, 420p. ISBN:0-8071-0823-5, ISBN13: 978-0-8071-0823-9. Dewey:920. LCCN:58-007551.
Audience: **l,u,f.** B

Wiley, Bell I. **E607**
The Life of Johnny Reb: The Common Soldier of the Confederacy. Trade Cloth. Louisiana State University Press. Baton Rouge, LA. 1971. 444p. ISBN:0-8071-1909-1, ISBN13: 978-0-8071-1909-9. Dewey:973.742. LCCN:71-162618.
Audience: **l,u,f.**

Williams, T. Harry **E467.1.B38W5 1995**
P. G. T. Beauregard: Napoleon in Gray. Trade Cloth. Louisiana State University Press. Baton Rouge, LA. 1995. 346p. Southern Biography Ser. ISBN:0-8071-1974-1, ISBN13: 978-0-8071-1974-7. Dewey:973.7/42. LCCN:55-007362.
Audience: **l,u,f.** B

Williams, Thomas H. **E467.W5 1976**
McClellan, Sherman, and Grant. Trade Cloth. Greenwood Publishing Group, Inc. Portsmouth, NH. 1976. ISBN:0-8371-9280-3, ISBN13: 978-0-8371-9280-2. Dewey:973.7/0922. LCCN:76-029654.
Audience: **l,u,f.**

United States > American History, by Period > Civil War Period (1861-1865) > Political History, 1861-1865

Abbott, Richard H. **E415.9.W6A64**
Cobbler in Congress: The Life of Henry Wilson, 1812-1875. Trade Cloth. University Press of Kentucky. Lexington, KY. 1972. 308p. ISBN:0-8131-1249-4, ISBN13: 978-0-8131-1249-7. Dewey:973.8/2/0924. LCCN:70-147856.
Audience: **l,u,f.** B

Anderson, John Q. (Editor) **E487.H74 1995**
Brokenburn: The Journal of Kate Stone, 1861-1868. Trade Cloth. Louisiana State University Press. Baton Rouge, LA. 1995. xl, 400p. Library of Southern Civilization ISBN:0-8071-2017-0, ISBN13: 978-0-8071-2017-0. Dewey:973.782. LCCN:95-170176.
Audience: **u,f.**

Belz, Herman **E459**
Reconstructing the Union: Theory and Policy During the Civil War. Trade Cloth. Greenwood Publishing Group, Inc. Portsmouth, NH. 1979. 336p. ISBN:0-313-20862-X, ISBN13: 978-0-313-20862-1. Dewey:973.7/1. LCCN:78-021311.
Audience: **l,u,f.** B

Bogue, Allan G. **JK2357 1861**
The Earnest Men: Republicans of the Civil War Senate. Book, Other. Cornell University Press. Ithaca, NY. 1981. 368p. ISBN:0-8014-1357-5, ISBN13: 978-0-8014-1357-5. Dewey:328.73/073. LCCN:81-067176.
Audience: **l,u,f.** B

Capers, Gerald Mortimer **E415.9.D73C28**
Stephen A. Douglas, Defender of the Union. Paper Text. Textbook Publishers. Temecula, CA. 2003. 239p. ISBN:0-7581-9680-6, ISBN13: 978-0-7581-9680-4. Dewey:923.273.
Audience: **l,u,f.** B

Catton, William & Catton, Bruce **E459**
Two Roads to Sumter. Trade Cloth. Book Sales, Inc. Edison, NJ. 2004. 304p. ISBN:0-7858-1597-X, ISBN13: 978-0-7858-1597-6. Dewey:973.911.
Audience: **l,u,f.**

Chase, Salmon Portland **E415.9.C4A3**
Inside Lincoln's Cabinet: The Civil War Diaries of Salmon P. Chase. Paper Text. Textbook Publishers. Temecula, CA. 2003. ix, 342p. ISBN:0-7581-9462-5, ISBN13: 978-0-7581-9462-6. Dewey:973.71.
Audience: **u,f.**

Chesnut, Mary Boykin Miller **E487**
Mary Chesnut's Civil War. C. Vann Woodward (Editor). Cloth over Boards. Yale University Press. Cumberland, RI. 1981. 892p. ISBN:0-300-02459-2, ISBN13: 978-0-300-02459-3. Dewey:973.7/82. LCCN:80-036661.
Audience: **u,f.** B

Commager, Henry Steele (Editor) **E464.B56**
The Blue and the Gray: From the Nomination of Lincoln to the Eve of Gettysburg. Trade Paper. Penguin Group (USA) Inc. New York, NY. 1995. 640p. ISBN:0-452-01144-2, ISBN13: 978-0-452-01144-1. Dewey:973.7/8. LCCN:94-018223.
Audience: **l,u,f.**

Connelly, Thomas L. & Jones, Archer **E487.C8**
The Politics of Command. Trade Cloth. Louisiana State University Press. Baton Rouge, LA. 1973. xvi, 235p. ISBN:0-8071-0228-8, ISBN13: 978-0-8071-0228-2. Dewey:973.7/3013. LCCN:72-089113.
Audience: **l,u,f.** B

Current, Richard Nelson **E415.9.S84C8 1980**
Old Thad Stevens: A Story of Ambition. Library Binding. Greenwood Publishing Group, Inc. Portsmouth, NH. 1980. v, 344p. ISBN:0-313-22569-9, ISBN13: 978-0-313-22569-7. Dewey:328.73/092/4. LCCN:80-015189.
Audience: **l,u,f.** B

Dana, Richard Henry Jr. **E0415.9.D15**
The Journal, Vol. 1. Robert Francis Lucid (Editor). Trade Paper. Books on Demand. Ann Arbor, MI. 460p. ISBN:0-598-23381-4, ISBN13: 978-0-598-23381-3. Dewey:818/.3/03. LCCN:68-014264.
Audience: **u,f.** B

Davis, Jefferson **E487**
The Rise and Fall of the Confederate Government. Earl S. Miers (Foreword by). Trade Cloth. Peter Smith Publisher, Inc. Magnolia, MA. 1990. ISBN:0-8446-0074-1, ISBN13: 978-0-8446-0074-1. Dewey:973.7/13.
Audience: **l,u,f.**

Degler, Carl N. **E487**
The Other South: Southern Dissenters in the Nineteenth Century. Cloth Text. Northeastern University Press. Boston, MA. 1983. 403p. ISBN:0-930350-33-2, ISBN13: 978-0-930350-33-8. Dewey:326/.8/097509034. LCCN:82-014429.
Audience: **l,u,f.**

Donald, David **E415.9.S9D6 1981**
Charles Sumner and the Coming of the Civil War. Paper Text. University of Chicago Press. Chicago, IL. 1981. ISBN:0-226-15633-8, ISBN13: 978-0-226-15633-0. Dewey:973.7/092/4. LCCN:81-011612.
Audience: **l,u,f.**

Donald, David **E415.9.S9**
Charles Sumner and the Rights of Man. Trade Cloth. Random House Children's Books. New York, NY. 1970. ISBN:0-394-41899-9, ISBN13: 978-0-394-41899-5. Dewey:973.7/0924. LCCN:60-009144.
Audience: **l,u,f.**

Douglas, Stephen Arnold **E415.9.D73**
The Letters of Stephen a Douglas. Paper Text. Textbook Publishers. Temecula, CA. 2003. xxxi, 558p. ISBN:0-7581-2230-6, ISBN13: 978-0-7581-2230-8. Dewey:923.273.
Audience: **u,f.**

Durden, Robert F. **E415.9.P53**
James Shepherd Pike: Republicanism and the American Negro 1850-1882. Trade Paper. Duke University Press. Durham, NC. 1957. v, 249p. ISBN:0-8223-0348-5, ISBN13: 978-0-8223-0348-0. Dewey:973.71. LCCN:57-006284.
Audience: **l,u,f.** B

Eaton, Clement **E487.E15**
A History of the Southern Confederacy. Paper Text. Textbook Publishers. Temecula, CA. 2003. 351p. ISBN:0-7581-8920-6, ISBN13: 978-0-7581-8920-2. Dewey:973.713.
Audience: **l,u,f.** B

Egan, Ferol **E415.9.F8E33 1985**
Fremont: Explorer for a Restless Nation. Richard Dillon (Foreword by). Trade Paper. University of Nevada Press. Reno, NV. 1985. 612p. Vintage West Ser. ISBN:0-87417-096-6, ISBN13: 978-0-87417-096-2. Dewey:979/.02/0924. LCCN:85-008492.
Audience: **l,u,f.**

Flick, Alexander C. & Lobrano, Gustav **E415.9.T5F5 1973**
Samuel Jones Tilden: A Study in Political Sagacity. Trade Cloth. Greenwood Publishing Group, Inc. Portsmouth, NH. 1973. 597p. ISBN:0-8371-6912-7, ISBN13: 978-0-8371-6912-5. Dewey:973.8/0924. LCCN:73-007103.
Audience: **l,u,f.**

Hesseltine, William B. (Editor) **E464.H4**
The Tragic Conflict. Trade Cloth. George Braziller Inc. New York, NY. 1988. American Epochs Ser. ISBN:0-8076-0169-1, ISBN13: 978-0-8076-0169-3. Dewey:973.7. LCCN:62-009693.
Audience: **l,u,f.**

Hyman, Harold Melvin **E458.8.H9**
Era of the Oath: Northern Loyalty Tests During the Civil War and Reconstruction. Paper Text. Textbook Publishers. Temecula, CA. 2003. 229p. ISBN:0-7581-1620-9, ISBN13: 978-0-7581-1620-8. Dewey:973.78.
Audience: **l,u,f.** B

Johannsen, Robert W. **E415.9.D73J55 1997**
Stephen A. Douglas. Trade Paper. University of Illinois Press. Champaign, IL. 1997. 993p. ISBN:0-252-06635-9, ISBN13: 978-0-252-06635-1. Dewey:973.6/8/092. LCCN:96-044592.
Audience: **l,u,f.** B

Klement, Frank L. **E458.8**
Dark Lanterns: Secret Political Societies, Conspiracies and Treason Trials in the Civil War. Trade Paper. Louisiana State University Press. Baton Rouge, LA. 1984. 263p. ISBN:0-8071-1567-3, ISBN13: 978-0-8071-1567-1. Dewey:973.71. LCCN:84-000834.
Audience: **l,u,f.**

Logsdon, Joseph **E415.9**
Horace White, Nineteenth Century Liberal. Trade Cloth. Greenwood Publishing Group, Inc. Portsmouth, NH. 1971. 418p.

Contributions in American History Ser., No. 10 ISBN:0-8371-3309-2, ISBN13: 978-0-8371-3309-6. Dewey:973.8/0924. LCCN:77-105982.

Audience: **l,u,f.**

Owsley, Frank Lawrence **E488.O85**
King Cotton Diplomacy: Foreign Relations of the Confederate States of America. Paper Text. Textbook Publishers. Temecula, CA. 2003. xxiii, 614p. ISBN:0-7581-2509-7, ISBN13: 978-0-7581-2509-5. Dewey:973.721.

Audience: **l,u,f.**

Patrick, Rembert W. **E487.P3**
Jefferson Davis and His Cabinet. Trade Cloth. Louisiana State University Press. Baton Rouge, LA. 1976. 411p. ISBN:0-8071-0642-9, ISBN13: 978-0-8071-0642-6. Dewey:973.716. LCCN:44-009637.

Audience: **l,u,f.**

Potter, David M. **E459**
Impending Crisis. Trade Paper. HarperCollins Publishers. New York, NY. 1977. 672p. New American Nation Ser. ISBN:0-06-131929-5, ISBN13: 978-0-06-131929-7. Dewey:973.7/11.

Audience: **l,u,f.**

Ramsdell, Charles W. **E487.R2 1997**
Behind the Lines in the Southern Confederacy. Wendell H. Stephenson (Editor). Trade Paper. Louisiana State University Press. Baton Rouge, LA. 1997. xxviii, 136p. Walter Lynwood Fleming Lectures ISBN:0-8071-2186-X, ISBN13: 978-0-8071-2186-3. Dewey:973.7/13. LCCN:96-045592.

Audience: **l,u,f.**

Roland, Charles P. **E487**
The Confederacy. Trade Paper. University of Chicago Press. Chicago, IL. 1962. 228p. History of American Civilization Ser. ISBN:0-226-72451-4, ISBN13: 978-0-226-72451-5. Dewey:973.713. LCCN:60-012573.

Audience: **l,u,f.**

Sewell, Richard H. **E0415.9.H15**
John P. Hale and the Politics of Abolition. Trade Paper. Books on Demand. Ann Arbor, MI. 308p. ISBN:0-7837-4472-2, ISBN13: 978-0-7837-4472-8. Dewey:923.273. LCCN:65-013849.

Audience: **l,u,f.**

Stampp, Kenneth M. **E458.S825**
The Imperiled Union: Essays on the American Civil War. Trade Cloth. Oxford University Press, Inc. New York, NY. 1980. 320p. ISBN:0-19-502681-0, ISBN13: 978-0-19-502681-8. Dewey:973.7/1. LCCN:79-020276.

Audience: **u,f.**

Strong, George Templeton **E415.9.S86**
Diary. Paper Text. Textbook Publishers. Temecula, CA. 2003. ISBN:0-7581-8900-1, ISBN13: 978-0-7581-8900-4. Dewey:974.71.

Audience: **u,f.**

Tatum, Georgia L. **E487.T176 2000**
Disloyalty in the Confederacy. David Williams (Introduction by). Trade Cloth. University of Nebraska Press. Lincoln, NE. 2000. 176p. ISBN:0-8032-9441-7, ISBN13: 978-0-8032-9441-7. Dewey:973.7/13. LCCN:99-049788.

Audience: **l,u,f.**

Thomas, Emory M. **E487**
Confederate Nation 1861-1865. Richard B. Morris & Henry Steele Commager (Editors). Trade Paper. HarperCollins Publishers. New York, NY. 1981. 416p. New American Nation Ser. ISBN:0-06-131965-1, ISBN13: 978-0-06-131965-5. Dewey:973.7/13. LCCN:76-026255.

Audience: **l,u,f.**

Vandiver, Frank E. **F213**
Their Tattered Flags: The Epic of the Confederacy. Trade Cloth. HarperCollins Publishers. New York, NY. 1970. ISBN:0-06-129125-0, ISBN13: 978-0-06-129125-8. Dewey:975/.03. LCCN:77-096018.

Audience: **l,u,f.**

Woodward, C. Vann & Muhlenfeld, Elisabeth (Editors) **E487.C525 1984**
The Private Mary Chesnut: The Unpublished Civil War Diaries. Trade Cloth. Oxford University Press, Inc. New York, NY. 1984. 320p. ISBN:0-19-503511-9, ISBN13: 978-0-19-503511-7. Dewey:973.7/82. LCCN:84-012219.

Audience: **u,f.**

Zornow, William Frank **E458.4.Z6 1972**
Lincoln and the Party Divided. Trade Cloth. Greenwood Publishing Group, Inc. Portsmouth, NH. 1972. xi, 264p. ISBN:0-8371-6054-5, ISBN13: 978-0-8371-6054-2. Dewey:973.7/1. LCCN:73-152619.

Audience: **l,u,f.**

United States > American History, by Period > Civil War Period (1861-1865) > Civil War, 1861-1865

E468.7.D5
Divided We Fought: A Pictorial History of the War 1861. Paper Text. Textbook Publishers. Temecula, CA. 2003. viii, 454p. ISBN:0-7581-9239-8, ISBN13: 978-0-7581-9239-4. Dewey:973.7084.

Audience: **l,u,f.**

Barney, William L. **E468.B32 1980**
Flawed Victory: A New Perspective on the Civil War. Trade Cloth. University Press of America, Inc. Lanham, MD. 1980. 225p. ISBN:0-8191-1273-9, ISBN13: 978-0-8191-1273-6. Dewey:973.7. LCCN:80-068972.

Audience: **l,u,f.**

Berlin, Ira (Editor), et al. **E540.N3F74 1998**
Freedom's Soldiers: The Black Military Experience in the Civil War. Joseph P. Reidy & Leslie S. Rowland (Editors). Trade Cloth. Cambridge University Press. New York, NY. 1998. 208p. ISBN:0-521-63258-7, ISBN13: 978-0-521-63258-4. Dewey:973.7/415. LCCN:98-149583.

Audience: **l,u,f.**

Boatner, Mark M. III **E468.B7**
The Civil War Dictionary. Trade Cloth. David McKay Company, Inc. New York, NY. 1980. ISBN:0-679-50013-8, ISBN13: 978-0-679-50013-1. Dewey:973.703. LCCN:59-012267.

Audience: **u,f.** *Choice, 1989.*

Boyer, Richard O. **E451.B77**
The Legend of John Brown. Trade Cloth. Random House Children's Books. New York, NY. 1973. ISBN:0-394-46124-X, ISBN13: 978-0-394-46124-3. Dewey:973.7/116/092. LCCN:69-010672.
Audience: **l,u,f.** B

Bruce, Robert V. **E491.B7 1989**
Lincoln and the Tools of War. Benjamin P. Thomas (Foreword by). Trade Cloth. University of Illinois Press. Champaign, IL. 1989. 400p. ISBN:0-252-01665-3, ISBN13: 978-0-252-01665-3. Dewey:973.7/092. LCCN:89-004830.
Audience: **l,u,f.** B

Catton, Bruce **E468**
America Goes to War: The Civil War and Its Meaning in American Culture. Trade Paper. Wesleyan University Press. Middletown, CT. 1992. 128p. ISBN:0-8195-6016-2, ISBN13: 978-0-8195-6016-2. Dewey:973.7. LCCN:58-013602.
Audience: **l,u,f.**

Catton, Bruce **E474.85**
Glory Road. Trade Cloth. Peter Smith Publisher, Inc. Magnolia, MA. 1994. ISBN:0-8446-6790-0, ISBN13: 978-0-8446-6790-4. Dewey:973.7/33.
Audience: **l,u,f.**

Catton, Bruce **E491**
Mr. Lincoln's Army. Trade Cloth. Peter Smith Publisher, Inc. Magnolia, MA. 1994. ISBN:0-8446-6791-9, ISBN13: 978-0-8446-6791-1. Dewey:973.7/41.
Audience: **l,u,f.** B

Catton, Bruce **E470.2.C39 2000**
A Stillness at Appomattox. Trade Cloth. Holt, Rinehart & Winston. Austin, TX. 2000. 500p. ISBN:0-03-055622-8, ISBN13: 978-0-03-055622-7. Dewey:973.7/38. LCCN:2001-268807.
Audience: **l,u,f.** B

Catton, Bruce **E468.C3 1998**
This Hallowed Ground. Trade Cloth. Wordsworth Editions, Ltd. Ware, 1998. 448p. Military History Ser. ISBN:1-85326-696-5, ISBN13: 978-1-85326-696-6. Dewey:973.7. LCCN:00-559979.
Audience: **l,u,f.**

Cornish, Dudley T. **E540.N3C77 1987**
The Sable Arm: Black Troops in the Union Army, 1861-1865. Herman Hattaway (Foreword by). Trade Cloth. University Press of Kansas. Lawrence, KS. 2004. xviii, 342p. Modern War Studies ISBN:0-7006-0328-X, ISBN13: 978-0-7006-0328-2. Dewey:973.7/415. LCCN:87-050106.
Audience: **l,u,f.**

Davis, William C. **E473.2**
Duel Between the First Ironclads. Ed. 2. Trade Cloth. Stackpole Books. Mechanicsburg, PA. 1994. 240p. Davis Ser. ISBN:0-8117-0536-6, ISBN13: 978-0-8117-0536-3. Dewey:973.7/52. LCCN:93-026867.
Audience: **l,u,f.** B

Donald, David (Editor) **E468.D65**
Why the North Won the Civil War. U. S. Grant (Introduction by). Trade Cloth. Louisiana State University Press. Baton Rouge, LA. 1960. ISBN:0-8071-0435-3, ISBN13: 978-0-8071-0435-4. Dewey:973.7. LCCN:61-013170.
Audience: **l,u,f.**

Faust, Patricia L. (Editor) **E468**
The Historical Times Illustrated Encyclopedia of the Civil War. Trade Cloth. HarperCollins Publishers. New York, NY. 1991. 1056p. ISBN:0-06-271535-6, ISBN13: 978-0-06-271535-7. Dewey:973.7. LCCN:86-045095.
Audience: **u,f.**

Franklin, John H. **E453.F8 1995**
The Emancipation Proclamation. Ed. 3. Trade Paper. Harlan Davidson Inc. Wheeling, IL. 1995. 200p. ISBN:0-88295-907-7, ISBN13: 978-0-88295-907-8. Dewey:973.7/14. LCCN:94-038153.
Audience: **l,u,f.**

Fredrickson, George M. **E468.9.F83 1993**
The Inner Civil War: Northern Intellectuals and the Crisis of the Union. Trade Paper. University of Illinois Press. Champaign, IL. 1993. 296p. ISBN:0-252-06274-4, ISBN13: 978-0-252-06274-2. Dewey:973.7/15. LCCN:92-036773.
Audience: **u,f.** B

Freeman, Douglas Southall **E470.2.F7 1997**
Lee's Lieutenants: A Study in Command, Gettysburg to Appomattox. Trade Cloth. Simon & Schuster. New York, NY. 1997. 912p. A Study in Command, Vol. 3 ISBN:0-684-83785-4, ISBN13: 978-0-684-83785-7. Dewey:973.7/3. LCCN:97-151696.
Audience: **l,u,f.**

Freeman, Douglas Southall **E470.2.F7 1997**
Lee's Lieutenants: A Study in Command Manassas to Malvern Hill. Trade Cloth. Simon & Schuster. New York, NY. 1997. 832p. Classics Ser. ISBN:0-684-83783-8, ISBN13: 978-0-684-83783-3. Dewey:973.7/3. LCCN:97-151696.
Audience: **l,u,f.**

Freeman, Douglas Southall **E470.2.F7 1997**
Lee's Lieutenants: A Study in Command, Cedar Mountain to Chancellorsville. Trade Cloth. Simon & Schuster. New York, NY. 1997. 800p. A Study in Command, Vol. 2 ISBN:0-684-83784-6, ISBN13: 978-0-684-83784-0. Dewey:973.7/3. LCCN:97-151696.
Audience: **l,u,f.**

Freeman, Douglas Southall **E470.2**
Lee's Lieutenants. Stephen Sears (Abridged by), James M. McPherson (Introduction by). Trade Cloth. William S. Konecky Associates, Inc. Old Saybrook, CT. 2005. 910p. ISBN:1-56852-509-5, ISBN13: 978-1-56852-509-9. Dewey:973.73.
Audience: **l,u,f.**

Fuller, J. F. C. **E468.F96**
Grant and Lee: A Study in Personality and Generalship. Trade Cloth. Indiana University Press. Bloomington, IN. 1957. 336p. ISBN:0-253-13400-5, ISBN13: 978-0-253-13400-4. Dewey:973.7. LCCN:57-010723.
Audience: **l,u,f.**

Gara, Larry **E450.G22 1996**
The Liberty Line: The Legend of the Underground Railroad. Trade Paper. University Press of Kentucky. Lexington, KY. 1996. 216p. ISBN:0-8131-0864-0, ISBN13: 978-0-8131-0864-3. Dewey:973.7/115. LCCN:95-026336.
Audience: **l,u,f.** B

Gardner, Alexander **E468.7.G19**
Gardner's Photographic Sketch Book of the Civil War. Trade Cloth. Peter Smith Publisher, Inc. Magnolia, MA. 1979. ISBN:0-8446-0104-7, ISBN13: 978-0-8446-0104-5. Dewey:973.79.
Audience: **l,u,f.**

Higginson, Thomas W. **E540.N3**
Army Life in a Black Regiment. Trade Cloth. Digital Scanning, Inc. Scituate, MA. 2001. 302p. ISBN:1-58218-359-7, ISBN13: 978-1-58218-359-6. Dewey:973.7/415.
Audience: **l,u,f.**

Hoehling, A. A. **E473.2.H57**
Thunder at Hampton Roads. Trade Cloth. Prentice-Hall. Upper Saddle, NJ. 1976. xvi, 231p. ISBN:0-13-920652-3, ISBN13: 978-0-13-920652-8. Dewey:973.7/52. LCCN:76-018261.
Audience: **l,u,f.** B

Katz, Jonathan **E450.K28 1974**
Resistance at Christiana; the Fugitive Slave Rebellion, Christiana, Pennsylvania, September 11, 1851: A Documentary Account. Trade Cloth. Collier Macmillan Canada, Inc. Cambridge, ON. 1974. viii, 359p. ISBN:0-690-00307-2, ISBN13: 978-0-690-00307-9. Dewey:974.8/15/03. LCCN:73-021907.
Audience: **l,u,f.** B

Leech, Margaret **E565.5**
Reveille in Washington, 1860-1865. Trade Paper. Simon Publications, Inc. 2001. 484p. ISBN:1-931313-23-7, ISBN13: 978-1-931313-23-0. Dewey:973.7/4/53. LCCN:41-014492.
Audience: **l,u,f.** B

McPherson, James M. **E468.M23 1992**
Ordeal by Fire: The Civil War and Reconstruction. Ed. 2. Trade Cloth. McGraw-Hill Companies, The. New York, NY. 1991. 713p. ISBN:0-07-045842-1, ISBN13: 978-0-07-045842-0. Dewey:973.7. LCCN:81-011832.
Audience: **l,u,f.**

Murdock, Eugene C. **E491**
One Million Men: The Civil War Draft in the North. Trade Cloth. Greenwood Publishing Group, Inc. Portsmouth, NH. 1980. 366p. ISBN:0-313-22502-8, ISBN13: 978-0-313-22502-4. Dewey:973.7/41. LCCN:80-014431.
Audience: **l,u,f.**

National Historical Society Staff **E487.E52 1982**
Embattled Confederacy: The Image of War, 1861-1865. Trade Cloth. Doubleday Publishing. New York, NY. 1982. 464p. Image of Wars Ser., Vol. 3 ISBN:0-385-15468-2, ISBN13: 978-0-385-15468-0. Dewey:973.7/022/2. LCCN:81-043240.
Audience: **l,u,f.**

National Historical Society Staff & Davis, Jenny **E468.7.S5**
Shadows of the Storm: The Image of War, 1861-1865. William C. Davis & Bell I. Wiley (Editors). Trade Cloth. Doubleday Publishing. New York, NY. 1981. 464p. Image of Wars Ser., Vol. 1 ISBN:0-385-15466-6, ISBN13: 978-0-385-15466-6. Dewey:973.7/022/2. LCCN:80-001659.
Audience: **l,u,f.**

National Historical Society Staff **E470.G87**
The Guns of '62: The Image of War, 1861-1865. William C. Davis (Editor). Trade Cloth. Doubleday Canada, Ltd. Toronto, ON. 1982. 464p. Image of Wars Ser., Vol. 2 ISBN:0-385-15467-4, ISBN13: 978-0-385-15467-3. Dewey:973.7/3. LCCN:81-043151.
Audience: **l,u,f.**

National Historical Society Staff & Davis, William C. **E470.E52 1984**
The End of an Era: The Image of War, 1861-1865. Bell I. Wiley (Editor). Trade Cloth. Doubleday Publishing. New York, NY. 1984. 496p. Image of Wars Ser., Vol. 6 ISBN:0-385-18282-1, ISBN13: 978-0-385-18282-9. Dewey:973.7. LCCN:82-045884.
Audience: **l,u,f.**

National Historical Society Staff **E468.7.F53 1983**
Fighting for Time: The Image of War, 1861-1865. William C. Davis & Bell I. Wiley (Editors). Trade Cloth. Doubleday Publishing. New York, NY. 1983. 464p. Image of Wars Ser., Vol. 4 ISBN:0-385-18280-5, ISBN13: 978-0-385-18280-5. Dewey:973.7. LCCN:82-045363.
Audience: **l,u,f.**

National Historical Society Staff & Davis, William C. **E470.S76 1983**
The South Besieged: The Image of War, 1861-1865. Bell I. Wiley (Editor). Trade Cloth. Doubleday Publishing. New York, NY. 1983. 464p. Image of Wars Ser., Vol. 5 ISBN:0-385-18281-3, ISBN13: 978-0-385-18281-2. Dewey:973.7/3/0222. LCCN:82-045399.
Audience: **l,u,f.**

Nevins, Allan **E415.7**
The War for the Union: War Becomes Revolution, 1862-1863, Vol. 6. Children's Board Books. Simon & Schuster. New York, NY. 1960. ISBN:0-684-10427-X, ISBN13: 978-0-684-10427-0. Dewey:973.
Audience: **l,u,f.**

Nevins, Allan **E468.N43**
The War for the Union: The Organized War to Victory, 1864-1865, Vol. 8. Trade Cloth. Simon & Schuster. New York, NY. 1971. ISBN:0-684-10429-6, ISBN13: 978-0-684-10429-4. Dewey:973.7. LCCN:59-003690.
Audience: **l,u,f.** B

Nevins, Allan **E468**
War for the Union: 1861-1862. Trade Cloth. William S. Konecky Associates, Inc. Old Saybrook, CT. 448p. ISBN:1-56852-296-7, ISBN13: 978-1-56852-296-8. Dewey:973.7.
Audience: **l,u,f.**

Nevins, Allan **E415.7**
The War for the Union: The Organized War, 1863-1864, Vol. 7. Trade Cloth. Simon & Schuster. New York, NY. 1971. ISBN:0-684-10428-8, ISBN13: 978-0-684-10428-7. Dewey:973.
Audience: **l,u,f.**

Oates, Stephen B. **E451.O17 1984**
To Purge This Land with Blood: A Biography of John Brown. Ed. 2. Trade Paper. University of Massachusetts Press. Amherst, MA. 1984. 448p. ISBN:0-87023-458-7, ISBN13: 978-0-87023-458-3. Dewey:973.6/8/0924. LCCN:84-002635.
Audience: **l,u,f.** B

Parish, Peter J. **E468.P27**
The American Civil War. Trade Cloth. Holmes & Meier Publishers, Inc. Teaneck, NJ. 1975. 728p. ISBN:0-8419-0176-7, ISBN13: 978-0-8419-0176-6. Dewey:973.7. LCCN:74-084660.
Audience: **l,u,f.** B

Porter, David Dixon **E792.W577**
The Naval History of the Civil War: Illustrated from Original Sketches Made by Rear-Admiral Walke and Others. Trade Cloth. Library Reprints, Inc. Temecula, CA. 843p. ISBN:0-7222-8207-9, ISBN13: 978-0-7222-8207-6. Dewey:973.91/5/0924.
Audience: **l,u,f.**

Quarles, Benjamin (Editor) **E451.Q37**
Blacks on John Brown. Trade Paper. Books on Demand. Ann Arbor, MI. 180p. ISBN:0-8357-7306-X, ISBN13: 978-0-8357-7306-5. Dewey:322.4/4/0924. LCCN:72-188132.
Audience: **l,u,f.** B

Quarles, Benjamin **E540.N3Q3**
Negro in the Civil War. Trade Cloth. Russell & Russell Publishers. New York, NY. 1968. ISBN:0-8462-1052-5, ISBN13: 978-0-8462-1052-8. Dewey:973.71/5/30145196. LCCN:68-010941.
Audience: **l,u,f.** B

Randall, James G. & Donald, David Herbert **E468.R26 1969**
The Civil War and Reconstruction. Ed. 2. Paper Text. Houghton Mifflin Company Trade & Reference Division. Boston, MA. 1969. 866p. ISBN:0-669-06428-9, ISBN13: 978-0-669-06428-5. Dewey:973.7.
Audience: **l,u,f.**

Ross, Alexander M. **E450.R82**
Recollections and Experiences of an Abolitionist, from 1855 to 1865. Library Binding. Reprint Services Company. Temecula, CA. 1991. 224p. American Biography Ser. ISBN:0-7812-8331-0, ISBN13: 978-0-7812-8331-1. Dewey:322.4/4/0924.
Audience: **u,f.**

Sears, Stephen **E474.65**
Landscape Turned Red: The Battle of Antietam. Trade Cloth. Houghton Mifflin Company. New York, NY. 1983. 431p. ISBN:0-89919-172-X, ISBN13: 978-0-89919-172-0. Dewey:973.7/336. LCCN:82-019519.
Audience: **l,u,f.** B

Spencer, Warren **E596**
Confederate Navy in Europe. Trade Paper. University of Alabama Press. Tuscaloosa, AL. 1997. 288p. ISBN:0-8173-0861-X, ISBN13: 978-0-8173-0861-2. Dewey:973.757. LCCN:81-023283.
Audience: **l,u,f.**

Starr, Stephen Z. **E492.5**
Union Cavalry in the Civil War: The War in the East, from Gettysburg to Appomattox, 1863-1865. Trade Cloth. Louisiana State University Press. Baton Rouge, LA. 1981. xvi, 568p. ISBN:0-8071-0859-6, ISBN13: 978-0-8071-0859-8. Dewey:973.7/3. LCCN:78-026751.
Audience: **u,f.**

Starr, Stephen Z. **E492.5**
Union Cavalry in the Civil War: The War in the West, 1861-1865. Trade Cloth. Louisiana State University Press. Baton Rouge, LA. 1985. xv, 616p. ISBN:0-8071-1209-7, ISBN13: 978-0-8071-1209-0. Dewey:973.7/41. LCCN:78-026751.
Audience: **u,f.** *Choice, 1986.*

Starr, Stephen Z. **E492.5.S7**
Union Cavalry in the Civil War: From Fort Sumter to Gettysburg. Trade Cloth. Louisiana State University Press. Baton Rouge, LA. 1979. xiv, 536p. ISBN:0-8071-0484-1, ISBN13: 978-0-8071-0484-2. Dewey:973.7/41. LCCN:78-026751.
Audience: **u,f.** B

Vandiver, Frank E. **E545.V3 1993**
Rebel Brass: The Confederate Command System. Trade Paper. Louisiana State University Press. Baton Rouge, LA. 1993. 143p. ISBN:0-8071-1862-1, ISBN13: 978-0-8071-1862-7. Dewey:973.713. LCCN:56-009169.
Audience: **l,u,f.** B

Villard, Oswald Garrison **E451.V72**
John Brown, 1800-1859: Biography Fifty Years After. Trade Cloth. New Library Press.Net. Murrieta, CA. 1910. 738p. ISBN:0-7950-0823-6, ISBN13: 978-0-7950-0823-8. Dewey:973.680924.
Audience: **l,u,f.**

Wiley, Bell I. **E607**
The Life of Billy Yank: The Common Soldier of the Union. Trade Cloth. Louisiana State University Press. Baton Rouge, LA. 1971. 480p. ISBN:0-8071-1908-3, ISBN13: 978-0-8071-1908-2. Dewey:973.741. LCCN:75-162619.
Audience: **l,u,f.**

Williams, David **E468.9.W56 2005**
A People's History of the Civil War: Struggles for the Meaning of Freedom. Trade Cloth. New Press, The. New York, NY. 2005. 528p. A New Press People's History Ser. ISBN:1-59558-018-2, ISBN13: 978-1-59558-018-4. Dewey:973.7. LCCN:2005-043873.
Audience: **g,l,u,f.** *Choice, 2006.*

Williams, T. Harry **E457.905**
Lincoln and His Generals. Trade Cloth. DIANE Publishing Company. Collingdale, PA. 2003. 363p. ISBN:0-7567-6655-9, ISBN13: 978-0-7567-6655-9. Dewey:973.7/092.
Audience: **l,u,f.** B

United States > American History, by Period > Late 19th Century (1865-1900) > Diplomatic History

Adams, Ephraim D. **E469.A25**
Great Britain and the American Civil War. Trade Cloth. Peter Smith Publisher, Inc. Magnolia, MA. 1978. ISBN:0-8446-1005-4, ISBN13: 978-0-8446-1005-4. Dewey:973.722.
Audience: **l,u,f.**

Campbell, Charles S. **E661.7.C36 1976**
The Transformation of American Foreign Relations, 1865-1900. Trade Cloth. HarperCollins Publishers. New York, NY. 1976. 352p. New American Nation Ser. ISBN:0-06-010618-2, ISBN13: 978-0-06-010618-8. Dewey:327.73. LCCN:75-023877.
Audience: **l,u,f.** B

Crook, D. P. **E469**
The North the South, and the Powers. Cloth Text. John Wiley & Sons, Inc. Hoboken, NJ. 1974. 405p. ISBN:0-471-18855-7, ISBN13: 978-0-471-18855-1. Dewey:973.7/2. LCCN:73-016355.
Audience: **l,u,f.** *B*

Dobson, John M. **E661.7.D62**
America's Ascent: The United States Becomes a Great Power, 1880-1914. Trade Cloth. Northern Illinois University Press. DeKalb, IL. 1978. 251p. ISBN:0-87580-070-X, ISBN13: 978-0-87580-070-7. Dewey:327.73. LCCN:77-090754.
Audience: **l,u,f.** *B*

Foner, Philip S. **E469.8.F66 1981**
British Labor and the American Civil War. Trade Cloth. Holmes & Meier Publishers, Inc. Teaneck, NJ. 1981. 130p. ISBN:0-8419-0671-8, ISBN13: 978-0-8419-0671-6. Dewey:973.7. LCCN:80-026162.
Audience: **l,u,f.** *B*

Jenkins, Brian **E469.8.J46**
Britain and the War for the Union, Vol. 2. Trade Cloth. McGill-Queen's University Press. Montreal, PQ. 1980. 480p. ISBN:0-7735-0354-4, ISBN13: 978-0-7735-0354-0. Dewey:973.7/2. LCCN:74-077503.
Audience: **l,u,f.** *B*

Lafeber, Walter **E661.7.L2 1998**
New Empire: An Interpretation of American Expansion, 1860-1898. Trade Paper. Cornell University Press. Ithaca, NY. 1998. 480p. Cornell Paperbacks Ser. ISBN:0-8014-8595-9, ISBN13: 978-0-8014-8595-4. Dewey:973.8. LCCN:99-160552.
Audience: **u,f.**

May, Ernest R. **E661.7.M3 1991**
American Imperialism: A Speculative Essay. Trade Cloth. Imprint Publications, Inc. Chicago, IL. 1991. xxxv, 239p. ISBN:1-879176-03-3, ISBN13: 978-1-879176-03-4. Dewey:327.73.220. LCCN:91-073252.
Audience: **u,f.** *B*

Monaghan, Jay **E469.M75 1972**
Diplomat in Carpet Slippers: Abraham Lincoln Deals with Foreign Affairs. Trade Cloth. Ayer Company Publishers, Inc. Manchester, NH. 1977. Select Bibliographies Reprint Ser. ISBN:0-8369-6802-6, ISBN13: 978-0-8369-6802-6. Dewey:973.7/2. LCCN:79-039200.
Audience: **l,u,f.** *B*

Plesur, Milton **E661.7.P55**
America's Outward Thrust: Approaches to Foreign Affairs, 1865-1890. Trade Cloth. Northern Illinois University Press. DeKalb, IL. 1971. 276p. ISBN:0-87580-019-X, ISBN13: 978-0-87580-019-6. Dewey:327.73. LCCN:76-137882.
Audience: **l,u,f.** *B*

Pletcher, David M. **HF1456.5.P3P56 2001**
The Diplomacy of Involvement: American Economic Expansion across the Pacific, 1784-1900. Trade Paper. University of Missouri Press. Columbia, MO. 2001. 416p. ISBN:0-8262-1315-4, ISBN13: 978-0-8262-1315-0. Dewey:337.7309. LCCN:2001-018917.
Audience: **u,f.** *Choice, 2002.*

Pletcher, David M. **HF1456.5.W45P55 1998**
The Diplomacy of Trade and Investment: American Economic Expansion in the Hemisphere, 1865-1900. Trade Cloth. University of Missouri Press. Columbia, MO. 1998. 440p. ISBN:0-8262-1127-5, ISBN13: 978-0-8262-1127-9. Dewey:337.73. LCCN:97-038825.
Audience: **u,f.**

Warren, Gordon H. **E469.W3**
Fountain of Discontent: The Trent Affair and Freedom of the Sea. Cloth Text. Northeastern University Press. Boston, MA. 1981. 316p. ISBN:0-930350-12-X, ISBN13: 978-0-930350-12-3. Dewey:973.7/2. LCCN:80-024499.
Audience: **l,u,f.** *B*

Winks, Robin W. **E469.W5 1998**
The Civil War Years: Canada and the United States. Ed. 2. Trade Cloth. McGill-Queen's University Press. Montreal, PQ. 1998. 456p. ISBN:0-7735-1819-3, ISBN13: 978-0-7735-1819-3. Dewey:973.7/2. LCCN:00-340505.
Audience: **l,u,f.**

United States > American History, by Period > Late 19th Century (1865-1900) > Biography

Adams, Charles Francis **PT1828.B6**
Charles Francis Adams 1835-1915: An Autobiography. Trade Cloth. Library Reprints, Inc. Temecula, CA. 224p. ISBN:0-7222-8980-4, ISBN13: 978-0-7222-8980-8. Dewey:832.6.
Audience: **l,u,f.**

Cherny, Robert W. **E664.B87C47**
A Righteous Cause. Oscar Handlin (Editor). Trade Cloth. Little Brown & Company. New York, NY. 1985. 256p. ISBN:0-318-79429-2, ISBN13: 978-0-318-79429-7. Dewey:973.91/092/4. LCCN:84-019434.
Audience: **l,u,f.**

Clark, Champ **E664.C49C4**
My Quarter Century of American Politics. Trade Cloth. Library Reprints, Inc. Temecula, CA. ISBN:0-7222-7522-6, ISBN13: 978-0-7222-7522-1. Dewey:973.8.
Audience: **l,u,f.** *B*

Coletta, Paolo E. **E664.B87C55**
William Jennings Bryan: Political Puritan, 1915-1925. Cloth Text. University of Nebraska Press. Lincoln, NE. 1969. xiv, 334p. ISBN:0-8032-0024-2, ISBN13: 978-0-8032-0024-1. Dewey:973.91/0924 B. LCCN:64-011352.
Audience: **u,f.**

Cooling, Benjamin Franklin III **E664.T72.C66**
Benjamin Franklin Tracy: Father of the Modern American Fighting Navy. Trade Cloth. Shoe String Press, Inc. North Haven, CT. 1973. xvi, 211p. ISBN:0-208-01336-9, ISBN13: 978-0-208-01336-1. Dewey:353.7. LCCN:73-006645.
Audience: **l,u,f.** *B*

Glad, Paul W. **E664.B87G55**
The Trumpet Soundeth: William Jennings Bryan and His Democracy 1896. Paper Text. Textbook Publishers. Temecula, CA. 2003. xii, 242p. ISBN:0-7581-1907-0, ISBN13: 978-0-7581-1907-0. Dewey:923.273.
Audience: **l,u,f.** *B*

Hay, John M. & Burlingame, Michael **E664.H41A4 2000**
At Lincoln's Side: John Hay's Civil War Correspondence and Selected Writings. Trade Cloth. Southern Illinois University Press. Carbondale, IL. 2000. 320p. ISBN:0-8093-2293-5, ISBN13: 978-0-8093-2293-0. Dewey:973.7/092. LCCN:99-031085.
Audience: **u,f.** *Choice, 2001, 1996.*

Hay, John M. **E664.H41A3 1988**
Lincoln and the Civil War. Tyler Dennett (Editor), Henry Steele Commager (Introduction by). Trade Paper. Da Capo Press, Inc. Cambridge, MA. 1988. 370p. Quality Paperbacks Ser. ISBN:0-306-80340-2, ISBN13: 978-0-306-80340-6. Dewey:973.7/092/4. LCCN:88-017072.
Audience: **l,u,f.** B

Hughes, Charles E. **E664.H86.A32**
The Autobiographical Notes of Charles Evans Hughes. David J. Danelski & Joseph S. Tulchin (Editors). Trade Cloth. Harvard University Press. Cambridge, MA. 1973. 383p. Studies in Legal History ISBN:0-674-05325-7, ISBN13: 978-0-674-05325-0. Dewey:973.91/092/4. LCCN:72-088130.
Audience: **u,f.** B

Jessup, Philip C. **E664.R7J5**
Elihu Root, Set. Library Binding. Reprint Services Company. Temecula, CA. 1993. History of the United States Ser. ISBN:0-7812-4908-2, ISBN13: 978-0-7812-4908-9. Dewey:923.273.
Audience: **l,u,f.** B

Jordan, David M. **E664.C75**
Roscoe Conkling of New York: Voice in the Senate. Trade Cloth. Cornell University Press. Ithaca, NY. 1971. 486p. ISBN:0-8014-0625-0, ISBN13: 978-0-8014-0625-6. Dewey:328.73/0924. LCCN:76-148021.
Audience: **l,u,f.** B

Klingman, Peter D. **E664.W19.K54**
Josiah Walls: Florida's Black Congressman of Reconstruction. Trade Cloth. University Press of Florida. Gainesville, FL. 1976. 157p. ISBN:0-8130-0399-7, ISBN13: 978-0-8130-0399-3. Dewey:975.9/06/0924. LCCN:75-045206.
Audience: **l,u,f.** B

La Follette, Robert M. **E664.L16L16**
La Follette's Autobiography: A Personal Narrative of Political Experiences. Paper Text. Textbook Publishers. Temecula, CA. 2003. 349p. ISBN:0-7581-1392-7, ISBN13: 978-0-7581-1392-4. Dewey:923.273.
Audience: **u,f.** B

Leopold, Richard W. **E664.R7L4**
Elihu Root and the Conservative Tradition. Paper Text. Textbook Publishers. Temecula, CA. 2003. 222p. ISBN:0-7581-9656-3, ISBN13: 978-0-7581-9656-9. Dewey:923.273.
Audience: **l,u,f.**

Maxwell, Robert S. **E664.L16M3**
La Follette and the Rise of the Progressives in Wisconsin. Paper Text. Textbook Publishers. Temecula, CA. 2003. viii, 271p. ISBN:0-7581-3406-1, ISBN13: 978-0-7581-3406-6. Dewey:923.273.
Audience: **l,u,f.**

McGeary, M. Nelson **E664.P62M2 1979**
Gifford Pinchot: Forester-Politician. Frank Freidel (Editor). Library Binding. Garland Publishing, Inc. New York, NY. 1979. 481p. History of the United States Ser., Vol. 12 ISBN:0-8240-9700-9, ISBN13: 978-0-8240-9700-4. Dewey:329/.0092/4. LCCN:78-066552.
Audience: **l,u,f.** B

Nevins, Allan **E664.F52N44**
Hamilton Fish: The Inner History of the Grant Administration. Trade Cloth. Continuum International Publishing Group, Ltd. London, 1957. American Classics ISBN:0-8044-1676-1, ISBN13: 978-0-8044-1676-4. Dewey:973.82. LCCN:57-009967.
Audience: **l,u,f.** B

Nixon, Raymond B. **E664G73 N5**
Henry W. Grady, Spokesman of the New South. Trade Cloth. Russell & Russell Publishers. New York, NY. 1969. ISBN:0-8462-1289-7, ISBN13: 978-0-8462-1289-8. Dewey:070.9/24. LCCN:68-027076.
Audience: **u,f.** B

Parks, Joseph H. **E664.B8613.P37**
Joseph E. Brown of Georgia. Trade Cloth. Louisiana State University Press. Baton Rouge, LA. 1977. xvi, 612p. Southern Biography Ser. ISBN:0-8071-0189-3, ISBN13: 978-0-8071-0189-6. Dewey:975.8/03/0924. LCCN:74-027192.
Audience: **l,u,f.** B

Pinchot, Gifford **E664.P62A3 1998**
Breaking New Ground. George T. Frampton 2nd, Char Miller & Alaric Sample (Introduction by). Trade Paper. Island Press. Washington, DC. 1998. 542p. ISBN:1-55963-670-X, ISBN13: 978-1-55963-670-4. Dewey:333.7/5/0924. LCCN:98-012418.
Audience: **l,u,f.** B

Ridge, Martin **E664.D68R5**
Ignatius Donnelly: The Portrait of a Politican. Trade Cloth. University of Chicago Press. Chicago, IL. 1962. ISBN:0-226-71480-2, ISBN13: 978-0-226-71480-6. Dewey:928.1. LCCN:62-019937.
Audience: **l,u,f.**

Robinson, William A. **E664.R3R66**
Thomas B. Reed, Parliamentarian. Library Binding. Reprint Services Company. Temecula, CA. 1992. 423p. History of the United States Ser. ISBN:0-7812-6200-3, ISBN13: 978-0-7812-6200-2. Dewey:923.273.
Audience: **l,u,f.**

Schurz, Carl **E664.S3**
The Autobiography of Carl Schurz. Library Binding. Reprint Services Company. Temecula, CA. 1991. 331p. American Biography Ser. ISBN:0-7812-8344-2, ISBN13: 978-0-7812-8344-1. Dewey:921.
Audience: **u,f.** B

Simkins, Francis Butler **E664.T57S5 2002**
Pitchfork Ben Tillman, South Carolinian. University of South Carolina, Institute for Southern Studies Staff & South Caroliniana Society Staff (Contribution by). Trade Paper. University of South Carolina Press. Columbia, SC. 2002. xliii, 584p. ISBN:1-57003-477-X, ISBN13: 978-1-57003-477-0. Dewey:975.7/041/092. LCCN:2002-074251.
Audience: **l,u,f.** B

Trefousse, Hans L. **E664.S39T7 1998**
Carl Schurz: A Biography. Trade Cloth. Fordham University Press. Bronx, NY. 1998. 386p. The North's Civil War Ser., No. 5: ISBN:0-8232-1854-6, ISBN13: 978-0-8232-1854-7. Dewey:328.73/092. LCCN:97-044229.
Audience: **l,u,f.** B

Urofsky, Melvin I. **E664.B819.U7**
A Mind of One Piece; Brandeis and American Reform. Trade Cloth. Simon & Schuster. New York, NY. 1971. xiii, 210p. ISBN:0-684-12368-1, ISBN13: 978-0-684-12368-4. Dewey:347/.7326/34. LCCN:74-143945.
Audience: **u,f.**

Welch, Richard E. Jr. **E664.H65**
George F. Hoar and the Half-Breed Republicans. Trade Cloth. Harvard University Press. Cambridge, MA. 1971. 376p. ISBN:0-674-34876-1, ISBN13: 978-0-674-34876-9. Dewey:329.6/00924. LCCN:70-133214.
Audience: **l,u,f.**

Widenor, William C. **E664.L7**
Henry Cabot Lodge and the Search for an American Foreign Policy. Trade Cloth. University of California Press. Berkeley, CA. 1980. xi, 389p. ISBN:0-520-03778-2, ISBN13: 978-0-520-03778-6. Dewey:327.73. LCCN:78-062863.
Audience: **l,u,f.**

Woodward, C. Vann **E664.W337W6**
Tom Watson: Agrarian Rebel. Cloth Text. University Press of Virginia. Charlottesville, VA. 1982. 430p. ISBN:0-8139-0952-X, ISBN13: 978-0-8139-0952-3. Dewey:320.9/758/04. LCCN:73-077845.
Audience: **l,u,f.**

United States > American History, by Period > Late 19th Century (1865-1900) > By Presidential Administration

Barnard, Harry **E682**
Rutherford B. Hayes: And His America. Katherine E. Speirs (Editor). Trade Cloth. American Political Biography. Newtown, CT. 1992. 606p. Signature Ser. ISBN:0-945707-05-3, ISBN13: 978-0-945707-05-9. Dewey:973.8/3/0924. LCCN:92-073458.
Audience: **l,u,f.**

Beale, Howard K. **E668.B354**
Critical Year: A Study of Andrew Johnson and Reconstruction. Trade Cloth. Continuum International Publishing Group, Ltd. London, 1958. ISBN:0-8044-1085-2, ISBN13: 978-0-8044-1085-4. Dewey:973.81. LCCN:58-009332.
Audience: **l,u,f.**

Beisner, Robert L. **E713.B47 1992**
Twelve Against the Empire: The Anti-Imperialists, 1898-1900. Trade Paper. Imprint Publications, Inc. Chicago, IL. 1992. 336p. ISBN:1-879176-10-6, ISBN13: 978-1-879176-10-2. Dewey:327.73. LCCN:93-158081.
Audience: **l,u,f.**

Benedict, Michael L. **E668.B46**
A Compromise of Principle: Congressional Republicans and Reconstruction 1863-1869. Trade Cloth. W. W. Norton & Company, Inc. New York, NY. 1975. 493p. ISBN:0-393-05524-8, ISBN13: 978-0-393-05524-5. Dewey:973.8/1. LCCN:74-010645.
Audience: **l,u,f.**

Benedict, Michael L. **E666.B46 1973**
The Impeachment and Trial of Andrew Johnson. Trade Cloth. W. W. Norton & Company, Inc. New York, NY. 1973. 224p. Essays in American History Ser. ISBN:0-393-05473-X, ISBN13: 978-0-393-05473-6. Dewey:973.8/1/0924. LCCN:72-010883.
Audience: **l,u,f.**

Brown, Harry J. & Williams, Frederick D. (Editors) **E660.G223**
The Diary of James A. Garfield, Vols. I-IV. Trade Cloth. Michigan State University Press. East Lansing, MI. 1967. ISBN:0-87013-302-0, ISBN13: 978-0-87013-302-2. Dewey:973.8/4/0924 B.
Audience: **u,f.**

Carter, Dan T. **E668.C28 1985**
When the War Was Over: The Failure of Self-Reconstruction in the South, 1865-1867. Paper Text. Louisiana State University Press. Baton Rouge, LA. 1985. xvi, 286p. ISBN:0-8071-1204-6, ISBN13: 978-0-8071-1204-5. Dewey:975/.041. LCCN:84-021315.
Audience: **l,u,f.** *Choice, 1985.*

Cashman, Sean D. **E661.C38 1988**
America in the Gilded Age: From Abraham Lincoln to Theodore Roosevelt. Ed. 2. Cloth Text. New York University Press. New York, NY. 1988. 416p. ISBN:0-8147-1417-X, ISBN13: 978-0-8147-1417-1. Dewey:973.8. LCCN:88-001241.
Audience: **l,u,f.**

Castel, Albert **E666.C23**
The Presidency of Andrew Johnson. Trade Cloth. University Press of Kansas. Lawrence, KS. 1979. x, 262p. American Presidency Ser. ISBN:0-7006-0190-2, ISBN13: 978-0-7006-0190-5. Dewey:973.8/1/0924. LCCN:79-011050.
Audience: **l,u,f.**

Catton, Bruce **E470**
Grant Moves South. Trade Cloth. Book Sales, Inc. Edison, NJ. 2000. 564p. ISBN:0-7858-1264-4, ISBN13: 978-0-7858-1264-7. Dewey:973.7/3.
Audience: **l,u,f.**

Catton, Bruce **E467.1.L4**
Grant Takes Command. Trade Cloth. Book Sales, Inc. Edison, NJ. 2000. 556p. ISBN:0-7858-1263-6, ISBN13: 978-0-7858-1263-0. Dewey:973.73/0924.
Audience: **l,u,f.**

Catton, Bruce **E672.C3**
U. S. Grant and the American Military Tradition. Trade Cloth. Amereon, Ltd. Mattituck, NY. 1985. ISBN:0-8488-0279-9, ISBN13: 978-0-8488-0279-0. Dewey:355/.0092.
Audience: **l,u,f.**

Cleveland, Grover **E0697.C63**
Letters of Grover Cleveland, 1850-1908. Allan Nevins (Editor). Trade Paper. Books on Demand. Ann Arbor, MI. 662p. ISBN:0-598-69225-8, ISBN13: 978-0-598-69225-2. Dewey:973.8/5/0924. LCCN:33-035003.
Audience: **u,f.**

Cosmas, Graham A. **E725.3.C6**
An Army for Empire: The United States Army in the Spanish American War. Trade Cloth. University of Missouri Press. Columbia, MO. 1971. 352p. ISBN:0-8262-0107-5, ISBN13: 978-0-8262-0107-2. Dewey:973.8/93. LCCN:76-149010.
Audience: **l,u,f.**

Croly, Herbert D. **E664.H24C9**
Marcus Alonzo Hanna: His Life and Work. Trade Cloth. New Library Press.Net. Murrieta, CA. 495p. ISBN:0-7950-2068-6, ISBN13: 978-0-7950-2068-1. Dewey:923.273.
Audience: **l,u,f.**

Crunden, Robert M. **E661.C945 1982**
Ministers of Reform: The Progressives' Achievement in American Civilization, 1889-1920. Cloth Text. Basic Books. New York, NY. 1982. 400p. ISBN:0-465-04631-2, ISBN13: 978-0-465-04631-7. Dewey:973.91. LCCN:82-070848.
Audience: **l,u,f.** B

Davison, Kenneth E. **E682**
The Presidency of Rutherford B. Hayes. Trade Cloth. Greenwood Publishing Group, Inc. Portsmouth, NH. 1972. 266p. Contributions in American Studies, No. 3 ISBN:0-8371-6275-0, ISBN13: 978-0-8371-6275-1. Dewey:973.8/3/0924. LCCN:79-176289.
Audience: **u,f.** B

Doenecke, Justus D. **E686.D63**
The Presidencies of James A. Garfield and Chester A. Arthur. Trade Cloth. University Press of Kansas. Lawrence, KS. 1981. xiv, 230p. American Presidency Ser. ISBN:0-7006-0208-9, ISBN13: 978-0-7006-0208-7. Dewey:973.8/4. LCCN:80-018957.
Audience: **l,u,f.** B

Dorris, Jonathon T. **KF7221.D6 1977**
Pardon and Amnesty under Lincoln and Johnson: The Restoration of the Confederates to Their Rights and Privileges, 1861-1898. J. C. Randall (Introduction by). Trade Cloth. Greenwood Publishing Group, Inc. Portsmouth, NH. 1977. 459p. ISBN:0-8371-9646-9, ISBN13: 978-0-8371-9646-6. Dewey:343/.73/012. LCCN:77-005940.
Audience: **l,u,f.**

Du Bois, W. E. B. **E668**
Black Reconstruction in America 1860-1880: An Essay Toward a History of the Part Which Black Folk Played in the Attempt to Reconstruct Democracy in America. Cedric Robinson (Introduction by). Library Binding. University of Notre Dame Press. Notre Dame, IN. 2001. 776p. The African American Intellectual Heritage Ser. ISBN:0-268-02165-1, ISBN13: 978-0-268-02165-8. Dewey:973.8.
Audience: **g,l,u,f.**

Dunning, William A. **E668.D927**
Essays on the Civil War and Reconstruction. David Donald (Introduction by). Trade Cloth. Peter Smith Publisher, Inc. Magnolia, MA. 1990. ISBN:0-8446-0600-6, ISBN13: 978-0-8446-0600-2. Dewey:320.9/73/08.
Audience: **u,f.**

Faulkner, Harold U. **E661.F3**
Politics, Reform and Expansion: 1890-1900. Cloth Text. HarperCollins Publishers. New York, NY. 1959. New American Nation Ser. ISBN:0-06-011210-7, ISBN13: 978-0-06-011210-3. Dewey:973.8.
Audience: **l,u,f.**

Fleming, Walter Lynwood **E668**
Documentary History of Reconstruction: Political, Military, Social, Religious, Educational and Industrial. Trade Cloth. Peter Smith Publisher, Inc. Magnolia, MA. 1979. ISBN:0-8446-1184-0, ISBN13: 978-0-8446-1184-6. Dewey:973.81082.
Audience: **u,f.**

Foner, Eric & Brown, Joshua **E668.F655 2005**
Forever Free: The Story of Emancipation and Reconstruction. Trade Cloth. Alfred A. Knopf Inc. New York, NY. 2005. 304p. ISBN:0-375-40259-4, ISBN13: 978-0-375-40259-3. Dewey:973.8. LCCN:2005-040706.
Audience: **g,l,u,f.**

Franklin, John H. **E668.F7**
Reconstruction after the Civil War. Library Binding. University of Chicago Press. Chicago, IL. 1961. Chicago History of American Civilization Ser. ISBN:0-226-26075-5, ISBN13: 978-0-226-26075-4. Dewey:973.8. LCCN:61-015931.
Audience: **l,u,f.** B

Garraty, John A. **E661**
New Commonwealth, 1877-1890. Trade Paper. HarperCollins Publishers. New York, NY. 1968. xv, 364p. New American Nation Ser. ISBN:0-06-131410-2, ISBN13: 978-0-06-131410-0. Dewey:973.8.
Audience: **l,u,f.**

Gillette, William **E668**
Retreat from Reconstruction: 1869-1879. Cloth Text. Louisiana State University Press. Baton Rouge, LA. 1980. xiv, 463p. ISBN:0-8071-0569-4, ISBN13: 978-0-8071-0569-6. Dewey:973.8/2. LCCN:79-012450.
Audience: **l,u,f.** B

Goldman, Eric F. **E661.G58 2001**
Rendezvous with Destiny: A History of Modern American Reform. Trade Paper. Ivan R. Dee Publisher. Blue Ridge Summit, PA. 2001. 560p. ISBN:1-56663-369-9, ISBN13: 978-1-56663-369-7. Dewey:973.8. LCCN:00-050437.
Audience: **l,u,f.**

Goodwyn, Lawrence **E661.G67**
Democratic Promise: The Populist Moment in America. Oxford University Press, Inc. 1976. ISBN:0-19-501996-2, ISBN13: 978-0-19-501996-4.
Audience: **l,u,f.** B

Gould, Lewis L. **E711.G68**
The Presidency of William McKinley. Trade Cloth. University Press of Kansas. Lawrence, KS. 1981. xiv, 294p. American Presidency Ser. ISBN:0-7006-0206-2, ISBN13: 978-0-7006-0206-3. Dewey:973.8/8/0924. LCCN:80-016022.
Audience: **l,u,f.** B

Hamilton, Holman **E422.H32**
Zachary Taylor. Trade Cloth. Shoe String Press, Inc. North Haven, CT. 1966. ISBN:0-208-00608-7, ISBN13: 978-0-208-00608-0. Dewey:973.6/3/092.
Audience: **l,u,f.** B

Hays, Samuel P. **HC105.H35 1995**
The Response to Industrialism, 1885-1914. Ed. 2. Daniel J. Boorstin (Editor). Trade Cloth. University of Chicago Press. Chicago, IL. 1995. 280p. Chicago History of American Civilization Ser. ISBN:0-226-32163-0, ISBN13: 978-0-226-32163-9. Dewey:330.973. LCCN:95-018562.
Audience: **l,u,f.** B

Hirshson, Stanley P. **E661**
Farewell to the Bloody Shirt: Northern Republicans and the Southern Negro 1877. Paper Text. Textbook Publishers. Temecula, CA. 2003. 334p. ISBN:0-7581-6770-9, ISBN13: 978-0-7581-6770-5. Dewey:973.8.
Audience: **l,u,f.** B

Hollingsworth, Joseph Rogers **E0661.H72**
The Whirligig of Politics: The Democracy of Cleveland and Bryan. Trade Paper. Books on Demand. Ann Arbor, MI. 275p. ISBN:0-598-15468-X, ISBN13: 978-0-598-15468-2. Dewey:973.87. LCCN:63-018846.
Audience: **l,u,f.**

Jensen, Ronald J. **E669**
The Alaska Purchase and Russian-American Relations. Cloth Text. University of Washington Press. Seattle, WA. 1975. 196p. ISBN:0-295-95376-4, ISBN13: 978-0-295-95376-2. Dewey:979.8/02. LCCN:74-023716.
Audience: **l,u,f.**

Josephson, Matthew **E661.J85**
The Politicos. Trade Paper. Harcourt Trade Publishers. New York, NY. 1963. 760p. ISBN:0-15-672799-4, ISBN13: 978-0-15-672799-0. Dewey:973.8. LCCN:38-027301.
Audience: **l,u,f.**

Keller, Morton **JK246.K45 2000**
Affairs of State: Public Life in Late Nineteenth Century America, 1977. Trade Cloth. Lawbook Exchange, Limited, The. Clark, NJ. 2000. ix, 631p. ISBN:1-58477-086-4, ISBN13: 978-1-58477-086-2. Dewey:973.8. LCCN:99-087921.
Audience: **l,u,f.**

Klein, Philip S. **E437**
President James Buchanan: A President. Katherine E. Speirs (Editor). Trade Cloth. American Political Biography. Newtown, CT. 1995. 506p. Signature Ser. ISBN:0-945707-11-8, ISBN13: 978-0-945707-11-0. Dewey:973.6/8/092. LCCN:95-079749.
Audience: **l,u,f.**

Leech, Margaret **E711.6**
In the Days of McKinley: William McKinley. Trade Cloth. American Political Biography. Newtown, CT. 1999. 686p. Signature Ser. ISBN:0-945707-24-X, ISBN13: 978-0-945707-24-0. Dewey:973.8/8/095. LCCN:99-076373.
Audience: **l,u,f.**

Lewis, Lloyd **E672.L48 1991**
Captain Sam Grant, 1822-1861. Trade Paper. Little Brown & Company. New York, NY. 1991. ISBN:0-316-52348-8, ISBN13: 978-0-316-52348-6. Dewey:973.6/092 B. LCCN:90-027738.
Audience: **l,u,f.**

Long, E. B. **E672**
Personal Memoirs of U. S. Grant. William S. McFeely (Introduction by), Jean Edward Smith (Foreword by). Trade Paper. Da Capo Press, Inc. Cambridge, MA. 2001. 648p. ISBN:0-306-81061-1, ISBN13: 978-0-306-81061-9. Dewey:973.8/2/092.
Audience: **u,f.**

Mantell, Martin E. **E666**
Johnson, Grant, and the Politics of Reconstruction. Cloth Text. Columbia University Press. New York, NY. 1973. 209p. ISBN:0-231-03507-1, ISBN13: 978-0-231-03507-1. Dewey:973.8/1. LCCN:72-013452.
Audience: **l,u,f.**

McFeely, William S. **E467.1.L4**
Grant: A Biography. Katherine E. Speirs (Editor). Trade Cloth. American Political Biography. Newtown, CT. 1996. 492p. Signature Ser. ISBN:0-945707-15-0, ISBN13: 978-0-945707-15-8. Dewey:973.8/2/0924. LCCN:96-085992.
Audience: **l,u,f.**

McKitrick, Eric L. **E668.M156 1988**
Andrew Johnson and Reconstruction. Trade Paper. Oxford University Press, Inc. New York, NY. 1988. 544p. ISBN:0-19-505707-4, ISBN13: 978-0-19-505707-2. Dewey:973.8/1/0924. LCCN:88-023509.
Audience: **l,u,f.**

Millis, Walter **E715.M76 1979**
The Martial Spirit. Richard H. Kohn (Editor). Library Binding. Ayer Company Publishers, Inc. Manchester, NH. 1980. American Military Experience Ser. ISBN:0-405-11866-X, ISBN13: 978-0-405-11866-1. Dewey:973.88. LCCN:78-022389.
Audience: **l,u,f.**

Morgan, H. Wayne **E711.6.M7 2003**
William McKinley and His America. Ed. 2. Trade Cloth. Kent State University Press. Kent, OH. 2003. 496p. ISBN:0-87338-765-1, ISBN13: 978-0-87338-765-1. Dewey:973.8/8/092 B. LCCN:2002-011850.
Audience: **l,u,f.**

Morgan, Howard W. **E715.M85**
America's Road to Empire: The War with Spain and Overseas Expansion. Paper Text. John Wiley & Sons, Inc. Hoboken, NJ. 1965. 124p. America in Crisis Ser. ISBN:0-471-61520-X, ISBN13: 978-0-471-61520-0. Dewey:973.891. LCCN:64-008714.
Audience: **l,u,f.**

Morgan, Howard W. **E660.M6**
From Hayes to McKinley: National Party Politics, 1877-1896. Trade Paper. Books on Demand. Ann Arbor, MI. 678p. ISBN:0-608-15201-3, ISBN13: 978-0-608-15201-1. Dewey:329/.02/0973. LCCN:69-017074.
Audience: **l,u,f.**

Nevins, Allan **F483.S6**
Grover Cleveland: A Study in Courage, Vol. 2. Katherine E. Speirs (Editor). Trade Cloth. American Political Biography. Newtown, CT. 2001. 425p. Signature Ser. ISBN:0-945707-29-0, ISBN13: 978-0-945707-29-5. Dewey:977/.01. LCCN:00-135878.
Audience: **u,f.**

Perman, M. **E487**
Reunion Without Compromise: The South and Reconstruction, 1865-1868. Cloth Text. Cambridge University Press. New York, NY. 1973. 383p. ISBN:0-521-20044-X, ISBN13: 978-0-521-20044-8. Dewey:320.9/75/04. LCCN:72-086418.
Audience: **l,u,f.**

Peskin, Allan & Davis, Jim **E687.P47 1999**
Garfield. Trade Cloth. Kent State University Press. Kent, OH. 1998. 720p. ISBN:0-87338-210-2, ISBN13: 978-0-87338-210-6. Dewey:973.8/4/092 B. LCCN:77-015630.
Audience: **l,u,f.**

Pletcher, David M. **E686**
Awkward Years: American Foreign Relations Under Garfield and Arthur. Trade Cloth. University of Missouri Press. Columbia, MO. 1962. 400p. ISBN:0-8262-0143-1, ISBN13: 978-0-8262-0143-0. Dewey:973.84. LCCN:62-015589.
Audience: **l,u,f.**

Polakoff, Keith I. **E680.P73**
The Politics of Inertia: The Election of 1876 and the End of Reconstruction. Trade Cloth. Louisiana State University Press. Baton Rouge, LA. 1973. xiv, 344p. ISBN:0-8071-0210-5,

ISBN13: 978-0-8071-0210-7. Dewey:329/.023/73082. LCCN:72-096400.
Audience: **l,u,f.** *B*

Pratt, Julius **E713.P895**
Expansionists of 1898: The Acquisition of Hawaii and the Spanish Islands. Trade Cloth. Peter Smith Publisher, Inc. Magnolia, MA. 1985. ISBN:0-8446-1364-9, ISBN13: 978-0-8446-1364-2. Dewey:973.88.
Audience: **l,u,f.**

Reeves, Thomas C. **E687**
Gentleman Boss: The Life of Chester Alan Arthur. Katherine E. Speirs (Editor). Trade Cloth. American Political Biography. Newtown, CT. 1991. 500p. Signature Ser. ISBN:0-945707-03-7, ISBN13: 978-0-945707-03-5. Dewey:973.8/4/0924. LCCN:91-071714.
Audience: **l,u,f.** *B*

Roark, James L. **E668.R64 1977**
Masters Without Slaves. Trade Cloth. W. W. Norton & Company, Inc. New York, NY. 1977. xii, 273p. ISBN:0-393-05562-0, ISBN13: 978-0-393-05562-7. Dewey:976/.04. LCCN:76-047689.
Audience: **l,u.** *B*

Sefton, James E. **E668.S46 1980**
The United States Army and Reconstruction, 1865-1877. Trade Cloth. Greenwood Publishing Group, Inc. Portsmouth, NH. 1980. 284p. ISBN:0-313-22602-4, ISBN13: 978-0-313-22602-1. Dewey:973. LCCN:80-015136.
Audience: **l,u,f.** *B*

Sievers, Harry J. **E83.89**
Benjamin Harrison: Hoosier Statesman. Katherine E. Speirs (Editor). Trade Cloth. American Political Biography. Newtown, CT. 1997. 502p. Signature Ser. ISBN:0-945707-17-7, ISBN13: 978-0-945707-17-2. Dewey:973.86. LCCN:96-078888.
Audience: **u,f.**

Sievers, Harry J. **B1203**
Benjamin Harrison: Hoosier Warrior. Katherine E. Speirs (Editor). Trade Cloth. American Political Biography. Newtown, CT. 1997. 344p. Signature Ser., Vol. 1 ISBN:0-945707-16-9, ISBN13: 978-0-945707-16-5. Dewey:192. LCCN:96-078887.
Audience: **u,f.**

Sievers, Harry J. **E702**
Benjamin Harrison: Hoosier President: The White House and After 1889-1901. Katherine E. Speirs (Editor). Trade Cloth. American Political Biography. Newtown, CT. 1997. 320p. Signature Ser. ISBN:0-945707-18-5, ISBN13: 978-0-945707-18-9. Dewey:973.8/6/0924. LCCN:96-078889.
Audience: **u,f.**

Singletary, Otis A. **E668**
Negro Militia and Reconstruction. Trade Cloth. Greenwood Publishing Group, Inc. Portsmouth, NH. 1984. 181p. ISBN:0-313-24573-8, ISBN13: 978-0-313-24573-2. Dewey:973.8. LCCN:84-010733.
Audience: **l,u,f.** *B*

Smith, Theodore Clarke **E687.S66 1968**
Life and Letters of James Abram Garfield. Trade Cloth. Shoe String Press, Inc. North Haven, CT. 1968. ISBN:0-208-00667-2, ISBN13: 978-0-208-00667-7. Dewey:973.8/4/0924. LCCN:68-026935.
Audience: **u,f.** *B*

Socolofsky, Homer E. & Spetter, Allan **E701.S62 1987**
The Presidency of Benjamin Harrison. Trade Cloth. University Press of Kansas. Lawrence, KS. 1987. xii, 268p. American Presidency Ser. ISBN:0-7006-0320-4, ISBN13: 978-0-7006-0320-6. Dewey:973.8/6/0924. LCCN:86-032592.
Audience: **l,u,f.** *Choice, 1987.*

Sproat, John G. **E661**
The Best Men: Liberal Reformers in the Gilded Age with a New Preface. Paper Text. University of Chicago Press. Chicago, IL. 1982. 376p. Phoenix Ser. ISBN:0-226-76990-9, ISBN13: 978-0-226-76990-5. Dewey:973.8. LCCN:82-010948.
Audience: **l,u,f.** *B*

Stampp, Kenneth M. **E668**
Era of Reconstruction, 1865-1877. Trade Paper. Knopf Publishing Group. New York, NY. 1967. 256p. ISBN:0-394-70388-X, ISBN13: 978-0-394-70388-6. Dewey:973.81.
Audience: **l,u,f.** *B*

Trachtenberg, Alan **E169.1.T72 1982**
The Incorporation of America: Culture and Society in the Gilded Age. Trade Paper. Farrar, Straus & Giroux. New York, NY. 1982. 262p. American Century Ser. ISBN:0-8090-0145-4, ISBN13: 978-0-8090-0145-3. Dewey:973.8. LCCN:81-013339.
Audience: **u,f.** *B*

Trask, David F. **E715.T7 1996**
The War with Spain in 1898. Trade Cloth. University of Nebraska Press. Lincoln, NE. 1996. 654p. ISBN:0-8032-9429-8, ISBN13: 978-0-8032-9429-5. Dewey:973.8/9. LCCN:96-021710.
Audience: **l,u,f.** *B*

Trelease, Allen W. **E668**
White Terror: The Ku Klux Klan Conspiracy and Southern Reconstruction. Trade Cloth. Greenwood Publishing Group, Inc. Portsmouth, NH. 1979. 557p. ISBN:0-313-21168-X, ISBN13: 978-0-313-21168-3. Dewey:973.8. LCCN:78-012864.
Audience: **l,u,f.** *B*

Welch, Richard E. Jr. **E696.W45 1988**
The Presidencies of Grover Cleveland. Trade Cloth. University Press of Kansas. Lawrence, KS. 1988. xviii, 246p. American Presidency Ser. ISBN:0-7006-0355-7, ISBN13: 978-0-7006-0355-8. Dewey:973.8/5. LCCN:88-000268.
Audience: **l,u,f.** *Choice, 1988.*

Welch, Richard E. Jr. **E721.W4**
Response to Imperialism: The United States and the Philippine-American War, 1899-1902. Trade Cloth. University of North Carolina Press. Chapel Hill, NC. 1987. xvi, 215p. ISBN:0-8078-1348-6, ISBN13: 978-0-8078-1348-5. Dewey:959.9/031. LCCN:78-011403.
Audience: **l,u,f.** *B*

Wiebe, Robert H. **E661**
The Search for Order, 1877-1920. Trade Paper. Farrar, Straus & Giroux. New York, NY. 1966. 336p. Making of America Ser. ISBN:0-8090-0104-7, ISBN13: 978-0-8090-0104-0. Dewey:973.8. LCCN:66-027609.
Audience: **l,u,f.** *B*

Williams, R. Hal **E701.W54**
Years of Decision American Politics 1890. Cloth Text. John Wiley & Sons, Inc. Hoboken, NJ. 1978. 219p.

ISBN:0-471-94877-2, ISBN13: 978-0-471-94877-3. Dewey:320.9/73/08. LCCN:78-006407.
Audience: **l,u,f.**

Woodward, C. Vann **E83.877**
Reunion and Reaction: The Compromise of 1877 and the End of Reconstruction. Trade Cloth. Peter Smith Publisher, Inc. Magnolia, MA. 1995. ISBN:0-8446-6871-0, ISBN13: 978-0-8446-6871-0. Dewey:973.8/3.
Audience: **l,u,f.**

United States > American History, by Period > 20th Century

Badger, Anthony J. **E806.B24**
The New Deal: The Depression Years, 1933-1940. Trade Paper. Farrar, Straus & Giroux. New York, NY. 1989. 360p. ISBN:0-8090-7260-2, ISBN13: 978-0-8090-7260-6. Dewey:973.917.
Audience: **l,u,f.**

Barber, William J. **HC106.8**
From New Era to New Deal: Herbert Hoover, the Economists, and American Economic Policy, 1921-1933. Craufurd D. Goodwin (Contribution by). Trade Paper. Cambridge University Press. New York, NY. 1989. 256p. Historical Perspectives on Modern Economics Ser. ISBN:0-521-36737-9, ISBN13: 978-0-521-36737-0. Dewey:330.973/0915.
Audience: **u,f.** *Choice, 1986.*

Beschloss, Michael R. **E807.B46 2003**
The Conquerors: Roosevelt, Truman and the Destruction of Hitler's Germany, 1941-1945. Trade Paper. Simon & Schuster. New York, NY. 2003. 400p. ISBN:0-7432-4454-0, ISBN13: 978-0-7432-4454-1. Dewey:940.5/3144/0943.
Audience: **u,f.**

Blum, John M. **E743.B6135 1980**
Progressive Presidents: Theodore Roosevelt, Woodrow Wilson, Franklin D. Roosevelt, Lyndon B. Johnson. Trade Cloth. W. W. Norton & Company, Inc. New York, NY. 1980. 221p. ISBN:0-393-01330-8, ISBN13: 978-0-393-01330-6. Dewey:353.03/2. LCCN:79-022866.
Audience: **l,u,f.**

Blum, John M. **E757.B65 1977**
The Republican Roosevelt. Ed. 2. Trade Cloth. Harvard University Press. Cambridge, MA. 1977. 177p. ISBN:0-674-76301-7, ISBN13: 978-0-674-76301-2. Dewey:973.91/1/0924. LCCN:54-005182.
Audience: **g,l,u,f.**

Blum, John Morton **E835**
Years of Discord: American Politics and Society, 1961-1974. Trade Paper. W. W. Norton & Company, Inc. New York, NY. 1992. 540p. ISBN:0-393-30910-X, ISBN13: 978-0-393-30910-2. Dewey:973.9/21.
Audience: **l,u,f.** *Choice, 1992.*

Branch, Taylor **E185.61.B7914 1989**
Parting the Waters: America in the King Years, 1954-1963. Trade Paper. Simon & Schuster. New York, NY. 1989. 1088p. ISBN:0-671-68742-5, ISBN13: 978-0-671-68742-7. Dewey:973/.0496073. LCCN:97-130525.
Audience: **g,l,u.** *Choice, 1989.*

Brinkley, Alan **E806.B75 1982**
Voices of Protest: Huey Long, Father Coughlin and the Great Depression. Trade Cloth. Alfred A. Knopf Inc. New York, NY. 1982. xiii, 348p. ISBN:0-394-52241-9, ISBN13: 978-0-394-52241-8. Dewey:973.917. LCCN:81-048121.
Audience: **u,f.**

Brownlee, W. Elliot & Graham, Hugh Davis (Editors) **E876.R4117 2003**
The Reagan Presidency: Pragmatic Conservatism and Its Legacies. Trade Cloth. University Press of Kansas. Lawrence, KS. 2003. xii, 404p. ISBN:0-7006-1268-8, ISBN13: 978-0-7006-1268-0. Dewey:973.927. LCCN:2003-007158.
Audience: **u,f.** *Choice, 2004.*

Bundy, William P. **E855.B85**
A Tangled Web: The Making of Foreign Policy in the Nixon Presidency. Trade Paper. Farrar, Straus & Giroux. New York, NY. 1999. 672p. ISBN:0-8090-1624-9, ISBN13: 978-0-8090-1624-2. Dewey:327.73.
Audience: **l,u,f.** *Choice, 1998.*

Burner, David **E802.B87 1979**
Herbert Hoover: The Public Life. Trade Cloth. Alfred A. Knopf Inc. New York, NY. 1979. xii, 433p. ISBN:0-394-46134-7, ISBN13: 978-0-394-46134-2. Dewey:973.91/6/0924. LCCN:78-054912.
Audience: **f.**

Burner, David **JK2316.B8 1986**
The Politics of Provincialism: The Democratic Party in Transition, 1918-1932. Trade Paper. Harvard University Press. Cambridge, MA. 1986. 320p. ISBN:0-674-68940-2, ISBN13: 978-0-674-68940-4. Dewey:324.736/09. LCCN:85-024832.
Audience: **l,u,f.**

Burton, David H. **E757.B9717 1997**
Theodore Roosevelt, American Politician: An Assessment. Trade Cloth. Fairleigh Dickinson University Press. Cranbury, NJ. 1997. 176p. ISBN:0-8386-3727-2, ISBN13: 978-0-8386-3727-2. Dewey:[B]. LCCN:96-029718.
Audience: **u,f.** *Choice, 1997.*

Burton, David Henry **E757.B9714 2005**
Taft, Roosevelt, and the Limits of Friendship. Trade Cloth. Fairleigh Dickinson University Press. Cranbury, NJ. 2004. 160p. ISBN:0-8386-4042-7, ISBN13: 978-0-8386-4042-5. Dewey:973.91/1/0922 B. LCCN:2004-005457.
Audience: **u,f.**

Burton, William **E762.B869 2004**
William Howard Taft, Confident Peacemaker: The Evolution Idea: World Ordered Diplomacy. Trade Cloth. Saint Joseph's University Press. Philadelphia, PA. 2004. 224p. ISBN:0-916101-51-7, ISBN13: 978-0-916101-51-0. Dewey:973.91/2/092. LCCN:2004-012433.
Audience: **f.** *Choice, 2005.*

Chafe, William Henry **E806.M63 2002**
The Achievement of American Liberalism: The New Deal and Its Legacies. Trade Paper. Columbia University Press. New York, NY. 2002. 350p. ISBN:0-231-11213-0, ISBN13: 978-0-231-11213-0. Dewey:973.917. LCCN:2002-073366.
Audience: **u,f.** *Choice, 2003.*

Chalmers, David M. **E743.C45 1970**
Social and Political Ideas of the Muckrakers. Trade Cloth. Ayer Company Publishers, Inc. Manchester, NH. 1977. Essay Index

Reprint Ser. ISBN:0-8369-1745-6, ISBN13: 978-0-8369-1745-1. Dewey:301.15/3. LCCN:70-117765.
Audience: **u,f.**

Chomsky, Noam **DS558.C5 1993**
Rethinking Camelot: JFK, the Vietnam War, and U. S. Political Culture. Trade Cloth. South End Press. Cambridge, MA. 1993. 172p. ISBN:0-89608-459-0, ISBN13: 978-0-89608-459-9. Dewey:959.704/3373. LCCN:93-000297.
Audience: **u,f.** *Choice, 1993.*

Clements, Kendrick A. **HC110.C6C53 2000**
Hoover, Conservation and Consumerism: Engineering the Good Life. Trade Cloth. University Press of Kansas. Lawrence, KS. 2000. xiv,330p. ISBN:0-7006-1033-2, ISBN13: 978-0-7006-1033-4. Dewey:333.7/0973. LCCN:00-028316.
Audience: **l,u,f.** *Choice, 2001.*

Cohen, Warren I. **E785.C64 1987**
Empire Without Tears: America's Foreign Relations, 1921-1933. Trade Cloth. Temple University Press. Philadelphia, PA. 1987. 152p. ISBN:0-87722-490-0, ISBN13: 978-0-87722-490-7. Dewey:327.73. LCCN:87-050219.
Audience: **u,f.**

Cooper, John M. **E757**
The Warrior and the Priest: Woodrow Wilson and Theodore Roosevelt. Trade Cloth. Harvard University Press. Cambridge, MA. 1983. 448p. ISBN:0-674-94750-9, ISBN13: 978-0-674-94750-4. Dewey:973.91/092/2. LCCN:83-006021.
Audience: **l,u,f.** B

Cooper, John Milton Jr. **E756.C78 1990**
Pivotal Decades: The United States, 1900-1920. Trade Paper. W. W. Norton & Company, Inc. New York, NY. 1990. 432p. ISBN:0-393-95655-5, ISBN13: 978-0-393-95655-9. Dewey:973.91. LCCN:89-003397.
Audience: **u,f.**

Davis, Kenneth S. **E807**
F. D. R.: Into the Storm, 1937-1940. Trade Paper. Random House Adult Trade Publishing Group. New York, NY. 1995. 708p. ISBN:0-8129-9205-9, ISBN13: 978-0-8129-9205-2. Dewey:973.917/092.
Audience: **l,u,f.** *Choice, 1993.*

Degler, Carl N. **E178**
Out of Our Past: The Forces That Shaped Modern America. Trade Cloth. HarperCollins Publishers. New York, NY. 1970. ISBN:0-06-011012-0, ISBN13: 978-0-06-011012-3. Dewey:973.
Audience: **g,u,f.** B

Deloria, Vine Jr. (Editor) **E93.A44 1985**
American Indian Policy in the Twentieth Century. Trade Cloth. University of Oklahoma Press. Norman, OK. 1985. 272p. ISBN:0-8061-1897-0, ISBN13: 978-0-8061-1897-0. Dewey:323.1/197/073. LCCN:85-001057.
Audience: **u,f.**

Dickinson, Matthew J. **JK518.D54 1997**
Bitter Harvest: FDR, Presidential Power and the Growth of the Presidential Branch. Trade Paper. Cambridge University Press. New York, NY. 1999. 280p. ISBN:0-521-65395-9, ISBN13: 978-0-521-65395-4. Dewey:351.7/3.
Audience: **u,f.** *Choice, 1997.*

Divine, Robert A. (Editor) **E846.J64 1987**
The Johnson Years: Vietnam, the Environment, and Science. Trade Paper. University Press of Kansas. Lawrence, KS. 1987. xii, 272p. ISBN:0-7006-0464-2, ISBN13: 978-0-7006-0464-7. Dewey:973.923. LCCN:86-032443.
Audience: **u,f.** *Choice, 1987.*

Fearon, Peter **HC106.2.F42 1987**
War, Prosperity and Depression: The U. S. Economy, 1917-1945. Trade Cloth. University Press of Kansas. Lawrence, KS. 1988. x, 294p. ISBN:0-7006-0348-4, ISBN13: 978-0-7006-0348-0. Dewey:330.973/091. LCCN:87-021571.
Audience: **u,f.** *Choice, 1988.*

Ferrell, Robert H. **E791.F47 1998**
The Presidency of Calvin Coolidge. Trade Cloth. University Press of Kansas. Lawrence, KS. 2004. xii, 244p. American Presidency Ser. ISBN:0-7006-0892-3, ISBN13: 978-0-7006-0892-8. Dewey:973.91/5/092. LCCN:97-051128.
Audience: **u,f.** *Choice, 1998.*

Ferrell, Robert H. **E176.1.F475 2005**
Presidential Leadership: From Woodrow Wilson to Harry S. Truman. Trade Cloth. University of Missouri Press. Columbia, MO. 2005. 184p. ISBN:0-8262-1623-4, ISBN13: 978-0-8262-1623-6. Dewey:973.091/09/9. LCCN:2005-023511.
Audience: **u,f.**

Ferrell, Robert H. **D619.F34 1985**
Woodrow Wilson and World War I, 1917-1921. Trade Cloth. HarperCollins Publishers. New York, NY. 1985. 312p. ISBN:0-06-011229-8, ISBN13: 978-0-06-011229-5. Dewey:940.3/73. LCCN:84-048160.
Audience: **u,f.** *Choice, 1985.*

Frankel, Max **E841.F68 2004**
High Noon in the Cold War: Kennedy, Khrushchev, and the Cuban Missile Crisis. Trade Cloth. Ballantine Books. New York, NY. 2004. 224p. ISBN:0-345-46505-9, ISBN13: 978-0-345-46505-4. Dewey:327.47073/09/046. LCCN:2004-046159.
Audience: **f.** *Choice, 2005.*

Freidel, Frank **E807.F75 1990**
Franklin D. Roosevelt: Rendezvous with Destiny. Trade Cloth. Little Brown & Company. New York, NY. 1990. viii, 710p. ISBN:0-316-29260-5, ISBN13: 978-0-316-29260-3. Dewey:973.917/092. LCCN:89-012580.
Audience: **u,f.**

Frum, David **JC573.2.U6**
Dead Right: The End of the Conservativism of Hope and the Rise of the Conservativism of Fear. Trade Paper. Basic Books. New York, NY. 1995. 256p. ISBN:0-465-09825-8, ISBN13: 978-0-465-09825-5. Dewey:320.5/2/0973.
Audience: **u,f.** *Choice, 1995.*

Galbraith, John Kenneth **HB37171929.G32**
The Great Crash 1929. Trade Cloth. Houghton Mifflin Company. New York, NY. 1988. ISBN:0-395-13935-X, ISBN13: 978-0-395-13935-6. Dewey:338.5/4/0973. LCCN:72-002285.
Audience: **u,f.** B

Gardner, Lloyd C. **DS558.G37 1995**
Pay Any Price: Lyndon Johnson and the Wars for Vietnam. Trade Cloth. Ivan R. Dee Publisher. Blue Ridge Summit, PA.

1995. 610p. ISBN:1-56663-087-8, ISBN13: 978-1-56663-087-0. Dewey:959.704/3373. LCCN:95-013208.
Audience: **l,u,f.** *Choice, 1996.*

Garza, Hedda (Compiled by) **KF27.J8**
The Watergate Investigation Index: House Judiciary Committee Hearings and Report on Impeachment. Fred L. Israel (Introduction by). Book, Other. Rowman & Littlefield Publishers, Inc. Lanham, MD. 1985. 261p. ISBN:0-8420-2186-8, ISBN13: 978-0-8420-2186-9. Dewey:364.1/32/0973. LCCN:85-002040.
Audience: **l,u,f.** *Choice, 1985.*

Giglio, James N. **E841.G54 1991**
The Presidency of John F. Kennedy. Trade Paper. University Press of Kansas. Lawrence, KS. 1991. x, 334p. American Presidency Ser. ISBN:0-7006-0520-7, ISBN13: 978-0-7006-0520-0. Dewey:973.922/092. LCCN:91-016841.
Audience: **g,l,u,f.** *Choice, 1992.*

Goldberg, David J. **E784.G65 1999**
Discontented America: The United States in the 1920s. Stanley I. Kutler (Foreword by). Trade Cloth. Johns Hopkins University Press. Baltimore, MD. 1999. 224p. The American Moment Ser. ISBN:0-8018-6004-0, ISBN13: 978-0-8018-6004-1. Dewey:973.91. LCCN:98-036310.
Audience: **l,u,f.** *Choice, 1999.*

Goodman, James **KF224.S34G66 1994**
Stories of Scottsboro. Trade Cloth. Knopf Publishing Group. New York, NY. 1994. 465p. ISBN:0-679-40779-0, ISBN13: 978-0-679-40779-9. Dewey:345.761/02532 347.61. LCCN:93-005589.
Audience: **u,f.**

Goossen, Rachel W. **D810.C82G66 1997**
Women Against the Good War: Conscientious Objection and Gender on the American Home Front, 1941-1947. Trade Paper. University of North Carolina Press. Chapel Hill, NC. 1997. 200p. Gender and American Culture Ser. ISBN:0-8078-4672-4, ISBN13: 978-0-8078-4672-8. Dewey:940.53/162. LCCN:97-009885.
Audience: **u,f.** *Choice, 1998.*

Gould, Lewis L. **E176.1**
The Modern American Presidency. Richard Norton Smith (Foreword by). Trade Paper. University Press of Kansas. Lawrence, KS. 2004. xvi, 302p. ISBN:0-7006-1330-7, ISBN13: 978-0-7006-1330-4. Dewey:973.9/092/2.
Audience: **g,l,u,f.** *Choice, 2003.*

Graebner, William **E169.1.G698 1990**
The Age of Doubt: American Thought and Culture in the 1940s. Trade Paper. Thomson Gale. Farmington Hills, MI. 1990. 216p. ISBN:0-8057-9070-5, ISBN13: 978-0-8057-9070-2. Dewey:973.917. LCCN:90-042941.
Audience: **l,u,f.** *Choice, 1991.*

Graham, Otis L. **E743.G72**
The Great Campaigns: Reform and War in America, 1900-1928. Trade Cloth. Prentice-Hall. Upper Saddle, NJ. 1971. xiii, 386p. ISBN:0-13-363572-4, ISBN13: 978-0-13-363572-0. Dewey:973.91. LCCN:79-135756.
Audience: **u,f.** *B*

Graubard, Stephen **E176.1.G815 2004**
Command of Office: How War, Secrecy and Deception Transformed the Presidency, from Theodore Roosevelt to George W. Bush. Cloth Text. Basic Books. New York, NY. 2004. 744p. ISBN:0-465-02757-1, ISBN13: 978-0-465-02757-6. Dewey:973/.09/9 B. LCCN:2004-007706.
Audience: **l,u,f.** *Choice, 2005.*

Handlin, Oscar **JV6450**
The Uprooted: The Epic Story of the Great Migrations That Made the American People. Ed. 2. Book, Other. University of Pennsylvania Press. Philadelphia, PA. 2002. 344p. ISBN:0-8122-1788-8, ISBN13: 978-0-8122-1788-9. Dewey:304.8/73. LCCN:2001-048096.
Audience: **u,f.**

Harrison, Robert **JK1041.H37 2004**
Congress, Progressive Reform, and the New American State. Trade Cloth. Cambridge University Press. New York, NY. 2004. 310p. ISBN:0-521-82789-2, ISBN13: 978-0-521-82789-8. Dewey:320/.6/097309041. LCCN:2003-055310.
Audience: **u,f.** *Choice, 2004.*

Hawley, Ellis W. **E784.H38**
The Great War and the Search for a Modern Order. Paper Text. St. Martin's Press. Gordonville, VA. 1979. Twentieth Century United States History Ser. ISBN:0-312-34681-6, ISBN13: 978-0-312-34681-2. Dewey:973.91. LCCN:78-071723.
Audience: **l,u,f.**

Hendin, Josephine **PS225.C66 2004**
A Concise Companion to Postwar American Literature and Culture. Trade Paper. Blackwell Publishing, Inc. Malden, MA. 2004. 448p. Blackwell Concise Companions to Literature and Culture Ser. ISBN:1-4051-2180-7, ISBN13: 978-1-4051-2180-4. Dewey:810.9/0054. LCCN:2003-020731.
Audience: **u,f.** *Choice, 2005.*

Hofstadter, Richard **E784**
Age of Reform: From Bryan to F. D. R. Trade Cloth. Alfred A. Knopf Inc. New York, NY. 1955. ISBN:0-394-41442-X, ISBN13: 978-0-394-41442-3. Dewey:973.91.
Audience: **g,l,u,f.** *B*

Hofstadter, Richard **E743.H632 1996**
The Paranoid Style in American Politics: And Other Essays. Trade Paper. Harvard University Press. Cambridge, MA. 1996. 352p. ISBN:0-674-65461-7, ISBN13: 978-0-674-65461-7. Dewey:320.973. LCCN:96-165819.
Audience: **u,f.** *B*

Hofstadter, Richard **HM22.U5H6 1992**
Social Darwinism in American Thought. Eric Foner (Introduction by). Trade Paper. Beacon Press. Boston, MA. 1992. 288p. ISBN:0-8070-5503-4, ISBN13: 978-0-8070-5503-8. Dewey:301/.0973. LCCN:91-045525.
Audience: **f.** *B*

Horowitz, David A. **E743.H679 1997**
Beyond Left and Right: Insurgency and the Establishment. Trade Cloth. University of Illinois Press. Champaign, IL. 1997. 472p. ISBN:0-252-02266-1, ISBN13: 978-0-252-02266-1. Dewey:306.2/0973. LCCN:96-010032.
Audience: **l,u,f.** *Choice, 1997.*

Houghton, David **E183.8.I55H68 2001**
U. S. Foreign Policy and the Iran Hostage Crisis. Thomas Biersteker, Chris Brown & Phil Cerny (Contribution by). Cloth

Text. Cambridge University Press. New York, NY. 2001. 270p. Studies in International Relations, Vol. 75 ISBN:0-521-80116-8, ISBN13: 978-0-521-80116-4. Dewey:955.05/42. LCCN:00-045453.
Audience: **l,u,f.** *Choice, 2002.*

Houghton, David **E183.8.I55H68 2001**
U. S. Foreign Policy and the Iran Hostage Crisis. Thomas Biersteker, Chris Brown, Phil Cerny, Joseph Grieco, A. J. R. Groom, Richard Higgott, G. John Ikenberry, Caroline Kennedy-Pipe, Steve Lamy & Steve Smith (Contribution by). Trade Paper. Cambridge University Press. New York, NY. 2001. 270p. Studies in International Relations, Vol. 75 ISBN:0-521-80509-0, ISBN13: 978-0-521-80509-4. Dewey:955.05/42. LCCN:00-045453.
Audience: **l,u,f.** *Choice, 2002.*

Johnson, Haynes **E885.J63**
The Best of Times: America in the Clinton Years. Trade Cloth. DIANE Publishing Company. Collingdale, PA. 2004. 610p. ISBN:0-7567-7912-X, ISBN13: 978-0-7567-7912-2. Dewey:973.929.
Audience: **g,u,f.** *Choice, 2002.*

Josephson, Matthew **E743.J65**
President Makers, Eighteen Ninety-Six to Nineteen Nineteen. Trade Cloth. Continuum International Publishing Group, Ltd. London, 1964. American Classics ISBN:0-8044-1460-2, ISBN13: 978-0-8044-1460-9. Dewey:973.91. LCCN:64-008722.
Audience: **u,f.**

Kaiser, David E. **DS558**
American Tragedy: Kennedy, Johnson, and the Origins of the Vietnam War. Trade Paper. Harvard University Press. Cambridge, MA. 2002. 576p. Belknap Press Ser. ISBN:0-674-00672-0, ISBN13: 978-0-674-00672-0. Dewey:959.704/3373.
Audience: **u,f.** *Choice, 2000.*

Kaplan, Leonard V. & Moran, Beverly I. (Editors) **E886.2.A44 2001**
Aftermath: The Clinton Impeachment and the Presidency in the Age of Political Spectacle. Trade Cloth. New York University Press. New York, NY. 2001. 384p. Critical America Ser. ISBN:0-8147-4742-6, ISBN13: 978-0-8147-4742-1. Dewey:973.929. LCCN:2001-001549.
Audience: **u,f.** *Choice, 2002.*

Karaagac, John **E876.K348 2000**
Between Promise and Policy: Ronald Reagan and Conservative Reformism. Trade Cloth. Lexington Books. Lanham, MD. 2000. 320p. ISBN:0-7391-0094-7, ISBN13: 978-0-7391-0094-3. Dewey:973.927/092. LCCN:99-052930.
Audience: **u,f.** *Choice, 2000.*

Kennedy, David M. **D570**
Over Here: The First World War and American Society. Trade Cloth. Oxford University Press, Inc. New York, NY. 1980. 416p. ISBN:0-19-502729-9, ISBN13: 978-0-19-502729-7. Dewey:940.3/73. LCCN:80-011753.
Audience: **l,u,f.** B

Kort, Michael G. **E744.K696 1998**
The Columbia Guide to the Cold War. Trade Cloth. Columbia University Press. New York, NY. 1998. 420p. Columbia Guides to American History and Cultures ISBN:0-231-10772-2, ISBN13: 978-0-231-10772-3. Dewey:973.9. LCCN:98-007154.
Audience: **g,l,u,f.** *Choice, 1999.*

Kraut, Alan M. **JV6450.K7 2001**
The Huddled Masses: The Immigrant in American Society, 1880-1921. Ed. 2. Abraham S. Eisenstadt & John H. Franklin (Editors). Trade Cloth. Harlan Davidson Inc. Wheeling, IL. 2003. 267p. The American History Ser. ISBN:0-88295-934-4, ISBN13: 978-0-88295-934-4. Dewey:304.8/73/009034. LCCN:00-047505.
Audience: **l,u,f.**

Kutler, Stanley I. **E740.7.E53 1996**
Encyclopedia of America in the Twentieth Century, 1. Trade Cloth. Prentice Hall PTR. Upper Saddle River, NJ. 1996. 1941p. ISBN:0-13-307190-1, ISBN13: 978-0-13-307190-0. Dewey:973/.003. LCCN:95-022696.
Audience: **g,l,u,f.** *Choice, 1996.*

Kutler, Stanley I. **E740.7.E53 1996**
Encyclopedia of America in the Twentieth Century, 3. Trade Cloth. Prentice Hall PTR. Upper Saddle River, NJ. 1995. xxxix, 1941p. ISBN:0-13-307216-9, ISBN13: 978-0-13-307216-7. Dewey:973/.003. LCCN:95-022696.
Audience: **g,l,u,f.** *Choice, 1996.*

Kutler, Stanley I. **E740.7.E53 1996**
Encyclopedia of America in the Twentieth Century, 2. Trade Cloth. Prentice Hall PTR. Upper Saddle River, NJ. 1996. xxxix, 1941p. ISBN:0-13-307208-8, ISBN13: 978-0-13-307208-2. Dewey:973/.003. LCCN:95-022696.
Audience: **g,l,u,f.** *Choice, 1996.*

Larson, Edward J. **KF224.S3**
Summer for the Gods: The Scopes Trial and America's Continuing Debate over Science and Religion. Trade Paper. Harvard University Press. Cambridge, MA. 1998. 336p. ISBN:0-674-85429-2, ISBN13: 978-0-674-85429-1. Dewey:345.73/0288. LCCN:97-009648.
Audience: **u,f.** *Choice, 1997.*

Leuchtenburg, William E. **E806.L474 1995**
The FDR Years: On Roosevelt and His Legacy. Trade Cloth. Columbia University Press. New York, NY. 1995. 377p. ISBN:0-231-08298-3, ISBN13: 978-0-231-08298-3. Dewey:973.917/092. LCCN:95-013282.
Audience: **u,f.** *Choice, 1996.*

Leuchtenburg, William E. **E806**
Franklin D. Roosevelt and the New Deal 1932-1940. Trade Cloth. HarperCollins Publishers. New York, NY. 1963. New American Nation Ser. ISBN:0-685-11865-7, ISBN13: 978-0-685-11865-8. Dewey:973.917. LCCN:63-012053.
Audience: **l,u,f.**

Leuchtenburg, William E. **HC106.3.L3957 1993**
The Perils of Prosperity, 1914-1932. Ed. 2. Daniel J. Boorstin (Foreword by). Trade Cloth. University of Chicago Press. Chicago, IL. 1993. 332p. Chicago History of American Civilization Ser. ISBN:0-226-47370-8, ISBN13: 978-0-226-47370-3. Dewey:330.9730913. LCCN:92-044912.
Audience: **g,u,f.**

Link, Arthur S. **E768.L67**
Woodrow Wilson: Revolution, War and Peace. Trade Paper. Harlan Davidson Inc. Wheeling, IL. 2003. 152p. ISBN:0-88295-798-8, ISBN13: 978-0-88295-798-2. Dewey:973.91/3/0924. LCCN:79-050909.
Audience: **f.** B

Link, William A. **F215.L56**
The Paradox of Southern Progressivism, 1880-1930. Trade Paper. University of North Carolina Press. Chapel Hill, NC. 1997. 458p. Fred W. Morrison Series in Southern Studies ISBN:0-8078-4589-2, ISBN13: 978-0-8078-4589-9. Dewey:306.2/0975. LCCN:92-001328.
Audience: **f.** *Choice, 1993.*

Lyons, James **F899.S45**
Selling Seattle: Representing Contemporary Urban America. Trade Cloth. Wallflower Press. London, 2004. 226p. ISBN:1-903364-96-5, ISBN13: 978-1-903364-96-3. Dewey:979.7772.
Audience: **f.** *Choice, 2005.*

May, Ernest R. & Zelikow, Philip D. (Editors) **E841.K4655 1997**
The Kennedy Tapes: Inside the White House During the Cuban Missile Crisis. Trade Cloth. Harvard University Press. Cambridge, MA. 1997. 800p. ISBN:0-674-17926-9, ISBN13: 978-0-674-17926-4. Dewey:973.922. LCCN:97-014216.
Audience: **u,f.** *Choice, 1998.*

May, Lary (Editor) **E169.12.R43 1989**
Recasting America: Culture and Politics in the Age of Cold War. Trade Paper. University of Chicago Press. Chicago, IL. 1988. 320p. ISBN:0-226-51176-6, ISBN13: 978-0-226-51176-4. Dewey:973.92. LCCN:88-021618.
Audience: **u,f.** *Choice, 1989.*

Mayhew, David R. **KF4945.Z9**
Divided We Govern: Party Control, Lawmaking and Investigations, 1946-1990. Trade Paper. Yale University Press. Cumberland, RI. 1993. 240p. ISBN:0-300-04837-8, ISBN13: 978-0-300-04837-7. Dewey:328.73/077.
Audience: **u,f.** *Choice, 1992.*

McDonogh, Gary (Editor), et al. **E169.12.E49 2001**
Encyclopedia of Contemporary American Culture. Robert Gregg & Cindy Hing-Yuk Wong (Editors). Paper over Boards. Routledge. New York, NY. 2001. 880p. Encyclopedias of Contemporary Culture Ser. ISBN:0-415-16161-4, ISBN13: 978-0-415-16161-9. Dewey:973.92/03. LCCN:00-055326.
Audience: **g,l,u,f.** *Choice, 2001.*

McElvaine, Robert S. (Editor) **E806.E63 2004**
Encyclopedia of the Great Depression. Trade Cloth. Thomson Gale. Farmington Hills, MI. 2003. lix, 1134p. ISBN:0-02-865687-3, ISBN13: 978-0-02-865687-8. Dewey:973.91/6/03. LCCN:2003-010292.
Audience: **g,l,u,f.** *Choice, 2004.*

McJimsey, George **E806.M46 2000**
The Presidency of Franklin Delano Roosevelt. Trade Cloth. University Press of Kansas. Lawrence, KS. 2000. xvi, 356p. American Presidency Ser. ISBN:0-7006-1012-X, ISBN13: 978-0-7006-1012-9. Dewey:973.917/092. LCCN:99-055956.
Audience: **u,f.** *Choice, 2000.*

Mencken, H. L. (Author, Editor) **E169.M5195 2004**
Mencken's America. Trade Paper. Ohio University Press. Athens, OH. 2004. 400p. ISBN:0-8214-1532-8, ISBN13: 978-0-8214-1532-0. Dewey:973.8. LCCN:2003-056755.
Audience: **f.** *Choice, 2004.*

Milkis, Sidney M. & Mileur, Jerome M. (Editors) **JC574.2.U6N48 2002**
The New Deal and the Triumph of Liberalism. Trade Cloth. University of Massachusetts Press. Amherst, MA. 2002. 304p. The Political Development of the American Nation Ser., :Studies in Politics and History ISBN:1-55849-320-4, ISBN13: 978-1-55849-320-9. Dewey:973.917. LCCN:2001-055501.
Audience: **u,f.** *Choice, 2003.*

Morris, Edmund **E757**
The Rise of Theodore Roosevelt. Trade Cloth. Penguin Group (USA) Inc. New York, NY. 1979. ISBN:0-698-10783-7, ISBN13: 978-0-698-10783-0. Dewey:973.91/1/092 B. LCCN:78-023789.
Audience: **g,l.** B

Mowry, George E. & Brownell, Blaine A. **E741**
The Urban Nation: 1920-1980. Trade Paper. Farrar, Straus & Giroux. New York, NY. 1990. 360p. ISBN:0-8090-9541-6, ISBN13: 978-0-8090-9541-4. Dewey:973.9.
Audience: **f.**

Murray, Robert K. **E786.M8**
Harding Era: Warren G. Harding and His Administration. Trade Cloth. University of Minnesota Press. Minneapolis, MN. 1969. ISBN:0-8166-0541-6, ISBN13: 978-0-8166-0541-5. Dewey:973.91/4/0924. LCCN:74-091797.
Audience: **u,f.**

Murray, Robert K. **E743.5.M8 1980**
Red Scare: A Study in National Hysteria, 1919-1920. Trade Cloth. Greenwood Publishing Group, Inc. Portsmouth, NH. 1980. xii, 337p. ISBN:0-313-22673-3, ISBN13: 978-0-313-22673-1. Dewey:973.913. LCCN:80-018184.
Audience: **u,f.**

Noble, David W. **PS78.N63 2002**
Death of a Nation: American Culture and the End of Exceptionalism. Trade Paper. University of Minnesota Press. Minneapolis, MN. 2002. 260p. Critical American Studies ISBN:0-8166-4081-5, ISBN13: 978-0-8166-4081-2. Dewey:801/.95/09730904. LCCN:2002-009538.
Audience: **l,u,f.** *Choice, 2003.*

O'Neill, William L. **D769.O64**
A Democracy at War: America's Fight at Home and Abroad in World War II. Trade Paper. Harvard University Press. Cambridge, MA. 1998. 512p. ISBN:0-674-19737-2, ISBN13: 978-0-674-19737-4. Dewey:940.540973.
Audience: **l,u,f.** *Choice, 1994.*

Pendergast, Sara & Pendergast, Tom (Editors) **E169.1.S764 2000**
St. James Encyclopedia of Popular Culture, Set. Jim Cullen (Introduction by). Trade Cloth. Thomson Gale. Farmington Hills, MI. 1999. 3065p. ISBN:1-55862-400-7, ISBN13: 978-1-55862-400-9. Dewey:973.9. LCCN:99-046540.
Audience: **g,l,u,f.** *Choice, 2000.*

Perry, Barbara A. **E843.K4P47 2004**
Jacqueline Kennedy: First Lady of the New Frontier. Trade Cloth. University Press of Kansas. Lawrence, KS. 2004. 270p. Modern First Ladies Ser. ISBN:0-7006-1343-9, ISBN13: 978-0-7006-1343-4. Dewey:973.922/092. LCCN:2004-006224.
Audience: **u,f.** *Choice, 2005.*

Peterson, Mark A. **JK585.P48**
Legislating Together: The White House and Capitol Hill from Eisenhower to Reagan. Trade Paper. Harvard University Press. Cambridge, MA. 1990. 358p. ISBN:0-674-52416-0, ISBN13: 978-0-674-52416-3. Dewey:320.473.
Audience: **u,f.** *Choice, 1991.*

Piper, Paul (Editor) **F209.S68 2004**
The Greenwood Encyclopedia of American Regional Cultures. William Ferris (Foreword by). Trade Cloth. Greenwood Publishing Group, Inc. Portsmouth, NH. 2004. 3200p. ISBN:0-313-33266-5, ISBN13: 978-0-313-33266-1. Dewey:977/.003. LCCN:2004-056060.
Audience: **g,l,u,f.** *Choice, 2005.*

Preston, William Jr. **E743.5.P7 1994**
Aliens and Dissenters: Federal Suppression of Radicals, 1903-1933. Ed. 2. Paul Buhle (Foreword by). Trade Paper. University of Illinois Press. Champaign, IL. 1994. 384p. ISBN:0-252-06452-6, ISBN13: 978-0-252-06452-4. Dewey:322.4/2/097309041. LCCN:94-027501.
Audience: **f.** B

Regier, C. C. **E741.R34**
The Era of the Muckrakers. Trade Cloth. Peter Smith Publisher, Inc. Magnolia, MA. 1983. ISBN:0-8446-1380-0, ISBN13: 978-0-8446-1380-2. Dewey:973.91.
Audience: **f.**

Rodgers, Daniel T. **HD8072**
The Work Ethic in Industrial America, 1850-1920. Trade Paper. University of Chicago Press. Chicago, IL. 1979. 316p. ISBN:0-226-72352-6, ISBN13: 978-0-226-72352-5. Dewey:301.5/5. LCCN:77-081737.
Audience: **u,f.**

Romasco, Albert U. **HC106.3**
The Politics of Recovery: Roosevelt's New Deal. Trade Cloth. Oxford University Press, Inc. New York, NY. 1983. 288p. ISBN:0-19-503248-9, ISBN13: 978-0-19-503248-2. Dewey:330.973/0917. LCCN:82-014499.
Audience: **u,f.**

Schlesinger, Arthur M. Jr. **E807**
The Coming of the New Deal, 1933-1935. Trade Cloth. Houghton Mifflin Company. New York, NY. 1959. The Age of Roosevelt Ser., Vol. 2 ISBN:0-395-08160-2, ISBN13: 978-0-395-08160-0. Dewey:973.917/092.
Audience: **u,f.**

Schlesinger, Arthur M. Jr. **E784.S36**
The Crisis of the Old Order, 1919-1933. Trade Cloth. Houghton Mifflin Company. New York, NY. 1957. The Age of Roosevelt Ser., Vol. 1 ISBN:0-395-08159-9, ISBN13: 978-0-395-08159-4. Dewey:973.91.
Audience: **u,f.**

Schlesinger, Arthur M. Jr. **E806.S347 1988**
The Politics of Upheaval, 1935-1936. Trade Paper. Houghton Mifflin Company. New York, NY. 1988. The Age of Roosevelt Ser., Vol. 3 ISBN:0-395-48904-0, ISBN13: 978-0-395-48904-8. Dewey:973.917. LCCN:88-008207.
Audience: **u,f.**

Schmitz, David F. (Editor) **E748.S883S36 2001**
Henry L. Stimson: The First Wise Man. Book, Other. Rowman & Littlefield Publishers, Inc. Lanham, MD. 2001. 222p. Biographies in American Foreign Policy Ser., No. 5 ISBN:0-8420-2631-2, ISBN13: 978-0-8420-2631-4. Dewey:973.91/092. LCCN:00-032190.
Audience: **f.** *Choice, 2001.*

Schwartz, Richard A. **E169.12.S39 1997**
Cold War Culture: Media and the Arts, 1945-1990. Trade Cloth. Facts On File, Inc. New York, NY. 1997. 384p. Cold War America Ser. ISBN:0-8160-3104-5, ISBN13: 978-0-8160-3104-7. Dewey:973.92/03. LCCN:96-029642.
Audience: **u,f.** *Choice, 1998.*

Shaw, Stephen K. (Editor), et al. **KF8742.F73 2003**
Franklin D. Roosevelt and the Transformation of the Supreme Court. William D. Pederson & Frank J. Williams (Editors). Trade Cloth. M. E. Sharpe Inc. Armonk, NY. 2004. 280p. Library of Franklin D. Roosevelt Studies, Vol. 3 ISBN:0-7656-1032-9, ISBN13: 978-0-7656-1032-4. Dewey:347.73/26/09. LCCN:2002-066944.
Audience: **u,f.** *Choice, 2004.*

Shull, Steven A. **E185.615.S5 1993**
A Kinder, Gentler Racism?: The Reagan-Bush Civil Rights Legacy. Paper Text. M. E. Sharpe Inc. Armonk, NY. 1993. 256p. American Political Institutions and Public Policy Ser. ISBN:1-56324-240-0, ISBN13: 978-1-56324-240-3. Dewey:323.1/196073. LCCN:93-002785.
Audience: **u,f.** *Choice, 1994.*

Small, Melvin **E855.S63 1999**
The Presidency of Richard Nixon. Trade Paper. University Press of Kansas. Lawrence, KS. 2003. xx, 388p. American Presidency Ser. ISBN:0-7006-1255-6, ISBN13: 978-0-7006-1255-0. Dewey:973.924/092. LCCN:99-013148.
Audience: **g,l,u,f.** *Choice, 2000.*

Sonenshein, Raphael **JS1003.A2S66 2004**
The City at Stake: Secession, Reform, and the Battle for Los Angeles. Trade Cloth. Princeton University Press. Princeton, NJ. 2004. 328p. ISBN:0-691-11590-7, ISBN13: 978-0-691-11590-0. Dewey:320.9794/94. LCCN:2004-044253.
Audience: **f.** *Choice, 2005.*

Stearns, Peter N. **HQ769.S76 2002**
Anxious Parents: A History of Modern Childrearing in America. Trade Cloth. New York University Press. New York, NY. 2003. 263p. ISBN:0-8147-9829-2, ISBN13: 978-0-8147-9829-4. Dewey:649/.1/0973. LCCN:2002-152802.
Audience: **l,u,f.** *Choice, 2003.*

Sullivan, Patricia **E185.61.S93 1996**
Days of Hope: Race and Democracy in the New Deal. Trade Paper. University of North Carolina Press. Chapel Hill, NC. 1996. 352p. ISBN:0-8078-4564-7, ISBN13: 978-0-8078-4564-6. Dewey:975/.00496073. LCCN:95-000365.
Audience: **u,f.** *Choice, 1996.*

Tentler, Leslie W. **HD6095.T44**
Wage-Earning Women: Industrial Work and Family Life in the United States, 1900-1930. Trade Cloth. Oxford University Press, Inc. New York, NY. 1979. 290p. ISBN:0-19-502627-6, ISBN13: 978-0-19-502627-6. Dewey:331.4/0973. LCCN:79-012802.
Audience: **u,f.** B

Tindall, George B. **F215.T59**
Emergence of the New South, 1913-1945. Cloth Text. Louisiana State University Press. Baton Rouge, LA. 1967. xvi, 808p.

History of the South Ser., Vol. 10 ISBN:0-8071-0010-2, ISBN13: 978-0-8071-0010-3. Dewey:975. LCCN:67-024551.
Audience: **f.**

Trachtenberg, Alan **E98.P99T73 2004**
Shades of Hiawatha: Staging Indians, Making Americans, 1880-1930. Cloth over Boards. Farrar, Straus & Giroux. New York, NY. 2004. 400p. ISBN:0-374-29975-7, ISBN13: 978-0-374-29975-0. Dewey:323.173. LCCN:2004-042438.
Audience: **u,f.** *Choice, 2005.*

Trani, Eugene P. & Wilson, David L. **E785.T7**
The Presidency of Warren G. Harding. Trade Cloth. University Press of Kansas. Lawrence, KS. 1977. xii, 232p. American Presidency Ser. ISBN:0-7006-0152-X, ISBN13: 978-0-7006-0152-3. Dewey:973.91/4/0924. LCCN:76-026110.
Audience: **u,f.**

Vandiver, Frank E. **DS558.V38 1997**
Shadows of Vietnam: Lyndon Johnson's Wars. Trade Cloth. Texas A&M University Press. College Station, TX. 1997. 432p. ISBN:0-89096-747-4, ISBN13: 978-0-89096-747-8. Dewey:959.704/3373. LCCN:96-050121.
Audience: **f.** *Choice, 1997.*

Varon, Jeremy **HN90.R3V37 2004**
Bringing the War Home: The Weather Underground, the Red Army Faction, and Revolutionary Violence in the Sixties and Seventies. Trade Paper. University of California Press. Berkeley, CA. 2004. 432p. ISBN:0-520-24119-3, ISBN13: 978-0-520-24119-0. Dewey:322.4/2/0943. LCCN:2003-019002.
Audience: **u,f.** *Choice, 2005.*

Walsh, Lawrence E. **DS318.85**
Firewall: The Iran-Contra Conspiracy and Cover-Up. Trade Paper. DIANE Publishing Company. Collingdale, PA. 1997. 544p. ISBN:0-7567-6493-9, ISBN13: 978-0-7567-6493-7. Dewey:955.05/42.
Audience: **u,f.** *Choice, 1997.*

Weinstein, James **E743.W44 1981**
The Corporate Ideal in the Liberal State: 1900-1918. Trade Cloth. Greenwood Publishing Group, Inc. Portsmouth, NH. 1981. 263p. ISBN:0-313-22709-8, ISBN13: 978-0-313-22709-7. Dewey:973.91. LCCN:80-022211.
Audience: **f.**

Welles, Benjamin **E748.W442W44 1997**
Sumner Welles: FDR's Global Strategist: A Biography. Cloth over Boards. Palgrave Macmillan. New York, NY. 1997. 464p. Franklin and Eleanor Roosevelt Institute Series on Diplomatic and Econ Ser. ISBN:0-312-17440-3, ISBN13: 978-0-312-17440-8. Dewey:327.73/092. LCCN:97-011579.
Audience: **f.** *Choice, 1998.*

Wiebe, Robert H. **E661**
The Search for Order, 1877-1920. Trade Paper. Farrar, Straus & Giroux. New York, NY. 1966. 336p. Making of America Ser. ISBN:0-8090-0104-7, ISBN13: 978-0-8090-0104-0. Dewey:973.8. LCCN:66-027609.
Audience: **l,u,f.**

Woods, Randall Bennett (Editor) **DS558.V476 2003**
Vietnam and the American Political Tradition: The Politics of Dissent. Trade Paper. Cambridge University Press. New York, NY. 2003. 332p. ISBN:0-521-01000-4, ISBN13: 978-0-521-01000-9. Dewey:959.704/3373. LCCN:2002-025619.
Audience: **u,f.** *Choice, 2003.*

Zinn, Howard & Arnove, Anthony (Editors) **E178**
Voices of a People's History of the United States. Trade Cloth. Seven Stories Press. New York, NY. 2004. 665p. ISBN:1-58322-647-8, ISBN13: 978-1-58322-647-6. Dewey:973. LCCN:2004-018173.
Audience: **l,u,f.** *Choice, 2005.*

United States > American History, by Period > 20th Century > Political History

Allen, Frederick L. **E784.A63 1986**
Since Yesterday: The 1930's in America, September 3, 1929 to September 3, 1939. Trade Paper. HarperCollins Publishers. New York, NY. 1986. 400p. ISBN:0-06-091322-3, ISBN13: 978-0-06-091322-9. Dewey:973.91. LCCN:86-045060.
Audience: **u.**

Allen, Frederick Lewis **E784.A6 2000**
Only Yesterday: An Informal History of the 1920's. Trade Paper. HarperCollins Publishers. New York, NY. 2000. 352p. Perennial Classics Ser. ISBN:0-06-095665-8, ISBN13: 978-0-06-095665-3. Dewey:973.91/3. LCCN:00-028345.
Audience: **u,f.**

Allen, Frederick Lewis **E0741.A66**
Since Yesterday: The Nineteen-Thirties in America, September 3, 1929-September 3 1939. Trade Paper. Books on Demand. Ann Arbor, MI. 377p. ISBN:0-598-99162-X, ISBN13: 978-0-598-99162-1. Dewey:973.9.
Audience: **l,u,f.**

Barker, Lucius Jefferson & Walters, Ronald W. (Editors) **E879.J47 1989**
Jesse Jackson's 1984 Presidential Campaign: Challenge and Change in American Politics. Trade Cloth. University of Illinois Press. Champaign, IL. 1989. 272p. ISBN:0-252-01537-1, ISBN13: 978-0-252-01537-3. Dewey:324.973/0927. LCCN:88-005097.
Audience: **u,f.** *Choice, 1989.*

Bell, Daniel (Editor, Afterword by) **E835.B4 2002**
The Radical Right. Ed. 3. David Plotke (Introduction by). Trade Paper. Transaction Publishers. Somerset, NJ. 2001. 526p. ISBN:0-7658-0749-1, ISBN13: 978-0-7658-0749-6. Dewey:320.973/09/045. LCCN:00-062927.
Audience: **u,f.**

Bentley, Eric (Editor) **E743.5**
Thirty Years of Treason. Trade Paper. Avalon Publishing Group. New York, NY. 2001. 991p. ISBN:1-56025-368-1, ISBN13: 978-1-56025-368-6. Dewey:322.4/2/097309045. LCCN:2002-278330.
Audience: **f.**

Blum, John Morton **E743**
Progressive Presidents: Theodore Roosevelt, Woodrow Wilson, Franklin D. Roosevelt, Lyndon B. Johnson. Trade Paper. W. W. Norton & Company, Inc. New York, NY. 1982. 224p.

ISBN:0-393-00063-X, ISBN13: 978-0-393-00063-4. Dewey:353.03/2.
Audience: **u,f.**

Brands, H. W. Jr. **E743.B68 2001**
The Strange Death of American Liberalism. Cloth over Boards. Yale University Press. Cumberland, RI. 2001. 224p. ISBN:0-300-09021-8, ISBN13: 978-0-300-09021-5. Dewey:320.51/3/0973. LCCN:2001-025867.
Audience: **u,f.** *Choice, 2002.*

Brinkley, Alan **E743.B755 1998**
Liberalism and Its Discontents. Trade Cloth. Harvard University Press. Cambridge, MA. 1998. 384p. ISBN:0-674-53017-9, ISBN13: 978-0-674-53017-1. Dewey:320.51/3/0973. LCCN:97-040654.
Audience: **u,f.**

Brinkley, Alan **E806.B75 1982**
Voices of Protest: Huey Long, Father Coughlin and the Great Depression. Trade Cloth. Alfred A. Knopf Inc. New York, NY. 1982. xiii, 348p. ISBN:0-394-52241-9, ISBN13: 978-0-394-52241-8. Dewey:973.917. LCCN:81-048121.
Audience: **u,f.** B

Broesamle, John J. **E743**
Reform and Reaction in Twentieth Century American Politics. Trade Cloth. Greenwood Publishing Group, Inc. Portsmouth, NH. 1990. 500p. Contributions in American History Ser., No. 137 ISBN:0-313-26799-5, ISBN13: 978-0-313-26799-4. Dewey:320.973. LCCN:89-011751.
Audience: **f.**

Bronner, Stephen Eric **E895.B74 2005**
Blood in the Sand: Imperial Fantasies, Right-Wing Ambitions, and the Erosion of American Democrary. Saddle Stitched, Cloth over Boards, Dust Jacket. University Press of Kentucky. Lexington, KY. 2005. 207p. ISBN:0-8131-2367-4, ISBN13: 978-0-8131-2367-7. Dewey:327.730090511. LCCN:2005-009207.
Audience: **f.** *Choice, 2006.*

Brown, Seyom **E895.B76 2003**
The Illusion of Control: Force and Foreign Policy in the 21st Century. Trade Cloth. Brookings Institution Press. Washington, DC. 2001. 196p. ISBN:0-8157-0262-0, ISBN13: 978-0-8157-0262-7. Dewey:327.73/009/0511. LCCN:2003-002604.
Audience: **u,f.** *Choice, 2004.*

Buckley, William F. **E743.5.B82**
The Committee and Its Critics: A Calm Review of the House Committee on Un-American Activities. Paper Text. Textbook Publishers. Temecula, CA. 2003. 352p. ISBN:0-7581-5236-1, ISBN13: 978-0-7581-5236-7. Dewey:328.36.
Audience: **f.** B

Buckley, William F. Jr. **E743.K39 1988**
Keeping the Tablets: Modern American Conservative Thought. Charles R. Kesler (Editor). Trade Cloth. HarperCollins Publishers. New York, NY. 1988. 544p. ISBN:0-06-055128-3, ISBN13: 978-0-06-055128-5. Dewey:320.5/2/0973. LCCN:86-046049.
Audience: **u,f.**

Busch, Andrew E. **JK5261980.B87 2005**
Reagan's Victory: The Presidential Election of 1980 and the Rise of the Right. Saddle Stitched, Cloth over Boards, Dust Jacket. University Press of Kansas. Lawrence, KS. 2005. 237p. American Presidential Elections Ser. ISBN:0-7006-1407-9, ISBN13: 978-0-7006-1407-3. Dewey:324.973/0926. LCCN:2005-020859.
Audience: **u,f.** *Choice, 2006.*

Cashman, Sean D. **E743.C277 1998**
America Ascendant: From Theodore Roosevelt to FDR in the Century of American Power, 1901-1945. Trade Cloth. New York University Press. New York, NY. 1998. 561p. ISBN:0-8147-1565-6, ISBN13: 978-0-8147-1565-9. Dewey:973.91. LCCN:97-045320.
Audience: **l,u,f.**

Caute, David **E743.5.C35**
The Great Fear. Trade Cloth. Simon & Schuster. New York, NY. 1978. ISBN:0-671-22682-7, ISBN13: 978-0-671-22682-4. Dewey:322.4/2. LCCN:77-013000.
Audience: **g,u,f.**

Chalmers, David M. **E743.C45 1970**
Social and Political Ideas of the Muckrakers. Trade Cloth. Ayer Company Publishers, Inc. Manchester, NH. 1977. Essay Index Reprint Ser. ISBN:0-8369-1745-6, ISBN13: 978-0-8369-1745-1. Dewey:301.15/3. LCCN:70-117765.
Audience: **u,f.**

Chambers, Whittaker & Fox, John **E743.5.C47 1997**
Witness. Trade Cloth. Regnery Publishing, Incorporated, An Eagle Publishing Company. Washington, DC. 1978. 808p. ISBN:0-89526-571-0, ISBN13: 978-0-89526-571-5. Dewey:324.273/75/092 B. LCCN:96-050336.
Audience: **g,u,f.**

Cohen, Warren I. **E785.C64 1987**
Empire Without Tears: America's Foreign Relations, 1921-1933. Trade Cloth. Temple University Press. Philadelphia, PA. 1987. 152p. ISBN:0-87722-490-0, ISBN13: 978-0-87722-490-7. Dewey:327.73. LCCN:87-050219.
Audience: **u,f.**

Degler, Carl N. **E178**
Out of Our Past: The Forces That Shaped Modern America. Trade Cloth. HarperCollins Publishers. New York, NY. 1970. ISBN:0-06-011012-0, ISBN13: 978-0-06-011012-3. Dewey:973.
Audience: **g,u,f.** B

Deloria, Vine Jr. (Editor) **E93.A44 1985**
American Indian Policy in the Twentieth Century. Trade Cloth. University of Oklahoma Press. Norman, OK. 1985. 272p. ISBN:0-8061-1897-0, ISBN13: 978-0-8061-1897-0. Dewey:323.1/197/073. LCCN:85-001057.
Audience: **u,f.**

Ellis, Lewis Ethan **E791.E5**
Frank B. Kellogg and American Foreign Relations 1925-1929. Paper Text. Textbook Publishers. Temecula, CA. 2003. 303p. ISBN:0-7581-4304-4, ISBN13: 978-0-7581-4304-4. Dewey:327.73.
Audience: **f.**

Fausold, Martin L. **E801.F25 1985**
The Presidency of Herbert C. Hoover. Trade Cloth. University Press of Kansas. Lawrence, KS. 1985. xii, 292p. American Presidency Ser. ISBN:0-7006-0259-3, ISBN13: 978-0-7006-0259-9. Dewey:973.91/6/0924. LCCN:84-017252.
Audience: **u,f.** B

Fearon, Peter **HC106.2.F42 1987**
War, Prosperity and Depression: The U. S. Economy, 1917-1945. Trade Cloth. University Press of Kansas. Lawrence, KS. 1988. x, 294p. ISBN:0-7006-0348-4, ISBN13: 978-0-7006-0348-0. Dewey:330.973/091. LCCN:87-021571.
Audience: **u,f.** *Choice, 1988.*

Ferrell, Robert H. **E791.F47 1998**
The Presidency of Calvin Coolidge. Trade Cloth. University Press of Kansas. Lawrence, KS. 2004. xii, 244p. American Presidency Ser. ISBN:0-7006-0892-3, ISBN13: 978-0-7006-0892-8. Dewey:973.91/5/092. LCCN:97-051128.
Audience: **u,f.** *Choice, 1998.*

Freidel, Frank **E807.F75 1990**
Franklin D. Roosevelt: Rendezvous with Destiny. Trade Cloth. Little Brown & Company. New York, NY. 1990. viii, 710p. ISBN:0-316-29260-5, ISBN13: 978-0-316-29260-3. Dewey:973.917/092. LCCN:89-012580.
Audience: **u,f.**

Fried, Albert **E743.5.F668 1997**
McCarthyism, the Great American Red Scare: A Documentary History. Paper Text. Oxford University Press, Inc. New York, NY. 1996. 240p. ISBN:0-19-509701-7, ISBN13: 978-0-19-509701-6. Dewey:973.9/21. LCCN:96-007280.
Audience: **f.**

Fried, Richard M. **E743.5.F67 1990**
Nightmare in Red: The McCarthy Era in Perspective. Trade Cloth. Oxford University Press, Inc. New York, NY. 1990. 256p. ISBN:0-19-504360-X, ISBN13: 978-0-19-504360-0. Dewey:973.9/21. LCCN:89-032891.
Audience: **f.** *Choice, 1990.*

Galbraith, John Kenneth **HB37171929.G32**
The Great Crash 1929. Trade Cloth. Houghton Mifflin Company. New York, NY. 1988. ISBN:0-395-13935-X, ISBN13: 978-0-395-13935-6. Dewey:338.5/4/0973. LCCN:72-002285.
Audience: **u,f.** B

Germond, Jack W. & Witcover, Jules **E884.G47 1993**
Mad As Hell: Revolt at the Ballot Box, 1992. Trade Cloth. Warner Books, Inc. New York, NY. 1993. 544p. ISBN:0-446-51650-3, ISBN13: 978-0-446-51650-1. Dewey:324.973/098. LCCN:92-050533.
Audience: **f.**

Germond, Jack W. & Witcover, Jules **E880**
Whose Broad Stripes and Bright Stars?: The Trivial Pursuit of the Presidency, 1988. Mass Market. Warner Books, Inc. New York, NY. 1990. ISBN:0-446-39187-5, ISBN13: 978-0-446-39187-0. Dewey:324.973/0927.
Audience: **f.**

Goldberg, David J. **E784.G65 1999**
Discontented America: The United States in the 1920s. Stanley I. Kutler (Foreword by). Trade Cloth. Johns Hopkins University Press. Baltimore, MD. 1999. 224p. The American Moment Ser. ISBN:0-8018-6004-0, ISBN13: 978-0-8018-6004-1. Dewey:973.91. LCCN:98-036310.
Audience: **l,u,f.** *Choice, 1999.*

Goldberg, Ronald Allen **E784.G656 2003**
America in the Twenties. Trade Cloth. Syracuse University Press. Syracuse, NY. 2003. 248p. America in the Twentieth Century Ser. ISBN:0-8156-3008-5, ISBN13: 978-0-8156-3008-1. Dewey:973.91/5. LCCN:2003-015312.
Audience: **u,f.** *Choice, 2004.*

Goldman, Eric F. **E813.G6 1981**
The Crucial Decade: America, 1945-1955. Trade Cloth. Greenwood Publishing Group, Inc. Portsmouth, NH. 1982. 298p. ISBN:0-313-23147-8, ISBN13: 978-0-313-23147-6. Dewey:973.918. LCCN:81-013399.
Audience: **u,f.**

Goldman, Eric F. **E661.G58 2001**
Rendezvous with Destiny: A History of Modern American Reform. Trade Paper. Ivan R. Dee Publisher. Blue Ridge Summit, PA. 2001. 560p. ISBN:1-56663-369-9, ISBN13: 978-1-56663-369-7. Dewey:973.8. LCCN:00-050437.
Audience: **l,u,f.**

Graham, Otis L. **E743.G72**
The Great Campaigns: Reform and War in America, 1900-1928. Trade Cloth. Prentice-Hall. Upper Saddle, NJ. 1971. xiii, 386p. ISBN:0-13-363572-4, ISBN13: 978-0-13-363572-0. Dewey:973.91. LCCN:79-135756.
Audience: **u,f.** B

Hamby, Alonzo L. **E743.H237 1992**
Liberalism and Its Challengers: From F. D. R. to Bush. Ed. 2. Trade Paper. Oxford University Press, Inc. New York, NY. 1992. 446p. ISBN:0-19-507030-5, ISBN13: 978-0-19-507030-9. Dewey:973.9. LCCN:91-016469.
Audience: **u,f.**

Handlin, Oscar **JV6450**
The Uprooted: The Epic Story of the Great Migrations That Made the American People. Ed. 2. Book, Other. University of Pennsylvania Press. Philadelphia, PA. 2002. 344p. ISBN:0-8122-1788-8, ISBN13: 978-0-8122-1788-9. Dewey:304.8/73. LCCN:2001-048096.
Audience: **u,f.**

Harvey, David **E895.H375 2005**
New Imperialism. Trade Paper. Oxford University Press, Inc. New York, NY. 2005. 288p. Clarendon Lectures in Geography and Environmental Studies ISBN:0-19-927808-3, ISBN13: 978-0-19-927808-4. Dewey:973.93. LCCN:2005-271656.
Audience: **f.**

Herspring, Dale R. **E745.H47 2005**
The Pentagon and the Presidency: Civil-Military Relations from FDR to George W. Bush. Trade Cloth. University Press of Kansas. Lawrence, KS. 2005. 512p. Modern War Studies ISBN:0-7006-1355-2, ISBN13: 978-0-7006-1355-7. Dewey:322/.5/09730904. LCCN:2004-025537.
Audience: **f.**

Hertzke, Allen D. **E880.H47 1992**
Echoes of Discontent: Jesse Jackson, Pat Robertson, and the Resurgence of Populism. Paper Text. Congressional Quarterly, Inc. Washington, DC. 1992. 280p. ISBN:0-87187-640-X, ISBN13: 978-0-87187-640-9. Dewey:973.927. LCCN:92-029842.
Audience: **u,f.** *Choice, 1993.*

Hofstadter, Richard **E743**
Age of Reform: From Bryan to F. D. R. Mass Market. Knopf Publishing Group. New York, NY. 1960. 352p. Vintage Ser. ISBN:0-394-70095-3, ISBN13: 978-0-394-70095-3. Dewey:973.91.
Audience: **l,u,f.** B

Hofstadter, Richard **E743.H632 1996**
The Paranoid Style in American Politics: And Other Essays. Trade Paper. Harvard University Press. Cambridge, MA. 1996. 352p. ISBN:0-674-65461-7, ISBN13: 978-0-674-65461-7. Dewey:320.973. LCCN:96-165819.
Audience: **u,f.** B

Hofstadter, Richard (Editor) **E743.P76 1986**
The Progressive Movement, 1900-1915. Trade Paper. Simon & Schuster. New York, NY. 1986. 192p. ISBN:0-671-62824-0, ISBN13: 978-0-671-62824-6. Dewey:973.91. LCCN:86-014018.
Audience: **u,f.**

Hogan, Michael J. (Editor) **E743.R47 2003**
Rhetoric and Reform in the Progressive Era: Rhetorical History of the United States. Trade Cloth. Michigan State University Press. East Lansing, MI. 2002. 700p. A Rhetorical History of the United States Ser., Vol. 6 ISBN:0-87013-637-2, ISBN13: 978-0-87013-637-5. Dewey:973.91. LCCN:2002-008953.
Audience: **f.**

Ikenberry, G. John (Editor) **E895.A44 2002**
America Unrivaled: The Future of the Balance of Power. Trade Paper. Cornell University Press. Ithaca, NY. 2005. 336p. Cornell Studies in Security Affairs ISBN:0-8014-8802-8, ISBN13: 978-0-8014-8802-3. Dewey:327.73. LCCN:2002-004120.
Audience: **u,f.** *Choice, 2003.*

Karl, Barry D. **E741**
The Uneasy State: The United States from 1915 to 1945. Trade Paper. University of Chicago Press. Chicago, IL. 1985. 268p. ISBN:0-226-42520-7, ISBN13: 978-0-226-42520-7. Dewey:973.91. LCCN:83-009134.
Audience: **u,f.** B

Kennedy, David M. **E173.094**
Freedom from Fear: The American People in Depression and War, 1929-1945. Trade Paper. Oxford University Press, Inc. New York, NY. 2001. 992p. Oxford History of the United States Ser., Vol. 9 ISBN:0-19-514403-1, ISBN13: 978-0-19-514403-1. Dewey:973.91. LCCN:98-049580.
Audience: **g,l,u,f.** *Choice, 1999.*

Kolko, Gabriel **E895.K65 2002**
Another Century of War. Trade Paper. New Press, The. New York, NY. 2002. 176p. ISBN:1-56584-758-X, ISBN13: 978-1-56584-758-3. Dewey:327.73/001/12. LCCN:2002-025512.
Audience: **f.**

Kutler, Stanley I. **KF4850.K87 1982**
The American Inquisition: Justice and Injustice in the Cold War. Trade Cloth. Farrar, Straus & Giroux. New York, NY. 1982. 285p. American Century Ser. ISBN:0-8090-2475-6, ISBN13: 978-0-8090-2475-9. Dewey:345.73/0231. LCCN:82-011976.
Audience: **f.**

Latham, Earl **E743.5**
The Communist Controversy in Washington: From the New Deal to McCarthy. Trade Paper. Books on Demand. Ann Arbor, MI. 460p. ISBN:0-608-16137-3, ISBN13: 978-0-608-16137-2. Dewey:335.430973. LCCN:66-014447.
Audience: **f.**

Leuchtenburg, William E. **E806.L474 1995**
The FDR Years: On Roosevelt and His Legacy. Trade Cloth. Columbia University Press. New York, NY. 1995. 377p. ISBN:0-231-08298-3, ISBN13: 978-0-231-08298-3. Dewey:973.917/092. LCCN:95-013282.
Audience: **u,f.** *Choice, 1996.*

Leuchtenburg, William E. **E806**
Franklin D. Roosevelt and the New Deal 1932-1940. Trade Cloth. HarperCollins Publishers. New York, NY. 1963. New American Nation Ser. ISBN:0-685-11865-7, ISBN13: 978-0-685-11865-8. Dewey:973.917. LCCN:63-012053.
Audience: **l,u,f.**

Leuchtenburg, William E. **E743.L49 1989**
In the Shadow of FDR: From Harry Truman to Ronald Reagan. Book, Other. Cornell University Press. Ithaca, NY. 1989. 378p. ISBN:0-8014-2341-4, ISBN13: 978-0-8014-2341-3. Dewey:973.92. LCCN:88-043301.
Audience: **g,u,f.** B

Leuchtenburg, William E. **HC106.3.L3957 1993**
The Perils of Prosperity, 1914-1932. Ed. 2. Daniel J. Boorstin (Foreword by). Trade Cloth. University of Chicago Press. Chicago, IL. 1993. 332p. Chicago History of American Civilization Ser. ISBN:0-226-47370-8, ISBN13: 978-0-226-47370-3. Dewey:330.9730913. LCCN:92-044912.
Audience: **g,u,f.**

Leuchtenburg, William E. **HC106.3.L3957 1993**
The Perils of Prosperity, 1914-1932. Ed. 2. Daniel J. Boorstin (Foreword by). Trade Paper. University of Chicago Press. Chicago, IL. 1993. 332p. Chicago History of American Civilization Ser. ISBN:0-226-47371-6, ISBN13: 978-0-226-47371-0. Dewey:330.9730913. LCCN:92-044912.
Audience: **g,u,f.**

Link, Arthur S. & McCormick, Richard L. **E743.L56 1983**
Progressivism. Abraham S. Eisenstadt & John H. Franklin (Editors). Trade Paper. Harlan Davidson Inc. Wheeling, IL. 2003. 164p. The American History Ser. ISBN:0-88295-814-3, ISBN13: 978-0-88295-814-9. Dewey:322.4/4/0973. LCCN:82-015857.
Audience: **l,u.** B

Link, William A. **F215.L56**
The Paradox of Southern Progressivism, 1880-1930. Trade Paper. University of North Carolina Press. Chapel Hill, NC. 1997. 458p. Fred W. Morrison Series in Southern Studies ISBN:0-8078-4589-2, ISBN13: 978-0-8078-4589-9. Dewey:306.2/0975. LCCN:92-001328.
Audience: **f.** *Choice, 1993.*

Margulies, Phillip (Editor) **E784.R63 2004**
The Roaring Twenties. Trade Paper. Thomson Gale. Farmington Hills, MI. 2004. 267p. Turning Points in World History Ser. ISBN:0-7377-1810-2, ISBN13: 978-0-7377-1810-2. Dewey:973.91/5. LCCN:2003-049370.
Audience: **l,u,f.**

McCoy, Donald R. **E784**
Coming of Age: The United States During the 1920s and 1930s. Trade Paper. Penguin Group (USA) Inc. New York, NY. 1973. 368p. History of the United States Ser. ISBN:0-14-021245-0, ISBN13: 978-0-14-021245-7. Dewey:973.91. LCCN:73-076027.
Audience: **u,f.**

McGinniss, Joe **E851.M3 1988**
The Selling of the President. Trade Paper. Penguin Group (USA) Inc. New York, NY. 1988. 272p. ISBN:0-14-011240-5, ISBN13: 978-0-14-011240-5. Dewey:329/.023/0973. LCCN:88-002501.
Audience: **u,f.**

Mencken, H. L. **E784.M46 1996**
On Politics: A Carnival of Buncombe. Malcolm Moos (Editor). Trade Paper. Johns Hopkins University Press. Baltimore, MD. 1996. 377p. Maryland Paperback Bookshelf Ser. ISBN:0-8018-5342-7, ISBN13: 978-0-8018-5342-5. Dewey:324.973/091. LCCN:96-010531.
Audience: **u,f.**

Miller, Nathan **E784.M555 2004**
New World Coming: The 1920s and the Making of Modern America. Trade Paper. Da Capo Press, Inc. Cambridge, MA. 2004. 448p. ISBN:0-306-81379-3, ISBN13: 978-0-306-81379-5. Dewey:973.91/5. LCCN:2004-056140.
Audience: **u,f.**

Miller, Nathan **E784.M555 2003**
New World Coming: The 1920's and the Making of Modern America. Trade Cloth. Simon & Schuster. New York, NY. 2003. 448p. ISBN:0-684-85295-0, ISBN13: 978-0-684-85295-9. Dewey:973.91. LCCN:2003-046001.
Audience: **u,f.**

Morgan, Ted **E743.5.M578 2003**
Reds: McCarthyism in Twentieth-Century America. Trade Cloth. Random House of Canada, Ltd. Mississauga, ON. 2003. 704p. ISBN:0-679-44399-1, ISBN13: 978-0-679-44399-5. Dewey:320.973. LCCN:2003-046509.
Audience: **g,u,f.** *Choice, 2004.*

Mowry, George E. & Brownell, Blaine A. **E741**
The Urban Nation: 1920-1980. Trade Paper. Farrar, Straus & Giroux. New York, NY. 1990. 360p. ISBN:0-8090-9541-6, ISBN13: 978-0-8090-9541-4. Dewey:973.9.
Audience: **f.**

Murray, Robert K. **E786.M8**
Harding Era: Warren G. Harding and His Administration. Trade Cloth. University of Minnesota Press. Minneapolis, MN. 1969. ISBN:0-8166-0541-6, ISBN13: 978-0-8166-0541-5. Dewey:973.91/4/0924. LCCN:74-091797.
Audience: **u,f.**

Murray, Robert K. **E743.5.M8**
Red Scare: A Study in National Hysteria 1919. Paper Text. Textbook Publishers. Temecula, CA. 2003. 337p. ISBN:0-7581-1975-5, ISBN13: 978-0-7581-1975-9. Dewey:973.91/3.
Audience: **u,f.**

Murray, Robert K. **E743.5.M8 1980**
Red Scare: A Study in National Hysteria, 1919-1920. Trade Cloth. Greenwood Publishing Group, Inc. Portsmouth, NH. 1980. xii, 337p. ISBN:0-313-22673-3, ISBN13: 978-0-313-22673-1. Dewey:973.913. LCCN:80-018184.
Audience: **u,f.**

Nash, George H. **E743.N37 1996**
The Conservative Intellectual Movement in America since 1945. Ed. 2. Trade Cloth. ISI Books. Wilmington, DE. 1996. 467p. ISBN:1-882926-12-9, ISBN13: 978-1-882926-12-1. Dewey:320.52/0973/09045. LCCN:96-075872.
Audience: **u,f.**

Nash, George H. **E743.N37 1998**
The Conservative Intellectual Movement in America since 1945. Trade Paper. ISI Books. Wilmington, DE. 1998. 467p. ISBN:1-882926-20-X, ISBN13: 978-1-882926-20-6. Dewey:320.52/0973/09045. LCCN:98-070719.
Audience: **u,f.**

Ogden, August R. **E743**
The Dies Committee: A Study of the Special House Committee for the Investigation of Un-American Activities, 1938-1944. Trade Cloth. Greenwood Publishing Group, Inc. Portsmouth, NH. 1984. 318p. ISBN:0-313-24567-3, ISBN13: 978-0-313-24567-1. Dewey:328.73/07658. LCCN:84-010736.
Audience: **f.**

Ogden, August R. **E743**
Dies Committee, a Study of the Special House Committee for the Investigation of Un-American Activities, 1938-1944. Library Binding. Reprint Services Company. Temecula, CA. 1993. 318p. History of the United States Ser. ISBN:0-7812-4816-7, ISBN13: 978-0-7812-4816-7. Dewey:328.73/07658.
Audience: **f.**

Parrish, Michael E. **E784.P37 1992**
The Anxious Decades: America in Prosperity and Depression 1920-1941. Trade Cloth. W. W. Norton & Company, Inc. New York, NY. 1992. 560p. ISBN:0-393-03394-5, ISBN13: 978-0-393-03394-6. Dewey:973.91. LCCN:92-003735.
Audience: **u,f.** *Choice, 1993.*

Powers, Richard G. **E743.5.P65 1995**
Not Without Honor: The History of American Anti-Communism. Trade Cloth. Simon & Schuster. New York, NY. 1996. 400p. ISBN:0-02-925301-2, ISBN13: 978-0-02-925301-4. Dewey:335.4/0973. LCCN:94-045953.
Audience: **f.** *Choice, 1996.*

Preston, William Jr. **E743.5.P7 1994**
Aliens and Dissenters: Federal Suppression of Radicals, 1903-1933. Ed. 2. Paul Buhle (Foreword by). Trade Paper. University of Illinois Press. Champaign, IL. 1994. 384p. ISBN:0-252-06452-6, ISBN13: 978-0-252-06452-4. Dewey:322.4/2/097309041. LCCN:94-027501.
Audience: **f.**

Ranney, Austin (Editor) **E879.A44 1985**
The American Elections of 1984. Trade Cloth. Duke University Press. Durham, NC. 1985. xii, 368p. At the Polls Ser. ISBN:0-8223-0230-6, ISBN13: 978-0-8223-0230-8. Dewey:324.973/0927. LCCN:85-024573.
Audience: **f.** *Choice, 1986.*

Regier, Cornelius C. **E741.R34**
The Era of the Muckrackers. Paper Text. Textbook Publishers. Temecula, CA. 2003. xi, 254p. ISBN:0-7581-6479-3, ISBN13: 978-0-7581-6479-7. Dewey:973.9.
Audience: **f.**

Rodgers, Daniel T. **HD8072**
The Work Ethic in Industrial America, 1850-1920. Trade Paper. University of Chicago Press. Chicago, IL. 1979. 316p. ISBN:0-226-72352-6, ISBN13: 978-0-226-72352-5. Dewey:301.5/5. LCCN:77-081737.
Audience: **u,f.**

Rovere, Richard H. **E743**
The American Establishment and Other Reports, Opinions, and Speculations. Trade Cloth. Greenwood Publishing Group, Inc.

Portsmouth, NH. 1981. 308p. ISBN:0-313-22646-6, ISBN13: 978-0-313-22646-5. Dewey:973.92.219. LCCN:80-022247.
Audience: **f.**

Schlesinger, Arthur M. Jr. **E807**
The Coming of the New Deal, 1933-1935. Trade Cloth. Houghton Mifflin Company. New York, NY. 1959. The Age of Roosevelt Ser., Vol. 2 ISBN:0-395-08160-2, ISBN13: 978-0-395-08160-0. Dewey:973.917/092.
Audience: **u,f.**

Schlesinger, Arthur M. Jr. **E784.S36 2003**
The Crisis of the Old Order, 1919-1933. Trade Paper. Houghton Mifflin Company Trade & Reference Division. Boston, MA. 2003. 576p. The Age of Roosevelt Ser., Vol. 1 ISBN:0-618-34085-8, ISBN13: 978-0-618-34085-9. Dewey:973.91. LCCN:2003-047884.
Audience: **u,f.**

Schlesinger, Arthur M. Jr. **E784.S36 1988**
The Crisis of the Old Order, 1919-1933. Trade Paper. Houghton Mifflin Company. New York, NY. 1988. 576p. The Age of Roosevelt Ser., Vol. 1 ISBN:0-395-48903-2, ISBN13: 978-0-395-48903-1. Dewey:973.91. LCCN:88-008210.
Audience: **u,f.**

Schlesinger, Arthur M. Jr. **E784.S36**
The Crisis of the Old Order, 1919-1933. Trade Cloth. Houghton Mifflin Company. New York, NY. 1957. The Age of Roosevelt Ser., Vol. 1 ISBN:0-395-08159-9, ISBN13: 978-0-395-08159-4. Dewey:973.91.
Audience: **u,f.**

Schlesinger, Arthur M. Jr. **E806.S347 1988**
The Politics of Upheaval, 1935-1936. Trade Paper. Houghton Mifflin Company. New York, NY. 1988. The Age of Roosevelt Ser., Vol. 3 ISBN:0-395-48904-0, ISBN13: 978-0-395-48904-8. Dewey:973.917. LCCN:88-008207.
Audience: **u,f.**

Schrecker, Ellen **E743.5.S366 2002**
The Age of McCarthyism: A Brief History with Documents. Ed. 2. Cloth over Boards. Palgrave Macmillan. New York, NY. 2002. 304p. ISBN:0-312-29425-5, ISBN13: 978-0-312-29425-0. Dewey:973.918. LCCN:2001-089428.
Audience: **u,f.**

Skillen, James W. **E895.S58 2005**
With or Against the World?: America's Role among the Nations. Book, Other. Rowman & Littlefield Publishers, Inc. Lanham, MD. 2005. 208p. ISBN:0-7425-3521-5, ISBN13: 978-0-7425-3521-3. Dewey:327.73/009/0511. LCCN:2004-018458.
Audience: **u,f.**

Steinberg, Peter L. **E743**
The Great "Red Menace": United States Prosecution of American Communists, 1947-1952. Trade Cloth. Greenwood Publishing Group, Inc. Portsmouth, NH. 1984. 311p. Contributions in American History Ser., No. 107 ISBN:0-313-23020-X, ISBN13: 978-0-313-23020-2. Dewey:973.918. LCCN:84-003832.
Audience: **f.**

Sullivan, Mark **E741.S92**
Our Times: The United States, 1900-1925. Paper Text. Classic Textbooks. Murrieta, CA. 1926. ISBN:1-4047-6215-9, ISBN13: 978-1-4047-6215-2. Dewey:973.91.
Audience: **f.**

Tanenhaus, Sam **E743.5.T36 1997**
Whittaker Chambers: A Biography. Trade Cloth. Random House, Inc. New York, NY. 1997. 638p. ISBN:0-394-58559-3, ISBN13: 978-0-394-58559-8. Dewey:973.91/092. LCCN:96-036087.
Audience: **u,f.** *Choice, 1997.*

Tindall, George B. **F215.T59**
Emergence of the New South, 1913-1945. Cloth Text. Louisiana State University Press. Baton Rouge, LA. 1967. xvi, 808p. History of the South Ser., Vol. 10 ISBN:0-8071-0010-2, ISBN13: 978-0-8071-0010-3. Dewey:975. LCCN:67-024551.
Audience: **f.**

Trani, Eugene P. & Wilson, David L. **E785.T7**
The Presidency of Warren G. Harding. Trade Cloth. University Press of Kansas. Lawrence, KS. 1977. xii, 232p. American Presidency Ser. ISBN:0-7006-0152-X, ISBN13: 978-0-7006-0152-3. Dewey:973.91/4/0924. LCCN:76-026110.
Audience: **u,f.**

Traxel, David **E743.T73 2005**
Crusader Nation: The United States in Peace and the Great War, 1898-1920. Trade Cloth. Alfred A. Knopf Inc. New York, NY. 2006. 432p. ISBN:0-375-41078-3, ISBN13: 978-0-375-41078-9. Dewey:973.8/9. LCCN:2004-063246.
Audience: **u,f.** *Choice, 2006.*

Weinstein, Allen **E748.H59W44 1997**
Perjury: The Hiss-Chambers Case. Book, Other. David McKay Company, Inc. New York, NY. 1997. xxv, 622p. ISBN:0-679-77338-X, ISBN13: 978-0-679-77338-2. Dewey:345/.73/0234. LCCN:98-141978.
Audience: **u,f.**

Weinstein, James **E743.W44 1981**
The Corporate Ideal in the Liberal State: 1900-1918. Trade Cloth. Greenwood Publishing Group, Inc. Portsmouth, NH. 1981. 263p. ISBN:0-313-22709-8, ISBN13: 978-0-313-22709-7. Dewey:973.91. LCCN:80-022211.
Audience: **f.** B

White, Theodore H. **E837.7W48**
The Making of the President, 1960. Library Binding. Buccaneer Books, Inc. Cutchogue, NY. 1993. ISBN:1-56849-143-3, ISBN13: 978-1-56849-143-1. Dewey:324.6.
Audience: **u,f.**

United States > American History, by Period > 20th Century > Diplomatic History

Acheson, Dean **E744.A2174**
Present at the Creation: My Years in the State Department. Trade Cloth. W. W. Norton & Company, Inc. New York, NY. 1987. 848p. ISBN:0-393-07448-X, ISBN13: 978-0-393-07448-2. Dewey:327.73. LCCN:69-014692.
Audience: **u,f.** B

Adler, Selig **E744.A26 1974**
Isolationist Impulse: Its Twentieth Century Reaction. Trade Cloth. Greenwood Publishing Group, Inc. Portsmouth, NH. 1974. 538p. ISBN:0-8371-7822-3, ISBN13: 978-0-8371-7822-6. Dewey:327.73. LCCN:74-015551.
Audience: **u,f.**

Agar, Herbert **E744.A3**
The Price of Power: America Since 1945. Paper Text. Textbook Publishers. Temecula, CA. 2003. 199p. ISBN:0-7581-2540-2, ISBN13: 978-0-7581-2540-8. Dewey:327.73.
Audience: **u,f.**

Almond, Gabriel Abraham **E813.A73**
The American People and Foreign Policy. Paper Text. Textbook Publishers. Temecula, CA. 2003. 269p. ISBN:0-7581-6188-3, ISBN13: 978-0-7581-6188-8. Dewey:301.15/43/32773.
Audience: **f.**

Ambrose, Stephen E. & Brinkley, Douglas **E744.A477 1997**
Rise to Globalism: American Foreign Policy since 1938. Ed. 8. Trade Paper. Penguin Group (USA) Inc. New York, NY. 1997. 480p. ISBN:0-14-026831-6, ISBN13: 978-0-14-026831-7. Dewey:327.73. LCCN:90-044958.
Audience: **l,u,f.**

Aron, Raymond **E744.A7613**
The Imperial Republic; the United States and the World, 1945-1973. Trade Cloth. Prentice-Hall. Upper Saddle, NJ. 1974. xxxviii, 339p. ISBN:0-13-451781-4, ISBN13: 978-0-13-451781-0. Dewey:327.73. LCCN:74-001389.
Audience: **f.**

Briggs, Philip J. **E744.B698 1994**
Making American Foreign Policy: President - Congress Relations from the Second World War to the Post-Cold War Era. Ed. 2. Trade Cloth. Rowman & Littlefield Publishers, Inc. Lanham, MD. 1994. 352p. ISBN:0-8476-7945-4, ISBN13: 978-0-8476-7945-4. Dewey:327.73. LCCN:94-016780.
Audience: **u,f.**

Brown, Seyom **E840.B768 1994**
The Faces of Power: United States Foreign Policy from Truman to Clinton. Ed. 2. Trade Cloth. Columbia University Press. New York, NY. 1994. 676p. ISBN:0-231-09668-2, ISBN13: 978-0-231-09668-3. Dewey:327.73. LCCN:93-041945.
Audience: **u,f.**

Brown, Seyom **E744**
The Faces of Power: Constancy and Change in United States Foreign Policy from Truman to Reagan. Ed. 2. Paper Text. Columbia University Press. New York, NY. 1983. 672p. ISBN:0-231-04737-1, ISBN13: 978-0-231-04737-1. Dewey:327.73. LCCN:83-001861.
Audience: **f.**

Challener, Richard D. **E0744.C42**
Admirals, Generals, and American Foreign Policy, 1898-1914. Trade Paper. Books on Demand. Ann Arbor, MI. 1973. 443p. ISBN:0-7837-0556-5, ISBN13: 978-0-7837-0556-9. Dewey:327.73. LCCN:72-000732.
Audience: **f.**

Chomsky, Noam **E744.C514 2002**
American Power and the New Mandarins. Ed. 2. Trade Paper. New Press, The. New York, NY. 2002. 416p. ISBN:1-56584-775-X, ISBN13: 978-1-56584-775-0. Dewey:327.7/3.
Audience: **u,f.**

Chomsky, Noam **E840.C49 2003**
Towards a New Cold War: U. S. Foreign Policy from Vietnam to Reagan. Trade Paper. New Press, The. New York, NY. 2003. 496p. ISBN:1-56584-859-4, ISBN13: 978-1-56584-859-7. Dewey:327.73/009/045. LCCN:2004-274455.
Audience: **u,f.**

Cottrell, Leonard S. & Eberhart, Sylvia **E744**
American Opinion on World Affairs in the Atomic Age. Trade Cloth. Greenwood Publishing Group, Inc. Portsmouth, NH. 1969. 152p. ISBN:0-8371-0361-4, ISBN13: 978-0-8371-0361-7. Dewey:320.52/0973. LCCN:69-013867.
Audience: **f.**

Crabb, Cecil V. Jr. & Mulcahy, Kevin V. **E744.C82 1986**
Presidents and Foreign Policy Making: From FDR to Reagan. Cloth Text. Louisiana State University Press. Baton Rouge, LA. 1986. xiv, 359p. Political Traditions in Foreign Policy Ser. ISBN:0-8071-1329-8, ISBN13: 978-0-8071-1329-5. Dewey:327.73. LCCN:86-007508.
Audience: **u,f.**

Dulles, Foster R. **E744.D8**
America's Rise to World Power: 1898-1954. Mass Market. HarperCollins Publishers. New York, NY. 1983. ISBN:0-06-133021-3, ISBN13: 978-0-06-133021-6. Dewey:327.73.
Audience: **u,f.**

Ehrman, John **E744.E36 1995**
The Rise of Neoconservatism: Intellectuals and Foreign Affairs, 1945-1994. Cloth over Boards. Yale University Press. Cumberland, RI. 1995. 256p. ISBN:0-300-06025-4, ISBN13: 978-0-300-06025-6. Dewey:327.73/009/045. LCCN:94-028386.
Audience: **f.** *Choice, 1995.*

Ferrell, Robert H. **E744.F48 1988**
American Diplomacy: The Twentieth Century. Ed. 4. Trade Paper. W. W. Norton & Company, Inc. New York, NY. 1987. 444p. ISBN:0-393-95609-1, ISBN13: 978-0-393-95609-2. Dewey:327.73. LCCN:87-007667.
Audience: **u,f.**

Foster, H. S. **E744.F7698 1983**
Activism Replaces Isolationism: U. S. Public Attitudes 1940-1975. Trade Cloth. Foxhall Press. Los Altos, CA. 1983. 420p. ISBN:0-9611128-1-6, ISBN13: 978-0-9611128-1-3. Dewey:327.73. LCCN:83-081284.
Audience: **f.**

Fromkin, David **E744.F865 1995**
In the Time of the Americans: FDR, Truman, Eisenhower, Marshall, MacArthur - The Generation That Changed America's Role in the World. Trade Cloth. Alfred A. Knopf Inc. New York, NY. 1995. 618p. ISBN:0-394-58901-7, ISBN13: 978-0-394-58901-5. Dewey:327.73. LCCN:94-030100.
Audience: **u,f.** *Choice, 1995.*

Fulbright, J. William **E744.F886**
The Arrogance of Power. UK-Trade Paper. Random House Adult Trade Publishing Group. New York, NY. 1967. 284p.

ISBN:0-8129-9262-8, ISBN13: 978-0-8129-9262-5. Dewey:327.73.
Audience: **u,f.** BCL3

Gaddis, John Lewis **E744.G24 2004**
Strategies of Containment. Ed. 2. Trade Cloth. Oxford University Press, Inc. New York, NY. 2005. 512p. ISBN:0-19-517448-8, ISBN13: 978-0-19-517448-9. Dewey:327.73/009/045. LCCN:2004-065459.
Audience: **u,f.**

Gaddis, John Lewis **E744.G25 2000**
The United States and the Origins of the Cold War, 1941-1947. Ed. 2. Trade Paper. Columbia University Press. New York, NY. 2000. 432p. ISBN:0-231-12239-X, ISBN13: 978-0-231-12239-9. Dewey:327.73/009/044. LCCN:00-056980.
Audience: **u,f.**

Gardner, Lloyd C. **E744.G3425 1984**
A Covenant with Power: America and World Order from Wilson to Reagan. Trade Cloth. Oxford University Press, Inc. New York, NY. 1984. 268p. ISBN:0-19-503357-4, ISBN13: 978-0-19-503357-1. Dewey:327.73. LCCN:83-013149.
Audience: **u,f.** BCL3

George, Alexander L. & Smoke, Richard **E744**
Deterrence in American Foreign Policy: Theory and Practice. Cloth Text. Columbia University Press. New York, NY. 1974. 666p. ISBN:0-231-03837-2, ISBN13: 978-0-231-03837-9. Dewey:327.7/3. LCCN:74-007120.
Audience: **f.**

Gibert, Stephen P. **E744.G49 1977**
Soviet Images of America. Trade Cloth. Bow Historical Books. New Providence, NJ. 1977. viii, 167p. ISBN:0-8448-1018-5, ISBN13: 978-0-8448-1018-8. Dewey:301.15/43/32773047. LCCN:76-028569.
Audience: **f.** BCL3

Goldwater, Barry M. **E744.G57 1980**
Why Not Victory?: A Fresh Look at American Foreign Policy. Trade Cloth. Greenwood Publishing Group, Inc. Portsmouth, NH. 1980. 201p. ISBN:0-313-22316-5, ISBN13: 978-0-313-22316-7. Dewey:327.73. LCCN:79-028300.
Audience: **u,f.**

Graebner, Norman A. (Editor) **E747.G68 1980**
An Uncertain Tradition: American Secretaries of State in the Twentieth Century. Trade Cloth. Greenwood Publishing Group, Inc. Portsmouth, NH. 1980. 341p. McGraw-Hill Series in American History ISBN:0-313-22317-3, ISBN13: 978-0-313-22317-4. Dewey:353.1/092/2. LCCN:79-026791.
Audience: **g,u,f.** BCL3

Graebner, Norman Arthur **E744**
Cold War Diplomacy: American Foreign Policy, 1945-1975. Ed. 2. Trade Paper. Van Nostrand Reinhold (International) Professional & Reference. Andover, 1977. viii, 248p. ISBN:0-442-22788-4, ISBN13: 978-0-442-22788-3. Dewey:327.73. LCCN:76-020843.
Audience: **f.**

Hannigan, Robert E. **E744.H353 2002**
The New World Power: American Foreign Policy, 1898-1917. Book, Other. University of Pennsylvania Press. Philadelphia, PA. 2002. 384p. ISBN:0-8122-3666-1, ISBN13: 978-0-8122-3666-8. Dewey:327.73. LCCN:2002-020424.
Audience: **f.** *Choice, 2003.*

Hogan, Michael J. (Editor) **E744.A475 1999**
The Ambiguous Legacy: U. S. Foreign Relations in the "American Century". Trade Cloth. Cambridge University Press. New York, NY. 1999. 548p. ISBN:0-521-77019-X, ISBN13: 978-0-521-77019-4. Dewey:327.73. LCCN:99-035709.
Audience: **u,f.**

Hogan, Michael J. (Editor) **E744.A486 1995**
America in the World: The Historiography of U. S. Foreign Relations since 1941. Trade Paper. Cambridge University Press. New York, NY. 1996. 624p. ISBN:0-521-49807-4, ISBN13: 978-0-521-49807-4. Dewey:327.73. LCCN:95-023512.
Audience: **f.** *Choice, 1996.*

Hook, Steven W. & Spanier, John **E744.H646 2003**
American Foreign Policy since World War II. Ed. 16. Trade Paper. CQ Press. Washington, DC. 2003. 448p. ISBN:1-56802-818-0, ISBN13: 978-1-56802-818-7. Dewey:327.73009/045. LCCN:2003-010424.
Audience: **l,u,f.**

Hunt, Michael H. **E744.H885 1996**
Crisis in U. S. Foreign Policy: An International History Reader. Cloth over Boards. Yale University Press. Cumberland, RI. 1996. 460p. ISBN:0-300-06368-7, ISBN13: 978-0-300-06368-4. Dewey:327.73. LCCN:95-022560.
Audience: **u,f.** *Choice, 1996.*

Johnson, Robert D. **E744.J658 1995**
The Peace Progressives and American Foreign Relations. Trade Cloth. Harvard University Press. Cambridge, MA. 1995. 464p. Harvard Historical Studies, Vol. 119 ISBN:0-674-65917-1, ISBN13: 978-0-674-65917-9. Dewey:327.73. LCCN:94-025609.
Audience: **f.** *Choice, 1995.*

Jonas, Manfred **E744.J667 1990**
Isolationism in America, 1935-1941. Paper Text. Imprint Publications, Inc. Chicago, IL. 1990. 336p. ISBN:1-879176-01-7, ISBN13: 978-1-879176-01-0. Dewey:327.73/009/043. LCCN:90-084058.
Audience: **u,f.**

Kaplan, Lawrence S. **E744**
The Long Entanglement: The United States and NATO after Fifty Years. Trade Cloth. Greenwood Publishing Group, Inc. Portsmouth, NH. 1999. 280p. ISBN:0-275-96418-3, ISBN13: 978-0-275-96418-4. Dewey:327.73. LCCN:98-037152.
Audience: **f.** *Choice, 1999.*

Kennan, George F. **E744.K3 1984**
American Diplomacy. Library Binding. University of Chicago Press. Chicago, IL. 1985. 186p. Walgreen Foundation Lectures ISBN:0-226-43146-0, ISBN13: 978-0-226-43146-8. Dewey:327.73. LCCN:84-024085.
Audience: **g,u,f.**

Kissinger, Henry A. **JZ1480.K57 2002**
Does America Need a Foreign Policy?: Toward a Diplomacy for the 21st Century. Trade Paper. Simon & Schuster. New York, NY. 2002. 352p. ISBN:0-684-85568-2, ISBN13: 978-0-684-85568-4. Dewey:327.73. LCCN:2003-276300.
Audience: **f.**

Kissinger, Henry A. **DS558.K59 2002**
Ending the Vietnam War: A History of America's Involvement in and Extrication from the Vietnam War. Trade Paper. Simon & Schuster. New York, NY. 2003. 640p. ISBN:0-7432-1532-X, ISBN13: 978-0-7432-1532-9. Dewey:959.704/32. LCCN:2002-017996.
Audience: **l,u,f.**

Kissinger, Henry A.
Diplomacy, Pt. 2. Jonathan Reese (Read by). Audio Cassette. Books on Tape, Inc. New York, NY. 1995. Dewey:327.7/3.
Audience: **u,f.**

Kolko, Gabriel **E744.K63 1988**
Confronting the Third World: United States Foreign Policy, 1945-1980. Trade Cloth. Knopf Publishing Group. New York, NY. 1988. ISBN:0-394-57138-X, ISBN13: 978-0-394-57138-6. Dewey:327.730173/4. LCCN:88-042600.
Audience: **u,f.**

Kolko, Gabriel **E744.K65 1990**
Politics of War: The World. Trade Paper. Knopf Publishing Group. New York, NY. 1990. 691p. ISBN:0-679-72757-4, ISBN13: 978-0-679-72757-6. Dewey:327.73. LCCN:89-043238.
Audience: **u,f.**

Kolko, Joyce **E744.K64 1972**
The Limits of Power: The World and United States Foreign Policy, 1945-1954. Trade Cloth. Harper & Row Ltd. London, 1972. xii, 820p. ISBN:0-06-012447-4, ISBN13: 978-0-06-012447-2. Dewey:327.73. LCCN:70-156530.
Audience: **u,f.**

LaFeber, Walter **E744**
The American Age: U. S. Foreign Policy at Home and Abroad, from 1750 to the Present. Trade Cloth. W. W. Norton & Company, Inc. New York, NY. 1989. xx, 759p. ISBN:0-393-02629-9, ISBN13: 978-0-393-02629-0. Dewey:327.73. LCCN:88-032688.
Audience: **u,f.** *Choice, 1989.*

Lake, David A. **E744.L27 1999**
Entangling Relations: American Foreign Policy in Its Century. Cloth Text. Princeton University Press. Princeton, NJ. 1999. 312p. Princeton Studies in International History and Politics ISBN:0-691-05990-X, ISBN13: 978-0-691-05990-7. Dewey:327.73. LCCN:98-037330.
Audience: **f.** *Choice, 2000.*

Langer, William L. & Gleason, S. Everett **E744.L3**
The Challenge to Isolation: The World Crisis of 1937-1940 and American Foreign Policy. Trade Cloth. Peter Smith Publisher, Inc. Magnolia, MA. 1990. ISBN:0-8446-0759-2, ISBN13: 978-0-8446-0759-7. Dewey:327.73.
Audience: **f.**

Leebaert, Derek **E744.L426 2003**
The Fifty-Year Wound: How America's Cold War Victory Shapes Our World. Trade Paper. Little Brown & Company. New York, NY. 2003. 784p. ISBN:0-316-16496-8, ISBN13: 978-0-316-16496-2. Dewey:973.92. LCCN:2003-542561.
Audience: **u,f.**

Leffler, Melvyn P. **E744.L432 1994**
The Specter of Communism: The United States and the Origins of the Cold War, 1917-1953. Eric Foner (Editor). Trade Paper. Farrar, Straus & Giroux. New York, NY. 1994. 144p. Critical Issue Ser. ISBN:0-8090-1574-9, ISBN13: 978-0-8090-1574-0. Dewey:327.73. LCCN:94-013419.
Audience: **f.**

May, Ernest R. **E744**
The Lessons of the Past: The Use and Misuse of History in American Foreign Policy. Trade Paper. Oxford University Press, Inc. New York, NY. 1975. 236p. ISBN:0-19-501890-7, ISBN13: 978-0-19-501890-5. Dewey:327.73. LCCN:73-082670.
Audience: **f.**

Millis, Walter **E181.M699**
Arms and Men: A Study in American Military History. Paper Text. Textbook Publishers. Temecula, CA. 2003. 382p. ISBN:0-7581-5253-1, ISBN13: 978-0-7581-5253-4. Dewey:973.
Audience: **f.**

Morgenthau, Hans J. **JX1391.M6 1978**
Politics among Nations: The Struggle for Power and Peace. Ed. 5. Trade Cloth. Alfred A. Knopf Inc. New York, NY. 1978. ISBN:0-394-50085-7, ISBN13: 978-0-394-50085-0. Dewey:327. LCCN:77-026277.
Audience: **f.**

Morgenthau, Hans J. **E813.M64 1982**
In Defense of the National Interest: A Critical Examination of American Foreign Policy. Kenneth W. Thompson (Introduction by). Trade Paper. University Press of America, Inc. Lanham, MD. 1983. 306p. ISBN:0-8191-2846-5, ISBN13: 978-0-8191-2846-1. Dewey:327.73. LCCN:82-018295.
Audience: **f.**

Morgenthau, Hans J. **E743.M597 1982**
The Purpose of American Politics. Kenneth W. Thompson (Introduction by). Trade Cloth. University Press of America, Inc. Lanham, MD. 1983. 382p. ISBN:0-8191-2847-3, ISBN13: 978-0-8191-2847-8. Dewey:973.91. LCCN:82-020057.
Audience: **f.**

Nevins, Allan **E173.C55**
The New Deal and World Affairs, Vol. 56. Other. U. S. Publishers Association. Pelham, NY. ISBN:0-911548-55-6, ISBN13: 978-0-911548-55-6. Dewey:327.73.
Audience: **f.**

Niebuhr, Reinhold **E744.N53 1974**
The World Crisis and American Responsibility. Ernest W. Lefever (Editor). Trade Cloth. Greenwood Publishing Group, Inc. Portsmouth, NH. 1974. 128p. ISBN:0-8371-7649-2, ISBN13: 978-0-8371-7649-9. Dewey:327.73. LCCN:74-010643.
Audience: **f.**

Offner, Arnold A. **E744.O43 1986**
The Origins of the Second World War: American Foreign Policy and World Politics, 1917-1941. Cloth Text. Krieger Publishing Company. Melbourne, FL. 1986. 288p. ISBN:0-89874-924-7, ISBN13: 978-0-89874-924-3. Dewey:940.53/112. LCCN:85-023928.
Audience: **u,f.**

Paterson, Thomas G. **E744.P3118 1988**
Meeting the Communist Threat: Truman to Reagan. Trade Cloth. Oxford University Press, Inc. New York, NY. 1988. 336p. ISBN:0-19-504533-5, ISBN13: 978-0-19-504533-8. Dewey:327.73. LCCN:87-020433.
Audience: **u,f.** *Choice, 1988.*

Paterson, Thomas G. **E744.P312 1992**
On Every Front: The Making and Unmaking of the Cold War. Ed. 2. Trade Cloth. W. W. Norton & Company, Inc. New York, NY. 1992. 256p. ISBN:0-393-03060-1, ISBN13: 978-0-393-03060-0. Dewey:327.73047. LCCN:92-001174.
Audience: **g,u,f.** *Choice, 1993.*

Radosh, Ronald **E744.R32**
Prophets on the Right: Profiles of Conservative Critics of American Globalism. Ed. 2. Perfect. Cybereditions Corporation Ltd. Christchurch, 2002. 280p. ISBN:1-877275-36-0, ISBN13: 978-1-877275-36-4. Dewey:327.73.
Audience: **f.** B

Robin, Ron **E744.R63 2003**
The Making of the Cold War Enemy: Culture and Politics in the Military-Intellectual Complex. Trade Paper. Princeton University Press. Princeton, NJ. 2003. 296p. ISBN:0-691-11455-2, ISBN13: 978-0-691-11455-2. Dewey:973.9/2/019.
Audience: **u,f.**

Rosenberg, Emily S. **E744.R82 1982**
Spreading the American Dream: American Economic and Cultural Expansion, 1890-1945. Trade Paper. Farrar, Straus & Giroux. New York, NY. 1982. 264p. American Century Ser. ISBN:0-8090-0146-2, ISBN13: 978-0-8090-0146-0. Dewey:973.9. LCCN:81-013250.
Audience: **f.**

Schmitz, David F. & Jespersen, T. Christopher (Editors) **E744.A73 2000**
Architects of the American Century: Individuals and Institutions in Twentieth-Century U.S. Foreign Policymaking. Trade Paper. Imprint Publications, Inc. Chicago, IL. 1999. 199p. Imprint Studies in International Relations, Vol. 4 ISBN:1-879176-35-1, ISBN13: 978-1-879176-35-5. Dewey:327.73/009/04. LCCN:00-134183.
Audience: **u,f.**

Schulzinger, Robert D. **E744.S399 2002**
U. S. Diplomacy since 1900. Ed. 5. Paper Text. Oxford University Press, Inc. New York, NY. 2001. 446p. ISBN:0-19-514221-7, ISBN13: 978-0-19-514221-1. Dewey:327.73/009/04. LCCN:2001-032880.
Audience: **u,f.**

Schulzinger, Robert D. **E744**
The Wise Men of Foreign Affairs: The History of the Council on Foreign Relations. Cloth Text. Columbia University Press. New York, NY. 1984. 326p. ISBN:0-231-05528-5, ISBN13: 978-0-231-05528-4. Dewey:353.0089. LCCN:83-027321.
Audience: **f.** B

Siracusa, Joseph M. **E744.S5637 1993**
New Left Diplomatic Histories and Historians: The American Revisionists. Trade Cloth. Regina Books. Claremont, CA. 1993. 132p. Topics in Diplomatic History Ser. ISBN:0-941690-46-6, ISBN13: 978-0-941690-46-1. Dewey:327.73. LCCN:95-153675.
Audience: **f.** B

Skolnikoff, Eugene B. **E744.S57**
Science, Technology, and American Foreign Policy. Trade Paper. MIT Press. Cambridge, MA. 1969. ISBN:0-262-69019-5, ISBN13: 978-0-262-69019-5. Dewey:327.73.
Audience: **u,f.** B

Smith, Tony **E744.S589 2000**
Foreign Attachments: The Power of Ethnic Groups in the Making of American Foreign Policy. Trade Cloth. Harvard University Press. Cambridge, MA. 2000. 208p. ISBN:0-674-00294-6, ISBN13: 978-0-674-00294-4. Dewey:327.73. LCCN:00-027288.
Audience: **f.**

Sobel, Richard **E744.S747 2001**
The Impact of Public Opinion on U. S. Foreign Policy since Vietnam: Constraining the Colossus. Cloth Text. Oxford University Press, Inc. New York, NY. 2001. 288p. ISBN:0-19-510527-3, ISBN13: 978-0-19-510527-8. Dewey:327.73. LCCN:00-037506.
Audience: **u,f.**

Sobel, Richard **E744.S747 2001**
The Impact of Public Opinion on U. S. Foreign Policy since Vietnam. Trade Paper. Oxford University Press, Inc. New York, NY. 2001. 288p. ISBN:0-19-510528-1, ISBN13: 978-0-19-510528-5. Dewey:327.73. LCCN:00-037506.
Audience: **u,f.**

Steel, Ronald **E744**
Pax Americana. Trade Paper. Penguin Group (USA) Inc. New York, NY. 1977. 384p. ISBN:0-14-004664-X, ISBN13: 978-0-14-004664-9. Dewey:327.73. LCCN:77-022626.
Audience: **u,f.**

Stoessinger, John G. **E744**
Crusaders and Pragmatists: Movers of Modern American Foreign Policy. Trade Cloth. W. W. Norton & Company, Inc. New York, NY. 1979. xvii, 334p. ISBN:0-393-01284-0, ISBN13: 978-0-393-01284-2. Dewey:327.73. LCCN:79-016698.
Audience: **u,f.**

Williams, William Appleman **E183.8.R9W63**
American: Russian Relations 1781. Paper Text. Textbook Publishers. Temecula, CA. 2003. 367p. ISBN:0-7581-7445-4, ISBN13: 978-0-7581-7445-1. Dewey:327.73047.
Audience: **f.**

Williams, William Appleman (Editor) **E183.7.W72**
From Colony to Empire: Essays in the History of American Foreign Relations. Trade Cloth. Books on Demand. Ann Arbor, MI. 518p. ISBN:0-8357-9895-X, ISBN13: 978-0-8357-9895-2. Dewey:327.73. LCCN:72-000545.
Audience: **f.** B

Williams, William Appleman **E744.W56 1988**
The Tragedy of American Diplomacy. Trade Paper. W. W. Norton & Company, Inc. New York, NY. 1988. 342p. ISBN:0-393-30493-0, ISBN13: 978-0-393-30493-0. Dewey:327.73.
Audience: **u,f.** B

Williams, William Appleman (Editor), et al. **DS558**
America in Vietnam: A Documentary History. Thomas McCormick, Lloyd C. Gardner & Walter LaFeber (Editors). Trade Paper. W. W. Norton & Company, Inc. New York, NY. 1989. 360p. ISBN:0-393-30555-4, ISBN13: 978-0-393-30555-5. Dewey:959.704/3.
Audience: **u,f.**

United States > American History, by Period > 20th Century > Collective Biography

Boxer, Barbara & Women of the Senate Members **E747.N56 2000**
Nine and Counting: American Politics as Seen by the Most Influential Women Who Make and Shape It. Trade Cloth. HarperCollins Publishers. New York, NY. 2000. 256p. ISBN:0-06-019767-6, ISBN13: 978-0-06-019767-4. Dewey:328.73/092/2 B. LCCN:00-709176.
Audience: **u,f.**

Collier, Peter **E747.C66 1994**
The Roosevelts: An American Saga. Trade Cloth. Simon & Schuster. New York, NY. 1994. 544p. ISBN:0-671-65225-7, ISBN13: 978-0-671-65225-8. Dewey:929.7/0973. LCCN:94-005729.
Audience: **g,u,f.**

Collier, Peter & Horowitz, David **E747.C64**
The Rockefellers. Trade Cloth. Henry Holt & Company. New York, NY. 1976. 746p. ISBN:0-03-008371-0, ISBN13: 978-0-03-008371-6. Dewey:973.9/092/2. LCCN:75-005465.
Audience: **g,u,f.** B

Isaacson, Walter & Thomas, Evan **E747.I77 1986**
The Wise Men: Architects of the American Century. Trade Cloth. Simon & Schuster. New York, NY. 1986. 816p. ISBN:0-671-50465-7, ISBN13: 978-0-671-50465-6. Dewey:327.2/092/2. LCCN:86-011860.
Audience: **f.** *Choice, 1987.*

Lippmann, Walter **E747**
Men and Destiny. Paul Roazen (Illustrator). Trade Paper. Transaction Publishers. Somerset, NJ. 2003. 264p. ISBN:0-7658-0514-6, ISBN13: 978-0-7658-0514-0. Dewey:920.073/09/04. LCCN:2003-042637.
Audience: **f.**

Maier, Thomas **E843.M35 2004**
The Kennedys: America's Emerald Kings: A Five-Generation History of the Ultimate Irish-Catholic Family. Paper Text. Basic Books. New York, NY. 2004. 736p. ISBN:0-465-04318-6, ISBN13: 978-0-465-04318-7. Dewey:973.922/092/2 B. LCCN:2003-010426.
Audience: **g,u,f.**

Weisberger, Bernard A. **E747.W3 1994**
The La Follettes of Wisconsin: Love and Politics in Progressive America. Trade Cloth. University of Wisconsin Press. Chicago, IL. 1994. 384p. ISBN:0-299-14130-6, ISBN13: 978-0-299-14130-1. Dewey:973.9/092/2. LCCN:93-032286.
Audience: **f.** *Choice, 1994.*

United States > American History, by Period > 20th Century > Individual Biography

Abramson, Rudy **E748.H35A64 1992**
Spanning the Century: The Life of W. Averell Harriman, 1891-1986. Trade Cloth. HarperCollins Publishers. New York, NY. 1992. 779p. ISBN:0-688-04352-6, ISBN13: 978-0-688-04352-0. Dewey:973.9/092. LCCN:91-042483.
Audience: **u,f.** *Choice, 1993.*

Ashby, Leroy **E748.B7**
The Spearless Leader. Trade Cloth. University of Illinois Press. Champaign, IL. 1972. 325p. ISBN:0-252-00220-2, ISBN13: 978-0-252-00220-5. Dewey:973.91/092/4. LCCN:74-170963.
Audience: **f.**

Axelrod, Alan **E745.P3A97 2006**
Patton: A Biography. Wesley C. Clark (Foreword by). Cloth over Boards. Palgrave Macmillan. New York, NY. 2006. 224p. Great Generals Ser. ISBN:1-4039-7139-0, ISBN13: 978-1-4039-7139-5. Dewey:355/.0092 B. LCCN:2005-051452.
Audience: **u,f.**

Baldwin, Charles **E748.B267**
An Ambassador's Journey: An Exploration of People and Culture. Kenneth Thompson (Introduction by). Trade Paper. University Press of America, Inc. Lanham, MD. 1984. 148p. American Values Projected Abroad Ser., Vol. XV ISBN:0-8191-3807-X, ISBN13: 978-0-8191-3807-1. Dewey:303.4/8273. LCCN:83-027359.
Audience: **f.**

Baruch, Bernard **E741**
Baruch: My Own Story. Library Binding. Buccaneer Books, Inc. Cutchogue, NY. 1993. ISBN:1-56849-095-X, ISBN13: 978-1-56849-095-3. Dewey:973.9.
Audience: **f.**

Bass, Jack & Thompson, Marilyn W. **E748.T58B37 1998**
Ol' Strom: An Unauthorized Biography of Strom Thurmond. Book, Other. Longstreet Press, Inc. Athens, GA. 1998. 272p. ISBN:1-56352-523-2, ISBN13: 978-1-56352-523-0. Dewey:973.9/092 B. LCCN:98-066360.
Audience: **g,u,f.**

Bayley, Edwin R. **E748.M143**
Joe McCarthy and the Press. Trade Cloth. University of Wisconsin Press. Chicago, IL. 1981. 282p. ISBN:0-299-08620-8, ISBN13: 978-0-299-08620-6. Dewey:973.918/092/4. LCCN:81-050824.
Audience: **f.**

Beschloss, Michael **E807.B46 2002**
The Conquerors: Roosevelt, Truman and the Destruction of Hitler's Germany, 1941-1945. Trade Cloth. Simon & Schuster. New York, NY. 2002. 400p. ISBN:0-684-81027-1, ISBN13: 978-0-684-81027-0. Dewey:940.53/144/0943. LCCN:2002-030331.
Audience: **u,f.** *Choice, 2003.*

Beschloss, Michael R. **E807**
Kennedy and Roosevelt: The Uneasy Alliance. James M. Burns (Introduction by). Trade Cloth. W. W. Norton & Company, Inc.

New York, NY. 1980. 318p. ISBN:0-393-01335-9, ISBN13: 978-0-393-01335-1. Dewey:973.917/092/4. LCCN:79-024548.
Audience: **u,f.** BCL3

Blum, John M. **E748.T84.B6 1969**
Joe Tumulty and the Wilson Era. Trade Cloth. Shoe String Press, Inc. North Haven, CT. 1969. xiii, 337p. ISBN:0-208-00736-9, ISBN13: 978-0-208-00736-0. Dewey:973.91/3/0924. LCCN:69-015787.
Audience: **u,f.** BCL3

Blumenson, Martin **E745.P293B553 1985**
Patton: The Man Behind the Legend, 1885-1945. Trade Cloth. HarperCollins Publishers. New York, NY. 1985. 325p. ISBN:0-688-06082-X, ISBN13: 978-0-688-06082-4. Dewey:355/.0092/4 B. LCCN:85-015301.
Audience: **g,u,f.**

Blumenson, Martin **E745.P3.B55**
Patton Papers, 1885 to 1940, Vol. 1. Trade Cloth. Houghton Mifflin Company. New York, NY. 1972. 1024p. ISBN:0-395-12706-8, ISBN13: 978-0-395-12706-3. Dewey:355.3/31/0924. LCCN:76-156490.
Audience: **f.**

Bohlen, Charles E. **E748.B64.A38**
Witness to History, 1929-1969. Trade Cloth. Norton. Farnborough, 1973. xiv, 562p. ISBN:0-393-07476-5, ISBN13: 978-0-393-07476-5. Dewey:327.47/073. LCCN:72-013407.
Audience: **f.** BCL3

Braeman, John **E748.B48**
Albert J. Beveridge: American Nationalist. Library Binding. University of Chicago Press. Chicago, IL. 1971. xii, 370p. ISBN:0-226-07060-3, ISBN13: 978-0-226-07060-5. Dewey:973.91/0924. LCCN:75-142041.
Audience: **f.** BCL3

Brinkley, Douglas **E748.A15B75**
Dean Acheson: The Cold War Years, 1953-71. Trade Paper. Yale University Press. Cumberland, RI. 1994. 446p. ISBN:0-300-06075-0, ISBN13: 978-0-300-06075-1. Dewey:973.92092.
Audience: **u,f.** *Choice, 1993.*

Brinkley, Douglas **E748.A15D43 1993**
Dean Acheson and the Making of U. S. Foreign Policy. Trade Cloth. Palgrave Macmillan. New York, NY. 1993. xxv, 271p. ISBN:0-312-05016-X, ISBN13: 978-0-312-05016-0. Dewey:327.73. LCCN:91-018101.
Audience: **u,f.**

Brinkley, Douglas **F334.M753P373 2000**
Rosa Parks. Trade Cloth. Penguin Group (USA) Inc. New York, NY. 2000. 256p. Penguin Lives Ser. ISBN:0-670-89160-6, ISBN13: 978-0-670-89160-3. Dewey:323/.092 B. LCCN:00-035916.
Audience: **g,l,u,f.**

Broadwater, Jeff **E748.S84B65 1994**
Adlai Stevenson and American Politics: The Odyssey of a Cold War Liberal. Trade Cloth. Thomson Gale. Farmington Hills, MI. 1994. 304p. Twayne's Twentieth Century American Biography Ser. ISBN:0-8057-7798-9, ISBN13: 978-0-8057-7798-7. Dewey:973.921/092. LCCN:93-043000.
Audience: **f.** *Choice, 1994.*

Brodsky, Alyn **E748.L23B76 2003**
The Great Mayor: Fiorello La Guardia and the Making of the City of New York. Cloth over Boards. St. Martin's Press. Gordonville, VA. 2003. 544p. ISBN:0-312-28737-2, ISBN13: 978-0-312-28737-5. Dewey:974.7/1042/092. LCCN:2003-041007.
Audience: **u,f.**

Broesamle, John J. **E748.M**
William Gibbs McAdoo: A Passion for Change, 1863-1917. Trade Cloth. Associated Faculty Press, Inc. New York, NY. 1974. 320p. ISBN:0-8046-9043-X, ISBN13: 978-0-8046-9043-0. Dewey:973.91/3/0924. LCCN:73-083261.
Audience: **f.**

Brown, Eugene **E748.F88B76 1985**
J. William Fulbright: Advice and Dissent. Trade Cloth. University of Iowa Press. Iowa City, IA. 1985. 181p. ISBN:0-87745-130-3, ISBN13: 978-0-87745-130-3. Dewey:973.9/092/4. LCCN:84-016134.
Audience: **f.** *Choice, 1985.*

Buhite, Russell D. **E748.H96**
Patrick J. Hurley and American Foreign Policy. Trade Cloth. Cornell University Press. Ithaca, NY. 1973. 342p. ISBN:0-8014-0751-6, ISBN13: 978-0-8014-0751-2. Dewey:327/.2/0924. LCCN:72-010917.
Audience: **f.**

Burns, James M. **E807.B836**
Roosevelt: The Soldier of Freedom, 1940-1945. Trade Cloth. Harcourt Trade Publishers. New York, NY. 1970. xiv, 722p. ISBN:0-15-178871-5, ISBN13: 978-0-15-178871-2. Dewey:940.532/2/730924. LCCN:71-095877.
Audience: **u,f.** BCL3

Butt, Archibald W. **E748.B94.A4 1971**
Taft and Roosevelt. Trade Cloth. Associated Faculty Press, Inc. New York, NY. 1971. xxv, 862p. American History and Culture in the Twentieth Century Ser. ISBN:0-8046-1425-3, ISBN13: 978-0-8046-1425-2. Dewey:973.91/1/0924. LCCN:71-137968.
Audience: **u,f.**

Byrnes, James Francis **D0815.B9**
Speaking Frankly. Trade Paper. Books on Demand. Ann Arbor, MI. 338p. ISBN:0-598-85830-X, ISBN13: 978-0-598-85830-6. Dewey:940.53/14. LCCN:47-011175.
Audience: **f.** BCL3

Carter, Jimmy **E873.A3 1996**
Why Not the Best? Doug Brinkley (Introduction by). Trade Paper. University of Arkansas Press. Fayetteville, AR. 2003. xxi, 166p. ISBN:1-55728-418-0, ISBN13: 978-1-55728-418-1. Dewey:973.926/092. LCCN:96-017579.
Audience: **u,f.**

Cassella-Blackburn, Michael **E748**
The Donkey, the Carrot, and the Club: William C. Bullitt and Soviet-American Relations, 1917-1948. Trade Cloth. Greenwood Publishing Group, Inc. Portsmouth, NH. 2004. 304p. ISBN:0-275-96820-0, ISBN13: 978-0-275-96820-5. Dewey:327.73047/092. LCCN:2004-047961.
Audience: **f.** *Choice, 2005.*

Chace, James **E814**
[Ebook] Acheson: The Secretary of State Who Created the American World. E-Book. Simon & Schuster. New York, NY. 2000.

ISBN:0-684-86482-7, ISBN13: 978-0-684-86482-2. Dewey:973.9/18/092.
Audience: **g,u,f.**

Chace, James **E748.A15C43 1998**
Acheson: The Secretary of State Who Created the American World. Trade Cloth. Simon & Schuster. New York, NY. 1998. 512p. ISBN:0-684-80843-9, ISBN13: 978-0-684-80843-7. Dewey:973.9/18/092. LCCN:98-003801.
Audience: **u,f.**

Clarke, Jeanne Nienaber **E748.I28C53 1996**
Roosevelt's Warrior: Harold L. Ickes and the New Deal. Trade Cloth. Johns Hopkins University Press. Baltimore, MD. 1970. 423p. ISBN:0-8018-5094-0, ISBN13: 978-0-8018-5094-3. Dewey:973.917/092. LCCN:95-044493.
Audience: **f.** *Choice, 1996.*

Clinton, Hillary Rodham **E887.C55.C55 2003**
Living History. Trade Cloth. Simon & Schuster. New York, NY. 2003. 576p. ISBN:0-7432-2224-5, ISBN13: 978-0-7432-2224-2. Dewey:973.929/092. LCCN:2003-276264.
Audience: **g,u,f.**

Cohodas, Nadine **E748.T58.C64 1993**
Strom Thurmond: And the Politics of Southern Change. Trade Cloth. Simon & Schuster. New York, NY. 1993. 576p. ISBN:0-671-68935-5, ISBN13: 978-0-671-68935-3. Dewey:973.9/092. LCCN:92-032417.
Audience: **u,f.** *Choice, 1993.*

Coit, Margaret L. **E748.B32C6 2000**
Mr. Baruch. Trade Paper. Beard Books, Inc. Chevy Chase, MD. 2000. xii, 698p. ISBN:1-58798-021-5, ISBN13: 978-1-58798-021-3. Dewey:973.91/3/092. LCCN:00-040404.
Audience: **f.** B

Cole, Wayne S. **E748.N9C6 1980**
Senator Gerald P. Nye and American Foreign Relations. Library Binding. Greenwood Publishing Group, Inc. Portsmouth, NH. 1980. 293p. ISBN:0-313-22660-1, ISBN13: 978-0-313-22660-1. Dewey:327.73. LCCN:80-017370.
Audience: **u,f.** B

Cray, Ed **E745.M37C73 2000**
General of the Army: George C. Marshall, Soldier and Statesman. Trade Paper. Cooper Square Publishers, Inc. New York, NY. 2000. 876p. ISBN:0-8154-1042-5, ISBN13: 978-0-8154-1042-3. Dewey:973.918/092. LCCN:00-030725.
Audience: **f.**

Creel, George **E748.C937A3**
Rebel at Large, Recollections of Fifty Crowded Years. Paper Text. Classic Textbooks. Murrieta, CA. 1947. 409p. ISBN:1-4047-4921-7, ISBN13: 978-1-4047-4921-4. Dewey:923.273.
Audience: **f.** B

Davis, Kenneth S. **E807.D37 1986**
F. D. R.: The New Deal Years, 1933-1937. Trade Cloth. Random House, Inc. New York, NY. 1986. 756p. ISBN:0-394-52753-4, ISBN13: 978-0-394-52753-6. Dewey:973.917/092/4. LCCN:85-031704.
Audience: **g,u,f.** *Choice, 1987.*

Davis, Kenneth S. **E807.D34 1993**
F. D. R.: Into the Storm, 1937-1940. Trade Cloth. Random House, Inc. New York, NY. 1993. 691p. ISBN:0-679-41541-6, ISBN13: 978-0-679-41541-1. Dewey:973.917/092. LCCN:92-021640.
Audience: **g,u,f.** *Choice, 1993.*

Davis, Kenneth S. **E807.D38 2000**
FDR: The War President, 1940-1943: A History. Trade Cloth. Random House, Inc. New York, NY. 2000. 864p. ISBN:0-679-41542-4, ISBN13: 978-0-679-41542-8. Dewey:973.917/081. LCCN:00-028194.
Audience: **g,u,f.**

Davis, Kenneth S. **E807.D35 1985**
F. D. R.: The New York Years, 1928-1933. Trade Cloth. Random House, Inc. New York, NY. 1985. 516p. ISBN:0-394-51671-0, ISBN13: 978-0-394-51671-4. Dewey:973.917/0924. LCCN:84-042529.
Audience: **g,u,f.** *Choice, 1986.*

Davis, Kenneth Sydney **E807.D36 1972**
FDR: The Beckoning of Destiny, 1882-1928: A History. Trade Cloth. Penguin Group (USA) Inc. New York, NY. 1972. 936p. ISBN:0-399-10998-6, ISBN13: 978-0-399-10998-0. Dewey:973.917/092/4. LCCN:72-079519.
Audience: **g,u,f.**

D'Este, Carlo **E745.P3D46 1995**
Patton: A Genius for War. Trade Paper. HarperCollins Publishers. New York, NY. 1996. 1024p. ISBN:0-06-092762-3, ISBN13: 978-0-06-092762-2. Dewey:355/.0092. LCCN:95-038433.
Audience: **g,u,f.**

Dewey, Thomas E. **E748.D48.A37**
Twenty Against the Underworld. Trade Cloth. Doubleday Publishing. New York, NY. 1974. xv, 504p. ISBN:0-385-01904-1, ISBN13: 978-0-385-01904-0. Dewey:973.91/092/4. LCCN:74-003546.
Audience: **f.**

Dirksen, Everett M. **E748.D557A3 1998**
The Education of a Senator. Trade Cloth. University of Illinois Press. Champaign, IL. 1998. 312p. ISBN:0-252-02414-1, ISBN13: 978-0-252-02414-6. Dewey:328.73/092. LCCN:97-046696.
Audience: **f.** *Choice, 1999.*

Drukman, Mason **E748.M76D78 1997**
Wayne Morse: A Political Biography. Trade Cloth. Oregon Historical Society Press. Portland, OR. 2000. 557p. ISBN:0-87595-263-1, ISBN13: 978-0-87595-263-5. Dewey:328.73/092. LCCN:97-003380.
Audience: **f.** *Choice, 1997.*

Elliott, Lawrence **E748.L23.E44 1983**
Little Flower: The Life and Times of Fiorello la Guardia. Trade Cloth. HarperCollins Publishers. New York, NY. 1983. 256p. ISBN:0-688-02057-7, ISBN13: 978-0-688-02057-6. Dewey:974.7/104/0924. LCCN:82-023964.
Audience: **f.** B

Farrell, John A. **E840.8.O54F37 2001**
Tip O'Neill and the Democratic Century: A Biography. Trade Cloth. Little Brown & Company. New York, NY. 2001. 784p. ISBN:0-316-26049-5, ISBN13: 978-0-316-26049-7. Dewey:328.73/092. LCCN:00-058005.
Audience: **u,f.** *Choice, 2001.*

Finan, Christopher M. **E748.S63F56 2002**
Alfred E. Smith: The Happy Warrior. Cloth over Boards. Farrar, Straus & Giroux. New York, NY. 2002. 368p. ISBN:0-8090-3033-0, ISBN13: 978-0-8090-3033-0. Dewey:973.91/5/092 B. LCCN:2002-019476.
Audience: **f.**

Fite, Gilbert C. **E748.R944F57 1991**
Richard B. Russell, Jr., Senator from Georgia. Trade Cloth. University of North Carolina Press. Chapel Hill, NC. 1991. 582p. Fred W. Morrison Series in Southern Studies ISBN:0-8078-1937-9, ISBN13: 978-0-8078-1937-1. Dewey:328.73/092. LCCN:90-040277.
Audience: **f.** *Choice, 1991.*

Fite, Gilbert C. **E748.R944F57**
Richard B. Russell, Jr., Senator from Georgia. Trade Cloth. University of North Carolina Press. Chapel Hill, NC. 2002. 582p. ISBN:0-8078-5465-4, ISBN13: 978-0-8078-5465-5. Dewey:328.73/092.
Audience: **f.** *Choice, 1991.*

Fleming, Thomas J. **E807.F54 2001**
[e] The New Dealers' War: Franklin D. Roosevelt and the War Within World War II. E-Book. NetLibrary, Inc. Boulder, CO. 2001. ISBN:0-585-41776-8, ISBN13: 978-0-585-41776-9. Dewey:973.917/092.
Audience: **f.**

Fontenay, Charles L. **E748.K314**
Estes Kefauver: A Biography. Trade Cloth. University of Tennessee Press. Knoxville, TN. 440p. ISBN:1-57233-258-1, ISBN13: 978-1-57233-258-4. Dewey:973.90924.
Audience: **f.**

Freidel, Frank **E807.F75 1990**
Franklin D. Roosevelt: Rendezvous with Destiny. Trade Cloth. Little Brown & Company. New York, NY. 1990. viii, 710p. ISBN:0-316-29260-5, ISBN13: 978-0-316-29260-3. Dewey:973.917/092. LCCN:89-012580.
Audience: **u,f.**

Fried, Richard M. **E748.M143**
Men Against McCarthy. Cloth Text. Columbia University Press. New York, NY. 1977. 428p. Contemporary American History Ser. ISBN:0-231-03872-0, ISBN13: 978-0-231-03872-0. Dewey:320.973. LCCN:75-040447.
Audience: **u,f.** [BCL3]

Gellermann, William **E743.5.D55.G4 1972**
Martin Dies. Paper Text. Da Capo Press, Inc. Cambridge, MA. 1972. 310p. Civil Liberties in American History Ser. ISBN:0-306-70200-2, ISBN13: 978-0-306-70200-6. Dewey:328.73/0924. LCCN:77-151620.
Audience: **u,f.** [BCL3]

Glad, Betty **E748.P6G53 1986**
Key Pittman. Trade Cloth. Columbia University Press. New York, NY. 1986. 388p. ISBN:0-231-06112-9, ISBN13: 978-0-231-06112-4. Dewey:328.73/092/4. LCCN:82-025455.
Audience: **f.**

Goldberg, Robert A. **E748.G64G65 1995**
Barry Goldwater. Cloth over Boards. Yale University Press. Cumberland, RI. 1995. 478p. ISBN:0-300-06261-3, ISBN13: 978-0-300-06261-8. Dewey:973.9/2/092. LCCN:94-046848.
Audience: **g,u,f.** *Choice, 1996.*

Goldwater, Barry M. **JK271.A75**
The Conscience of a Conservative. Paper Text. Textbook Publishers. Temecula, CA. 2003. 123p. ISBN:0-7581-0954-7, ISBN13: 978-0-7581-0954-5. Dewey:320.5/2/0973.
Audience: **g,u,f.** [BCL3]

Goldwater, Barry M. **E748.G64.A37**
With No Apologies: The Personal and Political Memoirs of United States Senator Barry M. Goldwater. Trade Cloth. HarperCollins Publishers. New York, NY. 1979. 320p. ISBN:0-688-03547-7, ISBN13: 978-0-688-03547-1. Dewey:328.73/092/4. LCCN:79-016823.
Audience: **g,u,f.**

Goodwin, Doris Kearns **E807.G66 1994**
No Ordinary Time: Franklin and Eleanor Roosevelt: The Home Front in World War II. Trade Paper. Simon & Schuster. New York, NY. 1995. 768p. ISBN:0-684-80448-4, ISBN13: 978-0-684-80448-4. Dewey:973.917/092/2. LCCN:94-082565.
Audience: **g,u,f.**

Gorman, Joseph B. **E748.K314.G6**
Kefauver: A Political Biography. Trade Cloth. Oxford University Press, Inc. New York, NY. 1971. 444p. ISBN:0-19-501481-2, ISBN13: 978-0-19-501481-5. Dewey:973.9/0924. LCCN:77-159645.
Audience: **f.** [BCL3]

Grew, Joseph C. **E748.G835.A3 1970**
Turbulent Era: A Diplomatic Record of Forty Years, 1904-1945, Set. Walter Johnson (Editor). Trade Cloth. Ayer Company Publishers, Inc. Manchester, NH. 1977. Select Bibliographies Reprint Ser. ISBN:0-8369-5284-7, ISBN13: 978-0-8369-5284-1. Dewey:327.2/0924. LCCN:72-114880.
Audience: **f.**

Griffith, Robert **E748.M143G7 1987**
The Politics of Fear: Joseph R. McCarthy and the Senate. Ed. 2. Trade Paper. University of Massachusetts Press. Amherst, MA. 1987. 392p. ISBN:0-87023-555-9, ISBN13: 978-0-87023-555-9. Dewey:973.918/092/4. LCCN:87-013766.
Audience: **u,f.**

Grose, Peter L. **E748.D86G46 1996**
Gentleman Spy: The Life of Allen Dulles. Trade Paper. University of Massachusetts Press. Amherst, MA. 1996. 672p. ISBN:1-55849-044-2, ISBN13: 978-1-55849-044-4. Dewey:327.12/092. LCCN:96-019010.
Audience: **f.** *Choice, 1995.*

Handlin, Oscar **E748.S63H16**
Al Smith and His America. Paper Text. Textbook Publishers. Temecula, CA. 2003. 207p. ISBN:0-7581-9740-3, ISBN13: 978-0-7581-9740-5. Dewey:923.273.
Audience: **f.** [BCL3]

Hardeman, D. B. & Bacon, Donald C. **E748.R24H37 1989**
Rayburn: A Biography. Trade Paper. Madison Books, Inc. New York, NY. 1989. 600p. ISBN:0-8191-7294-4, ISBN13: 978-0-8191-7294-5. Dewey:328.73/092. LCCN:89-007985.
Audience: **f.**

Haskins, James **E748.P86H37 1993**
Adam Clayton Powell: Portrait of a Marching Black. Trade Cloth. Africa World Press. Trenton, NJ. 1992. 166p. ISBN:0-86543-339-9, ISBN13: 978-0-86543-339-7. Dewey:973.92/092. LCCN:91-078317.
Audience: **f.**

Heinrichs, Waldo H. Jr. **E748.G835H4 1986**
American Ambassador: Joseph C. Grew and the Development of the United States Diplomatic Tradition. Trade Paper. Oxford University Press, Inc. New York, NY. 1986. 480p. ISBN:0-19-504159-3, ISBN13: 978-0-19-504159-0. Dewey:327.2/092/4. LCCN:86-016184.
Audience: **f.**

Hiss, Alger **E743.5.H544 1988**
Recollections of a Life. Trade Cloth. Henry Holt & Company. New York, NY. 1988. 256p. ISBN:0-8050-0612-5, ISBN13: 978-0-8050-0612-4. Dewey:973.91/0924. LCCN:87-028482.
Audience: **u,f.** *Choice, 1988.*

Hixson, Walter L. **E748.K37H58 1989**
George F. Kennan: Cold War Iconoclast. Trade Cloth. Columbia University Press. New York, NY. 1989. 381p. Contemporary American History Ser. ISBN:0-231-06894-8, ISBN13: 978-0-231-06894-9. Dewey:327.2/092. LCCN:89-035671.
Audience: **g,u,f.** *Choice, 1990.*

Hodgson, Godfrey **E748.S883H63 1990**
The Colonel: The Life and Wars of Henry Stimson, 1867-1950. Trade Cloth. Alfred A. Knopf Inc. New York, NY. 1990. 402p. ISBN:0-394-57441-9, ISBN13: 978-0-394-57441-7. Dewey:973.91/092. LCCN:89-043474.
Audience: **f.** *Choice, 1991.*

Hoopes, Townsend & Brinkley, Douglas **E748.F68H66 2000**
Driven Patriot: The Life and Times of James Forrestal. Trade Paper. Naval Institute Press. Annapolis, MD. 2000. 608p. Bluejacket Bks. ISBN:1-55750-334-6, ISBN13: 978-1-55750-334-3. Dewey:973.917/092. LCCN:00-040188.
Audience: **f.**

Hoover, Herbert **E802.A35 1979**
The Memoirs of Herbert Hoover. Trade Cloth. Garland Publishing, Inc. New York, NY. 1979. ISBN:0-8240-9703-3, ISBN13: 978-0-8240-9703-5. Dewey:973.91/6/0924. LCCN:78-066527.
Audience: **f.**

Hu, Shizhang **E748**
Stanley K. Hornbeck and the Open Door Policy, 1919-1937. Trade Cloth. Greenwood Publishing Group, Inc. Portsmouth, NH. 1995. 280p. Contributions to the Study of World History Ser., No. 48 ISBN:0-313-29394-5, ISBN13: 978-0-313-29394-8. Dewey:327.73051/09/041. LCCN:94-029834.
Audience: **f.** *Choice, 1995.*

Hull, Cordell **E748.H93A3**
The Memoirs of Cordell Hull, Set. Library Binding. Reprint Services Company. Temecula, CA. 1993. History of the United States Ser. ISBN:0-7812-4811-6, ISBN13: 978-0-7812-4811-2. Dewey:923.273.
Audience: **f.** B

Hulsey, Byron C. **E748.D557H85 2000**
Everett Dirksen and His Presidents: How a Senate Giant Shaped American Politics. Trade Cloth. University Press of Kansas. Lawrence, KS. 2000. x, 342p. ISBN:0-7006-1036-7, ISBN13: 978-0-7006-1036-5. Dewey:328.73/092. LCCN:00-027279.
Audience: **f.** *Choice, 2001.*

Humphrey, Hubert H. **E748.H945A3 1991**
The Education of a Public Man: My Life and Politics. Norman Sherman (Editor). Trade Paper. University of Minnesota Press. Minneapolis, MN. 1991. 416p. ISBN:0-8166-1897-6, ISBN13: 978-0-8166-1897-2. Dewey:973.923/092. LCCN:90-019647.
Audience: **f.**

Hutchinson, William T. **F0546.L92**
Lowden of Illinois - The Life of Frank O. Lowden: Nation and Countryside, Vol. 2. Trade Paper. Books on Demand. Ann Arbor, MI. 393p. Midway Reprint Ser. ISBN:0-608-09407-2, ISBN13: 978-0-608-09407-6. Dewey:923.273. LCCN:57-006274.
Audience: **f.**

Hutchinson, William T. **F0546.L92**
Lowden of Illinois - The Life of Frank O. Lowden: City and State. Trade Paper. Books on Demand. Ann Arbor, MI. 396p. Midway Reprint Ser. ISBN:0-608-09406-4, ISBN13: 978-0-608-09406-9. Dewey:923.273. LCCN:57-006274.
Audience: **f.**

Ickes, Harold L. & Sternsher, Bernard **E748**
The Autobiography of a Curmudgeon. Trade Cloth. Greenwood Publishing Group, Inc. Portsmouth, NH. 1985. 350p. ISBN:0-313-24988-1, ISBN13: 978-0-313-24988-4. Dewey:973.917/092/4. LCCN:85-014850.
Audience: **f.** B

Immerman, Richard H. **E748.D868I46 1998**
John Foster Dulles: Piety, Pragmatism and Power in U. S. Foreign Policy. Book, Other. Rowman & Littlefield Publishers, Inc. Lanham, MD. 1998. 221p. Biographies in American Foreign Policy Ser., Vol. 2 ISBN:0-8420-2600-2, ISBN13: 978-0-8420-2600-0. Dewey:973.921/092. LCCN:98-028869.
Audience: **f.** *Choice, 1999.*

Iverson, Peter **E748.G64I94 1997**
e Barry Goldwater: Native Arizonan. E-Book. University of Oklahoma Press. Norman, OK. 1997. ISBN:0-8061-7071-9, ISBN13: 978-0-8061-7071-8. Dewey:973.92/092.
Audience: **g,u,f.**

Iverson, Peter J. **E748.G64**
Barry Goldwater: Native Arizonan. Trade Paper. University of Oklahoma Press. Norman, OK. 1998. 288p. Oklahoma Western Biographies Ser., No. 15 ISBN:0-8061-2997-2, ISBN13: 978-0-8061-2997-6. Dewey:973.92/092. LCCN:97-002996.
Audience: **g,u,f.**

Kennan, George F. **E748**
Sketches from a Life. Trade Paper. W. W. Norton & Company, Inc. New York, NY. 2000. 400p. ISBN:0-393-32139-8, ISBN13: 978-0-393-32139-5. Dewey:327.2/092/4. LCCN:88-043282.
Audience: **f.**

Kennan, George Frost **E748.K374.A3 1968**
Memoirs, 1925-1950. Trade Cloth. Random House. London, 1968. 583p. ISBN:0-09-085800-X, ISBN13: 978-0-09-085800-2. Dewey:327.73. LCCN:68-082616.
Audience: **f.**

Kissinger, Henry A. **E855.K57**
The White House Years. Trade Cloth. Little Brown & Company. New York, NY. 1999. ISBN:0-316-49659-6, ISBN13: 978-0-316-49659-9. Dewey:327.73.
Audience: **g,u,f.** B

Kissinger, Henry A. **E748.G64**
Years of Renewal. Trade Paper. Simon & Schuster. New York, NY. 2000. 1152p. ISBN:0-684-85572-0, ISBN13: 978-0-684-85572-1. Dewey:973.9/2/092.
Audience: **g,u,f.** *Choice, 1999.*

Kissinger, Henry A. **E840.8.K58.A38**
Years of Upheaval. Trade Cloth. Little Brown & Company. New York, NY. 1982. xxi, 1283p. ISBN:0-316-28591-9, ISBN13: 978-0-316-28591-9. Dewey:973.924/092/4. LCCN:81-086320.
Audience: **g,u,f.** B

Landis, Mark **E748.M143L26 1987**
Joseph McCarthy: The Politics of Chaos. Trade Cloth. Susquehanna University Press. Cranbury, NJ. 1987. 176p. ISBN:0-941664-19-8, ISBN13: 978-0-941664-19-6. Dewey:973.918/092/4. LCCN:85-063422.
Audience: **u,f.** *Choice, 1987.*

Lash, Joseph P. **E807.1.R574**
Eleanor: The Years Alone. Franklin D. Roosevelt Jr. (Foreword by). Trade Cloth. W. W. Norton & Company, Inc. New York, NY. 1972. 368p. ISBN:0-393-07361-0, ISBN13: 978-0-393-07361-4. Dewey:973.917/092/4. LCCN:72-002674.
Audience: **u,f.** B

Lattimore, Owen **E743.5.L36**
Ordeal by Slander. Trade Paper. Avalon Publishing Group. New York, NY. 2003. 288p. ISBN:0-7867-1133-7, ISBN13: 978-0-7867-1133-8. Dewey:973.91.
Audience: **f.** B

Leary, William M. (Editor) **E745.M3M23 2003**
MacArthur and the American Century: A Reader. Trade Cloth. University of Nebraska Press. Lincoln, NE. 2005. 566p. ISBN:0-8032-8020-3, ISBN13: 978-0-8032-8020-5. Dewey:355/.0092. LCCN:00-044736.
Audience: **u,f.**

Long, Huey P. **E748.L86A3 1996**
Every Man a King: The Autobiography of Huey P. Long. T. Harry Williams (Introduction by). Trade Paper. Da Capo Press, Inc. Cambridge, MA. 1996. 412p. ISBN:0-306-80695-9, ISBN13: 978-0-306-80695-7. Dewey:328.73/92/4. LCCN:95-042402.
Audience: **g,u,f.**

Lower, Richard Coke **E748.J73L68 1993**
A Bloc of One: The Political Career of Hiram W. Johnson. Trade Cloth. Stanford University Press. Palo Alto, CA. 1993. xiv, 442p. ISBN:0-8047-2081-9, ISBN13: 978-0-8047-2081-6. Dewey:973.91/092. LCCN:93-006975.
Audience: **f.** *Choice, 1994.*

Lowitt, Richard **E748.N65**
George W. Norris: The Persistence of a Progressive, 1913-1933. Trade Cloth. University of Illinois Press. Champaign, IL. 1971. 605p. ISBN:0-252-00176-1, ISBN13: 978-0-252-00176-5. Dewey:973.91/092/4. LCCN:76-147923.
Audience: **u,f.** B

Lowitt, Richard **E748.N65 L622**
George W. Norris: The Triumph of a Progressive, 1933-1944. Trade Cloth. University of Illinois Press. Champaign, IL. 1978. 493p. ISBN:0-252-00223-7, ISBN13: 978-0-252-00223-6. Dewey:328.73/092/4. LCCN:78-002033.
Audience: **u,f.**

Lowitt, Richard & Norris, George W. **E748**
George W. Norris: The Making of a Progressive, 1861 to 1912. Trade Cloth. Greenwood Publishing Group, Inc. Portsmouth, NH. 1980. 341p. ISBN:0-313-22103-0, ISBN13: 978-0-313-22103-3. Dewey:328.73/092/4.. LCCN:79-018826.
Audience: **u,f.**

MacArthur, Douglas **E745.M28 2001**
Reminiscences. Trade Paper. Naval Institute Press. Annapolis, MD. 2001. 472p. Bluejacket Bks. ISBN:1-55750-483-0, ISBN13: 978-1-55750-483-8. Dewey:355/.0092. LCCN:00-051530.
Audience: **u,f.**

MacLean, Elizabeth K. **E748**
Joseph E. Davies: Envoy to the Soviets. Trade Cloth. Greenwood Publishing Group, Inc. Portsmouth, NH. 1992. 264p. ISBN:0-275-93580-9, ISBN13: 978-0-275-93580-1. Dewey:327.2/092. LCCN:91-044445.
Audience: **f.**

Maddox, Robert J. **E748.B7M6**
William E. Borah and American Foreign Policy. Trade Cloth. Louisiana State University Press. Baton Rouge, LA. 1969. xxi, 272p. ISBN:0-8071-0907-X, ISBN13: 978-0-8071-0907-6. Dewey:327.73. LCCN:74-086429.
Audience: **u,f.**

Maney, Patrick J. **E748.L22**
Young Bob La Follette: A Biography of Robert M. La Follette, Jr. 1895-1953. Trade Cloth. University of Missouri Press. Columbia, MO. 1978. 352p. ISBN:0-8262-0230-6, ISBN13: 978-0-8262-0230-7. Dewey:973.91/092/4. LCCN:77-024991.
Audience: **f.**

Marshall, George Catlett **E745.M37**
The Papers of George Catlett Marshall: The Soldierly Spirit, December 1880 - June 1939. Larry I. Bland & Fred L. Hadsel (Editors). Trade Cloth. Johns Hopkins University Press. Baltimore, MD. 1981. 776p. The Papers of George Catlett Marshall Ser. ISBN:0-8018-2552-0, ISBN13: 978-0-8018-2552-1. Dewey:355.3/31/0924. LCCN:81-047593.
Audience: **f.**

Marshall, George Catlett **E745.M37**
We Cannot Delay, July 1, 1939-December 6, 1941, Vol. 2. Larry I. Bland, Sharon R. Ritenour & Clarence E. Wunderlin Jr. (Editors). Trade Cloth. Johns Hopkins University Press. Baltimore, MD. 1991. 840p. The Papers of George Catlett Marshall Ser. ISBN:0-8018-2553-9, ISBN13: 978-0-8018-2553-8. Dewey:355.3/31/0924. LCCN:81-047593.
Audience: **f.**

May, Gary **E748.V564.M39**
China Scapegoat, the Diplomatic Ordeal of John Carter Vincent. Trade Cloth. New Republic Books. Washington, DC. 1979. 370p. ISBN:0-915220-49-0, ISBN13: 978-0-915220-49-6. Dewey:327/.2/0973. LCCN:79-004129.
Audience: **f.** B

McAdoo, William G. **E748.M14.M2 1971**
Crowded Years. Trade Cloth. Associated Faculty Press, Inc. New York, NY. 1971. x, 542p. American History and Culture in the Twentieth Century Ser. ISBN:0-8046-1430-X, ISBN13: 978-0-8046-1430-6. Dewey:973.91/3/0924. LCCN:74-137974.
Audience: **f.** B

McCoy, Donald R. **F686.L26**
Landon of Kansas. Trade Paper. Books on Demand. Ann Arbor, MI. 631p. ISBN:0-8357-3807-8, ISBN13: 978-0-8357-3807-1. Dewey:329.6/00924. LCCN:65-016190.
Audience: **f.** B

McFarland, Linda **E748**
Cold War Strategist: Stuart Symington and the Search for National Security. Trade Cloth. Greenwood Publishing Group, Inc. Portsmouth, NH. 2001. 240p. ISBN:0-275-97190-2, ISBN13: 978-0-275-97190-8. Dewey:328.73/092. LCCN:2001-016318.
Audience: **f.**

McJimsey, George **E748.H67M35 1987**
Harry Hopkins: Ally of the Poor and Defender of Democracy. Trade Cloth. Harvard University Press. Cambridge, MA. 1987. 304p. ISBN:0-674-37287-5, ISBN13: 978-0-674-37287-0. Dewey:973.917/092/4. LCCN:86-022764.
Audience: **f.** *Choice, 1987.*

Miscamble, Wilson D. **E748.K374M57 1992**
George F. Kennan and the Making of American Foreign Policy, 1947-1950. Trade Paper. Princeton University Press. Princeton, NJ. 1993. 440p. Studies in International History and Politics ISBN:0-691-02483-9, ISBN13: 978-0-691-02483-7. Dewey:327.73.
Audience: **f.** *Choice, 1992.*

Mosley, Leonard **E748.D87.M67**
Dulles: A Biography of Eleanor, Allen and John Foster Dulles and Their Family Network. Trade Cloth. Dell Distributing. Toronto, ON. 1978. xii, 530p. ISBN:0-8037-1744-X, ISBN13: 978-0-8037-1744-2. Dewey:929/.2/0973. LCCN:77-019042.
Audience: **u,f.** B

Neal, Steve **E748.W7N43 1989**
Dark Horse: A Biography of Wendell Wilkie. Trade Cloth. University Press of Kansas. Lawrence, KS. 1989. xii, 371p. ISBN:0-7006-0454-5, ISBN13: 978-0-7006-0454-8. Dewey:973.917/092. LCCN:89-022614.
Audience: **f.**

Norton-Smith, Richard **E748.D48.S65 1982**
Thomas E. Dewey and His Times. Trade Cloth. Simon & Schuster. New York, NY. 1982. 672p. ISBN:0-671-41741-X, ISBN13: 978-0-671-41741-3. Dewey:973.91/092/4. LCCN:82-000370.
Audience: **u,f.** B

Ohl, John K. **E748.J735O37 1985**
Hugh S. Johnson and the New Deal. Trade Cloth. Northern Illinois University Press. DeKalb, IL. 1985. 374p. ISBN:0-87580-110-2, ISBN13: 978-0-87580-110-0. Dewey:973.917/092/4. LCCN:85-010456.
Audience: **f.** *Choice, 1986.*

Olson, James C. **E748.S95O47 2004**
Stuart Symington: A Life. Trade Cloth. University of Missouri Press. Columbia, MO. 2005. 560p. Missouri Biography Ser. ISBN:0-8262-1503-3, ISBN13: 978-0-8262-1503-1. Dewey:328.73/092 B. LCCN:2003-017200.
Audience: **f.** *Choice, 2004.*

O'Neill, Thomas P. Jr. & Novak, William **DS706.T4**
Man of the House: The Life and Political Memoirs of Speaker Tip O'Neill. Mass Market. St. Martin's Press. Gordonville, VA. 1988. 480p. ISBN:0-312-91191-2, ISBN13: 978-0-312-91191-1. Dewey:303.48/251073.
Audience: **u,f.**

Oshinsky, David M. **E748.M143O82 2005**
A Conspiracy So Immense: The World of Joe Mccarthy. Trade Paper, Perfect. Oxford University Press, Inc. New York, NY. 2005. 611p. ISBN:0-19-515424-X, ISBN13: 978-0-19-515424-5. Dewey:973.921/092 B. LCCN:2005-010664.
Audience: **u,f.**

Patterson, James T. **E748.T2.P37**
Mr. Republican; a Biography of Robert A. Taft. Trade Cloth. Houghton Mifflin Company. New York, NY. 1972. xvi, 749p. ISBN:0-395-13938-4, ISBN13: 978-0-395-13938-7. Dewey:328.73/092/4. LCCN:72-000516.
Audience: **f.** B

Patton, George S. **E745**
War As I Knew It. Mass Market. Bantam Books. New York, NY. 1983. 416p. War Ser. ISBN:0-553-25991-1, ISBN13: 978-0-553-25991-9. Dewey:940.5/48173.
Audience: **f.** B

Patton, George S. & Blumenson, Martin **E745.P3B55 1996**
Patton Papers: 1940-1945. Trade Paper. Da Capo Press, Inc. Cambridge, MA. 1996. 944p. ISBN:0-306-80717-3, ISBN13: 978-0-306-80717-6. Dewey:355.3/31/092. LCCN:96-015251.
Audience: **f.**

Perkins, Dexter **E748**
Charles Evans Hughes and American Democratic Statesmanship. Oscar Handlin (Editor). Trade Cloth. Greenwood Publishing Group, Inc. Portsmouth, NH. 1978. 200p. The Library of American Biography ISBN:0-313-20463-2, ISBN13: 978-0-313-20463-0. Dewey:973.91/092/4. LCCN:78-005919.
Audience: **f.** B

Perret, Geoffrey **E745.M3P42 1997**
Old Soldiers Never Die: The Life of Douglas MacArthur. Paper Text. Adams Media Corporation. Avon, MA. 1997. 688p. ISBN:1-55850-723-X, ISBN13: 978-1-55850-723-4. Dewey:355.3/31/092. LCCN:97-008759.
Audience: **g,u,f.** *Choice, 1996.*

Perry, Barbara A. **E843.K4P47 2004**
Jacqueline Kennedy: First Lady of the New Frontier. Trade Cloth. University Press of Kansas. Lawrence, KS. 2004. 270p. Modern First Ladies Ser. ISBN:0-7006-1343-9, ISBN13: 978-0-7006-1343-4. Dewey:973.922/092. LCCN:2004-006224.
Audience: **u,f.** *Choice, 2005.*

Pogue, Forrest C. **E745.M37P6 1989**
George C. Marshall: Statesman, 1945-1959. Trade Paper. Penguin Group (USA) Inc. New York, NY. 1989. 640p. ISBN:0-14-011909-4, ISBN13: 978-0-14-011909-1. Dewey:973.918/092/4 B. LCCN:88-025419.
Audience: **u,f.** *Choice, 1987.*

Powell, Colin L. & Persico, Joseph E. **E840.5.P68**
My American Journey: An Autobiography. Trade Cloth. Random House, Inc. New York, NY. 1995. 656p. ISBN:0-679-43296-5, ISBN13: 978-0-679-43296-8. Dewey:355/.0092 B. LCCN:95-017119.
Audience: **g,u,f.**

Reeves, Thomas C. **E748.M143R37 1997**
The Life and Times of Joe McCarthy: A Biography. Trade Paper. Madison Books, Inc. New York, NY. 1997. 420p. ISBN:1-56833-101-0, ISBN13: 978-1-56833-101-0. Dewey:973.918/092/4. LCCN:97-026679.
Audience: **g,f.**

Robertson, David **E748.B975R63 1994**
Sly and Able: A Political Biography of James F. Byrnes. Trade Cloth. W. W. Norton & Company, Inc. New York, NY. 1994. xiii, 639p. ISBN:0-393-03367-8, ISBN13: 978-0-393-03367-0. Dewey:975.7043092. LCCN:93-019329.
Audience: **f.** *Choice, 1995.*

Roosevelt, Eleanor **E807.1.R36 1984**
The Autobiography of Eleanor Roosevelt. Trade Cloth. Thomson Gale. Farmington Hills, MI. 1984. xxv, 454p. ISBN:0-8398-2851-9, ISBN13: 978-0-8398-2851-8. Dewey:973.917/092/2. LCCN:84-009093.
Audience: **f.**

Roosevelt, Eleanor & Black, Allida M. **E807.1.R48A3 1999**
[e] Courage in a Dangerous World: The Political Writings of Eleanor Roosevelt. E-Book. Columbia University Press. New York, NY. ISBN:0-231-50003-3, ISBN13: 978-0-231-50003-6. Dewey:973.917/092.
Audience: **f.** *Choice, 1999.*

Roosevelt, Eleanor **E807.1**
It Seems to Me: Selected Letters of Eleanor Roosevelt. Leonard C. Schlup & Donald W. Whisenhunt (Editors). Trade Paper, Perfect. University Press of Kentucky. Lexington, KY. 2005. 296p. ISBN:0-8131-9133-5, ISBN13: 978-0-8131-9133-1. Dewey:973.917092. LCCN:00-012277.
Audience: **f.**

Roosevelt, Elliott **E807.R64 1974**
As He Saw It. Eleanor Roosevelt (Foreword by). Library Binding. Greenwood Publishing Group, Inc. Portsmouth, NH. 1974. 170p. ISBN:0-8371-7609-3, ISBN13: 978-0-8371-7609-3. Dewey:973.917. LCCN:74-009044.
Audience: **f.** B

Rovere, Richard H. **E748.M143R62 1995**
Senator Joe McCarthy. Arthur M. Schlesinger Jr. (Foreword by). Trade Paper. University of California Press. Berkeley, CA. 1996. 296p. ISBN:0-520-20472-7, ISBN13: 978-0-520-20472-0. Dewey:973.921/092. LCCN:95-040975.
Audience: **u,f.**

Rusk, Dean & Rusk, Richard **E748.R94A3 1990**
As I Saw It. Daniel S. Papp (Editor). Trade Cloth. W. W. Norton & Company, Inc. New York, NY. 1990. 672p. ISBN:0-393-02650-7, ISBN13: 978-0-393-02650-4. Dewey:973.92/092. LCCN:89-034461.
Audience: **f.** *Choice, 1990.*

Russell, Jan Jarboe **E847**
Lady Bird: A Biography of Mrs. Johnson. Trade Paper. Taylor Trade Publishing. Blue Ridge Summit, PA. 2004. 368p. ISBN:1-58979-097-9, ISBN13: 978-1-58979-097-1. Dewey:973.923/092.
Audience: **u,f.**

Schapsmeier, Edward L. & Schapsmeier, Frederick H. **E748.D557.S33 1985**
Dirksen of Illinois: Senatorial Statesman. Barry Goldwater (Foreword by). Trade Cloth. University of Illinois Press. Champaign, IL. 1985. 292p. ISBN:0-252-01100-7, ISBN13: 978-0-252-01100-9. Dewey:328.73/092/4. LCCN:83-021578.
Audience: **f.** B *Choice, 1985.*

Schmitz, David F. (Editor) **E748.S883S36 2001**
Henry L. Stimson: The First Wise Man. Book, Other. Rowman & Littlefield Publishers, Inc. Lanham, MD. 2001. 222p. Biographies in American Foreign Policy Ser., No. 5 ISBN:0-8420-2631-2, ISBN13: 978-0-8420-2631-4. Dewey:973.91/092. LCCN:00-032190.
Audience: **f.** *Choice, 2001.*

Schwarz, Jordan A. **E748.B47S38 1987**
Liberal: Adolf A. Berle and the Vision of an American Era. Trade Cloth. Simon & Schuster. New York, NY. 1987. 550p. ISBN:0-02-929170-4, ISBN13: 978-0-02-929170-2. Dewey:973.9/092/4. LCCN:87-015147.
Audience: **f.** *Choice, 1988.*

Scobie, Ingrid W **E748.D677S36 1992**
Center Stage: Helen Gahagan Douglas - A Life. Oxford University Press, Inc. 1992. ISBN:0-19-506896-3, ISBN13: 978-0-19-506896-2.
Audience: **f.**

Sherman, Janann **E748.S667S54 2000**
No Place for a Woman: A Life of Senator Margaret Chase Smith. Trade Cloth. Rutgers University Press. Piscataway, NJ. 2000. ix, 298p. Rutgers Series on Women and Politics Ser. ISBN:0-8135-2722-8, ISBN13: 978-0-8135-2722-2. Dewey:328.73/092. LCCN:99-012901.
Audience: **f.** *Choice, 2000.*

Sherwood, Robert E. **E807**
Roosevelt and Hopkins: An Intimate History. Trade Paper. Enigma Books. New York, NY. 2001. 900p. Ser. ISBN:1-929631-04-9, ISBN13: 978-1-929631-04-9. Dewey:973.9/17/0922.
Audience: **u,f.**

Slayton, Robert A. **E748.S63S57 2001**
Empire Statesman: The Rise and Redemption of Al Smith. Trade Cloth. Simon & Schuster. New York, NY. 2001. 496p. ISBN:0-684-86302-2, ISBN13: 978-0-684-86302-3. Dewey:974.7/04/092. LCCN:00-060011.
Audience: **f.**

Smith, Alfred Emanuel **E748.S63S6**
Up to Now: An Autobiography. Paper Text. Classic Textbooks. Murrieta, CA. 1929. 434p. ISBN:1-4047-6216-7, ISBN13: 978-1-4047-6216-9. Dewey:973.9150924.
Audience: **f.**

Smith, Gene **E181.P57S64 1998**
Until the Last Trumpet Sounds: The Life of General of the Armies John J. Pershing. Trade Cloth. John Wiley & Sons, Inc. Hoboken, NJ. 1998. 384p. ISBN:0-471-24693-X, ISBN13: 978-0-471-24693-0. Dewey:355/.0092. LCCN:97-033033.
Audience: **u,f.**

Smith, Richard Norton **PN4874.M48395S64**
The Colonel: The Life and Legend of Robert R. McCormick, 1880-1955. Trade Paper. Northwestern University Press. Evanston, IL. 2003. 640p. ISBN:0-8101-2039-9, ISBN13: 978-0-8101-2039-6. Dewey:070.5/092. LCCN:2003-044240.
Audience: **f.**

Smythe, Donald **U0053.P4S69**
Pershing, General of the Armies. Trade Paper. Books on Demand. Ann Arbor, MI. 413p. ISBN:0-7837-3727-0, ISBN13: 978-0-7837-3727-0. Dewey:355.3320924. LCCN:85-042529.
Audience: **u,f.**

Solberg, Carl **E748.H945S65 1984**
Hubert Humphrey: A Political Biography. Trade Cloth. W. W. Norton & Company, Inc. New York, NY. 1984. 352p. ISBN:0-393-01806-7, ISBN13: 978-0-393-01806-6. Dewey:973.923/092/4. LCCN:84-001641.
Audience: **u,f.** B

Solberg, Carl **E748.H945**
Hubert Humphrey: A Biography. Trade Paper. Minnesota Historical Society Press. Saint Paul, MN. 2003. 572p. ISBN:0-87351-473-4, ISBN13: 978-0-87351-473-6. Dewey:973.923/092.
Audience: **f.**

Stephanson, Anders **E748.K374S73 1989**
Kennan and the Art of Foreign Policy. Trade Cloth. Harvard University Press. Cambridge, MA. 1989. 424p. ISBN:0-674-50265-5, ISBN13: 978-0-674-50265-9. Dewey:327.2/092/4. LCCN:88-021810.
Audience: **f.** *Choice, 1989.*

Sternsher, Bernard **E0806.S79**
Rexford Tugwell and the New Deal. Trade Paper. Books on Demand. Ann Arbor, MI. 549p. ISBN:0-598-06445-1, ISBN13: 978-0-598-06445-5. Dewey:338.973. LCCN:63-015522.
Audience: **f.**

Stimson, Henry L. & Bundy, McGeorge **E748.S883A3 1971**
On Active Service in Peace and War. Library Binding. Hippocrene Books, Inc. New York, NY. 1971. xxii, 698p. ISBN:0-374-97627-9, ISBN13: 978-0-374-97627-9. Dewey:973.91/0924. LCCN:79-159230.
Audience: **f.**

Stoler, Mark A. **E745.M37S75 1989**
George C. Marshall: Soldier-Statesman of the American Century. Trade Paper. Macmillan Publishing Company, Inc. Old Tappan, NJ. 1989. 272p. Twayne's Twentieth Century American Biography Ser., No. 10 ISBN:0-8057-7785-7, ISBN13: 978-0-8057-7785-7. Dewey:973.91/092/4. LCCN:88-029474.
Audience: **f.** *Choice, 1989.*

Stratton, David H. **E748.F22S77 1998**
Tempest over Teapot Dome: The Story of Albert B. Fall. Trade Cloth. University of Oklahoma Press. Norman, OK. 1998. 400p. Oklahoma Western Biographies Ser., No. 16 ISBN:0-8061-3078-4, ISBN13: 978-0-8061-3078-1. Dewey:364.1/323. LCCN:97-051347.
Audience: **f.** *Choice, 1998.*

Tanenhaus, Sam **E743.5.T36 1997**
Whittaker Chambers: A Biography. Trade Cloth. Random House, Inc. New York, NY. 1997. 638p. ISBN:0-394-58559-3, ISBN13: 978-0-394-58559-8. Dewey:973.91/092. LCCN:96-036087.
Audience: **u,f.** *Choice, 1997.*

Taylor, Maxwell D. **E745.T317 1972**
Swords and Plowshares. Trade Cloth. W. W. Norton & Company, Inc. New York, NY. 1972. 434p. ISBN:0-393-07460-9, ISBN13: 978-0-393-07460-4. Dewey:355/.0092. LCCN:70-152677.
Audience: **f.**

Tuchman, Barbara W. **E745.S68T8 2001**
Stilwell and the American Experience in China, 1911-45. Trade Paper. Grove/Atlantic, Inc. New York, NY. 2001. 624p. ISBN:0-8021-3852-7, ISBN13: 978-0-8021-3852-1. Dewey:940.54/25/0924. LCCN:2001-040154.
Audience: **u,f.** B

Vandiver, Frank E. **E181.P575**
Black Jack: The Life and Times of John J. Pershing, Set. Trade Cloth. Texas A&M University Press. College Station, TX. 1977. 1246p. ISBN:0-89096-024-0, ISBN13: 978-0-89096-024-0. Dewey:355.3/31/0924. LCCN:76-051729.
Audience: **u,f.**

Walker, J. Samuel & Wallace, Henry A. **E748**
Henry A. Wallace and American Foreign Policy. Trade Cloth. Greenwood Publishing Group, Inc. Portsmouth, NH. 1976. 224p. Contributions in American History Ser., No.50 ISBN:0-8371-8774-5, ISBN13: 978-0-8371-8774-7. Dewey:327.73. LCCN:75-044658.
Audience: **f.**

Wallace, Patricia W. & McCormick, N. **E748**
Politics of Conscience: A Biography of Margaret Chase Smith. Trade Cloth. Greenwood Publishing Group, Inc. Portsmouth, NH. 1995. 272p. ISBN:0-275-95130-8, ISBN13: 978-0-275-95130-6. Dewey:328.73/092. LCCN:95-004288.
Audience: **f.** *Choice, 1996.*

Ward, Geoffrey C. **E807.W328 1989**
A First Class Temperament: The Emergence of Franklin Roosevelt. Trade Cloth. HarperCollins Publishers. New York, NY. 1989. xvii, 889p. ISBN:0-06-016066-7, ISBN13: 978-0-06-016066-1. Dewey:973.917/092/4. LCCN:88-045908.
Audience: **g,u,f.** *Choice, 1990.*

Watkins, T. H. **E748.I28W37 1990**
Righteous Pilgrim: The Life and Times of Harold L. Ickes, 1874-1952. Trade Cloth. Henry Holt & Company. New York, NY. 1990. 1024p. ISBN:0-8050-0917-5, ISBN13: 978-0-8050-0917-0. Dewey:973.917/092. LCCN:89-035746.
Audience: **f.**

Watson, James D. **QH450.2.W37 1998**
The Double Helix: A Personal Account of the Discovery of the Structure of DNA. Trade Cloth. Simon & Schuster. New York, NY. 1998. 256p. Scribner Classics Ser. ISBN:0-684-85279-9, ISBN13: 978-0-684-85279-9. Dewey:572.8/633. LCCN:98-136787.
Audience: **g,l,u,f.** B

Watts, Steven **HD9710.U52F6684 2005**
The People's Tycoon: Henry Ford and the American Century. Trade Cloth. Knopf Publishing Group. New York, NY. 2005. 640p. ISBN:0-375-40735-9, ISBN13: 978-0-375-40735-2. Dewey:338.7/6292/092. LCCN:2004-048594.
Audience: **g,u,f.** *Choice, 2006.*

Weatherson, Michael A. & Bochin, Hal W. **E748.J73W435 1995**
Hiram Johnson: Political Revivalist. Trade Cloth. University Press of America, Inc. Lanham, MD. 1995. 254p. ISBN:0-8191-9904-4, ISBN13: 978-0-8191-9904-1. Dewey:973.91/092. LCCN:95-001069.
Audience: **f.**

Weinstein, Allen **E748.H59W44 1997**
Perjury: The Hiss-Chambers Case. Book, Other. David McKay Company, Inc. New York, NY. 1997. xxv, 622p. ISBN:0-679-77338-X, ISBN13: 978-0-679-77338-2. Dewey:345/.73/0234. LCCN:98-141978.
Audience: **u,f.**

Welles, Benjamin **E748.W442W44 1997**
Sumner Welles: FDR's Global Strategist: A Biography. Cloth over Boards. Palgrave Macmillan. New York, NY. 1997. 464p. Franklin and Eleanor Roosevelt Institute Series on Diplomatic and Econ Ser. ISBN:0-312-17440-3, ISBN13: 978-0-312-17440-8. Dewey:327.73/092. LCCN:97-011579.
Audience: **f.** *Choice, 1998.*

Wheeler, Burton K. & Healy, Paul F. **E748.W5.A3 1977**
Yankee from the West. Library Binding. Hippocrene Books, Inc. New York, NY. 1977. 436p. ISBN:0-374-98405-0, ISBN13: 978-0-374-98405-2. Dewey:328.73/092/4. LCCN:77-011011.
Audience: **f.**

White, Graham & Maze, John **E748.W23W48 1995**
Henry A. Wallace: His Search for a New World Order. Trade Cloth. University of North Carolina Press. Chapel Hill, NC. 1995. 420p. ISBN:0-8078-2189-6, ISBN13: 978-0-8078-2189-3. Dewey:973.917/092. LCCN:94-027199.
Audience: **f.** *Choice, 1995.*

White, Richard D. Jr. **E748.L86W47 2005**
Kingfish: The Reign of Huey P. Long. Trade Cloth. Random House, Inc. New York, NY. 2006. 384p. ISBN:1-4000-6354-X, ISBN13: 978-1-4000-6354-3. Dewey:976.3/062/092. LCCN:2005-048590.
Audience: **u,f.**

Williams, T. Harry **E748.L86**
Huey Long. Trade Paper. Knopf Publishing Group. New York, NY. 1981. 944p. Vintage Ser. ISBN:0-394-74790-9, ISBN13: 978-0-394-74790-3. Dewey:976.3/06/0924. LCCN:81-040091.
Audience: **u,f.** *B*

Wills, Garry **E843.W54 2003**
The Kennedy Imprisonment: A Meditation on Power. Trade Paper. Houghton Mifflin Company Trade & Reference Division. Boston, MA. 2002. 336p. ISBN:0-618-13443-3, ISBN13: 978-0-618-13443-4. Dewey:973.922/092/2. LCCN:2002-191295.
Audience: **f.** *B*

Woods, Randall Bennett **E748.F88W66 1995**
Fulbright: A Biography. Cloth Text. Cambridge University Press. New York, NY. 1995. 733p. ISBN:0-521-48262-3, ISBN13: 978-0-521-48262-2. Dewey:973.9/092. LCCN:94-046347.
Audience: **f.**

Wunderlin, Clarence E. **E748.T2W86 2005**
Robert A. Taft: Ideas, Tradition, and Party in U.S. Foreign Policy. Book, Other. Rowman & Littlefield Publishers, Inc. Lanham, MD. 2005. 272p. Biographies in American Foreign Policy Ser., No. 12 ISBN:0-7425-4489-3, ISBN13: 978-0-7425-4489-5. Dewey:328.73092. LCCN:2004-023941.
Audience: **f.** *Choice, 2006.*

United States > American History, by Period > 20th Century > By Presidential Administration

Alexander, Charles C. **E835**
Holding the Line: The Eisenhower Era, 1952-1961. Trade Cloth. Indiana University Press. Bloomington, IN. 1975. 352p. ISBN:0-253-32840-3, ISBN13: 978-0-253-32840-3. Dewey:973.921. LCCN:74-011714.
Audience: **u,f.** *B*

Allison, Graham **E841.A44**
Essence of Decision: Explaining the Cuban Missile Crisis. Trade Cloth. Benjamin-Cummings Publishing Company. San Francisco, CA. 1998. ISBN:0-321-00497-3, ISBN13: 978-0-321-00497-0. Dewey:973.923.
Audience: **u,f.**

Alperovitz, Gar **E813.A75 1994**
Atomic Diplomacy: Hiroshima and Potsdam: The Use of the Atomic Bomb and the American Confrontation with Soviet Power. Ed. 2. Pluto Press. 1995. ISBN:0-7453-0948-8, ISBN13: 978-0-7453-0948-4.
Audience: **u,f.** *B*

Ambrose, Stephen E. **E836.A828 1990**
Eisenhower. Trade Cloth. Simon & Schuster. New York, NY. 1990. 635p. ISBN:0-671-70107-X, ISBN13: 978-0-671-70107-9. Dewey:973.921/092. LCCN:90-009701.
Audience: **g,u,f.**

Ambrose, Stephen E. **E856.A72 1988**
Nixon: The Education of a Politician, 1913-1962. Trade Paper. Simon & Schuster. New York, NY. 1988. 768p. ISBN:0-671-65722-4, ISBN13: 978-0-671-65722-2. Dewey:973.924/092/4. LCCN:86-026126.
Audience: **g,u,f.** *Choice, 1987.*

Ambrose, Stephen E. **E856.A72 1987**
Nixon: The Triumph of a Politician, 1962-1972. Trade Cloth. Simon & Schuster. New York, NY. 1989. 736p. ISBN:0-671-52837-8, ISBN13: 978-0-671-52837-9. Dewey:973.924/092/4. LCCN:86-026126.
Audience: **g,u,f.**

Ambrose, Stephen E. **E856.A72 1987**
Nixon: Ruin and Recovery, 1973-1990. Trade Cloth. Simon & Schuster. New York, NY. 1991. 656p. ISBN:0-671-69188-0, ISBN13: 978-0-671-69188-2. Dewey:973.924/092/4. LCCN:86-026126.
Audience: **g,u,f.** *Choice, 1992.*

Ambrose, Stephen E. **E836.A83 1999**
The Supreme Commander: The War Years of Dwight D. Eisenhower. Trade Paper. University Press of Mississippi. Jackson, MS. 1999. xii, 732p. ISBN:1-57806-206-3, ISBN13: 978-1-57806-206-5. Dewey:355/.0092. LCCN:99-043264.
Audience: **u,f.**

Ambrosius, Lloyd E. **D619.A6495 1991**
Wilsonian Statecraft: Theory and Practice of Liberal Internationalism During World War One. Book, Other. Rowman & Littlefield Publishers, Inc. Lanham, MD. 1991. 170p. America in the Modern World Ser. ISBN:0-8420-2393-3, ISBN13: 978-0-8420-2393-1. Dewey:940.3/22. LCCN:91-004766.
Audience: **f.** *Choice, 1992.*

Ambrosius, Lloyd E. **E768.A44 2002**
Wilsonianism: Woodrow Wilson and His Legacy in American Foreign Relations. Trade Paper. Palgrave Macmillan. New York, NY. 2002. 256p. ISBN:1-4039-6009-7, ISBN13: 978-1-4039-6009-2. Dewey:973.91/3/092. LCCN:2002-074849.
Audience: **u,f.** *Choice, 2003.*

Ambrosius, Lloyd E. **E768.A44 2002**
Wilsonianism: Woodrow Wilson and His Legacy in American Foreign Relations. Cloth over Boards. Palgrave Macmillan. New York, NY. 2002. 256p. ISBN:1-4039-6008-9, ISBN13: 978-1-4039-6008-5. Dewey:973.91/3/092. LCCN:2002-074849.
Audience: **u,f.** *Choice, 2003.*

Anderson, Patrick **E868.A53 1994**
Electing Jimmy Carter: The Campaign of 1976. Trade Cloth. Louisiana State University Press. Baton Rouge, LA. 1994. ix, 192p. ISBN:0-8071-1916-4, ISBN13: 978-0-8071-1916-7. Dewey:324.973/0925. LCCN:94-028320.
Audience: **f.**

Auchincloss, Louis **E767.A88 2000**
Woodrow Wilson. Trade Cloth. Penguin Group (USA) Inc. New York, NY. 2000. 144p. Penguin Lives Ser. ISBN:0-670-88904-0, ISBN13: 978-0-670-88904-4. Dewey:973.91/3/092. LCCN:99-046890.
Audience: **l,u,f.**

Baker, James A. III & DeFrank, Thomas M. **E881.B35 1995**
The Politics of Diplomacy: Revolution, War and Peace, 1989-1992. Trade Cloth. Penguin Group (USA) Inc. New York, NY. 1995. 687p. ISBN:0-399-14087-5, ISBN13: 978-0-399-14087-7. Dewey:327.73/009/048. LCCN:95-012465.
Audience: **f.**

Beard, Charles Austin **E806.B42 1968**
American Foreign Policy in the Making, 1932-1940: A Study in Responsibilities. Trade Cloth. Shoe String Press, Inc. North Haven, CT. 1968. 336p. ISBN:0-208-00610-9, ISBN13: 978-0-208-00610-3. Dewey:327.73. LCCN:68-008011.
Audience: **f.**

Beard, Charles Austin **E806.B434 2003**
President Roosevelt and the Coming of the War, 1941: Appearances and Realities. Trade Paper. Transaction Publishers. Somerset, NJ. 2003. 614p. ISBN:0-7658-0998-2, ISBN13: 978-0-7658-0998-8. Dewey:327.73/009/044. LCCN:2002-029104.
Audience: **f.**

Bell, Coral **E876.B45 1989**
The Reagan Paradox: U. S. Foreign Policy in the 1980s. Cloth Text. Rutgers University Press. Piscataway, NJ. 1989. 224p. ISBN:0-8135-1473-8, ISBN13: 978-0-8135-1473-4. Dewey:327.73. LCCN:89-033722.
Audience: **f.** *Choice, 1990.*

Bell, Daniel (Editor, Afterword by) **E835.B4 2002**
The Radical Right. Ed. 3. David Plotke (Introduction by). Trade Paper. Transaction Publishers. Somerset, NJ. 2001. 526p. ISBN:0-7658-0749-1, ISBN13: 978-0-7658-0749-6. Dewey:320.973/09/045. LCCN:00-062927.
Audience: **u,f.**

Bennett, William J. **E886.2.B47 1999**
The Death of Outrage: Bill Clinton and the Assault on American Ideals. Trade Paper. Simon & Schuster. New York, NY. 1999. 176p. ISBN:0-684-86403-7, ISBN13: 978-0-684-86403-7. Dewey:973.929/092. LCCN:99-461904.
Audience: **u,f.**

Benson, Michael **E842.9.B45 2002**
Encyclopedia of the JFK Assassination. Trade Cloth. Facts On File, Inc. New York, NY. 2002. 368p. Facts on File Library of American History ISBN:0-8160-4476-7, ISBN13: 978-0-8160-4476-4. Dewey:973.922. LCCN:2001-053212.
Audience: **g,u,f.**

Benson, Michael T. **E814**
Harry S. Truman and the Founding of Israel. Trade Cloth. Greenwood Publishing Group, Inc. Portsmouth, NH. 1997. 240p. ISBN:0-275-95807-8, ISBN13: 978-0-275-95807-7. Dewey:327.73/009/044. LCCN:96-054017.
Audience: **f.** *Choice, 1998.*

Berman, Larry (Editor) **E876.L66 1990**
Looking Back on the Reagan Presidency. Trade Cloth. Johns Hopkins University Press. Baltimore, MD. 1990. 324p. ISBN:0-8018-3921-1, ISBN13: 978-0-8018-3921-4. Dewey:973.927. LCCN:89-039972.
Audience: **f.** *Choice, 1991.*

Berman, William C. **E885.B467 2001**
From the Center to the Edge: The Politics and Policies of the Clinton Presidency. Trade Cloth. Rowman & Littlefield Publishers, Inc. Lanham, MD. 2001. 176p. ISBN:0-8476-9614-6, ISBN13: 978-0-8476-9614-7. Dewey:979.929/092. LCCN:2001-019406.
Audience: **f.** *Choice, 2002.*

Bernstein, Carl & Woodward, Bob **E860.B47 1987**
All the President's Men. Ed. 2. Trade Paper. Simon & Schuster. New York, NY. 1994. 352p. ISBN:0-671-89441-2, ISBN13: 978-0-671-89441-2. Dewey:320.973. LCCN:87-012938.
Audience: **g,l,u,f.**

Bernstein, Carl & Woodward, Bob **E860.B47 1999**
All the President's Men. Trade Cloth. Simon & Schuster. New York, NY. 1999. 352p. Simon and Schuster Classic Editions ISBN:0-684-86355-3, ISBN13: 978-0-684-86355-9. Dewey:320.973. LCCN:98-054773.
Audience: **g,l,u,f.**

Bernstein, Carl & Woodward, Bob **E861**
The Final Days. Trade Paper, Perfect. Simon & Schuster, Inc. New York, NY. 2005. 470p. ISBN:0-7432-7406-7, ISBN13: 978-0-7432-7406-7. Dewey:364.1/323/0973.
Audience: **g,l,u,f.**

Beschloss, Michael **E807.B46 2003**
The Conquerors: Roosevelt, Truman and the Destruction of Hitler's Germany, 1941-1945. Trade Cloth. Thorndike Press. Waterville, ME. 2005. ISBN:0-7862-5171-9, ISBN13: 978-0-7862-5171-1. Dewey:940.53/144/0943. LCCN:2002-044740.
Audience: **f.** *Choice, 2003.*

Best, Gary D. **E802.B46 1983**
Herbert Hoover: The Postpresidential Years, 1933-1964, Set. Trade Cloth. Hoover Institution Press. Stanford, CA. 1983.

538p. Publication Ser., No. 276 ISBN:0-8179-7761-9, ISBN13: 978-0-8179-7761-0. Dewey:973.91/6/0924. LCCN:82-023212.
Audience: **u,f.**

Best, Gary D. **E802**
The Politics of American Individualism: Herbert Hoover in Transition, 1918-1921. Trade Cloth. Greenwood Publishing Group, Inc. Portsmouth, NH. 1975. 202p. ISBN:0-8371-8160-7, ISBN13: 978-0-8371-8160-8. Dewey:320.9/73/0913. LCCN:75-016960.
Audience: **u,f.**

Best, Gary D. **E806**
Pride, Prejudice, and Politics: Roosevelt Versus Recovery, 1933-1938. Trade Cloth. Greenwood Publishing Group, Inc. Portsmouth, NH. 1990. 288p. ISBN:0-275-93524-8, ISBN13: 978-0-275-93524-5. Dewey:973.917. LCCN:90-038841.
Audience: **u,f.** *Choice, 1991.*

Blair, Clay & Blair, Joan **E842.B58 1976**
The Search for JFK. Other. Penguin Group (USA) Inc. New York, NY. 1976. 608p. ISBN:0-399-11418-1, ISBN13: 978-0-399-11418-2. Dewey:973.922/092/4. LCCN:76-008257.
Audience: **f.** B

Blaney, Joseph L. & Benoit, William L. **E886**
The Clinton Scandals and the Politics of Image Restoration. Trade Cloth. Greenwood Publishing Group, Inc. Portsmouth, NH. 2001. 184p. Praeger Series in Political Communication ISBN:0-275-97106-6, ISBN13: 978-0-275-97106-9. Dewey:973.929/092. LCCN:00-044130.
Audience: **f.** *Choice, 2001.*

Blum, John M. **E806.B58**
V Was for Victory: Politics and American Culture During World War 2. Trade Cloth. Harcourt Trade Publishers. New York, NY. 1976. 384p. ISBN:0-15-194080-0, ISBN13: 978-0-15-194080-6. Dewey:973.917. LCCN:75-038730.
Audience: **u,f.** B

Blum, John M. **E767.B64**
Woodrow Wilson and the Politics of Morality. Trade Paper. Longman Publishing. Boston, MA. 1997. 215p. Library of American Biography Ser. ISBN:0-673-39321-6, ISBN13: 978-0-673-39321-0. Dewey:973.91/3/092.
Audience: **u,f.**

Blum, John Morton **E743**
Progressive Presidents: Theodore Roosevelt, Woodrow Wilson, Franklin D. Roosevelt, Lyndon B. Johnson. Trade Paper. W. W. Norton & Company, Inc. New York, NY. 1982. 224p. ISBN:0-393-00063-X, ISBN13: 978-0-393-00063-4. Dewey:353.03/2.
Audience: **u,f.**

Blum, John Morton **E841.B59 1991**
Years of Discord: American Politics and Society, 1961-1974. Trade Cloth. W. W. Norton & Company, Inc. New York, NY. 1991. 608p. ISBN:0-393-02969-7, ISBN13: 978-0-393-02969-7. Dewey:973.9/21. LCCN:90-049242.
Audience: **u,f.** *Choice, 1992.*

Blumenthal, Sidney **E885.B58 2003**
The Clinton Wars. Cloth over Boards. Farrar, Straus & Giroux. New York, NY. 2003. 832p. ISBN:0-374-12502-3, ISBN13: 978-0-374-12502-8. Dewey:973.929. LCCN:2003-044066.
Audience: **u,f.** *Choice, 2004.*

Bornet, Vaughn D. **E847.B63 1983**
The Presidency of Lyndon B. Johnson. Trade Cloth. University Press of Kansas. Lawrence, KS. 1984. xvi, 416p. American Presidency Ser. ISBN:0-7006-0237-2, ISBN13: 978-0-7006-0237-7. Dewey:973.923/092/4. LCCN:83-012560.
Audience: **l,u,f.**

Boyer, Paul (Editor) **E876.R3929 1990**
Reagan As President: Contemporary Views of the Man, His Politics and His Policies. Trade Paper. Ivan R. Dee Publisher. Blue Ridge Summit, PA. 2002. 281p. ISBN:0-929587-28-6, ISBN13: 978-0-929587-28-8. Dewey:973.927/092. LCCN:89-078111.
Audience: **u,f.**

Brandon, Henry **E855.B67**
The Retreat of American Power. Trade Cloth. Doubleday Publishing. New York, NY. 1973. xiii, 368p. ISBN:0-385-01655-7, ISBN13: 978-0-385-01655-1. Dewey:327.73. LCCN:72-090969.
Audience: **f.** B

Brands, H. W. Jr. **E835.B684 1988**
Cold Warriors: Eisenhower's Generation and American Foreign Policy. Trade Cloth. Columbia University Press. New York, NY. 1988. 247p. Contemporary American History Ser. ISBN:0-231-06526-4, ISBN13: 978-0-231-06526-9. Dewey:327.73. LCCN:87-017900.
Audience: **f.** *Choice, 1988.*

Brands, H. W. Jr. (Editor) **E846.F59 1999**
Foreign Policies of Lyndon Johnson: Beyond Vietnam. Trade Cloth. Texas A&M University Press. College Station, TX. 1999. 224p. Foreign Relations and the Presidency Ser., Vol. 1 ISBN:0-89096-873-X, ISBN13: 978-0-89096-873-4. Dewey:327.73/009/046. LCCN:98-046981.
Audience: **u,f.** *Choice, 2000.*

Brands, H. W. & Schlesinger, Arthur M. Jr. **E767.B76 2003**
Woodrow Wilson: 1913-1921. Cloth over Boards. Henry Holt & Company. New York, NY. 2003. 192p. The American Presidents Ser. ISBN:0-8050-6955-0, ISBN13: 978-0-8050-6955-6. Dewey:973.91/3/092. LCCN:2002-041393.
Audience: **u,f.**

Brinkley, Alan **E806.B747 1995**
The End of Reform: New Deal Liberalism in Recession and War. Trade Cloth. Alfred A. Knopf Inc. New York, NY. 1995. x, 371p. ISBN:0-394-53573-1, ISBN13: 978-0-394-53573-9. Dewey:973.917. LCCN:94-021478.
Audience: **f.** *Choice, 1995.*

Brinkley, Alan **E806.B75 1982**
Voices of Protest: Huey Long, Father Coughlin and the Great Depression. Trade Cloth. Alfred A. Knopf Inc. New York, NY. 1982. xiii, 348p. ISBN:0-394-52241-9, ISBN13: 978-0-394-52241-8. Dewey:973.917. LCCN:81-048121.
Audience: **u,f.** B

Brinkley, Douglas (Introduction by) **E889.A145 2001**
36 Days: The Complete Chronicle of the 2000 Presidential Election Crisis. Trade Paper. Henry Holt & Company. New York, NY. 2001. 400p. ISBN:0-8050-6850-3, ISBN13: 978-0-8050-6850-4. Dewey:324.973/0929. LCCN:2002-512382.
Audience: **g,u,f.**

Brooks, David **E885.B33 1996**
Backward and Upward: The New Conservative Writing. Trade Paper. Knopf Publishing Group. New York, NY. 1996. 352p. ISBN:0-679-76654-5, ISBN13: 978-0-679-76654-4. Dewey:973.929. LCCN:95-023867.
Audience: **f.**

Buehrig, Edward H. **HQ793.W26 1979**
Woodrow Wilson and the Balance of Power. Trade Cloth. Peter Smith Publisher, Inc. Magnolia, MA. 1990. ISBN:0-8446-0522-0, ISBN13: 978-0-8446-0522-7. Dewey:305.235.
Audience: **u,f.** *B*

Bundy, William P. **E855.B85 1998**
A Tangled Web: The Making of Foreign Policy in the Nixon Presidency. Trade Cloth. Farrar, Straus & Giroux. New York, NY. 1998. 768p. ISBN:0-8090-9151-8, ISBN13: 978-0-8090-9151-5. Dewey:327.73. LCCN:97-035585.
Audience: **u,f.** *Choice, 1998.*

Burner, David **E802.B87 1979**
Herbert Hoover: The Public Life. Trade Cloth. Alfred A. Knopf Inc. New York, NY. 1979. xii, 433p. ISBN:0-394-46134-7, ISBN13: 978-0-394-46134-2. Dewey:973.91/6/0924. LCCN:78-054912.
Audience: **f.** *B*

Burton, David Henry **E762.B88 2003**
Taft, Wilson, and World Order. Trade Paper. Fairleigh Dickinson University Press. Cranbury, NJ. 2003. 144p. ISBN:0-8386-3969-0, ISBN13: 978-0-8386-3969-6. Dewey:973.91/2/092. LCCN:2002-071287.
Audience: **u,f.**

Busby, Robert **E876.B857 1998**
Reagan and the Iran-Contra Affair: The Politics of Presidential Recovery. Trade Cloth. Palgrave Macmillan. New York, NY. 1999. 236p. ISBN:0-312-21982-2, ISBN13: 978-0-312-21982-6. Dewey:973.9/27/092. LCCN:98-038451.
Audience: **u,f.**

Bush, George Herbert Walker & Scowcroft, Brent **E881.B86 1998**
A World Transformed: The Collapse of the Soviet Empire, the Unification of Germany, Tiananmen Square, the Gulf War. Trade Cloth. Alfred A. Knopf Inc. New York, NY. 1998. 576p. ISBN:0-679-43248-5, ISBN13: 978-0-679-43248-7. Dewey:327.7/3. LCCN:98-013499.
Audience: **u,f.**

Califano, Joseph A. Jr. **E847.C32 2000**
The Triumph and Tragedy of Lyndon Johnson: The White House Years. Trade Paper. Texas A&M University Press. College Station, TX. 2000. 416p. Joseph V. Hughes, Jr., and Holly O. Hughes Series in the Presidency and Leadership Studies, Vol. 8 ISBN:0-89096-960-4, ISBN13: 978-0-89096-960-1. Dewey:973.923/092. LCCN:00-036413.
Audience: **f.**

Campbell, Colin B. & Rockman, Bert A. **E881.B87 1991**
The Bush Presidency: First Appraisals. Trade Cloth. Seven Bridges Press, LLC. New York, NY. 1991. 320p. ISBN:0-934540-90-X, ISBN13: 978-0-934540-90-2. Dewey:973.928. LCCN:91-018333.
Audience: **f.** *Choice, 1991.*

Campbell, Colin B. & Rockman, Bert A. (Editors) **E886.C576 1999**
The Clinton Legacy. Trade Paper. CQ Press. Washington, DC. 2000. 368p. ISBN:1-889119-14-8, ISBN13: 978-1-889119-14-4. Dewey:973.929/092. LCCN:99-006299.
Audience: **f.** *Choice, 2000.*

Campbell, Colin B. & Rockman, Bert A. **E885.C55 1996**
The Clinton Presidency: First Appraisals. Trade Cloth. Seven Bridges Press, LLC. New York, NY. 1995. 416p. American Politics Ser. ISBN:1-56643-013-5, ISBN13: 978-1-56643-013-5. Dewey:973.929/092. LCCN:95-022611.
Audience: **f.** *Choice, 1996.*

Cannon, Lou **E877.C35 2000**
President Reagan: The Role of a Lifetime. Trade Paper. PublicAffairs. New York, NY. 2000. 912p. ISBN:1-891620-91-6, ISBN13: 978-1-891620-91-1. Dewey:973.927/092. LCCN:99-088017.
Audience: **g,l,u,f.**

Carey, Charles W. **E842.9.K46 2005**
The Kennedy Assassination. Trade Cloth. Thomson Gale. Farmington Hills, MI. 2004. 208p. Interpreting Primary Documents Ser. ISBN:0-7377-2112-X, ISBN13: 978-0-7377-2112-6. Dewey:364.152/4/097309046. LCCN:2004-040610.
Audience: **u,f.**

Caro, Robert A. **E847.C34 1982**
Master of the Senate: The Years of Lyndon Johnson. Trade Paper. Knopf Publishing Group. New York, NY. 2003. 1232p. Years of Lyndon Johnson Ser., Vol. 3 ISBN:0-394-72095-4, ISBN13: 978-0-394-72095-1. Dewey:328.73/092. LCCN:2002-282796.
Audience: **u,f.**

Caro, Robert A. **E847.C34 1983**
Means of Ascent: The Years of Lyndon Johnson. UK-Trade Paper. Knopf Publishing Group. New York, NY. 1991. 592p. Years of Lyndon Johnson Ser., Vol. 2 ISBN:0-679-73371-X, ISBN13: 978-0-679-73371-3. Dewey:973.923/092. LCCN:90-050483.
Audience: **u,f.**

Caro, Robert A. **E847.C34 1982**
The Path to Power. Trade Cloth. Alfred A. Knopf Inc. New York, NY. 1982. 960p. Years of Lyndon Johnson Ser., Vol. 1 ISBN:0-394-49973-5, ISBN13: 978-0-394-49973-4. LCCN:90-201781.
Audience: **g,u,f.** *B*

Carter, Jimmy **E873.A3 1995**
Keeping Faith: Memoirs of a President. Trade Paper. University of Arkansas Press. Fayetteville, AR. 2003. 640p. ISBN:1-55728-330-3, ISBN13: 978-1-55728-330-6. Dewey:973.926/092. LCCN:95-009691.
Audience: **g,l,u,f.**

Carter, Jimmy **E873.A3 1996**
Why Not the Best? Doug Brinkley (Introduction by). Trade Paper. University of Arkansas Press. Fayetteville, AR. 2003. xxi, 166p. ISBN:1-55728-418-0, ISBN13: 978-1-55728-418-1. Dewey:973.926/092. LCCN:96-017579.
Audience: **u,f.**

Chace, James **E765.C47 2004**
1912: Wilson, Roosevelt, Taft and Debs - The Election That Changed the Country. Trade Cloth. Simon & Schuster. New York, NY. 2004. 336p. ISBN:0-7432-0394-1, ISBN13: 978-0-7432-0394-4. Dewey:324.973/0912. LCCN:2004-041660.
Audience: **u,f.** *Choice, 2005.*

Chafe, William Henry **E806.M63 2002**
The Achievement of American Liberalism: The New Deal and Its Legacies. Trade Paper. Columbia University Press. New York, NY. 2002. 350p. ISBN:0-231-11213-0, ISBN13: 978-0-231-11213-0. Dewey:973.917. LCCN:2002-073366.
Audience: **u,f.** *Choice, 2003.*

Chalmers, David **E841.C46 1996**
And the Crooked Places Made Straight: The Struggle for Social Change in the 1960s. Ed. 2. Trade Paper. Johns Hopkins University Press. Baltimore, MD. 1986. 264p. The American Moment Ser. ISBN:0-8018-5334-6, ISBN13: 978-0-8018-5334-0. Dewey:973. LCCN:95-045588.
Audience: **f.** *Choice, 1992.*

Chang, Laurence & Kornbluh, Peter (Editors) **E841**
The Cuban Missile Crisis 1962: A National Security Archive Documents Reader. Ed. 2. Robert S. McNamara (Foreword by). Trade Paper. New Press, The. New York, NY. 1999. 464p. National Security Archive Documents Reader Ser. ISBN:1-56584-474-2, ISBN13: 978-1-56584-474-2. Dewey:973.922. LCCN:92-053734.
Audience: **u,f.**

Chayes, Abram **E841.C48 1987**
The Cuban Missile Crisis: International Crises and the Role of Law Published under the Auspices of the American Society of International Law. Trade Cloth. University Press of America, Inc. Lanham, MD. 1988. 172p. ISBN:0-8191-6717-7, ISBN13: 978-0-8191-6717-0. Dewey:972.91/064. LCCN:87-028051.
Audience: **f.**

Chomsky, Noam **E881.C48 1991**
Deterring Democracy. Trade Cloth. Analytical Psychology Club of San Francisco, Inc. San Francisco, CA. 1991. 384p. ISBN:0-86091-318-X, ISBN13: 978-0-86091-318-4. Dewey:327.73. LCCN:91-008125.
Audience: **f.** *Choice, 1991.*

Clements, Kendrick A. **E766.C44 1992**
The Presidency of Woodrow Wilson. Trade Cloth. University Press of Kansas. Lawrence, KS. 1992. xvi, 304p. American Presidency Ser. ISBN:0-7006-0523-1, ISBN13: 978-0-7006-0523-1. Dewey:973.91/3/092. LCCN:91-030591.
Audience: **l,u,f.** *Choice, 1992.*

Clinton, Bill **E886.A3 2004**
My Life. Trade Cloth. Alfred A. Knopf Inc. New York, NY. 2004. 1008p. ISBN:0-375-41457-6, ISBN13: 978-0-375-41457-2. Dewey:973.929092. LCCN:2004-107564.
Audience: **g,l,u,f.**

Coffman, Edward M. **D570.C6 1998**
The War to End All Wars: The American Military Experience in World War I. Trade Paper. University Press of Kentucky. Lexington, KY. 1998. 440p. ISBN:0-8131-0955-8, ISBN13: 978-0-8131-0955-8. Dewey:940.4/12/73. LCCN:98-015563.
Audience: **l,u,f.** B

Cohen, Warren I. **E768.C6**
The American Revisionists: The Lessons of Intervention in World War I. Trade Paper. Books on Demand. Ann Arbor, MI. 266p. ISBN:0-8357-5397-2, ISBN13: 978-0-8357-5397-5. Dewey:327.73. LCCN:66-020594.
Audience: **f.** B

Cohen, Warren I. & Tucker, Nancy B. (Editors) **E846.L95 1994**
Lyndon Johnson Confronts the World: American Foreign Policy, 1963-1968. Trade Cloth. Cambridge University Press. New York, NY. 1995. 352p. ISBN:0-521-41428-8, ISBN13: 978-0-521-41428-9. Dewey:327.73. LCCN:94-017951.
Audience: **f.**

Cole, Wayne S. **E806.C594 1983**
Roosevelt and the Isolationists, 1932-1945. Trade Cloth. University of Nebraska Press. Lincoln, NE. 1983. xii, 698p. ISBN:0-8032-1410-3, ISBN13: 978-0-8032-1410-1. Dewey:327.73. LCCN:82-008624.
Audience: **f.** B

Coletta, Paolo E. **E761.C64**
The Presidency of William Howard Taft. Trade Cloth. University Press of Kansas. Lawrence, KS. 1973. xii, 308p. American Presidency Ser. ISBN:0-7006-0096-5, ISBN13: 978-0-7006-0096-0. Dewey:973.91/2/0924. LCCN:97-050019.
Audience: **l,u,f.** B

Congressional Quarterly, Inc. Staff **E859.C62 1973**
Watergate: Chronology of a Crisis. Trade Cloth. Bow Historical Books. New Providence, NJ. 1973. v.p. ISBN:0-87187-059-2, ISBN13: 978-0-87187-059-9. Dewey:364.1/32/0973. LCCN:73-012792.
Audience: **l,u,f.** B

Conkin, Paul Keith **E806.C6 1975**
The New Deal. Trade Cloth. Collier Macmillan Canada, Inc. Cambridge, ON. 1967. xiii, 118p. ISBN:0-690-00810-4, ISBN13: 978-0-690-00810-4. Dewey:973.917. LCCN:67-014297.
Audience: **u,f.** B

Cooper, John M. Jr. **E766**
The Vanity of Power: American Isolationism and the First World War, 1914-1917, 3. Trade Cloth. Greenwood Publishing Group, Inc. Portsmouth, NH. 1970. 271p. Contributions in American History Ser., No. 3 ISBN:0-8371-2342-9, ISBN13: 978-0-8371-2342-4. Dewey:327.73. LCCN:70-095508.
Audience: **u,f.**

Cooper, John M. Jr. **E176.1**
The Warrior and the Priest: Woodrow Wilson and Theodore Roosevelt. Trade Paper. Harvard University Press. Cambridge, MA. 1983. 480p. ISBN:0-674-94751-7, ISBN13: 978-0-674-94751-1. Dewey:973.9/1/0922.
Audience: **u,f.**

Cooper, John Milton Jr. **E768.C66 2001**
Breaking the Heart of the World: Woodrow Wilson and the Fight for the League of Nations. Trade Cloth. Cambridge University Press. New York, NY. 2001. 464p. ISBN:0-521-80786-7, ISBN13: 978-0-521-80786-9. Dewey:973.91/3. LCCN:2001-025489.
Audience: **u,f.** *Choice, 2002.*

Dallek, Robert **E847.D26 1998**
Flawed Giant: Lyndon Johnson and His Times, 1961-1973. Trade Cloth. Oxford University Press, Inc. New York, NY. 1998. 784p. ISBN:0-19-505465-2, ISBN13: 978-0-19-505465-1. Dewey:973.923/092. LCCN:97-039084.
Audience: **g,u,f.** *Choice, 1998.*

Dallek, Robert **E806.D33 1995**
Franklin D. Roosevelt and American Foreign Policy, 1932-1945: With a New Afterword. Ed. 2. Trade Paper. Oxford University Press, Inc. New York, NY. 1995. 684p. ISBN:0-19-509732-7, ISBN13: 978-0-19-509732-0. Dewey:327.73. LCCN:97-118779.
Audience: **u,f.**

Dallek, Robert **E847.D25 1991**
Lone Star Rising: Lyndon Johnson and His Times, 1908-1960, Vol. 1. Trade Cloth. Oxford University Press, Inc. New York, NY. 1991. 736p. ISBN:0-19-505435-0, ISBN13: 978-0-19-505435-4. Dewey:973.9/23/092. LCCN:90-039830.
Audience: **g,u,f.** *Choice, 1992.*

Dallek, Robert **E877.D34 1999**
Ronald Reagan: The Politics of Symbolism. Trade Paper. Harvard University Press. Cambridge, MA. 1999. 256p. ISBN:0-674-77941-X, ISBN13: 978-0-674-77941-9. Dewey:973.927092. LCCN:98-050782.
Audience: **u,f.**

Dallek, Robert **E842.D28 2003**
An Unfinished Life: John F. Kennedy, 1917-1963. Trade Cloth. Little Brown & Company. New York, NY. 2003. 848p. ISBN:0-316-17238-3, ISBN13: 978-0-316-17238-7. Dewey:973.922/092. LCCN:2002-116388.
Audience: **g,l,u,f.** *Choice, 2004.*

Dalton, Kathleen **E757.D24 2002**
Theodore Roosevelt: A Strenuous Life. Trade Paper. Knopf Publishing Group. New York, NY. 2004. 752p. ISBN:0-679-76733-9, ISBN13: 978-0-679-76733-6. Dewey:973.91/1/092. LCCN:2002-022857.
Audience: **g,l,u,f.**

Dean, John **E860**
Blind Ambition: The White House Years. Trade Cloth. Simon & Schuster. New York, NY. 1976. 415p. ISBN:0-671-22438-7, ISBN13: 978-0-671-22438-7. Dewey:364.1/323/0973. LCCN:76-026488.
Audience: **u,f.** B

D'Este, Carlo **E836**
Eisenhower: A Soldier's Life. Cloth over Boards. Henry Holt & Company. New York, NY. 2002. 672p. ISBN:0-8050-5686-6, ISBN13: 978-0-8050-5686-0. Dewey:355/.0092. LCCN:2002-020152.
Audience: **g,u,f.**

Divine, Robert A. **E835.D54**
Eisenhower and the Cold War. Trade Paper. Oxford University Press, Inc. New York, NY. 1981. 182p. ISBN:0-19-502824-4, ISBN13: 978-0-19-502824-9. Dewey:327.73/0092/4. LCCN:80-020600.
Audience: **u,f.** B

Divine, Robert A. **E806.D58**
The Illusion of Neutrality. Paper Text. Textbook Publishers. Temecula, CA. 2003. xi, 370p. ISBN:0-7581-2358-2, ISBN13: 978-0-7581-2358-9. Dewey:327.73.
Audience: **u,f.** B

Divine, Robert A. **E846.J64 1987**
(Editor)
The Johnson Years: LBJ at Home and Abroad. Trade Cloth. University Press of Kansas. Lawrence, KS. 1994. xii, 294p. ISBN:0-7006-0655-6, ISBN13: 978-0-7006-0655-9. Dewey:973.923. LCCN:86-032443.
Audience: **f.**

Divine, Robert A. **E846.J64 1987**
(Editor)
The Johnson Years: Vietnam, the Environment, and Science. Trade Cloth. University Press of Kansas. Lawrence, KS. 1987. xii, 272p. ISBN:0-7006-0327-1, ISBN13: 978-0-7006-0327-5. Dewey:973.923. LCCN:86-032443.
Audience: **f.** *Choice, 1987.*

Divine, Robert A. **D753**
The Reluctant Belligerent: American Entry into World War II. Ed. 2. Paper Text. McGraw-Hill Higher Education. Burr Ridge, IL. 1979. 179p. ISBN:0-07-554672-8, ISBN13: 978-0-07-554672-6. Dewey:940.532.
Audience: **u,f.** B

Divine, Robert A. **E846.J64 1987**
(Editor, Preface by)
The Johnson Years: Foreign Policy, the Great Society, and the White House. Trade Paper. University Press of Kansas. Lawrence, KS. 1987. viii, 280p. ISBN:0-7006-0326-3, ISBN13: 978-0-7006-0326-8. Dewey:973.923. LCCN:86-032443.
Audience: **f.**

Donovan, Robert J. **E813.D6 1996**
Conflict and Crisis: The Presidency of Harry S. Truman, 1945-1948. Trade Paper. University of Missouri Press. Columbia, MO. 1996. 512p. Give 'em Hell Harry Ser. ISBN:0-8262-1066-X, ISBN13: 978-0-8262-1066-1. Dewey:973.918. LCCN:96-011937.
Audience: **u,f.** B

Donovan, Robert J. **E835.D6**
Eisenhower: The Inside Story. Trade Paper. Books on Demand. Ann Arbor, MI. 456p. ISBN:0-598-47302-5, ISBN13: 978-0-598-47302-8. Dewey:973.92. LCCN:56-009653.
Audience: **f.** B

Donovan, Robert J. **E813.D63 1996**
Tumultuous Years: The Presidency of Harry S. Truman, 1949-1953. Trade Paper. University of Missouri Press. Columbia, MO. 1996. 448p. ISBN:0-8262-1085-6, ISBN13: 978-0-8262-1085-2. Dewey:973.918. LCCN:96-020042.
Audience: **u,f.** B

Drew, Elizabeth **E886.D74 1994**
On the Edge: The Clinton Presidency. Trade Cloth. Simon & Schuster. New York, NY. 1994. 496p. ISBN:0-671-87147-1, ISBN13: 978-0-671-87147-5. Dewey:973.929092. LCCN:94-034873.
Audience: **u,f.**

Drew, Elizabeth **E885.D74 1997**
Showdown: The Struggle Between the Gingrich Congress and the Clinton White House. Trade Paper. Simon & Schuster. New York, NY. 1997. 400p. ISBN:0-684-82551-1, ISBN13: 978-0-684-82551-9. Dewey:973.929. LCCN:97-193528.
Audience: **f.** *Choice, 1996.*

Drew, Elizabeth **E860.D73**
Washington Journal: A Diary of the Events of 1973-1974. Trade Cloth. Random House, Inc. New York, NY. 1975. 448p.

ISBN:0-394-49575-6, ISBN13: 978-0-394-49575-0. Dewey:973.924. LCCN:75-009803.
Audience: **f.** BCL3

D'Souza, Dinesh **E876.D83 1997**
Ronald Reagan: How an Ordinary Man Became an Extraordinary Leader. Trade Paper. Simon & Schuster. New York, NY. 1999. 304p. ISBN:0-684-84823-6, ISBN13: 978-0-684-84823-5. Dewey:973.927/092. LCCN:97-031396.
Audience: **u,f.**

Duffy, Michael & Goodgame, Dan **E881.D84 1992**
Marching in Place: The Status Quo Presidency of George Bush. Trade Cloth. Simon & Schuster. New York, NY. 1992. 320p. ISBN:0-671-73720-1, ISBN13: 978-0-671-73720-7. Dewey:973.928/092. LCCN:92-020036.
Audience: **u,f.** *Choice, 1993.*

Dugger, Ronnie **E847**
The Politician: The Life and Times of Lyndon Johnson. Trade Cloth. W. W. Norton & Company, Inc. New York, NY. 1982. 544p. ISBN:0-393-01598-X, ISBN13: 978-0-393-01598-0. Dewey:973.923/092/4. LCCN:81-022507.
Audience: **f.** BCL3

Dumbrell, John **E872.D86 1995**
The Carter Presidency: A Re-Evaluation. Cloth Text. Manchester University Press. Manchester, 1995. 248p. ISBN:0-7190-4693-9, ISBN13: 978-0-7190-4693-3. Dewey:353.0081/1. LCCN:95-203172.
Audience: **f.** *Choice, 1994.*

Dunar, Andrew J. **E814.D86 1984**
[Ebook] The Truman Scandals and the Politics of Morality. E-Book. University of Missouri Press. Columbia, MO. 1984. ISBN:0-8262-6036-5, ISBN13: 978-0-8262-6036-9. Dewey:973.918/0924.
Audience: **f.** BCL3

Ehrlichman, John D. **E855.E35 1982**
Witness to Power: The Nixon Years. Trade Cloth. Simon & Schuster. New York, NY. 1982. 432p. ISBN:0-671-24296-2, ISBN13: 978-0-671-24296-1. Dewey:973.924. LCCN:81-018432.
Audience: **u,f.**

Ehrman, John **E876.E344 2005**
The Eighties: America in the Age of Reagan. Cloth over Boards. Yale University Press. Cumberland, RI. 2005. 304p. ISBN:0-300-10662-9, ISBN13: 978-0-300-10662-6. Dewey:973.927. LCCN:2004-024715.
Audience: **u,f.** *Choice, 2005.*

Eisenhower, Dwight D. **E836.E38 1991**
Eisenhower at War, 1943-1945. Trade Cloth. Random House Value Publishing. New York, NY. 1991. 1040p. ISBN:0-517-06501-0, ISBN13: 978-0-517-06501-3. Dewey:973.921/092/4. LCCN:91-023108.
Audience: **f.** BCL3 *Choice, 1987.*

Eisenhower, Dwight D. **E836**
The Eisenhower Diaries. Robert H. Ferrell (Editor). Trade Cloth. W. W. Norton & Company, Inc. New York, NY. 1981. xvii, 445p. ISBN:0-393-01432-0, ISBN13: 978-0-393-01432-7. Dewey:973.921/092/4. LCCN:80-027866.
Audience: **f.** BCL3

Eisenhower, John S. D. **D570.E37 2001**
Yanks: The Epic Story of the American Army in World War I. Trade Cloth. Simon & Schuster. New York, NY. 2001. 368p. ISBN:0-684-86304-9, ISBN13: 978-0-684-86304-7. Dewey:940.4/1273. LCCN:2001-023124.
Audience: **u,f.**

Ervin, Sam J. Jr. **E860.E78**
The Whole Truth: The Watergate Conspiracy by Sam Ervin. Trade Cloth. Random House, Inc. New York, NY. 1980. xvi, 320p. ISBN:0-394-48029-5, ISBN13: 978-0-394-48029-9. Dewey:364.1/32/0973. LCCN:78-021821.
Audience: **f.** BCL3

Esposito, David M. **D619**
The Legacy of Woodrow Wilson: American War Aims in World War I. Trade Cloth. Greenwood Publishing Group, Inc. Portsmouth, NH. 1996. 176p. ISBN:0-275-95493-5, ISBN13: 978-0-275-95493-2. Dewey:940.4/0973. LCCN:95-043729.
Audience: **u,f.**

Evans, Rowland **E855.E9**
Nixon in the White House: The Frustration of Power. Trade Cloth. Random House, Inc. New York, NY. 1971. viii, 431p. ISBN:0-394-46273-4, ISBN13: 978-0-394-46273-8. Dewey:973.924/0924. LCCN:75-140702.
Audience: **f.** BCL3

Evans, Rowland & Novak, Robert **E876.E93 1981**
The Reagan Revolution: An Inside Look at the Transformation of the U. S. Government. Trade Cloth. Penguin Group (USA) Inc. New York, NY. 1981. 288p. ISBN:0-525-18970-X, ISBN13: 978-0-525-18970-1. Dewey:973.927/092/4. LCCN:81-005553.
Audience: **f.**

Farber, David R. & Bailey, Beth L. **E841.C575 2001**
[Ebook] The Columbia Guide to America in the 1960s. E-Book. Columbia University Press. New York, NY. ISBN:0-231-50476-4, ISBN13: 978-0-231-50476-8. Dewey:973.923.
Audience: **l,u,f.**

Fausold, Martin L. **E801.F25 1985**
The Presidency of Herbert C. Hoover. Trade Cloth. University Press of Kansas. Lawrence, KS. 1985. xii, 292p. American Presidency Ser. ISBN:0-7006-0259-3, ISBN13: 978-0-7006-0259-9. Dewey:973.91/6/0924. LCCN:84-017252.
Audience: **u,f.** BCL3

Ferrell, Robert H. **E814.F46 1994**
[Ebook] Harry S. Truman: A Life. E-Book. University of Missouri Press. Columbia, MO. 1994. ISBN:0-8262-6045-4, ISBN13: 978-0-8262-6045-1. Dewey:973.9/18/092.
Audience: **g,u,f.** *Choice, 1995.*

Ferrell, Robert H. **E791.F47 1998**
The Presidency of Calvin Coolidge. Trade Cloth. University Press of Kansas. Lawrence, KS. 2004. xii, 244p. American Presidency Ser. ISBN:0-7006-0892-3, ISBN13: 978-0-7006-0892-8. Dewey:973.91/5/092. LCCN:97-051128.
Audience: **u,f.** *Choice, 1998.*

Ferrell, Robert H. **D619.F34 1985**
Woodrow Wilson and World War I, 1917-1921. Trade Paper. HarperCollins Publishers. New York, NY. 1986. 336p. New

American Nation Ser. ISBN:0-06-091216-2, ISBN13: 978-0-06-091216-1. Dewey:940.3/73. LCCN:84-048160.
Audience: **l,u,f.** *Choice, 1985.*

Fink, Gary M. & Graham, Hugh Davis (Editors) **E872.C38 1998**
The Carter Presidency: Policy Choices in the Post-New Deal Era. Trade Cloth. University Press of Kansas. Lawrence, KS. 1998. x, 310p. ISBN:0-7006-0895-8, ISBN13: 978-0-7006-0895-9. Dewey:973.926/092. LCCN:98-009967.
Audience: **u,f.** *Choice, 1999.*

FitzGerald, Frances **E876.F58 2000**
Way Out There in the Blue: Reagan, Star Wars and the End of the Cold War. Trade Cloth. Simon & Schuster. New York, NY. 2000. 592p. ISBN:0-684-84416-8, ISBN13: 978-0-684-84416-9. Dewey:973.927/092. LCCN:99-059913.
Audience: **u,f.**

Fleming, Thomas J. **D570.A456 2004**
The Illusion of Victory: America in World War I. Trade Paper. Basic Books. New York, NY. 2004. 576p. ISBN:0-465-02469-6, ISBN13: 978-0-465-02469-8. Dewey:940.3/73. LCCN:2003-002616.
Audience: **u,f.**

Frankel, Max **E841.F68 2004**
High Noon in the Cold War: Kennedy, Khrushchev, and the Cuban Missile Crisis. Trade Cloth. Ballantine Books. New York, NY. 2004. 224p. ISBN:0-345-46505-9, ISBN13: 978-0-345-46505-4. Dewey:327.47073/09/046. LCCN:2004-046159.
Audience: **f.** *Choice, 2005.*

Fraser, Steve & Gerstle, Gary (Editors) **E806.R57 1989**
The Rise and Fall of the New Deal Order, 1930-1980. Trade Paper. Princeton University Press. Princeton, NJ. 1990. 337p. ISBN:0-691-00607-5, ISBN13: 978-0-691-00607-9. Dewey:353.07209. LCCN:88-039842.
Audience: **f.** *Choice, 1989.*

Freeland, Richard M. **E813.F74 1985**
The Truman Doctrine and the Origins of McCarthyism: Foreign Policy, Domestic Policy, and Internal Security, 1946-48. Cloth Text. New York University Press. New York, NY. 1985. 448p. ISBN:0-8147-2575-9, ISBN13: 978-0-8147-2575-7. Dewey:973.918. LCCN:84-029562.
Audience: **f.**

Garrison, Jim **E842.9.G35 1988**
On the Trail of the Assassins: My Investigation and Prosecution of the Murder of President Kennedy. Carl Oglesby (Afterword by). Trade Cloth. Institute for Media Analysis, Inc. New York, NY. 1988. 336p. ISBN:0-941781-02-X, ISBN13: 978-0-941781-02-2. Dewey:973.924/092/4. LCCN:88-024002.
Audience: **f.**

Gelfand, Lawrence E. (Editor) **D570.1.H38**
Herbert Hoover: The Great War and Its Aftermath, 1914-23. Cloth Text. University of Iowa Press. Iowa City, IA. 1979. 254p. Herbert Hoover Centennial Seminar Ser. ISBN:0-87745-095-1, ISBN13: 978-0-87745-095-5. Dewey:940.3/14. LCCN:79-010139.
Audience: **f.**

Giglio, James N. **E841.G54 1991**
The Presidency of John F. Kennedy. Trade Cloth. University Press of Kansas. Lawrence, KS. 1991. x, 334p. American Presidency Ser. ISBN:0-7006-0515-0, ISBN13: 978-0-7006-0515-6. Dewey:973.922/092. LCCN:91-016841.
Audience: **u,f.** *Choice, 1992.*

Glad, Betty **E873.G56 1980**
Jimmy Carter: In Search of the Great White House. Trade Cloth. W. W. Norton & Company, Inc. New York, NY. 1980. 546p. ISBN:0-393-07527-3, ISBN13: 978-0-393-07527-4. Dewey:973.926/092/4. LCCN:80-014744.
Audience: **f.**

Goldman, Eric F. **E813.G6 1981**
The Crucial Decade: America, 1945-1955. Trade Cloth. Greenwood Publishing Group, Inc. Portsmouth, NH. 1982. 298p. ISBN:0-313-23147-8, ISBN13: 978-0-313-23147-6. Dewey:973.918. LCCN:81-013399.
Audience: **u,f.**

Goodwin, Doris Kearns **E847.G64 1991**
Lyndon Johnson and the American Dream. Trade Paper. St. Martin's Press. Gordonville, VA. 1991. 448p. ISBN:0-312-06027-0, ISBN13: 978-0-312-06027-5. Dewey:973.923/092. LCCN:90-028429.
Audience: **g,l,u,f.**

Gould, Lewis L. **E756.G62 1991**
The Presidency of Theodore Roosevelt. Trade Cloth. University Press of Kansas. Lawrence, KS. 1991. xii, 356p. American Presidency Ser. ISBN:0-7006-0435-9, ISBN13: 978-0-7006-0435-7. Dewey:973.91/1. LCCN:90-011184.
Audience: **l,u,f.** *Choice, 1991.*

Gould, Lewis L. **E756.G63 1996**
Reform and Regulation: American Politics from Roosevelt to Wilson. Ed. 3. Paper Text. Waveland Press, Inc. Prospect Heights, IL. 1996. 243p. ISBN:0-88133-899-0, ISBN13: 978-0-88133-899-7. Dewey:973.91. LCCN:97-205873.
Audience: **f.**

Greenberg, David **E856.G747 2003**
Nixon's Shadow: The History of an Image. Trade Cloth. W. W. Norton & Company, Inc. New York, NY. 2003. 384p. ISBN:0-393-04896-9, ISBN13: 978-0-393-04896-4. Dewey:973.924/092. LCCN:2003-008421.
Audience: **u,f.** *Choice, 2004.*

Greene, John R. **E865.G74 1995**
The Presidency of Gerald R. Ford. Trade Cloth. University Press of Kansas. Lawrence, KS. 1995. xvi, 256p. American Presidency Ser. ISBN:0-7006-0638-6, ISBN13: 978-0-7006-0638-2. Dewey:973.925/092. LCCN:94-020037.
Audience: **u,f.** *Choice, 1995.*

Greene, John Robert **E867.F67G74 2004**
Betty Ford: Candor and Courage in the White House. Trade Cloth. University Press of Kansas. Lawrence, KS. 2004. 176p. Modern First Ladies Ser. ISBN:0-7006-1354-4, ISBN13: 978-0-7006-1354-0. Dewey:973.925/092. LCCN:2004-013586.
Audience: **u,f.**

Greene, John Robert **E881.G74 2000**
The Presidency of George Bush. Trade Cloth. University Press of Kansas. Lawrence, KS. 2000. xiv, 250p. American Presidency Ser. ISBN:0-7006-0993-8, ISBN13: 978-0-7006-0993-2. Dewey:973.928/092. LCCN:99-035836.
Audience: **u,f.**

Greene, John R. **E855.G7 1992**
The Limits of Power: The Nixon and Ford Administrations. Warren F. Kimball (Foreword by). Trade Cloth. Indiana University Press. Bloomington, IN. 1992. 324p. ISBN:0-253-32637-0, ISBN13: 978-0-253-32637-9. Dewey:973.924. LCCN:91-047014.
Audience: **u,f.** *Choice, 1993.*

Greenstein, Fred I. **E836.G73 1994**
The Hidden-Hand Presidency: Eisenhower as Leader. Trade Paper. Johns Hopkins University Press. Baltimore, MD. 1994. 312p. ISBN:0-8018-4901-2, ISBN13: 978-0-8018-4901-5. Dewey:973.921092. LCCN:94-007281.
Audience: **u,f.**

Haig, Alexander M. **E876.H34 1984**
Caveat. Clare Boothe Luce (Contribution by). Children's Board Books. Simon & Schuster. New York, NY. 1984. 367p. ISBN:0-02-547370-0, ISBN13: 978-0-02-547370-6. Dewey:327.73. LCCN:84-000936.
Audience: **u,f.** B

Halberstam, David **E881**
War in a Time of Peace: Bush, Clinton, and the Generals. Trade Paper. Simon & Schuster. New York, NY. 2002. 560p. ISBN:0-7432-2323-3, ISBN13: 978-0-7432-2323-2. Dewey:327.73.
Audience: **u,f.**

Halberstam, David **E841.H25 2001**
The Best and the Brightest. John McCain (Foreword by). Trade Cloth. Random House Adult Trade Publishing Group. New York, NY. 2001. 816p. ISBN:0-679-64099-1, ISBN13: 978-0-679-64099-8. Dewey:973.92. LCCN:2001-031261.
Audience: **g,l,u,f.** B

Hallas, James H. (Editor) **D570.D68 2000**
Doughboy War: The American Expeditionary Force in World War I. Library Binding. Lynne Rienner Publishers, Inc. Boulder, CO. 1999. 352p. ISBN:1-55587-855-5, ISBN13: 978-1-55587-855-9. Dewey:940.3/73. LCCN:99-028754.
Audience: **u,f.**

Hamby, Alonzo L. **E813**
Beyond the New Deal: Harry S. Truman and American Liberalism. Paper Text. Columbia University Press. New York, NY. 1976. 655p. Contemporary American History Ser. ISBN:0-231-08344-0, ISBN13: 978-0-231-08344-7. Dewey:320.9/73/0918. LCCN:73-007593.
Audience: **f.** B

Hamby, Alonzo L. **E806.H293 2004**
For the Survival of Democracy: Franklin Roosevelt and the World Crisis of the 1930's. Trade Cloth. Simon & Schuster. New York, NY. 2003. 512p. ISBN:0-684-84340-4, ISBN13: 978-0-684-84340-7. Dewey:909.82/3. LCCN:2003-061807.
Audience: **f.**

Hamby, Alonzo L. (Editor) **E813.H27 1974**
Harry S. Truman and the Fair Deal. Paper Text. Houghton Mifflin Company Trade & Reference Division. Boston, MA. 1974. 223p. Problems in American Civilization Ser. ISBN:0-669-87080-3, ISBN13: 978-0-669-87080-0. Dewey:320.9/73/0918. LCCN:73-022759.
Audience: **f.**

Hamby, Alonzo L. **E814.H28 1995**
Man of the People: A Life of Harry S. Truman. Trade Cloth. Oxford University Press, Inc. New York, NY. 1995. 800p. ISBN:0-19-504546-7, ISBN13: 978-0-19-504546-8. Dewey:973.9/18/092. LCCN:94-043806.
Audience: **u,f.** *Choice, 1996.*

Hamilton, Nigel **E842.H275 1992**
JFK: Reckless Youth. Trade Cloth. Random House, Inc. New York, NY. 1992. xxiv, 898p. ISBN:0-679-41216-6, ISBN13: 978-0-679-41216-8. Dewey:973.9/22/092. LCCN:92-008207.
Audience: **g,u,f.** *Choice, 1993.*

Harbaugh, William H. **E757**
Power and Responsibility: The Life and Times of Theodore Roosevelt. Katherine E. Speirs (Editor). Trade Cloth. American Political Biography. Newtown, CT. 1997. 542p. Signature Ser. ISBN:0-945707-13-4, ISBN13: 978-0-945707-13-4. Dewey:973.9110924. LCCN:97-073117.
Audience: **u,f.**

Harris, John F. **E886.H37 2005**
The Survivor: Bill Clinton in the White House. Trade Cloth. Random House, Inc. New York, NY. 2005. 544p. ISBN:0-375-50847-3, ISBN13: 978-0-375-50847-9. Dewey:973.929/092. LCCN:2004-062893.
Audience: **g,u,f.** *Choice, 2005.*

Hill, Samuel S. & Owen, Dennis E. **E872.H54 1982**
The New Religious-Political Right in America. Trade Cloth. Abingdon Press. Nashville, TN. 1982. 160p. ISBN:0-687-27867-8, ISBN13: 978-0-687-27867-1. Dewey:261.7/0973. LCCN:81-020661.
Audience: **f.** B

Hoff, Joan **E856.H64 1994**
Nixon Reconsidered. Trade Cloth. Basic Books. New York, NY. 1994. 496p. ISBN:0-465-05107-3, ISBN13: 978-0-465-05107-6. Dewey:973.924/092. LCCN:94-012598.
Audience: **f.** *Choice, 1995.*

Hogan, Michael J. **E813.H58 1998**
A Cross of Iron: Harry S. Truman and the Origins of the National Security State, 1945-1954. Cloth Text. Cambridge University Press. New York, NY. 1998. 554p. ISBN:0-521-64044-X, ISBN13: 978-0-521-64044-2. Dewey:973.9/18. LCCN:98-015865.
Audience: **f.**

Hoover, Herbert **E802.A35 1979**
The Memoirs of Herbert Hoover. Trade Cloth. Garland Publishing, Inc. New York, NY. 1979. ISBN:0-8240-9703-3, ISBN13: 978-0-8240-9703-5. Dewey:973.91/6/0924. LCCN:78-066527.
Audience: **f.**

Hoover, Herbert **E767.H78 1992**
The Ordeal of Woodrow Wilson. Mark Hatfield (Introduction by). Trade Paper. Woodrow Wilson Center Press. Washington, DC. 1992. 352p. ISBN:0-943875-41-2, ISBN13: 978-0-943875-41-5. Dewey:973.91/3/092. LCCN:92-023528.
Audience: **f.** B

Houston, David Franklin **E766.H72**
Eight Years with Wilson's Cabinet, 1913 to 1920. Paper Text.

Classic Textbooks. Murrieta, CA. 1926. ISBN:1-4047-6223-X, ISBN13: 978-1-4047-6223-7. Dewey:973.91/3/0924.
Audience: **f.**

Hyland, William G. **E885**
Clinton's World: Remaking American Foreign Policy. Trade Cloth. Greenwood Publishing Group, Inc. Portsmouth, NH. 1999. 232p. ISBN:0-275-96396-9, ISBN13: 978-0-275-96396-5. Dewey:327.73/009/049. LCCN:98-037155.
Audience: **f.** *Choice, 1999.*

Isserman, Maurice & Kazin, Michael **E841.I87 2003**
America Divided: The Civil War of the 1960s. Ed. 2. Paper Text. Oxford University Press, Inc. New York, NY. 2003. 383p. ISBN:0-19-516047-9, ISBN13: 978-0-19-516047-5. Dewey:973.923. LCCN:2002-044968.
Audience: **f.** *Choice, 2000.*

Johnson, Haynes **E885.J63 2001**
The Best of Times: America in the Clinton Years. Cloth over Boards. Harcourt Trade Publishers. New York, NY. 2001. 624p. ISBN:0-15-100445-5, ISBN13: 978-0-15-100445-4. Dewey:973.929. LCCN:2001-024753.
Audience: **u,f.** *Choice, 2002.*

Johnson, Haynes **E872.J63**
In the Absence of Power: Governing America. Trade Cloth. Penguin Group (USA) Inc. New York, NY. 1980. 339p. ISBN:0-670-20548-6, ISBN13: 978-0-670-20548-6. Dewey:320.9/73/0926. LCCN:79-003625.
Audience: **u,f.** B

Johnson, Haynes **E876.J64 2003**
Sleepwalking Through History: America in the Reagan Years. Trade Paper. W. W. Norton & Company, Inc. New York, NY. 2003. 544p. ISBN:0-393-32434-6, ISBN13: 978-0-393-32434-1. Dewey:973.927. LCCN:2003-042083.
Audience: **g,u,f.**

Johnson, Haynes B. **E885**
Divided We Fall: Gambling with History in the Nineties. Trade Paper. W. W. Norton & Company, Inc. New York, NY. 1995. 480p. ISBN:0-393-31306-9, ISBN13: 978-0-393-31306-2. Dewey:973.929. LCCN:93-045713.
Audience: **u,f.**

Johnson, Lyndon B. **E846.J58**
The Vantage Point; Perspectives of the Presidency, 1963-1969. Trade Cloth. Holt, Rinehart & Winston. Austin, TX. 1971. x, 636p. ISBN:0-03-084492-4, ISBN13: 978-0-03-084492-8. Dewey:973.923. LCCN:74-102146.
Audience: **g,l,u,f.** B

Kaplan, Leonard V. & Moran, Beverly I. (Editors) **E886.2.A44 2001**
Aftermath: The Clinton Impeachment and the Presidency in the Age of Political Spectacle. Trade Cloth. New York University Press. New York, NY. 2001. 384p. Critical America Ser. ISBN:0-8147-4742-6, ISBN13: 978-0-8147-4742-1. Dewey:973.929. LCCN:2001-001549.
Audience: **u,f.** *Choice, 2002.*

Kaufman, Burton I. **E872.K38 1993**
The Presidency of James Earl Carter, Jr. Trade Cloth. University Press of Kansas. Lawrence, KS. 1993. x, 246p. American Presidency Ser. ISBN:0-7006-0572-X, ISBN13: 978-0-7006-0572-9. Dewey:973.926. LCCN:92-018134.
Audience: **u,f.** *Choice, 1993.*

Kengor, Paul & Schweizer, Peter **E876.R41164 2005**
The Reagan Presidency: Assessing the Man and His Legacy. Book, Other. Rowman & Littlefield Publishers, Inc. Lanham, MD. 2005. 240p. ISBN:0-7425-3414-6, ISBN13: 978-0-7425-3414-8. Dewey:973.927/092. LCCN:2004-029779.
Audience: **u,f.** *Choice, 2005.*

Kennan, George F. **E0835.K4**
Realities of American Foreign Policy. Trade Paper. Books on Demand. Ann Arbor, MI. 130p. ISBN:0-598-89737-2, ISBN13: 978-0-598-89737-4. Dewey:327.73. LCCN:54-009021.
Audience: **f.**

Kennan, George Frost **E865.K46**
The Cloud of Danger: Current Realities of American Foreign Policy. Trade Cloth. Little Brown & Company. New York, NY. 1977. xiii, 234p. ISBN:0-316-48844-5, ISBN13: 978-0-316-48844-0. Dewey:327.73. LCCN:77-079616.
Audience: **f.** B

Kennedy, David M. **D570.1.K43 2004**
Over Here: The First World War and American Society. Ed. 25. Trade Paper. Oxford University Press, Inc. New York, NY. 2004. 440p. ISBN:0-19-517399-6, ISBN13: 978-0-19-517399-4. Dewey:940.3/73. LCCN:2004-054789.
Audience: **l,u,f.** B

Kennedy, Robert F. **E841.K459 2001**
Thirteen Days: A Memoir of the Cuban Missile Crisis. Trade Cloth. Thorndike Press. Waterville, ME. 2001. 208p. American History Ser. ISBN:0-7838-9356-6, ISBN13: 978-0-7838-9356-3. Dewey:973.922. LCCN:00-051238.
Audience: **u,f.** B

Klein, Joe **E886.K64 2002**
The Natural: The Misunderstood Presidency of Bill Clinton. Trade Cloth. Doubleday Canada, Ltd. Toronto, ON. 2002. 240p. ISBN:0-385-50619-8, ISBN13: 978-0-385-50619-9. Dewey:973.929/092. LCCN:2001-047428.
Audience: **g,u,f.** *Choice, 2003, 2002.*

Knock, Thomas J **E767.1.K56 1992**
To End All Wars: Woodrow Wilson and the Quest for a New World Order. Oxford University Press, Inc. 1992. ISBN:0-19-507501-3, ISBN13: 978-0-19-507501-4.
Audience: **u,f.**

Kolb, Charles **E881.K65 1994**
White House Daze: The Unmaking of Domestic Policy in the Bush Years. Trade Cloth. Simon & Schuster. New York, NY. 1993. 377p. ISBN:0-02-917495-3, ISBN13: 978-0-02-917495-1. Dewey:973.928. LCCN:93-033175.
Audience: **f.** *Choice, 1994.*

Kunz, Diane B. (Editor) **E841.D46 1994**
The Diplomacy of the Crucial Decade: American Foreign Relations During the 1960s. Trade Cloth. Columbia University Press. New York, NY. 1994. 372p. ISBN:0-231-08176-6, ISBN13: 978-0-231-08176-4. Dewey:327.73. LCCN:93-037995.
Audience: **f.** *Choice, 1994.*

Kutler, Stanley I. **E860.A26 1998**
Abuse of Power: The New Nixon Tapes. Trade Paper. Simon & Schuster. New York, NY. 1998. 704p. ISBN:0-684-85187-3, ISBN13: 978-0-684-85187-7. Dewey:973.924/092. LCCN:98-215240.
Audience: **f.** *Choice, 1998.*

LaFeber, Walter **E851.L33 2005**
The Deadly Bet: LBJ, Vietnam, and the 1968 Election. Trade Cloth. Rowman & Littlefield Publishers, Inc. Lanham, MD. 2005. 240p. Vietnam Ser. ISBN:0-7425-4391-9, ISBN13: 978-0-7425-4391-1. Dewey:324.973/0923. LCCN:2004-020834.
Audience: **u,f.** *Choice, 2006.*

Lang, Gladys E. & Lang, Kurt **E860**
The Battle for Public Opinion: The President, the Press and the Polls During Watergate. Paper Text. Columbia University Press. New York, NY. 1983. 360p. ISBN:0-231-05549-8, ISBN13: 978-0-231-05549-9. Dewey:364.1/323/0973. LCCN:82-012791.
Audience: **f.** B

Leuchtenburg, William E. **E806.L474 1995**
The FDR Years: On Roosevelt and His Legacy. Trade Cloth. Columbia University Press. New York, NY. 1995. 377p. ISBN:0-231-08298-3, ISBN13: 978-0-231-08298-3. Dewey:973.917/092. LCCN:95-013282.
Audience: **u,f.** *Choice, 1996.*

Leuchtenburg, William E. **E806**
Franklin D. Roosevelt and the New Deal 1932-1940. Trade Paper. HarperCollins Publishers. New York, NY. 1963. 432p. New American Nation Ser. ISBN:0-06-133025-6, ISBN13: 978-0-06-133025-4. Dewey:973.917. LCCN:63-012053.
Audience: **u,f.**

Leuchtenburg, William E. **E176.1**
Herbert Hoover. Trade Cloth. Henry Holt & Company. New York, NY. The American Presidents Ser. ISBN:0-8050-6958-5, ISBN13: 978-0-8050-6958-7. Dewey:973/.09/9.
Audience: **g,u,f.**

Leuchtenburg, William Edward **E747.L48 2005**
The White House Looks South: Franklin D. Roosevelt, Harry S. Truman, Lyndon B. Johnson. Saddle Stitched, Cloth over Boards, Dust Jacket. Louisiana State University Press. Baton Rouge, LA. 2005. 668p. Walter Lynwood Fleming Lectures in Southern History ISBN:0-8071-3079-6, ISBN13: 978-0-8071-3079-7. Dewey:973.91/092/2. LCCN:2004-029192.
Audience: **u,f.**

Leuchtenburg, William E. **HC106.3.L3957 1993**
The Perils of Prosperity, 1914-1932. Ed. 2. Daniel J. Boorstin (Foreword by). Trade Paper. University of Chicago Press. Chicago, IL. 1993. 332p. Chicago History of American Civilization Ser. ISBN:0-226-47371-6, ISBN13: 978-0-226-47371-0. Dewey:330.9730913. LCCN:92-044912.
Audience: **g,u,f.**

Levin, N. Gordon Jr. **E768.L62**
Woodrow Wilson and World Politics: America's Response to War and Revolution. Trade Paper. Oxford University Press, Inc. New York, NY. 1970. 352p. ISBN:0-19-500803-0, ISBN13: 978-0-19-500803-6. Dewey:327.73. LCCN:68-015893.
Audience: **f.**

Liebovich, Louis W. **E856**
Richard Nixon, Watergate, and the Press: A Historical Retrospective. Trade Cloth. Greenwood Publishing Group, Inc. Portsmouth, NH. 2003. 160p. ISBN:0-313-03921-6, ISBN13: 978-0-313-03921-8. Dewey:973.924/092.
Audience: **f.**

Lingeman, Richard **E806.L568 2003**
Don't You Know There's a War On?: The American Home Front, 1941-1945. Trade Paper. Avalon Publishing Group. New York, NY. 2003. 300p. Nation Bks. ISBN:1-56025-465-3, ISBN13: 978-1-56025-465-2. Dewey:973.917. LCCN:2003-047311.
Audience: **u,f.**

Link, Arthur S. **E748.G835**
Wilson the Diplomatist: A Look at His Major Foreign Policies. Paper Text. Textbook Publishers. Temecula, CA. 2003. xvi, 165p. ISBN:0-7581-7783-6, ISBN13: 978-0-7581-7783-4. Dewey:327/.2/0924.
Audience: **f.**

Link, Arthur S. **E768.L67**
Woodrow Wilson: Revolution, War and Peace. Trade Paper. Harlan Davidson Inc. Wheeling, IL. 2003. 152p. ISBN:0-88295-798-8, ISBN13: 978-0-88295-798-2. Dewey:973.91/3/0924. LCCN:79-050909.
Audience: **f.** B

Link, Arthur S. (Editor) **E768.W66 1982**
Woodrow Wilson and a Revolutionary World, 1913-1921. Trade Cloth. University of North Carolina Press. Chapel Hill, NC. 1982. viii, 244p. Supplementary Volumes to the Papers of Woodrow Wilson ISBN:0-8078-1529-2, ISBN13: 978-0-8078-1529-8. Dewey:973.91/3/0924. LCCN:82-002565.
Audience: **u,f.**

Lippmann, Walter **E766.L574 2000**
Force and Ideas: The Early Writings. Arthur M. Schlesinger Jr. (Introduction by, Annotations by). Trade Paper. Transaction Publishers. Somerset, NJ. 2000. 356p. ISBN:0-7658-0620-7, ISBN13: 978-0-7658-0620-8. Dewey:320.973/09/041. LCCN:99-046898.
Audience: **f.**

Litwak, Robert S. **E855**
Detente and the Nixon Doctrine: American Foreign Policy and the Pursuit of Stability, 1969-1976. Cloth Text. Cambridge University Press. New York, NY. 1984. 240p. International Studies ISBN:0-521-25094-3, ISBN13: 978-0-521-25094-8. Dewey:327.73. LCCN:83-015053.
Audience: **u,f.**

Lodge, Henry Cabot **E835.L57 1976**
As It Was: An Inside View of Politics and Power in the Fifties and Sixties. Trade Cloth. W. W. Norton & Company, Inc. New York, NY. 1976. 224p. ISBN:0-393-05597-3, ISBN13: 978-0-393-05597-9. Dewey:973.921/092/4. LCCN:76-017615.
Audience: **f.** B

Lukas, J. Anthony **E860.L84 1999**
Nightmare: The Underside of the Nixon Years. Ed. 3. Joan Hoff (Contribution by). Trade Paper. Ohio University Press. Athens, OH. 1999. 640p. ISBN:0-8214-1287-6, ISBN13: 978-0-8214-1287-9. Dewey:973.924. LCCN:99-031513.
Audience: **u,f.**

Maga, Timothy P. **E872.M238 1995**
The World of Jimmy Carter: U. S. Foreign Policy, 1977-1981. Thomas Katsaros (Editor). Paper Text. University of New Haven Press. West Haven, CT. 1994. 200p. ISBN:0-936285-23-0, ISBN13: 978-0-936285-23-8. Dewey:327.73. LCCN:94-060806.
Audience: **u,f.**

Manchester, William **E806.M34 1988**
The Glory and the Dream: A Narrative History of America, 1932-1972. Trade Paper. Bantam Books. New York, NY. 1984. 1408p. ISBN:0-553-34589-3, ISBN13: 978-0-553-34589-6. Dewey:973.9. LCCN:89-017671.
Audience: **g,f.**

Maraniss, David **E886.M29 1996**
First in His Class: A Biography of Bill Clinton. Trade Paper. Simon & Schuster. New York, NY. 1996. 512p. ISBN:0-684-81890-6, ISBN13: 978-0-684-81890-0. Dewey:973.929092. LCCN:95-044894.
Audience: **g,u,f.**

March, Peyton C. **D570.M35 1970**
Nation at War. Trade Cloth. Greenwood Publishing Group, Inc. Portsmouth, NH. 1970. 407p. ISBN:0-8371-4269-5, ISBN13: 978-0-8371-4269-2. Dewey:940.4/12/73. LCCN:72-109779.
Audience: **f.**

Marks, Frederick W. III **E835**
Power and Peace: The Diplomacy of John Foster Dulles. Trade Cloth. Greenwood Publishing Group, Inc. Portsmouth, NH. 1993. 296p. ISBN:0-275-94497-2, ISBN13: 978-0-275-94497-1. Dewey:327.730092. LCCN:92-042442.
Audience: **f.** *Choice, 1993.*

Marks, Frederick W. III **E756**
Velvet on Iron: The Diplomacy of Theodore Roosevelt. Paper Text. University of Nebraska Press. Lincoln, NE. 1979. 247p. ISBN:0-8032-8115-3, ISBN13: 978-0-8032-8115-8. Dewey:327.73/0092/4. LCCN:79-001216.
Audience: **f.**

Matthews, Christopher **E842.1.M38 1996**
Kennedy and Nixon: The Rivalry That Shaped Postwar America. Trade Cloth. Simon & Schuster. New York, NY. 1996. 384p. ISBN:0-684-81030-1, ISBN13: 978-0-684-81030-0. Dewey:973.9/2/0922. LCCN:96-015677.
Audience: **f.** *Choice, 1996.*

Matusow, Allen J. **E841**
The Unraveling of America: A History of Liberalism in the 1960s. Trade Paper. HarperCollins Publishers. New York, NY. 1986. 560p. New American Nation Ser. ISBN:0-06-132058-7, ISBN13: 978-0-06-132058-3. Dewey:973.92. LCCN:83-048019.
Audience: **u,f.**

May, Ernest R. & Zelikow, Philip D. (Editors) **E841.K4655 1997**
The Kennedy Tapes: Inside the White House During the Cuban Missile Crisis. Trade Cloth. Harvard University Press. Cambridge, MA. 1997. 800p. ISBN:0-674-17926-9, ISBN13: 978-0-674-17926-4. Dewey:973.922. LCCN:97-014216.
Audience: **u,f.** *Choice, 1998.*

McCoy, Donald R. **E814.M38 1984**
The Presidency of Harry S. Truman. Trade Cloth. University Press of Kansas. Lawrence, KS. 1986. xii, 356p. American Presidency Ser. ISBN:0-7006-0252-6, ISBN13: 978-0-7006-0252-0. Dewey:973.918/092/4. LCCN:84-003624.
Audience: **g,u,f.**

McCoy, Donald R. **E792**
Calvin Coolidge: The Quiet President. Katherine E. Speirs (Editor). Trade Cloth. American Political Biography. Newtown, CT. 1999. 472p. Signature Ser. ISBN:0-945707-23-1, ISBN13: 978-0-945707-23-3. Dewey:973.91/5. LCCN:98-074526.
Audience: **u,f.**

McCullough, David **E757.M45 2001**
Mornings on Horseback: The Story of an Extraordinary Family, a Vanished Way of Life, and the Unique Child Who Became Theodore Roosevelt. Trade Cloth. Simon & Schuster. New York, NY. 2001. 464p. ISBN:0-7432-1738-1, ISBN13: 978-0-7432-1738-5. Dewey:973.91/1/092. LCCN:2001-027005.
Audience: **g,l,u,f.**

McCullough, David **E814.M26 1992**
Truman. Trade Paper. Simon & Schuster. New York, NY. 1993. 1120p. ISBN:0-671-86920-5, ISBN13: 978-0-671-86920-5. Dewey:973.9/18/092. LCCN:92-005245.
Audience: **g,l,u,f.**

McElvaine, Robert S. **E806.M43 1993**
The Great Depression: America, 1929-1941. Book, Other. Random House, Inc. New York, NY. 1993. 432p. ISBN:0-8129-2327-8, ISBN13: 978-0-8129-2327-8. Dewey:973.91/6. LCCN:94-100756.
Audience: **f.** *Choice, 1985.*

McFarlane, Robert C. & Smardz, Zofia **E876.M394 1994**
Special Trust: Pride, Principle and Politics Inside the White House. Trade Cloth. Cadell & Davies. New York, NY. 1994. xiii, 399p. ISBN:1-56977-880-9, ISBN13: 978-1-56977-880-7. Dewey:955.05/4. LCCN:94-032882.
Audience: **f.**

McGovern, James R. **E806**
And a Time for Hope: Americans in the Great Depression. Trade Cloth. Greenwood Publishing Group, Inc. Portsmouth, NH. 2000. 368p. ISBN:0-275-96786-7, ISBN13: 978-0-275-96786-4. Dewey:973.917. LCCN:99-041959.
Audience: **f.** *Choice, 2000.*

McJimsey, George **E806.M46 2000**
The Presidency of Franklin Delano Roosevelt. Trade Cloth. University Press of Kansas. Lawrence, KS. 2000. xvi, 356p. American Presidency Ser. ISBN:0-7006-1012-X, ISBN13: 978-0-7006-1012-9. Dewey:973.917/092. LCCN:99-055956.
Audience: **u,f.** *Choice, 2000.*

McMahan, Jeff **E876.M4 1985**
Reagan and the World: Imperial Policy in the New Cold War. Trade Paper. Monthly Review Press. New York, NY. 1985. 320p. ISBN:0-85345-678-X, ISBN13: 978-0-85345-678-0. Dewey:327.73. LCCN:85-005028.
Audience: **f.** *Choice, 1985.*

Meese, Edwin III **E877.2.M44 1992**
With Reagan: The Inside Story. Trade Cloth. Regnery Publishing, Incorporated, An Eagle Publishing Company. Washington, DC. 1992. 362p. ISBN:0-89526-522-2, ISBN13: 978-0-89526-522-7. Dewey:973.927/092. LCCN:92-004222.
Audience: **f.**

Mervin, David **E881.M47 1996**
George Bush and the Guardianship Presidency. Cloth over Boards. Palgrave Macmillan. New York, NY. 1996. 280p. ISBN:0-312-12961-0, ISBN13: 978-0-312-12961-3. Dewey:973.9/28/092. LCCN:95-053273.
Audience: **f.** *Choice, 1996.*

Mieczkowski, Yanek **E866.M54 2005**
Gerald Ford and the Challenges of The 1970s. Trade Cloth. University Press of Kentucky. Lexington, KY. 2005. 456p.

ISBN:0-8131-2349-6, ISBN13: 978-0-8131-2349-3. Dewey:973.925/092. LCCN:2004-026890.
Audience: **f.** *Choice, 2006.*

Milkis, Sidney M. (Editor), et al. **E756.P77 1999**
Progressivism and the New Democracy. James J. Mileur & Jerome M. Mileur (Editors). Cloth Text. University of Massachusetts Press. Amherst, MA. 1999. 312p. The Political Development of the American Nation Ser., :Studies in Politics and History ISBN:1-55849-192-9, ISBN13: 978-1-55849-192-2. Dewey:320.973/09/041. LCCN:99-019459.
Audience: **f.** *Choice, 2000.*

Miller, Merle **E847.M54 1980**
Lyndon: An Oral Biography. Trade Cloth. Penguin Group (USA) Inc. New York, NY. 1980. xix, 645p. ISBN:0-399-12357-1, ISBN13: 978-0-399-12357-3. Dewey:973.923/092/4. LCCN:80-000273.
Audience: **u,f.** B

Miller, Merle **E814.M54 1974**
Plain Speaking Biography of H. S. Truman. Trade Cloth. Penguin Group (USA) Inc. New York, NY. 1974. 448p. ISBN:0-399-11261-8, ISBN13: 978-0-399-11261-4. Dewey:973.918/092/4. LCCN:73-087198.
Audience: **u,f.** B

Miroff, Bruce **E841.M54 1979**
Pragmatic Illusions: The Presidential Politics of John F. Kennedy. Paper Text. Longman Publishing Group. White Plains, NY. 1976. 334p. ISBN:0-582-28130-X, ISBN13: 978-0-582-28130-1. Dewey:973.922/092/4. LCCN:79-016453.
Audience: **f.** B

Moley, Raymond **E806.M67 1972**
After Seven Years. Paper Text. Da Capo Press, Inc. Cambridge, MA. 1972. 446p. FDR and the Era of the New Deal Ser. ISBN:0-306-70327-0, ISBN13: 978-0-306-70327-0. Dewey:973.917. LCCN:71-168390.
Audience: **f.** B

Morgan, Iwan **E856.M665 2002**
Nixon. Trade Paper. Oxford University Press, Inc. New York, NY. 2002. 224p. Reputations Ser. ISBN:0-340-76032-X, ISBN13: 978-0-340-76032-1. Dewey:973.9/24/092. LCCN:2002-510274.
Audience: **u,f.**

Morley, Morris H. (Editor) **E876.C74 1988**
Crisis and Confrontation: Ronald Reagan's Foreign Policy. Book, Other. Rowman & Littlefield Publishers, Inc. Lanham, MD. 1988. 264p. ISBN:0-8476-7432-0, ISBN13: 978-0-8476-7432-9. Dewey:327.73. LCCN:87-016020.
Audience: **u,f.**

Morris, Dick **E886.2.M67 1999**
Behind the Oval Office: Getting Reelected Against All Odds. Ed. 2. Trade Paper. St. Martin's Press. Gordonville, VA. 1998. 392p. ISBN:1-58063-053-7, ISBN13: 978-1-58063-053-5. Dewey:324.973/0929. LCCN:99-168749.
Audience: **u,f.**

Morris, Kenneth E. **E873.M67 1996**
Jimmy Carter: An American Moralist. Trade Cloth. University of Georgia Press. Athens, GA. 1996. 432p. ISBN:0-8203-1862-0, ISBN13: 978-0-8203-1862-2. Dewey:973.926. LCCN:96-006350.
Audience: **u,f.** *Choice, 1997.*

Morris, Roger **E886.2**
Partners in Power: The Clintons and Their America. Trade Paper. Regnery Publishing, Incorporated, An Eagle Publishing Company. Washington, DC. 1999. 526p. ISBN:0-89526-302-5, ISBN13: 978-0-89526-302-5. Dewey:973.929/092/2.
Audience: **u,f.**

Morris, Roger **E856.M67 1990**
Richard Milhous Nixon: The Rise of an American Politician. Trade Cloth. Henry Holt & Company. New York, NY. 1989. 89p. ISBN:0-8050-1121-8, ISBN13: 978-0-8050-1121-0. Dewey:973.924/092. LCCN:89-007451.
Audience: **u,f.**

Morris, Roger **E855.M67 1977**
Uncertain Greatness: Henry Kissinger and American Foreign Policy. Trade Cloth. HarperCollins Publishers. New York, NY. 1977. viii, 312p. ISBN:0-06-013097-0, ISBN13: 978-0-06-013097-8. Dewey:327.2/092/4. LCCN:75-030339.
Audience: **u,f.** B

Morton, Andrew **E886.2.L5.M67 1999**
Monica's Story. Mass Market. St. Martin's Press. Gordonville, VA. 1999. 385p. ISBN:0-312-97362-4, ISBN13: 978-0-312-97362-9. Dewey:973.9/29/092. LCCN:00-265242.
Audience: **g,l,u,f.**

Murphy, Donald J. **D619.A6497 2005**
America's Entry into World War I. Library Binding. Thomson Gale. Farmington Hills, MI. 2005. At Issue in History Ser. ISBN:0-7377-1791-2, ISBN13: 978-0-7377-1791-4. Dewey:940.3/73. LCCN:2003-049495.
Audience: **l,u,f.**

Murray, Robert K. **E786.M83**
The Politics of Normalcy: Governmental Theory and Practice in the Harding-Coolidge Era. Trade Cloth. Norton. Farnborough, 1973. xii, 162p. ISBN:0-393-05474-8, ISBN13: 978-0-393-05474-3. Dewey:973.91/4/0924. LCCN:72-008354.
Audience: **u,f.** B

Murray, Robert K. **E786**
The Harding Era: Warren G. Harding and His Administration. Katherine E. Speirs (Editor). Trade Cloth. American Political Biography. Newtown, CT. 2000. 626p. Signature Ser. ISBN:0-945707-27-4, ISBN13: 978-0-945707-27-1. Dewey:973.91/4/0924. LCCN:00-133989.
Audience: **u,f.**

Myers, William Starr **E0801.M93**
The Foreign Policies of Herbert Hoover 1929-1933. Trade Paper. Books on Demand. Ann Arbor, MI. 271p. ISBN:0-598-72331-5, ISBN13: 978-0-598-72331-4. Dewey:327.73. LCCN:40-009670.
Audience: **f.**

Nash, George H. **E802**
The Life of Herbert Hoover: The Humanitarian, 1914-1917, Vol. 2. Trade Paper. W. W. Norton & Company, Inc. New York, NY. 1988. 3p. Life of Herbert Hoover Ser., Vol. 2 ISBN:0-393-02550-0, ISBN13: 978-0-393-02550-7. Dewey:973.91/6/0924. LCCN:82-014521.
Audience: **u,f.** *Choice, 1989.*

Nash, George H. **E802**
The Life of Herbert Hoover: The Engineer, 1874-1914. Trade Cloth. W. W. Norton & Company, Inc. New York, NY. 1983. xii, 768p. ISBN:0-393-01634-X, ISBN13: 978-0-393-01634-5. Dewey:973.91/6/0924. LCCN:82-014521.
Audience: **u,f.**

Nash, George H. **E802.N37 1983**
The Life of Herbert Hoover: Master of Emergencies, 1917-1918. Trade Cloth. W. W. Norton & Company, Inc. New York, NY. 1996. 704p. Life of Herbert Hoover Ser., Vol. 3 ISBN:0-393-03841-6, ISBN13: 978-0-393-03841-5. Dewey:973.916092. LCCN:82-014521.
Audience: **u,f.** *Choice, 1997.*

Nash, Gerald D. **E806.N28 1992**
The Crucial Era: The Great Depression and WWII, 1929-1945. Ed. 2. Paper Text. St. Martin's Press. Gordonville, VA. 1991. 213p. Twentieth Century United States History Ser. ISBN:0-312-03631-0, ISBN13: 978-0-312-03631-7. Dewey:973.917. LCCN:90-063553.
Audience: **u,f.**

Neack, Laura **E895.N43 2002**
The New Foreign Policy: U. S. and Comparative Foreign Policy in the 21st Century. Book, Other. Rowman & Littlefield Publishers, Inc. Lanham, MD. 2002. 256p. New Millennium Books in International Studies ISBN:0-7425-0146-9, ISBN13: 978-0-7425-0146-1. Dewey:327.73/009/049. LCCN:2002-002373.
Audience: **f.** *Choice, 2003.*

Nessen, Ron **E865.N47**
It Sure Looks Different from the Inside. Trade Cloth. Bow Historical Books. New Providence, NJ. 1978. xv, 367p. ISBN:0-87223-500-9, ISBN13: 978-0-87223-500-7. Dewey:973.925. LCCN:78-008185.
Audience: **f.** B

Ninkovich, Frank A. **E806.N56 1995**
The Diplomacy of Ideas: U. S. Foreign Policy and Cultural Relations, 1938-1950. Trade Paper. Imprint Publications, Inc. Chicago, IL. 1995. 253p. ISBN:1-879176-23-8, ISBN13: 978-1-879176-23-2. Dewey:327.73. LCCN:95-078628.
Audience: **f.** B

Nixon, Richard M. **E856.A3 1990**
RN: The Memoirs of Richard Nixon. Trade Paper. Simon & Schuster. New York, NY. 1990. 1136p. Richard Nixon Library ISBN:0-671-70741-8, ISBN13: 978-0-671-70741-5. Dewey:973.924/092 B. LCCN:90-031641.
Audience: **g,l,u,f.**

O'Brien, Michael **E842.O23 2005**
John F. Kennedy: A Biography. Cloth over Boards. St. Martin's Press. Gordonville, VA. 2005. 992p. ISBN:0-312-28129-3, ISBN13: 978-0-312-28129-8. Dewey:973.922/092. LCCN:2004-056209.
Audience: **g,l,u,f.** *Choice, 2006.*

Ochoa, George **E881.O23 2005**
America in the 1990s. Trade Cloth. Facts On File, Inc. New York, NY. 2005. 128p. Decades of American History Ser. ISBN:0-8160-5645-5, ISBN13: 978-0-8160-5645-3. Dewey:973.929. LCCN:2005-012439.
Audience: **u,f.**

Offner, Arnold A. **E813.O36 2002**
Another Such Victory: President Truman and the Cold War, 1945-1953. Trade Cloth. Stanford University Press. Palo Alto, CA. 2002. xv, 626p. Stanford Nuclear Age Ser. ISBN:0-8047-4254-5, ISBN13: 978-0-8047-4254-2. Dewey:973.918/092. LCCN:2001-049130.
Audience: **u,f.**

Olson, James S. (Editor) **E841057**
The Historical Dictionary of the 1960s. Book, Other. Greenwood Publishing Group, Inc. Portsmouth, NH. 1999. 560p. ISBN:0-313-29271-X, ISBN13: 978-0-313-29271-2. Dewey:973.923. LCCN:97-002231.
Audience: **u,f.** *Choice, 2000.*

O'Neill, William L. **E813.O55 1986**
American High: The Years of Confidence, 1945-1960. Trade Cloth. Simon & Schuster. New York, NY. 1987. ISBN:0-02-923680-0, ISBN13: 978-0-02-923680-2. Dewey:973.9. LCCN:86-018404.
Audience: **g,u,f.** *Choice, 1987.*

Oppenheimer, Jerry **E886.2.O66 2000**
State of a Union: Inside the Complex Marriage of Bill and Hillary Clinton. Trade Cloth. HarperCollins Publishers. New York, NY. 2000. 320p. ISBN:0-06-019392-1, ISBN13: 978-0-06-019392-8. Dewey:973.929/092/2. LCCN:00-044892.
Audience: **u,f.**

Pach, Chester J. Jr. & Richardson, Elmo **E835.P26 1991**
The Presidency of Dwight D. Eisenhower. Trade Cloth. University Press of Kansas. Lawrence, KS. 1991. xiv, 290p. American Presidency Ser. ISBN:0-7006-0436-7, ISBN13: 978-0-7006-0436-4. Dewey:973.921/092. LCCN:90-045952.
Audience: **u,f.**

Palmer, Frederick **D570.P32**
Newton D. Baker: America at War. Trade Cloth. Periodicals Service Company. Germantown, NY. 1969. ISBN:0-527-69300-6, ISBN13: 978-0-527-69300-8. Dewey:940.373. LCCN:31-028311.
Audience: **f.**

Paper, Lewis J. **E841.P35 1975**
The Promise and the Performance: The Leadership of John F. Trade Cloth. Crown Publishing Group. New York, NY. 1975. xi, 408p. ISBN:0-517-52342-6, ISBN13: 978-0-517-52342-1. Dewey:973.922/092/4. LCCN:75-019456.
Audience: **f.** B

Parenti, Michael J. **E876.P37 1989**
The Sword and the Dollar. Cloth over Boards. St. Martin's Press. Gordonville, VA. 1988. 240p. ISBN:0-312-02295-6, ISBN13: 978-0-312-02295-2. Dewey:327.73. LCCN:88-018162.
Audience: **u,f.** *Choice, 1989.*

Parmet, Herbert S. **E835.P3 1999**
Eisenhauer and the American Crusades. Trade Paper. Transaction Publishers. Somerset, NJ. 1998. 660p. American Presidents Ser. ISBN:0-7658-0437-9, ISBN13: 978-0-7658-0437-2. Dewey:973.92/1/092. LCCN:98-005460.
Audience: **u,f.**

Parmet, Herbert S. **E882.P37 2000**
George Bush: The Life of a Lone Star Yankee. Ed. 2. Trade Paper. Transaction Publishers. Somerset, NJ. 2000. 576p.

ISBN:0-7658-0730-0, ISBN13: 978-0-7658-0730-4. Dewey:973.928/092. LCCN:00-042597.
Audience: **g,u,f.**

Parmet, Herbert S. **E842.P33**
Jack: The Struggles of John F. Trade Cloth. Dell Distributing. Toronto, ON. 1980. xvii, 586p. ISBN:0-8037-4452-8, ISBN13: 978-0-8037-4452-3. Dewey:973.922/092/4. LCCN:80-010506.
Audience: **g,u,f.**

Parmet, Herbert S. **E856.P35 1990**
Richard Nixon and His America. Trade Cloth. Little Brown & Company. New York, NY. 1990. xii, 755p. ISBN:0-316-69232-8, ISBN13: 978-0-316-69232-8. Dewey:973.924/092. LCCN:89-038072.
Audience: **g,u,f.** *Choice, 1990.*

Paterson, Thomas G. **E841.K466 1989**
Kennedy's Quest for Victory: American Foreign Policy, 1961-1963. Trade Paper. Oxford University Press, Inc. New York, NY. 1989. 422p. ISBN:0-19-504584-X, ISBN13: 978-0-19-504584-0. Dewey:973.922/092/4. LCCN:88-022739.
Audience: **l,u,f.** *Choice, 1989.*

Patterson, James T. **E806.P365 1981**
Congressional Conservatism and the New Deal: The Growth of the Conservative Coalition in Congress, 1933 to 1939. Trade Cloth. Greenwood Publishing Group, Inc. Portsmouth, NH. 1981. 369p. ISBN:0-313-22676-8, ISBN13: 978-0-313-22676-2. Dewey:353.03/72. LCCN:81-004195.
Audience: **u,f.**

Perkins, Dexter **E806.P465**
The New Age of Franklin Roosevelt, 1932-1945. Paper Text. Textbook Publishers. Temecula, CA. 2003. 193p. ISBN:0-7581-2575-5, ISBN13: 978-0-7581-2575-0.
Audience: **u,f.**

Perret, Geoffrey **E836.P47 1999**
Eisenhower. Trade Cloth. Random House, Inc. New York, NY. 1999. 704p. ISBN:0-375-50046-4, ISBN13: 978-0-375-50046-6. Dewey:973.921/092. LCCN:99-020101.
Audience: **g,u,f.** *Choice, 2000.*

Perret, Geoffrey **E842.P47 2001**
Jack: A Life Like No Other. Trade Cloth. Random House, Inc. New York, NY. 2001. 480p. ISBN:0-375-50363-3, ISBN13: 978-0-375-50363-4. Dewey:973.922/092. LCCN:2001-019392.
Audience: **g,f.**

Perrett, Geoffrey **E806.P466 1985**
Days of Sadness, Years of Triumph: The American People, 1939-1945. Trade Paper. University of Wisconsin Press. Chicago, IL. 1985. 512p. ISBN:0-299-10394-3, ISBN13: 978-0-299-10394-1. Dewey:973.917. LCCN:72-087594.
Audience: **g,u,f.**

Pershing, John J. **D640.P454 1995**
My Experiences in the First World War. Frank E. Vandiver (Introduction by). Trade Paper. Da Capo Press, Inc. Cambridge, MA. 1995. 624p. ISBN:0-306-80616-9, ISBN13: 978-0-306-80616-2. Dewey:940.4/81/73. LCCN:94-048774.
Audience: **f.**

Reagan, Nancy & Novak, William **E878.R43A3 1989**
My Turn: The Memoirs of Nancy Reagan. Trade Cloth. Random House, Inc. New York, NY. 1989. 400p. ISBN:0-394-56368-9, ISBN13: 978-0-394-56368-8. Dewey:973.927/092. LCCN:89-042786.
Audience: **g,u,f.**

Reagan, Ronald **E877.R33 1990**
An American Life: The Autobiography. Trade Cloth. Simon & Schuster. New York, NY. 1990. 736p. ISBN:0-671-69198-8, ISBN13: 978-0-671-69198-1. Dewey:973.923/092. LCCN:90-010093.
Audience: **g,u,f.**

Reeves, Richard **E866.R46**
A Ford, Not a Lincoln. Trade Cloth. Harcourt Trade Publishers. New York, NY. 1975. 212p. ISBN:0-15-132302-X, ISBN13: 978-0-15-132302-9. Dewey:973.925/092/4. LCCN:75-022195.
Audience: **f.** B

Reeves, Richard **E856**
President Nixon: Alone in the White House. Trade Paper. Simon & Schuster. New York, NY. 2002. 704p. ISBN:0-7432-2719-0, ISBN13: 978-0-7432-2719-3. Dewey:973.924/092. LCCN:2001-034417.
Audience: **f.** *Choice, 2002.*

Reeves, Thomas C. (Editor) **E842.J638 1990**
John F. Kennedy: The Man, the Politician, the President. Trade Paper. Krieger Publishing Company. Melbourne, FL. 1990. 178p. ISBN:0-89464-371-1, ISBN13: 978-0-89464-371-2. Dewey:973.922/092. LCCN:89-033503.
Audience: **f.**

Reichley, A. James **E855.R44**
Conservatives in an Age of Change: The Nixon and Ford Administrations. Trade Cloth. Brookings Institution Press. Washington, DC. 1981. 482p. ISBN:0-8157-7380-3, ISBN13: 978-0-8157-7380-1. Dewey:973.9. LCCN:81-001672.
Audience: **f.** B

Renshon, Stanley A. **E885.R464 1996**
High Hopes: The Clinton Presidency and the Politics of Ambition. Trade Cloth. New York University Press. New York, NY. 1996. 320p. ISBN:0-8147-7463-6, ISBN13: 978-0-8147-7463-2. Dewey:973.9/29. LCCN:95-050236.
Audience: **f.**

Roosevelt, Franklin D. **E806.R7424 1972**
The Complete Presidential Press Conferences of Franklin Delano Roosevelt 1933-1945. Paper Text. Da Capo Press, Inc. Cambridge, MA. 1973. 7000p. FDR and the Era of the New Deal Ser. ISBN:0-306-77500-X, ISBN13: 978-0-306-77500-0. Dewey:973.917. LCCN:78-155953.
Audience: **u,f.** B

Roosevelt, Theodore **E757.A4 2004**
Theodore Roosevelt: Letters and Speeches. Louis Auchincloss (Editor). Trade Cloth. Library of America, The. New York, NY. 2004. 960p. Library of America, Vol. 154 ISBN:1-931082-66-9, ISBN13: 978-1-931082-66-2. Dewey:973.91/1/092. LCCN:2004-044205.
Audience: **f.**

Roosevelt, Theodore **E757.A37 1985**
Theodore Roosevelt: An Autobiography. Elting E. Morison (Introduction by). Trade Paper. Da Capo Press, Inc. Cambridge, MA. 1985. 636p. Quality Paperbacks Ser. ISBN:0-306-80232-5, ISBN13: 978-0-306-80232-4. Dewey:973.91/1/0924. LCCN:84-029218.
Audience: **f.**

Rose, Lisle A. **E813.R56 1999**
The Cold War Comes to Main Street: America in 1950. Trade Cloth. University Press of Kansas. Lawrence, KS. 1999. 416p. ISBN:0-7006-0928-8, ISBN13: 978-0-7006-0928-4. Dewey:973.918. LCCN:98-024677.
Audience: **u,f.** *Choice, 1999.*

Rose, Lisle Abbott **E806.R83 1973**
After Yalta. Trade Cloth. Simon & Schuster. New York, NY. 1973. vi, 216p. ISBN:0-684-13189-7, ISBN13: 978-0-684-13189-4. Dewey:327.73. LCCN:72-007866.
Audience: **f.**

Ross, Irwin **E815**
The Loneliest Campaign: The Truman Victory of 1948. Trade Cloth. Greenwood Publishing Group, Inc. Portsmouth, NH. 1977. 304p. ISBN:0-8371-8353-7, ISBN13: 978-0-8371-8353-4. Dewey:329/.023/730918. LCCN:75-022761.
Audience: **f.**

Rozell, Mark J. & Barilleaux, Ryan J. **E881.R686 2004**
Power and Prudence: The Presidency of George H. W. Bush. Trade Cloth. Texas A&M University Press. College Station, TX. 2004. 224p. The Presidency and Leadership Ser., 17 ISBN:1-58544-291-7, ISBN13: 978-1-58544-291-1. Dewey:973.928/092. LCCN:2003-015131.
Audience: **u,f.** *Choice, 2004.*

Rozell, Mark J. & Wilcox, Clyde (Editors) **E886.C5784 2000**
The Clinton Scandal and the Future of American Government. Trade Paper. Georgetown University Press. Washington, DC. 2000. xxii, 269p. ISBN:0-87840-777-4, ISBN13: 978-0-87840-777-4. Dewey:973.929/092. LCCN:99-036836.
Audience: **f.** *Choice, 2000.*

Safire, William **E855.S23 2005**
Before the Fall: An Inside View of the Pre-Watergate White House. Trade Paper. Transaction Publishers. Somerset, NJ. 2005. 704p. ISBN:1-4128-0466-3, ISBN13: 978-1-4128-0466-0. Dewey:973.924/092. LCCN:2005-041717.
Audience: **f.**

Salinger, Pierre **E842.1.S25 2000**
John F. Kennedy: Commander in Chief: A Profile in Leadership. Trade Cloth. Random House Value Publishing. New York, NY. 2000. 160p. ISBN:0-517-16209-1, ISBN13: 978-0-517-16209-5. Dewey:973.922/092 B. LCCN:00-024506.
Audience: **f.**

Schaller, Michael **E876.S29 1992**
Reckoning with Reagan: America and Its President in the 1980s. Trade Cloth. Oxford University Press, Inc. New York, NY. 1992. 208p. ISBN:0-19-506915-3, ISBN13: 978-0-19-506915-0. Dewey:973.927. LCCN:91-038021.
Audience: **u,f.** *Choice, 1992.*

Schapsmeier, Edward L. & Schapsmeier, Frederick H. **E866.S33 1989**
Gerald R. Ford's Date with Destiny: A Political Biography. Cloth Text. Peter Lang Publishing, Inc. New York, NY. 1989. XXI, 351p. American University Studies, Ser. IX, Vol. 74:History ISBN:0-8204-0961-8, ISBN13: 978-0-8204-0961-0. Dewey:973.925/092/4. LCCN:89-002410.
Audience: **l,u,f.** *Choice, 1990.*

Schell, Jonathan **E855.S36 1976**
The Time of Illusion. Trade Paper. Alfred A. Knopf Inc. New York, NY. 1975. ISBN:0-685-02841-0, ISBN13: 978-0-685-02841-4. Dewey:320.9.
Audience: **f.**

Schier, Steven E. (Editor) **E885.P67 2000**
The Postmodern Presidency: Bill Clinton's Legacy in U. S. Politics. Trade Paper. University of Pittsburgh Press. Pittsburgh, PA. 2000. 304p. Political Science Ser. ISBN:0-8229-5742-6, ISBN13: 978-0-8229-5742-3. Dewey:973.929/092. LCCN:00-009650.
Audience: **f.** *Choice, 2001.*

Schlesinger, Arthur M. Jr. **E806.S344 1988**
The Coming of the New Deal. Ed. 1. Trade Paper. Houghton Mifflin Company Trade & Reference Division. Boston, MA. 1988. 688p. American Heritage Library, Vol. 2 ISBN:0-395-48905-9, ISBN13: 978-0-395-48905-5. Dewey:973.917. LCCN:88-008209.
Audience: **u,f.**

Schlesinger, Arthur M. Jr. **E806.S344 2003**
The Coming of the New Deal: 1933-1935, the Age of Roosevelt. Trade Paper. Houghton Mifflin Company Trade & Reference Division. Boston, MA. 2003. 688p. The Age of Roosevelt Ser., Vol. 2 ISBN:0-618-34086-6, ISBN13: 978-0-618-34086-6. Dewey:973.917/092. LCCN:2003-047859.
Audience: **u,f.**

Schlesinger, Arthur M. Jr. **E806.S347 2003**
The Politics of Upheaval: 1935-1936, the Age of Roosevelt. Trade Paper. Houghton Mifflin Company Trade & Reference Division. Boston, MA. 2003. 768p. The Age of Roosevelt Ser., Vol. 3 ISBN:0-618-34087-4, ISBN13: 978-0-618-34087-3. Dewey:973.917. LCCN:2003-047889.
Audience: **u,f.**

Schlesinger, Arthur M. Jr. **E841.S3 2002**
A Thousand Days: John F. Kennedy in the White House. Trade Paper. Houghton Mifflin Company Trade & Reference Division. Boston, MA. 2002. 1087p. ISBN:0-618-21927-7, ISBN13: 978-0-618-21927-8. Dewey:973.922/092. LCCN:2002-032296.
Audience: **g,l,u,f.**

Schulzinger, Robert D. **E855.S365 1989**
Henry Kissinger: Doctor of Diplomacy. E-Book. NetLibrary, Inc. Boulder, CO. 1989. ISBN:0-585-38273-5, ISBN13: 978-0-585-38273-9. Dewey:327.73.
Audience: **f.**

Schweizer, Peter **E877.2.S35 2002**
Reagan's War: The Epic Story of His Forty Year Struggle and Final Triumph over Communism. Trade Paper. Knopf Publishing Group. New York, NY. 2003. 368p. ISBN:0-385-72228-1, ISBN13: 978-0-385-72228-5. Dewey:327.73. LCCN:2002-067393.
Audience: **u,f.** *Choice, 2003.*

Scott, James M. **E876.S36 1996**
Deciding to Intervene: The Reagan Doctrine and American Foreign Policy. Cloth Text. Duke University Press. Durham, NC.

1996. 344p. ISBN:0-8223-1780-X, ISBN13: 978-0-8223-1780-7. Dewey:327.73. LCCN:95-053041.
Audience: **u,f.** *Choice, 1997.*

Sick, Gary G. **E875.S48 1992**
October Surprise: America's Hostages in Iran and the Election of Ronald Reagan. Trade Paper. Crown Publishing Group. New York, NY. 1992. 306p. ISBN:0-8129-2087-2, ISBN13: 978-0-8129-2087-1. Dewey:973.926.220. LCCN:92-032028.
Audience: **u,f.**

Skidmore, David G. **E872.S556 1996**
Reversing Course: Carter's Foreign Policy, Domestic Politics, and the Failure of Reform. Trade Cloth. Vanderbilt University Press. Nashville, TN. 1996. 256p. ISBN:0-8265-1273-9, ISBN13: 978-0-8265-1273-4. Dewey:327.73/009/047. LCCN:95-045293.
Audience: **u,f.** *Choice, 1996.*

Small, Melvin **E855.S63 1999**
The Presidency of Richard Nixon. Trade Cloth. University Press of Kansas. Lawrence, KS. 1999. xx, 388p. American Presidency Ser. ISBN:0-7006-0973-3, ISBN13: 978-0-7006-0973-4. Dewey:973.924/092. LCCN:99-013148.
Audience: **u,f.** *Choice, 2000.*

Smith, Daniel M. **E768.S62**
The Great Departure: The United States and World War I, 1914-1920. Paper Text. John Wiley & Sons, Inc. Hoboken, NJ. 1965. 221p. America in Crisis Ser. ISBN:0-471-80006-6, ISBN13: 978-0-471-80006-4. Dewey:940.373. LCCN:65-019813.
Audience: **u,f.** B

Smith, Daniel M. **E768.L32.S58 1972**
Robert Lansing and American Neutrality, 1914-1917. Paper Text. Da Capo Press, Inc. Cambridge, MA. 1972. 254p. American Scene, Comments and Commentators Ser. ISBN:0-306-70057-3, ISBN13: 978-0-306-70057-6. Dewey:327/.2/0924. LCCN:79-126610.
Audience: **u,f.**

Smith, Gaddis **E872.S66 1986**
Morality, Reason, and Power: American Diplomacy in the Carter Years. Trade Cloth. Farrar, Straus & Giroux. New York, NY. 1986. 256p. American Century Ser. ISBN:0-8090-7017-0, ISBN13: 978-0-8090-7017-6. Dewey:327.73. LCCN:86-000317.
Audience: **f.** *Choice, 1986.*

Smith, Gene **E801.S6 1984**
The Shattered Dream: Herbert Hoover and the Great Depression. Paper Text. McGraw-Hill Companies, The. New York, NY. 1984. 288p. ISBN:0-07-058474-5, ISBN13: 978-0-07-058474-7. Dewey:973.91/6. LCCN:84-010080.
Audience: **u,f.**

Smith, Richard N. **E802.S68 1984**
An Uncommon Man: The Triumph of Herbert Hoover. Trade Cloth. Simon & Schuster. New York, NY. 1988. 448p. ISBN:0-671-46034-X, ISBN13: 978-0-671-46034-1. Dewey:973.91/6/0924. LCCN:83-027175.
Audience: **u,f.** B

Smythe, Donald **U53.P4S69 1986**
Pershing: General of the Armies. Trade Cloth. Indiana University Press. Bloomington, IN. 1986. 414p. ISBN:0-253-34381-X, ISBN13: 978-0-253-34381-9. Dewey:355/.0092/4. LCCN:85-042529.
Audience: **u,f.**

Sobel, Robert **E792**
Coolidge: An American Enigma. Trade Paper. Regnery Publishing, Incorporated, An Eagle Publishing Company. Washington, DC. 2000. 462p. ISBN:0-89526-247-9, ISBN13: 978-0-89526-247-9. Dewey:973.91/5/092. LCCN:98-014826.
Audience: **u,f.**

Sorensen, Theodore C. **E842.S56 1988**
Kennedy. Trade Paper. HarperCollins Publishers. New York, NY. 1988. 800p. ISBN:0-06-091530-7, ISBN13: 978-0-06-091530-8. Dewey:973.922/092/4. LCCN:88-045175.
Audience: **f.** B

Starr, Kenneth **KF5076.C57S728 1998**
Starr Report: The Findings of Independent Counsel Kenneth Starr on President Clinton and the Lewinsky Affair. Washington Post Staff (Commentaries by). Trade Paper. PublicAffairs. New York, NY. 1998. 480p. ISBN:1-891620-24-X, ISBN13: 978-1-891620-24-9. Dewey:364.1/34. LCCN:98-068030.
Audience: **g,l,u,f.**

Strober, Deborah H. & **E876.S773 2003**
Strober, Gerald S. (Translators)
The Reagan Presidency: An Oral History of the ERA. Trade Paper. Potomac Books, Inc. Dulles, VA. 2003. 640p. ISBN:1-57488-583-9, ISBN13: 978-1-57488-583-5. Dewey:973.927/092. LCCN:2003-004964.
Audience: **u,f.**

Tansill, Charles C. **E806.T3 1975**
Back Door to War: The Roosevelt Foreign Policy 1933-1941. Trade Cloth. Greenwood Publishing Group, Inc. Portsmouth, NH. 1975. 690p. ISBN:0-8371-7990-4, ISBN13: 978-0-8371-7990-2. Dewey:327.73. LCCN:75-001121.
Audience: **f.**

Terkel, Studs **E806**
Hard Times: An Oral History of the Great Depression in America. Trade Paper. New Press, The. New York, NY. 2005. 480p. ISBN:1-56584-656-7, ISBN13: 978-1-56584-656-2. Dewey:973.91. LCCN:86-005077.
Audience: **g,u,f.** B

Theoharis, Athan G. **E813.T48**
Seeds of Repression: Harry S. Truman and the Orgins of McCarthyism. Trade Cloth. Random House, Inc. New York, NY. 1971. xi, 238p. ISBN:0-8129-0169-X, ISBN13: 978-0-8129-0169-6. Dewey:973.918. LCCN:71-116089.
Audience: **u,f.** B

Thornton, Richard C. **E855.T52 2001**
Nixon-Kissinger Years: The Reshaping of American Foreign Policy. Ed. 2. Trade Paper. Paragon House Publishers. Saint Paul, MN. 2001. 428p. ISBN:0-88702-068-2, ISBN13: 978-0-88702-068-1. Dewey:327.73/009/047. LCCN:2001-041430.
Audience: **f.**

Toobin, Jeffrey **E889.T66 2001**
Too Close to Call: The Thirty-Six-Day Battle to Decide the 2000 Election. Trade Cloth. Random House, Inc. New York, NY. 2001. 320p. ISBN:0-375-50708-6, ISBN13: 978-0-375-50708-3. Dewey:324.973/0929. LCCN:2001-277527.
Audience: **g,u,f.**

Toobin, Jeffrey **E886.2.T66 2000**
A Vast Conspiracy: The Real Story of the Sex Scandal That Nearly Brought down a President. Trade Paper. Simon &

Schuster. New York, NY. 2000. 448p. ISBN:0-7432-0413-1, ISBN13: 978-0-7432-0413-2. Dewey:973.929/092. LCCN:00-059524.
Audience: **u,f.**

Trani, Eugene P. & Wilson, David L. **E785.T7**
The Presidency of Warren G. Harding. Trade Cloth. University Press of Kansas. Lawrence, KS. 1977. xii, 232p. American Presidency Ser. ISBN:0-7006-0152-X, ISBN13: 978-0-7006-0152-3. Dewey:973.91/4/0924. LCCN:76-026110.
Audience: **u,f.**

Trask, David F. **D544.T68 1993**
The AEF and Coalition Warmaking, 1917-1918. Trade Cloth. University Press of Kansas. Lawrence, KS. 1993. 248p. Modern War Studies ISBN:0-7006-0619-X, ISBN13: 978-0-7006-0619-1. Dewey:940.4. LCCN:93-007992.
Audience: **u,f.** *Choice, 1994.*

Traxel, David **E743.T73 2005**
Crusader Nation: The United States in Peace and the Great War, 1898-1920. Trade Cloth. Alfred A. Knopf Inc. New York, NY. 2006. 432p. ISBN:0-375-41078-3, ISBN13: 978-0-375-41078-9. Dewey:973.8/9. LCCN:2004-063246.
Audience: **u,f.** *Choice, 2006.*

Truman, Harry S. **E814.A327 1986**
Memoirs of Harry S. Truman: Years of Trial and Hope. Paper Text. Da Capo Press, Inc. Cambridge, MA. 1987. 326p. Quality Paperbacks Ser. ISBN:0-306-80297-X, ISBN13: 978-0-306-80297-3. Dewey:973.918/092/4. LCCN:85-031215.
Audience: **f.**

Truman, Harry S. **E814.A327 1986**
Memoirs, 1945: Year of Decisions. Paper Text. Da Capo Press, Inc. Cambridge, MA. 1986. 304p. Quality Paperbacks Ser. ISBN:0-306-80266-X, ISBN13: 978-0-306-80266-9. Dewey:973.918/092/4. LCCN:85-031215.
Audience: **f.**

Truman, Harry S. & Koenig, Louis W. **E813**
The Truman Administration, Its Principles and Practice. Trade Cloth. Greenwood Publishing Group, Inc. Portsmouth, NH. 1979. 394p. ISBN:0-313-21186-8, ISBN13: 978-0-313-21186-7. Dewey:320.9/73/0918. LCCN:78-012249.
Audience: **f.**

Tumulty, Joseph P. **E767.T9 1970**
Woodrow Wilson As I Know Him. Trade Cloth. A M S Press, Inc. New York, NY. 1970. xvi, 553p. ISBN:0-404-06527-9, ISBN13: 978-0-404-06527-0. Dewey:973.91/3/0924. LCCN:71-127912.
Audience: **f.**

Ungar, Sanford J. **KF224.N39.U54 1972**
The Papers and the Papers; an Account of the Legal and Political Battle over the Pentagon Papers. Trade Cloth. Penguin Group (USA) Inc. New York, NY. 1972. 319p. ISBN:0-525-17455-9, ISBN13: 978-0-525-17455-4. Dewey:323.44/5/0973. LCCN:77-190699.
Audience: **u,f.**

Unger, Irwin & Unger, Debi **E847.U48 1999**
LBJ: A Life. Trade Cloth. John Wiley & Sons, Inc. Hoboken, NJ. 1999. 592p. ISBN:0-471-17602-8, ISBN13: 978-0-471-17602-2. Dewey:973.9/23/092. LCCN:99-022475.
Audience: **u,f.**

Vance, Cyrus R. **E872.V36 1983**
Hard Choices: Four Critical Years in Managing America's Foreign Policy. Trade Cloth. Simon & Schuster. New York, NY. 1983. 320p. ISBN:0-671-44339-9, ISBN13: 978-0-671-44339-9. Dewey:327.73. LCCN:83-000592.
Audience: **u,f.**

Vandiver, Frank E. **E181.P575**
Black Jack: The Life and Times of John J. Pershing, Set. Trade Cloth. Texas A&M University Press. College Station, TX. 1977. 1246p. ISBN:0-89096-024-0, ISBN13: 978-0-89096-024-0. Dewey:355.3/31/0924. LCCN:76-051729.
Audience: **u,f.**

Walsh, Lawrence E. **E876.W33 1997**
Firewall: The Iran-Contra Conspiracy and Cover-Up. Trade Cloth. W. W. Norton & Company, Inc. New York, NY. 1997. 544p. ISBN:0-393-04034-8, ISBN13: 978-0-393-04034-0. Dewey:955.05/42. LCCN:96-048443.
Audience: **f.** *Choice, 1997.*

Walsh, Lawrence E. **E876.W35 1994**
Iran-Contra: The Final Report. Trade Paper. Crown Publishing Group. New York, NY. 1994. 592p. ISBN:0-8129-2456-8, ISBN13: 978-0-8129-2456-5. Dewey:973.927. LCCN:94-007172.
Audience: **f.** *Choice, 1994.*

Weisbrot, Robert **E841.W44 2001**
Maximum Danger: Kennedy, the Missiles, and the Crisis of American Confidence. Trade Cloth. Ivan R. Dee Publisher. Blue Ridge Summit, PA. 2001. 288p. ISBN:1-56663-392-3, ISBN13: 978-1-56663-392-5. Dewey:973.922. LCCN:2001-037220.
Audience: **f.** *Choice, 2002.*

Westbrook, Robert B. **E806.W4545 2004**
Why We Fought: Forging American Obligations in World War II. Trade Cloth. Smithsonian Institution Press. Washington, DC. 2004. 208p. ISBN:1-58834-130-5, ISBN13: 978-1-58834-130-3. Dewey:940.53/73. LCCN:2004-041670.
Audience: **f.**

White, John Kenneth **E885.W48 1998**
Still Seeing Red: How the Cold War Shapes the New American Politics. Trade Paper. Westview Press. Boulder, CO. 1998. 448p. Transforming American Politics Ser. ISBN:0-8133-1889-0, ISBN13: 978-0-8133-1889-9. Dewey:320.973/09/049. LCCN:98-028936.
Audience: **f.** *Choice, 1998.*

White, William Allen **JC423**
A Puritan in Babylon: The Story of Calvin Coolidge. Trade Paper. Simon Publications, Inc. 2001. 460p. ISBN:1-931541-52-3, ISBN13: 978-1-931541-52-7. Dewey:321.8.
Audience: **f.**

Wicker, Tom **E882.W53 2004**
George Herbert Walker Bush: A Penguin Life. Trade Cloth. Penguin Group (USA) Inc. New York, NY. 2004. 240p. ISBN:0-670-03303-0, ISBN13: 978-0-670-03303-4. Dewey:973.928/092. LCCN:2003-057633.
Audience: **g,u,f.**

Wicker, Tom **E842.W54 1991**
JFK and LBJ: The Influence of Personality upon Prejudice. Trade Paper. Ivan R. Dee Publisher. Blue Ridge Summit, PA. 1991. 297p. ISBN:0-929587-59-6, ISBN13: 978-0-929587-59-2. Dewey:973.922/092/2. LCCN:90-027786.
Audience: **f.**

Wicker, Tom **E856.W52 1995**
One of Us: Richard Nixon and the American Dream. Trade Cloth. Alfred A. Knopf Inc. New York, NY. 1995. 731p. ISBN:0-679-75817-8, ISBN13: 978-0-679-75817-4. Dewey:973.924/092. LCCN:95-135810.
Audience: **u,f.** *Choice, 1991.*

Wills, Garry **E856**
Nixon Agonistes: The Crisis of the Self-Made Man. Trade Paper. Houghton Mifflin Company Trade & Reference Division. Boston, MA. 2002. 640p. ISBN:0-618-13432-8, ISBN13: 978-0-618-13432-8. Dewey:973.924/092. LCCN:2002-191291.
Audience: **f.**

Wilson, Joan H. **E802.W53**
Herbert Hoover: Forgotten Progressive. Paper Text. Waveland Press, Inc. Prospect Heights, IL. 1992. 307p. ISBN:0-88133-705-6, ISBN13: 978-0-88133-705-1. Dewey:973.916092.
Audience: **u,f.**

Witcover, Jules **E868.W57 1977**
Marathon: The Pursuit of the Presidency, 1972-1976. Trade Cloth. Penguin Group (USA) Inc. New York, NY. 1977. xvii, 684p. ISBN:0-670-45461-3, ISBN13: 978-0-670-45461-7. Dewey:329/.023/730925. LCCN:77-004387.
Audience: **f.**

Wolf, Thomas P. (Editor), et al. **E806.F6915 2001**
Franklin D. Roosevelt and Congress: The New Deal and Its Aftermath. William D. Pederson & Byron W. Daynes (Editors), Richard Lowitt, Dennis N. Mihelich, Matthew Ware Coulter, Marc J. Dollinger, Nancy Beck Young, James P. Richards, Joseph Edward Lee, Stefano Luconi, Arthur R. Williams, Karl F. Johnson & Michael P. Barrett (Contribution by). Trade Cloth. M. E. Sharpe Inc. Armonk, NY. 2001. 212p. Library of Franklin D. Roosevelt Studies, Vol. 2 ISBN:0-7656-0622-4, ISBN13: 978-0-7656-0622-8. Dewey:973.917. LCCN:99-087719.
Audience: **f.**

Woodward, Bob **E885.W66 1994**
The Agenda: Inside the Clinton White House. Trade Cloth. Thomson Gale. Farmington Hills, MI. 1994. 16p. ISBN:1-56895-122-1, ISBN13: 978-1-56895-122-5. Dewey:973.9/29. LCCN:94-035160.
Audience: **g,u,f.**

Woodward, Bob **E888**
The Choice. Trade Paper. Simon & Schuster, Inc. New York, NY. 2005. 480p. ISBN:0-7432-8514-X, ISBN13: 978-0-7432-8514-8. Dewey:324.9/73/0929.
Audience: **u,f.**

Woodward, Bob **E881.W66 1991**
The Commanders. Trade Cloth. Simon & Schuster. New York, NY. 1991. 384p. ISBN:0-671-41367-8, ISBN13: 978-0-671-41367-5. Dewey:973.928/092. LCCN:91-013037.
Audience: **u,f.**

Wynn, Neil A. **E780.W96 1986**
From Progressivism to Prosperity: World War I and American Society. Trade Cloth. Holmes & Meier Publishers, Inc. Teaneck, NJ. 1986. 268p. ISBN:0-8419-0767-6, ISBN13: 978-0-8419-0767-6. Dewey:940.3/73. LCCN:86-019568.
Audience: **u,f.** *Choice, 1987.*

Young, Roland A. **E806.Y69 1972**
Congressional Politics in the Second World War. Paper Text. Da Capo Press, Inc. Cambridge, MA. 1972. 282p. FDR and the Era of the New Deal Ser. ISBN:0-306-70442-0, ISBN13: 978-0-306-70442-0. Dewey:320.9/73/0917. LCCN:70-038757.
Audience: **f.** B

Zelikow, Philip **E841.K4655 2002**
The Kennedy Tapes. Trade Paper. W. W. Norton & Company, Inc. New York, NY. 2002. 320p. ISBN:0-393-32259-9, ISBN13: 978-0-393-32259-0. Dewey:973.922. LCCN:2001-044484.
Audience: **f.**

Zinn, Howard (Editor) **E806.N425 2003**
New Deal Thought. Trade Cloth. Hackett Publishing Company, Inc. Indianapolis, IN. 2003. 431p. ISBN:0-87220-686-6, ISBN13: 978-0-87220-686-1. Dewey:320.973. LCCN:2003-056164.
Audience: **u,f.**

United States > American History, by Period > 21st Century

Allman, T. D. **E902.A445 2004**
Rogue State: America at War with the World. Trade Paper. Avalon Publishing Group. New York, NY. 2004. 416p. ISBN:1-56025-562-5, ISBN13: 978-1-56025-562-8. Dewey:327.73/009/0511. LCCN:2003-064671.
Audience: **u,f.**

Bacevich, Andrew J. **E902.I57 2003**
The Imperial Tense: Prospects and Problems of American Empire. Trade Cloth. Ivan R. Dee Publisher. Blue Ridge Summit, PA. 2003. 288p. ISBN:1-56663-532-2, ISBN13: 978-1-56663-532-5. Dewey:327.73. LCCN:2003-048484.
Audience: **f.** *Choice, 2004.*

Bolton, M. Kent **E902.B65 2004**
U. S. Foreign Policy and International Politics: George W. Bush, 9/11, and the the Global Terrorist Hydra. Trade Paper. Prentice Hall PTR. Upper Saddle River, NJ. 2004. 224p. Prentice Hall Studies in International Relations ISBN:0-13-117439-8, ISBN13: 978-0-13-117439-9. Dewey:327.73/009/0511. LCCN:2004-015994.
Audience: **u,f.**

Burke, John P. **E903.3.B86 2004**
Becoming President: The Bush Transition, 2000-2003. Library Binding. Lynne Rienner Publishers, Inc. Boulder, CO. 2004. 250p. ISBN:1-58826-292-8, ISBN13: 978-1-58826-292-9. Dewey:973.931/092. LCCN:2004-001255.
Audience: **f.** *Choice, 2005.*

Campbell, Colin B. & Rockman, Bert A. (Editors) **E902.G47 2004**
The George W. Bush Presidency: Appraisals and Prospects. Trade Paper. CQ Press. Washington, DC. 2003. 376p. ISBN:1-56802-909-8, ISBN13: 978-1-56802-909-2. Dewey:973.931/092. LCCN:2003-025522.
Audience: **u,f.**

Caraley, Demetrios (Editor) **E902.S47 2002**
September 11, Terrorist Attacks, and U. S. Foreign Policy. Perfect. Academy of Political Science. New York, NY. 2002. x, 200p. ISBN:1-884853-01-3, ISBN13: 978-1-884853-01-2. Dewey:327.73/009/0511. LCCN:2002-010120.
Audience: **f.**

Crotty, William J. (Editor) **E902.P65 2004**
The Politics of Terror: The U. S. Response to 9/11. Trade Cloth. Northeastern University Press. Boston, MA. 2003. 256p. The Northeastern Series on Democratization and Political Development ISBN:1-55553-577-1, ISBN13: 978-1-55553-577-3. Dewey:973.931. LCCN:2003-010692.
Audience: **u,f.** *Choice, 2004.*

Dolan, Chris J. & Glad, Betty (Editors) **E902.S77 2004**
Striking First: The Preventive War Doctrine and the Reshaping of U. S. Foreign Policy. Trade Cloth. Palgrave Macmillan. New York, NY. 2004. 240p. ISBN:1-4039-6548-X, ISBN13: 978-1-4039-6548-6. Dewey:327.73/009/0511. LCCN:2004-049759.
Audience: **f.**

Dyer, Gwynne **E903.D93 2003**
Ignorant Armies: Sliding into War in Iraq. Trade Paper. McClelland & Stewart. Toronto, ON. 2003. 200p. ISBN:0-7710-2977-2, ISBN13: 978-0-7710-2977-6. Dewey:956.7044/3. LCCN:2003-430421.
Audience: **u,f.**

Friedman, George **E902.F76 2004**
America's Secret War: Inside the Hidden Worldwide Struggle Between the United States and Its Enemies. Trade Cloth. Doubleday Canada, Ltd. Toronto, ON. 2004. 368p. ISBN:0-385-51245-7, ISBN13: 978-0-385-51245-9. Dewey:327.73009/0511. LCCN:2004-055287.
Audience: **f.** *Choice, 2005.*

Friedman, Thomas L. **HM846.F74 2005**
The World Is Flat: A Brief History of the Twenty-First Century. Oliver Wyman (Read by). Cloth over Boards. Farrar, Straus & Giroux. New York, NY. 2005. 496p. ISBN:0-374-29288-4, ISBN13: 978-0-374-29288-1. Dewey:303.48/33. LCCN:2004-028685.
Audience: **g,u,f.** *Choice, 2006.*

Frum, David **E903.F78 2005**
The Right Man: An Inside Account of the Bush White House. Trade Paper. Random House Adult Trade Publishing Group. New York, NY. 2005. 352p. ISBN:0-8129-7490-5, ISBN13: 978-0-8129-7490-4. Dewey:973.931/092.
Audience: **u,f.**

Gokay, Bulent & Walker, R. B. J. (Editors) **E902**
11 September 2001: War, Terror and Judgement. Ed. 2. Trade Cloth. Taylor & Francis Group. Abingdon, 2003. 160p. ISBN:0-7146-5505-8, ISBN13: 978-0-7146-5505-5. Dewey:973.931. LCCN:2003-043984.
Audience: **f.**

Greenstein, Fred I. **E902.G46 2003**
The George W. Bush Presidency: An Early Assessment. Trade Cloth. Johns Hopkins University Press. Baltimore, MD. 2003. 336p. ISBN:0-8018-7845-4, ISBN13: 978-0-8018-7845-9. Dewey:973.931/092. LCCN:2003-017428.
Audience: **u,f.** *Choice, 2004.*

Gregg, Gary L. & Rozell, Mark J. (Editors) **E902.C66 2003**
Considering the Bush Presidency. Cloth Text. Oxford University Press, Inc. New York, NY. 2003. 224p. ISBN:0-19-516681-7, ISBN13: 978-0-19-516681-1. Dewey:973.931/092. LCCN:2003-048638.
Audience: **u,f.**

Haass, Richard N. **E902.H22 2005**
The Opportunity: America's Moment to Alter History's Course. Saddle Stitched, Cloth over Boards, Dust Jacket. PublicAffairs. New York, NY. 2005. 242p. ISBN:1-58648-276-9, ISBN13: 978-1-58648-276-3. Dewey:327.73/009/051. LCCN:2005-045807.
Audience: **f.**

Hersh, Seymour M. **DS79.76.H465 2004**
Chain of Command: The Road from 9/11 to Abu Ghraib. Trade Cloth. HarperCollins Publishers. New York, NY. 2004. 416p. ISBN:0-06-019591-6, ISBN13: 978-0-06-019591-5. Dewey:956.7044/37. LCCN:2004-541382.
Audience: **g,u,f.**

Jervis, Robert **E902.J47 2005**
American Foreign Policy in a New Era. Paper over Boards. Routledge. New York, NY. 2005. 200p. ISBN:0-415-95100-3, ISBN13: 978-0-415-95100-5. Dewey:327.73. LCCN:2004-028638.
Audience: **f.**

Kilpatrick, Joel **E903.3.M3635 2004**
The Faith of George W. Bush. Trade Cloth. Strang Communications Company. Lake Mary, FL. 2004. 128p. ISBN:1-59185-456-3, ISBN13: 978-1-59185-456-2. Dewey:973.931/092. LCCN:2003-027770.
Audience: **f.**

Lennon, Alexander T. J. (Editor) **E902.T48 2002**
What Does the World Want from America?: International Perspectives on U. S. Foreign Policy. Trade Paper. MIT Press. Cambridge, MA. 2002. 200p. A Washington Quarterly Reader Ser. ISBN:0-262-62167-3, ISBN13: 978-0-262-62167-0. Dewey:327.73/09/0511. LCCN:2002-026486.
Audience: **f.**

Lindsay, James M. & Daalder, Ivo H. **E902.D23 2005**
America Unbound: The Bush Revolution in Foreign Policy. Trade Paper, Perfect. John Wiley & Sons, Inc. Hoboken, NJ. 2005. 272p. ISBN:0-471-74150-7, ISBN13: 978-0-471-74150-3. Dewey:327.73/009/0511. LCCN:2005-013207.
Audience: **f.**

Lindsay, James & Daalder, Ivo **E902.D23 2003**
America Unbound: The Bush Revolution in Foreign Policy. Trade Cloth. Brookings Institution Press. Washington, DC. 2003. 246p. ISBN:0-8157-1688-5, ISBN13: 978-0-8157-1688-4. Dewey:327.73. LCCN:2003-016767.
Audience: **u,f.** *Choice, 2004.*

Mann, James **E902.M345 2004**
Rise of the Vulcans: The History of Bush's War Cabinet. Trade Cloth. Penguin Group (USA) Inc. New York, NY. 2004. 400p.

ISBN:0-670-03299-9, ISBN13: 978-0-670-03299-0. Dewey:327.73/0092/2. LCCN:2003-065765.
Audience: **u,f.**

McMahon, Kevin J. (Editor), et al. **E902.T7 2004**
Transformed by Crisis: The Presidency of George W. Bush and American Politics. Jon Kraus & David M. Rankin (Editors). Cloth over Boards. Palgrave Macmillan. New York, NY. 2004. 224p. ISBN:1-4039-6592-7, ISBN13: 978-1-4039-6592-9. Dewey:973.931/092. LCCN:2004-040008.
Audience: **f.** *Choice, 2005.*

Moens, Alexander **E902.M625 2004**
The Foreign Policy of George W. Bush: Values, Strategy and Loyalty. Trade Cloth. Ashgate Publishing, Ltd. Aldershot, 2004. 236p. ISBN:0-7546-4274-7, ISBN13: 978-0-7546-4274-9. Dewey:327.73/009/0511. LCCN:2004-013268.
Audience: **f.** *Choice, 2005.*

Moore, James **E902.M64 2004**
Bush's War for Reelection: Iraq, the White House, and the People. E-Book. John Wiley & Sons, Inc. Hoboken, NJ. 2004. 352p. ISBN:0-471-67512-1, ISBN13: 978-0-471-67512-9. Dewey:956.7044/3.
Audience: **f.**

Rozell, Mark J. & Barilleaux, Ryan J. **E881.R686 2004**
Power and Prudence: The Presidency of George H. W. Bush. Trade Cloth. Texas A&M University Press. College Station, TX. 2004. 224p. The Presidency and Leadership Ser., 17 ISBN:1-58544-291-7, ISBN13: 978-1-58544-291-1. Dewey:973.928/092. LCCN:2003-015131.
Audience: **u,f.** *Choice, 2004.*

Schier, Steven E. (Editor) **E902.H54 2004**
High Risk and Big Ambition: The Presidency of George W. Bush. Trade Cloth. University of Pittsburgh Press. Pittsburgh, PA. 2004. 256p. ISBN:0-8229-4234-8, ISBN13: 978-0-8229-4234-4. Dewey:973.931/092. LCCN:2003-027967.
Audience: **u,f.** *Choice, 2005.*

Schweizer, Peter & Schweizer, Rochelle **E904.B87S39 2004**
The Bushes: Portrait of a Dynasty. Trade Cloth. Doubleday Canada, Ltd. Toronto, ON. 2004. 592p. ISBN:0-385-49863-2, ISBN13: 978-0-385-49863-0. Dewey:929/.2/0973. LCCN:2004-045122.
Audience: **g,u,f.**

Street, Paul **E902**
Empire and Inequality (H): America and the World Since 9/11. Library Binding. Paradigm Publishers. Boulder, CO. 2004. 208p. ISBN:1-59451-058-X, ISBN13: 978-1-59451-058-8. Dewey:327.73009051.
Audience: **f.**

Unger, Craig **E903.3.U54 2004**
House of Bush, House of Saud: The Secret Relationship Between the World's Two Most Powerful Dynasties. Trade Cloth. Simon & Schuster. New York, NY. 2004. 368p. ISBN:0-7432-5337-X, ISBN13: 978-0-7432-5337-6. Dewey:327.730538. LCCN:2004-274217.
Audience: **u,f.**

Woodward, Bob **E902**
Bush at War: Inside the Bush White House. Trade Cloth. Simon & Schuster. New York, NY. 2002. 400p. ISBN:0-7432-0473-5, ISBN13: 978-0-7432-0473-6. Dewey:973.931. LCCN:2002-042829.
Audience: **g,u,f.**

Woodward, Bob **DS79.76**
Plan of Attack. Trade Cloth. Simon & Schuster, Inc. New York, NY. 2004. 480p. ISBN:0-7432-5547-X, ISBN13: 978-0-7432-5547-9. Dewey:956.7044/31. LCCN:2004-351204.
Audience: **g,u,f.**

United States > U.S. Local History

Riedling, Marlow (Compiled by) **E180.I58 2005**
Internet Sources on Each U. S. State: Selected Sites for Classroom and Library. Paper Text. McFarland & Company, Incorporated Publishers. Jefferson, NC. 2005. 383p. ISBN:0-7864-2108-8, ISBN13: 978-0-7864-2108-4. Dewey:025.06/973. LCCN:2005-003511.
Audience: **g,l,u,f.**

Thomson Gale Staff **E174**
Worldmark Encyclopedia of the States. Ed. 7. Trade Cloth. Thomson Gale. Farmington Hills, MI. 2006. 900p. ISBN:1-4144-1058-1, ISBN13: 978-1-4144-1058-6. Dewey:973.003.
Audience: **g,l,u,f.**

United States > U.S. Local History > New England

Adair, John Eric **BX9334.2**
Founding Fathers: The Puritans in England and America. Trade Cloth. J. M. Dent & Sons. London, 1982. xii, 302p. ISBN:0-460-04421-4, ISBN13: 978-0-460-04421-9. Dewey:285/.9/0942. LCCN:82-194357.
Audience: **u,f.**

Bremer, Francis J. **F7.B77 1995**
The Puritan Experiment: New England Society from Bradford to Edwards. Trade Paper. University Press of New England. Lebanon, NH. 1995. 283p. ISBN:0-87451-728-1, ISBN13: 978-0-87451-728-6. Dewey:974/.02. LCCN:95-018209.
Audience: **u,f.**

Conforti, Joseph A. **F4.C76 2001**
Imagining New England: Explorations of Regional Identity from the Pilgrims to the Mid-Twentieth Century. Trade Cloth. University of North Carolina Press. Chapel Hill, NC. 2001. 400p. ISBN:0-8078-2625-1, ISBN13: 978-0-8078-2625-6. Dewey:974. LCCN:2001-027027.
Audience: **u,f.** *Choice, 2002.*

Deetz, James **E78.N5**
In Small Things Forgotten: The Archaeology of Early American Life. Trade Paper. Doubleday Publishing. New York, NY. 1996. 304p. ISBN:0-385-48399-6, ISBN13: 978-0-385-48399-5. Dewey:974/.01. LCCN:96-001739.
Audience: **f.**

Federal Writers' Project Staff & Writers Program Staff **F2.3**
Here's New England: A Guide to Vacationland. Library Binding. Reprint Services Company. Temecula, CA. 1989. American Guide Ser. ISBN:0-7812-1063-1, ISBN13: 978-0-7812-1063-8. Dewey:917.4/04/4.
Audience: **f.**

Foster, Stephen **F7.F758**
The Long Argument: English Puritanism and the Shaping of New England Culture, 1570-1700. Trade Paper. University of North Carolina Press. Chapel Hill, NC. 1996. 415p. ISBN:0-8078-4583-3, ISBN13: 978-0-8078-4583-7. Dewey:974/.02. LCCN:90-041564.
Audience: **f.** *Choice, 1991.*

Gura, Philip F. **F7.G87 1984**
A Glimpse of Sion's Glory: Puritan Radicalism in New England, 1620-1660. Trade Cloth. Wesleyan University Press. Middletown, CT. 1990. 417p. ISBN:0-8195-5095-7, ISBN13: 978-0-8195-5095-8. Dewey:974/.02. LCCN:83-021831.
Audience: **f.** B

Haffenden, Philip Spencer **E183.8.G7**
New England in the English Nation, 1689-1713. Trade Cloth. Oxford University Press, Inc. New York, NY. 1974. xiii, 326p. ISBN:0-19-821124-4, ISBN13: 978-0-19-821124-2. Dewey:301.29/74/042. LCCN:74-188338.
Audience: **u,f.** B

Jennings, Francis **F7J46 1976**
The Invasion of America: Indians, Colonialism, and the Cant of Conquest. Trade Paper. W. W. Norton & Company, Inc. New York, NY. 1976. 384p. Norton Library, Vol. N830 ISBN:0-393-00830-4, ISBN13: 978-0-393-00830-2. Dewey:974/.02. LCCN:76-025451.
Audience: **u,f.** B

Johnson, Claudia Durst **F7**
Daily Life in Colonial New England. Cloth Text. Greenwood Publishing Group, Inc. Portsmouth, NH. 2002. 248p. Daily Life Through History Ser. ISBN:0-313-32678-9, ISBN13: 978-0-313-32678-3. Dewey:974/.02. LCCN:00-061721.
Audience: **l,u,f.**

Jones, James W. **F7.J66**
The Shattered Synthesis: New England Puritanism Before the Great Awakening. Trade Paper. Books on Demand. Ann Arbor, MI. 219p. ISBN:0-8357-8320-0, ISBN13: 978-0-8357-8320-0. Dewey:974.4/02/0922. LCCN:73-077154.
Audience: **f.**

Mather, Cotton (Editor) **F7.M42**
Magnalia Christi Americana;. Trade Cloth. Scholarly Publishing Office, University of Michigan Library. Ann Arbor, MI. 2004. ISBN:1-4181-3257-8, ISBN13: 978-1-4181-3257-6. Dewey:974/.02.
Audience: **f.**

Miller, Perry G. **F7.M54 1983**
The New England Mind: From Colony to Province. Trade Paper. Harvard University Press. Cambridge, MA. 1983. 528p. ISBN:0-674-61301-5, ISBN13: 978-0-674-61301-0. Dewey:974. LCCN:82-020740.
Audience: **u,f.**

Miller, Perry G. **F7.M56 1983**
The New England Mind: The Seventeenth Century. Trade Paper. Harvard University Press. Cambridge, MA. 1983. 542p. ISBN:0-674-61306-6, ISBN13: 978-0-674-61306-5. Dewey:974/.02. LCCN:82-023291.
Audience: **u,f.**

Morgan, Edmund S. **F7.M8 1980**
The Puritan Family: Religion and Domestic Relations in Seventeenth-Century New England. Trade Cloth. Greenwood Publishing Group, Inc. Portsmouth, NH. 1980. 196p. ISBN:0-313-22703-9, ISBN13: 978-0-313-22703-5. Dewey:974/.02. LCCN:80-018819.
Audience: **u,f.**

Morison, Samuel Eliot **F7.M817 1980**
The Intellectual Life of Colonial New England. Trade Cloth. Greenwood Publishing Group, Inc. Portsmouth, NH. 1980. 288p. ISBN:0-313-22032-8, ISBN13: 978-0-313-22032-6. Dewey:974. LCCN:79-020246.
Audience: **u,f.** B

Parks, Roger (Editor) **Z1251.E1N454 1995**
Bibliographies of New England History: Further Additions, to 1994. Library Binding. University Press of New England. Lebanon, NH. 1995. 319p. Bibliographies of New England History Ser., No. 9 ISBN:0-87451-714-1, ISBN13: 978-0-87451-714-9. Dewey:016.974. LCCN:95-015340.
Audience: **f.**

Parks, Roger (Editor) **Z1251.E1N454 1989**
New England: Additions to the 6 State Bibliographies. Library Binding. University Press of New England. Lebanon, NH. 1989. 632p. Bibliographies of New England History Ser., Vol. 8 ISBN:0-87451-497-5, ISBN13: 978-0-87451-497-1. Dewey:016.974. LCCN:89-040232.
Audience: **f.** *Choice, 1990.*

Parks, Roger (Editor) **Z1251.E1N452 1989**
New England: A Bibliography of Its History. David D. Hall & Alan Taylor (Contribution by). Library Binding. University Press of New England. Lebanon, NH. 1989. 264p. Bibliographies of New England History Ser., Vol. 7 ISBN:0-87451-496-7, ISBN13: 978-0-87451-496-4. Dewey:016.974. LCCN:89-040231.
Audience: **f.** *Choice, 1990.*

Russell, Howard S. **HD1773.A2R87**
A Long, Deep Furrow: 3 Centuries of Farming in New England. Trade Cloth. Books on Demand. Ann Arbor, MI. 688p. ISBN:0-608-16641-3, ISBN13: 978-0-608-16641-4. Dewey:338.1/0974. LCCN:73-091314.
Audience: **u,f.**

Shipton, Clifford K. **F3.S43 1995**
New England Life in the 18th Century. Trade Paper. Harvard University Press. Cambridge, MA. 1995. 656p. ISBN:0-674-61251-5, ISBN13: 978-0-674-61251-8. Dewey:974/.02/0922. LCCN:95-220885.
Audience: **f.**

Sletcher, Michael (Editor) **F4.N47 2004**
New England: The Greenwood Encyclopedia of American Regional Cultures. William Ferris (Foreword by). Trade Cloth. Greenwood Publishing Group, Inc. Portsmouth, NH. 2004. 400p. The Greenwood Encyclopedia of American Regional Cultures

Ser. ISBN:0-313-32753-X, ISBN13: 978-0-313-32753-7. Dewey:974/.003. LCCN:2004-056058.
Audience: **g,l,u,f.**

Vaughan, Alden T. **F7.V3 1995**
New England Frontier: Puritans and Indians, 1620-1675. Ed. 3. Trade Paper. University of Oklahoma Press. Norman, OK. 1995. 492p. ISBN:0-8061-2718-X, ISBN13: 978-0-8061-2718-7. Dewey:974/.02. LCCN:94-035277.
Audience: **u,f.** B

Vaughan, Alden T. (Editor) **F7.P987 1997**
The Puritan Tradition in America, 1620-1730. Trade Paper. University Press of New England. Lebanon, NH. 1997. 384p. Library of New England ISBN:0-87451-852-0, ISBN13: 978-0-87451-852-8. Dewey:285/.9/0974. LCCN:97-023558.
Audience: **u,f.** B

Warren, Austin **F3.W3**
New England Saints. Paper Text. Textbook Publishers. Temecula, CA. 2003. v, 192p. ISBN:0-7581-2122-9, ISBN13: 978-0-7581-2122-6. Dewey:917.4.
Audience: **f.** B

United States > U.S. Local History > New England > Maine. New Hampshire. Vermont

Clark, Charles E. (Editor), et al. **F24**
Maine in the Early Republic: From Revolution to Statehood. James S. Leamon & Karen Bowden (Editors). Trade Paper. University Press of New England. Lebanon, NH. 1989. 280p. ISBN:0-87451-506-8, ISBN13: 978-0-87451-506-0. Dewey:974.1/03. LCCN:87-040510.
Audience: **u,f.**

Daniell, Jere R. **F37.D25 1981**
Colonial New Hampshire: A History. Library Binding. Kraus International Publications. Hackensack, NJ. 1982. 279p. History of the American Colonies Ser. ISBN:0-527-18715-1, ISBN13: 978-0-527-18715-6. Dewey:974.2/02. LCCN:81-006046.
Audience: **u,f.** B

Duffy, John J. (Editor), et al. **F47.V46 2003**
The Vermont Encyclopedia. Samuel B. Hand & Ralph H. Orth (Editors). Trade Cloth. University Press of New England. Lebanon, NH. 2005. xvi, 330p. ISBN:1-58465-086-9, ISBN13: 978-1-58465-086-7. Dewey:974.3/003. LCCN:2003-010744.
Audience: **l,u,f.** *Choice, 2004.*

Duffy, John & Feeney, Vincent **F49.D84 2000**
Vermont: An Illustrated History. Trade Cloth. American Historical Press. Sun Valley, CA. 2000. 296p. ISBN:1-892724-08-1, ISBN13: 978-1-892724-08-3. Dewey:974.3. LCCN:00-106471.
Audience: **l,u,f.**

Duncan, Roger **F27.A75D86 2002**
Coastal Maine: A Maritime History. Trade Paper. Countryman Press. Woodstock, VT. 2002. 576p. ISBN:0-88150-555-2, ISBN13: 978-0-88150-555-9. Dewey:974.1/00946. LCCN:2002-067310.
Audience: **f.**

Federal Writers' Project Staff & Writers Program Staff **F39**
New Hampshire: A Guide to the Granite State. Library Binding. Reprint Services Company. Temecula, CA. 1989. American Guide Ser. ISBN:0-7812-1028-3, ISBN13: 978-0-7812-1028-7. Dewey:917.42/04/4.
Audience: **f.**

Graffagnino, J. Kevin **F49.G78 1983**
The Shaping of Vermont: From the Wilderness to the Centennial 1749-1877. David W. Dangremond (Foreword by). Trade Cloth. Vermont Heritage Press. Rutland, VT. 1983. 180p. ISBN:0-911853-01-4, ISBN13: 978-0-911853-01-8. Dewey:974.1/02. LCCN:82-084526.
Audience: **f.**

Horwitz, Richard P. **F29.W9.H67**
Anthropology Toward History: Culture and Work in a 19th-Century Maine Town. Library Binding. Wesleyan University Press. Middletown, CT. 1978. xiii, 197p. ISBN:0-8195-5014-0, ISBN13: 978-0-8195-5014-9. Dewey:974.1/6. LCCN:77-074560.
Audience: **f.** B

Jager, Ronald & Jager, Grace **F34.J325 2000**
The Granite State: New Hampshire, an Illustrated History. Trade Cloth. American Historical Press. Sun Valley, CA. 2000. 232p. ISBN:1-892724-15-4, ISBN13: 978-1-892724-15-1. Dewey:974.2. LCCN:00-108799.
Audience: **l,u,f.**

Klyza, Christopher M. & Trombulak, Stephen C. **F49.K59 1999**
The Story of Vermont: A Natural and Cultural History. Ed. 2. Trade Paper. University Press of New England. Lebanon, NH. 1999. 254p. Middlebury Bicentennial Series in Environmental Studies ISBN:0-87451-936-5, ISBN13: 978-0-87451-936-5. Dewey:974.3. LCCN:99-019489.
Audience: **u,f.** *Choice, 1999.*

Leamon, James S. **E263.M4**
Revolution Downeast: The War for American Independence in Maine. Trade Paper. University of Massachusetts Press. Amherst, MA. 1995. 320p. ISBN:0-87023-959-7, ISBN13: 978-0-87023-959-5. Dewey:973.3/09741. LCCN:92-017757.
Audience: **u,f.** *Choice, 1993.*

Morrissey, Charles T. **F49.M67 1984**
Vermont: Bicentennial and History Guide. Trade Paper. W. W. Norton & Company, Inc. New York, NY. 1984. 235p. States and the Nation Ser. ISBN:0-393-30223-7, ISBN13: 978-0-393-30223-3. Dewey:974.3. LCCN:84-014895.
Audience: **f.**

Turner, Lynn W. **F0038.T87**
The Ninth State: New Hampshire's Formative Years. Trade Paper. Books on Demand. Ann Arbor, MI. 493p. ISBN:0-7837-0309-0, ISBN13: 978-0-7837-0309-1. Dewey:974.2/03. LCCN:82-013386.
Audience: **u,f.** B

Ulrich, Laurel Thatcher **HQ1438.N35U47 1991**
Good Wives: Image and Reality in the Lives of Women in Northern New England, 1650-1750. Trade Paper. Random House, Inc. New York, NY. 1991. 336p. ISBN:0-679-73257-8, ISBN13: 978-0-679-73257-0. Dewey:305.42/0974. LCCN:90-055673.
Audience: **u,f.**

United States > U.S. Local History > New England > Massachusetts

F67 .M4213 V.1
Diary of Cotton Mather Vol. 1: 1681-1709. Library Binding. Higginson Book Company. Salem, MA. 1995. 604p. ISBN:0-8328-4497-7, ISBN13: 978-0-8328-4497-3. Dewey:974.4.
Audience: **f.**

F67 .M4213 V.2
Diary of Cotton Mather Vol. 2: 1709-1724. Library Binding. Higginson Book Company. Salem, MA. 1995. 860p. ISBN:0-8328-4496-9, ISBN13: 978-0-8328-4496-6. Dewey:974.4.
Audience: **f.**

Bailyn, Bernard **E278.C67**
The Ordeal of Thomas Hutchinson. Trade Paper. Harvard University Press. Cambridge, MA. 1976. 458p. ISBN:0-674-64161-2, ISBN13: 978-0-674-64161-7. Dewey:973.3/14/0924. LCCN:73-076379.
Audience: **u,f.**

Bradford, William **F68**
Bradford's History of Plymouth Plantation, 1606-1646. Trade Paper. Adamant Media. Chestnut Hill, MA. 2001. 470p. ISBN:1-4021-9594-X, ISBN13: 978-1-4021-9594-5. Dewey:974.48.
Audience: **f.**

Bremer, Francis J. **F67.W79B74 2003**
John Winthrop: America's Forgotten Founding Father. Trade Cloth. Oxford University Press, Inc. New York, NY. 2003. 512p. ISBN:0-19-514913-0, ISBN13: 978-0-19-514913-5. Dewey:974.402092. LCCN:2002-038143.
Audience: **u,f.** *Choice, 2004.*

Brown, Richard D. & Tager, Jack **F64.B86 2000**
Massachusetts: A Concise History. Trade Cloth. University of Massachusetts Press. Amherst, MA. 2000. 400p. ISBN:1-55849-248-8, ISBN13: 978-1-55849-248-6. Dewey:974.4. LCCN:00-028629.
Audience: **l,u,f.**

Brown, Robert Eldon **F67.B86**
Middle: Class Democracy and the Revolution in Massachusetts 1691. Paper Text. Textbook Publishers. Temecula, CA. 2003. ix, 458p. ISBN:0-7581-4467-9, ISBN13: 978-0-7581-4467-6. Dewey:974.402.
Audience: **f.**

Dunn, Richard S. **F67.W7957**
Puritans and Yankees: The Winthrop Dynasty of New England 1630. Paper Text. Textbook Publishers. Temecula, CA. 2003. xi, 379p. ISBN:0-7581-5800-9, ISBN13: 978-0-7581-5800-0. Dewey:974.402.
Audience: **f.**

Graham, Judith S. **F7**
Puritan Family Life: The Diary of Samuel Sewall. Trade Paper. Northeastern University Press. Boston, MA. 2005. 296p. ISBN:1-55553-593-3, ISBN13: 978-1-55553-593-3. Dewey:974/.008825.
Audience: **f.** *Choice, 2000.*

Handlin, Oscar **F73.9.A1H3 1991**
Boston's Immigrants, 1790-1880: A Study in Acculturation. Trade Paper. Harvard University Press. Cambridge, MA. 1991. 400p. Belknap Press Ser. ISBN:0-674-07986-8, ISBN13: 978-0-674-07986-1. Dewey:305.8/00974461. LCCN:91-012808.
Audience: **l,u,f.**

Hutchinson, Thomas **F67**
History of the Colony of Massachusetts Bay. Trade Cloth. Ayer Company Publishers, Inc. Manchester, NH. 1972. Research Library of Colonial Americana ISBN:0-405-03291-9, ISBN13: 978-0-405-03291-2. Dewey:974.4/02. LCCN:77-141090.
Audience: **f.**

Labaree, Benjamin W. **F67.L34**
Colonial Massachusetts: A History. Library Binding. Kraus International Publications. Hackensack, NJ. 1979. 349p. History of the American Colonies Ser. ISBN:0-527-18714-3, ISBN13: 978-0-527-18714-9. Dewey:974.4/02. LCCN:79-000033.
Audience: **l,u,f.**

Langdon, George D. **F68.L25**
Pilgrim Colony: A History of New Plymouth, 1620-1691. Trade Paper. Books on Demand. Ann Arbor, MI. 268p. Yale Publications in American Studies, No. 12 ISBN:0-8357-8268-9, ISBN13: 978-0-8357-8268-5. Dewey:974.402. LCCN:66-021526.
Audience: **f.**

Middlekauff, Robert **F67.M47M53 1999**
Mathers: Three Generations of Puritan Intellectuals, 1596-1728. Trade Paper. University of California Press. Berkeley, CA. 1999. 460p. ISBN:0-520-21930-9, ISBN13: 978-0-520-21930-4. Dewey:285/.8/0922744. LCCN:98-050840.
Audience: **f.**

Morgan, Edmund S. **F67.W79M66 2006**
The Puritan Dilemma. Ed. 2. Trade Paper. Longman Publishing Group. White Plains, NY. 2005. 320p. Weekend Biographies Ser. ISBN:0-321-32886-8, ISBN13: 978-0-321-32886-1. Dewey:974.4/02/092 B. LCCN:2005-297441.
Audience: **u,f.**

Morison, Samuel Eliot **F67.M86**
Builders of the Bay Colony. Trade Paper. Kessinger Publishing, LLC. Whitefish, MT. 2004. ISBN:1-4179-0907-2, ISBN13: 978-1-4179-0907-0. Dewey:974.4/02.
Audience: **u,f.**

Murdock, Kenneth Ballard **F67.M477**
Increase Mather, the Foremost American Puritan. Paper Text. Textbook Publishers. Temecula, CA. 2003. xv, 442p. ISBN:0-7581-4423-7, ISBN13: 978-0-7581-4423-2. Dewey:974.4.
Audience: **f.**

O'Connor, Thomas H. **F73.3.O26 2001**
The Hub: Boston Past and Present. Trade Cloth. Northeastern University Press. Boston, MA. 2005. 310p.

ISBN:1-55553-474-0, ISBN13: 978-1-55553-474-5. Dewey:974.4/61. LCCN:00-068974.
Audience: **l,u,f.** *Choice, 2001.*

Richards, Leonard L. **F69.R63 2002**
Shay's Rebellion: The American Revolution's Final Battle. Trade Cloth. University of Pennsylvania Press. Philadelphia, PA. 2002. 216p. ISBN:0-8122-3669-6, ISBN13: 978-0-8122-3669-9. Dewey:974.4/03. LCCN:2001-058417.
Audience: **f.** *Choice, 2003.*

Silverman, Kenneth **F67.M43 S57**
The Life and Times of Cotton Mather. Trade Paper. Welcome Rain Publishers. New York, NY. 2001. 480p. ISBN:1-56649-206-8, ISBN13: 978-1-56649-206-5. Dewey:285.8/32/0924.
Audience: **f.** B

Walmsley, Andrew S. **F67.H982W35 1999**
Thomas Hutchinson and the Origins of the American Revolution. Trade Cloth. New York University Press. New York, NY. 1998. 288p. American Social Experience Ser., Vol. 38 ISBN:0-8147-9341-X, ISBN13: 978-0-8147-9341-1. Dewey:973.3/14/092 B. LCCN:98-025531.
Audience: **f.** *Choice, 1999.*

Yazawa, Melvin (Editor) **F67.S516 1998**
The Diary and Life of Samuel Sewall. Cloth over Boards. Palgrave Macmillan. New York, NY. 1998. 274p. Bedford Series in History and Culture ISBN:0-312-17771-2, ISBN13: 978-0-312-17771-3. Dewey:974.4/02. LCCN:97-074975.
Audience: **f.**

United States > U.S. Local History > New England > Regions. Cities

Brown, Richard D. **F73.4**
Revolutionary Politics in Massachusetts: The Boston Committee of Correspondence and the Towns, 1772-1774. Trade Cloth. Harvard University Press. Cambridge, MA. 1970. 298p. ISBN:0-674-76781-0, ISBN13: 978-0-674-76781-2. Dewey:320.9/744/02. LCCN:71-119072.
Audience: **f.** B

Connolly, James J. **F73.5.C745 1998**
The Triumph of Ethnic Progressivism: Urban Political Culture in Boston, 1900-1925. Trade Cloth. Harvard University Press. Cambridge, MA. 1998. 272p. ISBN:0-674-90950-X, ISBN13: 978-0-674-90950-2. Dewey:974.4/61. LCCN:97-038662.
Audience: **u,f.** *Choice, 1999.*

Formisano, Ronald P. **F73**
Boston, Seventeen Hundred to Nineteen Eighty: The Evolution of Urban Politics. Constance K. Burns (Editor). Trade Cloth. Greenwood Publishing Group, Inc. Portsmouth, NH. 1984. 296p. Contributions in American History Ser., No. 106 ISBN:0-313-23336-5, ISBN13: 978-0-313-23336-4. Dewey:320.9744/61. LCCN:83-018415.
Audience: **u,f.**

Frisch, Michael H. **F74.S8 F7**
Town into City: Springfield, Massachusetts, and the Meaning of Community, 1840-1880. Trade Paper. Harvard University Press. Cambridge, MA. 1980. 317p. Studies in Urban History ISBN:0-674-89826-5, ISBN13: 978-0-674-89826-4. Dewey:301.36/3/0974426. LCCN:72-178075.
Audience: **f.** B

Greven, Philip J. Jr. **F74.A6 G7**
Four Generations: Population, Land, and Family in Colonial Andover, Massachusetts. Book, Other. Cornell University Press. Ithaca, NY. 1972. 349p. ISBN:0-8014-9134-7, ISBN13: 978-0-8014-9134-4. Dewey:923.273.
Audience: **f.**

Gross, Robert A. **F74.C8G76 2001**
The Minutemen and Their World. Alan M. Taylor (Foreword by). Trade Paper. Farrar, Straus & Giroux. New York, NY. 2001. 280p. American Century Ser. ISBN:0-8090-0120-9, ISBN13: 978-0-8090-0120-0. Dewey:974.2/72. LCCN:2001-272032.
Audience: **l,u,f.** B

Handlin, Oscar **F73.9.A1H3 1991**
Boston's Immigrants, 1790-1880: A Study in Acculturation. Trade Paper. Harvard University Press. Cambridge, MA. 1991. 400p. Belknap Press Ser. ISBN:0-674-07986-8, ISBN13: 978-0-674-07986-1. Dewey:305.8/00974461. LCCN:91-012808.
Audience: **l,u,f.** B

Horton, James O. & **F73.9.N4H67 1999**
Horton, Lois E.
Black Bostonians: Family Life and Community Struggle in the Antebellum North. Ed. 2. Trade Cloth. Holmes & Meier Publishers, Inc. Teaneck, NJ. 1999. xxv, 198p. ISBN:0-8419-1379-X, ISBN13: 978-0-8419-1379-0. Dewey:305.896074461. LCCN:99-034883.
Audience: **f.** B

Lukas, J. Anthony **F73.9.A1L85 1986**
Common Ground: A Turbulent Decade in the Lives of Three American Families. Trade Paper. Knopf Publishing Group. New York, NY. 1986. 688p. Vintage Ser. ISBN:0-394-74616-3, ISBN13: 978-0-394-74616-6. Dewey:370.19/342. LCCN:86-040132.
Audience: **g,l,u,f.** B *Choice, 1986.*

Morrison, Dane A. & **F74.S1S33 2004**
Schultz, Nancy Lusignan (Editors)
Salem: Place, Myth and Memory. Trade Cloth. Northeastern University Press. Boston, MA. 2004. 312p. ISBN:1-55553-609-3, ISBN13: 978-1-55553-609-1. Dewey:974.4/02. LCCN:2003-023134.
Audience: **u,f.** *Choice, 2005.*

Powell, Sumner C. **F74.S94**
Puritan Village: The Formation of a New England Town. Trade Paper. Wesleyan University Press. Middletown, CT. 1982. 255p. ISBN:0-8195-6014-6, ISBN13: 978-0-8195-6014-8. Dewey:977.44. LCCN:63-008862.
Audience: **f.**

Rutman, Darrett Bruce **F73.4 .R8**
Winthrop's Boston: Portrait of a Puritan Town, 1630-1649. Trade Cloth. University of North Carolina Press. Chapel Hill, NC. 1969. Institute of Early American History and Culture Ser. ISBN:0-8078-0942-X, ISBN13: 978-0-8078-0942-6. Dewey:974.46. LCCN:65-013667.
Audience: **f.**

Seelye, John **F74.P8S44 1998**
Memory's Nation: The Place of Plymouth Rock. Trade Cloth. University of North Carolina Press. Chapel Hill, NC. 1998. 720p. ISBN:0-8078-2415-1, ISBN13: 978-0-8078-2415-3. Dewey:974.4/82. LCCN:97-040784.
Audience: **u,f.** *Choice, 1999.*

Thoreau, Henry David **F72.M7T5 2004**
A Week on the Concord and Merrimack Rivers. Carl F. Hovde, William L. Howarth & Elizabeth Hall Witherell (Editors), John McPhee (Introduction by). Trade Paper. Princeton University Press. Princeton, NJ. 2004. 440p. Writings of Henry D. Thoreau Ser. ISBN:0-691-11878-7, ISBN13: 978-0-691-11878-9. Dewey:917.42/720444.
Audience: **g,l,u,f.**

Whitehill, Walter Muir (Author, Illustrator) **F73.3.W57 2000**
Boston: A Topographical History. Ed. 3. Trade Cloth. Harvard University Press. Cambridge, MA. 2000. 432p. Belknap Press Ser. ISBN:0-674-00267-9, ISBN13: 978-0-674-00267-8. Dewey:974.461. LCCN:99-086597.
Audience: **u,f.**

Wilson, Lori Lee **BF1575.W613 1997**
The Salem Witch Trials. Trade Cloth, Library Binding. Lerner Publishing Group. Minneapolis, MN. 1997. 112p. How History Is Invented Ser. ISBN:0-8225-4889-5, ISBN13: 978-0-8225-4889-8. Dewey:133.4/3/097445. LCCN:96-021371.
Audience: **u,f.**

Young, Christine A. **F0074.S1Y68**
From "Good Order" to Glorious Revolution: Salem, Massachusetts, 1628-1689. Robert Berkhofer (Editor). Trade Paper. Books on Demand. Ann Arbor, MI. 1980. 271p. Studies in American History and Culture, Vol. 19 ISBN:0-8357-1101-3, ISBN13: 978-0-8357-1101-2. Dewey:974.4/5. LCCN:80-020118.
Audience: **f.**

United States > U.S. Local History > New England > Rhode Island. Connecticut

Bushman, Richard L. **F97 .B89**
From Puritan to Yankee: Character and the Social Order in Connecticut, 1690-1765. Trade Paper. Harvard University Press. Cambridge, MA. 1967. 352p. Center for the Study of the History of Liberty in America Ser. ISBN:0-674-32551-6, ISBN13: 978-0-674-32551-7. Dewey:917.46/03/2.
Audience: **f.**

Federal Writers' Project Staff **F79.F38**
Rhode Island: A Guide to the Smallest State. Trade Cloth. Somerset Publishers, Inc. Santa Barbara, CA. 1937. 500p. American Guidebook Ser. ISBN:0-403-02188-X, ISBN13: 978-0-403-02188-8. Dewey:917.45/04/4. LCCN:37-028463.
Audience: **f.**

Federal Writers' Project Staff & Writers Program Staff **F100 .F45**
Connecticut: A Guide to Its Roads, Lore and People. Library Binding. Reprint Services Company. Temecula, CA. 1989. American Guide Ser. ISBN:0-7812-1007-0, ISBN13: 978-0-7812-1007-2. Dewey:917.46.
Audience: **f.**

James, Sydney V. **F82.J33 2000**
The Colonial Metamorphoses in Rhode Island: A Study of Institutions in Change. Sheila L. Skemp & Bruce C. Daniels (Editors). Library Binding. University Press of New England. Lebanon, NH. 2000. 350p. Revisiting New England Ser. ISBN:1-58465-017-6, ISBN13: 978-1-58465-017-1. Dewey:974.5/02. LCCN:99-039782.
Audience: **f.** *Choice, 2000.*

Jeffries, John W. **F0100.J43**
Testing the Roosevelt Coalition: Connecticut Society and Politics in the Era of World War II. Trade Paper. Books on Demand. Ann Arbor, MI. 327p. Twentieth-Century America Ser. ISBN:0-7837-1318-5, ISBN13: 978-0-7837-1318-2. Dewey:320.9/746/04. LCCN:78-014550.
Audience: **f.**

Kellner, George & Lemons, J. Stanley **F79.K45 2004**
Rhode Island, the Ocean State: An Illustrated History. Trade Cloth. American Historical Press. Sun Valley, CA. 2004. 280p. ISBN:1-892724-40-5, ISBN13: 978-1-892724-40-3. Dewey:974.5. LCCN:2004-105458.
Audience: **l,u,f.**

McLoughlin, William G. **F79 .M324 1986**
Rhode Island: Bicentennial and History Guide. Trade Paper. W. W. Norton & Company, Inc. New York, NY. 1986. 240p. States and the Nation Ser. ISBN:0-393-30271-7, ISBN13: 978-0-393-30271-4. Dewey:974.5. LCCN:85-005132.
Audience: **u,f.**

Roth, David M. **F94.R67**
Connecticut. Trade Cloth. W. W. Norton & Company, Inc. New York, NY. 1979. 224p. States and the Nation Ser. ISBN:0-393-05676-7, ISBN13: 978-0-393-05676-1. Dewey:974.6. LCCN:79-016262.
Audience: **u,f.**

Roth, David M. & Meyer, Freeman **F94.S45**
From Revolution to Constitution: Connecticut, 1763 to 1818, Vol. 2. Trade Cloth. Center for Connecticut Studies. Willimantic, CT. 1975. ix, 111p. ISBN:0-87106-129-5, ISBN13: 978-0-87106-129-4. Dewey:974.6. LCCN:73-083257.
Audience: **f.**

Taylor, Robert J. **F97.T25**
Colonial Connecticut: A History. Library Binding. Kraus International Publications. Hackensack, NJ. 1979. 285p. History of the American Colonies Ser. ISBN:0-527-18710-0, ISBN13: 978-0-527-18710-1. Dewey:974.6/02. LCCN:79-001099.
Audience: **f.**

Winslow, Ola Elizabeth **F82 .W855**
Master Roger Williams, a Biography. Paper Text. Textbook Publishers. Temecula, CA. 2003. xi, 328p. ISBN:0-7581-7456-X, ISBN13: 978-0-7581-7456-7. Dewey:923.273.
Audience: **f.**

United States > U.S. Local History > Atlantic States

Evans, Mari-Lynn (Editor), et al. **F106.A59 2004**
The Appalachians: America's First and Last Frontier. Robert Santelli & Holly George-Warren (Editors). Trade Cloth. Random

House Adult Trade Publishing Group. New York, NY. 2004. 288p. ISBN:1-4000-6186-5, ISBN13: 978-1-4000-6186-0. Dewey:974. LCCN:2004-041162.
Audience: **u,f.**

Marzec, Robert P. **F106.M586 2004**
The Mid-Atlantic Region. Trade Cloth. Greenwood Publishing Group, Inc. Portsmouth, NH. 2004. xxiii, 469p. The Greenwood Encyclopedia of American Regional Cultures Ser. ISBN:0-313-32954-0, ISBN13: 978-0-313-32954-8. Dewey:974/.003. LCCN:2004-056059.
Audience: **u,f.**

United States > U.S. Local History > New York

Benson, Lee **F0123.B49**
The Concept of Jacksonian Democracy: New York As a Test Case. Trade Paper. Books on Demand. Ann Arbor, MI. 367p. ISBN:0-608-06402-5, ISBN13: 978-0-608-06402-4. Dewey:974.703. LCCN:61-006286.
Audience: **u,f.** B

Ellis, David M. **F119**
New York: State and City. Trade Cloth. Cornell University Press. Ithaca, NY. 1979. 267p. ISBN:0-8014-1180-7, ISBN13: 978-0-8014-1180-9. Dewey:974.7. LCCN:78-015759.
Audience: **f.** B

Ellis, Edward Robb **F128.3.E65 1997**
The Epic of New York City: A Narrative History. Trade Cloth. Kodansha America, Inc. New York, NY. 1997. 640p. ISBN:1-56836-204-8, ISBN13: 978-1-56836-204-5. Dewey:974.7/1. LCCN:97-025483.
Audience: **f.**

Federal Writers' Project Staff **F124.W89 1974**
New York State: A Guide to the Empire State. Trade Cloth. Somerset Publishers, Inc. Santa Barbara, CA. 1940. 782p. American Guidebook Ser. ISBN:0-403-02151-0, ISBN13: 978-0-403-02151-2. Dewey:917.47/04/4. LCCN:72-084496.
Audience: **f.**

Gergel, Thomas **F118 .E57 1982**
Encyclopedia of New York: A Reference Guide to the Empire State. Library Binding. Somerset Publishers, Inc. Santa Barbara, CA. 1983. 743p. Encyclopedia of the United States Ser. ISBN:0-403-09994-3, ISBN13: 978-0-403-09994-8. Dewey:974.7/003/21. LCCN:81-085115.
Audience: **l,u,f.**

Kammen, Michael G. **F122.K27**
Colonial New York: A History. Trade Cloth. Simon & Schuster. New York, NY. 1975. xix, 426p. ISBN:0-684-14325-9, ISBN13: 978-0-684-14325-5. Dewey:974.7/1/02. LCCN:75-005693.
Audience: **f.** B

Klein, Milton M. (Editor) **F119.E48 2001**
The Empire State: A History of New York. New York State Historical Association Staff (Contribution by). Book, Other. Cornell University Press. Ithaca, NY. 2005. 864p. ISBN:0-8014-3866-7, ISBN13: 978-0-8014-3866-0. Dewey:974.7. LCCN:2001-001669.
Audience: **l,u,f.** *Choice, 2002.*

United States > U.S. Local History > New York > New York City

Ackerman, Kenneth D. **F128.47.T96A28 2005**
Boss Tweed: The Rise and Fall of the Corrupt Pol Who Conceived the Soul of Modern New York. Trade Cloth. Avalon Publishing Group. New York, NY. 2005. 400p. ISBN:0-7867-1435-2, ISBN13: 978-0-7867-1435-3. Dewey:974.7/1041/092 B. LCCN:2005-042090.
Audience: **u,f.** *Choice, 2006.*

Boyd, Herb **F128.68.H3H33 2003**
The Harlem Reader: A Celebration of New York's Most Famous Neighborhood, from the Renaissance Years to the 21st Century. Trade Paper. Crown Publishing Group. New York, NY. 2003. 336p. ISBN:1-4000-4681-5, ISBN13: 978-1-4000-4681-2. Dewey:974.7/1. LCCN:2002-151280.
Audience: **u,f.**

Browne, Arthur, et al. **F128.54.K63B76 1985**
I, Koch: A Decidedly Unauthorized Biography of the Mayor of New York City. Dan Collins & Michael Goodwin (Authors). Trade Cloth. W. Clement Stone, P M A Communications, Inc. Northbrook, IL. 1985. 384p. ISBN:0-396-08647-0, ISBN13: 978-0-396-08647-5. Dewey:974.7/1043/0924 B. LCCN:85-006893.
Audience: **u,f.**

Burrows, Edwin G. & Wallace, Mike **F128.3.W35 1998**
Gotham: A History of New York City to 1898. Trade Cloth. Oxford University Press, Inc. New York, NY. 1998. 1,408p. The History of NYC Ser. ISBN:0-19-511634-8, ISBN13: 978-0-19-511634-2. Dewey:974.7/1. LCCN:97-039308.
Audience: **u,f.** *Choice, 1999.*

Cannato, Vincent J. **F128.54.L55**
The Ungovernable City: John Lindsay and His Struggle to Save New York. Trade Paper. Basic Books. New York, NY. 2002. 720p. ISBN:0-465-00844-5, ISBN13: 978-0-465-00844-5. Dewey:974.7104309.
Audience: **u,f.**

Erenberg, Lewis A. **F128.5.E65 1984**
Steppin' Out: New York Nightlife and the Transformation of American Culture. Trade Paper. University of Chicago Press. Chicago, IL. 1984. 312p. ISBN:0-226-21515-6, ISBN13: 978-0-226-21515-0. Dewey:974.7/1041. LCCN:84-002770.
Audience: **f.**

Federal Writers' Project Staff **F128.18**
The WPA Guide to New York City. William H. Whyte (Introduction by). Trade Paper. New Press, The. New York, NY. 1995. 736p. ISBN:1-56584-321-5, ISBN13: 978-1-56584-321-9. Dewey:917.47/10443. LCCN:82-047898.
Audience: **f.** B

Hammack, David C. **F128.47.H2 1982**
Power and Society: Greater New York at the Turn of the Century. Trade Cloth. Russell Sage Foundation. New York, NY. 1982. 450p. ISBN:0-87154-348-6, ISBN13: 978-0-87154-348-6. Dewey:974.7/1041. LCCN:81-066977.
Audience: **u,f.** B

Jackson, Kenneth T. (Editor) **F128.3.E75 1995**
Encyclopedia of New York City. Cloth over Boards. Yale University Press. Cumberland, RI. 1995. 1392p. ISBN:0-300-05536-6, ISBN13: 978-0-300-05536-8. Dewey:974.7/1/003. LCCN:95-002811.
Audience: **g,l,u,f.** *Choice, 1996.*

Kirtzman, Andrew **F128.57.G58K57 2000**
Rudy Giuliani: Emperor of the City. Trade Cloth. HarperCollins Publishers. New York, NY. 2000. 352p. ISBN:0-688-17492-2, ISBN13: 978-0-688-17492-7. Dewey:974.7/1043/092 B. LCCN:00-708709.
Audience: **g,l,u,f.**

Lankevich, George **F128**
New York City: A Short History. Ed. 2. Trade Cloth. New York University Press. New York, NY. 2002. 288p. ISBN:0-8147-5185-7, ISBN13: 978-0-8147-5185-5. Dewey:974.71. LCCN:98-011251.
Audience: **u,f.**

McKay, Claude **F0128**
Harlem: Negro Metropolis. Trade Paper. Books on Demand. Ann Arbor, MI. 277p. ISBN:0-598-56484-5, ISBN13: 978-0-598-56484-9. Dewey:917.471. LCCN:40-032205.
Audience: **l,u,f.**

Shorto, Russell **F128.4.S56 2004**
The Island at the Center of the World: The Epic Story of Dutch Manhattan and the Forgotten Colony That Shaped America. Trade Cloth. Thorndike Press. Waterville, ME. 2004. 622p. ISBN:0-7862-6835-2, ISBN13: 978-0-7862-6835-1. Dewey:974.7/102. LCCN:2004-053746.
Audience: **u,f.**

Tiedemann, Joseph S. **F128.4.T54 1997**
Reluctant Revolutionaries: New York City and the Road to Independence, 1763-1776. Book, Other. Cornell University Press. Ithaca, NY. 1997. 352p. ISBN:0-8014-3237-5, ISBN13: 978-0-8014-3237-8. Dewey:974.7/107. LCCN:96-035249.
Audience: **f.** *Choice, 1997.*

United States > U.S. Local History > New York > Other Cities, A-Z

Gonzalez, Evelyn Diaz **F128.68.B8G66 2004**
The Bronx: A History. Trade Cloth. Kegan Paul International, Ltd. London, 2004. 304p. Columbia History of Urban Life Ser. ISBN:0-231-12114-8, ISBN13: 978-0-231-12114-9. Dewey:974.7/275. LCCN:2003-055206.
Audience: **u,f.** *Choice, 2005.*

Immerso, Michael **F129.C75I46 2002**
Coney Island: The People's Playground. Trade Cloth. Rutgers University Press. Piscataway, NJ. 2005. 208p. ISBN:0-8135-3138-1, ISBN13: 978-0-8135-3138-0. Dewey:974.7/23. LCCN:2002-020159.
Audience: **g,u,f.** *Choice, 2003.*

Yans-McLaughlin, Virginia **F129.B89I8**
Family and Community: Italian Immigrants in Buffalo, 1880-1930. Trade Paper. University of Illinois Press. Champaign, IL. 1982. 288p. ISBN:0-252-00916-9, ISBN13: 978-0-252-00916-7. Dewey:305.8/51/074797. LCCN:81-011475.
Audience: **f.**

United States > U.S. Local History > New Jersey

Federal Writers' Project Staff & Writers Program Staff **F132.3 .F43**
New Jersey: A Guide to Its Present and Past. Library Binding. Reprint Services Company. Temecula, CA. 1989. American Guide Ser. ISBN:0-7812-1029-1, ISBN13: 978-0-7812-1029-4. Dewey:917.49/04/4.
Audience: **f.**

Fleming, Thomas J. **F134.F54 1984**
New Jersey: Bicentennial and History Guide. Trade Paper. W. W. Norton & Company, Inc. New York, NY. 1984. 214p. States and the Nation Ser. ISBN:0-393-30180-X, ISBN13: 978-0-393-30180-9. Dewey:974.9. LCCN:84-004143.
Audience: **u,f.**

Sheridan, Eugene R. **F0137.M63S4**
Lewis Morris, 1671-1746: A Study in Early American Politics. Trade Paper. Books on Demand. Ann Arbor, MI. 1981. 269p. A New York State Study Ser. ISBN:0-608-07626-0, ISBN13: 978-0-608-07626-3. Dewey:974.9/02/0924. LCCN:81-014531.
Audience: **f.**

Tice, George A. **F144.P4.T5**
Paterson. Trade Cloth. Rutgers University Press. Piscataway, NJ. 1972. ISBN:0-8135-0711-1, ISBN13: 978-0-8135-0711-8. Dewey:917.49/24/00222. LCCN:79-163964.
Audience: **f.**

United States > U.S. Local History > Pennsylvania

Buck, Solon J. & Buck, Elizabeth H. **F149 .B83**
Planting of Civilization in Western Pennsylvania. Trade Cloth. Brown Book Company. Miami, FL. 1939. ISBN:0-910294-28-3, ISBN13: 978-0-910294-28-7. Dewey:974.8. LCCN:39-025307.
Audience: **f.**

Dixon, Hepworth **BX7740.D6**
William Penn: An Historical Biography Founded on Family and State Papers. Trade Paper. Kessinger Publishing, LLC. Whitefish, MT. 2004. ISBN:1-4179-5913-4, ISBN13: 978-1-4179-5913-6. Dewey:974.802.
Audience: **u,f.**

Downey, Dennis B. & Bremer, Francis J. (Editors) **F149**
A Guide to the History of Pennsylvania: Reference Guides to State History and Research. Cloth Text. Greenwood Publishing Group, Inc. Portsmouth, NH. 1993. 504p. Reference Guides to State History and Research Ser. ISBN:0-313-25085-5, ISBN13: 978-0-313-25085-9. Dewey:016.9748. LCCN:93-000305.
Audience: **u,f.** *Choice, 1994.*

Federal Writers' Project Staff & Writers Program Staff **F147.3**
Pennsylvania: A Guide to the Keystone State. Library Binding. Reprint Services Company. Temecula, CA. 1989. American Guide Ser. ISBN:0-7812-1037-2, ISBN13: 978-0-7812-1037-9. Dewey:917.48/04/4.
Audience: **f.**

Geiter, Mary K. **F152.2.G42 2000**
William Penn. Trade Cloth. Longman Publishing Group. White Plains, NY. 2001. 224p. ISBN:0-582-29901-2, ISBN13: 978-0-582-29901-6. Dewey:974.8/02/092 B. LCCN:00-042826.
Audience: **g,l,u,f.** *Choice, 2001.*

Hanna, William S. **F0152.H37**
Benjamin Franklin and Pennsylvania Politics. Trade Cloth. Stanford University Press. Palo Alto, CA. 1964. x, 239p. ISBN:0-8047-0209-8, ISBN13: 978-0-8047-0209-6. Dewey:974.802.
Audience: **f.** B

Horle, Craig W. (Editor) **F152.2 .P3956**
The Papers of William Penn, 1701-1718, Vol. IV. Book, Other. University of Pennsylvania Press. Philadelphia, PA. 1987. 840p. ISBN:0-8122-8050-4, ISBN13: 978-0-8122-8050-0. Dewey:974.8/02/0924 B. LCCN:80-054052.
Audience: **f.**

Illick, Joseph E. **F152 .I44**
Colonial Pennsylvania: A History. Library Binding. Kraus International Publications. Hackensack, NJ. 1976. 359p. History of the American Colonies Ser. ISBN:0-527-18719-4, ISBN13: 978-0-527-18719-4. Dewey:974.8/02. LCCN:75-037551.
Audience: **u,f.**

Klein, Philip S. & Hoogenboom, Ari **GT4803**
History of Pennsylvania. Ed. 2. Trade Paper. Pennsylvania State University Press. University Park, PA. 1980. 648p. ISBN:0-271-01934-4, ISBN13: 978-0-271-01934-5. Dewey:394.26973. LCCN:79-001731.
Audience: **u,f.**

Miller, Randall M. & Pencak, William A. (Editors) **F149**
Pennsylvania: A History of the Commonwealth. Trade Cloth. Pennsylvania State University Press. University Park, PA. 2002. 672p. ISBN:0-271-02213-2, ISBN13: 978-0-271-02213-0. Dewey:974.8. LCCN:2002-005457.
Audience: **l,u,f.** *Choice, 2003.*

Nash, Gary B. **F152 .N25 1993**
Quakers and Politics: Pennsylvania, 1681-1726. Ed. 2. Paper Text. Northeastern University Press. Boston, MA. 1993. 384p. ISBN:1-55553-166-0, ISBN13: 978-1-55553-166-9. Dewey:974.8/02. LCCN:93-021914.
Audience: **u,f.** B

United States > U.S. Local History > Pennsylvania > Philadelphia

Bridenbaugh, Carl & Bridenbaugh, Jessica **F158.4 .B6 1978**
Rebels and Gentlemen: Philadelphia in the Age of Franklin. Trade Cloth. Greenwood Publishing Group, Inc. Portsmouth, NH. 1978. 393p. ISBN:0-313-20300-8, ISBN13: 978-0-313-20300-8. Dewey:974.8/11/02. LCCN:78-000657.
Audience: **u,f.**

Clark, Dennis **F158.9.I6 C55 1981**
The Irish in Philadelphia: Ten Generations of Urban Experience. Trade Paper. Temple University Press. Philadelphia, PA. 1982. 264p. ISBN:0-87722-227-4, ISBN13: 978-0-87722-227-9. Dewey:974.8/110049162. LCCN:81-018343.
Audience: **u,f.** B

Nash, Gary B. **F158.3.N37 2001**
First City: Philadelphia and the Forging of Historical Memory. Book, Other. University of Pennsylvania Press. Philadelphia, PA. 2001. 400p. Early American Studies ISBN:0-8122-3630-0, ISBN13: 978-0-8122-3630-9. Dewey:974.8/11. LCCN:2001-047082.
Audience: **u,f.** *Choice, 2002.*

Nash, Gary B. **F158.9.N4**
Forging Freedom: The Formation of Philadelphia's Black Community, 1720-1840. Trade Paper. Harvard University Press. Cambridge, MA. 1991. 372p. ISBN:0-674-30933-2, ISBN13: 978-0-674-30933-3. Dewey:974.8/1100496073. LCCN:87-023696.
Audience: **u,f.** *Choice, 1988.*

Warner, Sam Bass Jr. **F158.3.W18 1987**
Private City: Philadelphia in Three Periods of Its Growth. Ed. 2. Trade Cloth. University of Pennsylvania Press. Philadelphia, PA. 1987. 266p. ISBN:0-8122-8061-X, ISBN13: 978-0-8122-8061-6. Dewey:974.8/11. LCCN:68-021557.
Audience: **f.** B

Weigley, Russell F. (Editor) **F158.3**
Philadelphia: A Three Hundred Year History. Trade Cloth. W. W. Norton & Company, Inc. New York, NY. 1982. 852p. Barra Bks. ISBN:0-393-01610-2, ISBN13: 978-0-393-01610-9. Dewey:974.8/11. LCCN:82-008220.
Audience: **u,f.** B

United States > U.S. Local History > Pennsylvania > Other Cities, A-Z

Bodnar, John, et al. **F159.P69**
Lives of Their Own: Blacks, Italians, and Poles in Pittsburgh, 1900-1960. Roger Simon & Michael P. Weber (Authors). Trade Paper. University of Illinois Press. Champaign, IL. 1983. 312p. The Working Class in American History Ser. ISBN:0-252-01063-9, ISBN13: 978-0-252-01063-7. Dewey:974.8/86004. LCCN:81-003382.
Audience: **f.** B

Lorant, Stefan, et al. **F159.P657L67 1999**
Pittsburgh, the Story of an American City: The Millennium Edition. Ed. 5. Bruce D. Campbell, Henry Steele Commager, J. Cutler Andrews, John M. Blum, Gerald W. Johnson, Oscar Handlin, Sylvester K. Stevens, Henry David & David Lawrence (Authors). Trade Cloth. Derrydale Press, The. Lanham, MD. 1999. 776p. ISBN:0-9674103-0-4, ISBN13: 978-0-9674103-0-2. Dewey:974.8/86. LCCN:99-066641.
Audience: **u,f.**

Morawska, Ewa **F159.J7M83**
"For Bread with Butter": The Life-Worlds of East Central Europeans in Johnstown, Pennsylvania, 1890-1940. Robert Fogel & Stephan Thernstrom (Contribution by). Trade Paper. Cambridge University Press. New York, NY. 2004. 447p. Interdisciplinary Perspectives on Modern History Ser. ISBN:0-521-53063-6, ISBN13: 978-0-521-53063-7. Dewey:974.8/004918.
Audience: **f.** B

United States > U.S. Local History > Delaware. Maryland. District of Columbia

Arnett, Earl, et al. **F179.3.A66 1999**
Maryland: A New Guide to the Old Line State. Ed. 2. Robert J. Brugger & Edward C. Papenfuse (Authors), John Hopkins (Conducted by). Trade Paper. Johns Hopkins University Press. Baltimore, MD. 1999. 672p. ISBN:0-8018-5980-8, ISBN13: 978-0-8018-5980-9. Dewey:917.5204/43. LCCN:98-046982.
Audience: **u.**

Browne, William H. **F184.B88 1973**
Maryland, the History of a Palatinate. Trade Cloth. A M S Press, Inc. New York, NY. 1973. xii, 381p. American Commonwealths Ser., No. 3 ISBN:0-404-57203-0, ISBN13: 978-0-404-57203-7. Dewey:975.2/02. LCCN:72-003758.
Audience: **u,f.**

Federal Writers' Project Staff & Writers Program Staff **F164**
Delaware: A Guide to the First State. Library Binding. Reprint Services Company. Temecula, CA. 1989. American Guide Ser. ISBN:0-7812-1008-9, ISBN13: 978-0-7812-1008-9. Dewey:917.51.
Audience: **f.** B

Federal Writers' Project Staff & Writers Program Staff **F204.W5**
Washington D. C.: A City and Capital. Library Binding. Reprint Services Company. Temecula, CA. 1989. American Guide Ser. ISBN:0-7812-1061-5, ISBN13: 978-0-7812-1061-4. Dewey:975.3.
Audience: **f.**

Freidel, Frank & Pencak, William (Editors) **F204.W5W65 1994**
The White House: The First Two Hundred Years. John M. Cooper Jr. (Introduction by). Cloth Text. Northeastern University Press. Boston, MA. 1993. 288p. ISBN:1-55553-170-9, ISBN13: 978-1-55553-170-6. Dewey:975.3. LCCN:93-031360.
Audience: **g,l,u,f.**

Green, Constance McLaughlin **F194**
Washington. Paper Text. Textbook Publishers. Temecula, CA. 2003. ISBN:0-7581-5773-8, ISBN13: 978-0-7581-5773-7. Dewey:917.53.
Audience: **u,f.** B

Hoffecker, Carol E. **F164.H62**
Delaware, a Bicentennial History. Trade Cloth. W. W. Norton & Company, Inc. New York, NY. 1977. xvi, 221p. States and the Nation Ser. ISBN:0-393-05620-1, ISBN13: 978-0-393-05620-4. Dewey:975.1. LCCN:76-053844.
Audience: **u,f.** B

Hoffecker, Carol E. (Editor) **F164 .H63**
Readings in Delaware History. Trade Cloth. University of Delaware Press. Newark, DE. 220p. ISBN:0-87413-107-3, ISBN13: 978-0-87413-107-9. Dewey:917.51/03. LCCN:74-160876.
Audience: **f.**

Land, Aubrey C. **F184.L34**
Colonial Maryland: A History. Library Binding. Kraus International Publications. Hackensack, NJ. 1981. 367p. History of the American Colonies Ser. ISBN:0-527-18713-5, ISBN13: 978-0-527-18713-2. Dewey:975.2/02. LCCN:80-021732.
Audience: **u,f.** B

Lewis, David Levering **F194.L48**
District of Columbia: A Bicentennial History. Trade Cloth. W. W. Norton & Company, Inc. New York, NY. 1976. 208p. States and the Nation Ser. ISBN:0-393-05601-5, ISBN13: 978-0-393-05601-3. Dewey:975.3. LCCN:76-028397.
Audience: **u,f.** B

Munroe, John A. **F164.M83 2001**
History of Delaware. Ed. 4. Trade Cloth. University of Delaware Press. Newark, DE. 2001. 304p. ISBN:0-87413-772-1, ISBN13: 978-0-87413-772-9. Dewey:975.1. LCCN:2001-027438.
Audience: **u,f.**

Passonneau, Joseph **F194.P37 2004**
Washington Through Two Centuries. Trade Cloth. Monacelli Press, Inc. New York, NY. 2004. 288p. ISBN:1-58093-091-3, ISBN13: 978-1-58093-091-8. Dewey:975.3. LCCN:2003-024057.
Audience: **u,f.**

Steiner, Bernard C. **F184 .S813**
Maryland under the Commonwealth: A Chronicle of the Years, 1649-1658. Library Binding. Reprint Services Company. Temecula, CA. 1991. 178p. BCL1 - United States Local History Ser. ISBN:0-7812-6282-8, ISBN13 - 978-0-7812-6282-8. Dewey:975.2/02.
Audience: **f.**

United States > U.S. Local History > Southern States: General

Boles, John B. **F209.B65 1995**
The South Through Time: A History of an American Region. Ed. 1. Cloth Text. Prentice Hall PTR. Upper Saddle River, NJ. 1994. 640p. ISBN:0-13-825050-2, ISBN13: 978-0-13-825050-8. Dewey:975. LCCN:94-003343.
Audience: **l,u,f.**

Cash, W. J. **F209 .C3 1991**
The Mind of the South. Bertram Wyatt-Brown (Introduction by). Trade Paper. Knopf Publishing Group. New York, NY. 1991. 496p. ISBN:0-679-73647-6, ISBN13: 978-0-679-73647-9. Dewey:975. LCCN:91-050042.
Audience: **g,l,u,f.**

Cobb, James C. **F209.C597 2005**
Away down South: A History of Southern Identity. Trade Cloth. Oxford University Press, Inc. New York, NY. 2005. 416p. ISBN:0-19-508959-6, ISBN13: 978-0-19-508959-2. Dewey:975. LCCN:2005-017126.
Audience: **u,f.** *Choice, 2006.*

Cooper, William C. & Terrill, Thomas E. **F209.C64 2002**
The American South: A History. Ed. 3. Paper Text. McGraw-Hill Higher Education. Burr Ridge, IL. 2001. 432p. ISBN:0-07-246059-8, ISBN13: 978-0-07-246059-9. Dewey:975. LCCN:2001-044088.
Audience: **u,f.**

Dabney, Virginius **F209.D16 1970**
Liberalism in the South. Trade Cloth. A M S Press, Inc. New York, NY. 1970. xix, 456p. BCL Ser. II ISBN:0-404-00146-7, ISBN13: 978-0-404-00146-9. Dewey:309.1/75. LCCN:77-128983.
Audience: **f.**

Doyle, Don H. **HT123.5.S6D69 1990**
New Men, New Cities, New South: Atlanta, Nashville, Charleston, Mobile, 1860-1910. Trade Paper. University of North Carolina Press. Chapel Hill, NC. 1990. 391p. Fred W. Morrison Series in Southern Studies ISBN:0-8078-4270-2, ISBN13: 978-0-8078-4270-6. Dewey:307.76/0975. LCCN:89-034924.
Audience: **u,f.** *Choice, 1990.*

Eagles, Charles W. (Editor) **F209.C3M56 1992**
The Mind of the South: Fifty Years Later. Trade Cloth. University Press of Mississippi. Jackson, MS. 1992. 192p. Chancellor's Symposium on Southern History Ser. ISBN:0-87805-580-0, ISBN13: 978-0-87805-580-7. Dewey:975.0072. LCCN:92-017130.
Audience: **u,f.**

Gaston, Paul **F209**
The New South Creed: A Study in Southern Mythmaking. Trade Cloth. NewSouth, Inc. Montgomery, AL. 2001. 308p. ISBN:1-58838-053-X, ISBN13: 978-1-58838-053-1. Dewey:975.
Audience: **f.**

Genovese, Eugene D. **F209.5.G46 1994**
The Southern Tradition: The Achievement and Limitations of an American Conservatism. Trade Cloth. Harvard University Press. Cambridge, MA. 1994. 154p. The William E. Massey Sr. Lectures in the History of American Civilization Ser. ISBN:0-674-82527-6, ISBN13: 978-0-674-82527-7. Dewey:320.9/75. LCCN:94-004586.
Audience: **u,f.** *Choice, 1995.*

Mark, Rebecca & Vaughan, Robert **F209.S68 2004**
The South. Trade Cloth. Greenwood Publishing Group, Inc. Portsmouth, NH. 2004. xxii, 532p. The Greenwood Encyclopedia of American Regional Cultures Ser. ISBN:0-313-32734-3, ISBN13: 978-0-313-32734-6. Dewey:975/.003. LCCN:2004-056057.
Audience: **g,l,u,f.**

O'Brien, Robert & Martin, Harold (Editors) **F207**
The Encyclopedia of the South (To 1984). Cloth Text. DIANE Publishing Company. Collingdale, PA. 2000. 568p. ISBN:0-7881-6918-1, ISBN13: 978-0-7881-6918-2. Dewey:975/.003/21.
Audience: **g,l,u,f.**

Phillips, Ulrich Bon **F209.P56**
Life and Labor in the Old South. Trade Paper. Kessinger Publishing, LLC. Whitefish, MT. 2005. ISBN:0-7661-9894-4, ISBN13: 978-0-7661-9894-4. Dewey:975.
Audience: **f.**

Rubin, Louis Decimus Jr. (Editor) **F0209.5.A47**
The American South: Portrait of a Culture. Trade Paper. Books on Demand. Ann Arbor, MI. 1980. 389p. Southern Literary Studies ISBN:0-7837-9873-3, ISBN13: 978-0-7837-9873-8. Dewey:975/.04. LCCN:79-012316.
Audience: **f.**

Sellers, Charles Grier **F209 .S44**
The Southerner As American. Paper Text. Textbook Publishers. Temecula, CA. 2003. ix, 216p. ISBN:0-7581-1880-5, ISBN13: 978-0-7581-1880-6. Dewey:917.5.
Audience: **f.**

Taylor, William R. **F213 .T39 1993**
Cavalier and Yankee: The Old South and American National Character. Trade Paper. Oxford University Press, Inc. New York, NY. 1993. 400p. ISBN:0-19-508284-2, ISBN13: 978-0-19-508284-5. Dewey:975.03. LCCN:93-009623.
Audience: **f.**

Wilson, Charles Reagan, et al. **F209.N47 2006**
New Encyclopedia of Southern Culture: Religion. James G. Thomas & Ann J. Abadie (Authors), University of Mississippi, Center for the Study of Southern Culture Staff (Contribution by). Trade Cloth. University of North Carolina Press. Chapel Hill, NC. 2006. 272p. ISBN:0-8078-3003-8, ISBN13: 978-0-8078-3003-1. Dewey:975.003. LCCN:2005-024807.
Audience: **g,l,u,f.** *Choice, 2006.*

Woodward, C. Vann **F209.5 .W66 1993**
The Burden of Southern History. Ed. 3. Cloth Text. Louisiana State University Press. Baton Rouge, LA. 1993. xviii, 280p. ISBN:0-8071-1894-X, ISBN13: 978-0-8071-1894-8. Dewey:975. LCCN:93-029604.
Audience: **u,f.**

Wyatt-Brown, Bertram **F209.W9 1982**
Southern Honor: Ethics and Behavior in the Old South. Trade Cloth. Oxford University Press, Inc. New York, NY. 1982. 597p. ISBN:0-19-503119-9, ISBN13: 978-0-19-503119-5. Dewey:975. LCCN:81-022448.
Audience: **u,f.**

United States > U.S. Local History > Southern States: General > Early to 1865

Abernethy, Thomas Perkins **F213.A2**
The South in the New Nation 1789-1819. Paper Text. Textbook Publishers. Temecula, CA. 2003. xvi, 529p. ISBN:0-7581-9412-9, ISBN13: 978-0-7581-9412-1. Dewey:975.
Audience: **f.**

Alden, John Richard **F213 .A39**
The First South. Paper Text. Textbook Publishers. Temecula, CA. 2003. vii, 144p. ISBN:0-7581-6774-1, ISBN13: 978-0-7581-6774-3. Dewey:975.
Audience: **f.**

Alden, John Richard **F213.A4**
The South in the Revolution: 1763. Paper Text. Textbook Publishers. Temecula, CA. 2003. 442p. ISBN:0-7581-9414-5, ISBN13: 978-0-7581-9414-5. Dewey:975.
Audience: **f.**

Cooper, William J. Jr. **F213.C68 2000**
Liberty and Slavery: Southern Politics to 1860. Trade Paper. University of South Carolina Press. Columbia, SC. 2000. vi,

309p. ISBN:1-57003-387-0, ISBN13: 978-1-57003-387-2. Dewey:975/.02. LCCN:00-048851.
Audience: **f.** B

Cooper, William J. Jr. **F213**
The South and the Politics of Slavery, 1828-1856. Paper Text. Louisiana State University Press. Baton Rouge, LA. 1978. 420p. ISBN:0-8071-0775-1, ISBN13: 978-0-8071-0775-1. Dewey:326/.0975. LCCN:78-000751.
Audience: **f.**

Craven, Avery O. **QA184.2.L39**
The Growth of Southern Nationalism, 1848-1861. Trade Cloth. Louisiana State University Press. Baton Rouge, LA. 1953. x, 434p. A History of the South Ser., Vol. 6 ISBN:0-8071-0006-4, ISBN13: 978-0-8071-0006-6. Dewey:512/.55. LCCN:53-011470.
Audience: **u,f.** B

Craven, Wesley Frank **DR476.Z4**
The Southern Colonies in the Seventeenth Century, 1607-1689. Trade Cloth. Louisiana State University Press. Baton Rouge, LA. 1949. xvi, 452p. A History of the South Ser., Vol. 1 ISBN:0-8071-0001-3, ISBN13: 978-0-8071-0001-1. Dewey:327.56. LCCN:49-003595.
Audience: **f.** B

Davis, Richard B. **F212.D28**
Intellectual Life in the Colonial South, 1585-1763, Set. Trade Cloth, Box or Slipcased. University of Tennessee Press. Knoxville, TN. 1978. 1892p. ISBN:0-87049-210-1, ISBN13: 978-0-87049-210-5. Dewey:975/.01. LCCN:77-001370.
Audience: **u,f.** B

Dodd, William E. **F213.D64**
The Cotton Kingdom: A Chronicle of the Old South. Library Binding. Reprint Services Company. Temecula, CA. 1991. 161p. BCL1 - United States Local History Ser. ISBN:0-7812-6287-9, ISBN13: 978-0-7812-6287-3. Dewey:975/.03.
Audience: **f.**

Eaton, Clement **F213 .E18**
Growth of Southern Civilization, 1790-1860. Mass Market. HarperCollins Publishers. New York, NY. 1984. New American Nation Ser. ISBN:0-06-133040-X, ISBN13: 978-0-06-133040-7. Dewey:975.
Audience: **u,f.** B

Eaton, Clement **JA66 .F7**
Mind of the Old South. Paper Text. Louisiana State University Press. Baton Rouge, LA. 1964. x, 348p. Walter Lynwood Fleming Lectures ISBN:0-8071-0120-6, ISBN13: 978-0-8071-0120-9. Dewey:320/.01. LCCN:67-011648.
Audience: **u,f.** B

Eaton, Clement **F0215.E15**
The Waning of the Old South Civilization, 1860-1880's. Trade Paper. Books on Demand. Ann Arbor, MI. 207p. Mercer University. Lamar Memorial Lectures, Vol. 10 ISBN:0-598-11501-3, ISBN13: 978-0-598-11501-0. Dewey:917.5/03/4. LCCN:67-027141.
Audience: **u,f.**

Franklin, John H. **F213.F75 2002**
The Militant South, 1800-1861. Trade Paper. University of Illinois Press. Champaign, IL. 2002. 336p. ISBN:0-252-07069-0, ISBN13: 978-0-252-07069-3. Dewey:975.03. LCCN:2001-054011.
Audience: **u,f.** B

O'Brien, Michael **F213.O27 2004**
Conjectures of Order: Intellectual Life and the American South, 1810-1860. Trade Cloth. University of North Carolina Press. Chapel Hill, NC. 2004. 1456p. ISBN:0-8078-2800-9, ISBN13: 978-0-8078-2800-7. Dewey:975/.03. LCCN:2003-011163.
Audience: **f.** *Choice, 2004.*

Olmsted, Frederick Law **F213.O53 1996**
The Cotton Kingdom: A Traveller's Observations on Cotton and Slavery in the American Slave States, 1853-1861. Arthur M. Schlesinger Jr. (Editor). Trade Paper. Da Capo Press, Inc. Cambridge, MA. 1996. 716p. ISBN:0-306-80723-8, ISBN13: 978-0-306-80723-7. Dewey:975/.03. LCCN:96-024350.
Audience: **f.**

Osterweis, Rollin Gustav **F0213.O8**
Romanticism and Nationalism in the Old South. Trade Paper. Books on Demand. Ann Arbor, MI. 285p. ISBN:0-598-05852-4, ISBN13: 978-0-598-05852-2. Dewey:917.5033. LCCN:49-007620.
Audience: **f.**

Owsley, Frank Lawrence **HD8083.S9**
Plain Folk of the Old South. Grady McWhiney (Foreword by). Paper Text. Louisiana State University Press. Baton Rouge, LA. 1982. 234p. Walter Lynwood Fleming Lectures ISBN:0-8071-1063-9, ISBN13: 978-0-8071-1063-8. Dewey:305.5/62/0973. LCCN:82-009903.
Audience: **f.** B

Potter, David M. **F0214.P6**
The South and the Sectional Conflict. Trade Paper. Books on Demand. Ann Arbor, MI. 1968. 335p. ISBN:0-7837-8531-3, ISBN13: 978-0-7837-8531-8. Dewey:975. LCCN:68-008941.
Audience: **u,f.** B

Rose, Lisle Abbott **F0213.R83**
Prologue to Democracy: The Federalists in the South, 1789-1800. Trade Paper. Books on Demand. Ann Arbor, MI. 344p. ISBN:0-598-22010-0, ISBN13: 978-0-598-22010-3. Dewey:329/.1/009033. LCCN:67-029342.
Audience: **f.** B

Smith, Mark M. (Editor) **F213.O43 2001**
The Old South. Trade Paper. Blackwell Publishing, Inc. Malden, MA. 2000. 320p. Blackwell Readers in American Social and Cultural History Ser., Vol. 4 ISBN:0-631-21927-7, ISBN13: 978-0-631-21927-9. Dewey:975/.03. LCCN:00-037829.
Audience: **u,f.**

Snapp, J. Russell **F212.S7S65 1996**
John Stuart and the Struggle for Empire on the Southern Frontier. Cloth Text. Louisiana State University Press. Baton Rouge, LA. 1996. 288p. ISBN:0-8071-2024-3, ISBN13: 978-0-8071-2024-8. Dewey:975/.02/092 B. LCCN:95-047384.
Audience: **f.** *Choice, 1997.*

Sydnor, Charles S. **F213.S92**
The Development of Southern Sectionalism, 1819-1848. Trade Cloth. Louisiana State University Press. Baton Rouge, LA. 1948. xii, 432p. History of the South Ser., Vol. 5 ISBN:0-8071-0005-6, ISBN13: 978-0-8071-0005-9. Dewey:975. LCCN:48-007627.
Audience: **f.** B

Volo, James M. & Volo, Dorothy Denneen **F213**
Encyclopedia of the Antebellum South. Cloth Text. Greenwood Publishing Group, Inc. Portsmouth, NH. 2000. 408p. ISBN:0-313-30886-1, ISBN13: 978-0-313-30886-4. Dewey:975/.03/03. LCCN:99-028797.
Audience: **g,l,u,f.** *Choice, 2000.*

Wiley, Bell Irvin **F214.W56 2000**
Plain People of the Confederacy. Paul D. Escott (Introduction by). Trade Cloth. University of South Carolina Press. Columbia, SC. 2000. xxxix, 104p. Southern Classics Ser. ISBN:1-57003-362-5, ISBN13: 978-1-57003-362-9. Dewey:973.7/13. LCCN:00-028622.
Audience: **u,f.** BCL3

Wyatt-Brown, Bertram **F213.W957 2001**
The Shaping of Southern Culture: Honor, Grace, and War, 1760s-1880s. Trade Cloth. University of North Carolina Press. Chapel Hill, NC. 2001. 440p. ISBN:0-8078-2596-4, ISBN13: 978-0-8078-2596-9. Dewey:975.03. LCCN:00-069952.
Audience: **f.**

United States > U.S. Local History > Southern States: General > 1865-

Applebome, Peter **F216.2.A67 1997**
Dixie Rising: How the South Is Shaping American Values, Politics, and Culture. Trade Paper. Harcourt Trade Publishers. New York, NY. 1997. 416p. Harvest Book Ser. ISBN:0-15-600550-6, ISBN13: 978-0-15-600550-0. Dewey:973.929. LCCN:97-027787.
Audience: **u,f.**

Ayers, Edward L. **F215.A94 1992**
The Promise of the New South: Life after Reconstruction. Trade Cloth. Oxford University Press, Inc. New York, NY. 1992. 592p. ISBN:0-19-503756-1, ISBN13: 978-0-19-503756-2. Dewey:975/.041. LCCN:91-033070.
Audience: **u,f.** *Choice, 1993.*

Ayers, Edward L. **F215.A943 1995**
Southern Crossing: A History of the American South, 1877-1906. Trade Paper. Oxford University Press, Inc. New York, NY. 1995. 298p. ISBN:0-19-508689-9, ISBN13: 978-0-19-508689-8. Dewey:975/.041. LCCN:94-009755.
Audience: **f.**

Biles, Roger **F215.B55 1994**
The South and the New Deal. Trade Cloth. University Press of Kentucky. Lexington, KY. 1994. 216p. New Perspectives on the South Ser. ISBN:0-8131-1836-0, ISBN13: 978-0-8131-1836-9. Dewey:975.042. LCCN:93-020816.
Audience: **f.** *Choice, 1994.*

Boles, John B. & Johnson, Bethany L. (Editors) **F215.W85 2003**
Origins of the New South Fifty Years Later: The Continuing Influence of a Historical Classic. Trade Cloth. Louisiana State University Press. Baton Rouge, LA. 2003. 304p. ISBN:0-8071-2905-4, ISBN13: 978-0-8071-2905-0. Dewey:975/.041. LCCN:2003-047645.
Audience: **f.** *Choice, 2004.*

Clark, Thomas Dionysius **F215.C6 1964**
Pills, Petticoats, and Plows; the Southern Country Store. Trade Cloth. University of Oklahoma Press. Norman, OK. 1964. 306p. ISBN:0-8061-0593-3, ISBN13: 978-0-8061-0593-2. Dewey:917.5. LCCN:64-011333.
Audience: **f.** BCL3

Dailey, Jane Elizabeth (Editor), et al. **F215.J86 2000**
Jumpin' Jim Crow: Southern Politics from Civil War to Civil Rights. Glenda Elizabeth Gilmore & Bryant Simon (Editors). Trade Cloth. Princeton University Press. Princeton, NJ. 2000. 280p. ISBN:0-691-00192-8, ISBN13: 978-0-691-00192-0. Dewey:975/.04. LCCN:00-027861.
Audience: **u,f.**

Daniels, Jonathan (Introduction by) **F215.D257**
A Southerner Discovers the South. Paper Text. Da Capo Press, Inc. Cambridge, MA. 1970. xix, 346p. American Scene Ser. ISBN:0-306-71011-0, ISBN13: 978-0-306-71011-7. Dewey:917.5. LCCN:68-016228.
Audience: **f.** BCL3

Dollard, John **E185.92.D65 1988**
Caste and Class in a Southern Town. Daniel Moynihan (Foreword by). Paper Text. University of Wisconsin Press. Chicago, IL. 1989. 486p. ISBN:0-299-12134-8, ISBN13: 978-0-299-12134-1. Dewey:975/.004. LCCN:88-040430.
Audience: **f.** BCL3

Grantham, Dewey W. **F215.G739**
The Regional Imagination: The South and Recent American History. Trade Paper. Books on Demand. Ann Arbor, MI. 283p. ISBN:0-608-18734-8, ISBN13: 978-0-608-18734-1. Dewey:975/.04. LCCN:78-026556.
Audience: **u,f.**

Grantham, Dewey W. **F215.G75 2001**
The South in Modern America: A Region at Odds. Trade Paper. University of Arkansas Press. Fayetteville, AR. 2003. 406p. ISBN:1-55728-710-4, ISBN13: 978-1-55728-710-6. Dewey:975.04. LCCN:2001-021353.
Audience: **u,f.**

Hale, Grace E. **F215.H18 1998**
Making Whiteness: The Culture of Segregation in the South, 1890-1940. Trade Cloth. Knopf Publishing Group. New York, NY. 1998. 448p. ISBN:0-679-44263-4, ISBN13: 978-0-679-44263-9. Dewey:305.8/00973. LCCN:97-040906.
Audience: **f.** *Choice, 1998.*

Key, V. O. Jr. **F215.K45 1984**
Southern Politics in State and Nation. Alexander Heard (Introduction by). Paper Text. University of Tennessee Press. Knoxville, TN. 1984. 752p. ISBN:0-87049-435-X, ISBN13: 978-0-87049-435-2. Dewey:324.975/04. LCCN:84-003665.
Audience: **f.** BCL3

Lamis, Alexander P. (Editor) **JK2356.S72 1999**
Southern Politics in the 1990s. Trade Cloth. Louisiana State University Press. Baton Rouge, LA. 1999. xviii, 462p. ISBN:0-8071-2374-9, ISBN13: 978-0-8071-2374-4. Dewey:324.275/04/09049. LCCN:98-050424.
Audience: **u,f.** *Choice, 2000.*

Link, William A. **F215.L56 1992**
The Paradox of Southern Progressivism, 1880-1930. Cloth Text. University of North Carolina Press. Chapel Hill, NC. 1993. xviii, 440p. Fred W. Morrison Series in Southern Studies ISBN:0-8078-2040-7, ISBN13: 978-0-8078-2040-7. Dewey:306.2/0975. LCCN:92-001328.
Audience: **u,f.** *Choice, 1993.*

McGill, Ralph **F215 .M49 1992**
The South and the Southerner. Eugene Patterson (Foreword by). Trade Paper. University of Georgia Press. Athens, GA. 1992. 328p. Brown Thrasher Bks. ISBN:0-8203-1443-9, ISBN13: 978-0-8203-1443-3. Dewey:975. LCCN:92-006038.
Audience: **f.**

O'Brien, Michael **F215**
The Idea of the American South: 1920-1941. Trade Cloth. Johns Hopkins University Press. Baltimore, MD. 1990. 296p. The Johns Hopkins University Studies in Historical and Political Sciences Ser. ISBN:0-8018-2166-5, ISBN13: 978-0-8018-2166-0. Dewey:975/.04. LCCN:78-012250.
Audience: **f.**

Perman, Michael **F216.P47**
The Road to Redemption: Southern Politics, 1869-1879. Trade Paper. University of North Carolina Press. Chapel Hill, NC. 1985. 368p. Fred W. Morrison Series in Southern Studies ISBN:0-8078-4141-2, ISBN13: 978-0-8078-4141-9. Dewey:973.8/2. LCCN:83-012498.
Audience: **f.**

Potter, David M. **F215.P66**
The South and the Concurrent Majority. Don E. Fehrenbacher & Carl N. Degler (Editors). Trade Cloth. Louisiana State University Press. Baton Rouge, LA. 1972. viii, 90p. Walter Lynwood Fleming Lectures ISBN:0-8071-0229-6, ISBN13: 978-0-8071-0229-9. Dewey:320.9/75/04. LCCN:72-084123.
Audience: **f.**

Roland, Charles P. **F216.2 .R64 1976**
The Improbable Era: The South since World War II. Trade Paper. University Press of Kentucky. Lexington, KY. 1982. 240p. ISBN:0-8131-0139-5, ISBN13: 978-0-8131-0139-2. Dewey:975/.04. LCCN:76-046033.
Audience: **f.**

Scher, Richard K. **F215.S34 1997**
Politics in the New South: Republicanism, Race, and Leadership in the Twentieth Century. Ed. 2. Cloth Text. M. E. Sharpe Inc. Armonk, NY. 1997. 432p. ISBN:1-56324-847-6, ISBN13: 978-1-56324-847-4. Dewey:320.975. LCCN:96-030362.
Audience: **f.**

Sosna, Morton **F215**
In Search of the Silent South: Southern Liberals and the Race Issue. Cloth Text. Columbia University Press. New York, NY. 1977. xviii, 275p. Contemporary American History Ser. ISBN:0-231-03843-7, ISBN13: 978-0-231-03843-0. Dewey:305.8/96073/075. LCCN:77-004965.
Audience: **f.**

Thornton, R. Gordon **F216.2.T48 2000**
The Southern Nation: The New Rise of the Old South. Trade Paper. Pelican Publishing Company, Inc. Gretna, LA. 2000. 256p. ISBN:1-56554-697-0, ISBN13: 978-1-56554-697-4. Dewey:975/.043. LCCN:99-051592.
Audience: **f.**

Tindall, George B. **F215.T59**
Emergence of the New South, 1913-1945. Cloth Text. Louisiana State University Press. Baton Rouge, LA. 1967. xvi, 808p. History of the South Ser., Vol. 10 ISBN:0-8071-0010-2, ISBN13: 978-0-8071-0010-3. Dewey:975. LCCN:67-024551.
Audience: **f.**

Woodward, C. Vann **F215**
Origins of the New South, 1877-1913. Trade Cloth. Louisiana State University Press. Baton Rouge, LA. 1951. xiv, 656p. History of the South Ser., Vol. 9 ISBN:0-8071-0009-9, ISBN13: 978-0-8071-0009-7. Dewey:975/.041. LCCN:77-014582.
Audience: **g,l,u,f.**

United States > U.S. Local History > Southern States: General > Regions, A-Z

Abramson, Rudy & Haskell, Jean (Editors) **F106.E53 2006**
Encyclopedia of Appalachia. Cloth Text. University of Tennessee Press. Knoxville, TN. 2006. 1800p. ISBN:1-57233-456-8, ISBN13: 978-1-57233-456-4. Dewey:974/.003. LCCN:2005-017102.
Audience: **g,l,u,f.**

Adams, Shelby L. **F217.A65 A24 1998**
Appalachian Legacy. Trade Cloth. University Press of Mississippi. Jackson, MS. 1998. 128p. ISBN:1-57806-048-6, ISBN13: 978-1-57806-048-1. Dewey:974. LCCN:97-042794.
Audience: **u,f.**

Drake, Richard B. **F106.D73**
A History of Appalachia. Trade Cloth. University Press of Kentucky. Lexington, KY. 2003. 320p. ISBN:0-8131-9060-6, ISBN13: 978-0-8131-9060-0. Dewey:974.
Audience: **u,f.** *Choice, 2001.*

Dunaway, Wilma A. **HC107.A127D86 1996**
The First American Frontier: Transition to Capitalism in Southern Appalachia, 1700-1860. Trade Paper. University of North Carolina Press. Chapel Hill, NC. 1996. 468p. Fred W. Morrison Series in Southern Studies ISBN:0-8078-4540-X, ISBN13: 978-0-8078-4540-0. Dewey:330.974. LCCN:95-002790.
Audience: **f.** *Choice, 1996.*

Edwards, Grace Toney (Editor), et al. **F106.H23 2006**
A Handbook to Appalachia: An Introduction to the Region. JoAnn Aust Asbury & Ricky L. Cox (Editors). Trade Paper. University of Tennessee Press. Knoxville, TN. 2006. 336p. ISBN:1-57233-459-2, ISBN13: 978-1-57233-459-5. Dewey:974. LCCN:2005-019799.
Audience: **g,l,u,f.**

Inscoe, John C. (Editor) **E185.912**
Appalachians and Race: The Mountain South from Slavery to Segregation. Trade Paper. University Press of Kentucky. Lexington, KY. 2005. 344p. ISBN:0-8131-9127-0, ISBN13: 978-0-8131-9127-0. Dewey:974.004/96/073. LCCN:00-028311.
Audience: **f.** *Choice, 2001.*

Jones, Loyal **BR535.J66 1999**
Faith and Meaning in the Southern Uplands. Trade Cloth. University of Illinois Press. Champaign, IL. 1999. 288p.

ISBN:0-252-02431-1, ISBN13: 978-0-252-02431-3. Dewey:277.69. LCCN:98-025359.
Audience: **f.**

McCauley, Deborah V. **BR535.M38 1995**
Appalachian Mountain Religion: A History. Trade Paper. University of Illinois Press. Champaign, IL. 1995. 584p. ISBN:0-252-06414-3, ISBN13: 978-0-252-06414-2. Dewey:277.4/08. LCCN:94-018247.
Audience: **u,f.** *Choice, 1995.*

Pudup, Mary B. (Editor), et al. **F217.A65A654 1995**
Appalachia in the Making. Dwight Billings & Altina L. Waller (Editors). Trade Cloth. University of North Carolina Press. Chapel Hill, NC. 1995. 402p. ISBN:0-8078-2229-9, ISBN13: 978-0-8078-2229-6. Dewey:975. LCCN:94-047135.
Audience: **u,f.** *Choice, 1996.*

Shackelford, Laurel & Weinberg, Bill (Editors) **F217.A65**
Our Appalachia: An Oral History. Trade Paper. University Press of Kentucky. Lexington, KY. 1988. 408p. ISBN:0-8131-0184-0, ISBN13: 978-0-8131-0184-2. Dewey:975 B. LCCN:76-048625.
Audience: **u,f.**

Shapiro, Henry D. **77-2301**
Appalachia on Our Mind: The Southern Mountains and Mountaineers in the American Consciousness, 1870-1920. Trade Paper. University of North Carolina Press. Chapel Hill, NC. 1986. 397p. ISBN:0-8078-4158-7, ISBN13: 978-0-8078-4158-7. Dewey:301.29/74. LCCN:77-002301.
Audience: **f.** B

Straw, Richard Alan & Blethen, Tyler **F106.H46 2004**
High Mountains Rising: Appalachia in Place and Time. Trade Paper. University of Illinois Press. Champaign, IL. 2004. 256p. ISBN:0-252-07176-X, ISBN13: 978-0-252-07176-8. Dewey:975/.68. LCCN:2003-019701.
Audience: **f.** *Choice, 2005.*

Whisnant, David E. **F217.A65W47 1983**
All That Is Native and Fine: The Politics of Culture in an American Region. Trade Paper. University of North Carolina Press. Chapel Hill, NC. 1986. 355p. ISBN:0-8078-4143-9, ISBN13: 978-0-8078-4143-3. Dewey:306/.0974. LCCN:82-024851.
Audience: **f.** B

Williams, John Alexander **F106.W68 2002**
Appalachia: A History. Trade Paper. University of North Carolina Press. Chapel Hill, NC. 2002. 496p. ISBN:0-8078-5368-2, ISBN13: 978-0-8078-5368-9. Dewey:974. LCCN:2001-052761.
Audience: **g,l,u,f.**

Yarnell, Susan L. **F217.A65**
The Southern Appalachians: A History of the Landscape. Paper Text. DIANE Publishing Company. Collingdale, PA. 1999. 45p. ISBN:0-7881-4116-3, ISBN13: 978-0-7881-4116-4. Dewey:630.75.
Audience: **l,u,f.**

United States > U.S. Local History > Southern States: General > Population

Cole, Stephanie & Parker, Alison M. (Editor, Translator, Introduction by) **F220.A1B49 2003**
Beyond Black and White: Race, Ethnicity, and Gender in the U. S. South and Southwest. Laura F. Edwards (Editor). Trade Cloth. Texas A&M University Press. College Station, TX. 2004. 224p. Walter Prescott Webb Memorial Lectures, Vol. 35 ISBN:1-58544-297-6, ISBN13: 978-1-58544-297-3. Dewey:305.8/00975. LCCN:2003-010130.
Audience: **u,f.**

Evans, Eli **F220.J5E82 2005**
The Provincials: A Personal History of Jews in the South. Willie Morris (Foreword by). Trade Cloth. University of North Carolina Press. Chapel Hill, NC. 2005. 416p. ISBN:0-8078-2958-7, ISBN13: 978-0-8078-2958-5. Dewey:975/.004924. LCCN:2004-063767.
Audience: **u,f.**

Gallegos, Eloy J. **F220.M44G35 1997**
The Spanish Pioneers in United States History the Melungeons: The Pioneers of the Interior Southeastern U. S., 1526-1997. Perfect. Tennessee Valley Publishing. Knoxville, TN. 1997. 203p. Spanish Pioneer Ser. ISBN:1-882194-32-2, ISBN13: 978-1-882194-32-2. Dewey:975/.004044. LCCN:97-061691.
Audience: **u,f.**

Gleeson, David T. **F220.I6G58 2001**
e The Irish in the South, 1815-1877. E-Book. University of North Carolina Press. Chapel Hill, NC. ISBN:0-8078-7563-5, ISBN13: 978-0-8078-7563-6. Dewey:975/.0049162.
Audience: **u,f.** *Choice, 2002.*

Gleeson, David T. **F220.I6G58 2001**
The Irish in the South, 1815-1877. Trade Cloth. University of North Carolina Press. Chapel Hill, NC. 2001. 296p. ISBN:0-8078-2639-1, ISBN13: 978-0-8078-2639-3. Dewey:975/.0049162. LCCN:2001-027544.
Audience: **f.** *Choice, 2002.*

Rosen, Robert N. **F220.J5R67 2000**
The Jewish Confederates. Trade Cloth. University of South Carolina Press. Columbia, SC. 2000. xxiii, 517p. ISBN:1-57003-363-3, ISBN13: 978-1-57003-363-6. Dewey:975.004/924. LCCN:00-009492.
Audience: **u,f.** *Choice, 2001.*

Tindall, George B. **F220.A1T56 1995**
Natives and Newcomers: Ethnic Southerners and Southern Ethnics. Trade Cloth. University of Georgia Press. Athens, GA. 1994. 64p. Georgia Southern University Jack N. and Addie D. Averett Lecture Ser., No. 3 ISBN:0-8203-1655-5, ISBN13: 978-0-8203-1655-0. Dewey:305.8/00975. LCCN:94-005970.
Audience: **f.**

United States > U.S. Local History > South Atlantic States > Virginia

Ayers, Edward L. & Willis, John C. (Editors) **F230.E34 1991**
The Edge of the South: Life in Nineteenth-Century Virginia. Cloth Text. University Press of Virginia. Charlottesville, VA.

1991. 288p. ISBN:0-8139-1298-9, ISBN13: 978-0-8139-1298-1. Dewey:975.5. LCCN:90-012825.
Audience: **f.**

Bacon, Lisa **F226.B33 2004**
Virginia: A Commonwealth Comes of Age: An Illustrated History. Trade Cloth. American Historical Press. Sun Valley, CA. 2004. 368p. ISBN:1-892724-43-X, ISBN13: 978-1-892724-43-4. Dewey:975.5. LCCN:2004-110806.
Audience: **l,u,f.**

Beeman, Richard R. **F230.B43**
The Old Dominion and the New Nation, 1788-1801. Trade Cloth. University Press of Kentucky. Lexington, KY. 1972. 296p. ISBN:0-8131-1269-9, ISBN13: 978-0-8131-1269-5. Dewey:320.9/755/03. LCCN:76-190531.
Audience: **u,f.** B

Billings, Warren M. (Editor) **F229.B615**
The Old Dominion in the Seventeenth Century: A Documentary History of Virginia, 1606-1689. Trade Cloth. University of North Carolina Press. Chapel Hill, NC. 1975. xxiv, 324p. Institute of Early American History and Culture Ser. ISBN:0-8078-1234-X, ISBN13: 978-0-8078-1234-1. Dewey:975.5/02. LCCN:74-008302.
Audience: **f.** B

Breen, T. H. **F229.B8 2001**
Tobacco Culture: The Mentality of the Great Tidewater Planters on the Eve of Revolution. Trade Paper. Princeton University Press. Princeton, NJ. 2001. 246p. ISBN:0-691-08914-0, ISBN13: 978-0-691-08914-0. Dewey:975.5/02. LCCN:2001-019854.
Audience: **f.** B *Choice, 1986.*

Breen, T. H. & Innes, Stephen **F232.E2B73 2004**
Myne Owne Ground: Race and Freedom on Virginia's Eastern Shore, 1640-1676. Ed. 25. Trade Cloth. Oxford University Press, Inc. New York, NY. 2004. 168p. ISBN:0-19-517538-7, ISBN13: 978-0-19-517538-7. Dewey:975.5/100496073. LCCN:2004-054798.
Audience: **f.** B

Bridenbaugh, Carl **F234.J3.B7**
Jamestown, 1544 to 1699. Oxford University Press, Inc. 1980. ISBN:0-19-502650-0, ISBN13: 978-0-19-502650-4.
Audience: **u,f.** B

Bridenbaugh, Carl **F234.W7 W7**
Seat of Empire: The Political Role of Eighteenth. Paper Text. Textbook Publishers. Temecula, CA. 2003. 85p. ISBN:0-7581-1468-0, ISBN13: 978-0-7581-1468-6. Dewey:975.5425.
Audience: **f.** B

Byrd, William **F229.B9715 1972**
The Secret Diary of William Byrd of Westover, 1709-1712. Trade Cloth. Arno Press. New York, NY. 1972. xxviii, 622p. ISBN:0-405-03304-4, ISBN13: 978-0-405-03304-9. Dewey:975.5/02/0924. LCCN:72-141097.
Audience: **f.**

Craven, Wesley F. **F229**
The Virginia Company of London, 1606-1624. Trade Paper. Clearfield Company. Baltimore, MD. 1997. 70p. ISBN:0-8063-4555-1, ISBN13: 978-0-8063-4555-0. Dewey:975.503.
Audience: **f.**

Dabney, Virginius **F226 .D32 1983**
Virginia: The New Dominion, a History from 1607 to the Present. Paper Text. University Press of Virginia. Charlottesville, VA. 1983. 629p. ISBN:0-8139-1015-3, ISBN13: 978-0-8139-1015-4. Dewey:975.5. LCCN:83-018232.
Audience: **l,u,f.**

Emerson, Everett H. **F229.S7 E44 1993**
Captain John Smith. Trade Cloth. Thomson Gale. Farmington Hills, MI. 1993. 180p. Twayne's United States Authors Ser. ISBN:0-8057-3989-0, ISBN13: 978-0-8057-3989-3. Dewey:973.2/1/092. LCCN:92-029055.
Audience: **u,f.**

Furgurson, Ernest B. **F234.R557**
Ashes of Glory: Richmond at War. Trade Paper. Knopf Publishing Group. New York, NY. 1997. 464p. ISBN:0-679-74660-9, ISBN13: 978-0-679-74660-7. Dewey:975.5/451043.
Audience: **f.**

Hall, Granville Davisson **F226.H17 2000**
The Rending of Virginia: A History. John Edmund Stealey III (Introduction by). Paper Text. University of Tennessee Press. Knoxville, TN. 2000. 672p. Appalachian Echoes Ser. ISBN:1-57233-070-8, ISBN13: 978-1-57233-070-2. Dewey:975.5. LCCN:99-050734.
Audience: **g,l,u,f.**

Hoobler, Dorothy & Hoobler, Thomas **F229.S7H66 2006**
Captain John Smith: Jamestown and the Birth of the American Dream. Trade Cloth. John Wiley & Sons, Inc. Hoboken, NJ. 2005. 288p. ISBN:0-471-48584-5, ISBN13: 978-0-471-48584-1. Dewey:975.5/02/092 B. LCCN:2005-017411.
Audience: **u,f.** *Choice, 2006.*

Horn, James **F234.J3H66 2005**
A Land As God Made It: Jamestown and the Birth of America. Trade Cloth. Basic Books. New York, NY. 2005. 352p. ISBN:0-465-03094-7, ISBN13: 978-0-465-03094-1. Dewey:975.5/4251. LCCN:2005-013054.
Audience: **u,f.** *Choice, 2006.*

Isaac, Rhys **F229.I8 1999**
The Transformation of Virginia, 1740-1790. Trade Cloth. University of North Carolina Press. Chapel Hill, NC. 1982. 462p. Institute of Early American History and Culture Ser. ISBN:0-8078-1489-X, ISBN13: 978-0-8078-1489-5. Dewey:975.5/02. LCCN:81-010393.
Audience: **f.** B

Jefferson, Thomas **F230 .J5102**
Notes on the State of Virginia. Paper Text. Textbook Publishers. Temecula, CA. 2003. xxv, 315p. ISBN:0-7581-5411-9, ISBN13: 978-0-7581-5411-8. Dewey:917.55.
Audience: **u,f.** B

Jeffries, Judson L. **F231.3.W55J44 2000**
Virginia's Native Son: The Election and Administration of Governor L. Douglas Wilder. Trade Cloth. Purdue University Press. West Lafayette, IN. 2000. xxiv, 148p. ISBN:1-55753-200-1, ISBN13: 978-1-55753-200-8. Dewey:975.5/043/092. LCCN:99-045649.
Audience: **u,f.**

Kolp, John G. **F229.K75 1998**
Gentlemen and Freeholders: Electoral Politics in Colonial Virginia. Trade Cloth. Johns Hopkins University Press. Baltimore, MD. 1998. 264p. Early America Ser. ISBN:0-8018-5843-7, ISBN13: 978-0-8018-5843-7. Dewey:324.9755/02. LCCN:97-049956.
Audience: **f.** *Choice, 1999.*

Kopper, Philip **F234.W7K67 1986**
Colonial Williamsburg. Trade Cloth. Harry N. Abrams, Inc. New York, NY. 1986. 320p. ISBN:0-8109-0787-9, ISBN13: 978-0-8109-0787-4. Dewey:975.5/4252. LCCN:86-001252.
Audience: **f.**

Kupperman, Karen O. **F229.K9 1984**
Roanoke: The Abandoned Colony. Trade Cloth. Rowman & Littlefield Publishers, Inc. Lanham, MD. 1984. 200p. ISBN:0-8476-7127-5, ISBN13: 978-0-8476-7127-4. Dewey:975.6/175. LCCN:83-024419.
Audience: **f.** B

Lockridge, Kenneth A. **F229.B978 1987**
The Diary and Life of William Byrd II of Virginia, 1674-1744. Trade Cloth. University of North Carolina Press. Chapel Hill, NC. 1987. xiv, 202p. Institute of Early American History and Culture Ser. ISBN:0-8078-1736-8, ISBN13: 978-0-8078-1736-0. Dewey:975.5/02/0924 B. LCCN:86-040425.
Audience: **f.** *Choice, 1987.*

Maddex, Jack P. **F231.M2**
The Virginia Conservatives, 1867-1879; a Study in Reconstruction Politics. Trade Cloth. University of North Carolina Press. Chapel Hill, NC. 1970. xx, 328p. ISBN:0-8078-1140-8, ISBN13: 978-0-8078-1140-5. Dewey:320.9/755. LCCN:76-109465.
Audience: **f.** B

Moger, Allen W. **F0231.M66**
Virginia: Bourbonism to Byrd, 1870-1925. Trade Paper. Books on Demand. Ann Arbor, MI. 414p. ISBN:0-7837-4349-1, ISBN13: 978-0-7837-4349-3. Dewey:975.5. LCCN:68-008538.
Audience: **f.** B

Morgan, Edmund S. **F229.M6**
Virginians at Home: Family Life in the Eighteenth Century. Trade Paper. Colonial Williamsburg Foundation. Williamsburg, VA. 1952. 101p. America Ser., Vol. 2 ISBN:0-910412-52-9, ISBN13: 978-0-910412-52-0. Dewey:975.502. LCCN:52-014250.
Audience: **u,f.**

Morton, Richard Lee **F229 .M75**
Colonial Virginia. Paper Text. Textbook Publishers. Temecula, CA. 2003. ISBN:0-7581-5333-3, ISBN13: 978-0-7581-5333-3. Dewey:975.502.
Audience: **f.** B

Rubin, Louis Decimus Jr. **F226.R7**
Virginia: A History. Trade Cloth. W. W. Norton & Company, Inc. New York, NY. 1977. xii, 228p. States and the Nation Ser. ISBN:0-393-05630-9, ISBN13: 978-0-393-05630-3. Dewey:975.5. LCCN:77-003250.
Audience: **g,l,u,f.** B

Smith, J. Douglas **F235.A1S65 2003**
Managing White Supremacy: Race, Politics, and Citizenship in Jim Crow Virginia. Trade Paper. University of North Carolina Press. Chapel Hill, NC. 2002. 384p. ISBN:0-8078-5424-7, ISBN13: 978-0-8078-5424-2. Dewey:305.896/0730755. LCCN:2002-006437.
Audience: **f.** *Choice, 2003.*

Smith, John **F229.S592 1988**
Captain John Smith: A Select Edition of His Writings. Karen O. Kupperman (Editor). Trade Cloth. University of North Carolina Press. Chapel Hill, NC. 1988. 304p. Institute of Early American History and Culture Ser. ISBN:0-8078-1778-3, ISBN13: 978-0-8078-1778-0. Dewey:975.5/02. LCCN:87-021485.
Audience: **f.**

Stick, David **F229**
Roanoke Island: The Beginnings of English America. Trade Cloth. University of North Carolina Press. Chapel Hill, NC. 1983. xiii, 266p. ISBN:0-8078-1554-3, ISBN13: 978-0-8078-1554-0. Dewey:975.6/175. LCCN:83-007014.
Audience: **f.** B

Tillson, Albert H. Jr. **F229.T58 1991**
Gentry and Common Folk: Political Culture on a Virginia Frontier, 1740-1789. Cloth Text. University Press of Kentucky. Lexington, KY. 1991. 240p. ISBN:0-8131-1749-6, ISBN13: 978-0-8131-1749-2. Dewey:973.2. LCCN:91-008181.
Audience: **f.** *Choice, 1992.*

Tyler, Lyon G. **F225.E53 1998**
Encyclopedia of Virginia Biography, Set. Trade Cloth. Genealogical Publishing Company, Inc. Baltimore, MD. 1998. 2575p. ISBN:0-8063-1552-0, ISBN13: 978-0-8063-1552-2. Dewey:920.0755. LCCN:97-077441.
Audience: **g,l,u,f.**

Vaughan, Alden T. **QE507**
American Genesis: Captain John Smith and the Founding of Virginia. Trade Paper. Longman Publishing Group. White Plains, NY. 1997. 207p. Library of American Biography Ser. ISBN:0-673-39355-0, ISBN13: 978-0-673-39355-5. Dewey:551.6/09/012.
Audience: **f.** B

Ward, Harry M. **F0234.R557W**
Richmond During the Revolution, 1775-83: Harry M. Ward and Harold E. Greer, Jr. Trade Paper. Books on Demand. Ann Arbor, MI. 219p. ISBN:0-598-03437-4, ISBN13: 978-0-598-03437-3. Dewey:975.5/451/03. LCCN:77-022586.
Audience: **f.**

Washburn, Wilcomb E. **F229 .W28**
The Governor and the Rebel: A History of Bacon's Rebellion in Virginia. Paper Text. Textbook Publishers. Temecula, CA. 2003. xv, 248p. ISBN:0-7581-5416-X, ISBN13: 978-0-7581-5416-3. Dewey:975.5.
Audience: **f.** B

Webb, Stephen S. (Author, Preface by) **F229.W36 1995**
1676: The End of American Independence. Trade Paper. Syracuse University Press. Syracuse, NY. 1995. 460p. ISBN:0-8156-0361-4, ISBN13: 978-0-8156-0361-0. Dewey:973.2/4. LCCN:95-023883.
Audience: **f.** B

Wertenbaker, Thomas Jefferson **F229 .W49**
Patrician and Plebian in Virginia: Or, the Origin and Development of the Social Classes of the Old Dominion. Paper

Text. Textbook Publishers. Temecula, CA. 2003. vii, 239p. ISBN:0-7581-4367-2, ISBN13: 978-0-7581-4367-9. Dewey:975.502.

Audience: **f.**

Wertenbaker, Thomas Jefferson **F229.W493**
The Planters of Colonial Virginia. Paper Text. Textbook Publishers. Temecula, CA. 2003. 260p. ISBN:0-7581-4378-8, ISBN13: 978-0-7581-4378-5. Dewey:975.502.

Audience: **f.**

Wilkinson, J. Harvie **F0231.2.W5**
Harry Byrd and the Changing Face of Virginia Politics, 1945-1966. Trade Paper. Books on Demand. Ann Arbor, MI. 423p. ISBN:0-7837-8671-9, ISBN13: 978-0-7837-8671-1. Dewey:320.9/755. LCCN:68-022731.

Audience: **f.**

Workers of the WPA Writers Program Staff (Compiled by) **F226.V894 1992**
Virginia: A Guide to the Old Dominion. Trade Cloth. Library of Virginia, The. Richmond, VA. 1992. ISBN:0-88490-173-4, ISBN13: 978-0-88490-173-0. Dewey:917.5504/43. LCCN:92-028334.

Audience: **u,f.**

Wright, Louis B. **F 0229.W7**
The First Gentlemen of Virginia: Intellectual Qualities of the Early Colonial Ruling Class. Trade Paper. Books on Demand. Ann Arbor, MI. 383p. ISBN:0-608-17949-3, ISBN13: 978-0-608-17949-0. Dewey:975.5. LCCN:40-008029.

Audience: **f.**

United States > U.S. Local History > South Atlantic States > West Virginia

Hennen, John **F241.H54 1996**
The Americanization of West Virginia: Creating a Modern Industrial State, 1916-1925. Cloth Text. University Press of Kentucky. Lexington, KY. 1996. 248p. ISBN:0-8131-1960-X, ISBN13: 978-0-8131-1960-1. Dewey:975.4/042. LCCN:95-032714.

Audience: **f.** *Choice, 1996.*

Rice, Otis K. & Brown, Stephen W. **F241.R515 1993**
West Virginia: A History. Ed. 2. Trade Cloth. University Press of Kentucky. Lexington, KY. 1993. 376p. ISBN:0-8131-1854-9, ISBN13: 978-0-8131-1854-3. Dewey:975.4. LCCN:93-017819.

Audience: **g,l,u,f.** *Choice, 1985.*

Williams, John Alexander **F241**
West Virginia: A History. Ed. 2. Trade Cloth. West Virginia University Press. Morgantown, WV. 2001. 248p. ISBN:0-937058-56-4, ISBN13: 978-0-937058-56-5. Dewey:975.4. LCCN:2001-093429.

Audience: **g,l,u,f.**

Writers Program Staff **F241.W85 1974**
West Virginia, a Guide to the Mountain State. Trade Cloth. Oxford University Press, Inc. New York, NY. 1974. xxxi, 559p. ISBN:0-403-02197-9, ISBN13: 978-0-403-02197-0. Dewey:917.54/04/4. LCCN:72-084516.

Audience: **u,f.**

United States > U.S. Local History > South Atlantic States > North Carolina. South Carolina

F254.E53 1992
Encyclopedia of North Carolina: A Reference Guide to the Tar Heel State. Library Binding. Somerset Publishers, Inc. Santa Barbara, CA. 1993. 542p. Encyclopedia of the United States Ser. ISBN:0-403-09905-6, ISBN13: 978-0-403-09905-4. Dewey:975.6/003. LCCN:92-006032.

Audience: **g,l,u,f.**

Cecelski, David S. & Tyson, Timothy B. (Editors) **F264.W7D46 1998**
Democracy Betrayed: The Wilmington Race Riot of 1898 and Its Legacy. John H. Franklin (Foreword by). Trade Cloth. University of North Carolina Press. Chapel Hill, NC. 1998. 320p. ISBN:0-8078-2451-8, ISBN13: 978-0-8078-2451-1. Dewey:975.627041. LCCN:98-003467.

Audience: **f.**

Click, Patricia C. **F262.R4C58 2001**
A Time Full of Trial: The Roanoke Island Freedmen's Colony, 1862-1867. Trade Cloth. University of North Carolina Press. Chapel Hill, NC. 2001. 328p. ISBN:0-8078-2602-2, ISBN13: 978-0-8078-2602-7. Dewey:975.6/175. LCCN:00-069951.

Audience: **f.** *Choice, 2002.*

Crane, Verner W. **F212.C67 2004**
The Southern Frontier, 1670-1732. Steven C. Hahn (Introduction by). Trade Paper. University of Alabama Press. Tuscaloosa, AL. 2004. 424p. ISBN:0-8173-5082-9, ISBN13: 978-0-8173-5082-6. Dewey:976/.01. LCCN:2003-016903.

Audience: **f.**

Decredico, Mary A. **F273.C54D43 1995**
Mary Boykin Chestnut: A Confederate Woman's Life. Trade Cloth. Rowman & Littlefield Publishers, Inc. Lanham, MD. 1996. 212p. American Profiles Ser. ISBN:0-945612-46-X, ISBN13: 978-0-945612-46-9. Dewey:975.7/041/092 B. LCCN:95-011155.

Audience: **u,f.** *Choice, 1997.*

Drescher, John **F260.D74 2000**
Triumph of Good Will: How Terry Sanford Beat a Champion of Segregation and Reshaped the South. Trade Cloth. University Press of Mississippi. Jackson, MS. 2000. xxi, 316p. ISBN:1-57806-310-8, ISBN13: 978-1-57806-310-9. Dewey:975.6/043/092. LCCN:00-035925.

Audience: **u,f.** *Choice, 2001.*

Edgar, Walter B. **F269.E34 1998**
South Carolina: A History. Trade Cloth. University of South Carolina Press. Columbia, SC. 1998. 761p. ISBN:1-57003-255-6, ISBN13: 978-1-57003-255-4. Dewey:975.7. LCCN:98-019679.

Audience: **g,l,u,f.** *Choice, 1999.*

Egerton, Douglas **F279**
He Shall Go Out Free: The Lives of Denmark Vesey. Book, Other. Rowman & Littlefield Publishers, Inc. Lanham, MD. 2004. 296p. ISBN:0-7425-4222-X, ISBN13: 978-0-7425-4222-8. Dewey:975.7/91503/092. LCCN:2006-272498.

Audience: **u,f.**

Faust, Drew G. **F273.H25 F38**
James Henry Hammond and the Old South: A Design for Mastery. Paper Text. Louisiana State University Press. Baton Rouge, LA. 1982. xx, 407p. Southern Biography Ser. ISBN:0-8071-1248-8, ISBN13: 978-0-8071-1248-9. Dewey:975.7/03/0924. LCCN:82-008939.
Audience: **f.** B

Federal Writers' Project Staff & Writers Program Staff **F259 .F44**
North Carolina: A Guide to the Old North State. Library Binding. Reprint Services Company. Temecula, CA. 1989. American Guide Ser. ISBN:0-7812-1032-1, ISBN13: 978-0-7812-1032-4. Dewey:917.56.
Audience: **f.**

Federal Writers' Project Staff & Writers Program Staff **F269**
South Carolina: A Guide to the Palmetto State. Library Binding. Reprint Services Company. Temecula, CA. 1989. American Guide Ser. ISBN:0-7812-1039-9, ISBN13: 978-0-7812-1039-3. Dewey:917.57.
Audience: **f.**

Grimsley, Wayne **F260.42.H86G75 2003**
James B. Hunt: A North Carolina Progressive. Trade Paper. McFarland & Company, Incorporated Publishers. Jefferson, NC. 2003. 293p. ISBN:0-7864-1607-6, ISBN13: 978-0-7864-1607-3. Dewey:975.6/043/092 B. LCCN:2003-008661.
Audience: **u,f.**

Kidder, Chris **F262.O96K53 2005**
The Outer Banks. Outer Banks History Center Associates (As told to). Trade Paper. Arcadia Publishing. Mount Pleasant, SC. 2005. 128p. Postcard History Ser. ISBN:0-7385-1768-2, ISBN13: 978-0-7385-1768-1. Dewey:975.6/100222. LCCN:2004-117374.
Audience: **f.**

Lefler, Hugh Talmage **F257.L52**
Colonial North Carolina; a History. Trade Cloth. Simon & Schuster. New York, NY. 1973. xvi, 318p. ISBN:0-684-13536-1, ISBN13: 978-0-684-13536-6. Dewey:975.6/02. LCCN:73-005188.
Audience: **l,u,f.** B

Lesser, Charles H. **F272.L57 1995**
South Carolina Begins: The Records of a Proprietary Colony, 1663-1721. Trade Paper. South Carolina Department of Archives & History. Columbia, SC. 1995. 540p. ISBN:1-880067-31-5, ISBN13: 978-1-880067-31-4. Dewey:975.7/02. LCCN:95-622449.
Audience: **f.**

Merrens, H. Roy (Editor) **F272.C73**
The Colonial South Carolina Scene: Contemporary Views 1697-1774. Trade Cloth. University of South Carolina Press. Columbia, SC. 1977. xii, 296p. Tricentennial Edition Ser., No. 7 ISBN:0-87249-261-3, ISBN13: 978-0-87249-261-5. Dewey:975.7/02/08. LCCN:76-054972.
Audience: **f.** B

Paludan, Phillip Shaw **F262**
Victims: A True Story of the Civil War. Ed. 2. Trade Paper. University of Tennessee Press. Knoxville, TN. 2004. 176p. ISBN:1-57233-325-1, ISBN13: 978-1-57233-325-3. Dewey:973.7/33.
Audience: **u,f.**

Powell, William S. **F254.P63 1989**
North Carolina Through Four Centuries. Trade Cloth. University of North Carolina Press. Chapel Hill, NC. 1989. 670p. ISBN:0-8078-1846-1, ISBN13: 978-0-8078-1846-6. Dewey:975.6. LCCN:88-007691.
Audience: **g,l,u,f.**

Ready, Milton **F254.R43 2005**
The Tar Heel State: A History of North Carolina. Trade Cloth. University of South Carolina Press. Columbia, SC. 2005. 384p. ISBN:1-57003-591-1, ISBN13: 978-1-57003-591-3. Dewey:975.6. LCCN:2005-009660.
Audience: **g,l,u,f.**

Rose, Willie L. **F279.P6R67 1998**
Rehearsal for Reconstruction: The Port Royal Experiment. Trade Paper. University of Georgia Press. Athens, GA. 1999. 464p. Brown Thrasher Bks. ISBN:0-8203-2061-7, ISBN13: 978-0-8203-2061-8. Dewey:975.7/99. LCCN:98-003851.
Audience: **g,l,u.**

Sinha, Manisha **F273.S64 2000**
The Counterrevolution of Slavery: Politics and Ideology in Antebellum South Carolina. Trade Cloth. University of North Carolina Press. Chapel Hill, NC. 2000. 384p. ISBN:0-8078-2571-9, ISBN13: 978-0-8078-2571-6. Dewey:975.7/03. LCCN:00-032590.
Audience: **f.** *Choice, 2001.*

Sirmans, Marion E. **F 0272.S5**
Colonial South Carolina: A Political History, 1663-1763. Trade Paper. Books on Demand. Ann Arbor, MI. 414p. ISBN:0-8357-3918-X, ISBN13: 978-0-8357-3918-4. Dewey:975.702. LCCN:66-025363.
Audience: **u,f.**

Stick, David **F229**
Roanoke Island: The Beginnings of English America. Trade Paper. University of North Carolina Press. Chapel Hill, NC. 1983. 279p. ISBN:0-8078-4110-2, ISBN13: 978-0-8078-4110-5. Dewey:975.6/175. LCCN:83-007014.
Audience: **l,u,f.** B

Weir, Robert M. **F272.W46 1997**
Colonial South Carolina: A History. Trade Paper. University of South Carolina Press. Columbia, SC. 1997. 430p. Understanding Contemporary American Literature Ser. ISBN:1-57003-189-4, ISBN13: 978-1-57003-189-2. Dewey:975.7/02. LCCN:97-001517.
Audience: **g,l,u,f.**

Zuczek, Richard **F274.Z83 1996**
State of Rebellion: Reconstruction in South Carolina. Cloth Text. University of South Carolina Press. Columbia, SC. 1996. 260p. ISBN:1-57003-105-3, ISBN13: 978-1-57003-105-2. Dewey:975.704. LCCN:95-050219.
Audience: **u,f.** *Choice, 1997.*

United States > U.S. Local History > South Atlantic States > Georgia

Anderson, William **F291.T3.A52**
The Wild Man from Sugar Creek: The Political Career of Eugene Talmadge. Trade Cloth. Louisiana State University Press. Baton Rouge, LA. 1975. xviii, 268p.

ISBN:0-8071-0088-9, ISBN13: 978-0-8071-0088-2. Dewey:975.8/04/0924. LCCN:74-082002.

Audience: **u,f.** B

Bartley, Numan V. **F291.B26 1990**
The Creation of Modern Georgia. Ed. 2. Trade Paper. University of Georgia Press. Athens, GA. 1990. 312p. Brown Thrasher Bks. ISBN:0-8203-1178-2, ISBN13: 978-0-8203-1178-4. Dewey:975.8/04. LCCN:90-030699.

Audience: **f.** B

Bayor, Ronald H. **F294.A89N424**
Race and the Shaping of Twentieth-Century Atlanta. Trade Paper. University of North Carolina Press. Chapel Hill, NC. 2000. 350p. Fred W. Morrison Series in Southern Studies ISBN:0-8078-4898-0, ISBN13: 978-0-8078-4898-2. Dewey:305.8/009758/231. LCCN:95-039552.

Audience: **f.** *Choice, 1996.*

Carey, Anthony G. **F290.C37 1997**
Parties, Slavery, and the Union in Antebellum Georgia. Trade Cloth. University of Georgia Press. Athens, GA. 1997. 336p. ISBN:0-8203-1898-1, ISBN13: 978-0-8203-1898-1. Dewey:324.2758/009/034. LCCN:96-030786.

Audience: **f.**

Cimbala, Paul A. **F291.C56 1997**
Under the Guardianship of the Nation: The Freedmen's Bureau and the Reconstruction of Georgia, 1865-1870. Trade Cloth. University of Georgia Press. Athens, GA. 1997. 336p. ISBN:0-8203-1891-4, ISBN13: 978-0-8203-1891-2. Dewey:975.8/041. LCCN:96-031225.

Audience: **f.**

Coleman, Kenneth **F290.C55**
The American Revolution in Georgia, 1763-1789. Paper Text. Textbook Publishers. Temecula, CA. 2003. viii, 352p. ISBN:0-7581-2286-1, ISBN13: 978-0-7581-2286-5.

Audience: **u,f.**

Coleman, Kenneth **F289.C64**
Colonial Georgia: A History. Trade Cloth. Simon & Schuster. New York, NY. 1976. xviii, 331p. ISBN:0-684-14556-1, ISBN13: 978-0-684-14556-3. Dewey:975.8/02. LCCN:75-037534.

Audience: **g,l,u,f.** B

Coleman, Kenneth (Editor) **F286.H58 1991**
A History of Georgia. Ed. 2. Trade Paper. University of Georgia Press. Athens, GA. 1991. 464p. ISBN:0-8203-1269-X, ISBN13: 978-0-8203-1269-9. Dewey:975.8. LCCN:90-041759.

Audience: **g,l,u,f.**

Federal Writers' Project Staff **F291.G45 1990**
Georgia: The WPA Guide to Its Towns and Countryside. Phinizy Spalding (Introduction by). Cloth Text. University of South Carolina Press. Columbia, SC. 1990. 606p. ISBN:0-87249-706-2, ISBN13: 978-0-87249-706-1. Dewey:917.58/0443. LCCN:89-077068.

Audience: **f.**

Flynn, Charles L. Jr. **F291**
White Land, Black Labor: Caste and Class in Late Nineteenth-Century Georgia. Cloth Text. Louisiana State University Press. Baton Rouge, LA. 1983. xi, 196p. ISBN:0-8071-1097-3, ISBN13: 978-0-8071-1097-3. Dewey:975.8/041. LCCN:83-000721.

Audience: **f.** B

Henderson, Harold P. & Roberts, Gary L. (Editors) **F291.G43 1988**
Georgia Governors in an Age of Change: From Ellis Arnall to George Busbee. Trade Paper. University of Georgia Press. Athens, GA. 1988. 304p. ISBN:0-8203-1005-0, ISBN13: 978-0-8203-1005-3. Dewey:973.8/043. LCCN:87-023293.

Audience: **u,f.**

Hyatt, Richard **F291.3.M55H93 1997**
Zell: The Governor Who Gave Georgia Hope. Trade Cloth. Mercer University Press. Macon, GA. 2004. xv, 497p. ISBN:0-86554-577-4, ISBN13: 978-0-86554-577-9. Dewey:975.8/043/092 B. LCCN:97-018269.

Audience: **f.**

Johnson, Michael P. **F290**
Toward a Patriarchal Republic: The Secession of Georgia. Cloth Text. Louisiana State University Press. Baton Rouge, LA. 1977. 244p. ISBN:0-8071-0270-9, ISBN13: 978-0-8071-0270-1. Dewey:973.7/13. LCCN:77-003029.

Audience: **f.** B

Konter, S. **F287.G27**
Vanishing Georgia: Photographs from the Vanishing Georgia Collection, Georgia Department of Archives and History. Trade Paper. University of Georgia Press. Athens, GA. 1994. 240p. Brown Thrasher Bks. ISBN:0-8203-1631-8, ISBN13: 978-0-8203-1631-4. Dewey:917.580443. LCCN:82-004764.

Audience: **u,f.**

McCash, William B. **F290.C67M37 2004**
Thomas R. R. Cobb: The Making of a Southern Nationalist. Trade Paper. Mercer University Press. Macon, GA. 2004. 356p. ISBN:0-86554-858-7, ISBN13: 978-0-86554-858-9. Dewey:975.8/03/0924. LCCN:2004-558369.

Audience: **f.**

Short, Bob **F291.3.M3S56 1999**
Everything Is Pickrick: The Life of Lester Maddox. Trade Cloth. Mercer University Press. Macon, GA. 2004. 400p. ISBN:0-86554-662-2, ISBN13: 978-0-86554-662-2. Dewey:975.8/043/092 B. LCCN:99-052166.

Audience: **u,f.**

Spalding, Phinizy **F289.O367**
Oglethorpe in America. Library Binding. University of Chicago Press. Chicago, IL. 1977. xi, 207p. ISBN:0-226-76846-5, ISBN13: 978-0-226-76846-5. Dewey:975.8/02/0924. LCCN:76-008092.

Audience: **f.** B

Spalding, Phinizy (Author, Editor) **F289.O37O37 1989**
Oglethorpe in Perspective: Georgia's Founder after Two Hundred Years. Harvey H. Jackson (Editor). Trade Cloth. University of Alabama Press. Tuscaloosa, AL. 1989. 256p. ISBN:0-8173-0386-3, ISBN13: 978-0-8173-0386-0. Dewey:975.8/02/0924 B. LCCN:87-019121.

Audience: **f.** *Choice, 1989.*

United States > U.S. Local History > Gulf States > Florida. Alabama. Mississippi

Abernethy, Thomas P. **F326.A14 1990**
The Formative Period in Alabama, 1815-1828. Ed. 2. David T. Morgan (Introduction by). Trade Paper. University of Alabama Press. Tuscaloosa, AL. 1995. 232p. Library of Alabama Classics ISBN:0-8173-0486-X, ISBN13: 978-0-8173-0486-7. Dewey:976.1/04. LCCN:89-020612.
Audience: **f.**

Barney, William L. (Author, Introduction by) **F326.B3 2004**
The Secessionist Impulse: Alabama and Mississippi in 1860. Trade Paper. University of Alabama Press. Tuscaloosa, AL. 2004. 386p. The Library of Alabama Classics ISBN:0-8173-5089-6, ISBN13: 978-0-8173-5089-5. Dewey:973.7/13. LCCN:2003-016915.
Audience: **f.**

Bond, Bradley G. **F341.B76 1995**
Political Culture in the 19th-Century South: Mississippi, 1830-1900. Cloth Text. Louisiana State University Press. Baton Rouge, LA. 1995. xvi, 392p. ISBN:0-8071-1976-8, ISBN13: 978-0-8071-1976-1. Dewey:306.2/09762/09034. LCCN:95-011134.
Audience: **f.** *Choice, 1996.*

Brown, James S. Jr. (Editor) **F326.U65 1997**
Up Before Daylight: Life Histories from the Alabama Writers' Project, 1938-1939. Trade Paper. University of Alabama Press. Tuscaloosa, AL. 1982. 280p. ISBN:0-8173-0099-6, ISBN13: 978-0-8173-0099-9. Dewey:976.1/062. LCCN:81-021988.
Audience: **f.** B

Burns, Stewart (Editor) **F334.M79N39 1997**
Daybreak of Freedom: The Montgomery Bus Boycott. Trade Cloth. University of North Carolina Press. Chapel Hill, NC. 1997. 392p. ISBN:0-8078-2360-0, ISBN13: 978-0-8078-2360-6. Dewey:305.8/00976147. LCCN:97-007909.
Audience: **u,f.** *Choice, 1998.*

Busbee, Westley F. **F341.B93 2005**
Mississippi: A History. Trade Paper. Harlan Davidson Inc. Wheeling, IL. 2005. 445p. ISBN:0-88295-227-7, ISBN13: 978-0-88295-227-7. Dewey:976.2. LCCN:2004-025954.
Audience: **g,l,u,f.**

Carter, Dan T. **F330.3.W3C37 2000**
The Politics of Rage: George Wallace, the Origins of the New Conservatism and the Transformation of American Politics. Ed. 2. Trade Paper. Louisiana State University Press. Baton Rouge, LA. 2000. 580p. ISBN:0-8071-2597-0, ISBN13: 978-0-8071-2597-7. Dewey:976.1/063/092 B. LCCN:99-054330.
Audience: **u,f.** *Choice, 1996.*

Croucher, Sheila L. **F319.M6C76 1997**
Imagining Miami: Ethnic Politics in a Postmodern World. Cloth Text. University Press of Virginia. Charlottesville, VA. 1997. 250p. Race, Ethnicity and Politics Ser. ISBN:0-8139-1704-2, ISBN13: 978-0-8139-1704-7. Dewey:305.8/009759/381. LCCN:96-041357.
Audience: **u,f.**

Danese, Tracy E. **F316.B19D36 2000**
Claude Pepper and Ed Ball: Politics, Purpose and Power. Raymond Arsenault & Gary R. Mormino (Foreword by). Trade Cloth. University Press of Florida. Gainesville, FL. 2000. 320p. Florida History and Culture Ser. ISBN:0-8130-1744-0, ISBN13: 978-0-8130-1744-0. Dewey:975.9/06/092 B. LCCN:99-035314.
Audience: **u,f.** *Choice, 2000.*

Federal Writers' Project Staff **F341.F45 1988**
Mississippi: The WPA Guide to the Magnolia State. Robert McElvaine (Introduction by). Cloth Text. University Press of Mississippi. Jackson, MS. 1988. 545p. ISBN:0-87805-368-9, ISBN13: 978-0-87805-368-1. Dewey:917.62/0462. LCCN:88-023327.
Audience: **f.**

Federal Writers' Project Staff & Writers Program Staff **F316 .F44**
Florida: A Guide to the Southern-Most State. Library Binding. Reprint Services Company. Temecula, CA. 1989. American Guide Ser. ISBN:0-7812-1009-7, ISBN13: 978-0-7812-1009-6. Dewey:917.59.
Audience: **f.**

Flynt, Wayne **F326.F754 2004**
Alabama in the Twentieth Century. Trade Cloth. University of Alabama Press. Tuscaloosa, AL. 2004. 624p. The Modern South Ser. ISBN:0-8173-1430-X, ISBN13: 978-0-8173-1430-9. Dewey:976.1/063. LCCN:2004-002841.
Audience: **g,l,u,f.** *Choice, 2005.*

Gannon, Michael **F311.G34 2003**
Florida: A Short History. Trade Cloth. University Press of Florida. Gainesville, FL. 2003. 192p. Columbus Quincentenary Ser. ISBN:0-8130-2681-4, ISBN13: 978-0-8130-2681-7. Dewey:975.9. LCCN:2004-268993.
Audience: **g,l,u,f.**

Gannon, Michael V. (Editor) **F311.5.N49 1996**
The New History of Florida. Trade Cloth. University Press of Florida. Gainesville, FL. 1996. 492p. ISBN:0-8130-1415-8, ISBN13: 978-0-8130-1415-9. Dewey:975.9. LCCN:95-011055.
Audience: **g,l,u,f.**

George, Paul S. (Editor) **Z1271**
A Guide to the History of Florida. Cloth Text. Greenwood Publishing Group, Inc. Portsmouth, NH. 1989. 312p. Reference Guides to State History and Research Ser. ISBN:0-313-24911-3, ISBN13: 978-0-313-24911-2. Dewey:016.9759. LCCN:88-038080.
Audience: **l,u,f.**

Hamilton, Virginia Van der Veer **F326.H26**
Alabama, a Bicentennial History. Trade Cloth. W. W. Norton & Company, Inc. New York, NY. 1977. xv, 189p. States and the Nation Ser. ISBN:0-393-05621-X, ISBN13: 978-0-393-05621-1. Dewey:976.1. LCCN:76-054517.
Audience: **f.** B

Harris, William C. **F341.H298**
The Day of the Carpetbagger: Republican Reconstruction in Mississippi. Trade Cloth. Louisiana State University Press. Baton Rouge, LA. 1979. xvi, 776p. ISBN:0-8071-0366-7, ISBN13: 978-0-8071-0366-1. Dewey:976.2/06. LCCN:78-018779.
Audience: **f.** B

Jahoda, Gloria Love **F311.J334 1984**
Florida: Bicentennial and History Guide. Trade Paper. W. W. Norton & Company, Inc. New York, NY. 1984. States and the Nation Ser. ISBN:0-393-30178-8, ISBN13: 978-0-393-30178-6. Dewey:975.9. LCCN:84-003177.
Audience: **f.**

Kirwan, Albert D. **F341 .K5**
Revolt of the Rednecks: Mississippi Politics. Paper Text. Textbook Publishers. Temecula, CA. 2003. x, 328p. ISBN:0-7581-6780-6, ISBN13: 978-0-7581-6780-4. Dewey:976.206.
Audience: **f.**

Lyon, Eugene **E78.F6**
The Enterprise of Florida: Pedro Menendez de Aviles and the Spanish Conquest of 1565-1568. Trade Paper. University Press of Florida. Gainesville, FL. 1976. 253p. ISBN:0-8130-0777-1, ISBN13: 978-0-8130-0777-9. Dewey:975.9/01. LCCN:76-029612.
Audience: **f.**

Metress, Christopher (Editor) **F350.N4L96 2002**
The Lynching of Emmett Till: A Documentary Narrative. Trade Cloth. University Press of Virginia. Charlottesville, VA. 2002. 372p. The American South Ser. ISBN:0-8139-2121-X, ISBN13: 978-0-8139-2121-1. Dewey:305.8/00975. LCCN:2002-002337.
Audience: **l,u,f.**

Portes, Alejandro **F319.M6**
City on the Edge: The Transformation of Miami. Trade Paper. University of California Press. Berkeley, CA. 1994. 298p. ISBN:0-520-08932-4, ISBN13: 978-0-520-08932-7. Dewey:305.8009759381.
Audience: **u,f.** *Choice, 1993.*

Rogers, William W., et al. **F326.A553 1994**
Alabama: The History of a Deep South State. Robert D. Ward, Leah R. Atkins & Wayne Flynt (Authors). Trade Cloth. University of Alabama Press. Tuscaloosa, AL. 1994. 768p. ISBN:0-8173-0712-5, ISBN13: 978-0-8173-0712-7. Dewey:976.1. LCCN:93-027240.
Audience: **g,l,u,f.** *Choice, 1995.*

Shofner, Jerrell H. **F316.S56**
Nor Is It over Yet: Florida in the Era of Reconstruction, 1863-1877. Trade Cloth. University Press of Florida. Gainesville, FL. 1974. 412p. ISBN:0-8130-0353-9, ISBN13: 978-0-8130-0353-5. Dewey:975.9/06. LCCN:70-186325.
Audience: **u,f.**

Tebeau, Charlton W. & Marina, William **F311**
A History of Florida. Ed. 3. Trade Paper. University of Miami Press. Edison, NJ. 1999. xiv, 616p. Copeland Studies in Florida History, No. 1 ISBN:0-87024-338-1, ISBN13: 978-0-87024-338-7. Dewey:957.9. LCCN:96-061201.
Audience: **g,l,u,f.**

Webb, Samuel L. & Armbrester, Margaret E. (Editors) **F326.A543 2001**
Alabama Governors: A Political History of the State. Albert P. Brewer (Foreword by). Trade Cloth. University of Alabama Press. Tuscaloosa, AL. 2001. 376p. ISBN:0-8173-1082-7, ISBN13: 978-0-8173-1082-0. Dewey:976.1/009/9. LCCN:00-012559.
Audience: **l,u,f.**

Weeks, William Earl **F314 .W44**
John Quincy Adams and American Global Empire. Trade Paper. University Press of Kentucky. Lexington, KY. 2002. 250p. ISBN:0-8131-9058-4, ISBN13: 978-0-8131-9058-7. Dewey:973.5/5/092.
Audience: **f.**

Wiggins, Sarah W. **F326.W53**
The Scalawag in Alabama Politics, 1865-1881. Trade Cloth. University of Alabama Press. Tuscaloosa, AL. 1977. 240p. ISBN:0-8173-5233-3, ISBN13: 978-0-8173-5233-2. Dewey:320.9/761/06. LCCN:76-056833.
Audience: **f.**

Williamson, Edward C. **F316.2.W54**
Florida Politics in the Gilded Age, 1877-1893. Trade Cloth. University Press of Florida. Gainesville, FL. 1976. 234p. ISBN:0-8130-0365-2, ISBN13: 978-0-8130-0365-8. Dewey:320.9/759/06. LCCN:75-030634.
Audience: **f.**

Writers Program Staff **F326.W68 2000**
The WPA Guide to 1930s Alabama. Harvey H. Jackson III (Introduction by). Trade Paper. University of Alabama Press. Tuscaloosa, AL. 2000. 580p. ISBN:0-8173-1028-2, ISBN13: 978-0-8173-1028-8. Dewey:976.1/062. LCCN:99-048891.
Audience: **f.**

United States > U.S. Local History > Gulf States > Mississippi Valley. Middle West

Alvord, Clarence Walworth **F352 .A47**
The Mississippi Valley in British Politics: A Study of the Trade, Land Speculation and Experiments in Imperialism Culminating in the American Revolution. Paper Text. Textbook Publishers. Temecula, CA. 2003. ISBN:0-7581-4389-3, ISBN13: 978-0-7581-4389-1. Dewey:977.
Audience: **f.**

Atherton, Lewis E. **F354**
Main Street on the Middle Border. Trade Cloth. Indiana University Press. Bloomington, IN. 1984. 464p. Midwestern History and Culture Ser. ISBN:0-253-33655-4, ISBN13: 978-0-253-33655-2. Dewey:977/.03. LCCN:54-007970.
Audience: **l,u,f.**

Barry, John M. **F354.B47 1997**
Rising Tide: The Great Mississippi Flood of 1927 and How It Changed America. Trade Cloth. Simon & Schuster. New York, NY. 1997. 528p. ISBN:0-684-81046-8, ISBN13: 978-0-684-81046-1. Dewey:977/.03. LCCN:96-040077.
Audience: **g,l,u,f.**

Barry, John M. **F354**
Rising Tide: The Great Mississippi Flood of 1927 and How It Changed America. Trade Paper. Simon & Schuster. New York, NY. 1998. 528p. ISBN:0-684-84002-2, ISBN13: 978-0-684-84002-4. Dewey:977/.03. LCCN:96-040077.
Audience: **g,u,f.**

Carpenter, Allan **F351.C33 1989**
The Encyclopedia of the Midwest. Trade Cloth. Facts On File, Inc. New York, NY. 1989. 544p. ISBN:0-8160-1660-7, ISBN13: 978-0-8160-1660-0. Dewey:977/.003/21. LCCN:88-027410.
Audience: **g,l,u,f.** *Choice, 1989.*

Fremling, Calvin R. **F351.F84 2004**
Immortal River: The Upper Mississippi in Ancient and Modern Times. Trade Cloth. University of Wisconsin Press. Chicago, IL. 2005. 472p. ISBN:0-299-20290-9, ISBN13: 978-0-299-20290-3. Dewey:977. LCCN:2004-005381.
Audience: **f.**

Geus, Theodor **F351.G3813 1989**
Mississippi. Trade Cloth. University Press of Kentucky. Lexington, KY. 1989. 184p. ISBN:0-8131-1713-5, ISBN13: 978-0-8131-1713-3. Dewey:977. LCCN:89-016466.
Audience: **u,f.**

Gjerde, Jon **F358.G58 1997**
[e] The Minds of the West: Ethnocultural Evolution in the Rural Middle West, 1830-1917. E-Book. University of North Carolina Press. Chapel Hill, NC. 1997. ISBN:0-8078-6167-7, ISBN13: 978-0-8078-6167-7. Dewey:306/.0978.
Audience: **f.** *Choice, 1997.*

Harris, Eddy L. **F355.H37 1998**
Mississippi Solo: A River Quest. Trade Paper. Henry Holt & Company. New York, NY. 1998. 256p. ISBN:0-8050-5903-2, ISBN13: 978-0-8050-5903-8. Dewey:917.704/33. LCCN:98-024706.
Audience: **u,f.**

Hudson, John C. **F351.H858 1994**
[e] Making the Corn Belt: A Geographical History of Middle-Western Agriculture. E-Book. Indiana University Press. Bloomington, IN. 1994. 129p. Midwestern History and Culture Ser. ISBN:0-253-32832-2, ISBN13: 978-0-253-32832-8. Dewey:917.8. LCCN:93-035723.
Audience: **f.** *Choice, 1995.*

Jensen, Richard **F354.J4**
Winning of the Midwest: Social and Political Conflict, 1888-1896. Library Binding. University of Chicago Press. Chicago, IL. 1971. xvii, 357p. ISBN:0-226-39825-0, ISBN13: 978-0-226-39825-9. Dewey:320.9/77. LCCN:71-149802.
Audience: **f.** B

Johnson, AnnMae **F358.2.G3J64 2000**
Unsung Heroes: A History of American Immigrants. Trade Paper. Galde Press, Inc. Lakeville, MN. 2000. 192p. ISBN:1-880090-98-8, ISBN13: 978-1-880090-98-5. Dewey:977.004/31. LCCN:00-037633.
Audience: **u,f.**

Madison, James H. (Editor) **F351.H35 1988**
Heartland: Comparative Histories of the Midwestern States. Trade Cloth. Indiana University Press. Bloomington, IN. 1988. 318p. Midwestern History and Culture Ser. ISBN:0-253-31423-2, ISBN13: 978-0-253-31423-9. Dewey:977. LCCN:87-045835.
Audience: **f.** *Choice, 1988.*

Merrill, Horace S. **F354 .M45**
Bourbon Democracy of the Middle West, 1865-1896. Trade Paper. University of Washington Press. Seattle, WA. 1969. Americana Library Ser., No. 2 ISBN:0-295-95032-3, ISBN13: 978-0-295-95032-7. Dewey:977. LCCN:53-008592.
Audience: **f.**

Rhodes, Richard **F351.R58 1991**
The Inland Ground: An Evocation of the American Middle West. Bill Greer (Illustrator). Trade Cloth. University Press of Kansas. Lawrence, KS. 1991. xvi, 328p. ISBN:0-7006-0498-7, ISBN13: 978-0-7006-0498-2. Dewey:977. LCCN:91-026020.
Audience: **u,f.**

Selcraig, James T. **F0354.S44**
The Red Scare in the Midwest, 1945-1955. Robert Berkhofer (Editor). Trade Paper. Books on Demand. Ann Arbor, MI. 1982. 226p. Studies in American History and Culture, Vol. 36 ISBN:0-8357-1380-6, ISBN13: 978-0-8357-1380-1. Dewey:322.4. LCCN:82-017545.
Audience: **f.** B

Shortridge, James R. **F351.S5 1989**
The Middle West: Its Meaning in American Culture. Trade Cloth. University Press of Kansas. Lawrence, KS. 1989. xiv, 202p. ISBN:0-7006-0388-3, ISBN13: 978-0-7006-0388-6. Dewey:977. LCCN:88-029991.
Audience: **u,f.** *Choice, 1989.*

Twain, Mark **F351**
Life on the Mississippi (1883). James M. Cox (Notes by). Trade Paper. Penguin Group (USA) Inc. New York, NY. 1985. 448p. Penguin American Library ISBN:0-14-039050-2, ISBN13: 978-0-14-039050-6. Dewey:818/.409. LCCN:84-001194.
Audience: **g,l,u,f.**

Usner, Daniel H. Jr. **F352.U86 1992**
Indians, Settlers, and Slaves in a Frontier Exchange Economy: The Lower Mississippi Valley Before 1783. Trade Cloth. University of North Carolina Press. Chapel Hill, NC. 1992. 314p. Institute of Early American History and Culture Ser. ISBN:0-8078-2014-8, ISBN13: 978-0-8078-2014-8. Dewey:977. LCCN:91-026689.
Audience: **f.** *Choice, 1992.*

Walton, Anthony **F350.N4W35 1996**
Mississippi: An American Journey. Trade Cloth. Alfred A. Knopf Inc. New York, NY. 1996. 304p. ISBN:0-679-44600-1, ISBN13: 978-0-679-44600-2. Dewey:976.2/00496073. LCCN:95-032031.
Audience: **g,l,u,f.**

Watts, Edward **F351.W35 2002**
An American Colony: Regionalism and the Roots of Midwestern Culture. Trade Cloth. Ohio University Press. Athens, OH. 2002. 328p. ISBN:0-8214-1432-1, ISBN13: 978-0-8214-1432-3. Dewey:977. LCCN:2001-058819.
Audience: **f.** *Choice, 2003.*

Weddle, Robert S. **F352.W42 1999**
Wilderness Manhunt: The Spanish Search for la Salle. Trade Paper. Texas A&M University Press. College Station, TX. 1999. 320p. ISBN:0-89096-910-8, ISBN13: 978-0-89096-910-6. Dewey:977/.01. LCCN:99-038277.
Audience: **f.**

Whitaker, Arthur P. **F352 .W56**
The Mississippi Question, 1985 to 1803. Trade Cloth. Peter Smith Publisher, Inc. Magnolia, MA. 1990. ISBN:0-8446-1476-9, ISBN13: 978-0-8446-1476-2. Dewey:977.
Audience: **f.**

United States > U.S. Local History > Gulf States > Louisiana

Binder, Wolfgang (Editor) **F372.C74 1998**
Creoles and Cajuns: French Louisiana - La Louisiane Francaise. Paper Text. Peter Lang Publishing, Inc. New York, NY. 1998. XIII, 344p. ISBN:0-8204-3244-X, ISBN13: 978-0-8204-3244-1. Dewey:976.3. LCCN:98-205648.
Audience: **f.**

Brasseaux, Carl A. **F380.F8B735 2005**
French, Cajun, Creole, Houma: A Primer on Francophone Louisiana. Saddle Stitched, Cloth over Boards, Dust Jacket. Louisiana State University Press. Baton Rouge, LA. 2005. 159p. ISBN:0-8071-3036-2, ISBN13: 978-0-8071-3036-0. Dewey:976.3/0097541. LCCN:2004-019011.
Audience: **f.**

Cummins, Light Townsend, et al. **F369.L883 2002**
Louisiana: A History. Ed. 4. Judith Kelleher Schafer & Edward F. Haas (Authors), Bennett H. Wall (Editor), Michael L. Kurtz (Contribution by). Trade Paper. Harlan Davidson Inc. Wheeling, IL. 2002. 450p. ISBN:0-88295-964-6, ISBN13: 978-0-88295-964-1. Dewey:976.3. LCCN:2001-039298.
Audience: **g,l,u,f.**

Dawson, Joseph G. III (Editor) **F368.L68 1990**
Louisiana Governors: From Iberville to Edwards. Cloth Text. Louisiana State University Press. Baton Rouge, LA. 1990. 360p. ISBN:0-8071-1527-4, ISBN13: 978-0-8071-1527-5. Dewey:976.3/0092/2 B. LCCN:89-027333.
Audience: **u,f.** *Choice, 1990.*

Giraud, Marcel **F372 .G5**
Histoire de la Louisiane Francaise. Paper Text. Textbook Publishers. Temecula, CA. 2003. ISBN:0-7581-5840-8, ISBN13: 978-0-7581-5840-6. Dewey:976.3.
Audience: **f.**

Jackson, Joy J. **F379.N557**
New Orleans in the Gilded Age: Politics and Urban Progress, 1880-1896. Ed. 2. Trade Cloth. University of Louisiana at Lafayette, Center for Louisiana Studies. Lafayette, LA. 1998. 326p. ISBN:1-887366-16-4, ISBN13: 978-1-887366-16-8. Dewey:309.1/763/355. LCCN:96-084965.
Audience: **u,f.** B

Kuzenski, John C., et al. **F376.3.D84D38 1995**
e David Duke and the Politics of Race in the South. Charles S. Bullock & Ronald Keith Gaddie (Authors). E-Book. NetLibrary, Inc. Boulder, CO. 1995. ISBN:0-585-03310-2, ISBN13: 978-0-585-03310-5. Dewey:320.9763/09/049.
Audience: **u,f.**

McCrary, Peyton **F374**
Abraham Lincoln and Reconstruction: The Louisiana Experiment. Trade Cloth. Princeton University Press. Princeton, NJ. 1979. 448p. ISBN:0-691-04660-3, ISBN13: 978-0-691-04660-0. Dewey:976.3/05. LCCN:78-051181.
Audience: **f.** B

McKinney, Louise **F379.N55M39 2005**
New Orleans: A Cultural History. Trade Cloth. Oxford University Press, Inc. New York, NY. 2006. 272p. Cityscapes Ser. ISBN:0-19-530135-8, ISBN13: 978-0-19-530135-9. Dewey:976.3/35. LCCN:2005-049878.
Audience: **u,f.**

Reeves, Miriam G. **F368.R4 1998**
Governors of Louisiana. Ed. 5. Trade Cloth. Pelican Publishing Company, Inc. Gretna, LA. 1998. 136p. Pelican Governors Ser. ISBN:1-56554-425-0, ISBN13: 978-1-56554-425-3. Dewey:976.3/0099 B. LCCN:98-234669.
Audience: **u,f.**

Reeves, William D. **F369.R42 2003**
Historic Louisiana: An Illustrated History. Trade Cloth. Historical Publishing Network. San Antonio, TX. 2003. 144p. ISBN:1-893619-32-X, ISBN13: 978-1-893619-32-6. Dewey:976.3. LCCN:2003-102315.
Audience: **g,l,u,f.**

Sacher, John M. **F374.S24 2003**
A Perfect War of Politics: Parties, Politicians, and Democracy in Louisiana, 1824-1861. Trade Cloth. Louisiana State University Press. Baton Rouge, LA. 2003. xvi, 331p. ISBN:0-8071-2848-1, ISBN13: 978-0-8071-2848-0. Dewey:320.9763/09/034. LCCN:2002-015276.
Audience: **f.**

Schott, Matthew & Conrad, Glenn R. (Editors) **F375.L9438 2000**
Louisiana Politics and the Paradoxes of Reaction and Reform, 1877-1928. Cloth Text. University of Louisiana at Lafayette, Center for Louisiana Studies. Lafayette, LA. 2001. 706p. The Louisiana Purchase Bicentennial Series in Louisiana History, Vol. 7 ISBN:1-887366-39-3, ISBN13: 978-1-887366-39-7. Dewey:976.3/06. LCCN:2002-279161.
Audience: **f.**

Shugg, Roger W. **F0374.S5819**
Origins of Class Struggle in Louisiana: A Social History of White Farmers and Laborers During Slavery and After, 1840-1875. Trade Paper. Books on Demand. Ann Arbor, MI. 388p. ISBN:0-608-13748-0, ISBN13: 978-0-608-13748-3. Dewey:309.1763. LCCN:74-001055.
Audience: **f.** B

Sindler, Allan P. & Long, Huey Pierce Jr. **F375 .S59 1980**
Huey Long's Louisiana: State Politics, 1920-1952. Trade Cloth. Greenwood Publishing Group, Inc. Portsmouth, NH. 1980. 316p. ISBN:0-313-22692-X, ISBN13: 978-0-313-22692-2. Dewey:976.3/062. LCCN:80-019447.
Audience: **u,f.** B

Taylor, Joe G. **F369.T29**
Louisiana: A Bicentennial History. Trade Cloth. W. W. Norton & Company, Inc. New York, NY. 1976. xi, 194p. States and the Nation Ser. ISBN:0-393-05602-3, ISBN13: 978-0-393-05602-0. Dewey:976.3. LCCN:76-024848.
Audience: **f.** B

Taylor, Joe G **F0375.T23**
Louisiana Reconstructed, 1863-1877. Trade Paper. Books on Demand. Ann Arbor, MI. 1974. 574p. ISBN:0-7837-8504-6, ISBN13: 978-0-7837-8504-2. Dewey:976.3/06. LCCN:74-077327.
Audience: **u,f.**

Tregle, Joseph G. Jr. **F374.T74 1999**
Louisiana in the Age of Jackson: A Clash of Cultures and Personalities. Trade Cloth. Louisiana State University Press. Baton Rouge, LA. 1999. 344p. History Ser. ISBN:0-8071-2292-0, ISBN13: 978-0-8071-2292-1. Dewey:976.3/05. LCCN:98-024708.
Audience: **f.** *Choice, 1999.*

Worth, Richard **F372.W67 2005**
Louisiana, 1682-1803. Trade Cloth. National Geographic Society. Washington, DC. 2006. 112p. Voices from Colonial America Ser. ISBN:0-7922-6544-0, ISBN13: 978-0-7922-6544-3. Dewey:976.3/01. LCCN:2005-016225.
Audience: **u,f.**

United States > U.S. Local History > Gulf States > Texas

Acosta, Teresa Palomo & Winegarten, Ruthe **F395.M5A75 2003**
Las Tejanas: 300 Years of History. Trade Cloth. University of Texas Press. Austin, TX. 2003. 456p. Jack and Doris Smothers Series in Texas History, Life, and Culture, No. 10 ISBN:0-292-74710-1, ISBN13: 978-0-292-74710-4. Dewey:976.4004/6872. LCCN:2002-009360.
Audience: **u,f.**

Barb, Alwyn **F391.B27 1999**
Reconstruction to Reform: Texas Politics, 1876-1906. Hal Williams (Foreword by). Paper Text. Southern Methodist University Press. Dallas, TX. 1999. 340p. ISBN:0-87074-444-5, ISBN13: 978-0-87074-444-0. Dewey:320.9764/09/034. LCCN:99-041948.
Audience: **f.**

Brands, H. W. **F390.B833 2004**
Lone Star Nation: The Epic Story of the Battle for Texas Independence. Trade Paper. Knopf Publishing Group. New York, NY. 2005. 608p. ISBN:1-4000-3070-6, ISBN13: 978-1-4000-3070-5. Dewey:976.4/03. LCCN:2003-061921.
Audience: **g,l,u,f.**

Campbell, Randolph B. **F386.C268 2004**
Gone to Texas: A History of the Lone Star State. Trade Cloth. Oxford University Press, Inc. New York, NY. 2003. 512p. ISBN:0-19-513842-2, ISBN13: 978-0-19-513842-9. Dewey:976.4. LCCN:2002-041657.
Audience: **g,l,u,f.** *Choice, 2004.*

Cantrell, Gregg **F389.A942C36 1999**
Stephen F. Austin: Empresario of Texas. Cloth over Boards. Yale University Press. Cumberland, RI. 1999. 512p. ISBN:0-300-07683-5, ISBN13: 978-0-300-07683-7. Dewey:976.4/03/092 B. LCCN:98-051176.
Audience: **u,f.** *Choice, 2000.*

Chipman, Donald E. **F389.C44 1992**
Spanish Texas, 1519-1821. Trade Paper. University of Texas Press. Austin, TX. 1992. 359p. ISBN:0-292-77659-4, ISBN13: 978-0-292-77659-3. Dewey:976.4/02. LCCN:92-006116.
Audience: **f.** *Choice, 1993.*

Crisp, James E. **F390.C79 2004**
Sleuthing the Alamo: Davy Crockett's Last Stand and Other Mysteries of the Texas Revolution. Trade Cloth. Oxford University Press, Inc. New York, NY. 2004. 220p. New Narratives in American History Ser. ISBN:0-19-516349-4, ISBN13: 978-0-19-516349-0. Dewey:976.4/03. LCCN:2004-049255.
Audience: **u,f.**

Davis, William C. **F390.D2757 2004**
Lone Star Rising: The Revolutionary Birth of the Texas Republic. Trade Cloth. Simon & Schuster. New York, NY. 2003. 368p. ISBN:0-684-86510-6, ISBN13: 978-0-684-86510-2. Dewey:976.4/03. LCCN:2003-065051.
Audience: **l,u,f.** *Choice, 2004.*

De Leon, Arnoldo **F395.M5D37 1999**
Mexican Americans in Texas: A Brief History. Ed. 2. Trade Paper. Harlan Davidson Inc. Wheeling, IL. 2003. 186p. ISBN:0-88295-948-4, ISBN13: 978-0-88295-948-1. Dewey:976.4/0046872073. LCCN:98-054219.
Audience: **l,f.**

De León, Arnoldo **F395.M5 D43 1983**
They Called Them Greasers: Anglo Attitudes Toward Mexicans in Texas, 1821-1900. Trade Paper. University of Texas Press. Austin, TX. 1983. 167p. ISBN:0-292-78054-0, ISBN13: 978-0-292-78054-5. Dewey:976.4/0046872. LCCN:82-024850.
Audience: **f.**

Fehrenbach, T. R. **F386.3.F44 2003**
Lone Star: The Story of Texas. American Heritage Publishing Staff (Contribution by). Trade Cloth. Prentice Hall PTR. Upper Saddle River, NJ. 2003. xxxii, 600p. ISBN:0-13-058625-0, ISBN13: 978-0-13-058625-4. Dewey:976.4. LCCN:2002-514683.
Audience: **g,l,u,f.**

Frantz, Joe B. **F386.F72**
Texas. Trade Cloth. W. W. Norton & Company, Inc. New York, NY. 1976. xiv, 222p. States and the Nation Ser. ISBN:0-393-05580-9, ISBN13: 978-0-393-05580-1. Dewey:976.4. LCCN:76-023132.
Audience: **f.** B

García, Mario T. **F394.E4**
Desert Immigrants: The Mexican of el Paso, 1880-1920. Trade Paper. Yale University Press. Cumberland, RI. 1982. 318p. Western Americana Ser., No. 32 ISBN:0-300-02883-0, ISBN13: 978-0-300-02883-6. Dewey:976.4. LCCN:80-036862.
Audience: **u,f.**

Haley, James L. **F386.H2355 2006**
Passionate Nation: The Epic History of Texas. Trade Cloth. Simon & Schuster. New York, NY. 2006. 656p. ISBN:0-684-86291-3, ISBN13: 978-0-684-86291-0. Dewey:976.4. LCCN:2005-058062.
Audience: **g,l,u,f.**

Haley, James L. **F390.H84H34 2001**
Sam Houston. Trade Cloth. University of Oklahoma Press. Norman, OK. 2002. 544p. ISBN:0-8061-3405-4, ISBN13: 978-0-8061-3405-5. Dewey:976.4/04/092 B. LCCN:2001-045108.
Audience: **l,u,f.**

Hatch, Thom **F390.H33 1999**
Encyclopedia of the Alamo and the Texas Revolution. Cloth Text. McFarland & Company, Incorporated Publishers. Jefferson, NC. 1999. 237p. ISBN:0-7864-0593-7, ISBN13: 978-0-7864-0593-0. Dewey:976.4/03. LCCN:99-35608.
Audience: **l,u,f.** *Choice, 2000.*

Horgan, Paul **F392.R5H65 1991**
Great River: The Rio Grande in North American History. Vol. 1, Indians and Spain. Vol. 2, Mexico and the United States. Ed. 4. Trade Paper. Wesleyan University Press. Middletown, CT. 1991. 1038p. ISBN:0-8195-6251-3, ISBN13: 978-0-8195-6251-7. LCCN:91-013753.
Audience: **u,f.**

Hoyt, Edwin P. **F390.H915**
The Alamo: An Illustrated History. Trade Paper. Taylor Trade Publishing. Blue Ridge Summit, PA. 2003. 192p. ISBN:0-87833-288-X, ISBN13: 978-0-87833-288-5. Dewey:976.4/351.
Audience: **g,l,u,f.**

Lich, Glen E. (Editor) **F391.2.R44 1992**
Regional Studies: The Interplay of Land and People. Trade Cloth. Texas A&M University Press. College Station, TX. 1992. 198p. Elma Dill Russell Spencer Series in the West and Southwest, No. 12 ISBN:0-89096-477-7, ISBN13: 978-0-89096-477-4. Dewey:976.4/06. LCCN:91-004133.
Audience: **f.**

Lind, Michael **F391.2**
Made in Texas: George W. Bush and the Southern Takeover of American Politics. Trade Paper. Basic Books. New York, NY. 2004. 224p. A New America Book Ser. ISBN:0-465-04122-1, ISBN13: 978-0-465-04122-0. Dewey:306.2/0973. LCCN:2004-541372.
Audience: **u,f.** *Choice, 2003.*

Meinig, D. W. **F386.M35**
Imperial Texas; an Interpretive Essay in Cultural Geography. Trade Cloth. University of Texas Press. Austin, TX. 1969. 145p. ISBN:0-292-78381-7, ISBN13: 978-0-292-78381-2. Dewey:301.29/764. LCCN:69-018807.
Audience: **f.**

Minutaglio, Bill **F391.4.B87M56 2001**
First Son: George W. Bush and the Bush Family Dynasty. UK-Trade Paper. Crown Publishing Group. New York, NY. 2001. 400p. ISBN:0-609-80867-2, ISBN13: 978-0-609-80867-2. Dewey:976.404/63/092. LCCN:2002-278404.
Audience: **u,f.** *Choice, 2000.*

Moneyhon, Carl H. **F391.M636 2004**
Texas after the Civil War: The Struggle of Reconstruction. Trade Cloth. Texas A&M University Press. College Station, TX. 2004. 352p. Texas A. & M. Southwestern Studies, No. 14 ISBN:1-58544-361-1, ISBN13: 978-1-58544-361-1. Dewey:976.4/05. LCCN:2004-003675.
Audience: **f.**

Olmsted, Frederick Law **F391.O512 2004**
A Journey Through Texas: Or a Saddle-Trip on the Southwestern Frontier. Witold M. Rybczynsk (Introduction by). Trade Cloth. University of Nebraska Press. Lincoln, NE. 2005. 560p. ISBN:0-8032-8620-1, ISBN13: 978-0-8032-8620-7. Dewey:917.6404/5. LCCN:2004-012904.
Audience: **f.**

Rathjen, Frederick **F392.P168R37 1998**
Texas Panhandle Frontier. Trade Paper. Texas Tech University Press. Lubbock, TX. 1998. 288p. Double Mountain Bks., :Classic Reissues of the American West ISBN:0-89672-399-2, ISBN13: 978-0-89672-399-3. Dewey:976.4/8. LCCN:98-008399.
Audience: **f.**

Richardson, Rupert Norval, et al. **F386.T434 2005**
Texas: The Lone Star State. Ed. 9. Adrian Anderson, Ernest Wallace & Cary D. Wintz (Authors). Trade Paper. Prentice Hall PTR. Upper Saddle River, NJ. 2004. 480p. ISBN:0-13-183550-5, ISBN13: 978-0-13-183550-4. Dewey:976.4. LCCN:2004-040012.
Audience: **g,l,u,f.**

Sanford, William R. & Green, Carl R. **F391.K535 1997**
Richard King: Texas Cattle Rancher. Library Binding. Enslow Publishers, Inc. Berkeley Heights, NJ. 1997. 48p. Legendary Heroes of the Wild West Ser. ISBN:0-89490-673-9, ISBN13: 978-0-89490-673-2. Dewey:976.4/061/092 B. LCCN:96-001892.
Audience: **u,f.**

Silbey, Joel H. **F390.S558 2005**
Storm over Texas: The Annexation Controversy and the Road to Civil War. Trade Cloth. Oxford University Press, Inc. New York, NY. 2005. 256p. Pivotal Moments in American History Ser. ISBN:0-19-513944-5, ISBN13: 978-0-19-513944-0. Dewey:976.4/04. LCCN:2005-040636.
Audience: **f.**

Timmons, W. H. **F394.E4**
El Paso: A Borderlands History. Trade Cloth. Texas Western Press. El Paso, TX. 1990. 387p. ISBN:0-87404-207-0, ISBN13: 978-0-87404-207-8. Dewey:976.4/96. LCCN:88-050545.
Audience: **f.**

Utley, Robert Marshall **F391.U9 2002**
Lone Star Justice: The First Century of the Texas Rangers. Trade Cloth. Oxford University Press, Inc. New York, NY. 2002. 416p. ISBN:0-19-512742-0, ISBN13: 978-0-19-512742-3. Dewey:976.4. LCCN:2001-036405.
Audience: **l,u,f.** *Choice, 2002.*

Wallace, Ernest, et al. **F386.W32 1994**
Documents of Texas History (1528-1993). David M. Vigness & George B. Ward (Authors). Trade Cloth. State House Press. Austin, TX. 1994. 349p. ISBN:1-880510-08-1, ISBN13: 978-1-880510-08-7. Dewey:976.4. LCCN:94-012996.
Audience: **u,f.**

Webb, Walter Prescott **F391 .W43**
Texas Rangers. Library Binding. Reprint Services Company. Temecula, CA. 1993. ISBN:0-7812-5981-9, ISBN13: 978-0-7812-5981-1. Dewey:976.4.
Audience: **f.**

Williams, John H. **F390.H84W55 1992**
Sam Houston: A Biography of the Father of Texas. Trade Cloth. Simon & Schuster. New York, NY. 1993. 448p. ISBN:0-671-74641-3, ISBN13: 978-0-671-74641-4. Dewey:976.4/04/092. LCCN:92-035418.
Audience: **l,u,f.** *Choice, 1993.*

Writers' Program of the Work Projects Administration in th Staff **F391.W95 1969**
Texas; a Guide to the Lone Star State. Trade Cloth. Hastings House Daytrips Publishers. Winter Park, FL. 1969. xxxiv, 717p. ISBN:0-8038-7055-8, ISBN13: 978-0-8038-7055-0. Dewey:917.64/04/6. LCCN:68-031690.
Audience: **f.**

United States > U.S. Local History > Old Southwest. Lower Mississippi Valley

Atherton, Lewis E. **F596.A8**
The Cattle Kings. Trade Paper. University of Nebraska Press. Lincoln, NE. 1972. 324p. ISBN:0-8032-5759-7, ISBN13: 978-0-8032-5759-7. Dewey:978. LCCN:61-013722.
Audience: **u,f.**

Dick, Everett **F396 .D5 1993**
The Dixie Frontier: A Social History of the Southern Frontier from the First Transmontaine Beginnings to the Civil War. Trade Paper. University of Oklahoma Press. Norman, OK. 1993. 422p. ISBN:0-8061-2385-0, ISBN13: 978-0-8061-2385-1. Dewey:976. LCCN:92-054144.
Audience: **f.**

Doherty, Kieran **F396.D64 2001**
Ranchers, Homesteaders and Traders: Frontiersmen of the South-Central States. Sylvia A. Johnson & Jenna Anderson (Editors). Library Binding. Oliver Press, Inc. Minneapolis, MN. 2001. 176p. Shaping America Ser., Vol. No. 4 ISBN:1-881508-53-6, ISBN13: 978-1-881508-53-3. Dewey:976/.009/9 B. LCCN:00-052864.
Audience: **f.**

Foreman, Grant **F396.F72 1994**
Pioneer Days in the Early Southwest. Donald E. Worcester (Introduction by). Trade Paper. University of Nebraska Press. Lincoln, NE. 1994. 345p. ISBN:0-8032-6883-1, ISBN13: 978-0-8032-6883-8. Dewey:976/.03. LCCN:93-045372.
Audience: **f.**

Herda, D J **F396.H52 1991**
Ethnic America: The South Central States. Millbrook Press, Inc. 1991. American Scene Ser. ISBN:1-56294-017-1, ISBN13: 978-1-56294-017-1.
Audience: **f.**

United States > U.S. Local History > Old Southwest. Lower Mississippi Valley > Arkansas. Tennessee

Abernethy, Thomas P. **F436.A17 1979**
From Frontier to Plantation in Tennessee: A Study in Frontier Democracy. Trade Cloth. Greenwood Publishing Group, Inc. Portsmouth, NH. 1979. 392p. Southern Historical Publications, No. 12 ISBN:0-313-21124-8, ISBN13: 978-0-313-21124-9. Dewey:976.8. LCCN:78-012038.
Audience: **f.**

Arnow, Harriette Louisa Simpson **F442.2.A69 1996**
Flowering of the Cumberland. Margaret R. Wolfe (Introduction by). Trade Cloth. University of Nebraska Press. Lincoln, NE. 1996. 443p. ISBN:0-8032-5928-X, ISBN13: 978-0-8032-5928-7. Dewey:976.8/5. LCCN:96-011178.
Audience: **u,f.**

Bolton, S. Charles **F411.B72 1998**
Arkansas, 1800-1860: Remote and Restless. Elliott West (Editor). Cloth Text. University of Arkansas Press. Fayetteville, AR. 1998. 224p. Histories of Arkansas Ser., No. 2 ISBN:1-55728-518-7, ISBN13: 978-1-55728-518-8. Dewey:976.7/03. LCCN:98-016180.
Audience: **f.** *Choice, 1999.*

Capers, Gerald M. Jr. **F444.M557**
The Biography of a River Town: Memphis—Its Heroic Age. Ed. 2. Trade Cloth. Burke's Book Store, Inc. Memphis, TN. 1980. 318p. ISBN:0-937130-10-9, ISBN13: 978-0-937130-10-0. Dewey:976.8191.
Audience: **f.**

Corlew, Robert E. **F436.C78**
Tennessee: A Short History. Ed. 2. Paper Text. University of Tennessee Press. Knoxville, TN. 1981. 652p. ISBN:0-87049-647-6, ISBN13: 978-0-87049-647-9. Dewey:976.8. LCCN:80-013553.
Audience: **g,l,u,f.** B

Crockett, David **F436.C9395 1987**
A Narrative of the Life of David Crockett of the State of Tennessee. Paul A. Hutton (Introduction by). Trade Cloth. University of Nebraska Press. Lincoln, NE. 1987. 211p. ISBN:0-8032-6325-2, ISBN13: 978-0-8032-6325-3. Dewey:976.8/04/0924 B. LCCN:87-016226.
Audience: **u,f.** B

Dykeman, Wilma **F436.D983 1975**
Tennessee. Trade Cloth. W. W. Norton & Company, Inc. New York, NY. 1975. 224p. States and the Nation Ser. ISBN:0-393-05555-8, ISBN13: 978-0-393-05555-9. Dewey:976.8. LCCN:75-025873.
Audience: **g,l,u,f.** B

Federal Writers' Project Staff **F436.F45 1949**
Tennessee: A Guide to the State. Trade Cloth. Somerset Publishers, Inc. Santa Barbara, CA. 1939. 558p. ISBN:0-403-02191-X, ISBN13: 978-0-403-02191-8. Dewey:917.68. LCCN:49-005822.
Audience: **f.** B

Fletcher, John G. **F411.F5**
Arkansas. Lucas Carpenter (Editor), Harry S. Ashmore (Introduction by). Trade Paper. University of Arkansas Press. Fayetteville, AR. 1995. 368p. ISBN:1-55728-379-6, ISBN13: 978-1-55728-379-5. Dewey:976.7. LCCN:88-017188.
Audience: **g,l,u,f.**

Johnson, Ben F. III **F411.J64 2000**
Arkansas in Modern America, 1930-1999. Trade Paper. University of Arkansas Press. Fayetteville, AR. 2003. xiv, 275p. Histories of Arkansas Ser., No. 3 ISBN:1-55728-618-3, ISBN13: 978-1-55728-618-5. Dewey:976.7/053. LCCN:00-009325.
Audience: **u,f.**

Kirk, John A. **F419.L7K57 2002**
Redefining the Color Line: Black Activism in Little Rock, Arkansas, 1940-1970. Trade Cloth. University Press of Florida. Gainesville, FL. 2002. xx, 256p. New Perspectives on the History of the South Ser. ISBN:0-8130-2496-X, ISBN13: 978-0-8130-2496-7. Dewey:323.1/196073076773. LCCN:2002-019472.
Audience: **f.** *Choice, 2003.*

Langsdon, Phillip R. **F436.L34 2000**
Tennessee: A Political History. Trade Cloth. Providence Publishing Corporation. Franklin, TN. 2000. xii, 436p.

ISBN:1-57736-125-3, ISBN13: 978-1-57736-125-1. Dewey:976.8. LCCN:98-075681.
Audience: **l,u,f.**

Majors, William R. **F436.B86.M34 1982**
End of Arcadia: Gordon Browning and Tennessee Politics. Trade Cloth. Memphis State University Press. Memphis, TN. 1982. viii, 263p. ISBN:0-87870-098-6, ISBN13: 978-0-87870-098-1. Dewey:976.8/05/0924. LCCN:82-003412.
Audience: **f.**

Moneyhon, Carl H. **F411.M74 1997**
Arkansas and the New South, 1874-1929. Trade Cloth. University of Arkansas Press. Fayetteville, AR. 2003. 208p. Histories of Arkansas Ser. ISBN:1-55728-489-X, ISBN13: 978-1-55728-489-1. Dewey:976.7/05. LCCN:97-026932.
Audience: **u,f.** *Choice, 1998.*

Reed, Roy **F415.3.F37R43 1997**
Faubus: The Life and Times of an American Prodigal. Trade Paper. University of Arkansas Press. Fayetteville, AR. 2003. 408p. ISBN:1-55728-467-9, ISBN13: 978-1-55728-467-9. Dewey:976.7/053/092 B. LCCN:96-053868.
Audience: **g,l,u,f.**

Shackford, James A. **F436.C95S47 1994**
David Crockett: The Man and the Legend. John B. Shackford (Editor), Michael A. Lofaro (Introduction by). Trade Paper. University of Nebraska Press. Lincoln, NE. 1994. 338p. ISBN:0-8032-9230-9, ISBN13: 978-0-8032-9230-7. Dewey:976.8/04/0924 B. LCCN:94-021656.
Audience: **g,l,u,f.**

Tucker, David M. **F411.T83 1985**
Arkansas: A People and Their Reputation. Trade Cloth. Memphis State University Press. Memphis, TN. 1985. 176p. ISBN:0-87870-211-3, ISBN13: 978-0-87870-211-4. Dewey:976.7. LCCN:85-015511.
Audience: **g,l,u,f.** *Choice, 1986.*

Van West, Carroll (Editor) **F436.T53 1998**
Tennessee History: The Land, the People, and the Culture. Cloth Text. University of Tennessee Press. Knoxville, TN. 1998. 488p. ISBN:1-57233-003-1, ISBN13: 978-1-57233-003-0. Dewey:976.8. LCCN:97-021170.
Audience: **g,l,u,f.**

Whayne, Jeannie M. **F411.A772 2002**
Arkansas: A Narrative History. Trade Cloth. University of Arkansas Press. Fayetteville, AR. 2002. 416p. ISBN:1-55728-724-4, ISBN13: 978-1-55728-724-3. Dewey:976.7. LCCN:2002-002104.
Audience: **g,l,u,f.**

United States > U.S. Local History > Old Southwest. Lower Mississippi Valley > Kentucky

Appleton, Thomas H. Jr. (Editor), et al. **F451.K417 1998**
Kentucky: Land of Tomorrow. Melba P. Hay, James C. Klotter & Thomas E. Stephens (Editors). Trade Cloth. Kentucky Historical Society. Frankfort, KY. 2001. 256p. ISBN:0-916968-25-1, ISBN13: 978-0-916968-25-0. Dewey:976.9. LCCN:98-226808.
Audience: **g,l,f.**

Blakey, George T. **F0456.B53**
Hard Times and New Deal in Kentucky, 1929-1939. Trade Paper. Books on Demand. Ann Arbor, MI. 1986. 268p. ISBN:0-7837-9580-7, ISBN13: 978-0-7837-9580-5. Dewey:976.9/042. LCCN:86-001513.
Audience: **f.** *Choice, 1986.*

Davenport, Francis Garvin **F455.D36 1983**
Ante-Bellum Kentucky: A Social History, 1800-1860. Trade Cloth. Greenwood Publishing Group, Inc. Portsmouth, NH. 1983. 238p. Annals of America Ser., No. 5 ISBN:0-313-24113-9, ISBN13: 978-0-313-24113-0. Dewey:976.9/03. LCCN:83-010871.
Audience: **f.**

Harrison, Lowell H. (Editor) **F450.K44 2004**
Kentucky's Governors. Trade Cloth. University Press of Kentucky. Lexington, KY. 2004. 304p. ISBN:0-8131-2326-7, ISBN13: 978-0-8131-2326-4. Dewey:976.9/009/9. LCCN:2004-017747.
Audience: **l,u,f.**

Harrison, Lowell H. & Klotter, James C. **F451.H315 1997**
New History of Kentucky. Trade Cloth. University Press of Kentucky. Lexington, KY. 1997. 464p. ISBN:0-8131-2008-X, ISBN13: 978-0-8131-2008-9. Dewey:976.9. LCCN:96-035904.
Audience: **g,l,u,f.**

Klotter, James C. **F451.O94 2000**
Our Kentucky: A Study of the Bluegrass State. Ed. 2. Trade Cloth. University Press of Kentucky. Lexington, KY. 2000. 400p. ISBN:0-8131-2145-0, ISBN13: 978-0-8131-2145-1. Dewey:976.9. LCCN:99-047987.
Audience: **g,l,u,f.**

Lofaro, Michael A. **F454.B66L628 2003**
Daniel Boone: An American Life. Trade Cloth. University Press of Kentucky. Lexington, KY. 2003. 192p. ISBN:0-8131-2278-3, ISBN13: 978-0-8131-2278-6. Dewey:976.9/02/092 B. LCCN:2003-008805.
Audience: **g,l,u,f.** *Choice, 2004.*

Pearce, John E. **F456.P42 1987**
Divide and Dissent: Kentucky Politics, 1930-1963. Trade Paper. University Press of Kentucky. Lexington, KY. 1987. 256p. ISBN:0-8131-0804-7, ISBN13: 978-0-8131-0804-9. Dewey:976.9/043. LCCN:86-028978.
Audience: **f.** *Choice, 1987.*

Simon, Kevin (Editor) **F451.F45 1996**
The WPA Guide to Kentucky. Trade Cloth. University Press of Kentucky. Lexington, KY. 1996. 608p. ISBN:0-8131-1997-9, ISBN13: 978-0-8131-1997-7. Dewey:976.9. LCCN:96-024751.
Audience: **f.**

United States > U.S. Local History > Old Southwest. Lower Mississippi Valley > Missouri

Aron, Stephen **F466.A76 2006**
American Confluence: The Missouri Frontier from Borderland to Border State. Perfect, Paper over Boards, Dust Jacket. Indiana University Press. Bloomington, IN. 2005. 301p. A History of the Trans-Appalachian Frontier Ser. ISBN:0-253-34691-6, ISBN13: 978-0-253-34691-9. Dewey:977.8/01. LCCN:2005-018951.
Audience: **f.**

Christensen, Law & Kremer, Gary **F466.H58**
History of Missouri, Vol. 4. Trade Paper. University of Missouri Press. Columbia, MO. 2004. 296p. ISBN:0-8262-1559-9, ISBN13: 978-0-8262-1559-8. Dewey:977.8. LCCN:76-155844.
Audience: **f.**

Dorsett, Lyle W. **F0474.K257.**
The Pendergast Machine. Trade Paper. Books on Demand. Ann Arbor, MI. 179p. A Bison Bk. ISBN:0-7837-0225-6, ISBN13: 978-0-7837-0225-4. Dewey:352.0778/411. LCCN:80-011581.
Audience: **u,f.**

Federal Writers' Project Staff **F466.W85 1973**
Missouri: A Guide to the "Show Me" State. Trade Cloth. Somerset Publishers, Inc. Santa Barbara, CA. 1981. 652p. American Guidebook Ser. ISBN:0-403-02175-8, ISBN13: 978-0-403-02175-8. Dewey:917.78/04/4. LCCN:72-084486.
Audience: **f.**

Ferrell, Robert H. **E814.F483 1999**
Truman and Pendergast. Trade Cloth. Thomson Gale. Farmington Hills, MI. 1999. 278p. American History Ser. ISBN:0-7838-8758-2, ISBN13: 978-0-7838-8758-6. Dewey:973.918/092. LCCN:99-041471.
Audience: **u,f.** *Choice, 2000.*

Gilmore, Robert K. **F472.O9 G55**
Ozark Baptizings, Hangings, and Other Diversions: Theatrical Folkways of Rural Missouri, 1885-1910. Robert Flanders (Foreword by). Trade Paper. University of Oklahoma Press. Norman, OK. 1990. 294p. ISBN:0-8061-2270-6, ISBN13: 978-0-8061-2270-0. Dewey:977.8/835. LCCN:83-040324.
Audience: **u,f.**

Kirkendall, Rich **F466.H58**
History of Missouri, Vol. 5. Trade Paper. University of Missouri Press. Columbia, MO. 2004. 448p. ISBN:0-8262-1560-2, ISBN13: 978-0-8262-1560-4. Dewey:977.8. LCCN:76-155844.
Audience: **u,f.**

Larsen, Lawrence H. & Hulston, Nancy J. **F474.K253P465 1997**
Pendergast!. William E. Foley (Contribution by). Trade Cloth. University of Missouri Press. Columbia, MO. 1997. 256p. Biography Ser. ISBN:0-8262-1145-3, ISBN13: 978-0-8262-1145-3. Dewey:977.8/411042/092 B. LCCN:97-033391.
Audience: **u,f.** *Choice, 1998.*

Nagel, Paul C. **F466.N3**
Missouri: A History. Trade Paper. University Press of Kansas. Lawrence, KS. 1988. xiv, 210p. ISBN:0-7006-0386-7, ISBN13: 978-0-7006-0386-2. Dewey:977.8. LCCN:88-027761.
Audience: **g,l,u,f.**

Parrish, William E. **F466.P27 1992**
Missouri: The Heart of the Nation. Ed. 2. Trade Paper. Harlan Davidson Inc. Wheeling, IL. 2003. 423p. ISBN:0-88295-887-9, ISBN13: 978-0-88295-887-3. Dewey:977.8.220. LCCN:91-044286.
Audience: **g,l,u,f.**

Sandweiss, Lee Ann (Editor) **F474.S2S38 2000**
Seeking St. Louis: Voices from a River City, 1670-2000. Trade Cloth. Missouri Historical Society Press. Saint Louis, MO. 2000. 1200p. ISBN:1-883982-11-1, ISBN13: 978-1-883982-11-9. Dewey:977.8/66. LCCN:00-045591.
Audience: **f.**

Schirmer, Sherry Lamb **F474.K29A27 2002**
A City Divided: The Racial Landscape of Kansas City, 1900-1960. Trade Cloth. University of Missouri Press. Columbia, MO. 2002. 272p. ISBN:0-8262-1391-X, ISBN13: 978-0-8262-1391-4. Dewey:305.8/0097708. LCCN:2002-017953.
Audience: **f.**

United States > U.S. Local History > Old Northwest. Northwest Territory

Bond, Beverley W. Jr. **F479 .B69**
Civilization of the Old Northwest. Library Binding. Reprint Services Company. Temecula, CA. 1993. ISBN:0-7812-5341-1, ISBN13: 978-0-7812-5341-3. Dewey:390.1/77.
Audience: **u,f.**

Buley, R. Carlyle **F484.3.B94 1983**
The Old Northwest: Pioneer Period, 1815-1840. Trade Cloth. Indiana University Press. Bloomington, IN. 1983. 1344p. ISBN:0-253-34168-X, ISBN13: 978-0-253-34168-6. Dewey:977. LCCN:83-048117.
Audience: **f.**

Cayton, Andrew R. & Onuf, Peter S. **F479.C34 1990**
The Midwest and the Nation: Rethinking the History of an American Region. Trade Cloth. Indiana University Press. Bloomington, IN. 1990. 192p. Midwestern History and Culture Ser. ISBN:0-253-31525-5, ISBN13: 978-0-253-31525-0. Dewey:977. LCCN:89-045479.
Audience: **u,f.** *Choice, 1990.*

Kellogg, Louise Phelps **LA226.H53**
Early Narratives of the Northwest, 1634-1699. Trade Paper. Clearfield Company. Baltimore, MD. 2002. xiv, 382p. ISBN:0-8063-5187-X, ISBN13: 978-0-8063-5187-2. Dewey:378.73.
Audience: **f.**

Kohlmeier, Albert L. **F484.3 .K798**
The Old Northwest As the Keystone of the Arch of American Federal Union: A Study in Commerce and Politics. Trade Cloth. Johnson Reprint Corporation. New York, NY. 1970. History of American Economy Ser. ISBN:0-384-30070-7, ISBN13: 978-0-384-30070-5. Dewey:977. LCCN:38-002230.
Audience: **f.**

Ogg, Federick Austin **F479 .O34**
The Old Northwest. Trade Paper. 1st World Publishing, Inc. Fairfield, IA. 2005. 164p. ISBN:1-4218-0125-6, ISBN13: 978-1-4218-0125-4. Dewey:977. LCCN:2004117754.
Audience: **f.**

Power, Richard L. **F484.3 .P6 1983**
Planting Corn Belt Culture: The Impress of the Upland Southerner and Yankee in the Old Northwest. Trade Cloth. Greenwood Publishing Group, Inc. Portsmouth, NH. 1983. 196p. Indiana Historical Society Publications Ser. ISBN:0-313-24060-4, ISBN13: 978-0-313-24060-7. Dewey:977. LCCN:83-008491.
Audience: **f.**

Rohrbough, Malcolm J. **F484.3.R64 1990**
The Trans-Appalachian Frontier: People, Societies, and Institutions, 1775-1850. Trade Cloth. Thomson Wadsworth. Belmont, CA. 1989. 403p. ISBN:0-534-12336-8, ISBN13: 978-0-534-12336-9. Dewey:977/.02. LCCN:89-034083.
Audience: **f.**

Slade, Joseph W. & Lee, Judith Yaross **F351.M59 2004**
The Midwest. Trade Cloth. Greenwood Publishing Group, Inc. Portsmouth, NH. 2004. xxx, 584p. The Greenwood Encyclopedia of American Regional Cultures Ser. ISBN:0-313-32493-X, ISBN13: 978-0-313-32493-2. Dewey:977/.003. LCCN:2004-056060.
Audience: **g,l,u,f.**

Sosin, Jack M. **E748.S84B72**
Whitehall and the Wilderness: The Middle West in British Colonial Policy 1760. Paper Text. Textbook Publishers. Temecula, CA. 2003. xi, 307p. ISBN:0-7581-1915-1, ISBN13: 978-0-7581-1915-5. Dewey:973.921/092.
Audience: **f.**

United States > U.S. Local History > Ohio. Ohio Valley

Cayton, Andrew R. **F495**
The Frontier Republic: Ideology and Politics in the Ohio Country, 1780-1825. Trade Paper. Kent State University Press. Kent, OH. 1989. 209p. ISBN:0-87338-409-1, ISBN13: 978-0-87338-409-4. Dewey:977.1/03. LCCN:86-004706.
Audience: **f.** *Choice, 1987.*

Cayton, Andrew R. L. **F491.C39 2002**
Ohio: The History of a People. Trade Cloth. Ohio State University Press. Columbus, OH. 2002. vii, 472p. ISBN:0-8142-0899-1, ISBN13: 978-0-8142-0899-1. Dewey:977.1. LCCN:2001-007350.
Audience: **g,l,u,f.** *Choice, 2002.*

Federal Writers' Project Staff & Writers Program Staff **F496 .W96**
Ohio: The Ohio Guide. Library Binding. Reprint Services Company. Temecula, CA. 1989. American Guide Ser. ISBN:0-7812-1034-8, ISBN13: 978-0-7812-1034-8. Dewey:917.71/04/4.
Audience: **f.**

Havighurst, Walter **F491.H4 2001**
Ohio: A History. Trade Paper. University of Illinois Press. Champaign, IL. 2001. 224p. ISBN:0-252-07017-8, ISBN13: 978-0-252-07017-4. Dewey:977.1. LCCN:2001-027666.
Audience: **g,l,u,f.**

Hurt, R. Douglas **F495.H94**
The Ohio Frontier: Crucible of the Old Northwest, 1720-1830. Trade Paper. Indiana University Press. Bloomington, IN. 1998. 440p. A History of the Trans-Appalachian Frontier Ser. ISBN:0-253-21212-X, ISBN13: 978-0-253-21212-2. Dewey:977.1. LCCN:95-053278.
Audience: **u,f.**

Jakle, John A. **F517.J28**
Images of the Ohio Valley: A Historical Geography of Travel. Miklos Pinther (Illustrator). Trade Cloth. Oxford University Press, Inc. New York, NY. 1977. viii, 217p. ISBN:0-19-502240-8, ISBN13: 978-0-19-502240-7. Dewey:977/.02. LCCN:77-009570.
Audience: **f.**

Knepper, George W. **F491.K63 2003**
Ohio and Its People. Ed. 3. Trade Paper. Kent State University Press. Kent, OH. 2003. 519p. ISBN:0-87338-791-0, ISBN13: 978-0-87338-791-0. Dewey:977.1. LCCN:2003-051950.
Audience: **g,l,u,f.** *Choice, 1990.*

Linkon, Sherry Lee & Russo, John **F499.Y8L56 2002**
Steeltown U. S. A.: Work and Memory in Youngstown. Trade Cloth. University Press of Kansas. Lawrence, KS. 2002. viii, 288p. Culture America Ser. ISBN:0-7006-1161-4, ISBN13: 978-0-7006-1161-4. Dewey:977.1/39. LCCN:2001-006342.
Audience: **f.** *Choice, 2003.*

Maizlish, Stephen E. **F0495.M34**
The Triumph of Sectionalism: The Transformation of Ohio Politics, 1844-1856. Trade Paper. Books on Demand. Ann Arbor, MI. 325p. ISBN:0-7837-1353-3, ISBN13: 978-0-7837-1353-3. Dewey:977.1/03. LCCN:83-011255.
Audience: **f.**

Miller, Carol P. & Wheeler, Robert **F499.C657M55 1997**
Cleveland: A Concise History, 1796-1996. Ed. 2. Trade Cloth. Indiana University Press. Bloomington, IN. 1997. 240p. Encyclopedia of Cleveland History Ser. ISBN:0-253-33336-9, ISBN13: 978-0-253-33336-0. Dewey:977.1/32. LCCN:97-009916.
Audience: **u,f.**

Moore, Leonard N. **F499.C653S866 2002**
Carl B. Stokes and the Rise of Black Political Power. Trade Cloth. University of Illinois Press. Champaign, IL. 2002. 264p. ISBN:0-252-02760-4, ISBN13: 978-0-252-02760-4. Dewey:977.1/32043/092 B. LCCN:2001-007063.
Audience: **u,f.** *Choice, 2003.*

Roseboom, Eugene Holloway **F591.K7**
A History of Ohio. Paper Text. Textbook Publishers. Temecula, CA. 2003. xiii, 443p. ISBN:0-7581-7368-7, ISBN13: 978-0-7581-7368-3. Dewey:978.
Audience: **g,l,u,f.**

Van Tine, Warren R. & Pierce, Michael D. (Editors) **F491.6.B85 2003**
Builders of Ohio: A Biographical History. Trade Cloth. Ohio

State University Press. Columbus, OH. 2003. xi, 338p. ISBN:0-8142-0951-3, ISBN13: 978-0-8142-0951-6. Dewey:977.1/009/9. LCCN:2003-017391.

Audience: **u,f.**

Wade, Richard C. **F518**
The Urban Frontier: The Rise of Western Cities, 1790-1830. Trade Cloth. Harvard University Press. Cambridge, MA. 1959. 372p. Historical Monographs, No. 41 ISBN:0-674-93075-4, ISBN13: 978-0-674-93075-9. Dewey:977/.009732. LCCN:59-009285.

Audience: **f.** B

United States > U.S. Local History > Indiana

Barnhart, John D. & Riker, Dorothy L. **F526 .H55 VOL. 1**
Indiana to Eighteen Sixteen: The Colonial Period. Trade Cloth. Indiana Historical Society. Indianapolis, IN. 1971. 520p. History of Indiana Ser. ISBN:0-253-37018-3, ISBN13: 978-0-253-37018-1. Dewey:977.2.

Audience: **u,f.**

Bigham, Darrel E. (Editor) **F526.5.I54 2001**
Indiana Territory, 1800-2000: A Bicentennial Perspective. Trade Cloth. Indiana Historical Society. Indianapolis, IN. 2001. xi, 196p. ISBN:0-87195-155-X, ISBN13: 978-0-87195-155-7. Dewey:977.2/03. LCCN:2001-039311.

Audience: **u,f.**

Carmony, Donald F. **F526.C295 1998**
Indiana, 1816 to 1850: The Pioneer Period. Trade Cloth. Indiana Historical Society. Indianapolis, IN. 1998. xiv, 924p. History of Indiana Ser., Vol. 2 ISBN:0-87195-124-X, ISBN13: 978-0-87195-124-3. Dewey:977.2. LCCN:97-036392.

Audience: **u,f.**

Cayton, Andrew R. **F526.C35 1996**
Frontier Indiana. Trade Cloth. Indiana University Press. Bloomington, IN. 1996. 360p. A History of the Trans-Appalachian Frontier Ser. ISBN:0-253-33048-3, ISBN13: 978-0-253-33048-2. Dewey:977.2. LCCN:95-026443.

Audience: **f.** *Choice, 1997.*

Esslinger, Dean R. **F534.S7.E77**
Immigrants and the City: Ethnicity and Mobility in a 19th Century Midwestern City. Trade Cloth. Associated Faculty Press, Inc. New York, NY. 1975. xii, 156p. ISBN:0-8046-9108-8, ISBN13: 978-0-8046-9108-6. Dewey:301.32/9/77289. LCCN:75-015947.

Audience: **u,f.** B

Federal Writers' Project Staff & Writers Program Staff **F526**
Indiana: A Guide to the Hoosier State. Library Binding. Reprint Services Company. Temecula, CA. 1989. American Guide Ser. ISBN:0-7812-1013-5, ISBN13: 978-0-7812-1013-3. Dewey:917.72.

Audience: **f.**

Madison, James H. **F526 .H55 VOL. 5**
Indiana Through Tradition and Change: A History of the Hoosier State and Its People, 1920-1945. Trade Cloth. Indiana Historical Society. Indianapolis, IN. 1982. xx, 453p. History of Indiana Ser., Vol. 5 ISBN:0-87195-043-X, ISBN13: 978-0-87195-043-7. Dewey:977.2 s 977.2/042.

Audience: **u,f.** B

Mohl, Raymond A. & Betten, Neil **F534.G2M64 1986**
Steel City: Urban and Ethnic Patterns in Gary, Indiana, 1906-1950. Trade Cloth. Holmes & Meier Publishers, Inc. Teaneck, NJ. 1986. 227p. ISBN:0-8419-1010-3, ISBN13: 978-0-8419-1010-2. Dewey:977.2/99. LCCN:85-000963.

Audience: **f.** *Choice, 1986.*

Peckham, Howard H. **F526.P43 2003**
Indiana: A History. Trade Paper. University of Illinois Press. Champaign, IL. 2003. 224p. ISBN:0-252-07146-8, ISBN13: 978-0-252-07146-1. Dewey:977.2. LCCN:2003-041013.

Audience: **g,l,u,f.**

Phillips, Clifton J. **F526 .H55 V.4**
Indiana in Transition, 1880-1920. Trade Cloth. Indiana Historical Society. Indianapolis, IN. 1968. xiv, 674p. History of Indiana Ser., Vol. 4 ISBN:0-87195-092-8, ISBN13: 978-0-87195-092-5. Dewey:917.72/03/4.

Audience: **u,f.**

Stampp, Kenneth Milton **E0506.S73**
Indiana Politics During the Civil War. Trade Paper. Books on Demand. Ann Arbor, MI. 312p. Indiana Historical Collections, Vol. 31 ISBN:0-598-81113-3, ISBN13: 978-0-598-81113-4. Dewey:320.9/772/03. LCCN:49-045273.

Audience: **f.**

Thornbrough, Emma L. **F526.H55**
Indiana in the Civil War Era, 1850-1880. Trade Cloth. Indiana University Press. Bloomington, IN. 1995. xii, 758p. History of Indiana Ser., Vol. 3 ISBN:0-253-37020-5, ISBN13: 978-0-253-37020-4. Dewey:977.2. LCCN:66-063323.

Audience: **u,f.** B

United States > U.S. Local History > Illinois

Adams, Jane **F547.U5A34 1994**
The Transformation of Rural Life: Southern Illinois, 1890-1990. Trade Cloth. University of North Carolina Press. Chapel Hill, NC. 1994. 352p. Studies in Rural Culture ISBN:0-8078-2168-3, ISBN13: 978-0-8078-2168-8. Dewey:977.3/99504. LCCN:94-004176.

Audience: **f.** *Choice, 1995.*

Biles, Roger **F541.3.B55 2006**
Illinois: A History of the Land and Its People. Saddle Stitched, Cloth over Boards, Dust Jacket. Northern Illinois University Press. DeKalb, IL. 2005. 341p. ISBN:0-87580-349-0, ISBN13: 978-0-87580-349-4. Dewey:977.3. LCCN:2005-007279.

Audience: **g,l,u,f.** *Choice, 2006.*

Bogue, Margaret B. **HD211.I3 B6 1979**
Patterns from the Sod. Stuart Bruchey (Editor). Library Binding. Ayer Company Publishers, Inc. Manchester, NH. 1979. Management of Public Lands in the U. S. Ser. ISBN:0-405-11318-8, ISBN13: 978-0-405-11318-5. Dewey:333/.009773. LCCN:78-056691.

Audience: **f.**

Brown, Stuart Gerry **QP303.H35**
Conscience in Politics: Adlai E. Stevenson in the 1950's. Paper Text. Textbook Publishers. Temecula, CA. 2003. 313p. ISBN:0-7581-3336-7, ISBN13: 978-0-7581-3336-6. Dewey:612.7/6.
Audience: **f.** B

Federal Writers' Project Staff **F546**
Illinois - Collected Works of Federal Writers Project, Set. Library Binding. Reprint Services Company. Temecula, CA. 1991. ISBN:0-7812-5558-9, ISBN13: 978-0-7812-5558-5. Dewey:917.73/04/4.
Audience: **f.**

Hoffmann, John (Editor) **Z1277**
A Guide to the History of Illinois: Reference Guides to State History and Research. Cloth Text. Greenwood Publishing Group, Inc. Portsmouth, NH. 1991. 360p. Reference Guides to State History and Research Ser. ISBN:0-313-24110-4, ISBN13: 978-0-313-24110-9. Dewey:016.9773. LCCN:90-036776.
Audience: **u,f.**

Jensen, Richard J. **F541.J46 2001**
Illinois: A History. Trade Paper. University of Illinois Press. Champaign, IL. 2001. 216p. ISBN:0-252-07021-6, ISBN13: 978-0-252-07021-1. Dewey:977.3. LCCN:2001-027665.
Audience: **g,l,u,f.** B

United States > U.S. Local History > Illinois > Chicago

Algren, Nelson **F548.3.A43 2001**
Chicago: City on the Make. David Schmittgens & Bill Savage (Annotations by). Trade Paper. University of Chicago Press. Chicago, IL. 2001. 135p. ISBN:0-226-01385-5, ISBN13: 978-0-226-01385-5. Dewey:977.3/11. LCCN:2001-035158.
Audience: **f.**

Bales, Richard F. **F548.42.B23 2002**
The Great Chicago Fire and the Myth of Mrs. O'Leary's Cow. Trade Cloth. McFarland & Company, Incorporated Publishers. Jefferson, NC. 2002. 350p. ISBN:0-7864-1424-3, ISBN13: 978-0-7864-1424-6. Dewey:977.3/11041. LCCN:2002-010361.
Audience: **u,f.**

Biles, Roger **F548.5.K44.B54 1984**
Big City Boss in Depression and War: Mayor Edward J. Kelly of Chicago. Trade Cloth. Northern Illinois University Press. DeKalb, IL. 1984. 219p. ISBN:0-87580-098-X, ISBN13: 978-0-87580-098-1. Dewey:977.3/11042/0924. LCCN:83-019391.
Audience: **f.** B

Biles, Roger **F548.54.D34B55 1995**
Richard J. Daley: Politics, Race, and the Governing of Chicago. Trade Cloth. Northern Illinois University Press. DeKalb, IL. 2003. 302p. ISBN:0-87580-199-4, ISBN13: 978-0-87580-199-5. Dewey:977.3/11043/092 B. LCCN:94-048268.
Audience: **u,f.** *Choice, 1995.*

Byrne, Jane **F548.54.B97A3 1992**
My Chicago. Trade Cloth. W. W. Norton & Company, Inc. New York, NY. 1992. 352p. ISBN:0-393-03073-3, ISBN13: 978-0-393-03073-0. Dewey:352/.00092 B. LCCN:91-025422.
Audience: **u,f.**

Cutler, Irving **F548.9.J5C87 1996**
The Jews of Chicago: From Shtetl to Suburb. Trade Cloth. University of Illinois Press. Champaign, IL. 1996. 336p. The Ethnic History of Chicago Ser. ISBN:0-252-02185-1, ISBN13: 978-0-252-02185-5. Dewey:977.3/11004924. LCCN:94-047591.
Audience: **f.** *Choice, 1996.*

Farber, David **F548.52.F37 1988**
Chicago '68. Trade Cloth. University of Chicago Press. Chicago, IL. 1988. 334p. ISBN:0-226-23800-8, ISBN13: 978-0-226-23800-5. Dewey:977.3/11043. LCCN:87-019071.
Audience: **u,f.** *Choice, 1988.*

Ginger, Ray **F548.5.G45 1986**
Altgeld's America: The Lincoln Ideal Versus Changing Realities. Ed. 2. Garry Gerstle (Introduction by). Paper Text. Markus Wiener Publishers, Inc. Princeton, NJ. 1986. 400p. History Syllabi Ser. ISBN:0-910129-48-7, ISBN13: 978-0-910129-48-0. Dewey:977.3/11031. LCCN:86-040364.
Audience: **f.** B

Green, Paul M. (Editor, Afterword by) **F548.25.M39 1995**
The Mayors: The Chicago Political Tradition. Melvin G. Holli (Editor). Trade Cloth. Southern Illinois University Press. Carbondale, IL. 1994. 311p. ISBN:0-8093-1961-6, ISBN13: 978-0-8093-1961-9. Dewey:977.3/11/0099 B. LCCN:94-005734.
Audience: **u,f.** *Choice, 1987.*

Grossman, James R. (Editor), et al. **F548.3.E53 2004**
The Encyclopedia of Chicago. Ann Durkin Keating & Janice L. Reiff (Editors), Newberry Librar & Chicago Histori (Contribution by). Trade Cloth. University of Chicago Press. Chicago, IL. 2004. 1152p. ISBN:0-226-31015-9, ISBN13: 978-0-226-31015-2. Dewey:977.3/11/003. LCCN:2004-003487.
Audience: **g,l,u,f.**

Holli, Melvin G. & Jones, Peter d' A. (Editors) **F548.9.A1E85 1994**
Ethnic Chicago: A Multicultural Portrait. Ed. 4. Trade Paper. William B. Eerdmans Publishing Company. Grand Rapids, MI. 1995. 656p. ISBN:0-8028-7053-8, ISBN13: 978-0-8028-7053-7. Dewey:305.8/009773/11. LCCN:95-003130.
Audience: **f.**

Kantowicz, Edward **F548.9.P7**
Polish-American Politics in Chicago, 1888-1940. Arthur Mann (Editor). Trade Cloth. University of Chicago Press. Chicago, IL. 1975. 267p. ISBN:0-226-42380-8, ISBN13: 978-0-226-42380-7. Dewey:323.1/19/185077311. LCCN:74-016682.
Audience: **f.**

Karamanski, Theodore **F548.4**
Rally 'Round the Flag: Chicago and the Civil War. Trade Cloth. Rowman & Littlefield Publishers, Inc. Lanham, MD. 1993. 328p. ISBN:0-8304-1295-6, ISBN13: 978-0-8304-1295-2. Dewey:977.3. LCCN:92-024197.
Audience: **f.** *Choice, 1993.*

Kleppner, Paul **F548.52.W36K54 1985**
Chicago Divided: The Making of a Black Mayor. Trade Paper. Northern Illinois University Press. DeKalb, IL. 1985. 313p. ISBN:0-87580-532-9, ISBN13: 978-0-87580-532-0. Dewey:324.9773/11043. LCCN:84-025531.
Audience: **u,f.** B *Choice, 1985.*

Mayer, Harold M. & Wade, Richard C. **F548.3.M37**
Chicago: Growth of a Metropolis. Trade Cloth. University of Chicago Press. Chicago, IL. 2001. 522p. ISBN:0-226-51273-8, ISBN13: 978-0-226-51273-0. Dewey:917.73/11/03. LCCN:68-054054.
Audience: **u,f.** *B*

Merriner, James L. **F548.3.M47 2004**
Grafter and Goo Goos: Corruption and Reform in Chicago, 1833-2003. Trade Cloth. Southern Illinois University Press. Carbondale, IL. 2004. 344p. ISBN:0-8093-2571-3, ISBN13: 978-0-8093-2571-9. Dewey:977.3/11. LCCN:2003-015588.
Audience: **f.** *Choice, 2004.*

Nelli, Humbert S. **F548.9.I8**
The Italians in Chicago, 1880-1930: A Study in Ethnic Mobility. Paper Text. Oxford University Press, Inc. New York, NY. 1973. 320p. The Urban Life in America Ser. ISBN:0-19-501674-2, ISBN13: 978-0-19-501674-1. Dewey:301.453/45/077311.
Audience: **f.** *B*

Philpott **F548.9.N4 P47**
The Slum and the Ghetto. Trade Paper. Thomson Wadsworth. Belmont, CA. Adaptable Courseware-Softside Ser. ISBN:0-534-15922-2, ISBN13: 978-0-534-15922-1. Dewey:305.896/073077311.
Audience: **f.**

Pierce, Bessie Louise **F548.3.A8 2004**
As Others See Chicago: Impressions of Visitors, 1673-1933. Perry R. Duis (Foreword by). Trade Paper. University of Chicago Press. Chicago, IL. 2004. 548p. ISBN:0-226-66821-5, ISBN13: 978-0-226-66821-5. Dewey:977.3/111. LCCN:2003-026813.
Audience: **f.**

Royko, Mike (Author, Introduction by) **F548.54.D34K68 1988**
Boss: Richard J. Daley of Chicago. Trade Paper. Penguin Group (USA) Inc. New York, NY. 1988. 224p. ISBN:0-452-26167-8, ISBN13: 978-0-452-26167-9. Dewey:352/.000924. LCCN:88-022495.
Audience: **g,l,u,f.**

Taylor, Elizabeth & Cohen, Adam **F548.54.D34C64 2000**
American Pharaoh: Mayor Richard J. Daley: His Battle for Chicago and the Nation. Trade Cloth. Little Brown & Company. New York, NY. 2000. 624p. ISBN:0-316-83403-3, ISBN13: 978-0-316-83403-2. Dewey:977.3/11043/092 B. LCCN:99-042157.
Audience: **u,f.**

Travis, Dempsey J. **F548.54.W36T73 1989**
Harold: The People's Mayor. Trade Cloth. Urban Research Press, Inc. Chicago, IL. 1989. 349p. ISBN:0-941484-08-4, ISBN13: 978-0-941484-08-4. Dewey:977.3/11043/0924 B. LCCN:88-014225.
Audience: **u,f.**

Tuttle, William M. Jr. **F548.9.N4T88 1996**
Race Riot: Chicago in the Red Summer of 1919. Trade Paper. University of Illinois Press. Champaign, IL. 1996. 320p. Blacks in the New World Ser. ISBN:0-252-06586-7, ISBN13: 978-0-252-06586-6. Dewey:977.3/1100496073. LCCN:96-007602.
Audience: **f.** *B*

United States > U.S. Local History > Great Lakes

Sobol, Julie Macfie & Sobol, Ken **F555.S626 2004**
Lake Erie: A Pictorial History. Trade Cloth. Boston Mills Press. Erin, ON. 2004. 224p. ISBN:1-55046-361-6, ISBN13: 978-1-55046-361-3. Dewey:977.1/2. LCCN:2004-381460.
Audience: **u,f.**

United States > U.S. Local History > Michigan

F566.E53 1999
The Encyclopedia of Michigan: A Reference Guide to the Wolverine State, Set. Ed. 4. Trade Cloth. Somerset Publishers, Inc. Santa Barbara, CA. 2001. 600p. ISBN:0-403-09322-8, ISBN13: 978-0-403-09322-9. Dewey:977.4/003/21.
Audience: **g,l,u,f.**

Catton, Bruce **F566.C3 1984**
Michigan: Bicentennial and History Guide. Ed. 2. Trade Paper. W. W. Norton & Company, Inc. New York, NY. 1984. 204p. ISBN:0-393-30175-3, ISBN13: 978-0-393-30175-5. Dewey:977.4. LCCN:83025416.
Audience: **g,l,u,f.**

Cohen, Irwin J. **F574.D49J533 2002**
Jewish Detroit. Trade Paper. Arcadia Publishing. Mount Pleasant, SC. 2001. 128p. Images of America Ser., :Michigan ISBN:0-7385-1996-0, ISBN13: 978-0-7385-1996-8. Dewey:977.4/34004924/00222. LCCN:2002-106084.
Audience: **f.**

Dunbar, Willis F. & May, George S. **F566.D84 1995**
Michigan: A History of the Wolverine State. Ed. 3. Trade Cloth. William B. Eerdmans Publishing Company. Grand Rapids, MI. 1995. 781p. ISBN:0-8028-7055-4, ISBN13: 978-0-8028-7055-1. Dewey:977.4. LCCN:95-013128.
Audience: **g,l,u,f.**

Federal Writers' Project Staff **F566.W9 1973**
Michigan: A Guide to the Wolverine State. Trade Cloth. Somerset Publishers, Inc. Santa Barbara, CA. 1981. xxxvi, 682p. American Guidebook Ser. ISBN:0-403-02172-3, ISBN13: 978-0-403-02172-7. Dewey:917.74/04/4. LCCN:72-084482.
Audience: **f.** *B*

Kestenbaum, Justin L. (Editor) **F566.M35 1990**
Making of Michigan, 1820-1860: A Pioneer Anthology. Trade Cloth. Wayne State University Press. Detroit, MI. 1990. 422p. Great Lakes Bks. ISBN:0-8143-1918-1, ISBN13: 978-0-8143-1918-5. Dewey:977.4/03. LCCN:89-005457.
Audience: **f.**

Rubenstein, Bruce A. & Ziewacz, Lawrence E. **F566.R8 2002**
Michigan: History of a Great Lakes State. Ed. 3. Trade Paper. Harlan Davidson Inc. Wheeling, IL. 2002. 300p. ISBN:0-88295-967-0, ISBN13: 978-0-88295-967-2. Dewey:977.4. LCCN:2001-039433.
Audience: **g,l,u,f.**

Sugrue, Thomas J. **F574.D49N4835 2005**
The Origins of the Urban Crisis: Race and Inequality in Postwar Detroit. Ed. 2. I. R. A. Katznelson, Martin Shefter & Theda Skocpol (Editors). Trade Paper, Perfect. Princeton University Press. Princeton, NJ. 2005. 416p. Princeton Studies in American Politics ISBN:0-691-12186-9, ISBN13: 978-0-691-12186-4. Dewey:305.8/00977434. LCCN:2005-047695.
Audience: **l,u,f.** *Choice, 1997.*

Thompson, Heather Ann **F574.D457T48 2001**
Whose Detroit?: Politics, Labor, and Race in a Modern American City. Book, Other. Cornell University Press. Ithaca, NY. 2002. 304p. ISBN:0-8014-3520-X, ISBN13: 978-0-8014-3520-1. Dewey:306/.09774/34. LCCN:2001-003940.
Audience: **f.** *Choice, 2002.*

Welch, Susan, et al. **F574.D49 A27 2001**
Race and Place: Race Relations in an American City. Timothy Bledsoe, Michael W. Combs & Lee Sigelman (Authors), Dennis Chong & James H. Kuklinski (Contribution by). Trade Paper. Cambridge University Press. New York, NY. 2001. 224p. Studies in Political Psychology and Public Opinion ISBN:0-521-79655-5, ISBN13: 978-0-521-79655-2. Dewey:305.8/009774/34. LCCN:2001-025035.
Audience: **u,f.**

Widick, B. J. **F574.D49A28 1989**
Detroit: City of Race and Class Violence. Horace Sheffield (Introduction by). Trade Paper. Wayne State University Press. Detroit, MI. 1989. 292p. Great Lakes Bks. ISBN:0-8143-2104-6, ISBN13: 978-0-8143-2104-1. Dewey:305.8/009774/34. LCCN:88-033761.
Audience: **u,f.**

Woodford, Arthur M. **F574.D457W66 2001**
This Is Detroit, 1701-2001. Trade Cloth. Wayne State University Press. Detroit, MI. 2001. xiii, 268p. Great Lakes Bks. ISBN:0-8143-2914-4, ISBN13: 978-0-8143-2914-6. Dewey:977.4/34. LCCN:2001-000689.
Audience: **f.**

United States > U.S. Local History > Wisconsin

Current, Richard Nelson **F581.C87 2001**
Wisconsin: A History. Trade Paper. University of Illinois Press. Champaign, IL. 2001. 240p. ISBN:0-252-07018-6, ISBN13: 978-0-252-07018-1. Dewey:977.5. LCCN:2001-027664.
Audience: **g,l,u,f.** B

Federal Writers' Project Staff & Writers Program Staff **F586.M35**
Wisconsin: A Guide to the Badger State. Library Binding. Reprint Services Company. Temecula, CA. 1989. American Guide Ser. ISBN:0-7812-1048-8, ISBN13: 978-0-7812-1048-5. Dewey:917.75.
Audience: **f.**

Glad, Paul W. **F581.H68**
The History of Wisconsin. Paul Hass & Jack Holzhueter (Editors). Trade Cloth. Wisconsin Historical Society. Madison, WI. 1990. 664p. History of Wisconsin Ser. ISBN:0-87020-122-0, ISBN13: 978-0-87020-122-6. Dewey:977.5. LCCN:72-012941.
Audience: **g,l,u,f.** B *Choice, 1989.*

Kellogg, Louise T. **F584.K26 1971**
British Regime in Wisconsin and the Northwest. Paper Text. Da Capo Press, Inc. Cambridge, MA. 1971. xvii, 361p. American Scene Ser. ISBN:0-306-71047-1, ISBN13: 978-0-306-71047-6. Dewey:977.5/02. LCCN:74-124927.
Audience: **f.** B

Margulies, Herbert F. **F586.M35**
The Decline of the Progressive Movement in Wisconsin, 1890-1920. Trade Cloth. Wisconsin Historical Society. Madison, WI. 1968. 310p. ISBN:0-87020-060-7, ISBN13: 978-0-87020-060-1. Dewey:320.5/09775. LCCN:68-063073.
Audience: **u,f.** B

Miller, John E. **F586.L3.M54 1982**
Governor Philip F. LaFollette: The Wisconsin Progressives, and the New Deal. Trade Cloth. University of Missouri Press. Columbia, MO. 1982. 240p. ISBN:0-8262-0371-X, ISBN13: 978-0-8262-0371-7. Dewey:977.5/042/0924. LCCN:82-001982.
Audience: **f.** B

Mollenhoff, David V. **F589.M157M64 2004**
Madison: A History of the Formative Years. Ed. 2. Trade Cloth. University of Wisconsin Press. Chicago, IL. 2003. 512p. ISBN:0-299-19980-0, ISBN13: 978-0-299-19980-7. Dewey:977.5/83. LCCN:2003-022546.
Audience: **u,f.**

Nesbit, Robert C. **F581.N47 2004**
Wisconsin: A History. Ed. 2. William F. Thompson (Revised by, Contribution by). Trade Paper. University of Wisconsin Press. Chicago, IL. 2004. 630p. ISBN:0-299-10804-X, ISBN13: 978-0-299-10804-5. Dewey:977.5. LCCN:89-022650.
Audience: **g,l,u,f.** B

Rippley, La Vern J. **F590.A1 R56 1985**
The Immigrant Experience in Wisconsin. Trade Cloth. Thomson Gale. Farmington Hills, MI. 1985. Immigrant Heritage of America Ser. ISBN:0-8057-8424-1, ISBN13: 978-0-8057-8424-4. Dewey:977.5. LCCN:84-019820.
Audience: **u,f.** *Choice, 1985.*

Thelen, David P. **F586.T47**
The New Citizenship: Origins of Progressivism in Wisconsin, 1885-1900. Trade Cloth. University of Missouri Press. Columbia, MO. 1972. 352p. ISBN:0-8262-0111-3, ISBN13: 978-0-8262-0111-9. Dewey:320.9/775/03. LCCN:79-158075.
Audience: **f.** B

Thompson, A. M. **JK2295.W7 T4**
Political History of Wisconsin. Library Binding. Brookhaven Press. LaCrosse, WI. 1998. ISBN:1-58103-071-1, ISBN13: 978-1-58103-071-6. Dewey:324.
Audience: **g,l,u,f.**

Wisconsin Cartographers Guild Staff & Wisc Cart Guild Staff **F581.W57 1998**
Wisconsin's Past and Present: A Historical Atlas. Zoltan Grossman (Contribution by). Trade Cloth. University of Wisconsin Press. Chicago, IL. 1998. 144p. ISBN:0-299-15940-X, ISBN13: 978-0-299-15940-5. Dewey:977.5. LCCN:98-024580.
Audience: **g,l,u,f.**

United States > U.S. Local History > The West: General

Billington, Ray Allen **F591.B55 1995**
Far Western Frontier, 1830-1860. Trade Paper. University of New Mexico Press. Albuquerque, NM. 1995. 355p. ISBN:0-8263-1585-2, ISBN13: 978-0-8263-1585-4. Dewey:978. LCCN:95-005306.
Audience: **u,f.** BCL3

Brown, Dee Alexander **F591.B88**
The Westerners. Trade Cloth. Holt, Rinehart & Winston. Austin, TX. 1974. 288p. ISBN:0-03-088360-1, ISBN13: 978-0-03-088360-6. Dewey:917.8/03/0922. LCCN:73-015456.
Audience: **f.** BCL3

Brown, Dee **F591.B86 1994**
The American West. Martin F. Schmitt (Editor). Trade Paper. Simon & Schuster. New York, NY. 1995. 448p. ISBN:0-684-80441-7, ISBN13: 978-0-684-80441-5. Dewey:978. LCCN:94-037444.
Audience: **g,l,u,f.**

Dick, Everett **F591 .D54**
Sod-House Frontier. Trade Cloth. J. & L. Lee Company. Lincoln, NE. 550p. ISBN:0-934904-38-3, ISBN13: 978-0-934904-38-4. Dewey:978/.02.
Audience: **f.**

Etulain, Richard W. (Editor) **F591.W88 2002**
Writing Western History: Essays on Major Western Historians. Glenda Riley (Foreword by). Trade Paper. University of Nevada Press. Reno, NV. 2002. 392p. ISBN:0-87417-517-8, ISBN13: 978-0-87417-517-2. Dewey:978/.0072. LCCN:2002-006426.
Audience: **f.** *Choice, 1992.*

Frazier, Ian **F591.F83 1990**
The Great Plains. Trade Paper. Penguin Group (USA) Inc. New York, NY. 1990. 304p. ISBN:0-14-013170-1, ISBN13: 978-0-14-013170-3. Dewey:978. LCCN:89-029894.
Audience: **g,u,f.**

Greever, William S. **F593**
Bonanza West: The Story of the Western Mining Rushes 1848-1900. Trade Paper. University of Idaho Press. Moscow, ID. 1986. 444p. ISBN:0-89301-116-9, ISBN13: 978-0-89301-116-1. Dewey:979/.02. LCCN:63-008991.
Audience: **f.** BCL3

Gressley, Gene M. (Editor) **F591.O624 1997**
Old West, New West. Trade Paper. University of Oklahoma Press. Norman, OK. 1997. 208p. ISBN:0-8061-2962-X, ISBN13: 978-0-8061-2962-4. Dewey:978/.0072. LCCN:97-009215.
Audience: **f.**

Hine, Robert V. & Faragher, John **F591.H662 2000**
American West: A New Interpretive History. Cloth over Boards. Yale University Press. Cumberland, RI. 2000. 632p. ISBN:0-300-07833-1, ISBN13: 978-0-300-07833-6. Dewey:978. LCCN:99-043653.
Audience: **g,l,u,f.** *Choice, 2000.*

Iber, Jorge & De Leon, Arnoldo **F596.3.S75I24 2005**
Hispanics in the American West. Scott C. Zeman (Editor). Saddle Stitched, Cloth over Boards. ABC-CLIO, Inc. Santa Barbara, CA. 2005. 447p. Cultures in the American West Ser. ISBN:1-85109-679-5, ISBN13: 978-1-85109-679-4. Dewey:978/.00468. LCCN:2005-022932.
Audience: **g,l,u,f.**

Kraenzel, Carl Frederick **BS192.2.A1**
The Great Plains in Transition. Paper Text. Textbook Publishers. Temecula, CA. 2003. xiv, 428p. ISBN:0-7581-1775-2, ISBN13: 978-0-7581-1775-5. Dewey:220.6/6.
Audience: **f.** BCL3

Lamar, Howard R. (Editor) **F591.N46 1998**
The New Encyclopedia of the American West. Cloth over Boards. Yale University Press. Cumberland, RI. 1998. 1344p. ISBN:0-300-07088-8, ISBN13: 978-0-300-07088-0. Dewey:978/.003. LCCN:98-006231.
Audience: **g,l,u,f.** *Choice, 1999.*

Limerick, Patricia Nelson **F591.L57 2000**
Something in the Soil: Field-Testing the New Western History. Trade Cloth. W. W. Norton & Company, Inc. New York, NY. 2000. 352p. ISBN:0-393-03788-6, ISBN13: 978-0-393-03788-3. Dewey:978. LCCN:99-047246.
Audience: **u,f.**

Limerick, Patricia N. (Editor), et al. **F591.T683 1991**
Trails: Toward a New Western History. Charles Rankin & Clyde A. Milner Jr. (Editors). Trade Paper. University Press of Kansas. Lawrence, KS. 1991. xvi, 296p. ISBN:0-7006-0501-0, ISBN13: 978-0-7006-0501-9. Dewey:978/.0072. LCCN:91-025640.
Audience: **u,f.**

Milner, Clyde A. II (Editor), et al. **F591.O95 1994**
The Oxford History of the American West. Carol A. O'Connor & Martha A. Sandweiss (Editors). Trade Cloth. Oxford University Press, Inc. New York, NY. 1994. 904p. ISBN:0-19-505968-9, ISBN13: 978-0-19-505968-7. Dewey:978. LCCN:93-038829.
Audience: **g,l,u,f.**

Morgan, Ted **F591.M865 1995**
A Shovel of Stars: The Settling of the North American Continent 1850-1994. Trade Cloth. Simon & Schuster. New York, NY. 1995. 560p. ISBN:0-671-79439-6, ISBN13: 978-0-671-79439-2. Dewey:978. LCCN:94-043838.
Audience: **g,u,f.** *Choice, 1995.*

Nash, Gerald D. **F591.N37 1991**
Creating the West: Historical Interpretations, 1890-1990. Trade Paper. University of New Mexico Press. Albuquerque, NM. 1991. 318p. Calvin P. Horn Lectures in Western History and Culture ISBN:0-8263-1267-5, ISBN13: 978-0-8263-1267-9. Dewey:978/.0072. LCCN:91-008584.
Audience: **f.** *Choice, 1992.*

Nugent, Walter & Ridge, Martin (Editors) **F591.A425 1999**
The American West: The Reader. Cloth Text. Indiana University

Press. Bloomington, IN. 1999. 352p. ISBN:0-253-33530-2, ISBN13: 978-0-253-33530-2. Dewey:978. LCCN:99-019404.
Audience: **u,f.**

Paul, Rodman W. **F591.P3 2001**
Mining Frontiers of the Far West, 1848-1880. Ed. 2. Trade Paper. University of New Mexico Press. Albuquerque, NM. 2001. 340p. Histories of the American Frontier Ser. ISBN:0-8263-2771-0, ISBN13: 978-0-8263-2771-0. Dewey:978/.02. LCCN:2001-026718.
Audience: **f.**

Phillips & Axelrod **F591.E485 1996**
Encyclopedia of the American West, Vol. 4. Trade Cloth. Macmillan Publishing Company, Inc. Old Tappan, NJ. 1996. ISBN:0-02-897499-9, ISBN13: 978-0-02-897499-6. Dewey:978. LCCN:96-001685.
Audience: **g,l,u,f.**

Rees, Amanda **F591**
The Great Plains. Cloth Text. Greenwood Publishing Group, Inc. Portsmouth, NH. 2004. 512p. The Greenwood Encyclopedia of American Regional Cultures Ser. ISBN:0-313-32733-5, ISBN13: 978-0-313-32733-9. Dewey:978/.003. LCCN:2004-056069.
Audience: **g,l,u,f.**

Riegel, R. E. & Athearn, R. G. **F591**
America Moves West. Ed. 5. Cloth Text. Holt, Rinehart & Winston, Inc. Austin, TX. 1971. xvi, 599p. ISBN:0-03-084316-2, ISBN13: 978-0-03-084316-7. Dewey:978. LCCN:72-113832.
Audience: **f.**

Smith, Henry N. **F591.S65 1971**
Virgin Land: The American West as Symbol and Myth. Trade Paper. Harvard University Press. Cambridge, MA. 1970. 328p. Harvard Paperbacks Ser. ISBN:0-674-93955-7, ISBN13: 978-0-674-93955-4. Dewey:917.8/03/2. LCCN:50-006230.
Audience: **f.**

Walsh, Margaret **F591.W258 2004**
The American West.Visions and Revisions. Maurice Kirby (Contribution by). Cloth Text. Cambridge University Press. New York, NY. 2004. 180p. New Studies in Economic and Social History Ser. ISBN:0-521-59333-6, ISBN13: 978-0-521-59333-5. Dewey:978. LCCN:2004-051855.
Audience: **f.** *Choice, 2006.*

Ward, Geoffrey C. (Contribution by, Narrated by) **F591.W27 1996**
The West: An Illustrated History. Dayton Duncan (Contribution by). Trade Cloth. Little Brown & Company. New York, NY. 1996. 528p. ISBN:0-316-92236-6, ISBN13: 978-0-316-92236-4. Dewey:978. LCCN:96-004323.
Audience: **g,l,u,f.**

Webb, Walter Prescott **F591**
The Great Plains. Paper Text. University of Nebraska Press. Lincoln, NE. 1981. 525p. ISBN:0-8032-9702-5, ISBN13: 978-0-8032-9702-9. Dewey:978/.01. LCCN:81-001821.
Audience: **f.**

Wishart, David J. **F591.E4856 2004**
Encyclopedia of the Great Plains. Trade Cloth. University of Nebraska Press. Lincoln, NE. 2004. 958p. ISBN:0-8032-4787-7, ISBN13: 978-0-8032-4787-1. Dewey:978/.003. LCCN:2003-021037.
Audience: **g,l,u,f.** *Choice, 2005.*

United States > U.S. Local History > The West: General > By Period

Abbott, Carl **F595.A24 1993**
The Metropolitan Frontier: Cities in the Modern American West. Trade Cloth. University of Arizona Press. Tucson, AZ. 1993. 244p. Modern American West Ser. ISBN:0-8165-1129-2, ISBN13: 978-0-8165-1129-7. Dewey:978.033. LCCN:93-011035.
Audience: **u,f.** *Choice, 1994.*

Ambrose, Stephen E. **F592.7.A49 1996**
Undaunted Courage: Meriwether Lewis, Thomas Jefferson and the Opening of the American West. Trade Cloth. Simon & Schuster. New York, NY. 1996. 512p. ISBN:0-684-81107-3, ISBN13: 978-0-684-81107-9. Dewey:917.8/042. LCCN:95-037146.
Audience: **g,l,u,f.**

Argersinger, Peter H. **F595.A74 1995**
The Limits of Agrarian Radicalism: Western Populism and American Politics. Trade Cloth. University Press of Kansas. Lawrence, KS. 1995. 312p. ISBN:0-7006-0702-1, ISBN13: 978-0-7006-0702-0. Dewey:324.2732/7. LCCN:94-023556.
Audience: **f.** *Choice, 1995.*

Carter, Robert A. **F594.B63C37 2000**
Buffalo Bill Cody: The Man Behind the Legend. Trade Cloth. John Wiley & Sons, Inc. Hoboken, NJ. 2000. 512p. ISBN:0-471-31996-1, ISBN13: 978-0-471-31996-2. Dewey:978/.02/092 B. LCCN:00-020368.
Audience: **g,u,f.**

Clark, Ella E. & Edmonds, Margot **F592.7.S123**
Sacagawea of the Lewis and Clark Expedition. Trade Cloth. University of California Press. Berkeley, CA. 1979. viii, 171p. ISBN:0-520-03822-3, ISBN13: 978-0-520-03822-6. Dewey:917.8/04/20924. LCCN:78-065466.
Audience: **u,f.**

Crutchfield, James A. **F592.C93 1997**
Mountain Men of the American West. Trade Paper. Tamarack Books, Inc. Boise, ID. 1997. 200p. ISBN:1-886609-07-1, ISBN13: 978-1-886609-07-5. Dewey:978/.01/0922 B. LCCN:97-185712.
Audience: **u,f.**

Custer, George Armstrong **F594**
My Life on the Plains: Or, Personal Experiences with Indians. Trade Paper. University of Oklahoma Press. Norman, OK. 1977. 446p. Western Frontier Library, No. 52 ISBN:0-8061-1357-X, ISBN13: 978-0-8061-1357-9. Dewey:973.8/2/092 B.
Audience: **g,u,f.**

De Voto, Bernard A. **F592.D38 1989**
The Year of Decision. Trade Paper. Houghton Mifflin Company. New York, NY. 1989. 538p. ISBN:0-395-50079-6, ISBN13: 978-0-395-50079-8. Dewey:978/.02. LCCN:88-032014.
Audience: **f.**

De Voto, Bernard Augustine **F592.D36 1947**
Across the Wide Missouri. Trade Cloth. Houghton Mifflin Company. New York, NY. 1947. xxvii, 483p.

ISBN:0-8335-2272-8, ISBN13: 978-0-8335-2272-6. Dewey:978. LCCN:48-003175.
Audience: **f.**

Devoto, Bernard (Editor) **F592.4 1997**
The Journals of Lewis and Clark. Stephen E. Ambrose (Foreword by). Trade Paper. Houghton Mifflin Company Trade & Reference Division. Boston, MA. 1997. 576p. ISBN:0-395-85996-4, ISBN13: 978-0-395-85996-4. Dewey:917.804/2. LCCN:97-001518.
Audience: **u,f.**

Fremont, John C. **F592.F874 1988**
The Exploring Expedition to the Rocky Mountains. Herman J. Viola & Ralph Ehrenburg (Introduction by). Trade Paper. Smithsonian Institution Press. Washington, DC. 1988. 360p. Exploring the American West Ser. ISBN:0-87474-439-3, ISBN13: 978-0-87474-439-2. Dewey:917.8/042. LCCN:87-051511.
Audience: **f.**

Fresonke, Kris & Spence, Mark David (Editors) **F592.7 .L6945 2004**
Lewis and Clark: Legacies, Memories, and New Perspectives. Trade Paper. University of California Press. Berkeley, CA. 2004. 298p. ISBN:0-520-23822-2, ISBN13: 978-0-520-23822-0. Dewey:917.804/2. LCCN:2003-005228.
Audience: **f.** *Choice, 2004.*

Hafen, Leroy R. (Editor) **F592.M742 1997**
French Fur Traders and Voyageurs in the American West. Janet Lecompte (Introduction by). Trade Paper. University of Nebraska Press. Lincoln, NE. 1997. 333p. ISBN:0-8032-7302-9, ISBN13: 978-0-8032-7302-3. Dewey:[B]. LCCN:96-053858.
Audience: **f.**

Hill, William E. **F593.H553 1996**
The Mormon Trail: Yesterday and Today. Trade Paper. Utah State University Press. Logan, UT. 1996. 240p. ISBN:0-87421-202-2, ISBN13: 978-0-87421-202-0. Dewey:978. LCCN:95-050223.
Audience: **u,f.**

Howard, Harold P. **F592.7.S1233 2002**
Sacajawea. Trade Paper. University of Oklahoma Press. Norman, OK. 1979. 224p. ISBN:0-8061-1578-5, ISBN13: 978-0-8061-1578-8. Dewey:978/.004974/0092 B. LCCN:2001-054625.
Audience: **g,u,f.**

Hoy, Jim & Isern, Tom **F595.2.H68 1987**
Plains Folk: A Commomplace of the Great Plains. Don Johnson (Illustrator). Trade Cloth. University of Oklahoma Press. Norman, OK. 1987. 214p. ISBN:0-8061-2064-9, ISBN13: 978-0-8061-2064-5. Dewey:978. LCCN:87-005082.
Audience: **f.** *Choice, 1988.*

Jackson, Donald (Editor) **F592.7**
Letters of the Lewis and Clark Expedition, with Related Documents, 1783-1854. Ed. 2. Trade Cloth. University of Illinois Press. Champaign, IL. 1979. 872p. ISBN:0-252-00697-6, ISBN13: 978-0-252-00697-5. Dewey:917.8/04/20922. LCCN:78-015288.
Audience: **f.**

Lewis, Meriwether & Clark, William **F592.42002**
The Definitive Journals of Lewis and Clark, Vol. 7. Gary E. Moulton (Editor). Trade Paper. University of Nebraska Press. Lincoln, NE. 2002. 3404p. ISBN:0-8032-8016-5, ISBN13: 978-0-8032-8016-8. Dewey:917.8/042.
Audience: **f.**

Parkman, Francis **F592.P284 1994**
The Oregon Trail. E. N. Feltskog (Editor). Trade Cloth. University of Nebraska Press. Lincoln, NE. 1994. 758p. ISBN:0-8032-8739-9, ISBN13: 978-0-8032-8739-6. Dewey:917.804/2. LCCN:94-019303.
Audience: **u,f.**

Pike, Zebulon M. **F592**
Zebulon Pike's Arkansas Journal: In Search of the Southern Louisiana Purchase Boundary Line. Stephen H. Hart & Archer B. Hulbert (Editors). Trade Cloth. Greenwood Publishing Group, Inc. Portsmouth, NH. 1972. 200p. ISBN:0-8371-5629-7, ISBN13: 978-0-8371-5629-3. Dewey:917.8/04/2. LCCN:72-138172.
Audience: **f.**

Roberts, David **F592.C33R58 2000**
A Newer World: Kit Carson, John C. Fremont and the Claiming of the American West. Trade Cloth. Simon & Schuster. New York, NY. 2000. 320p. ISBN:0-684-83482-0, ISBN13: 978-0-684-83482-5. Dewey:978/.02. LCCN:99-041816.
Audience: **f.**

Slaughter, Thomas P. **F592.7.S67 2003**
Exploring Lewis and Clark: Reflections on Men and Wilderness. Trade Cloth. Alfred A. Knopf Inc. New York, NY. 2003. 256p. ISBN:0-375-40078-8, ISBN13: 978-0-375-40078-0. Dewey:917.804/2. LCCN:2002-069376.
Audience: **u,f.** *Choice, 2003.*

Tubbs, Stephenie Ambrose & Jenkinson, Clay Straus **F592.7.T83 2003**
The Lewis and Clark Companion: An Encyclopedic Guide to the Voyage of Discovery. Cloth over Boards. Henry Holt & Company. New York, NY. 2003. 368p. ISBN:0-8050-6725-6, ISBN13: 978-0-8050-6725-5. Dewey:917.804/2/03. LCCN:2002-037992.
Audience: **g,l,u,f.**

Turner, Frederick Jackson **F592 .T87**
Rise of the New West 1819 To 1829. Trade Paper. Kessinger Publishing, LLC. Whitefish, MT. 2004. ISBN:1-4191-4504-5, ISBN13: 978-1-4191-4504-9. Dewey:973.54.
Audience: **u,f.**

Unruh, John D. Jr. **E166**
The Plains Across: The Overland Emigrants and the Trans-Mississippi West, 1840-60. Trade Paper. University of Illinois Press. Champaign, IL. 1993. 592p. ISBN:0-252-06360-0, ISBN13: 978-0-252-06360-2. Dewey:917.3/04/6. LCCN:93-013751.
Audience: **u,f.** B

Utley, Robert Marshall **F592.U87 1997**
A Life Wild and Perilous: Mountain Men and the Path to the Pacific. Trade Cloth. Henry Holt & Company. New York, NY. 1997. 416p. ISBN:0-8050-3304-1, ISBN13: 978-0-8050-3304-5. Dewey:978. LCCN:97-000006.
Audience: **f.**

United States > U.S. Local History > The West: General > Frontier and Pioneer Life

Allen, Charles W. **F596.A3795 1997**
From Fort Laramie to Wounded Knee: In the West That Was. Richard E. Jensen (Editor). Trade Cloth. University of Nebraska Press. Lincoln, NE. 1997. 296p. ISBN:0-8032-1045-0, ISBN13: 978-0-8032-1045-5. Dewey:978. LCCN:97-020276.
Audience: **u,f.**

Billington, Ray A. **F596**
Land of Savagery, Land of Promise: The European Image of the American Frontier. Trade Cloth. W. W. Norton & Company, Inc. New York, NY. 1981. xv, 364p. ISBN:0-393-01376-6, ISBN13: 978-0-393-01376-4. Dewey:978/.01. LCCN:80-000291.
Audience: **f.**

Carlson, Paul H. **F596.C8773 2000**
Cowboy Way: An Exploration of History and Culture. Trade Cloth. Texas Tech University Press. Lubbock, TX. 1999. 256p. ISBN:0-89672-425-5, ISBN13: 978-0-89672-425-9. Dewey:978. LCCN:99-040584.
Audience: **g,u,f.** *Choice, 2000.*

Casper, Scott E. & Long, Lucinda (Editors) **F596.M696 2001**
Moving Stories: Migration and the American West, 1850-2000. Trade Paper. University of Nevada Press. Reno, NV. 2001. 250p. Halcyon Ser. ISBN:1-890591-08-4, ISBN13: 978-1-890591-08-3. Dewey:978/.02. LCCN:2002-485442.
Audience: **f.**

Clayton, Lawrence, et al. **F596.C437 2001**
Vaqueros, Cowboys, and Buckaroos: The Genesis and Life of the Mounted North American Herders. Jim Hoy & Jerald Underwood (Authors). Trade Cloth. University of Texas Press. Austin, TX. 2001. 296p. M.K. Brown Range Life Ser., No. 20 ISBN:0-292-71238-3, ISBN13: 978-0-292-71238-6. Dewey:978. LCCN:2001-027992.
Audience: **u,f.**

Dary, David **F597.D37 2004**
The Oregon Trail: An American Saga. Trade Cloth. Knopf Publishing Group. New York, NY. 2004. 432p. ISBN:0-375-41399-5, ISBN13: 978-0-375-41399-5. Dewey:978/.02. LCCN:2004-046512.
Audience: **f.** *Choice, 2005.*

Dykstra, Robert R. **HD9433.U5 K215 1983**
The Cattle Towns. Paper Text. University of Nebraska Press. Lincoln, NE. 1983. 412p. ISBN:0-8032-6561-1, ISBN13: 978-0-8032-6561-5. Dewey:978.1/031. LCCN:83-006485.
Audience: **u,f.**

Frantz, Joe Bertram **F596 .F75**
The American Cowboy: The Myth and the Reality. Paper Text. Textbook Publishers. Temecula, CA. 2003. 232p. ISBN:0-7581-1749-3, ISBN13: 978-0-7581-1749-6. Dewey:978.
Audience: **g,l,u,f.**

Holt, Marilyn Irvin **F596.H6835 2003**
Children of the Western Plains: The Nineteenth-Century Experience. Trade Cloth. Ivan R. Dee Publisher. Blue Ridge Summit, PA. 2003. 256p. American Childhoods Ser. ISBN:1-56663-540-3, ISBN13: 978-1-56663-540-0. Dewey:978/.02/083. LCCN:2003-046050.
Audience: **u,f.** *Choice, 2004.*

Iber, Jorge & De León, Arnoldo **F596.3.S75I24 2006**
[e] Hispanics in the American West. Scott C. Zeman (Editor). E-Book. ABC-CLIO, Inc. Santa Barbara, CA. 2005. xv, 445p. Cultures in the American West Ser. ISBN:1-85109-684-1, ISBN13: 978-1-85109-684-8. Dewey:978/.00468. LCCN:2005-022932.
Audience: **u,f.**

Luchetti, Cathy **F596.L85 2004**
Men of the West: Life on the American Frontier. Trade Cloth. W. W. Norton & Company, Inc. New York, NY. 2004. 288p. ISBN:0-393-05905-7, ISBN13: 978-0-393-05905-2. Dewey:978/.02/081. LCCN:2003-020698.
Audience: **u,f.**

Luebke, Frederick C. (Editor) **F596.2.E86**
Ethnicity on the Great Plains. Cloth Text. University of Nebraska Press. Lincoln, NE. 1980. 237p. ISBN:0-8032-2855-4, ISBN13: 978-0-8032-2855-9. Dewey:301.45/1/0978. LCCN:79-017743.
Audience: **f.** B

Peavy, Linda S. & Smith, Ursula **F596.P4 1998**
Pioneer Women: The Lives of Women on the Frontier. Trade Paper. University of Oklahoma Press. Norman, OK. 1998. 144p. ISBN:0-8061-3054-7, ISBN13: 978-0-8061-3054-5. Dewey:978/.0082. LCCN:97-040684.
Audience: **u,f.** *Choice, 1998.*

Riley, Glenda **F596.R56 2004**
Confronting Race: Women and Indians on the Frontier, 1815-1915. Trade Cloth. University of New Mexico Press. Albuquerque, NM. 2004. 326p. ISBN:0-8263-3632-9, ISBN13: 978-0-8263-3632-3. Dewey:978/.02. LCCN:2004-009064.
Audience: **f.** *Choice, 2005.*

Sandoz, Mari **F596**
The Buffalo Hunters: The Story of the Hide Men. Trade Cloth. University of Nebraska Press. Lincoln, NE. 1978. 372p. ISBN:0-8032-5883-6, ISBN13: 978-0-8032-5883-9. Dewey:978/.02. LCCN:77-014079.
Audience: **u,f.**

Tate, Michael L. **F596.T36 1999**
Frontier Army in the Settlement of the West. Trade Cloth. University of Oklahoma Press. Norman, OK. 1999. 416p. ISBN:0-8061-3173-X, ISBN13: 978-0-8061-3173-3. Dewey:978/.02. LCCN:99-036276.
Audience: **f.** *Choice, 2000.*

Thrapp, Dan L. **F596.T515 1991**
Encyclopedia of Frontier Biography, Set. Trade Paper. University of Nebraska Press. Lincoln, NE. 1991. ISBN:0-8032-9417-4, ISBN13: 978-0-8032-9417-2. Dewey:920.078. LCCN:91-015482.
Audience: **g,l,u,f.**

United States > U.S. Local History > The West: General > Missouri Valley

Hafen, Leroy R. **F598.F87 1995**
Fur Traders, Trappers and Mountain Men of the Upper Missouri. Scott Eckberg (Introduction by). Trade Paper. University of Nebraska Press. Lincoln, NE. 1995. 142p. ISBN:0-8032-7269-3, ISBN13: 978-0-8032-7269-9. Dewey:978. LCCN:94-039598.
Audience: **f.**

McNeese, Tim **F598.M36 2004**
The Missouri River. Trade Cloth. Facts On File, Inc. New York, NY. 2004. 120p. Rivers in American Life and Times Ser. ISBN:0-7910-7724-1, ISBN13: 978-0-7910-7724-5. Dewey:978. LCCN:2003-023057.
Audience: **u,f.**

Thorne, Tanis C. **F598.T48 1996**
The Many Hands of My Relations: French and Indians on the Lower Missouri. Trade Cloth. University of Missouri Press. Columbia, MO. 1996. 320p. ISBN:0-8262-1083-X, ISBN13: 978-0-8262-1083-8. Dewey:978. LCCN:96-031899.
Audience: **u,f.** *Choice, 1997.*

United States > U.S. Local History > Northwestern States > Minnesota. Iowa

Blegen, Theodore Christian **F606.B668 2005**
Minnesota, a History of the State. Ed. 2. Trade Paper. University of Minnesota Press. Minneapolis, MN. 2005. ISBN:0-8166-3983-3, ISBN13: 978-0-8166-3983-0. Dewey:977.6. LCCN:2005-001586.
Audience: **g,l,u,f.**

Chrislock, Carl H. **F606 .C477**
The Progressive Era in Minnesota, 1899-1918. Trade Cloth. Minnesota Historical Society Press. Saint Paul, MN. 1971. xiii, 242p. Public Affairs Center Publications ISBN:0-87351-067-4, ISBN13: 978-0-87351-067-7. Dewey:320.9/776/05. LCCN:79-178677.
Audience: **f.** B

Federal Writers' Project Staff & Writers Program Staff **F621 .F45**
Iowa: A Guide to the Hawkeye State. Library Binding. Reprint Services Company. Temecula, CA. 1989. American Guide Ser. ISBN:0-7812-1014-3, ISBN13: 978-0-7812-1014-0. Dewey:917.77/04/3.
Audience: **f.**

Federal Writers' Project Staff & Writers Program Staff **F604.3**
Minnesota: A State Guide. Library Binding. Reprint Services Company. Temecula, CA. 1989. American Guide Ser. ISBN:0-7812-1022-4, ISBN13: 978-0-7812-1022-5. Dewey:917.76/04/5.
Audience: **f.**

Lass, William E. **F606**
Minnesota Bicenntenial and History Guide. Ed. 2. Trade Paper. W. W. Norton & Company, Inc. New York, NY. 2000. 336p. ISBN:0-393-31971-7, ISBN13: 978-0-393-31971-2. Dewey:977.6. LCCN:97-034650.
Audience: **g,l,u,f.**

Mayer, George H. **F606.O484 1987**
The Political Career of Floyd B. Olson. Russell W. Fridley (Introduction by). Trade Paper. Minnesota Historical Society Press. Saint Paul, MN. 1987. xxii, 329p. Borealis Bks. ISBN:0-87351-206-5, ISBN13: 978-0-87351-206-0. Dewey:977.6/052/0924 B. LCCN:86-033332.
Audience: **u,f.**

Ostler, Jeffrey **F621.O88 1993**
Prairie Populism: The Fate of Agrarian Radicalism in Kansas, Nebraska, and Iowa, 1880-1892. Trade Cloth. University Press of Kansas. Lawrence, KS. 1993. 272p. Rural America Ser. ISBN:0-7006-0606-8, ISBN13: 978-0-7006-0606-1. Dewey:320.978. LCCN:93-014828.
Audience: **u,f.** *Choice, 1994.*

Riley, Glenda (Editor) **F621.F76 1996**
Prairie Voices: Iowa's Pioneering Women. Paper Text. Blackwell Publishing Professional. Ames, IA. 1996. 300p. ISBN:0-8138-2595-4, ISBN13: 978-0-8138-2595-3. Dewey:977.7/02/082. LCCN:96-024258.
Audience: **f.**

Risjord, Norman K. **F606.R58 2005**
A Popular History of Minnesota. Trade Cloth. Minnesota Historical Society Press. Saint Paul, MN. 2004. 256p. ISBN:0-87351-531-5, ISBN13: 978-0-87351-531-3. Dewey:977.6. LCCN:2004-025294.
Audience: **g,l,u,f.**

Sage, Leland L. **F621.S15**
History of Iowa. Trade Cloth. Blackwell Publishing Professional. Ames, IA. 1974. xii, 376p. ISBN:0-8138-0840-5, ISBN13: 978-0-8138-0840-6. Dewey:977.7. LCCN:73-014984.
Audience: **g,l,u,f.** B

Schwieder, Dorothy **F621.S38 1996**
Iowa: The Middle Land. Cloth Text. Blackwell Publishing Professional. Ames, IA. 1996. 328p. ISBN:0-8138-2307-2, ISBN13: 978-0-8138-2307-2. Dewey:977.7. LCCN:95-045200.
Audience: **g,l,u,f.** *Choice, 1996.*

Valelly, Richard M. **JK2391.F32M68 1989**
Radicalism in the States: The Minnesota Farmer-Labor Party and the American Political Economy. Martin Shefter (Foreword by). Trade Cloth. University of Chicago Press. Chicago, IL. 1989. 276p. American Politics and Political Economy Ser. ISBN:0-226-84535-4, ISBN13: 978-0-226-84535-7. Dewey:324.2776/02. LCCN:88-036843.
Audience: **u,f.**

Wall, Joseph Frazier **F621.W17**
Iowa. Trade Cloth. W. W. Norton & Company, Inc. New York, NY. 1978. xviii, 212p. States and the Nation Ser. ISBN:0-393-05671-6, ISBN13: 978-0-393-05671-6. Dewey:977.7. LCCN:77-017546.
Audience: **g,l,u,f.** B

United States > U.S. Local History > Northwestern States > North Dakota. South Dakota

Federal Writers' Project Staff **F656**
South Dakota: A Guide to the State. Trade Cloth. Somerset

Publishers, Inc. Santa Barbara, CA. 1938. 421p. American Guidebook Ser. ISBN:0-403-02190-1, ISBN13: 978-0-403-02190-1. Dewey:917.83.
Audience: **f.**

Federal Writers' Project Staff & Writers Program Staff **F636 .F45**
North Dakota: A Guide to the Northern Prairie State. Library Binding. Reprint Services Company. Temecula, CA. 1989. American Guide Ser. ISBN:0-7812-1033-X, ISBN13: 978-0-7812-1033-1. Dewey:917.84.
Audience: **f.**

Handy-Marchello, Barbara **HQ1438.N9H36 2005**
Women of the Northern Plains: Gender and Settlement on the Homestead Frontier, 1870-1930. Trade Cloth. Minnesota Historical Society Press. Saint Paul, MN. 2005. 240p. ISBN:0-87351-521-8, ISBN13: 978-0-87351-521-4. Dewey:305.43/63/09784. LCCN:2004-021947.
Audience: **u,f.** *Choice, 2005.*

Hoover, Herbert T. **F651.N49 2005**
A New South Dakota History. Trade Cloth. Center for Western Studies. Sioux Falls, SD. 2005. xiv, 648p. ISBN:0-931170-84-2, ISBN13: 978-0-931170-84-3. Dewey:978.3. LCCN:2005-051320.
Audience: **g,l,u,f.** *Choice, 2006.*

Lamar, Howard Roberts **F0655.L25**
Dakota Territory, 1861-1889: A Study of Frontier Politics. Trade Paper. Books on Demand. Ann Arbor, MI. 324p. Yale Historical Publications. Miscellany, Vol. 64 ISBN:0-598-36523-0, ISBN13: 978-0-598-36523-1. Dewey:978.3. LCCN:56-010098.
Audience: **f.**

Lysengen, Janet D. & Rathke, Ann M. (Editors) **F636.5 .C46**
The Centennial Anthology of North Dakota History: Journal of the Northern Plains. Trade Paper. State Historical Society of North Dakota. Bismarck, ND. 1996. xv, 526p. ISBN:1-891419-03-X, ISBN13: 978-1-891419-03-4. Dewey:978.4.
Audience: **f.**

Milton, John R. **F651**
South Dakota: A History. Trade Paper. W. W. Norton & Company, Inc. New York, NY. 1989. ISBN:0-393-30571-6, ISBN13: 978-0-393-30571-5. Dewey:978.3.
Audience: **g,l,u,f.**

Norris, Kathleen **F656.2.N66 1993**
Dakota: A Spiritual Geography. Trade Cloth. Houghton Mifflin Company. New York, NY. 1993. 192p. ISBN:0-395-63320-6, ISBN13: 978-0-395-63320-5. Dewey:978.4/03. LCCN:92-030820.
Audience: **u,f.**

Robinson, Doane **F0650.R6**
History of South Dakota, Vol. 2. Trade Paper. Books on Demand. Ann Arbor, MI. 955p. ISBN:0-598-27658-0, ISBN13: 978-0-598-27658-2. Dewey:978.3.
Audience: **f.**

Robinson, Elwyn B. **F636.R6 1995**
History of North Dakota. D. Jerome Tweton (Preface by), David B. Danbom (Contribution by). Trade Paper. North Dakota State University, Institute for Regional Studies. Fargo, ND. 1995. 610p. ISBN:0-911042-43-1, ISBN13: 978-0-911042-43-6. Dewey:978.4. LCCN:95-068420.
Audience: **f.**

Schell, Herbert Samuel **F651.S29 2004**
History of South Dakota. Ed. 4. John E. Miller (Revised by). Trade Paper. South Dakota State Historical Society. Pierre, SD. 2004. 425p. ISBN:0-9715171-3-4, ISBN13: 978-0-9715171-3-4. Dewey:978.3. LCCN:2004-049141.
Audience: **g,l,u,f.**

Sherman, William C. & Thorson, Playford V. (Editors) **F645.A1P53 1988**
Plains Folk: North Dakota's Ethnic History. Trade Cloth. North Dakota State University, Institute for Regional Studies. Fargo, ND. 1986. 419p. ISBN:0-911042-35-0, ISBN13: 978-0-911042-35-1. Dewey:978.4/004. LCCN:86-063088.
Audience: **u,f.**

Wilkins, Robert P. & Wilkins, Wynona H. **F636.W49**
North Dakota. Trade Cloth. W. W. Norton & Company, Inc. New York, NY. 1977. xii, 218p. States and the Nation Ser. ISBN:0-393-05655-4, ISBN13: 978-0-393-05655-6. Dewey:978.4. LCCN:77-022102.
Audience: **f.**

United States > U.S. Local History > Northwestern States > Oklahoma

Blakey, Ellen Sue & Geiger, Rita **F694.B57 2001**
Oklahoma: The History of an American State. Trade Cloth. Clairmont Press, Inc. Montgomery, AL. 2001. ix, 454p. ISBN:1-56733-056-8, ISBN13: 978-1-56733-056-4. Dewey:372.89766. LCCN:2002-265069.
Audience: **g,l,u,f.**

Brophy, Alfred L. **F704.T92B76 2003**
Reconstructing the Dreamland: The Tulsa Riot of 1921: Race, Reparations, and Reconciliation. Randall Kennedy (Foreword by). Trade Paper. Oxford University Press, Inc. New York, NY. 2003. 208p. ISBN:0-19-516103-3, ISBN13: 978-0-19-516103-8. Dewey:976.6/86.
Audience: **f.**

Federal Writers' Project Staff **F694.O38 1986**
The WPA Guide to 1930s Oklahoma. Trade Paper. University Press of Kansas. Lawrence, KS. 1986. xxxviii, 442p. ISBN:0-7006-0294-1, ISBN13: 978-0-7006-0294-0. Dewey:917.66/0453. LCCN:86-050226.
Audience: **f.**

Gibson, Arrell M. **F694.G49 1981**
Oklahoma: A History of Five Centuries. Ed. 2. Trade Cloth. University of Oklahoma Press. Norman, OK. 1981. 328p. ISBN:0-8061-1758-3, ISBN13: 978-0-8061-1758-4. Dewey:976.6. LCCN:81-040284.
Audience: **g,l,u,f.**

Goble, Danney **F699.G6**
Progressive Oklahoma: The Making of a New Kind of State. Trade Cloth. University of Oklahoma Press. Norman, OK. 1980. 288p. ISBN:0-8061-1510-6, ISBN13: 978-0-8061-1510-8. Dewey:320.9/766. LCCN:79-004734.
Audience: **u,f.**

Morgan, H. Wayne & Morgan, Anne H. **F694.M8175**
Oklahoma: A History. Trade Cloth. W. W. Norton & Company, Inc. New York, NY. 1977. xv, 190p. States and the Nation Ser. ISBN:0-393-05642-2, ISBN13: 978-0-393-05642-6. Dewey:976.6. LCCN:77-007052.
Audience: **f.** BCL3

Rister, Carl C. **F697.P35 R57 1975**
Land Hunger: David L. Payne and the Oklahoma Boomers. Trade Cloth. Ayer Company Publishers, Inc. Manchester, NH. 1975. Mid-American Frontier Ser. ISBN:0-405-06884-0, ISBN13: 978-0-405-06884-3. Dewey:976.6/04/0924. LCCN:75-000118.
Audience: **f.**

Scales, James R. & Goble, Danny **F694.S28 1982**
Oklahoma Politics: A History. Trade Cloth. University of Oklahoma Press. Norman, OK. 1982. 375p. ISBN:0-8061-1824-5, ISBN13: 978-0-8061-1824-6. Dewey:976.6/05. LCCN:82-040328.
Audience: **f.** BCL3

Stein, Howard F. & Hill, Robert F. (Editors) **F694.5.C84 1993**
The Culture of Oklahoma. Fred R. Harris (Foreword by). Trade Cloth. University of Oklahoma Press. Norman, OK. 1993. xxvii, 264p. ISBN:0-8061-2498-9, ISBN13: 978-0-8061-2498-8. Dewey:976.6. LCCN:92-050722.
Audience: **u,f.**

Wickett, Murray R. **F705.A1W53 2000**
Contested Territory: Whites, Native Americans and African Americans in Oklahoma. Trade Cloth. Louisiana State University Press. Baton Rouge, LA. 2000. xvii, 240p. ISBN:0-8071-2584-9, ISBN13: 978-0-8071-2584-7. Dewey:976.6004/96073. LCCN:00-032122.
Audience: **u,f.** *Choice, 2001.*

United States > U.S. Local History > Northwestern States > Nebraska. Kansas

Atherton, Lewis E. **F596.A8**
The Cattle Kings. Trade Paper. University of Nebraska Press. Lincoln, NE. 1972. 324p. ISBN:0-8032-5759-7, ISBN13: 978-0-8032-5759-7. Dewey:978. LCCN:61-013722.
Audience: **u,f.**

Bader, Robert S. **F686.B33 1988**
Hayseeds, Moralizers, and Methodists: The Twentieth Century Image of Kansas. Trade Cloth. University Press of Kansas. Lawrence, KS. 1988. x, 214p. ISBN:0-7006-0360-3, ISBN13: 978-0-7006-0360-2. Dewey:978.1/03. LCCN:88-000097.
Audience: **u,f.**

Cherny, Robert W. **F666.C49**
Populism, Progressivism, and the Transformation of Nebraska Politics, 1885-1915. Trade Cloth. University of Nebraska Press. Lincoln, NE. 1981. xviii, 227p. ISBN:0-8032-1407-3, ISBN13: 978-0-8032-1407-1. Dewey:320.9782. LCCN:80-011151.
Audience: **f.** BCL3

Davis, Kenneth S. **F681.D37**
Kansas: A Bicentennial History. Trade Cloth. W. W. Norton & Company, Inc. New York, NY. 1976. xiii, 226p. States and the Nation Ser. ISBN:0-393-05593-0, ISBN13: 978-0-393-05593-1. Dewey:978.1. LCCN:76-021674.
Audience: **f.** BCL3

Federal Writers' Project Staff **F664.3 .F42 1979**
Nebraska: A Guide to the Cornhusker State. Trade Paper. University of Nebraska Press. Lincoln, NE. 1979. 424p. ISBN:0-8032-6851-3, ISBN13: 978-0-8032-6851-7. Dewey:917.820434. LCCN:78-026756.
Audience: **f.**

Federal Writers' Project Staff **F686.K164 1984**
The WPA Guide to 1930s Kansas. James R. Shortridge (Introduction by). Trade Paper. University Press of Kansas. Lawrence, KS. 1984. xxxiv, 540p. ISBN:0-7006-0249-6, ISBN13: 978-0-7006-0249-0. Dewey:917.81/0433. LCCN:84-051694.
Audience: **f.**

Ise, John **F687.O7I84 1996**
Sod and Stubble: The Unabridged and Annotated Edition. Von Rothenberger (Annotations by). Trade Cloth. University Press of Kansas. Lawrence, KS. 1996. xx, 446p. Kansas and the Region Ser. ISBN:0-7006-0774-9, ISBN13: 978-0-7006-0774-7. Dewey:978.1/21503/092 B. LCCN:96-003722.
Audience: **f.**

Johnsgard, Paul A. **QH105.N2J64 1995**
This Fragile Land: A Natural History of the Nebraska Sandhills. Trade Cloth. University of Nebraska Press. Lincoln, NE. 1995. 256p. ISBN:0-8032-2578-4, ISBN13: 978-0-8032-2578-7. Dewey:508.782. LCCN:94-036409.
Audience: **u,f.** *Choice, 1996.*

Malin, James **F685.B877.M3 1971**
John Brown and the Legend of Fifty-Six, Set. Library Binding. M. S. G. Haskell House. Brooklyn, NY. 1970. Studies in History and Culture, No. 54 ISBN:0-8383-1021-4, ISBN13: 978-0-8383-1021-2. Dewey:973.6/8/0924. LCCN:70-117588.
Audience: **u,f.** BCL3

Miner, Craig **F681.5**
West of Wichita: Settling the High Plains of Kansas, 1865-1890. Trade Paper. University Press of Kansas. Lawrence, KS. 2004. viii, 304p. Kansas and the Region Ser. ISBN:0-7006-0364-6, ISBN13: 978-0-7006-0364-0. Dewey:978.1/031. LCCN:85-026013.
Audience: **f.** BCL3 *Choice, 1986.*

Miner, H. Craig **F681.M54 2002**
Kansas: The History of the Sunflower State, 1854-2000. Trade Cloth. University Press of Kansas. Lawrence, KS. 2002. xviii, 534p. Kansas and the Region Ser. ISBN:0-7006-1215-7, ISBN13: 978-0-7006-1215-4. Dewey:978.1. LCCN:2002-007025.
Audience: **g,l,u,f.** *Choice, 2003.*

Olson, James C. & Naugle, Ronald C. **F666.O48 1997**
History of Nebraska. Ed. 3. Trade Paper. University of Nebraska Press. Lincoln, NE. 1997. 506p. ISBN:0-8032-8605-8, ISBN13: 978-0-8032-8605-4. Dewey:978.2. LCCN:96-027320.
Audience: **g,l,u,f.** BCL3

Olson, James C. & Naugle, Ronald C. **F666.O48 1997**
History of Nebraska. Ed. 3. Trade Cloth. University of Nebraska

Press. Lincoln, NE. 1997. 506p. ISBN:0-8032-3559-3, ISBN13: 978-0-8032-3559-5. Dewey:978.2. LCCN:96-027320.
Audience: **g,l,u,f.**

Sandoz, Mari **F666.S34 1985**
Old Jules: 50th Anniversary Edition. Ed. 50. Cloth Text. University of Nebraska Press. Lincoln, NE. 1985. 438p. ISBN:0-8032-4164-X, ISBN13: 978-0-8032-4164-0. Dewey:978.2 B. LCCN:85-001114.
Audience: **u,f.**

Socolofsky, Homer E. **F680.S63 1990**
Kansas Governors. Trade Cloth. University Press of Kansas. Lawrence, KS. 1990. xiv, 258p. ISBN:0-7006-0421-9, ISBN13: 978-0-7006-0421-0. Dewey:978.1/00992 B. LCCN:89-029123.
Audience: **f.** *Choice, 1990.*

United States > U.S. Local History > Rocky Mountain States

Ferguson, Gary **F721.F46 2004**
The Great Divide: The Rocky Mountains in the American Mind. Trade Cloth. W. W. Norton & Company, Inc. New York, NY. 2004. 288p. ISBN:0-393-05072-6, ISBN13: 978-0-393-05072-1. Dewey:978. LCCN:2004-002566.
Audience: **u,f.**

Haines, Aubrey L. **F722.H17 1996**
The Yellowstone Story: A History of Our First National Park. E-Book. NetLibrary, Inc. Boulder, CO. 1996. ISBN:0-585-03043-X, ISBN13: 978-0-585-03043-2. Dewey:978.7/52.
Audience: **g,l,u,f.**

Lavender, David **F721.L3 2003**
The Rockies. Duane A. Smith (Introduction by). Trade Cloth. University of Nebraska Press. Lincoln, NE. 2005. 432p. ISBN:0-8032-8019-X, ISBN13: 978-0-8032-8019-9. Dewey:978/.02. LCCN:2002-075096.
Audience: **g,l,u,f.**

Newby, Rick **F721.R74 2004**
The Rocky Mountains Region. Trade Cloth. Greenwood Publishing Group, Inc. Portsmouth, NH. 2004. xxi, 473p. The Greenwood Encyclopedia of American Regional Cultures Ser. ISBN:0-313-32817-X, ISBN13: 978-0-313-32817-6. Dewey:978/.003. LCCN:2004-056066.
Audience: **g,l,u,f.**

Peirce, Neal R. **F721.P45 1972**
The Mountain States of America: People, Politics and Power in the Eight Rocky Mountain States. Trade Cloth. W. W. Norton & Company, Inc. New York, NY. 1971. 320p. ISBN:0-393-05255-9, ISBN13: 978-0-393-05255-8. Dewey:917.8/03/3. LCCN:72-000437.
Audience: **f.**

Smith, Duane A. **F721.S65 1992**
Rocky Mountain West: Colorado, Wyoming, and Montana, 1859-1915. Trade Cloth. University of New Mexico Press. Albuquerque, NM. 1992. 304p. Histories of the American Frontier Ser. ISBN:0-8263-1339-6, ISBN13: 978-0-8263-1339-3. Dewey:978. LCCN:91-041638.
Audience: **f.** *Choice, 1992.*

Wyckoff, William & Dilsaver, Lary M. (Editors) **F721.M65 1995**
The Mountainous West: Explorations in Historical Geography. Trade Cloth. University of Nebraska Press. Lincoln, NE. 1995. 422p. ISBN:0-8032-9759-9, ISBN13: 978-0-8032-9759-3. Dewey:978. LCCN:94-031183.
Audience: **u,f.**

United States > U.S. Local History > Rocky Mountain States > Montana. Idaho

Beal, Merrill D. **F746 .B335**
History of Idaho. Paper Text. Textbook Publishers. Temecula, CA. 2003. ISBN:0-7581-9918-X, ISBN13: 978-0-7581-9918-8. Dewey:979.6.
Audience: **g,l,u,f.**

Federal Writers' Project Staff **F746**
Idaho - Collected Works of Federal Writers Project. Library Binding. Reprint Services Company. Temecula, CA. 1991. ISBN:0-7812-5554-6, ISBN13: 978-0-7812-5554-7. Dewey:917.96.
Audience: **f.**

Federal Writers' Project Staff & Writers Program Staff **F732 .W65**
Montana: A State Guide Book. Library Binding. Reprint Services Company. Temecula, CA. 1989. American Guide Ser. ISBN:0-7812-1025-9, ISBN13: 978-0-7812-1025-6. Dewey:917.8604/32.
Audience: **f.**

Fritz, Harry W. **F731.F75 2001**
Montana: Land of Contrast. Trade Cloth. American Historical Press. Sun Valley, CA. 2001. 220p. ISBN:1-892724-22-7, ISBN13: 978-1-892724-22-9. Dewey:978.6. LCCN:2001-095442.
Audience: **g,l,u,f.**

Graves, Lee **F731.G73 1994**
Montana's Fur Trade Era. Trade Paper. Farcountry Press. Helena, MT. 1994. 64p. ISBN:1-56037-054-8, ISBN13: 978-1-56037-054-3. Dewey:978.6/01. LCCN:94-011761.
Audience: **u,f.**

Howard, Joseph Kinsey **F731.H86 2003**
Montana: High, Wide, and Handsome. A. B. Guthrie Jr. (Produced by), William Kittredge (Introduction by). Trade Cloth. University of Nebraska Press. Lincoln, NE. 2005. 372p. ISBN:0-8032-7339-8, ISBN13: 978-0-8032-7339-9. Dewey:978.6. LCCN:2003-050770.
Audience: **g,l,u,f.**

Malone **F731.M339 1991**
Montana: History of 2 Centuries. Ed. 2. Trade Paper. University of Washington Press. Seattle, WA. 1991. 480p. ISBN:0-295-97129-0, ISBN13: 978-0-295-97129-2. Dewey:978.6. LCCN:91-021742.
Audience: **g,l,u,f.**

Malone, Michael P. **F746 .M3**
C. Ben Ross and the New Deal in Idaho. Trade Cloth. University of Washington Press. Seattle, WA. 1970. 217p.

ISBN:0-295-95060-9, ISBN13: 978-0-295-95060-0. Dewey:320.9/796 B. LCCN:69-014207.
Audience: **f.** B

Spence, Clark C. **F731.S62 1978**
Montana: A History. Trade Cloth. W. W. Norton & Company, Inc. New York, NY. 1978. xi, 211p. States and the Nation Ser. ISBN:0-393-05679-1, ISBN13: 978-0-393-05679-2. Dewey:978.6. LCCN:77-018829.
Audience: **f.** B

Spence, Clark C. **F0731.S63**
Territorial Politics and Government in Montana, 1864-89. Trade Paper. Books on Demand. Ann Arbor, MI. 339p. ISBN:0-598-15381-0, ISBN13: 978-0-598-15381-4. Dewey:320.9/786/02. LCCN:75-028343.
Audience: **f.** B

Toole, K. Ross **F731.T66**
e Twentieth-Century Montana: A State of Extremes. E-Book. NetLibrary, Inc. Boulder, CO. 1972. ISBN:0-585-27126-7, ISBN13: 978-0-585-27126-2. Dewey:978.6/03.
Audience: **u,f.** B

United States > U.S. Local History > Rocky Mountain States > Wyoming. Colorado

Abbott, Carl, et al. **F776.A22 2005**
Colorado: A History of the Centennial State. Ed. 4. Stephen J. Leonard & Thomas J. Noel (Authors). Trade Paper. University Press of Colorado. Boulder, CO. 2005. 576p. ISBN:0-87081-800-7, ISBN13: 978-0-87081-800-4. Dewey:978.8. LCCN:2005-006600.
Audience: **g,l,u,f.**

Federal Writers' Project Staff **F761 .W58 1981**
Wyoming: A Guide to Its History, Highways, and People. Trade Paper. University of Nebraska Press. Lincoln, NE. 1981. 555p. ISBN:0-8032-6854-8, ISBN13: 978-0-8032-6854-8. Dewey:917.87/0433. LCCN:80-023038.
Audience: **f.**

Federal Writers' Project Staff & Writers Program Staff **F774.3.W74**
Colorado: A Guide to the Highest State. Library Binding. Reprint Services Company. Temecula, CA. 1989. American Guide Ser. ISBN:0-7812-1006-2, ISBN13: 978-0-7812-1006-5. Dewey:917.88/04/3.
Audience: **f.** B

Gould, Lewis L. **F761 .G63 1989**
Wyoming: From Territory to Statehood. Trade Cloth. High Plains Publishing Company, Inc. Worland, WY. 1989. 298p. ISBN:0-9623333-0-1, ISBN13: 978-0-9623333-0-9. Dewey:978.7. LCCN:90-172741.
Audience: **g,l,u,f.**

Hafen, Leroy R. **F776.H13 1970**
Colorado: The Story of a Western Commonwealth. Trade Cloth. A M S Press, Inc. New York, NY. 1970. 328p. ISBN:0-404-00604-3, ISBN13: 978-0-404-00604-4. Dewey:978.8. LCCN:78-100528.
Audience: **g,l,u,f.**

Larson, T. A. **F761.L3**
History of Wyoming. Ed. 2. Jack Brodie (Illustrator). Paper Text. University of Nebraska Press. Lincoln, NE. 1978. 695p. ISBN:0-8032-7936-1, ISBN13: 978-0-8032-7936-0. Dewey:978.7. LCCN:78-005633.
Audience: **g,l,u,f.** B

Larson, T. A. **F761.L3 1978**
History of Wyoming. Ed. 2. Jack Brodie (Illustrator). Trade Cloth. University of Nebraska Press. Lincoln, NE. 1978. 695p. ISBN:0-8032-2851-1, ISBN13: 978-0-8032-2851-1. Dewey:978.7. LCCN:78-005633.
Audience: **g,l,u,f.** B

Monnett, John H. & McCarthy, Michael **F776.M65 1996**
Colorado Profiles: Men and Women Who Shaped the Centennial State. Trade Paper. University Press of Colorado. Boulder, CO. 1996. 329p. ISBN:0-87081-439-7, ISBN13: 978-0-87081-439-6. Dewey:978.8. LCCN:96-031144.
Audience: **u,f.**

Sprague, Marshall **F776 .S76 1984**
Colorado: Bicentennial and History Guide. Trade Paper. W. W. Norton & Company, Inc. New York, NY. 1984. 204p. States and the Nation Ser. ISBN:0-393-30138-9, ISBN13: 978-0-393-30138-0. Dewey:978.8. LCCN:83-005328.
Audience: **f.**

Ubbelohde, Carl, et al. **F776.U195 2001**
A Colorado History. Ed. 8. Maxine Benson & Duane Smith (Authors). Trade Paper. Pruett Publishing Company. Boulder, CO. 2001. 464p. ISBN:0-87108-923-8, ISBN13: 978-0-87108-923-6. Dewey:978.8. LCCN:2001-041894.
Audience: **g,l,u,f.** B

United States > U.S. Local History > New Southwest. Colorado River

Barra, Allen **F786.E12**
Inventing Wyatt Earp: His Life and Many Legends. Trade Cloth. Book Sales, Inc. Edison, NJ. 2005. 448p. ISBN:0-7858-1494-9, ISBN13: 978-0-7858-1494-8. Dewey:978/.02/092 B.
Audience: **u,f.**

Busby, Mark **F786.S747 2004**
The Southwest. Trade Cloth. Greenwood Publishing Group, Inc. Portsmouth, NH. 2004. xxviii, 469p. The Greenwood Encyclopedia of American Regional Cultures Ser. ISBN:0-313-32805-6, ISBN13: 978-0-313-32805-3. Dewey:979/.003. LCCN:2004-056067.
Audience: **g,l,u,f.**

Chavana, Herminia B. **F790.S75C43 1996**
Biographies of Noble Hispanics. Trade Cloth. Pine Hill Press, Inc. Sioux Falls, SD. 1996. 200p. ISBN:1-57579-048-3, ISBN13: 978-1-57579-048-0. Dewey:920/.009268079 B. LCCN:96-092993.
Audience: **g,l,u,f.**

Chavez, John R. & Platts-Mills, John **E184.M5**
The Lost Land: The Chicano Image of the Southwest. Trade Paper. University of New Mexico Press. Albuquerque, NM. 1984. 207p. ISBN:0-8263-0750-7, ISBN13: 978-0-8263-0750-7. Dewey:979/.0046872. LCCN:84-011950.
Audience: **u,f.** B

Culley, John H. **F786.C92 1984**
Cattle, Horses and Men of the Western Range. Trade Paper. University of Arizona Press. Tucson, AZ. 1984. 337p. ISBN:0-8165-0865-8, ISBN13: 978-0-8165-0865-5. Dewey:979/.03. LCCN:84-002769.
Audience: **f.**

Dary, David **F786.D37 2000**
The Santa Fe Trail: Its History, Legends, and Lore. Trade Cloth. Alfred A. Knopf Inc. New York, NY. 2000. 400p. ISBN:0-375-40361-2, ISBN13: 978-0-375-40361-3. Dewey:978. LCCN:00-023276.
Audience: **u,f.**

Davenport, John **F786.D375 2004**
The U. S.-Mexico Border. Trade Cloth. Facts On File, Inc. New York, NY. 2004. 112p. Arbitrary Borders Ser., :Political Boundaries in World History ISBN:0-7910-7833-7, ISBN13: 978-0-7910-7833-4. Dewey:972/.1. LCCN:2004-003391.
Audience: **f.**

Del Castillo, Richard G. **F790.M5G75 1984**
La Familia: Chicano Families in the Urban Southwest, 1848 to the Present. Paper Text. University of Notre Dame Press. Notre Dame, IN. 1984. 224p. ISBN:0-268-01273-3, ISBN13: 978-0-268-01273-1. Dewey:306.8/50896872073. LCCN:84-040356.
Audience: **u,f.** B

Fregoso, Rosa Linda **F790.M5 F75 2003**
Mexicana Encounters: The Making of Social Identities on the Borderlands. Trade Cloth. University of California Press. Berkeley, CA. 2003. 246p. American Crossroads Ser., Vol. 12 ISBN:0-520-22997-5, ISBN13: 978-0-520-22997-6. Dewey:305.48/868720721. LCCN:2003-000594.
Audience: **u,f.** *Choice, 2004.*

Gómez-Quiñones, Juan **F790.M5G65 1994**
Roots of Chicano Politics, 1600-1940. Trade Paper. University of New Mexico Press. Albuquerque, NM. 1994. 540p. ISBN:0-8263-1431-7, ISBN13: 978-0-8263-1431-4. Dewey:979/.0046872073. LCCN:93-031940.
Audience: **l,u,f.** *Choice, 1995.*

Jackson, Robert H. (Editor) **F786.N49 1998**
New Views of Borderlands History. Trade Cloth. University of New Mexico Press. Albuquerque, NM. 1998. 242p. ISBN:0-8263-1937-8, ISBN13: 978-0-8263-1937-1. Dewey:972/.1. LCCN:98-024572.
Audience: **u,f.**

Lamar, Howard Roberts **F786.L27 2000**
The Far Southwest, 1846-1912: A Territorial History. Trade Cloth. University of New Mexico Press. Albuquerque, NM. 2000. ISBN:0-8263-2288-3, ISBN13: 978-0-8263-2288-3. Dewey:979. LCCN:00-029883.
Audience: **u,f.** B

Martínez, Oscar J. **F787**
Troublesome Border. Trade Paper. University of Arizona Press. Tucson, AZ. 1989. 177p. Profmex Ser. ISBN:0-8165-1104-7, ISBN13: 978-0-8165-1104-4. Dewey:972/.1. LCCN:87-034294.
Audience: **u,f.** *Choice, 1988.*

Martínez, Oscar J. (Editor) **F786.U13 1995**
U. S. - Mexico Borderlands: Historical and Contemporary Perspectives. Book, Other. Rowman & Littlefield Publishers, Inc. Lanham, MD. 1996. 264p. Jaguar Books on Latin America, No. 11 ISBN:0-8420-2447-6, ISBN13: 978-0-8420-2447-1. Dewey:972/.1. LCCN:95-021781.
Audience: **u,f.**

McWilliams, Carey & Meier, Matt S. **E184**
North from Mexico: The Spanish-Speaking People of the United States. Paper Text. Greenwood Publishing Group, Inc. Portsmouth, NH. 1990. 372p. ISBN:0-275-93224-9, ISBN13: 978-0-275-93224-4. Dewey:973.046872. LCCN:89-038043.
Audience: **u,f.**

Meinig, Donald W. **F790.A1**
Southwest: Three Peoples in Geographical Change, 1600-1970. Cloth Text. Oxford University Press, Inc. New York, NY. 1971. 164p. Historical Geography of North America Ser. ISBN:0-19-501289-5, ISBN13: 978-0-19-501289-7. Dewey:911.78. LCCN:71-125508.
Audience: **l,u,f.**

Powell, John W. **F788.P886 2002**
The Exploration of the Colorado River and Its Canyons. UK-Trade Paper. National Geographic Society. Washington, DC. 2002. 288p. National Geographic Adventure Classics Ser. ISBN:0-7922-6636-6, ISBN13: 978-0-7922-6636-5. Dewey:917.91/3044. LCCN:2002-025072.
Audience: **f.**

Sheridan, Thomas E. **F786.S554 1998**
A History of the Southwest: The Land and Its People. Trade Paper. Western National Parks Association. Tucson, AZ. 1998. ISBN:1-877856-76-2, ISBN13: 978-1-877856-76-1. Dewey:979. LCCN:97-040075.
Audience: **l,u,f.**

Spener, David & Staudt, Kathleen (Editors) **F787.U66 1998**
The U.S.-Mexico Border: Transcending Divisions, Contesting Identities. Library Binding. Lynne Rienner Publishers, Inc. Boulder, CO. 1998. 264p. ISBN:1-55587-796-6, ISBN13: 978-1-55587-796-5. Dewey:303.48/2730721. LCCN:98-029810.
Audience: **u,f.**

Thompson, Linda **F786.T46 2004**
The Santa Fe Trail. Trade Cloth. Rourke Publishing, LLC. Vero Beach, FL. 2004. 48p. ISBN:1-59515-226-1, ISBN13: 978-1-59515-226-8. Dewey:978. LCCN:2004-010034.
Audience: **u,f.**

Torrans, Thomas **F786.T68 2000**
Forging the Tortilla Curtain: Cultural Drift and Change along the United States-Mexico Boarderlands from the Spanish Conquest to the Present. Trade Cloth. Texas Christian University Press. Fort Worth, TX. 2000. xi, 424p. ISBN:0-87565-231-X, ISBN13: 978-0-87565-231-3. Dewey:972/.1. LCCN:00-030245.
Audience: **u,f.** *Choice, 2001.*

Tuska, Jon **F786**
Billy the Kid: His Life and Legend. Ed. 2. Cloth Text. Greenwood Publishing Group, Inc. Portsmouth, NH. 1994. 320p. ISBN:0-313-28589-6, ISBN13: 978-0-313-28589-9. Dewey:364.1/552/092. LCCN:93-040176.
Audience: **l,u,f.**

Utley, Robert Marshall **F786.U85 1996**
Changing Course: The International Boundary, U. S. and Mexico, 1848-1963. Trade Paper. Western National Parks Association. Tucson, AZ. 1996. 128p. ISBN:1-877856-29-0, ISBN13: 978-1-877856-29-7. Dewey:327.73072. LCCN:96-014212.
Audience: **f.**

Velez-Ibanez, Carlos G. **F790.M5V45 1996**
Border Visions: Mexican Cultures of the Southwest United States. Trade Cloth. University of Arizona Press. Tucson, AZ. 1996. xii, 360p. ISBN:0-8165-1422-4, ISBN13: 978-0-8165-1422-9. Dewey:305.868/72073. LCCN:96-010100.
Audience: **l,u,f.** *Choice, 1997.*

Vila, Pablo (Editor) **F787.E89 2003**
Ethnography at the Border. Trade Cloth. University of Minnesota Press. Minneapolis, MN. 2003. 320p. Cultural Studies of the Americas, Vol. 13 ISBN:0-8166-4033-5, ISBN13: 978-0-8166-4033-1. Dewey:305.8/00972/1. LCCN:2002-152987.
Audience: **f.**

Weber, David J. **F786**
Myth and the History of the Hispanic Southwest: Essays. Trade Paper. University of New Mexico Press. Albuquerque, NM. 2002. 180p. Calvin P. Horn Lectures in Western History and Culture ISBN:0-8263-1194-6, ISBN13: 978-0-8263-1194-8. Dewey:972/.1. LCCN:88-012035.
Audience: **u,f.**

Worster, Donald **F786.W87 2004**
Dust Bowl: The Southern Plains in the 1930s. Ed. 25. Trade Cloth. Oxford University Press, Inc. New York, NY. 2004. 304p. ISBN:0-19-517489-5, ISBN13: 978-0-19-517489-2. Dewey:978/.032. LCCN:2004-054703.
Audience: **u,f.** B

United States > U.S. Local History > New Southwest. Colorado River > New Mexico. Arizona

Bolton, Herbert E. **F799**
Spanish Exploration in the Southwest, 1542-1706. Library Binding. Reprint Services Company. Temecula, CA. 1993. ISBN:0-7812-5867-7, ISBN13: 978-0-7812-5867-8. Dewey:973.16.
Audience: **f.**

Chavez, Thomas E. **F797.C47 2002**
An Illustrated History of New Mexico. Trade Paper. University of New Mexico Press. Albuquerque, NM. 2002. 253p. ISBN:0-8263-3051-7, ISBN13: 978-0-8263-3051-2. Dewey:978.9. LCCN:2002-067306.
Audience: **g,l,u,f.**

Etulain, Richard W. (Editor) **F801.2.C66**
Contemporary New Mexico, 1940-1990. Trade Paper. Books on Demand. Ann Arbor, MI. 222p. ISBN:0-608-20972-4, ISBN13: 978-0-608-20972-2. Dewey:978.9/05. LCCN:93-032426.
Audience: **l,u,f.**

Etulain, Richard W. (Editor) **F796.5.N49 2002**
New Mexican Lives: Profiles and Historical Stories. Trade Cloth. University of New Mexico Press. Albuquerque, NM. 2002. 334p. ISBN:0-8263-2432-0, ISBN13: 978-0-8263-2432-0. Dewey:978.9. LCCN:2001-006432.
Audience: **g,l,u,f.**

Federal Writers' Project Staff & Writers Program Staff **F811.W87**
Arizona: A State Guide. Library Binding. Reprint Services Company. Temecula, CA. 1989. American Guide Ser. ISBN:0-7812-1003-8, ISBN13: 978-0-7812-1003-4. Dewey:917.91.
Audience: **f.**

Hammond, George Peter **F799 .H3**
Don Juan de Onate, Colonizer of New Mexico 1595: 1628. Paper Text. Textbook Publishers. Temecula, CA. 2003. ISBN:0-7581-1892-9, ISBN13: 978-0-7581-1892-9. Dewey:978.9.
Audience: **f.**

Hyslop, Stephen G. **F800.H97 2002**
Bound for Santa Fe: The Road to New Mexico and the American Conquest, 1806-1848. Trade Cloth. University of Oklahoma Press. Norman, OK. 2002. 528p. ISBN:0-8061-3389-9, ISBN13: 978-0-8061-3389-8. Dewey:978. LCCN:2001-052268.
Audience: **f.** *Choice, 2003.*

Jones, Oakah L. Jr. **F799.J75 1996**
Los Paisanos: Spanish Settlers on the Northern Frontier of New Spain. Trade Paper. University of Oklahoma Press. Norman, OK. 1996. 368p. ISBN:0-8061-2885-2, ISBN13: 978-0-8061-2885-6. Dewey:979. LCCN:96-017090.
Audience: **u,f.** B

Luckingham, Bradford **E99.H68**
Phoenix: The History of a Southwestern Metropolis. Trade Paper. University of Arizona Press. Tucson, AZ. 1995. 316p. ISBN:0-8165-1116-0, ISBN13: 978-0-8165-1116-7. Dewey:979.1/73. LCCN:88-024276.
Audience: **l,u,f.** *Choice, 1989.*

Sheridan, Thomas E. **F811.S465 1995**
Arizona: A History. Trade Cloth. University of Arizona Press. Tucson, AZ. 1995. 434p. ISBN:0-8165-1515-8, ISBN13: 978-0-8165-1515-8. Dewey:979.1. LCCN:94-018712.
Audience: **g,l,u,f.** *Choice, 1995.*

Simmons, Marc **F796.S54 1988**
New Mexico: An Interpretive History. Trade Paper. University of New Mexico Press. Albuquerque, NM. 1988. 228p. ISBN:0-8263-1110-5, ISBN13: 978-0-8263-1110-8. Dewey:978.9. LCCN:88-021623.
Audience: **g,l,u,f.**

Simmons, Marc **F794.3.N49 1989**
The WPA Guide to 1930s New Mexico. WPA Staff (Compiled by). Trade Paper. University of Arizona Press. Tucson, AZ. 1989. 458p. ISBN:0-8165-1102-0, ISBN13: 978-0-8165-1102-0. Dewey:917.890. LCCN:88-027891.
Audience: **f.**

Sonnichsen, Charles L. **E99.H68**
Tucson: The Life and Times of an American City. Donald H. Bufkin (Illustrator). Trade Paper. University of Oklahoma Press. Norman, OK. 1987. 383p. ISBN:0-8061-2042-8, ISBN13: 978-0-8061-2042-3. Dewey:979.1/77. LCCN:82-040329.
Audience: **u,f.** B

Vigil, Ralph H. (Editor), et al. **F799.S69 1994**
Spain and the Plains: Myths and Realities of Spanish Exploration and Settlement on the Great Plains. Frances W. Kaye & John R. Wunder (Editors). Trade Cloth. University Press of Colorado. Boulder, CO. 1994. 192p. ISBN:0-87081-352-8, ISBN13: 978-0-87081-352-8. Dewey:978/.01. LCCN:94-027335.
Audience: **f.** *Choice, 1995.*

Weber, David J. **F786**
The Mexican Frontier, 1821-1846: The American Southwest under Mexico. Trade Paper. University of New Mexico Press. Albuquerque, NM. 1982. 440p. Histories of the American Frontier Ser. ISBN:0-8263-0603-9, ISBN13: 978-0-8263-0603-6. Dewey:979/.02. LCCN:82-008200.
Audience: **f.**

United States > U.S. Local History > New Southwest. Colorado River > Utah. Nevada

Alexander, Thomas G. **F826.A43 1996**
Utah, the Right Place: The Official Centennial History. Trade Paper. Gibbs Smith, Publisher. Layton, UT. 1996. 488p. ISBN:0-87905-767-X, ISBN13: 978-0-87905-767-1. Dewey:979.2. LCCN:96-007575.
Audience: **g,l,u,f.**

Bagley, Will **F826**
Blood of the Prophets: Brigham Young and the Massacre at Mountain Meadows. Trade Paper. University of Oklahoma Press. Norman, OK. 2004. 544p. ISBN:0-8061-3639-1, ISBN13: 978-0-8061-3639-4. Dewey:979.2/47.
Audience: **u,f.**

Bowers, Michael W. **F841.B593 2002**
The Sagebrush State: Nevada's History, Government and Politics. Ed. 2. Paper Text. University of Nevada Press. Reno, NV. 2002. 256p. Wilbur S. Shepperson Series in History and Humanities ISBN:0-87417-516-X, ISBN13: 978-0-87417-516-5. Dewey:979.3. LCCN:2002-004788.
Audience: **g,l,u,f.**

Denton, Sally **F826.D44 2003**
American Massacre: The Tragedy at Mountain Meadows, September 1857. Trade Cloth. Alfred A. Knopf Inc. New York, NY. 2003. 336p. ISBN:0-375-41208-5, ISBN13: 978-0-375-41208-0. Dewey:979.2/47. LCCN:2002-043085.
Audience: **u,f.** *Choice, 2004.*

Denton, Sally & Morris, Roger **F849.L35D46 2001**
The Money and the Power: The Making of Las Vegas and Its Hold on America, 1947-2000. Trade Cloth. Alfred A. Knopf Inc. New York, NY. 2001. 496p. ISBN:0-375-40130-X, ISBN13: 978-0-375-40130-5. Dewey:979.3/135. LCCN:00-062011.
Audience: **l,u,f.** *Choice, 2001.*

Elliott, Russell R. (Foreword by) **F841.N495 1991**
The WPA Guide to 1930s Nevada. Trade Paper. University of Nevada Press. Reno, NV. 1991. 408p. Vintage West Reprints Ser. ISBN:0-87417-170-9, ISBN13: 978-0-87417-170-9. Dewey:917.9304/33. LCCN:90-025810.
Audience: **f.**

Elliott, Russell R. & Rowley, William D. **F841.E43 1987**
History of Nevada. Ed. 2. Trade Cloth. University of Nebraska Press. Lincoln, NE. 1987. 504p. ISBN:0-8032-6715-0, ISBN13: 978-0-8032-6715-2. Dewey:979.3. LCCN:86-007064.
Audience: **g,l,u,f.**

Federal Writers' Project Staff & Writers Program Staff **F826.W75**
Utah: A Guide to the State. Library Binding. Reprint Services Company. Temecula, CA. 1989. American Guide Ser. ISBN:0-7812-1043-7, ISBN13: 978-0-7812-1043-0. Dewey:917.92.
Audience: **f.**

Hulse, James **F841.H83 1998**
The Silver State. Ed. 2. Paper Text. University of Nevada Press. Reno, NV. 1998. 392p. Wilbur S. Shepperson Series in History and Humanities ISBN:0-87417-318-3, ISBN13: 978-0-87417-318-5. Dewey:979.3. LCCN:98-021770.
Audience: **g,l,u,f.**

Kelen, Leslie G. & Stone, Eileen Hallet **F835.A1K45 2000**
Missing Stories: An Oral History of Ethnic and Minority Groups in Utah. Trade Paper. Utah State University Press. Logan, UT. 2000. 528p. ISBN:0-87421-293-6, ISBN13: 978-0-87421-293-8. Dewey:979.2/004. LCCN:00-027521.
Audience: **u,f.**

Land, Myrick E. & Land, Barbara N. **F849.R4L35 1995**
A Short History of Reno. Trade Paper. University of Nevada Press. Reno, NV. 1995. 136p. ISBN:0-87417-262-4, ISBN13: 978-0-87417-262-1. Dewey:979.3/55. LCCN:94-032428.
Audience: **f.**

Land, Myrick & Land, Barbara **F849**
A Short History of Las Vegas. Ed. 2. Trade Paper. University of Nevada Press. Reno, NV. 2004. 288p. ISBN:0-87417-564-X, ISBN13: 978-0-87417-564-6. Dewey:979.3/135. LCCN:2004-268966.
Audience: **l,u,f.**

Laxalt, Robert **F841.L39 1991**
Nevada: A Bicentennial History. Trade Paper. University of Nevada Press. Reno, NV. 1991. 176p. ISBN:0-87417-179-2, ISBN13: 978-0-87417-179-2. Dewey:979.3. LCCN:91-031281.
Audience: **f.**

Lyman, Edward L. **F826.L95 1986**
Political Deliverance: The Mormon Quest for Utah Statehood. Trade Cloth. University of Illinois Press. Champaign, IL. 1986. 352p. ISBN:0-252-01239-9, ISBN13: 978-0-252-01239-6. Dewey:979.2/02. LCCN:85-001204.
Audience: **f.** *Choice, 1987.*

May, Dean **F826.M29 1987**
Utah: A People's History. Trade Paper. University of Utah Press. Salt Lake City, UT. 1987. 210p. Bonneville Bks. ISBN:0-87480-284-9, ISBN13: 978-0-87480-284-9. Dewey:979.2. LCCN:87-017898.
Audience: **g,l,u,f.**

Morgan, Dale L. **F832.G7M6 1995**
The Great Salt Lake. Harold Schindler (Foreword by). Trade Paper. University of Utah Press. Salt Lake City, UT. 1995. 440p.

ISBN:0-87480-478-7, ISBN13: 978-0-87480-478-2. Dewey:979.2/42. LCCN:94-044127.
Audience: **f.**

Peterson, Charles S. **F826.P48 1984**
Utah Bicentennial and History. Trade Paper. W. W. Norton & Company, Inc. New York, NY. 1984. 213p. ISBN:0-393-30221-0, ISBN13: 978-0-393-30221-9. Dewey:979.2. LCCN:84-016535.
Audience: **u,f.**

Smart, William B. **F826.S644 1995**
Utah: A Portrait. John Telford (Photographer). Trade Cloth. University of Utah Press. Salt Lake City, UT. 1995. 256p. ISBN:0-87480-451-5, ISBN13: 978-0-87480-451-5. Dewey:979.2. LCCN:94-048005.
Audience: **g,l,u,f.**

United States > U.S. Local History > Pacific States

F859.E52 1994
The Encyclopedia of California: A Reference Guide to the Golden State. Ed. 3. Trade Cloth. Somerset Publishers, Inc. Santa Barbara, CA. 1994. Encyclopedia of the United States Ser. ISBN:0-403-09964-1, ISBN13: 978-0-403-09964-1. Dewey:979.4/003. LCCN:94-007024.
Audience: **g,l,u,f.**

Cook, Warren L. **F851.5**
Flood Tide of Empire: Spain and the Pacific Northwest, 1543-1819. Trade Cloth. Yale University Press. Cumberland, RI. 1973. 672p. Western Americana Ser., No. 24 ISBN:0-300-01577-1, ISBN13: 978-0-300-01577-5. Dewey:979.5/01. LCCN:72-075187.
Audience: **f.** B

Dietrich, William **F853.D54 1995**
Northwest Passage: The Great Columbia River. Trade Cloth. Simon & Schuster. New York, NY. 1995. 448p. ISBN:0-671-79650-X, ISBN13: 978-0-671-79650-1. Dewey:979.7. LCCN:94-041920.
Audience: **u,f.**

Fuller, George W. **F851.F96 1976**
A History of the Pacific Northwest. Trade Cloth. A M S Press, Inc. New York, NY. 1976. xvi, 483p. ISBN:0-404-14664-3, ISBN13: 978-0-404-14664-1. Dewey:979. LCCN:75-041106.
Audience: **l,u,f.**

Goggans, Jan & Di Franco, Aaron **F851.P1955 2004**
The Pacific Region. Trade Cloth. Greenwood Publishing Group, Inc. Portsmouth, NH. 2004. xxiv, 475p. The Greenwood Encyclopedia of American Regional Cultures Ser. ISBN:0-313-33043-3, ISBN13: 978-0-313-33043-8. Dewey:979/.003. LCCN:2004-056061.
Audience: **g,l,u,f.**

Hitchman, James H. **F851.H659 1990**
A Maritime History of the Pacific Coast, 1540-1980. Trade Cloth. University Press of America, Inc. Lanham, MD. 1990. 226p. ISBN:0-8191-7816-0, ISBN13: 978-0-8191-7816-9. Dewey:917.904. LCCN:90-034399.
Audience: **f.**

Koepplin, Leslie **F852.K64 1990**
A Relationship of Reform: Immigrants and Progressives in the Far West. Paper over Boards. Garland Publishing, Inc. New York, NY. 1990. 224p. European Immigrants and American Society Ser. ISBN:0-8240-0259-8, ISBN13: 978-0-8240-0259-6. Dewey:979.5. LCCN:90-003253.
Audience: **f.**

Meinig, Donald W. **F853**
The Great Columbia Plain: A Historical Geography, 1805-1910. Trade Paper. University of Washington Press. Seattle, WA. 1995. 598p. Weyerhaeuser Environmental Classics Ser. ISBN:0-295-97485-0, ISBN13: 978-0-295-97485-9. Dewey:911/.797. LCCN:95-035777.
Audience: **l,u,f.**

Morrissey, Katherine G. **F852.M67 1997**
Mental Territories: Mapping the Inland Empire. Book, Other. Cornell University Press. Ithaca, NY. 1997. 240p. ISBN:0-8014-3250-2, ISBN13: 978-0-8014-3250-7. Dewey:979.7/37. LCCN:97-023223.
Audience: **f.** *Choice, 1998.*

Peirce, Neal R. **F851.P43 1972**
The Pacific States of America; People, Politics, and Power in the Five Pacific Basin States. Trade Cloth. W. W. Norton & Company, Inc. New York, NY. 1972. 387p. ISBN:0-393-05272-9, ISBN13: 978-0-393-05272-5. Dewey:917.9/03. LCCN:72-002333.
Audience: **u,f.** B

Pomeroy, Earl S. **F851.P57 2003**
The Pacific Slope: A History of California, Oregon, Washington, Idaho, Utah, and Nevada. Elliott West (Foreword by). Paper Text. University of Nevada Press. Reno, NV. 2003. 488p. ISBN:0-87417-518-6, ISBN13: 978-0-87417-518-9. Dewey:979. LCCN:2002-013109.
Audience: **u,f.** B

Schwantes, Carlos A. **F851.S34 1996**
The Pacific Northwest: An Interpretive History. Ed. 2. Paper Text. University of Nebraska Press. Lincoln, NE. 1996. 570p. ISBN:0-8032-9228-7, ISBN13: 978-0-8032-9228-4. Dewey:979.5. LCCN:95-031650.
Audience: **g,l,u,f.** *Choice, 1989.*

United States > U.S. Local History > Pacific States > California

Bouvier, Virginia **F864**
Women and the Conquest of California 1542-1840. Trade Cloth. University of Arizona Press. Tucson, AZ. 2004. 266p. ISBN:0-8165-2446-7, ISBN13: 978-0-8165-2446-4. Dewey:979.4/02/082.
Audience: **f.**

Brands, H. W. **F865 .B76 2002**
The Age of Gold: The California Gold Rush and the New American Dream. Trade Paper. Knopf Publishing Group. New York, NY. 2003. 592p. ISBN:0-385-72088-2, ISBN13: 978-0-385-72088-5. Dewey:979.4/04. LCCN:2002-023776.
Audience: **g,l,u,f.** *Choice, 2003.*

Cleland, Robert Glass (Editor) **F867.C6 1951**
The Cattle on a Thousand Hills: Southern California, 1850-1880. Ed. 2. Trade Cloth. Huntington Library Press. San Marino, CA. 1990. 384p. ISBN:0-87328-006-7, ISBN13: 978-0-87328-006-8. Dewey:979.4/904. LCCN:89-049490.
Audience: **f.** *B*

Daniels, Roger **D769.8.A6**
The Politics of Prejudice: The Anti-Japanese Movement in California and the Struggle for Japanese Exclusion. Ed. 2. Trade Paper. University of California Press. Berkeley, CA. 1999. 182p. ISBN:0-520-21950-3, ISBN13: 978-0-520-21950-2. Dewey:323.1195607.
Audience: **u,f.** *B*

Deverell, William **F869.L89 M515**
Whitewashed Adobe: The Rise of Los Angeles and the Remaking of Its Mexican Past. Trade Cloth. University of California Press. Berkeley, CA. 2005. 349p. ISBN:0-520-24667-5, ISBN13: 978-0-520-24667-6. Dewey:979.4/94046872. LCCN:2003-065066.
Audience: **f.**

Federal Writers' Project Staff & Writers Program Staff **F859.3 .F4**
California: A Guide to the Golden State. Library Binding. Reprint Services Company. Temecula, CA. 1989. American Guide Ser. ISBN:0-7812-1005-4, ISBN13: 978-0-7812-1005-8. Dewey:917.94/04/5.
Audience: **f.**

Fogelson, Robert M. **F869.L857 F64 1993**
The Fragmented Metropolis: Los Angeles, 1850-1930. Trade Paper. University of California Press. Berkeley, CA. 1993. 396p. Classics in Urban History Ser., Vol. 3 ISBN:0-520-08230-3, ISBN13: 978-0-520-08230-4. Dewey:979.494. LCCN:92-029078.
Audience: **u,f.**

Garcia, Matthew **F869.L89A253 2002**
A World of Its Own: Race, Labor, and Citrus in the Making of Greater Los Angeles, 1900-1970. Trade Cloth. University of North Carolina Press. Chapel Hill, NC. 2002. 352p. Studies in Rural Culture ISBN:0-8078-2658-8, ISBN13: 978-0-8078-2658-4. Dewey:305.8/009794/94. LCCN:2001-035879.
Audience: **u,f.** *Choice, 2002.*

Harlow, Neal **F864**
California Conquered: The Annexation of a Mexican Province, 1846-1850. Trade Paper. University of California Press. Berkeley, CA. 1982. 544p. ISBN:0-520-06605-7, ISBN13: 978-0-520-06605-2. Dewey:979.403. LCCN:81-007588.
Audience: **u,f.**

Holliday, J. S. & Swain, William **F865.H695 2002**
The World Rushed In: The California Gold Rush Experience. Trade Paper. University of Oklahoma Press. Norman, OK. 2002. 568p. ISBN:0-8061-3464-X, ISBN13: 978-0-8061-3464-2. Dewey:917.94/044. LCCN:2002-069594.
Audience: **l,u,f.**

Horne, Gerald **F869.L89N4 1995**
Fire This Time: The Watts Uprising and the 1960's. Trade Cloth. University Press of Virginia. Charlottesville, VA. 1995. 448p. Carter G. Woodson Institute Series in Black Studies ISBN:0-8139-1626-7, ISBN13: 978-0-8139-1626-2. Dewey:979.4/94053. LCCN:95-001630.
Audience: **l,u,f.** *Choice, 1996.*

Johnson, Susan Lee **F865.J675 2000**
Roaring Camp: The Social World of the California Gold Rush. Trade Cloth. W. W. Norton & Company, Inc. New York, NY. 2000. 352p. ISBN:0-393-04812-8, ISBN13: 978-0-393-04812-4. Dewey:979.4/04. LCCN:99-033684.
Audience: **u,f.** *Choice, 2000.*

Lavender, David **F861.L38 1987**
California: Land of New Beginnings. Trade Paper. University of Nebraska Press. Lincoln, NE. 1987. 480p. ISBN:0-8032-7924-8, ISBN13: 978-0-8032-7924-7. Dewey:979.4. LCCN:86-030929.
Audience: **l,u,f.**

Olin, Spencer C. **F866.O47**
California's Prodigal Sons: Hiram Johnson and the Progressives, 1911-1917. Trade Paper. Books on Demand. Ann Arbor, MI. 267p. ISBN:0-8357-7975-0, ISBN13: 978-0-8357-7975-3. Dewey:979.4/05. LCCN:68-011968.
Audience: **f.**

Rawls, James J. & Bean, Walton **F861.R38 2003**
California: An Interpretive History. Ed. 8. Paper Text. McGraw-Hill Companies, The. New York, NY. 2003. 600p. ISBN:0-07-242438-9, ISBN13: 978-0-07-242438-6. Dewey:979.4. LCCN:2002-021272.
Audience: **g,l,u,f.**

Rice, Richard, et al. **F861.R49 2002**
The Elusive Eden: A New History of California. Ed. 3. William Bullough & Richard Orsi (Authors). Paper Text. McGraw-Hill Higher Education. Burr Ridge, IL. 2001. 704p. ISBN:0-07-241810-9, ISBN13: 978-0-07-241810-1. Dewey:979.4. LCCN:2001-044905.
Audience: **g,l,u,f.**

Rorabaugh, W. J. **F869.B5**
Berkeley at War: The 1960s. Trade Paper. Oxford University Press, Inc. New York, NY. 1990. 336p. ISBN:0-19-506667-7, ISBN13: 978-0-19-506667-8. Dewey:979.467.
Audience: **f.**

Schuparra, Kurt **F866.2.S39 1998**
Triumph of the Right: The Rise of the California Conservative Movement, 1945-1966. Glen Jeansonne (Foreword by). Cloth Text. M. E. Sharpe Inc. Armonk, NY. 1998. 250p. Right Wing in America Ser. ISBN:0-7656-0277-6, ISBN13: 978-0-7656-0277-0. Dewey:324.9794/93043. LCCN:98-002897.
Audience: **f.** *Choice, 1999.*

Starr, Kevin **F861 .S82**
Americans and the California Dream, 1850-1915. Trade Cloth. Oxford University Press, Inc. New York, NY. 1973. 512p. Americans and the California Dream Ser. ISBN:0-19-501644-0, ISBN13: 978-0-19-501644-4. Dewey:917.94/03/4. LCCN:72-092299.
Audience: **u,f.**

Starr, Kevin **F861.S83 2005**
California: A History. Trade Cloth. Random House, Inc. New York, NY. 2005. 400p. ISBN:0-679-64240-4, ISBN13: 978-0-679-64240-4. Dewey:979.4. LCCN:2005-043857.
Audience: **g,l,u,f.**

Starr, Kevin **F866.2.S73 2004**
Coast of Dreams: California on the Edge, 1990-2003. Trade Cloth. Alfred A. Knopf Inc. New York, NY. 2004. 784p. ISBN:0-679-41288-3, ISBN13: 978-0-679-41288-5. Dewey:979.4/053. LCCN:2003-060577.
Audience: **u,f.** *Choice, 2005.*

Starr, Kevin **F866.S78 1997**
The Dream Endures: California Enters the 1940s. Trade Cloth. Oxford University Press, Inc. New York, NY. 1997. 512p. Americans and the California Dream Ser. ISBN:0-19-510079-4, ISBN13: 978-0-19-510079-2. Dewey:979.4/052. LCCN:96-017087.
Audience: **u,f.** *Choice, 1997.*

Starr, Kevin **F866.S786 2002**
Embattled Dreams: California in War and Peace, 1940-1950. Trade Paper. Oxford University Press, Inc. New York, NY. 2003. 416p. Americans and the California Dream Ser. ISBN:0-19-516897-6, ISBN13: 978-0-19-516897-6. Dewey:979.4/052. LCCN:2001-036047.
Audience: **u,f.** *Choice, 2003.*

Starr, Kevin **HB3717 1929.S73 1996**
Endangered Dreams: The Great Depression in California. Trade Cloth. Oxford University Press, Inc. New York, NY. 1996. 432p. Americans and the California Dream Ser. ISBN:0-19-510080-8, ISBN13: 978-0-19-510080-8. Dewey:979.4/052. LCCN:95-002662.
Audience: **u,f.** *Choice, 1996.*

Starr, Kevin **F867**
Inventing the Dream: California Through the Progressive Era. Trade Paper. Oxford University Press, Inc. New York, NY. 1986. 391p. Americans and the California Dream Ser., No. 2 ISBN:0-19-504234-4, ISBN13: 978-0-19-504234-4. Dewey:979.4/9.
Audience: **u,f.** B *Choice, 1985.*

Starr, Kevin **F867.S82 1990**
Material Dreams: Southern California Through the 1920s. Trade Cloth. Oxford University Press, Inc. New York, NY. 1990. 458p. Americans and the California Dream Ser. ISBN:0-19-504487-8, ISBN13: 978-0-19-504487-4. Dewey:979.4/9. LCCN:89-016122.
Audience: **u,f.** *Choice, 1990.*

Winchester, Simon **F869.S357W56 2005**
A Crack in the Edge of the World: America and the Great California Earthquake of 1906. Trade Cloth. HarperCollins Publishers. New York, NY. 2005. 480p. ISBN:0-06-057199-3, ISBN13: 978-0-06-057199-3. Dewey:979.4/61051. LCCN:2005-046009.
Audience: **l,u,f.**

United States > U.S. Local History > Pacific States > Oregon. Washington

Dodds, Gordon **F876.D57 1986**
The American Northwest: A History of Washington and Oregon. Trade Cloth. Forum Press. Wheeling, IL. 1986. 374p. ISBN:0-88273-238-2, ISBN13: 978-0-88273-238-1. Dewey:979.5. LCCN:85-002072.
Audience: **g,l,u,f.**

Federal Writers' Project Staff **F874.3.W73 1972**
Oregon: End of the Trail. Trade Cloth. Somerset Publishers, Inc. Santa Barbara, CA. 1941. 548p. American Guidebook Ser. ISBN:0-403-02186-3, ISBN13: 978-0-403-02186-4. Dewey:917.95/04/4. LCCN:72-084501.
Audience: **f.**

Federal Writers' Project Staff **F874.3.F4 1972**
The Oregon Trail: The Missouri River to the Pacific Ocean. Trade Cloth. Somerset Publishers, Inc. Santa Barbara, CA. 1971. xii, 244p. American Guidebook Ser. ISBN:0-403-01290-2, ISBN13: 978-0-403-01290-9. Dewey:917.8/04. LCCN:70-145012.
Audience: **f.** B

Federal Writers' Project Staff **F889.3 .W74 1972**
Washington: A Guide to the Evergreen State. Trade Cloth. Somerset Publishers, Inc. Santa Barbara, CA. 1941. 688p. ISBN:0-403-02196-0, ISBN13: 978-0-403-02196-3. Dewey:917.97/04/4. LCCN:72-084515.
Audience: **f.**

Ficken, Robert E. & LeWarne, Charles P. **F891.F49 1988**
Washington: A Centennial History. Trade Cloth. University of Washington Press. Seattle, WA. 1988. 232p. ISBN:0-295-96693-9, ISBN13: 978-0-295-96693-9. Dewey:979.7. LCCN:88-020459.
Audience: **g,u,f.**

Golay, Michael **F880.G65 2003**
e The Tide of Empire: America's March to the Pacific. E-Book. John Wiley & Sons, Inc. Hoboken, NJ. 2004. ISBN:0-471-69039-2, ISBN13: 978-0-471-69039-9. Dewey:978.02.
Audience: **l,u,f.** *Choice, 2004.*

May, Dean L. **F882.W6 M39 1994**
Three Frontiers: Family, Land, and Society in the American West, 1850-1900. Robert Fogel & Stephan Thernstrom (Contribution by). Trade Cloth. Cambridge University Press. New York, NY. 1994. 329p. Interdisciplinary Perspectives on Modern History Ser. ISBN:0-521-43499-8, ISBN13: 978-0-521-43499-7. Dewey:979. LCCN:93-043560.
Audience: **u,f.** *Choice, 1995.*

Merk, Frederick **F0880.M537**
The Oregon Question: Essays in Anglo-American Diplomacy and Politics. Trade Paper. Books on Demand. Ann Arbor, MI. 443p. ISBN:0-7837-2300-8, ISBN13: 978-0-7837-2300-6. Dewey:327.73/042. LCCN:67-014345.
Audience: **f.** B

Peterson del Mar, David **F876.3.P48 2003**
Oregon's Promise: An Interpretive History. Trade Cloth. Oregon State University Press. Corvallis, OR. 2003. 320p. ISBN:0-87071-558-5, ISBN13: 978-0-87071-558-7. Dewey:979.5. LCCN:2003-007845.
Audience: **g,l,u,f.** *Choice, 2004.*

Ritter, Harry **F891.R58 2005**
Washington's History: The People, Land, and Events of the Far Northwest. Trade Paper. Graphic Arts Center Publishing Company. Portland, OR. 2003. 144p. ISBN:1-55868-641-X,

ISBN13: 978-1-55868-641-0. Dewey:979.7.
LCCN:2002-013466.
Audience: **g,l,u,f.**

Stratton, David H. (Editor) **F891.5.W36 1992**
Washington Comes of Age: The State in the National Experience. Trade Cloth. Washington State University Press. Pullman, WA. 1993. 171p. Reprint Ser. ISBN:0-87422-093-9, ISBN13: 978-0-87422-093-3. Dewey:979.7/04. LCCN:92-033109.
Audience: **u,f.**

United States > U.S. Local History > Pacific States > Alaska

Berton, Pierre **F1095.K5**
The Klondike Fever: The Life and Death of the Last Great Gold Rush. Trade Paper. Avalon Publishing Group. New York, NY. 2003. 496p. ISBN:0-7867-1317-8, ISBN13: 978-0-7867-1317-2. Dewey:971.9/1.
Audience: **l,u,f.**

Black, Lydia T. **F907.B53 2004**
Russians in Alaska: 1732-1867. Trade Cloth. University of Alaska Press. Fairbanks, AK. 2004. 344p. ISBN:1-889963-05-4, ISBN13: 978-1-889963-05-1. Dewey:979.8/02. LCCN:2003-024662.
Audience: **f.** *Choice, 2004.*

Borneman, Walter R. **F904.B75 2003**
Alaska: Saga of a Bold Land. Trade Cloth. HarperCollins Publishers. New York, NY. 2003. 624p. ISBN:0-06-050306-8, ISBN13: 978-0-06-050306-2. Dewey:979.8. LCCN:2002-027271.
Audience: **g,l,u,f.**

Federal Writers' Project Staff & Writers Program Staff **F909**
Alaska: A Guide to Alaska, Last American Frontier. Library Binding. Reprint Services Company. Temecula, CA. 1989. American Guide Ser. ISBN:0-7812-1002-X, ISBN13: 978-0-7812-1002-7. Dewey:917.98/04/4.
Audience: **f.**

Haycox, Stephen W. **F904.5.A42 1996**
Alaska Anthology: Interpreting the Past. Trade Paper. University of Washington Press. Seattle, WA. 1996. 480p. ISBN:0-295-97495-8, ISBN13: 978-0-295-97495-8. Dewey:979.8. LCCN:96-010463.
Audience: **f.** *Choice, 1997.*

Hunt, William R. **F904.H84**
Alaska: A Bicentennial History. Trade Cloth. W. W. Norton & Company, Inc. New York, NY. 1976. xiv, 200p. States and the Nation Ser. ISBN:0-393-05604-X, ISBN13: 978-0-393-05604-4. Dewey:979.8. LCCN:76-044422.
Audience: **f.**

James, James Alton **F0907.J3**
The First Scientific Exploration of Russian America and the Purchase of Alaska. Trade Paper. Books on Demand. Ann Arbor, MI. 303p. Northwestern University Studies in the Social Sciences, No. 4 ISBN:0-598-22443-2, ISBN13: 978-0-598-22443-9. Dewey:979.8. LCCN:42-050931.
Audience: **f.**

Moore, Denton R. **F909.M76 1995**
Alaska's Lost Frontier: Life in the Days of Homesteads, Dog Teams, and Sailboat Fisheries. Jim Hogan (Illustrator, Introduction by). Trade Cloth. Prospector Press. Bellingham, WA. 1995. 448p. ISBN:0-9628828-9-5, ISBN13: 978-0-9628828-9-0. Dewey:979.8/04/092. LCCN:94-067836.
Audience: **u,f.**

Morse, Kathryn Taylor **F1095.K5M67 2003**
The Nature of Gold: An Environmental History of the Klondike Gold Rush. Trade Cloth. University of Washington Press. Seattle, WA. 2003. 304p. Weyerhaeuser Environmental Bks. ISBN:0-295-98329-9, ISBN13: 978-0-295-98329-5. Dewey:971.9/1. LCCN:2003-048411.
Audience: **u,f.** *Choice, 2004.*

Muir, John **F908**
Travels in Alaska. Edward Hoagland (Introduction by). Trade Paper. Random House, Inc. New York, NY. 2002. 272p. ISBN:0-375-76049-0, ISBN13: 978-0-375-76049-5. Dewey:917.9804/3.
Audience: **f.**

Naske, Claus M. & Slotnick, Herman E. **F904 .N37**
Alaska: A History of the 49th State. Ed. 2. Trade Paper. University of Oklahoma Press. Norman, OK. 1994. 368p. ISBN:0-8061-2573-X, ISBN13: 978-0-8061-2573-2. Dewey:979.8. LCCN:87-040215.
Audience: **g,l,u,f.**

Whitehead, John S. **F909.W53 2004**
Completing the Union: Alaska, Hawai'i, and the Battle for Statehood. Trade Cloth. University of New Mexico Press. Albuquerque, NM. 2004. 438p. Histories of the American Frontier Ser. ISBN:0-8263-3636-1, ISBN13: 978-0-8263-3636-1. Dewey:979.8/03. LCCN:2004-013685.
Audience: **l,u,f.** *Choice, 2005.*

United States > U.S. Local History > Pacific States > Hawaii

Bell, Roger J. **DU627.5.B44 1984**
Last among Equals: Hawaiian Statehood and American Politics. Cloth Text. University of Hawaii Press. Honolulu, HI. 1984. 388p. ISBN:0-8248-0847-9, ISBN13: 978-0-8248-0847-1. Dewey:996.9/03. LCCN:83-024330.
Audience: **u,f.**

Buck, Elizabeth **DU624.65.B83 1993**
Paradise Remade: The Politics of Culture and History in Hawai'i. Trade Cloth. Temple University Press. Philadelphia, PA. 1993. 288p. ISBN:0-87722-978-3, ISBN13: 978-0-87722-978-0. Dewey:996.9. LCCN:92-000310.
Audience: **g,l,u,f.** *Choice, 1993.*

Coffman, Tom **DU627.5.C64 2003**
The Island Edge of America: A Political History of Hawaii. Trade Cloth. University of Hawaii Press. Honolulu, HI. 2003. 440p. ISBN:0-8248-2625-6, ISBN13: 978-0-8248-2625-3. Dewey:996.9/03. LCCN:2002-074240.
Audience: **l,u.** *Choice, 2003.*

Hopkins, Gerard Manley **DU625**
Hawaii: The Past, Present, and Future of Its Island-Kingdom: An Historic Account of the Sandwich Islands of Polynesia. Ed. 2. Trade Cloth. Kegan Paul International, Ltd. London, 2003. 552p. ISBN:0-7103-0781-0, ISBN13: 978-0-7103-0781-1. Dewey:996.902.
Audience: **g,l,u,f.**

Kuykendall, Ralph S. **DU625.K778**
Hawaii: A History, from Polynesian Kingdom to American State. Paper Text. Textbook Publishers. Temecula, CA. 2003. 331p. ISBN:0-7581-6072-0, ISBN13: 978-0-7581-6072-0. Dewey:996.9.
Audience: **g,u,f.**

Kuykendall, Ralph S. **DU627**
The Hawaiian Kingdom: Foundation and Transformation, 1778-1854. Trade Cloth. University of Hawaii Press. Honolulu, HI. 1938. 462p. ISBN:0-87022-431-X, ISBN13: 978-0-87022-431-7. Dewey:996.902.
Audience: **u,f.**

Melendy, H. Brett **DU627.5.M45 1999**
Hawaii, America's Sugar Territory 1898-1959. Trade Cloth. Edwin Mellen Press, The. Lewiston, NY. 1999. 360p. Studies in American History, Vol. 25 ISBN:0-7734-7998-8, ISBN13: 978-0-7734-7998-2. Dewey:996.9/03. LCCN:99-026436.
Audience: **f.**

Osborne, Thomas J. **DU0627.4.O83**
Empire Can Wait: American Opposition to Hawaiian Annexation, 1893 - 1898. Trade Paper. Books on Demand. Ann Arbor, MI. 197p. ISBN:0-7837-0501-8, ISBN13: 978-0-7837-0501-9. Dewey:996.9/028. LCCN:81-008156.
Audience: **u,f.**

Russ, William A. Jr. **DU627.2.R79 1992**
The Hawaiian Republic, 1894-98: And Its Struggle to Win Annexation. Pauline N. King (Introduction by). Trade Cloth. Susquehanna University Press. Cranbury, NJ. 1993. 416p. ISBN:0-945636-44-X, ISBN13: 978-0-945636-44-1. Dewey:996.9/028. LCCN:91-043886.
Audience: **f.**

Tabrah, Ruth M. **DU625 .T24 1984**
Hawaii: Bicentennial and History Guide. Trade Paper. W. W. Norton & Company, Inc. New York, NY. 1984. 233p. States and the Nation Ser. ISBN:0-393-30220-2, ISBN13: 978-0-393-30220-2. Dewey:996.9. LCCN:84-016534.
Audience: **f.**

Canada > Reference Works

CT283.D52 1978
The Macmillan Dictionary of Canadian Biography. Trade Cloth. C D G Books Canada, Inc. Toronto, ON. 1978. 914p. ISBN:0-7705-1462-6, ISBN13: 978-0-7705-1462-4. Dewey:920/.071. LCCN:79-308717.
Audience: **g,l,u,f.** B

Cook, G. Ramsay **F1005**
Dictionary of Canadian Biography, Vol. 14. Trade Cloth. University of Toronto Press. Toronto, ON. 1998. 2280p. ISBN:0-8020-3476-4, ISBN13: 978-0-8020-3476-2. Dewey:920/.071.
Audience: **g,l,u,f.**

Cook, G. Ramsay (Editor) **F1005**
Dictionary of Canadian Biography, 1901-1910 - Dictionnaire Biographique du Canada, 1901-1910, Vol. 13. Jean Hamelin (Contribution by). Cloth over Boards. University of Toronto Press. Toronto, ON. 1994. 1295p. ISBN:0-8020-3998-7, ISBN13: 978-0-8020-3998-9. Dewey:920/.071.
Audience: **g,l,u,f.**

Gough, Barry M. **F1026.G69 1999**
Historical Dictionary of Canada. Trade Cloth. Scarecrow Press, Inc. Lanham, MD. 1999. 320p. ISBN:0-8108-3541-X, ISBN13: 978-0-8108-3541-2. Dewey:971/.003. LCCN:99-025103.
Audience: **g,l,u,f.** *Choice, 2000.*

Halpenny, Francess (Editor) **PS3513.L34Z75 1982**
Dictionary of Canadian Biography, Vols. I-XII. Trade Cloth. University of Toronto Press. Toronto, ON. ISBN:0-318-56149-2, ISBN13: 978-0-318-56149-3. Dewey:813/.52 B. LCCN:66-031909.
Audience: **g,l,u,f.**

Magocsi, Paul R. (Editor) **F1006.E66 1999**
Encyclopedia of Canada's Peoples. Trade Cloth. University of Toronto Press. Toronto, ON. 1998. 2756p. ISBN:0-8020-2938-8, ISBN13: 978-0-8020-2938-6. Dewey:305.8/0097103. LCCN:99-226153.
Audience: **g,l,u,f.**

University of Toronto Press (Created by) **F1005**
Dictionary of Canadian Biography: 1921 to 1930, Vol. 15. Book, Other. University of Toronto Press. Toronto, ON. 2005. 1266p. ISBN:0-8020-9087-7, ISBN13: 978-0-8020-9087-4. Dewey:920/.071.
Audience: **g,l,u,f.**

Canada > Description. Civilization

Angus, Ian **F1021.2.A64 1997**
A Border Within: National Identity, Cultural Plurality and Wilderness. Trade Cloth. McGill-Queen's University Press. Montreal, PQ. 1997. 280p. ISBN:0-7735-1652-2, ISBN13: 978-0-7735-1652-6. Dewey:971.064/8. LCCN:98-152232.
Audience: **u,f.**

Bailey, Alfred Goldsworthy **F1021.B25 1969**
The Conflict of European and Eastern Algonkian Cultures 1504-1700: A Study in Canadian Civilization. Trade Cloth. University of Toronto Press. Toronto, ON. 1969. xxiii, 218p. ISBN:0-8020-1506-9, ISBN13: 978-0-8020-1506-8. Dewey:917.1/03/1. LCCN:78-434310.
Audience: **f.** B

Berton, Pierre **G640.B47 2000**
The Arctic Grail: The Quest for the Northwest Passage and the North Pole, 1818-1909. Trade Paper. Globe Pequot Press, The. Guilford, CT. 2000. 672p. ISBN:1-58574-116-7, ISBN13: 978-1-58574-116-8. Dewey:910/.91632. LCCN:00-712425.
Audience: **f.** *Choice, 1989.*

Bone, Robert M. **F1011.3.B66 2005**
The Regional Geography of Canada. Ed. 3. Trade Cloth. Oxford University Press, Inc. New York, NY. 2005. 592p. ISBN:0-19-541933-2, ISBN13: 978-0-19-541933-7. Dewey:917.1. LCCN:2005-274366.
Audience: **l,u,f.**

Cormier, Jeffrey **F1021.2.C67 2004**
The Canadianization Movement: Emergence, Survival, and Success. Trade Cloth. University of Toronto Press. Toronto, ON. 2004. 380p. ISBN:0-8020-8815-5, ISBN13: 978-0-8020-8815-4. Dewey:971.064/4. LCCN:2004-541273.
Audience: **u,f.** *Choice, 2005.*

Frye, Northrop **F1021.2.F79 1982**
Divisions on a Ground: Essays on Canadian Culture. James Polk (Introduction by). Trade Paper. House of Anansi Press. Toronto, ON. 1989. 208p. ISBN:0-88784-093-0, ISBN13: 978-0-88784-093-7. Dewey:971. LCCN:82-180003.
Audience: **f.** B

Howarth, William L. **F1017.H68 1987**
Traveling the Trans-Canada: From Newfoundland to British Columbia. Donald J. Crump (Editor). Trade Cloth. National Geographic Society. Washington, DC. 1995. 200p. Special Publications Series 22, No. 3 ISBN:0-87044-626-6, ISBN13: 978-0-87044-626-9. Dewey:917.1/046. LCCN:87-028145.
Audience: **u,f.**

Hutchison, Bruce **F1015 .H96 1977**
The Unknown Country: Canada and Her People. Trade Cloth. Greenwood Publishing Group, Inc. Portsmouth, NH. 1977. 420p. ISBN:0-8371-9451-2, ISBN13: 978-0-8371-9451-6. Dewey:971.06. LCCN:76-058025.
Audience: **g,l,u,f.** B

Konrad, Victor **F1011.3.K66 1996**
Geography of Canada. Ed. 2. Trade Paper. Michigan State University Press. East Lansing, MI. 1996. 50p. ACSUS Papers Ser. ISBN:0-87013-397-7, ISBN13: 978-0-87013-397-8. Dewey:917.1. LCCN:97-127563.
Audience: **l,u,f.**

Lower, Arthur R. **F1021 .L67 1981**
Canadians in the Making: A Social History of Canada. Trade Cloth. Greenwood Publishing Group, Inc. Portsmouth, NH. 1981. 475p. ISBN:0-313-23037-4, ISBN13: 978-0-313-23037-0. Dewey:971. LCCN:81-004142.
Audience: **u,f.**

MacLennan, Hugh **F1016.M25**
The Rivers of Canada. Trade Paper. Books on Demand. Ann Arbor, MI. 182p. ISBN:0-598-88443-2, ISBN13: 978-0-598-88443-5. Dewey:917.1. LCCN:62-010401.
Audience: **l,u,f.**

McKillop, A. B. **F1021**
Contours of Canadian Thought. Cloth Text. University of Toronto Press. Toronto, ON. 1987. 163p. ISBN:0-8020-5740-3, ISBN13: 978-0-8020-5740-2. Dewey:971.
Audience: **f.** *Choice, 1988.*

McKillop, A. B. **F1021.M346 2001**
A Disciplined Intelligence: Critical Inquiry and Canadian Thought in the Victorian Era. Trade Cloth. McGill-Queen's University Press. Montreal, PQ. 2000. 287p. Carleton Library Ser. ISBN:0-7735-2141-0, ISBN13: 978-0-7735-2141-4. Dewey:191.
Audience: **f.** B

Morton, Desmond **F1017.M67 2000**
Canada: A Millennium Portrait. Trade Paper. Edgar Kent Incorporated, Publishers. Ontario, ON. 1999. 106p. ISBN:0-88866-647-0, ISBN13: 978-0-88866-647-5. Dewey:971. LCCN:00-340263.
Audience: **g,l,u,f.**

Sherman, George **F1011.3.S48 1995**
O Canada: It's Geography, History and the People Who Call It Home. Richard Beach (Editor). Cloth Text. State University of New York, Plattsburgh, Center for the Study of Canada. Plattsburgh, NY. 260p. ISBN:1-885468-00-8, ISBN13: 978-1-885468-00-0. Dewey:971. LCCN:94-071904.
Audience: **g,l,u,f.**

Wright, Robert A. **F1021.2.W75 2004**
Virtual Sovereignty: Nationalism, Culture and the Canadian Question. Trade Paper. Canadian Scholars' Press, Inc. Toronto, ON. 2004. 300p. ISBN:1-55130-258-6, ISBN13: 978-1-55130-258-4. Dewey:971.064/8. LCCN:2004-381977.
Audience: **f.** *Choice, 2005.*

Canada > History

Balthazar, Louis **F1027.B25 1996**
French-Canadian Civilization. Ed. 2. Trade Paper. Michigan State University Press. East Lansing, MI. 1996. 50p. ACSUS Papers Ser. ISBN:0-87013-395-0, ISBN13: 978-0-87013-395-4. Dewey:971/.004114. LCCN:97-127553.
Audience: **u,f.**

Berger, Carl **F1024**
The Writing of Canadian History: Aspects of English-Canadian Historical Writing 1900-1970. Ed. 2. Cloth Text. University of Toronto Press. Toronto, ON. 1986. 376p. ISBN:0-8020-2546-3, ISBN13: 978-0-8020-2546-3. Dewey:971/.0072.
Audience: **f.**

Bothwell, Robert **F1027.B66 1995**
Canada and Quebec: One Country, Two Histories. Trade Cloth. University of Washington Press. Seattle, WA. 1995. 288p. ISBN:0-7748-0524-2, ISBN13: 978-0-7748-0524-7. Dewey:971.4. LCCN:95-198077.
Audience: **u,f.**

Bothwell, Robert **F1027.B66 1998**
e Canada and Quebec: One Country, Two Histories. E-Book. NetLibrary, Inc. Boulder, CO. 1998. ISBN:0-585-31850-6, ISBN13: 978-0-585-31850-9. Dewey:971.4.
Audience: **l,u,f.**

Brown, Craig (Editor) **F1026.I43 2002**
The Illustrated History of Canada. Ed. 4. Trade Paper. Key Porter Books. Toronto, ON. 2003. 640p. ISBN:1-55263-508-2, ISBN13: 978-1-55263-508-7. Dewey:971. LCCN:2004-380652.
Audience: **g,l,u,f.** *Choice, 2003.*

Bumsted, Jack & Bumsted, J. M. **F1026**
The Peoples of Canada: A Post-Confederation History. Ed. 2. Trade Paper. Oxford University Press, Inc. New York, NY. 2004. 656p. ISBN:0-19-541690-2, ISBN13: 978-0-19-541690-9. Dewey:971. LCCN:2003-278310.
Audience: **g,l,u,f.**

Burns, Ronald M. **F1027.O5**
One Country or Two? John J. Deutsch (Introduction by). Trade Paper. Books on Demand. Ann Arbor, MI. 297p. ISBN:0-608-16143-8, ISBN13: 978-0-608-16143-3. Dewey:301.29/71/0714. LCCN:76-174566.
Audience: **f.**

Chaput, Marcel **F1027.C443**
Why I Am a Separatist. Robert A. Taylor (Translator). Trade Paper. Books on Demand. Ann Arbor, MI. 112p. ISBN:0-598-64650-7, ISBN13: 978-0-598-64650-7. LCCN:63-004553.
Audience: **f.** B

Chennels, David W. **F1026.C54 2001**
The Politics of Nationalism in Canada: Cultural Conflict since 1760. Trade Cloth. University of Toronto Press. Toronto, ON. 2000. 732p. ISBN:0-8020-4224-4, ISBN13: 978-0-8020-4224-8. Dewey:320.54/0971. LCCN:2001-273337.
Audience: **l,u,f.** *Choice, 2002.*

Clark, Samuel D. **F1026.C6**
Movements of Political Protest in Canada, 1640-1840. Trade Paper. Books on Demand. Ann Arbor, MI. 528p. Social Credit in Alberta Ser., No. 9 ISBN:0-608-13755-3, ISBN13: 978-0-608-13755-1. Dewey:971.01. LCCN:60-000029.
Audience: **f.** B

Cook, Ramsay **F1027.C76**
Canada and the French-Canadian Question. Trade Cloth. C D G Books Canada, Inc. Toronto, ON. 1966. 219p. ISBN:0-7705-0054-4, ISBN13: 978-0-7705-0054-2. Dewey:301.29/71. LCCN:67-079220.
Audience: **u,f.** B

Creighton, Donald **F1026.C74 2002**
The Empire of the St. Lawrence: A Study in Commerce and Politics. Trade Paper. University of Toronto Press. Toronto, ON. 2001. 441p. Reprints in Canadian History Ser. ISBN:0-8020-8418-4, ISBN13: 978-0-8020-8418-7. Dewey:971. LCCN:2002-279886.
Audience: **f.**

Finkel, Alvin **HV108**
Social Policy and Practice in Canada: A History. Trade Paper. Wilfrid Laurier University Press. Waterloo, ON. 2005. 396p. ISBN:0-88920-475-6, ISBN13: 978-0-88920-475-1. Dewey:361.6/10971.
Audience: **l,u,f.**

Hallowell, Gerald (Editor) **F1026**
The Oxford Companion to Canadian History. Trade Cloth. Oxford University Press, Inc. New York, NY. 2005. 782p. ISBN:0-19-541559-0, ISBN13: 978-0-19-541559-9. Dewey:971.
Audience: **g,l,u,f.**

Harris, R. Cole & Warkentin, John **F1027.5.H37 1991**
Canada Before Confereration: A Study in Historical Geography, No. 166. Paper Text. Bow Historical Books. New Providence, NJ. 362p. ISBN:0-88629-137-2, ISBN13: 978-0-88629-137-2. Dewey:911/.71. LCCN:93-112521.
Audience: **u,f.**

Morton, Desmond **F1026.M73 2001**
A Short History of Canada. Ed. 5. Trade Cloth. McClelland & Stewart/Tundra Books. Plattsburgh, NY. 2001. 408p. ISBN:0-7710-6508-6, ISBN13: 978-0-7710-6508-8. Dewey:971. LCCN:2001-347793.
Audience: **g,l,u,f.**

Silver, A. I. **F1027.S562 1997**
The French-Canadian Idea of Confederation, 1864-1900. Ed. 2. Trade Paper. University of Toronto Press. Toronto, ON. 1996. 460p. ISBN:0-8020-7928-8, ISBN13: 978-0-8020-7928-2. Dewey:971.004114. LCCN:97-224453.
Audience: **u,f.**

Vallieres, Pierre **F1027.V313 1971**
White Niggers of America. Trade Cloth. McClelland & Stewart. Toronto, ON. 1971. 278p. ISBN:0-7710-8670-9, ISBN13: 978-0-7710-8670-0. Dewey:322.4/2/0924. LCCN:72-180519.
Audience: **f.** B

Wade, Mason **F1027.W14**
Canadian Dualism: Studies of French-English Relations. Trade Paper. Books on Demand. Ann Arbor, MI. 452p. ISBN:0-598-05560-6, ISBN13: 978-0-598-05560-6. Dewey:917.1. LCCN:61-003019.
Audience: **f.** B

Wade, Mason **F1027 .W15 1982**
The French-Canadian Outlook: A Brief Account of the Unknown North Americans. Trade Cloth. Greenwood Publishing Group, Inc. Portsmouth, NH. 1982. 192p. ISBN:0-313-23496-5, ISBN13: 978-0-313-23496-5. Dewey:971/.004114. LCCN:82-011802.
Audience: **u,f.** B

Winks, Robin W. **F1026.6.W56 1988**
The Relevance of Canadian History: U. S. and Imperial Perspectives. Trade Paper. University Press of America, Inc. Lanham, MD. 1988. 116p. ISBN:0-8191-6831-9, ISBN13: 978-0-8191-6831-3. Dewey:971. LCCN:87-032181.
Audience: **f.**

Canada > History > Nationalism. French Canadians

F1027.5
Canadian Boundary. Ed. 3. Trade Cloth. Irish Academic Press. Dublin, ISBN:0-7165-0679-3, ISBN13: 978-0-7165-0679-9. Dewey:320.1/2.
Audience: **f.**

Harris, R. Cole & Warkentin, John **F1027.5.H37 1991**
Canada Before Confereration: A Study in Historical Geography, No. 166. Paper Text. Bow Historical Books. New Providence, NJ. 362p. ISBN:0-88629-137-2, ISBN13: 978-0-88629-137-2. Dewey:911/.71. LCCN:93-112521.
Audience: **u,f.**

Nicholson, Norman **F1027.5.N52 1979**
The Boundaries of the Canadian Confederation. Trade Paper. Gage Learning Corporation. Scarborough, ON. 1979. 252p. ISBN:0-7705-1742-0, ISBN13: 978-0-7705-1742-7. Dewey:911/.71. LCCN:80-450098.
Audience: **u,f.** B

Canada > Military and Diplomatic History

Balawyder, A. **F1029.5.E852**
Road to Freedom: On the Canadian-East European Relations, 1963-1991. Trade Cloth. Eastern European Monographs. Bradenton, FL. 2005. 200p. ISBN:0-88033-567-X, ISBN13: 978-0-88033-567-6. Dewey:327.47071.
Audience: **f.**

Berton, Pierre **F1028.B47 2001**
Marching As to War: Canada's Turbulent Years, 1899-1953. Trade Cloth. Doubleday Canada, Ltd. Toronto, ON. 2001. 640p. ISBN:0-385-25725-2, ISBN13: 978-0-385-25725-1. Dewey:971.06. LCCN:2001-431506.
Audience: **u,f.**

Canada in World Affairs Staff **F1029.C3**
Canada in World Affairs, the Pre-War Years. Trade Paper. Books on Demand. Ann Arbor, MI. 357p. ISBN:0-598-94626-8, ISBN13: 978-0-598-94626-3. Dewey:327.71. LCCN:56-002289.
Audience: **u,f.**

Chartrand, Rene **F1028.C48 1993**
Canadian Military Heritage: 1000-1754. Trade Cloth. Editions Art Global. Outremont, PQ. 1997. 240p. Canadian Military Heritage Ser., Vol. 1 ISBN:2-920718-49-5, ISBN13: 978-2-920718-49-4. Dewey:355/.00971. LCCN:96-103723.
Audience: **u,f.**

Chartrand, Rene **F1028.C48 1993**
Canadian Military Heritage: 1755-1871. Trade Cloth. Editions Art Global. Outremont, PQ. 1997. 240p. Canadian Military Heritage Ser., Vol. 2 ISBN:2-920718-50-9, ISBN13: 978-2-920718-50-0. Dewey:355/.00971. LCCN:96-103723.
Audience: **u,f.**

Cooper, Andrew F. **F1029.C32**
Canadian Culture: International Dimensions. Trade Paper. Books on Demand. Ann Arbor, MI. 1985. 168p. Contemporary Affairs Ser., Vol. 50 ISBN:0-608-04225-0, ISBN13: 978-0-608-04225-1. Dewey:306/.4/0971. LCCN:86-105590.
Audience: **u,f.**

Granatstein, Jack L. **F1029.5 U6**
Yankee Go Home?: Canadians and Anti-Americanism. Trade Paper. HarperCollins College. New York, NY. 1998. 336p. ISBN:0-00-638541-9, ISBN13: 978-0-00-638541-7. Dewey:327.71073.
Audience: **u,f.**

Graves, Donald E., et al. **F1028.F54 2000**
Fighting for Canada: Seven Battles, 1758-1945. Ian M. McCulloch, Robert Malcomson, Brian A. Reid, John R. Grodzinski & Michael R. McNorgan (Authors). Trade Cloth. Robin Brass Studio, Inc. Toronto, ON. 2000. 446p. ISBN:1-896941-15-X, ISBN13: 978-1-896941-15-8. Dewey:971. LCCN:00-691175.
Audience: **u,f.**

James, Patrick, et al. **F1029.H27 2006**
Handbook of Canadian Foreign Policy. Nelson Michaud & Marc O'Reilly (Authors). Trade Cloth. Lexington Books. Lanham, MD. 2006. 648p. ISBN:0-7391-0694-5, ISBN13: 978-0-7391-0694-5. Dewey:327.71. LCCN:2005-030657.
Audience: **f.**

McKercher, B J; Aronsen, Lawrence **F1029.5.U6N67 1996**
The North Atlantic Triangle in a Changing World: Anglo-American-Canadian Relations, 1902-1956. B. J. McKercher (Editor) ; Lawrence Aronsen (Editor). University of Toronto Press. 1995. ISBN:0-8020-0520-9, ISBN13: 978-0-8020-0520-5.
Audience: **f.**

Morton, Desmond **F1028.M68 1999**
A Military History of Canada: From Champlain to Kosovo. Ed. 4. Trade Paper. McClelland & Stewart/Tundra Books. Plattsburgh, NY. 1999. 352p. ISBN:0-7710-6514-0, ISBN13: 978-0-7710-6514-9. Dewey:971. LCCN:00-361357.
Audience: **u,f.**

Morton, William Lewis **F1029.**
The Canadian Identity. Ed. 2. Trade Paper. Books on Demand. Ann Arbor, MI. 1972. 174p. ISBN:0-608-01974-7, ISBN13: 978-0-608-01974-1. Dewey:971/.008. LCCN:73-187505.
Audience: **u,f.**

Stacey, C. P. **F1029.S73**
Canada and the Age of Conflict: A History of Canadian External Policies. Trade Cloth. C D G Books Canada, Inc. Toronto, ON. 1977. ISBN:0-7705-1428-6, ISBN13: 978-0-7705-1428-0. Dewey:327.71. LCCN:78-306832.
Audience: **l,u,f.** B

Canada > History, by Period. > 1763-1867

Bearor, Bob **F1030.B35 2002**
Leading by Example: Partisan Fighters and Leaders of New France, 1660-1760. Trade Cloth. Heritage Books. Westminster, MD. 2002. ISBN:0-7884-2348-7, ISBN13: 978-0-7884-2348-2. Dewey:971.4/014/0922 B. LCCN:2002-283565.
Audience: **f.**

Bishop, Morris **F1030.1.B6**
Champlain, the Life of Fortitude. Trade Paper. Books on Demand. Ann Arbor, MI. 393p. ISBN:0-598-68730-0, ISBN13: 978-0-598-68730-2. Dewey:923.971. LCCN:48-008873.
Audience: **f.** B

Choquette, Leslie **F1030.C57 1997**
Frenchmen into Peasants: Modernity and Tradition in the Peopling of French Canada. Trade Cloth. Harvard University Press. Cambridge, MA. 1997. 409p. Frenchmen Into Peasants Ser., Vol. 123 ISBN:0-674-32315-7, ISBN13: 978-0-674-32315-5. Dewey:304.871. LCCN:96-040089.
Audience: **f.**

Dale, Ronald J. **F1030.9.D35 2004**
The Fall of New France: How the French Lost a North American Empire. Trade Paper. James Lorimer & Company Ltd., Publishers. Toronto, ON. 2004. 96p. ISBN:1-55028-840-7, ISBN13: 978-1-55028-840-7. Dewey:971.01/8. LCCN:2004-478148.
Audience: **u,f.**

De Champlain, Samuel **F1030.1C494**
Voyages of Samuel de Champlain, 1604-1618. Library Binding. Reprint Services Company. Temecula, CA. 1991. 374p. BCL1 - History - Canada Ser. ISBN:0-7812-6351-4, ISBN13: 978-0-7812-6351-1. Dewey:971.011.
Audience: **u,f.**

Dix, Edwin Asa **F1030.1.D61**
Champlain, the Founder of New France. Trade Paper. Books on Demand. Ann Arbor, MI. 256p. Appleton's Historic Lives Ser. ISBN:0-598-86749-X, ISBN13: 978-0-598-86749-0. Dewey:971.0113092. LCCN:32-009867.
Audience: **u,f.**

Du Creux, Francois **F1030**
History of Canada, or New France, Vol. 1. James B. Conacher (Editor), Percy J. Robinson (Translator). Trade Cloth. Greenwood Publishing Group, Inc. Portsmouth, NH. 1969. 404p. Champlain Society Publication ISBN:0-8371-5070-1, ISBN13: 978-0-8371-5070-3. Dewey:971.01/1. LCCN:69-014507.
Audience: **u,f.**

Eccles, William J. **F1030 .E312 1983**
The Canadian Frontier, 1534-1760. Trade Paper. University of New Mexico Press. Albuquerque, NM. 1983. 258p. Histories of the American Frontier Serie Ser. ISBN:0-8263-0706-X, ISBN13: 978-0-8263-0706-4. Dewey:971.01. LCCN:83-005753.
Audience: **f.**

Greer, Allan **F1030.G79 1997**
The People of New France. Cloth over Boards. University of Toronto Press. Toronto, ON. 1997. 130p. Themes in Canadian Social History Ser. ISBN:0-8020-0826-7, ISBN13: 978-0-8020-0826-8. Dewey:971.01/8. LCCN:98-112694.
Audience: **f.**

Johnson, Donald **F1030.5.J85 2002**
La Salle: A Perilous Odyssey from Canada to the Gulf of Mexico. Trade Cloth. Cooper Square Publishers, Inc. New York, NY. 2002. 296p. ISBN:0-8154-1240-1, ISBN13: 978-0-8154-1240-3. Dewey:977/.01. LCCN:2002-004683.
Audience: **u,f.**

Litalien, Raymonde & Vaugeois, Denis (Editors) **F1030**
Champlain: The Birth of French America. Trade Cloth. McGill-Queen's University Press. Montreal, PQ. 2004. 402p. ISBN:0-7735-2850-4, ISBN13: 978-0-7735-2850-5. Dewey:971.01/13/092.
Audience: **u,f.**

Moogk, Peter M. **F1030.M793 2000**
La Nouvelle France: The Making of French Canada - A Cultural History. Trade Paper. Michigan State University Press. East Lansing, MI. 2000. 320p. ISBN:0-87013-528-7, ISBN13: 978-0-87013-528-6. Dewey:971.01. LCCN:00-008122.
Audience: **l,u,f.** *Choice, 2001.*

Muhlstein, Anka **F1030.5.M8413 1994**
La Salle: Explorer of the North American Frontier. Willard Wood (Translator). Trade Cloth. Arcade Publishing, Inc. New York, NY. 1994. 244p. ISBN:1-55970-219-2, ISBN13: 978-1-55970-219-5. Dewey:977/.01/092 B. LCCN:94-047991.
Audience: **u,f.**

Parkman, Francis **F1030.P261 1996**
Pioneers of France in the New World. Colin G. Calloway (Introduction by). Trade Cloth. University of Nebraska Press. Lincoln, NE. 1996. 473p. ISBN:0-8032-8744-5, ISBN13: 978-0-8032-8744-0. Dewey:970.01/8. LCCN:96-017586.
Audience: **f.**

Parkman, Francis **F1030.7.P24 1997**
The Jesuits in North America in the Seventeenth Century. Conrad E. Heidenreich & Jose A. Brandao (Introduction by). Trade Cloth. University of Nebraska Press. Lincoln, NE. 1997. 587p. ISBN:0-8032-8746-1, ISBN13: 978-0-8032-8746-4. Dewey:971.01/62. LCCN:97-030487.
Audience: **f.**

Parkman, Francis & Morison, Samuel Eliot **F1030.P246 1998**
Francis Parkman Reader. Trade Paper. Da Capo Press, Inc. Cambridge, MA. 1998. 552p. ISBN:0-306-80823-4, ISBN13: 978-0-306-80823-4. Dewey:971.01. LCCN:97-042967.
Audience: **u,f.**

Parkman, Francis **F1030**
La Salle and the Discovery of the Great West. William R. Taylor (Editor). Trade Cloth. Greenwood Publishing Group, Inc. Portsmouth, NH. 1986. 377p. ISBN:0-313-24223-2, ISBN13: 978-0-313-24223-6. Dewey:917.7041092. LCCN:86-022763.
Audience: **l,u,f.**

Parkman, Francis **F1030.P2472 2001**
The Battle for North America. John Tebbel (Editor). Saddle Stitched. Phoenix Press, WC2. London, 2001. 800p. Phoenix Press Ser. ISBN:1-84212-416-1, ISBN13: 978-1-84212-416-1. Dewey:971.01. LCCN:2001-430965.
Audience: **f.**

Savelle, Max **F1030.S28**
The Diplomatic History of the Canadian Boundary, 1749-1763. Trade Paper. Books on Demand. Ann Arbor, MI. 202p. ISBN:0-598-80224-X, ISBN13: 978-0-598-80224-8. Dewey:327.71/073. LCCN:40-035105.
Audience: **u,f.** B

Stewart, Gordon T. **F1030.S85 1996**
History of Canada Before 1867. Trade Paper. Michigan State University Press. East Lansing, MI. 1996. 50p. ACSUS Papers Ser. ISBN:0-87013-398-5, ISBN13: 978-0-87013-398-5. Dewey:971. LCCN:97-127561.
Audience: **g,l,u,f.**

Canada > History, by Period. > 1867-1914

Ajzenstat, Janet (Editor), et al. **F1032.**
Canada's Founding Debates. Paul Romney, Ian Gentles & William D. Gairdner (Editors). Trade Paper. University of Toronto Press. Toronto, ON. 2003. 502p. ISBN:0-8020-8607-1, ISBN13: 978-0-8020-8607-5. Dewey:971.04/9.
Audience: **u,f.**

Bothwell, Robert **F1033.B765 1996**
History of Canada since 1867. Trade Paper. Michigan State University Press. East Lansing, MI. 1996. 50p. ACSUS Papers Ser. ISBN:0-87013-399-3, ISBN13: 978-0-87013-399-2. Dewey:971.05. LCCN:97-127555.
Audience: **g,l,u,f.**

Buckingham, William & Ross, George William **F1033**
The Hon. Alexander MacKenzie, His Life and Times. Ed. 5. Trade Paper. Books on Demand. Ann Arbor, MI. 682p. ISBN:0-608-34901-1, ISBN13: 978-0-608-34901-5. Dewey:971.05/0924. LCCN:16-025919.
Audience: **u,f.**

Coupland, Reginald **F1032 .C85**
The Quebec Act: A Study in Statesmanship. Library Binding. Reprint Services Company. Temecula, CA. 1991. 224p. BCL1 - History - Canada Ser. ISBN:0-7812-6357-3, ISBN13: 978-0-7812-6357-3. Dewey:325.3/42/09714.
Audience: **f.**

Creighton, Donald G. **F1033.M126 C7 1998**
John A. MacDonald: The Young Politician and the Old Chieftain. Trade Paper. University of Toronto Press. Toronto, ON. 1998. 1536p. Reprints in Canadian History Ser. ISBN:0-8020-7164-3, ISBN13: 978-0-8020-7164-4. Dewey:971.05/092. LCCN:98-147627.
Audience: **u,f.**

Creighton, Donald G. **F1032 .C9 1976**
The Road to Confederation: The Emergence of Canada, 1863-1867. Trade Cloth. Greenwood Publishing Group, Inc. Portsmouth, NH. 1976. 489p. ISBN:0-8371-8435-5, ISBN13: 978-0-8371-8435-7. Dewey:971.04. LCCN:75-027652.
Audience: **u,f.**

Dawson, Robert MacGregor **F1033.K53.D3**
William Lyon Mackenzie King. Trade Cloth. University of Toronto Press. Toronto, ON. 1958. v.p. ISBN:0-8020-1083-0, ISBN13: 978-0-8020-1083-4. Dewey:923.271. LCCN:59-000347.
Audience: **u,f.**

Durham, John George Lambton **F1032**
The Durham Report: An Abridged Version with an Introduction and Notes by Sir Reginald Coupland. Trade Paper. Books on Demand. Ann Arbor, MI. 257p. ISBN:0-598-63600-5, ISBN13: 978-0-598-63600-3. Dewey:971.038. LCCN:48-004760.
Audience: **u,f.**

English, John **F1033.B76.E53**
Borden: His Life and World. Trade Cloth. McGraw-Hill Ryerson, Ltd. Whitby, ON. 1977. 223p. ISBN:0-07-082303-0, ISBN13: 978-0-07-082303-7. Dewey:971.06/12/0924. LCCN:78-304660.
Audience: **f.** B

Ged, Martin **F1032.M37 1995**
Britain and the Origins of Canadian Confederation, 1837-1867. Trade Cloth. University of British Columbia Press. Vancouver, BC. 1995. 400p. ISBN:0-7748-0488-2, ISBN13: 978-0-7748-0488-2. Dewey:971.04/9. LCCN:95-166843.
Audience: **f.** *Choice, 1995.*

Granatstein, J. L. **F1033.K53.G73**
Mackenzie King: His Life and World. Trade Cloth. McGraw-Hill Ryerson, Ltd. Whitby, ON. 1977. 202p. ISBN:0-07-082304-9, ISBN13: 978-0-07-082304-4. Dewey:971.06/22/0924. LCCN:78-304849.
Audience: **l,u,f.** B

Guillet, Edwin Clarence **F1032.G89**
The Lives and Times of the Patriots: An Account of the Rebellion in Upper Canada, 1837-1838, and of the Patriot Agitation in the United States, 1837-1842. Trade Paper. Books on Demand. Ann Arbor, MI. 320p. ISBN:0-598-18480-5, ISBN13: 978-0-598-18480-1. Dewey:971.03/8. LCCN:68-115557.
Audience: **f.** B

Hall, D. J. **F1033.S59 H254**
Clifford Sifton: A Lonely Eminence, 1901-1929, Vol. 2. Trade Cloth. University of British Columbia Press. Vancouver, BC. 1985. 459p. ISBN:0-7748-0209-X, ISBN13: 978-0-7748-0209-3. Dewey:971.05/6/0924. LCCN:81-201998.
Audience: **f.** *Choice, 1985.*

Hall, D. J. **F1033.S59.H254**
Clifford Sifton: Young Napoleon, 1861-1900. Trade Cloth. University of British Columbia Press. Vancouver, BC. 1981. 385p. ISBN:0-7748-0135-2, ISBN13: 978-0-7748-0135-5. Dewey:971.056092. LCCN:81-201998.
Audience: **f.** B

Hardy, Henry R. **F1033.K53 H36**
Mackenzie King of Canada: A Biography. Trade Cloth. Greenwood Publishing Group, Inc. Portsmouth, NH. 1970. 390p. ISBN:0-8371-5164-3, ISBN13: 978-0-8371-5164-9. Dewey:971.06/0924. LCCN:77-135245.
Audience: **l,u,f.**

Hincks, Francis **F1032**
The Political History of Canada Between 1840 and 1855. Trade Paper. Books on Demand. Ann Arbor, MI. 88p. ISBN:0-598-48193-1, ISBN13: 978-0-598-48193-1. Dewey:971.04.
Audience: **f.**

Kilbourn, William **F1032 .M148 1977**
The Firebrand: William Lyon Mackenzie and the Rebellion in Upper Canada. Trade Paper. General Distribution Services, Inc. Niagara Falls, NY. 1977. 259p. ISBN:0-7720-1179-6, ISBN13: 978-0-7720-1179-4. Dewey:971.03/8. LCCN:98-224657.
Audience: **u,f.** B

Kinchen, Oscar Arvle **F1032**
Lord Russell's Canadian Policy, a Study in British Heritage and Colonial Freedom. Trade Paper. Books on Demand. Ann Arbor, MI. 248p. Texas Technological College Research Publication Ser., No. 13 ISBN:0-598-67650-3, ISBN13: 978-0-598-67650-4. Dewey:923.242. LCCN:47-004340.
Audience: **f.**

Lawson, Philip **F1032.L2 1989**
The Imperial Challenge: Quebec and Britain in the Age of the American Revolution. Trade Cloth. McGill-Queen's University Press. Montreal, PQ. 1989. 208p. ISBN:0-7735-0698-5, ISBN13: 978-0-7735-0698-5. Dewey:325/.341/09714. LCCN:90-171126.
Audience: **f.** *Choice, 1990.*

Lindsey, Charles **F1032**
The Life and Times of William Lyon MacKenzie: With an Account of the Canadian Rebellion of 1837, Vol. 2. Trade Paper. Books on Demand. Ann Arbor, MI. 420p. ISBN:0-598-52368-5, ISBN13: 978-0-598-52368-6. Dewey:971.038. LCCN:43-006343.
Audience: **f.**

Penlington, Norman **F1033.P4**
Canada and Imperialism, 1896-1899. Trade Paper. Books on Demand. Ann Arbor, MI. 302p. ISBN:0-598-15861-8, ISBN13: 978-0-598-15861-1. Dewey:971.05. LCCN:65-001619.
Audience: **l,u,f.**

Read, Colin **F1032.R27**
The Rising in Western Upper Canada, 1837-38: The Duncombe Revolt and After. Trade Paper. Books on Demand. Ann Arbor, MI. 339p. ISBN:0-8357-6366-8, ISBN13: 978-0-8357-6366-0. Dewey:971.03/8. LCCN:82-168779.
Audience: **f.** B

Robeson, Virginia R. (Author, Editor) **F1033.D28**
Debates about Canada's Future, 1868-1896. Trade Paper. Books on Demand. Ann Arbor, MI. 124p. Ontario Institute for Studies in Education. Curriculum Ser., Vol. 24 ISBN:0-598-13183-3, ISBN13: 978-0-598-13183-6. Dewey:971.05. LCCN:78-307873.
Audience: **f.**

Samuels, Raymond II (Editor) **F1033.P75 2002**
Prime Ministers of Canada: Selected Speeches 1867-2002, Profiles, Bibliography with Editorial Commentary. Trade Paper. Agora Publishing Consortium. Ottawa, ON. 2006. 515p. ISBN:1-894839-19-6, ISBN13: 978-1-894839-19-8. Dewey:971.05/092/2 B. LCCN:2002-491802.
Audience: **u,f.**

Saunders, Edward Manning **B770.P6**
Three Premiers of Nova Scotia: The Honorable J.W. Johnstone, the Hon. Joseph Howe, the Hon. Charles Tupper. Trade Cloth. Library Reprints, Inc. Temecula, CA. 628p. ISBN:0-7222-6886-6, ISBN13: 978-0-7222-6886-5. Dewey:108.
Audience: **f.**

Skelton, Oscar D. **F1033 .L386**
Life and Letters of Sir Wilfrid Laurier. Paper Text. Classic Textbooks. Murrieta, CA. 1922. ISBN:1-4047-6366-X, ISBN13: 978-1-4047-6366-1. Dewey:354.71.
Audience: **f.**

Stacey, C. P. **F1033.K53.S72**
A Very Double Life: The Private World of Mackenzie King. Trade Cloth. C D G Books Canada, Inc. Toronto, ON. 1976. 256p. ISBN:0-7705-1390-5, ISBN13: 978-0-7705-1390-0. Dewey:971.06/22/0924. LCCN:76-366908.
Audience: **u,f.** B

Stacey, Charles P. **F1029**
Canada and the Age of Conflict: A History of Canadian External Policies, 1921-1948 - The Mackenzie King Era. Trade Paper. University of Toronto Press. Toronto, ON. 1981. 680p. ISBN:0-8020-6420-5, ISBN13: 978-0-8020-6420-2. Dewey:327.71.
Audience: **g,l,u,f.**

Stacey, Charles P. **F1029**
Canada and the Age of Conflict: A History of Canadian External Policies, 1867-1921. Trade Paper. University of Toronto Press. Toronto, ON. 1984. 567p. ISBN:0-8020-6560-0, ISBN13: 978-0-8020-6560-5. Dewey:327.71.
Audience: **g,l,u,f.**

Stacey, Charles P. **F1032.S78**
Canada and the British Army, 1846-1871: A Study in the Practice of Responsible Government. Trade Paper. Books on Demand. Ann Arbor, MI. 312p. ISBN:0-8357-7988-2, ISBN13: 978-0-8357-7988-3. Dewey:971.04. LCCN:64-007285.
Audience: **f.** B

Waite, P. B. **F1032.W16 2001**
The Life and Times of Confederation, 1864-1867: Politics, Newspapers and the Union of British North America. Ed. 3. Trade Cloth. Robin Brass Studio, Inc. Toronto, ON. 2001. 468p. ISBN:1-896941-23-0, ISBN13: 978-1-896941-23-3. Dewey:971.04/9. LCCN:2002-318307.
Audience: **u,f.**

Waite, Peter B. **F1033.W15**
Canada 1874-1896: Arduous Destiny. Trade Cloth. McClelland & Stewart. Toronto, ON. 1971. xii, 340p. ISBN:0-7710-8800-0, ISBN13: 978-0-7710-8800-1. Dewey:971.05. LCCN:76-597589.
Audience: **u,f.** B

Waite, Peter B. **F1033.M135**
Macdonald: His Life and World. Trade Cloth. McGraw-Hill Ryerson, Ltd. Whitby, ON. 1975. 224p. ISBN:0-07-082301-4, ISBN13: 978-0-07-082301-3. Dewey:971.05/1/0924. LCCN:76-355909.
Audience: **f.** B

Wilson, George Earl **F1032.B22**
The Life of Robert Baldwin, a Study in the Struggle for Responsible Government. Trade Paper. Books on Demand. Ann Arbor, MI. 320p. ISBN:0-598-96496-7, ISBN13: 978-0-598-96496-0. Dewey:928/.271. LCCN:33-036988.
Audience: **f.** B

Canada > History, by Period. > 1914-

Azzi, Stephen **F1034.3.G67A98 1999**
Walter Gordon and the Rise of Canadian Nationalism. Trade Cloth. McGill-Queen's University Press. Montreal, PQ. 1999. xv, 300p. ISBN:0-7735-1840-1, ISBN13: 978-0-7735-1840-7. Dewey:971.064/3/092 B. LCCN:00-364119.
Audience: **f.** *Choice, 2000.*

Blanchette, Arthur E. **F1034.2.C323 2000**
Canadian Foreign Policy, 1945-2000: Major Documents and Speeches. Trade Paper. Golden Dog Press. Kemptville, ON. 2004. 262p. Rideau Ser., Vol. 1 ISBN:0-919614-89-2, ISBN13: 978-0-919614-89-5. Dewey:327.71. LCCN:2002-318930.
Audience: **l,u,f.**

Bothwell, Robert **F1034.2.B67**
Canada since 1945: Power, Politics, and Provincialism. Trade Cloth. University of Toronto Press. Toronto, ON. 1981. xii, 489p. ISBN:0-8020-2417-3, ISBN13: 978-0-8020-2417-6. Dewey:971.06. LCCN:81-152041.
Audience: **u,f.** B

Bothwell, Robert **F1034.3.P4.B67**
Pearson, His Life and World. Trade Cloth. McGraw-Hill Ryerson, Ltd. Whitby, ON. 1978. 223p. ISBN:0-07-082305-7, ISBN13: 978-0-07-082305-1. Dewey:971.06/43/0924. LCCN:78-322388.
Audience: **u,f.** B

Cohen, Andrew **F1034.3.T7**
Trudeau's Shadow: The Life and Legacy of Pierre Elliott Trudeau. Jack L. Granatstein (Editor). Trade Paper. Random House, Inc. New York, NY. 1999. 416p. ISBN:0-679-31006-1, ISBN13: 978-0-679-31006-8. Dewey:971.064/4/092.
Audience: **u,f.**

Eayrs, James George **F1034.E17**
In Defence of Canada: From the Great War to Thegreat Depression. Trade Paper. Books on Demand. Ann Arbor, MI. 396p. Studies in the Structure of Power, Vol. 1 ISBN:0-598-13062-4, ISBN13: 978-0-598-13062-4. Dewey:355/.033/071.
Audience: **f.**

English, John **F1034.3.P4 E54 1989**
Shadow of Heaven: The Life of Lester Pearson. Trade Cloth. Bow Historical Books. New Providence, NJ. 1989. ISBN:0-88619-169-6, ISBN13: 978-0-88619-169-6. Dewey:971.064/3/092. LCCN:90-135093.
Audience: **u,f.**

Finkel, Alvin **F1034.2.F56 1997**
Our Lives: Canada since 1945. Cloth Text. James Lorimer & Company Ltd., Publishers. Toronto, ON. 1997. 423p. ISBN:1-55028-550-5, ISBN13: 978-1-55028-550-5. Dewey:971.064. LCCN:98-119286.
Audience: **g,l,u,f.**

Fox, Annette B. **F1034.2.F69 1996**
Canada in World Affairs. Trade Paper. Michigan State University Press. East Lansing, MI. 1996. 50p. ACSUS Papers Ser. ISBN:0-87013-391-8, ISBN13: 978-0-87013-391-6. Dewey:327.71. LCCN:97-127564.
Audience: **f.**

Granatstein, Jack L. **F1034.2.G697 1986**
Canada, 1957-1967: The Years of Uncertainty and Innovation. Trade Cloth. McClelland & Stewart/Tundra Books. Plattsburgh, NY. 1986. 375p. Canadian Centenary Ser., Vol. 19 ISBN:0-7710-3515-2, ISBN13: 978-0-7710-3515-9. Dewey:971.064/2. LCCN:85-099058.
Audience: **u,f.**

Granatstein, Jack L. & Hillmer, Norman **F1033.H655 1994**
Empire to Umpire: Canada and the World to the 1990s. Trade Paper. Addison-Wesley Longman, Inc. Boston, MA. 1994. 350p. ISBN:0-7730-5439-1, ISBN13: 978-0-7730-5439-4. Dewey:327.71/009/04. LCCN:95-112949.
Audience: **u,f.**

Hillmer, Norman (Editor) **F1034.3.P4P44 1999**
Pearson: The Unlikely Gladiator. Jean Chretien (Foreword by). Trade Cloth. McGill-Queen's University Press. Montreal, PQ. 1998. x, 213p. ISBN:0-7735-1768-5, ISBN13: 978-0-7735-1768-4. Dewey:971.064/3/092. LCCN:2001-369785.
Audience: **u,f.**

Keating, Tom **F1034.2.K43 2002**
Canada and World Order: The Multilateralist Tradition in Canadian Foreign Policy. Ed. 2. Paper Text. Oxford University Press, Inc. New York, NY. 2001. 272p. ISBN:0-19-541529-9, ISBN13: 978-0-19-541529-2. Dewey:327.71. LCCN:2002-278424.
Audience: **f.**

Laforest, Guy **F1034.3.T7L3413 1995**
Trudeau and the End of a Canadian Dream. Paul L. Browne & Michelle Weinroth (Translators). Trade Cloth. University of Toronto Press. Toronto, ON. 1995. 224p. ISBN:0-7735-1300-0, ISBN13: 978-0-7735-1300-6. Dewey:971.064/4/092. LCCN:95-217903.
Audience: **u,f.** *Choice, 1995.*

Martin, Lawrence **F1034.3.C47M38 2003**
Iron Man: The Defiant Reign of Jean Chrétien. Ed. 2. Trade Cloth. Penguin Group (USA) Inc. New York, NY. 2003. 400p. ISBN:0-670-04310-9, ISBN13: 978-0-670-04310-1. Dewey:971.064/8/092 B. LCCN:2003-495292.
Audience: **f.**

McRoberts, Kenneth (Editor) **F1034.2.M36 1997**
Misconceiving Canada: The Struggle for National Unity. Paper Text. Oxford University Press, Inc. New York, NY. 1997. 416p. ISBN:0-19-541233-8, ISBN13: 978-0-19-541233-8. Dewey:971.064. LCCN:97-183213.
Audience: **f.**

Melakopides, Costas **F1034.2.M45 1998**
Pragmatic Idealism: Canadian Foreign Policy, 1945-1995. Trade Cloth. McGill-Queen's University Press. Montreal, PQ. 1998. 248p. ISBN:0-7735-1722-7, ISBN13: 978-0-7735-1722-6. Dewey:971.064. LCCN:00-503331.
Audience: **f.**

Michaud, Nelson & Nossal, Kim Richard (Editors) **F1034.2.D585 2001**
Diplomatic Departures: The Conservative Era in Canadian Foreign Policy, 1984-1993. Trade Cloth. University of British Columbia Press. Vancouver, BC. 2001. 336p. Canada and International Relations Ser., Vol. 14 ISBN:0-7748-0864-0, ISBN13: 978-0-7748-0864-4. Dewey:327.71/009/048. LCCN:2002-491575.
Audience: **f.**

Pearson, Lester B. **F1034.3.P4A**
Mike: The Memoirs of the Right Honourable Lester B. Pearson, Vol. 1. Trade Paper. Books on Demand. Ann Arbor, MI. 323p. ISBN:0-598-16035-3, ISBN13: 978-0-598-16035-5. Dewey:971.06/43/0924. LCCN:72-088037.
Audience: **f.**

Radwanski, George **F1034.3.T7.R32 1978**
Trudeau. Trade Cloth. Taplinger Publishing Company, Inc. Marlboro, NJ. 1978. xii, 372p. ISBN:0-8008-7897-3, ISBN13: 978-0-8008-7897-9. Dewey:971.06/44/0924. LCCN:78-067827.
Audience: **u,f.** B

Simpson, Jeffrey **F1034.2.S53**
Discipline of Power: The Conservative Interlude and the Liberal Restoration. Trade Cloth. Bow Historical Books. New Providence, NJ. 1980. xiv, 369p. ISBN:0-920510-24-8, ISBN13: 978-0-920510-24-7. Dewey:971.064/5. LCCN:81-133616.
Audience: **f.** B

Smith, Dennis **F1034.S64 1988**
Diplomacy of Fear: Canada and the Cold War, 1941-1948. Cloth Text. University of Toronto Press. Toronto, ON. 1988. 300p. ISBN:0-8020-5770-5, ISBN13: 978-0-8020-5770-9. Dewey:327.71. LCCN:88-198113.
Audience: **f.** *Choice, 1988.*

Trudeau, Pierre E. **F1034.3.T7A3 1993**
Memoirs. Trade Cloth. McClelland & Stewart/Tundra Books. Plattsburgh, NY. 1993. 379p. ISBN:0-7710-8588-5, ISBN13: 978-0-7710-8588-8. Dewey:971.064/4/092 B. LCCN:94-121141.
Audience: **u,f.**

Trudeau, Pierre E. **F1034.3.T7A25 1998**
The Essential Trudeau. Ron Graham (Editor). Trade Cloth. McClelland & Stewart/Tundra Books. Plattsburgh, NY. 1998. 216p. ISBN:0-7710-8591-5, ISBN13: 978-0-7710-8591-8. Dewey:971.064. LCCN:98-210519.
Audience: **u,f.**

Canada > Elements in the Population

Abella, Irving M. & Troper, Harold **F1035.J5.A23 1983**
None Is Too Many: Canada and the Jews of Europe, 1933-1948. Trade Cloth. Random House, Inc. New York, NY. 1983. 368p. ISBN:0-394-53328-3, ISBN13: 978-0-394-53328-5. Dewey:325/.2/08992404. LCCN:83-042864.
Audience: **f.** B

Breton, Raymond **F1035**
The Governance of Ethnic Communities: Political Structures and Processes in Canada, 26. Trade Cloth. Greenwood Publishing Group, Inc. Portsmouth, NH. 1990. 208p. Contributions in Ethnic Studies Ser., No. 26 ISBN:0-313-27417-7, ISBN13: 978-0-313-27417-6. Dewey:305.8/00971. LCCN:90-038423.
Audience: **f.** *Choice, 1991.*

Brown, Michael G. **F1035.J5B76**
Jew or Juif? Jews, French Canadians, and Anglo-Canadians, 1759-1914. Trade Paper. Books on Demand. Ann Arbor, MI. 368p. ISBN:0-598-03157-X, ISBN13: 978-0-598-03157-0. Dewey:305.8/924/0714. LCCN:86-010564.
Audience: **f.**

Bumsted, J. M. **F1035.A1**
Canada's Diverse Peoples: A Reference Sourcebook. Elliott Robert Barkan (Editor). Library Binding. ABC-CLIO, Inc. Santa Barbara, CA. 2003. 315p. Ethnic Diversity Within Nations Ser. ISBN:1-57607-672-5, ISBN13: 978-1-57607-672-9. Dewey:305.8/00971. LCCN:2003-011077.
Audience: **g,l,u,f.**

Day, Richard **F1035.A1D39 2000**
Multiculturalism and the History of Canadian Diversity. Cloth over Boards. University of Toronto Press. Toronto, ON. 2000. 288p. ISBN:0-8020-4231-7, ISBN13: 978-0-8020-4231-6. Dewey:971.004. LCCN:00-703155.
Audience: **l,u,f.** *Choice, 2000.*

Driedger, Leo **F1035.A1R32 2000**
Race and Racism: Canada's Challenge. Trade Cloth. McGill-Queen's University Press. Montreal, PQ. 2000. 328p. ISBN:0-88629-362-6, ISBN13: 978-0-88629-362-8. Dewey:305.8/00971. LCCN:2001-369748.
Audience: **u,f.**

Elliott, Jean Leonard **F1035.A1.T85**
Two Nations, Many Cultures: Ethnic Groups in Canada. Ed. 2. Trade Cloth. Prentice Hall Canada. Scarborough, ON. 1978. xiii, 395p. ISBN:0-13-935205-8, ISBN13: 978-0-13-935205-8. Dewey:301.45/1/0971. LCCN:79-311705.
Audience: **f.** B

Houston, Cecil J. & Smyth, William J. **F1035.I6.H68 1990**
Irish Emigration and Canadian Settlement: Patterns, Links, and Letters. Trade Cloth. University of Toronto Press. Toronto, ON. 1990. 387p. ISBN:0-8020-5829-9, ISBN13: 978-0-8020-5829-4. Dewey:305.89162071. LCCN:91-149616.
Audience: **f.** *Choice, 1990.*

Iacovetta, Franca **F1035.A1N366 1998**
Nation of Immigrants: Readings in Canadian History, 1840-1960. Trade Cloth. University of Toronto Press. Toronto, ON. 1998. 918p. ISBN:0-8020-0466-0, ISBN13: 978-0-8020-0466-6. Dewey:971. LCCN:98-213289.
Audience: **u,f.**

Li, Peter S. **F1035.A1R3 1999**
Race and Ethnic Relations in Canada. Ed. 2. Paper Text. Oxford University Press, Inc. New York, NY. 1999. 424p. ISBN:0-19-541477-2, ISBN13: 978-0-19-541477-6. Dewey:305.8/00971. LCCN:99-461879.
Audience: **u,f.** *Choice, 1991.*

Mensah, Joseph **F1035.N3M46 2002**
Black Canadians: History, Experience, Social Conditions. Trade Paper. Fernwood Publishing Company, Ltd. Peterborough, ON. 2004. 280p. ISBN:1-55266-090-7, ISBN13: 978-1-55266-090-4. Dewey:971/.00496. LCCN:2002-489704.
Audience: **u,f.** *Choice, 2003.*

Satzewich, V. **F1035.A1R337 1998**
Racism and Social Inequality in Canada: Concepts, Controversies and Strategies of Resistance. Trade Paper. Thompson Educational Publishing. Toronto, ON. 1998. 354p. ISBN:1-55077-100-0, ISBN13: 978-1-55077-100-8. Dewey:305.8/00971. LCCN:98-183063.
Audience: **f.**

Winks, Robin W. **F1035.N3W5 1997**
The Blacks in Canada: A History. Ed. 2. Trade Cloth. McGill-Queen's University Press. Montreal, PQ. 1997. 576p. Carleton Library, Vol. 192 ISBN:0-7735-1631-X, ISBN13: 978-0-7735-1631-1. Dewey:971/.04/96. LCCN:98-122722.
Audience: **u,f.** B

Canada > Regions. Provinces > Maritime Provinces

Beck, J. Murray **F1038.H82B43 1982**
Joseph Howe: Conservative Reformer, 1804-1848. Trade Cloth. McGill-Queen's University Press. Montreal, PQ. 1982. 400p. ISBN:0-7735-0387-0, ISBN13: 978-0-7735-0387-8. Dewey:971.6/02/0924 B. LCCN:83-185321.
Audience: **f.** B

Benedict, William H. **F144.N5**
New Brunswick in History. Trade Paper. Heritage Books. Westminster, MD. 2001. 391p. ISBN:0-7884-1709-6, ISBN13: 978-0-7884-1709-2. Dewey:974.942.
Audience: **g,u,f.**

Buckner, Phillip A. & Reid, John C. (Editors) **F1035.8.A78 1994**
The Atlantic Region to Confederation: A History. Trade Cloth. University of Toronto Press. Toronto, ON. 1994. 1030p. ISBN:0-8020-0553-5, ISBN13: 978-0-8020-0553-3. Dewey:971.5. LCCN:94-176925.
Audience: **g,l,u,f.**

Clark, Andrew H. **F1047.C57**
Three Centuries and the Island: A Historical Geography of Settlement and Agriculture in Prince Edward Island, Canada. Trade Paper. Books on Demand. Ann Arbor, MI. 300p. ISBN:0-608-13300-0, ISBN13: 978-0-608-13300-3. Dewey:911.717. LCCN:59-002157.
Audience: **u,f.**

Conrad, Margaret R. & Hiller, James K. **FC2005**
Atlantic Canada: A Concise History. Trade Paper. Oxford University Press, Inc. New York, NY. 2006. 256p. ISBN:0-19-541829-8, ISBN13: 978-0-19-541829-3. Dewey:971.5.
Audience: **g,l,u,f.**

Forbes, E. R. & Muise, D. A. (Editors) **F1035.8.A765 1993**
The Atlantic Provinces in Confederation. Trade Cloth. University of Toronto Press. Toronto, ON. 1993. 1210p. ISBN:0-8020-5886-8, ISBN13: 978-0-8020-5886-7. Dewey:971.5. LCCN:92-095005.
Audience: **f.**

Forbes, Ernest R. **F1035.8.F59**
The Maritime Rights Movement, 1919-1927: A Study in Canadian Regionalism. Trade Paper. Books on Demand. Ann Arbor, MI. 258p. ISBN:0-7837-1021-6, ISBN13: 978-0-7837-1021-1. Dewey:320.9/71. LCCN:79-308545.
Audience: **f.** B

Griffiths, N. E. S. **F1038 .G855 2005**
From Migrant to Acadian: A North American Border People, 1604-1755. Trade Cloth. McGill-Queen's University Press. Montreal, PQ. 2005. 640p. ISBN:0-7735-2699-4, ISBN13: 978-0-7735-2699-0. Dewey:971.5/017.
Audience: **g,l,u,f.** *Choice, 2006.*

Griffiths, Naomi E. **F1038.G853 1992**
The Contexts of Acadian History, 1686-1784. Trade Cloth. McGill-Queen's University Press. Montreal, PQ. 1992. 160p. ISBN:0-7735-0883-X, ISBN13: 978-0-7735-0883-5. Dewey:971.6/01. LCCN:93-125253.
Audience: **f.**

Harvey, Daniel Cobb **F1048**
The French Regime in Prince Edward Island. Trade Paper. Books on Demand. Ann Arbor, MI. 281p. ISBN:0-598-61368-4, ISBN13: 978-0-598-61368-4. Dewey:971.7. LCCN:26-003408.
Audience: **f.**

Laws, Gordon D. & Laws, Lauren M. **F1035.8.L39 2004**
The Maritime Provinces. Trade Cloth. Thomson Gale. Farmington Hills, MI. 2003. 112p. ISBN:1-59018-335-5, ISBN13: 978-1-59018-335-9. Dewey:971.5. LCCN:2003-005440.
Audience: **u,f.**

Pryke, Kenneth G. **F1038.P83**
Nova Scotia and Confederation, 1864-74. Trade Paper. Books on Demand. Ann Arbor, MI. 252p. Canadian Studies in History and Government, No. 15 ISBN:0-608-15418-0, ISBN13: 978-0-608-15418-3. Dewey:971.6/03. LCCN:79-322022.
Audience: **f.**

Sharpe, Errol **F1047.S43**
A People's History of Prince Edward Island. Trade Cloth. Bow Historical Books. New Providence, NJ. 1976. 252 p. :p. ISBN:0-88791-003-3, ISBN13: 978-0-88791-003-6. Dewey:971.7. LCCN:77-353480.
Audience: **l,u,f.**

Canada > Regions. Provinces > Quebec

Basham, Richard Dalton **F1053.B29 1978**
Crisis in Blanc and White: Urbanization and Ethnic Identity in French Canada. Trade Cloth. Thomson Gale. Farmington Hills, MI. 1978. x, 287p. ISBN:0-8161-8251-5, ISBN13: 978-0-8161-8251-0. Dewey:971/.004/41. LCCN:78-016950.
Audience: **u,f.** B

Carment, David (Editor), et al. **F1053**
The International Politics of Quebec Secession: State Making and State Breaking in North America. Frank P. Harvey & John F. Stack Jr. (Editors). Trade Cloth. Greenwood Publishing Group, Inc. Portsmouth, NH. 2001. 200p. Praeger Studies on Ethnic and National Identities in Politics ISBN:0-275-97051-5, ISBN13: 978-0-275-97051-2. Dewey:971.4. LCCN:00-042769.
Audience: **u,f.**

Clift, Dominique **F1053.C57 1982**
Quebec Nationalism in Crisis. Trade Cloth. Bow Historical Books. New Providence, NJ. 1982. viii, 155p. ISBN:0-7735-0381-1, ISBN13: 978-0-7735-0381-6. Dewey:971.4/04. LCCN:82-197673.
Audience: **u,f.** B

Dickinson, John Alexander & Young, Brian **F1052**
A Short History of Quebec. Ed. 3. Cloth Text. McGill-Queen's University Press. Montreal, PQ. 2002. 400p. ISBN:0-7735-2393-6, ISBN13: 978-0-7735-2393-7. Dewey:971.4. LCCN:2003-269861.
Audience: **g,l,u,f.**

Gougeon, Gilles (Editor) **F1052.95.G6813 1994**
A History of Quebec Nationalism. Cloth Text. James Lorimer & Company Ltd., Publishers. Toronto, ON. 118p. ISBN:1-55028-441-X, ISBN13: 978-1-55028-441-6. Dewey:971.4. LCCN:94-232071.
Audience: **u,f.**

Guindon, Hubert **F1053.G85 1988**
Quebec Society: Tradition, Modernity and Nationhood. John McMullan (Editor), Roberta Hamilton (Introduction by). Trade Paper. University of Toronto Press. Toronto, ON. 1988. 340p. ISBN:0-8020-6671-2, ISBN13: 978-0-8020-6671-8. Dewey:971.4/04. LCCN:88-207551.
Audience: **u,f.** *Choice, 1989.*

Handler, Richard **F1053.2.H36 1988**
Nationalism and the Politics of Culture in Quebec. Trade Paper. University of Wisconsin Press. Chicago, IL. 1988. 240p. New Directions in Anthropological Writing Ser. ISBN:0-299-11514-3, ISBN13: 978-0-299-11514-2. Dewey:306.4/09714. LCCN:87-040362.
Audience: **f.** *Choice, 1988.*

Klement, Alice **F1054.5.M83K58 1995**
Montreal. Trade Paper. Houghton Mifflin Company. New York, NY. 1995. 108p. Insight Pocket Guides ISBN:0-395-71058-8, ISBN13: 978-0-395-71058-6. Dewey:917.14/28044. LCCN:95-141011.
Audience: **g.**

Linteau, Paul-Ande, et al. **F1052.L662513 1983**
Quebec: A History: 1867-1929. Rene Durocher & Jean-Claude Robert (Authors). Trade Paper. James Lorimer & Company Ltd., Publishers. Toronto, ON. 1983. 602p. ISBN:0-88862-604-5, ISBN13: 978-0-88862-604-2. Dewey:971.4/03. LCCN:83-165011.
Audience: **l,u,f.**

Mackey, Frank **F1054.5.M89N36 2004**
Black Then: Blacks and Montreal, 1780-1880's. Trade Cloth. McGill-Queen's University Press. Montreal, PQ. 2004. 216p. ISBN:0-7735-2735-4, ISBN13: 978-0-7735-2735-5. Dewey:971.4/2800496071. LCCN:2004-484702.
Audience: **f.**

Prevost, Robert **F1054.5.M857P74 1993**
Montreal: A History. McClelland & Stewart/Tundra Books. 1993. ISBN:0-7710-7034-9, ISBN13: 978-0-7710-7034-1.
Audience: **g,l,u,f.**

Saywell, John T. **F1053.S29**
Quebec 70: A Documentary Narrative. Trade Paper. Books on Demand. Ann Arbor, MI. 156p. Canadian University Paperbooks Ser., Vol. 113 ISBN:0-598-09728-7, ISBN13: 978-0-598-09728-6. Dewey:320.9/714/04. LCCN:76-030964.
Audience: **f.**

Thoreau, Henry David **F1052**
A Yankee in Canada, with Anti-Slavery and Reform Papers. Trade Cloth. Greenwood Publishing Group, Inc. Portsmouth, NH. 1970. 286p. ISBN:0-8371-2044-6, ISBN13: 978-0-8371-2044-7. Dewey:081. LCCN:69-014117.
Audience: **f.** B

Trofimenkoff, Susan Mann **F1053.T84**
Action Francaise: French Canadian Nationalism in the Twenties. Trade Paper. Books on Demand. Ann Arbor, MI. 169p. ISBN:0-598-11158-1, ISBN13: 978-0-598-11158-6. Dewey:322.4/4/09714. LCCN:74-079990.
Audience: **f.**

Young, Robert A. **F1053.2.Y68 1999**
The Struggle for Quebec. Trade Cloth. McGill-Queen's University Press. Montreal, PQ. 1999. 210p. ISBN:0-7735-1851-7, ISBN13: 978-0-7735-1851-3. Dewey:971.064/8. LCCN:00-503645.
Audience: **u,f.** *Choice, 2000.*

Canada > Regions. Provinces > Ontario

Baskerville, Peter A. **F1058**
Sites of Power: A Concise History of Ontario. Trade Paper, Perfect. Oxford University Press, Inc. New York, NY. 2005. 304p. ISBN:0-19-541892-1, ISBN13: 978-0-19-541892-7. Dewey:971.3.
Audience: **g,l,u,f.** *Choice, 2006.*

Careless, James M. (Editor) **F1056.8.P73**
The Pre-Confederation Premiers: Ontario Government Leaders, 1841-1867. Trade Paper. Books on Demand. Ann Arbor, MI. 358p. Ontario Historical Studies Ser. ISBN:0-608-16708-8, ISBN13: 978-0-608-16708-4. Dewey:971.3/02/0922. LCCN:80-501684.
Audience: **f.**

English, John & McLaughlin, Kenneth **F1059.5.K6E54 1996**
Kitchener: An Illustrated History. Trade Cloth. Robin Brass Studio, Inc. Toronto, ON. 1996. 240p. ISBN:1-896941-01-X, ISBN13: 978-1-896941-01-1. Dewey:971.3/45. LCCN:97-165385.
Audience: **f.** B

Glazebrook, G.P.De T. **F1059.5.T6857.G55**
The Story of Toronto. Trade Cloth. University of Toronto Press. Toronto, ON. 1971. xi, 310p. ISBN:0-8020-1791-6, ISBN13: 978-0-8020-1791-8. Dewey:971.3/541. LCCN:78-163815.
Audience: **u,f.** B

Greenhill, Pauline **F1059.7.E53.G74 1994**
Ethnicity in the Mainstream: Three Studies of English Canadian Culture in Ontario. Trade Cloth. McGill-Queen's University Press. Montreal, PQ. 1994. 208p. McGill-Queen's Studies in Ethnic History ISBN:0-7735-1173-3, ISBN13: 978-0-7735-1173-6. Dewey:305.811/20713. LCCN:95-160937.
Audience: **f.** *Choice, 1994.*

Guillet, Edwin Clarence **F1058.G872**
Pioneer Settlements in Early Canada. Trade Paper. Books on Demand. Ann Arbor, MI. 154p. ISBN:0-598-05573-8, ISBN13: 978-0-598-05573-6. Dewey:971.3.
Audience: **u,f.**

Johnson, J. K. **F1056.8 .J64 1989**
Becoming Prominent: Regional Leadership in Upper Canada, 1791-1841. Trade Cloth. McGill-Queen's University Press. Montreal, PQ. 1988. 288p. ISBN:0-7735-0641-1, ISBN13: 978-0-7735-0641-1. Dewey:971.3/02/0922. LCCN:89-198085.
Audience: **f.** *Choice, 1989.*

Mcnair, Jeffrey L. **F1058.M36 2000**
The Capacity to Judge: Public Opinion and Deliberative Democracy in Upper Canada, 1791-1854. Trade Cloth. University of Toronto Press. Toronto, ON. 2000. 854p. ISBN:0-8020-4360-7, ISBN13: 978-0-8020-4360-3. Dewey:320.9713/09/034. LCCN:2001-280330.
Audience: **f.**

Noel, S. J. **F1058**
Patrons, Clients, Brokers: Ontario Society and Politics, 1791-1896. Cloth Text. University of Toronto Press. Toronto, ON. 1990. 328p. ISBN:0-8020-5858-2, ISBN13: 978-0-8020-5858-4. Dewey:971.3/02.
Audience: **f.**

Shatzer, Robert **F1059.5.T685T67 2001**
Toronto: The World Within a City. Edwin Mirvish & David Mirvish (Introduction by). Trade Cloth. Towery Publishing, Inc. Memphis, TN. 2001. 317p. Urban Tapestry Ser. ISBN:1-881096-97-1, ISBN13: 978-1-881096-97-9. Dewey:971.3/541. LCCN:2001-035151.
Audience: **u,f.**

Wilton, Carol **F1058.W54 2000**
Popular Politics and Political Culture in Upper Canada, 1800-1850. Trade Cloth. McGill-Queen's University Press. Montreal, PQ. 2001. 320p. ISBN:0-7735-2053-8, ISBN13: 978-0-7735-2053-0. Dewey:971.3/02. LCCN:2001-277110.
Audience: **f.**

Canada > Regions. Provinces > Canadian Northwest (General)

F1060.P7
The Prairie West to 1905: A Canadian Sourcebook. Trade Cloth. Oxford University Press, Inc. New York, NY. 1975. xiii, 360p. ISBN:0-19-540249-9, ISBN13: 978-0-19-540249-0. Dewey:971.2. LCCN:76-375608.
Audience: **u,f.** B

Campbell, Marjorie Wilkins **F1060 .C18**
The North West Company. Paper Text. Textbook Publishers. Temecula, CA. 2003. 295p. ISBN:0-7581-3578-5, ISBN13: 978-0-7581-3578-0. Dewey:971.2.
Audience: **u,f.** B

Collins, Robert **F1060.C66 2003**
Prairie People: A Celebration of My Homeland. Trade Cloth. McClelland & Stewart. Toronto, ON. 2003. 360p. ISBN:0-7710-2257-3, ISBN13: 978-0-7710-2257-9. Dewey:971.2. LCCN:2003-501455.
Audience: **l,u,f.**

Conway, John **F1060.9.C7 1994**
The West: The history of a region in Confederation. Ed. 2. Trade Cloth. James Lorimer & Company Ltd., Publishers. Toronto, ON. 1994. 372p. ISBN:1-55028-408-8, ISBN13: 978-1-55028-408-9. Dewey:971.2. LCCN:94-211748.
Audience: **g,l,u,f.**

Elofson, W. M. **F1060.9.E46 2000**
Cowboys, Gentlemen and Cattle Thieves: Ranching on the Western Frontier. Trade Cloth. McGill-Queen's University Press. Montreal, PQ. 2000. 224p. ISBN:0-7735-2100-3, ISBN13: 978-0-7735-2100-1. Dewey:971.2/02. LCCN:2002-327879.
Audience: **u,f.**

Flanagan, Tom **F1060.9.F58 2000**
Riel and the Rebellion: 1885 Reconsidered. Ed. 2. Trade Cloth. University of Toronto Press. Toronto, ON. 2000. 256p. ISBN:0-8020-4708-4, ISBN13: 978-0-8020-4708-3. Dewey:971.05/4. LCCN:00-266114.
Audience: **f.**

Gough, Barry **F1060.7.M1783G68**
First Across the Continent: Sir Alexander Mackenzie. Trade Cloth. University of Oklahoma Press. Norman, OK. 1997. 264p. Oklahoma Western Biographies Ser., Vol. 14 ISBN:0-8061-2944-1, ISBN13: 978-0-8061-2944-0. Dewey:971.2/01/092. LCCN:97-002942.
Audience: **u,f.** *Choice, 1998.*

Gray, James Henry **F1060.9.G684**
The Roar of the Twenties. Trade Cloth. C D G Books Canada, Inc. Toronto, ON. 1975. 358p. ISBN:0-7705-1276-3, ISBN13: 978-0-7705-1276-7. Dewey:971.2/02. LCCN:75-324708.
Audience: **f.** B

Hearne, Samuel **F1060**
Journey from Prince of Wales's Fort in Hudson's Bay to the Northern Ocean in the Years 1769-1772. J. G. Tyrell (Illustrator). Trade Cloth. Greenwood Publishing Group, Inc. Portsmouth, NH. 1969. 437p. Champlain Society Publication, Vol. 6 ISBN:0-8371-5045-0, ISBN13: 978-0-8371-5045-1. Dewey:971.2/01. LCCN:68-028601.
Audience: **f.**

Howard, Joseph Kinsey **F1060.9 .H7**
Strange Empire, a Narrative of the Northwest. Paper Text. Textbook Publishers. Temecula, CA. 2003. xii, 601p. ISBN:0-7581-8023-3, ISBN13: 978-0-7581-8023-0. Dewey:971.051.
Audience: **l,u,f.** B

Huber, Thomas P. & Huber, Carole J. **F1060.92.H83 2000**
The Alaska Highway: A Geographical Discovery. Trade Cloth. University Press of Colorado. Boulder, CO. 2000. xiii, 168p. ISBN:0-87081-600-4, ISBN13: 978-0-87081-600-0. Dewey:917.9804/5. LCCN:00-056802.
Audience: **l,u,f.**

Innis, Harold Adams **F1060.I58 1999**
The Fur Trade in Canada. A. J. Ray (Introduction by). Trade Paper. University of Toronto Press. Toronto, ON. 1999. 496p. ISBN:0-8020-8196-7, ISBN13: 978-0-8020-8196-4. Dewey:380.1/456753/0971. LCCN:99-203946.
Audience: **u,f.**

Leduc, Joanne (Editor) **F1060.8.M39 1981**
Overland from Canada to British Columbia: By Mr. Thomas McMicking of Queenston, Canada West. Trade Cloth. University of British Columbia Press. Vancouver, BC. 1981. 165p. ISBN:0-7748-0136-0, ISBN13: 978-0-7748-0136-2. Dewey:917.1/044. LCCN:82-108332.
Audience: **f.** B

Mackie, Richard **F1060.8.S56M33 1997**
Trading Beyond the Mountains: The British Fur Trade on the Pacific, 1793-1843. Trade Cloth. University of Washington Press. Seattle, WA. 1997. 440p. ISBN:0-7748-0559-5, ISBN13: 978-0-7748-0559-9. Dewey:971.1/02. LCCN:97-144799.
Audience: **u,f.** *Choice, 1997.*

Nuffield, Edward W. **F1060.7.N82 1998**
Bay of the North: The Struggle for Control of Hudson Bay, 1686-1713. Trade Paper. Haro Books. Vancouver, BC. 1998. ISBN:0-9680288-1-0, ISBN13: 978-0-9680288-1-0. Dewey:971.01. LCCN:99-488478.
Audience: **f.**

Oliver, Peter **F1058.F466.O43**
G. Howard Ferguson: Ontario Tory. Cloth Text. University of Toronto Press. Toronto, ON. 1977. 1049p. Ontario Historical Studies ISBN:0-8020-3346-6, ISBN13: 978-0-8020-3346-8. Dewey:971.3/03/0924. LCCN:77-378936.
Audience: **f.** B

Owram, Doug **F1060.9.O94**
Promise of Eden: The Canadian Expansionist Movement and the Idea of the West, 1856-1900. Trade Cloth. University of Toronto Press. Toronto, ON. 1980. x, 264p. ISBN:0-8020-5483-8, ISBN13: 978-0-8020-5483-8. Dewey:971.2/01. LCCN:80-491231.
Audience: **f.** B

Phillips, R. A. J. **F1060.P5**
Canada: The Story of the Yukon and Northwest Territories. Trade Paper. Books on Demand. Ann Arbor, MI. 132p. ISBN:0-608-32858-8, ISBN13: 978-0-608-32858-4. Dewey:917.12. LCCN:66-006450.
Audience: **l,u,f.**

Spry, Irene M. **F1060.8.S75 1995**
The Palliser Expedition: The Dramatic Story of Western Canadian Exploration, 1857-1860. Ed. 2. Trade Cloth. Fifth House Publishers. Calgary, AB. 1995. 315p. Western Canadian Classics Ser. ISBN:1-895618-52-5, ISBN13: 978-1-895618-52-5. Dewey:917.1204/1. LCCN:96-136123.
Audience: **f.**

Stanley, George F. G. **F1060.9.S79**
The Birth of Western Canada: A History of the Riel Rebellions. Ed. 2. Thomas Flanagan (Introduction by). Trade Paper. University of Toronto Press. Toronto, ON. 1992. 690p. Reprints in Canadian History Ser. ISBN:0-8020-6931-2, ISBN13: 978-0-8020-6931-3. Dewey:971.05. LCCN:93-137741.
Audience: **f.**

Van Kirk, Sylvia **F1060**
Many Tender Ties: Women in Fur-Trade Society, 1670-1870. Trade Paper. University of Oklahoma Press. Norman, OK. 1983. 314p. ISBN:0-8061-1847-4, ISBN13: 978-0-8061-1847-5. Dewey:305.4/09712. LCCN:82-040457.
Audience: **f.** B

Wardhaugh, Robert A. **F1060.9.W294 2000**
MacKenzie King and the Prairie West. Printed Dust Jacket. University of Toronto Press. Toronto, ON. 2000. 350p. ISBN:0-8020-4733-5, ISBN13: 978-0-8020-4733-5. Dewey:971.2/02. LCCN:2001-268417.
Audience: **u,f.**

Canada > Regions. Provinces > Manitoba. Saskatchewan. Alberta

Coates, Kenneth S. **HF3229.M36**
Manitoba: The Keystone Province: An Illustrated History. Trade Cloth. American Historical Press. Sun Valley, CA. 1988. 192p. ISBN:0-89781-257-3, ISBN13: 978-0-89781-257-3. Dewey:330.97127. LCCN:89-113684.
Audience: **g,l,u,f.**

Friesen, Gerald **F1062.F74**
The Canadian Prairies: A History. Trade Paper. University of Toronto Press. Toronto, ON. 1987. 820p. ISBN:0-8020-6648-8, ISBN13: 978-0-8020-6648-0. Dewey:971.2.
Audience: **g,l,u,f.** B

Laws, Gordon D. & Laws, Lauren M. **F1062.4.L39 2003**
Manitoba. Trade Cloth. Thomson Gale. Farmington Hills, MI. 2002. 112p. Exploring Canada Ser. ISBN:1-59018-047-X, ISBN13: 978-1-59018-047-1. Dewey:971.27. LCCN:2002-014364.
Audience: **l,u,f.**

MacGregor, James G. **F1078 .M32 1981**
The History of Alberta. Trade Cloth. McClelland & Stewart. Toronto, ON. 1999. ISBN:0-88830-196-0, ISBN13: 978-0-88830-196-3. Dewey:971.23. LCCN:82-113208.
Audience: **g,l,u,f.**

McAllister, James A. **F1063.M39 1984**
The Government of Edward Schreyer: Democratic Socialism in Manitoba. Trade Paper. McGill-Queen's University Press. Montreal, PQ. 1984. 224p. ISBN:0-7735-0437-0, ISBN13: 978-0-7735-0437-0. Dewey:328.7127. LCCN:85-160930.
Audience: **f.**

Palmer, Howard **F1078.P35 1990**
Alberta: A New History. Trade Cloth. McClelland & Stewart. Toronto, ON. 1999. x, 422 p. :p. ISBN:0-88830-340-8, ISBN13: 978-0-88830-340-0. Dewey:971.23. LCCN:92-220855.
Audience: **g,l,u,f.**

Canada > Regions. Provinces > British Columbia. Northwest Territories. Arctic

Barman, Jean **F1088.B24 1996**
The West Beyond the West: A History of British Columbia. Ed. 2. Trade Paper. University of Toronto Press. Toronto, ON. 1996. 450p. ISBN:0-8020-7185-6, ISBN13: 978-0-8020-7185-9. Dewey:971.1. LCCN:96-215678.
Audience: **g,l,u,f.** *Choice, 1991.*

Bocking, Richard C. **F1089.F7B63 1997**
Mighty River: A Portrait of the Fraser. Trade Cloth. University of Washington Press. Seattle, WA. 1998. 304p. ISBN:0-295-97670-5, ISBN13: 978-0-295-97670-9. Dewey:971.1/3. LCCN:97-023760.
Audience: **l,u,f.** *Choice, 1998.*

Carty, Ken (Editor) **F1088.P65 1996**
Politics, Policy, and Government in British Columbia. Trade Cloth. University of Washington Press. Seattle, WA. 1996. 396p. ISBN:0-7748-0582-X, ISBN13: 978-0-7748-0582-7. Dewey:971.1/04. LCCN:96-221740.
Audience: **u,f.**

Cherrington, John **F1089.F7C48 1992**
The Fraser Valley: A History. Trade Cloth. Harbour Publishing Company, Ltd. Madeira Park, BC. 392p. ISBN:1-55017-068-6, ISBN13: 978-1-55017-068-9. Dewey:971.1/3. LCCN:93-134156.
Audience: **u,f.**

Coates, Ken S. & Morrison, William **F1090.5.C62 1992**
The Forgotten North: A History of Canada's Provincial North. Trade Cloth. James Lorimer & Company Ltd., Publishers. Toronto, ON. 144p. ISBN:1-55028-391-X, ISBN13: 978-1-55028-391-4. Dewey:971.9. LCCN:93-100635.
Audience: **l,u,f.**

Coates, Ken S. & Powell, Judith **F1090.5.C63 1989**
The Modern North: People, Politics and the Rejection of Colonialism. Trade Cloth. James Lorimer & Company Ltd., Publishers. Toronto, ON. 168p. ISBN:1-55028-122-4, ISBN13: 978-1-55028-122-4. Dewey:971.9. LCCN:89-197150.
Audience: **f.**

Cooke, Alan **F1090.5.C67**
The Exploration of Northern Canada, 500 to 1920: A Chronology. Trade Cloth. Bow Historical Books. New Providence, NJ. 1978. 549p. ISBN:0-7710-2265-4, ISBN13: 978-0-7710-2265-4. Dewey:917.1/04/0202. LCCN:80-457979.
Audience: **l,u,f.** B

Diubaldo, Richard J. **F1090.5.D58**
Stefansson and the Canadian Arctic. Trade Paper. Books on Demand. Ann Arbor, MI. 296p. ISBN:0-7837-1020-8, ISBN13: 978-0-7837-1020-4. Dewey:971.902092. LCCN:79-304078.
Audience: **f.** B

Ficken, Robert E. **F1089.F7F53 2003**
Unsettled Boundaries: Fraser Gold and the British-American Northwest. Trade Paper, Pictures or Photographs. Washington State University Press. Pullman, WA. 2003. 208p. ISBN:0-87422-268-0, ISBN13: 978-0-87422-268-5. Dewey:971.1/302. LCCN:2003-022359.
Audience: **f.** *Choice, 2004.*

Grace, Sherrill E. **F1090.5.G725 2001**
Canada and the Idea of North. Trade Cloth. McGill-Queen's University Press. Montreal, PQ. 2002. 368p. ISBN:0-7735-2247-6, ISBN13: 978-0-7735-2247-3. Dewey:971. LCCN:2002-512066.
Audience: **u,f.** *Choice, 2002.*

Hamilton, John D. **F1090.5.H356 1994**
Arctic Revolution: A Political and Social History of the Northwest Territories, 1935-1993. Trade Paper. Dundurn Group, The. Toronto, ON. 2004. 298p. ISBN:1-55002-206-7, ISBN13: 978-1-55002-206-3. Dewey:971.9/203. LCCN:95-108851.
Audience: **u,f.** *Choice, 1995.*

Harbord, Heather **F1089.N8H37 1996**
Nootka Sound: And the Surrounding Waters of Maquinna. Trade Paper. Heritage House Publishing Company, Ltd. Surrey, BC. 1996. 128p. ISBN:1-895811-03-1, ISBN13: 978-1-895811-03-2. Dewey:917.11/2. LCCN:97-112036.
Audience: **f.**

Morrison, William R. **F1093.M67 1998**
True North: The Yukon and Northwest Territories. Trade Paper. Oxford University Press, Inc. New York, NY. 1998. 212p. Illustrated History of Canada Ser. ISBN:0-19-541045-9, ISBN13: 978-0-19-541045-7. Dewey:971.9. LCCN:98-202744.
Audience: **g,l,u,f.**

Morse, Kathryn Taylor **F1095.K5M67 2003**
The Nature of Gold: An Environmental History of the Klondike Gold Rush. Trade Paper. University of Washington Press. Seattle, WA. 2003. ISBN:0-295-98330-2, ISBN13: 978-0-295-98330-1. Dewey:971.9/1. LCCN:2003-048411.
Audience: **g,l,u,f.** *Choice, 2004.*

Resnick, Philip **F1088.R47 2000**
The Politics of Resentment: British Columbia Regionalism and Canadian Unity. Cloth Text. University of British Columbia Press. Vancouver, BC. 2000. 184p. ISBN:0-7748-0804-7, ISBN13: 978-0-7748-0804-0. Dewey:971.1/04. LCCN:2001-430834.
Audience: **f.** *Choice, 2001.*

Stefansson, Vihjalmur **G640.S75 1974**
Northwest to Fortune: The Search of Western Man for a Commercially Practical Route to the Far East. Trade Cloth. Greenwood Publishing Group, Inc. Portsmouth, NH. 1974. 356p. ISBN:0-8371-5729-3, ISBN13: 978-0-8371-5729-0. Dewey:919.8. LCCN:73-020881.
Audience: **f.**

Sterne, Netta **F1088.S85 1998**
Fraser Gold 1858!: The Founding of British Columbia. Trade Cloth, Pictures or Photographs. Washington State University Press. Pullman, WA. 1998. 200p. ISBN:0-87422-165-X, ISBN13: 978-0-87422-165-7. Dewey:917.12. LCCN:98-014831.
Audience: **l,u,f.**

Wynn, Graeme & Oke, Timothy **F1089.5.V22V34 1992**
Vancouver and Its Region. Trade Cloth. University of British Columbia Press. Vancouver, BC. 1992. 344p. ISBN:0-7748-0407-6, ISBN13: 978-0-7748-0407-3. Dewey:917.11/33. LCCN:92-220463.
Audience: **g,l,u,f.** *Choice, 1992.*

Canada > Regions. Provinces > Newfoundland. Labrador

Hiller, James & Neary, Peter (Editors) **F1122.5.N48**
Newfoundland in the Nineteenth and Twentieth Centuries: Essays in Interpretation. Trade Paper. Books on Demand. Ann Arbor, MI. 297p. ISBN:0-608-16860-2, ISBN13: 978-0-608-16860-9. Dewey:971.8. LCCN:80-506730.
Audience: **f.**

Ingstad, Helge **F1122.9**
The Norse Discovery of America, Vol. 2. Ed. 2. Oxford University Press, Inc. 1986. ISBN:82-00-07039-5, ISBN13: 978-82-00-07039-9.
Audience: **g,l,u,f.**

Jackson, Lawrence **F1122.4.J33 1995**
Newfoundland and Labrador. Library Binding. Lerner Publications. Minneapolis, MN. 1995. 76p. Hello Canada Ser. ISBN:0-8225-2757-X, ISBN13: 978-0-8225-2757-2. Dewey:971.8. LCCN:94-028964.
Audience: **l,u,f.**

Mayell, Mark **F1122.4.M395 2004**
Newfoundland. Trade Cloth. Thomson Gale. Farmington Hills, MI. 2003. 112p. ISBN:1-59018-048-8, ISBN13: 978-1-59018-048-8. Dewey:971.8. LCCN:2003-002060.
Audience: **l,u,f.**

O'Flaherty, Patrick **F1123.O45 1999**
Old Newfoundland: A History to 1843. Trade Paper. Long Beach Press. Saint John's, NF. 1999. ISBN:0-9680998-2-3, ISBN13: 978-0-9680998-2-7. Dewey:971.8/01. LCCN:00-300523.
Audience: **u,f.** *Choice, 2000.*

Pendgracs, Doreen & Chafe, Dawn **F1122.7**
Newfoundland and Labrador. Trade Paper. John Wiley & Sons, Inc. Hoboken, NJ. 2004. 240p. Frommer's Complete Ser. ISBN:0-470-83223-1, ISBN13: 978-0-470-83223-3. Dewey:917.1/8/044.
Audience: **l,u,f.**

Rompkey, Bill **F1136**
Story of Labrador. Trade Cloth. McGill-Queen's University Press. Montreal, PQ. 2003. 360p. ISBN:0-7735-2574-2, ISBN13: 978-0-7735-2574-0. Dewey:971.8/2. LCCN:2004-478115.
Audience: **g,l,u,f.**

Author Index

A

B

C

D

E

F

G

H

I

J

K

L

M

N

O

P

Q

R

S

T

U

V

W

X

Y

Z

Title Index

A

B

C

D

E

F

G

H

I

J

K

M

N

O

P

Q

R

S

T

U

V

W

X

Y

Z

Numeric Titles